COMPANY DIRECTORS

COMPANY DIRECTORS

Duties, Liabilities, and Remedies

THIRD EDITION

Edited by

SIMON MORTIMORE QC

OXFORD
UNIVERSITY PRESS

OXFORD
UNIVERSITY PRESS

Great Clarendon Street, Oxford, OX2 6DP,
United Kingdom

Oxford University Press is a department of the University of Oxford.
It furthers the University's objective of excellence in research, scholarship,
and education by publishing worldwide. Oxford is a registered trade mark of
Oxford University Press in the UK and in certain other countries

© Oxford University Press 2017

The moral rights of the author have been asserted

Second Edition published in 2013
Third Edition published in 2017

Impression: 1

Published in the United States of America by Oxford University Press
198 Madison Avenue, New York, NY 10016, United States of America

British Library Cataloguing in Publication Data

Data available

Library of Congress Control Number: 2017930577

ISBN 978–0–19–875439–8

Printed and bound by
CPI Group (UK) Ltd, Croydon, CR0 4YY

Links to third party websites are provided by Oxford in good faith and
for information only. Oxford disclaims any responsibility for the materials
contained in any third party website referenced in this work.

PREFACE

Much has happened in the law relating to directors' duties during the four years since the second edition of this work, which attempted to state the law at 1 August 2012. The most significant development has been the enactment of the Small Business, Enterprise and Employment Act 2015, which, among miscellany of provisions relating to voluntary and community bodies, pubs, and education, included the first major reform of company law since the Companies Act 2006. The reforms in Part 7 are designed to improve transparency: the introduction of a register of people with significant control, the abolition of bearer shares, the requirement for all company directors to be natural persons (unless exceptions apply), modification of the definition of 'shadow director', and clarification of the application of general duties to shadow directors (so, it may be hoped, resolving the uncertainties that emerged in *Ultraframe (UK) Ltd v Fielding* [2005] EWHC 1638 (Ch) and *Vivendi SA v Richards* [2013] BCC 771). Part 8 simplifies filing requirements and replaces the annual return with an annual confirmation of accuracy of information on the companies register. Part 9 contains a major reform of the directors' disqualification regime and has led to an almost entirely new Chapter 31 on disqualification proceedings, contributed by Robert Amey. Part 10 makes reforms to insolvency law, including making wrongful and fraudulent trading proceedings available to administrators and facilitating the assignment of such claims as well as undervalue and preference claims.

Since 2012 there have been several Supreme Court decisions of relevance to directors and their duties; *Prest v Petrodel Resources Ltd* [2013] 2 AC 415 (use of companies to conceal ownership of property), *Bilta (UK) Ltd v Nazir (No 2)* [2016] AC 1 (attribution of a director's conduct or knowledge to the company and the non-availability of the *ex turpi causa* defence where the company was the victim of the wrongdoing and sues through a liquidator for the benefit of creditors), *Eclairs Group Ltd v JKX Oil & Gas plc* [2015] Bus LR 1395 (the duty to act for proper purposes), and *FHR European Ventures LLP v Cedar Capital Partners LLC* [2015] AC 250 (availability of a proprietary remedy to recover a bribe or secret commission).

Three recent High Court decisions have explored issues of great practical relevance to directors. In his long and illuminating judgment in *Madoff Securities International Ltd v Raven* [2013] EWHC 3147 (Comm) Popplewell J considered whether directors of an English company owned by Bernard Madoff were liable for breach of duty for making payments in accordance with his instructions at a time when they believed him to be an experienced businessman of unimpeachable integrity, when, unbeknown to them, through Bernard L Madoff Investment Securities, he was running the largest Ponzi scheme fraud in history.

In the second case, *BTI 2014 LLC v Sequana SA* [2016] EWHC 1686 (Ch), one of the issues that Rose J had to consider was whether directors were in breach of duty for declaring large dividends, which were lawful under the Companies Act, at a time when the company had an uncertain indemnity liability for environmental clean-up costs, which might turn out to be larger than the provision in its accounts. The judge found that the directors were protected by parent company consent, unless, at the relevant time, their duty under s 172 required them to consider creditors' interests and that was not the case while there was no more than a risk that there would be insufficient assets to meet the indemnity liability. This decision reflects a commercial judicial response to a problem frequently encountered by directors of a company with an uncertain liability (eg for product liability or for making good a potential pension fund deficiency).

It had been supposed that the statutory derivative claim under Part 11 of the 2006 Act had replaced the common law derivative claim, which was bedevilled by high cost and complexity, associated with the rule in *Foss v Harbottle* and its exceptions. In a closely reasoned judgment in the third case, *Universal Project Management Services Ltd v Fort Gilkicker Ltd* [2013] Ch 551, Briggs J found that Part 11 does not apply to what are called double or multiple derivative claims, where a shareholder of a parent entity complains of breach of duty towards some other group company, but that the common law continues to apply to them. His decision was followed by David Richards J in *Abouraya v Sigmund* [2015] BCC 503. Since the circumstances giving rise to double or multiple derivative claims are by no means uncommon, it seems that there is a lot of life left in the old common law derivative claim.

The second edition of this work introduced a new chapter on the taxation of directors' earnings and benefits. For the third edition there is a new chapter on civil penalties for market abuse, contributed by Glen Davis QC and Robert Amey. This is a topic which should be of interest to those advising directors in the financial services sector. In what may be one of the last incursions of European law into the UK, on 3 July 2016 the new European Market Abuse Regulation came into force, replacing provisions in FSMA 2000, which were based on the 2005 Market Abuse Directive and which had given rise to several reported cases, some of which are noted in Chapter 32.

Stuart Hill of Wynterhill LLP has made extensive revisions to his chapter on Insurance to reflect the Insurance Act 2015, which, as he says, brought about the most radical reform of insurance law for over a century. This chapter also discusses the issues that may arise when a D&O claim goes to arbitration. I am very grateful to Robert Turner and Nicola Dyke of Simmons & Simmons LLP for sharing with us their experience of these types of claim and identifying some of the issues that may arise.

Finally, I would like to say what a pleasure it has been to work with the contributors to this book and with the team from OUP, led from the beginning by Rachel Mullaly. When this book was first proposed and I began assembling my team of contributors, I was the only QC engaged in the project. Now we have nine QCs. I rather doubt whether participation in this work assisted their passage to Silk, but what is clear is that the knowledge and expertise of all the contributors has contributed enormously to the excellent reputation this work enjoys among practitioners and academics.

This third edition attempts to state the law at 1 September 2016, but Chapter 33 identifies the rules in the Insolvency (England and Wales) Rules 2016, which will apply after 6 April 2017.

LIST OF CONTRIBUTORS

Adam Al-Attar *Chapter 23*

BA (Oxon), BCL, called to the Bar 2007; practises at South Square, Gray's Inn; specializes in insolvency and company law, banking and financial law, and the law of trusts.

Robert Amey *Chapter 31, and Chapter 32 with Glen Davis QC*

MA (Oxon), called to the Bar 2012; practises at South Square, Gray's Inn; specializes in insolvency/restructuring, banking, and commercial and company law.

Mark Arnold QC *Chapters 10, 12 (Section E), 14, and 15 (Section E)*

MA (Cantab) (Downing College), called to the Bar (Middle Temple) 1988; QC 2013; practises at South Square, Gray's Inn; specializes in insolvency and restructuring law, company law, and commercial and financial law.

Edward Brown *Chapters 7 and 8*

BA (Cantab), LLM (LSE), MA (Siena), called to the Bar (Lincoln's Inn) 2002; practises at Essex Court Chambers; specializes in employment and commercial law.

Thomas Chacko *Chapter 9*

MA (Cantab), Dip Law (City), BCL (Oxon), called to the Bar (Inner Temple) 2007; practises at Pump Court Tax Chambers; specializes in tax practice covering all areas of revenue law.

Charlotte Cooke *Chapters 33 and 34*

MA MPhil (Cantab), BCL (Oxon), called to the Bar (Middle Temple) 2008; practises at South Square, Gray's Inn; specializes in insolvency and restructuring, banking and financial law, company and business law, and commercial litigation.

Glen Davis QC *Chapter 30, and Chapter 32 with Robert Amey*

MA (Oxon), Dip Law (City), called to the Bar (Middle Temple) 1992; QC 2011; practises at South Square, Gray's Inn; specializes in insolvency and reconstruction law, company law, and commercial, financial, and financial services law; called to the BVI Bar and for specific cases to the Bars of Gibraltar and the Cayman Islands; Member, Insolvency Rules Committee 2002–2012.

Andrew Feld *Chapter 20 with Blair Leahy*

BA (Oxon), MSc, called to the Bar (Inner Temple) 2013; practises at 20 Essex Street; specializes in commercial disputes, insolvency and restructuring, competition law, and shipping and commodities.

Adam Goodison *Chapters 3 and 4*

Called to the Bar (Middle Temple) 1990; practises at South Square, Gray's Inn; specializes in insolvency and reconstruction law, company law, and commercial law.

Martin Griffiths QC *Chapter 6*

MA (Oxon), Dip Law (City), called to the Bar (Inner Temple) 1986; QC 2006; practises at Essex Court Chambers; specializes in employment and commercial law; Member, Bar Council; Committee Member, Employment Law Bar Association.

Marcus Haywood *Chapters 11, 12 (Sections A–D), 13, 15 (Sections A–D), 16, and Chapter 17 with Lloyd Tamlyn*

BA (Oxon), called to the Bar (Lincoln's Inn) 2002. Barrister practising at South Square, Gray's Inn; specializes in all aspects of company law with a particular emphasis on corporate insolvency.

Stuart Hill *Chapter 21*

MA (Cantab); solicitor (1993), solicitor advocate (2001); since 2002, Partner in Wynterhill LLP specializing in insurance and reinsurance litigation.

Lexa Hilliard QC *Chapter 24*

LLB (LSE), called to the Bar (Middle Temple) 1987; QC 2009; practises at Wilberforce Chambers, Lincoln's Inn; specializes in insolvency and reconstruction law, company law, and commercial and financial law.

Blair Leahy *Chapter 20 with Andrew Feld*

Called to the Bar (Inner Temple) 2001; practises at 20 Essex Street; specializes in insolvency and restructuring, company law, civil fraud, and general commercial litigation.

Henry Legge QC *Chapter 29*

BA (Oxon), Dip Law (City) called to the Bar (Middle Temple) 1993 and for specific cases to the Cayman Bar; QC 2012; practises from 5 Stone Buildings, Lincoln's Inn, specializing in trust and pensions law.

Simon Mortimore QC *Consultant editor, contributor of Chapters 1 and 2*

LLB (Exon), called to the Bar (Inner Temple) 1972; QC 1991; practises at South Square, Gray's Inn; specializes in insolvency and reconstruction law, company law, commercial and financial law; called to the BVI Bar, 1991; accredited CEDR mediator.

Georgina Peters *Chapter 22*

MA (Cantab) History (Christ's College), called to the Bar (Lincoln's Inn) 2005; practises at South Square, Gray's Inn; specializes in commercial, and financial law, including corporate insolvency and reconstructing, banking and finance, commercial litigation, and company law.

Stephen Robins *Chapters 26 and 27*

BA Hons (Oxon), called to the Bar (Lincoln's Inn) 2001; practises at South Square, Gray's Inn; specializes in insolvency law, company law, banking and financial law, and commercial litigation.

Clare Sibson QC *Chapter 35*

MA (Cantab) (Foundation Scholar, Corpus Christi), called to the Bar 1997; QC 2016; practises at Cloth Fair Chambers; specializes in criminal law.

Tom Smith QC *Chapters 28 and 36*

MA, LLM (Cantab), called to the Bar (Middle Temple) 1999; QC 2014; practises at South Square, Gray's Inn; specializes in banking law, insolvency and reconstruction law, company law, and commercial and financial law.

Lloyd Tamlyn *Chapter 17 with Marcus Haywood, and Chapter 18*

BA (Cantab), called to the Bar (Gray's Inn) 1991; practises at South Square, Gray's Inn; specializes in insolvency and reconstruction law, company law, and commercial and financial law.

Hannah Thornley *Chapter 25*

MA (Cantab), BCL (Oxon), called to the Bar (Middle Temple) 2003; practises at South Square, Gray's Inn primarily in the fields of commercial litigation, corporate and personal insolvency, and company law.

William Willson *Chapter 5*

MA (Oxon), CPE (City), called to the Bar (Lincoln's Inn) 2006; practises at South Square, Gray's Inn; specializes in commercial law, financial law, company law, and insolvency and reconstruction law.

Antony Zacaroli QC *Chapter 19*

BA, BCL (Oxon), called to the Bar (Middle Temple) 1987; QC 2006; practises at South Square, Gray's Inn, specializing in insolvency and reconstruction, company, commercial, and banking and financial law; called to the BVI Bar, 2004; called for specific cases to the Cayman Bar and the Bahamas Bar.

CONTENTS—SUMMARY

I. INTRODUCTION

II. THE OFFICE OF DIRECTOR

III. THE GENERAL DUTIES OF DIRECTORS

IV. LIABILITIES OF DIRECTORS

V. DIRECTORS' PARTICULAR FUNCTIONS AND DUTIES

CONTENTS—DETAILED

I. INTRODUCTION

II. THE OFFICE OF DIRECTOR

3. Directors and Other Officers: Requirement and Definitions
Adam Goodison

4. Directors' Powers and Responsibilities
Adam Goodison

III. THE GENERAL DUTIES OF DIRECTORS

10. General Duties of Directors
Mark Arnold QC

11. Duty to Act Within Powers
Marcus Haywood

12. Duty to Promote the Success of the Company

Mark Arnold QC and Marcus Haywood

13. Duty to Exercise Independent Judgment

Marcus Haywood

IV. LIABILITIES OF DIRECTORS

19. The Company's Remedies for Breach of Directors' General Duties
Antony Zacaroli QC

V. DIRECTORS' PARTICULAR FUNCTIONS AND DUTIES

25. Decision-making by Members
Hannah Thornley

26. Accounting Records and Disclosure Requirements
Stephen Robins

28. Reorganizations and Takeovers

Tom Smith QC

29. Pension Schemes

Henry Legge QC

32. Civil Penalties for Market Abuse

Glen Davis QC and Robert Amey

35. Criminal Liability of Directors

Clare Sibson QC

VII. DIRECTORS OF FOREIGN COMPANIES

36. Duties and Liabilities of Directors of Foreign Companies
Tom Smith QC

TABLE OF CASES

TABLE OF STATUTES

TABLE OF STATUTORY INSTRUMENTS

PRACTICE DIRECTIONS

TABLE OF EUROPEAN COUNCIL DIRECTIVES AND REGULATIONS

REGULATIONS

TABLE OF INTERNATIONAL LEGISLATION

GLOSSARY

The following table sets out the abbreviations used in this work. Reference should also be made to the Companies Act 2006, Schedule 8[1] which is an index of expressions defined in that Act. In addition, the Insolvency Act 1986,[2] the Company Directors Disqualification Act 1986,[3] and the Financial Services and Management Act 2000[4] contain interpretation sections.

Expression	Meaning
1844 Act	The Act for the Registration, Incorporation, and Regulation of Joint Stock Companies (7&8 Vic, c 110)
1844 Winding Up Act	The Act for facilitating the winding up of the Affairs of Joint Stock Companies unable to meet their pecuniary Engagements (7&8 Vic, c 111)
1856 Act	The Joint Stock Companies Act 1856
1862 Act	The Companies Act 1862
1908 Act	The Companies (Consolidation) Act 1908
1929 Act	The Companies Act 1929
1948 Act	The Companies Act 1948
1967 Act	The Companies Act 1967
1980 Act	The Companies Act 1980
1981 Act	The Companies Act 1981
1985 Act	The Companies Act 1985
1989 Act	The Companies Act 1989
2006 Act	The Companies Act 2006, also called the Companies Act
2006 Act Commencement Order No 1	The Companies Act 2006 (Commencement No 1, Transitional Provisions and Savings) Order 2006 (SI 2006/3428)
2006 Act Commencement Order No 2	The Companies Act 2006 (Commencement No 2, Consequential Amendments, Transitional Provisions and Savings) Order 2007 (SI 2007/1093)
2006 Act Commencement Order No 3	The Companies Act 2006 (Commencement No 3, Consequential Amendments, Transitional Provisions and Savings) Order 2007 (SI 2007/2194)

---

[1] Introduced by s 1174.

[2] Sections 247–251 for the first group of Parts, concerning company insolvency and companies' winding up, and ss 435–436A which are of general application.

[3] s 22.

[4] ss 102A–103 which contain interpretative provisions for Part VI concerning official listing and s 417 which contains definitions used in FSMA.

Expression	Meaning
2006 Act Commencement Order No 4	The Companies Act 2006 (Commencement No 4 and Commencement No 3 (Amendment)) Order 2007 (SI 2007/2607)
2006 Act Commencement Order No 5	The Companies Act 2006 (Commencement No 5, Transitional Provisions and Savings) Order 2007 (SI 2007/3495)
2006 Act Commencement Order No 6	The Companies Act 2006 (Commencement No 6, Saving and Commencement Nos 3 and 5 (Amendment)) Order 2008 (SI 2008/674)
2006 Act Commencement Order No 7	The Companies Act 2006 (Commencement No 7 and Transitional Provisions) Order 2008 (SI 2008/1886)
2006 Act Commencement Order No 8	The Companies Act 2006 (Commencement No 8, Transitional Provisions and Savings) Order 2008 (SI 2008/2860)
AGM	Annual General Meeting
AIM	Alternative Investment Market of the London Stock Exchange
Bankruptcy Act	The Bankruptcy Act 1914
BEIS	Department for Business, Energy and Industrial Strategy, also called DBEIS[5]
BERR	Department for Business, Enterprise, and Regulatory Reform, also called DBERR[6]
BIS	Department for Business, Innovation and Skills, also called DBIS[7]
Cadbury Committee	The Committee on the Financial Aspects of Corporate Governance, chaired by Sir Adrian Cadbury, which reported in June 1992
C(AICE) Act 2004	The Companies (Audit, Investigations and Community Enterprise) Act 2004
CDDA	Company Directors Disqualification Act 1986
CIB	Companies Investigation Branch of Departments for BERR and BIS
CJA	Criminal Justice Act 1987
CLR	The Company Law Review set up by the Secretary of State for Trade and Industry on 4 March 1998 under the auspices of the Company Law and Reporting Commission and/or The Company Law Review Steering Group
CLR: *The Strategic Framework*	Modern Company Law For a Competitive Economy, The Strategic Framework, a Consultation Document published by the Company Law Review Steering Group in February 1999 (URN 99/654)

---

[5] Formed in July 2016 from the merger of the Departments for BIS and of Energy and Climate Change.

[6] Formerly the DTI; merged into Department for BIS, June 2009.

[7] Created June 2009 from a merger of Department for BIS and Department for Innovation, Universities and Skills.

Expression	Meaning
CLR: *Developing the Framework*	Modern Company Law For a Competitive Economy, Developing the Framework, a Consultation Document published by the Company Law Review Steering Group in March 2000 (URN 00/656)
CLR: *Completing the Structure*	Modern Company Law For a Competitive Economy, Completing the Structure, a Consultation Document published by the Company Law Review Steering Group in March 2000 (URN 00/1335)
CLR: *Final Report*	Modern Company Law For a Competitive Economy, Final Report published by the Company Law Review Steering Group in July 2001 (URN 01/942, 943)
CMA	Competition and Markets Authority
Code	UK Corporate Governance Code issued by the FRC
Cohen Committee	The Committee on Company Law Amendment under the chairmanship of Cohen J, whose report was presented to Parliament in June 1945 (Cmd 6659)
COMI	Centre of Main Interests
Companies Act	Companies Act 2006, also called the 2006 Act
Cork Committee	The Committee on Insolvency Law and Practice under the chairmanship of Sir Kenneth Cork
Cork Report	Report of the Cork Committee, presented to Parliament in June 1982 (Cmnd 8558) The Principles of Good Governance and Code of Best Practice, prepared by the Hampel Committee and published in June 1998, amended and updated in July 2003, June 2006, and June 2008
Corporate Governance Rules	Rules made by the FCA under FSMA, Part 6 relating to the corporate governance of issuers who have requested or approved admission of their securities to trading on a regulated market
CPR	Civil Procedure Rules 1998 applicable to proceedings in the High Court and the County Courts
CSIP	Company Share Incentive Plan
CVA	Company voluntary arrangement
D&O Insurance	Directors and officers liability insurance
Davey Committee	The Committee on Company Law Amendment under the chairmanship of Lord Davey, whose report was presented to Parliament in 1895 (C 7779)
DBIS	See BIS

Expression	Meaning
Disclosure Rules	Rules made by the FCA under FSMA, Part 6 relating to disclosure of information in respect of financial instruments which have been admitted to trading on a regulated market or for which a request for admission to trading on such a market has been made
DTI	Department of Trade and Industry[8]
EBT	Employee Benefit Trust
EC	European Community
ECHR	European Convention on Human Rights
EC Insolvency Regulation	EC Regulation on Insolvency Procedings (1346/2000/EC)
EEA	European Economic Area
EEC	European Economic Community
EEIG	European Economic Interest Grouping
EGM	Extraordinary General Meeting
EIM	Employment Income Manual
EMI	Enterprise Management Incentive
ERA	Employment Rights Act 1996
EU	European Union
FCA	Financial Conduct Authority
Former Companies Acts	The Companies Acts 1862–1985
FRC	Financial Reporting Council
FRRP	Financial Reporting Review Panel
FSA	Financial Services Authority
FSMA	Financial Services and Markets Act 2000
GAAP	Generally accepted accounting practice
GC100	The Association for the General Counsel and Company Secretaries of FTSE100 Companies
Greenbury Committee	The Study Group on Directors' Remuneration, chaired by Sir Richard Greenbury, which reported in June 1995
Greene Committee	The Committee on Company Law Amendment under the chairmanship of Sir Wilfred Greene KC, whose report was presented to Parliament in 1926 (Cmd 2657)
Hampel Committee	The Committee on Corporate Governance, chaired by Sir Ronald Hampel
Higgs Report	Report on the Effectiveness of Non-executive Directors of a committee chaired by Sir Derek Higgs
HMRC	Her Majesty's Revenue and Customs
IAS	International Accounting Standards
Insolvency Act	Insolvency Act 1986
Insolvency Rules	Insolvency Rules 1986
IR 2016	Insolvency (England and Wales) Rules 2016 (SI 2016/1024)
ITEPA	Income Tax (Earnings and Pensions) Act 2003

---

[8] 1983–2007 when it became Department for BERR.

Expression	Meaning
Jenkins Committee	The Company Law Committee under the chairmanship of Lord Jenkins, whose report was presented to Parliament in June 1962 (Cmnd 1749)
Listing Rules	The rules made by the FCA as UK Listing Authority under FSMA, Part 6 relating to the official list
Loreburn Committee	The Committee on Company Law Amendment under the original chairmanship of Sir Robert Reid KC (later Lord Loreburn), whose report was presented to Parliament in 1906 (cd 3052)
MAD	Market Abuse Directive (2003/6/EC)
MAR	Market Abuse Regulation (EC Reg 596/2014)
MFR	Minimum funding requirement (concerning pensions)
MiFID	Markets in Financial Instruments Directive (Directive 2004/39/EC)
Model Articles (pclg)	Model articles for private companies limited by guarantee, prescribed by the Model Articles Regulations
Model Articles (pcls)	Model articles for private companies limited by shares, prescribed by the Model Articles Regulations
Model Articles (plc)	Model articles for public companies, prescribed by the Model Articles Regulations
Model Articles Regulations	The Companies (Model Articles) Regulations 2008 (SI 2008)
NED	Non-executive Director
NIC	National Insurance Contribution
OFR	Operating and Financial Review
OFT	Office of Fair Trading
PACE	Police and Criminal Evidence Act 1984
Panel	Panel on Takeovers and Mergers
PILON	Payment in lieu of notice
POS Regulations	Public Offers of Securities Regulations
PPER Act	Political Parties, Elections and Referendums Act 2000
PRA	Prudential Regulatory Authority
Prospectus Rules	Rules made by the FCA under FSMA, Part 6 relating to transferrable securities
PSC register	Register of people with significant control
PSM	Professional Securities Market of the London Stock Exchange
Registrar	The Registrar of Companies for England and Wales
RIS	Regulatory Information Service
SCE	European Co-operative Society
SE	Societas Europaea (a European Company)
SFO	Serious Fraud Office (concerning crime)
SFO	Statutory Funding Objective (concerning pensions)

Expression	Meaning
Table A	Table A, regulations for the management of a company limited by shares, prescribed by the Companies (Tables A to F) Regulations 1985 (SI 1985/805)
Tables A to F Amendment Regulations 2007 and 2008	The Companies (Tables A to F) (Amendment) Regulations 2007 (SI 2007/2541), The Companies (Tables A to F) (Amendment) (No 2) Regulations 2007 (SI 2007/2826) and The Companies (Tables A to F) (Amendment) Regulations 2008 (SI 2008/739)
Takeover Code	City Code on Takeovers and Mergers, published by the Panel
Transparency Rules	Rules made by the FCA under FSMA, Part 6 to give effect to the Transparency Directive (Directive 2004/109/EC)
UCITS	Undertakings for Collective Investment in Transferable Securities
UKLA	United Kingdom Listing Authority
White Paper: *Company Law Reform*	White Paper, *Company Law Reform*, presented to Parliament by the Secretary of State for Trade and Industry, March 2005 (CM 6456)
White Paper: *Modernising Company Law*	White Paper, *Modernising Company Law*, presented to Parliament by the Secretary of State for Trade and Industry, July 2002 (CM 5553-1)

Part I

INTRODUCTION

1

HISTORICAL INTRODUCTION TO THE LAW RELATING TO THE DUTIES AND LIABILITIES OF DIRECTORS

Simon Mortimore QC

A. Introduction

Directors of a company are identified by their functions, rather than their descriptive title. **1.01** The Joint Stock Companies Act 1844, the first of the Victorian statutes on company law, defined directors as 'the persons having the direction, conduct, management, or superintendence of the affairs of the company'.[1] The Companies Act 1862 did not provide definitions, but since 1908 the Companies Acts have provided that in those Acts a director 'includes any person occupying the position of director, by whatever name called', so including de facto directors.[2] Whereas the 1844 Act made it clear that the directors, not the shareholders, had the conduct of the ordinary management of the company, with power to make contracts, execute documents, and hire employees and agents,[3] subsequent Companies Acts have imposed duties on directors, but left it to the company's constitution to provide for the directors' functions and powers.

---

[1] 1844 Act, s 3.
[2] 1908 Act, s 285; 1929 Act, s 380; 1948 Act, s 455; 1985 Act, s 741(1); and 2006 Act, s 250.
[3] 1844 Act, s 27.

1.02 Directors occupy a central position in the structure of company law, made up of statutory provisions supported by common law rules and equitable principles. The structure reflects three purposes.[4] The first purpose is that companies are formed and managed by the directors for the benefit of shareholders. This is achieved through the fiduciary obligations of directors and their duties of care, skill, and diligence, remedies at law for their breach, and by the shareholders' powers of dismissal.[5] That purpose is subject to the second purpose, which is that there should be safeguards for the benefit of actual and potential creditors. This is achieved through directors' duties, insolvency law, and special provisions or rules about, for example, capital maintenance. Finally, as reflected in accounting and disclosure requirements, company law operates for the benefit of the community as a whole, including actual and potential shareholders and creditors.

1.03 The following sections of this chapter trace the changing functions and obligations of directors as reflected in the default articles prescribed for companies, identify the common law rules and equitable principles which support the statutory framework, and finally outline the changes in statute law as they have affected the functions, duties, and liabilities of directors. These matters are discussed in more detail in later chapters.

B. Articles of Association Relating to Directors

1.04 The Companies Acts of 1862, 1908, 1929, and 1948 prescribed articles of association in the form of Table A, which would stand as the default articles for companies unless excluded or modified, as was frequently the case. Table A for the 1985 Act and the Model Articles for the 2006 Act have been prescribed by statutory instruments.[6] Under the 2006 Act there are separate Model Articles for private companies limited by shares (pcls), private companies limited by guarantee (plg), and public companies (plc). Many companies, particularly larger ones, adopt bespoke articles which depart to a greater or lesser extent from the Table A model or the 2006 Model Articles.

1.05 The 1862 Act, Table A established the essential features of the office of director which, with modifications, were repeated in the 1908, 1929, 1948, and 1985 Tables.[7] The significant developments have concerned directors with executive functions and conflict of interest. The first directors were appointed by the subscribers and thereafter by the company in general meeting, subject to a power of the board to fill casual vacancies. Directors received remuneration determined by the company in general meeting. There were provisions for directors to retire by rotation, but a director could only be removed by special resolution. The directors managed the business of the company and could exercise all its powers except for those reserved by the Act or the articles to the company in general meeting. They would

---

[4] CLR: *The Strategic Framework* at paras 5.1.4–5.1.7.

[5] This traditional relationship between directors and shareholders is described by Lord Oliver in *Caparo plc v Dickman* [1990] 2 AC 605, 630, HL.

[6] Companies (Tables A to F) Regulations 1985 (SI 1985/805); Companies (Tables A to F) (Amendment) Regulations 2007 (SI 2007/2541); and Companies (Tables A to F) (Amendment) (No 2) Regulations 2007 (SI 2007/2826) which apply to companies incorporated between 1 October 2007 and 30 September 2009; Companies (Model Articles) Regulations 2008 (SI 2008/3229) which apply to companies incorporated after 1 October 2009.

[7] 1862 Act, Table A, regs 52–94; 1908 Act, Table A, regs 68–108; 1929 Act, Table A, regs 64–101; 1948 Act, Table A, regs 75–129, 136; 1985 Act, Table A, regs 64–110, 118.

dispatch the business of the company at board meetings, but could delegate their powers to a committee of one or more directors. They could recommend the payment of dividends out of profits subject to the sanction of the company in general meeting. They were responsible for keeping accounts and in each year having them audited and laid before the company in general meeting.

Under the 1862 Act, Table A a director automatically vacated office if 'he holds any other **1.06** office or place of profit under the company', or 'if he is concerned in or participates in the profits of any contract with the company'; subject to the proviso that he should not vacate office 'by reason of his being a member of any company which has entered into contracts with or done any work for the company of which he is director; nevertheless he shall not vote in respect of such contract or work; and if he does so vote his vote shall not be counted'.[8] It was not envisaged, therefore, that a director would be a full-time executive, remunerated under a contract of employment; hence references in the cases to the intermittent nature of the office. By the turn of the century this had begun to change and the role of executive directors who devoted the whole or a substantial amount of their time to the company's affairs was recognized in the 1908 Act, Table A. Under it the directors could appoint one or more of their body to the office of managing director or manager on terms and at remuneration fixed by the directors and a director so appointed was not subject to the rotation provisions and did not automatically vacate his office as director.[9]

The 1948 Act, Table A acknowledged the obligations, expenses, and risks of the office of **1.07** director by providing that in addition to remuneration directors might be paid all expenses properly incurred in attending meetings of directors, committees of directors, or general meetings of the company or in connection with the business of the company and that they were entitled to an indemnity in respect of all liabilities incurred in successfully defending civil or criminal proceedings or applying for relief under the 1948 Act, s 448.[10] Although a director's remuneration was to be determined by the company in general meeting, the directors could determine the terms, including remuneration, on which a director held other offices or places of profit under the company or provided professional services.[11] The 1985 Act, Table A for the first time expressly stated that the directors' powers of management were subject to any directions given by special resolution.[12]

Under the 1948 Act, Table A conflict of interest was no longer a ground for vacating office. **1.08** Instead a director who was in any way directly or indirectly interested in a contract or proposed contract with the company was to declare his interest to a meeting of the directors in accordance with the 1948 Act, s 199. With certain exceptions he was not to vote on the contract. The 1985 Act, Table A went further: a director could be directly or indirectly interested in transactions or arrangements with the company or in which the company was interested and was not accountable for benefits, provided that he disclosed the nature and extent of his interest to the directors.

---

[8] reg 57. He also vacated office if he became bankrupt or insolvent.
[9] regs 72 and 77, which also provided for a director to vacate office if he 'is found lunatic or becomes of unsound mind'.
[10] 1948 Act, Table A, regs 76 and 136.
[11] 1948 Act, Table A, regs 76, 84, 88. Also 1985 Act, Table A, regs 85 and 94. 1985 Act, Table A, reg 87, gave the directors power to provide gratuities and pensions to former executive directors and their families.
[12] 1985 Act, Table A, reg 70.

1.09   The 2006 Act Model Articles give directors more powers in relation to appointment and remuneration and more flexibility in decision-making. They are responsible for managing the company's business, subject to directions given by special resolution, and they have full power to delegate to any person or committee.[13] Directors' decisions are to be taken collectively, either at a meeting or by written resolution.[14] Since the 2006 Act, ss 175, 177, and 182 deal expressly with conflicts of interest and interests in actual and proposed transactions, the Model Articles simply deal with the mechanics of decision-making in cases of conflict.[15] Directors may be appointed by ordinary resolution or by decision of the directors.[16] A director's remuneration for services as director and for any other service undertaken for the company is to be decided by the directors.[17]

C. Common Law Rules and Equitable Principles Relating to the Management of Companies

(1) The ultra vires doctrine

1.10   The memorandum of association of a company incorporated under the Companies Acts 1862 to 1985 had to state the objects of the company with some degree of particularity.[18] Two consequences, of particular relevance to directors, followed from this. The first was that any transaction outside the scope of the company's objects, or what may fairly be regarded as incidental or consequential upon the stated objects, was void and incapable of ratification by shareholders.[19] A director who caused the company's property to be applied for purposes outside its objects would be personally liable for any loss caused.[20] The courts developed the ultra vires rule to protect investors in the company and creditors from loss resulting from the unauthorized use of company funds. A company could avoid the rigours of the rule by including in its memorandum a long list of objects, each of which was stated to be as an independent object, not limited or restricted by any other object.[21] The second consequence was that since the funds of a company were made by statute applicable only for the specific purposes set out in the memorandum, those funds were impressed with the qualities of a trust fund.[22] Directors were therefore considered to be in a position comparable to that of a trustee, although account had to be taken of the commercial nature of their engagement.[23]

---

[13]   Model Articles (pcls, plg, and plc) 3–6.

[14]   Model Articles (pcls and plg) 7–13, 15, 16 and Model Articles (plc) 7–15, 17–19.

[15]   Model Article (pcls and plg) 14 and Model Article (plc) 16.

[16]   Model Article (pcls and plg) 17 and Model Article (plc) 20. Retirement by rotation only applies to directors of public companies (Model Article (plc) 21). Model Article (pcls and plg) 18 and Model Article (plc) 22 deal with automatic vacation of office for disqualification, bankruptcy, etc.

[17]   Model Article (pcls and plg) 19 and Model Article (plc) 23. The company may also pay a director's reasonable expenses: Model Article (pcls and plg) 20 and Model Article (plc) 24.

[18]   1985 Act, s 2(1)(c). Also 1862 Act, s 10; 1908 Act, s 3; 1929 Act, s 2; 1948 Act, s 2(1)(c); *Re Crown Bank* (1890) 44 Ch D, 634, 644.

[19]   *Eastern Counties Railway v Hawkes* (1855) 5 HLC 331, 346, 348; *The Ashbury Railway Carriage and Iron Co v Riche* (1875) LR 7 HL 653, 672, 673, 679, 689, 694; *A-G v Great Eastern Railway Co* (1880) 5 AC 473, 478, 481, 486.

[20]   *Joint Stock Discount Co v Brown* (1869) LR 8 Eq 376; *Hardy v Metropolitan Land Co* (1872) 7 Ch App 427; *Great Eastern Railway Co v Turner* (1872) 8 Ch App 149; *Russell v Wakefield Waterworks Co* (1875) LR 20 Eq 474, 479; *Cullerne v London and Suburban Building Society* (1890) 25 QBD 485; *Re George Newman & Co* [1895] 1 Ch 674, CA; *Re Claridge's Patent Asphalt Co Ltd* [1921] 1 Ch 543, CA.

[21]   In *Cotman v Brougham* [1918] AC 514, 523 Lord Wrenbury deprecated the use of 'independent objects' clauses, but acknowledged that they were effective.

[22]   *Selangor United Rubber Estates v Cradock* (No 3) [1968] 1 WLR 1555, 1575.

[23]   Para 1.19 below.

The ultra vires doctrine has now largely disappeared from view as a result of statutory reforms **1.11** beginning in 1972 by which a company's capacity is no longer limited by the objects stated in its memorandum.[24] The 2006 Act, s 39(1) provides that 'the validity of an act done by a company shall not be called into question on the ground of lack of capacity by reason of anything in the company's constitution'.[25]

Also, the objects clause has been liberalized. The 2006 Act, s 31(1) reverses the traditional **1.12** rule that the memorandum must positively state the company's objects. Instead it provides that 'unless a company's articles specifically restrict the objects of the company, its objects are unrestricted'.[26]

(2) The indoor management rule

Royal British Bank v Turquand[27] established that, although it was to be assumed that a person **1.13** dealing with a company had read the company's public documents[28] and satisfied himself that the proposed transaction was not inconsistent with them, such a person was not required to inquire whether internal procedures had been duly carried out. The rule is supplemented by the rules of agency that a director or other officer may bind the company if he has ostensible or apparent authority to do so.[29]

The rule has been superseded by statutory provision now contained in the 2006 Act, s 40(1), **1.14** which provides that, in favour of a person dealing with a company in good faith, the power of the directors to bind the company, or authorize others to do so, is deemed to be free of any limitation under the company's constitution.[30] For this purpose s 40(2) provides that a person dealing with a company, through being a party to any transaction or other act to which the company is a party (i) is not bound to enquire as to any limitation on the powers of the directors to bind the company or authorize others to do so, (ii) is presumed to have acted in good faith unless the contrary is proved, and (iii) is not to be regarded as acting in bad faith by reason only of his knowing that an act is beyond the powers of the directors under the company's constitution. Section 40(5) provides that the section does not affect any

---

[24] The reforms began with the European Communities Act 1972, s 9 (giving effect to Article 9 of Council Directive 68/151/EEC), which became 1985 Act, s 35. A new s 35 was inserted into the 1985 Act by 1989 Act, s 108(1) as from 4 February 1991 to remove the limit of the protection in the original s 35, which only applied to third parties acting in good faith and to transactions decided on by the directors. The purpose of the 1972 Act and the directive 'is to enable people to deal with a company in good faith without being adversely affected by any limits on the company's capacity or its rules for internal management'; per Sir Nicholas Browne-Wilkinson V-C in *TCB Ltd v Gray* [1986] Ch 621, 635.

[25] There are special rules for charitable companies: 2006 Act, ss 39(2) and 42. 2006 Act s 39 replaced the 1985 Act, s 35(1) and (4) without material change. 1985 Act, s 35(2) and (3), concerning proceedings by members to restrain an act beyond the company's capacity and the duty of directors to observe limitations on their powers flowing from the company's memorandum and ratification were repealed and not replaced.

[26] 2006 Act, s 31(1) replaced 1985 Act, s 3A, which provided that where a company's memorandum stated that the object of the company was to carry on business as a general commercial company, then its object was to carry on any trade or business whatsoever, and it had power to do all such things as were incidental or conducive to the carrying on of any trade or business by it. 1985 Act, s 3A had been inserted by 1989 Act, s 110 with effect from 4 February 1991.

[27] (1856) 6 El & Bl 327. In *Mahony v East Holyford Mining Co* (1875) LR 7 HL 869, 898 Lord Hatherley used the phrase 'the indoor management' in this context.

[28] eg its memorandum of association, articles of association, and special resolutions delivered to the Registrar.

[29] *Freeman & Lockyer v Buckhurst Park Properties (Mangal) Ltd* [1964] 2 QB, 480, CA.

[30] 2006 Act, s 40 replaced without material change 1985 Act, ss 35A and 35B, which had been inserted by 1989 Act, s 108 with effect from 4 February 1991 in place of the original s 35. In their original form these provisions were introduced by European Communities Act 1972, s 9.

liability incurred by the directors, or any other person, by reason of the directors exceeding their powers.

(3) Attribution

1.15 In numerous civil and criminal contexts the court may have to determine whether the knowledge, mental state (malice, dishonesty), or intentions of its directors, other officers, or employees are to be attributed to the company. In the leading case of *Lennard's Carrying Company v Asiatic Petroleum Ltd*[31] the House of Lords attributed the managing director's default to the company on the ground that he was the 'directing mind and will' or alter ego of the company. Where wrongdoing is attributed to the company, the maxim *ex turpi causa* may prevent it from obtaining indemnity from the wrongdoers[32] or insurers.[33]

1.16 In *Meridian Global Funds Management Asia Ltd v Securities Commission*[34] Lord Hoffmann reviewed the rules of attribution. The primary rules are generally found in the company's constitution (eg a decision of the directors is a decision of the company) and those primary rules are supported by principles of agency law. If it is apparent that a particular rule of law is intended to apply to companies, but insistence on the primary rules would defeat that intention, it becomes necessary to apply a special rule of attribution. The court's task is to interpret the rule in order to determine whose act, knowledge, or state of mind is to be attributed to the company; that person may be the person entrusted with conduct of the particular matter.

(4) The duties of directors

1.17 From the earliest times the duties of directors have been identified by comparing directors with trustees. In 1742, in *The Charitable Corporation v Sutton*,[35] Lord Hardwicke LC found that the corporation's affairs were a 'great scene of iniquity' in which its funds, rather than being applied for the relief of the industrious poor, had been misapplied in fraudulent and fictitious loans and other improper transactions, causing loss to the corporation of more than £350,000. The corporation brought proceedings to recover its losses from some 50 committeemen, directors, and other officers on the ground that they 'had been guilty of manifest breaches of trust, or at least of such supine and gross negligence of their duty'. Lord Hardwicke held that the office of director (or committeeman) was in the nature of a private trust, so that such officers were liable to the corporation for 'breaches of trust, either by commissions or omissions, for acts of misfeasance or nonfeasance' and that where 'there is a series of neglects, and breaches of trust are occasioned by their absence, then they are answerable for the misfeasance of others'. Even though the office of director is voluntary, it had to be discharged with 'fidelity, integrity, and diligence'. The five conspirators who had been directly responsible for the misapplication of the funds were primarily liable to make good the losses, but the other directors could be liable in the second degree if they connived in the affair by

---

[31] [1915] AC 705, HL.

[32] *Stones & Rolls v Moore Stephens* [2009] AC 1391, HL; *Safeway Stores Ltd v Twigger* [2011] Bus LR 1629, CA. See the observations of Lord Neuberger on these cases in *Bilta (UK) Ltd v Nazir (No 2)* [2016] AC 1, SC, at paras 21–31.

[33] *KR v Royal & Sun Alliance plc* [2007] Bus LR 139, CA.

[34] [1995] 2 AC 500, 506–12, PC. See also *Bilta (UK) Ltd v Nazir (No 2)* [2016] AC 1, SC, at paras 7–9, per Lord Neuberger, paras 35–52, per Lord Mance, paras 65–78, per Lord Sumption, and paras 82–97, per Lords Toulson and Hodge.

[35] (1742) 2 Atk 400; 9 Mod Rep 349. There are differences between the two reports and the quotations in this paragraph are taken from both reports.

signing the false notes under which monies were misapplied, or if they failed to make use of 'the proper power invested in them by the charter, in order to prevent the ill consequences arising from such a confederacy'. Inquiries were ordered to determine the liability of the directors in the second degree. Thus *The Charitable Corporation v Sutton* established that directors owed the company fiduciary duties (fidelity and integrity) and a duty of diligence.

In relation to fiduciary duties the courts have always imposed exacting standards. Directors were liable to restore misapplied company property, whether they were recipients of the property or participants in the misapplication[36] and to account for secret profits and bribes.[37] A director's fiduciary duty to promote the interests of the company precluded him from entering on behalf of the company into a contract with himself or a firm or company of which he was a member, regardless of the fairness or unfairness of the contract.[38] He could only be released from his position of conflict or duty to account by the assent of the members.[39] The fiduciary duties of a director were reflected in the 1862 Act, s 165, which gave the court a summary power, where a company was being wound up, to assess damages against a delinquent director or officer who had 'misapplied or retained or become liable or accountable for any moneys or property of the company, or been guilty of any misfeasance or breach of trust in relation to the company'.[40]   **1.18**

The position of a director could not be equated entirely with that of a trustee. In 1878 Jessel MR said: 'Directors have sometimes been called trustees, or commercial trustees, and sometimes they have been called managing partners, it does not matter what you call them so long as you understand what their true position is, which is that they are really commercial men managing a trading concern for the benefit of themselves and all other shareholders in it', and that 'they are so bound to use fair and reasonable diligence in the management of the company's affairs, and to act honestly'.[41] In *City Equitable Fire Insurance Co*[42] Romer J said that he found the analogy with trustees wholly misleading. Directors stood in a fiduciary relationship to the company, but there was little resemblance between their duties and those of a trustee of a will or marriage settlement. The duties that a director owes to the company are determined by the functions he undertakes to perform, the nature of the company's business, and the way in which work is properly distributed among the directors and other officers.   **1.19**

In 1998 the Law Commission, chaired by Arden J, identified six heads of fiduciary duties owed by a director to the company:[43] (i) a duty of loyalty (to act in the best interests of the company),[44] (ii) a duty to act for proper purposes (to exercise powers for the purpose   **1.20**

---

[36] *Benson v Heathorn* (1842) 1 Y&CC 326.

[37] *The York and North-Midland Railway Co v Hudson* (1853) 16 Beav 485.

[38] *Aberdeen Railway Co v Blaikie Bros* (1854) 1 Macq 461, HL.

[39] *Regal (Hastings) Ltd v Gulliver* (1942) [1967] 2 AC 134n, 150, HL.

[40] As restated by Companies (Winding Up) Act 1890, s 10. *Palmer's Handbook on Company Law*, 4th edn (1902), pp 170, 172 took the view that breach of trust was generally confined to misapplication of company funds (eg application for an ultra vires purpose), whereas misfeasance covered other breaches of duty (eg the allotment of shares to an infant, taking a bribe, or committing a fraudulent preference).

[41] *Re Forest of Dean Coal Mining Co* (1878) 10 Ch D 450, 451, 452; *Re Lands Allotment Co* [1894] 1 Ch 616, 631, CA, per Lindley LJ.

[42] [1925] Ch 407, 426–30.

[43] Law Commission Company Directors: Regulating Conflicts of Interest and Formulating a Statement of Duties (Consultation Paper No 153) at paras 11.4–11.20.

[44] Directors must act in good faith in what they consider to be in the best interests of the company: *Re Smith and Fawcett Ltd* [1942] Ch 304, 306, CA. If they do so, it does not matter that their decision also promotes

for which those powers were conferred),[45] (iii) a duty not to fetter their discretion,[46] (iv) the no conflict and no profit rules (under which a director could not keep profits from information, property, or opportunities that belong to the company),[47] (v) a duty to act in accordance with the company's constitution, and (vi) a duty to act fairly as between different shareholders.[48]

1.21 The amount of diligence expected of a nineteenth-century director was distinctly modest. A director who, by taking no part in the company's affairs and not attending board meetings, was unaware of wrongdoing or breaches of the company's constitution could escape liability to compensate the company for losses suffered.[49] Since a director could hold office while being largely ignorant of the company's affairs, he was free to take office as a director of a rival company.[50]

1.22 Consistently with the low standard of diligence tolerated by the court, a director could be found liable to compensate the company for breach of a duty of care and skill in relation to business decisions only if a high degree of negligence was shown. The negligence had to amount to *crassa negligentia*,[51] or 'it must be in a business sense culpable and gross'.[52] The standard of care was essentially subjective and dependent on the director's own capabilities: a director was required to show the degree of skill to be reasonably expected of a person with his knowledge and experience and to take such a care as an ordinary man might be expected to take on his own behalf, but he was not bound to give continuous attention to the affairs of the company and, in the absence of grounds for suspicion, was entitled to trust his fellow

their own interests: *Hirsche v Sims* [1894] AC 654, 660, 661, PC. The best interests of the company may require account to be taken of the interests of creditors (Ch 12, Section E below) and employees (*Hutton v West Cork Railway Co* (1883) 23 Ch D 654, 672, 673, CA, where Bowen LJ said 'The law does not say that there are to be no cakes and ale, but there are to be no cakes and ale except such as are required for the benefit of the company', and 1985 Act, s 309).

   [45] *Howard Smith Ltd v Ampol Petroleum Ltd* [1974] AC 821, 835, PC; also *Spackman v Evans* (1868) LR 3 HL 171,186; *Alexander v Automatic Telephone Co* [1890] 2 Ch 233; *Re a Company (No 00370 of 1987), ex p Glossop* [1988] BCLC 570, 577; *Re BSB Holdings Ltd (No 2)* [1996] 1 BCLC 155, 243–6.
   [46] *Fulham Football Club Ltd v Cabra Estates plc* [1994] 1 BCLC 363, 392, CA.
   [47] *Regal (Hastings) Ltd v Gulliver* [1967] 2 AC 131n; *Industrial Development Consultants Ltd v Cooley* [1972] 1 WLR 443; *Movitex Ltd v Bullfield* [1988] BCLC 104, where Vinelott J said that the no profit rule imposed a disability not a duty; *Island Export Finance Ltd v Umunna* [1986] BCLC 460.
   [48] *Mutual Life Insurance v Rank Organisation Ltd* [1985] BCLC 11, 21; *Re BSB Holdings Ltd (No 2)* [1996] 1 BCLC 155, 246–9.
   [49] *Re Cardiff Savings Bank, the Marquis of Bute's Case* [1892] 2 Ch 100; *Re Denham* (1883) 25 Ch D 752.
   [50] *Re London and Mashonaland Exploration Co v New Mashonaland Exploration Co* [1891] WN 165; discussed in *In Plus Group Ltd v Pyke* [2002] 2 BCLC 201, CA and *Jason v Chen* [2016] HKFCA 23 at [92]–[106]. In fact the New Mashonaland Exploration Co soon collapsed into insolvent liquidation and the director whose appointment had been in dispute was fortunate to escape liability for misfeasance in making negligent loans of company money: *Re New Mashonaland Exploration Co* [1892] 3 Ch 577.
   [51] *Overend, Gurney & Co v Gibb* (1872) LR 5 HL 480, 487, HL; Lord Hatherley explained that directors would be guilty of *crassa negligentia* if 'they were cognisant of circumstances of such a character, so plain, so manifest, and so simple of appreciation, that no men with any ordinary degree of prudence, acting on their own behalf, would have entered into such a transaction as they entered into'.
   [52] *Lagunas Nitrate Co v Lagunas Syndicate* [1899] 2 Ch 392, 435, CA. In *Re Brazilian Rubber Plantations and Estates Ltd* [1911] 1 Ch 425 the directors, who somewhat surprisingly were acquitted of negligence and were in any event entitled to rely on an exemption clause in the articles, consisted of a baronet who was 'absolutely ignorant of business', a banker from Bath who was 'seventy-five years of age and very deaf', a rubber broker who understood that his only function was to value the rubber if and when it arrived in England, and a businessman who joined because he considered that the banker and rubber broker were 'good men'.

officers.[53] Therefore shareholders and creditors had to put up with the blunders of foolish and unwise directors[54] or of a board comprising 'a set of amiable lunatics'.[55]

Subsequent changes to the Companies Acts, including provisions to enforce fair dealing, to **1.23** strengthen the duties of directors, to maintain sufficient accounting records, and for the disqualification of unfit directors, have required directors to be more conscientiously involved in a company's affairs. This has encouraged the court to apply an objective standard of care, skill, and diligence and to adopt the twofold test in the Insolvency Act, s 213(4) (wrongful trading).[56]

Now the general duties of directors are codified by the 2006 Act and these duties are but- **1.24** tressed by provisions requiring directors to disclose interests in existing transactions and to obtain the approval of members for certain transactions in which they are interested.[57] The statutory statement of directors' fiduciary duties includes elements of reform in relation to the duty to promote the success of the company and in permitting the independent directors to authorize a matter in which a director has a conflict of interest.[58]

(5) Shareholders' remedies

Where directors have misapplied company property or otherwise caused the company loss, **1.25** the company can sue to recover its property or to obtain compensation even though it was party to the impugned transaction.[59] If the wrongdoers are in control of the company, they will be able to prevent it from suing. To prevent this injustice, in *Hichens v Congreve*,[60] decided in 1828, Lord Lyndhurst LC held that shareholders could sue on behalf of themselves and the other shareholders for the purpose of compelling the directors to refund monies improperly withdrawn by them. The limits of Lord Lyndhurst's decision were soon exposed by the well-known case of *Foss v Harbottle*,[61] decided in 1843, which established (i) the 'proper plaintiff' principle, by which prima facie the corporation is the proper claimant in proceedings in respect of a wrong alleged to have been done to it, and (ii) the 'majority rule' principle, by which an individual shareholder will not be allowed to pursue proceedings on behalf of himself and all other shareholders if the alleged wrong was within the powers of the company, since, in those circumstances, the majority of the shareholders might ratify the allegedly wrongful transaction; if they did not, they would be able to put the company in motion to bring the necessary proceedings.

The rule in *Foss v Harbottle* did not apply to claims to enforce a shareholder's personal rights, **1.26** as distinct from rights belonging to the company. Nor did the rule prevent an individual shareholder from bringing proceedings (later called a 'derivative action') in respect of a wrong

---

[53] *Re City Equitable Fire Insurance Co* [1925] Ch 407, 428, 429; *Dorchester Finance Co Ltd v Stebbing* (1977) [1989] BCLC 498, 501, 502. As to relying on other officers: *Dovey v Corey* [1901] AC 477, 485, HL.
[54] *Turquand v Marshall* (1869) LR 4 Ch App 376, 386.
[55] In argument in *Pavlides v Jensen* [1956] Ch 565, 570.
[56] *Norman v Theodore Goddard* [1991] BCLC 1028, 1030, 1031, 1037, 1038; *Bishopsgate Investment Management Ltd v Maxwell* [1994] 1 All ER 261, CA; *Re D'Jan of London Ltd* [1994] 1 BCLC 561, 563.
[57] The general duties of directors are in 2006 Act, ss 170–81 and the supporting disclosure and transparency obligations are in ss 182–231.
[58] 2006 Act, s 175.
[59] *AG v Wilson* (1840) Cr & Ph 1, 24.
[60] (1828) 4 Russ 562.
[61] (1843) 2 Hare 461. Followed in *Mozley v Alston* (1847) 1 Ph 790.

done by the directors to the company where (i) the transaction in question was beyond the powers of the company or illegal, (ii) there had been a fraud on the minority shareholders and the wrongdoers were in control, or (iii) the act required the sanction of a special majority which could not be obtained.[62] In relation to the 'fraud on the minority' exception the law was 'complex and obscure'.[63] Litigation could become protracted, expensive, and damaging to the company, which could be 'killed by kindness'.[64] Rules of court were introduced to control the procedure.[65]

1.27   In 1980 a new remedy, now contained in the 2006 Act, ss 994–9, was introduced to protect members from unfair prejudice.[66] The new remedy meant that minority shareholders would seldom need to resort to a derivative action. The 2006 Act has reformed this area of the law in two further ways. First, s 239 prevents the director and those connected with him from voting on a resolution to ratify his own wrong. Secondly, Part 11, ss 260–4, has introduced a new statutory code for derivative actions, which replaces the rule in *Foss v Harbottle* and its exceptions.[67]

(6) Decision-making of members

1.28   A company's articles invariably provide that the directors have unfettered powers of management which cannot be interfered with by the members except by altering the articles, giving directions pursuant to a special resolution, or by removing and replacing directors.[68] The directors may need to obtain a resolution of the members, whether to alter the constitution; to consent to, approve, or authorize some transaction or arrangement; or to ratify acts of directors or for some other purpose. In this connection the courts have developed three rules. First, the notice of the meeting to consider the resolution (or statement accompanying the proposed written resolution) must give 'a fair and candid and reasonable explanation' of the proposed business and must not be misleading or tricky.[69] If it does not, any resolution purportedly passed will be invalid. This rule remains relevant to the provisions of the 2006 Act, Part 13, about resolutions and meetings.

---

[62] *Burland v Earle* [1902] AC 83, 93, HL, per Lord Davey; *Edwards v Halliwell* [1950] 2 All ER 1064, 1067, CA; *Daniels v Daniels* [1978] Ch 406, 408, 414, where Templeman J said that the minority could sue 'where directors use their powers, intentionally or unintentionally, fraudulently or negligently, in a manner which benefits themselves at the expense of the company'; *Prudential Assurance Co Ltd v Newman Industries Ltd* [1982] Ch 204, 210, CA; *Estmanco (Kilner House) Ltd v Greater London Council* [1982] 1 WLR 2, 12; *Smith v Croft (No 2)* [1988] Ch 114, 173. The minority have not been allowed to proceed on an allegation of mere negligence without fraud: *Pavlides v Jensen* [1956] Ch 565; *Heyting v Dupont* [1964] 1 WLR 843, CA.

[63] Law Commission Consultation Paper No 142 *Shareholder Remedies* at para 1.6.

[64] *Prudential Assurance Co Ltd v Newman Industries Ltd* [1982] Ch 204, 221, CA.

[65] RSC Order 15, rule 12A, replaced by CPR 19.9. In *Barrett v Duckett* [1995] 1 BCLC 243, 249, 250, CA, Peter Gibson LJ stated the general principles governing such actions.

[66] 1980 Act, s 75, which was replaced by 1985 Act, s 459. On 1 October 2007 the 2006 Act, Part 30, ss 994–9 came into force and replaced 1985 Act, s 459. 1980 Act, s 75 replaced 1948 Act, s 210, which provided the first statutory remedy for oppression, but in terms that were too onerous on the applicant.

[67] The common law principles continue to apply to double derivative claims, as discussed in Chapter 22; see *Universal Project Management Services Ltd v Fort Gilkicker Ltd* [2013] Ch 551; *Abouraya v Sigmund* [2015] BCC 503 at paras 13–16; *Bhullar v Bhullar* [2016] 1 BCLC 106. They also apply to derivative claims in respect of foreign companies: *Novatrust Ltd v Kea Investments Ltd* [2014] EWHC 4061 (Ch).

[68] Table A, reg 70; Model Article (pcls) 3 and Model Article (plc) 4.

[69] *Kaye v Croydon Tramways Co* [1898] 1 Ch 358, 373, CA; *Tiessen v Henderson* [1899] 1 Ch 861; *Baillie v Oriental Telephone and Electric Co Ltd* [1915] 1 Ch 503, CA; *Pacific Coast Coal Mines Ltd v Arbuthnot* [1917] AC 607, 618, PC; *Clarkson v Davies* [1923] AC 100, PC.

Secondly, there is an equitable rule that, in order for a resolution to be effective, the voting **1.29** rights of the members in support of it must be exercised in good faith in the interests of the company as a whole.[70] The CLR said the rule was rather 'rather ill-defined' and limited it to alterations of articles and class right cases,[71] but in *British America Nickel Corp Ltd v MJ O'Brien Ltd*[72] Lord Haldane referred to 'a general principle, which is applicable to all authorities conferred on majorities of classes enabling them to bind minorities; namely, that the power given must be exercised for the purpose of benefiting the class as a whole, and not merely individual members only'. In cases where the rule does apply, the court would only find that voting rights had been invalidly exercised if it is satisfied that no reasonable person could have considered the resolution to be for the benefit of the company.[73]

Thirdly, there is a rule that the company is bound by the unanimous agreement of its mem- **1.30** bers entitled to attend and vote on the matter without the need for a formal resolution, whether in writing or at a meeting.[74] This rule, which is expressly preserved by the 2006 Act, ss 239(6)(a) and 281(4), is subject to exceptions, the scope of which is not clearly marked out, where a transaction is beyond the powers of the company, such as a gift to directors out of capital,[75] or where the company is insolvent or nearly so.[76]

(7) Accounts

Like any other fiduciary a director is liable to account to the company. The 1844 Act stated the **1.31** obligation of directors to keep books of account, prepare accounts to be laid before the members, and have them audited. The 1862 Act left those matters to Table A,[77] but the twentieth-century Companies Acts have regulated those obligations and provided for the public filing of accounts. The provisions concerning accounts, reports, and audit are now contained in the 2006 Act, Parts 15 and 16. Any failure of a director to comply with his statutory duties in

---

[70] *Allen v Gold Reefs of West Africa Ltd* [1900] 1 Ch 656, 671, CA. Also: *Blisset v Daniel* (1853) 10 Hare 493 (a partnership case); *Menier v Hooper's Telegraph Works* (1874) 9 Ch App 350; *Dominion Cotton Mills Co v Amyot* [1912] AC 546, 551–3, PC; *Cook v Deeks* [1916] 1 AC 554, 564, PC; *Greenhalgh v Arderne Cinemas Ltd* [1951] Ch 286, 291, CA; *Re Holders Investment Trust Ltd* [1971] 1 WLR 583; *Estmanco (Kilner House) Ltd v Greater London Council* [1982] 1 WLR 2, 16; *Smith v Croft (No 2)* [1988] Ch 114, 186.

[71] CLR: *Developing the Framework* at para 4.142. In CLR: *Completing the Structure* at paras 5.94–5.101, 5.110 the CLR proposed retaining the rule, but only in relation to changes to the constitution and class rights and cases where the votes of the majority are tainted. The CLR recommended the reforms in 2006 Act, s 239 to deal with this area: CLR: *Final Report* at paras 7.52–7.62.

[72] [1927] AC 369, 371, PC; *Redwood Master Fund Ltd v TD Bank Europe Ltd* [2006] 1 BCLC 149 (both cases concerning the power to modify debentures or loan notes). Briggs J reviewed these authorities in *Assengon Asset Management SA v Irish Bank Resolution Corp Ltd* [2012] EWHC 2090 (Ch) at paras 41–9. For a summary of the principles, see *Re Charterhouse Capital Ltd* [2015] 2 BCLC 627, CA, at para 90.

[73] *Shuttleworth v Cox Bros & Co (Maidenhead) Ltd* [1927] 2 KB 9, 18, 23, CA; *Greenhalgh v Arderne Cinemas Ltd* [1951] Ch 286, 291, CA; *Citco Banking Corp NV v Pusser's Ltd* [2007] 2 BCLC 483, PC. In *Standard Chartered Bank v Walker* [1992] 1 WLR 561 Vinelott J invoked the court's Mareva jurisdiction to restrain a shareholder from causing wilful damage to the value of his shares by voting his shares to block a restructuring proposal.

[74] *Re Duomatic Ltd* [1969] 2 Ch 365, 373; *Cane v Jones* [1981] 1 WLR 1451. The informal unanimous decision is attributed to the company: *Multinational Gas and Petrochemical Co v Multinational Gas and Petrochemical Services Ltd* [1983] Ch 258, 269, 288–90, CA; *Meridian Global Funds Management Asia v Securities Commission* [1995] 2 AC 500, 506, PC.

[75] *Re George Newman & Co* [1895] 1 Ch 674, 686, CA; *Cook v Deeks* [1916] 1 AC 554, 564, PC.

[76] *Kinsela v Russell Kinsela Pty Ltd* (1986) 4 NSWLR 722, 730; approved in *West Mercia Safetywear Ltd v Dodd* [1988] BCLC 250, 252, 253, CA.

[77] 1862 Act, Table A, regs 78–94.

relation to accounts is to be taken into consideration in determining his fitness to be a director for the purposes of disqualification proceedings.[78]

1.32 In addition, if a company becomes subject to insolvency proceedings (administration, administrative receivership, or liquidation) or proposes a voluntary arrangement, directors become subject to additional duties to provide a statement of affairs and provide information to the office-holder or the official receiver.[79] Furthermore directors may be called to account in a private or public examination.[80] If in the winding up it is found that directors have failed to keep proper books of account or have falsified or destroyed them, a criminal offence is committed which is punishable by imprisonment.[81]

(8) Maintenance of capital

1.33 In their management of the company, directors are bound by the fundamental common law principle of maintenance of capital, breach of which exposes the directors responsible to liability for damages for breach of duty. Since, in most cases the liability of members is limited, the paid up share capital is the fund of last resort available to meet the claims of creditors. The principle of maintenance of capital is therefore a principle for the protection of creditors.[82] Maintenance of capital is now entirely regulated by statute,[83] but at common law it was manifest in four rules. First, shares could not be issued at a discount: the company must not be entitled to receive less than the nominal amount of the share, par value, in consideration for its allotment.[84] Secondly, a person who retained his shares, which he had been induced to take by fraud, could not claim damages, because that would infringe the principle of maintenance of capital. His only remedy was to rescind the contract on the ground of fraud and recover his money, provided he did so before the company went into liquidation.[85] Now, by the 2006 Act, s 655 holding or having held shares is not a bar to obtaining damages or other compensation from a company.[86] Thirdly, a company could not return capital to its members except by a reduction of capital in accordance with the provisions of the Companies Acts.[87] Now the 2006 Act contains detailed provisions for the reduction of capital and the circumstances in which a company may redeem or purchase its own shares.[88] Fourthly, although the

---

[78] CDDA, s 12C and Sch 1, paras 1 and 6 (which came into force on 1 October 2015 and replaced s 9 and the original Sch 1, which were repealed).

[79] Statement of affairs: Insolvency Act, ss 2(3)47, 99, 131. Sch B1, paras 47 and 48; Insolvency Rules 1.5, 1.56, 2.28–2.32, 3.3–3.7, 4.32–4.42 (and IR 2016, rr 2.6, 2.7, 3.28–3.34, 4.6–4.11, 6.2–6.7 and 7.40–7.45 after 6 April 2017).

[80] Private examinations are provided for by the Insolvency Act 1986, s 236 and can be traced back to the 1844 Winding Up Act, s 15. Public examination is provided for by the Insolvency Act, s 133 and can be traced back to the Companies (Winding Up) Act 1890, s 8.

[81] Insolvency Act, ss 206–11.

[82] *Trevor v Whitworth* (1887) 12 App Cas 409, 423, HL; *The Ooregum Gold Mining Company of India Ltd v Roper* [1892] AC 125, 133, HL.

[83] 2006 Act, Parts 17, 18, and 23.

[84] This principle is governed by statutory provision: 2006 Act, ss 580–609, 1150, 1153.

[85] *Houldsworth v City of Glasgow Bank* (1880) 5 App Cas 317; *Re Addlestone Linoleum Co* (1887) 37 Ch D 191, CA. The principle also applied to claims under Misrepresentation Act 1967, s 2(2). It did not apply to purchases in the after-market: *Soden v British & Commonwealth Holdings plc* [1998] AC 298, HL. Note the departure from the principle taken by the High Court of Australia in *Sons of Gwalia Ltd v Margaretic* [2007] HCA 1 and the subsequent amendment to the Australian Corporations Act, made by the Corporations (Sons of Gwalia) Act 2010.

[86] On 1 October 2009 this section replaced 1985 Act, s 111A, which was inserted by 1989 Act, s 131.

[87] *Trevor v Whitworth* (1887) 12 App Cas 409.

[88] 2006 Act, ss 641–723. Since 1 October 2008 private companies no longer have to obtain court sanction for a reduction of capital.

way in which a company distributes its profits is a matter for its constitution, it could not pay dividends or make other distributions out of capital, since that would involve an unlawful distribution of capital.[89] The rules controlling the making of distributions are contained in the 2006 Act, ss 829–53.

D. The Development of Statute Law Affecting Directors before the Companies Act 2006

The Companies Acts provide for the incorporation of companies and lay down the frame-   **1.34** work for their operation. To an ever-increasing extent, in order to protect members and persons dealing with a company and improve standards of corporate governance, the Companies Acts have imposed restrictions on the management of companies, required public disclosure of information about the company, and imposed sanctions and provided remedies for default. The techniques adopted have included: (i) making certain conduct a criminal offence (eg fraudulent trading and some contraventions of the Companies Acts); (ii) disqualifying bankrupts and fraudulent or unfit persons from being directors or concerned in the management of a company; (iii) making some transactions unlawful (eg financial assistance in the purchase of a company's own shares and formerly tax-free payments to directors and loans to directors); and (iv) to protect the interests of members, making some transactions with directors unlawful unless approved by the members (payments for loss of office and transactions with directors) and providing members with a statutory remedy for unfair prejudice (formerly oppression).

Since 1844 winding up has been the process through which directors have been brought   **1.35** to account for their management of the company. Since 1890 the procedures have been strengthened to give creditors more control of the winding up where the company is insolvent, to improve the means of calling directors to account, and to make directors personally liable for fraudulent trading. The procedures have been extensively modernized by the Insolvency Act 1986, which has made directors personally liable for wrongful trading and contravention of the 'phoenix company' provisions.

Since the 1856 Act the Board of Trade, or its successor Department, has had power, on the   **1.36** application of a specified proportion of members, to appoint inspectors to examine the affairs of the company. The 1967 Act extended these powers and enabled the Board of Trade to appoint inspectors whenever it had good reason to do so. Now the powers are held by the Secretary of State for the Department of Business, Energy and Industrial Strategy (BEIS) and the provisions are contained in the 1985 Act, Part XIV, ss 431–7, 439–53, as amended by the 2006 Act, Part 32.

(1) Legislation for companies 1844 to 1890

The Joint Stock Companies Act 1844 provided the first general statutory scheme for compa-   **1.37** nies to obtain corporate personality through registration with the Registrar of Companies. It suffered from two serious defects. First, the process of registration was cumbersome and the company could not enjoy the benefits of the Act until it was complete. Secondly, members

---

[89] *MacDougall v Jersey Imperial Hotel Co* (1864) 2 Hem & M 528; *Dovey v Corey* [1901] AC 477; *Ammonia Soda Co v Chamberlain* [1918] 1 Ch 266, 292, CA.

were personally liable for the debts of the company.[90] In order to protect the members who were at risk, their approval was required for the purchase and sale of shares by directors, loans to directors, and contracts with directors outside the ordinary course of business and at least two directors had to sign larger contracts and bills.[91] Directors were responsible for maintaining the company's books of account and having the accounts confirmed by an auditor.

1.38 The 1844 Winding Up Act provided for the winding up of companies unable to meet their debts and was intended 'to make better provision for discovery of the abuses that may have attended the formation or management of the affairs' of companies and 'for ascertaining the causes of their failure'. Members would be the principal beneficiaries of these provisions since they were personally liable for the company's debts. Directors were obliged to produce a balance sheet, provide information on which they would be examined, and hand over company property.[92] The court would make a report on the causes of failure which could lead to criminal prosecution.[93]

1.39 The main defect of the 1844 Act, the failure to provide for limited liability, was remedied by the Limited Liability Act 1855, which allowed a company to be incorporated with limited liability if its name included the word 'limited'. The 1855 Act contained a number of provisions to protect persons dealing with the company, including one, which continued to be used in subsequent Companies Acts until repealed by the 2006 Act, making directors personally liable on all bills and other documents on which its correct name did not appear.[94]

1.40 The Joint Stock Companies Act 1856 consolidated and amended the law relating to companies, including winding up. It omitted many of the sanctions in the 1844 and 1855 Acts,[95] but included, for the first time, provisions for inspectors to examine the affairs of the company, either appointed by the Board of Trade on the application of members or by special resolution of members.[96]

1.41 The 1862 Act is generally regarded as the Act that 'laid down the foundation upon which subsequent legislation relating to companies has been built'.[97] The underlying philosophy was that a company should be free to determine the way in which it would be managed and administered, although default articles in the form of Table A were provided. A director could only be removed by special resolution.[98] Directors and managers were liable for a fine, along with the company, if they knowingly and willfully authorized or permitted contravention of certain provisions for record-keeping and transparency.[99]

1.42 Among the provisions of the 1862 Act for winding up companies were provisions for the court to order officers and others to deliver up monies, books, papers, and other property to

---

[90] 1844 Act, s 25.
[91] 1844 Act, ss 27, 29, 44–6.
[92] 1844 Winding Up Act, ss 12–15.
[93] 1844 Winding Up Act, ss 26 and 27.
[94] Limited Liability Act 1855, ss 4, 5, 9, 10, 13. The provision referred to last appeared as 1985 Act, s 349, which was repealed on 1 October 2008 by the 2006 Act Commencement Order No 5, Art 8(b) and Sch 3.
[95] 1856 Act, ss 14 and 31.
[96] 1856 Act, ss 48–52.
[97] Report of the Cork Committee at para 75.
[98] 1862 Act, s 51 and Table A, reg 65. That remained the position until 1948 Act, s 184 gave an overriding power to remove directors by ordinary resolution.
[99] 1862 Act, ss 25, 27, 32, 34, 43, 44, 46, 53, 54, 58, 60.

which the company is entitled,[100] for the private examination of, and production of books by, officers and others,[101] and for the court to assess damages against delinquent directors and officers.[102] If a director or other person was found to have falsified the company's books he was guilty of an offence, punishable by imprisonment.[103] There were also provisions for the prosecution of a director who had committed an offence in relation to the company, but on terms that the court could order that the costs and expenses of the prosecution could be paid out of the company's assets.[104]

The Companies Act 1867 amended the 1862 Act[105] and included a new provision for the   **1.43** memorandum of a company with limited liability to provide for directors, managers, or managing directors to have unlimited liability and for the memorandum to be altered by special resolution to render unlimited the liability of those officers. Although the provision was seldom, if ever, used, it was retained in the successive Companies Acts until it was repealed on 1 October 2009[106] and it is reflected in the Insolvency Act, s 75.

In 1890 there were two major reforming statutes affecting directors. The first was the   **1.44** Companies (Winding Up) Act 1890, which was 'clearly aimed at fraudulent and dishonest company promoters and directors'.[107] It improved the statutory powers for investigating the affairs of the company by requiring directors to make out and submit to the official receiver a statement of affairs and providing machinery for the public examination of promoters, directors, and officers of the company and gave the court somewhat wider powers to assess damages against delinquent directors and promoters than had been contained in the 1862 Act, s 165.[108] The second reforming statute was the Directors' Liability Act 1890, which was a prompt legislative response to the refusal by the House of Lords in *Derry v Peek*[109] to hold that a director could be personally liable for negligent misstatement in a prospectus. Section 3 made directors and others responsible for issuing a prospectus personally liable to subscribers for any false statement unless they could show that the untrue statement was made by an expert on whom they could reasonably rely or by an official person in a public document, or was one that they had reasonable grounds for believing was true.[110]

---

[100] 1862 Act, s 100. This section was the derivation of 1948 Act, s 258 and is the predecessor of Insolvency Act, s 234, which uses broader language.

[101] 1862 Act, ss 115–17. These sections were the derivation, subject to amendment by the 1928 Act, of 1948 Act, s 268 and are the predecessors of Insolvency Act, ss 236 and 237.

[102] 1862 Act, s 165. See para 1.18 above. This section was replaced by the Companies (Winding Up) Act 1890, s 10, which was the derivation, subject to amendment by the 1893 and 1928 Acts, of 1948 Act, s 333 and is the predecessor of Insolvency Act, s 212, whose provisions are significantly broader.

[103] 1862 Act, s 166. This section was the derivation, subject to amendment by the 1947 Act, of 1948 Act, s 329, and is the predecessor of Insolvency Act, s 209.

[104] 1862 Act, ss 167 and 168. These sections were the derivation, subject to amendment by the 1928 and 1947 Acts (to remove the provision for the costs and expenses of prosecution to be borne by the company), of 1948 Act, s 334 and are the predecessors of Insolvency Act, ss 218 and 219.

[105] The most significant amendments were provisions enabling a company to reduce its capital. 1867 Act, s 37 re-enacted 1856 Act, s 41 (which had been inadvertently omitted from the 1862 Act) and provided for the ways in which contracts on behalf of the company could be made.

[106] 1985 Act, ss 306 and 307 were repealed by 2006 Act Commencement Order No 8, para 4 and Sch 1.

[107] Cork Report at para 78.

[108] Companies (Winding Up) Act 1890, ss 7, 8, 10.

[109] (1889) 14 App Cas 337. Directors were personally liable for their own deceits: *Barwick v English Joint Stock Bank* (1867) 2 Exch 259; *Standard Chartered Bank v Pakistan Shipping Corp* [2003] 1 AC 959, 968, HL.

[110] This section was the derivation, subject to amendments made by the 1928 and 1947 Acts, of 1948 Act, ss 40, 43, 46 and 1985 Act, ss 61, 62, 67–9, 71. Those sections were repealed by Financial Services Act 1986, s 212(3) and Sch 17, Part I and were replaced by s 150 of that Act. The current provision is FSMA, s 90.

(2) The Companies Acts 1900 to 1985

1.45 In the period between the end of the nineteenth century and the UK joining the European Community in 1972 a pattern of company law reform emerged under which a committee would be appointed to report on amendments to company law, a Companies Act would give effect to the recommendations adopted by the government, and a consolidating statute would follow. The committees' recommendations invariably responded to recently exposed scandals and mischief arising from the lack of regulation in the original 1862 Act. Thus in 1895 a committee under the chairmanship of Lord Davey reported on what amendments to the Companies Acts were necessary 'with a view to the better prevention of fraud in relation to the formation and management of companies'.[111] Some of its recommendations, mainly concerning control of the abuse of the prospectus and registration of charges, were included in the 1900 Act.[112] The Loreburn Committee[113] reported in 1906. Its recommendations were enacted by the 1907 Act and consolidated with the surviving provisions of the Companies Acts 1862–1900 into the Companies (Consolidation) Act 1908. The Greene Committee, under the chairmanship of Wilfred Greene KC (later Lord Greene MR), published its report in 1926. Its recommendations were enacted by the Companies Act 1928 and brought into effect by the consolidating Companies Act 1929. Similarly the Cohen Committee, under the chairmanship of Cohen J (later Lord Cohen) reported in June 1945. Its recommendations were enacted by the Companies Act 1947 and its provisions consolidated into the Companies Act 1948. In June 1962 the Jenkins Committee, of which Lord Jenkins was chairman, published its report. The previous pattern of implementing recommendations was somewhat broken, because the Companies Act 1967 only implemented some of the Jenkins Committee recommendations (eg disclosure and accounts). Its recommendation for reform to give minority shareholders meaningful relief from unfair prejudice was not enacted until 1980, and a consolidating statute did not follow until 1985, by which time there had been several other reforming statutes.

1.46 The four twentieth-century Committees proceeded on the basis that the great majority of companies were honestly and conscientiously managed and that, in the words of the Greene Committee, it was 'most undesirable, in order to defeat an occasional wrongdoer, to impose restrictions which would seriously hamper the activities of honest men and would inevitably re-act upon the commerce and prosperity of the country'.[114] The Cohen Committee took a more interventionist view, believing that the fullest practicable disclosure of information concerning a company's affairs should be made to shareholders, creditors, and the general public, that the requirements of the Companies Acts should be enforced more rigorously, and that improper or dishonest conduct should be investigated and prosecuted.[115]

---

[111] The committee was a distinguished one and included Chitty J, Vaughan Williams J, Mr HB Buckley QC, and Mr F Palmer.

[112] Companies Act 1900, ss 14–16 contained new provisions for registration of charges. The Davey Committee also recommended reforms to the law concerning qualification shares of directors and the particulars to be stated in a prospectus, which were enacted by the Companies Act 1900. In 1906 the Loreburn Committee found that these requirements were so stringent that they discouraged the use of a prospectus and deterred honest and prudent men from accepting directorships (para 16(3) of its Report). They were repealed and replaced by the less onerous requirements of the 1907 Act.

[113] The Loreburn Committee included Mr Gore-Browne and Messrs Palmer and Waterhouse who had been members of the Davey Committee.

[114] Report of the Loreburn Committee at para 8; Report of the Greene Committee at paras 7 and 9; Report of the Cohen Committee at para 5; Report of the Jenkins Committee at paras 11–14.

[115] Report of the Cohen Committee at paras 5 and 6.

None of the Committees made any recommendations in relation to a company's capacity, **1.47** the ultra vires rule, or the power of directors to bind the company.[116] Reform in that area had to await the implementation of the First EEC Directive on Harmonisation of Company Law (paragraph 1.11 above).

The process of reform resumed with the Insolvency Act 1976, s 9, and the Companies Acts **1.48** 1976, 1980, and 1981 (the latter two Acts also giving effect to the Second and Fourth EEC Directives on Harmonisation of Company Law). The reforms made by those Acts were consolidated into the 1985 Act with provisions from the 1948 and 1967 Acts. The following paragraphs provide a brief summary of the course of the reform of the law relating to directors, following the order in which these matters are addressed in this work.

Appointment and removal of directors

On the recommendation of the Cohen Committee every company had to have at least one **1.49** director and a secretary;[117] the appointment of a director was to be voted on individually, and the members were given an overriding power to remove a director by ordinary resolution, but without prejudice to the director's right to claim compensation and protest his removal.[118] Except that a private company need not have a secretary, these provisions were adopted by the 2006 Act.[119]

Directors' duties

In response to the unsatisfactory state of the law in relation to a director's duty of care **1.50** (paragraph 1.22 above), the Davey Committee recommended a statutory statement of this duty in objective terms: 'Every director shall be under an obligation to the company to use reasonable care and prudence in the exercise of his powers, and shall be liable to compensate the company for any damage incurred by reason of neglect to use such care and prudence.'[120] This recommendation was not adopted and the Loreburn Committee did not repeat it. Instead the Loreburn Committee recommended, and the government accepted, that the

---

[116] The Cohen Committee considered that 'the doctrine of ultra vires is an illusory protection for the shareholders and yet may be a pitfall for third parties dealing with the company' and favoured its abolition (para 12), but the Jenkins Committee disagreed (paras 35–41). On the recommendation of the Cohen Committee (para 12) a company could change its objects by special resolution without the need for court sanction; 1947 Act, s 76; 1948 Act, s 5.

[117] Report of the Cohen Committee at para 55 and 1948 Act, ss 177–9.

[118] Report of the Cohen Committee at para 130 and 1948 Act, ss 183 and 184. The Committee also recommended a compulsory retirement age of 70 for directors of public companies: Report at para 131 and 1948 Act, ss 185 and 186, which were re-enacted as 1985 Act, ss 293 and 294 (repealed by the 2006 Act on 1 October 2009). Instead the 2006 Act is concerned to prevent the appointment of under-age directors: ss 157–9.

[119] 2006 Act, ss 155, 160, 168, 270, 271.

[120] Report of the Davey Committee at para 32 and draft clause 10(2). The Davey Committee recognized that the draft law went beyond any actual decision of the courts. In an appendix to the report (pp 19 and 20) Dr Schuster compared the amount of diligence expected of a director under English law with German law:

> German law requires the diligence of a prudent trader, and presumes negligence in case of loss. English law recognises a shadowy liability for 'crassa negligentia' and presumes diligence. German law makes a director liable for non-attendance to his duties; according to English law a director who never attends any board meetings cannot come under any liability, and a director who votes for a resolution sanctioning an 'ultra vires' expenditure of the company's funds is not liable for such expenditure if he has not actually signed the cheque by which such expenditure is effected. [Referring implicitly to *Re Cardiff Savings Bank* [1892] 2 Ch 100 and explicitly to *Cullerne v London and Suburban BS* (1890) 25 QBD 485, CA.]

court should have a statutory power to relieve directors who have acted honestly and reasonably, from liability for negligence or breach of trust.[121]

1.51 The Greene Committee said that 'to attempt by statute to define the duties of directors would be a hopeless task', but it observed that provisions in the articles or contract exempting directors from liability for negligence or breach of trust gave 'a quite unjustifiable protection to directors' and recommended that they should be void. It found the general law of negligence satisfactory, but recommended that, in exercising its power to relieve a director, the court should take into account all the circumstances of his appointment.[122] These recommendations were adopted in the 1929 Act, ss 152 and 372 and, in modified form continue in effect in the 2006 Act.[123]

1.52 The Cohen Committee did not address the issue of directors' duties, except to advocate strengthening their civil and criminal liability for false and misleading statements in a prospectus.[124]

1.53 The Jenkins Committee rejected the suggestion that the existing law on directors' duties should be codified, because of the danger that there might be gaps in the law as codified. Instead, it favoured a statement of the basic principles underlying the fiduciary relationship of a director to his company; namely a duty to observe the utmost good faith and act honestly and a duty not to make, and to account for, secret profits.[125] Attempts were made to include a statutory statement of a director's fiduciary duties in Companies Bills of 1973 and 1978, but both were lost because of general elections. Instead, the 1980 Act, s 46 introduced a duty owed by a director to the company to have regard to the interests of the company's employees as well as the interests of its members.[126]

Transactions with directors

1.54 Following the recommendation of the Greene Committee, the 1929 Act, s 128 required a company's accounts laid before the company in general meeting to contain particulars of loans to, and remuneration of, directors other than managing directors.[127] The 1929 Act included other new provisions to compel transparency in directors' dealings. A director had a duty to disclose his interests in a contract or proposed contract to the board and in default was liable to a fine.[128] It was not lawful for a director to receive a payment for loss of office in

---

[121] Report of the Loreburn Committee at para 24. The recommendation, modelled on Judicial Trustees Act 1896, s 3(1)(a), was enacted as Companies Act 1907, s 32, which is the derivation, with amendments made by the 1928 and 1947 Acts, of 1985 Act, s 727 and of the current 2006 Act, s 1157. Mr Edgar Speyer, a businessman and member of the Committee, added a note on para 24 of the Report in which he said that 'the immunity of directors from liability for negligence lies at the seat of the deplorable abuses in company matters in this country' and urged a statutory statement of a director's personal liability for negligence in the discharge of his duties.

[122] Report of the Greene Committee at paras 46 and 47. Reference was made to *Re Brazilian Rubber Estates Ltd* [1911] 1 Ch 425.

[123] 1929 Act, s 152 is the derivation of 1985 Act, s 310 (as originally enacted). 2006 Act, ss 232–8 deal with provisions protecting directors from liability.

[124] Report of the Cohen Committee at paras 41–6 and 1948 Act, ss 43 and 44.

[125] Report of the Jenkins Committee at paras 86, 87, 99(a).

[126] This was re-enacted by 1985 Act, s 309. Employees' interests are now a factor to be considered in the duty to promote the success of the company (2006 Act, s 172(1)(b)).

[127] Report of the Greene Committee at paras 48–50. These provisions were the tentative precursors of provisions in 1985 Act, Part X, underpinning directors' duties and the provisions in the 2006 Act, Part 10, Chapter 4 (Ch 18 of this work). A company could avoid the need to disclose directors' remuneration by appointing all its directors as managing directors: Cohen Report at para 89.

[128] 1929 Act, s 149, the precursor of 1985 Act, s 317; now 2006 Act, ss 177 and 182.

connection with a transfer of all or part of the company's undertaking or property without the approval of the company.[129]

On the recommendation of the Cohen Committee, the tax-free payment of fees and salaries to directors and loans to directors were made unlawful and absolutely prohibited,[130] and a payment to a director as compensation for loss of office was not lawful unless approved by the company.[131] The Cohen Committee also recommended that there should be more disclosure of share transactions by directors and that all directors' remuneration should be disclosed, including that earned as managing director or executive, and pensions.[132] These disclosure requirements have been enhanced by subsequent Acts requiring details of remuneration to be disclosed in annual accounts and providing for directors' service contracts to be available for inspection. **1.55**

The Jenkins Committee recommended the prohibition of directors' dealing in options to buy or sell quoted shares or debentures of his company or its associated companies and made other recommendations for reform in relation to compensation for directors' loss of office, disclosure of directors' other interests, and loans to directors. The 1967 Act gave effect to these recommendations by making dealings by directors in options an offence, requiring directors' service contracts to be open to inspection by members, and imposing a duty on directors to notify the company of their interests in shares or debentures of the company or associated companies.[133] **1.56**

As 'a hasty legislative response' to a number of financial scandals in the 1970s,[134] the 1980 Act, ss 47–61 provided that certain transactions in which directors had a conflict of interest were invalid unless disclosed to and approved by the members; namely contracts of employment, substantial property transactions, and loans.[135] These provisions, which applied to shadow directors,[136] and the surviving provisions of the 1948 Act concerning transactions with directors were incorporated into the 1985 Act, Part X.[137] **1.57**

---

[129] 1929 Act, s 150, the precursor of 1985 Act, s 312; now 2006 Act, ss 215 and 217.

[130] Report of the Cohen Committee at paras 88 and 90 and 1948 Act, ss 189 and 190. The corresponding sections in 1985 Act (ss 311, 330–42) have been repealed by 2006 Act and replaced in the case of loans by a requirement of members' approval (2006 Act, ss 197–214).

[131] Report of the Cohen Committee at para 92 and 1948 Act, s 191. This provision, with the related provisions brought into effect by the 1929 Act, were included in 1985 Act, Part X. The corresponding provisions in the 2006 Act, but in different terms, are ss 215–22. Since the provisions concerning payment for loss of office did not apply to covenanted payments (*Taupo Totara Timber Co Ltd v Rowe* [1978] AC 537, PC), they were riddled with loopholes and easily evaded: Law Commission Joint Consultation Paper *Company Directors: Regulating Conflicts of Interest and Formulating a Statement of Duties* (No 153) at para 4.19.

[132] Report of the Cohen Committee at paras 89, 90, 93 and 1948 Act, s 196.

[133] Report of the Jenkins Committee at paras 92–8, 99(b)–(p); 1967 Act, ss 25–32; and 1976 Act, ss 24–7. The provisions about options and interests in shares, which were replaced by 1985 Act, ss 323–9 have been repealed by the 2006 Act.

[134] Law Commission Consultation Paper *Company Directors: Regulating Conflicts of Interest and Formulating a Statement of Duties* (No 153) at para 1.9.

[135] 1948 Act, s 190 was repealed.

[136] The concept of a 'shadow director' was not new to companies legislation. Its features had been used in the Companies (Particulars as to Directors) Act 1917, although the phrase 'shadow director' was not used. After 1980 more extensive use was made of the concept.

[137] 2006 Act, ss 188–226 are the corresponding provisions.

Shareholders' remedies

1.58   The Cohen Committee recognized the need to provide an alternative remedy to winding up for cases of minority oppression, particularly in private companies. The court should have power, if satisfied that a minority of shareholders was being oppressed and that a winding-up order would not do justice to the minority, to make such order as the court thought just, including an order that the minority be bought out at a fair price.[138] This recommendation was brought into effect by the 1948 Act, s 210, but, as interpreted by the court, the threshold test of oppression proved too onerous to give the section much practical value.[139] The Jenkins Committee doubted whether s 210 was intended to be interpreted so restrictively and recommended that the section be replaced by one that extended the court's powers and made it clear that it applied to isolated acts as well as to a course of conduct and to the conduct of the affairs of the company in a manner unfairly prejudicial to the interests of some part of the members and not merely in an oppressive manner.[140] The 1980 Act, s 75 replaced the 1948 Act, s 210 in the wide terms advocated by the Jenkins Committee and without reference to making a winding-up order.[141]

Accounts

1.59   The Davey Committee recommended that there should be statutory obligations to prepare annual accounts, which should be laid before the shareholders, and to appoint auditors, but it did not favour an obligation to file the accounts with the Registrar.[142] The 1900 Act, in ss 22 and 23, only adopted the recommendation for the appointment of auditors. The Loreburn Committee recommended that private companies should be distinguished from public companies and exempt from the requirement to file with the Registrar an annual return and balance sheet, which was brought in by the 1907 Act, s 21.

1.60   After noting that there was no statutory obligation to keep proper accounts, the Greene Committee recommended that the law be changed to make the keeping of such accounts compulsory, that a profit and loss account and balance sheet, with directors' report, should be laid before the general meeting every year, and that willful default should be punishable by imprisonment. The recommendation was brought into effect by the 1929 Act, ss 122, 123.[143] The Cohen Committee recommended that the Companies Act should state the form and contents of a company's accounts and identify the matters to be stated in the auditors' report.[144] The provisions in the 1948 Act, which gave effect to the recommendations of the Cohen Committee, were substantially recast by the 1967 Act, on the recommendation of the Jenkins Committee, and further amended by the 1976 and 1981 Acts.[145] Failure to keep

---

[138]   Report of the Cohen Committee at paras 60, 152, 153.

[139]   *Scottish Co-operative Wholesale Society v Meyer* [1959] AC 324, 342, HL. In that case the claim for relief under s 210 succeeded. The only other reported successful application is *Re HR Harmer Ltd* [1959] 1 WLR 62.

[140]   Report of the Jenkins Committee at paras 199–212.

[141]   This was replaced by 1985 Act, s 459, which was amended by 1989 Act, s 145 and Sch 19, para 11 and replaced by 2006 Act, Part 30, ss 994–9.

[142]   Report of the Davey Committee at paras 51–5.

[143]   Report of the Greene Committee at paras 67 and 72. The current provisions are 2006 Act, ss 386–9, 393–426.

[144]   Report of the Cohen Committee at paras 96–114.

[145]   Report of the Jenkins Committee at paras 330–435; 1967 Act, ss 3–14; 1976 Act, ss 1–20; 1981 Act, ss 1–21.

accounts and file returns is a factor to be taken into account in determining whether a director should be disqualified on the ground of unfitness.[146]

Maintenance of capital

The only reform recommended by any of the four Committees concerning maintenance **1.61**
of capital was the prohibition on a company giving financial assistance in the purchase of
its own shares. From the spectacular corporate collapses during and after the First World
War,[147] the Greene Committee identified the 'highly improper' practice of a syndicate
agreeing to buy from existing shareholders sufficient shares to acquire control of a company
and arranging for the company to lend them the purchase money. Such a practice appeared
to the Committee 'to offend against the spirit if not the letter of the law which prohibits a
company from trafficking in its own shares and the practice is open to the gravest abuses'.
The Committee recommended that a company should be prohibited from giving direct
or indirect assistance in the purchase of their own shares.[148] This recommendation was
adopted in the 1929 Act, s 45.[149] A director who caused or procured a company to misapply its money in contravention of the prohibition was in breach of his duties and liable
to compensate the company for its loss and was also liable to criminal prosecution and
imprisonment.[150]

The Jenkins Committee referred to dissatisfaction with the provision, which had become **1.62**
the 1948 Act, s 54, and recommended that it be recast so that financial assistance could be
given if sanctioned by a special resolution and if a declaration of solvency was filed with the
Registrar, thereby protecting the interests of creditors.[151] This recommendation was eventually adopted in the 1981 Act, but under the 2006 Act the restriction on giving financial assistance only applies to public companies.[152] The 1981 Act also, for the first time, permitted a
company to purchase or redeem its own shares provided that it complied with provisions for
the protection of creditors.[153]

Meanwhile the 1980 Act, ss 39–45 for the first time imposed statutory restrictions on the **1.63**
distribution of profits and assets, so that distributions to members could only be made out
of profits available for the purpose.[154]

---

[146] CDDA, s 12C and Sch 1, paras 1 and 6 (which came into force on 1 October 2015 and replaced s 9 and
the original Sch 1, which were repealed). See the observations of Sir Donald Nicholls V-C in *Re Swift 736 Ltd*
[1993] BCLC 896, 900.
[147] *Re Jubilee Cotton Mills Ltd* [1922] 1 Ch 100; [1923] 1 Ch 1, CA; [1924] AC 958, HL, is a well-known
example.
[148] Report of the Greene Committee at paras 30 and 31. Lord Greene described the offensive practice that
the prohibition was designed to prevent in *Re VGM Holdings Ltd* [1942] Ch 235, 239, CA. In *Steen v Law*
[1964] AC 287, 301, PC, Lord Radcliffe referred to the 'notorious objections' to the practice.
[149] With amendments made by the 1947 Act, this section was re-enacted as 1948 Act, s 54.
[150] *Re VGM Holdings Ltd* [1942] Ch 235, CA; *Steen v Law* [1964] AC 287, PC; *Selangor United Rubber
Estates Ltd v Cradock (No 3)* [1968] 1 WLR 1555, 1652–9; *Wallersteiner v Moir* [1974] 1 WLR 991, CA. As to
criminal liability: *R v Lorang* (1931) 22 Cr App Rep 167.
[151] Report of the Jenkins Committee at paras 170–86, 187(d).
[152] 1981 Act, ss 42–4, which became 1985 Act, ss 151–3, 155–8. The current provisions, 2006 Act, ss 677–
83, only apply to public companies. By the 2006 Act Commencement Order No 5, Arts 5(2) and 8(b) and Sch
3 1985 Act, ss 151–3, 155–8 ceased to apply to private companies on 1 October 2008.
[153] 1981 Act, ss 46–62. Provisions for purchase and redemption of a company's own shares are in 2006 Act,
ss 684–737.
[154] These provisions are now in 2006 Act, ss 829–53.

Disqualification

1.64   The Greene Committee discovered that undischarged bankrupts used companies through which to carry on business and incur credit, to the great risk of persons dealing with the company. It recommended that an undischarged bankrupt should be disqualified from being a director of a company or in any way concerned in its management without the leave of the bankruptcy court and that contravention of this prohibition should be an offence punishable with imprisonment. The recommendation was implemented in the 1929 Act, s 142 and continues in force as the CDDA, ss 11 and 13.[155]

1.65   Also, on the recommendation of the Greene Committee, the 1929 Act gave the court power to disqualify a person from being a director or concerned in the management of a company for up to five years, but it limited the power to cases of fraudulent trading and other frauds in relation to the promotion or management of the company.[156] On the recommendation of the Cohen Committee the circumstances justifying disqualification were extended to cases of breach of trust and conviction of an offence in relation to companies.[157] The Jenkins Committee recommended further extensions to cover persons convicted on indictment of any offence involving fraud or dishonesty, persons who had been persistently in default in complying with the provisions of the Companies Act, and persons who had shown themselves to be unfit to be concerned in the management of companies through improper, reckless, or incompetent conduct.[158] Those recommendations were partially implemented by the Insolvency Act 1976, s 9 (disqualification for unfitness), the Companies Act 1976, s 28, and the 1981 Act, ss 93 and 94, which, with the disqualification provisions from the 1948 Act, were consolidated in the 1985 Act.[159]

Winding up

1.66   The Davey Committee recommended radical reform to protect unsecured creditors through provisions making directors personally liable for debts incurred when there was no reasonable expectation that the company would be able to pay them, and also liable to the company for misfeasance for being party to a fraudulent preference and for pledging or disposing of property obtained on credit.[160] None of this was adopted at the time.

1.67   The Greene Committee recommended the introduction of a provision to deal with fraudulent trading. There was evidence of persons in control of a company taking a floating charge over all its assets, obtaining goods on credit to 'fill up' the security, and then appointing a receiver who would pay them the sale proceeds. The recommendation was accepted. Directors responsible for carrying on the business of the company in fraud of creditors faced three sanctions: (i) personal liability for the debts and liabilities of the company, with the personal liability being charged on any debts owed to, or security held by, the director, (ii) imprisonment for a criminal offence, and (iii) disqualification for up to five years.[161]

---

[155]   Report of the Greene Committee at paras 56 and 57. 1929 Act, s 142 was re-enacted, with modifications, as 1948 Act, s 187 and 1985 Act, s 302 (repealed when the CDDA came into force).

[156]   Report of the Greene Committee at paras 61 and 62 and 1929 Act, ss 217 and 275.

[157]   Report of the Cohen Committee at paras 150 and 153 and 1948 Act, s 188.

[158]   Report of the Jenkins Committee at paras 80–5.

[159]   1985 Act, ss 295–302.

[160]   Report of the Davey Committee at para 33 and draft clause 11. In *Re Washington Diamond Mining Co* [1893] 3 Ch 95 the Court of Appeal had held that a director was personally liable for misfeasance for causing the company to make a fraudulent preference.

[161]   1929 Act, s 275, which is the precursor of the civil liability in Insolvency Act, s 213 and the criminal offence in 2006 Act, s 993 (which replaced 1985 Act, s 458).

Also, on the recommendation of the Greene Committee, the 1929 Act provided that officers **1.68**
of a company in liquidation were liable for a range of offences, punishable with imprisonment, covering fraud and failure to keep proper accounts, and enforcing cooperation with
the official receiver or liquidator.[162]

The Jenkins Committee referred to widespread criticism that the Companies Act did not **1.69**
deal adequately with fraudulent or incompetent directors. It recommended more use of
public examinations and extending the fraudulent trading section to reckless conduct, the
misfeasance section to cover actionable negligence, and disqualification to cover acting as a
receiver or liquidator.[163]

Restructuring of the 1985 Act

The 1985 Act had only been in force for a little over one year when many of its sections were **1.70**
repealed and replaced by provisions in other Acts. Provisions about capital issues, including liability for false and misleading statements in listing particulars[164] were moved to the
Financial Services Act 1986 and the new provisions are now in the Financial Services and
Markets Act 2000 (FSMA). Provisions about disqualification[165] were repealed and are now
in the Company Directors Disqualification Act 1986 (CDDA). Provisions about receivers
and winding up[166] were repealed and replaced by provisions in the Insolvency Act 1986.

(3) The Insolvency Act and CDDA

As regards insolvency and disqualification, the catalyst for the restructuring of the 1985 Act **1.71**
was the Report of the Cork Committee on Insolvency Law and Practice, published in June
1982. The Insolvency Act 1985 enacted the reforms made in light of the recommendations
of the Cork Committee. The new provisions about insolvent companies were then brought
into effect by the Insolvency Act 1986, which also included provisions from the 1985 Act
about receivers and winding up. The new provisions about disqualification were included in
the CDDA, which also includes disqualification provisions from the 1985 Act.[167]

The Cork Committee promoted the 'rescue culture',[168] but it also addressed the public **1.72**
interest in the conduct of the management of companies, which included being satisfied
(i) whether or not there is any fault or blame attaching to that conduct, (ii) if the conduct
merits it, that those responsible for the management are suitably punished, (iii) that the
opportunity to repeat that conduct is curtailed or restricted, and (iv) whether or not others are responsible for the insolvency. It found that the treatment of directors of insolvent
companies was unduly lenient.[169] It recommended, among other measures, a new wrongful
trading provision, automatic disqualification in certain cases, a general strengthening of the

---

[162] Report of the Greene Committee at paras 58, 60, 67, 72 and 1929 Act, ss 271, 273, 274. The corresponding provisions are in Insolvency Act, ss 206–11.

[163] Report of the Jenkins Committee at paras 496–503.

[164] 1985 Act, Part III, ss 56, 57, 61, 63–79.

[165] 1985 Act, Part IX, ss 295–302.

[166] 1985 Act, Parts XIX and XX, ss 488–650.

[167] These Acts have been amended by the Insolvency Act 1994, the Insolvency (No 2) Act 1994, the
Insolvency Act 2000, the Enterprise Act 2002, Part 10, and by the Small Business, Enterprise and Employment
Act 2015 (SBEE Act 2015), Part 9 (which substantially amends the CDDA) and Part 10 (which amends the
Insolvency Act).

[168] Report of the Cork Committee at paras 495 and 1980; *Bristol Airport v Powdrill* [1990] Ch 744, 756,
758, CA; *Powdrill v Watson* [1995] 2 AC 394, 441, 442, HL.

[169] Report of the Cork Committee at paras 1735, 1737, 1739.

existing disqualification regime, and measures to deal with repeated abuse of limited liability through phoenix companies.[170]

1.73 The reforms in the Insolvency Act of particular relevance to directors are the provisions requiring them to provide information and assistance to office-holders (including ss 235 and 236), the new public examination provision (s 133), the new misfeasance section (s 212), personal liability for wrongful trading (s 214), the restriction on reuse of company names and personal liability for debts in the event of contravention (ss 216, 217), and the new transaction at undervalue, preference, and transactions defrauding creditors provisions (ss 238, 239, and 423). The CDDA, s 6 introduced a new and widely used power to disqualify unfit directors of an insolvent company for up to 15 years.

(4) Reforms to the 1985 Act regime

1.74 In the period after 1986 there were several strands in the reform and modernization of company law and governance under the 1985 Act regime. One strand concerned reform of parts of the 1985 Act. The 1989 Act, which implemented the Seventh and Eighth EC Company Law Harmonisation Directives, made a number of miscellaneous reforms of particular relevance to directors, which have been mentioned earlier in this chapter.[171] It also provided a measure of deregulation for private companies by enabling them to pass written resolutions,[172] made reforms in relation to company contracts and the execution of documents,[173] and made it clear that the 1985 Act, s 310 did not prevent a company from purchasing and maintaining insurance for officers and auditors.[174] The Political Parties, Elections and Referendums Act 2000 prohibited political donations unless authorized by resolution of the company in general meeting and made directors personally liable for damages in respect of any unauthorized donations.[175] The Companies (Acquisition of Own Shares) (Treasury Shares) Regulations 2003 enabled a company to hold shares in its own capital that it had duly purchased as treasury shares.[176] The Companies (Audit, Investigations and Community Enterprise) Act 2004 was a response to weaknesses exposed by the accounting scandals associated with the US companies Enron and WorldCom. Of particular relevance to directors, it inserted new provisions restricting and controlling the indemnification of directors and auditors.[177]

---

[170] Report of the Cork Committee at paras 1758–66 and 1807–37.

[171] 1989 Act, ss 108–10 inserted into 1985 Act, new ss 3A (statement of company's objects: general commercial company), 35 (a company's capacity not limited by its memorandum), 35A (power of directors to bind the company), 35B (no duty to inquire as to capacity of company or authority of directors), 36, 36A–C (company contracts, execution of documents), 322A (preserving the invalidity of certain transactions with directors). Section 131 inserted a new 1985 Act, s 111A (member's right to damages).

[172] 1989 Act, ss 113 and 114 inserting 1985 Act, ss 381A, 381B, 381C, 382A, and Sch 15A.

[173] Section 130 inserted new 1985 Act, ss 36, 36A–36C (company contracts, execution of documents, pre-incorporation deeds and documents).

[174] 1989 Act, s 137 replaced 1985 Act, s 310(3) with a new provision and inserted a new para 5A in Sch 7.

[175] Section 139 and Sch 19 inserted these provisions into the 1985 Act as ss 347A–347K. These provisions were recommended by the report of the Committee on Standards in Public Life, chaired by Lord Neill of Bladen, published in October 1998. They were replaced, with some minor changes, by 2006 Act, Part 14, ss 362–79.

[176] SI 2003/1116. These provisions were 1985 Act, ss 162A–162G and are now in 2006 Act, ss 724–32.

[177] The C(AICE) Act replaced 1985 Act, s 310 with new 1985 Act, ss 309A–309C and 310 (provisions protecting directors from liability, qualifying third party indemnity provision, disclosure of qualifying third party indemnity provisions, and provisions protecting auditors from liability). The corresponding provisions of the 2006 Act are ss 232–8 in relation to directors and ss 532–8 in relation to auditors' liability.

A second strand concerned improvements in corporate governance. Following reports on the **1.75** role of non-executive directors[178] and directors' remuneration,[179] a Committee on Corporate Governance, chaired by Sir Ronald Hampel, published a *Final Report of the Committee on Corporate Governance* (1998) and drew up a Combined Code, stating a set of principles of corporate governance and a Code of Best Practice. The Financial Reporting Council amends and updates the UK Corporate Governance Code.[180] The Code is not legally binding,[181] but listed companies are expected to comply with it or explain departures. The Code requires listed companies to maintain a sound system of internal control to safeguard shareholders' investments and the company's assets.

The third and most important strand of reform has been the work of the Law Commission **1.76** on shareholder remedies and directors' duties and the work of the Company Law Review in setting out a framework for the fundamental modernization and restatement of company law now found in the 2006 Act.

E. Genesis of the Companies Act 2006

In 1992 the Department of Trade and Industry began a review of a number of areas of **1.77** company law. In February 1995 it asked the Law Commission to review shareholder remedies and make recommendations. The Law Commission, chaired by Arden J, published a Consultation Paper on *Shareholder Remedies* (1996, No 142) and a Report (1997, No 246). Among its recommendations was a new derivative action governed by court rules. This was not implemented at the time, because the issue of shareholder remedies was absorbed into the wider work of the Company Law Review described below.

In order to contribute to the work of the CLR, the Law Commission, chaired by Arden **1.78** J, went on to review the 1985 Act, Part X (enforcement of fair dealing by directors) and consider the case for a statutory statement of directors' duties. In August 1998 the Law Commission published a Consultation Paper, *Company Directors: Regulating Conflicts of Interests and Formulating a Statement of Duties* (No 153). In September 1999 the Law Commission, then chaired by Carnwath J, published its Report (No 261), recommending a statutory statement, in broad and non-exhaustive terms, of a director's main fiduciary duties and duty of care and skill.[182] The terms of the statement reflected the duties identified by the Law Commission from case law (paragraph 1.20 above). Thus a director could only make use of the company's property, information, or opportunities or have a position of conflict of interest if permitted by the company's constitution or if there has been disclosure to and approval by the company in general meeting. The Law Commission also recommended that a director's duty of skill, care, and diligence should be set out in the statute, that the test should be both objective (the knowledge and experience that may reasonably be expected of a person in the same position as the director) and subjective (the director's

---

[178] *Report of the Committee on the Financial Aspects of Corporate Governance* chaired by Sir Adrian Cadbury (1992).

[179] *Directors' Remuneration: Report of a Study Group* chaired by Sir Richard Greenbury (1995).

[180] The current version is dated April 2016.

[181] Nor do departures constitute unfair prejudice for the purpose of a petition under 2006 Act, Part 30: *Re Astec (BSR) plc* [1998] 2 BCLC 556, 590.

[182] Report at para 4.48; Appendix A.

own knowledge and experience), and that regard should be had to the particular functions of the director and the circumstances of the company, but there was no need for a statutory business judgment rule or statement in relation to delegation or reliance on others.[183] The Law Commission also recommended the redrafting and simplifying of the 1985 Act, Part X and the repeal of prohibitions on tax-free payments to directors and option dealing by them, as well as the exemption from disclosure of directors' service contracts in respect of overseas employment.[184]

1.79   In March 1998 the Department of Trade and Industry launched a wide-ranging review of core company law by an independent steering group, the CLR. The foreword to the consultation paper *Modern Company Law for a Competitive Economy* described the then current framework of company law as 'a patchwork of regulation that is immensely complex and seriously out of date'. The CLR's goal was a framework that was up to date and competitive and which facilitated enterprise and promoted transparency and fair dealing.[185] This could be achieved through clarifying the language and structure of the legislation, removing obsolescent and ineffective provisions, and making full use of electronic communication.

1.80   Under the general heading *Modern Company Law for a Competitive Economy* the CLR produced three consultation papers: *The Strategic Framework* (February 1999, URN 99/654), *Developing the Framework* (March 2000, URN 00/656), *Completing the Structure* (November 2000, URN 00/1335), and a *Final Report*, with suggested draft clauses (July 2001, URN 01/942, 943).[186] The overall approach of the CLR was that modern company law should be in 'a coherent and accessible form, providing maximum freedom for participants to perform their proper functions, but recognizing the case for high standards and for ensuring appropriate protection for all interested parties'.[187]

1.81   One of the core policies of the CLR was the 'think small first' approach to private company regulation and legislative structure.[188] To this end the CLR proposed simplifying and modernizing the law for private companies, by (a) simplifying decision-making procedures (more use of written resolutions), (b) streamlining internal procedures (no need for AGMs or a secretary, and a simpler form of constitution), (c) reducing the burden of financial reporting and audit (extending the small companies regime and raising the audit exemption level), and (d) removing the ban on private companies giving financial assistance in the purchase of their own shares.[189]

---

[183] Report at paras 5.6, 5.20, 5.29, 5.37. This was accepted by the CLR (CLR: *Developing the Framework* at para 3.87).

[184] Report at paras 7.99, 11.3–11.7 deal with recommended repeals. The provisions about option dealing were repealed, because of duplication with the Criminal Justice Act 1993. For general recommendations about 1985 Act, Part X, see paras 16.07–16.58.

[185] The CLR's terms of reference are set out in the CLR: *Final Report*, Annex A, p 335.

[186] In addition the CLR published consultation papers on Company General Meetings and Shareholder Communication, Company Formation and Capital Maintenance, and Reforming the Law Concerning Overseas Companies (October 1999, URN/1144–6), Capital Maintenance (June 2000, URN 00/880), Registration of Company Charges (October 2000, URN 00/1213), and Trading Disclosures (October 2000).

[187] CLR: *Strategic Framework* at Executive Summary, para 2.

[188] CLR: *Strategic Framework* at Executive Summary, para 2 and paras 2.25 and 5.2.33; CLR: *Final Report* at paras 1.52–1.55.

[189] CLR: *Strategic Framework* at Executive Summary, para 8; CLR: *Final Report* at paras 2.15–2.19, 2.21, 2.28–2.37, 4.3–4.7, 4.13–4.37, 10.06.

Another core policy was to provide an inclusive, open, and flexible regime for corporate governance. To this end the CLR proposed a statutory statement of directors' duties and a clarification and updating of the 1985 Act, Part X, dealing with conflicts of interest. The duty of loyalty, by which directors are bound to promote the success of the company, should be informed by 'enlightened shareholder value', so that directors manage the business of the company in the long-term interests of shareholders, but in an enlightened and inclusive way, enabling the company to achieve productive relations with a range of interested parties, such as employees, suppliers, and customers. The CLR rejected the 'pluralist' approach by which the interests of shareholders are merely balanced with the interests of others affected by the company.[190] **1.82**

To protect the interests of shareholders the CLR recommended a statutory form of derivative action,[191] and that members with an interest in facilitating or condoning misconduct should be disenfranchised.[192] The CLR also made a number of recommendations to make sanctions more effective.[193] **1.83**

The government's response is contained in two White Papers *Modernising Company Law* (July 2002, Cm 5553) and *Company Law Reform* (March 2005, Cm 6456). The government broadly adopted the approach of the CLR. There would be a statutory statement of directors' duties which would replace the existing common law and equitable rules and which would embed the concept of 'enlightened shareholder value' (but without codifying a duty to creditors). One change was that a director would be able to exploit a corporate opportunity with the consent of independent directors.[194] The government did not agree to codify the *Duomatic* rule.[195] **1.84**

On 1 November 2005 a Company Law Reform Bill was introduced into the House of Lords. The Under-Secretary of State, Department of Trade and Industry (Lord Sainsbury) said it had four key objectives: 'enhancing shareholder engagement and a long-term investment culture; ensuring better regulation and a "think small first" approach; making life easier to set up and run a company; and providing flexibility for the future'.[196] After extensive revision and a change of name to the Companies Bill, the bill received Royal Assent on 8 November 2006. The 2006 Act also repeals all the provisions of the Companies Act 1985, except for the provisions about investigations contained in Parts XIV and XV, which were amended. **1.85**

---

190 CLR: *Strategic Framework* at Executive Summary, paras 5, 5.1.11–5.1.33; CLR: *Developing the Framework* at paras 2.7–2.26, 3.17–3.20, 3.37–3.58, 3.82; CLR: *Final Report* at paras 2.20, 3.5–3.11, 3.21–3.27, 4.8, 4.9, 6.2–6.16.
191 CLR: *Final Report* at paras 2.23–2.26, 7.41–7.51.
192 CLR: *Final Report* at paras 7.52–7.62.
193 CLR: *Final Report* at paras 1.17, 15.1–15.77.
194 2005 White Paper at para 3.3.
195 This was recommended by the CLR in the *Final Report* at paras 2.14, 7.17–7.26; 2005 White Paper at para 4.2. The CLR had recommended codifying a duty to creditors: *Developing the Framework* at paras 3.72, 3.73, 3.81; *Final Report* at paras 3.12–3.20.
196 Hansard, HL Debate, vol 677, col 182 (11 January 2006). In relation to flexibility for the future, Part 31 of the original Bill gave the Secretary of State wide law-making powers, but this Part was withdrawn. Instead the 2006 Act contains many provisions for the law to be stated in delegated legislation under the negative and affirmative resolution procedures or by the instrument being approved after being made; see ss 1288–92.

F. Reforms Made by the Companies Act 2006

1.86 Although it was intended to be more accessible (eg by differentiating the provisions that apply to private and public companies), it must be accepted that the 2006 Act is a daunting piece of legislation. As originally enacted, it had 1,300 sections and 16 schedules. It is supported by more than 50 statutory instruments. The following paragraphs highlight the reforms of most concern to directors.

Parts 1–7: The fundamentals of a company

1.87 These provisions concern types of company, company formation, a company's constitution, its capacity to act, its name, its registered office, and change of status.[197] There are new provisions, which simplify the procedure for forming a company and its constitution (Parts 2 and 3). Now a single person may form a private or public company.[198] By s 9,[199] to form a company there must be delivered to the Registrar (a) the memorandum of association in the prescribed form authenticated by the subscribers;[200] (b) an application for registration containing prescribed information about the company, including particulars of its proposed share capital (if any) and its first directors and secretaries, with consents to act;[201] (c) a copy of the proposed articles unless the applicable Model Article is to apply;[202] and (d) a statement of compliance in accordance with s 13.

1.88 The main change from the procedure under the 1985 Act is that under the 2006 Act the memorandum is a simple document which provides a historical record evidencing the intention of the founder members to form the company and become members. It therefore underpins the statutory contract between members and the company.[203] It cannot be changed or updated, but there is no need to do so. The memorandum does not state the company's objects and much of the information that used to be contained in it is now contained in the application for registration.

1.89 There are also changes to a company's constitution. The 1985 Act did not refer to a company's constitution as such. Under the 2006 Act, s 17, unless the context otherwise requires, a company's constitution includes its articles[204] and also any resolutions or agreements

---

[197] As Sir John Vinelott put it in 'Individual Insolvency: The Insolvency Acts 1985 and 1986' (1987) 40 *Current Legal Problems* 1, 11: 'A company, like a good soldier has a name, a number and a place.'

[198] Under 1985 Act, s 1(3A), inserted by the Companies (Single Member Private Limited Companies) Regulations 1992 (SI 1992/1699) with effect from 15 July 1992, a single person was able to form a private company, but not a public company.

[199] See also the Companies (Registration) Regulations 2008 (SI 2008/3014) and the Companies (Shares and Share Capital) Order 2009 (SI 2009/388).

[200] 2006 Act, s 8.

[201] 2006 Act, ss 9–12. For public companies the statement about the company's share capital is linked to Art 2 of the Second Company Law Directive (77/91/EC). For unregistered companies, see the Unregistered Companies Regulations 2009 (SI 2009/2436), regulation 3 and Sch 1, paras 1–3. For companies not formed under companies legislation but authorized to register pursuant to the 2006 Act, s 1040, see Companies (Companies Authorised to Register) Regulations 2009 (SI 2009/2437).

[202] Pursuant to 2006 Act, s 19, the Companies (Model Articles) Regulations 2008 (SI 2008/3229) prescribe default model articles for private companies limited by shares, private companies limited by guarantee, and public companies.

[203] 2006 Act, s 33(1).

[204] 2006 Act, ss 18–20.

which affect its constitution.[205] The constitution may now include entrenched provisions, which can only be amended or repealed by procedures more restrictive than a special resolution.[206] Another change is that a company's objects are unrestricted, giving it the same plenary capacity as an individual, unless specifically restricted by its articles.[207] The provisions of the constitution 'bind the company and its members to the same extent as if there were covenants on the part of the company and each member to observe those provisions'.[208]

There are new rules about choice of name and trading disclosures (Part 5). These provi-   **1.90**
sions should be considered with the supporting regulations[209] and Part 41, which contains new provisions about business names and provisions derived from the Business Names Act 1985, with changes. One matter of particular significance to directors is that they are no longer personally liable if the company's name is not correctly stated on its contracts and bills, because the 1985 Act, s 349 was repealed with effect from 1 October 2008.[210]

Part 9: Exercise of members' rights

In recognition of the fact that shares are often held through nominees, there are new provi-   **1.91**
sions, which enable the registered member to nominate another person to exercise members' rights where the company's articles so provide,[211] or to nominate another person to enjoy information rights where the company is a traded company.[212]

Part 10: A company's directors

As originally enacted, the 2006 Act provided that every company had to have one natural   **1.92**
director, but it will soon be the case that all directors must be natural persons unless certain exceptions apply.[213] A person who is under the age of 16 cannot be appointed a director, but there are no upper age limits.[214] There are new restrictions on the disclosure of directors' residential addresses.[215]

---

[205] 2006 Act, s 29. An informal agreement of the type considered in *Cane v Jones* [1980] 1 WLR 1451 would be part of the constitution and subject to the rules about forwarding to the Registrar (s 30) and being provided to members (s 32).

[206] 2006 Act, s 22 and for alteration of articles: ss 21–7.

[207] 2006 Act, ss 31 and 39. For charitable companies, see s 42.

[208] 2006 Act, s 33(1). Unlike its predecessor (the 1985 Act, s 14(1)), s 33 expressly refers to the company. For cases on former provisions, see *Welton v Saffery* [1897] AC 299, 315 and *Hickman v Romney Marsh Sheep-Breeders Association* [1915] 1 Ch 881. Section 33 (like 1985 Act, s 14) is excepted from the general principle set out in the Contracts (Rights of Third Parties) Act 1999, s 1 and so the provisions of a company's constitution will not confer any rights on persons other than the company and its members.

[209] The supporting regulations are: the Company, Limited Liability Partnership and Business (Names and Trading Disclosures) Regulations 2015 (SI 2015/17) (which replaced the Companies (Trading Disclosures) Regulations 2008 (SI 2008/495) and the Company and Business Names (Miscellaneous Provisions) Regulations 2009 (SI 2009/1085) with effect from 31 January 2015), the Company Names Adjudicator Rules 2008 (SI 2008/1738). Also see the Companies (Unregistered Companies) Regs 2009 (SI 2009/2436) and the Companies (Companies Authorised to Register) Regulations 2009 (SI 2009/2437).

[210] 2006 Act Commencement Order No 5, Art 8(b) and Sch 3.

[211] 2006 Act, s 145.

[212] 2006 Act, ss 146–53.

[213] 2006 Act, s 155, which will be repealed by the SBEE Act, s 87 from a day to be appointed when the new ss 156A–156C come into force.

[214] 2006 Act, ss 157–9.

[215] 2006 Act, Part 10, Chapter 8, ss 240–6.

1.93   There is a statutory statement of directors' general duties and independent directors are given power to authorize a director to have a conflict of interest or take the benefit of a corporate opportunity.[216]

1.94   There are changes to the rules about directors declaring their interests in existing transactions and about transactions with directors requiring approval of members.[217] Certain restrictions on transactions with directors, formerly contained in the 1985 Act, Part X (enforcement of fair dealing by directors), have been repealed and not replaced by provisions in the 2006 Act.[218]

1.95   There are new provisions about qualifying pension scheme indemnity provision in respect of directors' liabilities and ratification of a director's wrongful conduct by independent members.[219]

Part 11: Derivative claims

1.96   There is a new statutory procedure for derivative claims by members arising from a breach of duty by directors[220]

Part 12: Company secretaries

1.97   There is no need for private companies to have a secretary.[221]

Part 13: Resolutions and meetings

1.98   The way in which companies pass resolutions is simplified. The reforms include the following: (a) there are now only ordinary and special resolutions (extraordinary resolutions have been abolished),[222] (b) written resolutions are the normal procedure for private companies,[223] (c) all company meetings are convened on 14 days' notice, except public company AGMs which require 21 days,[224] (d) communications in relation to company meetings may be sent electronically,[225] (e) private companies are no longer obliged to hold AGMs,[226] and (f) there are new provisions for polls for quoted companies.[227]

---

[216]   2006 Act, Part 10, Chapter 2, ss 170–81.

[217]   2006 Act, Part 10, Chapters 3–6, ss 182–231.

[218]   The provisions of 1985 Act, Part X, concerning transactions with directors, that have been repealed and not replaced are s 311 (prohibition on tax-free payments to directors), ss 323 and 327 (prohibition on directors dealing in share options), ss 324–6, 328, 329, and Sch 13, Parts 2–4 (register of directors' interests), s 342 (criminal liability for loans to directors), and ss 343 and 344 (special procedure for disclosure by banks). The government repealed the provisions about the register of directors' interests because the FSA (and, as from 1 April 2013, the FCA) requires disclosure by traded companies to comply with the EU Market Abuse Directive (2003/6/EC and, as from 3 July 2016, the Market Abuse Regulation (596/2014)) and the government did not wish to extend those requirements to other companies. Because 2006 Act, s 413 makes special provision for disclosure requirements by banking companies, the provisions of 1985 Act, ss 343 and 344 were no longer required.

[219]   2006 Act, Part 10, Chapter 7, ss 232–9.

[220]   2006 Act, Part 11, ss 260–4 (claims in England and Wales or Northern Ireland).

[221]   2006 Act, Part 12, ss 270–80.

[222]   2006 Act, ss 281–3.

[223]   2006 Act, ss 288–300.

[224]   2006 Act, s 307.

[225]   2006 Act, s 333.

[226]   The provisions about AGMs for public companies are in 2006 Act, ss 336–40.

[227]   2006 Act, ss 341–54.

The Companies (Shareholders' Rights) Regulations 2009 have made amendments to Part 13 **1.99**
to facilitate the exercise of shareholders' rights in traded companies.[228]

Part 15: Accounts and reports

Directors are under a new duty not to approve accounts unless they give a true and fair **1.100**
view.[229] There are new requirements for a company's annual accounts to disclose information
about directors' benefits and for a business review in the directors' report for all companies
other than those subject to the small companies regime.[230] The annual accounts of quoted
companies must be published on their website.[231] The time for filing accounts and reports
with the Registrar is reduced from ten months after the end of the relevant accounting reference period to nine months for private companies and six months for public companies.[232]
There is a new provision making a director liable to compensate the company for any loss
suffered by it as a result of an untrue or misleading statement in, or omission from the directors' report, the directors' remuneration report, or any summary financial statement derived
from them.[233]

Part 16: Audit

There are new provisions to improve the accountability of auditors, including (a) provisions **1.101**
relating to the appointment of auditors of private companies and the disclosure of the terms
of an auditor's appointment,[234] (b) a requirement that an auditor's report given by a firm
must be signed by an individual as senior statutory auditor,[235] (c) provisions about offences
relating to the audit report,[236] (d) obligations of the auditor and the company to notify the
appropriate audit authority if the auditor ceases to hold office by providing it with a statement of reasons,[237] (e) a right of shareholders in a quoted company to raise audit concerns at
an accounts meeting of a quoted company,[238] and (f) provisions relating to indemnity and
limitation of auditors' liability.[239]

*Parts 17 and 18: A company's share capital and acquisition by a limited company of
its own shares*

There are two relaxations in the capital maintenance rules for private companies. First, a **1.102**
private company may reduce its capital without a court order, provided that the directors
make a solvency statement.[240] Secondly, the prohibition on giving financial assistance in the

---

228 SI 2009/1632; implementing Directive 2007/36/EC of the European Parliament and of the Council of
11 July 2007.
229 2006 Act, s 393.
230 2006 Act, ss 412, 413, 417.
231 2006 Act, s 430.
232 2006 Act, s 442.
233 2006 Act, s 463.
234 2006 Act, ss 485(2)–(5), 487, 488, 493, 514.
235 2006 Act, ss 503, 504, 506.
236 2006 Act, ss 507 and 508.
237 2006 Act, ss 522–5, as amended by the Deregulation Act 2015, s 18 with effect from 1 October 2015.
238 2006 Act, ss 527–31.
239 2006 Act, ss 532–8.
240 2006 Act, ss 641(1)(a) and (2)–(6), 642–4, 652(1) and (3), 654. See also the Companies (Reduction of
Share Capital) Order 2008 (SI 2008/1915), which prescribes the form of solvency statement and provides for
the treatment of reserves as distributable profits, unless, where the court confirms the reduction, it orders that
it is not distributable.

purchase of its own shares no longer applies to a private company (and the 'whitewash' provisions no longer apply to them).[241]

1.103 Other new provisions provide that (a) companies no longer have an authorized capital, but shares must have a nominal value and cannot be in the form of stock;[242] (b) directors of a private company with only one class of shares may allot shares without prior approval of members (as had been required by the 1985 Act, s 80) unless prohibited by the company's articles;[243] and (c) a company may redenominate the currency of its share capital.[244]

Part 21: Certification and transfer of securities

1.104 There is a new provision, which makes clear the directors' duties when a transfer of shares in or debentures of a company is lodged.[245] As soon as reasonably practicable and in any event within two months after the date of lodgment the company must either register the transfer or give the transferee notice of refusal with reasons. The requirement for reasons is new. If the section is not complied with the company and every officer in default commits an offence.

Part 23: Distributions

1.105 The 2006 Act, s 845 provides a solution to a problem in making an inter-group transfer of a non-cash asset at book value, which was thought to have been caused by the decision in *Aveling Barford Ltd v Perion Ltd*.[246] The new section enables a company, which has distributable profits, to sell or transfer a non-cash asset to a member of its group at book value without being treated as having made a distribution.

Part 31: Dissolution and restoration to the register

1.106 There are new provisions for restoring a dissolved company to the register, either administratively by the Registrar on the application of a former director or member if certain conditions are met, or by the court on the application of a former director and others, provided that the application is made within six years of dissolution (unless the application is for the purpose of bringing a claim against the company for damages for personal injury).[247] Under the 1985 Act a former director did not have standing to apply to restore a dissolved company to the register.

---

[241] 2006 Act, ss 677–83 only apply to public companies. Commencement Order No 5, Arts 5(2) and 8(b) and Sch 3 repealed 1985 Act, ss 151–3, 155–8 as regards private companies with effect from 1 October 2008. Paragraph 52 of Sch 4 to that Commencement Order makes it clear that the repeal could not have the effect that a case of financial assistance given by a private company might be impugned under the rule of law derived from *Trevor v Whitworth* (1887) 12 App Cas 409, HL (see commentary in para 7 of the Explanatory Memorandum to Commencement Order No 5).

[242] 2006 Act, ss 540(2)–(3), 542, 545, 546.

[243] 2006 Act, s 550. The directors' power of allotment is of course subject to any pre-emption rights of existing shareholders, which in the case of a private company may be excluded by the articles or disapplied by the articles or special resolution (ss 567 and 569).

[244] 2006 Act, ss 622–8.

[245] 2006 Act, s 771.

[246] [1989] BCLC 626. The CLR recommended that there should be provision enabling solvent companies to make inter-group transfers at book value: CLR: *Capital Maintenance: Other Issues* (URN 00/880) at paras 24–43 and CLR: *Completing the Structure* at para 7.21.

[247] 2006 Act, ss 1024–32. The CLR recommended administrative restoration to the register in *Final Report* at paras 11.17–11.20.

G. Reforms Made by the Small Business, Enterprise and Employment Act 2015

Among the disparate reforms made by the Small Business, Enterprise and Employment Act 2015 (SBEE Act 2015) there are some which are significant for directors. **1.107**

To give effect to 'the G8 Action Plan Principles to prevent the misuse of companies and legal arrangements' of June 2013, SBEE Act 2015, Part 7 contains provisions to enhance company transparency by (i) requiring companies, except DTR5 issuers and other companies specified by the Secretary of State, to obtain information about people with significant control over them and to maintain a register of such people;[248] (ii) abolishing bearer shares;[249] (iii) requiring all company directors to be natural persons, subject to certain exceptions;[250] and (iv) clarifying the application of directors' general duties to shadow directors.[251] **1.108**

The SBEE Act 2015, Part 8, contains provisions to make company filing requirements less burdensome. Rather than filing an annual return, companies are to deliver to the registrar an annual confirmation of accuracy of information on the register.[252] Private companies are given the option of keeping certain information on the register kept by the registrar instead of keeping it on their own registers.[253] Section 96 amends the 2006 Act, Part 35, to protect information about the date of birth of a director and certain other persons.[254] Sections 100–2 are headed 'Director Disputes' and make amendments to the 2006 Act covering company filing requirements in relation to consent to act as a director or secretary, the registrar's duty to inform new directors of entry in the register, and removal from the register of material about directors.[255] **1.109**

The SBEE Act 2015, Part 9, ss 104–16 make substantial changes to the CDDA to modernize and strengthen the director disqualification regime.[256] The principal changes are (i) a new power to disqualify persons subject to certain convictions abroad,[257] (ii) a new power **1.110**

---

[248] SBEE Act 2015, ss 81–3 and Sch 3, inserting a new Part 21A into the 2006 Act. These provisions came fully into force on 30 June 2016 and are supported by The Register of People with Significant Control Regulations 2016 (SI 2016/339). These provisions are discussed further in Chapter 27, Section E, below.

[249] SBEE Act 2015, ss 84, 85, and Sch 4 abolish bearer shares by (i) inserting a new s 779(4) in the 2006 Act which prevents a company from issuing bearer shares after 26 May 2015; (ii) making arrangements for bearer shares to be converted into registered shares or cancelled; and (iii) making provision for the amendment of a company's articles to reflect the abolition of bearer shares.

[250] SBEE Act 2015, ss 87, from a day to be appointed, amends the 2006 Act by deleting s 155 (which requires a company to have at least one director who is a natural person) and inserting s 156A (which states that each director is to be a natural person), s 156B (which enables the Secretary of State to make regulations, providing for exceptions from the requirement that each director be a natural person), and s 156C (which deals with existing directors who are not natural persons). These provisions are discussed in Chapter 6, Section C, below.

[251] SBEE Act 2015, s 89 (which amends the 2006 Act, s 170 by inserting a new s 170(5) and provides for the Secretary of State to make regulations) and s 90 (which amends the definitions of 'shadow director' in Insolvency Act, s 251, CDDA, s 22, and 2006 Act, s 251. These provisions are discussed in Chapter 10, Section C, below.

[252] SBEE Act 2015, s 92 substitutes a new Part 24 of the 2006 Act, as discussed in Chapter 26, Section F, below.

[253] SBEE Act 2015, ss 94, 95.

[254] SBEE Act 2015, s 96.

[255] These provisions came into force on 10 October 2015 and are discussed further in Chapter 6, Section F, below.

[256] These provisions came into force on 1 October 2015 and are discussed further in Chapter 31 below.

[257] CDDA, s 5A.

to disqualify persons who instruct an unfit director of an insolvent company,[258] (iii) changes to the determination of unfitness,[259] and (iv) new provisions for compensation orders and undertakings,[260]

1.111 The SBEE Act 2015, Part 10 contains a variety of amendments to the Insolvency Act, including provisions designed to make it easier to bring proceedings against directors and persons who benefited from avoidable transactions. These provisions are discussed in more detail in Chapter 34 below. An administrator may now bring fraudulent or wrongful trading proceedings.[261] An administrator or liquidator is given power to assign a right of action (including the proceeds of an action) for fraudulent or wrongful trading, transaction at undervalue, preference or extortionate credit transaction.[262] It is made clear that the proceeds of such claims, whether brought by the administrator, liquidator, or assignee are not caught by any floating charge.[263] Finally a liquidator no longer needs to obtain sanction before starting such proceedings.[264]

---

[258] CDDA, ss 8ZA–8ZE.

[259] Amendments to CDDA, ss 6, 7, and 8, insertion of a new s 7A (office-holder's report on conduct of directors, omission of s 9 and insertion of s 12C with a new Sch 1 (matters to be taken into account for determining unfitness and disqualifications),

[260] CDDA, s 15A–15C.

[261] Insolvency Act ss 246ZA–246ZC, which came into force on 1 October 2015.

[262] Insolvency Act, s 246ZD, which came into force on 1 October 2015.

[263] Insolvency Act s 176ZB, which came into force on 1 October 2015.

[264] SBEE Act 2015, s 120, which amends the Insolvency Act, ss 165, 167, and Sch 4. This section came into force on 26 May 2015.

2

THE CURRENT LEGAL FRAMEWORK RELATING TO DIRECTORS

Simon Mortimore QC

A. Introduction

This work attempts to state the law of England and Wales relating to the duties and liabilities **2.01** of directors of companies, both civil and criminal.[1] The most important elements of the legal framework affecting these matters are the company's constitution and the Companies Act 2006, but particular aspects of a director's conduct may engage other statutory provisions (eg Insolvency Act 1986 or criminal legislation). Common law rules and equitable principles provide the background that informs the interpretation of the legislation and the assessment by the court of a director's conduct. Also relevant are 'industry standards' such as the UK Corporate Governance Code, which applies to listed companies, and guidance from the Financial Conduct Authority (FCA) for companies subject to its regulation.[2]

Section B of this chapter discusses the meaning of 'company' and related expressions that **2.02** appear in the Companies Act and other legislation. Section C outlines the statutory framework and supporting materials to which directors of companies are subject. Sections D and E discuss the interpretation of the Companies Act and a company's constitution.

Immediately preceding Chapter 1 is a Glossary of expressions used in this work, which **2.03** includes some definitions in the 2006 Act, s 1174 and Schedule 8.

---

[1] It does not consider limited liability partnerships, open-ended investment companies, industrial and provident societies, friendly societies, European Economic Interest Groupings, or European Public Limited Liability Companies.

[2] On 1 April 2013 the FCA took over the functions of the Financial Services Authority (FSA) in relation to conduct of business as a result of the coming into effect of amendments made to FSMA by the Financial Services Act 2012.

B. Companies and Other Bodies

(1) Company

The Companies Act

2.04 The 2006 Act, s 1(1) provides that in the Companies Acts, unless the context otherwise requires, 'company' means a company formed and registered under the 2006 Act; that is to say (i) a company formed and registered after 1 October 2009, when the 2006 Act, Part 1, came into effect,[3] or (ii) a company formed and registered before that date under the 1985 Act or the Companies (Northern Ireland) Order 1986, or an existing company for the purposes of that Act or Order and which are treated as if formed and registered under the 2006 Act.[4]

2.05 The 2006 Act, s 895(2) provides a special definition of 'company' for arrangements and reconstructions under Part 26. The power of the court to facilitate reconstructions or amalgamations under s 900 only applies to companies within the meaning of the 2006 Act (ie as described in the preceding paragraph), but the power of the court to sanction a scheme or compromise is broader, because it applies to 'any company liable to be wound up under the Insolvency Act 1986' (paragraphs 2.08 and 2.09 below). This is logical because a liquidator or administrator may apply to the court under ss 896(2) and 899(2). Chapter 28, Section B(1) below explains that these arrangement and reconstruction provisions are available to foreign companies that are capable of being wound up under Part 5 of the Insolvency Act.

Insolvency Act

2.06 Parts 1–7 of the Insolvency Act concerning company insolvency used to adopt the definitions in the relevant Companies Act, including the definition of 'company'.[5] Now each Part identifies the companies to which it may apply.[6] Broadly, there are three regimes for corporate insolvency.

2.07 The procedures for company voluntary arrangements under Part 1 and administration under Part 2 and Schedule B1 are potentially available to the following companies:[7]

(1) a company registered under the 2006 Act in England and Wales or Scotland;[8]

---

[3] 2006 Commencement Order No 8, Art 3(a).

[4] By the 2006 Act, s 1(2) and Parts 33 and 34, ss 1040–59 certain provisions of that Act may also extend to companies authorized to register under the 2006 Act, unregistered companies incorporated in and having a principal place of business in the UK, and overseas companies.

[5] Insolvency Act, s 251 (as it was until the material references to the Companies Act were repealed on 1 October 2009 by Companies Act 2006 (Consequential Amendments, Transitional Provisions and Savings) Order 2009, SI 2009/1941, Art 2(1), Sch 1, para 77(1), (4); subject to transitional provisions and savings in Art 8, Sch 1, para 84).

[6] In part this was the consequence of the EC Regulation on Insolvency Proceedings (1346/2000/EC), but changes were also made to reverse expansive interpretations by the court of 'company', under which the powers of an administrative receiver were extended to receivers appointed in respect of property of a Liberian company (*Re International Bulk Commodities Ltd* [1993] Ch 77) and an association incorporated by royal charter was made subject to an administration order (*Re Salvage Association* [2004] 1 WLR 174).

[7] 2006 Act, s 1(4) for company voluntary arrangements and Sch B1, para 111(1A) for administration. There are special administration regimes for certain utilities, insurers and banks, for which the relevant regulations should be consulted. Note also special provisions for companies incorporated outside the UK with a principal place of business in Northern Ireland in s 1(6) and Sch B1, para 111A.

[8] These procedures are not available to a provident society (*Re Dairy Farmers of Great Britain Ltd* [2010] Ch 63) or a club (*Panter v Rowellian Football Social Club* [2012] Ch 125).

(2) a company incorporated in an EEA state other than the UK; but a company with its COMI[9] within the EU (other than Denmark) may not enter administration;[10] and

(3) a company not incorporated in an EEA state but having its COMI in a member state other than Denmark.[11]

Part 3, concerning receivership, and Part 4, concerning winding up, apply only to companies **2.08** registered under the 2006 Act in England and Wales or Scotland.[12]

Part 5, concerning the winding up of unregistered companies, applies to any association and **2.09** any company with the exception of a company registered under the Companies Act 2006 in any part of the UK.[13]

CDDA

For the purposes of the Company Directors Disqualification Act (CDDA) 'company' **2.10** means a company registered under the 2006 Act in Great Britain or an unregistered company that may be wound up under Part 5 of the Insolvency Act.[14] The CDDA also applies to building societies, incorporated friendly societies, NHS foundation trusts, and registered societies as defined in the Co-operative and Community Benefit Societies Act 2014.[15] Some provisions now also apply to disqualification for conduct in relation to overseas companies.[16]

(2) Types of company

The types of companies that may be formed under the 2006 Act are: **2.11**

(1) limited or unlimited companies; limited companies being limited by shares or by guarantee, but a company cannot be limited by guarantee with a share capital; and[17]

---

[9] In relation to a company, 'centre of main interests' or COMI has the same meaning as in the EC Insolvency Regulation and, in the absence of proof to the contrary, is presumed to be the place of its registered office: Insolvency Act, s 1(5) and Sch B1, para 111(1B) and see *Re Eurofood IFSC Ltd* [2006] Ch 508, ECJ at paras 29–34; *Re Stanford International Bank Ltd* [2011] Ch 33, CA at paras 30–67.

[10] This is the effect of Art 3 of the EC Insolvency Regulation.

[11] Thus administration is available to a company incorporated in the USA with its COMI in England: *Re BRAC Rent-A-Car International Inc* [2003] 1 WLR 1421.

[12] Insolvency Act, s 28 for receivership and s 73 for winding up.

[13] Insolvency Act, s 220, as substituted with effect from 1 October 2009 by Companies Act 2006 (Consequential Amendments, Transitional Provisions and Savings) Order 2009, SI 2009/1941, Art 2(1) and Sch 1, para 76(1) and (2). Foreign companies may be, and frequently are, wound up under Part 5, but a members' association is not an association that can be wound up under that Part: *Re Witney Town Football and Social Club* [1994] 2 BCLC 487.

[14] CDDA, s 22(2).

[15] CDDA, ss 22A–22C and 22E. Section 22E, which applies the CDDA to registered societies, came into force on 6 April 2014. Section 22D, which applied the CDDA to open-ended investment companies within the meaning of FSMA, s 236, has been repealed by the SBEE Act 2015, s 111, Sch 7, Part 1, paras 1, 21 as from 1 October 2015.

[16] By CDDA, s 22(2A) an 'overseas company' is a company incorporated or formed outside Great Britain. The sections that apply to overseas companies are s 3 (persistent breaches of companies legislation), s 5 (summary conviction), s 5A (certain convictions abroad), ss 6–8 (unfitness), and s 10 (wrongful trading). These provisions were inserted by SBEE Act 2015, Part 9 with effect from 1 October 2015.

[17] 2006 Act, ss 3 and 5.

(2) private and public companies;[18] the two main differences being that a private company is prohibited from making a public offer, and a public company must have a minimum share capital of £50,000 or the euro equivalent.[19]

2.12 For certain provisions of the 2006 Act it is necessary to identify particular types of company.

Subsidiary, holding company, and parent

2.13 Sometimes the reason is to identify the relationship between companies. The 2006 Act uses two groups of overlapping expressions. One group is 'subsidiary', 'holding company', and 'wholly-owned subsidiary'.[20] These expressions are used in the prohibition of a subsidiary being a member of its holding company,[21] concerning members' approval of payments to a director for loss of office,[22] the prohibition of a public company giving financial assistance for the purchase of its own shares,[23] and takeovers.[24] The core definitions, given in s 1159 are:

> (1) A company is a 'subsidiary' of another company, its 'holding company', if that other company—
>   (a) holds a majority of voting rights in it, or
>   (b) is a member of it and has the right to appoint or remove a majority of its board of directors, or
>   (c) is a member of it and controls alone, pursuant to an agreement with other members, a majority of the voting rights in it,
>   or if it is a subsidiary of a company that is itself a subsidiary of that other company.
> (2) A company is a 'wholly-owned subsidiary' of another company if it has no members except that other and that other's wholly-owned subsidiaries or persons acting on behalf of that other or its wholly-owned subsidiaries.

2.14 The other group is 'parent company', 'parent undertaking', and 'subsidiary undertaking',[25] which are used in the 2006 Act, Part 15 about accounts and reports, which derive from the Seventh Company Law Directive 83/349/EEC, and in FSMA.[26] A 'parent company' is a 'parent undertaking'[27] and s 1162(2) gives the core definitions of a 'parent undertaking':

> (2) An undertaking is a parent undertaking in relation to another undertaking, a subsidiary undertaking, if—
>   (a) it holds a majority of the voting rights in the undertaking, or
>   (b) it is a member of the undertaking and has the right to appoint or remove a majority of its board of directors, or
>   (c) it has the right to exercise a dominant influence over the undertaking—
>   (i) by virtue of provisions contained in the undertaking's articles, or
>   (ii) by virtue of a control contract, or

---

[18] 2006 Act, s 4.

[19] 2006 Act, Part 20, ss 755–60 (prohibition of public offers by private companies, of which ss 757–9 are new) and ss 761–7 (minimum share capital requirement for public companies, of which ss 765 and 766 are new).

[20] 2006 Act, s 1159 and Sch 6. This definition may be amended by regulations: s 1160. A company is not a subsidiary where the holding company charges the shares in its subsidiary and the chargee, or its nominee, is registered as the member: *Enviroco Ltd v Farstad Supply A/S* [2011] 1 WLR 921, SC.

[21] 2006 Act, ss 136–44.

[22] 2006 Act, ss 217 and 219.

[23] 2006 Act, ss 677–83.

[24] 2006 Act, s 988.

[25] 2006 Act, ss 1162, 1173(1), and Sch 7. By s 1161(1) an 'undertaking' is (a) a body corporate or partnership, or (b) an unincorporated association carrying on a trade or business, with or without a view to profit.

[26] FSMA, s 420.

[27] 2006 Act, s 1173(1).

(d) it is a member of the undertaking and controls alone, pursuant to an agreement with other shareholders or members, a majority of the voting rights in the undertaking.

Listed, quoted, and traded companies

Another group of overlapping expressions applies to companies whose securities are traded on some form of regulated market. **2.15**

A 'listed company' is a company that has any class of its securities listed in an official list maintained by the FCA under FSMA, Part 6.[28] A listed company is subject to the disclosure, prospectus, transparency, and corporate governance rules made by the FCA pursuant to that Part. Some of the Listing Rules apply to companies with a Premium Listing. **2.16**

The expression 'quoted company' is used in the 2006 Act, Part 13 (resolutions and meetings) and Part 15 (accounts and reports) and also in relation to the right of members of a quoted company to raise audit concerns at an accounts meeting.[29] In Part 15 a quoted company is one whose equity share capital (a) has been included in the official list in accordance with FSMA, Part 6; (b) is officially listed in an EEA state; or (c) is admitted to dealing on the New York Stock Exchange or the Nasdaq exchange.[30] **2.17**

The expression 'traded company' is used in Part 9 (exercise of members' rights), where it means a company whose shares are admitted to trading on a regulated market,[31] and in Part 13 (resolutions and meetings), where it means a company 'any shares of which (a) carry rights to vote at general meetings, and (b) are admitted to trading on a regulated market in an EEA state by or with the consent of the company'.[32] **2.18**

Distinctions in accounting and reporting requirements

Accounting and reporting requirements vary, depending on whether the company is a small company, so as to qualify for the small companies regime,[33] a micro-entity,[34] a medium-sized company,[35] or a quoted company.[36] **2.19**

Geographical distinctions

There are also geographical distinctions. There are special provisions for overseas companies, being companies incorporated outside the UK.[37] There are also distinctions depending on where the company was incorporated within the UK.[38] **2.20**

---

[28] FCA Listing Rules, Glossary.
[29] 2006 Act, ss 527–31.
[30] 2006 Act, s 385(2). This definition is adopted in ss 361 (for the purposes of Part 13) and 531 (for the purposes of the right of members to raise audit concerns at accounts meeting). The definition may be amended or replaced by regulations (ss 385(4)–(6) and 531(2)).
[31] 2006 Act, s 146(1). By s 1173(1) 'regulated market' has the same meaning as in Directive 2004/39/EC of the European Parliament and of the Council on markets in financial instruments.
[32] 2006 Act, s 360C.
[33] 2006 Act, ss 381–4. For eligibility for the small companies regime, see Ch 26, paras 26.04–26.07 below.
[34] 2006 Act, ss 384A, 384B.
[35] 2006 Act, ss 465–7; see Ch 26 at paras 26.09–26.11 below.
[36] By 2006 Act, s 385.
[37] 2006 Act, s 1044. For the CDDA, s 22(2A) defines an overseas company as 'a company incorporated or formed outside Great Britain', since that Act does not apply to Northern Ireland (except for s 11(1) and (2A)).
[38] 2006 Act, s 88 (Welsh company), ss 861(5) and 879(6) in relation to registration of company charges, and s 1158 (UK-registered company).

Activities

2.21 The activity of a company may determine whether particular provisions of the Companies Acts apply to it and whether it is subject to other forms of regulation.

2.22 There are special rules for distributions by investment companies, by which they may make distributions out of accumulated revenue profits.[39] For this purpose an investment company is a public company which has given notice to the Registrar of its intention to carry on business as an investment company and which, since the date of that notice, carries on the business of investing its funds in shares, land, or other assets, with the aim of spreading risk and giving members of the company the benefit of the results of the management of its funds.

2.23 Banks and banking companies,[40] insurance companies,[41] and open-ended investment companies[42] are regulated in the conduct of their business by the FCA.

2.24 The Companies Act is modified for charitable companies, including modifications in relation to constitutional limitations, directors' duties, and transactions with directors. Also charitable companies are subject to oversight by the Charity Commissioners.[43]

2.25 Community interest companies are subject to the Companies (Audit, Investigations and Community Enterprise) Act 2004 (C(AICE) Act 2004), Part 2.[44]

Other entities

2.26 Some organizations have similarities to companies, but are not companies unless they exercise statutory powers to convert into companies:

(1) Building societies are regulated by the Building Societies Acts 1986 and 1997 and supervised by the FCA.[45] They are not companies, but are managed by directors and can convert into public companies.[46]

(2) Cooperatives (such as consumer, agricultural, or housing cooperatives) and credit unions may be organized as companies, subject to the Companies Acts, but are more

---

[39] 2006 Act, ss 832–3, as amended by the Companies Act 2006 (Amendment of Part 23) (Investment Companies) Regulations 2012, (SI 2012/952) with effect from 6 April 2012.

[40] 2006 Act, s 1164.

[41] 2006 Act, s 1165.

[42] FSMA, Part XVII (collective investment schemes) and in particular ss 236, 262; the Open-Ended Investment Companies Regulations 2001 (SI 2001/1228), as amended by the Open-Ended Investment Companies (Amendment) Regulations 2005 (SI 2005/923) and 2009 (SI 2009/553). Open-ended investment companies can buy back their shares free of the restrictions that apply to ordinary companies. The FCA refers to them as 'investment companies with variable capital'.

[43] 2006 Act, s 42 (constitutional limitations: companies that are charities) and s 181 (modification of ss 175 and 180(2)(b) in relation to charitable companies). The Charity Commissioners have power to authorize dealings with charity property and what would otherwise be a breach of a director's general duties under the 2006 Act, Part 10, ss 170–80 (Charities Act 2011, s 105). The prior written consent of the Charity Commissioners is required for certain transactions that require the approval of members under the 2006 Act, Part 10, Chapter 4 (Charities Act 2011, s 201).

[44] By 2006 Act, s 6, a company may be formed as a community interest company. Also see the Community Interest Company Regulations 2005 (SI 2005/1788), as amended.

[45] Unless they are authorized and regulated by the Prudential Regulation Authority; Building Societies Act 1986, s 119.

[46] See Building Societies Act 1986, Part VII, and Building Societies Act 1997, Part III.

frequently organized as societies and registered under the Co-operative and Community Benefit Societies Act 2014. A registered society may convert to a company.[47]

(3) Friendly Societies (such as workmen's clubs) could not be companies until the Friendly Societies Act 1992 enabled them to establish as, or convert to, companies.

(3) 'Body corporate' and 'corporation'

The 2006 Act, s 1173(1) provides that the expressions 'body corporate' and 'corporation' include 'a body incorporated outside the United Kingdom,[48] but do not include (a) a corporation sole,[49] or (b) a partnership that, whether or not a legal person, is not regarded as a body corporate under the law by which it is governed'. A 'body corporate' in the 2006 Act is a corporation aggregate; ie 'a body of persons which is recognized by the law as having personality which is distinct from the separate personalities of the members of the body or the personality of the individual holder of the office in question for the time being'.[50]   **2.27**

The expressions 'body corporate' and 'corporation' may include: **2.28**

(1) a company formed and registered under the Companies Act 2006;[51]

(2) a company incorporated in the UK, but not formed and registered, or treated as formed and registered under the 2006 Act (ie by royal charter,[52] private or local Act of Parliament,[53] or special public Act of Parliament[54]), to which the 2006 Act applies either because it is entitled to and does register under that Act,[55] or because its provisions apply to it as an unregistered company;[56]

(3) limited liability partnerships under the Limited Liability Partnerships Act 2000, since such partnerships are bodies corporate with unlimited capacity;[57]

---

[47] Co-operative and Community Benefit Societies Act 2014, s 112. Unless it converts into a company, it is not a company for the purposes of the Insolvency Act (in the absence of a contrary statutory intention): *Re Devon and Somerset Farmers Ltd* [1994] Ch 57.

[48] FSMA, s 417(1) provides that in that Act a 'body corporate' includes a body corporate constituted under the law of a country or territory outside the UK.

[49] An individual constitutes a corporation sole by virtue of holding a particular office (the Sovereign, an Archbishop, or the Public Trustee), so the property of the office passes to the successive holders of the office by virtue of appointment or succession without the need for conveyance: Law Commission, *The Execution of Deeds and Documents by or on Behalf of Bodies* (1998, No 253) at para 4.23; also see *Halsbury's Laws of England*, 5th edn (LexisNexis Butterworths, 2010), vol 24, para 314.

[50] Law Commission, *The Execution of Deeds and Documents by or on Behalf of Bodies* (1998, No 253) at para 4.1; also see *Halsbury's Laws of England*, 5th edn (LexisNexis Butterworths, 2010), vol 24, para 312.

[51] This is made explicit by 2006 Act, s 16(2) and (3), and see s 1(1), which treats a company formed and registered under the Companies Act 1985 or the Companies (Northern Ireland) Order 1986 or which was an existing company for the purposes of that Act or Order as if it was formed and registered under the 2006 Act.

[52] At common law these companies, unlike others incorporated by Act of Parliament, have unlimited capacity: *Sutton's Hospital Case* (1612) 10 Co Re 1a, 23a, 30b; *Baroness Wenlock v River Dee Co* (1883) 36 Ch D 675, 685, per Bowen LJ (upheld on appeal at (1885) 10 AC 354). Examples of companies incorporated by Royal Charter are the Institute of Chartered Accountants and the Institute of Chartered Secretaries and Administrators, incorporated in 1880 and 1902 respectively.

[53] These were usually incorporated to undertake public utilities and few remain in existence.

[54] These were usually formed for public-sector activity, but few of them remain following the government's privatization programme, which began with the Telecommunications Act 1984.

[55] 2006 Act, ss 1040–2; the Companies (Companies Authorised to Register) Regulations 2009 (SI 2009/2437).

[56] 2006 Act, s 1043; the Unregistered Companies Regulations 2009 (SI 2009/2436).

[57] Limited Liability Partnerships Act 2000, s 1.

(4) companies incorporated outside the UK, to which the 2006 Act, Part 34 may apply;[58]

(5) European Economic Interest Groupings (EEIG), which if registered in Great Britain are bodies corporate;[59]

(6) European companies or Societas Europaea (SE), intended to facilitate cross-border mergers, which may be set up within the Community in the form of a European public limited-liability company with legal personality;[60] and

(7) European Co-operative Societies (SCE) which have separate legal personality and may be formed to further members' economic and social activities.[61]

2.29 Whereas 'corporation' is only used in the 2006 Act in connection with the representation of a corporation at a company meeting,[62] the expression 'body corporate' is used to enable provisions of the 2006 Act to reach corporations other than companies as defined above,[63] or so that a provision in the 2006 Act may apply to a corporate entity with dealings or connections with a company as:

(1) a member,[64] holding company,[65] associated body corporate,[66] subsidiary undertaking or company,[67] or a person interested in shares in a company;[68]

(2) a director, secretary, or person authorized to certify share transfers on behalf of the company;[69]

(3) an entity in which a director is interested,[70] with which a director is connected,[71] or which is controlled by a director;[72]

(4) a person associated for the purposes of independence requirements;[73]

---

[58] 2006 Act, ss 1044–59 provides a new regime for overseas companies, as discussed in Ch 36 below. Other sections of the Act specifically apply to overseas companies: ss 1066 (company's registered numbers), 1067 (registered numbers of UK establishments of overseas company), 1084 (retention by registrar of records relating to companies that have been dissolved etc), 1139 (service of documents on company) and the 1985 Act, s 453 (Department of BIS investigations). Sections 1044–59 are supported by the Overseas Companies Regulations 2009 (SI 2009/1801) and the Overseas Companies (Execution of Documents and Registration of Charges) Regulations 2009 (SI 2009/1917).

[59] Council Regulation (EEC) No 2137/85. An EEIG may be formed with legal personality (Art 1(3) and reg 3) by existing firms or undertakings in Member States to provide cross-border non-profit-making ancillary services for its members on the basis of unlimited liability (Art 24). An EEIG may be wound up under the Insolvency Act as an unregistered company (regs 7 and 8) and, if wound up, the CDDA applies (reg 20).

[60] Council Regulation 2157/2001; Directive 2001/86; the European Public Limited Company Regulations 2004 (SI 2004/2326). An SE may be wound up under the Insolvency Act if its registered office is in Great Britain (Art 63).

[61] Council Regulation 1435/2003; Directive 2003/72. An SCE may be wound up under the Insolvency Act if it is registered.

[62] 2006 Act, ss 318 and 323.

[63] 2006 Act, s 995(4) (petition by Secretary of State on the ground of unfair prejudice to members), 1985 Act, Parts XIV and XV, as amended by 2006 Act, ss 1035–9, in particular 1985 Act, s 453 (investigation by Secretary of State or inspectors appointed by him of overseas companies carrying on business in Great Britain); 2006 Act, ss 949(3), 1123, 1127 (offences by companies); and 2006 Act, s 1148, applying to ss 1144–8 and Schs 4 and 5 (companies subject to the company communication provisions).

[64] 2006 Act, ss 136(1)(a), 137(1), 148(3)(b), 384(2)(b), 467(2)(b).

[65] 2006 Act, ss 251(3) (shadow director) and 1159.

[66] 2006 Act, ss 176(2), 203(1), 208(1) and (2), 220(2), 256.

[67] 2006 Act, ss 499(2)(a), 500(1), 532(4), 1159, 1161.

[68] 2006 Act, s 823(1) and (2).

[69] 2006 Act, ss 164, 165(6), 278(1), 775(4)(b).

[70] 2006 Act, s 185(2), (3).

[71] 2006 Act, ss 252(2), 254, 255.

[72] 2006 Act, ss 255 and 412(b).

[73] 2006 Act, ss 345(2)(b), 937(2)–(4), 1150, 1152.

(5) an organization in relation to the provisions about political donations and expenditure; and[74]

(6) an entity with whom the company is proposing to merge or enter into an arrangement to allot shares.[75]

The expression 'body corporate' is also used to identify the bodies corporate in respect of which members do not have to approve transactions with directors.[76]

C. The Companies Act 2006 and Other Legislation

(1) The Companies Act

The 2006 Act extends to the whole of the UK including Northern Ireland, unless the context otherwise requires.[77] As originally enacted, it consisted of 47 Parts and 1,300 sections. It also has 16 schedules and is supplemented by more than 50 statutory instruments. It has replaced the provisions of the Companies Act 1985, except for the 1985 Act, Parts XIV and XV, ss 431–57 (investigation of companies and their affairs; requisition of documents; and orders imposing restrictions on shares under the 1985 Act, s 445), as amended by the 2006 Act, Part 32, ss 1035–9, which remain in force.[78] **2.30**

The 2006 Act was enacted on 8 November 2006 and was brought into force by eight Commencement Orders, the last of which took effect on 1 October 2009.[79] In its approach to implementing the 2006 Act the government had three main objectives: (a) the new law should apply in the same way to existing companies and companies formed under the 2006 Act, (b) existing bargains should not be overridden, and (c) it should be as easy as possible for existing companies to take advantage of the new freedoms in the 2006 Act.[80] **2.31**

The 2006 Act s 2(1) defines the Companies Acts as: **2.32**

(1) the company law provisions of the 2006 Act, being Parts 1–39, ss 1–1181, and the provisions of Parts 45–47, ss 1284–1300, as they apply for the purposes of those parts, with Schedules 1–9 and 16;[81]

---

[74] 2006 Act, s 379(1).

[75] 2006 Act, ss 93(6), 594(6), 595, 616.

[76] 2006 Act, ss 188(6), s 190(4), 198(6), 200(6), 201(6), 203(5), 217(4), 218(4).

[77] 2006 Act, ss 1284–7, 1299. In contrast the 1985 Act did not extend to Northern Ireland or apply to companies registered or incorporated in Northern Ireland or outside Great Britain, except where expressly provided—eg the Companies (Northern Ireland) Order 1986 (SI 1986/1032 (NI 6)), the Companies Consolidation (Consequential Provisions) (Northern Ireland) Order 1986 (SI 1986/1035 (NI 9)), and Part 3 of the Companies (Audit, Investigations and Community Enterprise) Order 2005 (SI 2005/1967 (NI 17)).

[78] These provisions were not included in the 2006 Act, because they can go beyond companies and apply to other types of organization.

[79] The 2006 Act Commencement Order No 8 brought into force all the provisions of the 2006 Act not then in force, except for s 22(2) (delayed implementation because of a possible difficulty in relation to the creation or amendment of class rights) and ss 327(2)(c) and 330(6)(c) (both repealed by the Deregulation Act 2015, s 19, Sch 6, Part 8, paras 29 and 30 as from 26 May 2015).

[80] *Implementation of the Companies Act 2006*, a DTI Consultative Document (February 2007) at para 4.6. The government's approach is supported by *Yew Bon Tew v Kenderaan Bas Mara* [1983] 1 AC 553, 562, 563, PC, per Lord Brightman; *Wilson v First County Trust Ltd (No 2)* [2004] 1 AC 816, HL at paras 18 and 19, per Lord Nicholls; at para 98, per Lord Hope; at paras 153 and 154, per Lord Scott; at paras 186–202, per Lord Rodger.

[81] The Parts of the 2006 Act that are not company law provisions are: Part 40, ss 1182–91 (Company Directors: Foreign Disqualification etc); Part 41, ss 1192–208 (Business Names); Part 42, ss 1209–64 (Statutory Auditors); Part 43, ss 1265–73 (Transparency Obligations and Related Matters); Part 44, ss

(2) the Companies (AICE) Act 2004, Part 2, ss 26–67, concerning community interest companies;

(3) the provisions of the 1985 Act, which remain in force, namely Parts XIV and XV, ss 431–457 (investigation of companies and their affairs; requisition of documents; and orders imposing restrictions on shares under the 1985 Act, s 445[82]), as amended by the 2006 Act, Part 32, ss 1035–1039; and

(4) the provisions of the Companies Consolidation (Consequential Provisions) Act 1985, which remain in force, concerning old public companies, as defined by s 1, and miscellaneous savings and amendments relating to the 1985 Act.

Those provisions are considered to be core provisions of company law in that they are concerned with the way companies are formed and run.

The UK Corporate Governance Code

2.33 Since 1992 the Financial Reporting Council has produced a code to promote good corporate governance among listed companies. The current UK Corporate Governance Code[83] applies to all companies with a Premium Listing[84] of equity shares whether they are incorporated in the UK or elsewhere. These companies are expected to comply with the Code or explain any departures. The Listing Rules require companies to apply the main principles of the Code and to report to shareholders how they have done so.

2.34 The main principles of the Code concern (a) leadership for which the chairman is responsible; (b) an effective board with independent non-executive directors and nomination, audit and remuneration committees; (c) accountability of the board, which should present a balanced and understandable assessment of the company's position and prospects; (d) the levels of remuneration of directors, including performance-related elements; and (e) relations with shareholders.

The Takeover Code

2.35 The rules in the Takeover Code, which has been developed since 1968, now have statutory effect and support the 2006 Act, Part 28.[85] The current form of the Takeover Code is published on the Takeover Panel's website.[86] The Code reflects appropriate business standards in relation to takeovers and seeks to achieve fairness to shareholders and to provide an orderly framework for takeovers.

(2) Other legislation

2.36 Other statutes of direct relevance to directors are considered to be on the fringe of core company law. These are statutory provisions, including those formerly included in the 1985 Act about disqualification of directors (CDDA)[87] and insolvency (Insolvency Act).

1274–83 (Miscellaneous Provisions); the related Schs 10–15. Parts 45–7 (ss 1284–300) contain extensions of the Companies Acts and other enactments to Northern Ireland, general supplementary and final provisions.

[82] These provisions were not included in the 2006 Act, because they can go beyond companies and apply to other types of organization.

[83] September 2014, published on the Financial Reporting Council website.

[84] See the Listing Rules in the FCA Handbook.

[85] 2006 Act, s 943, giving effect to the Takeover Directive 2004/25/EC. It also applies to the Isle of Man, Jersey, and Guernsey.

[86] The 11th edition was published on 20 May 2013.

[87] Although foreign disqualification orders are in the 2006 Act, Part 40.

The provisions of FSMA, Part 6 dealing with the official listing of companies are also con- **2.37** sidered to be on the fringe of core company law. These provisions are supported by Part 6 rules made by the FCA, which apply to listed companies. These rules, published in the FCA handbook,[88] comprise listing, disclosure, prospectus, transparency, and corporate govern-ance rules. The provisions in FSMA, Part 8, concerning penalties for market abuse, and Part 25, concerning injunctions and restitution for market abuse, are of particular relevance to directors (see Chapter 32 below).

D. Interpretation of the Companies Act 2006

The government's intention was that the Companies Act 2006 should be drafted 'in clear, **2.38** concise and unambiguous language which can be readily understood by those involved in business enterprise'.[89] The 2006 Act not only includes the new reforming provisions, described in Chapter 1, Section F above, but also restates some of the provisions of the 1985 and 1989 Acts, rewriting them to make them simpler and easier to understand.[90] To assist in understanding the 2006 Act, the government published Explanatory Notes on the Act and tables of derivations and destinations.

The table of derivations identifies (a) provisions that have been re-enacted in the 2006 Act **2.39** without change; (b) provisions that have been re-enacted with one or more primary, and not just consequential, changes, which are indicated by the word 'changed'; (c) new provisions of a mechanical or editorial nature (such as a definition used to avoid repetition), which are indicated by the word 'drafting'; and (d) provisions which have no predecessor in the repealed legislation or which are fundamentally different from their predecessors, which are indicated by the word 'new'. The table of destinations uses the word 'repealed' to identify provisions in the 1985 Act, the Business Names Act 1985, and the 1989 Act, in force on 8 November 2006, which were repealed by the 2006 Act and not re-enacted, even in amended form.

Despite the government's intentions and the assistance in understanding the 2006 Act it has **2.40** provided, it is to be expected that unusual factual situations will expose difficulties of con-struction. In order to understand the background to, and objective of, particular provisions, reference may be made to the reports of the Law Commission, the reports of the CLR and the White Papers, which have been described in Chapter 1, Section E above, and also to the Explanatory Notes on the Act.[91]

To give guidance on the new statutory statement of duties of company directors, in June **2.41** 2007 the government published extracts of statements made by ministers in Parliament during the passage of the bill. Whether or not any of these statements may be admissible in court proceedings under the rule established by *Pepper v Hart*[92] the statements are likely to be a useful guide to understanding the 2006 Act and so many of them are quoted in this work.

---

[88] The FCA Handbook is published on the FCA website.
[89] *Modern Company Law for a Competitive Economy* (March 1998) at para 5.2(c).
[90] Explanatory memorandum to the 2006 Act Commencement Order No 1 at para 4.1.
[91] The court may refer to this material in order to interpret the Act: *Wilson v First County Trust Ltd (No 2)* [2004] 1 AC 816, HL, per Lord Nicholls at para 56; and for explanatory notes *R (Westminster County Court) v National Asylum Service* [2002] 1 WLR 2956, HL, per Lord Steyn at paras 4–6.
[92] [1993] AC 593, HL.

2.42 It is clear that the 2006 Act is intended to mark a new chapter in company law, freed from many of the restrictions and complications of the previous law. Since the 2006 Act combines old and new provisions, difficulties of interpretation or of application of the provisions to particular circumstances may arise. If there are any ambiguities, the court will no doubt prefer the interpretation which furthers rather than hinders the government's stated aim of providing a framework which 'facilitates enterprise and promotes transparency and fair dealing'.[93]

2.43 In relation to interpretation issues, the 2006 Act may be compared with the Insolvency Act 1986, since the latter Act includes not only reforms made by the Insolvency Act 1985 in the light of the report of the Cork Committee,[94] but also provisions about insolvency which derived from the Companies Act 1985 and some provisions about personal bankruptcy which derived from the Bankruptcy Act 1914. The approach of the court to issues of inter-pretation of the Insolvency Act may be instructive in relation to the 2006 Act.

2.44 In *Smith v Braintree District Council*[95] Lord Jauncey of Tullichettle (with whom the other Lords agreed) construed a section of the Insolvency Act 'as a piece of new legislation without regard to 19th century authorities or similar provisions of repealed Bankruptcy Acts', having regard to changes in policy shown by the new Act in relation to that provision.

2.45 In *Re a Debtor (No 784 of 1991)*[96] Hoffmann J, having referred to Lord Jauncey's speech in *Smith* and other authorities, said:

> Those authorities show that, in approaching the language of the Act of 1986, one must pay particular attention to the purposes and policies of its own provisions and be wary of simply carrying over uncritically meanings which had been given to similar words in the earlier Act. It does not, however, mean that the language of the new Act comes to one entirely free of any of the intellectual freight which was carried by words and phrases in earlier bankruptcy or other legislation.

Where there is nothing in the policy of the new Act to indicate that words taken from the old Act should bear a different meaning, they should be interpreted in the same way as in the old Act.

2.46 In *Bishopsgate Investment Ltd v Maxwell*,[97] a case concerning an application for a private examination under s 236, Dillon LJ said:

> there can be no doubt that the primary task of the court is to construe the Insolvency Act 1986 as it stands, without regard to the legislative histories of its various components ... Even so, I have found it essential in the present case to consider the legislative antecedents of the Act of 1986, and the cases decided under them, partly to see how certain provisions of the Act of 1986 can, in the light of previous decisions under the earlier statutes, be expected to fit together, but even more to see what the mischief was in the old law which the Act of 1986 was intended to cure.

---

[93] Foreword of the President of the Board of Trade (Margaret Beckett) to *Modern Company Law for a Competitive Economy* (March 1998); also paras 3.1, 3.8, 5.1, 5.2.
[94] 1982, Cmnd 6659.
[95] [1990] 2 AC 215, 238, HL.
[96] [1992] Ch 554, 558, 559; cited with approval by Ferris J in *Woodland-Ferrari v UCL Group Retirement Scheme* [2003] Ch 115 at para 41.
[97] [1993] Ch 1, 21, CA.

E. Interpretation of the Company's Constitution

If the company was incorporated before 1 October 2009, it will have a memorandum of **2.47** association. It is very rare for an issue of construction to arise in relation to the memorandum, given the nature of matters stated in it. The articles could not be referred to in order to alter or vary what would be the result of the memorandum standing alone,[98] but, in relation to matters not required by statute to be stated in the memorandum, the articles could be read with the memorandum in order to resolve an ambiguity or to supplement the memorandum on a matter on which it is silent.[99] Now, by the 2006 Act, s 28 provisions in a company's memorandum are treated as provisions of the company's articles. Such provisions will therefore be interpreted in the same way as provisions in the articles.

Issues of interpretation of a company's articles of association are also unusual. This is partly **2.48** because most companies have adopted, with or without modification, the form of Table A in force at the time of their registration.[100] It is to be expected that most companies incorporated after 1 October 2009 will adopt, in whole or in part, the relevant model articles.[101] Where a company's articles adopt in part Table A or the relevant model article, they must be construed together and effect given, so far as possible, to every provision; it is only if the express articles are inconsistent with the incorporated regulations of Table A or the model articles that the former will override the latter.[102] Ambiguities, gaps, or errors of drafting may arise in bespoke provisions of a company's articles. Where such deficiencies are revealed, the articles may be amended by special resolution.[103] The court is only likely to be troubled with an issue of interpretation where the issue cannot be resolved by amendment.

Where issues of interpretation of a company's articles do come before a court, they are to be **2.49** resolved in the same way as an issue about the interpretation of any other written contract or instrument.[104] The question for the court is 'what a reasonable person having all the background knowledge which would have been available to the parties would have understood them to be using the language in the contract to mean'.[105] In *Arnold v Britton*,[106] a case concerning the interpretation of provisions in leases, Lord Neuberger quoted that passage with approval and explained that the court focuses on the meaning of the relevant words of the

---

[98] *Guinness v Land Corporation of Ireland* (1882) 22 Ch D 349, 376, CA.

[99] *Angostura Bitters (Dr JGB Siegert and Sons) Ltd v Kerr* [1933] AC 550, 554, PC; *Re Duncan Gilmour & Co Ltd* [1952] 2 All ER 871, 874.

[100] 1985 Act, s 8; 1948 Act, s 8.

[101] 2006 Act, s 20.

[102] *Stothers v William Steward (Holdings) Ltd* [1994] 2 BCLC 266, 273, CA. Since the Interpretation Act 1978 applies to Table A, it will apply to the express articles as well: *Fell v Derby Leather Co Ltd* [1931] 2 Ch 252 (a case on the Interpretation Act 1889).

[103] 2006 Act, s 21. The amendment must be made in good faith in the interests of the company as a whole: *Allen v Gold Reefs of West Africa Ltd* [1900] 1 Ch 656, 671, CA.

[104] The articles have contractual effect: 2006 Act, s 33. *AG of Belize v Belize Telecom Ltd* [2009] 1 WLR 1988, PC at para 16; *Cream Holdings Ltd v Davenport* [2010] EWHC 3096 (Ch) at para 27; *Cosmetic Warriors Ltd v Gerrie* [2015] EWHC 3718 (Ch) at para 7.

[105] *Chartbrook Ltd v Persimmon Homes Ltd* [2009] AC 1101, HL at para 14, per Lord Hoffmann; also *Investors Compensation Scheme Ltd v West Bromwich Building Society* [1998] 1 WLR 896, 912H, HL, per Lord Hoffmann; *Rainy Sky SA v Kookmin Bank* [2011] 1 WLR 2900, SC at paras 14 and 21.

[106] [2015] AC 1619, SC, at para 15 (with whom Lords Sumption, Hughes, and Hodge agreed).

clause in issue in their documentary, factual, and commercial context and assesses its meaning in the light of:

> (i) the natural and ordinary meaning of the clause, (ii) any other relevant provisions of the lease, (iii) the overall purpose of the clause and the lease, (iv) the facts and circumstances known or assumed by the parties at the time that the document was executed, and (v) commercial common sense, but (vi) disregarding evidence of any party's intentions.

2.50 Lord Neuberger emphasized the paramount importance of the language used, which should not be undervalued by invocation of commercial common sense or reference to the surrounding circumstances. The clearer the natural meaning of the words used, the more difficult it is to justify departing from it. The court should not search for, let alone construct, drafting infelicities in order to facilitate a departure from the natural meaning. Nor should the court reject the natural meaning of a provision, because it appears to be a very imprudent term for a party to have agreed. The purpose of interpretation is to identify what the parties have agreed (ie what the provision means), not what they should have agreed.[107]

2.51 While commercial common sense is an important factor to take into account when interpreting an instrument, it should not be invoked retrospectively.[108] In the case of a company's articles, it is only relevant to the extent of how matters would have been perceived by reasonable people at the time they were adopted.[109]

2.52 The general rule is that the contract or other instrument should be interpreted in the context of the relevant background known to all the parties,[110] but where an instrument applies to a number of parties over a period of time, background facts have a more limited part to play. Rather, the instrument should be interpreted as a whole in the light of the commercial intention which may be inferred from the face of the instrument and from the nature of the relevant party's business.[111] Articles of association are the paradigm example of such an instrument. For the purposes of construing articles or considering the implication of a term,

---

[107] *Arnold v Britton* [2015] AC 1619, SC, at paras 17, 18. Also *Chartbrook Ltd v Persimmon Homes Ltd* [2009] AC 1101, HL at para 20, per Lord Hoffmann; *ING Bank NV v Ros Roca* [2011] EWCA Civ 353 at para 110, per Rix LJ; *Rainy Sky SA v Kookmin Bank* [2011] 1 WLR 2900, SC at para 23.

[108] *Arnold v Britton* [2015] AC 1619, SC, at paras 19, 20. *Pink Floyd Music Ltd v EMI Records Ltd* [2010] EWCA Civ 1429 at para 18, per Lord Neuberger MR. Knowledge of established legal principles would be attributed to reasonable people: *Spencer v Secretary of State for Defence* [2012] EWHC 120 (Ch) at paras 74 and 96.

[109] This follows from *Arnold v Britton* [2015] AC 1619, SC, at para 19.

[110] *Investors Compensation Scheme Ltd v West Bromwich Building Society* [1998] 1 WLR 896, 912H-913A, HL, per Lord Hoffmann; *Bank of Credit and Commerce International SA v Ali* [2002] 1 AC 251 at para 39, per Lord Hoffmann; *Arnold v Britton* [2015] AC 1619, SC, at paras 15 and 21. It is not necessary to find an ambiguity in language to justify looking at the background: *R (Westminster City Council) v National Asylum Support Service* [2002] 1 WLR 2956 at para 5, per Lord Steyn (quoted by Lord Clarke in *Oceanbulk Shipping SA v TMT Ltd* [2011] 1 AC 662, HL at para 36).

[111] *Re Sigma Finance Corporation* [2010] 1 All ER 571, SC at paras 10 and 12, per Lord Mance; at para 37, per Lord Collins; *BAI (Run-Off) Ltd v Durham* [2012] 1 WLR 867, SC at para 41, per Lord Mance; *Cherry Tree Investments Ltd v Landmain Ltd* [2013] Ch 305, CA, at paras 99, 124-30, per Lewison LJ, and para 149, per Longmore LJ; *BNY Mellon Corporate Trustee Services Ltd v LBG Capital No 1 plc* [2016] Bus LR 725, SC at paras 30-2.

the courts have declined to take account of circumstances extrinsic to the articles[112] other than the general nature of the company's business.[113]

The court has always taken a commercial approach to the interpretation of articles. In *Holmes* **2.53** *v Keyes*[114] Jenkins LJ said:

> I think that the articles of association of the company should be regarded as a business document and should be construed so as to give them reasonable business efficacy, where a construction tending to that result is admissible on the language of the articles, in preference to a result which would or might prove unworkable.

This approach accords with the commercial common sense approach taken by the court **2.54** where a provision appears to be ambiguous or where it suggested that something has gone wrong with the language or syntax. In these cases, the court adopts an iterative approach, testing the plausibility of a given construction by examining what the consequences may be.[115]

In a case of ambiguity, where there are two possible constructions, the court is entitled to prefer **2.55** the construction which is consistent with business common sense and to reject the other.[116] This may result in the court expressing its interpretation in language which is quite different to that used in the instrument.[117] The court should only depart from the natural and ordinary meaning where it is clear that something has gone wrong with the language and it is also clear what a reasonable person would have understood the parties or the draftsman to have meant.[118]

---

[112] *Egyptian Salt and Soda Co Ltd v Port Said Salt Assoc Ltd* [1931] AC 677, 682, PC; *Bratton Seymour Service Co Ltd v Oxborough* [1992] BCLC 693, 698, and 699; approved in *HSBC Bank Middle East v Clarke* [2006] UKPC 31 at paras 4 and 5. See also *Re Blue Arrow Ltd* [1987] BCLC 585, 590; *Folkes Group plc v Alexander* [2002] 2 BCLC 254 at para 6 (where the court took into account an earlier form of the company's articles); *Cosmetic Warriors Ltd v Gerrie* [2015] EWHC 3718 (Ch) at paras 14–28. For similar reasons the court has no jurisdiction to rectify articles on the ground of mistake: *Scott v Frank F Scott (London) Ltd* [1940] Ch 794, CA. Australian courts have taken a slightly more generous approach to the consideration of the background as an aid to the interpretation of a company's constitution: *Lion Nathan Australia Pty Ltd v Coopers Brewery Ltd* [2006] FCAFC 144.

[113] *Equitable Life Assurance Society v Hyman* [2002] 1 AC 408, 459, per Lord Steyn, HL; *AG of Belize v Belize Telecom Ltd* [2009] 1 WLR 1988, PC at paras 35–7, per Lord Hoffmann.

[114] [1959] Ch 199, 215, CA. *Rayfield v Hands* [1960] Ch 1 shows the application of this principle and the maxim 'validate if possible' in relation to directors' obligation to buy shares at fair value. In *Cream Holdings Ltd v Davenport* [2009] BCC 183, CA, the Court of Appeal gave a commercial meaning to badly drafted articles dealing with the procedure for valuing shares on the removal of a director.

[115] *Charter Reinsurance Co v Fagan* [1997] AC 313, 326 (in the judgment of Mance J), 384–6, per Lord Mustill; *Re Sigma Finance Corporation* [2009] BCC 393, CA at para 98, per Lord Neuberger; [2010] 1 All ER 571, SC at para 12, per Lord Mance; *Al Sanea v Saad Investment Co Ltd* [2012] EWCA Civ 313 at para 31; *Arnold v Britton* [2015] AC 1619, SC, at para 77, per Lord Hodge.

[116] *Rainy Sky SA v Kookmin Bank* [2011] 1 WLR 2900, SC at paras 20 and 21, per Lord Clarke; *BAI (Run-Off) Ltd v Durham* [2012] 1 WLR 867, SC at para 26; *Barclays Bank plc v HHY Luxembourg SARL* [2011] 1 BCLC 336, CA at paras 25 and 26. There is a distinction between cases of ambiguity and mistake; in the former case, the court has more flexibility to adopt a commercial interpretation; see also *Pink Floyd Music Ltd v EMI Records Ltd* [2010] EWCA Civ 1420 at para 20; *LB Re Financing No 3 Ltd v Excalibur Funding No 1 plc* [2011] EWHC 2111 (Ch) at para 46.

[117] *Chartbrook Ltd v Persimmon Homes Ltd* [2009] AC 1101, HL at para 21 per Lord Hoffmann.

[118] *Investors Compensation Scheme Ltd v West Bromwich Building Society* [1998] 1 WLR 896, 913D–F, HL, per Lord Hoffmann; *Chartbrook Ltd v Persimmon Homes Ltd* [2009] AC 1101, HL at para 25, per Lord Hoffmann; *ING Bank NV v Ros Roca* [2012] 1 WLR 472, CA at paras 22, 24, 25, per Carnwath LJ; at paras 80–3, per Rix LJ; *Thompson v Goblin Hills Hotels Ltd* [2011] 1 BCLC 587, PC; *Arnold v Britton* [2015] AC 1619, SC, at paras 18, per Lord Neuberger.

2.56 In *AG of Belize v Belize Telecom Ltd*,[119] a case concerning the implication of a term in a company's articles, Lord Hoffmann said that the implication of a term is an exercise in the construction of the instrument as a whole and observed that '[t]here is only one question; is that what the instrument, read as a whole against the relevant background, would reasonably be understood to mean?'.

2.57 In *Marks and Spencer plc v BNP Paribas Securities Services Trust Company (Jersey) Ltd*[120] Lord Neuberger summarized the law relating to the implication of a term into a particular contract in light of the express terms, commercial common sense, and the facts known to both parties at the time the contract was made. He went on to make two points about Lord Hoffmann's observation in the *Belize* case.[121] The first point was that Lord Hoffmann's observation was acceptable provided that (i) the reasonable reader is treated as reading the contract at the time it is made, since the question whether a term is to be implied is to be judged at the date the contract is made, and (ii) the reasonable reader would consider the term to be so obvious as to go without saying or to be necessary to give business efficacy to the contract, since no term will be implied unless one or other of those conditions is satisfied.[122] The second point was that interpreting the express words of a contract and implying additional words are different processes governed by different rules, since the question of whether a term should be implied only arises after the express terms have been construed and involves the interpolation of terms for which the parties have made no provision.[123]

2.58 As noted in paragraph 2.52 above, the background to interpretation of a company's articles or the implication of a term in them is usually restricted to the general nature of the company's business which would be known to everyone dealing with it. Even so, there have been several cases where the court has been able to imply a term in articles—usually where the scheme laid down in the articles would not work without such a term.[124] On the other hand, in *McKillen v Misland (Cyprus) Investments Ltd* there was an apparent error in the articles, but no term could be implied, since the court was not satisfied as to the nature of the error and the suggested term would affect other parties' rights.[125]

---

[119] [2009] 1 WLR 1988, PC at paras 16–21.

[120] [2016] AC 742, SC at paras 14–21 (Lords Clarke, Sumption, and Hodge agreed with Lord Neuberger).

[121] At paras 22–31.

[122] In this respect Lord Neuberger approved *BP Refinery (Westernport) Pty Ltd v President, Councillors and Ratepayers of the Shire of Hastings* (1977) 52 ALJR 20, 26, PC, per Lord Simon and *Philips Electronique Grand Public SA v British Sky Broadcasting Ltd* [1995] EMLR 472, 481, 482, CA, per Sir Thomas Bingham MR. For other cases showing that a term will only be implied if it is strictly necessary to do so, see *Mediterranean Salvage & Towage Ltd v Seamar Trading & Commerce Inc* [2009] 2 Lloyd's Rep 639, CA at paras 15–18; *Eastleigh Borough Council v Town Quay Developments Ltd* [2009] EWCA Civ 1391 at para 30.

[123] In this respect Lord Neuberger approved the *Philips* case at 481.

[124] The *Belize* case itself (implied term that a director would vacate office when there was no longer an appropriate shareholder to authorize his appointment); *Equitable Life Assurance Society v Hyman* [2002] 1 AC 408 (implied term preventing directors from exercising discretion to defeat guaranteed annuities); *Tett v Phoenix Property and Investment Co Ltd* [1986] BCLC 149, CA (implied term requiring service of notice of intention to transfer shares); *Cream Holdings Ltd v Davenport* [2012] 2 BCLC 365, CA (implied term that members would cooperate to make share valuation process effective); *Cosmetic Warriors Ltd v Gerrie* [2015] EWHC 3718 (Ch) at paras 90–2 (implied terms as to provision of information to valuer). The court declined to imply a term that reasonable steps should be taken to have the company's accounts audited prior to the issue of a share transfer notice, alternatively prior to the auditors carrying out a valuation of the shares: *Dashfield v Davidson (No 2)* [2008] BCC 662 at paras 82–4.

[125] [2012] BCC 575, CA.

Part II

THE OFFICE OF DIRECTOR

3

DIRECTORS AND OTHER OFFICERS: REQUIREMENT AND DEFINITIONS

Adam Goodison

A. The Requirement for a Company to Have Directors

Every private company must have at least one director and every public company must have at **3.01** least two directors.[1] The Model Articles[2] do not provide for minimum or maximum numbers of directors, leaving that matter to the Companies Act, but Table A, reg 64 provides: 'Unless otherwise determined by ordinary resolution, the number of directors (other than alternate directors) shall not be subject to any maximum but shall not be less than two.'

As originally enacted, the 2006 Act stated[3] that every company must have at least one direc- **3.02** tor who is a natural person, although the requirement was met if the office of director is held by a natural person as a corporation sole[4] or otherwise by virtue of an office. The Small Business, Enterprise and Employment Act 2015 (SBEE Act 2015) has amended the 2006 Act, so that it is no longer permissible to appoint corporate directors, save in circumstances prescribed by regulation.[5] As a result, there is now a general requirement that company

---

[1] 2006 Act, s 154; in force 1 October 2007.

[2] For companies registered before 1 October 2007, Table A of the Companies Act 1985 (SI 1985/805) continues to apply. For companies registered on or after 1 October 2007 (but before 1 October 2009), Table A with the amendments made by SI 2007/2541 and SI 2007/2826 applies.

[3] 2006 Act, s 155; in force 1 October 2008.

[4] eg the Archbishop of Canterbury.

[5] SBEE Act 2015, s 87 (2), which deleted s 155 of the 2006 Act, and inserted ss 156A–156 C into the 2006 Act. The amendment comes into effect on a date to be appointed. It is anticipated that pension trustee

directors must be natural persons (individuals, which will include a natural person who is a corporation sole or otherwise is a director by virtue of an office). An appointment made in contravention of s 156A (for example the appointment of a corporate director) is void.[6] If at the date when the amendment comes into effect, where a person who is not a natural person holds office as a director, and the case is not one excepted from that section by regulations under s 156B, that person shall cease to be a director on the day after the end of the period of 12 months beginning on the day on which section 156A came into force.[7] A non-natural person can still be found to have acted as a de facto director or shadow director and be liable as such.[8]

3.03   Section 156[9] gives the Secretary of State power to require a company to comply with s 154 (requirements as to number of directors). The Secretary of State's direction must specify (a) the statutory requirement the company appears to be in breach of, (b) what the company must do in order to comply with the direction, and (c) the period within which it must do so. That period must be not less than one month or more than three months after the date on which the direction is given.[10] The company must comply with the direction by making the necessary appointments and giving notice of them to the Registrar of Companies before the end of the period specified in the direction,[11] or if the company has already made the necessary appointment or appointments (or so far as it has done so), it must comply with the direction by giving notice of them under s 167 before the end of the period specified in the direction. If a company fails to comply with a direction, an offence is committed by the company and by every officer of the company who is in default (and for this purpose a shadow director is treated as an officer of the company).[12]

3.04   The civil consequences of the number of directors falling below the statutory minimum are discussed in Ch 6 at paragraphs 6.04 and 6.05 below.

B. The Statutory Meaning

3.05   Section 250 provides: 'In the Companies Acts "director" includes any person occupying the position of director, by whatever name called.'[13] Thus the name or description of the role or position is not relevant in deciding whether someone is a director, and instead the court will examine the substance of the person's activities to decide whether he occupies the position of director. By s 1173 a director is an officer of a company.

---

companies and other companies engaged in high value and low risk activities will be included among the companies for which the regulations will make exceptions.

  [6] 2006 Act, s 156A (3). See s 156A (1) and (2).
  [7] 2006 Act, s 156 C (2).
  [8] 2006 Act, s 156A (4).
  [9] In force 1 October 2008. This section also gives the Secretary of State power to compel compliance with s 155 until its repeal by SBEE Act 2015 takes effect.
  [10] 2006 Act, s 156(2).
  [11] 2006 Act, ss 156(4) and 167.
  [12] 2006 Act, s 156(6).
  [13] The definitions in the Model Article (plc) 1 and Model Article (pcls) 1 use similar wording stating that 'director' means a director of the company, and includes any person occupying the position of director, by whatever name called. Insolvency Act, s 251 and CDDA s 22(4) both adopt the same inclusive meaning of 'director'.

The 1844 Act defined the word 'directors' as meaning 'the persons having the direction, conduct, **3.06** management, or superintendence of the affairs of the company'. Subsequent Companies Acts have not included such a description of the 'position of director'. Instead the articles of the company have identified the directors' functions and powers. Thus Table A, reg 70 provides that, subject to the provisions of the 1985 Act, 'the business of the company shall be managed by the directors who may exercise all the powers of the company'. Model Article (plc) 3 and Model Article (pcls) 3 both provide: 'Subject to the articles, the directors are responsible for the management of the company's business, for which purpose they may exercise all the powers of the company.'[14]

The phrase 'by whatever name called' (s 250) covers alternative descriptions in a company's **3.07** constitution of the office of director, such as 'governor' or 'manager'.[15] Other descriptions of the persons managing the affairs of a company, occasionally found in company constitutions, are 'council', 'managing committee', or 'managers'. Such descriptions of persons occupying the position of directors are now unusual. The directors of charitable companies are often called 'trustees'.

C. Types of Director

(1) Appointed directors

Anyone may be appointed to act as a director if willing to act, unless prohibited by law. As to **3.08** those prohibited from acting as directors, see Chapter 6 below (for appointment, minimum age requirements, disqualification, etc) and note also paragraphs 3.01 and 3.02 above.

Model Article (pcls) 17 provides that for private companies, any person who is willing to act **3.09** as a director, and is permitted by law to do so, may be appointed to be a director by ordinary resolution of the shareholders or by a decision of the directors. Model Article (plc) 20 is in identical terms for public companies.

(2) De facto directors

Persons who undertake the functions of directors, even though not formally appointed as **3.10** such, are called de facto directors. Since a de facto director is within the definition of a 'director', he will owe to the relevant company all the general duties of a director specified in ss 171–7, and will have all the other responsibilities and liabilities of a director under the 2006 Act and under the Insolvency Act 1986.[16]

---

[14] In its response to consultation on the model articles (URN 07/1227) the government commented as regards Model Article 3:

> As set out in the February consultation document, previous wording used in the drafting of this article arguably gave rise to doubts as to whether the directors could dispose of the company's business without the consent of shareholders—we changed it to put this beyond doubt. One respondent to the February consultation considered that the article as drafted would not be applicable to dormant companies. We do not agree. The directors are still responsible for the activity of a company even if it is dormant—in deciding that it should be dormant and when it would cease to be dormant—therefore they are still managing the business. We do not therefore propose to change the drafting of this article. [Para 17, July 2007 response.]

[15] *Re Lo-Line Electric Motors Ltd* [1988] Ch 477, 488.

[16] *Revenue and Customs Commissioners v Holland, Re Paycheck Services 3 Ltd* (*Paycheck*) [2010] 1 WLR 2793, SC, at para 25, per Lord Hope; at para 56, per Lord Collins; at para 136, per Lord Clarke; *Re Canadian Land Reclaiming and Colonizing Co* (1880) 14 Ch D 660, 670; *Ultraframe (UK) Ltd v Fielding* [2004] RPC 24 at para 39; *Primelake Ltd v Matthews Associates* [2007] 1 BCLC 666 at para 284.

3.11 The modern law about de facto directors begins with *Re Lo-Line Ltd*[17] where Sir Nicholas Browne-Wilkinson V-C held that a former director who carried on running the company as manager could be disqualified under the CDDA, since a person was a director, for purposes of the CDDA, 'whether validly appointed, invalidly appointed, or assuming to act as a director without any appointment at all'. That case and all the earlier cases about de facto directors concerned persons whose appointment was defective or who had been, but had ceased to be, directors.[18]

3.12 Where it was alleged that a person was a de facto director, even though he had never even purportedly been appointed a director, it became necessary for the court to look closely at the conduct that might make a person a de facto director. In *Re Hydrodam (Corby) Ltd*[19] Millett J described a de facto director as:

> a person who assumes to act as a director. He is held out as a director by the company, claims and purports to be a director, although never actually or validly appointed as such. To establish that a person was a de facto director of a company it is necessary to plead and prove that he undertook functions in relation to the company which could probably be discharged only by a director. It is not sufficient to show that he was concerned in the management of a company's affairs or undertook tasks in relation to its business which can probably be performed by a manager below board level. A de facto director, I repeat, is one who claims to act and purports to act as director although not validly appointed as such.
>
> Attendance at board meetings and voting, with others, may in certain limited circumstances expose a director to personal liability to the company of which he is a director or its creditors. But it does not, without more, constitute him a director of any company of which his company is a director.

3.13 Millett J's exposition was applied in several subsequent cases prior to the decision of the Supreme Court in the *Paycheck* case.[20] To determine whether a person was a de facto director, the court took into account all the relevant factors, not merely statutory functions, including at least (a) directing others, (b) committing the company to major obligations, or (c) participating on an equal level in collective decisions made by the board, (d) whether or not there was a holding out by the company of the individual as a director, (e) whether the individual used the title 'director', (f) whether the individual had proper information (eg management accounts) on which to base decisions, and (g) whether the individual had to make major decisions.[21]

3.14 In the *Paycheck* case[22] the Paycheck companies, which only had a corporate director (a situation now prohibited by the 2006 Act, s 155), went into insolvent liquidation and the

---

[17] [1988] Ch 477, 490.
[18] The early cases are reviewed in the judgment of Lord Collins in the *Paycheck* case at [2010] 1 WLR 2793 at paras 58–81.
[19] [1994] 2 BCLC 180, 183, 184.
[20] *Secretary of State for Trade and Industry* [1998] 1 BCLC 333; *Re Kaytech International plc* [1999] 2 BCLC 351, CA; *Ultraframe (UK) Ltd v Fielding* [2005] EWHC 1638 (Ch) at paras 1255–7; *Secretary of State for Trade and Industry v Hollier* [2007] BCC 11; *Re Mea Corporation Ltd, Secretary of State for Trade and Industry v Aviss* [2007] 1 BCLC 618; *Secretary of State for Trade and Industry v Hall* [2009] BCC 190 (expressly overruled by the *Paycheck* case); *Gemma Ltd v Davies* [2008] 2 BCLC 281; *Secretary of State for BERR v Poulter* [2009] BCC 608.
[21] *Secretary of State for Trade and Industry v Tjolle* [1998] 1 BCLC 333, 343.
[22] [2010] 1 WLR 2793, SC.

liquidator brought misfeasance proceedings under the Insolvency Act, s 212 against the individual who was a director of the corporate director on the grounds that he was a de facto director of each of the Paycheck companies and was responsible for the payment by them of unlawful dividends. By a majority of three to two the Supreme Court held that the individual was not a de facto director of the Paycheck companies.

Lord Hope (in the majority) commended the 'without more' approach taken by Millett J in **3.15** *Re Hydrodam (Corby) Ltd*, quoted at paragraph 3.12 above, and said:

> The words 'without more' are important. They indicate that the mere fact of acting as a director of a corporate director will not be enough for that individual to become a de facto director of the subject company.[23]

Lord Hope agreed with Millett J that it is possible to obtain some guidance by looking at the purpose of the Insolvency Act, s 212 under which:

> liability is imposed on those who were in a position to prevent damage to creditors by taking proper steps to protect their interests. As he put it, those who assume to act as directors and who thereby exercise the powers and discharge the functions of a director, whether validly appointed or not, must accept the responsibilities of the office. So one must look at what the person actually did to see whether he assumed those responsibilities in relation to the subject company.[24]

After referring to the need to recognize the separate legal personality of the corporate director (*Salomon v A Salomon & Co Ltd*)[25] Lord Hope stated the guiding principle that applied where it was alleged that a director of a corporate director was a de facto director:

> So long as the relevant acts are done by the individual entirely within the ambit of the discharge of his duties and responsibilities as a director of the corporate director, it is to that capacity that his acts must be attributed.[26]

Lord Collins (also in the majority) identified the question as one of principle: **3.16**

> whether fiduciary duties can be imposed, in relation to a company whose sole director is a corporate director, on a director of that corporate director when all of his relevant acts were done as a director of the corporate director and can be attributed in law solely to the activities of the corporate director.[27]

After a full review of the authorities, Lord Collins concluded that, in the context of the fiduciary duty not to misapply the company's assets, the crucial question is whether the person assumed the duties of a director, ie whether he was 'part of the corporate governing structure' and whether 'he assumed a role in the company sufficient to impose on him a fiduciary duty to the company to make him responsible for the misuse of its assets'.[28] Applying that test the claim failed. Lord Walker, in a powerful dissent, agreed with Lord Collins that 'assumption of responsibility' is the appropriate test to determine whether a person is a de facto director, but found that the test was satisfied on the facts of the *Paycheck* case.[29]

---

[23] [2010] 1 WLR 2793, SC, at para 29.
[24] [2010] 1 WLR 2793, SC, at para 39.
[25] [1897] AC 22.
[26] [2010] 1 WLR 2793, SC, at para 42.
[27] [2010] 1 WLR 2793, SC, at para 53.
[28] [2010] 1 WLR 2793, SC, at para 93.
[29] [2010] 1 WLR 2793, SC, at para 121 (and paras 114 and 115). Lord Clarke agreed with Lord Walker's reasons (para 126).

3.17 In *Re Mumtaz Properties Ltd*[30] the Court of Appeal applied the Supreme Court's decision in the *Paycheck* case to an informally run family company in order to determine whether a member of the family was liable as a de facto director for breach of fiduciary duty. The Court of Appeal found that the individual was liable, because the totality of the evidence showed that he was 'part of the corporate governance structure' and 'one of the nerve centres from which the activities of the Company radiated'.[31]

3.18 By contrast, in *Smithton Ltd v Naggar*[32], the Court of Appeal again applied the Supreme Court's decision[33] in holding that the director of a former holding company was not a de facto director of the subsidiary in circumstances where the subsidiary had suffered trading losses on trades introduced by him to the subsidiary. Arden LJ identified a number of points to assist in determining whether a person is a de facto director.[34]

(1) The concepts of shadow director and de facto director are different but there is some overlap.

(2) A person may be a de facto director even if there was no invalid appointment. The question is whether he has assumed responsibility to act as a director.

(3) To answer that question, the court may have to determine in what capacity the director was acting.

(4) The court will in general also have to determine the corporate governance structure of the company so as to decide in relation to the company's business whether the defendant's acts were directorial in nature.

(5) The court is required to look at what the director actually did and not any job title actually given to him.

(6) A defendant does not avoid liability if he shows that he in good faith thought he was not acting as a director. The question whether or not he acted as a director is to be determined objectively and irrespective of the defendant's motivation or belief.

(7) The court must look at the cumulative effect of the activities relied on. The court should look at all the circumstances 'in the round'.

(8) It is also important to look at the acts in their context. A single act might lead to liability in an exceptional case.

(9) Relevant factors include: (i) whether the company considered him to be a director and held him out as such; (ii) whether third parties considered that he was a director.

(10) The fact that a person is consulted about directorial decisions or his approval does not in general make him a director because he is not making the decision.

---

[30] [2012] BCLC, CA. Also see *Re Idessa (UK) Ltd* [2012] 1 BCLC 80 at paras 35–40; *McKillen v Misland (Cyprus) Investments Ltd* [2012] EWHC 521 (Ch); *Re Snelling House Ltd* [2012] EWHC 440 (Ch) at paras 23–39.

[31] [2012] 2 BCLC 109, CA at para 47, per Arden LJ.

[32] [2015] 1 WLR 189, CA.

[33] See also *Elsworth Ethanol Co Ltd v Hartley* [2015] 1 BCLC 221 where the High Court held that there was no single test by which a de facto director could be defined, however, the principles of whether an individual was acting on an equal footing with the true directors of a company, whether he held himself out as a director, and whether he was part of the corporate governing structure of a company would all be relevant in the decision. In *Energenics Holdings Pte Ltd v Hazarika* [2014] EWHC 1845 (Ch) the High Court held that the court should take into account all the relevant factors in deciding whether a person at the relevant time assumed to act as a director or exercised the powers and discharged the functions of a director so as to be a de facto director (see para 88 of the judgment). And see *International Cat Manufacturing Pty Ltd v Rodrick* [2013] QSC 91, paras 152 to 190 (court deciding that investor was a de facto director, taking account of his involvement in the company's affairs) (the finding as regards the de facto directorship issue was not appealed: see [2013] QCA 372, paras 20–5).

[34] [2015] 1 WLR 189 at paras 33–45, CA.

(11) Acts outside the period when he is said to have been a de facto director may throw light on whether he was a de facto director in the relevant period.

A de facto director is not to be regarded as a director for all purposes of the Companies Act.[35] Since a de facto director is within the definition of a director in s 251 he is subject to all the provisions in the 2006 Act, Part 10 about a company's directors, but the application of those provisions to a particular de facto director may depend on the circumstances.   **3.19**

(3) Shadow directors

The Companies Act

Section 251 defines 'shadow director':[36]   **3.20**

(1) In the Companies Acts 'shadow director', in relation to a company, means a person in accordance with whose directions or instructions the directors of a company are accustomed to act.

(2) A person is not to be regarded as a shadow director by reason only that the directors act—
   (a) on advice given by that person in a professional capacity;
   (b) in accordance with instructions, a direction, guidance or advice given by that person in the exercise of a function conferred by or under an enactment;
   (c) in accordance with guidance or advice given by that person in that person's capacity as a Minister of the Crown (within the meaning of the Ministers of the Crown Act 1975).

(3) A body corporate is not to be regarded as a shadow director of any of its subsidiary companies for the purposes of—
   Chapter 2 (general duties of directors),
   Chapter 4 (transactions requiring members' approval), or
   Chapter 6 (contract with sole member who is also a director), by reason only that the directors of the subsidiary are accustomed to act in accordance with its directions or instructions.

The concept of a 'shadow director' was introduced by the 1980 Act, s 63 to strengthen the new provisions of Part IV of that Act, concerning duties of directors and conflicts of interest, which were later incorporated into Part X of the 1985 Act and have been replaced by provisions in the Companies Act, Part 10, Chapters 3–6.[37] 'Shadow director' therefore fulfils a statutory purpose.   **3.21**

The Companies Act makes clear when and how a provision applies to a shadow director: **3.22**

(1) A shadow director is treated as an officer of the company for the purpose of committing an offence on default in relation to provisions in:
   (a) Part 5 concerning a company's name;[38]
   (b) Part 10, Chapter 1, concerning (i) a direction from the Secretary of State to appoint a director,[39] (ii) the register of directors,[40] (iii) the register of directors' residential addresses,[41] and (iv) the duty to notify the Registrar of changes; and[42]

---

[35] *Re Lo-Line Electric Motors Ltd* [1988] BCLC 698, 706, 707.

[36] As amended, as regards sub-s (2), by SBEE Act 2015, s 90(3) with effect from 26 May 2015.

[37] The philosophy behind 'shadow director' can be traced back to the First World War, when Companies (Particulars as to Directors) Act 1917 was enacted to provide for the disclosure of 'certain particulars respecting the Directors of Companies'. Section 3 provided that 'the expression "director" shall include any person who occupies the position of a director and any person in accordance with whose directions or instructions the directors of a company are accustomed to act'. The actual phrase 'shadow director' was not used in that 1917 Act.

[38] 2006 Act, ss 63(2), 68(5), 75(5), 76(5).

[39] 2006 Act, s 156(6).

[40] 2006 Act, s 162(6).

[41] 2006 Act, s 165(4).

[42] 2006 Act, s 167(4).

(c) Part 12, concerning (i) a direction from the Secretary of State to a public company to appoint a secretary,[43] (ii) the register of secretaries,[44] and (iii) the duty to notify the Registrar of changes.[45]

(2) A person under the age of 16 who acts a shadow director may be liable under any provision of the Companies Acts even though he could not be validly appointed a director.[46]

(3) The scope and nature of general duties of directors, set out in Part 10, Chapter 2, apply to shadow directors 'where and to the extent that they are capable of so applying'.[47]

(4) A shadow director is under the duty in s 182 to disclose an interest in an existing transaction or arrangement, but the declaration must be made by notice, including a general notice, in writing.[48]

(5) A shadow director is treated as a director for the purposes of the provisions of Part 10, Chapter 4–6 concerning:[49]

(a) transactions requiring members approval;[50]

(b) remuneration and loss of office payments to directors of quoted companies (but loss of office does not include loss of a person's status as a shadow director);[51]

(b) disclosure of directors' service contracts; and[52]

(c) contracts with a sole member who is a director.[53]

(6) A shadow director is treated as a director for the purposes of the provisions of Chapter 7, s 239 concerning ratification by a company of acts of directors.[54]

(7) A resolution of directors is not sufficient sanction for payments to or for the benefit of shadow directors under s 247, which gives directors power to make provision for employees on cessation or transfer of business in accordance with that section (so that such payments must be authorized by the members).

(8) A shadow director is treated as a director for the purposes of derivative claims in England and Wales and Northern Ireland under Part 11.[55]

(9) The expression 'director' includes a shadow director for the purposes of Part 14, concerning the control of political donations and expenditure.[56]

---

[43] 2006 Act, s 272(6).

[44] 2006 Act, s 275(6).

[45] 2006 Act, s 276(3).

[46] 2006 Act, s 157(5).

[47] 2006 Act, s 170(5). The 2005 Act, s 170 (5) originally provided that the general duties owed by directors applied to shadow directors where, and to the extent that, the corresponding common law rules or equitable principles applied. The SBEE Act 2015 replaced this provision with the new s 170 (5) in the 2006 Act, effective from 26 May 2015, to resolve previous uncertainty as to whether shadow directors owed common law duties to creditors: see *Vivendi SA v Richards* 2013 BCC 771. The general duties are discussed in Chs 10–17 below.

[48] 2006 Act, s 187. This duty is discussed in Ch 17 below.

[49] Discussed in Ch 18 below.

[50] 2006 Act, s 223(2).

[51] 2006 Act, s 226A(9). Chapter 4A was inserted by the Enterprise and Regulatory Reform Act 2013, s 80 as from 1 October 2013.

[52] 2006 Act, s 230.

[53] 2006 Act, s 231(5).

[54] 2006 Act, s 239(5)(c). Discussed in Ch 20 below.

[55] 2006 Act, s 260. Discussed in Ch 22 below.

[56] 2006 Act, s 379. Discussed in Ch 22 below.

Part 28 concerns takeovers and the Takeover Panel. The Takeover Code provides: 'Directors **3.23** include persons in accordance with whose instructions the directors or a director are accustomed to act.'[57]

Insolvency Act

For the purposes of the Insolvency Act, Parts I–VII, s 251 of that Act gives substantially the **3.24** same definition of 'shadow director' as is contained in s 251(1) and (2) of the Companies Act.[58]

Under the Insolvency Act: **3.25**

(1) The expression 'officer' includes a shadow director for the purposes of liability for criminal offences for fraud in anticipation of winding up, misconduct in the course of the winding up, material omissions from any statement relating to the company's affairs, and false representations to creditors.[59]

(2) Section 214 provides that in that section, concerning directors' liability for wrongful trading, the expression 'director' includes a shadow director for the purpose of liability for wrongful trading.[60]

(3) A shadow director who contravenes the provisions of s 216 concerning the reuse of a prohibited company name commits a criminal offence.[61]

It should be noted that a person who is only a 'shadow director' is not amenable to a sum- **3.26** mary remedy for misfeasance under the Insolvency Act, s 212.[62] For that purpose the shadow director would also have to be an officer of the company or to have taken part in its promotion, formation, or management. Nor is a person who is merely a shadow director necessarily liable for fraudulent trading under the Insolvency Act, s 213. For that purpose the shadow director must also have been knowingly party to the carrying on of the company's fraudulent business.

The Insolvency Act, s 249 also provides that a person is connected with a company if he is a **3.27** shadow director. Under the Insolvency Act:

(1) A liquidator who exercises his powers to dispose of any property of the company to a person connected with the company is obliged to give notice of that exercise of his powers to the liquidation committee if there is one.[63]

(2) In the case of a preference given to a person connected with the company: (a) it is presumed, unless the contrary is shown, that the company was influenced in deciding to give it by such a desire as is mentioned in subs 239(5);[64] and (b) the relevant time is extended from six months to two years.

(4) In the case of a transaction at undervalue entered into by a company with a person connected with the company, it is presumed, unless the contrary is shown, that the company

---

[57] The Takeover Code, (11th edn, 20 May 2013), 'Definitions' at page C9.
[58] Insolvency Act, s 251 was amended by the SBEE Act 2015, s 90(1) with effect from 26 May 2015 so that the definition is the same as in the 2006 Act, s 251.
[59] Insolvency Act, ss 206(3), 208(3), 210(3), 211(2). Criminal offences under the Insolvency Act are discussed in Ch 35, Section J below.
[60] Insolvency Act, s 214(7). Sections 214 and 216 are discussed in Ch 34, Sections C and D below.
[61] Insolvency Act, s 216(1).
[62] The *Paycheck* case [2010] 1 WLR 2793 at para 22, per Lord Hope; at para 55, per Lord Collins.
[63] Insolvency Act, ss 165(6) and 167(2)(a).
[64] Insolvency Act, s 239(6), unless the only connection is being an employee.

was at the time unable to pay its debts within the meaning of the Insolvency Act, s 123, or became unable to pay its debts within the meaning of that section in consequence of the transaction.[65]

(5) In the case of a floating charge created in favour of a person connected with the company, the relevant time for avoidance is extended from one to two years, without the need to prove that the company was unable to pay its debts or became unable to pay its debts in consequence of the creation of the charge.[66]

CDDA

3.28 The Company Directors Disqualification Act 1986, s 22(5) also adopts substantially the same definition of shadow director as is contained in the Companies Act, s 251(1) and (2).[67]

3.29 A shadow director is liable to be disqualified:

(1) for fraud in relation to a company being wound up;[68]

(2) for conduct as a director of an insolvent company, which makes him unfit to be concerned in the management of a company;[69]

(3) if, after an investigation, it is expedient in the public interest that a disqualification order should be made; [70] and

(4) for competition infringements.[71]

FSMA

3.30 In FSMA 'director', in relation to a body corporate, includes a person in accordance with whose directions or instructions (not being advice given in a professions capacity) the directors of that body are accustomed to act.[72]

Judicial comment

3.31 In *Re Hydrodam (Corby) Ltd* Millett J described the characteristics of a shadow director in contrast to a de facto director:

> A shadow director, by contrast, does not claim or purport to act as a director. On the contrary, he claims not to be a director. He lurks in the shadows, sheltering behind others who, he claims, are the only directors of the company to the exclusion of himself. He is not held out as a director by the company. To establish that a defendant is a shadow director of a company it is necessary to allege and prove: (1) who are the directors of the company, whether de facto or

---

[65] Insolvency Act, s 240(2).

[66] Insolvency Act, s 245(3)(a) and (4).

[67] CDDA, s 22(5) was amended by the SBEE Act 2015, s 90(2) with effect from 26 May 2015 so that the definition is the same as in the 2006 Act, s 251.

[68] CDDA, s 4(2). Disqualification is discussed in Ch 31 below.

[69] CDDA, s 6(3C). By CDDA, s 7A(12), in s 7A 'director' includes shadow director for the purposes of an office-holder's report on conduct of directors (inserted by SBEE Act 2015, s 107(1), (2), in force from 6 April 2016). Note that CDDA, ss 8ZA–8ZE (order disqualifying a person instructing an unfit director; inserted by SBEE Act 2015, s 105, in force from 1 October 2015) does not apply where the disqualification order was made against, or undertaking given by, a shadow director; see ss 8ZA(1)(a)(i), 8ZC(1)(a)(i), 8ZD(1)(a)(i), and 8ZE(a)(i). But of course the person instructing the unfit director may be a shadow director.

[70] CDDA, s 8(1), (2A).

[71] CDDA, s 9E(5).

[72] FSMA, s 417(1), which also provides that a 'body corporate' includes a body corporate constituted under the law of a country or territory outside the UK. The FCA Handbook gives the same definition of 'director' as given in the Companies Act.

de jure; (2) that the defendant directed those directors how to act in relation to the company or that he was one of the persons who did so; (3) that those directors acted in accordance with such directions; and (4) that they were accustomed so to act. What is needed is first, a board of directors claiming and purporting to act as such; and secondly, a pattern of behaviour in which the board did not exercise any discretion or judgment of its own, but acted in accordance with the directions of others.[73]

In *Re Kaytech International plc* Robert Walker LJ commented on Millett J's contrast between **3.32** the characteristics of de facto and shadow directors and observed that they may have features in common in that 'an individual who was not a *de jure* director is alleged to have exercised real influence (otherwise than as a professional adviser) in the corporate governance of a company. Sometimes that influence may be concealed and sometimes it may be open. Sometimes it may be something of a mixture, as the facts of the present case show.'[74] In *obiter* remarks in the *Paycheck* case[75] Lord Walker returned to this point. He said that a shadow director may not necessarily be someone lurking in the shadows. He may do so, especially if he has a bad commercial reputation or has been disqualified as a director. But he may be the chief executive of a group of companies who openly gives directions to the board of a subsidiary company on which he does not sit. Also, it was not the case that the concepts of de facto director and shadow director are fundamentally different, and always, or nearly always, to be regarded as mutually exclusive categories.

The meaning of shadow director was considered by the Court of Appeal in *Secretary of State* **3.33** *for Trade and Industry v Deverell*.[76] Morritt LJ summarized the law in a number of propositions as follows:

(1) The definition of a shadow director is to be construed in the normal way to give effect to the parliamentary intention ascertainable from the mischief to be dealt with and the words used. In particular, as the purpose of the Act is the protection of the public and as the definition is used in other legislative contexts, it should not be strictly construed merely because it also has quasi-penal consequences in the context of the Company Directors Disqualification Act 1986.

(2) The purpose of the legislation is to identify those, other than professional advisers, with real influence in the corporate affairs of the company. But it is not necessary that such influence should be exercised over the whole field of its corporate activities.

(3) Whether any particular communication from the alleged shadow director, whether by words or conduct, is to be classified as a direction or instruction must be objectively ascertained by the court in the light of all the evidence. In that connection it is not necessary to prove the understanding or expectation of either giver or receiver. In many, if not most, cases it will suffice to prove the communication and its consequence. Evidence of such understanding or expectation may be relevant but it cannot be conclusive. Certainly the label attached by either or both parties then or thereafter cannot be more than a factor in considering whether the communication came within the statutory description of direction or instruction.

---

[73] [1994] 2 BCLC 180, 183.
[74] [1999] 2 BCLC 351, 424c, CA.
[75] [2010] 1 WLR 2793, SC, paras 109–10.
[76] [2001] Ch 340, CA at para 35. See also *Secretary of State for Trade and Industry v Becker* [2003] 1 BCLC 555 at paras 24–5; *McKillen v Misland (Cyprus) Investments Ltd* [2012] EWHC 521 (Ch); See also *Re Mea Corporation Ltd* [2007] 1 BCLC 618 at paras 86–91; *McKillen v Misland (Cyprus) Investments Ltd* [2012] EWHC 521 (Ch). See also Temple, 'Misfeasance: Shadow Director Versus De Facto Director' (2011) 24(1) Insolvency Intelligence 4–5 and Griffin, 'Confusion Surrounding the Characteristics, Identification and Liability of a Shadow Director' (2011) 24(3) Insolvency Intelligence 44–7.

(4) Non-professional advice may come within that statutory description. The proviso except-
ing advice given in a professional capacity appears to assume that advice generally is or
may be included. Moreover the concepts of 'direction' and 'instruction' do not exclude the
concept of 'advice' for all three share the common feature of 'guidance'.

(5) It will, no doubt, be sufficient to show that in the face of 'directions or instructions'
from the alleged shadow director the properly appointed directors or some of them cast
themselves in a subservient role or surrendered their respective discretions. But it is not
necessary to do so in all cases. Such a requirement would be to put a gloss on the statutory
requirement that the board are 'accustomed to act' 'in accordance with' such directions or
instructions.[77]

3.34 In addition, Morritt LJ said that if (a) the directors usually took the advice of the putative
shadow director, it is irrelevant that on the occasions when he did not give advice the board
did exercise its own discretion; and (b) if the board were accustomed to act on the directions
or instructions of the putative shadow director it is not necessary to demonstrate that their
action was mechanical rather than considered.[78]

3.35 In *Ultraframe (UK) Ltd v Fielding* Lewison J considered the phrase 'accustomed to act' in the
definition of shadow director and concluded that (a) a person is capable of being a shadow
director if a governing majority of the board is accustomed to act at his direction, (b) if a
person becomes a shadow director as a result of the board being accustomed to act on his
instructions or directions, transactions entered into before it can be said that the board is so
accustomed cannot be retrospectively invalidated, and (c) the mere giving of instructions
does not make someone a shadow director; it is only when they are translated into action
by the board that the question can arise.[79] There needs to be a pattern of conduct in which
a *de jure* director of a company is accustomed to act on the instructions or directions of the
shadow director, rather than instructions or directions for a single event.[80]

3.36 The question whether a director is a shadow director is a question of fact and degree for the
court to assess.[81] Although it is possible for a bank, financier, or other creditor to be a shadow
director, so far attempts to establish that such a person is a shadow director have been unsuccessful.[82] This is because the court readily accepts that a creditor is entitled to protect his
own interests, by imposing conditions of continued support, without necessarily becoming
a shadow director. Such a creditor is not dictating how the company is run, even if the directors have little choice but to accept his terms.[83]

Professional advice

3.37 Section 251(2)(a) provides a measure of protection for professional advisers since '[a] person
is not to be regarded as a shadow director by reason only that the directors act on advice
given by him in a professional capacity'. Morritt LJ's fourth proposition in the *Deverell* case

---

[77] Adopted by Lewison J in *Ultraframe (UK) Ltd v Fielding* [2005] EWHC 1638 (Ch) at paras 1260–1. See
also *Re Mea Corporation Ltd* [2007] 1 BCLC 618 at paras 86–91.
[78] *Secretary of State for Trade and Industry v Deverell* [2001] Ch 340, CA at para 59.
[79] [2005] EWHC 1638 (Ch) at paras 1270–8.
[80] *Secretary of State for Trade and Industry v Becker* [2003] 1 BCLC 555 at para 42.
[81] *Smithton Ltd v Naggar* [2015] 1 WLR 189, CA, para 45.
[82] *Re a Company (No 005009 of 1987)* (1988) 4 BCC 424 (where the claim of shadow directorship against
a bank was abandoned at trial); *Re MC Bacon Ltd* [1990] BCLC 324, 325; and *In Re PTZFM Ltd* [1995] 2
BCLC 354.
[83] *Ultraframe (UK) Ltd v Fielding* [2005] EWHC 1638 (Ch) at paras 1264–9.

(paragraph 3.33 above)[84] shows that advice is capable of being a 'direction' or 'instruction' since they are all forms of 'guidance'. While lawyers who give legal advice to the board should be in no danger of being shadow directors, the same is not true of those who give financial advice, since in that context the dividing line between an adviser giving advice in a professional capacity and a shadow director may be difficult to draw.[85]

Statutory functions and ministers

Section 251(2)(b) and (c) make it clear that where a Minister of the Crown or a person exercising a function conferred by or under an enactment (such as a regulator)[86] gives instructions, a direction, guidance, or advice to the directors he does not thereby become a shadow director and exposed to liability as such. **3.38**

Parent company

Since a parent company may well give directions and instructions to the directors of its subsidiaries, the parent is capable of being a shadow director within s 251(1). **3.39**

Section 251(3) goes on to limit the statutory provisions for which a body corporate may be regarded as a shadow director of any of its subsidiaries. First, the parent is not to be regarded as a shadow director for the purposes of Part 10, Chapter 2 (general duties of directors). Without this provision, it could be argued that parent companies owe fiduciary duties and duties of care to their subsidiaries, thereby undermining the separate corporate personalities of group companies. Secondly, the parent is not to be regarded as a shadow director of any of its subsidiary companies for the purposes of Part 10, Chapter 4 (transactions requiring members' approval) and Chapter 6 (contract with sole member who is also a director). These provisions are needed, because otherwise any group transaction between a subsidiary and a holding company might be classed as a transaction between the subsidiary company and a shadow director and so subject to the controls imposed by the relevant sections in those Chapters. **3.40**

(4) Alternate directors

Save where a company's articles make special provision, a directorship is a personal office and responsibility.[87] The 1985 Act Table A, regs 65–9 make provision for the appointment of alternate directors. Alternate directors can be appointed in relation to any company, but are usually found in public companies. Thus Model Articles (plc) 25–7 contain provisions for public companies for the appointment, rights, and responsibilities of alternate directors and for termination of an alternate directorship.[88] The Model Articles (pcls) do not include provision for private companies for alternate directors, because the government considered it unlikely that directors of most private companies would want to appoint alternate directors.[89] Private companies that wish to adopt articles providing for the appointment of alternate directors may adopt the model articles for public companies or draft their own articles appropriately. **3.41**

---

[84] *Secretary of State for Trade and Industry v Deverell* [2001] Ch 340, CA at para 35.
[85] *Re Tasbian Ltd (No 3)* [1991] BCLC 792, 802 (affd [1992] BCLC 297, CA).
[86] As defined by 2006 Act, s 1293.
[87] A director therefore cannot delegate his powers under a power of attorney: *Mancini v Mancini* (1999) 17 ACLC 1, 570, SC (NSW).
[88] See Ch 6, paras 6.65 and 6.66 below.
[89] *Implementation of the Companies Act 2006*, a DTI Consultative Document (February 2007) at para 3.107.

3.42 The appointment of an alternate director does not replace the appointing director who remains in office. An alternate director is a person appointed by a director to (a) exercise that director's powers, and (b) carry out that director's responsibilities in relation to the taking of decisions by the directors in the absence of the alternate's appointor.[90] The alternate director has the same rights in relation to any directors' meeting or directors' written resolution as the alternate's appointor.[91] Alternate directors are deemed for all purposes to be directors; they are personally liable for their own acts and omissions; they are subject to the same restrictions as their appointors; and they are not deemed to be agents of or for their appointors.[92]

3.43 An alternate director's appointment as an alternate terminates (a) when his appointor revokes his appointment by notice to the company in writing specifying when it is to terminate and (b) on the occurrence in relation to the alternate of any event which, if it occurred in relation to the alternate's appointor, would result in the termination of the appointor's appointment as director. The appointment of the alternate also terminates when his appointor dies or when the directorship of the appointor terminates (except that an alternate's appointment as an alternate does not terminate when the appointor retires by rotation at a general meeting and is then reappointed as a director at the same general meeting).[93] An alternate director can only act where his appointor is not present and the alternate director has no powers, rights, or duties when the director for whom he is alternate is acting.[94]

(5) Nominee directors

3.44 Whereas an alternate director is appointed by a director, a nominee director is appointed a director by a shareholder or, perhaps, by a major creditor. The shareholder may have the right to appoint a nominee director pursuant to a right attaching to shares or a contractual right in a joint venture or shareholders' agreement. The mere fact of appointment as a nominee director does not impose any duty on the director owed to his nominator.[95]

3.45 A nominee director has the same duties to the company as any other director.[96] He will risk breaching his duties to the company if he is bound to act on the instructions of his appointor.[97]

---

[90] Model Article (plc) 25(1).

[91] Model Article (plc) 26(1).

[92] Model Article (plc) 26(2) and compare Table A, regs 66 and 69. The alternate director is not imputed with knowledge of a matter known to his appointor: *Re Associated Tool Industries Ltd* (1963) 5 FLR 55, 68 (SC (NSW)). The alternate director is not required to disclose an adverse interest in a transaction or disqualified from voting if the interest is not his own but that of his appointor: *Anaray Ltd v Sydney Futures Exchange Ltd* (1988) 6 ACLR 271 (SC (NSW)). It therefore follows that the alternate director will be disqualified from voting if he (the alternate director) has an adverse interest, even though his appointor has no adverse interest: *ASIC v Doyle* (2001) 38 ACSR 606, SC (WA).

[93] Model Article (plc) 27.

[94] *Strathmore Group Ltd v Fraser* (1991) 5 NZCLC 67, 163 HC (NZ).

[95] *Re Neath Rugby Ltd (No 2), Hawkes v Cuddy* [2009] 2 BCLC 427, CA at paras 32 and 33.

[96] *Re Neath Rugby Ltd (No 2), Hawkes v Cuddy* [2009] 2 BCLC 427, CA at paras 32 and 33.

[97] *Scottish Co-operative Wholesale Society v Meyer* [1959] AC 324, 366, 367, HL, per Lord Denning; *Boulting v Association of Cinematograph Television and Allied Technicians* [1963] 2 QB 606, 626–7, CA, per Lord Denning MR; *Kuwait Asia Bank EC v National Mutual Life Nominees Ltd* [1991] 1 AC 187, 222 (where Lord Lowry said that the nominee directors 'were bound to ignore the interests and wishes of their employer, the bank'); *Re Neath Rugby Ltd, Hawkes v Cuddy (No 2)* [2008] BCC 390 at paras 186–91, [2009] BCLC 427, CA, at paras 32, 33.

(6) Managing and executive directors

A company's articles invariably give the board power to delegate powers to a manag- **3.46** ing director or to other executive directors.[98] Such persons are usually employed under contracts of employment. Delegation of powers to a managing director is discussed in Chapter 5 below.[99]

(7) The chairman of a listed company

The chairman of a listed company has more responsibilities than presiding over meetings of **3.47** directors and shareholders, as discussed in Chapter 5, Section D(2) and Chapter 25, Section D(4) below. A main principle of the UK Corporate Governance Code (September 2014), which applies to listed companies, is that there should be a clear division of responsibilities at the head of the company between the running of the board and the executive responsibility for the running of the company's business. No one individual should have unfettered powers of decision.[100] Therefore the Code states:[101]

> The roles of chairman and chief executive should not be exercised by the same individual. The division of responsibilities between the chairman and chief executive should be clearly established, set out in writing and agreed by the board.

The Code goes on to state what is expected of the chairman of a listed company. He should **3.48** personally satisfy the independence criteria for non-executive directors.[102]

He is responsible for leadership of the board and ensuring the overall effectiveness of all **3.49** aspects of the board's role.[103] Where the board's evaluation of its own performance and that of its committees and individual directors reveal strengths and weaknesses, the chairman should recognize them, if necessary by proposing that new members be appointed to the board and seeking the resignation of directors.[104] The chairman also has particular responsibilities for ensuring that new directors receive a full, formal and tailored induction on joining the board and he should regularly review and agree with each director their training and development needs.[105]

The chairman is responsible for setting the board's agenda and ensuring that adequate time is **3.50** available for discussion of all agenda items, in particular strategic issues.[106] He is responsible for ensuring that the directors receive accurate, timely, and clear information.[107]

---

[98] Model Article (pcls) 5; Model Article (plc) 5; Table A, reg 72.
[99] At paras 5.61–5.63.
[100] A.2.
[101] A.2.1.
[102] The criteria under para B.1.1 are described in Ch 6 at para 6.75 below. Paragraph A.3.1 deals with the question of whether the chief executive of a listed company can go on to become chairman, and recommends that a chief executive should not go on to be chairman of the same company. If the board decides to take the exceptional course of proposing the appointment of the chief executive as chairman, it should consult the major shareholders in advance and should set out its reasons to shareholders at the time of the appointment and also in the next annual report (but these reporting requirements only apply in the year in which the appointment is made).
[103] A.3 and A.3.1 and Preface, para 7.
[104] B.6.
[105] B.4.1 and B.4.2.
[106] A.3.
[107] B.5.

3.51 He is also responsible for promoting a culture of openness and debate by facilitating the effective contribution of non-executive directors and ensuring constructive relations between executive and non-executive directors.[108]

3.52 The chairman should ensure effective communication between the board and shareholders;[109]

(8) Non-executive directors

3.53 The Companies Act does not distinguish between executive and non-executive directors. Nor do the Insolvency Act and the CDDA. In small private companies the practical distinction is between the directors who manage the daily business of the company and receive remuneration for their executive services, so that they are employees of the company, and those who do not. Similar arrangements may apply in many public companies.

3.54 It is with listed companies that a formal distinction is drawn between executive and non-executive directors under the provisions of the UK Corporate Governance Code discussed below. The former are executives, employed under service contracts, to work full time for the company. A non-executive director is a director who is not employed under a contract of service. He may be a director of several unconnected companies and his role is to provide the company with the benefit of his advice and expertise on a part-time basis. The non-executive director of a listed company has an important role in providing independent supervision of the management of the executive directors, participating in nomination, audit and remuneration committees, and liaising with shareholders.

3.55 Both executive and non-executive directors participate in decision-making by directors as members of the same board and they have the same access to the company's books and accounting records.

General duties of non-executive directors

3.56 Non-executive directors have the same general and particular duties under the Companies Act as executive directors, although the latter may owe additional duties by virtue of their contracts of service.[110] While non-executive directors owe the same duty of care, skill, and diligence, the 2006 Act, s 174 indicates that the content of the duty depends on the functions carried out by the director. Thus the extent of a director's duty to participate depends on 'how the particular company's business is organised and the part the director can reasonably be expected to play'.[111] Chapter 14, Section F below discusses how the duty of care, skill, and diligence applies to non-executive directors and the extent to which they can safely delegate to executives or other members of the board.

---

[108] Under A.4.2 the chairman should hold meetings with the non-executive directors without the executives being present. If a non-executive director resigns and has concerns about the running of the company or a proposed action, he should provide a written statement to the chairman for circulation to the board (A.4.3).

[109] E.1. By E.1.1 the chairman should discuss governance and strategy with major shareholders.

[110] In *Dorchester Finance Co Ltd v Stebbing* [1989] BCLC 498, decided in 1977, Foster J rejected the proposition that non-executive directors had no duties to perform. In *Re Wimbledon Village Restaurant Ltd* [1994] BCC 753 a non-executive director was criticized, in the same way as executive directors, for failure to file accounts but no disqualification order was made.

[111] *Bishopsgate v Maxwell* [1994] 1 All ER 261, 264, CA, per Hoffmann LJ.

Listed companies

The UK Corporate Governance Code,[112] on a comply or explain basis, deals with the role of **3.57** non-executive directors and indicates what level of commitment is to be expected of them.

The main Principle of the Code under the heading 'Leadership' is: 'Every company should **3.58** be headed by an effective board, which is collectively responsible for the success of the company.'[113] As part of their role as members of a unitary board, non-executive directors should constructively challenge and help develop proposals on strategy. They should scrutinize the performance of management in meeting agreed goals and objectives and monitor the reporting of performance. They should satisfy themselves on the integrity of financial information and that financial controls and systems of risk management are robust and defensible. They are responsible for determining appropriate levels of remuneration of executive directors and have a prime role in appointing, and where necessary removing, executive directors, and in succession planning.[114]

The board should appoint one of the independent non-executive directors to be senior inde- **3.59** pendent director to provide a sounding board for the chairman and to serve as an intermediary for the other directors when necessary. The senior independent director should be available to shareholders if they have concerns that have not been resolved through contact with the chairman, chief executive, or other executive directors.[115]

The non-executive directors should hold meetings with the chairman without executives **3.60** present. They should also meet together under the leadership of the senior independent director at least annually, without the chairman present, to appraise the chairman's performance and on such other occasions as they consider appropriate.[116]

If directors have unresolved concerns about the running of the company, they should ensure **3.61** that their concerns are recorded in the board minutes. On resignation a non-executive director should provide a written statement to the chairman, for circulation to the board, if they have any concerns about the running of the company.[117]

Under the heading 'Effectiveness' the main principle is: 'The board and its committees **3.62** should have the appropriate balance of skills, experience, independence, and knowledge of the company to enable them to discharge their respective duties and responsibilities effectively.' To this end, 'the board should include an appropriate combination of executive and non-executive directors (and in particular independent non-executive directors) such that no individual or small group of individuals can dominate the board's decision taking'.[118]

The Code identifies particular attributes and functions of non-executive directors. **3.63**

(1) They are expected to comprise the membership of the nomination, audit, and remuneration committees.[119]

---

[112] April 2016. The Code applies to companies with a Premium listing of equity shares regardless of whether they are incorporated in the UK or elsewhere.
[113] A.1.
[114] A.4.
[115] A.4.1.
[116] A.4.2.
[117] A.4.3.
[118] B.1.
[119] B1, B.2, C3, D1, and Chs 5, Section H, and 6, Section D(3) below.

(2) They are expected to meet certain independence requirements.[120]

(3) They should be appointed for specified terms and, in the normal way, should not serve for more than six years and should be subject to regular re-election.[121]

(4) Their terms and conditions of appointment should be made available for inspection.[122] The letter of appointment should set out the expected time commitment. Non-executive directors should undertake that they will have sufficient time to meet what is expected of them. Their other significant commitments should be disclosed to the board before appointment, with a broad indication of the time involved and the board should be informed of subsequent changes.[123]

(5) They should receive induction on joining the board and regular updates to develop their skills and the knowledge and familiarity with the company to fulfil their roles.[124]

(6) Directors should be supplied with timely information and non-executive directors should have access to independent professional advice at the company's expense.[125]

(7) Their performance should be evaluated on an annual basis and the non-executive directors should be responsible for performance evaluation of the chairman, taking into account the views of executive directors.[126]

(8) They should be submitted for re-election at regular intervals, subject to satisfactory performance.[127]

(9) Their remuneration should reflect the time commitment and responsibilities of the role and should not include performance-related elements.[128]

(10) They should be offered the opportunity to attend meetings with major shareholders and should expect to attend them if requested by major shareholders.[129]

D. Persons Connected with a Director

3.64 Sections 252–5 and Schedule 1 identify, for the purposes of Part 10, those persons, and only those persons, who are connected with a director of a company or a director being connected with a person.[130] This identification is material to provisions (for all of which a shadow director is treated as a director) in:

(1) Chapter 4 concerning substantial property transactions,[131] loans, quasi-loans, and credit transactions,[132] and payments for loss of office; and[133]

---

[120] B.1.1 and Ch 6 at paras 6.75 and 6.76 below.
[121] B.2.3, B.7 and Ch 6 at paras 6.77–6.79 below.
[122] They should be made available for inspection by any person at the company's registered office during normal business hours and at the AGM (for 15 minutes prior to the meeting and during the meeting).
[123] B.3.2.
[124] B.4 and Ch 6 at para 6.80 below.
[125] B.5, B.5.1.
[126] B.6 and B.6.3.
[127] B.7 and Ch 6 at para 6.77 below.
[128] D.1.3 and Ch 8, Section E below.
[129] E.1.1.
[130] Note that Insolvency Act, ss 249 and 435 explain for the purposes of Parts I–VII of that Act the meanings of 'connected' with a company and 'associate'.
[131] 2006 Act, ss 190, 194, 195.
[132] 2006 Act, ss 197, 200, 201, 203, 204, 210, 213.
[133] 2006 Act, s 215.

(2) Chapter 7 concerning ratification of acts of directors giving rise to liability.[134]

Section 252(2) identifies five categories of persons who are regarded as connected with a **3.65** director for the purposes of Part 10 if, but only if, they meet the requirements of the statutory definitions: (a) members of a director's family, (b) companies, (c) trustees, (d) partners, and (e) firms. Section 252(3) provides that for those purposes a person connected with a director of a company does not include a person who is himself a director of the company. Section 239(5)(d), however, provides that s 252(3) does not apply for the purposes of s 239, which is concerned with the power of the company to ratify acts of directors giving rise to liability.

(1) Family members

Section 253 defines what is meant by references to members of a director's family who are **3.66** connected to him. Reflecting recommendations of the Law Commission the categories of family members has been extended.[135] The members of a director's family who are connected with him are:

(1) the director's spouse or civil partner;
(2) any other person (whether of a different sex or the same sex) with whom the director lives as partner in an enduring family relationship, but not where the person with whom the director lives is the director's grandparent or grandchild, sister, brother, aunt or uncle, or nephew, or niece;[136]
(3) the director's children or step-children;
(4) any children or step-children of a person within (2) above (and who are not children or step-children of the director) who live with the director and have not attained the age of 18; and
(5) the director's parents.

(2) Connected companies

Section 254, read with s 255 and Schedule 1, defines what is meant by references in Part 10 **3.67** to a director being 'connected with a body corporate'. This is the case if, but only if, he and the persons connected with him together either (a) 'are interested in shares comprised in the equity share capital of that body corporate of a nominal value equal to at least 20 per cent of that share capital', or (b) 'are entitled to exercise or control the exercise of more than 20 per cent of the voting power at any general meeting of that body'. Those tests, based on interests in shares and voting power require considerable elaboration, as discussed in the following paragraphs.

For the purposes of ss 254 and 255 the provisions of Schedule 1 (references to interest in **3.68** shares or debentures) have effect.[137] The general provisions of Schedule 1 are that a reference to an interest in shares includes any interest of any kind whatsoever in shares, and any restraints or restrictions to which the exercise of any right attached to the interest is or may be

---

[134] 2006 Act, s 239.
[135] *Company Directors: Regulating Conflicts of Interests and Formulating a Statement of Duties* (Law Commission No 261) Part 14. Under 1985 Act, s 346 family members were limited to the director's spouse, child, or step-child. The Law Commission's recommendation to include a director's siblings was not adopted in the 2006 Act.
[136] The exception is made by s 253(3).
[137] 2006 Act, s 254 (3); Sch 1 applies to interests in debentures as well as shares.

subject shall be disregarded; it is immaterial that the shares in which a person has an interest are not identifiable; and persons having a joint interest in shares are deemed each of them to have that interest.[138] Schedule 1, paragraphs 3–6 provide that a person is taken to have an interest in shares if:

(1) he enters into a contract to acquire them;[139]

(2) he has a right to call for delivery of the shares to himself or his order, or he has a right to acquire, or an obligation to take, an interest in shares (whether the right or obligation is absolute or conditional);[140]

(3) not being the registered holder, he is entitled to exercise or control the exercise of rights conferred by the holding of the shares;

(4) a body corporate is interested in them and (a) the body corporate or its directors are accustomed to act in accordance with his directions or instructions, or (b) he is entitled to exercise or control the exercise of more than one-half of the voting power at general meetings of the body corporate; and[141]

(5) he is a beneficiary of a trust, the property of which includes an interest in shares, subject to the provisions of paragraph 6.[142]

3.69 Section 255 explains what is meant by references to a director 'controlling' a body corporate.[143] A director of a company is taken to control a body corporate if, but only if, (a) he or any person connected with him is interested in any part of the equity share capital of that body, or is entitled to exercise or control the exercise of any part of the voting power at any general meeting of that body; and (b) he, the persons connected with him, and the other directors of that company, together are interested in more than 50 per cent of that share capital, or are entitled to exercise or control the exercise of more than 50 per cent of that voting power.[144] The rules set out in Schedule 1 apply.[145]

3.70 For both tests (interest in shares and control of the exercise of voting power), additional rules apply:

(1) References to voting power the exercise of which is controlled by a director include voting power whose exercise is controlled by a body corporate controlled by him.[146]

(2) Shares in a company held as treasury shares, and any voting rights attached to such shares, are disregarded.[147]

(3) To avoid circularity in the application of s 252(a) a body corporate with which a director is connected is not treated for the purposes of s 254 as connected with him by virtue

---

[138] Sch 1, para 2.

[139] Sch 1, para 3(1).

[140] Sch 1, para 3(2). Para 3(3) and (4) contains further provisions for determining when a person is taken to have an interest in shares.

[141] Sch 1, para 5(2) contains further provisions for determining when voting power is taken to be exercisable.

[142] Under para 6(a) an interest in the shares in reversion or remainder is disregarded so long as a person is entitled to receive, during the lifetime of himself or another, income from trust property comprising shares; (b) a person is treated as not interested in shares if and so long as he holds them as bare trustee or custodian trustee; (c) there shall be disregarded any interest of a person subsisting by virtue of certain unit trust and charitable church schemes.

[143] 2006 Act, s 255(1).

[144] 2006 Act, s 255(2).

[145] 2006 Act, s 255(3).

[146] 2006 Act, ss 254(4) and 255(4).

[147] 2006 Act, ss 254(5) and 255(5).

of s 252(2)(c) or (d) (connection as trustee or partner), and (b) a trustee of a trust the beneficiaries of which include (or may include) a body corporate with which a director is connected is not treated for the purposes of s 254 as connected with a director by reason only of that fact.[148]

(3) Trusts

A person is connected with a director of a company if he is acting in his capacity as trus- **3.71** tee of a trust (not being a trust for the purposes of an employees' share scheme or pension scheme) (a) the beneficiaries of which include the director or a person who by virtue of (1) or (2) above is connected with him, or (b) the terms of which confer a power on the trustees that may be exercised for the benefit of the director or any such person.[149]

(4) Partners

A person is connected with a director of a company if he is acting in his capacity as partner **3.72** (a) of the director, or (b) of a person who is connected with that director by virtue of s 252(2) (a), (b), or (c) (family, company, or trust connection).[150]

(5) Firms

A firm that is a legal person under the law by which it is governed is connected with a director **3.73** of a company if it is one in which (a) the director is a partner, (b) a partner is a person who, by virtue of s 252(2)(a), (b), or (c) (family, company, or trust connection) is connected with the director, or (c) a partner is a firm in which the director is a partner or in which there is a partner who, by virtue of s 252(2)(a), (b), or (c) (family, company, or trust connection) is connected with the director.[151]

E. The Secretary

Part 12 of the Companies Act is concerned with company secretaries. The word 'secretary' is **3.74** not defined in the Companies Act or the Model Articles. Table A, reg 1 states that in Table A, 'secretary' means 'the secretary of the company or any other person appointed to perform the duties of the secretary of the company, including a joint, assistant or deputy secretary'.

Although the office of secretary is not defined, his functions are usually regarded as ministe- **3.75** rial and administrative, rather than managerial. He acts under the direction of the directors and it is for them to decide on his role and functions.[152] Outside Part 12 there are few references to the secretary:

---

[148] 2006 Act, ss 254(6) and 255(6).

[149] 2006 Act, s 252(2)(c). Note *Re Kilnoore Ltd* [2006] Ch 489, where Lewison J held that a bare trustee of shares is not a person entitled to exercise the voting power attached to those shares, because the verb 'entitled' governed both the exercise of voting power and the control of voting power (Insolvency Act, s 435).

[150] 2006 Act, s 252(2)(d).

[151] 2006 Act, s 252(2(e).

[152] The traditional view of a secretary was: 'A secretary is a mere servant; his position is that he is to do what he is told, and no person can assume that he has authority to represent anything at all ...', per Lord Esher MR in *Barnett, Hoares & Co v South London Tramways Co* (1887) 18 QBD 815, 817, CA, approved in *George Whitechurch Ltd v Cavanagh* [1902] AC 117, 124, HL, and supported by *Ruben v Great Fingall Consolidated* [1906] AC 439, HL. However, see also *Panorama Developments (Guildford) Ltd v Fidelis Furnishing Fabrics Ltd* [1971] 2 QB 711, CA, referred to in para 3.76 below.

(1) Sections 12 and 16 contain provisions for the appointment of the first secretary or joint secretaries (see below).

(2) By s 44 he is an authorized signatory for the execution of documents by a company.[153]

(3) In the case of quoted companies, the secretary is required to provide an independent assessor, appointed to report on a poll, with information and explanations for the purposes of the report.[154]

(4) His signature on the record of a resolution of members passed otherwise than at a general meeting is evidence of the passing of the resolution.[155]

(5) He is an officer of the company for the purpose of being liable for offences committed by 'every officer of the company who is in default' in the event of contravention of an enactment in relation to a company,[156] and generally in the Companies Acts.[157]

(6) On the application of the Director of Public Prosecutions, the Secretary of State, or a chief officer of police, he may be ordered by a judge of the High Court to produce documents where there is reasonable cause to believe that any person has, while an officer of a company, committed an offence in connection with the management of the company's affairs.[158]

(7) He is a person on whom a document may be served by leaving it at, or sending it by post to, the secretary's registered address, whatever the purpose of the document in question.[159]

3.76 The secretary will be regarded as having ostensible authority to make contracts concerning the administration of the company.[160] As an officer and, invariably an employee, of the company, the secretary will owe the company fiduciary duties and duties of skill, care, and diligence.[161]

(1) Private companies

3.77 The principal change from the 1985 Act is that private companies are not required to have a secretary.[162] The reasons for removing the requirement for private companies were explained in the White Paper, *Modernising Company Law*:

> The requirement represents a regulatory burden on small private companies, particularly those with only one director, which are forced to contract out the role to external advisers or appoint a family member, friend or associate to fill the position. While a company secretary can, for many companies, perform a highly valuable function, the specific role is not essential to good corporate governance; that is properly the responsibility of directors. It will, of course

---

[153] 2006 Act, s 44(2)(a), (3) and (7).

[154] 2006 Act, s 349(2).

[155] 2006 Act, s 356(2).

[156] 2006 Act, ss 1121 and 1123.

[157] 2006 Act, s 1173. This makes the secretary an officer for the purposes of the Insolvency Act; see s 251 of that Act.

[158] 2006 Act, s 1132.

[159] 2006 Act, s 1140.

[160] *Panorama Developments (Guildford) Ltd v Fidelis Furnishing Fabrics Ltd* [1971] 2 QB 711, CA. Indeed his authority may involve managerial matters; see *Re Maidstone Buildings Ltd* [1971] 1 WLR 1085, 1093. Whether a secretary has actual authority to enter into a transaction on behalf of the company is an issue of fact; see *UBAF Ltd v European American Banking Corp* [1984] QB 713 CA.

[161] For fiduciary duties, see *McKay's Case* (1876) 2 Ch D 1, CA, and *De Ruvigne's Case* (1877) 5 Ch D 306, CA. For a 'knowing assistance' claim against a company secretary, see *Brown v Bennett* [1999] 1 BCLC 649, CA.

[162] 2006 Act, s 270.

be open to private companies to appoint company secretaries if they choose, on the basis of the value that they add to the company; indeed, the Government believes that many companies will do so, and this will certainly be welcome.[163]

A private company may keep a secretary if it wishes.[164] Anyone may be appointed a secretary **3.78** of a private company. If a private company appoints a secretary the provisions of ss 274–80, described below, apply.[165] Where a private company is to be formed and a person is to be the first secretary (or joint secretaries) of the company the required particulars must be given in the statement of the company's proposed officers and, on registration of the company, that person or persons will be deemed to have been appointed.[166] The Model Articles (pcls) do not contain any articles in relation to secretaries, but Table A, reg 99 provided 'the secretary shall be appointed by the directors for such term, at such remuneration and upon such conditions as they may think fit; and any secretary so appointed may be removed by them'.

The removal by s 270(1) of the requirement for private companies to have a secretary neces- **3.79** sitated modifications in relation to services and acts required or authorized to be done by or to the secretary. Where a private company is without a secretary (a) anything authorized or required to be given or sent to, or served on, the company by being sent to its secretary (i) may be given or sent to, or served on, the company itself, and (ii) if addressed to the secretary shall be treated as addressed to the company; and (b) anything else required or authorized to be done by or to the secretary of the company may be done by or to (i) a director, or (ii) a person authorized generally or specifically in that behalf by the directors.[167]

(2) Public companies

Public companies are required to have a secretary.[168] Where a public company is to be formed **3.80** and a person is, or persons are, to be the first secretary (or joint secretaries) of the company the required particulars must be given in the statement of the company's proposed officers and, on registration of the company, that person or persons will be deemed to have been appointed.[169] The Model Articles (plc) do not contain any provisions in relation to secretaries. Table A, reg 99 provides for the directors to appoint the secretary.

The Companies Act imposes a duty on directors of a public company to appoint a secretary. **3.81** It does so in two ways. First, if it appears that a public company is in breach of the requirement to have a secretary the Secretary of State can use enforcement powers in s 272 to require it to appoint a secretary. If the company fails to comply with the requirement, the company and every officer in default is guilty of an offence.[170] Secondly, the directors of a public company are under a duty to take all reasonable steps to secure that the secretary, or each joint

---

[163] Para 6.6. See also Lord Sainsbury (Hansard, col 185 (11 Jan 2006)).

[164] As recommended by the Company Law Review Steering Group (CLR) in *Final Report*, paras 4.6 and 4.7. See also CLR: *Developing the Framework* at paras 7.34–7.36 and CLR: *Completing the Structure* at paras 2.18–2.22.

[165] 2006 Act, ss 274A and 279A to 279F (inserted by the SBEE Act 2015, s 94 and Schedule 5, from 30 June 2016) allow private companies the option of keeping information about secretaries on the register kept by the registrar instead of keeping it on their own registers (for the commencement date see the SBEE Act 2015 Commencement No 4 Regulations, SI 2016 / 321, reg 6 (c)).

[166] 2006 Act, ss 12(1)(b) and 16(6)(b).

[167] 2006 Act, s 270(3).

[168] 2006 Act, s 271.

[169] 2006 Act, ss 12(1)(c) and 16(6)(b).

[170] 2006 Act, s 272(6) and (7).

secretary, (a) is a person who appears to them to have the requisite knowledge and experience to discharge the functions of secretary of the company, and (b) has one or more of the specified qualifications.[171]

3.82 If there is a vacancy in office of the secretary, or there is for any other reason no secretary capable of acting, anything required or authorized to be done by or to the secretary may be done (a) by or to an assistant or deputy secretary (if any), or (b) if there is no assistant or deputy secretary or none capable of acting, by or to any person authorized generally or specifically in that behalf by the directors.[172]

3.83 A company must keep a register of its secretaries, containing the required particulars and which is available for inspection at the place notified to the Registrar.[173]

F. Officers

3.84 Section 1173(1) defines an 'officer' in relation to a body corporate, as including a director, manager, or secretary. Although not mentioned in this definition, an auditor, appointed under s 485, is an officer of the company,[174] but not for the purposes of the independence requirements for acting as a statutory auditor.[175] A receiver and manager appointed by directors is not a manager within the definition of 'officer', since he does not manage on behalf of the company, but to enforce security over the company's property.[176] A liquidator, administrator, or administrative receiver would not be regarded as a manager within the definition of officer, since, although they have powers of management, they are separately identified in the Insolvency Act, s 212.

3.85 In the Act, the word 'officer' is used as a generic term for the directors and secretaries of a company.[177] Its most important function, however, is to identify persons who are guilty of an offence for contravention of the provisions of the Act. The Companies Act contains numerous offences, most of which provide a sanction for contravention of provisions requiring companies to maintain specified records, to make records available for inspection, and returns to be made to the Registrar. Criminal offences are discussed in Chapter 35 below. Directors, secretaries, and managers (and in some specified cases shadow directors) are all

---

[171] 2006 Act, s 273. The qualifications specified by s 273(2) and (3) are: (a) holding office as secretary of a public company for at least three of the immediately preceding five years; (b) membership of specified bodies (Institute of Chartered Accountants of England and Wales, Institute of Chartered Accountants of Scotland, Association of Chartered Certified Accountants, Institute of Chartered Accountants of Ireland, Institute of Chartered Secretaries and Administrators, Chartered Institute of Management Accountants, Chartered Institute of Public Finance and Accountancy); (c) UK barrister, advocate, or solicitor; (d) being a person who, by virtue of his holding or having held any other position or being a member of another body, appears to the directors to be capable of discharging the functions of secretary of the company.

[172] 2006 Act, s 274.

[173] 2006 Act, ss 275–9.

[174] *R v Shacter* [1960] 2 QB 252, CA. *Mutual Reinsurance Co Ltd v Peat Marwick Mitchell & Co (A Firm)* [1996] BCC 1010. *Re Sasea Finance Ltd v KPMG* [1998] BCC 216, 222–3. An auditor may therefore be subject to misfeasance proceedings under Insolvency Act, s 212; see *Re London and General Bank Ltd (No 2)* [1895] 2 Ch 166; *Re Kingston Cotton Mill Co* [1896] 1 Ch 6 and *(No 2)* [1896] 2 Ch 279, CA; *Re Thomas Gerrard Ltd* [1968] Ch 455.

[175] 2006 Act, s 1214(5).

[176] *Re B Johnson & Co (Builders) Ltd* [1955] Ch 634, CA.

[177] 2006 Act, ss 9(4), 12, 16, 1078, 1189.

potentially liable as officers to criminal punishment for default by the company in complying with these requirements.

Section 1121 deals with the criminal liability of an officer in default.[178] It provides: **3.86**

(1) This section has effect for the purposes of any provision of the Companies Acts to the effect that, in the event of contravention of an enactment in relation to a company, an offence is committed by every officer of the company who is in default.
(2) For this purpose 'officer' includes—(a) any director, manager or secretary, and (b) any person who is to be treated as an officer of the company for the purposes of the provision in question.
(3) An officer is 'in default' for the purposes of the provision if he authorises or permits, participates in, or fails to take all reasonable steps to prevent, the contravention.

For particular provisions shadow directors and liquidators are treated as officers.[179] It should also be noted that s 1121(3) extends criminal liability to officers who (a) authorize, (b) permit, or (c) fail to take all reasonable steps to prevent the contravention, whereas the 1985 Act, s 730(5) only applied to officers who knowingly and wilfully authorized or permitted the contravention.

Section 1122 deals with the position where a company is an officer of another company. It   **3.87**
provides:

(1) Where a company is an officer of another company, it does not commit an offence as an officer in default unless one of its officers is in default.
(2) Where any such offence is committed by a company the officer in question also commits the offence and is liable to be proceeded against and punished accordingly.
(3) In this section 'officer' and 'in default' have the meanings given by section 1121.

The other uses of the word 'officer' in the Companies Act are to identify the persons (a) who   **3.88**
may be ordered to provide information in connection with a shareholders' action to enforce directors' liabilities for unauthorized political donations or expenditure,[180] (b) who are entitled to inspect the company's accounting records,[181] (c) who may be required by an auditor of a company to provide information or explanations,[182] (d) who may certify on behalf of a company an instrument of transfer of shares,[183] (e) who may be required to give information in relation to an expert's report on a merger or division of a public company,[184] (f) who may be served with process where the company has no registered office,[185] and (g) in respect of whom the court may grant relief under s 1157 (discussed in Chapter 19, Section D below).

---

[178] 2006 Act s 1121. By s 1123, s 1121 also applies to bodies other than companies.
[179] As regards shadow directors, see ss 63(2), 68(5), 75(5), 76(6), 84(2), 156(6), 162(6), 165(4), 167(4), 272(6), 275(6), 276(3). As regards liquidators, see ss 30(4) and 36(5).
[180] 2006 Act, s 373.
[181] 2006 Act, s 388.
[182] 2006 Act, ss 499 and 500.
[183] 2006 Act, s 775.
[184] 2006 Act, ss 909 and 924.
[185] 2006 Act, s 1002, concerning striking off.

4

DIRECTORS' POWERS AND RESPONSIBILITIES

Adam Goodison

A. Introduction

This chapter deals with the management of the company by its directors, acting collectively **4.01** if there is more than one director. It is concerned with the directors' authority under the constitution, the company's capacity to transact business and the way it does so.[1]

Although the Companies Act 2006 contains much more provision about the nature of direc- **4.02** tors' responsibilities than is found in previous Companies Acts, it does not state what the directors actually do. The only Act to have done so was the 1844 Act, which identified the directors as 'the persons having the direction, conduct, management, or superintendence of the affairs of the company'.[2] It has always been well understood that those are the functions of a director and that they have an internal and an external aspect. Internally, as between the directors and the shareholders, the directors' powers of management are left to the company's articles, as has always been the case since the 1856 Act. The exercise of the directors' powers is not solely a matter to be regulated by articles, since the conduct of a company's affairs affects wider

---

[1] The relevant statutory provisions are in 2006 Act, s 31 (statement of company's objects) and Part 4, ss 39–52 (a company's capacity and related matters); in force 1 October 2009.

[2] 1844 Act, s 3.

interests. For this reason the Companies Acts have imposed particular responsibilities on directors. These internal aspects of the directors' powers and responsibilities are considered in Section B of this chapter. The external aspects of the management of a company, its dealings with third parties, are considered in Sections C and D.

4.03 Section E deals with the important topic of when the conduct, knowledge, or mental state of a director or other persons may be attributed to the company.

B. Directors' Authority to Manage Companies

(1) Directors' general authority

Table A, reg 70

4.04 A company limited by shares and incorporated under the 1985 Act,[3] whether private or public, must have articles of association prescribing its regulations, which may be in the form registered with the Registrar, or in default of registration, the company is deemed to have adopted Table A.[4] Companies that registered their own bespoke articles invariably adopted at least some of the provisions of Table A for reasons of convenience and certainty. A company limited by guarantee and not having a share capital and an unlimited company having a share capital had to register their articles with the Registrar, which had to be as near to the forms of Tables C and E respectively as the circumstances admitted.[5] Tables C and E adopt the provisions of Table A concerning the management of a company by directors and need not be considered further in this chapter.

4.05 Table A, reg 70 states the powers of directors in these terms:

> Subject to the provisions of the Act, the memorandum and the articles and to any directions given by special resolution, the business of the company shall be managed by the directors who may exercise all the powers of the company. No alteration of the memorandum or articles and no such direction shall invalidate any prior act of the directors which would have been valid if that alteration had not been made or that direction had not been given. The powers given by this regulation shall not be limited by any special power given to the directors by the articles and a meeting of directors at which a quorum is present may exercise all powers exercisable by the directors.

4.06 The first sentence of reg 70 gives the directors the responsibility for managing the business of the company, for which purpose they may exercise all the company's powers. Case law suggested some limits on the otherwise broad expression 'business of the company'. It was held not to cover fixing the directors' own remuneration,[6] but Table A goes on to provide expressly for the fixing of directors' remuneration. In general it is to be determined by ordinary resolution (reg 82), but by reg 84 the directors have power to determine the remuneration of the managing and executive directors.

---

[3] Which was the case until 1 October 2009; 2006 Act Commencement Order No 8, Arts 3(a)–(d).

[4] 1985 Act, ss 7 and 8. For companies registered before 1 October 2007, 1985 Act, Table A (SI 1985/805) continues to apply. For companies registered on or after 1 October 2007 (but before 1 October 2009), Table A (SI 1985/805) is amended by SI 2007/2541 and SI 2007/2826, to achieve consistency with provisions of the 2006 Act in force after that date.

[5] 1985 Act, ss 7 and 8.

[6] *Foster v Foster* [1916] 1 Ch 532.

The second sentence of reg 70 prevents an alteration of the company's memorandum or art- **4.07**
icles or any direction given by special resolution from retrospectively invalidating the prior
exercise by the directors of their powers of management.[7] This provision protects directors as
well as third parties, since directors owe a duty to obey the constitution of the company and
could find themselves exposed to a breach of duty claim if the members could retrospectively
interfere with the exercise of their powers. The third and final sentence of reg 70 makes clear
that the breadth of the directors' powers under reg 70 is not limited by any special powers
given to them in the articles and that a board meeting at which a quorum is present may
exercise all such powers.

Model Article 3

Companies are now, and have been since 1 October 2009, incorporated under the 2006 Act. **4.08**
Such a company must have articles of association prescribing its regulations, which are either
those registered by it or the applicable Model Articles, which apply in default of registering
articles.[8] Pursuant to the 2006 Act, s 19, the Companies (Model Articles) Regulations 2008[9]
prescribe Model Articles for (a) private companies limited by shares (Model Article (pcls)),
(b) private companies limited by guarantee (Model Article (pclg)), and public companies
(Model Article (plc)). Companies not incorporated under the 2006 Act are able to adopt
the Model Articles or provisions in them if they wish. It is likely that public companies will
regard the Model Articles (plc) as containing a template of suitable provisions and will continue to have bespoke articles which adopt some but not all of the provisions of the Model
Articles (plc).

The Model Articles (pcls), (pclg), and (plc) 3 each provide for the directors' general authority **4.09**
in the same terms:

> Subject to the articles, the directors are responsible for the management of the company's busi-
> ness, for which purpose they may exercise all the powers of the company.

Model Article 3 is derived from Table A, reg 70, but uses simpler and clearer language to **4.10**
establish the directors' responsibility to manage the company's business and the breadth of
their powers to do so, unless there are specific provisions to the contrary in the articles. Such
a provision is Model Article 4, which states the shareholders' reserve power to intervene by
special resolution, contained in Model Article 4.[10]

Model Article 3 does not include anything comparable to the second sentence of Table A, reg **4.11**
70. This is because each Model Article 4(2) prevents a special resolution from having retrospective effect. Nor does it include anything comparable to the third sentence, since Model
Articles (pcls) and (pclg) contain express provisions for directors of a private company to
make decisions unanimously without a meeting[11] and Model Articles (plc) contains express
provision for directors to make decisions by written resolution.[12]

---

[7] This reflects the view of Buckley LJ in *Gramophone and Typewriter Ltd v Stanley* [1908] 2 KB 89, 105, 106, CA.
[8] 2006 Act, ss 18–20.
[9] SI 2008/3229.
[10] The same Art 4 applies to each of Model Article (pcls), (pclg), and (plc).
[11] Model Articles (pcls) and (pclg) 7 and 8.
[12] Model Articles (plc) 7, 17, and 18.

4.12 Finally, Model Article 3 does not state that the directors' authority is subject to the company's memorandum of association, because under the 2006 Act that document is simply a record of the basis on which the company was incorporated. It is not part of the company's constitution and does not regulate the affairs of the company.[13]

The company's objects

4.13 Companies incorporated under the 2006 Act have unlimited capacity, since their objects are not restricted. The 2006 Act, s 31(1) provides:

> Unless a company's articles specifically restrict the objects of the company, its objects are unrestricted.

Charitable companies and community interest companies may restrict their objects, but it is unlikely that any commercial company would do so. Where there are restrictions, persons dealing with a company may have the benefit of statutory protections (see Section C below).[14] Even so, directors who exceed the company's powers may be exposed to personal liability for breach of the duty under the 2006 Act, s 171(a) to act in accordance with the company's constitution.

4.14 Where the company has unrestricted capacity, Model Article 3 provides that the directors' authority to exercise its powers is similarly unrestricted. There should therefore be no question of the directors being unable to close down or dispose of all or part of the company's business.[15]

4.15 The capacity of a company incorporated under the 1985 Act or earlier Companies Acts was controlled by the objects for which it was incorporated as stated in its memorandum.[16] In practice such companies achieved almost unlimited capacity by adopting one of two forms of memorandum. Under one form, in order to avoid the risk of acting ultra vires, the company was given the widest possible range of objects in the form of a long list, each of which was stated to be an independent object, not limited or restricted by any other object. Alternatively the company's memorandum could state that its object was to carry on business as a general commercial company,[17] so that the 1985 Act, s 3A applied to it. This provided:

> Where the company's memorandum states that the object of the company is to carry on business as a general commercial company—
> (a) the object of the company is to carry on any trade or business whatsoever, and
> (b) the company has the power to do all such things as are incidental or conducive to the carrying on of any trade or business by it.

---

[13] 2006 Act, ss 8 and 17.

[14] 2006 Act, ss 39–42.

[15] This was certainly the government's view of Model Article 3: *Implementation of Companies Act 2006* (Consultative Document, February 2007) at paras 3.46 and 3.47.

[16] The memorandum must (a) be subscribed by the persons forming the company (s 1); (b) state, among other things, the objects of the company, which can be altered in accordance with the 1985 Act (ss 2–6); and (c) be delivered to the Registrar for him to issue a certificate of incorporation (ss 10–13). From the moment the company is incorporated it is able to exercise all the functions of an incorporated company (s 13(3)).

[17] Some companies were reluctant to adopt the stand-alone objects clause provided by 1985 Act, s 3A due to uncertainties about a general objects clause (eg whether such a clause would allow a company to sell its entire undertaking or carry on charitable activities). Many preferred to continue with the established practice of adopting extensive express objects clauses.

As from 1 October 2009 the objects clauses in the memorandum of a company incorporated **4.16** under the 1985 Act or earlier Companies Acts are treated as provisions of the company's articles.[18] Therefore such companies enjoy the same unlimited capacity as companies incorporated under the 2006 Act, unless the articles contain provisions which specifically restrict the objects, which may be the case with charities and community interest companies.

Limits on powers of management

The directors' power to manage the business of the company is subject to three limita- **4.17** tions: (a) the provisions of the 2006 Act, which provide that certain matters can only be undertaken by the company in general meeting, eg alterations of capital;[19] (b) restrictions contained in the company's constitution, which may impose limits on what the directors can do, either at all or without approval of the members; and (c) directions given by special resolution.

There are some more general limits on the power of management that should be mentioned. **4.18** It is axiomatic that a director's power of management does not give him actual authority to defraud his company.[20] Also, the directors' powers of management are limited to actions on behalf of the company and they do not have authority on behalf of members to give assurances or understandings as to the management of the company that could give rise to equitable considerations of the kind required for a petition under the 2006 Act, Part 30 (unfair prejudice).[21]

It used to be the law that the power to manage the business did not give the directors power **4.19** to destroy it by presenting a winding-up petition,[22] but now directors have a statutory power to put a company into administration or present a winding-up petition.[23] As stated in paragraph 4.14 above, now there should be no question that the directors have power to close it down if that is the appropriate course.

(2) Shareholders' reserve power

Where, as with Table A, reg 70, and each Model Article 3, the articles confer on the **4.20** directors power to manage the company's business, the shareholders cannot compel the directors, by ordinary resolution, to manage the business in a particular way.[24] On the

---

[18] 2006 Act, s 28. The articles can be amended by special resolution to remove unnecessary objects clauses.

[19] Ch 25 below identifies matters required by the 2006 Act to be done by the members.

[20] *Lexi Holdings v Pannone and Partners* [2009] EWHC 2590 (Ch), para 69. See also *Bilta (UK) Ltd v Nazir (No 2)* [2014] Ch 52, CA, at para 20, per Patten LJ; *Bilta (UK) Ltd v Nazir (No 2)* [2016] AC 1, SC 23, at paras 6–8, per Lord Neuberger and paras 71, 89, and 90, per Lord Sumption.

[21] *Re Benfield Greig Group plc* [2000] 2 BCLC 488 at para 43(7).

[22] *Smith v Duke of Manchester* (1883) 24 Ch D 611; *Re Emmadart Ltd* [1979] Ch 540. Although this is largely academic, it might be thought unduly restrictive to limit carrying on of business to active trading, not least because many companies are not trading companies. Also in bankruptcy it was well understood that a person carried on business until all his debts were paid: *Theophile v The Solicitor General* [1950] AC 186, HL; *Morphitis v Bernasconi* [2003] Ch 552, CA, para 41.

[23] For administration: Insolvency Act, Sch B1, paras 12(1)(b) and 22(2). For winding up: Insolvency Act, s 124(1). See also *Re Instrumentation Electrical Services Ltd* [1988] BCLC 550; *Re Equiticorp International plc* [1989] 1 WLR 1010. The rules of internal management of the company must be complied with where administrators are appointed out of court by the directors: *Minmar (929) Ltd v Khalatschi* [2011] BCC 485 (held that there had been an invalid appointment of administrators where no proper board meeting of the directors was held).

[24] *Automatic Self-Cleansing Filter Syndicate Co Ltd v Cunninghame* [1906] 2 Ch 34, CA; *Gramophone and Typewriter Ltd v Stanley* [1908] 2 KB 89, CA; *Salmon v Quin & Axtens* [1909] 1 Ch 311, 320, CA (affd in *Quin & Axtens Ltd v Salmon* [1909] AC 442, HL); *John Shaw and Sons (Salford) Ltd v Shaw* [1935] 2 KB 113, 134,

other hand the shareholders can by ordinary resolution consent to, approve, or authorize the exercise of the directors' powers in accordance with the 2006 Act, s 180, or they may ratify their acts so as to protect them from complaint by the company in accordance with the 2006 Act, s 239.[25] In these circumstances there is no conflict between the directors and the shareholders.

4.21 Where the shareholders wish to intervene in the management of the company and the directors do not agree, four courses of action may be open to the shareholders. First, by ordinary resolution they may remove and replace the directors of whom they disapprove: 2006 Act, s 168.[26] The targeted director may be protected from removal from office by entrenched rights contained in the articles[27] or by weighted voting rights in favour of himself or shareholders who support him.[28]

4.22 Secondly, they may pass a special resolution directing the directors to take or refrain from taking specified action. This power is stated in the first sentence of Table A, reg 70, but the second sentence states that the special resolution cannot purport to operate retrospectively.[29] Each Model Article (pcls), (pclg), and (plc) 4 provides to the same effect:

(1) The shareholders may, by special resolution, direct the directors to take, or refrain from taking, specified action.
(2) No such special resolution invalidates anything which the directors have done before the passing of the resolution.

Again, the ability of shareholders to intervene by special resolution may be restricted by provisions for entrenchment in the articles or by weighted voting rights.[30]

4.23 Thirdly, the shareholders may pass a special resolution to alter the company's articles to control or restrict the directors' powers of management, either generally or in relation to a particular matter.[31] Again, the altered article could not have retrospective effect.

4.24 Fourthly, if they are unanimous, the shareholders may informally take over the management of the company for themselves.[32] The CLR expressed the principle in this way:

> The courts have established a rule that the members of a company may, by their unanimous agreement, bind or empower the company and its organs to do anything within its capacity, regardless of any limitations in the articles. This implies that the members may even decide

---

CA; *Scott v Scott* [1943] 1 All ER 582; *Breckland Group Holdings Ltd v London and Suffolk Properties Ltd* [1989] BCLC 100.

[25] *Hogg v Crampthorn Ltd* [1967] Ch 254, 269; *Bamford v Bamford* [1970] Ch 212, CA. Consent, approval, and authorization is discussed in Ch 10, Section D below, and ratification is discussed in Ch 20 below.
[26] Ch 7, Section A(2) below.
[27] 2006 Act, s 22.
[28] *Bushell v Faith* [1970] AC 1099, HL; *Russell v Northern Bank Development Corporation Ltd* [1992] 1 WLR 588, HL. But see *Jackson v Dear* [2014] 1 BCLC 186, CA, where directors could exercise a power in the articles to remove a director even though the sole shareholder was bound by an agreement to appoint and not remove him.
[29] Reflecting the judgment of Buckley LJ in *Gramophone and Typewriter Ltd v Stanley* [1908] 2 KB 89, 105, 106, CA.
[30] 2006 Act, s 22. *Bushell v Faith* [1970] AC 1099, HL; *Russell v Northern Bank Development Corporation Ltd* [1992] 1 WLR 588, HL.
[31] 2006 Act, s 21.
[32] *Re Duomatic Ltd* [1969] 2 Ch 365; *Bilta (UK) Ltd v Nazir (No 2)* [2016] AC 1, SC, at para 187. See further Ch 25, Section B(4) below.

unanimously to dispense with the division of powers between themselves and the directors and run the company themselves.[33]

The principle there stated is well supported by authority.[34] In *Multinational Gas and Petrochemical Co v Multinational Gas and Petrochemical Services Ltd*[35] the Court of Appeal held that the company, which had a functioning board, was bound by the unanimous decision of its shareholders that it should enter into contracts from which it suffered losses.[36]

In *Re Frontsouth (Witham) Ltd*,[37] Henderson J was referred to the treatment of this issue **4.25** in the first edition of this work and, without the benefit of citation of further authority, expressed the provisional view that shareholders cannot decide that the company should apply for an administration order or enter administration out of court where there is a functioning board. It is respectfully suggested that Henderson J's doubts are misplaced, because the Insolvency Act makes express provision for the company (by decision of its members), as an alternative to the directors, to make the application to court or to make the company enter administration out of court,[38] although the formalities involved in those steps would require the unanimous decision or resolution to be recorded in writing.[39] Nor should there be confusion because the board is bound to act in accordance with a unanimous decision of the shareholders.

If for some reason the directors are incapable of acting or the board has ceased to exist, **4.26** the company, through its shareholders, has a residual power to appoint new or additional directors to enable the company to function.[40] It will seldom be necessary to resort to this principle, since articles invariably give shareholders power to appoint directors by ordinary resolution.[41]

The foregoing paragraphs have described the steps that may be open to all or a majority **4.27** of the shareholders. If there is deadlock or if a minority shareholder complains of unfair prejudice in the management of a company, the aggrieved member may present a petition for relief under the 2006 Act, Part 30 (or less likely for winding up on the just and equitable ground) in which the court may grant appropriate interim relief, including injunctions and the appointment of a receiver.[42]

---

[33] CLR: *Developing the Framework* (March 2000) at para 4.21.

[34] The CLR only cited *Re Duomatic Ltd* [1969] 2 Ch 365.

[35] [1983] Ch 258, CA, 269, per Lawton LJ; 289, 290, per Dillon LJ; applying *Salomon v A Salomon & Co Ltd* [1897] AC 22, 57, HL, per Lord Davey.

[36] The principle stated in the *Multinational* case was expressly approved in *Meridian Global Funds Management Asia Ltd v Securities Commission* [1995] 2 AC 500, 506, PC per Lord Hoffmann.

[37] [2011] BCC 635 at paras 31–4.

[38] Insolvency Act, Sch B1, paras 12(1)(a) and 22(1).

[39] As was the case in *Re Barry Artist Ltd* [1985] 1 WLR 1305 (unanimous resolution to reduce capital in place of special resolution).

[40] *Barron v Potter* [1914] 1 Ch 895; *Foster v Foster* [1916] 1 Ch 532; *Alexander Ward & Co v Samyang Navigation Co Ltd* [1975] 1 WLR 673, 679, HL.

[41] Table A, reg 78; Model Article (pcls) and (pclg) 17(1)(a) and Model Article (plc) 20(a). See Ch 6, Section D below. If necessary the court can direct that a meeting of the company be held for this purpose: 2006 Act, s 306; see Ch 25, Section D(1) below.

[42] As to interim relief, see *Re a Company (No 00596 of 1986)* [1987] BCLC 133; *Weir, Petitioners* [1990] BCC 761; *Re Milgate Developments Ltd* [1993] BCLC 291; *Wilton-Davies v Kirk* [1998] 1 BCLC 274; *Re Worldhams Park Golf Course Ltd* [1998] 1 BCLC 554.

(3) Particular responsibilities of directors

4.28 In exercising their powers to manage the business of the company, directors must comply with their general duties under the Companies Act, Part 10, including, where necessary, obtaining the approval of a transaction from the members.[43] In addition, the Act imposes on directors numerous specific functions and duties to secure compliance with provisions of the Act. If the obligation is not complied with a director may be an officer in default and guilty of a criminal offence. The offences are for the most part intermediate or quasi-regulatory and triable summarily and punishable by a fine.[44]

4.29 Many of these responsibilities concern record-keeping, and, where required, delivering information to the Registrar or making the company's records open to inspection. These records include constitutional documents,[45] the register of the company's members,[46] with an index if necessary,[47] the register of directors,[48] directors' service and indemnity contracts,[49] minutes of meetings of directors,[50] the register of secretaries,[51] records of company meetings and decisions of members,[52] information about interests in shares in a public company,[53] and the register of charges.[54] Model Article (plc) 82 gives a public company the right to destroy old documents relating to shares and dividends.

4.30 The 2006 Act has been amended by the Small Business, Enterprise and Employment Act 2015 (SBEE Act), s 94 and Sch 5[55] to give private companies the option of keeping information on the central register kept by the registrar under the 2006 Act, s 1080 instead of keeping it in its own register of members,[56] register of directors or directors' residential addresses,[57] and register of secretaries.[58] The elections to take up these options may be made by the subscribers wishing to form a private company under the Act or by the private company itself once it is formed and registered.[59] Relevant information must be delivered to the registrar as soon as reasonably practicable after the company becomes aware of it and, in any event, no later than the time by which the company would have been obliged to notify the

---

[43] See Chapters 10–18 below.

[44] See Ch 35, Section I below for a discussion of offences under the Companies Act.

[45] 2006 Act, ss 26, 30, 32, 34–6, and (following relief under Part 30) 998, 999.

[46] *Intellimedia Technologies Ltd v Richards* [2015] EWHC 1200 (Ch) (rectification of the register granted under 2006 Act, s 125 where a director had wrongly entered himself as shareholder in place of previous registered shareholder). Rectification under s 125 is a summary remedy which is not suitable where there is no clear legal right to rectification: *Nilon Ltd v Royal Westminster Investments SA* [2015] 2 BCLC 1, PC.

[47] 2006 Act, ss 113–15, 118, 120, 123, 130, 132, 135.

[48] 2006 Act, ss 162, 165, 167, 246

[49] 2006 Act, ss 228, 229, 231, 237, 238.

[50] 2006 Act, s 248.

[51] 2006 Act, ss 275 and 276.

[52] 2006 Act, ss 355, 357, 358.

[53] 2006 Act, ss 806–10, 813, 815, 819.

[54] 2006 Act, s 877.

[55] In force from 30 June 2016 (SBEE Act 2015 (Commencement No 4) Regulations, SI 2016 / 321, reg 6 (c)).

[56] 2006 Act, Part 8, Ch 2A, ss 128A–128K. This option applies to the register of overseas members; SBEE Act, Sch 5, para 4.

[57] 2006 Act, ss 161A, 167A–167E.

[58] 2006 Act, ss 274A, 279A–279F.

[59] 2006 Act, ss 112A, 128A, and 128B; 2006 Act, ss 161A, 167A, and 167B; 2006 Act, ss 274A, 279A, and 279B. The election takes effect so long as the company is a private company and it may be withdrawn by notice sent to the registrar: 2006 Act, ss 128C, 128 J, 167B, 167E, 279B, and 279E.

registrar of the changes.[60] The Secretary of State is permitted to extend these central register options to public companies by regulation.[61]

Directors are responsible for securing compliance by the company with directions from the Secretary of State in relation to the company's name,[62] the appointment of directors,[63] and the appointment of a secretary of a public company.[64]

4.31

In addition the directors are responsible for the proper conduct of company meetings.[65] They are responsible for maintaining proper accounting records and the preparation of accounts, reports, audit, and annual return.[66] They have a range of duties and responsibilities in relation to capital.[67] They also have particular responsibilities in relation to reorganizations and takeovers.[68] In each case default is a criminal offence.

4.32

Directors are also persons referred to in the Civil Procedure Rules as persons holding a senior position in the company who are included in the category of persons who may sign a statement of truth on behalf of the company (alongside other senior persons such as the treasurer, the secretary, the chief executive, a manager or other officer of the company).[69]

4.33

Where a company, or any of its subsidiaries, is ceasing to carry on or is transferring the whole or any part of its business, the directors have power to make provision for the employees or former employees of the company, provided that payments are made before the company goes into liquidation and are made out of distributable profits. The directors have power to make this provision with the sanction of an ordinary resolution of the company or if so authorized by the company's memorandum or articles.[70] But the directors cannot use this power for the benefit of themselves, former directors, or shadow directors without the sanction of a resolution of the company.[71] The Model Articles include provisions authorizing the directors to make provision for employees and former employees, other than directors, former directors, and shadow directors.[72]

4.34

(4) Directors' powers and responsibilities in relation to dissolution

Thus far this chapter has considered the powers and responsibilities of directors while a company is in operation, whether or not it is actively carrying on business (but not when it is subject to insolvency proceedings). Directors also have powers to have a company dissolved or to take steps to have it restored to life after it has been dissolved in accordance with the 2006 Act, Part 31.[73]

4.35

---

[60] 2006 Act, ss 128E (4), 167, 167D (3), 276, and 279D (3).

[61] 2006 Act, ss 128K, 167F, and 279F (inserted by SBEE Act 2015, Sch 5).

[62] 2006 Act, ss 63, 64, 68, 75, 76, 84.

[63] 2006 Act, s 156.

[64] 2006 Act, s 272.

[65] Ch 25 below.

[66] Ch 26 below.

[67] Ch 27 below.

[68] Ch 28 below.

[69] Civil Procedure Rules, Part 22, and see in particular 22PD.3, paras 3.4 and 3.5. Cf also *Kirby v Centro Properties Ltd (No 2)* [2012] FCA 70, 87 ACSR 229 (direction that the company secretary shall make inquiries and answer interrogatories on behalf of the company).

[70] 2006 Act, s 247; in force 1 October 2009. 2006 Act, s 247(3) makes special provision for charities.

[71] 2006 Act, s 247(5)(b), which was introduced on the recommendation of the CLR: *Final Report* at para 6.5.

[72] Model Article (pcls) 51; Model Article (pclg) 37; Model Article (plc) 84.

[73] In force 1 October 2009.

4.36 A company's existence is brought to an end when it is dissolved either because the Registrar takes steps to strike off the register a company that appears to be defunct,[74] or because the company, by its directors or a majority of them, takes the initiative and applies to be struck off the register and dissolved.[75] The procedure for dissolution on the application of the company has a number of safeguards to protect the interests of persons with dealings with the company: (a) three months must have elapsed since publication of notice of the proposed striking off was given in the Gazette, (b) the company must have been inactive for three months before the application for voluntary striking off, (c) the company must not be subject to ongoing insolvency proceedings or proceedings in relation to a scheme of compromise or arrangement, and (d) seven days' notice of the application for voluntary striking off must be given to members, employees, creditors, directors, pension fund trustees, and other persons specified by regulation.

4.37 Whether the company is struck off by the Registrar or dissolved voluntarily, any liability of directors, managing officers, and members of the company continues and may be enforced as if the company had not been dissolved.[76]

4.38 The consequence of the company being dissolved is that all its property and rights vest in the Crown as *bona vacantia*, but subject to a power of the Crown to disclaim and a power of the court to make a vesting order in favour of a person with an interest in the disclaimed property.[77] Sometimes it is necessary to have a company which has been struck off the register or dissolved restored to the register. The most common reason for this is where it is discovered that the company had some valuable property. It used to be the case that a restoration was also sought where a third party needed to establish the company's liability for the purposes of making a claim against an insurer under the Third Parties (Rights against Insurers) Act 1930, but it is no longer necessary to restore the company since the coming into force of the Third Parties (Rights Against Insurers) Act 2010, which Act allows for establishing the insured claim within proceedings against only the insurer, without the requirement to restore or join the company.[78]

4.39 Under the 1985 Act a person who was simply a former director of the dissolved company could not apply for it to be restored to the register. Unless he was also a member or creditor, he did not have a sufficient interest to apply for the dissolution to be declared void under the 1985 Act, s 651,[79] and only the company, a member, or

---

[74] 2006 Act, ss 1000 and 1002. The Registrar has a similar power where the company is in liquidation and he has reasonable cause to believe that no liquidator is acting or that the affairs of the company are fully wound up: 2006 Act, ss 1001 and 1002.

[75] 2006 Act, ss 1003–11. The voluntary striking-off procedure is now extended to public companies.

[76] 2006 Act, ss 1000(7)(a) and 1003(6)(a). By SBEE Act, s 103 the one-month period referred to in s 1000 (2) and (3)(b) of the 2006 Act is reduced to 14 days, and the three-month period referred to in ss 1000 (3), 1001, and 1003 is reduced to two months, to provide for accelerated strike off (in force from 10 October 2015 pursuant to SI 2015 / 1689, reg 4).

[77] 2006 Act, ss 1012–19 and apply provisions similar to those in the Insolvency Act, ss 180–2 to Crown disclaimer.

[78] Asset overlooked: *Stanhope Pension Trust Ltd v Registrar of Companies* [1994] 1 BCLC 628; *Re Oakleague Ltd* [1995] 2 BCLC 624. Insured claims: under the old law (Third Parties (Rights Against Insurers) Act 1930, see *Re Harvest Lane Motor Bodies Ltd* [1969] 1 Ch 457; *Re Priceland Ltd* [1997] 1 BCLC 467; *Re Philip Powis Ltd* [1998] 1 BCLC 440, CA. For the new law see the 2010 Act, brought into force from 1 August 2016 (the Third Parties (Rights Against Insurers) Act 2010 (Commencement Order) 2016).

[79] *Re Waterbury Nominees Pty Ltd* (1986) 11 ACLR 348, SC (WA).

creditor could apply to the court under s 653 for the company to be restored to the register.[80]

Under the provisions of the 2006 Act there are two ways of having a dissolved company **4.40** restored to life; one is an administrative procedure and the other is by application to the court. Both may be invoked by a former director. Under the new administrative procedure an application for the restoration of the company to the register may be made to the Registrar by a former director or member of the company within six years of the date of dissolution provided that (a) the company was carrying on business or in operation at the time of striking off, (b) in respect of any property vested as *bona vacantia* the Crown consents, and (c) records to be delivered to the Registrar are brought up to date and any penalties paid.[81] The general effect of administrative restoration to the register is that the company is deemed to have continued in existence as if it had not been dissolved or struck off the register.[82] The court may give such directions and make such provision as seems just for placing the company and all other persons in the same position (as nearly as may be) as if the company had not been dissolved or struck off the register.[83]

If the administrative procedure is not available, the court has power to restore the company **4.41** to the register under the 2006 Act, ss 1029–32. These provisions extend the classes of applicants to include, among others, former directors,[84] but limit the time to six years from the date of dissolution (rather than 20 years under s 653),[85] unless the application is for the purpose of bringing proceedings against the company for damages for personal injury, in which case it can be brought at any time (unless it appears that the claim is bound to fail).[86] The court may order the restoration of the company to the register if (a) it was struck off as a defunct company, but was, at the time of striking off, carrying on business or in operation, (b) it was struck of voluntarily, but the requirements for striking off were not complied with, or (c) the court considers it just to do so.[87] The general effect of an order by the court for restoration to the register is that the company is deemed to have continued in existence as if it had not been dissolved or struck off the register.[88] The court may give such directions and make such provision as seems just for placing the company and all other persons in the same position (as nearly as may be) as if the company had not been dissolved or struck off the register.[89]

---

[80] In *Witherdale v Registrar of Companies* [2008] 1 BCLC 174 it was held that a bankrupt director had no locus to procure the company to apply for restoration because his agency as a director terminated upon bankruptcy. In *Kaye v Zeital* [2010] 2 BCLC 1, CA, para 17, Rimer LJ questioned the locus of the applicant seeking to restore the company in circumstances where the applicant had purported to self-appoint as a director of the dissolved company, and made a declaration of membership despite not being entered on the share register as a member.

[81] 2006 Act, ss 1024–8. These provisions were recommended by the CLR: *Final Report* at paras 11.17–11.20.

[82] 2006 Act, s 1028 (1).

[83] 2006 Act, s 1028 (3).

[84] 2006 Act, s 1029(2)(b).

[85] 2006 Act, s 1030(4).

[86] 2006 Act, s 1030(1)–(3).

[87] 2006 Act, s 1031(1).

[88] 2006 Act, s 1032 (1). In *Joddrell v Peaktone Ltd* [2013] 1 WLR 784, CA, it was held that where a company was restored to the register pursuant to s 1029, retrospective validation of proceedings issued against the company when the company was dissolved was the proper course due to the provisions of s 1032 (1) of the 2006 Act (and its deeming provisions as if the company had continued in existence while dissolved or struck off).

[89] 2006 Act, s 1032 (3).

C. Power of Directors to Bind the Company

4.42 A transaction will be binding on the company if (a) it has capacity to make it (ie it is within its power), (b) it is made by the company directly (ie under its seal) or on its behalf by persons capable of binding the company, and (c) it is formally valid. This had been an area of the law bedevilled by technicality, but reforms to the Companies Acts have greatly simplified it and there is less scope for companies avoiding their obligations on what might be seen as technical grounds. This Section C is concerned with capacity and the power of directors to bind the company. Section D considers formal validity.

(1) A company's capacity

4.43 Under the ultra vires doctrine developed by the courts, a company only had capacity to enter into transactions within the scope of its objects, set out in its memorandum of association. A transaction outside those objects was ultra vires and void and could not even be ratified by the unanimous assent of all the members.[90] The ultra vires doctrine was an impediment to the development of a company's business and so companies adopted a wide range of objects, usually stated to be separate objects, which enabled them to pursue an unlimited range of business activities with unrestricted powers.

4.44 As explained in paragraphs 4.14–4.16 above, the capacity of a company is not restricted by its objects unless there are specific restrictions in its articles. This is the effect of the 2006 Act, s 28 for companies incorporated before 1 October 2009, and s 31 for those incorporated after that date. The 2006 Act, s 31(1) provides that 'unless a company's articles specifically restrict the objects of the company, its objects are unrestricted'. In practice, the only companies that are likely to restrict their objects are charitable companies and community interest companies.

4.45 It became necessary to reform and largely do away with the ultra vires doctrine when the UK joined the EEC, because the First EEC Company Law Directive[91] states:

> 9.1 Acts done by the organs of the company shall be binding upon it even if those acts are not within the objects of the company, unless such acts exceed the powers that the law confers or allows to be conferred on those organs. However, Member States may provide that the company shall not be bound where such acts are outside the objects of the company, if it proves that the third party knew that the act was outside those objects or could not in view of the circumstances have been unaware of it; disclosure of the statutes shall not of itself be sufficient proof thereof.
>
> 9.2 The limits on the powers of the organs of the company, arising under the statutes or from a decision of the competent organs, may never be relied upon as against third parties, even if it had been disclosed.

Those provisions are now reflected in the 2006 Act, ss 39–42.[92] The manifest purpose of these provisions is to enable people to deal with a company in good faith without

---

[90] *Ashbury Railway Carriage and Iron Company Ltd v Riche* (1875) LR 7 HL 653; *AG v Great Eastern Railway* (1880) 5 AC 473, HL.

[91] 1968/151/EEC.

[92] The first attempt to meet the requirements of the directive was the European Communities Act, s 9, later consolidated into 1985 Act, s 35. 1989 Act, ss 108 and 109, replaced the original s 35 with ss 35, 35A, 35B

being adversely affected by any limits on the company's capacity or its rules of internal management.[93]

The 2006 Act, s 39(1) deals with a company's capacity and provides: **4.46**

> The validity of an act done by a company shall not be called into question on the ground of lack of capacity by reason of anything in the company's constitution.

In most cases, by reason of s 31(1), the company will have unlimited capacity and there will be no scope for challenging validity on the ground of lack of capacity. If, however, the objects are restricted, as in the case of a company which is a charity, the directors' powers are also restricted, and they are under a duty, stated in s 171(a), to act in accordance with the company's constitution.[94]

The 2006 Act, s 39(2) states that s 39 has effect subject to s 42 which contains special provisions for charities (paragraph 4.63 below). **4.47**

(2) The power of the directors to bind the company

Under the 'indoor management rule' third parties who dealt in good faith with a company were entitled to assume that the company's internal procedures had been complied with.[95] As mentioned above, Article 9 of the First EEC Company Law Directive required reforms to be made in this respect. The 2006 Act, s 40(1) states the power of the directors to bind the company in these terms: **4.48**

> In favour of a person dealing with a company in good faith, the power of the directors to bind the company, or authorise others to do so, is deemed to be free of any limitation under the company's constitution.

It has been suggested that the change from 'the power of the board of directors to bind the company' in the 1985 Act, s 35A(1) to 'the power of the directors to bind the company' in s 40(1) is a change of substance enabling a third party to rely on a transaction not decided on by the board, because, for example, it was inquorate.[96] It is respectfully suggested that there is no such change. First, none is indicated in the Explanatory Notes or Table of Derivations and none was suggested in the White Paper, *Modernising Company Law*[97] when commenting on its draft bill: 'The basic rule … as under the present law, is that those doing business with the company are entitled to assume that the board of directors has authority to enter into **4.49**

---

with effect from 4 February 1991. The new provisions, 2006 Act, ss 39–42, came into force on 1 October 2009. 1985 Act, s 35 applies to acts of a company before that date: 2006 Act Commencement Order No 8, Sch 2, para 15. Similarly 1985 Act, ss 35A and 35B apply, instead of 2006 Act, s 40, to dealings prior to that date: *Ford v Polymer Vision Ltd* [2009] 2 BCLC 160 at para 70.

[93] *TCB Ltd v Gray* [1986] Ch 621, 635, per Sir Nicholas Browne-Wilkinson V-C (whose judgment was upheld on appeal: [1987] Ch 458).

[94] Explanatory Notes to 2006 Act, s 39.

[95] *Royal British Bank v Turquand* (1856) 6 E & B 327. In *TCB Ltd v Gray* [1986] Ch 621, 635 Sir Nicholas Browne-Wilkinson V-C (whose judgment was upheld on appeal: [1987] Ch 458) said that the old doctrine of constructive notice of the company's memorandum and articles, mitigated by the *Turquand* case, caused commercial inconvenience and injustice and was largely swept away by the provisions giving effect to Art 9 First EEC Company Law Directive.

[96] *Palmer's Company Law Annotated Guide to the Companies Act 2006* (Sweet and Maxwell, 2007) where it is suggested that such a change would reflect the view expressed by Robert Walker LJ in *Smith v Henniker-Major* [2003] Ch 182, CA at paras 23, 41–43.

[97] Paras 28 and 29.

commitments on the company's behalf and to authorise others to do so. They do not need therefore to worry about what is in the company's constitution.' Secondly, the deletion of the reference to the board is merely a return to the language used in the original European Communities Act, s 9. Thirdly, the Model Articles, like Table A, are drafted on the basis that directors take decisions collectively, unless a matter has been delegated.[98] Finally the Insolvency Act, s 124(1) and Schedule B1, paragraphs 12(1)(b) and 22(1), dealing with presentation of winding-up petitions and administration, refer to 'the directors' and it is well established that the taking of those steps must be decided on by the board.[99]

4.50 The phrase 'or authorise others to do so' indicates that the directors acting collectively may delegate the transaction to a managing director, committee,[100] or other agents.[101] A person dealing with the company to whom s 40 applies will be entitled to proceed on the basis that the delegation was valid. As discussed in paragraph 4.66 below, the default position is that a managing director has all the implied powers that would ordinarily be exercisable by a managing director in his position.[102]

4.51 The 2006 Act, s 40(2) explains what is meant by a person dealing with the company in good faith in s 40(1):

> For this purpose—
> (a) a person 'deals with' a company if he is a party to any transaction or other act to which the company is a party;
> (b) a person dealing with a company—
>   (i) is not bound to enquire as to any limitation on the powers of the directors to bind the company or authorise others to do so,
>   (ii) is presumed to have acted in good faith unless the contrary is proved, and
>   (iii) is not to be regarded as acting in bad faith by reason only of his knowing that an act is beyond the powers of the directors under the company's constitution.

4.52 The reference to a 'person dealing with a company' is wide enough to include insiders such as a director of the company,[103] but in such a case the provisions of s 40 are subject to s 41, discussed below.[104] It does not include a company's members as such.[105] To be 'dealing' with

---

[98] Table A, regs 70–2, 84, 87–98, 102, 108, 110 (all of which refer to the directors, not the board); Model Articles (pcls) 5, 7–16; Model Articles (plc) 5, 7–19.

[99] *Re Equiticorp International plc* [1989] 1 WLR 1010; *Minmar (929) Ltd v Khalastchi* [2011] BCC 485.

[100] In *Newcastle International Airport Ltd v Eversheds LLP* [2014] 1 WLR 3073, CA, the company was bound by the decision of its remuneration committee, even though its chairman (a non-executive director) was in breach of duty and failed in its claim against negligent solicitors because the true cause of its loss was the behaviour of the remuneration committee and its chairman (see Rimer LJ at paras 100 and 102).

[101] *Kelly v Fraser* [2013] 1 AC 450, PC at paras 2–8 (company acting as agent of pension trustees was bound by the apparent authority of an employee).

[102] *Smith v Butler* [2012] BCC 645, CA, at para 28, per Arden LJ.

[103] *Smith v Henniker-Major* [2003] Ch 182, CA at paras 45–52, 109, 125.

[104] In *Cooperatieve Rabobank 'Vecht en Plassengebied' BA v Minderhoud* [1998] 1 WLR 1025 it was held that it was possible for directors to be treated differently by national law provisions and Art 8 of Council Directive 68/151/EEC should be so construed.

[105] *EIC Services Ltd v Phipps* [2005] 1 WLR 1377, CA, where the Court of Appeal decided that a bonus issue could not be validated by 1985 Act, s 35A(1) because shareholders receiving bonus shares were not persons 'dealing with the company'. At para 35 Peter Gibson LJ said that s 35A contemplated a bilateral transaction between the company and the person dealing with the company, and as a matter of ordinary language and having regard to the nature of a bonus issue and the fact that it was an internal arrangement in which there was no diminution or increase in the assets or liabilities of the company, a shareholder receiving bonus shares could not be regarded as a person dealing with the company.

the company a person must be a party to any transaction 'or other act' to which the company is a party. The provisions therefore refer to wider arrangements than just contracts (because of the words 'or other act').[106]

The requirement that the dealing must be 'in good faith' ensures that a defence based on absence of notice would not be available to someone who has not acted genuinely and honestly in his dealings with the company.[107] However, the statutory language means that it is possible for a person to act in good faith despite knowing that an act is beyond the powers of the directors under the company's constitution.[108] Further, the person dealing is also protected by the statutory presumption that he acted in good faith unless the contrary is proved. **4.53**

Good faith is unlikely to be established by a person who knows or has reason to believe that the contract or transaction is contrary to the commercial interests of the company; it is likely to be very difficult for the person to assert with any credibility that he believed the agent did have actual authority, and lack of such a belief would be fatal to a claim that the agent had apparent authority.[109] Nor will good faith be established if there are suspicious circumstances putting the person contracting with the company on inquiry,[110] or where the person contracting with the company is dishonest or irrational, which includes turning a blind eye or being reckless.[111] **4.54**

The 2006 Act, s 40(3) explains what is meant by limitations on the directors' powers under the company's constitution: **4.55**

> The references above to limitations on the directors' powers under the company's constitution include limitations deriving—
> (a) from a resolution of the company or of any class of shareholders, or
> (b) from any agreement between the members of the company or of any class of shareholders.

---

[106] Thus, for example, a gratuitous act would presumably be included. See also *International Sales and Agencies Ltd v Marcus* [1982] 3 All ER 551; *EIC Services Ltd v Phipps* [2005] 1 WLR 1377, CA. Contracts such as the grant of a debenture or grant of an option are within the section: *Ford v Polymer Vision Ltd* [2009] 2 BCLC 160 at para 74.

[107] See *Barclays Bank v TOSG Trust Fund* [1984] BCLC 1, 18; *Smith v Henniker-Major & Co* [2003] Ch 182, CA at para 108, where Carnwath LJ said that the general policy of the section 'seems to be that, if a document is put forward as a decision of the board by someone appearing to act on behalf of the company, in circumstances where there is no reason to doubt its authenticity, a person dealing with the company in good faith should be able to take it at face value'. A third party cannot rely on apparent authority if his belief is dishonest or irrational, which includes turning a blind eye or being reckless: see *Thanakharn v Akai Holdings Ltd (No 2)* [2011] 1 HKC 357, as applied by the English Court of Appeal in *Quinn v CC Automotive Group Ltd* [2011] 2 All ER (Comm) 584, CA, para 23. See also *LNOC Ltd v Watford AFC Ltd* [2013] EWHC 3615 at paras 90–2; *Acute Property Developments Ltd v Apostolou* [2013] EWHC 200 (Ch), at para 39; and *PEC Ltd v Asia Golden Rice Co Ltd* [2014] EWHC 1583 (Comm) at para 73.

[108] *Ford v Polymer Vision Ltd* [2009] 2 BCLC 160 illustrates this. There was no arguable case of absence of good faith even if a third party knew that the board meeting at which his debenture was approved was defective under the company's constitution, because notice to persons entitled to it was not given and it was deemed to have been held in the UK (para 78). As Blackburne J said, at para 73, good faith is 'the touchstone'.

[109] *Criterion Properties plc v Stratford UK Properties LLC* [2004] 1 WLR 1846, HL at para 31 per Lord Scott. See also *Re Capitol Films Ltd* [2011] 2 BCLC 359 (third party could not rely on apparent authority of a director of the company in circumstances where the third party acquired most of the company's assets for uncertain consideration at a time when the company was in severe financial difficulties and where the director of the company was also a director of the third party).

[110] *Wrexham Association Football Club Ltd v Crucialmove Ltd* [2008] 1 BCLC 508 at paras 47 and 48.

[111] *Thanakharn v Akai Holdings Ltd (No 2)* [2011] 1 HKC 357; applied in *Quinn v CC Automotive Group Ltd* [2011] 2 All ER (Comm) 584, CA, para 23. See also *LNOC Ltd v Watford AFC Ltd* [2013] EWHC 3615 at paras 90–2; *Acute Property Developments Ltd v Apostolou* [2013] EWHC 200 (Ch), at para 39; *PEC Ltd v Asia Golden Rice Co Ltd* [2014] EWHC 1583 (Comm) at para 73.

The limitations are therefore wider than limitations contained in the articles or imposed by special resolution.

4.56 The 2006 Act, s 40(4) and (5) goes on to state the internal consequences of acts or intended acts beyond the directors' powers.

> (4) This section does not affect any right of a member of the company to bring proceedings to restrain the doing of an action which is beyond the powers of the directors. But no such proceedings lie in respect of an act to be done in fulfilment of a legal obligation arising from a previous act of the company.
>
> (5) This section does not affect any liability incurred by the directors, or any other person, by reason of the directors' exceeding their powers.

Subsection (4) reflects the fact that a member has a right to see that the company's constitution is obeyed.[112] Subsection (5) preserves the directors' liability for breach of duty, including breach of the 2006 Act, s 171(a) and is without prejudice to the ability of the independent members to ratify the directors' conduct under s 239.

4.57 Finally the 2006 Act, s 40(6) restricts the application of the section to directors and their associates and to charitable companies (Section C(4) below).

(3) Transactions involving directors or their associates

4.58 The 2006 Act, s 41 applies to a transaction between the company and its directors or their associates if or to the extent that its validity depends on the 2006 Act, s 40 (because the transaction exceeded any limitation on the directors' powers under the company's constitution).[113] The effect of s 41 is that the company may avoid transactions with directors and their associates and claim accounts and indemnity. Other remedies may be pursued as well, for example a derivative claim under the 2006 Act, Part 11, because the sections are not to be read as excluding the operation of any other enactment or rule of law by virtue of which the transaction may be called in question or any liability to the company may arise.[114]

4.59 The 2006 Act, s 41(2) provides that the transaction is voidable at the instance of the company where:

> (a) the company enters into such a transaction,[115] and
> (b) the parties to the transaction include—
>> (i) a director of the company or of its holding company,[116] or
>> (ii) a person connected with any such director.[117]

As explained below, avoiding the transaction may cease to be an available option for the company.

4.60 Whether or not the transaction is avoided, three categories of person may be personally liable to the company: (i) any director of the company or its holding company who was a party

---

[112] *Smith v Croft (No 2)* [1988] Ch 114, 169.
[113] 2006 Act, s 41(1). By s 40(6), s 40 is subject to s 41.
[114] 2006 Act, s 41(1).
[115] ie one within s 41(1). By s 41(7) a 'transaction' includes any act.
[116] Holding company is defined by 2006 Act, s 1159.
[117] Under 2006 Act, s 41(7), the reference to a person connected with a director has the same meaning as in Part 10, ss 252–7, which are discussed in Ch 3, Section D above.

to the transaction, (ii) any person who was a party to the transaction and who is connected with such a director, and (iii) any director of the company who authorized the transaction.[118] Such persons are liable:

(a) to account to the company for any gain they have made directly or indirectly by the transaction, and

(b) to indemnify the company for any loss or damage resulting from the transaction.[119]

But a person other than a director of the company is not liable to account or indemnify if he shows that at the time the transaction was entered into he did not know that the directors were exceeding their powers.[120]

There are limitations on the company's ability to avoid a transaction to which the 2006 Act, s 41 applies. The first limitation, stated in s 41(4), is that: **4.61**

The transaction ceases to be voidable if—

(a) restitution of any money or other asset which was the subject-matter of the transaction is no longer possible, or

(b) the company is indemnified for any loss or damage resulting from the transaction, or

(c) rights acquired bona fide for value and without actual notice of the directors' exceeding their powers by a person who is not party to the transaction would be affected by the avoidance, or

(d) the transaction is affirmed by the company.

The list is not exhaustive and a company may be prevented from avoiding the transaction by laches. Paragraphs (a)–(c) may be compared with the 2006 Act, s 195 concerning the civil consequences of a contravention of the provisions of s 190 (substantial property transactions with directors). Paragraph (d) enables the members to affirm the transaction, with the support of votes of the directors who exceeded their powers,[121] but these votes could not be used to ratify the conduct of the directors in excess of their powers to save them from liability for breach of duty.[122] If the directors are unable to obtain ratification of their conduct they may obtain relief from the court under the 2006 Act, s 1157.

The second limitation on the power of the company to avoid the transaction is where a party to the transaction itself is not a director of the company or its holding company or connected with such a director.[123] In such a case the transaction would have been valid under the 2006 Act, s 39 if the party had entered into the transaction on his own in good faith. His rights are not affected by s 41(1)–(5), even though persons within s 41(2) were party to the transaction, but the court has power, on the application of the company or the independent party, to make an order affirming, severing, or setting aside the transaction on such terms as appear to the court to be just.[124] In effect the court has to identify the justice of the case where the transaction is valid in favour of the independent party under s 40, but voidable at the **4.62**

---

118 2006 Act, s 41(3) and (7). See n 100 above.
119 2006 Act, s 41(3). These provisions may be compared with 2006 Act, s 195(3).
120 2006 Act, s 41(5). These provisions may be compared with 2006 Act, s 195(7).
121 *North West Transportation Co v Beatty* (1887) 12 App Cas 589, PC.
122 2006 Act, s 239.
123 2006 Act, s 41(2)(b) and (6).
124 2006 Act, s 41(6).

instance of the company under s 41(2).[125] In *Re Torvale Group Ltd*[126] Neuberger J considered the circumstances and the policy of the statutory provisions and affirmed a debenture issued to the trustees of a pension scheme as security for a loan to the company, where one of the trustees was a director and party to the debenture.

(4) Charities

4.63 The 2006 Act, s 42 makes special provisions for constitutional limitations of companies which are charities so as to qualify ss 39 and 40.[127] Section 42(1) provides that the 2006 Act, ss 39 and 40:

> do not apply to the acts of a company that is a charity except in favour of a person who—
> (a) does not know at the time the act is done that the company is a charity, or
> (b) gives full consideration in money or money's worth in relation to the act in question and does not know (as the case may be)—
>   (i) that the act is not permitted by the company's constitution, or
>   (ii) that the act is beyond the powers of the directors.

The title of a person who subsequently acquires property, or any interest in it, which was transferred outside the charity's constitutional limitations is not affected provided that he gave full consideration and did not have actual notice of the circumstances affecting the validity of the company's act.[128] The burden of proving that a person knew that the company was a charity and that the act was not permitted by the company's constitution or was beyond the powers of the directors lies on the person who asserts that fact.[129]

4.64 One of the circumstances in which a transaction may no longer be avoidable at the instance of the company is where the company affirms it.[130] Where the company is a charity, s 42(4) provides that the affirmation is ineffective without the prior written consent of the Charity Commission.

(5) Transactions of individual directors

Actual authority, express or implied

4.65 The directors, (as the organ of the company vested with actual authority to manage its affairs), may delegate their authority to a committee of directors, a managing director, or any other director, so as to confer express actual authority and allow the company to be bound by such delegate.[131]

4.66 The directors may also confer implied actual authority on a director when they appoint one of their number to be managing director. He will have implied actual authority to do all such things as fall within the usual scope of that office.[132] The default position is that a managing director has the implied powers that would ordinarily be exercisable by a managing director

---

[125] A conflict that was made explicit by 1985 Act, s 322A(7).
[126] [1992] 2 BCLC 605, 621, 622, a case on 1985 Act, s 322A(7).
[127] 2006 Act, s 42 restates the Charities Act 1993, s 65, with effect from 1 October 2009.
[128] 2006 Act, s 42(2).
[129] 2006 Act, s 42(3).
[130] 2006 Act, s 41(4)(d).
[131] eg Table A, reg 72; Model Article (pcls) (pcg) (plc) 5. *Hely-Hutchison v Brayhead Ltd* [1968] 1 QB 549, 583, CA, per Lord Denning MR. See Ch 5, Section D below.
[132] *Hely Hutchison v Brayhead Ltd*, see n 131 above, 583, per Lord Denning MR.

and those powers extend to carrying out those functions on which he does not need to obtain specific directions of the board.[133] Persons dealing in good faith with a managing director are entitled to assume that he has all the powers that he purports to exercise, if they are powers which a managing director could have under the company's constitution.[134] In *Kreditbank Cassel GmbH v Schenkers Ltd* Atkin LJ said:[135]

> If you are dealing with a director in a matter in which normally a director would have power to act for the company you are not obliged to inquire whether or not the formalities required by the articles have been complied with before he exercises that power. Those are matters of internal management which an outsider is not obliged to investigate.

The same considerations apply to the appointment of a director with any other title such as finance director[136] or marketing director. Since directors should take decisions together,[137] an individual director, who has not been appointed to a particular office, will have little, if any, usual authority to act on behalf of the company beyond executing documents.[138] But if the board is to be taken to have impliedly authorized an individual director to deal with a particular matter he will have all the powers of the company that could have been delegated to him under the constitution and those powers are likely to be unlimited.[139] Thus an individual director may be able to bind the company to a bill signed by him.[140] A company may be bound by contract made on its behalf by a director who was bankrupt director (and thus disqualified under the CDDA s 11).[141] **4.67**

The directors may of course extend or restrict the authority of a director whom they have appointed to a particular office, but the extension will not assist, or the restriction prejudice, a third party unless he is aware of them.[142] If a director exceeds his authority, the board may ratify his conduct, but if the matter was beyond the powers of the board (which would be unusual) or involved a breach of duty, only the members could ratify under the 2006 Act, s 239.[143] **4.68**

A director's actual authority is limited to acting in the interests of the company, so that a director who acts not for the benefit of the company (fulfilling his duty to promote the success of the company under the 2006 Act, s 172), but for his own benefit, or in fraud of the company, is acting outside his authority.[144] The transaction is therefore void, as being outside the director's authority unless the third party can rely on apparent authority.[145] **4.69**

---

133 *Smith v Butler* [2012] EWCA Civ 314, [2012] BCC 645, at para 28, per Arden LJ.

134 *Biggerstaff v Rowatt's Wharf Ltd* [1897] 2 Ch 93, CA. Under Table A, reg 72 and Model Article (pcls) and (plc) 5 all the powers of the directors may be delegated to a managing director, with the consequence that he can exercise all the powers of the company.

135 [1927] 1 KB 826, 844, CA.

136 *Kreditbank Kassel v Schenkers Ltd* [1927] 1 KB 826, CA; *British Bank of the Middle East v Sun Life Assurance Co of Canada Ltd* [1983] 2 Lloyd's Rep 9, HL.

137 Table A, regs 70 and 88; Model Article (pcls) and (plc) 7.

138 *Rama Corporation Ltd v Proved Tin & General Investments Ltd* [1952] 2 QB 147, following *Houghton & Co v Nothard, Lowe & Wills Ltd* [1927] 1 KB 246, CA (affd on other grounds [1927] AC 1, HL) and *Kreditbank Kassel v Schenkers Ltd* [1927] 1 KB 826, CA.

139 Table A, reg 72 and Model Article (pcls) and (plc) 5.

140 *Re Land Credit Company of Ireland* (1869) 4 Ch App 460, 473, per Sir GM Giffard LJ; *Dey v Pullinger Engineering Co* [1921] 1 KB 77.

141 *Hill v Secretary of State for the Environment, Food and Rural Affairs* [2006] 1 BCLC 601.

142 *Houghton & Co v Nothard, Lowe & Wills Ltd* [1927] 1 KB 246, CA.

143 See Ch 20 below.

144 *Lysaght Bros & Co Ltd v Falk* (1905) 2 CLR 421, 430, per Griffiths CJ; *Lexi Holdings v Pannone and Partners* [2009] EWHC 2590 (Ch), para 69.

145 *Hopkins v TL Dallas Group Ltd* [2005] 1 BCLC 543 at para 88.

4.70 A third party who deals with the company through the delegate so appointed is protected by the 2006 Act, ss 39 and 40 as discussed above. Furthermore, the third party has the protection of the 2006 Act, s 161, which provides:

(1) The acts of a person acting as a director are valid notwithstanding that it is afterwards discovered—
   (a) that there was a defect in his appointment;
   (b) that he was disqualified from holding office;
   (c) that he had ceased to hold office;
   (d) that he was not entitled to vote on the matter in question.
(2) This applies even if the resolution for his appointment is void under section 160 (appointment of directors of public company to be voted on individually).

The only limit on the scope of s 161 is that a person who did not act in good faith may not rely on it.[146]

Ostensible or apparent authority

4.71 In *Freeman & Lockyer v Buckhurst Park Properties (Magnal) Ltd* Diplock LJ described the features of apparent or ostensible authority in these terms:[147]

> An 'apparent' or 'ostensible' authority … is a legal relationship between the principal and the contractor created by a representation, made by the principal to the contractor, intended to be and in fact acted upon by the contractor, that the agent has authority to enter on behalf of the principal into a contract of a kind within the scope of the 'apparent' authority, so as to render the principal liable to perform any obligations imposed upon him by such contract. To the relationship so created the agent is a stranger. He need not be (although he generally is) aware of the existence of the representation but he must not purport to make the agreement as principal himself. The representation, when acted upon by the contractor by entering into a contract with the agent, operates as an estoppel, preventing the principal from asserting that he is not bound by the contract. It is irrelevant whether the agent had actual authority to enter into the contract.

Diplock LJ went on to summarize four conditions which must be fulfilled to entitle a contractor to enforce against a company a contract entered into on behalf of the company by an agent who had no actual authority to do so:[148]

(1) that a representation that the agent had authority to enter on behalf of the company into a contract of the kind sought to be enforced was made to the contractor;
(2) that such representation was made by a person or persons who had 'actual' authority to manage the business of the company either generally or in respect of those matters to which the contract relates;
(3) that he (the contractor) was induced by such representation to enter into the contract, that is, that he in fact relied upon it; and
(4) that under its memorandum or articles of association the company was not deprived of the capacity either to enter into a contract of the kind sought to be enforced or to delegate authority to enter into a contract of that kind to the agent.

4.72 The first two conditions concern the representation on behalf of the company as to the agent's authority. The representation will usually involve, not words, but permitting the

---

[146] *Channel Collieries Trust Ltd v Dover, St Margaret's and Martin Mill Light Railway Co* [1914] 2 Ch 506, CA.
[147] [1964] 2 QB 480, 503, CA.
[148] [1964] 2 QB 480, 506, CA. See also paras 4.48 to 4.57 above.

director or other officer to conduct the company's business with a third party.[149] That permitted conduct will entail a representation that the director or officer has all authority of an agent in that position. In the *Freeman & Lockyer* case the board allowed a director to deal with a project as if he was managing director, although never so appointed. A managing director would have authority to retain architects on behalf of the company and accordingly the company was liable to pay the architects' fees. While an agent cannot make an effective representation as to his own authority,[150] he may have been put in a position where he can make some other a representation on behalf of the company as to the authority of others.[151] Thus, although a branch manager of a bank may not have ostensible authority to agree a large loan facility, he may have such authority to communicate his superiors' approval of the loan to the prospective borrower.[152]

As to the third condition, the third party would not be entitled to rely on the representation if he knew or ought reasonably to have appreciated that it was not made to him or for his benefit.[153] **4.73**

It will seldom be necessary to consider the fourth condition, since the 2006 Act, s 40(1) provides that in favour of a person dealing with a company in good faith, the power of the directors to bind the company, or authorize others to do so, is deemed to be free of any limitation under the company's constitution (see Section C(2) above). **4.74**

D. Formalities of Doing Business

This section deals with company contracts and the execution of documents by or on behalf of a company. The 2006 Act, ss 43–7, 49, 50, and 52 contain provisions about the formalities of doing business by companies under the law of England and Wales or Northern Ireland, which replace provisions in the 1985 Act, ss 36, 36A, 36AA, 37–40.[154] **4.75**

Among this group of sections is 2006 Act, s 51,[155] which deals with pre-incorporation contracts, deeds, and obligations. A contract purportedly made on behalf of a company before it is formed takes effect, subject to any agreement to the contrary, as one made by the person purporting to act for the company or as agent for it, and he is personally liable on the contract accordingly. Since this topic gives rise to personal liability, it is discussed in Chapter 24, **4.76**

---

[149] *Freeman & Lockyer v Buckhurst Park Properties (Mangal) Ltd* [1964] 2 QB 480, 503, CA; *Hely-Hutchinson v Brayhead Ltd* [1968] 1 QB 549, 583, CA, per Lord Denning MR; *AMB Generali Holding AG v SEB TRYGG LIV* [2006] 1 Lloyd's Rep 318, CA at paras 31 and 32, per Buxton LJ.

[150] *Armagas Ltd v Mundogas SA* [1986] AC 717, HL. See also *Hudson Bay Apparel Brands LLC v Umbro International Ltd* [2011] 1 BCLC 259, CA, where the Court of Appeal held that the president of a US subsidiary, Umbro US, who was not a director or employee of the parent, Umbro UK, did not have actual or ostensible authority on behalf of the parent to agree a variation to a contract made between Umbro UK and Hudson Bay Apparel, even though she had had authority to negotiate the contract for Umbro UK and to operate it.

[151] *ING Re (UK) Ltd V R&V Verssicherung AG* [2007] 1 BCLC 108 at paras 100 and 101.

[152] *First Energy (UK) Ltd v Hungarian International Bank Ltd* [1993] 2 Lloyd's Rep 194, CA.

[153] *ING Re (UK) Ltd V R&V Verssicherung AG* [2007] 1 BCLC 108 at para 104.

[154] 1985 Act, s 41 (authentication of documents) was repealed on 6 April 2007 and is not replaced (2006 Act Commencement Order No 1, art 4(2)(b)). 1985 Act, s 42 (events affecting a company's status) was replaced by 2006 Act, s 1079 on 1 January 2007 (2006 Act Commencement Order No 1, Arts 2(1)(d) and 7(a)). The new provisions came into effect on 1 October 2009, except that the 2006 Act, s 44 (execution of documents) replaced the 1985 Act, s 36A on 6 April 2008.

[155] 2006 Act, s 51 came into effect on 1 October 2009.

Section C(2) below. If the company wishes to be bound by the contract it must novate it or take an assignment of its benefit; it cannot simply ratify it.[156]

(1) Company contracts

4.77 The 2006 Act, s 43(1) provides that there are two ways in which the directors may procure a company to make a contract: one directly by the company and the other through the agency of authorized persons on its behalf. It provides:

> Under the law of England and Wales or Northern Ireland a contract may be made—
> (a) by a company, by writing under its common seal, or
> (b) on behalf of a company, by a person acting under its authority, express or implied.

A contract within (b) may be made orally or in writing. Whether the contract is with the company or the director personally is a question of the proper construction of the contract.[157]

4.78 Section 43(2) goes on to provide that any formalities required by law in the case of a contract made by an individual also apply, unless a contrary intention appears, to a contract made by or on behalf of a company. A guarantee given by a company must therefore be in writing and duly signed on its behalf.[158] Contracts for the sale or other disposition of an interest in land must be in writing in a document incorporating all the terms which the parties have expressly agreed, which is signed by or on behalf of each party or, where contracts are exchanged, in each exchanged document one of which must be signed by or on behalf of each party.[159]

4.79 Section 43(1) is modified for overseas companies as regard the formalities of their doing business under the law of England and Wales and Northern Ireland in three respects.[160] First, s 43(1)(a) is extended so that a contract may be made by an overseas company 'in any manner permitted by the laws of the territory in which the company is incorporated for the execution of documents by such a company'. Secondly, s 43(1)(b) is modified so that a contract may be made on behalf of an overseas company 'by any person who, in accordance with the laws of the territory in which the company is incorporated, is acting under the authority (express or implied) of the company'. Therefore where an overseas company is proposing to make a contract otherwise than under its common seal, the other party will be well advised to check that it is doing so in a manner that is valid under the law of the place of its incorporation. Section 43(2) also applies to overseas companies.

---

[156] *Kelner v Baxter* (1866) LR 2 CP 174; *Howard v Patent Ivory Manufacturing Co* (1888) 38 Ch D 156; *Natal Land and Colonization Co Ltd v Pauline Colliery and Development Syndicate Ltd* [1904] AC 120, PC.

[157] *Hamid v Francis Bradshaw Partnership* [2013] EWCA Civ 470 (contract partly written, partly oral, held contracting party was the director personally); contrast with *Badgerhill Properties Ltd v Cottrell* [1991] BCC 463.

[158] Statute of Frauds 1677, s 4. The court may not find an estoppel, so as to enforce the guarantor's liability, which is founded on an informal agreement which does not comply with s 4: *Actionstrength Ltd v International Glass Engineering IN.GL.EN SpA* [2003] 2 AC 541, HL.

[159] Law of Property (Miscellaneous Provisions) Act 1989, s 2. It is first necessary to identify the contract and then determine whether it falls within s 2: *Kilcarne Holdings Ltd v Target Follow (Birmingham) Ltd* [2004] EWHC 2547 (Ch) at paras 189, 190 and also 200–4. See also *Spiro v Glencrown Properties Ltd* [1991] Ch 537 (option agreement); *United Bank of Kuwait plc v Sahib* [1997] Ch 107 (equitable charge by deposit of title deeds must comply with s 2); *McCausland v Duncan Lawrie Ltd* [1997] 1 WLR 38, CA (variations must also comply with s 2); *Dolphin Quays Development Ltd v Mills* [2006] EWHC 931, Ch (side letter).

[160] Overseas Companies (Execution of Documents etc) Regulations 2009 (SI 2009/917), para 4 (made pursuant to CA 2006, s 1045).

(2) Execution of documents: the company seal

The 2006 Act, s 44 prescribes the two ways in which a company may itself execute a document, **4.80** whether the document embodies a contract or is any other document required for a formal legal purpose.[161] The section applies to a document executed by a company in the name of or on behalf another person, whether or not that person is also a company.[162]

One way that a company may execute a document (including a contract made by the company **4.81** 'by writing under its common seal')[163] is by affixing its common seal.[164] Similarly a document is executed by an overseas company by the affixing of its common seal.[165]

It may not be possible for a company to make a contract directly under seal, because there is no **4.82** requirement for it to have a common seal.[166] Where a company does not have a common seal its documents are executed in the manner described in paragraphs 4.90 *et seq* below. The advantages of a seal are that (a) it provides a greater degree of authenticity than execution by the officers alone; (b) since execution under seal involves more formality, it may help focus the attention of the company's officers on the transaction proposed; (c) provisions dealing with the safekeeping of the seal and maintenance of a seal register may enhance internal controls; (d) foreign jurisdictions may require documents to be executed under seal; and (e) execution under seal may offer greater flexibility because the range of persons authorized to attest the sealing may be extended by the articles to persons other than directors and the secretary, such as solicitors.[167]

If the company does have a common seal, its name must be engraved on it in legible charac- **4.83** ters; otherwise an offence is committed, by the company, and every officer of the company who is in default.[168] However, a contract made by a company with a non-compliant seal may be enforced against it.[169]

Authority to use the seal

The authority to use the common seal is a matter for the company's articles, which usually **4.84** provide that it may only be used by the authority of the directors. Table A, reg 101 provides:

> The seal shall only be used by the authority of the directors or of a committee of directors authorised by the directors. The directors may determine who shall sign any instrument to which the seal is affixed and unless otherwise so determined it shall be signed by a director and by the secretary or by a second director.

---

[161] *Hilmi Ltd v 20 Pembridge Villas Freehold Ltd* [2010] 1 WLR 2750, CA, at para 31 (and see *Re Armstrong Brands Ltd* [2015] EWHC 3303 (Ch), at para 17).

[162] 2006 Act, s 44(8).

[163] 2006 Act, s 43 (1).

[164] 2006 Act, s 44(1). By s 44(8) the company may execute a document by affixing its seal where it executes it in the name and on behalf of another person whether or not that person is also a company.

[165] Overseas Companies (Execution of Documents etc) Regulations 2009 (SI 2009/917), para 4.

[166] 2006 Act, s 45(1).

[167] The Law Commission in *The Execution of Deeds and Documents by or on Behalf of Bodies Corporate* (1996) Consultation Paper, No 143 and Report No 253 (1998), para 3.24.

[168] 2006 Act, s 45(2). Also an officer of the company, or a person acting on behalf of the company, commits an offence, punishable by a fine, if he uses, or authorizes the use of, a seal purporting to be a seal of the company on which its name is not engraved as required by 2006 Act, s 45(2); see s 45(4), (5).

[169] *OTV Birwelco Ltd v Technical and General Guarantee Co Ltd* [2002] 4 All ER 668 at paras 45–59, where the company's trade name, not its registered name, was engraved on the seal.

Where the instrument is so signed its validity cannot be contested by the company.[170]

4.85 In relation to the common seal the Model Articles give more flexibility as to the signing of the document to which the seal is affixed. Model Article 49 (pcls) states:[171]

(1) Any common seal may only be used by the authority of the directors.

(2) The directors may decide by what means and in what form any common seal is to be used.

(3) Unless otherwise decided by the directors, if the company has a common seal and it is affixed to a document, the document must also be signed by at least one authorised person in the presence of a witness who attests the signature.

(4) For the purposes of this article, an authorised person is—

(a) any director of the company;

(b) the company secretary (if any); or

(c) any person authorised by the directors for the purpose of signing documents to which the common seal is applied.

Execution of deeds

4.86 A document executed by the company by the affixing of its common seal satisfies one of the two requirements for valid execution as a deed for the purposes of the Law of Property (Miscellaneous Provisions) Act 1989, s 1(2)(b); the other requirement being delivery as a deed.[172] A document is presumed to be delivered as a deed upon its being executed, unless the contrary is proved.[173] Delivery in this context does not mean 'handed over', but doing an act so as to evince an intention to be bound.[174]

Protection of purchaser

4.87 Those requirements for authority to affix the common seal to a document are consistent with the Law of Property Act 1925, s 74, which provides protection for purchasers where an instrument has been executed by a corporation (including a company) under seal:[175]

(1) In favour of a purchaser an instrument shall be deemed to have been duly executed by a corporation aggregate if a seal purporting to be the corporation's seal purports to be affixed to the instrument in the presence of and attested by—

(a) two members of the board of directors, council or other governing body of the corporation, or

(b) one such member and the clerk, secretary or other permanent officer of the corporation or his deputy.

(1A) Subsection (1) of this section applies in the case of an instrument purporting to have been executed by a corporation aggregate in the name or on behalf of another person whether or not that person is also a corporation aggregate.

---

[170] *County of Gloucester Bank v Rudry Merthyr Steam and House Coal Colliery Co* [1895] 1 Ch 629, CA; *Duck v Tower Galvanising Co* [1901] 2 KB 314, CA.

[171] Model Article (pclg) 35 is in the same terms; as is Model Article (plc) 81(1)–(4), except that Art 81(2) also refers to the securities seal and Art 81(4)(b) omits the words '(if any)'.

[172] 2006 Act, s 46. This section, in unmodified form, applies to the execution of deeds by an overseas company: Overseas Companies (Execution of Documents etc) Regulations 2009 (SI 2009/917), para 4.

[173] 2006 Act, s 46(2). This effectively overrules the view expressed by Peter Gibson LJ in *Bolton Metropolitan BC v Torkington* [1994] Ch 66, CA at para 46 that to speak of a rebuttable presumption at common law may be going too far.

[174] *Vincent v Premo Enterprises Ltd* [1969] 2 QB 609, 619, CA, per Lord Denning MR.

[175] With effect from 15 September 2005 s 74 was amended by the Regulatory Reform (Execution of Deeds and Documents) Order 2005 (SI 2005/1906), Art 3.

(1B) For the purposes of subsection (1) of this section, a seal purports to be affixed in the presence of and attested by an officer of the corporation, in the case of an officer which is not an individual, if it is affixed in the presence of and attested by an individual authorised by the officer to attest on its behalf.

Other matters relating to company seals

A company may also have two other official seals, which when duly affixed to a document **4.88** have the same effect as the common seal. It may have a seal for use outside the UK. This seal must be a facsimile of the company's common seal, with the addition on its face of the place or places where it is to be used.[176] A company having an official seal for use outside the UK may, by writing under its common seal, authorize any person appointed for the purpose to affix the official seal to any deed or other document to which the company is a party. Model Article 81(5) (plc) provides that the company's official seal for use abroad may only be affixed to a document if its use on that document, or documents of a class to which it belongs, has been authorized by a decision of the directors. As between the company and a person dealing with such an agent, the agent's authority continues during the period mentioned in the instrument conferring the authority, or if no period is mentioned, until notice of the revocation or termination of the agent's authority has been given to the person dealing with him.[177] The agent affixing the official seal must certify in writing on the deed or other document to which the seal is affixed the date on which, and place at which, it is affixed.[178]

The other official seal that a company may have is a seal for use for sealing securities issued **4.89** by the company or for sealing documents creating or evidencing securities so issued. This seal must be a facsimile of the company's common seal, but with the addition on its face of the word 'Securities'.[179] Model Article 81(6) (plc) provides that the company's securities seal may only be affixed to securities by the company secretary or a person authorized to apply it to securities by the company secretary.[180]

(3) Execution of deeds and documents otherwise than under seal

Execution by signature

Where the directors want to execute a document on behalf of the company (including **4.90** where it executes the document on behalf of another person)[181] the alternative to affixing the company's common seal (as discussed in paragraphs 4.80–4.86 above) is by signature in accordance with s 44(2).[182] The purpose of these provisions is to facilitate the formalities of

---

[176] 2006 Act, s 49(1)–(3).
[177] 2006 Act, s 49(5).
[178] 2006 Act, s 49(6).
[179] 2006 Act, s 50.
[180] By Model Article 81(7) (plc) 'For the purposes of the articles, references to the securities seal being affixed to any document include the reproduction of the image of that seal on or in a document by any mechanical or electronic means which has been approved by the directors in relation to that document or documents of a class to which it belongs.'
[181] 2006 Act, s 44(8). Thus, for example, a company if acting as an agent for an individual (eg to effect a contract for that individual) must comply with the provisions of s 44.
[182] 2006 Act, 44(1)(b). The main change from 1985 Act, s 36A is the new s 44(2)(b), which allows one director to execute a document in the presence of a witness who attests the signature. In respect of the execution of documents at a virtual signing or closing, see the Law Society's Practice Note: Execution of Documents at a Virtual Signing or Closing, 16 February 2010, in relation to issues arising from *Koenigsblatt v Sweet* [1923] 2 Ch 314 and *R (Mercury Tax Group) v Revenue and Customs Comrs* [2008] EWHC 2721 (Admin) at paras 34–43. With regard to electronic signatures see *Chitty on Contracts*, 32nd edn (Sweet and Maxwell, 2015), vol 1, paras 5–008–5–009.

the execution of documents by companies by allowing signatures either of two authorized signatories or of one director, if attested to count as execution by a company under its common seal.[183]

4.91 Section 44(2) and (3) sets out how and by whom a document may be signed on behalf of a company:

> (2) A document is validly executed by a company if it is signed[184] on behalf of the company—
>   (a) by two authorised signatories,[185] or
>   (b) by a director of the company in the presence of a witness who attests the signature.
> (3) The following are 'authorised signatories' for the purposes of subsection (2)—
>   (a) every director of the company, and
>   (b) in the case of a private company with a secretary or a public company, the secretary (or any joint secretary) of the company.

4.92 Where a person signs a document on behalf of more than one company, it will not be duly signed by that person for the purposes of this section unless he signs it separately in each capacity.[186] Thus the same person can sign the document as agent for different companies, but separate entries will have to be made on the document for the names of each of the companies and to make clear that he is signing it separately in each capacity. A person can sign a contract once, both in his personal capacity and in his capacity of a director of a company in compliance with s 44(2) of the Act, if both the person as individual and the company are defined as parties to the contract, albeit it is preferable if it is made clear in what capacity each person is executing a contract to avoid uncertainty.[187]

4.93 Section 44(4) provides that a document signed in accordance with subsection (2) and expressed, in whatever words, to be executed by the company has the same effect as if executed under the common seal of the company. Therefore a document executed by signature in accordance with s 44(2) may be validly executed as a deed if it is delivered as a deed.[188]

---

[183] In *Redcard Ltd v Williams* [2011] 2 BCLC 350, CA, the signatures of two sellers of their leasehold interests in a block of flats were construed as signatures made in their own individual capacities (as individual vendors of their leasehold interests), and as signatures of two directors on behalf of the other seller as defined in the sale contract, being the company which owned and was selling the freehold, and thus the sale contract was enforceable against the purchaser as a contract executed by the company in compliance with s 44 (2) of the Act. In *Hilmi Ltd v 20 Pembridge Villas Freehold Ltd* [2010] 1 WLR 2750, CA, a case under 1985 Act, s 36A, a notice was invalid because it was not under seal and it was only signed by one director. Now such a notice would be valid under s 44(2)(b), provided the director's signature is attested by a witness.

[184] Section 44(7) makes provision for where an office is held by a firm which is the signatory. It provides: 'References in this section to a document being (or purporting to be) signed by a director or secretary are to be read, in a case where that office is held by a firm, as references to its being (or purporting to be) signed by an individual authorised by the firm to sign on its behalf.'

[185] Provided two authorized signatories sign, it does not matter if the transaction completes subsequently and when one of the authorized signatories is no longer an authorized signatory (2006 Act, s 44 (2)(a), and s 46 (2) which presumes simultaneous execution and delivery unless a contrary intention is proved): see *Re Armstrong Brands Ltd* [2015] EWHC 3303 (Ch) at paras 14 and 24.

[186] 2006 Act, s 44(6).

[187] *Redcard Ltd v Williams* [2011] 2 BCLC 350, CA, at paras 1, 3, 9, 11, 12, 14, 15, 25–30.

[188] 2006 Act, s 46, which applies to overseas companies: Overseas Companies (Execution of Documents etc) Regulations 2009 (SI 2009/917), para 4.

In *Redcard Ltd v Williams*[189] the Court of Appeal accepted that the phrase 'expressed in **4.94** whatever words to be executed by the company' in s 44(4) added something to the provision in s 44(2) that a document is validly executed by a company if it is signed on behalf of the company by two authorized signatories. It was not necessary for there to be words expressly stating that the signatures were 'by or on behalf of' the company; it was sufficient that the company's name appeared on the document as the party to the contract or the person on whose behalf the document was made.

Overseas company

The provisions of s 44(1)(b)–(4) are modified for overseas companies.[190] Under s 44(1) a **4.95** document is executed by an overseas company:

> (b) if it is executed in any manner permitted by the laws of the territory in which the company is incorporated for the execution of documents by such a company.

For overseas companies the provision in s 44(2)–(4) are replaced by the following provisions **4.96** of s 44(2):[191]

> A document which—
> (a) is signed by a person who, in accordance with the laws of the territory in which an overseas company is incorporated, is acting under the authority (express or implied) of the company, and
> (b) is expressed (in whatever form of words) to be executed by the company, has the same effect in relation to the company as it would have in relation to a company incorporated in England and Wales or Northern Ireland if executed under the common seal of a company so incorporated.

The effect of signature on behalf of an overseas company is the same as for an English company. The critical question is whether the person who signs has authority under the law of the place of incorporation. If he has, it is not necessary for his signature to be attested.

Protection of purchaser

It is therefore logical to find that s 44(5) gives the same protection to purchasers as the Law **4.97** of Property Act 1925, s 74(1)–(1B) does for documents under seal:[192]

> In favour of a purchaser a document is deemed to have been duly executed by a company if it purports to be signed in accordance with subsection (2).
>
> A 'purchaser' means a purchaser in good faith for valuable consideration and includes a lessee, mortgagee or other person who for valuable consideration acquires an interest in property.

The word 'purports' in s 44(5) is a wide word which refers to the impression the document **4.98** conveys. Thus it validates, in favour of a purchaser, a document erroneously signed by a

---

[189] [2011] 2 BCLC 350, CA at paras 23–8. In this case it was held that two individuals, who were directors of the company, could sign a contract for the sale of freehold land for the company while also, by the same signatures, signing a contract for the sale of their individual leasehold interests in the same property.

[190] Overseas Companies (Execution of Documents etc) Regulations 2009 (SI 2009/917), para 4.

[191] The provisions about signing on behalf of more than one overseas company and firms in 2006 Act, s 44(4) and (5) as modified for overseas companies (Overseas Companies (Execution of Documents etc) Regulations 2009 (SI 2009/917), para 4) are the same as s 44(6) and (7) for English companies.

[192] 2006 Act, s 44(3), as modified for overseas companies is to the same effect: Overseas Companies (Execution of Documents etc) Regulations 2009 (SI 2009/917), para 4.

person who it styles as a director, but who is not in fact a director.[193] In *Lovett v Carson County Homes Ltd* one of the two directors' signatures on a debenture was forged.[194] Davis J favoured the view that a purchaser could obtain the protection of s 44(5) where there was fraud or forgery if the document purports to be signed in accordance with s 44(2),[195] but he was able to find that the company was bound by the debenture since the director who signed the debenture had ostensible or apparent authority to warrant that the formalities had been complied with and that both signatures were genuine.[196] Section 44 reflects common law principles and so, in favour of a purchaser, extends to a document purporting to be signed by two directors in circumstances of apparent authority on the part of one of them.[197]

Execution of deeds

4.99 A document validly executed by signature in accordance with s 44 is duly executed as a deed for the purposes of the Law of Property (Miscellaneous Provisions) Act 1989, s 1(2)(b) and will take effect as a deed if delivered as a deed.[198]

4.100 Rather than having a deed or document executed under seal or by signature of its directors or secretaries, the directors may wish to have it executed by someone else on its behalf. The 2006 Act, s 47 provides:

(1) Under the law of England and Wales or Northern Ireland a company may, by instrument executed as a deed, empower a person, either generally or in respect of specified matters, as its attorney to execute deeds or other documents on its behalf.

(2) A deed or other document so executed, whether in the United Kingdom or elsewhere, has effect as if executed by the company.

4.101 The appointment of the attorney may be made by instrument executed as a deed, rather than under seal, since the 2006 Act, s 44(4) provides that a document executed by signature has the same effect as if executed under the common seal of the company. The appointment must be executed as a deed whether the attorney is appointed to execute documents or deeds and whether the deeds and documents are to be executed in the UK outside it.

4.102 In addition, the Law of Property Act 1925, s 74(2) gives the directors power, by resolution or otherwise, to appoint an agent either generally or in a particular case, to execute on its behalf any agreement or other instrument which is not a deed in relation to any matter within the powers of the company.[199]

Bills of exchange and promissory notes

4.103 The 2006 Act, s 52 provides that a bill of exchange or promissory note is deemed to have been made, accepted, or endorsed on behalf of the company if made, accepted, or endorsed in the name of, or by or on behalf or on account of, the company by a person acting under its authority. The company is bound by the bill or promissory note signed by a director, consistently with the company's articles, even though the director did not in fact have authority from the board to issue the bill.[200]

---

[193] *Lovett v Carson Country Homes Ltd* [2009] 2 BCLC 186 at paras 79 and 80.
[194] [2009] 2 BCLC 186.
[195] [2009] 2 BCLC 186, at para 80, 98–102.
[196] [2009] 2 BCLC 186, at paras 92–6.
[197] [2009] 2 BCLC 186, at para 97.
[198] 2006 Act, s 46. See para 4.86 above.
[199] Law of Property Act 1925, s 74(3) and (4) deals with the conveyance of property by an attorney.
[200] *Dey v Pullinger Engineering Co* [1921] 1 KB 77.

E. Attribution

For certain purposes it may be necessary for the court to determine whether the conduct, **4.104**
knowledge, mental state, or intentions of its directors, other officers, or employees are to
be attributed to it. This issue may arise in civil contexts, as discussed in the following paragraphs, and also in relation to the question whether the company has the necessary mental
state (malice, dishonesty, or intention) to commit a criminal (or quasi-criminal) offence.[201]

To begin with the courts adopted a metaphysical approach to the issue. In *Lennard's Carrying* **4.105**
Company v Asiatic Petroleum Ltd,[202] in a well-known passage, Lord Haldane said:

> My Lords, a corporation is an abstraction. It has no mind of its own any more than it has a
> body of its own; its active and directing will must consequently be sought in the person of
> somebody who for some purposes may be called an agent, but who is really the directing mind
> and will of the corporation, the very ego and centre of the personality of the corporation. That
> person may be under the direction of the shareholders in general meeting; that person may be
> the board of directors itself, or it may be, and in some companies it is so, that that person has
> an authority co-ordinate with the board of directors given to him under the articles of associa-
> tion, and is appointed by the general meeting of the company, and can only be removed by the
> general meeting of the company.

In *HL Bolton (Engineering) Co Ltd v TJ Graham & Sons Ltd*,[203] a case concerning the intention of a company, Denning LJ said:

> A company may in many ways be likened to a human body. It has a brain and nerve centre
> which controls what it does. It also has hands which hold the tools and act in accordance with
> the directions from the centre. Some of the people in the company are mere servants and
> agents who are nothing more than hands to do the work and cannot be said to represent the
> mind or will. Others are directors and managers who represent the directing mind and will
> of the company, and control what it does. The state of mind of these managers is the state of
> mind of the company and is treated by the law as such. So you will find that in cases where the
> law requires personal fault as a condition of liability in tort, the fault of the manager will be
> the personal fault of the company.

In accordance with that principle the directors would normally be regarded as the directing
mind and will of a company by virtue of their position under the company's constitution.

(1) The rules of attribution

The modern law about attribution starts with the judgment of Lord Hoffmann in *Meridian* **4.106**
Global Funds Management Asia Ltd v Securities Commission.[204] In that case the issue was
whether the company was liable for breach of the obligation under New Zealand securities

---

[201] *DPP v Kent & Sussex Contractors Ltd* [1944] KB 146, DC; *R v ICR Haulage* [1944] KB 551, 559, CA;
Moore v Bresler Ltd [1944] 2 All ER 515, DC; *Melias Ltd v Preston* [1957] 2 QB 380, DC; *R v McDowell* [1966]
1 QB 233; *Tesco Supermarkets v Nattrass* [1972] AC 155, HL; *Knowles Transport v Russell* [1975] RTR 87, DC;
Re Supply of Ready Mixed Concrete (No 2) [1995] 1 AC 456, HL; *Re AG's Reference (No 2 of 1999)* [2000] 2
BCLC 257, 261, CA.

[202] [1915] AC 705, 713, HL.

[203] [1957] 1 QB 159, 172, CA.

[204] [1995] 2 AC 500, 506–12, PC. Lord Hoffmann's analysis has been approved and applied on many occasions, including in *Bilta (UK) Ltd v Nazir (No 2)* [2016] AC 1,SC, at paras 7–9, 20, 65–78, 82–97. (See also
Stone & Rolls Ltd v Moore Stephens [2009] AC 1391 at paras 39–42 of the speech of Lord Phillips, although the
reasoning in *Stone & Rolls* should now be approached with caution: see *Jetivia*, at paras 21–30.)

legislation to give notice to the Securities Commission of the acquisition of certain shares. The shares had been acquired for the company by the senior portfolio manager without the knowledge of the managing director or the board. It was held that for the purposes of the legislation the knowledge of the manager was to be attributed to the company. In explaining why the company was liable for breach of the legislation Lord Hoffmann identified three rules of attribution applicable to companies: (i) the primary rules, (ii) the general rules, and (iii) the special rules.[205]

4.107   The primary rules of attribution are generally found in the company's constitution. The articles usually give conduct of the management of the business to the company, with a power for the board to delegate to a managing director or committee. These rules include the principle of company law under which the unanimous decision of the shareholders binds the company.[206]

4.108   Secondly, there are the general rules of attribution, which apply to natural persons as well as companies; namely the rules of agency. By a combination of the general principles of agency and the company's primary rules of attribution, the acts of its servants or agents become the acts of the company. As a result the company may make itself contractually liable under general rules such as estoppel or ostensible authority or vicariously liable in tort.[207] Liability in these cases depends on the wrongful act or omission of the agent or employee himself for which the company is held responsible as principal or employer; it does not depend on attribution to the company of another's state of mind.[208]

4.109   Thirdly, there are special rules of attribution, which apply where it is clear that a particular substantive rule was intended to apply to companies, but the primary and general rules do not provide a satisfactory solution. Then the court must interpret the rule to determine whose state of mind, knowledge, or act was to count as the company's, given that the rule was intended to apply to companies.[209] The *Meridian* case concerned a rule in legislation, but the special rules of attribution also apply to a court order[210] or contractual provisions.[211]

4.110   In *Bilta (UK) Ltd v Nazir (No 2)*, Lord Mance considered the rules of attribution and observed that the key to any question of attribution is ultimately always to be found in consideration of context and purpose.[212]

> Rules of attribution are as relevant to individuals as to companies. An individual may him- or herself do the relevant act or possess the relevant state of mind. Equally there are many contexts in which an individual will be attributed with the actions or state of mind of another, whether an agent or, in some circumstances, an independent contractor. But in relation to companies there is the particular problem that a company is an artificial construct,

---

205 [1995] 2 AC 500, 506, 507.
206 [1995] 2 AC 500, 506C–E.
207 [1995] 2 AC 500, 506E–G.
208 *MAN Nutzfahrzeuge AG v Freightliner Ltd* [2005] EWHC 2347 (Comm) at para 154 (misstatements as financial reports as a result of financial controller's fraud; knowledge of fraud not attributed to company).
209 [1995] 2 AC 500, 507B–G.
210 *Re Supply of Ready Mixed Concrete (No 2)* [1995] 1 AC 456, HL.
211 *KR v Royal & Sun Alliance plc* [2007] Bus LR 139, CA.
212 [2016] AC 1 at paras 39–41, as expressly approved by Lord Neuberger at para 9. See also *Bilta* at paras 7, 65–78, and 82–97.

and can only act through natural persons. It has no actual mind, despite the law's persistent anthropomorphism[213] ...

As Lord Hoffmann pointed out in *Meridian Global* at pp 506–507, the courts' task in all such situations is to identify the appropriate rules of attribution, using for example general rules like those governing estoppel and ostensible authority in contract and vicarious liability in tort. It is well-recognised that a company may as a result of such rules have imputed to it the conduct of an ordinary employee, and this is so also in the context of illegality. By acquiescing in the overloading of the hauliers' lorries in *Ashmore, Benson, Pease & Co Ltd v A V Dawson Ltd* [1973] 1 WLR 828 the consignors' assistant transport manager and his assistant made the haulage contract unenforceable at the instance of the consignors, who were unable to recover when a lorry toppled over damaging the goods being carried. But it is not always appropriate to apply general rules of agency to answer questions of attribution, and this is particularly true in a statutory context. Particular statutory provisions may indicate that a particular act or state of mind should only be attributed when undertaken or held by a company's 'directing mind and will'[214]... In contrast in *Meridian Global* itself the company was for criminal purposes attributed with the conduct and knowledge of the senior portfolio manager who, without knowledge of the board or managing director, had entered into the relevant transaction of which the company had failed to give notice as required by the legislation.

As Lord Hoffmann made clear in *Meridian Global*, the key to any question of attribution is ultimately always to be found in considerations of context and purpose. The question is: whose act or knowledge or state of mind is *for the purpose* of the relevant rule to count as the act, knowledge or state of mind of the company? Lord Walker said recently in *Moulin Global*, para 41 that: 'One of the fundamental points to be taken from *Meridian* is the importance of context in any problem of attribution'. Even when no statute is involved, some courts have suggested that a distinction between the acts and state of mind of, on the one hand, a company's directing mind and will or 'alter ego' and, on the other, an ordinary employee or agent may be relevant in the context of third party relationships. This is academically controversial[215] ... Any such distinction cannot in any event override the need for attention to the context and purpose in and for which attribution is invoked or disclaimed.

(2) Conduct of director attributed to company

Cases where the question is whether the conduct of a director or other person should be **4.111** attributed to the company are now regarded as being cases for the application of special rules of attribution. Under these rules the company may find itself liable for the unauthorized acts of employees[216] and it is a question of construction of the rule whether instructions issued, or precautions taken, by the board are sufficient to protect the company from liability.[217]

---

[213] See Lord Hoffmann in *Meridian Global Funds Management Asia Ltd v Securities Commission* [1995] 2 AC 500, 507A, and 509G–H as to the absence of any 'ding an sich'; Professor Eilis Ferran in 'Corporate Attribution and the Directing Mind and Will' (2011) 127 LQR 239, 239–40 as to the distracting effect of references to a company's 'brain and nerve centre' or 'hands'.

[214] *Lennard's Carrying Co Ltd v Asiatic Petroleum Co Ltd* [1915] AC 705 and *Tesco Supermarkets Ltd v Nattrass [1972] AC 153*, cited in *Meridian Global* at pp 507–9.

[215] Professor Peter Watts, 'The Company's Alter Ego: An Impostor in Private Law' (2000) LQR 525; Campbell and Armour, 'Demystifying the Civil Liability of Corporate Agents' (2003) CLJ 290.

[216] *Re Supply of Ready Mixed Concrete (No 2)* [1995] 1 AC 456, 465, 475, 481, HL (unauthorized breach of injunction by employees attributed to company).

[217] *Tesco Supermarkets Ltd v Nattrass* [1972] AC 153, HL (breaches of Trade Descriptions Act as a result of negligence of shop manager, but precautions taken by the board were acts of the company under the Act, whereas the manager's negligence was not attributed to it).

4.112   In the *Meridian* case Lord Hoffmann identified *Lennard's Carrying Co Ltd v Asiatic Petroleum Co Ltd*[218] as such a case. The question was whether the ship-owner company had a defence under the Merchant Shipping Act to a claim by a cargo owner for nondelivery on the ground that it acted without fault or privity. Mr Lennard was a director of both the ship-owner company and the company that managed the ship. In the latter capacity he was responsible for monitoring the condition of the ship, receiving reports from the master and ship's agents, and authorizing repairs. Accordingly (and not because he was a director of the ship-owner) Lord Haldane described Mr Lennard as the 'directing mind and will' of the ship-owner, to whom his fault and privity was attributed for the purposes of the Act.

4.113   In *KR v Royal & Sun Alliance plc*[219] the issue was whether, under the Third Party (Rights against Insurers) Act 1930, victims of sexual abuse at children's care homes formerly operated by a company, which had gone into liquidation, could recover damages under an insurance policy maintained by the company. That turned on whether the claims fell within the exception in the policy for deliberate acts of the insured. The sexual abuse had been committed by the chief executive and managing director of the company. Applying the special rules of attribution to the claim under the policy, the conduct of the director was attributed to the company, with the result that the claims came within the exception for deliberate acts and the victims could not recover.

4.114   Other conduct of directors or other persons that has been attributed to a company include actions in contempt of injunction under Restrictive Trade Practices Act 1976 by employees even though breach prohibited by the board,[220] breach of notification requirements under securities legislation,[221] infringement of Competition Act 1998 by directors and employees,[222] and perjury by a company's key witness and a member of the claims handling team.[223]

(3) Intention of director attributed to company

4.115   The fraudulent conduct and intention of a director, de facto director, or shadow director towards third parties may be attributed to the company, so that it is primarily and not just vicariously liable to the victim.[224] Also the intentions of the directors as to the company's actions will be attributed to the company as its intentions.[225]

---

[218] [1915] AC 705, HL. See the *Meridian* case at [1995] 2 AC 500, 509. At 510 and 511 Lord Hoffmann explains why under the special rules of attribution in *The Truculent* [1952] P 1 the conduct of the Third Sea Lord was attributed to the Crown, and in *The Lady Gwendolen* [1965] P 294, 355, CA, the conduct of the traffic manager was attributed to the ship-owner company.

[219] [2007] Bus LR 139, CA. Note that the 2010 Act is now in force: see para 4.38 above.

[220] *Re Supply of Ready Mixed Concrete (No 2)* [1995] 1 AC 456, HL.

[221] *Meridian Global Funds Management Asia Ltd v Securities Commission* [1995] 2 AC 500, PC.

[222] *Safeway Stores Ltd v Twigger* [2010] Bus LR 974, [2011] Bus LR 1629, CA.

[223] *Odyssey Re (London) Ltd v OIC Run-Off Ltd*, 13 March 2000, CA, The Times, 17 March 2000.

[224] *Stone & Rolls Ltd v Moore Stephens* [2009] AC 1391, HL at paras 49–56 of the speech of Lord Phillips, at paras 132–6 in the speech of Lord Walker, and para 197 in the speech of Lord Brown. *Stone & Rolls* should be treated with caution as regards the illegality defence until further consideration by the Supreme Court: *Bilta (UK) Ltd v Nazir (No 2)* [2016] AC 1 at paras 13–31 per Lord Neuberger. As to attribution, see *Bilta* at paras 7–9, per Lord Neuberger, paras 80 and 91 per Lord Sumption), and paras 204 and 207 per Lords Toulson and Hodge). See also *Royal Brunei Airlines Sdn Bhd v Tan* [1995] 2 AC 378, 393, where Lord Nicholls said of the defendant director, who owned and managed the company: 'The defendant was the company, and his state of mind is to be imputed to the company.' In *Mahmud v Bank of Credit and Commerce International SA* [1998] AC 20, 34, Lord Nicholls explained that corruption and dishonesty within BCCI was such that the bank could be identified with the dishonesty.

[225] *Bolton (Engineering) Co Ltd v Graham & Sons* [1957] 1 QB 159, CA (intention of directors who ran the company's business between board meetings, that it should occupy premises for the purposes of the Landlord

The dishonest intent of the directors will not, however, be attributed to the company where **4.116** the fraud is committed upon the company and the company sues the wrongdoing direc-tors.[226] This exception was referred to as the *Hampshire Land* principle.[227] In *Bilta (UK) Ltd v Nazir (no 2)* Lord Neuberger summarized the proposition:[228]

> Where a company has been the victim of wrong-doing by its directors, or of which its directors had notice, then the wrong-doing, or knowledge, of the directors cannot be attributed to the company as a defence to a claim brought against the directors by the company's liquidator, in the name of the company and/or on behalf of its creditors, for the loss suffered by the company as a result of the wrong-doing, even where the directors were the only directors and sharehold-ers of the company, and even though the wrong-doing or knowledge of the directors may be attributed to the company in many other types of proceedings.

Lord Neuberger went on to suggest that the expression 'the fraud exception' be abandoned, as it is certainly not limited to cases of fraud in that it is not so much an exception to a general rule as part of a general rule.[229]

(4) Knowledge of director attributed to company

Cases where knowledge obtained by a single director or other officer has been attributed **4.117** to the company, even though the knowledge has not been shared with the other directors, also involve the application of special rules of attribution. *El Ajou v Dollar Land Holdings plc*[230] involved a claim to recover the proceeds of a fraud from the defendant company. Mr Ferdman, who received the money for the company for a construction project, knew that the money was the proceeds of a fraud. His knowledge was attributed to the company. He was chairman of the company and in relation to the construction project he was the directing mind and will of the company. It did not matter that the managing director was unaware of the source of the money.

In *Jafarini-Fini v Skillglass Ltd*,[231] a case where one director had knowledge of payment of a **4.118** bribe and his knowledge was attributed to the company, Moore-Bick LJ stated the general position:[232]

> The question in the present case is whether information which comes to the attention of one director, but which he has not shared with the rest of the board, is to be treated as informa-tion in the possession of the company … In general … I think that information relevant to

---

and Tenant Act 1954 attributed to the company; since reference was made to 'directing mind and will', this could be a case within the special rules of attribution).

[226] *Re Hampshire Land Co* [1896] 2 Ch 743, 749, CA; *JC Houghton & Co v Nothard, Lowe and Wills Ltd* [1928] AC 1, 15, 19, HL; *Belmont Finance Corp v Williams Furniture Ltd* [1979] Ch 250, 261, 262, CA; *Stone & Rolls Ltd v Moore Stephens* [2009] AC 1391, HL at paras 39–56, 132–6; *Safeway Stores Ltd v Twigger* [2011] Bus LR 1629, CA at para 28 (where Longmore LJ said that it was arguable that the exception extends to 'acts of an agent which are in breach of his duty to his principal and which have, in fact, resulted in harm to his principal').

[227] *Safeway Stores Ltd v Twigger* [2011] Bus LR 1629, CA at para 28.

[228] [2016] AC 1, SC, at para 7. This was the effect of Lord Sumption's speech at paras 65–78 and 82–97 and of the speech of Lords Toulson and Hodge at paras 182–209.

[229] [2016] AC 1, SC, at para 9.

[230] [1994] 2 All ER 685, 695–8, 699, 700, 705, CA.

[231] [2007] EWCA Civ 261.

[232] At para 98. Approved and applied in *Lebon v Aqua Salt Co* [2009] 1 BCLC 549, PC at para 24 (know-ledge of the promotor, director, and substantial shareholder of prior interest in land attributed to the company for the purpose of the acquisition of its interest).

the company's affairs that comes into possession of one director, however that may occur, can properly be regarded as information in the possession of the company itself.

4.119   In *Real Estate Opportunities Ltd v Aberdeen Asset Managers Jersey Ltd*,[233] having said that 'a company is in general deemed to have notice of anything of which any of its directors obtains knowledge in the course of his duties', Arden LJ went on to consider whether a company can be said to retain knowledge of something once known by a director who had vacated office or forgotten it. Arden LJ did not have to decide the point, but appeared to favour the view that those circumstances would not necessarily mean that the company ceased to possess the knowledge.[234]

4.120   For some purposes the knowledge of a person below the rank of director will count as knowledge of the company. In *Re Bank of Credit and Commerce International SA (No 15)*[235] a senior manager at Bank of India's knowledge of fraud at BCCI was attributed to Bank of India so that it was knowingly party to fraudulent trading by BCCI for the purposes of a claim under the Insolvency Act, s 213.[236]

(5) Director of more than one company

4.121   There is a problem of attribution where a person is a director of two companies. Knowledge received by a person as a director of one company will not be attributed to another company of which he is director, unless he owed both a duty to the second company to receive it and a duty to the first company to communicate it.[237]

(6) *Ex turpi causa non oritur actio*

4.122   As the cases on attribution discussed in the previous paragraphs illustrate, the consequences of conduct, intention, or knowledge being attributed to a company are wide ranging— sometimes beneficial and sometimes harmful. One particular consequence is the rule of policy known as *ex turpi causa* which prevents a claimant from using the court to obtain benefits from his own unlawful conduct.[238] The rule only applies to a company is the unlawful conduct is attributed to it and that will not be the case where the company if the victim of wrongdoing by its directors (paragraph 4.116 above).[239] The scope of the *ex turpi causa* defence to a claim by the company against a director is discussed further in Chapter 19, Section E(4) below.

---

[233] [2008] 2 BCLC 116, CA at para 49.

[234] [2008] 2 BCLC 116, CA at para 50.

[235] [2005] 2 BCLC 328, CA at paras 93–6, 114–20.

[236] In *FCA v Da Vinci Invest Ltd* [2015] EWHC 2401 (Ch) the market abuse of traders was attributed to the company on agency principles, even though their conduct was not directed by directors.

[237] *Re Hampshire Land Co* [1896] 2 Ch 743, 748; *Re Fenwick Stobart & Co Ltd* [1902] 1 Ch 507, 511; *Re David Payne & Co Ltd* [1904] 2 Ch 608, 616, 618–20, CA; *JC Houghton and Co v Nothard, Lowe and Wills Ltd* [1928] AC 1, 15, 19, PC; *El Ajou v Dollar Land Holdings Ltd* [1994] 2 All ER 685, 695–8, 699, 700, 705, CA.

[238] *Gray v Thames Trains Ltd* [2009] 1 AC 1339, HL at para 32, per Lord Hoffmann (stating the rule in its narrower and wider forms); *Safeway Stores Ltd v Twigger* [2011] Bus LR 1629, CA at para 16.

[239] *Bilta (UK) Ltd v Nazir (No 2)* [2016] AC 1, SC, at paras 7, 38, 41, 42, 89, and 206.

5

DIRECTORS' DECISION-MAKING
AND DELEGATION

William Willson

A. Introduction

Chapter 4 explained how management powers are vested in directors. This Section A explains **5.01** how directors, acting as a board or by delegation, take decisions to carry out those functions. The Companies Acts have always left the procedure for decision-making by directors to the constitution of the company, but have required records of decisions to be kept.[1]

The company's articles of association provide the rules regulating decision-making by direc- **5.02** tors, a managing director, and committees to whom particular functions have been delegated. Sometimes the articles will contain special rules designed to meet the needs of the particular company: eg prescribing that certain matters cannot be done without the assent of particular directors. More often the company's articles adopt, with or without adaptation, the default articles prescribed by the Companies Acts, or at least those articles that deal with decision-making by directors. They do so for reasons of certainty and convenience. The discussion in this chapter therefore focuses on the procedures in those default articles.

For companies incorporated under the 1985 Act (which was the case until 1 October 2009), **5.03** Table A, regs 88–98 deal with proceedings of directors.[2] For companies incorporated after

---

[1] 2006 Act, ss 248 and 249, which came into force on 1 October 2007. These sections can be traced back, with changes, to 1862 Act, s 67.

[2] For companies incorporated between 1 October 2007 and 1 October 2009 these have been amended by the Companies (Tables A–F) (Amendment) Regulations 2007 (SI 2007/2541), the Companies Act (Tables A–F) (Amendment) (No 2) Regulations 2007 (SI 2007/2826), and the Companies (Tables A–F) (Amendment) Regulations 2008 (SI 2008/739). These amendments enable Table A to conform to the provisions of the 2006 Act brought into force before 1 October 2009, but none of the amendments affect the regulations of Table

1 October 2009, the 2006 Act, s 19 provides that the Model Articles are the default articles.[3] The Model Articles are significantly different to Table A. They are designed to promote efficiency of decision-making and to reflect more closely the commercial world in which private and public companies operate today.

5.04   The Model Articles (pcls) for private companies limited by shares and the Model Articles (pclg) for private companies limited by guarantee are in the same terms in relation to delegation to committees (Articles 5 and 6) and decision-making by directors (Articles 7–16), so Model Articles (pclg) are not mentioned again in this chapter. The Model Articles (plc) for public companies, so far as they relate to those matters (Articles 5–19) are broadly the same as those for private companies. One important difference is that the directors of a private company may take unanimous decisions on an informal basis (Article 8), whereas for the directors of a public company the written resolution procedure is rather more formal (Articles 17 and 18). The Model Articles (plc) are likely to be used as a drafting source for public companies, which are more likely to adopt tailor-made articles.[4]

B. Decisions to Be Taken Collectively

5.05   Table A and the Model Articles reflect two general principles. The first is that decisions of directors are to be taken collectively, either by written decision, taken or agreed to by all directors, or made by a majority at a meeting, duly convened and held.[5] Once the decision has been taken, the directors, including dissenters, are bound by the decision and must carry it into effect (or resign).[6] This principle is expressly stated in Model Article (pcls) 7:

(1) The general rule about decision-making by directors is that any decision of the directors must be either a majority decision at a meeting or a decision taken in accordance with article 8.

(2) If—

(a) the company only has one director, and

(b) no provision of the articles requires it to have more than one director, the general rule does not apply, and the director may take decisions without regard to any of the provisions of the articles relating to directors' decision-making.

Model Article (plc) 7 is in different terms:

(1) Decisions of the directors may be taken—

(a) at a directors' meeting, or

(b) in the form of a directors' written resolution.

A considered in this chapter. Different versions of Table A apply to companies incorporated under the 1948 Act or earlier Companies Acts.

[3] These are set out in the Companies (Model Articles) Regulations (SI 2008/3229).

[4] *Implementation of the Companies Act 2006, a Consultation Paper* (DTI, February 2007) at paras 3.31 and 3.32.

[5] *Minmar (929) Ltd v Khalastchi* [2011] BCC 485. This was a case on articles in the form of Model Articles (pcls) 7(1), 8(1), (2) and (4), 9(1)–(3) and Insolvency Act, Sch B1, para 105, in which it was held that a majority of the directors could not validly appoint administrators without holding a validly convened meeting. At para 51 Sir Andrew Morritt C held that *Re Equiticorp* [1989] 1 WLR 1010 must be considered as a case where the majority applied for the appointment of administrators following a validly convened board meeting. See also *Baker v London Bar Co Ltd* [2012] BCC 69. A company's articles may provide for a decision of the directors to be taken when a majority of those eligible to vote on the matter have agreed to a written resolution.

[6] *Re Equiticorp International plc* [1989] 1 WLR 1010.

The two articles' results are different because the unanimous decision procedure is not available for directors of public companies and a private company may have only one director, but a public company must have at least two.[7] Model Article (pcls) 7 does not require a private company which is entitled to have, and only has, one director to go through the fiction of requiring the sole director to have a meeting with himself.[8] The sole director must comply with his obligations under the 2006 Act, Part 10, Chapters 4–6, concerning transactions with directors requiring approval of members, directors' service contracts, and contracts with the sole member who is also a director (Chapter 18 below).

5.06 The second general principle is that, subject to the provisions of the company's articles, which can only be altered by special resolution, 'the directors may regulate their proceedings as they see fit' (Table A, reg 88). This wording was 'generally taken to refer to fixing the timing of periodic meetings, the circulation of agendas and other administrative matters'.[9] Wording in terms of reg 88 does not enable a casual meeting of the only two directors of a company to be treated as a board meeting at the option of one, against the will of the other.[10]

5.07 Model Article (pcls) 16 and Model Article (plc) 19 both state the principle more explicitly:

> Subject to the articles, the directors may make any rule which they think fit about how they take decisions, and about how such rules are to be recorded or communicated to directors.

The new wording is intended to make clear that the directors are able to 'fill in the gaps' which there may in particular circumstances turn out to be in the Model Articles' provisions on directors' decision-making.[11]

C. Private Companies: Unanimous Decisions

5.08 Directors have always been able to take unanimous decisions on uncontentious matters in an informal way. In *Charterhouse Investment Trust Ltd v Tempest Diesels Ltd* Hoffmann J held that the informal acquiescence of all the directors sufficed for a binding resolution.[12] Table A, reg 93, however, required unanimous decisions not taken at a meeting to be in writing signed by all the directors.[13] Unanimity is essential to the validity of informal decisions. If there is dissent or if the express assent of one or more directors cannot be obtained, the matter must be decided at a meeting. Such a meeting must be properly convened, because an informal meeting cannot take place against the will of one of the directors who happens to be present.[14] Nor is it sufficient to obtain the separate authority of a sufficient number of

---

[7] 2006 Act, s 154, which came into force on 1 October 2007.

[8] Cf *Neptune (Vehicle Washing Equipment) Ltd v Fitzgerald* [1996] Ch 274.

[9] *Implementation of the Companies Act 2006, a Consultative Document* (DTI, February 2007) at para 3.84.

[10] *Barron v Potter* [1914] 1 Ch 895. See para 5.08 below.

[11] *Implementation of the Companies Act 2006, a Consultative Document* (DTI, February 2007) at paras 3.85–3.86.

[12] *Charterhouse Investment Trust Ltd v Tempest Diesels Ltd* [1986] BCLC 1, 9. See also *Re Bonelli's Telegraph Co, Collie's Claim* (1871) LR 12 Eq 246, 258; *Runciman v Walter Runciman Plc* [1992] BCLC 1084, 1092; *Hunter v Senate Support Services Ltd* [2005] 1 BCLC 175, 208.

[13] See para 5.46 below for written resolutions of directors of public companies.

[14] *Barron v Potter* [1914] 1 Ch 895; *Glatzer and Warwick Shipping Ltd v Bradston Ltd* [1997] 1 Lloyd's Rep 449, 471, 472. However, there is a narrow dividing line. In *Smith v Paringa Mines Ltd* [1906] 2 Ch 193 one of the only two directors did not attend a meeting, though he had received proper notice. The other director met

directors to constitute a quorum.[15] Where the matter has not been validly decided, the defect may be cured by ratification by a duly passed resolution at a meeting,[16] or indeed, by a later valid unanimous decision.

5.09   Model Article (pcls) 8 now gives directors of private companies more flexibility in decision-making, because they are not required to do so simultaneously. They can do so over a period of time by an exchange of emails or text messages. It provides:

> (1) A decision of the directors is taken in accordance with this article when all eligible directors indicate to each other by any means that they share a common view on a matter.
> (2) Such a decision may take the form of a resolution in writing, copies of which have been signed by each eligible director or to which each eligible director has otherwise indicated agreement in writing.
> (3) References in this article to eligible directors are to directors who would have been entitled to vote on the matter had it been proposed as a resolution at a director's meeting.
> (4) A decision may not be taken in accordance with this article if the eligible directors would not have formed a quorum at such a meeting.

5.10   Model Article (pcls) 8(1) indicates that a director may assent orally to the decision, perhaps by telephone. Furthermore, Model Article 8(2) is permissive: the unanimous decision may take the form of a written resolution. Model Article 8(3) and (4) reflects the fact that by the 2006 Act, s 175(5) a director with a conflict of interest is not counted in the quorum and his vote is not counted.[17] While all the eligible directors must agree to the resolution, they can do so by signing it or in any other way (ie orally).

5.11   By Model Article (pcls) 15 the directors must ensure that the company keeps a record of every unanimous decision for at least ten years. This is consistent with the required period stated by the 2006 Act, s 248 for keeping minutes of proceedings at directors' meetings.

D. Decisions Taken at Meetings

5.12   Where the decision cannot be taken unanimously, it must be taken at a meeting, properly called and constituted.

(1) Calling the meeting

5.13   Table A, reg 88 provides for the calling of a meeting of directors in these terms:

> A director may, and the secretary at the request of a director shall, call a meeting of the directors. It shall not be necessary to give notice of the meeting to a director who is absent from the United Kingdom.[18]

---

him in the corridor and proposed a resolution. He objected, whereby the other declared it passed by his casting vote (as chairman). The resolution was held to have been duly passed.

[15] *D'Arcy v Tanner, Kit Hill and Callington Railway Co* (1867) LR 2 Exch 158; *Re Haycraft Gold Reduction and Mining Co* [1900] 2 Ch 230, 235.

[16] *Re Portuguese Consolidated Copper Mines Ltd* (1890) 45 Ch D 16, CA; *Municipal Mutual Insurance Ltd v Harrop* [1998] 2 BCLC 540.

[17] The position is the same at meetings; see paras 5.22, 5.23, 5.40–5.45 below.

[18] Formerly 1948 Table A, Art 98: 'a director may, and the secretary on the requisition of a director shall, at any time summon a meeting of the directors. It shall not be necessary to give notice of a meeting of directors to any director for the time being absent from the United Kingdom.'

Table A, reg 111 does not require notice of directors' meetings to be given in writing.[19] The **5.14**
Model Articles follow Table A in providing that any director may call a meeting by giving
notice and that the secretary is to give notice on the request of a director. The language of the
Model Articles (pcls) and (plc) is slightly different, reflecting the fact that a private company
need not have a secretary. Model Article (pcls) 9(1) provides:

> Any director may call a directors' meeting by giving notice of the meeting to the directors or
> by authorising the company secretary (if any) to give such notice.

Model Article (plc) 8 explains who[20] can or must call a directors' meeting in these terms:

> (1) Any director may call a directors' meeting.
> (2) The company secretary must call a directors' meeting if a director so requests.
> (3) A directors' meeting is called by giving notice of the meeting to the directors.

Model Article (pcls) 9(2)–(4) and Model Article (plc) 8(4)–(6) provide for the giving of **5.15**
notice of the directors' meeting in the same terms. Model Article 9(2) provides:

> (2) Notice of any directors' meeting must indicate—
>   (a) its proposed date and time;
>   (b) where it is to take place; and
>   (c) if it is anticipated that directors participating in the meeting will not be in the same
>   place, how it is proposed that they should communicate with each other during the
>   meeting.
> (3) Notice of a directors' meeting must be given to each director, but need not be in writing.
> (4) Notice of a directors' meeting need not be given to directors who waive their entitlement
>   to notice of that meeting, by giving notice to that effect to the company not more than
>   7 days after the date on which the meeting is held. Where such notice is given after the
>   meeting has been held, that does not affect the validity of the meeting, or of any business
>   conducted at it.

Unlike Table A, reg 88, the Model Articles require the notice to give directors information **5.16**
about the arrangements for the meeting. Although there is no requirement for notice of the
meeting to be given in writing,[21] that will be a sensible precaution in case there may be an
issue about the validity of decisions taken at the meeting. There is no need for the notice to
indicate the subject matter of the meeting.[22]

Unlike Table A, reg 88, the Model Articles make no exception for directors absent from **5.17**
the UK.[23] This exception is no longer appropriate given modern communications technology.[24] The Model Articles recognize that in the days of mobile phones and email, the
circumstances in which a director can be said to be out of reach have shrunk dramatically.[25]

---

[19] *Browne v La Trinidad* (1887) 37 Ch D 1, 9, CA.
[20] In *Sneddon v MacCullum* [2011] CSOH 59 the Outer House, Court of Session concluded that an individual who was neither a director nor an alternate director did not have capacity to call a meeting of directors.
[21] *Browne v La Trinidad* (1887) 37 Ch D 1, 9, CA.
[22] *La Compagnie de Mayville v Whitley* [1896] 1 Ch 788, 797, CA.
[23] Even if a director is abroad and out of reach of notices, the meeting will be invalid if his absence means
there is no quorum: *Davidson & Begg Antiques Ltd v Davidson* [1997] BCC 77, CS, Outer House.
[24] *Implementation of Companies Act 2006, a Consultative Document* (DTI, February 2007) at para 3.63.
[25] In *Halifax Sugar Refining Co Ltd v Francklyn* (1890) 59 LJ Ch 591, 593 a meeting was held to be valid
where a director was genuinely 'out of reach'. In *Implementation of Companies Act 2006, a Consultative Document*
(DTI, February 2007) at para 3.63, the DTI compared notification of a director on business in New York and
a director 'holidaying on a remote island', but in the days of the BlackBerry and iPad, that may no longer be a
distinction of substance.

The Model Articles give effect to the general principle that each director is entitled to notice of the meeting.[26] Instead the Model Articles allow a director to waive his right to notice, by giving notice to the company not more than seven days after the date on which the meeting is held.[27]

5.18 As with Table A, reg 88, the Model Articles do not specify a minimum length of notice. The case law has laid down various principles. Each board member should have reasonable notice of every meeting.[28] What is 'reasonable' may be determined by the board's previous course of conduct.[29] Reference should also be made to relevant circumstances such as urgency, subject matter, and location. In *Re Homer District Consolidated Gold Mines* three hours' notice was enough: in *Browne v La Trinidad* five minutes' notice was sufficient. If a director wishes to object to the shortness of notice, he should do so at once.[30]

5.19 Like Table A, reg 88, the Model Articles are silent about the effect of failure to give notice. Though the practical consequences of this will most likely be limited, case law has established the following principles. A director cannot lawfully be excluded from a board meeting, and an excluded director can obtain an injunction restraining his continued exclusion (unless he is about to be removed, in which case an injunction would be pointless).[31] Where notice is not received by every director so entitled, business done at that meeting does not bind the company[32] and 'the failure to give requisite notice is an irregularity'.[33] This is so, even where directors without notice could not have changed the result.[34] Where a directors' meeting is rendered irregular, the irregularity will not prejudice persons acting in good faith.[35] An irregularity can be ratified at a subsequent board meeting.[36]

---

[26] *Smyth v Darley* (1849) 2 HL Cas 789; *Re Homer District Consolidated Gold Mines, ex p Smith* (1888) 39 Ch D 546.

[27] Cf *Re Portuguese Consolidated Copper Mines Limited* (1890) 42 Ch D 160, 168, CA, where Lord Esher MR said of a director that 'he could not waive his right to notice'; *Young v Ladies' Imperial Club* [1920] 2 KB 523, 528, 534, 536, CA. The approach in those cases is to be contrasted with that in *Browne v La Trinidad* (1887) 37 Ch D 1, 9, CA; *Bentley-Stevens v Jones* [1974] 1 WLR 638, 641.

[28] *Re Homer District Consolidated Gold Mines* (1888) 39 Ch D 546.

[29] *Toole v Flexihire Pty Ltd* (1991) 6 ACSR 455, 461.

[30] *Browne v La Trinidad* (n 27 above) at 9.

[31] *Pulbrook v Richmond Consolidated Mining Co* (1878) 9 Ch D 610, 612; *Hayes v Bristol Plant Hire Ltd* [1957] 1 WLR 499; *Choudhury v Bhattar* [2009] 2 BCLC 108 at para 28. In *Bentley-Stevens v Jones* [1974] 1 WLR 638 the court would not grant an injunction in respect of irregularities which could be cured by going through the right process (following *Browne v La Trinidad*). However, the board may exclude a director where the company has by resolution declared that it does not desire the director to act: *Bainbridge v Smith* (1889) 41 Ch D 462, 474, CA.

[32] *Re Homer District Consolidated Gold Mines* (1888) 39 Ch D 546. For more recent cases where meetings were invalidated because of failure to give notice, see *Minmar (929) Ltd v Khalastchi* [2011] BCC 485; *Baker v London Bar Co Ltd* [2012] BCC 69; *Orr v DS Orr & Sons (Holdings) Ltd* [2011] CSOH 116.

[33] *Re Oriental Gas Co Ltd* [1999] BCC 237, 251, per Ferris J.

[34] *Young v Ladies' Imperial Club Limited* [1920] 2 KB 523. There is some debate as to whether notice must be given to a director with no vote under the articles: *John Shaw & Sons (Salford) v Shaw* [1935] 2 KB 113, CA (per Greer LJ at 133, per Slesser LJ at 138).

[35] 2006 Act, s 40. A director will not be able to rely on this section if the irregularity arose from his own failure to ensure that the transaction was properly authorized: *Smith v Henniker-Major & Co* [2003] Ch 182, CA. See Ch 4, Section C above.

[36] *Re Portuguese Consolidated Copper Mines Limited* (1890) 42 Ch D 160, 166, CA; *Re State of Wyoming Syndicate* [1901] 2 Ch 431, 437; *Breckland Group Holdings Ltd v London and Suffolk Properties Ltd* [1989] BCLC 100, 103; *Municipal Mutual Insurance Ltd v Harrop* [1996] 2 BCLC 540, 550–3.

(2) Conduct of the meeting

Participation

Whereas Table A, reg 88 assumes that the directors will meet in the same place, Model Article **5.20**
(pcls) 10 and Model Article (plc) 9 recognize improvements in communication technology
(such as conference calls[37] and video conferencing) and provide in the same terms for the directors to be in different locations from where they can communicate with each other. Model
Article (pcls) 10 provides:

> (1) Subject to the articles, directors participate in a directors' meeting or part of a directors'
>   meeting when—
>   (a) the meeting has been called and takes place in accordance with the articles, and
>   (b) they can each communicate to the others any information or opinions they have on any
>   particular item of the business of the meeting.
> (2) In determining whether directors are participating in a directors' meeting, it is irrelevant
>   where any director is or how they communicate with each other.
> (3) If all the directors participating in a meeting are not in the same place, they may decide that a
>   meeting is to be treated as taking place wherever any of them is.

Quorum

Where a private company has only one director and is not required to have more, the provisions **5.21**
in the company's articles regulating meetings of directors have no application. The following
discussion assumes that the company has, or must have, at least two directors. In such cases
the articles usually provide for a quorum to be present, failing which business cannot be conducted. In the rare cases where the articles do not prescribe a quorum, the court has regarded
the number of directors who usually conduct the company's business as being a de facto quorum.[38] In any event the business may be conducted by the majority of the directors.[39] Where
business is conducted by one or more directors, being less than the quorum, the court may be
entitled to infer that such business has been delegated to those directors as a committee.[40]

Table A, reg 89 states that: **5.22**

> The quorum for the transaction of the business of the directors may be fixed by the directors
> and unless so fixed at any other number shall be two. A person who holds office only as an
> alternate director shall, if his appointor is not present, be counted in the quorum.

In such a case the alternate director will be entitled to vote. In fact, entitlement to vote is
a prerequisite to being counted in the quorum; a director who is not entitled to vote on a
resolution (usually on the ground of conflict of interest) cannot be counted in the quorum
for the purposes of the resolution.[41] Table A, reg 95 provides:

---

[37] In *Sneddon v MacCallum* [2011] CSOH 59 at para 275, the Court of Session discussed the importance
of having speakerphone capability so that all participants can hear and be heard where there is participation by
speakerphone.

[38] *Lyon's Case* (1866) 35 Beav 646; *Re Tavistock Iron Works Co, Lyster's Case* (1867) 4 Eq 233; *Re Regent's Canal
Iron Co* [1867] WN 79.

[39] *York Tramways Co v Willows* (1882) 8 QBD 685, CA.

[40] Table A, reg 72; Model Articles (pcls) and (plc) 5 and 6; *Totterdell v Fareham Blue Brick and Tile Co* (1866)
LR 1 CP 674; *Re Barned's Banking Co, ex p Contract Corp* (1867) 3 Ch App 105, 116; *Re Fireproof Doors Ltd*
[1916] 2 Ch 142.

[41] *Re Greymouth-Point Elizabeth Railway and Coal Co Ltd* [1904] 1 Ch 32, 34; *Victors Ltd v Lingard* [1927]
1 Ch 323; *Re Cleadon Trust* [1939] Ch 286, CA; *Colin Gwyer & Associates Ltd v London Wharf (Limehouse) Ltd*
[2003] 2 BCLC 153, 176.

A director shall not be counted in the quorum present at a meeting in relation to a resolution on which he is not entitled to vote.

5.23 Model Article (pcls) 11(1) and (2) and Model Article (plc) 10 set out the quorum requirements for private and public companies in the same terms: Model Article (pcls) 11(1) and (2) provides:

> (1) At a directors' meeting, unless a quorum is participating, no proposal is to be voted on, except a proposal to call another meeting.
> (2) The quorum for directors' decision-making may be fixed from time to time by a decision of the directors, but it must never be less than two, and unless otherwise fixed it is two.

Model Article (pcls) 14(1) and Model Article (plc) 16(1) both provide that a director with a conflict of interest and who cannot vote is not included for quorum purposes (paragraph 5.43 below). Since Model Article (plc) 15 provides for an alternate director to be entitled to vote, he can be included for quorum purposes. It was not considered necessary for the Model Articles to include the second sentence of Table A, reg 89. The directors are free to alter the quorum provision, provided that it is never less than two. If the members want to fix the quorum provision in a way that the directors cannot alter their remedy is to make an appropriate alteration of the articles.

5.24 The general rule is that where there is no quorum, the board is unable to act.[42] Further, the quorum must be satisfied both at the time the meeting opens, as well as when the resolution is voted upon.[43] As noted in paragraphs 5.22 and 5.23 above a director who cannot vote because of a conflict of interest is not to be counted for the quorum. This consequence cannot be evaded by splitting one resolution into two resolutions (in respect of each of which only one director is conflicted) or by reducing the quorum for a specific purpose.[44] It has been held (*obiter*) that where a director breaches his fiduciary duty in voting for a resolution, he is not included for quorum purposes.[45]

5.25 A company's articles will usually provide that where the company has directors, but less than the number required to transact business, the remaining directors may act for limited purposes, such as appointing new directors or calling a general meeting.[46] Table A, reg 90 provides:

---

[42] *Re Greymouth-Point Elizabeth Railway and Coal Co Ltd* [1904] 1 Ch 32, 34. In *Re Copal Varnish Co* [1917] 2 Ch 349 one of the company's two directors attempted to block the transfer of certain shares through non-attendance of board meetings (the quorum for the transaction of business being two). It was held that the transferees were entitled to an order directing the company to register the transfers. For recent cases where a meeting was held to be invalid due to (amongst other things) lack of quorum, see *Minmar (929) Ltd v Khalastchi* [2011] BCC 485 and *Re Melodious Corp* [2015] 1 BCLC 518.

[43] However, in *Re Hartley Baird Ltd* [1955] Ch 143, it was held that an article which provided that 'the quorum shall be two directors present when the meeting proceeds to business' did not require two directors to be present throughout the meeting.

[44] *Re North Eastern Insurance Co* [1919] 1 Ch 198, 205.

[45] In *Colin Gwyer & Associates Ltd v London Wharf (Limehouse) Ltd* [2003] 2 BCLC 153 the directors were found to have acted in their own, rather than the company's interests. The court held (*per curiam*) that where a director is shown to have acted in breach of his fiduciary duty, he should be treated as being incapable of voting on the business before the board, and not taken into account for quorum purposes. For new statutory provisions on directors' conflicts of interest, see 2006 Act, s 175, discussed in Ch 15.

[46] *Channel Collieries Trust v Dover Light Railway Co* [1914] 2 Ch 506, CA. It is arguable that without such an article, the continuing directors may not be able to act: *York Tramways Co v Willows* (1883) 8 QBD 685, CA; *Re Bank of Syria* [1900] 2 Ch 272, 278; [1901] 1 Ch 115, 120, CA.

The continuing directors or a sole continuing director may act notwithstanding any vacancies in their number, but, if the number of directors is less than the number fixed as the quorum, the continuing directors or director may act only for the purpose of filling vacancies or of calling a general meeting.

An article in these terms does not validate the acts of a board that was originally less than the prescribed minimum.[47] However, where an article, like reg 90, allows continuing directors to act notwithstanding vacancies, and the board was originally competent to transact business, the continuing directors (being less than the prescribed minimum) could act so as to bind the company.[48] But where there is no equivalent of reg 90 and the articles prescribe a constitutional minimum, acts done by the directors when their number is reduced below that prescribed will be invalid.[49]

Model Article (pcls) 11(3) makes similar provision: **5.26**

If the total number of directors for the time being is less than the quorum required, the directors must not take any majority decision other than a decision—
(a) to appoint further directors, or
(b) to call a general meeting so as to enable the shareholders to appoint further directors.

This article recognizes that the remaining directors may make a decision unanimously at the meeting, since they could do so informally under Model Article (pcls) 8.

Model Article (plc) 11 makes slightly different provision for public companies where the   **5.27**
total number of directors is less than the quorum, depending on whether there is one or more than one director in office at the time:

(1) This article applies where the total number of directors for the time being is less than the quorum for directors' meetings.
(2) If there is only one director, that director may appoint sufficient directors to make up a quorum or call a general meeting to do so.
(3) If there is more than one director—
(a) a directors' meeting may take place, if it is called in accordance with the articles and at least two directors participate in it, with a view to appointing sufficient directors to make up a quorum or call a meeting to do so, and
(b) if a directors' meeting is called but only one director attends at the appointed date and time to participate in it, that director may appoint sufficient directors to make up a quorum or call a meeting to do so.

Where there are no directors at all, or they are unwilling to fill the vacancies, the com-   **5.28**
pany in general meeting may make appointments until the board is properly reconstituted.[50] In *Alexander Ward v Samyang Navigation Co* the House of Lords held that the absence of validly appointed directors did not prevent a company taking proceedings to recover its debts on the authority of an individual whose conduct was ratified by the members.[51]

---

[47] *Re Sly, Spink & Co* [1911] 2 Ch 430.
[48] *Re Scottish Petroleum Co* (1883) 23 Ch D 413, 431, CA.
[49] *Bottomley's Case* (1880) 16 Ch D 681.
[50] *Isle of Wight Railway Co v Tahourdin* (1883) 25 Ch D 320, 332, 335, CA; *Barron v Potter* [1914] 1 Ch 895, 902; *Foster v Foster* [1916] 1 Ch 532, 551.
[51] [1975] 1 WLR 673, HL.

Chairman

5.29 The articles usually provide for the directors to have power to appoint a chairman to conduct their meetings. A director does not have a common law right to hold the office of chairman during his period of office as a director.[52] The directors may terminate a chairman's appointment without any particular formality.[53] The chairman's role is limited to the conduct of meetings and it does not, as such, give him any particular power to transact business on behalf of the company.[54] The chairman must carry out his functions in good faith for the purpose for which he was appointed. There are special rules about the chairman of a listed company which are described in paragraphs 5.33–5.34 below.

5.30 Table A, reg 91 deals with the appointment of the chairman:

> The directors may appoint one of their number to be the chairman of the board of directors and may at any time remove him from that office. Unless he is unwilling to do so, the director so appointed shall preside at every meeting of directors at which he is present. But if there is no director holding that office, or if the director holding it is unwilling to preside or is not present within five minutes after the time appointed for the meeting, the directors present may appoint one of their number to be chairman of the meeting.

5.31 One of the chairman's important functions is to determine the eligibility of directors to vote on particular matters, having regard to conflict of interest issues. Table A, reg 98 gives the chairman the power to rule conclusively on such matters:

> If a question arises at a meeting of directors or of a committee of directors as to the right of a director to vote, the question may, before the conclusion of the meeting, be referred to the chairman of the meeting and his ruling in relation to any director other than himself shall be final and conclusive.

5.32 Subject to two minor variations, Model Article (pcls) 12 and Model Article (plc) 12 deal with the appointment of chairman in the same terms. The directors do not have to appoint a chairman. Model Article (pcls) 12 provides:

(1) The directors may appoint a director to chair their meetings.
(2) The person so appointed for the time being is known as the chairman.
(3) The directors may terminate the chairman's appointment at any time.
(4) If the chairman is not participating in a directors' meeting within ten minutes of the time at which it was to start, the participating directors must appoint one of themselves to chair it.

Model Article (plc) 12(3) enables the directors of a public company 'to appoint other directors as deputy or assistant chairmen to chair directors' meetings in the chairman's absence'.[55] This leads to Model Articles (plc) 12(4) providing for the termination of the appointment of the deputy or assistant chairman and 12(5) adapting the language of Model Article (pcls) 12(4) to refer to the absence of both the chairman and any director appointed under Model Article (plc) 12(3). One difference between Table A, reg 91 and both Model Article (pcls) 12(4) and Model Article (plc) 12(5) is that under the Model Articles the chairman must

---

[52] *Foster v Foster* [1916] 1 Ch 532, 551.
[53] *Cane v Jones* [1980] 1 WLR 1451.
[54] *Bell Houses Ltd v Wall Properties Ltd* [1966] 2 QB 656, 688, CA; *Hely-Hutchinson v Brayhead Ltd* [1968] 1 QB 549, CA.
[55] This was inserted in response to requests from consultees: *Implementation of the Companies Act 2006, a Consultation Document* (DTI, February 2007) at para 3.74.

be more than ten minutes late (not five minutes) before the directors present may appoint another chairman.

Chairman of a listed company

The chairman of a listed company has more responsibilities than presiding over meetings of **5.33** directors and shareholders. The personal qualities expected of him and the broader role that he should fulfil are described in more detail in Chapter 3, Section C(7).

He is responsible for leadership of the board and ensuring the overall effectiveness of all **5.34** aspects of the board's role.[56] In relation to board meetings, the chairman is responsible for (i) setting the agenda and ensuring that adequate time is available for discussion of all agenda items, in particular strategic issues;[57] (ii) ensuring that the directors receive accurate, timely and clear information;[58] and (iii) promoting a culture of openness and debate by facilitating the effective contribution of non-executive directors and ensuring constructive relations between executive and non-executive directors.[59]

Voting

Table A, reg 88 provides that 'questions arising at a meeting shall be decided by a majority **5.35** of votes'. The Model Articles (pcls) do not prescribe any rules about voting, but assume that each director has one vote and that decisions are decided on a majority basis, subject to the chairman's casting vote and directors with conflicts of interest being disqualified from voting.[60]

On the other hand, Model Article (plc) 13 does prescribe general rules for voting at meetings **5.36** of directors of public companies:

(1) Subject to the articles, a decision is taken at a directors' meeting by a majority of the votes of the participating directors.
(2) Subject to the articles, each director participating in a directors' meeting has one vote.
(3) Subject to the articles, if a director has an interest in an actual or proposed transaction or arrangement with the company—
    (a) that director and that director's alternate may not vote on any proposal relating to it, and
    (b) this does not preclude the alternate from voting in relation to that transaction or arrangement on behalf of another appointor who does not have such an interest.

The references to 'subject to the articles' would seem to be to Model Articles (plc) 14–16, dealing with the chairman's casting vote, votes of alternate directors, ineligibility to vote on the ground of conflict of interest, and any particular provisions restricting or enlarging directors' voting rights in the articles adopted by the company.

It is common for the chairman to have a casting vote to prevent the company being paralysed **5.37** by deadlock. At common law a chairman does not have a second casting vote.[61] Where the

---

[56] UK Corporate Governance Code (April 2016), paras A.3, A.3.1, and Preface, para 7.
[57] A.3.
[58] B.5.
[59] A.3. Under A.4.2 the chairman should hold meetings with the non-executive directors without the executives being present. If a non-executive director resigns and has concerns about the running of the company or a proposed action, he should provide a written statement to the chairman for circulation to the board (A.4.3).
[60] Model Articles (pcls) 13 and 14.
[61] *Nell v Longbottom* [1894] 1 QB 767, 771; *Re Hackney Pavilion Ltd* [1924] 1 Ch 276, 280.

company is formed as a joint venture with shareholders having equal rights, a casting vote may not be appropriate.[62] Table A, reg 88 provides: 'In the case of an equality of votes, the chairman shall have a second or casting vote.' Similarly both Model Article (pcls) 13 and Model Article (plc) 14 make provision, in the same terms, for the chairman's casting vote at directors' meetings:

(1) If the number of votes for and against a proposal are equal, the chairman or other director chairing the meeting has a casting vote.
(2) But this does not apply if, in accordance with the articles, the chairman or other director is not to be counted as participating in the decision-making process for quorum, or voting purposes.

5.38 Table A, reg 66 provides that an alternate director is entitled to vote at a directors' meeting at which his appointor is not personally present. The Model Articles (pcls) do not deal with alternate directors on the ground that they are not frequently found in private companies.[63] Model Article (plc) 15 deals with the voting rights of a director who is also an alternate director for another director:

A director who is also an alternate director has an additional vote on behalf of each appointor who is—
(a) not participating in a directors' meeting, and
(b) would have been entitled to vote if they were participating in it.

5.39 Table A, reg 92 is a general provision validating acts done at a meeting of directors, which operates as between the members themselves as well as being for the benefit of outsiders.[64] There is no comparable provision in the Model Articles, perhaps because the statutory protection given to outsiders dealing with the company, the 2006 Act, s 161 (validity of acts of directors), and the finality of the chairman's decision on directors' voting rights makes such a provision unnecessary.

Conflicts of interest

5.40 Articles have always contained detailed restrictions on participation by directors on matters in which they are conflicted.[65] The purpose is to ensure that the other directors are able to give their unbiased consideration to the matter and so discharge their duties to the company. The articles discussed below must be considered alongside the provisions of the 2006 Act regulating directors' duties: (a) s 175 (duty to avoid conflicts of interest, but subject to authorization by the directors), (b) s 177 (duty to declare interest in a proposed transaction or arrangement), and (c) s 182 (duty to declare interest in an existing transaction or arrangement).[66]

---

[62] In *Fusion Interactive Communications Solutions Ltd v Venture Investments Placement Ltd (No 2)* [2005] 2 BCLC 571, at para 49, the court refused to allow two directors to block a resolution to commence proceedings against a company in which they were interested, since to vote in that way would be a breach of their fiduciary duties. Now the position is governed by 2006 Act, s 175 under which a director is ineligible to vote on a matter in which he is interested.

[63] *Implementation of the Companies Act 2006, a Consultation Document* (DTI, February 2007) at para 3.26. Alternate directors are discussed in Ch 3, Section C(4) above.

[64] *Dawson v African Consolidated Land and Trading Co* [1898] 1 Ch 6. For further discussion of such provisions, see *British Asbestos Co v Boyd* [1903] 2 Ch 439; *Morris v Kanssen* [1946] AC 459, HL.

[65] There can be no conflict arising from the office of bare trustee, which involves no duties: *Cowan de Groot Properties Ltd v Eagle Trust Ltd* [1991] BCLC 1045, 1115.

[66] Chs 15 and 17 below.

Table A, reg 94 provides that: **5.41**

Save as otherwise provided by the articles, a director shall not vote at a meeting of directors of a committee of directors on any resolution concerning a matter in which he has, directly or indirectly, an interest or duty which is material and which conflicts or may conflict with the interests of the company unless his interest or duty arises only because the case falls within one or more of the following paragraphs—

(a) the resolution relates to the giving to him of a guarantee, security, or indemnity in respect of money lent to, or an obligation incurred by him for the benefit of, the company or any or its subsidiaries;

(b) the resolution relates to the giving to a third party of a guarantee, security, or indemnity in respect of an obligation of the company or any of its subsidiaries for which the director has assumed responsibility in whole or part and whether alone or jointly with others under a guarantee or indemnity or by the giving of security;

(c) his interest arises by virtue of his subscribing or agreeing to subscribe for any shares, debentures or other securities of the company or any of its subsidiaries, or by virtue of his being, or intending to become, a participant in the underwriting or sub-underwriting of an offer of any such shares, for subscription, purchase or exchange;

(d) the resolution relates in any way to a retirement benefits scheme which has been approved, or is conditional upon approval, by the Board of the Inland Revenue for taxation purposes.

For the purpose of this regulation, an interest of a person who is, for any purpose of the Act (excluding any statutory modification thereof not in force when this regulation becomes binding on the company), connected with a director shall be treated as an interest of the director and, in relation to an alternate director, an interest of his appointer shall be treated as an interest of the alternate director without prejudice to any interest which the alternate director has otherwise.

As already noted, if by reason of conflict a director cannot vote he is not counted in the quo-   **5.42**
rum and the question whether the director may vote is to be determined by the chairman, whose decision is final and conclusive[67] Table A, reg 96 gives the company the power to relax voting restrictions:

A company may by ordinary resolution suspend or relax to any extent, either generally or in respect of any particular manner, any provision of the articles prohibiting a director from voting at a meeting of directors or of a committee of directors.

Model Article (pcls) 14 makes provision for directors' conflicts of interest in relation to   **5.43**
actual and proposed transactions or arrangements of the company. They complement the 2006 Act, ss 177 and 182, which require a director to disclose his interest in such transactions or arrangements. Model Article (plc) 16 makes almost identical provision for public companies. Model Article (pcls) 14 provides:

(1) If a proposed decision of the directors is concerned with an actual or proposed transaction or arrangement with the company in which a director is interested, that director is not to be counted as participating in the decision-making process for quorum or voting purposes.

(2) But if paragraph (3) applies, a director who is interested in an actual or proposed transaction or arrangement with the company is to be counted as participating in the decision-making process for quorum and voting purposes.

(3) This paragraph applies when—

---

[67] Table A, regs 95 and 98.

    (a) the company by ordinary resolution disapplies the provision of the articles which would otherwise prevent a director from being counted as participating in the decision-making process;

    (b) the director's interest cannot reasonably be regarded as likely to give rise to a conflict of interest; or

    (c) the director's conflict of interest arises from a permitted cause.

(4) For the purposes of this article, the following are permitted causes—

    (a) a guarantee given, or to be given, by or to a director in respect of an obligation incurred by or on behalf of the company or any of its subsidiaries;

    (b) subscription, or an agreement to subscribe, for shares or other securities of the company or any of its subsidiaries, or to underwrite, sub-underwrite, or guarantee subscription for any such shares or securities; and

    (c) arrangements pursuant to which benefits are made available to employees and directors or former employees and directors of the company or any of its subsidiaries which do not provide special benefits for directors or former directors.

(5) For the purposes of this article, references to proposed decisions and decision-making processes include any directors' meeting or part of a directors' meeting.

(6) Subject to paragraph (7), if a question arises at a meeting of directors or of a committee of directors as to the right of a director to participate in the meeting (or part of the meeting) for voting or quorum purposes, the question may, before the conclusion of the meeting, be referred to the chairman whose ruling in relation to any director other than the chairman is to be final and conclusive.

(7) If any question as to the right to participate in the meeting (or part of the meeting) should arise in respect of the chairman, the question is to be decided by a decision of the directors at that meeting, for which purpose the chairman is not to be counted as participating in the meeting (or that part of the meeting) for voting or quorum purposes.

5.44 Issues may arise as to the materiality of the interest of the director which is said to give rise to a conflict. That will be for the chairman to determine and the finality of his decision severely limits the scope for challenging his decision. In practice the better course may be to refer the matter to the members if that is possible. Where the director is permitted to vote in spite of his conflict he must do so in what he honestly considers to be the company's best interests.[68]

5.45 Unlike the 2006 Act, s 175 (which concerns conflicts of interest arising otherwise than in relation to a transaction or arrangement with the company), ss 177 and 181 do not seek to restrict the interested director's participation for quorum or voting purposes. Company articles frequently provide that a director may vote and be counted in the quorum on proposed decisions on an actual or proposed transaction or arrangement in which he is interested, provided that he has declared his interest. The 1948 Act, Table A, reg 84 is an example of such a provision. Provisions of this type may be appropriate for a private company with few directors. If an interested director abuses his voting rights to the prejudice of minority shareholders they may have remedies in the form of a derivative claim or unfair prejudice petition.[69] On the other hand, Model Article (pcls) 14 reflects the fact that it makes for better corporate governance if decisions are taken only by directors who have no personal interest in the transaction or arrangement.

---

[68] *Breckland Group Ltd v London and Suffolk Properties Ltd* [1989] BCLC 100.
[69] Chs 22 and 23 below.

E. Public Companies: Written Resolutions

The Model Articles (plc) 17 and 18 contain provisions for directors of public companies to **5.46** make decisions by written resolution. These provisions may be compared with provisions in the 1985 Act, Table A, reg 93, which enabled directors to make decisions by a written resolution signed by all of them. Reg 93 provides:

> A resolution in writing signed by all the directors entitled to receive notice of a meeting of directors or of a committee of directors shall be as valid and effectual as if it had been passed at a meeting of directors or (as the case may be) a committee of directors duly convened and held and may consist of several documents in the like form each signed by one or more directors; but a resolution signed by an alternate director need not also be signed by his appointor and, if it is signed by a director who has appointed an alternate director, it need not be signed by the alternate director in that capacity.[70]

A resolution passed pursuant to Table A, reg 93 would appear to be invalid where the number of directors 'entitled to receive notice' is less than the number required for a quorum.[71] Though the oral assent of a majority does not amount to a valid resolution, the defect may be ratified at a subsequent board meeting.[72]

The Model Articles (plc) contain a more detailed procedure for written resolutions of public **5.47** companies, but in more permissive terms than Table A, reg 93. Model Article (plc) 17 deals with the means of giving notice of the proposed written resolution to the directors other than the director who proposes it:

(1) Any director may propose a directors' written resolution.
(2) The company secretary[73] must propose a directors' written resolution if a director so requests.
(3) A director's written resolution is proposed by giving notice of the proposed resolution to the directors.
(4) Notice of a proposed directors' written resolution must indicate—
   (a) the proposed resolution, and
   (b) the time by which it is proposed that the directors should adopt it.
(5) Notice of a proposed directors' written resolution must be given in writing to each director.
(6) Any decision which a person giving notice of a proposed directors' written resolution takes regarding the process of adopting that resolution must be taken reasonably in good faith.

Model Article (plc) 18 provides for the adoption of the written resolutions proposed by a **5.48** director under Model Article (plc) 17:

(1) A proposed directors' written resolution is adopted when all the directors who would have been entitled to vote on the resolution at a directors' meeting have signed one or more copies of it, provided that those directors would have formed a quorum at such a meeting.

---

[70] Unlike its predecessor (the 1948 Table A, reg 106), reg 93 allows for the resolution to be contained within several documents, and can be applied to meetings of a committee of directors as well as meetings of the full board.

[71] *Hood Sailmakers Ltd v Axford* [1997] 1 WLR 625.

[72] *Municipal Mutual Insurance Ltd v Harrop* [1998] 2 BCLC 540, 551 (applying *Re Portuguese Consolidated Copper Mines Ltd* (1890) 42 Ch D 160, CA).

[73] Unlike a private company, a public company must have a secretary: 2006 Act, ss 270 and 271 (which came into force on 6 April 2008).

(2) It is immaterial whether any director signs the resolution before or after the time by which the notice proposed that it should be adopted.

(3) Once a directors' written resolution has been adopted, it must be treated as if it had been a decision taken at a directors' meeting in accordance with the articles.

(4) The company secretary must ensure that the company keeps a record, in writing, of all directors' written resolutions for at least ten years from the date of their adoption.

5.49   The procedure under Model Articles (plc) 17 and 18 is similar to that under Model Articles (pcls) 8, in that they both enable decisions to be taken by directors when some are travelling. The person giving notice of the proposed written resolution must give notice in writing to each director, but he may exercise a judgment as to how that notice may conveniently be given. Sending notice by email or fax to the place where the director is believed to be may be sufficient.

5.50   There are material differences between the directors' written resolution procedure for public companies and unanimous decision-making by directors of private companies. Under Model Article (pcls) 8(1) the decision is taken when the directors indicate to each other their common view, whereas under Model Article (plc) 18(1) the decision is not adopted until all the directors have signed copies of the resolution. Also under Model Article (pcls) 8(2) the unanimous decision need not be in the form of a written resolution, but under Model Article (plc) 18 it must be.

5.51   A public company's articles may provide for directors to take a decision by written resolution which is agreed to be a majority of directors eligible to vote.

F. Records of Decisions

5.52   The 2006 Act, s 248 requires minutes of directors' meetings to be kept for at least ten years, failing which every officer of the company in default commits an offence.[74] The substantive obligation is:

(1) Every company must cause minutes of all proceedings at meetings of its directors to be recorded.

(2) The records must be kept for at least ten years from the date of the meeting.

By the 2006 Act, s 1135, 'company records'[75] may be kept in hard-copy or electronic form, though where they are stored electronically they must be capable of being reproduced in hard-copy form.

5.53   The 2006 Act, s 249 provides for the minutes to be evidence:

(1) Minutes recorded in accordance with section 248, if purporting to be authenticated by the chairman of the meeting or by the chairman of the next directors' meeting, are evidence … of the proceedings at the meeting.[76]

(2) Where minutes have been made in accordance with that section of the proceedings of a meeting of directors, then, until the contrary is proved—

---

[74] 2006 Act, s 248(3) and (4).

[75] 2006 Act, s 1134 includes board minutes in its definition of 'company records'.

[76] In order for a trust of shares to be created, there is no requirement for a board minute approving or recording the declaration of such a trust: *Singh v Anand* [2007] EWHC 3346 (Ch).

    (a) the meeting is deemed duly held and convened,

    (b) all proceedings at the meeting are deemed to have duly taken place, and

    (c) all appointments at the meeting are deemed valid.

The Model Articles complement the 2006 Act, s 248 by imposing on directors a simi- **5.54** lar obligation, which is owed to the company and enforceable by members, to preserve records of informal unanimous decisions and written resolutions. Model Article (pcls) 15 provides that:

> The directors must ensure that the company keeps a record, in writing, for at least 10 years from the date of the decision recorded, of every unanimous or majority decision taken by the directors.

Model Article (plc) 18(4) contains a similar obligation for written resolutions of directors of public companies.

Table A also provides for records of proceedings of directors to be kept. Regulation 100 **5.55** provides that:

> Directors shall cause minutes to be made in books kept for the purpose—
>
> …
>
> (b) of all proceedings at meeting … of the directors, and of committees of directors, including the names of the directors present at each such meeting.[77]

A written resolution of directors under Table A, reg 93 is treated as if it had been passed at a meeting so as to fall within the obligation in reg 100.

Keeping records of decisions made by directors and of the factors taken into account has an **5.56** additional significance in light of the duty under s 172 to promote the success of the company (Chapter 12 below). It is generally thought that this section will encourage detailed minutes, outlining the factors taken into account, as well as the decisions taken. It is possible to adduce evidence of decisions taken but not recorded in the minutes.[78] Draft minutes may also be admitted as evidence if supported by other evidence that they accurately reflect decisions made at the directors' meeting.[79]

G. Delegation

At common law the board may not delegate any of the powers conferred on it to a manager **5.57** or committee, unless the articles permit it to do so.[80] In practice a company's articles always give a power of delegation, because, except for companies with only one or two directors, it would be impractical for the board to have to exercise all powers of management itself. Where there is a power of delegation, the directors may always revoke it or alter the terms of the delegation to the individual or committee and the board will be treated as having done

---

[77] Formerly 1948 Table A, Art 86, though omitting the requirement of that article that every director present at any meeting of directors or committee of directors should sign his name in a book kept for the purpose.

[78] *Re Fireproof Doors Ltd* [1916] 2 Ch 142.

[79] *R (on the application of IRC) v Kingston Crown Court* [2001] 4 All ER 721.

[80] *Re County Palatine Loan and Discount Co, Cartmell's Case* (1874) 9 Ch App 691, 695; *Re Leeds Banking, Howard's Case* (1866) 1 Ch App 561; *Boschoek Proprietary Co v Fuke* [1906] 1 Ch 148, 159; *Nelson v James Nelson & Sons* [1914] 2 KB 770, 779, CA.

so where it exercises the delegated power itself.[81] This is because a board cannot deprive itself of the power to control the company's business.[82]

5.58 Model Article (pcls) 5 and Model Article (plc) 5 give the directors power to delegate any of their powers to an individual or a committee in the broadest terms:

    (1) Subject to the articles, the directors may delegate any of the powers which are conferred on them under the articles—
        (a) to such person or committee;
        (b) by such means (including by power of attorney);
        (c) to such an extent;
        (d) in relation to such matters or territories; and
        (e) on such terms and conditions; as they think fit.
    (2) If the directors so specify, any such delegation may authorise further delegation of the directors' powers by any person to whom they are delegated.
    (3) The directors may revoke any delegation in whole or part, or alter its terms and conditions.

5.59 Table A includes distinct powers of delegation to an agent, to a committee, and to a managing director or other director. Table A, reg 71 gives the directors power to delegate any of their powers to an agent:[83]

The directors may, by power of attorney or otherwise, appoint any person to be the agent of the company for such purposes and on such conditions as they determine, including authority for the agent to delegate all or any of his powers.

5.60 Table A, reg 72 gives the directors power to delegate to a committee or managing director or other director (eg a finance director or marketing director):

The directors may delegate any of their powers to any committee consisting of one or more directors. They may also delegate to any managing director or any director holding any other executive office such of their powers as they consider desirable to be exercised by him. Any such delegation may be made subject to any conditions the directors may impose, and either collaterally with or to the exclusion of their own powers and may be revoked or altered. Subject to any such conditions, the proceedings of a committee with two or more members shall be governed by the articles regulating the proceedings of directors so far as they are capable of applying.[84]

(1) Managing director

5.61 Where the articles give directors the power to appoint a managing director, as they usually do, the shareholders cannot make the appointment.[85] But the shareholders may intervene by passing a special resolution directing the directors to make the appointment.[86] The shareholders may make the appointment by ordinary resolution where the board has shown itself unable or unwilling to act.[87]

---

[81] *Huth v Clarke* (1890) 25 QBD 391, 394 (per Lord Coleridge CJ); *Gordon, Dadds & Co v Morris* [1945] 2 All ER 616, 622.

[82] *Horn v Henry Faulder & Co* (1908) 99 LT 524.

[83] Such a power was introduced for the first time by the 1948 Table A, reg 81. It enables the board to appoint an overseas representative.

[84] Formerly 1948 Table A, Arts 103 and 109.

[85] *Macari v Celtic Football and Athletic Co Ltd* [1999] SLT 138.

[86] Table A, reg 70; Model Article (pcls) 4; Model Article (plc) 4.

[87] *Barron v Potter* [1914] 1 Ch 895; *Foster v Foster* [1916] 1 Ch 532.

The appointment to the office of managing director is dependent on the person being a **5.62**
director.[88] He is an ordinary director to whom certain powers are delegated.[89] So where a
person is removed from office as a director he ceases to be managing director.[90] He will also
cease to be managing director where the articles provide for directors to retire at the next
AGM and he is not re-elected a director.[91] Where a managing director is removed from office
as director or managing director, he may have a claim for damages for breach of contract if
there is a distinct contract of service,[92] but not where the appointment is solely made under
the articles.[93]

The managing director, or chief executive officer, will usually be given very wide powers of **5.63**
management on behalf of the company and persons dealing with him in good faith may
assume that he is authorized to do everything that falls within the usual scope of that office.[94]
A managing director's implied powers are those that would ordinarily be exercisable by a
managing director in his position, so that his powers extend to carrying out those functions
on which he need not obtain the specific directions of the board.[95] The managing director is
expected to work within the strategy set by the board and his powers do not extend to sus-
pending the duly appointed chairman.[96] There is no reason why the board may not restrict
his powers to particular areas or companies within the group.[97] A managing director does
not necessarily have power by virtue of his appointment to commence proceedings on behalf
of the company.[98]

(2) Committee

Subject to the construction of the articles, the delegation may be to a committee with a single **5.64**
member.[99] Where the articles give a power to delegate, it is a fiduciary power. It may not be
used for an improper purpose, such as excluding one or more directors from the decision-
making process.[100]

---

[88] *Southern Foundries (1926) Ltd v Shirlaw* [1940] AC 701, 721, HL, per Lord Wright; *Shindler v Northern Raincoat Co Ltd* [1960] 1 WLR 1038, 1042. Whether a person is in fact an executive director is a question of fact, and may depend on the company's constitution or the conduct of the board: *Jacques v AIG Australia Ltd* [2014] VSC 269.

[89] *Re Newspaper Proprietary Syndicate Ltd* [1900] 2 Ch 349, 350; *Foster v Foster* [1916] 1 Ch 532, 543.

[90] *Read v Astoria Garage (Streatham) Ltd* [1952] Ch 637.

[91] *Bluett v Stuchbury's Ltd* (1908) 24 TLR 469, CA.

[92] *Nelson v James Nelson & Sons* [1914] 2 KB 770, CA; *Fowler v Commercial Timber Co Ltd* [1930] 2 KB 1, CA; *Southern Foundries (1926) Ltd v Shirlaw* [1940] AC 701, HL; *Shindler v Northern Raincoat Co* [1960] 1 WLR 1308; *Yetton v Eastwoods Froy Ltd* [1967] 1 WLR 104. The managing director's remedies for breach of contract are discussed in more detail in Ch 7, Section D below.

[93] *Read v Astoria Garage (Streatham) Ltd* [1952] Ch 637, CA.

[94] *Hely-Hutchinson v Brayhead Ltd* [1968] 1 QB 549, 583, CA, per Lord Denning MR (guarantee of loans to subsidiary); *Biggerstaff v Rowatt's Wharf Ltd* [1896] 2 Ch 93, 102, 104, 106, CA (borrow money and give security); *Dey v Pullinger Engineering Co* [1921] 1 KB 77 (sign cheques and bills of exchange).

[95] *Smith v Butler* [2012] BCC 645, CA at para 28, per Arden LJ.

[96] *Smith v Butler* (n 95 above) at paras 30 and 31, per Arden LJ.

[97] *Harold Holdsworth & Co (Wakefield) Ltd v Caddies* [1955] 1 WLR 352, HL.

[98] *Mitchell & Hobbs (UK) Ltd v Mills* [1996] 2 BCLC 102, 107, 108; *Fusion Interactive Communication Solutions Ltd v Venture Investment Placement* [2005] 2 BCLC 250 at para 254; *Fusion Interactive Communication Solutions Ltd v Venture Investment Placement (No 2)* [2005] 2 BCLC 571 at para 46 (but the court would not allow two directors to breach their fiduciary duties by blocking proceedings brought by the company through solicitors instructed by the other two directors; see para 49).

[99] *Re Taurine Co* (1884) 25 Ch D 118, CA; *Re Fireproof Doors Ltd* [1916] 2 Ch 142.

[100] *Pulbrook v Richmond Consolidated Mining Co* (1878) 9 Ch D 610; *Trounce and Wakefield v NCF Kaiapoi Ltd* (1985) 2 NZCLC 99.

5.65   A committee must take care not to act beyond the powers of delegation granted (as a matter of construction) by its articles. In the leading case of *Guinness plc v Saunders*,[101] the House of Lords found that a committee's powers did not extend to fixing the remuneration for one of its members.

5.66   The last sentence of Table A, reg 72 (paragraph 5.60 above) provides that where a committee consists of two or more members, the articles governing proceedings of directors apply so far as they are capable of applying. Model Article (pcls) 6 and Model Article (plc) 6 adopt the same default position, but give the directors power to stipulate special rules of procedure for a committee. They provide in identical terms:

(1)   Committees to which the directors delegate any of their powers must follow procedures which are based as far as they are applicable on those provisions of the articles which govern the taking of decisions by directors.
(2)   The directors may make rules of procedure for all or any committees, which prevail over rules derived from the articles if they are not consistent with them.

H.   Listed Companies: Committees

5.67   The rest of this chapter reflects the UK Corporate Governance Code (April 2016) ('the Code'),[102] which contains non-statutory requirements for listed companies to establish nomination, audit, and remuneration committees.[103] The Code is a guide to a number of key components of effective board practice, and is based on the underlying principles of good governance: accountability, transparency, probity, and focus on the sustainable success of an entity over the longer term. The board and its committees should have the appropriate balance of skill, experience, independence, and knowledge of the company to enable them to discharge their respective duties and responsibilities effectively.[104] The Code applies on a 'comply or explain' basis to all companies with a Premium Listing of equity shares regardless of whether they are incorporated in the UK or elsewhere. Smaller listed companies, in particular those new to listing, may judge that some of the provisions are disproportionate or less relevant in their case.[105]

(1)   Nomination committee

5.68   The Code spells out the principle underlying board appointments: there should be a formal, rigorous, and transparent procedure for the appointment of new directors.[106]

5.69   There are two supporting principles.[107] First, 'the search for board candidates should be conducted, and appointments made, against objective criteria and with due regard for the

---

[101]   [1990] 2 AC 663, HL. In *UK Safety Group Ltd v Heane* [1998] 2 BCLC 208, 215, it was held (as a matter of construction) that the power to grant special terms of employment to a committee member cannot be delegated.
[102]   This version of the Corporate Governance Code replaces the Corporate Governance Code of June 2010, which was referred to in the previous edition of this work
[103]   The Association of British Insurers and the National Association of Pension Funds have also provided guidance on matters covered by the Code.
[104]   Code at B.1.
[105]   'Comply or Explain', para 5. A smaller company is one that is below the FTSE 350 throughout the year immediately prior to the reporting year.
[106]   B.2.
[107]   B.2.1.

benefits of diversity on the board, including gender'. Secondly, 'the board should satisfy itself that plans are in place for orderly succession for appointments to the board and to senior management, so as to maintain an appropriate balance of skills and experience within the company and on the board'. These principles are discussed in Chapter 6, Section C(2) below.

The Code then sets out various provisions on board appointments.[108] There should be a **5.70** nomination committee, which should lead the process for board appointments and make recommendations to the board. A majority of members of the nomination committee should be independent non-executive directors. The chairman or an independent non-executive director should chair the committee, but the chairman should not chair the nomination committee when it is dealing with the appointment of a successor to the chairmanship. The nomination committee should make available[109] its terms of reference, explaining its role and the authority delegated to it by the board. The nomination committee should evaluate the balance of skills, experience, independence, and knowledge on the board and, in the light of this evaluation, prepare a description of the role and capabilities required for a particular appointment.[110]

The work of the nomination committee should be described in a separate section of the **5.71** company's annual report. This should include a description of the process used in relation to board appointments and an explanation if neither an external search consultancy nor open advertising was used in the appointment of a chairman or a non-executive director.[111]

The Code states that the main principle in the appointment of the chairman, non-executive **5.72** directors, and full-time executive directors is 'commitment': all directors should be able to allocate sufficient time to the company to discharge their responsibilities effectively.[112] The nomination committee is specifically responsible for preparing a job specification for the appointment of a chairman, including an assessment of the time commitment expected, recognizing the need for availability in the event of crises.[113] The Code goes on to provide for the chairman and non-executive directors to disclose their other significant commitments so that the board can assess their impact on effectiveness.[114] Finally, the board should not agree to a full-time executive director being a non-executive director or chairman of more than one FTSE 100 company.[115]

(2) Audit committee

The Code[116] lays down two bases for accountability and audit. As to financial and busi- **5.73** ness reporting, the board should present a balanced and understandable assessment of the

---

[108] B.2.1 *et seq.*
[109] The requirement to make the information available would be met by including the information on a website that is maintained by or on behalf of the company.
[110] B.2.2.
[111] B.2.4.
[112] B.3.
[113] B.3.1.
[114] B.3.1; B.3.2.
[115] B.3.3.
[116] Section C.3 of the Code should be read alongside the Financial Reporting Council's 'Guidance on Audit Committees' (also known as the 'Smith Guidance'), which suggests means of applying this part of the Code. Copies are available on the FRC website.

company's position and prospects. As to risk management and internal control, the board is responsible for determining the nature and extent of the significant risks it is willing to take in achieving its strategic objectives. The board should maintain sound risk management and internal control systems. It requires that 'the board should establish formal and transparent arrangements for considering how they should apply the financial reporting and internal control principles and for maintaining an appropriate relationship with the company's auditors'.[117]

5.74 The Code then sets out how this should be achieved through the audit committee.[118] The board should establish an audit committee of at least three, or in the case of smaller companies,[119] two members, who should all be independent non-executive directors. The board should satisfy itself that at least one member of the audit committee has recent and relevant financial experience.

5.75 The main role and responsibilities of the audit committee should be set out in written terms of reference, and should include:[120]

(1) to monitor the integrity of the financial statements of the company, and any formal announcements relating to the company's financial performance, reviewing significant financial reporting judgments contained in them;

(2) to review the company's internal financial controls and, unless expressly addressed by a separate board risk committee composed of independent directors, or by the board itself, to review the company's internal control and risk management systems;

(3) to monitor and review the effectiveness of the company's internal audit function;

(4) to make recommendations to the board, for it to put to the shareholders for their approval in general meeting, in relation to the appointment, re-appointment, and removal of the external auditor and to approve the remuneration and terms of engagement of the external auditor;

(5) to review and monitor the external auditor's independence and objectivity and the effectiveness of the audit process, taking into consideration relevant UK professional and regulatory requirements;

(6) to develop and implement policy on the engagement of the external auditor to supply non-audit services, taking into account relevant ethical guidance regarding the provision of non-audit services by the external audit firm; and to report to the board, identifying any matters in respect of which it considers that action or improvement is needed and making recommendations as to the steps to be taken;

(7) to report to the board on how it has discharged its responsibilities.

5.76 The terms of reference of the audit committee, including its role and the authority delegated to it by the board, should be made available.[121] Where requested by the board, the audit committee should provide advice on whether the annual report and accounts, taken as a whole, is fair, balanced, and understandable and provides the information necessary for shareholders to assess the company's position and performance, business model, and strategy.

---

[117] 'Main Principles of the Code', Section C.

[118] C.3.1 *et seq.*

[119] A smaller company is one that is below the FTSE 350 throughout the year ending prior to the reporting year.

[120] C.3.2.

[121] C.3.3. The requirement to make information available would be met by including the information on a website that is maintained by or on behalf of the company.

Other functions of the audit committee are: **5.77**

(1) to review arrangements by which staff of the company may, in confidence, raise concerns about possible improprieties in matters of financial reporting or other matters,
so as to ensure that arrangements are in place for the proportionate and independent
investigation of such matters and for appropriate follow-up action;[122]
(2) to monitor and review the effectiveness of the internal audit activities, and where there is
no internal audit function, the audit committee should consider annually whether there
is a need for an internal audit function and make a recommendation to the board, and
the reasons for the absence of such a function should be explained in the relevant section
of the annual report; and[123]
(3) to have primary responsibility for making a recommendation on the appointment, reappointment, and removal of the external auditors. FTSE 350 companies should put the external audit contract out to tender at least every ten years. If the board does not accept the audit
committee's recommendation, it should include in the annual report, and in any papers
recommending appointment or re-appointment, a statement from the audit committee
explaining the recommendation and should set out reasons why the board has taken a different position.[124]

A separate section of the annual report should describe the work of the committee in dis-   **5.78**
charging its responsibilities. The report should include: the significant issues that the committee considered in relation to the financial statements and how these issues were addressed;
an explanation of how it has assessed the effectiveness of the external report process and the
approach taken to the appointment or reappointment of the external auditor, and information on the length of tenure of the current audit firm and when a tender was last conducted;
and if the external auditor provides non-audit services, an explanation of how auditor objectivity and independence are safeguarded.

(3) Remuneration committee

The Code sets out the following main principle with regard to remuneration: **5.79**

> Executive directors' remuneration should be designed to promote the long-term success of the com-
> pany. Performance-related elements should be transparent, stretching and rigorously applied.[125]

This main principle is supplemented by a supporting principle: **5.80**

> The remuneration committee should judge where to position their company relative to other
> companies. But they should use such comparisons with caution, in view of the risk of an
> upward ratchet of remuneration levels with no corresponding improvement in corporate or
> individual performance, and should avoid paying more if necessary. They should also be sensi-
> tive to pay and employment conditions elsewhere in the group, especially when determining
> annual salary increases.

There are detailed Code provisions about the level and components of remuneration (see   **5.81**
Chapter 8, Section E below).[126] As to those matters: (i) the remuneration committee should

---

[122] C.3.5.
[123] C.3.6.
[124] C.3.7.
[125] D.1.
[126] D.1.1–D.1.5.

follow the provisions of Schedule A to the Code when designing performance-related remuneration for executive directors, (and schemes for performance-related remuneration should include provisions that would enable the company to recover sums paid or withhold the payment of any sum, and specify the circumstances in which it would be appropriate to do so);[127] (ii) where a company releases an executive director to serve as a non-executive director elsewhere, the remuneration report should include a statement as to whether or not the director will retain such earnings and if so what the remuneration is; (iii) levels of remuneration for non-executive directors should reflect the time, commitment, and responsibilities of the role; (iv) the remuneration committee should carefully consider what compensation commitments (including pension contributions and all other elements) their directors' terms of appointment would entail in the event of early termination, with a view to avoiding rewarding poor performance.[128]

5.82 Having set out detailed provisions on remuneration policy, the Code goes on to deal with procedure. The main principle is that: 'there should be a formal and transparent procedure for developing policy on executive remuneration and for fixing the remuneration packages of individual directors. No director should be involved in deciding his or her own remuneration.'[129]

5.83 There are two supporting principles:

(1) The remuneration committee should take care to recognize and manage conflicts of interest when receiving views from executive directors or senior management, or consulting the chief executive about its proposals. The remuneration committee should also be responsible for appointing any consultants in respect of executive director remuneration.

(2) The chairman of the board should ensure that the company maintains contact as required with its principal shareholders about remuneration.[130]

5.84 The Code then sets out further provisions on remuneration committees. The board should establish a remuneration committee of at least three, or in the case of smaller companies two, independent non-executive directors. The company chairman may also be a member of, but not chair, the committee if he or she was considered independent on appointment as chairman. The remuneration committee should make available its terms of reference, explaining its role and the authority delegated to it by the board. Where remuneration consultants are appointed, a statement should be made available of whether they have any other connection with the company.[131]

5.85 The remuneration committee should have delegated responsibility for setting remuneration for all executive directors and the chairman, including pension rights and any compensation payments (taking into account the matters in paragraph 5.81 above). The committee should also recommend and monitor the level and structure of remuneration for senior management. The definition of 'senior management' for this purpose should be determined by the board but should normally include the first layer of management below board level.[132]

---

[127] D.1.1.
[128] D.1.4.
[129] D.2.
[130] D.2.
[131] At D.2.1. In *Newcastle International Airport Ltd v Eversheds LLP* [2012] EWHC 2648 (Ch) Proudman J reviewed the responsibility of non-executive members of the remuneration committee to executive directors' remuneration packages (appeal allowed: [2014] 1 WLR 3073, CA).
[132] D.2.3.

Finally the Code goes on to deal with the approval of remuneration in accordance with the   **5.86**
constitution. The board itself or, where required by the articles of association, the shareholders should determine the remuneration of the non-executive directors within the limits
set in the articles of association. Where permitted by the articles, the board may delegate
this responsibility to a committee, which might include the chief executive.[133] Shareholders
should be invited specifically to approve all new long-term incentive schemes (as defined in
the Listing Rules) and significant changes to existing schemes, save in circumstances provided by the Listing Rules.

---

[133] Further provisions on the design of performance-related remuneration are contained in Schedule A of
the Corporate Governance Code.

6

APPOINTMENT OF DIRECTORS

Martin Griffiths QC

A. Introduction

This chapter deals with directors who are formally appointed to the role (including cases where the **6.01** formal process is defective). It does not consider de facto or shadow directors. It describes the rules relating to the required numbers of directors, their eligibility for appointment, the appointment process, and the publicity rules relating to the appointment. Appointed directors may be either executive or non-executive directors. The relevant statutory provisions are now found in Part 10 of the Companies Act. The sections about the appointment of directors are ss 154–61.[1] The sections about publicity, concerning the register of directors and directors' residential addresses, are ss 162–7 and 240–6.[2] Reference should also be made to the company's own constitution.

B. Numbers of Directors

There must be at least one director in every private company.[3] A sole director may **6.02** serve also as company secretary.[4] There must be at least two directors in every public

---

[1] 2006 Act, ss 154, 160, 161 came into force on 1 October 2007 and ss 155–9 came into force on 1 October 2008. Under the SBEE Act 2015, s 87 from a date to be appointed, s 155 is to be repealed and replaced by new ss 156A–C and by s 94 and Sch 5 new ss 167A–F and new s 246(3A), (4A), and (5) are inserted with effect from 30 June 2016.

[2] 2006 Act, ss 162–7, 240–6 came into force on 1 October 2009.

[3] 2006 Act, s 154(1).

[4] This is because 1985 Act, s 283(2) has not been re-enacted.

company.[5] Every company must at present have at least one director who is a natural person.[6] But, from a date to be appointed, all new directors must be natural persons[7] (although there will be power to provide for exceptions[8]) and existing directors who are not natural persons will, 12 months after the appointed day, automatically lose their office.[9] A natural person who is a corporation sole, or who serves by virtue of holding some other office, will still qualify as a natural person for the purpose of eligibility for office;[10] examples might be 'the Bishop of Winchester' (who is both a corporation sole and a natural person) or 'the Chairman of the Board of Governors of Anytown School' (who is a natural person but not a corporation sole).[11] These requirements were noted earlier (see Chapter 3, Section A). Chapter 3, Section C explains the difference between appointed directors (the subject of this chapter), de facto directors, shadow directors, alternate directors, nominee directors, and executive and non-executive directors. These categories are not mutually exclusive.

6.03   Although the Companies Act imposes a minimum number of directors, it does not impose any maximum. The UK Corporate Governance Code[12] says that 'it should not be so large as to be unwieldy' but there should be a balance of skills, experience, independence, and knowledge of the company and 'The board should be of sufficient size that the requirements of the business can be met and that changes to the board's composition and that of its committees can be managed without undue disruption.'[13] Table A, reg 64 gives the members the power to determine any maximum number of directors by ordinary resolution, but provides that there is no maximum number until such a resolution is passed. The Model Articles (pcls) and (plc) do not contain any similar provision. It is not unusual for a limit to be specified in public company articles, although typically this may be increased by ordinary rather than special resolution. In a joint venture company, such a provision might be used in order to preserve a balance of voting power between the joint venture partners. However, balance is usually achieved in joint venture companies by having different classes of directors, with a requirement for a resolution to be supported by all classes.

6.04   The common law rule was that, if the number of directors fell below the fixed minimum, the remaining directors could not, on the face of it, act at all.[14] But the articles may empower the continuing directors to act even when there is a vacancy or even if the number has fallen below the minimum.[15] Typically the articles provide that the quorum is two, unless set at

---

[5]   2006 Act, s 154(2). This is so even in the case of public companies registered before 1 November 1929, because the exception formerly contained in 1985 Act, s 282(2) has not been re-enacted.

[6]   2006 Act, s 155(2).

[7]   2006 Act, s 156A.

[8]   2006 Act, s 156B. Even with exceptions, at least one director will have to be a natural person: s156B(4).

[9]   2006 Act, s 156C.

[10]   2006 Act, ss 155(2), 156A(2).

[11]   For the corporation sole, see *Halsbury's Laws of England* (4th edn) (2006 Reissue), Vol 9(2), paras 1111 and 1112.

[12]   The UK Corporate Governance Code (April 2016) applies (on a 'comply or explain' basis) to all companies with a Premium (formerly Primary) Listing on the London Stock Exchange with effect from the accounting period beginning on or after 1 October 2014 but incorporates good practice which is also more generally applicable. It replaces the UK Corporate Governance Code (2010) discussed in the previous edition of this work.

[13]   UK Code B.1.

[14]   *Re Alma Spinning Co* (1880) 16 Ch D 681.

[15]   *Re Scottish Petroleum Co* (1883) 23 Ch D 413; *Re Bank of Syria* [1900] 2 Ch 272, [1901] 1 Ch 115, CA.

some other number, and that where this quorum is not met, the remaining directors may only act for the purposes of appointing further directors or calling a general meeting.[16]

Even when the articles do not, strictly, empower the continuing directors to act in the event **6.05** of a lack of numbers,[17] their acts will still be valid in favour of a person dealing with the company in good faith, even if that person knows that the directors are acting beyond their powers under the company's constitution.[18] This will not, however, be the case when there are transactions with the directors themselves or with connected persons.[19] When the company is a charity, the terms of the good faith exemption are drawn more strictly.[20]

When the directors cannot act because the articles do not permit them to do so, or because **6.06** there are no directors (for example, the directors all resign), or because they are deadlocked, the default position is that their powers revert to the members.[21] Model Articles (pcls) 17(2) and (3) also give power to the personal representative of the last surviving shareholder in cases where there are no directors and no shareholders who might otherwise make the relevant appointment.

When the maximum number of directors prescribed by the articles has been reached, any **6.07** appointments over and above the prescribed limit will be void. However, the persons purportedly appointed might act as de facto or shadow directors if they purport to take up the void appointment. An appointment made by ordinary resolution may take effect as a valid appointment provided the articles allow the maximum to be increased by ordinary resolution; the resolution is taken to be an exercise of that power.[22] A resolution to reduce the maximum number of directors does not affect any existing directors (even in excess of the maximum) during the remainder of their current terms of office.[23] However, it prevents new directors being appointed until the number of directors has fallen below the new maximum.

If a company finds itself with no directors at all, it will be in breach of the 2006 Act, ss 154 **6.08** and 155. It will be directed to appoint directors by the Secretary of State by virtue of s 156. The direction so given must include: (1) a statement of the section the company is in breach of; (2) the action the company must take in order to comply; and (3) the period within which the company must comply with the direction.[24]

C. Eligibility for Appointment as a Director

(1) Private and public companies

A significant aspect of the control of companies for the public interest is the prohibition of **6.09** certain people (as a class, or specifically) from acting as company directors. Certain general

---

[16] Table A, regs 89 and 90; Model Article (pcls) 11; and Model Articles (plc) 10 and 11.
[17] Table A, regs 89 and 90; Model Article (pcls) 11; and Model Articles (plc) 10 and 11.
[18] 2006 Act, s 40.
[19] 2006 Act, s 41.
[20] 2006 Act, s 42.
[21] *Barron v Potter* [1914] 1 Ch 895, per Warrington J.
[22] *Worcester Corsetry Ltd v Witting* [1936] Ch 640, CA.
[23] *Foster v Greenwich Ferry Co Ltd* (1888) 5 TLR 16; *Worcester Corsetry Ltd v Witting* [1936] Ch 640, CA.
[24] Under s 156(2) that period must be no less than one month or more than three months after the date on which the direction is given.

disqualifications apply. These are considered below. In addition, the courts may declare specific individuals disqualified from directing or managing companies. This is done by making disqualification orders or accepting disqualification undertakings under CDDA (see Chapter 31).

6.10   In all these cases, third parties are protected: s 161(1) will render the acts of such persons, as directors, valid notwithstanding that there was a defect in their appointment, that they were disqualified from holding office, or that they had ceased to hold office. The purpose of s 161 is to protect third parties against a company relying on a person's lack of entitlement in order to avoid obligations. Its wording is more expansive than that contained in its predecessor section.[25]

Age limits

6.11   Section 157 imposes a mandatory rule that persons under the age of 16 years may not be appointed as directors of a company unless the appointment is not to take effect until the age of sixteen is reached. Appointments in breach of the rule are void. An under-age person may nevertheless be liable as a de facto or shadow director.[26]

6.12   The Secretary of State has power to make regulations providing for exceptions from the minimum age requirement but has not done so.[27]

6.13   Anyone under the age of 16 who was a director when the age requirement came into force on 1 October 2008, and who was not exempted by regulations, automatically ceased to be a director.[28] The company's own register must be altered accordingly, but, interestingly, it is specified that there is no obligation to give notice to the Registrar of the change. The change will not appear on the register at Companies House until the Registrar is alerted in some other way.[29]

6.14   An under-age person is therefore prohibited by law from being a director for the purposes of the company's articles.[30] If under-age persons continue to act after their appointment is automatically terminated, then their acts remain valid,[31] and they may be liable as de facto or shadow directors. The section expressly preserves the liability of any de facto or shadow director who is under the age of 16.[32]

6.15   The Companies Act does not impose any maximum age for directors. The upper age limit of 70 years imposed by the 1985 Act, s 293 in relation to directors of public

---

[25]   This provision replaces 1985 Act, s 285, which was applicable only where there was a procedural defect in the appointment of a director and not when there was no appointment at all (*Morris v Kanssen* [1946] AC 459, HL) or where a director had vacated office but continued to act.

[26]   2006 Act, s 157(5).

[27]   2006 Act, s 158. In Annex B to the Consultative Document *Implementation of the Companies Act 2006* (February 2007), the government indicated that it did not intend to make regulations under s 158 and no such regulations have been made or published as a draft for consultation.

[28]   2006 Act, s 159(2). Although the government indicated that it would consider making transitional provisions to deal with special circumstances, relating to existing under-age directors (HC Comm D 6/7/06, col 501, HC Report Stage 17/10/06, col 815), it did not do so.

[29]   2006 Act, s 159(3), (4).

[30]   Model Article (pcls) 17(1), Model Article (plc) 20 and Table A, reg 81(a).

[31]   2006 Act, s 161 (validity of acts of directors).

[32]   2006 Act, s 157(5).

companies and their private company subsidiaries has been repealed as from 6 April 2007.[33]

Disqualification

A person is prohibited by law from being a director of a company if he is subject to a dis- **6.16** qualification order or undertaking under the CDDA, or is otherwise prohibited by law from acting as a director (see the detail below).[34] Under the CDDA,[35] the courts may declare specific individuals disqualified from directing or managing companies. This is done by making disqualification orders or accepting disqualification undertakings on the grounds of the following types of misconduct (see Chapter 31 for details):

(1) conviction of an indictable offence in connection with the promotion, formation, management, liquidation, or striking off of a company, or with the receivership of a company's property or with being an administrative receiver (CDDA, s 2);

(2) persistent breaches of the companies legislation (CDDA, s 3);

(3) fraudulent trading, any fraud in relation to the company, or breach of duty as an officer of the company, where the company has gone into liquidation (CDDA, s 4);

(4) summary conviction for failure to comply with statutory requirements for delivering documents or providing information to the Registrar (CDDA, s 5);

(5) conviction abroad of certain offences in relation to companies (CDDA, s 5A);

(6) unfitness to be concerned in the management of a company as shown by conduct of a company that has gone into insolvent liquidation, administration, or administrative receivership (CDDA, s 6);

(7) unfitness to be concerned in the management of a company as revealed by investigation of a company (CDDA, s 8);

(8) instructing an unfit director of an insolvent company (CDDA, s 8ZA);

(9) unfitness to be concerned in the management of a company as revealed by breaches of competition law (CDDA, s 9A); and

(10) participation in fraudulent or wrongful trading under the Insolvency Act, ss 213 or 214 (CDDA, s 10).

Substantial additional restrictions (subject to some limited exceptions) have been imposed **6.17** by the Insolvency Act, s 216 to prevent the 'phoenix syndrome'.[36] The goal is to prevent directors (including shadow directors) of companies that have gone into insolvent liquidation[37] from being directors, or promoting or managing or being involved in a company or an unincorporated business, that uses the same or substantially the same registered or trading name as that used by the insolvent company during the 12 months preceding insolvency. By the Insolvency Act, s 216 breach of this restriction is an offence punishable by fine or imprisonment or both.[38] Section 216(1) states that the section applies where a company

---

[33] 2006 Act, s 1295, Sch 16; 2006 Act Commencement Order No 1, Art 4(2)(c).

[34] 2006 Act, Part 40 contains provisions for disqualifying a person who is subject to a foreign disqualification order, but no regulations have been made bringing this Part into effect (see Chs 31 and 36 below).

[35] As amended by SBEE Act 2015, ss 104, 105 with effect from 1 October 2015.

[36] See Ch 33, Section D below for further discussion of these provisions.

[37] The restrictions apply to directors and shadow directors who held office at any time during the 12 months before the insolvent company went into liquidation, and apply for five years from that date, unless leave is obtained from the court (see Insolvency Rule 4.227) or certain prescribed circumstances exist (Insolvency Rules 4.228–4.230, and IR 2016, rr 22.1–22.7 after 6 April 2017).

[38] Insolvency Act, s 216(4).

(known as the liquidating company) has gone into insolvent liquidation. It does not apply to the company itself, but rather to any person who has been a director or shadow director of that company at any time in the period of 12 months ending with the day before it went into liquidation. Under s 216(3) the ex-director or shadow director must not, during the period of five years beginning with the day on which the company went into insolvent liquidation: (a) be a director of any other company that is known by a prohibited name; (b) in any way, whether directly or indirectly, be concerned or take part in the promotion, formation, or management of any such company; or (c) in any way, whether directly or indirectly, be concerned in the carrying on of a business under a prohibited name. A prohibited name is not only the name by which the company was actually known in the 12 months before its liquidation, but also a name which is so similar as to suggest an association with that company.[39] The test is not limited to an abstract comparison of the names themselves, but engages consideration of 'the context of all the circumstances in which they were actually used or likely to be used'.[40] In addition, by the Insolvency Act, s 217, the individual may be personally liable for the debts and liabilities incurred by the company during the period that he is involved in its management. Liability is strict and ignorance is no defence.[41] A person who is involved in the management of a company and acts on instructions given by someone he knows is in contravention of these restrictions may similarly incur personal liability.

6.18 The legislature has also imposed restrictions on bankrupts acting as directors. Under the CDDA, ss 11 and 13, it is a criminal offence for an undischarged bankrupt to act as a director or to participate in or be concerned in the management of a company, whether directly or indirectly, except by leave of the court that made the bankruptcy order.[42] The offence of acting as a company director while bankrupt or subject to a bankruptcy restrictions order is an offence of strict liability (see Chapter 35, Section J).[43] The court may not give leave unless notice of the intention to apply is served on the official receiver in bankruptcy. It is his duty, if he is of the opinion that it is contrary to the public interest that the application should be granted, to attend the hearing of the application and oppose it.[44] 'Company', for the purposes of the section, includes an unregistered company and a company incorporated outside Great Britain which has an established place of business within Great Britain.[45] A defaulting director is liable to imprisonment or a fine, or both.[46]

6.19 In addition, under the Insolvency Act, s 281A and Schedule 4A restrictions may be imposed on individuals beyond the period of bankruptcy by bankruptcy restriction orders or undertakings operating for periods from two to 15 years. These are similar to director

---

[39] Insolvency Act, s 216(2).

[40] Per Mummery LJ in *Ricketts v Ad Valorem Factors Ltd* [2004] 1 All ER 894, CA at para 22; *Revenue & Customs Commissioners v Walsh* [2006] BCC 431, CA.

[41] *Thorne v Silverleaf* [1994] 2 BCLC 1637, CA; *Ricketts v Ad Valorem Factors Ltd* [2004] 1 All ER 894, CA; *Archer Structures v Griffiths Ltd* [2004] 1 BCLC 201; *Revenue & Customs Commissioners v Walsh* [2006] BCC 431, CA; *ESS Production Ltd v Sully* [2005] 2 BCLC 547, CA; *Revenue & Customs Commissioners v Benton-Diggins* [2006] 2 BCLC 255; *First Independent Factors Ltd v Churchill* [2007] 1 BCLC 293, CA.

[42] CDDA, s 11(1). Courts are unlikely to give leave: *Re McQuillan* (1988) 5 BCC 137; *Re Altim Pty Ltd* [1968] 2 NSWR 762; *Re Kingsgate Rare Metals Pty Ltd* [1940] QWN 42.

[43] *R v Doring* (2002) Crim LR 817.

[44] CDDA, s 11(3).

[45] CDDA, s 22.

[46] CDDA, ss 11(1) and 13.

disqualification orders and undertakings under the CDDA. It is an offence for a person subject to such restrictions or undertakings to act as a director or, directly or indirectly, to take part in or be concerned in the promotion, formation, or management of a company, without the leave of the court which adjudged the bankrupt.[47]

Finally, if an administration order (under which an individual's estate is administered by a court under the County Courts Act 1984, Part VI) is revoked because the individual has failed to make a payment required by the order, the court may order that CDDA, s 12 is to apply to that individual for a period not exceeding one year.[48] The individual is then prohibited from acting as a director of, or directly or indirectly taking part or being concerned in the management of, a company without leave of the court which ordered CDDA, s 12 to apply. **6.20**

In addition to these legislative provisions, a company's own articles usually provide that the office of director will be vacated automatically in certain events, such as the director becoming bankrupt or making arrangements with creditors. Model Article (pcls) 18 and Model Article (plc) 22, both provide that a person ceases to be a director of the company as soon as '(b) a bankruptcy order is made against that person; (c) a composition is made with that person's creditors generally in satisfaction of that person's debts'. Similarly the 1985 Act, Table A, reg 81 provided for the office of director to be vacated if '(b) he becomes bankrupt or makes any arrangement or composition with his creditors generally'. Articles in the above form do not prevent directors from holding office merely because they are in fact unable to pay their debts.[49] Articles may go further, and provide that bankrupts may not be appointed as directors, and that any purported appointments are void. **6.21**

Some commentators suggest that where a bankrupt is disqualified from *acting* as a director, but is not expressly disqualified from being appointed or holding office, then the bankrupt might continue to hold office, so preventing the appointment of new directors to fill the vacancy.[50] This is, however, inconsistent with the modern understanding of a director's continuing duties and obligations whilst in office. A director could not remain in office on the basis that he could and would do nothing at all, without being permanently in breach of all his duties as director. The assumption of duty which goes with the office must be associated with a power to act. Since a bankrupt lacks such power, he cannot properly serve in the office of director. **6.22**

Share qualification

It used to be common for a company's articles to require its directors to hold a certain number of shares in the company. The 1985 Act, s 291[51] forced directors who failed to **6.23**

---

[47] CDDA, ss 11 and 13, as amended by SBEE Act, s 113 with effect from 1 October 2015; Insolvency Act, Sch 4A, para 8.

[48] Insolvency Act, s 429(2)(b). No day has been appointed for this provision to be replaced by a new s 429(2) (Tribunals, Courts and Enforcement Act 2007, s 106(2), Sch 16, para 3(1) and (2)) but, in any event, although the new s 429(2A) specifies the grounds on which an administration order under the County Courts Act 1984, Part VI may be revoked, it retains the existing power to make a disqualification order at the time of revocation for a period not exceeding one year.

[49] Old cases are unlikely to have any continuing relevance: *London & Counties Assets Co v Brighton Grand Concert Hall* [1915] 2 KB 493, CA; *James v Rockwood Colliery Co* (1912) 106 LT 128; *Sissons & Co v Sissons* (1910) 54 SJ 802.

[50] They refer to *Dawson v African Consolidated Land and Trading Co* [1898] 1 Ch 6, CA; *Re Northwestern Autoservices Ltd* [1980] 2 NZLR 302, CA (NZ).

[51] 1985 Act, s 291 required a director who was subject to qualification shares provisions to obtain his qualification shares within two months after his appointment, or such shorter time as may be fixed by the company's

comply with this requirement to vacate their office and made them liable to a fine. But share qualifications are now much less common, and the 2006 Act repealed these provisions as obsolete.[52] Share qualifications are not mentioned in the 1985 Act, Table A, or the Model Articles. The rationale behind the original requirement was to ensure that the director had a personal financial interest in the success of the company beyond his salary. However, although share qualifications are now rare as a formal obligation, in the context of public companies, shareholders may in practice expect directors (including non-executive directors) to hold shares as a demonstration of their commitment to the company and so as to align their financial interests with those of the shareholders. Shareholders will sometimes raise this issue at an AGM, or in correspondence with the company, with a view to embarrassing directors into making such investment. Many directors' compensation schemes include a Long Term Incentive Plan or Short Term Incentive Plan which will result in a holding of shares, and which may place restrictions upon disposal of those shares for a certain period. Alternatively, share options may be granted, or shadow options, both of which will depend for their value on share performance, although, in the case of share options, exercise is usually followed immediately by sale, in order to realize the difference between the share option strike price and the market value, with the result that the shares themselves are not retained for any significant period of time. In the case of shadow options, actual shares are not held at any time, although the rewards of the shadow option scheme will follow the performance of the shares.

6.24 If such qualifications exist, they must be imposed by the articles. The articles must then provide time limits for compliance with the qualification, and state the consequences should the qualification never be complied with, or cease to be complied with. Where the articles do impose such a requirement, the following principles have been established:

(1) Articles which state that no person shall be 'eligible' as a director or 'qualified to become' a director, unless he hold[53] so many shares, impose a condition precedent to appointment. As a result, any appointment of a person not *already* holding such shares will be invalid.[54] Ratification is not possible (unless the articles are altered).[55]

(2) If, on the other hand (as is more usual), the provision is that '[a] director's qualification shall be' so many shares, this does not impose a condition precedent.[56] The articles should then make it clear when the condition should be complied with, with

---

articles. If the director failed to obtain the requisite number of shares within the prescribed time period he would cease to hold office automatically. If he continued to act whist being disqualified under s 291, he would be liable to a fine.

[52] 2006 Act, s 1295 and Sch 16; 2006 Act Commencement Order No 8.

[53] To 'hold' means to be registered as holder: *Spencer v Kennedy* [1926] 1 Ch 125. In *Pulbrook v Richmond Consolidated Mining Co* (1878) 9 Ch D 610 the articles required the person to hold the shares 'as registered member in his own right'. It was held that it was not necessary that he should also be the beneficial owner of the shares; cf *Venture Acceptance Corpn Ltd v Kirton* (1985) 9 ACLR 390, SC (NSW), affd on other grounds (1986) 10 ACLR 347, CA (NSW).

[54] *Barber's Case* (1877) 5 Ch D 963, CA; *Jenner's Case* (1877) 7 Ch D 132, CA.

[55] *Boschoek Proprietary Co v Fuke* [1906] 1 Ch 148.

[56] *Re Issue Co, Hutchinson's Case* [1895] 1 Ch 226, 234; *Brown's Case* (1873) 9 Ch App 102, 109 where Mellish LJ said 'according to the ordinary understanding of mankind it would be quite sufficient if a person acquired shares before he acted as a director'. But he must acquire them before acting: *Miller's Case* (1876) 3 Ch D 661, 665 (unless the articles otherwise provide).

words such as 'A director may act before acquiring his qualification, but shall acquire the same within two months' or some other limited time.[57]

(3) The articles may authorize a director to act before acquiring his qualification, but, if they do not, it is his duty to qualify before he acts as a director,[58] and, in any event, within a reasonable time after his appointment.[59]

(4) Even if the articles authorize a director to act before acquiring his qualification, he automatically loses his office and his power to act in office if, upon expiry of the deadline, he has still failed to acquire the qualification.[60] However, s 161 validates the acts of de facto directors notwithstanding any defect which may subsequently be discovered.[61] The provision is wide enough to cover an appointment vacated by reason of failure to qualify. Typically, the articles themselves will also provide that the acts of an unqualified director are valid until the defect is discovered.[62]

(5) If, after a director has acquired his qualification, the amount required to qualify is increased, and he fails to acquire the additional amount, he retains his office but is deemed to have contracted to acquire the necessary qualification within a reasonable time.[63]

Companies as directors

A company or other corporation may, as matters stand, be appointed as director.[64] A company proposing to accept such an appointment should ensure that it is not ultra vires the company's constitution. At least one director, however, must be a natural person.[65] From a future date to be appointed, all new directors will have to be natural persons.[66] Any non-natural persons, such as companies or other corporate bodies, who are already directors, will cease to be so 12 months later.[67] A natural person will remain eligible to act as a director, however, even if he or she does so as a corporation sole or otherwise by virtue of an office.[68]   **6.25**

Conflicting offices or professional roles

Very few express restrictions operate to prevent those occupying certain offices, or undertaking certain professional roles for the company, from being appointed as directors of that company. Of more concern for professionals is the possibility that, because of their professional activities, they may be deemed to be shadow directors of the company,[69] with all   **6.26**

---

[57] 1985 Act, s 291 made two months the maximum time for compliance although it allowed the articles to prescribe a shorter period.

[58] *Miller's Case* (1876) 3 Ch D 661, 665, per Sir George Jessel MR.

[59] *Re Issue Co, Hutchinson's Case* [1895] 1 Ch 226, 234; *Molineaux v London, Birmingham and Manchester Insurance Co* [1902] 2 KB 589, CA, where signing a prospectus issued to the public was held to be acting as a director.

[60] *Craven-Ellis v Canons Ltd* [1936] 2 KB 403, CA.

[61] *Essendon Land & Finance Assn Ltd v Kilgour* (1897) 24 VLR 136, 146, 147, SC (Vic); *Oliver v Elliott* (1960) 23 DLR (2d) 486, SC (Alta); *Re Northwestern Autoservices Ltd* [1980] 2 NZLR 302, CA (NZ).

[62] See 1985 Act, Table A, reg 92.

[63] *Molineaux v London, Birmingham, and Manchester Insurance Co* [1902] 2 KB 589.

[64] *Re Bulawayo Market and Offices Co Ltd* [1907] 2 Ch 58. *Revenue and Customs Comrs v Holland* [2010] 1 WLR 2793, SC, is a well-known illustration of an individual using the appointment of a corporate director to protect himself from liability. The government gave careful consideration to the question whether a company should be eligible to be appointed a director; see further Ch 3, para 3.02 above.

[65] 2006 Act, s 155.

[66] 2006 Act, s 156A, subject to exceptions to be made under s 156B; both introduced by SBEE Act 2015, s 87(4).

[67] 2006 Act, s 156C.

[68] 2006 Act, s 156A(2), which will replace s 155(2), to the same effect. Examples are given in para 6.02 above.

[69] A shadow director is any person in accordance with whose directions or instructions the directors of the company are accustomed to act, 2006 Act, s 251(1).

the potential liabilities that flow from that. However, a person will not be regarded as a shadow director by reason only that the directors act on advice given by him in a professional capacity.[70] This provision applies only to advice given in a professional capacity, so that the protection does not apply to commercial or other advice which may be given by a professional not acting in his professional capacity. This (limited) protection may, however, assist auditors, solicitors and, in particular circumstances, company doctors and venture capital providers from being deemed to be shadow directors. This issue is discussed in more detail in Chapter 3, Section C(3) above.

6.27 Directors may accept office with more than one company, but must in that event recognize that they owe exactly the same general and fiduciary duties to each company (including those imposed by the 2006 Act, ss 170–7). Some disapplication or relaxation of duties is permitted by the 2006 Act, s 175 and s 180(4). However, subject to that, any dual appointment raises a question of possible conflicts of interest and duty which must be borne in mind in every such case. In some cases, the conflict of interest may be irreconcilable which would place the director in an impossible position. In addition, employment contracts may restrict or prohibit the acceptance of outside directorships. Breaches of duty may result in liability to one or even both companies. They would not, however, affect the validity of the appointment.

6.28 Previously a sole director could not also be secretary of the company.[71] This restriction was abolished in the 2006 Companies Act (see Chapter 3, Section E above). Nevertheless, it remains the case that a provision requiring or authorizing a thing to be done by or to a director *and* the secretary is not satisfied by its being done by or to the *same person* acting both as director and as, or in place of, the secretary.[72]

6.29 An individual cannot act as both auditor and director. The 2006 Act, s 1214 restates the 1989 Act, s 27 and prescribes circumstances where a person must not act as a statutory auditor on grounds of lack of independence.[73] Indeed, an auditor cannot be an officer or employee (or a partner or employee of such an officer or employee) of the company or of any of its parent or subsidiary undertakings. For these purposes, and notwithstanding a company's articles, an auditor in his capacity as such is not regarded as an officer or employee of a company.[74]

6.30 Solicitors are not expressly prohibited from acting as directors, but a solicitor's first responsibility is to his client.[75] A solicitor who accepts an appointment as a company director must ensure that any possible conflict with other members of the board or with his employer or partners or other clients is clearly identified and understood by all concerned. If a conflict does arise, the solicitor must resolve it either by ceasing to act for the client or by resigning or declining office as director.[76]

---

[70] 2006 Act, s 251(2).
[71] 1985 Act, s 283.
[72] 2006 Act, s 280.
[73] 2006 Act, s 1214 came into force on 6 April 2008.
[74] 2006 Act, s 1214(5). Section 1173(1) defines 'officer' in the Companies Acts as including 'any director, manager or secretary', but s 1121(1) extends the definition of 'officer in default' to include not only those persons, but also 'any person who is to be treated as an officer of the company for the purposes of the provision in question' (which does, in particular cases, include for the purposes of liability a shadow director or a liquidator as an officer).
[75] Solicitors Regulation Authority Code of Conduct 2011, Principle 4.
[76] Solicitors Regulation Authority Code of Conduct 2011, Ch 3.

It is increasingly common for people with appropriate skills or experience to be appointed **6.31** on a short-term basis to rescue or turn around a company which is in difficulties.[77] Such directors are known as 'company doctors' or 'turnaround professionals'. Company doctors may be formally appointed as directors. However, they may also be appointed on a consultancy basis, without becoming directors, thereby avoiding the duties and liabilities of the directorship of what may be a failing company or allowing them to align themselves exclusively with the interests of a particular lender or shareholder,[78] provided they do not assume the position of a de facto or shadow director. A company doctor who does not wish to assume the obligations of a director must ensure that all decisions are made, ultimately, by the duly appointed directors, and should take care that his role is demonstrably advisory and not executive.[79]

Beneficed clergy of the Church of England have only recently become entitled to serve as **6.32** company directors. This follows repeal of the prohibition in the Pluralities Act 1838, s 29, by the Statute Law (Repeals) Act 2004.

(2) Additional requirements for listed companies

The UK Corporate Governance Code does not suggest (even on a 'comply or explain' **6.33** basis) that directors of listed companies ought to have particular qualifications. It simply states that 'The board and its committees should have the appropriate balance of skills, experience, independence and knowledge of the company to enable them to discharge their respective duties and responsibilities effectively.'[80] The UK Corporate Governance Code does, however, contain detailed provisions about the eligibility of those appointed as independent non-executive directors,[81] who are to make up at least half of the board (excluding the chairman) of FTSE 350 companies and to number not less than two on the board of smaller companies.[82] It doubts the propriety of a chief executive going on to be chairman of the company and states that the chairman should, on first appointment, satisfy the independence criteria.[83] It states that all directors are to be appointed on objective criteria and with due regard for the benefits of diversity on the board, including gender.[84]

D. The Appointment of Directors

(1) Private companies

Introduction

At the time the company is registered, the Companies Act requires delivery to the Registrar **6.34** of a statement of the company's proposed officers, and their consents to act.[85] More generally,

---

[77] Finch, 'Doctoring in the Shadows of Insolvency' [2005] JBL 690–708.
[78] Fennell and Dingly, 'Working with Companies in Financial Difficulties—Will You be Paid' (2006) 19(4) Insolvency Intelligence 49–53.
[79] *Re Tasbian Ltd (No 3)* [1992] BCLC 297, CA.
[80] B.1 Main Principle.
[81] B.1.1, considered in more detail in section D(2) below.
[82] B.1.2.
[83] A.3.1.
[84] B.2 Supporting Principles.
[85] 2006 Act, s 12, which came into force on 1 October 2009.

the Companies Act also requires particular details of all appointments to be registered and/or made available to the public.[86]

6.35 The Companies Act does not prescribe who is responsible for appointing the directors of the company. That is left to the articles. Even when the Secretary of State acts under s 156 against a company which does not have the required number of directors, or which does not have the required minimum of one director who is a natural person, it is the company itself which is directed to make the appointment, and, in default of appointment, the remedy is enforcement against the company, and/or officers of the company (including shadow directors) by fines.

6.36 Appointment of a person as a director of a company requires the proper agreement of the appointee before it takes effect.[87] Upon election, a director wishing to withdraw can only resign and create a casual vacancy which must be filled by a new process; he cannot make way for the runner-up in the election once he has been elected.[88]

6.37 A person who has not been properly appointed but who nevertheless acts as a director may be sued by a member in order to restrain him from continuing to act.[89] Likewise, if a director who has been properly appointed is wrongly prevented from acting, he or any member may bring an action to enforce his right to act,[90] but not if the remedy would be pointless, because the director could and would be lawfully removed from office anyway.[91] A director who is improperly appointed may be removed by mandatory injunction on the application of an interested third party so as to restore the board to its correct constitution.[92]

Persons entitled to appoint a director

6.38 Provision for the appointment of directors, other than upon the company's registration, is normally made in the company's articles. Model Article (pcls) 17 and Model Article (plc) 20 both provide simply that willing and qualified candidates may be appointed directors, either by ordinary resolution of the shareholders, or by decision of the directors. There are more detailed provisions in Table A, regs 73–80, but regs 73–5 and 80 do not apply to companies incorporated after 1 October 2007.[93] Table A, reg 76 requires advance notice to be given between 14 and 35 days before any general meeting of the company at which it is proposed to appoint a director who is not recommended by the existing directors, and reg 77 provides for this notice to be disseminated to those entitled to notice of the meeting. Table A, regs 73–5 and 80 provide for retirement by rotation (subject to any reappointment), and for retirement of all the original directors at the first AGM (also subject to any reappointment).

---

[86] See Section F, below.
[87] *Re British Empire Match Co Ltd* (1888) 59 LT 291.
[88] *Hedges v NSW Harness Racing Club Ltd* (1991) 5 ACSR 291, SC (NSW).
[89] *Kraus v Lloyd* [1965] VR 232, SC (Vic).
[90] *Pulbrook v Richmond Consolidated Mining Co* (1878) 9 Ch D 610; *Choudhury v Bhattar* [2009] 2 BCLC 108 at para 28.
[91] *Bentley-Stevens v Jones* [1974] 1 WLR 638; *Conway v Petronius Clothing Co Ltd* [1978] 1 WLR 72.
[92] *Royal Bank of Scotland v Hicks* [2010] EWHC 2568 (Ch). The injunction was granted on the application of a bank with a contractual interest in the composition of the board.
[93] Companies (Tables A to F) (Amendment) Regulations 2007 (SI 2007/2541).

If the articles give exclusive power to appoint directors to a specific person or group (such **6.39** as the board of directors, the vendor of a business,[94] or a major investor), then the general meeting has no power of appointment, although the general meeting does have the power to change the articles. If the articles make no provision, the inherent power to appoint directors lies with the general meeting by ordinary resolution.[95]

First directors

As noted above, the 2006 Act requires delivery to the Registrar at the time the company is **6.40** registered of particulars of the company's first director or directors, and their consents to act.[96] The persons so named are deemed to have been appointed directors on the company's incorporation.[97] The articles may provide that none of the first directors can continue in office beyond the first AGM[98] without being approved by the members.

Subsequent directors

It will eventually be necessary to make further appointments after the first directors have **6.41** been appointed, either to fill vacancies when a director vacates office for any reason, or to increase the size of the board. Depending upon the company's articles, these appointments may be made either by the directors or by the members. Special rules may apply to the appointment of alternate directors and nominee directors (as discussed in Chapter 3). These issues are discussed below.

Appointment by the directors

It is usual for the articles to empower the directors to appoint other directors, whether by **6.42** board resolution or decision.[99]

Even if there is only one director, he may exercise this power to increase the number of direc- **6.43** tors to the minimum required by statute or by the articles, or to constitute a quorum.[100] Sometimes directors are given power to fill vacancies which is exclusive, excluding, in particular, the usual power of appointment in the general meeting.[101] But the general meeting is always entitled to act to fill vacancies if the board cannot or will not act, even when an exclusive provision suggests otherwise.[102] Similarly, the general meeting has power to act if the directors are unable to appoint a managing director.[103]

The directors can only make appointments that are consistent with their powers. They must, **6.44** therefore, respect any procedural requirements set out in the articles: for example, requirements

---

[94] See eg *British Murac Syndicate Ltd v The Alperton Rubber Co* [1915] 2 Ch 186, and the court may enforce acceptance of the appointee by injunction unless the appointee is unsuitable on personal grounds.

[95] *Worcester Corsetry Ltd v Witting* [1936] Ch 640, CA.

[96] 2006 Act s 12.

[97] 2006 Act, s 16.

[98] The Model Articles (pcls), do not do this, but see Table A, reg 73 and Model Article (plc) 21(1), which retain this provision for public companies.

[99] See eg Table A, reg 79, Model Article (pcls) 17(1)(b) and Model Article (plc) 20(b).

[100] *Channel Collieries Trust Ltd v Dover St Margaret's and Martin Mill Light Railway Co* [1914] 2 Ch 506.

[101] *Blair Open Hearth Furnace Co v Reigart* (1913) 108 LT 665. Where power is given to the remaining directors to fill a casual vacancy, they may act by a majority: *Logan v Settlers Steamship Co* (1906) 26 NZLR 193, SC (NZ). Clear language is needed if the articles are to be construed so as to take away this inherent power: *Integrated Medical Technologies Ltd v Macel Nominees Pty Ltd* (1988) 13 ACLR 110, SC (NSW).

[102] *Barron v Potter* [1914] 1 Ch 895; *Isle of Wight Railway Co v Tahourdin* (1883) 25 Ch D 320.

[103] *Foster v Foster* [1916] 1 Ch 532.

that they give notice.[104] In addition, any appointee must, at the time of the appointment, meet the necessary qualifications for the role.[105]

6.45 In addition, the power to appoint must no doubt be exercised by the directors in a manner consistent with their general duties, including their fiduciary duties. Abuse of the power which causes unfair prejudice to any member of the company may justify a petition under s 994.[106]

Appointment by the members

6.46 The members have inherent power to appoint directors, unless the articles provide otherwise.[107] In fact, the articles usually give them this power explicitly.[108]

6.47 In exercising this power, the members must act in accordance with the terms of the power granted to them. They must comply with any general or specific provisions in the Act or the company's articles relating to the general conduct of meetings or to the conduct of meetings specifically for the election or re-election of directors. For example, if the members can only appoint persons recommended by the board, this recommendation must be given by a properly constituted board meeting. It will not be sufficient that a majority of the board are present at the general meeting and assent to the appointment then.[109] Members must also comply with any contractual or third party rights limiting their powers of appointment.[110]

6.48 The power of the majority to appoint directors must 'be exercised for the benefit of the company as a whole and not to secure some ulterior advantage'.[111] The general meeting must, therefore, act for proper purposes. In *Theseus Exploration NL v Mining and Associated Industries Ltd*,[112] the court issued an interim injunction to prevent members of the company electing certain persons as directors, because there was sufficient evidence that those persons intended to use the company's assets solely for the benefit of the majority shareholder.[113]

Appointment by a nominated third party

6.49 In rare cases, a company's articles may give a third party (not even a shareholder) the right to appoint one or more directors[114] or may authorize the delegation of the power of appointment to a third party.[115] It seems, however, that the right may not be enforced by specific performance.[116] Moreover, the articles bind the company and the shareholders between themselves and do not constitute a covenant with the named third party.[117] They do not,

---

[104] *Catesby v Burnet* [1916] 2 Ch 325. The relevant articles need to be interpreted carefully.

[105] *Jenner's Case* (1877) 7 Ch D 132, CA; *Spencer v Kennedy* [1926] 1 Ch 125 (both on share qualifications).

[106] *Re Malaga Investments* (1987) 3 BCC 569.

[107] *Munster v Cammell Co* (1882) 21 Ch D 183; *Isle of Wight Railway Co v Tahourdin* (1883) 25 Ch D 320, 333, 335, CA; *Barron v Potter* [1914] 1 Ch 895; *Worcester Corsetry v Witting* [1936] Ch 640, CA.

[108] See eg Model Article (pcls) 17(1)(a), Model Article (plc) 20(a) and Table A, reg 78.

[109] *Barber's Case* (1877) 5 Ch D 963, CA.

[110] *Royal Bank of Scotland v Hicks* [2010] EWHC 2568 (Ch).

[111] *Re HR Harmer Ltd* [1959] 1 WLR 62, 82.

[112] [1973] QdR 81.

[113] The case was considered more recently in *Remrose Pty Ltd v Allsilver Holdings Pty Ltd*, 2005 WASC 251 and *Minecom Australia Pty Ltd v Mine Radio Systems Inc*, 1999 TASC 116.

[114] *Woodlands Ltd v Logan* [1948] NZLR 230, SC (NZ). Such a power, even if conferred on a named shareholder, is not constrained by any fiduciary or similar obligation and may be exercised in the shareholder's own interests: *Santos Ltd v Pettingell* (1979) 4 ACLR 110, SC (NSW).

[115] *British Murac Syndicate v Alperton Rubber Co* [1915] 2 Ch 186.

[116] *Plantations Trusts v Bila (Sumatra) Rubber Lands* (1916) 85 LJ Ch 801. See, however, *Royal Bank of Scotland v Hicks* [2010] EWHC 2568 (Ch) in which a mandatory injunction was granted to enforce the rights of a third party in relation to the composition of the board.

[117] 2006 Act, s 33(1).

therefore, confer rights on third parties which are directly enforceable against the company. This is confirmed by the Contracts (Rights of Third Parties) Act 1999, s 6(2), which provides that 'Section 1 [which states the general principle of enforcement of third party rights] confers no rights on a third party in the case of any contract binding on a company and its members under section 14 of the Companies Act 1985.' If the relevant third party is to be sure that his right to appoint or remove a director is to be respected, he should seek a direct contractual undertaking from the shareholders in the company, confirming that they will act on his instructions. Finally it should be noted that, even if the agreement as to appointment is honoured, the shareholders have a statutory right to remove a director by ordinary resolution under the 2006 Act, s 168, notwithstanding any provision of the company's articles or any agreement between the company and the director.

A shareholder who is not an executive director and who has a significant investment in a **6.50** private company, usually ensures that he has the right to appoint one or more directors. This is typically done by dividing the company's shares into different classes, and amending the articles to provide that the different classes may appoint and remove a specific number of directors. This creates class rights, which must be operated in accordance with s 334, and which can be altered only with the written consent of at least 75 per cent of the shareholders of that class by nominal value, or by a special resolution at a separate general meeting of the shareholders of that class, unless, which is unusual, the articles otherwise provide.[118] The shareholder's power to appoint a director could be protected by a provision for entrenchment in the company's articles.[119]

Formerly, when sole traders incorporated, the sole trader and vendor of the business to the **6.51** company was typically appointed a director by the articles. He frequently had conferred upon him all the powers of a board of directors, with a right from time to time to appoint and remove other directors, and with a power to appoint a successor during his life, or by his will, or for his legal personal representatives to make such appointment after his death. Such powers appear to be effective as grants or delegations of the power to appoint new directors (rather than as powers to assign office).[120] Modern sole-trader businesses which incorporate, however, are more likely simply to adopt Table A or the Model Articles and to exercise control through the shares. As control over the shares changes (for example, upon sale of the business), so would control over the board, and this would likely be required by any purchaser of the shares, who would not ordinarily expect an entrenched power over the board to exist independently.

When the shareholders alone have the right to appoint, then the directors cannot by agree- **6.52** ment with a stranger give the latter a power to appoint a director.[121]

Nominee directors: appointment

The Companies Act does not provide specifically for nominee directors,[122] and nor **6.53** do the various Model Articles. Nevertheless, it is common for large shareholders to

---

[118] 2006 Act, s 630.

[119] 2006 Act, s 22.

[120] In any event, 2006 Act repealed, with effect from 1 October 2009, 1985 Act, s 308, which rendered the assignment of the office of director as such to another person of no effect unless and until approved by a special resolution of the company.

[121] *James v Eve* (1873) LR 6 HL 335.

[122] There is no statutory definition of the term 'nominee director'. Nor is there recognition of a nominee director as distinct from any other director for the purposes of the Companies Act, Part 10.

have the right, under the articles, to appoint one or more directors to the board.[123] A nominee director may be either executive or non-executive. Although he reports to his appointor as to the activities of the company, he should not identify the interests of his appointor with those of the company.[124] He may take the interests of his nominator into account, but his decisions as director must be in what he genuinely considers to be the best interests of the company.[125] Every director owes his fiduciary duties to the company and, in the absence of a specific disapplication or relaxation of those duties, they will override any duties the director may owe to the appointing shareholder.

Alternate directors: appointment

6.54 There are no provisions in the Companies Act relating to alternate directors, nor in the draft model articles for private companies.[126] Nevertheless, a private company's articles may include provisions permitting a director to appoint an alternate; ie a person who is typically authorized to attend meetings in place of the appointing director, and who may also be generally authorized to act in place of the appointing director. Companies which have adopted Table A will have the benefit of such a provision (regs 65–9), but companies that adopt the Model Articles (pcls) will not.

Retirement by rotation

6.55 Articles of a private company may provide for a scheme of retirement by rotation, although the Model Articles (pcls) do not.[127] Table A, regs 73–80 formerly made provision for automatic retirement by rotation (subject to reappointment) but, for companies incorporated after 1 October 2007, regs 73–5 and 80 are deleted, and references to rotation are excised from regs 76–9.[128]

(2) Additional rules for public companies

Introduction

6.56 All of the powers and rules already described in relation to private companies also apply to public companies. Model Article (plc) 20 (methods of appointing directors) is drafted in the same terms as Model Article (pcls) 17(1).

6.57 The two principal differences in the regime applied to the appointment of directors of public companies are in respect of rotation and the appointment of alternates. For those public companies which are also listed companies, the UK Corporate Governance Code imposes further requirements.[129] The goal is to ensure, as far as possible, that the process is fair and transparent, and provides for appropriate renewal of talent and expertise, and that the boards of listed companies are sufficiently independent and well qualified for the task of managing the company.

---

[123] Nominees are also discussed in Ch 3, Section C(5) above.

[124] *Scottish Co-Operative Wholesale Society Limited v Meyer* [1959] AC 324, HL.

[125] *Re Neath Rugby Ltd* [2009] EWCA Civ 291, [2009] 2 BCLC 427.

[126] For public companies, and the provisions of Model Articles 25–7 in relation to alternate directors, see below.

[127] But contrast Model Article (plc) 21 for public companies.

[128] Companies (Tables A to F) (Amendment) Regulations 2007 (SI 2007/2541).

[129] See paras 6.67–6.80 below.

Appointment by directors

As in the case of private companies, the articles usually give power to the directors of a public **6.58** company to appoint additional directors,[130] typically exercisable by board decision or resolution. Any express limitations must be heeded. For example, the appointment may terminate automatically unless the appointee is reappointed by the members at the next annual meeting,[131] or appointments may be limited from the outset in that they can be made only in specified circumstances.[132]

Appointment by the members

As with private companies, the members have inherent power to appoint directors, but are **6.59** usually given such power explicitly in the articles.[133] In exercising this power, the members must comply with any general or specific provisions in the Act or the company's articles relating to the general conduct of meetings or to the conduct of meetings specifically for the election or re-election of directors.

Section 160 has already been considered above. It provides that a public company in general **6.60** meeting may not consider a single motion for the appointment of two or more directors unless it has first been agreed by the meeting, without any vote being cast against the proposal, that a single resolution is acceptable. In the absence of such unanimous agreement, a separate resolution must be proposed for the appointment of each candidate. Any resolution moved in contravention of the requirement is void, whether or not any objection was raised at the time. This statutory rule overrides any contrary provisions in the company's constitution.[134] Section 160 applies even if the resolution is for approving an appointment already made, or nominates a person for appointment, rather than making the appointment directly (s 160(3)). There is no corresponding ban on removing a number of directors by a single resolution.[135]

Although a resolution in contravention of s 160 is void, whether or not it was objected to at **6.61** the time, it may still have some result. First, s 161(2) provides that the acts of a director shall be valid notwithstanding any defect afterwards discovered in his appointment, specifically including defects arising by virtue of s 160 (void resolution to appoint). Secondly, s 160(2) specifically disapplies the application of any provision in the articles for the automatic reappointment of retiring directors in default of another appointment. Thus, if A and B retire under the articles, and a single resolution purports to pass for the election of C and D in their place, that resolution is void under the provisions of s 160, but the result will *not* be that A and B are automatically re-elected even if there is an article providing that, in default of an election to the vacated offices, the retiring directors shall be deemed to have been re-elected.[136] Finally, s 160(4) specifically provides that nothing in the section is to apply to a resolution altering the articles, so it would not apply to a special resolution to introduce

---

[130] See eg Model Article (plc) 20(b); and Table A, reg 79.

[131] Model Article 21(2).

[132] See eg Table A, reg 79 limits appointments to those necessary to fill a vacancy or as an additional director. Model Article (plc) 20(b) contains no such limitation.

[133] Model Article (plc) 20(a); and Table A, reg 78.

[134] The requirements of the predecessor of s 160 (1985 Act, s 292) were considered in *PNC Telecom plc v Thomas* [2004] 1 BCLC 88.

[135] *NRMA Ltd v Scandrett* (2002) 43 ACSR 401, SC (NSW).

[136] See eg Table A, reg 73; Model Article (plc) 21 is more restrictive.

an article providing that both X and Y should be directors of the company, even when the proposal is made in a single resolution. In this case, s 160 does not make the resolution void at all because it does not apply.

Retirement by rotation

6.62 In the case of public companies only, Model Article (plc) 21 provides for the retirement of directors by rotation. All directors must retire from office at the first AGM unless specifically reappointed (Model Article (plc) 21(1)). All directors appointed by the directors since the last AGM must retire from office unless specifically reappointed (Model Article (plc) 21(2) (a)). All directors not appointed at one of the preceding two AGMs must retire from office unless specifically reappointed (Model Article (plc) 21(2)(b)). This effectively requires directors to offer themselves for reappointment at least every three years. However, it applies to each individually, rather than providing for a bloc of one-third of directors to retire at every AGM as was the case with Table A, regs 73–5 (now deleted for companies incorporated after 1 October 2007 adopting Table A).

6.63 Regulation 73 of Table A, where applicable, provides that at every AGM subsequent to the first one, one-third of directors subject to retirement by rotation (or if their number is not three or a multiple of three the number nearest one-third) shall retire from office and may put themselves up for re-election. In order to determine which of the directors are to retire at any particular AGM from amongst those eligible, companies are directed by reg 74 to select for retirement those directors who have been in office longest since their last appointment or reappointment. If more than the required number of directors were last appointed or reappointed at the same time, those to retire are determined by lot, unless they agree amongst themselves who is to stand for re-election in that year.[137]

6.64 Where the articles provide for such a scheme of retirement by rotation, they typically also provide that a retiring director who is willing to act may be reappointed.[138] They may go further and provide that such a director will be deemed to have been reappointed if, at the general meeting at which the retirement takes effect, the company does not appoint someone else to fill the vacancy, unless the retiring director's reappointment was put to the meeting and rejected, or the meeting expressly resolves not to fill the vacancy.[139]

Alternate directors

6.65 Model Articles (plc) 25–7 provide for public companies to have alternate directors. Any director may appoint an alternate to act in his absence (Model Article (plc) 25) and the appointment may last (unless revoked) as long as, although no longer than, his own appointment (Model Article (plc) 27). The alternate director has the same rights, and owes the same responsibilities, as his appointor and is deemed to be a director for all purposes and not the agent of or for his appointor (Model Article (plc) 26). The appointment or removal of an alternate must be notified to the company in writing signed by the appointor, or in any other manner approved by the directors (Model Article (plc) 25). The notice must identify the

---

[137] Table A, reg 74.

[138] Model Article (plc) 21; see also Table A, reg 80 (abolished for companies incorporated after 1 October 2007).

[139] Model Articles (plc) do not, but see Table A, reg 75 (abolished for companies incorporated after 1 October 2007).

alternate and contain his signed willingness to act (Model Article (plc) 25). Alternates are considered above at Chapter 3, paragraphs 3.39–3.41.

Table A, regs 65–9 also provide for the appointment of alternate directors[140] to substantially **6.66** the same effect. The first principal difference between the provisions of Table A and the corresponding provisions of Model Articles (plc) is that whereas Table A, reg 66 provides that the role of the alternate extends to all his appointor's functions, Model Article (plc) 25(1) stipulates that his appointment is 'in relation to the taking of decisions by the directors'. Model Article (plc) 26(1) also gives the alternate the appointor's rights 'in relation to any directors' meeting or directors' written resolution'. However, these provisions must be read with Model Article (plc) 26(2)(a), which provides that (except as the articles specify otherwise), alternate directors 'are deemed for all purposes to be directors'. The second principal difference is that whereas Table A, reg 66, provides that an alternate director is not entitled to any remuneration, Model Article (plc) 26(4) provides that the alternate's appointor may in writing direct the company to pay part of his own remuneration to the alternate.

(3) Additional requirements for listed companies

The UK Corporate Governance Code

The UK Corporate Governance Code[141] contains a number of requirements (on a 'comply or **6.67** explain' basis) relating to the appointment of directors of listed companies.

The appointment procedure must be 'formal, vigorous and transparent'.[142] Appointments **6.68** are to be on merit and against objective criteria.[143] If a chairman or non-executive director is appointed without using an external search consultancy or open advertising, an explanation should be included in the annual report.[144] The board should have plans in place for orderly succession and for progressive refreshing of the board.[145]

The lead in the process for board appointments should be taken by a nomination commit- **6.69** tee making recommendations to the board.[146] The nomination committee should contain a majority of independent, non-executive directors.[147] The nomination committee is to be chaired by the chairman of the board (but not when dealing with the chairman's successor) or an independent non-executive director.[148] The annual report should describe the work of the nomination committee and set out the board appointment process.[149]

The nomination committee should prepare a description of the role and capabilities **6.70** required.[150] For the appointment of a chairman, the nomination committee should prepare a job specification, including the time commitment expected.[151] The terms and conditions

---

[140] No change is made to these by any of the Companies (Tables A to F) (Amendment) Regulations 2007 (SI 2007/2541).
[141] See n 12 above.
[142] B.2 Main Principle.
[143] B.2 Supporting Principles.
[144] B.2.4.
[145] B.2 Supporting Principles. See also B.7.1.
[146] B.2.1.
[147] B.2.1.
[148] B.2.1.
[149] B.2.4.
[150] B.2.2.
[151] B.3.1.

of appointment of non-executive directors should be made available for inspection by any person at the registered office and also at the AGM.[152] They should include the time commitment expected.[153]

6.71 There should be due regard for 'the benefits of diversity' on the board 'including gender'.[154] Other forms of diversity are not explicitly referred to in the UK Corporate Governance Code, but any appointment will be unlawful if it discriminates against candidates on the grounds of age, disability, gender reassignment, marriage and civil partnership, pregnancy and maternity, race, religion or belief, or sexual orientation, as well as gender.[155]

6.72 The roles of chairman and chief executive should not be combined.[156] The division of responsibilities between the chairman and the chief executive should be agreed by the board and set out in writing.[157] The chief executive should not go on to be chairman but, if he does, the reasons for this should be provided to shareholders and also set out in the annual report.[158]

6.73 The board should appoint one of the independent non-executive directors to be the senior independent director. His role is to provide a sounding board for the chairman, to act as intermediary for the other directors, and to be available to shareholders who have concerns which have not been resolved or cannot appropriately be resolved through the normal channels of chairman, chief executive, or other executive directors.[159]

6.74 The board should include a combination of executive and independent non-executive directors such that no individual or small group of individuals can dominate the board's decision-making.[160]

6.75 Independent non-executive directors should be identified in the annual report by the board.[161] An independent director will be independent 'in character and judgement' and the board must also consider relationships or circumstances which are likely to or could appear to affect the director's judgment.[162] Specific examples, calling for explanation should the director nevertheless be identified as independent, include: employment by the company or group within the last five years; a material business relationship with the company within the last three years (either directly, or as a partner, shareholder, director, or other senior employee of a body that has had such a relationship); remuneration (past or present) apart from a director's fee; participation in the company's share option or performance-related pay scheme; membership of the company's pension scheme; close family ties with any of the company's directors, senior employees, or advisers; significant links with other directors through involvement in other companies or bodies; representation of a significant shareholder; or more than nine years' service on the board since first election.[163]

---

152 B.3.2.
153 B.3.2.
154 B.2 Supporting Principles.
155 Equality Act 2010, s 4.
156 A.2.1.
157 A.2.1.
158 A.3.1.
159 A.4.1.
160 B.1 Supporting Principles.
161 B.1.1.
162 B.1.1.
163 B.1.1.

Non-executive directors determined by the board to be independent should make up at **6.76** least half the board (excluding the chairman) of FTSE 350 companies.[164] Smaller companies should have at least two independent non-executive directors.[165]

All directors of FTSE 350 companies should be subject to annual election by shareholders.[166] **6.77** All other directors should be subject to election by shareholders at the first AGM after their appointment, and to re-election at least every three years.[167] Non-executive directors who have served longer than nine years should be subject to annual re-election[168] and their independence will, after nine years service, be in question.[169]

Shareholders should be given biographical and other information about directors up for **6.78** election or re-election so that they can make an informed decision.[170] In the case of the election of a non-executive director, shareholders should have a board paper giving reasons for the election of that individual,[171] and re-election should be supported by confirmation from the chairman of a formal and satisfactory performance evaluation.[172]

Notice or contract periods should be set at one year or less and, if longer periods are neces- **6.79** sary to recruit new directors from outside, they should reduce to one year or less after the initial period.[173] This may be achieved by limiting the appointment to a fixed term (which will shorten and expire by effluxion of time) or to an initial minimum term combined with a notice period of not more than one year expiring at or after expiry of the initial minimum term.[174]

All directors should receive induction on joining the board[175] which is 'full, formal and tai- **6.80** lored'.[176] The directors must have appropriate knowledge of the company and access to its operations and staff.[177] New directors should also meet major shareholders.[178]

The Listing Rules
The Listing Rules, LR 9.8.6R(5) and (6), require a listed company to include two governance- **6.81** related statements in its annual report and accounts. The first must indicate how the company has applied the *Main Principles* set out in the UK Corporate Governance Code, in a manner that would enable shareholders to evaluate how the principles have been applied.

---

[164] B.1.2.
[165] B.1.2.
[166] B.7.1.
[167] B.7.1.
[168] B.7.1.
[169] B.1.1 final bullet point.
[170] B.7.1.
[171] B.7.2.
[172] B.7.2.
[173] D.1.5.
[174] Fixed-Term Employees (Prevention of Less Favourable Treatment) Regulations 2002 (SI 2002/2034), reg 8, will in certain cases of successive contracts leading to more than four years' service result in a permanent contract, which makes provision for a notice period in addition to the fixed term particularly important in such cases.
[175] B.4 Main Principle.
[176] B.4.1. The chairman should continue to review and agree training and development needs with each director after appointment: B.4.2.
[177] B.4 Supporting Principles.
[178] B.4.1.

The second is a statement as to whether the company has complied with all relevant provisions set out in the UK Corporate Governance Code throughout the accounting period being reported upon, or a statement it has not so complied, together with details of, and reasons for, any non-compliance.

E. Validity of Acts and Defective Appointments

6.82 Section 161 provides for the validity of acts of directors. In particular, the acts of a person acting as a director are valid notwithstanding that it is afterwards discovered (a) that there was a defect in his appointment; or (b) that he was disqualified from holding office; or (c) that he had ceased to hold office; or (d) that he was not entitled to vote on the matter in question. Section 161(2) applies these provisions even if the resolution for his appointment is void under s 160 (appointment of directors of public company to be voted on individually).[179]

6.83 Despite all the preceding comment on the appropriate process for the appointment of directors and the eligibility rules for such appointments, the acts undertaken by those acting as directors are generally valid. It follows that third parties dealing with the company are generally protected, and the company's remedy is to take action, if appropriate, against those responsible for the appointments and those acting improperly as directors.

6.84 Section 161 replaces the more limited provision in the 1985 Act, s 285, which was typically supplemented in the articles by wider terms such as those now appearing in s 161.[180] Third parties could only rely on the 1985 Act, s 285 if they had acted in good faith.[181] The material words in the new section are identical, so presumably the same limitation will apply.

6.85 Where a director has been properly appointed, he may obtain an injunction to restrain the company or other directors from preventing him acting as a director.[182] A director's shareholding and the possibility that he may be paid directors' fees may give him a sufficient interest for the court to have jurisdiction.[183] But whether the court exercises its discretion to grant the injunction is another matter. The wishes of the members of the company, expressed in general meeting, are highly material in this respect.[184] and it may also be relevant that he was appointed pursuant to some class right, but, in general, the court will not intervene when those able to remove the director wish to do so, since there is no point in merely making them go through the motions.[185]

6.86 Where it is not clear whether a director is entitled to act (ie whether he was properly appointed, or whether he remains a director), then, rather than litigating that preliminary issue, it seems preferable for the directors to convene an extraordinary general meeting to

---

[179] It has been said in a different context that 'the effect of an appointment for an improper purpose is that the exercise of the power is void, not voidable'—*Roadchef (Employee Benefits Trustees) Ltd v Hill* [2014] EWHC (Ch) per Proudman J at para 131), but s 161(2) avoids any difficulty.

[180] See eg Table A, reg 92, the provisions of which are codified by s 161.

[181] *Channel Collieries Trust Ltd v Dover, St Margaret's and Martin Mill Light Rly Co* [1914] 2 Ch 506, CA; *British Asbestos Co Ltd v Boyd* [1903] 2 Ch 439.

[182] *Pulbrook v Richmond Consolidated Mining Co* (1878) 9 Ch D 610; *Munster v Cammell Co* (1882) 21 Ch D 183; *Choudhury v Bhattar* [2009] 2 BCLC 108 at para 28.

[183] *Hayes v Bristol Plant Hire Ltd* [1957] 1 WLR 499.

[184] *Harben v Phillips* (1883) 23 Ch D 14; *Bainbridge v Smith* (1889) 41 Ch D 462.

[185] *Bentley-Stevens v Jones* [1974] 1 WLR 638.

consider a resolution to dismiss the director under s 168, even if the resolution for dismissal is expressed to be conditional on the question of whether the person is indeed presently a director.[186]

The purpose of s 161 is to protect third parties (both members[187] and outsiders) against a company relying on a person's lack of entitlement to act as a director in order to avoid obligations. The predecessor section, the 1985 Act, s 285, referred only to 'any defect that may afterwards be discovered in his appointment or qualification', and specifically mentioned void resolutions to appoint (as in the new sub-s (2)). That wording had been interpreted narrowly so as to apply only when there is a procedural defect in the appointment, not when there has been no appointment at all,[188] or where a director had vacated office but continued to act.[189] The new section is explicitly more expansive, and, for example, covers directors who have vacated office, and acts of under-age directors, notwithstanding that their appointment is void (by virtue of sub-s (1)(b)) or that they have been removed from office as a consequence of s 159 (by virtue of sub-s (1)(c)). Nevertheless, it would still seem that there must, at some stage, have been a purported appointment of the person to the role of director, and to that extent the words of Lord Simonds in *Morris v Kanssen*[190] remain apt: **6.87**

> There is, as it appears to me, a vital distinction between (a) an appointment in which there is a defect or, in other words, a defective appointment, and (b) no appointment at all. In the first case it is implied that some act is done which purports to be an appointment but is by reason of some defect inadequate for the purpose; in the second case, there is not a defect, there is no act at all. The section does not say that the acts of a person acting as director shall be valid notwithstanding that it is afterwards discovered that he was not appointed a director.

F. Publication of Appointment of Directors

(1) Register of directors, etc

Under the 2006 Act, the register of directors and secretaries becomes two separate registers, and only public companies are required to keep a register of secretaries.[191] The Secretary of State has power to amend by regulation the required registered particulars of directors.[192] The three significant changes from the 1985 Act, s 289, are: (i) the director's address need not be a residential address but must be a service address (see below on the rules about residential addresses); (ii) particulars of any other directorships held are no longer required to be registered; and (iii) there is no longer an exception from the requirement for registering details of 'former names' for married women's maiden names.   **6.88**

---

[186] *Browne v Panga Pty Ltd* (1995) 120 FLR 34; but contrast *Currie v Cowdenbeath Football Club Ltd* 1992 SLT 407, where Lord Penrose allowed the alleged directors an interim interdict (interim injunction) against the holding of the meeting, saying this usurped the court's jurisdiction over the dispute and that it was not possible to pass a contingent resolution under the predecessor of s 168.

[187] *Dawson v African Consolidated Land and Trading Co* [1898] 1 Ch 6.

[188] *Morris v Kanssen* [1946] AC 459, HL.

[189] *Morris v Kanssen* [1946] AC 459, HL; *Tyne Mutual Steamship Insurance Association v Brown* (1896) 74 LT 283.

[190] [1946] AC 459, 471.

[191] 2006 Act, ss 162 and 275.

[192] 2006 Act, s 166. The Secretary of State decided not to make regulations on commencement of ss 162–7: *Implementation of the Companies Act 2006, a Consultative Document*, Annex B (February 2007).

6.89   The reason for applying registration requirements to directors is that 'it is essential that the identities of those who control companies ... should have their record in the public domain'[193] and 'to prevent the easy evasion of the legislation by persons who control companies but who either do not wish to be appointed to the board or, more typically, cannot be appointed because they are undischarged bankrupts or the subject of disqualification orders'.[194]

6.90   To this end s 162 provides for the company to keep a register of directors, which is open to inspection by members without charge and by other persons on payment of the prescribed fee.[195] The location of the register is ordinarily the registered office (but it may be at alternative inspection location)[196] and must be notified to the Registrar. Failure to comply with the section is an offence, and the court may also enforce it by order compelling immediate inspection where there has been a refusal. An alternative regime gives private companies the right to opt out of keeping their own registers, substituting, instead, an obligation to keep the Registrar updated with the relevant information, so that it can be held centrally.[197] This option may in future also be extended to some or all public companies.[198]

6.91   In the case of individuals, under s 163, the register of directors must contain various particulars: name and any former name, a service address (which may be 'the company's registered office'), country or state (including part of the UK where applicable) of usual residence, nationality, business occupation (if any), and date of birth. Under s 163, it is no longer necessary to give particulars of the director's other directorships and a former name need be given only if it was one by which the individual was known for business purposes.[199] Even that does not have to be provided if it relates to names used before the age of 16 years, or to activities conducted more than 20 years ago, or (in the case of the holder of a British title such as a peerage) to names pre-dating acquisition of the title.[200] The exception in relation to a woman's name before marriage has been removed.

6.92   Section 164 provides for a similar list in the case of 'a body corporate, or a firm that is a legal person under the law by which it is registered' including, in every case, the corporate or firm name, the registered or principal office, the register in which entered (if applicable), including details of the state and of the registration number, and, except in the case of registration in an EEA state, the legal form of the company or firm and the law by which it is governed.

6.93   Section 165 provides for maintenance by the company of a separate register of individual directors' residential addresses which is not open for inspection, whether to shareholders or the public. The information in the register is subject to the new provisions of ss 240–6, which protect directors' residential addresses from disclosure (see below). This separate register is

---

[193]   HC Comm D 6/7/07, cols 515–18.
[194]   HL GC Day 2, Hansard, HL 678, col 170 (1 February 2006).
[195]   Companies (Fees for Inspection of Company Records) Regulations 2008 (SI 2008/3007).
[196]   Under the 2006 Act, s 1136, the Companies (Company Records) Regulations 2008 (SI 2008/3006), reg 3 provides that a company can specify a place situate in the part of the UK in which it is registered, which is the same place for all the relevant provisions and which has been notified to the Registrar, as an alternative inspection location.
[197]   2006 Act, ss 167A–E, introduced by SBEE Act 2015, s 94 and Sch 5, Pt 1, paras 5, 7 with effect from 30 June 2016.
[198]   2006 Act, s 167F.
[199]   2006 Act, s 163(3).
[200]   2006 Act, s 163(4).

necessary because directors' residential addresses no longer have to be included in the company's register of directors.[201] Section 165(4) makes it a criminal offence not to comply with this section, and liability extends to shadow directors.

(2) Filing requirements with the Registrar of Companies

Within a period of 14 days from the date on which a person becomes or ceases to be a direc- **6.94**
tor, or from the occurrence of any change in the particulars contained in its register of directors, or its register of directors' residential addresses, the company must give notice to the Registrar of Companies of the change and the date it occurred. Such notice must contain (in the case of the appointment of a new director) a statement of the particulars of the new director that are required to be included in the company's registers, as well as the consent of the new director to act in that capacity.[202]

The Registrar must notify newly-named directors that they have been named as directors of **6.95**
the company and 'include such information relating to the office and duties of a director…
as the Secretary of State may from time to time direct the registrar to include'.[203] The 2006 Act, s 1095 enables the Registrar to remove the name of a person who did not consent to being appointed a director.[204]

The company and its defaulting officers (including shadow directors) are liable to fines on **6.96**
conviction for any failure to comply with these provisions, and in the event of a refusal to allow inspection of the register, the court may order an immediate inspection.[205]

The court must have regard to the extent of a person's responsibility for the company's failure **6.97**
to comply with the duty to keep a register of directors and secretaries in accordance with these provisions in deciding whether that person's conduct as a director or shadow director of the company makes him unfit to be concerned in the management of a company.[206]

(3) Directors' residential addresses: protection from disclosure

The protection of directors' residential addresses from disclosure, despite the continuing **6.98**
requirement that they should be registered, is new in the 2006 Act. The reason for limiting disclosure of directors' residential addresses is simple. Directors have become increasingly concerned that public disclosure of their residential addresses endangers them and their families, in particular because of tactics used by campaigners and activists, for example, seeking to prevent the use of animals in biomedical research. In 2002, a limited system of confidentiality orders to protect directors who could demonstrate risk was introduced into the 1985 Act as ss 723B–723E, which remained in force until 1 October 2009.[207] Under the 1985 Act an individual had to apply to the Secretary of State for a confidentiality order protecting disclosure of his residential address on the ground that disclosure exposed him and persons living with him to a serious risk of violence or intimidation. By contrast, the

---

[201] 2006 Act, s 163(1)(b), requires only a service address.
[202] 2006 Act, s 167(2).
[203] 2006 Act, s 1079B, inserted with effect from 10 October 2015 by SBEEA 2015 s 101(1).
[204] 2006 Act, s 1095(4A)–(4D), inserted by SBEE Act, s 102 as from 6 April 2016.
[205] 2006 Act, s 162(6)–(8).
[206] CDDA, s 9 and Sch 1, para 4(c).
[207] 1985 Act, ss 723B–723E were introduced by the Criminal Justice and Police Act 2001. The provisions of 2006 Act, ss 240–6 replaced them on 1 October 2009.

2006 Act, ss 240–6, contains a complete system of confidentiality for all directors' residential addresses.[208] The confidential register satisfies the need, considered to be important, to give creditors, the police, and regulatory authorities some ability to locate company directors. There is no requirement for the register of directors' residential addresses to be open for inspection. Although any change in a company's register of directors' residential addresses must be reported to Companies House (unless it concerns a shadow director), the information is subject to the confidentiality requirements of ss 240–6.

6.99   The usual residential address of a director is 'protected information' within the meaning of s 240. It remains protected information after the director ceases to hold office.

6.100   There are specific restrictions on use by companies and by the Registrar of Companies, and also specific exceptions to these restrictions.

6.101   By s 241(1), a company must not use or disclose protected information about any of its directors except: (a) for communicating with the director concerned, (b) in order to comply with any requirement of the Companies Acts as to particulars to be sent to the Registrar, or (c) in accordance with s 244 (which provides for disclosure under court order). A company is not, however, prohibited from using or disclosing protected information if it has the consent of the director concerned.[209]

6.102   Companies House must withhold from public inspection all the information that has been supplied to it as protected information. This includes directors' residential addresses provided to the Registrar of Companies after the relevant provisions of the Act come into force. Section 242(2)(b) provides that the Registrar is not obliged to omit anything from the public register that was registered before Chapter 8 (containing ss 240–6) came into force on 1 October 2009. Previously registered information will remain subject to any limited confidentiality orders applicable to that information under the former confidentiality regime.

6.103   The Registrar of Companies may disclose this information only (a) as permitted by s 243 or (b) in accordance with a court order for disclosure under s 244. Section 243 allows the Registrar to use protected information for communicating with the director in question, and to disclose protected information to a public authority specified by regulations, or to a credit reference agency. Disclosure is subject to conditions and procedures set out in the Companies (Disclosure of Address) Regulations 2009.[210]

6.104   Section 244 sets out the circumstances in which a court order may be granted for disclosure of protected information. These are that (a) there is evidence that service of documents at a service address other than the director's usual residential address is not effective to bring them to the notice of the director, or (b) it is necessary or expedient for the information to be provided in connection with the enforcement of an order or decree of the court (and the court is otherwise satisfied that it is appropriate to make the order). An order for disclosure by the Registrar is to be made only if the company does not have the director's usual residential address, or has been dissolved. Application for the order may only be made by a person

---

[208] The bill originally included provisions to 'opt-in' to protection, but during the passage of the bill through Parliament this was changed to the 'opt-out' scheme for reasons explained by Lord Sainsbury (Hansard, HL Report Stage, cols 873–4 (9 May 2006)).

[209] 2006 Act, s 241(2).

[210] SI 2009/214; as amended by Companies (Disclosure of Address) (Amendment) Regulations 2010 (SI 2010/2156).

'appearing to the court to have a sufficient interest' but application by a liquidator, creditor, or member of the company is permitted expressly. Any order has to specify the persons to whom, and purposes for which, disclosure is authorized.

Section 245 establishes a procedure by which the Registrar of Companies can put a director's **6.105** residential address on the public record, provided that the director and every company of which he is a director are notified and account is taken of representations made. The power to invoke this procedure is given to Companies House when (a) communications sent by the Registrar to the director and requiring a response within a specified period remain unanswered, or (b) there is evidence that service of documents at a service address provided in place of the director's usual residential address is not effective to bring them to the notice of the director. The Registrar's notice of the proposal to the director and to every company of which he is a director must state the grounds on which it is proposed to put the director's usual residential address on the public record, and specify a period within which representations may be made before that is done. It must be sent to the director at his usual residential address, unless it appears to the Registrar that service at that address may be ineffective to bring it to the individual's notice, in which case it may be sent to any service address provided in place of that address.

Once the Registrar has decided to make this change, he must notify the director and the **6.106** company, and the company must change its own registers. Failure to do so constitutes an offence committed by the company and every officer.[211] For directors whose residential addresses are put on the public record in this way, the publicity cannot be avoided by registering a service address other than the residential address for a period of five years from the Registrar's decision.[212]

Section 242 sets out the extent of the Registrar's duty to guard against disclosure of protected **6.107** information. The Registrar must omit protected information from the material on the register available for inspection where it is contained in a document delivered to him in which such information is required to be stated, and, in the case of a document having more than one part, it is contained in a part of the document in which such information is required to be stated. But he is not obliged to check other documents or (as the case may be) other parts of the document to ensure the absence of protected information. He is also not obliged to omit from the material that is available for public inspection anything registered before ss 240–6 come into force.

(4) Additional publicity rules applying to listed companies

The Listing Rules require a listed company to notify its Regulated Information Service[213] of **6.108** any change in its board of directors. This is taken to include any important change in the role, functions, or responsibilities of the director (LR 9.6.11R(3)).

Whenever a new director is appointed, a listed company must notify its Regulated **6.109** Information Service of the director's name and whether the position is executive, non-executive, or chairman, and the nature of any specific function or responsibility of the position (LR 9.6.11R(1)). This notification is required as soon as possible, and in any event by

---

[211] 2006 Act, s 246(5)–(6).
[212] 2006 Act, s 246(7).
[213] Such as the London Stock Exchange's Regulatory News Service.

the end of the business day following the decision, or receipt of notice, about the change by the company.

6.110 Further information about a new director is required to be notified as soon as possible following the decision to appoint, and in any event within five business days of the decision, namely (LR 9.6.13R):

(1) details of all directorships held in any other publicly quoted company at any time in the previous five years, including whether the position is still held;

(2) any unspent convictions in relation to indictable offences;

(3) details of any receiverships, administrations, liquidations or other arrangements with creditors suffered by any company of which he was an executive director, or of any partnership in which he was a partner, at the time of or within the 12 months preceding such events;

(4) details of any public criticism of the director by statutory or regulatory (including professional) authorities; and

(5) whether he has ever been disqualified by a court from acting as a director or from acting in the management or conduct of the affairs of any company.

6.111 Notification is also required of any change in these details (including any new directorships in any other publicly quoted company) in relation to an existing director (LR 9.6.14R).

7

TERMINATION OF APPOINTMENT
OF DIRECTORS

Edward Brown

A. Termination of Appointment of Directors of Private Companies

(1) Introduction

It is an essential feature of the management of any company that directors' appointments are capable of termination, either voluntarily or upon the occurrence of some specified event, such as a resolution of the company. Termination provisions may be relied upon for a number of reasons: a director may be removed as part the process of accountability to company shareholders; a director may become incapacitated or otherwise unable to perform his duties; or from time to time a director may simply resign and move on or retire. This chapter considers the provisions of the Companies Act and company articles that govern termination, together with the rights and liabilities that arise in the event of termination.

7.01

(2) Vacation of office under the Companies Act

In some circumstances it will be necessary for a company to remove a director against his will, in particular because of unsatisfactory performance or behaviour. Under the provisions of the Companies Act, s 168,[1] a director[2] can be removed by an ordinary resolution of the shareholders at any time. Section 168 provides:

7.02

---

[1] 2006 Act, s 168(1) includes the phrase 'at a meeting' to make it clear that the written resolution procedure cannot be used to remove a director.

[2] Or more than one director or all of the company's directors simultaneously: *Taylor v McNamara* [1974] 1 NSWLR 164, SC (NSW); *Claremont Petroleum NL v Indosuez Nominees Pty Ltd* (1986) 10 ACLR 520, FC (Qld); *NRMA Ltd v Scandrett* (2002) 43 ACSR 401, SC (NSW). If the resolution takes effect from the election

(1) A company may by ordinary resolution at a meeting remove a director before the expiration of his period of office, notwithstanding anything in any agreement between it and him.

(2) Special notice is required of a resolution to remove a director under this section or to appoint somebody instead of a director so removed at the meeting at which he is removed.

(3) A vacancy created by the removal of a director under this section, if not filled at the meeting at which he is removed, may be filled as a casual vacancy.

(4) A person appointed director in place of a person removed under this section is treated, for the purpose of determining the time at which he or any other director is to retire, as if he had become director on the day on which the person in whose place he is appointed was last appointed a director.

(5) This section is not to be taken—

    (a) as depriving a person removed under it of compensation or damages payable to him in respect of the termination of his appointment as director or of any appointment terminating with that as director, or

    (b) as derogating from any power to remove a director that may exist apart from this section.

Section 168 is highly significant as part of the accountability of a company's directors to its owners. The power given to shareholders is unfettered[3] and may therefore be used for a number of aims. In particular, the power allows shareholders to remove directors who are performing poorly; but also to remove directors acting competently and within their powers, but in a way that may be contrary to the wishes of the shareholders. Further, the existence of the s 168 power has an influential effect upon the appointment of directors. There is little point in the directors' attempting to override the hostility of shareholders, as any appointment may subsequently be terminated by a s 168 resolution. In short, s 168 constitutes an effective remedy for preserving the interests of shareholders as against directors.

7.03 The power under the Companies Act to remove a director applies irrespective of any written agreement in the service contract.[4] As such, a resolution will override any notice period or other provision in the contract.[5] However, s 168(5)(a) preserves any rights that a director may have in the event of termination to compensation[6] under the service agreement or to damages for breach of contract.[7]

7.04 The statutory power under s 168 expressly preserves any other right that a company may have to dismiss a director, under common law or the articles. Further, even where a director, in his capacity as a member, may be entitled to petition for a just and equitable winding up[8] on the principles stated by the House of Lords in *Re Westbourne Galleries*,[9] he may still

---

of the succeeding directors or if there is a small delay prior to the appointment of new directors, there will be no breach of the statutory requirement prescribing a minimum number of directors (see paras 3.01 and 6.02 above).

  [3] Although the shareholders are entitled to fetter their discretion by contract, and can agree not to use the s 168 power.

  [4] 2006 Act, s 168(1). Removal of a director under s 168 will also override anything to the contrary in the articles.

  [5] See paras 7.39 *et seq* below.

  [6] Breach of a fiduciary duty is not inherently repudiatory. So a director's right to compensation may survive even such a breach: *Crocs Europe BV v Anderson* [2012] EWCA Civ 1400, [2013] 1 Lloyd's Rep 1, at para 47 (an agency case); see further Ch 19 Section B below.

  [7] In particular the right to payment for notice under ERA, s 86 will be preserved.

  [8] Pursuant to Insolvency Act, s 122(1)(g).

  [9] [1973] AC 360.

be dismissed from the board by a resolution within s 168.[10] As reflected in s 168(5)(b), the articles may, however, provide for the dismissal of a director without following the procedure under s 168 or s 169.[11] In *Re Siteburn Ltd*,[12] it was considered doubtful that an estoppel by convention could arise in circumstances where directors were removed under this procedure but treated as remaining in office.

Director's right to protest his removal

The Companies Act contains stringent procedural requirements, which are intended to pro- **7.05** vide a director with a degree of protection. These are contained in s 169, which provides:

(1) On receipt of notice of an intended resolution to remove a director under section 168, the company must forthwith send a copy of the notice to the director concerned.

(2) The director (whether or not a member of the company) is entitled to be heard on the resolution at the meeting.

(3) Where notice is given of an intended resolution to remove a director under that section, and the director concerned makes with respect to it representations in writing to the company (not exceeding a reasonable length) and requests their notification to members of the company, the company shall, unless the representations are received by it too late for it to do so—

(a) in any notice of the resolution given to members of the company state the fact of the representations having been made; and

(b) send a copy of the representations to every member of the company to whom notice of the meeting is sent (whether before or after receipt of the representations by the company).

(4) If a copy of the representations is not sent as required by subsection (3) because received too late or because of the company's default, the director may (without prejudice to his right to be heard orally) require that the representations shall be read out at the meeting.

(5) Copies of the representations need not be sent out and the representations need not be read out at the meeting if, on the application either of the company or of any other person who claims to be aggrieved, the court is satisfied that the rights conferred by this section are being abused.

(6) The court may order the company's costs (in Scotland, expenses) on an application under subsection (5) to be paid in whole or in part by the director, notwithstanding that he is not a party to the application.

The procedural requirements apply whenever a notice of a shareholders' resolution under **7.06** s 168 is given. However, they do not apply where removal occurs pursuant to the articles,[13] which may provide for effective removal without any special protections for the director.[14]

Special notice is required of a resolution to remove a director under s 168, or to appoint **7.07** somebody instead of a director so removed at the meeting at which he is removed.[15] When the company receives notice of an intended resolution to remove a director under s 168, it must immediately send a copy of the notice to the director concerned.[16] The director has the right to protest his removal. He is entitled to be heard on the resolution at the meeting,

---

[10] *Bentley-Stevens v Jones* [1974] 1 WLR 638.
[11] *Browne v Panga Pty Ltd* (1995) 120 FLR 34.
[12] [2006] BPIR 1009.
[13] See paras 7.14 *et seq* below.
[14] *Browne v Panga Pty Ltd* (1995) 120 FLR 34. Removal pursuant to the articles is effective by reason of s 168(5)(b).
[15] 2006 Act, s 168(2).
[16] 2006 Act, s 169(1).

even if he is not a member of the company.[17] In addition, provided the right is not abused,[18] a director is entitled to make representations in writing to the company (not exceeding a reasonable length) and request their notification to the members of the company. Unless the representations are received too late, the company must state that representations have been made and send a copy of the representations to every member of the company to whom notice of the meeting is sent (whether before or after receipt of the representations by the company).[19] If a copy of the representations is not sent either because received too late or because of the company's default, the director may (without prejudice to his right to be heard orally) require that the representations shall be read out at the meeting.[20] Copies of the representations need not be sent out and need not be read out at the meeting if, on the application either of the company or of any other person who claims to be aggrieved, the court is satisfied that the rights conferred by this section are being abused.[21] In these circumstances, the court may order the company's costs of such an application under sub-s (5) to be paid in whole or in part by the director, notwithstanding that he is not a party to the application.[22]

7.08 Unless these procedures are complied with, a removal pursuant to s 168 is likely to be ineffective. But if the company is able to cure the defects, the court will not make an order reinstating the ousted director and it would be pointless to complain about the defective procedure.[23] The special procedures permitting members of private companies to agree to written resolutions, in Part 13 of the 2006 Act, are expressly excluded from applying to resolutions under s 168.[24]

Implied qualifications to s 168

7.09 As with the equivalent provisions in the earlier Companies Acts, the power under s 168 is subject to certain implied qualifications, alongside the express procedural obligations set out above.

7.10 First, any removal of a director will not affect his rights under any agreement with the company. As such, the service agreement itself may contain certain rights or liabilities, which arise when the s 168 power is used. The risk in such circumstances is that a director may have entrenched himself, such that any exercise of the power of removal would result in significant financial liabilities. These are considered in paragraphs 7.39 *et seq* below.

7.11 Secondly, although s 168 overrides any contrary provision in a service agreement or the articles, there is no objection to shareholders agreeing by contract not to use s 168,[25] either between themselves or in any agreement with a director. In appropriate circumstances, the court may intervene to uphold such an agreement by way of injunctive relief.[26] The

---

[17] 2006 Act, s 169(2), and see below.
[18] 2006 Act, s 169(5).
[19] 2006 Act, s 169(3).
[20] 2006 Act, s 169(4).
[21] 2006 Act, s 169(5).
[22] 2006 Act, s 169(6).
[23] *Bentley-Stevens v Jones* [1974] 1 WLR 638.
[24] 2006 Act, s 288(2)(1).
[25] See eg *Bonham-Carter v Situ Ventures Ltd* [2013] EWCA Civ 47, [2014] BCC 125 where the share purchase agreement went so far as to provide (effectively) that vendors ceased to be directors if 'requested by the purchaser'; *Holmes v Life Funds of Australia Ltd* [1971] 1 NSWLR 860.
[26] *Walker v Standard Chartered Bank plc* [1992] BCLC 535, CA.

ordinary principles of contractual interpretation, eg as to implied terms, apply to such questions.[27]

Thirdly, it is possible in private companies to put in place weighted voting rights that can **7.12** make it difficult or impossible for the ordinary shareholders to use the power in s 168. In *Bushell v Faith*,[28] the articles of a private company provided that 'in the event of a resolution being proposed at any general meeting for the removal from office of any director any shares held by that director shall on a poll in respect of such resolution carry the right of three votes per share'. The House of Lords, by a majority,[29] held that this was not an infringement of the rights of members under the equivalent of what is now s 168, and did not contravene the principle that any director may be removed by ordinary resolution despite any contrary provision in the articles. Lord Upjohn described the distinction between voting rights attached to shares and the policy of the Act as follows:[30]

> Parliament has never sought to fetter the right of the company to issue a share with such rights or restrictions as it may think fit. There is no fetter which compels the company to make the voting rights or restrictions of general application and it seems clear that such rights or restrictions can be attached to special circumstances and to particular types of resolution. This makes no mockery of [s 168]; all that Parliament was seeking to do thereby was to make an ordinary resolution sufficient to remove a director. Had Parliament desired to go further and enact that every share carrying an entitlement to vote should be deprived of its special right under the articles it should have said so in plain terms by making the vote on a poll one vote one share.

The literal approach favoured by the majority of the House in theory constitutes a major **7.13** limitation to the effect of s 168. In his forceful dissenting speech, Lord Morris of Borth-y-Gest[31] considered the decision to make a mockery of the law, in that its unconcealed effect, where the articles were so drafted, would be to make a director irremovable.[32] Lord Donovan,[33] justified the decision by reference to the need to protect shareholder–directors in small companies, which are 'conducted in practice as though they were little more than partnerships, particularly family companies running a family business', as, his Lordship held: 'it is, unfortunately, sometimes necessary to provide some safeguard against family quarrels having their repercussions in the boardroom'. In practice, the effect of the decision in *Bushell v Faith* is restricted to small private companies of this nature and has little widespread effect. Such articles are very rare in public companies (presumably because they render the shares unattractive to potential shareholders) and are prohibited in many sets of listing rules. As

---

[27] *Jackson v Dear* [2013] EWCA Civ 89, [2014] 1 BCLC 186 (Court of Appeal rejected director's submission that shareholders' agreement contained an implied term precluding recourse to articles' mechanism for removing him; referred to with approval by Lord Carnwath in *Marks and Spencer plc v BNP Paribas Securities Services Trust Co (Jersey) Ltd* [2016] AC 742, SC). See also *Liberty Investing Ltd v Sydow* [2015] EWHC 608 (Comm).

[28] [1970] AC 1099. Cf *Swerdlow v Cohen* 1977 (3) SA 1050, PD (Tvaal) (article giving named individual a veto). In *James North (Zimbabwe) (Pvt) Ltd v Mattinson* 1990 (2) SA 228, HC (Zim) the articles conferred on the 'A' shareholders and the 'B' shareholders separate rights to appoint and remove their own representative directors. It was held that only the 'B' shareholders could vote on a resolution to remove a director representing that class, notwithstanding a statutory provision equivalent to 1985 Act, s 303.

[29] Lord Morris of Borth-y-Gest dissenting.

[30] [1970] AC 1099 at 1109.

[31] At 1106.

[32] See also the criticism of Prentice (1969) 32 MLR 693.

[33] At 1110.

such, notwithstanding the strength of the criticism of *Bushell v Faith*, the 2006 Act does not reverse its effect.

(3) Termination under the articles

Vacation of office on occurrence of specified events

7.14   Articles may and usually do provide that the office of director is to be vacated upon the occurrence of certain specified events. Regulation 81 of Table A provides:

> The office of a director shall be vacated if—
> (a) he ceases to be a director by virtue of any provision of the Act or he becomes prohibited by law from being a director; or
> (b) he becomes bankrupt or makes any arrangement or composition with his creditors generally; or
> (c) he is, or may be, suffering from mental disorder and either—
>   (i)   he is admitted to hospital in pursuance of an application for admission for treatment under the Mental Health Act 1983 or, in Scotland, an application for admission under the Mental Health (Scotland) Act 1960, or
>   (ii) an order is made by a court having jurisdiction (whether in the United Kingdom or elsewhere) in matters concerning mental disorder for his detention or for the appointment of a receiver, curator bonis or other person to exercise powers with respect to his property or affairs; or
> (d) he resigns his office by notice to the company; or
> (e) he shall for more than six consecutive months have been absent without permission of the directors from meetings of directors held during that period and the directors resolve that his office be vacated.

7.15   Model Article (pcls) 18 provides that:

> A person ceases to be a director as soon as:
> (a) that person ceases to be a director by virtue of any provision of the Companies Act 2006 or is prohibited from being a director by law;
> (b) a bankruptcy order is made against that person;[34]
> (c) a composition is made with that person's creditors generally in satisfaction of that person's debts;
> (d) a registered medical practitioner who is treating that person gives a written opinion to the company stating that that person has become physically or mentally incapable of acting as a director and may remain so for more than three months;
> (e) by reason of that person's mental health, a court makes an order which wholly or partly prevents that person from personally exercising any powers or rights which that person would otherwise have;
> (f) a notification is received by the company from the director that the director is resigning or retiring from office as director and such resignation or retirement has taken effect in accordance with its terms.

7.16   Model Article (plc) 22 is in identical terms to that article.

7.17   Further, a company's articles may provide that the office of director will be vacated for any number of specified circumstances considered inappropriate or inconsistent with the role. In the past articles have provided that a director may be removed if he is concerned or interested

---

[34] This does not bar from holding office an individual whose bankruptcy dates from the time of their appointment: *Dawson v African Consolidated Land and Trading Co* [1898] 1 Ch 6, CA; *Re Northwestern Autoservices Ltd* [1980] 2 NZLR 302, CA (NZ).

in contracts made with the company,[35] accepts or holds an office of profit under the company,[36] or fails to acquire share qualification within a stated time or ceases to hold necessary share qualification. Those provisions are unlikely to be considered suitable for modern companies, since few have share qualification requirements and the 2006 Act provides other means of dealing with conflicts of interest.[37] Articles may also provide for vacation of office if a director is convicted of an indictable offence,[38] or is absent from meetings of directors for a long period.

Interpretation of the particular provision for automatic vacation of office can be crucial. For **7.18** example, in interpreting the words 'if he absents himself' (from board meetings), the courts have held that this means voluntary absence, and absence through sickness would not result in disqualification.[39] In interpreting articles providing for disqualification 'if he is concerned in any contract', it has been held that a director would be disqualified even though the contract he is concerned in is one that he could not profit from.[40]

If the articles provide for automatic vacation[41] when certain circumstances arise, the vacation **7.19** is effective without a resolution and cannot be waived by the directors.[42] However, a person who is automatically removed from office by virtue of the company's articles may be reappointed when the disqualifying circumstances no longer apply.[43] Where circumstances (such as bankruptcy) arise after a company has been dissolved, the office is in any event vacated from the time of the bankruptcy as it would be illogical for a director's agency to terminate if the company had not been dissolved but to survive after the company had been dissolved.[44]

In *Smith v Butler*,[45] the Court of Appeal held that the implied delegated authority provided **7.20** to a managing director did not include the authority to suspend the chairman (and majority shareholder) of the company. The managing director's powers extended to carrying out those functions on which he did not need to obtain the specific directions of the board, but the suspension of the chairman was a matter on which he needed the instructions of the board.

Resignation of directors

The company's articles and the director's contract of service generally specify the terms for **7.21** retirement or resignation. Subject to those terms, however, the general rule is that a director is entitled to resign at any time by giving notice to the company. Resignation is effected by the giving of notice, and does not depend upon acceptance by the company. Even if the

---

[35] This may apply where the director holds shares in a contracting company: *Turnbull v West Riding Club* (1894) 70 LT 92; *Todd v Robinson* (1884) 14 QBD 739; *Dimes v Grand Junction Canal Co* (1852) 3 HLC 759. However, modern articles commonly permit interests in contracts.

[36] *Astley v New Tivoli Ltd* [1899] 1 Ch 151; cf *Iron Ship Coating Co v Blunt* (1868) LR 3 CP 484 in which a director appointed as an unpaid company secretary was not disqualified. Modern articles now usually permit such activities, other than that of auditor.

[37] See Chs 15 and 17 below.

[38] Even if the indictable offence is tried summarily: *Hastings & Folkestone Glassworks v Kalson* [1949] 1 KB 214, CA.

[39] *Mack's Claim* [1900] WN 114; *McConnell's Case* [1901] 1 Ch 728.

[40] *Star Steam Laundry Co v Dukas* [1913] WN 39.

[41] For example where the articles provide that 'a director's office is vacated in the following circumstances …'.

[42] *Re Bodega Co Ltd* [1904] 1 Ch 276.

[43] *Re Bodega Co Ltd* [1904] 1 Ch 276.

[44] *Witherdale v Registrar of Companies* [2008] 1 BCLC 174.

[45] [2012] Bus LR 1836, CA, at paras 27–31, per Arden LJ; affirming [2012] 1 BCLC 444.

articles provide that notice of resignation is to be in writing, oral resignation is effective if accepted,[46] as is the submission of the appropriate form[47] to the Registrar by the resigning director, with resignation acknowledged in the annual return.[48] Once notice has been given, it cannot be withdrawn except by agreement with the company.[49] No minimum period of notice is required to resign the position of director.[50]

7.22 A director may resign his office at any time, even if the articles do not provide such a power. The only exception is where the articles contain positive conditions for resignation. The resignation is complete when notice is given to the company (even though no acceptance has taken place) and it cannot subsequently be withdrawn except with the consent of the company.

7.23 Even though a person's resignation from the directorship of a company may seriously damage the company, it is not in breach of the director's fiduciary duty to the company.[51] However, an executive director who breaches his service contract by leaving without giving the required period of notice may be liable to the company for damages suffered as a result.[52] Further, although the general position is that a director who no longer wishes to perform his duties or finds it impossible to do so may resign,[53] he may be required to deal with pressing matters before he goes or, exceptionally, put relevant information into the hands of the proper organs of the company if he is not satisfied that the continuing directors will deal properly with the matter of concern (eg a fellow director's criminal convictions).[54]

7.24 As noted, sometimes a company's articles will specify a procedure to be followed for giving effect to a resignation from office of a director. Model Article (pcls) 18(f) and Model Article (plc) 22(f), for instance, provide that the office of a director shall be vacated upon the company receiving notice that he is resigning and such resignation has taken effect in accordance with its terms.[55] In such circumstances, resignation will be effective upon the completion of the notice period.

7.25 Provisions for vacation of office on the unanimous decision of the other directors and for retirement or resignation by rotation are more often found in public companies and are considered in Section B below.

B. Additional Rules for Public Companies

(1) Dismissal by unanimous decision of directors

7.26 Earlier drafts of the Model Articles (plc) included provision for the directors of a public company to remove a director by unanimous decision, but this was not included in the final

---

[46] *Latchford Premier Cinema Ltd v Ennion* [1931] 2 Ch 409.
[47] Form 288b.
[48] *Aberdeen Water Technologists v Henderson* 2000 GWD 20-783 (Sheriff Court).
[49] *Glossop v Glossop* [1907] 2 Ch 370.
[50] *OBC Caspian Ltd v Thorp* 1998 SLT 653. Notice may, however, be required under the service contract. See paras 7.41 *et seq* below.
[51] *CMS Dolphin Ltd v Simonet* [2001] 2 BCLC 704.
[52] *CMS Dolphin Ltd v Simonet* [2001] 2 BCLC 704.
[53] *Re Galeforce Pleating Co Ltd* [1999] 2 BCLC 704, 716.
[54] *Lexi Holdings plc v Luqman* [2008] 2 BCLC 725 at para 39, reversed [2009] 2 BCLC 1, CA, but not on this point.
[55] Table A, reg 81(d) provides for a director to vacate office if he resigns his office by notice to the company.

version. The rationale behind the inclusion of such a provision is that it allows directors, when acting unanimously, to deal with disruptive directors without the publicity and procedural difficulties of the Companies Act, s 168. Similar articles will often allow a company to detail procedures to remove a director by conferring a power of removal upon all, or a specified majority, of the directors. However, in the absence of such a power, the board has no inherent right to remove a director from office, and a company will be obliged to use the power in s 168. Directors must act in the best interests of the company, and not for an ulterior motive, when issuing such a notice, although the fact that they are acting for an ulterior motive does not itself invalidate a notice.[56]

(2) Retirement by rotation

Private companies rarely choose to include articles providing for retirement of directors by rotation and there is no such provision in the Model Articles (pcls). Table A, regs 73–7 contain detailed provisions for the retirement of directors by rotation, which are seldom of relevance or benefit to private companies. However, public companies often do include an article providing for retirement by rotation. This is reflected in Model Article (plc) 21, which provides for retirement of directors by rotation: **7.27**

(1) At the first annual general meeting all the directors must retire from office.
(2) At every subsequent annual general meeting any directors—
    (a) who have been appointed by the directors since the last annual general meeting, or
    (b) who were not appointed at one of the preceding two annual general meetings,
        must retire from office and may offer themselves for reappointment by the members.

As such, the Model Articles envisage a period of office of no more than three years for any director, before he may offer himself for reappointment by the members. Further, any director appointed outside of the AGM must offer himself for reappointment at the next AGM, ensuring that shareholders have the opportunity to sanction any appointment at an early stage. **7.28**

Articles which provide for retirement by rotation usually make special provision for the choice of the directors who will retire, and for the process of election of new directors. In every case, the articles are interpreted strictly. For example, where an article provides for the retirement of one-third of the directors (or the nearest number to one-third), and there are only two directors subject to such provision, neither is bound to retire.[57] Equally, a provision that a retiring director be deemed re-elected will operate notwithstanding that an express resolution to re-elect a retiring director has been defeated, even if a resolution, which proves to be invalid, is passed to appoint some other person in his place.[58] If a retiring director is re-elected, or deemed to be re-elected, his retirement does not constitute a vacation of office.[59] **7.29**

(3) Listed companies

Section B.7 of the UK Corporate Governance Code[60] states the general principle that all directors of listed companies should be submitted for re-election at regular intervals subject **7.30**

---

[56] *Lee v Chou Wen Hsien* [1984] 1 WLR 1202, PC. Also see Ch 12 below.
[57] *Re David Moseley & Sons* [1939] Ch 719.
[58] *Holt v Catterall* (1931) 47 TLR 322; *Grundt v Great Boulder Proprietary Mines* [1948] Ch 145, CA, disapproving *Robert Batcheller & Son v Batcheller* [1945] Ch 169.
[59] *Walker v Kenns* [1937] 1 All ER 566, CA.
[60] April 2016, issued by the Financial Reporting Council.

to continued satisfactory performance. These rules are described in Chapter 6, Section D(3) above. The shareholders have the opportunity to consider the election or re-election of directors at regular intervals. If they decline to elect or re-elect the director, he thereupon vacates office.

7.31   Paragraph B.7.1 provides that directors of listed companies must be submitted for election or re-election by shareholders as follows:

(1) all directors of FTSE 350 companies should be subject to annual election;

(2) all other directors should be subject to election at the first AGM after their appointment, and to re-election thereafter at intervals of no more than three years;

(3) non-executive directors who have served longer than nine years should be subject to annual re-election.

7.32   Shareholders should be provided with sufficient biographical details and other relevant information about the directors submitted for election or re-election to enable them to make an informed decision on their election.[61] The proposed election or re-election of a non-executive director should be supported by the positive recommendation of the board and the chairman.[62]

(4) Financial institutions: special rules

7.33   The provisions of the Financial Services (Banking Reform) Act 2013 governing the approval of senior managers (including directors) are dealt with in Chapter 6. For the purposes of this chapter, it is relevant to note that the 2013 Act inserts a new section 64C into the Financial Services and Markets Act 2000 which requires a 'relevant authorised person' under the 2000 Act to notify the appropriate regulator if such a director is inter alia suspended or dismissed.[63]

C. Effect of Termination of Appointment

7.34   Where directors continue to act as directors after their office is vacated, for whatever reason, their acts will continue to bind the company.[64]

7.35   Although a director may be validly removed as a matter of company law, he may still have the benefit of certain rights by reason of his status as an employee or worker of the company.[65] In *Mountain Spring Water Co Ltd v Colesby (No 2)*,[66] the Employment Appeal Tribunal held that the effect of Regulation 84 of Table A was that a director who was appointed to an executive office, as opposed to a director who was merely providing services beyond his ordinary director's duties, would have his employment terminated when he was removed as director. In any event, many company articles expressly provide that the appointment of a managing director terminates if he ceases to be a director of the company.[67] In such circumstances, a company may incur liability to the director under his service contract. Further, a director employed under a service contract will have the benefit of statutory employment rights,

---

[61] UK Corporate Governance Code, para B.7.1.
[62] UK Corporate Governance Code, para B.7.2.
[63] In force 25 July 2014 for the purpose of making rules, otherwise 7 March 2016.
[64] 2006 Act, s 161(1)(c); *Muir v Forman's Trustees* (1903) 5 F 546, IH (Scotland).
[65] See Ch 8 below regarding the employment status of a director.
[66] EAT, UKEAT/0855/04 RN, 18 April 2005.
[67] See *Southern Foundries Ltd v Shirlaw* [1940] AC 701, HL.

which may apply in the event of his removal. As such, a valid removal of a director under the Companies Act or articles of association may still result in liabilities to the director under contract or statute.

Conversely, depending on the terms of his service contract, a director may still remain a company director despite being dismissed under the terms of his service agreement, until he resigns or is removed from office. **7.36**

Where a director is removed from office, his right to inspect the company's books termi-nates.[68] This is because the right exists in order to allow a director to perform his duties, which lapse upon removal. **7.37**

Where the articles include a provision requiring a director to serve a transfer notice in respect of his shares following resignation or termination, the effect of the service of the transfer notice will be irrevocable.[69] **7.38**

D. Rights and Liabilities in the Event of Termination

In the event of removal, a company may have liabilities to a director arising under the terms of the service contract and by reason of employment legislation. Similarly, where a director resigns in breach of contract, he may also have liabilities to the company. **7.39**

(1) Rights arising under the service contract

Service contracts for directors often make detailed provision regarding the consequences of termination. This section considers notice periods (statutory and contractual notice, PILON, and garden leave clauses), summary dismissal for gross misconduct, and remedies for wrongful dismissal. The next section of this chapter considers statutory rights in the event of termination. **7.40**

Notice periods

Directors who are employed under service contracts are, normally,[70] entitled to minimum periods of notice, either under statute or under the terms of the contract itself (either through express provision or by an implied term). However, no notice is required to terminate a ser-vice contract by reason of gross misconduct, as discussed below.[71] **7.41**

A significant exception to this principle applies when the service contract is silent as to notice and the articles of association at the time of appointment[72] provide that the **7.42**

---

[68] *Oxford Legal Group Ltd v Sibbasbridge Services plc* [2008] 2 BCLC 381, CA; *Conway v Petronius Clothing Co* [1978] 1 WLR 72.

[69] *Doughty Hanson & Co Ltd v Roe* [2008] 1 BCLC 404.

[70] There may be no entitlement to notice where the parties agree to immediate termination or the direc-tor is engaged to perform a specific task which, upon completion, discharges the contract through perfor-mance: *Wiltshire County Council v NATFHE* [1980] ICR 455, per Lord Denning MR. Further, there will be no entitlement to notice where the service contract is frustrated (which may occur for example when a director is imprisoned): *C Shepherd & Co Ltd v Jerrom* [1987] QB 301, CA. See also *G F Sharp & Co Ltd v McMillan* [1998] IRLR 632, EAT.

[71] At para 7.54.

[72] If a company changes its articles to grant itself a power to dismiss which is contrary to the service agree-ment, it will be in breach of contract if it exercises the power: *Southern Foundries v Shirlaw* [1940] AC 701, HL; *Shindler v Northern Raincoat Co Ltd* [1960] 1 WLR 1038.

contract shall terminate automatically upon ceasing to be a director. In such circumstances, if a company exercises its power under s 168, or any other power under the articles, and removes a director, this will be effective to bring the service contract to an end immediately.[73]

7.43 Under normal contractual principles, the giving of notice is operative to terminate the contract. As such, once notice is given by either side, there is no unilateral right to rescind, notwithstanding that the director may remain in employment whilst he serves his notice period.[74] Whether a director has in fact given notice will not always be apparent. Where there is ambiguity, the issue of whether a director has resigned must be determined objectively by reference to the understanding of a reasonable recipient.[75]

Statutory minimum periods of notice

7.44 A director who has been employed for a month or longer is entitled to a minimum period of notice, based upon length of service. Directors who have been continuously employed for longer than one month are entitled to a notice period of one week, increasing by an additional week for each additional continuous year of service up to a maximum of 12 weeks.[76] As the statutory right to notice takes effect as an implied term of the service agreement, it can be enforced as an action for breach of contract.

7.45 A company also has a right to a minimum notice period of one week from a director who has been continuously employed for longer than one month.[77]

Contractual notice periods

7.46 Depending on the terms of his service agreement, a director may (and usually will) be entitled to a longer period of notice than that provided by statute. Any termination by either party without the relevant period of notice is effective to terminate the contract, but will amount to a breach of contract (and therefore give rise to an action for damages).

7.47 Occasionally, a service contract will be silent as to the relevant period of notice. In such circumstances, the court will infer that the contract is capable of termination upon reasonable notice.[78] Factors that the court will take into account when determining what is reasonable in any given set of circumstances include seniority, nature of employment, and length of service.[79] Further, courts may take into account the frequency of salary payments[80] or any existing custom of the trade.[81] Any notice period implied by contract cannot, however, be less than the statutory minimum.[82]

---

[73] *Read v Astoria Garage (Streatham) Ltd* [1952] Ch 637, CA.

[74] *Riordan v War Office* [1959] 1 WLR 1046 (affd [1960] 1 WLR 210, CA).

[75] *Quarter Master UK Ltd v Pyke* [2005] 1 BCLC 245, applying *Mannai Investment Co Ltd v Eagle Star Life Assurance Co Ltd* [1997] AC 749, HL.

[76] ERA, s 86.

[77] ERA, s 86(2).

[78] *Baxter v Nurse* (1844) 6 Man & G 935; *McClelland v Northern Ireland General Health Service Board* [1957] 1 WLR 594, per Lord Oaksey at 599; *Reda v Flag Ltd* [2002] IRLR 747, per Lord Millett at para 57.

[79] *CMS Dolphin Ltd v Simonet* [2001] 2 BCLC 704 (three months for an executive director of an advertising agency).

[80] *Marshall v English Electric Co Ltd* [1945] 1 All ER 653 (hourly); *Baxter v Nurse* (1844) 6 Man & G 935 (weekly); see also *Nokes v Doncaster Amalgamated Collieries Ltd* [1940] AC 1014, 1028 per Lord Atkin.

[81] See *Nokes v Doncaster Amalgamated Collieries Ltd* [1940] AC 1014, 1028.

[82] *Hill v C A Parsons & Co Ltd* [1972] Ch 305, CA.

PILON clauses

Directors' service agreements will often include a clause allowing the company to make **7.48** a payment in lieu of notice (PILON) clause. The effect of a PILON clause is a matter of contractual construction in any given case. Typically, a PILON clause will confer upon the company a discretion to dismiss a director immediately, upon payment of the full amount of notice period salary as a lump sum.[83] Alternatively, a company may summarily dismiss the director, having previously agreed to offer a payment in lieu of notice (even where the service agreement does not confer an express right). In such circumstances, the parties have agreed to vary the contract and the payment is lawful.[84]

If the contract does not contain a PILON clause, there is no common law right to tender **7.49** payment in lieu of notice without the agreement of the director.[85] As such, payment of salary in lieu of notice without agreement would normally constitute wrongful dismissal on the part of the employer. There are potential implications for a company that takes this step. A director may still have suffered loss in such circumstances if, for example, he would have been entitled to a contractual bonus during the notice period.[86] Further, wrongful dismissal may have the effect of releasing a director from any restrictive covenants to which he would otherwise have been bound.[87]

Garden leave

Many directors' service contracts include an express provision allowing the employer to sus- **7.50** pend a director from his normal duties for the duration of his notice period. Alternatively, in the absence of a written provision in the service contract, the parties may agree that a director is not required to carry out any work. An express contractual suspension of this nature is commonly referred to as 'garden leave', as the director in question is expected not to carry out any work at all, and therefore might choose to spend his time in his garden. The benefit is that the director cannot enter into employment with a competitor for the period of garden leave, providing the company with an opportunity to recruit a successor (if no succession plan is in place). Further, any confidential information that the director might otherwise take to a rival is more likely to go stale if the director no longer has access to the company premises and records.

In certain circumstances, a service contract may include an implied right to place a director **7.51** on garden leave. However, whether it will be possible in any given instance depends upon the nature of the director's position together with the express terms of the service agreement. In *William Hill v Tucker*,[88] the Court of Appeal held that there was no implied right to place a senior employee on garden leave in circumstances where his seniority, unique position, and

---

[83] *Delaney v Staples* [1992] 1 AC 687, 692, HL per Lord Browne-Wilkinson. A PILON clause takes effect only after the employee is notified that it has been or will be exercised: *Geys v Société Générale, London Branch* [2012] UKSC 63, [2013] 1 AC 523.

[84] *Delaney v Staples* [1992] 1 AC 687, HL.

[85] See the decision of the Scottish Inner House of the Court of Session in *Morrish v NTL Group* [2007] CSIH 56, rejecting an argument that a PILON clause could be implied into a financial director/company secretary's service contract.

[86] *Morrish v NTL Group* [2007] CSIH 56. Where a bonus requires a director to be in employment at the time that the bonus is payable, he is not entitled to payment if his employment was terminated before that time and without notice upon the making of a PILON: *Locke v Candy & Candy Ltd* [2011] IRLR 163, CA.

[87] See para 8.68 below.

[88] [1999] ICR 291, CA.

the presence of contractual terms encouraging development of personal skills, meant that the employee had a 'right to work'. However, as noted by the Court of Appeal in *Tucker*, where the service contract contains an express contractual provision allowing garden leave, there would be no need to consider whether the company had an implied right to place a director on garden leave. As such, to avoid this difficulty, garden leave clauses are now commonly found in directors' service contracts.

7.52 Where the service contract does not contain a garden leave clause, a company may still have an implied right to place a director on garden leave where the director is himself in prior breach of contract. In *SG&R Valuation Service v Boudrais*,[89] Cranston J held that a company was entitled to place two directors on garden leave in the absence of an express power, where their earlier competitive activity had made it impossible for the company to offer continuing work.

7.53 Conversely, an express garden leave clause may be indirectly 'whittled down' by the grant of an injunction covering less than its full term.[90]

Summary dismissal for gross misconduct

7.54 The main exception to the principle that notice must be given before termination of a service agreement applies where the company dismisses a director for gross misconduct. Gross misconduct is the term used in employment law to describe any conduct on the part of the employee sufficiently serious to justify termination without notice[91] (including the statutory minimum period of notice).

7.55 The categories of gross misconduct have developed over time to reflect changing values.[92] As held in *Neary v Dean of Westminster*[93] whether particular misconduct justifies summary dismissal is a question of fact. The character of the company, the role played by the director in the company, and the degree of trust required of the director vis-à-vis the company must all be considered in determining the extent of the duty of trust and the seriousness of any breach thereof.[94] Any director (and in particular a director occupying a central role in the management of the company, such as a managing director) will normally therefore be held to a higher standard than a mere employee.

7.56 A breach of fiduciary duty will inevitably constitute gross misconduct, whether or not it was known to the employer at the time of dismissal.[95] However, a director will not be guilty of gross misconduct merely by indicating his intention to set up in competition in the future,[96] providing any steps that he takes to do so do not go beyond preparatory steps.[97] A company must act reasonably promptly when dismissing an employee on account of gross misconduct,

---

[89] [2008] IRLR 770, QB. Approved in *Standard Life Health Care Ltd v Gorman* [2010] IRLR 233, CA.
[90] *J M Finn & Co Ltd v Holliday* [2013] EWHC 3450 (QB), [2014] IRLR 102.
[91] *Laws v London Chronicle (Indicator Newspapers) Ltd* [1959] 1 WLR 698, CA; *Wilson v Racher* [1974] ICR 428, CA.
[92] *Laws v London Chronicle (Indicator Newspapers) Ltd* [1959] 1 WLR 698, CA.
[93] [1999] IRLR 288, per Lord Jauncey sitting as Special Commissioner.
[94] [1999] IRLR 288. See also *Crocs Europe BV v Anderson* [2012] EWCA Civ 1400, [2013] 1 Lloyd's Rep 1.
[95] *Item Software v Fassihi* [2005] 2 BCLC 91, CA.
[96] *Adamson v B & L Cleaning Services Ltd* [1995] IRLR 193, EAT.
[97] *Shepherds Investments v Walters* [2007] IRLR 110; *Helmet Integrated Systems Ltd v Tunnard* [2007] IRLR 126; *Ranson v Customers Systems plc* [2012] EWCA Civ 841; [2012] IRLR 769.

as prolonged delay may be taken as amounting to an implied affirmation of the contract of employment.

Constructive dismissal

Not all dismissals occur when a director is sacked by the company. A director is entitled to treat **7.57** himself as having been dismissed, where he resigns in response to some sufficiently serious conduct on the part of the company (known as 'constructive dismissal').[98] However, mere unreasonable conduct is not enough; rather the conduct must be sufficient to constitute a breach of the service contract so as to justify the director treating the contract as at an end.[99] Further, the director must leave in response to the breach[100] and must not delay unreasonably doing so.[101] If these conditions are not met, the director will be taken to have resigned.

The acts that may constitute constructive dismissal are wide and varied. Examples include **7.58** subjecting an employee to insulting language;[102] imposing a disproportionate disciplinary sanction for a minor incident;[103] and arbitrarily imposing an inferior pay rise as compared to other employees.[104] Notably, any attempt to impose changes in conditions which are not permitted by the terms of the service contract may amount to a constructive dismissal, including changing a place of work without a mobility clause;[105] cutting pay;[106] or requiring an employee to relinquish his job in favour of another role.[107] The making of hostile comments in the boardroom cannot, however, constitute constructive dismissal, as the board is the controlling mind of the company and representations between individuals on the board are merely equivalent to the company thinking aloud to itself, which may include even negative and unworthy thoughts about a director.[108]

In *RDF Media Group plc v Clements*,[109] the court held that a director is not entitled to claim **7.59** constructive dismissal, even where he meets all of the conditions discussed above, if he is himself in repudiatory breach of contract at the time of his resignation.[110] This reasoning is highly doubtful; an unaccepted repudiation by a party does not normally bring a contract to an end, but rather gives the innocent party a right of election to treat the contract as terminated.[111] However, unless and until *Clements* is overturned, a company faced with a constructive dismissal claim may be able to take advantage of any anterior repudiatory breaches on the part of their former director. *Clements* was not followed in *SG&R Valuation Service Ltd v Boudrais*,[112] *Tullett Prebon v BGC Brokers*,[113] or *Brandeaux Advisers (UK) v*

---

[98] See also ERA, s 95(1)(c).
[99] *Western Excavating (ECC) Ltd v Sharp* [1978] ICR 221.
[100] *Meikle v Nottinghamshire County Council* [2004] EWCA Civ 859, [2005] ICR 1 (disapproving the 'effective cause' test suggested by the EAT in *Jones v F Sirl & Son (Furnishers) Ltd* [1997] IRLR 493); *Wright v North Ayrshire Council* [2014] ICR 77, EAT.
[101] *Walker v Josiah Wedgwood & Sons Ltd* [1978] IRLR 105.
[102] *Palmanor Ltd v Cedron* [1978] ICR 1008.
[103] *Stanley Cole (Wainfleet) Ltd v Sheridan* [2003] IRLR 52.
[104] *FC Gardner Ltd v Beresford* [1978] IRLR 63.
[105] *Aparu v Iceland Frozen Foods plc* [1996] IRLR 119.
[106] *Cantor Fitzgerald v Callaghan* [1999] IRLR 234.
[107] *Hilton v Shiner Ltd Builders Merchants* [2001] IRLR 727.
[108] *RDF Media Group plc v Clements* [2008] IRLR 207 at para 113.
[109] [2008] IRLR 207.
[110] [2008] IRLR 207.
[111] See *State Trading Corporation of India v Golodetz* [1989] 2 Lloyd's Rep 277 at 285, per Kerr LJ.
[112] [2008] IRLR 775, QBD.
[113] [2010] EWHC 484 (QB); upheld on other grounds: [2011] IRLR 420, CA.

Chadwick.[114] It had been applied by the Scottish Employment Appeal Tribunal in *Aberdeen CC v McNeill*,[115] but the EAT's decision was overturned on appeal to the Inner House of the Court of Session.[116] On a related point, in *Item Software (UK) Ltd v Fassihi*,[117] the court held that the director's breach of fiduciary duty could justify his dismissal irrespective of whether the breach was known to the company at the time of his dismissal and irrespective of whether his dismissal was otherwise justified.

Remedies for wrongful dismissal

7.60 Where a director is dismissed without due notice, he may bring a claim for damages[118] for wrongful dismissal. Normal principles of contract law apply to the measure of damages, meaning that a director will be entitled to damages equivalent to the amount of salary that he would otherwise have earned,[119] subject to the duty to mitigate his loss.

7.61 Further, in assessing damages, it is to be assumed that a company would exercise any power available to it to bring the contract to an end in the way most beneficial to itself.[120] In *Laverack v Woods of Colchester*[121] a majority of the Court of Appeal held that the dismissed employee was not entitled to damages in respect of bonuses, which the directors of the company had made available from time to time, but which did not form part of his contractual entitlement. However, where a director's service contract provides for a discretionary annual pay rise or bonus, the director will be entitled to damages equivalent to the amount that he would have received if the company had exercised its discretion (which it cannot exercise capriciously or in bad faith).[122] A director's service agreement will often provide that there is no entitlement to a bonus if employment has terminated or notice has been given by either side and in such circumstances, no damages will be recoverable.[123]

7.62 Where a director is dismissed in breach of a contractual dismissal procedure, the court will calculate loss for the period during which the procedure would have been operated, together with damages for the notice period under the contract.[124]

7.63 A director who is wrongfully dismissed is under a duty to take reasonable steps to mitigate his loss. However, the concept of reasonableness means that a director is not obliged to accept

---

114 [2011] IRLR 224 (QB).
115 [2010] IRLR 374.
116 [2013] CSIH 102.
117 [2005] 2 BCLC 91, CA.
118 A claim may also be brought for debt if the contract includes a PILON clause: *Abrahams v Performing Rights Society* [1995] IRLR 486, unless the payment in lieu is at the discretion of the company: *Cerberus Software Ltd v Rowley* [2001] IRLR 160, CA. An action for debt does not require the director to mitigate his loss and is therefore a valuable alternative remedy.
119 Therefore taking account of matters such as any income tax, national insurance, or pension contributions that would have been payable on the outstanding salary and, if necessary, 'grossing up' to take account of any tax payable on the award of damages (payable where the award is in excess of £30,000 pursuant to Income Tax (Earnings and Pensions) Act 2003, s 403: *Shove v Downs Surgical plc* [1984] ICR 532.
120 *Laverack v Woods of Colchester Ltd* [1967] 1 QB 278.
121 [1967] 1 QB 278.
122 *Clark v BET plc* [1997] IRLR 348; *Clark v Nomura International plc* [2000] IRLR 766; *Horkulak v Cantor Fitzgerald International* [2005] ICR 402.
123 *Keen v Commerzbank AG* [2007] ICR 623. The Supreme Court in *Braganza v BP Shipping Ltd* [2015] UKSC 17, [2015] 1 WLR 1661 referred with approval to this case and those in the preceding note.
124 *Gunton v Richmond-upon-Thames LBC* [1980] ICR 755; *Dietman v Brent LBC* [1987] ICR 737; *Boyo v Lambeth LBC* [1995] IRLR 50.

a position which would involve a significant loss of pay, seniority, or status.[125] Any salary, fees, or state benefits received after dismissal will go to reduce the amount payable by the company in damages.[126] Further, damages will be reduced to reflect the fact that damages are payable as a single lump sum and to reflect the potential for future salary to be curtailed by the 'vicissitudes of life'.[127]

A claim for wrongful dismissal on the part of the director may be brought as an action for **7.64** breach of contract in the High Court or county court, or in the employment tribunals. However, damages in the employment tribunals are limited to £25,000 and a director cannot bring a further claim in the High Court or county court for the balance of any outstanding sums.[128] There is no objection to a director's pursuing a claim for unfair dismissal in the employment tribunals and a separate claim for wrongful dismissal in the High Court or county court. Any damages awarded will be subject to the principles of double recovery.[129] However, it is for the company to demonstrate that compensation awarded for unfair dismissal is attributable to the notice period for which damages for wrongful dismissal have been ordered. As the Court of Appeal made clear in *O'Laoire v Jackel International Ltd*,[130] this will only be the case when it is made clear from the judgment of the employment tribunal.

The provisions of the Companies Act regulating payments for loss of office are considered in **7.65** Chapter 18, Section E below.

(2) Statutory rights in the event of termination

A director who is removed from office may also have the benefit of certain other protective **7.66** rights, set out in the legislation. In particular, subject to certain qualifying requirements and the details of the relevant statutory provision, a director is entitled to protection in the event of unfair dismissal, redundancy, and discrimination on certain specified grounds.

Unfair dismissal

A company that dismisses a director may have liability for unfair dismissal.[131] The concept of **7.67** 'unfairness' in the legislation is not assessed by reference to the reasonable man on the street; rather protection under the legislation applies to breach of the statutory tests of fairness as developed by the courts.[132] The statutory provisions impose a number of qualifying requirements for a claim, which can only be brought in the employment tribunals. Unless the reason for dismissal is one of a number of reasons specified in the legislation, the compensation that an employment tribunal can award is subject to a statutory cap.[133] Although rarely used in

---

[125] *Yetton v Eastwoods Froy Ltd* [1967] 1 WLR 104, where a managing director was entitled to reject an offer of the position of assistant managing director with the same salary, because of the loss of status that would entail.

[126] *Shove v Downs Surgical plc* [1984] ICR 532.

[127] ie if payment for the whole notice period may not actually have happened in certain circumstances. In *Bold v Brough Nicholson & Hall Ltd* [1964] 1 WLR 201 credit was given for the possibility of early lawful termination for illness.

[128] *Fraser v HLMAD Ltd* [2006] ICR 1395, CA.

[129] *O'Laoire v Jackel International Ltd* [1990] ICR 197. However, a basic award (as opposed to a compensatory award) for unfair dismissal does not fall to be deducted: *Shove v Downs Surgical plc* [1984] ICR 532.

[130] [1990] ICR 197.

[131] For a comprehensive account of the law of unfair dismissal, see *Harvey on Industrial Relations and Employment Law* (LexisNexis, looseleaf), section DI.

[132] *W Devis & Sons Ltd v Atkins* [1976] 2 All ER 822, 828, per Phillips J, affd by [1977] AC 931.

[133] Calculated by reference to a statutory basic award and compensatory award, capped at £78,335 from 6 April 2015: ERA, s 124.

practice, an employment tribunal can order a company to reinstate the director to his previous position[134] or re-engage him elsewhere in the company.[135]

Redundancy

7.68   If a director becomes surplus to the requirements of the business in which he is employed, he may be dismissed on account of redundancy.[136] Although the term 'redundancy' is often used in practice when dismissing a director, he will only be redundant for the purposes of the legislation if the statutory definition is met.[137] The company is under specific duties prior to making a director redundant, notably the duty to consult at the earliest possible opportunity. A complaint of unfair redundancy can be enforced as a claim for unfair dismissal in the employment tribunals.[138]

7.69   Subject to his qualifying for the right, a director who is dismissed on account of redundancy will be entitled to a statutory redundancy payment.[139] If a service contract provides for enhanced terms in the event of redundancy (that is, beyond the statutory minimum) the director will be entitled to enforce his entitlement by way of a claim for damages for breach of contract.

Discriminatory termination[140]

7.70   A company will also be liable to a director where a termination is discriminatory because of one or more of the following protected characteristics: age, disability, gender reassignment, marriage and civil partnership, pregnancy and maternity, race, religion or belief, sex or sexual orientation.[141] Liability may also arise where a director is removed on the grounds of trade union membership or non-membership.[142] A claim for discrimination can be brought in the employment tribunals, which have the power to award unlimited compensation, usually awarded in respect of lost earnings and injury to feelings.[143] Further, discrimination legislation may protect non-executive directors who fall within the restricted definition of an office-holder[144] from discriminatory removal from office.

---

[134] ERA, s 114.

[135] ERA, s 115.

[136] For a comprehensive account of redundancy law, see *Harvey on Industrial Relations and Employment Law*, Division E.

[137] ERA, s 139.

[138] See para 7.67 above.

[139] ERA, s 135.

[140] For a comprehensive account of discrimination law, see *Harvey on Industrial Relations and Employment Law*, Division L.

[141] Equality Act 2010, s 4.

[142] Trade Unions and Labour Relations (Consolidation) Act 1992, s 152.

[143] In line with the guidelines set out in *Vento v Chief Constable of West Yorkshire Police (No 2)* [2003] ICR 318, CA.

[144] Equality Act 2010, s 49.

8

DIRECTORS' TERMS OF SERVICE

Edward Brown

A. Introduction

The terms of service of a director will usually be a matter for negotiation between the parties and incorporated within a written service agreement. The Companies Act imposes certain restrictions and controls upon directors' service agreements, which are discussed in Chapter 18. Chapter 26, Section C discusses the rules requiring quoted companies[1] to disclose details of directors' remuneration in a directors' remuneration report, which must be approved by the members. This chapter considers the rights and duties of directors which result from their contractual obligations, as opposed to the general duties (as now codified within the 2006 Act) which are discussed in Chapters 10 to 17. It examines the tests that the courts will apply to determine whether a director is employed under a service agreement, together with the sources of contractual rights. It also considers the typical contractual rights and restrictions that apply in service agreements, including the rights to remuneration and expenses, confidentiality, and post-termination restrictions. **8.01**

B. Employment Status of Directors

Depending on the nature of his role in the company, a director may, in addition to holding the office of director, be employed by the company.[2] However, holding the office of director **8.02**

---

[1] By 2006 Act, s 385 a quoted company is a company whose equity share capital has been included in the official list in accordance with FSMA, Part 6, or is officially listed in an EEA state, or is admitted to dealing in either the New York Stock Exchange or Nasdaq.

[2] *Dunstan v Imperial Gas Light Co* (1832) 3 B & Ad 125; *Hutton v West Cork Railway* (1883) 23 Ch D 654, CA. See *Johnson v Ryan* [2000] ICR 236, explaining that office-holders may also be employees.

does not in itself confer employment status.[3] In *Ranson v Customer Systems plc*[4] the Court of Appeal said:

> The appointment of a person as a company director does not make that person an employee of the company. A director is the holder of an office. Nor does appointment as a company director of itself bring into existence any contract between the director and the company. Many directors will have contracts of service running in parallel with their status as officers of the company. But they are distinct legal relationships.

The company articles usually contemplate that directors may be appointed to executive office under the terms of a service agreement and receive remuneration.[5] In such circumstances, the director will also be an employee of the company. This will be the case with managing and other executive directors of most companies. However, in some instances, a director will not have the benefit of a written service agreement, but may still have the status of an employee, for the purposes of, inter alia, unfair dismissal and redundancy rights.[6] A contract of employment may be formed partly expressly and partly impliedly.[7] Further, if a director does not have the status of an employee, he may still be classified as a worker, a status that has the benefit of limited protection under employment legislation.

8.03   The significance of the following discussion is that both company and director will have different rights and obligations depending on the status of the director. For instance, the company's liability for tax and national insurance contributions will depend upon the director's position as an employee (see Chapter 9). Further, a company may make certain pension rights and share option schemes available to employees. Debts to employees may also constitute preferential debts in the event of a winding up of the company. Further, an employed director has certain protective rights, such as unfair dismissal, redundancy protection, maternity or paternity rights, and protection in the event of a transfer of undertaking, which a director who is not employed will not have. This section discusses the main tests that the courts apply to determine whether a director should also be considered an employee or worker.

8.04   The tests of employment have been the subject of continuing common law development. In many cases, the courts draw across a range of statutes and the common law itself in order to determine the status of an individual in question.[8] It should not, however, be concluded that a director who is not treated as an employee for tax purposes will not be treated as an employee under employment legislation or for the purposes of a company's pension scheme. It is possible for a director to be considered an employee in respect of, for example, a tax statute, but not an employee for the purposes of claiming unfair dismissal or redundancy payments.[9]

8.05   The courts will take as their starting point the question of whether there is a contract of employment between the company and director. Under ERA, s 230, a contract of employment is

---

[3] *McMillan v Guest* [1942] AC 561, HL.
[4] [2012] EWCA Civ 841 at para 21, [2012] IRLR 769.
[5] Table A, Art 84; Model Article (pcls) 19, Model Article (plc) 22.
[6] See Ch 7, paras 7.66–7.69 above.
[7] *Stack v Ajar-Tec Ltd* [2015] EWCA Civ 46, [2015] IRLR 474, CA.
[8] See eg the decision of Nolan LJ in the tax case of *Hall v Lorimer* [1994] 1 WLR 209, CA.
[9] See eg *Road Transport Industry Training Board v Readers Garage Ltd* (1969) 4 ITR 195, Div Ct.

defined as a contract of service whether express or implied and (if it is express) whether oral or in writing. Applying the statutory definition, the existence of a written service agreement invariably confers employment status upon a director. Similarly, although unusual in the context of a director, where the court finds that a contract has been agreed orally between the parties, the director will be held to be an employee. The main difficulty arises in circumstances where the parties have not expressly agreed that a director is to be employed.

In order to determine whether a contract may be implied in such circumstances, the courts **8.06** apply a number of notoriously complicated common law tests.[10] Such tests include control of the director by the company;[11] integration into the workforce;[12] the economic reality of the relationship;[13] and an obligation on the director to provide work personally (and not through a substitute).[14]

Application of the control test presents certain difficulties in the case of directors. For **8.07** instance, a director will rarely be subject to control, in the sense of the company deciding the thing to be done, the means to be employed, and the time and place for doing it.[15] Rather, it will be the director himself, acting as the mind of the company, who controls the activities and it is unreal to suggest that a director is subject to his own, or his fellow directors' control. Application of the other tests will present little difficulty in cases where a director does not act under a service contract, but carries out certain duties on behalf of the company on a full-time basis in return for a salary. Usually, the courts will presume that a contract of employment exists.[16] However, this will not always be the case and in *Albert J Parsons & Sons Ltd v Parsons*[17] the Court of Appeal held that it was not possible to imply a service contract in respect of a full-time director, as he received remuneration by way of fees, was not treated as an employee for national insurance purposes, and no record of a service contract had been kept.[18]

There is no reason why a director, who is also the controlling or sole shareholder, cannot **8.08** also be an employee of a company.[19] Whether he will be an employee in any given case is a question of fact. The starting point for analysing this issue is the decision of the Court of

---

[10] For a comprehensive discussion of this area, see Deakin and Morris, *Labour Law*, 6th edn (Hart, 2012), Ch 3. See also *Autoclenz Ltd v Belcher* [2011] UKSC 41; [2011] 4 All ER 745.

[11] *Yewens v Noakes* (1880) 6 QBD 530, CA; *Montgomery v Johnson Underwood Ltd* [2001] ICR 819.

[12] *Stevenson, Jordan & Harrison v MacDonald & Evans* [1952] 1 TLR 101, CA, per Denning LJ.

[13] *Market Investigations Ltd v Minister of Social Security* [1969] 2 QB 173.

[14] *Express and Echo Publications v Tanton* [1999] IRLR 367; a limited power to appoint substitutes is not inconsistent with an obligation of personal service: *Byrne Bros (Formwork) Ltd v Baird* [2002] IRLR 96.

[15] *Ready Mixed Concrete (South East) Ltd v Minister for Pensions and National Security* [1968] 2 QB 497, 515.

[16] *Trussed Steel Concrete Co Ltd v Green* [1946] Ch 115, per Cohen J; *Folami v Nigerline (UK) Ltd* [1978] ICR 277, EAT.

[17] [1979] ICR 271, CA.

[18] As then required under 1967 Act, s 26(1). See now 2006 Act, s 228.

[19] *Lee v Lee's Air Farming Ltd* [1961] AC 12, PC, referring to *Salomon v Salomon & Co* [1897] AC, 22, HL in holding that this was the case even in relation to one-man companies. See also *Secretary of State for Trade and Industry v Bottrill* [1999] ICR 592, doubting *Buchan v Secretary of State for Employment* [1997] IRLR 80; *Fleming v Secretary of State for Trade and Industry* [1997] IRLR 682; *Sellars Arenascene Ltd v Connolly* [2001] ICR 760; *Gladwell v Secretary of State for Trade and Industry* [2007] ICR 264, EAT; *Nesbitt v Secretary of State for Trade and Industry* [2007] IRLR 847, EAT; *Clark v Clark Construction Initiatives Ltd* [2008] ICR 635; *Neufeld v Secretary of State for BERR* [2009] 3 All ER 790, CA.

Appeal in *Secretary of State for Trade and Industry v Bottrill* and the following guidance of Lord Woolf MR:[20]

> We are anxious not to lay down rigid guidelines for the factual inquiry which the tribunal of fact must undertake in the particular circumstances of each case, but we hope that the following comments may be of assistance.
>
> The first question which the tribunal is likely to wish to consider is whether there is or has been a genuine contract between the company and the shareholder. In this context how and for what reasons the contract came into existence (for example, whether the contract was made at a time when insolvency loomed) and what each party actually did pursuant to the contract are likely to be relevant considerations.
>
> If the tribunal concludes that the contract is not a sham, it is likely to wish to consider next whether the contract, which may well have been labelled a contract of employment, actually gave rise to an employer/employee relationship. In this context, of the various factors usually regarded as relevant ... the degree of control exercised by the company over the shareholder employee is always important. This is not the same question as that relating to whether there is a controlling shareholding. The tribunal may think it appropriate to consider whether there are directors other than or in addition to the shareholder employee and whether the constitution of the company gives that shareholder rights such that he is in reality answerable only to himself and incapable of being dismissed. If he is a director, it may be relevant to consider whether he is able under the articles of association to vote on matters in which he is personally interested, such as the termination of his contract of employment. Again, the actual conduct of the parties pursuant to the terms of the contract is likely to be relevant. It is for the tribunal as an industrial jury to take all relevant factors into account in reaching its conclusion, giving such weight to them as it considers appropriate.

8.09 The approach set out by Lord Woolf in *Bottrill* requires the court or tribunal to consider all of the relevant circumstances, including the existence of a controlling shareholding (which may or may not be determinative), whether the contract of employment was genuine or instead designed to confer employment status so as to take advantage of statutory rights, and whether the conduct of the parties is consistent with an employment relationship.

8.10 In *Nesbitt v Secretary of State for Trade and Industry*,[21] Underhill J, considering the *Bottrill* guidance, suggested that the key issue would be whether or not the company is a 'mere simulacrum' defined as: 'something having merely the form or appearance of a certain thing, without possessing its substance or proper qualities', which applies 'where it appears that there is no real intention to vest the business in the company in question or, therefore, to distinguish between the two roles of director and employee'. This approach suggests that employment should always be treated as valid where the arrangement is not a sham.

8.11 In *Clark v Clark Construction Initiatives Ltd*,[22] Elias J (as he then was) gave further guidance[23] as to whether or not there is a genuine, not sham, contract of employment, which was approved by the Court of Appeal,[24] per Sedley LJ, as a 'comprehensive overview ... which

---

[20] [1999] ICR 592, CA at 604.
[21] [2007] IRLR 847, EAT at paras 12 and 27.
[22] [2009] BCC 665; [2008] ICR 635, EAT.
[23] At para 98.
[24] [2008] EWCA Civ 1446, [2008] ICR 718. Appeal dismissed on other grounds.

practitioners will find of considerable assistance in this difficult terrain'. Elias J's guidance was as follows:

(1) Where there is a contract ostensibly in place, the onus is on the party seeking to deny its effect to satisfy the court that it is not what it appears to be. This is particularly so where the individual has paid tax and national insurance as an employee; he has on the face of it earned the right to take advantage of the benefits which employees may derive from such payments.

(2) The mere fact that the individual has a controlling shareholding does not of itself prevent a contract of employment arising. Nor does the fact that he in practice is able to exercise real or sole control over what the company does [*Lee v Lee's Air Farming Ltd*].

(3) Similarly, the fact that he is an entrepreneur, or has built the company up, or will profit from its success, will not be factors militating against a finding that there is a contract in place. Indeed, any controlling shareholder will inevitably benefit from the company's success, as will many employees with share option schemes [*Sellars Arenascene Ltd v Connolly*].

(4) If the conduct of the parties is in accordance with the contract that would be a strong pointer towards the contract being valid and binding. For example, this would be so if the individual works the hours stipulated or does not take more than the stipulated holidays.

(5) Conversely, if the conduct of the parties is either inconsistent with the contract … or in certain key areas where one might expect it to be governed by the contract is in fact not so governed, that would be a factor, and potentially a very important one, militating against a finding that the controlling shareholder is in reality an employee.

(6) In that context, the assertion that there is a genuine contract will be undermined if the terms have not been identified or reduced into writing [*Fleming v Secretary of State for Trade and Industry*]. This will be powerful evidence that the contract was not really intended to regulate the relationship in any way.

(7) The fact that the individual takes loans from the company or guarantees its debts could exceptionally have some relevance in analysing the true nature of the relationship, but in most cases such factors are unlikely to carry any weight. There is nothing intrinsically inconsistent in a person who is an employee doing these things. Indeed, in many small companies it will be necessary for the controlling shareholder personally to have to give bank guarantees precisely because the company assets are small and no funding will be forthcoming without them. It would wholly undermine the [*Lee v Lee's Air Farming*] approach if this were to be sufficient to deny the controlling shareholder the right to enter into a contract of employment.

(8) Although the courts have said that the fact of there being a controlling shareholding is always relevant and may be decisive, that does not mean that the fact alone will ever justify a tribunal in finding that there was no contract in place. That would be to apply the [*Buchan v Secretary of State for Employment*] test which has been decisively rejected. The fact that there is a controlling shareholding is what may raise doubts as to whether that individual is truly an employee, but of itself that fact alone does not resolve those doubts one way or another.

In *Secretary of State for Business Enterprise and Regulatory Reform v Neufeld*,[25] the Court of **8.12**
Appeal held that directors with 90 per cent and 100 per cent shareholdings respectively in their companies were employees. Following a review of the case law discussed above, Rimer LJ approved Elias J's guidance in *Clark* with the following additional comments:

(1) guideline (1) does not constitute a formal reversal of the burden of proof on to the party denying employment status. In cases where the putative employee is asserting the

---

[25] [2009] 3 All ER 790, CA.

existence of an employment contract, it will be for him to prove it. If challenged, it may still be necessary for the putative employee to do more than produce an employment contract or other document to satisfy the tribunal;

(2) guideline (6) may have been expressed in too negative terms. The lack of a written contract will be an important consideration, but the parties' conduct may still point to the existence of a true contract of employment.

8.13 A separate difficulty may arise where a director holds executive positions at a number of companies. Assuming the various appointments are all intended to operate over a period of time, the likely classification is that the director acts as an employee of each of the separate companies for which he acts.[26] Non-executive directors who do not provide labour or services to the company under a service agreement will rarely be employees, even if they receive written terms of appointment.

8.14 If a director is not classified as an employee, he may still be classified as a worker under ERA. A worker is defined under ERA as any individual who works under a contract of employment (meaning that all employees are also workers) or any other contract 'whereby the individual undertakes to do or perform personally any work or services for another party to the contract whose status is not by virtue of the contract that of a client or customer of any profession or undertaking carried on by the individual'.[27] The concept of worker is used in relation to a number of statutes, including the unlawful deductions from wages provisions of ERA,[28] public interest disclosure (whistleblowing) protection,[29] the national minimum wage,[30] working time protection,[31] and the right to be accompanied to disciplinary hearings.[32] The Supreme Court has held, in the context of a whistleblowing member of an LLP, that being a worker did not necessarily depend on any element of subordination to the undertaking.[33] If, therefore, an executive director is not an employee upon application of the tests discussed above, he will in all likelihood meet the definition of a worker and have the benefit of these protective rights.

(1) Personal service companies

8.15 Where an individual is providing work through a personal service company the key consideration is whether he might additionally be an employee of the company to which the services are provided. The use of such a company has become less attractive with the introduction of the 'IR35' tax regime, removing the key tax benefits of the device. In appropriate cases, employment tribunals have been prepared to pierce the corporate veil and find that a contract of employment exists between the individual acting through the personal service company, and the company itself.[34]

---

[26] This is consistent with the decision in *McMeechan v Secretary of State for Employment* [1997] ICR 549.
[27] ERA, s 230(3).
[28] ERA, Part II.
[29] ERA, Part IVA.
[30] National Minimum Wage Act 1998, s 54.
[31] Working Time Regulations 1998, reg 2.
[32] ERA, s 13.
[33] *Clyde and Co LLP v Bates van Winkelhof* [2014] 1 WLR 2047, SC.
[34] *Catamaran Cruisers v Williams* [1994] IRLR 386; cf *Hewlett Packard v O'Murphy* [2002] IRLR 4; *Lanksford v Business Post Ltd* [2004] All ER (D) 46 (Aug). See also, in a different context, *Prest v Petrodel Resources Ltd* [2013] 2 AC 415, SC.

C. Sources of Contractual Terms

In most cases, the contract of a managing or other executive director will be set out in a **8.16** detailed service agreement.[35] However, the written service agreement will rarely be the sole document that evidences terms and conditions and it will often be amended or supplemented by other sources, such as a company handbook, set of work rules, company policies, collective agreement, letters from the company, oral promises, or the conduct of the parties as time passes by, which the court will consider in order to determine the terms agreed by the parties.[36] In *Attrill v Dresdner Kleinwort Ltd*,[37] the Court of Appeal held that a company could make legally binding promises by making an announcement at a Town Hall meeting (approved by the board), which was subsequently repeated on the company intranet. Further, the court held that the promise to establish a minimum bonus pool was legally binding even though at that time an individual employee could not point to any specific amount payable to him out of that pool.

Whether the terms of any written document form part of the contract is a question of **8.17** fact in any given set of circumstances. In particular, the terms of the service agreement may expressly state that a certain document, such as disciplinary or grievance policy, is not intended to have contractual effect, which will negate the possibility of it being incorporated into the contract. A service agreement may contain an 'entire agreement' clause, excluding reliance by either party on any other sources. Whether such a clause is conclusive will depend upon whether in all the circumstances the parties really intended the written instrument to reflect their whole bargain.[38]

As is particularly the case in relation to oral promises, the courts will consider whether any **8.18** statement was intended to have legal effect (as distinct from words of comfort). As such, in *Judge v Crown Leisure*[39] the Court of Appeal upheld a finding that a casual conversation in the 'convivial spirit' of the Christmas party did not amount to a contractual promise.

A contract of employment will contain terms implied under normal contractual principles.[40] **8.19** A term will be implied into a director's service agreement where it is obvious,[41] necessary for business efficacy,[42] or part of the custom of the industry or workplace in question.[43] Certain terms (particularly in relation to pay) are also implied by legislation.[44]

---

[35] Companies have a statutory obligation to provide all employed directors with a written statement of terms and conditions: ERA, Part I.

[36] See *Carmichael v National Power plc* [1999] 1 WLR 2042, HL, per Lord Hoffmann at 2048 *et seq.*

[37] [2011] EWCA Civ 229; [2011] IRLR 613.

[38] *Bushaway v Royal National Lifeboat Institution* [2005] IRLR 674, EAT, in which the EAT held that the tribunal was entitled to look beyond the clause as there were inconsistencies between the contract and the parties' previous dealings; cf *White v Bristol Rugby Ltd* [2002] IRLR 204, in which the clause was held to be effective.

[39] [2005] IRLR 823.

[40] As to which see *Marks & Spencer Plc v BNP Paribas Securities Services Trust Co (Jersey) Ltd* [2016] AC 742, SC.

[41] *Shirlaw v Southern Foundries (1926) Ltd* [1939] 2 KB 206.

[42] *The Moorcock* (1889) 14 PD 64; *Reigate v Union Manufacturing Co (Ramsbottom) Ltd* [1918] 1 KB 592; *Marshall v Alexander Sloan & Co Ltd* [1981] IRLR 264.

[43] *Sagar v H Ridehalgh & Son Ltd* [1931] 1 Ch 310. For an example of custom being used as an aid to interpretation of an express term, see *Dunlop Tyres Ltd v Blows* [2001] IRLR 629.

[44] See para 8.41 below.

8.20   Of particular importance is the implied term of mutual trust and confidence (otherwise described as the duty of fair dealing),[45] implied into all service agreements.[46] The term, recognized by the House of Lords in *Malik v Bank of Credit and Commerce International SA*,[47] is that a company must not without reasonable and proper cause, conduct itself in a manner calculated or likely to destroy or seriously damage the relationship of confidence and trust between itself and an employed director. In *Malik*, the House of Lords held that the term meant that the defendant bank was under an implied obligation not to conduct a dishonest or corrupt business. Any breach of the implied trust and confidence term by a company will be sufficient for a director to resign on account of constructive dismissal.[48]

8.21   The overarching trust and confidence term regulates both a director's performance of his duties and a director's own contractual rights. Where an executive director carries out the managerial functions of the company itself, he must take care to do so in a manner that does not breach the trust and confidence term. Usually this will present little difficulty, as the director's fiduciary duty to act in the best interests of the company will in most cases require him to act consistently with the implied trust and confidence term, vis-à-vis the employees.[49]

8.22   The trust and confidence term will often regulate discretionary clauses, commonly found in directors' service agreements. In particular, it will regulate express contractual provisions that purport to give the company a discretionary power, for instance in relation to pension provision,[50] a mobility clause,[51] and bonuses,[52] or to change duties.[53] Further, the duty may oblige a company to investigate complaints made by a director[54] or prevent its officers or employees from subjecting a director to foul and abusive language.[55]

8.23   As an implied term, there is no reason in principle why the term cannot be excluded by a properly worded express term in a service contract. In practice, such exclusion may arise either directly or indirectly. An example of direct exclusion would be where the company purports to exclude the term itself; whereas indirect exclusion may arise where the terms of the contract provide that any discretionary power may be exercised on any basis whatsoever, whether irrationally or capriciously. Alternatively, the service contract might seek to deem otherwise repudiatory acts (such as a removal of duties or changing of status) as not constituting a repudiation of contract. It is unlikely that the courts would take a strong objection to any such terms (for example on public policy grounds) in the service agreements of directors, given their relatively strong bargaining power. Of greater significance may be the fact that any such term can indirectly cause the director to contract out of his protective rights, and may therefore be void.[56]

---

[45] Usually described as such in the context of termination: see *Johnson v Unisys Ltd* [2003] 1 AC 518, HL, per Lord Steyn at para 24.

[46] *Malik v Bank of Credit and Commerce Interational SA* [1998] AC 20, HL.

[47] [1998] AC 20, HL.

[48] *Morrow v Safeway Stores plc* [2002] IRLR 9.

[49] See in particular the duty contained in 2006 Act, 172(1)(b), discussed in Ch 12.

[50] *Imperial Group Pension Trust Ltd v Imperial Tobacco Ltd* [1991] 1 WLR 589.

[51] *United Bank Ltd v Akhtar* [1989] IRLR 507.

[52] See *Horkulak v Cantor Fitzgerald* [2005] IRLR 502, CA.

[53] See *Land Securities Trillium v Thornley* [2005] IRLR 765, in which the duty applied notwithstanding a broadly worded flexibility clause.

[54] *British Airways Corpn v Austin* [1978] IRLR 332.

[55] *Horkulak v Cantor Fitzgerald* [2005] ICR 502, CA, in which the court also held that high levels of remuneration cannot be used as justification for poor treatment.

[56] ERA, s 230.

D. Terms of Employment

At common law, company and director are free to enter into a service agreement for any **8.24** specified period of time or for an unlimited duration. Termination of service agreements is considered in Chapter 7. The provisions of the Companies Act regarding disclosure of details of long-term service agreements are discussed in Chapter 18 below. Quoted companies[57] have further obligations to disclose details of directors' remuneration in a directors' remuneration report, which must be approved by the members (Chapter 26, Section C below).

(1) Remuneration

The remuneration of directors comes from two separate sources. First, the directors (and **8.25** in particular non-executive directors of public companies) may receive fees for acting as a director. Secondly, a director's service agreement, if there is one, will provide for payment of a salary and other benefits.

The provisions contained within Part 10 of the Companies Act for the prior approval by mem- **8.26** bers of certain long-term service contracts and for directors' service contracts to be available for inspection are considered in Chapter 18, Section B. Chapter 26, Section C(4) describes the requirement in Part 15 of the Companies Act for a quoted company to prepare in each financial year a directors' remuneration report, which must be approved by the board. The UK Corporate Governance Code sets out standards for the level and components of the remuneration of directors of listed companies, which are described in Section E of this chapter.

Remuneration permitted by the company articles

Under most company articles, members must approve fees payable for holding office as **8.27** directors, but directors may fix remuneration under the service agreement for executive functions.

Regulation 82 of Table A provides as follows: **8.28**

> The directors shall be entitled to such remuneration as the company may by ordinary resolution determine and, unless the resolution provides otherwise, the remuneration shall be deemed to accrue from day to day.

Regulation 84 of Table A provides as follows: **8.29**

> Subject to the provisions of the Act, the directors may appoint one or more of their number to the office of managing director or to any other executive office under the company and may enter into an agreement or arrangement with any director for his employment by the company or for the provision by him of any services outside the scope of the ordinary duties of a director. Any such appointment, agreement or arrangement may be made upon such terms as the directors determine and they may remunerate any such director for his services as they think fit. Any appointment of a director to an executive office shall terminate if he ceases to be a director but without prejudice to any claim to damages for breach of the contract of service between the director and the company. A managing director and a director holding any other executive office shall not be subject to retirement by rotation.

---

[57] By 2006 Act, s 385 a quoted company is a company whose equity share capital has been included in the official list in accordance with the FSMA, Part 6, or is officially listed in an EEA state, or is admitted to dealing in either the New York Stock Exchange or Nasdaq.

8.30   Model Article (pcls) 19 and Model Article (plc) 23 give authority to the directors to determine directors' remuneration and provide:

> (1) Directors may undertake any services for the company that the directors decide.
> (2) Directors are entitled to such remuneration as the directors determine—
> > (a) for their services to the company as directors, and
> > (b) for any other service which they undertake for the company.
> (3) Subject to the articles, a director's remuneration may—
> > (a) take any form, and
> > (b) include any arrangements in connection with the payment of a pension, allowance or gratuity, or any death, sickness or disability benefits, to or in respect of the director.
> (4) Unless the directors decide otherwise, directors' remuneration accrues from day to day.
> (5) Unless the directors decide otherwise, directors are not accountable to the company for any remuneration which they receive as directors of the company's subsidiaries or of any other body corporate in which the company is interested.

8.31   As such, the Model Articles provide for wide powers as to the form of any remuneration at the discretion of the directors, with such power delegated to the board.

8.32   However, in the absence of a service contract, provision in the company articles or other approval by members,[58] a director does not have a right to be remunerated for services performed as a director for the company,[59] whether as a *quantum meruit* or otherwise.[60] As expressed by Bowen LJ in *Hutton v West Cork Railway*[61] a 'director is not a servant; he is a person doing business for the company, but not upon ordinary terms. It is not implied from the mere fact that he is a director that he is to be paid for it.' This general rule is an aspect of the fiduciary principle that a director is not allowed to make a profit unless expressly permitted.[62] In *Deir v Al Athel*[63] the court held that a company had agreed to pay fees to a director (in addition to his written service contract) notwithstanding that the agreement was not evidenced in writing. However, the court found that the fees would only be payable where the director had carried out more than merely nominal duties. Where a director also provides services as a manager or otherwise, he will be entitled to remuneration on a *quantum meruit* basis.[64]

8.33   Provided that remuneration is bona fide and not an improper return of capital to shareholders,[65] the court will not intervene in the company's exercise of discretion because 'it is not for the courts to manage the company'.[66] As such, there is no obligation to pay a 'going rate',[67]

---

[58] *Re George Newman and Co* [1895] 1 Ch 674, CA.
[59] *Dunstan v Imperial Gas Light Co* (1832) 3 B & Ad 125; *Hutton v West Cork Railway* (1883) 23 Ch D 654, CA; *Guinness plc v Saunders* [1990] 2 AC 663, HL; *Knopp v Thane Investments Ltd* [2003] 1 BCLC 380 at para 140.
[60] See also *Re George Newman and Co* [1895] 1 Ch 674, CA; *Dunstan v Imperial Gas Light Co* (1832) 3 B & Ad 125; *Ex p Cannon* (1885) 30 Ch D 629; *In re Richmond Gate Property Co Ltd* [1965] 1 WLR 335; *Tayplan Ltd v Smith* [2012] BCC 523, CS at para 25.
[61] (1883) 23 Ch D 654, 671.
[62] '[E]very fiduciary is under a duty not to make a profit from his position (unless such profit is authorised)': *Henderson v Merrett Syndicates* [1995] 2 AC 145, HL, per Lord Browne-Wilkinson at 206. *Hutton v West Cork Railway* (1883) 23 Ch D 654.
[63] [2011] EWHC 354 (QB).
[64] On the calculation of which see *Benedetti v Sawiris* [2014] AC 938, SC.
[65] A disguised gift repaid out of capital is ultra vires: *Re Halt Garage (1964) Ltd* [1984] 3 All ER 1016.
[66] *Re Halt Garage (1964) Ltd* [1982] 3 All ER 1016, 1039, per Oliver J.
[67] *Secretary of State for Trade and Industry v Van Hengel* [1995] 1 BCLC 545.

nor a restriction on high salaries. However, a failure by the directors to ensure that the board fixes salaries that are affordable by the company may show the directors' unfitness and be a ground for a disqualification order.[68] In addition, the payment of excessive remuneration bearing no reasonable relation to the services performed may be open to challenge by members in a derivative claim or unfair prejudice petition.[69] Finally, excessive remuneration awarded when the company is in financial difficulties may be open to challenge by a liquidator under the misfeasance provision contained in the Insolvency Act.[70]

Remuneration is consideration for work done or to be done and as such it may take different forms. It will normally take the form of a salary, and may be supplemented by commissions, fees, or bonuses.[71] In every case, the entitlement that arises is a question of construction of the articles and any duly authorized agreement. Where a sum is dependent upon the performance of the company (for example by reference to profits), then the director is not entitled to any sum where no profits are made.[72] However, where a sum is not dependent upon performance or any other measure, it will be payable irrespective of whether or not the company is making a profit.[73] In practical terms, a decrease in profits may result in the members resolving to cut or cancel directors' fees. However, absent express provision in the service agreement, any attempt to reduce contractual benefits will constitute a breach of contract, irrespective of the motive (and may amount to a repudiation of the agreement, entitling the director to resign on account of constructive dismissal). Sale of the bulk of the company's assets, so that the directors' duties are greatly reduced, does not disentitle them to their full remuneration.[74]   **8.34**

If the articles are silent, the company in general meeting may vote remuneration; but in such case the remuneration is a gratuity, and not a matter of right.[75] In a going company, the general meeting may vote a gratuity at will,[76] but upon liquidation this cannot be done.[77]   **8.35**

The 2006 Act has repealed an earlier provision[78] that made it unlawful for a company to agree to pay the director a certain sum net of tax, or to vary the director's income in line with changes in income tax rates.   **8.36**

---

[68] *Secretary of State for Trade and Industry v Van Hengel* [1995] 1 BCLC 545.

[69] See Chs 22 and 23 below. Cases on 'fraud on the minority' including allegations of excessive remuneration: *Nolan v Parsons* [1942] OR 358, CA (Ont); *Smith v Croft* [1986] 1 WLR 580; *Smith v Croft (No 2)* [1988] Ch 114 where the court rejected the excessive remuneration allegation.

[70] Insolvency Act, s 212; *Re Halt Garage (1964) Ltd* [1982] 3 All ER 1016; *Re Nixon & Hope Ltd, Power v Hodges* [2015] EWHC 2983 (Ch) [2016] BPIR 162.

[71] *Currencies Direct Ltd v Ellis* [2002] 2 BCLC 482, 487, per Mummery LJ.

[72] Remuneration as a percentage of profits does not include a share of the profit made on the sale of the whole business of the company: *Frames v Bulfontein Mining Co* [1891] 1 Ch 140. It will include profits which exist in specie, even though these would not be converted into cash except on liquidation: *Re Spanish Prospecting Co* [1911] 1 Ch 92, CA.

[73] *Re Lundy Granite Co, Lewis's Case* (1872) 26 LT 673; *Nell v Atlanta Gold and Silver Consol Mines* (1895) 11 TLR 407, CA.

[74] *Re Consolidated Nickel Mines* [1914] 1 Ch 883.

[75] *Re Geo Newman and Co* [1895] 1 Ch 674, CA; *Dunstan v Imperial Gas Light Co* (1832) 3 B&Ad 125; *Ex p Cannon* (1885) 30 Ch D 629; *Putaruru Pine & Pulp Co (NZ) Ltd v MacCulloch* [1934] NZLR 639. Alternatively, in such a case, it may be paid with the unanimous consent of the shareholders: *D'Amore v McDonald* [1973] 1 OR 845 at 864, HC (Ont), affd (1974) 1 OR (2d) 370, CA (Ont).

[76] *Re Lundy Granite Co, Lewis's Case* (1872) 26 LT 673; *Re Geo Newman & Co* [1895] 1 Ch 674.

[77] *Hutton v West Cork Railway Co* (1883) 23 Ch D 654; *Stroud v Royal Aquarium, etc, Society* [1903] WN 143.

[78] 1985 Act, s 311.

Position of directors with invalid appointments

8.37 If a director's appointment is not valid, he cannot recover remuneration as a director in accordance with the articles, even though he may have served for a long period.[79] However, depending on the terms of the service agreement, an invalid appointment will not necessarily affect the contractual position, which may be effective irrespective of the lack of a valid appointment. As noted below, however, compensation in all but name may often be recovered by an action for unjust enrichment if the director acted in accordance with an implied invitation, one of the terms of which was for remuneration at the rate specified.[80]

8.38 In the unlikely event that it is discovered that fees have been paid after a director had vacated office, for whatever reason, and where the facts negative the probability of an intention to grant remuneration, the company can recover the amounts as money paid by mistake.[81]

Agreement to forego fees

8.39 It is open to directors by a resolution to renounce the right to future remuneration under such implied contracts.[82] An agreement by all the directors inter se and with the company to renounce the right to remuneration is binding on each director even at the suit of the company.[83] A resolution to forego fees may, however, be rescinded by a subsequent resolution, and if this is done, remuneration will be payable as from the date of the rescinding resolution.[84]

The right to pay under the service agreement

8.40 Under the terms of the service agreement, the entitlement to pay may comprise a number of different benefits, usually wider than those expressly referred to in the company articles. Almost always, the principal benefit will comprise salary, and will often be supplemented by further benefits such as bonuses, share options, a pension, medical care, company car, expenses incurred by reason of employment, sick pay, holiday pay, or any other specified entitlement. Service agreements are likely to give directors the right to be considered for a salary increase, rather than a right to a particular increase in itself.

8.41 Legislation (other than the Companies Act) imposes two restrictions upon the level of remuneration provided under a service contract. First, an equality clause will be implied into all service agreements, providing that a female director carrying out equal work is entitled to be paid the same as her male counterparts.[85] In *Villalba v Merrill Lynch & Co Inc*,[86] a former managing director brought a claim for equal pay alleging that her bonus payments constituted a breach of the implied equality clause.[87] For the purposes of the right to equal pay at least, the concept is wide enough to encompass all of the benefits listed above which

---

[79] *Woolf v East Nigel Gold Mining Co* (1905) 21 TLR 660.

[80] *Swabey v Port Darwin Gold Mining Co* (1889) 1 Meg 385; *Isaacs' Case* [1892] 2 Ch 158; *Re Peruvian Guano Co* [1894] 3 Ch 690; *Re New British Iron Co, ex p Beckwith* [1898] 1 Ch 324; *Craven-Ellis v Canons* [1936] 2 KB 403, CA; *Re Richmond Gate Property Co* [1965] 1 WLR 335.

[81] *Re Bodega Co* [1904] 1 Ch 276. In this case the director was disqualified for having secretly participated in contracts with the company.

[82] *McConnell's Claim, re London and Northern Bank* [1901] 1 Ch 728.

[83] *West Yorkshire Darracq Agency v Coleridge* [1911] 2 KB 326.

[84] *Re Consolidated Nickel Mines* [1914] 1 Ch 883.

[85] Equality Act 2010, ss 64–6; the right to equal pay also applies by reason of Art 157 of the TFEU, which the European Court of Justice in Case 43/75 *Defrenne v SA Belge de Navigation Aérienne* [1976] ECR 455 held to be directly effective in English law.

[86] [2006] IRLR 437.

[87] See also *Barton v Investec Henderson Crosthwaite Securities* [2003] IRLR 332.

are payable as a condition of employment.[88] Secondly, where the director has the status of worker,[89] his contract will contain an implied term that he is entitled to the national minimum wage.

Discretionary bonuses and share options

The entitlement to a bonus will often form the principal part of a director's remuneration. **8.42** Such clauses are commonly described as discretionary and provide that an employer has an absolute discretion as to whether to award an employee a bonus, and, if it decides to make such an award, as to the amount and form of that bonus. In *Clark v Nomura International plc*,[90] Burton J held that such a clause provided the employee with a right to have the discretion exercised, and that the discretion was subject to an implied obligation that it not be exercised irrationally or perversely. Further, the precise wording of the clause would constitute a 'contractual straitjacket' as to the factors that could be taken into consideration when exercising discretion.[91] Burton J went on to hold that, in determining damages, the court should put itself in the position of the company as far as possible in order to reach a conclusion as to what position the employee would have been in had the employer performed its obligation. The Court of Appeal has since gone on to adopt the *Clark* test in a number of cases,[92] and the Supreme Court referred to it with approval in *Braganza v BP Shipping Ltd*.[93] In the analogous context of a discretionary share option scheme, Peter Smith J in *McCarthy v McCarthy & Stone plc*[94] held that where a discretion had not been lawfully exercised (because of an absence of good faith) the court may conclude it to be a nullity and as a result may direct that the employer or the committee should reconsider the decision on a lawful basis. In the Court of Appeal,[95] it was recognized that whereas the decision could be remitted to the committee, if there was only one possible outcome then the court was entitled to exercise the decision itself.

In *Commerzbank AG v Keen*,[96] the Court of Appeal recognized that a higher threshold **8.43** would apply in cases where the company had exercised its discretion and determined the amount of the discretionary bonus (as opposed to deciding to make a nil award as in *Clark v Nomura International plc*).[97] There, Mr Keen sought to challenge bonus awards in the region of €3 million (making him amongst the highest paid employees of the company internationally) on the grounds of irrationality and perversity. Mummery LJ held that the burden upon an individual in such circumstances is a 'very high one' and would require an 'overwhelming case' to succeed.[98] As set out by Moses LJ, it is for the director to establish the irrationality of the decision, and he must, therefore, be able to demonstrate some feature of

---

[88] See *Barber v Guardian Royal Exchange Assurance Group* [1990] IRLR 240 in which the European Court of Justice held that the concept covered an occupational pension scheme.

[89] As defined in National Minimum Wage Act 1998, s 54.

[90] [2000] IRLR 766.

[91] As such, in *Clark v Nomura*, the discretionary bonus was based upon 'individual performance', which restricted the company from taking other factors into account.

[92] See eg *Mallone v BPB Industries Ltd* [2002] ICR 1045, CA and *Horkulak v Cantor Fitzgerald International* [2005] ICR 402, CA.

[93] [2015] UKSC 17, [2015] 1 WLR 1661.

[94] [2006] 4 All ER 1127.

[95] [2008] 1 All ER 221.

[96] [2007] ICR 623, CA.

[97] [2000] IRLR 766.

[98] At 632.

the award, or the circumstances in which it was made, which tends to show its perversity. However, in circumstances where the director has made out a prima facie case of irrationality, the company must meet that case by identifying the decision-maker and the reason for the decision.[99]

8.44 It is presently unclear whether a director may have a claim in circumstances where he is dismissed with the object of avoiding a bonus payment. The question arises as it is common for discretionary bonuses to provide that the director is in employment on the date that payment falls due. In *Commerzbank AG v Keen*,[100] the Court of Appeal rejected an argument that such clauses were unenforceable by reason of the Unfair Contract Terms Act 1977, as that Act has no application to service agreements. In *Clark v Nomura International plc*,[101] Burton J held that dismissal with the aim of avoiding payment of a bonus might be ineffective, meaning that the director would either be able to keep the contract alive until the payment date or bring a claim for damages. Similarly, in *Reda v Flag Ltd*[102] the Privy Council was willing to assume that if employees had been capriciously or arbitrarily singled out for dismissal in order to deprive them of an entitlement to participate in a stock option plan, this might well constitute a breach of the implied term of trust and confidence and that an employee would not necessarily be without a remedy because the mechanism of victimization took the form of dismissal. That approach would have allowed the employees to pursue a free-standing contractual claim in respect of their non-participation in a stock option plan as damages for breach of the implied term of trust and confidence rather than a claim for damages for wrongful dismissal (that is, for a free-standing anterior breach of contract). The Privy Council held that there had been no breach of the implied term of trust and confidence in that case because the employers were justified in treating the employees differently and less favourably for commercially legitimate and objectively defensible reasons. In *Takacs v Barclays Services Jersey Ltd*,[103] a High Court Master considered it arguable that an employer owed a contractual duty (by reason of the implied term of mutual trust and confidence) not to frustrate an employee's ability to earn a contractual bonus, notwithstanding that his employment had been lawfully terminated before the right to a bonus arose.

8.45 Remuneration may also take the form of a right to participate in a share option scheme. Such schemes typically allow for a director to purchase shares at a fixed price at a set time in the future, and therefore provide an incentive for a director to remain in service, perform well, and to improve the company's share price for the benefit of shareholders. The contractual provisions that govern any such scheme will follow the same principles of construction as apply to other contractual provisions regarding remuneration, such as bonuses. In *Hopkin v Financial Security Assurance (UK) Ltd*[104] the Court of Appeal held that an employee was not entitled to be allocated performance shares under a share scheme as his employment had been terminated by reason of redundancy prior to the vesting of such rights.

---

[99] At 639.
[100] [2007] ICR 623, CA.
[101] [2000] IRLR 766.
[102] [2002] IRLR 747.
[103] [2006] IRLR 877.
[104] [2011] EWCA Civ 243.

Apportionment of remuneration

8.46 Under Table A, reg 82 and Model Article (pcls) 19(4) and Model Article (plc) 23(4) a director's remuneration accrues from day to day. As noted in *Item Software Ltd v Fassihi*,[105] the same outcome would apply under the Apportionment Act 1870, unless the parties otherwise stipulated in the service agreement.

Remedies for breach of payments provisions

8.47 A claim for non-payment of any contractual benefit can be enforced by way of an action for debt or damages for breach of contract.[106] If the claim is for unpaid wages, it can be enforced in the employment tribunals, and there is no limit on compensation.[107] If the company goes into administration or liquidation, a director ranks as an ordinary creditor for any unpaid remuneration or other claims against the company.[108]

(2) Expenses

8.48 Regulation 83 of Table A provides:

> The directors may be paid all travelling, hotel, and other expenses properly incurred by them in connection with their attendance at meetings or committees of directors or general meetings or separate meetings of the holders of any class of shares or of debentures of the company or otherwise in connection with the discharge of their duties.

8.49 Model Article (pcls) 20 and Model Article (plc) 24 each provide:

> The company must pay any reasonable expenses which the directors properly incur in connection with their attendance at—
> (a) meetings of directors or committees of directors,
> (b) general meetings, or
> (c) separate meetings of the holders of any class of shares or of debentures of the company, or otherwise in connection with the exercise of their powers and the discharge of the their responsibilities in relation to the company.

8.50 Similar provisions are likely to be included within the service agreement, which may impose a procedure for reclaiming expenses. Where a director fails to claim expenses in accordance with an agreed contractual formula, they cannot be recovered.

8.51 Directors, as agents, are by law entitled to an indemnity in respect of all liabilities properly incurred by them in the management of the company's business.[109] No express provision is necessary, although the articles often give rights that are more extensive than those implied by law. This indemnity does not necessarily cover all expenses. Unless specially authorized by the articles or by resolution of a general meeting, expenses of travelling to or from board meetings must not be paid in addition.[110]

---

[105] [2005] 2 BCLC 91, CA.

[106] Non-payment of salary will not necessarily constitute a repudiatory breach: *WPM Retail Ltd v Laing* [1978] ICR 787, EAT; *Gillies v Richard Daniels & Co Ltd* [1979] IRLR 457, EAT; *Cantor Fitzgerald International v Callaghan* [1999] ICR 639, CA. By contrast, denial of contractual obligations to pay normally will constitute a repudiation: *F Hill Ltd v Mooney* [1981] IRLR 258.

[107] However, a claim for a discretionary bonus cannot be enforced under the provisions of ERA, Part II where the discretion has not been exercised and the figure is not therefore quantifiable and due: *Coors Brewery v Adcock* [2007] ICR 983; *Tradition Securities and Futures SA v Mouradian* [2009] EWCA Civ 60.

[108] *Re Dale & Plant* (1889) 43 Ch D 255; *Re New British Iron Co* [1898] 1 Ch 324; *Re A1 Biscuit Co* [1899] WN 115.

[109] *Re German Mining Co* (1853) 4 De GM & G 19; *James v May* (1873) LR 6 HL 328.

[110] *Young v Naval and Military Co-operative Society* [1905] 1 KB 687; *Marmor v Alexander* 1908 SC 78.

(3) Confidentiality

8.52 A director will invariably be subject to a duty of confidentiality in respect of the company's trade secrets and confidential information.[111] Inevitably, there will be a significant degree of overlap between the duties imposed under the service agreement (whether expressly or impliedly) and a director's statutory duties under the 2006 Act.[112]

8.53 Typically, a service agreement will include an express confidentiality clause which will give contractual force to the director's statutory duties. In any event, all directors employed under service agreements are subject to an implied term not to disclose trade secrets or confidential information obtained by reason of employment[113] and not to use any information obtained as a result of employment to the detriment of the company.[114] Such clauses can be enforced by an injunction, both before and after termination of the service agreement.[115] However, contractual clauses regarding confidentiality cannot restrict a director from making a public interest disclosure within the meaning of the whistleblowing provisions of the ERA.[116]

8.54 Such clauses will often be used to protect trade secrets and confidential information. In *Herbert Morris v Saxelby*,[117] a distinction was drawn between information that properly belongs to the company, and that forming part of the director's own general knowledge. A company director will often have experience in and knowledge about the relevant industry in which his company operates, which he is entitled to use for the benefit of a future company. The burden rests upon the company to show that any specific body of information is outside that falling within the director's own general knowledge.[118] Further, the company must be able to show that the information is such as to have the nature of confidentiality. In *Thomas Marshall (Exports) Ltd v Guinle*,[119] Megarry V-C held that the issue of confidentiality should be judged by reference to the potential injury to the company or advantage to a competitor, the reasonable belief of the company, and the nature of the trade in question.

8.55 Often, a service contract will seek to impose more onerous restrictions upon a director, both in relation to the categories of information that should be treated as confidential, and in relation to restrictions after termination. Any attempt by a company to deem specific information as confidential, which would not otherwise be confidential (for example as forming part of the director's skill and general knowledge or not otherwise having the nature

---

[111] See Goulding, *Employee Competition*, 2nd edn (Oxford University Press, 2011), Ch 3.

[112] See Ch 15 below.

[113] *Amber Size and Chemical Co v Menzel* [1913] 2 Ch 239; *Alperton Rubber Co v Manning* (1917) 86 LJ Ch 377; *British Industrial Plastics v Ferguson* [1940] 1 All ER 479; *Initial Services Ltd v Putterill* [1968] 1 QB 396; *Thomas Marshall Ltd v Guinle* [1979] Ch 227.

[114] *Merryweather v Moore* [1892] 2 Ch 518; *Bent's Brewery Co v Hogan* [1945] 2 All ER 570; *Cranleigh Precision Engineering Ltd v Bryant* [1965] 1 WLR 1293.

[115] An injunction may be granted where the breach of the duty of confidentiality or the duty of good faith has occurred during the course of the employment even if the consequences of this only occur after the employment has ended and, had it not been for the breach during the course of the employment, the employee would have been free to use it afterwards: see *Roger Bullivant Ltd v Ellis* [1987] ICR 464, CA.

[116] ERA, Part IVA.

[117] [1916] 1 AC 688, HL.

[118] *FSS Travel and Leisure Systems Ltd v Johnson* [1998] IRLR 382, CA. In *PennWell Publishing (UK) Ltd v Ornstien* [2008] 2 BCLC 246 the court granted an injunction preventing a former employee making use of the company's contact except for his own key personal contacts and those that he had made before his employment began.

[119] [1979] Ch 227.

of confidentiality)[120] is ineffective.[121] However, such a clause may be useful as an aid in determining whether any information should properly be considered confidential.

Many companies will also seek to impose restrictions on the use of confidential information **8.56** after termination of a service agreement. Absent an express clause, the duty will continue in any event after employment.[122] This position is now enshrined in the 2006 Act, s 170(2)(a), which provides that the director's duty to avoid conflicts of interest as regards the exploitation of property, information, or opportunity of which he became aware at a time when he was a director[123] continues when he ceases to be a director. Notwithstanding the existence of the duty, express contractual clauses are often useful as they will identify the restriction with precision and are more likely to be known to the director.

There is no objection to the parties' expressly identifying the category of information that is **8.57** considered to be confidential.[124] However, where a deeming clause of this nature is so wide ranging as to be in restraint of trade,[125] it will not be enforced, and it cannot be used as an alternative to an appropriate non-solicitation or non-competition clause.[126] As such, in circumstances where there is doubt as to whether the information in question would constitute a trade secret, a company would be well advised to include a well-drafted provision identifying the relevant information with precision and an appropriate duration for which it would remain confidential.

(4) Restrictive covenants

The importance of a director to the success of the company means that it will often be com- **8.58** mon to include covenants restricting competition with the company after termination.[127] Notably, a director will also be subject to s 170(2)(b) which prevents him from receiving benefits from third parties as regards things done or omitted before he ceased to be a director.[128] This may conceivably apply to remuneration received from a competitor company for whom a director subsequently goes to work.

As restrictive covenants restrict a director's ability to work, they will constitute an invalid **8.59** restraint of trade unless reasonable and necessary to protect the company's legitimate business interests.[129] Restrictive covenants may be enforced by the company by way of a claim for damages in the event of breach or by way of an injunction, either before or after the termination of employment.

The legitimate business interests of the company are determined by reference to the nature **8.60** of its activities and the director's role in those activities.[130] The company can primarily use a restrictive covenant to protect trade secrets and confidential information, a director's

---

[120] See *Faccenda Chicken Ltd v Fowler* [1987] Ch 117.
[121] *Ixora Trading Inc v Jones* [1990] FSR 251.
[122] See *Printers and Finishers Ltd v Holloway (No 2)* [1965] 1 WLR 1.
[123] 2006 Act, s 175.
[124] *Lansing Linde v Kerr* [1990] ICR 428.
[125] *Intelsec Systems v Grech-Chini* [2000] 1 WLR 1190.
[126] See *Balston v Headline Filters* [1987] FSR 330, 351–2.
[127] For a comprehensive discussion of this area, see Goulding, *Employee Competition*, 3rd edn (Oxford University Press, 2016), Ch 5.
[128] 2006 Act, s 176.
[129] *Nordenfelt v Maxim Nordenfelt & Co* [1894] AC 535, HL.
[130] *Herbert Morris Ltd v Saxelby* [1916] 1 AC 688, HL.

connections, and workforce skills. However, the categories of legitimate interests are not closed and a reasonable covenant can be used in respect of any further legitimate interest that a company may have.[131]

8.61 The business interests so far recognized as potentially requiring protection fall into three categories. First, as discussed above, the courts will act to protect confidential information and trade secrets that properly form part of the employer's property and not the general knowledge of the director. The prevailing view is that confidential information is not proprietary as such,[132] though a company's property in documents may be separately protected by remedies such as delivery up.[133]

8.62 Secondly, typically, the director's contacts with customers and clients will constitute an asset of the company. This is particularly true in respect of companies offering professional services, where client relationships constitute a significant part of the company's income. It has long been the case that a company cannot restrict a director from soliciting clients with whom he has had no significant contact.[134] However, where a director has had significant contact, there will be little difficulty in most cases in establishing the legitimate interests capable of protection.[135] In *Threlfall v ECD Insight Ltd*[136] the court refused to enforce a non-solicitation and non-competition clause where it related to a category of work which the company had performed only during, and because of, the now former senior employee's presence.

8.63 Thirdly, the courts have held that a company will have a legitimate interest in protecting the stability of its workplace. This interest is usually protected by way of a covenant restricting the solicitation or 'poaching' of existing directors or employees of the company. As such in *Alliance Paper Group plc v Prestwich*,[137] the court granted an injunction to prevent a managing director from attempting to recruit senior staff. In *Dawnay Day & Co Ltd v D'Alphen*,[138] the Court of Appeal held that the restriction of such a clause to 'senior' staff was reasonable and therefore could be enforced. However, in *TSC Europe (UK) Ltd v Massey*[139] the court held that a similar non-solicitation clause constituted a legitimate interest, but on the facts of the case, the covenant was unenforceable as it extended to all employees of the company (including employees who had been recruited since the employee had departed) and was therefore too wide.

8.64 The reasonableness of the covenant will depend very much upon the nature of the restriction. The courts are more likely to uphold restrictions in directors' service agreements for two reasons. First, as a high-status employee, a director is more likely to have the knowledge and contacts that constitute a legitimate interest of the company. As such a restriction against competition entirely may be the only way of protecting the company's interest.[140] Secondly, a

---

[131] *Dawnay Day & Co Ltd v D'Alphen* [1998] ICR 1068, 1106, 1107, per Evans LJ.

[132] *Phillips v News Group Newspapers Ltd* [2012] UKSC 28, [2013] 1 AC 1.

[133] *Fairstar Heavy Transport NV v Adkins* [2013] EWCA Civ 886, [2013] 2 CLC 272.

[134] *Herbert Morris Ltd v Saxelby* [1916] 1 AC 688, HL.

[135] *Beckett Investment Management Group Ltd v Hall* [2007] ICR 1539; *Le Puy Ltd v Potter* [2015] EWHC 193 (QB), [2015] IRLR 554.

[136] [2012] EWHC 3543 (QB), [2013] IRLR 185.

[137] [1996] IRLR 25, Ch D.

[138] [1998] ICR 1068.

[139] [1999] IRLR 22, Ch D.

[140] *TFS Derivatives Ltd v Morgan* [2005] IRLR 246 at paras 15–17, 84, per Cox J; *Thomas v Farr plc* [2007] ICR 932, CA.

director, in contrast to a junior employee, is more likely to be able to protect his own interests when entering into an agreement and does not need the protection of the court.[141]

However, notwithstanding the position of a director within the company, a court will still strike down a covenant or any severable part of a covenant[142] where the restriction is more than is reasonably necessary to protect the interest of the company.[143] Covenants for longer durations and of wider scope will necessarily be more difficult to justify.[144] As such, care should be taken when deciding the interaction between area, duration, and specified restricted activities. In *Office Angels Ltd v Rainer-Thomas*,[145] the court struck down a 1-km area restriction in the contracts of a branch manager and consultant where the effect would be to restrict competition throughout most of the City of London. In *Beckett Investment Management v Hall*,[146] the Court of Appeal held that a 12-month non-competition clause was reasonable as it reflected the time required to recruit, organize, train, and project a suitable replacement director, and was consistent with industry practice. The enforceability of the covenants in any given case will turn upon its own facts.[147] **8.65**

Any covenant must have been valid from the outset.[148] However, even where a covenant was reasonable and necessary at the time of agreement, the court has a discretion as to whether to enforce it, which it is unlikely to exercise in respect of a covenant that has become obsolete. For this reason, continued review of the restrictive covenants in directors' service agreements will improve the likelihood that the restrictions remain reasonable and necessary. When drafting such clauses, it is useful to bear in mind Sedley LJ's comment in *Wincanton Ltd v Cranny*[149] that restrictive covenants are 'drafted with the comprehensive particularity of a conveyancer, and one of the morals of the many decided cases in this field of law is that those who live by this mode of drafting may find, when it comes to litigation, that they perish by it'. **8.66**

Group companies

Directors are often employed under a service agreement with one company, but in fact perform their duties for a related company within the same group. In many cases, the director may be subject to a covenant that purports to restrict competition against an associated company, or any company within the group. In *Henry Leetham & Sons Ltd v Johnstone-White*,[150] the Court of Appeal refused to uphold a covenant against competition against the group on the grounds that it was wider than necessary for the company which actually employed the director. However, in *Stenhouse Australia Ltd v Phillips*,[151] the court upheld a similar **8.67**

---

[141] 'A managing director can look after himself': *M and S Drapers v Reynolds* [1957] 1 WLR 9, CA, per Denning LJ. See also *Hanover Insurance Brokers Ltd v Schapiro* [1994] IRLR 82.

[142] On severance, see *Mason v Provident Clothing and Supply Co Ltd* [1913] AC 724, HL; *Rex Stewart Jeffries Parker Ginsberg Ltd v Parker* [1988] IRLR 483, CA; *Attwood v Lamont* [1920] 3 KB 571.

[143] *Nordenfelt v Maxim Nordenfelt & Co* [1894] AC 535, HL; *Mason v Provident Clothing Co* [1913] AC 724, HL; *Herbert Morris v Saxelby* [1916] 1 AC 688, HL.

[144] *Herbert Morris v Saxelby* [1916] 1 AC 688, 715, HL; *Safetynet Security Ltd v Coppage* [2013] EWCA Civ 1176; [2013] IRLR 970.

[145] [1991] IRLR 214, CA.

[146] [2007] ICR 1539.

[147] *Dairy Crest Ltd v Pigott* [1989] ICR 92, CA.

[148] *Gledhow Autoparts Ltd v Delaney* [1965] 1 WLR 1366.

[149] [2000] IRLR 716 at para 29.

[150] [1907] 1 Ch 322, CA.

[151] [1974] AC 391, PC.

covenant where subsidiary companies were agencies, handling the business of the parent. In *Beckett Investment Management v Hall*,[152] the Court of Appeal overturned a finding that a covenant was ineffective by reason that it applied to a holding company, notwithstanding the fact that the business in question was carried out by a subsidiary. Maurice Kay LJ referred back to the words of Lord Denning MR in *Littlewoods Organisation Ltd v Harris*[153] that the law should 'have regard to the realities of big business' and held that the parent did have an interest capable of protection, notwithstanding that the actual activities were performed by subsidiaries.

Repudiation of restrictive covenants

8.68 Where the company repudiates the service agreement of a director, he will be released from the restrictive covenants contained within the agreement.[154] In such circumstances, a director may be entitled to any damages caused by the repudiation and, additionally, be released from otherwise enforceable restrictions. As such, the rule is of particular importance where the company may have committed a repudiatory breach, such as breach of the implied term of mutual trust and confidence, which would entitle the director to treat himself as constructively dismissed. However, a director will not be released from any enforceable covenants merely because he is unfairly (as opposed to wrongfully) dismissed.[155]

E. Listed Companies: Control of Remuneration

8.69 The Enterprise and Regulatory Reform Act 2013 amended the Companies Act 2006 to introduce significant new means of scrutinizing directors' remuneration. Section 420 of the 2006 Act requires directors of quoted companies to prepare remuneration reports. The 2013 Act inserts a new subsection 421(2A) into the 2006 Act,[156] requiring such reports to contain a separate part specifying information as to the policy of the company with respect to the making of remuneration payments and payments for loss of office. It further inserts a new section 422A,[157] which provides:

422A Revisions to directors' remuneration policy
(1) The directors' remuneration policy contained in a company's directors' remuneration report may be revised.
(2) Any such revision must be approved by the board of directors.
(3) The policy as so revised must be set out in a document signed on behalf of the board by a director or the secretary of the company. ...
(6) In this section, '*directors' remuneration policy*' means the policy of a company with respect to the matters mentioned in section 421(2A).

The detailed requirements for remuneration reports are contained in the Large and Medium-sized Companies and Groups (Accounts and Reports) Regulations 2008 (as amended), made under section 421(1) of the 2006 Act.

---

[152] [2007] ICR 1539.
[153] [1978] 1 All ER 1026, CA.
[154] *General Billposting v Atkinson* [1909] AC 118, HL. See, however, the doubts expressed upon this decision in *Rock Refrigeration v Jones* [1997] ICR 938, per Phillips LJ at 959–60.
[155] *Lonmar Global Risks Ltd v West* [2011] IRLR 138.
[156] Effective as from 25 April 2013 (re power to make regulations) and otherwise from 1 October 2013.
[157] Effective as from 25 April 2013 (re power to make regulations) and otherwise from 1 October 2013.

Further, a new section 439A supplements the existing section 439, which requires a quoted **8.70**
company to give notice of its intention to move at the accounts meeting, as an ordinary resolution, its approval of the directors' remuneration report for the financial year (other than the
part containing the directors' remuneration policy).

Section 439A provides as follows: **8.71**

439A Quoted companies: members' approval of directors' remuneration policy
(1) A quoted company must give notice of the intention to move, as an ordinary resolution,
a resolution approving the relevant directors' remuneration policy—
  (a) at the accounts meeting held in the first financial year which begins on or after the
day on which the company becomes a quoted company, and
  (b) at an accounts or other general meeting held no later than the end of the period
of three financial years beginning with the first financial year after the last
accounts or other general meeting in relation to which notice is given under this
subsection.
(2) A quoted company must give notice of the intention to move at an accounts meeting,
as an ordinary resolution, a resolution approving the relevant directors' remuneration
policy if—
  (a) a resolution required to be put to the vote under section 439 was not passed at the last
accounts meeting of the company, and
  (b) no notice under this section was given in relation to that meeting or any other general
meeting held before the next accounts meeting.
(3) Subsection (2) does not apply in relation to a quoted company before the first meeting in
relation to which it gives notice under subsection (1).
(4) A notice given under subsection (2) is to be treated as given under subsection (1) for
the purpose of determining the period within which the next notice under subsection
(1) must be given.
(5) Notice of the intention to move a resolution to which this section applies must be given,
prior to the meeting in question, to the members of the company entitled to be sent notice
of the meeting.
(6) Subsections (2) to (4) of section 439 apply for the purposes of a resolution to which this
section applies as they apply for the purposes of a resolution to which section 439 applies,
with the modification that, for the purposes of a resolution relating to a general meeting
other than an accounts meeting, subsection (3) applies as if for 'accounts meeting' there
were substituted 'general meeting'.
(7) For the purposes of this section, the relevant directors' remuneration policy is—
  (a) in a case where notice is given in relation to an accounts meeting, the remuneration policy contained in the directors' remuneration report in respect of which
a resolution under section 439 is required to be put to the vote at that accounts
meeting;
  (b) in a case where notice is given in relation to a general meeting other than an accounts
meeting—
    (i) the remuneration policy contained in the directors' remuneration report in
respect of which such a resolution was required to be put to the vote at the last
accounts meeting to be held before that other general meeting, or
    (ii) where that policy has been revised in accordance with section 422A, the policy
as so revised.
(8) In this section—
  (a) 'accounts meeting' means a general meeting of the company before which the company's annual accounts for a financial year are to be laid;
  (b) 'directors' remuneration policy' means the policy of the company with respect to the
matters mentioned in section 421(2A).

8.72   A crucial limitation of the statutory scheme is that, under section 439(5), 'No entitlement of a person to remuneration is made conditional on the resolution being passed by reason only of the provision made by this section.' However, failure to observe the requirements of section 439 is punishable by fine.

8.73   Beyond those legislative requirements, the UK Corporate Governance Code sets out standards for the level and components of remuneration which should be observed, on a 'comply or explain' basis by the remuneration committee when fixing the remuneration of directors of a listed company.[158] The main principles are (i) that executive directors' remuneration should be designed to promote the long-term success of the company and (ii) performance-related elements should be transparent, stretching, and rigorously applied.[159]

8.74   Schedule A of the Code gives further guidance about the design of performance-related elements for executive directors. If there are annual bonuses, they should be relevant, stretching, and designed to promote the long-term success of the company and they should be subject to disclosed upper limits. If there are share options, they should not be offered at a discount save as permitted by the Listing Rules, they should not normally be exercisable for less than three years, and directors should be encouraged to hold the shares for a further period after vesting. Shareholders should be invited to approve new incentive schemes. In general only basic salary should be pensionable.

8.75   Remuneration of non-executive directors should not include share options or other performance-related elements. If exceptionally share options are granted to a non-executive director, advance shareholder approval should be obtained and the terms should require the director to hold the shares for at least a year after he leaves the board.[160]

8.76   Notice and contract periods should be set at one year or less. If it is necessary to offer longer notice or contract periods to new directors recruited from outside, the periods should reduce to one year or less after the initial period.[161]

8.77   Lastly, the Investment Association publishes its own Principles of Remuneration.[162] These are aimed primarily at companies with a main market listing, but also relevant to companies on public markets and other entities. The Principles of Remuneration set out the Association's views on quantum of remuneration generally, as well as on fixed and variable remuneration in particular. The overriding principles include, most significantly, (i) that remuneration structures should be aligned with strategy and agreed risk appetite, reward success fairly, and avoid paying more than is necessary;[163] (ii) that remuneration policies should encourage the underlying sustainable financial health of the business and promote sound risk management for the benefit of all investors, including shareholders and creditors;[164] and complexity of remuneration is discouraged.[165]

---

[158]   The Code of April 2016 applies to all companies with a Premium (formerly Primary) Listing on the London Stock Exchange with effect from the accounting period beginning on or after 1 October 2014 but incorporates good practice which is also more generally applicable.

[159]   Corporate Governance Code, D.1.

[160]   Corporate Governance Code, D.1.3

[161]   Corporate Governance Code, D.1.5.

[162]   Most recently on 11 November 2015.

[163]   Principle 3.b.

[164]   Principle 4.b.

[165]   Principle 5.b.

9

TAXATION OF DIRECTORS' EARNINGS AND BENEFITS

Thomas Chacko

A. Introduction

This chapter outlines the tax issues that arise in the context of directorships. The great majority of these concern the director's income tax liability, which is in most circumstances the same as that of any other employee. However, there are a number of more elaborate ways of remunerating employees which are likely to be encountered in the context of directors, both because they are often among the higher-paid employees of a business and because their employers often wish to link their remuneration to performance. This chapter therefore covers 'golden hellos' and termination payments, other ways of benefiting an employee (including the reimbursement of expenses and making them loans), and pension contributions, before outlining the tax implications of various share schemes that might be used. More complex remuneration planning is mentioned in Section D, but the wider area of remuneration structures is outside the scope of this work. **9.01**

This chapter then moves on to tax issues concerned with the status of directors: principally, the various close company charges which arise when a company is controlled by a small number of individuals, the circumstances in which directors may be personally liable for failures by their company, and the tax consequences of a director receiving funds in breach of duty. **9.02**

B. Directors as Employees: General

(1) Income tax and National Insurance

9.03 Directors are office-holders. Whether they are also employees or not, any income from their position will be charged as employment income under the Income Tax (Earnings and Pensions) Act 2003 (ITEPA), s 62. ITEPA, s 66(4) specifically includes 'employment as a director of a company' as a form of employment for these purposes, and s 5 provides that office-holders are treated as employees generally.

9.04 There is no distinction between executive and non-executive directors, or full and part-time appointments. If a non-executive director works for one hour per month and also supplies services as a self-employed consultant to the company, then his director's fees (and, as explained below, any reimbursed expenses incurred as a director) will be charged as if he were an employee.

9.05 ITEPA, s 67 expands the meaning of 'director' for the purposes of the benefits code, defining it as follows:

(a) in relation to a company whose affairs are managed by a board of directors or similar body, a member of that body
(b) in relation to a company whose affairs are managed by a single director or similar person, that person
(c) in relation to a company whose affairs are managed by the members themselves, a member.

The expression 'director' also includes any person 'in accordance with whose directions or instructions the directors of the company (as defined above) are accustomed to act'. This catches 'shadow directors'. A person is not taken to be a shadow director simply because the directors act upon his professional advice.[1]

9.06 In *R v Allen*[2] the House of Lords explained that this expanded definition applies to deem a shadow director to hold an office such that the benefits in kind he receives will necessarily be taxable. While the definition is only extended for the purposes of the benefits code, if a cash sum were paid to a shadow director this would be almost certainly taxable under the benefits code as a 'benefit or facility of any kind' (see 9.52 below) even if it were not taxed as ordinary earnings. A similar expanded meaning of 'director' also applies for National Insurance.[3]

9.07 It is sometimes in the interest of a taxpayer to argue that he is a de facto or shadow director, such as where it would help him to satisfy the requirements of entrepreneurs' relief.[4]

9.08 There are exceptions for National Insurance, which disregards earnings of a director in three situations:[5]

(1) Where the director is a partner in a professional firm, serving as a director being a normal incident of that firm's business and that profession, the director is required by the

---

[1] ITEPA, s 67(2).
[2] [2002] 1 AC 509, 537 at para 19.
[3] Social Security (Contributions) Regulations 2001 (SI 2001/1004), reg 1(2). This definition matches that in ITEPA, s 67 except that it does not contain point (c) in the text at para 9.05 above.
[4] See eg *HMRC v Hirst* [2014] UKFTT 9243 (TC).
[5] Social Security (Contributions) Regulations 2001, reg 27.

partnership to account to the firm for his earnings from the directorship and those earnings form an insubstantial part of the firms' gross returns.

(2) Where the director was appointed by another company which has the right to appoint directors (by virtue of a shareholding or an agreement with the company employing the director in question), the director is required to account for those earnings to the company that appointed him (by agreement with that company), and those earnings are chargeable to corporation or income tax in the hands of that company.

(3) Where the director was appointed by another company which does not have the right to appoint directors by virtue of a shareholding or an agreement with the directed company, but (2) would otherwise apply if the director and persons connected to him (spouses, parents, children, sons- and daughters-in-law) do not control the company that appointed him.

For income tax, there is no analogous statutory provision but Her Majesty's Revenue and **9.09** Customs (HMRC) apply extra-statutory concession A37. This applies in the situation described in paragraph 9.08(1) above where the fees are pooled for division between the partners (this probably means the same thing as the director being required to account to the partnership for the fees) but only applies if the partnership request this treatment from HMRC. The requirements for the situations described in paragraphs 9.08(2) and (3) are the same for income tax as for National Insurance.

Tax on a director's earnings will generally be dealt with under the Pay as you Earn ('PAYE') **9.10** system as for any other employee, with the company required to deduct tax from payments to the director and account for it to HMRC. There is special provision in ITEPA, s 223 for directors where a company accounts for tax to HMRC but does not accordingly reduce the director's take-home pay (ie does not deduct the tax that the company is paying). The director is treated as earning (as an addition to his pay) the amount of tax that should have been deducted. This only applies where the director has a material interest in the company and does not apply if the director is a 'full time working director' (see the definitions used in the 'benefits code' at 9.27 below) or the company is non-profit making (does not trade and its functions do not consist wholly or mainly in the holding of investments or other property) or charitable. Note, though, that if the true salary agreed with the director is that he gets, for example, £100,000 free of tax, then for income tax purposes his earnings are £100,000 plus tax, ie the amount that, after the employer has paid the tax, leaves £100,000. Section 223 merely makes it easier for HMRC to get to this result when dealing with those directors where the company is more likely to fail to deduct the tax from their pay informally.

Class 1 National Insurance contributions (NICs) will be due because an 'employed earner' **9.11** is defined in the Social Security (Contributions and Benefits) Act 1992, s 2 as 'a person who is gainfully employed in Great Britain either under a contract of service or in an office … with earnings'. A director's earnings period is (unusually compared to the treatment of other employees) treated as being either a full year (April 6 to April 5) or if appointed during the tax year, the remainder of that year.[6] This means that a director would only become liable to make contributions at the point in the year when his earnings reached the annual minimum threshold, with a higher rate of NICs thereafter. However, payments may be made on account so this can be spread across the year in the normal fashion.[7]

---

[6] Social Security (Contributions) Regulations 2001, reg 8.
[7] Social Security (Contributions) Regulations 2001, reg 8(6).

9.12 By concession earnings are disregarded if the director only attends board meetings in Great Britain or Northern Ireland and the director attends a maximum of ten board meetings in a tax year and each visit lasts no more than two nights at a time; or the director only attends one board meeting in a tax year and the visit lasts no more than two weeks.[8] These criteria are applied strictly.

9.13 ITEPA, s 18 defines when earnings become taxable as the earliest of:

(1) when payment is made of or on account of the earnings

(2) when the employee becomes entitled to payment of or on account of the earnings

(3) when sums on account of the earnings are credited in the company's accounts or records, whether or not the director is immediately free to draw those sums

(4) if the earnings for a certain period are determined by the end of that period, when that period ends, whether or not the director is free to call for that money

(5) if the earnings for a certain period are determined after the end of that period, when they are determined, whether or not the director is free to call for that money.

Paragraphs (3)–(5) above are rules applying only to directors.

9.14 For the purposes of ITEPA, s 18 a payment is made on account of earnings where payment is made in respect of *already earned* money before it would normally fall due. So, if a director's fee is payable quarterly in arrears, but after one month he gets an 'advance' of a month's fee, this counts as payment of earnings as he has earned the money and does not owe it to the company. Conversely, a true advance against future fees is not a payment on account of earnings, but a loan by the company. HMRC take the view that where directors do not have a salary but rather vote themselves remuneration at the end of the year, any drawings they make before that vote are not payments on account but rather loans.[9] The position on NICs is different: if a payment in advance is made in respect of a director's remuneration, it is chargeable at that point (and the later fee set off against the debt to the company is not charged to NICs).[10]

(2) Golden hellos and termination payments

9.15 The general charge on earnings is charged on earnings 'from being or becoming an employee'.[11] Therefore payments to induce someone to join a company before they begin work fall into charge. Where earnings are earned before the first tax year in which the employee is employed, they are treated as earnings for the first tax year of employment.[12]

9.16 The same rule applies to payments made after leaving employment if the right to those payments arose from being an employee. For example, if the employment contract provided for a payment in the event of dismissal, while the immediate cause of that payment would be the director's dismissal, he would have obtained the right to that by working for the company, and it would count as general earnings. If earnings are earned after the last tax year in which the employee is employed, they are treated as earnings for that last tax year.[13]

---

[8] National Insurance Manual at para 12013.

[9] Employment Income Manual at para 42280 ('EIM42280').

[10] This is the consequence of Social Security (Contributions) Regulations 2001, reg 22(2).

[11] *Shilton v Wilmshurst* [1991] 1 AC 684, 689, per Lord Templeman.

[12] ITEPA 2003, s 17(2).

[13] ITEPA 2003, s 17(3).

However, where payments to induce someone to leave are negotiated around their leaving, **9.17**
these are not something they get for working but rather for ceasing to work. They are not general earnings, but are taxed under ITEPA, s 401. This taxes any payments or benefits given in connection with the termination of employment, or any change in the nature of the job or its pay, where the payment would otherwise not be taxed. ITEPA, s 17(3) does not apply to these payments and they are treated as income of the year in which they are received.[14]

The scope of ITEPA, s 401 is wide. It catches payments 'in any way connected with' the end **9.18**
of employment.[15] The payment need not be made by the employer and can be made long after the end of employment. It is taxable whether or not the former director is still UK resident. The payment is taxable if received by the employee, their spouse, blood relative, or dependent or if paid on behalf of the employee or to their order.

Payments made on the employee's behalf into a registered pension scheme or an employee **9.19**
financed retirement benefits scheme are not taxed,[16] and neither are payments to an employee's solicitor for the costs of taking action against the employer (subject to the terms of ITEPA s 413A), or the costs of outplacement counselling.[17]

Payments and benefits are only taxable under s 401 to the extent that they exceed £30,000.[18] **9.20**

It should be noted that if the payment in respect of the termination of employment is made **9.21**
under previously agreed contractual (or customary) terms HMRC consider it to be general earnings taxable under ITEPA, s 62 and that the £30,000 threshold will not apply. Redundancy payments are an exception to this, and are taxed under s 401 (with the £30,000 threshold) whether or not they are provided for in the contract. Redundancy is defined in the Employment Rights Act 1996, s 139 as follows:

(1) ... an employee who is dismissed shall be taken to be dismissed by reason of redundancy if the dismissal is wholly or mainly attributable to—

  (a) the fact that his employer has ceased, or intends to cease—
    (i) to carry on the business for the purposes of which the employee was employed by him, or
    (ii) to carry on that business in the place where the employee was so employed, or
  (b) the fact that the requirements of that business—
    (i) for employees to carry out work of a particular kind, or
    (ii) for employees to carry out work of a particular kind in the place where the employee was employed by the employer,
  have ceased or diminished or are expected to cease or diminish.

There are also exceptions from the charge under s 401 if the termination is due to the death **9.22**
of the employee, or the payment is in respect of injury or disablement of the employee, or where the payment is made by a registered pension scheme.[19]

---

[14] ITEPA, s 403(2).

[15] *HMRC v Colquhoun* [2011] STC 394. In *HMRC v Crompton* [2009] UKFTT 71 (TC), it was held that compensation received by Mr Crompton for failings in considering his applications for alternative employment was not connected with the termination of his employment, which ended in its ordinary course.

[16] ITEPA, s 408. For discussion of such retirement schemes, see para 9.64 below.

[17] ITEPA, s 310.

[18] ITEPA, s 403.

[19] ITEPA, ss 406 and 407. In *Moorthy v HMRC* [2016] UKUT 13 (TCC), currently under appeal to the Court of Appeal, the Upper Tribunal held that s 406 did not apply to compensation for injury to feelings or

9.23 Where a director agrees as part of his compromise agreement that he will not work for a competitor, any payment made in return for that commitment will be charged to tax under ITEPA, s 225. This applies when any payment is made (whoever it is made to) in respect of a restrictive undertaking in connection with current, future, or past employment.

9.24 Where a lump sum is provided under an unregistered pension scheme (an employer financed retirement benefits scheme) on retirement, this will usually be taxed under ITEPA, s 394.

(3) Reimbursement of expenses and alternative forms of remuneration

9.25 Other provision made for a director, apart from pay, may be charged to tax under the 'benefits code'.[20] This charges such things as travel, accommodation, loans, and expenses.

9.26 Until the tax year 2015–16, the benefits code did not apply to employees earnings under £8,500 per year, unless they were directors.[21] Some directors, however, were excluded: those who, as well as earning under £8,500, did not own a 'material interest' in the company (broadly speaking, over 5 per cent, including shareholdings owned by relatives) and either worked full time (in a managerial or technical capacity), or worked for a company which was either charitable or non-profit-making, in the sense that it did not trade and did not mainly exist to hold investments or land.[22] Where the director held more than one employment with the same employer or with employers that controlled each other or were under common control, the sum of his earnings had to be less than £8,500.[23] For 2016–17 onwards, all directors (and in fact, all employees except some low-paid ministers of religion) are subject to the benefits code.[24]

9.27 The effect of this is that all part-time directors will be taxable under the full benefits code: if a non-executive director attends for meetings once a year and draws no fee, any expenses payments may still be subject to tax.

9.28 The Finance Act 2016 makes provision for an exemption for trivial benefits, which are (generally) non-cash benefits of less than £50 in cost, not being part of a salary–sacrifice arrangement, with (broadly speaking) a £300 annual limit for directors of close companies (see 9.123 below) and their families.[25]

Expenses

9.29 Payments in respect of expenses are charged under the benefits code. Sums paid to directors as expenses or paid for them to pay their expenses therefrom are treated as earnings.[26] However, there may be a corresponding deduction against the director's employment income.

---

discrimination, though noting that compensation for discrimination at work might not be taxable (following *A v HMRC* [2015] UKFTT 0189 (TC)); meaning that some discrimination awards might need to be apportioned between damages for treatment at work and damages for discriminatory termination of employment.

[20] ITEPA, Part 3, Chapters 2–10.
[21] ITEPA, s 217.
[22] ITEPA, ss 68 and 216.
[23] ITEPA, s 220.
[24] ITEPA, Part 3, Chapter 11 was repealed by Finance Act 2015 s 13.
[25] The Finance Act inserts ITEPA 2003, ss 323A, 323B.
[26] ITEPA, ss 70–2.

If a director is simply given an allowance towards expenses, that is earnings in its own right **9.30** (irrespective of the benefits code).[27] Similarly the employee receives earnings where he incurs a debt (for example a hotel bill) which the employer then meets.

However, sums paid as reimbursement, or handed to the employee for him to spend on **9.31** expenses with an expectation that the remainder is returned, are taxed under ITEPA, s 70. As long as the employee is employed during the same tax year, it does not matter that the reimbursement or (in the second situation) expenditure happens when the employee is not employed.

ITEPA, s 336 allows for a deduction where the employee (or director) is obliged to incur and **9.32** pay the expense as holder of the employment, and the amount is incurred wholly, exclusively, and necessarily in the performance of his duties.

The deductions rule is restrictive. An expense is only deductible if *any* director doing that **9.33** job would need to incur it.[28] It should be noted that the requirement of necessity refers to the nature of the expense, not the amount.[29] So, if a director buys a first-class ticket for a necessary journey, that will still be deductible, though a standard-class ticket would have been cheaper. The fact that the employer requires the employee to incur the expense does not make it necessary.

To be deductible the expense must be incurred in the performance of the director's duties, **9.34** not merely in putting the director in a position to do so. The fact that something is required by the director's contract does not necessarily mean that that thing is something he does in the performance of his duties: this test was expressed by Rowlatt J in *Nolder v Walters*[30] as expense incurred 'in doing the work of the office, in doing the things which it is his duty to do while doing the work of the office'. For example, arranging childcare so that a director can come into work is not deductible[31] and (apart from the specific deduction explained below at 9.38) travel expenses will not be deductible, as they are incurred in getting to work, not in doing the work. Nor (generally) will training expenses, even where the training is a requirement of the director's contract.[32]

The expense must be wholly and exclusively for the purposes of the employment. Where an **9.35** expense has several purposes, some of which are irrelevant to the employment or generally beneficial to the employee, there can be no deduction. For example, ordinary clothing worn at work may be necessary for the job but is also seen as necessary for ordinary life. The cost of a uniform or protective clothing may be a deductible expense.[33]

However, if cost can be split into fractions, as with a telephone bill, then the expense can be **9.36** apportioned between employment and private use.

---

[27] *Fergusson v Noble* (1919) 7 TC 176.
[28] *Ricketts v Colquhoun* (1925) 10 TC 118.
[29] *Pook v Owen* (1969) 45 TC 571.
[30] (1930) 15 TC 380.
[31] *Halstead v Condon* (1970) 46 TC 289. On the other hand, in some circumstances, employer-provided childcare, which is in principle a taxable benefit, will fall out of charge: ITEPA, ss 318–318D.
[32] *HMRC v Decadt* [2008] STC 1103; *HMRC v Banerjee (No 1)* [2010] STC 2318, where (unusually) training costs were deductible because the employment in question was essentially a training post.
[33] *Sian Williams v Revenue & Customs* [2010] UKFTT 86 (TC); *Mallalieu v Drummond* [1983] 2 AC 861.

9.37   There is a general prohibition on the deductibility of entertainment expenses in s 356. However, to prevent double-charging, where a director has paid for entertainment and been reimbursed this by the company, if the director is then charged to tax on that reimbursement,[34] but that reimbursement cannot be deducted by the company for corporation tax purposes (being for entertainment), then the expense can be deducted by the director.[35] Deductions are also permitted where the entertainment or gifts are for other employees, or where gifts include conspicuous advertising, are not food, drink, tobacco, vouchers, or tokens and have a total value per recipient of no more than £50.[36]

Travel expenses

9.38   Travel expenses have their own rules for deduction. The full cost of travel is allowed for journeys in the course of a director's duties, but not if that is for travel from home to the director's permanent workplace.[37] If a director is required to go to a different site for a temporary project, that site may be a temporary workplace and travel from home to it may be deductible.[38]

9.39   Where a director has several employments with unrelated companies, there is no deduction for travel between them.[39] However, where a director or employee of two or more companies in the same group travels between them, that travel is deductible.[40] Where a director is a director of several 'linked' companies, his travel between them is also deductible.[41]

9.40   There are specific allowances for mileage when driving (or cycling) and workplace parking.[42]

9.41   Where a director is unpaid and works for a company not managed with a view to dividends, his travel expenses are not taxed.[43]

9.42   Where a director travels abroad for work and takes his spouse because the director's health requires this, the spouse's travel expenses are eligible for deduction.[44]

Indemnities and insurance

9.43   Directors may be sued for their conduct as directors. In principle, if the company reimburses or meets their liabilities or expenses, this would be earnings, and if the company pays their insurance premiums this would be a benefit in kind.

9.44   However, ITEPA, ss 346–50 provide for a deduction against the director's employment income where either the director has paid out the liability or paid for the insurance, or where the employer has paid this and thereby created a charge to tax (where this is not a tax avoidance arrangement).

---

[34]   Under ITEPA, s 70.
[35]   ITEPA, s 357.
[36]   ITEPA, s 358.
[37]   ITEPA, ss 337–9.
[38]   ITEPA, s 338.
[39]   *Parikh v Sleeman* (1990) 63 TC 75.
[40]   ITEPA, s 340.
[41]   ITEPA, s 340A: this applies where the director of one company was appointed because of the shareholding or financial interest of the other company by which he is also employed (not necessarily as a director).
[42]   See ITEPA, ss 229–36 (mileage), 237 (parking).
[43]   ITEPA, s 241A.
[44]   Historically this was dealt with under ESC A4(d), but HMRC now take the view that it follows from the basic rules on necessary expenses: Employment Income Manual at EIM31985, which also sets out other situations where HMRC consider that a deduction for the expenses of the spouse's travel should be allowed.

The liability (or expenses or expenses of related proceedings) must arise from acting or failing **9.45**
to act in the director's capacity as an employee or director, or in any other capacity in which
he acted in the performance of his duties.[45]

There can be no deduction where it would be illegal to insure against the liability, ie for a **9.46**
penalty, for deliberate misconduct, or for fraud.[46]

If insurance is paid for, it must only relate to such liabilities and associated costs, or vicarious **9.47**
liability for another, or for the liability of the company to indemnify the employee. Its period
must not exceed two years (though it can be renewed) and there must be no requirement to
renew it. It must confer no other benefit unless that benefit cannot have a significant part of
the premium attributed to it.[47]

Further, the insurance must not be connected with any other contract. This is explained in **9.48**
ITEPA, s 350 as applying when two contracts are entered into (not necessarily at the same
time) and one is entered into by reference to the other or with a view to facilitating entry into
the other, and that this has significantly affected the terms. However, this does not apply if
the difference is a reduction in premium because of the contract being a renewal (or containing a right to renew), or because it has been entered into along with another contract (or
several) and there is a discount for buying them together.

HMRC take the view that connection with an 'ordinary' contract of employment does **9.49**
not disqualify insurance.[48] They do not explain their basis for this or for qualifying it by
'ordinary'—the provisions say nothing about contracts of employment not counting, but
it appears correct to exclude them because otherwise the deduction would almost never be
allowed. What HMRC mean by 'ordinary' in this case is unclear.

Where an overarching insurance contract is taken out (for example to cover all employees **9.50**
and the company itself) then relief is still available on an apportioned part of the premium.[49]
HMRC point out that it will not normally be necessary to calculate this apportionment as
the relief will be the same as the benefit in kind charge.[50]

If the employee has left employment, similar relief can be obtained in the following six tax **9.51**
years under ITEPA, s 555. This amount (being the cost of insurance, the cost of defending
proceedings, or the liability itself) can be set against general earnings and capital gains.

Other expenses

There are specific charges on the provision of cars and accommodation. There is also a gen- **9.52**
eral charge in ITEPA, s 201 on any 'benefit or facility of any kind' provided by reason of
employment to the director or a member of his family or household. As long as the benefit
is provided in a tax year when the director is employed, it does not matter that he has left
or not started work. The amount charged to tax is the cost to the company of providing the
benefit. *Pepper v Hart*[51] made clear that this is the actual cost to the company, not the amount

---

[45] ITEPA, s 348.
[46] ITEPA, s 346(2).
[47] ITEPA, s 349.
[48] EIM 30517.
[49] ITEPA, s 346(3)(b).
[50] EIM 30519.
[51] [1993] AC 593.

the company would expect to charge a third party for providing that benefit. In that case a school provided education to the children of teachers, and they were taxed on the marginal cost of educating those children, not the fees the school would have charged to a third party.

9.53 If what would otherwise be an expense is in fact incurred for the employee by the employer and met by the employer, so that no money is ever paid over to the employee, this is not an expense payment; but the service which has been procured for the employee may be chargeable under the general benefits provisions.

(4) Loans

9.54 These are dealt with in Chapter 7 of Part 3 of ITEPA, which is targeted at the provision of cheap loans to employees and the possibility of their being written off.

9.55 The 'loans' caught include any form of credit, including an (unearned) advance to a director,[52] or a company allowing a director to defer payment for goods he has bought from the company.[53] It also applies to various alternative finance arrangements such as purchases and resales or diminishing share ownership arrangements.[54] ITEPA s 173 has been amended by s 7 of the Finance Act 2016 for the tax years 2016–17 onwards, to state that it is immaterial for these purposes whether or not the loan represents a fair bargain: if it falls within Chapter 7, it is treated as a benefit whether or not it is actually beneficial.

9.56 The benefits code taxes 'employment-related' 'taxable cheap loans'. A loan is a taxable cheap loan if it is outstanding for all or part of the year in which the employee is employed, and any interest paid is less than the official rate prescribed by the Treasury, which fell to 4 per cent on 6 April 2010.[55] The difference between the interest paid and the official rate is charged to income tax.

9.57 To be 'employment-related', the loan must be made by the employer or a prospective employer, but this includes arranging, guaranteeing, adopting, and in any way facilitating the loan. HMRC consider that where, for example, an employee benefit trust (EBT), being a trust established by an employer where the employees are beneficiaries, lends money to a director, this will have been facilitated by the employer if the employer ultimately provided the EBT's funding. Where the EBT was provided with a sum of money which was generally intended to be lent to that director, this seems correct: but if HMRC are correct it would also apply if the EBT was funded with an aggregate sum and the money was lent without any indication by the employer that they wished for this to happen. The point is now probably academic because in most cases a loan by an EBT will be caught by the new provisions of ITEPA Part 7A (see paragraph 9.119 below) and taxed in full as income.

9.58 Any lending of money by a third party where the employer has provided funding should be considered very carefully as it may well fall within ITEPA, Part 7A provisions, leading to the whole sum of the loan being treated as the director's income. For this reason it would usually be prudent for lending to be done by the employer directly so that the tax charge, if it arises, will only be on interest that should have been charged.

---

[52] See eg *Williams v Todd* (1988) 60 TC 727, where the taxpayer was a Revenue inspector who had been advanced money by the Inland Revenue to help him move to London.

[53] *Grant v Watton* (1999) 71 TC 333.

[54] ITEPA, s 173A.

[55] ITEPA, s 175(2). The 'official rate' is that applicable under Finance Act 1989, s 178: ITEPA, s 181(1).

Loans are also caught if made by a company controlling, controlled by, or under the same **9.59** control as the employer, and if made by someone with a material interest in a close company which is the employer (or controls, is controlled by, or is in the same control as the employer).[56] There is an exception for loans made by an individual employer in the course of their personal relationships.[57]

Loans are also caught if made to the director's relatives, which (unusually) include parents, **9.60** children, siblings and remoter ancestors and descendants of spouses, and spouses of relatives:[58] but they are not so caught if the employee derives no benefit from the loan.[59]

Finally, if the loan is written off this will usually bring the whole sum into tax.[60]   **9.61**

There are various exemptions to the charge: **9.62**

(1) if any interest charged would be deductible against the trade or property income of the director[61]
(2) if the total amount (not including interest until it is due to be paid) outstanding on beneficial loans is no more than £10,000 at any point in the year[62]
(3) if the total amount goes above £10,000, but if, ignoring any loans which are at least partly entered into to fund a trade or property business such that a deduction would be allowed against the director's trade or property income, the remainder does not go above £10,000[63]
(4) if a loan is made to a relative but the director can show they derived no benefit from it[64]
(5) if the loan is for a fixed period at a fixed rate, and when entered into that rate was not below the official rate[65]
(6) where advances (not exceeding £1,000) are made to the director to cover expenses and are spent within six months, with the director regularly accounting to the company for that spending[66]
(7) where the person making the loan did so in the ordinary course of their business, the loan being comparable to those available to other borrowers at the time, a substantial proportion of whom were members of the public.[67]

The most significant exemption for small businesses with outstanding director's loan **9.63** accounts will be the exemption for loans under £10,000 and for expenses advances.

---

[56] ITEPA, s 174(2).
[57] ITEPA, s 174(5)(a).
[58] ITEPA, s 174(1)(a) and (6).
[59] ITEPA, s 174(5)(b).
[60] ITEPA, s 188. Section 189 relieves the employee from double taxation where the amount written off is taxed under other provisions. Section 190 provides that there is no charge on the writing off of a loan after the death of the employee.
[61] ITEPA, s 178. HMRC consider that this cannot apply to an overdrawn director's current account because overdrafts cannot be deductible—see EIM26505.
[62] ITEPA, s 180.
[63] ITEPA, s 180.
[64] ITEPA, s 174(5)(b).
[65] ITEPA, s 177.
[66] ITEPA, s 179.
[67] ITEPA, s 176.

(5) Pensions

9.64 Contributions into a registered pension scheme[68] have a number of tax advantages. Providing they are made wholly and exclusively for the purposes of the trade, they will generally be deductible expenses of the company in the year they are paid (whatever the accounting treatment), though if they are unusually large they may be required to be spread over up to four years.[69] Pension contributions are also subject to the same controls regarding excessive remuneration as salary generally.[70] HMRC's view is that where a controlling director or an employee connected to someone who controls the company gives contributions that are significantly out of line with those made for similar but unconnected employees or directors, they may challenge deductibility.

9.65 When the director is an active member of a pension scheme (ie he is accruing benefits under it), who is either a UK resident, pays UK tax on his earnings, or meets certain other residence conditions,[71] and makes a pension contribution before he is 75, he should get income tax relief.[72] The relief can only be used in the year in which the contribution is made. It cannot be carried forward or back, and is capped at the director's earnings for the year or £3,600, whichever is higher.[73] The relief can also be claimed where a third party (not the employer) makes a contribution on behalf of the director. In some circumstances, relief can also be claimed for contributions to overseas pension schemes.[74]

9.66 There are three ways in which relief can be granted. These depend on the rules of the pension scheme—the director does not have a choice.

(1) The primary system is 'Relief at source', where the director makes a contribution to the scheme but keeps hold of basic rate tax: for example, if he wants to contribute £100 he pays over £80 and keeps £20. He does not pay the £20 to HMRC. The scheme then claims the tax back from HMRC. If the director is taxed at the higher rate, he claims relief so as to increase his basic rate limit by the amount he has contributed (in the example, by £100, not by £80). If this system is used, the director can claim 'relief' even if he earns less than £3,600 in taxable UK income, as he would still pay over up to £2,880 to the scheme and the scheme would be able to claim up to £720 in 'tax' back from HMRC, even though the director had not in fact paid that much tax in the UK.

(2) Where the scheme allows it (usually for occupational pension schemes), the director may use a 'net pay arrangement' to make contributions. The employer will pay over part of the director's salary to the pension scheme, and will treat the salary as if reduced by that sum for PAYE.

(3) The final alternative is for the contribution to be made gross to the scheme, and for the director to make a claim for a tax refund/reduction.

---

[68] A scheme approved by HMRC under the Finance Act 2004, s 153.
[69] Finance Act 2004, ss 196–200.
[70] See 9.132 below.
[71] Finance Act 2004, s 189.
[72] Finance Act 2004, s 188.
[73] Finance Act 2004, s 190.
[74] See the Finance Act 2004, Schs 33 and 44; and *TMF Trustees Singapore Ltd v HMRC* [2012] EWCA Civ 192.

If 'pension inputs' are made over the 'annual allowance', however, a tax charge is levied on the excess at the individual's marginal rate.[75] If this charge is over £2,000, it may in some circumstances be payable by the pension scheme.[76] **9.67**

For the tax year 2014–15 the annual allowance was £40,000. Unused annual allowances can in some circumstances be carried forward. **9.68**

Pension inputs are not solely confined to contributions into the pension fund and are supposed to represent the general increase in the value of the pension, taking account of inflation. Different rules relate to different kinds of pension scheme.[77] **9.69**

The operation of the annual allowance charge is a complex area beyond the scope of this work. It has also been subject to frequent legislative change in recent years. **9.70**

Contributions into a registered pension scheme or an overseas scheme are not taxed as benefits in kind.[78] **9.71**

Contributions into a non-registered pension scheme (referred to as an employee financed retirement benefits scheme, or 'EFRBS') have less-favoured treatment than registered schemes. They are subject to similar controls to EBTs, and the employer cannot claim a deduction until the employee is charged to tax. This applies whether the employer actually funds a separate scheme or merely makes provision in their accounts for liabilities that they themselves will later pay out to the employee. **9.72**

However, in as much as the contribution is made for benefits to be paid to the director or his family in the event of retirement or death, ITEPA, s 307 provides that there is no benefit in kind charge whether or not this is under a registered pension scheme. There may in some circumstances still be a Part 7A charge, as discussed below under 'Remuneration involving third parties' (see 9.119). **9.73**

The taxation of sums coming out of a pension scheme is a complex area, not within the scope of this work. **9.74**

C. Rewarding the Director with Shares

(1) Share schemes

Where a director acquires shares in the company that employs him these shares will frequently be 'employment related securities' governed by ITEPA, Part 7. This applies when the right to acquire the shares (or any interest in securities)[79] is available by reason of the employment (including a former or prospective employment). Where the right is made available by the employer, this will always be 'by reason of the employment' unless they are made available by an employer who is an individual in the course of his personal relationships. **9.75**

---

[75] Finance Act 2004, s 227. The marginal rate is calculated as if the excess formed part of the director's income: ie if the director's other income (after reliefs) is £5,000 below the basic rate limit, and there is an excess of £10,000, then half of that is charged at the basic rate and half at the higher rate.

[76] Finance Act 2004, ss 237A–237F.

[77] Finance Act 2004, ss 229–37.

[78] ITEPA, ss 308–308A.

[79] Note that these provisions are not limited to shares, applying also to eg loan stock, debentures, units in a collective investment scheme, and a wide range of other securities: ITEPA, s 420.

9.76 Employment-related securities retain this status until sale to an unconnected person, death, or seven years after the end of the employment (or certain other employments).[80]

9.77 There are a number of income tax consequences of holding employment-related securities. The rules here are complex and beyond the scope of this work, but the discussion below indicates some points that should be borne in mind.

9.78 Some of the charges detailed below (those on restricted securities, convertible securities, and securities acquired below market value) will not apply where the securities have been acquired in a public offer, unless there was an intention to avoid tax.[81]

Restricted securities: ITEPA, Part 7, Chapter 2

9.79 Where there is some sort of arrangement or condition (including provisions for forfeiture and restrictions on transfer)[82] that reduces the current market value of the shares, they will usually be classified as restricted securities.

9.80 Where there is a forfeiture (or similar) provision with a time limit of no more than five years, there is no immediate tax charge on acquiring the securities unless the employee and employer elect otherwise, except for certain charges that can arise when they were acquired by conversion, at below market value or pursuant to a securities option. This will avoid the charge to general earnings on the value of the shares if the director remains liable to forfeit them.

9.81 When a restriction is lifted or varied, a charge to income tax will arise essentially charging the increase in the value of the shares.

9.82 The employer and employee may elect not to apply the restricted securities rules.[83] If they do this the employee is taxed on acquisition as if there were no restrictions, but no later charge will arise when the restrictions are lifted. If the shares have been acquired with a tax-avoidance motive, the employer and employee are deemed to have made such an election.

Convertible securities: ITEPA, Part 7, Chapter 3

9.83 Where shares (or other securities) carry a right to convert them into other securities, they will generally be taxed on acquisition as if they had no such right, but a further tax charge will arise if they are converted, sold, the right to convert is released, or if the holder receives something in connection with that right.

Securities with artificially depressed market value: ITEPA, Part 7, Chapter 3A

9.84 Where something has been done for non-commercial purposes which depresses the market value of shares when they are acquired, an additional tax charge equivalent to that reduction will be levied when the employee acquires the shares (see Part 7, Chapter 3A).

Artificially enhancing market value: ITEPA, Part 7, Chapter 3B

9.85 Where something is done for non-commercial purposes to increase the market value of employment-related securities, this will usually create a tax charge on that increase in value.

---

[80] ITEPA, s 421B.
[81] ITEPA, s 421F.
[82] Defined in ITEPA, s 423.
[83] ITEPA, s 431.

Securities acquired for less than market value: ITEPA, Part 7, Chapter 3C

Where securities are acquired for less than their market value, the company is treated as hav- **9.86** ing made a notional loan of the difference to the employee to fund that purchase, which is taxed as an employment-related loan.

Securities disposed of for more than market value: ITEPA, Part 7, Chapter 3D

Where employment-related securities are disposed of for more than their market value, this **9.87** chapter can give rise to an income tax charge.

Other benefits

The value of any other benefit received in connection with employment-related securities **9.88** is taxed under Part 7, Chapter 4 unless there is no tax-avoidance motive, the same benefit is received by all holders of a class of shares, and either the company is employee controlled or the majority of the shares in that class are not employment related.

Exemptions: ITEPA, Part 7, Chapter 4A

There are exemptions from many of these charges for shares in spin-out companies from **9.89** research institutions, where the person holding the shares is involved in the research being done.

(2) Share options

Where share options are made available by reason of employment, ITEPA, Part 7, Chapter 5 **9.90** applies. Under s 475, there is no charge to general earnings on the value of the option when it is granted. Tax arises later, under s 476, when the option is exercised or assigned, or a benefit is received in connection with it. If the option is exercised the charge will be on the market value of the shares acquired under the option (at the time of exercise) less the price, any consideration given for the option at the time of grant, and related expenses.

Share incentive schemes with tax relief

There are various share incentive schemes encouraged by the tax code. Share incentive plans **9.91** (SIPs) and SAYE schemes need to be available to all employees on similar terms and cannot be used selectively to benefit directors or senior employees, so are outside the scope of this work. Company share option plans (CSOPs), which are provided for under ITEPA, ss 521–6 and Schedule 4, and enterprise management incentives (EMI) schemes, which are provided for under ITEPA, ss 527–41 and Schedule 5, are particularly relevant to directors as, unlike SIPs, they can be applied selectively to particular employees or directors at the discretion of the company.

Company share option plan (CSOP)

There is no income tax charged on the grant of a CSOP option unless (as generally will not **9.92** happen due to the statutory requirements of the CSOP scheme) the price of exercise is lower than the market value of the shares at the time of the grant, in which case that difference in value will be charged to tax under ITEPA, s 526.

Provided the scheme is not being used for tax avoidance, where an option under a CSOP **9.93** is exercised over three years and under ten from its grant, or where it is exercised at an earlier date because the director has left for an approved reason (injury, disability, redundancy, retirement, or certain corporate reconstructions), and the option is exercised within six months of the director's departure, there should be no income tax charge. If a later event causes the shares to increase in value in such a way that employment-derived shares would normally incur an additional tax charge (such as the removal of restrictions) then CSOP shares also avoid this charge as a s 431 election is treated as having been made.[84]

9.94 If the options were acquired on or after 10 April 2003, then when the shares are finally sold, capital gains tax is charged on their value less the consideration given for the option and the exercise price, along with any sum charged to tax under s 526.

9.95 Despite the general prohibition on transfer, a CSOP scheme may provide that on the death of the holder, options can be exercised by their personal representatives within 12 months. HMRC consider that this exercise is free of income tax,[85] though it is not obvious that s 524 makes provision for that.

Requirements for a CSOP

9.96 The scheme can be open to employees generally, but can only include full-time directors.[86] HMRC consider this to mean working time of at least 25 hours per week as the director's only full-time job. If the director is also engaged as a self-employed consultant by the company, he must receive PAYE remuneration for his work as a director (ie not as a consultant) in respect of at least 25 hours of work per week, being more time than he spends on his work for the company as a self-employed consultant.[87]

9.97 No director may be granted options where the market value of the shares to be acquired *at the date of the grant* exceeds £30,000. This is aggregated across each separate grant under the CSOP, ignoring options which have been exercised. However, the value of the shares for this purpose is fixed at the date of the grant. For example, if a director is granted options over shares worth £15,000, and a year later the shares have doubled in value, that director may still be granted options over another £15,000 of shares.[88]

9.98 The option must have an exercise price not manifestly lower than the market price for the shares at the time of the grant.

9.99 There are restrictions on the type of company whose shares can be used for a CSOP, in order to reduce the risk of value manipulation. The shares can be in the employing company, in a company that controls it (in the sense of being able to secure that the employing company directs its affairs as the controlling company wishes), or in a consortium company (owning, together with the rest of the consortium, 75 per cent of the employer and, on its own, at least 5 per cent). However, where the employing company is controlled by another company (in the above sense) the employing company's shares may only be used if it is listed.[89]

9.100 The shares must be fully paid up and non-redeemable.[90] CSOP options cannot be transferred by the director (except on death, to their personal representatives).[91] Until 17 July 2013, there were prohibitions on the kind of restrictions that could be imposed on the

---

84 ITEPA, s 431A.
85 HMRC's Employee Tax Advantaged Share Scheme User Manual at ETASSUM 42210.
86 ITEPA, Sch 4, para 8.
87 ETASSUM 42170.
88 ITEPA, Sch 4, para 6.
89 ITEPA, Sch 4, paras 16, 17.
90 ITEPA, Sch 4, para 18.
91 ITEPA, Sch 4, para 23.

option shares, but these have been removed.[92] The class of shares involved must either be a class which gives the employees and directors control of the company, or must be a class where the majority of the shares are held by people who did not acquire them through being employees or directors. This does not apply where there is only one class of shares.[93]

The purpose of the scheme must be to provide benefits for employees and directors in the form of share options, and it must not provide benefits which fall outside the terms of ITEPA, Schedule 4. In particular, it must not provide cash alternatives to share options.[94]   **9.101**

CSOP options cannot be issued where the director owns (or has owned in the last 12 months) more than 30 per cent of the company and the company is 'close' (broadly, controlled by five or fewer shareholders, or by shareholders who are also directors).[95] This also applies where the director together with his relatives, the trustees of a settlement the director has founded or of which the director is a beneficiary,[96] owns more than 30 per cent of the company, assuming that any share options they (but not others) hold have been exercised. There are special provisions when the director is a beneficiary of an employee benefit trust, as otherwise employee benefit trusts owning significant numbers of shares would routinely prevent the use of CSOP or EMI schemes by any employees. Subject to certain conditions, where a director is a beneficiary of an EBT but does not hold over 30 per cent of the company (together with his other associates) he is only attributed ownership of a fraction of the EBT's holding based on the proportion of the trustees' dividend income that has been used to provide benefits to him in the previous 12 months. Shares appropriated to the director under a SIP are taken into account, but he is not treated as associated with the ownership of unappropriated SIP shares.[97]   **9.102**

Provision may be made for issuing replacement options on a company reorganization.   **9.103**

Enterprise management incentives (EMIs)

EMIs are a more generous option scheme available to a more restricted range of companies.   **9.104**

EMI options must be granted 'for genuine commercial reasons, to recruit or retain an employee'.[98] They do not qualify if granted as part of an arrangement to avoid tax. They cannot be assigned.[99]   **9.105**

No income tax or NI is charged on the grant of an EMI option.   **9.106**

Provided the option is exercised within ten years (and there has been no 'disqualifying event'), there will only be income tax charged on the difference between the exercise price and the (higher) market value of the shares at the time of the grant, if there was one. If the   **9.107**

---

92 ITEPA, Sch 4, para 19.
93 ITEPA, Sch 4, para 20.
94 ITEPA, Sch 4, para 5.
95 Close companies are discussed below in Section E under 'Companies where the directors are extremely influential' (see 9.123).
96 The director can cease his association with the trustees of a discretionary trust if he disclaims any eligibility to benefit or is excluded by the trustees, immediately after that disclaimer no associate of his is eligible to benefit, and they and their associates received no benefits in the 12 months preceding the disclaimer or exclusion: see Sch 4, para 14.
97 ITEPA, Sch 4, paras 9–14.
98 ITEPA, Sch 5, para 4.
99 ITEPA, Sch 5, para 38.

option was granted with a lower exercise price than market value but the shares have dropped in value, then tax is charged on the difference between the price and current market value.[100]

9.108 If a disqualifying event occurs, the director has 90 days to exercise the option and preserve its advantages. The following are disqualifying events:[101]

(1) loss of independence (see paragraph 9.115 below);
(2) the company ceasing to meet the trading activities requirement (see paragraph 9.116 below);
(3) the employee ceasing to be eligible (either ceasing employment or dropping below 25 hours per week and 75 per cent of his working time);
(4) changes to the terms of the option which increase the value of the shares or mean that the general requirements for the EMI scheme are no longer met;
(5) alterations to the share capital of the company which affect the value of the shares, consisting of or including the creation, variation, or removal of a right relating to the shares, the imposition of a restriction on any of the shares, or the variation or removal of such a restriction; provided that either (a) the change is not made for commercial reasons, (b) the change is made for the purposes of increasing the market value of the option shares, or (c) the change causes the general EMI scheme requirements to cease to be met;
(6) a conversion of shares (subject to some exceptions); and
(7) grant of a CSOP option that takes the option holder over the £250,000 limit.

9.109 Where an option is exercised over 90 days after the disqualifying event, tax (and, if the shares are readily convertible assets—broadly speaking, those listed on a recognized exchange or for which there are trading arrangements—National Insurance) is charged on any increase in value since the disqualifying event (as well as any discount on the issue of the option which would have been chargeable in any event as described above).

9.110 EMI shares may be subject to restrictions such that a tax charge would arise when the restrictions are lifted. As with ordinary restricted securities, it is possible to make a s 431 election to treat the restrictions as lifted for tax purposes. If the option is exercised and no income tax charge arises, this election is treated as having been made,[102] so that no charge arises when the restrictions are actually lifted. If the option is exercised over 90 days after a disqualifying event, then when calculating the tax, the market value at the date of the disqualifying event is taken to be the restricted market value (whether or not an election has been made) but the market value at exercise will be the restricted value if no election has been made (meaning that a later charge will arise if the restriction is lifted) or the unrestricted value if the election has been made.

9.111 Capital gains tax on the shares when sold will take into account the exercise price and any amount paid for the grant of the option.

Requirements for an EMI

9.112 While the CSOP limit is £30,000, the EMI limit is currently £250,000.[103] This includes any unexercised CSOP options. If the shares are restricted, their unrestricted value is used

---

[100] ITEPA, ss. 530–1.
[101] ITEPA, ss 532–9.
[102] ITEPA, s 431A.
[103] ITEPA, Sch 5, para 5.

for this purpose. Once the £250,000 limit has been reached (including exercised options), no further EMI options can be granted for another three years.[104] This can be capricious: if a director is granted options of £250,000 in year one, which he exercises at the end of year three, he can take another £250,000 in year four. If he had been granted £240,000 in year one and £10,000 in year three, he cannot take any options until three years after the grant of the year-three options. Options over shares in other group companies are also taken into account.

The total unrestricted market value of unexercised EMI option shares issued by the company (to all employees), calculated at the various dates of grant, cannot exceed £3 million.[105] **9.113**

HMRC take the view that it is permissible to grant parallel EMI options, where only one of the pair can be exercised: for example, a company might grant options at (original) market value with low performance targets, and options at a large discount with high performance targets. Only the option with the higher amount of available shares will be taken into account for the financial limits.[106] **9.114**

There are restrictions on the companies that can use EMI:[107] **9.115**

(1) The company must be independent: it must not be controlled by another company (with its connected persons) or be its 51 per cent subsidiary, and there must be no arrangements by virtue of which it could come under such control.[108]
(2) All the company's subsidiaries must be controlled and 51 per cent owned by the company. If a subsidiary has a business wholly or mainly of holding or managing land (or property deriving its value from land), it must be 90 per cent owned by the company.[109]
(3) The company's gross assets must not exceed £30 million.[110]
(4) The company must have fewer than 250 full-time (or equivalent) employees, including those of its subsidiaries.[111]
(5) The company must either have a permanent establishment in the UK or the subsidiary that fulfils the primary trading requirement in paragraph 9.116(2) below must do so.[112]

There are also requirements regarding the company's trade.[113] **9.116**

(1) If the company is not part of a group, it must exist wholly for the purpose of carrying on a qualifying trade, and be doing so or preparing to do so.
(2) If the company is a parent company, then at least one group company must satisfy the above requirement, and the business of the group as a whole does not consist even to a

---

[104] ITEPA, Sch 5, para 6.
[105] ITEPA, Sch 5, para 7.
[106] ETASSUM 51070.
[107] ITEPA, Sch 5, paras 8–23.
[108] ITEPA, Sch 5, para 9. This is treated as satisfied if the company is subject to an employee–ownership trust.
[109] ITEPA, Sch 5, paras 10–11B.
[110] ITEPA, Sch 5, para 12.
[111] ITEPA, Sch 5, para 12A.
[112] ITEPA, Sch 5, para 14A.
[113] ITEPA, Sch 5, paras 13, 14, 15–23.

substantial part in carrying out non-qualifying activities (being excluded or non-trading activities).[114]

(3) Qualifying trades must be conducted on a commercial basis with a view to profit, and not consist in excluded activities.

9.117 A disqualifying event can be avoided in some circumstances (such as an appropriate company reorganization) by the issue of a suitable replacement option.

9.118 The director must be employed by the company or its subsidiary, and must work for at least 25 hours a week or (if less) 75 per cent of his total working time, and cannot have a material interest (above 30 per cent) in the company.[115]

D. Remuneration Involving Third Parties

9.119 In 2011 ITEPA, Part 7A was introduced to combat a range of tax avoidance schemes.[116] It contains extremely broad provisions which can result in unexpectedly punitive taxation.

9.120 Broadly speaking, where an employer enters into an arrangement which is in essence to do with rewarding an employee, and a third party (not usually including other companies in the same group as the employer) takes a 'relevant step', tax is charged. A 'relevant step' includes 'earmarking' assets or funds with an eye to doing another relevant step later, payment of a sum or transfer of an asset to the employee or someone chosen by him, or making an asset available to the employee or someone chosen by him. Payment by way of loan counts as payment.[117] The results can be severe: for example, if a company transfers £100,000 to trustees who lend that money to a director, the director is charged as if he received £100,000 absolutely, and gets no relief if he repays the loan. If the trustees spend the £100,000 on a house and let the director live in it, the director is treated as receiving the value of the house. In fact, if the house is there to be used by the director, he is taxed on it even if he never uses it, and if it is still there to be used two years after his employment ceases he is taxed on its full value even if he was never given full use of it, for example if he had to share use of it with other staff.

9.121 There are exceptions for contributions to registered pension schemes and to contributions to an employee financed retirement benefits scheme (EFRBS) that purely exist to provide retirement provision.

9.122 Part 7A largely puts an end to the simple EBTs litigated in *Macdonald v Dextra Associates*[118] and *Sempra Metals*,[119] where companies would settle funds into trust (originally in the belief that this would be deductible for corporation tax) and those funds would be lent out to directors on an indefinite basis without any tax arising. Any use of an EFRBS or an EBT (including actions taken by EBTs that predate Part 7A) should be considered very carefully in the light of this code.

---

[114] ITEPA, Sch 5, paras 16–23 defines 'excluded activities'.
[115] ITEPA, Sch 5, paras 24–33.
[116] Inserted by the Finance Act 2011, s 26, Sch 2.
[117] ITEPA, ss 554B–554D, 554Z(7).
[118] (2005) 77 TC 146.
[119] [2008] STC (SCD) 1062.

E. Companies Where Directors Are Extremely Influential

(1) Close companies

Special rules apply where a company is under the control of a small number of individu- **9.123**
als. A 'close company' is a company under the control of five or fewer 'participators' or
participators who are also directors.[120] For these purposes, directors include any manager
of the company who (with his associates) owns or controls at least 20 per cent of the
company.[121]

A 'participator' is any person with a share or interest in the capital or income of the company, **9.124**
specifically including:[122]

(1) a person who possesses or is entitled to acquire (such as under share options) share capital or voting rights;
(2) a loan creditor of the company, being a creditor in respect of redeemable loan capital or
in respect of a debt incurred for money borrowed by the company, capital assets acquired
by the company, a right to receive income in favour of the company, or incurred for
consideration which at the time of incurring the debt was substantially less valuable to
the company than the amount of the debt;
(3) a person who possesses or is entitled to acquire a right to receive or participate in distributions or payments by the company to loan creditors; and
(4) a person who is entitled to secure that income or assets of the company will be applied
directly or indirectly for his benefit.

When calculating whether the company is controlled by directors, or by five or fewer partici- **9.125**
pators, the rights of associates and nominees of the director and of companies controlled by
the director (and his associates and nominees) are attributed to the director.[123]

Associates for these purposes are: spouses, parents or remoter ancestors, children or remoter **9.126**
issue, siblings, and partners (in business partnership rather than relationship sense); trustees
of a settlement founded by the participator (or a relative of theirs); trustees of a settlement
where the participator is a beneficiary; if the participator is a company, any other company
which has an interest in shares or obligations (of a company) which the participator has an
interest in under a trust or as part of the estate of a deceased person; and if the participator
has an interest in shares or obligations of a company which are part of the estate of a deceased
person, that person's personal representatives.[124]

Control of the company means control under any of five tests. These are possession of:[125] **9.127**

(1) the ability to direct the company's affairs;
(2) the greater part of the voting power of the company;
(3) the greater part of the share capital of the company;

---

[120] Corporation Tax Act 2010, s 439.
[121] Corporation Tax Act 2010, s 452.
[122] Corporation Tax Act 2010, s 454.
[123] Corporation Tax Act 2010, s 451.
[124] Corporation Tax Act 2010, s 448.
[125] Corporation Tax Act 2010, s 450.

(4) such share capital as would mean that is all income were distributed, produce the greater part of that income; and

(5) such rights as would, if the company were wound up, provide the greater part of the distributed assets.

9.128 There are various exclusions from close status, such as where the Crown controls the company.[126]

9.129 A company will not be close where it is controlled by non-close companies and where it could not be treated as close without including a non-close company as one of the five or fewer participators.[127] It will also not be close where the only reason it is close is by reference to the distribution of assets under a winding up, and that is only satisfied by including as participators non-close companies who are loan creditors.[128] Shares held by a registered pension scheme are treated as held by a non-close company if that pension scheme is not for the benefit of the staff (or their dependents) of a close company, the company being tested, a company associated with it, or a company controlled by directors of the company being tested or their associates.[129]

9.130 A company will not be close if at least 35 per cent of the shares are held by the public, meaning held by a non-close company, a registered pension scheme, or anyone who is not a principal member.[130]

Consequences of a company being a close company

9.131 Where a company is close, benefits provided to a participator may be taxed as if a distribution (meaning that there will be no deduction for the company).[131] However, this does not apply to certain benefits taxed to employment income.[132] HMRC state that they do not consider that this charge applies where a participator is paid cash at what seems to be a commercial rate.[133]

9.132 Where a loan is made to a participator (or to a number of related persons, such as associates, co-trustees with the participator, trustees for the participator, or partners with the participator) by a close company (or the participator incurs a debt to them or their debt is assigned to them), this gives rise to a corporation tax charge against the company.[134]

(1) This does not apply where the participator holds less than 5 per cent of the company, works full time for the company and the loan is less than £15,000. It also does not apply where the debt is incurred for the supply to the participator of goods or services

---

[126] Corporation Tax Act 2010, ss 442–7.
[127] Corporation Tax Act 2010, s 444(2).
[128] Corporation Tax Act 2010, s 444(3).
[129] Corporation Tax Act 2010, s 445.
[130] Corporation Tax Act 2010, s 446.
[131] Corporation Tax Act 2010, s 1064: this applies to the provision of accommodation, entertainment, services, and any other benefits or facilities.
[132] Car and van benefits, payments of a director's tax liability, living accommodation, and death or retirement benefits: Corporation Tax Act 2010, s 1065.
[133] Company Taxation Manual at CTM 60670.
[134] Corporation Tax Act 2010, s 455.

by the close company in the course of its trade, and the credit does not last for longer than six months (or, if shorter, the normal period allowed to the close company's trade debtors).

(2) The tax charge is reversed when the loan is repaid, released, or written off.

A similar charge is made when the close company makes a loan that does not fall within **9.133** s 455 and some other person pays, transfers property to, or discharges a liability of the participator.[135]

A similar charge is also made on benefits conferred on participators as part of tax avoidance **9.134** arrangements.[136]

(2) Excessive remuneration

Whether a company is close or not, if the director is a powerful figure within it, HMRC are **9.135** likely to scrutinize his remuneration to see if it is so excessive that it does not seem a plausible reward for his services. If this appears to be the case, they will refuse the company a corporation tax deduction because they will say that some of that salary has not been expended wholly and exclusively for the purposes of the company's trade.

HMRC state that they will allow that excess to be repaid to the company and the income tax **9.136** to be avoided,[137] although this goes against the strict letter of ITEPA, s 18 which would tax it even though it had been waived, if it had been paid or fallen due.

(3) Personal expenditure

Where a director is very close to the operation of a company, HMRC are likely to scrutinize **9.137** expenditure which benefits him or his family but is claimed to be for the company's trade. For example, in *Executive Network (Consultants) Ltd v O'Connor*,[138] a company sponsored the horse-riding school run by the wife of one of the directors. The Special Commissioners accepted that this was done for advertising purposes and in fact was useful to that end, but held that it was also done to benefit the riding school for personal reasons and could not be allowed as a deduction.

This is a highly fact-specific area. In one case, sponsorship of a motor rallying team was **9.138** not allowed as a deduction because it was seen as partly for the private enjoyment of the sole director of the company;[139] in another the expense of participating in motor rallying for the purposes of advertising was allowed with the enjoyment the director in question gained seen as peripheral.[140] The actual purpose of the expenditure is crucial and the reasoning behind any decisions should be accurately and fully documented at the time the decisions are taken. A major reason why the taxpayer lost in the former case was that the taxpayer refused to give evidence explaining the sponsorship decision.

---

[135] Corporation Tax Act 2010, s 459.
[136] Corporation Tax Act 2010, s 464A.
[137] EIM 42730.
[138] [1996] STC (SCD) 29.
[139] *HMRC v Protec International Ltd* [2010] UKFTT 628 (TC).
[140] *McQueen v HMRC* [2007] STC (SCD) 457.

F. Liabilities of Directors

(1) Failure to pay PAYE and National Insurance contributions

9.139 If a company fails to account for tax on a director's earnings under PAYE, there are a number of circumstances in which the director can be made personally liable. He could be liable under the PAYE Regulations,[141] regs 72, 72F, or 81.

9.140 Regulation 72 applies either where the company satisfies HMRC that it (not the director receiving the money) took reasonable care to deduct properly and failed to do so by reason of an error in good faith, or where the director knew that the company wilfully failed to deduct tax. The director can appeal against this direction, whether or not he disputes the tax liability itself.

9.141 Regulation 72F applies in certain situations where tax was not deducted but some of the tax (but not enough) was accounted for in other ways, ie has been self-assessed, paid on account, or has been deducted under various subcontractors' liability provisions.[142]

9.142 Regulation 81 applies where HMRC have issued a direction to the company asking for payment but it has not been paid, and either:

(1) the tax due was tax on a notional payment (where the earnings charged are not a payment from which tax could have been deducted, so that the employer is required to deduct from other payments of cash) but there were not enough other payments made to the director for deduction to be applied so that the employer was required to account for tax without making a deduction, or

(2) the director knew that the company had wilfully failed to deduct tax.

9.143 It has been held that knowledge in this test means actual knowledge; it is not sufficient that the employee ought to have known.[143] Wilful failure to pay the tax means deliberate failure, knowing that the tax should be paid. As put by Nolan J, there must be 'evidence of culpability or blameworthiness or wrong, deliberately or intentionally carried out'.[144]

9.144 It will of course be easier for HMRC to show that a director knew of the failure than it might be for other employees.

9.145 Where a company has failed to pay National Insurance contributions, the directors can be made personally liable to pay these (including those of other employees). Where the failure to pay can be attributed to the fraud or neglect of officers of the company, the Social Security Administration Act 1992, s 121C provides for this. While this provision was introduced in 1998 to combat 'phoenix companies' where the company would run up NIC debts and liquidate but the directors would soon appear in a new company running the same business, it is not limited to that situation.

---

[141] SI 2003/2682.
[142] SI 2003/2682, reg 72E.
[143] *R v IRC ex p Chisholm* [1981] STC 253, per McNeill J; *R v IRC ex p Cook* [1987] STC 434, per Nolan J.
[144] *R v IRC ex p Cook* [1987] STC 434.

Fraudulent failure to pay National Insurance contributions is a criminal offence. Any person **9.146** knowingly concerned in this, and, where a company commits the offence, any director, is shown to have consented to, connived at, or allowed the offence through neglect, may be liable to up to seven years' imprisonment or a fine.[145]

Where a company fails to pay its tax, or notify HMRC that it is liable to do so, or submits **9.147** inaccurate documents to HMRC, it may be liable for a penalty. The Finance Act 2007, Schedule 24, paragraph 19 provides that where there is a deliberate inaccuracy attributable to an officer of the company, that officer may be required to pay some or all of that penalty. The Finance Act 2008, Schedule 41, paragraph 22 makes similar provision for VAT and Excise duties.

This work does not deal with the taxation of employment through intermediaries (such **9.148** as personal service companies). However, it should be noted that if the managed service company legislation in ITEPA 2003, Part 2, Chapter 9 applies, and the managed service company fails to pay its PAYE liabilities, directors of the managed service company, of the MSC provider, and of a company actively involved in the provision of the worker's services (which might in some circumstances include a client) can be made liable to pay the PAYE debt.[146]

The Finance Act 2016 introduces new restrictions on the deductibility of travel expenses for **9.149** certain work carried out through an intermediary. Where this gives rise to PAYE debt which is unpaid, it (and any penalty or interest) will be recoverable from the directors of various companies, such as employment intermediaries or companies which have been required to account for the PAYE. They would be so required if they issued a fraudulent document to avoid the application of the provisions restricting deduction.[147]

(2) Receipts by a director in breach of duty

Where a director takes money from his company in breach of duty, whether or not that is **9.150** taxed in his hands will depend on the circumstances. A series of cases dealing with moneys taken from pension schemes in breach of their terms has probably settled on the position that where someone receives money in breach of trust such that they are liable to return it, and that the recipient is able and prepared to do so, they will not be taxed.[148] In *Thorpe v HMRC*[149] Sir Edward Evans-Lombe departed from the Court of Appeal in *Venables v Hornby*,[150] which had suggested that such payments would necessarily be taxable, at least in the context of the specific pensions provisions. Sir Edward decided he was not bound by that case as the Court of Appeal had been overturned on another ground by the House of Lords.

However, if the director does not appear likely to return the money, it would be very surpris- **9.151** ing if the courts overturned an assessment to tax on it as employment income. Obtaining

145 Social Security Administration Act 1992, ss 114–15.
146 ITEPA, s 688A; PAYE Regulations (SI 2003/2682) 97A–97L.
147 The Finance Act inserts ITEPA 2003, ss 339A, 688B.
148 *Thorpe v HMRC* [2009] STC 2107 (approved by the Court of Appeal [2010] STC 964).
149 See n 148 above.
150 [2002] STC 1248.

money by fraud can be a trade whose profits are taxed despite the fact that all those profits are matched by liabilities to the defrauded parties.[151] It would be very surprising if fraud by an employee was not treated similarly. The courts have not yet addressed the relationship between these cases and the situation in *Martin v HMRC*[152] where a contractual payment by the employee to the employer was held to be 'negative earnings' rather than having retrospectively reduced the employee's income.

---

[151] *Forbes v Director of the Assets Recovery Agency* [2007] STC (SCD) 1 at [13].
[152] [2015] STC 478.

PART III

THE GENERAL DUTIES OF DIRECTORS

10

GENERAL DUTIES OF DIRECTORS

Mark Arnold QC

A. Scope and Nature of General Duties

(1) Introduction

The general duties owed to a company by its directors are to be found in Part 10, Chapter 2 **10.01**
of the Companies Act 2006. Their codification followed the recommendation of the Law
Commission and the Scottish Law Commission in their report in 1999,[1] which itself was but
the latest in a distinguished line of reports spanning the previous 100 years, most of which
had recommended the introduction of a statutory statement of directors' duties in one form
or another,[2] and several previous attempts to do so, each of which had been unsuccessful.[3]
As explained by Lord Goldsmith, the Attorney General, the purpose of codification is 'to
make what is expected of directors clearer and to make the law more accessible to them and
to others'.[4]

---

[1] *Company Directors: Regulating Conflicts of Interest and Formulating a Statement of Duties* (Law Com
No 261).
[2] The Davey Committee (1895), the Greene Committee (1926), and the Jenkins Committee (1962). Of
these, only the Greene Committee did not recommend the introduction of a statutory statement, concluding
at para 46 of its report that '[t]o attempt by statute to define the duties of directors would be a hopeless task'.
[3] The Companies Bill 1973, which was lost due to the general election the following year, and the Companies
Bill 1978, which was lost in similar circumstances in 1979.
[4] Lords Grand Committee, 6 February 2006, col 254.

10.02 The general duties are identified as:

(1) the duty to act within powers (s 171);
(2) the duty to promote the success of the company (s 172);
(3) the duty to exercise independent judgment (s 173);
(4) the duty to exercise reasonable care, skill, and diligence (s 174);
(5) the duty to avoid conflicts of interest (s 175);
(6) the duty not to accept benefits from third parties (s 176); and
(7) the duty to declare an interest in a proposed transaction or arrangement (s 177).[5]

These duties are considered separately in the chapters following.

10.03 As they are formulated, the general duties specified in this part of the 2006 Act are based on, and take effect in place of, certain common law rules and equitable principles as they apply to directors.[6] Accordingly, the general duties are to be interpreted and applied in the same way as common law rules and equitable principles, and in interpreting and applying them, regard is to be had to the corresponding common law rules and equitable principles.[7] This suggests that they may continue to develop over time, in the same way as they have been allowed to develop in the past, rather than remaining static and immutable according to the position reached by the time the Act came into force. It was certainly the government's intention that the statement of general duties should be sufficiently flexible as to enable the law to respond to changing business circumstances and needs.[8]

10.04 The statutory statement is, then, intended to be a codification of the existing position at common law, at least in so far as the general duties in their statutory form reflect the common law rules and equitable principles on which they are based. The codification does not, however, provide a complete code of the conduct to be expected of directors. This was confirmed by Lord Goldsmith, Attorney General, who said:

> The statement of general duties ... is not intended to be an exhaustive list of all the duties owed by a director to his company. The directors may owe a wide range of duties to their companies in addition to the general duties listed. Those are general, basic duties which it is seen as right and important to set out in this way. The statement that these are the general duties does not allow a director to escape any other obligation he has, including obligations under the Insolvency Act 1986.[9]

10.05 One significant duty that remains uncodified, although its existence (or, at least, the possibility of its existence) is recognized in s 172(3), is the duty owed to the company by directors to consider the interests of creditors when the company is insolvent or facing the threat of insolvency.[10] This is considered further in Chapter 12, Section E below. Another is the duty not to defraud the company, although this will in practice overlap with the duty to act within powers and the duty to promote the success of the company.[11] In the same vein, there is no

---

[5] The duties set out in ss 170–4, 178–81 came into force on 1 October 2007: 2006 Act Commencement Order No 3, Art 2(1)(d). The duties set out in ss 175–7 came into force on 1 October 2008: 2006 Act Commencement Order No 5, Art 5(1)(d).

[6] 2006 Act, s 170(3).

[7] 2006 Act, s 170(4); *Eclairs Group Ltd v JKX Oil & Gas plc* [2015] Bus LR 1395, SC, at para 14, per Lord Sumption.

[8] White Paper: Company Law Reform at p 21.

[9] Lords Grand Committee, 6 February 2006, col 249.

[10] *Bilta (UK) Ltd v Nazir (No 2)* [2014] Ch 52, CA, per Patten LJ at paras 22 and 37; *Bilta (UK) Ltd v Nazir (No 2)* [2016] AC 1, SC at paras 123–27, per Lords Toulson and Hodge.

[11] *Lexi Holdings plc v Pannone and Partners* [2009] EWHC 2590 (Ch) at para 69.

express mention of the principle that directors are to be regarded as trustees of property belonging to the company which is in their hands or under their control, nor of their duties to account for, and not to misapply, such property.[12] So, too, there is no express mention of the director's duty to disclose his own misconduct, although this will usually arise in the context of his duty to promote the interests of the company.[13] These matters are considered further below.

The general duties apply to directors appointed as such (*de jure* directors). They also apply **10.06** to de facto directors,[14] although it is to be noted that an individual who does nothing more than perform his functions as a *de jure* director of the corporate director of a company will not thereby become a de facto director of that company: it is necessary in such a case to consider whether the individual has assumed to act as a director of the company by exercising the powers and discharging the functions associated with that office.[15] It follows that the general duties will apply to nominee directors as well, as they will be either *de jure* or de facto directors of the company. In addition, following recent amendment, they now apply to shadow directors where and to the extent that they are capable of so applying:[16] see Section C below. Certain of the duties, namely the duties to avoid conflicts of interest and not to accept benefits from third parties, also apply to former directors in the manner described in Chapter 15, Section E.[17]

The general duties are owed to the company, but the question whether and in what circum- **10.07** stances a director may owe a duty to someone other than the company is neither addressed nor affected by the 2006 Act. This is discussed further below.

(2) Distinction between fiduciary duties and other duties

Directors occupy a fiduciary position in relation to the company and owe duties as such. **10.08** A distinction has traditionally been drawn between fiduciary duties on the one hand, and other duties (including the duty to exercise reasonable care, skill, and diligence) on the other. The distinction is important because the duties are fundamentally different. In particular, not every breach of duty by a fiduciary is a breach of fiduciary duty,[18] and the consequences will be different.

---

[12] Citing this passage in *Akai Holdings Ltd v Everwin Dynasty Ltd (No 2)* [2016] 3 HKC 307 at para 59, Bharwaney J said: 'It is difficult to conceive of a more fundamental breach of duty by a fiduciary than the dishonest misappropriation of funds under his care.' In *Re Paycheck Services 3 Ltd, HMRC v Holland* [2010] 1 WLR 2793, SC, Lord Hope at para 49 inclined to the view that a director who causes the company's assets to be misapplied is in principle strictly liable to make good the misapplication, subject to the court's discretion under the Insolvency Act, s 212 and his right to claim relief under 2006 Act, s 1157. Lord Walker, at para 119, agreed with Rimer LJ in the Court of Appeal that liability for payments that should never have been made was strict and Lord Clarke agreed with Lord Walker (para 146). Ultimately, however, it was not necessary to decide the question in that case. See also *Progress Property Co Ltd v Moore* [2011] 1 WLR 1, SC, at para 32, and *Madoff Securities International Ltd v Raven* [2013] EWHC 3147 (Comm) per Popplewell J, at paras 195–200.
[13] See *Item Software (UK) Ltd v Fassihi* [2005] 2 BCLC 91; the discussion in *GHLM Trading Ltd v Maroo* [2012] 2 BCLC 369 at paras 192–95; and *First Subsea Ltd v Balltec Ltd* [2014] EWHC 866 (Ch), per Norris J at paras 191, 192.
[14] The statutory definition of 'director' in 2006 Act, s 250 includes a de facto director.
[15] *Re Paycheck Services 3 Ltd, HMRC v Holland* [2010] 1WLR 2793, SC.
[16] 2006 Act, s 170(5), as amended by the SBEE Act 2015, s 89(1), which came into force on 26 May 2015.
[17] 2006 Act, s 170(2).
[18] *Bristol and West Building Society v Mothew* [1998] Ch 1, 16D, CA, per Millett LJ.

10.09 It is necessary first to determine what a fiduciary is. In what has come to be regarded as a classic statement, Millett LJ explained the position in *Bristol and West Building Society v Mothew*:[19]

> A fiduciary is someone who has undertaken to act for or on behalf of another in a particular matter in circumstances which give rise to a relationship of trust and confidence. The distinguishing obligation of a fiduciary is the obligation of loyalty. The principal is entitled to the single-minded loyalty of his fiduciary. This core liability has several facets. A fiduciary must act in good faith; he must not make a profit out of his trust; he must not place himself in a position where his duty and his interest may conflict; he may not act for his own benefit or the benefit of a third person without the informed consent of his principal. This is not intended to be an exhaustive list, but it is sufficient to indicate the nature of fiduciary obligations.

10.10 The badge of a fiduciary and, accordingly, of a fiduciary duty, therefore, is loyalty. As Millett LJ went on to say in *Mothew*:

> The various obligations of a fiduciary merely reflect different aspects of his core duties of loyalty and fidelity. Breach of fiduciary obligation, therefore, connotes disloyalty or infidelity. Mere incompetence is not enough. A servant who loyally does his incompetent best for his master is not unfaithful and is not guilty of a breach of fiduciary duty.[20]

10.11 Mr Jonathan Crow, sitting as a deputy judge of the Chancery Division, summarized the position in similar terms in *Extrasure Travel Insurance Ltd v Scattergood*, where he said:

> Fiduciary duties are concerned with concepts of honesty and loyalty, not with competence. In my view, the law draws a clear distinction between fiduciary duties and other duties that may be owed by a person in a fiduciary position. A fiduciary may also owe tortious and contractual duties to the cestui que trust: but that does not mean that those duties are fiduciary duties. Bearing all that in mind, I find nothing surprising in the proposition that crass incompetence might give rise to a claim for breach of a duty of care, or breach of contract, but not for a breach of fiduciary duty … The fact that his alleged belief was unreasonable may provide evidence that it was not in fact honestly held at the time: but if, having considered all the evidence, it appears that the director did honestly believe that he was acting in the best interests of the company, then he is not in breach of his fiduciary duty merely because that belief appears to the trial judge to be unreasonable, or because his actions happen, in the event, to cause injury to the company.[21]

10.12 The 2006 Act, s 178 perpetuates the distinction between fiduciary duties and other duties. It specifically excludes from the former the duty to exercise reasonable care, skill, and diligence (s 174), and confirms that the civil consequences of breach will fall to be determined according to different principles. This does not mean that there can be no interaction between fiduciary and other duties. As the 2006 Act, s 179 recognizes, more than one of the general duties may apply in any given case. This raises, for example, the possibility of the duty to exercise reasonable care, skill, and diligence arising in the performance of other duties,

---

[19] [1998] Ch 1, 18A; *Sinclair Investments (UK) Ltd v Versailles Trade Finance Ltd* [2012] Ch 453, CA, per Lord Neuberger MR at para 35.

[20] [1998] Ch 1, 18E–F. See also *GHLM Trading Ltd v Maroo* [2012] 2 BCLC 369 at para 203, where Newey J said that an allegation of non-disclosure involves an allegation of breach of the duty of good faith and, hence, of dishonesty.

[21] [2003] 1 BCLC 598, 617–18. See also *Ultraframe (UK) Ltd v Fielding* [2005] EWHC 1638 (Ch), per Lewison J at para 1300; for the content of the duty of loyalty in the United States, see *Item Software (UK) Ltd v Fassihi* [2005] 2 BCLC 91, per Arden LJ at para 42.

including the duty to promote the interests of the company (s 172), as discussed in paragraphs 10.32–10.35 below.

It is worth emphasizing that, despite the adoption of similar terminology in the case law, **10.13** the director's fiduciary duty of loyalty to the company is different from, and more extensive than, the duty of fidelity owed by employees to their employer. As Arden LJ has pointed out:

> … the duties of a director are in general higher than those imposed by law on an employee. This is because a director is not simply a senior manager of the company. He is a fiduciary and with his fellow directors he is responsible for the success of the company's business.[22]

Unlike a director, an employee will not, merely by reason of his status as an employee, assume fiduciary obligations to his employer. That is not to say that fiduciary duties cannot arise out of the employment relationship. Where they do so, however, this is not simply the ordinary consequence of the employment relationship but of the fact that, within that relationship, the employee may undertake specific contractual obligations where equity imposes the more rigorous fiduciary duties in addition to the contractual obligations. Absent any such fiduciary duty, the employee's duty is one of fidelity, founded in contract. Whereas the duty owed by the director as a fiduciary is a single-minded duty of loyalty, meaning that he must subjugate his interests to those of the company, the employee's contractual duty of fidelity requires merely that he must have regard to the interests of the company, rather than subjugating his own interests to them.[23]

(3) The relevance of common law rules and equitable principles

Questions of honesty and loyalty affect the conscience, which has traditionally been the pre- **10.14** serve of equity. As Lord Templeman once said, 'Equity is not a computer. Equity operates on the conscience …'.[24] Such questions do not arise in relation to directors alone. They relate to all fiduciaries, including trustees and agents as well, with whose position that of directors has often been compared. The influence of equity has thus been keenly felt in the development of the nature and scope of fiduciary duties owed by directors and other fiduciaries. That it continues to do so in more modern times is clear from Millett LJ's judgment in *Bristol and West Building Society v Mothew* referred to at paragraphs 10.08–10.10 above, as well as *Ultraframe (UK) Ltd v Fielding*[25] considered below.

In contrast, the rules relating to duties of skill and care, even ones owed by fiduciaries, have **10.15** been developed at common law. As will be seen in the context of the discussion of the general duty to exercise reasonable care, skill, and diligence in Chapter 14, the nature and scope of such duties developed over the course of the last century as the functions of, and the role played by, directors changed, and as the legislature recognized that more was to be expected of those who sought to take advantage of the benefits of trading with limited liability in

---

[22] *Item Software (UK) Ltd v Fassihi* [2005] 2 BCLC 91, per Arden LJ at para 34.

[23] *Ranson v Customer Systems plc* [2012] EWCA Civ 841, [2012] IRLR 769. See the comprehensive discussion of this topic in the judgment of Lloyd LJ at paras 20–61, in which he acknowledged the masterly judgment of Elias J in *University of Nottingham v Fishel* [2000] ICR 1462. For a helpful distillation of the employee's contractual duty of fidelity, see *QBE Management Services (UK) Ltd v Dymoke* [2012] EWHC 80 (QB), per Haddon-Cave J at para 169, referred to in *Re-use Collections Ltd v Sendall* [2014] EWHC 3852 (QB) and *Allfiled v Eltis* [2016] FSR 11, per Hildyard J at para 111. For the position in Australia, see *Prestige Lifting Service Pty Ltd v Williams* [2015] FCA 1063.

[24] *Winkworth v Edward Baron Development Co Ltd* [1986] 1 WLR 1512, HL, at p 1516.

[25] [2005] EWHC 1638 (Ch).

the modern commercial world (apparent not only from the wrongful trading and other provisions of the Insolvency Act, but also from the enactment of the Company Directors Disqualification Act).

10.16 The general duties in their codified form are based on these common law rules and equitable principles as they apply in relation to directors, and take effect in place of those rules and principles as regards the duties owed to a company by a director.[26] As already stated, those general duties are to be interpreted and applied in the same way as common law rules and equitable principles, and regard is to be had to the corresponding common law rules and equitable principles in interpreting and applying them.[27] Despite the apparent conflict between the concept of the general duties as codified having effect 'in place of' the relevant common law rules and equitable principles, while at the same time requiring those duties to be interpreted having regard to such rules and principles, the intended effect of s 170(3) and (4) must be that the courts should interpret and give effect to the general duties by reference not only to the relevant rules and principles as they existed at the time of enactment, but as they continue to develop in the future. This recognizes the possibility, for example, that the rules and principles relating to agents, trustees, and other fiduciaries may develop over time, and enables the courts to have regard to such developments. This was confirmed by Lord Goldsmith, the Attorney General:

> Although the duties in relation to directors have developed in a distinctive way, they are often manifestations of more general principles. Subsection (4) is intended to enable the courts to continue to have regard to developments in the common law rules and equitable principles applying to these other types of fiduciary relationship. The advantage of that is that it will enable the statutory duties to develop in line with relevant developments in the law as it applies elsewhere.[28]

10.17 Just how much regard shall be had to such rules and principles in any given case, however, is likely to depend upon the nature of the duty under consideration, and the extent to which the terms in which it is expressed in its codified form coincide with the corresponding rule or principle. In certain respects, the general duties in their codified form depart from existing common law duties or equitable principles. This is the case, for example, in relation to certain aspects of the general duty to promote the success of the company (s 172), the new conflict rules (s 175), and the new rules relating to disclosure of interests in proposed transactions or arrangements (s 177). Each of these general duties is discussed in the following chapters. Where these provisions change the law, the scope for having regard to the corresponding common law rules and equitable principles is obviously limited.

(4) Directors as trustees

10.18 The position of a director has historically been likened to that of a trustee. Since both are fiduciaries, their positions are analogous.[29] Strictly speaking, however, a director is not a trustee, although he may become subject to the same liabilities as a trustee in certain circumstances.

---

[26] 2006 Act, s 170(3).
[27] 2006 Act, s 170(4).
[28] Lords Grand Committee, 6 February 2006, cols 243–5.
[29] *Re Duckwari plc* [1999] Ch 253, 262, CA, per Nourse LJ; *Bairstow v Queens Moat Houses plc* [2001] 2 BCLC 531, CA, per Robert Walker LJ at paras 50–1; *Sinclair Investments v Versailles Trade Finance Ltd* [2012] Ch 453, CA, per Lord Neuberger MR at para 34; *Ranson v Customer Systems plc* [2012] IRLR 769, CA, per Lloyd LJ at para 20.

It is the actual control of assets belonging beneficially to a company which causes the law to treat directors as analogous to trustees of those assets.[30] As Lindley LJ put it in *Re Lands Allotment Company*:

> Although directors are not properly speaking trustees, yet they have always been considered and treated as trustees of money which comes to their hands or which is actually under their control; and ever since joint stock companies were invented directors have been held liable to make good moneys which they have misapplied upon the same footing as if they were trustees ...[31]

Chadwick LJ expanded on this in *JJ Harrison (Properties) Ltd v Harrison*,[32] identifying four **10.19** propositions which he considered to be beyond argument, namely:

> (i) that a company incorporated under the Companies Acts is not trustee of its own property; it is both legal and beneficial owner of that property; (ii) that the property of a company so incorporated cannot lawfully be disposed of other than in accordance with the provisions of its memorandum and articles of association; (iii) that the powers to dispose of the company's property, conferred upon the directors by the articles of association, must be exercised by the directors for the purposes, and in the interests, of the company; and (iv) that, in that sense, the directors owe fiduciary duties to the company in relation to those powers and a breach of those duties is treated as a breach of trust.

Directors, therefore, are under a duty not to misapply the company's property (or, put **10.20** another way, they must account for the company's property and apply it for proper purposes).[33] Their conduct in relation to the company's property may therefore engage the duty only to exercise their powers for the purposes for which they were conferred under s 171(b), as discussed in Chapter 11 below. The onus is upon them, as fiduciaries, to account for their dealings with company property by providing such explanations as may be necessary.[34] Misapplication may, as noted by Chadwick LJ, take the form of disposal otherwise than in accordance with the company's articles, but it might also take the form of disposal which is contrary to any statutory provision or rule of law. There is an issue as to whether a director's liability for misapplication of company property for an improper purpose is strict or fault based, so that the director is not liable unless he knows that the purpose is improper or of the facts which make the purpose improper. In *Madoff Securities International Ltd v Raven*[35]

---

[30] *Ultraframe (UK) Ltd v Fielding* [2005] EWHC 1638 (Ch), per Lewison J at para 1253; *Sinclair Investments v Versailles Trade Finance Ltd* [2012] Ch 453, CA, per Lord Neuberger MR at para 34.

[31] [1894] 1 Ch 616, 631.

[32] [2002] 1 BCLC 162 at para 25.

[33] *Statek Corp v Alford* [2008] BCC 266 at para 107 (applying the duty stated by Lord Esher MR in *Soar v Ashwell* [1893] 2 QB 390, 394, CA, to a de facto director).

[34] *Re Idessa (UK) Ltd* [2012] 1 BCLC 80; *Re Snelling House Ltd, Alford v Barton* [2012] EWHC 440 (Ch) where Gabriel Moss QC, sitting as a deputy judge of the High Court, also cited *Gilman & Soame Ltd v Young* [2007] EWHC 1245 (Ch), *Sinclair Investments (UK) Ltd v Versailles Trade Finance* [2012] Ch 453 at para 34, *Re Mumtaz Properties Ltd* [2012] 2 BCLC 109 (CA), *GHLM Trading Ltd v Maroo* [2012] 2 BCLC 369 at paras 143–9 and *Ross River Ltd v Waverley Commercial Ltd* [2014] 1 BCLC 545, CA at paras 64 and 94. In *Psycare Ltd v Mundy* [2013] EWHC 4573 (Ch), the director failed to discharge the onus of demonstrating any proper entitlement to remuneration in the face of the company's claim against him for what Carr J found to be 'a systemic misuse of company funds' (para 20). The results were similar in *Fern Advisers Ltd v Burford* [2014] BPIR 581. In both *Mundy* and *Burford*, the company obtained summary judgment against the director.

[35] [2013] EWHC 3147 (Comm) at paras 195–200, discussing the two Supreme Court decisions, *Re Paycheck Services 3 Ltd* [2010] 1 WLR 2793 at paras 44–7, 124, and 146, and *Progress Property Co Ltd v Moore* [2011] 1 WLR 1 at para 32.

Popplewell J discussed this question and inclined to the view that liability was fault based, but did not have to decide it.

10.21 Similarly, the dealing with company property may take the form of a disposal by the directors in bad faith or otherwise than in accordance with their duty to act in the way they consider in good faith would be most likely to promote the success of the company (now embodied in s 172 and discussed in Chapter 12 below).

10.22 What constitutes the company's property for these purposes is not always easy to determine. It is clear that the director's duty does not simply arise in relation to money which comes into the director's hands; rather it applies to all property coming under the directors' control in their capacity as such. As Kay LJ said in *Re Lands Allotment Company*:

> They are only trustees qua the particular property which is put into their hands or under their control.[36]

Property is not confined to tangible assets, however, but will include opportunities and rights which are properly to be regarded as belonging to the company.[37]

10.23 That is not to say that directors are to be treated, nor are they expected to behave, in the same way as trustees in every circumstance. Where the trustee may be expected to exercise caution in the conduct of trust affairs, the direction and control of a trading company as a commercial profit-making enterprise will frequently call for a more robust exercise of commercial judgment at a strategic level as well as on a day-to-day basis. The courts have traditionally adopted a more relaxed attitude to the taking of commercial risk by directors in the exercise of their business judgment. This is perhaps most clearly demonstrated by the so-called business judgment rule.[38] As Kay J explained in *In re Faure Electric Accumulator Co*:

> However, it is quite obvious that to apply to directors the strict rules of the Court of Chancery with respect to ordinary trustees might fetter their action to an extent which would be exceedingly disadvantageous to the companies they represent.[39]

Stirling J explained the position in *Sheffield and South Yorkshire Permanent Building Society v Aizlewood*,[40] in the following terms:

> In my judgment, directors are not under an obligation to avoid investments attended with hazard, but may, in the absence of anything to the contrary in the rules or articles of association, act in the same manner as business men of ordinary prudence.

---

[36] [1894] 1 Ch 616, 639. See also *Re Forest of Dean Mining Co* (1878) LR 10 Ch 450, per Sir George Jessel MR at 453.

[37] *Sinclair Investments (UK) Ltd v Versailles Trade Finance Ltd* [2012] Ch 453, CA, per Lord Neuberger MR at para 88. As regards directors, the effect of the decision of the Supreme Court in *FHR European Ventures LLP v Cedar Capital Partners LLC* [2015] AC 250, is that a director is liable to account *in specie* for any benefit obtained from his directorship or breach of his fiduciary duties, as the benefit should be treated as the property of the company: see para 30 *et seq*, relying on the authorities cited at paras 14 and 19. See also *Ball v Eden Project Ltd* [2002] 1 BCLC 313, in which Laddie J decided the trademark in 'The Eden Project' was a fundamental part of the company's business, so that by registering it in his own name and for his own benefit, the director deprived the company of the opportunity to benefit from the goodwill generated by its own efforts.

[38] See Chapter 12, Section B and Chapter 14, Section D below.

[39] (1888) 40 Ch D 141 at 151, cited with approval by Lord Russell in *Regal (Hastings) Ltd v Gulliver* [1967] 2 AC 134 at 147.

[40] (1889) 44 Ch D 412 at 454.

The modern approach to the different functions of trustees on the one hand and directors on the other can be illustrated by reference to *Daniels v Anderson*, in which two members of the New South Wales Court of Appeal described the position in the following way: **10.24**

> [W]hile the duty of a trustee is to exercise a degree of restraint and conservatism in investment judgments the duty of a director may be to display entrepreneurial flair and accept commercial risks to produce a sufficient return on the capital invested.[41]

More recently still, Norris J expressly recognized in *Roberts v Frohlich*[42] that 'risk is an inherent part of economic activity'. That begs the question as to when the risk will become too great. According to Norris J, the risk would be too great where the particular activity becomes speculative 'in the sense of being, in all the circumstances, too risky for a competent board to embark upon it'.[43] If, for example, the company were insolvent or of doubtful solvency, where a long-term view is unrealistic, acts which a competent director or board of directors might justifiably undertake in relation to a solvent company might be wholly inappropriate.[44]

(5) The duties are owed to the company

The 2006 Act, s 170(1) provides as follows: **10.25**

> The general duties specified in sections 171 to 177 are owed by a director of the company to the company.

This reflects the position long recognized at common law that a director owes fiduciary duties and a duty to exercise reasonable care, skill, and diligence to the company and, in the absence of special circumstances,[45] to the company alone. Lord Goldsmith, the Attorney General, explained that 'as in existing law, the general duties are owed by the director to the company. It follows that, as now, only the company can enforce them. Directors are liable to the company for loss to the company, and not more widely.'[46] A distinction is to be drawn here between the company and, in particular, its shareholders, which emanates from the company's separate legal personality. As Dillon LJ said in *Multinational Gas and Petrochemical Co Ltd v Multinational Gas and Petrochemical Services Ltd*:

> The directors indeed stand in a fiduciary relationship to the company, as they are appointed to manage the affairs of the company and they owe fiduciary duties to the company though not to the creditors, present or future, or to individual shareholders.[47]

Historically, the interests of the company have fallen to be determined by reference primar- **10.26**
ily to the interests of the shareholders (both present and future) as a general body, at least when the company is solvent. Even before the 2006 Act came into force, however, this was not exclusively so. The 1985 Act, s 309 obliged directors, in the performance of their functions, to have regard to the interests of the company's employees in general. In addition, in circumstances where the company was in financial difficulties so that its creditors were at

---

[41] [1995] 13 ACLC 614, 657.
[42] [2011] 2 BCLC 625 at para 105.
[43] [2011] 2 BCLC 625 at para 105.
[44] [2011] 2 BCLC 625 at para 98. See the discussion at Chapter 12, Section E below.
[45] See the discussion at paras 10.27–10.29 below.
[46] Lords Grand Committee, 6 February 2006, col 242.
[47] [1983] Ch 258, 288, CA. Also *Percival v Wright* [1902] 2 Ch 421; *Colin Gwyer v London Wharf* [2003] 2 BCLC 153 at para 72; *Secretary of Trade for Trade and Industry v Goldberg* [2004] 1 BCLC 597 at para 29.

risk, even if it was not technically insolvent, the interests of the company were extended so as to encompass the interests of the company's creditors as a whole, as well as those of its shareholders.[48] Whether and to what extent interests other than those of the members are to be taken into account must now be considered in the light of the 2006 Act, s 172 (as to which see Chapter 12 below).

10.27 It is important to note, however, that the question whether and in what circumstances a director may owe a duty to someone other than the company, and what the nature and extent of any such duty may be, is neither addressed nor affected by the 2006 Act. To the extent that any such duty existed before the 2006 Act was enacted, therefore, it will continue to apply. Further, to the extent that a director may by his acts or representations render himself liable to someone other than the company even in the absence of a duty (where, for example, he is guilty of deceit),[49] such liability is unaffected by the 2006 Act.

10.28 Although as a general rule, fiduciary duties owed by a director to the company do not necessarily extend to members, either individually or generally, the fact that a director owes fiduciary duties to the company does not necessarily preclude the coexistence of additional duties owed by the directors in special circumstances. Mummery LJ summarized the position in the following way in *Peskin v Anderson*:[50]

> The fiduciary duties owed to the company arise from the legal relationship between the directors and the company directed and controlled by them. The fiduciary duties owed to the shareholders do not arise from that legal relationship. They are dependent on establishing a special factual relationship between the directors and the shareholders in the particular case. Events may take place which bring the directors of the company into direct and close contact with the shareholders in a manner capable of generating fiduciary obligations, such as a duty of disclosure of material facts to the shareholders, or an obligation to use confidential information and valuable commercial and financial opportunities, which have been acquired by the directors in that office, for the benefit of the shareholders, and not to prefer and promote their own interests at the expense of the shareholders.
>
> These duties may arise in special circumstances which replicate the salient features of well-established categories of fiduciary relationships. Fiduciary relationships, such as agency, involve duties of trust, confidence and loyalty. Those duties are, in general, attracted by and attached to a person who undertakes, or who, depending on all the circumstances, is treated as having assumed, responsibility to act on behalf of, or for the benefit of, another person. That other person may have entrusted or, depending on all the circumstances, may

---

[48] *West Mercia Safetywear Ltd v Dodd* [1988] BCLC 250, 252, CA; *Facia Footwear v Hinchcliffe* [1998] 1 BCLC 218, 228; *MDA Investment Management Ltd* [2004] 1 BCLC 217; *Bilta (UK) Ltd v Nazir (No 2)* [2014] Ch 52, CA at para 22, per Patten LJ; *Bilta (UK) Ltd v Nazir (No 2)* [2016] AC 1, SC at paras 123–7, per Lords Toulson and Hodge. See further the discussion in Chapter 12, Section E below.

[49] *Standard Chartered Bank v Pakistan National Shipping Corp* [2003] 1 AC 959, HL.

[50] [2001] 1 BCLC 372, CA at paras 33–4. See also *Allen v Hyatt* (1914) 30 TLR 444 (where the Privy Council held that the directors had held themselves out to the shareholders as acting as agents on their behalf and, accordingly, that they were liable to account to the shareholders for the profits they had made); *Howard Smith Ltd v Ampol Petroleum Ltd* [1974] AC 821, PC (directors' use of fiduciary power of allotment of shares for a different purpose than that for which it was granted, and so as to dilute the voting power of the majority shareholding of issued shares); *Coleman v Myers* [1977] 2 NZLR 225; *Heron International Ltd v Lord Grade* [1983] BCLC 244; *Re a Company (No 005136 of 1986)* [1987] BCLC 82; *Dawson International plc v Coats Patons plc* [1988] 4 BCC 305; *Re Chez Nico (Restaurants) Ltd* [1992] BCLC 192; *Platt v Platt* [1999] 2 BCLC 745. For a recent review of the authorities in this area, see *Sharp v Blank* [2015] EWHC 3220 (Ch) (Nugee J) at paras 9–13.

be treated as having entrusted, the care of his property, affairs, transactions or interests to him.

Mummery LJ then gave a number of examples of circumstances in which a direct fiduciary duty to shareholders might arise:

There are, for example, instances of the directors of a company making direct approaches to, and dealing with, the shareholders in relation to a specific transaction and holding themselves out as agents for them in connection with the acquisition or disposal of shares; or making material representations to them; or failing to make material disclosure to them of insider information in the context of negotiations for a take-over of the company's business; or supplying to them specific information and advice on which they have relied. These events are capable of constituting special circumstances and of generating fiduciary obligations, especially in those cases in which the directors, for their own benefit, seek to use their position and special inside knowledge acquired by them to take improper and unfair advantage of the shareholders.

In *Peskin v Anderson* itself, both Neuberger J at first instance and the Court of Appeal held **10.29** that directors of the Royal Automobile Club Ltd, who were contemplating a sale of the company's motoring services business, did not owe a fiduciary duty to members who had resigned, or not renewed, their membership in ignorance of the proposals and who had thus missed out on substantial payments made to those who were members when the transaction completed, there being 'nothing special' in the factual relationship between the directors and members, and no relevant dealings or negotiations between them.

In *Sharp v Blank*[51] the directors accepted that they owed a duty to provide sufficient informa- **10.30** tion to the shareholders of Lloyds Bank in the context of its acquisition of HBOS, but denied that this meant they owed fiduciary duties to the shareholders. Nugee J agreed; he considered that the duty to provide sufficient information was a rule of ordinary fairness rather than a duty of loyalty, and that the circumstances were not such as to give rise to any fiduciary duty to act generally in the shareholders' best interests or in good faith. The fact that the directors had vastly superior knowledge was not enough.

In the case of nominee directors, the mere fact of nomination of itself does not operate to **10.31** impose a duty on the part of the director to his nominator.[52] Such duties may arise out of the fact that the nominee director is an employee or officer of the person nominating him, or has a separate agreement with that person. Even where such duties arise, however, they will not detract from his duties to the company of which he is a director.[53] Appointment as a nominee director may lead to difficulties in relation to the duty to exercise independent judgment and conflict of interest, as discussed in Chapters 13 and 15 of this work.

(6) More than one of the general duties may apply

The 2006 Act, s 179 is in the following terms: **10.32**

Except as otherwise provided, more than one of the general duties may apply in any given case.

This provision makes it clear that the general duties are normally to be regarded as cumu- **10.33** lative. Thus, when performing his duty to promote the success of the company (s 172),

---

[51] [2015] EWHC 3220 (Ch).
[52] *Re Neath Rugby Ltd (No 2), Hawkes v Cuddy* [2009] 2 BCLC 427, CA, per Stanley Burnton LJ at para 32.
[53] *Re Neath Rugby Ltd (No 2), Hawkes v Cuddy* [2009] 2 BCLC 427, CA at para 32.

a director must presumably do so in compliance with his duty to exercise independent judgment (s 173) and with reasonable care, skill, and diligence, in accordance with his duty under s 174. Likewise, a director who accepts a bribe from a third party may simultaneously act in breach not only of the duty not to accept benefits from third parties (s 176), but also the duty to avoid conflicts of interest (s 175), and to promote the success of the company (s 172).

10.34 To take another example: a director who causes the company to sell property at an undervalue to a company in which he holds shares may find himself in simultaneous breach of more than one of the general duties. He may be in breach of his duty to act within powers (s 171) to the extent that he does not exercise his powers for a legitimate purpose. He may be in breach of his duty to promote the success of the company (s 172). It may even be that he acts in breach of his duty to take account of the interests of the company's creditors (recognized by s 172(3)) if the company is insolvent or becomes insolvent as a result of the sale. He may act in breach of his duty to exercise reasonable care, skill, and diligence (s 174) to the extent that the undervalue results from negligence on his part. Similarly, he may be in breach of his duty to avoid conflicts of interest (s 175). If he receives a payment or other benefit from the recipient company, he may be in breach of his duty not to accept benefits from third parties (s 176), although it is unclear whether the fact that the value of his shareholding in the recipient company may increase would suffice for these purposes. Finally, he may also be in breach of his duty to declare an interest in a proposed transaction or arrangement (s 177).

10.35 The general rule will not apply where provision is made to the contrary. Thus the duty to avoid conflicts of interest (s 175) does not apply to a conflict of interest arising in relation to a transaction or arrangement with the company, to which the duty to declare an interest (s 177) will apply instead.[54]

B. The Application of the General Duties to Former Directors

10.36 Section 170(2) provides that:

A person who ceases to be a director continues to be subject—
(a) to the duty in section 175 (duty to avoid conflicts of interest) as regards the exploitation of any property, information or opportunity of which he became aware at a time when he was a director, and
(b) to the duty in section 176 (duty not to accept benefits from third parties) as regards things done or omitted by him before he ceased to be a director.

To that extent those duties apply to a former director as to a director, subject to any necessary adaptations.

10.37 The duties to avoid conflicts of interest and not to accept benefits from third parties are the only general duties capable of subsisting after a person has ceased to be a director and to be concerned in the management of a company. The application of these duties to former directors is discussed in Chapter 15, Section E and Chapter 16, Section E.

---

[54] 2006 Act, s 175(3).

C. The Application of the General Duties to Shadow Directors

The 2006 Act, s 170(5) originally provided as follows: **10.38**

> The general duties apply to shadow directors where, and to the extent that, the corresponding common law rules or equitable principles so apply.

Following amendment by the Small Business, Enterprise and Employment (SBEE) Act 2015,[55] it now provides as follows:

> The general duties apply to a shadow director of a company where and to the extent that they are capable of so applying.

The original formulation intentionally left the applicability of the general duties to shadow directors[56] to be determined by the courts, by reference to existing rules and principles, without any steer from the legislature. As the Attorney General, Lord Goldsmith said:

> The law is still developing. It would not be right for the general duties not to apply at all to shadow directors, but the law may develop in such a way that some do and some don't. It is right to leave those areas, as now, to the courts …[57]

Although the amendment is relatively slight, it is significant: the default position now appears to be that the general duties do apply to shadow directors and will only not do so to the extent that they cannot do so, subject only to regulations yet to be made which may prescribe adaptations or disapply certain general duties.[58]

Initially, it seems to have been assumed, in what little authority there was on the subject, that   **10.39** shadow directors owed the same fiduciary and other duties as *de jure* directors. In *Yukong Line v Rendsburg Investments*,[59] for example, Toulson J expressed himself in terms which do not appear to admit the possibility of debate:

> As to an unlawful means conspiracy, Mr [Y] undoubtedly owed a fiduciary duty to [the company]. Although he was not formally a director, he was a 'shadow director' and controlled the company's activities. To remove the funds in [the company's] bank account when it had a probable liability to [the Claimant] far in excess of its assets involved a clear breach of that fiduciary duty: *West Mercia Safetywear Ltd (in liq) v Dodd* [1988] BCLC 250.

Toulson J did not explain his reasoning and expressed his view in the context of the duty owed by a director to a company, which was insolvent, to take into account the interests of its creditors.[60] As appears from the discussion in Chapter 12, Section E below, while such a duty exists at common law, the circumstances giving rise to it and its scope remain uncertain, and it is not one which has been codified in the 2006 Act, ss 171–7.

In *John v PriceWaterhouseCoopers*,[61] Ferris J was minded to accept that a shadow director   **10.40** owed a duty of care to the company, as appears from the following paragraph in his judgment:

---

[55] SBEE Act 2015, s 89(1), which came into force from 26 May 2015.
[56] As to who qualifies as a shadow director, see the discussion in Chapter 3, Section 3(C) above.
[57] Lords Grand Committee, 9 May 2006, col 828.
[58] SBEE Act 2015, s 89(2) and (3).
[59] [1998] 2 BCLC 485, 502h.
[60] In *Ultraframe*, Lewison J referred to Toulson J's judgment in *Yukong*, but considered that he must be cautious before accepting that a shadow director 'undoubtedly' owes fiduciary duties to the company.
[61] Unreported, 11 April 2001 at para 319.

> The case against Mr Haydon was that he was in breach of a duty of care owed by him to Bong as a shadow director and, to the extent that the salaries and expenses were debited to Bondi, in breach of a duty of care owed by him to Bondi. For reasons which I have already stated, I am satisfied that Mr Haydon did owe such a duty of care to Bondi. If it is correct that he was a shadow director of Bong I would accept that he owed a similar duty of care to Bong.

In the result, however, Ferris J concluded that Mr Haydon was not a shadow director of Bong. Accordingly, what he said in relation to a duty of care being owed by a shadow director was, strictly, *obiter*.

10.41 In neither case does it appear that the point was fully argued. The same cannot be said of *Ultraframe (UK) Ltd v Fielding*,[62] decided before the 2006 Act came into force. In that case, it was alleged, and Lewison J held, that Mr Fielding was a shadow director of two companies. It was argued that this meant that he owed the same fiduciary obligations to those two companies as if he had been a *de jure* director of both of them. Lewison J disagreed. He concluded that the mere fact that a person falls within the statutory definition of 'shadow director' was not enough to impose upon him the same fiduciary duties to the relevant company as are owed by a *de jure* or de facto director,[63] but that on the facts of a particular case the activities of a shadow director may go beyond the mere exertion of indirect influence and subject him to particular fiduciary duties.[64]

10.42 The essential premise of the reasoning[65] which led Lewison J to this conclusion was that the statutory definition of 'shadow director' was enacted for specific purposes of company legislation (including many prohibitions relating to transactions between companies and their directors, duties of disclosure, liability for wrongful trading, or to the making of disqualification orders). However, there was no specific statutory provision that said that a shadow director owes the same duties to a company as a *de jure* or de facto director.

10.43 Lewison J considered that the real question at issue[66] was this: in what circumstances will equity impose fiduciary obligations on a person with regard to property belonging to another? After considering the authorities, he accepted the proposition that the key component of a fiduciary duty is the obligation of loyalty, and that he must look for facts which supported the inference that the company was in a direct relation of trust and confidence with the putative fiduciary.[67] Lewison J accepted that, on the facts of a particular case, the activities of a shadow director may go beyond the mere exertion of indirect influence. As sole signatory on the company's bank account, for example, it was indisputable that the shadow director was not entitled to draw on the account for his personal benefit. Taking it upon himself to assume control of an asset belonging to another carried with it a duty to use the asset for the benefit of the company, a duty which was properly called a fiduciary duty. Lewison J emphasized, however, that this fact alone did not mean that wider fiduciary duties were imposed upon him, and that the indirect influence exerted by a paradigm shadow director who does not directly deal with or claim the right to deal directly with the company's assets would not usually be enough to impose fiduciary duties upon him.[68]

---

[62] [2005] EWHC 1638 (Ch).
[63] [2005] EWHC 1638 (Ch) at paras 1284 and 1289.
[64] [2005] EWHC 1638 (Ch) at paras 1289–90.
[65] [2005] EWHC 1638 (Ch) at paras 1279–84.
[66] [2005] EWHC 1638 (Ch) at para 1285.
[67] [2005] EWHC 1638 (Ch) at paras 1286–8.
[68] [2005] EWHC 1638 (Ch) at paras 1289–90.

Just as the 1985 Act did not extend the definition of 'director' so as to include shadow direc- **10.44** tor, neither does the 2006 Act.[69] As matters stand following amendment, however, the 2006 Act does now provide that the general duties apply to shadow directors where, and to the extent that, they are capable of so applying. It follows, therefore, that the essential premise of Lewison J's reasoning set out in paragraph 10.42 above has fallen away.

Even prior to the amendment, however, it is doubtful whether the position as described by **10.45** Lewison J in *Ultraframe* was that which was envisaged at the time the statutory statement of general duties was being considered and formulated. For example, having referred to the statement in the edition of Pennington's *Company Law* current at the time, to the effect that shadow directors are not subject to the common law or equitable duties of directors, the Law Commission and the Scottish Law Commission said the following:

> However, the better view is that the shadow director is to be regarded as akin to a de facto director and that he can incur the liability of a de jure director under the general law where he effectively acts as a director through the people whom he can influence.[70]

They also considered that Toulson J had been correct to proceed on the basis that a shadow director could be in breach of fiduciary duties as a director, in *Yukong Line Ltd v Rendsburg Investments Corporation (No 2)*.[71]

It is also fair to say that this part of the *Ultraframe* decision had a mixed reception,[72] and **10.46** when the issue arose for determination in *Vivendi SA v Richards*,[73] Newey J adopted a different approach, observing that he thought that *Ultraframe* had understated the extent to which shadow directors owe fiduciary duties. He identified the idea at the heart of Lewison J's judgment as being that the imposition of fiduciary duties depends on the person concerned having undertaken or assumed responsibility. Newey J considered by reference to the authorities that the question whether there was such an undertaking or assumption had to be determined objectively, rather than by reference to the shadow director's subjective intentions, and that the taking on of a role must be capable of implying an undertaking or assumption of responsibility.[74] Adopting that approach, he considered that a person who gives directions or instructions to a company's *de jure* directors in the belief that they will be acted on could fairly be described as assuming responsibility for the company's affairs, at least as regards the directions or instructions he gives. Applying by analogy the position relating to promoters,[75] he observed that a shadow director could also be said to choose to make use of powers which 'greatly affect the interests of the corporation'. He concluded, therefore, that a shadow director will typically owe fiduciary duties in relation at least to the directions or

---

[69] 2006 Act, s 250(1).

[70] Law Commission, *Company Directors: Regulating Conflicts of Interests and Formulating a Statement of Duties*, at para 17.15 (Consultation Paper No 153, Scottish Law Commission Discussion Paper No 105).

[71] [1998] 1 WLR 294; Joint Consultation Paper at para 17.15.

[72] See Prentice and Payne (2006) 122 LQR 558; Kershaw, *Company Law in Context*, 2nd edn (OUP, 2012) at 330; Gower & Davies, *Principles of Modern Company Law*, 9th edn (eds), Davies and Worthington, Sweet & Maxwell, 2012.

[73] [2013] BCC 771.

[74] [2013] BCC 771, at para 139.

[75] [2013] BCC 771, at para 140, referring to *Erlanger v New Sombrero Phosphate Co* (1878) LR 3 App Cas 1218.

instructions he gives to the *de jure* directors, including more particularly the duty of good faith when giving such directions and instructions.[76]

10.47 CA 2006, section 170(5), following amendment, does not in terms state whether it applies only prospectively, or retrospectively as well so as to extend the general duties to shadow directors in respect of their conduct before 27 May 2015. Its language is wide enough to operate retrospectively. The intention behind the amendment seems to have been to correct and redirect the narrow course adopted in *Ultraframe*. As already stated, the purpose of this part of the 2006 Act, Chapter 10 was to replace existing common law rules and equitable principles as regards duties owed to a company by a director. Against that background, there is no obvious unfairness in treating shadow directors as being subject to general duties even in respect of pre-amendment conduct, for that was the course adopted at common law in *Vivendi* itself; nor is there any vested interest that requires protection. It is suggested, therefore, that the section as amended will apply to define the duties owed by shadow directors in the period prior to amendment as well as after, subject to any adaptation or regulation the Secretary of State may make.[77] If that is right, it should not be necessary in future to consider which of *Ultraframe* or *Vivendi* correctly states the position at common law. If and to the extent that it does become necessary to consider the position at common law, however, it is suggested that *Vivendi* is to be preferred, not simply as the later decision in which the relevant authorities were fully considered,[78] but because its reasoning is the more persuasive.[79]

10.48 The position following the statutory amendment appears more straightforward: while the precise extent of the capability of the general duties applying to shadow directors may give rise to some debate, the starting point will be that shadow directors owe those duties, subject to any adaptation or regulation to the contrary which the Secretary of State may see fit to make.[80]

D. Consent, Approval, or Authorization by Members

(1) The general rule

10.49 The 2006 Act, s 180 contains provisions concerning the manner in which members of the company may give their consent, approval, or authorization, or where they may not be required to do so, in relation to the directors' general duties.

10.50 Three general propositions are to be derived from the provisions of the 2006 Act, s 180. First, the application of the general duties is not affected by the fact that the case also falls

---

[76] [2013] BCC 771, at para 143. In *Vivendi SA v Richards* itself, there was an additional reason for concluding that the shadow director owed fiduciary duties, namely the fact that he had undertaken express obligations of loyalty when he entered into a consultancy agreement with the company: para 144.

[77] See the approach adopted in *L'Office Cherfien des Phosphates v Yamashita-Shinnihon Steamship Co Ltd* [1994] 1 AC 486 and *Odelola v Secretary of State for the Home Department* [2009] 1 WLR 1230, and the discussion in *Ng v Charalambos* [2015] 1 WLR 3018, CA.

[78] This would operate only at first instance, and was the course adopted by Sir James Munby P in *R v R & others* [2014] Fam Law 454, at paras 9–10.

[79] In *Sukhoruchkin v Bekestein* [2014] EWCA Civ 399, the appellate court noted the differing decisions but found it unnecessary to decide between them: per Sir Terence Etherton C at para 41.

[80] SBEE Act 2015, s 89(2) and (3).

within the 2006 Act, Part 10, Chapter 4 (transactions requiring approval of members) or 4A (directors of quoted companies).[81] In other words, the general duties and those set out in Chapters 4 and 4A are generally to be regarded as being cumulative (save to the extent that the 2006 Act, s 180 otherwise provides, as discussed below), so that the general duties will apply even if either Chapter 4 or 4A also applies. It follows that compliance with the general duties does not remove the need for approval under any applicable provision of Chapter 4 or 4A.[82]

Secondly, the general duties have effect subject to any rule of law enabling the company to give authority, specifically or generally, for anything to be done (or omitted) by the directors, or any of them, that would otherwise be a breach of duty.[83] This means that members may still authorize what would otherwise constitute a breach of a general duty, for example by giving their unanimous consent informally,[84] such that the act becomes the act of the company itself.[85] However, it also means that such limitations as already exist on such powers to authorize acts or omissions by directors will remain. Thus consent, to be effective, must be properly informed.[86] Members could not authorize an act or omission that would be unlawful, or (possibly) for an improper purpose,[87] or in fraud of the company, or dishonest,[88] or would constitute a breach of a statutory provision, the underlying purpose of which extends beyond the protection of members.[89] For similar reasons, members cannot authorize acts or omissions which are likely to affect the interests of the company's creditors, in circumstances where the company is insolvent or on the verge of insolvency.[90]

10.51

---

[81] 2006 Act, s 180(2), as amended (with effect from 1 October 2013) by the Enterprise and Regulatory Reform Act, s 81. 2006 Act, Part 10, Chapters 4 and 4A are discussed in Ch 18 below.

[82] 2006 Act, s 180(3) as amended (with effect from 1 October 2013) by the Enterprise and Regulatory Reform Act, s 81.

[83] 2006 Act, s 180(4)(a).

[84] *Re Duomatic Ltd* [1969] 2 Ch 365; *Wright v Atlas Wright (Europe) Ltd* [1999] 2 BCLC 301, CA.

[85] *Multinational Gas v Multinational Services* [1983] Ch 258 at 269A–E, per Lawton LJ; at 288D–G, per Dillon LJ; *Meridian Global Funds Management Asia Ltd v Securities Commission* [1995] 2 AC 500, 506, PC, per Lord Hoffmann.

[86] *Kaye v Croydon Tramways Co* [1989] 1 Ch 358, CA.

[87] *Madoff Securities International Ltd v Raven* [2013] EWHC 3147 (Comm) at para 269. However, the view there expressed by Popplewell J makes no reference to, and takes no account of, the *obiter* remarks to the contrary made by Slade LJ in *Rolled Steel Ltd v British Steel Corpn* [1986] Ch 246, at 296G–297A. While Browne-Wilkinson LJ expressed no view on the question either way, and Lawton LJ made no express reference to it, the view expressed by Popplewell J remains in doubt.

[88] *AG for Canada v Standard Trust* [1911] AC 498, 505, per Viscount Haldane LC; *Cox v Cox* [1979] Ch 250; *Multinational Gas Ltd v Multinational Services Ltd* [1983] Ch 258 at 268E–H, CA, per Lawton LJ; *Bowthorpe Holdings v Ellis* [2003] 1 BCLC 226; *Architects of Wine v Barclays Bank* [2007] 1 Lloyds Rep 55 (reversed on appeal on other grounds); *Madoff Securities International Ltd v Raven* [2013] EWHC 3147 (Comm) at paras 266–9. In the *Madoff* case, Popplewell J decided that, insofar as making or permitting the relevant (MSIL Kohn) payments constituted a breach by the directors of a duty to act in what they perceived to be the interests of the company, or a failure to exercise reasonable care skill and diligence, the transactions were ratified by the unanimous approval of the voting shareholders. That applied to those directors who addressed their minds to whether the payments were in the interests of MSIL, as well as to those who did not.

[89] *Wright v Atlas Wright (Europe) Ltd* [1999] 2 BCLC 301, CA.

[90] *West Mercia Safetywear Ltd v Dodd* [1988] BCLC 250, 252h–253b, CA, per Dillon LJ (citing and adopting *Kinsela v Russell Kinsela* (1986) 4 NSWLR 822, a decision of the Court of Appeal for New South Wales, itself approving and applying the statement of Cooke J to like effect in *Nicholson v Permakraft (NZ) Ltd* [1985] 1 NZLR 242 at 250); *Official Receiver v Stern* [2002] 1 BCLC 119 at para 32; *Bowthorpe Holdings v Ellis* [2003] 1 BCLC 226; *Architects of Wine v Barclays Bank* [2007] 1 Lloyd's Rep 55 (reversed on appeal on other grounds); *Lexi Holdings plc v Luqman* [2007] EWHC 2652 (Ch), Briggs J at para 191; *Vivendi SA v Richards* [2013] BCC 771, per Newey J at para 148. For a recent application of *Kinsela* in Australia, see *Australasia Annuities Pty Ltd v Rowley Super Fund Pty Ltd* (2015) 318 ALR 302.

10.52   Careful consideration will have to be given, however, to the terms of the authority given by the members. The mere fact that directors may be authorized to act in a certain way, for example to enter into a certain transaction, will not obviate the need for them to continue to exercise reasonable care, skill, and diligence (2006 Act, s 174) when doing so, or to reconsider whether the transaction would promote the success of the company (2006 Act, s 172), if there were to be a material change of circumstances after authorization had been obtained.[91]

10.53   The 2006 Act, s 180(4)(a) must be read with the 2006 Act, s 239 (ratification of acts of directors), which is discussed in Chapter 20, Section D. The limitations on ratification by informal shareholder approval in accordance with the *Duomatic* principle were recently considered and restated by Newey J in *Secretary of State for Business, Innovation and Skills v Doffman (No 2)*,[92] a disqualification case. The principle will not apply, for example, if the shareholders did not address their minds to the matter in question, unless at least it has become inequitable for them to deny that they have given their approval. It will not be enough if they would probably have authorized or ratified the act if they had known or thought about it.[93] Further, the principle does not permit shareholders to do informally what they could not have done formally by way of written resolution or at a meeting.[94] Thus it will not extend to ultra vires transactions, such as unlawful distributions[95] or, possibly, the exercise of powers for an improper purpose,[96] and its application may also be precluded where the company is insolvent or on the verge of insolvency'.[97]

10.54   It will be seen that there are, as is to be expected, many similarities in the approach to be adopted in cases where members authorize or ratify the acts of directors. Certain differences arising from the statutory provisions should, however, be borne in mind. The obvious difference is that ratification may only follow after the relevant act or omission that would otherwise constitute a breach of duty, whereas the 2006 Act, s 180(4)(a) contemplates prior authority being given. Subject to this, the essential distinction between the two is that, where ratification is sought, the vote of the director in breach of duty (if he is a member) and any member connected with him will be disregarded for the purposes of ascertaining whether the resolution has been passed by the requisite majority.[98] This is not so if the act or omission is authorized in advance. The reason for this is that an act or omission previously authorized cannot give rise to a breach of duty. On the other hand, the ratification of an act or omission which was not so authorized and which constitutes a breach of duty involves the company giving up a claim against the director concerned. It is to be noted that, whether the act or

---

[91]   eg *In re Brazilian Rubber Plantations and Estates Ltd* [1911] 1 Ch 425, 437 (a case where the company's articles conferred a discretion on the directors, which Neville J considered the directors were bound to exercise).

[92]   [2011] 2 BCLC 541 at paras 37–45. Also *Re D'Jan of London Ltd* [1994] 1 BCLC 561.

[93]   *Re D'Jan of London Ltd* [1994] 1 BCLC 561.

[94]   *Re New Cedos Engineering Co Ltd [1994] 1 BCLC 797*, 814g–h; *Atlas Wright (Europe) Ltd v Wright [1999] BCC 163*, 174G–H.

[95]   *Aveling Barford Ltd v Perion Ltd* [1989] BCLC 626. See also *Progress Property Co Ltd v Moorgath Group Ltd* [2010] 1 BCLC 1, CA.

[96]   *Madoff Securities International Ltd v Raven* [2013] EWHC 3147 at para 269; but see fn 87 above.

[97]   *West Mercia Safetywear Ltd v Dodd* [1988] BCLC 250; *Colin Gwyer & Associates Ltd v London Wharf (Limehouse) Ltd* [2003] 2 BCLC 153; *Re MDA Investment Management Ltd* [2004] 1 BCLC 217; *Madoff Securities International Ltd v Raven* [2013] EWHC 3147 (Comm) at paras 272, 273. See also *Goldtrail Travel Ltd v Aydin* [2015] 1 BCLC 89 (not affected on this point by the judgment on appeal by some defendants: [2016] EWCA Civ 371).

[98]   2006 Act, s 239(4).

omission is previously authorized or subsequently ratified, a member will not be permitted to pursue a derivative claim against the director in respect of that act or omission.[99]

The third general proposition set out in the 2006 Act, s 180 is that the general duties other- **10.55** wise (ie subject to the other provisions of that section) have effect notwithstanding any enactment or rule of law, except as otherwise provided or where the context otherwise requires.[100] An example of an exception is s 247, which provides that directors may make provision for employees on the cessation or transfer of a company's business even if this would otherwise constitute a breach of the general duty to promote the success of the company.[101]

What the 2006 Act, s 180 also does, however, is make special provision in respect of cases **10.56** which are concerned with the duty to avoid conflicts of interest (2006 Act, s 175), the duty not to accept benefits from third parties (2006 Act, s 176), and the duty to declare an interest in a proposed transaction or arrangement with the company (2006 Act, s 177). These are addressed separately below.

(2) The duty to avoid conflicts of interest

As more fully discussed in Chapter 15, the 2006 Act, s 175 contains a statutory statement of **10.57** the duty to avoid conflicts of interest, which will include a conflict of interest and duty and a conflict of duties. It does not apply to a conflict of interest arising in relation to a transaction or arrangement with the company,[102] to which the 2006 Act, s 177 and Chapters 3–6 apply instead. The duty is not infringed if the particular transaction or arrangement has been properly authorized by the directors.[103] Where this authorization has been obtained, the 2006 Act, s 180(1)(a) provides that the transaction or arrangement is not liable to be set aside by virtue of any common law rule or equitable principle requiring the consent or approval of the members of the company. However, if any other enactment requires the consent or approval of the members in respect of the particular transaction or arrangement, or if such consent or approval is required by the company's constitution, then it must be sought and obtained.[104]

The 2006 Act, Part 10, Chapter 4 deals with transactions with directors which require the **10.58** approval of members.[105] Where the transaction or arrangement under consideration falls within the provisions of Chapter 4, and either approval is given under that chapter or it is provided that approval is not needed, it is not necessary also to comply with s 175.[106] Otherwise, the application of the general duty to avoid conflicts of interest is not affected by the fact that the case also falls within Chapter 4.[107] This is an exception to the first general proposition discussed in paragraph 10.50 above. Conversely, however, the mere fact that the director complies with his general duty under s 175 does not remove the need for approval

---

[99] 2006 Act, s 263(2)(c).

[100] 2006 Act, s 180(5). See the discussion of s 180(5) at first instance in *Bilta (UK) Ltd v Nazir (No 2)* [2014] Ch 52, where Sir Andrew Morritt C accepted the submission that it demonstrated that there is no limitation of the duty imposed by s 172(3) in the case of 'one man' companies.

[101] Explanatory Notes to 2006 Act, para 320.

[102] 2006 Act, s 175(3).

[103] 2006 Act s 175(4)(b), (5), and (6).

[104] 2006 Act, s 180(1).

[105] The provisions of 2006 Act, Part 10, Chapter 4 are fully discussed in Ch 18 below.

[106] 2006 Act, s 180(2).

[107] 2006 Act, s 180(2).

under any applicable provision of Chapter 4.[108] The same analysis applies to the requirements of the 2006 Act, Part 10, Chapter 4A in relation to directors of quoted companies.[109]

10.59 Finally, in this context, it is to be noted that the general duties are not infringed by any act or omission on the part of the directors, when done (or omitted) in accordance with provisions contained in the company's articles for dealing with conflicts of interest.[110] It is suggested that this means that a director will not be in breach of a general duty merely by reason of a conflict of interest, if he acts (or omits to act) in accordance with the company's articles dealing with conflicts of interest. It is improbable, however, that the director will by virtue of this provision avoid liability for breach of one of the general duties altogether if, for example, he fails to exercise reasonable care, skill, and diligence; acts outside his powers; or fails to promote the success of the company.

(3) The duty to declare an interest in a proposed transaction or arrangement

10.60 With an important qualification, the 2006 Act, s 180 makes similar provision in relation to those cases which concern the duty to declare an interest in a proposed transaction or arrangement with the company. The duty is set out in the 2006 Act, s 177, which is fully discussed in Chapter 17. The section states that the declaration must be made before the company enters into the transaction or arrangement,[111] and explains how it may be made.[112] Where the requirements of s 177 are complied with, the transaction or arrangement is not liable to be set aside by virtue of any common law rule or equitable principle requiring the consent or approval of the members of the company.[113] Once again, however, if any other enactment requires the consent or approval of the members in respect of the particular transaction or arrangement, or if such consent or approval is required by the company's constitution, then it must be sought and obtained.[114]

10.61 Where the approach to this duty differs from the duty to avoid conflicts of interest, however, is in the application of the 2006 Act, s 180(2), which contains no exception in relation to a case to which the 2006 Act, s 177 applies. This means that, as with the remaining general duties (with the exception of the duty not to accept benefits from third parties discussed below), the application of the duty to declare an interest is not affected by the fact that the case also falls within Chapter 4 or 4A. In other words, the requirements of the 2006 Act, s 177 will apply even if the provisions of Chapter 4 or 4A also apply and are complied with, just as compliance with s 177 will not remove the need for approval under either Chapter 4 or 4A.

(4) The duty not to accept benefits from third parties

10.62 The 2006 Act, s 176 sets out the general duty on the part of a director not to accept benefits from third parties.[115] The 2006 Act, s 180(2) provides that where the transaction or

---

[108] 2006 Act, s 180(3).

[109] 2006 Act, s 180(2) and (3) as amended (with effect from 1 October 2013) by the Enterprise and Regulatory Reform Act, s 81. The provisions of the 2006 Act, Part 10, Chapter 4A are discussed in Chapter 18, Section F below.

[110] 2006 Act, s 180(4)(b).

[111] 2006 Act, s 177(3).

[112] 2006 Act, s 177(2). See generally the discussion in Ch 17, Section B(2) below.

[113] 2006 Act, s 180(1)(a).

[114] 2006 Act, s 180(1).

[115] 2006 Act, s 176 is discussed in Ch 16 below.

arrangement under consideration falls within the provisions of either Chapter 4 or 4A, and either approval is given under the applicable chapter or it is provided that approval is not needed, it is not necessary also to comply with s 176.[116] This is the second exception to the general rule discussed in paragraph 10.51 above. Otherwise, however, the application of the general duty not to accept benefits from third parties is unaffected by the fact that the case also falls within either Chapter 4 or 4A.[117] Furthermore, the mere fact that the director complies with his general duty under s 176 does not remove the need for approval under any applicable provision of Chapter 4 or 4A.[118]

E. Modifications for Charitable Companies

The 2006 Act, s 181(1), (2), and (3) (which do not extend to Scotland[119]) provide that, in their application to a company that is a charity, the provisions of s 175 (the duty to avoid conflicts of interest) and s 180(2)(b) are modified in certain respects.[120] In all other respects, the provisions of Chapter 10 of the 2006 Act apply to companies that are charities in the same way as they apply to companies that are not.   **10.63**

The effect of the 2006 Act, s 181(2) is that s 175(3) and (5) (which impose the general duty to avoid conflicts of interest) are modified in so far as they relate to a company that is a charity. In the first place, the duty does not apply to a conflict of interest arising in relation to a transaction or arrangement with the company if or to the extent that the company's articles allow that duty to be so disapplied, which they may do only in relation to descriptions of transaction or arrangement specified in the company's articles.[121] Secondly, while the duty will not be infringed if the matter has been authorized by the directors,[122] such authorization may only be given by the directors where the company's constitution includes provision enabling them to authorize the matter, and the matter is proposed to, and authorized by, them in accordance with the company's constitution.   **10.64**

Section 181(3) provides as follows: **10.65**

> Section 180(2)(b) (which disapplies certain duties under this Chapter in relation to cases excepted from requirement to obtain approval by members under Chapter 4) applies only if or to the extent that the company's articles allow those duties to be so disapplied, which they may do only in relation to descriptions of transaction or arrangement specified in the company's articles.

The Charities Act 2011, s 105(1)[123] confers powers on the Charities Commission to sanction any action proposed or contemplated in the administration of a charity if it is expedient in   **10.66**

---

[116] 2006 Act, s 180(2), as amended (with effect from 1 October 2013) by the Enterprise and Regulatory Reform Act, s 81.

[117] 2006 Act, s 180(2), as amended (with effect from 1 October 2013) by the Enterprise and Regulatory Reform Act, s 81.

[118] 2006 Act, s 180(3), as amended (with effect from 1 October 2013) by the Enterprise and Regulatory Reform Act, s 81.

[119] 2006 Act, s 181(5).

[120] 2006 Act, s 181(4), which inserted a new s 26(5A) in the Charities Act 1993 was repealed by the Charities Act 2011, s 354, Schedule 10 with effect from 14 March 2012.

[121] 2006 Act, s 181(2)(a).

[122] 2006 Act, s 175(4)(b).

[123] In force 14 March 2012.

the interests of the charity, whether or not it would otherwise be within the powers exercisable by the charity trustees in the administration of the charity. The Charities Act 2011, s 105(9) provides that an order under that section may authorize an act notwithstanding that it involves the breach of a duty imposed on a director of the company under Chapter 2 of Part 10 of the Companies Act 2006 (general duties of directors).[124]

---

[124] The Charities Act 2011 repeals the Charities Act 1993 in its entirety (including s 26, the predecessor of s 105) and also the Companies Act 2006, s 181(4) (which is replaced by s 105(9)).

11

DUTY TO ACT WITHIN POWERS

Marcus Haywood

A. Introduction

Section 171 of the Companies Act provides that:[1] **11.01**

> A director of a company must—
> (a) act in accordance with the company's constitution, and
> (b) only exercise powers for the purposes for which they are conferred.

Paragraph (a) of the duty states a director's overriding duty of obedience to the constitu- **11.02**
tion.[2] A director will act other than in accordance with the company's constitution and will
breach this duty if he causes the company to do something beyond its powers or if he fails to
comply with the company's internal regulations. Paragraph (b) requires a director to observe
the spirit as well as the letter of the constitution by which his powers of management are
conferred. Whether there is a breach of paragraph (a) is to be determined objectively, whereas
paragraph (b) concerns the subjective intentions of the director.

The duty stated in s 171 applies to shadow directors to the extent that the common law rules **11.03**
or equitable principles corresponding to the duty to act within powers applied to shadow
directors (see Chapter 10, Section C above).[3]

---

[1] In force 1 October 2007.

[2] CLR: *Final Report*, explanatory note 10 at p 350. Also see the Law Commission: *Company
Directors: Regulating Conflicts of Interest and Formulating a Statement of Duties* (Consultation Paper, No 153;
Scottish Law Commission Discussion Paper No 105) at paras 11.6–11.10, 11.18.

[3] 2006 Act, s 170(5).

11.04   A director who, in relation to a particular transaction, wishes to be protected from the risk of being in breach of the duty to act within powers may obtain the prior consent, approval, or authorization of the members, as recognized by s 180(4)(a) (see Chapter 10, Section D above) or the subsequent ratification of his conduct under s 239 (Chapter 20, Section D below).

B. Duty to Act in Accordance with the Company's Constitution

11.05   The 2006 Act, s 171(a) codifies the director's duty to comply with the company's constitution. To the extent that the directors exceed their constitutional power in breach of s 171(a) they will be liable accordingly.

(1) Meaning of the company's constitution

11.06   The constitution is defined for the purpose of the general duties by the 2006 Act, ss 17 and 257 and therefore includes:[4]

(1)   the company's articles (s 17(a));

(2)   any resolutions and agreements affecting a company's constitution (s 29), that is to say:
  (a)   any special resolution;
  (b)   any resolution or agreement agreed to by all the members of a company that, if not so agreed to, would not have been effective for its purpose unless passed as a special resolution;
  (c)   any resolution or agreement agreed to by all the members of a class of shareholders that, if not so agreed to, would not have been effective for its purpose unless passed by some particular majority or otherwise in some particular manner;
  (d)   any resolution or agreement that effectively binds all members of a class of shareholders though not agreed to by all those members; and
  (e)   any other resolution or agreement to which Chapter 3 applies by virtue of any enactment;[5]

(3)   in addition to (1) and (2): '(a) any resolution or other decision come to in accordance with the constitution, and (b) any decision by the members of the company, or a class of members, that is treated by virtue of any enactment or rule of law as equivalent to a decision by the company' (s 257).

11.07   It is important to note that the definitions of the term 'company's constitution' set out in ss 17 and 257 are non-exhaustive. In addition to the matters set out in those sections, the Companies Act clearly contemplates that the contents of certain other documents may be of constitutional relevance for certain purposes. What those other documents may encompass is presently unclear. Their ambit is, however, unlikely to be extensive. One example of an additional document that might be of constitutional relevance for certain purposes would be the company's certificate of incorporation, provision for which is made in the 2006 Act, s 15.

---

[4]   2006 Act, s 257 came into force on 1 October 2007, as did s 17 for certain purposes. Section 17 came into force fully on 1 October 2009. 2006 Act Commencement Order No 3, para 2(3)(a) made transitional provisions relating to the application of s 17 in connection with 2006 Act, ss 170–81.

[5]   2006 Act, s 29(2) provides that references to a member of a company, or a class of members of a company, do not include the company itself where it is such a member by virtue only of its holding shares as treasury shares.

This summarizes key information as to whether the company has been registered as a limited company or a public company and where the company is limited, whether it is limited by shares or by guarantee.

The company's articles

The provisions of the 1985 Act Table A and the Model Articles (pcls) and (plc) are drafted **11.08** such that the restrictions placed on the powers of directors to act are relatively limited. Of most relevance to this duty are those provisions concerning the procedure for declaring and paying dividends[6] and those concerning the participation of a director in the decision-making process for quorum, voting, or agreement purposes in circumstances where that director has a conflict of interest.[7]

Companies may, however, through their articles go further than the statutory duties by plac- **11.09** ing more onerous requirements on their directors (eg by requiring shareholder authorization of the remuneration of the directors). The articles may not, however, dilute the duties except to the extent that this is permitted by the following sections:[8]

(1) Section 173 provides that a director will not be in breach of the duty to exercise independent judgment if he has acted in a way that is authorized by the constitution.
(2) Section 175 permits authorization of some conflicts of interest by independent directors, subject to the constitution.
(3) Section 180(4)(a) preserves any rule of law enabling the company to give authority for anything that would otherwise be a breach of duty and complements s 239.[9]
(4) Section 180(4)(b) provides that a director will not be in breach of duty if he acts in accordance with any provisions in the company's articles for dealing with conflicts of interest.
(5) Section 232 places restrictions on the provisions that may be included in the company's articles. But nothing in that section prevents companies from including in their articles any such provisions as are currently lawful for dealing with conflicts of interest.

Subject to the constraints imposed by the statutory regime, a provision conferring power on **11.10** the directors should be given as broad an operation as is reasonably available on the language and without imposing procedural constraints on the board, absent some contextual indication or purpose requiring the language to be so construed.[10]

Resolutions and agreements

Where a company passes a resolution or enters into an agreement affecting a company's **11.11** constitution of the type listed in the 2006 Act, s 29, it must forward a copy of the resolution or agreement to the Registrar of Companies for registration within 15 days of the date on which the resolution was passed. If a company fails to do this, the company, and every

---

[6] Table A, regs 102–8; Model Articles (pcls) 30–6; Model Articles (plc) 70–7.
[7] Table A, reg 85; Model Article (pcls) 14; Model Article (plc) 16. See also Ch 15 below.
[8] 2006 Act, s 232.
[9] As to which see Ch 20 below. Note also that s 239(7) preserves the rule of uncertain ambit as to matters incapable of ratification because of prejudice to creditors where the company is insolvent or in the zone of insolvency. The relevant principles in this regard are discussed in full in Ch 12, Section E below.
[10] *Dome Resources NL v Silver* [2008] NSWCA 322, (2008) 68 ACSR 458 at para 12.

officer of it who is in default, commits an offence. Where a resolution or agreement which affects a company's constitution is not in writing, the company is required to provide the Registrar with a written memorandum setting out the terms of the resolution or agreement in question.[11]

11.12　In this context, the directors should also have regard to those provisions (if any) of the company's articles which concern the shareholders' reserve power to control the actions of the directors by means of a special resolution. Model Article (pcls) 4 and Model Article (plc) 4 both provide that the shareholders may, by special resolution, direct the directors to take, or refrain from taking, specified action.[12] Such a direction might be in general terms, for example relating to transactions of a particular class, or it might relate to a specific transaction, either requiring it to be carried out or prohibiting it.

Informal unanimous consent

11.13　The 2006 Act, s 257 broadens the definition of the company's constitution for the purposes of the general duties still further, by making it plain that informal unanimous decisions by the members are included.[13] The principle established in *Re Duomatic Ltd* provides that if all of the shareholders entitled to vote on a matter have informally assented to it then the formalities required by the Companies Act or by the company's articles can be dispensed with. The principle has been extended further in recent case law.[14]

11.14　In *Euro Brokers Holdings Ltd v Monecor (London) Ltd*[15] the Court of Appeal considered whether the principle could be extended to a situation in which the procedural requirements existed outside the articles, specifically in a separate shareholders' agreement. The shareholders' agreement in question detailed how further financing of a joint venture should take place, setting out stated procedural requirements for the company to follow if it wished to make a capital call on the shareholders. The company did not follow these procedures, but sent out an email request instead. Both shareholders nevertheless agreed to this request, albeit that at a later stage one of the parties failed to pay the entire amount it had promised. That party argued that the capital call was invalid because it had not followed the procedure set out in the shareholders' agreement. It argued that the *Duomatic* principle was irrelevant because that principle only applied to internal corporate governance and to the issue of whether acts could be described as those of the company or not. The Court of Appeal disagreed, allowing the application of the *Duomatic* principle to an act done with the consent of the shareholders and yet not in procedural compliance with a shareholders' agreement. The Court of Appeal rejected the appellant's attempts to confine *Duomatic* to 'internal governance' and to procedures placed in the articles of association. There was no difference between the contractual nature of the articles of association and a separate shareholders' agreement. It was the unanimous consent of the shareholders which was the key to the application of the principle and not the basis of the formal procedural requirement which it waived.[16]

---

[11]　2006 Act, s 30, which came into force on 1 October 2007.
[12]　See also the provisions of Table A, reg 70.
[13]　*Re Duomatic Ltd* [1969] 2 Ch 365.
[14]　See Ch 25, Section B(4) below. Also see Ch 4, Section B(2) above.
[15]　[2003] 1 BCLC 506, CA.
[16]　Cf *Russell v Northern Bank Development Corp Ltd* [1992] 1 WLR 588, HL (NI).

The *Duomatic* principle does not, however, permit shareholders to do informally what they **11.15** could not have done formally by way of written resolution or at a meeting.[17] Accordingly the principle cannot apply to relieve the directors of liability in respect of transactions which are ultra vires (and, possibly, where there has been the exercise of powers for an improper purpose).[18] In each case the shareholders in general meeting could not lawfully do that which they have approved the directors in doing.

(2) Ultra vires

Where a director causes the company to act beyond its powers he will be in breach of the **11.16** duty contained in s 171(a). This aspect of the duty set out in s 171(a) is not, however, one that has featured greatly in recent case law. In *Rolled Steel Products (Holdings) Ltd v British Steel Corporation*[19] Slade LJ said that ultra vires was used by company lawyers in two senses: (i) primarily to describe acts which are beyond the capacity of a company, and (ii) also to describe acts which are not beyond the capacity of the company, but simply beyond the authority of either the board of directors or a majority of shareholders. Acts within the second sense are considered in paragraphs 11.29–11.32 below.

An act may be beyond a company's capacity because it is outside the company's objects as set **11.17** out in its constitution or because the act is something that the company cannot lawfully do.

Beyond the company's objects

Where directors cause the company to do something beyond its objects, they will be person- **11.18** ally liable for any loss caused to the company. There are many old cases that illustrate this.[20] Furthermore, the shareholders were unable to ratify the directors' conduct.[21]

The risk that directors might cause the company to do something beyond its objects was **11.19** greatly reduced by most commercial companies adopting extremely wide objects in the memoranda of association, each of which was described as a separate object. If the particu- lar act was of a category which, on a true construction of the company's memorandum, was capable of being performed as reasonably incidental to the attainment or pursuit of its objects, it would not be rendered ultra vires the company merely because in a particular instance the directors, in performing the act in the company's name, were in fact acting for a purpose other than that set out in the memorandum.[22] Therefore the subjective intentions

---

[17] *Re New Cedos Engineering Co Ltd* [1994] 1 BCLC 797, 814g–h; *Atlas Wright (Europe) Ltd v Wright* [1999] BCC 163, 174G–H; *Madoff Securities International Ltd v Raven* [2013] EWHC 3147 (Comm) at para 269 per Popplewell J.

[18] *Madoff Securities International Ltd v Raven* [2013] EWHC 3147 (Comm) at para 269 per Popplewell J. However, as noted in fn 87 to para 10.51 above: the view expressed by Popplewell J in *Madoff* makes no refer- ence to, and takes no account of, the *obiter* remarks to the contrary made by Slade LJ in *Rolled Steel Ltd v British Steel Corp* [1986] Ch 246, at 296G–297A. While Browne-Wilkinson LJ expressed no view on the question either way, and Lawton LJ made no express reference to it, the view expressed by Popplewell J remains in doubt.

[19] [1986] Ch 246, 286, 287, CA. Browne-Wilkinson LJ took the same approach at 302, 303.

[20] *Joint Stock Discount Co v Brown* (1869) LR 8 Eq 376; *Hardy v Metropolitan Land Co* (1872) 7 Ch App 427; *Great Eastern Railway Co v Turner* (1872) 8 Ch App 149; *Russell v Wakefield Waterworks Co* (1875) LR 20 Eq 474, 479; *Cullerne v London and Suburban Building Society* (1890) 25 QBD 485; *Re Lands Allotment Co* [1894] 1 Ch 616; *Re George Newman & Co* [1895] 1 Ch 674, CA; *Re Claridge's Patent Asphalt Co Ltd* [1921] 1 Ch 543, CA.

[21] *Eastern Counties Railway v Hawkes* (1855) 5 HLC 331, 346, 348; *The Ashbury Railway Carriage and Iron Co v Riche* (1875) LR 7 HL 653, 672, 673, 679, 689, 694; *A-G v Great Eastern Railway Co* (1880) 5 AC 473, 478, 481, 486.

[22] *Rolled Steel Products (Holdings) Ltd v British Steel Corporation* [1986] Ch 246, 295, CA, per Slade LJ.

of the directors responsible for the act was irrelevant to the question of whether the act was beyond the powers of the company, but those intentions would be highly relevant to the question of breach of paragraph (b) of s 171.

11.20 Now the role of the memorandum of association is significantly reduced under the 2006 Act. Under the 2006 Act the purpose of the memorandum of association is to provide evidence of the intention of the subscribers to the memorandum to form a company and become members of that company on formation.[23] Information regarding the company's objects, as well as internal allocation of powers between the directors and members, will now be found in the company's articles of association. Provisions in the memoranda of companies formed under the 1985 Act and its predecessors will be treated as provisions in the articles if they are of a type that will not now be in the memoranda of companies formed under the Companies Act.[24]

11.21 The 2006 Act, s 31 also provides for a new approach to the question of a company's objects. Under the 1985 Act all companies were required to have objects which were to be specified in the memorandum. With effect from 4 February 1991 the 1985 Act was amended to make specific provision for a company's memorandum to state that its object is to carry on business as a general commercial company, so that it had power to carry on any trade or business and to do anything incidental or conducive to the carrying on of any trade or business by it.[25] Based on a recommendation of the Company Law Review Steering Group (CLR)[26] under the 2006 Act a different approach is taken. Instead of companies being required to specify their objects, companies will have unrestricted objects unless the objects are specifically restricted by the articles. This will mean that unless a company makes a deliberate choice to restrict its objects, which will be the case with charitable companies, the objects will have no bearing on what it can do.

11.22 Even where the company's constitution does restrict its objects, it is unlikely to constitute a breach of duty for the directors to authorize expenditure of the company's money on investigating proposals to amend the constitution to remove the relevant restriction. In *Peskin v Anderson*[27] a claim for damages for breach of duty was brought by former full members of the Royal Automobile Club against the committee of the club (who were also directors of the holding company) and against its holding company in relation to the sale by the holding company of its motoring services business. Clause 4 of the memorandum of association of the holding company contained a prohibition on distributions to members. Clause 4 of the memorandum of the motoring services business contained a similar prohibition with a further provision which prohibited any addition, alteration, or amendment to clause 4 of the memorandum. The Court of Appeal held that the directors were not acting ultra vires by authorizing the expenditure of the company's money on investigating proposals to sell the motor services business or on proposals to demutualize the company. On its true construction, the prohibition in clause 4 did not extend to attempts to alter the company's constitution by means of a scheme of arrangement so as to permit what was previously prohibited. In substance, the expenditure complained of was no different to expenditure on changing

---

[23] 2006 Act, s 8.
[24] 2006 Act, s 28.
[25] 1985 Act, s 3A; inserted by the 1989 Act, s 110(1).
[26] *Final Report*, para 9.10.
[27] [2001] 1 BCLC 372, CA.

the objects in the memorandum so as to allow the company to carry on a different business, which was impliedly prohibited until the objects were changed.

Unlawful acts

A transaction which is ultra vires in the sense that the company cannot lawfully do it will also **11.23** involve a breach by the directors of their duties to the company. Examples of such unlawful acts, for which directors responsible have been made personally liable for breach of duty, are payment of dividends out of capital,[28] paying interest on share capital when there were no profits,[29] and causing the company to give unlawful financial assistance in the acquisition of its own shares.[30]

Another example is *MacPherson v European Strategic Bureau Ltd*[31] where the Court of Appeal **11.24** held that it was a breach of the duties owed by the directors to the company or alternatively an act which was ultra vires the company for them to enter into an arrangement which sought to achieve a distribution of assets to shareholders, as if on a winding up, without making proper provision for creditors, since to do so amounted to an attempt to circumvent the protection which the 1985 Act, s 263 (now 2006 Act, s 830) aimed to provide. Such an arrangement failed the test of validity of a distribution of assets because it could not be described as being either for the benefit of the company or reasonably incidental to the carrying on of the company's business. Since the distribution of assets as if on a winding up but without making proper provision for creditors was not permitted by the 1985 Act, s 263 it was also an act outside the directors' powers.

Whether an act is unlawful and ultra vires the company is a matter of substance, not form, **11.25** and does not depend on the label attached by the parties to the transaction.[32] Thus payments described as being in respect of interest, which were out of proportion to the amount of principal, may be characterized as unlawful and gratuitous dispositions of company property.[33] Payment of remuneration to a director who performs no services for the company may be characterized as an unlawful gift of company money.[34] A sale of company property to a company connected with the director and beneficial owner of the company at what was known to be an undervalue may be characterized as an unlawful distribution and so incapable of being authorized or ratified by the shareholders.[35]

---

[28] *Flitcroft's Case* (1882) 21 Ch D 519; *Re Kingston Cotton Mill Co (No 2)* [1896] 1 Ch 331; *Dovey v Corey* [1901] AC 477, HL; *Ammonia Soda Co v Chamberlain* [1918] 1 Ch 266, 292, CA; *Precision Dippings Ltd v Precision Dippings Marketing Ltd* [1986] Ch 447; *Bairstow v Queens Moat Houses plc* [2000] 1 BCLC 549, 559, 560; [2001] 2 BCLC 531, CA; *Re Loquitur Ltd* [2003] 2 BCLC 442. Had Mr Holland been a de facto director, he would have been personally liable for breach of duty in causing the companies to pay unlawful dividends: *Revenue and Customs Commissioners v Holland, Re Paycheck Service 3 Ltd* [2010] 1 WLR 2793, SC.

[29] *Re Sharpe* [1892] 1 Ch 154, CA (where the articles permitted payment of interest on share capital).

[30] *Re VGM Holdings Ltd* [1942] Ch 235, CA; *Steen v Law* [1964] AC 287, PC; *Selangor United Rubber Estates Ltd v Cradock (No 3)* [1968] 1 WLR 1555, 1652–9; *Wallersteiner v Moir* [1974] 1 WLR 991, CA.

[31] [2000] 2 BCLC 683, CA.

[32] *Progress Property Co Ltd v Moore* [2011] 1 WLR 1, SC at paras 24–33, per Lord Walker; at para 42, per Lord Mance (a case concerning an allegedly unlawful distribution, which was in fact a genuine commercial sale).

[33] *Ridge Securities Ltd v Inland Revenue Commissioners* [1964] 1 WLR 479.

[34] *Re Halt Garage (1964) Ltd* [1982] 3 All ER 1016.

[35] *Aveling Barford Ltd v Perion Ltd* [1989] BCLC 626. This case is discussed by Lord Walker in *Progress Property Co Ltd v Moore* [2011] 1 WLR 1, SC at paras 20–3 and by Lord Mance at para 42. Note 2006 Act, s 845, which deals with distributions in kind.

11.26 There is a question as to whether the liability of a director responsible for an unlawful act is strict or whether it depends on knowledge and intention. In *Bairstow v Queens Moat Houses plc* the director was strictly liable to restore the unlawful dividends that he had deliberately made.[36] In the *Paycheck* case Lord Hope said that he considered the better view to be that where a director had caused the payment of an unlawful dividend his liability was strict, subject to a claim for relief under section 1157 of the Companies Act (but he found it unnecessary to decide the point).[37]

11.27 However, in *Progress Property Co Ltd v Moore*[38] Lord Walker approved the following statement of principle which suggests that a director will not always be strictly liable to restore company money where he has been responsible for an unlawful transaction:[39]

> It is plain, in my view, that directors are liable only if it is established that in effecting the unlawful distribution they were in breach of their fiduciary duties (or possibly of contractual obligations, though that does not arise in the present case). Whether or not they were so in breach will involve consideration not only of whether or not the directors knew at the time that what they were doing was unlawful but also of their state of knowledge at that time of the material facts. In reviewing the then authorities Vaughan Williams J in *Re Kingston Cotton Mill Co (No 2)* said at [1896] 1 Ch, 347: 'In no one of [the cases cited] can I find that directors were held liable unless the payments were made with actual knowledge that the funds of the company were being misappropriated or with knowledge of the facts that established the misappropriation.' Although this case went to the Court of Appeal, this aspect of the decision was not quarreled with (see [1896] 2 Ch 279).

11.28 This leaves uncertain the circumstances in which the knowledge and intention of a director will be relevant to his liability in circumstances where he has been responsible for an unlawful transaction. In *Madoff Securities International Ltd v Raven* Popplewell J referred to the relevant passages in *Paycheck* and *Progress Property* and, without deciding the point, said:[40]

> I incline to the view that such liability is fault based: a director's liability in relation to misapplication of a company's property by exercising a power otherwise than that for which it was conferred cannot arise unless he knows that it is an improper purpose or of the facts which make the purpose improper.

(3) Breach of the company's constitution

Acts beyond the authority of the board

11.29 As a result of the 'indoor management rule' established by *Royal British Bank v Turquand*[41] and the enactment of the statutory predecessors to the 2006 Act, ss 39 and 40,[42] breach of a director's duty to comply with the company's constitution seldom affects third parties who

---

[36] [2001] 2 BCLC 531 at paras 53 and 54, per Walker LJ.

[37] *Revenue and Customs Commissioners v Holland, Re Paycheck Services 3 Ltd* [2010] 1 WLR 2793, SC at para 47, per Lord Hope; see also [2008] 2 BCLC 613 at para 218, per Mark Cawson QC; [2010] 2 BCLC 309, CA, at para 98, per Rimer LJ, paras 121–36; at para 125, per Elias LJ; [2010] 1 WLR 2793, SC at paras 45–50, per Lord Hope; at paras 119 and 124, per Lord Walker; at para 146, per Lord Clarke.

[38] [2011] 1 WLR 1, SC at para 32.

[39] *Clydebank Football Club Ltd v Steedman* [2002] SLT 109 at para 79, per Lord Hamilton.

[40] [2013] EWHC 3147 (Comm) at para 200.

[41] (1856) 6 El & Bl 327.

[42] 1985 Act, ss 35(1) and 35A, which were replaced by 2006 Act, ss 39 and 40 on 1 October 2009. The provisions of 1985 Act, s 35A did not protect dealings with directors and their associates, to which 1985 Act, s 322A applied. For further discussion, see Ch 4, Section C above.

deal with it. The 2006 Act, s 40 provides that, in favour of a person dealing with a company in good faith, the power of the directors to bind the company, or authorize others to do so, is deemed to be free of any limitation under the company's constitution.[43] In addition, s 39 provides that the validity of an act done by the company shall not be called into question on the ground of lack of capacity by reason of anything in the company's constitution.[44] Taken together the two provisions mean that a third party dealing with a company in good faith need not concern itself about whether the company is acting within its constitution and will be able to enforce an obligation incurred by the company even where a director causes the company to act in contravention of its constitution. The sections only operate to protect third parties dealing with the company or its directors. They do not alter any liability of a director to the company where he acts in excess of his constitutional powers in breach of s 171(a).

Accordingly, where a director purports to enter into an agreement on behalf of the company knowing that he has no authority to do so, because the authority he has been given was granted at a board meeting which was not quorate, it is likely he would be in breach of the duty contained in s 171(a).[45] Furthermore, where a director prevents his company from functioning properly by refusing to attend board meetings in order to render them inquorate, arguably that would also amount to a breach of section 171(a).[46] **11.30**

Re Oxford Benefit Building and Investment Society[47] is an example of a case where directors were liable for failing to act in accordance with the provisions in the articles to the effect that no dividends should be payable except out of realized profits and that no remuneration should be paid to the directors until a dividend of 7 per cent had been paid to the shareholders. The business of the company consisted chiefly in lending money to builders on mortgages payable by instalments, and the directors treated, as part of the profits available for dividends, the value (upon an estimate made by their surveyor who was also their secretary) of the instalments of principal and interest remaining unpaid by each mortgagor. Upon this footing the directors caused the company to pay out dividends and remuneration to themselves. The court held that the directors, having treated estimated profits as realized profits, had acted outside their constitutional powers and were jointly and severally liable to repay the dividends and remuneration. **11.31**

Similarly, directors may be liable where they have authorized payments to themselves or another other person in circumstances where they have no power to do so. For example, in *Guinness plc v Saunders*[48] a committee of the board of Guinness had authorized payment of remuneration to Mr Ward, who was a director. However, the articles of association of the company did not give authority to a committee of the board (as opposed to the full board) to **11.32**

---

[43] 2006 Act, s 40 is subject to the constitutional limitations concerning transactions involving directors or their associates to which s 41 applies (replacing 1985 Act, s 322A).

[44] This section has effect subject to 2006 Act, s 42 which relates to companies that are charities.

[45] *Stimpson v Southern Private Landlords Association* [2010] BCC 387 at para 33.

[46] *Stimpson v Southern Private Landlords Association* (n 45 above) at para 44. The case concerned an application for permission to continue a derivative claim. Accordingly, it was not necessary for the court to reach a firm conclusion on the point.

[47] (1886) 35 Ch D 502. For an example of a disqualification order being made in circumstances where the directors had acted in contravention of the articles of association of the company (and where they had used their powers for improper purposes), see *Re AG (Manchester) Plc, Official Receiver v Watson* [2008] 1 BCLC 321.

[48] [1990] 2 AC 663, HL.

authorize such a payment. The House of Lords dismissed an appeal by Mr Ward for recovery of the payment on the basis that it was made in breach of his fiduciary duty as a director. Lord Templeman said as follows:[49]

> Equity forbids a trustee to make a profit out of his trust. The articles of association of Guinness relax the strict rule of equity to the extent of enabling a director to make a profit provided that the board of directors contracts on behalf of Guinness for the payment of special remuneration or decides to award special remuneration. Mr. Ward did not obtain a contract or a grant from the board of directors. Equity has no power to relax its own strict rule further than and inconsistently with the express relaxation contained in the articles of association. A shareholder is entitled to compliance with the articles. A director accepts office subject to and with the benefit of the provisions of the articles relating to directors. No one is obliged to accept appointment as a director. No director can be obliged to serve on a committee. A director of Guinness who contemplates or accepts service on a committee or has performed outstanding services for the company as a member of a committee may apply to the board of directors for a contract or an award of special remuneration. A director who does not read the articles or a director who misconstrues the articles is nevertheless bound by the articles. … In these circumstances there are no grounds for equity to relax its rules further than the articles of association provide. Similarly, the law will not imply a contract between Guinness and Mr. Ward for remuneration on a quantum meruit basis awarded by the court when the articles of association of Guinness stipulate that special remuneration for a director can only be awarded by the board.

C. Duty to Only Exercise Powers for the Purposes for Which They Are Conferred

11.33 The Companies Act, s 171(b) codifies the 'proper purpose rule', by which a director may only exercise his powers for the purposes for which they are conferred. The duty is closely connected with the duty under the 2006 Act, s 172 to act in good faith in the interests of the company. While, in a given case, it may be difficult to separate the considerations that go to each of them they remain separate duties.[50] Accordingly, a power may be exercised for an improper purpose notwithstanding that the directors bona fide believe it is being exercised in the company's best interests.[51]

11.34 The proper purpose rule has its origin in the equitable doctrine of 'fraud on a power'. The use of the word 'fraud' does not denote fraud in the common law sense of 'dishonest' or 'immoral'.[52] For a number of purposes, the early Court of Chancery attached the consequences of fraud to acts which were honest and unexceptionable at common law but unconscionable according to equitable principles. In particular, it set aside dispositions under

---

[49] At 692.

[50] Although there were prior indications of the existence of the duty separate from the duty to act in good faith in the interests of the company, it is arguable that the duty was only established as a distinct duty in *Hogg v Cramphorn Ltd* [1967] Ch 254. The independent existence of the duty was confirmed in *Howard Smith Ltd v Ampol Petroleum Ltd* [1974] AC 821, 834–7.

[51] *Hogg v Cramphorn Ltd* [1967] 1 Ch 254, 266G–269A; *Madoff Securities International Ltd v Raven* [2013] EWHC 3147 (Comm) at para 195 per Popplewell J; *Eclairs Group Ltd v JKX Oil & Gas plc* [2015] Bus LR 1395, SC.

[52] *Vatcher v Paull* [1915] AC 372, 378.

powers conferred by trust deeds if, although within the language conferring the power, they were outside the purpose for which it was conferred.[53]

The proper purpose rule (now codified in s 171(b)) imposes a duty upon the directors to **11.35** exercise each of the powers conferred on them only for their proper purpose. The rule is not concerned with excess of power by doing an act which is beyond the scope of the instrument creating it as a matter of construction or implication. It is concerned with abuse of power, by doing acts which are within its scope but done for an improper reason.[54] In *The Bell Group Ltd v Westpac Banking Corporation*[55] Owen J of the Supreme Court of Western Australia explained the duty as follows:

> The limited powers of directors can only be exercised for the purpose for which they are granted. Any exercise of a power for an extraneous purpose is a fraud on the power. The concept of fraud on a power was explained by Lord Parker in *Vatcher v Paull* [1915] AC 372, 378. It does not necessarily denote conduct on the part of the appointor amounting to fraud in the common law meaning of the word or any conduct that could properly be termed dishonest or immoral. It simply means that the power has been exercised for a purpose, or with an intention, beyond the scope of, or not justified by, the instrument creating the power.

A proper purpose is one which, on a true construction of the constitution of the company, **11.36** the power can be said to have been conferred.[56] It will not usually be possible to lay down in advance all of the exact limits beyond which directors must not exercise a particular power, since the variety of situations facing directors of different types of company in different situations cannot be anticipated. Instead, the court approaches the question of whether a director has exercised his powers for an improper purpose in stages. The first task of the court is to construe the power and to determine the limits within which it may be exercised. This is a question of law. Having done that, the court turns to a question of fact; namely whether, in all of the circumstances, the purported exercise goes beyond the constitutional powers of the company or is otherwise an abuse of the power so construed. Put simply, the court must identify the nature and scope of the power and the purpose for which it was exercised and then decide whether the purpose was permissible or impermissible.

The tasks that a court is required to perform were described in the leading case, *Howard* **11.37** *Smith Ltd v Ampol Petroleum Ltd*,[57] where Lord Wilberforce said as follows:

> In their Lordships' opinion it is necessary to start with a consideration of the power whose exercise is in question, in this case a power to issue shares. Having ascertained, on a fair view, the nature of this power, and having defined as can best be done in the light of modern conditions the, or some, limits within which it may be exercised, it is then necessary for the court, if a particular exercise of it is challenged, to examine the substantial purpose for which it was exercised, and to reach a conclusion whether that purpose was proper or not. In doing so it

---

[53] See eg *Lane v Page* (1754) Amb 233; *Aleyn v Belchier* (1758) 1 Eden 132, 138; *Duke of Portland v Topham* (1864) 11 HLC 32.

[54] *Eclairs Group Ltd v JKX Oil & Gas plc* [2015] Bus LR 1395, SC at para 15, per Lord Sumption.

[55] [2008] WASC 239 at para 4458. This statement of principle was not criticized on appeal: [2012] WASCA 257.

[56] *Smith v Fawcett* [1942] Ch 304, 306, per Lord Greene MR. See also the discussion of the meaning of 'proper purpose' as used in 2006 Act, s 117(3) (which concerns the right to inspect and require a copy of a company's register of members) in *Re Burry & Knight Ltd* [2014] 1 WLR 4046, CA at paras 18–20 per Arden LJ. In that context, Arden LJ said that 'Where there were multiple purposes—some proper and some not— ... a proper purpose is not necessarily tainted by being coupled to an improper purpose'.

[57] [1974] AC 821, 835, PC.

will necessarily give credit to the bona fide opinion of the directors, if such is found to exist, and will respect their judgment as to matters of management; having done this, the ultimate conclusion has to be as to the side of a fairly broad line on which the case falls.[58]

Accordingly, in that case the court set aside an allotment of additional shares made by the company's directors to a minority shareholder in order to constitute it a majority share-holder, thereby promoting the success of its takeover bid, which the directors had recommended. The court did this notwithstanding the fact that the directors had been acting in good faith in what they considered to be in the best interests of the company.

11.38   In *Extrasure Travel Insurance Ltd v Scattergood*[59] the deputy judge was able to say that the law was clear and described the court's task in this way:

> It is unnecessary for a claimant to prove that a director was dishonest, or that he knew he was pursuing a collateral purpose. In that sense, the test is an objective one. It was suggested by the parties that the court must apply a three-part test, but it may be more convenient to add a fourth stage. The court must: (i) identify the power whose exercise is in question; (ii) identify the proper purpose for which that power was delegated to the directors; (iii) identify the substantial purpose for which the power was in fact exercised; and (iv) decide whether that purpose was proper. Finally, it is worth noting that the third stage involves a question of fact. It turns on the actual motives of the directors at the time: *Re A Company (No 00370 of 1987) ex p Glossop* [1988] BCLC 570 at 577.

11.39   Many of the cases concerning a breach by directors of their duty to use their powers for proper purposes concern situations where a section of the company's membership is given a special advantage or subjected to undue disadvantage, or where the directors act principally for their own benefit.[60] Some examples are considered below.

(1) Misapplication of company funds

11.40   An example of a situation where directors act principally for their own benefit is where they misappropriate or misapply company funds. Although directors are not strictly speaking trustees of a company's assets they are considered and treated as trustees of the company's property which comes into their hands or which is under their control.[61] In this regard, it is clear they owe a fiduciary duty to the company to apply its assets only for the proper purposes of the company. As Ungoed-Thomas J said in *Selangor United Rubber Estates Ltd v Cradock (No 3)*:[62]

> property in [directors'] hands or under their control is theirs for the company, ie, for the company's purposes in accordance with their duties, powers and functions. However much

---

[58]   Compare the position that has been adopted in Canada in *Teck Corpn Ltd v Millar* (1972) 33 DLR (3d) 288 where it was held that the directors' honest belief that the action was in the company's best interests was paramount. That decision does not, however, represent the law of England.

[59]   [2003] 1 BCLC 598 at paras 92–3. See also *Madoff Securities International Ltd v Raven* [2013] EWHC 3147 (Comm) at para 196 per Popplewell J.

[60]   Nominee directors, in particular, are at risk in this regard given the temptation to use their powers to advance the interests of their nominator, not the interest of the company itself: see eg *Scottish Co-operative Wholesale Society Ltd v Meyer* [1959] AC 324.

[61]   *Russell v Wakefield Waterworks Co* (1875) LR 20 Eq 474, 479; *Re Forest of Dean Coal Mining Co* (1879) 10 Ch D 450, 453; *Re Faure Electric Accumulator Co* (1888) 40 Ch D 141; *Flitcroft's Case* (1882) 21 Ch D 519, CA; *Re Sharpe, Re Bennett, Masonic and General Life Assurance Co v Sharpe* [1892] 1 Ch 154; *Belmont Finance Corpn Ltd v Williams Furniture Ltd (No 2)* [1980] 1 All ER 393, 404, CA, per Buckley LJ; *International Sales and Agencies Ltd v Marcus* [1982] 3 All ER 551; *Simtel Communications v Rebak* [2006] 2 BCLC 571 at para 15.

[62]   [1968] 1 WLR 1555, 1575.

the company's purposes and the directors' duties, powers and functions may differ from the purposes of a strict settlement and the duties, powers and functions of its trustees, the directors and such trustees have this indisputably in common—that the property in their hands or under their control must be applied for the *specified purposes of the company or the settlement*; and to apply it otherwise is to misapply it in breach of the obligation to apply it to those purposes for the company or the settlement beneficiaries. So, even though the scope and operation of such obligation differs in the case of directors and strict settlement trustees, the nature of the obligation with regard to property in their hands or under their control is identical, namely, to apply it to specified purposes for others beneficially.

More recently in *The Bell Group Ltd v Westpac Banking Corporation*[63] Owen J of the Supreme **11.41** Court of Western Australia explained the role of a director in relation to the assets of the company as follows:[64]

> There are various organs that influence the decision-making processes of a corporation and which are involved in corporate governance. But primary governance responsibility lies with the board of directors. In formal terms the directors are appointed by, and are accountable to, the body of shareholders. As a general rule it is the directors who are 'the directing mind and will of the corporation, the very ego and centre of the personality of the corporation': *Lennard's Carrying Co Ltd v Asiatic Petroleum Co Ltd* [1915] AC 705, at 713. The power to manage the business of the company has been delegated to the directors. The delegation arises as part of, or by virtue of, the contract between the shareholders and the company represented by the Articles of association.
>
> With the power to manage a business comes (necessarily) an element of control over the assets that are employed in the operation. When a corporation that conducts a business acquires assets, those assets belong to it. They do not belong to those (such as directors) who manage the corporation. Yet the individuals who manage the corporation have effective control over those assets and can affect the interests of the corporation by the way in which they use the assets. The individuals who manage the corporation are, in a real sense, stewards of those assets on behalf of the corporation and, in an indirect sense, other persons or entities (such as shareholders) who have a legitimate interest in the affairs of the corporation.
>
> In my view the notion of stewardship is a key factor in understanding the role of directors. This is borne out by what was said in the Cadbury Report, produced by a specialist corporate committee in the United Kingdom during the early 1990s. It emphasised the trinity of 'openness, integrity and accountability' as prerequisites for sound financial reporting. In my view, those principles are not confined to financial reporting. They apply to corporate governance generally and, consequently, to the role of directors.

Accordingly, a director will breach this duty where he gives away company assets, in the form **11.42** of shares held by the company as trustee of a number of pension funds, for no consideration to a private family company of which he was a director.[65] Similarly it has been held that it is a misapplication for directors knowingly to pay or to recommend the unlawful payment of dividends,[66] or to make payments to selected individuals (including the directors themselves) when the company is insolvent.[67]

---

[63] [2008] WASC 239.
[64] At paras 4365–7. This statement of principle was not criticized on appeal: [2012] WASCA 257.
[65] *Bishopsgate Investment Management Ltd v Maxwell (No 2)* [1994] 1 All ER 261, CA.
[66] *Re Exchange Banking Co, Flitcroft's Case* (1882) 21 Ch D 536.
[67] *Re HLC Environmental Projects Ltd* [2014] BCC 337.

(2) Issue of shares

11.43 An issue or allotment of shares by the directors under exclusive powers conferred in the articles, to themselves or their nominees, not for the purposes of raising further capital but to obtain or retain voting control at general meetings, may constitute a breach of duty.[68] Accordingly, in *Howard Smith Ltd v Ampol Petroleum Ltd*[69] the Privy Council held that while in some circumstances it might be proper to issue shares for purposes other than to raise capital for the company 'it must be unconstitutional for directors to use their fiduciary powers over the shares in the company purely for the purpose of destroying an existing majority or creating a new majority which did not previously exist'.[70] Similarly, in *Percy v S Mills & Co*[71] Peterson J said that 'directors are not entitled to use their powers of issuing shares merely for the purpose of maintaining their control or the control of themselves and their friends over the affairs of the company, or merely for the purpose of defeating the wishes of the existing majority of shareholders'. At the other extreme, where directors unquestioningly follow the instructions of a majority of members without realistically exercising their discretion, which might have been exercised for the benefit of the company as a whole, they are in breach of this duty.[72]

11.44 The *Howard Smith* case was distinguished in *CAS (Nominees) Ltd v Nottingham Forest Football Club plc*.[73] In that case, the claimants presented an unfair prejudice petition[74] claiming that an agreement between Nottingham Forest plc, which operated the football club, and a new investor, was unfairly prejudicial to their interests. This agreement involved an injection of cash by the new investor in return for control of the club and was arranged in a manner designed to avoid any opposition from the claimants, who held almost 25 per cent of the issued share capital and could effectively block any special resolution. The restructuring of the company which followed had the inevitable effect of reducing their stake and removing this power. The power exercised by the board of the company in order to implement the transaction was the power of general management conferred by Article 110 of the company's articles. Hart J held that given the genuine desire on the part of the directors to raise capital for the club, it could not be said that the company's powers to reconstitute the board of the club and to increase and allot share capital in the club were being exercised for a purpose foreign to their proper ambit.[75]

11.45 The provisions of the Companies Act, s 171(b) and the decision in *Howard Smith* were considered by Lord Glennie in *Re West Coast Capital (Lios) Ltd*,[76] a Scottish case. In that case, a minority shareholder sought an interim injunction, in the context of a petition under

---

[68] *Punt v Symons & Co Ltd* [1903] 2 Ch 506; *Piercy v S Mills & Co* [1920] 1 Ch 77; *Hogg v Cramphorn Ltd* [1967] Ch 254; *Re Looe Fish Ltd* [1993] BCLC 1160; *Re Zetnet Ltd* [2011] EWHC 1518 (Ch).

[69] [1974] AC 821, PC.

[70] At 837. Note also the provisions in 2006 Act, Part 17, Chapter 2 about the allotment of shares, which came into force on 1 October 2009.

[71] [1920] 1 Ch 77 at 84.

[72] *Scottish Co-operative Wholesale Society Ltd v Meyer* [1959] AC 324, 367 (at least where the majority are known not to be acting in the interests of the company and its members as a whole).

[73] [2002] 1 BCLC 613.

[74] Now 2006 Act, Part 30.

[75] 2006 Act, ss 632–3.

[76] [2008] CSOH 72. Compare also in the context of an application for an interim injunction to restrain the issue of shares the approach taken by the Court of Appeal in *Cayne v Global Natural Resources plc* [1984] 1 All ER 225.

the 2006 Act, s 996, preventing the board of the company from putting to the vote at the company's annual general meeting a resolution which, amongst other things, would increase the company' authorized share capital. It was submitted by the minority shareholder that the proposed resolution was not motivated by a genuine desire to raise money. Rather it was a device to force the minority shareholder out of the company by presenting it with a 'no win' situation: either to pay a significant sum of money to preserve its proportionate shareholding; or refuse to take up its entitlement and see its interest in the company diminished. Lord Glennie said[77] that the relevant test was 'essentially one of looking at the purpose or purposes for which the directors were exercising their powers, ie their motivation. If an improper motivation can be shown, if only by inference from an objective assessment of all the surrounding circumstances, the basis of a case of unfairly prejudicial conduct might be established.' However, on the facts Lord Glennie held that no such case had been made out.

(3) Restrictions on shares

In *Eclairs Group Ltd v JKX Oil & Gas plc*,[78] the Supreme Court has now decided (following disagreement in the courts below) that the proper purpose rule applies to a decision by directors to exercise a power in a public company's articles to impose restrictions on shares following what they believed to be failure to comply with a notice under the 2006 Act, s 793 requiring information about interests in its shares.[79] **11.46**

In outline the facts of the *Eclairs* case were as follows. The directors of JKX Oil & Gas plc suspected that it was about to become subject to a 'corporate raid' under which the persons behind two minority blocks of its shares would seek to obtain management or voting control. The directors therefore exercised their power under s 793 to send disclosure notices to elicit information about interests in, and agreements or arrangements relating to, the two minority blocks. After the responses to the first batch of disclosure notices had been received, the directors convened the AGM, at which a number of resolutions would be proposed, including two special resolutions, which were designed to help protect the company and its shareholders from the 'raid'. The directors appreciated that the special resolutions would not be passed if the two blocks of shares were raiders voted against them. The directors then caused the company to send out a second batch of disclosure notices, requesting further information about interests in and agreements and arrangements relating to the two blocks of shares. The responses asserted that there was no agreement or arrangement. At the board meeting to consider the responses, the directors decided that they had reasonable cause to believe that the information provided in the responses to the disclosure notices was materially incorrect, so that they had power under the company's articles to issue restriction notices in respect of the two blocks of shares, and that restriction notices should be issued. The minutes recorded that the directors considered that the issue of restriction notices would promote the success of the company for the benefit of the members as a whole, having regard to the factors set out in the 2006 Act, s 173. There was no mention of the duty under section 171(b). The legal owners of the blocks of shares issued proceedings, challenging the validity of the restriction notices. **11.47**

---

[77] At para 21.
[78] [2015] Bus LR 1395, SC. See Mortimore, 'The Proper Purpose Rule Under the Spotlight in the Supreme Court' (2016) 31(3) Butterworths Journal of International Banking & Financial Law, 142–5.
[79] For further discussion about s 793, see Chapter 27, Section E below.

11.48 At the trial,[80] Mann J rejected all of the grounds for challenging the restriction notices except one: he held that, even though the directors had acted bona fide in what they considered to be the best interests of the company, they had acted for an improper purpose. The restriction notices would be set aside since they had not been issued in order to encourage the relevant shareholders to provide truthful information (or as a sanction for failing to do so), but in order to thwart the suspected raiders. As Mann J put it, a majority of the directors:[81]

> did not have in mind the protection of the company pending the provision of the information; they had in mind protecting the company full stop. The restrictions were thus a useful weapon to be used against the 'raiders'. The disenfranchisement of the 'raiders' at the AGM was not just an incidental effect of the imposition of restrictions; it was the positively desired effect, seen as beneficial to the company in the long term.

11.49 Mann J went on to note that, even if the directors had put the improper purpose out of their minds and had only taken account of proper considerations, they would probably have issued the restriction notices anyway. However, since the company had neither pleaded that point, nor adduced any evidence in support of it, but had simply argued that the proper purpose rule did not apply to the decision to issue restriction notices, Mann J did not allow the company to take the point.

11.50 By a majority, the Court of Appeal allowed the company's appeal,[82] giving three overlapping reasons why the proper purpose rule had a very limited part to play in such circumstances.[83] First, the shareholder had only himself to blame: he could avoid a restriction notice by simply complying with the disclosure notice. Secondly, the issue of a restriction notice was the very thing permitted by the mandatory disclosure regime. Once a shareholder had failed to comply with a disclosure notice, the directors had an unfettered power to issue a restriction notice. Thirdly, neither the 2006 Act, Pt 22, nor the relevant provisions of the company's articles, contained any express or implied reference to the proper purpose rule. At a time of controversy in a company's affairs, the directors would naturally want to see corporate raiders disenfranchised, and the draftsmen of the Act and the articles were unlikely to have intended a detailed enquiry into the minds of directors 'in what may often be a rapidly changing scene'. The shareholders appealed.

11.51 The Supreme Court unanimously allowed the shareholders' appeal,[84] restoring the order of Mann J. Lord Sumption, giving the main judgment, dealt with the three arguments given by the majority in the Court of Appeal as follows.[85]

11.52 First, the fact that the shareholder only had to comply with the disclosure notice in order to avoid a restriction notice did not lead to the conclusion that the proper purpose rule should not apply. The limitation of the power to issue a restriction notice derives from its fiduciary character. If its exercise would otherwise be an abuse, it is no answer to say that the person against whom it is directed had only himself to blame. Moreover, other shareholders (who may be entirely unblameworthy) might be adversely affected, since they might be deprived of votes which might have been cast in their favour.

---

80 [2014] 1 BCLC 202.
81 At para 200. See also paras 189 and 227.
82 [2014] 2 BCLC 164, CA (Longmore LJ and Sir Robin Jacob, Briggs LJ dissenting).
83 At paras 136, 138, 141–3.
84 [2015] Bus LR 1395, SC.
85 At paras 37–40.

Secondly, the failure to comply with a disclosure notice was not to be treated as a 'gateway' **11.53** which then empowered the directors to take whatever action was permitted by the articles, regardless of the purpose for which they were truly acting. The issuing of a restriction notice had three permissible purposes, as Lord Sumption explained:[86]

> The first is to induce the shareholder to comply with a disclosure notice ... Secondly ... to protect the company and its shareholders against having to make decisions about their respective interests in ignorance of relevant information ... Thirdly, the restrictions have a punitive purpose. They are imposed as sanctions on account of the failure or refusal of the addressee of a disclosure notice to provide the information for as long as it persists, on the footing that a person interested in shares who has not complied with obligations attaching to that status should not be entitled to the benefits attaching to the shares ... These three purposes are all directly related to the non-provision of information requisitioned by a disclosure notice. None of them extends to influencing the outcome of resolutions at a general meeting. That may well be a consequence of a restriction notice. But it is no part of its proper purpose. It is not itself a legitimate weapon of defence against a corporate raider, which the board is at liberty to take up independently of its interest in getting the information.

Thirdly, the proper purpose rule is not a term of a contract and does not necessarily depend **11.54** on any limitation on the scope of the power as a matter of construction. It is a principle by which equity controls the exercise of a fiduciary's powers in respects which are not, or not necessarily, determined by the instrument. Moreover, the rule is fundamental to the constitutional distinction between the respective domains of the board and the shareholders. These considerations are particularly important when the company is in play between competing groups seeking to control or influence its affairs. The Court of Appeal was wrong to think that this was a factor militating against the application of the proper purpose rule. If anything, it is a strong factor in favour of the rule's application.

(4) Other examples

Other powers to which the duty has been held applicable include the forfeiture of shares,[87] **11.55** making calls on shares,[88] approving transfers of shares,[89] refusing to register a share transfer,[90] bonus agreements,[91] and causing the company to enter into an agreement which deprived the directors of the managerial powers in circumstances where those directors knew the shareholders shortly intended to appoint new directors.[92]

(5) Extent to which court will substitute its own view for that of the director

More recent cases decided before the enactment of the 2006 Act have shown a greater ten- **11.56** dency on the part of the court to intervene in corporate decision-making than was previously

---

[86] At para 32.

[87] *Re Agriculturist Cattle Insurance Co, Stanhope's Case* (1866) 1 Ch App 161; *Re London and Provincial Starch Co, Gower's Case* (1868) LR 6 Eq 77; *The European Assurance Society Arbitration, Manisty's Case* (1873) 17 SJ 745.

[88] *Galloway v Hallé Concerts Society* [1915] 2 Ch 233.

[89] *Bennett's Case* (1867) 5 De GM&G 284.

[90] *Mactra Properties Ltd v Morshead Mansions Ltd* [2009] BCC 335, where the claim failed.

[91] *Re McCarthy Sufacing Ltd* [2009] 1 BCLC 622 at paras 73–7 (where the court held that bonus agreements dividing the net profits of a major contract among the directors were not entered into for a proper purpose as they were a device deliberately designed to ensure that none of the profits would be available to the shareholders of the company).

[92] *Lee Panavision Ltd v Lee Lighting Ltd* [1992] BCLC 22, CA.

the case. In particular, the courts have done so by applying the *Wednesbury* principle familiar in public and administrative law. The application of the *Wednesbury* principle to the duties of a director is probably now better seen as an aspect of the duty to only exercise powers for the purposes for which they are conferred (although it may also be relevant to whether there has been a breach by a director of his duty to act in the best interest of the company under section 172 of the 2006 Act). The *Wednesbury* principle is derived from the decision of Lord Greene in *Associated Provincial Picture Houses Ltd v Wednesbury Corp*, a case of judicial review of the exercise of a public duty by a local licensing authority, in which Lord Greene MR summarized the principle as follows:[93]

> The court is entitled to investigate the action of the local authority with a view to seeing whether they have taken into account matters which they ought not to take into account, or, conversely, have refused to take into account or neglected to take into account matters which they ought to take into account. Once that question is answered in favour of the local authority, it may be still possible to say that, although the local authority have kept within the four corners of the matters which they ought to consider, they have nevertheless come to a conclusion so unreasonable that no reasonable authority could ever have come to it. In such a case, again, I think the court can interfere.

11.57 In *Byng v London Life Association Ltd*[94] the defendant company's AGM was convened at a location which proved of wholly inadequate capacity for the number of members who attended. The chairman adjourned the meeting until later that day at a different location with a greater capacity. The question then arose of whether the chairman exercised that discretion validly. As to that the Vice-Chancellor said:

> The chairman's decision will not be declared invalid unless on the facts which he knew or ought to have known he failed to take into account all relevant factors, took into account irrelevant factors, or reached a conclusion which no reasonable chairman, properly directing himself as to his duties, could have reached, ie the test is the same as that applicable on judicial review in accordance with the principles of *Associated Provincial Picture Houses Ltd v Wednesbury Corp*.[95]

11.58 Another example of the application of a concept familiar in public and administrative law to this aspect of a director's duty is the extent to which the exercise by a director of his discretion will be void if he has failed to take into account a material consideration and that consideration might have materially affected his decision. Thus in *Hunter v Senate Support Services Ltd*[96] the deputy judge held that although the decisions of the directors to forfeit the claimant's shares for non-payment of a call and to transfer the forfeited shares to the group holding company were not made for any improper purpose they were nevertheless flawed because the directors had proceeded on the mistaken basis that the only course available to them was forfeiture of the shares. The directors regarded forfeiture as the inevitable result of non-payment of the second call notice and had acted without giving any consideration to possible alternative courses of action or exercising a genuine discretion whether to forfeit, as they were bound to do. In particular, they could have informed the claimant that his shares

---

[93] [1948] 1 KB 223, 233 to 234, CA.

[94] [1990] Ch 170.

[95] At 189. See also *Re a Company, ex p Glossop* [1988] BCLC 570, 577; *Hunter v Senate Support Services Ltd* [2005] 1 BCLC 175 at paras 165–79; *Edge v Pensions Ombudsman* [2000] Ch 602, 627–8, per Chadwick LJ. Cf *Oxford Legal Group Ltd v Sibbasbridge Services plc* [2008] 2 BCLC 381, CA (inspection of books by director under 1985 Act, s 222 (2006 Act, s 389) refused where purpose was improper).

[96] [2005] 1 BCLC 175.

would not be forfeited but in the absence of payment he would be excluded from any future dividend. Their failure to consider the exercise of such a discretion amounted to a failure to take into account matters they ought reasonably to have taken into account and the evidence showed that had they done so they would or might have reached a different decision. The directors' decision to forfeit the claimant's shares was therefore voidable at the instance of the claimant. It appears that the deputy judge saw the case as an application of what is sometimes referred to as the rule in *Hastings-Bass*. However, this principle is probably now better seen as an aspect of the duty to only exercise powers for the purposes for which they are conferred.[97]

This more interventionist approach is likely to continue after the enactment of the 2006 Act **11.59** and is reflected in the positive formulation of the duty imposed by s 171(b) which provides that directors '*must* exercise their powers for the purposes for which they are conferred'.[98] This is to be contrasted with the negative formulation of the test used in some earlier cases.[99]

Section 171(b) does not seek to spell out all the characteristics of the duty and a number of **11.60** questions have been left open for interpretation by the courts. In particular, questions will continue to arise where the board exercises a particular power for several reasons, only one of which is improper. There are differing views as to whether the dominant motive must be improper or whether it is sufficient that any causative motive was improper. The traditional test has been that the court will seek to ascertain what was the primary or substantial purpose for which the power was exercised. This has been variously described as the 'dominant'[100] or 'substantial'[101] purpose. In *Howard Smith Ltd v Ampol Petroleum Ltd*[102] the Privy Council held that when a dispute arises as to whether the directors of a company made a particular decision for one purpose or for another, or whether there being more than one purpose, one or another purpose was the substantial or primary purpose, the court is entitled to look at the situation objectively in order to estimate how critical or pressing or substantial an alleged requirement may have been. If it finds that a particular requirement, though real, was not urgent or critical at the relevant time, it may have reason to doubt or discount the assertions of individuals. However, a stricter formulation of the principle has been suggested in Australia in *Whitehouse v Carlton Hotel Pty Ltd* where it has been suggested that it is not necessary to show that the dominant motive of the directors was improper, only that the improper purpose was a causative motive, in the sense that but for its presence the power would not have been exercised.[103]

In *Eclairs Group Ltd v JKX Oil & Gas plc*,[104] Lord Sumption (with whom Lord Hodge **11.61** agreed) reviewed the authorities that had considered multiple concurrent purposes. His Lordship considered that, while a director would breach his duty if he allowed himself to

---

[97] See also in this regard *Edge v Pension Ombudsman* [2000] Ch 602 at 627–8, CA.

[98] See *The Bell Group v Westpac Banking Corporation* [2012] WASCA 257 at para 2029 where Drummond AJA cited the views referred to in the equivalent paragraph of the previous edition of this work with approval. However, not all concepts familiar to public and administrative law will be directly applicable to this duty: see *Gaiman v National Association for Mental Health* [1971] Ch 317 where Megarry J held that the principles of natural justice were not applicable to the exclusion of a person from membership of company limited by guarantee.

[99] eg *Re Smith & Fawcett Ltd* [1942] Ch 304, 306 where Lord Greene MR referred to the duty not to act for any collateral purpose.

[100] *Whitehouse v Carlton Hotel Pty Ltd* (1987) 162 CLR 285, 294.

[101] *Howard Smith Ltd v Ampol Petroleum Ltd* [1974] AC 821, 835.

[102] [1974] AC 821, 832D–G.

[103] *Whitehouse v Carlton Hotel Pty Ltd* (1987) 162 CLR 285 at 294.

[104] [2015] Bus LR 1395, SC at paras 17–24.

be influenced by *any* improper purpose, the impugned decision would be allowed to stand if the director would have reached the same outcome even in the absence of the improper purpose. Correspondingly, if without the improper purpose the impugned decision would not have been made, then it would be irrational to allow the decision to stand simply because the directors had other, proper considerations in mind to which perhaps they attached greater importance.[105] Lords Mance, Neuberger, and Clarke expressed mixed views on Lord Sumption's analysis, while declining to give a firm determination on the point, which was not determinative of the appeal and on which the Supreme Court had not heard oral argument.[106]

11.62 Unlike the duty imposed by the 2006 Act, s 172(1), it will be no defence to an action that alleges that a director has acted in breach of s 171(1)(b) for the director to assert that he bona fide believed his conduct to be in the best interests of the company.[107]

(6) Effect of breach of the duty

11.63 Where a director enters into a transaction in breach of his duty to act for proper purposes it will have both internal and external consequences. In so far as the transaction concerns the director himself or a third party not dealing in good faith with the company the transaction may be set aside. Accordingly, in the case of an improper allotment of shares or remuneration to a director the transaction may be set aside or declared invalid.[108] However, where the transaction involves a third party dealing with the company in good faith the question of whether or not the agreement will be binding on the company will depend upon the principles of the law of agency with appropriate regard for the 2006 Act, ss 39 and 40.[109] In *Criterion Properties plc v Stratford UK Properties LLC*[110] the House of Lords held that the principles of 'knowing receipt' and 'dishonest assistance' do not apply to a contract entered into with a company in breach of the directors' duty to act for a proper purpose. 'Receipt' in 'knowing receipt' referred to the receipt by one person from another of assets. The creation by a contract of contractual rights did not constitute a receipt of assets in that sense. This position will remain the same under the 2006 Act.

---

[105] Paragraph 21.

[106] At paras 46, 50–55.

[107] *Hardy v Metropolitan Land and Finance Co* (1872) 7 Ch App 427; *Great Eastern Rly Co v Turner* (1872) 8 Ch App 149; *Russell v Wakefield Waterworks Co* (1875) LR 20 Eq 474, 479; *Howard Smith Ltd v Ampol Petroleum Ltd* [1974] AC 821, 832; *Hogg v Cramphorn* [1967] Ch 254, 266–8; *Ultraframe (UK) Ltd v Fielding* [2005] EWHC 1638 (Ch) at paras 1292–5; *Eclairs Group Ltd v JKX Oil & Gas plc* [2015] Bus LR 1395, SC.

[108] *Hogg v Cramphorn Ltd* [1967] Ch 254; *Howard Smith Ltd v Ampol Petroleum Ltd* [1974] AC 821.

[109] As to which see para 11.29 above.

[110] [2004] 1 WLR 1846, HL.

12

DUTY TO PROMOTE THE SUCCESS OF THE COMPANY

Mark Arnold QC and Marcus Haywood

A. Introduction

The Companies Act, s 172 provides that: **12.01**

(1) A director of a company must act in the way he considers, in good faith, would be most likely to promote the success of the company for the benefit of its members as a whole and in doing so have regard to (amongst other matters)—

    (a) the likely consequences of any decision in the long term,

    (b) the interests of the company's employees,

    (c) the need to foster the company's business relationship with suppliers, customers and others,

    (d) the impact of the company's operation on the community and the environment,

    (e) the desirability of the company maintaining a reputation for high standards of business conduct, and

    (f) the need to act fairly as between members of the company.

(2) Where to the extent that the purposes of the company consist of or include purposes other than the benefit of its members, subsection (1) has effect as if the reference to promoting the success of the company for the benefit of its members were to achieving those purposes.

(3) The duty imposed by this section has effect subject to any enactment or rule of law requiring directors, in certain circumstances, to consider or act in the interest of the creditors of the company.[1]

12.02 The Companies Act, s 172 codifies the duty of a director to act in the way he considers, in good faith, would be most likely to promote the success of the company for the benefit of its members as a whole. The section is one of the more controversial in the Companies Act as can be gleaned from the considerable periods of time that debate surrounding the provisions of the section took up during the passage of the bill through Parliament. In its review, the Company Law Review Steering Group (CLR) considered the issues surrounding the enactment of this section to be of central importance.[2] It identified two possible approaches: 'the shareholder-value approach' and 'the pluralist approach'. The shareholder-value approach recognizes that companies are managed with the ultimate objective of generating maximum value for shareholders and advocates this as the best means of achieving overall prosperity and welfare. The pluralist approach argues that the ultimate objective of maximizing shareholder value will not necessarily achieve maximum prosperity and welfare. Advocates of the pluralist approach argue that company law should be modified to ensure that a company is required to serve a wider range of interests, not subordinate to, or as a means of achieving, shareholder value but as valuable in their own right. The approach advocated by the CLR was referred to as an 'enlightened shareholder-value approach'. This approach is based upon the shareholder-value approach and involves directors having to act in the collective best interests of shareholders but does not focus on the exclusive consideration of short-term financial benefits but instead on the factors that will maximize shareholder value in the long term. The enlightened shareholder-value approach was adopted by the government in its White Papers, the Companies Bill, and ultimately in the Companies Act. One reason for this choice was that the pluralist approach risked leaving directors accountable to no one, since there would be no clear yardstick for judging their performance.[3]

12.03 The adoption of the enlightened shareholder-value approach is reflected in the language of s 172(1). The director must act in the way he considers, in good faith, would be most likely to promote the success of the company '*for the benefit of its members as a whole*'. This language clearly relates the success of the company to the interests of the members as a whole not to any individual shareholder or indeed the majority shareholder or shareholders. It follows that a director would be in breach of the duty if he were to promote the interests of only one section or class of shareholders.[4] This approach was advocated by the CLR:[5]

> We believe there is value in inserting a reference to the success of the company, since what is in view is not the individual interests of members, but their interests as members of an association with the purposes and the mutual arrangements embodied in the constitution; the

---

[1] The section came into force on 1 October 2007: 2006 Act Commencement Order No 3, Art 2(d).

[2] CLR: *The Strategic Framework*, para. 5.1.1.

[3] CLR: *Final Report*, para.1.17.

[4] See the speech of Lord Goldsmith in the second passage quoted in para 12.23 below: Hansard, HL, vol 678, col 256 (6 February 2006).

[5] CLR: *Developing the Framework*, para 3.51.

objective is to be achieved by the directors successfully managing the complex of relationships and resources which comprise the company's undertaking.

Accordingly, in those rare cases where the interests of the company conflict with the interests **12.04** of the members as a whole, or at least some of them, it would appear that the interests of the company should be preferred. This is akin to the approach that was adopted by Owen J of the Supreme Court of Western Australia in *The Bell Group Ltd v Westpac Banking Corporation*:[6]

> What is often overlooked in the writings on this subject is that while the fundamental nature of the duty is a constant, its content may vary from case to case depending on the circumstances of the company and on the type of decisions that the directors are called upon to make. It does no damage to the doctrine of separate corporate personality to recognise that a reflection of the interests of the company may be seen in the interest of shareholders. ...
>
> This does not mean that the general body of shareholders is always and for all purposes the embodiment of 'the company as a whole'. It will depend on the context, including the type of company and the nature of the impugned activity or decision. And it may also depend on whether the company is a thriving ongoing entity or whether its continued existence is problematic. In my view the interests of shareholders and the interests of the company may be seen as correlative not because the shareholders *are* the company but, rather, because the interests of the company and the interests of the shareholders intersect. ...
>
> It is, in my view, incorrect to read the phrases 'acting in the best interests of the company' and 'acting in the best interests of the shareholders' as if they meant exactly the same thing. To do so is to misconceive the true nature of the fiduciary relationship between a director and the company. And it ignores the range of other interests that might (again, depending on the circumstances of the company and the nature of the power to be exercised) legitimately be considered. On the other hand, it is almost axiomatic to say that the content of the duty may (and usually will) include a consideration of the interests of shareholders. But it does not follow that in determining the content of the duty to act in the interests of the company, the concerns of shareholders are the only ones to which attention need be directed or that the legitimate interests of other groups can safely be ignored.

The duty to promote the success of the company is closely related to the other general **12.05** duties owed by a director to the company. Indeed, the duty has been described as 'the fundamental duty to which a director is subject'.[7] In a sense, it is the duty from which the other fiduciary duties of a director flow. Accordingly, where a director acts in breach of one of the other general duties, he will often also be in breach of his duty under s 172(1). In particular, the duty is closely related to the duty under s 175 to avoid conflicts of interests. So, in *Newgate Stud Co v Penfold* David Richards J held that where on the facts there exists a real risk of conflict between duty and personal loyalties the burden is on the director to show that the transaction in question was demonstrably in the best interests of the company.[8]

The common law principle from which the duty contained in s 172 derives was a broad one **12.06** that has been described as 'dynamic and capable of application in cases where it has not previously been applied but the principle or rationale of the rule applies'.[9]

---

[6] [2008] WASC 239 at paras 4391–5. This statement of principle was not criticized on appeal: [2012] WASCA 257.

[7] *Item Software (UK) Ltd Fassihi* [2005] 2 BCLC 91 at para 41, per Arden LJ.

[8] [2008] 1 BCLC 46 at para 242.

[9] *Item Software (UK) Ltd Fassihi* [2005] 2 BCLC 91 at para 41, per Arden LJ. Accordingly, in that case the duty was broad enough to impose an obligation upon a director to disclose his own misconduct.

12.07 The duty stated in s 172 applies to shadow directors to the extent that they are capable of so applying (see Chapter 10, Section C).[10]

12.08 A director who, in relation to a particular transaction, wishes to be protected from the risk of being in breach of the duty to promote the success of the company may obtain the consent, approval, or authorization of the members, as recognized by s 180(4)(a) (see Chapter 10, Section D) or ratification of his conduct under s 239 (Chapter 20, Section D).

B. The Director's Judgment

12.09 The decision as to what will promote the success of the company is one for the director's good-faith judgment. The onus of showing that the directors did not act in the best interests of the company is on the party challenging the impugned decision.[11] Section 172(1) gives an unfettered discretion to the directors, provided that they act in a way that they consider, in good faith, to be most likely to promote the success of the company.

(1) Subjectivity

12.10 This reflects the position at common law, the classic statement of which is that of Lord Greene MR in *Re Smith and Fawcett Ltd*: 'The [directors] must exercise their discretion bona fide in what they consider—not what a court may consider—is in the interests of the company …'[12] It has been said that the 'perhaps old-fashioned phrase acting "bona fide in the interests of the company" is reflected in the statutory words [of s 172] … They come to the same thing with the modern formulation giving a more readily understood definition of the scope of the duty.'[13]

12.11 Prior to the enactment of s 172 Jonathan Parker J referred to the relevant test in *Re Regentcrest plc v Cohen* as follows:

> The duty imposed on directors to act bona fide in the interests of the company is a subjective one. The question is not whether, viewed objectively by the court, the particular act or omission which is challenged was in fact in the interests of the company; still less is the question whether the court, had it been in the position of the director at the relevant time, might have acted differently. Rather, the question is whether the director honestly believed that his act or omission was in the interests of the company. The issue is as to the director's state of mind. No doubt, where it is clear that the act or omission under challenge resulted in substantial detriment to the company, the director will have a harder task persuading the court that he honestly believed it to be in the company's interest; but that does not detract from the subjective nature of the test.[14]

---

[10] 2006 Act, s 170(5) as amended by SBEE Act 2015, s 89(1) with effect from 25 May 2015.

[11] *The Bell Group Ltd v Westpac Banking Corporation* [2008] WASC 239 at para 4596; and on appeal: [2012] WASCA 257 at para 1992.

[12] [1942] Ch 304, 306, CA. See also *Charles Forte Investments Ltd v Amanda* [1964] Ch 240, CA.

[13] *Re Southern Counties Fresh Foods Ltd, Cobden Investments Ltd v RWM Langport Ltd* [2008] EWHC 2810 (Ch) at para 52, per Warren J.

[14] [2001] 2 BCLC 80 at 120. Applied in *Re Onslow Ditchling Ltd, Roberts v Frohlich* [2011] 2 BCLC 625 at para 84. See also *Re Southern Counties Fresh Foods Ltd, Cobden Investments Ltd v RWM Langport Ltd* [2008] EWHC 2810 (Ch) at paras 52–3.

Accordingly, in *Extrasure Travel Insurance Ltd v Scattergood* Jonathan Crow, sitting as a dep- **12.12** uty High Court judge, rejected an argument that a director acts in breach of his fiduciary duty if he honestly, but unreasonably and mistakenly, believed that he is pursuing the company's best interests.[15]

A recent illustration of this aspect of the duty is *Madoff Securities International Ltd v Raven*.[16] **12.13** That case involved a claim by the liquidators of an English company, which had been founded by Bernard Madoff, against former directors to recover certain payments which were said to have been improper. All the payments were made at the direction of Mr Madoff, who was a director, chief executive officer, and majority shareholder of the company. Following the exposure of Mr Madoff's notorious Ponzi scheme, the English company went into liquidation. It was accepted that it had its own legitimate business. Popplewell J said as follows in relation to the duty to promote the success of the company:[17]

> … corporate management often requires the exercise of judgement on which opinions may legitimately differ, and requires some give and take. A board of directors may reach a decision as to the commercial wisdom of a particular transaction by a majority. A minority director is not thereby in breach of his duty, or obliged to resign and to refuse to be party to the implementation of the decision. Part of his duty as a director acting in the interests of the company is to listen to the views of his fellow directors and to take account of them. He may legitimately defer to those views where he is persuaded that his fellow directors' views are advanced in what they perceive to be the best interests of the company, even if he is not himself persuaded. A director is not in breach of his core duty to act in what he considers in good faith to be the interests of a company merely because if left to himself he would do things differently.

Applying those principles to the facts, the judge held that none of the defendant directors **12.14** had acted in breach of their duties. In particular, he emphasized that directors bring different experience and expertise to the joint exercise of corporate management.[18] On the facts of the case, the judge held that it would have been unfair and unrealistic to expect any of the defendant directors to have done anything other than attach great weight to the views of Mr Madoff in deciding what was in the interests of the company.

(2) Rationality

Notwithstanding the emphasis of the subjective nature of the test in relation to the duty to **12.15** act in good faith in the best interests of the company, there are suggestions in some cases that the courts can go further than a mere appraisal of the director's belief about his or her state of mind.[19] In *Hutton v West Cork Railway Co*[20] Bowen LJ said:

> Bona fides cannot be the sole test, otherwise you might have a lunatic conducting the affairs of the company, and paying away its money with both hands in a manner perfectly bona fide yet perfectly irrational.

---

[15] [2003] 1 BCLC 598 at para 89. The relevant paragraph is quoted in Ch 10 at para 10.11.
[16] [2013] EWHC 3147 (Comm); see also Chapter 13 at para 13.08 to 13.10 for a discussion of this case in context of a director's duty to exercise independent judgment.
[17] [2013] EWHC 3147 (Comm), at paras 191 and 193.
[18] At para 220.
[19] For a discussion of the nature of the relevant test see Keay, 'Good Faith and Directors' Duty to Promote the Success of their Company' (2011) 32 *The Company Lawyer* 138.
[20] (1883) LR 23 Ch D 654 at 671.

12.16 And more recently, in *The Bell Group Ltd v Westpac Banking Corporation*[21] Owen J of the Supreme Court of Western Australia said that in deciding upon the state of mind of the directors the court should take into account surrounding circumstances and that this may involve objective considerations:

> Unless the party challenging the conduct in question can demonstrate a justifiable basis for asserting that the directors did not believe bona fide that the transactions were in the interest of the companies there is no breach of this duty. If the challenging party can show that there are no reasonable grounds on which the decision could have been made or the conduct undertaken, then an element of objectivity is introduced into the equation. But it seems to me that the objective considerations relate back to the question whether the directors honestly believed the transaction to be in the best interests of the company, not to whether (regardless of what the directors believed) it did not benefit the company. ...
>
> It follows that to regard the test as being solely subjective would be wrong. But it is important to bear in mind the critical task with which the court is confronted. The court must ascertain whether the directors have breached their duties by, for example, committing the company to a particular transaction. It is not part of the court's function to decide whether the transaction was commercially good, bad or indifferent, although ... it may be necessary to look at that question as part of the reasoning process by which a court carries out its critical task and arrives at a conclusion in relation to it. The enquiry cannot be entirely subjective.

12.17 A requirement of some degree of objectivity is consistent with the duty of a director to exercise reasonable skill, care, and diligence in assembling the relevant material to enable him to make his decision. Although this is a developing area, two strands of analysis appear to have emerged. The first is where there is absence of good faith or where the interests of the company are disregarded. Here the courts have applied an objective standard of reasonableness. The second is where regard was had to the interests of the company; in which case the courts will only interfere if the decision is irrational or perverse.

Absence of good faith or disregard of the interests of the company

12.18 In *Charterbridge Corp Ltd v Lloyds Bank Ltd*,[22] Pennycuick J said that where the director had failed to consider whether the action that was the subject of complaint would be in the best interests of the company, the proper test was whether an intelligent and honest man in the position of a director of the company concerned could, in the whole of the existing circumstances, have reasonably believed that the transaction was for the benefit of the company. This reasoning has been applied subsequently both in England and Australia.[23]

---

[21] [2008] WASC 239 at paras 4598–603. But see the observations of Drummond AJA on appeal: [2012] WASCA 257 at para 1998 (who considered that the law was correctly stated by Jonathan Parker J in *Regentcrest plc (in liq) v Cohen* [2001] 2 BCLC 80 at para 120 (as set out in para 12.11 above).

[22] [1970] Ch 62 at 74. Applied in *Extrasure Travel Insurances Ltd v Scattergood* [2003] 1 BCLC 598 at para 138; *Re HLC Environmental Projects Ltd* [2014] BCC 337 at paras 92 and 93.

[23] eg *Reid Murray Holdings Ltd v David Murray Holdings Pty Ltd* (1972) 5 SASR 386; *Australian National Industries Ltd v Greater Pacific Investments Pty Ltd (in liq) (No 3)* (1992) 7 ACSR 176; *Colin Gwyer & Associates Ltd v London Wharf (Limehouse) Ltd* [2003] 2 BCLC 153 at para 73; *Extrasure Travel Insurance Ltd v Scattergood* [2003] 1 BCLC 598 at para 91; *Simtel Communications Ltd v Rebak* [2006] 2 BCLC 571 at para 104; but see the reservations expressed about the *Charterbridge* test in *Equiticorp Finance Ltd v Bank of New Zealand* (1993) 32 NSWLR 50 at 147–8; with which Lee AJA agreed in *The Bell Group Ltd (in liquidation) v Westpac Banking Corporation* [2012] WASCA 257 at para 1012; but see also the observations of Carr AJA at paras 2881 to 2902 of that case.

Certainly, where it can be demonstrated that the director's belief that he was acting in the best **12.19**
interest of the company was not well founded the court will be willing to interfere. Accordingly,
in *Re W & M Roith Ltd*[24] the court accepted that the onus was on the liquidator to show that the
service agreement in question was not entered into bona fide in the interests of the company,
but that the presumption was displaced by the following matters: (i) the director concerned had
been in office for more than 30 years without a service contract, and the late change was only
referable to his desire to benefit someone other than himself; (ii) while the director remained
alive there was no benefit to the company resulting from the existence of the contract; and (iii)
when the director took legal advice as to how to secure his widow's position, it was considered
immaterial which of the companies with which he was associated was actually to provide the
pension.[25] Accordingly, notwithstanding no actual dishonesty or secret profit, the interests of
the company were subordinated by the transaction and the test of bona fides was not satisfied.
It is clear in this regard that a finding of bad faith does not require a finding of dishonesty.[26]

Similarly, in *Knight v Frost*[27] Hart J held that the directors had not acted bona fide in the inter- **12.20**
ests of the company when they caused it to make loans to a third party corporation associated
with one of the directors in circumstances where: (i) no steps had been taken to ensure that
the company was entitled to a commercial rate of interest or to record or agree the currency in
which repayment would be made; (ii) the third party had no assets of any significance apart
from the one of the director's services which he could choose to provide on his own terms; and
(iii) looked at from the company's viewpoint it stood to gain nothing from the transactions
beyond a chance that it might be repaid if the third party flourished in the future.

Perverse or irrational decisions

It is suggested that where a director acts perversely or irrationally in considering what step **12.21**
would be most likely to promote the success of the company he will also be in breach of
his duties under s 172 (and perhaps also under ss 171(b), or 174). This is consistent with a
growing tendency on the part of the court to intervene in corporate or contractual decision-
making to prevent abuse by applying principles familiar in public and administrative law.[28]
In *Hayes v Willoughby*,[29] Lord Sumption said:

> Rationality is a familiar concept in public law. It has also in recent years played an increasingly
> significant role in the law relating to contractual discretions, where the law's object is also to

---

[24] [1967] 1 WLR 432.
[25] As to the burden of proof in the absence of a satisfactory explanation by a director as to the reasons for a
payment, see *Re Idessa (UK) Ltd* [2012] 1 BCLC 80 at paras 24–8. Depending on the other evidence, it may be
that the absence of a satisfactory explanation drives the court to conclude that there was no proper justification
for the payment.
[26] *Wrexham Association Football Club Ltd v Crucialmove Ltd* [2008] 1 BCLC 508, CA at para 37.
[27] [1999] 1 BCLC 364.
[28] See Ch 11 at 11.56–11.62 above. Compare also the position in relation to administrators as described
in Lightman and Moss, *The Law of Receivers and Administrators of Companies*, 5th edn (Sweet and Maxwell,
2011), paras 12–038–12–040. For a detailed exposition of the administrator's duty to act rationally, see Mokal,
Corporate Insolvency Law: Theory and Application (Oxford University Press, 2005), Ch 7; Armour and Mokal,
'Reforming the Governance of Corporate Rescue: The Enterprise Act 2002' [2005] LMCLQ 32. Note, however, that the so-called rule in *Re Hastings Bass* [1975] Ch 25, CA has since been comprehensively restated and
clarified: see *Pitt v Holt* [2013] 2 AC 108, SC.
[29] [2013] 1 WLR 935 at para 14 (in the context of the Protection from Harassment Act 1997); citing
Ludgate Insurance Co Ltd v Citibank NA [1998] Lloyds Rep IR 221, para 35 and *Socimer International Bank Ltd
v Standard Bank Ltd* [2008] Bus LR 1304, para 66. Also see *Braganza v BP Shipping* [2015] 1 WLR 1661, SC at
paras 22, 23 per Baroness Hale, para 53, per Lord Hodge, and para 103 per Lord Neuberger.

limit the decision-maker to some relevant contractual purpose … Rationality is not the same as reasonableness. Reasonableness is an external, objective standard applied to the outcome of a person's thoughts or intentions. The question is whether a notional hypothetically reasonable person in his position would have engaged in the relevant conduct for the purpose of preventing or detecting crime. A test of rationality, by comparison, applies a minimum objective standard to the relevant person's mental processes. It imports a requirement of good faith, a requirement that there should be some logical connection between the evidence and the ostensible reasons for the decision, and (which will usually amount to the same thing) an absence of arbitrariness, of capriciousness or of reasoning so outrageous in its defiance of logic as to be perverse.

12.22 *Re a Company, ex p Glossop*[30] is an example of a case where express reference was made to the *Wednesbury* principle. Harman J had before him an application to amend a petition for relief under the 1985 Act, s 459 (unfair prejudice) and in the alternative for a just and equitable winding up, to add allegations concerning the directors' alleged failure to recommend payment of a dividend. The application succeeded in part. Harman J said:

> It is, in my judgment, vital to remember that actions of boards of directors cannot simply be justified by invoking the incantation 'a decision taken bona fide in the interests of the company' … If it were to be proved that directors resolved to exercise their powers to recommend dividends to a general meeting … without regard to the right of members to have profits distributed so far as was commercially possible, I am of opinion that the directors' decision would be open to challenge. This is an application, in a sense, of the principle affirmed in so many local government cases and usually called 'the *Wednesbury* principle'.[31]

(3) Success of the company

12.23 Similar principles also apply as to what constitutes the 'success of the company'. The Companies Act does not seek to lay down any definition of this phrase. Instead, the decision as to what constitutes success is one for the members and directors using their good-faith judgment.[32] Two extracts from a speech of Lord Goldsmith during the passage of the Companies Bill through Parliament are instructive in this regard:

> What is success? The starting point is that it is essentially for the members of the company to define the objective they wish to achieve. Success means what the members collectively want the company to achieve. For a commercial company, success will usually mean long-term increase in value. For certain companies, such as charities and community interest companies, it will mean the attainment of the objectives for which the company has been established. …
>
> … it is for the directors, by reference to those things we are talking about—the objective of the company—to judge and form a good faith judgement about what is to be regarded as success for the members as a whole … they will need to look at the company's constitution, shareholder decisions and anything else that they consider relevant in helping them to reach that judgement … the duty is to promote the success for the benefit of the members as a whole—that is, for the members as a collective body—not only to benefit the majority shareholders,

---

[30] [1988] BCLC 570.

[31] [1988] BCLC 570 at 577. See also *Byng v London Life Association Ltd* [1989] BCLC 400 considered in para 11.57 above; and *Equitable Life Assurance Society v Hyman* [2002] 1 AC 408 at paras 17–21. But see *Progress Property Co Ltd v Moorgarth Group Ltd* [2011] 1 WLR 1, SC: sale of shares at an undervalue but in genuine belief that it is a proper commercial sale and is not a disguised unlawful distribution.

[32] Explanatory Notes to the Companies Act, para 327.

or any particular shareholder or section of shareholders, still less the interests of directors who might happen to be shareholders themselves. That is an important statement of the way in which directors need to look at this judgement they have to make.[33]

In this regard, it is permissible for directors to promote their own interests[34] or those of anybody else where to do so is in the company's interest (subject to any internal limitations on their powers). This permits the promoting of employees' interests under the 2006 Act, s 172(1)(b) or those of a group of companies of which the director is one.[35] **12.24**

(4) Duty to report

A director is not strictly speaking the agent of his co-directors. The mere fact that a particular director is liable to the company for a breach of duty is not enough of itself to render the remaining directors liable as well. Accordingly, it has been held that, in the absence of negligence, a director is not liable for a breach of duty by other directors of which he was ignorant, or which occurred before he became a director.[36] **12.25**

However, in certain circumstances the director's duty to promote the success of the company for the benefit of the members as a whole will require him to report breaches of duty either of his fellow directors or himself.[37] Thus in *British Midland Tool Ltd v Midland International Tooling Ltd*[38] Hart J held that the director's duty to act so as to promote the best interests of his company includes a duty to inform the company of any activity, actual or threatened, which damages those interests. This in itself includes a duty to inform the company of any breaches of duty being carried out and perhaps even contemplated by other directors. Similarly, in *Item Software (UK) Ltd v Fassihi* the Court of Appeal held that a director was under a duty to disclose his own misconduct.[39] **12.26**

Where a director is also a 'worker' with the meaning of the Employment Rights Act 1996, s 230[40] he or she will be protected from dismissal or victimization in certain circumstances where he brings wrongdoing to the attention of his or her employers. This is commonly referred to as 'whistle-blowing'. 'Qualifying disclosures' in respect of which such protection arises under the Employment Rights Act 1996 are disclosures of information where **12.27**

---

[33] Hansard, HL, vol 678, cols 255–6 (6 February 2006).

[34] *Hirsche v Sims* [1894] AC 654 at 660, per Lord Selborne.

[35] See paras 13.14–13.17 below and *Charterbridge Corporation Ltd v Lloyds Bank Ltd* [1970] Ch 62. As to the position of nominee directors see *Re Neath Rugby Ltd (No 2), Hawkes v Cuddy* [2009] 2 BCLC 427, CA and paras 13.18–13.25 below.

[36] *Cullerne v London and Suburban General Permanent Building Society* (1890) 25 QBD 485. Cf *Green v Walkling* [2008] 2 BCLC 332: director not liable for breach of duty when he acted on legal advice and could not have done more to prevent misappropriation by others.

[37] *Madoff Securities International Ltd v Raven* [2013] EWHC 3147 (Comm) at para 192, citing: *Walker v Stones* [2001] QB 902, 921D-E; *Gidman v Barron* [2003] EWHC 153 (Ch) at para 131; *Neville v Krikorian* [2007] 1 BCLC 1, CA at paras 49–51; and *Lexi Holdings v Luqman (No. 1)* [2007] EWHC 2652 (Ch) at paras 201–5.

[38] [2003] 2 BCLC 523 at para 89.

[39] [2005] 2 BCLC 91, CA. See also *Tesco Stores Ltd v Pook* [2003] EWHC 823; *Shepherds Investments Ltd v Walters* [2006] 2 BCLC 202 at paras 104–8, per Etherton J.

[40] Which defines a 'worker' as 'an individual who has entered into or works under (or, where the employment has ceased, worked under): (a) a contract of employment, or (b) any other contract, whether express or implied and (if it is express) whether oral or in writing, whereby the individual undertakes to do or perform personally any work or services for another party to the contract whose status is not by virtue of the contract that of a client or customer of any profession or business undertaking carried on by the individual'.

the worker reasonably believes making the disclosure will tend to show one or more of the following:[41]

    (a) that a criminal offence has been committed, is being committed or is likely to be committed,

    (b) that a person has failed, is failing or is likely to fail to comply with any legal obligation to which he is subject,

    (c) that a miscarriage of justice has occurred, is occurring or is likely to occur,

    (d) that the health or safety of any individual has been, is being or is likely to be endangered,

    (e) that the environment has been, is being or is likely to be damaged, or

    (f) that information tending to show any matter falling within any one of the preceding paragraphs has been, is being or is likely to be deliberately concealed.

12.28 Where the decision is taken by the board to expel another director that decision too must be exercised in good faith and in the best interests of the company.[42]

(5) Non-executive directors

12.29 The considerations discussed in the paragraph above are particularly important in the context of non-executive directors. In the case of a non-executive director, the question of whether there has been a breach of the duty imposed by s 172 involves consideration of 'how the particular company's business is organised and the part which the director could reasonably have been expected to play'.[43] A non-executive director who places 'unquestioning reliance upon others to do their job' may not be able to show that he has considered what step is most likely to promote the success of the company. In this regard 'a company may reasonably at least look to non-executive directors for independence of judgment and supervision of the executive management'.[44]

C. Matters to which the Directors Should Have Regard

12.30 Section 172(1) lays down a list of matters to which directors are to have regard when they exercise their duty to promote the success of the company. Whilst the wording of s 172(1) is mandatory (directors '*must* act … and in doing so *have* regard to') the list is not exhaustive, but is said to highlight areas of particular importance which reflect wider expectations of responsible business behaviour, such as the interests of the company's employees and the impact of the company's operations on the community and the environment.[45] The list is not ordered in any type of priority.

---

[41] Employment Rights Act 1996, ss 43A to 43L; and for cases considering these provisions see *Northbrook Laboratories (GB) Ltd v Shaw* [2014] ICR 540; *Bates van Winkelhof v Clyde & Co LLP* [2014] 1 W.L.R. 2047, SC; and *Blackbay Ventures Ltd v Gahir* [2014] ICR 747.

[42] *Lee v Chou Wen Hsien* [1984] 1 WLR 1202, 1206, PC.

[43] *Bishopsgate Investment Management Ltd v Maxwell* [1994] 1 All ER 261, CA at 264.

[44] *Equitable Life v Bowley* [2004] 1 BCLC 180 at para 41. Further guidance is to be found in *Re Barings plc* [1999] 1 BCLC 433, [2000] 1 BCLC 523, CA. See *Lexi Holdings plc v Luqman* [2009] 2 BCLC 1, CA, where two sisters were liable to pay damages to the company, because they failed to supervise their dishonest brother or report their concerns to the auditors; and see *Madoff Securities International Ltd v Raven* [2013] EWHC 3147 (Comm) discussed in paragraph 12.13 above and in Chapter 13 at paras 13.08–13.10.

[45] Explanatory Notes to the Companies Act, para 326. During the passage of the bill through Parliament Lord Goldsmith said 'we have included the words "amongst other matters". We want to be clear that the list of factors is not exhaustive' (Hansard, HL Grand Committee, col 846 (9 May 2006)).

It is also important to note that the factors set out in s 172(1) are subsidiary to the overall **12.31** duty to promote the success of the company. Where the different matters to which the director must have regard suggest a conflicting course of action the director must take that action which he bona fide believes is consistent with the overarching duty to promote the success of the company.

The duty is not owed to any of the persons specified in the subsection directly (eg employ- **12.32** ees, suppliers, customers) but to the company.[46] Accordingly the duty to have regard to the interests of employees, suppliers, and customers is not enforceable by those individuals. The same is true of the duty to act fairly as between the members of the company. The duty is one owed to the company not to individual shareholders, although, as with other fiduciary duties owed to the company it may be enforced indirectly by shareholders by a derivative claim, or, where the relevant breach of duty is unfairly prejudicial to the interests of those shareholders within the meaning of the 2006 Act, s 994, by petition under that section. When having regard to the factors listed in s 172(1), a director must also act in accordance with his duty to exercise reasonable care, skill, and diligence (2006 Act, s 174).[47] Where a director fails to properly take account one of the factors set out in the list he may act in breach of his duty under s 174.[48]

There is no statutory explanation of what the term 'have regard to' means in this context. An **12.33** indication of how the government intended the expression to be interpreted was given by Margaret Hodge, Minister of State for Industry and the Regions:

> The words 'have regard to' mean 'think about'; they are absolutely not about just ticking boxes. If 'thinking about' leads to the conclusion, as we believe it will in many cases, that the proper course is to act positively to achieve the objectives in the clause, that will be what the director's duty is. In other words 'have regard to' means 'give proper consideration to' …[49]

Accordingly, where a director fails utterly to have regard to any of the specific matters set out in sub-s (1) it appears likely he will act in breach of the duty.

However, where a director gives those matters due consideration and concludes in good **12.34** faith that the relevant action is likely to promote the success of the company he will not act in breach of the duty. The weight to be given to the specific factors will be a matter for the director's good-faith judgment. This is confirmed by Lord Goldsmith:

> We want the director to give such consideration to the factors identified as is necessary for the decision that he has to take, and no more than that. We do not intend a director to be required to do more than good faith and the duty of skill and care require, nor do we want it to be possible for a director acting in good faith to be held liable for a process failure where it could not have affected the outcome.[50]

Similarly Margaret Hodge said:

> Consideration of the factors will be an integral part of the duty to promote the success of the company for the benefit of its members as a whole. The clause makes it clear that a director is

---

[46] 2006 Act, s 170(1).
[47] See Ch 14 below.
[48] See also para 12.21 above.
[49] Hansard, HC, vol 450, col 789 (17 October 2006).
[50] Hansard, HL Grand Committee, col 846 (9 May 2006).

to have regard to the factors in fulfilling that duty. The decisions taken by a director and the weight given to the factors will continue to be a matter for his good faith judgment.[51]

12.35 One perhaps unintended consequence of this approach is that the list of factors may be used by directors increasingly as a defence to an action by the company. For instance, where a director in good faith and in order to promote the success of the company for the benefit of its members as a whole makes a decision in the wider interests of the community or the environment it may be arguable that he will be protected from reproach.

12.36 Few of the factors set out in s 172(1) had ever specifically been recognized in case law prior to the enactment of the Companies Act.[52] However, they are clearly reconcilable with that case law. Indeed, one of the strengths of the common law duty was that it was expressed in very general terms and capable of application in cases where it has not previously been applied.

(1) Likely consequences of any decision in the long term

12.37 Section 172(1)(a) reflects the importance placed by the government on the long-term as opposed to the short-term approach that should be taken by directors. It provides that the directors are to have regard to the likely consequences of any decision in the long term. This is arguably what the general law required anyway, namely that directors should, in appropriate circumstances, seek to balance short-term considerations against long-term considerations. The subsection does not of course mean that directors are not allowed to have regard to the consequences in the short or medium term. Indeed in many circumstances short-term consequences may well outweigh long-term consequences. As Lord Goldsmith pointed out during the passage of the bill through Grand Committee, 'a particular decision may be an excellent long-term decision if only you could pay for it, but if you try to pay for it today you may go completely bust'.[53] The important point is that directors are only to have *regard* to the likely consequences of a decision in the long term. If a director has regard to such long-term consequences but in good faith considers that other short-term factors outweigh those consequences the court will not interfere with his decision.

(2) The interests of the company's employees

12.38 In requiring directors to have regard to the interests of employees, s 172(1)(b) replaces the 1985 Act, s 309.[54] This provided that the matters to which the directors of a company were to have regard in the performance of their functions include the interests of the company's employees in general, as well as the interests of its members. The employees' interests are various and may include non-discriminatory policies and safe systems of work, as well as job security and financial benefits. Although the 1985 Act, s 309 was cited in a number of

---

[51] Hansard, HC, col 789 (17 October 2006).

[52] The Law Commission identified the relevant duties as (a) a duty of loyalty, to act in good faith in the best interests of the company, (b) a duty to have regard to the interests of the company's employees in general and its members, and (c) a duty to act fairly as between members: *Company Directors: Regulating Conflicts of Interest and Formulating a Statement of Duties*, Consultation Paper No 153 at paras 11.4–11.20; Report No 261 at Appendix A.

[53] Hansard, HL Grand Committee, col GC271 (6 February 2006).

[54] 1985 Act, s 309 re-enacted 1980 Act, s 46 which was the first statutory expression of the duty of directors to have regard to interests of employees. 1980 Act, s 74 for the first time gave a company power to provide for employees on cessation of business, so reversing *Parke v Daily News Ltd* [1962] Ch 927. Section 74 was re-enacted as 1985 Act, s 719 and was replaced by 2006 Act, s 247 on 1 October 2009: 2006 Act Commencement Order No 8, Art 3(i).

cases,[55] 'it has not been fully considered in any of these cases'.[56] In particular the courts have not expressed a view on the question of whether s 309 required directors in exercising their functions to have regard to the interests of employees in general even if their interests are not the same as those of the company.

In *Fulham Football Club Ltd v Cabra Estates plc*,[57] the Court of Appeal *obiter* were minded to reject an argument that the company was bound by undertakings merely because all the shareholders had signed them on the basis that the duties owed by directors are to their company and the company is more than the sum of its members. The Court of Appeal held that creditors, both present and potential, were also interested, while the 1985 Act, s 309 imposed a specific duty on directors to have regard to the interests of the company's employees in general. The Court of Appeal's decision could be read as suggesting that s 309 was not limited to requiring directors to have regard to the interests of employees when to do so is conducive to the interests of the company.[58] In so far as this is an acceptable reading of the *Fulham Football Club* case it is submitted that it should not be adopted in relation to s 172(1)(b). As noted above, the requirement that the director have regard to the interest of the company's employees is only a factor to which the company is to have regard. The overriding duty is to act in the way the director considers in good faith would be most likely to promote the success of the company for the benefit of its members as a whole. Often the interests of employees will be in conflict with the interests of the members as a whole—eg in a question as to whether to close an unprofitable factory (but in such a case employees' interests will be respected by redundancy payments).[59]   **12.39**

The statutory duty of a director to ensure compliance by his company with health and safety legislation was considered in *Brumder v Motornet Service and Repair Ltd*.[60] That case concerned a claim by the sole director and shareholder of a company against the company for damages for personal injury caused by defective equipment. Although the company was in breach of its absolute statutory duty to ensure that work equipment 'is maintained in an efficient state, in efficient working order and in good repair'[61] and that the defective equipment caused the accident, the Court of Appeal held that the director could not bring a claim against the company in circumstances where he was in breach of his own obligations to it to exercise reasonable care to enable the company to fulfil its health and safety obligations.   **12.40**

---

[55] *Fulham Football Club Ltd v Cabra Estates plc* [1994] 1 BCLC 363, CA; *Re Saul D Harrison & Sons plc* [1995] 1 BCLC 14, CA; *Dawson International plc v Coats Paton plc* [1989] BCLC 233, Ct of Sess; *Re London Life Association Ltd* (21 February 1989, unreported) (Hoffmann J); *Re A company, ex p Burr* [1992] BCLC 724 at 734.

[56] *Company Directors Regulating Conflicts of Interests and Formulating a Statement of Duties* (Law Com Paper No 153) at para 11.28. As to the circumstances in which the directors may cause the company to grant gratuities to the company's employees see *Hampson v Price's Patent Candle Co* (1876) 45 LJ Ch 437; *Hutton v West Cork Rly Co* (1883) 23 Ch D 654, CA; *Kaye v Croydon Tramways Co* [1898] 1 Ch 358, 367, CA; *Parke v Daily News Ltd* [1962] Ch 927; *Re W and M Roith Ltd* [1967] 1 WLR 432; and *Re Halt Garage* [1982] 3 All ER 1016.

[57] [1994] 1 BCLC 363, CA.

[58] *Company Directors Regulating Conflicts of Interests and Formulating a Statement of Duties* (Law Com Paper No 153) at para 11.28.

[59] Margaret Hodge said: 'We do not, however, claim that the interests of the company and of its employees will always be identical; regrettably, it will sometimes be necessary, for example, to lay off staff. The drafting … must therefore clearly point directors towards their overarching objective' (Hansard, HC, col 789 (17 October 2006)).

[60] [2013] 2 BCLC 58.

[61] Provision and Use of Work Equipment Regulations 1998, reg 5.

Whilst the Court of Appeal analysed the case by reference to the director's obligation to exercise reasonable care and skill, in an appropriate case the duty to have regard to the interests of the company's employees imposed by s 172(1)(b) could be equally applicable. Beatson LJ said as follows in that case:[62]

> As a general rule the remedy for breach of a director's duty of care is compensation for the harm caused to the company by the director's negligence. That would have been the position in this case had the person injured been an employee or another person, for example a visitor who was assisting Mr Lewis. The harm to the company would in principle be the damages payable to the injured person and the company would in principle be able to recover that sum from the defaulting director. Here, the injured person was also the director. ....

> Unless there is a particular policy reason which precludes the company from suing the director, the employer would be entitled to recover damages against the director in the sum which the director was supposedly entitled to recover against the employer. ...

> There is in my judgment no such precluding policy in the situation before us and no reason for protecting a director who, like the claimant in this case, has made no efforts in respect of the company's health and safety duties, in a situation where it is only that person who is able to act on behalf of the company.

12.41 The power to make provision for employees on cessation or transfer of the company's business is exercisable notwithstanding the general duty imposed by s 172.[63]

(3) The need to foster the company's business relationships with suppliers, customers, and others

12.42 Section 172(1)(c) provides that a director must have regard to the need to foster the company's business relationships with suppliers, customers, and others. In most cases the application of this duty will be relatively obvious. A reputation for bad commercial practices (eg late payment of bills and providing poor quality goods and services) can damage the company's business. Even prior to the enactment of s 172 the importance of maintaining a good relationship with customers and suppliers was something to which most directors would ordinarily have had regard. Such consideration will obviously be of crucial importance in maintaining the ongoing success of the company.[64]

(4) The impact of the company's operations on the community and the environment

12.43 Section 172(1)(d) provides that the directors must have regard to the impact of the company's operations on the community and the environment. It is perhaps in this section that the 'pluralist approach' to directors' duties is most apparent. In many cases it may not be

---

[62] [2013] 2 BCLC 58, at paras 49–51.

[63] 2006 Act, s 247, replacing 1985 Act, s 719.

[64] It may be arguable that on the facts of a case such as *Secretary of State for BIS v Aaron* [2009] EWHC 3263 (Ch) the directors would now be regarded as being in breach of their duty under s 172 for failing to have regard to this matter. The case—which pre-dated the enactment of s 172—was argued on the basis that a disqualification order should have been made because there was a breach of the duty of care and skill and specifically not on the basis of a breach of fiduciary duty. However, Proudman J's conclusion in finding the defendants were unfit to act as directors was that (at para 109): 'It flies in the face of common sense to say that these two individuals were, despite all this, fit to act as directors. Whilst I stress there was no dishonesty, it seems to me that the wrong balance was struck between marketing considerations and the interests of the consumer.'

obviously apparent to a director how the impact of a company's operations on the wider community and the environment will be referable to the success of the company for the benefit of its members as a whole. However, the approach taken by the 2006 Act is that it is only if a director has regard to such factors that a company can ensure the success of the company particularly in the long term. There may also be short-term considerations in relation to this aspect of the duty. For example, where a director takes a decision which pays no regard to this consideration and this results in a fine or a claim for damages, for example because of some breach of environmental legislation, it is possible that the director could be held to be liable to the company for the loss caused by the fine or claim for damages.

The limits of s 172(1)(d) are apparent from *R (on the application of People & Planet) v HM*   **12.44**
Treasury.[65] In that case, the claimant action group applied for permission to bring judicial review proceedings in relation to the policy adopted by HM Treasury in respect of the handling of its majority shareholding in the Royal Bank of Scotland. The claimant wished to see a policy adopted which required HM Treasury to seek to persuade or require the bank to adopt lending practices and policies which did not support ventures or businesses which were harmful to the environment or insufficiently respectful of human rights. The question was whether HM Treasury should have sought to impose its own policy in relation to combating climate change and promoting human rights on the board of the bank, contrary to the judgment of the board. Sales J held that there was no such obligation on HM Treasury and that such a policy would have had a tendency to come into conflict with, and hence would cut across, the duties of the bank's board as set out in s 172(1). It would also have given rise to a real risk of litigation by minority shareholders seeking to complain that the value of their shares had been detrimentally affected by the government seeking to impose its policy on the bank. Decisions regarding the management of the bank were matters for the judgment of its directors. A shareholder could only influence directors to act within the limits imposed under s 172 (which include considerations other than the impact of the company's operations on the community and the environment).

(5) The desirability of the company maintaining a reputation for high standards of business conduct

Section 172(1)(e) provides that a director is to have regard to the desirability of the com-   **12.45**
pany maintaining a reputation for high standards of business conduct. As with the need to foster the company's business relationships with suppliers, customers, and others the application of this aspect of the duty will be relatively obvious. Directors who cause their company not to maintain a high standard of business conduct are unlikely to be promoting the success of the company for the benefit of its members as a whole. As with s 172(1)(d) consideration will need to be had as to the circumstances in which this subsection could lead to personal liability on the part of the director. In particular, where a director takes a decision which pays no regard to this consideration and this results in, for example, the production by the company of poorly manufactured goods, it is possible that he may be held liable for any fines or claims for damages arising in respect of those goods. Similarly, where the directors cause the company to fail to comply with its statutory[66] or

---

[65] [2009] EWHC 3020 (Admin).
[66] See eg in the context of the failure of a director to implement correctly the now repealed procedure set out in the 1985 Act, ss 155–8 under which, before 1 October 2008, a private company could give financial

reporting[67] obligations that may amount to a breach of section 172.

(6) Need to act fairly as between members of the company

12.46 The duty on the part of a director to have regard to the need to act fairly as between different shareholders set out in s 172(1)(f) was identified in *Mutual Life v The Rank Organisation (No 2)*[68] and subsequently applied by Arden J in *Re BSB (Holdings) Ltd (No 2)*.[69] In *Mutual Life v The Rank Organisation* it was held that the directors were not in breach of their duty when after proper investigation they decided that it was in the interests of the company to proceed to make a rights issue to some only of the holders of ordinary shares. In *Re BSB (Holdings) Ltd* Arden J said 'the law did not require the interests of the company to be sacrificed in the particular interests of a group of shareholders'.[70] However, there would be a breach of the relevant duty where the directors fail completely to consider whether a proposal which is under consideration will be fair as between different groups of shareholders. Accordingly, it has been held that the directors must not use their powers of allotment, making calls, forfeiting shares, and so on to favour themselves above other shareholders,[71] or to favour particular classes of shareholders.[72] Likewise, where, before any dividend is declared, the directors cause the company to set aside a portion of profits to form a reserve, they should have regard to how the reserve may affect the respective rights of the preference and ordinary shareholders, particularly in cases where the preference dividend is not cumulative. In such cases, if the articles authorize the creation of a reserve, 'it will always be the duty of the directors to fix the amount of the fund to be retained with reference to the general interest of all classes of shareholders, and not to favour any one class at the expense of the other'.[73]

12.47 Similarly, where the directors are considering exercising their discretionary power under a company's articles of association to refuse to register any transfer of shares they may only do so if they are acting in good faith in the best interests of the company. An example of a case where the directors were held to be so acting was *Mactra Properties Ltd v Morshead Mansions Ltd*.[74] In that case, the articles of a company, which managed a block of leasehold flats, provided that a leasehold owner who sold his flat was required to transfer his share in the company to the new owner, but that the directors were entitled to refuse to register any transfer of shares. The claimant, which owned several long leases of flats in the building, disputed levies imposed by the company in respect of its flats. The claimant then sold two of its flats

---

assistance for the acquisition of its own shares or those of its holding company (the 'whitewash' procedure): *Cook v Green* [2009] BCC 204; and *Re In a Flap Envelope Co Ltd* [2003] BCC 487.

[67] In the context of a director's duty to make an assessment of whether the company is a 'going concern' when preparing annual and half-yearly financial statements see the Financial Reporting Council's, *Going Concern and Liquidity Risk: Guidance for Directors of UK Companies 2009*.

[68] [1985] BCLC 11 at 21.

[69] [1996] 1 BCLC 155 at 246–9.

[70] [1996] 1 BCLC 155 at 251.

[71] *Hirsche v Sims* [1894] AC 654, PC (allotment); but cf *Re Jermyn Street Turkish Baths Ltd* [1971] 1 WLR 1042, CA; *Shaw v Holland* [1900] 2 Ch 305 (allotment to directors at an undervalue); *Harris v North Devon Rly Co* (1855) 20 Beav 384 (forfeiture); *Bennett's Case* (1854) 5 De GM & G 284 at 297; *Re National Provincial Marine Insurance Co, Gilbert's Case* (1870) 5 Ch App 559 (calls); *Re European Central Railway Co, Sykes' Case* (1872) LR 13 Eq 255 (payments in advance of calls); *Parker v McKenna* (1875) 10 Ch App 96; *Alexander v Automatic Telephone Co* [1900] 2 Ch 56, 72–3, CA (payments on application and allotment).

[72] *Howard Smith Ltd v Ampol Petroleum Ltd* [1974] AC 821, PC.

[73] *Henry v Great Northern Railway* (1857) 1 De G&J 606 at 638, per Lord Cranworth LC.

[74] [2009] 1 BCLC 179.

and assigned the leases to them, but the company refused to register a transfer of the shares relating to the two flats on the ground that the claimant had not paid the levies on the two flats. In the light of undisputed evidence that the company operated a policy of refusing to register share transfers following lease assignments in all cases where the outgoing leaseholders owed money to the company, the court held that claimant had not established that the directors had acted in bad faith in refusing to register the share transfers.

Furthermore, when some question of importance, is to be brought before a meeting of **12.48** a company (for example where a general meeting is summoned following a request from members pursuant to the 2006 Act, ss 303 and 304) it is not only legitimate but is expressly the duty of the directors to take such steps as are necessary to secure the best expression of the corporate voice, and to lay before shareholders, and even press them to support, the policy which the directors, acting in good faith, consider to be in the best interests of the company. The expense of so doing, including the issue of a circular, of printing and issuing proxy forms, and paying postage may, if reasonably necessary, be paid out of the corporate funds.[75]

The principle embodied within s 172(1)(f) accords with the general principle that the fiduci- **12.49** ary relationship of a director exists with the company not individual shareholders.[76] Directors will only be in a fiduciary relationship with individual shareholders in certain 'special circumstances'. The 'special circumstances' approach to the question of whether directors owe fiduciary duties to individual shareholders was endorsed by the Court of Appeal in *Peskin v Anderson*.[77] In that case the Court of Appeal refused to apply the principle so as to require directors to disclose to individual members plans, which had not yet become firm, for the selling of a major business of the company, simply because the interests of the individual shareholders would have been furthered by such disclosure. This was particularly the case where there had been no dealing between the directors and the members in relation to those plans.

However, where the directors seek to influence the exercise by the shareholders of their rights **12.50** they may assume duties in relation to those shareholders. For example, where a company meeting has been summoned directors owe a specific duty in equity to give sufficient information to shareholders for them to make an informed decision about proposals to be put to them in the meeting.[78] Similarly, the courts have held directors to be under a duty of good faith when giving advice whether to accept a takeover offer for their shares[79] or whether to sanction a scheme for the purchase of a large bloc of assets from another company.[80] Having given advice, if there is a change of circumstances it would normally be prudent for the directors to send out a circular in which they honestly state their views in the light of the change.[81] In *Prudential Assurance* this duty was classified as arising in tort and being 'no

---

[75] *Peel v London and North Western Rly Co* [1907] 1 Ch 5.
[76] See Ch 10 at paras 10.25–10.32 above; *Peskin v Anderson* [2001] 1 BCLC 372, CA; *Percival v Wright* [1902] 2 Ch 421. As to the application of s 172 in the context of a derivate application see *Franbar Holdings Ltd v Patel* [2009] 1 BCLC 1; *Kiani v Cooper* [2010] 2 BCLC 427; *Iesini v Westrip Holdings Ltd* [2011] 1 BCLC 498; *Stainer v Lee* [2011] 1 BCLC 537; *Kleanthous v Paphitis* [2011] EWHC 2287 (Ch); and Ch 22 below.
[77] [2001] 1 BCLC 372, CA.
[78] *Residues Treatment & Trading Co Ltd v Southern Resources Ltd* (1988) 14 ACLR 375 at 377–8, per White J; approved in RAC *Motoring Services Ltd* [2000] 1 BCLC 307 at 326–7.
[79] *Gething v Kilner* [1972] 1 WLR 337; *John Crowther Group plc v Carpets International plc* [1990] BCLC 460; cf. *Goldex Mines Ltd v Revill* (1974) 54 DLR (3rd edn) 672.
[80] *Prudential Assurance Co Ltd v Newman Industries Ltd (No 2)* [1981] Ch 257, per Vinelott J.
[81] *Rackham v Peek Foods Ltd* [1990] BCLC 895.

more than a particular application, to directors who assume responsibility for giving advice to shareholders, of the general duty to act honestly and with due care'.[82] However, in *Re a Company*[83] Hoffmann J was prepared to hold that, although directors were not obliged to give shareholders advice on whether to accept or reject a takeover offer, if such advice were given it should not only be accurate but 'given with a view to enabling the shareholders to sell, if they so wish at the best price and not in order to persuade the shareholders to accept or reject a bid which the directors, for their own reasons, wished to have accepted or rejected'.[84] This language echoes that used in the case law relating to the common law duty to promote the success of the company.

12.51　It has also been held that where directors have decided that it is in the interests of a company that it should be taken over, and where there are two or more bidders, it is the duty of the director to obtain the best price available.[85]

(7) Practical effect on boardroom practice

12.52　There has been some debate as to the extent to which s 172 will alter practice in the boardroom, in particular, with regard to the documentation of board decisions.[86] Certainly in some cases it may be necessary for the board to review their decision-making processes to ensure that proper attention is given to each of the factors set out in s 172(1) and that such considerations are properly documented. However, in most cases this will not be necessary. Also, the board should not concentrate on the duty under s 172 and the factors listed in s 172(1) to the extent of failing to have regard to the other general duties.[87]

12.53　The 2006 Act places no positive obligation on the board to evidence the thought processes that influence their thinking. Indeed, Margaret Hodge, the Minister for Trade and Industry, emphasized during the passage of the bill through Parliament that 'the clause does not impose a requirement on directors to keep records ... in any circumstances in which they would not have to do so now'.[88] Likewise, the Attorney General, Lord Goldsmith, said in the Lords:

> There is nothing in this Bill that says there is a need for a paper trail ... I do not agree that the effect of passing this Bill will be that directors will be subject to a breach if they cannot demonstrate that they have considered every element. It will be for the person who is asserting breach of duty to make that case good ...[89]

---

[82] [1981] Ch 257 at 302. Directors who fail to give factually accurate advice or who give advice otherwise than in the interests of the shareholders may also, in appropriate circumstances, expose themselves to a petition on grounds of unfairly prejudicial treatment: *Re a Company* [1986] BCLC 382.

[83] [1986] BCLC 382.

[84] See also rule 23 of the City Code on Take-overs and Mergers which states that:
Shareholders must be given sufficient information and advice to enable them to reach a properly informed decision as to the merits or demerits of an offer. Such information must be available to shareholders early enough to enable them to make a decision in good time. No relevant information should be withheld from them. The obligation of the offeror in these respects towards the shareholders of the offeree company is no less than an offeror's obligation towards its own shareholders.

[85] See eg *Heron International Ltd v Lord Grade* [1983] BCLC 244, 265, CA.

[86] See in particular The Association for the General Counsel and Company Secretaries of FTSE100 Companies' ('GC100') guidance on the Companies Act 2006 (Directors' Duties) dated 7 February 2007.

[87] In *Eclairs Group Ltd v JKX Oil & Gas plc* [2015] Bus LR 1395, SC, at para 43 (where the directors were in breach of the proper purpose duty under s 171(b) and the board minute referred to s 172, but not s 171(b): [2014] 1 BCLC 202 at para 80).

[88] Hansard, HC Committee, col 592 (11 July 2006).

[89] Hansard, HL, col 841 (9 May 2006).

A pragmatic and proportionate approach should be taken. In some cases, particularly in   **12.54**
relation to a very significant decision being taken by the board, it may be appropriate for
board minutes to state that each of the factors set out in s 172(1) have been considered. In
situations where litigation is possible or likely such an approach may even help to protect
directors from criticism. However, in most other cases it will not be necessary to take such
an approach. In particular, where one particular factor has been significant in causing the
board to reach a decision it may be sufficient simply to note this. Each case will, however,
depend upon its facts. GC100[90] has issued best practice guidelines for companies expressing
concern that the 2006 Act potentially increases bureaucracy, makes the decision-making
process more cumbersome, and potentially increases the liability of directors. The approach
suggested by GC100 is that:

(1) Companies should ensure that all directors are aware of their duties under the 2006 Act.
(2) Where the nature of the decision being taken by directors is such that it is supported
     by a formal process, that process need only specifically record consideration of those
     duties where the particular circumstances make it particularly necessary or relevant. The
     default position should be not to include these references. In this regard, GC100 empha-
     sizes the importance of the preparation of briefing or background papers (the prepara-
     tion of which can be properly delegated) in relation to important board decisions.
(3) When decisions are taken by directors in circumstances other than at a formal board
     meeting, it should be for the company concerned to decide, in its particular circum-
     stances, the best approach to be adopted. Where there is a clear scheme of delegation
     and a decision is to be taken by an individual director, it is unlikely to be appropriate for
     a paper to be prepared as described above. It has to be recognized that many decisions,
     even if taken in accordance with a formal scheme of delegation, have to be taken within
     a timeframe which does not allow for preparation of a formal paper; or for a formal
     minute of the decision. It is important that best practice recognizes this—lack of formal
     process should not lead to any inference that factors have not been properly considered.

It should, however, be emphasized that the duty imposed by s 172 relates not only to a direc-   **12.55**
tor's activities in the boardroom, but also to all aspects of a director's activities in connection
with the company. Whether a director is assessing a substantial investment opportunity or
dealing with a more routine matter, he is required always to be acting in what he considers
to be in the company's best interests. The point was made succinctly by Stanley Burnton LJ
in *Re Neath Rugby Ltd (No 2), Hawkes v Cuddy*,[91] in the context of a discussion of this duty:

> The fiduciary duties of a director do not begin or end at the door to the (actual or notional)
> boardroom. They apply to him whenever he is acting as an officer of the company or in relation
> to its assets or affairs.

D. Special Purpose Companies

Section 172(2) provides that where or to the extent that the purposes of the company consist   **12.56**
of or include purposes other than the benefit of its members, the duty contained in sub-s
(1) has effect as if the reference to promoting the success of the company for the benefit of its

---

[90] See n 86 above.
[91] [2009] 2 BCLC 427, CA at para 39.

members were to achieving those purposes. This addresses the question of altruistic, or partly altruistic, companies. Where the purpose of the company is something other than the benefit of its members, the directors must act in the way they consider, in good faith, would be most likely to achieve that purpose. It is a matter for the good-faith judgment of the director as to what those purposes are, and, where the company is operated partially for the benefit of its members and partly for other purposes, the extent to which those other purposes apply in place of the benefit of the members. In the case of a company with mixed objects, where there is a conflict between promoting the success of the company for the benefit of its members and the achievement of the other objectives, a balancing exercise will be required.[92]

E. The Duty to Take Account of the Interests of Creditors

12.57 The 2006 Act, s 172(3) provides that the duty to promote the success of the company 'has effect subject to any enactment or rule of law requiring directors, in certain circumstances, to consider or act in the interests of creditors of the company'.

12.58 It might be thought that, of all the situations in which directors and their advisors would want to know as precisely as possible the nature and extent of their duties to the company, where the company is insolvent or at risk of insolvency would be amongst the most significant. At first blush, therefore, it may seem surprising that the 2006 Act does not contain a statutory statement of any such duty.

(1) Consideration by the CLR and government

12.59 The principal reason for the omission appears from the CLR's Final Report. Initially, the inclination of the CLR had been not to include in the statement of general duties reference to an obligation to have regard separately to the interests of creditors where the company was insolvent or threatened with insolvency, since the cases seemed capable of resolution on the basis of other principles and such a statement would cut across the Insolvency Act. Subsequently, they stated that it was generally agreed that the general duties must be subject to the overriding duties of directors towards creditors in an insolvency situation 'but also that it is undesirable to lay down any detailed new rule in this area: the law is developing and there is already a carefully balanced statutory provision, which operates *ex post* in a liquidation, in the Insolvency Act 1986 section 214 (wrongful trading)'.[93]

12.60 In the Final Report the CLR considered that the wrongful trading rule should be included in the statement of general duties.[94] However, on the question whether reference should also be made to a special duty to take into account creditors' interests at an earlier stage when there was a substantial probability of an insolvent liquidation, at which point the directors should carry out a balancing exercise, they were unable to reach agreement.[95] On the one hand, it was said that such a rule would reflect what good directors should do, so that even where insolvency was less than inevitable but the risk substantial, directors should consider the interests of members and creditors together.[96] On the other hand, it was feared that such

---

[92] *Stimpson v Southern Private Landlords Association* [2010] BCC 387 at paras 24–9.
[93] CLR: *Completing the Structure* at para 3.12.
[94] CLR: *Final Report* at para 3.16.
[95] CLR: *Final Report* at para 3.20.
[96] CLR: *Final Report* at para 3.18.

a 'balanced judgment' test would have a 'chilling effect', such that the directors might run down or abandon a going concern at the first hint of insolvency:

> The balanced judgement demanded is a difficult and indeterminate one. Fears of personal liability may lead to excessive caution. Small company directors in particular may feel driven to take expensive professional advice which may well be likely to err on the side of caution, with personal liabilities involved. Liquidation can, where there are means of saving the going concern, be as damaging to creditors as to shareholders. Break-up destroys value and employment. Arguably the first, 'no reasonable prospect', test will, in practice, influence directors to act more cautiously on the approach of insolvency.[97]

In its White Paper *Modernising Company Law*, the government rejected the suggestion that **12.61** any duties in relation to creditors should be included in the statutory statement of general duties. It considered that it would be inappropriate and unhelpful to make reference to a special duty arising where there is no reasonable prospect of avoiding insolvent liquidation, having regard to the provisions of the Insolvency Act.[98] As regards the suggestion that reference should be made to a special duty arising in circumstances where the company was likely to become insolvent and which would require the directors to carry out a balancing exercise, the government stated that:

> Directors would need to take a finely balanced judgement, and fears of personal liability might lead to excessive caution. This would run counter to the 'rescue culture' which the Government is seeking to promote through the Insolvency Act 2000 and the Enterprise Bill now before Parliament.[99]

As it had not then been fully worked out at what point such a duty was triggered, nor how **12.62** the director could be expected to act in a situation where insolvent liquidation was short of inevitable, nor whether in such circumstances the interests of creditors were to be regarded as paramount, trumping all others, it was right that they be left to the courts to develop on a case-by-case basis. Since then some progress has been made on these issues, at least at first instance, but they have yet to be addressed authoritatively at appellate level.

(2) The interests of creditors

For the purposes of the discussion that follows, it is useful to have clearly in mind just what **12.63** the interests of creditors are. They are, quite simply, to be paid, in full, and on time. It follows that their interests will or may be adversely affected if anything occurs that will or may compromise the company's ability to discharge its debts when it is supposed to or, in other words, prejudice the creditors' entitlement and expectation to be paid. Such a statement is not to be interpreted literally, however, for to require directors to take into account the interests of creditors when there is a mere possibility that they will be affected would be likely to act as an unwelcome fetter on enterprise. Business necessarily involves risk. It is suggested, therefore, that what is required is a real risk of prejudice such that the inquiry becomes: whether, having regard to the financial position of the company, there is a real and not remote risk of prejudice to the company's ability to pay its creditors on time if a certain course of action is taken. As will be seen, this reflects the approach largely adopted at first instance by the English courts, taking their lead from recent Australian decisions. Exactly

---

[97] CLR: *Final Report* at para 3.19.
[98] White Paper: *Modernising Company Law* at paras 3.12–3.13.
[99] White Paper: *Modernising Company Law* at para 3.11.

when the risk to creditors' interests becomes sufficient will vary from case to case. The most recent case emphasizes, however, that for the company merely to be at risk of insolvency at some indefinite point in the future will not suffice, at least where proper provision has been made in the company's accounts.[100]

(3) Enactments requiring consideration of interests of creditors

12.64   Turning to the 2006 Act, the reference in s 172(3) to 'any enactment … requiring directors, in certain circumstances, to consider or act in the interests of creditors of the company' must be a reference to the Insolvency Act, the most directly relevant provision of which is that relating to wrongful trading (ss 214 and 246ZB[101]).

12.65   Strictly speaking, ss 214 and 246ZB only apply to fix a director with liability once a company has gone into insolvent administration or insolvent liquidation. Even where the company does go into insolvent administration or insolvent liquidation, it may not be a straightforward matter for the liquidator to satisfy the requirements of s 214 or 246ZB so as to fix the director with liability. Nevertheless, the provisions of those sections, which are to substantially the same effect, will inform the well-advised director how he should act before insolvent administration or insolvent liquidation actually intervenes. This is because the possibility of liability is triggered as soon as the director knows or ought to conclude that there is no reasonable prospect that the company will avoid going into insolvent administration or insolvent liquidation.[102] The facts which a director ought to know or ascertain and the conclusions he ought to reach are to be determined by reference to the matters set out in ss 214(4) and (5) and 246ZB(4) and (5), discussed at Chapter 34, Section C(3) below.

12.66   In the context of the duty to promote the success of the company imposed by the 2006 Act, s 172, therefore, the effect of the proviso in s 172(3) is to render the duty to take every step to minimize the potential loss to the company's creditors paramount, in circumstances where the wrongful trading provisions apply, supplanting the matters listed in s 172(1). In other words, once the position is reached that the company has no reasonable prospect of avoiding insolvent liquidation, the mere fact that the director can show that he acted in a way which he considered, in good faith, would be most likely to promote the success of the company for the benefit of its members as a whole, having regard to the matters referred to in s 172(1), will not enable him to avoid liability for wrongful trading, if he failed to take every step that he ought to have taken to minimize the potential loss to the company's creditors.

12.67   Sections 214 and 246ZB are the only provisions within the Insolvency Act which expressly require directors to consider or act in the interests of creditors in certain circumstances. There are other provisions, however, which have as their clear purpose the protection of creditors' interests, most notably those which permit the court to set aside antecedent transactions in certain circumstances,[103] even though they do not in terms require separate consideration to be given to creditors' interests. The provisions relating to transactions at an undervalue and preferences are contained in the Insolvency Act, ss 238–41, which are discussed in Chapter 34, Sections E(1) and (2) below. The underlying purpose of the undervalue provisions is to prevent the assets of the company, which should properly be made available for

---

[100]   *BTI 2014 LLC v Sequana SA* [2016] EWHC 1686 (Ch).
[101]   Inserted by SBEE Act 2015, s 117(1), (2) with effect from 1 October 2015.
[102]   Insolvency Act, s 214(2)(b); s 246ZB(2)(b).
[103]   Insolvency Act, ss 238–41.

distribution amongst the company's creditors in satisfaction of their debts, being improperly depleted. The evident purpose of the preference provisions is to ensure that, when the company is not in a position to pay all its creditors in full, the position of one or more of them is not improved to the detriment of the others.

Transactions or transfers may be vulnerable to being impugned as transactions at an under-value or preferences if they take place within the relevant time as defined by the Insolvency Act, s 240. Even if the transaction or transfer would otherwise be regarded as taking place within the relevant period of six months or two years (as appropriate) ending with the onset of insolvency (as defined), however, it will still not be regarded as having taken place at a relevant time unless the company is at that time unable to pay its debts within the meaning of the Insolvency Act, s 123, or becomes unable to do so in consequence of the transaction or transfer.[104] Ascertaining whether the company is unable to pay its debts within the meaning of s 123, which includes both a cash-flow test and a balance sheet test for insolvency, will require a fact specific inquiry, which will depend on the circumstances of the case. As a matter of general approach, however, it will be necessary to have regard to the guidance given in three recent cases, which are considered below. **12.68**

In *Re Cheyne Finance plc*,[105] Briggs J considered that it is necessary to have regard to future **12.69** debts for the purposes of the cash-flow or commercial test of insolvency, such that a company may fail the test, even if it is currently able to pay its debts then due, if it is already apparent that it will not be able to pay its debts in the reasonably near future. What the 'reasonably near future' may be will depend on the circumstances of the case. In the context of his review of Australian authorities, based on legislation which does not make provision for a balance sheet test, he contrasted a momentary inability to pay as a result of temporary lack of liquidity soon to be remedied with an endemic shortage of working capital which would lead to inevitable failure, even if it could survive for a period of weeks or months in the meantime. The implication seems to be that the former would not constitute an inability to pay debts for the purposes of the s 123 cash-flow or commercial test whereas the latter would. It will also be important to consider how the company is able to pay its debts as they fall due: if it can do so only by increasing its indebtedness, that will not suffice.[106]

In *Eurosail*,[107] the Supreme Court considered the test for balance sheet insolvency, which is **12.70** satisfied when the company's liabilities, including its contingent and prospective liabilities, exceed its assets. This test is the one to be applied when it is impossible to foresee with any reasonable degree of certainty what lies within the 'reasonably near future', such that the application of the cash-flow test would be merely speculative. It requires a comparison of present assets against future liabilities, discounted for contingencies and deferment. The Supreme Court roundly rejected the inquiry whether the company has reached 'the point of no return' as the applicable test, as the Court of Appeal had suggested.[108] As the Court of Appeal subsequently pointed out in *Re Casa Estates (UK) Ltd*,[109] both the cash-flow and the

---

[104] Insolvency Act, s 240(2).
[105] [2008] 1 BCLC 741, referred to with approval in *BNY Corporate Trustee Services Ltd v Eurosail-UK 2007-3BL plc* [2013] 1 WLR 1408, SC, per Lord Walker at paras 33, 34.
[106] *Re Casa Estates (UK) Ltd* [2014] 2 BCLC 49, CA at para 31, per Lewison LJ.
[107] *BNY Corporate Trustee Services Ltd v Eurosail-UK 2007-3BL plc* [2013] 1 WLR 1408, SC.
[108] *BNY Corporate Trustee Services Ltd v Eurosail-UK 2007-3BL plc* [2013] 1 WLR 1408, SC, per Lord Walker at paras 42, 48.
[109] [2014] 2 BCLC 49, CA at paras 27, 29, per Lewison LJ.

balance sheet tests for insolvency are concerned with what is, in essence, the same question, namely: is the company able to pay its debts, on the balance of the probabilities?

12.71   It follows that, when considering whether the company should enter into a particular transaction or make a particular payment, the starting-point must be that the director must ensure that he has satisfied himself as to the company's financial position. He must then have proper regard for the interests of creditors so as to ensure that such interests are not prejudiced, even if the company is actually solvent immediately before the transaction or payment, if it would in consequence become insolvent in the sense explained in either *Cheyne Finance* or *Eurosail*. When deciding whether the company should enter into a transaction when it is insolvent, or will become insolvent as a result of doing so, therefore, the directors must ensure that the company will receive full value. Alternatively, if the company will not receive full value, or may not do so, the directors must satisfy themselves in good faith that the purpose of entering into the transaction is to enable the company to carry on its business and that there are reasonable grounds for believing that the transaction will benefit the company. In addition, the directors must ensure that the effect of the transaction or payment is not to prefer any of the company's creditors over the others. If the directors do not act in this way, they are at risk of being held in breach of their duty to take account of the interests of the company creditors, at least if the company then goes into administration or liquidation within the relevant period.[110]

12.72   In summary, therefore, it is clear from these provisions of the Insolvency Act that directors (i) must act so as to minimize the potential loss to creditors once it has become clear, or ought to have become clear, that there is no reasonable prospect of the company avoiding insolvent administration or insolvent liquidation; and (ii) must consider or act in the interests of creditors so as to cause the company to avoid entering into a transaction at an undervalue or giving a preference, when the company either is insolvent or will become insolvent in consequence of the transaction or preference, in either sense as explained in *Cheyne Finance* and *Eurosail*. In such circumstances, the duty so to act will displace or, at the very least, take precedence over the duty to promote the interests of the company under the 2006 Act, s 172(1).

12.73   The question arises whether the directors of a company come under a duty to consider or act in the interests of creditors at any earlier stage and, if so, in what circumstances that duty arises and how it is to be fulfilled. The Insolvency Act itself provides two instances where such a duty may arise even if, at the time, the company is solvent. The first is fraudulent trading. Sections 213 and 246ZA[111]enable the administrator or liquidator to pursue a claim for fraudulent trading against anyone (including any director) who was knowingly a party to the carrying on of the business of the company with (amongst other things) intent to defraud creditors of the company. The condition for relief under these sections is not insolvency, but the presence of the intent to defraud creditors, which involves knowingly or recklessly exposing them to the risk that their debts will not be paid (see further Chapter 34, Section C(2)). The second is s 423, which applies in the event that the company enters into a transaction at an undervalue for the purpose of putting assets beyond the reach of a person (including a creditor) who is making, or may at some time make, a claim against the company,

---

[110]   *Re Washington Diamond Mining Co* [1893] 3 Ch 95, CA; *West Mercia Safetywear Ltd v Dodd* [1988] BCLC 250, CA; *Re Cityspan Ltd* [2007] 2 BCLC 522.
[111]   Inserted by SBEE Act 2015, s 117(1), (2) with effect from 1 October 2015.

or otherwise prejudicing the interests of such a person in relation to such a claim. In such circumstances, s 423 permits the liquidator or administrator of the company or, in any other case, a victim of the transaction to seek relief. The condition for relief is not insolvency, but the presence of the purpose of defrauding creditors as defined by s 423(3) (see further Chapter 34, Section E(4)).[112]

Apart from these two instances, however, the Insolvency Act is silent, and it is necessary **12.74** to look to the authorities for further guidance. As will appear from the discussion below, while the authorities recognize the existence of a duty to take into account the interests of the company's creditors in circumstances where the company itself is insolvent or at risk of insolvency, what triggers that duty, and its scope when it does arise, is still being worked out.

(4) Rule of law requiring consideration of interests of creditors

In Australia Mason J adverted to the directors' duty to consider the interests of creditors in **12.75** *Walker v Wimborne*,[113] noting that a failure on the part of the directors to take account of the interests of creditors would have adverse consequences for the company as well as for them, but he did not elaborate on this.

In *Lonrho Ltd v Shell Petroleum Ltd*,[114] Lord Diplock observed, in the context of a request to **12.76** allow inspection of the company's documents, that it was the duty of the board to consider whether to accede to the request would be in the best interests of the company, and that these were not exclusively those of the shareholders but might include those of its creditors as well. In *Winkworth v Baron Development Ltd*,[115] Lord Templeman described the position in the following terms:

> But a company owes a duty to its creditors, present and future. The company is not bound to pay off every debt as soon as it is incurred, and the company is not obliged to avoid all ventures which involve an element of risk but the company owes a duty to its creditors to keep its property inviolate and available for the repayment of its debts. The conscience of the company, as well as its management, is confided to its directors. A duty is owed by the directors to the company and to the creditors of the company to ensure that the affairs of the company are properly administered and that its property is not dissipated or exploited for the benefit of the directors themselves to the prejudice of the creditors.[116]

Lord Templeman considered that breach of any such duty would not have mattered if the **12.77** solvency of the company had been maintained.[117] It is nevertheless implicit that he considered such a duty would exist even if the company were solvent. The fact that a duty to consider the interests of creditors exists even if the company is solvent, albeit that the interests of creditors in such circumstances should not count for very much, is supported by the following passage in the judgment of Nourse LJ in *Brady v Brady*:[118]

---

[112] A transfer of property could be set aside under the Fraudulent Conveyances Act 1571 where the debtor was solvent at the time of the transfer but was about to embark on a hazardous venture and wanted to put the property out of the reach of his future creditors: *Crossley v Elworthy* (1871) 12 Eq 158; *Mackay v Douglas* (1872) 14 Eq 106; *Re Butterworth* (1882) 19 Ch D 588, CA.
[113] (1976) 137 CLR 1 at 6–7.
[114] [1980] 1 WLR 627 at 634F, HL.
[115] [1986] 1 WLR 1512, HL.
[116] [1986] 1 WLR 1512 at 1516E–F.
[117] [1986] 1 WLR 1512 at 1516G.
[118] [1988] BCLC 40g–h, CA (reversed on different grounds: [1989] AC 755).

The interests of a company, an artificial person, cannot be distinguished from the interests of the persons who are interested in it. Who are those persons? Where a company is both going and solvent, first and foremost come the shareholders, present and no doubt future as well. How material are the interests of creditors in such a case? Admittedly existing creditors are interested in the assets of the company as the only source for the satisfaction of their debts. But in a case where the assets are enormous and the debts minimal it is reasonable to suppose that the interests of the creditors ought not to count for very much. Conversely, where the company is insolvent, or even doubtfully solvent, the interests of the company are in reality the interests of existing creditors alone.

12.78 The reference to a company being 'doubtfully solvent' echoes language Templeman LJ had used in *Re Horsley & Weight Ltd.*[119] In that case, the directors caused the company to grant a pension to one of its directors, in the absence of any resolution of the board or of the company in general meeting. The Court of Appeal held that it was within the objects of the company to grant such a pension, that the grant could be ratified by the members, and that it had been. The liquidator's misfeasance claim against the recipient director was accordingly dismissed. While agreeing with the result, Templeman LJ considered what the position would have been if the company had been 'doubtfully solvent' at the time the pension was granted, which he described in the following words:

> If the company had been doubtfully solvent at the date of the grant to the knowledge of the directors, the grant would have been both a misfeasance and a fraud on the creditors for which the directors would remain liable.[120]

Even in the absence of fraud, Templeman LJ considered that there could have been gross negligence amounting to misfeasance (although, in the event, there was not):

> If the company could not afford to pay out £10,000 and was doubtfully solvent so that the expenditure threatened the continued existence of the company, the directors ought to have known the facts and ought at any rate to have postponed the grant of the pension until the financial position of the company was assured.[121]

12.79 Two judgments in New Zealand and Australia have developed recognition in England of a rule of law requiring directors to take account of the interests of creditors when a company is insolvent or near insolvency. Cooke J adopted similar language to Templeman LJ in *Nicholson v Permakraft (NZ) Ltd,*[122] where he said that:

> On the facts of particular cases this may require the directors to consider inter alia the interests of creditors. For instance creditors are entitled to consideration, in my opinion, if the company is insolvent, or near-insolvent, or of doubtful solvency, or if a contemplated payment or other course of action would jeopardise its solvency.[123]

12.80 In Australia in *Kinsela v Russell Kinsela Pty Ltd,*[124] Street CJ adverted to the same principle, summarizing the position in two passages in his judgment, which have had a marked influence on the development of the duty in this country:

---

[119] [1982] Ch 442, CA.
[120] [1982] Ch 442 at 455C–D.
[121] [1982] 1 Ch 442 at 455E.
[122] [1985] 1 NZLR 242.
[123] [1985] 1 NZLR 242 at 249.
[124] (1986) 4 NSWLR 722 at 730, 733. See also *Australasia Annuities Pty Ltd v Rowley Super Fund Pty Ltd* (2015) 318 ALR 302.

In a solvent company the proprietary interests of the shareholders entitle them as a general body to be regarded as the company when questions of the duty of directors arise. If, as a general body, they authorise or ratify a particular action of the directors, there can be no challenge to the validity of what the directors have done. But where a company is insolvent the interests of the creditors intrude. They become prospectively entitled, through the mechanism of liquidation, to displace the power of the shareholders and the directors to deal with the company's assets. It is in a practical sense their assets and not the shareholders' assets that, through the medium of the company, are under the management of the directors pending either liquidation, return to solvency, or the imposition of some alternative administration ...

...

I hesitate to attempt to formulate a general test of the degree of financial instability which would impose upon directors an obligation to consider the interests of creditors. For present purposes, it is not necessary to draw upon *Nicholson v Permakraft* as authority for any more than the proposition that the duty arises when a company is insolvent inasmuch as it is the creditors' money which is at risk, in contrast to the shareholders' proprietary interests. It needs to be borne in mind that to some extent the degree of financial instability and the degree of risk to the creditors are inter-related. Courts have traditionally and properly been cautious indeed in entering boardrooms and pronouncing upon the commercial justification of particular executive decisions. Wholly differing value considerations might enter into an adjudication upon the justification for a particular decision by a speculative mining company of doubtful stability on the one hand, and, on the other hand, by a company engaged in a more conservative business in a state of comparable financial instability. Moreover, the plainer it is that it is the creditors' money that is at risk, the lower may be the risk to which the directors, regardless of the unanimous support of all the shareholders, can justifiably expose the company.

12.81 In *West Mercia Safetywear v Dodd* the Court of Appeal cited with approval the first of these passages from *Kinsela*.[125] In *West Mercia*, which was a pre-Insolvency Act case, the director had caused the company to make a payment to its parent, the effect of which (while reducing the debt owed by the company to the parent) was to reduce the parent's overdraft, which the director had guaranteed. The Court of Appeal concluded that the transfer constituted a fraudulent preference (under the pre-1986 legislation) and that the director was liable for misfeasance, on the basis of its earlier decision in *Re Washington Diamond Mining Co*.[126]

12.82 Pausing in the review of the jurisprudence at this stage, it is to be noted that the duty to take account of the interests of creditors gives rise to three fundamental questions, namely (i) when the duty arises and whether it is triggered at a point short of inevitable insolvency; (ii) what behaviour on the part of the director will constitute a breach of the duty and what will not; and (iii) whether, when the duty arises, the interests of creditors are to be considered to the exclusion of other interests, or whether a balance is to be drawn. It is useful to bear these issues in mind when considering those cases which have followed *West Mercia*.[127]

---

[125] [1988] BCLC 250 at 252h–253b, CA, per Dillon LJ. See also *Bowthorpe Holdings v Hills* [2003] 1 BCLC 220 at paras 48–52. This passage in Dillon LJ's judgment, as well as the first passage in *Kinsela* set out in para 12.80 above, were cited with approval by Lords Toulson and Hodge in *Bilta (UK) Ltd v Nazir (No 2)* [2016] AC 1, at paras 123, 124.

[126] [1893] 3 Ch 95, CA.

[127] *Facia Footwear v Hinchcliffe* [1998] 1 BCLC 218; *Knight v Frost* [1999] 1 BCLC 364; *Official Receiver v Stern* [2002] 1 BCLC 119, CA at para [32]; *Bowthorpe Holdings* [2003] 1 BCLC 226 at paras 48–52; *Colin Gwyer & Associates Ltd v London Wharf (Limehouse) Ltd* [2003] 2 BCLC 153 at para 74; *Re Arena Corporation* [2004] BPIR 475 at para 118; *Ultraframe (UK) Ltd v Fielding* [2005] EWHC 1638 (Ch) at para 1304; *Re MDA Investment Management Ltd* [2004] 1 BCLC 217 at paras 69, 70, 75; *Re Cityspan Ltd* [2007] 2 BCLC 522 at

(5) When the duty to consider the interests of creditors arises

12.83   As to the first of these questions, the principles expressed in *Walker v Wimborne, Nicholson v Permakraft (NZ) Ltd, Kinsela v Russell Kinsela Pty Ltd*, and *West Mercia Safetywear v Dodd*, and set out above, were considered sufficient to justify the submission in *Facia Footwear v Hinchcliffe*[128] that the directors owed a duty to take into account the interests of creditors in circumstances where the company, and the group of which it was a member, were in a 'very dangerous' or 'parlous' financial position such that the future of the group probably depended on satisfactory refinancing arrangements becoming available.

12.84   While later cases have repeated the formulation adopted in *Facia Footwear v Hinchcliffe*, however, it is fair to say that they provide only limited guidance on the all-important question when the duty to take account of the interests of creditors is triggered, short of the company's actual insolvency (in the sense of being unable to pay its debts on a cash-flow or balance sheet basis). While it was accepted in *Re MDA Investment Management Ltd*[129] that the duty arose when the company was in a 'dangerous' or 'precarious' financial position, the court also found that the company in that case was insolvent anyway (albeit in the context of the transaction at an undervalue claim, which failed for other reasons).[130] The company was also insolvent in *West Mercia Safetywear v Dodd*,[131] *Official Receiver v Stern*,[132] *Colin Gwyer & Associates Ltd v London Wharf (Limehouse) Ltd*,[133] *Re Cityspan Ltd*,[134] *GHLM Trading Ltd v Maroo*,[135] and *Bilta (UK) Ltd v Nazir (No 2)*.[136]

12.85   In any event, the words 'dangerous' and 'precarious' or even 'near-insolvent' or 'of doubtful solvency', when applied to the financial position of a company, are imprecise terms. What will constitute a 'dangerous' or 'precarious' financial position sufficient to trigger the duty is likely to differ from case to case. The CLR sought to meet the problem by suggesting that the duty arose in circumstances where the directors 'know or ought to recognise that there is *a substantial probability* of an insolvent liquidation'.[137] The CLR's suggested clause, however, put the position more generally, such that the duty would arise '[a]t a time when the director of a company knows, or would know but for a failure of his duty to exercise due care and skill, that it is more likely than not that the company will at some point be unable to pay its

---

para 31; *Singla v Hedman* [2010] 2 BCLC 61 at para 33; *Re Capitol Films Ltd; Rubin v Cobalt* [2011] 2 BCLC 359 at paras 49–50; *Roberts v Frohlich* [2011] 2 BCLC 625 at para 85; *GHLM Trading Ltd v Maroo* [2012] 2 BCLC 369; *Bilta (UK) Ltd v Nazir (No 2)* [2016] AC 1; *Re HLC Environmental Projects Ltd* [2014] BCC 337; *Vivendi SA v Richards* [2013] BCC 771; *Goldtrail Travel Ltd v Aydin* [2015] 1 BCLC 89 (not affected by the outcome of the appeal, [2016] 1 BCLC 635); *Caliendo v Mishcon de Reya* [2016] EWHC 150 (Ch); and *BTI 2014 LLC v Sequana SA* [2016] EWHC 1686 (Ch).

[128]   [1998] 1 BCLC 218 at 228b.
[129]   [2004] 1 BCLC 217 at para 75.
[130]   [2004] 1 BCLC 217 at paras 119–21, 122–4.
[131]   [1988] BCLC 250.
[132]   [2002] 1 BCLC 119.
[133]   [2003] 2 BCLC 153 at para 80.
[134]   [2007] 2 BCLC 522 at para 31.
[135]   [2012] 2 BCLC 369, in which Newey J concluded (at para 173) that the company was insolvent or at any rate 'of doubtful solvency or on the verge of insolvency'. On the evidence, it was admitted there was insufficient cashflow to pay salaries and expenses.
[136]   [2016] AC 1, per Lords Toulson and Hodge at paras 115, 116. The case concerned a 'missing trader' fraud. As the company was at all material times insolvent the directors were at all times required to consider or act in the interests of creditors.
[137]   CLR: *Final Report*, para 3.17.

debts as they fall due'. As already explained,[138] the government rejected the suggestion that any such duty should be formulated and included in the statutory statement.

Cases where a breach of duty claim is made against directors solely on the basis of their **12.86** actions or inaction when the company was in the danger zone (rather than, for example, wrongful trading or for breach of duty in circumstances giving rise to undervalue or preference claims) may be expected to be few and far between. Nevertheless, recent authorities suggest that, for the purposes of determining whether the duty has arisen, the court will focus on the degree of risk of insolvency and of prejudice to creditors in consequence: the duty will arise when there is a real and not remote risk that the creditors' expectations and entitlement to be paid will be prejudiced if the directors cause the company to make a certain decision or embark on a certain course of action.

In his monumental judgment in *The Bell Group Ltd v Westpac Banking Corporation*,[139] Owen **12.87** J cited the passages from Street CJ's judgment in *Russell Kinsela* set out above[140] and stated:

> [I]n my view Street CJ was right when he pointed out that the degree of financial instability and the degree of risk to the creditors are interrelated. This ties back into the ability of the company to continue its existence. The same can be said for the statement that the plainer it is that the creditors' money ... is at risk, the lower may be the level of risk to which the directors can justifiably expose the company.[141]

Owen J concluded that on the facts of the case before him the company was actually insolvent at the relevant time so that the point at which the duty arose did not strictly fall to be determined. Nevertheless, he stated (*obiter*) the basic principle in the following terms:

> [A] decision that has adverse consequences for creditors might also be adverse to the interests of the company. Adversity might strike short of actual insolvency and might propel the company towards an insolvency administration. And that is where the interests of creditors come to the fore.[142]

Owen J also adopted the following statement of principle by Giles JA (with whom Ipp and **12.88** Basten JJA agreed) in *Kalls Enterprises Pty Ltd v Baloglow*:[143]

> It is sufficient for present purposes that, in accord with the reason for regard to the interests of creditors, the company need not be insolvent at the time and the directors must consider their interests if there is a real and not remote risk that they will be prejudiced by the dealing in question.[144]

The question of whether there is a 'real and not remote risk of prejudice to creditors' is a helpful objective test to determine whether (i) the directors are required to consider the interests of creditors in relation to a proposed transaction and (ii) the directors may be protected by prior authorization or subsequent ratification by the shareholders. As such, it is a test

---

[138] Para 12.61 above.
[139] [2008] WASC 239.
[140] Para 12.80 above.
[141] [2008] WASC 239 at para 4419.
[142] [2008] WASC 239 at para 4445. On appeal there was no challenge to the finding of insolvency: [2012] WASCA 257, per Lee AJA at para 917.
[143] [2007] NSWCA 191, (2007) 25 ACLC 1094.
[144] [2007] NSWCA 191 at para 162. On appeal in *Bell*, Drummond AJA endorsed Owen J's adoption of this statement of principle: [2012] WASCA 257, at paras 2039–40.

which, as appears below, has now been adopted at first instance by the courts of England and Wales, albeit with some qualification.

12.89 Although Giles JA's test was not directly referred to, the 'real and not remote risk of prejudice to creditors' approach was adopted in *Roberts v Frohlich*.[145] In that case, in considering whether the directors of a property development company acted in breach of duty in commencing and continuing the development, Norris J asked the question whether the development was speculative in the sense of being, in all the circumstances, too risky for a competent board to embark upon it.[146] He concluded that at the initial stage it was not, but once it became clear that further funding was required but was unavailable, it was speculative for the directors to carry on, with the result that they acted in breach of duty: no reasonably competent director in their position would have continued with the project because 'he would have appreciated that the time horizon for the company was extremely short'.[147] He also concluded, for good measure, that the directors were liable for wrongful trading from the same date.

12.90 In *Re HLC Environmental Projects Ltd*,[148] John Randall QC (sitting as a deputy judge of the High Court) referred to the various different formulations, both Australian (including that of Giles JA) and English, and could detect no difference in principle. He went on:

> The underlying principle is that the directors are not free to take action which puts at real (as opposed to remote) risk the creditors' prospects of being paid, without first having considered their interests rather than those of the company and its shareholders. If, on the other hand, the company is going to be able to pay its creditors in any event, *ex hypothesi* there need be no such constraint on the directors.[149]

12.91 In *Vivendi SA v Richards*,[150] decided just a few weeks later, Newey J also referred with approval to Giles JA's statement of principle in *Kalls Enterprises*, as well as that of Owen J in *Bell*. Rose J adopted the same approach in *Goldtrail Travel Ltd v Aydin*,[151] albeit without express reference to those paragraphs of Newey J's judgment in which he cited the recent Australian cases; so too did Arnold J in *Caliendo v Mishcon de Reya*.[152]

12.91A Rose J considered the position again in *BTO 2014 LLC v Sequana SA*.[153] In that case, the company's balance sheet showed no net deficiency and 'there were no unpaid creditors

---

[145] [2011] 2 BCLC 625.
[146] [2011] 2 BCLC 625 at para 105.
[147] [2011] 2 BCLC 625, at para 102.
[148] [2014] BCC 337.
[149] [2014] BCC 337, at para 89. In that case, the director caused certain payments to be made without giving any consideration to the interests of creditors when he should have done, as the company was insolvent, having net liabilities, no live projects or revenue stream, and no realistic prospect of gaining any. As no intelligent and honest man in the director's position would have concluded that making the payments was for the benefit of the creditors (adopting the approach in *Charterbridge Corp Ltd v Lloyds Bank Ltd* [1970] Ch 62, at 74E–F), the director was found to have acted in breach of duty.
[150] [2013] BCC 771, at paras 148–50. The company was found to be actually insolvent when the directors caused certain payments to be made, primarily for their own benefit. Newey J considered that it did not matter that the directors were not aware of the company's insolvency (at least initially), as they clearly appreciated its vulnerability, having large rental and other obligations and no income, and no potential new source of future income.
[151] [2015] 1 BCLC 89 (not affected by the outcome of the appeal, [2016] 1 BCLC 635).
[152] [2016] EWHC 150 (Ch), at para 688.
[153] [2016] EWHC 1686 (Ch), at paras 456–84.

knocking at [the] door'. The directors had made an estimated provision in the company's accounts in relation to a long-term liability under an indemnity in respect of environmental clean-up costs in the USA. The directors had then reduced the capital of the company and made a distribution to its shareholder. The judge rejected the argument that the distribution was unlawful. She also rejected an alternative argument that, when making the distribution, the directors acted in breach of their duty to take account of the interests of creditors. Having reviewed the authorities referred to above, she agreed that all the various formulations to be found in them were simply different expressions of the same test. She did not accept, however, that they establish that the duty arises whenever a company is 'at risk' of becoming insolvent at some indefinite point in the future. She saw no justification for subjecting directors to such a duty where they made proper provision for a liability in the company's accounts, even if there was a real risk that the provision would turn out to be inadequate. In the particular circumstances of that case, therefore, the duty to take account of creditors' interests was found not to have arisen.[154]

(6) Conduct required of the directors when the duty arises

As the decision in *Facia Footwear v Hinchcliffe*[155] demonstrates, the manner in which the **12.92** directors must act in the interests of creditors and whether the directors have acted in such a way as to be in breach of their duty by causing the company to continue trading, must inevitably depend upon the facts of the particular case. *Facia Footwear v Hinchcliffe* concerned a claim for breach of duty against directors for making payments to or for the benefit of group companies at a time when it was claimed there was no realistic expectation that the group companies would be able to repay. One of the directors' defences was that at the time of the payments they considered that the group had a reasonable chance of weathering its financial difficulties.[156] In relation to that defence Sir Richard Scott V-C did not consider that the answer would always be clear cut:

> It is clear enough that in continuing to trade … [the directors] were taking a risk. But the boundary between an acceptable risk that an entrepreneur may properly take and an unacceptable risk the taking of which constitutes misfeasance is not always, perhaps not usually, clear cut … I accept that, given the parlous financial state of the group, the directors had to have regard to the interests of creditors. But the creditors of the group, and of [the company] in particular, would clearly have been best served by a refinancing that could support a continuation of profitable trading. The cessation of trading followed by the disposal of the assets of the companies on a forced sale basis would, it was always realised, lead to heavy losses for the creditors. The creditors' only chance of being paid in full lay in a continuation of trading. A continuation of trading might mean a reduction in the dividend eventually payable to creditors but it represented the creditors' only chance of full payment. It is, therefore, not in the least obvious that in continuing to trade … the directors were ignoring the interests of creditors.[157]

In *Facia Footwear v Hinchcliffe* itself, which was an application for summary judgment, the court concluded that a trial was necessary in order to determine this issue, so that the application must fail.

---

[154] [2016] EWHC 1686 (Ch), at paras 456–84.
[155] [1998] 1 BCLC 218.
[156] [1998] 1 BCLC 218 at 225c–226a.
[157] [1998] 1 BCLC 218 at 228d–h.

12.93   Subsequent cases afford at least some guidance as to the type of conduct which has been found to constitute, or which might arguably constitute, a breach of duty on the part of the director. Examples from the cases of conduct amounting to a breach of duty include causing the company to make payments to the directors in excess of those properly payable,[158] or by way of preference,[159] or for the primary purpose of extracting the company's remaining cash before it failed or by making unlawful distributions;[160] causing the company to make payments to third parties which it was not contractually obliged to make in order to facilitate the payment by them to the director personally of sums they were contractually obliged to pay,[161] or to discharge the debts of others;[162] causing the company to make payments to assist a connected company, directly or as guarantor of the company's indebtedness;[163] the sale to a director of the company's shares in another company for substantially less than their market value;[164] causing the company to compromise on terms that meant the company would release valuable contractual rights against one of its members for no consideration;[165] diverting consideration received from the sale of the company's business away from the company and causing the company to make payments to associated persons, which constituted preferences;[166] causing the company to continue with the development of property after it has become clear the required funding is not available in circumstances which also render the directors liable for wrongful trading;[167] and pursuing uncertain litigation in the name of the company when that company has no assets and would be unable to discharge liabilities to creditors thereby created.[168]

12.94   *Knight v Frost*[169] provides an example of conduct which was found not to constitute a breach of the duty. In that case, in reliance on *West Mercia Safetywear v Dodd*[170] and *Re Washington Diamond Milling Co*,[171] it was alleged that the de facto director had acted in breach of duty by causing payments to be made by the insolvent company to one of its creditors, which payments were said to involve an unlawful or improper preference of that creditor as against the plaintiff, another creditor. Although the court accepted that the company was insolvent

---

[158] *Official Receiver v Stern* [2002] 1 BCLC 119 at paras 51–4.

[159] *Re Cityspan Ltd* [2007] 2 BCLC 522. In *E-Clear (UK) plc v Elia* [2013] 2 BCLC 455, the CA decided that the question whether payments made by the company to the director in discharge of pre-existing debt could amount to a breach of fiduciary duty, even if not a preference, was not suitable for summary determination in circumstances where the company's insolvency was not (as the judge had held) beyond reasonable doubt, and should be investigated at trial. Patten LJ observed that, absent actual or imminent insolvency, the payments would be unobjectionable: para 24.

[160] *Vivendi SA v Richards* [2013] BCC 771. See also *BAT Industries plc v Windward Prospects Ltd* [2013] EWHC 3612 (Comm) in which the court appointed a receiver to pursue a claim for breach of duty for making unlawful distributions.

[161] *Goldtrail Travel Ltd v Aydin* [2015] 1 BCLC 89 (not affected by the outcome of the appeal: [2016] EWCA Civ 371).

[162] *Re HLC Environmental Projects Ltd* [2014] BCC 337.

[163] *Re HLC Environmental Projects Ltd* [2014] BCC 337.

[164] *Bowthorpe Holdings Ltd v Hills* [2003] 1 BCLC 220.

[165] *Colin Gwyer & Associates Ltd v London Wharf (Limehouse) Ltd* [2003] 2 BCLC 153.

[166] *Re MDA Investment Management Ltd* [2004] 1 BCLC 217.

[167] *Roberts v Frohlich* [2011] 2 BCLC 625.

[168] *Eastford Ltd v Gillespie* [2012] BCC 303 (Court of Session, Inner House).

[169] [1999] 1 BCLC 364. In *Re Pro4sport Ltd* [2016] 1 BCLC 207, the director had caused the company to transfer its assets on the eve of its liquidation for a deferred consideration and without (as a director of the transferee) providing a guarantee. As he had done so acting on advice and the liquidator had subsequently adopted the contract, however, he was found not to have acted in breach of duty.

[170] [1988] BCLC 250.

[171] [1893] 3 Ch 95.

at the time of the payment, it did not accept that the payments constituted preferences made in breach of duty because they had not been made within the relevant statutory period prior to the commencement of a winding up.[172] It is to be noted, however, that the contrary view was expressed in *GHLM Trading Ltd v Maroo*, in which Newey J considered that the fact the conditions laid down by the preference provisions were not all met should not, of itself, preclude a finding of breach of duty, although it may have a bearing on what, if any, remedy is available for that breach.[173]

Although the authorities referred to above give some guidance on the behaviour to be **12.95** expected of directors, the question whether particular conduct will or will not attract liability will depend on the circumstances of each case. Where the conduct falls foul of well-known prohibitions on preferences and transactions at an undervalue the position is likely to be straightforward. Where the conduct complained of is more general, however, such as causing the company to continue to trade, the position is likely to be much less clear cut. Even in the wrongful trading context, it is accepted that directors may, depending on the circumstances, properly decide that, although insolvent, the company can continue to trade out of its difficulties, that some loss-making trading may be acceptable in anticipation of future profitability,[174] and that there is scope for error without liability.[175]

Any attempt at an exhaustive guide to the manner in which directors may be expected **12.96** to act would be futile given that what needs to be done will inevitably depend on the particular circumstances. Generally, however, directors may be expected to take such steps as are necessary to ensure that all information relating to the company is adequate and up to date so that they are each properly informed as to its financial position. They should convene regular meetings to consider the company's financial position and ensure that such meetings are carefully minuted, providing fully reasoned explanations for decisions made. If the company has a liquidity problem, they should consider whether it is temporary and soon to be remedied (for example, by the sale of an asset). If the company is insolvent, they should ask whether it can properly continue to trade on the basis that there is a realistic prospect of recovery. Even if the company is able to pay its debts as they fall due in the short term, they should consider whether it has access to adequate working capital to enable it to do so in the longer term, taking a realistic view of its contingent and prospective liabilities. If they cannot answer any of these questions affirmatively, they must take every step available to them to minimize any loss to creditors, which is likely in most cases to involve embarking on some form of restructuring

---

[172] [1999] 1 BCLC 364 at 381f–382e. Park J took the same view in *Re Continental Assurance Co of London plc (No 4)* [2007] 2 BCLC 287, at para 420.

[173] *GHLM Trading Ltd v Maroo* [2012] 2 BCLC 369, at paras 168–9. As to the appropriate remedy in that case, Newey J concluded that, where a director has caused his company to enter into a contract in pursuit of his own interests, and not in the interests of the company, its members or (where appropriate) its creditors as a class, and the other contracting party had notice of that fact, the contract is void rather than voidable: para 171. In the absence of loss to the company or profit to the director, he declared the company's contract of sale of stock to a third party, which had such notice, to be void, with the result that the third party was liable to account for the sums it had itself received when it sold the stock on: para 179.

[174] *Re CS Holdings Ltd* [1997] 1 WLR 407, 414 per Chadwick J; *Re Continental Assurance* [2001] BPIR 733 at paras 106–8 per Park J; *Hawkeshill Publishing Co Ltd* [2007] BCC 937 at para 28 per Lewison LJ; and *Re Ralls Builders Ltd* [2016] Bus LR 555 at paras 168–79 per Snowden J.

[175] *Robin Hood Centre plc, Brooks v Armstrong* [2015] BCC 661.

or other insolvency process. At the very least, directors should consider whether it is appropriate for the company to continue trading. They should also consider whether to seek professional advice, both legal and financial, which they must then consider and apply exercising their own judgment: it will not avail them to seek such advice if they then follow it blindly.[176]

12.97 Where the directors conclude that the company has temporary financial difficulties but that creditors' interests are nevertheless at risk, they should keep the position under review. Before committing the company to a particular transaction, they should satisfy themselves that it is appropriate to enter into it having regard to the effect it will have on the company's solvency, the value to be derived from it, the benefits that will accrue to the company's business, and any potential prejudice to creditors' interests generally that may ensue. Generally in such cases, it will be important to be able to demonstrate proper consideration of professional advice or other evidence as to valuation. Similarly, before causing the company to make payments to certain creditors, the directors should consider whether they are necessary in the interests of the company having regard to the interests of creditors generally. Where it is necessary to give guidance or instructions to others for payments to be made, the directors should ensure that such instructions are clearly expressed and properly documented; that they are actually communicated to, and properly understood by, those who need to implement them; and that implementation is adequately supervised so as to ensure that the instructions are properly carried out.

(7) Weight to be given to creditors' interests

12.98 The third issue concerns the degree to which directors must consider or act in the interests of creditors, in circumstances where the company is in a dangerous or precarious financial position short of actual insolvency. The question arises whether the interests of creditors are to be considered to the exclusion of all other matters, or whether a balancing exercise is to be undertaken such that creditors' interests form just one of a number of matters to which the directors ought to have regard.

12.99 Some members of the CLR advocated that directors should perform a balancing exercise, such that 'the greater the risk of insolvency in terms of probability and extent, the more directors should take account of creditors' needs and the less those of members'.[177] As explained above, however, this view was not universally held and was not adopted in the legislation. Nevertheless, such an approach is supported by the decision of the Supreme Court of Western Australia in *The Bell Group Ltd v Westpac Banking Corporation*,[178] in which Owen J concluded that the interests of creditors were not necessarily determinative or paramount although, depending on the circumstances, they may be.[179] He summarized the position in the following terms:

> I have previously mentioned that circumstances will wax and wane. It may be, therefore, that in particular circumstances the only reasonable conclusion to draw, once the interests of creditors have been taken into account, is that a contemplated transaction will be so prejudicial

---

[176] *Re Ralls Builders Ltd* [2016] EWHC 243 (Ch) at paras 176–9 per Snowden J.
[177] CLR: *Final Report*, para 3.17.
[178] [2008] WASC 239.
[179] [2008] WASC 239 at paras 4436–40.

to creditors that it could not be in the interests of the company as a whole. But that will be because of the particular circumstances and not because a general principle has mandated that the treatment of the creditors' interests is paramount.[180]

Conversely, the view so far taken by the English courts, at least at first instance, is that the **12.100** interests of creditors are paramount when they fall to be taken into account. Nourse LJ provided some guidance (albeit strictly *obiter*) in *Brady v Brady*, when he said that 'where the company is insolvent, or even doubtfully solvent, the interests of the company are in reality the interests of existing creditors alone'.[181] In reliance on this dictum, in *Colin Gwyer & Associates Ltd v London Wharf (Limehouse) Ltd* Leslie Kosmin QC (sitting as a deputy judge of the High Court) stated the position as follows:

> When a company is insolvent or of doubtful solvency or on the verge of insolvency and it is the creditors' money which is at risk the directors, when carrying out their duty to the company, must consider the interests of the creditors as paramount and take those into account when exercising their discretion.[182]

That passage in *Colin Gwyer* has since been cited with apparent approval on a number of occasions, including in *GHLM Trading Ltd v Maroo*,[183] *Roberts v Frohlich*,[184] *Re HLC Environmental Projects Ltd*,[185] *Vivendi SA v Richards*,[186] and *Goldtrail Travel Ltd v Aydin*.[187] It is to be noted, however, that in all these cases, including *Colin Gwyer* itself, the company was found to be actually insolvent. Strictly, therefore, these statements must be taken as *obiter* in so far as they suggest that creditors' interests are paramount even when the company is not yet insolvent although it is likely to become so.

(8) Authorization and ratification

Issues concerning the duty to consider the interests of the company's creditors are often **12.101** coupled with issues as to whether the relevant transaction or conduct has been, or is capable of being, consented to, approved, authorized, or ratified by the members of the company. Questions of consent, approval, and authorization are considered in Chapter 10, Section D and ratification is considered in Chapter 20, Section D.

---

[180] [2008] WASC 239 at para 4440. On appeal, Drummond AJA endorsed Owen J's approach but went on to state that he would prefer to say that if there is a real risk that creditors of a company in an insolvency context would suffer significant prejudice if the directors undertook a certain course of action, that is sufficient to show that the contemplated course of action is not in the interests of the company: [2012] WASCA 257 at para 2046.

[181] [1988] BCLC 40g-h (reversed on appeal on different grounds: [1989] AC 755).

[182] [2003] 2 BCLC 153, at para 74.

[183] [2012] 2 BCLC 369, at para 165.

[184] [2011] 2 BCLC 265 at para 85.

[185] [2014] BCC 337 at para 92.

[186] [2013] BCC 771 at para 149.

[187] [2015] 1 BCLC 89 at para 114 (not affected by the outcome of the appeal, [2016] 1 BCLC 207).

13

DUTY TO EXERCISE INDEPENDENT JUDGMENT

Marcus Haywood

A. Introduction

Section 173 of the Companies Act provides that: **13.01**

(1) A director of a company must exercise independent judgment.
(2) This duty is not infringed by his acting—
   (a) in accordance with an agreement duly entered into by the company that restricts the future exercise of discretion by its directors, or
   (b) in a way authorised by the company's constitution.

The 2006 Act, s 173(1) codifies the established principle of law under which directors must **13.02** exercise their powers independently, without subordinating their powers to the will of others, whether by delegation or otherwise (unless authorized by or under the constitution to do so).

The duty stated in s 173(1) applies to shadow directors to the extent that it is capable of so **13.03** applying (see Chapter 10, Section C above).[1]

A director who, in relation to a particular transaction, wishes to be protected from the risk **13.04** of being in breach of the duty to exercise independent judgment may obtain the consent, approval, or authorization of the members, as recognized by s 180(4)(a) (see Chapter 10, Section D above) or ratification of his conduct under s 239 (see Chapter 20, Section D below).

---

[1] s 170(5), as amended by SBEE Act 2015, s 89(2) as from 26 May 2015.

B. The Duty

13.05   In the conduct of the management of its affairs, a company is entitled to the benefit of collective decision-making by its directors acting as a board, save to the extent that decisions have been duly delegated.[2] Breach of the duty to exercise independent judgment compromises collective decision-making. This duty under s 173(1) may be regarded as supporting the core duty to promote the success of the company, as stated in s 172, which used to be described as the duty to act in good faith in the interests of the company.[3]

13.06   Breach of the duty under s 173(1) invariably arises when a director's relationship with a third party puts him in a position of conflict of interest. It is therefore closely linked with the director's duty under the 2006 Act, s 175(1) to avoid conflicts of interest and the duty under s 177 to declare his interest in proposed transactions or arrangements with the company.[4] For example, where a director makes a prior agreement to vote in a third party's interests on a particular transaction, thereby leaving himself no independent discretion as to how to act, he will be in breach of s 173(1).[5]

13.07   This duty under s 173(1) is also closely connected with the duty in s 174 to exercise reasonable skill, care, and diligence.[6] A director who merely does what he is told or who leaves the decision to others, may find it difficult to show that he acted in the manner required under s 174.

13.08   A recent illustration of the scope of this duty and its interrelationship with the duty to promote the success of the company is *Madoff Securities International Ltd v Raven*.[7] That case involved a claim by the liquidators of an English company, which had been founded by Bernard Madoff, against former directors to recover certain payments which were said to have been improper. All the payments were made at the direction of Mr Madoff, who was a director, chief executive officer, and majority shareholder of the company. Following the exposure of Mr Madoff's notorious Ponzi scheme, the English company went into liquidation. It was accepted that it had its own legitimate business. The judge, Popplewell J, said as follows in relation to the duty to exercise independent judgment:[8]

> It is legitimate, and often necessary, for there to be division and delegation of responsibility for particular aspects of the management of a company. Nevertheless each individual director owes inescapable personal responsibilities. He owes duties to the company to inform himself of the company's affairs and join with his fellow directors in supervising them. It is therefore a breach of duty for a director to allow himself to be dominated, bamboozled or manipulated by a dominant fellow director where such involves a total abrogation of this responsibility... . Similarly it is the duty of each director to form an independent judgment as to whether acceding to a shareholder's request is in the best interests of the company: *Lonrho Ltd v Shell Petroleum* [1980] 1 WLR 627, 634F. The duty to exercise independent judgment is now reflected in s. 173 Companies Act 2006. ...

---

[2]   Model Article (pcls) 7; Model Article (plc) 7.
[3]   Ch 12 above.
[4]   Chs 15 and 17 below.
[5]   *Re Englefield Colliery Co* (1878) 8 Ch D 388.
[6]   Ch 14 below.
[7]   [2013] EWHC 3147 (Comm).
[8]   At paras 191 and 193.

In fulfilling this personal fiduciary responsibility, a director is entitled to rely upon the judgment, information and advice of a fellow director whose integrity skill and competence he has no reason to suspect: see *Dovey v Cory* [1901] AC 477 at 486, 492. Moreover, corporate management often requires the exercise of judgement on which opinions may legitimately differ, and requires some give and take. A board of directors may reach a decision as to the commercial wisdom of a particular transaction by a majority. A minority director is not thereby in breach of his duty, or obliged to resign and to refuse to be party to the implementation of the decision. Part of his duty as a director acting in the interests of the company is to listen to the views of his fellow directors and to take account of them. He may legitimately defer to those views where he is persuaded that his fellow directors' views are advanced in what they perceive to be the best interests of the company, even if he is not himself persuaded. A director is not in breach of his core duty to act in what he considers in good faith to be the interests of a company merely because if left to himself he would do things differently.

Applying those principles to facts, the judge held that none of the defendant directors had acted in breach of their duties. In particular, he emphasized that directors bring different experience and expertise to the joint exercise of corporate management.[9] Whilst each is required to exercise his independent judgment, he may legitimately defer to the views of those with greater experience or expertise than him. Where there is a director who has a record and reputation for outstanding skill and experience in the company's business activity, his fellow directors are entitled to accord a high degree of deference and trust to his views as to what is in the company's best interests. In that regard, on the facts of the case, the judge held that it would have been unfair and unrealistic to expect any of the defendant directors to have done anything other than attach great weight to the views of Mr Madoff in deciding what was in the interests of the company. For those directors to have taken the view that Mr Madoff knew best, was not a dereliction of their duty to exercise independent judgment. It was merely a legitimate recognition of Madoff's then high standing in the financial world. **13.09**

Accordingly, the case draws a line between directors who are manipulated and dominated by others, who would be in breach of their duty to exercise independent judgment through complete abrogation of the duties, and those who act honestly and reasonably in the best interests of a company where there is a dominant director to whom they justifiably defer due to his reputation and (apparent) expertise. It will not, however, always be easy to see where that line lies and careful analysis will be required in each case. These themes are considered further below. **13.10**

(1) Obedience to controllers

A director will fail to exercise independent judgment if he merely does what he is told to do by the majority of the board, or the dominant personality on it, or if he unthinkingly accedes to the demands of those who control the company. As Lord Diplock explained in *Lonrho Ltd v Shell Petroleum Co Ltd*,[10] if a company receives a request to do something from its shareholders, it is the duty of the board to consider whether to accede to the request would be in the best interests of the company. These interests are not exclusively those of its shareholders and may include the interests of creditors. **13.11**

---

[9] At para 220.
[10] [1980] 1 WLR 627, 634, HL.

13.12   *Scottish Co-operative Wholesale Society Ltd v Meyer*[11] is an example of a case where directors who were nominees of the majority shareholder implemented the instructions of the majority shareholder to transfer the company's business to a new department within the parent company, thereby forcing down the value of the company's shares to the prejudice of the minority shareholders. The House of Lords held that the interest of the minority had been oppressed by the majority and they were entitled to relief under what was then the 1948 Act, s 210.[12] In doing so, it was said that the nominee directors were in breach of their duty to the subsidiary through their failure to take any positive steps to protect the subsidiary against the oppressive policy of the holding company.[13] This can be seen as an application of the duty to exercise independent judgment. There was also a conflict between the nominee directors' duty to the holding company and their duty to the subsidiary.[14]

13.13   Similarly a family member, who simply signs what the relative who runs the company asks him or her to sign, abdicates responsibility and breaches the duty to exercise independent judgment.[15]

(2) Group companies

13.14   Similar principles apply where the company is a member of a group. In *Charterbridge Corporation Ltd v Lloyds Bank Ltd* Pennycuick J said that 'each company in the group is a separate legal entity and the directors of a particular company are not entitled to sacrifice the interest of that company'.[16] It follows that the directors of a holding company do not owe any duties to its subsidiary, at least if the subsidiary has different directors;[17] and that a director of a subsidiary owes his duties as such only to the subsidiary and cannot be compelled to exercise his powers in accordance with the holding company's wishes.[18] This is particularly the case where the subsidiary is not wholly owned by the parent. In such a case, where the directors of the subsidiary act in the interest of the parent and wholly without regard for the interests of the minority, issues of unfair prejudice may be relevant.[19] An example of such a case is *Scottish Co-operative Wholesale Society Ltd v Meyer* (the facts of which are set out in paragraph 13.12 above) where Viscount Simonds approved the statement of Lord President Cooper that: '[t]he truth is that, whenever a subsidiary is formed as in this case with an independent minority of shareholders, the parent company must, if it is engaged in the same class

---

[11] [1959] AC 324, HL. See also *Gardner v Parker* [2004] 1 BCLC 417 at paras 18–19, per Blackburne J (affd [2004] 2 BCLC 554, CA).

[12] A more restricted predecessor of 2006 Act, Part 30.

[13] [1959] AC 324, 341, per Viscount Simonds; 347, per Lord Morton; 367, per Lord Denning.

[14] [1959] AC 324, 366, per Lord Denning.

[15] *Bishopsgate Investment Management Ltd v Maxwell (No 2)* [1994] 1 All ER 261, 265, CA (where Hoffmann LJ said that the company was entitled to have two officers decide independently whether it was proper to sign a transfer); *Lexi Holdings plc v Luqman* [2009] 2 BCLC 1, CA (where the inactivity of sisters of the managing director exposed them to personal liability). In Australia the metaphor 'sexually transmitted debt' is used to describe the liability of wives who accept appointment as directors and who unquestioningly sign what their husband asks them to sign: Australian Law Reform Commission Report: *Equality before the Law: Women and Equality* (1994) Rep No 69. For an example of a wife's liability: *Deputy Commissioner of Taxation v Clark* [2003] NSWCA 91.

[16] [1970] Ch 62, 74. See also *Wallersteiner v Moir* [1974] 1 WLR 991, 1013, CA.

[17] *Lindgren v L & P Estates Limited* [1968] Ch 572, 595D–E, 604D–F.

[18] *Pergamon Press Limited v Maxwell* [1970] 1 WLR 1167, 1172; *Lonrho Ltd v Shell Petroleum Co Ltd* [1980] 1 WLR 627, 634, HL.

[19] Ch 23 below.

of business, accept as a result of having formed such a subsidiary an obligation so to conduct what are in a sense its own affairs as to deal fairly with its subsidiary'.[20]

In practice, however, it may be possible for the directors of a subsidiary to take into account **13.15** the interests of the group more than the *Charterbridge* case suggests. Certainly, if the intended measure is likely to promote the success of the company for the benefit of its members as a whole, it is not a breach of duty for the director to take into account the benefit to the group as a whole. Group companies are often dependent on group-based financing which may be routed through a parent company and distributed by it to subsidiaries. In such a case a director of a subisdiary is likely to be able to discharge his duty to act in the interests of each subsidiary if he decides that it should provide securities or guarantees to support the group borrowing.

Moreover, in the case of a solvent company the interests of the subsidiary are likely to include **13.16** the interests of its shareholders generally.[21] In the case of a wholly-owned subsidiary, the interests of the subsidiary will therefore include its holding company. Accordingly, in *The Bell Group Ltd v Westpac Banking Corporation*[22] Owen J of the Supreme Court of Western Australia said that:

> The law does not require directors of a group of companies to ignore the interests of the wider group. But it does demand that where one or more companies in a group enter into a transaction or transactions, consideration must be given to the interests of that company or those companies. Most commercial transactions involve both benefits and detriments and, in considering the interests of the participants and those affected by the transaction, it will usually be a case of balancing the two.

In addition, where directors of a wholly-owned solvent subsidiary enter into a transaction **13.17** which might prima facie amount to a breach of duty, the potential for a breach can in many cases be removed by prior authorization, approval, or consent of the holding company, given by resolution or unanimously and informally, and an actual breach may be cured by subsequent ratification.[23] Difficulties may, however, arise in the case where the subsidiary is insolvent or in financial difficulties. In such circumstances, the holding company's ability to ratify a breach of duty by the directors is limited.[24]

(3) Nominee directors

The duty is particularly important in the context of nominee directors. Particular examples **13.18** of such directors include where a holding company has nominee directors on the board of its subsidiary or when a particular class of shareholder or a debenture holder has the right to appoint one or more directors on the board to represent their interests. There is nothing

---

[20] [1959] AC 324, 343, HL.

[21] See 2006 Act, s 172 (considered in Ch 12 above) which codifies the duty of a director to act in the way he considers, in good faith, would be most likely to promote the success of the company for the *benefit of its members as a whole*; see also *Greenhalgh v Arderne Cinemas* [1951] Ch 286, 291.

[22] [2008] WASC 239 at para 4621. This statement of principle was not criticized on appeal: [2012] WASCA 257.

[23] As to prior authorization etc, see Ch 10, Section D above, and as to ratification of breaches of duty, see Ch 20, Section D below.

[24] As to directors' duties in the case of an insolvent company or company in financial difficulties, see Ch 12, Section E above. For authorization and ratification where the duty to consider creditors' interests applies, see Ch 10, Section D above and Ch 20, Section D below.

unlawful for a director to act in such a capacity. A director who, without concealment of his position and with the consent of the company,[25] represents the interests of a third party on the board does not thereby breach his duty to the company. However, directors in such a position must take care to ensure that they continue to exercise their judgment independently and that no conflict of interest arises between their duty to the company and their obligations to their appointor. The law draws no distinction between the position of a nominee director and any other director. A nominee owes the same duties to the company and cannot blindly follow the judgment of those who appointed them. A nominee director may not plead any instruction from his appointor as a defence to an allegation of breach of duty.[26]

13.19 The first of the more modern cases to consider the duties of nominee directors is *Scottish Co-operative Wholesale Society v Meyer*.[27] Lord Denning said as follows:[28]

> What, then, is the position of the nominee directors here? Under the articles of association of the textile company the co-operative society was entitled to nominate three out of the five directors, and it did so. It nominated three of its own directors and they held office, as the articles said, 'as nominees' of the co-operative society. These three were therefore at one and the same time directors of the co-operative society—being three out of 12 of that company— and also directors of the textile company—three out of five there. So long as the interests of all concerned were in harmony, there was no difficulty. The nominee directors could do their duty by both companies without embarrassment. But, so soon as the interests of the two companies were in conflict, the nominee directors were placed in an impossible position … It is plain that, in the circumstances, these three gentlemen could not do their duty by both companies, and they did not do so. They put their duty to the co-operative society above their duty to the textile company in this sense, at least, that they did nothing to defend the interests of the textile company against the conduct of the co-operative society. They probably thought that 'as nominees' of the co-operative society their first duty was to the co-operative society. In this they were wrong. By subordinating the interests of the textile company to those of the co-operative society, they conducted the affairs of the textile company in a manner oppressive to the other shareholders.

13.20 Lord Denning MR returned to this theme in *Boulting v Association of Cinematograph Television and Allied Technicians*[29] when he said (in the course of a dissenting judgment):[30]

> Or take a nominee director, that is, a director of a company who is nominated by a large shareholder to represent his interests. There is nothing wrong in it. It is done every day. Nothing wrong, that is, so long as the director is left free to exercise his best judgment in the interests of the company which he serves. But if he is put upon terms that he is bound to act in the affairs of the company in accordance with the directions of his patron, it is beyond doubt unlawful (see *Kregor v Hollins* by Avory J), or if he agrees to subordinate the interests of the company to the interests of his patron, it is conduct oppressive to the other shareholders for which the patron can be brought to book: see *Scottish Co-operative Wholesale Society Ltd v Meyer*.

13.21 In *Kuwait Asia Bank EC v National Mutual Life Nominees Ltd*[31] Kuwait Asia appointed two of its employees (House and August) as directors of a company in which it had a 40 per cent

---

[25] *Kregor v Hollins* (1913) 109 LT 225, 231, CA.
[26] *Kuwait Asia Bank EC v National Mutual Life Nominees Ltd* [1991] 1 AC 187, 222, PC.
[27] [1959] AC 324, HL.
[28] At 366–7.
[29] [1963] 2 QB 606, CA.
[30] At 626–7.
[31] [1991] 1 AC 187, PC.

interest. In a brief discussion of the duties of those directors Lord Lowry, giving the advice of the Privy Council said:[32]

> In the performance of their duties as directors and in the performance of their duties imposed by the trust deed, House and August were bound to ignore the interests and wishes of their employer, the bank.

These cases point towards the conclusion that the duties of a director, even a nominee **13.22** director, are owed to the company alone. That is confirmed by the most recent Court of Appeal decision on the issue, *Re Neath Rugby Ltd (No 2), Hawkes v Cuddy (No 2)*.[33] In a judgment given at a preliminary hearing of an unfair prejudice petition,[34] HH Judge Havelock-Allen QC said that a nominee director's primary loyalty is to the company of which he is a director; he is obliged to act in its best interests, but is quite entitled to have regard to the interests or requirements of his appointor to the extent those interests are not incompatible with his duty to act in the best interests of the company. At the trial[35] Lewison J also considered the duties of a nominee director and reached a similar conclusion:[36] the company was entitled to the best independent judgment of the director in deciding where its interests lay; the nominee director was not required to prefer the interests of his appointor where they conflicted with the interests of the company. In that case the nominee director could fulfil his duty to consult his appointor. That did not mean that the appointor had a right of veto; provided the appointor's views were taken into account, the duty to consult him was satisfied.

When the matter came before the Court of Appeal following the trial, Stanley Burnton LJ **13.23** said as follows:[37]

> In my judgment, the fact that a director of a company has been nominated to that office by a shareholder does not, of itself, impose any duty on the director owed to his nominator. The director may owe duties to his nominator if he is an employee or officer of the nominator, or by reason of a formal or informal agreement with his nominator, but such duties do not arise out of his nomination, but out of a separate agreement or office. Such duties cannot however, detract from his duty to the company of which he is a director when he is acting as such ...
>
> ... an appointed director, without being in breach of his duties to the company, may take the interests of his nominator into account, provided that his decisions as a director are in what he genuinely considers to be the best interests of the company; but that is a very different thing from his being under a duty to his nominator by reason of his appointment by it.

Accordingly, where a nominee director is placed in a position where the interests of his **13.24** appointer directly conflict with the interests of the company he may need to consider whether to vote against the interests of his appointer or to resign his position.

---

[32] At 194. This case was discussed in *Diary Containers Ltd v NZI Bank Ltd* [1995] 2 NZLR 30.

[33] [2009] 2 BCLC 427, CA.

[34] [2008] 1 BCLC 327. At paras 26–7, HH Judge Havelock-Allen QC discussed three Australian authorities on nominee directors: *Re Broadcasting Station 2 GB Pty Ltd* [1964–65] NSWR 1648, 1663; *Re News Corp Ltd* (1987) 70 ALR 419, 437; *CanWest Global Communications Corp v Australian Broadcasting Authority* (1997) 24 ACSR 405. The appeal from this judgment does not consider nominee directors: [2008] BCC 125.

[35] [2008] BCC 390 at paras 182–97. In *Re Southern Counties Fresh Foods Ltd* [2008] EWHC 2810 (Ch) at paras 57–69 Warren J reached similar conclusions; see para 13.36 below.

[36] At paras 194 and 195.

[37] [2009] 2 BCLC 427, CA at paras 32–33.

13.25   The provisions of s 173(2)(b) which provide that the duty is not infringed by a director when he is acting in a way authorized by the company's constitution are also highly relevant to nominee directors. The purpose of s 173(2)(b) appears to have been to allow the position of nominee directors to be enshrined in a company's constitution and, provided the relevant provisions of the company's constitution are properly worded, for the nominee director to be released from the duty imposed by s 173(1). The nominee director will, however, remain obliged to comply with his other duties to the company, including his duty to promote the success of the company. The particular issues highlighted above in relation to nominee directors will, therefore, continue to arise. The provisions of s 173(2)(b) are considered in further detail in Section D below.

(4) Delegation

13.26   The company's constitution invariably contains power for the directors (ie the board) to delegate their powers.[38] Equally an individual director may delegate his functions to others where it is appropriate to do so. In particular, he must take reasonable care and skill in making his decision to whom to delegate his functions. However, where it is appropriate for the director to delegate he will not be expected to supervise every aspect of the delegate's activities.[39]

13.27   The problem of delegation arises with larger companies where it is not possible for an individual director to be familiar with all aspects of the company's business. He has to delegate functions to other directors or managers and, absent grounds for inquiry, he should be able to rely on their reports. Similarly non-executive directors are not expected to be directly concerned in management and may have to contribute to decisions on the basis of information obtained from the executive directors and other members of the management team. That is acceptable, because the content of a director's duty depends on 'how the particular company's business is organized and the part which the director could reasonably have been expected to play'.[40] As the cases in the following paragraphs show, what is not acceptable is abdication.

13.28   In *Re Barings plc (No 5), Secretary of State for Trade and Industry v Baker (No 5)* the Court of Appeal approved the following statement by Jonathan Parker J:[41]

> (i) Directors have, both collectively and individually, a continuing duty to acquire and maintain a sufficient knowledge and understanding of the company's business to enable them properly to discharge their duties as directors.
>
> (ii) Whilst directors are entitled (subject to the articles of association of the company) to delegate particular functions to those below them in the management chain, and to trust their competence and integrity to a reasonable extent, the exercise of the power of delegation does not absolve a director from the duty to supervise the discharge of the delegated functions.
>
> (iii) No rule of universal application can be formulated as to the duty referred to in (ii) above. The extent of the duty, and the question whether it has been discharged, must

---

[38] Table A, reg 72; Model Article (pcls) 5; Model Article (plc) 5.
[39] *Dovey v Cory* [1901] AC 477; *Re City Equitable Fire Insurance Co Ltd* [1925] Ch 407; *Norman v Theodore Goddard* [1991] BCLC 1028; *Daniels v Anderson* (1995) 13 ACLC; *Ultraframe (UK) Ltd v Fielding* [2005] EWHC 1638 (Ch) at paras 1296–301.
[40] *Bishopsgate Investment Management Ltd v Maxwell (No 2)* [1994] 1 All ER 261, 264, CA, per Hoffmann LJ.
[41] [2000] 1 BCLC 523, 536, CA.

depend on the facts of each particular case, including the director's role in the management of the company.

Similarly, in *Re Westmid Packing Services Ltd* Lord Woolf MR said:[42] **13.29**

> A proper degree of delegation and division of responsibility is of course permissible, and often necessary, but total abrogation of responsibility is not. A board of directors must not permit one individual to dominate them and use them …

Equitable Life Assurance Society v Bowley[43] involved a negligence claim against non- **13.30**
executive directors. After referring to the passage from the *Barings* judgment quoted in paragraph 13.28 above, Langley J said that in the modern world non-executive directors could not adopt the position of 'unquestioning reliance upon others to do their job' and that it was at least arguable that 'a company may reasonably at least look to non-executive directors for independence of judgment and supervision of the executive management'.[44]

(5) Acting on advice

Similar principles apply in respect of advice received by a director. There is little doubt that **13.31**
a failure to take appropriate advice could, in an appropriate case constitute a breach of, for example, the duty to promote the company's success or the duty to exercise reasonable care, skill, and diligence.[45] However, a director should not accept advice without applying his own judgment to it. If, having considered the advice carefully and concluded that it is sensible (and from a trustworthy source), he proceeds to follow it, he can normally be satisfied that he has complied with his duty to exercise independent judgment.

The duty was expressed by Lord Goldsmith in the Lords Grand Committee stage of the **13.32**
Companies Bill as follows:

> the clause does not mean that a director has to form his judgment totally independently from anyone or anything. It does not actually mean that the director has to be independent himself. He can have an interest in the matter … It is the exercise of the judgment of a director that must be independent in the sense of it being his own judgment … The duty does not prevent a director from relying on the advice or work of others, but the final judgment must be his responsibility. He clearly cannot be expected to do everything himself. Indeed, in certain circumstances directors may be in breach of their duty if they fail to take appropriate advice—for example, legal advice. As with all advice, slavish reliance is not acceptable, and the obtaining of outside advice does not absolve directors from exercising their judgment on the basis of such advice.[46]

There is an analogy with cases on the extent to which a solicitor may rely on the advice of **13.33**
counsel. Adapting the statement of principle of Sir Thomas Bingham MR, giving the judgment of the Court of Appeal in *Ridehalgh v Horsefield*[47] to a director relying on legal advice,

---

[42] [1998] 2 BCLC 646, 653, CA.

[43] [2004] 1 BCLC 180.

[44] [2004] 1 BCLC 180 at para 41.

[45] See eg *Re Sunrise Radio Ltd* [2010] 1 BCLC 36, where HH Judge Purle QC commented at para 256 that the directors in question should have sought legal advice in connection with a transaction between the company and one of their number.

[46] Hansard, HL, vol 678, col 282 (6 February 2006).

[47] [1994] Ch 205, 237, CA.

the position is this: a director does not abdicate his responsibilities when he seeks legal advice. He must apply his mind to the advice received (he cannot unquestioningly rely on it). But the more specialist the nature of the advice, the more reasonable is it likely to be for the director to accept it and act on it.[48] Of course legal advice will not protect a director where it is obvious that it is wrong,[49] based on inadequate information, or where it impinges on the commercial decision that is the director's responsibility.

C. Contracts Restricting Future Exercise of Discretion

13.34 The duty imposed by s 173(1) will preclude a director from fettering his discretion by entering into a contract with a third party as to how he will exercise his discretion.[50] To do so would prevent the director from exercising an independent judgment at the appropriate time. However, the duty does not preclude the company from entering into, in good faith and in the interests of the company, a contract to take such further action as is necessary to carry out that contract. In *Fulham Football Club Ltd v Cabra Estates plc* the Court of Appeal stated:[51]

> It is trite law that directors are under a duty to act bona fide in the interests of their company. However, it does not follow from that proposition that directors can never make a contract by which they bind themselves to the future exercise of their powers in a particular manner, even though the contract taken as a whole is manifestly for the benefit of the company. Such a rule could well prevent companies from entering into contracts which were commercially beneficial to them.

The Court of Appeal went on to hold:

> The true rule was stated by the High Court of Australia in *Thorby v Goldberg* (1964) 112 CLR 597. The relevant part of the headnote reads: 'If, when a contract is negotiated on behalf of a company, the directors bona fide think it in the interests of the company as a whole that the transaction should be entered into and carried into effect they may bind themselves by the contract to do whatever is necessary to effectuate it.'[52]

13.35 This position is confirmed by s 173(2)(a) which provides that the duty to exercise independent judgment is not infringed by the director if he is acting in accordance with an agreement duly entered into by the company that restricts the future exercise of discretion by the directors.

---

[48] *Green v Walkling* [2008] 2 BCLC 332 is an example of a case where a director was not liable for breach of duty where he had acted in accordance with legal advice in a specialist area, even though the advice might have been wrong.

[49] Cf *Davy-Chiesman v Davy-Chiesman* [1984] Fam 48, CA.

[50] *Re Englefield Colliery Co* (1878) 8 Ch D 388; and see *Re London and South-Western Canal Ltd* [1911] 1 Ch 346, where directors were held liable for 'misfeasance' for holding their qualification shares on trust for promoters and giving them blank transfers, so that the promoters could dismiss them at any time.

[51] [1994] 1 BCLC 363 at 392. In so far as the cases of *Rackham v Peek Foods Ltd (1977)* [1990] BCLC 895 and *John Crowther Group plc v Carpets International plc* [1990] BCLC 460 can be read as laying down a general proposition that directors can never bind themselves as to the future exercise of their fiduciary powers, they would be wrong: *Fulham Football Club Ltd v Cabra Estates plc* at 393 per Neill LJ.

[52] [1994] 1 BCLC 363, 392.

D. Authorization by the Constitution

In *Re Southern Counties Fresh Foods Ltd*[53] Warren J had to consider whether, at common **13.36**
law, a nominee director could be released from his duties to the company and stated seven
propositions, the first three of which are consistent with the decisions in *Re Neath Rugby Ltd*
(discussed in paragraphs 13.22 and 13.23 above):[54]

(1) A nominee director owes the same duties to the company as any other director.
(2) A nominee director owes his duties as a director to the company alone.
(3) A company is entitled to expect from the director his best independent judgment.
(4) Those duties can be qualified in the case of a nominee director just as they can be quali-
     fied in the case of any other director; in particular such duties (except perhaps for certain
     core duties) can be qualified by the unanimous assent of the shareholders.
(5) It is doubtful whether it is possible to release a director from his general duty to act in the
     best interests of the company.
(6) Even if it is possible to do so, it would require strong evidence to demonstrate that that
     had been done, ideally an express written agreement signed by all the shareholders; the
     onus is on those who say that the general rule has been attenuated or relaxed to demon-
     strate that such approval has been given and the extent to which the general rule has been
     relaxed.
(7) There is no reason in principle why, in relation to specific areas of interest, a director
     should not be released from his fiduciary duty to give his best independent judgment to
     the company. So the shareholder may unanimously agree that a nominee director may
     negotiate an agreement with the company on behalf of his appointor, provided that the
     nominee director is excluded from discussions of the board relating to the negotiations
     and does not vote on the issue.

The fourth to seventh propositions stated by Warren J need to be considered in the light of **13.37**
the statutory statement of directors' duties which provides a framework for the board to deal
with conflicts of interest by way of authorization given by the director (see s 175(4)(b) and
(5) of the 2006 Act which is discussed in Chapter 15 below).

Now the 2006 Act, s 173(2)(b) provides that the duty to exercise independent judgment is **13.38**
not infringed by the director acting in a way authorized by the company's constitution.[55] The
Solicitor General explained the purpose of the subsection during consideration of the bill in
Standing Committee as follows:[56]

> subsection (2)(b) will allow the status of the nominee director to be enshrined in the com-
> pany's constitution so that the nominee is able to follow the instructions of the person who
> appointed him without breaching that duty. The extent to which that is possible under the
> existing law was unclear, but we have now made it clear. However, even when a nominee
> follows instructions, he must still comply with all his other duties—there may well be other
> duties—such as a duty to act broadly in the interests of the company.

---

[53] [2008] EWHC 2810 (Ch) at paras 57–69.
[54] At para 67.
[55] As to the meaning of the company's 'constitution' see CA 2006, ss 17 and 257 and Ch 10, paras
11.06–11.07 above.
[56] See the answer by the Solicitor General, HC Official Report, SC D (Company Law Reform Bill), col 601
(11 July 2006).

13.39 Accordingly, when considering the appointment of nominee directors it will also be necessary to consider some amendment to the company's constitution in order to ensure that such directors are given the full protection afforded by s 173(2)(b). However, as the passage from the speech of the Solicitor General set out above makes clear, even where a nominee or other director is released from the duty imposed by s 173(1) by a provision in the company's constitution he will remain under a duty to comply with his other duties.

14

DUTY TO EXERCISE REASONABLE CARE, SKILL, AND DILIGENCE

Mark Arnold QC

A. Introduction

The 2006 Act, s 174 provides that: **14.01**

(1) A director of a company must exercise reasonable care, skill and diligence.
(2) This means the care, skill and diligence that would be exercised by a reasonably diligent person with—
  (a) the general knowledge, skill and experience that may reasonably be expected of a person carrying out the functions carried out by the director in relation to the company, and
  (b) the general knowledge, skill and experience that the director has.

The 2006 Act, s 174 thus codifies the director's duty to exercise reasonable care, skill, and **14.02** diligence. It reflects the current position at common law, which itself reflects the tests laid down in the context of wrongful trading, as set out in the Insolvency Act, s 214. Indeed, the wording of this section of the 2006 Act is substantially the same as that of the Insolvency Act, s 214(4).

Whether a director has complied with the duty in any particular case will require an assess- **14.03** ment of his conduct which is both objective and subjective. It is objective in the sense that the director's conduct will be compared with that which may reasonably be expected of a person carrying out the same functions as those carried out by the director in relation to the company. If the director's conduct thus compared falls short of this standard, objectively ascertained, then he will have breached the duty. The fact that, having regard to the general knowledge, skill, and experience of the director concerned, nothing better could perhaps have been expected of him, will be nothing to the point. The objective standard may thus be regarded as imposing a minimum standard to be expected of all directors, which cannot be reduced further by reference to the general knowledge, skill, and experience of the particular director concerned. As Beatson LJ has said, 'this objective standard sets the floor'.[1]

14.04   The mere fact that the particular director meets the objective standard, however, will not mean that he has acted in accordance with his duty. In order to ascertain whether or not he has, it is also necessary to have regard to the general knowledge, skill, and experience of the director himself. It is in this respect that the assessment is subjective. If the director has greater knowledge, skill, and experience than might ordinarily be expected of someone carrying out the same functions as he carries out in relation to the company, a higher standard of conduct may be expected of him, and he must satisfy that higher standard.[2] If he does not, he will have acted in breach of his duty. It will not suffice that he has reached the standard reasonably to be expected of someone carrying out the same functions but who does not have his greater knowledge, skill, and experience.

14.05   The dual assessment required by the duty as codified by the 2006 Act, s 174 thus confirms the rejection by the courts in the early 1990s[3] of the standard which had been prevalent earlier in the twentieth century, which did not require directors to exhibit a greater degree of skill than could reasonably be expected from a person with their knowledge and experience and which gave rise merely to a subjective assessment of the director's conduct in this respect.[4]

14.06   The duty to exercise care, skill, and diligence in its codified form replaces the common law rules and equitable principles upon which it is based.[5] Nevertheless, it is intended that it will be interpreted and applied in the same way as those corresponding common law rules and equitable principles which it replaces.[6]

14.07   It has been consistently emphasized by the courts on numerous occasions that the question whether a director has in fact acted in breach of his duty of care can only be determined upon consideration of the facts and circumstances of the particular case.[7] In order to ascertain whether a breach has occurred, it is first necessary to determine the extent of the duty. That depends on 'how the particular company's business is organized and the part which the director could reasonably have been expected to play'.[8] Conduct which may be acceptable (in the sense that it does not give rise to actionable complaint) in one case may constitute an actionable breach of duty in another. Acts which a competent director may undertake in relation to a solvent company, for example, may be wholly inappropriate in relation to a company which is insolvent or of doubtful solvency, where a long-term view is unrealistic and if, in all the circumstances, the acts are too risky for a competent board to embark on.[9]

---

[1]   *Brumder v Motornet Services and Repairs Ltd* [2013] 1 WLR 2783, CA, at para 46.

[2]   In *Robin Hood Centre plc, Brooks v Armstrong* [2015] BCC 661 the director's experience in a different retail field did not raise the standard expected of him.

[3]   *Re D'Jan of London Ltd, Copp v D'Jan* [1994] 1 BCLC 561 (Hoffmann LJ, sitting as an additional judge of the Chancery Division), 563d. In *Norman v Theodore Goddard* [1991] BCLC 1028, the same was assumed by Hoffmann J, but without argument: 1031b. See also *Lexi Holdings plc v Luqman* [2008] 2 BCLC 725 at paras 36 and 37, and *Brumder v Motornet Service and Repairs Ltd* [2013] 1 WLR 2783, CA, per Beatson LJ at paras 45–6.

[4]   *Lagunas Nitrate Co v Lagunas Syndicate* [1899] 2 Ch 392; *Re Brazilian Rubber Plantations and Estates Ltd* [1911] 1 Ch 425; *Re City Equitable Fire Insurance Co* [1925] Ch 407; *Huckerby v Elliott* [1970] 1 All ER 189.

[5]   2006 Act, s 170(3).

[6]   2006 Act, s 170(4).

[7]   *Brumder v Motornet Service and Repairs Ltd* [2013] 1 WLR 2783, CA, per Beatson LJ at para 54.

[8]   *Bishopsgate Management Co Ltd v Maxwell (No 2)* [1994] 1 All ER 261, 264, CA, per Hoffmann LJ.

[9]   *Roberts v Frohlich* [2011] 2 BCLC 625 at paras 98 and 105. See the discussion of this decision in Ch 12, at para 12.89, and Section E generally.

In the event that concern arises as to the conduct of a director, therefore, it will be necessary to form a clear understanding of the factual context so as to be able to identify the extent of the duty owed by the director and the manner in which it was breached, in order both to formulate the claim properly and determine whether it can be substantiated. It is likely to be necessary to have regard to the size of the company, and the nature of its business. It may also be necessary to have regard to the effect changes in the economy are likely to have on the company's business, and to the regulatory regime affecting the industry in which it operates. As far as the director himself is concerned, it will be necessary to ascertain the basis upon which his services have been retained by the company and, with an appropriate degree of precision, the functions he has been charged to undertake in relation to the company. It will be necessary to consider whether the director has any particular skill or skills, and the degree to which those skills relate, or were reasonably expected to relate, to the discharge of his functions. Likewise it will be necessary to have regard to the director's experience, both recent and over the course of his entire working life.

14.08

As conduct may constitute a breach of the director's duty of care in one case but not in another, and since each case must therefore be considered on its own facts, it follows that the guidance to be derived from the authorities is necessarily limited. It is further to be noted, however, that even if the director would otherwise be liable for negligently exposing the company to a penalty or other liability, if the circumstances are such that the company (to the exclusion of the director) is thereby rendered personally liable for criminal or quasi-criminal conduct, the maxim *ex turpi causa non oritur actio* may operate to prevent any action by it to recover its losses from the director concerned.[10]

14.09

Finally, subject to certain exceptions, it remains the position in England and Wales that any provision by which a company purports to exempt a director from, or directly or indirectly indemnifies him against, any liability that would otherwise attach to him for any negligence, default, breach of duty, or breach of trust in relation to the company, is void.[11] It follows that issues relating to the scope of such provisions where they are permitted and operate, save in cases of fraud or wilful default, notably in various offshore and other common law jurisdictions, do not arise.[12]

14.10

---

[10] In *Safeway Stores Ltd v Twigger* [2011] 2 All ER 841, CA, a number of senior directors and employees caused the company to contravene the Competition Act 1998, s 2. As that Act imposed the prohibition and the resulting penalty only on the company, such that their acts must be attributed to the company for these purposes, the CA concluded that to allow the company to recover the penalty from the individuals concerned would be inconsistent with the statutory scheme. The reasoning, but not the result, was criticized by Lords Toulson and Hodge JJSC, with whose criticisms Lord Mance sympathized, in *Bilta (UK) v Nazir (No 2)* [2016] AC 1; however, no concluded view was expressed. The *Bilta* case is discussed in detail in Ch 19 section E(4) below. For the current position on the ex turpi causa defence, see *Patel v Mirza* [2016] 3 WLR 399, SC.

[11] 2006 Act, s 232. See the discussion of ss 232–9 in Chapter 20.

[12] eg the Cayman Islands, the BVI, Bermuda, and the Channel Islands, as well as Delaware and a number of other US States. For the position in the Cayman Islands, see *Weavering Macro Fixed Income Fund Ltd v Peterson*, decided by the Court of Appeal of the Cayman Islands on 12 February 2015, which is currently subject to appeal to the Privy Council. The CICA decided that, in the context of such a clause, 'wilful default' requires (i) a deliberate and conscious decision to act or fail to act in knowing breach of duty, such that negligence is not enough; or (ii) reckless carelessness, in the sense of not caring whether the act or omission is or is not a breach of duty, for which purpose it is sufficient to show that the director appreciated his conduct might be a breach of duty but made a conscious decision to act or refrain from acting without regard to the consequences.

B. Nature of the Duty

14.11 The duty of care is not recognized at common law as a fiduciary duty and is not enforceable as such. This is expressly recognized by the 2006 Act, s 178(2), which identifies the duty to exercise reasonable care, skill, and diligence as an exception to the rule that the duties codified in ss 171–7 are enforceable in the same way as any other fiduciary duty owed to a company by its directors.

14.12 The duty comprises three elements, namely care, skill, and diligence, which will often overlap in practice. For the purposes of analysis, however, it may be helpful to distinguish between them. On the basis of the authorities discussed below, it is suggested that care is to be understood as carefulness, though not caution; skill denotes ability, while diligence may be understood as requiring the director to apply himself conscientiously to the affairs of the company and, in particular, the matter in hand.

C. Scope of the Duty

14.13 In common with his fiduciary duties, in the absence of special circumstances which demonstrate the assumption of a wider duty, the director's duty to exercise reasonable care, skill, and diligence is one owed to the company rather than to its individual shareholders or creditors or other stakeholders. In the same way, the directors of a trust company do not owe a duty to exercise reasonable care, skill, and diligence directly to the trust itself or to the beneficiaries of the trust, and nor do such duties as the directors owe to the trust company constitute trust property, so that no indirect (or 'dog leg') claim lies against them at the instance of the beneficiaries.[13]

14.14 Historically, it was considered that directors would only be liable for breach of their duty of care if guilty of 'gross' negligence, or *crassa negligentia*. Some eminent judges regarded the use of the word 'gross' as unnecessary. In *Wilson v Brett*,[14] for example, Baron Rolfe (later Lord Cranworth) said that he 'could see no difference between negligence or gross negligence; that it was the same thing, with the addition of a vituperative epithet'. Others, however, considered that it was 'certainly not without its significance' and that it could usefully be retained.[15] In *Giblin v McMullen*, Lord Chelmsford considered that for the bank to have been negligent, it would need to have shown 'the want of that ordinary diligence which men of common prudence generally exercise about their own affairs'.

14.15 The House of Lords adopted the same approach in relation to directors in *Overend & Gurney Co v Gibb*,[16] where Lord Hatherley LC identified the question in the following terms:

> [W]hether if [the directors] did not so exceed their powers they were cognisant of circumstances of such a character, so plain, so manifest, and so simple of appreciation, that no men with any ordinary degree of prudence, acting on their own behalf, would have entered into such a transaction as they entered into? Was there *crassa negligentia* on their part ...?[17]

---

[13] *Gregson v HAE Trustees Ltd* [2008] 2 BCLC 542.
[14] (1843) 11 M & W 113 (a case about the management of a horse).
[15] *Giblin v McMullen* (1868) 2 LR 2 PC 317, 336, 337, per Lord Chelmsford.
[16] (1872) LR 5 HL 480.
[17] (1872) LR 5 HL 480, 487.

In *Lagunas Nitrate Company v Lagunas Syndicate*,[18] Lindley MR stated the position as **14.16** follows:

> If directors act within their powers, if they act with such care as is reasonably to be expected from them, having regard to their knowledge and experience, and if they act honestly for the benefit of the company they represent, they discharge both their equitable as well as their legal duty to the company.[19]

He found that the amount of care to be taken was difficult to define. He continued:

> [B]ut it is plain that directors are not liable for all the mistakes they may make, although if they had taken more care they might have avoided them: see *Overend, Gurney & Co. v Gibb.* Their negligence must be not the omission to take all possible care; it must be much more blameable than that: it must be in a business sense culpable or gross. I do not know how better to describe it.[20]

In *In re Brazilian Rubber Plantation and Estates Limited*,[21] Neville J explained the position in **14.17** memorable terms by reference to the management of a rubber company:

> A director's duty has been laid down as requiring him to act with such care as is reasonably to be expected from him, having regard to his knowledge and experience. He is, I think, not bound to bring any special qualifications to his office. He may undertake the management of a rubber company in complete ignorance of everything connected with rubber, without incurring responsibility for the mistakes which may result from such ignorance; while if he is acquainted with the rubber business he must give the company the advantage of his knowledge when transacting the company's business. He is not, I think, bound to take any definite part in the conduct of the company's business, but so far as he does undertake it he must use reasonable care in its despatch.
>
> Such reasonable care must, I think, be measured by the care an ordinary man might be expected to take in the same circumstances on his own behalf. He is clearly, I think, not responsible for damages occasioned by errors of judgment.

This set the stage for Romer J's classical exposition in *Re City Equitable Fire Insurance Co* **14.18** *Ltd*.[22] He began by emphasizing the need to investigate all the relevant circumstances:

> In order, therefore, to ascertain the duties that a person appointed to the board of an established company undertakes to perform, it is necessary to consider not only the nature of the company's business, but also the manner in which the work of the company is in fact distributed between the directors and the other officials of the company, provided always that this distribution is a reasonable one in the circumstances, and is not inconsistent with any express provisions of the articles of association. In discharging the duties of his position thus ascertained a director must, of course, act honestly: but he must also exercise some degree of both skill and diligence. To the question of what is the particular degree of skill and diligence required of him, the authorities do not, I think, give any very clear answer. It has been laid down that so long as a director acts honestly he cannot be made responsible in damages unless guilty of gross or culpable negligence in a business sense.[23]

---

[18] [1899] 2 Ch 392, 422, CA.
[19] [1899] 2 Ch 392, 435, CA.
[20] [1899] 2 Ch 392, CA.
[21] [1911] 1 Ch 425, 437.
[22] [1925] Ch 407.
[23] [1925] Ch 407, 427.

14.19   Romer J felt some difficulty in understanding the difference between negligence and gross negligence, and the distinction has not been maintained in the context of directors' liability.[24] Following the approach adopted in the *Lagunas* and *Brazilian Rubber* cases, Romer J agreed that a director had to display reasonable care to be measured by the care an ordinary man might be expected to take in the circumstances on his own behalf, not all possible care. He continued:

> There are, in addition, one or two other general propositions that seem to be warranted by the reported cases: (1) A director need not exhibit in the performance of his duties a greater degree of skill than may reasonably be expected from a person of his knowledge and experience. A director of a life insurance company, for instance, does not guarantee that he has the skill of an actuary or of a physician … It is perhaps only another way of stating the same proposition to say that directors are not liable for mere errors of judgment. (2) A director is not bound to give continuous attention to the affairs of his company. His duties are of an intermittent nature to be performed at periodical board meetings, and at meetings of any committee of the board upon which he happens to be placed. He is not, however, bound to attend all such meetings though he ought to attend, whenever, in the circumstances, he is reasonably able to do so. (3) In respect of all duties that, having regard to the exigencies of business, and the articles of association, may properly be left to some other official, a director is, in the absence of grounds for suspicion, justified in trusting that official to perform such duties honestly …

14.20   Three general observations may be made before considering separately care, skill, and diligence as they have developed since *City Equitable*. First, the courts were reluctant historically to formulate detailed rules for the guidance of directors in the conduct of business affairs. In the words of Lord Macnaghten in *Dovey v Cory*:[25]

> I do not think it desirable for any tribunal to do that which Parliament has abstained from doing—that is, to formulate precise rules for the guidance or embarrassment of business men in the conduct of business affairs. There never has been, and I think there never will be, much difficulty in dealing with any particular case on its own facts and circumstances: and, speaking for myself, I rather doubt the wisdom of attempting to do more.

14.21   Secondly, although (as will appear from the discussion below) the standard of conduct to be expected of directors is no longer in all respects the same as that suggested by Romer J, it was the case then—and remains the case now—that the scope of the duty and, in particular, whether it has been discharged or breached, required a detailed consideration of all the relevant facts in any particular case. As the position was described more recently by the Supreme Court of New South Wales in *Daniels v Anderson*:[26]

---

[24] Although the term 'gross negligence' is often found in commercial documents, it has never been accepted by English civil law as a concept distinct from civil negligence: *Tradigrain SA v Intertek Testing Services (ITS) Canada* [2007] EWCA Civ 154 per Moore-Bick LJ at para 23. Where the term does appear in commercial documents, its meaning falls to be determined by reference to ordinary canons of construction. In that context, it is generally intended to represent something more fundamental than failure to exercise proper skill and/or care constituting negligence: see *Red Sea Tankers Ltd v Papachristidis, the Hellespont Ardent* [1997] 2 Lloyds Rep 547, 586, per Mance J; *Camerata Property Inc v Credit Suisse Securities (Europe) Ltd* [2011] 2 BCLC 54, per Andrew Smith J at para 161.

[25] [1901] AC 477, 488, HL.

[26] (1995) 16 ACSR 607, 668 cited and adopted by Jonathan Parker J in *Re Barings plc (No 5)* [1999] 1 BCLC 433, 488, para B5. This approach was adopted in *Weavering Capital (UK) Ltd v Peterson* [2012] EWHC 1480 (Ch) at para 162. See also *Brumder v Motornet Services and Repairs Ltd* [2013] 1 WLR 2783, CA, at para 54. For a recent review of relevant Australian authorities see *ASIC v Healey* [2011] FCA 717 and *Trilogy Funds Management Ltd v Sullivan* [2015] FCA 1452.

A person who accepts the office of director of a particular company undertakes the responsibility of ensuring that he or she understands the nature of the duty a director is called upon to perform. That duty will vary according to the size and business of the particular company and the experience or skills that the director held himself or herself out to have in support of appointment to the office. None of this is novel. It turns upon the natural expectations and reliance placed by shareholders on the experience and skill of a particular director ... The duty includes that of acting collectively to manage the company.

Finally, it is also fair to say that, if an issue arises as to the extent of a director's duties and **14.22** responsibilities in any particular case, the level of reward he is entitled to receive may be a relevant factor in resolving that issue. As Jonathan Parker J put it in *Re Barings plc (No 5)*,[27] echoing what Sir Richard Scott V-C had previously said in *Re Barings plc, Secretary of State for Trade and Industry v Baker*:[28]

> The point is that the higher the level of reward, the greater the responsibilities which may reasonably be expected (prima facie, at least) to go with it.

(1) Care

The requirement that a director should exercise reasonable (though not all possible) care necessarily introduced objective criteria in determining the standard of care he should exercise, the director's behaviour being compared with that to be expected of an ordinary man acting on his own behalf in similar circumstances. This is how Foster J interpreted the position in *Dorchester Finance Co Ltd v Stebbing*.[29] In that case, it was held that non-executive directors who were either qualified accountants or had considerable accountancy and business experience, and who had signed blank cheques, thereby allowing the managing director to misappropriate the company's money, had been negligent. Foster J distinguished between the duty of care, in relation to which a director was required to take such care in the performance of his duties as an ordinary man might be expected to take on his own behalf, and the duty of skill, which was to be determined subjectively.

It is unlikely to have been a coincidence that this distinction was one drawn in the draft **14.24** Companies Bill 1978,[30] published the year after *Dorchester Finance Co v Stebbing* was decided. As will be seen below, however, such a distinction did not survive *D'Jan of London Ltd, Copp v D'Jan*,[31] with the adoption of the test provided for by the Insolvency Act, s 214(4).

(2) Skill

To the extent that Romer J identified the standard of skill required as a matter to be deter- **14.25** mined subjectively, that is to say by reference only to the personal qualities of the director concerned, what he said was entirely consistent with the authorities at that time. As

---

[27] [1999] 1 BCLC 433, para [B6].

[28] [1998] BCC 583, 586.

[29] [1989] BCLC 498, 501c–502a (actually decided in July 1977).

[30] Clause 45(1) of the Companies Bill 1978 provided as follows: '(1) In the exercise of the powers and the discharge of the duties of his office in circumstances of any description, a director of a company owes a duty to the company to exercise such care and diligence as could reasonably be expected of a reasonably prudent person in circumstances of that description and to exercise such skill as may reasonably be expected of a person of his knowledge and experience.'

[31] [1994] 1 BCLC 561, 563d.

demonstrated by *Dorchester Finance Co Ltd v Stebbing*,[32] the test remained a subjective one into the late 1970s as Foster J accepted the proposition that a director is required to exhibit in the performance of his duties such a degree of skill as may reasonably be expected from a person with *his* knowledge and experience.

14.26   Within 16 years of Foster J's decision, however, the skill to be expected of a director fell to be determined not simply by reference to the knowledge and experience of the director himself (a subjective standard) but also by reference to an objective standard. In *D'Jan of London Ltd, Copp v D'Jan*,[33] Hoffmann LJ (sitting as an additional judge of the Chancery Division) made the following statement as to the duty of care owed by a director at common law:

> In my view, the duty of care owed by a director at common law is accurately stated in section 214(4) of the Insolvency Act 1986. It is the conduct of—
>
> 'a reasonably diligent person having both—(a) the general knowledge, skill and experience that may reasonably be expected of a person carrying out the same functions as are carried out by that director in relation to the company, and (b) the general knowledge, skill and experience that that director has.'

14.27   It is not easy to discern the basis for this development of the standard of skill from the authorities of the time. It is true that Hoffmann J had himself previously stated the position in similar terms in *Norman v Theodore Goddard*.[34] In that case, however, he did not hear argument on the point as he was willing to assume that was the relevant test. In *D'Jan* itself, Romer J's judgment in *Re City Equitable Fire Insurance Co* appears not to have been cited, perhaps because it was thought unnecessary by reason of its familiarity, and Hoffmann LJ did not elaborate on the reasoning which led him to take the view he did. It is also the case that in *Bishopsgate Investment Management Ltd v Maxwell (No 2)*,[35] Hoffmann LJ recognized that the law might be evolving in response to changes in public attitudes to corporate governance, but this statement was *obiter*.

14.28   Nevertheless the development was plainly consistent with the changing role of directors and the legislature's recognition that more was to be expected of those who sought to take advantage of the benefits of trading with limited liability in the modern commercial world, apparent not only from the specific terms of s 214 and other provisions of the Insolvency Act itself, but also from the enactment of CDDA of the same year. These legislative developments had been intended to meet concerns which had been voiced increasingly vociferously over previous decades, including by the Jenkins Committee in its Report delivered in 1962 and the Report of the Cork Committee, delivered in 1982.[36] As Henry LJ said in *Re Grayan Building Services Ltd*:[37]

---

[32] [1989] BCLC 498, 501 (actually decided in July 1977). In that case, it was held that non-executive directors who were either qualified accountants or had considerable accountancy and business experience had been negligent in signing blank cheques, thereby allowing the managing director to misappropriate the company's money.

[33] [1994] 1 BCLC 561, 563d.

[34] [1991] BCLC 1028, 1030h–1b.

[35] [1994] 1 All ER 261, 264b, CA.

[36] Report of the Jenkins Committee at paras 497–500, 503; report of the Cork Committee at Chapter 45.

[37] [1995] Ch 241, 257–8, CA. In *Blackspur Group plc (No 2)* [1998] 1 BCLC 676, 680, CA, Lord Woolf MR described the purposes of the directors' disqualification legislation as 'the protection of the public, by means of prohibitory remedial action, by anticipated deterrent effect on further misconduct and by encouragement of higher standards of honesty and diligence in corporate management, from those who are unfit to be concerned in the management of a company'.

The concept of limited liability and the sophistication of our corporate law offers great privileges and great opportunities for those who wish to trade under that regime. But the corporate environment carries with it the discipline that those who avail themselves of those privileges must accept the standards laid down and abide by the regulatory rules and disciplines in place to protect creditors and shareholders. And while some significant corporate failures will occur despite the directors exercising best managerial practice, in many too many [cases] there have been serious breaches of those rules and disciplines, in situations where the observance of them would or at least might have prevented or reduced the scale of the failure and consequent loss to creditors and investors. Reliable figures are hard to come by, but it seems that losses from corporate fraud and misman-agement have never been higher. At the same time the regulatory regime has never been more stringent—on paper even if not in practice. The Parliamentary intention to improve managerial safeguards and standards for the long term good of employees, creditors and investors is clear ... The statutory corporate climate is stricter than it has ever been, and those enforcing it should reflect the fact that Parliament has seen the need for higher standards.

Such a development leads to a result which is both consistent and coherent, in the sense **14.29** that the standard to be expected falls to be determined in the same way whether the company is carrying on business as usual or whether it is approaching, and has no rea-sonable prospect of avoiding, insolvent liquidation. This was recognized by the Law Commission.[38]

Regardless of the basis in authority for the position adopted in *D'Jan*, therefore, the decision **14.30** to require the standard of skill to be ascertained by reference to objective (as well as subjec-tive) criteria is obviously sensible,[39] both in principle and as a matter of policy. As the CLR subsequently recognized,[40] '[t]he community as a whole suffers if companies are run with less than objective standards of competence and it is appropriate to impose a mandatory standard'.

The dual test expounded in *D'Jan* has subsequently been widely recognized and applied by **14.31** the courts,[41] including in the context of directors' disqualification cases.[42] It is no longer suf-ficient, therefore, for directors to bring to the performance of their functions the degree of skill they actually possess. Both collectively and individually, they have a continuing duty to acquire and maintain a sufficient knowledge and understanding of the company's business

---

[38] *Company Directors: Regulating Conflicts of Interests and Formulating a Statement of Duties* (Consultation Paper No 153, 1998), paras 15.27 and 15.29.

[39] According to the Law Commission, the movement in the case law to a dual subjective/objective test was a 'remarkable example of the modernisation of the law by the judges, facilitated of course by the changes in the insolvency legislation made by Parliament'. (*Company Directors: Regulating Conflicts of Interests and Formulating a Statement of Duties* (Consultation Paper No 153, 1998), para 14.19).

[40] CLR: *Developing the Framework* (March 2000) at para 3.68.

[41] *Cohen v Selby* [2001] 1 BCLC 176, CA at paras 10 and 21; *Re Westlowe Storage and Distribution Ltd* [2000] 2 BCLC 590, 611; *Bairstow v Queens Moat Houses plc* [2000] 1 BCLC 549, 559c–e; *Re Loquitur Ltd, IRC v Richmond* [2003] 2 BCLC 442 at para 241; *Equitable Life Assurance Society v Bowley* [2004] 1 BCLC 180 at paras 36 and 37; *Swan v Sandhu* [2005] EWHC 2743 (Ch), at para 44; *Lexi Holdings plc v Luqman* [2008] 2 BCLC 725 at paras 36 and 37, [2009] 2 BCLC 1, CA, at para 18; *Roberts v Frohlich* [2011] 2 BCLC 625, at para 99; *Brumder v Motornet Services and Repairs Ltd* [2013] 1 WLR 2783, CA.

[42] *Re Landhurst Leasing plc* [1999] 1 BCLC 286 at 344e–h.

to enable them properly to discharge their duties as directors.[43] As Jonathan Parker J noted in *Re Barings plc (No 5)*:

> It is a truism that if a manager does not properly understand the business which he is seeking to manage, he will be unable to take informed management decisions in relation to it.[44]

(3) Diligence

14.32 Romer J's summary of the position in relation to the degree of diligence to be expected of directors was not in practice a very exacting one. Apart from the authorities already referred to, perhaps the best-known illustration of the results to which such an unexacting requirement might lead was the *Marquis of Bute's Case*.[45] In that case, the bank went into liquidation following the discovery of a fraud perpetrated by its paid officer. The Marquis of Bute had been appointed president of the bank at the age of six months and attended only one board meeting in 39 years. He was found not liable for breach of duty. Stirling J distinguished between the failure to attend meetings and a neglect or omission of a duty which ought to be performed at those meetings. Even if he had read the reports sent to him, the Marquis would have been led to believe that the bank's affairs were being conducted in accordance with its rules.

14.33 Romer J's statement of the diligence to be expected of a director no longer accurately reflects modern standards or expectations save, possibly, in relation to non-executive directors. In practice, executive directors will generally be subject to contractual obligations which require that they give their constant and undivided attention to the affairs of the company in any event. The general expectation is that, so long as a director holds office and receives remuneration, it is incumbent upon that director to keep himself informed as to its financial affairs and to play an appropriate role in its management.[46]

---

[43] *Re Barings plc (No 5)* [1999] 1 BCLC 433, 489, per Jonathan Parker J at para B7(i), and endorsed by the CA at [2000] 1 BCLC 523, 553–6 at para 36.

[44] *Re Barings plc (No 5)* [1999] 1 BCLC 489, 528g–h, per Jonathan Parker J. See *Weavering Capital (UK) Ltd v Peterson* [2012] EWHC 1480 (Ch); [2015] BCC 741 CA. In that case, one director (Mrs Peterson) was found to have been negligent in approving the company's swaps trading policy, another (Mr Dabhia) by failing to satisfy himself as to the details and propriety of the swaps. Proudman J concluded that both directors had failed to acquire a sufficient knowledge and understanding of the company's business: paras 177 and 188. The CA dismissed Mr Dabhia's appeal. See also *Brumder v Motornet Services and Repairs Ltd* [2013] 1 WLR 2783, CA: the fact that the director was neither a mechanic nor skilled in the operation of a workshop did not mean he could escape liability for adopting a cavalier attitude and approach to health and safety issues, to which he paid no attention whatsoever (para 58). For a recent statement of the position in Australia see *ASIC v Healey* [2011] FCA 717.

[45] *Re Cardiff Savings Bank* [1892] 2 Ch 100. See also *Re Denham & Co* (1884) 25 Ch D 752, in which a director who was a 'country gentleman not a skilled accountant' was not liable for recommending payment of a dividend out of capital.

[46] *Re Galeforce Pleating Co Ltd* [1999] 2 BCLC 704, a disqualification case in which it was held that it was no answer to say, as the director had, that she 'had virtually a most negligible actual involvement in the running of the company' (716a). There is a useful discussion by Briggs J of the duty to take reasonable steps to prevent and detect fraud and other irregularities in *Lexi Holdings plc v Luqman* [2008] 2 BCLC 725 at paras 30–9, but note that the CA reversed the Judge on the question of causation. If, consistently with his duty to the company, a director should have performed a particular action then he is liable for the consequences of not doing it. It is no answer to prove that he would have done something else for that would be to enable one breach of duty to be used to excuse another: [2009] 2 BCLC 1, per Sir Andrew Morritt C at para 38.

D. Errors of Judgment

It has long been the case that directors are not to be held liable for 'mere errors of judgment'.[47] **14.34**
'Misjudgment is not of itself negligence.'[48] The courts historically have been reluctant to
second-guess commercial decisions taken by the directors in good faith in what they honestly consider to be the best commercial interests of the company. They will certainly not
be prepared to do so simply because, with the benefit of hindsight, the decision taken has
turned out to be wrong.[49] Any lingering doubt the court may have in such a case is likely to
be resolved in favour of the director. As Lord Wilberforce said in *Howard Smith Ltd v Ampol
Petroleum Ltd*[50] (in relation to the raising of finance):

> [Their Lordships] accept that it would be wrong for the court to substitute its opinion for
> that of the management, or indeed to question the correctness of the management's decision,
> on such a question, if bona fide arrived at. There is no appeal on merits from management
> decisions to courts of law; nor will courts assume to act as a kind of supervisory board over
> decisions within the powers of management honestly arrived at.

That is not to say that the court will always refuse to investigate the position. Indeed it will **14.35**
be necessary for it to determine whether what is complained of is a mere error of judgment
or negligence amounting to breach of duty. It is implicit from what Lord Hatherley LC said
in *Overend & Gurney Co v Gibb*[51] that his conclusion would have been different had he considered that the directors were 'cognisant of circumstances of such a character, so plain, so
manifest, and so simple of appreciation, that no men with any ordinary degree of prudence,
acting on their own behalf, would have entered into such a transaction as they entered into'.
In modern times, and having regard to the 2006 Act, s 174, it is suggested that the courts' traditional reluctance to criticize errors of judgment will not extend to acts or omissions which
no reasonable director or one possessing the particular director's expertise would have made.

The hurdle is necessarily a high one. This is emphasized perhaps by the high burden of proof **14.36**
which falls to be discharged if the only complaint in support of an application for a director's
disqualification is that he was incompetent.[52] Some caution is to be exercised in seeking to

---

[47] *Overend & Gurney Co v Gibb* (1872) LR 5 HL 480, 494, per Lord Hatherley LC; *Lagunas Nitrate Company
v Lagunas Syndicate* [1899] 2 Ch, 392, 435, CA, per Lindley MR; *In re Brazilian Rubber Plantations and Estates
Limited* [1911] 1 Ch 425, 437; *In re City Equitable Fire Insurance Company Limited* [1925] 1 Ch 407, 429.

[48] *Roberts v Frohlich* [2011] 2 BCLC 625, at para 108 (Norris J). The position is Australia is similar: see *ASIC
v Vines* [2005] NSWSC 738, [2007] NSWCA 75 (on appeal); *ASIC v Rich* [2009] NSWSC 1229; and *ASIC
v Healey* [2011] FCA 717.

[49] See eg *Richmond Pharmacology Ltd v Chester Overseas Ltd* [2014] Bus LR 1110. In that case, confidential
information was disclosed when shares in the company were marketed, in reliance by the director on an interpretation of the shareholders' agreement and new articles which the deputy judge rejected. Nevertheless, he
accepted that the director's interpretation had been a reasonable one, as a reasonable person in his position at the
relevant time could properly have taken a different view from that ultimately taken by the judge.

[50] [1974] AC 821, 832. See also *Re Smith & Fawcett Ltd* [1942] Ch 304; *Devlin v Slough Estates Ltd and
ors* [1983] BCLC 497, 504; *Runciman v Walter Runciman plc* [1992] BCLC 1084; *Re Tottenham Hotspur plc*
[1994] BCLC 655, 660.

[51] (1872) LR 5 HL 480, 487.

[52] *Re Sevenoaks Stationers (Retail) Ltd* [1991] Ch 164, 184, CA; *Re Barings plc (No 5)* [1999] 1 BCLC 433,
483–4 (para [A7]); *Re Cubelock* [2001] BCC 523, 535–6 (paras 50–3); *Re Bradcrown Ltd* [2001] 1 BCLC 547
at para 10; *Secretary of State for Trade and Industry v Walker* [2003] 1 BCLC 363 at paras 48–50. Though high,
the degree of incompetence should not be exaggerated given the ability of the court to grant the director leave
to act, notwithstanding the making of a disqualification order: *Re Barings plc (No 5)* [2000] 1 BCLC 523, CA
at para 35.

draw parallels in the context of disqualification, however. What may constitute a breach of duty in civil proceedings against the director, though it is a matter to which the court must have regard,[53] will not necessarily justify a finding of unfitness for the purposes of making a disqualification order against him, just as the director may be unfit even though no breach of duty is proved against him.[54] The position was perhaps best summed up by Jonathan Parker J in another passage in his judgment in *Re Barings plc (No 5)*:[55]

> Although in considering the question of unfitness the court had to have regard (among other things) to 'any misfeasance or breach of any fiduciary or other duty' by the respondent in relation to the company ... it is not in my judgment a prerequisite of a finding of unfitness that the respondent should have been guilty of misfeasance or breach of duty in relation to the company. Unfitness may, in my judgment, be demonstrated by conduct which did not involve a breach of any statutory or common law duty: for example, trading at the risk of creditors may found a finding of unfitness even though it might not amount to wrongful trading under s 214 of the Insolvency Act 1986. Nor, in my judgment, would it necessarily be an answer to a charge of unfitness founded on allegations of incompetence that the errors which the respondent made can be characterised as errors of judgment rather than as negligent mistakes. It is, I think, possible to envisage a case where a respondent had shown himself so completely lacking in judgment as to justify a finding of unfitness, notwithstanding that he had not been guilty of misfeasance or breach of duty. Conversely, in my judgment, the fact that a respondent may have been guilty of misfeasance or breach of duty does not necessarily mean that he is unfit. As Sch 1 makes clear, there were a number of matters to which the court was required to have regard in considering the question of unfitness, in addition to misfeasance and breach of duty.

14.37 The Law Commission considered whether, in the event that a statutory duty of care were to be introduced, there would also need to be a statutory statement of the principle of non-interference by the courts in commercial decisions made in good faith,[56] but concluded that it would be unnecessary and also difficult to formulate so as to avoid narrowing the principle or making it too rigid.[57] The CLR agreed and likewise were opposed to a legislative business-judgment rule. As they observed:

> Directors are employed to take risks, often under severe time pressures which prevent the fullest examination of all relevant factors. Some of these risks will not pay off. The directors' key skill is one of balancing the risk and time factors, recognising that their company's success and failure will depend on their not being unduly cautious as well as avoiding foolhardiness. What risks are appropriate will depend on a multitude of factors, including the ethos of the company and the character of its business and markets.[58]

While they recognized a danger that the courts might apply hindsight, they noted that the courts had in fact shown 'a proper reluctance to enter into the merits of commercial decisions'.[59]

14.38 In the event, the Act contains no statement of the principle, nor is any reference made to it.

---

[53] CDDA, s 9 and Sch 1, Part I, para 1.
[54] *Re Barings plc (No 5)* [2000] 1 BCLC 523, CA at para 35.
[55] [1999] 1 BCLC 433, 486.
[56] Law Commission, *Company Directors: Regulating Conflicts of Interests and Formulating a Statement of Duties* (Consultation Paper No 153, 1998), paras 15.31 and 15.41.
[57] Law Commission, *Company Directors: Regulating Conflicts of Interests and Formulating a Statement of Duties* (Report No 261, 1999), paras 5.28–5.29.
[58] CLR: *Developing the Framework*, para 3.69.
[59] CLR: *Developing the Framework*, para 3.70.

E. Delegation to and Reliance on Others

The 2006 Act contains no statement to the effect that directors may delegate to, and **14.39** rely on, third parties, nor any description of the circumstances in which they may do so. This follows the recommendation of the Law Commission that there should be no such statement, because the law was still developing, such a statement was likely to be too restrictive and, in any event, their research did not reveal any undue concern on the question. In the absence of a statutory statement, therefore, the position remains as it is at common law.

The classical exposition of the position at common law, to be found in Romer J's third **14.40** general proposition in *City Equitable*, is set out in paragraph 14.19 above. That statement has since been relied on, perhaps unfairly, in order to support the contention that the modern director is entitled to place unquestioning reliance upon others to do their job. That contention was decisively rejected, however, by Langley J in *Equitable Life Assurance Society v Bowley*.[60] The most authoritative summary of the modern position is to be found in the following extract from the judgment of Jonathan Parker J in *Re Barings plc (No 5)*,[61] in terms subsequently adopted verbatim by the Court of Appeal in that case:[62]

   (i) Directors have, both collectively and individually, a continuing duty to acquire and maintain a sufficient knowledge and understanding of the company's business to enable them properly to discharge their duties as directors.

   (ii) Whilst directors are entitled (subject to the articles of association of the company) to delegate particular functions to those below them in the management chain, and to trust their competence and integrity to a reasonable extent, the exercise of the power of delegation does not absolve a director from the duty to supervise the discharge of the delegated functions.

   (iii) No rule of universal application can be formulated as to the duty referred to in (ii) above. The extent of the duty, and the question whether it has been discharged, must depend on the facts of each particular case, including the director's role in the management of the company.

The duty to supervise is thus a continuing duty, which cannot be avoided. The extent of the **14.41** supervision required will depend on all the circumstances. In some cases, the circumstances will be such that it will be incumbent on the director to take the initiative in satisfying himself that matters of concern have been properly dealt with and that delegated functions have been properly carried out, rather than expecting a colleague or senior subordinate charged with implementing improvements to raise any continuing concerns he may have.[63] In an extreme case, the degree of supervision required by extensive delegation of management to others may of itself mean that the director simply cannot in any practical sense discharge his duty. Such was the position in *Re London Citylink*,[64] where the sole director of hundreds

---

[60] [2004] 1 BCLC 180 at para 41.
[61] [1999] 1 BCLC 433, 489, following *Re Westmid Packing Services Ltd* [1998] 2 BCLC 646, CA.
[62] [2000] 1 BCLC 523, CA at para 36.
[63] *Re Barings plc (No 5)* [1999] 1 BCLC 433, 519c–h.
[64] [2005] EWHC 2875 (Ch), per Pumfrey J at para 37.

of companies, by powers of attorney, delegated their management to the beneficial owners, who had to be, but could not possibly be, supervised by him.

14.42 Directors can delegate functions. Their ability to do so, however, does not mean that they can delegate responsibility, nor that they are no longer under any duty in relation to the discharge of the particular function delegated, notwithstanding that the person to whom the function has been delegated may appear both trustworthy and capable of discharging it. As Sir Richard Scott V-C put it, in the context of disqualification proceedings following the collapse of Barings plc:[65]

> Overall responsibility is not delegable. All that is delegable is the discharge of particular functions. The degree of personal blameworthiness that may attach to the individual with the overall responsibility, on account of a failure by those to whom he has delegated a particular task, must depend on the facts of each particular case. Sometimes there may be a question whether the delegation has been made to the appropriate person; sometimes there may be a question of whether the individual with overall responsibility should have checked how his subordinates were discharging their delegated functions. Sometimes the system itself, in which the failures have taken place, is an inadequate system for which the person with overall responsibility must take some blame.

14.43 It will frequently be the case that directors will of necessity delegate and divide responsibility as between themselves. There is nothing wrong with that so long as it is done to a proper degree and does not involve total abrogation of responsibility.[66] Likewise a director may legitimately defer to the views of a fellow director whom he reasonably considers to have greater experience and expertise than himself, even one with whose views he might disagree. Where, for example, there is a director who has a record and reputation for outstanding skill and experience in the company's business activity, as Bernard Madoff once did, his fellow directors are entitled to accord a high degree of deference and trust to his views as to what is in the company's best interests.[67] In circumstances where one or more of the directors allow themselves to be dominated or manipulated, dazzled or bamboozled by one of their number, however, they will have gone beyond the boundaries of what is proper, and will be in breach of duty.[68] Similarly, a director will not be able to escape liability by saying she only had a limited role in the management of a small company owned and controlled by her husband.[69]

---

[65] Cited by Jonathan Parker J in *Re Barings plc (No 5)* [1999] 1 BCLC 433, 487 (para B3); *Re Queens Moat Houses plc (No 2)* [2005] 1 BCLC 136 at para 27.

[66] *Re Westmid Packing Services Ltd* [1998] 2 BCLC 646, 653c, CA, per Lord Woolf MR.

[67] *Madoff Securities International Ltd v Raven* [2013] EWHC 3147 (Comm). In that case, Popplewell J concluded that the directors were entitled to defer to the views expressed by Bernard Madoff as to what was in the interests of MSIL. See also the discussion of the duty to exercise independent judgment in Chapter 13.

[68] *Re Westmid Packing Services Ltd* [1998] 2 BCLC 646, 653c, 654g, CA, per Lord Woolf MR; *Lexi Holdings v Luqman* [2009] 2 BCLC 1, CA, per Sir Andrew Morritt C at para 37. See also *Weavering Capital (UK) Ltd v Peterson* [2012] EWHC 1480 (Ch). In that case, one director (Mr Dabhia) had allowed himself to be taken in by the apparently plausible explanations of another director, Mr Peterson. The judge concluded that, had he probed the information he had been given, as he should have done, Mr Dabhia would have been able to see the explanations were deficient. Accordingly, he had acted in breach of duty, a decision upheld by the CA on appeal: [2015] BCC 741 at para 34.

[69] *Weavering Capital (UK) Ltd v Peterson* [2012] EWHC 1480 (Ch). In that case, Mrs Peterson, another director, was found to have been negligent in approving the company's swaps trading policy. Proudman J concluded that if the director had acquired a sufficient knowledge and understanding of the company's business, she would have known that she could not, consistently with her duties, have given such approval.

In applying to the management and custodianship of the company's property and affairs **14.44** the same degree of care as he might reasonably be expected to apply in the management and custodianship of his own, it is to be expected that a director will frequently seek and then rely upon advice. That is not to say that it will always be necessary to seek advice, or that failure to do so will necessarily amount to a breach of duty.[70] Nevertheless, failure to seek advice when it should have been sought may amount to a breach of duty by the director.[71] If the director seeks appropriate advice and then acts upon it to the best of his ability, believing it to be correct, he will prima facie have discharged his duty.[72] The advice may be right or wrong, or it may be that a different advisor would have given different, possibly better, advice, but this will not affect the question whether the director, by so acting, has discharged his duty.[73] The director must, however, exercise reasonable care in determining what advice it is, in all the circumstances, reasonable to seek. Moreover, he cannot rely on it slavishly or blindly, as to do so would be inconsistent not only with his duty to exercise reasonable care, skill, and diligence but also his duty to exercise independent judgment.[74]

It follows from these statements of the law that the question whether, in any given case, **14.45** delegation or reliance by the director is appropriate, will depend upon all the circumstances of that case, and what may be appropriate in one case will not necessarily be appropriate in another.[75]

F. Non-executive Directors

The 2006 Act, s 174 does not distinguish between executive directors and non-executive **14.46** directors: each owes the same duty to exercise reasonable care, skill, and diligence. The scope of the duty, however, will necessarily vary. What may reasonably be expected of an executive director, bound by the terms of his service contract to devote himself full-time to the business of the company, would be unrealistic to expect of a non-executive director. Moreover the purpose behind the appointment of non-executive directors to the board of the company, and the functions they will perform, are obviously different.

---

[70] *ARB International Ltd v Baillie* [2014] CLC 255. In that case, the director permitted insurance business to go to another company on the basis that post-transfer commission would go to that company. Robin Knowles QC, sitting as a deputy judge of the High Court, concluded that the director was not to be criticized for not seeking advice to establish the company's rights prior to the transfer, as there had been no suggestion from lawyers previously involved that advice should be taken and, even if it had been, it could easily have been less than conclusive.

[71] *Equitable Life Assurance Society v Bowley* [2004] 1 BCLC 180 at paras 70–3.

[72] *Green v Walkling* [2008] 2 BCLC 332 at paras 34–8. See also *Re Pro4Sport Ltd* [2016] 1 BCLC 207. In that case, acting on the advice of the firm of insolvency practitioners, a partner in which was subsequently appointed liquidator of the company, the director had transferred the company's assets on the eve of its liquidation for a deferred consideration and without (as a director of the transferee) providing a guarantee. He was found not to have acted in breach of duty, the fact that he had sought and relied on advice being an important factor (para 46), as was the fact that the liquidator had adopted the contract.

[73] *Green v Walkling* [2008] 2 BCLC 332 at para 38.

[74] 2006 Act, s 173.

[75] For the position in Australia, see *ASIC v Adler* [2002] NSWSC 171, [2003] NWSCA 131 (on appeal); *ASIC v Vines* (2007) 62 ACSR 1; *ASIC v Healey* [2011] FCA 717; and *Trilogy Funds Management Ltd v Sullivan* [2015] FCA 1452. For the position in New Zealand, see *Dairy Containers Ltd v NZI Bank Ltd* [1995] 2 NZLR 30.

14.47   In modern times, the company may reasonably look to non-executive directors for independence of judgment and supervision of the executive management.[76] *In Equitable Life Assurance Society v Bowley*[77] Langley J accepted that the duty owed by a non-executive director will in expression be the same as the duty owed by an executive director, but in application the duty may and usually will differ. He went on to conclude that (a) a non-executive director could not place unquestioning reliance on others to do their job, (b) the extent to which a non-executive director may reasonably rely on the executive directors and other professionals to perform their duties is a developing area of the law and one which is 'fact sensitive',[78] and (c) it is arguable that a company may reasonably look to non-executive directors for independence of judgment and supervision of executive management.

14.48   It is a main principle of the UK Corporate Governance Code April 2016 that non-executive directors should 'constructively challenge and help develop proposals on strategy'. It goes on:

> Non-executive directors should scrutinise the performance of management in meeting agreed goals and objectives and monitor the reporting of performance. They should satisfy themselves on the integrity of financial information and that financial controls and systems of risk management are robust and defensible. They are responsible for determining appropriate levels of remuneration of executive directors and have a prime role in appointing and, where necessary, removing executive directors, and in succession planning.[79]

More detailed guidance is then given as to the manner in which the non-executive directors should perform their functions and communicate any concerns:

> A.4.1 The board should appoint one of the independent non-executive directors to be the senior independent director to provide a sounding board for the chairman and to serve as an intermediary for the other directors when necessary. The senior independent director should be available to shareholders if they have concerns which contact through the normal channels of chairman, chief executive or other executive directors has failed to resolve or for which such contact is inappropriate.

> A.4.2 The chairman should hold meetings with the non-executive directors without the executives present. Led by the senior independent director, the non-executive directors should meet without the chairman present as least annually to appraise the chairman's performance and on such other occasions as are deemed appropriate.

> A.4.3 Where directors have concerns which cannot be resolved about the running of the company or a proposed action, they should ensure that their concerns are recorded in the board minutes. On resignation, a non-executive director should provide a written statement to the chairman, for circulation to the board, if they have any such concerns.

14.49   Day-to-day involvement with the company will not generally be expected, and is unlikely in any event to be possible or desirable. Just how much time and attention the non-executive director must devote to the company will inevitably depend on the facts and will vary from

---

[76] *Equitable Life Assurance Society v Bowley* [2004] 1 BCLC 180 at para 41.

[77] [2004] 1 BCLC 180 at paras 35–41. In reaching these conclusions Langley J found helpful the statement of Jonathan Parker J, [1999] 1 BCLC 433, 489, approved by Morritt LJ in *Re Barings plc (No 5), Secretary of State for Trade and Industry v Baker (No 5)* [2000] 1 BCLC 523, 535–6, CA at para 36, quoted in para 14.39 above. For the position in Australia, see *ASIC v Healey* [2011] FCA 717.

[78] This dictum was referred to with apparent approval in *Brumder v Motornet Services and Repairs Ltd* [2013] 1 WLR 2783, CA, per Beatson LJ at para 55.

[79] The UK Corporate Governance Code April 2016, A.4 Non-executive Directors (supporting principle).

case to case. Nevertheless the diligence with which he will be expected to attend to the affairs of the company will be that which, in all the circumstances, is reasonably necessary to enable him properly to ensure that the judgment he exercises is not only independent but also properly informed, and to ensure that his supervision of the executive management is effective. The UK Corporate Governance Code April 2016 provides further guidance in this respect. In common with executive directors, non-executive directors 'should be able to allocate sufficient time to the company to discharge their responsibilities effectively'. In particular:

> B.3.2 … The letter of appointment should set out the expected time commitment. Non-executive directors should undertake that they will have sufficient time to meet what is expected of them. Their other significant commitments should be disclosed to the board before appointment, with a broad indication of the time involved and the board should be informed of subsequent changes.

It goes on to state that non-executive directors should be offered the opportunity to attend scheduled meetings with major shareholders and should expect to attend meetings if requested by major shareholders, to help develop a balanced understanding of their concerns.[80]

14.50 Typically, the non-executive director will be appointed to the company's board by virtue of his particular knowledge, skill, and experience. He must take care to apply such skills. Indeed the subjective element of the requirement laid down by the 2006 Act, s 174 requires him to do so. It is no part of the non-executive director's function, for example, to accept without question the reliability of management accounts and financial information presented to him. In order properly to supervise the executive management, it is to be expected that he would probe the financial information provided in order to test its reliability, deploying the care and skill reasonably to be expected of him, both subjectively and objectively ascertained in accordance with the requirements of the 2006 Act, s 174. To underline the importance of maintaining an appropriate relationship with the company's auditors, the Code recommends that the board should establish an audit committee comprising non-executive director, at least one of which should have recent and relevant financial experience.[81]

14.51 In other cases, however, particularly where the company is effectively used as a vehicle for fraud or other illegal activity by a dominant director, it may be that it is the very absence of any particular knowledge, skill, or experience on the part of the non-executive directors marks them out for appointment. That will not lessen the rigour with which their conduct will be examined if, through culpable failures on their part, the frauds committed by the dominant director continue and cause the company loss. In *Lexi Holdings plc v Luqman*,[82] for example, two sisters who were non-executive directors of a property company operated as a vehicle for fraud by their brother, who was managing director, were found liable to compensate the company for losses caused by his fraud, which could have been prevented if they had not been negligent. Their negligence consisted in their failure to heed and act on signs of dishonesty, when they knew of his past convictions for theft and that he required supervision in the management of the company; their failure to take sufficient interest in the company's affairs to inquire into a false account, which showed continuing dishonesty on a large scale; and allowing themselves to be dominated and bamboozled by him.

---

[80] The UK Corporate Governance Code April 2016, E.1.1.
[81] The UK Corporate Governance Code April 2016, C.3.1.
[82] [2009] 2 BCLC 1, CA.

14.52   It has been said that such duties do not require non-executive directors to overrule the specialist directors, like the finance director, in their specialist fields.[83] Generally speaking, that may be so. What is to be expected of the non-executive director, however, will depend upon the facts and it is conceivable that the circumstances may be such as to require him so to act in an exceptional case. As Lord Woolf has put it, a non-executive director should act as a guard dog and be prepared to bark when necessary.[84]

[83] *Re Continental Assurance of London plc* [2007] 2 BCLC 287 at para 399.
[84] In response to a question from the audience following the COMBAR Annual Lecture 2008, 'Global companies can and should have the highest ethical standards', delivered by Lord Woolf on 21 October 2008.

15

DUTY TO AVOID CONFLICTS OF INTEREST

Mark Arnold QC and Marcus Haywood

A. Introduction

The 2006 Act, s 175, quoted in paragraph 15.09 below,[1] sets out the duty to avoid conflicts of interest. That duty is one of the paradigm manifestations of a director's fiduciary duty of loyalty to the company. As Lord Upjohn said in *Phipps v Boardman*: '[T]he fundamental rule of equity [is] that a person in a fiduciary capacity must not make a profit out of his trust which is part of the wider rule that a trustee must not place himself in a position where his duty and his interest may conflict.'[2]   **15.01**

(1) The 'no conflict rule' and the 'no profit rule'

The court came to recognize that the duty of a fiduciary, such as a director, concerning conflicts of interest had two strands: the 'no conflict rule' and the 'no profit rule',[3] which were   **15.02**

---

[1] Section 175 came into force on 1 October 2008.

[2] [1967] 2 AC 46, 123, HL.

[3] The two strands were identified by Deane J in the High Court of Australia in *Chan v Zacharia* (1984) 154 CLR 178, 198, cited with approval in England in *Don King Productions Inc v Warren* [2000] Ch 291, 340, 341, CA. The Law Commission recognized the two strands when discussing a statutory statement of directors' fiduciary duties: *Company Directors: Regulating Conflicts of Interest and Formulating a Statement of Duties* (No 153, 1998), paras 11.13–11.17.

to be considered separately.[4] The two rules remain relevant to the discussion of s 175.[5] That section states the 'no conflict rule' and also includes the 'no profit rule'.

15.03 Under the 'no conflict rule', as it applies to a company director, the director has to account to the company for any benefit or gain obtained or received by him in circumstances where there existed a conflict of personal interest and fiduciary duty or a significant possibility of such conflict. This strict rule was imposed in order to prevent the director from being swayed by considerations of personal interest in the exercise of those powers which were his to exercise in a fiduciary capacity.[6] The rule did not apply (a) if the company gave its informed consent to the director being in a position of conflict,[7] (b) to the activities of a director after he had ceased to hold office and had no powers to exercise,[8] and (c) where the director was entirely excluded from all decision-making and participation in the company's affairs.[9]

15.04 Under the 'no profit rule', as it applies to a company director, a director is required to account to the company for any benefit or gain obtained or received by reason of or by use of his fiduciary position or of opportunity or knowledge resulting from it, without the informed consent of the company to the benefit or gain. The purpose of the rule is to prevent the director from actually misusing his position for personal advantage.[10]

(2) Reform

15.05 In March 2000 the CLR described the law relating to directors' conflict of interest as one of the most difficult areas of company law.[11] By then the Companies Acts had intervened to regulate many aspects of a director's dealings with the company, making some dealings unlawful (loans) and requiring others to be subject to approval by members (substantial property transactions) or to be disclosed to the board (interests in contracts).[12] These statutory interventions did not affect the underlying principle, which the CLR identified in these terms:[13]

---

[4] *Ultraframe (UK) Ltd v Fielding* [2005] EWHC 1638 (Ch) at para 1306. That is how they were treated in the most significant recent cases on the application of these rules to company directors under the pre-2006 Act law: *Wilkinson v West Coast Capital* [2007] BCC 717 at paras 245–319 and *Re Allied Business and Financial Consultants Ltd* [2009] 2 BCLC 666, CA.

[5] *Premier Waste Management Ltd v Towers* [2012] 1 BCLC 67, CA at paras 5, 7–12.

[6] *Chan v Zacharia* (1984) 154 CLR 178, 198; *Ultraframe (UK) Ltd v Fielding* [2005] EWHC 1638 (Ch) at para 1305, 1308.

[7] *Bristol and West Building Society v Mothew* [1998] Ch 1, 18, CA, per Millett LJ; *Ultraframe (UK) Ltd v Fielding* [2005] EWHC 1638 (Ch) at para 1317.

[8] *Ultraframe (UK) Ltd v Fielding* [2005] EWHC 1638 (Ch) at para 1309, citing *CMS Dolphin Ltd v Simonet* [2001] 2 BCLC 704; *British Midland Tool Ltd v Pyke* [2003] 2 BCLC 523; *Quarter Master UK Ltd v Pyke* [2005] 1 BCLC 245, 264. See also *Wilkinson v West Coast Capital* [2007] BCC 717 at para 251 where Warren J makes the point that a former director remains liable under the 'no profit rule'.

[9] *In Plus Group Ltd v Pyke* [2002] 2 BCLC 201, CA at paras 71–7, per Brooke LJ; at para 90, per Sedley LJ; at paras 92 and 94, per Jonathan Parker LJ (where the director did not exploit the company's property or confidential information); *Ultraframe (UK) Ltd v Fielding* [2005] EWHC 1638 (Ch) at para 1310.

[10] *Chan v Zacharia* (1984) 154 CLR 178, 198; *Ultraframe (UK) Ltd v Fielding* [2005] EWHC 1638 (Ch) at paras 1305 and 1318. Also see: *Furs Ltd v Tomkies* (1936) 54 CLR 583, 592 (High Court of Australia); *Regal Hastings Ltd v Gulliver* (1941) [1967] 2 AC 134n, 144, HL; *Gwembe Valley Development Co Ltd v Koshy* [2004] 1 BCLC 131, CA at paras 44 and 45; *Wilkinson v West Coast Capital* [2007] BCC 717 at para 255.

[11] CLR: *Modern Company Law for a Competitive Economy: Developing the Framework* at para 3.61.

[12] 1985 Act, Part X, now replaced by 2006 Act, Part 10, Chapter 4, which is discussed in Ch 18 below.

[13] CLR: *Modern Company Law for a Competitive Economy: Developing the Framework* at para 3.61.

Unless the constitution of the company permits it, a director may not engage in any transaction where his personal interest is involved, nor receive a personal benefit in connection with his functions, whether or not the company's best interests are damaged thereby.

The CLR identified three areas where this principle applies: (a) where the company enters **15.06** into a contract or other transaction in which the director has an interest;[14] (b) where the director uses or exploits an asset, including a business opportunity, which is considered to belong to the company, for his own purposes or for the purpose of someone other than the company;[15] and (c) where a director receives an undisclosed benefit in some other way, such as a bribe or commission, in connection with the exercise of his powers.[16] The CLR recommended a statutory statement of directors' duties relating to conflict of interest which reflected the three areas it had identified.[17]

The area that caused most concern to the CLR concerned the personal exploitation of corpo- **15.07** rate opportunities. The CLR identified three kinds of case, where the company, acting by its members or the board, might permit a director to exploit for his personal benefit or for the benefit of some other person a business opportunity which he had encountered as a director: (a) where the company could not exploit the opportunity itself in any event; (b) where the company had already decided to abandon the opportunity; and (c) where the company did not wish to exploit it and was content for the director to do so. The CLR considered that the requirement for approval by members in all those cases was unduly strict. It recommended that the board of a private company and the board of a public company, if expressly authorized under its constitution, should be able to waive the company's rights and approve the transaction provided that (i) the board acts independently of any conflicted director, so that the authorization is given only by directors who are genuinely independent in the sense that they have no interest, direct or indirect, in the transaction, (ii) the transaction should subsequently be disclosed in the company's annual report and accounts, and (iii) the authorization should be specific to the proposal.[18]

The government accepted these recommendations[19] and the 2006 Act deals with conflicts of **15.08** interest in three distinct ways:

(1) in s 175, which applies to the duty to avoid conflicts of interest which do not arise in relation to a transaction or arrangement with the company (the subject of this chapter);

(2) in s 176, which applies to the duty not to accept benefits from third parties (the subject of Chapter 16 below); and

---

[14] *Modern Company Law for a Competitive Economy: Developing the Framework* at para 3.62. *Aberdeen Railway Co v Blaikie Bros* (1854) 1 Macq 461, HL, is a well-known example of this type of conflict. There, at the instance of the company, the court set aside a contract with a partnership of which a director was a member.

[15] CLR: *Modern Company Law for a Competitive Economy: Developing the Framework* at para 3.63. *Cook v Deeks* [1916] 1 AC 554, PC, and *Regal Hastings Ltd v Gulliver* (1941) [1967] 2 AC 134n, HL are much-cited examples. In both cases directors were held liable to account to the company for profits from dealings with third parties which came to them from their position as directors.

[16] CLR: *Modern Company Law for a Competitive Economy: Developing the Framework* at para 3.64. *AG for Hong Kong v Reid* [1994] 1 AC 324, PC is a well-known example, which, in relation to personal and proprietary remedies, is discussed in detail in Ch 19 and also in paras 16.35ff below.

[17] CLR: *Modern Company Law for a Competitive Economy: Completing the Structure* at paras 3.25–3.28; *Final Report* at paras 3.5–3.12.

[18] CLR: *Modern Company Law for a Competitive Economy: Final Report* at paras 3.21–3.27.

[19] White Paper: *Company Law Reform* (Cm 6456, March 2005) at p 21.

(3) in s 177, which obliges a director to declare to the board his interest in a proposed transaction or arrangement with the company (with the duty in s 182 to declare to the board his interest in an existing transaction or arrangement with the company, the subject of Chapter 17 below).

B. The Scope of the Duty to Avoid Conflicts of Interest

15.09 The 2006 Act, s 175 provides that:

(1) A director of a company must avoid a situation in which he has, or can have, a direct or indirect interest that conflicts, or possibly may conflict, with the interests of the company.

(2) This applies in particular to the exploitation of any property, information or opportunity (and it is immaterial whether the company could take advantage of the property, information or opportunity).

(3) This duty does not apply to a conflict of interest arising in relation to a transaction or arrangement with the company.

(4) This duty is not infringed—
  (a) if the situation cannot reasonably be regarded as likely to give rise to a conflict of interest; or
  (b) if the matter has been authorised by the directors.

(5) Authorisation may be given by the directors—
  (a) where the company is a private company and nothing in the company's constitution invalidates such authorisation, by the matter aabeing proposed to and authorised by the directors; or
  (b) where the company is a public company and its constitution includes provision enabling the directors to authorise the matter, by the matter being proposed to and authorised by them in accordance with the constitution.

(6) The authorisation is effective only if—
  (a) any requirement as to the quorum at the meeting at which the matter is considered is met without counting the director in question or any other interested director, and
  (b) the matter was agreed to without their voting or would have been agreed to if their votes had not been counted.

(7) Any reference in this section to a conflict of interest includes a conflict of interest and duty and a conflict of duties.

15.10 The duty stated in s 175 applies not only to a director, but also to a former director as regards the exploitation of any property, information, or opportunity of which he became aware at a time when he was a director.[20] The application of the duty to former directors is discussed in Section E below.

15.11 The duty also applies to a shadow director to the extent that it is capable of so applying.[21]

15.12 The content of the duty to avoid conflicts of interest is stated in s 175(1) and (2), which should be read with sub-s (7), which explains that references in the section to a conflict of interest include both a conflict of interest and duty and a conflict of duties. These subsections

---

[20] 2006 Act, s 170(2).
[21] 2006 Act, s 170(5), as substituted by SBEE Act 2015, s 89(2) as from 26 May 2015. See Ch 10, Section C above.

are considered in Section C below. A breach by a director of his duty under s 175 will often also involve a breach of his other duties; eg his duty to promote the success of the company, to exercise independent judgment or to act within the scope of his powers.

Section 175(3) limits the scope of the duty, because it provides that the duty does not apply to a conflict of interest arising in relation to a proposed or existing transaction or arrangement with the company.[22] Matters such as a director's service contract or remuneration, loans between the company and the director, and contracts with a company of which the director is a shareholder are not within the scope of s 175 and fall to be considered under s 177 or under s 182 (as to which see Chapter 17 below). **15.13**

Section 175(3)–(6) explains the two circumstances where the duty is not infringed. One is where the situation cannot reasonably be regarded as likely to give rise to a conflict of interest. If that is not the case, the director who is in a position of conflict should bring himself within the second circumstance by obtaining the authorization of the directors. This latter circumstance is a reform recommended by the CLR, which enables a director to avoid the harsh consequences of the decision of the House of Lords in *Regal (Hastings) Ltd v Gulliver*.[23] If the director does not or cannot obtain authorization from the directors he may obtain the protection of the consent, approval, or authorization of the members.[24] **15.14**

C. Avoidance of Situations of Conflict

(1) The principle

By s 175(1) a director of a company must avoid any situation in which he has, or can have, a direct or indirect interest that conflicts, or possibly may conflict, with the interests of the company.[25] By s 175(2) this duty applies to any property, information or opportunity, whether or not the company could take advantage of it. When interpreting and applying these provisions, the court will have regard to the corresponding common law rule and equitable principles.[26] The statutory rule therefore applies to situations that were within the equitable 'no conflict rule' and/or 'no profit rule'. **15.15**

The situation to be avoided

The statutory duty is based upon the common law rule of equity that any person owing fiduciary duties must not put himself into a position in which he has or can have conflicting interests. The rule is a reformulation of the classic statement of the common law in *Aberdeen Railway Co v Blaikie Bros* by Lord Cranworth:[27] **15.16**

> [It] is a rule of universal application, that no one, having [fiduciary] duties to discharge, shall be allowed to enter into engagements in which he has, or can have, a personal

---

[22] For the meaning of 'transaction or arrangement', see Ch 17 below at para 17.20.
[23] [1967] 2 AC 134n, HL.
[24] 2006 Act, s 180(4)(a) (Ch 10, Section D above), or ratification under s 239 (Ch 20, Section D below).
[25] 2006 Act, s 175(1).
[26] 2006 Act, s 170(4); *Premier Waste Management Ltd v Towers* [2012] 1 BCLC 67, CA at para 5.
[27] (1854) 1 Macq 461, 471, HL. See also *Keech v Sandford* (1726) Sel Cas t King 61; *Bray v Ford* [1896] AC 44, 51, HL.

interest conflicting, or which may conflict, with the interests of those whom he is bound to protect. So strictly is this principle adhered to, that no question is allowed to be raised as to the fairness or unfairness of a contract so entered into.[28]

15.17   As is clear from the passage cited above the rule is strict.[29] As it relates to serving directors, it is 'an inflexible rule [which] must be applied inexorably by [the] court which is not entitled … to receive evidence, or suggestion, or argument as to whether the principal did or did not suffer any injury in fact by reason of the dealing of the agent'.[30] The rationale and justice of the strict rule, now embodied in s 175(1), is to protect the company whose interests are potentially at risk from a director who does not give his undivided loyalty to the company.[31] Since the rule is strict, it applies whether or not the director is aware that what he is doing is a breach of his duty;[32] and even though he thought that what he was doing was in the best interests of the company.[33]

15.18   The principle of equity did not involve any enquiry into whether there has been an actual conflict between the interests of the director and that of the company. Instead, it was sufficient for there to have been a breach of the rule that the director had placed himself in a position where there is a possibility that he has or can have an interest that conflicts with that of the company. The phrase 'possibly may conflict' was considered by Lord Upjohn in *Boardman v Phipps* when he said: 'the reasonable man looking at the relevant facts and circumstances of the particular case would think that there was a real sensible possibility of conflict; not that you could imagine some situation arising which might, in some conceivable possibility in events not contemplated as real sensible possibilities by any reasonable person, result in conflict'.[34] More recently in *Bhullar v Bhullar* Jonathan Parker LJ stated that the test was whether: 'reasonable men looking at the facts would think that there was a real sensible possibility of conflict'.[35]

15.19   This test has been reformulated in the 2006 Act, so that a director infringes his duty to avoid a situation of actual or possible conflict, unless (s 175(4)(a)) the situation cannot reasonably be regarded as likely to give rise to a conflict of interest.[36]

---

[28] This principle has been applied in numerous subsequent cases. See in particular: *Regal (Hastings) Ltd v Gulliver* [1967] 2 AC 134, 137–8, 147–50, 155–6, HL; *Boardman v Phipps* [1967] 2 AC 46, 94C–E, 112C–D, 123–5, HL; *Industrial Development Consultants Ltd v Cooley* [1972] 1 WLR 443, 447–53; *Canadian Aero Service v O'Malley* [1973] 40 DLR (3d) 371, 382ff and *Bhullar v Bhullar* [2003] 2 BCLC 241, CA at 27–42. It is also apparent in the first principle quoted in para 15.75 below.

[29] *Boardman v Phipps* [1967] 1 AC 46, 111; *New Zealand Netherlands Society 'Oranje' Inc v Keys* [1973] 1 WLR 1126, 1129–30, PC.

[30] *Parker v McKenna* (1874) LR 10 Ch App 96, 124–5, per James LJ, cited in *Regal (Hastings) Ltd v Gulliver* [1967] 2 AC 134n, 155, HL, per Lord Wright.

[31] *Premier Waste Management Ltd v Towers* [2012] 1 BCLC 67, CA at para 9, per Mummery LJ; citing *Boulting v Association of Cinematograph Television and Allied Technicians* [1963] 2 QB 606, 635–6, CA, per Upjohn LJ.

[32] *Richmond Pharmacology Ltd v Chester Overseas Ltd* [2014] Bus LR 1110 at paras 70–2, confirming that the rule is strict and does not depend on bad faith or the state of mind of the fiduciary.

[33] *Breitenfeld UK Ltd v Harrison* [2015] 2 BCLC 275 at para 70, citing *Bray v Ford* [1896] AC 44, 51.

[34] [1967] 2 AC 46, 124, HL.

[35] [2003] 2 BCLC 241, CA at para 42 and see discussion at paras 27–39; for other similar restatements see *Guinness v Saunders* [1990] 2 AC 663, HL, 689–92, per Lord Templeman; 700, per Lord Goff; *Neptune (Vehicle Washing Equipment) v Fitzgerald (No. 2)* [1995] BCC 1000, 1015–16.

[36] See Section D(1) below.

The interests of the company

The duty to avoid a situation of conflict is infringed by a director even though his conduct **15.20** has caused no loss to the company,[37] there is no unfairness,[38] the honesty of the director is not in question,[39] and the director does not directly or indirectly make a profit.[40] These matters are all irrelevant to the question of liability, given the strict nature of the principle, but may be relevant to remedy.

Section 175(1) applies to all situations where there is a conflict, or possible conflict, between **15.21** the interests of the company on the one hand and the direct or indirect interests of the director or duties owed by him to another person on the other hand. As the exploitation of opportunity cases, discussed in Sections C(6) and E below show, it is not necessary for the company to be the owner of, or have any legal rights over, the property, information, or opportunity referred to in s 175(2). The duty is engaged so long as, in relation to the property, information, or opportunity, the director has a duty of undivided loyalty to the company.

(2) Decision-making

A director owes the company a duty to consider a matter put before the board solely in the **15.22** company's interests. Where the matter concerns a proposed transaction or arrangement with the company, the situation is within s 177 (discussed in Chapter 17 below). An example of a situation where the duty to avoid a conflict of interest under s 175 is infringed is where a director votes at a board meeting in favour of certain corporate changes (eg change of control and compensation terms), which, if approved, will facilitate the sale of his own shares in the company to a third party. In such a case there is a conflict between the director's personal interest in selling his own shares and his duty to consider the terms of the proposed changes solely in the company's interests.[41]

A director who has been appointed as a nominee director for a shareholder or creditor will **15.23** often face particular difficulties in connection with conflicts or possible conflicts of interest. As explained in Chapter 13, Section B(3) there is nothing wrong with a director being appointed as a nominee, but he must comply with his general duties to the company. If a matter comes before the board which concerns his appointor, the nominee director will be in a position of conflict and would usually abstain from voting and obtain any necessary authorization from the other directors or approval from the members.

Similar considerations apply to directors of more than one company in a group, although **15.24** in such a situation it should be straightforward for the director to obtain the protection of approval of the members.

(3) Competing directorships

Section 175(7) provides that any reference in s 175 to a conflict of interest includes a conflict **15.25** of interest and duty and a conflict of duties. This provision raises a number of questions in

---

[37] *Aberdeen Railway Co v Blaikie Bros* (1854) 1 Macq 461, 472, HL; *Regal (Hastings) Ltd v Gulliver* [1967] 2 AC 134n, 153, HL; *Richmond Pharmacology Ltd v Chester Overseas Ltd* [2014] Bus LR 1110 at paras 70–2.
[38] *Aberdeen Railway Co v Blaikie Bros* (1854) 1 Macq 461, 471–2, HL.
[39] *Regal (Hastings) Ltd v Gulliver* [1967] 2 AC 134n, 153, HL; *Breitenfeld UK Ltd v Harrison* [2015] 2 BCLC. 275 at para 70.
[40] *Wilkinson v West Coast Capital* [2007] BCC 717 at para 252.
[41] *PNC Telecom plc v Thomas (No 2)* [2008] 2 BCLC 95 at para 42.

relation to the position where a director acts in relation to two or more companies which are in competition with each other. In such a situation the director does not prefer or potentially prefer his own interest to that of the company, but may prefer his duty to one company to his duty to the other. Similar questions may arise where a director holds shares in or enters into a transaction with a company which competes with the company of which he is a director.

15.26 The position in relation to fiduciaries generally was discussed by Millett LJ in *Bristol and West BS v Mothew*, where he said:[42]

> A fiduciary who acts for two principals with potentially conflicting interests without the informed consent of both is in breach of the obligation of undivided loyalty; he puts himself in a position where his duty to one principal may conflict with his duty to the other … This is sometimes described as 'the double employment rule'. Breach of the rule automatically constitutes a breach of fiduciary duty.

15.27 In so far as the position in relation to directors is concerned it was held by a majority of the Court of Appeal in *Plus Group Ltd v Pyke*[43] that there is no completely rigid rule that a director may not be involved in the business of a company which is in competition with another company of which he was a director.[44] This proposition was based upon the decision in *London and Mashonaland Exploration Co Ltd v New Mashonaland Exploration Co Ltd*,[45] which was approved *obiter* by Lord Blanesburgh in *Bell v Lever Bros Ltd*.[46] However, the *Mashonaland* decision has been subjected to criticism including by Sedley JL in *Re Plus Group*.[47] It is submitted that *Mashonaland* has to be understood as being a case of its time. The better view now is that, like other fiduciaries, a director must not act for two companies with potentially competing interests unless he does so with the informed consent of both companies or the authorization of the directors within the meaning of s 174(4)–(6).[48]

15.28 This was the view of Lord Goldsmith who said that:

> there is currently no absolute rule prohibiting directors from holding multiple directorships or even from engaging in business that competes with the company of which they are a director, but obviously a tension results from that degree of tolerance and the fiduciary duties which the director owes. The solution to it is … there is no prohibition of a conflict or potential conflict as long as it has been authorised by the directors in accordance with the requirements set out in the [Act].[49]

(4) Exploitation of property

15.29 Section 175(2) provides that the duty to avoid conflicts or possible conflicts of interest applies in particular to the exploitation of any property whether or not the company could have taken advantage of it.

---

42 [1998] Ch 1, 18, CA. Cf the position in relation to solicitors: *Clark Boyce v Mouat* [1994] 1 AC 428, PC; *Hilton v Barker Booth & Eastwood* [2005] 1 WLR 567, HL.
43 [2002] 2 BCLC 201.
44 [2002] 2 BCLC 201 at para 72.
45 [1891] WN 165.
46 [1932] AC 161, 195.
47 [2002] 2 BCLC 201 at paras 79–88; *First Subsea Ltd v Balltec Ltd* [2014] EWHC 866 (Ch) at paras 186–95 per Norris J; *Jason v Cheng* [2016] HKFCA 23 at paras 92–106 per Spigelman NPJ.
48 As to authorization by the company, see s 180 and Ch 10, Section D above. As to ratification, see 2006 Act, s 239 and Ch 20, Section D below.
49 Hansard, HL Grand Committee, col 288 (6 February 2006).

It is clear that misappropriation, diversion, or exploitation of the company's property by a **15.30** director will amount to a breach of the duty imposed by s 175(1). Although directors are not strictly speaking trustees of a company's assets they owe a duty not to misapply those assets.[50] As noted above, s 175(2) applies to property that does not belong to the company. It is sufficient that the director owes the company fiduciary duties in relation to the property.

Ball v Eden Project Ltd[51] concerned the personal exploitation of company property by a **15.31** director in a situation that would now be within s 175. While the company was developing the Eden Project, a director registered that name as a trade mark in his own name in respect of a range of goods and services. The court found that the name was part of the goodwill of the company. By registering the trade mark in his own name, the director was able to hold the company to ransom to force it to pay him what he considered he should be paid for work on the development of the project. The court found that the director's conduct put him in a situation of conflict between his personal interest and his fiduciary duties to the company and ordered him to assign the registered trade mark to the company.

Premier Waste Management Ltd v Towers[52] is a recent example of a director putting himself **15.32** in a position of conflict of interest in relation to the exploitation of property in which the company had an interest. In this case the director used for his personal affairs equipment that an employee of the company had obtained on hire from a third party without paying for the equipment or telling the board about these arrangements. As Mummery LJ held,[53] by breaching his duty to avoid a conflict between his duty to the company and his personal interest, the director disloyally deprived the company of the ability to consider whether or not it objected to the diversion of an opportunity to use the equipment away from itself to the director personally. The director was held liable to account to the company at the rate and for the period for which it had been charged by the owner of the equipment.

(5) Exploitation of information

By s 175(2) the duty to avoid situations of conflict of interest applies to the exploitation of **15.33** information, whether or not the company could take advantage of it. Arguably the juxtaposition of the term 'information' next to the term 'property' in s 175(2) suggests that there is an intention to treat information in a similar manner to property, even though in *Boardman v Phipps* Lord Upjohn said that 'in general information is not property at all' as 'it is normally open to all who have eyes to read and ears to hear'.[54] As with property and opportunities, information is within the section if the director owes fiduciary duties to the company in relation to the information.

Deciding whether information has been exploited in breach of a director's duty to avoid **15.34** conflict of interest will largely be a question of fact. No single factor is likely to be determinative. The court will need to decide whether, in the circumstances in which he acquired the

---

[50] *Cook v Deeks* [1916] AC 554, PC; *Selangor United Rubber Estates Ltd v Craddock* [1968] 1 WLR 1555, 1575–6; *CMS Dolphin Ltd v Simonet* [2001] 2 BCLC 704 at para 96. See also Ch 11 at paras 11.40–11.42 above.
[51] [2002] 1 BCLC 313.
[52] [2012] 1 BCLC 67, CA.
[53] [2012] 1 BCLC 67, CA at para 48.
[54] [1967] 2 AC 46, 127.

information, the director had duties to the company. If so he will put himself in a position of conflict if he exploits the information for himself or becomes subject to duties to someone else in relation to the same information.

15.35 In this regard the information exploited need not be confidential to fall within the scope of the duty. The legal rationale for the doctrine is separate from the doctrine of breach of confidence: 'The fact that breach of confidence … may itself afford a ground of relief does not make [it] a necessary ingredient of a successful claim for breach of a fiduciary duty.'[55] Thus it has been said: 'Whether or not the information is confidential, if the opportunity that arises by reason of the acquisition of the information puts the fiduciary in a position of conflict, he cannot take that opportunity.'[56] Of course a director will be in clear breach of his duty to avoid a situation of conflict if he exploits the company's confidential information for his own purposes or for the benefit of a third party in which the director is interested.[57]

15.36 By contrast where the information forms part of the general knowledge and expertise of the director acquired during the course of his work there is unlikely to be any conflict of interest.[58]

(6) Exploitation of an opportunity

15.37 By s 175(2) the duty to avoid situations of conflict of interest also applies to the exploitation of an opportunity, whether or not the company could have taken advantage of it.

The interest of the company in the maturing opportunity

15.38 In the subsection an opportunity is treated in the same way as property. This reflects the position at common law. In *CMS Dolphin Ltd v Simonet* Lawrence Collins J said:[59]

> In my judgment the underlying basis of the liability of a director who exploits after his resignation a maturing business opportunity of the company is that the opportunity is to be treated as if it were property of the company in relation to which the director had fiduciary duties. By seeking to exploit the opportunity after his resignation he is appropriating for himself that property.

---

[55] *Canadian Aero Service Ltd v O'Malley* (1973) 40 DLR (3d) 371, 390; this analysis was confirmed by Collins J in *CMS Dolphin v Simonet* [2001] 2 BCLC 704 at para 94. As to action for breach of confidence see eg *Saltman Engineering Co Ltd v Campbell Engineering Co Ltd* [1963] 3 All ER 413n, CA; *Printers and Finishers Ltd v Holloway* [1964] 3 All ER 731; and *Vestergaard Frandsen A/S v Bestnet Europe Ltd* [2013] 1 WLR 1556, SC.

[56] *Crown Dilmun v Sutton* [2004] 1 BCLC 468 at para 187, per Peter Smith J.

[57] It has been held that the principle that where a person has obtained confidential information from another he must not use that information to the prejudice of the person who gave it applies with particular force as between a director and his company by reason of the fiduciary character of the duty owed by the director: *Baker v Gibbons* [1972] 1 WLR 693, 700. See also *Cranleigh Precision Engineering Ltd v Bryant* [1965] 1 WLR 1293; *Thomas Marshall (Exports) Ltd v Guinle* [1979] Ch 227; *Dranez Anstalt v Hayek* [2002] 1 BCLC 693; *Energy Renewals Ltd v Borg* [2014] EWHC 2166 (Ch); *Richmond Pharmacology Ltd v Chester Overseas Ltd* [2014] Bus LR 1110; *Allfiled UK Ltd v Eltis* [2016] FSR 11. Where a director passes on confidential information this may also amount to a breach of his services agreement with the company (if one exists): cf eg *LC Services Ltd v Brown* [2003] EWHC 3024 (QB).

[58] *Islands Export Finance Ltd v Umunna* [1986] BCLC 460, 482. See also principle 6 quoted in para 15.75 below.

[59] [2001] 2 BCLC 704 at para 96 (applied in *Simtel Communications Ltd v Rebak* [2006] 2 BCLC 571 at para 80). See also *Cook v Deeks* [1916] 1 AC 554, 564, PC.

The duty to avoid conflicts of interest applies even though the company does not have some **15.39** kind of beneficial or proprietary interest in the maturing opportunity.[60] In *Bhullar v Bhullar*, a case on the 'no conflict rule', Jonathan Parker LJ said:[61]

> In a case such as the present, where a fiduciary has exploited a commercial opportunity for his own benefit, the relevant question, in my judgment, is not whether the party to whom the duty is owed (the company, in the instant case) had some kind of beneficial interest in the opportunity: in my judgment that would be too formalistic and restrictive an approach. Rather, the question is simply whether the fiduciary's exploitation of the opportunity is such as to attract the application of the rule.

Jonathan Parker LJ went on to stress that:[62]

> Whether the company could or would have taken that opportunity, had it been made aware of it, is not to the point: the existence of the opportunity was information which it was relevant for the company to know, and it follows that the appellants were under a duty to communicate it to the company.

Whether the company has a sufficient interest in the opportunity to engage the duty under **15.40** s 175 is largely a question of fact. The application of the 'no conflict rule' does not depend on establishing that the company has a proprietary interest in the business opportunity that has been diverted.[63] The court has to weigh all the relevant factors and decide whether the opportunity is sufficiently closely connected to the company to be considered an opportunity of the company.[64]

In this connection, in *Sharma v Sharma*[65] Jackson LJ provided a helpful summary of the scope **15.41** of the opportunities to which the principle applies:

> A company director is in breach of his fiduciary or statutory duty if he exploits for his personal gain (a) opportunities which come to his attention through his role as director or (b) any other opportunities which he could and should exploit for the benefit of the company.

---

[60] *Ultraframe (UK) Ltd v Fielding* [2005] EWHC 1638 (Ch) at para 1355.

[61] [2003] 2 BCLC 241, CA, at para 28; quoted and applied in *Ultraframe (UK) Ltd v Fielding* [2005] EWHC 1638 (Ch) at para 1348; *Wilkinson v West Coast Capital* [2007] BCC 717 at para 268; *Re Southern Counties Fresh Foods Ltd* [2008] EWHC 2810 (Ch) at para 54.

[62] At para 41.

[63] *Ultraframe (UK) Ltd v Fielding* [2005] EWHC 1638 (Ch) at para 1355. See also principle 8 quoted in para 15.75 below.

[64] *Canadian Aero v O'Malley* [1973] 40 DLR (3d) 371 at 390–1; *Regal (Hastings) Ltd v Gulliver* [1967] 2 AC 134n, 153E–F; *Pacifica Shipping Co Ltd v Andersen* [1986] 2 NZLR 328; *SEA Food Internal Pty Ltd v Lam* (1998) 16 ACLC 552, Australian FCA, at §137–§144. Compare also 'the line of business test' in the United States as formulated in *Guth v Loft, Inc* 5 A2d 503 (Del 1939) where it was held that an opportunity was a corporate opportunity if it was closely related to the corporation's existing or prospective activities.

[65] [2014] BCC 73, CA at para 52. Recent illustrations include *Re Allied Business and Financial Consultants Ltd* [2009] 2 BCLC 666, CA, which is discussed at paras 15.49 and 15.51 below; *Odyssey Entertainment Ltd v Kamp* [2012] EWHC 2316 (Ch) (where director took up an opportunity, having misled the board about the company's financial position and ability to pursue it); *Invideous Ltd v Thorogood* [2013] EWHC 3015 (Ch) (director of company involved in monetizing video content on the internet in breach of his duties where he had secretly set up a second company involved in the same field to which he diverted business opportunities); *Pennyfeathers Ltd v Pennyfeathers Property Co Ltd* [2013] EWHC 3530 (Ch) (company set up to exploit an option to buy land with potential development land; in breach of duty, two of the directors set up a new company which pursued the opportunity; held that the second company held the assets on trust for the first company).

15.42   Section 175(2) makes it clear that it is immaterial whether the company could take advantage of the property, information, or opportunity. Again, this reflects the position at common law.[66] A director 'must not be allowed to use his position as such to make a profit even if it was not open to the company, as for example, by reason of a legal disability, to participate in the transaction'.[67] The reasoning behind the rule is to act as a deterrent to discourage fiduciaries from placing themselves in a conflict of interest.[68]

15.43   Where the director acquires a benefit which came to his notice as a result of his fiduciary position, or pursuant to an opportunity which results from his fiduciary position, the equitable rule is that he is to be treated as having acquired the benefit on behalf of his company so that it is beneficially owned by the company. In such cases, the company has a proprietary remedy in addition to his personal remedy against the director, and the company can elect between the two remedies.[69] The company's remedies are discussed in Chapter 19, Section B below.

The nature of the duty

15.44   Under s 175, as under the common law, a director is precluded from 'obtaining for himself, either secretly or without the informed approval of the company … any property or business advantage either belonging to the company or for which it has been negotiating'.[70] This is especially the case where the director or officer is a participant in those negotiations.[71] If a director obtains or seeks to obtain such an advantage he infringes the 'no conflict rule', which is inherent in s 175, because he creates a situation of conflict between his personal interest and his duty of undivided loyalty to the company, which obliges him to protect and advance its interest.[72] If the opportunity produces a profit for the director, his conduct will also infringe the 'no profit rule' unless duly sanctioned by the directors or the company (Sections D(2)–(4) below), which continues to apply after the director has ceased to hold office.[73]

15.45   Determining which of the rules applies to the case may be relevant to remedy. If the 'no conflict rule' is engaged, the company may claim compensation or an account of profits, whereas if the 'no profit rule' is infringed, the company can only claim an account of profits and will have no remedy if no profits were earned. The following paragraphs discuss some of the more important maturing opportunity cases at common law concerning directors in terms of the two rules, although it is not always evident which rule was being applied by the court.

---

[66]   *Industrial Development Consultants v Cooley* [1972] 1 WLR 443, 453; *Regal (Hastings) Ltd v Gulliver*, [1967] 2 AC 134n, HL at 139; *Canadian Aero v O'Malley* [1973] 40 DLR (3d) 371 at 383–4; *Natural Extracts Pty Ltd v Stotter* (1997) 24 ASCR 10, 141; *Crown Dilmun v Sutton* [2004] 1 BCLC 704 at paras 49 and 182.

[67]   *Canadian Aero Service Ltd v O'Malley* (1973) 40 DLR (3d) 371, 383–4; see also Struan Scott, '*Corporate Opportunity Doctrine and Impossibility Arguments*' (2003) 66 MLR 852; Pearlie Koh, '*Principle 6 of the Proposed Statement of Directors Duties*' (2003) 66 MLR 894; D Prentice '*The Corporate Opportunity Doctrine*' (1974) 37 MLR 464.

[68]   *Murad v Al-Saraj* [2005] EWCA Civ 959 at para 74, per Arden LJ.

[69]   *FHR European Ventures LLP v Cedar Capital Partners LLC* [2015] AC 250, SC at para 7 per Lord Neuberger (as to bribes and secret commissions, see Chapter 16, Section B(1) below).

[70]   *CMS Dolphin v Simonet* [2001] 2 BCLC 704 at para 91.

[71]   *Canadian Aero Service Ltd v O'Malley* (1973) 40 DLR (3d) 371, 382, 391. See also the second principle quoted in para 15.75 below.

[72]   *Regal (Hastings) Ltd v Gulliver* [1967] 1 AC 134n, 137G, 149F; *IDC v Cooley*, [1972] 1 WLR 443, 452, 453; *Canadian Aero Service v O'Malley* (1973) 40 DLR (3d) 371, 382, 391; *CMS Dolphin Ltd v Simonet* [2001] 2 BCLC 704; *Ball v Eden Project Ltd* [2002] 1 BCLC 313; *Kingsley IT Consulting v McIntosh* [2006] BCC 875; *Simtel Communications v Rebak* [2006] 2 BCLC 571; *Berryland Books Ltd v BK Books Ltd* [2009] 2 BCLC 709.

[73]   2006 Act, s 170(2)(a) and Section E below.

The 'no conflict rule'

Cook v Deeks[74] was a derivative claim in which the directors of a construction company nego-   **15.46**
tiated a lucrative contract with a railway company, but then decided to form a new company
to take over the contract for their own benefit and to the exclusion of the company and its
other shareholders. This was a case where the company could have taken advantage of the
opportunity. The Privy Council held that (i) the directors were in breach of their fiduciary
duties, (ii) the shareholders could not ratify the breach, because the directors in effect made a
present to themselves of what should be regarded as company property, and (iii) the directors
were liable to account to the company for their profits. In giving the judgment of the Privy
Council, Lord Buckmaster said that the directors 'were not at liberty to sacrifice the interests
which they were bound to protect, and, while ostensibly acting for the company, divert in
their own favour business which should properly belong to the company they represent'.[75]
This analysis reflects the application of the 'no conflict rule',[76] but the outcome would have
been the same under the 'no profit rule'.

In *Industrial Development Consultants Ltd v Cooley*[77] the defendant was an architect who was   **15.47**
also the managing director of the plaintiff company, which was in a group supplying construction services. One of his duties was to procure new business, particularly in connection
with the gas industry and the gas boards. The company had unsuccessful negotiations with
one of the gas boards for a contract to design and build depots. Subsequently the deputy
chairman of the board approached the defendant in his private capacity about the design and
construction of new depots. In the course of the meeting, the defendant acquired knowledge
that the company did not have, and would have wanted to have. The defendant realized that
if he could obtain his release from his position with the company he could acquire a valuable
contract from the board. He falsely told the company that he was ill and obtained a release.
He was subsequently awarded a contract by the board. That contract was substantially the
same business as the company had been attempting to obtain. Roskill J found that there was
no doubt that Mr Cooley got the contract for himself as a result of work that he did while
still the company's managing director. He said:[78]

> Therefore, I feel impelled to the conclusion that when the defendant embarked on this course
> of conduct of getting information … using that information and preparing those documents
> … and sending them off … , he was guilty of putting himself into the position in which his
> duty to his employers, the plaintiffs, and his own private interests conflicted and conflicted
> grievously. There being the fiduciary relationship I have described, it seems to me plain that
> it was his duty once he got this information to pass it to his employers and not to guard it for
> his own personal purposes and profit. He put himself into the position when his duty and his
> interests conflicted.

Again, the reasoning of the judgment appears to reflect the 'no conflict rule', since the company had an interest in obtaining the knowledge that the defendant obtained while still in

---

[74] [1916] 1 AC 554, PC. Also see for a similar misuse of a maturing opportunity: *Canadian Aero Services Ltd v O'Malley* (1973) 40 DLR (3d) 371, discussed in *Ultraframe (UK) Ltd v Fielding* [2005] EWHC 1638 (Ch) at paras 1337–41 and in *Wilkinson v West Coast Capital* [2007] BCC 717 at paras 260, 293, 294. Also see the cases noted at paragraph 15.41 above.

[75] [1916] 1 AC 554, PC at p 563.

[76] *Ultraframe (UK) Ltd v Fielding* [2005] EWHC 1638 (Ch) at para 1334; *Wilkinson v West Coast Capital* [2007] BCC 717 at para 259.

[77] [1972] 1 WLR 443.

[78] [1972] 1 WLR 443, 452H–453B.

office as a director and which he was bound to pass on to the company.[79] The defendant was held liable to account to the company for his profits; a result that could equally have been achieved under the 'no profit rule'.

15.48 In *Wilkinson v West Coast Capital*[80] the minority shareholder in an unfair prejudice petition claimed that the directors obtained the opportunity to acquire another business in the course of carrying out their role as directors and that they breached both the 'no conflict' and 'no profit rules' by acquiring it for themselves. Warren J found that there had been no breach of the 'no conflict rule' because the company was subject to a legal impediment which prevented it from having an interest in the opportunity to buy the business.[81] Under the company's constitution it was not able to acquire the new business unless 65 per cent of the shareholders consented, which could not be obtained, since the directors who bought the business had a majority of the company's shares and they were entitled to vote their shares to prevent the company from acquiring the new business. In reaching this conclusion, Warren J accepted that the fact that the company is unable as a matter of fact to take up the opportunity does not exonerate a director from breach of the 'no conflict rule' if he takes the opportunity for himself,[82] but he relied on the decision of the Court of Appeal in *Aas v Benham*,[83] a partnership case, to support his conclusion that the position was different where there is a legal impediment in the company's constitution that meant that the majority shareholders could lawfully prevent the company from taking advantage of the opportunity. This line of reasoning did not apply to the breach of the 'no profit rule', but that claim failed on the facts because the new business was sold at a loss.

15.49 The decision of the Court of Appeal in *Re Allied Business and Financial Consultants Ltd*[84] is significant for its discussion of the 'no profit rule' (paragraph 15.50 below), but the 'no conflict rule' was also considered. The company, which operated as a financial intermediary, arranging bank loans, mortgages, and insurance was owned and managed by three individuals as a quasi-partnership. Two of the directors, while acting for the company, were approached to find a buyer for a property for a commission. They were unable to find a buyer for the property, but eventually found someone who would take a 50 per cent interest in the property on terms that the company would not receive a commission. The two directors put up the other 50 per cent. The acquisition of the property was profitable and the third director and shareholder brought an unfair prejudice petition, alleging that, in taking advantage of the opportunity to acquire an interest in the property, the other two directors had breached their fiduciary duties. The Court of Appeal held that the 'no conflict rule' was engaged, because there was a conflict between the two directors' duty to obtain a proper reward for the company for brokering the transaction and their personal interest in participating as purchasers.[85] By personally taking advantage of the opportunity, the directors deprived the

---

[79] *Ultraframe (UK) Ltd v Fielding* [2005] EWHC 1638 (Ch) at para 1336; *Wilkinson v West Coast Capital* [2007] BCC 717 at para 264.

[80] [2007] BCC 717.

[81] [2007] BCC 717 at paras 272–304.

[82] [2007] BCC 717 at paras 291 and 301. Warren J directed himself in relation to practical impossibility by reference to the decision in *Regal (Hastings) Ltd v Gulliver* (see paras 286–90), discussed below, but that was a no profit case, not a no conflict case.

[83] [1891] 2 Ch 244, CA. In *Re Southern Counties Fresh Foods Ltd* [2008] EWHC 2810 (Ch) at para 52 Warren J said that in *West Coast* 'I considered situations where a director could exercise his powers as a shareholder in a way which might be against the company's interests with particular reference to *Aas v Benham*.'

[84] [2009] 2 BCLC 666, CA.

[85] [2009] 2 BCLC 666, CA at paras 73–5.

company of the possibility of earning commission and infringed the 'no conflict rule'. There was no suggestion that the two directors had fiduciary duties to protect the company's interests in any other way.

The 'no profit rule'

Regal (Hastings) Ltd v Gulliver[86] is the leading case on the application of the 'no profit rule' **15.50** to companies.[87] The company formed a subsidiary to purchase additional cinemas, but was only able to subscribe for 2,000 of the 5,000 £1 shares in the subsidiary. The directors and an outsider subscribed for the remaining 3,000 shares. In due course the subsidiary was sold at a profit and the company brought proceedings to recover the profit from the directors.[88] It was accepted that in taking up shares in the subsidiary the directors had acted in good faith and in the best interests of the company, so that the 'no conflict rule' was not engaged.[89] On the other hand the conduct of the directors fell within the 'no profit rule' under which the directors 'may be liable to account for the profits which they have made, if, while standing in a fiduciary relationship to Regal, they have by reason and in course of that fiduciary relationship made a profit'.[90] Lord Russell went on to explain the rule:

> The rule of equity which insists on those, who by use of a fiduciary position make a profit, being liable to account for that profit, in no way depends on fraud, or absence of bona fides; or upon such questions or considerations as whether the profit would or should otherwise have gone to the plaintiff, or whether the profiteer was under a duty to obtain the source of the profit for the plaintiff, or whether he took a risk or acted as he did for the benefit of the plaintiff, or whether the plaintiff has in fact been damaged or benefitted by his action. The liability arises from the mere fact of a profit having, in the stated circumstances been made.

The consequence was that the directors were in a situation of conflict between their duty to account to the company for their profit and their personal interest in retaining it.[91] The directors could have relieved themselves of liability to account by obtaining the informed consent of the company.[92]

The main issue in *Re Allied Business and Financial Consultants Ltd*,[93] the facts of which have **15.51** been summarized in paragraph 15.49 above, was whether the two directors were in breach of the 'no profit rule'. Rimer LJ, with whom the other members of the Court of Appeal agreed, considered that the circumstances clearly engaged the 'no profit rule'. It was irrelevant that the opportunity was outside the scope of the company's business, since it had come to the directors in the course of acting as such for the company and they should have obtained the company's informed consent before taking personal advantage of it.[94] The directors' reliance

---

[86] (1941) [1967] 2 AC 134n, HL.

[87] This is how it is considered in *Wilkinson v West Coast Capital* [2007] BCC 717 at paras 286–91 and *Re Allied Business and Financial Consultants Ltd* [2009] 2 BCLC 666, CA at paras 58 and 59.

[88] The claims against one of the directors failed, because he arranged for third parties to take his shares and he did not make a profit, as did the claim against the third party, because he took his shares with the knowledge and consent of the company.

[89] [1967] 2 AC 134n, 137F, 143E, 153B, 154D–E, 158B. In terms of the 2006 Act there was no breach of the duty to promote the success of the company (s 172). The directors' only breach of duty was failing to account for their profits.

[90] [1967] 2 AC 134n, pp 143E, per Lord Russell. See also pp 137G, 153E, 154F–G, 157D, 158E–F.

[91] [1967] 2 AC 134n, p 137G.

[92] [1967] 2 AC 134n, pp 139E, 150A, 154D, 157A.

[93] [2009] 2 BCLC 666, CA.

[94] [2009] 2 BCLC 666, CA paras 54–60, 70.

on the partnership case, *Aas v Benham*[95] was misplaced, because in a partnership a partner's duties are circumscribed by the contract of partnership, whereas in a company directors' fiduciary duties are unlimited.[96] Rimer LJ summarized the position in these terms:[97]

> The point is that the existence of the opportunity is one that is relevant for the company to know and of which the director has a duty to inform it. It is not for the director to make his own decision that the company will not be interested and to proceed, without more, to appropriate the opportunity for himself. His duty is one of undivided loyalty and this is one manifestation of how that duty is required to be discharged.

If the director does not comply with his fiduciary duties in this way he will be exposed to a claim for an account of profits.[98]

15.52 Rimer LJ's conclusion that it is irrelevant to a claim based on breach of the 'no profit rule' that the opportunity is outside the scope of the company's business is consistent with s 175(2), which provides that it is immaterial that the company could not take advantage of the opportunity. It does not matter whether the company's inability stems from the commercial limits of the company's business or financial impossibility.

D. Situations Where the Duty Is Not Infringed

(1) Where there is no reasonable likelihood of a conflict

15.53 Section 175(4) provides that the duty is not infringed if the situation cannot reasonably be regarded as likely to give rise to a conflict of interest. This reflects the position at common law.[99]

15.54 In this regard, it has been held that there is no duty on a director to disclose competitive activity unless he had used his position to further that activity. To investigate the possibility of setting up a business in competition with the company does not, of itself, constitute a breach of fiduciary duty provided the director does not engage in any actual competitive activity.[100]

15.55 The precise point at which preparations by a departing director for the establishment of a competing business become unlawful will turn on the facts of the case. Merely making a decision to set up a competing business will not be sufficient, but soliciting customers would be in breach of the director's duties. In between, there is a wide spectrum of possible activity which must be considered on a case-by-case basis.[101]

---

[95] [1891] 2 Ch 244, CA.

[96] [2009] 2 BCLC 666 at paras 68–70. This is not inconsistent with *Wilkinson v West Coast Capital*, since Warren J did not rely on *Aas v Benham* when considering the 'no profit rule'.

[97] [2009] 2 BCLC 666 para 70.

[98] [2009] 2 BCLC 666, para 72.

[99] *Queensland Mines Ltd v Hudson* (1978) 52 ALJR 399, 400, PC ('a real sensible possibility of conflict'); and see *Peso Silver Mines Ltd v Cooper* (1966) 58 DLR (2d) 1. The later decision has, however, not been without criticism: Beck, 'The Saga of Peso Silver Mines: Corporate Opportunity Reconsidered' (1971) 49 *Can Bar Review* 80; see also Prentice, 'Regal Hastings Ltd v Gulliver: The Canadian Experience' (1967) 30 MLR 450; and VanDuzer, *The Law of Partnerships and Corporations*, 3nd edn (Concord, 2009), p 355–6.

[100] *Balston Ltd v Headline Filters Ltd* [1990] FSR 385; *Coleman Taymar Ltd v Oakes* [2001] 2 BCLC 749; *Framlington Group plc v Anderson* [1995] BCC 611, 629.

[101] *Shepherds Investments Ltd v Walters* [2006] 2 BCLC 202.

In *Wilkinson v West Coast Capital*[102] where Warren J instanced a case in which a director of a company selling fashion clothing could hardly be in breach of the 'no conflict rule' if he took a stake in a farm machinery company since there would be no 'real sensible possibility' of conflict. It would, however, be different if the fashion company had been actively considering diversification into farm machinery.[103] It would also be different if both companies were interested in acquiring offices in the same location.

15.56

In *Miller v Stonier*[104] Newey J held that there was no breach by a director of his duty under s 175 where the company had divested itself of the business in respect of which the relevant conflict was said to arise (trading in gas fires) and there was no prospect of it re-entering the market, but the position might well have been different had the company still been trading in gas fires.

15.57

The question of whether a situation can reasonably be regarded as likely to give rise to a conflict of interest is often a difficult one. Unless it is plain that the situation is covered by s 175(4)(a), the prudent course is for the director to disclose the matter to the board and seek authorization.

15.58

(2) Authorization by the directors

Section 175(4)(b) modifies the position at common law. It provides that the duty to avoid conflicts of interests will not be infringed if the matter has been authorized by the directors. The circumstances in which authorization may be granted are set out in s 175(5) and (6). Traditionally conflicts of interest could be resolved only by disclosure to and with the consent of the members of the company, although in practice standard articles often replaced this by a requirement of disclosure to the board of directors. The CLR were concerned that this strict requirement might stifle entrepreneurial activity and made the recommendations now found in these subsections.[105] The reform gives proper effect to the delegation of all powers of management to the directors found in the articles of most companies.[106]

15.59

As a result of the provisions of s 175(5) and (6) directors should be able to avoid the harsh consequences of the decision in *Regal (Hastings) Ltd v Gulliver* (paragraph 15.50 above), provided the provisions of those subsections are complied with.

15.60

Section 175(5) provides that authorization may be given by the directors (a) where the company is a private company and nothing in the company's constitution invalidates such authorization, by the matter being proposed to and authorized by the directors; or (b) where the company is a public company and its constitution includes provisions enabling the directors to authorize the matter, by the matter being proposed to and authorized by them in accordance with the constitution.[107]

15.61

---

[102] [2007] BCC 717 at [252]–[253].

[103] In *Re Allied Business and Financial Consultants Ltd* [2009] 2 BCLC 666 at para 39 Rimer LJ referred to this example but did not express a view about it.

[104] *Miller v Stonier* [2015] EWHC 2796 (Ch) at para 70.

[105] CLR: *Final Report* at paras 3.21–3.27; *Completing the Structure* at paras 3.26 and 3.27.

[106] Table A, reg 70; Model Article (pcls) 3; Model Article (plc) 3.

[107] On 18 January 2008 the Association of General Counsel and Company Secretaries of the FTSE 100 (the GC100) published a guidance paper on directors' conflicts of interest and the Companies Act 2006. The GC100 has concluded that most public companies will want to amend their articles of association to include a general power for directors to authorize conflicts.

15.62   The 2006 Act, s 180(1) makes clear that if s 175 is complied with any transaction or arrangement is not liable to be set aside by virtue of any common law rule or equitable principle requiring the consent or approval of the company in general meeting. However, if any other enactment requires the consent or approval of the members in respect of the particular transaction or arrangement, or if such consent or approval is required by the company's constitution, then it must be sought and obtained.[108]

15.63   Under s 175(6), board authorization is effective only if the conflicted directors or 'any other interested director' have not participated in the taking of the decision or if the decision would have been valid even without the participation of the conflicted directors: the votes of the conflicted directors in favour of the decision are ignored and the conflicted directors are not counted in the quorum. In this regard, what amounts to an interested director may well not always be clear, although it is to be expected that the court will give the expression 'interested director' a broad and commercially realistic interpretation. Therefore, in the context of smaller and family companies, it may be difficult to find any directors who are independent in the requisite sense. In such cases authorization or ratification by a majority of the shareholders of the company at a general meeting in accordance with the 2006 Act, ss 180 or 239 may well be required to obtain protection.[109]

15.64   The use of the word 'only' in s 175(6) makes it clear that these are the minimum procedural requirements for authorization. Any further rules imposed by the company's constitution or the common law must be complied with. As Lord Goldsmith said during the passage of the bill through Parliament:

> [A]ny requirements under the common law for what is necessary for a valid authorisation remain in force. I draw the Committee's attention to Clause 159(6), which says: 'The authorisation is effective only if'. It then sets out certain specific requirements. It deliberately does not say that if those requirements are met the authorisation is effective. There might be other conditions in relation to the authorisation that would be required—for example, the company's constitution may have some specific provision with which it would be necessary to comply. Those formalities and those conditions need to be complied with as well.[110]

(3)   Compliance with the company's articles

15.65   The Companies Act contains two provisions which confirm that a company's articles may contain provisions dealing with conflict of interest. Section 180(4)(b) provides that where the company's articles contain provisions for dealing with conflicts of interest, the general duties (including the duty under s 175) are not infringed by anything done or omitted by a director in accordance with those provisions. Also, s 232(4) provides that nothing in that section prevents a company's articles from making such provision as has previously been lawful for dealing with conflicts of interest. This is a departure from the general rule contained in s 232 which prohibits a company from exempting a director from, or indemnifying him against, any liability in connection with any negligence, default, breach of duty, or breach of trust by him in relation to the company.

---

[108]   2006 Act, s 180(1).
[109]   See *North-West Transportation Co Ltd v Beatty* (1887) 12 App Cas 589, 593–4, PC; *Boulting v Association of Cinematograph, Television and Allied Technicians* [1963] 2 QB 606; and Ch 10 and Ch 20, Section D of this work.
[110]   Hansard, HL, vol 678, col 326 (9 February 2006).

It has long been the practice, in this regard, for articles to provide that in certain circum-   **15.66**
stances, and subject to certain conditions, usually involving disclosure of the nature and
extent of the interest to the board, a director may put himself in a position of conflict or make
a profit from the use of the company's property, information, or opportunities.[111]

(4) Consent, approval, or authorization of members

One situation where it will be necessary to obtain the consent, approval, or authorization of   **15.67**
members to avoid infringement of the duty to avoid conflicts of interest within s 175(1) is
where it is not possible to obtain authorization from the directors under s 175(4)–(6). This
may be because a majority of the other directors are not willing to agree to authorization
being given, because provisions of the company's constitution prevent them from doing so,
or because none of the directors is without an interest in the matter. In such circumstances
the director can only avoid infringing s 175 if he obtains the consent, approval, or authorization of the members in advance of his becoming subject to a conflict of interest.

Section 180(4)(a) preserves the rule of law which enables the company, acting by its mem-   **15.68**
bers, to give authority, specifically or generally, for anything done or omitted by a director
that would otherwise be a breach of duty. As has been noted above, it was always the case that
the company's members could authorize or permit a director to be in a situation of conflict or
to make a profit from property, information, or opportunities. To obtain effective protection
the disclosure made by the director to the shareholders must be full and frank such that the
shareholders have full knowledge of the conflict.[112]

In *Sharma v Sharma*,[113] after describing the scope of the duty in relation to corporate oppor-   **15.69**
tunities, as described in paragraph 15.41 above, Jackson LJ went on to summarize what is
required to obtain effective authorization or consent of the members:

(ii) If the shareholders with full knowledge of the relevant facts consent to the director
exploiting those opportunities for his own personal gain, then that conduct is not a
breach of the fiduciary or statutory duty.

(iii) If the shareholders with full knowledge of the relevant facts acquiesce in the director's
proposed conduct, then that may constitute consent. However, consent cannot be
inferred from silence unless: (a) the shareholders know that their consent is required, or
(b) the circumstances are such that it would be unconscionable for the shareholders to
remain silent at the time and object after the event.

(iv) For the purposes of propositions (ii) and (iii) full knowledge of the relevant facts does
not entail an understanding of their legal incidents. In other words the shareholders need
not appreciate that the proposed action would be characterized as a breach of fiduciary or
statutory duty.

In *Sharma*, the Court of Appeal held that the shareholders in a claimant family company
set up to acquire dental practices had consented to or acquiesced in the sole director being
permitted to acquire some dental practices for her own benefit, so she was not in breach
of her duty to avoid a conflict of interest under s 175 when she acquired five practices for
herself.

---

[111] Table A, reg 85, discussed in Ch 17 below.
[112] *Kaye v Croydon Tramways Company* [1898] 1 Ch 358, CA; *Herrman v Simon* (1990) 8 ACLC 1094 at
1096–7; *Hurstanger Ltd v Wilson* [2007] 1 WLR 2351, CA.
[113] [2014] BCC 73, CA at para 52.

15.70 If the director is already in a situation of conflict of interest or if he is liable or potentially liable to account for profits, he may seek ratification under s 239, but then the votes of himself and persons connected with him are not counted (see Chapter 20, Section D).

15.71 The 2006 Act, Part 10, Chapter 4 deals with transactions with directors which require the approval of members.[114] Where the transaction or arrangement under consideration falls within the provisions of Chapter 4, and either approval is given under that Chapter or it is provided that approval is not needed, s 180(2) provides it is not necessary also to comply with s 175. Otherwise, the application of the general duties to avoid conflicts of interest and not to accept benefits from third parties are unaffected by the fact that the case also falls within Chapter 4.[115] Conversely, the mere fact that the director complies with his general duties under s 175 does not remove the need for approval under any applicable provision of Chapter 4.[116]

E. Application to Former Directors

15.72 Section 170(2) provides that:

A person who ceases to be a director continues to be subject—

(a) to the duty in section 175 (duty to avoid conflicts of interest) as regards the exploitation of any property, information or opportunity of which he became aware at a time when he was a director, …

To that extent those duties apply to a former director as to a director, subject to any necessary adaptations.

15.73 Once a director ceases to hold office, he no longer exercises the powers of a director.[117] To that extent the 'no conflict rule' is no longer engaged, but s 170(2)(a) preserves his liability under the 'no profit rule' in relation to the exploitation of any property, information, or opportunity of which the director became aware at a time when he was a director. The company may be able to obtain an injunction to restrain exploitation by the director and may require him to account for profits.

15.74 When determining whether a former director is in breach of his duty to avoid conflicts of interest, the court will be assisted by pre-2006 Act authorities, which adopted a nuanced approach by reference to the particular facts of each case.[118] It is clear that the incidence of

---

[114] The provisions of Chapter 4 are fully discussed in Ch 18 below.
[115] 2006 Act, s 180(2).
[116] 2006 Act, s 180(3).
[117] *Ultraframe (UK) Ltd v Fielding* [2005] EWHC 1638 (Ch) at para 1309, citing *CMS Dolphin Ltd v Simonet* [2001] 2 BCLC 704; *British Midland Tool Ltd v Pyke* [2003] 2 BCLC 523; *Quarter Master UK Ltd v Pyke* [2005] 1 BCLC 245, 264. See also *Wilkinson v West Coast Capital* [2007] BCC 717 at para 251 where Warren J makes the point that a former director remains liable under the 'no profit rule'.
[118] *Industrial Development Consultants v Cooley* [1972] 1 WLR 443; *Canadian Aero Service Ltd v O'Malley* (1973) 40 DLR (3d) 371; *Island Export Finance Ltd v Ummuna* [1986] BCLC 460; *Balston Ltd v Headline Filters Ltd* [1990] FSR 385; *Framlington Group plc v Anderson* [1995] 1 BCLC 475; *CMS Dolphin Ltd v Simonet* [2001] 2 BCLC 704; *Hunter Kane Ltd v Watkins* [2003] EWHC 186 (Ch); *In Plus Group Ltd v Pyke* [2002] 2 BCLC 201, CA; *British Midland Tool Ltd v Midland International Tooling Ltd* [2003] 2 BCLC 523; *Shepherds Investments Ltd v Walters* [2007] 2 BCLC 202; *Foster Bryant Surveying Ltd v Bryant* [2007] 2 BCLC 239, CA; *First Subsea Ltd v Balltec Ltd* [2014] EWHC 866 (Ch).

liability on the part of the former director does not depend upon the company being shown to have suffered loss; it would suffice if the former director had, directly or indirectly, made a profit, for which he would be made liable to account.[119]

(1) Common law authorities

A helpful starting point is the summary of the principles by Bernard Livesey QC, sitting as a **15.75** deputy judge of the High Court, in *Hunter Kane Ltd v Watkins*,[120] itself based on the earlier analysis of Lawrence Collins J in *CMS Dolphin Ltd v Simonet*,[121] and described as 'perceptive and useful' by the Court of Appeal in *Foster Bryant Surveying Ltd v Bryant* (subject to the qualification that each case will depend on its facts):[122]

1. A director, while acting as such, has a fiduciary relationship with his company. That is he has an obligation to deal towards it with loyalty, good faith and avoidance of the conflict of duty and self-interest.
2. A requirement to avoid a conflict of duty and self-interest means that a director is precluded from obtaining for himself, either secretly or without the informed approval of the company, any property or business advantage either belonging to the company or for which it has been negotiating, especially where the director or officer is a participant in the negotiations.
3. A director's power to resign from office is not a fiduciary power. He is entitled to resign even if his resignation might have a disastrous effect on the business or reputation of the company.
4. A fiduciary relationship does not continue after the determination of the relationship which gives rise to it. After the relationship is determined the director is in general not under the continuing obligations which are a feature of the fiduciary relationship.
5. Acts done by the directors while the contract of employment subsists but which are preparatory to competition after it terminates are *not necessarily* in themselves a breach of the implied term as to loyalty and fidelity.
6. Directors, no less than employees, acquire a general fund of skill, knowledge and expertise in the course of their work, which [it] is plainly in the public interest that they should be free to exploit [...] in a new position. After ceasing the relationship by resignation or otherwise a director is in general (and subject of course to any terms of the contract of employment) not prohibited from using his general fund of skill and knowledge, the 'stock in trade' of the knowledge he has acquired while a director, even including such things as business contacts and personal connections made as a result of his directorship.
7. A director is however precluded from acting in breach of the requirement at 2 above, even after his resignation where the resignation may fairly be said to have been prompted or influenced by a wish to acquire for himself any maturing business opportunities sought by the company and where it was his position with a company rather than a fresh initiative that led him to the opportunity which he later acquired.
8. In considering whether an act of a director breaches the preceding principle the factors to take into account will include the factor of position or office held, the nature of the corporate opportunity, its ripeness, its specificness and the director's relation to it, the amount of knowledge possessed, the circumstances in which it was obtained and whether it was

---

[119] *Foster Bryant Surveying Ltd v Bryant* [2007] 2 BCLC 239, per Rix LJ at para 88; per Buxton LJ at para 101.
[120] [2003] EWHC 186 (Ch).
[121] [2001] 2 BCLC 704.
[122] *Foster Bryant Surveying Ltd v Bryant* [2007] 2 BCLC 239, per Rix LJ at para 76. Mr Livesey QC's summary of the principles is quoted at para 8. The principles were summarized more briefly, but without modification, in *First Subsea Ltd v Balltec Ltd* [2014] EWHC 866 (Ch), per Norris J at para 186.

special or indeed private, the factor of time in the continuation of the fiduciary duty where the alleged breach occurs after termination of the relationship with the company and the circumstances under which the [relationship] was terminated, that is whether by retirement or resignation or discharge.

9. The underlying basis of the liability of a director who exploits after his resignation a maturing business opportunity of the company is that the opportunity is to be treated as if it were the property of the company in relation to which the director had fiduciary duties. By seeking [to] exploit the opportunity after resignation he is appropriating to himself that property. He is just as accountable as a trustee who retires without properly accounting for trust property.

10. It follows that a director will not be in breach of the principle set out as point 7 above where either the company's hope of obtaining the contract was not a 'maturing business opportunity' and it was not pursuing further business orders nor where the director's resignation was not itself prompted or influenced by a wish to acquire the business for himself.

11. As regards breach of confidence, although while the contract of employment subsists a director or other employee may not use confidential information to the detriment of his employer, after it ceases the director/employee may compete and may use know-how acquired in the course of his employment (as distinct from trade secrets—although the distinction is sometimes difficult to apply in practice).

15.76 The authorities have been concerned with a wide variety of differing circumstances and conduct, and were the subject of extensive review by the Court of Appeal in *Foster Bryant Surveying Ltd v Bryant* itself.[123] Rix LJ, who delivered the leading judgment in that case, was in no doubt that the underlying principles, namely that a director must act towards his company with honesty, good faith, and loyalty and must avoid any conflicts of interest 'are firmly in place, and are exacting requirements, exactingly enforced'.[124] Nevertheless, emphasizing that each case depended on its own facts and that it was difficult accurately to encapsulate the circumstances in which a retiring director may be found to have breached his fiduciary duty, Rix LJ considered that the courts had developed merits-based solutions, having regard to the fact that the circumstances in which directors retire are so various.[125]

15.77 *British Midland Tool Ltd v Midland International Tooling Ltd*[126] illustrates how the 'no conflict rule' does not apply after a director resigns. In that case one director resigned in order to compete with the company, while his three former colleagues remained in office and conspired with him to poach the company's employees. Hart J concluded that the director who had resigned had not acted in breach of fiduciary duty, but that the others had.

15.78 On the other hand there are many cases of former directors being liable for infringing the 'no profit rule'. While s 175, read with s 170(2)(a), applies where the former director exploits any property, information, or opportunity of which he became aware when he was a director, Rix LJ noted that in many of the cases where the director was liable for breach of duty at common law he had 'planned his resignation having in mind the destruction of the company or at least the exploitation of its property in the form of business opportunities' in which the director was currently involved.[127] *Industrial Development Consultants v Cooley*,[128] described

---

[123] [2007] 2 BCLC 239 at paras 48–77.
[124] [2007] 2 BCLC 239, per Rix LJ at para 76.
[125] [2007] 2 BCLC 239, per Rix LJ at para 77.
[126] [2003] 2 BCLC 523.
[127] *Foster Bryant Surveying Ltd v Bryant* [2007] 2 BCLC 239 at para 77.
[128] [1972] 1 WLR 443.

in paragraph 15.47 above, is an example of such a case. Two others he gave are those mentioned in the following two paragraphs.

In *Canadian Aero Service Ltd v O'Malley*,[129] the directors or senior officers had resigned in   **15.79**
order to take the benefit of a project for which they had been negotiating on behalf of their company. They were held to be in breach of duty. Laskin J summarized the position in the following terms:[130]

> An examination of the case law in this Court and in the Courts of other like jurisdictions on the fiduciary duties of directors and senior officers shows the pervasiveness of a strict ethic in this area of the law. In my opinion, this ethic disqualifies a director or senior officer from usurping for himself or diverting to another person or company with whom or with which he is associated a maturing business opportunity which his company is actively pursuing; he is also precluded from so acting even after his resignation where the resignation may fairly be said to have been prompted or influenced by a wish to acquire for himself the opportunity sought by the company, *or where it was his position with the company rather than a fresh initiative that led him to the opportunity which he later acquired.* [emphasis added][131]

In *CMS Dolphin Ltd v Simonet*,[132] the director had resigned (without notice) in order to profit   **15.80**
from the company's business. Having made plans beforehand, he immediately set up in competition after his resignation and set about poaching the company's staff and clients. The director was found to have acted in breach of duty: by resigning, he had exploited the company's maturing business opportunities. Lawrence Collins J found that the director had been prompted or influenced to resign by a wish to acquire for himself, directly or indirectly, the business opportunities which he had previously obtained or was actively pursuing with the company's clients, and which he had then actually diverted for his own profit. The judge emphasized that '[t]here must be some relevant connection or link between the resignation and the obtaining of the business'.[133]

In *Shepherds Investments Ltd v Walters*,[134] Etherton J concluded that the former directors had   **15.81**
acted in breach of duty by reason of what they did while still directors in anticipation of the competition they planned after their resignations. In that case, the directors had, prior to their respective resignations, formed the irrevocable intention to establish a business which they knew would fairly be regarded by the companies to which they owed fiduciary duties as a competitor to the business carried on by another company, for which those companies acted as manager (responsible for sales and marketing) and investment advisor. Nevertheless, the directors continued to take steps to bring into existence that rival business, contrary to what they knew to be the best interests of the companies, and without the consent of those companies after full disclosure of all material facts. After reviewing the authorities, Etherton J said the following:[135]

> What the cases show, and the parties before me agree, is that the precise point at which preparations for the establishment of a competing business by a director become unlawful

---

[129] (1983) 40 DLR (3d) 371.
[130] (1983) 40 DLR (3d) 371, p 382.
[131] It is to be noted in relation to the italicized part of this extract from Laskin J's judgment that the courts in this country have interpreted the 'or' as 'and'; see *Island Export Finance Ltd v Umunna* [1986] BCLC 460, 480a–b, 481c–e; *CMS Dolphin Ltd v Simonet* [2001] BCLC 704, per Lawrence Collins J at para 91.
[132] [2001] 2 BCLC 704.
[133] [2001] 2 BCLC 704 at para 91.
[134] [2007] 1 BCLC 202.
[135] [2007] 1 BCLC 202 at para 108.

will turn on the actual facts of any particular case. In each case, the touchstone for what, on the one hand, is permissible, and what, on the other hand, is impermissible unless consent is obtained from the company or employer after full disclosure, is what, in the case of a director, will be in breach of the fiduciary duties to which I have referred or, in the case of an employee, will be in breach of the obligation of fidelity. It is obvious, for example, that merely making a decision to set up a competing business at some point in the future and discussing such an idea with friends and family would not of themselves be in conflict with the best interests of the company and the employer. The consulting of lawyers and other professionals may, depending on all the circumstances, equally be consistent with a director's fiduciary duties and the employee's obligation of loyalty. At the other end of the spectrum, it is plain that soliciting customers of the company and the employer or the actual carrying on of trade by a competing business would be in breach of the duties of the director and the obligations of the employee. It is the wide range of activity and decision making between the two ends of the spectrum which will be fact sensitive in every case. In that context, Hart J may have been too prescriptive in saying, at paragraph [89] of his judgment, that the director must resign once he has irrevocably formed the intention to engage in the future in a competing business and, without disclosing his intentions to the company, takes any preparatory steps. On the facts of *British Midland Tool*, Hart J was plainly justified in concluding, in paragraph [90] of his judgment, that the preparatory steps had gone beyond what was consistent with the directors' fiduciary duty in circumstances where the directors were aware that a determined attempt was being made by a potential competitor to poach the company's workforce and they did nothing to discourage, and at worst actively promoted, the success of that process, whereas their duty to the company required them to take active steps to thwart the process.

15.82   In *Berrylands Books Ltd v BK Books Ltd*[136] the line between legitimate preparation for future competition and undertaking illegitimate competitive activity was crossed by the former director and employees where there had been a premeditated and seamless transformation of the company's business to a new corporate vehicle controlled and managed by the director, as part of which he appropriated maturing business opportunities.

15.83   By contrast, a former director was not liable to account to the company for profits which the court did not regard as being derived from an opportunity which came to him in the course of his former office. In *Island Export Finance Ltd v Umunna*,[137] the director, who had resigned because of his dissatisfaction with the company, and not in order to appropriate its business for himself, subsequently obtained an order from a client of the company. Hutchison J found that the director was not in breach of duty: the mere fact that his position as director led to a post-resignation opportunity was not sufficient to found a breach of duty (retreating from the apparent width of the italicized section of Laskin J's judgment in the *Canadian Aero* case set out in paragraph 15.79 above). Hutchison J adopted a practical commercial view of the issue when he said:[138]

> It would … be surprising to find that directors alone, because of the fiduciary nature of their relationship with the company, were restrained from exploiting after they had ceased to be such any opportunity of which they acquired knowledge while directors. Directors, no less

---

[136] [2009] 2 BCLC 709. See also *Penn Well Publishing v Ornstein* [2008] 2 BCLC 246, a case concerned with duty of good faith and fidelity owed by an employee.
[137] [1986] BCLC 460.
[138] [1986] BCLC 460, p 482.

than employees, acquire a general fund of knowledge and expertise in the course of their work, and it is plainly in the public interest that they should be free to exploit it in a new position.

The fact that the company hoped to obtain a repeat order from a customer did not make that hope a maturing business opportunity which the former director could not exploit after he resigned.

Balston Ltd v Headline Filters Ltd,[139] is another case where there was no maturing business **15.84** opportunity when the director resigned and it was nothing to the point that, before he resigned, he had taken preparatory steps to set up a company of his own in anticipation of engaging in competing activities. On the other hand, as an employee, he had acted in breach of his duty of good faith to the company by engaging in active competition (in the form of successful tendering for the business of a client of the company) before the notice terminating his employment had expired.

In *Framlington Group plc v Anderson*,[140] the directors of the company resigned and took up **15.85** employment with a competing company, to which the company had sold a fund management business. Under remuneration packages negotiated before their resignation from the company, the directors were to receive benefits from the competing company, which related to the value of the managed funds transferred. The company complained that it was unaware that the directors would receive such benefits from the competing company. It was held, however, that the directors were not in breach of duty: they had played no role in the negotiations for the sale of the business (indeed, they had been instructed not to), there was no duty to inform the company of their own arrangements, and they were free to negotiate whatever price they could from the competing company for their future services; there was no question of a secret bribe or commission, and nor had they diverted any kind of maturing business opportunity.

In *In Plus Group Ltd v Pyke*,[141] the director had set up his own company and began competing **15.86** with the company, even to the extent of working for its major client. On the facts, however, the Court of Appeal found the director had not acted in breach of duty, since he had been effectively expelled and could not function as a director, he did not use any of the company's property, and he did not make use of any confidential information which had come to him as a director of the company. In the words of Buxton LJ, the exclusion of the director from the company 'eliminates the duality of interest or duty which the law seeks to guard against … Quite exceptionally, the defendant's duty to the [company] had been reduced to vanishing point by the acts (explicable and even justifiable though they may have been) of his sole fellow director and fellow shareholder …'[142]

In *Foster Bryant Surveying Ltd v Bryant* itself, the Court of Appeal concluded that the former **15.87** director did not act in breach of fiduciary duty: his resignation had been forced upon him and had no ulterior purpose. The acceptance of an offer of future employment was innocent,

---

[139] [1990] FSR 385.
[140] [1995] 1 BCLC 475.
[141] [2002] 2 BCLC 201.
[142] [2002] 2 BCLC 201, per Buxton LJ at para 90. See also *Halcyon House Ltd v Baines* [2014] EWHC 2216 (QB) per HHJ Richard Seymour QC at paras 226–7, albeit the judge preferred to base his decision on the ground that, even if the director owed continuing fiduciary duties, she did not act in breach of them.

and there had been no diversion of any property or any maturing business opportunity from the company to him.

(2) Section 175 cases

15.88 In *Thermascan Ltd v Norman*[143] it was agreed that the provisions of ss 170(2) and 175 did not alter the pre-existing law.[144] The company sought interim injunctive relief to prevent a former director from canvassing, soliciting, or approaching its clients, even if this involved no use of confidential information. Contractual restrictions on the former director's conduct having expired, the company based its claim for an injunction on breach of the duty to avoid a situation of conflict under ss 170(2) and 175. Since a director, after he had resigned, was entitled to use his general skill and knowledge, including business contacts and personal connections made as a result of his directorship, it was necessary to demonstrate the existence of a maturing business opportunity at the time of resignation. It may not be necessary to show that formal negotiations were under way at that time, but it would be hard to demonstrate the existence of a maturing business opportunity if there had been no or no significant discussion of potential business.[145] On the facts, there had been no discussions at all at the relevant time. Interim injunctive relief was accordingly refused.

15.89 By contrast, in *Killen v Horseworld Ltd*,[146] the judge proceeded on the basis that s 170(2) effected statutory change to the equitable rules.[147] In that case, the company had secured the internet broadcast rights for Badminton in 2008 and wished to continue to do so. The successful bid for such rights made by the former director through another company, however, meant that it was unable to do so. Rather than considering directly whether the former director, who appeared in person, had diverted a maturing business opportunity, the judge appears to have focused more closely on the wording of s 170(2) itself. He concluded on the evidence that the former director had subsequently exploited an opportunity and information of which she had only become aware in her capacity as a director prior to her departure. That, it was held, constituted a breach of duty on the part of the former director, notwithstanding that some four months elapsed between her departure and the commencement of negotiations by her through her new company, especially when set against her earlier (unsuccessful) attempt to divert that opportunity. It is not apparent from the judgment whether the company itself was actually engaged in similar negotiations or discussions at the time the former director left; its clear wish to continue the project, however, must have been considered sufficient in this respect.

15.90 It remains to be seen whether *Killen v Horseworld Ltd* will be followed and, in particular, whether 'opportunity' has a broader meaning under ss 170(2) and 175(2) than it was considered to have at common law. It is suggested that the more orthodox approach was taken in *Thermascan Ltd v Norman*. For a company to succeed in a claim that a former director is in breach of the duty not to put himself in a position of conflict, it must either point to conduct putting the director in such a situation while he was in office or show that the opportunity that he exploited after he resigned was a maturing business opportunity as understood by the

---

[143] [2011] BCC 535, David Donaldson QC sitting as a deputy High Court judge.
[144] As set out in *CMS Dolphin Ltd v Simonet* [2001] 2 BCLC 74; *Hunter Kane Ltd v Watkins* [2003] EWHC 186 (Ch); *Foster Bryant Surveying Ltd v Bryant* [2007] 2 BCLC 239, CA.
[145] [2011] BCC 535 at para 16.
[146] [2012] EWHC 363 (QB), Judge Robinson sitting as a judge of the High Court.
[147] [2012] EWHC 363 (QB) at para 69.

common law authorities. There is nothing to suggest that s 170(2) was intended to restrict former directors in the exploitation of their general knowledge and expertise.

Allfiled UK Ltd v Eltis[148] was concerned not with the misuse of an opportunity, but with use of **15.91** the company's information (namely a personal data store, or PDS, system) by former directors. In that case, adopting the approach set out in *Foster Bryant* (although distinguishing it on its facts), Hildyard J concluded that it was sufficiently arguable that the PDS system was Allfiled's proprietary and confidential information, which the former directors had made use of otherwise than for its benefit, and from which they had sought to profit by enticing one of its former customers to contract instead with the new company, having encouraged and arranged for the migration of all Allfiled's UK staff to the new company, which (arguably) they set up for that very purpose. Accordingly, he granted interim injunctive relief.

F. Charitable Companies

The 2006 Act, s 181 reverses the relaxations made to the 'no conflict rule' as it applies to **15.92** the directors of charitable companies. Section 181(2)(a) replaces s 175(3) which excludes conflicts of interest arising out of transactions or arrangements with the company. The replacement excludes such conflicts of interest from the duty only if or to the extent that the charitable company's articles so allow. The articles must describe the transactions or arrangements which are to be so excluded from the duty.

Section 181(2)(b) replaces s 175(5) which allows authorization for conflicts of interest to be **15.93** given by the directors. The replacement only allows authorization to be given by the directors where the charitable company's constitution expressly allows them to do so.

Section 181(4) amends the Charities Act 1993 to give the Charity Commission the power to **15.94** authorize acts that would otherwise be in breach of the general duties. This was necessary to preserve the current power of the Charity Commissioners to do so, in the light of the statutory statement of the general duties.

---

[148] [2015] EWHC 1300 (Ch); [2016] FSR 11.

16

DUTY NOT TO ACCEPT BENEFITS
FROM THIRD PARTIES

Marcus Haywood

A. Introduction

The Companies Act, s 176 provides that: **16.01**

(1) A director of a company must not accept a benefit from a third party conferred by reason of—
   (a) his being a director, or
   (b) his doing (or not doing) anything as director.
(2) A 'third party' means a person other than the company, an associated body corporate or a person acting on behalf of the company or an associated body corporate.
(3) Benefits received by a director from a person by whom his services (as a director or otherwise) are provided to the company are not regarded as conferred by a third party.
(4) This duty is not infringed if the acceptance of the benefit cannot reasonably be regarded as likely to give rise to a conflict of interest.
(5) Any reference in this section to a conflict of interest includes a conflict of interest and duty and a conflict of duties.

The duty of a director not to accept benefits from a third party, now stated in the 2006 Act,   **16.02**
s 176, is part of the broader duty not to profit from his position as a director without the company's consent.[1] Acceptance of such a benefit inevitably places the director in a position of conflict of interest and duty, as is recognized by s 176(4) and (5), so that the director may be in breach of the duty to avoid conflicts of interest, stated in s 175 (discussed in Chapter 15 above), if the conflict does not arise in relation to a transaction or arrangement with the company, or of the duties in ss 177 or 182 (discussed in Chapter 17 below), if it does so arise. For

---

[1] *Regal (Hastings) Ltd v Gulliver* [1967] AC 134n, 144, 145, HL, per Lord Russell.

the purposes of s 176 it does not matter whether or not there is a proposed or actual transaction or arrangement with the company.

16.03   What distinguishes a benefit within s 176 from other dealings of a director within ss 175, 177, or 182 is the fact that a third party gives the benefit to the director because he is a director or to influence his conduct as a director.[2] As such, the giving of the benefit strikes at the core of the director's duty of 'undivided loyalty'.[3] It is perhaps for this reason that the Companies Act sets this duty apart from the other duties relating to conflicts of interest and does not enable the director to retain the benefit or avoid liability by declaring the benefit to the directors and obtaining their consent on behalf of the company.[4] Instead a director who receives a benefit within s 176 would have to disclose it to the members in the hope that they resolve to authorize him to keep it or release him from liability. Where the director has not disclosed the benefit to the other directors, as will usually be the case, he will be personally liable and it does not matter whether the breach is within ss 175 (or 177 or 182) or 176 or both.[5]

B. Scope of the Duty

16.04   This section codifies the rule prohibiting the exploitation of the position of director for personal benefit. Lord Goldsmith said that the section codifies the 'long-standing rule, prohibiting the exploitation of the position of director for personal benefit. It does not apply to benefits that the director receives from the company, or from any associated company, or from any person acting on behalf of those companies', and he added that 'benefits are prohibited by the duty only if their acceptance is likely to give rise to a conflict of interest'.[6]

16.05   Although ss 175 and 176 are both concerned with secret profits, there is a distinction between the two sections, deriving from the source of the benefit. Under s 176 the source of the property forming the benefit is usually the third party, whereas s 175 is concerned with the unauthorized use by the director of the company's property, information or opportunities.

16.06   A benefit within s 176 is usually called a secret commission or bribe, depending on whether it has a corrupt purpose. The essence of the matter is that the company does not know about it: 'the real evil is not the payment of the money, but the secrecy attending it'.[7] Any

---

[2]   2006 Act, s 176(1).

[3]   *Boulting v Association of Cinematograph, Television and Allied Technicians* [1963] 2 QB 606, 636, CA, per Upjohn LJ; quoted by Mummery LJ in *Towers v Premier Waste Management Ltd* [2012] BCLC 313, CA at para 9. Also see the agency case *Imageview Management Ltd v Jack* [2009] 1 BCLC 724, CA, where at para 6 Jacob LJ described an agent's duty to his client in terms that apply equally to directors and which are particularly relevant to the duty under s 176: 'An agent's own personal interests come entirely second to the interest of his client. If you undertake to act for a man you must act 100% body and soul, for him. You must act as if you were him. You must not allow your own interest to get in the way without telling him. An undisclosed but realistic possibility of conflict of interest is a breach of your duty of good faith to your client.'

[4]   2006 Act, ss 175(4)–(6), 177, 182.

[5]   This was the position in *Towers v Premier Waste Management Ltd* [2012] BCC 72, CA, where a customer of the claimant company made a personal loan of plant and equipment to a director without charge and the claim was brought successfully against the director under ss 172, 175, 176 for an account of profits equal to the amount of hire charges that the customer had attempted to charge the company.

[6]   Hansard, HL Grand Committee, col 330 (9 February 2006).

[7]   *Shipway v Broadwood* [1899] 1 QB 369, 373, CA, per Chitty LJ; *Logicrose Ltd v Southend United Football Club Ltd* [1988] 1 WLR 1256, 1262.

'surreptitious dealing' between a third party, a director, or other agent, on behalf of the company is necessarily a fraud on the company[8] and contrary to the broad principles of morality and law.[9]

The acceptance of the benefit by the director immediately places him in breach of his duty **16.07** under s 176 unless s 176(4) applies where the benefit is such that its acceptance cannot reasonably be regarded as likely to give rise to a conflict of interest and duty or conflict of duties.[10]

(1) Bribes

In *Hovenden & Sons v Milhoff*[11] Romer LJ described a bribe paid to an agent in terms that **16.08** apply equally to a director:

> If a gift be made to a confidential agent with a view of inducing the agent to act in favour of the donor in relation to transactions between the donor and the agent's principal and that gift is secret as between donor and agent—that is to say, without the knowledge and consent of the principal—then the gift is a bribe in the view of the law.

More recently in *Fiona Trust & Holding Corp v Privalov*[12] Andrew Smith J said: **16.09**

> English law takes a broad view of what constitutes a bribe for the purposes of civil claims. It considers that a bribe (or 'secret commission' or 'surreptitious payment') has been paid where '(i) ... the person making the payment makes it to the agent of another person with whom he is dealing; (ii) ... he makes it to that person knowing that that person is acting as the agent of the other person with whom he is dealing; and (iii) ... he fails to disclose to the other person with whom he is dealing that he has made that payment to the person he knows to be the other person's agent': *Industries & General Mortgage Co Ltd v Lewis*.[13] Thus, a bribe is 'commission or other inducement which is given by a third party to an agent as such, and which is secret from his principal': *Anangel Atlas Compagnia Naviera SA v Ishikawajima-Harima Heavy Industries Co Ltd*.[14]

As Lord Templeman has said:[15] 'Bribery is an evil practice which threatens the foundations **16.10** of any civilized society.' The bribe or secret commission 'is necessarily calculated to sap the fidelity of the agent towards his employer'.[16] Moreover, bribery corrupts not only the recipient but the giver of the bribe.[17] In *FHR European Ventures LLP v Cedar Capital Partners LLC* Lord Neuberger said '[s]ecret commissions are objectionable as they inevitably tend to undermine trust in the commercial world. ... Accordingly, one would expect the law to be particularly stringent in relation to a claim against an agent who has received a bribe or secret commission.'[18] The criminal law aspects of bribery that concern directors are discussed in Chapter 35, Section F below.

---

[8] *Panama and South Pacific Telegraph Co v India Rubber, Gutta Percha, and Telepgraph Works Co* (1875) LR 10 Ch App 515, 526, per James LJ.

[9] *Boston Deep Sea Fishing and Ice Co v Ansell* (1888) 39 Ch D 339, 368, 369, CA, per Fry LJ.

[10] 2006 Act, s 176(5).

[11] (1900) 83 LT 41, 43, CA.

[12] [2010] EWHC 3199 (Comm) at para 70.

[13] [1949] 2 All ER 573, 575G.

[14] [1990] 1 Lloyd's Rep 166, 169.

[15] *AG for Hong Kong v Reid* [1994] 1 AC 324, 330, PC.

[16] *Smith v Sorby* (1875) 3 QBD 552n, 554, per Cockburn CJ.

[17] *Daraydan Holdings Ltd v Solland International Ltd* [2005] Ch 119 at para 1, per Lawrence Collins J.

[18] [2015] AC 250 at para 42.

(2) Acceptance of a benefit

16.11 'Benefit' is generally a word of wide import.[19] The benefit may be financial or non-financial and may include gifts and hospitality. During the passage of the bill through Parliament the Solicitor General suggested that 'in using the word "benefit" we intend the ordinary dictionary meaning of the word. The Oxford English Dictionary defines it as a favourable or helpful factor, circumstance, advantage or profit.'[20] Earlier Lord Goldsmith made the same point when he said 'the word "benefit" … includes benefits of any description, including non-financial benefits'.[21]

16.12 It is the fact of acceptance of the benefit that places the director in breach of duty. The bribe or secret commission usually takes the form of a payment of money or the transfer of property. A director will also be in breach of duty if he accepts an offer or promise of a bribe or commission to be paid in the future (eg after completion of a transaction), since the offer is tantamount to payment of the bribe.[22] On the other hand a director would not be in breach of s 176 if he merely acknowledged a prediction that he would, or would be likely to, receive money in the future.[23] A director would also be in breach of his duty under s 176 if he agreed to an arrangement with the seller of goods to the company under which he received the benefit of the difference between the seller's actual price and the inflated price invoiced to the company or under which he took the benefit of a discounted price.[24]

16.13 Needless to say, the benefit need not be paid or transferred to the director. Invariably, in order to further concealment, a bribe or secret commission is paid to someone else, such as an offshore company.[25]

16.14 There is no breach of duty if the bribe or secret commission is offered but rejected or if, for example, money is transferred into the director's bank account without his knowledge. In such a case the director would have to return the money or transfer it to the company as soon as reasonably practicable after he found out about it.

(3) Third party

16.15 A third party is defined by s 176(2) as a person other than the company, an associated body corporate, or a person acting on behalf of the company or an associated body corporate.[26]

---

[19] See eg *Cronin v Grierson* [1968] AC 895, 909, per Lord Upjohn.

[20] Hansard, HC, cols 621–2 (11 July 2006).

[21] Hansard, HL Grand Committee, col 330 (9 February 2006).

[22] *Shipway v Broadwood* [1899] 1 QB 369, CA; *Grant v The Gold Exploration and Development Syndicate Ltd* [1900] 1 QB 233, CA; and cf *Shetty v Al Rushaid Petroleum Investment Co* [2013] EWHC 1152 at paras 120 and 163, per Floyd LJ. In that case payments by suppliers of equipment to a former director and an employee of a Saudi Arabian company were held to be secret commissions notwithstanding that the payments were made after the suppliers had been paid for the equipment (albeit that the relevant duties of the director and the employee in that case were governed by the law of Saudi Arabia). Now such an offer to a director would also come within s 177 where the transaction is with the company.

[23] *Donegal International Ltd v Republic of Zambia* [2007] 1 Lloyd's Rep 397 at para 275.

[24] Cf *Turnbull v Garden* (1869) 38 LJ Ch 331; *Kimber v Barber* (1872) LR 8 Ch App 56.

[25] As was the case in *Logicrose Ltd v Southend United Football Club Ltd* [1988] 1 WLR 1256; *Shell International Trading & Shipping Co Ltd v Tikhonov* [2010] EWHC 1399 (QB); and *Shetty v Al Rushaid Petroleum Investment Co* [2013] EWHC 1152 (where a Jersey company was set up by the director and employee to receive the relevant payments).

[26] As to the meaning of an associated body corporate, see 2006 Act, s 256.

Accordingly, benefits conferred by the company (and its holding company or subsidiaries) do not fall within this duty.

In addition, by s 176(3), benefits received by a director from a person by whom his services **16.16** (as a director or otherwise) are provided to the company are not regarded as conferred by a third party.

(4) By reason of his being a director or his conduct as a director

The use of the expression 'by reason of his being a director, or his doing (or not doing) **16.17** anything as director' is an important limitation on the duty contained in s 176(1). As Lord Goldsmith said 'the purpose of the clause … is to impose on a director a duty not to accept benefits from third parties. It applies only to benefits conferred because the director is a director of the company or because of something that the director does or doesn't do as director.'[27]

A benefit will come within s 176(1) if it is given to the director because he is a director, even **16.18** though there is no transaction in view at the time, since the payment may influence and taint the director's conduct in the future.[28] But, a benefit given to a director will not come within the subsection if it is given to him because he holds some other position outside the company. For example, in *Pullan v Wilson*[29] the remuneration received by a professional trustee who had also been appointed as a non-executive director of three companies in which the relevant trusts held substantial shareholdings was held to fall outside the scope of s 176. The judge held that the relevant benefits were conferred, not by reason of the defendant being a director, or doing anything as a director, but rather because he was a trustee and was acting as such.[30]

Alternatively, acceptance of the benefit will come within the subsection if it is conferred **16.19** by reason of the director doing or not doing something as a director. In other words the benefit is intended to influence the director's conduct and put him in a position of conflict of interest. It is, however, irrelevant, in the same way that it is irrelevant under the general law, (a) that the third party and the director did not realize that what they were doing was wrong,[31] or (b) that the director may be able to show that was he not in fact influenced by the benefit received or that he did not in fact fail to discharge his duties to the company.[32] Under the general law there is an irrebuttable presumption that the bribe did in fact influence the recipient.[33]

There are several nineteenth-century cases, concerning the formation of companies, where **16.20** directors accepted payments or paid-up shares from a third party (eg a promoter, vendor, or

---

[27] Hansard, HL Grand Committee, col 330 (9 February 2006).

[28] *Daradayan Holdings Ltd v Solland International Ltd* [2005] Ch 115 at para 112; *Fiona Trust & Holding Corp v Privalov* [2010] EWHC 3199 (Comm) at para 73(i).

[29] [2014] EWHC 126 (Ch).

[30] At para 74.

[31] *Re a Debtor* [1927] 2 Ch 367, 376, CA; *Fiona Trust & Holding Corp v Privalov* [2010] EWHC 3199 (Comm) at para 72.

[32] *Harrington v Victoria Graving Dock Co* (1878) 3 QBD 549.

[33] *Parker v McKenna* (1874) LR 10 Ch App 96, 118, 124, 125; *Harrington v Victoria Graving Dock Co* (1878) 3 QBD 549; *Shipway v Broadwood* [1899] 1 QB 369, CA; *Hovenden & Sons v Milhoff* (1900) 83 LT, 41, 43, CA; *Industries and General Mortgage Co v Lewis* [1949] 2 All ER 573, 578; *Logicrose Ltd v Southend United Football Club Ltd* [1988] 1 WLR 1256; *Donegal International Ltd v Republic of Zambia* [2007] 1 Lloyd's Rep 397 at para 275; *Fiona Trust & Holding Corp v Privalov* [2010] EWHC 3199 (Comm) at para 72.

purchaser of a business or property), which were offered to them because they were directors and because they agreed to the company entering into a transaction, which was beneficial to the third party and harmful to the company and its shareholders.[34] In these cases the terms of the arrangements, including the directors' benefits were not disclosed to shareholders and, by accepting the bribes or secret commissions, the directors were in breach of the duty now stated in s 176.

16.21 The well-known case *Boston Deep Sea Fishing and Ice Co v Ansell*[35] illustrates breaches by the managing director of a company, which operated a fishing fleet, of the duties now stated in ss 175 and 176. On behalf of the company he contracted with a shipbuilding company for the construction of some fishing-smacks and agreed to take a commission from the shipbuilder. His agreement to take the secret commission would now be a breach of s 176. Not only was he accountable to the company for it, but acceptance of the secret commission justified the director's summary dismissal. The director was also a shareholder in another company whose services the company employed. As a shareholder he received a bonus referable to the services used by the company and it was held that he was accountable to the company for the bonuses (as would be the case now as a breach of s 175).

C. Situations Where the Duty Is Not Infringed

16.22 By s 176(4) the duty is not infringed if the acceptance of the benefit cannot reasonably be regarded as likely to give rise to a conflict of interest. In this regard the reference to conflict of interest includes a conflict of interest and duty and a conflict of duties.[36]

16.23 This subsection sets an objective test. If the benefit is characterized as a bribe or secret commission, it will be conclusively presumed to have influenced the director and so given rise to a conflict of interest (paragraph 16.19 above). In considering whether some other form of benefit could not reasonably be regarded as likely to give rise to a conflict of interest, the court may be assisted by considering these features: (i) the size of the benefit, (ii) its timing, (iii) whether it was normal trade practice to give such a benefit, and (iv) whether it was disclosed to the company.

16.24 Some gifts or benefits may be too small to create even a real possibility of conflict of interest (or to be treated as a bribe).[37] This would apply to hospitality, such as taking the director out to dinner or to a sports event, which are part of everyday commercial life. The more lavish

---

[34] *Madrid Bank v Pelly* (1869) LR 7 Eq 442; *General Exchange Bank v Horner* (1969) 9 Eq 480; *Re Canadian Oil Works Corporation* (1875) LR 10 Ch App 593; *Re British Provident Life and Guarantee Association* (1877) 5 Ch D 306, CA; *Re West Jewell Tin Mining Co* (1879) 10 Ch D 579, CA; *Re Diamond Fuel Co* (1879) 13 Ch D 169, CA; *Re Carriage Co-Operative Supply Association* (1884) 27 Ch D 322; *Eden v Ridsdale Railway Lamp and Lighting Co Ltd* (1889) 23 QBD 368, CA; *Re North Australian Territory Co* [1892] 1 Ch 323, CA; *Re Postage Stamp Automatic Delivery Co* [1892] 3 Ch 566.

[35] (1888) 39 Ch D 339, CA.

[36] 2006 Act, s 176(5). Section 176(5) appears to explain s 176(4), which is the only subsection to refer to conflict of interest.

[37] *Fiona Trust & Holding Corp v Privalov* [2010] EWHC 3199 (Comm) at para 73(ii), where Andrew Smith J referred to *The Parkdale* [1897] P 53, 58, 59. *The Parkdale* was also discussed in *Towers v Premier Waste Management Ltd* [2012] BCLC 313, CA, at paras 49 and 50. In *The Parkdale* the cargo owner gave the master of a ship a customary tip for the efficient discharge of the cargo. The ship-owner was aware of the practice and the master was not accountable. The 'little gift' was not antagonistic to the owner's interest, since it encouraged good performance.

the hospitality or gift, the greater will be the risk that it might be regarded as giving rise to a conflict of interest. It is unlikely that a gift of money to a director could ever come within the s 176(4) exception, because, unlike small presents and hospitality, gifts of money are remote from normal commercial practice.

Timing is also a relevant consideration, because a gift given before a transaction is entered **16.25** into is more likely to influence the director's mind than one given afterwards. Even a post-transaction gift may fall outside the s 176(4) exception, because it may be designed to influence the director in relation to future transactions.[38]

With ordinary agents it may be possible to satisfy the court that it is normal market practice **16.26** to pay a commission;[39] for example, auctioneers may receive discounts on advertising costs for which they are not accountable.[40] A provision for a director to receive an indemnity may be sufficiently common for it not to give rise to reasonable likelihood of conflict of interest.[41] Otherwise, it is improbable that the court would ever be satisfied that normal market practice entailed giving gifts, other than small presents and hospitality to directors, as described above.

Whether or not the gift is disclosed to the company is likely to be the most important con- **16.27** sideration. This applies to even small gifts and hospitality, unless the benefit is really trivial. If the benefit is modest and if the director tells the other directors he has received, or expects to receive it, the benefit may not be regarded as likely to affect the director's undivided loyalty to the company. To be effective to bring the matter within s 176(4), the disclosure would have to be full and frank, not partial and vague.[42]

In the agency case *Imageview Management Ltd v Jack*[43] the defendant argued that there **16.28** were circumstances of 'harmless collaterality' where an agent could have a private separate arrangement with a third party, without being in breach of his fiduciary duties to his principal. Jacob LJ accepted the principle, but found that it did not apply on the facts. In Jacob LJ's view an undisclosed arrangement between an agent and a third party would only be acceptable if it did not give rise to a 'realistic possibility of conflict of interest', because it is that conflict that brings the agent's conscience into play. It is most unlikely that the court would find a benefit received by a director was harmlessly collateral to his functions and duties as a director, since a director has 'a general trusteeship or fiduciary position', so that there is no 'scope of business' limit on the company's interests.[44]

---

[38] See para 16.18 above. Compare *Smith v Sorby* (1875) 3 QBD 552n, where after an agreement for the supply of coal had been made, the purchaser agreed to pay the colliery owner's agent a commission, which was not disclosed to the owner. Later, at the request of the buyer the agent agreed a variation of the agreement, which was adverse to the interests of the owner. Because of the secret commission the owner was not bound by the variation. See also *Shetty v Al Rushaid Petroleum Investment Co* [2013] EWHC 1152 referred to in n 22 and 24 above.

[39] *Secretary of State for Justice v Topland Group plc* [2011] EWHC 983 (QB). In *The Parkdale* tipping was customary.

[40] *Hippisley v Knee Bros* [1905] 1 KB 1, CA.

[41] *Stimpson v Southern Private Landlords Association* [2010] BCC 387 at para 32.

[42] Cf paras 17.21 and 17.22 below. In *Stimpson v Southern Private Landlords Association* [2010] BCC 387 at para 32, payments made by a third party to directors for loss of office were described as 'so small and sufficiently widely known' as not to be reasonably regarded as likely to give rise to a conflict of interest.

[43] [2009] 1 BCLC 724, CA at paras 30–44.

[44] *Re Allied Business and Financial Consultants Ltd* [2009] 2 BCLC 666, CA at paras 52–72, per Rimer LJ. However, compare the remarks of Spigelman NPJ in the Hong Kong Court of Final Appeal in *Jason v Cheng* [2016] HKFCA 23, at paras 83 to 87, commenting that despite the authority of *Allied Business,* '[t]he facts and circumstances of a particular case may be such as to modify the subject matter to which the fiduciary

D. Consent, Approval, or Authorization of Members

16.29 Where a director has obtained a benefit from a third party in circumstances to which s 176 applies, he should disclose the benefit to the members of the company and seek their consent, approval, authorization,[45] or ratification.[46] Members' approval may also be required where the dealing falls within Chapter 4 of the Act (discussed in Chapter 18 below).[47]

16.30 Where the approval or ratification of members is sought, the director should give full and frank disclosure of the benefit if he is to obtain protection from liability.[48] It is not enough for the director to disclose that he has an interest or to disclose merely enough to put the company on enquiry.[49]

E. Application to Former Directors

16.31 Section 170(2) provides that:

> A person who ceases to be a director continues to be subject—
>
> …
>
> (b) to the duty in section 176 (duty not to accept benefits from third parties) as regards things done or omitted by him before he ceased to be a director.

To that extent those duties apply to a former director as to a director, subject to any necessary adaptations.

16.32 This means that a director will be liable for benefits received after he ceases to hold office, if the benefits relate to his conduct while he was in office.

F. Remedies

16.33 The company's remedies against the director are discussed in more detail in Chapter 19, but the following points should be noted where a director has been bribed.

16.34 By paying the bribe or secret commission the third party takes a high risk, because he cannot afterwards defend the transaction on the basis that he believed the director to be an honest

---

duties of a director apply.' His view was that such modification must be 'binding in the corporate context' but not necessarily formal in the sense of being part of the constitutive documents or a shareholders' resolution, 'so long as it is, in substance, equivalent to a formal modification' (para 87). On the facts of that case, the majority of the shareholders were not party to any such binding agreement so the director's duties were not so limited (para 114).

[45] 2006 Act, s 180(4); *Shipway v Broadwood* [1899] 1 QB 369, 373, CA, per Chitty LJ; *Rhodes v Macalister* (1924) 29 Com Cas 19, CA at 23, per Bankes LJ; at 27, per Scrutton LJ; at 29 and 30, per Atkin LJ; quoted and applied by Jacob LJ in *Imageview Management Ltd v Jack* [2009] 1 BCLC 724, CA at paras 20–6.

[46] 2006 Act, s 239, discussed in Ch 20 below.

[47] 2006 Act, s 180(2) contemplates that some dealings to which s 176 might apply would be within exceptions to Chapter 4 of the Act; in which case there will be no breach of s 176.

[48] See paras 17.21 and 17.22 below.

[49] *Hurstanger Ltd v Wilson* [2007] 1 WLR 2351, CA.

man who would disclose the benefit to the company.[50] Furthermore the bribe or secret commission is regarded as a gift by the third party to the company, so that the third party cannot recover it from the company.[51] The *ex turpi causa* rule discussed in Chapter 19, section E(4) below should prevent the third party from recovering the bribe from the director.[52]

The company can recover the bribe or secret commission from the director as money had **16.35** and received,[53] or seek an account of profits,[54] or compensation for loss.[55] The company can also recover from the third party the amount of the bribe or damages for any loss suffered in the transaction in respect of which the bribe was given.[56] There has been considerable controversy as to whether equity will require a director or other agent to hold a bribe on constructive trust, but it has recently been decided in FHR European Ventures LLP v Cedar Capital Partners LLC[57] that the bribe is so held.[58] Lord Neuberger MR said in that case:[59]

> The respondents' formulation of the rule has the merit of simplicity: any benefit acquired by an agent as a result of his agency and in breach of his fiduciary duty is held on trust for the principal. …
>
> A further advantage of the respondents' position is that it aligns the circumstances in which an agent is obliged to account for any benefit received in breach of his fiduciary duty and those in which his principal can claim the beneficial ownership of the benefit. …
>
> The notion that the rule should not apply to a bribe or secret commission received by an agent because it could not have been received by, or on behalf of, the principal seems unattractive. The whole reason that the agent should not have accepted the bribe or commission is that it puts him in conflict with his duty to his principal. Further, in terms of elementary economics, there must be a strong possibility that the bribe has disadvantaged the principal. … [I]t accords with common sense that it should often, even normally, be correct; indeed, in some cases, it has been assumed by judges that the price payable for the transaction in which the agent was acting was influenced pro rata to account for the bribe.

---

[50] *Grant v Gold Exploration and Development Syndicate Ltd* [1900] 1 QB 233, 249, 250, CA; *Logicrose Ltd v Southend United Football Club Ltd* [1988] 1 WLR 1256, 1262; *Daradayan Holdings Ltd v Solland International Ltd* [2005] Ch 119, 132.

[51] *Grant v Gold Exploration and Development Syndicate Ltd* [1900] 1 QB 233, 249, 251, CA; *Logicrose Ltd v Southend United Football Club Ltd* [1988] 1 WLR 1256, 1262, 1263; *Daradayan Holdings Ltd v Solland International Ltd* [2005] Ch 119, 132.

[52] Or from an allegedly negligent solicitor or agent: *Nayyar v Denton Wilde Sapte* [2009] EWHC 3218 (QB). For the current position on the *ex turpi causa* defence, see *Patel v Mirza* [2016] 3 WLR 399, SC.

[53] *Boston Deep Sea Fishing and Ice Co v Ansell* (1888) 39 Ch D 339; *Reading v AG* [1949] 2 KB 232; [1951] AC 507; *Mahesan v Malaysia Housing Society* [1979] AC 374, PC; *Logicrose Ltd v Southend United Football Club Ltd* [1988] 1 WLR 1256, 1263; *Daradayan Holdings Ltd v Solland International Ltd* [2005] Ch 119, 132; *Shell International Trading & Shipping Co Ltd v Tikhonov* [2010] EWHC 1399 (QB).

[54] *Towers v Premier Waste Management Ltd* [2012] BCLC 313, CA; *FHR European Ventures LLP v Cedar Capital Partners LLC* [2015] AC 250 at para 6, per Lord Neuberger MR.

[55] *Mahesan v Malaysia Housing Society* [1979] AC 374, PC; *Shell International Trading & Shipping Co Ltd v Tikhonov* [2010] EWHC 1399 (QB); *FHR European Ventures LLP v Cedar Capital Partners LLC* [2015] AC 250 at para 7 per Lord Neuberger MR.

[56] *Mahesan v Malaysia Housing Society* [1979] AC 374, 383, PC, per Lord Diplock.

[57] [2015] AC 250.

[58] Following *AG of Hong Kong v Reid* [1994] 1 AC 324, PC and overruling *Lister & Co v Stubbs* (1890) 45 Ch D 1 and *Sinclair Investments (UK) Ltd v Versailles Trade Finance Ltd* [2012] Ch 453, CA.

[59] At paras 35 to 37.

17

DUTY TO DECLARE INTEREST
IN TRANSACTION OR ARRANGEMENT

Lloyd Tamlyn and Marcus Haywood

A. Introduction

(1) The former law

One of the consequences of the common law principle that a director must avoid conflicts **17.01** of interest was that a director could not have an interest in a transaction with the company unless he had disclosed all material facts about the interest to the members and they had approved or authorized his having the interest.[1] Authorization by the board was not sufficient.[2] If the other party to the transaction had notice of the irregularity, the company might rescind the contract.[3] The director might also be liable for breach of duty and under a duty to account for profits obtained by reason of such dealings.[4]

---

[1] *Aberdeen Ry Co v Blaikie* (1854) 1 Macq 461, 471, 472, HL (SC); *North-West Transportation Co Ltd v Beatty* (1887) 12 App Cas 589, 593, 594, PC; *Transvaal Lands Company v New Belgium (Transvaal) Land and Development Company* [1914] 2 Ch 488; *Gwembe Valley Development Co Ltd v Koshy (No 3)* [2004] 1 BCLC 131, CA at para 65; *Newgate Stud Co v Penfold* [2008] 1 BCLC 46 at paras 218–56.

[2] *Benson v Heathorn* (1842) 1 Y&C Ch Cas 326, 341, 342; *Re Cardiff Preserved Coke and Coal Co* (1862) 32 LJ Ch 754; *Imperial Mercantile Credit Association v Coleman* (1871) 6 Ch App 556 at 567 (revd on other grounds (1873) LR 6 HL 189); *Gray v New Augarita Porcupine Mines Ltd* [1952] 3 DLR 1, 13, PC.

[3] The *Transvaal Lands Company* case, n 1 above.

[4] The *Transvaal Lands Company* case, n 1 above; *Hely-Hutchinson v Brayhead Ltd* [1968] 1 QB 549, 589, 590, CA per Lord Wilberforce; *Regal (Hastings) Ltd v Gulliver* [1967] 2 AC 134n.

17.02   There was some support in the case law for the proposition that a principle of equity disabled a director from entering into such dealings (without full disclosure), as opposed to his being under a fiduciary duty not to make a secret profit.[5]

Relaxation of the general rule in a company's articles

17.03   Company articles frequently relaxed the common law and equitable rules where the director disclosed his interest to the board and the transaction was approved by directors without an interest.[6] The effect of such articles was permissive, permitting a director to carry out dealings which would otherwise have been precluded under the general law. If the conditions were complied with, the director was not accountable to the company for any benefit which he derived from the transaction or arrangement, and the transaction or arrangement was not voidable on the basis of the director's interest.

17.04   Thus the 1985 Table A included these provisions:[7]

> 85.   Subject to the provisions of the Act, and provided that he has disclosed to the directors the nature and extent of any material interest of his, a director notwithstanding his office—
> (a)   may be a party to, or otherwise interested in, any transaction or arrangement with the company or in which the company is otherwise interested; …
> 86.   For the purposes of regulation 85—
> (a)   a general notice given to the directors that a director is to be regarded as having an interest of the nature and extent specified in the notice in any transaction or arrangement in which a specified person is interested shall be deemed to be a disclosure that the director has an interest in any such transaction of the nature and extent specified; and
> (b)   an interest of which a director has no knowledge and of which it is unreasonable to expect him to have knowledge shall not be treated as an interest of his.

Articles 94 and 95 prevented a director with a direct or indirect interest from voting or being counted in the quorum, except in specific circumstances.

1985 Act, s 317

17.05   The provision of the Act referred to in Table A, reg 94 was the 1985 Act, s 317,[8] which required a director who was in any way, whether directly or indirectly, interested in a contract or proposed contract with the company to declare the nature of his interest at a meeting of the directors of the company.

17.06   A director who failed to comply with the 1985 Act, s 317 was liable to a fine, but s 317 did not specify any other consequences of a failure to comply. Section 317(9) provided that nothing in the section prejudiced the operation of any rule of law restricting directors of a

---

[5] *Movitex Ltd v Bulfield* [1988] BCLC 104, 119–21, referring to *Tito v Waddell (No 2)* [1977] Ch 106. CLR: *Developing the Framework*, para 3.62, n 43, explained that the 'disability' analysis had been preferred due to the need to reconcile Table A, reg 85 with 1985 Act, s 309A (see now 2006 Act, s 232), which rendered void any provision purporting to exempt a director from liability for breach of duty. In *Gwembe Valley Development Co Ltd v Koshy* [2004] 1 BCLC 131 at paras 104–9 the Court of Appeal described the distinction between disability and duty in *Tito v Waddell* as 'a needless complication'.

[6] 1985 Table A, regs 85, 86, 94.

[7] 1985 Table A, reg 94 set out in paragraphs (a)–(d) four exceptions (concerning guarantees, subscriptions, and retirement benefits schemes), where the director could still vote. Reg 96 enabled the company by ordinary resolution to suspend or relax to any extent the prohibition on voting by interested directors. Compare 1948 Act, Table A, reg 84.

[8] Formerly 1948 Act, s 199.

company from having an interest in contracts with the company. Although not wholly free from doubt, the legal position under the 1985 Act, s 317 was, therefore, probably as follows:

(1) In and of itself, any failure by a director to comply with its provisions had no civil consequences. The effect of a failure by a director to comply with s 317 was merely that he thereby committed an offence.[9]

(2) The civil consequences of a director having an interest in a transaction, and his failure to disclose the same, were therefore determined exclusively by the general law and the company's articles of association. The general law prohibited a director, absent full disclosure of his interest to the members, from dealing on behalf of the company in respect of any transaction in which he had an interest, imposed a duty to account on the director if he did so, and rendered the contract entered into absent such disclosure potentially voidable.[10] A company's articles could, however, permit such dealings provided that certain preconditions relating to disclosure by the interested director were complied with. Those preconditions might (and, in the case of the 1985 Table A, reg 85, implicitly did) include compliance with s 317.[11]

(2) The new provisions in the 2006 Act

The legal landscape under the 2006 Act is very different. The general law prohibiting a direc- **17.07** tor from having an interest in contracts, transactions, or arrangements with a company, and rendering the contract or transaction voidable if the informed consent of the members has not been obtained, has been superseded by a combination of the Companies Act, ss 177, 178, and 180,[12] in relation to proposed transactions or arrangements with the company, and ss 182–7, in relation to existing transactions or arrangements.[13]

Section 177 imposes a general duty on a director to declare the nature and extent of his inter- **17.08** est in a proposed transaction or arrangement to the other directors. If the director complies

---

[9] *Hely-Hutchinson v Brayhead Ltd* [1968] 1 QB 549, 588–91, 594, CA, per Lord Wilberforce and Lord Pearson (Lord Denning at 585, 586 is equivocal); *Guinness plc v Saunders* [1990] 2 AC 663, 697, 698, HL, per Lord Goff, who approved the reasoning of Lord Pearson. At 694 Lord Templeman stated that the Court of Appeal in *Hely-Hutchinson* had held that s 317 rendered a contract voidable by the company if the director did not declare his interest. In *Lee Panavision Ltd v Lee Lighting Ltd* [1991] BCLC 575, 583, Harman J described Lord Templeman's observation as 'surprising', adding that 'quite plainly *Hely-Hutchinson* never said anything of the sort at all'. The Court of Appeal upheld the decision in *Lee Panavision* on other grounds ([1992] BCLC 22), but, at 33, refused to enter into the 'scholastic exercise' of discerning whether 'true doctrine' was to be discerned in the judgments of Lords Pearson and Wilberforce, as opposed to Lord Denning MR, in the *Hely-Hutchinson* case, or in the speech of Lord Templeman rather than Lord Goff in the *Guinness* case. In *Cowan de Groot Properties Ltd v Eagle Trust plc* [1991] BCLC 1045, 1113 Knox J stated that it was clear that the statutory duty of disclosure under the 1985 Act, s 317 and its predecessors did not of itself affect the validity of a contract. In *Re Marini Ltd* [2004] BCC 172, 195, 196 it was said to be common ground that a breach of the 1985 Act, s 317 rendered the contract voidable, though it is unclear from the limited references to the company's articles, at 176, whether this would have resulted from the company's articles in any event. Under s 317 a director was not liable for damages for breach of statutory duty if he failed to comply with its requirements: *Coleman Taymar Ltd v Oakes* [2001] 2 BCLC 749, 769; *Castlereagh Motels v Davies-Roe* (1967) 67 SR (NSW) 279.

[10] Para 17.01 above.

[11] However, see *Kleanthous v Paphitis* [2012] BCC 676, paras 47–50, where it was argued that 'the provisions of the Act' referred to in the opening words of Table A, reg 85, did not include section 317 of the 1985 Act, since then the words '… and provided that he has disclosed to the directors the nature and extent of any material interest of his …' would be otiose.

[12] As amended by the Enterprise and Regulatory Reform Act 2013, s 81(1), (2)(a)–(c), as from 1 October 2013: SI 2013/2227, art 2(h).

[13] These provisions came into force on 1 October 2008: 2006 Act, Commencement Order No 5, Art 4.

with that general duty, the transaction or arrangement is not liable to be set aside by reason of his not obtaining the consent or approval of the members of the company (as was the case previously under the general law).[14] Disclosure to the board, under the general duty embodied in s 177, is now key to the validity of the transaction, rather than disclosure to the members (or compliance with the company's articles).[15] If a director fails to comply with his general duty of disclosure under s 177, the consequence is that the transaction may be voidable, and the director accountable for breach of fiduciary duty.[16]

17.09 Section 182, read with ss 183–7, imposes a similar duty in relation to existing transactions or arrangements with the company.[17] A director who fails to declare an interest in a transaction or arrangement already entered into with the company as required by s 182 is guilty of an offence; a director who fails to declare an interest in a proposed transaction or arrangement is not.[18] On the other hand, whereas a breach of s 177 attracts civil consequences, a breach of s 182 does not. The reason for the distinction appears to be that a failure to make the relevant disclosure under s 177 has the potential to prejudice the company's decision to enter into a proposed transaction whereas a failure to make the relevant disclosure under s 183 has no such potential.[19]

17.10 One consequence of the change to the legal landscape is that while articles such as 1985 Table A, reg 85 will continue to be adopted, they will generally no longer play the crucial role they once did, ie of permitting that which would otherwise be prohibited. The Model Articles thus make reference to conflicts of interest only in the context of voting at board meetings.[20] The articles may, however, contain a provision requiring the consent or approval of the members to any proposed transaction in which a director has an interest.[21]

B. Duty in Relation to a Proposed Transaction or Arrangement

(1) Scope of the duty

17.11 The 2006 Act, s 177(1) provides that:

> (1) If a director of a company is in any way, directly or indirectly, interested in a proposed transaction or arrangement with the company, he must declare the nature and extent of that interest to the other directors.

---

[14] 2006 Act, s 180 (as amended: see n 12 above).

[15] Save where the company's constitution requires the consent or approval of members: s 180(1).

[16] 2006 Act, s 178. The imposition of a positive fiduciary duty to declare the relevant interest, in default of which the relevant transaction may be avoided and the director accountable for any profit, is in some ways a statutory formulation of the general law as, perhaps, it was expressed by Lord Denning MR in the *Hely-Hutchinson* case, [1968] 1 QB 549, 585.

[17] The provisions of 2006 Act, ss 182–7 replace the provisions of s 317 in so far as they relate to existing transactions with the company. See Section C below.

[18] 2006 Act, s 183.

[19] See eg Lord Goldsmith who said that s 177 'is deliberately intended to apply only to proposed transactions … if a company is told that a director has an interest in a proposed transaction, it can decide whether to enter into the transaction, on what terms and with what safeguards': Hansard, HL Grand Committee, col 334 (9 February 2006).

[20] See Model Article (plc) 16, Model Article (pcls) 14, and Model Article (pclg) 14.

[21] 2006 Act, s 180(1).

The duty

Section 177 replaces the equitable rule that directors may not have interests in transactions **17.12**
with the company unless the interest has been authorized by the members. As proposed
by the CLR, shareholder approval for the transaction is not a requirement of the statutory
duty.[22] The members of the company may, however, still impose requirements for shareholder approval in the articles. However, the statutory duty imposed by s 177 cannot be
ousted by the company's articles.[23]

Section 177 requires a director to disclose any interest, direct or indirect, that he has in rela- **17.13**
tion to a proposed transaction or arrangement[24] with the company. Any declaration required
by the section must be made before the company enters into the transaction or arrangement.[25] This is to allow the directors on behalf of the company to decide whether to enter
into the transaction, on what terms, and with what safeguards.

Provided a declaration has been made the conflicted director may, subject to the company's **17.14**
articles of association (see paragraph 17.10 above) and compliance with his other duties,
participate in decision-taking relating to such transactions with the company.

Direct and indirect interest

Case law relating to the 1985 Act, s 317 and the common law principles, discussed in the **17.15**
following paragraphs, has considered what constitutes a direct or indirect interest. That case
law is likely to continue to be instructive in considering what constitutes a direct or indirect
interest in a transaction or arrangement under s 177. However, care will obviously need to
be taken where the case law considers those parts of the 1985 Act, s 317 which do not form
part of s 177.

The director does not need to be a party to the transaction for the duty to apply. An interest **17.16**
of another person in a contract, transaction, or arrangement with the company may require
the director to make a disclosure under this duty, if the director's connection with that other
person gives the director a direct or indirect interest in the matter. For example, a director is
'interested' in a contract with a firm of which he was a member;[26] and a director is 'interested'
in a contract between the company of which he is director and another company in which
he owns shares, even though he holds such shares qua trustee.[27]

---

[22] CLR: *Final Report* at paras 3.21–3.27; *Completing the Structure* at paras 3.26 and 3.27.

[23] 2006 Act, s 232.

[24] The words 'transaction or arrangement' are not defined. Compare the broad inclusive definition of 'transaction' in Insolvency Act, s 436 and Ch 18 at para 18.37 below on 'arrangement' under the Companies Act,
s 190 (substantial property transactions). Whilst 'transaction or arrangement' are words of broad meaning, the
words themselves, and the requirement that the transaction or arrangement must have been 'entered into by' the
company, perhaps connote an element of mutual dealing and suggest that a gift, or any unilateral dealing, would
not fall within s 177: compare cases on the meaning of 'transaction' in the Insolvency Act: *Re Taylor Sinclair
(Capital) Ltd* [2001] 2 BCLC 176, 184; *Feakins v DEFRA* [2007] BCC 54, CA at para 78; *Clement v Henry
Hadaway Organisation Ltd* [2008] 1 BCLC 223 at para 31.The word 'arrangement' is wider than the word
'transaction': *Re British Basic Slag Ltd's Agreements* [1963] 1 WLR 727; *Re Duckwari plc* [1999] Ch 253, CA;
Murray v Leisureplay plc [2004] EWHC 1927 (QB) at para 106, per Stanley Burnton J (overruled by the Court
of Appeal [2005] EWCA Civ 963 but not on this point); *Granada Group Ltd v The Law Debenture Pension Trust
Corporation plc* [2015] 2 BCLC 604, para 40.

[25] 2006 Act, s 177(4); *Burns v The Financial Conduct Authority* [2014] UKUT 0509 (TCC), para 78.

[26] *Imperial Mercantile Credit Association v Coleman* (1873) LR 6 HL 189; *Aberdeen Rly Co v Blaikie Bros*
(1854) 1 Macq 461.

[27] *Transvaal Lands Co v New Belgium Co* [1914] 2 Ch 488.

17.17   A director is not automatically interested in a contract, or proposed contract, for the purposes of s 177 by reason of some interest in that contract or proposed contract held by a person 'connected' to him within the meaning of the 2006 Act, s 252: persons so connected with a director are not specifically mentioned in s 177. Clearly, however, sometimes such interests will fall within the terms of s 177 and consequently disclosure of such interests is advisable as a matter of caution.[28]

17.18   An expectation of benefit by reason of, rather than under, a contract or proposed contract can constitute an 'interest' in that contract though the strength of the expectation will be material in deciding whether it does in fact constitute such an interest. Under the 1985 Act it has been held that, for the purposes of s 317, an interest in a transaction or arrangement included real and substantial expectations.[29] Also, a director's expectation of some benefit as a result of the company rejecting a proposed contract could also result in the director having an interest in the contract.[30]

17.19   Under the 1985 Act, s 317 it was held to be irrelevant that the proposed contract would not otherwise come before the board for approval.[31] It is thought that the same position will be true under s 177.

Proposed transaction or arrangement with the company

17.20   Section 177 relates to proposed transactions or arrangements[32] *with* the company and is to be contrasted with the 2006 Act, s 175 which applies where there is no transaction or arrangement with the company: see Chapter 15 above. Sections 175 and 177 are mutually exclusive, since the duty in s 175(1) does not apply to a conflict of interest arising in relation to a transaction or arrangement with the company.[33] Therefore if there is no transaction or arrangement with the company, the fact that disclosure may have been made in accordance with s 177 is irrelevant[34]. It would seem that the proposed transaction or arrangement is one to be entered into by the board or other authorized persons on behalf of the company. So, in order to determine whether a case of alleged conflict is within ss 175 or 177, it is necessary to see if the company is to be made a party to the proposed transaction or arrangement.[35]

---

[28]   *Re Dominion International Group plc (No 2)* [1996] 1 BCLC 572, 597–8.

[29]   *Re Dominion International Group plc (No 2)* [1996] 1 BCLC 572, 597. Given that the expectation in that case was 'comparable to that of a healthy young person entitled as the sole next of kin on the prospective intestacy of an incurable lunatic in the last stages of a fatal disease', Knox J held that there was an interest which ought to have been disclosed under 1985 Act, s 317. It appears that even a nominal interest had to be disclosed: *Todd v Robinson* (1884) 14 QBD 739, CA, though this is now subject to s 182(6).

[30]   *Item Software (UK) Ltd v Fassihi* [2005] 2 BCLC 91, CA at para 36, per Arden LJ.

[31]   *Guinness plc v Saunders* [1988] BCLC 607, 612, per Fox LJ, CA; affd on other grounds [1990] 2 AC 663, HL suggests that disclosure 'at a meeting of the directors of the company' means disclosure to a duly convened meeting of the main board, rather than disclosure to a committee of the board. See also *Gwembe Valley v Koshy* [2004] 1 BCLC 131, CA at para 59 and *Re MDA Investment Management Ltd* [2004] 1 BCLC 217 at para 97. However, disclosure 'at a meeting of the directors of the company' does not necessarily entail disclosure to a meeting of the board at which all members of it are present.

[32]   As to the meaning of the words 'transaction or arrangement' see n 24 above.

[33]   2006 Act, s 175(3). *McKillen v Misland (Cyprus) Investments Ltd* [2012] EWHC 2343 (Ch), paras 583 and 584 (unaffected by the appeal at [2013] 2 BCLC 583); see also *Burns v The Financial Conduct Authority* [2014] UKUT 0509 (TCC), para 75.

[34]   *McKillen*, n 33 above.

[35]   Compare the issue in *Criterion Properties plc v Stratford UK Properties LLC* [2004] 1 WLR 1846, HL at paras 28–30, per Lord Scott.

Nature and extent to be disclosed

The requirement is for full and frank disclosure.[36] Disclosure must be for the purposes of allowing the board to consider and approve the contract, that is, it must be more than a mere presentation to the board of a fait accompli.[37] Similarly, informal disclosure made piecemeal, or proof of the knowledge of individual board members, does not comply with the formal requirements of disclosure to the board, which would involve an opportunity for consideration of the matter by the board as a body.[38]   **17.21**

Whereas s 317 required a director to declare merely the 'nature' of his interest to a meeting of the directors, the requirement in s 177 follows the phraseology of the 1985 Table A, reg 85 and is to declare the nature 'and extent' of that interest to the other directors. Authorities on the general law and the 1985 Act, s 317 indicate that what is required is a full and frank declaration by the director not of 'an' interest but of the precise nature of the interest.[39] Thus in *Movitex Ltd v Bulfield*[40] Vinelott J said that the disclosure must be such that the other director or directors can see 'what his interest is and how far it goes'. The burden is on the director to show that his declaration was adequate disclosure.[41]   **17.22**

(2) The declaration

Method of making declaration

Section 177(2) provides for how the declaration may be made: **17.23**

> (2) The declaration may (but need not) be made:
>   (a) at a meeting of the directors, or

---

[36] *Ultraframe (UK) Ltd v Fielding* [2005] EWHC 1638 at para 1432, citing *Neptune (Vehicle Washing Equipment) Ltd v Fitzgerald* [1996] Ch 274, 282; *Fine Industrial Commodities Ltd v Powling* (1954) 71 RPC 253, 259, 261–2. See also *FHR European Ventures LLP v Cedar Capital Partners LLC* [2015] AC 250 (SC), judgment of the Court at para 5: 'Because of the importance which equity attaches to fiduciary duties, such "informed consent" [ie of both principals where a fiduciary acts for two principals with potentially conflicting interests] is only effective if it is given after "full disclosure"', to quote Jessel MR in *Dunne v English* (1874) LR 18 Eq 524, 533.

[37] *Re a Company (No 00789 of 1987); Nuneaton Borough Association Football Club Ltd (No 2)* [1991] BCLC 267 44, 60D.

[38] *Gwembe Valley Development Co Ltd v Koshy (No 3)* [2004] 1 BCLC 131, CA at 59, per Mummery LJ; *Guinness plc v Saunders* [1988] 1 WLR 863, 868–9, CA, per Fox LJ (on appeal but not affected on this point [1990] 2 AC 663); *Neptune (Vehicle Washing Equipment) Ltd v Fitzgerald* [1996] Ch 274, 282–4; *Re MDA Investment Management Ltd* [2004] 1 BCLC 217. But cf *Lee Panavision Ltd v Lee Lighting Ltd* [1992] BCLC 22, CA (where the court hesitated to find that the failure formally to declare at a board meeting an interest common to all members and *ex hypothesi* already known to all of the members of the board was a breach of 1985 Act, s 317). See also *Runciman v Walter Runciman plc* [1992] BCLC 1084, 1093; *MacPherson v European Strategic Bureau Ltd* [1999] 2 BCLC 203, 219 (revsd but not on this point [2000] 2 BCLC 683, CA); *Re Marini Ltd* [2004] BCC 172 at paras 59–64.

[39] *Neptune (Vehicle Washing Equipment) Ltd v Fitzgerald* [1996] Ch 274, 282; *Ultraframe (UK) Ltd v Fielding* [2005] EWHC 1638 (Ch) at para 1432. Full disclosure was also required as a matter of general law: see *Imperial Mercantile Credit Association v Coleman* (1873) LR 6 HL 189, 201; *Gray v New Augarita Porcupine Mines Ltd* [1952] 3 DLR 1, 14, 15, PC; *New Zealand Netherlands Society Oranje Inc v Kuys* [1973] 1 WLR 1126, 1131, PC; *Gwembe Valley Development Co Ltd v Koshy* [1998] 2 BCLC 613, 620, 621, where Harman J said that disclosure had to be 'clear and precise' and that conveying 'a general understanding' was not adequate disclosure; *Gwembe Valley Development Co Ltd v Koshy (No 3)* [2004] 1 BCLC 131, CA at para 65.

[40] [1988] BCLC 104, 121, where there was sufficient disclosure, because two directors disclosed their interest in a company and it was self-evident to the third director that the two directors and their families owned that company; the proportions in which they did so was irrelevant.

[41] *Gray v New Augarita Porcupine Mines Ltd* [1952] 3 DLR 1, 14, 15, PC; *Gwembe Valley Development Co Ltd v Koshy* [1998] 2 BCLC 613, 620, 621.

      (b) by notice to the directors in accordance with:
         (i)   section 184 (notice in writing), or
         (ii) section 185 (general notice).

17.24   Section 177 does not impose any rules on how the declaration of an interest must be made, but sub-s (2) allows the declaration to be made (a) at a meeting of the directors, or (b) by notice to the directors in accordance with s 184 (notice in writing), or s 185 (general notice).[42] Disclosure to the members would not comply with the section. (For consent, approval or authorization by members, see Chapter 10, Section D above.)

Declaration at a meeting of directors

17.25   It had been held under the 1985 Act, s 317 that the requirement for disclosure at a meeting of the directors meant a duly convened meeting of directors.[43] The point is now largely irrelevant, since if there is disclosure to the directors making up the board outside a formally convened board meeting, there will be no duty to disclose at a formal board meeting by reason of s 177(6)(b). Under the 1985 Act, s 317, disclosure to a committee of the board was insufficient.[44] It is thought that it would also be insufficient for the purposes of s 177(2)(a).

Notice in writing

17.26   Where the declaration is made by notice in writing, the director must send the notice to the other directors.[45] The notice may be sent in hard copy form or, if the recipient has agreed to receive it by electronic means, in an agreed electronic form.[46] The notice may be sent by hand or by post or, if the recipient has agreed to receive it by electronic means, by agreed electronic means.[47] Where a director declares an interest by notice in writing in accordance with s 184, the making of the declaration is deemed to form part of the proceedings at the next meeting of the directors after the notice is given, and the provisions of s 248 (minutes of meetings of directors) apply as if the declaration had been made at that meeting.[48]

General notice

17.27   General notice is notice given to the directors of the company to the effect that the director has an interest (as member, officer, employee, or otherwise) in a specified body corporate or firm and is to be regarded as interested in any transactions or arrangement that may, after the date of the notice, be made with that body corporate or firm, or is connected with a specified body (other than a body corporate or firm) and is to be regarded as interested in any transaction or arrangement that may, after the date of the notice, be made with that person.[49] The notice must state the nature and extent of the director's interest in the body corporate or firm

---

[42] 2006 Act, s 177(2).

[43] *Guinness plc v Saunders* [1988] 1 WLR 863, 868, CA (appeal to the House of Lords dismissed on other grounds: [1990] 2 AC 663); *Gwembe Valley Development Co Ltd v Koshy (No 3)* [2004] 1 BCLC 131, CA at para 59; *Re MDA Investment Management Ltd* [2004] 1 BCLC 217, 255, 6. In *Re Marini Ltd* [2004] BCC 172, 194, it was held that 1985 Act, s 317 did not require disclosure at a formal board meeting, but the decision of the Court of Appeal in the *Guinness* case was not, it appears, cited.

[44] *Guinness plc v Saunders* [1988] 1 WLR 863, CA, 868 (the point was not addressed when the case went to the House of Lords: [1990] 2 AC 663); *Gwembe Valley Development Co Ltd v Koshy* [2004] 1 BCLC 131, CA at paras 51 and 59.

[45] 2006 Act, s 184(2).

[46] 2006 Act, s 184(3).

[47] 2006 Act, s 184(4).

[48] 2006 Act, s 184(5).

[49] 2006 Act, s 185(2).

or, as the case may be, the nature of his connection with the person.[50] General notice is not effective unless it is given at a meeting of the directors, or the director takes reasonable steps to secure that it is brought up and read at the next meeting of the directors after it is given.[51] Where general notice is given in accordance with these provisions, it is a sufficient declaration of interest in relation to the matters to which it relates.[52]

Inaccurate or incomplete declaration

Where the declaration is inaccurate or incomplete, s 177(3) provides for a further declaration to be made: **17.28**

> If a declaration of interest under this section proves to be, or becomes, inaccurate or incomplete, a further declaration must be made.

However, a further declaration is only necessary if the company has not yet entered into **17.29** the transaction or arrangement at the time the director becomes aware of the inaccuracy or incompleteness of the earlier declaration (or ought reasonably to have become so aware). Where the company has entered into the transaction or arrangement, there is no longer a proposed transaction or arrangement and the provisions of the 2006 Act, ss 182–7 apply.

When the declaration must be made

Section 177(4) deals with timing: **17.30**

> Any declaration required by this section must be made before the company enters into the transaction or arrangement.

(3) Where a declaration is not required

Section 177(5) and (6) identifies circumstances where a declaration is not required: **17.31**

> (5) This section does not require a declaration of an interest of which the director is not aware or where the director is not aware of the transaction or arrangement in question. For this purpose a director is treated as being aware of matters of which he ought reasonably to be aware.
>
> (6) A director need not declare an interest:
>
> > (a) if it cannot reasonably be regarded as likely to give rise to a conflict of interest;
> > (b) if, or to the extent that, the other directors are already aware of it (and for this purpose the other directors are treated as aware of anything of which they ought reasonably to be aware); or
> > (c) if, or to the extent that, it concerns terms of his service contract that have been or are to be considered:
> > > (i) by a meeting of the directors, or
> > > (ii) by a committee of the directors appointed for the purpose under the company's constitution.

Lack of knowledge

Those subsections provide various exemptions from the duty to make a declaration pursuant **17.32** to s 177. Under s 177(5) a director is not required to make a declaration if he is not aware

---

[50] 2006 Act, s 185(3).
[51] 2006 Act, s 185(4).
[52] 2006 Act, s 185(1). These provisions re-enact, with some modifications, 1985 Act, s 317(3) and (4). Also see the provision about general notice in 1985 Table A, reg 86(a).

that he has an interest or if he is not aware of the transaction or arrangement in question. For this purpose a director is treated as being aware of matters of which he ought reasonably to be aware.[53] Accordingly, a director will breach the duty if he fails to declare something he ought reasonably to have known, but no declaration is required where the director is not aware of his interest or of the transaction or arrangement.[54]

17.33   Section 177(5) provides for an objective test.[55] The Solicitor General said:[56]

> The Government take the view that directors have some substantial obligations and that they ought to declare those things about which they should reasonably have been aware. That is an objective test applied to directors concerned. So it will take into account any relevant circumstances relating to that director; it will focus on the individual director. This is the question that will be asked: what is it reasonable to expect a director in those circumstances to have been aware of? For example, a non-executive director might be expected generally to be less aware of the individual transactions or arrangements entered into by a company. I repeat that directors are not expected to disclose things that they do not know. One of the purposes of the clause is to ensure that the board is aware of anything that might influence a director's decision. The director can disclose only what he is aware of, and if he is aware of it, he ought to declare it. The clause will therefore be clear enough, but anyone who wants clarification can read the notes on the clause or, on the basis of *Pepper v Hart*, read my comments in Hansard.

17.34   Section 177(6) identifies three circumstances where a declaration need not be made.[57] This express provision should make it unnecessary for the court to have to consider whether mere technical breaches of disclosure requirements have substantive consequences.[58]

No reasonable likelihood of conflict

17.35   First, by s 177(6)(a) a director need not declare an interest if it cannot reasonably be regarded as likely to give rise to a conflict of interest.[59] The test is not whether the interest is in fact likely to give rise to a conflict of interest, but whether it cannot reasonably be regarded as likely to give rise to such an interest, a narrower limitation on the duty. The test has no subjective component. The word 'likely' has several different shades of meaning, varying from

---

[53]   2006 Act, s 177(5).

[54]   Following the Law Commission recommendation: Law Commission, *Company Directors: Regulating Conflicts of Interest and Formulating a Statement of Duties*, No 261, para 8.57. Under 1985 Table A, reg 85, an interest of which the director had no knowledge, and of which it was unreasonable to expect him to have knowledge, was not treated as an interest of his which needed to be disclosed if he was to take advantage of the permission in reg 85: see reg 86(b).

[55]   This was the view of Lord Goldsmith. Hansard, HL GC Day 4, vol 678, col 334 (9 February 2006).

[56]   Hansard HC Standing Committee D, col 628 (11 July 2006).

[57]   Again a recommendation of the Law Commission: Law Commission, *Company Directors: Regulating Conflicts of Interest and Formulating a Statement of Duties*, No 261, paras 8.33, 8.44, 8.45.

[58]   This issue was considered in a number of cases all concerned with prospective transactions: *Runciman v Walter Runciman plc* [1992] BCLC 1084, 1093, 1095–6; *Lee Panavision Ltd v Lee Lighting Ltd* [1992] BCLC 22, 33, CA; *Re Dominion International Group plc (No 2)* [1996] 1 BCLC 572, 598–600 (a directors' disqualification case); *MacPherson v European Strategic Bureau Ltd* [1999] 2 BCLC 203, 219; *Re Marini Ltd* [2004] BCC 172, 194–6. In each case, no substantive effect was given where the breach was merely technical by refusing to grant any equitable remedy even where recognized defences such as acquiescence, delay, and impossibility of *restitutio in integrum* were not available. A strict approach to construction was adopted in *Neptune (Vehicle Washing Equipment) Ltd v Fitzgerald* [1996] Ch 274, and followed through to trial ([1995] BCC 1000). No declaration would be necessary if the facts of *Neptune* were to recur in the context of the Act ss 182 or 177: see below at paras 17.43 and 17.61–17.63.

[59]   This is to some degree a reflection of Table A, reg 85, which required disclosure only of any 'material' interest of the director.

'more likely than not' to 'may well'.[60] Given the importance which the law has traditionally ascribed to the need to avoid conflict of duty and interest,[61] it is thought that s 182(6)(a) should be interpreted narrowly, and a director under a duty to disclose the interest even where the possibility of a conflict is somewhat remote.

Other directors aware

Secondly, by s 177(6)(b) a director also need not declare an interest if, or to the extent that, **17.36** the other directors are already aware of it (and for this purpose the other directors are treated as aware of anything of which they ought reasonably to be aware). It appears, therefore, that a director who knows or suspects that his fellow directors are in fact unaware of his interest (even though they ought to know of it) is, on a strict reading of s 177(6)(b), under no duty to disclose it.

Service contracts

Thirdly, s 177(6)(c) makes special provision for service contracts[62] that are considered by a **17.37** meeting of the directors or a committee appointed for the purpose (such as a remuneration committee). It provides that a director need not declare an interest if, or to the extent that, it concerns terms of his service contract that have been or are to be considered (i) by a meeting of the directors, or (ii) by a committee of the directors appointed for the purpose under the company's constitution.[63]

It was thought to be the law under the predecessors of s 177 (and s 182) that the section did **17.38** not apply solely to contracts which were to go before the board for approval.[64] This is, to some extent, implicitly confirmed by s 177(6)(c)(ii), since it limits the duty to disclose in circumstances in which the relevant contract has been or is to be approved by a committee of the board, and not the board itself.[65]

It is likely that, ordinarily, a director who fails to disclose his interest in respect of his service **17.39** contract or a variation of it will not be required to disclose that interest in any event, because the other directors will normally be aware of his interest with the consequence that s 177(6)(b) will apply. However, where the service contract or variation to it is not agreed by the board, but, for example, the chief executive alone, or a remuneration committee of the directors, or the composition of the board changes, directors other than the chief executive or members of the committee may not be aware of the relevant transaction or arrangement or of the director's interest in it. In those circumstances, s 177(6)(b) would not, it seems, apply. Thus, a further limitation on the duty to disclose is created by s 177(6)(c), so that there is no duty of disclosure where the relevant interest concerns terms of his service contract that have been or are to be considered by a meeting of directors or a remuneration committee.

---

[60] *Cream Holdings Ltd v Banerjee* [2005] 1 AC 253, 259, HL, per Lord Nicholls.

[61] In *Guinness plc v Saunders* [1990] 2 AC 663, 694 Lord Templeman said 'section 317 [of the 1985 Act] shows the importance which the legislature attaches to the principle that a company should be protected against a director who has a conflict of interest and duty'.

[62] As to the meaning of the terms 'service contract' see 2006 Act, s 227.

[63] As was held in respect of 1948 Act, s 199, the predecessor of 1985 Act, s 317. In *Runciman v Walter Runciman plc* [1992] BCLC 1084. Simon Brown J, at 1095, was much struck by the absurdity of a director having to disclose his interest in a service contract at a meeting of directors, when all other directors were plainly aware of the director's interest in his own service contract—an absurdity now removed by s 177(6)(b).

[64] *Neptune (Vehicle Washing Equipment) Ltd v Fitzgerald* [1996] Ch 274, 283.

[65] In line with the Law Commission's recommendation: Law Commission, *Company Directors: Regulating Conflicts of Interest and Formulating a Statement of Duties*, No 261, para 8.38.

(4) Decision of the directors

17.40 A company's constitution usually provides that, if a proposed decision of the directors is concerned with an actual or proposed transaction or arrangement with the company, a director with a direct or indirect interest is not entitled to vote at the meeting of directors, or be counted in the quorum,[66] unless (a) the company by ordinary resolution disapplies the prohibition, (b) the interest cannot reasonably be regarded as giving rise to a conflict of interest, or (c) the director's conflict of interest arises from a permitted cause.[67] A director with an interest in the transaction or arrangement is free to vote on it if the company's constitution does not include provisions preventing him from doing so.

17.41 For the purposes of those provisions of a company's constitution, the permitted causes where the director is entitled to vote and be counted in the quorum despite his conflict of interest concern (a) a guarantee given, or to be given, by or to a director in respect of obligations incurred by or on behalf of the company or any of its subsidiaries; (b) subscription, or any agreement to subscribe, for securities of the company or any of its subsidiaries, or to underwrite, sub-underwrite, or guarantee subscription for any such securities; and (c) arrangements pursuant to which benefits are made available to employees and directors or former employees and directors of the company or any of its subsidiaries which do not provide special benefits for directors or former directors.[68]

17.42 If a question arises at a meeting of directors or a committee of directors as to the right of a director to participate, the constitution may provide for the chairman to give a final and conclusive ruling unless the conflict concerns him; in which case his entitlement to participate is to be decided by the other directors.[69]

(5) Companies with a sole director

17.43 As the duty requires disclosure to be made to the other directors, no disclosure is required where the company has only one director.[70]

(6) Shadow directors

17.44 The duty stated in s 177 applies to shadow directors to the extent that the common law rules or equitable principles corresponding to the duty to declare an interest in a proposed transaction or arrangement applied to shadow directors (see Chapter 10, Section C).[71]

---

[66] 1985 Table A, reg 95.

[67] 1985 Table A, regs 94–6; Model Article 14(1)–(3) (pcls); Model Article 14(1)–(3) (pclg); Model Article 16(1)–(3) (plc).

[68] Model Article 14(4) (pcls); Model Article 14(4) (pclg); Model Article 16(4) (plc). Compare 1985 Table A, reg 94(a)–(d).

[69] Model Article 14(6)–(7) (pcls); Model Article 14(6)–(7) (pclg); Model Article 16(5)–(6) (plc). Compare 1985 Table A, reg 98.

[70] See the Explanatory Notes to the Companies Act, para 352. Compare the position under 1985 Act, s 317: *Neptune (Vehicle Washing Equipment) Ltd v Fitzgerald* [1996] Ch 274 (followed in *Neptune (Vehicle Washing Equipment) Ltd v Fitzgerald (No 2)* [1995] BCC 1000), and see 17.61–17.63 below. However, note the provisions of 2006 Act, s 231 which impose obligations where a director who is its only member contracts with the company.

[71] 2006 Act, s 170(5).

(7) Consent, approval, or ratification of members

If s 177 is complied with, the transaction or arrangement is not liable to be set aside for fail- **17.45**
ure to obtain the consent or approval of the members. Section 180(1) of the Companies Act
makes clear that if s 177 is complied with any transaction or arrangement is not liable to be
set aside by virtue of any common law rule or equitable principle requiring the consent or
approval of the company in general meeting. However, if any other enactment requires the
consent or approval of the members in respect of the particular transaction or arrangement,
or if such consent or approval is required by the company's constitution, then it must be
sought and obtained.[72]

The application of the general duty to declare an interest in the proposed transaction or **17.46**
arrangement is not affected by the fact that the case also falls within the 2006 Act, Chapter 4
(transactions with directors requiring approval of members).[73] Conversely, in such a case,
compliance with the general duty under s 177 does not remove the need for approval under
any applicable provisions of Chapter 4.[74]

Where s 177 has not been complied with, the director may obtain the protection of ratifica- **17.47**
tion by the members under s 239 (discussed in Chapter 20, Section D).

(8) Civil consequences of failure to declare

Where a director fails to comply with the provisions of s 177 two consequences follow. **17.48**
First, as with the 1985 Act, s 317, the failure to comply will not render the contract void or
unenforceable, but only voidable at the instance of the company against any party thereto
who has notice of the breach of duty,[75] so that, if it is no longer possible to restore the parties
to their former position, rescission is impossible.[76] Secondly, any profit which the director
derives from the contract is recoverable from him by the company.[77] This is so even if he can
show that the transaction was fair and reasonable and/or that he would have made the same
amount of profit after disclosure.[78]

---

[72] 2006 Act, s 180(1).
[73] 2006 Act, s 180(2).
[74] 2006 Act, s 180(3).
[75] *Transvaal Lands Co v New Belgium (Transvaal) Land and Development Co* [1914] 2 Ch 488, CA;
Boulting v ACTAT [1963] 2 QB 606, 648, CA; *Hely-Hutchinson v Brayhead Ltd* [1968] 1 QB 549,
585 CA, per Lord Denning MR; *Guinness plc v Saunders* [1990] 2 AC 663, 697, HL, per Lord Goff
of Chieveley; *Cowan de Groot Properties Ltd v Eagle Trust plc* [1991] BCLC 1045, 1116, 1117; *Craven
Textile Engineers Ltd v Batley Football Club Ltd* [2001] BCC 679, 688; *Re Marini Ltd* [2004] BCC 172
at paras 62–6.
[76] *Erlanger v New Sombrero Phosphate Co* (1878) 3 App Cas 1218, HL; *Victors Ltd v Lingard* [1927] 1
Ch 323.
[77] Formerly, under 1985 Act, s 317 a failure to comply with the statute did not give a separate right of
action to the company for damages against a director. Such liability depended upon a breach of the director's fiduciary obligations: *Coleman Taymar Ltd v Oakes* [2001] 2 BCLC 749. However, since 2006 Act, s
177 replaces both 1985 Act, s 317 and the common law rules such a distinction is no longer likely to be
relevant.
[78] *Costa Rica Ry Co v Forwood* [1901] 1 Ch 746, 761, CA. In fashioning the account the court may have
regard to just allowances for the time, skill, labour, or assumption of business risk undertaken by the director
in relation to the transaction: *O'Sullivan v Management Agency and Music Ltd* [1985] QB 428, CA; *Ultraframe
(UK) Ltd v Fielding* [2005] EWHC 1638 (Ch) at para 1588.

C. Duty in Relation to an Existing Transaction or Arrangement

(1) Scope of the duty

Introduction

17.49 The Companies Act, Part 10, Chapter 3 contains provisions requiring a director to declare his interest in existing transactions or arrangements of the company unless any of the exceptions apply.[79] Section 182(1) provides:

> Where a director of a company is in any way, directly or indirectly, interested in a transaction or arrangement that has been entered into by the company, he must declare the nature and extent of the interest to the other directors in accordance with this section. This section does not apply if or to the extent that the interest has been declared under section 177 (duty to declare interest in proposed transaction or arrangement).

The nature and form of the required declaration are discussed in Section C(2) below. Section 182(5) and (6) identify the circumstances in which a declaration is not required or need not be made (see Section C(3) below).

Comparison with the 1985 Act, s 317 and with the 2006 Act, s 177

17.50 The provisions summarized above represent, substantially, a re-enactment of the 1985 Act, s 317.[80] That section applied to declarations of an interest not only in existing transactions or arrangements, but also in proposed transactions or arrangements. The duty to declare an interest in a proposed transaction or arrangement has been discussed in Section B above. Although s 177, one of the general duties of directors, is in similar terms to the duty in respect of actual transactions and arrangements set out above, the consequences of breach are different. A director who fails to declare an interest in a transaction or arrangement already entered into with the company as required by s 182 is guilty of an offence, a director who fails to declare an interest in a proposed transaction or arrangement is not. On the other hand, whereas a breach of s 177 attracts civil consequences, a mere breach of s 182 does not (except for liability for disqualification).[81]

17.51 The Attorney General has explained the reason for the different legal consequences of breaches of ss 177 and 182:[82]

---

[79] Sections 182–7 came into force on 1 October 2008: 2006 Act Commencement Order No 5, Art 5(1)(e) with the transitional provisions in Sch 4, Part 4, para 50.

[80] 1985 Act, s 317 derived from (i) 1948 Act, s 199, which in turn derived from 1947 Act, s 41(5) and 1929 Act, s 149 (introducing the provisions of 1928 Act, s 81), and (ii) 1980 Act, ss 60, 63(3), and Sch 3, para 25. A comparison of 1985 Act, s 317 with Companies Act, ss 177 and 182 suggests that the latter two sections are essentially a splitting up of the composite s 317 into separate sections dealing with proposed and actual transactions. Despite the similarity in wording, Companies Act, s 177, dealing with proposed transactions, has substantive effects which go well beyond those of 1985 Act, s 317. The table of origins of the 2006 Act gives 1985 Act, s 317 as the origin of s 182 but not of s 177.

[81] Failure to comply with s 182 may also be taken into account in proceedings taken against a director under Company Directors Disqualification Act 2004 (CDDA); see s 9 and Sch 1, Part 1, para 1. In *Re Dominion International Group plc (No 2)* [1996] 1 BCLC 572, 597–600 a breach of the disclosure requirements under 1985 Act, s 317 was relied on in disqualification proceedings, but was discounted as purely technical.

[82] Hansard, HL GC Day 4, vol 678, col 338 (9 February 2006).

As regards why the remedies are different … there is only one consequence of breach of [s 182]—because one is here concerned with an existing transaction or arrangement, the failure to declare cannot affect the validity of the transaction or give rise to any other civil consequences. That is to be contrasted with the position where there is the failure to disclose an interest in relation to a proposed transaction where the law can say that as a result of the failure to disclose that interest—and the company then enters into the transaction in ignorance of that—consequences can follow. The transaction may be voidable, to be set aside. The company may wish to claim financial redress in one form or another as a result of what has taken place. But, as I say, that is different from a failure to declare an interest in an existing transaction where those considerations probably cannot arise. That is why a criminal offence is created.

Section 182 will primarily apply in two contexts: **17.52**

(1) Where a new director, interested in a transaction or arrangement already entered into by the company, joins the board. Mere non-disclosure of the director's interest could not, of itself, give the company a civil remedy in respect of the contract itself or against the director. A criminal sanction is imposed by s 183 to compel disclosure of the director's interest in the transaction or arrangement in order to enable the other directors to preserve the integrity of their decision-making and to protect the company's position, eg by protecting its confidential information. If, while concealing his interest in the transaction or arrangement, the director's conduct causes the company harm, it may have civil remedies for breach of the director's general duties under ss 171–4 or 176[83] or possibly arising from any related breach of its articles.

(2) Where a director has failed to declare his interest in a proposed transaction or arrangement under s 177 and the company has since entered into that transaction or arrangement. The company will or may have remedies by reason of the breach of s 177 itself. Continuing non-disclosure of the director's interest after the company has entered into the transaction or arrangement will expose the director to criminal sanction under s 183.

Reference should be made to paragraphs 17.15–17.22 above for discussion about direct and **17.53** indirect interests, what is meant by a transaction or arrangement with the company and the nature and extent of the required disclosure.

(2) The declaration

As to the form, accuracy and completeness of the declaration and timing, s 182(2)–(4) **17.54** provides:

(2) The declaration must be made—
  (a) at a meeting of the directors, or
  (b) by notice in writing (see section 184), or
  (c) by general notice (see section 185).
(3) If a declaration of interest under this section proves to be, or becomes, inaccurate or incomplete, a further declaration must be made.
(4) Any declaration required by this section must be made as soon as is reasonably practicable.

---

[83] Compare cases under the previous law: *Neptune (Vehicle Washing Equipment) Ltd v Fitzgerald (No 2)* [1995] BCC 1000; *Ultraframe (UK) Ltd v Fielding* [2005] EWHC 1638 (Ch) at para 1436. By s 175(3), the general duty to avoid conflicts of interest does not apply to conflicts of interest arising in relation to a transaction or arrangement with the company.

Method of making the declaration

17.55 The provisions of s 182(2) are identical to those in s 177(2), which have been discussed in paragraphs 17.23–17.27 above.

Inaccurate or incomplete declaration

17.56 Section 182(3), which is in the same terms as s 177(3) (paragraphs 17.28 and 17.29 above), provides that, if a declaration of interest proves to be or becomes inaccurate or incomplete, a further declaration must be made. Since the duty is to disclose both the nature and the extent of the interest, a director who is, for example, interested in a contract between the company and a third party by reason of his holding of shares in that third party will be obliged to make a new declaration if and when his shareholding in that third party increases or, it appears, decreases.

When the declaration must be made

17.57 Any declaration must be made as soon as is reasonably practicable, but failure to make the declaration as soon as reasonably practicable does not affect the underlying duty to make the declaration.[84]

(3) Where a declaration is not required

17.58 As already noted, the 2006 Act, s 182 does not apply if and to the extent that the interest has already been declared under s 177. Further, the requirement to disclose an interest in an existing transaction or arrangement is subject to the same qualifications, set out in s 182(5) and (6), as apply to the duty to disclose an interest in a proposed transaction or arrangement under s 177(5) and (6), which have been discussed in paragraphs 17.31–17.39 above.[85] These qualifications are entirely new, having no equivalent under the 1985 Act. For the most part, the qualifications have the sensible effect that no duty of disclosure is imposed where it would be pointless to impose such a duty. The possibility of a director being guilty of an offence by reason of a technical breach of the disclosure provisions is therefore significantly lessened, compared to the position under s 317.

(4) Decision of the directors

17.59 Although the declaration of a direct or indirect interest in an existing transaction or arrangement must be made as soon as reasonably practicable, it is plainly important that it is made before any decision, or further decision, is made by the directors in relation to the transaction or arrangement.

17.60 As discussed in paragraphs 17.40–17.42 above, the company's constitution is likely to exclude a director with a direct or indirect interest in an actual transaction or arrangement from voting or being counted in the quorum.

(5) Companies with a sole director

17.61 Where a director of a company is its sole director, and the company is not required to have more than one director, the sole director is under no obligation to declare any

---

[84] 2006 Act, s 182(4).
[85] The one difference is that the first line of s 182(6) includes the phrase 'under this section'.

interest in an existing transaction or arrangement under s 182 of the Act. The obligation under s 182 is to declare the interest to 'the other directors', and thus where there are no other directors, the section cannot apply.[86] This was confirmed by the Attorney General who said:[87]

> The Company Law Review recommended that the requirement should be disapplied in respect of a sole director. The Bill implements that recommendation, but only where the company legitimately has just one director ... this is a common-sense approach. Plainly, a requirement of a sole director to make disclosure to himself is a nonsense. But the position is different where, at that point in time, the company has only one director where it should have more than one—for example, if it were a public company. In that circumstance, [s 186] provides that the sole director must record in writing the nature and extent of his interest in any transaction or arrangement that has been entered into, and that the declaration has to form part of the proceedings at the next meeting of the directors after the notice has been given. The consequence is that there will be a record so that when another director comes along, as should be the case, the position is clear and has been seen. However, I repeat that if a sole director is entitled to be a sole director, the provision does not apply.

Thus, s 186 deals with the position where, at the time the company only has one director, it is required to have more than one director.[88] In such a case the sole director's duty to declare his interest is effectively the same as if the other directors had been appointed (except that s 182(6)(b) cannot apply). Section 186(1) provides that (a) the declaration must be recorded in writing, (b) the making of the declaration is deemed to form part of the proceedings at the next meeting of the directors after the notice is given, and (c) the provisions of s 248 of the Act (minutes of meetings of directors) apply as if the declaration had been made at that meeting. In this way the declaration will be made available to the new directors following their appointment.   **17.62**

Nothing in s 186 affects the operation of s 231 of the Act (contract with sole member who is also a director: terms to be set out in writing or recorded in minutes).[89]   **17.63**

(6) Shadow directors

Section 187 applies the provisions of Chapter 3 (ie ss 182–6) to shadow directors, but with modifications as to the means of giving the notice.[90] A shadow director may not declare his interest at a meeting of directors.[91] Instead there must be a written record of the declaration of the shadow director's interest. A shadow director may not give a general notice of   **17.64**

---

[86] The obligation under 1985 Act, s 317 was to declare the interest 'at a meeting of the directors of the company'. It had been held by Lightman J in *Neptune (Vehicle Washing Equipment) Ltd v Fitzgerald* [1996] Ch 274, 283 that a sole director of a company was under a duty to make the relevant declaration to himself at a duly convened meeting with himself 'and have the statutory pause for thought, though it may be that the declaration does not have to be out loud', and record the declaration in the minutes.

[87] Hansard, HL GC Day 4, cols GC 343–4 (9 February 2006).

[88] A public company is required to have at least two directors: s 154 of the Act.

[89] 2006 Act, s 186(2). See Ch 18, paras 18.193–18.201.

[90] Certain persons will not be considered shadow directors for the purposes of ss 188 and 189 in respect of Northern Rock Bank plc, Bradford & Bingley plc, Heritable Bank plc, and Dunfermline Building Society whilst those institutions are owned by the Treasury: SI 2008/432, Art 17, Sch, para 2(f); 2008/2546, Art 13(1), Sch, para 2(f); 2008/2644, Art 26, Sch, para 2(f); SI 2009/814, Art 6, Sch, para 2(g).

[91] 2006 Act, s 187(2).

his interest at a meeting of directors and a general notice is not effective unless given in writing.[92]

(7) Criminal consequences of failure to declare

17.65 Section 183 provides that a director who fails to comply with these requirements commits an offence, for which he is liable to a fine.[93]

---

[92] 2006 Act, s 187(3) and (4).
[93] By sub-s (2) on conviction on indictment the fine is unlimited, but on summary conviction the fine may not exceed the statutory maximum.

18

TRANSACTIONS WITH DIRECTORS REQUIRING APPROVAL OF MEMBERS

Lloyd Tamlyn

A. Introduction

This chapter covers the provisions in the Companies Act, Part 10, Chapters 4 and 4A,[1] **18.01** ss 188–230, which for the most part underpin the duties of directors by requiring certain transactions with directors to be approved by the members.[2] It also deals with the right to

---

[1] Chapter 4A (Directors of Quoted Companies: Special Provision), ie ss 226A–226F, were inserted by the Enterprise and Regulatory Reform Act 2013, s 80, with effect from 1 October 2013: SI 2013/2227, art 2(h). For transitional provisions, see para 18.172 below.

[2] These sections came into force on 1 October 2007: 2006 Act Commencement Order No 3, Art 2(1)(d).

inspect directors' service contracts or memoranda of their terms and the special rules, set out in s 231, that apply to contracts with a sole member who is a director.[3]

B. Directors' Service Contracts

(1) Requirement of approval of members

The substantive provisions

18.02   Section 188 of the Act requires the prior approval of members before a company enters into certain long-term service contracts. Section 189 sets out the civil consequences in the event that such approval is not obtained.[4]

18.03   Section 188(1)–(4) provides:

(1) This section applies to provision under which the guaranteed term of a director's employment—
   (a) with the company of which he is a director, or
   (b) where he is the director of a holding company, within the group consisting of that company and its subsidiaries,
   is, or may be, longer than two years.

(2) A company may not agree to such provision unless it has been approved—
   (a) by resolution of the members of the company, and
   (b) in the case of a director of a holding company, by resolution of the members of that company.

(3) The guaranteed term of a director's employment is—
   (a) the period (if any) during which the director's employment—
      (i) is to continue, or may be continued otherwise than at the instance of the company (whether under the original agreement or under a new agreement entered into in pursuance of it), and
      (ii) cannot be terminated by the company by notice, or can be so terminated only in specified circumstances, or
   (b) in the case of employment terminable by the company by notice, the period of notice required to be given,
   or, in the case of employment having a period within paragraph (a) and a period within paragraph (b), the aggregate of those periods.

(4) If more than six months before the end of the guaranteed term of a director's employment the company enters into a further service contract (otherwise than in pursuance of a right conferred, by or under the original contract, on the other party to it[5]), this section applies as if there were added to the guaranteed term of the new contract the unexpired period of the guaranteed term of the original contract.

Section 188(5) deals with approval by members (paragraph 18.18 below). Section 188(6) provides that no approval is required under s 188 on the part of the members of a body corporate that is not a UK-registered company, or is a wholly-owned subsidiary of another body corporate.

---

[3] This section also came into force on 1 October 2007: 2006 Act Commencement Order No 3, Art 2(1)(d).

[4] 2006 Act, ss 188 and 189 apply to agreements made on or after 1 October 2007: 2006 Act Commencement Order No 3, Sch 3, para 6(1); for transitional provisions, see paras 6(2) and (4).

[5] In such a case, there is no need for any provision such as s 188(4) to apply, as the contract will fall within s 188(3)(a)(i).

Under s 188(7), 'employment' for the purposes of s 188 means any employment under **18.04** a 'director's service contract', which for the purposes of the 2006 Act, Part 10, is defined by s 227:

(1) For the purposes of this Part a director's 'service contract', in relation to a company, means a contract under which—
   (a) a director of the company undertakes personally to perform services (as director or otherwise) for the company, or for a subsidiary of the company, or
   (b) services (as director or otherwise) that a director of the company undertakes personally to perform are made available by a third party to the company, or to a subsidiary of the company.
(2) The provisions of this Part relating to directors' service contracts apply to the terms of a person's appointment as a director of a company.
They are not restricted to contracts for the performance of services outside the scope of the ordinary duties of a director

This definition of 'service contract' expressly covers cases whereby the director's services are provided through a service company.

Lord Sainsbury explained the operation of s 227:[6] **18.05**

In line with the recommendations of the Law Commissioners and the Company Law Review, the definition of 'service contracts' is expressly extended so that, in addition to covering contracts of service and contracts for services, it includes letters of appointment to the office of director. As a result, it covers the terms under which a director is appointed to that office alone. It operates as follows; subs(1)(a) covers contracts of service such as any employment contract that the director may hold with a company or a subsidiary of the company of which he is a director, for example, as an executive director, or any contract for services that he personally undertakes to perform as such. Subsection (1)(b) covers the case where those services are made available to the company through a third party such as a personal services company. In either case, the contract must require the director personally to perform the service or services in question. Subsection (2) brings within the definition of a service contract letters of appointment to the office of director. Many directors will have no contract of service or for services with the company. Historically ... an office has been regarded as a kind of property, with the fees attaching to that office being regarded as an incident of that office. The second sentence of subs (2) ensures that the definition of 'service contracts' includes arrangements under which the director performs duties within the scope of the ordinary duties of the director, as well as contracts to perform duties outside the scope of the ordinary duties of a director. Without that, the term 'service contract' might be interpreted as applying only to the latter type of contract.

Under s 189, if a company agrees to provision in contravention of s 188, the provision is **18.06** void, to the extent of the contravention (s 189(a)), and the contract is deemed to contain a term entitling the company to terminate it at any time by the giving of reasonable notice (s 189(b)).[7]

For the purposes of ss 188 and 189, a shadow director is treated as a director.[8] **18.07**

---

[6] Hansard, HL GC Day 4, vol 678, cols 361, 362 (9 February 2006). Contrary to the apparent sense of the first clause of the quoted passage, no such recommendation appears to have been made by either the Law Commissioners or the CLR.

[7] See eg *Bain v The Rangers Football Club Plc* [2011] CSOH 158.

[8] 2006 Act, s 223(1) and also s 230. In respect of Northern Rock plc, Bradford & Bingley plc, Heritable Bank plc, and Dunfermline Building Society, whilst owned by the Treasury certain persons will not be considered

Changes made by the 2006 Act, ss 188 and 189

18.08   The Companies Act, ss 188 and 189 derive ultimately from the 1980 Act, ss 47 and 63(1), a White Paper having recommended that directors' service contracts for longer than five years should be approved by the company in general meeting.[9] The purpose of the immediate predecessor of ss 188 and 189 (1985 Act, s 319) was to ensure that a company should not be bound by an obligation to employ a director for more than (at that time) five years unless its members had considered and approved the relevant term, but the purpose was limited to protecting the shareholders.[10] A company is empowered by ordinary resolution at a meeting to remove a director before the expiration of his period of office, notwithstanding anything in any agreement between it and him;[11] but this power does not deprive a person removed of compensation or damages payable to him in respect of the termination of his appointment as director or of any appointment terminating with that as director.[12] Sections 188 and 189 seek to ensure that, save where the members have approved the director's long-term service contract, a company's hands are not tied in deciding whether to remove a director by the prospect of very considerable sums payable by the company by way of compensation or damages.

18.09   Sections 188 and 189 are, in large part, a re-enactment of the 1985 Act, s 319. Section 188 has been reworded with the aim of clarifying the law: in particular, the reference to 'guaranteed term' makes the essential purpose clearer. Four substantive changes should be noted.

18.10   First, the duration of the 'guaranteed term' has been significantly reduced from five to two years.[13]

18.11   Secondly, although broadly speaking the provisions of the 1985 Act, s 319 for determining when (under that legislation) the five-year limit was exceeded are repeated in s 188, there are new provisions dealing with the situation where the company is entitled to terminate the employment by notice. In such a case, the period of notice required to be given by the company is taken into account in determining the 'guaranteed term', hence whether the two-year limit is or may be exceeded. Under s 188(3)(b), where the director's employment is terminable by notice, the period of notice required to be given is the 'guaranteed term'. If the period of notice is, or may be, longer than two years, prior members' approval is necessary.

---

shadow directors for the purposes of ss 188 and 189: Northern Rock plc Transfer Order SI 2008/432, Art 17; Bradford & Bingley plc Transfer of Securities and Property etc Order 2008/2546, Art 13; Heritable Bank plc Transfer of Certain Rights and Liabilities Order 2008/2644, Art 26; Amendments to Law (Resolution of Dunfermline Building Society) Order 2009/814, Art 7.

[9] The Conduct of Company Directors (1977) Cmnd 7037.

[10] *Wright v Atlas Wright (Europe) Ltd* [1999] 2 BCLC 301, 310, 315, per Potter LJ.

[11] 2006 Act, s 168(1).

[12] 2006 Act, s 168(5).

[13] Despite recommendations of various shorter periods. The Law Commission (in *Company Directors: Regulating Conflicts of Interest and Formulating a Statement of Duties*, No 261, paras 9.30 and 9.35) recommended three years. CLR: *Final Report*, paras 6.10–6.14 generally recommended one year, which was consistent with the objective of one year stated in the Combined Code (now UK Corporate Governance Code (April 2016), para D.1.5). The Companies Bill started life by retaining the five-year period, but it was reduced to two years after an Opposition amendment proposed in House of Lords Grand Committee stage: Hansard, HL GC Day 4, vol 678, cols 344–345 (9 February 2006). Lord Hodgson of Astley Abbotts supporting the amendment and stated: 'Out there in UK plc or among the general public, if they were to see us considering long-term contracts of five years, they would consider it an amazing length of time. It would be laughable against the background of modern corporate governance and practice.'

A service contract for five years, terminable by the company on 12 months' notice, does not require prior members' approval. Under the final two clauses of s 188(3), in the case of employment having periods which fall within both paragraphs 188(3)(a) and 188(3)(b), the two periods are aggregated for the purposes of determining the 'guaranteed term'. Hence, if the relevant service contract were for three years, with a provision whereby the company could give the director notice of termination at the earliest 18 months from commencement, such notice period being 12 months, without the final two clauses of s 188(3) the guaranteed term of the employment would not exceed two years: the guaranteed term under s 188(3)(a) would be only 18 months (ie the period of the contract during which the company could not give notice), and the guaranteed term under s 188(3)(b) would be only 12 months (ie the requisite notice period). By virtue of the aggregation under the final two clauses of s 188(3), the 'guaranteed term' would be two years six months.

18.12 Thirdly, by means of the new definitions of 'employment' and 'director's service contract',[14] ss 188 and 189 apply to contracts under which a director undertakes to perform services as director or otherwise, apply to the terms of a person's appointment as a director of the company, and are not restricted to contracts for the performance of services outside the scope of the ordinary duties of a director. Under the 1985 Act, s 319(7), 'employment' was defined as including employment under a contract for services, and hence, explicitly at least, applied only to contracts of service and for services. The new Act will therefore cover, for example, letters of appointment to the office of director.[15]

18.13 Fourthly, the Companies Act largely re-enacts the provisions of the 1985 Act relating to approval given (in respect of private companies) by written resolution, and the requirement for a written memorandum incorporating the relevant provision to be sent or submitted to eligible members at or before the time that the proposed resolution is sent or submitted.[16] In a change to the law, the Companies Act, s 224 now provides that, subject to any provision of the company's articles, any accidental failure to send or submit the memorandum to one or more members shall be disregarded for the purpose of determining whether the requirement has been met.

18.14 The legal landscape underpinning ss 188 and 189 remains similar to that which obtained under the 1985 Act. At common law, a director is not entitled to remuneration for his services, as he is treated as a trustee and hence, prima facie, not entitled to profit from the trust.[17] That common law rule is abrogated where the articles of association so provide just as, in the case of a trustee *strictu sensu*, the trust instrument so provides.[18] Articles of Association almost invariably make such provision.[19] Section 188, however, prohibits the inclusion of provisions under which the guaranteed term of a director's employment exceeds two years unless the prior approval of the members is obtained, whilst s 189 renders the provision void to the extent of the contravention, and deems the contract to contain a term entitling the company to terminate it at any time by the giving of reasonable notice.[20]

---

[14] 2006 Act, ss 188(7) and 227, set out in para 18.04 above.

[15] Explanatory Notes, para 399.

[16] 2006 Act, s 188(5)(a), substantially re-enacting 1985 Act, Sch 15A, para 7.

[17] *Guinness plc v Saunders* [1990] 2 AC 663, 689, 700, HL, per Lord Templeman and Lord Goff. The legal position is the same in Scotland: *Tayplan Ltd v Smith* [2012] BCC 523.

[18] *Guinness plc v Saunders*, n 17 above.

[19] See eg Table A, reg 82, Model Article (pcls) 19 and Model Article (plc) 23.

[20] See eg *Bain v The Rangers Football Club Plc* [2011] CSOH 158.

18.15   A number of features of ss 188 and 189 may be noted. First, the director need not be a party to the relevant contract. A combination of ss 188(7) and 227(1)(b) make clear that the sections apply equally to a contract to which the director is not a party—for example where the director's services are provided by a service company which he controls.[21]

18.16   Secondly, the sections do not, it appears, apply to certain 'rolling contracts'.[22] The Law Commission had pointed out that the predecessor of ss 188 and 189 could be, and was in fact being, circumvented by the use of rolling contracts, and thus recommended that, as a matter of necessity, those contracts should be subject to the relevant statutory limit.[23] This recommendation appears not to have been adopted by Parliament.

18.17   Where the terms of a service contract are approved by the directors (or any of them), irrespective of ss 188 and 189 of the Act such directors owe general duties to the company as set out in the 2006 Act, Part 10, Chapter 2, breach of which may render them, as well as the relevant director whose terms of employment are under consideration, liable to the company if such duties are breached. For example, any director has a duty to promote the success of the company (s 172), a duty which applies equally to the agreement of a director's service contract.[24]

Approval of members

18.18   The resolution of the members of the company or holding company may be a written resolution or a resolution at a meeting,[25] but s 188(5) lays down certain requirements for a valid resolution under s 188(2):

> (5) A resolution approving provision to which this section applies must not be passed unless a memorandum setting out the proposed contract incorporating the provision is made available to members—
>
> (a) in the case of a written resolution, by being sent or submitted to every eligible[26] member at or before the time at which the proposed resolution is sent or submitted to him;
>
> (b) In the case of a resolution at a meeting, by being made available for inspection by members of the company both—
>
>> (i) at the company's registered office for not less than 15 days ending with the date of the meeting, and
>>
>> (ii) at the meeting itself.

Eligible members are those members entitled to vote on the resolution on the circulation date of the resolution (as itself defined in s 290).[27] As was the case under the 1985 Act, where the written resolution procedure is used, it is only those members entitled to vote who are

---

[21] See the quotation from Lord Sainsbury in para 18.05 above.

[22] Law Commission Consultation Paper *Company Directors: Regulating Conflicts of Interest and Formulating a Statement of Duties*, No 153, paras 4.161–4.162.

[23] *Company Directors: Regulating Conflicts of Interest and Formulating a Statement of Duties*, No 261, paras 9.33 and 9.35.

[24] See, under the old law where the equitable duty upon the directors was to act bona fide in the interests of the company: *Runciman v Walter Runciman plc* [1992] BCLC 1084, 1097–8.

[25] For resolutions of members, see Ch 25 below.

[26] For the definition of 'eligible member' see s 289: essentially, it means those members entitled to vote on the resolution on the circulation date of the resolution (as itself defined in s 290).

[27] 2006 Act, s 289 defines 'eligible member' and s 290 identifies the circulation date.

entitled to the memorandum: whereas, if an actual meeting is held, all members can inspect the memorandum. Subject to any provision of the company's articles, any accidental failure to send or submit the memorandum to one or more members shall be disregarded for the purpose of determining whether the requirement has been met.[28]

In relation to the 1985 Act, the Court of Appeal held that the properly informed unanimous **18.19** consent of all shareholders entitled to attend and vote at the general meeting of the company, given informally, overrode the statutory formalities for member approval under s 319, given that the sole purpose of s 319 was to protect the shareholders.[29] There is no reason to believe that the position has altered under the Act.

(2) Service contracts to be available for inspection

Section 228 provides for a copy of a director's service contract or memorandum of terms to **18.20** be available for inspection.[30] Section 228(1) provides:

> A company must keep available for inspection—
> (a) a copy of every director's service contract with the company or with a subsidiary of the company, or
> (b) if the contract is not in writing, a written memorandum setting out the terms of the contract.[31]

The obligation under s 228, to keep and allow inspection of a copy of the director's service **18.21** contract or memorandum of its terms, applies even though the director is required to work wholly or mainly outside the UK.[32] The obligation extends, it appears, in the case of a written contract only to documents which contain the terms of the contract, but where the contract is unwritten, the memorandum must contain all the terms of the contract.[33] The provisions apply to a variation of a director's service contract as they apply to the original contract.[34]

Lord Sainsbury explained that 'a memorandum is nothing more than a proper written record **18.22** of the terms of the contract or agreement', which is required to prevent avoidance of the requirements of ss 228 and 229 by use of an oral contract.[35]

---

[28] 2006 Act, s 224.

[29] *Wright v Atlas-Wright (Europe) Ltd* [1999] 2 BCLC 301, CA.

[30] 2006 Act, ss 228 and 229, which came into force on 1 October 2007, are substantially re-enactments of the 1985 Act, s 318, having their ultimate origin in the 1967 Act, s 26. For transitional provisions, see 2006 Act Commencement Order No 3, paras 13(1) and (4).

[31] A director includes a shadow director: s 230. 'Service contract' is defined by s 227.

[32] The Law Commission Report, *Company Directors: Regulating Conflicts of Interest and Formulating a Statement of Duties*, No 261, para 9.14 recommended the repeal of the 1985 Act, s 318(5), which provided that, where the contract required the director to work wholly or mainly outside the UK, the company was merely required to keep and allow inspection of a memorandum specifying the director's name, the provisions of the contract relating to its duration, and (if the contract was with a subsidiary) the name and place of incorporation of that subsidiary.

[33] Law Commission Consultation Paper, *Company Directors: Regulating Conflicts of Interest and Formulating a Statement of Duties*, No 153, paras 9.18–9.20. CLR: *Completing the Structure*, para 4.1, recommended the extension to such documents, apparently under the impression that the Law Commission had itself made that recommendation. Parliament did not act on the recommendation.

[34] 2006 Act, s 228(7).

[35] Hansard, HL GC Day 4, cols 362–3 (9 February 2006). There followed some debate in which certain members of the Committee expressed some doubts as to whether the requirement for a memorandum meant that all the terms of the contract had to be accurately set out: ibid, Lords Wedderburn and Freeman.

18.23   All such copies and memoranda must be available for inspection at the company's registered office, or a place specified in regulations.[36] The copies and memoranda must be retained by the company for at least one year from the date of termination or expiry of the contract and must be kept available for inspection during that time.[37] The company must give notice to the Registrar of Companies of the place at which the copies and memoranda are kept available for inspection, and of any change in that place, unless they have at all times been kept at the company's registered office.[38]

18.24   If default is made in complying with the provisions of s 228(1)–(3) (or in the case of the obligation to give notice to the registrar of companies under s 228(4), if default is made for 14 days in complying with that obligation), an offence is committed by every officer of the company who is in default.[39]

18.25   Section 229 states the right of every member to inspect and take a copy of a director's service contract or memorandum of terms.

(1)   Every copy or memorandum required to be kept under section 228 must be open to inspection by any member of the company without charge.

(2)   Any member of the company is entitled, on request and on payment of such fee as may be prescribed,[40] to be provided with a copy of any such copy or memorandum.

The copy must be provided within seven days after the request is received by the company.

18.26   If an inspection required under s 229(1) is refused, or default is made in complying with s 229(2), an offence is committed by every officer of the company who is in default.[41] In the case of any such refusal or default the court may by order compel an immediate inspection or, as the case may be, direct that the copy required be sent to the person requiring it.[42]

---

[36]   2006 Act, s 228(2): see the Companies (Company Records) Regulations 2008 (SI 2008/3006), reg 3, whereby the 'specified place' for the purposes of, inter alia, s 228(2) is a place that is situated in the part of the UK in which the company is registered, must be the same place for all relevant provisions (ie all provisions listed in s 1136(2)) and must have been notified to the registrar of companies as being the company's alternative inspection location.

[37]   2006 Act, s 228(3). Enacting a recommendation of the Law Commission: Law Commission Report, *Company Directors: Regulating Conflicts of Interest and Formulating a Statement of Duties*, No 261, para 9.17 to extend the period of retention. Under the 1985 Act, s 318(11) no copy had to be kept or inspection allowed of any copy of the contract or memorandum which had less than a year to run, or in relation to a contract which could be terminated by the company on 12 months' notice or less without payment of compensation.

[38]   2006 Act, s 228(4). See 2006 Act, s 1068 for delivery by electronic means.

[39]   2006 Act, s 228(5). Unlike 1985 Act, s 318(8) the company is not guilty of an offence. A person guilty of an offence is liable on summary conviction to a fine under s 228(6).

[40]   Companies (Fees for Inspection and Copying of Company Records) Regulations (SI 2007/2612), reg 4. The right under the 1985 Act, s 318 was simply to inspect, though by Companies (Inspection and Copying of Registers, Indices and Documents) Regulations 1991 (SI 1991/1998), reg 3(2)(b) and (3) the person inspecting was permitted to copy any information made available for inspection by means of taking notes or the transcription of the information and the company was obliged to provide facilities for the purpose.

[41]   2006 Act, s 229(3). Unlike 1985 Act, s 318(8) the company is not guilty of an offence. A person guilty of an offence is liable on summary conviction to a fine under s 229(4).

[42]   2006 Act, s 229(5). In *Pelling v Families Need Fathers Ltd* [2002] 1 BCLC 645, CA, the Court of Appeal considered the similarly worded provision relating to the enforcement of a member's right to inspect the register of members under 1985 Act, s 356(6) (replaced and substantially altered by 2006 Act, ss 116 and 117). The Court of Appeal there decided that the court's power to order inspection was discretionary. Although the court would normally make a mandatory order to give effect to a legal right (by analogy, the legal right of inspection or to a copy under s 229(1) and (2)), and although the criminal sanctions attaching to the failure to allow inspection (by analogy, the criminal sanctions contained in s 229(3)) underscored the importance of the right and obligation of the company, the grant of a mandatory order was not a matter of unqualified right, and in special

C. Substantial Property Transactions

(1) The substantive provisions

The Companies Act, Part 10, Chapter 4, ss 190–6 (as amended) contains provisions prohib- **18.27**
iting a company from entering into an arrangement under which a director of the company
or its holding company, or a person connected with such a director, directly or indirectly
acquires or is to acquire a 'substantial non-cash asset' from the company, or the company
acquires or is to acquire such an asset from such a person, unless the arrangement is approved
by resolution of the members.[43]

Section 190(1) provides: **18.28**

(1) A company may not enter into an arrangement under which—
    (a) a director of the company or of its holding company, or a person connected with[44]
       such a director, acquires or is to acquire from the company (directly or indirectly) a
       substantial non-cash asset, or
    (b) the company acquires or is to acquire a substantial non-cash asset (directly or indi-
       rectly) from such a director or a person so connected,
    unless the arrangement has been approved by a resolution of the members of the com-
    pany or is conditional on such approval being obtained.

For the purposes of this section a director includes shadow director.[45] The prohibition is
subject to a number of exceptions: see paragraphs 18.50–18.55 below.

'Non-cash asset' means 'any property or interest in property, other than cash', and 'cash' **18.29**
includes foreign currency.[46] A reference to the transfer or acquisition of a non-cash asset
includes '(a) the creation or extinction of an estate or interest in, or a right over, any property,
and (b) the discharge of the liability of any person, other than a liability for a liquidated
sum'.[47]

---

circumstances could be refused. The order could be made subject to terms and conditions; and see now, under
the 2006 Act, ss 116 and 117: *Re Burry and Knight Ltd* [2014] 1 WLR 4046, CA.

[43] 2006 Act, ss 190–6 apply to arrangements or transactions entered into on or after 1 October 2007: 2006
Act Commencement Order No 3, Sch 3, para 7(1); for transitional provisions, see, paras 7(2) and (3).

[44] 'Connected' for these purposes is defined in 2006 Act, s 252. The exclusion of a person acting in
his capacity as a trustee of a pension scheme under the predecessor of section 252(2)(c) was considered
in *Granada Group Ltd v The Law Debenture Pension Trust Corporation plc* [2015] 2 BCLC 604, paras
75–90, where 'pension scheme' was given its ordinary interpretation, consistently with analogous
legislation; aff'd on appeal at [2016] EWCA Civ 1289, paras 43–6.

[45] 2006 Act, s 223(1)(b). In respect of Northern Rock plc, Bradford & Bingley plc, Heritable Bank plc, and
Dunfermline Building Society, whilst owned by the Treasury certain persons will not be considered shadow
directors for the purposes of ss 190–6: see n 8 above. 'Holding company' is defined in 2006 Act, s 1159: see also
s 1160 and Sch 6. Section 252 explains when a person is connected with a director (see further Ch 3, Section
D above).

[46] 2006 Act, s 1163(1).

[47] 2006 Act, s 1163(2). It has been held under the predecessor of s 1163(2) that 'any person' does not include
the company itself, so that the predecessor of s 190 applied only where the company discharges the liability of
another person, not its own liability: *Gooding v Cater* (unreported) 13 March 1989, Edward Nugee QC. Save
where the relevant non-cash asset is held on trust for the director or a person connected with him by a person
other than the company, so that the director's or connected person's rights in respect of the non-cash asset were
merely rights against the trustee to the proper administration of the trust, section 320 of the 1985 Act did not
apply, save possibly where the trust was a bare trust: *Granada Group Ltd v The Law Debenture Pension Trust
Corporation plc* [2015] 2 BCLC 604, paras 47, 59; aff'd on appeal at [2016] EWCA Civ 1289.

18.30 'Substantial non-cash asset' is explained in s 191, whereby a non-cash asset is a substantial asset in relation to a company if its value exceeds 10 per cent of the company's asset value and is more than £5,000, or exceeds £100,000.[48] For this purpose, a company's 'asset value' at any time is the value of the company's net assets determined by reference to its most recent statutory accounts, or if no statutory accounts have been prepared, the amount of the company's called up-share capital.[49] Whether an asset is a substantial asset is to be determined as at the time the arrangement is entered into.[50]

18.31 If the director or connected person is a director of the company's holding company or a person connected with such a director, the arrangement must also have been approved by a resolution of the members of the holding company or conditional on such approval being obtained.[51]

18.32 The civil consequences of contravention of s 190 are set out in s 195: see paragraphs 18.62–18.75 below.

(2) Changes made by the 2006 Act, s 190

18.33 Section 190(1) and (2) very substantially re-enacts the 1985 Act, s 320(1). Three main changes have been made. First, the prohibition applies where the director or the person connected with the director acquires or is to acquire *directly or indirectly* the substantial non-cash asset from the company, and likewise where the company acquires or is to acquire the substantial non-cash asset *directly or indirectly* from a director or person connected.

18.34 Secondly, whereas the 1985 Act, s 320 required prior approval of the company in general meeting, a company may now enter into such an arrangement conditional on approval by members' resolution.[52] A company is not subject to any liability by reason of a failure to obtain approval required by s 190.[53]

18.35 Thirdly, by reason of s 190(5), an arrangement involving more than one non-cash asset, or an arrangement that is one of a series involving non-cash assets, is treated as if they involved a non-cash asset of a value equal to the aggregate value of all the non-cash assets involved in the arrangement or, as the case may be, the series. The purpose is to avoid the artificial structuring of arrangements and transactions so as to bring each individual arrangement or transaction under the financial minima set out in s 191, and hence outside the scope of the Act.[54]

---

[48] The Secretary of State has power to vary the sum under 2006 Act, s 258.

[49] A company's 'statutory accounts' means its annual accounts prepared in accordance with 2006 Act, Part 15, and by s 191(4) its 'most recent' statutory accounts are those in relation to which the time for sending them out to members under s 424 is most recent.

[50] 2006 Act, s 191(5).

[51] 2006 Act, s 190(2).

[52] 2006 Act, s 190(1). The Law Commission found that the requirement of prior members' approval under the 1985 Act placed the company at a commercial disadvantage if the other party to the arrangement was not willing to wait whilst approval was obtained: Law Commission Consultation Paper, *Company Directors: Regulating Conflicts of Interest and Formulating a Statement of Duties*, No 153, para 4.192.

[53] 2006 Act, s 190(3).

[54] In *Attwood v Maidment* [2011] EWHC 2186 (Ch), paras 180–4, it was held that s 190(5) clarified but did not substantively alter the position under the 1985 Act.

(3) The prohibition: essential elements

The similarity between the 1985 Act, ss 320–2 and the 2006 Act ss 190–6 suggests that **18.36** case law decided under the 1985 Act will generally continue to be authoritative. Sections 190–6 constitute the latest enactment of parts of a fasciculus of provisions first enacted in the 1980 and 1981 Acts intended to sharpen up the protections of companies against being improperly exploited to the companies' detriment.[55] The thinking behind the requirement for members' approval of substantial property transactions is that if a company by its directors enters into a substantial commercial transaction with one of their number, there is a danger that their judgment may be distorted by conflicts of interest. The requirement of members' approval is designed to protect a company against such distortions.[56]

An 'arrangement'

For s 190 to apply, first there must be an 'arrangement' within the meaning of s 190(1). The **18.37** question whether an 'arrangement' falls within the section must be asked on the basis of the arrangement as at its inception.[57] 'Arrangement' is not defined by the Act. It was decided under the 1985 Act that it was a word widely used by Parliament to include arrangements or understandings having no contractual effect.[58]

'Is to acquire'

Secondly, the arrangement entered into by the director, connected person, or company must **18.38** be one under which such person acquires or is to acquire a substantial non-cash asset. Section 190 does not apply in circumstances where under the arrangement the director, connected person, or company, merely *may* acquire the relevant asset: the director, connected person, or company must either acquire or be under an obligation to acquire the asset, as the words 'is to acquire' make clear.[59] The reference in s 190 to the acquisition of a non-cash asset is given a broad inclusive definition of 'acquire' given by s 1163(2) of the Act. The breadth of the definition is such that non-cash assets can, in certain circumstances, be deemed to have been acquired for the purposes of s 190 in circumstances where, as a matter of normal usage, no acquisition of the asset would be considered to have taken place at all.[60]

The interest that the director acquires or is to acquire need not be a proprietary interest; it **18.39** may include a right over the property such as an option or licence, or, more doubtfully, a

---

[55] *NBH Ltd v Hoare* [2006] 2 BCLC 649, 662, per Park J. A fasciculus means 'a group of sections or paragraphs [of an Act] marked by a cross-heading' (Bennion, *Statutory Interpretation*, 6th edn (Lexis/Nexis, 2010), s 257) and which, through its ultimate Latin root, has given us both fascism and faggot (in most of its current meanings, including the slang).

[56] *British Racing Drivers' Club v Hextall Erskine* [1997] 1 BCLC 182, 198, per Carnwath J, remarking that the requirement for members' approval did not necessarily mean that the members would exercise a better commercial judgment: but it did make it likely that the proposed arrangement would be more widely ventilated and a more objective decision reached. To similar effect: *Granada Group Ltd v The Law Debenture Pension Trust Corporation plc* [2015] 2 BCLC 604, paras 38 and 39; on appeal at [2016] EWCA Civ 1289, paras 22–3.

[57] *Smithton Ltd v Naggar* [2015] 1 WLR 189, CA, per Arden LJ at para 95.

[58] *Re Duckwari plc* [1998] Ch 253, 260, CA, per Nourse LJ; *Murray v Leisureplay plc* [2004] EWHC 1927 (QB), per Stanley Burnton J at para 106 referring to the Restrictive Trade Practices Act 1976 (not affected by the decision of the Court of Appeal [2005] IRLR 946, CA); *Granada Group Ltd v The Law Debenture Pension Trust Corporation plc* [2015] 2 BCLC 604, para 40, unaffected by the appeal at [2016] EWCA Civ 1289. Cf *Re Sky Land Consultants plc* [2010] EWHC 399 (Ch) per David Richards J at para 16 (meaning of 'arrangements' in FSMA, s 235).

[59] *Smithton Ltd v Naggar*, n 57 above, per Arden LJ at para 110.

[60] *Ultraframe (UK) Ltd v Fielding* [2005] EWHC 1638 (Ch) at paras 1369–87, referring to the acquisition of the licence in respect of intellectual property rights.

contractual right to purchase the asset, but it did not include the right of a beneficiary to compel due administration of a trust, at least where the trust was not a bare trust.[61]

18.40   In *Duckwari plc v Offerventure Ltd*,[62] a company (O) had agreed to purchase real property from a third party, and paid a 10 per cent deposit. Prior to completion of the sale, O agreed that another company (D) should take over the purchase contract. D was connected with one of the directors of O. The approval of the members of D was not obtained. After D had acquired the property, the property market fell and D sued O for breach of the 1985 Act, s 320, the predecessor of s 190. The precise legal nature of the 'taking over' was in dispute. O contended that, on its true analysis, the contract of purchase between the third party and O must have been novated in favour of D. The Court of Appeal decided that, as a matter of fact, the nature of the arrangement was a bilateral agreement whereby O agreed to allow D to acquire the rights under the contract by directing the third party to convey to D. Millett LJ, however, considered it arguable that even if the true nature of the arrangement had been a novation, this did not mean that there was no acquisition of an asset by D. By reason of the 1985 Act, s 739(2) (the predecessor of s 1163(2)), by which acquisition includes the 'extinction … of an estate or interest in, or right over, any property', a novation, which would necessarily involve the consent of the initial contracting party, might constitute the acquisition of an asset from that contracting party. The addition of the words 'directly or indirectly' in s 190(1)(a) suggests that, were an arrangement similar to that undertaken in the *Duckwari* case to occur now, but effected by a novation, such an arrangement would indeed fall within s 190(1).

18.41   Section 190 applies not only to arrangements whereby the company, director, or connected person actually acquires a substantial non-cash asset, but also to arrangements whereby such person is to acquire such an asset. The company may have remedies for non-compliance with s 190 even where the relevant asset is never in fact acquired by the company. Thus, if the company enters into an arrangement for the acquisition of an asset, the requisite members' approval under s 190 is not obtained, and the acquisition is never completed, the company may still be able to recover for any loss or damage suffered by it resulting from the arrangement, for example money spent on due diligence.[63]

'Non-cash asset'

18.42   Thirdly, the director, connected person, or company must acquire a 'non-cash asset'. The definition is given in s 1163(1) of the Act: see paragraph 18.29 above. In straightforward cases, the identification of the asset acquired will be obvious: if the arrangement is a contract of sale, for example. The characterization of the relevant assets in other arrangements may be more difficult. On the facts of *Duckwari*, the Court of Appeal held that the asset acquired was a single asset which could be described in one of two ways with equal accuracy, namely the benefit of the purchase contract, or company O's beneficial interest in the property subject of the purchase contract.[64]

---

[61]   *Granada Group Ltd v The Law Debenture Pension Trust Corporation plc* [2015] 2 BCLC 604, paras 41–7; aff'd on appeal at [2016] EWCA Civ 1289.

[62]   [1997] 2 BCLC 713, Ch and CA; discussed in *Smithton Ltd v Naggar*, n 57 above, Arden LJ at para 105.

[63]   *Murray v Leisureplay plc* [2005] IRLR 946, CA.

[64]   [1997] 2 BCLC 713, 724, 725, per Millett LJ. A similar conclusion was reached by Lewison J in *Ultraframe (UK) Ltd v Fielding* [2005] EWHC 1638 (Ch) at paras 1395–410, when considering whether 1985 Act, s 320 applied to the sale by a receiver of a company's charged assets. The judge held that in such circumstances, the relevant 'non-cash asset' for the purposes of s 320 was not the assets themselves, but the equity of redemption in

In *Lander v Premier Pict Petroleum Ltd*,[65] a director's service contract was amended so as to **18.43** provide that if control of the company's share capital was taken by a third party, the director had the option of terminating the service contract whereupon he would become entitled to payment of three times his annual salary from the company and various pension contributions. Following the exercise of the option by the director, he sued for payment of these various sums, and proceedings were defended on the basis, inter alia, that the amendment was voidable under the 1985 Act, s 320 since the option granted by the amendment was a non-cash asset. The Court of Session (Outer House) rejected that defence on several bases. The court held that since the option was incapable of assignment, it did not constitute 'property or [an] interest in property, other than cash' within the meaning of what is now s 1163(1); further, the rights granted under the option were rights to cash payments, so that the rights were not rights to property 'other than cash'.[66]

In *Ultraframe (UK) Ltd v Fielding*,[67] issues arose as to whether a number of different arrange-   **18.44** ments involved the acquisition of a 'non-cash asset' within the meaning of the 1985 Act, s 320. The grant by the directors of a company of a lease to that company was held to fall within s 320, and the relevant non-cash asset was the lease itself, not the right to possession granted to the company under the lease.[68] A licence to exploit certain intellectual property rights was held not to constitute 'any property or interest in property' within the meaning of what is now s 1163(1), on the basis that the licence was a mere authority and created no proprietary interest in the intellectual property rights. Nonetheless, Lewison J held that the grant of the licence did constitute the acquisition of a non-cash asset within the meaning of what is now s 1163(2), as the grant constituted 'the creation ... of ... a right over, any property' under what is now s 1163(2). Hence what is now s 190 applied.[69] By reason of the broad inclusive definition in s 1163(2), the meaning of the word 'acquire' is thus extended well beyond its typical application. In effect, Lewison J reasoned that whilst the licence itself was not property or an interest in property, and hence not itself a 'non-cash asset' under what is now s 1163(1), the trade marks in respect of which the licence was granted were undoubtedly property and thus non-cash assets. The grant of the licence in respect of that property (ie the trade marks) created a right over that property in favour of the licensee within the meaning of what is now s 1163(2)(a). Hence, for the purposes of what is now s 190, the trademarks themselves were acquired (within the meaning ascribed to that word by what is now s 1163(2)(b)) by the licensee by virtue of the grant of the licence.

---

the charged assets, since this alone was owned by the company: see para 18.46 below; also *Attwood v Maidment* [2011] EWHC 2186 (Ch), paras 177–9.

[65] [1998] BCC 248.

[66] [1998] BCC 248, 254. This conclusion is questionable. The definition in what is now s 1163 indicates that cash means cash (including foreign currency): the Court of Session's reasoning would suggest that a debt, for example, would not be a non-cash asset. Contrast *Sylfaen Constructions Ltd v Davies* (HHJ Nicholas Chambers QC, 18 August 2000, unreported) at para 16: 'The fact that an asset may be turned into cash does not make it a cash asset.'

[67] [2005] EWHC 1638 (Ch).

[68] *Ultraframe (UK) Ltd v Fielding* [2005] EWHC 1638 (Ch) at paras 1369–72. This led to the conclusion that the value of that asset was the capital value of the lease itself, not the value of the right to occupy: see para 18.50 below. In *Joint Receivers and Managers of Niltan Carson Ltd v Hawthorne* [1988] BCLC 298, decided under 1980 Act, s 48 (the predecessor of 1985 Act, s 320) the parties and Hodgson J assumed that the section applied to a lease.

[69] *Ultraframe* [2005] EWHC 1638 (Ch) at paras 1373–87. See also *Granada Group Ltd v The Law Debenture Trust Corporation Plc* [2016] EWCA Civ 1289, paras 27–8.

'Substantial' non-cash asset

18.45 The meaning of 'substantial' is explained in s 191 of the Act: see paragraph 18.30 above.[70] Whether an asset is a substantial asset is determined as at the time that the arrangement is entered into. The focus of s 190 is on the members approving the arrangement at inception,[71] and therefore if s 190 is to apply at all, the requisite value of the non-cash asset must be established at that time. Thus, if a company enters into a trading arrangement with one of its directors, under which the director is obliged to supply an indeterminate amount of, say, raw materials to the company, if the minimum value of those supplies determined as at the date of the arrangement cannot be shown to exceed the requisite values under s 191, the section will not apply and member approval is unnecessary.[72] For s 190 to apply, it is not necessary to establish what the value of the non-cash asset is: but it is necessary to establish that, at a minimum, its value exceeds those set out in s 191.[73] The burden of establishing that the value of the non-cash asset exceeds those minima lies on the party seeking relief.[74]

18.46 The value of the non-cash asset will, of course, depend on what non-cash asset is acquired, which may depend on the characterization of the arrangement or transaction by the court. Thus, for example, in the *Duckwari* case the non-cash asset was the benefit of the purchase contract or (another way of describing the same thing) the transferring company's beneficial interest in the property. Hence the value was the value of the property less the unpaid element of the purchase price, or (the same thing) the value of the property less the unpaid vendor's lien. In *Ultraframe*, as concerns the sale by a receiver of the assets of the company, the non-cash asset was the company's equity of redemption in those assets, and hence it was the value of that equity which had to be proven for the purposes of what is now s 191, not the value of the assets themselves.[75] Also in *Ultraframe*, concerning the creation of a lease by directors in favour of the company, the non-cash asset was the lease itself, not the right to possession acquired under the lease, and hence the relevant value was the capital value of the lease, not the value of the right to possession as evidenced by the rental covenant.[76]

18.47 Section 191 gives no guidance as to how the value of the non-cash asset is to be determined. There may be cases where the value of the non-cash asset to the company, and indeed its market value, is significantly less than the value of the non-cash asset to the acquiring director or connected person. For example, a strip of land transferred by the company to one of its directors may have little value in itself, but may have considerable value to the owner of adjoining land if the strip is necessary for the development of that other land. Similar circumstances came before the Court of Session (Outer House) in *Micro Leisure Ltd v County Properties &*

---

[70] Derived with changes from 1985 Act, s 320(2).

[71] *Smithton Ltd v Naggar,* [2015] 1 WLR 189, CA, per Arden LJ at para 95.

[72] Cf the *Ultraframe* case [2005] EWHC 1638 (Ch) at paras 1390–3.

[73] *Ultraframe* case (n 72 above) at para 1392; *Sylfaen Constructions Ltd v Davies* (HHJ Nicholas Chambers QC, 18 August 2000, unreported) at para 19. In *Granada Group Ltd v The Law Debenture Pension Trust Corporation plc* [2015] 2 BCLC 604, where it was held that the right of a director to compel the trustee of a pension scheme to administer the trust was incapable of valuation for the purpose of ascertaining whether the prescribed value was exceeded, Andrews J said at para 66: 'The more complex the valuation exercise and the more dependent that exercise is on assumptions that could be the subject of dispute, the more inherently unlikely it is that Parliament intended that the rights concerned should fall within the ambit of the section.' See also on appeal at [2016] EWCA Civ 1289.

[74] *Joint Receivers and Managers of Niltan Carson Ltd v Hawthorne* [1988] BCLC 298, 321.

[75] *Attwood v Maidment* [2011] EWHC 2186 (Ch) at para 179.

[76] In *Niltan Carson Ltd v Hawthorne*, n 74 above, Hodgson J reached the same conclusion at 321.

Developments Ltd.[77] The issue arose on an application to amend pleadings so as to allege that the value of land transferred by a company to entities connected with its directors was higher than the value of the land in isolation, by reason of its 'marriage value' with adjacent land also owned by the connected entities. Allowing the amendment, Lord Hamilton reasoned that since the purpose behind what is now s 190 was to afford protection to members in respect of transactions which might benefit directors to the detriment of the company, Parliament intended that the value of a non-cash asset had to be determined in the context of the particular circumstances of the arrangement, which circumstances would include the fact that the land had a particular increased value to the owners of adjacent land—at least where the board of the company was aware of that fact.[78] That reasoning is, it is submitted, correct.[79] It is further submitted that the knowledge of the directors is irrelevant.

In the *Ultraframe* case, the grant of a debenture by a company was held not to fall within the   **18.48**
1985 Act, s 320 on the basis that 'the company parts with nothing of value when it grants a debenture; and the consideration it receives is incapable of being valued in money or money's worth, and cannot therefore be a "non-cash asset" of the requisite value'.[80] In so deciding, Lewison J relied on the decision in *Re MC Bacon Ltd*,[81] where it was held on similar grounds that the grant of a debenture could not constitute a transaction at an undervalue within the meaning of Insolvency Act, s 238. It appears that Lewison J did not reason that the grant of a debenture in favour of a director or connected person was not the acquisition of a 'non-cash asset' within the meaning of what is now s 1163: rather, his reasoning was that no *value* could be ascribed to that non-cash asset (or to the consideration moving from the chargee), and hence there was no acquisition of a *substantial* non-cash asset. Indeed, in the context of s 1163(1), it is difficult to see why the interest of a chargee is not 'property or an interest in property',[82] or in any event (and following the reasoning of Lewison J on the licence issue, above) why the grant of a debenture by a company is not 'the creation of … a right over … any property' (the relevant property being the property which is charged to the chargee) within the meaning of s 1163(2). If so, the grant of debentures to a person could constitute the acquisition of a non-cash asset by that person within the meaning of s 190(1)(a).

Whether the grant of the debenture in *Ultraframe* could constitute the acquisition of a *sub-*   **18.49**
stantial non-cash asset by the chargee thus depended on whether the requisite value could be ascribed to the debenture for the purposes of what is now s 191. Relying on *MC Bacon*, Lewison J stated that 'the company parts with nothing of value when it grants a debenture'. This contention, which appears to have been conceded by counsel, is doubtful. Security is of

---

[77] [2000] BCC 872.

[78] [2000] BCC 872, 874, 875.

[79] *Granada Group Ltd v The Law Debenture Pension Trust Corporation plc* [2015] 2 BCLC 604, para 67.

[80] *Ultraframe* case [2005] EWHC 1638 (Ch), at paras 1388–9. The passage quoted deals with two different analyses whereby the grant of a debenture might fall within what is now s 190. First, the charge itself in favour of the chargee might constitute the acquisition of a substantial non-cash asset by the chargee (the first clause of the passage quoted); secondly, whatever consideration is given by the chargee might constitute the acquisition of a substantial non-cash asset by the company (the second clause). As to the latter, given that (as in *MC Bacon*) the consideration in question was constituted by such nebulous expectations as the forbearance of the creditor, it appears to have been inherently incapable of valuation on the facts: and in any event, it is difficult to see that any 'non-cash asset' was acquired by the company.

[81] [1990] BCLC 324.

[82] This is obviously so in the case of a mortgage or specific charge: and in the case of a floating charge, it creates a present proprietary interest albeit in a fund of circulating capital rather than over any specific asset: see eg *National Westminster Bank plc v Spectrum Plus Ltd* [2005] 2 AC 680, 729, 730, HL, per Lord Walker.

undoubted value to any creditor of a company, and hence the ability to grant security must have value. In *Hill v Spread Trustee Ltd*[83] Arden LJ stated that there was no reason why the value of a right to have recourse to security and to take priority over other creditors should be left out of account when considering the value of the consideration moving between the parties to a putative transaction defrauding creditors under Insolvency Act 1986, s 423.[84] If, therefore, a charge has value, the next issue is whether it can be ascribed a value in excess of one of the statutory minima found in s 191. There might in many cases be difficulties in proving that the value of a charge exceeded the statutory minima: though since, for example, a grant of security might be reflected in an interest rate differential between secured and unsecured lending, in principle a certain value in excess of the statutory minima might be ascribed.

(4) Exceptions to the requirements for member approval

18.50 No approval is required under s 190 on the part of the members of a body corporate that is not a UK-registered company or is a wholly-owned subsidiary of another body corporate.[85]

18.51 Section 190 does not apply to a transaction so far as it relates to anything to which a director of a company is entitled under his services contract, or to payment for loss of office as defined in s 215 (payments to which the requirements of Chapter 4 or 4A apply).[86] This provision is new, but probably merely clarifies rather than changes the law.[87]

18.52 By s 192 approval is not required under s 190:

    (a) for a transaction between a company and a person in his character as a member of that company, or

    (b) for a transaction between—

        (i) a holding company and its wholly-owned subsidiary, or

        (ii) two wholly-owned subsidiaries of the same holding company.[88]

Exception (a) was explained by Lord Sainsbury as being:

> intended to cover transactions such as the payment of the [sic] dividend in specie as well as the distribution of assets to a member of a company during the winding-up of the company and in satisfaction of his rights qua member in the liquidation. Likewise a duly sanctioned return of capital in the form of non-cash assets would fall within this exception. It is also intended to put beyond doubt that the issue of shares or other rights to a member does not require approval under the rules for substantial property transactions.[89]

---

[83] [2007] 1 WLR 2404, CA.

[84] [2007] 1 WLR 2404, CA at para 138. To some degree, the reasoning in *MC Bacon* was doubted. It is not clear to what extent Arden LJ relied on the fact that the relevant charges in the *Hill* case were by way of mortgage, though her reasoning on value would apply equally to a floating charge.

[85] 2006 Act, s 190(5); substantially a re-enactment of 1985 Act, s 321(1). For the meaning of 'subsidiary', see 2006 Act, s 1159, also s 1160 and Sch 6.

[86] 2006 Act, s 190(6), as amended by the Enterprise and Regulatory Reform Act 2013, s 81(1), (3), with effect from 1 October 2013; SI 2015/2227, art 2(h).

[87] *Gooding v Cater* (unreported) 13 March 1989; also *Lander v Premier Pict Petroleum Ltd* [1998] BCC 248.

[88] Substantially a re-enactment of 1985 Act, s 321(2)(a) and (3), although the scope of s 321(3) has been extended. For the definitions of 'holding company' and 'wholly-owned subsidiary' see 2006 Act, s 1159, also s 1160 and Sch 6.

[89] Hansard, HL GC Day 4, col 347 (9 February 2006).

By s 193, where a company is being wound up (unless the winding up is a members' volun- **18.53** tary winding up), or the company is in administration,[90] members' approval is not required under s 190 on the part of the members of a company or for an arrangement entered into by a company. The exception relating to a company which is being wound up is substantially a re-enactment of the 1985 Act, s 321(2)(b), albeit that its precise method of operation differs. The exception relating to a company in administration is new. If the purpose underlying s 190 is to protect a company against the danger that the directors' judgment may be distorted by conflicts of interest when the transaction is with one of their number, that danger does not exist where the company is in insolvent winding up or administration, nor is it likely that the shareholders have any interest in the transaction in any event. This was confirmed by Lord Sainsbury:[91]

> The point of the exception [ie under s 193] is that when a company is being wound up or is in administration, the conduct of the company's affairs is no longer in the hands of the members. If a liquidator or administrator is content with the substantial property transaction, it is not appropriate to require approval under [s 190], either by the members of the company being wound up or in administration, or by the members of its holding company.

There is no exception where the company is in administrative (or other) receivership.[92]

The absence of an exception for administrative or other receivership is unlikely to create prac- **18.54** tical difficulties, certainly as time passes. First, since the relevant provisions of the Enterprise Act 2002 came into force on 15 September 2003, the holder of a qualifying floating charge may now appoint an administrator, who will of course benefit from the statutory exemption. Secondly, Lewison J has decided in the *Ultraframe* case that the relevant 'non-cash asset' which is sold by an administrative receiver when he sells the business of a company in administrative receivership is the equity of redemption in those assets, not the assets unencumbered (paragraph 18.46 above).[93] If this decision is correct (as, it is submitted, it is in the result), members' approval under s 190 will only be required where the value of the equity of redemption exceeds one of the statutory minima in s 191.[94] This latter point applies equally, of course, to non-administrative receivers.

---

[90] Within the meaning of Insolvency Act, Sch B1.

[91] Hansard, HL Report Stage, vol 681, col 870 (9 May 2006).

[92] In *Demite Ltd v Protec Health Ltd* [1998] BCC 638, Park J had held that 1985 Act, s 320 applied to a sale of the business of a company in administrative receivership. The Law Commission considered whether there should be such an exception, first in the consultation paper on directors' duties, then in the Report itself. The Law Commission recommended that there should be no exemption for administrative receivers, apparently on the basis that a company in administrative receivership was not necessarily insolvent on a balance sheet basis (thus the shareholders might have a residual interest in the assets), and because of the possibility of abuse where the receiver was appointed by a director or connected person. Against this, the Law Commission recognized that often shareholders would have no residual interest, and the most appropriate buyer would sometimes be a connected person or director. The Law Commission sought to balance these factors by recommending the enactment of a power to apply to court for approval of a transaction where there is reason to believe that the company's assets are insufficient to make a payment to shareholders or for some other good reason, a proposal accepted in CLR: *Developing the Framework*, para 26. Parliament did not adopt this recommendation. It may be that such a power existed already by reason of Insolvency Act, s 35(2): see the *Demite* case [1998] BCC 638, 647.

[93] See also *Attwood v Maidment* [2011] EWHC 2186 (Ch) at para 179. This point was not argued in the *Demite* case.

[94] [2005] EWHC 1638 (Ch). Lewison J, at para 1409, considered that this result was appropriate as a matter of policy, given that shareholders should only have a veto on sale where there is the prospect of a surplus, and thus 'if ... there is the prospect of a surplus [*sc* after payment of the secured debt] which exceeds the requisite value, then there is every point in requiring the shareholders to approve the sale'. The dovetailing of s 320 with

18.55 By s 194(1), approval is not required under s 190 for a transaction on a recognized investment exchange effected by a director, or a person connected with him, through the agency of
a person who in relation to the transaction acts as an independent broker.[95]

(5) Approval by the members

18.56 In order to comply with s 190, the arrangement must have been approved by a resolution of
the members of the company or be conditional on such approval being obtained.[96]

18.57 Under the 1985 Act, s 320 it was eventually held that the *Duomatic* principle[97] applied to the
requirement for member approval so that the informal consent of members of the company
satisfied the requirement for prior approval of the arrangement.[98] It had been held, *obiter*,
that informal approval could not be given under the 1985 Act in circumstances where the
company was insolvent, the onus being on the party who sought to rely on informal approval
to prove solvency.[99]

(6) Subsequent affirmation

18.58 By s 196 where a transaction or arrangement is entered into by a company in contravention
of s 190 but, within a reasonable period, it is affirmed by resolution of the members of the
company (in the case of a contravention of s 190(1)) or of the holding company (in the case
of a contravention of s 190(2)), the transaction or arrangement may no longer be avoided
under s 195.

18.59 Section 196 is, substantially, a re-enactment of the 1985 Act, s 322(2)(c). One change should
be noted. Under the 1985 Act, s 320, as under s 190(1) and (2), where the arrangement
was with a director of the company's holding company (or a person connected with such a
director), there was a dual requirement of resolutions of both the members of the company

---

such policy arguments may not be exact. Where there is the prospect of a surplus after repayment of the secured
debt, but no prospect of a surplus for shareholders by reason of the existence of unsecured liabilities, as may
well be the case in a receivership, shareholders will have a right of veto by reason of s 190 even where they have
no interest in the assets sold.

[95] This exception is, very substantially, a re-enactment of 1985 Act, s 321(4). By s 194(2) 'independent broker' means 'a person who, independently of the director or any person connected with him, selects the person
with whom the transaction is to be effected' and 'recognised investment exchange' has the same meaning as in
FSMA, Part 18.

[96] 2006 Act, s 190(1).

[97] *Re Duomatic Ltd* [1969] 2 Ch 365, 373, per Buckley J: 'where it can be shown that all shareholders who
have a right to attend and vote at a general meeting of the company assent to some matter which a general meeting of the company could carry into effect, that assent is as binding as a resolution in general meeting would be'.

[98] *Re Conegrade Ltd* [2003] BPIR 358; *NBH Ltd v Hoare* [2006] 2 BCLC 649, 665, 666, following *Wright v
Atlas Wright (Europe) Ltd* [1999] 2 BCLC 301, CA, where the principle was applied in the context of 1985 Act,
s 319 (now s 188—Directors' long-term service contracts: requirement of members' approval). *Conegrade* was
not apparently cited in the *NBH* case, but the court came to the same conclusion. See Goddard, 'The Duomatic
Principle and ss 320–322 of the Companies Act' [2004] JBL 121.

[99] *Lexi Holdings Plc v Luqman* [2007] EWHC 2652, per Briggs J, paras 191–3 (applied in *Madoff Securities
International Ltd v Raven* [2013] EWHC 3147 (Comm), by Popplewell J at para 282); see also under s 190 of
the 2006 Act *Haig v Beasant* (unreported, 15/6/10), Registrar Jaques, *obiter*, paras 31–6. This issue is discussed
in Ch 20, Section D below. In *Walker v WA Personnel Ltd* [2002] BPIR 621, 639, 642, it was held to be seriously
arguable that the *Duomatic* principle did not operate where the company was insolvent: see para 18.60 below.
In *Re Conegrade Ltd* [2003] BPIR 358, the *Duomatic* principle was applied to an arrangement under 1985 Act,
s 320 notwithstanding that the company was insolvent at the time of the transaction (and thus the transaction
was set aside as a preference), but the possible non-application of the principle where the company was insolvent
does not appear to have been argued.

and of its holding company. Under s 322(2)(c), in order for the arrangement to be affirmed in such circumstances, there was a dual requirement that both the company and its holding company affirm the arrangement. A consequence of these dual requirements (presumably unintended) was that where the members of the company itself approved the arrangement before it was entered into, but the members of the holding company affirmed the arrangement within a reasonable period after it had been entered into, or vice versa, s 320 was not complied with.[100] Under s 190, this is no longer the case. Whilst there remains a requirement for dual approval, where s 190 is contravened solely by reason of the members of the company failing to approve the arrangement before it is entered into, the members of the company alone can affirm the arrangement under s 196(a), and likewise, where the contravention of s 190 arises by reason of the members of the holding company failing to approve the arrangement before it is entered into, the members of the holding company alone can affirm the arrangement under s 196(b).

18.60 Under the 1985 Act, s 322(2)(c) it had implicitly been held that it was seriously arguable that the ability of a company in general meeting to ratify the arrangement abated when the company was insolvent or close to insolvency.[101] It is submitted that the members of the company or holding company should be able to ratify the transaction in accordance with s 196 whether the company is solvent or not. The statutory wording contains no limit on the power to ratify, explicit or implicit. There can be no question but that the requisite approval at the time of the arrangement in question can be given whether or not the company is insolvent or near insolvent. Further, to introduce limitations into statutory wording based on indeterminate concepts such as near insolvency, or even insolvency itself, is to introduce uncertainty.

18.61 It appears that, in certain circumstances, the arrangement may be affirmed by a method outside of s 196. In the *Ultraframe* case, Lewison J held that an arrangement which was voidable through failure to comply with the 1985 Act, s 320 could be affirmed by the liquidator when the company subsequently entered insolvent liquidation.[102] The judge reasoned that failure to comply with the 1985 Act, s 320 rendered the arrangement voidable at the instance of the company, that this right to avoid was a chose in action within the control of the liquidator, and thus the liquidator could decide to affirm the arrangement. In the context of affirmation by a liquidator in an insolvent liquidation, the result is unexceptionable. The reasoning could lead to the conclusion that the right to affirm could be exercised by the board of the company, an absurd result: though apart from being implicit in s 196 that such affirmation is not possible, such affirmation itself might possibly be subject to s 195.

(7) Civil consequences of contravention

18.62 Section 195 states:[103]

> (1) This section applies where a company enters into an arrangement in contravention of section 190 ...

---

[100] *Sylfaen Constructions Ltd v Davies* (HHJ Nicholas Chambers QC, 18 August 2000, unreported) at paras 27–40.

[101] *Walker v WA Personnel Ltd* [2002] BPIR 621. The issue arose on an application for a continuation of an injunction, thus the court reached no concluded view as to the issue.

[102] *Ultraframe (UK) Ltd v Fielding* [2005] EWHC 1638 (Ch) at paras 1440 and 1441.

[103] 2006 Act, s 195 is very substantially a re-enactment of 1985 Act, s 322. The wording has been changed in places but not so as to change the substance.

(2) The arrangement, and any transaction entered into in pursuance of the arrangement (whether by the company or any other person), is voidable at the instance of the company, unless—

    (a) restitution of any money or other asset that was the subject matter of the arrangement or transaction is no longer possible,

    (b) the company has been indemnified in pursuance of this section by any other persons for the loss or damage suffered by it, or

    (c) rights acquired in good faith, for value and without actual notice of the contravention by a person who is not a party to the arrangement or transaction would be affected by the avoidance.

(3) Whether or not the arrangement or any such transaction has been avoided, each of the persons specified in subsection (4) is liable—

    (a) to account to the company for any gain that he has made directly or indirectly by the arrangement or transaction, and

    (b) (jointly and severally with any other person so liable under this section) to indemnify the company for any loss or damage resulting from the arrangement or transaction.

(4) The persons so liable are—

    (a) any director of the company or of its holding company with whom the company entered into the arrangement in contravention of section 190,

    (b) any person with whom the company entered into the arrangement in contravention of that section who is connected with a director of the company or of its holding company,

    (c) the director of the company or of its holding company with whom any such person is connected, and

    (d) any other director of the company who authorised the arrangement or any transaction entered into in pursuance of such an arrangement.

(5) Subsections (3) and (4) are subject to the following two subsections.

(6) In the case of an arrangement entered into by a company in contravention of section 190 with a person connected with a director of the company or of its holding company, that director is not liable by virtue of subsection (4)(c) if he shows that he took all reasonable steps to secure the company's compliance with that section.

(7) In any case—

    (a) a person so connected is not liable by virtue of subsection (4)(b), and

    (b) a director is not liable by virtue of subsection (4)(d),

    if he shows that, at the time the arrangement was entered into, he did not know the relevant circumstances constituting the contravention.

(8) Nothing in this section shall be read as excluding the operation of any other enactment or rule of law by virtue of which the arrangement or transaction may be called in question or any liability to the company may arise.

18.63 Broadly speaking, the remedies available under s 195 reflect those which would be available under the general law if s 190 stood alone, thus the remedies available in respect of a misapplication of the company's assets by its directors.[104] Section 195 is in very similar terms to s 213, which sets out the civil consequences of contravening the 2006 Act, ss 197, 198, 200, 201, and 203 (loans to directors, etc). Reference may therefore be made to the commentary on s 213 at paragraphs 18.119–18.123 below in addition to the following commentary.

---

[104] *Re Duckwari plc* [1999] Ch 253, 260–2, CA, per Nourse LJ, dealing specifically with the liability to account and indemnify under what is now s 195(3).

Avoidance

The first remedy which is, in principle, available to the company is to avoid the arrange- **18.64**
ment, and any transaction entered into in pursuance of the arrangement, under s 190(2).
The company may avoid the arrangement or any transaction unless, first, restitution of any
money or other asset that was the subject matter of the arrangement or transaction is no
longer possible. The statutory remedy is similar to, but not the same as, the right to rescind
in equity. For example, whereas in equity delay in exercising the right to rescind may provide
a defence to the purported exercise of that right, there is no limitation on the right to avoid
under s 195(2) arising by reason of lapse of time alone.[105]

Further, it has been held under the 1985 Act, s 322(1) and (2) that the company could avoid **18.65**
the arrangement or transaction notwithstanding that complete restitution of the assets transferred under the arrangement in question was no longer possible.[106] A purposive approach
to construction was adopted since otherwise the right to avoid granted by Parliament was
likely to be incapable of exercise in a large number of cases: and in the case of a business sale
agreement, where assets are necessarily changing from time to time as the business is carried on, the 1985 Act s 322(1) and (2) would have had no scope.[107] The word 'unless' which
now appears in s 195(2) was thus read in the sense of 'except to the extent that', so that the
arrangement or transaction could be avoided (and the transferred property ordered to be
returned) except to the extent that the property no longer existed.[108] It was further held that
an incident of the company's right to avoid is that the company must repay to the other party
to the arrangement or transaction the consideration which passed to the company: though if
complete restitution were not possible, the repayment would be reduced pro tanto.[109]

The right to avoid is otherwise lost when the company has been indemnified under s 195(3) **18.66**
and (4) (s 195(2)(b)), and when the avoidance would affect rights acquired by a person who
is not a party to the arrangement or transaction in good faith, for value and without actual
notice of the contravention (s 195(2)(c)). If 'unless' is read in the sense of 'except to the extent
that' for the purposes of s 195(2)(b) and (c) also, it may be that partial avoidance is possible.

Liability to account for any gain

Whether or not the arrangement or any transaction entered into in pursuance of the arrange- **18.67**
ment has been avoided, each of the persons specified in s 195(4) (the Specified Persons) is
liable to account to the company for any gain that he has made directly or indirectly by the
arrangement or transaction.

It was held under the similarly worded 1985 Act, s 322(3)(a) that this provision corre- **18.68**
sponded to s 320(1)(a) of that Act (now s 190(1)(a)).[110] Thus, where it is the director (or
connected person) that acquires the substantial non-cash asset, the relevant entitlement of
the company under s 195(3) is a right to an account of the gains made directly or indirectly
by the Specified Persons by the arrangement or transaction under s 195(3)(a). Where it is

---

[105] *Demite Ltd v Protec Health Ltd* [1998] BCC 638, 650.
[106] *Demite Ltd v Protec Health Ltd* [1998] BCC 638; *Demite Ltd v Protec Health Ltd (No 2)* (7 July 1998,
unreported, Park J) ('*Demite (No 2)*').
[107] *Demite (No 2)* (n 106 above).
[108] *Demite (No 2)* (n 106 above).
[109] *Demite (No 2)* (n 106 above).
[110] *Re Duckwari plc* [1999] Ch 253, 261, CA, per Nourse LJ; *NBH Ltd v Hoare* [2006] 2 BCLC 649,
667, 668.

the company that acquires the substantial non-cash asset under s 190(1)(b), the relevant entitlement of the company is to be indemnified for any loss or damage resulting from the arrangement or transaction under s 195(3)(b).

18.69 The use of the words 'directly or indirectly' in s 195(3)(a) means that Parliament intended to cast its net wide:[111] the liability to account is potentially extremely broad. The gain must, however, have been made by the arrangement or transaction, so the arrangement or transaction must, in some sense, have caused the gain.[112]

18.70 It is no answer to a case based on authorization under s 195(4)(d) that the director concerned did not trouble to ask himself what it was that he was authorizing; and provided that the director at least understood the basic nature of the transaction in question, there is no defence under s 195(7).[113] Authorization need not be express so that if, for example, specific authority is given in relation to a number of transactions, it may be that the court will find that other transactions were implicitly authorized.[114]

Liability to indemnify for loss or damage

18.71 Again, whether or not the arrangement or any transaction entered into in pursuance of the arrangement has been avoided, each of the Specified Persons is liable to indemnify the company for any loss or damage resulting from the arrangement or transaction. As stated above, the liability to indemnify arises where it is the company that has acquired the substantial non-cash asset under s 190(1)(b). The scope of the liability to indemnify under s 190(1)(b) was held, under the 1985 Act, to mirror in large part the scope of the liability of directors of a company to make good a company's losses arising from a misapplication by them of the company's assets.[115] Such liability treats the directors as if they were trustees of those assets.[116] Hence, prima facie, they (and other Specified Persons) are liable to make good any losses which the company would not have suffered *but for* the transaction which constitutes the misapplication.[117]

18.72 Therefore, if a company acquires a substantial non-cash asset of the requisite value from a director or person connected without complying with the formalities of s 190, and pays the market value for that asset, the Specified Persons will in principle be liable to indemnify the company under s 195(3)(b) in the event that the asset depreciates. But for the acquisition, the company would not have suffered the loss or damage which it in fact suffered by reason of the acquisition. In the *Duckwari* case,[118] the right to acquire a property was acquired by the company, and the company then completed the acquisition. The price paid was not, as at the date of acquisition, excessive. Property prices generally fell, and the value of the property fell far below the acquisition price. The court of first instance had concluded that in those

---

[111] *Murray v Leisureplay plc* [2004] EWHC 1927 (QB), per Stanley Burnton J (at first instance), para 110.

[112] *NBH Ltd v Hoare* [2006] 2 BCLC 649, 666.

[113] *Lexi Holdings plc v Luqman* [2008] 2 BCLC 725 per Briggs J at paras 176–8, decided under the equivalent provisions of the 1985 Act, and referring to *Bishopsgate Investment Management Ltd v Maxwell (No 2)* [1993] BCLC 1282 at 1285–7; and the appeal at [2009] 2 BCLC 1, CA.

[114] *Lexi Holdings plc v Luqman* [2008] 2 BCLC 725 at paras 178–9, 182, referring to *Neville v Krikorian* [2007] 1 BCLC 1, CA.

[115] *Re Duckwari plc* [1999] Ch 253, 260–2, CA, per Nourse LJ.

[116] *Duckwari* (n 110 above), 262.

[117] *Murray v Leisureplay plc* [2005] IRLR 946, CA, 960, per Arden LJ, referring to *Target Holdings Ltd v Redferns* [1996] AC 421, HL.

[118] [1999] Ch 253, CA.

circumstances, the Specified Persons were not liable to indemnify the company in respect of the loss in value which followed acquisition, stating that 'the mischief, and only mischief, addressed by these provisions [ie the 1985 Act, ss 320 *et seq*] is acquisition[s] by the company at an inflated value or disposals by the company at an undervalue'.[119] The Court of Appeal overruled that decision, holding the Specified Persons liable for the loss to the company caused by the fall in property values.

In order for the Specified Persons to be liable to indemnify under s 195(3)(b), the relevant **18.73** loss or damage suffered by the company must be loss or damage 'resulting from' the arrangement or transaction. This wording contrasts with that used in s 195(3)(a), where the liability of the Specified Persons to account for any gain is for any gain that he has made 'directly or indirectly' by the arrangement or transaction. In *Re Duckwari plc (No 2)*,[120] one of the issues was whether the borrowing costs incurred by the company for the purpose of acquiring the property, but before it had actually acquired the property, were recoverable under s 195(3) (b). The analysis of the Court of Appeal in *Re Duckwari plc*[121] itself, whereby the predecessor of s 195 was interpreted as reflecting the remedies which would have been available to a company against its directors in respect of a misapplication of the company's assets, suggested that the borrowing costs ought to be recoverable. But for the acquisition, the borrowing costs would not have been incurred. Notwithstanding, the Court of Appeal held that the borrowing costs were irrecoverable. The loss or damage recoverable under the predecessor of s 195(3)(b) was only that 'resulting from' the arrangement or transaction, and on the basis that the relevant arrangement or transaction was the actual acquisition of the property by the company, the borrowing costs were not recoverable. If the decision is correct, and the same interpretation placed on s 195(3)(b), the parallel between remedies under trust law and under s 195(3) is less than exact. Further, there is a marked contrast between the scope of the gain for which account must be made under s 195(3)(a) (which covers gains made directly or indirectly by the arrangement or transaction) and the scope of the indemnity under s 195(3) (b) (which would not include loss or damage resulting indirectly from the arrangement or transaction).[122]

Some doubt has been cast on the decision in *Duckwari (No 2)* by a differently constituted **18.74** Court of Appeal in *Murray v Leisureplay plc*.[123] Arden LJ stated that it was open to question whether the interpretation of the predecessor of s 195(3)(b) was consistent with the decision in the earlier *Duckwari* case as to the parallel between remedies under the statute and remedies for misapplication by directors. She nonetheless considered herself bound by *Duckwari (No 2)*. Buxton LJ also remarked that *Duckwari (No 2)* caused difficulties in interpreting the predecessor of s 195.[124] It remains to be seen whether s 195(3)(b) will ultimately be interpreted in line with *Duckwari (No 2)*. Although there is no change of substance to the wording in the new Act, it is possible that the courts will not consider themselves bound by *Duckwari (No 2)*.[125]

---

[119] *Re Duckwari plc* [1997] Ch 201, 206.
[120] [1999] Ch 268.
[121] [1999] Ch 253, CA. The Court of Appeal was identically constituted.
[122] See the comments of Arden LJ in *Murray v Leisureplay plc* [2005] IRLR 946, 960.
[123] [2005] IRLR 946.
[124] [2005] IRLR 946, 963–4.
[125] Cf *Power v Sharp Investments Ltd* [1994] 1 BCLC 111, 122, CA.

18.75 If the decision in *Duckwari (No 2)* is correct, greater importance is placed on defining the relevant arrangement or transaction at issue.[126] On the interpretation in that case, in order for loss and damage to result from an arrangement or transaction, the arrangement or transaction must pre-date the loss or damage. In *Duckwari (No 2)*, the Court of Appeal defined the relevant arrangement or transaction as the acquisition of the property itself, and hence the borrowing costs incurred to enable that acquisition were irrecoverable. Had the relevant arrangement been defined differently, it seems that the borrowing costs might have been recoverable.[127]

D. Loans and Quasi-loans, Credit Transactions, and Related Arrangements

18.76 The 2006 Act, ss 197–214 prohibit a company (in the case of loans to directors under s 197, and 'related arrangements' under s 203), or a public company or company associated with a public company (in the case of quasi-loans to directors under s 198, loans or quasi-loans to persons connected with directors under s 200, and credit transactions under s 201), from entering into loans to directors, quasi-loans to directors, quasi-loans to persons connected with directors, or credit transactions with directors or persons connected with such directors unless the prior approval of members has been obtained.[128] The prohibitions are subject to a number of exceptions.

18.77 The Law Commission described the statutory predecessors of these sections as 'complex and inaccessible'.[129] The CLR also identified the need to simplify the provisions.[130] Sections 197–214 of the Act have succeeded, to some limited extent, in this regard. In broad terms, ss 197–214 re-enact the 1985 Act, ss 330–44, subject to one significant change: whereas under the 1985 Act, loans etc made in breach of the Act were illegal, and attracted criminal penalties, the Act merely imposes a requirement of prior member approval (and under s 214 permits subsequent affirmation by the members).

(1) Loans to directors: requirement of members' approval

18.78 The substantive provisions are contained in s 197(1) and (2), which provide:

> (1) A company may not—
>   (a) make a loan to a director of the company or of its holding company, or

---

[126] See para 18.37 above.

[127] See in particular the judgment of Buxton LJ in *Murray v Leisureplay plc* [2005] IRLR 946, 963, 964.

[128] 2006 Act, ss 197–214 apply to transactions or arrangements entered into on or after 1 October 2007: 2006 Act Commencement Order No 3, Sch 3, para 8(1). A resolution passed before that date approving a transaction or arrangement is effective for the purposes of those sections if it complies with the requirements of those sections: ibid, para 8(2). 1985 Act, ss 330–42 continue to apply in relation to a contravention occurring before that date: ibid, para 8(3). Approval is not required under ss 197, 198, 200, or 201 for anything done by the company in pursuance of an agreement entered into before 1 October 2007 that, by virtue of 1985 Act, s 337A (funding of director's expenditure on defending proceedings), would not have required approval if done before that date: ibid, para 9. There are further specific transitional provisions relating to the application of 2006 Act, ss 204 and 205, noted under the relevant sections below.

[129] *Company Directors: Regulating Conflicts of Interest and Formulating a Statement of Duties*, A Joint Consultation Paper (No 153) para 6.6.

[130] CLR: *Developing the Framework*, Annex C, para 28.

> (b) give a guarantee[131] or provide security in connection with a loan made by any person to such a director,
>
> unless the transaction has been approved by a resolution of the members of the company.
>
> (2) If the director is a director of the company's holding company,[132] the transaction must also have been approved by a resolution of the members of the holding company.

For the purposes of s 197 the person for whom the transaction is entered into is the person to whom the loan is made or, in the case of a guarantee or security, the person for whom the transaction is made in connection with which the guarantee or security is entered into,[133] and a director includes a shadow director.[134]

Section 197(3) and (4) states the requirements for obtaining members' approval: **18.79**

> (3) A resolution approving a transaction to which this section applies must not be passed unless a memorandum setting out the matters mentioned in subsection (4) is made available to members—
>
> (a) in the case of a written resolution, by being sent or submitted to every eligible member at or before the time at which the proposed resolution is sent or submitted to him;
>
> (b) in the case of a resolution at a meeting, by being made available for inspection by members of the company both—
>
> (i) at the company's registered office for not less than 15 days ending with the date of the meeting, and
>
> (ii) at the meeting itself: s 197(3)(a).
>
> (4) The matters to be disclosed are—
>
> (c) the nature of the transaction,
>
> (d) the amount of the loan and the purpose for which it is required, and
>
> (e) the extent of the company's liability under the transaction connected with the loan.

Eligible members are those members entitled to vote on the resolution on the circulation date of the resolution (as itself defined in s 290).[135] As was the case under the 1985 Act, where the written resolution procedure is used, it is only those members entitled to vote who are entitled to the memorandum, whereas, if an actual meeting is held, all members can inspect the memorandum. The 2006 Act, s 224 applies where there is an accidental failure to send the memorandum.

By s 197(5) no approval is required under s 197 on the part of the members of a body corporate that is not a UK-registered company, or is a wholly-owned subsidiary[136] of another body corporate. There are also exceptions (discussed in paragraphs 18.101–18.118 below) for (a) expenditure on company business, (b) expenditure on defending proceedings, (c) expenditure in connection with regulatory action or investigation, (d) for minor and business transactions, (e) for intra-group transactions, and (f) for money-lending companies. **18.80**

---

[131] This is undefined. Section 331(2) of the 1985 Act provided: '"Guarantee" includes indemnity, and cognate expressions are to be construed accordingly.' Presumably the Act will be construed so as to apply to indemnities, if not through a wide reading of the word 'guarantee', then by interpreting 'security' as including personal security.

[132] Defined in 2006 Act, s 1159; and see s 1160 and Sch 6.

[133] 2006 Act, s 212(a) and (c).

[134] 2006 Act, s 223(1)(c). In respect of Northern Rock plc, Bradford & Bingley plc, Heritable Bank plc, and Dunfermline Building Society, whilst owned by the Treasury certain persons will not be considered shadow directors for the purposes of ss 197–214: see n 8 above.

[135] 2006 Act, s 289 defines 'eligible member' and s 290 identifies the circulation date.

[136] Defined in 2006 Act, s 1159; and see s 1160 and Sch 6.

18.81 'Loan' in s 197 is not defined; nor was it under s 330 of the 1985 Act. In *Champagne Perrier-Jouet SA v HH Finch Ltd*,[137] Walton J construed the word 'loan' for the purposes of a company's articles and the 1948 Act, s 190 (a predecessor of s 197). He held that the correct meaning of loan was to be found in the then current edition of the *Shorter Oxford English Dictionary*: 'A sum of money lent for a time, to be returned in money or money's worth ...' The judge held, therefore, that if a person paid money to B at the request of A, although A would be indebted to that person, there was no loan. The indebtedness would now be a 'quasi-loan' within the meaning of the 2006 Act, ss 198 and 199 (paragraphs 18.84–18.89 below). A contract of loan is a consensual transaction, and hence for there to be a loan the lender must, objectively, have consented to the lending.[138]

18.82 In practice, difficulties can arise in deciding whether a transaction entered into by a company with a director is indeed a loan (in which case the company will be able to recover the loan in the normal way, in addition to having the remedies now found in the 2006 Act, s 213 if the loan falls within s 218 and no relevant exception applies), or whether the relevant payment is by way of remuneration (in which case, prima facie, the company has no remedy), or a misapplication of company funds (in which case, the company has no remedies under any contract of loan nor under s 213, but has the usual remedies available to it in respect of a misapplication of company funds).[139]

18.83 Whether the members can approve the relevant transaction informally, under the *Duomatic* principle, is unclear.[140] Under the 1985 Act, given that the relevant transaction was illegal, there was no question of member approval, formal or informal. The answer may depend on whether the provisions of the Act are interpreted as being for the protection of members or for creditors also.[141]

---

137 [1982] 1 WLR 1359.

138 *Re Ciro Citterio Menswear plc* [2002] 1 BCLC 672.

139 See, under 1985 Act, *Currencies Direct Ltd v Ellis* [2002] 1 BCLC 193, Gage J, and [2002] 2 BCLC 482, CA (where the issue was whether certain payments were made by way of loan to the director, or by way of remuneration); *Re Westminster Property Management Ltd (No 3)* [2004] BCC 599 (where an issue arose as to whether certain payments were loans, and hence unlawful, or the misapplication of company funds); *Re Broadside Colours and Chemicals Ltd* [2011] 2 BCLC 597 (whether loans were in fact payments made by way of remuneration). Those cases illustrate that such issues can only be decided by a close analysis of the facts. It appears that the mere fact that a director has signed a company's accounts recording the relevant transaction as a loan will not necessarily bind him, since he will ordinarily have signed such accounts in his capacity as director, not borrower: *John Shaw and Sons (Salford) Ltd v Shaw* [1935] 2 KB 113; and see *Currencies Direct Ltd v Ellis* [2002] 1 BCLC 193 (where a certificate under s 232(3) of the 1985 Act bound the director). It appears that, as a mere admission out of court, a director could in any event explain and contradict such admission, unless the accounts constituted an account stated: *Camillo Tank Steamship Company Ltd v Alexandria Engineering Works* (1921) 38 TLR 134. In *Re DPR Futures Ltd* [1989] BCLC 634, 638, Millett J relied on the fact that the directors had acknowledged their indebtedness in a statement of affairs in concluding that it was difficult to see any possible defence to a claim for repayment of the loans.

140 *Re Duomatic Ltd* [1969] 2 Ch 365, and see paras 18.58–18.60 above.

141 See *Wright v Atlas-Wright (Europe) Ltd* [1999] 2 BCLC 301 (CA) decided under 1985 Act, s 319. The Law Commission interpreted the provisions of the 1985 Act as being for the protection of creditors as well as members, but that interpretation was based, in part at least, on the fact that the relevant transactions were illegal, and attracted criminal penalties: Joint Consultation Paper, *Company Directors: Regulating Conflicts of Interest and Formulating a Statement of Duties*, No 153, paras 6.33–6.43. Under the Act, the transactions are not illegal, no criminal sanctions attach, and whether the transactions can be entered into depends on member approval.

(2) Quasi-loans to directors: requirement of members' approval

Section 198 contains provisions in respect of 'quasi-loans', which are very similar to the provisions about loans in s 197, but s 198 applies only to a public company or a company associated with a public company.[142] Section 198(2) and (3) contain the substantive provisions:

> (2) A company to which this section applies may not—
>   (a) make a quasi-loan to a director of the company or of its holding company, or
>   (b) give a guarantee or provide security in connection with a quasi-loan made by any person to such a director,
> unless the transaction has been approved by a resolution of the members of the company.
> (3) If the director is a director of the company's holding company, the transaction must also have been approved by a resolution of the members of the holding company.

For the purposes of s 198 the person for whom the transaction is entered into is the person to whom the quasi-loan is made, or, in the case of a guarantee or security, the person for whom the transaction is made in connection with which the guarantee or security is entered into,[143] and a director includes a shadow director.[144]

Section 198(4) and (5), relating to the necessary resolution of members and disclosure to those members regarding the quasi-loan, mirror, *mutatis mutandis*, s 197(4) and (5) in the context of loans to directors, and s 224 (accidental failure to send memorandum) applies (paragraphs 18.79–18.80 above).

By s 198(6) no approval is required under s 198 on the part of the members of a body corporate that is not a UK-registered company, or is a wholly-owned subsidiary[145] of another body corporate. There are also exceptions (discussed in paragraphs 18.101–18.118 below) for (a) expenditure on company business, (b) expenditure on defending proceedings, (c) expenditure in connection with regulatory action or investigation, (d) for minor and business transactions, (e) for intra-group transactions, and (f) for money-lending companies.

Section 198 is in large part a re-enactment of the 1985 Act, s 330 so far as it applied to the making of quasi-loans to directors, but with the significant change that quasi-loans are not illegal, and attract no criminal penalties. Instead, members' approval is required, in default of which the civil consequences of contravention set out in s 213 apply (paragraphs 18.119–18.123 below).

The restriction of the prohibition on making quasi-loans to public companies and companies associated with public companies, as per s 198(1) of the Act, broadly re-enacts the restriction in the 1985 Act, s 330 to 'relevant' companies.[146]

'Quasi-loan' and related expressions are defined under s 199:[147]

18.84

18.85

18.86

18.87

18.88

18.89

---

[142] 2006 Act, s 198(1). For the meaning of 'associated', see s 256.

[143] 2006 Act, s 212(a) and (c).

[144] 2006 Act, s 223(1)(c).

[145] Defined in 2006 Act, s 1159; and see s 1160 and Sch 6.

[146] As defined by 1985 Act, s 331(6). The Government did not act on the recommendation of the Law Commission (Law Commission Report, *Company Directors: Regulating Conflicts of Interest and Formulating a Statement of Duties*, No 261, para 12.17) as endorsed by the CLR (CLR: *Developing the Framework*, Annex C, para 28) that the prohibitions contained in ss 198, 200, and 201 should apply to all companies. For the Government's explanation for not acting on these recommendations, see Hansard, HC Debates, cols 797–8 (17 October 2006), which may refer to a discussion in Committee in Hansard, HC Standing Committee D, cols 632–3.

[147] A re-enactment, without substantive change, of 1985 Act, s 331(3) and (4).

(1) A 'quasi-loan' is a transaction under which one party 'the creditor' agrees to pay, or pays otherwise than in pursuance of an agreement, a sum for another 'the borrower' or agrees to reimburse, or reimburses otherwise than in pursuance of an agreement, expenditure incurred by another party for another ('the borrower')—

    (a) on terms that the borrower (or a person on his behalf) will reimburse the creditor; or

    (b) in circumstances giving rise to a liability on the borrower to reimburse the creditor.

(2) Any reference to the person to whom a quasi-loan is made is a reference to the borrower.

(3) The liabilities of the borrower under a quasi-loan include the liabilities of any person who has agreed to reimburse the creditor on behalf of the borrower.

(3) Loans or quasi-loans to persons connected with directors: requirement of members' approval

18.90 Under s 200 of the Act, similar provisions to those in ss 197 and 198 apply to a public company or a company associated with a public company in respect of loans and quasi-loans made to persons connected with a director of the company or its holding company, and the giving of guarantees or provision of security in connection with such loans or quasi-loans.[148] Section 200(2) and (3) contains the substantive provisions:

(2) A company to which this section applies may not—

    (a) make a loan or quasi-loan to a person connected with[149] a director of the company or of its holding company, or

    (b) give a guarantee or provide security in connection with a loan or quasi-loan made by any person to a person connected with such a director,

    unless the transaction has been approved by a resolution of the members of the company.

(3) If the connected person is a person connected with a director of the company's holding company, the transaction must also have been approved by a resolution of the members of the holding company.

For the purposes of s 200, the person for whom a transaction is entered into is the person to whom the loan or quasi-loan is made, or, in the case of a guarantee or security, the person for whom the transaction is made in connection with which the guarantee or security is entered into,[150] and a director includes a shadow director.[151]

18.91 Section 200(4) and (5), relating to the necessary resolution of members and disclosure to those members regarding the loan or quasi-loan, mirror, *mutatis mutandis*, ss 197(4) and (5), and 198(4) and (5), in the context of loans and quasi-loans to directors.

18.92 By s 200(6) no approval is required under s 200 on the part of the members of a body corporate that is not a UK-registered company, or is a wholly-owned subsidiary[152] of another body corporate. There are also exceptions (discussed in paragraphs 18.101–18.118 below) for (a) expenditure on company business, (b) expenditure on defending proceedings, (c) expenditure in connection with regulatory action or investigation, (d) for minor

---

[148] 2006 Act, s 200 derives from s 330(3)(b) of the 1985 Act. The criminal sanctions applicable under the 1985 Act have been removed, and the prohibition under the 1985 Act replaced by a requirement for members' approval. Section 200(1) restricts the application of s 200 to public companies and companies associated with a public company. For the meaning of 'associated', see s 256. As with ss 198 and 201, the Law Commission and CLR had recommended that the provisions should apply to all companies (see n 146 above).

[149] For the definition of 'connected person' see s 252 (Persons connected with a director).

[150] 2006 Act, s 212(a) and (c).

[151] 2006 Act, s 223(1)(c).

[152] Defined in 2006 Act, s 1159; and see s 1160 and Sch 6.

and business transactions, (e) for intra-group transactions, and (f) for money-lending companies.

(4) Credit transactions: requirement of members' approval

Under s 201, similar provisions to those relating to loans and quasi-loans to directors or con- **18.93** nected persons apply in respect of a public company or a company associated with a public company entering into a 'credit transaction' with a director or person connected with a direc- tor.[153] Section 201(2) and (3) contain the substantive provisions:

> (2) A company to which this section applies may not—
>> (a) enter into a credit transaction as creditor for the benefit of a director of the company or of its holding company, or a person connected with such a director, or
>> (b) give a guarantee or provide security in connection with a credit transaction entered into by a person for the benefit of such a director, or a person connected with such a director,
>
> unless the transaction (that is, the credit transaction, the giving of the guarantee or the provision of security, as the case may be) has been approved by a resolution of the mem- bers of the company.
> (3) If the director or connected person is a director of its holding company or a person con- nected with such a director, the transaction must also have been approved by a resolution of the members of the holding company.

For the purposes of s 201 the person for whom a transaction is entered into is the person to whom goods, land, or services are supplied, sold, hired, leased, or otherwise disposed of under the transaction, or, in the case of a guarantee or security, the person for whom the transaction is made in connection with which the guarantee or security is entered into,[154] and a director includes a shadow director.[155]

Section 201(4) and (5) state the requirements for obtaining members' approval of the credit **18.94** transaction:

> (4) A resolution approving a transaction to which this section applies must not be passed unless a memorandum setting out the matters mentioned in subsection (5) is made avail- able to members[156]—
>> (a) in the case of a written resolution, by being sent or submitted to every eligible member at or before the time at which the proposed resolution is sent or submitted to him;
>> (b) in the case of a resolution at a meeting, by being made available for inspection by members of the company both—
>>> (i) at the company's registered office for not less than 15 days ending with the date of the meeting, and
>>> (ii) at the meeting itself.
> (5) The matters to be disclosed are—
>> (a) the nature of the transaction,

---

[153] 2006 Act, s 201 derives from 1985 Act, s 330(4). The prohibition under the 1985 Act has been replaced by the requirement of prior member approval and the criminal sanctions applicable under the 1985 Act have been removed. Section 201(1) restricts the application of s 201 to public companies and companies associated with a public company. For the meaning of 'associated', see s 256. As with ss 198 and 200, the Law Commission and CLR had recommended that the provisions should apply to all companies (see n 146 above).

[154] 2006 Act, s 212(b) and (c).

[155] 2006 Act, s 223(1)(c).

[156] Where there is an accidental failure to send the memorandum, s 224 applies.

    (b) the value of the credit transaction and the purpose for which the land, goods or services sold or otherwise disposed of, leased, hired or supplied under the credit transaction are required, and

    (c) the extent of the company's liability under any transaction connected with the credit transaction.

18.95 By s 201(6) no approval is required under s 201 on the part of the members of a body corporate that is not a UK-registered company, or is a wholly-owned subsidiary[157] of another body corporate. There are also exceptions (discussed in paragraphs 18.101–18.112 below) for (a) expenditure on company business, (b) expenditure on defending proceedings, and (c) expenditure in connection with regulatory action or investigation.

18.96 Section 202 gives the meaning of 'credit transaction':[158]

    (1) A 'credit transaction' is a transaction under which one party ('the creditor')—

        (a) supplies any goods or sells any land under a hire-purchase agreement or a conditional sale agreement,[159]

        (b) leases or hires any land or goods in return for periodical payments, or

        (c) otherwise disposes of land or supplies goods or services[160] on the understanding that payment (whether in a lump sum or instalments or by way of periodical payments or otherwise) is to be deferred.

    (2) Any reference to the person for whose benefit a credit transaction is entered into is to the person to whom goods, land or services are supplied, sold, leased, hired or otherwise disposed of under the transaction.

(5) Related arrangements: requirements of members' approval

18.97 Section 203 is an anti-avoidance provision,[161] which prevents a company from evading the requirements for members' approval by entering into an arrangement whereby another person gives the director a loan, quasi-loan, or credit transaction, and in return that person obtains a benefit from a company or subsidiary of the company.[162] For example, a 'back-to-back' arrangement, whereby a company agrees to make loans to the directors of another company in return for that other company making loans to its own directors, will be caught.

18.98 The substantive provisions of s 203 are:

    (1) A company may not—

        (a) take part in an arrangement[163] under which—

            (i) another person enters into a transaction that, if it had been entered into by the company, would have required approval under sections 197, 198, 200 or 201, and

            (ii) that person, in pursuance of the arrangement, obtains a benefit from the company or a body corporate associated with it, or

        (b) arrange for the assignment to it, or assumption by it, of any rights, obligations or liabilities under a transaction that, if it had been entered into by the company, would

---

[157] Defined in 2006 Act, s 1159; and see s 1160 and Sch 6.

[158] The definition is a re-enactment, without substantive change, of 1985 Act, s 331(7), (8), (9)(b), and (10).

[159] 'Conditional sale agreement' has the same meaning as in the Consumer Credit Act 1974: s 202(3).

[160] 'Services' means anything other than goods or land.

[161] It is derived from 1985 Act, s 330(6) and (7).

[162] Hansard, HL GC Day 4, vol 678, cols 349–50 (9 February 2006), Lord Sainsbury.

[163] 'Arrangement' is not defined. It is a word of wide import and, given the purpose of the section, it is thought that it will be widely construed: compare para 18.37 above, as to the meaning of 'arrangement' in the context of s 190 (substantial property transactions).

have required such approval, unless the arrangement in question has been approved by a resolution of the members of the company.

(2) If the director or connected person for whom the transaction is entered into is a director of its holding company or a person connected with such a director, the arrangement must also have been approved by a resolution of the members of the holding company. ...

(6) In determining for the purposes of this section whether a transaction is one that would have required approval under section 197, 198, 200 or 201 if it had been entered into by the company, the transaction shall be treated as having been entered into on the date of the arrangement.

For the purposes of s 203 the person for whom the arrangement is entered into is the person for whom the transaction is made to which the arrangement relates,[164] and a director includes a shadow director.[165]

Under s 203(4) and (5), a resolution approving an arrangement to which s 203 applies must not be passed unless a memorandum setting out the matters that would have to be disclosed if the company were seeking approval of the transaction to which the arrangement relates, the nature of the arrangement, and the extent of the company's liability under the arrangement or any transaction connected with it, is made available to members in the same way, *mutatis mutandis*, as under ss 197(3), 198(4), 200(4), and 201(4).[166] **18.99**

As under ss 197(3), 198(4), 200(4), and 201(4), no approval is required on the part of the members of a body corporate that is not a UK-registered company, or is a wholly-owned subsidiary of another body corporate. **18.100**

(6) Exceptions

Sections 204–9 create six exceptions from the requirement for member approval of loan and quasi-loan transactions, namely (a) for expenditure on company business (s 204), (b) for expenditure on defending proceedings etc (s 205), (c) for expenditure in connection with regulatory action or investigation (s 206), (d) for minor and business transactions (s 207), (e) for intra-group transactions (s 208), and (f) for money-lending companies (s 209). None of the exceptions applies to related arrangements. The exceptions apply to shadow directors.[167] **18.101**

Expenditure on company business

Section 204 provides as follows:[168] **18.102**

(1) Approval is not required under section 197, 198, 200 or 201 (requirement of members' approval for loans etc) for anything done by a company—

(a) to provide a director of the company or of its holding company, or a person connected with any such director, with funds to meet expenditure incurred or to be incurred by him—

(i) for the purposes of the company, or

(ii) for the purpose of enabling him properly to perform his duties as an officer of the company, or

(b) to enable any such person to avoid incurring such expenditure.

---

[164] 2006 Act, s 212(d).
[165] 2006 Act, s 223(1)(c).
[166] Where there is an accidental failure to send the memorandum s 224 applies.
[167] 2006 Act, s 223(1)(c).
[168] In force on 1 October 2007. For transitional provisions, see 2006 Act Commencement Order No 3, Sch 3, para 10(1)–(3).

(2) This section does not authorise a company to enter into a transaction if the aggregate of—
   (a) the value of the transaction in question, and
   (b) the value of any other relevant transactions or arrangements,[169] exceeds £50,000.[170]

18.103 Section 204 re-enacts the 1985 Act, s 337, with significant changes. Under the 1985 Act, s 337(3), the exception applied only if the members in general meeting had given prior approval to the loan etc, or the loan etc was made on condition that if such approval was not given at or before the next AGM, the loan was to be repaid, or any other liability arising under such transaction was discharged, within six months from the conclusion of that AGM. The 1985 Act, s 337(3) and (4) provided for the disclosure of certain matters at the relevant AGM. These limitations on the exception have now gone, with the result that a loan etc for expenditure on company business need not be repayable or disclosed, provided it is less than £50,000 in aggregate.

18.104 The provisions of ss 210 and 211 are material for determining whether the loan, quasi-loan, or credit transaction is within the £50,000 limit.[171] For this purpose it is necessary to add up the transaction in question and any other relevant existing transactions or arrangements.[172] Section 211 provides the rules for determining the value of a transaction or arrangement, of which sub-ss (2)–(5) and (7) are relevant to the value of the transaction in question (s 204(2)(a)):

(2) The value of a loan is the amount of its principal.
(3) The value of a quasi-loan is the amount, or maximum amount, that the person to whom the quasi-loan is made is liable to reimburse the creditor.
(4) The value of a credit transaction is the price that it is reasonable to expect could be obtained for the goods, services or land to which the transaction relates if they had been supplied (at the time the transaction is entered into) in the ordinary course of business and on the same terms (apart from price) as they have been supplied, or are to be supplied, under the transaction in question.
(5) The value of a guarantee or security is the amount guaranteed or secured.
(6) The value of an arrangement to which section 203 (related arrangements) applies is the value of the transaction to which the arrangement relates.
(7) If the value of a transaction or arrangement is not capable of being expressed as a specific sum of money—
   (a) whether because the amount of any liability arising under the transaction or arrangement is unascertainable, or for any other reason, and
   (b) whether or not any liability under the transaction or arrangement has been reduced,
   its value is deemed to exceed £50,000.

18.105 Section 204(2)(b) requires the value of any other relevant transactions or arrangements to be added to the value of the transaction in question. Other relevant transactions or arrangements are identified in accordance with s 210:

(2) Other relevant transactions or arrangements are those previously entered into, or entered into at the same time as the transaction or arrangement in question in relation to which the following conditions are met.

---

[169] See 2006 Act, s 210.
[170] The Secretary of State has power to increase this limit under 2006 Act, s 256.
[171] These sections derived from 1985 Act, ss 339 and 340 without material change.
[172] Lord Sainsbury, Hansard, HL GC Day 4, vol 678 (9 February 2006).

(3) Where the transaction or arrangement in question is entered into—
   (a) for a director of the company entering into it, or
   (b) for a person connected with such a director,
   the conditions are that the transaction or arrangement was (or is) entered into for that director, or a person connected with him, by virtue of the relevant exception by that company or by any of its subsidiaries.

(4) Where the transaction or arrangement in question is entered into—
   (a) for a director of the holding company of the company entering into it, or
   (b) for a person connected with such a director,
   the conditions are that the transaction or arrangement was (or is) entered into for that director, or a person connected with him, by virtue of the relevant exception[173] by the holding company or by any of its subsidiaries.

(5) A transaction or arrangement entered into by a company that at the time it was entered into—
   (a) was a subsidiary of the company entering into the transaction or arrangement in question, or
   (b) was a subsidiary of the company's holding company,
   is not a relevant transaction or arrangement if, at the time the question arises whether the transaction or arrangement in question falls within a relevant exception, it is no longer such a subsidiary.

18.106 Having determined whether a transaction or arrangement is relevant for the purposes of 204(2)(b) it is necessary to value it in accordance with s 211. By s 211(1)(b) its value is taken to be the value determined in accordance with sub-ss (2)–(7), reduced by any amount by which the liabilities of the person for whom the transaction or arrangement was made have been reduced.

Defending proceedings etc

18.107 Section 205 provides as follows:[174]

(1) Approval is not required under section 197, 198, 200 or 201 (requirement of members' approval for loans etc) for anything done by a company—
   (a) to provide a director of the company or of its holding company with funds to meet expenditure incurred or to be incurred by him—
      (i) in defending any criminal or civil proceedings in connection with any alleged negligence, default, breach of duty or breach of trust by him in relation to the company or an associated company,[175] or
      (ii) in connection with an application for relief (see subsection (5)), or
   (b) to enable any such director to avoid incurring such expenditure,
   if it is done on the following terms.

(2) The terms are—
   (a) that the loan is to be repaid, or (as the case may be) any liability of the company incurred under any transaction connected with the thing done is to be discharged, in the event of—
      (i) the director being convicted in the proceedings,
      (ii) judgment being given against him in the proceedings, or
      (iii) the court refusing to grant him relief on the application, and

---

[173] By s 210(1) 'the relevant exception' means the exception under ss 204–9 for the purposes of which it falls to be determined what are 'other relevant transactions or arrangements'.

[174] In force on 1 October 2007. For transitional provisions, see 2006 Act Commencement Order No 3, Sch 3, paras 9, 11(1) and (2).

[175] See 2006 Act, s 256.

    (b) that it is to be so repaid or discharged not later than—

        (i) the date when the conviction becomes final,

        (ii) the date when the judgment becomes final, or

        (iii) the date when the refusal of relief becomes final.

(3) For this purpose a conviction, judgment or refusal of relief becomes final—

    (a) if not appealed against, at the end of the period for bringing an appeal;

    (b) if appealed against, when the appeal (or any further appeal) is disposed of.

(4) An appeal is disposed of—

    (a) if it is determined and the period for bringing any further appeal has ended, or

    (b) if it is abandoned or otherwise ceases to have effect.

(5) The reference in subsection (1)(a)(ii) to an application for relief is to an application for relief under—

    section 661(3) or (4) (power of court to grant relief in case of acquisition of shares by innocent nominee), or

    section 1157 (general power of court to grant relief in case of honest and reasonable conduct).[176]

18.108 Section 205 largely re-enacts the exception in the 1985 Act, s 337A. Section 205 is complemented by s 206, an express exception for expenditure in connection with regulatory action or investigation. The exception applies not only in respect of expenditure incurred or to be incurred in actually defending criminal or civil proceedings but also, as appears from s 205(1)(b), expenditure incurred or to be incurred in respect of, for example, the instruction of legal advisers prior to the issue of any proceedings.

18.109 The reference to associated companies in s 205(1)(a)(i) makes clear that the exception applies, in principle, to loans made by one company to the director of another company in the same group.[177] Where the prohibition applies, the board of the associated company should not fall into the trap of thinking that, merely because the exception in s 205 extends to associated companies, a loan for the purposes set out in s 205 can be made by the associated company without further consideration. Hence, before authorizing the loan, the board of the associated company must consider their general duties and thus, for example, whether the making of the loan promotes the success of the lending company (see s 172 and Chapter 12 above).

18.110 There is no financial limit on the exception for expenditure on defending proceedings. The loan must be repaid if the defence is unsuccessful in that (a) the director is convicted in criminal proceedings, (b) judgment is given against him in civil proceedings, or (c) he is refused relief under s 1157. This is consistent with the provisions permitting third party indemnity provision and qualifying pension scheme indemnity provision under ss 234 and 235 (see Chapter 20 below). If civil proceedings against a director are settled, without

---

[176] 2006 Commencement Order No 3, Art 6, Sch 1, para 11 provides that in sub-s (5), for the words 'section 661(3)' to the end is to be substituted 'section 144(3) or (4) of the Companies Act 1985 …, or section 727 of the Companies Act 1985'.

[177] The government recognized the convenience of the extension, but was keen to emphasize that the exception 'should only be used for matters that are properly connected to the company. It would be inappropriate for the exceptions to be available for company funds to be used without member approval to defend a director against proceedings unconnected with company business': Hansard, HC Report Stage 17, col 799 (17 October 2006), Margaret Hodge. Hence, the exceptions are narrower than the circumstances in which a director can be granted a qualifying third party indemnity provision under s 234.

judgment being entered against him, it will not be necessary for the purposes of s 205 for the loan to be repaid. The directors may need to consider whether a loan on those terms is in the interests of the company or whether it should be repayable where the director has effectively 'lost'.

Regulatory action or investigation

Section 206 provides: **18.111**

> Approval is not required under section 197, 198, 200 or 201 (requirement of members' approval for loans etc) for anything done by a company—
> (a) to provide a director of the company or of its holding company with funds to meet expenditure incurred or to be incurred by him in defending himself—
> (i) in an investigation by a regulatory authority, or
> (ii) against action proposed to be taken by a regulatory authority,
> in connection with any alleged negligence, default, breach of duty or breach of trust by him in relation to the company or an associated company, or
> (b) to enable any such director to avoid incurring such expenditure.

Section 206 is new and complements s 205. It was introduced following Opposition calls **18.112** for clarification (the government considered that expenditure in connection with regulatory action or investigation fell within s 205 in any event). There is no financial limit on expenditure in relation to regulatory actions or investigations, nor need any loan be repaid even if the director is found to have been negligent, or in default, breach of duty, or breach of trust in relation to the company or an associated company.

Minor and business transactions

Section 207 provides: **18.113**

> (1) Approval is not required under section 197, 198 or 200 for a company to make a loan or quasi-loan, or to give a guarantee or provide security in connection with a loan or quasi-loan, if the aggregate of—
> (a) the value of the transaction, and
> (b) the value of any other relevant transactions or arrangements, does not exceed £10,000.[178]
> (2) Approval is not required under section 201 for a company to enter into a credit transaction, or to give a guarantee or provide security in connection with a credit transaction, if the aggregate of—
> (a) the value of the transaction (that is, of the credit transaction, guarantee or security), and
> (b) the value of any other relevant transactions or arrangements,
> does not exceed £15,000.
> (3) Approval is not required under section 201 for a company to enter into a credit transaction, or to give a guarantee or provide security in connection with a credit transaction, if—
> (a) the transaction is entered into by the company in the ordinary course of the company's business, and
> (b) the value of the transaction is not greater, and the terms on which it is entered into are not more favourable, than it is reasonable to expect the company would have offered to, or in respect of, a person of the same financial standing but unconnected with the company.

---

[178] The Secretary of State has power to increase this limit under 2006 Act, s 256.

18.114   Section 207 largely re-enacts the 1985 Act, ss 332, 334, and 335, with the exception extended to quasi-loans and including connected persons. The monetary limits have also been increased. In order to determine whether the loan, quasi-loan, guarantee, or security or credit transaction is within the relevant monetary limit, it is necessary to assess values under ss 210 and 211 as described in paragraph 18.106 above. A credit transaction may come within the exception even though it exceeds the £15,000 limit, provided that it is on normal business terms within sub-s 207(3).

Intra-group transactions

18.115   Section 208 provides:

> (1) Approval is not required under section 197, 198 or 200 for—
>   (a) the making of a loan or quasi-loan to an associated body corporate,[179] or
>   (b) the giving of a guarantee or provision of security in connection with a loan or quasi-loan made to an associated body corporate.
> (2) Approval is not required under section 201—
>   (a) to enter into a credit transaction as creditor for the benefit of an associated body corporate, or
>   (b) to give a guarantee or provide security in connection with a credit transaction entered into by any person for the benefit of an associated body corporate.

18.116   Section 208 re-enacts the 1985 Act, ss 333 and 336, though the exception is somewhat broader. Section 256 defines an 'associated body corporate'.

Money-lending companies

18.117   Section 209 provides:

> (1) Approval is not required under section 197, 198 or 200 for the making of a loan or quasi-loan, or the giving of a guarantee or provision of security in connection with a loan or quasi-loan, by a money-lending company if—
>   (a) the transaction (that is, the loan, quasi-loan, guarantee or security) is entered into by the company in the ordinary course of the company's business, and
>   (b) the value of the transaction is not greater, and its terms are not more favourable, than it is reasonable to expect the company would have offered to a person of the same financial standing but unconnected with the company.
> (2) A 'money-lending company' means a company whose ordinary business includes the making of loans or quasi-loans, or the giving of guarantees or provision of security in connection with loans or quasi-loans.
> (3) The condition specified in subsection (1)(b) does not of itself prevent a company from making a home loan—
>   (a) to a director of the company or of its holding company, or
>   (b) to an employee of the company,
> if loans of that description are ordinarily made by the company to its employees and the terms of the loan in question are no more favourable than those on which such loans are ordinarily made.
> (4) For the purposes of subsection (3) a 'home loan' means a loan—
>   (a) for the purpose of facilitating the purchase, for use as the only or main residence of the person to whom the loan is made, of the whole or part of any dwelling-house together with any land to be occupied and enjoyed with it,

---

[179] See 2006 Act, s 256.

   (b) for the purpose of improving a dwelling-house or part of a dwelling-house so used or any land occupied and enjoyed with it, or

   (c) in substitution for any loan made by any person and falling within paragraph (a) or (b).

Section 209 re-enacts the 1985 Act, s 338 with changes. Whereas s 338 imposed a financial **18.118** limit of £100,000 on the value of the aggregate of the loans etc, no such limit appears in s 209. The exception in respect of home loans in s 209(3) has been broadened by s 209(3) (b). The purpose of that exception is to allow directors to take advantage of any employee home loan schemes operated by a money-lending company on the same terms as are offered to employees. Whereas under the 1985 Act, s 338 the exception did not apply in respect of a home loan to an employee connected with a director, s 209 applies in such circumstances— the government considered it unfair for certain employees to be excluded from the benefit of schemes run by their employers for their benefit merely because of a connection with a director.[180]

(7) Civil consequences of contravention

Section 213 states: **18.119**

   (1) This section applies where a company enters into a transaction or arrangement in contravention of section 197, 198, 200, 201 or 203 (requirement of members' approval for loans etc).

   (2) The transaction or arrangement is voidable at the instance of the company, unless—

      (a) restitution of any money or other asset that was the subject matter of the transaction or arrangement is no longer possible,

      (b) the company has been indemnified for any loss or damage resulting from the transaction or arrangement, or

      (c) rights acquired in good faith, for value and without actual notice of the contravention by a person who is not a party to the arrangement or transaction would be affected by the avoidance.

   (3) Whether or not the transaction or arrangement has been avoided, each of the persons specified in subsection (4) is liable—

      (a) to account to the company for any gain that he has made directly or indirectly by the transaction or arrangement, and

      (b) (jointly and severally with any person so liable under this section) to indemnify the company for any loss or damage resulting from the transaction or arrangement.

   (4) The persons so liable are—

      (a) any director of the company or of its holding company with whom the company entered into the transaction or arrangement in contravention of section 197, 198, 201 or 203,

      (b) any person with whom the company entered into the transaction or arrangement in contravention of any of those sections who is connected with a director of the company or of its holding company,

      (c) the director of the company or of its holding company with whom any such person is connected, and

      (d) any other director of the company who authorised the transaction or arrangement.

   (5) Subsections (3) and (4) are subject to the following two subsections.

   (6) In the case of a transaction or arrangement entered into by a company in contravention of section 200, 201 or 203 with a person connected with a director of the company or of

---

[180] Hansard, HL GC Day 4, vol 678, col 353 (9 February 2006), Lord Sainsbury.

its holding company, that director is not liable by virtue of subsection (4) (c) if he shows that he took all reasonable steps to secure the company's compliance with the section concerned.

(7) In any case—

    (a) a person so connected is not liable by virtue of subsection (4)(b), and

    (b) a director is not liable by virtue of subsection (4)(d),

    if he shows that, at the time the arrangement was entered into, he did not know the relevant circumstances constituting the contravention.

(8) Nothing in this section shall be read as excluding the operation of any other enactment or rule of law by virtue of which the transaction or arrangement may be called in question or any liability to the company may arise.

18.120   Section 213 is in terms almost identical to s 195 (property transactions: civil consequences of contravention) and reference may be made to paragraphs 18.62–18.75 above on that section.[181]

18.121   The two main remedies created by s 213 are the right to avoid the transaction or arrangement (under s 213(2)) and the right, as against directors and others, to an account and indemnity (under s 213(3) and (4)). The right to avoid under s 213(2) is subject to there having been no subsequent affirmation under s 214: see paragraphs 18.124–18.125 below. It may not be necessary for the company to rely on the statutory remedies at all: for example, if a loan is made by a company to one of its directors without prior member approval, and thus in breach of s 197, the company may choose simply to sue on the loan rather than seeking to avoid it: see eg *Re Westminster Property Management Ltd (No 3)*.[182] In certain circumstances, however, even where the remedy sought is simply repayment of monies advanced by way of loan, there may be an advantage in avoiding first, for example where the debtor maintains that the loan is not yet repayable.[183] Under the 1985 Act, s 341, under which Act the making of a prohibited loan was illegal, it had been argued that any loan made in breach of s 330 of that Act was irrecoverable on grounds of illegality, a contention which was, naturally, rejected.[184]

18.122   Section 213(8) preserves remedies which might exist in respect of the transaction or arrangement outside of s 213.[185] In *Re Ciro Citterio Menswear plc*,[186] it was contended that a loan

---

[181] 2006 Act, s 213 derives from 1985 Act, s 341. There are no longer any criminal penalties for breach of ss 197, 198, 200, 201, or 203, as were previously contained, in relation to those sections' predecessors, in 1985 Act, s 342.

[182] [2004] BCC 599. Where a claim to an indemnity is made under s 213(3)(b), the limitation period expires six years from the day on which the loan was made: *Re Broadside Colours and Chemicals Ltd* [2011] 2 BCLC 597.

[183] See *Tait Conisbee (Oxford) Ltd v Tait* [1997] 2 BCLC 349, where the director alleged that the loan was repayable only out of dividends to be declared by the company. The Court of Appeal held that, were that the case, the letter of demand for repayment served by the company avoided the loan and hence the amount of the loan was in any event due to the company.

[184] *Currencies Direct Ltd v Ellis* [2002] 1 BCLC 193 (Gage J). The argument was not pursued on appeal: *Currencies Direct Ltd v Ellis* [2002] 2 BCLC 482, 484, CA. Under the Act, there are no criminal sanctions and the making of a loan is no longer illegal.

[185] See, therefore, *Re Mumtaz Properties Ltd* [2012] 2 BCLC 109, CA per Arden LJ at para 9: since the loans in that case had been made to the directors to allow them to meet personal expenditure, and it was common ground that the making of loans for that purpose was a breach of fiduciary duty, the liquidator had no cause to rely on the predecessor of s 213 since liability for breach of fiduciary duty was expressly preserved by the predecessor of s 213(8).

[186] [2002] 1 BCLC 672.

made to a director under s 330 of the 1985 Act was held by that director as constructive trustee for the company by reason solely of the fact that the loan was made in contravention of s 330. In the absence of facts rendering the making of the loan a breach of fiduciary duty by the directors of the company,[187] the argument was rejected.[188]

In *Neville v Krikorian*,[189] the Court of Appeal held that a director who authorized the practice of the company making loans to a fellow director (in breach of the 1985 Act, s 330), and who took no steps to cause the company to recover the indebtedness, was in breach of his duty as a director. In addition, despite the fact that it had not been proven that the director had known of each loan which the company advanced, since he had authorized the practice of making such loans, he was liable to indemnify the company for any loss or damage resulting from the loans under the 1985 Act, s 341(2)(b) (the predecessor of the 2006 Act, s 213(3) (b)).[190] Under s 341(2)(b), the director was liable to make good the difference between the amount outstanding to the company as at the date that he authorized the practice, and the amount ultimately outstanding when the company entered administration. The director who received the loans was unable to make any repayment. In respect of his breach of duty as director, the director was liable to pay to the company the difference between the sum which could have been recovered by the company if it had sought repayment of the loans when the director first got to know of them, and the amount recoverable at the date of judgment (the latter sum being nil).

18.123

(8) Effect of subsequent affirmation

Section 214 provides:

18.124

> Where a transaction or arrangement is entered into by a company in contravention of section 197, 198, 200, 201 or 203 (requirement of members' approval for loans etc) but, within a reasonable period, it is affirmed—
> (a) in the case of a contravention of the requirement for a resolution of the members of the company, by a resolution of the members of the company, and
> (b) in the case of a contravention of the requirement for a resolution of the members of the holding company, the transaction or arrangement may no longer be avoided under section 213.

---

[187] As may have been the case in *Budge v AF Budge (Contractors) Limited* [1997] BPIR 366, CA, discussed in *Ciro Citterio* at [2002] 1 BCLC 672, 688–9. In *Baker v Potter* [2005] BCC 855, at para 110, David Richards J held that a payment to a director potentially in breach of s 330 of the 1985 Act was made in breach of fiduciary duty not only because of the breach of s 330, but also because it was not made for a proper corporate purpose. On that basis the decision in *Ciro Citterio* was distinguished.

[188] This rejection did, however, involve a questionable treatment of dicta in *Wallersteiner v Moir* [1974] 1 WLR 991, 1015, CA, where Lord Denning MR stated that a director who authorized the lending of money to a company which was his 'puppet', in breach of 1948 Act, s 190 (a predecessor of 2006 Act, s 197), was guilty of misfeasance. The Master of the Rolls appears to have relied on the unlawfulness of the loan, however: under the Act, loans etc in breach of ss 197, 198, 200, and 201 are no longer unlawful. In *Re a Company (No 1641 of 2003)* [2004] 1 BCLC 210 it was held that a debtor in respect of a loan made in breach of 1985 Act, s 330 could not set off monies alleged to have been owing from the company to the debtor under rule 4.90 of the Insolvency Rules. However, this was on the basis that the taking of an unlawful loan was a misappropriation, and thus there was no 'dealing' within rule 4.90. Since a loan made without prior member approval is no longer unlawful, if the only circumstances relied upon were such failure to obtain approval, rule 4.90 would probably apply (and IR 2016, r 14.25 after 6 April 2017).

[189] [2007] 1 BCLC 1, CA.

[190] See also *Lexi Holdings plc v Luqman* [2008] 2 BCLC 725, at paras 178–9, 182; on appeal at [2009] 2 BCLC 1; *McGregor Glazing Ltd v McGregor* 2014 GWD 27–540 Sh Ct (Grampian) (Aberdeen).

18.125   This is a new provision, very similar to section 196 (property transactions: effect of subsequent affirmation): see paragraphs 18.58-18.60 above. Since the making of loans etc in contravention of s 330 of the 1985 Act was illegal, they were incapable of ratification by the shareholders.[191] In *Ultraframe (UK) Ltd v Fielding*,[192] Lewison J held that an arrangement which was voidable through failure to comply with the 1985 Act, s 320 (the predecessor of s 190) could be affirmed by the liquidator when the company subsequently entered insolvent liquidation: see paragraph 18.61 above. Similar reasoning may apply to transactions and arrangements entered into in breach of ss 197, 198, 200, and 201.

E.   Payments for Loss of Office

(1)   The meaning of 'payment for loss of office'

18.126   Sections 215–22 deal with payments for loss of office.[193] These are payments made to a director (or former director) to compensate him for ceasing to be a director, or for losing any other office or employment with the company or a subsidiary of the company. They also include payments made in connection with retirement. Members' approval is required for these payments.

18.127   With one exception,[194] and subject to transitional provisions,[195] nothing in ss 215–22 applies in relation to a payment for loss of office to a director of a quoted company.[196] Special provision is now made in respect of directors of quoted companies by Chapter 4A (Directors of Quoted Companies: Special Provisions), ss 226A–F: see 18.172 below.

18.128   Section 215(1) states that, for the purposes of these provisions, 'payment for loss of office' means a payment made to a director or past director of a company:[197]

    (a)   by way of compensation for loss of office as director of the company,

    (b)   by way of compensation for loss, while director of the company or in connection with his ceasing to be a director of it, of—

        (i)   any other office or employment in connection with the management of the affairs of the company, or

        (ii)   any office (as director or otherwise) or employment in connection with the management of the affairs of any subsidiary undertaking of the company,

    (c)   as consideration for or in connection with his retirement from his office as director of the company, or

    (d)   as consideration for or in connection with his retirement, while director of the company or in connection with his ceasing to be a director of it, from—

        (i)   any other office or employment in connection with the management of the affairs of the company, or

---

[191]   *Re DPR Futures Ltd* [1989] BCLC 634, 638.

[192]   [2005] EWHC 1638 (Ch) at paras 1440–1.

[193]   In force on 1 October 2007. For transitional provisions, see: 2006 Act Commencement Order No 3, Sch 3, paras 12(1) to (4).

[194]   ie a payment to which s 226C does not apply by virtue of s 226D(6): s 215(5), added by the Enterprise and Regulatory Reform Act 2013, s 81(4), with effect from 1 October 2013 (SI 2013/2227, art 2(h)) subject to transitional provisions in s 82(3)–(5) of the 2013 Act.

[195]   See para 18.172 below.

[196]   ie as defined in 2006 Act, Part 15 at s 385(2): s 226A(1).

[197]   2006 Act, s 215 is a new provision.

(ii) any office (as director or otherwise) or employment in connection with the management of the affairs of any subsidiary undertaking of the company.

By s 215(2) references to 'compensation' and 'consideration' include benefits otherwise than in cash and references to 'payment' have a corresponding meaning. By s 215(3) payment to a person connected with a director, or payment to any person at the direction of, or for the benefit of, a director or a person connected with him, is treated as payment to the director. By s 215(4) references to payment by a person include payment by another person at the direction of, or on behalf of, the person referred to. **18.129**

For the purposes of these provisions, references to a director include a shadow director, but any reference in those provisions to loss of office as a director does not apply in relation to loss of a person's status as a shadow director.[198] They also apply to former directors, so that it is not possible to evade the provisions by resigning prior to payment. The court would be expected to treat resignation and payment as part of a single operation.[199] **18.130**

There are three categories of payments, which categories may overlap: **18.131**

(1) Under s 217, members' approval is required if a company wishes to make a payment for loss of office to one of its directors or a director of its holding company.

(2) Under s 218, members' approval is required if any person (including the company or anyone else) wishes to make a payment for loss of office to a director of the company in connection with the transfer of the whole or any part of the undertaking of the property of the company or of a subsidiary of the company.

(3) Under s 219, in the case of a payment for loss of office to a director of the company in connection with the transfer of shares in the company or in a subsidiary of the company resulting from a takeover bid, approval is required of the holders of the shares to which the bid relates and of any other holder of shares of the same class. In what follows, payments by a company for loss of office under s 217 are dealt with first, followed by payments in connection with transfer of undertaking etc (s 218) and payment in connection with share transfer (s 219).

(2) Payments by company

Section 217 states the prohibition: **18.132**

(1) A company may not make a payment for loss of office to a director of the company unless the payment has been approved by a resolution of the members of the company.

(2) A company may not make a payment for loss of office to a director of its holding company unless the payment has been approved by a resolution of each of those companies.

Section 217(3) deals with the requirements for obtaining members' approval in much the same way as applied to ss 197, 198, 200, and 201:[200] **18.133**

(3) A resolution approving a payment to which this section applies must not be passed unless a memorandum setting out particulars of the proposed payment (including its amount) is made available to the members of the company whose approval is sought—

---

[198] 2006 Act, s 223(1)(d) and (2). In respect of Northern Rock plc, Bradford & Bingley plc, Heritable Bank plc, and Dunfermline Building Society, whilst owned by the Treasury certain persons will not be considered shadow directors for the purposes of ss 215–22: see n 8 above.

[199] Hansard, HL GC Day 4, vol 678, cols 355–6 (9 February 2006).

[200] For the meaning of 'eligible member' see Part 13, Chapter 2, s 289 and para 18.18 above. Where there has been an accidental failure to send the requisite memorandum s 224 applies.

(a) in the case of a written resolution, by being sent or submitted to every eligible member at or before the time at which the proposed resolution is sent or submitted to him;

(b) in the case of a resolution at a meeting, by being made available for inspection by the members both—

   (i) at the company's registered office for not less than 15 days ending with the date of the meeting, and

   (ii) at the meeting itself.

18.134 No approval is required under s 217 on the part of the members of a body corporate that is not a UK-registered company, or is a wholly-owned subsidiary of another body corporate.

18.135 The provisions requiring prior[201] approval of members before a company makes a payment for loss of office now embodied in s 217 are derived from the 1985 Act, ss 312 and 316(3).[202] The Act makes very significant amendments, bolstering considerably the protection that had been given by the 1985 Act. Some understanding of the law as it appeared to be under the 1985 Act assists in understanding the new provisions.

18.136 The 1985 Act, s 312 stated that:

> It is not lawful for a company to make to a director of the company any payment by way of compensation for loss of office, or as consideration for or in connection with his retirement from office, without particulars of the proposed payment (including its amount) being disclosed to members of the company and the proposal being approved by the company.

Very broadly (and somewhat inaccurately) speaking, s 312 thus covered, in abbreviated form, what is now included in s 217(1). By reason of the 1985 Act, s 316(3), such payments did not include 'any bona fide payment by way of damages for breach of contract or by way of pension in respect of past services'. Section 220 of the Act covers similar ground, though is much expanded from the 1985 Act, s 316(3).

18.137 The 1985 Act, ss 312 and 316(3) had never been interpreted by the House of Lords or Court of Appeal, and, it appears, had only twice been interpreted by the English courts at all.[203] A similar provision in New Zealand legislation had, however, come before the Privy Council in *Taupo Totara Timber Co Ltd v Rowe*.[204] The Privy Council interpreted that provision restrictively, apparently concluding, first, that the only payments which were covered by the equivalent of s 312 were payments made to the director for the loss of his office *as director*, and thus the section did not cover payments made, for example, in respect of the termination of a contract of service held by that director; and secondly, the provisions only

---

[201] The fact that approval must be given before payment is made is clear from the reference to 'proposed payment' in s 217(3). No provision is made in ss 215–22 for ratification or affirmation of a payment made without prior approval: compare and contrast s 196 of the Act regarding affirmation of substantial property transactions, and s 214 regarding affirmation of loans etc made without prior member approval. It might nonetheless be possible for the company (presumably acting in general meeting, and not by its board), or a liquidator or administrator, to waive any remedies that it holds arising from failure to comply with s 217: cf *Ultraframe (UK) Ltd v Fielding* [2005] EWHC 1638 (Ch) at paras 1440–1, decided under the predecessor of ss 190–6 of the Act (substantial property transactions) and discussed at para 18.61 above.

[202] They have their origin in Companies Act 1947, s 36(1).

[203] *Re Duomatic Ltd* [1969] 2 Ch 365 (considering 1948 Act, s 191, the predecessor of 1985 Act, s 312) and *Gooding v Cater* (unreported) 13 March 1989, Edward Nugee QC.

[204] [1978] AC 537.

applied to uncovenanted (ie voluntary) payments. Thus, if the company was legally liable to make certain payments under the contract or terms of office of the director, s 312 did not apply at all. This interpretation was adopted and applied by the English and Scottish Courts in deciding the scope of the 1985 Act, ss 312 and 316(3).[205]

The second finding in the *Taupo* case, that the provisions do not apply to uncovenanted pay- **18.138** ments, has been adopted, clarified, and expanded somewhat in the new legislation.[206] By reason of s 220(1)(a), approval is not required under s 217 for a payment made in good faith in discharge of an existing legal obligation.

As to the other conclusion in the *Taupo* case (ie the legislation covered only payments made **18.139** to the director for the loss of his office *as director*), this has been reversed by the new provisions. The limited operation of the previous legislation as reflected in the *Taupo* case is now covered by s 215(1)(a) (and s 215(1)(c) in respect of retirement). The broad wording of s 215(1)(b) (and in connection with retirement from office, 215(1)(d)) make clear that payments for loss of office include not only loss of office as director, but also loss of any other office or employment[207] in connection with the management of the affairs of the company. Section 215(1)(b)(ii) also covers payments made by way of compensation for loss of any office (as director or otherwise) or employment in connection with the management of the affairs of any subsidiary undertaking of the company. There will in all cases remain the preliminary question as to whether any payment is indeed made by way of compensation for loss of office etc or as consideration for or in connection with a director's retirement from office, as opposed, for example, to some new role which the director might be taking up with the company.[208]

The ambit of the provisions has been extended from those under the 1985 Act in several **18.140** other ways:

(1) By reason of s 217(2), payment for loss of office is prohibited where the payment is made to a director of the holding company, and in such case the members of both the company and the holding company must approve the payment. This covers the situation where a director of a holding company is employed by the subsidiary, as not infrequently occurs where one subsidiary in a group employs all employees in the group.

(2) Section 217 applies both to directors and to *past* directors of a company.[209] The wording is designed to close a possible loophole under the 1985 Act whereby, if the director resigned his office prior to payment, arguably members' approval was not required.

---

[205] In England in *Gooding v Cater* (unreported) 13 March 1989, Edward Nugee QC followed the second holding in the *Taupo* case. He also held that the payment of damages for wrongful dismissal or of an agreed sum in settlement of a right to compensation for premature termination of a contract of employment were payments which a company was legally obliged to make, and thus fell outside s 312. *Sed quaere*: such payments would have fallen within 1985 Act, s 316(3), now s 220. In Scotland: *Lander v Pict Petroleum Ltd* [1998] BCC 248, 253, 254, OH; *Mercer v Heart of Midlothian plc* [2002] SLT 945, 951–3, OH.

[206] By reason of the reference to 'good faith' in s 220(1), and the wording of s 220(1)(a), it appears that no members' approval will be required where the company in good faith but mistakenly miscalculates the extent of the existing legal obligation (s 220(1)(a)).

[207] 'Employment' is not defined: compare s 188(7) in the context of directors' long-term service contracts. The context suggests that 'employment' will be interpreted broadly.

[208] See *Mercer v Heart of Midlothian plc* [2002] SLT 945, 952, where the benefits to the retiring director were held referable not to his retirement, but to his new appointment as life president. Lord MacFayden held, following *Lincoln Mills (Aust) Ltd v Gough* [1964] VR 193, that the court must have regard to 'the nature and circumstances' of the payment in order to determine 'its true character'.

[209] 2006 Act, s 215(1).

(3) Section 217 treats payments to a person connected with a director, or payment to any person at the direction of, or for the benefit of, a director or a person connected with him, as payment to the director.[210]

(4) References to 'compensation' and 'consideration' include benefits[211] otherwise than in cash, and references to 'payment' in Part 10, Chapter 4 have a corresponding meaning.[212] Under the 1985 Act, it had been held that the focus of s 312 was on the depletion of assets of the company as opposed to the benefit received by the director.[213]

Exceptions

18.141 There are two main exceptions, namely (a) exception for payments in discharge of legal obligations etc and (b) exception for small payments.

18.142 Section 220(1) provides that members' approval is not required under s 217[214] for a payment[215] made in good faith:

(a) in discharge of an existing legal obligation ...,
(b) by way of damages for breach of such an obligation,
(c) by way of settlement or compromise in connection with the termination of a person's office or employment, or
(d) by way of pension in respect of past services.[216]

By s 220(2), in relation to a payment within s 217, 'an existing legal obligation' means 'an obligation of the company, or any body corporate associated with it, that was not entered into in connection with, or in consequence of, the event giving rise to the payment for loss of office'.[217] This definition applies where the payment is also within ss 218 or 219.[218] A payment part of which falls within s 220(1) and part of which does not is treated as if the parts were separate payments.[219]

---

[210] 2006 Act, s 215(3).

[211] During debates on what is now s 176 of the Act, the Solicitor General stated: 'In using the word "benefit", we intend the ordinary dictionary definition of the word. The "Oxford English Dictionary" defines it as a favourable or helpful factor, circumstance, advantage or profit' (HC Comm D, col 622 (11 July 2006)). Reference was also made to the wide interpretation of 'benefit' in another context in *Cronin v Grierson* [1968] AC 895, HL.

[212] 2006 Act, s 215(2). In *Mercer v Heart of Midlothian plc* [2002] SLT 945, 953, Lord MacFayden provisionally concluded that 'payment' under s 312 of the 1985 Act did not include solely transfers of money.

[213] The *Mercer* case, above. The benefits to the former director included two seats in the directors' box at Tynecastle on match days to watch Hearts, and Lord MacFayden concluded, perhaps unsurprisingly, that no cost to the company in allowing the director to enjoy such privileges was properly alleged.

[214] 2006 Act, s 220 applies also to payments under s 218 (payment in connection with transfer or undertaking etc) and s 219 (payment in connection with share transfer): see further below.

[215] By reason of 2006 Act, s 215(3), 'payment' in s 220 has the extended meaning given by s 215(2), and hence extends to the provision of benefits otherwise than in cash.

[216] The wording 'by way of pension in respect of past services' repeats the wording found in 1985 Act, s 316(3). 'Pension' was there defined as including 'any superannuation allowance, superannuation gratuity or similar payment'. The Act includes no definition of 'Pension', though it will doubtless be interpreted as covering all payments specifically mentioned in the former definition. The exception in s 220(1)(d) presumably applies where the director had no entitlement to any pension.

[217] The point of s 220(2) is to close a potential loophole whereby s 217 could be circumvented by the company entering into a binding agreement with the director shortly before his loss of office, and then making the payment in discharge of the company's legal obligations under that agreement. The possible existence of this loophole under the 1985 Act was discussed in *Mercer v Heart of Midlothian plc* [2002] SLT 945, 952, OH.

[218] 2006 Act, s 220(4).

[219] 2006 Act, s 220(5).

The wording of s 220(1)(c) will cover settlement or compromise of any statutory claims **18.143** for unfair dismissal and redundancy which were, it seems, outside the wording of the 1985 Act, s 316(3), which referred only to 'bona fide payment by way of damages for breach of contract'.

By s 221(1), which is a wholly new provision, approval is also not required under s 217 if: **18.144**

(a) the payment in question is made by the company or one of its subsidiaries, and
(b) the amount or value of the payment, together with the amount or value of any other relevant payments, does not exceed £200.[220]

In s 221, 'payment' has the extended meaning given in s 215(3) and (4) (paragraph 18.129 above). By s 221(2) 'other relevant payments' are payments for loss of office in relation to which, in relation to s 217, the conditions of s 221(3) are met, namely that the other payment was or is paid:

(a) by the company making the payment in question or any of its subsidiaries[221]
(b) to the director to whom that payment is made[222] and
(c) in connection with the same event.

Civil consequences of payments made without approval

By s 222, if a payment is made in contravention of s 217: **18.145**

(a) it is held by the recipient on trust for the company making the payment, and
(b) any director who authorised the payment is jointly and severally liable to indemnify the company that made the payment for any loss resulting from it.

If the payment is in contravention of s 217 and also of s 218 or 219, the civil consequences in respect of the latter provisions apply (paragraphs 18.160–18.162 and 18.170–18.171 below), unless, in the case of s 219, the court otherwise orders.[223]

The civil consequences of a payment made in contravention of s 217 have been spelt out for **18.146** the first time.[224] The provision whereby any payment is held on trust by the recipient for the company which made the payment (s 221(1)(a)) applies not only to any director recipient, but to any person who falls within s 215(3) of the Act.

(3) Payment in connection with transfer of undertaking etc

Section 218[225] requires members' approval of any payment for loss of office in connection **18.147** with the transfer of the whole or any part of the undertaking or property of the company. 'Payment for loss of office' has the meaning stated in s 215 (paragraphs 18.126–18.131 above).

---

[220] 2006 Act, s 221 applies also to payments under s 218 (payment in connection with transfer or undertaking etc) and s 219 (payment in connection with share transfer): see further below. The Secretary of State has the power to raise the £200 limit: s 258.

[221] See n 219 above.

[222] For these purposes, payment to a person connected with a director, or payment to any person at the direction of, or for the benefit of, a director or person connected with him, is treated as payment to the director: s 215(3).

[223] 2006 Act, s 222(4) and (5).

[224] Under the former law (where payment without prior approval was not lawful), the remedies available were those which applied to a misapplication of the company's funds: *Re Duomatic Ltd* [1969] 2 Ch 365, 374–5.

[225] 2006 Act, s 218 derives from 1985 Act, ss 313 and 316 and ultimately the Companies Act 1928.

18.148 Under s 216(1)[226] the provisions of sub-s (2) apply to identify amounts to be taken to be payments for loss of office where in connection with any transfer as is mentioned in s 218 a director of the company:

(a) is to cease to hold office, or

(b) is to cease to be the holder of—

    (i) any other office or employment in connection with the management of the affairs of the company, or

    (ii) any office (as director or otherwise) or employment in connection with the management of the affairs of any subsidiary undertaking of the company.

Subsection (2) provides:

If in connection with any such transfer—

(a) the price to be paid to the director for any shares in the company held by him is in excess of the price which could at the time have been obtained by other holders of like shares, or

(b) any valuable consideration is given to the director by a person other than the company, the excess or, as the case may be, the money value of the consideration is taken for the purposes of s 218[227] to have been a payment for loss of office.

18.149 Section 216 effectively ensures that certain 'disguised' payments for loss of office do not slip through the net, and require prior members' approval. Thus, where, in connection with a transfer of undertaking or property of a company,[228] a director is paid an inflated price in respect of shares held by him in the company (s 216(2)(a)), the excess value of the consideration is taken to have been a payment for loss of office; and if a person other than the company gives any valuable consideration to the director in connection with such a transfer, the value of the consideration is taken to have been a payment for loss of office (s 216(2)(b)).

18.150 The conditions for the requirement of members' approval are stated in s 218(1), (2), and (5):

(1) No payment for loss of office may be made by any person to a director of a company in connection with the transfer of the whole or any part of the undertaking or property of the company unless the payment has been approved by a resolution of the members of the company.

(2) No payment for loss of office may be made by any person to a director of a company in connection with the transfer of the whole or any part of the undertaking or property of a subsidiary of the company unless the payment has been approved by a resolution of the members of each of the companies. …

(5) A payment made in pursuance of an arrangement[229]—

    (a) entered into as part of the agreement for the transfer in question, or within one year before or two years after that agreement, and

---

[226] The section, which is substantially derived from 1985 Act, s 316(2), also applies to payments within s 219 (payment in connection with share transfer): see para 18.163 below.

[227] 2006 Act, s 216(2) also applies to s 219 (payment in connection with share transfer): see paras 18.163 *et seq* below.

[228] 2006 Act, s 216(2) in part achieves its expansive effect by applying wherever the excessive price for the shares, or the valuable consideration given by a person other than the company, is 'in connection with' the transfer identified in s 218—the payment need not, it appears, be by way of compensation etc as specified in the opening words of each of s 215(1)(a)–(b). It is not clear what the addition of the words 'by a person other than the company' are intended to add to s 216(2)(b): such words did not appear in s 316(2)(b) of the 1985 Act, and ss 218 and 219 apply to payments 'by any person'.

[229] On the meaning of 'arrangement' in the context of s 190 of the Act (substantial property transactions) see para 18.37 above.

(b) to which the company whose undertaking or property is transferred, or any person to whom the transfer is made, is privy,

is presumed, except in so far as the contrary is shown, to be a payment to which this section applies.

The requirements for members' approval in respect of payments for loss of office in connection with transfers of undertaking, set out in s 218(3), are the same as those applicable to payments for loss of office under s 217 (paragraph 18.133 above). Section 224, dealing with an accidental failure to send the requisite memorandum, also applies. **18.151**

Section 218(4) of the Act creates the same exception as s 217(4) in respect of members of a body corporate that is not a UK-registered company or is a wholly-owned subsidiary of another body corporate. **18.152**

By s 218(2) of the Act, the requirement for prior members' approval is extended so as now to cover payments to a director of a company in connection with the transfer of the whole or any part of the undertaking or property of the subsidiary of the company. In contrast to s 219, where a director or his associate are precluded from voting on the resolution, a transferee who also holds shares in the company, and his associates, are permitted to vote.[230] **18.153**

No reported decision had considered the 1985 Act, ss 313 and 316 in so far as they applied to company approval for payments for loss of or retirement from office. The case law cited at paragraphs 18.137–18.139 above, which considered statutory predecessors of the current s 216, was of persuasive authority on s 313. In particular, the decision of the Privy Council in *Taupo Totara Timber Co Ltd v Rowe*,[231] and those cases which followed its reasoning, suggested that s 313 did not apply to covenanted payments, reasoning which was endorsed by the Law Commission and CLR. Parliament followed this reasoning, and as with s 217, s 218 does not apply to covenanted payments: see s 220(1)(a). **18.154**

As to the other aspect of the decision in the *Taupo* case, limiting the scope of the 1985 Act, s 312 to payments made to the director for the loss of his office *as director*, it is doubtful that that reasoning ever applied to the predecessor of s 218 by reason of the wide wording of s 316(2)(b) of the 1985 Act. In any event, by reason of s 215 of the Act, the scope of s 218 extends to the offices and employment covered by the broad wording of s 215(1). It is further made express that s 218 applies to past directors (s 215(1)), that references to 'compensation' and 'consideration' include benefits otherwise than in cash, references to 'payment' having a corresponding meaning (s 215(2)), that s 218 includes payment to persons connected with the director, and to any person at the direction of, or for the benefit of, a director or a person connected with him (s 215(3)) and to any person at the direction of, or for the benefit of, a director or a person connected with him (s 215(3)) and that references to payment by a person include payment by another person at the direction of, or on behalf of, the person referred to (s 215(4)). **18.155**

---

[230] See Law Commission Report, *Company Directors: Regulating Conflicts of Interest and Formulating a Statement of Duties*, No 261, para 7.64 for the distinction between the two sections: the Law Commission considered that if the effect of a resolution under s 218 was to confer a benefit on the majority who caused it to be passed at the expense of the minority, the resolution was likely to be ineffective on the ground that it is a fraud on the minority.

[231] [1978] AC 537.

18.156 A rebuttable statutory presumption is created by s 218(5) whereby certain payments are presumed to be covered by s 218.[232] Despite the fact that s 218 applies to payments for loss of office to a director of a company in connection with the transfer of a subsidiary's undertaking or property, the presumption will apply only where, inter alia, the company whose undertaking or property is transferred (and not the company in respect of which the director holds office for the purposes of s 218(2)) is privy to the arrangement.[233]

Exceptions

18.157 As with payments falling within ss 217 and 219, there are two exceptions, namely exception for payments in discharge of legal obligations etc and exception for small payments, but with some modifications.

18.158 By s 220(1), members' approval is not required under s 218 for a payment made in good faith in discharge of 'an existing legal obligation', by way of damages for breach of such an obligation, by way of settlement or compromise in connection with the termination of a person's office or employment, or by way of pension in respect of past services (paragraph 18.142 above). However, in relation to payments within ss 218 and 219, the words 'an existing legal obligation' have a different meaning from that which applies in respect of payments within s 217. In relation to payments under ss 218 and 219, s 220(3) provides that 'an existing legal obligation' means 'an obligation of the person making the payment that was not entered into for the purposes of, in connection with or in consequence of, the transfer in question'. In the case of a payment within both ss 217 and 218, the definition in s 220(2) (paragraph 18.142 above) applies and s 220(3) does not apply.[234]

18.159 Section 221(1) provides that approval is not required under s 218 if the payment in question is made by the company or one of its subsidiaries, and the amount or value of the payment, together with the amount or value of any 'other relevant payments', does not exceed £200 (paragraph 18.144 above). However, where the payment is one to which s 218 applies, the conditions which must be met for a payment for loss of office to be 'other relevant payments' differ from the conditions applicable to payments falling within s 217 and are stated in s 221(4):[235]

> (4) Where the payment in question is one to which section 218 or 219 applies (payment in connection with transfer of undertaking, property or shares), the conditions are that the other payment was (or is) paid in connection with the same transfer—
> (a) to the director to whom the payment in question was made, and
> (b) by the company making the payment or any of its subsidiaries.

Civil consequences of payments made without approval

18.160 Section 222(2) provides:

---

[232] 2006 Act, s 218(5) is substantially a re-enactment of 1985 Act, s 316(1), in so far as that subsection applied to payments in respect of a transfer of undertaking or property. 1985 Act, s 316(1) was limited in its operation to proceedings for recovery of a payment received by any person in trust by virtue of s 313(2): s 218(5) is not so limited.

[233] 2006 Act, s 218(5)(b).

[234] 2006 Act, s 220(4).

[235] 2006 Act, s 221(2) and (4).

If a payment is made in contravention of section 218 …, it is held by the recipient on trust for the company whose undertaking or property is or is proposed to be transferred.[236]

Section 222(2) is substantially a re-enactment of the 1985 Act, s 313(2). The wording has been altered and expanded in line with the new provisions found in s 218(2) (ie members' approval is now required for payment to a director where it is a subsidiary's undertaking or property which is transferred) and s 215(3) (whereby payments to persons connected with the director, and payments to third parties at the direction of, or for the benefit of, a director or person connected with him, are now treated as payments to the director). In contrast to the civil consequences applicable where a payment is made in breach of s 217, directors who authorized the payment are not liable under any provision of the statute to indemnify the company in respect of any loss resulting from it.

18.161

If a payment is made in contravention of both ss 217 and 218, s 222(2) applies rather than s 222(1).[237] It is not wholly clear how this provision is intended to apply. Presumably the remedies set out in s 222 operate to the exclusion of remedies under the common law:[238] though since ss 217, 218, (and 219) prohibit payments without the requisite approval, it is not beyond argument that, where the payments are made by the company, the usual remedies apply where directors misapply a company's property, and s 222 does not specifically exclude this conclusion. Assuming that s 222 implicitly excludes such common law remedies, the surprising effect of s 222(4) appears to be that where a payment falls within both ss 217 and 218, the liability of directors under s 222(1)(b) which would arise if the payment fell within s 217 alone is excluded.

18.162

(4) Payment in connection with share transfer: requirement of members' approval

Section 219 deals with payment to a director for loss of office in connection with share transfers resulting from a takeover bid.[239] Payment for loss of office has the meaning in s 215, and s 216 also applies to determine the amounts to be taken to be payments for loss of office (paragraphs 18.126–18.146 above). Section 219(1), (2), and (7) provides:

18.163

(1) No payment for loss of office may be made by any person to a director of a company in connection with a transfer of shares in the company, or in a subsidiary of the company, resulting from a takeover bid[240] unless the payment has been approved by a resolution of the relevant shareholders.

(2) The relevant shareholders are the holders of the shares to which the bid relates and any holders of shares of the same class as any of those shares. …

---

[236] Compare and contrast s 222(1) at para 18.144 above, setting out the civil consequences of a payment made in contravention of s 217, where the payment is held on trust for the company making the payment, and any director who authorized the payment is jointly and severally liable to indemnify that company for any loss resulting from it.

[237] 2006 Act, s 222(4).

[238] Unlike eg s 195 (property transactions: civil consequences of contravention) and 213(8) (loans etc: civil consequences of contravention), s 222 does not specifically preserve remedies which might arise under the general law.

[239] 2006 Act, s 219 derives from 1985 Act, ss 314–16 and ultimately the Companies Act 1928.

[240] 'Takeover bid' is not defined for the purposes of s 219. The definition in s 971 applies only for the purposes of Part 28 Chapter 2 of CA 2006; and the definitions in ss 943 and 953 apply only for the purposes of those sections.

(7) A payment made in pursuance of an arrangement[241]—

    (a) entered into as part of the agreement for the transfer in question, or within one year before or two years after that agreement, and

    (b) to which the company whose shares are the subject of the bid, or any person to whom the transfer is made, is privy,

is presumed, except in so far as the contrary is shown, to be a payment to which s 219 applies.

18.164 The requirements for members' approval in respect of payments for loss of office in connection with share transfers, set out in s 219(3), are the same as those applicable to payments for loss of office under ss 217 and 218 (paragraphs 18.132–18.162 above). However, s 219(4) and (5) contain special provisions to protect shareholders by preventing the person making the offer and his associates from voting on the resolution to approve the payment to the director:[242]

    (4) Neither the person making the offer, nor any associate of his (as defined in section 988), is entitled to vote on the resolution, but—

        (a) where the resolution is proposed as a written resolution, they are entitled (if they would otherwise be so entitled) to be sent a copy of it, and

        (b) at any meeting to consider the resolution they are entitled (if they would otherwise be so entitled) to be given notice of the meeting, to attend and speak and if present (in person or by proxy) to count towards the quorum.

    (5) If at a meeting to consider the resolution a quorum is not present, and after the meeting has been adjourned to a later date a quorum is again not present, the payment is deemed to have been approved.

18.165 No approval is required under s 217 on the part of the members of a body corporate that is not a UK-registered company, or is a wholly-owned subsidiary of another body corporate.[243]

18.166 Under the 1985 Act, ss 314–16, where a takeover offer or similar conditional offer for shares was made in respect of shares in a company, a director to whom a payment was to be made by way of compensation for loss of office in connection with such offer was obliged to take all reasonable steps to secure that particulars of the proposed payment were included in any notice to the shareholders of the offer made for the shares.[244] If the director failed to comply with this duty, or the making of the payment was not approved by a meeting by the shareholders to whom the offer related (and those in the same class) the payment was held in trust for the shareholders who sold their shares as a result of the offer, and the costs of distributing the payment to such persons was again to be borne by the director. Section 219 removes the duty on the director to disclose particulars of a proposed payment for loss of office in connection with a share transfer to the target shareholders. The requirement that the relevant shareholders (ie the shareholders to whom the bid relates, or who are in the same class) should approve the proposed payment by resolution is retained, consonant with the similar requirements for prior approval in ss 217 and 218.[245] The rationale is to avoid the risk that

---

[241] On the meaning of 'arrangement' in the context of s 190 of the Act (substantial property transactions) see para 18.37 above.

[242] This was on the recommendation of the Law Commission (Hansard, HL GC Day 4, vol 678, cols 358, 359 (9 February 2006)).

[243] 2006 Act, s 219(6).

[244] 1985 Act, s 314(1) and (2).

[245] Under 1985 Act, s 314(3), if the director failed to take the steps set out in s 314 (ie inclusion of particulars of the proposed payment in the offer document), or any person properly required by the director to include such particulars failed to do so, they were liable to a fine. No such provision is included in the Act. Lord Sainsbury

directors may obtain advantageous payments from the persons launching the takeover bid which should in fact go towards the members in return for their shares.[246]

The observations in paragraphs 18.154–18.155 concerning the scope of s 218 apply equally to s 219. **18.167**

A rebuttable statutory presumption is created by s 219(7) whereby certain payments are presumed to be covered by s 219. Section 219(7) is substantially a re-enactment of the 1985 Act, s 316(1), in so far as that subsection applied to payments held on trust in consequence of a director's failure to disclose a payment for loss of office to be made in connection with a takeover.[247] **18.168**

Exceptions

As with payments falling within ss 217 and 218, there are two exceptions, namely an exception for payments in discharge of legal obligations etc (s 220) and an exception for small payments (s 221). In respect of both exceptions, the position under s 219 is the same as under s 218 (paragraphs 18.150–18.156 above). **18.169**

Civil consequence of payments made without approval

Section 222(3) provides: **18.170**

> (3) If a payment is made in contravention of section 219 …—
>   (a) it is held by the recipient on trust for persons who have sold their shares as a result of the offer made, and
>   (b) the expenses incurred by the recipient in distributing that sum amongst those persons are to be borne by him and not retained out of that sum.[248]

Section 222(3) is substantially a re-enactment of the 1985 Act, s 315(1). The wording has been altered and expanded in line with the new provisions found in s 215(3) (whereby payments to persons connected with the director, and payments to third parties at the direction of, or for the benefit of, a director or person connected with him, are now treated as payments to the director). In contrast to the civil consequences applicable where a payment is made in breach of s 217, directors who authorized the payment are not liable under any provision of the statute to indemnify the company in respect of any loss resulting from it. The 1985 Act imposed no such liability either.[249] If a payment is made in contravention of ss 217 and 219, s 222(3) applies rather than s 222(1), unless the court directs otherwise.[250] This provides clarification of the law: it is plainly **18.171**

---

described such a provision, and the duty cast upon a director under 314(2), as 'over-regulatory', and stated that the civil consequences of failure to obtain approval should be sufficient, in line with the removal of criminal sanction for all breaches in this Chapter of the Act: Hansard, HL GC Day 4, vol 678, cols 358–9 (9 February 2006).

[246] Per Lord Sainsbury, Hansard, HL GC Day 4, vol 678, col 358 (9 February 2006).

[247] 1985 Act, s 316(1) was limited in its operation to proceedings for recovery of a payment received by any person in trust by virtue of s 315(1): s 219(7) is not so limited.

[248] Compare and contrast s 222(1) at paras 18.145–18.146 above, setting out the civil consequences of a payment made in contravention of s 217, where the payment is held on trust for the company making the payment, and any director who authorized the payment is jointly and severally liable to indemnify that company for any loss resulting from it; and s 222(2) at paras 18.160–18.162 above, setting out the civil consequences of a payment made in contravention of s 218, where the payment is held on trust for the company whose undertaking is or is proposed to be transferred.

[249] 1985 Act, s 315(1). The Law Commission recommended that s 315(1) be expanded so as to impose liability on authorizing directors: Law Commission Report, *Company Directors: Regulating Conflicts of Interest and Formulating a Statement of Duties*, No 261, paras 7.81–7.86.

[250] 2006 Act, s 222(5).

right that where ss 217 and 219 both apply, it is the shareholders who have lost out who should be compensated, not the company as such (since of course benefit to the company will not benefit the shareholders who have sold their shares). For reasons similar to those above at paragraph 18.162, in certain respects it is not clear how s 222(5) will operate in practice.

F. Directors of Quoted Companies: Special Provision

18.172   Chapter 4A, ss 226A–226F,[251] restricts the circumstances in which a quoted company[252] may make a 'remuneration payment' to a person who is, or is to be, or has been, a director of the quoted company, or in which any person may make a 'payment for loss of office' to such a person. The broad scheme of Chapter 4A is:

(1) Section 226A contains certain key definitions, including 'remuneration payment', 'payment for loss of office' and 'directors' remuneration policy';

(2) Section 226B prohibits a quoted company from making a 'remuneration payment' to a person who is, or is to be, or has been, a director of the company unless the payment is consistent with the approved 'directors' remuneration policy' or the payment is approved by resolution of the members of the company;

(3) Section 226C prohibits any person from making a 'payment for loss of office' to a person who is, or is to be, or has been, a director of a quoted company unless, again, the payment is consistent with the approved 'directors' remuneration policy' or approved by a resolution of the members;

(4) Section 226D specifies, *inter alia*, the process which must be adopted if the 'remuneration payment' or 'payment for loss of office' is to be approved by the members;

(5) Section 226E sets out the civil consequences of making a payment in contravention of sections 226B or 226C;

(6) Section 226F deals with the interaction of Chapter 4 and Chapter 4A: Chapter 4A does not affect any requirement for member approval which applies in relation to the company under Chapter 4 (eg substantial property transactions, loans and certain credit transactions), but where the making of a payment to which s 226B or 226C applies requires member approval under Chapter 4, approval obtained for the purposes of Chapter 4 is to be treated as satisfying the members' approval requirements of section 226B or 226 C.[253]

(1) Definitions

18.173   Section 226A(1) contains four key definitions, namely 'directors' remuneration policy, 'quoted company', 'remuneration payment', and 'payment for loss of office'.

18.174   'Directors' remuneration policy' means the policy of a quoted company with respect to the making of remuneration payments and payments for loss of office. Under s 420 of the Act, the directors of a quoted company are obliged to prepare a directors' remuneration report for each

---

[251]   Inserted by the Enterprise and Regulatory Reform Act 2013, s 80 as from 1 October 2013. Section 82 of that Act introduced transitional provisions relevant to Chapter 4A. Chapter 4A does not apply in relation to remuneration payments or payments for loss of office that are required to be made under an agreement entered into before 27 June 2012 or in consequence of any other obligation arising before that date: (s 82(3)). An agreement entered into, or any other obligation arising, before 27 June 2012 that is modified or renewed on or after that date is to be treated for the purposes of s 82(3) as having been entered into or (as the case may be) as having arisen on the date on which it was modified or renewed: (s 82(4)). Where s 82(3) applies, then the amendment made by s 81(4) (adding a new s 215(5) to the Act) does not apply: (s 82(5)).

[252]   As defined in Part 15 of the 2006 Act, at s 385(2): s 226A(1).

[253]   ie of s 226B(1)(b) or s 226C(1)(b), as applicable.

of the financial years of the company. Under s 421, the Secretary of State may make provision by regulations as to the content of the report; and under s 421(2A),[254] the regulations must provide that any information required to be included in the report as to the policy of the company with respect to the making of remuneration payments and payments for loss of office (as defined in Chapter 4A) is to be set out in a separate part of the report. Parts 4 and 6 of Schedule 8 to the Large and Medium-Sized Companies and Groups (Accounts and Reports) Regulations 2008[255] specify the information which the directors' remuneration report must include in respect of the directors' remuneration policy and any revision of that policy, including, per para 24(3), all those matters for which the company requires approval under Chapter 4A. Section 422A[256] sets out requirements where the directors' remuneration policy set out in a quoted company's directors' remuneration report may be revised, and allows for regulations to make provision as to what information is to be contained and how it is to be set out (as referred to above). Section 439A[257] makes provision for the approval of the directors' remuneration policy.

'Quoted company' has the same meaning as in Part 15 of the Act (ie the meaning in section 385(2)). **18.175**

'Remuneration payment' means any form of payment or other benefit made to or otherwise conferred on a person as consideration for the person— **18.176**

(a) holding, agreeing to hold or having held office as a director of a company, or
(b) holding, agreeing to hold or having held, during a period when the person is or was such a director—
    (i) any other office or employment in connection with the management of the affairs of the company, or
    (ii) any office (as director or otherwise) or employment in connection with management of the company, or
other than a payment for loss of office.

'Payment for loss of office' in Chapter 4A has the same meaning as in Chapter 4 of Part 10 (ie as defined in section 215 of the Act: see 18.128 above): but that definition is extended in respect of 'relevant transfers' by section 226A(2)–(4). The extended definition is discussed below, 18.184, under s 226C (Loss of office payments). **18.177**

Section 226A(6)–(9) clarify and extend the meaning of other terms used in the course of Chapter 4A, and are considered as appropriate below. **18.178**

(2) Remuneration Payments

Section 226B(1) states: **18.179**
    (1) A quoted company may not make a remuneration payment to a person who is, or is to be or has been, a director[258] of the company unless—
        (a) the payment is consistent with the approved directors' remuneration policy, or
        (b) the payment is approved by resolution of the members of the company.

---

[254] Added by the Enterprise and Regulatory Reform Act 2013, s 79(1).
[255] SI 2008/410; as amended by SI 2013/1981.
[256] Added by the Enterprise and Regulatory Reform Act 2013, s 79(2).
[257] Added by the Enterprise and Regulatory Reform Act 2013, s 79(4).
[258] A director includes a shadow director: s 226A(9).

18.180 The approved directors' remuneration policy is the most recent remuneration policy to have been approved by a resolution passed by the members of the company in general meeting (ie in accordance with s 439A of the Act).[259]

18.181 The payment by a quoted company referred to in s 226B(1) includes a payment by another person at the direction of, or on behalf of, the company.[260]

18.182 Payment to a person (B) who is, has been or is to be, a director of the company includes a payment to a person connected with B,[261] or a payment to a person at the direction of, or for the benefit of, B or a person connected with B.[262]

18.183 Nothing in s 226B authorizes the making of a remuneration payment in contravention of the articles of the company concerned.[263] Nor does anything in s 226B apply in relation to a remuneration payment made to a person who is, or is to be, or has been, a director of a quoted company before the earlier of (a) the end of the first financial year of the company to begin on or after the day on which it becomes a quoted company, and (b) the date from which the company's first director's remuneration policy to be approved under s 439A of the Act takes effect.[264]

(3) Loss of Office Payments

18.184 Section 226C(1) states:

> No payment for loss of office may be made by any person to a person who is, or has been, a director[265] of a quoted company unless—
>
> (a) the payment is consistent with the approved directors' remuneration policy, or
> (b) the payment is approved by resolution of the members of the company.

18.185 As under s 226B(2), the approved directors' remuneration policy is the most recent remuneration policy to have been approved by a resolution passed by the members of the company in general meeting (ie in accordance with s 439A of the Act).[266]

18.186 Payment to a person (B) who is, or has been, a director of the company includes a payment to a person connected[267] with B,[268] or a payment to a person at the direction or, or for the benefit of, B or a person connected with B.[269]

18.187 As stated above, 'payment for loss of office' has the same meaning as in s 215, but the meaning is extended for certain purposes by s 226A(2)–(4). Those subsections apply in respect of

---

[259] 2006 Act, s 226B(2).

[260] 2006 Act, s 226A(6).

[261] 2006 Act, s 226A(7)(a). By s 226A(8), s 252 of the Act applies for the purpose of determining whether a person is connected with a person who has been, or is to be, a director of a company as it applies for the purposes of determining whether a person is connected with a director.

[262] 2006 Act, s 226A(7)(b).

[263] 2006 Act, s 226D(5).

[264] 2006 Act, s 226D(6).

[265] A director includes a shadow director but references to loss of office as a director do not include loss of a person's status as a shadow director: s 226A(9).

[266] 2006 Act, s 226C(2).

[267] Section 252 of the Act applies for the purpose of determining whether a person is connected with a person who has been a director of a company as it applies for the purposes of determining whether a person is connected with a director: s 226A(8).

[268] 2006 Act, s 226A(7)(a).

[269] 2006 Act, s 226A(7)(b).

a 'relevant transfer', which means (a) a transfer of the whole or any part of the undertaking or property of the company or a subsidiary of the company, or (b) a transfer of shares in the company, or in a subsidiary of the company, resulting from a takeover bid.[270] Under s 226A(2), where, in connection with a relevant transfer, a director of a quoted company is to cease to hold office as director, or to cease to be the holder of any other office or employment in connection with the management of the affairs of the company, or any office (as director or otherwise) or employment in connection with the management of the affairs of any subsidiary undertaking of the company, then s 226A(3) applies. Under s 226A(3), if in connection with the transfer (a) the price to be paid to the director for any shares in the company held by the director is in excess of the price which could at the time have been obtained by other holders of like shares, or (b) any valuable consideration is given to the director by a person other than the company, the excess or, as the case may be, the money value of the consideration is taken for the purposes of s 226C to have been a payment or loss of office. These provisions resemble, and are modelled on, ss 218 and 219 of the Act: see 18.148 above.

18.188 Nothing in s 226C authorizes the making of a payment for loss of office in contravention of the articles of the company concerned.[271] Nor does anything in s 226B apply in relation to a remuneration payment made to a person who is or has been, a director of a quoted company before the earlier of (a) the end of the first financial year of the company to begin on or after the day on which it becomes a quoted company, and (b) the date from which the company's first director's remuneration policy to be approved under s 439A of the Act takes effect.[272]

(4) Resolution to approve payments

18.189 A resolution approving a payment for the purposes of s 226B(1)(b) or 226C(1)(b) must not be passed until a memorandum setting out particulars of the proposed payment (including its amount) is made available for inspection by the members of the company at the company's registered office for not less than 15 days ending with the date of the meeting at which the resolution is to be considered, and at that meeting itself.[273] The memorandum must explain the ways in which the payment is inconsistent with the approved directors' remuneration policy.[274]

18.190 By s 226D(3) the company must ensure that the memorandum is made available on the company's website[275] from the first day on which the memorandum is made available for inspection under s 226D(1) until its next accounts meeting.[276] Failure to comply with s 226D(3) does not, however, affect the validity of the meeting at which a resolution is passed approving a payment to which the memorandum relates or the validity of anything done at the meeting.[277]

---

[270] 'Takeover bid' is not defined: see 18.163 above.
[271] 2006 Act, s 226D(5).
[272] 2006 Act, s 226D(6).
[273] 2006 Act, s 226D(1).
[274] 2006 Act, s 226D(2). The approved directors' remuneration policy is as defined in s 226B(2) or 226C(2), as applicable.
[275] ie the website on which the company makes material available under s 430 of the Act: s 226D(7).
[276] As to the meaning of 'accounts meeting', see s 439 of the Act.
[277] 2006 Act, s 226D(4).

(5) Civil consequences of payments without approval

18.191 Section 226E sets out the civil consequences of failure to comply with s 226B or 226C. It resembles (broadly) s 222 of the Act: see therefore the commentary at paragraphs 18.160–18.162 above. Section 226E(1), (2), and (5) applies, *prima facie*, to both s 226B and 226C. Section 226E(3) and (4) applies solely to s 226C.

18.192 An obligation, however arising, to make payment which would be in contravention of s 226B or 226C has no effect.[278] If a payment is made in contravention of s 226B or 226C it is held by the recipient on trust for the company or other person making the payment,[279] and in the case of a payment by a company,[280] any director who authorized the payment is jointly and severally liable to indemnify the company that made the payment for any loss resulting from it.[281]

18.193 If a payment for loss of office is made in contravention of s 226C to a director of a quoted company in connection with the transfer of the whole or any part of the undertaking or property of the company or a subsidiary of the company, then s 226E(2) does not apply, and the payment is held by the recipient on trust for the company whose undertaking or property is or is proposed to be transferred.[282] If a payment for loss of office is made in contravention of s 226C to a director of a quoted company in connection with the transfer of share in the company, or in a subsidiary of the company, resulting from a takeover bid, s 226E(2) does not apply, the payment is held by the recipient on trust for persons who have sold their shares as a result of the offer made, and the expenses incurred by the recipient in distributing that sum amongst those persons shall be borne by the recipient and not retained out of that sum.[283]

G. Contracts with Sole Members who Are Directors

18.194 The Companies Act, s 231[284] regulates contracts between a company and its sole member where:

    (a) a limited company having only one member enters into a contract with the sole member,

    (b) the sole member is also a director of the company, and

    (c) the contract is not entered into in the ordinary course of the company's business.[285]

---

[278] 2006 Act, s 226E(1).

[279] 2006 Act, s 226(2)(a).

[280] Including a payment by another person at the direction of, or on behalf of, the company: s 226A(6).

[281] 2006 Act, s 226E(2)(b). If in proceedings against a director for enforcement of a liability under s 226E(2)(b) the director shows that he or she has acted honestly or reasonably, and the court considers that, having regard to all the circumstances of the case, the director ought to be relieved of liability, the court may relieve the director, either wholly or in part, from liability on such terms as the court thinks fit: s 226E(5).

[282] 2006 Act, s 226E(3).

[283] 2006 Act, s 226E(4).

[284] 2006 Act, s 231 applies to contracts entered into on or after 1 October 2007. For transitional provisions, see 2006 Act Commencement Order No 3, Sch 3, para 14(2).

[285] 2006 Act, s 231(1). Section 3 defines limited and unlimited companies. For the purposes of s 231 a shadow director is treated as a director. In respect of Northern Rock plc, Bradford & Bingley plc, Heritable Bank plc, and Dunfermline Building Society, whilst owned by the Treasury certain persons will not be considered shadow directors for the purposes of ss 188 and 189: see n 8 above. The expression '*ordinary course of business*' as it appeared in the preference legislation of New Zealand was considered in *Countrywide Banking Corporation Ltd v Dean* [1998] AC 338, PC and in *Waikato Freight and Storage Ltd v Meltzer* [2001] NZCA 106 and the expression '*ordinary course of its business*', as it appeared in a facility agreement, was considered in

Where s 231 applies, s 231(2) provides: **18.195**

> The company must, unless the contract is in writing, ensure that the terms of the contract are
> either:
> (a) set out in a written memorandum, or
> (b) recorded in the minutes of the first meeting of the directors of the company following the
> making of the contract.

If a company fails to comply with the requirements set out above, every officer of the com-   **18.196**
pany who is in default commits an offence, which is punishable on summary conviction by
a fine.[286]

Failure to comply with s 231 in relation to a contract does not affect the validity of the con- **18.197**
tract.[287] Nothing in s 231 is to be read as excluding the operation of any other enactment or
rule of law applying to contracts between a company and a director of the company.[288]

Section 231 substantially re-enacts the 1985 Act, s 322B and gives effect to Article 5 of the   **18.198**
Twelfth EEC Company Law Directive.[289] That directive ultimately sought to harmonize
divergences that had occurred between Member States permitting single-member private
limited-liability companies, the aim being to encourage enterprise amongst small firms. The
preamble to the directive specifically provided for contracts between the company and sole
member to be recorded in writing.

The main change introduced by s 231 is that the section now applies to any limited com-   **18.199**
pany having only one member, and thus applies to a public limited company with only one
member.[290] A further change is that under s 231(3), the company itself commits no offence
if s 231 is not complied with, and hence is not itself liable to a fine.[291]

The purpose of s 231 is to ensure that records are kept in those cases where there is a high risk **18.200**
of the lines becoming blurred between where a person acts in his personal capacity and when
he acts on behalf of the company.[292] This may be of particular interest to a liquidator should
the company become insolvent.[293]

The purpose and scope of s 231 is thus rather different to the purpose and scope of the   **18.201**
provisions in the Companies Act, Part 10, Chapters 4 and 4A discussed in the previous
sections of this chapter. Section 231 only applies to contracts whereas the provisions in

---

Ashborder BV v Green Gas Power Ltd [2005] 1 BCLC 623. See also *Steen v Law* [1964] AC 287, PC at 302–3,
interpreting 'the ordinary business of a company'; *Sandhu v Jet Star Retail Ltd* [2011] EWCA Civ 459, CA, para
10; and *Board of the Pension Protection Fund v Trustees of the West of England Ship Owners Insurance Services Ltd
Retirement Benefits Scheme* [2014] Pens LR 167.

[286] 2006 Act, s 231(3) and (4).

[287] 2006 Act, s 231(6).

[288] 2006 Act, s 231(7).

[289] Which was inserted into the 1985 Act by the Companies (Single Member Private Limited Companies)
Regulations 1992 (SI 1992/1699), reg 2, Sch, para 3, as from 15 July 1992, so as to give effect to Art 5 of the
Twelfth EEC Company Law Directive (89/667/EEC) [1989] OJ L395/40.

[290] See the Explanatory Notes, para 422. Under 1985 Act, ss 1(1) and 24 a public limited company had to
have two members as a minimum. Such requirement in respect of private limited companies was removed by
the Twelfth EEC Company Law Directive as made clear by, inter alia, 1985 Act, s 1(3A).

[291] Explanatory Notes, para 424.

[292] Explanatory Notes, para 421.

[293] Explanatory Notes, para 421; a point repeated by the Attorney General: Hansard, HL GC Day 4, vol
678, col 344 (9 February 2006).

Part 10, Chapters 4 and 4A apply to transactions and arrangements. Section 231 applies to any contract outside the ordinary course of business and is not limited to service contracts, substantial property transactions, loans, quasi-loans and credit transactions, or payments for loss of office or remuneration payments. Since its purpose is limited to ensuring that there is a record of the contract, it does not apply to written contracts. Whereas Part 10, Chapters 4 and 4A set out the civil consequences of non-compliance, there are no civil consequences of non-compliance with s 231. This is not surprising since the sole member can consent to, authorize, approve, or ratify any contract into which the company may lawfully enter, so as to make it binding on the company and protect directors from personal liability. Compliance with s 231 is irrelevant to the merits of a claim under the provisions in the Insolvency Act for relief in respect of antecedent transactions.

18.202 Section 231 is complemented by the Companies Act, s 357,[294] which again applies to a company limited by shares or by guarantee that has only one member.[295] Where the member takes any decision that may be taken by the company in general meeting, and has effect as if agreed by the company in general meeting, he must (unless that decision is taken by way of a written resolution) provide the company with details of that decision.[296] A person who fails to comply with the section commits an offence, and is liable on summary conviction to a fine, but failure to comply with s 357 does not affect the validity of any decision taken where s 357 is not complied with.[297]

---

[294] 2006 Act, s 357 re-enacts s 382B of the Act, which again resulted ultimately from the Twelfth EEC Company Law Directive (n 289 above).

[295] 2006 Act, s 357(1).

[296] 2006 Act, s 357(2).

[297] 2006 Act, s 357(3)–(5).

Part IV

LIABILITIES OF DIRECTORS

19

THE COMPANY'S REMEDIES FOR BREACH OF DIRECTORS' GENERAL DUTIES

Antony Zacaroli QC

A. Introduction

The Companies Act 2006 has effected no change to the remedies which lie against a director for breach of duty. Section 178(1) provides that 'the consequences of breach (or threatened breach) of ss 171–7 are the same as would apply if the corresponding common law rule or equitable principle applied', and s 178(2) provides that the duties set out in ss 171–3 and 175–7 'are, accordingly, enforceable in the same way as any other fiduciary duty owed to a company by its directors'.[1] No separate express provision is made in respect of the duty to exercise reasonable care, skill, and diligence (set out in s 174), but it is clear that the remedies for breaches of that duty are those provided by the common law. **19.01**

This chapter is concerned with the remedies available to the company. They are also applicable to a derivative claim under Part 11 (Chapter 22 below). The company's remedies may be pursued in conjunction with contractual claims for breach of the director's service contract, which may contain additional obligations supplementing the general duties, and also with claims arising from a failure to obtain members' approval to a transaction in accordance with Part 10, Chapter 4, ss 188–226 (Chapter 18 above). **19.02**

In addition, where the director has been guilty of a breach of duty he may be removed from office under s 168 and the company's articles (Chapter 7 above). A breach of fiduciary duty **19.03**

---

[1] ss 170–4, 178 came into force on 1 October 2007: 2006 Act Commencement Order No 3, para 2(d). Sections 175–7 came into force on 1 October 2008: 2006 Act Commencement Order No 5, para 5(1)(d).

will constitute grounds for summary dismissal under his service contract without compensation, except for unpaid salary payable for the period up to the date of termination.[2]

B. Remedies for Breach of Fiduciary Duty

(1) Introduction

19.04 Breach by a director of a fiduciary duty owed to the company may give rise to a number of remedies. First, the company may avoid a transaction entered into as a result of the breach of fiduciary duty or it may obtain an injunction to prevent it from occurring or being carried into effect. Secondly, the company may pursue a proprietary claim to recover its property from a director or third party. Thirdly, the company may pursue personal claims against a director or third party for compensation or an account of profits.[3] In considering these claims, and the potential defences to them, it is important to keep in mind the nature of the fiduciary or trustee-like obligations of a director or a third party in relation to the company's property.

19.05 Directors are not trustees of the company's property, but a breach by a director of a fiduciary duty owed to the company is treated as a breach of trust. In *JJ Harrison (Properties) Limited v Harrison*,[4] Chadwick LJ identified the following four propositions which he regarded as beyond argument:

> (i) that a company incorporated under the Companies Acts is not a trustee of its own property; it is both legal and beneficial owner of that property; (ii) that the property of a company so incorporated cannot lawfully be disposed of other than in accordance with the provisions of its memorandum and articles of association; (iii) that the powers to dispose of the company's property, conferred upon the directors by the articles of association, must be exercised by the directors for the purposes, and in the interests, of the company; (iv) that, in that sense, the directors owe fiduciary duties to the company in relation to those powers and a breach of those duties is treated as a breach of trust.

---

[2] In *Boston Deep Sea Fishing and Ice Co Ltd v Ansell* (1889) 39 Ch D 339 a director was found to have accepted a secret commission in relation to a contract entered into by the company. The Court of Appeal held that this entitled the company summarily to dismiss him, since his conduct revealed that he was incompetent faithfully to discharge his duties to the company. Moreover, the Court of Appeal held that the director was not entitled to payment of any outstanding salary. In *Item Software (UK) Ltd v Fassihi* [2005] 2 BCLC 91 the Court of Appeal distinguished the *Boston* case and held that where the director was summarily dismissed for breach of fiduciary duty during a pay period he was entitled to be paid a proportionate part of his salary for the period up to his summary dismissal under the Apportionment Act 1870. In *Brandeaux Advisors (UK) Ltd v Chadwick* [2011] IRLR 224, at paras 46–57, Jack J followed *Fassihi* in concluding that no loss had been occasioned by an employee's failure to inform his employer of his breach of fiduciary duty. While the judge accepted that the consequences of having informed the employer would have been the earlier dismissal of the employee, the continued payment of the employee's salary did not constitute loss because the employer had had the benefit of the employee's work during that period.

[3] Worthington, 'Corporate Governance: Remedying and Ratifying Directors' Breaches' (2000) 116 LQR 638, 659–74, contains a discussion of the personal and proprietary remedies for breach of directors' fiduciary duties, and a discussion of the extent to which directors can be made liable to disgorge profits acquired in breach of duty.

[4] [2002] 1 BCLC 162, CA at para 25. See also *In re Forest of Dean Coal Mining Co* (1878) 10 Ch D 450, 453, per Sir George Jessel.

This has the effect of bringing into play certain remedies applicable to breaches of trust so that, for example, 'a person who receives that property with knowledge of the breach of duty is treated as holding it upon trust'.[5]

Millett LJ, in *Paragon Finance plc v Thakerar*,[6] identified two separate classes of constructive **19.06** trustee. The first covers the case where a person (though not expressly appointed a trustee) has assumed the duties of a trustee by a lawful transaction which was independent of and preceded the breach of trust and is not impeached by the beneficiary. A director will fall within this class, in relation to the company's property, since he assumes the duties of a trustee in relation to the company's property upon appointment to the office of director so that, if he subsequently takes possession of the company's property, his possession is 'coloured from the first by the trust and confidence by means of which he obtained it'.[7] In *Williams v Central Bank of Nigeria*,[8] in which the Supreme Court reaffirmed the existence of two classes of constructive trust, Lord Sumption JSC[9] said that this first category 'comprises persons who have lawfully assumed fiduciary obligations in relation to trust property, but without a formal appointment', and that it included, for example, trustees under trusts implied from common intention, but never formally created as such, and others, such as directors, who by virtue of their status are fiduciaries with very similar obligations.

The second class of constructive trustee covers the case where the trust obligation arises **19.07** as a direct consequence of the unlawful transaction which is impeached by the claimant, such as deceit. In this case the defendant is not a trustee at all, having never assumed the duties of a trustee, but because of his implication in a fraud he is held liable to account: he is liable to account as if he were a constructive trustee in respect of property which he has received adversely to the claimant by an unlawful transaction impugned by the claimant.[10] In *Williams v Central Bank of Nigeria*,[11] Lord Sumption described this second category as comprising persons 'who never assumed and never intended to assume the status of a trustee, whether formally or informally, but have exposed themselves to equitable remedies by virtue of their participation in the unlawful misapplication of trust assets.' It includes those who have dishonestly assisted in the misapplication of funds by a trustee, and those who have received trust property knowing that the transfer to them was in breach of trust.

(2) Avoiding the transaction

Internal matters

Where the consequence of a director's breach of fiduciary duty is a transaction between the **19.08** company and a third party, it will normally follow that the director acted in excess of the powers conferred on him by the company's constitution in causing the company to enter into the transaction.[12] This will typically be the consequence of a breach of s 171 (duty to act within powers and for proper purposes), but may also arise in case of breach of s 172 (duty to promote the success of the company).

---

[5] *JJ Harrison (Properties) Ltd v Harrison* [2002] 1 BCLC 162, CA at para 26, per Chadwick LJ.
[6] [1999] 1 All ER 400, CA. See *JJ Harrison* (n 5 above) at para 27, per Chadwick LJ.
[7] See *JJ Harrison* (n 5 above) at para 29.
[8] [2014] AC 1189.
[9] [2014] AC 1189, at para 9.
[10] *Gwembe Valley Development Ltd v Koshy* [2004] 1 BCLC 131, CA at paras 88 and 91, per Mummery LJ.
[11] [2014] AC 1189, at para 9.
[12] *Rolled Steel Products (Holdings) Ltd v British Steel Corporation* [1986] Ch 246, CA.

19.09   Following the House of Lords' decision in *Criterion Properties plc v Stratford UK Properties LLC*,[13] it is clear that the relevant question is whether or not the director who caused the company to enter into the transaction had actual or apparent authority to do so.[14] According to Lord Scott (with whom the remainder of their Lordships agreed) if the director had either actual or apparent authority then the transaction was enforceable by the third party, but otherwise it was not.[15]

19.10   Lord Nicholls (with whom Lord Walker agreed) explained the position as follows:[16]

> If a company (A) enters into an agreement with B under which B acquires benefits from A, A's ability to recover these benefits from B depends essentially on whether the agreement is binding on A. If the directors of A were acting for an improper purpose when they entered into the agreement, A's ability to have the agreement set aside depends upon the application of familiar principles of agency and common law. If, applying these principles, the agreement is found to be valid and is therefore not set aside, questions of 'knowing receipt' by B do not arise. So far as B is concerned there can be no question of A's assets having been misapplied. B acquired the assets from A, the legal and beneficial owner of the assets, under a valid agreement made between him and A. If, however, the agreement is set aside, B will be accountable for any benefits he may have received from A under the agreement. A will have a proprietary claim, if B still has the assets. Additionally, and irrespective of whether B still has the assets in question, A will have a personal claim against B for unjust enrichment, subject always to a defence of change of position. B's personal accountability will not be dependent upon proof of fault or 'unconscionable' conduct on his part. B's accountability, in this regard, will be 'strict'.[17]

19.11   If the court concludes that the director did not have authority, then it simply declares the transaction invalid. Other personal or proprietary remedies may follow and, if necessary, an injunction may be granted to prevent the transaction from being acted on.

19.12   This is a remedy which is frequently employed in the context of the improper issue or forfeiture of shares. Thus the court has:

(1)   declared invalid the following transactions in exercise of the powers to forfeit or buy back shares: an arrangement between the company and a shareholder that his shares should be forfeited on his retirement for non-payment of a call, as being beyond the powers of the directors;[18] the action of the directors in appropriating an amount uncalled upon their shares to pay their unpaid fees, as being a breach of duty to act in the proper interests of the company;[19] a transfer of shares following a purchase by the manager acting under his supposed delegated authority, where the purported delegation from the directors to a manager of authority to buy back shares was held to be beyond their powers;[20]

---

[13]   [2004] 1 WLR 1846, HL.

[14]   The House of Lords in this regard disagreed with the Court of Appeal in the same case, where the liability of the third party to disgorge benefits received under the transaction was assumed to depend upon the principles derived from the cases dealing with knowing receipt of property disposed of in breach of fiduciary duty.

[15]   [2004] 1 WLR 1846 at para 30. At para 31 he explained that a person who dealt with the director knowing or having reason to believe that the contract is contrary to the commercial interests of the company is unlikely to be able to assert with any credibility that he believed the director had actual authority, and lack of such a belief would be fatal to a claim that the agent had apparent authority.

[16]   [2004] 1 WLR 1846 at para 4.

[17]   See also *Ultraframe v Fielding* [2005] EWHC 1638 at paras 1492–4; *Allied Carpets Group PLC v Nethercott* [2001] BCC 81.

[18]   *Re Agriculturist Cattle Insurance, Stanhope's Case* (1866) 1 Ch App 161.

[19]   *Re European Central Rly Co, Sykes Case* (1872) 13 Eq 255.

[20]   *Re County Palatine Loan & Discount Co, Cartmell's Case* (1874) 9 Ch App 691.

the decision by the directors to forfeit shares for non-payment of a call, as being the product of a failure to take into account matters they ought to have taken into account;[21]

(2) declared invalid the following transactions in exercise of the power to issue new shares unless the issue was duly ratified: the purported exercise by the directors of a power to issue shares for the improper purpose of seeking to maintain control;[22] the purported issue of shares and a connected loan as having been made for an improper purpose, unless ratified by general meeting;[23] an allotment of shares for the improper purpose of blocking a takeover bid, but the allotment was saved from invalidity by subsequent ratification; and[24]

(3) granted an injunction to restrain: the holding of a meeting at which new shares were to be issued in breach of the directors' duty to act for the proper purposes of the company;[25] a call being made on certain shareholders where the exercise of the power to make calls was found to be invalid as carried out in breach of duty.[26]

It is also relevant in cases involving unlawful dividends or unlawful distributions of assets: see, **19.13** for example, *Macpherson v European Strategic Bureau Ltd*,[27] in which the Court of Appeal invalidated a transaction pursuant to which members of the company were paid an amount by way of remuneration which had the effect, at a time when the company was insolvent, of distributing the company's assets to them as members without making proper provision for creditors.

Similarly, the remedy has been employed to invalidate resolutions approving remuneration **19.14** or pension payments for directors. Thus the court has declared invalid: a resolution authorizing payments to directors for their services after the time at which the company had ceased as a going concern and only existed for the purpose of its winding up;[28] a pension granted in favour of the widow of a director on the grounds that the transaction was not one for the benefit of the company or reasonably incidental to the carrying on of its business;[29] proposed ex gratia payments to employees on the grounds that making the payments would be a breach of duty by the directors, as they were not reasonably incidental to the company's business;[30] and a service agreement with a director, on the ground that its sole purpose was to benefit the director's widow, by providing a pension after the director's death, and not the company.[31]

Transactions with third parties

Where the result of a director's breach of duty is a transaction with a third party, then the **19.15** ability of the third party to uphold the transaction is likely to depend on whether he can bring himself within the protection of the 2006 Act, s 40 (power of the directors to bind the company)[32] or s 44 (execution of documents by a company),[33] and whether he can avoid

---

[21] *Hunter v Senate Support Services Ltd* [2005] 1 BCLC 175.
[22] *Piercy v S Mills & Co Ltd* [1920] 1 Ch 77.
[23] *Hogg v Cramphorn Ltd* [1967] Ch 254.
[24] *Bamford v Bamford* [1970] Ch 212, CA.
[25] *Punt v Symons & Co* [1903] 2 Ch 506.
[26] *Galloway v Halle Concert Society* [1915] 2 Ch 233.
[27] [2000] 2 BCLC 683.
[28] *Hutton v West Cork Rly Co Ltd* (1883) 23 Ch D 654, CA.
[29] *Re Lee Behrens & Co Ltd* [1932] 2 Ch 46.
[30] *Parke v Daily News Ltd* [1962] Ch 927.
[31] *Re W&M Roith Ltd* [1967] 1 WLR 432.
[32] The protection of s 40 is subject to s 41 (transactions with directors or their associates) and s 42 (companies that are charities). For further discussion of these sections, see Ch 4, Section C.
[33] See Ch 4, Section D(2) and (3) above.

a finding of lack of good faith, or failure to make enquiries having been put on enquiry, as in *Wrexham Association Football Cub Ltd v Crucialmove Ltd*,[34] applying *Rolled Steel Products (Holdings) Ltd v British Steel Corporation*,[35] in which a guarantee entered into in breach of the directors' authority was held to be unenforceable, on the basis that a person dealing with a company on notice that the directors are exercising a power of the company for purposes other than the purpose of the company cannot rely on the ostensible authority of the directors and cannot hold the company to the transaction.

(3) Proprietary claims to recover the company's property

Recovery from a director

19.16   The question as to when a proprietary claim lies against a director, or other fiduciary, consequent upon a breach of fiduciary duty, has been the subject matter of intense debate and inconsistent decisions over the past 200 years. It is to be hoped that the controversy has largely been laid to rest by the recent unanimous decision of the panel of seven Supreme Court justices in *FHR European Ventures LLP v Cedar Capital Partners LLC*.[36] The case concerned the vexed question of when a bribe or secret commission obtained by a fiduciary is held on trust for its principal or beneficiary, but the decision deals more broadly with benefits received by a fiduciary in breach of its duties. The Supreme Court's conclusion was that where an agent acquired a benefit which came to his notice as a result of his fiduciary position, or through an opportunity resulting from that position, the general equitable rule was that he was treated as having acquired the benefit on behalf of his principal, so that the benefit was owned by the principal who had a proprietary as well as a personal remedy against the agent. Moreover, it concluded that the general principle extended to a bribe or secret commission obtained by an agent.

19.17   Lord Neuberger PSC delivered the judgment of the court. He first noted the well-established principle[37] that where an agent receives a benefit in breach of fiduciary duty, it is obliged to account to the principal for such benefit and to pay a sum equal to the profit by way of equitable compensation. The relief accorded by equity is 'primarily restitutionary or restorative rather than compensatory'.[38] He then noted that 'at least in some cases' where the agent acquires a benefit which came to its notice as a result of its fiduciary position, or pursuant to an opportunity which results from its fiduciary position, it is to be treated as having acquired the benefit on behalf of the principal, so that it is beneficially owned by the principal. The rule is strictly applied to cases which fall within its ambit.

19.18   An early example of the application of the rule is *Keech v Sandford*[39] in which a trustee who held a lease of a market in trust for an infant, having failed to negotiate a new lease on behalf of the infant, negotiated a lease for itself. The Court held that the infant was entitled to an assignment of the lease, a result which Lord Neuberger in *FHR European Ventures* said could only be justified on the basis that the new lease had been beneficially acquired for the infant beneficiary.

---

[34] [2007] BCC 139, CA.
[35] [1986] Ch 246, CA.
[36] [2015] AC 250. For a commentary on the case, see McGrath, 'FHR European Ventures LLP: the demise of Sinclair v Versailles and a welcome return to orthodoxy' (2014) CR&I 7(5), 175–8.
[37] [2015] AC 250, at para 6, citing *Regal (Hastings) Ltd v Gulliver (Note)* [1967] 2 AC 134.
[38] Citing *Bristol and West Building Society v Motthew* [1998] Ch 1, 18, per Millett LJ.
[39] (1726) Sel Cas Ch 61.

In the corporate sphere the rule has been applied in cases where a director makes an unauthorized profit by taking advantage of an opportunity which came to his attention as a result of his position. Examples include *Cook v Deeks*[40] where directors wrongfully obtained the benefit of a contract, which represented an opportunity belonging to the company, in their own names. In *Bhullar v Bhullar*[41] Jonathan Parker LJ considered that it was too formalistic and restrictive, in the context of a fiduciary wrongfully exploiting a commercial opportunity for his own benefit, to limit a proprietary remedy to those cases where the person to whom the duty is owed (eg the company in the case of a director's breach of duty) had some kind of pre-existing beneficial interest in the opportunity. The question was simply 'whether the fiduciary's exploitation of the opportunity is such as to attract the application of the rule' (ie the rule that a benefit acquired by a fiduciary as a result of its position is treated as having been acquired on behalf of his principal).

19.19

It is in relation to bribes and secret commissions that the application of the rule has proved most controversial. Lord Neuberger reviewed the many, often inconsistent, authorities, stretching back over 200 years, at paras 15 to 28 of *FHR European Ventures*. Immediately prior to the Supreme Court's decision, the position was the unsatisfactory one that while the Privy Council had concluded, in *Attorney General for Hong Kong v Reid*,[42] that bribes received by a corrupt government legal officer were held on trust for his principal, the English Court of Appeal, in *Sinclair Investments (UK) Ltd v Versailles Trade Finance Ltd*,[43] considered itself to be bound by the nineteenth-century Court of Appeal decision of *Lister & Co v Stubbs*,[44] where an agent of a company had accepted a bribe from one of its clients, and an interlocutory injunction was refused on the ground that the relationship between the company and its agent was that of creditor and debtor, not beneficiary and trustee.

19.20

In the end, in light of the inconsistent authorities, and the powerful arguments on both sides of the debate from numerous distinguished academics, Lord Neuberger concluded that 'it is not possible to identify any plainly right or plainly wrong answer to the issue of the extent of the rule, as a matter of pure legal authority'.[45] The Supreme Court, therefore, decided the issue by reference to principle and practicality. In summary, such considerations favoured the conclusion that applied the general equitable rule to the recipient of a bribe or secret commission because: (1) it is consistent with the fundamental principles of the law of agency, under which the agent owes a duty of undivided loyalty to the principle, and the principal is entitled to the entire benefit of the agent's acts in the course of the agency; (2) it has the benefit of simplicity, whereas if bribes and secret commissions were to be excepted from the general principle the fact that there is more than one way to identify the exception leads to uncertainty; (3) it aligns the circumstances in which an agent is obliged to account for any benefit received in breach of his fiduciary duty and those in which his principal can claim the beneficial ownership of the benefit; (4) in terms of elementary economics, there must be a strong possibility that a bribe will have disadvantaged the principle, since common sense suggests that in most cases the value of the bribe would otherwise have been received by the

19.21

---

[40] [1916] 1 AC 554, PC.
[41] [2003] 2 BCLC 241, CA, at para 28, cited with approval by the Supreme Court in *FHR European Ventures* [2015] AC 250 at paras 14 and 36.
[42] [1994] 1 AC 324, PC.
[43] [2012] Ch 453, CA.
[44] (1890) 45 Ch D 1, CA.
[45] [2015] AC 250, at para 32.

principal; (5) the opposite conclusion gave rise to artificialities and difficulties, such as where the issue whether a principal had a proprietary interest in a bribe to his agent depended upon the mechanism agreed between the briber and the agent for payment;[46] (6) it would be paradoxical if a principal whose agent receives a bribe or secret commission is worse off than a principal whose agent receives a benefit in far less opprobrious circumstances; (7) it is consistent with the wider policy considerations that 'bribery is an evil practice'[47] and that secret commissions inevitably tend to undermine trust in the commercial world; and (8) although the counter-argument—that affording the principal a proprietary remedy tends to prejudice the agent's unsecured creditors—has force, it is outweighed by the fact that a principal whose agent has obtained a bribe or secret commission should be able to trace the proceeds of the bribe or commission into other assets and follow them into the hands of knowing recipients.[48] Finally, Lord Neuberger noted that the conclusion reached by the Supreme Court was consistent with the conclusion reached in Australia, New Zealand, Canada, and Singapore, and it was 'highly desirable for all those jurisdictions to learn from each other, and at least to lean in favour of harmonising the development of the common law around the world'.[49]

19.22   It is clear from the Supreme Court's approval of the strict nature of the general equitable rule that a proprietary remedy lies against a director who has acquired an opportunity that belonged to the company irrespective of whether the opportunity is one the company could, would, or might have taken up, and irrelevant to enquire whether the opportunity fell within the company's scope of business.[50]

19.23   Where, however, the opportunity exploited in breach of fiduciary duty consists of a business, there is authority that it is not regarded as property belonging to the company (as opposed to where specific business assets—whether tangible, such as shares, or intangible, such as goodwill—are appropriated by the director). Whilst there is Australian authority going the other way,[51] in *Ultraframe (UK) Ltd v Fielding*[52] Lewison J held that a proprietary claim is not available in the case of an exploitation of a business opportunity and does not apply to profits made from such a business, pointing out that the process of fashioning an account of profits, including making just allowances or limiting the period within which profits from a business were to be accounted for, was inconsistent with a non-discretionary proprietary remedy. Lewison J also concluded that it was not possible to trace into the profits of a business, given that the identification of profits involved a balance of income and expenditure over an extended period, including notional items such as depreciation, whereas tracing depended upon the 'identification of specific inputs and outputs of substitution'.

---

[46]   Referring to the decision in *Whaley Bridge Calico Printing Co v Green* (1879) 5 QBD 109.
[47]   Citing Lord Templeman in *Attorney General for Hong Kong v Reid* [1994] 1 AC 324, 330H.
[48]   [2015] AC 250, at paras 33–44.
[49]   [2015] AC 250, at para 45.
[50]   [2015] AC 250, at para 40. See also *Re Allied Business and Financial Consultants Ltd* [2009] BCLC 666 at para 70, per Rimer LJ. In *Cheng Wait Tao v Poon Ka Man Jason* [2016] HKCFA 23, at paras 70–91, per Spigelman NPJ, the Hong Kong Court of Final Appeal considered that the reasoning of the court in *Allied Business* may have gone too far, and that it was indeed appropriate to apply a 'scope of business' test so as to modify the subject matter of the fiduciary duty owed by a director.
[51]   *Timber Engineering Co Pty Ltd v Anderson* [1980] 2 NSWLR 488.
[52]   [2005] EWHC 1638 at para 1547: 'a proprietary remedy is not available in the case of an alleged misappropriation of a business (as opposed to a proprietary claim to shares in a company or to a specific business asset, including an intangible but proprietary asset)'. See also *Warman v Dyer* [1994] 128 ALR 201.

One question that remains unresolved is whether a proprietary claim lies in circumstances   **19.24**
where a director's breach of duty consists of causing the company to make a payment in
discharge of an existing debt. It is clear that it may be a breach of duty by a director to cause
the company to pay a debt, for example where that payment would constitute a preference in
the event of a subsequent liquidation.[53] The question was raised, but not answered in *E-Clear
(UK) plc v Elia*.[54] The Court of Appeal, citing *Re Washington Diamond Mining Company*,[55]
noted that the payment of a debt owed to directors may constitute both a fraudulent preference and a misappropriation of company property for which the directors are accountable, but that the decision provided no guidance as to the type of remedy available. It was
contended that no proprietary claim could lie in respect of money that had been paid in
satisfaction of a debt. Without answering the point, Patten LJ considered that the answer
was likely to lie in the general rules governing tracing claims. For example, where money
is used to pay a debt, any proprietary claim would usually be lost because the recipient can
claim to be a purchaser in good faith for value without notice. That answer is unlikely to be
available, however, where the recipient was the defaulting director. The better view, it is suggested, is that the mere fact that the company's money was paid away in discharge of a debt,
if the payment of that debt constituted a breach of fiduciary duty, and the recipient is either
the defaulting director or someone with knowledge of the breach of duty, then the fact that
the payment was made in purported discharge of a debt does not prevent a proprietary claim
over the money or its traceable proceeds in the hands of the recipient.

Recovery from third parties

A proprietary claim may lie against a third party to whom property of the company has   **19.25**
been transferred and who still retains that property or its traceable proceeds.[56] The basic
principle is that the company, in the same way as the beneficiary of a trust, is entitled to a
continuing beneficial interest not merely in the trust property, but in its traceable proceeds.
Tracing in equity depends upon the existence of a fiduciary duty, a condition that is necessarily satisfied in the case of directors where the company seeks to trace property transferred
away as a consequence of the director's breach of fiduciary duty. Although often referred to
as a proprietary claim or remedy, tracing properly so-called is neither a claim nor a remedy,
but a process for identifying what has happened to the claimant's property.[57] There are three
aspects to the process of tracing: first, identifying the property belonging to the company
in the hands of the wrongdoer; secondly following the asset into the hands of subsequent
recipients of it; and thirdly, tracing into the proceeds of the misappropriated property which
remain in the hands of the wrongdoer after the property has been transferred on. So far as the
second of these aspects is concerned, the company may follow its property into the hands of
subsequent recipients unless and until the property is acquired by a bona fide purchaser for
value without notice of the company's claim.[58] Where the trust property has been mixed with
other property of the wrongdoing fiduciary, the onus is on the fiduciary to establish that the

---

[53] See Chapter 34 at para 34.149.
[54] [2013] 2 BCLC 455, per Patten LJ at paras 32–4.
[55] [1893] 3 Ch 95.
[56] In contrast, the mere fact that a third party has dishonestly assisted in a breach of fiduciary duty does not
lead to the imposition of a proprietary claim: *Sinclair Investment Holdings v Versailles Trading Finance Ltd* [2007]
2 All ER (Comm) 993.
[57] *Boscawen v Bajwa* [1996] 1 WLR 328, 334, CA.
[58] See eg *Foskett v McKeown* [2001] 1 AC 102, 127, HL, per Lord Millett. See further para 19.28 below.

property in the mixed fund is not trust property: *Sinclair Investments (UK) Ltd v Versailles Trade Finance Group plc*.[59]

19.26 It is not in every case necessary to identify each step in the transfer of property from the company to the defendant. Depending on the circumstances it may be possible to draw the inference that the payment to the defendant was the product of a series of transactions between a number of entities and across a number of bank accounts, cumulatively designed to achieve the result that funds derived from the company, pursuant to a breach of fiduciary duty by its directors, were paid to the defendant. Such an inference may be drawn from, for example, the close relationship (in time and amount) between the payments from the company and payments to the defendant, and from evidence that the payment to the defendant would not have been made but for the initial transfer from the company: see *Relfo Ltd v Varsani*.[60] In that case, it was claimed that money paid away from a company in breach of duty by its director was traceable into the hands of a third party recipient, notwithstanding that the claimant could not prove the complete chain of payments between the money leaving the company's account and arriving at the ultimate recipient and that at least in relation to a part of the chain of payments which could be established, a payment out (by an intermediate entity in the chain) was made before the payment to that entity of the funds deriving from the payment by the company. The Court of Appeal, following the earlier decision of Millett J in *El Ajou v Dollar Land Holdings plc*,[61] held that the funds could nevertheless be traced into the hands of the ultimate recipient. First, where there was an absence of evidence of a chain of direct payments, the court was nevertheless entitled to draw inferences from the surrounding circumstances, including the intention of the defaulting director, in authorizing the payment out of the company's account, that it should lead to the payment made to the ultimate recipient. While intention could not be enough by itself to establish the necessary link between the payment out of the company's account and the ultimate receipt of funds by the defendant, it was a factor which the court was permitted to take into account in determining whether it was possible to draw the necessary inference. Secondly, the critical feature is that there is an exchange of *value* of the claimant's property into the next product, on the basis that a chain of substitutions in reality consists of a series of debits and credits which are causally and transactionally linked and that what is traced is not the physical asset itself but the value inherent in it.[62] Third, it was not fatal to a tracing claim that an intermediate link in the chain paid funds on to the next link before itself being placed in funds, provided that the intermediate link paid out on the basis that reimbursement would be made to it from the trust funds.

19.27 A proprietary claim will lie against any person who retains the property, or its traceable proceeds, save for the bona fide purchaser for value without notice of the breach of fiduciary duty.[63]

19.28 The onus of establishing the defence of bona fide purchaser for value without notice is on the defendant.[64] The scope of the defence was reviewed by both Lewison J and the

---

[59] [2012] Ch 453, CA, per Lord Neuberger MR at para 141.
[60] [2015] 1 BCLC 14, CA.
[61] [1993] 3 All ER 717 (Millett J), and [1994] 2 All ER 685 (CA).
[62] Citing with approval *Foskett v McKeown* [2001] 1 AC 102, HL.
[63] *Re Loftus (deceased); Green v Gaul* [2005] 2 All ER 700 at paras 172–4.
[64] *Sinclair Investments (UK) Ltd v Versailles Trade Finance Ltd* [2011] 1 BCLC 202; [2012] Ch 453, CA, at para 94; *Re Nisbet & Potts' Contract* [1906] 1 Ch 386; *Barclays Bank plc v Boulter* [1998] 1 WLR 1, 8.

Court of Appeal in *Sinclair Investments (UK) Ltd v Versailles Trade Finance Ltd.*[65] The question of 'notice' is to be determined by asking what the defendant actually knew, and what further enquiries, if any, a reasonable person with the knowledge and experience of the defendant would have made and, in the light of that, whether it was, or should have been, obvious to the banks that the transaction was 'probably improper'.[66] The test thus involves a subjective element (what the defendant actually knew) and an objective element (what the defendant ought reasonably to have appreciated in light of that knowledge). The same test applies to considering the legal consequences of known facts. There is thus no simple rule that a defendant either is, or is not, taken to know the legal consequences of particular facts. Once a person is found to know certain facts, he is not treated as appreciating the legal consequences unless he either actually knew of those consequences, or, in all the circumstances, ought reasonably to have appreciated those consequences.[67]

An example of a proprietary remedy is *Clark v Cutland,*[68] where one of the directors of the **19.29** company misappropriated funds and transferred them to the trustees of a pension fund, the beneficiaries of which were the director and his family. The Court of Appeal held that the company was entitled to trace the payments into the pension fund assets and granted a charge over those assets, notwithstanding that the pension trustees were unaware of the breach of duty at the time of receipt of the funds.

Where the relevant property is transferred to a bona fide purchaser for value without **19.30** notice, and that purchaser further transfers the property on to another person, the fact that the ultimate purchaser has notice of the breach of fiduciary duty is irrelevant (unless that person was himself previously bound by the equity). If this were not so, it would unduly restrict the ability of the bona fide purchaser for value to deal with the property as his own.[69]

Whether a proprietary claim is brought against the director or against third parties, the **19.31** claimant company has within its armoury the possibility of obtaining a proprietary injunction to restrain dealings with the claimed property pending its right being established by action.[70]

(4) Personal remedies against a director

There are three categories of personal claim against a director who is guilty of actual, or **19.32** threatened, breach of fiduciary duty: (i) equitable compensation, (ii) an account of profits, and (iii) injunctive relief.

---

[65] [2012] Ch 453. *Sinclair* was followed in *Papadimitriou v Credit Agricole Corpn and Investment Bank* [2015] 1 WLR 4265, PC.

[66] [2012] Ch 453, per Lord Neuberger MR at para 100. See also *Barclays Bank v O'Brien* [1994] 1 AC 180, 195, per Lord Browne-Wilkinson and *Macmillan Inc v Bishopsgate Trust plc (No 3)* [1995] 1 WLR 978, 1014, per Millett J.

[67] *Sinclair* (n 64 above), per Lord Neuberger MR at para 104. Notice of the existence of a claim is not to be equated with notice of the existence of a right: see Lord Neuberger at para 108, citing *Carl Zeiss Stiftung v Herbert Smith & Co* [1969] 2 Ch 276, CA. In all cases it is necessary to identify the facts known to a person, and then consider the question by reference to the test summarized in the main text.

[68] [2003] 2 BCLC 393, CA. See also *LS Systems v David Scott* [2015] EWHC 1335 (Ch), at para 57.

[69] *Barrow's Case* (1880) 14 Ch D 432.

[70] See below at para 19.67.

Equitable compensation

19.33 Claims for equitable compensation are more likely to arise in cases of breach of the duties referred to in ss 171–3 (duties to act within powers, to promote the success of the company and to exercise independent judgment), as opposed to the conflict-based duties in ss 175–7.

19.34 Equitable compensation differs in material respects from a common law claim for damages, as explained by the House of Lords in *Target Holdings Ltd v Redferns*.[71] Whilst the House of Lords noted that the common law principles of causation and quantification do not apply to claims for equitable compensation, nevertheless two principles fundamental to an award of damages at common law are applicable as much in equity as at common law. Those principles are (1) the defendant's wrongful act must cause the damage complained of, and (2) the claimant is to be put 'in the same position as he would have been in if he had not sustained the wrong for which he is now getting compensation or reparation'.[72]

19.35 Lord Browne-Wilkinson described the approach of equity to ordering compensation for breach of fiduciary duty as follows.[73] The rules have developed in relation to traditional trusts 'where the only way in which all the beneficiaries' rights can be protected is to restore to the trust fund what ought to be there'. Accordingly, the basic rule is that a trustee in breach of trust must restore or pay to the trust estate either the assets which have been lost to the estate or compensation for such loss. 'If specific restitution of the trust property is not possible, then the liability of the trustee is to pay sufficient compensation to the trust estate to put it back to what it would have been had the breach not been committed.' Whilst the common law rules of remoteness of damage and causation do not apply, there must be some causal connection between the breach of trust and the loss to the trust estate for which compensation is recoverable, namely 'the fact that the loss would not have occurred but for the breach'.

19.36 Lord Browne-Wilkinson approved the following statement of the law by McLachlin J in *Canson Enterprises Ltd v Boughton & Co*:[74]

> In summary compensation is an equitable monetary remedy which is available when the equitable remedies of restitution and account are not appropriate. By analogy with restitution, it attempts to restore to the plaintiff what has been lost as a result of the breach, ie the plaintiff's loss of opportunity. The plaintiff's actual loss as a consequence of the breach is to be assessed with the full benefit of hindsight. Foreseeability is not a concern in assessing compensation, but it is essential that the losses made good are only those which, *on a common sense view of causation*, were caused by the breach.

The emphasis was added by Lord Browne-Wilkinson, who went on:[75] 'In my view this is good law. Equitable compensation for breach of trust is designed to achieve exactly what

---

[71] [1996] 1 AC 421, a case involving mortgage fraud, and not concerned specifically with breaches of duty by company directors. Nevertheless, the principles set out in the case relating to equitable compensation are of general application.

[72] At 432, per Lord Browne-Wilkinson. One respect in which equitable compensation for breach of fiduciary duty may differ from a damages claim at law is in respect of a director's breach of duty in exploiting a corporate opportunity. In *Goldtrail Travel Ltd v Aydin* [2016] 1 BCLC 635, CA, at para 43, Vos LJ considered, *obiter*, that because section 175(2) expressly provides that it is immaterial whether the company could have taken advantage of the property or the opportunity, if one were considering the compensation that the company was entitled to recover from the director, one would ignore the question of whether or not the company could in fact have availed itself of the opportunity that the director diverted to himself.

[73] At 434.

[74] (1991) 85 DLR (4th) 129, 163.

[75] At 438, 439.

the word compensation suggests: to make good loss in fact suffered by the beneficiaries and which, using hindsight and common sense, can be seen to have been caused by the breach.'

Writing extrajudicially, Lord Millett has criticized the reasoning of the House of Lords **19.37** in *Target Holdings*.[76] According to Lord Millett, it is wrong and misleading to speak of a breach of trust as if it were the equitable counterpart of breach of contract at common law, and equally wrong to regard equitable compensation as 'common law damages masquerading under a fancy name'.[77] Unlike a contracting party, whose primary obligation is to perform the contract and whose secondary obligation is to pay damages if he does not, a trustee's primary obligation is to account for his stewardship of the trust, so that the primary remedy of the beneficiary is to have an account taken, 'to surcharge and falsify the account, and to require the trustee to restore to the trust estate any deficiency which may appear when the account is taken'. The liability of the trustee is strict, and the account must be taken 'down to the date that it is rendered'. Lord Millett returned to this theme, when sitting on the Court of Final Appeal in Hong Kong in *Libertarian Investments Ltd v Hall*.[78]

Lord Millett's approach has the advantage of clarity and lends itself to a more consistent **19.38** application, in contrast to the less-principled approach of the House of Lords in *Target Holdings*. The 'common sense view' test for causation is necessarily more susceptible to inconsistent application.[79] In *AIB Group (UK) Ltd v Mark Redler & Co*,[80] the Supreme Court has, however, rejected Lord Millett's approach and, instead affirmed the decision and reasoning of Lord Brown Wilkinson in *Target v Redferns*. Lord Toulson JSC, with whom the other justices agreed, said:[81]

> There are arguments to be made both ways, as the continuing debate among scholars has shown, but absent fraud, which might give rise to other public policy considerations that are not present in this case, it would not in my opinion be right to impose or maintain a rule that gives redress to a beneficiary for loss which would have been suffered if the trustee had properly performed its duties.

In a concurring judgment, Lord Reed JSC referred[82] to the Supreme Court's comment, in **19.39** *FHR European Ventures*,[83] that it was highly desirable for common law jurisdictions to learn from each other, and noted that most other common law jurisdictions had taken the view that the correct approach to the assessment of equitable compensation for breach of trust

---

[76] 'Equity's Place in the Law of Commerce' (1998) 114 LQR 214.

[77] This approach nevertheless continues to be adopted: *Shepherds Investment Ltd v Walters* [2007] 2 BCLC 202, where Etherton J spoke in terms of 'damages' for breach of fiduciary duty. He does not appear to have been referred to *Target Holdings*.

[78] [2014] 1 HKC 368.

[79] In *Fyffes Group v Templeman* [2000] 2 Lloyd's Rep 643, Toulson J noted that it was accepted in that case that the same principles applied in assessing damages in tort for fraud as in assessing equitable compensation for knowingly assisting in a breach of fiduciary duty. See also *Queen's Moat Houses plc v Bairstow* [2001] 2 BCLC 531, where the Court of Appeal held that a case where directors had been guilty of dishonest payment of dividends was wholly different from the circumstances in *Target Holdings*. As such, no question of 'stopping the clock' arose (as in *Target*), and the directors were liable to pay compensation for their breach of fiduciary duty notwithstanding that the company could have paid the dividends lawfully had its relevant accounts been properly prepared.

[80] [2015] AC 1503.

[81] [2015] AC 1503, at para 62.

[82] [2015] AC 1503, at paras 120 to 133.

[83] [2015] AC 250. See para 19.21 above.

was that taken by McLachlin J in *Canson Enterprises*, which underpinned Lord Browne-Wilkinson's reasoning in *Target v Redferns*.

19.40   Where the breach of fiduciary duty consists of the removal of property from the beneficiary pursuant to an unauthorized transaction between the fiduciary and the beneficiary, then the above difficulties are largely avoided. In *Gidman v Barron & Moore*[84] Patten J held that in such a case the fiduciary is simply not entitled to enforce the transaction, the transaction can be set side, and the fiduciary is required to restore the property removed from the beneficiary. It is, in particular, not relevant to enquire whether the beneficiary nonetheless would have entered into the transaction if the fiduciary had not breached his duty (for example, in the case of a transaction between a director and the company, if the director had obtained the informed consent of the company before entering into the transaction). Even if it could be shown that the fiduciary's principal would have consented, if asked, the fiduciary is required to make restitution.

19.41   In *Gwembe Valley Development Co Ltd v Koshy*,[85] however, Mummery LJ drew a distinction in this regard between the remedies of account of profits or rescission on the one hand and the remedy of equitable compensation on the other. Where the relevant breach of fiduciary duty by the director consists of failing to disclose an interest in a transaction, then the strictness of the rule in equity that a fiduciary should not profit from a breach of trust means that the transaction should be set aside, or the director should be made to account for the profit made by him, irrespective of whether the company would have entered into the transaction if there had been proper disclosure. Where, on the other hand, equitable compensation was claimed, it was right, in asking whether compensation should be paid for the loss claimed to have been suffered as a result of the actionable non-disclosure, to consider what would have happened if disclosure had been made. On the facts, the Court of Appeal upheld the judge's decision to refuse to order equitable compensation where the evidence showed that the disclosure by the director would probably have made no difference.[86]

19.42   A director guilty of breach of fiduciary duty can be made liable to pay compensation for the loss caused by his own breach, but not for the loss attributable only to breaches of fiduciary duty committed by other directors.[87] Where, however, two or more directors are in breach of fiduciary duty which has caused the same loss to the company, then each of them is jointly and severally liable to pay equitable compensation[88] and any one of them who is required to repay the whole of the loss is entitled to proceed against the others for a contribution.

---

[84] [2003] EWHC 153 (Ch).

[85] [2004] 1 BCLC 131, CA at paras 142–7.

[86] See also *Murad v Al Saraj* [2005] EWCA Civ 959; *Condliffe v Sheingold* [2007] EWCA Civ 1043; *Fanmailuk.com v Cooper* [2011] EWHC 902 (Ch).

[87] *Lexi Holdings plc v Luqman* [2009] 2 BCLC 1, CA, demonstrates the importance of establishing, in relation to the particular director found guilty of breach of fiduciary duty, the loss that was caused by that breach of duty. This involves, among other things, distinguishing between what a director, acting consistently with his fiduciary duties, should have done, and what, in all probability, he would have done. Where it is established that a director ought to have done a particular thing, then he is liable for not having done it and it is irrelevant that he might have done something else.

[88] *Re Englefield Colliery Co* (1878) 8 Ch D 388; *Re Duckwari plc* [1999] Ch 253, 262. In both *Cullerne v London & Suburban Building Society* (1890) 25 QBD 485 and *Young v Naval, Military, and Civil Service Co-operative Society of South Africa* [1905] 1 KB 687 the court refused to impose liability on directors who, though they had been party to resolutions authorizing the company to make payments of a type which were held to be ultra vires, were not themselves privy to the actual payments made.

Although in *Gluckstein v Barnes*, the House of Lords recognized that it may be appropriate **19.43** to proceed against all the defaulting directors instead of proceeding against one, leaving it to that director to seek to recover against the others, on the facts, however, they refused to show any indulgence to the sole director against whom proceedings had been brought.[89] In *Gidman v Barron & Moore*,[90] Patten J refused to allow a contribution in favour of defaulting directors against another director whose alleged default was to permit the others to carry out their acts of default, saying:

> I have no difficulty in accepting that a director cannot sit in silence and allow his fellow directors to act in breach of duty, without making reasonable attempts to curtail their activities. But for the otherwise innocent director to become liable for the consequences of the breaches of duty by the other directors, there must be culpable inactivity on his part.

In many cases the company may have a claim either for an account of profits or for equitable **19.44** compensation. In those circumstances the company may elect which remedy to pursue.[91] An example of such a case is *Crown Dilmun v Sutton*[92] where Peter Smith J refused to force the claimant to elect whether to adopt a transaction entered into in breach of fiduciary duty and claim an account of profits, or claim equitable compensation, on the basis that the claimant did not yet have sufficient information to make an informed choice.

Examples of cases where directors have been ordered to pay equitable compensation to the **19.45** company for breach of fiduciary duty include those where directors have caused the company to make ultra vires payments (such as unauthorized payments out of capital),[93] to pay unlawful dividends,[94] or to enter into transactions which were unlawful, as being in breach of the financial assistance provisions of the Companies Acts.[95]

Examples of compensation ordered to be paid by directors guilty of breach of fiduciary **19.46** duty include: *Re Oxford Benefit Building and Investment Society*,[96] where directors were ordered to pay compensation to the company equal to the amount of dividends they had wrongly caused the company to pay out of capital, plus 4 per cent interest, and *Hirsche v Sims*,[97] where directors were ordered to pay compensation in the sum equal to the discount at which they had wrongly caused shares to be issued, and, in the absence of fraud or evidence of further damage to the company from the transaction, the compensation was limited to the amount of the discount and did not extend, for example, to the profit made by the directors from the sale of the shares. In *Knight v Frost*,[98] compensation was ordered in the sum which the director wrongly caused the company to loan to a company connected with the director, and which was subsequently irrecoverable. In *Extrasure Travel Insurance Ltd v Scattergood*,[99] where directors had, in breach of

---

[89] [1900] AC 240, 255, per Lord MacNaghten.

[90] [2003] EWHC 153 at para 131.

[91] *Sinclair Investment Holdings SA v Versailles Trade Finance Ltd* [2007] 2 All ER (comm) 993 at para 128, per Rimer J.

[92] [2004] 1 BCLC 468. See also *Breitenfeld Ltd v Harrison* [2015] 2 BCLC 275.

[93] *Re Sharpe* [1892] 1 Ch 154.

[94] *Queen's Moat House v Bairstow* [2001] 2 BCLC 531. See further paras 19.47 and 19.48 below in relation to unlawful dividends.

[95] *Selangor United Rubber Estates v Craddock (No 3)* [1968] 1 WLR 1555.

[96] (1886) 35 Ch D 502.

[97] [1894] AC 654, HL.

[98] [1999] 1 BCLC 364.

[99] [2003] 1 BCLC 598.

fiduciary duty, caused the company to transfer £200,000 to a company associated with the directors, without any honest belief that it benefited the transferring company, the court ordered (at least on a provisional basis) compensation to be assessed by reference to the amount by which the transferring company's assets had been diminished as a consequence of the wrongful transfer. Moreover, the court held that there was no duty to mitigate.

19.47 There are two competing lines of authority as to the nature of the director's liability in respect of unlawful dividends.[100] On the one hand, there are cases which appear to conclude that a director is under a strict liability to make good such a misapplication of the company's property.[101] On the other hand, there are cases which conclude that a director is only liable if he knew or ought reasonably to have known that it was a misapplication.[102] In *Revenue and Customs Commissioners v Holland; In re Paycheck Services 3 Ltd*[103] Lord Hope noted that the trend of modern authority supported the view that a director who caused a misapplication of a company's assets is in principle strictly liable to make good the misapplication, subject to his rights to make good, if he can, a claim to relief under the 2006 Act, s 1157.[104] While it was unnecessary to express a concluded view on this issue, he thought that this represented the better view.[105]

19.48 The established remedy for breach of duty in causing payment of an unlawful dividend is an order requiring the director to restore the full amount of the moneys wrongfully paid out. In *Revenue and Customs Commissioners v Holland*, however, Lord Hope (*obiter*, agreeing with the majority of the Court of Appeal) considered that it was open to the court, by reason of the discretion conferred by the word 'may' in s 212(3), to limit the amount which is payable by reference to the amount lost by a particular creditor where the claim was made by a party other than the liquidator. In circumstances, therefore, where the claim was brought by HMRC, which was the only creditor, and there was no evidence that anyone else would have been disadvantaged by limiting the liability, Lord Hope held that it would have been a proper exercise of discretion to limit the order for payment to the amount required to make up the deficiency of that creditor.[106] Lord Walker,[107] with whom Lord Clarke agreed,[108] considered, on the other hand, that the discretion conferred by s 212(3) is limited, and does not replicate the court's powers under what is now the 2006 Act, s 1175.[109]

---

[100] *Revenue and Customs Commissioners v Holland; In re Paycheck Services 3 Ltd* [2010] 1 WLR 2793, SC at paras 44–5, per Lord Hope.

[101] See eg *In re Loquitur Ltd* [2003] 2 BCLC 442, 471–2.

[102] See eg *In re City Equitable Fire Insurance Co Ltd* [1925] Ch 407, 426, per Romer J.

[103] [2010] 1 WLR 2793 at paras 46–7.

[104] Formerly 1985 Act, s 727.

[105] That was also the opinion of Lord Walker, at para 124, and Lord Clarke, at para 146, who approved the judgment of Rimer LJ in the Court of Appeal at [2009] 2 BCLC 309 at paras 82–112. See, however, *Madoff Securities International Ltd v Raven* [2014] Lloyd's Rep. FC 95 at paras 197–200, where Popplewell J inclined to the view that such liability was fault based.

[106] [2010] 1 WLR 2793, per Lord Hope at para 49. In the Court of Appeal at paras 129–35, per Elias LJ; at paras 139–43, per Ward LJ.

[107] [2010] 1 WLR 2793 at para 124, agreeing with Rimer LJ's dissenting judgment in the Court of Appeal.

[108] [2010] 1 WLR 2793 at para 146.

[109] In *Re D'Jan of London Ltd* [1994] 1 BCLC 561, Hoffmann LJ reduced the amount to be paid under what is now the 2006 Act, s 1157, not under the Insolvency Act, s 212.

Account of profits

Claims to an account of profits will usually involve a breach of ss 175–7 (duties to avoid con- **19.49**
flicts of interest, not to accept benefits from third parties and to declare interests in proposed
transactions or arrangements).

A defaulting fiduciary is liable to account for any unauthorized profit made by him. This is **19.50**
an aspect of the obligation of a trustee to account for his stewardship of the trust assets.[110]
Where it is established that there has been a transfer of property or payment to a director, the
burden lies on the director to establish that the transfer or payment was proper.[111] The fiduciary is treated as having made the unauthorized profit for the benefit of his principal (the
trust in the case of a trustee, and the company in the case of a director).[112] Where a director
acquires, as a consequence of the breach of duty, an asset which fluctuates in value, then he
can be made liable to account to the company for the value of the asset at its highest value in
the intervening period.[113]

The liability to account for profits is a personal liability of the defaulting fiduciary. A direc- **19.51**
tor is liable to account for (ie to pay over to the company) the profits made by him as a
consequence of his breach of duty whether or not he retains the profits (or their traceable
proceeds). Moreover, a director is liable to account for profit made by him irrespective of
whether the company suffered any loss. In *Premier Waste Management Ltd v Towers*[114] a director had accepted a loan of equipment from a customer of the company in breach of the 'no
conflict rule'. The Court of Appeal held that the absence of evidence that the company would
have taken up the opportunity itself, or suffered any loss as a result of the director's actions,
was irrelevant to the obligation to account for profits made.[115]

Each fiduciary is liable for the unauthorized profit made by him. The question whether a **19.52**
fiduciary is obliged to account for profit made by others was considered in *Regal (Hastings)
v Gulliver*. In that case, one of the director fiduciaries, Gulliver, who had himself made no
profit, had nevertheless participated in the acquisition of shares by others, upon which those
others made a profit. The House of Lords held that Gulliver, not having made any profit
himself, was not liable to account for the profit made by those others[116] (distinguishing, in
the process, cases where partners have been held liable to account for profits made by the

---

[110] Lord Millett, 'Equity's Place in the Law of Commerce' (1998) 114 LQR 214, 225: 'The primary obligation of a trustee is to account for his stewardship.' In *Ultraframe (UK) Ltd v Fielding* [2005] EWHC 1638 at
para 1550 Lewison J said: 'Where a fiduciary makes an unauthorised profit he is liable to account for that profit.
He is treated as having made the profit for the benefit of the trust; and hence the account may be surcharged
with that profit.' See also *Re Allied Business and Financial Consultants Ltd* [2009] 2 BCLC 666, CA.

[111] *Re Snelling House Ltd* [2012] EWHC 440 (Ch) at para 40. See also: *GHLM Trading Ltd v Maroo* [2012] 2
BCLC 369 at paras 143–9; *Burke v Morrison* [2011] BPIR 957; *Re Mumtaz Properties Ltd* [2012] 2 BCLC 109,
CA; *Gilman & Soame Ltd v Young* [2007] EWHC 1245 (Ch); *Sinclair Investments (UK) Ltd v Versailles Trade
Finance Ltd* [2012] Ch 453, CA at para 34.

[112] *Cook v Deeks* [1916] 1 AC 554, 565, PC; *Regal (Hastings) Ltd v Gulliver* [1967] 2 AC 134, 143, HL, per
Lord Russell of Killowen: '[the directors] may be liable to account for the profits which they have made, if, while
standing in a fiduciary relationship to Regal, they have by reason and in course of that fiduciary relationship
made a profit'; *Boardman v Phipps* [1967] 2 AC 46, HL.

[113] *Nant-y-glo and Blaina Ironworks Co v Grave* (1878) 12 Ch D 738; *Target Holdings Ltd v Redferns* [1996]
AC 421.

[114] [2012] 1 BCLC 67, CA.

[115] [2012] 1 BCLC 67, CA at para 51, per Mummery LJ.

[116] [1967] 2 AC 134, 151–2, per Lord Russell of Killowen.

partnership as a result of the breach by one of the partners of a fiduciary obligation owed to a third party).[117]

19.53 More recently, in *Ultraframe (UK) Ltd v Fielding* Lewison J reaffirmed that a fiduciary is only liable to account for profits that he himself has made and is not liable to account for profits made by a third party, save for the case where a company which is a mere cloak or alter ego of the fiduciary makes the relevant profit, in which case it may be appropriate to pierce the corporate veil and treat the company's receipt as the fiduciary's receipt.[118] Lewison J declined to follow, in this respect, a decision of Lawrence Collins J in *CMS Dolphin Ltd v Simonet*[119] to the effect that a fiduciary was liable to account for an unauthorized profit made by a company in which the fiduciary had a substantial interest.[120] Lawrence Collins J's reasoning, that directors are jointly liable with the corporate vehicle formed by them because they have 'jointly participated' in the breach of trust, was expressly disapproved by Lewison J, who considered that the concept of 'joint participation' in a breach of trust has no place in English law.[121]

19.54 Where the court orders an account of profits, the form of the account will vary depending upon the precise circumstances of the case.[122] 'In each case the form of inquiry to be directed is that which will reflect as accurately as possible the true measure of the profit or benefit obtained by the fiduciary in breach of duty.'[123] There is some debate in the authorities as to whether the court can order an account of less than the entire profit made by the defaulting fiduciary,[124] or whether the fiduciary is liable for the whole of the profit but the court is able to fashion the account by defining the profit by reference to the precise circumstances of the breach of duty.[125] In *Ultraframe (UK) Ltd v Fielding*[126] Lewison J derived the following principles from the authorities:

(i) The fundamental rule is that a fiduciary must not make an unauthorized profit out of his fiduciary position.

(ii) The fashioning of an account should not be allowed to operate as the unjust enrichment of the claimant.

---

[117] *Liquidators of Imperial Mercantile Credit Association v Coleman* (1873) LR 6 HL 189.

[118] [2005] EWHC 1638 at paras 1550–76. Cases in which the court has been willing to pierce the corporate veil and treat the profits of a company under the control of the defaulting fiduciary as having been made by the fiduciary include: *Trustor AB v Smallbone (No 2)* [2001] 1 WLR 1177; *Gencor ACP Ltd v Dalby* [2000] 2 BCLC 734.

[119] [2001] 2 BCLC 704; also *Quarter Master UK Ltd v Pyke* [2005] 1 BCLC 245.

[120] *Cook v Deeks* [1916] 1 AC 554 was said by Lawrence Collins J to support the proposition that directors could be jointly liable to account for profits made by a company under their control, even though it was not their alter ego. In contrast, Lewison J, in *Ultraframe* at para 1574 regarded *Cook v Deeks* as establishing no more than that the defaulting fiduciary was liable to account for his own profits.

[121] *Ultraframe (UK) Ltd v Fielding* [2005] EWHC 1638 at paras 1573 and 1574. The concepts of 'dishonest assistance' in a breach of trust and 'knowing receipt' of trust property are, in contrast, well known to English law.

[122] *Re Jarvis* [1958] 1 WLR 815, 820, per Upjohn J.

[123] *Hospital Products Ltd v United States Surgical Corp* (1984) 156 CLR 41, 110, per Mason J.

[124] In *Satnam Investments Ltd v Dunlop Heywood* [1999] 3 All ER 652 the Court of Appeal held that, in determining whether to order an account, the court should apply a principle of proportionality. In that case, because an account would have been a disproportionate response to the nature of the breach of duty committed, the Court of Appeal declined to order any account at all.

[125] *CMS Dolphin Ltd v Simonet* [2001] 2 BCLC 704, 732, per Lawrence Collins J.

[126] [2005] EWHC 1638 at para 1588.

(iii) The profits for which an account is ordered must bear a reasonable relationship to the breach of duty proved.

(iv) It is important to establish exactly what has been acquired.

(v) Subject to that, the fashioning of the account depends on the facts. In some cases it will be appropriate to order an account limited in time;[127] or limited to profits derived from particular assets or particular customers; or to order an account of all the profits of a business subject to just allowances for the fiduciary's skill, labour, and assumption of business risk.[128] In some cases it may be appropriate to order the making of a payment representing the capital value of the advantage in question, either in place of or in addition to an account of profits.[129]

For example: **19.55**

(1) In *Gwembe Valley Development Ltd v Koshy*[130] the Court of Appeal ordered a director guilty of a dishonest breach of fiduciary duty to account for all of the profits made by him, overturning the judge who, it was held, 'failed to follow through the consequences of his finding of dishonesty on the part of Mr Koshy when he declined to order an account against him of *all* the profits obtained by him from the pipeline loan transactions'. The order included profits that were made by the director indirectly through the increase in value of shares in a company which itself received profits, as well as profits that were made by him directly. 'The point', said Mummery LJ, 'is that Mr Koshy was not, as a fiduciary vis a vis GVDC, entitled to retain for his personal benefit any of the unauthorised profits dishonestly made from transactions between him and the company.'[131]

(2) In *Murad v Al Saraj*[132] the Court of Appeal ordered the defaulting fiduciary to account for the whole of the profit made as a consequence of the breach of duty; it was irrelevant that the consent of the beneficiary might have been forthcoming: 'it is only actual consent which obviates the liability to account'; moreover, liability to account did not depend on whether the beneficiary had suffered any loss.[133]

(3) In *Condliffe and Hilton v Sheingold*[134] a director sold, after liquidation of the company, a business which she had formerly run via the company. This was held to be a misappropriation of the goodwill of the business which belonged to the company. The court held that once the director had been found liable to account, it was up to her to raise any matter that could be raised as a proper deduction from profits she actually received. Having agreed, in the sale of the business, a price for the goodwill, the court decided

---

[127] *Warman v Dwyer* (1995) 182 CLR 544.

[128] But see *Guinness v Saunders* below, on whether it would ever be appropriate to permit a defaulting director an allowance by way of remuneration for the work carried out by him. In *FHR European Ventures LLP v Mankarious* [2012] 2 BCLC 39, per Simon J at paras 90–3 and 108, an equitable allowance was refused in the context of a claim against a fiduciary agent in respect of receipt of secret commission. The agent had opportunities to inform its principal of the commission agreement reached with the vendor, but it did not do so.

[129] *Lindsley v Woodfull* [2004] 2 BCLC 131, CA.

[130] [2004] 1 BCLC 131, CA.

[131] At para 137.

[132] [2005] EWCA Civ 959.

[133] Per Arden LJ at paras 71 and 80. Also see *Fanmailuk.com v Cooper* [2011] EWHC 902 (Ch).

[134] [2007] EWCA Civ 1043.

that the price so agreed on was the value of the goodwill, for the purpose of fixing the quantum of the obligation to account.

(4) In *Ross River Ltd v Waveley Commercial Ltd*,[135] the Court of Appeal ordered a defaulting joint venturer to account for all payments made out of the joint venture otherwise than payments authorized under its terms. In particular, the fiduciary was not entitled to exclude from the account payments made in circumstances where the fiduciary believed they would ultimately be justified by the net profits made in the future by the venture. The onus was on the defaulting fiduciary to justify any payment where there was any doubt as to whether it was properly made.[136]

19.56 In *Gencor ACP Ltd v Dalby*[137] Rimer J held that a director guilty of diverting a business opportunity in breach of fiduciary duty was liable to account for the benefit he received from that business, irrespective of whether the company would have been able to take up the opportunity. Rimer J also lifted the corporate veil in respect of an offshore company so that the benefits received by it were treated as benefits received by the director for which he had to account.[138]

19.57 In the case of trustee fiduciaries, it is open to the court to permit a fiduciary who is liable to account for unauthorized profits to claim an allowance for reasonable remuneration for work carried out in effecting the transaction giving rise to the secret profit. In *Boardman v Phipps*,[139] where it was found that the defaulting trustees acted in good faith throughout, the House of Lords agreed with the view of the trial judge that the trustees should be permitted an allowance 'on a liberal scale'.

19.58 In theory, the possibility exists of a similar allowance being permitted in the case of directors who act in breach of fiduciary duty. In *Guinness Plc v Saunders*,[140] however, the House of Lords drew an unfavourable contrast between directors and trustees. Lord Goff considered that to permit a fiduciary an allowance, even in the case of a trustee, was on its face irreconcilable with the 'fundamental principle that a trustee is not entitled to remuneration for services rendered by him to the trust except as expressly provided in the trust deed'. He considered, therefore, that:

> it can only be reconciled with it to the extent that the exercise of the equitable jurisdiction to permit an allowance does not conflict with the policy underlying the rule. And, as I see it, such a conflict will only be avoided if the exercise of the jurisdiction is restricted to those cases where it cannot have the effect of encouraging trustees in any way to put themselves in a position where their interests conflict with their duties as trustees.[141]

---

135 [2014] 1 BCLC 545, CA.

136 [2014] 1 BCLC 545, at para 96. The Court of Appeal also considered the ability of a defaulting fiduciary to expend costs in defending the claim against it. Ordinarily, it would be a striking proposition to say that a fiduciary should not be able to expend its own sums in defending a claim against it. The defaulting co-venturer, however, was a corporation owned by another defendant, who was also guilty of breaching a fiduciary duty owed to the claimant. The Court of Appeal concluded (at para 110) that the real contest was between the claimant and the individual defendant and that, while the corporate defendant was a necessary party, it had no separate interest to protect and it was therefore a breach of fiduciary duty to use its funds (which the court had already found were to be used only for the purposes of the joint venture) in defence of the proceedings.

137 [2000] 2 BCLC 734.

138 See also *Industrial Development Consultants v Cooley* [1972] 1 WLR 443.

139 [1967] 2 AC 46, 104, per Lord Cohen.

140 [1990] 2 AC 663.

141 At 701.

He expressly left open the question whether this was ever possible in the case of a director fiduciary, but could not see any possibility of an allowance being permitted to the director in the *Guinness* case itself. Lord Templeman, in the same case, could not envisage any circumstances in which a court of equity would exercise a power to award remuneration to a director when the relevant articles of association confided that power to the board of directors.[142]

It is to be noted, however, that in *Kingsley IT Consulting v McIntosh*,[143] an account of profits **19.59** was ordered against a former director who had diverted a corporate opportunity to himself, but an allowance of £3,000 per month was given to the former director for the work he had undertaken in exploiting the opportunity. In *Quarter Master UK v Pyke*,[144] on the other hand, Paul Morgan QC applied the approach of Lord Goff in the *Guinness* case (to the effect that the exercise of the jurisdiction to award an allowance was restricted to those cases where it could not have the effect of encouraging trustees or directors in any way to put themselves in a position where their interests conflict with their duties) and, on the facts, refused to make any allowance.

Interest

The power of the court to award interest was recently summarized by the Court of Appeal in **19.60** *Black v Davies*[145] as follows:

(1) The court has no power at common law to award interest.
(2) The statutory power to award interest, pursuant to the Senior Courts Act 1981, s 35A is limited to simple interest.
(3) The court had an equitable jurisdiction to award compound interest in certain cases, those cases being limited to (a) those involving the obtaining and retention of money by fraud and (b) the withholding or misapplication of money by a trustee or fiduciary who was liable to account for the profit made by him.[146]

The inability of the common law to award compound interest was addressed to a large extent by the House of Lords in *Sempra Metals v IRC*.[147] It was there decided that the common law jurisdiction to grant restitutionary relief permitted the court in an appropriate case to award compound interest as part of its restitutionary relief. The House of Lords also held that the court had jurisdiction at common law to award compound interest as damages for breach of any contractual or tortious duty.

In cases involving breach by misapplication of the company's money by a director in breach **19.61** of fiduciary duty, accordingly, the court may (and often will) award compound interest.[148] On the other hand, in *Knight v Frost*[149] the court refused to award compound interest on the basis that such an award is usually intended to ensure that as far as possible the defendant retains no profit for which he ought to account, and on the facts it was plain that the

---

[142] Above at 694.
[143] [2005] BCC 875.
[144] [2005] 1 BCLC 245, 271–2.
[145] [2005] EWCA Civ 531.
[146] *Westdeutsche Landesbank v Islington LBC* [1996] AC 669, HL; *Wallensteiner v Moir* [1975] QB 373, CA; *President of India v La Pintanda Compania Navigacion SA* [1985] AC 104, HL.
[147] [2008] AC 561, HL.
[148] *Bank of Credit and Commerce International SA v Saadi* [2005] EWHC 2256 (QB), Forbes J.
[149] [1999] 1 BCLC 364.

defendant had not retained any of the money transferred to it in breach of duty, but had immediately defrayed it on expenses.

19.62   In the case of liability for breach of an express trust, the Court of Appeal, in *Bartlett v Barclays Trust Co (No 2)*,[150] held that the appropriate rate of interest was that received from time to time on the courts' short-term investment account. In the case of breach of duty by directors, however, it would appear that the more commercial approach advocated in *Sempra Metals* (above) is appropriate; on this basis the rate of interest would be calculated by reference to the benefit actually received (if interest is awarded in a restitution context, eg where it is awarded in conjunction with an account of profits made) or by reference to the loss actually suffered by the company being kept out of its money (if interest is awarded in the context of an award for compensation).

Injunctions

19.63   The court has wide-ranging powers to grant injunctive relief against directors guilty of actual or threatened breaches of duty, both on a final and interlocutory basis.

19.64   A final injunction may take one of two forms, or a combination of both. Where it is established that particular proposed conduct on the part of a director would constitute a breach of fiduciary duty the court may grant a permanent injunction to restrain the director from committing the breach. This is an inherently less likely possibility, given the practical difficulties in identifying possible breaches of fiduciary duty before they are committed. Alternatively, where it is established that a director has committed a breach of fiduciary duty then injunctive relief may be available to prevent the director from continuing the breach. An injunction may be granted, for example, to restrain a director from continuing a business which it is proved constituted a corporate opportunity wrongly acquired by him in breach of duty, or to restrain a director from exploiting information acquired in breach of confidence.[151] Such an injunction may be granted on an interim basis, pending trial. One particular consideration which is likely to arise in such a case, however, is whether the grant of such an injunction would lead to the worst of both worlds: the destruction of the new business set up by the defaulting director (so as to remove any possibility of profits being made, and subsequently accounted for to the claimant in the event the claim succeeded), but without a corresponding benefit to the claimant, for example because the poached employees or customers did not return to the claimant. It was on this basis that an interim injunction was refused in *Wright v Pyke*.[152]

19.65   The most common form of interim injunction is the freezing order. This, as the name suggests, 'freezes' assets of the defendant (either particular assets, or assets up to the value of the

---

[150] [1980] Ch 515, CA.

[151] See the analogous line of cases dealing with misuse of confidential information or trade secrets by former employees: *Faccenda Chickens v Fowler* [1987] Ch 117; *Lancashire Fires Ltd v S A Lyons & Co Ltd* [1997] IRLR 117; *Take v BSM Marketing* [2006] EWHC 1085; *Dranez Anstalt v Hayek* [2002] 1 BCLC 693, in which Evans-Lombe J held that an ex-director who set up a competing business was in no worse position than an ex-employee so far as concerned his exploitation of the skills and experience acquired while he was a director (although the judge's decision on the facts was reversed by the Court of Appeal [2003] 1 BCLC 278). In *Hedgehog Golf Co Ltd v Hauser* [2011] EWHC 689 (Ch) the court granted a permanent injunction to restrain a former director from disclosing confidential information.

[152] [2013] BCC 300, CA. See also *Allfiled UK Limited v Eltis* [2015] EWHC 1300 (Ch), in which an interim injunction was granted so as to prevent the directors and employees from using confidential information in a new company.

claim), thereby preventing him from dealing with those assets in a way which would prevent them from being available to satisfy any judgment obtained by the claimant. This is not confined to cases in which a proprietary claim is made, but is potentially available wherever a judgment for the payment of money is sought against a defendant. A freezing order could therefore be relevant in any case where damages, equitable compensation, or an account of profits are sought against a director, whether the claim is for a breach of fiduciary duty or breach of a duty to exercise reasonable skill and care.

In essence, a freezing order may be granted where the court is satisfied that the claimant has **19.66** a good arguable case and there is a real risk that in the absence of an injunction any judgment ultimately obtained may go unsatisfied. A freezing order may also be obtained following judgment, to ensure that assets of the defendant against which the judgment could be executed are not dissipated pending enforcement of the judgment.[153]

In any case where a proprietary claim is made against a director or third party arising out of a **19.67** breach of fiduciary duty by the director, the court's equitable jurisdiction extends to granting an injunction to preserve the property over which the company claims a beneficial interest and correspondingly to restrain dealing with the particular asset. Such an injunction may be available in circumstances which would not satisfy a claim for a freezing order, for example because there is insufficient evidence of a risk of dissipation of the defendant's assets.[154]

As an adjunct to injunctive relief in the context of a proprietary claim, the court has, in a **19.68** number of cases, ordered the defendant to disclose the whereabouts of property or money claimed to belong in equity to the claimant.[155]

Where a simple freezing order is sought, it is common to permit the defendant to use his funds **19.69** (otherwise frozen) for payment of reasonable legal costs. Where an injunction is sought in support of a proprietary claim over specific funds of the defendant, then the position is more problematic. The court is naturally reluctant to permit a defendant to use funds which, if the claimant's claim turns out to be correct, belong beneficially to the claimant. On the other hand, the court is also reluctant to deprive a defendant of the ability to use funds which are only arguably subject to a proprietary claim in favour of the claimant, in order to defend that very claim. These competing considerations were discussed in *PCW (Underwriting Agencies) v Dixon*.[156] The proprietary claim in that case extended to the entirety of the defendant's assets. Lloyd J considered, in those circumstances, that it would be unjust to deprive the defendant of the use of his assets, notwithstanding the pending proprietary claim, and therefore held that the balance came down in favour of permitting the use of the funds in order to pay legal expenses. In the unreported case of *Sundt Wrigley & Co v Wrigley*,[157] Sir Thomas Bingham MR said that:

> a careful and anxious judgment has to be made in a case where a proprietary claim is advanced by the plaintiff as to whether the injustice of permitting the use of the funds by the defendant

---

[153] See Gee, *Commercial Injunctions*, 6th edn (Sweet and Maxwell, July 2016) for a full description of the circumstances in which freezing orders may be granted.

[154] *Polly Peck International plc v Nadir* [1992] 4 All ER 769, 784, CA.

[155] *Bankers Trust Co v Shapira* [1980] 1 WLR 1274; *A v C (No 1)* [1981] QB 956; *PCW (Underwriting Agencies) Ltd v Dixon* [1983] 2 Lloyd's Rep 197.

[156] [1983] 2 Lloyd's Rep 197.

[157] Court of Appeal, 23 June 1993.

is out-weighed by the possible injustice to the defendant if he is denied the opportunity of advancing what may of course turn out to be a successful defence.

In that case, the Court of Appeal did not interfere with the first-instance judge's decision to allow the defendant to use a very substantial portion of the claimed funds in order to pay his legal expenses.[158]

19.70 It was made clear by the Court of Appeal, however, in *Fitzgerald v Williams*,[159] that a defendant who wished to obtain permission to use funds covered by a 'proprietary' interim injunction would first have to satisfy the court, on proper evidence, that there were no funds or assets available to him to be utilized for the payment of his legal fees other than the assets to which the claimants maintained an arguable proprietary claim.

19.71 Moreover, in *United Mizrahi Bank Ltd v Doherty*,[160] it was held that even where the court (in the exercise of its discretionary jurisdiction relating to the grant of injunctions) does permit a defendant to use funds that are the subject of a proprietary claim to pay legal expenses incurred in defending proceedings, that merely precludes an action for contempt being brought against the defendant (since it would cause the use of the funds not to be a breach of the injunction). In particular, such an order of the court would not necessarily mean that third parties (eg the lawyers instructed to defend the proceedings) who received funds from the defendant could not be found to hold those funds on constructive trust for the claimant.

Delivery up of documents

19.72 A director is under a continuing liability to deliver up documents relating to the affairs of the company notwithstanding he has ceased to be a director. The liability arises from his position as agent of the company, and is not dependent on his fiduciary obligations. In *Fairstar Heavy Transport NV v Adkins*[161] a company sought to inspect and copy the content of emails on a former employee's computer relating to the company's business affairs. The Court of Appeal concluded: (1) the former relationship had been that of principal and agent; (2) it is as a general rule a legal incident of that relationship that a principal is entitled to require production by the agent of documents relating to the affairs of the principal; (3) 'documents' may include information recorded, stored, or held by other means than paper; (4) materials held on a computer, which may be displayed in readable form on a screen or printed out on paper are in principle covered by the same incidents of agency as apply to paper documents; (5) accordingly, and quite apart from the question whether the company had any proprietary right to the information, the former employee was under a duty to allow the company to inspect emails sent to or received by him and relating to its business.

(5) Personal claims against third parties

19.73 Personal claims against third parties arising out of a breach of fiduciary duty by a director fall into two categories: (i) dishonest assistance in breach of fiduciary duty and (ii) unconscionable receipt of trust property.

---

[158] In *Phillips v Symes*, 1 May 2001, Neuberger J said: 'it seems to me that the court should be very slow indeed before it makes an order the effect of which will be to deprive a party of the ability to obtain legal representation, especially in complex litigation involving large sums of money and a great deal of evidence such as the present case'.

[159] [1996] QB 657, CA.

[160] [1998] 1 WLR 435.

[161] [2013] EWCA Civ 886.

Dishonest assistance

A third party who dishonestly assists in a breach of fiduciary duty may be personally liable **19.74**
to pay compensation to the company.[162] The claim is a personal, fault-based one and has
nothing to do with the receipt of trust property.[163] In addition, an account of profits may be
ordered against the dishonest assister—even if the principal suffered no loss and the fiduciary
made no gains from his or her breach of duty.[164]

In order to impose liability on a defendant for dishonest assistance in a breach of fiduci- **19.75**
ary duty, three matters must be established. First, the fiduciary must have committed a
breach of fiduciary duty, although it is not necessary to show that the breach was committed
dishonestly.[165]

Secondly, the defendant must have assisted in that breach. The mere receipt of trust property **19.76**
does not count as assistance: *Brown v Bennett*.[166] In *Brink's Ltd v Abu-Saleh*,[167] the fact that
the wife of the defaulting fiduciary accompanied him on money laundering trips was not
considered sufficient assistance to impose liability on her.

Thirdly, the defendant must have acted 'dishonestly'. In *Royal Brunei Airlines Sdn Bhd v* **19.77**
Tan[168] Lord Nicholls defined dishonesty as 'simply not acting as an honest person would in
the circumstances' and explained that this involved both subjective and objective elements.
This appears to have been interpreted in *Twinsectra Ltd v Yardley*[169] as a twofold test: (a) that
what was done was dishonest by the standards of ordinary people, and (b) that the assistant knew that what he was doing was, by those standards, dishonest.[170] This precluded
the assistant from relying on his own (non-standard) concept of what was acceptable. In
Barlow Clowes International Ltd v Eurostrust International Ltd,[171] however, the Privy Council
disagreed with this twofold analysis of *Twinsectra*. According to Lord Hoffmann in *Barlow
Clowes*, the House of Lords in *Twinsectra* had not intended to depart in this respect from the

---

[162] *Royal Brunei Airlines Sdn Bhd v Tan* [1995] AC 378, PC; *Twinsectra Ltd v Yardley* [2002] 2 AC 164, HL
(explained in *Barlow Clowes International Ltd v Eurotrust International Ltd* [2006] 1 WLR 1476, PC). Rattee
J, in *Brown v Bennett* [1998] 2 BCLC 97, had held that liability for dishonest assistance was applicable only
in cases of breach of trust, and not breaches of fiduciary duty. The Court of Appeal in the same case, [1999]
1 BCLC 649, doubted that this was correct, but did not decide the point. The Privy Council in the *Tan* case
stated the principle as covering dishonest assistance both in a breach of trust and in a breach of fiduciary duty
(see [1995] AC 378, per Lord Nicholls at 392). Subsequent decisions have assumed that dishonest assistance
in the breach of a fiduciary duty attracts liability under this principle: see eg *Caring Together Ltd v Bauso* [2006]
EWHC 2345 (Ch); *AG of Zambia v Meer Care & Desai* [2008] EWCA Civ 1007, CA. In *JD Wetherspoon v
Van de Berg* [2009] EWHC 639, Peter Smith J concluded, at para 518, that it was unnecessary (in order to find
accessory liability for dishonest assistance) that there was any trust property: it was sufficient that the accessory
had assisted a breach by another in a fiduciary position.
[163] *Twinsectra Ltd v Yardley* [2002] 2 AC 164, 194, per Lord Millett; *Royal Brunei Airlines Sdn Bhd v Tan*
[1995] AC 378, 387, per Lord Nicholls.
[164] *Novoship (UK) Ltd v Nikitin* [2015] QB 499, CA, at paras 66–93 (a judgment described by Lord Mance
as 'penetrating'); see *Central Bank of Ecuador v Conticorp SA* [2015] UKPC 11 at para 185 (in the judgment on
interest). For further commentary on this case and *FHR European Ventures* see Davies, 'Gain-Based Remedies
for Dishonest Assistance' (2015) LQR 131 (Apr), 173–6.
[165] *Royal Brunei Airlines Sdn Bhd v Tan* [1995] AC 378, 384, 385, PC.
[166] [1999] 1 BCLC 649, 659, CA, per Morritt LJ.
[167] [1999] CLC 133.
[168] [1995] AC 378, 389, PC.
[169] [2002] 2 AC 164, HL.
[170] This was followed in *Ultraframe (UK) Ltd v Fielding* [2005] EWHC 1638 at para 1498.
[171] [2006] 1 WLR 1476, PC.

decision of the Privy Council in *Tan* and, in particular, the House of Lords in *Twinsectra* had not intended to suggest that an assistant must have had 'reflections' or 'thoughts' about what the normally acceptable standards of honest conduct were.[172]

19.78 Accordingly, in order to find a person liable for dishonest assistance it must be shown that he had knowledge of the elements of the transaction which rendered his participation contrary to ordinary standards of honest behaviour, but it did not require him to have reflections on what those normally acceptable standards were.[173] A person who deliberately shuts his eyes so as to avoid confirming a suspicion that the relevant facts exist is dishonest (provided that the suspicion is 'firmly grounded and targeted on specific facts'): *Manifest Shipping Co Ltd v Uni-Polaris Insurance Co Ltd*.[174]

Knowing receipt

19.79 A third party who receives property as a consequence of a director's breach of fiduciary duty may be liable to pay compensation to the company. This is a personal liability which is dependent upon *receipt* of the relevant property but not upon the *retention* of that property.[175] In order to impose liability, it must be established that:[176]

(1) there was a disposal of assets of the company in breach of fiduciary duty;
(2) there was beneficial receipt by the defendant of assets which are traceable as representing the assets of the company;[177] and
(3) the defendant acted with knowledge that the assets are traceable to a breach of fiduciary duty.

19.80 After considerable debate in the authorities,[178] the Court of Appeal in *Bank of Credit and Commerce International (Overseas) Ltd v Akindele*[179] held that there was a single test of 'knowledge' for the purposes of knowing receipt cases, namely that the defendant's state of knowledge should be such as to make it 'unconscionable' for him to retain the benefit of the receipt. Unconscionability is established if the third party had the

---

[172] See also *JD Wetherspoon v Van de Berg* [2009] EWHC 639, per Peter Smith J at para 503: 'whether the individual was aware that his conduct fell below the objective standard is not part of the test'.

[173] *Barlow Clowes International Ltd v Eurotrust International Ltd* [2006] 1 WLR 1476, PC. In *Abou-Rahmah v Abacha* [2007] 1 All ER (Comm) 827, CA, the majority of the Court of Appeal appear to have accepted that the *Barlow Clowes* decision must be taken as representing English law. Lewison J, in *Mullarkey v Broad* [2008] 1 BCLC 638, took the same view. See also: *Barnes v Tomlinson* [2006] EWHC 3115; *AG of Zambia v Meer Care & Desai* [2007] EWHC 952 (Ch); [2008] EWCA Civ 1007, CA; Sir Anthony Clarke MR, 'Claims against Professionals: Negligence, Dishonesty and Fraud' [2006] 22 *Professional Negligence* 70–85; Yeo, 'Dishonest Assistance: A Restatement from the Privy Council' [2006] 122 LQR 171–4.

[174] [2003] 1 AC 469, HL at para 116, per Lord Scott. In *Nolan v Minerva Trust* [2014] JRC 78A, the Royal Court of Jersey found a trust company guilty of dishonest assistance in a breach of trust where they paid money away on the instruction of the fraudster (their client), notwithstanding that they did not know he was a fraudster. For discussion of the case see Redgrave, 'Nolan v Minerva: A Jersey Perspective on Dishonest Assistance' (2015) PCB 1, 8–19.

[175] *Ultraframe (UK) Ltd v Fielding* [2005] EWHC 1638 at para 1486.

[176] *El Ajou v Dollar Land Holdings Ltd* [1994] 2 All ER 685, 700, CA, per Hoffmann LJ.

[177] The receipt must be the direct consequence of the breach of fiduciary duty: *Brown v Bennett* [1999] 1 BCLC 649, 655, CA.

[178] eg as to whether 'constructive knowledge' was sufficient: see *Re Montagu's Settlement Trusts* [1987] Ch 264; *Eagle Trust plc v SBC Securities Ltd* [1993] 1 WLR 484; *Cowan de Groot Properties Ltd v Eagle Trust plc* [1992] 4 All ER 700; *Baden v Société Générale pour Favoriser le Développement du Commerce et de l'Industrie en France SA* [1993] 1 WLR 509.

[179] [2001] Ch 437. Followed in *Charter plc v City Index Ltd* [2008] Ch 313, CA.

requisiste knowledge either when he acquired the property or at any time when he still retained it.[180]

The use of 'unconscionability' as the touchstone of liability is surprising in the light of the **19.81** following passage from Lord Nicholls' opinion in *Royal Brunei Airlines Sdn Bhd v Tan*:[181]

> It must be recognised, however, that unconscionable is not a word in everyday use by non-lawyers. If it is to be used in this context, and if it is to be the touchstone for liability as an accessory, it is essential to be clear on what, in this context, unconscionable means. If unconscionable means no more than dishonesty, then dishonesty is the preferable label. If unconscionable means something different, it must be said that it is not clear what that something different is. Either way, therefore, the term is better avoided in this context.

In *Criterion Properties plc v Stratford UK Properties LLC*[182] the House of Lords held that the test of **19.82** unconscionability had no application to a case where challenge was made to a transaction which a director had procured the company to enter into in breach of fiduciary duty. The question in such a case (see above at paragraph 19.15) was not one of knowing receipt at all, but related to the enforceability of a transaction entered into in excess of the directors' powers (see further below). The House of Lords did not, however, disapprove of the single test of 'unconscionability' for true cases of knowing receipt, and that test has been followed and applied in subsequent cases.[183]

There has been considerable academic debate[184] as to whether there is an alternative claim in **19.83** restitution against the recipient of property paid away by a company as a result of a breach of fiduciary duty by its director. If so, such a claim would not be dependent upon establishing fault, but the defendant would be able to assert any restitutionary defence, such as change of position, if available to him. The possibility of bringing a claim in restitution, as opposed to knowing receipt or dishonest assistance, was rejected by the Court of Appeal in *Bank of Credit and Commerce International (Overseas) Ltd v Akindele*.[185] In *Relfo Ltd v Varsani*,[186] however, Sales J (*obiter*) concluded that a proper ground for a personal claim in unjust enrichment was clearly made out where the company's consent to a transfer from it to a third party was procured through a breach of fiduciary duty by its director. On appeal from that decision,[187] the Court of Appeal agreed, concluding that as a matter of substance the defendant had been a direct recipient of a payment made by the company, and that this was sufficient causal connection to support a remedy of unjust enrichment. In Australia, an attempt to raise such an

---

[180] *Relfo Ltd v Varsani* [2012] EWHC 2168 (Ch), per Sales J at paras 79 and 80.

[181] [1995] 2 AC 378, 392, PC.

[182] [2004] 1 WLR 1846.

[183] *Pakistan v Zardari* [2006] EWHC 2411 (Comm); *Ultraframe (UK) Ltd v Fielding* [2005] EWHC 1638 (Ch); *Wexham Drinks v Corkery* [2005] EWHC 1731.

[184] Fuelled to some extent by an article by Lord Nicholls of Birkenhead in 'Knowing Receipt: The Need for a New Landmark' in Cornish et al (eds), *Restitution Past, Present and Future* (Hart Publishing, 1998), p 231.

[185] [2001] Ch 437, 456:

> No argument before us was based on the suggestions made in Lord Nicholls's essay. Indeed, at this level of decision, it would have been a fruitless exercise. We must continue to do our best with the accepted formulation of the liability in knowing receipt, seeking to simplify and improve it where we may. While in general it may be possible to sympathise with a tendency to subsume a further part of our law of restitution under the principles of unjust enrichment, I beg leave to doubt whether strict liability coupled with a change of position defence would be preferable to fault-based liability in many commercial transactions, for example where, as here, the receipt is of a company's funds which have been misapplied by its directors.

[186] [2012] EWHC 2168 (Ch) at para 883.

[187] [2015] 1 BCLC 14 (CA).

argument was rejected by the High Court,[188] primarily on the ground that the point had not been raised below and it would be unfair to allow it to be raised on appeal. The High Court also considered, however, that there were considerable difficulties in the way of such a claim, not least because it involved no recognized basis for reversing an unjust enrichment.

Interest

19.84   For the power of the court to award interest, see paragraph 19.60 above. A person who dishonestly receives and retains fiduciary property or who procures or assists a director to misapply it is just as much liable to pay compound interest as the director.[189]

C.   Remedies for Breach of Duty of Care

19.85   A director who breaches his duty to exercise reasonable skill and care is liable to pay damages for that breach, in accordance with the common law principles applicable to negligence claims, including the common law principles of causation, foreseeability, and quantification of damages.[190]

19.86   Examples of cases where directors have been ordered to pay damages for breach of a duty of care include: *Dorchester Finance Co v Stebbing*,[191] where an enquiry as to damages was ordered; *Re D'Jan of London*,[192] where, taking into account the defence available to the director under what is now the 2006 Act, s 1157, Hoffmann LJ ordered the director to pay compensation limited to an amount equal to any further dividends which he would otherwise have received from the company's liquidation; and *Re Simmons Box (Diamonds) Ltd, Cohen v Selby*,[193] a case under the Insolvency Act s 212, where the Court of Appeal emphasized that the amount which a director should be ordered to contribute under that section must be specifically related to the amount of damage which his breach of duty caused the company.

D.   Relief from Liability

19.87   The Companies Act, s 1157 re-enacts the 1985 Act, s 727 without change.[194] Section 1157(1) provides as follows:

> If in proceedings for negligence, default, breach of duty or breach of trust against—

---

[188]   *Farah Construction Pty Ltd v Say-Dee Pty Ltd* [2007] HCA 22.

[189]   *Central Bank of Ecuador v Conticorp SA* [2015] UKPC 11 at paras 185, 186 (following submissions on interest and not included in the report at [2016] 1 BCLC 26), applying the analysis of the Court of Appeal in *Novoship (UK) Ltd v Nikitin* [2015] QB 499, CA at paras 66–93, which held that the remedy of account of profits was available against a dishonest assister in a breach of fiduciary duty.

[190]   It is necessary to show eg that the loss claimed fell within the scope of the director's duty of care: see *South Australia Asset Management Corporation v York Montague Ltd* [1997] AC 191, 124, per Lord Hoffmann. Note that the Compensation Act 2006, s 1 modifies the common law by requiring a court—when considering whether a person ought to have taken particular steps to meet a standard of care—to have regard to the fact that a requirement that those steps be taken might prevent a desirable activity from being undertaken at all, or discourage persons from undertaking a desirable activity. This is unlikely, however, to have any material impact on the scope of duty owed by directors to the company itself.

[191]   [1989] BCLC 498.

[192]   [1994] 1 BCLC 561.

[193]   [2001] 1 BCLC 176.

[194]   s 1157 replaced 1985 Act, s 727 on 1 October 2008; 2006 Act Commencement Order No 5, para 5(1) (f).

(a) an officer[195] of a company, or

(b) a person employed by a company as auditor (whether or not he is an officer of the company),

it appears to the court hearing the case that the officer or person is or may be liable but that he acted honestly and reasonably, and that having regard to all the circumstances of the case (including those connected with his appointment) he ought fairly to be excused, the court may relieve him, either wholly or in part, from his liability on such terms as it thinks fit.

As the wording of the section makes plain, relief may be granted in relation to breaches of **19.88** fiduciary duty as much as in relation to breaches of a duty of care. It would include, therefore, relief against liability to account for profits made as a result of a breach of fiduciary duty.[196] It does not include, however, liability imposed on a director imposed by legislation other than that regulating his duties to the company.[197] It has also been held that the section cannot be used to relieve from a liability to repay, for example, remuneration wrongly received by a director, where the apparent contract under which the remuneration was paid was void: see *Guinness Plc v Saunders*,[198] where Lord Templeman noted that if s 727 were to apply it would have entitled the director to remuneration in circumstances where such entitlement depended on the authority of the board and there had in fact been no such authority. The section also does not apply to claims for wrongful trading under the Insolvency Act, s 214,[199] or to claims under ss 216 and 217 of that Act (liability for reuse of prohibited company name).[200]

In order to be relieved from liability a director must establish three things: (i) that he acted **19.89** honestly, (ii) that he acted reasonably, and (iii) that having regard to all the circumstances he ought fairly to be excused. The first of these is a subjective requirement, the second an objective requirement.[201]

It might be thought odd that a director could establish that he had acted reasonably in cir- **19.90** cumstances so as to relieve him of a liability in negligence where, by definition, the court will have found him to have breached a duty to act with reasonable skill and care. There is no doubt, however, that the court can grant relief under the section from liability in

---

[195] It was held in *Ultraframe (UK) Ltd v Fielding* [2005] EWHC 1638 at para 1452 that 'officer' did not include a shadow director, who was thus outside the scope of the section.

[196] *Coleman Taymar Ltd v Oakes* [2001] 2 BCLC 749.

[197] *Customs & Excise Commissioners v Hedon Alpha Ltd* [1981] 1 QB 818, CA, which related to liability under the Betting and Gaming Duties Act 1972. Cf the position in Australia: *Edwards v AG* (2004) 60 NSWLR 667.

[198] [1990] 2 AC 663.

[199] *Re Produce Marketing Consortium (No 1)* [1990] 1 WLR 745; *Re Brian D Pierson (Contractors) Ltd* [2001] 1 BCLC 275. In *IRC v McEntaggart* [2006] 1 BCLC 476, Patten J held that the section did not apply to relieve a person from liability under the CDDA, s 15 (which imposes liability on an undischarged bankrupt, who acts as a director of a company, for the debts of that company), because 'the provisions of s 727 applied only where the essential nature of the proceedings, whether they be brought in equity or under the provisions of the companies legislation, was to enforce, at the suit of or for the benefit of the company, the duties which the director owed to the company'. Whether or not the section can be used to grant relief from liability under the Insolvency Act, s 217 (which imposes liability on a director for use of a prohibited name) was expressly left open by the Court of Appeal in *ESS Production Ltd v Sully* [2005] 2 BCLC 547.

[200] *First Independent Factors Ltd v Mountford* [2008] 2 BCLC 297. At paras 31–33, it was held that s 727 did not apply to a claim under the Insolvency Act 1986, ss 216 and 217, because such a claim was not brought by or on behalf of the company of whom the defendant was a director and did not involve any consideration of his duties owed under the Companies Acts.

[201] *Coleman Taymar Ltd v Oakes* [2001] 2 BCLC 749, 770; *Re MDA Investment Management Ltd* [2004] 1 BCLC 217.

negligence.[202] In *Barings plc v Coopers & Lybrand*,[203] for example, Evans-Lombe J held that auditors whom he had found guilty of relatively technical breaches of a duty to take reasonable care were entitled to be partially relieved of liability in proceedings brought by the company's liquidators. Their conduct could be described as reasonable given that their breaches of duty were not 'pervasive and compelling'.[204] In *Green v Walkling*[205] the deputy judge had found that the defendant director was not guilty of breach of duty because, among other reasons, he had followed legal advice in continuing to act as a director after the discovery of a VAT fraud committed by his fellow director. The defendant director had reported the fraud to HMRC, but there had been significant delay on their part in taking action. The deputy judge nevertheless went on to consider the application of s 1157 in case his conclusion on breach of duty was set aside. In this regard, he held, in circumstances where the director had acted on legal advice, had reported the fraud to HMRC, and had not profited in any way from the breaches of duty, it would have been right to relieve him from liability under s 1157.

19.91 The burden of establishing honesty and reasonableness lies on the director.[206] In a case decided before the introduction of the new Civil Procedure Rules in England and Wales, it was held that the defence may be raised at trial, and that there was no requirement specifically to plead the defence, so that no particulars of the defence would be ordered.[207] It remains to be seen whether a court would require details of the facts and matters which a defendant sought to rely on in support of the defence pursuant to the court's powers to order further information or clarification of a party's case under CPR Part 18. In *Revenue and Customs Commissioners v Holland*[208] there was considerable debate as to the reasonableness of the conduct of a director who caused the company to make unlawful dividends. It was found at first instance[209] that the director had acted reasonably in causing the dividends to be made at least until such time as he received advice from Queen's Counsel in relation to the company's tax liability which had the consequence of rendering continued trading wrongful. There was no appeal against the conclusion that the director had acted reasonably until receipt of that advice. The deputy judge at first instance also held, however, that the director was allowed a period of grace from the receipt of the advice, in order to consider its impact, before it could be said he acted unreasonably in continuing to trade (and thus cause further dividends to be

---

[202] The words of the section make this plain; and see *Re D'Jan of London* [1994] 1 BCLC 561; *Re MDA Investment Management Ltd* [2004] 1 BCLC 217; *PNC Telecom plc v Thomas (No 2)* [2008] 2 BCLC 95.

[203] [2003] EWHC 1319, [2003] PNLR 34.

[204] See also *Maelor Jones Inv v Heywood-Smith* (1989) 54 SASR 285, where express consideration was given by Olsson J, in the South Australian Supreme Court, to whether there is any limitation (both in terms of scope and time frame) to the South Australian equivalent to s 727. He concluded (at 295) that: 'Whilst it may be that, in a particular situation, the very circumstances which give rise to a finding of negligence may be so pervasive and compelling as also to demand a conclusion that a person had acted unreasonably for the purposes of the exculpatory section, nevertheless that section is to be taken to directing its attention to a much wider area of concern—both in point of scope and time frame.'

[205] [2008] 2 BCLC 332. See also *Re Pro4sport Ltd* [2016] 1 BCLC 257 at paras 54–5 for an example of a further case where the court would have relieved the director from liabilty had it considered there was a breach of duty in the first place.

[206] *Bairstow v Queens Moat Houses plc* [2001] 2 BCLC 531, CA at para 58; *Re Loquitur Ltd* [2003] 2 BCLC 442 at para 228. *Re In A Flap Envelope Company Ltd* [2004] 1 BCLC 64 is an example of a case where the director's refusal to give oral evidence meant that he was unable to discharge the burden of establishing that he acted honestly.

[207] *Re Kirby's Coaches Ltd* [1991] BCLC 414.

[208] [2009] BCLC 309, CA; [2010] 1 WLR 2793, SC.

[209] [2008] 2 BCLC 613.

paid). Although the issue did not strictly arise for decision in the Court of Appeal, the majority agreed, considering the relevant question to be from when the director should be taken to have acted unreasonably so that the defence was no longer available. Rimer LJ's dissent on this point was based on his view that the director had not used the few days following the receipt of the advice to consider its impact but had 'put his head in the sand and adopted a "business as usual" policy'.[210] In the Supreme Court, Lord Hope agreed with the majority of the Court of Appeal.

It is only if both of the first two requirements are established that the court needs to consider the third requirement, that in all the circumstances the director ought fairly to be excused. 'All the circumstances' has been widely interpreted by the courts. In the Australian case of *AWA Ltd v Daniels*[211] Rogers CJ rejected a submission on behalf of the company that the phrase 'all the circumstances of the case' in the Australian equivalent of the section should be construed narrowly so as to limit it to a consideration of the way in which the default or breach occurred. He found that the phrase was broad enough to encompass the circumstances of a release given by a company to its former directors, in the context of a negligence claim by the company against its auditors. In *Re D'Jan of London Ltd*,[212] Hoffmann LJ, in exercising his discretion under the 1985 Act, s 727, took into account the fact that in light of the company's solvent position at the time of the breach of duty of care by the director and the fact that he and his wife owned all the shares in the company, he had been foreseeably putting only his and his wife's interests at risk. In *Re Barry and Staines Linoleum Ltd*[213] Maugham J considered that the current views of the shareholders and other directors of the company (which was solvent) would be relevant to the question whether the particular director found to be in breach of duty should be granted relief. Finally, in *Re Duomatic Ltd*,[214] Buckley J relieved a director from liability in respect of unauthorized drawings having regard to the fact that he was in control of the company, could have passed a resolution in general meeting permitting the drawings, and it was a mere oversight that he had not passed the requisite resolution.

19.92

Examples of successful applications under the predecessors of the 2006 Act, s 1157 in practice include the following. The court relieved directors, guilty of causing the company to enter into an ultra vires transaction, since they had acted in good faith having taken advice from counsel that the transaction was *intra vires*.[215] In a case where the directors of a company consisted of a husband and wife, but where the wife in fact undertook no executive management functions, the court relieved her from liability in respect of misfeasance claims involving the transfer of goodwill and other assets of the company shortly before its liquidation.[216]

19.93

More often than not the attempt to obtain relief is unsuccessful. Examples include the following. In a case involving the payment of an unlawful dividend, the court found that the directors had acted honestly and reasonably where they had taken advice before paying the dividend. Nevertheless the court refused to grant relief against liability imposed under

19.94

---

[210] [2009] BCLC 309 at para 87, per Rimer LJ.
[211] (1992) 7 ACSR 463.
[212] [1994] 1 BCLC 561.
[213] [1934] 1 Ch 227.
[214] [1969] 2 Ch 365.
[215] *Re Claridge's Patent Asphalte Co Ltd* [1921] 1 Ch 543.
[216] *Re Brian D Pierson (Contractors) Ltd* [2001] 1 BCLC 275.

the 1985 Act, s 263 where the consequences of granting relief would have been to leave the directors in enjoyment of benefits, at the expense of creditors, which they would never have received but for the default.[217] In a case where the court found that the companies' failure was the result of mismanagement and disastrous financial handling, most of which was the responsibility of the defendant director, the court would have refused to exercise its discretion to grant relief, even if it had found that the director's conduct was reasonable.[218] Similarly, in *Re Westlowe Storage and Distribution Ltd*[219] the court refused to grant relief where, although the director had acted in good faith and in what he believed to be the interests of the company in intermingling its affairs with a separate joint venture, his failure to put in place proper accounting procedures was not reasonable. Where directors acted blindly at the behest of the majority shareholders, who had appointed them to the board, in disposing of large sums without any regard for the minority shareholders, the court held that the directors had not acted reasonably even if they had been acting in good faith.[220]

19.95 Section 1157(2) enables directors or officers of a company to apply to the court for relief in advance of any finding of breach of duty against them. It provides as follows:

> If any such officer or person has reason to apprehend that a claim will or might be made against him in respect of negligence, default, breach of duty or breach of trust—
> (a) he may apply to the court for relief, and
> (b) the court has the same power to relieve him as it would have had if it had been a court before which proceedings against him for negligence, default, breach of duty or breach of trust had been brought.

It is only permissible to make an application for prospective relief, however, in circumstances where proceedings have not already been commenced against the director or officer for breach of the relevant duty.[221] By the Companies Act, ss 232 and 234(3)(iii) a company may not indemnify a director in respect of an application under s 1157 if the court refuses to grant him relief.

E. Defences

19.96 There are a number of potential defences open to directors against whom proceedings are brought for breach of duty. The following are considered in this section: (i) limitation, (ii) set-off, and (iii) contributory negligence.

(1) Limitation

19.97 A director may be entitled to plead limitation as a defence to a claim brought against him by the company or a derivative claim brought under Part 11 or pursuant to an order of the

---

[217] *Re Marini Ltd* [2004] BCC 172. 1985 Act, s 263 was replaced by 2006 Act, ss 829, 830, 849, 850 on 6 April 2008. In *Inn Spirit Ltd v Burns* [2002] 2 BCLC 780, Rimer J could not see that the court could or should grant relief from liability at the expense of creditors, but that it was arguable that the directors should be relieved from having to repay to the company any more than was necessary to enable creditors' claims to be paid in full.

[218] *Re MDA Investment Management Ltd* [2004] 1 BCLC 217.

[219] [2000] 2 BCLC 590.

[220] *Selangor United Rubber Estates Ltd v Craddock (No 3)* [1968] 1 WLR 1555. Recent examples of cases where relief has been refused include *Re Onslow Ditchling Ltd, Roberts v Frohlich* [2011] BCLC 625, ChD and *Tayplan v Smith* [2012] BCC 523 (CS).

[221] *Re Barry and Staines Linoleum Ltd* [1934] Ch 227.

court in proceedings under s 994 (proceedings for protection of members against unfair prejudice). Whether (and the extent to which) he will be able to do so depends on the nature of the claim brought against him.

Misfeasance claims brought by a liquidator pursuant to the Insolvency Act, s 212 in respect **19.98** of any breach of duty by a director of the company are no different, substantively, from claims by the company in respect of the same breach of duty. Section 212 merely provides an alternative procedure for asserting such claims, once the company is in liquidation. As such, even though a claim pursuant to s 212 cannot be brought until after the company has gone into liquidation, there is no new limitation period for such claims: the relevant limitation period is that which would have applied as if the claim had been brought by the company.[222]

Negligence

If the claim against a director is based on his failure to act with reasonable skill and care, then **19.99** the claim will be barred six years after the date on which it accrued. This is either because the claim is analogous to a claim in tort[223] or because the claim might be for breach of a term (express or implied) of the contract between the director and the company.[224]

Breach of fiduciary duty

A director's 'trustee-like' position has the consequence that the provisions of the Limitation **19.100** Act 1980, s 21 (dealing with actions against trustees) apply, either directly or by analogy to certain claims arising out of a breach of fiduciary duty by the director.[225]

Section 21 provides (materially) as follows: **19.101**

(1) No period of limitation prescribed by this Act shall apply to an action by a beneficiary under a trust, being an action—
    (a) in respect of any fraud or fraudulent breach of trust to which the trustee was a party or privy; or
    (b) to recover from the trustee trust property or the proceeds of trust property in the possession of the trustee, or previously received by the trustee and converted to his use
    …
(3) Subject to the preceding provisions of this section, an action by a beneficiary to recover trust property or in respect of any breach of trust, not being an action for which a period of limitation is prescribed by any other provision of this Act, shall not be brought after the expiration of six years from the date on which the right of action accrued.

The application of this section to proceedings against a director was considered by the Court **19.102** of Appeal in *JJ Harrison (Properties) Ltd v Harrison*,[226] in which the director had, as a result of a breach of fiduciary duty owed to the company, received land and then sold it on. There

---

[222] This was reaffirmed by Blackburne J in *Re Eurocruit Europe Ltd* [2007] 2 BCLC 598, following *Re Lands Allotment Company* [1894] 1 Ch 616, CA. See also *Canadian Land Reclaiming and Colonizing Company* (1880) 14 Ch D 660; *Cohen v Selby* [2001] 1 BCLC 176.

[223] Any claim in tort is statute barred six years after the cause of action accrued: Limitation Act 1980, s 2. Where a claim to equitable relief mirrors a common law claim, then the common law limitation period applies by analogy: the Limitation Act 1980, s 36 and *Cia Imperio v Heath Ltd* [2001] 1 WLR 112.

[224] Any claim in simple contract is also statute barred six years after the cause of action accrued: Limitation Act 1980, s 5.

[225] *Gwembe Valley Development Ltd v Koshy* [2004] 1 BCLC 131, CA at paras 111 and 112, per Mummery LJ.

[226] [2002] 1 BCLC 162. This case, and *Gwembe Valley* (see preceding footnote) were cited with approval by the Supreme Court in *Williams v Central Bank of Nigeria* [2014] AC 1189 at para 28, per Lord Sumption JSC.

was no claim to trace the proceeds of sale of the land in the director's hands. The Court of Appeal held as follows:

(1) A director who in breach of the fiduciary duty owed by him to the company had taken a transfer of the company's property to himself was a 'trustee' of property of which the company was the 'beneficiary' for the purposes of the Limitation Act 1980, s 21.[227]

(2) The action was not one to recover trust property or its proceeds in the possession of the director (since neither was retained by him).

(3) It was, however, an action to recover 'the proceeds of trust property previously received by the trustee and converted to his use'. In reaching this conclusion, Chadwick LJ applied the decision of Kekewich J in *In re Timmis, Nixon v Smith*[228] who considered that the intention of the provisions now found in the Limitation Act 1980, s 21 was:

> to give a trustee the benefit of the lapse of time when, although he had done something legally or technically wrong, he had done nothing morally wrong or dishonest, but it was not intended to protect him where, if he pleaded the statute, he would come off with something he ought not to have, ie money of the trust received by him and converted to his use.

19.103 The Court of Appeal's decision in *JJ Harrison* was premised on the finding that the director was a 'trustee' within the first of the two classes of constructive trustee identified by Millett LJ in *Paragon Finance v Thakerar*.[229] A constructive trustee within the first class is treated as a 'trustee' for the purposes of (and thus caught by the provisions of) the Limitation Act 1980, s 21, whereas a constructive trustee within the second class is not.[230] Accordingly, a proprietary claim to recover property held on constructive trust by a director of the company will fall within the Limitation Act 1980, s 21(1)(b) and will not therefore be subject to any statutory limitation period.

19.104 In the second class of case the defendant (not being a trustee at all) is liable to account as if he were a constructive trustee in respect of property which he has received adversely to the claimant by an unlawful transaction impugned by the claimant.[231] Claims against a 'constructive trustee' in the second category are therefore subject to limitation defences by analogy with common law claims.

19.105 This distinction was reaffirmed by the Supreme Court in *Williams v Central Bank of Nigeria*,[232] where it was held that the words 'trust' and 'trustee' in section 21(1) of the Limitation Act 1980 bore their orthodox meaning, with the consequence that (1) a 'trust' did not include a constructive trustee falling within the second of Millett LJ's categories in *Paragon Finance* and (2) a 'trustee' did not include someone who was liable to account in equity simply because he was a dishonest assistant in a breach of trust, or a knowing recipient

---

[227] [2002] 1 BCLC 162 at para 39, per Chadwick LJ.

[228] [1902] 1 Ch 176, 186.

[229] [1999] 1 All ER 400. See *JJ Harrison* (n 226 above) at para 27, per Chadwick LJ. The two classes described by Millett LJ are considered further at paras 19.06 and 19.07 above. In *Burnden Holdings (UK) Ltd v Fielding* [2016] EWCA Civ 557 at paras 34–7, per David Richards LJ, the Court of Appeal concluded that section 21(1)(b) applied not only to cases where a trustee directly and personally acquired the trust property, but extended to a case where the trust property was transferred to a company directly or indirectly controlled by the trustee. See also *Re Pantone* [2002] 1 BCLC 266, at paras 43–4 per Richard Field QC.

[230] *Gwembe Valley* (n 225 above) at para 157, per Mummery LJ.

[231] *Gwembe Valley* (n 225 above) at paras 88 and 91 of the judgment of Mummery LJ.

[232] [2014] AC 1189 at paras 7 to 9, per Lord Sumption JSC.

of trust assets. The rationale for the different treatment of true constructive trustees, and those who are liable to account as if they were constructive trustees, was explained by Lord Sumption JSC as follows:[233]

> Because of his fiduciary position, the true trustee's possession of trust assets was the beneficiary's possession and was entirely consistent with the beneficiary's interest. If the trustee misapplied the assets, equity would ignore the misapplication and simply hold him to account for the assets as if he had acted in accordance with his trust. There was thus nothing to make time start running against the beneficiary. That reasoning simply did not apply to someone who had not assumed responsibility as a trustee, whether expressly or de facto, at the time of the misapplication of the assets.

On this basis, a claim for recovery of property from a knowing recipient of trust property did not fall within s 21(1)(b) of the Limitation Act 1980 and was therefore subject to a six-year limitation period. Lord Mance, dissenting on this point, considered that a knowing recipient of trust property had possession in just the same way as an executor de son tort, and the latter was undoubtedly regarded as a true trustee for the purposes of limitation. **19.106**

Lord Sumption JSC recognized[234] that the wording of s 21(1)(a) of the Limitation Act 1980 ('*in respect of any fraud or fraudulent breach of trust to which the trustee was a party or privy*') was susceptible to two interpretations: it was either limited to actions against a trustee or it was extended to actions against a stranger who was not a trustee (such as a dishonest assistant or knowing recipient). He concluded, however, (as part of a three/two majority) that the narrower interpretation was the correct one.[235] There was, he considered, no rational reason why the draftsman of the legislation should have intended that the availability of limitation to a non-trustee should depend on a consideration which had no bearing on his liability, namely the honesty or dishonesty of the trustee. Lord Neuberger, agreeing, noted that dishonest assisters and knowing recipients were thus: (i) in the same position as those who are liable in common law for improper or dishonest conduct; and (ii) in a better position than trustees. The first was appropriate since there was no case for distinguishing between an action at fraud at common law and its counterpart in equity[236], and the second was plainly justifiable on the basis that trustees owed pre-existing fiduciary duties, whereas dishonest assisters and knowing recipients did not. **19.107**

In *Gwembe Valley* itself, a claim for an account of profits made by a fiduciary was held not to fall within the first class of constructive trust cases, and is therefore subject to the six-year limitation period under the Limitation Act 1980, s 21(3) unless there is some other reason for disapplying that period.[237] **19.108**

---

[233] [2014] AC 1189 at para 13.

[234] [2014] AC 1189 at para 32.

[235] In this respect the Supreme Court approved the decision of Richard Sheldon QC sitting as a deputy high court judge in *Cattley v Pollard* [2007] 2 All ER 1086 at paras 85–9, and the judgment of Lord Hoffmann sitting in the Court of Final Appeal in Hong Kong in *Peconic Industrial Development Limited v Lau Kwok Fai* [2009] 5 HKC 135. Conversely, the decision of Danckwerts J in *GL Baker Ltd v Medway Building and Supplies Ltd* [1958] 1 WLR 1216, 1222, and the decision of Evans-Lombe J in *Statek Corpn v Alford* [2008] BCC 266 were disapproved.

[236] [2014] AC 1189 at para 118, quoting Lord Millett in *Paragon Finance*.

[237] See *Gwembe Valley* (n 225 above) per Mummery LJ at para 91 of his judgment. Where a claim is based on the fraud of the defendant, or where facts material to the claim have been concealed, then the time period does not begin to run until the fraud or concealment could with reasonable diligence have been discovered: Limitation Act 1980, s 32. A fiduciary has a duty to disclose his own wrongdoing if either he thought it was in the interests of the principal/company to know of it, or he would have considered it was in its interests had

19.109   In *Gwembe Valley* the claim against the director was for an account of profits made by him from his fiduciary position. This claim was not dependent on showing that he had received any money or other property belonging to the company. He was, however, under a personal liability to account for the unauthorized profits made by him. The Court of Appeal analysed this as a constructive trust within the second of Millett LJ's two classes: the director's liability to account for profits did not depend on any pre-existing responsibility for any property of the company. The claim did not, therefore, fall within the Limitation Act 1980, s 21(1)(b) which would have disapplied the six-year limitation period otherwise applicable because of s 21(3).[238]

Statutory claims

19.110   Claims against a director pursuant to particular sections of the Companies Act[239] (or pursuant to any other statutory provision) are also governed by a six-year limitation period by virtue of the Limitation Act 1980, s 9.

Laches

19.111   It has long been a defence to a claim in equity that the claimant has through his conduct and neglect, whilst not constituting a waiver of the claim, put the defendant in a situation where it would not be reasonable to assert the claim against him.[240]

19.112   Although the doctrine of laches applies principally where the statute of limitations does not apply, it can do so even where the statute does apply, either directly or, possibly, by analogy.[241] The issue was considered recently by the Court of Appeal in *P&O Nedlloyd BV v Arab Metals Co.*[242] It was there held that the defence of laches might be available where an applicable limitation period was still extant, although it was likely that something more than mere delay was required in support of the laches defence.

---

he thought about it in good faith. A failure to disclose his own breach of fiduciary duty in such circumstances amounts to concealment within s 32(1)(b): *IT Human Resources PLC v David Land* [2014] EWHC 3812 (Ch) at paras 134–5, per Morgan J.

[238]   In fact, the Court of Appeal went on to hold that the director had acted dishonestly, such that the claim fell within s 21(1)(a) and the six-year limitation period was disapplied for that reason instead. A further example of a case which the court decided fell within the second category of constructive trust is *Halton International Inc v Guernroy Ltd* [2006] 1 BCLC 78, in which Patten J held at para 165 that a liability to account for shares received was based on the recipient's breach of fiduciary duty in circumstances 'which gave rise to what amounts to a remedial constructive trust' and was therefore outside the ambit of s 21. The Court of Appeal upheld his judgment; [2006] EWCA Civ 801. See also *Frawley v Neill* [2000] CP Reports 20, cited with approval in *Green v Gaul* [2007] 1 WLR 591.

[239]   eg pursuant to the following provisions of the Companies Act: s 41(3) (liability of directors to indemnify the company for loss suffered as a result of a transaction entered into in excess of the directors' powers); s 213 (liability to account for gains made by transactions in breach of ss 197, 198, 200, 201, or 203, relating to members' approval for loans etc); s 222 (liability to indemnify company in respect of payments made for loss of office in contravention of s 217); s 369 (liability to make good to the company the amount of an unauthorized political donation or expenditure, and to compensate the company for any loss suffered as a result thereof); s 767 (joint and several liability of the directors to indemnify the counterparty to a transaction entered into in contravention of s 761, which prohibits a public limited company from transacting business without a trading certificate); and s 847 (liability to repay an unauthorized distribution made in contravention of Part 23).

[240]   *The Lindsay Petroleum Co v Hurd* (1874) LR 5 PC 221, 240, per Lord Selborne LC.

[241]   See eg *Snell's Equity*, 33rd edn (Sweet and Maxwell, 2015), para 5–011. See also *Halsbury's Laws*, 5th edn (2008), vol 68 at para 906, citing the Limitation Act 1980, s 36(2) ('Nothing in this Act shall affect any equitable jurisdiction to refuse relief on the ground of acquiescence or otherwise').

[242]   [2007] 1 WLR 2288.

(2) Set-off

There are three kinds of set-off: (i) legal set-off, where both the claim and the cross-claim   **19.113**
are liquidated; (ii) equitable, or transaction set-off, which may operate in respect of unliquidated or even contingent claims, and which requires the cross-claim to flow out of and be
inseparably connected with the dealings and transactions which give rise to the claim;[243] and
(iii) insolvency set-off under either Insolvency Rule 4.90 (and IR 2016, r 14.25 after 6 April
2017), in the case of the liquidation of the company,[244] which operates in respect of mutual
credits, mutual debts, or other mutual dealings between the company and the director, or
Insolvency Act, s 323 in the case of the bankruptcy of the director.[245]

Prior to either the company going into liquidation (or administration and the administrator   **19.114**
giving notice of an intention to make a distribution to creditors) or the director becoming
bankrupt, there is unlikely to be much scope for set-off as between a claim for breach of duty
against a director and any claim which the director may have against the company. This is
because it is unlikely either that the claim against the director will be liquidated (which is
necessary for legal set-off to operate) or that the claim and cross-claim would be sufficiently
closely connected for equitable set-off to operate.

There is a further difficulty in relation to set-off as between a claim for breach of duty against   **19.115**
a director, and any cross-claim that the director may have against the company, once the
company has gone into liquidation. This is due to long-standing authority to the effect that
a director may not rely on a claim against the company by way of set-off against a claim in
misfeasance brought against him: *ex p Pelly*.[246] The various justifications offered for this rule
have not, however, been consistent or equally persuasive.

In *Pelly* itself, Brett LJ sought to justify the rule on the basis that set-off was only permissible   **19.116**
where there was an action at law, and a misfeasance claim (under what is now the Insolvency
Act s 212) is a summary remedy without an action. This is not satisfactory, however, since an
action at law is not a prerequisite of set-off under Insolvency Rule 4.90, or IR 2016, r 14.25
when it applies (which is the only applicable basis of set-off once a company is in liquidation).
An alternative justification, also referred to in *Pelly*, is that misfeasance was a creature of statute
and as a matter of statutory construction there was no reason to imply into the statutory remedy
of misfeasance a right of set-off under the separate statutory provision permitting insolvency
set-off.[247] If this is correct, then the rule could not have any application to a situation where the
claim was brought by way of action by the company prior to the liquidation of the company.[248]

---

[243] *Bank of Boston Connecticut v European Grain and Shipping Ltd* [1989] 1 AC 1056.

[244] Rule 4.90 (and IR 2016, r 14.25 after 6 April 2017) applies only if the company is in liquidation (the
Insolvency Act, s 323 is the comparable provision for bankruptcy). If the company is in administration then,
unless and until the administrator gives notice of an intention to make a distribution to creditors (pursuant to
Insolvency Rule 2.95, or IR 2016, r 14.29 after 6 April 2017 for administrations to which the IR 2016 apply)
then set-off between the company and a third party is governed by the principles relating to legal or equitable
set-off. Where, however, the administrator has given notice of an intention to make a distribution to creditors, then Insolvency Rule 2.85 provides for set-off of mutual credits, mutual debts, or other mutual dealings
in much the same way as Insolvency Rule 4.90 operates in respect of a company in liquidation (and IR 2016,
r 14.25 after 6 April 2017 for liquidations to which the IR 2016 apply).

[245] For a fuller treatment of the principles of legal and equitable set-off generally, see Derham, *Set-off*, 4th
edn (Oxford University Press, 2010).

[246] (1882) 21 Ch D 492. See, generally, Derham, *Set-off*, paras 8.80–8.87.

[247] (1882) 21 Ch D 492, per Brett LJ at 507, per Jessel MR at 502.

[248] In *Re Bassett* (1895) 2 Mans 177 it was indeed held that if an action is brought against a director or for breach
of duty by way of proceedings, as opposed to by way of summons for misfeasance, then set-off is available as a defence.

19.117   More recently, in *Manson v Smith*,[249] Millett LJ has offered two further justifications for the rule. First, that misappropriation of a company's assets is not a 'dealing' between the director and the company. This was expressly approved by the House of Lords in *Smith v Bridgend County Borough Council*.[250] Secondly, Millett LJ suggested that the rule can be justified on the basis that the misfeasance claim only arises after the company goes into liquidation. This is less convincing, because the Insolvency Act, s 212 does not create a new right, but is merely a procedure for enforcing an existing claim (paragraph 19.98 above).

19.118   A further explanation for the rule is found in the judgment of Maugham J in *Re Etic*.[251] He considered that the 1908 Act, s 215 (the equivalent then of the Insolvency Act, s 212) only applied to claims against officers in the nature of breach of trust. In so doing, he relied on the fact that set-off was not available in defence to a misfeasance claim: he reasoned that the section ought to be confined to cases in which set-off was not available. This reasoning is undermined by the fact that the wording of the Insolvency Act, s 212 is wider than the wording of the 1908 Act, s 215.[252] Moreover, the assumption that set-off is not available as a defence to claims in the nature of a breach of trust is incompatible with the notion that the defence would be available where a claim was pursued by a company by action, prior to liquidation.[253]

19.119   As a matter of principle, there is something to be said for limiting the non-availability of set-off to claims in misfeasance brought after the company has gone into liquidation, on the basis that a delinquent director ought to contribute to the insolvent estate formerly under his stewardship and be left to prove along with all other creditors for his debt. A good example of a case where the result accords with such a principle is provided by *Reliance Wholesale (Toys, Fancy Goods and Sports) Ltd*[254] in which the director had loaned £7,500 to the company on terms that it should be repaid as soon as the company could afford it. The director caused the company to pay him the balance owing by filling in and countersigning a cheque which had been signed in blank by his co-director. The director was found to be guilty of misfeasance and ordered to repay the money without set-off of his loan.

(3) Contributory negligence

19.120   A director guilty of dishonest breach of fiduciary duty would not be able to plead a defence of contributory negligence.[255] Whilst in theory a director might be entitled to raise a defence of contributory negligence as a defence to a claim that he failed to exercise reasonable skill and care, in reality it is difficult to envisage circumstances in which such a defence could operate, given the difficulty in practice of identifying any negligence on the part of the company that was not attributable to the actions of the defendant director.

---

[249]   [1997] 2 BCLC 161.

[250]   [2002] 1 AC 336 at para 35, per Lord Hoffmann. See also *Re a Company (No 1641 of 2003)* [2004] 1 BCLC 210 at paras 22–5, per HHJ Norris QC.

[251]   [1928] Ch 861.

[252]   The former section referred only to misfeasance or breach of trust, whereas s 212 extends to a breach of any other duty and therefore includes negligence under the Companies Act, s 174.

[253]   But see para 19.114 above as to the practical likelihood of set-off being available in respect of an unliquidated claim against a director prior to liquidation.

[254]   (1979) 76 Law Soc Gazette 731.

[255]   *Standard Chartered Bank v Pakistani National Shipping Corp* [2003] 1 AC 959. See also *Corpn nel Cobre de Chile v Sogernu* [1997] 1 WLR 1396.

(4) *Ex turpi causa*

The maxim *ex turpi causa* provides a potential defence against a claim by a person seeking **19.121**
damage where the claimant is guilty of a criminal or other sufficiently morally reprehensible
act. As explained by Lord Hoffmann in *Gray v Thames Trains Ltd*,[256] it has a wide and narrow
version: the wide version is that you cannot recover for damage which is the consequence
of your own criminal act, whereas the narrow version is that you cannot recover for damage
which is the consequence of a sentence imposed upon you for a criminal act. Lord Hoffmann
went on to explain that the narrow version is justified on the basis of inconsistency between
the criminal law, which imposes a penalty upon a person to reflect his own personal responsibility for the act, and the claim that the civil law should require someone else to compensate
him for that penalty. The main difference between the two versions is that there are no causation issues in connection with the narrow version.[257]

The rule is one of public policy, in essence that the court will not lend its aid to someone **19.122**
who founds his cause of action on an immoral or illegal act: see *Les Laboratoires Servier v
Apotex Inc*,[258] at para 131, per Lord Sumption JSC, citing Lord Mansfield CJ in *Holman v
Johnson*.[259] It raises three questions: (i) what acts constitute turpitude for the purposes of
the defence; (ii) what relationship must the turpitude have to the claim; and (iii) on what
principles should the turpitude of an agent be attributed to his principal, especially when the
principal is a corporation.[260]

So far as the first question is concerned, in the *Les Laboratoires Servier* case[261] Lord Sumption **19.123**
JSC held that, while the paradigm case of an illegal act engaging the defence is a criminal
offence, the defence also extends to acts which can conveniently be described as 'quasi-
criminal' because they engage the public interest in the same way. He interpreted Lord
Mansfield's reference to 'illegal or immoral' acts as embracing '*acts which engage the interests
of the state or, as we would put it today, the public interest*'. The additional category of non-
criminal acts includes cases of dishonesty or corruption, which have always been regarded as
engaging the public interest, even in the context of purely civil disputes. The defence does
not extend, however, to acts which are merely tortious or in breach of contract.[262] On the
facts of the *Les Laboratoires Servier* case, the defence was not engaged by conduct consisting
of a breach of patent. Although a patent was a public grant of the state, it did not follow that
the public interest was engaged by a breach of the patentee's rights. The effect of the grant was
simply to give rise to private rights of a character no different in principle from contractual
rights or rights founded on breach of statutory duty or other torts.[263] In contrast, in *Safeway
Stores v Twigger*[264] Flaux J held that anti-competitive acts in breach of the prohibition in

---

[256] [2009] AC 1339 at para 32.
[257] *Safeway Stores v Twigger* [2011] 2 All ER 841 CA at para 16, per Longmore LJ. See also *Les Laboratoires
Servier v Apotex Inc* [2015] AC 430 at para 19, per Lord Sumption JSC.
[258] [2015] AC 430.
[259] (1775) 1 Cowp 341, 343
[260] *Les Laboratoires Servier* (n 258 above) at par 22, per Lord Sumption JSC.
[261] *Les Laboratoires Servier* (n 258 above), at paras 21 to 25.
[262] *Les Laboratoires Servier* (n 258 above), at para 28.
[263] *Les Laboratoires Servier* (n 258 above), at para 30.
[264] [2010] 3 All ER 577 Flaux J, upheld on appeal [2011] 2 All ER 841 CA. See below, for further consideration of this case.

Chapter 1 of the Competition Act 1998, leading to the imposition of a civil penalty for the breach, was capable of engaging the defence.

19.124   More controversy surrounds the second and third of Lord Sumption's three aspects of the defence. On the one hand, the House of Lords in *Tinsley v Milligan*[265] unanimously rejected an attempt to transform the rule into a 'public conscience' test, or a mere power, whose exercise depended upon the the perceived equities of the case. This would, in the words of Lord Goff,[266] 'constitute a revolution in this branch of the law, under which what is in effect a discretion would become vested in the court to deal with the matter by a process of a balancing operation, in place of a system of rules, ultimately derived from the principle of public policy enunciated by Lord Mansfield in *Holman v Johnson*.' According to the majority in *Tinsley v Milligan*, the application of the defence was based on a 'reliance' test, such that the claim was barred only if the claimant needed to rely on (ie to assert, whether by way of pleading or evidence) facts which disclosed the illegality.[267]

19.125   In *Les Laboratoires Servier v Apotex Inc*,[268] Lord Sumption JSC referred to *Tinsley v Milligan* having 'decisively rejected' the public conscience test, and that observations of Lord Hoffmann in *Gray v Thames Trains Ltd*[269] to the effect that the *ex turpi causa* defence expressed not so much as a principle, but a policy, and a policy based on a group of reasons which varied according to circumstances, did not justify any departure from the conclusion reached in *Tinsley v Milligan*.

19.126   In *Bilta (UK) Ltd v Nazir (No 2)*,[270] Lord Sumption JSC[271] reiterated the view that the rule was as stated in *Tinsley v Milligan* and not a discretionary power.

19.127   On the other hand, Lord Toulson JSC and Lord Hodge JSC in *Bilta* considered that the application of the *ex turpi causa* defence in any given case depended upon whether the policy underlying the defence meant that it should defeat the claim, in accordance with the majority judgment of Lord Wilson JSC in *Hounga v Allen*.[272] This would involve balancing competing public policies. In *Bilta* itself, which involved a claim brought by a company in liquidation (acting by its liquidator) to recover damages from those alleged to have participated in a conspiracy with the directors, Lords Toulson and Hodge considered that it was sufficient to dispose of the case that the public interest which underlies the duty that the directors of an insolvent company owe for the protection of the interests of the company's creditors '… requires axiomatically that the law should not place obstacles in the way of its enforcement.'[273] Now see *Patel v Mirza* in which the majority of the Supreme Court endorsed this view.[274]

---

[265]   [1994] 1 AC 340.
[266]   Above, at p 363B.
[267]   The minority (Lords Goff and Keith of Kinkel) preferred a rule that barred any claim tainted by a sufficiently close factual connection with the illegal purpose.
[268]   [2015] AC 430 at paras 13–19.
[269]   [2009] AC 1339 at para 30.
[270]   [2016] AC 1. For comment on the decision see Fletcher, 'Fraudulent Trading, Ex Turpi Causa, and Directors' Duties' (2016) Insolv Int, 29(1) 12–15; and see Day, 'Attributing Illegalities' (2015) CLJ, 74(3), 409–12.
[271]   [2016] AC 1 at para 62.
[272]   [2014] 1 WLR 2889 at para 42.
[273]   [2016] AC 1 at para 129.
[274]   Now see *Patel v Mirza* [2016] 3 WLR 399 in which the majority of the Supreme Court endorsed this view.

The Supreme Court, in *Bilta*, was in the event unanimous in deciding that the defence of **19.128** *ex turpi causa* was not available to the defendants on the basis of their conclusion on the third of Lord Sumption's three aspects of the rule, namely that the wrongdoing of the directors was not to be attributed to the company (as to which see further below). In view of this, it was unnecessary to decide whether the application of the rule depended upon the reliance test, as favoured by Lord Sumption, or upon a balance of public policies, as favoured by Lord Toulson and Lord Hodge. Lord Neuberger PSC considered that the proper approach to the defence of illegality needed to be addressed by the Supreme Court (certainly with a panel of seven, and possibly nine, justices) as soon as appropriately possible, but that this was not the case in which it should be decided.[275]

One thing upon which the Supreme Court in *Bilta* was agreed upon was that the difficult **19.129** case of *Stone & Rolls Ltd v Moore Stephens*,[276] should be confined to its own facts. In the words of Lord Denning MR, quoted by Lord Neuberger at para 30, it should be put 'on one side in a pile and marked "not to be looked at again" '.[277]

The Court was, on the other hand, divided as to the correctness of the Court of Appeal's **19.130** decision in *Safeway Stores v Twigger*.[278] The Court of Appeal had held that an action by the company against its directors, to recover the amount of financial penalties imposed on it by the Office of Fair Trading, for anti-competitive activity, was barred by the illegality principle. Its reasoning was that the company's liability was 'personal' as opposed to vicarious, since the liability was imposed directly upon it, and not on its directors and employees. The claim against the directors and employees was thus based on its own wrongdoing and barred by illegality. Lord Toulson and Lord Hodge, at para 159 of *Bilta*, considered that this reasoning was flawed, preferring the conclusion of Professor Watts[279] that 'In the absence of some countervailing policy reason, it is not just for someone who falls foul of a statute by reason of the acts of its employees or other agents to add to its burdens and disabilities by depriving it of any recourse against those employees or other agents.'

Judicial opinion was divided over whether the defence involves the exercise of any discretion **19.131** by the court. In *Patel v Mirza*[280] the Supreme Court concluded that the public interest was best served by a principled and transparent assessment of the purpose behind the provision transgressed, other public policy considerations, and whether denial of the claim would be a proportionate response to the illegality.

So far as the third of Lord Sumption's three aspects of the rule is concerned, namely when **19.132** the wrongdoing of an agent will be attributed to its principal (in particular in the case of corporations) the Supreme Court in *Bilta* was unanimous in its decision. It concluded that there was no single rule for whether a director's wrongdoing would be attributed to the company. Instead, it depended upon the context and purpose for which the attribution was relevant. Where the purpose of the attribution was to apportion responsibility between

---

[275] Above, at para 15.
[276] [2009] AC 1391.
[277] See also Lord Toulson and Lord Hodge, at para 154: 'Stone & Rolls should be regarded as a case which has no majority ratio decidendi. It stands as authority for the point which it decided, namely that on the facts of that case no claim lay against the auditors, but nothing more.'
[278] [2011] 2 All ER 841.
[279] 'Illegality and Agency Law: Authorising Illegal Action' [2011] JBL 213.
[280] [2016] 3 WLR 399.

a company and its agents so as to determine their rights and liabilities to each other, the answer would not necessarily be the same as where the purpose was to apportion responsibility between the company and a third party. Where a company had been the victim of wrongdoing by its directors, such wrongdoing could not be attributed to the company in the context of an action by the liquidator of the company against the directors.[281]

19.133 Where an action is brought by the company against a third party, the attribution of the directors' wrongdoing to the company depends upon the nature of the claim. If the claim is against a third party accessory to the directors' wrongdoing, then that wrongdoing is not to be attributed to the company so as to bar the claim.[282] If the claim is brought against a third party who was not involved in the directors' wrongdoing, then such wrongdoing may be attributed to the company so as to provide a defence of illegality.[283] There remains disagreement as to whether the approach is the 'open' one described by Lord Neuberger PSC at para 9 (ie whether or not it is appropriate to attribute an action by, or a state of mind of, a company director or agent to the company or agent's principal in relation to a particular claim against the company or the principal must depend on the nature and factual context of the claim in question) or whether, as Lord Sumption JSC preferred, there is prima facie attribution of a director's knowledge to the company, subject to a 'breach of duty exception'. As Lord Mance JSC noted, however, at para 37, it made no difference on the facts of *Bilta*, and may well often make no difference in practice.

---

[281] [2016] AC 1, per Lord Neuberger PSC, at para 7. See also Lord Mance JSC at paras 38, 41, and 42, Lord Sumption JSC at para 89, and Lord Toulson JSC and Lord Hodge JSC at para 206.

[282] See Lord Sumption JSC at para 90, Lord Toulson JSC and Lord Hodge JSC at para 207.

[283] Above, per Lord Sumption JSC at para 91, Lord Toulson JSC and Lord Hodge JSC at para 207.

20

DIRECTORS' LIABILITIES: EXEMPTION, INDEMNIFICATION, AND RATIFICATION

Blair Leahy and Andrew Feld

A. Introduction

The 2006 Act, Part 10, Chapter 7, ss 232–9, contains provisions relating to exemption and **20.01** protection of directors from liabilities incurred in discharge of their functions.[1] Sections 232–4 and 236–8 largely restate or preserve the former law,[2] providing for general prohibitions on the exemption and indemnification of a director from liability or against liability that would otherwise attach to him in connection with any negligence, default, breach of trust, or breach of duty in relation to the company, subject, in the case of indemnification,[3] to specified exceptions relating to insurance and certain third party indemnity provision. Section 235 is a new provision dealing with the indemnification of a director of a company that is a trustee of an occupational pension scheme.

---

[1] These sections came into force on 1 October 2007: 2006 Act Commencement Order No 3, Art 2(1)(d).

[2] As contained in 1985 Act, ss 309A–309C. These sections were inserted in the 1985 Act by the Companies (Audit, Investigations and Community Enterprise) Act 2004 (C(AICE) Act), s 19(1), with effect from 6 April 2005. Until then 1985 Act, s 310 provided for a general prohibition on provisions exempting officers and auditors from liability attaching in respect of any negligence, default, breach of duty, or breach of trust in relation to the company. Section 310 derived from the 1948 Act, s 205, and was first brought into effect by 1929 Act, s 152. With effect from 6 April 2005 s 310 ceased to apply to officers of a company. In the 2006 Act, the provisions in s 310 relating to auditors have been replaced by the largely new provisions contained in Part 16, Chapter 6, ss 532–8.

[3] In *Firma C-Trade SA v Newcastle P & I Association* [1991] 2 AC 1 at 35, Lord Geoff said: 'A promise of indemnity is simply a promise to hold the indemnified person harmless against a specified loss or expense.'

20.02 Section 239 is another new provision which reforms the law as to the circumstances in which a company may ratify the conduct of a director amounting to negligence, default, breach of duty, or breach of trust. In effect the conduct can only be ratified if shareholders who are independent of the wrongdoer assent. Section 239 does, however, preserve the current law on the validity of decisions taken by unanimous consent of members, the power of the directors not to sue or to settle or release claims, and existing rules which impose additional requirements for ratification or render certain acts incapable of ratification.

20.03 This chapter deals with the general prohibition on exemptions and indemnities, qualifying third party and pension scheme indemnity provision, and ratification. The provision of insurance for directors, which is made lawful by s 233, is dealt with in Chapter 21.

B. General Prohibition on Exemptions and Indemnities

20.04 Section 232 sets out the general prohibition on the exemption and indemnification of directors in relation to their negligence, default, breach of duty, or breach of trust in relation to the company; identifies the exceptions to the general prohibition on indemnification (discussed in Sections C and D below); and preserves the effectiveness of provisions in a company's articles dealing with conflicts of interest. It provides:

(1) Any provision that purports to exempt a director of a company (to any extent) from any liability that would otherwise attach to him in connection with any negligence, default, breach of duty or breach of trust in relation to the company is void.

(2) Any provision by which a company directly or indirectly provides an indemnity (to any extent) for a director of a company, or of an associated company, against any liability attaching to him in connection with any negligence, default, breach of duty or breach of trust in relation to the company of which he is a director is void, except as permitted by—

    (a) section 233 (provision of insurance),

    (b) section 234 (qualifying third party indemnity provision), or

    (c) section 235 (qualifying pension scheme indemnity provision).

(3) This section applies to any provision, whether contained in a company's articles or in any contract with the company or other otherwise.

(4) Nothing in this section prevents a company's articles from making such provision as has previously been lawful for dealing with conflicts of interest.

20.05 Until the 1929 Act, s 152 brought into effect provisions recommended by the Greene Committee,[4] it was common for the articles of a company to exempt directors from loss except when it was due to their 'wilful neglect or default' or, in some cases, due to actual dishonesty, and the court gave effect to these exemptions from liability.[5] Since 1929 provisions for exemption or indemnification falling within the scope of the successive statutory provisions have been void.

20.06 The Attorney General, Lord Goldsmith, explained the principle underlying the prohibition on exempting and indemnifying directors for negligence, default, breach of duty, and breach of trust:[6]

---

[4] Report of the Greene Committee, paras 46 and 47.

[5] *Re Brazilian Rubber Plantations and Estates Ltd* [1911] 1 Ch 425; *Re City of London Insurance Co Ltd* (1925) 41 TLR 521; *Re City Equitable Fire Insurance Co Ltd* [1925] Ch 407; *Re Home and Colonial Insurance Co Ltd* [1930] 1 Ch 102.

[6] Hansard, Lords Grand Committee, col 364 (9 February 2006).

the starting point for our reform package was a principle ... that companies should be prohibited from exempting directors from, or indemnifying them against, liability for negligence, default, breach of duty or breach of trust in relation to the company. However the reform package also recognised that companies should be permitted to indemnify directors in respect of third party claims in most circumstances ... There are four main possible exceptions to indemnification: criminal penalties; penalties imposed by regulatory bodies; costs incurred by the director in defending criminal proceedings in which he is convicted; and costs incurred by the director in defending civil proceedings brought by the company in which final judgment is given against him.

Thus there is nothing to prevent a company from indemnifying a director for liability incurred through, for example, giving a guarantee. The company's articles usually contain provision for indemnification of directors to the extent it is not unlawful under the Companies Act.[7]

20.07 The conduct of a director to which s 232(1) and (2) applies is any negligence, default, breach of duty, or breach of trust in relation to the company. This formulation has been used since the 1929 Act, s 152, and is used also in Part 11, s 260(3), in relation to the new procedure for bringing derivative claims[8] and in s 1157 (power of court to grant relief in certain cases).[9] The misconduct described in s 232(1) and (2) may be compared with the misconduct in the Insolvency Act, s 212 (summary remedy against delinquent directors, liquidators, etc), which applies where a director 'has misapplied or retained, or become accountable for, any money or other property of the company, or has been guilty of any misfeasance or breach of any fiduciary or other duty in relation to the company'.[10] The words 'breach of any fiduciary or other duty' in s 212 replaced the words 'breach of trust' found in its predecessor, the 1948 Act, s 333, and are wide enough to include claims based on negligence.[11] Thus the difference in scope between the Companies Act, s 232, and the Insolvency Act, s 212, is that the former extends to defaults, whereas the latter does not. This is not surprising, since in the context of s 232 'default' would seem to apply to acts or omissions of a director, which expose him to liability to criminal penalty or penalty imposed by a regulatory authority. Those are matters for which a director might wish to be indemnified, but which are prohibited as a matter of policy.

20.08 The 1985 Act, s 309A, introduced by the C(AICE) Act 2004, made three changes from the language of the 1985 Act, s 310: (i) it deleted the phrase 'by virtue of any rule of law', so that there can be no question that statutory as well as common law liability is covered; (ii) it added the words in brackets 'to any extent' to make it clear that that partial exemption or indemnification was prohibited; and (iii) it extended the prohibition to indemnities to a director of an associated company. These changes are restated in s 232(1) and (2). Section 256 defines 'associated bodies corporate' for the purposes of Part 10:

For the purposes of this Part—

---

[7] Table A, reg 118; Model Article (pcls) 52; Model Article (plc) 85 (quoted in paras 20.17 and 20.18 below). Since directors are fiduciaries in respect of their powers, as a matter of general law, by analogy with the position of trustees, they may be entitled to an indemnity from the company for expenses incurred in good faith and for the benefit of the company: *Re German Mining Co* (1853) 4 De G M & G 19, 52, per Turner LJ (where the directors guaranteed ultra vires borrowing).

[8] Ch 22 below.

[9] Ch 19, Section D above.

[10] For discussion on Insolvency Act, s 212 see Ch 34, Section C(1) below.

[11] *Re D'Jan of London Ltd* [1994] BCLC 561. In *Re B Johnson & Co (Builders) Ltd* [1955] Ch 634, CA, the Court of Appeal had held that the language used in 1948 Act, s 333 did not cover negligence claims.

(a) bodies corporate are associated if one is a subsidiary of the other or both are subsidiaries of the same body corporate, and

(b) companies are associated if one is a subsidiary of the other or both are subsidiaries of the same body corporate.

The Attorney General, Lord Goldsmith, explained the significance of the extension of the prohibition of indemnification to associated companies:[12]

> The 2004 Act ... closed an important loophole concerning the indemnification of directors by third parties. It used to be the practice in some groups that one group company would indemnify the director of another group company. It was possible thereby in effect to circumvent the rule that the company could not indemnify its own directors. We take the view that that should continue to apply and that what we consider is an important prohibition—to continue to make directors properly accountable for what they do in relation to the company—should stand.

20.09   Section 232(3) makes it clear that the prohibitions in s 232 apply to exemptions and indemnities contained in the company's articles as well as to contracts.[13] Provisions in the company's articles are not automatically incorporated into a contract between the company and a director, but, if not expressly incorporated, relatively little may be required for an indemnity in the articles to be impliedly incorporated.[14] The words 'or otherwise' are limited to exemptions and indemnities given by the company and do not extend to indemnities given by third parties.[15]

20.10   Section 232(4) is a new provision, which preserves the existing law by which a company's articles may continue to make provision for dealing with conflicts of interest without them being void under s 232(1) and (2). Sections 175–7 deal with the duties of directors to avoid conflicts of interest, not to accept benefits from third parties, and to declare interests in a proposed transaction or arrangement. Section 180(4)(b) provides that, where the company's articles contain provisions for dealing with conflicts of interest, a director's general duties are not infringed by anything done or omitted by him in accordance with those provisions.[16] It

---

[12] Hansard, Lords Grand Committee, col 366 (9 February 2006). Lord Sainsbury of Turville explained why the government was not persuaded to provide a carve-out so that a parent company could indemnify a director of a subsidiary (Lords Report, col 724 (23 May 2006)):

> It is also important to remember that at the same time as the loophole was closed, important reforms were introduced that permit all companies to indemnify directors against third-party claims, subject to ... [certain] requirements. Although we agree that indemnification by a parent company of the directors is less likely to result in attempts at circumvention of the prohibition than indemnification by a wholly owned subsidiary company of the director of a holding company, we still believe there is scope for mischief. We cannot ... accept [any] amendment.

[13] Articles often include indemnity provisions: Table A, reg 118; Model Article (pcls) 52; Model Article (plc) 85.

[14] *John v Price Waterhouse* [2002] 1 WLR 953 at para 26; *Globalink Telecommunications Ltd v Wilmbury* [2003] 1 BCLC 145 at paras 29–31.

[15] *Burgoine v London Borough of Waltham Forest* [1997] 2 BCLC 612, 626.

[16] Table A, reg 85, Model Article (pcls) 14, and Model Article (plc) 16 all make express provision for dealing with conflicts of interest. In *Movitex Ltd v Bulfield* [1988] BCLC 104 Vinelott J resolved the apparent conflict between 1948 Act, Table A, regs 78 and 84 (now 1985 Act, Table A, reg 85) and 1948 Act, s 205 (a predecessor of s 232) by distinguishing (i) the self-dealing rule, which disabled a director from entering into contracts with the company, which could be modified by the articles, and (ii) liability for breach of trust, which could not be exempted by virtue of the 1948 Act, s 205. In *Gwembe Valley Development Co Ltd v Koshy (No 3)* [2004] 1 BCLC 131, CA at para 107 the Court of Appeal described this distinction as 'an unnecessary complication' and inconsistent with the exposition of the nature of fiduciary duties given by Millett LJ in *Bristol and West BS*

would seem that provisions in a company's articles that deal with conflicts of interest are not rendered void as exempting a director from liability for breach of duty or breach of trust, and that the director will not be liable to the company provided that he complies with the articles and the Companies Act, as the case may be. Section 232(4) does not apply to the directors' other duties under ss 171–4, namely to act within his powers, to promote the success of the company, to exercise independent judgment, and to exercise reasonable care, skill, and diligence.

Notwithstanding that s 232 renders void provisions in a contract, the articles, or otherwise **20.11** that purport to exempt or indemnify the director from or against liability before the relevant conduct has occurred, there are a number of ways in which a director may achieve practical exemption from liability to the company for negligence, default, breach of trust, or breach of duty:

(1) The directors may cause the company not to make a claim against him and in due course the claim will become barred by limitation. If the directors act in this way, they expose themselves to a claim for negligence, breach of duty, or breach of trust if the company suffers any loss from the non-pursuit of the claim.

(2) The directors may agree not to sue, or to settle or to release a claim made by them on behalf of the company.[17] In exercising their powers in this respect the directors must of course comply with their fiduciary duties and duty of care, skill, and diligence. If they do not and the wrongdoing director has the requisite knowledge of the other directors' breach of duty, the agreement may be set aside. Also, if creditors' interests are prejudiced, the agreement may be vulnerable under the Insolvency Act, ss 238 and 423.

(3) The company may ratify the director's conduct under s 239 or by informal unanimous consent and so release him from liability (but again subject to the impact on creditors' interests).[18]

(4) Finally by s 1157 the court has a discretion to relieve the director, either wholly or in part, from any liability for negligence, default, breach of duty, or breach of trust where it appears to the court that he has acted honestly and reasonably and ought fairly to be excused.[19]

C. Qualifying Indemnity Provision

(1) Qualifying third party indemnity provision

As foreshadowed by s 232(2)(b), s 234[20] provides an exemption from the general rule, con- **20.12** tained in s 232(2), making void any provision by which a company directly or indirectly provides an indemnity (to any extent) for a director of the company, or of an associated company, against any liability attaching to him in connection with any negligence, default, breach of duty, or breach of trust in relation to the company of which he is a director. Section

---

v Mothew [1998] Ch 1, CA, and *Paragon Finance plc v DB Thackerar & Co* [1999] 1 All ER 400, CA. In the context of the 2006 Act it should not be necessary to refer to this distinction.

[17] 2006 Act, s 239(6)(b).
[18] Section D below and Ch 25, Section B(4) below.
[19] 2006 Act, s 1157, which replaced 1985 Act, s 727. This is discussed in Ch 19, Section D above.
[20] It restates 1985 Act, s 309B without substantial change.

234(1) states that s 232(2) does not apply to a qualifying third party indemnity provision and s 234(2) and (3) explain what the requirements for that provision are:

> (2) Third party indemnity provision means provision for indemnity against liability incurred by the director to a person other than the company or an associated company. Such provision is qualifying third party indemnity provision if the following requirements are met.
>
> (3) The provision must not provide indemnity against—
>> (a) any liability of the director to pay—
>>> (i) a fine imposed in criminal proceedings, or
>>> (ii) a sum payable to a regulatory authority by way of a penalty in respect of noncompliance with any requirement of a regulatory nature (howsoever arising); or
>> (b) any liability incurred by the director—
>>> (i) in defending criminal proceedings in which he is convicted, or
>>> (ii) in defending civil proceedings brought by the company, or an associated company in which judgment is given against him,[21] or
>>> (iii) in connection with an application for relief (see subsection (6)) in which the court refuses to grant him relief.[22]

20.13 Therefore the first requirement for qualifying third party indemnity provision is that it does not indemnify the director against liability incurred by him to the company or an associate company[23] in connection with any negligence, default, breach of duty, or breach of trust in relation to the company of which he is director. The company may indemnify the director against liability incurred by him to any third party in connection with those wrongs, provided that the second requirement is met: the liability is not a criminal or civil liability within sub-s (3), as discussed in the following paragraphs. The liabilities against which the company may indemnify the director include liability to a third party under a guarantee or for misrepresentation in relation to the company, liabilities arising as a result of an accident relating to the company's affairs, and, as discussed below, liabilities for legal costs, so long as the indemnity is consistent with s 234.

20.14 Sections 234(3)(a)(i) and (b)(i) deal with criminal proceedings. A company may not indemnify a director against liability to pay a fine imposed in criminal proceedings or a liability incurred by him in defending criminal proceedings in which he is convicted (after exhausting all appeals). A company can, however, indemnify the director against costs liabilities incurred by him in successfully defending criminal proceedings.

20.15 Section 234(3)(a)(ii) prevents a company from indemnifying the director against liability to pay a penalty imposed by a regulatory authority in respect of non-compliance with any

---

[21] Subsection (4) explains that the references in sub-s (3)(b) to a conviction, judgment, or refusal of relief are to the final decision in the proceedings. Subsection (5) provides:

For this purpose—
(a) a conviction, judgment, or refusal of relief becomes final—(i) if not appealed against, at the end of the period for bringing an appeal, or (ii) if appealed against, at the time when the appeal (or any further appeal) is disposed of; and
(b) an appeal is disposed of—(i) if it is determined and the period for bringing any further appeal has ended, or (ii) if it is abandoned or otherwise ceases to have effect.

[22] Subsection (6) explains that the reference in sub-s (3)(b)(iii) to an application for relief is to an application for relief under s 661(3) or (4) (power of court to grant relief in case of acquisition of shares by innocent nominee), or s 1157 (general power of court to grant relief in case of honest and reasonable conduct).

[23] 'Associate company' is defined by s 256; see para 20.08 above.

requirement of a regulatory nature, but s 234(3)(b) does not in terms appear to prevent the company from indemnifying the director in respect of the costs of unsuccessfully defending the regulatory proceedings.

Sections 234(3)(b)(ii) and (iii) deal with liabilities incurred by the director in relation to **20.16** certain civil proceedings concerning the company. They prevent a company from indemnifying the director against any liability, including a liability to pay any costs, incurred by him in defending civil proceedings brought by the company or an associate company in which final judgment is given against him or in unsuccessfully applying for relief under ss 661(3) or (4) or 1157.[24] On the other hand the company may indemnify the director in respect of his costs, whether pursuant to an order or by agreement, if he succeeds in his defence of the proceedings brought against him by the company (or in the name of the company in a derivative action) or an associate company or if he succeeds in obtaining relief from the court under ss 661(3) or (4) or 1157. It may be difficult to apply s 234(3)(b) to a case where the director settles or compromises proceedings. By so doing he may avoid a final judgment, but can it be said that he has succeeded in his defence? Furthermore the director may be protected by indemnity under a directors' and officers' insurance policy as discussed in Chapter 21 below.

Director's right of indemnity

The 1985 Table A, reg 118 provides for indemnification of directors in respect of legal **20.17** defence costs, whether the claimant is the company or a third party:

> Subject to the provisions of the Act[25] but without prejudice to any indemnity to which a director may otherwise be entitled, every director or other officer or auditor of the company shall be indemnified out of the assets of the company against any liability incurred by him in defending any proceedings, whether civil or criminal, in which judgment is given in his favour or in which he is acquitted or in connection with any application in which relief is granted to him by the court from liability for negligence, default, breach of duty or breach of trust in relation to the affairs of the company.

If, pursuant to such an article, the company pays a director costs of defending legal proceedings during the course of the proceedings, which the director, in due course, loses, the director will be liable to repay to the company the costs that it had paid.

Although the drafting is different, the position is substantially the same under Model Articles **20.18** 52 (pcls) and 85 (plc), which provide:

(1) Subject to paragraph (2), a relevant director of the company or an associated company may be indemnified out of the company's assets against—
    (a) any liability incurred by that director in connection with any negligence, default, breach of duty or breach of trust in relation to the company or an associated company,
    (b) any liability incurred by that director in connection with the activities of the company or an associated company in its capacity as a trustee of an occupational pension scheme (as defined in section 235(6) of the Companies Act 2006),
    (c) any other liability incurred by that director as an officer of the company or an associated company.
(2) This article does not authorise any indemnity which would be prohibited or rendered void by any provision of the Companies Acts or by any provision of law.

---

[24] Applications for relief under s 1157 are discussed in Ch 19, Section D above.
[25] This includes the provisions of the 2006 Act: see reg 1, as substituted by the Companies (Tables A to F) (Amendment) Regulations 2007 (SI 2007/2541), reg 3.

(3) In this article:

    (a) companies are associated if one is a subsidiary of the other or both are subsidiaries of the same body corporate, and

    (b) a 'relevant director' means any director or former director of the company or an associated company.

20.19 As noted in paragraph 20.09 above, the indemnity provisions in the company's articles are not necessarily incorporated into any contract between the director and the company, although usually they are. The indemnity provisions in the Model Articles expressly apply to a former director and his contractual right to an indemnity cannot be prejudiced by a retrospective alteration of the articles.[26] Under normal contractual principles, a director who is in repudiatory breach of his contract with the company may be unable to enforce the indemnity provision.[27]

20.20 Although a company's ability to indemnify the director in respect of liabilities incurred in civil and criminal proceedings is controlled and restricted by s 234, it should be noted that a company may lend the director money to defend civil or criminal proceedings, provided that the requirements of the 2006 Act, s 205 are complied with.[28]

(2) Qualifying pension scheme indemnity provision

20.21 As foreshadowed by s 232(2)(c), s 235 enables a company that is a trustee of an occupational pension scheme to indemnify a director against liability for negligence, default, breach of duty, or breach of trust incurred in connection with the company's activities as trustee of the scheme in slightly broader terms than apply to third party indemnities. Section 235(6) provides that in s 235 'occupational pension scheme' means an occupational pension scheme as defined in the Finance Act 2004, s 150(5) that is established under a trust, namely:

> a pension scheme established by an employer or employers and having or capable of having effect so as to provide benefits to or in respect of any or all of the employees of—
>
> (a) that employer or those employers, or
>
> (b) any other employer, (whether or not it also has or is capable of having effect so as to provide benefits to or in respect of other persons).

The liabilities facing directors of companies that are trustees of such schemes are discussed in Chapter 29 below.

20.22 The section was introduced by the government at the committee stage in the House of Commons, in response to concerns expressed in the House of Lords as to the importance of the role performed by such directors, the limited protection currently offered by D&O Insurance policies, and the difficulties of recruiting high-quality directors for companies acting as trustees of occupational pension schemes.[29]

---

[26] See Australian cases: *Swabey v Port Darwin Co* (1889) 1 Meg 385, CA; *Bailey v New South Wales Medical Defence Union Ltd* (1995) 18 ACSR 521, HC (Aus) at paras 14–25 of the majority judgment; *NRMA Ltd v Snodgrass* (2001) 19 ACLC 769, NSWSC at para 23.

[27] *Boston Deep Sea Fishing and Ice Co Ltd v Ansell* (1889) 39 Ch D 339; *Neptune (Vehicle Washing Equipment) Ltd v Fitzgerald (No 2)* [1995] BCC 1,000; *Item Software (UK) Ltd v Fassihi* [2003] 2 BCLC 1, [2005] 2 BCLC 91, CA. The position is the same for any agent: *Bowstead & Reynolds on Agency*, 20th edn (Sweet and Maxwell, 2014), para 7–065, cross-referring to Art 62 of that work.

[28] Ch 18, Section D above.

[29] The Solicitor General explained why the government amended the Company Law Reform Bill by adding a clause in terms of s 235 (Hansard, HC Comm D, cols 636–7 (11 July 2006)):

Section 235(1) states that s 232(2) does not apply to a qualifying pension scheme **20.23**
indemnity provision and s 235(2) and (3) explains what the requirements for that
provision are:

> (2) Pension scheme indemnity provision means provision indemnifying a director of a company that is a trustee of an occupational pension scheme against liability incurred in connection with the company's activities as trustee of the scheme.
>
> Such provision is qualifying pension scheme indemnity provision if the following requirements are met.
>
> (3) The provision must not provide indemnity against—
>   (a) any liability of the director to pay—
>   (i) a fine imposed in criminal proceedings, or
>   (ii) a sum payable to a regulatory authority by way of a penalty in respect of non-compliance with any requirement of a regulatory nature (howsoever arising); or
>   (b) any liability incurred by the director in defending criminal proceedings in which he is convicted.

Subsections (4) and (5) explain that the reference to a conviction is to a final conviction after
any appeal process has been exhausted.[30]

Unlike a qualifying third party indemnity provision, a qualifying pension scheme indem- **20.24**
nity provision may indemnify the director against liability incurred by him in connection
with the company's activities as trustee of the scheme (1) to the company or an associate
company in connection with any negligence, default, breach of duty, or breach of trust;
(2) in defending civil proceedings brought by the company or associate company even if
judgment is given against him; and (3) in connection with an unsuccessful application for
relief under s 1157 (general power of court to grant relief in case of honest and reasonable
conduct). In connection with its activities as trustee of an occupational pension scheme,
a company may grant its directors effective immunity from suit. A company may also
indemnify the director against liability incurred by him to any third party in connection
with the company's activities as trustee of an occupational pension scheme, provided that
the liability is not a criminal or regulatory liability within sub-s (3). The position in respect
of criminal fines, regulatory penalties, and the costs of unsuccessfully defending criminal
proceedings is the same as for a qualifying third party indemnity provision (paragraphs
20.14 and 20.15 above).

> The amendments concern indemnification of a director of a company acting as a trustee of an occupational pension scheme. They deal with worries that were raised in another place. It was said that such directors perform a vital role, often for little direct financial reward, and that directors' and officers' liability insurance policies currently available afford limited protection. We made it clear in another place that the Government attach importance to the work of such directors and that we were aware that it can sometimes be difficult to recruit high-quality directors for companies acting as trustees of occupational pension schemes. In view of that, and following consultation with key stakeholders, we agreed in principle to table amendments that would permit companies to indemnify the directors of associated companies acting as trustees of occupational pension schemes.

[30] The language used in s 235(4) and (5) is the same as that used in s 234(4) and (5) (see n 21 above), except that s 235 is only concerned with criminal convictions.

(3) Disclosure and inspection of qualifying indemnity provision

20.25   Sections 236–8[31] impose requirements for disclosure of any qualifying third party or pension scheme indemnity provision in the directors' report, for copies of such provision to be available for general inspection, and for members' entitlement to inspect and be provided with copies. Breach of the requirements to have copies available for inspection and for members' entitlements is an offence.

20.26   If a qualifying indemnity provision[32] is in force for the benefit of one or more directors of the company (or an associated company) at the time of the directors' report, or was in force at any time during the financial year to which the report relates for the benefit of one or more persons who were then directors of the company (or an associated company), the directors' report must state that such provision is or was in force.[33]

20.27   A copy of the qualifying indemnity provision (or, if it is not in writing, a written memorandum setting out its terms) must be kept available for inspection at the company's registered office or a place specified in regulations under s 1136.[34] The copy or memorandum must be retained and kept available for inspection for a year after expiry or termination.[35] Unless the copy or memorandum has at all times been kept at the company's registered office, the company must give notice to the Registrar of the place where it is kept and of any changes to that place.[36] Every copy or memorandum required to be kept under s 237 must be open to inspection by any member without charge and any member is entitled, on request and on payment of the prescribed fee, to be provided with a copy of the copy or memorandum, to be supplied within seven days.[37] Default in complying with these provisions is an offence.[38] Further, the court may, in case of refusal or default in providing a requested copy, make an order for immediate inspection or direct dispatch of a copy to the person requesting it.[39]

D. Ratification of Acts of Directors

(1) The reform made by section 239

20.28   Section 239 is a new provision regulating the means by which a company may decide to ratify any conduct (ie acts or omissions) of a director, former director, or shadow director, which amount to negligence, default, breach of duty, or breach of trust in relation to the company. The section does not alter the law as to the acts or omissions of directors that are

---

[31] Except for ss 237(4) and (9) and 238(4), which are new, these sections derive, with minor changes, from 1985 Act, ss 309C and 318.

[32] Meaning qualifying third party indemnity provision and qualifying pension scheme indemnity provision (s 236(1)).

[33] 2006 Act, s 236(2) and (3) in relation to the company and s 236(3) and (4) in relation to an associated company.

[34] 2006 Act, s 237(2) and (3). By s 237(1), the section applies to the company (whether provision is made by the company or an associated company), and where the provision is made by as associated company, to that company.

[35] 2006 Act, s 237(4).

[36] 2006 Act, s 237(5).

[37] 2006 Act, s 238(1) and (2). The Companies (Fees for Inspection and Copying of Company Records) Regulations 2007 (SI 2007/2612) prescribe the fee.

[38] 2006 Act, s 237(6) and (7) and s 238(3) and (4).

[39] 2006 Act, s 238(5).

incapable of being ratified by the company.[40] Provided that the conduct is capable of being ratified by the company, the section gives the members, either unanimously or by a resolution in which the votes of the director and persons connected with him are not counted, the power to decide whether the company should relieve the director of liability in respect of his misconduct. If they do so decide, the company is bound by their decision and there is an absolute bar to the continuation of a derivative action under the Companies Act, Part 11.[41] If the untainted members do not agree to ratify the director's conduct, he will remain exposed to a claim by the company or a derivative action until the expiry of the relevant limitation period,[42] unless and to the extent that the court grants relief under s 1157 on the ground that he acted honestly and reasonably and ought fairly to be excused.[43]

Section 239 provides for the ratification of acts of directors as follows:　**20.29**

(1) This section applies to the ratification by a company of conduct by a director amounting to negligence, default, breach of duty or breach of trust in relation to the company.

(2) The decision of the company to ratify such conduct must be made by resolution of the members of the company.

(3) Where the resolution is proposed as a written resolution neither the director (if a member of the company) nor any member connected with him is an eligible member.

(4) Where the resolution is proposed at a meeting, it is passed if the necessary majority is obtained disregarding votes in favour of the resolution by the director (if a member of the company) and any member connected with him. This does not prevent the director or any such member from attending, being counted towards the quorum and taking part in proceedings at any meeting at which the decision is considered.

(5) For the purposes of this section—
   (a) 'conduct' includes acts or omissions;
   (b) 'director' includes a former director;
   (c) a shadow director is treated as a director; and
   (d) in section 252 (meaning of 'connected person'), subsection (3) does not apply (exclusion of person who is himself a director).

(6) Nothing in this section affects—
   (a) the validity of a decision taken by unanimous consent of the members of the company, or
   (b) any power of the directors to agree not to sue, or to settle or release a claim made by them on behalf of the company.

(7) This section does not affect any other enactment or rule of law imposing additional requirements for valid ratification or any rule of law as to acts that are incapable of being ratified by the company.

---

[40] 2006 Act, s 239(7); *Franbar Holdings Ltd v Patel* [2009] 1 BCLC 1 at paras 43 and 45. See paras 20.50 *et seq* below.

[41] 2006 Act, s 263(2)(c)(ii).

[42] By the Limitation Act 1980, ss 2, 5, 23 the limitation period for cases of negligence, breach of duty, or breach of trust is six years (eg *Re Lands Allotments Ltd* [1894] 1 Ch 616, CA), unless the claim is one in respect of fraud or trust property within s 21, for which there is no limitation period, or the limitation period is extended by s 32 on the ground of fraud, concealment, or mistake. For the proper scope of trust claims within s 21, see: *Paragon Finance plc v Thackerar & Co* [1999] 1 All ER 400, CA; *JJ Harrison (Properties) Ltd v Harrison* [2002] 1 BCLC 162, CA; *Gwembe Valley Development Co Ltd v Koshy* [2004] 1 BCLC 131, CA; *Halton International Inc v Guernroy Ltd* [2006] EWCA Civ 801, CA; *Re Southill Finance Ltd, Mullarkey v Broad* [2009] EWCA Civ 2; *Cedric Slack & Partners v Slack* [2010] EWCA Civ 204; *Central Bank of Nigeria v Williams* [2014] AC 1189, SC.

[43] Ch 19, Section D above.

20.30 Under the old law a director and persons connected with him were entitled to vote at a general meeting of the company to ratify his conduct or to approve a transaction procured through the director's breach of duty. If the meeting decided by the requisite majority, including the votes of the director and persons connected with him, to approve the transaction and ratify the director's conduct, the transaction would be binding on the company and the director relieved of liability.[44] This was an element of the rule in *Foss v Harbottle*[45] and was subject to exceptions, two of which are discussed in this chapter: (1) where the transaction was beyond the powers of the company, and (2) where the transaction was a fraud on the minority and the wrongdoers were in control.[46] The first exception is discussed in paragraphs 20.53–20.57 below and the second in the next two paragraphs.

20.31 The precise scope of the second exception was more difficult to identify. In *Burland v Earle* Lord Davy gave as an example of a fraudulent transaction within the second exception a case 'where the majority are endeavouring directly or indirectly to appropriate to themselves money, property, or advantages which belong to the company, or in which other shareholders are entitled to participate'.[47] Some cases took a broader view of the second exception, holding that it applied where the justice of the case required it,[48] or where there was a breach of duty from which the wrongdoing director and majority shareholder benefited.[49] These decisions have focused on the transaction or conduct of the director, rather than on the question whether the company in general meeting could properly exercise its authority to ratify.

20.32 Professor Sarah Worthington has argued that it is more profitable to concentrate on the decision by the company organ to authorize or ratify, rather than on the nature of the transaction or conduct in question. Her thesis is that a decision will not be effective to bind the company unless it is taken bona fide and for proper purposes.[50] This equitable restriction on the exercise of voting rights is recognized in the context of the alteration of a company's articles,[51] improper share issues,[52] and sometimes more generally in the 'fraud on the minority'

---

[44] *North West Transportation Co Ltd v Beatty* (1887) 12 AC 589, PC; *Burland v Earle* [1902] AC 83, 94, PC; *Cook v Deeks* [1916] 1 AC 554, 561, PC; *Bamford v Bamford* [1970] Ch 212, 239, CA. Third parties would in any event be able to rely on 2006 Act, ss 39 and 40 to uphold the validity of the transaction (which replaced 1985 Act, ss 35 and 35A on 1 October 2009).

[45] (1843) 2 Hare 461.

[46] For further discussion of the rule and its exceptions, see Ch 1, paras 1.25 and 1.26 above, and Ch 22 below.

[47] [1902] AC 83, 93, PC. Other cases on the 'fraud on the minority' exception are noted in the next two footnotes and also: *Atwool v Merryweather* (1867) LR 5 Eq 464n; *Gray v Lewis* (1873) LR 8 Ch App 1035; *Menier v Hooper's Telegraph Works* (1874) LR 9 Ch App 350; *MacDougall v Gardiner* (1875) 1 Ch D 13, 25; *Mason v Harris* (1879) 11 Ch D 97; *Cook v Deeks* [1916] 1 AC 554, 563–5, PC; *Edwards v Halliwell* [1950] 2 All ER 1064, 1067, CA; *Prudential Assurance Co Ltd v Newman Industries Ltd* [1982] Ch 204, 210, CA; *Estmanco (Kilner House) Ltd v Greater London Council* [1982] 1 WLR 2, 12; *Smith v Croft (No 2)* [1988] Ch 114. Mere negligence was not enough to bring the case within the exception: *Turquand v Marshall* (1869) LR 4 Ch App 376, 386; *Pavlides v Jensen* [1956] Ch 565; *Heyting v Dupont* [1964] I WLR 843, CA.

[48] *Russell v Wakefield Waterworks Co* (1875) LR 20 Eq 474, 480, 482; but see *Prudential Assurance Co Ltd v Newman Industries Ltd (No 2)* [1982] Ch 204, 221 CA.

[49] *Alexander v Automatic Telephone Co* [1900] 2 Ch 56, CA; *Daniels v Daniels* [1978] Ch 406, 408, 414; *Abouraya v Sigmund* [2015] BCC 503 at para 25.

[50] 'Corporate Governance: Remedying and Ratifying Directors' Breaches' (2000) 116 LQR 638, 646. See *British America Nickel Corp Ltd v MJ O'Brien* [1927] AC, 369, 371, PC; *Redwood Master Fund Ltd v TD Bank Europe Ltd* [2006] 1 BCLC 149 (both cases on modification of loan notes).

[51] *Allen v Gold Reefs of West Africa Ltd* [1900] 1 Ch 656, 671, CA; *Shuttleworth v Cox Bros & Co (Maidenhead) Ltd* [1927] 2 KB 9, 18, 23, 24, CA; *Greenhalgh v Arderne Cinemas Ltd* [1951] Ch 286, 291, CA; *Citco Banking Corp NV v Pusser's Ltd* [2007] 2 BCLC 483, PC; *Re Charterhouse Capital Ltd* [2015] 2 BCLC 627, CA, at para 90.

[52] *Hogg v Cramphorn Ltd* [1967] Ch 254; *Bamford v Bamford* [1970] Ch 212, CA (although this is not to say that any shareholder is disenfranchised); *Mason v Harris* (1879) 11 Ch D 97.

cases.[53] It does not mean that shareholders are subject to fiduciary obligations. They can vote in their own interests except where they would be using their voting power to achieve a purpose outside the scope of the power granted them to vote at general meetings. The court would only interfere if satisfied that no reasonable person could have considered the resolution would benefit the company.[54] The burden is on those who allege that a shareholder has or will cast his vote in bad faith or for an improper purpose.[55]

The new s 239 takes this approach a stage further by disenfranchising the wrongdoer and **20.33** persons connected with him in relation to the decision to ratify.[56] The Attorney General, Lord Goldsmith, said of the new provision:[57]

> It seeks to exclude the votes of the wrongdoer and those persons most likely to be biased in favour of the director or under his influence—namely, the persons connected with him—and make it easier to identify those persons when the votes are counted.

So, in relation to the decision whether or not to ratify a director's conduct, it is no longer necessary for minority shareholders to impugn the exercise of voting rights by the majority. By the section certain votes are excluded. It will seldom, if ever, be necessary to return to the difficult issues discussed in the preceding paragraphs. The second important change made by s 239 is that, provided that the transaction is within the powers of the company and creditors' interests are not affected, it ought no longer to be necessary to consider the nature of the director's conduct to determine whether or not it is capable of being ratified by the shareholders.[58] If the independent shareholders are content to ratify the director's conduct, he will be safe from a derivative action.[59]

(2) The effect of ratification

Section 239 is concerned with the decision of the company, by its members, to ratify the **20.34** conduct of a director, former director, or shadow director. It is not explicitly concerned with ratifying or adopting a transaction entered into or apparently entered into as a result of the acts or omissions of the director. Indeed it is possible for the company to affirm or adopt a transaction as against the other party to it, while preserving its breach of duty claims against the director who caused the company to enter into it.

The Companies Act does not define 'ratification', but an effective ratification is generally **20.35** understood to mean that the director's wrong is cured so that there is no cause of action in respect of which the company can bring proceedings and, equally, no derivative action may

---

[53] *Atwool v Merryweather* (1867) LR 5 Eq 464n; *Cook v Deeks* [1916] 1 AC 554, PC; *Smith v Croft (No 2)* [1988] Ch 114.

[54] *Shuttleworth v Cox Bros & Co (Maidenhead) Ltd* [1927] 2 KB 9, 18, 23, 24, CA; *Greenhalgh v Arderne Cinemas Ltd* [1951] Ch 286, 291, CA; *Citco Banking Corp NV v Pusser's Ltd* [2007] 2 BCLC 483, PC; *Assenagon Asset Management SA v Irish Bank Resolution Corp Ltd* [2013] Bus LR 266; *Re Charterhouse Capital Ltd* [2015] 2 BCLC 627, CA, at para 90.

[55] *Peter's American Delicacy Co Ltd v Heath* (1939) 61 CLR 457, 482, 511; *Citco Banking Corp NV v Pusser's Ltd* [2007] 2 BCLC 483, PC at para 18.

[56] This reform was recommended in the CLR *Final Report* at paras 7.52–7.62. In *Goldtrail Travel Ltd v Aydin* [2015] 1 BCLC 89 at para 25 Rose J described this provision as giving rise to a 'clear change in the previous law'.

[57] Hansard, HL Report Stage, cols 872–3 (9 May 2006).

[58] See, however, the discussion of *Madoff Securities International Ltd v Raven* [2013] EWHC 3147 (Comm) below at paras 20.56–20.57.

[59] 2006 Act, s 263(2)(c). Note that where the director's conduct has exposed the company to criminal or regulatory sanction, the *ex turpi causa* rule may prevent the company from claiming indemnity from the director and he will not need to obtain the protection of ratification: *Safeway Stores Ltd v Twigger* [2011] 2 All ER 841, CA; Ch 19, Section E(4) above.

be pursued by a minority shareholder.[60] In *Bamford v Bamford* Harman LJ said that where directors find that they have misconducted themselves 'such directors can, by making a full and frank disclosure and calling together the general body of shareholders, obtain absolution and forgiveness of their sins'.[61] In *Madoff Securities International Ltd v Raven* Popplewell J concluded:[62] 'Such ratification makes such acts the acts of the company, of which it can make no complaint against the directors, and is a complete defence to such allegations of breach.'

20.36 So long as the decision to ratify subsists, the director is certainly safe from proceedings by the company or a derivative action. But it is not entirely clear whether the decision of the company to ratify is, on its own, sufficient to protect the director at all times. Following a change of control or insolvency, the company may change its mind and wish to sue the director. A director would be well advised to obtain a deed of release or enter into a compromise agreement, including a release of claims.

20.37 A director may wish to obtain ratification of his conduct where he is exposed to the civil liability to the company as a consequence of a breach of his general duties (s 178).[63] A director will not be exposed to civil liability to the company for breach of the duty and will therefore not need to obtain ratification if:

(1) in relation to the director's conflict or possible conflict of interest, the matter is authorized by the directors in accordance with s 175;[64]

(2) the director duly declares the nature and extent of his interest in a proposed transaction or arrangement with the company to the other directors in accordance with s 177;[65]

(3) the director complies with any provisions in the company's articles dealing with conflicts of interest; and[66]

(4) the director obtains from the company, acting by its directors, an agreement not to sue or a settlement or release of a claim; provided of course that the directors act in accordance with their general duties in agreeing not to sue, to settle, or to release the claim.[67]

20.38 Finally a director will not need to resort to ratification if he acts in accordance with a specific or general authority of the company; as where the company, by its members, consents to, approves, or authorizes a transaction before it is entered into in accordance with s 180(4) (a).[68] But s 180(4)(a) appears to preserve any rule of law to the effect that a resolution of the members will not be valid if the vote was carried by votes that were not cast in good faith and for the proper purposes of the company. If it were otherwise, a director

---

[60] Law Commission, *Shareholder Remedies*, No 246 at para 6.80.

[61] [1970] Ch 212, 238, CA.

[62] [2013] EWHC 3147 (Comm) at para 288. See also para 268, in which Popplewell J summarized the effect of Lawton LJ's judgment in *Multinational Gas and Petrochemical Co v Multinational Gas and Petrochemical Services Ltd* [1983] Ch 258, 269E, CA.

[63] 2006 Act, s 178.

[64] Companies Act, s 180(1).

[65] Companies Act, s 180(1).

[66] Companies Act, s 180(4)(b); eg 1985 Table A, reg 84.

[67] 2006 Act, s 239(6)(b). There would have to be a deed of release unless there was consideration for the company's agreement to release or not pursue the claim.

[68] *Queensland Mines Ltd v Hudson* (1978) 18 ALR 1, PC; *Re Horsley & Weight Ltd* [1982] Ch 442, CA; *Multinational Gas and Petrochemical Co v Multinational Gas and Petrochemical Services Ltd* [1983] Ch 258, CA.

and the majority shareholders could use prior authorization as a means of avoiding the provisions of s 239.

(3) The decision of the company to ratify

There are three ways in which the company may decide to ratify a director's conduct: by written resolution, by resolution passed at a meeting, and unanimously. **20.39**

Ratification by resolution

Chapter 25, Section C below describes the written resolution procedure. Where the proposed resolution is for ratification of a director's conduct, s 239(3) varies the procedure in that the director (if a member of the company) and any member connected with him is not an eligible member within s 289. **20.40**

Chapter 25, Section D below describes the procedure where a decision is taken by resolution at a meeting of the members of the company. Where the proposed resolution is for ratification of a director's conduct, s 239(4) varies the procedure in that the votes in favour of the resolution by the director (if a member of the company) and any member connected with him are disregarded. **20.41**

Where ratification is sought by way of a written resolution or a resolution at a meeting, the relevant circumstances must be fully and frankly disclosed to the shareholders.[69] **20.42**

Section 252 identifies the persons connected with the director whose conduct is the subject of the proposed ratification, but, for the purposes of s 239 a person who is himself a director is included among those connected with the director.[70] Persons connected with the director are members of the director's family and certain companies, trustees, partners, and partnerships.[71] **20.43**

Section 253 identifies the members of a director's family as being: **20.44**

(a) the director's spouse or civil partner;
(b) any other person (whether of a different sex or the same sex) with whom the director lives as partner in an enduring family relationship, unless that person is the director's grandparent or grandchild, sister, brother, aunt or uncle, or nephew or niece;
(c) the director's children or step-children;
(d) any children or step-children of a person within (b), not being the children or step-children of the director, who live with the director and have not attained the age of 18; and
(e) the director's parents.

It follows that members of the director's broader family, such as his brothers and sisters, may be able to force a ratification of the director's conduct against the wishes of the wholly independent minority members, unless that minority could challenge the votes as not being cast in good faith and for proper purposes.[72]

---

[69] *Kaye v Croydon Tramway Co* [1898] 1 Ch 358, CA; *Tiessen v Henderson* [1899] 1 Ch 861; *Baillie v Oriental Telephone and Electric Co Ltd* [1915] 1 Ch 503, 514, CA; *New Zealand Netherlands Society 'Oranje' Inc v Kuys* [1973] 1 WLR 1126, PC; *Knight v Frost* [1999] 1 BCLC 364; *Re RAC Motoring Services Ltd* [2000] 1 BCLC 307; *Sharma v Sharma* [2014] BCC 73, CA, at para 47.
[70] 2006 Act, ss 239(5)(d) and 252(3).
[71] See also Ch 3, Section D above.
[72] Para 20.32 above.

20.45   A body corporate is connected with the director in the circumstances described in s 254 and Schedule 1. In essence a director is connected with a body corporate if the director and persons connected with him together (a) are interested in at least 20 per cent of the equity share capital or (b) are entitled to exercise or control the exercise of more than 20 per cent of the voting power at any general meeting.[73]

20.46   A member is also connected with the director if:

(1) he is a person acting in his capacity as trustee of a trust and (a) the beneficiaries of the trust include the director, a member of the director's family, or a connected body corporate connected, or (b) the terms of the trust confer a power on the trustees that may be exercised for the benefit of any such person;[74]

(2) he is acting in his capacity as a partner of (a) the director or (b) a member of the director's family, a connected body corporate, or a connected trustee; and[75]

(3) it is a firm that is a legal person under the law by which it is governed and in which (a) the director is a partner; (b) a partner is a member of the director's family, a connected body corporate, or a connected trustee; or (c) a partner is a firm in which the director is a partner or in which there is a partner who is a member of the director's family, a connected body corporate, or a connected trustee.[76]

Unanimous consent

20.47   The power of all the members of the company unanimously to consent to the director's conduct, so as to ratify it, is preserved by s 239(6)(a). The members may also unanimously consent to, approve, or authorize in advance a particular transaction or conduct, so that no question of breach of duty arises: the director simply carries out the company's will. Where a person relies on informal unanimous consent, approval, authorization, or ratification to uphold a particular transaction or to be excused from liability in respect of particular conduct, he is said to raise a *Duomatic* defence.[77]

20.48   The availability of the *Duomatic* defence is subject to the transaction or conduct being capable of ratification, as discussed in Section D(4) below. The established exceptions which prevent its availability are: (a) acts beyond the power of the company, such as unlawful distributions; (b) fraud; and (c) the company being insolvent or on the verge of insolvency.[78]

20.49   The unanimous consent procedure is discussed in Chapter 25, Section B below. In *Re D'Jan of London Ltd*[79] Hoffmann LJ said that the principle that the members could bind the company by unanimous consent to ratify a breach of duty or mandate particular conduct 'requires that the shareholders should have, whether formally or informally, mandated or ratified the

---

[73] See *Re Kilnoore Ltd* [2006] Ch 489 for discussion of the comparable provision in Insolvency Act, s 435(10).
[74] 2006 Act, s 252(2)(c).
[75] 2006 Act, s 252(2)(d).
[76] 2006 Act, s 252(2)(e).
[77] *Re Duomatic Ltd* 1969] 2 Ch 365.
[78] *Prest v Petrodel* [2013] 2 AC 415 at para 106 per Rimer LJ in the Court of Appeal and at para 41 per Lord Sumption in the Supreme Court; *Bilta (UK) Ltd v Nazir (No 2)* [2014] Ch 52, CA, at para 20 per Patten LJ; [2016] AC 1, SC, at paras 122–30, per Lords Toulson and Hodge; *Madoff Securities International Ltd v Raven* [2013] EWHC 3147 (Comm) at para 269; *Goldtrail Travel Ltd v Aydin* [2015] 1 BCLC 89 at paras 116–18; (not affected by appeal, [2016] 1 BCLC 635, CA).
[79] [1994] 1 BCLC 561, 564 (where Hoffmann LJ was sitting as an additional judge of the Chancery Division).

act in question. It is not enough that they probably would have ratified if they had known or thought about it before the liquidation removed their power to do so.' It might therefore be thought difficult to see what scope there could be for any attempt to establish ratification by acquiescence.[80] Nevertheless, in *Sharma v Sharma*,[81] a case concerning s 175 of the 2006 Act (duty to avoid conflicts of interest), the Court of Appeal held that ratification could be established by silence, even where shareholders were not aware of their legal rights, provided that the circumstances were such that it would be unconscionable for shareholders to remain silent and only raise objections later. Three of the propositions stated by Jackson LJ were:[82]

(ii) If the shareholders with full knowledge of the relevant facts consent to the director exploiting those opportunities for his own personal gain, then that conduct is not a breach of the fiduciary or statutory duty [to avoid conflicts of interest].

(iii) If the shareholders with full knowledge of the relevant facts acquiesce in the director's proposed conduct, then that may constitute consent. However, consent cannot be inferred from silence unless:

(a) the shareholders know that their consent is required, or

(b) the circumstances are such that it would be unconscionable for the shareholders to remain silent at the time and object after the event.

(iv) For the purposes of propositions (ii) and (iii) full knowledge of the relevant facts does not entail an understanding of their legal incidents. In other words the shareholders need not appreciate that the proposed action would be characterised as a breach of fiduciary or statutory duty.

(4) Limits on ratification

Section 239(7) preserves the existing law, firstly, as to additional requirements for a valid ratification and, secondly, as to acts that are incapable of being ratified by the company.[83] The Attorney General, Lord Goldsmith, explained that 'the requirements of this section are additional and not alternative to any other requirements as to ratification imposed by statute or under the common law'.[84]

20.50

The reference in sub-s (7) to additional requirements probably refers to acts which to be valid require a special resolution or the taking of some other procedural step. By way of exception to the rule in *Foss v Harbottle*, an individual shareholder was entitled to maintain an action where the resolution could only be passed by a special resolution (assuming the majority could not obtain it) or where the wrong done to the company infringed the individual's own rights.[85] Section 239 is not a means of avoiding the requirements of other provisions of the Companies Act.

20.51

The acts which are incapable of being ratified by the company so as to prevent the minority from suing have been described as being 'of a fraudulent character or beyond the powers of the company'.[86] Equally such acts could not be ratified so as to prevent a liquidator,

20.52

---

[80] Consider *Re Bailey Hay & Co Ltd* [1971] 1 WLR 1357.
[81] [2014] BCC 73, at paras 45–52. The Court of Appeal relied on *Re Home Treat* [1991] BCC 165 as establishing that acquiescence was as good as actual consent.
[82] [2014] BCC 73, at para 52.
[83] *Franbar Holdings Ltd v Patel* [2009] 1 BCLC 1 at paras 43–5.
[84] Hansard, HL Report Stage, col 873 (9 May 2006).
[85] *Edwards v Halliwell* [1950] 2 All ER 1064, 1066, 1067, CA, per Jenkins LJ; *Baillie v Oriental Telephone and Electric Co Ltd* [1915] 1 Ch 503, CA; *Cotter v National Union of Seamen* [1929] 2 Ch 58, 69, 70.
[86] Lord Davey in *Burland v Earle* [1902] AC 83, 93, PC.

administrator, or administrative receiver from suing or causing the company to sue. More recently the courts have identified a duty owed by directors to have regard to the interests of creditors and have developed from that the view that, where the company is insolvent or on the verge of insolvency,[87] the members are not able to ratify a director's breach of duty which adversely affects the interests of creditors, as discussed in Chapter 12, Section E above.

Acts beyond the power of the company

20.53 It is plain that an act which is beyond the corporate capacity of the company cannot be ratified,[88] but given the unrestricted objects of a modern company, this issue will seldom arise.[89] The principle also applies to acts which infringe statutory or common law rules as to the preservation of capital and which are therefore unlawful. Thus the members cannot ratify a distribution paid out of capital in breach of ss 830 and 831 or an act constituting financial assistance given by a public company in breach of the s 678.[90] At common law it was established that the shareholders could not authorize or ratify the payment of gifts to directors out of capital or money borrowed by the company, for, as Lindley LJ explained:[91] 'Such money cannot be lawfully divided amongst shareholders themselves, nor can it be given away by them for nothing to their directors so as to bind the company in its corporate capacity.'

20.54 The court may recharacterize a transaction as being a disguised distribution to or at the direction of the shareholders which is unlawful and incapable of being ratified if not made out of distributable profits.[92] The Supreme Court, in *Progress Property Co Ltd v Moorgarth Group Ltd*,[93] has affirmed that whether a transaction should be so recharacterized is a matter of substance, not form. In rejecting an exclusively objective approach, Lord Walker said:[94]

> the court's real task is to inquire into the true purpose and substance of the impugned transaction. That calls for an investigation of all the relevant facts, which sometimes include the state of mind of the human beings who are orchestrating the corporate activity.
>
> Sometimes their states of mind are totally irrelevant. A distribution described as a dividend but actually paid out of capital is unlawful, however technical the error and however well-meaning the directors who paid it. The same is true of a payment which is on analysis the equivalent of a

---

[87] For the purposes of the Insolvency Act, 'insolvency' refers to the process (s 247(1)). That Act, s 123, refers instead to a company being unable to pay its debts on either a balance-sheet basis (liabilities exceed assets) or a cash-flow basis (inability to pay debts as they fall due).

[88] *Rolled Steel Ltd v British Steel Corpn* [1986] Ch 246, 296, CA.

[89] 2006 Act, s 31(1) (and formerly 1985 Act, s 3A).

[90] *Precision Dippings Ltd v Precision Dippings Marketing Ltd* [1986] Ch 447, CA (an unlawful distribution of profits). 2006 Act, s 678 replaced 1985 Act, s 151 on 1 October 2009, but the private company exemptions came into force on 1 October 2008.

[91] *Re George Newman & Co* [1895] 1 Ch 674, 686, CA; *Official Receiver v Stern* [2002] 1 BCLC 119, CA at para 32.

[92] *Ridge Securities v Inland Revenue Commissioners* [1964] 1 WLR 479, 495 (interest payments recharacterized as distributions); *Re W & M Roith Ltd* [1964] 1 WLR 432 (widow's pension in a service contract a disguised distribution at the direction of the shareholder); *Re Halt Garage Ltd* [1982] 3 All ER 1016 (excessive remuneration paid to a director who performed no services treated as a disguised distribution); *Sasea Finance Ltd v KPMG* [2002] BCC 574 at paras 25–31 (circular transaction involving loan for purchase of shares); *Progress Property Co Ltd v Moorgarth Group Ltd* [2011] 1 WLR 1, SC (sale of shares at an undervalue but in the genuine belief that the sale is a proper commercial sale is not a disguised distribution).

[93] [2011] 1 WLR 1, SC at para 16.

[94] [2011] 1 WLR 1, SC at paras 27–9.

dividend[95] … Where there is a challenge to the propriety of a director's remuneration the test is objective …,[96] but probably subject in practice to what has been called, in a recent Scottish case,[97] a 'margin of appreciation'…. If a controlling shareholder simply treats a company as his own property, as the domineering master-builder did in *Re George Newman & Co*[98] … his state of mind (and that of his fellow-directors) is irrelevant. It does not matter whether they were consciously in breach of duty, or just woefully ignorant of their duties. What they do is enough by itself to establish the unlawful character of the transaction.

The participant's subjective intentions are however sometimes relevant, and a distribution disguised as an arm's length commercial transaction is the paradigm example. If a company sells to a shareholder at a low value assets which are difficult to value precisely, but which are potentially very valuable, the transaction may call for close scrutiny, and the company's financial position, and the actual motives and intentions of the directors, will be highly relevant. There may be questions to be asked as to whether the company was under financial pressure compelling it to sell at an inopportune time, as to what advice was taken, how the market was tested, and how the terms of the deal were negotiated. If the conclusion is that it was a genuine arm's length transaction then it will stand, even if it may, with hindsight, appear to have been a bad bargain. If it was an improper attempt to extract value by the pretence of an arm's length sale, it will be held to be unlawful. But either conclusion will depend on a realistic assessment of all relevant facts, not simply a retrospective valuation exercise in isolation of all other inquiries.[99]

20.55 This type of inquiry, taking into account both objective facts and factors inviting suspicion, is exemplified by the decision of Hoffmann J in *Aveling Barford Ltd v Perion Ltd*,[100] which concerned 'a sale at a gross undervalue for the purpose of enabling a profit to be realised by an entity controlled and put forward by [the company's] sole beneficial shareholder'. The company did not have sufficient distributable profits and so the sale could not be validated by the unanimous approval of the shareholder. Hoffmann J went on to say that: '[i]t was the fact that it was known and intended to be a sale at an undervalue which made it an unlawful distribution'.[101]

20.56 In *Madoff Securities International Ltd v Raven*[102] Popplewell J, held that directors were entitled to rely on a *Duomatic* defence to claims that, in relation to certain impugned payments, they had breached their duties to act in what they considered to be the interests of the company and to exercise reasonable skill and care.[103] He was satisfied that all the shareholders were aware of and approved the impugned payments.[104] He accepted that a *Duomatic* defence would not be available if the company was not insolvent or of doubtful insolvency,[105]

---

95 The cases of this type referred to by Lord Walker were *Re Walters' Deed of Guarantee* [1933] Ch 321 (claim by guarantor of preference dividends); *British & Commonwealth Holdings plc v Barclays Bank plc* [1996] 1 WLR 1, CA (claim for damages for contractual breach of scheme for redemption of shares).

96 *Re Halt Garages (1964) Ltd* [1982] 3 All ER 1016.

97 *Clydebank Football Club Ltd v Steedham* [2002] SLT 109 at para 76. At paras 31 and 32 Lord Walker expressly approved passages in the judgment of Lord Hamilton at paras 76 and 79.

98 [1895] 1 Ch 674, CA.

99 See also the useful summary of the characterization process given by Popplewell J in *Madoff Securities International Ltd v Raven* [2013] EWHC 3147 (Comm) at [204].

100 [1989] BCLC 626, 632, 633. Discussed and approved by Lord Walker at paras 20–2, 30.

101 Note the reform made by 2006 Act, s 845.

102 [2013] EWHC 3147 (Comm) at paras 266–88.

103 2006 Act, ss 172 and 174.

104 [2013] EWHC 3147 (Comm) at paras 270–1.

105 [2013] EWHC 3147 (Comm) at paras 272–3.

but on the facts that was not the case.[106] In his judgment, Popplewell J explored the limits of the *Duomatic* defence:[107]

> It follows that the *Duomatic* principle does not permit shareholders to do informally what they could not have done formally by way of written resolution or at a meeting.[108] Accordingly the principle cannot apply to relieve the directors of liability in respect of transactions which are ultra vires in either the narrow or the wider sense in which the expression is used (see *Rolled Steel*)[109]… Therefore this defence would not be capable of applying to breaches which amounted to unlawful payment of dividends[110]… Nor can it provide a defence where there has been the exercise of powers for an improper purpose: *Rolled Steel*[111]… In each case the shareholders in general meeting could not lawfully do that which they have approved the directors in doing. In the current case the principle would therefore only be of potential application to breaches by the directors of their duty to act in what they considered to be the interests of the company, or their duty to exercise reasonable care, skill and due diligence.

20.57 It is respectfully suggested that Popplewell J was wrong to say, *obiter*, that the *Duomatic* defence is not available where directors have exercised their powers for an improper purpose in breach of s 171. The passages from *Rolled Steel* on which he specifically relied were summaries of passages in, or a quotation from, the judgment of Vinelott J, which was heavily criticized by Slade and Browne-Wilkinson LJJ in the Court of Appeal in *Rolled Steel* itself. Both Slade and Browne-Wilkinson LJJ made it clear that an exercise of a company's powers for improper purposes would be capable of ratification by shareholders at a general meeting.[112] That was established in *Hogg v Cramphorn Ltd*,[113] where it was held that the issue of shares for an improper purpose could be ratified at a general meeting (with the improperly issued shares not voting). Moreover, the resurrection of '*ultra vires in either the narrow or the wider sense in which the expression is used*' is not helpful, since companies now have unlimited capacity.[114] On the other hand, the exercise by directors of a power in the company's constitution for an improper purpose affecting members' rights may be incapable of ratification under s 239.[115]

Fraudulent transactions

20.58 A fraudulent transaction necessarily involves a victim.[116] In the present context that may be the company itself or its constituents: ie its shareholders and creditors. A company which

---

[106] [2013] EWHC 3147 (Comm) at paras 280–4.

[107] [2013] EWHC 3147 (Comm) at para 269.

[108] Popplewell J relied on *Re New Cedos Engineering Co Ltd* [1994] 1 BCLC 797, at 814g–h and *Atlas Wright (Europe) Ltd v Wright* [1999] BCC 163, at 174G–H.

[109] *Rolled Steel Products (Holdings) Ltd v British Steel Corpn* [1986] Ch 246 at 276–8, 302–3.

[110] *Aveling Barford Ltd v Perion Ltd* [1989] BCLC 626 at 630–1, 632; *Re Stakefield (Midlands) Ltd* [2011] 2 BCLC 541 at para 41.

[111] Popplewell J referred to *Rolled Steel Products (Holdings) Ltd v British Steel Corpn* [1986] Ch 246 at 277C, per Slade LJ, reciting the judgment of Vinelott J below.

[112] *Rolled Steel Products (Holdings) Ltd v British Steel Corpn* [1986] Ch 246 at 296E–297D, per Slade LJ, and 304D–F, per Browne-Wilkinson LJ.

[113] [1967] Ch 254.

[114] 2006 Act, ss 31 and 39.

[115] An example might be the improper service of a restriction notice on a shareholder under a power contained in the company's constitution in order to disenfranchise him at a meeting. It is difficult to see why the other shareholders should be able to ratify the breach of duty and so validate the restriction. Consider the circumstances of *Eclairs Group Ltd v JKX Oil & Gas plc* [2015] UKSC 71; [2015] Bus LR 1395.

[116] In *Welham v Director of Public Prosecutions* [1961] AC 103, 123, HL Lord Radcliffe said: 'Now, I think that there are one or two things that can be said with confidence about the meaning of the word "defraud". It requires a person as its object: that is, defrauding involves doing something to someone. Although in the nature of things it is almost invariably associated with the obtaining of an advantage for the person who commits the

has been defrauded by its directors and shareholders may pursue a claim against them for compensation.[117] Similarly a company may be the victim of a theft committed by all its shareholders and it is no defence for the shareholders to say that they all agreed to take the company's property.[118] In these cases the shareholders' participation in the conspiracy or theft could not be regarded as a corporate act equivalent to a resolution authorizing or ratifying the directors' conduct.

If a director defrauds some of the shareholders by misapplying company property available **20.59** for distribution to shareholders, the question whether his conduct is capable of being ratified needs to be reconsidered in the light of s 239. If the director seeks ratification, he will have to disclose his misconduct to the shareholders and it will be for the shareholders who are not connected with the director to decide whether or not to grant ratification. If the majority of the independent shareholders agree to ratify, then, unless their votes were cast in bad faith or for an improper purpose,[119] there seems no reason why there should not be ratification.

More often the creditors are the direct or indirect victims of the fraud. Where the transac- **20.60** tion or conduct of the directors involves a fraud on creditors the members have no power to cause the company to authorize or ratify it.[120] The courts have given a flexible meaning to the concept of fraud on creditors, so that conduct amounting to 'sharp practice' may be considered fraudulent.[121]

In *Madoff Securities International Ltd v Raven*,[122] Flaux J held that, as a matter of public **20.61** policy, the shareholders of a solvent company could not ratify directors' acts, where they, the shareholders, were acting dishonestly and using the company as a vehicle for fraud or wrongdoing (in that case as a money laundering vehicle to disguise and distribute proceeds of fraud).[123] Flaux J's decision arose on a challenge to jurisdiction and an application for an interim injunction. The question was therefore whether the state of the authorities was such that there was a serious issue to be tried on the point. Giving judgment after the trial of the

---

fraud, it is the effect upon the person who is the object of the fraud that ultimately determines its meaning.' That passage was quoted by Lord Lane CJ in the fraudulent trading case *R v Grantham* [1984] QB 675, 683, CA.

[117] *Belmont Finance Corporation Ltd v Williams Furniture Ltd* [1979] Ch 250, CA; *Bilta (UK) Ltd v Nazir (No 2)* [2014] Ch 52, [2016] AC 1.

[118] *AG's Reference (No 2 of 1982)* [1984] QB 624, CA; *Prest v Petrodel Resources Ltd* [2013] 2 AC 415 at para 106 per Rimer LJ in the Court of Appeal and at para 41 per Lord Sumption JSC; *Bilta (UK) Ltd v Nazir (No 2)* [2014] Ch 52 at para 20 per Patten LJ; *Bilta (UK) Ltd v Nazir (No 2)* [2016] AC 1 at paras 122–30 per Lords Toulson and Hodge. Fraud prevents valid authorization or ratification by unanimous consent: *AG for Canada v Standard Trust Company of New York* [1911] AC 498, 504, 505, PC, per Viscount Haldane; *Re Express Engineering Works Ltd* [1920] 1 Ch 466, 471, CA, per Younger LJ; *Multinational Gas and Petrochemical Co v Multinational Gas and Petrochemical Services Ltd* [1983] Ch 258, 280, CA, per May LJ.

[119] See para 20.32 above. The majority of shareholders not connected with the director in accordance with s 252 might nevertheless have close associations with the director; eg as brothers or sisters or as business associates. As a result they might have had some collateral reason for voting to ratify.

[120] *Re Halt Garages (1964) Ltd* [1982] 3 All ER 1016, 1037; *Rolled Steel Ltd v British Steel Corp* [1986] Ch 246, 296, CA.

[121] *Lloyds Bank Ltd v Marcan* [1973] 1 WLR 1387, CA; *Agricultural Mortgage Corp Ltd v Woodward* [1995] 1 BCLC 1, CA. See also Ch 34, Section E(4) below.

[122] [2012] 2 All ER (Comm) 634 at paras 105–13.

[123] Flaux J found support for that principle in *Bowthorpe Holdings Ltd v Hills* [2003] 1 BCLC 226 at paras 51 and 52 and see also *AG for Canada v Standard Trust Company of New York* [1911] AC 498, 505, PC, per Lord Haldane; *Multinational Gas and Petrochemical Co v Multinational Gas and Petrochemical Services Ltd* [1983] Ch 258, 268, 269, CA, per Lawton LJ; *Architects of Wine Ltd v Barclays Bank plc* [2007] 1 Lloyd's Rep 55 at para 19; *Cox v Cox* [2006] EWHC 1077 (Ch) at para 58.

same case,[124] Popplewell J declined, since the legal issue did not arise on the facts, to decide whether shareholders could ratify the acts of directors in circumstances where (a) the directors were acting honestly but (b) the shareholders purporting to have ratified the directors' acts were acting dishonestly for the purposes of furthering a fraud.

Insolvency and the interests of creditors

20.62 There are two distinct, albeit connected, matters to consider. The first is whether, and in what circumstances, a director owes the company a duty to consider or act in the interests of creditors of the company.[125] The second is whether insolvency or harm to creditors prevents the members from authorizing or ratifying a breach of duty by a director, whether the breach is in respect of the duty to have regard to the interests of creditors or any other breach of the general duties of a director.[126]

20.63 Section 172 states the duty of a director to promote the success of the company for the benefit of its members as a whole, but sub-s (3) provides that the duty imposed by that section 'has effect subject to any enactment or rule of law requiring directors, in certain circumstances, to consider or act in the interests of creditors of the company'. The Insolvency Act, s 214 (wrongful trading) is an enactment requiring directors to take every step with a view to minimizing the potential loss to the company's creditors, but that section only applies when the company has reached the point when there is no reasonable prospect that the company will avoid going into insolvent liquidation. A number of cases have recognized a rule of law to the effect that a director has a duty to the company to consider and act in the interests of its creditors when it is insolvent or on the verge of insolvency.[127] The duty is owed to the company, not directly to creditors.[128]

20.64 In *Re Horsley & Weight Ltd*[129] Cumming-Bruce and Templeman LLJ said, *obiter*, that it would be surprising and unsatisfactory if the members of an insolvent company could ratify conduct of its directors which amounted to serious but not fraudulent misconduct so as to provide the directors with a defence to a breach of duty claim. But *obiter dicta* of Slade LJ

---

[124] *Madoff Securities International Ltd v Raven* [2013] EWHC 3147 (Comm) at paras 285–7.

[125] This aspect is discussed in more detail in Ch 12, Section E above.

[126] These issues have been considered by the CLR in *Developing the Framework* at paras [3.72], [3.73], [3.79]–[3.81] and in the *Final Report* at paras 3.12–3.20. Also see the White Paper, *Modernising Company Law* (July 2002) at paras 3.8–3.14 and articles by Andrew Keay: 'The Director's Duty to Take into Account the Interests of Company Creditors: When Is it Triggered?' [2001] MULR 11 and 'Directors' Duties to Creditors: Contrarian Concerns Relating to Efficiency and Over-protection of Creditors' (2003) 66 MLR 665.

[127] This duty has been referred to in: *Walker v Wimborne* (1976) 137 CLR 1 at para 13; *Lonrho Ltd v Shell Petroleum Co Ltd* [1980] 1 WLR 627, 634, HL, per Lord Diplock; *Nicholson v Permakraft (NZ) Ltd* (1985) 3 ACLC 453; *Kinsela v Russell Kinsela Pty Ltd* (1986) 4 NSWLR 722; *Winkworth v Edward Baron Development Ltd* [1986] 1 WLR 1512, 1516, HL; *Brady v Brady* (1987) 3 BCC 535, 552, CA; *West Mercia Safetywear Ltd v Dodd* [1988] BCLC 250, CA; *Facia Footwear Ltd v Hinchcliffe* [1998] 1 BCLC 218, 228; *Knight v Frost* [1999] 1 BCLC 364, 381, 382; *Re Pantone 485 Ltd* [2002] 1 BCLC 266 at para 70; *Colin Gwyer Associates Ltd v London Wharf (Limehouse) Ltd* [2003] 2 BCLC 153 at para 74; *Re MDA Investment Management Ltd* [2004] 1 BCLC 217 at para 70; *GHLM Trading Ltd v Maroo* [2012] EWHC 61 (Ch) at paras 164–169; *Westpac Banking Corp v Bell Group Ltd* [2012] WASCA 157; *Vivendi SA v Richards* [2013] BCC 731 at paras 148–50; *Re HLC Environmental Projects* [2014] BCC 337 at paras 88–9; *Bilta (UK) Ltd v Nazir (No 2)* [2016] AC 1 at paras 123–6; *BTI 2014 LLC v Sequana SA* [2016] EWHC 1686 (Ch) at paras 456-479. For further discussion of these cases, see Ch 12, Section E above.

[128] *Re Horsley & Weight Ltd* [1982] Ch 442, 454, per Buckley LJ; *Kuwait Asia Bank EC v National Mutual Life Nominees Ltd* [1991] 1 AC 187, 219, PC; *Yukong Line Ltd v Rendsburg Investments Corp (No 2)* [1998] 1 WLR 294, 311, 312.

[129] [1982] Ch 442, 455, 456, CA.

in *Rolled Steel Ltd v British Steel Corp*[130] tend to support the view that the limitation on the power of members to ratify acts which are within the power of a company is restricted to frauds on creditors. He said:

> However the clear general principle is that any act that falls within the corporate capacity of a company will bind it if it is done with the unanimous consents of all the shareholders or is subsequently ratified by such consents ... This last-mentioned principle certainly is not an unqualified one. In particular, it will not enable the shareholders of a company to bind the company itself to a transaction which constitutes a fraud on its creditors.

In the Australian case *Kinsela v Russell Kinsela Pty Ltd*[131] the court had to determine **20.65** whether the members of a company could effectively authorize or ratify a transaction which occurred at a time when the company was insolvent or on the verge of insolvency and prejudiced creditors. In that case, at a time when the company was in severe financial difficulties and shortly before the court made a winding-up order, the directors caused the company to grant them a lease of its property at a rent that was substantially below the market rate. The liquidator did not allege that the lease was a fraud on creditors. Although all the members assented to the lease, the New South Wales Court of Appeal held that it was void, since the members of a company did not have power to authorize or ratify conduct which is or, but for the members' assent, would be a breach of a director's duty and which has the effect of prejudicing the company's creditors. In two influential paragraphs Street CJ distinguished between the power of the members to authorize or ratify conduct of the directors when the company is solvent and the position when it is not:[132]

> In a solvent company the proprietary interests of the shareholders entitle them as a general body to be regarded as the company when questions of the duty of directors arise. If, as a general body, they authorise or ratify a particular action of the directors, there can be no challenge to the validity of what the directors have done. But where a company is insolvent the interests of the creditors intrude. They become prospectively entitled, through the mechanism of liquidation, to displace the power of the shareholders and directors to deal with the company's assets. It is in a practical sense their assets and not the shareholders' assets that, through the medium of the company, are under the management of the directors pending either liquidation, return to solvency or the imposition of some alternative administration.

> It is, to my mind, legally and logically acceptable to recognise that, where directors are involved in a breach of duty to the company affecting the interests of shareholders, then shareholders can either authorise that breach in prospect or ratify it in retrospect. Where, however, the interests at risk are those of creditors I see no reason in law or logic to recognise that the shareholders can authorise the breach. Once it is accepted, as in my view it must be, that the directors' duty to a company as a whole extends in an insolvency context to not prejudicing the interests of creditors ... the shareholders do not have the power or authority to absolve the directors from that breach.

---

[130] [1986] Ch 246, 296, CA.

[131] (1986) 4 NSWLR 722, New South Wales Court of Appeal.

[132] At 730 and 732. Hope and McHugh JJA agreed with Street CJ who drew support from the *obiter dicta* of Cumming-Bruce and Templeman LLJ in *Re Horsley & Weight Ltd* [1982] Ch 442, 455, 456, CA and the judgment of Cooke J in *Nicholson v Permakraft (NZ) Ltd* (1985) 3 ACLC 453, 457–60, New Zealand Court of Appeal.

20.66 In *West Mercia Safetywear Ltd v Dodd*[133] the English Court of Appeal approved the first of those paragraphs in the judgment of Street CJ in support of its decision that a director was liable for breach of duty for causing a company to make a payment in fraudulent preference of a related company, when he knew both companies were insolvent and had been advised by the prospective liquidator not to operate the bank accounts.

20.67 The second of those paragraphs in the judgment of Street CJ has also been quoted with approval by Sir Andrew Morritt V-C in *Bowthorpe Holdings Ltd v Hills*,[134] when holding that the company had an arguable claim to rescind a sale of shares on terms that gave rise to a deficiency against its creditors.

20.68 Thus English law endorses the proposition that where a company's financial position is such that creditors' interests are at risk, shareholders cannot authorize what would otherwise be a breach of duty by directors or ratify a past breach of duty, so as to release directors from liability.[135] It is not so clear whether this is because of a rule of public policy,[136] or because the ratification was not in good faith and for the proper purposes of the company.[137] There is much to be said for the latter justification. If the ratification resolution has been passed by the votes of members other than the director and members connected with him, there may well be a good reason for ratifying the directors' conduct. On the other hand, a unanimous resolution passed by members including the director and members connected with him would be viewed differently; such a resolution is much more likely to have been passed to protect the director from liability in a future administration or liquidation.

20.69 There is also a degree of uncertainty as to whether, and if so to what extent, application of the principle is affected by the state of mind of the directors said to be in breach. In *Madoff Securities International v Raven*[138] Popplewell J expressed the view that it was irrelevant whether the directors honestly and reasonably believed that the company was solvent; what mattered was the objective solvency at the relevant time. However, he declined to express a concluded view on the point because the company was objectively solvent at the relevant time.[139]

---

[133] [1988] BCLC 250, CA, a decision on the pre-Insolvency Act law. The director does not appear to have defended the claim on the ground that the payment was authorized or ratified by all the shareholders. Instead his defence was that he was not in breach of duty in causing the company to pay a due debt. The defence failed because it was a breach of duty and fraud on the creditors for a director to cause a company to make a fraudulent preference: *Re Washington Diamond Mining Co* [1893] 3 Ch 95, 115, CA. The first paragraph from Street CJ's judgment has since been quoted with approval in a number of English cases. See for example: *Official Receiver v Stern* [2002] 1 BCLC 119, CA at paras 32, 51, 52 per Sir Andrew Morritt V-C; *Vivendi v Richards* [2013] BCC 771 at para 148; *Bilta (UK) Ltd v Nazir (No 2)* [2016] AC 1 at para 123 per Lords Hodge and Toulson JJSC. See also Rose J's review of the English and Commonwealth authorities in *BTI 2014 LLC v Sequana SA* [2016] EWHC 1686 (Ch) at paras 456–79.

[134] [2003] 1 BCLC 226 at paras 51–5. His judgment was followed by Flaux J in *Madoff Securities International Ltd v Raven* [2012] 2 All ER (Comm) 364 at paras 106–13.

[135] For applications of the proposition to the facts see, eg: *Madoff Securities International Ltd v Raven* [2013] EWHC 3147 (Comm) at para 272 (where the allegation of actual or potential insolvency failed on the facts); *Oxford Fleet Management Ltd v Brown* [2014] EWHC 3065 (Ch) at paras 105–9; *Goldtrail Travel Ltd v Aydin* [2015] 1 BCLC 89 at paras 113–15; *Re Finch (UK) Plc* [2015] EWHC 2430 (Ch) at para 28.

[136] Cf *Madoff Securities International Ltd v Raven* [2012] 2 All ER (Comm) 634 at paras 105–12, a case on the fraud exception.

[137] See para 20.32 above.

[138] [2013] EWHC 3147 (Comm) at paras 272–3.

[139] Popplewell J took support from *Lexi Holdings Ltd v Luqman (No. 1)* [2007] EWHC 2652 (Ch) and the Hong Kong Court of Final Appeal decision in *Tradepower (Holdings) Ltd v Tradepower (Hong Kong) Ltd* [2010] 1 HKC 380. Cf the approach taken by John Randall QC, also *obiter*, in *Re HLC Environmental Projects Ltd*

Where the company goes into administration or liquidation the transaction entered into **20.70** as a result of a director's breach of duty may be within the reach of the provisions of the Insolvency Act for adjusting prior transactions on the grounds of transaction at undervalue, preference, or defrauding creditors.[140] Even if the transaction is liable to be adjusted under one or other of those provisions, it does not necessarily follow that the director responsible is liable for breach of duty, although he may well be.[141] If, at the time of the transaction, the company was unable to pay its debts within s 240 of the Insolvency Act or had the purpose of defrauding creditors within s 423, the court is likely to be satisfied that the company was objectively insolvent or on the verge of insolvency for the purpose of denying the director a *Duomatic* or ratification defence.

[2014] BCC 337 at para 95 (duty to consider interests of creditors only arises where directors know of the facts establishing the actual or potential insolvency of the company).

[140] Insolvency Act, ss 238–41, 423–5. Had the circumstances of *Kinsela* been brought before an English court after 1986, the lease could have been set aside under the Insolvency Act, s 238 and/or s 423. As to s 239, see *Re Washington Diamond Mining Co* [1893] 3 Ch 95 CA. As to s 423, consider *Agricultural Mortgage Corp Plc v Woodward* [1995] 1 BCLC 1, CA and *Lloyd's Bank Ltd v Marcan* [1973] 1 WLR 1387, CA.

[141] In *Re Brian D Pierson (Contractors) Ltd* [2001] 1 BCLC 275, 299 it was held that a director responsible for a preference vulnerable under s 239 of the Insolvency Act did not necessarily commit a breach of duty. On the other hand, a director may be liable for breach of duty for causing a preferential payment made outside the relevant period under s 240 of the Insolvency Act; see *GHLM Trading Ltd v Maroo* [2012] 2 BCLC 369 at paras 168–72.

21

DIRECTORS' LIABILITIES: PROVISION OF INSURANCE

Stuart Hill

A. Introduction

The Companies Act, s 233 deals with the provision of insurance as a valid means of indemnifying a director against liability attaching to him in connection with any negligence, default, breach of duty, or breach of trust.[1] It provides: **21.01**

> Section 232(2) (voidness of provisions for indemnifying directors) does not prevent a company from purchasing and maintaining for a director of the company, or of an associated company, insurance against any such liability as is mentioned in that subsection.

Section 233 permits, but does not oblige, a company to purchase and maintain insurance **21.02** for a director of the company or an associated company, against any liability attaching to the director in connection with any negligence, default, breach of duty, or breach of trust in relation to the company of which he is a director. The rationale for permitting liability

---

[1] s 233 came into force on 1 October 2007: 2006 Act Commencement Order No 3, Art 2(1)(d). It restates without change the provisions in 1985 Act, s 309A(5), which were inserted with effect from 6 April 2005 by C(AICE) Act, s 19(1). Until then the relevant provision was contained in 1985 Act, s 310 which applied to directors as well as officers. With effect from 1 April 1990 the 1985 Act was amended by 1989 Act, s 137 to make it clear that s 310 did not prevent a company from purchasing and maintaining for any officer or auditor insurance against liability which by virtue of any rule of law would attach to him in respect of any negligence, default, breach of duty, or breach of trust. The original form of s 310 contained provisions first brought into effect by 1929 Act, s 152 and there had been some doubt as to whether a company was permitted to provide liability insurance for its officers without breaching the general prohibition on exempting from liability or indemnifying against liability any officer of the company.

insurance for the directors of companies can be seen from the White Paper, *Company Law Reform* (2005), where it was explained that:

> the law on directors' liability needs to strike a careful balance: on the one hand, the law must be firm and robust to deal fairly with cases where something has gone wrong, as a result of either negligence or of dishonesty; on the other, Britain needs a diverse pool of high-quality individuals willing to assume the role of company director, and a willingness by directors to take informed and rational risks.[2]

Furthermore, the government agreed with the CLR that 'ultimately it [was] a matter for the board [of a company] to determine the conditions of employment of senior employees'.[3]

21.03 The Model Articles for public and private companies contain a short permissive article dealing with the provision of insurance to directors and former directors of a company.[4]

(1) The directors may decide to purchase and maintain insurance, at the expense of the company, for the benefit of any relevant director in respect of any relevant loss.
(2) In this article—
   (a) a 'relevant director' means any director or former director of the company or an associated company,
   (b) a 'relevant loss' means any loss or liability which has been or may be incurred by a relevant director in connection with that director's duties or powers in relation to the company, any associated company or any pension fund or employees' share scheme of the company or an associated company, and
   (c) companies are associated if one is a subsidiary of the other or both are subsidiaries of the same body corporate.

It is open to the company to adopt more detailed articles regulating the circumstances in which the directors of a company are permitted to purchase Directors and Officers Liability Insurance (D&O Insurance) in accordance with the provisions of the Companies Act.[5] The 2006 Act does not contain any restriction on providing such insurance to officers, as opposed to directors. A company can therefore purchase D&O Insurance for its officers without reference to ss 232 and 233.

B. The Policy

(1) Available cover

21.04 D&O Insurance is a product. It is subject to fluctuations in price and to variations in the terms and conditions that insurers are prepared and permitted to offer. Insurance against certain risks may be permissible in one jurisdiction but prohibited in another.[6] Competition

---

[2] Ch 3 (Enhancing Shareholder Engagement and a Long Term Investment Culture), p 23.
[3] Hansard, Standing Committee A, col 9 (14 September 2004).
[4] Model Article (pcls) 53 and Model Article (plc) 86.
[5] 1985 Act, Table A does not contain any provision about purchasing or maintaining insurance for directors or other officers.
[6] The prohibition may be a matter of law driven by public policy or a matter of regulation. It is a particular concern where an English law policy provides cover for a UK company with subsidiaries in overseas jurisdictions in which jurisdictions there are restrictions on coverage that may not match the legal and regulatory assumptions upon which the English law policy is drafted. This is one of the issues which has produced a London Market practice whereby the London Market policy operates as an 'umbrella' policy and 'local' policies appropriate to local conditions are issued in individual overseas jurisdictions. Claims paid under the local

for business between insurers, and factors such as loss history (both an insured's own and the insurance industry's as a whole), may lead to terms differing materially from year to year and from insured to insured. The terms of any D&O Insurance will depend upon the commercial circumstances in which it is negotiated. The discussion that follows is intended to highlight the key concepts and issues around which the commercial discussion will revolve.

(2) The risks covered

The purpose of D&O Insurance is, in broad terms, to provide indemnity for liabilities incurred by directors and officers (and, in most cases, specified categories of employee) as a result of their acting in the course of the business of a company. Such liabilities can arise from breach of duty to the company and from breach of duty to third parties. A third category of potential liability is that arising from regulatory investigation. In most cases cover will extend not only to the amount of any judgment or settlement, but also to legal and certain other costs incurred by the insured individual in defending claims and otherwise seeking to avoid liability. **21.05**

The range of duties which may be owed to a company by a director or officer are covered elsewhere in this book. It is usual for the insuring clause, which specifies the general scope of the policy cover, to be cast in wide terms, with insurers then specifically excluding matters which they are not prepared to cover:[7] **21.06**

(1) Exclusions may relate to issues specific to the insured, such as exclusions of cover for the financial consequences of problems of which the insured was aware prior to the commencement of cover.

(2) Exclusions may also relate to general issues of concern to the insurance market, such as claims arising out of incidents involving pollution of the environment.

(3) Insurers will usually look to exclude liabilities arising from wilful misconduct. It will be a matter of interpreting the specific policy language to determine whether any exclusion for deliberate wrongful acts is intended to reflect only the public policy prohibition on insurance against the consequences of criminal conduct or is intended to go further. Any uncertainty as to coverage can be exacerbated by the nature of the claim which a director faces. It is unusual for policies to specify expressly that cover is provided for contributions to company assets which directors guilty of wrongful trading may be ordered to make pursuant to the Insolvency Act, s 214. The observation of Knox J in *Re Produce Marketing Consortium Ltd (No 2)*[8] that 'In my judgment the jurisdiction under s 214 is primarily compensatory rather than penal' states the problem from a D&O Insurance perspective rather than resolves it. The majority of conduct subject to sanctions under s 214 is likely to be of a type squarely within the ambit of standard D&O cover. Where

---

policies should erode both the local policy's limit and the limit of the umbrella policy, otherwise insurers will be providing a bigger limit of indemnity than they intended.

[7] The normal principles for the interpretation of written contracts or instruments apply to the interpretation of the policy (see Ch 2, paras 2.49 *et seq* above). Where the form of the insurance contract has been proposed by one of the parties, the *contra proferentum* rule, under which ambiguities are construed against the person who drafts or puts forward the provision, may be applied. Thus the court is disposed to adopt a narrow interpretation of an exclusion clause and is reluctant to allow a condition precedent to extinguish or reduce the basic cover: *Tektol Ltd v International Insurance Co of Hanover Ltd* [2005] 1 All ER (Comm) 132, CA; *Royal & Sun Alliance Insurance plc v Dornoch Ltd* [2005] 1 All ER (Comm) 590, CA.

[8] [1989] BCLC 520, 554.

the alleged conduct flirts with the borderline between wrongful trading under s 214 and fraudulent trading under s 213 then a definitive opinion on coverage may not be possible pending the court's decision as to the nature of the director's acts.

(4) Insurers will also seek to exclude losses arising out of breaches of duty which result in an individual making a personal profit.[9]

21.07   The provision of cover against regulatory intervention is an increasingly important component of the protections available to individuals working for companies operating in regulated industries. Depending on its powers, a regulator may be involved in the investigation of an individual in respect of alleged breaches of duty to the company, breaches of duty to third parties, and breaches of the regulators' own rules. Regulators may impose restrictions on the extent to which it is permissible to insure against the consequences of their interventions: pursuant to General Provision 6.1.5 of the FCA Handbook no FCA or PRA-regulated firm may 'enter into, arrange, claim on or make a payment under a contract of insurance that is intended to have, or has or would have, the effect of indemnifying' an FCA or PRA-regulated person (including both natural and legal persons) against all or part of a financial penalty imposed by the FCA or the PRA. The prohibition does not extend to insurance in respect of defence costs incurred in defending enforcement action nor to insuring against having to pay the regulator's costs of such action.[10]

(3) The period of cover

21.08   Most D&O Insurance is written with a policy period of one year. D&O Insurance is also usually written on the so-called 'claims made' basis. In broad terms the effect of this is that the coverage provided by the policy applies to those claims of which the insured becomes aware during the policy period.[11]

21.09   The first key feature to note about the 'claims made' concept is that it does not matter when the conduct complained of took place, or when the claimant suffered the loss out of which his claim arises. It is the making of the claim against the insured within the policy period that potentially triggers the operation of the cover.

21.10   The second key feature of the 'claims made' concept is that the insured being aware of the claim will not usually, in and of itself, be sufficient to trigger policy coverage. An insured must also notify his insurer of the claim within a prescribed time of the insured becoming aware of it. Because of this, it might be more accurate to refer to such insurances as 'claims made and notified' policies. That each element is significant can, for example, be seen in the context of a time-barred claim against the insured which comes to the insured's attention for the first time during the policy period. The fact that a claim is or may be time-barred is not usually a justification for failing to notify insurers of it, nor is it necessarily wise for an insured to fail in such circumstances to seek to activate policy coverage by notification: failing to notify will mean that the insured loses the ability to recover from insurers the costs of

---

[9] Insurers have traditionally proved reluctant to treat the giving up of a profit as financial 'loss'. This has a necessary impact on the availability of cover for certain breaches of fiduciary duty.

[10] FCA Handbook, Gen 6.1.7, G

[11] The standard, but now rarely used in liability insurance, alternative to 'claims made' policies are so-called 'losses occurring during' policies which are triggered when the conduct potentially giving rise to liability occurs during the policy period, even if no claim is advanced until after the policy period has expired.

striking out any time-barred claim pursued by an unwise claimant. Both the 'claims made' and the 'notified' elements merit further consideration.[12]

What is a 'claim' and when is it 'made'? A well-drafted policy will make this clear. Both **21.11** insurer and insured risk considerable uncertainty in the operation of the policy if they are unable to identify what constitutes a claim being made. Service of suit upon the insured is the clearest indication that a claim has been made. However, policies do not usually set the threshold so high that actual service of proceedings is the sole determinant of whether a claim has been 'made'. A more informal intimation of an actual or potential dispute may suffice. That said, the policy will normally require some form of communication of intent by the potential claimant to the insured. The nature of that communication, and the nature of the intention evidenced thereby, are matters which the insurer and insured may wish to specify in order to introduce maximum certainty into their obligations. For instance, some policies will treat the receipt of a pre-action demand as the making of a claim and, indeed, in certain cases the receipt of a complaint seeking redress will be deemed a claim even though litigation is not expressly threatened.

Once a claim has been made, the insured will be obliged to notify the insurer of that claim. **21.12** The policy will specify a period which is permitted to elapse between the insured becoming aware of the claim and the receipt by the insurer of notification of it. If a specific number of days or weeks is identified then the deadline is likely to be relatively tight. Alternatively, the policy may stipulate the time in which the insurer must be notified by reference to concepts such as 'as soon as reasonably practicable' after the insured becomes aware of the claim. This allows potentially greater flexibility, while still permitting an objective assessment of whether the requirement has been met. Much will depend on commercial considerations but also on what is realistic in terms of how quickly news of claims will percolate through an organization. This is a particular concern in the context of D&O Insurance where it cannot be assumed that any individual who has the benefit of the cover will be conversant with the subtleties of what the policy regards as a claim, or familiar with his notification obligations. Ensuring that the covered individuals are sufficiently aware of the steps necessary to satisfy their policy obligations is one of the risk management challenges associated with D&O Insurance.

The consequences which flow from a failure to notify within the permitted period will **21.13** depend on the policy language. Frequently the obligation to notify the insurer of a claim is expressed as a condition precedent to the insurer's liability. Condition precedent language necessitates strict compliance with the term in question: any failure to meet the deadline, no matter how narrow the margin of failure, will entitle the insurer to refuse to meet the claim, even though the insurer has in no way been prejudiced by the delay.[13] The need for speed and

---

[12] An exhaustive discussion of this difficult subject is beyond the scope of this chapter. What follows is by way of introduction only.

[13] See eg *Pioneer Concrete (UK) Ltd v National Employers' Mutual General Insurance Association* [1985] 2 All ER 395. In this case the policy required the insured to give immediate notice of 'any accident or claim or proceedings' as to which Bingham J observed at 400: 'On ordinary principles of contract, it would seem to me that the insurer could rely on this breach of condition whether the breach caused him prejudice or not and whether the refusal of payment in those circumstances was in general terms meritorious or unmeritorious.' It should be noted that use of conditions precedent in insurance policies is not confined to claims notification provisions and conditions precedent should always be treated with exceptional care due to the potential for the consequences of breach to be wholly disproportionate to the nature and scale of the breach.

care is underscored whenever there is the potentially dangerous combination of an obligation phrased in terms which are inherently open to interpretation—'as soon as reasonably practicable'—coupled with a severe sanction for non-compliance triggered by the slightest failure.

21.14 The position may be complicated further if a policy imposes a requirement that, notwithstanding any specified period for notification, the notification must in any event be made before the end of the policy period. A claim may emerge at a time when the remainder of the policy period is less than the amount of time usually permitted to elapse between the insured becoming aware of a claim and his effecting notification of it. In view of this, well-drafted policies will allow a period of time after the expiry of the policy in which claims may be notified. However, insurers will seek to ensure that the claim must still have been made during the policy period. Otherwise they will be extending the period for which the policy provides cover.

21.15 What of matters of which the insured becomes aware during the policy period, and which suggest that he may face a claim in the future, but which do not mature during the policy period so as to meet the threshold for a 'claim' being treated as 'made'? It is common for policies to give the insured the option to notify such matters, but without subjecting the insured to an obligation so to do. If the insured exercises the option then the policy will cover any claim which subsequently emerges out of the notified matter, even if that claim does not emerge until after the end of the policy period. However, the option to notify such matters is not a 'blank cheque'. Insurers will wish to specify a test for the likelihood of a future claim which needs to be satisfied as a precondition of the exercise of the insured's option. Coupled with the imposition of such a test, therefore, is the insurers' right to say that the matter did not satisfy the test at the time of notification, such that policy cover does not apply to any claim which subsequently emerges.

21.16 In setting that test the insurer and the insured are balancing legitimate commercial concerns. A prime commercial consideration influencing insurers to write policies on the 'claims made' basis is that, at the end of the policy period, insurers will have a complete list of their sources of potential exposure and so can quantify and manage them. Allowing an insured to notify everything of which they became aware during the policy year that might conceivably become a problem, no matter how unclear the concern or its basis might be, would leave insurers in a significant, and commercially unappealing state of uncertainty. In order to prevent this, the insurer will wish the insured to be able to show some identifiable and objectively verifiable basis for concern. The insurer will also desire some clarity as to the subject matter of the notification: at the very least he will want details of the facts which are causing the concern. In addition, the insurer will want to impose some relatively close connection between the facts notified and any subsequent claim in order for that claim to be covered: the insurer will, for example, want the claim to 'arise out of' or 'relate to' the notified matters. In the absence of clear delineation of what qualifies for notification, and a clear link between that and the subsequent claim, insurers face the potential for a wider than anticipated range of subsequent claims to be brought under the policy by reference to the notification. To put it in extreme terms in order to make the point, there is unlikely to be a policy wording which would accept 'We are bound to have done something wrong this year' as a valid notification of something which could lead to a claim.

Insurers' legitimate commercial objectives potentially pose problems for the insured and, in this regard, the insured has to exercise particular care. When entering into a policy for any one year he will be in no position to know what exclusions he may face as and when he comes to buy his cover for the following year. He will not wish to encounter a position where an emerging matter which does not qualify as a 'claim' under the current policy might also fall within an exclusion to be imposed in a successor policy. If that happens then he will be without cover. Therefore, his objective will be to secure the maximum scope for notifying problems which have not yet matured into claims.   **21.17**

The difficulty of defining what, short of a claim, may be notified is reflected in the arcane law which has developed around the phrases which have sought to give expression to the concept. For instance, defining such matters as 'circumstances likely to give rise to a claim' has been held to create a different threshold for notification than wording which requires notification of 'circumstances which may give rise to a claim'.[14]   **21.18**

(4) The structure of D&O Insurance

D&O Insurance may be purchased to provide protection to individuals, or to companies, or to both.   **21.19**

The coverage offered to individuals is widely known by the shorthand 'Side A Cover'. The cover available to companies is, broadly, of two distinct types. One type, often referred to as 'Side B Cover', provides an indemnity to a company to the extent that it has indemnified certain individuals against specified liabilities. Side B Cover does not operate in respect of a company's own liability to third parties: it is triggered by the company's performance of an obligation to indemnify the insured individuals against their own liabilities. Whether a particular indemnity is recoverable from insurers via Side B Cover will hinge upon the nature of the underlying conduct indemnified against, not the scope of the company's agreement to indemnify. If an insurer would not be prepared to insure an individual directly for a particular liability, it is unlikely to be prepared to insure a company against having to indemnify that individual for such liability.   **21.20**

The second type of cover available to companies is generally known as 'Entity Cover' and is offered in respect of a company's own liability to third parties. As insurers offer a range of specific products tailored to cover the third party liabilities of companies, any Entity Cover element of D&O Insurance may be restricted: most usually it is confined to liabilities arising from so-called 'Securities Claims'. In essence, these are claims by investors in the shares of a company. Such claims generally arise when investors allege that, due to the concealment of information by the company, the price they paid for their shares was in excess of the true value of those shares. Such claims are usually triggered by a decline in the share price of the company. As Securities Claims are frequently pursued against both a company and its directors, the inclusion of Entity Cover against such claims in a D&O Insurance policy has a certain logic.   **21.21**

---

[14] The former has been held to mean that a claim was more likely than not, so that the mere possibility that a claim will be made is not sufficient to trigger the option to notify; see *Layher v Lowe* [2000] Lloyd's Rep IR 510, CA. The latter is a weaker test, and has been held to be satisfied where 'it was at least possible' that a claim would arise; see *J Rothschild v Collyear* [1999] Lloyd's Rep IR 6.

21.22　It is not necessary to purchase Side A Cover, Side B Cover, and Entity Cover in the same policy. Side A and Side B Covers are often bought on a stand-alone basis. The decision as to what to purchase and in what combinations will be a commercial one driven by the risk profile and coverage requirements of a company and its directors. However, the combinations in which these covers are purchased can have very significant implications for the scope and efficacy of cover. Those implications are dealt with later in this chapter.

(5) The level of cover

21.23　D&O Insurance will provide cover subject to a policy 'limit of liability'. That limit will almost certainly be expressed to represent the maximum amount for which insurers will be liable under the policy for all claims by all insureds. It is sometimes assumed, incorrectly, that the limit of liability represents an amount which is available in full to each insured in respect of his own liabilities. In certain circumstances that may be the case. It is not, however, the norm. Usually, the limit of liability is a single 'pot' of money to be divided up between the claims of all insureds. Once it is exhausted by payments there will be no further funds available to any insured. Subject to certain modifications which may appear in the wording of the policy,[15] claims are met in the order in which the insureds' liabilities are established by judgment or settlement, not in the order in which the claims were made or notified. Furthermore, it is the norm for payments by insurers in respect of defence costs to reduce the 'pot' such that, in exceptional circumstances or because a low limit of liability has been purchased, the entire amount of insurance available may have been expended on defence costs before any liability to pay compensation is established or agreed.

21.24　The size of a policy's limit of liability is a decision influenced by a number of factors. One factor will be the insurer's willingness to provide cover and the price it wishes to charge for it. From the purchaser's perspective, the amount of cover needed will be determined by such factors as the insureds' appetite for retaining risk and the scale of the company's operations, particularly in jurisdictions where the potential for claims is seen as significant. There are also corporate governance questions to be weighed: is there a point at which the availability of D&O Insurance may cease to be reassuring but, rather, come to be seen as a licence to take risks in the management of the company? Will a company wish to purchase a level of D&O cover which may induce complacency or unnecessary risk-taking on the part of directors? Will purchasing a significant limit of D&O cover render the directors a more likely target of litigation if the potentially deep pockets of insurers may become exposed to the claimants?

21.25　The decision as to whom and what to cover may also be influenced by simple economics. The more individuals who have the benefit of the cover, the more potential claimants upon the limit of liability, and so the more thinly spread the contents of the 'pot' may become. This can also influence which covers to buy. In a Side A only policy, the covered individuals know that only they have the potential to make a claim under the policy. Once Side B Cover is added, indemnifying companies have potential claims on the policy funds. This may not seem to matter to the directors who have been indemnified by those companies, but the reduction in the amount of insurance otherwise available after a Side B payment might give them pause for thought about future claims in respect of which corporate indemnity may be prohibited. Some may form the view that it is preferable to have the benefit of a corporate indemnity to

---

[15] Often in policies involving both Side A and Side B there is a provision whereby the policyholder may elect for all Side A claims to be paid prior to settlement of any Side B claims.

the extent it can be given, plus a Side A only policy for all other eventualities. The number of potential demands on the limit of liability is thrown into even sharper relief if Entity Cover is purchased: the directors may be surprised to discover that a policy which, on the face of it, has been purchased for their benefit is, as it turns out, completely exhausted by a claim against the company.

(6) The insured under the policy

The companies in respect of which cover is provided

Which individuals within an organization will have the benefit of D&O Insurance? The **21.26** process of answering that question begins with identifying the 'organization'. The principal purpose of D&O Insurance is, in broad terms, to provide indemnity for liabilities incurred by individuals as a result of their holding office as director or acting in the course of the business of a company. Consequently, the policy needs to identify accurately the company or companies whose directors, officers, and employees are to be insured.

If a single company is purchasing D&O Insurance then this question is easily answered. In **21.27** the context of D&O Insurance purchased for a group of companies the position is more complex. The usual way of resolving the issue is to identify one company as the 'policyholder'. The policyholder is normally identified as having responsibility for a number of administrative functions under the policy, not least paying the premium. The policyholder is also usually the entity which forms the basis of the policy's definition of the companies whose directors, officers, and employees are intended to be insured.

A standard policy may identify the 'company' in respect of which the insurance is provided **21.28** as the 'policyholder and its subsidiaries'. Two basic issues flow from this. The first is the need to check that the definition of 'subsidiaries' is sufficiently comprehensive to encompass all of the entities to which the cover is intended to apply.[16] The second is that any cover which operates by reference to 'the policyholder and its subsidiaries' contains an inherent assumption that the 'policyholder' is at the apex of the corporate structure pyramid. If the policyholder is not the ultimate holding company, and there are companies of which it is a subsidiary and to which it is intended that the D&O Insurance should apply, then either the identity of the policyholder will need to be changed or the means of defining the 'group' modified.

'Outside entities'

D&O Insurance frequently distinguishes between the cover provided to individuals act- **21.29** ing on behalf of 'group' companies (ie the policyholder and its subsidiaries) and the cover provided for directors, officers, and employees of group companies when acting in roles for companies which fall outside the group as defined. Such companies are frequently referred to as 'outside entities'. A company may appoint one of its directors, officers, or employees to sit on the board of a company in which it has invested, but the nature or scale of that investment may mean that the company to which the appointment is made does not satisfy the test by which the policy identifies members of the 'group'. In those circumstances, because the individual is taking up that appointment in furtherance of the interests of the appointing

---

[16] Policies issued in the London insurance market have tended to adopt as the policy definition of 'subsidiary' that used in the Companies Acts and which now appears in Companies Act, s 1159. But note that a company is not a subsidiary if its shares are charged and the chargee is registered as the member: *Enviroco Ltd v Farstad Supply A/S* [2011] 1 WLR 921, SC.

company, it would seem appropriate that he should be covered under the D&O Insurance purchased by the appointing company for any liabilities that he incurs in the capacity he assumes by way of that appointment.[17]

21.30   If such cover is provided, most D&O Insurances draw some important distinctions between activities undertaken on behalf of companies regarded as part of the 'group' and those undertaken for 'outside entities'. One of the more obvious distinctions is as to which individuals are covered. All of the members of a board of a 'group' company will be covered by the D&O Insurance, unless specifically excluded by the policy. However, the D&O Insurance of the group will only cover board members of an outside entity if they have been appointed to that outside entity by or with the consent of the insurance buying group.[18]

21.31   In addition, the policy may limit the type of companies which it is prepared to regard as qualifying automatically as 'outside entities'. The insurer may not be prepared to offer automatic cover to someone who undertakes their 'outside entity' role with a company that has a share listing in the United States of America or which is engaged in an area of commercial activity regarded by insurers as high risk. Often a company will not qualify as an 'outside entity' unless and until identified in a schedule or endorsement to the policy. This may cause considerable difficulties if, for instance, a claim is made against an individual who has been appointed to an 'outside entity' but that entity has accidentally been omitted from the relevant policy schedule.

21.32   In order to obtain cover as an 'outside entity' director an individual will often not only have to show that the company to which he is appointed meets the definition of 'outside entity', but also that he meets any policy requirement as to the reason for and the form of his appointment to that role. For example, the policy may only cover appointments to outside entities if those appointments are made either for certain limited purposes or by certain formal means. The policy may not provide cover where the role has nothing to do with the business of the group that purchased the policy. A director of a group company who has directorships with non-group companies should not therefore assume that those roles will be covered automatically by the 'outside entity' provisions of the D&O Insurance which the group arranges. Furthermore, there may be procedural requirements, such that the appointment be in writing, which do not reflect the reality of how individuals come to join those outside boards. It is important to ensure that the outside entity cover is not defeated by some specified procedural requirement in relation to an appointment that is not met in practice.

---

[17] The interaction between any D&O Insurance of the outside entity of which the individual has the benefit and the 'group' insurance is considered below at para 21.43.

[18] This is an important consideration when companies are determining how wide they wish to cast the definition of what constitutes the 'group' for the purposes of a D&O policy. Because of the limitations upon cover for roles with outside entities there may be a temptation to bring all such entities within the scope of the 'group' for the purpose of the policy definitions. However, the company purchasing the policy may thereby bring within the scope of its cover numerous individuals who, as board members of the outside entity with no other link to the group, would not otherwise be covered as directors of 'outside entities'. The increase in the number of potential claimants on the policy limit may thereby prejudice the coverage available for the 'group' directors. Furthermore, those individuals may thereby become 'insureds' subject to obligations imposed by or in relation to the policy, the performance of which the 'group' may not be able to monitor effectively, thereby potentially prejudicing the cover for the other directors.

Covered individuals

Once the relevant companies have been identified, which individuals within those compa- **21.33**
nies have the benefit of cover? As one would expect, 'directors' and 'officers' are usually covered. However, elaboration on what constitutes a 'director' or 'officer' is often not provided.
Consideration needs to be given as to whether the policy language should make clear that
both de facto and *de jure* appointments will be covered.[19] Another refinement, of particular
relevance in the 'claims made' policy context, is ensuring that cover is provided for directors
who have already retired when the policy commences, but against whom a claim may be
made during the policy period in respect of conduct undertaken when in office.

It is a question for the company purchasing the insurance to decide to what extent it requires **21.34**
cover for employees who are not directors or officers. Some individuals may, as a result of
seniority, face potential exposures equivalent to those of directors and officers. Indeed, in
a heavily regulated industry, all employees or a significant number thereof may be subject
to the jurisdiction of the regulator and it may be necessary to extend the cover to them to
provide some protection in the case of regulatory investigation, primarily in relation to the
payment of any legal fees. Further, those appointed to 'outside entity' boards may not be
directors or officers of their 'home' organization. A crucial consideration for the company is
how wide it wishes to cast the net of potential claimants upon the policy, thereby potentially
reducing the policy funds available to senior executives.

C. Pre-contractual Disclosure

One of the unusual features of insurance is the obligation imposed upon potential insureds to **21.35**
give disclosure of certain matters to an insurer in advance of the policy becoming binding. The
law in this area has undergone the most radical reform in over a century with the coming into
effect, on 12 August 2016, of the main provisions of the Insurance Act 2015 ('the 2015 Act').[20]

In large part the 2015 Act carries out the recommendations made by a joint report of the **21.36**
Law Commission and the Scottish Law Commission ('the Report').[21] In relation to pre-
contractual disclosure, the Report expressed the view that commercial insurances had fallen
out of step with the realities of the modern commercial environment, general commercial
law and insurance law insofar as it applies to policies provided to consumers.[22] Of particular
concern was the serious and inflexible remedy of avoidance (ie treating the policy as if it had
never existed) available to the insurer if the insured failed to disclose to the insurer a 'material'
circumstance or made a 'material' representation to the insurer that was untrue. The remedy

---

[19] That is, those occupying the position of director, whether or not formally appointed.

[20] 2015 Act, s 23(2).

[21] Insurance Contract Law: Business Disclosure; Warranties; Insurers' Remedies for Fraudulent Claims; and
Late Payment (Law Com No 353; Scot Law Com No 238).

[22] The 2015 Act applies in part to both 'consumer insurance contracts' and also 'non-consumer insurance
contracts' while some of it applies to one or the other form of contract. The 2015 Act, s 1 defines 'consumer
insurance contract' as having the same meaning as in the Consumer Insurance (Disclosure and Representations)
Act 2012 ('CIDRA') and also defines 'non-consumer insurance contract' as one that is 'not a consumer insurance contract'. CIDRA, s 1 defines a 'consumer insurance contract' as an insurance contract between an insurer
(being a person who carries on the business of insurance and enters into the contract by way of that business)
and 'an individual who enters into the contract wholly or mainly for purposes unrelated to the individual's
trade, business or profession'.

of avoidance was available even if the non-disclosure or misrepresentation was made wholly innocently and without fault on the part of the insured.

21.37   The 2015 Act combines abolition of aspects of the pre-existing law, retention—sometimes with, sometimes without, modification—of other aspects of the pre-existing law, and the introduction of new law.[23] A description and evaluation of the 2015 Act, even only insofar as it affects the provision of pre-contractual disclosure, is beyond the scope of this work. For present purposes, the following summary is offered of the disclosure regime now applicable to non-consumer insurance contracts:[24]

(1)   Before the policy is entered into, the proposed insured must provide information to the proposed insurer such as to satisfy 'the duty of fair presentation' in respect of the risk to be insured.[25]

(2)   Subject to certain exceptions relating to circumstances which reduce the risk, or of which the insurer knows or should know, [26] a 'fair presentation' is one that:

   (a)   discloses every material circumstance;[27]

   (b)   which the insured knows or ought to know; [28] or

   (c)   failing that, gives the insurer sufficient information to put a prudent insurer on notice of the need to make further enquiries for the purpose of revealing those material circumstances; [29] and

   (d)   which makes the disclosure in a manner which would be reasonably clear and accessible to a prudent insurer; [30] and

---

[23]   The 'Explanatory Notes' which accompanied the version of the 2015 Act which came before the House of Lords as a bill on 15 January 2015 described the Marine Insurance Act 1906 (from which the 2015 Act departs in many significant respects) as 'written in clear, forthright terms which can constrain the courts' ability to develop the law': an observation which is both intriguing in its seeming distaste for clarity in statutes, and also pregnant with the suggestion that the 2015 Act is designed to be elusive in meaning and pliable in application.

[24]   The content of n 22 above demonstrates that a D&O Insurance Policy is unequivocally a 'non-consumer insurance contract'.

[25]   2005 Act s 3(1) and (2).

[26]   2015 Act, s 3(5).

[27]   What constitutes a circumstance and makes it 'material' is dealt with at s 7(2) to 7(4). What is 'material' is expressed in similar if different terms to those deployed in the Marine Insurance Act 1906 but, for all practical purposes, the 2015 Act keeps the insured in the position in which it was under the pre-existing law: ie obliged to compile its disclosure by having to asses what might be 'material' in the eyes of the notional 'prudent insurer'.

[28]   The assessment of what the insured knows, is presumed to know, and is deemed to know is dealt with in detail at s 4 as supplemented by s 6(1). The novelty introduced by the 2015 Act is the imposition on the insured of what is, for all practical purposes, a duty to conduct a 'reasonable search' for information to be included in the 'fair presentation'. Under the pre-existing law the court was primarily concerned with the significance, or otherwise, of what had been omitted from disclosure or allegedly misrepresented: as the intent or fault of the insured in relation to any misrepresentation or non-disclosure was irrelevant, then so was any consideration of how the insured had gone about compiling the material which was placed before the insurers by way of pre-contract disclosure. The 2015 Act opens up the potential for the courts being faced with conducting exhaustive analyses of reconstructed information-gathering exercises, raising interesting questions for the insured as to their approach to documenting that exercise for potential use in the event of a dispute. Further, and by virtue of s 6(1), knowledge of any individual extends beyond what they actually know to encompass matters which the individual 'suspected, and of which the individual would have had knowledge but for deliberately refraining from confirming them or enquiring about them'.

[29]   The language of the 2015 Act is interesting in this regard. It would appear that it is insufficient to put the insurer on enquiry generally as to the possible inadequacy of the disclosure but, rather, the insurer must be put on enquiry as to the particular circumstances that subsequently are alleged not to have been disclosed. This may be the only means of reconciling the keeping alive of the insured's potential to argue that the insurer was put on enquiry, on the one hand, with the aspect of the duty of fair presentation articulated at s 3(3)(b), on the other.

[30]   2015 Act, s 3(3)(b).

(e) in which every material representation as to a matter of fact is substantially correct; [31] and

(f) in which every material representation as to a matter of expectation or belief is made in good faith. [32]

(3) If the insured is in breach of the duty of fair presentation then the insurer has a remedy but only if he shows that, but for the breach, he would not have entered into the contract of insurance at all, or he would have done so only on different terms. [33] A breach that gives rise to a remedy on the part of the insurer is known as a 'qualifying breach'. [34]

(4) The remedy available to the insurer will depend on the nature of the 'qualifying breach'.

(a) If the breach was deliberate or reckless [35] the insurer may avoid the policy, refuse all claims and retain the premium paid; [36]

(b) If the breach was neither deliberate nor reckless then;

(i) if the insurer would not have entered into the policy in the absence of the breach then he may avoid the policy and refuse all claims but must return the premium paid; [37] or,

(ii) if he would have entered into the policy but on different terms then he may require the policy to be treated as if it had been entered into on those different terms [38] and, alternatively or additionally, reduce the amount of any claim payment in an amount proportionate to any additional premium he would have charged in the absence of the breach. [39]

What happens if an insured is guilty of non-disclosure: are insurers entitled to avoid the **21.38** policy in respect of all those intended to be covered by the policy, or just in respect of the party who is guilty of the non-disclosure? This will depend on whether the policy is construed to be a 'joint' insurance or a 'composite' insurance. A joint insurance treats all those covered as if they were one, with the result that a non-disclosure by one renders the policy voidable against all. A composite insurance proceeds on the basis that each of those with the benefit of the cover is insured individually for their own interest, with the result that a non-disclosure by one of those covered can only result in the avoidance of their cover and not that of the others.

Whether a policy is to be construed as a joint or a composite insurance can often turn upon **21.39** detailed and difficult analysis of the intention behind its provisions. [40] In order to circumvent this analysis, policies will often include a provision intended to make the insurance

---

[31] The assessment of whether it is 'substantially correct' is to be conducted in accordance with s 7(5).

[32] The concept of 'good faith' survives the 2015 Act's abolition of any rule of law allowing avoidance of a contract of insurance on the grounds that the *utmost* good faith has not been observed by one of the parties (see s 14(1) in particular).

[33] 2015 Act, s 8(1).

[34] 2015 Act, s 8(3).

[35] The test for 'deliberate' and 'reckless' is set out at s 8(5).

[36] 2015 Act, Sch 1, para 2.

[37] 2015 Act, Sch 1, para 4.

[38] 2015 Act, Sch 1, para 5.

[39] 2015 Act, Sch 1, para 6(1), with the claim reduction formula being specified at para 6(2).

[40] As to the complications that may arise, see eg *New Hampshire Insurance Co Ltd v MGN Ltd* [1997] LRLR 24, CA.

composite. Whether the provision achieves that will turn upon the detail of its wording which will need to be construed with care.[41]

21.40   Care will also be needed to ensure that such provisions are not limited to pre-contractual disclosure. Although the duty of fair presentation ceases at the moment the policy becomes binding,[42] it can revive to a degree during the course of the life of a policy in certain instances: for example, if new insureds are to be added to the policy.[43] It is therefore important to ensure that any provisions seeking to modify or mitigate the rules relating to disclosure are drafted to apply to any revival of the duty of fair presentation post-inception.[44] Indeed, all provisions seeking to modify the duty or to mitigate the consequence of breach, or to achieve both, need to be approached with care to ensure that all relevant obligations are catered for and that the mitigation is adequate and permissible.[45]

D. The Interaction between D&O Insurance and Indemnities from the Company

21.41   A director who has the benefit of indemnities from the company of which he is a director, and who also has D&O Insurance in respect of that directorship, may feel that he is in a fortunate position. However, he needs to be conscious of how those protections will interrelate.

21.42   One of the advantages of Side A Cover is that it is usually provided to directors on the basis that they will have to meet no part of any loss from their own pocket. This absence of any self-insured retention or excess is of considerable value to directors. However, because insurers will pay Side A claims without the benefit of any self-insured retention, they are keen to limit the scope of claims which will fall within Side A. The most effective way of achieving this is for the insurer to look at the indemnities which are, or which could be, available to a director to meet a loss which is otherwise within the scope of the insurance. Insurers can seek to limit their Side A exposures by the inclusion in the policy of a 'presumption of indemnity'.

---

[41] These provisions often deal with, or are accompanied by a provision which addresses pre-contractual disclosure by excluding or restricting the attribution of knowledge of any covered party to any other covered party. Any such provision may need to be revisited with care in light of the Act in order to ensure that the provision does not leave room for application of some or all of the rules of attribution of knowledge set out at 2015 Act, s 4. Those rules are detailed, arguably equivocal in some respects, and certainly untested.

[42] See 2015 Act, ss 3(1) and 7(6).

[43] 2015 Act, s 2(2) makes clear that the rules governing the duty of fair presentation (2015 Act, ss 2 to 8) and the other parts of the Act referred to therein) apply to variations in non-consumer insurance contracts in respect of 'changes in the risk relevant to the proposed variation'. In light of the fact that the policy is not tainted from the outset by a breach in the context of a post-inception revival of the duty of fair presentation, a specific set of remedies for such breach are set out at 2015 Act, Sch 1, Pt 2.

[44] One potential solution is to anticipate certain changes in risk and provide for them in advance. A company may make acquisitions during a policy year or create new subsidiaries, potentially bringing new individuals into the scope of the D&O Insurance. The policy may automatically extend cover to new subsidiaries, but care will need to be taken in the drafting to ensure that such an automatic extension provision is read as preventing the revival of the duty of fair presentation as opposed, for example, to being limited to preventing the imposition of an additional premium.

[45] As to the difficulties that can arise in the drafting of clauses modifying and mitigating the law relating to disclosure, see *HIH Casualty & General Ins Ltd v Chase Manhattan Bank* [2003] 1 All ER (Comm) 349, HL; *Arab Bank Ltd v Zurich Insurance Co* [1999] 1 Lloyd's Rep 262. Although these cases may not now be directly applicable to the disclosure rules and terminology in the wake of the Act, there is no reason to believe that the conceptual questions they consider regarding the efficacy of the drafting of such mitigation clauses do not remain relevant.

In essence, this is a stipulation that whenever a particular loss could have been recovered by an individual insured under another indemnity then, for policy purposes, he shall be deemed to have effected such recovery. The Side A Cover will only respond to the extent that the deeming provision does not apply. The most obvious other source of indemnity is an indemnity from the company; but a presumption of indemnity will not necessarily be limited to such indemnities and may call into account all and any other potential sources of indemnification.

While a presumption of indemnity can apply in a stand-alone Side A Cover, it affects fun-   **21.43**
damentally the operation of a policy combining Side A Cover with Side B Cover. By way of contrast with the Side A Cover, the Side B Cover is likely to have a significant reten-tion: companies who have the benefit of the Side B Cover will have to bear for themselves a portion of the financial consequences of their decision to indemnify their directors. In such circumstances, the insurer is exposed 'from the ground up' on Side A but not exposed via Side B until the insured loss exceeds the retention.

A presumption of indemnity may not be limited to stipulating that an insured cannot   **21.44**
recover under the insurance any part of his loss which has actually been paid by an alterna-tive source of indemnity. The presumption may treat that alternative source of indemnity as having responded to the claim whether or not it actually has done. In such circumstances, a director may find a gap opening up in his protections between the amount of indemnity he actually receives from the company, if any, and the amount of indemnity which, for policy recovery purposes, he is deemed to have received. If the latter exceeds the former then the director will find himself personally responsible for the amount of the gap between the two. This is a genuine practical concern. For example, the company which is supposed to be providing the relevant indemnity may be insolvent. An important feature of the commercial negotiation between the parties to a D&O Insurance will be whether, and to what extent, insurers will be prepared to modify the presumption of indemnity to reflect directors' dif-ficulties should other sources of indemnity prove unwilling or unable to pay. The position can be particularly complex in relation to outside directorship roles: a policy may presume indemnification of an individual not only by the company appointing but also by the outside entity in which he serves. Indeed, the policy may say it operates only after performance by any outside entity directorship indemnity and also by any D&O Insurance available by way of the outside directorship. The outside entity's insurance and indemnification arrangements can thereby operate as a bar to access to the cover available via the appointing company unless the Side A Cover arranged by that company permits the outside entity's arrange-ments to be overlooked in certain circumstances (such as insolvency or denial of liability in the context of the outside entity's arrangements) or any Side B Cover respects a decision of the appointing company to step in and indemnify should the outside entity's arrangements prove ineffective.

A well-drafted policy will override any presumption of indemnity in the event that the   **21.45**
potentially indemnifying company is insolvent. However, could directors make use of the Third Parties (Rights against Insurers) Act 2010 if the policy does not permit the directors to claim under it in respect of a loss indemnifiable by the company? To put it another way, with the company liable to them by way of their indemnity arrangements, but not paying, could they use the Act to compel any Side B Cover to perform for their benefit?

(1) The 2010 Act, s 1 provides that where certain insolvent individuals and corporate bodies (being a 'relevant person'[46]) incur, either before or after insolvency, a liability for which they are insured under a contract of insurance, then the relevant person's rights against the insurer under the contract of insurance are transferred to the third party to whom the liability is or was incurred. The third party is thereby entitled to pursue the relevant person's rights against the insurer under the insurance.[47] By virtue of s 16 of the Act this transfer of rights is effective even where the relevant person voluntarily incurred the liability against which they are insured. Therefore, the Act potentially opens the door to directors accessing Side B Cover when the potentially indemnifying company is insolvent and the policy otherwise appears to give them no access to cover.[48]

(2) Unfortunately for directors the Act does not apply universally following its coming into force.[49] Where the relevant person both incurred the liability and also became insolvent prior to 1 August 2016 then the Third Parties (Rights against Insurers) Act 1930 will continue to apply.[50] It has been held the 1930 Act does not apply to voluntarily incurred liabilities such as those created by contract.[51] This will defeat any claim founded upon the insolvent company's indemnity arrangements with directors.

That said, the Third Parties Rights legislation in either incarnation still provides less than perfect protection for directors. The legislation will only be relevant where there is a Side B element of cover and, as explained, a key difference between Side A and Side B is the level of the self-insured retention. While both Acts allow the director to enforce the company's rights, the enforcement is only of such rights as the company has and no more. As such, a director who relied on the legislation, and succeeded, would still be left meeting out of his own pocket his liabilities to the extent of the, potentially significant, self-insured retention that the company had agreed to bear in relation to its Side B Cover.

21.46   Many policies contain deeming provisions which operate not by reference to the indemnity which the company has actually agreed to give to the individual, but by reference to the indemnity which the company could have given had it provided the maximum indemnity permitted by law. If the company has agreed to indemnify, but stopped short of agreeing to indemnify to the maximum extent which the law permits, then a gap in the protections available will also emerge.[52] This is a particular concern for officers. It is unusual for a D&O

---

[46] The categories of relevant person are specified by sections 4 to 7 of the Act.

[47] Subject, of course, to requirements set out in the Act which are not of immediate relevance to this discussion.

[48] There remains, at the very least, the potentially interesting question of whether the obligation to indemnify on the part of the company is the kind of liability for which the company is 'insured' as contemplated by the Act in the case of Side B cover. It is possible to contemplate an argument that Side B is not insurance at all: the insured event is the incurring of liability by the director, a necessary condition of the operation of both Side A and Side B. Looked at from that perspective Side B is no more than a payment mechanism by which the insurer pays out to the company the amount due from the insurer to the director in circumstances where the company has agreed to indemnify against the same liability. The answer to that question may not turn on first principles but, rather, depend on the particular language of the relevant policy on the facts of each case.

[49] On 1 August 2016, see The Third Parties (Rights against Insurers) Regulations 2016, made on 28 April 2016.

[50] Paragraph 3 of Schedule 3 to the 2010 Act.

[51] *Tarbuck v Avon Insurance plc* [2001] 2 All ER 503.

[52] It should not be assumed that a company will agree to provide directors with the maximum indemnity that the law will allow.

Insurance to make any distinction of substance between its treatment of directors and its treatment of officers. However, English law permits companies to indemnify their officers to a much greater extent than they are permitted to indemnify their directors.[53] In determining the extent to which it is appropriate to indemnify directors and officers, companies may take the decision that officers should not be placed in a more advantageous position than directors, notwithstanding that the company is legally entitled to put them in such a position. In such circumstances, and where a policy has a presumption of indemnity expressed by reference to 'the maximum extent permitted by law', the danger of a gap opening up in the protections available is even more acute for officers of an English company than it is for directors.

E. The Policy in Operation

(1) Claims by the company

The circumstances in which a company can indemnify one of its own directors against a claim by the company are now very restricted.[54] Consequently, Side A D&O Insurance is all the more important to directors. It may be their principal, or sole, protection against the financial consequences of such claims. That said, the policy may not provide unqualified cover against them.   **21.47**

Insurers argue that claims by a company against its own directors are of particular concern to them. The essence of the concern is that a company may wish to institute a weak or hopeless claim against its own directors with a view to extracting a settlement from insurers. Insurers do not wish their policy to be exploited in this way so as to become a potential source of income for the company.[55] Insurers consider that they are at risk of such conduct because the board represents both a potential object of litigation by the company and also the principal decision-making body of the company. Put another way, the board has the ability to launch claims against itself.   **21.48**

It is clearly not the case that directors will only face claims by the company brought at the instigation of a board on which they sit. Claims by a company can be brought by a successor board after the retirement of an insured director, or by way of derivative action, or at the behest of an administrator or liquidator. In none of these instances will the director have been in a position to influence the decision to bring proceedings against himself and the specific basis of the insurer's concern ought not to be allowed to influence the policy's approach to all and any claims by the company.   **21.49**

---

[53] Companies Act, s 232 applies to directors, not to officers.

[54] Companies Act, ss 232–6; see Ch 20 above.

[55] It should be some comfort to insurers that there are certain kinds of corporate liability that the court considers inappropriate for the company to pass on to its directors and their insurers. In *Safeway Stores Ltd v Twigger* [2011] 2 All ER 841, CA, a company sought to recover damages or equitable compensation from its directors in respect of an OFT fine. While the case was decided as a matter of interpretation of the statutory provisions conveying the power to fine, at p 853 Pill LJ referred to relevant public policy considerations: 'The policy of the 1998 Act is to protect the public and to do so by imposing obligations on the undertaking specifically. The policy of the statute would be undermined if undertakings were able to pass on the liability to their employees, or the employee's D&O insurers.'

21.50 Some D&O policies start from the position that any claim by a company against its own directors is excluded.[56] Whether the director has cover at all will then depend on his being able to bring himself within any exceptions to that exclusion. The exceptions will usually preserve cover in the event of actions brought at the behest of administrators or liquidators or by way of derivative action. Any exclusion will need to be read with care in order to understand its scope and in order to ensure that the exceptions to the exclusion identify ways of proceeding that are practicable. For instance, it may be that a policy will exclude all claims against the directors brought by the company except in so far as the directors can show that they have not been party to a decision to bring the claim or have not in some way incited or solicited the claim. However, in order to take advantage of an exception drafted in such terms, the directors necessarily assume the considerable burden of proving a negative. Such a burden should not be assumed lightly.

(2) The funding of a director's defence

21.51 How and when the policy will fund the legal costs of individuals incurred in dealing with actual or potential claims against them is one of the most important aspects of D&O Insurance. Directors of major companies are exceptionally unlikely to be able to find sufficient affordable insurance to cover the full financial consequences of that company becoming insolvent by reason of their actions. Not all risks are capable of being laid off in their entirety to the insurance market. However, no director will wish to be forced to liquidate his own assets to meet legal costs incurred in defending a claim for which the ultimate liability may be well within the policy limits, especially if the director has a good defence to that claim. Directors will want to ensure that the policy provides an adequate mechanism for paying regularly invoiced and potentially significant lawyers' fees.

21.52 It is not unusual for a policy to provide that insurers will 'advance' defence costs prior to the resolution of the claim. While that will be of some comfort to individual insureds, it falls short of a commitment that lawyers' invoices will be paid as and when submitted. In order to ensure proper protection for the individual insureds the policy should provide a clear mechanism for the submission, agreement, and payment of legal fees as and when they are incurred.

21.53 Some policies do provide that, in respect of certain types of claim, defence costs will be advanced pending a finding of liability against the insured notwithstanding that some or all of that liability, if established, will be excluded by the policy terms and conditions. Particular care will need to be exercised in the drafting of such provisions.[57] In the absence of specific provision an insurer is unlikely to agree to advance defence costs in circumstances where the insurer is denying liability for reasons other than the application of a particular exclusion or is challenging policy validity generally. By performing the contract the insurer will risk waiving its rights to refuse to pay or to avoid the policy. Further, it will assume the credit risk of not recovering the amount of the advanced costs if it is ultimately found not to be liable. This latter consideration is fundamental to why, except in limited circumstances, insurers are

---

[56] At present, it is more likely than not that the exclusion will be limited to claims brought in the United States of America.

[57] The legal issues underpinning and resulting from such drafting have been explored by the High Court of Australia in *Rich v CGU Insurance Limited* and *Silberman v CGU Insurance Limited* [2005] HCA 16 and in *Wilkie v Gordian Runoff Ltd* [2005] HCA 17.

unlikely to be prepared to agree policy wordings which allow insureds to receive policy funds while insurer's liability to indemnify is unresolved.

Usually legal costs will be covered in so far as they are incurred with the insurer's prior written **21.54** consent.[58] This is, on the whole, an adequate arrangement when insured individuals are faced with a claim which is proceeding through the courts in the usual way. Notwithstanding the advances which have been made in the light of the CPR, court proceedings generally progress at a pace which allows for advance communication with insurers as to steps which are required and, perhaps most importantly in this respect, court proceedings have a relatively predictable course.

Where a D&O Insurance provides cover for the costs incurred in connection with regu- **21.55** latory action it will be necessary for it to recognize the practicalities for companies and individuals operating in a regulated environment. It is not unusual for regulators to have significant powers of intervention and coercion. An invitation to attend an interview with a regulator at short notice may not be an invitation that an individual will be able, or will wish, to ignore. The individual may have time to consult with his lawyers in advance of the meeting, but possibly not with his insurers.[59] However, on the traditional approach to policy drafting, he will be at risk of having his claim for any legal costs incurred in preparing for that meeting denied for want of prior written consent from the insurer. One solution is to have a predetermined level of costs which can be spent pending consent in emergency situations.

Any insureds who are looking to buy cover to deal with potential regulatory action need **21.56** to take account of the realities of operating in a regulated industry, in order to ensure that the policy will respond as they wish to the situations which they may face. The potential difficulties are not confined to costs cover. Regulators may, for instance, require that, at the initial stage of an investigation, the matter be treated as so confidential that not even communication with the insurers of the person under investigation is permitted. This can lead to breaches of the obligation to notify insurers of claims.[60] Similarly, a regulator may require companies and individuals to self-report breaches of the regulator's rules, again potentially placing the insured in breach of any policy prohibition on the admission of liability. In the course of negotiating policy terms the insured may be able to cater for such scenarios, but it is an essential precondition to any such exercise that the insured understands the respects in which their regulatory obligations may conflict with their policy obligations.

---

[58] It is not out of the question that the obtaining of consent will be expressed or construed as a condition precedent to insurer's liability. Further, as a matter of construction, that condition precedent may be applicable not just to the costs incurred but to any liability at all on the part of insurers for the claim in connection with which the costs are incurred. This is a particularly important respect in which the insured needs to be aware of ongoing obligations under the policy and organized so as to be in a position to comply with them. See *Eagle Star Insurance Co Ltd v Cresswell* [2004] 2 All ER (Comm) 244, CA.

[59] Whether this is an issue will depend upon the scope of the cover for costs incurred in connection with regulatory action. Some policies will only provide cover once formal regulatory enforcement action commences. Depending on the industry in which the insured operates this may mean that some regulatory action in relation to which it is necessary to take legal advice will not be covered and so the associated legal costs will not be paid by insurers. It will be for the organization to satisfy itself where its directors' exposures may arise and engage in debate with insurers as to whether appropriate cover can be provided.

[60] As to the consequences of which see paragraph 21.13 above.

(3) Continuing obligations of the company

21.57 The policy is likely to include ongoing obligations and other terms of which the insured must take note in the event that significant developments in the company's business take place during the period in which the policy is in force. Examples of such terms include the following:

(1) Cover for outside entity appointments may be conditional upon the names of the relevant outside entities being notified to the insurer. If that obligation exists, then means will need to be put in place to monitor appointments to ensure that the necessary details are conveyed to the insurers to ensure that cover is effective from the date of appointment.

(2) While the policy may grant an automatic extension of cover to directors and officers of newly acquired subsidiaries this is likely to be subject to thresholds. In particular, policies are unlikely to confirm cover automatically in respect of subsidiaries whose capital exceeds certain limits or whose operations involve certain jurisdictions, particularly the USA. Acquisitions will need to be monitored to determine whether an extension of cover for the new subsidiary needs to be specifically negotiated.

(3) Some mergers and acquisitions may terminate cover. The policy may specify that if the company engages in transactions of a particular kind or scale then, as of the effective date of that transaction, the policy will cease to cover claims made except in so far as they arise out of conduct which took place prior to the effective date of the transaction.

(4) During the course of any policy year any number of directors, officers, and employees will resign and retire. The retirement or resignation will not bring to an end their potential liability for conduct which took place before they left the company. They will be exposed to the risk of claims up until such time as any relevant periods of limitation take effect. A director may resign or retire at a time when the D&O Insurance of his company provides cover for claims made against former directors. However, if the policy is an annual contract then its terms and conditions may change from year to year. The company may decide in future not to purchase cover for former directors. The director will need to consider, prior to his departure, whether he needs to extract a contractual commitment from the company to ensure that future D&O policies include cover designed to respond to claims he may face after he leaves.

(4) Conduct of claims

21.58 While all of the above issues are important, it is in the defence of potentially covered claims that the policy will impose ongoing obligations which individual insureds may regard as of greatest significance to them.

21.59 A familiar feature of liability policies is the requirement that an insured who is defending a claim shall consult with the insurers as to the conduct of the insured's defence. It is self-evident that insurers have an interest in the conduct of that defence: they are probably paying for it and they may well find themselves having to meet the ultimate liability if the defence is unsuccessful. The mechanics of that relationship and the respective degrees of control which the insurer and insured will have over the litigation are matters for which the policy ought to make specific provision.

21.60 It may be helpful if the policy specifies when, and in what respects, the insured is obliged to consult his insurers as to the conduct of the litigation. Certain decisions, in particular the admission of liability or the agreement to a settlement, will almost certainly be specified as matters requiring the input of insurers. It is not unusual to see a 'QC clause' whereby any dispute between the insured and insurers as to whether an offer to settle should be put or accepted is referred to the binding decision of a QC.[61]

In the context of D&O Insurance two potential consequences of a claim merit particular comment. The first is that policies will often contain an 'allocation' provision to regulate what happens when a claim is made for which some of the defendants are insured under the policy and some are not and, or alternatively, where some of the causes of action advanced against the insured are covered and some are not. Insurers will wish to be able to determine the extent to which they are obliged to contribute to a damages award or settlement encompassing insured and uninsured individuals and causes of action, and to the costs of defending a claim where the lawyers' fees may not identify with precision on whose behalf and on what issues those fees were incurred. Allocation provisions can confer a very broad discretion on insurers to determine what their contribution should be: in extreme cases, that discretion may come perilously close to a unilateral right on the part of the insurer to determine whether or not it makes any payment at all. However, seeking to provide for every eventuality in advance may lead to tortuous drafting or to the policy not catering for unexpected developments. The extent to which the policy prescribes the allocation process will, largely, depend on personal taste. The key consideration from the perspective of insureds is to try to achieve a means of ensuring an objective and legally binding determination of the extent of insurers' obligation to contribute. **21.61**

The second consequence arises from the fact that in most cases the D&O Insurance will have been purchased for the directors by the company. The day-to-day administration of the policy will be performed by the company. Indeed, and as recognized above, the policy normally confers upon a corporate 'policyholder' the right and obligation to act on behalf of all insureds when dealing with insurers. From an administrative perspective such arrangements are perfectly sensible. However, a key risk against which the policy may provide cover is claims against directors by the policyholder. In the event that such a claim arises there will be a clear conflict of interest between the party authorized to deal with insurers on the director's behalf and the director. As with allocation, this is an area in respect of which it may be problematic to be too prescriptive as to what will happen in the event that a conflict emerges. However, those negotiating the policy will need to consider to what extent they wish to recognize the potential for conflicts and make provision for them, at the very least in providing that the policyholder's authority on behalf of an individual insured will terminate in the event that a claim is brought against that insured by the policyholder. **21.62**

F. Conclusions

The operation of D&O Insurance has not been subject to extensive exploration by the English courts. That said, the policies involve terms, conditions, and features of other forms of liability policy in respect of which the courts have given considerable guidance over time, **21.63**

---

[61] Where the policy provides cover for companies with international operations it may not always be appropriate to have reference to an English QC. For multinational operations it is often prudent to 'internationalize' the QC clause to allow referral to a senior lawyer in any relevant jurisdiction.

although it remains to be seen just what impact the Insurance Act 2015 will have upon the guidance to be derived from existing case law as to the matters in respect of which the Act has effected change. It remains to be seen whether a detailed examination of a D&O Insurance policy by the courts will produce conclusions which take the insurance industry and its customers by surprise. For present purposes, the drafting and operation of those policies remains guided by general principles of insurance law and common sense. At the heart of these lie perhaps two fundamental questions:

(1) What are the exposures which the policy will cover?

(2) Will the policy provide the insured with the funds the insured needs at the time he needs them?

21.64 The first of the above questions is a risk management issue for the insured and a product development issue for insurers. Both parties need to explore what risks need to be covered. However, the insured should not rely upon his insurer to tell him what cover he needs. The second question is one of policy mechanics and necessitates consideration of what will happen when a claim arises. The insured may have negotiated a policy which covers every conceivable risk that he might face. However, that cover will be of no use to him if, as a matter of practical mechanics, the policy leaves the insurer with the option of whether and when he might pay. Both insureds and insurers have entirely legitimate interests to protect. In reaching their bargain it is essential that each of them understands what is expected of them, and that each of them has an adequate contractual means of enforcing his expectations of the other.

22

MEMBERS' PERSONAL AND DERIVATIVE CLAIMS

Georgina Peters

A. Introduction

22.01 This chapter is concerned with proceedings brought by members who have suffered or may suffer damage or prejudice to their shareholding arising out of the conduct of directors.

22.02 Section B deals briefly with personal claims by shareholders against directors and the principle of reflective loss, which affects most such claims.

22.03 Section C deals with common law derivative claims, which remain relevant to an understanding of the new statutory procedure, introduced by the 2006 Act, Part 11, Chapter 1, ss 260–4,[1] for bringing a derivative claim or action arising out of an act or omission (or threatened act or omission) involving negligence, default, breach of duty, or breach of trust by a director, which is described in Section D. Those provisions, for the first time, placed on a statutory footing derivative claims brought by members of a company against wrongdoing directors. This change followed the recommendations of the Law Commission and the Company Law Review Steering Group (CLR),[2] the terms of which were adopted to a

---

[1] Part 11 came into effect on 1 October 2007. The old law applies to cases where the claimant has applied for permission to continue the claim before that date. Where the claim arises out of acts or omissions occurring before that date, the court must not allow a claim to continue which would not have been allowed under the previous law. See 2006 Act Commencement Order No 3, para 20.

[2] *Shareholder Remedies* (Law Com No 246, 1997), which was preceded by a Consultation Paper No 142 (1996); CLR: *Developing the Framework* at paras 4.65–4.144; CLR: *Final Report* at paras 7.46–7.51.

significant extent. As described in Section D, there is now a body of case law, which reveals the court's approach to the exercise of its powers under Part 11.

22.04 Section E sets out the circumstances, prescribed by the 2006 Act, Part 14, ss 362–79, in which shareholders may enforce directors' liabilities for unauthorized political donations or expenditure. These provisions largely restate provisions in the 1985 Act.[3] There have been no reported cases under these provisions.

B. Personal Claims: Reflective Loss

22.05 The 2006 Act does not affect the law relating to when a member can bring a personal action to enforce his individual rights against the company. Section 260(1) defines a derivative claim in terms which preclude a cause of action vesting in a person other than the company.[4] As such, the new statutory procedure under Part 11 does not extend to a member seeking to enforce personal rights which derive from the articles of association of the company.

22.06 Nor do the new provisions in Part 11 affect the rare cases where a member has a direct claim against a director or cases where a member has a claim against a third party in relation to his shares in the company. Such claims invariably raise difficult issues and are almost always defeated by the 'reflective loss principle'. That principle dictates that where a company suffers loss caused by a breach of duty owed to it, only the company may sue in respect of that loss. No action lies at the suit of a member suing in that capacity to make good a diminution in the value of his shareholding, where it is merely a reflection of the loss suffered by the company.[5]

22.07 The interplay between personal claims and derivative claims was considered at length by the House of Lords in *Johnson v Gore Wood & Co*.[6] In that case, claims were brought against a firm of solicitors by a majority (and virtually the only) shareholder and the company. The plaintiff was in principle entitled to recover damages in respect of all heads of non-consequential loss,

---

[3] 1985 Act, ss 347A–K. Those sections were inserted into the 1985 Act by the Political Parties, Elections and Referendums Act 2000, Sch 19, to control political donations and political expenditure by companies. The provisions of the 2006 Act came into force on 1 October 2007, except for the provisions in relation to independent election candidates, which came into force on 1 October 2008.

[4] By contrast, s 265(6)(a) expressly recognizes the non-application of those provisions to the personal rights of a member to raise proceedings and obtain a remedy on his own behalf, in relation to Scotland.

[5] *Prudential Assurance Co Ltd v Newman Industries Ltd (No 2)* [1982] Ch 204, 222–3, CA, as cited by Lord Bingham in *Johnson v Gore Wood & Co* [2002] 2 AC 1, 35, HL. The principle of reflective loss has been applied to claims brought by *shareholders*. In *International Leisure Ltd v First National Trustee Co UK Ltd* [2013] Ch 346, the Deputy Judge declined to extend the principle to a claim brought by a secured creditor of a company, who had suffered loss as the result of a breach of duty owed by an administrative receiver both to the secured creditor and the company.

[6] [2002] 2 AC 1, 35, 62, HL. For subsequent cases, see: *Ellis v Property Leeds (UK) Ltd* [2002] 2 BCLC 175, CA; *Barings plc v Cooper & Lybrand (a firm) (No 1)* [2002] 2 BCLC 364; *Giles v Rhind* [2003] Ch 618, CA; *Shaker v Al-Bedrawi* [2003] Ch 350, CA; *Gardner v Parker* [2004] 2 BCLC 554, CA; *Perry v Day* [2005] 2 BCLC 405; *Waddington v Thomas* [2009] 2 BCLC 82, HK FCA; *Renova Resources Private Equity Ltd v Gilbertson* [2009] CILR 268, 295–7; *Webster v Sandersons Solicitors (a firm)* [2009] 2 BCLC 542, CA; *Gaetano Ltd v Obertor Ltd* [2009] EWHC 2653 (Ch); *Towler v Wills* [2010] EWHC 1209 (Comm); *Stevenson v London Borough of Southwark* [2011] EWHC 108 (QB); *Barclay Pharmaceuticals Ltd v Waypharm LP* [2013] 2 BCLC 551; *Energenics Holdings Pte Ltd v Hazarika* [2014] EWHC 1845 (Ch); *Novatrust Ltd v Kea Investments Ltd* [2014] EWHC 4061 (Ch); *Malhotra v Malhotra* [2015] 1 BCLC 428; *Sivagbaham v Barclays Bank Plc* [2015] EWHC 3985 (Comm); *Bank Mellat v HM Treasury* [2016] EWCA Civ 452.

arising in relation to duties owed to him personally as shareholder, but his claims in respect of losses which merely reflected losses suffered by the company were struck out. Lord Bingham stated the general principle:[7]

> Where a company suffers loss caused by a breach of duty owed to it, only the company may sue in respect of that loss. No action lies at the suit of a shareholder suing in that capacity and no other to make good a diminution in the value of the shareholder's shareholding where that merely reflects the loss suffered by the company. A claim will not lie by a shareholder to make good a loss which would be made good if the company's assets were replenished through action against the party responsible for the loss, even if the company, acting through its con-stitutional organs, has declined or failed to make good that loss.

Lord Millett explained the rationale of the principle:[8]

> If the shareholder is allowed to recover in respect of such loss, then either there will be double recovery at the expense of the defendant or the shareholder will recover at the expense of the company and its creditors and other shareholders. Neither course can be permitted. This is a matter of principle; there is no discretion involved. Justice to the defendant requires the exclu-sion of one claim or the other; protection of the interests of the company's creditors requires that it is the company which is allowed to recover to the exclusion of the shareholder.

On that broad proposition, the reflective loss is not limited to the diminution in value of the shareholding. Rather, Lord Millett said that it includes a loss of dividends and all other pay-ments which a member might have obtained from the company if it had not been deprived of its funds.[9]

In *Giles v Rhind*[10] the Court of Appeal found that there was an exception to the principle **22.08** that a shareholder cannot sue where his loss is merely reflective of the loss suffered by the company where, by reason of the wrong done to it, the company is unable to pursue its own claim against the wrongdoer. The Court of Appeal permitted a shareholder's action to recover what it accepted was reflective loss, on the basis that the company in administrative receivership had been stifled from pursuing proceedings against the wrongdoing director by reason of the director's own actions.

In the Hong Kong Final Court of Appeal in *Waddington v Thomas*[11] Lord Millett criticized **22.09** *Giles v Rhind*, saying that its outcome produced precisely the result that he had identified as unacceptable in *Johnson v Gore Wood & Co*. Lord Millett confirmed that the principle in *Johnson v Gore Wood & Co* applies not only where the company has the right to sue, but also where it has declined or failed to sue. However, in the subsequent case of *Webster v Sandersons*

---

[7] [2002] 2 AC 1, 35, HL. The general principle was supported by, among other cases, *Prudential Assurance Co Ltd v Newman Industries Ltd (No 2)* [1982] Ch 204, 222–3, CA. Lords Goff, Cooke, Hutton, and Millett agreed with Lord Bingham: pp 41, 43, 55, and 62.

[8] [2002] 2 AC 1, 62E, HL.

[9] [2002] 2 AC 1, 66H, HL.

[10] [2003] Ch 618, CA. *Giles v Rhind* was followed in *Perry v Day* [2005] 2 BCLC 405 and referred to in *Day v Cook* [2002] 1 BCLC 1, CA, *Gardner v Parker* [2004] 2 BCLC 554, CA, and *Barnett v Creggy* [2015] PNLR 13, paras 92–9. In *Barnett v Creggy* the claims of the (sole) shareholders for equitable compensation against a solicitor found to be in breach of duty in respect of certain unauthorized transfers out of the compa-nies' accounts were not barred by the reflective loss principle. The defence had been raised after the trial of the factual evidence, such that the evidence was incomplete and an additional factual inquiry might have brought the claims within the exception in *Giles v Rhind*. In those circumstances, the Judge considered that it would be contrary to fairness to hold that the reflective loss principle applied.

[11] [2009] 2 BCLC 82 at paras 81–8, HK FCA.

Solicitors,[12] the English Court of Appeal held that there was no proper basis on which the court should decline to follow *Giles v Rhind*, although the court made it clear that the fact that the company is in liquidation will not, of itself, bring a case within the exception to the reflective loss principle.

22.10 Accordingly, a personal claim may only be brought by a member where he can demonstrate (a) a breach of a duty owed to him personally, and crucially (b) personal loss separate and distinct from that suffered by the company.[13] That notwithstanding, it is difficult to conceive of circumstances in which a member would have a personal claim against the directors which was not defeated by reflective loss. The shareholder's appropriate remedy in such a case is a derivative claim (Section D below) or unfair prejudice petition (Chapter 23 below). A notable exception would be where the shareholder has a claim against the directors and/or company in deceit or negligence which arises out of the issue of a false prospectus.[14] That is dealt with in Chapter 24 below.

C. Derivative Claims at Common Law

(1) The nature of a derivative claim

22.11 A derivative claim or derivative action is an action commenced by a shareholder seeking relief on behalf of the company in respect of a wrong done to the company: the shareholder's rights are 'derived' from the company. The expression 'derivative action' in the context of shareholders' actions has been used in the United States since the nineteenth century and was first used in that context in England by Lord Denning MR in *Wallersteiner v Moir (No 2)*.[15] As explained by Lord Millett in *Waddington v Thomas* a derivative action is necessarily an exception to the rule in *Foss v Harbottle*:[16]

> A company is a legal entity separate and distinct from its members. It has its own assets and liabilities and its own creditors. The company's property belongs to the company and not to its shareholders. If the company has a cause of action, this represents a legal chose in action which represents part of its assets. Accordingly, where a company suffers loss as a result of an actionable wrong done to it, the cause of action is vested in the company and the company alone can sue. This is the first rule in *Foss v Harbottle*.[17] No action lies at the suit of a shareholder suing as such, although exceptionally he may be permitted to bring a derivative action in right of the company and recover damages on its behalf: see *Wallersteiner v Moir (No 2)*;[18] *Prudential Assurance Co Ltd v Newman Industries Ltd (No 2)*;[19] *Johnson v Gore Wood & Co*.[20]

---

[12] [2009] 2 BCLC 542, CA.

[13] *Johnson v Gore Wood & Co* [2002] 2 AC 1, 35H, HL.

[14] Cf *Prudential Assurance Co Ltd v Newman Industries Ltd (No 2)* [1982] Ch 204, CA. In that case, the claim against the directors involved inter alia a claim for conspiracy arising out of the distribution of a false circular to shareholders. The Court of Appeal considered that the directors owed the shareholders a duty to give advice in good faith and not fraudulently. It went on to accept that if directors convened a meeting on the basis of a fraudulent circular, a shareholder would have a right of action to recover any loss which he had been personally caused as a result, for example, of the expense of attending the meeting.

[15] [1975] QB 373, 390, CA; *Roberts v Gill & Co* [2011] 1 AC 240, SC at para 60, per Lord Collins.

[16] [2009] 2 BCLC 82, HK FCA at para 47. See also *Prudential Assurance Co Ltd v Newman Industries Ltd* [1982] Ch 204, 210D–211B, CA.

[17] (1843) 2 Hare 461.

[18] [1975] QB 373, 390, CA.

[19] [1982] Ch 204, 210, CA.

[20] [2002] 2 AC 1, 62, HL.

A derivative action may be analysed as two claims, one against the company for failure to take **22.12** action and the other being the claim by the company against the wrongdoer.[21]

The common law principles relating to derivative actions are of continuing relevance to **22.13** derivative claims under Part 11.[22] They also apply to multiple or double derivative claims[23] and to derivative claims in respect of foreign companies,[24] both of which are outside the scope of Part 11. It is therefore worthwhile to describe the rule in *Foss v Harbottle* and its exceptions in more detail.

(2) The rule in *Foss v Harbottle* and its exceptions

The proper plaintiff and majority rule principles

The case of *Foss v Harbottle*[25] established two general propositions: (i) the 'proper plaintiff' **22.14** principle, by which prima facie the corporation is the only proper claimant in proceedings in respect of a wrong alleged to have been done to it or to recover money or damages alleged to be due to it; and (ii) the 'majority rule' principle, by which an individual shareholder will not be allowed to pursue proceedings on behalf of himself and all other shareholders if the alleged wrong was within the powers of the corporation, since, in those circumstances, the majority of the shareholders might lawfully ratify the allegedly wrongful transaction; if they did not, they would be able to put the corporation in motion to bring the necessary proceedings.

Minority shareholders could not complain of irregularities in the conduct of the company's **22.15** internal affairs if the irregularity was one which could be cured by a vote of the company in general meeting.[26] As such, the rule prevented the court from interfering with the internal management of a company at the instance of a minority shareholder, dissatisfied with the conduct of the company's affairs by the majority or the board of directors.[27] In *Edwards v Halliwell*[28] Jenkins LJ explained the relationship between those two propositions. The assertion that the company is prima facie the proper plaintiff in an action the subject of which is the company's affairs, is equivalent to holding that the majority have the sole right to determine whether or not the action shall be brought.

---

[21] *Roberts v Gill & Co* [2011] 1 AC 240, SC at para 60 per Lord Collins, citing *Nurcombe v Nurcombe* [1985] 1 WLR 370, 378, CA; *Konamaneni v Rolls Royce Industrial Power (India) Ltd* [2002] 1 WLR 1269 at para 50.

[22] The judgment in *Iesini v Westrip Holdings Ltd* [2011] 1 BCLC 498 is a clear illustration of this.

[23] *Universal Project Management Services Ltd v Fort Gilkicker Ltd* [2013] Ch 551, per Briggs J, in which the common law principles relevant to the grant of permission to continue the derivative claim were considered and applied at paras 53–63. See further the discussion at para 22.66 below.

[24] *Abouraya v Sigmund* [2015] BCC 503, which followed *Fort Glilkicker* and concerned both a multiple derivative claim and a foreign company.

[25] (1843) 2 Hare 461. In that case, an action was brought by two minority shareholders against the directors for misapplication, alienation, and waste of company property. Sir James Wigram VC considered (at 491) the only question to be whether the facts of the case justified a departure from the rule which prima facie would require the company to sue in its own name (or that of its representative). He observed (at 494) that a simple majority of shareholders in general meeting had the power to bind the entire body of shareholders, and thus waive the complaints against the directors. His reasoning was that the shareholders were the ultimate proprietors of the company and in most cases would act by majority rule. Accordingly, were the court to allow the minority shareholder action to proceed, the company could defeat the judgment by way of majority vote. Its power to do so demonstrated that the action was not sustainable. Only where it could be demonstrated that 'there is no such power' on the part of the majority, could the action be pursued.

[26] *Prudential Assurance Co Ltd v Newman Industries Ltd* (No 2) [1982] Ch 204, 210–11, CA.

[27] See also *Mozley v Alston* (1847) 1 Ph 790; *Burland v Earle* [1902] AC 83, PC; *Pavlides v Jensen* [1956] Ch 565.

[28] [1950] 2 All ER 1064, 1066H, CA.

22.16   In its essential features the rule in *Foss v Harbottle* is a salutary one. It reflects the separate corporate personality of the company, it gives effect to the constitution of the company and the democratic rights of its shareholders, and it avoids multiplicity of suits.[29]

Exceptions to the rule in Foss v Harbottle

22.17   It was soon recognized, however, that the principle of majority rule could not be equitably applied in the case of wrongdoing directors who were, or formed part of, the majority shareholders. The effect would be to allow the majority to 'cure' by way of ratification a breach of duty committed by the majority. In relation to the proper plaintiff principle, it was also recognized that reliance on the shareholders in general meeting to bring a claim in the name of the company would be unrealistic in such circumstances. In this way, an otherwise meritorious claim could be stultified by reason of wrongdoer control. As such, it was thought that an individual member ought in certain (limited) circumstances to be allowed to bring a derivative action. Several exceptions to the rule in *Foss v Harbottle* consequently grew up, of which the most significant turned on whether the action taken was a 'fraud on the minority'. The exceptions dictated the circumstances in which a derivative action could be brought.

22.18   In *Burland v Earle*[30] Lord Davey considered the development of the exceptions to the rule and said:

> [it] is mere matter of procedure in order to give a remedy for a wrong which would otherwise escape redress, and it is obvious that in such an action the plaintiffs cannot have a larger right to relief than the company itself would have if it were plaintiff, and cannot complain of acts which are valid if done with the approval of the majority of the shareholders, or are capable of being confirmed by the majority. The cases in which the minority can maintain such an action are, therefore, confined to those in which the acts complained of are of a fraudulent character or beyond the powers of the company.

22.19   The rule thus evolved to recognize certain limited situations in which a member could bring a derivative action. Specifically, the claimant was required to prove that the case came within one of three exceptions to the rule:[31] (i) the nature of the wrong committed by the directors was beyond the powers of the company or illegal (hence it could not be ratified),[32] (ii) the wrong constituted a fraud on the minority shareholders and the alleged wrongdoers had control of the general meeting which was or would be exercised to preclude the bringing of an action against the wrongdoers, or (iii) the act required the sanction of a special majority

---

[29]   For judicial justification of the rule by reference to practical considerations, see *Gray v Lewis* (1873) 8 Ch App 1035, 1051, CA; *MacDougall v Gardiner* (1875) 1 Ch D 13, 25, CA; *Prudential Assurance Co Ltd v Newman Industries Ltd* (No 2) [1982] Ch 204, 224A–B, CA. In *MacDougall v Gardiner*, Mellish LJ considered that 'if something has been done irregularly which the majority are entitled to do regularly, or if something has been done illegally which the majority of the company are entitled to do legally, there can be no use having litigation about it the ultimate end of which is that a meeting is called and then ultimately the majority gets its wishes'. As such, ignoring the majority's power to ratify was futile.

[30]   *Burland v Earle* [1902] AC 83, 93, PC.

[31]   The three exceptions are stated by Jenkins LJ in *Edwards v Halliwell* [1950] 2 All ER 1064, 1067, CA; described as the 'classic definition' in *Prudential Assurance Co Ltd v Newman Industries Ltd (No 2)* [1982] Ch 204, 210–11, CA.

[32]   See eg *Smith v Croft (No 2)* [1988] Ch 114, 164, 165 (unlawful financial assistance in the acquisition of shares); *Australian Agricultural Co v Oatmont Pty Ltd* (1992) 8 ACSR 255, CA.

which could not be obtained.[33] It is now clear that there is no fourth exception based on the interests of justice.[34]

In *Barrett v Duckett*[35] Peter Gibson LJ summarized the established general principles applicable **22.20** to actions in respect of wrongs done to a company or irregularities in the conduct of its affairs, the first three of which are relevant to this stage of the discussion:[36]

1. The proper plaintiff is prima facie the company.
2. Where the wrong or irregularity might be made binding on the company by a simple majority of its members, no individual shareholder is allowed to maintain an action in respect of that matter.
3. There are however recognized exceptions, one of which is where the wrongdoer has control which is or would be exercised to prevent a proper action being brought against the wrongdoer: in such a case the shareholder may bring a derivative action (his rights being derived from the company) on behalf of the company.

The 'fraud on the minority' exception to the rule (paragraph 22.19(ii) above and Peter Gibson **22.21** LJ's third principle) that alleged wrongdoers who control the majority of shares may prevent the company from bringing an action by refusing to authorize proceedings in the company's name merits particular attention. If the court denied the minority the right to bring proceedings 'their grievance could never reach the court because the wrongdoers themselves, being in control, would not allow the company to sue'.[37] The principal question therefore became: 'Is the plaintiff being improperly prevented from bringing these proceedings on behalf of the company?'[38]

In *Burland v Earle*[39] Lord Davey illustrated a typical case of a fraudulent kind where the **22.22** minority could sue: 'A familiar example is where the majority are endeavouring directly or indirectly to appropriate to themselves money, property, or advantages which belong to the company, or in which the other shareholders are entitled to participate.' Cases where fraud was alleged were within the principle,[40] as were cases of equitable fraud, where the majority secure for themselves an improper advantage at the expense of the company or the minority, as was the case in *Cook v Deeks*.[41] A claim based on an allegation of negligence

---

[33] *Prudential Assurance Co Ltd v Newman Industries Ltd (No 2)* [1982] Ch 204, 210–11, CA: 'because a simple majority cannot confirm a transaction which requires the concurrence of a greater majority'.

[34] *Prudential Assurance Co Ltd v Newman Industries Ltd (No 2)* [1982] Ch 204, 221, CA; *Konamaneni v Rolls Royce Industrial Power (India) Ltd* [2002] 1 WLR 1269 at para 47.

[35] [1995] 1 BCLC 243, 249, 250, CA.

[36] Principles 4–6 are quoted in paras 22.27 and 22.41 below.

[37] *Prudential Assurance Co Ltd v Newman Industries Ltd (No 2)* [1982] Ch 204, 210–11, CA. Also *Wallersteiner v Moir (No 2)* [1975] QB 373, 390, CA, per Lord Denning MR.

[38] *Smith v Croft (No 2)* [1988] Ch 114, 185B.

[39] [1902] AC 83, 93, PC.

[40] Examples of cases alleging fraud are *Atwool v Merryweather* (1867) LR 5 Eq 464n; *Clinch v Financial Corporation* (1868) LR 5 Eq 450; *Duckett v Gover* (1877) 6 Ch D 82; *Mason v Harris* (1879) 11 Ch D 97.

[41] [1916] 1 AC 554, PC. Other cases of this type include *Menier v Hooper's Telegraph Works* (1874) LR 9 Ch App 350; *Alexander v Automatic Telephone Co* [1900] 2 Ch 56, CA; and *Estmanco (Kilner House) Ltd v Greater London Council* [1982] 1 WLR 2, 12, where Megarry V-C said: 'Apart from the benefit to themselves at the company's expense, the essence of the matter seems to be being used as comprising not only fraud at common law but also fraud in the wider equitable sense of that term, as in the equitable concept of a fraud on a power.' More recently, see *Universal Project Management Services Ltd v Fort Gilkicker Ltd* [2013] Ch 551, paras 18 and 54, per Briggs J (misappropriation of valuable business opportunity by director for his personal benefit), and *Abouraya v Sigmund* [2015] BCC 503, paras 18–22, per David Richards J (misappropriation of funds and diversion of a business opportunity by director, but no loss being borne by the wronged company or claimant shareholder).

could not be brought within the fraud on the minority exception.[42] In *Daniels v Daniels*,[43] Templeman J reviewed the authorities and found that a non-fraudulent breach of duty by a director (whether a breach of fiduciary duty or of the duty to exercise reasonable skill, care, and diligence) which harms the company could be brought within the exception to the rule in *Foss v Harbottle* if the defendant director benefited from his breach of duty.

No constitutional impediment to the claim

22.23   Where those seeking to bring a derivative claim in fact controlled the company, such that they were in a position to cause the company to bring the claim itself, any such claim was judged wholly misconceived.[44] Similarly shareholders were not allowed to bring a derivative claim where the company was no longer in the hands of the wrongdoers; as where a liquidator had been appointed.[45]

A substantive right?

22.24   Although Lord Davey described a shareholder's ability to bring a derivative claim as a 'mere matter of procedure' (paragraph 22.18 above),[46] the right of a shareholder to be protected from the wrongs described in paragraph 22.22 above, which are all in the nature of equitable fraud, has been recognized as being substantive in nature.[47]

(3) Procedural restrictions on bringing a derivative claim

Prima facie case

22.25   In order to prevent a company from being subjected to an unwanted derivative claim the Court of Appeal in the *Prudential* case said that:[48]

> In our view, whatever may be the properly defined boundaries of the exception to the rule, the plaintiff ought at least to be required before proceeding with his action to establish a prima facie case (i) that the company is entitled to the relief claimed, and (ii) that the action falls within the proper boundaries of the exception to the rule in *Foss v Harbottle*.

22.26   At the time of the *Prudential* case there was no procedural rule, restricting a plaintiff's ability to proceed with a derivative action to trial.[49] The burden was therefore on the defendant to raise the prima facie case issue on an application to strike out the claim or by challenging the plaintiff's standing as a preliminary issue.[50]

---

[42] *Pavlides v Jensen* [1956] Ch 565 (approved in *Multinational Gas and Petrochemical Co v Multinational Gas and Petrochemical Services Ltd* [1983] Ch 258, CA); *Heyting v Dupont* [1964] 1 WLR 843, CA; *Jackson v Dear*, unreported, The Royal Court of the Island of Guernsey, Lieutenant Bailiff Patrick Talbot QC, 6 March 2013; *Universal Project Management Services Ltd v Fort Gilkicker Ltd* [2013] Ch 551, para 18, per Briggs J.

[43] [1978] Ch 406.

[44] *Watts v Midland Bank plc* [1986] BCLC 15, where there was no obstacle to the company bringing the action.

[45] *Ferguson v Wallbridge* [1935] 3 DLR 66, 83, PC, per Lord Blanesburgh; *Fargro Ltd v Godfroy* [1986] 1 WLR 1134, 1136, per Walton J.

[46] See also *Nurcombe v Nurcombe* [1985] 1 WLR 370, 376, CA, per Lawton LJ.

[47] *Konamaneni v Rolls Royce Industrial Power (India) Ltd* [2002] 1 WLR 1269 at paras 45–50, per Lawrence Collins J; *Base Metal Trading v Shamurin* [2005] 1 WLR 1157, CA at paras 67 and 68, per Arden LJ; *Waddington v Thomas* [2009] 2 BCLC 82, HK FCA at para 55, per Lord Millett.

[48] [1982] Ch 204, 221H–222B, CA.

[49] For a description of earlier procedural filters, see Lord Millett's judgment in *Waddington v Thomas* [2009] 2 BCLC 82, HK FCA at paras 49–51.

[50] *Prudential Assurance Co Ltd v Newman Industries Ltd (No 2)* [1982] Ch 204, 211B–212E, 217G, 219F–H, 221B–G, CA; *Smith v Croft (No 2)* [1988] Ch 114, 127F, 138D–139C; *Waddington v Thomas* [2009]

In *Barrett v Duckett* Peter Gibson LJ stated two principles in relation to the court's decision **22.27**
on whether the plaintiff should be allowed to proceed with his derivative action:[51]

4. Where a challenge is made to the right claimed by a shareholder to bring a derivative action
on behalf of the company, it is the duty of the court to decide as a preliminary issue the
question whether or not the plaintiff should be allowed to sue in that capacity.
5. In taking that decision it is not enough for the court to say that there is no plain and obvious
case for striking out; it is for the shareholder to establish to the satisfaction of the court that
he should be allowed to sue on behalf of the company.

In 1994 Rules of the Supreme Court were adopted which required the plaintiff in a deriva- **22.28**
tive action to apply to court for permission to continue his claim and to support his application with evidence.[52]

Prima facie case that the company is entitled to the relief claimed

By selecting the 'prima facie case' standard the Court of Appeal indicated that the plaintiff had **22.29**
to demonstrate that the allegations in the statement of claim were supported by evidence.[53]
Further, the Court of Appeal made it clear that an application challenging the plaintiff's standing was not to be determined 'on the hypothesis that all the allegations in the statement of
claim of "fraud" and "control" are facts, as they would be on the trial of a preliminary point
of law'.[54] In *Waddington v Thomas* Lord Millett said that the plaintiff had to establish a prima
facie case 'that the company would be likely to succeed if it brought the action'.[55]

In the Cayman Islands case *Renova Resources Private Equity Ltd v Gilbertson* Foster Ag J **22.30**
agreed with Lord Millett[56] and went on to describe the prima facie test in these terms:[57]

For the plaintiff to obtain leave to continue with the action, I consider that I must be satisfied
in the exercise of my discretion that its case is not spurious or unfounded, that it is a serious as
opposed to speculative case, that it is a case brought *bona fide* on reasonable grounds, on behalf
of and in the interests of the company and that it is sufficiently strong to justify granting leave
for the action to continue rather than dismissing it at this preliminary stage.

At common law the prima facie test had therefore come to be described in terms similar to **22.31**
what is now the test for summary judgment under the CPR Part 24—ie the plaintiff had
to show positively that his claim had a 'real prospect of succeeding': that it was better than
merely arguable.[58]

---

2 BCLC 82, HK FCA at paras 53 and 54, per Lord Millett; *Jackson v Dear*, unreported, The Royal Court of the
Island of Guernsey, Lieutenant Bailiff Patrick Talbot QC, 6 March 2013.

[51] [1995] 1 BCLC 243, 249, CA (a case prior to the introduction of RSC Ord 15, r 12A).
[52] By adding RSC Ord 15, r 12A (later CPR 19.9 and now s 260 of the 2006 Act).
[53] See the discussion of the meaning of 'prima facie case' in *American Cyanamid Co v Ethicon Ltd* [1975] AC
396, 404, 405, 407, HL.
[54] [1982] Ch 204, 221G–H, CA.
[55] [2009] 2 BCLC 82, HK FCA at para 54.
[56] [2009] CILR 268 at para 30.
[57] [2009] CILR 268 at para 35.
[58] In *Smith v Croft (No 2)* [1988] Ch 114, 157–65 Knox J assessed the four heads of claim. He found that
the plaintiff had failed to establish a prima facie case on two of the heads of claim, excessive remuneration and
improper expenses, but there was a prima facie case in respect of payments to associated companies, which could
be but had not been effectively ratified, and also in respect of a breach of the financial assistance provisions,
which involved an ultra vires act, which could not be ratified. More recently, see *Abouraya v Sigmund* [2015]
BCC 503, paras 53–7, per David Richards J; *Bhullar v Bhullar* [2016] 1 BCLC 106, paras 20–4, per Morgan J.

Views of the hypothetical independent board of directors

22.32 In *Wallersteiner v Moir (No 2)*[59] the Court of Appeal held that, since the minority shareholder brought the derivative claim for the benefit of the company, he was, in principle, entitled to be indemnified for his costs out of the assets of the company. This was so even if the plaintiff was not without means and did not need the indemnity in order to proceed with the action.[60] In the *Wallersteiner* case Buckley LJ said that the plaintiff should be entitled to an indemnity if it would have been reasonable for an independent board, exercising the standard of care that a prudent businessman would exercise in his own affairs, to continue the action to judgment.[61]

22.33 In *Smith v Croft*[62] Walton J applied Buckley LJ's reasonable independent board test, when refusing the plaintiff an indemnity for costs.

22.34 In *Mumbray v Lapper*,[63] decided after the RSC and CPR had introduced a permission application requirement, HHJ Robert Reid QC applied the test to the question of whether the plaintiff should be permitted to proceed with the derivative action, when he said that the central question was: 'Would an independent board sanction pursuit of the proceedings?'

22.35 In *Airey v Cordell*[64] Warren J reviewed the authorities and concluded that the hypothetical independent board test was the relevant standard, even where a prima facie case on the merits could be shown:

> My conclusion in agreement with Judge Reid is that the appropriate test for bringing proceedings is indeed the view of the hypothetical independent board of directors, but I am also of the view that it is not for the court to assert its own view of what it would do if it were the board, but it merely has to be satisfied that a reasonable board of directors could take the decision that the minority shareholder applying for permission to proceed would like it to take, and I do not think it would be right to shut out the minority shareholder on the basis of the court's, perhaps inadequate, assessment of what it would do rather than a test which is easier to apply, which is whether any reasonable board could take that decision.
>
> If no reasonable board would bring the proceedings, even though there is a *prima facie* case, then the court should not sanction the minority shareholder's action.

22.36 However, in *Bhullar v Bhullar*[65] Morgan J drew a distinction between the nature of the hypothetical board test to be applied to granting permission to continue a derivative claim, and the test which is applicable to the grant of an indemnity for costs, once it has been established that the derivative claim should be permitted. He characterized the test in respect of a pre-emptive costs order as being whether an independent reasonable board of directors *should* bring the claim, rather than whether the reasonable independent board *could think that it should* bring the claim.[66]

---

[59] [1975] QB 373, CA.

[60] *Jaybird Group Ltd v Greenwood* [1986] BCLC 319, 327, 328.

[61] [1975] QB 373, 404A–B, CA.

[62] [1986] 1 WLR 580.

[63] [2005] BCC 990 at para 5.

[64] [2007] BCC 785 at paras 75 and 76; followed in *Bhullar v Bhullar* [2016] 1 BCLC 106, para 38, per Morgan J.

[65] [2016] 1 BCLC 106, paras 47–71.

[66] Morgan J, despite granting permission for certain elements of the claim to continue, refused to grant an indemnity for costs in favour of the claimant. He emphasized the 'high degree of assurance' of which the court must be satisfied, that such an indemnity would be the proper order to make following a trial on the merits of the claim.

The independent board test is now found in the 2006 Act, s 263(2)(a), as discussed in para- **22.37**
graph 22.99 below.[67] At common law, the independent board test was applied if the plaintiff
had established a prima facie case that the company was entitled to the relief claimed.

Views of independent shareholders

The plaintiff in a derivative action also had to satisfy the court that there was a prima facie **22.38**
case that the action fell within the proper boundaries of the exception to the rule in *Foss v
Harbottle*. The company would not be under the control of the wrongdoers if there was an
independent organ of the company capable of deciding whether or not the claim should be
pursued.[68]

In *Smith v Croft (No 2)* Knox J struck out the claim based on illegal financial assistance, **22.39**
which could not be ratified and as to which there was a prima facie case on the merits,
because he was satisfied that the majority of the independent shareholders were opposed to
the continuation of the action and that their votes were cast for reasons genuinely thought to
be for the company's advantage and not just to favour the defendant directors.[69]

Under the 2006 Act, s 239 a vote to ratify conduct of a director can only be passed if assented **22.40**
to by a majority of members who are not connected to the director.[70] Under Part 11, the
views of unconnected members are of critical importance to the court's decision whether or
not a derivative claim should be permitted to proceed.[71]

Good faith and alternative remedy

These two matters are invariably connected and in his sixth principle in *Barrett v Duckett* **22.41**
Peter Gibson LJ dealt with them together:[72]

> 6. The shareholder will be allowed to sue on behalf of the company if he is bringing the action
>   bona fide for the benefit of the company for wrongs to the company for which no other
>   remedy is available. Conversely if the action is brought for an ulterior purpose or if another
>   adequate remedy is available, the court will not allow the action to proceed.

The conduct of the plaintiff may mean that he is not a proper person to bring the claim **22.42**
or that it is unjust for him to be allowed to do so.[73] Now the good faith of the claimant is
a factor to be taken into account under Part 11.[74]

---

[67] In *Renova Resources Private Equity Ltd v Gilbertson* [2009] CILR 268 at para 30 Foster Ag J declined to
follow *Airey v Cordell* on the question whether permission should be given to pursue a derivative claim, saying
that the test only applied to an application for an indemnity for costs.

[68] *Prudential Assurance Co Ltd v Newman Industries Ltd (No 2)* [1982] Ch 204, 212, 221, CA.

[69] [1988] Ch 114, 177, 186, 189.

[70] See Ch 20, Section D above.

[71] 2006 Act, s 263(2)(b), (c)–(e), and (4).

[72] [1995] 1 BCLC 243, 249.

[73] *Nurcombe v Nurcombe* [1985] 1 WLR 370, 377, 378, CA. In divorce proceedings the plaintiff had accepted
a lump sum award on the basis that the profits of a transaction were at her husband's disposition, knowing that
he was in breach of fiduciary duty, whereas in the derivative claim she was alleging that the profits belonged to the
company. The derivative claim was struck out. In *Barrett v Duckett* [1995] 1 BCLC 243 the derivative claim was
struck out because the plaintiff was pursuing the claim for an ulterior purpose, concerning her daughter's divorce
from the defendant. More recently, in *Abouraya v Sigmund* [2015] BCC 503, paras 26, 59, and 60, permission to
continue a multiple derivative claim was refused where the real purpose of the claim was to advance the interests
of the claimant in his capacity as an alleged creditor of the parent company, it being considered an improper use
of the derivative procedure. Also see *Konamaneni v Rolls Royce Industrial Power (India) Ltd* [2002] 1 WLR 1269
at para 28; *Harley Street Capital Ltd v Tchigirinsky* [2006] BCC 209 at paras 134–41.

[74] 2006 Act, s 263(3)(a).

22.43 The availability of an alternative remedy was recognized as a factor which might lead the court in the exercise of its discretion to refuse permission to continue the claim. In *Barrett v Duckett*[75] the action was struck out because liquidation of the company was an adequate alternative remedy. The alternative remedy could be an offer in appropriate terms which was capable of acceptance.[76] Under Part 11 the existence of an alternative remedy is a factor to be taken into account.[77]

(4) The need for reform

22.44 The need to protect the interests of the company and all persons interested in its affairs means that derivative claims pose difficult problems of case management for the court. The requirement for a permission stage was a response to the need to protect those interests, but a permission stage necessarily adds to the costs and complexity of the proceedings.[78] Therefore it is not surprising that derivative claims were rarely brought and few were successful.

22.45 It is in that context that in 1997 reform was recommended by the Law Commission and the CLR.[79] It was considered that the rule in *Foss v Harbottle*, which could only be found in case law, was 'complicated and unwieldy'. The scope of the exception to the rule was uncertain. Further, the way in which a member was required to prove *locus standi* as a preliminary issue by evidence which shows a prima facie case on the merits, could amount to a mini-trial which increased the length and cost of litigation.[80] Rather than determining the availability of the derivative claim by reference to a set of rules which defined whether the claim could be brought at all, it was proposed to transfer that discretion to the court.

22.46 The statutory derivative procedure proposed by the Law Commission envisaged the imposition of criteria for determining whether a shareholder may pursue a claim, which were 'more modern, flexible and accessible'.[81] In this way, the Law Commission considered that the proposals would put the derivative action on a much clearer and more rational basis and, further, that the proposals would give courts the flexibility to allow cases to proceed in appropriate circumstances, while giving advisers and shareholders the necessary guidance on matters which the court would take into account in deciding whether to grant leave.[82] It was further considered that a statutory procedure would give greater transparency to the requirements for a claim, in that it would alert shareholders, directors, and other interested parties to the existence of the provision and would ensure (along with the unfair prejudice remedy) that the Companies Act constituted a complete code with regard to shareholders' remedies.[83]

---

[75] [1995] 1 BCLC 243, CA. Also see *Konamaneni v Rolls Royce Industrial Power (India) Ltd* [2002] 1 WLR 1269 at para 29; *Jafarini-Fini v Skillglass Ltd* [2005] BCC 842, CA (available personal claim); *Mumbray v Lapper* [2005] BCC 990 (liquidation more appropriate).

[76] *Airey v Cordell* [2007] BCC 785 at paras 80–7.

[77] 2006 Act, s 263(3)(f).

[78] Other cases, which foundered at the permission stage, not so far mentioned, include *Jafari-Fini v Skillglass Ltd* [2005] BCC 842, CA, and *Reeves v Sprecher* [2007] 2 BCLC 614, where Lewison J refused leave to continue a derivative claim on the basis that the English court was not the appropriate forum. In *Portfolios of Distinction Ltd v Laird* [2004] 2 BCLC 741 the court would not hear a summary judgment application until after the court had given permission to proceed.

[79] Law Com No 246, which was preceded by a Consultation Paper No 142 (1996).

[80] Law Com No 246 at para 6.4.

[81] Law Com No 246 at para 6.15.

[82] Law Com No 246 at para 6.14.

[83] Law Com No 246 at paras 6.16–6.18. The Law Commission also considered that it was important to remain consistent with the legislation of other jurisdictions such as Canada, New Zealand, and Australia, cf

D. Derivative Claims under Part 11

(1) Introduction

A derivative claim within Part 11 is a claim by a member of a company in respect of a cause **22.47**
of action vested in the company and seeking relief on behalf of the company, which arises
out of an act or omission (actual or proposed) involving negligence, default, breach of
duty, or breach of trust by a director.[84] Such a claim is now subject to a successful application to the court for permission under the statute, since s 260(2) states that a derivative
claim may only be brought under Part 11 or pursuant to a court order in proceedings
under s 994. To that extent, the rule in *Foss v Harbottle*,[85] described in Section C above, is
displaced.

However, the substantive change to the existing rules should not be overstated. Part 11, Chapter 1 **22.48**
does not introduce a substantive rule to replace the rule in *Foss v Harbottle*. Rather, it introduces a
new statutory procedure for bringing a derivative claim by way of exception to that rule[86] which
is supplemented by a new CPR 19.9.

The changes made by Part 11 are intended to provide a more easily deducible statutory **22.49**
guide according to which the court may conduct its determination of whether a derivative
claim ought to be allowed to proceed, although obtaining permission has remained a very
substantial challenge. Part 11 contains provisions which adopt the Law Commission's proposals to a significant extent.[87] For example, it is now not necessary to demonstrate control
of the general meeting by wrongdoing directors (ie that the defendant director(s) control
the majority of shares in the company). This will nevertheless remain a relevant factor to be
considered by the court in its determination of whether to grant permission to continue a
derivative claim.[88]

Although more derivative claims have been commenced since the enactment of Part 11 than **22.50**
was the case before, they remain relatively rare in comparison with unfair prejudice proceedings under Part 30.[89]

Canadian Business Corporation Act 1975, s 239; New Zealand Companies Act 1993, ss 165–8; and Australian
Corporations Act 2001, Part 2F.1A, ss 236–42.

[84] 2006 Act, s 260(1), (3).

[85] (1843) 2 Hare 461.

[86] It is to be noted that Chapter 11 of the Act uses the term 'derivative claim' and assumes that there is already
a right to bring such claims in England and Wales and Northern Ireland. It therefore regulates the conduct of a
derivative claim rather than conferring the right to bring a claim.

[87] *Final Report* at para 7.46. That notwithstanding, a certain amount of unease was expressed over the prescription by statute of the substantive criteria according to which a claim may be brought. In this respect Part 11
extends further than envisaged by the Commission. During the bill's passage through Parliament, amendments
were effected so as to prescribe yet further the circumstances in which the court's discretion could be exercised
(681 HL Official Report (5th series) col 883 (9 May 2006)).

[88] *Stimpson v Southern Private Landlords Association* [2010] BCC 387, 405; *Cinematic Finance v Ryder*
[2012] BCC 797.

[89] In 'Litigating Domestic Disputes within Companies: Continuity or Change?' (Sweet and Maxwell
Company Law Newsletter, Issue 220 (22/2007) 1, 2) David Milman contended that the wider range of directors' duties under ss 170 *et seq* may open up greater opportunities for shareholder litigation. He concluded,
however, that the new statutory procedure would be unlikely to lead to a flood of shareholder litigation, but
merely an enhanced opportunity to launch derivative claims.

(2) Scope of Part 11

22.51   Section 260 identifies derivative claims to which Part 11, Chapter 1 applies:

> (1) This Chapter applies to proceedings in England and Wales or Northern Ireland by a member of a company—
>   (a) in respect of a cause of action vested in the company, and
>   (b) seeking relief on behalf of the company.
> This is referred to in this Chapter as a 'derivative claim'.
> (2) A derivative claim may only be brought—
>   (a) under this Chapter, or
>   (b) in pursuance of an order of the court in proceedings under section 994 (proceedings for protection of members against unfair prejudice).
> (3) A derivative claim under this Chapter may be brought only in respect of a cause of action arising from an actual or proposed act or omission involving negligence, default, breach of duty, or breach of trust by a director of the company.
> The cause of action may be against the director or another person (or both).
> (4) It is immaterial whether the cause of action arose before or after the person seeking to bring or continue the derivative claim became a member of the company.
> (5) For the purposes of this Chapter—
>   (a) 'director' includes a former director;
>   (b) a shadow director is treated as a director; and
>   (c) references to a member of a company include a person who is not a member but to whom shares in the company have been transferred or transmitted by operation of law.

Proceedings by a member

22.52   A derivative claim may be brought by a member[90] and, by virtue of the extended meaning of member in s 260(5)(c), also by a person to whom shares have been transferred or a person to whom shares have been transmitted by operation of law. The same extended meaning of member applies to unfair prejudice petitions. Reference should be made to Chapter 23 at paragraphs 23.05 and 23.06 for a discussion of who is a member for the purposes of entitlement to bring a derivative claim.

22.53   In practice, the member is most likely to be a minority shareholder unable to persuade the company to bring proceedings. This may include a 50 per cent shareholder, where he can be treated as being under the same disability as a minority shareholder.[91] A majority shareholder will only be granted permission to bring a derivative claim in exceptional circumstances.[92]

22.54   No minimum shareholding is stipulated.[93] In theory, therefore, the putative claimant could purchase one share for the purpose of bringing a derivative claim. Concern was voiced

---

[90] By 2006 Act, s 112 the members of a company are the subscribers of its memorandum and every other person who agrees to become a member of a company and whose name is entered in its register of members.

[91] *Barrett v Duckett* [1995] 1 BCLC 243, 250, CA. More recently, see *Renova Resources Private Equity Ltd v Gilbertson* [2009] CILR 268; *Parry v Bartlett* [2012] BCC 700; *Universal Project Management Services Ltd v Fort Gilkicker Ltd* [2013] Ch 551, paras 18 and 54, per Briggs J; *Abouraya v Sigmund* [2015] BCC 503, para 17, per David Richards J.

[92] *Cinematic Finance v Ryder* [2012] BCC 797 at para 14.

[93] Cf *Seaton v Grant* (1867) 2 Ch App 459.

during the parliamentary debates that vulture funds, environmentalists, animal rights activists, and US litigators would seek to take advantage of the absence of any such provision, and that this would be damaging to commercial activity.[94] Those fears were somewhat allayed by the potential disadvantages to any such litigant. Specifically, any recovery will inure to the benefit of the company and the claimant will risk being penalized in costs in the absence of an indemnity order. Such differences in incentive were viewed as preventing American-style class actions. The reported cases brought under Part 11 to date suggest that this concern was not justified.[95]

By s 260(4) it is not necessary for the person seeking to bring or continue the derivative **22.55** claim to have been a member when the cause of action arose. This preserves the common law rule.[96] It also reflects the fact that the rights being enforced are those of the company rather than the member. It is also commercially realistic. If the company receives a windfall from previous events just after a shareholder disposes of shares, it is the new shareholder who takes the benefit. Similarly, it is the new shareholder who will suffer detriment where the company suffers an unexpected loss arising out of past events.

The cause of action

By s 260(1) a derivative claim is in respect of a cause of action vested in the company, seek- **22.56** ing relief on its behalf. The nature of the cause of action is then explained in s 260(3): it is a claim arising from an actual or proposed act or omission involving negligence, default, breach of duty, or breach of trust by a director of the company.[97] In both form and substance this is a significant change from the common law. The ability to bring a derivative claim is no longer restricted to causes of action grounded on equitable fraud, as discussed in paragraph 22.22 above. The element of wrongdoer control is replaced by the court controls in ss 261 and 263, discussed below.[98] As a result, the ambit of the derivative claim is now much wider than under the previous regime and extends to any cause of action falling within the four categories of conduct stated in s 260(3). Three points should be noted.

First, a derivative claim may now be brought in respect of negligence. It was previously the **22.57** case that no such action would lie where mere negligence on the part of the directors was alleged.[99] The CLR noted, however, that a general concern had been voiced in relation to breaches of the duty of care and skill.[100] The CLR considered that 'the developments in the law in relation to directors' duties of skill and care should have their counterpart in policing procedures'.[101] Against that it was argued that the court should adopt a restrictive approach,

---

[94] 679 HL Official Report (5th Series) cols GC11–13 (27 February 2006).

[95] See evaluation by Hannigan in 'Board Failures in the Financial Crisis: Tinkering with Codes and the Need for Wider Corporate Governance Reforms' (2011) 32(12) *Comp Law* 363–71 and by Keay and Loughrey in 'Derivative Proceedings in a Brave New World' [2010] JBL 151.

[96] Cf *Seaton v Grant* (1867) 2 Ch App 459. See further Law Com No 246 at para 6.98 and 679 HL Official Report (5th Series) col GC15 (27 February 2006).

[97] The same language is used in 2006 Act, s 239. See the discussion in Ch 20, Section D above.

[98] It was considered that the requirement of wrongdoer control may make it impossible for a derivative claim to be brought successfully by a member of a widely held company: 681 HL Official Report (5th series) col 883 (9 May 2006) (Lord Goldsmith).

[99] *Pavlides v Jensen* [1956] Ch 565 (approved in *Multinational Gas and Petrochemical Co v Multinational Gas and Petrochemical Services Ltd* [1983] Ch 258, CA); *Heyting v Dupont* [1964] 1 WLR 843, CA.

[100] CLR: *Final Report* at para 7.47. See also Law Com No 246 at paras 6.38–6.41 in relation to the risks of extending the scope of derivative claims to include negligence of directors.

[101] CLR: *Developing the Framework* at para 4.127.

since the board is responsible for management, and problems may arise where there is a clear breach of duty by a director but the board takes a commercial decision not to pursue it. The CLR did not consider this latter suggestion to pose any difficulties. If an untainted majority of the board takes the decision, in compliance with their duties, then it should stand. If not, then whether an action should proceed would be determined in accordance with the principles on directors' duties.[102] In practice, therefore, it will be a matter for the courts to distinguish between commercial misjudgement and negligent conduct.

22.58 The second important change is that a claim may now be brought in respect of a breach of duty, including negligence, without having to prove some personal benefit accruing to the alleged wrongdoers. The position at common law was that as a mere breach of a fiduciary duty owed to the company is ratifiable, a derivative action could not be brought in respect of any such breach.[103] Only (in the absence of fraud) where the directors and majority shareholders were guilty of a breach of duty which not only harms the company but *benefits* themselves, could a derivative claim be brought.[104]

22.59 Finally, it might be thought that the inclusion of 'breach of duty' is no more than a reference to breaches of the general duties set out in Part 10, Chapter 2 of the Act. However, the section does not so provide in terms and the general thrust of the text is to widen the ambit of the derivative claim.[105] Moreover, the inclusion of 'default' as a ground for a derivative claim is a direct reference to a breach of other statutory obligations, which cause loss to the company (eg through being fined).[106]

The company

22.60 Part 11 applies to a company formed and registered under the Companies Act in accordance with s 1. It does not apply to foreign companies, which could be the subject of a derivative claim in England (as to which, see Chapter 36, Section G(1) below).[107] Nor does Part 11 apply to other bodies corporate and trade unions, which may be the subject of a derivative claim under the common law and the procedure in CPR 19.9C.[108]

Director and third parties

22.61 For the purposes of Part 11 the definition of 'director' is extended by s 260(5)(a) and (b) to a former director[109] and a shadow director.[110] A director will usually be a defendant.

---

[102] In a similar vein, the Law Commission took the view that, whilst investors take the risk that those who manage companies may make mistakes, they do not have to accept that directors will fail to comply with their duties (Law Com No 246 at para 6.41).

[103] *Burland v Earle* [1902] AC 83, PC; *Pavlides v Jensen* [1956] Ch 565; *Heyting v Dupont* [1964] 1 WLR 843, CA.

[104] *Daniels v Daniels* [1978] Ch 406, 414; *Estmanco v Greater London Council* [1982] 1 WLR 2.

[105] 679 HL Official Report (5th Series) col GC2 (27 February 2006).

[106] But this is subject to the *ex turpi causa* principle, as discussed in Ch 19, Section E(4) above.

[107] *Abouraya v Sigmund* [2015] BCC 503.

[108] For an example of a derivative claim in respect of a trade union, see *Ritchie v Union of Construction, Allied Trades and Technicians* [2011] EWHC 3613 (Ch).

[109] 2006 Act, s 170(2) provides that a person who ceases to be a director continues to be subject to the duty to avoid conflicts of interests in s 175 as regards the exploitation of any property, information, or opportunity of which he became aware at the time he was a director. He also continues to be subject to the duty in s 176 (duty not to accept benefits from third parties) as regards things done or omitted by him before he ceased to be a director.

[110] How significant this will be in practice is not clear, since it cannot be said with any certainty that shadow directors owe fiduciary duties to the company. See Ch 10, Section C above. The extension of s 260 to shadow directors was recommended by the Law Commission in *Shareholder Remedies* (Law Com No 246, 1997) at para

Section 260(3) makes it clear that it is not necessary to make a director a defendant if the **22.62** real target is a third party, as where a third party has knowingly received corporate property as a result of a breach of duty by a director. In this context, the common law rules relating to dishonest assistance or knowing receipt of corporate property remain applicable.[111] For a derivative claim to be brought against the third party it must arise out of the negligence, default, breach of duty, or breach of trust of a director.[112] If the claim does not fall within the definition of a derivative claim contained in s 260(3) then the claim can only be brought pursuant to a court order in proceedings under s 994.[113]

The restriction

Section 260(2) delineates the scope for bringing a derivative claim. It makes the statutory **22.63** remedy under s 260 the exclusive procedure for bringing the claim, save for orders granted in proceedings under s 994 of the Companies Act. In practice, however, a successful petitioner under s 994 is most unlikely to seek such an order under s 996(2)(c), since a buy-out order will usually be more appropriate (see Chapter 23 below).[114]

The multiple derivative claim

It has been decided by recent first-instance authority that the description of the derivative **22.64** claim under s 260(1) operates to exclude a derivative claim being brought by a shareholder in a parent company on behalf of a subsidiary company to whom the duty is owed (known as a double derivative claim), or by a shareholder in a parent company on behalf of a sub-subsidiary company to whom the duty is owed, where the corporate structure contains one or more sub-subsidiary companies interposed in the structure (known as a multiple derivative claim): *Universal Project Management Services Ltd v Fort Gilkicker Ltd*.[115]

The *Fort Gilkicker* case has also decided two very significant issues of principle in respect of **22.65** the multiple derivative action.[116] First, it is the first English authority expressly to decide that such a claim was known to English common law before the coming into force of Part 11.[117]

6.36. This was on the basis that it should be possible to base a claim against a shadow director on the grounds of breach of a statutory obligation (eg for non-compliance with Part 10, where many of the provisions do apply to shadow directors). Naturally the derivative claimant will still need to satisfy the court that the putative defendant is in fact a shadow director.

[111] *Iesini v Westrip Holdings Ltd* [2011] 1 BCLC 498 at para 75; *Stimpson v Southern Private Landlords Association* [2010] BCC 387.

[112] *Iesini v Westrip Holdings Ltd* [2011] 1 BCLC 498 at para 75; *Stainer v Lee* [2011] BCC 537.

[113] *Iesini v Westrip Holdings Ltd* [2011] 1 BCLC 498 at para 75.

[114] Attempts were made during the bill's passage through Parliament to remove the provision under s 260(2)(b) (679 HL Official Report (5th series) col GC6 (27 February 2006)). The government rejected them and accepted the view of the Law Commission that, despite the fact that a shareholder is unlikely to use s 996(2)(c) to bring a derivative claim, the better approach is to maintain both routes (Law Com No 246 at para 6.55). Furthermore, where relief is given under s 996 to bring a derivative claim, the threshold for permission to continue the claim laid down in s 261 will not apply.

[115] [2013] Ch 551, para 31. The Law Commission considered that it would be neither helpful nor practicable to include such claims (Law Com No 246 at para 6.110). However, the Commission at the same time considered that the question was best left to the courts to resolve, if necessary using its remedial power upon a successful unfair prejudice petition to allow the commencement of derivative proceedings.

[116] The decision has been subsequently applied in two further first-instance decisions: *Abouraya v Sigmund* [2015] BCC 503, paras 12–14, per David Richards J, and *Bhullar v Bhullar* [2016] 1 BCLC 106, para 19 per Morgan J. In *Abouraya v Sigmund*, para 14, the Judge expressly endorsed the conclusions and reasoning of Briggs J in *Fort Gilkicker*.

[117] The circumstances in which cases under the old law were decided suggest that such a claim would have been allowed to proceed if the point had been taken by a defendant and the relevant thresholds were

Prior to *Fort Gilkicker*, in *Waddington v Thomas* in the Hong Kong Court of Final Appeal[118] Lord Millett found that a shareholder could maintain a multiple derivative action at common law on behalf of a subsidiary of a company of which he was a member. He characterized the question as simply one of *locus standi*, and the justification behind permitting the 'simple' derivative claim as equally applicable in the case of a double or multiple derivative claim.[119]

22.66 In *Fort Gilkicker* Briggs J adopted an identical approach, in finding that a 50 per cent shareholder could maintain a double derivative action at common law on behalf of a subsidiary of an LLP of which he was a member.[120] He similarly characterized the issue as one of *locus standi,* and considered that: [121]

> Once it is recognized that the derivative action is merely a procedural device designed to prevent a wrong going without a remedy (see *Nurcombe v Nurcombe* [1985] 1 WLR 370, 376A)[122] then it is unsurprising to find the court extending locus standi to members of the wronged company's holding company, where the holding company is itself in the same wrongdoer control. The would-be claimant is not exercising some right inherent in its membership, but availing itself of the court's readiness to permit someone with a sufficient interest to sue as the company's representative claimant, for the benefit of all its stakeholders.

He thus concluded:[123]

> In my judgment the common law procedural device called the derivative action was, at least until 2006, clearly sufficiently flexible to accommodate as the legal champion or representative of a company in wrongdoer control a would-be claimant who was either (and usually) a member of that company or (exceptionally) a member of its parent company where that parent company was in the same wrongdoer control. I would not describe that flexibility in terms of separate forms of derivative action, whether headed 'ordinary', 'multiple' or 'double'. Rather it was a single piece of procedural ingenuity designed to serve the interests of justice in appropriate cases calling for the identification of an exception to the rule in *Foss v Harbottle.*

22.67 Secondly, *Fort Gilkicker* is also authority for the proposition that such a claim has survived the coming into force of Part 11 and is permitted as a matter of common law.[124] The rationale for Briggs J's decision was essentially twofold: first, he did not consider the multiple derivative action, as it existed as a matter of common law prior to the enactment of Part 11, to constitute a 'separate derivative action', but simply an example of 'the efficient application of the procedural device designed to avoid injustice, to different factual circumstances'. Secondly, as a matter of language, s 260 applied Part 11 only to that part of the common law device

---

satisfied: see eg *Wallersteiner v Moir (No 2)* [1975] QB 373; *Halle v Trax BW Ltd* [2000] BCC 1020; *Trumann Investment Group Ltd v Societe Generale SA* [2002] EWHC 2621; *Airey v Cordell* [2007] BCC 785.

[118] [2009] 2 BCLC 82.

[119] *Waddington v Thomas* [2009] 2 BCLC 82, 100–5 at 104, per Lord Millett: 'if wrongdoers must not be allowed to defraud a parent company with impunity, they must not be allowed to defraud its subsidiary with impunity'. In that case, the provisions of s 168BC of the Hong Kong Companies Ordinance were found not to extend to multiple derivative claims, but the proceedings were permitted to continue as a multiple derivative claim governed by the common law. See also *Renova Resources Private Equity Ltd v Gilbertson* [2009] CILR 268 at paras 62–6.

[120] *Universal Project Management Services Ltd v Fort Gilkicker Ltd* [2013] Ch 551, paras 16–26.

[121] *Universal Project Management Services Ltd v Fort Gilkicker Ltd* [2013] Ch 551, para 24.

[122] See, however, para 22.24 above, as to the right of a shareholder to be protected by means of the derivative action as being substantive in nature.

[123] *Universal Project Management Services Ltd v Fort Gilkicker Ltd* [2013] Ch 551, para 26.

[124] *Universal Project Management Services Ltd v Fort Gilkicker Ltd* [2013] Ch 551, paras 27–49, in which Briggs J considered the competing constructions of s 260(1) in some detail.

labelled a 'derivative claim', leaving other instances of its application unaffected. Absent the express abolition of the 'whole of the common law derivative action in relation to companies', Briggs J could not conclude, as a matter of construction, that a multiple derivative claim at common law has been restricted by Part 11.

Finally, the facts of *Fort Gilkicker* resulted in an additional point of principle being decided **22.68** for the first time: namely, that the precise nature of the corporate body which owned the wronged company's shares is of no legal relevance, provided that it is itself in wrongdoer control and has some members who are interested in seeing the wrong done to the company put right.[125]

(3) Application for permission to continue the claim

The permission application: the first stage

Section 261 places the procedure for an application for permission to continue a derivative **22.69** claim on a statutory footing. It sets out the procedure to be observed once a claimant has initiated a derivative action. Subsection (1) requires a member of a company who brings a derivative claim to apply to the court for permission to continue it.[126] Part 11 thus assumes that the claimant may commence the claim without any court intervention, but must then seek permission to continue.

The new CPR 19.9[127] supplements the substantive provisions of Part 11 and requires the **22.70** derivative claimant to apply for permission to continue.[128] By CPR 19.9(2) the claim is commenced by the issue of a claim form, which must be headed 'Derivative claim'.[129] Rule 19.9(3) provides that the company for the benefit of which a remedy is sought must be made a defendant to the claim. After the issue of the claim form, the claimant must not take any further step in the proceedings without the permission of the court, other than: (a) a step permitted or required by rule 19.9A or (b) making an urgent application for interim relief.[130]

Rule 19.9A deals with the application for permission. When the claim form is issued, the **22.71** claimant must file an application notice under Part 23 for permission to continue the claim and the written evidence on which he relies in support of the permission application.[131] The claimant must not make the company a respondent to the permission application.[132] As such, the claim form may be issued without any prior notice or request to the company. However, the claimant must notify the company of the claim and permission application by sending to the company as soon as reasonably practicable after the claim form is issued: (a) a notice in the form set out in the practice direction supplement to r 19.9,[133] (b) copies of the

---

[125] *Universal Project Management Services Ltd v Fort Gilkicker Ltd* [2013] Ch 551, paras 51 and 52. The claimant was a member of an LLP, which was itself the parent company of the wronged company. Briggs J held to be irrelevant the fact that the LLP's members had no recourse to a statutory derivative claim, relating as it did to the remedies for wrongs done to the LLP, rather than to the company which it owned.

[126] The court is defined by s 1156 as the High Court and also a county court in England and Wales, subject to the power of the Lord Chancellor to redefine the jurisdictions of the county courts for the purposes of the Companies Acts.

[127] Brought into effect by SI 2007/2204 on 1 October 2007.

[128] Which came into force on 1 October 2007.

[129] Practice Direction 19C, para 2(1).

[130] CPR 19.9(4).

[131] CPR 19.9A(2).

[132] CPR 19.9A(3).

[133] Practice Direction 19C sets down further details on certain procedural requirements.

claim form and the particulars of claim, (c) the application notice, and (d) a copy of the evidence filed by the claimant in support of the permission application.[134] The claimant must file a witness statement confirming that he has notified the company in accordance with the rule.[135] The requirement for notice to be given to the company is subject to the court's discretion to permit notification to be delayed where it would be likely to frustrate some part of the remedy sought.[136]

22.72 Although the company is notified of the permission application, it is not expected to make submissions or attend any oral hearing and if it does so it will not normally be allowed any costs.[137] The purpose of notifying the company of the first stage of the permission application is so that it may inform the court of a simple answer to the claim, if one exists, which can be considered on paper.

22.73 The permission application is allocated to a judge.[138] His task is to decide whether the application and the supporting evidence make out a prima facie case. Section 261(2) provides:

> If it appears to the court that the application and the evidence filed by the applicant in support of it do not disclose a prima facie case for giving permission … , the court—
>
> (a) must dismiss the application, and
>
> (b) may make any consequential order it considers appropriate.

This provision was introduced after debate in the House of Lords, with a view to reducing the burden on directors in defending unmeritorious cases.[139] As Lewison J noted in *Iesini v Westrip Holdings Ltd*[140] the requirement of a prima facie case for giving permission 'necessarily entails a decision that there is a prima facie case both that the company has a good cause of action and that the cause of action arises out of a director's default, breach of duty (etc)', which is 'precisely the decision that the Court of Appeal required in *Prudential*'.[141] The court's power to dismiss the application at this stage is reinforced by s 261(2)(b) which

---

[134] CPR 19.9A(4).

[135] CPR 19.9A(6). Interestingly the Law Commission also recommended that a shareholder wishing to bring a derivative claim be required to serve a notice on the company at least 28 days before the commencement of the proceedings, specifying the grounds of the proposed claim (Law Com No 246 at paras 6.58–6.59). That recommendation was not followed, despite such a requirement being imposed under 2006 Act, s 371 (unauthorized political donations). During the bill's passage through Parliament it was also proposed that a derivative claim be allowed to be brought only where the directors have been requested by a member of the company to bring a claim and have refused to do so (679 HL Official Report (5th Series) cols GC6–7 (27 February 2006)). That proposed amendment was designed to decrease the number of unmeritorious claims being brought for tactical reasons. It was, however, similarly rejected. The government stressed that it did not wish to reintroduce an element of the 'wrongdoer control' test—one of the very reasons the Law Commission proposed a new statutory remedy (679 HL Official Report (5th Series) cols GC7–8 (27 February 2006)). Lord Goldsmith felt that this may create scope for directors to spin out the claim in order to buy time and, further, that that is an issue better dealt with by the court when exercising its discretion under s 263(3).

[136] CPR 19.9A(7). Such an application may be made without notice (r 19.9A(8)).

[137] Practice Direction 19C, para 5.

[138] Practice Direction 19C, para 6.

[139] 681 HL Official Report (5th Series) cols 883 (9 May 2006). As to earlier concerns that the reform would burden companies with frivolous or unmeritorious claims, see 679 HL Official Report (5th series) col GC14 (27 February 2006); 681 HL Official Report (5th Series) cols 883–4 (9 May 2006). This power to dismiss the claim subsists alongside the ability of a defendant to apply to have the claim struck out under CPR 3.4. The principal difference is that an application to strike out requires a positive response from the company, whereas s 261(2) requires the court to dismiss the application without hearing from the company.

[140] [2011] 1 BCLC 498 at para 78. For the procedure in Scotland, see *Wishart, Petitioner* [2010] BCC 161.

[141] [1982] Ch 204, 221, CA.

enables the court to penalize an applicant with costs orders or deter a nuisance applicant with a civil restraint order.

CPR 19.9A(9) contemplates that the first stage is dealt with by the court as a paperwork **22.74** exercise without a hearing.[142] Where the court dismisses the claimant's application, because the judge is not satisfied that the application and evidence disclose a prima facie case for giving permission, the court notifies the claimant and (unless the court orders otherwise) the company of that decision.[143]

If the application is dismissed on paper, the claimant may ask for an oral hearing to **22.75** reconsider the decision to dismiss the permission application, provided that the claimant makes the request in writing within seven days of being notified of the decision.[144] The claimant must notify the company in writing, as soon as reasonably practicable, of that request unless the court orders otherwise.[145] If the court dismisses the permission application at the oral hearing, it will notify the claimant and the company of its decision.[146]

The permission application: the second stage

Where a prima facie case for giving permission is made out and the application is not dis- **22.76** missed at the first stage under s 261(2), the court gives directions for the hearing of the permission application. Section 261(3) provides:

> If the application is not dismissed under subsection (2), the court—
> (a) may give directions as to the evidence to be provided by the company, and
> (b) may adjourn the proceedings to enable the evidence to be obtained.

This provision enables the court to obtain from the company any evidence that may be required so that it can decide what order to make on the permission application.

For the second stage of the permission application the court will: (a) order that the company **22.77** and any other appropriate party must be made respondents to the permission application, and (b) give directions for the service on the company and other appropriate party of the application notice and the claim form.[147] It should be noted that the court will not necessarily require all the defendants to the derivative claim to be made respondents to the permission application.

The purpose of the second stage is for the court to determine whether or not permission to **22.78** continue the claim should be given, having regard to the provisions of s 263, discussed in Sections D(5) and (6) below. At this stage the court will have before it the evidence of the claimant member, the company, and the respondents who have served with the application,

---

[142] Sometimes the parties may agree to telescope the first stage into the second stage; see *Mission Capital plc v Sinclair* [2010] 1 BCLC 304; *Franbar Holdings Ltd v Patel* [2009] 1 BCL 1 at para 24; *Stimpson v Southern Private Landlords Association* [2010] BCC 387 at para 3; the Scottish case *Wishart, Petitioner* [2010] BCC 161 at para 9 in the judgment of Lord Reed; and *Bridge v Daley* [2015] EWHC 2121 (Ch) at paras 8–9. For a warning about departing from the statutory two-stage process, see *Langley Ward Ltd v Trevor* [2011] EWHC 1893 (Ch) at paras 61–2.

[143] CPR 19.9A(9).

[144] CPR 19.9A(10)(a).

[145] CPR 19.9A(10)(b).

[146] CPR 19.9A(11).

[147] CPR 19.9A(12).

who will usually include the defendant directors. It is clear that at the hearing the court should not embark on a 'mini-trial'.[148]

22.79 Although the company is made a respondent to the permission application as a matter of course and may be directed to serve evidence, it does not necessarily follow that the company should actively participate in the second stage of the permission application. Whether it should do so largely turns on whether the company has a distinct interest in so doing.[149] In the *Prudential* case, the Court of Appeal considered that the company might have a distinct interest in having an unwanted derivative claim dismissed.[150] Apart from any commercial damage or disruption that the derivative claim may cause the company, it may be ordered to indemnify the claimant for his costs if permission is granted to continue the claim.[151] In *Smith v Croft (No 2)* the company made its own application to strike out a derivative claim and actively participated in the hearing of its successful application.[152] In *Harley Street Capital Ltd v Tchigirinsky*[153] serious, but unfounded, allegations were made against the company in a derivative claim. It actively participated at the permission stage, when the claim was dismissed, and obtained an order for costs.[154] The company actively participated in the permission application without criticism in *Iesini v Westrip Holdings Ltd*[155] and *Kleanthous v Paphitis*.[156] Where the derivative claim can be characterized as in substance a shareholders' dispute, as will be the case with many derivative claims, it is not appropriate for company money to be spent on active participation (see the discussion in relation to a company's participation in an unfair prejudice petition in Chapter 23 at paragraphs 23.98–23.100 below).[157]

Orders on the permission application

22.80 Section 261(4) affords the court a very wide discretion to manage the case in the manner it deems appropriate at the second stage of the permission application. It provides:

> On hearing the application, the court may—
> (a) give permission to continue the claim on such terms as it thinks fit,[158]
> (b) refuse permission … and dismiss the claim, or
> (c) adjourn the proceedings on the application and give such directions as it thinks fit.

---

[148] *Fanmailuk.com Ltd v Cooper* [2008] BCC 877 at para 2; *Iesini v Westrip Holdings Ltd* [2011] 1 BCLC 498 at para 79.

[149] See *Carlisle & Cumbria United Supporters Society v Story* [2010] EWCA Civ 463, CA at paras 22 and 24; *Power v Ekstein* (2010) 77 ACSR 302 at paras 109–21 (a case on the role of the company after permission had been granted).

[150] [1982] Ch 204, 212D–E, 221A–G, CA. Also see the observations of Lord Scott in *Re Chime Corporation* [2004] HK FCA 73 at paras 53, 59, 62.

[151] *Iesini v Westrip Holdings Ltd* [2011] 1 BCLC 498 at para 126. See para 22.82 below.

[152] [1988] Ch 114.

[153] [2005] BCC 209.

[154] [2005] BCC 209. See judgment on costs at paras 5–8.

[155] [2011] 1 BCLC 498. The application was refused in respect of all heads of claim except one, as to which the application was adjourned so that the board could reconsider its position.

[156] [2012] BCC 676, where the claimant unsuccessfully challenged the participation of the defendant directors (but not the company) (paras 43 and 44) and permission was refused.

[157] See also *Singh v Anand* (17 March 2006, unreported) at paras 10 and 11; *Smith v Butler* [2012] 1 BCLC 444, [2012] Bus LR 1836, CA (improper use of company funds in a shareholders' dispute under s 306 CA 2006, where the Court of Appeal observed, at para 47, that the company could avoid any significant expenditure by simply filing a defence that it would abide by the order made by the court).

[158] This will presumably include the power to make an order for costs under CPR 19.9E (see para 22.82 below).

Where the court gives permission

Paragraph 261(4)(a) gives the court discretion to give permission to continue the claim where provisions in sub-s 263(2) do not apply and, taking into account the matters set out in s 263(3) and (4), the court concludes that it is just and equitable for the claim to be continued, either unconditionally or on terms.[159] In exercise of this power the court has limited permission to continue the claim down to disclosure in the proceedings, when the facts and strength of the case may be clearer and at which point the claimant may be required to apply for further permission.[160]   **22.81**

The court may also make an order that the company for whose benefit the derivative claim is brought indemnifies the claimant against liability for costs incurred in the permission application or in the derivative claim or both.[161] Indeed, once the court has decided that the claim ought to proceed, it ought normally to order the company to indemnify the claimant against his costs.[162] The company's potential indemnity liability is therefore a proper consideration for the court in deciding whether to allow the derivative claim to proceed[163] and may be a factor leading to refusal of permission.[164] The court may decide to limit or control the extent of the indemnity.[165]   **22.82**

The court may grant an injunction preventing the company's funds from being used to defend the derivative claim as it proceeds to trial, save in respect of particular matters affecting its interests.[166] The court may also order a director defendant to reimburse the company for costs it should not have incurred.[167] On the other hand the company may make loans to a director in respect of his own costs of the proceeds on terms that the loan is to be repaid if judgment is given against him.[168] The company may even indemnify a director against his own defence costs, subject to the same liability to return the money if judgment is given against him.[169]   **22.83**

Where the court has given permission to continue a derivative claim, it may order that the claim may not be discontinued, settled, or compromised without the permission of the court.[170] Such an order may be appropriate to protect members who are not party to the proceedings.   **22.84**

---

[159] Examples are: *Kiani v Cooper* [2010] 2 BCLC 427; *Stainer v Lee* [2011] 1 BCLC 537; *Parry v Bartlett* [2012] BCC 700; and the Scottish case *Wishart, Petitioner* [2010] BCC 161.

[160] *Kiani v Cooper* [2010] 2 BCLC 427 at paras 45 and 46; *Stainer v Lee* [2011] 1 BCLC 537 at paras 48 and 55.

[161] CPR 19.9E. This reflects the practice established at common law by *Wallersteiner v Moir (No 2)* [1975] QB 373, CA; *Jaybird Group Ltd v Greenwood* [1986] BCLC 319. Indemnity was refused, having regard to the merits in *Smith v Croft* [1986] 1 WLR 580. It was also refused in cases of partnership break-up: *Halle v Trax BW Ltd* [2000] BCC 1020; *Mumbray v Lapper* [2005] BCC 990.

[162] *Iesini v Westrip Holdings Ltd* [2011] 1 BCLC 498 at para 125.

[163] *Iesini v Westrip Holdings Ltd* [2011] 1 BCLC 498 at para 126.

[164] *Stimpson v Southern Private Landlords Association* [2010] BCC 387 at para 39; *Langley Ward Ltd v Trevor* [2011] EWHC 1893 (Ch) at para 21.

[165] *Kiani v Cooper* [2010] 2 BCLC 427 at paras 47–9; *Stainer v Lee* [2011] 1 BCLC 537 at para 56.

[166] *Power v Ekstein* (2010) 77 ACSR 302 at paras 109–21, 131. See further Ch 23 at paras 23.87–23.89 below.

[167] *Carlisle & Cumbria United Independent Supporters' Society Ltd v CUFC Holdings Ltd* [2010] EWCA Civ 463, CA at paras 21–8.

[168] 2006 Act, s 205. See Ch 18 at paras 18.107–18.110 above.

[169] 2006 Act, s 234. See Ch 20, Section C(1) above.

[170] CPR 19.9F; Practice Direction 19C, para 7.

Refusal or adjournment of the permission application

22.85 The court is obliged to refuse permission and dismiss the application at the second stage under s 261(4)(b) if it finds that the provisions in s 263(2) apply (Section D(5) below).[171] The court may refuse permission and dismiss the claim where the provisions in s 263(2) do not apply, but taking into account the matters set out in s 263(3) and (4), the court concludes that the claim should not be continued.[172]

22.86 Section 264(4)(c) gives the court power to adjourn the permission application. An adjournment may be appropriate: (i) to allow the company to seek authorization or ratification of the wrong doing,[173] (ii) to enable the board to reconsider its position in relation to a claim which the court has decided could be pursued,[174] (iii) to await the outcome of related proceedings,[175] or (iv) to enable the parties to reach a settlement.

(4) Change of carriage of claim

Permission to take over company's claim by members

22.87 If the company has brought a claim against a director, there should be no reason for a member to have to resort to a derivative claim. However, sometimes it may be necessary, for example where the directors have caused the company to institute the claim in order to frustrate the member and prevent a successful claim being brought,[176] or where a change of control in the company results in the board wanting to discontinue the claim. Section 262 deals with the circumstances in which a member may take over a claim initiated by the company. By s 262(1), it applies where: '(a) a company has brought a claim, and (b) the cause of action on which the claim is based could be pursued as a derivative claim under [Part 11]'.[177]

22.88 By s 262(2) a member may apply to court for permission to continue the claim as a derivative claim on the ground that:

  (a) the manner in which the company commenced or continued the claim amounts to an abuse of the process of the court,
  (b) the company has failed to prosecute the claim diligently, and
  (c) it is appropriate for the member to continue the claim as a derivative claim.

22.89 Section 262(3)–(5) repeats the provisions of s 261(2)–(4). Accordingly, the application to the court is treated in the same way as if the member was applying from the outset to bring a derivative claim under s 261. The same two-stage process applies. CPR 19.9B applies to permission applications under s 262(1) the provisions of CPR19.9A, except for paras (1),

---

[171] See eg *Stimpson v Southern Private Landlords Association* [2010] BCC 387 at para 40; *Iesini v Westrip Holdings Ltd* [2011] 1 BCLC 498 as to all claims apart from the trust claim (paras 102, 104, 111, 135); *Langley Ward Ltd v Trevor* [2011] EWHC 1893 (Ch) as to some of the claims.

[172] See eg *Mission Capital plc v Sinclair* [2010] 1 BCLC 304; *Franbar Holdings Ltd v Patel* [2009] 1 BCLC 1; *Kleanthous v Paphitis* [2012] BCC 676.

[173] Cf the guidance given by the Court of Appeal in *Prudential Assurance Co Ltd v Newman Industries Ltd (No 2)* [1982] Ch 204, 222, CA.

[174] *Iesini v Westrip Holdings Ltd* [2011] 1 BCLC 498 at paras 107–10, 135.

[175] *Fanmailuk.com Ltd v Cooper* [2008] BCC 877.

[176] See Law Com No 246 at para 6.63. The Law Commission considered that any such action on the part of the directors would amount to an abuse of the process of the court for the purposes of the new rule.

[177] There is no equivalent provision for a company seeking to take over a claim commenced by a member, since the company always has this right: 679 HL Official Report (5th Series) col GC34 (27 February 2006).

(2), (4)(b), and para (12)(b) so far as it applies to the claim form and references in rule 19.9A are to be read as references to the person who seeks to take over the claim.

The effect is that even if the requirements of s 262(2) are met, the member may still be pre- **22.90**
cluded from taking over the claim if it cannot satisfy the court that permission would have been granted if the claim had originally been brought as a derivative action. That interpretation is also borne out by the wording of s 262(1)(b): 'the cause of action on which the claim is based could be pursued as a derivative claim under this Chapter'.

Permission to take over derivative claim brought by another member

In a similar vein, s 264 deals with the circumstances in which a member may take over a **22.91**
claim already commenced by another member. By s 264(1) this will extend to the situation where 'a member of a company ("the claimant"): (a) has brought a derivative claim; (b) has continued as a derivative claim a claim brought by the company; or (c) has continued a derivative claim under this section'. The grounds upon which the member may seek to take over the claim and the attendant procedure are set out in s 264(2) and (3), and are the same as those set out for the taking over of an action commenced by the company under s 262. CPR 19.9B applies to permission applications under s 264(1) the provisions of CPR19.9A in the same way as it does to permission applications under s 262(1) (paragraph 22.89 above). The court's powers under s 264(5) are the same as under s 261(4).

There is one significant difference between ss 262 and 264. The court is not, when proceeding **22.92**
under s 264, formally required to take the additional step of exercising its discretion under s 263. Section 263 does not refer to s 264, presumably because s 264 assumes that the original claimant has already obtained permission to continue under s 263. However, s 264(1) applies where a member has *brought* a derivative claim and this may simply mean that the member has instituted the claim. It is therefore possible to invoke the s 264 procedure before the original claimant obtained permission. This might be appropriate if a limitation issue was relevant.

(5) Whether permission must be refused

Section 263 sets out the criteria to which the court should have regard in determining leave on **22.93**
a ss 261 or 262 application. Two types of criteria are stipulated: (i) those laid out in s 263(2) which *require* the court to refuse leave to commence or continue the claim, and (ii) those set out in s 263(3) which contain a list of factors the court must take into account if it does not refuse permission under s 263(2). This prescription of the substantive criteria according to which a claim may be brought is an important innovation. By s 263(5)–(7) the Secretary of State is given power to alter or add to the circumstances in s 263(2) and the matters in s 263(3).

The factors in s 263(2) thus constitute an absolute bar to the court giving permission to con- **22.94**
tinue the derivative claim. By sub-s (2), permission must be refused if the court is satisfied:

    (a) that a person acting in accordance with section 172 (duty to promote the success of the company) would not seek to continue the claim, or

    (b) where the cause of action arises from an act or omission that is yet to occur, that the act or omission has been authorised by the company,[178] or

---

[178] ie whoever has the right to decide matters for the company, be they directors or members; see 679 HL Official Report (5th Series) col GC29 (27 February 2006).

    (c) where the cause of action arises from an act or omission that has already occurred, that the
        act or omission—

        (i) was authorised by the company before it occurred, or

        (ii) has been ratified by the company since it occurred.

Strength of the claim

22.95 One notable omission from the matters mentioned in s 263(2) and (3) is a requirement that the claimant's claim and evidence should disclose a prima facie case that the company is entitled to the relief claimed.[179] But as Lewison J noted in *Iesini v Westrip Holdings Ltd*,[180] doing the best it can on the material before it 'the court will have to form a view on the strength of the claim in order properly to consider the requirements of s 263(2)(a) and 263(3)(b)'. In fact he considered that something more than a prima facie case was required. This reflects the judgment of Warren J in *Airey v Cordell* (a common law case),[181] when he found that satisfying the hypothetical reasonable director test was a higher threshold than disclosing a prima facie case on the merits.

22.96 In *Stainer v Lee*[182] Roth J noted that the court might revise its view on the prima facie case issue after it had received evidence and argument from the respondents. In remarks more directed towards s 263(3)(b) than s 263(2)(a), Roth J went on to express the view that, rather than a particular standard of proof requiring to be satisfied, the court should simply consider the range of factors considered on the application to reach 'an overall view' and the evaluation should not be 'mechanistic'.

22.97 In subsequent cases, a less strict approach has been adopted in respect of the importance of the merits of the claim. In *Kleanthous v Paphitis*[183] Newey J said that 'the Court can potentially grant permission for a derivative claim to be continued without being satisfied that there is a strong case. The merits of the claim will be relevant to whether permission should be given, but there is no set threshold.' In *Certain Limited Partners in Henderson PFI Secondary Fund II LP v Henderson PFI Secondary Fund II LLP*,[184] Cooke J considered that 'in the context of a preliminary issue of the kind with which I am concerned, merits can play little part unless the merits are very strongly in favour of one party or the other. If the claimant had no realistic prospects of success, it could be said that there were no special circumstances which would justify the bringing of the derivative claim. If the merits were strongly in favour of the claimant, this would be a factor forming part of the assessment of special circumstances and the root question of whether injustice would be caused if no derivative claim was allowed.'

22.98 While it is clear that nothing in s 263 requires the claimant to satisfy the court that the claim is a strong one, it is inherent in Lewison J's judgment in the *Iesini* case that the claimant

---

[179] One of the requirements stated by the Court of Appeal in *Prudential Assurance Co Ltd v Newman Industries Ltd* [1982] Ch 204, 221, 222, CA.

[180] [2011] 1 BCLC 498 at para 79. Followed by Proudman J in *Kiani v Cooper* [2010] 2 BCLC 427 at paras 13, 14, 31, 35, where there was a strong breach of duty claim, which had not been answered.

[181] [2007] BCC 785 at paras 70, 75, 76. See para 22.35 above.

[182] [2011] 1 BCLC 537 at para 29; followed in *Hughes v Weiss* [2012] EWHC 2363 (Ch) at para 33. The same approach was taken in relation to s 268(2)(b), the Scottish equivalent of s 263(3)(b), in *Wishart, Petitioner* [2010] BCC 161 at paras 39–40, per Lord Reed.

[183] *Kleanthous v Paphitis* [2012] BCC 676 at paras 39–42.

[184] [2013] QB 934 at para 37.

should at the least satisfy the court, on the basis of the material before it, that there is a prima facie case that the company is entitled to the relief claimed, namely that the claim has a real prospect of success and is not fanciful or speculative.[185]

The s 172 test

By s 263(2)(a) the court must dismiss the claim if it is satisfied that a person acting in accord- **22.99** ance with s 172 would not seek to continue the claim. By s 172 a director must act in the way he considers, in good faith, would be most likely to promote the success of the company for the benefit of its members as a whole.[186] This test embodies in substance the hypotheti-cal reasonable independent board test, first stated by Buckley LJ in *Wallersteiner v Moir (No 2)*[187] and applied to common law permission applications in *Mumbray v Lapper*[188] and *Airey v Cordell*.[189] As discussed in more detail in Chapter 12 above, the duty in s 172 is not solely subjective, but involves a requirement for the director to act rationally.[190] Buckley LJ's test included both a requirement of reasonableness and the exercise of the appropriate standard of care.

Before a hypothetical director can decide whether continuing a claim is most likely to pro- **22.100** mote the success of the company, he would at the very least be expected to investigate the claim with due skill, care, and diligence and take legal advice about its prospects of success. He would also consider a range of other factors, as mentioned in the next paragraph. In rela-tion to assessing the strength of the claim on the permission application, the court is as well placed as the hypothetical director in that it has the benefit of the evidence and arguments put before it by the parties.

The application of the s 172 test is not limited to a consideration of the merits of the claim, **22.101** but also takes into account a range of factors applicable to the particular circumstances of the company.[191] In *Iesini v Westrip Holdings Ltd* Lewison J outlined some of the matters that an independent director would take into account when exercising his duty under s 172 and which are relevant to s 263(2)(a):[192]

> the size of the claim; the strength of the claim; the cost of the proceedings; the company's ability to fund the proceedings; the ability of the potential defendants to satisfy a judgment;

---

[185] See the position at common law as described in paras 22.29–22.31 above. This appears to be consistent with the recommendation of the Law Commission in *Shareholder Remedies* (No 246, October 1997), which at paras 6.71 and 6.72 recommended that there should be no threshold test on the merits, but said 'it would clearly be wrong for the court to allow an obviously hopeless case to proceed'. In that context the footnote referred to the proposed CPR rule by which the court would have power to dismiss a claim that had no realistic prospect of success (ie the present summary judgment test).

[186] Proposals to draft this requirement in terms merely of a director acting in good faith in what he consid-ers to be in the interests of the company were rejected (679 HL Official Report (5th Series) cols GC23–4 (27 February 2006)). The scope of the duty is modified where the purposes of the company consist of or include purposes other than the benefit of its members; see *Stimpson v Southern Private Landlords Association* [2010] BCC 387, 398–9, a case concerning a derivative claim.

[187] [1975] QB 373, 404A–B, CA.

[188] [2005] BCC 990 at para 5.

[189] [2007] BCC 785 at para 75.

[190] See paras 12.15 *et seq* above.

[191] A test which operates by reference to the decision-making of a hypothetical individual will inevitably give rise to much debate between the parties to the claim. See Peters, 'Hypothesizing the Hypothetical Director: An Unpredictable Opponent', *Law Society Gazette*, 30 July 2009.

[192] [2011] 1 BCLC 498 at para 85. This list of factors derives from the factors listed by William Trower QC in *Franbar Holdings Ltd v Patel* [2009] 1 BCLC 1 at para 36, with reference to s 263(3)(b).

the impact on the company if it lost the claim and had to pay not only its own costs but the defendant's as well; any disruption to the company's activities while the claim is pursued; whether the prosecution of the claim would damage the company in other ways (eg by losing the services of a valuable employee or alienating a key supplier or customer) and so on. The weighing of all these considerations is essentially a commercial decision, which the court is ill-equipped to take, except in a clear case.

Different factors, or a differently balanced range of factors, may be relevant if the company is not a trading company or is a non-profit making company.[193]

22.102   The court also recognizes that, in weighing these or other relevant factors, directors may reach different tactical decisions. Some may wish to investigate the claim further, while others would consider it beneficial to start proceedings straight away or to continue the claim at least for the time being.[194]

22.103   In these circumstances the court will only refuse permission under s 263(2)(a) if it is satisfied that no director acting in accordance with s 172 would seek to continue the claim and that if some directors would and others would not seek to continue the claim the case is one for the application of s 263(3)(b).[195] In other words, s 263(2)(a) only applies if continuing the claim is outside the range of reasonable decisions an independent director might take. Examples of such cases are where the claim is extremely weak,[196] particularly where it is against a director who did not personally benefit,[197] or where it has costs consequences which would be damaging to the company.[198] Nor would such a director pursue a derivative claim which served no useful purpose, because it was duplicative of existing proceedings.[199]

Authorization or ratification by the company

22.104   This ground for refusing permission should be straightforward to apply, since the court simply has to see if the act or omission giving rise to the cause of action has been validly authorized or ratified.[200] The provisions of s 263(2)(b) and (c) reflect established principles, which the Law Commission recommended should not be changed.[201] The rule in *Foss v Harbottle* was premised on the ratifiability of the wrongful act or omission: ratifiability by simple majority remains fundamental. If the act has been duly authorized or ratified, it no longer

---

[193] *Stimpson v Southern Private Landlords Association* [2010] BCC 387 at para 39.

[194] *Franbar Holdings Ltd v Patel* [2009] 1 BCLC 1 at para 30, where William Trower QC observed that:

[d]irectors are often in the position of having to make what is no more than a partially informed decision on whether or not the institution of legal proceedings is appropriate, without having a very clear idea of how the proceedings will turn out. Some directors might wish to spend more time investigating and strengthening the company's case before issuing process, while others would wish to press on with proceedings straight away; in a case such as this one, both approaches would be entirely appropriate.

Also see *Iesini v Westrip Holdings Ltd* [2011] 1 BCLC 498 at para 85; *Stainer v Lee* [2011] 1 BCLC 537 at para 27.

[195] *Iesini v Westrip Holdings Ltd* [2011] 1 BCLC 498 at para 86, agreeing with *Airey v Cordell* [2007] BCC 785 at para 75; *Franbar Holdings Ltd v Patel* [2009] 1 BCLC 1 at para 30. Followed in *Langley Ward Ltd v Trevor* [2011] EWHC 1893 (Ch) at para 9; *Kleanthous v Paphitis* [2012] BCC 676 at para 38.

[196] *Iesini v Westrip Holdings Ltd* [2011] 1 BCLC 498 at para 102; *Langley Ward Ltd v Trevor* [2011] EWHC 1893 (Ch); *Brannigan v Style* [2016] EWHC 512 (Ch) (difficult claim and not cost effective).

[197] *Kleanthous v Paphitis* [2012] BCC 676 at para 70.

[198] *Stimpson v Southern Private Landlords Association* [2010] BCC 387.

[199] *Mission Capital plc v Sinclair* [2010] 1 BCLC 304 at para 41.

[200] *Singh v Singh* [2014] 1 BCLC 649 at para 39; *Brannigan v Style* [2016] EWHC 512 (Ch).

[201] See Law Com No 246 at 6.85–6.86.

constitutes a wrong on the part of the director. Either the director never was liable to the company or his liability is extinguished.[202] If the act or omission has not yet been authorized or ratified, but might be, the court will consider that as a discretionary factor under s 263(3) (c) and (d) and may adjourn the permission application under ss 261(4)(c) or 262(5)(c).

22.105 Two points should be noted in relation to ratification and authorization. The first is that the act or omission must be one capable of being authorized or ratified by the members. Section 239(7) recognizes that some acts or omissions are incapable of being ratified, but, as discussed in Chapter 20, Section D above, there are few acts or omissions affecting members' interests that are incapable of being ratified. Acts which are beyond the power of the company cannot be ratified. Since most companies have unrestricted objects, the acts which are incapable of ratification are likely to be limited to acts which are unlawful (eg unlawful distributions or financial assistance). The other acts which are incapable of ratification concern transactions which prejudice creditors. But if the company is insolvent or on the verge of insolvency a member would have difficulty in showing a tangible interest in pursuing the derivative claim and it might be dismissed on that ground.[203]

22.106 The second point to note is a difference between authorization and ratification. Section 180(4)(a) preserves the rule of law under which the company may give authority, specifically or generally, for anything to be done or omitted by the directors or any of them, that would otherwise be a breach of duty. If there is such authorization there could be no breach of duty and a derivative claim alleging breach of duty could not succeed. In relation to authorization, there is no restriction on the voting rights of any member. Where the act or omission has occurred without prior authorization, so that the directors require the protection of ratification, s 239(3) and (4) prevents the director and members connected with him from voting.[204] If a member is prevented from bringing a derivative claim by reason of prior authorization, he may be able to obtain relief by application under Part 30.[205]

(6) Whether permission should be given: discretionary factors

22.107 Even where the claim is not prohibited by s 263(2), a discretion still resides in the court to refuse permission under s 263(3). A non-exhaustive list of factors is set out in that subsection. By s 263(3), in considering *whether to* give permission the court must take into account, '*in particular*':

(a) whether the member is acting in good faith in seeking to continue the claim;
(b) the importance that a person acting in accordance with section 172 (duty to promote the success of the company) would attach to continuing it;
(c) where the cause of action results from an act or omission that is yet to occur, whether the act or omission could be, and in the circumstances would be likely to be—
    (i) authorised by the company before it occurs, or
    (ii) ratified by the company after it occurs;

---

[202] For authorization and disclosure of conflicts of interest under ss 175, 177, 182, see Chs 15 and 17 above; for authorization generally in accordance with s 180(4), see Ch 10, Section D above; for ratification of acts of directors under s 239, see Ch 20, Section D above.

[203] Cf *Re Rica Goldwashing Co* (1879) 11 Ch D 36, 42, 43 CA; *Cavendish-Bentinck v Fenn* (1887) 12 App Cas 652, HL; *Deloitte & Touche v Johnson* [1999] 1 WLR 1605, PC.

[204] This changes the law as stated in cases such as *MacDougall v Gardiner* (1875) 1 Ch D 13, 25, CA; *North West Transport Co Ltd v Beatty* (1887) 12 AC 589, PC; *Burland v Earle* [1902] AC 83, 93–4, PC.

[205] The aggrieved member could also consider applying to restrain an act which is beyond the powers of the directors: 2006 Act, s 40(4).

(d) where the cause of action arises from an act or omission that has already occurred, whether the act or omission could, and in the circumstances would be likely to be, ratified by the company;

(e) whether the company has decided not to pursue the claim;

(f) whether the act or omission in respect of which the claim is brought gives rise to a cause of action that the member could pursue in his own right rather than on behalf of the company.

The factors are non-exhaustive and, in considering whether a prima facie case is established, the court is bound to have regard to any other relevant considerations.[206]

22.108   Section 263(4) requires the court to have regard to the views of independent members when deciding whether to grant leave. It provides:

> In considering whether to give permission … the court shall have particular regard to any evidence before it as to the views of members of the company who have no personal interest, direct or indirect, in the matter.[207]

The good faith of the member

22.109   The good faith requirement in s 263(3)(a) is designed to prevent frivolous, vexatious, or abusive claims from being brought. In most cases the court will be satisfied as to the claimant's good faith where the claim appears to have merit. The problem arises where it is alleged that the claim is being advanced to pursue personal interests of the member as distinct from the company. It is suggested that provided that a successful outcome would bring benefits to the company, the claim should not be excluded on good faith grounds. If the member brings a derivative claim for the benefit of the company, he will not be disqualified from doing so if there are other benefits which he will derive from the claim.[208] The Law Commission did not intend that an interest in the commercial benefits of litigation should rule out a claim if the court otherwise considers that it is in the company's interests.[209]

22.110   Under the common law the member had to satisfy the court that he was acting in good faith, pursuing the interests of the company and not some personal agenda,[210] and the defendant could raise against the claimant any defence which could have been raised had the action been one brought by the shareholder personally.[211] A person could be prevented from bringing a derivative claim if he participated in the wrong of which he complained, and it would count against a member if the action was brought to escape the consequences of his own misdeeds.[212] Accordingly, under the new law, the court may refuse to allow a claim to proceed

---

[206] *Stimpson v Southern Private Landlords Association* [2010] BCC 387 at para 46 (claimant could requisition EGM to consider replacing the board); *Langley Ward Ltd v Trevor* [2011] EWHC 1893 (Ch) at paras 13–20 (liquidation).

[207] As with certain other requirements in Part 11, this provision was added to the bill during its passage through the House of Lords with a view to deterring vexatious claims. See 681 HL Official Report (5th series) cols 883–4 (9 May 2006).

[208] *Iesini v Westrip Holdings Ltd* [2011] 1 BCLC 498 at para 121; *Hughes v Weiss* [2012] EWHC 2363 (Ch) at para 47. In *Iesini v Westrip Holdings,* Lewison J concluded that the dominant purpose of the action was to benefit the company, and it could not be said that, but for the collateral purposes, the claim would not have been brought at all. The claim was consequently judged to have been brought in good faith.

[209] See Law Com No 246 at para 6.76.

[210] *Barrett v Duckett* [1995] 1 BCLC 243, 250, CA.

[211] *Nurcombe v Nurcombe* [1985] 1 WLR 370, CA.

[212] *Nurcombe v Nurcombe* (n 211 above); *Central Estates (Belgravia) Ltd v Woolgar* [1972] 1 QB 48.

where the behaviour of the minority shareholder would render it inequitable for the claim to succeed (ie he has not come to court with 'clean hands').[213]

Experience of recent cases suggests that it will be difficult to persuade the court to refuse **22.111** permission on the ground of the claimant's bad faith or ulterior motive.[214] It may be more profitable for defendants to focus their fire on alternative remedies within s 263(3)(f).

The importance a director would attach to continuing the claim

Section 263(3)(b) requires the court to take into account the importance that a person (a **22.112** director) acting in accordance with s 172 (duty to promote the success of the company) would attach to continuing the claim. This factor is to be considered on the footing that the court has not been satisfied under s 263(2)(a), negatively, that such a person would not seek to continue the claim. Section 263(3)(b) therefore enables the court to give some weight, when exercising its discretion under the section, to the broader commercial considerations for and against continuing the claim.[215]

The court will look again at the factors that may have been considered in relation to s 263(2) **22.113** (a) (paragraph 22.101 above) and may find, for example that the weight attached to the benefit to the company and its members as a whole is reduced because the claim is a weak one or insufficiently strong to outweigh other factors, such as disruption and damage to the business and the availability of an alternative remedy.[216] On the other hand where the case is stronger and the potential benefits from pursuing the claim to the company and its members as a whole are clearer, there will be more reason for the court to give permission to continue the claim.[217] The fact that the company is dormant or no longer trading will not of itself result in the refusal of permission to continue a derivative claim, but it may mean that certain of the factors that will often be important under s 172 do not apply.[218]

---

[213] *Stimpson v Southern Private Landlords Association* [2010] BCC 387 at para 44; *Iesini v Westrip Holdings Ltd* [2011] 1 BCLC 498 at para 122.

[214] *Mission Capital plc v Sinclair* [2010] 1 BCLC 304 at para 42; *Franbar Holdings Ltd v Patel* [2009] 1 BCLC 1 at paras 32–4; *Kiani v Cooper* [2010] 2 BCLC 427 at para 36; *Stainer v Lee* [2011] 1 BCLC 537 at para 49; *Hughes v Weiss* [2012] EWHC 2363 (Ch) at para 47; *Cullen Investments Ltd v Brown* [2015] BCC 539 at para 53. However, in *Singh v Singh* [2014] 1 BCLC 649, in which the claim failed on the ground of authorization or ratification of the relevant conduct, an alternative reason for the refusal of permission was that the real motivation of the claimant was his animosity towards the defendant, rather than genuinely seeking to promote the best interests of the company (para 44).

[215] In *Developing the Framework*, the CLR suggested that the best test of whether the action should proceed was whether the minority's views were the best available evidence of what was in the best interests of the company. Reactions to that proposal were mixed. Thus the CLR went on to suggest conferring on the court a discretion to consider all the circumstances in determining whether a derivative action should proceed, and in so doing pay particular regard to the issue of whether it was in the best interests of the company in accordance with the criterion set out in the principles on directors' duties (CLR: *Final Report* at para 7.48). In practice, the considerations under s 263(3)(b) and (4) may well be the same; cf the statement of Lord Goldsmith: 'What is success? The starting point is that it is essentially for the members of the company to define the objective they wish to achieve. Success means what the members collectively want the company to achieve.' (678 HL Official Report (5th series) col GC255 (6 February 2006)).

[216] *Mission Capital plc v Sinclair* [2010] 1 BCLC 304 at para 43 (alleged damage speculative); *Franbar Holdings Ltd v Patel* [2009] 1 BCLC 1 at paras 35–7 (where a director would take into account that an offer had been made to buy out the minority); *Kleanthous v Paphitis* [2012] BCC 676 at paras 71–3, 85 (pursuit of claim likely to lead loss of directors and other adverse commercial consequences).

[217] *Kiani v Cooper* [2010] 2 BCLC 427 at paras 43–5; *Stainer v Lee* [2011] 1 BCLC 537 at paras 29 and 48. Also see the Scottish case *Wishart, Petitioner* [2010] BCC 161 at paras 44–6, per Lord Reed.

[218] *Hughes v Weiss* [2012] EWHC 2363 (Ch) at paras 49–55; *Cullen Investments Ltd v Brown* [2015] BCC 539 at paras 54–5. In *Hughes v Weiss* His Honour Judge Keyser QC considered that the fact that the company

22.114 If the court can only be confident that the hypothetical director would decide to continue the proceedings, until the stage of disclosure in the proceedings only, then the grant of permission will be limited to that extent.[219]

Authorization or ratification by the company

22.115 Where there has not been authorization or ratification so as to constitute an absolute bar to continuance of the claim under s 263(2)(b) or (c), the court is required by s 263(3)(c) and (d) to consider how, on the evidence before it, the members would be likely to vote, if asked to authorize or ratify the act or omission. As to that, the court may prefer to adjourn the permission application to enable the matter to be put to the vote of the members. The subsections presuppose that any such resolution of the members to authorize or ratify the conduct complained of would be valid[220] and, as discussed in paragraph 22.105 above, certain conduct is incapable of being ratified.

22.116 Even if satisfied that the members would authorize or ratify the act or omission, the court retains a discretion to permit the claim to continue. It might take the view that pursuit of the claim plainly furthered the interests of the company and that the majority of members would be acting irrationally in voting against it. Also the court might take the view that a majority against continuing the claim would be made up of persons favouring the defendant director and hostile to the claimant, even though not sufficiently connected to the director to have their votes excluded under s 239(3) and (4) (eg the director's brothers and sisters).

Decision of the company not to pursue the claim

22.117 The court is required by s 263(3)(e) to take account of any decision by the company not to pursue the claim. Such a decision may have been taken by the board or by resolution of the members.

22.118 If the directors have decided that the company should not pursue the claim, the court may take the view that they are in a better position than the court to determine what would best satisfy the company's commercial interests.[221] In considering that decision the court would have regard to the independence, or otherwise, of the directors who took the decision and the reasons why they took it.[222] If the directors had taken the decision on the basis of professional advice, the court is likely to attach considerable weight to their decision.[223] If possible an independent committee of directors should be appointed to consider and respond to the claim. If the decision had been taken some time previously and had not been challenged, that might be a factor against permitting the claim to continue.

---

in that case was not to resume trading was not a compelling objection to the conclusion that a person acting in accordance with s 172 would attach importance to continuing the proceedings, and he considered that the fair distribution of the benefits of litigation to the company's members was within the scope of s 172 (para 54). In *Cullen Investments v Brown* it was considered that the question which the hypothetical director would ask is whether and to what extent the company's funds available for distribution to its members were likely to be enhanced or diminished by continuing the litigation (para 55).

[219] Cf *Kiani v Cooper* [2010] 2 BCLC 427 at para 45.
[220] *Franbar Holding Ltd v Patel* [2009] 1 BCLC 1 at paras 38–47.
[221] 679 HL Official Report (5th series) col GC29 (27 February 2006). See *Kleanthous v Paphitis* [2012] BCC 676 at paras 74–5.
[222] Law Com No 246 at para 6.87.
[223] *Kleanthous v Paphitis* [2012] BCC 676 at paras 74–5.

Similar considerations apply to a decision by the members that the company should not pursue the claim. More weight would be given to such a decision than to a decision by the directors, at least where the decision was supported by independent members. It should be noted that such a decision is different from a decision to authorize or ratify the act or omission. The members can decide or approve a board decision that the company should not pursue the claim even though the act or omission was incapable of being ratified. The decision not to pursue the claim does not affect the liability of the director to the company until the claim becomes barred by limitation.

22.119

Alternative remedy

Section 263(3)(f) enables the court to stop a derivative claim where the member has a personal claim that could be pursued without involving the company.[224] In particular this factor brings into question the interplay between a derivative claim and an unfair prejudice petition under s 994 of the Act. It is clear that the availability of an alternative remedy is not an absolute bar to granting permission to continue the derivative claim,[225] although it will be an important factor considered by the court in deciding whether to grant permission.[226] Where it is clear that the claimant could have arranged for the company to commence proceedings in its own right against the defendant, by reason of the terms of a shareholders' agreement operating between the parties, this may be decisive in causing the court to refuse permission.[227] However, where the claimant's extant personal proceedings against the defendant under a joint venture agreement, founded on identical alleged wrongdoing, might fail for reasons affecting the personal proceedings alone, the subsequent commencement of a derivative claim was held to be a 'conventional response to the risk' that the company and not the claimant may be entitled to the relief claimed.[228]

22.120

---

[224] At common law the availability of an alternative remedy was a discretionary factor for refusing permission; see para 22.43 above. The Law Commission recommended that the court should take into account the availability of alternative remedies, but that their availability should not necessarily be conclusive on the issue of leave: see Law Com No 246 at 6.91. The government resisted an amendment which would have required the court to address the question whether an alternative remedy exists. This was on the basis that: (i) an offer to buy the claimant's shares is not an appropriate remedy in the circumstances of a derivative claim; and (ii) such a provision could encourage vulture funds to tell companies that they must either buy them out or face a possible derivative claim. See further 682 HL Official Report (5th series) cols 726–8 (23 May 2006).

[225] *Iesini v Westrip Holdings Ltd* [2011] 1 BCLC 498 at paras 123–6; *Kiani v Cooper* [2010] 2 BCLC 427 at paras 39–41; *Stainer v Lee* [2011] 1 BCLC 537 at paras 50–52; *Parry v Bartlett* [2011] EWHC 3146 (Ch) at para 96; *Phillips v Fryer* [2013] BCC 176 at paras 9–24; *Certain Limited Partners in Henderson PFI Secondary Fund II LP v Henderson PFI Secondary Fund II LLP* [2013] QB 934 at para 39; *Cullen Investments Ltd v Brown* [2015] BCC 539 at paras 58–61.

[226] See *Mission Capital Plc v Sinclair* [2010] 1 BCLC 304; *Franbar Holdings Ltd v Patel* [2009] 1 BCLC 1; *Wishart, Petitioner* [2010] BCC 161 at paras 44–6; *Ritchie v Union of Construction, Allied Trades and Technicians* [2011] EWHC 3613 (Ch) at para 61; *Kleanthous v Paphitis* [2012] BCC 676 at paras 80–1; *Phillips v Fryer* [2013] BCC 176 at paras 9–24; *Certain Limited Partners in Henderson PFI Secondary Fund II LP v Henderson PFI Secondary Fund II LLP* [2013] QB 934 at para 39; *Cullen Investments Ltd v Brown* [2015] BCC 539 at paras 58–61.

[227] *Bamford v Harvey* [2013] Bus LR 589 at paras 6–32. In that case, Roth J declined to grant permission on this basis, but was careful to make clear that the foundation for this decision was not that wrongdoer control of the company was an absolute condition for a derivative claim. He said: 'It is not elevating "wrongdoer control" to a preclusive condition for the court to hold that when proceedings clearly can be brought in the name of the company and there is no objection raised on that ground, they should be brought in the name of the company. The first "guiding principle" set out by the Law Commission that is quoted in *Cinematic Finance Ltd v Ryder* [2012] BCC 797, para 12, remains applicable.' See para 22.49 above.

[228] *Cullen Investments Ltd v Brown* [2015] BCC 539 at paras 58–61.

22.121 Section 263(3)(f) is engaged where the act or omission which gives rise to the breach of duty claim also gives rise to a claim for unfair prejudice, even though the respondents to the two proceedings might be different.[229] The court has regarded the availability of an unfair prejudice claim as a powerful reason for refusing permission to continue the derivative claim where the court found that the claimant could achieve all that it could properly want through a s 994 petition[230] and, even more so, where most of the fruits of a successful derivative claim would be for the benefit of the defendants as shareholders.[231] Liquidation of the company may also be regarded as the appropriate alternative remedy.[232] On the other hand the availability of relief under s 994 has not been considered to be a compelling reason for refusing permission to continue a derivative claim where a s 994 petition would be an indirect or less satisfactory means of obtaining relief from which the claimant would benefit.[233]

The views of independent members

22.122 The requirement in s 263(4) applies whether or not the conduct giving rise to the derivative claim has been or might be authorized or ratified or whether the company has decided not to pursue the claim.[234] Section 263(4) applies even though the conduct cannot be validly authorized or ratified. As such, it builds upon the decision of Knox J in *Smith v Croft (No 2)*,[235] who said that if the bringing of proceedings is prevented by an expression of the corporate will of the company by an appropriate independent organ, then the plaintiff is not improperly but properly prevented. He did not consider that a just result would be achieved by a single minority shareholder having the right to involve a company in a derivative action

---

[229] *Franbar Holdings Ltd v Patel* [2009] 1 BCLC 1 at para 50.

[230] *Mission Capital plc v Sinclair* [2010] 1 BCLC 304 at para 46; *Franbar Holdings Ltd v Patel* [2009] 1 BCLC 1 at paras 49–54; *Iesini v Westrip Holdings Ltd* [2011] 1 BCLC 498 at paras 123–6; *Kleanthous v Paphitis* [2012] BCC 676 at paras 76–81, 85. In both *Franbar* and *Kleanthous* there was evidence that the claimant was interested in being bought out.

[231] *Kleanthous v Paphitis* [2012] BCC 676 at para 85.

[232] *Langley Ward Ltd v Trevor* [2011] EWHC 1893 (Ch). In that case, the company had 'run its course' and was almost certain to be wound up eventually.

[233] *Kiani v Cooper* [2010] 2 BCLC 427 at paras 39 and 40; *Stainer v Lee* [2011] 1 BCLC 537 at paras 50–2; *Parry v Bartlett* [2012] BCC 700; *Phillips v Fryer* [2013] BCC 176, paras 9–24; *Hughes v Weiss* [2012] EWHC 2363 (Ch) at para 66. In *Kiani v Cooper* and *Stainer v Lee,* the claimant did not want to be bought out and would not obtain permission to bring civil proceedings under s 996(2)(c) until unfair prejudice had been established, which was less satisfactory than pursuing a direct derivative claim. In *Parry v Bartlett* the judge did not consider that a s 994 petition was a realistic alternative remedy where there was a strong prima facie case of breach of duty, which was not ratifiable. In *Phillips v Fryer*, the claimant had already commenced proceedings under s 994 in which he sought, inter alia, an order enabling him to be bought out; in those circumstances, the Deputy Judge considered that the onus was on the claimant to show why he should be permitted to bring a derivative action in addition to the petition (para 18). The issue was treated as a matter of case management, the Deputy Judge being influenced by the fact that there were grounds for making a summary judgment application, being the most effective means of getting the case quickly and economically before the court (para 20). Also see the Scottish case *Wishart, Petitioner* [2010] BCC 161 at paras 44–6, per Lord Reed.

[234] For an illustration of s 263(4) precluding a derivative claim, see *Bridge v Daley* [2015] EWHC 2121 (Ch) at paras 73, 74, and 80 (public limited company, in respect of which the Judge considered that the shareholders required protection from a minor minority individual shareholder seeking to pursue a claim on behalf of the company when the shareholders did not wish the company's assets to be applied for that purpose).

[235] [1988] Ch 114, 166, 183. At p 186 Knox said that votes should be disregarded only if the court is satisfied either that the vote or its equivalent is actually cast with a view to supporting the defendants rather than securing benefit to the company, or that the situation of the person whose vote is considered is such that there is a substantial risk of that happening; further, that the court should not substitute its own opinion but should assess whether the decision-making process is vitiated by being or being likely to be directed to an improper purpose.

if all the other minority shareholders are, for disinterested reasons, satisfied that the proceedings will be productive of more harm than good. The court thus looked to an independent 'majority within the minority' to reach its conclusion on grounds generally thought to advance the company's interests.

Although s 263(4) makes it clear that the views of independent members will carry great weight with the court,[236] there are some problems. The first is one of interpretation. Since all the members of a company have an obvious, financial interest in any claim brought on the company's behalf, 'personal interest' within the meaning of s 263(4) must mean a personal interest, not in the question whether or not to give permission, but in the alleged default etc of the directors out of which the cause of action has arisen.[237] The court must be as satisfied as it can be that such members are not financially interested in the outcome (beyond their interest as shareholders in the company). Secondly, if the claimant is genuinely pursuing a claim for the benefit of members as a whole, should his views be included among those of independent members? Thirdly, it may not be practical to obtain the views of members of a large quoted company on directors' commercial decisions.[238] Fourthly, there may be issues as to whether particular shareholders are 'persons who have no personal interest, direct or indirect, in the matter'. Finally, the court considers views, including the reasons for the views, and does not merely count heads.[239]   **22.123**

Other matters

One factor not mentioned in s 263 is that the company is in or is about to enter liquidation or administration. A member may wish to pursue a derivative claim in these circumstances in the hope that the relief obtained may restore the company to solvency or enable the company to be rescued as a going concern. Under the common law a claim did not lie once the company was in liquidation.[240] It was the impossibility of relief being obtained for the company in any other manner which had originally persuaded the courts to allow derivative claims to be brought. It follows that once the right to bring a claim in the name of the company has passed to an administrator or liquidator, then the premise on which such a claim was allowed disappears.[241] There is no reason to think that under the new Part 11 regime the court would allow a claim to continue if the company was in administration or liquidation (solvent or insolvent) or about to enter into one of those proceedings.[242] If the company is insolvent but not in liquidation or administration, the court might permit a shareholder to   **22.124**

---

[236] See *Stimpson v Southern Private Landlords Association* [2010] BCC 387 at para 42. In that case, at the first hearing of the application for permission to continue the derivative claim, the judge adjourned the matter and directed that a questionnaire be sent to members of the company to elicit their views.

[237] *Iesini v Westrip Holdings Ltd* [2011] 1 BCLC 498 at para 129.

[238] 681 HL Official Report (5th series) col 884 (9 May 2006).

[239] Cf cases on the Insolvency Act, s 190 and its predecessors, such as *Re JD Swain Ltd* [1965] 1 WLR 909, CA.

[240] *Ferguson v Wallbridge* [1935] 3 DLR 66, PC; *Fargo Ltd v Godfroy* [1986] 3 All ER 279; *Barrett v Duckett* [1995] 1 BCLC 243, 250–2, CA.

[241] Insolvency Act, Sch B1, para 60 and Sch 1, para 5 gives the administrator power to bring proceedings in the name of the company. A liquidator has the same power under the Insolvency Act, s 165 and Sch 4, para 4, subject to directions of the court under ss 112 or 167(3) giving conduct to a creditor or member.

[242] See *Cinematic Finance v Ryder* [2012] BCC 797 at para 22 and *Langley Ward Ltd v Trevor* [2011] EWHC 1893 (Ch) at para 20. See also 'Can Derivative Proceedings Be Commenced when a Company Is in Liquidation?' (2008) 21 *Insolvency Intelligence* 49, in which Andrew Keay concludes that the arguments for allowing permission to be given to members in these circumstances are evenly balanced.

bring a derivative claim in order to obtain the benefit of recovering a debt, provided the debt was closely connected to the shareholding.[243]

E. Unauthorized Political Donations or Expenditure

(1) The requirement for authorization by resolution of the members

22.125 The 2006 Act, Part 14, re-enacts the law on the liability of directors to compensate the company for unauthorized political donations. As originally enacted the rationale of these provisions was to regulate conflicts of interest. The government did not consider it acceptable for directors to support political parties that promote policies with which they personally agree, rather than policies that will benefit the company.[244] In October 1998 the Neill Committee (Committee on Standards in Public Life) recommended that a company intending to make a donation (whether in cash or in kind, and including any sponsorship, loans, or transactions at a favourable rate) to a political party or organization should be required to have the prior authority of its shareholders.[245] The government accepted that recommendation. It was implemented principally through the Political Parties, Elections and Referendums Act 2000 (the 'PPER Act'), by inserting a new regime for the control of political donations and expenditure as Part XA of the 1985 Act.

22.126 Part 14 largely restates the provisions of the 1985 Act, Part XA, in a manner consistent with other sections of the Companies Act. Of greatest import for directors are the provisions of s 369, which make directors personally liable for unauthorized political donations and expenditure, and ss 370–3, which enable a shareholder to bring proceedings to enforce that liability. Part 14 makes two changes to provide greater flexibility from the perspective of the company.[246] A holding company may seek authorization in respect of both itself and one or more subsidiaries through a single approval resolution. In addition, the provision preventing subsequent ratification from nullifying a contravention of the 1985 Act, Part XA has been repealed.[247]

22.127 Part 14 governs: (a) political donations made by companies to political parties,[248] to other political organizations,[249] and to independent election candidates;[250] and (b) political expenditure incurred by companies (s 362). In relation to a political party or other political organization, a 'political donation' is defined by reference to the PPER Act, ss 50–2 as anything that in accordance with those sections constitutes a donation for the purposes of

---

[243] *Gamlestaden Fastigheter AB v Baltic Partners Ltd* [2007] 4 All ER 164, PC.

[244] See 678 HL Official Report, cols GC139–40 (1 March 2006).

[245] 678 HL Official Report, cols GC139–40 (1 March 2006). See also the Explanatory Notes at para 611.

[246] See 678 HL Official Report, cols GC139–40 (1 March 2006).

[247] 1985 Act, s 347C(5).

[248] By 2006 Act, s 363(1) a party is a 'political party' if: (a) it is registered under the PPER Act, Part 2; or (b) it carries on, or proposes to carry on, activities for the purposes of or in connection with the participation of the party in any election or elections to public office held in a Member State other than the UK.

[249] By 2006 Act, s 363(2) an organization is a 'political organization' if it carries on, or proposes to carry on, activities that are capable of being reasonably regarded as intended: (a) to affect public support for a political party to which, or an independent election candidate to whom, Part 14 applies; or (b) to influence voters in relation to any national or regional referendum held under the law of the United Kingdom or another Member State.

[250] By 2006 Act, s 363(3) Part 14 applies to an 'independent election candidate' at any election to public office held in the UK or another Member State.

Chapter 1 of Part 4 of the PPER Act (control of donations to registered parties) or would constitute such a donation reading references in those sections to a registered party as references to any political party or other political organization.[251] A similar definition applies to a political donation to an independent election candidate.[252]

In relation to a company, 'political expenditure' means expenditure, not being a political donation incurred by the company on:[253]   **22.128**

    (a) the preparation, publication or dissemination of advertising or other promotional or publicity material—

        (i) of whatever nature, and

        (ii) however published or otherwise disseminated,

        that, at the time of publication or dissemination, is capable of being reasonably regarded as intended to affect public support for a political party or other political organisation, or an independent election candidate; or

    (b) activities on the part of the company that are capable of being reasonably regarded as intended—

        (i) to affect public support for a political party or other political organisation, or an independent election candidate, or

        (ii) to influence voters in relation to any national or regional referendum held under the law of a member State.

A loan at a commercial rate will not fall within the ambit of Part 14.[254] It also seems that payment to a political party for the promotion or advertisement of that company's product or services would not be construed as a political donation if it is genuinely commensurate with the value of the service provided by the political party.[255]   **22.129**

By reason of s 366(1) a company must not: (a) make a political donation to a political party or other political organization, or to an independent election candidate; or (b) incur any political expenditure, unless the donation or expenditure is authorized in accordance with s 366(2)–(5). Section 366(2)(a) institutes the general rule that the donation or expenditure must be authorized, in the case of a company that is not a subsidiary of another company, by a resolution of the members of the company. It must be passed before the donation is made or the expenditure incurred (s 366(5)(b)).[256] Where the donation or expenditure is to   **22.130**

---

[251] 2006 Act, s 364(2)(a). By s 364(2)(b) the PPER Act, s 53 applies, in the same way, for the purpose of determining the value of a donation.

[252] 2006 Act, s 364(3). This is a new provision.

[253] 2006 Act, s 365.

[254] This is because 2006 Act, s 364(4) provides that the PPER Act, ss 50 and 53 (definition of 'donation' and value of donations) shall be treated as if the amendments to those sections made by the Electoral Administration Act 2006 had not been made. Lord McKenzie explained that the amendment ensures that the scope of s 364 is not altered by the changes to the PPER Act made by the Electoral Administration Act: 'In other words, [Part 14] of this Bill will continue to apply only to political donations, which are defined as including loans at a non-commercial rate' (HL Report Stages, col 912, (10 May 2006)).

[255] Lord McKenzie said that the PPER Act, Part IV already recognizes that companies may interact with political parties on commercial terms, and that s 50(2) of that Act states that 'donation' means 'any gift of money or other property' (678 HL Official Report, cols GC145–6 (1 March 2006)).

[256] 2006 Act, s 366(5)(b). During the Company Law Reform Bill's passage through Parliament, there was a debate as to why a director cannot make a political donation or incur political expenditure without a resolution if he considers it would promote the success of the company, or why board authorization is not sufficient. The government responded by emphasizing the nuisance that Part 14 is trying to avoid, namely the need to regulate donations that might be seen to reflect the director's personal viewpoint rather than the interests of the company (678 HL Official Report, col 149 (1 March 2006)).

be made or incurred by a subsidiary company it must be authorized by (i) a resolution of the members of the company and (ii) a resolution of the members of any relevant holding company.[257] However, no resolution is required on the part of a company that is a wholly-owned subsidiary of a UK-registered company.[258] In spite of these provisions it seems that a breach of the rules may be ratified in accordance with the 2006 Act, s 239 and a director may apply for relief under s 1157 (power of court to grant relief in certain cases).[259]

22.131 Section 367 deals with the form of authorizing resolutions. There are four matters to be addressed in the resolution.

(1) It should identify the company or companies to which it relates.[260] A holding company may seek authorization of political donations and expenditure in respect both of itself and one or more of its subsidiaries, including non-wholly-owned subsidiaries, in a single approval resolution. Subsection 367(2) provides that a resolution may be expressed to relate to all companies that are subsidiaries of the company passing the resolution without identifying them individually.[261]

(2) The resolution may authorize the following heads of donations or expenditure: '(a) donations to political parties or independent election candidates; (b) donations to political organizations other than political parties; (c) political expenditure'.[262] The resolution is to be expressed in general terms conforming with sub-s (3) and must not purport to authorize particular donations or expenditure.[263]

(3) The donations or expenditure must be authorized up to a specified amount.[264] A holding company is permitted to state one aggregate amount to cover the total amounts paid or incurred by all the companies for, on the one hand, political donations and, on the other, political expenditure.[265]

(4) The period of authorization must be specified. That is, a period of four years beginning with the date on which it is passed unless the directors determine, or the articles require, that it is to have effect for a shorter period beginning with that date.[266]

22.132 Sections 374–8 set out various exemptions to the requirement for shareholder authorization of political donations and expenditure. In broad terms, those exceptions relate to trade unions, membership of trade associations, all-party parliamentary groups, political

---

[257] 2006 Act, s 366(2)(b). A 'relevant holding company' is a company that, at the time the donation was made or the expenditure was incurred: (a) was a holding company of the company by which the donation was made or the expenditure was incurred, (b) was a UK-registered company, and (c) was not a subsidiary of another UK-registered company (s 366(4)).

[258] 2006 Act, s 366(3).

[259] Lord McKenzie stated: 'It is our intention—and we believe the effect of these clauses—that members will be able to ratify an unauthorised donation or political expenditure and that, in such cases, the director will not continue to have any liability for the failure to obtain authorisation. Similarly [Part 14] will not prevent a director applying for relief under section 1157.' (678 HL Official Report, col 149 (1 March 2006)).

[260] 2006 Act, s 367(1), (2), (4), and (5).

[261] Further, the resolution may relate to companies that are subsidiaries of the company passing the resolution (a) at the time the resolution is passed, or (b) at any time during the period for which the resolution has effect.

[262] 2006 Act, s 367(3), (4).

[263] 2006 Act, s 367(5).

[264] 2006 Act, s 367(6), (7).

[265] 2006 Act, s 367(6), (7). Subsection (3) details the three different heads under which donations or expenditure may be authorized.

[266] 2006 Act, ss 367(6) and 368.

expenditure exempted by order of the Secretary of State, and donations amounting to not more than £5,000 in any 12-month period.

(2) Enforcement of directors' liability

Section 369 provides that where a company has made a political donation or incurred political expenditure without the authorization required by Part 14[267] the directors[268] in default are jointly and severally liable: '(a) to make good to the company the amount of the unauthorised donation or expenditure, with interest,[269] and (b) to compensate the company for any loss or damage sustained by it as a result of the unauthorised donation or expenditure having been made'.

22.133

Pursuant to s 369(3), the directors in default are:

22.134

(a) those who, at the time the unauthorised donation was made or the unauthorised expenditure was incurred, were directors of the company by which the donation was made or the expenditure was incurred, and

(b) where—
  (i) that company was a subsidiary of a relevant holding company, and
  (ii) the directors of the relevant holding company failed to take all reasonable steps to prevent the donation being made or the expenditure incurred,
  the directors of the relevant holding company.[270]

Section 370 gives the right to enforce a director's liability for contravention of Part 14 to an authorized group of members[271] of the company or holding company subject to the controls in s 371. This right is necessary, because the directors responsible for the unauthorized donation or expenditure control the relevant board. It is, however, additional to the company's own right to enforce the liability[272] and to any member's right to bring or continue a derivative claim under Part 11.[273] Section 370(1) provides:

22.135

Any liability of a director under section 369 is enforceable—
(a) in the case of a liability of a director of a company to that company, by proceedings brought under [s 370] in the name of the company by an authorised group of its members;
(b) in the case of a liability of a director of a holding company to a subsidiary, by proceedings brought under [s 370] in the name of the subsidiary by—
  (i) an authorized group of members of the subsidiary, or
  (ii) an authorized group of members of the holding company.

---

[267] 2006 Act, s 369(6) provides that where only part of a donation or expenditure was unauthorized, s 369 applies only to so much of it as was unauthorized.

[268] By s 379(1), this includes a shadow director.

[269] That means interest on the amount of the unauthorized donation or expenditure so far as not made good to the company (a) in respect of the period beginning with the date when the donation was made or the expenditure was incurred, and (b) at such rate as the Secretary of State may prescribe by regulations (s 369(5)); namely Companies (Interest on Unauthorised Political Donation or Expenditure) Regulations 2007 (SI 2007/2242).

[270] 2006 Act, s 369(4) defines 'relevant holding company' in terms that are consistent with earlier sections: 'a company that, at the time the donation was made or the expenditure was incurred—(a) was a holding company of the company by which the donation was made or the expenditure was incurred, (b) was a UK-registered company, and (c) was not a subsidiary of another UK-registered company'.

[271] By s 370(3) an 'authorized group' of members of a company means—'(a) the holders of not less than 5% in nominal value of the company's issued share capital, (b) if the company is not limited by shares, not less than 5% of its members, or (c) no less than 50 of the company's members'.

[272] 2006 Act, s 370(2).

[273] 2006 Act, s 370(5).

22.136 By s 371 the court[274] is afforded a supervisory role. Section 371(1) contains certain procedural formalities to be observed in relation to the giving of notice to the company. Section 371(2) allows any director to apply to the court within 28 days of the giving of the notice for an order directing that the proposed proceedings shall not be brought on one or more of the following grounds:

    (a) that the unauthorized amount has been made good to the company;

    (b) that proceedings to enforce the liability have been brought, and are being pursued with due diligence, by the company;

    (c) that the members proposing to bring proceedings do not constitute an authorized group.

In relation to s 371(2)(b), s 371(3) permits the court as an alternative to direct: (a) that such proceedings may be brought on such terms and conditions as the court thinks fit; and (b) that the proceedings brought by the company (i) shall be discontinued or (ii) may be continued on such terms and conditions as the court thinks fit.

22.137 For the purpose of enforcing the director's liability the authorized group may apply to the court for an order directing the company to indemnify them in respect of their costs.[275] The group is not entitled to be paid any such costs out of the assets of the company except by virtue of such a court order.[276] If no such order is made, the group is entitled to be paid any costs of the proceedings awarded or agreed to be paid to the company and the group is liable to pay any costs awarded or agreed to be paid to a defendant.[277]

22.138 The authorized group of members is bound to need information from the company in order to pursue the claim. Section 373 obliges the company to provide the group 'with all information relating to the subject matter of the proceedings that is in the company's possession or under its control or which is reasonably obtainable by it'.[278]

---

[274] The court is defined by s 1156 as the High Court and also a county court in England and Wales, subject to the power of the Lord Chancellor to redefine the jurisdictions of the county courts for the purposes of the Companies Acts.

[275] 2006 Act, s 372(1) and (2).

[276] 2006 Act, s 372(3).

[277] 2006 Act, s 372(4).

[278] 2006 Act, s 373.

23

MEMBERS' UNFAIR PREJUDICE CLAIMS AND WINDING-UP PETITIONS

Adam Al-Attar

A. Unfair Prejudice Petition

(1) Introduction

The 2006 Act, Part 30, ss 994–9 contains the provisions protecting members from unfair **23.01** prejudice arising from the conduct of the affairs of the company. These provisions came into force on 1 October 2007 and replaced provisions in the 1985 Act, ss 459–61 without change, except for the introduction of the 2006 Act, s 999, which contains new supplementary provisions where the company's constitution is altered. With effect from 6 April 2008 a new s 994(1A) was inserted which provides that the removal from office of the company's auditor should in certain circumstances be treated as unfairly prejudicial to the interests of some part of the members.[1]

Part 30 derives from the 1948 Act, s 210, which was brought into force on the recommenda- **23.02** tion of the Cohen Committee[2] to provide minority shareholders who were being oppressed with an alternative remedy to winding up. Where the conditions of the section were satisfied the court had power to make such order as it thought just, including an order that the minority be bought out at a fair price. Under s 210 the applicant had to show that 'the affairs of the company are being conducted in a manner oppressive to some part of the members (including himself)' and that a winding-up order would not do justice to the minority. The court interpreted the reference to oppression as requiring the applicant to satisfy it that

---

[1] Inserted by reg 42(1) of Statutory Auditors and Third Country Auditors Regs 2007 (SI 2007/3494). See further para 23.59 below.

[2] Report of the Cohen Committee at paras 60, 152, 153.

the majority were exercising their powers in a manner that was 'burdensome, harsh and wrongful'.[3] As a result there were only two reported successful applications under s 210.[4] The Jenkins Committee doubted whether this restrictive interpretation had been intended, preferring the meaning of oppression given by Lord Cooper in *Elder v Elder & Watson Ltd*:[5]

> the essence of the matter seems to be that the conduct complained of should at the lowest involve a visible departure from the standards of fair dealing, and a violation of the conditions of fair play on which every shareholder who entrusts his money to a company is entitled to rely.

The Jenkins Committee recommended that s 210 be replaced by a section based on unfair prejudice and which did not require the applicant to show that winding up would not be a just remedy.[6]

23.03 After some delay the 1980 Act, s 75 was enacted to replace s 210 in the terms recommended by the Jenkins Committee. The provisions of s 75 were re-enacted as the 1985 Act, ss 459–61. These sections and the current Part 30 have been widely used. The availability of a statutory remedy for unfair prejudice is significant for directors, because their conduct of the affairs of the company or their acts or omissions may justify a member's application for relief. Where the petition is well founded the court has wide powers to give relief in ways which may affect the directors. As described in Section A(6) below, the court may, and frequently does, order the respondents (who are usually directors and shareholders) to buy the petitioner's shares at a fair price. The court can also sanction a derivative action and may even short-circuit the process by ordering compensation to be paid or property restored to the company.

(2) The statutory provisions

Petition by company member

23.04 Section 994(1) provides:

> A member of a company may apply to the court[7] by petition for an order under this Part on the ground—
>
> (a) that the company's affairs are being or have been conducted in a manner that is unfairly prejudicial to the interests of members generally or some part of its members (including at least himself),[8] or
>
> (b) that an actual or proposed act or omission of the company (including an act or omission on its behalf) is or would be so prejudicial.

23.05 The normal meaning of 'member of a company' applies to s 994(1). By the 2006 Act, s 112[9] a member of a company is either a subscriber of its memorandum or a person who

---

[3] *Scottish Co-operative Wholesale Society Ltd v Meyer* [1959] AC 324, 342, HL (Sc), per Lord Simonds.

[4] The *Scottish Co-operative* case (n 3 above) and *Re HR Harmer Ltd* [1959] 1 WLR 62, CA. Also see *Re Beladon Silk Ltd* [1965] 1 WLR 1051.

[5] [1952] SC 49, referred to by Hoffmann LJ in *Re Saul D Harrison & Sons Plc* [1995] 1 BCLC 14, 18, CA.

[6] Report of the Jenkins Committee at paras 199–212.

[7] The court is defined by s 1156 as the High Court and also a county court in England and Wales, subject to the power of the Lord Chancellor to redefine the jurisdictions of the county courts for the purposes of the Companies Acts.

[8] With effect from 4 February 1991 the 1989 Act, s 145 and Sch 19, para 11 substituted the phrase 'unfairly prejudicial to the interests of members generally or some part of its members' for the phrase in 1985 Act, s 459 'unfairly prejudicial to the interests of some part of the members' in order to make it clear that the section was engaged where all members were harmed, so avoiding the outcome of *Re a Company (No 00370 of 1987), ex p Glossop* [1988] 1 WLR 1068. In fact *ex p Glossop* was not followed on this point by Peter Gibson J in *Re Sam Weller & Sons Ltd* [1990] Ch 682.

[9] On 1 October 2009, 2006 Act, s 112 replaced 1985 Act, s 22 with minor changes.

agreed to become a member and whose name is entered on its register of members. For this purpose it is sufficient for a person to have consented to become a member, provided his name is entered on the register; a binding contract to become a member is not required.[10] A registered member who has agreed to transfer his shares still has standing to petition,[11] but his interest may be limited to receiving the agreed purchase price.[12] A beneficial owner of shares, who does not come within the provisions of s 994(2), does not have standing to petition.[13] In *Re Starlight Developers Ltd*[14] Briggs J refused to strike out an unfair prejudice petition on the ground that the petitioner was not a registered member, because the petitioner claimed to be entitled to shares by allotment and he was satisfied that the petitioner had a reasonable case for retrospective rectification. Instead Briggs J stayed the petition pending determination of the rectification claim. In *Re I Fit Global Ltd*[15] Roth J made an order for retrospective rectification of the share register at the trial of the petition, where he was satisfied that the petitioner had agreed to become a member, but his name had not been entered on the register because none existed.

Section 994(2) extends the provisions of Part 30 to 'a person who is not a member of a   **23.06** company but to whom shares have been transferred or transmitted by operation of law' in the same way as they apply to a member of a company. A person to whom shares have been transferred is a person to whom a properly executed instrument of transfer has been delivered, but whose name has not been entered on the register of members.[16] A mere agreement that shares would be transferred to the petitioner is not enough to give standing to petition.[17] A trustee in bankruptcy or executor is a person to whom shares have been transmitted by operation of law.[18]

Section 994(3) explains that in s 994 and other provisions of Part 30 applicable to that sec-   **23.07** tion 'company' means a company within the meaning of the 2006 Act and a statutory water company. As with the statutory provisions for derivative claims, s 994 therefore does not apply to foreign companies.[19]

The grounds to support an unfair prejudice petition are discussed in Sections A(3)–(6)   **23.08** below.

---

[10] *Re Nuneaton Borough Association Football Club Ltd* [1989] BCLC 454, CA; *Jaber v Science and Information Technology Ltd* [1992] BCLC 764.

[11] *Atlasview Ltd v Brightview Ltd* [2004] 2 BCLC 191 (where it was considered arguable that the interests of the nominee shareholder included the interests of the beneficial owner); *Re McCarthy Surfacing Ltd* [2006] EWHC 832 (Ch).

[12] *Baker v Potter* [2005] BCC 855 (where specific performance of the sale and purchase agreement was ordered).

[13] *Re a Company (No 007828 of 1985)* (1986) 2 BCC 98,951, 98,954; *Atlasview Ltd v Brightview Ltd* [2004] 2 BCLC 191 at para 31. The position is the same for derivative claims under Part 11 of the 2006 Act (Ch 22 at para 22.52). For standing to present a winding-up petition, see para 23.102 below.

[14] [2007] BCC 929. See also *Re Garage Door Ltd* [1984] 1 WLR 35.

[15] [2014] 2 BCLC 116.

[16] *Re a Company (No 3160 of 1986)* [1986] BCLC 391, 393; *Re McCarthy Surfacing Ltd* [2006] EWHC 832 (Ch).

[17] *Re Quickdome Ltd* [1988] BCLC 370.

[18] *Murray's Judicial Factor* [1992] BCC 596. A person claiming to be the beneficiary of a constructive trust is not a person to whom shares have been transmitted by operation of law: *Re a Company (No 007828 of 1985)* (1986) 2 BCC 98,951, 98,954.

[19] See Ch 22 at para 22.60.

Petition by Secretary of State

23.09 The 2006 Act, s 995(2) gives the Secretary of State power to present a petition for an order under Part 30 on the same grounds of unfair prejudice to members as are set out in s 994(1), where (a) the Secretary of State has received an inspector's report under the 1985 Act, s 437; (b) the Secretary of State has exercised his powers to require documents or information or to enter and search premises under the 1985 Act, ss 447 or 448; (c) the Secretary of State, the FCA, PRA, or the Bank of England has exercised his or its powers under FSMA, Part 11 (information gathering and investigations); or (d) the Secretary of State has received a report from an investigator appointed by him, the FCA, PRA, or the Bank of England under FSMA, Part 11.[20] The Secretary of State may present such a petition in addition to, or instead of, presenting a petition for the winding up of the company.[21] In s 995 'company' means any body corporate that is liable to be wound up under the Insolvency Act.[22] Unlike s 994, the scope of s 995 therefore extends to foreign companies. It is not thought that the Secretary of State has ever used the power now contained in s 995.[23]

Powers of the court under Part 30

23.10 Section 996 provides for the orders that may be made on a well-founded petition under Part 30:

(1) If the court is satisfied that a petition presented under this Part is well founded, it may make such order as it thinks fit for giving relief in respect of the matters complained of.

(2) Without prejudice to the generality of subsection (1), the court's order may—
    (a) regulate the company's affairs in the future;
    (b) require the company—
        (i) to refrain from doing or continuing an act complained of, or
        (ii) to do an act that the petitioner has complained it has omitted to do;
    (c) authorise civil proceedings to be brought in the name and on behalf of the company by such person or persons and on such terms as the court may direct;
    (d) require the company not to make any, or any specified, alterations in its articles without the leave of the court;
    (e) provide for the purchase of the shares of any members of the company by other members or by the company itself and, in the case of a purchase by the company itself, the reduction of the company's capital accordingly.

Relief for unfair prejudice is discussed below in Section A(7) of this chapter. The remedies are not dependent on a case being made for winding up the company. Rather, s 996 gives the court a full range of powers to apply 'an appropriate remedy during the continuing life of the company'.[24]

23.11 Section 998(1) and (2) provides for a copy of an order affecting the company's constitution[25] to be delivered to the Registrar within 14 days from making the order or such longer period as the court may allow. Section 999, which is a new section, adds that (a) the copy of the

---

[20] 2006 Act, s 995(1), as amended by Financial Services Act 2012, s 114(1), Sch 18, Pt 2, paras 110, 120 as from 1 April 2013.
[21] 2006 Act, s 995(3).
[22] 2006 Act, s 995(4).
[23] Or its predecessors, 1980 Act, s 75(2) and (10) and 1985 Act, s 460.
[24] *Re a Company (No 00314 of 1989), ex p Estate Acquisition and Development Ltd* [1991] BCLC 154, 161, per Mummery J; approved by Lord Hoffmann in *O'Neill v Phillips* [1999] 1 WLR 1092, 1100, HL.
[25] By s 17 a company's constitution includes its articles and the resolutions and agreements identified in s 29.

order altering the company's constitution delivered to the Registrar must be accompanied by a copy of the company's articles or the resolution or agreement in question, and (b) every copy of a company's articles issued by it after the order is made must be accompanied by a copy of the order unless the effect of the order has been incorporated into the articles by amendment.[26] If the company makes default in complying with these sections, it and every officer in default commits an offence and is liable for a fine.[27]

Procedure

Section 997 provides for rules to be made under the Insolvency Act, s 411. The rules so made to govern the procedure for Part 30 petitions are the Companies (Unfair Prejudice Applications) Proceedings Rules 2009[28] and, subject to them, the Civil Procedure Rules.[29] Particular points on procedure of concern to directors are discussed in Section A(8) below. These points include applications to strike out or stay the petition and the role of the company. **23.12**

(3) The concept of unfair prejudice

The grounds to support an unfair prejudice petition have been the subject of authoritative explanation by Hoffmann LJ in *Re Saul D Harrison Ltd*[30] and later as Lord Hoffmann in the leading case of *O'Neill v Phillips*.[31] It is convenient to identify the statements of principle made in these cases before turning to the detail of the grounds in Sections A(4) and (6) of this chapter. **23.13**

In those cases Lord Hoffmann considered what was required to show unfairly prejudicial conduct: **23.14**

(1) The concept of unfair prejudice was chosen 'to free the court from technical considerations of legal right and to confer a wide power to do what appeared just and equitable'.[32]

(2) The court applies an objective standard of fairness.[33] 'The concept of fairness must be applied judicially and the content which it is given by the courts must be based on rational principles.'[34]

(3) Fairness is considered in a commercial context in which the company's articles govern the relationships of the shareholders with the company and each other. Sometimes there are collateral agreements between shareholders. The starting point is therefore to ask whether the conduct complained of was in accordance with the articles or the collateral agreement.[35]

(4) Therefore 'a member of a company will not ordinarily be entitled to complain of unfairness unless there has been some breach of the terms on which he agreed that the affairs of the company should be conducted'.[36]

---

[26] Section 999(1)–(3).

[27] Sections 998(3) and (4) and 999(4) and (5).

[28] SI 2009/2469, which replaced the Companies (Unfair Prejudice Applications) Rules 1986 (SI1986/2000).

[29] Companies (Unfair Prejudice Applications) Proceedings Rules 2009, r 2.2.

[30] [1995] 1 BCLC 14, CA.

[31] [1999] 1 WLR 1092, HL. See the description of Lord Hoffmann's speech given by Arden LJ *Re Tobian Properties Ltd* [2013] 2 BCLC 567, CA at para 21. Also see *Re Coroin Ltd (No 2)* [2013] 2 BCLC 583 at paras 632, 632 per David Richards J and in the CA at para 17 per Arden LJ.

[32] [1999] 1 WLR 1092, 1098D.

[33] [1995] 1 BCLC 14, 17f–g.

[34] [1999] 1 WLR 1092, 1098E.

[35] [1995] 1 BCLC 14, 17i–18a; [1999] 1 WLR 1092, 1098G–H.

[36] [1999] 1 WLR 1092, 1098H–1099A.

(5) Whether there has been some such breach may turn on the exercise by the directors of the fiduciary powers entrusted to them under the articles. A breach of their fiduciary duties may entitle a shareholder to a remedy under the unfair prejudice section even though, as a matter of general law, the directors would be protected by the principle of majority rule. This is because 'enabling the court in an appropriate case to outflank the rule in *Foss v Harbottle* was one of the purposes of the section'.[37]

(6) Not every breach of the articles or breach of duty will amount to unfairly prejudicial conduct. Trivial or technical infringements should not give rise to an unfair prejudice petition.[38]

(7) On the other hand 'there will be cases in which equitable considerations make it unfair for those conducting the affairs of the company to rely upon their strict legal rights'.[39] In this part of the analysis Lord Hoffmann asserted the role of equity 'to restrain the exercise of strict legal rights in certain relationships in which it considered it to be contrary to good faith'[40] and drew support from the speech of Lord Wilberforce in *Ebrahimi v Westbourne Galleries Ltd*[41] (quoted in paragraph 23.60 below).

(8) In the interests of legal certainty the control of the exercise of legal rights should be governed by established principles of equity, rather than some 'indefinite notion of fairness'.[42] As to the concept of 'legitimate expectations' used in *Re Saul D Harrison & Sons Plc*,[43] Lord Hoffmann said that 'it was probably a mistake to use this term' and that 'the concept of legitimate expectation should not be allowed to lead a life of its own, capable of giving rise to equitable restraints in circumstances to which the traditional equitable principles have no application'.[44]

(9) The application of equitable principles may mean that:

there may be some event which puts an end to the basis upon which the parties entered into association with each other, making it unfair that one shareholder should insist upon the continuance of the association. The analogy of contractual frustration suggests itself. The unfairness may arise not from what the parties have positively agreed but from a majority using its legal powers to maintain the association in circumstances to which the minority can reasonably say it did not agree.[45]

(10) It follows that it is not fair for a member who has been excluded from participation in management to keep his assets locked up in the company. There should therefore be an offer to buy the excluded member's shares at a fair price or some other fair arrangement.[46]

(11) A fair price will ordinarily be at a value representing an equivalent proportion of the total issued share capital without any discount on account of it being a minority holding. If the price is not agreed it should be fixed by an expert acting as such, with the

---

[37] [1995] 1 BCLC 14, 18a–g.
[38] [1995] 1 BCLC 14, 18g–i.
[39] [1995] 1 BCLC 14, 19a–20b; [1999] 1 WLR 1092, 1099A.
[40] [1999] 1 WLR 1092, 1098H.
[41] [1973] AC 360, 379.
[42] [1999] 1 WLR 1092, 1099F–H.
[43] [1995] 1 BCLC 14, 19. It was used in many other cases.
[44] [1999] 1 WLR 1092, 1102E–F.
[45] [1999] 1 WLR 1092, 1101H–1102A.
[46] [1999] 1 WLR 1092, 1104G, 1107B.

parties having equal access to information. The majority shareholder should have a reasonable time to make an offer before being at risk as to costs.[47]

(12) Lord Hoffmann emphatically rejected the idea of 'no-fault divorce' as running counter to the contractual basis underlying the shareholders' relationship. Accordingly 'a member who has not been dismissed or excluded [cannot] demand that his shares be purchased simply because he feels that he has lost trust and confidence in the others'.[48]

(13) He also affirmed that 'the requirement that prejudice must be suffered as a member should not be too narrowly or technically construed'.[49]

In *Grace v Biagioli*[50] the Court of Appeal deduced the following principles from Lord **23.15** Hoffmann's speech in *O'Neill v Phillips*:

(1) The concept of unfairness, although objective in its focus, is not to be considered in a vacuum. An assessment that conduct is unfair has to be made against the legal background of the corporate structure under consideration. This will usually take the form of the articles of association and any collateral agreements between shareholders which identify their rights and obligations as members of the company. Both are subject to established equitable principles which may moderate the exercise of strict legal rights when insistence on the enforcement of such rights would be unconscionable.

(2) It follows that it will not ordinarily be unfair for the affairs of a company to be conducted in accordance with the provisions of its articles or any other relevant and legally enforceable agreement, unless it would be inequitable for those agreements to be enforced in the particular circumstances under consideration. Unfairness may, to use Lord Hoffmann's words, 'consist in a breach of the rules or in using the rules in a manner which equity would regard as contrary to good faith' (see [1999] 2 BCLC 1 at 8, [1999] 1 WLR 1092 at 1099); the conduct need not therefore be unlawful, but it must be inequitable.

(3) Although it is impossible to provide an exhaustive definition of the circumstances in which the application of equitable principles would render it unjust for a party to insist on his strict legal rights, those principles are to be applied according to settled and established equitable rules and not by reference to some indefinite notion of fairness.

(4) To be unfair, the conduct complained of need not be such as would have justified the making of a winding-up order on just and equitable grounds as formerly required under s 210 of the Companies Act 1948.

(5) A useful test is always to ask whether the exercise of the power or rights in question would involve a breach of an agreement or understanding between the parties which it would be unfair to allow a member to ignore. Such agreements do not have to be contractually binding in order to found the equity.

(6) It is not enough merely to show that the relationship between the parties has irretrievably broken down. There is no right of unilateral withdrawal for a shareholder when trust and confidence between shareholders no longer exist. It is, however, different if

---

[47] [1999] 1 WLR 1092, 1107C–1108B. But see further paras 23.81–23.87 below.
[48] [1999] 1 WLR 1092, 1104G–1105B.
[49] [1999] 1 WLR 1092, 1105G.
[50] [2006] 2 BCLC 70, CA at para 61. There is a useful analysis of Lord Hoffmann's speech by Jonathan Parker J in *Re Guidezone Ltd* [2000] 2 BCLC 321 at paras 175 and 176 and another summary by Auld LJ in *Re Phoenix Office Supplies Ltd* [2003] 1 BCLC 76, CA at para 19.

that breakdown in relations then causes the majority to exclude the petitioner from the management of the company or otherwise to cause him prejudice in his capacity as a shareholder.

23.16 The CLR considered, but rejected, submissions that the 1985 Act, s 459 should be amended to give the court more flexibility to grant relief to minority shareholders than Lord Hoffmann's analysis permitted.[51] The CLR agreed with the House of Lords in *O'Neill v Phillips* that 'the basis for a claim should be a departure from an agreement, broadly defined, between those concerned, to be identified by their words or conduct. This is necessary in the interests of certainty and the containment of the scope of section 459 actions.' The government agreed and hence Part 30 re-enacts without change the comparable provisions of the 1985 Act.

23.17 Although section 994 emphasizes the need for a connection between the conduct complained of and the relief sought (so distinguishing unfair prejudice petitions from derivative claims),[52] the jurisdiction is statutory and it is necessary to consider each component of that jurisdiction before consideration of remedies. In *Re Coroin Ltd (No 2)* David Richards said that in order to be entitled to a remedy the petitioner must establish:[53]

> first, that the matters of which he complains are either actual or proposed acts or omissions of the company or consist of the conduct of the company's affairs; secondly, that those matters caused prejudice to his interests as a member of the company; and thirdly, that the prejudice is unfair.

(4) The company's affairs

23.18 The conduct complained of as being unfairly prejudicial must concern 'the affairs of the company', which is a phrase of the 'widest import'.[54] The phrase is extremely wide and should be construed liberally, having regard to the business realities, and should not be confined to a narrow legalistic view; it extends to all matters that may come, or are capable of coming, before the board for consideration.[55] The flexibility of the expression 'affairs of the company' has enabled the court to hold that when a company which held 75 per cent of the shares in the company, the subject of the petition, withheld payments due to the company it was conducting the affairs of the company.[56]

23.19 Complaints about the conduct of a company's affairs usually concern a course of conduct.[57] Section 994(1)(b) makes it clear, however, that individual acts or omissions, actual or

---

[51] *Final Report* at para 7.41.
[52] *Re Charnley Davies Ltd (No 2)* [1990] BCLC 760, 783, 784 (a case on the Insolvency Act, s 27).
[53] *Re Coroin Ltd (No 2)* [2013] 2 BCLC 583, 732 at para 625.
[54] *Rackind v Gross* [2005] 1 WLR 3505, CA at para 26, per Sir Martin Nourse.
[55] *Re Neath Rugby Ltd (No 2), Hawkes v Cuddy (No 2)* [2009] 2 BCLC 427, CA at paras 48 and 50. It would include a refusal by the board to convene a general meeting. The affairs of the company encompass matters which must go to the company in general meeting, rather than the board, for consideration: *Re Coroin Ltd (No 2)* [2013] 2 BCLC 583 at para 629, per David Richards J.
[56] *Nicholas v Soundcraft Electronics Ltd* [1993] BCLC 360, 364, 368, CA. In that case the group was in financial difficulties and payment by the parent to the company was withheld in order to support the group, from which the company would benefit. Accordingly there was no unfair prejudice.
[57] *Re Macro (Ipswich) Ltd* [1994] 2 BCLC 354, 406.

proposed, are capable of being the subject of legitimate complaint.[58] Threats of acts or omissions may not be enough to persuade the court to act.[59]

Notwithstanding the width of the statutory language, some matters are outside the scope of the **23.20** affairs of the company.[60] These include the payment by a respondent shareholder from his own money of a debt owed by the company to its bank,[61] and theft, or unauthorized taking, by a director of company money or property (but the failure by the directors to take steps to recover the money or property would be within the scope of Part 30).[62] Also acts of a shareholder in dealing with his shares (such as refusing to sell his shares to another member) are outside the affairs of a company.[63] Similarly an offer by one member to buy another's shares is outside the conduct of the company's affairs;[64] as is the failure by a shareholder to serve a transfer notice in respect of his shares,[65] or breach by a shareholder of a pre-emption agreement.[66] The line is often a fine one, because the company will necessarily be involved in giving effect to the transfer of shares.

An unsuccessful attempt by the majority shareholder in a listed company through its nomi- **23.21** nee directors to persuade the board to stop dividend payments and support its offer to buy the remaining shares was not conduct of the affairs of the company, since the company's affairs were reflected in the decision of the board; nor was an announcement by the majority shareholder of its desired dividend policy conduct of the affairs of the company.[67]

While the general position is that the complaint must concern the conduct of the affairs **23.22** of the company which is the subject of the petition and not the conduct of directors of a connected company or trustees of a pension scheme,[68] or the conduct of the affairs of some other company, which holds shares in it or supplies it with goods,[69] a more flexible approach is necessary where the subject company is the parent of a company whose management is the subject of complaint. In *Rackind v Gross*[70] the Court of Appeal held that the affairs of a company can include the affairs of a subsidiary, in a case where the two companies had common directors. Sir Martin Nourse held that 'the expression "the affairs of the company" is one of the widest import which can include the affairs of a subsidiary'.[71] In *Re*

---

[58] *Re Legal Costs Negotiators Ltd* [1999] 2 BCLC 171, 200, CA. Proposed acts were taken into account in *Re Kenyon Swansea Ltd* [1987] BCLC 514 and *Re a Company (No 00314 of 1989), ex p Estates Acquisition and Development Ltd* [1991] BCLC 154, 160 (threats to alter articles to remove director/shareholder).

[59] Cases where threats were not enough are: *Re Astec (BSR) plc* [1998] 2 BCLC 556, 571; *Re John Reid & Sons (Strucsteel) Ltd* [2003] 2 BCLC 319.

[60] *Re Charterhouse Capital Ltd* [2015] 2 BCLC 627, CA at para 45.

[61] *Re a Company (No 001761 of 1986)* [1987] BCLC 141, 144, 145.

[62] *Re a Company (No 001761 of 1986)* (n 61 above),148. See the observations of Sales J in *Oak Investment Partners XII, LLP v Boughtwood* [2009] 1 BCLC 453 at para 15 (appeal dismissed, [2010] 2 BCLC 459).

[63] *Re Unisoft Group Ltd (No 3)* [1994] 1 BCLC 609, 623; *Re Leeds United Holdings plc* [1996] 2 BCLC 545; 559, 560; *Re Legal Costs Negotiators Ltd* [1999] 2 BCLC 171, 196, 197, CA.

[64] *Re Estate Acquisition & Development Ltd* [1995] BCC 338, 349.

[65] In *Re Coroin Ltd (No 2)* [2013] 2 BCLC 583 at para 626 David Richards J discussed the distinction between activities of shareholders among themselves, which are governed by the law of contract and tort, and acts or omissions of the company or the conduct of its affairs. At para 639 he held that failure by a shareholder to serve a transfer notice was not within s 994. The Court of Appeal agreed; see 755, 776, and 781 at paras 55, 145, and 168.

[66] *Graham v Every* [2015] 1 BCLC 41, CA, at paras 30, 31, and 37 per Arden LJ.

[67] *Re Astec (BSR) plc* [1998] 2 BCLC 556.

[68] *Re Blackwood Hodge plc* [1997] 2 BCLC 650, 673.

[69] *Arrow Nominees Inc v Blackledge* [2000] 2 BCLC 167, CA at para 23.

[70] [2005] 1 WLR 3505, CA. Also see *Re Coroin Ltd* [2012] EWHC 2343 (Ch) at para 628.

[71] [2005] 1 WLR 3505 at para 26. Keene and Jacob LJJ agreed. In *Waddington v Thomas* [2009] 2 BCLC 82, a decision of the Hong Kong FCA, at para 77 Lord Millett applied this statement of the law.

Grandactual Ltd[72] the judge limited that statement to cases where a company controls, or is controlled by, another company, so that a petitioner for relief in respect of one company could not complain about the affairs of another company which the respondent shareholders controlled.

(5) Prejudice

23.23   The conduct complained of must be prejudicial to the interests of the petitioner as a member.[73] In order to establish his standing as a member it may be necessary for the petitioner to combine the petition with an application for rectification of the register of members.[74]

23.24   The court does not take a narrow or technical approach to the interests of which account is taken.[75] The core case of prejudice to the petitioner's interest as a member is damage to the financial position of a member. In *Re Coroin Ltd (No 2)*[76] David Richards J said:

> The prejudice may be damage to the value of his shares but may also extend to other financial damage which in the circumstances of the case is bound up with his position as a member. So, for example, removal from participation in the management of a company and the resulting loss of income or profits from the company in the form of remuneration will constitute prejudice in those cases where the members have rights recognised in equity, if not at law, to participate in that way. Similarly, damage to the financial position of a member in relation to a debt due to him from the company can in appropriate circumstances amount to prejudice. The prejudice must be to the petitioner in his capacity as a member but this is not to be strictly confined to damage to the value of his shareholding.

23.25   Insolvency complicates the unfair prejudice remedy but the courts take a wide view of prejudice. Shares in an insolvent company in liquidation are clearly valueless unless the value of any claims which the company has against the respondents to the petition will eliminate the deficiency and produce a surplus for members. If there is a real prospect that those claims might succeed and restore value to the petitioner's shareholding, the petition will be allowed to proceed.[77]

23.26   As David Richards J said in the passage quoted at paragraph 23.24 above, damage to the financial position of a member in relation to a debt due to him from the company can in the appropriate circumstances amount to prejudice. In *R & H Electric Ltd v Haden Bill Electrical Ltd*[78] Robert Walker J took into account a member's legitimate expectation of participation in management in a company so long as loans made to that company by another company with which he was connected remained unpaid. In *Gamlestaden Fastigher AB v Baltic Partners Ltd*[79] Lord Scott followed the approach in *R & H Electric Ltd* and held that a shareholder

---

[72] [2006] BCC 73 at para 29. This case and *Rackind v Gross* were considered by Lewison J in *Hawkes v Cuddy (No 2)* [2008] BCC 390 at paras 208–13.

[73] *Re Saul D Harrison & Sons Plc* [1995] 1 BCLC 14, 31, CA, per Neill LJ.

[74] *Re I Fit Global Ltd* [2014] 2 BCLC 116. See para 23.05 above.

[75] *O'Neill v Phillips* [1999] 1 WLR 1092, 1105G, HL, per Lord Hoffmann.

[76] [2013] 2 BCLC 583 at para 630.

[77] *Re Tobian Properties Ltd* [2013] 2 BCLC 56, CA, paras 11–13, 46–8, 55, and 57, per Arden LJ (claims against a director for drawing excessive remuneration and failing to obtain value for the company's trading name on a sale of its business might restore value to petitioner's shares).

[78] [1995] 2 BCLC 280, 292–4, where Robert Walker J said that he would order the purchase of the petitioner's shares at a fair price without discount and that the loans should be repaid as soon as reasonably possible. Robert Walker J's broad approach to a member's interests was endorsed by Lord Hoffmann in *O'Neill v Phillips* [1999] 1 WLR 1092, 1105G, HL.

[79] [2007] 4 All ER 164, PC, a case on the Jersey equivalent of Part 30.

who was also a loan creditor could obtain relief which, because of the company's insolvency, could only benefit it as loan creditor and not as shareholder. Such relief would amount to 'a real financial benefit' for the petitioner.[80]

Prejudice need not be financial in character. Unlawful conduct, such as breach of the articles, **23.27** breach of a shareholders' agreement, or breach of duty, even though without any financial consequences, may amount to prejudice falling within the section. This is because the wrongful conduct may cause the petitioner to have a justifiable loss of confidence in management,[81] or because his rights as a shareholder are prejudiced.[82] Even so, where the acts complained of have no adverse financial consequences, it may be more difficult to establish relevant prejudice.[83]

Where the company is a quasi-partnership company it may not be appropriate to separate a **23.28** member's expectation of participation in management from his shareholding,[84] but where the company is not a quasi-partnership the court may be able to distinguish a person's interest as a shareholder from his interest as an executive director under a service contract. A director of a public company would not be able to complain of unfair prejudice simply because he had been dismissed from office. Similarly, in the case of a private company which is not a quasi-partnership, there may be no unfair prejudice to a minority shareholder who was dismissed as a director for genuine reasons and who refused the majority's demand that he transfer his shares.[85] On the other hand, even in such a case, there may be unfair prejudice where there is a combination of proposals for the removal of the minority shareholder as a director, the appointment of new directors, the alteration of the company's constitution and an offer to purchase shares without providing information about value or the running of the company.[86]

Part 30 is not to be used as a means of enforcing rights which are distinct from the mem- **23.29** ber's shares such as enforcing a member's consultancy agreement against the company,[87] or obtaining possession of property let by the member to the company.[88]

---

[80] *Gamlestaden Fastigher AB v Baltic Partners Ltd* [2007] 4 All ER 164, PC at para 36. In *Re Tobian Properties Ltd* [2013] 2 BCLC 567, CA, at paras 11–13, Arden LJ followed *Gamlestaden*.

[81] *Re Baumler (UK) Ltd* [2005] 1 BCLC 92 at paras 180–1, per Mr George Bompas QC. See also *Loch v John Blackwood Ltd* [1924] AC 783, 788, PC, a winding-up case, where Lord Shaw said that 'whenever the lack of confidence is rested on lack of probity in the conduct of the company's affairs, then the former is justified by the latter and it is, under the statute, just and equitable that the company be wound up.'

[82] *Re Kenyon Swansea Ltd* [1987] BCLC 514 (para 23.65 below) and the cases on the fiduciary duty to act within powers discussed in paras 23.43–23.45 below.

[83] *Re Coroin Ltd (No 2)* [2013] 2 BCLC 583 at para 631 per David Richards J, discussing *Rock Nominees Ltd v RCO (Holdings) plc* [2004] 1 BCLC 439, CA, where the alleged breach of duty had caused no loss to the company or prejudice to the petitioner and the petition was struck out.

[84] *Re a Company (No 00477 of 1986)* [1986] BCLC 376, 379. In *Re Phoenix Office Supplies Ltd* [2003] 1 BCLC 76, CA, there was no unfair prejudice entitling the petitioner to have his shares bought at a non-discounted price where he had voluntarily severed his connection with the company and had thereafter been wrongly treated as having resigned as a director and been excluded from the company.

[85] *Re John Reid & Sons (Strucsteel) Ltd* [2003] 2 BCLC 319.

[86] *Re a Company (No 00314 of 1989), ex p Estate and Acquisition and Development Ltd* [1991] BCLC 154, 160.

[87] *Re a Company (No 003843 of 1986)* [1987] BCLC 562, 572, 573; *Re a Company (No 005685 of 1988), ex p Schwarcz* [1989] BCLC 424, 442.

[88] *Re JE Cade & Son Ltd* [1992] BCLC 213, 228, 229.

(6) Unfairness

23.30   The words 'unfairly prejudicial' are general words to be applied flexibly to meet the circumstances of the particular case.[89] As Arden J put it in *Re BSB Holdings Ltd (No 2)* 'the categories of unfair prejudice are not closed'.[90] Moreover the concept of unfairness 'cuts across the distinction between acts which do or do not infringe rights attaching to the shares by the constitution of the company'.[91]

23.31   The conduct of which complaint typically is made involves (a) breach of the company's constitution or a shareholders' agreement, (b) breach of directors' duties, or (c) lawful conduct which in the particular circumstances is restrained by equity. Whether the petitioner is able to show that the conduct of which he complains is unfair may depend on his personal position.

The position of the petitioner

23.32   The petitioner is entitled to complain about conduct before he became a member,[92] even though he was aware of it when he acquired his shares,[93] and about matters arising after the petition was presented.[94]

23.33   Although the language of s 994 does not preclude the possibility of a majority shareholder petitioning for relief, such a procedure is most unlikely to be necessary or appropriate, because the majority shareholder can readily put an end to the unfair prejudice alleged.[95]

23.34   The petitioner does not have to come to court with clean hands, but his own conduct may prevent him from establishing the grounds of the petition in that it may render the conduct of the other parties, even if prejudicial, not unfair, and it may affect the relief, if any, that the court is prepared to grant.[96] Illegality may amount to unfair prejudice, but a person cannot rely on his own illegal conduct in order to found relief.[97] Delay may be a bar to relief,[98] as may fraudulent conduct or abuse of the process of the court.[99]

---

[89]   *Re Saul D Harrison & Sons plc* [1995] 1 BCLC 14, 30, CA, per Neill LJ.

[90]   [1996] 1 BCLC 155, 243; quoted and discussed in *Re Sunrise Radio Ltd* [2010] 1 BCLC 367 at paras 13 and 14. See also Arden LJ's statement of the principles in *Maidment v Attwood* [2012] EWCA Civ 998 at para 21.

[91]   *Re a Company (No 008699 of 1985)* [1986] BCLC 382, 387, per Hoffmann J.

[92]   *Lloyd v Casey* [2002] 1 BCLC 454.

[93]   *Bermuda Cablevision Ltd v Colica Trust Co Ltd* [1998] AC 198, PC.

[94]   *Cobden Investments Ltd v RWM Langport Ltd* [2007] EWHC 3048 (Ch).

[95]   *Re Legal Costs Negotiators Ltd* [1999] 2 BCLC 171, 200, 201, CA, where Peter Gibson LJ discusses the cases of *Re Baltic Real Estate Ltd (No 1)* [1993] BCLC 498 and *Re Baltic Real Estate Ltd (No 2)* [1993] BCLC 503, where this issue had been raised. In each of those cases the petitioner, who was the majority shareholder, unsuccessfully attempted to use 1985 Act, s 459 as a means of forcing the minority shareholder to sell his shares.

[96]   *Re London School of Electronics Ltd* [1986] Chs 211, 222; *Re Baumler (UK) Ltd* [2005] 1 BCLC 92 at para 181; *Richardson v Blackmore* [2006] BCC 277, CA at para 53; *Moxon v Litchfield* [2013] EWHC 3957 (Ch) (petitioner was a bad leaver, so there was no unfairness in him being bought out under the terms of the articles); *Re J&S Insurance & Financial Consultants Ltd* [2014] EWHC 2206 (Ch) (where despite the petitioner's conduct the exclusion could not be objectively justified). Also see *Vujnovich v Vujnovich* [1990] BCLC 227, PC (a winding-up case).

[97]   *Re Neath Rugby Club Ltd (No 2), Hawkes v Cuddy (No 2)* [2008] BCC 390 at para 238.

[98]   *Re Grandactual Ltd* [2006] BCC 73 (where the delay was nine years). In *Re a Company (No 5134 of 1986), ex p Harries* [1989] BCLC 383 the delay did not prevent the petitioner from obtaining relief. In *Rahman v Malik* [2008] 2 BCLC 403, 425 there had been considerable delay, but it had not prejudiced the respondents and did not justify excluding the petitioner from any remedy to which he might otherwise be entitled.

[99]   *Arrow Nominees Inc v Blackledge* [2000] 2 BCLC 167, CA. Also see *Rock (Nominees) Ltd v RCO (Holdings) Plc* [2004] 1 BCLC 439, CA, where at para 81 Jonathan Parker LJ considered that the petition was being used as a 'weapon in a tactical battle' and might have been struck out as an abuse.

On the other hand, prejudice may be unfair even though the petitioner could have discov-   **23.35**
ered the conduct complained of (eg payment of excessive remuneration) if he had read the
accounts. To hold otherwise would be to impose a new restriction on the manner in which
shareholders could enforce the liability of directors for wrongs to their company, and meant
that minority shareholders were at risk of losing their rights if they did not read their company's filed accounts.[100]

A petitioner may be prevented from obtaining relief under Part 30 where the matters com-   **23.36**
plained of are within the scope of an arbitration agreement.[101]

Conduct that is ratified by all the shareholders will not amount to unfairly prejudicial con-   **23.37**
duct. This is a problem peculiar to the situation where, at the relevant time, shares are held in
trust and the trustees ratify the conduct in question contrary, it may transpire, to the interests
or wishes of the person ultimately beneficially entitled. The trustees might well be liable for
breach of trust, but the affairs of the company have regularly been conducted.[102]

Breach of the company's constitution or shareholders' agreement

The company's articles of association and memorandum, and any shareholders' agreements,   **23.38**
govern the relationships of the shareholders with the company and each other. As such,
unfairness may consist in a breach of the articles or the terms of any such agreement. A failure by the directors to recognize the appointment of a director by a shareholder pursuant to
its entitlement under a shareholders' agreement would be unfairly prejudicial conduct.[103]
A repeated failure to hold AGMs and lay accounts before the company depriving the members of their right to consider and question those accounts and to consider the affairs of the
company, may amount to conduct unfairly prejudicial to the interests of all the members.[104]
The holding of extraordinary general meetings, which have been invalidated by short notice,
may also be unfairly prejudicial to shareholders who subscribed for shares which did not exist
because of the procedural irregularity.[105] Breach by a shareholder of an agreement between
shareholders for prompt payment of trade debts to the company and for giving business
opportunities to the company may constitute unfairly prejudicial conduct.[106]

---

[100] *Re Tobian Properties Ltd* [2013] 2 BCLC 567, CA at paras 31, 32.

[101] Para 23.97 below.

[102] *Re Batesons Hotels (1958) Ltd* [2014] 1 BCLC 507. Cf *Bermuda Cablevision Ltd v Colica Trust Co Ltd*
[1998] 1 BCLC 1 in which the conduct complained of was a criminal offence and, as such, incapable of
ratification.

[103] *Re A&BC Chewing Gum Ltd* [1975] 1 WLR 579 (a winding-up case, where these facts entitled the petitioner to a winding-up order).

[104] *Re a Company (No 00789 of 1987), ex p Shooter* [1990] BCLC 384. In that case, the repeated failure to
hold AGMs deprived the company of any proper board of directors. Harman J observed that one instance of
such failure might not be enough; here, the resultant absence of any proper authority to look after the company's
affairs was prejudicial to the interests of members. In *Fisher v Cadman* [2006] 1 BCLC 499 the respondents
had failed to hold regular AGMs without valid reason. As a result, they deliberately frustrated the petitioner's
reasonable efforts to obtain information about the conduct of the company's business and allowed the inclusion
of (what was held to be) unreasonable directors' remuneration in the company accounts which had not been
approved by the company in general meeting.

[105] *Re a Company (No 00789 of 1987), ex p Shooter* [1990] BCLC 384, in which Harman J's finding that
the majority shareholder was unfit to control the company led him to order the majority shareholder to sell his
shares to the petitioner.

[106] *Re Southern Counties Fresh Foods Ltd, Cobden Investments Ltd v RWM Langport Ltd* [2008] EWHC
2810 (Ch).

23.39   The interests of members may also be unfairly prejudiced where the majority ignore an agreement made or an understanding reached between shareholders and on which the minority has acted in reliance.[107] In *Re Guidezone Ltd* Jonathan Parker J, in analysing Lord Hoffmann's speech in *O'Neill v Phillips*, held that:[108]

> Applying traditional equitable principles, equity will not hold the majority to an agreement, promise or understanding which is not enforceable at law unless and until the minority has acted in reliance on it. In the case of an agreement, promise or understanding made or reached when the company was formed, that requirement will almost always be fulfilled, in that the minority will have acted on the agreement, promise or understanding in entering into association with the majority and taking the minority stake. But the same cannot be said of agreements, promises or understandings made or reached subsequently, which are not themselves enforceable at law. In such a case, the majority will not as a general rule be regarded in equity as having acted contrary to good faith unless and until it has allowed the minority to act in reliance on such an agreement, promise or understanding. Absent some special circumstances, it will only be at that point, and not before, that equity will intervene by providing a remedy to the minority which is not available at law.

23.40   Deadlock between the members under the company's constitution as a result of which it is unable to carry on its business does not without more constitute unfairness. Conduct of the affairs of the company that caused any breakdown of trust and confidence and gave rise to the deadlock may be unfairly prejudicial conduct as may a party's reaction to the deadlock.[109]

Breach of fiduciary duties

23.41   The breach by a director of his fiduciary duties, whether or not the breaches were ratifiable under the rule in *Foss v Harbottle*, may amount to unfairly prejudicial conduct for the purposes of s 994 as a breach of the bargain between shareholders and the company.[110] 'Enabling the court in an appropriate case to outflank the rule in *Foss v Harbottle* was one of the purposes of [Part 30].'[111] The codification of directors' general duties in the 2006 Act, Part 10, Chapter 2[112] will affect directors in that any alleged unfairly prejudicial conduct arising out of a breach of duty will be identified with greater ease. Invariably the conduct complained of in a Part 30 petition amounts to a breach of more than one of the general duties of directors. As Arden observed in *Re Tobian Properties Ltd*,[113] non-compliance by respondent shareholders with their general duties as directors will generally indicate that unfair prejudice has occurred.

---

[107]   *Re Regional Airports Ltd* [1999] 2 BCLC 30 (decided before *O'Neill v Phillips*; breach of common understandings as to the way that the company should be run, which were based on the relationship of mutual trust and confidence between the parties); *Re Guidezone Ltd* [2000] 2 BCLC 321 (alleged failure to sell property in breach of understanding); *Re Phoneer Ltd* [2002] 2 BCLC 241 (breach of shareholders' agreement that the petitioner should continue to manage and develop the company's business and act as its managing director, when the petitioner withdrew from management and wanted to renegotiate the basis of an agreed salary); *Rahman v Malik* [2008] 2 BCLC 403 (breach of agreement in failing to appoint petitioner as director and thereafter excluding him from real and effective participation in the affairs of the company).

[108]   [2002] 2 BCLC 321 at para 175. See *Yeomans Row Management Ltd v Cobbe* [2008] 1 WLR 1752, HL for a discussion of the application of equitable principles to incomplete agreements and understandings.

[109]   *Re Neath Rugby Ltd (No 2), Hawks v Cuddy (No 2)* [2009] 2 BCLC 427, CA at paras 101–8, overruling *Re Guidezone Ltd* [2000] 2 BCLC 321 at paras 177–80.

[110]   *O'Neill v Phillips* [1999] 1 WLR 1098H–1099A, HL.

[111]   *Re Saul D Harrison Ltd* [1995] 1 BCLC 14, 18g–i, CA.

[112]   See Chs 10–17 above.

[113]   [2013] 2 BCLC 567, CA at para 22.

It is not enough to prove a breach of fiduciary duty to establish a claim for relief under **23.42** Part 30; it must also cause unfair prejudice to the interest of the petitioner as member.[114] It is necessary in each case to show that the breach of fiduciary duty constitutes unfairly prejudicial management of the affairs of the company, since the petition will seek 'relief from mismanagement, not a remedy for misconduct'.[115] Usually the unfairness to the petitioner or shareholders will be inherent in the nature of the breach of duty complained of and the harm caused to the company and thereby to shareholders.[116] As the following discussion shows the breaches of duty which constitute unfairly prejudicial conduct invariably involve dishonesty, concealment, conflict of interest, or partisan or discriminatory behaviour. Where those breaches occur the petitioner will have good grounds for saying he has lost trust and confidence in the management of the company. On the other hand a breach which is trivial or technical may not be enough to support an unfair prejudice petition.[117] Nor is it likely to be enough to point to bad business decisions or acts of incompetence, because every shareholder takes the risk that they will occur (paragraph 23.58 below).

The fiduciary duty to act within powers

Directors of a company must act in accordance with the company's constitution and only **23.43** exercise powers for the purposes for which they are conferred.[118] The corollary of that rule is that they must not exercise those powers for an improper or collateral purpose.[119] A rights issue may be unfairly prejudicial conduct if the directors had a collateral purpose or if it discriminates against the minority.[120] As HHJ Purle QC observed in *Re Sunrise Radio Ltd*, the power to allot shares is a fiduciary one and the decision whether or not capital is needed is different from the determination of the proper price at which the new shares should be offered; in the latter connection the directors' fiduciary duties may require them to give proper consideration to the impact the issue and the price may have on particular shareholders.[121] An allotment of shares in breach of statutory pre-emption rights and an unequal allotment in breach of fiduciary duty which discriminates between shareholders *inter se* have both been found to be conduct amounting to unfair prejudice.[122] Where, however, capital

---

[114] *Re Saul D Harrison & Sons plc* [1995] 1 BCLC 14, 31, CA, per Neill LJ; *Re Blackwood Hodge plc* [1997] 2 BCLC 650, 673.

[115] *Re Charnley Davies Ltd (No 2)* [1990] BCLC 760, 783, 784, per Millett J (a case on the Insolvency Act, s 27); see also the judgment of Lord Scott in *Re Chime Corp Ltd* [2004] HKFCA 7 at para 47.

[116] *Anderson v Hogg* [2002] BCC 923.

[117] *Re Saul D Harrison Ltd* [1995] 1 BCLC 14, 18g–i, CA.

[118] 2006 Act, s 171. Discussed in Ch 11 above.

[119] *McGuiness, Petitioner* (1988) 4 BCC 161 (directors exercising power to postpone EGM at which resolutions to change the constitution of the board were to be considered; held capable of being unfairly prejudicial conduct).

[120] *Re a Company* [1985] BCLC 80, 82; *Re a Company (No 007623 of 1984)* [1986] BCLC 362, 366, 367 (directors proposed a rights issue at par to raise capital that the company needed, but this was arguably unfairly prejudicial conduct, because the shares were worth more than par and the directors knew the minority shareholder could not afford to subscribe for his shares). Both these cases were considered in *West Coast Capital (Lios) Ltd, Petitioner* [2008] CSOH 72 and by HHJ Purle QC in *Re Sunrise Radio Ltd* [2010] 1 BCLC 367 at paras 76–96. See also: *Re a Company (No 002612 of 1984)* (1986) 2 BCC 99,453, 99,478–99,480; on appeal as *Re Cumana Ltd* [1986] BCLC 430, 434, CA (rights issue to depress petitioner's stake); *Jesner v Jarrad Properties Ltd* [1993] BCLC 1032 (threatened use of company's assets to pay the liabilities of an associated company, in which the petitioner had a smaller shareholding); *Re Zetnet Ltd* [2011] EWHC 1518 (Ch).

[121] [2010] 1 BCLC 367 at paras 79, 95, 96. Presumably the relevant fiduciary duty is under s 172(1)(f) (para 23.46 below).

[122] *Re a Company (No 005134 of 1986), ex p Harries* [1989] BCLC 383; *Dalby v Bodilly* [2005] BCC 627 (breach of duty in the allotment of shares to himself by a controlling director).

has been raised legitimately and there is no unfairness in the subsequent allotment of share capital, there will be no finding of unfair prejudice.[123] A proposed act which affects the rights of different groups of shareholders *inter se* might amount to unfairly prejudicial conduct where the directors have not exercised their powers fairly as between the different groups.[124]

23.44 Directors of a company have a duty to consider what proportion of a company's trading profits they can properly distribute to members, as the owners of the company, and a failure to pay reasonable dividends may, in the particular circumstances of the company, support an allegation of unfair prejudice,[125] albeit one that may be difficult to make good. Such an allegation is invariably accompanied by an allegation that the directors have paid excessive remuneration to themselves or paid other benefits to the majority shareholders.[126]

23.45 Where the directors use their powers as such to enable the majority shareholders to sell their shares, they may breach their fiduciary duties and their obligations of good faith to the minority shareholder and director from whom they deliberately concealed the sale.[127]

The fiduciary duty to promote the success of the company

23.46 Directors have an overriding duty to act in good faith in what they consider to be the interests of the company[128] and are not bound to pursue the interests of minority shareholders contrary to those interests. A director of a company must act in the way he considers, in good faith, would be most likely to promote the success of the company for the benefit of its members as a whole.[129] The breaches of this duty capable of sustaining an unfair prejudice petition are likely to involve conflict of interest or discriminatory treatment of shareholders.[130] Where

---

[123] *CAS (Nominees) Ltd v Nottingham Forest FC plc* [2002] 1 BCLC 613 (shares allotted without infringing the company's articles of association and where the directors could not be said to have exercised their powers for an improper purpose).

[124] 2006 Act, s 172(1)(f); *Re BSB Holdings Ltd (No 2)* [1996] 1 BCLC 155; cf *Mutual Life Insurance Co of New York v Rank Organisation Ltd* [1985] BCLC 11.

[125] *Re a Company (No 00370 of 1987), ex p Glossop* [1988] 1 WLR 1068, 1076–7 (allegation by a minority shareholder that the directors of the company had failed to pay reasonable dividends out of the very large profits accruing to the company could justify a winding-up order, but held in *Re Saul D Harrison Ltd* [1995] 1 BCLC 14, CA, per Hoffmann LJ to apply to an unfair prejudice petition as well). In *Sikorski v Sikorski* [2012] EWHC 1613 (Ch) the unfair prejudice claim succeeded where the company had been managed so as to depress profits and prevent dividends from being paid.

[126] In *Re Sam Weller & Sons Ltd* [1990] Ch 682 it was held that the payment of the same derisory dividend over many years and the failure of the majority shareholders of a family company to pay reasonable dividends, whilst continuing to draw an income from the company and to accumulate profits and cash in hand, combined with a proposed significant capital expenditure, could amount to conduct unfairly prejudicial to the interests of the minority shareholders. Also: *Re a Company (No 004415 of 1996)* [1997] 1 BCLC 479, 489; *Grace v Baglioli* [2006] 2 BCLC 70, CA (failure to pay dividends and distribution of profits by majority shareholders to themselves under the guise of management expenses in breach of profit sharing agreement); *Irvine v Irvine (No 1)* [2007] 1 BCLC 349; *Re McCarthy Surfacing Ltd* [2009] 1 BCLC 622 at paras 77–84 (unfairly prejudicial conduct where the directors had paid themselves substantial bonuses while failing to consider whether or not they should declare dividends).

[127] *Richardson v Blackmore* [2006] BCC 277, CA at paras 23, 24, 65. In that case, the sale altered the petitioner's position in the company from that of being an equal shareholder with two people who had been partners (or quasi partners in the context of the company), to that of being a true minority shareholder with an individual who was a competitor of the company's business. In respect of a number of the individual steps involved in completing the sale, the directors were held to have breached their duties of good faith to the company and their conduct was held to be unfairly prejudicial.

[128] *Re Saul D Harrison Ltd* [1995] 1 BCLC 14, 18; *Mutual Life Insurance Co of New York v Rank Organisation Ltd* [1985] BCLC 11. This duty has been codified in 2006 Act, s 172.

[129] 2006 Act, s 172. Discussed in Ch 12 above.

[130] The conduct in *Scottish Co-operative Wholesale Society Ltd v Meyer* [1959] AC 324, HL (Sc), a case under the 1948 Act, s 210, is an example of a breach of the duty to promote the success of the company which would

a proposed act will have an effect not only on the company itself, but also on the interest of some of the shareholders, the duty to act in the best interests of the company requires them also within limits to act fairly as between different groups of shareholders.[131] Where the act has different effects on different groups of shareholders, however, the directors must consider whether this is justified in the particular circumstances by the overriding need to act in the interests of the company: they are not bound to pursue the interests of minority shareholders contrary to the interests of the company itself.[132]

The need to act in the interests of the company pervades all transactions into which the **23.47** directors propose to enter.[133] The duty is subject to the company's constitution. If a transaction required the approval of a particular majority of shareholders, which could not be obtained, the failure by the company to enter into the transaction could not put the directors in breach of the duty to promote the success of the company or amount to unfair prejudice.[134]

Where the directors take the view that it is in the interests of the company for all the shares to **23.48** be transferred to an outside bidder, their fiduciary duty extends to not misleading shareholders, when advising shareholders on rival takeover bids, and providing them with sufficient information to reach a properly informed decision, and a breach of this duty is prima facie capable of founding an unfair prejudice petition.[135]

In *Re Blackwood Hodge plc*[136] the petitioners, who held preference shares, established **23.49** that the former directors had breached their duties to the company by failing to give adequate consideration to the terms of a merger of the company's pension scheme with the pension scheme of the company that bought all its ordinary share capital, but failed to establish unfair prejudice, because they could not show that the company had suffered any loss.

Where the petition alleges that the directors are continuing to trade when the company is **23.50** trading at a loss and when it should have been apparent that there was no real prospect that the company would return to profitability, the court would conclude that its affairs were being conducted in a manner unfairly prejudicial to its members if it is able to infer that the

---

amount to unfairly prejudicial conduct. There the director deliberately ran down the company so that another company in which he was interested could prosper.

[131] 2006 Act, s 172(1)(f); *Re BSB Holdings Ltd (No 2)* [1996] 1 BCLC 155.

[132] In *Re BSB Holdings Ltd (No 2)* [1996] 1 BCLC 155 Arden J held that had the directors considered and detected the effects on different groups of shareholders, they would doubtless have taken the view that it was imperative to approve the proposed act in the interests of the company having regard to the urgency of the situation and the almost certain absence of other sources of funding.

[133] *Re Metropolis Motor Cycles Ltd* [2007] 1 BCLC 520 (alleged non-disclosure of information material to transaction at the time of its implementation and allegedly unfair cessation of drawings in breach of arrangement between former partners where there were insufficient profits to support those drawings); *Bermuda Cablevision Ltd v Colica Trust Co Ltd* [1998] AC 198, PC (application to strike out petition dismissed where petitioner alleged that the carrying on of the business of the company unlawfully constituted unfairly prejudicial conduct).

[134] *Wilkinson v West Coast Capital* [2007] BCC 717 at paras 295–304.

[135] *Re a Company (No 008699 of 1985)* [1986] BCLC 382 (motion to strike out petition dismissed since it was arguable that chairman's circular to shareholders was misleading and impaired their chances of being able to sell their shares to the highest bidder).

[136] [1997] 2 BCLC 650.

directors' decision was improperly influenced by their desire to continue in office and to draw remuneration and other benefits for themselves and that no reasonable board would consider it to be in the interests of the company and its members for it to continue to trade.[137]

The fiduciary duty to avoid conflicts of interest

23.51 The strict and inflexible rule of equity that a director must not place himself in a position of conflict of interest and duty may found an allegation of unfairly prejudicial conduct,[138] as may a breach of the 'no profit rule'.[139] Unfair prejudice in this context may consist in diversion of the company's business by the majority shareholders to another business owned by them,[140] charging the company's assets to support another company connected with the directors,[141] misapplication of the company's assets for the personal benefit of its director and his family and friends,[142] misappropriation by a director of the company's business and assets for the benefit of a new business in which he is interested,[143] payment of 'management charges' which had no commercial justification to a company wholly owned by the majority shareholder and his wife,[144] unlawful loans to directors and excessive remuneration,[145] a transfer of company property to majority shareholders at an undervalue,[146] the sale of the company's business to a company connected with the director without obtaining anything for its name,[147] and competing with the company, using a domain intended for the company.[148] Subjecting a company to a loan on onerous and uncommercial terms from a company connected with directors and without obtaining shareholder approval as had been agreed could amount to unfairly prejudicial conduct.[149] It has also been held that a director will be placed in a position of conflict with his duties as a director where he attempts to

---

[137] *Re a Company, ex p Burr* [1992] BCLC 724; on appeal, reported as *Re Saul D Harrison Ltd* [1995] 1 BCLC 14. The Court of Appeal found that the evidence did not support the allegation that the directors had carried on the business with no or no substantial expectation that they would succeed in making a profit which would reflect the value of the assets employed. Nor could the court accept the allegation that the directors had carried on the business simply to further their own interests.

[138] Now codified under 2006 Act, ss 175–7 in the form of three distinct duties. These duties are discussed in Chs 15 and 16 above. See *Bhullar v Bhullar* [2003] 2 BCLC 241 at paras 27–39 for a detailed exposition of the 'no conflict rule'.

[139] *Re Allied Business and Financial Consultants Ltd* [2009] 2 BCLC 666, CA at paras 52–76 where Rimer LJ discusses the 'no profit' and the 'no conflict' rules in the context of an unfair prejudice petition.

[140] *Re London School of Electronics Ltd* [1986] Ch 211; *Re a Company (No 002612 of 1984)* (1986) 2 BCC 99,453, 99,477, 99,478; on appeal as *Re Cumana Ltd* [1986] BCLC 430, 434, CA; *Lowe v Fahey* [1996] 1 BCLC 262.

[141] *Re Brenfield Squash Racquets Club Ltd* [1996] 2 BCLC 184.

[142] *Re Elgindata Ltd* [1991] BCLC 959 (notwithstanding that there was no serious diminution in value of the minority's shares); see *Bhullar v Bhullar* [2003] 2 BCLC 241 as to the relevant question being simply whether the circumstances attract application of the rule against conflicts of interest.

[143] *Allmark v Burnham* [2006] 2 BCLC 43 at para 96. See also *Whillock v Henderson* [2009] BCC 314.

[144] *Wilson v Jaymarke Estates Ltd* [2007] BCC 883, HL (Sc).

[145] *Fowler v Gruber* [2010] 1 BCLC 563.

[146] *Re Little Olympian Each-Ways Ltd (No 3)* [1995] 1 BCLC 636 (transfer of company's business at an undervalue to a company under the same de facto control as part of a hiving up operation, depriving the petitioner of any further interest in those assets); *Guinness Peat Group plc v British Land Co plc* [1999] 2 BCLC 243, CA (petition based on an alleged transfer by the company of its sole asset at an undervalue was not struck out, as the questions of valuation of the minority shareholding merited a full hearing in order to determine whether prejudice had in fact been suffered by the petitioner).

[147] *Re Tobian Properties Ltd* [2013] 2 BCLC 567, CA at paras 51–5.

[148] *Re Via Servis Ltd* [2014] EWHC 3069 (Ch).

[149] *Atlasview Ltd v Brightview Ltd* [2004] 2 BCLC 191.

negotiate the purchase of a potential competitor, without any disclosure or discussion with his fellow directors and shareholders, and attempts to conceal the negotiations.[150]

A prima facie conflict of interest on the part of the directors will not constitute unfair preju-   **23.52**
dice to the interests of the minority, where the transaction the subject of the complaint did not harm the company, because it was for a legitimate commercial purpose or was not at an undervalue.[151] Similarly non-voting minority shareholders, who complained about a sale of the company's assets (indirectly) to its directors under a transaction which gave rise to a prima facie conflict of interest, were unable to establish unfair prejudice where the company had complied with both the provisions of the articles of association and the Companies Act dealing with conflicts of interest,[152] and no other agreement or understanding of the share-holders *inter se* is demonstrated.[153]

A shareholders' agreement may in certain circumstances preclude a finding of unfair preju-   **23.53**
dice even though there has been a prima facie breach of a director's fiduciary duties. In *North Holdings Ltd v Southern Tropics Ltd*[154] the shareholders' agreement provided that the majority shareholders were free to engage in any other business for their own benefit or set up any competing business using a specified trading name. The Court of Appeal held that, notwith-standing the fact that the majority's development and promotion of a competing business was not a breach of their fiduciary duties as directors of the company, it was arguable that they had acted in breach of their fiduciary duties by using the company's assets for their own benefit as shareholders in the competing business.

That notwithstanding, the putative petitioner must still satisfy the court that he has suffered   **23.54**
some prejudice in consequence of the breach of fiduciary duty, which is unfair. In *Wilkinson v West Coast Capital*[155] the shareholders had made an agreement to the effect that no other company or business would be acquired without the consent of 65 per cent of the holders of issued shares. Warren J interpreted the shareholders' agreement as evincing an intention that the company was to be a single purpose vehicle. As such, he held that a director's pursuit of a corporate opportunity in his personal capacity did not amount to a breach of the 'no conflict rule' since the company was prevented by its constitution from taking up the same opportu-nity. Accordingly, no prejudice for the purposes of s 994 could be said to exist.

---

[150] *Grace v Biagioli* [2006] 2 BCLC 70, CA at paras 64–70, in which such misconduct was held to justify the removal of the petitioner as a director of the company.

[151] *Nicholas v Soundcraft Electronics Ltd* [1993] BCLC 360, CA (no 'unfair' prejudice because the decision to withhold payments was a reasonable commercial judgment necessary to support the group); *Re Blackwood Hodge plc* [1997] 2 BCLC 650 (no prejudice caused by directors' treatment of employees' pension schemes fol-lowing a takeover in breach of fiduciary duties); *Re Grandactual Ltd* [2006] BCC 73, para 31 (no unfair preju-dice where alleged diversion of the company's assets to the benefit of the majority was in fact a valid payment of licence fees to a related company, which was necessary to keep the company subject to the petition in business). See also *Rock Nominees Ltd v RCO (Holdings) plc* [2004] 1 BCLC 439, CA at paras 73 *et seq* (sale by the directors of the company's subsidiary was not found to be at an undervalue and in consequence the petitioner had not suffered prejudice; the Court of Appeal considered it inappropriate to make a finding of a breach of fiduciary duty in the abstract, notwithstanding that the directors were in a position of conflict). See the discussion of this case by David Richard J in *Re Coroin Ltd (No 2)* [2013] 2 BCLC 583 at paras 631 and 648.

[152] Now 2006 Act, ss 175(4)(b), 177, 180, 182, and Part 10, Chapter 4 of the Act.

[153] *Re Posgate and Denby (Agencies) Ltd* [1987] BCLC 8 (shareholder approval as required by 1985 Act, s 320 having been obtained).

[154] [1999] 2 BCLC 625, CA.

[155] [2007] BCC 717 at paras 305–13.

Transactions with directors

23.55 A director who is in any way, directly or indirectly, interested in a proposed or existing transaction or arrangement with the company must declare the nature and extent of that interest to the other directors.[156] Service contracts, substantial property transactions, loans, quasi-loans and credit transactions, and payments for loss of office all require the approval of members.[157]

23.56 Conduct consisting in the drawing of excessive levels of remuneration and other benefits,[158] payment of unauthorized remuneration,[159] the procurement by a director of consultancy fees and remuneration in breach of the articles of association,[160] the payment by directors of company money for their own personal expenditure,[161] and gifts described as bonuses and payment to assist a shareholder to pay calls[162] may all amount to unfair prejudice on the part of the directors. In *Re Tobian Properties Ltd*,[163] Arden LJ said that the appropriate level of remuneration should be determined by objective criteria and that excessive remuneration did not cease to be unfair, because it was disclosed in publicly available accounts. In *Re Regional Airports Ltd*,[164] the conduct complained of concerned inter alia an excessive claim to remuneration and the proposal of a rights issue by the majority shareholder and director. It was found that his proposal of the rights issue was motivated by a desire to achieve a situation where: (a) he stood a good chance of being able to increase his proportionate equity stake at effectively no cost to himself; (b) certain desirable aspects of his remuneration package would be settled retrospectively subject only to upwards renegotiation in the future; and (c) the remaining shareholders and directors would be forced either to increase their financial investment in the company or allow their existing stakes to be significantly diluted.

---

[156] 2006 Act, ss 177, 182–7. Discussed in Ch 17 above.

[157] 2006 Act, ss 188–226. Discussed in Ch 18 above.

[158] *Re a Company (No 004415 of 1996)* [1997] 1 BCLC 479; *Irvine v Irvine (No 1)* [2007] 1 BCLC 349 (payment of excessive levels of remuneration by a director to himself without seeking the approval of the company in general meeting and without reference to the board of directors, thus depriving the petitioner of his dividend entitlement); *Re McCarthy Surfacing Ltd* [2009] 1 BCLC 622 (unjustified bonuses); *Re Tobian Properties Ltd* [2013] 2 BCLC 567, CA at paras 30–6, 44–50 (excessive remuneration). In such circumstances the court may hear expert evidence as to 'objective commercial criteria' to determine whether the remuneration was in fact excessive and thus founds an allegation of unfair prejudice. Note the observations on remuneration levels in *Smith v Croft* [1986] 1 WLR 580, 592, and *Smith v Croft (No 2)* [1988] Ch 114, 159, 160. See also: *Re Phoneer Ltd* [2002] 2 BCLC 241(an attempt by the majority shareholder and director to renegotiate an agreed salary structure and his simultaneous withdrawal from management of the company); *Allmark v Burnham* [2006] 2 BCLC 437 at para 96.

[159] *Clark v Cutland* [2003] 2 BCLC 393, CA; *Anderson v Hogg* [2002] BCC 923 (where the payments were described as redundancy payments).

[160] *Re Ravenhart Service (Holdings) Ltd* [2004] 2 BCLC 376 at para 86; cf *Guinness plc v Saunders* [1990] 2 AC 663.

[161] *Re Jayflex Construction Ltd* [2004] 2 BCLC 145 at para 71. In that case it was held that such payments by both directors of the company were improper and a breach of the duty of each to the company as a director. Such payments, albeit to a minor degree, prejudiced the company and, therefore, the shareholders. However, on the facts Sir Donald Rattee found that since both directors had adopted a practice of making such payments (and there were no other shareholders), neither could complain as against the other that the making of such payments was unfairly prejudicial conduct. Even though the aggregate quantum of payments to each director was not equal, the judge found that there was an understanding as between the directors that an equalization process would be carried out in the future.

[162] *Re Hailey Group Ltd* [1993] BCLC 459, 471.

[163] [2013] 2 BCLC 567, CA at paras 31–3 and 36 (approving *Irvine v Irvine (No 1)* [2007] 1 BCLC 349 at paras 267–8).

[164] [1999] 2 BCLC 30.

Breach of duty of care, skill, and diligence

A director of a company must exercise the care, skill, and diligence that may reasonably be **23.57** expected of a person carrying out the functions carried out by the director in relation to the company and the general knowledge, skill, and experience that the director has.[165]

It is unlikely that a simple breach of this duty will be sufficient to make out a complaint of **23.58** unfair prejudice. In *Re Elgindata Ltd*[166] Warner J identified two reasons for this. The first is the general reluctance of the court to resolve disputes over particular managerial decisions. Not only is the court ill-qualified to do so, but 'there can be no unfairness to the petitioners in those in control of the company's affairs taking a different view from theirs on such matters'. Secondly, shareholders acquire their shares knowing that their value will depend on the competence of management. They take a risk that management will make mistakes. The position might be different if, for example, a director known to be incompetent was kept in office for family reasons. In *Re Macro (Ipswich) Ltd*[167] Arden J applied Warner J's analysis and held there was a distinction between a difference of opinion on commercial decisions and serious mismanagement. The latter could justify intervention under Part 30, particularly where steps were not taken to prevent or rectify it.

Removal of the auditor

By the 2006 Act, s 994(1A) the removal of the company's auditor from office on the grounds **23.59** of divergence of opinions on accounting treatments or audit procedures or on any other improper grounds is to be treated as being unfairly prejudicial to the interests of some part of the company's members for the purposes of s 994(1)(a). Where the auditor is removed in such circumstances, regardless of whether there has been a good faith dispute about accounting treatments or audit procedures, the court must find that unfair prejudice has been established, but it need not necessarily consider it appropriate to grant relief.[168]

Equitable restraints on lawful conduct

As Lord Hoffmann explained in *Re Saul D Harrison Ltd*[169] and *O'Neill v Phillips*[170] equitable prin- **23.60** ciples may make it unfair for those in control of the company to exercise their legal rights in a particular way. The company may remove a director by ordinary resolution,[171] but if the director is a minority shareholder, it may be unfair to remove him without making a fair offer for his shares. To identify the considerations that make equitable principles applicable in the context of unfair prejudice petitions, Lord Hoffmann applied the reasoning of Lord Wilberforce in *Ebrahimi v Westbourne Galleries Ltd*[172] (a contributory's winding-up petition on the just and equitable ground):

> The words ['just and equitable'] are a recognition of the fact that a limited company is more than a mere legal entity, with a personality in law of its own: that there is room in company law

[165] 2006 Act, s 174. Discussed in Ch 14 above.
[166] [1991] BCLC 959, 993, 994.
[167] [1994] 2 BCLC 354, 405, 406. See also *Re Saul D Harrison & Sons plc* [1995] 1 BCLC 14, 31, per Neill LJ; *F&C Alternative Investments (Holdings) Ltd v Barthelemy* [2011] EWHC 1731 (Ch) at paras 254, 593, 594 (partially reported at [2012] Ch 613).
[168] *Re Sunrise Radio Ltd* [2010] 1 BCLC 367 at para 10.
[169] [1995] 1 BCLC 14, 19a–20b, CA.
[170] [1999] 1 WLR 1092, 1098H–1099A, 1104G, 1107B, HL.
[171] 2006 Act, s 168.
[172] [1973] AC 360, 379, HL. Lord Hoffmann quoted the first paragraph of the quotation and referred to the second paragraph of the quotation at [1999] 1 WLR 1092, 1099. He quoted both passages in *Re Saul D Harrison & Sons plc* [1995] 1 BCLC 14 at pp 19 and 20, CA.

for recognition of the fact that behind it, or amongst it, there are individuals with rights, expectations and obligations inter se which are not necessarily submerged in the company structure. That structure is defined by the Companies Act and by the articles of association by which shareholders agree to be bound. In most companies and in most contexts, this definition is sufficient and exhaustive, equally so whether the company is large or small. The 'just and equitable' provision does not, as the respondents suggest, entitle one party to disregard the obligation he assumes by entering a company, nor the court to dispense him from it. It does, as equity always does, enable the court to subject the exercise of legal rights to equitable considerations; considerations, that is, of a personal character arising between one individual and another, which may make it unjust, or inequitable, to insist on legal rights, or to exercise them in a particular way.

It will be impossible, and wholly undesirable, to define the circumstances in which these considerations may arise. Certainly the fact that the company is a small one, or a private company, is not enough. There are very many of these where the association is a purely commercial one, of which it can safely be said that the basis of association is adequately and exhaustively laid down in the articles. The superimposition of equitable considerations requires something more …

23.61   Where the company is a public company with many shareholders it is improbable that equitable considerations will apply.[173] In relation to listed companies the public dealing in the market for the company's shares must be entitled to proceed 'on the footing that the constitution of the company is as it appears in the company's public documents, unaffected by any extraneous equitable considerations and constraints'.[174]

23.62   Equally with private companies there may be no scope for equitable considerations to be applied. *Re Saul D Harrison Ltd*[175] was a case where there was 'nothing more' to prevent the board from exercising its powers of management. In *Posgate and Denby Agencies Ltd*[176] Hoffmann J rejected the petitioner's case that certain property could not be sold without shareholder approval as being inconsistent with (a) the directors' powers of management conferred by the articles, (b) a particular article dealing with conflicts of interest, and (c) the fact shareholders must be taken to accept that the best commercial decisions may not be taken. Similarly the existence of detailed agreements may preclude any expectation inhibiting the exercise of legal rights.[177]

23.63   As Lord Hoffmann explained in *O'Neill v Phillips*[178] it is usually unfair for a member who has been removed from participation in management to keep his investment locked

---

[173] *Re Blue Arrow plc* [1987] BCLC 585, 590 (petition of president of quoted company to prevent it from altering its articles to remove her was struck out); *Re Tottenham Hotspur plc* [1994] 1 BCLC 655, 659 (no expectation that nominee of minority shareholder in quoted company would retain office as chief executive); *Re Leeds United Holdings plc* [1996] 2 BCLC 556, 559; *Re Benfield Greig Group plc* [2000] 2 BCLC 488, 507, 508; *Re CAS (Nominees) Ltd v Nottingham Forest FC plc* [2002] 1 BCLC 613 at para 37.

[174] *Re Astec (BSR) plc* [1998] 2 BCLC 556, 589, 590 (where the judge rejected the petitioner's submission that it had a legitimate expectation that the listed company would comply with the Listing Rules, the City Code, and the Cadbury Code).

[175] [1995] 1 BCLC 14, 20, CA. In that case the complaint, which was dismissed, was that the directors were continuing a loss-making business in order to earn remuneration, whereas a reasonable board would stop trade and sell the company's property.

[176] [1987] BCLC 8, 14.

[177] *Re a Company (No 005685), ex p Schwarcz* [1989] BCLC 427, 440, 441 (no expectation that a director would not be removed from office in a case where there were detailed agreements covering the relationship between the parties). Also see *Re Elgindata Ltd* [1991] BCLC 959, 985; *Re Estate Acquisition & Development Ltd* [1995] BCC 338, 345–9, 355.

[178] [1999] 1 WLR 1092, 1104F–H, HL (where the petitioner unsuccessfully relied on loss of confidence in management in support of a petition to be bought out).

up in the company, but 'that does not mean that a member who has not been dismissed or excluded can demand that his shares be purchased simply because he feels that he has lost trust and confidence in the others'.[179] In *Re Neath Rugby Ltd (No 2), Hawkes v Cuddy (No 2)* the Court of Appeal held that a mere allegation of deadlock between shareholders without more did not constitute unfairly prejudicial conduct for the purposes of a Part 30 petition, although it might justify a winding up order on the just and equitable ground.[180]

The 'something more' referred to by Lord Wilberforce (paragraph 23.60 above) may typi- **23.64**
cally include one, or probably more of the following elements:

> (i) an association formed or continued on the basis of a personal relationship, involving mutual trust and confidence ... ; (ii) an agreement, or understanding, that all, or some (for there may be 'sleeping' members), of the shareholders shall participate in the conduct of the business; (iii) restriction upon the transfer of the member's interest in the company—so that if confidence is lost, or one member is removed from management, he cannot take out his stake and go elsewhere.[181]

As a convenient shorthand an association in a company which has these features is usually called a 'quasi-partnership'. Relationships in relation to a company may change so that it may become a quasi-partnership,[182] or cease to be one.[183] The fact that the minority shareholder is employed by the company under a service agreement does not preclude a quasi-partnership relationship, although the dividing line between a master and servant relationship and the more equal one of quasi-partnership may be a fine one.[184] Where a person who began working for the company as an employee, but later became a director and shareholder, claimed relief from unfair prejudice on the footing that the company was a quasi-partnership, the question to be answered is whether, if the company had been incorporated at the time it was alleged to have become a quasi-partnership, it would have been formed on the basis of a personal relationship involving mutual confidence with one or more of the three elements described above.[185]

---

[179] In *Re a Company (No 004475 of 1982)* [1983] Ch 178, 191 Lord Granchester said that he did not consider that the unfair prejudice section was enacted 'so as to enable a "locked-in" minority shareholder to require the company to buy him out at a price which he considered adequately to reflect the value of the underlying assets referable to his shareholding, providing the company held sufficient resources so to do'. Also see *Re Jayflex Construction Ltd* [2004] 2 BCLC 145 at para 55.

[180] [2009] 2 BCLC 427 at paras 101–8, per Stanley Burnton LJ, reversing the judgment of Lewison J on this point ([2008] BCC 390 at para 231, a case containing a full review of the authorities at paras 198–242) and overruling *Re Guidezone Ltd* [2000] 2 BCLC 321 at paras 177–80.

[181] [1973] AC 360, 379; summarized by Lord Hoffmann in *O'Neill v Phillips* [1999] 1 WLR 1092, 1102, HL and by Lord Millett in *CVC/Opportunity Equity Partners Ltd v Demarco Almeida* [2002] 2 BCLC 108, PC (a just and equitable winding-up case) at para 32.

[182] As was the case in *O'Neill v Phillips* [1999] 1 WLR 1092, HL.

[183] *Re a Company (No 005134 of 1986)* [1989] BCLC 383; *Re McCarthy Surfacing Ltd* [2009] 1 BCLC 622 at paras 95–9.

[184] There was a quasi-partnership relationship in *Quinlan v Essex Hinge Co Ltd* [1996] 2 BCLC 417; *Richards v Lundy* [2000] 1 BCLC 376; *Brownlow v GH Marshall Ltd* [2000] 2 BCLC 655; *Croly v Good* [2010] 2 BCLC 569; but not in the Scottish case *Third v North East Ice & Cold Storage Co Ltd* [1998] BCC 242. Nor was there a quasi-partnership relationship in *Re Migration Solutions Holdings Ltd* [2016] EWHC 523 (Ch).

[185] *Strahan v Wilcock* [2006] 2 BCLC 555, CA at para 21.

23.65 There have been many cases of exclusion from management where, in the absence of a fair offer to buy the petitioner's shares, the court has taken into account equitable considerations and given the petitioner relief from unfair prejudice by ordering the purchase of his shares at a fair price.[186] In *Re Kenyon Swansea Ltd*[187] the petitioner was a minority shareholder and managing director of the company and had an option to buy the majority shareholder's shares. The court refused to strike out a petition which complained that the majority shareholder was taking steps to alter the company's articles to prevent the option from being exercisable and to have the petitioner removed from office.

23.66 The petitioner's misconduct or threatened breach or departure from the company's constitution or associated agreements may prevent him from complaining that his exclusion from management was unfair.[188] Even in a case of a quasi-partnership, if a director voluntarily resigns for personal reasons, or indicates his wish to do so, it is not unfair for him to be excluded from management and such a departing director cannot force a purchase of his shares at their full undiscounted value when he had no contractual right to do so.[189]

23.67 As Lord Hoffmann also explained in *O'Neill v Phillips*,[190] 'there may be some event which puts an end to the basis upon which the parties entered into association with each other, making it unfair that one shareholder should insist upon the continuance of the association'. Thus where the parties joined together to operate a nightclub, which was sold, it may be unfair to the minority shareholder, who wished to recover his investment, for the directors and majority shareholders to use their powers to invest the proceeds in another club or business.[191] Similarly, where a company paid management charges to one of its shareholder's companies while both shareholders were engaged in management, it may be unfair to continue to do so after the relationship in the business has ended.[192] The court would only find that a breakdown in the relationship of trust and confidence had been caused by unfairly prejudicial

---

[186] *Re a Company (No 00477 of 1986)* [1986] BCLC 376; *Tay Bok Choon v Tahansan Sdn Bdh* [1987] 1 WLR 413, PC (a just and equitable winding-up case); *Re Ghill Beck Driving Range Ltd* [1993] BCLC 1126; *R&H Electric Ltd v Haden Bill Electrical Ltd* [1995] 2 BCLC 280, 295 (participation through a representative); *Quinlan v Essex Hinge Co Ltd* [1996] 2 BCLC 417; *Re a Company (No 002015 of 1996)* [1997] 2 BCLC 1 (even though there were formal agreements between the parties); *Richards v Lundy* [2000] 1 BCLC 376; *Brownlow v GH Marshall Ltd* [2000] 2 BCLC 655 (even though the director had a service agreement); *Parkinson v Eurofinance Group Ltd* [2001] 1 BCLC 720; *Richardson v Blackmore* [2006] BCC 276, CA at paras 64–8; *Strahan v Wilcock* [2006] 2 BCLC 555, CA at paras 27–30; *Re Abbington Hotels Ltd* [2012] 1 BCLC 410 (Ch); *Moxon v Litchfield* [2013] EWHC 3957 (Ch) (petitioner was a bad leaver so no unfairness in him being bought out under the terms of the articles); *Re J&S Insurance & Financial Consultants Ltd* [2014] EWHC 2206 (Ch) (where notwithstanding the petitioner's conduct, the exclusion could not be objectively justified and no fair offer was made).

[187] [1987] BCLC 514.

[188] *Re London School of Electronics Ltd* [1986] Ch 211, 222; *Parkinson v Eurofinance Group Ltd* [2001] 1 BCLC 720 at para 87; *Mears v R Mears & Co (Holdings) Ltd* [2002] 2 BCLC 1 at paras 34–6; *Grace v Biagioli* [2006] 2 BCLC 70, CA at para 64 (petitioner's removal justified by putting himself in a position of conflict and attempted concealment of actions); *Shah v Shah* [2010] EWHC 313 (Ch); [2010] EWCA Civ 1408 (misconduct insufficient to prevent exclusion from being unfair). Where a director tipped off a customer about the company's unlawful collusive practices, he was not in breach of his duty under 2006 Act, s 172 and his subsequent exclusion was unfairly prejudicial conduct: *Re Phoenix Contracts (Leicester) Ltd* [2010] EWHC 2375 (Ch).

[189] *Re Guidezone Ltd* [2000] 2 BCLC 321 at paras 185–92; *Mears v R Mears & Co (Holdings) Ltd* [2002] 2 BCLC 1; *Re Phoenix Office Supplies Ltd* [2003] 1 BCLC 76, CA; *Re Jayflex Construction Ltd* [2004] 2 BCLC 145; *Re Flex Associates Ltd* [2009] EWHC 3690 (Ch).

[190] [1999] 1 WLR 1092, 1101H–1102A, HL.

[191] See the facts of *Virdi v Abbey Leisure Ltd* [1990] BCLC 342, CA, which were considered by Lord Hoffmann at [1999] 1 WLR 1092, 1101H–1102A, HL.

[192] *Wilson v Jaymarke Estates Ltd* [2007] BCC 883, HL (Sc).

conduct in the form of the way one party behaved in dealing with the other if there was particularly strong and clearly unacceptable behaviour and there was a clear preponderance of fault on one side.[193] This was the position in *Re Home & Office Fire Extinguishers Ltd*,[194] where the company was owned and managed by two brothers, one of whom committed a serious assault on the other, aggravated by failure to apologize and denial. The court found that this breached the implied understanding that the brothers would act properly and in good faith towards each other, made it impossible for them to continue their association and caused prejudice to the management of the business. The court ordered the guilty party to sell his shares to his brother on a non-discounted basis.

Where it was understood or agreed that a shareholder would participate in management and the **23.68** venture for which the association between the parties was formed has come to an end, it will ordinarily be unfair for the shareholder's investment to be locked into the company. In *O'Neill v Phillips*[195] Lord Hoffmann explained that fairness required the purchase of the shareholder's shares at a price fixed pro rata to the value of the company without any discount and that, if the parties could not agree on price, an independent expert should be appointed to fix it (paragraph 23.14(10) and (11) above). If the other shareholders offer to buy out the (potential) petitioner in accordance with the principles stated by Lord Hoffmann there will be no unfairness and no need for any relief to be granted by the court. Any petition presented by the shareholder will be struck out.[196]

Sometimes the company's articles provide a mechanism for the purchase of shares, but in a **23.69** case where equitable considerations apply and the shareholder is not a willing seller, the court will not expect him to invoke the procedures in the articles if their terms are, or may be in their implementation, less favourable to him than the principles stated by Lord Hoffmann.[197] Where, however, the articles provide a mechanism which conforms to Lord Hoffmann's principles, it would normally be an abuse of the process of the court for the excluded shareholder to proceed with a Part 30 petition rather than invoking the articles.[198] Indeed, where, by the articles or otherwise, the excluded shareholder has contractually bound himself to sell his shares on agreed terms in the applicable circumstances, the other shareholders' case for the petition being an abuse is stronger.[199] The two exceptions to this, which would justify

---

[193] *F&C Alternative Investments (Holdings) Ltd v Barthelemy* [2011] EWHC 1731 (Ch) at para 668 (this para is not reported at [2012] Ch 613).

[194] *Re Home & Office Fire Extinguishers Ltd* [2012] EWHC 917 (Ch).

[195] [1999] 1 WLR 1092, 1104G, 1107C–H. Also *Re Bird Precision Bellows Ltd* [1984] Ch 419, CA. A discounted basis will usually be appropriate where the company is not a quasi-partnership; see para 23.84 below.

[196] *Re a Company (No 003843 of 1986)* [1987] BCLC 562; *Re a Company (No 005685 of 1988), ex p Schwarcz* [1989] BCLC 427, 437; *West v Blanchet* [2000] 1 BCLC 795; *Re Belfield Furnishings Ltd* [2006] 2 BCLC 707; *Harbourne Road Nominees Ltd v Greenway* [2011] EWHC 2214 (Ch) (petition will only be struck out if the offer gives the petitioner all the advantages he could reasonably expect to receive in the proceedings).

[197] *Re Boswell & Co (Steels) Ltd* (1989) 5 BCC 145; *Virdi v Abbey Leisure Ltd* [1990] BCLC 342, 349, CA; *Re a Company (No 00330 of 1991) ex p Holden* [1991] BCLC 597; *Re Benfield Greig Group plc* [2000] 2 BCLC 488, CA.

[198] *Re Belfield Furnishings Ltd* [2006] 2 BCLC 705 at para 38(1). This is so where the articles have been amended to include a compulsory buy-out provision in circumstances where the amendment was lawful and consistent with a shareholders' agreement: *Re Charterhouse Capital Ltd* [2015] 2 BCLC 627, CA.

[199] *Re Belfield Furnishings Ltd* (n 198 above) at para 38(2). See also *Re a Company (No 007623 of 1984)* [1986] BCLC 362; *Re a Company No 004377 of 1986)* [1987] 1 WLR 102; *Re a Company (No 003096 of 1987)* (1988) 4 BCC 80; *Re a Company (No 006834 of 1988), ex p Kremer* [1989] BCLC 365; *Re Castleburn Ltd* [1991] BCLC 89; *Re Migration Solutions Holdings Ltd* [2016] EWHC 523 (Ch). Indeed in *Holt v Faulks* [2000] 2 BCLC 816 the minority shareholder was bound to sell his shares in accordance with the articles, since their terms applied expressly to a shareholder who had been wrongfully dismissed. In relation to his ability to

Chapter 23: Members' Unfair Prejudice Claims

pursuing a Part 30 petition are where (a) there has been misapplication of company assets which might affect the value of the shares, unless it is agreed that the value of the misapplied assets is restored for the purposes of valuation, or (b) there is an issue as to the independence of the valuer.[200]

(7) Remedies

23.70 A petitioner will usually succeed in obtaining relief if he shows that 'the value of his share-holding in the company has been seriously diminished or at least seriously jeopardized by reason of a course of conduct on the part of those persons who have had de facto control of the company, which has been unfair to him'.[201] But those are not the only reasons why the court may consider it just to grant relief. Relief may be granted provided the applicant is a member and the court is satisfied that the affairs of the company have been conducted in a manner unfairly prejudicial to his interests.[202] Even if the petition is well founded, the petitioner's conduct may affect the relief given to him (paragraph 23.34 above).

23.71 The relief cannot be granted under s 996 until the court is satisfied that the petition is well founded.[203] It must be appropriate at the time the court decides what, if any, relief to grant.[204] In formulating the relief to be granted the court may take into account the interests of other members and creditors and may even grant relief that the petitioner did not seek.[205]

23.72 The assessment of the seriousness or otherwise of the unfairly prejudicial conduct and appropriate remedy are matters of judgment. The latter decision is for the discretion of the trial judge and the Court of Appeal will be slow to interfere with his decisions on those matters unless it is shown that (i) his decision was based on legal error or on unsustainable findings of fact, (ii) he failed to take a relevant matter into account, (iii) he took an irrelevant matter into account, or (iv) his decision was one that he could not sensibly have reached.[206]

The general power

23.73 Most unfair prejudice petitions concern closely held private companies. If successful, the court invariably makes an order for the purchase of the petitioner's shares, exercising its power under s 996(2)(e), but the power of the court to grant relief is not limited. Section 996(1) provides:

---

petition under Part 30, such a shareholder would seem to be in the position described in *Baker v Potter* [2005] BCC 855 (para 23.05 above).

[200] *Re Benfield Greig Group plc* [2000] 2 BCLC 488, CA; *Re Belfield Furnishings Ltd* [2006] 2 BCLC 705 at para 38(3).

[201] *Re Bovey Hotels Ltd* (31 July 1981, unreported), per Slade J; adopted and applied by Nourse J in *Re RA Noble & Sons (Clothing) Ltd* [1983] BCLC 273; by Warner J in *Re Elgindata Ltd* [1991] BCLC 959, 984; and by Hart J in *Re Regional Airports Ltd* [1999] 2 BCLC 30, 79.

[202] *Gamlestaden Fastigher AB v Baltic Partners Ltd* [2007] 4 All ER 164, PC at para 24.

[203] Para 23.90 below.

[204] *Re Hailey Group Ltd* [1993] BCLC 459, 473. In this case the relief sought in the petition was no longer appropriate, since the company had become insolvent for reasons unconnected with the matters complained of and receivers had been appointed. A buy-out order would amount to a fine on the respondents since there was nothing of value to buy. The position might have been different if the petitioner had been prevented from selling his shares before the onset of insolvency.

[205] *Re Neath Rugby Ltd (No 2), Hawkes v Cuddy (No 2)* [2009] 2 BCLC 427, CA at paras 84–91; *Fulham Football Club (1987) Ltd v Richards* [2012] Ch 333, CA at para 46.

[206] *Re Neath Rugby Ltd (No 2), Hawkes v Cuddy (No 2)* [2009] 2 BCLC 427, CA at para 80.

616

If the court is satisfied that a petition under this Part is well founded, it may make such order as it thinks fit for giving relief in respect of the matters complained of.

In *Re a Company (No 005287 of 1985)*[207] Hoffmann J said of similar words in the predecessor of s 996(1): 'Those words appear to give the widest possible discretion.' Similarly in *Re Bird Precision Bellows Ltd*[208] Oliver LJ said of the same section that it confers on the court 'a very wide discretion to do what is considered fair and equitable in all the circumstances of the case, in order to put right and cure for the future the unfair prejudice which the petitioner has suffered at the hands of the other shareholders of the company'. The court's powers of granting relief are not limited to the particular heads of relief identified in s 996(2). Nor need the relief be directed solely towards remedying the particular things that have happened.[209] In appropriate circumstances a declaration may be granted.[210]

Thus where the conduct complained of is misappropriation of company property or other **23.74** conduct causing it loss, the court may order a party before it to make a payment to the company.[211] This short-circuits a derivative claim, as mentioned in s 996(2)(c). However, in *Re Chime Corporation Ltd*[212] Lord Scott of Foscote NPJ said that such a claim should not be included in an unfair prejudice petition, as distinct from a derivative claim, unless it is clear at the pleading stage that the claim can be dealt with conveniently in the petition, so that, if the claim is upheld, the company receives the amount, if any, to which it is entitled and the person liable receives a good discharge as against the company.

In *Atlasview Ltd v Brightview Ltd*[213] the deputy judge considered that the provision now in s **23.75** 996(1) would enable the court to order the person liable to the company to make a payment direct to the petitioner. In *Re Chime Corporation Ltd*[214] Lord Scott of Foscote NPJ pointed out that this could only be done in a winding up or by a distribution duly made, in each case having regard to creditors' interests.

Where the respondent director and shareholder had misappropriated the company's **23.76** business leaving the company in an uncertain financial position, in addition to ordering him to buy the petitioner's shares at fair value, the court may make him jointly and

---

[207] [1986] 1 WLR 281, 283; *Re Little Olympian Each-Ways Ltd* [1994] 2 BCLC 420, 423, 424; *Re Neath Rugby Ltd (No 2), Hawkes v Cuddy (No 2)* [2008] BCC 390 at paras 243–7; [2009] 2 BCLC 427, CA at para 92.

[208] [1986] Ch 658, 669, CA.

[209] *Re Hailey Group Ltd* [1993] BCLC 459, 472.

[210] *Re Castleburn Ltd* [1991] BCLC 89, 102; *Clark v Cutland* [2004] 1 WLR 783, CA at para 34 (declaration that company entitled to charge over assets in respondent's pension fund); *Re Neath Rugby Ltd* [2008] 1 BCLC 527 at para 92 (although the Court of Appeal held that the grant of declaratory relief was premature; [2008] BCC 125 at paras 21 and 22).

[211] *Lowe v Fahey* [1996] 1 BCLC 262; *Anderson v Fahey* [2002] BCC 923; *Clark v Cutland* [2003] 2 BCLC 393; *Atlas Ltd v Brightview Ltd* [2004] 2 BCLC 191 at paras 56 and 63; *Re Chime Corporation Ltd* [2004] HKFCA 73 at para 49, per Lord Scott of Foscote NPJ; *Gamlestaden Fastigher AB v Baltic Partners Ltd* [2007] 4 All ER 164, PC at para 28; *Rahman v Malik* [2008] 2 BCLC 403, 426–7 (reconciliation of funds diverted to respondent's company, as well as payment to petitioner of his proper share of profits and of dividends and buy-out order).

[212] [2004] HKFCA 73 at para 62.

[213] [2004] 2 BCLC 191 at para 63.

[214] [2004] HKFCA 73 at para 46. In *Richardson v Blackmore* [2006] BCC 276 the Court of Appeal set aside an order under which £60,000 of company money was to be applied towards payment for the petitioner's shares as being unlawful financial assistance. On the restriction at common law and 2006 Act, ss 829 and 830 on distributions to shareholders otherwise than by way of payment for services or an asset, see *Progress Property Co Ltd v Moorgarth* [2010] 1 BCLC, CA at para 23; [2011] 1 WLR 1, SC at paras 15 and 16; *Re TXU Europe Group plc* [2012] BCC 363.

severally liable with the company to repay a loan made by the petitioner to the company and order him to indemnify the petitioner as guarantor of the company's lease and bank overdraft.[215]

Regulation of the affairs of the company

23.77 Section 996(2)(a), (b), and (d) (quoted in paragraph 23.10 above) gives the court wide powers to regulate the affairs of the company and put right the matters complained of. In a case under the 1948 Act, s 210, *Re HR Harmer Ltd*,[216] the court ordered the principal respondent not to interfere in the affairs of the company otherwise than in accordance with valid decisions of the board. The power has been used to prevent the issue and allotment of shares and the company disposing of property pending a meeting[217] or to order the convening of an extraordinary general meeting for the purpose of replacing directors who were considered to be incompetent.[218]

23.78 These powers have been little used, however, because a buy-out order is usually the most satisfactory means of disposing of a successful unfair prejudice petition. In *Grace v Biagioli*[219] the directors had breached their duties by withholding a dividend from the petitioner and paying themselves management fees. The Court of Appeal took the view that relations between the parties had broken down to such an extent that making good the default by paying the petitioner the dividends he should have been paid was not sufficient and that the respondents should be ordered to buy the petitioner's shares.

23.79 In *Re Neath Rugby Ltd (No 2), Hawkes v Cuddy (No 2)*,[220] Lewison J considered that an order that one member should sell his shares to the other was disproportionate to the unfair prejudice that had been established; instead the court would make an order regulating the affairs of the company in a way that gave the other member a more effective role in the company's affairs. The Court of Appeal dismissed the appeal from this order, observing that the judge's order was workable and probably the least bad solution.[221]

Derivative claim

23.80 The power under s 996(2)(c) to 'authorise civil proceedings to be brought in the name and on behalf of the company by such person or persons and on such terms as the court may direct' has also been little used.[222] Where the petitioner's purpose is to obtain relief for the benefit of the company and the intended defendant to the derivative claim is a respondent to the Part 30 petition, the court, if satisfied that the petition is well founded, may make an immediate order in favour of the company, so avoiding the cost and delay of a derivative claim (see paragraph 23.74 above).

---

[215] *Allmark v Burnham* [2006] 2 BCLC 437.
[216] [1959] 1 WLR 62, CA.
[217] *Malaga Investments Ltd, Petitioners* (1987) 3 BCC 569.
[218] *McGuinness v Bremner plc* [1988] BCLC 673.
[219] [2006] 2 BCLC 70, CA. See also *Fowler v Gruber* [2010] 1 BCLC 563.
[220] [2008] BCC 390 at paras 290–1.
[221] [2009] 1 BCLC 427 at paras 80–92.
[222] In *Music Sales Ltd v Shapiro Bornstein & Co Ltd* [2006] 1 BCLC 371 an alternative head of relief was authority to bring certain proceedings in New York. The judge dismissed an application to strike out the petition, but, at para 16, expressed surprise that neither side sought a buy-out order. In *Moordene Ltd v Trans Global Chartering Ltd* [2006] EWHC 1407 Ch a petition seeking such relief was dismissed.

Buy-out orders

The usual order made on a successful unfair prejudice petition is an order that the **23.81** respondent(s) buy the petitioner's shares at a fair price. The respondent ordered to buy the shares need not have been involved in the conduct complained of.[223] Exceptionally the court may order the respondent to sell his shares to the petitioner.[224] A buy-out order must be proportionate to the matters complained of and it will be refused where such an order would be disproportionate[225] or no longer appropriate at the time of the hearing.[226]

The overriding requirement is that the valuation should be fair on the facts of the case.[227] **23.82** There are two principal issues relevant to the fairness of a valuation: its basis (pro rata or discounted) and the date of valuation.

Usually the fair price will represent a pro rata share of the total value of the company, with- **23.83** out any discount on account of minority holding.[228] In quasi-partnership cases, a valuation on a non-discounted basis is well established.[229] In *CVC/Opportunity Equity Partners Ltd v Almeida*[230] Lord Millett explained that the reason for this rule derived from the law of partnership under which the value of the outgoing partner's interest was 'based on a notional sale of the business as a whole to an outside purchaser' and that in the case of a quasi-partnership company:

> the majority can exclude the minority only if they offer to pay them a fair price for their shares. In order to be free to manage the company's business without regard to the relationship of trust and confidence which formerly existed between them, they must buy the whole, part from themselves and part from the minority, thereby achieving the same freedom to manage the business as an outside purchaser would enjoy.

These considerations do not apply where the company is not a quasi-partnership. Then a fair **23.84** price may include a discount on account of a minority interest. Indeed Arden LJ has said: 'It is difficult to conceive of circumstances in which a non-discounted basis of valuation would be appropriate where there was unfair prejudice for the purposes of the 1985 Act but such a relationship [of quasi-partnership] did not exist.'[231] In *Irvine v Irvine (No 2)*[232] Blackburne J summarized the position:

---

[223] *Re Little Olympian Each-Ways Ltd (No 3)* [1995] 1 BCLC 636, 666.

[224] *Re a Company (No 00789 of 1987), ex p Shooter* [1990] BCLC 384, 394, 395; *Re a Company (No 00789 of 1987), ex p Shooter (No 2)* [1991] BCLC 267; *Re Brenfield Squash Racquets Club Ltd* [1996] 2 BCLC 184, 190; *Re Home & Office Fire Extinguishers Ltd* [2012] EWHC 917 (Ch).

[225] *Re Full Cup International Trading Ltd* [1995] BCC 682; on appeal *Antoniades v Wong* [1997] 2 BCLC 419, CA (no order made in a case where a winding-up order would have been the appropriate remedy, but was not sought); *Re Metropolis Motorcycles Ltd* [2007] 1 BCLC 520 (no order made); *Hawkes v Cuddy (No 2)* [2008] BCC 390 (see para 23.79 above).

[226] *Re Hailey Group Ltd* [1993] BCLC 459 (see para 23.71 above).

[227] *Re London School of Economics Ltd* [1986] Ch 211, 224; *Re Bird Precision Bellows Ltd* [1986] Ch 658, 669, CA; *Shah v Shah* [2011] EWHC 1902 (Ch) at para 6.

[228] *O'Neill v Phillips* [1999] 1 WLR 1092, 1107C–1108B, HL. If necessary the price may be fixed by an expert.

[229] *Re Bird Precision Bellows Ltd* [1984] Ch 419, 431 (affd [1986] Ch 658, CA); *Strahan v Wilcock* [2006] 2 BCLC 555, CA at para 55; *Rahman v Malik* [2008] 2 BCLC 403, 426.

[230] [2002] 2 BCLC 108, PC at paras 41 and 42.

[231] *Strahan v Wilcock* [2006] 2 BCLC 555, CA at para 17.

[232] [2007] 1 BCLC 445 at para 11. Nevertheless in *Re Sunrise Radio Ltd* [2010] 1 BCLC 367, a case where the company was not a quasi-partnership, at paras 289–308 HHJ Purle QC considered the relevant authorities and ordered that the petitioner be bought out on a non-discounted basis.

> A minority shareholding, even one where the extent of the minority is as slight as in this case, is to be valued for what it is, a minority shareholding, unless there is some good reason to attribute to it a pro rata share of the overall value of the company. Short of a quasi-partnership or some other exceptional circumstance, there is no good reason to accord to it a quality it lacks.

A discounted basis is also appropriate where the quasi-partnership relationship has ceased and the petitioner has determined to remain as a minority shareholder.[233]

23.85   Subsequently, in *Re Annacott Holdings Ltd*[234] Arden LJ said that there is no inflexible rule that a buy-out order valued on a non-discounted going concern basis is available only in a quasi-partnership case. In that case, concerning a company which had been formed to make capital profits from disposal of properties, it was fair to value the petitioner's shares on that basis, since a discounted break-up basis would produce a windfall for the respondent who retained the benefit of the properties.

23.86   The selection of the date of valuation is informed by two considerations.[235] One consideration is that the shares should be valued at a date as close as possible to the date of sale; ie the date on which the shares are ordered to be purchased.[236] The other consideration favours the date of the petition as being the date when the petitioner elected to treat the unfair conduct as destroying the basis on which he agreed to continue as a shareholder.[237] If an early date is chosen the court has power under s 996 to include a sum equivalent to interest.[238] In *Profinance Trust SA v Gladstone*[239] Robert Walker LJ concluded that the starting point was that the valuation date should be the date of the order to purchase, but that in the interests of fairness to one side or the other a different date might be selected. He illustrated the circumstances where that might be appropriate:

(i)   Where a company has been deprived of its business, an early valuation date (and compensating adjustments) may be required in fairness to the claimant.[240]

(ii) Where a company has been reconstructed or its business has changed significantly, so that there is a new economic identity, an early valuation date may be required in fairness to one or both parties.[241] But an improper alteration in the issued share capital, unaccompanied by any change in the business, will not necessarily have that outcome.[242]

---

[233]   *Re a Company (No 005134 of 1986)* [1989] BCLC 383, 399; *Re McCarthy Surfacing Ltd* [2009] 1 BCLC 622 at paras 95–9 (petitioners had ended the quasi-partnership by launching unsuccessful proceedings); *Fowler v Gruber* [2010] 1 BCLC 563.

[234]   [2013] 2 BCLC 46, CA at paras 11–15.

[235]   *Profinance Trust SA v Gladstone* [2002] 1 WLR 1024, CA at paras 33–45, per Robert Walker LJ.

[236]   *Re London School of Electronics Ltd* [1986] Ch 211, 224; *Re a Company (No 005134 of 1986)* [1989] BCLC 383, 399; *Re Elgindata Ltd* [1991] BCLC 959; *Re Regional Airports Ltd* [1999] 2 BCLC 30, 83.

[237]   *Re a Company (No 002612 of 1984)* (1986) 2 BCC 99, 453, 492–9; on appeal as *Re Cumana Ltd* [1986] BCLC 430, 436, 445, CA; *Re OC (Transport) Services* [1984] BCLC 251, 258.

[238]   *Profinance Trust SA v Gladstone* [2002] 1 WLR 1024, CA at paras 31 and 32, where Robert Walker LJ said that the power to include interest was to be exercised sparingly and that a petitioner had to plead the claim and support it with evidence to persuade the court that including interest produced a fair result. Valuation may include an interest element to compensate the petitioner for delayed valuation and payment where the respondent had enjoyed benefit of company: *Re Southern Counties Fresh Foods Ltd* [2010] EWHC 3334 (Ch). In *Re Annacott Holdings Ltd* [2013] 2 BCLC 46, CA at para 27 Arden LJ said that the power to award interest ought to be exercised only on a proper evidential basis.

[239]   [2002] 1 WLR 1024, CA at paras 60 and 61.

[240]   *Scottish Co-operative Wholesale Society Ltd v Meyer* [1959] AC 324, HL (Sc).

[241]   *Re OC (Transport) Services* [1984] BCLC 251; *Re London School of Electronics Ltd* [1986] Ch 211.

[242]   *Re a Company (No 005134 of 1986)* [1989] BCLC 383.

(iii) Where a minority shareholder has a petition on foot and there is a general fall in the market, the court may in fairness to the claimant have the shares valued at an early date, especially if it strongly disapproves of the majority shareholder's prejudicial conduct.[243]

(iv) But a claimant is not entitled to what the deputy judge called a one-way bet, and the court will not direct an early valuation date simply to give the claimant the most advantageous exit from the company, especially where severe prejudice has not been made out.[244]

(v) All these points may be heavily influenced by the parties' conduct in making and accepting or rejecting offers either before or during the course of the proceedings.[245]

23.87 Valuing the shares in a private company as a going concern on the open market is not a straightforward task, since there is no known applicable price/earnings ratio to be applied to the company's maintainable profits.[246] The valuation may add back losses caused by the unfairly prejudicial conduct[247] where the facts are clear.[248] An asset, such as a claim for use of a trade name, should not be left out of account unless it is clear that the cost of valuation is disproportionate to its value.[249] But it is appropriate to deduct or leave out of account bank debt and debts owing to or by connected parties that a purchaser of the company would not take on and would expect to be discharged before completing the purchase.[250] Where an issue affecting valuation is not clear, the issue should be determined by the court, not the valuer.[251]

23.88 The court may also adjust the value in the light of the unfairly prejudicial conduct complained of.[252] Where the unfairly prejudicial conduct included failure to consider paying dividends, the value may compensate the petitioner for having lost the chance to receive pro rata dividends.[253]

23.89 Although the court will be reluctant to reach such a conclusion, it is possible that difficulties in the way of valuing the shares mean that a fair price is not ascertainable; in such a case no order for purchase will be made and a winding-up order may be the only appropriate relief.[254]

Interim orders

23.90 The court does not have power to make an interim order in exercise of its jurisdiction under Part 30, s 996 until it is satisfied that the petition is well founded.[255] Once an order

---

[243] *Re Cumana Ltd* [1986] BCLC 430, CA; *Re Phoenix Contracts (Leicester) Ltd* [2011] EWHC 2375 (Ch) at paras 153 and 154 (valuation at date of exclusion where company had subsequently gone into administration).

[244] *Re Elgindata Ltd* [1991] BCLC 959.

[245] *O'Neill v Phillips* [1999] 1 WLR 1092, HL.

[246] *Re Planet Organic Ltd* [2000] 1 BCLC 366; *Parkinson v Eurofinance Group Ltd* [2001] 1 BLC 720.

[247] *Lloyd v Casey* [2002] 1 BCLC 454; *Wilson v Jaymarke Estates Ltd* [2007] BCC 883, HL (Sc) (where improper management charges were added back); *Re Scitec Ltd* [2011] 1 BCLC 277. For later proceedings, see [2012] EWHC 661 (Ch).

[248] *Macro v Thompson (No 3)* [1997] 2 BCLC 36, 72.

[249] *Re Tobian Properties Ltd* [2013] 2 BCLC 567, CA at para 55.

[250] *Re Sunrise Radio Ltd* [2014] 1 BCLC 427, CA at paras 31–6.

[251] *North Holdings Ltd v Southern Tropics Ltd* [1999] 2 BCLC 625, 637, CA.

[252] *Birdi v Specsavers Optical Group Ltd* [2015] EWHC 2870 (Ch) at paras 361–5 in which Nugee J adjusted the share price to take account of the effect of breaches of fiduciary duty.

[253] *Re McCarthy Surfacing Ltd* [2009] 1 BCLC 622 at paras 100 and 101.

[254] *Re Full Cup International Trading Ltd* [1995] BCC 682; on appeal *Antoniades v Wong* [1997] 2 BCLC 419, 427, CA.

[255] *Re Bird Precision Bellows Ltd* [1986] Ch 658, 670, CA; *Re a Company (No 007623 of 1984)* [1986] BCLC 362, 368; *Re a Company (No 004175 of 1986)* [1987] 1 WLR 585 (where Scott J noted that what is now the Insolvency Act, s 125(1) gives the court power to make an interim order on hearing a winding-up

for the purchase of shares has been made, the court can order an interim payment on account.[256]

23.91 In a petition under Part 30, the court may grant an interim injunction in exercise of its general jurisdiction under the Senior Courts Act 1981, s 37.[257] In the context of a Part 30 petition the court's normal consideration of issue to be tried, adequacy of damages and balance of convenience[258] has to be modified to a consideration of whether there is an adequate remedy at the end of the day for the petitioner.[259] Since in general the petitioner will be compensated in the price he receives for his shares, it is seldom necessary for the court to grant injunctions imposing controls on the management of the company.[260] Nevertheless the court frequently grants injunctions to prevent use of company funds on its participation in what is usually in substance a shareholders' dispute (paragraphs 23.98 and 23.99 below).

23.92 Under the same jurisdiction (the Senior Courts Act, s 37) the court may appoint a receiver in a quasi-partnership case where it is not clear which party will be ordered to buy out the other and there is evidence of mismanagement by the respondents.[261] In most cases it is clear who will be bought out if the petition succeeds and there is no need for an order interfering with management by the party who will retain control of the company.

23.93 A freezing order may be made in a Part 30 petition to prevent dissipation of the company's assets[262] or against individual respondents after they have been ordered to purchase the petitioner's shares.[263] There are difficulties in making a freezing order against the individual respondents before the court is satisfied that the petition is well founded, because the general principle is that a freezing order can only be made in support of an existing cause of action.[264]

---

petition). Harman J followed this decision in *Re a Company (No 004502 of 1988), ex p Johnson* [1992] BCLC 701, 706, 707, when refusing to make an interim order that the respondent shareholders restore to the company its money, which had been wrongly used by them in responding to the unfair prejudice petition. *Malaga Investments Ltd, Petitioners* (1987) 3 BCC 569 appears to be a case where the injunction was granted on the footing that the petition was well founded.

[256] *Re Clearsprings (Management) Ltd* [2003] EWHC (Ch) 2516 at paras 43–5 (recording that the court's power to make such an order was common ground).

[257] *Re a Company (No 2612 of 1984)* [1985] BCLC 80 (interim injunction to restrain majority from voting at a general meeting to increase capital and confer a power of allotment on directors); *Re a Company (No 00330 of 1991), ex p Holden* [1991] BCLC 597 (interim injunction to restrain individual respondents from implementing compulsory purchase of petitioner's shares); *Rutherford, Petitioner* [1994] BCC 876 (interim injunction to restrain the company from proceeding with a buy-back of its shares was discharged on the balance of convenience); *Jones v Jones* [2003] BCC 226, CA (interim injunction to restrain the company from pursuing a separate action against the petitioner until after the disposal of the unfair prejudice petition); *Re Ravenhart Service (Holdings) Ltd* [2004] 2 BCLC 376 (interim injunction to restrain the company from making payments to directors of fees and remuneration); *Re RSM Industries Ltd* [2004] EWHC 601 (Ch) (interim injunction to restrain removal of petitioner as a director where he sought an order that the respondents sell their shares to him).

[258] *American Cyanamid Co v Ethicon Ltd* [1975] AC 396, HL.

[259] *Re Posgate & Denby (Agencies) Ltd* [1987] BCLC 8, 15, 16; *Pringle v Callard* [2008] 2 BCLC 505, CA at para 27.

[260] *Re Posgate* (n 259 above); *Trident European Fund v Coats Holdings Ltd* [2003] EWHC 2471 (Ch); *Pringle v Callard* [2008] 2 BCLC 505, CA; *Mission Capital plc v Sinclair* [2010] 1 BCLC 304 (interim reinstatement of directors refused); *Re Canterbury Travel (London) Ltd* [2010] EWHC 1464 (Ch).

[261] *Re a Company (No 00596 of 1986)* [1987] BCLC 133; *Wilton-Davies v Kirk* [1998] 1 BCLC 274.

[262] *Re Ravenhart Service (Holdings) Ltd* [2004] 2 BCLC 376 at para 102.

[263] *Re a Company (No 2612 of 1984)* (1985) 1 BCC 99, 485, CA.

[264] *Veracruz Transportation Inc v VC Shipping Inc* [1992] 1 Lloyd's Rep 353, CA; *Zucker v Tyndall Holdings plc* [1992] 1 WLR 1127, CA. But note the dissenting speech of Lord Nicholls in *Mercedes Benz AG v Leiduck* [1996] AC 284, 310–12, PC under the heading 'Causes of action and prospective rights'. The principle has

In *Re Premier Electronics (GB) Ltd*[265] Pumfrey J applied this principle when refusing to make a freezing order against the respondents in support of relief in an unfair prejudice petition, which alleged that the respondents as directors of the company had conducted its affairs in an unfairly prejudicial manner by misappropriating £250,000 of the company's money. In the meantime the company had gone into administration. It is not clear from the report what relief was sought in the petition. If it was an order that the respondents buy the petitioner's shares, it was rightly disregarded as a basis for a freezing order, since the respondents would have no liability to the petitioner until the order was made (and then only if there was a real risk that the respondents would deal with their assets so as to avoid paying the petitioner). It seems, however, that the petitioner sought to justify the freezing order by reference to the respondents' liabilities to the company, but, as the judge observed, they had not brought, or obtained leave to bring, a derivative claim in the name of the company under what is now s 996(2)(c).[266] A freezing order might have been justifiable if the petitioner had sought direct payment by the respondents to the company (paragraph 23.74 above), but that relief would have been a matter for the administrator to pursue.

(8) Procedure

As mentioned in paragraph 23.12 above, the Companies (Unfair Prejudice Applications) **23.94** Proceedings Rules 2009 govern the procedure for Part 30 Petitions.[267] Paragraph 3 of these rules provides for the petition, in the form set out in the Schedule to the Rules, to 'specify the grounds on which it is presented and the nature of the relief which is sought by the petitioner' and for the petition to be filed at court, which fixes a return day. The petitioner should not include a petition for winding up as an alternative to relief under s 996 unless the petitioner prefers winding up or considers it to be the only relief to which he is entitled.[268] By paragraph 4 the petition is to be served on the company and every respondent named in the petition. On the return day, by paragraph 5, the court gives directions for the conduct of the petition, including any directions required for pleadings and evidence.[269] By paragraph 5(c) the court may, but usually does not, give directions for advertisement of the petition.[270] By paragraph 6 the court may direct advertisement of the order made on the petition.

---

been eroded by the Civil Jurisdiction and Judgments Act 1982, s 25 and the Civil Jurisdiction and Judgments Act 1982 (Interim Relief) Order 1997.

[265] [2002] 2 BCLC 634, 638.

[266] This is consistent with the view expressed by Harman J in *Re a Company (No 004502 of 1988), ex p Johnson* [1992] BCLC 701, 707.

[267] A claim under Part 30 brought otherwise than by petition (eg by claim form) will be struck out: *Re Osea Road Camp Sites Ltd* [2005] 1 WLR 760.

[268] *Practice Direction—Order under Section 127 Insolvency Act 1986* (supplementing CPR Part 49), para 1 (*Civil Procedure* (Vol 2) at para 2G-47; [1999] BCC 741). There are cases where the facts support a winding-up order, but not relief under s 996: *Re Full Cup International Trading Ltd* [1995] BCC 682, on appeal *Antoniades v Wong* [1997] 2 BCLC 419; *Re Copeland & Craddock Ltd* [1997] BCC 294, CA; *Re Neath Rugby Ltd (No 2), Hawkes v Cuddy (No 2)* [2009] 2 BCLC 427, CA at paras 104 and 108.

[269] As to pleadings, see *Re Unisoft Group Ltd* [1994] 1 BCLC 609. As to disclosure, see *Arrow Trading & Investments Est 1920 v Edwardian Group Ltd* [2005] 1 BCLC 696, referring at para 24 to the general rule that a shareholder is entitled to disclosure of all documents obtained by the company in the course of its administration, including advice by solicitors to the company about its affairs; but not where the advice relates to hostile proceedings between the company and its shareholders: *Re Hydrosan Ltd* [1991] BCLC 418; *CAS (Nominees) Ltd v Nottingham Forest plc* [2002] 1 BCLC 613. As to disclosure of connected company documents, see *Re Technion Investments Ltd* [1985] BCLC 434, CA.

[270] *Re a Company (No 002015 of 1996)* [1997] 2 BCLC 1 (breach of rules relating to advertisement may in a serious case lead to order striking out petition).

23.95 While the petitioner must be a member of the company or a person within s 994(2) (paragraphs 23.05 and 23.06 above), there is flexibility as to the joinder of respondents. That is inherent in the broad language of Part 30.[271] In deciding who are proper respondents, the court considers both the allegations of unfairly prejudicial conduct and who may be affected by the relief sought.[272] A former member may be joined as a respondent,[273] but only if relief may properly be claimed against him.[274] On the other hand the petitioner is not obliged to join as respondents all the other shareholders or all persons whose conduct is criticized.[275]

Application to strike out or stay the petition

23.96 A common response to service of an unfair prejudice petition is an application to strike it out, either on the ground that it is plainly and obviously unsustainable (and many of the issues discussed in Sections A(4)–(6) have arisen on strike-out applications) or on the ground that it is an abuse, a fair offer having been made (paragraph 23.68 above). In relation to the former ground Hoffmann LJ has said:[276]

> I accept that the notoriously burdensome nature of s 459 proceedings does not lighten the burden on the respondent who applies to have the petition struck out. He must still satisfy the court that the petitioner's case is plainly and obviously unsustainable. But I think that the consequences for the company mean that a court should be willing to scrutinize with care the allegations in a s 459 petition and, if necessary, the evidence proposed to be adduced in support, in order to see whether the petitioner really does have an arguable case. This is particularly so when the petition rests on allegations of bad faith akin to fraud: see Sir George Jessel MR in *Re Rica Gold Washing Co* (1879) 11 Ch D 36.

23.97 Where the issues raised in the petition are within the scope of an arbitration agreement binding on the petitioner and other parties the court will stay the proceedings under s 9 of the Arbitration Act 1996.[277]

The role of the company

23.98 One matter affecting the directors is what role, if any, the company should play in the proceedings. In the normal case where the petitioner is seeking relief against the respondent shareholders, so that as a matter of substance the dispute is between shareholders, it is well established that the company should not be involved or incur costs in relation to the proceedings and that the directors would be in breach of their duties if they applied company money for such a purpose. Where it is clear that there is no proper reason for company participation the court will grant an injunction to restrain its funds being spent on the proceedings, except for giving disclosure and attendance on judgment which might concern it.[278]

---

[271] *Re Little Olympian Each-Ways Ltd* [1994] 2 BCLC 420, 429.

[272] *Re BSB Holdings Ltd* [1993] BCLC 246 (where a party was properly joined since it had been involved in the transactions complained of and would be affected by the relief sought).

[273] *Re a Company (No 005287 of 1985)* [1986] 1 WLR 281.

[274] *Re Baltic Real Estate Ltd (No 1)* [1993] BCLC 498 (petition of majority shareholder sought purchase of the minority's shares; former shareholders wrongly joined). As to service out of the jurisdiction, see *Re Baltic Real Estate Ltd (No 2)* [1993] BCLC 503.

[275] *Re Ravenhart Service (Holdings) Ltd* [2004] 2 BCLC 376 at para 103.

[276] *Re Saul D Harrison & Sons plc* [1995] 1 BCLC 14, 22, CA.

[277] *Fulham Football Club (1987) Ltd v Richards* [2012] Ch 333, CA (also see judgment of Vos J at [2011] Ch 208), overruling *Exeter Football Club Ltd v Football Conference Ltd* [2004] 1 WLR 2910, and approving *Re Vocam Europe Ltd* [1998] BCC 396.

[278] *Re Crossmore Electrical and Civil Engineering Ltd* [1989] BCLC 137; *Re Hydrosan Ltd* [1991] BCLC 418, 420; *Re a Company (No 004502 of 1988), ex p Johnson* [1992] BCLC 701; *Re Milgate Developments Ltd* [1993]

The court will also restrain the company from funding an individual respondent's defence to the petition.[279] Where the petitioner also seeks a winding up order in relation to a company which is carrying on business, it will be necessary to obtain an order under the Insolvency Act, s 127 validating expenditure in the ordinary course of business. Expenditure on company participation in the shareholders' dispute will not be protected as being within the ordinary course of business, but the court may permit the company to protect itself from being wound up.[280] Further, improper participation can be taken into account when fixing the price at which shares are to be purchased.[281]

In *Re a Company (No 001126 of 1992)*[282] Lindsay J reviewed the authorities on company par- **23.99**
ticipation in and expenditure on an unfair prejudice petition and concluded that (i) 'there is no rule that necessarily and in all cases such active participation and such expenditure is improper'; (ii) 'the test of whether such expenditure is proper is whether it is necessary or expedient in the interests of the company as a whole', which would now seem to equate with a test of whether the directors would comply with their duty under the 2006 Act, s 172 to promote the success of the company if they caused it to participate or incur the expenditure; (iii) 'in considering that test the court's starting point is a sort of rebuttable distaste for such participation and expenditure, initial scepticism as to its necessity or expediency'; so that (iv) there is a heavy onus on the company to justify past participation or expenditure already incurred and it is very unlikely that the court will approve future participation or expenditure in the absence of 'the most compelling circumstances proven by cogent evidence'. In *Arrow Trading & Investment Est. 1920 v Edwardian Group Ltd*[283] the court restrained the company from participating in order to defend its remuneration policy which had benefited the individual respondents.

Active participation may be justified when the relief sought challenges the com- **23.100**
pany's decision-making processes, its constitution, or regulations by which it is bound,[284] where the relief sought is ostensibly for the benefit of the company (direct payment to the company of damages for breach of duty),[285] or where serious allegations are made against the company itself.[286] Also, where the relief sought in the

---

BCLC 291; *Arrow Trading & Investment Est 1920 v Edwardian Group Ltd* [2004] BCC 955. As to disclosure of documents in an unfair prejudice petition, see *Re Technion Investments Ltd* [1985] BCLC 434, CA.

[279] *Corbett v Corbett* [1993] BCC 93; *Singh v Anand*, HHJ Norris QC, 17 March 2006 (injunction to restrain company funds from being used to support shareholder's defence to a claim to ownership of shares).

[280] *Re Crossmore Electrical and Civil Engineering Ltd* [1989] BCLC 137 (separate creditor's petition); *Re a Company (No 005685 of 1988), ex p Schwarcz* [1989] BCLC 424 (shareholders' winding-up petition; the court deferred consideration of the question until after it had determined the outcome of a strike out application; subsequently the petition was struck out: *Re a Company (No 005685 of 1988), ex p Schwarcz (No 2)* [1989] BCLC 427).

[281] *Re Kenyon Swansea Ltd* [1987] BCLC 514, 521

[282] [1994] 2 BCLC 146, 155, 156.

[283] [2004] BCC 955 at paras 17 and 22.

[284] *Power v Ekstein* [2010] NSWSC 137 at paras 109–21. In *CAS (Nominees) Ltd v Nottingham Forest FC plc* [2002] 1 BCLC 613 the company was represented at the trial in a case where the petition impugned a resolution passed at an EGM. Similarly in *Fulham Football Club (1987) Ltd v Richards* [2011] Ch 208; [2012] Ch 333, CA, the company, The Football Association Premier League Ltd, successfully applied with the respondent member for a stay of an unfair prejudice petition under the Arbitration Act 1996, s 9 on the ground that the claim was subject to arbitration under regulations binding on the company and its members.

[285] *Re Chime Corporation Ltd* [2004] HKFCA 73 at paras 53–5, 59 per Lord Scott of Foscote NPJ.

[286] *Harley Street Capital Ltd v Tchigirinsky* [2006] BCC 209, 231 (a derivative claim).

petition directly affects the company, it will be appropriate for the company actively to participate.[287]

B. Just and Equitable Winding Up

23.101 By the Insolvency Act, s 122(1)(g) a company[288] may be wound up by the court[289] if 'the court is of the opinion that it is just and equitable that the company should be wound up'.[290] A member or members (referred to as a contributory[291]) may petition the court for the company to be wound up[292] on this ground provided that he satisfies a statutory condition and a common law condition. The company's articles cannot restrict the ability of a member to petition.[293]

(1) Standing to petition

23.102 The statutory condition, contained in s 124(2), prevents a member from presenting a winding-up petition unless either (a) the number of members is reduced below two,[294] or (b) the shares in respect of which he is a contributory, or some of them, either were originally allotted to him, or have been held by him, and registered in his name, for at least 6 months during the 18 months before the commencement of the winding up,[295] or have devolved on him through the death of a former holder. For the requirement that the member is a registered shareholder, reference should be made to paragraph 23.05 above. In *Alipour v Ali*[296] the Court of Appeal took a more flexible approach than had been shown in the past[297] to disputes as to standing in a member's winding-up petition, saying that such issues could

---

[287] *Re Posgate & Denby (Agencies) Ltd* [1987] BCLC 8 (injunction to restrain company and directors from executing agreement for sale of company's assets without the approval of a majority of the shareholders); *Re Blue Arrow plc* [1987] BCLC 585 (injunction to restrain quoted company from putting to AGM a special resolution to alter its articles so that the petitioner could be removed as director); *Re Tottenham Hotspur plc* [1994] 1 BCLC 655 (petitioner sought order for sale of shares to it and injunction restraining company from acting on directors' resolution to determine a director's service contract).

[288] For the jurisdiction of the English court to wind up a solvent foreign company on the application of a member, reference should be made to the discussion in Dicey and Morris, *The Conflict of Laws*, 15th edn (Thomson, Sweet and Maxwell, 2012), at rule 176.

[289] By the Insolvency Act, s 117 the High Court has jurisdiction to wind up any company registered in England and Wales and the county court has concurrent jurisdiction where the company's paid up share capital does not exceed £120,000 (subject to increase under s 117(3)) and its registered office is situated in the district of the county court.

[290] The other grounds for petitioning for a winding-up order specified in s 124(1) that might be of relevance to a member are in fact almost never invoked and are not discussed in this chapter.

[291] Defined by the Insolvency Act, s 79(1) as 'every person liable to contribute to the assets of a company in the event of it being wound up', but does include the holder of fully paid shares: *Re National Savings Bank Association* (1866) 1 Ch App 547.

[292] Insolvency Act, s 124(1).

[293] *Re Peveril Gold Mines Ltd* [1898] 1 Ch 122. In *Fulham Football Club (1987) Ltd v Richards* [2011] Ch 1055 at para 59 Vos J described this as a difficult decision (the Court of Appeal did not refer to it: [2012] Ch 333, CA).

[294] This does not apply where the company has always had only one member: *Re Pimlico Capital Ltd* [2002] 2 BCLC 544. This condition reflects s 122(1)(e).

[295] In *Re Gattopardo Ltd* [1969] 1 WLR 619 a premature petition was struck out.

[296] [1997] 1 WLR 534, 546, CA. Subsequently the court refused to summarily dismiss the petition on the ground that the petitioner had a viable argument to be a contributory: *Alipour v UOC Corp* [2002] 2 BCLC 770. At the trial the petition was dismissed, the judge finding that the petitioner's claim to be a contributory was founded on a forged share certificate: [2002] EWHC 530 (Ch).

[297] *Re JN 2 Ltd* [1978] 1 WLR 183.

be determined in the petition if in all the circumstances it was convenient to do so and not harmful to the company.

The common law condition is that the member must have a legitimate interest in obtaining a **23.103** winding-up order.[298] For this purpose he must satisfy the court that there is a real prospect of a surplus being available for distribution to members.[299] The court will, however, allow a member to proceed where he complains that accounts or information to which he is entitled have not been provided, so that he does not know whether or not the company is solvent.[300] Outside quasi-partnership cases, this relaxation of the rule is limited by the fact that members do not have a general right to information from a company or to access to its documents.

(2) The just and equitable ground

The leading authority on the just and equitable ground is the speech of Lord Wilberforce in **23.104** *Ebrahimi v Westbourne Galleries Ltd*[301] part of which has been quoted in paragraph 23.60 above. Lord Wilberforce went on to describe the typical elements, summarized in paragraph 23.64 above, that may make the relationship of the parties a quasi-partnership and one to which equitable considerations apply. Where the relationship breaks down or a member is removed from management, he may petition for winding up on the just and equitable ground, provided he was not the cause of the removal or breakdown.[302]

As noted in paragraph 23.94 above a member should not petition for winding up unless he **23.105** prefers winding up to the relief that may be granted under the Companies Act, Part 30 or he considers it to be the only relief to which he is entitled. The reasons why members' winding-up petitions are discouraged are that (a) they put the company to the cost of applying for relief under the Insolvency Act, s 127, and (b) the court is limited to imposing a 'death sentence' on the company, whereas under Part 30 'the appropriate remedy [can be] applied during the course of the continuing life of the company'.[303] Since the remedies available under Part 30, including an order that one member purchases the shares of another, are more flexible and responsive to the needs of the parties, a petition under Part 30 alone is the invariable practice. The court will strike out an unnecessary claim for a winding-up order.[304]

In *Re Guidezone Ltd*[305] Jonathan Parker J had held that the jurisdiction to wind up a company **23.106** on the just and equitable ground is no wider than the jurisdiction under Part 30. In *Re Neath*

---

[298] *Deloitte & Touche AG v Johnson* [1999] 1 WLR 1605, PC.

[299] *Re Rica Gold Washing Co* (1879) 11 Ch D 36, CA; *Re WR Willcocks* [1974] Ch 163; *Re Chesterfield Catering Co Ltd* [1977] Ch 373; *Re Martin Coulter Enterprises Ltd* [1988] BCLC 12, 18.

[300] *Re Newman and Howard Ltd* [1962] Ch 257; *Re Chesterfield Catering Co Ltd* [1977] Ch 373; *Re Commercial and Industrial Insulation Ltd* [1986] BCLC 191; *Re Wessex Computer Stationers Ltd* [1992] BCLC 366; *Re a Company (No 007936 of 1994)* [1995] BCC 705, 713.

[301] [1973] AC 360, 379, 380, HL. Also see *Loch v John Blackwood Ltd* [1924] AC 783, 788, PC; *Re A & BC Chewing Gum Ltd* [1975] 1 WLR 579 (breach of shareholders' agreement as to participation in management); *Re a Company (No 00370 of 1987)*, *ex p Glossop* [1988] 1 WLR 1068, 1076.

[302] *Ebrahimi v Westbourne Galleries Ltd* [1973] AC 360, 387f, per Lord Cross; *Re RA Noble (Clothing) Ltd* [1983] BCLC 273, 290; *Vujnovich v Vujnovich* (1989) 5 BCC 740, 744, PC.

[303] *Re a Company (No 00314 of 1989)*, *ex p Estates Acquisition and Development Ltd* [1991] BCLC 154, 161.

[304] *Re a Company (No 004415 of 1996)* [1997] 1 BCLC 479; *Re Woven Rugs Ltd* [2008] BCC 903. There are also cases where the court has refused to strike out the claim for winding up on the ground that it was not plain and obvious it would not succeed: *Re a Company (No 001363 of 1988) ex p S-P* [1989] BCLC 579; *Re Copland & Craddock Ltd* [1997] BCC 294, 299, CA.

[305] [2000] 2 BCLC 321 at para 179.

Rugby Club Ltd (No 2)[306] the Court of Appeal overruled this decision, holding that there are cases where the court might make a winding up order, but where the circumstances might not amount to unfair prejudice so as to give the court jurisdiction to make an order under the 2006 Act, s 996. Such cases include deadlock and inability to trade,[307] loss of substratum and failure of objects,[308] or disposal of the business for which company was formed.[309] The court may also make a winding-up order in preference to an order under Part 30 where the circumstances of the company are such that none of the parties wants to carry on the business of the company and buy out another party and it is not fair for the court to make an order that one party buys out another.[310]

23.107   The court may make a winding-up order on a minority shareholder's petition where the majority has placed the company in voluntary liquidation.[311]

(3) Alternative remedy

23.108   The Insolvency Act, s 125(2) restricts the power of the court to make a winding-up order on a member's petition on the just and equitable ground. It provides:

> If the petition is presented by members of the company as contributories on the ground that it is just and equitable that the company should be wound up, the court, if it is of the opinion—
> (a) that the petitioners are entitled to relief either by winding up the company or by some other means, and
> (b) that in the absence of any other remedy it would be just and equitable that the company should be wound up, shall make a winding-up order; but this does not apply if the court is also of the opinion both that some other remedy is available to the petitioners and that they are acting unreasonably in seeking to have the company wound up instead of pursuing that other remedy.

23.109   The approach of the court under this provision is much the same as its approach to fair offers in the context of Part 30 petitions (as to which see the principles stated by Lord Hoffmann in *O'Neill v Phillips* summarized in paragraph 23.14(10) and (11) and their application as discussed in paragraphs 23.68 and 23.69 above).[312]

(4) Procedure

23.110   The procedure for presentation of a winding-up petition by a contributory is dealt with under rules 4.22–4.24 of the Insolvency Rules 1986 (or IR 2016, rr 7.25–7.32 after

---

[306] *Re Neath Rugby Club Ltd (No 2), Hawkes v Cuddy (No 2)* [2009] 2 BCLC 427, CA at paras 101–8.

[307] *Re Yenidje Tobacco Co Ltd* [1916] 2 Ch 426, CA.

[308] *Re German Date Coffee Co* (1882) 20 Ch D 169, CA; *Re Perfectair Holdings Ltd* [1990] BCLC 423, 435.

[309] *Virdi v Abbey Leisure Ltd* [1990] BCLC 342, CA.

[310] Cases where the court has made a winding-up order rather than making an order giving relief from unfair prejudice are: *Re Perfectair Holdings Ltd* [1990] BCLC 423; *Jesner v Jarrad Properties Ltd* [1993] BCLC 1032; *Re Worldhams Park Golf Course Ltd* [1998] 1 BCLC 554. Also see *Re Full Cup International Trading Ltd* [1995] BCC 682; on appeal *Antoniades v Wong* [1997] 2 BCLC 419, CA, where the court regarded winding up as the appropriate remedy and refused to give relief for unfair prejudice. See also observations of Warren J in *Amin v Amin* [2009] EWHC 3356 (Ch) at paras 612–14.

[311] *Re Internet Investment Corp Ltd* [2010] 1 BCLC 458.

[312] Further cases on the exercise of this power not mentioned in the footnotes to paras 23.68 and 23.69 are: *Re a Company (No 002567 of 1982)* [1983] 1 WLR 927; *Re a Company (No 001363 of 1988)* [1989] BCLC 579, 586, 587; *Fuller v Cyracuse Ltd* [2001] 1 BCLC 187; *CVC/Opportunity Equity Partners Ltd v Demarco Almeida* [2002] 2 BCLC 108, PC; *Apcar v Aftab* [2003] BCC 510.

6 April 2017). They are broadly the same as those applicable to Part 30 petitions discussed in paragraph 23.94 above. Usually the petition is not advertised.[313]

Unlike the position in relation to Part 30 petitions, the court has jurisdiction under the **23.111** Insolvency Act, s 125(1) to make an interim order.

The presentation of a just and equitable winding-up petition brings into operation the **23.112** Insolvency Act, s 127, which has an impact on the management of the affairs of the company. The petition must state whether the petitioner consents or objects to an order under s 127 in the standard form. If the petitioner consents, or consents to an order in a modified form, the Registrar will make the order without further inquiry. If the petitioner objects, the company may apply to the judge for an order under s 127.[314] For further discussion of this section, see Chapter 33 at paragraphs 33.81–33.87.

Usually it will be a breach of the directors' duties to cause it to participate actively or incur **23.113** expenditure in a member's winding-up petition, relying on the just and equitable ground.[315]

---

[313] *Re a Company (No 00687 of 1991)* [1991] BCC 210 ('advertised' means 'notified'); *Re Doreen Boards Ltd* [1996] 1 BCLC 501 (premature advertisement an abuse).
[314] *Practice Direction 49B—Order under Section 127 Insolvency Act 1986* (supplementing CPR Part 49); *Civil Procedure* (vol 2) at para 2G-47; [1999] BCC 741.
[315] See cases in paras 23.98–23.100 above; see also *Re A & BC Chewing Gum Ltd* [1975] 1 WLR 579, 592.

24

LIABILITIES OF DIRECTORS TO THIRD PARTIES

Lexa Hilliard QC

A. Introduction

A principal purpose of incorporating a company with limited liability is to avoid the personal liability that otherwise attaches to an individual if he trades without the protection of the corporate form. Incorporation with limited liability undoubtedly shields a director from the routine liabilities associated with carrying on business when that business is carried on by a company rather than by him as an individual. Legally, the business is then the company's business, not the director's business and therefore any contracts concluded or obligations undertaken in relation to the business are, ordinarily, contracts or obligations of the company.

24.01

In *Ferguson v Wilson*[1] Cairns LJ said:

24.02

> What is the position of directors of a public company? They are merely agents of a company. The company itself cannot act in its own person, for it has no person; it can only act through directors, and the case is, as regards those directors, merely the ordinary case of principal and

---

[1] (1866) LR 2 Ch App 77, 89–90.

agent. Wherever an agent is liable those directors would be liable; where the liability would attach to the principal, and the principal only, the liability is the liability of the company.

Despite this statement of general principle there are a variety of circumstances in which a director may find himself liable to third parties in connection with the business of the company.

24.03   This chapter focuses on those circumstances. The liabilities are, for the most part, the creation of the common law. However, statute has an increasing role to play where, for reasons of policy, the imposition of personal liability upon a director to a third party has been deemed appropriate. This chapter also addresses the circumstances in which a director can be held liable for costs incurred by the successful party in litigation where the company has sued or been sued. Finally, the exposure of a director to proceedings for contempt of court is discussed where a company has breached a judgment or order of the court.

B.   Piercing the Veil

24.04   In *Salomon v A Salomon & Co Ltd*[2] a unanimous House of Lords reached a clear and principled decision that a legally incorporated company must be treated like any other independent person with rights and liabilities appropriate to itself whatever may have been the ideas of those who brought it into existence.[3] In spite of this substantial obstacle to extending liability to those associated with the company, for well over a century there have been a number attempts to do so on the basis that the so-called 'veil of incorporation' should be pierced so that the separate legal personality of the company is disregarded. The relevant case law was recently extensively examined by the Supreme Court in *Prest v Petrodel Resources Ltd*.[4] The Supreme Court concluded that the jurisdiction to pierce the corporate veil had been misunderstood and misapplied in most of the cases; that there was a power to pierce the corporate veil but the power was an extremely limited one to be exercised only in rare cases. Such cases would be if a person under an existing legal obligation or liability or being subject to an existing legal restriction sought to deliberately evade, or the enforcement of which he deliberately sought to frustrate, by the interposition of a company under his control. In such circumstances the court could pierce the corporate veil for the purpose, and only for the purpose, of depriving the person of the advantage that he would otherwise have obtained by the company's separate legal personality.[5]

24.05   In *Prest*, Lord Sumption analysed the previous cases where the court had considered itself justified in piercing the corporate veil as being either cases within the concealment principle, where a company is interposed to conceal the identity of the real actors,[6] or within

---

[2] [1897] AC 22.

[3] *Salomon v A Salomon & Co Ltd* (n 2 above) per Lord Halsbury LC at pp 30–1.

[4] [2013] 2 AC 415.

[5] *Prest* (n 4 above) at para 35, per Lord Sumption, para 81, per Lord Neuberger. Baroness Hale (at para 92), with whom Lord Wilson agreed, was not sure that it was possible to classify all cases where the courts have been prepared to disregard the separate legal personality of a company as cases of concealment or evasion. Lord Mance (at para 100) and Lord Clarke (at para 103) did not think it right to close off the possibility that other rare circumstances might justify piercing the corporate veil; see also Lord Walker at para 106.

[6] *Prest* (n 4 above) at para 28. In these cases the corporate veil is not pierced; rather the court looks behind the façade to discover the real facts which the corporate structure is concealing. Examples, where a director used a company to hold misappropriated assets are *Gencor ACP Ltd v Dalby* [2000] 2 BCLC 734 and *Trustor AB v*

the evasion principle, where a company is interposed to defeat or frustrate enforcement of a legal right.[7] Those situations apart, the effect of *Prest*[8] is that for the time being, at least, the situations in which the law attributes the acts of a company to those who control it, will invariably require the application of conventional principles taking into account the separate legal personality of the company.

C. Liabilities of Directors in Relation to Contracts

(1) Company contracts

A director, being an agent, is not personally liable to third parties on contracts between the third party and his company. This is the position even if the director had no authority to bind the company to the contract although in such circumstances he could be liable for breach of warranty of authority.[9] The director is also not liable even if the company's failure to perform the contract is due entirely to the fault of the director or if the company could not, at the time of the contract, fulfil it.[10] A director is also not liable in tort at the suit of a third party, if acting in good faith within the scope of his authority, he procures or causes the company to breach a contract with the third party.[11]   **24.06**

Prior to *Prest*[12] an increasing number of attempts had been made to pierce the corporate veil so as to make controllers of companies, including directors, personally liable in relation to a contract to which the company was a party.[13] Those attempts came to an end with *VTB Capital Plc v Nutritek International Corpn*.[14] The Supreme Court held that, even assuming it was possible to pierce the corporate veil in certain circumstances, they did not extend to holding the person controlling the company liable as if he had been a co-contracting party with the company where the company was a party but the controller was not. The reasoning which underpinned this conclusion was that it made no sense for the controller to be treated as if he were, or had been, a co-contracting party with the company even though neither the controller nor any of the contracting parties ever intended the controller to be a party.[15]   **24.07**

The mere fact that a person describes himself as a director does not necessarily lead to the conclusion that a person did not intend to contract personally.[16] A director may contract so as to make himself personally liable to a third party by, for example, expressly guaranteeing   **24.08**

Smallbone (No 2) [2001] 1 WR 1177 (per Lord Sumption at paras 22, 31–3; per Lord Neuberger at para 68). See also *Pennyfeathers Ltd v Pennyfeathers Property Co Ltd* [2013] EWHC 3530 (Ch).

[7] *Prest* (n 4 above) at para 28. *Gilford Motor Co Ltd v Horne* [1933] Ch 935, where a director used a company to evade a restrictive covenant is an example of a case within the evasion principle (per Lord Sumption at paras 29–30; per Lord Neuberger at paras 70–2).

[8] *Prest v Petrodel Resources Ltd* (n 4 above).

[9] *Firbank's Executors v Humphreys* (1886) 18 QBD 54, CA.

[10] *Elkington & Co v Hurter* [1892] 2 Ch 452.

[11] *Said v Butt* [1920] 3 KB 496, 506; see also *G Scammel & Nephew Ltd v Hurley* [1929] KB 419, 443, 449; *DC Thompson & Co Ltd v Deakin* [1952] Ch 646, 680–1, CA; *Welsh Development Agency v Export Finance Co Ltd* [1992] BCLC 148, 171–3, 179–82, 191, CA. This issue is also discussed at para 24.28 below.

[12] *Prest v Petrodel Resources Ltd* [2013] 2 AC 415.

[13] *Antonio Gramsci Shipping Corp v Stepanovs* [2012] BCC 182; *Alliance Bank JSC v Aquatic Corp* [2012] 1 Lloyd's Rep 181; *Linsen International Ltd v Humpuss Sea Transport Pte Ltd* [2012] 1 BCLC 651.

[14] [2013] 2 AC 337.

[15] *VTB Capital plc v Nutritek International Corpn* (n 14 above), at para 131 per Lord Neuberger PSC.

[16] *McCollin v Gilpin* (1881) 6 QBD 516, CA.

in his capacity as a director the performance of a contract between the third party and the company. More difficult are cases where a director has not expressly guaranteed performance but the question is whether, having regard to the terms of the contract and the circumstances, the director must be regarded as having contracted personally. There can be difficulties, in particular, where the contract is an oral one and there has been no express statement by the director as to the capacity in which he is intending to contract.[17] It will be necessary, in such event, to consider the surrounding circumstances in order to determine whether the contract was made with the director personally or with the company. Where the contract is in writing and it is signed in the director's own name without any reference to the company of which he is a director, there is obviously a substantial risk that the director will be found to have contracted personally.[18] By contrast if the company's name appears on the contractual document and the director signs it 'for and on behalf' of the company, there will be no doubt that it is the company who is the party to the contract, not the director.[19]

24.09   Until 2006 the Companies Acts had since 1856[20] imposed personal liability on directors for company contracts where the company's name was incorrectly stated in the contractual document. Historically, great importance was attached to this statutory liability.[21] It was applied strictly and there were numerous reported cases where directors were found liable.[22] In 2001 the CLR concluded that the personal statutory liability attaching to directors was unduly harsh.[23] In particular, concern was expressed that the civil sanctions could provide a windfall to someone who had not been misled or suffered loss by the misstatement of the name but through some other cause such as the insolvency of the company. The CLR recommended that civil sanctions should be targeted more closely at those who were really responsible for the breach and on cases where there was a genuine causal link between the misstatement and any loss suffered by the relevant third party.

24.10   The 2006 Act removed the personal liability that formerly attached to a director for misstating the name of a company.[24] The Company, Limited Liability Partnership and Business (Names and Trading Disclosures) Regulations 2015,[25] made under the 2006 Act, s 82 still

---

[17] *Hamid v Francis Bradshaw Partnership* [2013] BLR 447, CA where it was held that the contract was not with the company when the contract was partly oral and partly in writing and it was signed by an individual (without describing himself as a director) above the trading name (which was different from the registered name) of the company of which the individual was a director. Cf *Badgerhill Properties Ltd v Cottrell* [1991] BCLC 805, CA where it was held that the contract was with the company when the individual signed the contract as a director but the name of the company was misspelt.

[18] *Re International Contract Company* (1871) 6 Ch App 525; *Gadd v Houghton* (1876) LR 1 Ex D 357; cf *Aggs v Nicholson* (1856) 1 H&N 165.

[19] *Universal Steam Navigation Co v James McKelvie & Co* [1923] AC 492 HL.

[20] 1856 Act, s 31.

[21] In *Atkin v Wardle* (1889) 5 TLR 734 CA Lindley LJ described the 1862 Act, ss 41 and 42 as two of the most important sections and that the court should take care not to relax them.

[22] See eg *Durham Fancy Goods v Michael Jackson (Fancy Goods)* [1968] 2 QB 839; *Lindholst & Co A/S v Fowler* [1988] BCLC 166; *Blum v OCP Repartition SA* [1988] BCLC 170, CA; *Oshkosh B'gosh Inc v Dan Marbel Inc Ltd* [1989] BCLC 507, CA; *Novaknit Hellas SA v Kumar Bros International Ltd* [1998] CLC 971; cf *Banque de L'Indochine et de Suez SA v Euroseas Group Finance Co Ltd* [1981] 3 All ER 198; *Jenice Ltd v Dan* [1993] BCLC 1349.

[23] CLR: *Final Report* at para 11.57.

[24] By the repeal of 1985 Act, s 349 on 1 October 2008: 2006 Act Commencement Order No 5, Art 8(b) and Sch 3.

[25] SI 2015/17. The regulations are concerned, inter alia, with restrictions relating to the registered name of a company and to business names and imposing requirements relating to trading disclosures both at the

require the registered name of a company to be stated in a contract and other company documents and communications.[26] However, the civil sanction contained in s 83 for failure to make the required disclosure no longer attaches to directors. Section 83, as recommended by the CLR, targets the company in breach of the regulations rather than the individual responsible for the breach. If a company in proceedings seeks to enforce a right arising out of a contract made in the course of a business in respect of which the company was, at the time the contract was made, in breach of the regulations, the proceedings may be dismissed unless the court before which the proceedings are brought is satisfied that it is just and equitable to permit the proceedings to continue. The requirements of justice and equity tend to suggest that proceedings would not be dismissed where the defendant has received a benefit under a contract made in breach of the regulations or there is no suggestion that the defendant has been misled in any way by the breach. Importantly, there is no longer any provision for the imposition of personal liability on a director or any other person who signs or authorizes to be signed an instrument where the company's registered name is not properly stated. However, s 83(3) preserves any other rights available to a person affected by a failure of a company to comply with the regulations. Thus the right of a third party to sue a director personally who signs a cheque as a director without stating the company's name continues unaffected.[27]

Although a director no longer incurs personal civil liability for misstating a company's name on a company contract, there may be criminal sanctions. Where a company fails, without reasonable excuse, to comply with the requisite trading disclosures set out in the Company, Limited Liability Partnership and Business (Names and Trading Disclosures) Regulations 2015,[28] the company and every officer of the company who is in default commits an offence and can be liable on summary conviction to a fine.[29] An officer for the purposes of the regulation includes a shadow director.[30]   **24.11**

(2) Pre-incorporation contracts

Until a company has been incorporated it has no legal existence. It cannot make a valid contract, nor can it be bound by contracts purported to have been entered into on its behalf. However, frequently contracts are entered into by the promoters of a company in anticipation of being able to commence business immediately upon a company's incorporation. Typically, one or more of the promoters of a company will become its first directors.   **24.12**

Common law

At common law: **24.13**

(1) If the company was not in existence when the contract was signed, there was no contract with the company.[31]

---

company's registered office and other locations and in business communications, business letters, order forms, and websites.

[26] The Company, etc (Names and Trading Disclosures) Regs 2015 (SI 2015/17), regs. 24–7.
[27] Bills of Exchange Act 1882 s 26(2); *Rafsanjan Pistachio Producers Co-operative v Reiss* [1990] BCLC 352.
[28] SI 2015/17, regs 20–7.
[29] Company, etc (Names and Trading Disclosures) Regs 2015 (SI 2015/17), reg 28(2). A person guilty of an offence is liable on summary conviction to (a) a fine not exceeding level 3 on the standard scale; and (b) for continued contravention, a daily default fine not exceeding one-tenth of level 3 on the standard scale.
[30] Reg 28(3).
[31] *Kelner v Baxter* (1866) LR 2 CP 174.

(2) There could, however, be a contract with anyone who had made the contract purportedly on behalf of the non-existent company.[32]

(3) Whether there was such a contract depended upon the capacity in which the maker of the contract was found to have acted.

(4) Where a person was found to have made a contract, solely in his capacity as agent, he could not thereafter sue or be sued upon it. However, where a person was found to have contracted as principal, he could sue or be sued.[33]

24.14 In *Kelner v Baxter*[34] the individual defendant promoters of a company which had not yet been incorporated signed a contract for the purchase of a supply of wine 'on behalf of the proposed Gravesend Alexandra Hotel Company (Limited)'. There, notwithstanding the use of that phrase, the judgment proceeded upon the basis that the reality of the matter was that the parties signing were acting as principals and that therefore they, not the company, were liable. This was so despite reference being made to a company which was in contemplation and not incorporated when the contract was signed. It was further held that the contract was not capable of ratification by the company once it had been incorporated as ratification was not available where the ratifying party was not in existence at the time of the contract.

24.15 *Kelner v Baxter* was distinguished in *Newborne v Sensolid (Great Britain) Ltd*.[35] The case concerned a contract for the sale of goods by a company that had not been incorporated at the time of the contract. The company's name was appended to the contract as 'Leopold Newborne (London) Ltd' and underneath the individual promoter, Leopold Newborne, signed his name. The market fell and the purchasers refused to accept delivery. Mr Newborne sought to enforce the contract in his own name on the basis that as the company had not been in existence at the date of the contract, the claim could not be advanced by the company. It was held that Mr Newborne never purported to sell the goods, either as principal or agent. The contract was purportedly made by the, albeit non-existent, company. Mr Newborne had merely added his name to verify that the company was a party. The contract was therefore a nullity and could not be enforced by Mr Newborne.

Legislation

24.16 The Jenkins Committee considered *Newborne's Case* and recommended that (a) a company should be able to adopt, unilaterally, contracts that purport to be made on the company's behalf prior to incorporation so that it would thereby become a party to the same extent as if the contract had been entered into after incorporation and (b) until the company did adopt such a contract the persons who purported to act for the company should be entitled to sue and be liable to be sued on the contract.[36] Implementation of these recommendations was overtaken by the UK becoming a member of the European Community. On accession the UK was obliged to implement the First Company Law Directive,[37] and in particular, Article 7.

---

[32] *Kelner v Baxter* (n 31 above).
[33] *Newborne v Sensolid (Great Britain) Ltd* [1954] 1 QB 45, 51, per Lord Goddard CJ.
[34] (1866) LR 2 CP 174.
[35] [1954] 1 QB 45.
[36] Report of the Jenkins Committee, paras 44 and 54(b).
[37] First Council Directive on Harmonisation of Company Law (EC) 68/151/EEC.

Article 7 first found expression in the European Communities Act 1972, s 9(2) and later in **24.17** the 1985 Act, s 36(4). The 1989 Act[38] amended the 1985 Act, s 36(4) in the form of a new s 36C.[39] This provision is now restated without material change in the 2006 Act, s 51(1) which provides:[40]

> A contract that purports to be made by or on behalf of a company at a time when the company has not been formed has effect, subject to any agreement to the contrary, as one made with the person purporting to act for the company or as agent for it, and he is personally liable on the contract accordingly.

The cases on the various statutory formulations of this provision have established the follow- **24.18** ing principles:

(1) Even where both parties to the contract know at the date of the contract that the company is not in existence the party who signs 'for and on behalf of' the proposed company is personally liable to repay an advance made pursuant to the contract. The phrase 'any agreement to the contrary' cannot be inferred from the knowledge of the parties. Any agreement must be express.[41]

(2) Although the provision initially applied only to companies incorporated under English law, [42] it now also applies to foreign companies.[43]

(3) The provision does not impose personal liability on a director where the company exists, but is merely misdescribed in the contract.[44]

(4) The provision does not impose personal liability on a director where the company has been incorporated but its change of name has not been registered.[45]

(5) The provision does not permit a director who makes a contract purportedly on behalf of a company that has been dissolved to enforce the contract in his own name or in the name of a new company set up for the purpose.[46]

(6) The provision permits the maker of the contract to enforce it for his benefit as well as be sued on it.[47]

The effect of the 2006 Act, s 51(1) and its predecessors is to protect third parties from the **24.19** consequences if the company is not incorporated. However, this protection does not require that third parties should benefit from an uncovenanted windfall. It follows that where an individual makes a contract as a director on behalf of a company that has not yet been formed, although he will be liable on the contract, he can also enforce it for the benefit of the company. The other contracting party will not be able to avoid the consequences of the

---

[38] 1989 Act, s 130(4).

[39] The main change was that liability was extended to pre-incorporation deeds and under the law of Scotland the undertaking of an obligation: see s 36C(2)(a) and (b).

[40] 2006 Act, s 51 came into force on 1 October 2009: 2006 Act Commencement Order No 8, Art 3(d).

[41] *Phonogram Ltd v Lane* [1982] QB 938, CA, *Royal Mail Estates Ltd v Maple Teesdale* [2016] 1 WLR 942 at paras 51–2.

[42] *Rover International Ltd v Cannon Film Sales Ltd* [1987] BCLC 540.

[43] Overseas Companies (Execution of Documents and Registration of Charges) Regs 2009/1917, reg 16. Prior to 1 October 2009 the relevant provision was contained in the Foreign Companies (Execution of Documents) Regulations 1994/950. See also *Royal Mail Estates Limited v Maple Teesdale* at para 17 (n 41 above).

[44] *Badgerhill Properties Ltd v Cottrell* [1991] BCLC 805, CA.

[45] *Oshkosh B'Gosh Inc v Dan Marbel Inc Ltd* [1989] BCLC 507, CA.

[46] *Cotronic (UK) Ltd v Dezonie* [1991] BCLC 721, CA.

[47] *Braymist Ltd v The Wise Finance Co Ltd* [2002] Ch 273, CA.

contract on the basis only of the technicality that the company was not incorporated at the date of the contract.

(3) Breach of warranty of authority

24.20 A company will itself be liable if a director has actual or implied authority to cause the company to enter into a contract with a third party.[48] Actual authority is given by express words, such as when a board of directors passes a resolution that authorizes two of their number to sign cheques. Authority is implied when it is inferred from the conduct of the parties and the circumstances of the case, such as when the board of directors appoints one of its number to be managing director. The board thereby impliedly authorizes that person to do all such things as fall within the usual scope of that office.[49] A company can also be liable if it has been bound by a director's ostensible authority. Ostensible authority is the authority of a director as it appears to others and may in some cases coincide with, and in most cases will overlap, actual or implied authority.[50]

24.21 If a director commits his company to a contract with a third party, the director impliedly represents to the third party that he has authority to cause his company to enter into the transaction. At common law a director who committed a company to a contract without any authority to do so was personally liable for breach of warranty of authority.[51] However, the provision now contained in the 2006 Act, s 40 has reduced the significance of this liability in respect of third parties dealing with a company in good faith.[52] Section 40(1), which is discussed in Chapter 4, Section B(2) of this work, provides that the power of the board of directors to bind the company or to authorize others to do so is deemed to be free of any limitation under the company's constitution. Thus unless the third party is dealing in bad faith,[53] the company will be bound by a transaction which was beyond the power of a director. The scope for a claim against the director by the third party for breach of warranty of authority has therefore been virtually eliminated. A claim against the director by the company would, however, still lie for the director's breach of duty in exceeding his corporate authority.[54]

D. Liabilities of Directors in Relation to Torts

(1) Introduction

24.22 A director's position in relation to torts is similar to his position in relation to contracts. The orthodox position is that the separate legal personality of a limited company means that a

---

[48] *Hely-Hutchinson v Brayhead Ltd* [1966] 1 QB 549, CA; *Newcastle International Airport Ltd v Eversheds LLP* [2012] EWHC 2648 (Ch), [2013] PNLR 5 at para 92 (judgment on this point upheld: [2014] 1 WLR 3073, CA, at para 76).

[49] *Hely-Hutchinson v Brayhead Ltd* (n 48 above), per Lord Denning MR, 583; *Smith v Butler* [2012] EWCA Civ 314.

[50] *Hely-Hutchinson v Brayhead Ltd* (n 48 above), per Lord Wilberforce, 588; per Lord Pearson, 593; *Armagas Ltd v Mundogas SA* [1986] 1 AC 717, 777, HL, per Lord Keith of Kinkel.

[51] *Collen v Wright* (1857) 8 E&B 647, 657–8.

[52] The provision was introduced by 1989 Act, s 108, which inserted 1985 Act, s 35A. 2006 Act, s 40 which does not apply to companies that are charities, replaced s 35A on 1 October 2009: 2006 Act Commencement Order No 8, Art 3(d).

[53] 2006 Act, s 40(2)(b). As to bad faith, see *Barclays Bank Ltd v TOSG Trust Fund Ltd* [1984] BCLC 1, 18.

[54] 2006 Act, s 40(5).

director is not liable for the torts of the company of which he is a director.[55] This does not mean, however, that there are no circumstances in which a director could find himself liable for torts committed whilst a director of the company. The issue in such circumstances will be whether the tort was properly one to be attributed to the company alone or whether the tort was also committed by the director personally.

In recent years both in England and in the Commonwealth, courts have seen repeated **24.23** challenges to the boundaries of a director's liability in tort with claims being made against directors for deceit, negligent misstatement, infringement of copyright, and conversion.[56] The cases illustrate a tension between company and common law doctrines. Company law dictates that a non-natural entity should, ordinarily, be responsible for actions committed on its behalf by human actors. The common law focuses on the person who committed the wrongful act.

There is an obvious jurisprudential distinction to be drawn between those who by choice **24.24** enter into contractual arrangements with a corporate entity and should thus be taken to have accepted limited liability and those who have had no dealings with a company and whose only interest is not to be harmed by the conduct of anyone.[57] Perhaps this distinction explains the apparent greater readiness to find a director liable in tort (frequently in conjunction with the company) where there is no pre-existing contractual relationship with the company.

A director will be personally liable in three circumstances where events occur in relation to **24.25** the company. The director is, of course, responsible for his own tortious acts or omissions which are unrelated to the affairs of the company:

(1) A director is personally liable for his own torts committed in relation to the company's affairs, whilst acting as a director or employee of the company. In such circumstances the company will also be vicariously liable for the director's torts.
(2) A director can be liable as a joint tortfeasor with the company where he assumes personal responsibility for the acts or omissions of the company which render the company liable in tort.
(3) A director can be liable as a joint tortfeasor with the company where he procures or directs the acts or omissions of the company which render the company liable in tort.

(2) Liability for the director's own torts

If a director commits a tort whilst carrying out duties for his company, the director will, on **24.26** general principles, be personally liable for his own tort. Whether the director is personally liable depends on whether all the elements of the tort can be established against him. Thus a director will be personally liable in tort if, when driving on company business, he causes personal injury to another person in an accident caused by his negligent or dangerous driving. In such a case all the ingredients of the relevant tort are established against the director

---

[55] *Williams v Natural Life Health Foods* [1998] 1 WLR 830, 835, HL, per Lord Steyn; and *Forster v Action Aviation Ltd* [2014] EWCA Civ 1368. See also Lo, 'Liability of Directors as Joint Tortfeasors' [2009] JBL 109; Grantham and Rickett, 'Directors' Tortious Liability: Contract, Tort or Company Law?' (1999) 62 MLR 133, 134.

[56] Armour, 'Demystifying the Civil Liability of Corporate Agents' (2003) CLJ 290.

[57] *Johnson Matthey (Aust) Pty Ltd v Dascorp Pty Ltd* [2003] VSC 291, per Redlich J at para 199.

and the fact that he was driving on company business is irrelevant to his personal liability. It is, however, relevant to the company's vicarious liability.

24.27 General principles were momentarily forgotten in *Standard Chartered Bank v Pakistan National Shipping Corporation (No 2)*[58] when the Court of Appeal failed to distinguish the elements of the tort of deceit from those of the tort of negligent misstatement. The Court of Appeal held that a director who made a fraudulent statement whilst acting in the course of the business of his company was not himself liable for deceit unless he had voluntarily assumed personal responsibility for the accuracy of the statement. In reaching this surprising conclusion the Court of Appeal was heavily influenced by the decision of the House of Lords in *Williams v Natural Life Health Foods Ltd*,[59] which was concerned with the different tort of negligent misstatement made by a director for which an assumption of responsibility is a necessary element.[60] The House of Lords overturned the judgment in the Court of Appeal and returned to the conventional orthodoxy that a director, just like anyone else, is liable for those torts, including the tort of deceit, that he commits personally.[61] In particular, the House of Lords held that a director cannot avoid liability by claiming that he was acting on behalf of the company. As Lord Hoffmann pointed out: 'No one can escape liability for his fraud by saying: "I wish to make it clear that I am committing this fraud on behalf of someone else and I am not to be personally liable".'[62]

24.28 An apparent exception to the conventional orthodoxy is the rule first enunciated by McCardie J in *Said v Butt*[63] that a director or other agent is not liable to an action in tort for wrongful interference with contract where, acting bona fide within the scope of his authority, the director procures a breach of contract between his company and a third party.[64] In *Welsh Development Agency v Export Finance Co Ltd*[65] the Court of Appeal expressed considerable doubt about McCardie J's reasoning in *Said v Butt*. In particular, Dillon LJ pointed out that the decision was inconsistent with the principle that an agent or employee is normally

---

[58] [2001] 1 Lloyd's Rep 218, CA.

[59] [1988] 1 WLR 830 HL.

[60] See paras 24.31–24.34 below.

[61] *Standard Chartered Bank v Pakistan National Shipping (Nos 2 and 4)* [2003] 1 AC 959, HL, in particular at paras 21 and 22, per Lord Hoffmann; at para 39, per Lord Rodger. Cases reflecting the conventional approach, affirmed by the House of Lords are *Barwick v English Joint Stock Bank* (1867) LR 2 Ex 259, 265; *Yuille v B & B Fisheries (Leigh) Ltd* [1958] 2 Lloyd's Rep 596, 619, per Willmer LJ; *Fairline Shipping Corp v Adamson* [1975] QB 180, 190–1; *Noel v Poland* [2001] 2 BCLC 645; *Contex Drouzhba Ltd v Wiseman* [2008] 1 BCLC 631, CA: *Wirecard Bank AG v Scott* [2010] EWHC 451 (QB); *Sean Lindsay v Jared O'Loughnane* [2012] BCC 153; *Al Khudairi v Abbey Brokers Ltd* [2010] EWHC 1486 (Ch).

[62] *Standard Chartered Bank v Pakistan National Shipping (Nos 2 and 4)* (n 61 above), 968, paras 21 and 22, per Lord Hoffmann. Thus where a document executed by a director on behalf of a company contained a fraudulent representation as to the company's credit, the director's signature on the document was sufficient evidence in writing by the director so as to impose personal liability on him pursuant to Statute of Frauds (Amendment) Act 1828, s 6 (Lord Tenterden's Act): *Contex Drouzhba Ltd v Wiseman* [2008] 1 BCLC 631, CA. Note also that although s 6 provides a director with a defence to a claim in deceit in respect of an oral false representation to obtain money or goods on credit for a company, it provides no defence where the oral representation is made after the credit has already been provided; *Roder UK Ltd v Titan Marquees Ltd* [2012] QB 752, CA.

[63] [1920] 3 KB 497.

[64] McCardie J's conclusion on this point was accepted as correct in *G Scammell & Nephew Ltd v Hurley* [1929] 1 KB 419, 443 and 449, CA. See also *D C Thomson & Co Ltd v Deakin* [1952] Ch 646, 680–1, CA, per Evershed MR; *Telemetrix plc v Modern Engineers of Bristol (Holdings) plc* [1985] BCLC 213, 217. A director may be personally liable for inducing a breach of contract between the claimant and a person other than the company of which he is director: *Lewis v Yeeles* [2010] EWCA Civ 326.

[65] [1992] BCLC 148, CA, 173, per Dillon LJ; 179, per Ralph Gibson LJ; 191, per Staughton LJ.

personally liable for any tortious acts he does to third parties in the course of that agency or employment. Nevertheless the Court of Appeal was unwilling to interfere with a judgment that had stood for so long and was so widely accepted.

Another apparent exception is conversion. A director will not be liable for the tort of conver-   **24.29**
sion of goods in the possession or control of his company merely because the director has de facto control over the company's staff and could instruct the staff to release the goods.[66] In such a case the possession or control is the possession or control of the company, not the director. No liability can, therefore, lie against the director for wrongful interference with goods.[67]

In cases where a director does incur personal liability for his own tort, his company will be   **24.30**
liable vicariously for this tort where the director commits the tort whilst acting as a director within the scope of his authority.[68] A company will not be vicariously liable for the torts of its director where:

(1) the tort was not committed in the course of the person carrying out his duties as a director; and

(2) it is established that the company is in fact the agent of the director for the purposes of committing the tort or that the company was merely a 'cloak' or sham under cover of which the tort was committed;[69] in this latter case the company does not escape liability. Its liability, however, is primary, not secondary.

(3) Assumption of responsibility for the company's torts

A director may assume personal responsibility for the company's performance by giving a   **24.31**
contractual guarantee. It is rare, however, for him to assume personal liability in tort.

In *Fairline Shipping Corpn v Adamson*[70] a director of a company that had contracted to store   **24.32**
a customer's goods, wrote to the customer and rendered an invoice in such a way as to create the clear impression that the director was undertaking to be personally answerable for the goods. When the goods were damaged through negligent storage it was held that the director was liable in negligence to the customer.

In *Williams v Natural Life Ltd*[71] an attempt was made to impose liability on a director of a   **24.33**
company for inaccurate statements negligently made in the company's promotional litera-ture. The company was insolvent. The claim was rejected by the House of Lords because there had been no exchanges between the director and the claimants or conduct crossing the line which could have conveyed the impression to the claimants that the director was willing

---

[66] *Joiner v George* [2002] EWHC 90 (Ch), per Park J at paras 22–6; *Thunder Air Ltd v Hilmarsson* [2008] EWHC 355 (Ch).

[67] But see para 24.35 below. The director could be liable for procuring the tort of conversion by the company.

[68] See generally *Dubai Aluminium Co Ltd v Salaam* [2003] 2 AC 366, HL. See also *Barings plc v Coopers & Lybrand (No 2)* [2002] 2 BCLC 410, paras 155–7.

[69] *Rainham Chemical Works Ltd v Belvedere Fish Guano Co* [1921] 2 AC 465, 475, HL, per Lord Buckmaster; see also *Townsend v Haworth* (1875) 48 LJ Ch 770 where Sir George Jessel MR described the company in such circumstances as the 'mere tool' or 'cat's paw' of the individual director. See also *British Thomson-Houston Company, Limited v Sterling Accessories, Limited* [1924] 2 Ch 33, 37–8.

[70] [1975] 1 QB 180.

[71] [1998] 1 WLR 830, HL.

to assume personal responsibility to them.[72] From Lord Steyn's speech, with which the other Lords agreed, several principles may be identified:

(1) In order to render a director of a company liable for a misstatement, the director, as opposed to the company, must have assumed responsibility so as to create a special relationship. Lord Steyn said that 'the inquiry must be whether the director, or anybody on his behalf, conveyed directly or indirectly to the prospective franchisees that the director assumed personal responsibility towards the prospective franchisees'.[73]

(2) An objective test is to be applied in deciding whether the director has assumed responsibility and the main enquiry must be into the exchanges between the director and the claimant.[74]

(3) The assumption of responsibility test is not confined to statements but applies to the provision of services.[75]

(4) The other party must have relied on the assumption of responsibility by the director and the reliance must have been reasonable. Lord Steyn said: 'The test is not simply reliance in fact. The test is whether the plaintiff could reasonably rely on the assumption of personal responsibility by the individual who performed the services on behalf of the company.'[76]

24.34   *Williams v Natural Life Ltd* illustrates that it will rarely be possible to impose liability on directors at common law for negligent statements made by them whilst they are acting as directors. The fact of the office itself will mean that a statement will seldom be treated as a statement made in a director's personal capacity. Likewise, once the statement is treated as having been made by the company, absent evidence of reliance by the claimant on a personal assurance by a director to be answerable for the statement made by the company, no liability will lie.[77]

(4) Liability for the company's torts procured or directed by the director

24.35   The fact that a person is a director of a limited liability company does not, by itself, render him liable for torts committed by the company during the period of his directorship.[78] However, a director can be liable as a joint tortfeasor with his company without himself committing the tortious wrong that causes the damage if he procures or directs the company to

---

[72] *Williams v Natural Life Ltd* [1998] 1 WLR 830, 837–8, HL. The position might have been different if the statements had been made by an employed professional who was also a director: see *Merrett v Babb* [2001] QB 1174, CA; *Phelps v Hillingdon LBC* [2001] 2 AC 619, HL.

[73] *Williams v Natural Life Ltd* [1998] 1 WLR 830, HL, 835H. Direct contact between the director and the claimant will not necessarily be sufficient: see *Trevor Ivory Ltd v Anderson* [1992] 2 NZLR 517 which was approved in *Williams v Natural Life Ltd*.

[74] *Williams v Natural Life Ltd* [1998] 1 WLR 830, at 835F–G, HL.

[75] *Williams v Natural Life Ltd* [1998] 1 WLR 830, at 834F, HL; *Henderson v Merrett Syndicates Ltd* [1995] AC 145 HL. It seems that the mere supply of information by directors in the course of a takeover pursuant to the provisions of the Code and the Rules cannot without some additional indication of assumed responsibility for the supply of information be sufficient to found liability: see *Partco Group Ld v Wragg* [2002] 1 BCLC 323, CA, at para 51, per Potter LJ; however, see *Gilbert v Holms* [2014] EWHC 482 (Ch) at paras 28–9.

[76] *Williams v Natural Life Ltd* [1998] 1 WLR 830, 837, HL.

[77] The distinction may be one between mere reliance in fact and reasonable reliance on the director's pocket book: *London Drugs Ltd v Kuehne & Nagel International Ltd* [1992] 3 SCR 299, 387, per La Forest J; and *Edgeworth Construction Ltd v N D Lea Associates Ltd* [1993] SCR 206 referred to by Lord Steyn in *Williams v Natural Life Ltd* [1998] 1 WLR 830, 836. See also *Ojjeh v Waller* (14 December 1998, unreported) Buckley J.

[78] *Rainham Chemical Works Ltd v Belvedere Fish Guano Co Ltd* [1921] 2 AC 465, 488, HL, per Lord Parmoor; *Prichard & Constance (Wholesale) Ltd v Amata Ltd* (1924) 42 RPC 63.

commit the tort. The courts have been careful to control strictly the circumstances in which a director is exposed to personal liability in this way, because of the danger of undermining the principle of the separate corporate personality of the company and prejudicing the benefits of limited liability.

The principles applicable to liability in these circumstances are as follows: 24.36

(1) A director of a company is not automatically to be identified with the company for the purpose of the law of tort, however small the company may be and however powerful his control over its affairs.[79]

(2) In every case where it is sought to make a director liable for his company's torts it is necessary to examine with care what part he personally played in regard to the act or acts complained of. Mere management of the trade that results in the tortious act is insufficient; the director must procure or direct the commission of the tort by his company.[80]

(3) Where the director procures or directs the commission of the tort by the company, it is no defence to a conspiracy claim for causing loss by unlawful means that the director was the sole controlling mind of the corporate co-conspirator.[81]

(4) Further a director will not be made liable where he did no more than carry out his constitutional role in the governance of the company by, for example, voting at board meetings or, if he is a controlling shareholder, exercising his power of control through passing resolutions to appoint directors.[82] On the other hand, a director may be personally liable as a joint tortfeasor where his participation goes beyond the exercise of constitutional control.[83]

(5) Evidence is not required that the director expressly procured or directed the wrongful act that caused the damage. The director will be liable if he impliedly procured or directed the wrongful act.[84]

(6) Unless knowledge is an essential ingredient of the tort alleged, it is not necessary for the director to know that the acts procured or directed were tortious or that the director was reckless as to whether or not they were likely to be tortious.[85] The focus of the inquiry

---

[79] *C Evans Ltd v Spritebrand Ltd* [1985] 1 WLR 317, 329A–B, CA, per Slade LJ; see also *Campbell v Peter Gordon Joiners Ltd* [2016] AC 1513, SC, where the Supreme Court held (by a majority) that the imposition of criminal liability on a director for his company's breach of its statutory obligation to insure did not result in him also being personally liable in tort, thereby confirming the general rule that a person does not have a civil right of action in respect of another's failure to comply with a statutory obligation where the statute imposes a criminal penalty for non-compliance.

[80] *Rainham Chemical Works Ltd v Belvedere Fish Guano Co* [1921] 2 AC 465, 476, HL, per Lord Buckmaster; see also *Performing Right Society Ltd v Ciryl Theatrical Syndicate Ltd* [1924] 1 KB 1, 14, CA, per Atkin LJ.

[81] *Barclay Pharmaceutical Ltd v Waypharm LP* [2012] EWHC 306 (Comm) paras 220–9.

[82] *MCA Records Inc v Charly Records Ltd* [2003] 1 BCLC 93, CA, at para 49, per Chadwick LJ; *Società Esplosivi Industriali Spa v Ordnance Technologies (UK) Ltd* [2008] 2 BCLC 428 at paras 75–9.

[83] *MCA Records Inc v Charly Records Ltd* [2003] 1 BCLC 93, CA, at para 50, per Chadwick LJ; *Società Esplosivi Industriali Spa v Ordnance Technologies (UK) Ltd* [2008] 2 BCLC 428 at para 80; see also *Ottercroft Ltd v Scandia Care Ltd* [2016] EWCA 86 where at para 24 the role of the joint tortfeasor director was described as being 'decisive in driving the project through' on behalf of the company. Where the defendant is a sole director, a finding that he did no more than carry out his constitutional role and did not authorize the tort is unlikely: *Omnibill (Pty) Ltd v EGPSXXX Ltd* [2014] EWHC 3762 (IPEC) where the tort was infringement of the claimant's copyright.

[84] *Performing Right Society v Ciryl Theatrical Syndicate* [1924] 1 KB, 1 CA.

[85] *British Sky Broadcasting Group plc v Digital Satellite Warranty Cover Ltd* [2012] EWHC 2642 (Ch), para 42: for a director to be jointly liable with the company for trademark infringement or passing off, the director must have at least that degree of knowledge and intention which would suffice to bind his conscience if the wrong in question was a breach of confidence.

must be the degree of the director's personal involvement in the tort alleged and each case depends on its own particular facts.[86]

24.37 Thus a director of a company in the business of manufacturing high explosives will not be liable for procuring the tort of nuisance by his company merely because he had control of the business which resulted in the tort.[87] Likewise, a director of a theatre company will not be liable where without his knowledge and in his absence from the theatrical premises works are performed by independent contractors in breach of copyright.[88]

24.38 However, a director might be liable where his company infringes a third party's copyright where the evidence discloses that the director instructed the company's employees to carry out the infringing acts, but the employees themselves did not know that the acts were tortious.[89] Whether the director is personally liable for a tort relating to intellectual property depends on whether he 'intends and procures and shares a common design that the infringement takes place'.[90]

E. Liabilities of Directors and Contribution

24.39 Where a third party is the subject of a claim by a company to make good loss suffered by it, there may be circumstances where the third party can claim against the directors of the company for contribution under the Civil Liability (Contribution) Act 1978. By s 2(1) of the 1978 Act, the right of contribution turns on whether it is just and equitable to order it.[91]

24.40 In *Charter plc v City Index Ltd*,[92] the defendant settled a claim by the claimant for knowing receipt of the claimant's monies that had been misappropriated by the claimant's treasury manager to finance his spread betting activities with the defendant. The defendant then brought Part 20 proceedings against, inter alia, the directors of the claimant seeking contribution and indemnity under the 1978 Act on the ground that the directors had breached their duties to the claimant by causing the unauthorized transfers to continue undetected and so caused or contributed to the claimant's loss. The defendant accepted that it would have to repay to the company any money or profits retained by it before apportionment under the 1978 Act took place.[93] The Court of Appeal held that, on a broad interpretation of the 1978 Act, the defendant's claim against the directors was in respect of a liability to make compensation in respect of damage within the 1978 Act which could not be summarily dismissed.

---

[86] *C Evans Ltd v Spritebrand Ltd* [1985] 1 WLR 317, CA, where the Court of Appeal refused to follow earlier first-instance decisions to the effect that knowledge was required: eg *Hoover plc v George Hulme (Stockport) Ltd* (1982) 8 FSR 565, 596–7, per Whitford J; *White Horse Distillers Ltd v Gregson Associates Ltd* [1984] RPC 61, 91–2, per Nourse J; *Fairfax Dental Ltd v SJ Filhol Ltd* (unreported) 20 July 1984.

[87] *Rainham Chemical Works Ltd v Belvedere Fish Guano Co* [1921] 2 AC 465, HL.

[88] *Performing Right Society v Ciryl Theatrical Syndicate* [1924] 1 KB 1, CA.

[89] *C Evans Ltd v Spritebrand Ltd* [1985] 1 WLR 317, CA.

[90] *CBS Songs Ltd v Amstrad Consumer Electronics plc* [1988] AC 1013, 1058, HL, per Lord Templeman; *MCA Records Inc v Charly Records Ltd* [2003] 1 BCLC 93, CA at para 51, per Chadwick LJ; *Società Esplosivi Industriali Spa v Ordnance Technologies (UK) Ltd* [2008] 2 BCLC 428 at para 82.

[91] *Dawson v Bell* [2016] EWCA Civ 96; it was not just and equitable for a director who had misappropriated funds for his own exclusive benefit to obtain contribution from another director who was aware of his misappropriations and, in breach of her fiduciary duties had done nothing to stop it.

[92] [2008] Ch 313, CA.

[93] [2008] Ch 313, CA at para 36.

F. Liabilities of Directors Created by Statute

There are a variety of miscellaneous statutory provisions that impose personal liability on **24.41** directors to third persons. These provisions which are discussed below are to be found in:

(1) the Companies Acts: breach of pre-emption requirements, public company allotments, and trading certificates;

(2) FSMA: untrue and misleading statements in prospectuses and listing particulars;

(3) tax statutes: failure of a company to account to HMRC for certain taxes;

(4) the Insolvency Act: being concerned in the management of a company with a prohibited name; and

(5) the CDDA: disqualification.

(1) The Companies Acts

Pre-emption requirements

The 2006 Act, ss 560–77 contains provisions requiring a company that is proposing to allot **24.42** equity securities to offer them to existing shareholders and to communicate pre-emption offers to shareholders, unless, in the case of a private company those provisions are excluded by a provision contained in the company's memorandum or articles or pre-emption rights are disapplied by special resolution.[94] By the 2006 Act, s 563, where there has been a contravention of the shareholder's right of pre-emption or a failure to communicate a pre-emption offer to the shareholder, every officer of the company who knowingly authorized or permitted the contravention is jointly and severally liable with the company to compensate any person to whom an offer should have been made or communicated for any loss, damage, costs, and expenses which the person has sustained by reason of the contravention.[95] However, there is a two-year time limit for the commencement of any proceedings.[96]

Public companies: allotment where issue not fully subscribed

The 2006 Act, s 578(1) provides that a public company may not allot shares for subscription **24.43** or as wholly or partly payable otherwise than in cash unless the issue is subscribed for in full or the offer is made on terms that the shares subscribed for may be allotted in any event or if specified conditions are met and they are met. If the requirements for an allotment are not fulfilled within 40 days after the first making of the offer all money received from applicants for shares must be repaid to them forthwith without interest.[97] Furthermore, s 579(1) provides that an allotment made by a public company to an applicant in contravention of s 578 is voidable at the instance of the applicant within one month after the date of the allotment and not later.[98] This is so even if the company is in the course of being wound up.[99]

---

[94] These provisions apply to offers made on or after 1 October 2009: Companies Act 2006 (Commencement No 8 Transitional Provisions and Savings) Order (SI 2008/2860). Note substituted wording to ss 560(2)–(3), 562(4), 566, 573(1) and the repeal of s 561(3) with effect from 1 October 2009 made by the Companies Act 2006 (Allotment of Shares and Rights of Pre-emption) (Amendment) Regulations 2009 (SI 2009/2561), reg 2.

[95] 2006 Act, s 563(2).

[96] 2006 Act, s 563(3).

[97] 2006 Act, s 578(2). Section 578 came into force on 1 October 2009, when it replaced 1985 Act, s 84.

[98] 2006 Act, s 579(1), which came into force on 1 October 2009, when s 579 replaced 1985 Act, s 85.

[99] 2006 Act, s 579(2).

24.44 The provisions of ss 578 and 579 expose the directors of a public company to two forms of personal liability:

(1) If the company is prohibited by s 578(1) from allotting shares and all money received from applicants for shares has not been repaid within 48 days after the first making of the offer, the directors of the company are jointly and severally liable to repay the sums with interest, but a director can avoid liability if he proves that the default in the repayment of the money was not due to any misconduct or negligence on his part.[100]

(2) A director of a public company who knowingly contravenes or permits or authorizes the contravention of any provision of s 578 with respect to allotment is liable to compensate the company and the allottee for any loss, damage, costs or expenses they may have sustained or incurred.[101] But no proceedings may be brought more than two years after the date of the allotment.[102]

Public company: minimum share capital requirement and trading certificate

24.45 Under the 2006 Act, s 761(1) a company that is a public company, unless it is one that has been re-registered as a public company,[103] must have been issued with a trading certificate by the Registrar of Companies before it does any business or exercises any powers of borrowing.[104] If a trading certificate has not been issued and a company carries on business or borrows money and fails to comply with its obligations in connection with the transaction within 21 days from being called upon to do so, any directors of the company at the time of the relevant transaction are jointly and severally liable to indemnify any other party to the transaction in respect of any loss or damage suffered by him by reason of the company's failure to comply with its obligations.[105]

(2) Financial Services and Markets Act 2000

24.46 Statements made by directors in prospectuses and other fundraising documents are an area deserving of particular attention. In the nineteenth century, when the issue of prospectuses first became a feature of commercial life, the common law allowed an investor who incurred financial loss after investing in reliance on the contents of a false or misleading prospectus to bring a claim in damages but only if he could establish the tort of deceit. In *Derry v Peek*[106] the House of Lords rejected an attempt to extend liability to negligent statements. The rejection was met with considerable public disquiet and in the following year the Directors' Liability Act 1890[107] was passed.[108] Section 3 of that Act imposed liability for the first time on directors and others for negligent statements in a prospectus. The provisions of the 1890

---

[100] 2006 Act, s 578(3).

[101] 2006 Act, s 579(3).

[102] 2006 Act, 579(4).

[103] As defined by Companies Act 2006, s 4(2).

[104] 2006 Act, s 761 which replaces, without substantive change, the 1985 Act provisions in s 117, came into force on 6 April 2008; 2006 Act Commencement Order No 5, Art 3(1)(h).

[105] 2006 Act, s 767(3). By s 767(1) and (2) the company and officers of the company also commit an offence. It was unclear whether the reference to 'obligations' in 1985 Act, s 117(8) referred to the company's obligation to obtain a trading certificate or to its obligations in relation to the transaction. 2006 Act, s 767(3) makes it clear that the requirement to indemnify relates to loss suffered in connection with the transaction.

[106] (1889) 14 App Cas 337, HL.

[107] 53 & 54 Vict c 64.

[108] Lobban, 'Nineteenth Century Frauds in Company Formation: Derry v Peek in Context' (1996) 112 LQR 287, which contains a general discussion of the commercial and legal environment at that time.

Act were brought into the mainstream of companies' legislation in 1908 and remained there until 1986 when they were moved to the securities legislation of the Financial Services Act 1986.[109]

A prospectus is an invitation issued to the public to subscribe for shares. It is not an invitation **24.47** to purchase shares in the market.[110] From time to time attempts have been made at common law to extend protection to purchasers in the after-market without much success.[111] In 1990 Mervyn Davies J struck out a claim by purchasers of shares in the after-market against directors for negligent misstatement in a prospectus.[112] More recently the merits of this decision have been doubted. In *Possfund Custodian Trustee Ltd v Diamond*[113] Lightman J accepted that it was arguable that persons responsible for the issue of a modern prospectus owed a duty of care to purchasers in an after-market of unlisted securities. Lightman J was impressed by the fact that modern prospectuses often contain statements that their purpose is to lead to an admission to listing on the Stock Exchange.[114] The prospectus in *Possfund* expressly stated that the shares in question would be traded on the Unlisted Securities Market. This point was sufficiently persuasive to allow the case to go to trial.

Compensation for misleading statements

Current statutory protection is to be found in FSMA, s 90[115] which provides for the payment **24.48** of statutory compensation where loss is suffered by a person as a result of untrue or misleading statements in either prospectuses or listing particulars[116] where securities are to be offered to the public in the UK or admitted to trading on a regulated market operating in the UK or if the securities are to be admitted to the official list.[117]

Compensation is payable by 'any person responsible' for the relevant document.[118] **24.49** Unsurprisingly, directors are included within this term.[119] In the case of prospectuses, the FCA applies different rules to (1) equity shares, warrants, or options to subscribe for equity shares which are issued by the issuer of the shares and other securities having similar characteristics to such shares, warrants, and options; and (2) any other securities, including debt and convertible securities. Directors are exposed to liability only in relation to the

---

[109] The statutory successors to the Directors' Liability Act 1890, s 3 are 1908 Act, s 84; 1929 Act, s 37; 1948 Act, s 45; 1985 Act, s 58; and Financial Services Act 1986, s 166.

[110] See *Peek v Gurney* (1873) LR 6 HL 377.

[111] *Andrews v Mockford* [1896] 1 QB 372; see also *Scott v Dixon* (1859) 29 LJ Ex 62n.

[112] *Al-Nakib Investments (Jersey) Ltd v Longcroft* [1990] 1 WLR 1390 where he applied the principle that had been recently formulated by the House of Lords in *Caparo Industries plc v Dickman* [1990] 2 AC 605 to restrict liability to persons who knew or ought to have known that the claimant would rely on the statement for a specific purpose.

[113] [1996] 1 WLR 1351.

[114] [1996] 1 WLR 1351, 1366.

[115] As amended by the Prospectus Regulations 2005 (SI 2005/1433), Sch 1, para 6 and the Prospectus Regulations 2012 (SI 2012/1538), reg 7.

[116] 'Listing particulars' are particulars issued prior to listing, including supplementary listing particulars (see s 90(10)) which are issued after preparation of the listing particulars but before the commencement of dealings in the securities following their admission to the official list (see s 81(1)). Announcements in breach of the 'Listing Rules' if not listing particulars do not give rise to a private law right of action under s 90: see *Hall v Cable & Wireless plc* [2010] 1 BCLC 95 per Teare J at para 20.

[117] The official list as maintained by the FCA: see FSMA, s 103(1).

[118] FMSA s 90(1).

[119] See, for listing particulars, Financial Services and Markets Act 2000 (Official Listing of Securities) Regulations 2001 (SI 2001/2956), reg 6(1)(c); for prospectuses, the FCA Handbook Prospectus Rules 5.5.

first classification concerning equity shares unless they expressly accept responsibility for the prospectus in relation to the latter classification.[120] Those who are potentially liable are (i) directors of the issuer at the date of the prospectus; (ii) each person who has authorized himself to be named, and is named as having agreed to become a director of the issuer either immediately or in the future;[121] (iii) directors of the offeror if the company making the offer is a selling shareholder; and (iv) the directors of the company requesting admission, if not the issuer.[122] In the case of listing particulars existing and future directors of the company seeking a listing are potentially liable for statements made in the particulars.[123]

24.50 Four features of the statutory liability to pay compensation under s 90 deserve comment.

(1) First, to be actionable the statement only needs to have been untrue or misleading in fact. Fraud or dishonest intention is not a requirement.

(2) Secondly, the statutory liability does not appear to require the person who acquired the securities to have relied on the statement or the omission as long as the statement or omission caused the loss. On this basis a claim might lie even if the claimant did not read the prospectus or listing particulars.

(3) Thirdly, although compensation is payable to the person who acquired the securities there is no reference to the person from whom the securities were acquired. Thus s 90 does not seem to be confined to the original offer but can be used by later market purchasers. This logically flows from the liability extending not just to prospectuses in connection with a public offer but also to an admission to trading without any public offer.[124] It is also a logical consequence of the developing principles of common law illustrated by *Possfund*.[125]

(4) Fourthly, the section provides no guidance as to the appropriate measure of compensation. It is unclear whether the compensation is to be determined on the basis of loss (tort) or expectation (contract). Arguably, the term 'compensation' suggests that the tortious measure of loss should be used. On the other hand since, generally, the object of purchasing shares is to make a profit, it might be said that the expectation measure equates more to a claimant's idea of compensation.

24.51 There are a number of important exclusions from or defences to liability of directors in connection with statements made in prospectuses and listing particulars.[126] The most important of these is where the director shows that at the time the document was submitted for publication he reasonably believed, having made all such enquiries as were reasonable, that the statements were true and not misleading or the matter whose omission caused the loss was properly omitted and that:

---

[120] FCA Handbook Prospectus Rules 5.5.4R.

[121] It is common in recommended takeover offers, for example, to state that certain directors of the target company will join the board of the offeror upon the offer becoming unconditional. Those directors will thereby become responsible for the information concerning the offeror as well as the information concerning their own company.

[122] FCA Handbook Prospectus Rules 5.5.3R.

[123] Financial Services and Markets Act 2000 (Official Listing of Securities) Regulations 2001 (SI 2001/2956), reg 6.

[124] FSMA, Sch 10, para 6.

[125] *Possfund Custodian Trustee Ltd v Diamond* [1996] 1 WLR 1351.

[126] See generally FSMA, s 90(2) and (5) and Sch 10; Financial Services and Markets Act 2000 (Official Listing of Securities) Regulations 2001 (SI 2001/2956), reg 6 in relation to listing particulars; FCA Handbook Prospectus Rules 5.5 R in relation to prospectuses.

(1) the director continued in that belief until the securities were acquired or the securities were acquired before it was reasonably practicable to bring a correction to the attention of those persons likely to acquire them; or

(2) before the securities were acquired the director had taken all reasonable steps to secure that a correction was brought to the attention of those persons likely to acquire them; or

(3) the directors continued in that belief until after the commencement of dealings in the securities following their admission to the official list or regulated market and the securities were acquired after such a lapse of time that the director ought reasonably to be excused;[127] or

(4) where the person suffering the loss acquired the securities with knowledge that the statement was false or misleading.

Statutory liability for inaccurate statements in listing particulars and prospectuses does not apply to offers that are exempt.[128] Exempt offers are those made to qualified investors, those directed at fewer than 50 persons other than qualified investors, where the minimum consideration paid by the person acquiring the securities is at least €100,000 or where the total consideration for the securities being offered does not exceed €100,000.[129] It follows that where there is an exempt offer the common law applicable to misstatements will continue to apply.   **24.52**

From 1 October 2010, s 90A FSMA, which was originally introduced by the 2006 Act, s 1270, has been amended to include a detailed framework for liability contained in a new Schedule 10A.[130] Section 90A encompasses all official announcements issued by UK and overseas companies whose securities are traded on a UK securities market and UK companies whose securities are traded on any overseas securities market. Securities markets in the UK cover both regulated markets and multilateral trading facilities such as AIM and ISDX. A statutory tort is created in relation to: **24.53**

(1) any untrue or misleading statement in an official announcement where any director knew or was reckless as to the error;

(2) any omission of required information from an official announcement where any director knew the omission to be dishonest concealment; and

(3) any delay in the official publication of information where any director acted dishonestly in delaying publication. Unlike s 90, liability is confined to the issuer.

The Davies Review[131] whose recommendations resulted in the revised s 90A took the view that imposing liability on directors was unnecessary and potentially counter-productive because: **24.54**

(1) the sanctions and censure of what is now the FCA and market operators themselves would act as a powerful deterrent against directors making untrue and misleading statements;

---

[127] FSMA 2000, Sch 10, para 1.
[128] FSMA, s 86. For collective investment schemes, see also s 90ZA.
[129] FSMA, s 86.
[130] Added by the Financial Services and Markets Act 2000 (Liability of Issuers) Regulations 2010 (SI 2010/1192), reg 2(2) (subject to transitional provisions specified in reg 3).
[131] Professor Paul Davies QC, 'Davies Review of Issuer Liability—Final Report' (HMSO, June 2007) formed the basis for the introduction of Sch 10A.

(2) exposing directors personally to large compensation claims is likely to induce extreme and undesirable caution in order to avoid liability;

(3) D&O insurance may shift the loss from directors back to the company;

(4) the company has the ability to seek compensation from directors for breach of duty, if the company is held liable for the untrue and misleading statement; and

(5) shareholders could bring an action against the directors under the new derivative action procedures in the CA 2006.[132]

However, as Professor Davies acknowledged,[133] even without statutory liability, directors who are responsible for a statement or omission that was known by the directors to be fraudulent could still be liable at common law for the tort of deceit.[134]

Injunctions and restitution orders

24.55 A director may be an insider for the purposes of the provisions of FSMA, Part 8, which imposes penalties for market abuse within s 118. Under FSMA, the FCA also has power to apply for an injunction to restrain persons, including directors, from engaging in market abuse and to obtain restitution orders against persons, including directors, who have engaged in market abuse.[135] Directors' liability for market abuse is discussed in Chapter 32 below.

24.56 The FCA has similar powers to apply for injunctions to restrain contravention of requirements imposed by FSMA[136] and to obtain restitution orders where there has been such a contravention.[137]

(3) Tax statutes

24.57 A director of a company that fails to pay national insurance contributions may be personally liable to pay the amount of unpaid tax if the failure appears to the Inland Revenue to be attributable to the fraud or neglect of the director.[138] In such circumstances the Inland Revenue can issue a personal liability notice against the director for the amount of the unpaid tax. In *HMRC v O'Rorke*,[139] it was held in a First Tier Tribunal tax case that 'neglect' involved a subjective element of the director knowing that the amount of tax had not been paid. The judgment was overturned on appeal to the Upper Tribunal.[140] Mr Justice Hildyard held that the ordinary objective test which usually applies where neglect or negligence is in issue should apply.

24.58 In the context of agency work, under Chapter 7, Part 2 of the Income Tax (Earnings and Pensions) Act 2003, the responsibility for deducting income tax and national insurance contributions and paying the tax to HMRC is on the agency that has the relationship with the worker. The legislation is designed to tackle false self-employment where an agency is used to evade employment taxes and obligations by disguising the employment as self-employment. Where Chapter 7 Part 2 applies and the corporate agent does not account to HMRC for such

---

132 See Davies Final Report (n 131 above), paras 54–8.
133 See Davies Final Report (n 131 above), para 55.
134 *Standard Chartered Bank v Pakistan National Shipping (Nos 2 and 4)* [2003] 1 AC 959, HL.
135 FSMA, ss 381, 383, and 384.
136 FSMA, s 380.
137 FSMA, s 382; *Financial Services Authority v Shepherd*, Chancery Division, 22 May 2009.
138 Social Security Administration Act 1992, s 121C.
139 [2011] UKFTT 839(TC).
140 [2013] UKUT 49 (TCC).

taxes, HMRC may serve a personal liability notice on the directors of the corporate agent for the unpaid tax.[141]

(3) The Insolvency Act

Under the Insolvency Act claims may be brought for the benefit of creditors against directors **24.59** or former directors of a company by a liquidator for misfeasance and by an administrator or liquidator for fraudulent or wrongful trading.[142] However, such claims are not claims by third parties against directors. They are claims brought by the liquidator of the company to enforce, for the benefit of creditors, the directors' duties owed to the company or to obtain a contribution to the company's assets for distribution in its winding up. These claims are discussed in more detail in Chapter 34, Section C below.

Third parties do, however, have direct rights of action under the Insolvency Act, s 217 against **24.60** a director who, in contravention of s 216 of that Act, becomes involved in the management of a new company with a name that is the same as or similar to the name of a company that went into insolvent liquidation at any time in the previous 12 months. In such circumstances the director is personally liable for the debts of the new company. These provisions are discussed in detail in Chapter 34, Section D below.

(4) The Company Directors Disqualification Act 1986

Disqualification of directors is discussed in Chapter 31 below. Section G of that chapter **24.61** discusses in more detail the circumstances in which, under the CDDA, a person, including a director, may be liable for the debts and liabilities of a company.

In brief there are two circumstances. First, the CDDA, s 15(1)(a) and (2) makes a person **24.62** responsible for all relevant debts of the company, jointly and severally with the company and any other person responsible for those debts, if he is involved in the management of the company in contravention of (a) a disqualification order or disqualification undertaking under the CDDA, ss 1 or 1A or (b) the CDDA, s 11. By the CDDA, s 11[143] it is an offence for a person to act as a director of a company or directly or indirectly to take part in or be concerned in the promotion, formation, or management of a company, without the leave of the court, at a time when (a) he is an undischarged bankrupt, (b) a bankruptcy restrictions order or undertaking is in force in respect of him, (c) a debt relief restrictions order or undertaking is in force in respect of him, or (d) a moratorium period under a debt relief order applies in relation to him.[144] Such a person is personally liable for such debts and other liabilities of the company that are incurred at a time when he was involved in the management of the company.[145]

---

[141] Income Tax (Pay As You Earn) Regulations 2003/2682, regs 97ZA–97ZF.

[142] Claims under Insolvency Act, ss 212, 213, 214 and, with effect from 1 October 2015, ss 246ZA and 246ZB. The official receiver, a creditor, or contributory may be the applicant under s 212(3). Claims for fraudulent and wrongful trading of the proceeds may now be assigned; s 246ZD.

[143] As amended by the SBEE Act 2015, s 113 with effect from 1 October 2015.

[144] These orders and undertakings are made or given under the IA 1986, in relation to England and Wales, the Bankruptcy (Scotland) Act 1985, and the Insolvency (Northern Ireland) Order 1989. The liability continues to attach to a bankrupt even if he subsequently obtains an annulment: *IRC v McEntaggart* [2006] 1 BCLC 476.

[145] CDDA, s 15(3)(a). The question of when a debt or liability is incurred depends on the circumstances of the case and the nature of the liability: see *Wirecard Bank AG v Scott* [2010] EWHC 451 (QB), para 104.

24.63 Secondly, a person is also personally responsible for all relevant debts, jointly and severally with the company and any other person responsible for those debts, if he is involved in the management of the company and acts or is willing to act on instructions given, without leave of the court, by a person whom he knows at the time to be the subject of a disqualification order or disqualification undertaking or to be an undischarged bankrupt.[146] Such a person is personally liable for such debts and liabilities of the company as were incurred when that person was acting or willing to act on the instructions of the person whilst he was disqualified.[147]

24.64 Also, by CDDA s 15A,[148] the court may make a compensation order against a person on the application of the Secretary of State, or the Secretary of State may accept a compensation undertaking if (a) the person is subject to a disqualification order or undertaking under the CDDA, and (b) the conduct for which the person is subject to the order or undertaking has caused loss to one or more creditors of an insolvent company of which the person has at any time been a director.[149] By s 15A the amount of the compensation takes into account the amount of the loss caused and the person's conduct and is to be paid as a contribution to the assets of the company for the benefit of the creditor or creditors, or class or classes of creditor specified in the order or undertaking.

G. Liabilities of Directors Arising from Legal Proceedings

24.65 A director may incur personal liability from legal proceedings relating to the company. First, a director may be personally liable for costs payable to other parties in proceedings where the company, but not the director, is a party. Secondly, a director may be liable to punishment for contempt for breach of an order made by a court, even if he is not a party to the proceedings or even named in the order.

(1) Costs

24.66 The Senior Courts Act 1981, s 51(3) gives the courts full power to determine by whom and to what extent costs of court proceedings are to be paid. In *Aiden Shipping Co Ltd v Interbulk Ltd*[150] it was held that this provision was not confined to orders against parties to the relevant proceedings but could apply to non-parties. In the last few years the section has often been used against directors where their company has been the unsuccessful party to proceedings and is then unable to meet an adverse order for costs.

---

[146] CDDA, s 15(1)(b), (2). Interestingly, a person who acts on the instructions given by a person whom he knows is subject to a bankruptcy restrictions order or undertaking, a debt relief restrictions order or undertaking, or to whom a moratorium period under a debt relief order applies, is not included in the class of persons who are personally liable under CDDA, s 15.

[147] CDDA, s 15(3)(b).

[148] Inserted by SBEE Act 2015, s 110 with effect from 1 October 2015 (SI 2015/1689).

[149] CDDA, s 15A(3). By s 15A(4) an insolvent company is a company that is or has been insolvent and a company becomes insolvent if (a) it goes into liquidation at a time when its assets are insufficient for the payment of its debts and other liabilities and the expenses of the winding up, (b) it enters administration, or (c) an administrative receiver of it is appointed. By s 15A(5) the Secretary of State may apply for a compensation order at any time before the end of the period of two years beginning with the date when the disqualification order was made or the disqualification undertaking was accepted.

[150] [1986] AC 965, HL. In *Symphony Group plc v Hodgson* [1994] QB 179, CA the CA set out guidelines at pp 192–4. See also *Murphy v Young & Co's Brewery plc* [1997] 1 WLR 1591, CA; *Hamilton v Al Fayed (No 2)* [2003] QB 1175, CA; *Dymocks Franchise Systems (NSW) Pty Ltd v Todd* [2004] 1 WLR 2807, PC; *Deutsche Bank AG v Sebastian Holding Inc* [2016] 4 WLR 17, CA.

The power to award costs against a non-party has particular relevance where the unsuccessful **24.67** claimant or defendant is a company which is insolvent. Case law has established a number of principles which are relevant to the exercise of the power to award costs against a director of a company which cannot pay costs that it is ordered to pay:

(1) The jurisdiction applies not only for the benefit of those who have been unsuccessfully sued by an insolvent company but also for the benefit of claimants who are successful,[151] although the case of a company which is forced to defend a claim is not necessarily the same as the case of a company that initiates a claim.[152]

(2) The jurisdiction is exceptional.[153]

(3) The ultimate question in the exceptional case is whether in all the circumstances it is just to make the order.[154]

(4) A director's knowledge that his company will not be able to meet an adverse costs order should the company prove to be the unsuccessful party in the litigation is, by itself, insufficient to trigger the exercise of the jurisdiction.[155]

(5) Lack of good faith may be sufficient although it is not a necessary condition to trigger the section.[156] Pursuit of speculative litigation may amount to impropriety for this purpose.[157]

(6) The question is whether the litigation is being conducted in the interests of the company (its shareholders or, if insolvent, its creditors) or whether the director is the 'real party' for whose benefit the litigation is being conducted.[158]

(7) The conduct of the director must have been the cause of the applicant incurring the costs it seeks to recover.[159]

---

[151] *Taylor v Pace Developments Ltd* [1991] BCC 406, CA; *Europeans Ltd v HMRC* [2011] BCC 527 (director ordered to pay the costs of an appeal by the company that was withdrawn).

[152] *Goodwood Recoveries Ltd v Breen* [2006] 1 WLR 2723, CA, at para 48.

[153] *Metalloy Supplies Ltd v MA (UK) Ltd* [1997] 1 WLR 1613, 1620, CA, per Millett LJ; although exceptional in this context means no more than outside the ordinary run of things, *Deutsche Bank AG v Sebastian Holdings Inc* [2014] EWHC 2073 (Comm) (affirmed in CA [2016] 4 WLR 17), citing *Dymocks Franchise Systems (NSW) Pty Ltd v Todd* [2004] 1 WLR 2807 PC.

[154] *Dymocks Franchise Systems (NSW) Pty Ltd v Todd* (n 153 above) at para 25.

[155] *Goodwood Recoveries Ltd v Breen* [2006] 1 WLR 2723 CA, per Rix LJ at para 59.

[156] *Goodwood Recoveries Ltd v Breen* (n 155 above).

[157] *Goodwood Recoveries Ltd v Breen* (n 155 above), referring to *Dymocks Franchise Systems (NSW) Pty Ltd v Todd* [2004] 1 WLR 2807 at para 33; *BE Studios Ltd v Smith & Williamson Ltd* [2006] 2 All ER 811 at paras 16–19.

[158] *Dymocks Franchise Systems (NSW) Pty Ltd v Todd* (n 153 above) at para 29; *BE Studios Ltd v Smith & Williamson Ltd* [2006] 2 All ER 811; *Petromec Inc v Petroleo Brasiliero SA Petrobras (No 4)* [2006] EWCA Civ 1038, per Longmore LJ at para 10; *Sims v Hawkins* [2007] EWCA Civ 1175; *Chantrey Vellacott v Convergence Group plc* [2007] EWHC 1774; *DNA Productions (Europe) Ltd v Manoukian* [2008] EWHC 2627 (Ch); *Systemcare (UK) Ltd v Services Design Technology Ltd* [2012] 1 BCLC 14, *Trident Australasia Pty Ltd and Versabuild LLC v Cox* [2015] EWHC 2890 (Comm). For earlier cases, see *Re North West Holding plc, Secretary of State for Trade and Industry v Backhouse* [2001] 1 BCLC 468; *Metalloy Supplies Ltd v MA (UK) Ltd* [1997] 1 WLR 1613, 1620, CA, per Millett LJ; *Re Aurum Marketing Ltd* [2000] 2 BCLC 645 where a director, for his own personal interests, caused the company to contest a winding-up petition. *Lingfield Properties (Darlington) v Padgett Lavender Associates* [2008] EWHC 2795 (QB) and *Equitas Ltd v Horace Holman & Co Ltd* [2009] 1 BCLC 662 are cases where the application against the director failed. An application to make administrative receivers personally liable for costs of unsuccessful litigation failed in *Mills v Birchall* [2008] 1 WCR 1829, CA.

[159] *Goodwood Recoveries Ltd v Breen* [2006] 1 WLR 2723, CA, per Rix LJ at paras 60–6; although *quaere* whether costs have to be caused by all factors which render the case an exception: *Globe Equities Ltd v Globe Legal Services Ltd* [1999] BLR 232, 241, per Morritt LJ.

(8) The fact that the applicant had previously obtained an order for security for costs is not a reason, in itself, for refusing to make an order against a non-party director, if the amount of the security turns out to be inadequate.[160]

(9) The importance of a warning being given to the non-party director of the possibility of an application for costs will vary from case to case; it may be of little consequence where the non-party has controlled the conduct of the litigation, but more significant where the non-party is just a witness.[161]

24.68 If a successful party wishes to seek a costs order against a director who was not a party to the proceedings then under CPR 46.2[162] the director must be added as a party to the proceedings for the purposes of obtaining a costs order against him. The director must also be given a reasonable opportunity to attend a hearing and make representations against an order being made. Judicial findings in one set of proceedings are generally inadmissible as evidence of the facts upon which they were based in a different set of proceedings between one of the parties to those proceedings and a stranger. However, in the summary procedure for the determination of the liability of a non-party director to pay costs there can be a departure from this principle if the connection of the director with the main proceedings was so close that he does not suffer any injustice by allowing an exception to the general rule. The connection will be sufficiently close if the director is a majority shareholder of the company, he funded the litigation, and has a real interest in the outcome of the litigation both in his capacity as majority shareholder and in his capacity as director.[163]

(2) Civil contempt

24.69 A court order binds the person to whom it is addressed,[164] but does not in general compel compliance by other persons.[165] So if an order is made against a company, restraining it from performing an act by itself, its officers, servants, or agents, the effect is not to bind the officers, servants, or agents directly but to make it plain to the company that it will contravene the order if it performs the act through those other persons.[166] The company will be liable for contempt for a breach of the order committed by its officers or servants even if they have been instructed not to contravene the order, provided that the contravention occurs during the course of employment.[167]

---

[160] *Petromec Inc v Petroleo Brasiliero SA Petrobras (No 4)* [2006] EWCA Civ 1038 per Longmore LJ at paras 13 and 14.

[161] *Deutsche Bank AG v Sebastian Holdings Inc* [2016] 4 WLR 17, CA at paras 32, 34.

[162] Enacted by the Civil Procedure (Amendment) Rules 2013 (SI 2013/262) which came into effect on 1 April 2013.

[163] *Brampton Manor (Leisure) Ltd v McClean (No 2)* [2009] BCC 30, paras 17–20; *Deutsche Bank AG v Sebastian Holdings Inc* [2016] 4 WLR 17, CA at para 27.

[164] So a director, like any other person, commits a contempt if he is served with an order and fails to comply with it or he gives an undertaking to the court and does not comply with it: see eg *Re Hartmayes Ltd* [2013] EWHC 4624 (Ch); *Khawaja v Popat* [2016] EWCA Civ 362 (directors procuring company's breach of freezing injunction and failing to comply with requirement to provide information); *Sports Direct International plc v Rangers International Football plc* [2016] EWHC 85 (Ch) (committal refused, for failure to prove beyond reasonable doubt that chairman had breached confidentiality order).

[165] *Lord Wellesley v Earl of Mornington* (1848) 11 Beav 180; *Marengo v Daily Sketch* [1948] 1 All ER 406; *AG v Newspaper Publishing plc* [1988] Ch 333, 366, 367, 377, 384, CA. More recently courts have been prepared to grant injunctions *contra mundum* to protect identity or confidence; *Venables v New Group Newspapers Ltd* [2001] Fam 430.

[166] *Marengo v Daily Sketch* [1948] 1 All ER 406; *AG v Newspaper Publishing plc* [1988] Ch 333, 366, CA.

[167] *Re Supply of Ready Mixed Concrete (No 2)* [1995] 1 AC 456, 465, 481, HL. For a recent application of the principle, see *Back Office Ltd v Percival* [2013] EWHC 1385 (QB); [2013] EWHC 3776 (QB).

A director may, however, be liable for contempt of court in respect of an order made against a **24.70** company in two situations: (1) he knowingly aids and abets a breach of the order by the company, or (2) with knowledge of the order he does an act which deliberately interferes with the course of justice by frustrating the purpose for which the order was made.[168] The latter contempt is described as criminal contempt and its essential nature is interference with justice. Deliberate interference with the course of proceedings, by destroying disclosable documents or interfering with witnesses is punishable as a contempt, even without a court order.[169]

Special factors apply to directors even though they are also agents and often employees as **24.71** well. This is because CPR Part 81.4(1) and (3) provide that where a company or other corporation is required by a judgment or order to do an act within the time fixed by the judgment or order or disobeys a judgment or order not to do an act, a committal order may be made against any director or other officer of that company or corporation. A copy of the judgment or order, endorsed with a penal notice, must be personally served on the director or other officer before the end of the time fixed for doing the act.[170] The purpose of this rule is to focus the minds of directors on ensuring that the company complies with its obligations. The rule applies not only where an order has been made against a company but also where the company has given an undertaking to the court to do or abstain from doing something on the basis that an undertaking to the court is equivalent to an injunction.[171] A director is under a duty to take reasonable steps to ensure that the company obeys the order.[172] In *Biba Ltd v Stratford Investments Ltd*[173] it was held that even if a director adopted a purely passive role and did not aid and abet a contempt in any way, he could be held liable for contempt in consequence of a breach of an undertaking given by the company of which he was a director.

In *AG for Tuvalu v Philatelic Distribution Corp*[174] the Court of Appeal explained the position **24.72** of a director where an order is made against a company or an undertaking is given by it:

> In our view where a company is ordered not to do certain acts or gives an undertaking to like effect and a director of that company is aware of the order or undertaking he is under a duty to take reasonable steps to ensure that the order or undertaking is obeyed, and if he wilfully fails to take those steps and the order or undertaking is breached he can be punished for contempt. We use the word 'wilful' to distinguish the situations where the director can reasonably believe some other director is taking those steps.

Where a foreign company has submitted to the jurisdiction of the English court, a director, **24.73** whether or not resident in the jurisdiction, may be held liable for contempt if they cause the foreign company to commit a contempt.[175] In *Dar Al Arkan Real Estate Development Co v Al Refai*,[176] the Court of Appeal held that the exercise of a court's contempt jurisdiction in such

---

[168] *AG v Times Newspapers Ltd* [1992] 1 AC 191, 217, 218, 222, HL; *AG v Punch Ltd* [2003] 1 AC 1046, HL at 39, 66, 87; *Customs & Excise Commissioners v Barclays Bank plc* [2007] 1 AC 181, HL at paras 29, 56–9. For freezing orders, see *Z Ltd v A-Z* [1982] QB 558, 578, CA.

[169] *British Steel Corporation v Granada Television* [1981] AC 1096, 1127, 1142, CA.

[170] CPR 81.5(2); CPR 81.6; 81PD para 2. In the case of a judgment or order requiring a person not to do an act, the court may dispense with personal service: CPR 81.8. See also *Iberian Trust Ltd v Founders Trust and Investment Co Ltd* [1932] 2 KB 87.

[171] CPR 81.4(4).

[172] *Public Joint Stock Company, Vseukrainskyi Aktsionernyi Bank v Sergey Maksimov* [2014] EWHC 3771 (Comm) at para 127.

[173] [1973] 1 Ch 281.

[174] [1990] 1 WLR 926, 936, CA.

[175] *Dar Al Arkan Real Estate Development Co v Al Refai* [2015] 1 WLR 135, CA.

[176] (n 175 above).

circumstances was not tantamount to permitting the enforcement of English penal law in another jurisdiction since it merely enabled the enforcement in England of an order made by an English court in proceedings against companies which were properly before it. The latter case is to be contrasted with *Masri v Consolidated Contractors Int (UK) Ltd (No 4)*,[177] where it was held that there was no jurisdiction to order the examination of a director of a judgment corporate debtor as to its assets where the director resided outside the jurisdiction. The difference in treatment in both cases can best be explained by the fact that in *Dar Al Arkan* the issue was the public interest in upholding the authority of the court by enforcement of its orders against the directors through whom the companies acted, whereas *Masri* was concerned with the pursuit of private rights and interests in seeking information from foreign directors for the purposes of enforcing a judgment against a corporate defendant.[178]

24.74 A non-executive director may be justified in believing that the directors responsible for managing the company are taking the necessary steps to secure compliance with the order.[179] In the ordinary case the necessary steps will include taking adequate and continuing steps to ensure that those to whom the director has delegated the handling of matters which fall within the scope of the order or undertaking did not forget, misunderstand, or overlook the obligations imposed by the order.[180] A director would not be liable if the company was unable to comply with the order, for example because it lacked the resources to comply. However, a court would undoubtedly subject such a defence to close scrutiny.[181]

24.75 Where a judgment has been entered against a company, the judgment creditor may apply to court for an order requiring an officer of the company (including a director) to attend court to provide information about the company's assets or any other matter about which information is needed to enforce the judgment.[182] A director who fails to comply with the order is liable to be committed to prison for contempt.[183] A person who alleges that the director is in contempt of court must prove breach of the order beyond reasonable doubt.

---

[177] [2010] 1 AC 90 HL.

[178] *Dar Al Arkan Real Estate Development Co v Refai* (n 175 above) per Beatson LJ at paras 42–4.

[179] *Director General of Fair Trading v Buckland* [1990] 1 WLR 920, 925.

[180] *AG for Tuvalu v Philatelic Distribution Corp* [1990] 1 WLR 926, CA, per Woolf LJ at 938F, explaining *Director General of Fair Trading v Buckland* (n 179 above).

[181] *Lewis v Pontypridd Caerphilly and Newport Railway Co* (1895) 11 TLR 203.

[182] CPR Part 71.2(1). No order may be made against a director to provide information or to attend court for cross-examination about a foreign judgment debtor company's assets when the director is resident outside the jurisdiction: see *Masri v Consolidated Contractors Int (UK) Ltd (No 4)* [2010] 1 AC 90 HL.

[183] CPR Part 71.2(7).

PART V

DIRECTORS' PARTICULAR FUNCTIONS AND DUTIES

25

DECISION-MAKING BY MEMBERS

Hannah Thornley

A. Introduction

(1) Overview

This chapter describes the ways in which members make decisions for a company and the **25.01** procedures for obtaining their decisions. The members of the company are the subscribers and any other person who agrees to become a member, by allotment or transfer, and whose name is entered on the register of members.[1] The company is required to keep a register of members, which the court has power to rectify.[2] Alternatively, the company will in due course

---

[1] 2006 Act, s 112. A person agrees to become a member if he assents; a binding contract is not required: *Re Nuneaton Borough Association Football Club Ltd* [1989] BCLC 454, CA. The 2006 Act, ss 136–44 contain provisions prohibiting a subsidiary from being a member of its holding company, which came into force on 1 October 2009. The 2006 Act, ss 549–609 contain provisions about allotment of shares, pre-emption rights, and payment for shares, which also came into force on 1 October 2009. The 2006 Act, ss 544, 768–90 contain provisions about share certificates, transfers including paperless transfers, and warrants, which came into force on 6 April 2008.

[2] 2006 Act, ss 113–35, which came into force on 1 October 2009, except that ss 116–19 came into force on 1 October 2007 and ss 121 and 128 came into force on 6 April 2008.

be able to opt to keep information on a central register in order to avoid the need for a register of members.[3]

25.02 Directors are concerned with decision-making by members, because (a) the Companies Act provides that certain transactions must be authorized or approved by the company, acting by the decision of its members, (b) a company's articles may require other transactions to be authorized or approved by decision of the members, (c) in other cases the directors may wish to have a transaction authorized, approved, or ratified by the company, in order to protect themselves from criticism or liability, (d) members may use the procedures to change or influence the management of the company,[4] (e) the directors have duties and powers in relation to the obtaining and recording of members' decisions, and (f) directors may face criminal liability for certain defaults.

25.03 The necessary procedures and requirements by which the directors may obtain the authorization, approval, or ratification of the company are to be found primarily in the Companies Act, Part 13, ss 281–361[5] and the company's articles of association.[6] The Companies Act reflects a structural change in that some provisions that formerly appeared in Table A are now included in the Companies Act.[7] The rule of law by which the company is bound by certain decisions taken by informal unanimous consent of the members of the company is preserved by s 281(4).

(2) Types of company

25.04 The Companies Act, Part 13 makes provisions about decision-making by members for four distinct types of company: (i) private companies, (ii) public companies, (iii) quoted companies, and (iv) traded companies.

25.05 A private company is any company that is not a public company.[8] Such a company may use the written resolution procedure and does not need to hold AGMs unless it is a traded company.

25.06 A public company is a company limited by shares or limited by guarantee and having a share capital whose certificate of incorporation states that it is a public company and in

---

[3] Part 8, Ch 2A of 2006 Act, ss112A, 128A–128K, inserted by SBEE Act 2015, s.94 and Schedule 5 with effect from a day to be appointed. These new provisions are to save a company from having to keep a register of members.

[4] By 2006 Act, s 518 a resigning auditor also has the right to requisition a general meeting to explain the circumstances of his resignation (Ch 26, paras 26.139–26.147 below).

[5] Part 13 came into force on 1 October 2007, except for ss 308, 309, 333, which came into force on 20 January 2007, and ss 327(2)(c) and 330(6)(c), which did not come into force and were repealed by the Deregulation Act 2015, s.19, Schedule 6, Part 8, paras 29, 30 as from 26 May 2015.

[6] Decision-making by members is dealt with by Model Articles (pcls) 37–47, Model Articles (pclg) 23–33, which are in the same terms, and Model Articles (plc) 28–42. By the Companies Act, s 17, these are the default articles for companies incorporated after 1 October 2009. Table A, regs 36–63 contain provisions dealing with general meetings for companies incorporated under the 1985 Act. With effect from 1 October 2007 Table A was amended for companies incorporated under the 1985 Act on or after that date by the 2007 Tables A to F Amendment Regulations.

[7] 2006 Act, s 284 derives in part from Table A, reg 54; s 302 derives from Table A, reg 37; ss 310 and 311 derive in part from Table A, reg 38; s 313 derives from Table A, reg 39; and s 320 derives in part from Table A, regs 47 and 48.

[8] 2006 Act, s 4(1). The main differences between a private company and a public company are set out in Part 20 and concern the prohibition of public offers by private companies and the minimum share capital requirement for public companies.

relation to which the requirements of the 2006 or the former Companies Acts have been complied with.[9]

A quoted company is a company whose equity share capital has been included in the official **25.07**
list in accordance with FSMA, Part 6, or is officially listed in an EEA state, or is admitted to dealing on either the New York Stock Exchange or Nasdaq.[10] There are additional requirements for polls for quoted companies.

A traded company is a company any shares of which carry rights to vote at general meetings **25.08**
and are admitted to trading on a regulated market in an EEA state by or with the consent of the company.[11] Traded companies are subject to the provisions about information rights in Part 9 and additional requirements about notices of general meetings, answering questions at general meetings, AGMs, and polls.

(3) Reforms

The reforms to decision-making by members made by the Companies Act, Part 13, had two **25.09**
broad purposes, both recommended by the CLR: (i) the deregulation and simplification of procedures for private companies, and (ii) the improvement of communications with members.[12] The main changes made by the 2006 Act to the law relating to decision-making by members may be summarized as follows:

(1) Private companies no longer have to hold AGMs.[13]

(2) The written resolution procedure is now only available to private companies, but may be used to pass a resolution by a simple resolution rather than unanimously.[14]

(3) The concept of extraordinary resolutions has been abolished and only ordinary and special resolutions remain.

(4) All company meetings may be convened on 14 days' notice, including a meeting to consider a special resolution, but a company's articles may require a longer period of notice and public company AGMs require 21 days' notice.[15] For private companies 90 per cent, rather than 95 per cent, of the members can agree to short notice.[16]

(5) The use of electronic communication and record-keeping in relation to meetings has been extended.[17]

(6) There are reforms in relation to corporate representation at meetings and proxies.[18]

(7) In order to improve confidence in the integrity and effectiveness of voting processes and to promote greater transparency, quoted companies are required to publish the results

---

[9] 2006 Act, s 4(2).

[10] 2006 Act, ss 361 and 385.

[11] 2006 Act, s 360C, inserted by the Companies (Shareholders' Rights) Regulations 2009 (SI 2009/1632), reg 21(1).

[12] CLR: *Company General Meetings and Shareholder Communications* at paras 24–7, 51, 52; CLR: *Developing the Framework* at paras 4.19–4.64, 7.6–7.15; the CLR: *Final Report* at paras 2.15, 4.3, 6.39, 7.5–7.26; White Paper: *Modernising Company Law* at paras 2.6–2.35; White Paper: *Company Law Reform* at paras 3.1 and 4.2.

[13] The provisions about AGMs apply only to public companies: ss 336–40. White Paper: *Company Law Reform* at para 4.2 rejected the CLR's recommendation that public companies should be able to opt out of having to hold AGMs.

[14] 2006 Act, s 281(1) and (2) and ss 288–300.

[15] 2006 Act, s 307. Note that special notice requires 28 days.

[16] 2006 Act, s 307.

[17] 2006 Act, ss 296, 308, 309, 314, 333, 338, 1143–8, and Schs 4 and 5.

[18] 2006 Act, ss 323–31.

of a poll on a website and there are provisions for an independent audit of a poll taken in general meeting.[19]

25.10 Two other reforms made by the 2006 Act which concerned decision-making by members should be mentioned here. First, the 2006 Act, s 22 enables a company's articles to contain entrenched provisions if they are made in the company's articles on formation or if an amendment to the articles to include them is made with the agreement of all the members of the company.[20] Once a provision has been entrenched it can only be amended by agreement of all the members of the company or by order of a court or other authority having power to alter the company's articles.[21]

25.11 Secondly, the Companies Act, Part 9, ss 145–53, set out important new rights for indirect investors, whose shares are held through nominees, to enable them to play a greater role in company proceedings.[22] These apply where the company's articles make provision enabling a member to nominate another person or persons as entitled to enjoy or exercise specified rights of the member in relation to the company.[23] A member of a traded company who holds shares on behalf of another person may nominate that person to enjoy information rights, which include the right to receive communications that the company sends to its members generally or to any class of its members that includes the person making the nomination.[24] The member may enforce the information rights against the company for the benefit of the nominated person.[25] When the company sends notice of a meeting to a nominated person it must provide information as to possible rights in relation to voting at the meeting.[26] Subject to the requirements of s 153(2) a nominated person may be included among the 100 persons for the purposes of determining whether the company is required to (a) circulate a members' statement under s 314, (b) circulate a resolution for a public company AGM under s 338, (c) include matters in business to be dealt with at a traded company AGM under s 338A, or (d) have an independent report on a poll under s 342.

25.12 The Companies (Shareholders' Rights) Regulations 2009[27] makes significant reforms to Part 13, in order to implement Directive 2007/36/EC of the European Parliament and of the Commission of 11 July 2007 on the exercise of certain rights of shareholders in listed companies. The purposes of this directive are (i) to facilitate the exercise of basic shareholders' rights, and (ii) to solve problems in the cross-border exercise of those rights, particularly voting rights, in respect of companies traded on regulated markets.

---

[19] 2006 Act, ss 341–51. See the comments of Lord Sainsbury in Hansard, HL, col 185 (11 January 2006).

[20] CLR: *Final Report* recommended provisions for entrenchment at paras 16.68–16.70.

[21] 2006 Act, s 22(3).

[22] For discussion of the need for these provisions, see the DTI paper: *Modern Company Law for a Competitive Economy* (March 1998) at para 3.7; CLR: *Developing the Framework* at paras 4.7–4.18; CLR: *Final Report* at paras 7.1–7.4 and 7.13; White Paper: *Company Law Reform* (2005) at para 3.2, and the DTI and Treasury Consultative document: *Private Shareholders: Corporate Governance Rights* (November 2006). Regarding exercise of rights by beneficial owners under s 145, see *Re DNick Holding plc* [2014] Ch 196.

[23] 2006 Act, s 145.

[24] 2006 Act, s 146. The company's articles should provide for it to recognize nominations and keep records of them; 2006 Act, s 145.

[25] 2006 Act, s 150.

[26] 2006 Act, s 149.

[27] SI 2009/1632, which came into force on 3 August 2009.

B. General Provisions about Resolutions

(1) Means of passing resolutions

Section 281 identifies or recognizes three means by which a resolution of the members of a **25.13** company may be passed: (i) as a written resolution, (ii) at a meeting of the members, or (iii) by informal unanimous assent. Section 281(1) gives private companies the option of passing a resolution as a written resolution or at a meeting, unless the decision concerns the removal of a director or auditor.[28] The attractions of the written resolution procedure (described in Section C of this chapter) should mean that private companies will seldom need to convene meetings of members. In contrast s 281(2) insists that public companies must pass resolutions of members at meetings.[29] These subsections provide:

> (1) A resolution of the members (or of a class of members) of a private company must be passed—
>   (a) as a written resolution in accordance with Chapter 2, or
>   (b) at a meeting of the members (to which the provisions of Chapter 3 apply).
> (2) A resolution of the members (or of a class of members) of a public company must be passed at a meeting of the members (to which the provisions of Chapter 3 and, where relevant, Chapter 4 of this Part apply).

Although both sub-ss 281(1) and (2) are expressed in mandatory terms, they are subject to **25.14** the provisions of sub-s (4) which preserves two established rules of law, by which decisions of members may be effective and binding on the company: (i) the informal unanimous consent or *Duomatic*[30] principle, and (ii) the principle that in certain circumstances a person may be precluded from alleging that a resolution has not been duly passed.[31] Section 281(4) provides:

> Nothing in this Part affects any enactment or rule of law as to—
>   (a) things done otherwise than by passing a resolution,
>   (b) circumstances in which a resolution is or is not treated as having been passed, or
>   (c) cases in which a person is precluded from alleging that a resolution has not been duly passed.

(2) Ordinary resolutions

The ordinary resolution is the normal means for making decisions of members of a com- **25.15** pany. A company's articles may provide for certain matters to be decided on by ordinary resolution.[32] The Companies Acts expressly provide for certain matters to be decided on by

---

[28] 2006 Act, s 288(2).

[29] This represents a change in the law; see para 25.09(2) above.

[30] *Re Duomatic Ltd* [1969] 2 Ch 365.

[31] See *Re Bailey, Hay & Co Ltd* [1971] 1 WLR 1357, in which the shareholders who abstained from voting did not object to the passing of the resolution.

[32] (i) The issue of different classes of shares (Table A, reg 2, Model Article (pcls) 22 and Model Article (plc) 43); (ii) appointment of directors (Table A, reg 78, Model Article (pcls) 17 and Model Article (plc) 20); (iii) payment of dividends recommended by directors (Table A, reg 102, Model Article (pcls) 31 and Model Article (plc) 72); (iv) authorization of inspection by member of accounting records and other records or documents (Table A, reg 109, Model Article (pcls) 50 and Model Article (plc) 83); (v) capitalization of profits (Table A, reg 110, Model Article (pcls) 36 and Model Article (plc) 78); (vi) amendment of special resolution in cases of obvious error (Model Article (pcls) 47(2) and Model Article (plc) 40(2)).

ordinary resolution[33] and in other cases merely require a resolution of a company, without specifying what kind of resolution is required.[34] In those cases, s 281(3) provides that what is required is an ordinary resolution, unless the company's articles require a higher majority or unanimity. The following matters of particular relevance to directors require an ordinary resolution:

(1) A company's articles invariably provide that a director may be appointed by ordinary resolution.[35]

(2) During a director's period of office, certain transactions between him and the company require the approval of an ordinary resolution (as discussed in Chapter 18),[36] and an ordinary resolution is one of the ways in which a company may ratify conduct of a director amounting to negligence, default, breach of duty, or breach of trust, as discussed in Chapter 20, Section D.[37]

(3) By s 168(1) an ordinary resolution is the means for removing a director before the expiration of his period of office, notwithstanding anything in any agreement between the company and him.[38] Special notice of the resolution to remove the director must be given and the written resolution procedure may not be used, since the director has a right to protest against his removal.[39] Although a director cannot rely on any provision in the company's constitution or agreement with the company to override the right of the members to remove him by ordinary resolution, in *Bushell v Faith* the House of Lords held that a provision in the company's articles giving weighted voting rights could be relied on to entrench the director in office and defeat his removal by ordinary resolution.[40]

---

[33] (i) The removal of a director (2006 Act, s 168(1)); (ii) quoted company: approval of directors' remuneration report (2006 Act, s 439(1)); (iii) appointment and removal of auditors and fixing their remuneration (2006 Act, ss 485(4), 489(4), 492(1), 510(2)); (iv) public company: approval of the transfer of a non-cash asset as consideration for shares (2006 Act, s 601(1)); (v) reconversion by limited company of stock into shares (2006 Act, s 620(2)); (vi) terms and manner of redemption of shares in limited company (2006 Act, s 685(2)); (vii) the adoption of arrangements under which title to securities is required to be evidenced or transferred (or both) without a written instrument (2006 Act, s 786(1)); (viii) approval of the articles of the new transferee company in case of merger or division (2006 Act, ss 912 and 928).

[34] (i) Transactions with directors requiring approval (2006 Act, Part 10, Chapter 4); (ii) ratification of acts of directors (2006 Act, s 239); (iii) power to make provision for employees on cessation or transfer of business (2006 Act, s 247); (iv) authorization of political donations and expenditure (2006 Act, ss 366–8, 377, 378); (v) omission of name of auditor in published copies of auditor's report (2006 Act, s 506); (vi) authorization of limited liability agreement with auditor (2006 Act, s 536); (vii) subdivision or consolidation of shares (2006 Act, s 618); (viii) authorization for market purchase of a company's own shares (2006 Act, s 701).

[35] 1985 Act, Table A, reg 78; Model Article (pcls) 17(1)(a); Model Article (plc) 20(1)(a).

[36] These transactions are long-term service contracts, substantial property transactions, loans, and quasi-loans to directors or persons connected with them, credit transactions for the benefit of directors or persons connected with them, related arrangements, and payments for loss of office as director (2006 Act, ss 188, 190, 196–8, 200, 201, 203, 214, 217–19, 224, 225).

[37] s 239. The other ways are unanimous consent of members and an agreement made by the directors of the company not to sue, or to settle or release a claim made by them on behalf of the company (s 239(6)).

[38] Ch 7 above.

[39] 2006 Act, ss 168(2), 169, and 288(2)(a). It is doubtful whether an informal decision of all the members to remove a director from office would comply with ss 168, 169, 288(2)(a), but the director would gain nothing by challenging the lack of formality of the procedure for his removal, since the company could cure any defects by ratification and the court would not grant an injunction; *Bentley-Stevens v Jones* [1974] 1 WLR 638.

[40] [1970] AC 1099, HL. Applying *Bushell v Faith*, a Hong Kong court has held that an unqualified agreement not to remove a particular person as a director constitutes an unlawful fetter on the statutory power of removal (*Muir v Lampl* [2004] 4 HKC 626 in respect of s 157B of the Companies Ordinance).

Section 282 describes what is meant by an ordinary resolution:[41]   **25.16**

(1) An ordinary resolution of the members (or of a class of members) of a company means a resolution that is passed by a simple majority.

(2) A written resolution is passed by a simple majority if it is passed by members representing a simple majority of the total voting rights of eligible members (see Chapter 2).

(3) A resolution passed at a meeting on a show of hands is passed by a simple majority if it is passed by a simple majority of the votes cast by those entitled to vote.

(4) A resolution passed on a poll taken at a meeting is passed by a simple majority if it is passed by members representing a simple majority of the total voting rights of members who (being entitled to do so) vote in person, by proxy or in advance (see section 322A) on the resolution.

(5) Anything that may be done by ordinary resolution may also be done by special resolution.

Subsection (2) changes the law to enable private companies to use the written resolution procedure to pass a resolution by a simple majority, rather than unanimously as had been the case under the 1985 Act, ss 381A–381C.

A proposal may be made to amend an ordinary resolution if the amendment does not materi-   **25.17**
ally alter the scope of the resolution, but the company's articles may restrict amendments to those of which notice has been given before the meeting.[42] If there is an irregularity in the passing of an ordinary resolution, it can be cured by subsequent ratification.

Special notice of the intention to move an ordinary resolution is required to be given to the   **25.18**
company if the resolution is: (i) to remove a director under s 168 or to appoint somebody instead of a director so removed at the meeting at which he is removed;[43] (ii) to remove an auditor from office under s 510;[44] and (iii) in certain cases, to appoint a person as auditor in place of an auditor whose term of office has ended or is to end.[45] Since special notice is for the protection of the director or auditor who is to be removed, members cannot waive compliance with the requirements for special notice set out in s 312 (paragraph 25.72 below).[46]

---

[41] Amended by the Companies (Shareholders' Rights) Regulations 2009 (SI 2009/1632), regs 2(1) and 5(2)). Previous Companies Acts defined extraordinary and special resolutions, but not ordinary resolutions. At common law an ordinary resolution was passed by a simple majority of the persons present and entitled to vote. In *AG v Davy* (1741) 2 Atk 212 Lord Hardwicke CJ said: 'It cannot be disputed, that wherever a certain number are incorporated, a major part of them may do any corporate act; so if all are summoned, and part appear, a major part of those that appear may do a corporate act, though nothing be mentioned in the charter of the major part.' Also see *Grant v United Kingdom Switchback Railways Co* (1880) 40 Ch D 135; *Merchants of the Staple v Bank of England* (1887) 21 QB 160, 165. 'Eligible members' are those entitled to vote on the resolution: s 289.

[42] Model Article (pcls) 47(1) and Model Article (plc) 40(1) provide that an ordinary resolution may be amended if (i) notice of the proposed amendment is given to the company in writing by a person entitled to vote at the general meeting at which it is to be proposed 48 hours before the meeting is to take place, or at such time as the chairman of the meeting may direct and (ii) the proposed amendment does not, in the reasonable opinion of the chairman, materially alter the scope of the resolution. For the general law relating to amendments of ordinary resolutions: *Clinch v Financial Corporation* (1868) LR 5 Eq 450, 481; *Wright's Case* (1871) LR 12 Eq 335n, 341n; *Henderson v Bank of Australasia* (1890) 45 Ch D 330, CA; *Wall v London and Northern Assets Corp (No 1)* [1898] 2 Ch 469, 483, CA; *Re Teede & Bishop Ltd* (1901) 70 LJ Ch 409; *Stroud v Royal Aquarium Soc* (1903) 89 LT 243; *Betts & Co v Macnaghten* [1910] 1 Ch 430; *Baillie v Oriental Telephone and Electric Co Ltd* [1915] 1 Ch 503, CA.

[43] 2006 Act, s 168(2).

[44] 2006 Act, s 511.

[45] 2006 Act, s 515 (as amended by the Deregulation Act 2015, s 18(5) and Sch 5, Pt 2, paras 13, 15(1), (2) as from 1 October 2015). Where the written resolution procedure is adopted, s 514 (as amended by the Deregulation Act 2015, s 18(5) and Sch 5, Pt 2, paras 13, 14(1), (2) with effect from 1 October 2015) applies.

[46] The director has a right to protest his removal under s 169 and the auditor has rights under ss 502 and 513.

(3) Special resolutions

25.19   The Companies Act requires the sanction of a special resolution for amendment of a company's articles,[47] and changes to the name,[48] status,[49] and share capital of a company[50] and also for a change of the registered office of a Welsh company[51] and for takeovers.[52] A special resolution is required to put a company into voluntary liquidation or, in the case of a company proposed to be, or being, wound up voluntarily, to sanction the transfer of the whole or part of the company's business or property to another company in consideration for shares, policies, and like interests in the transferee company for distribution among the members of the transferor company.[53] The court may wind up a company if it has by special resolution resolved that it be wound up by the court.[54] The company's articles may provide that where the members wish to direct the directors to take or refrain from taking specified action they can do so by special resolution.[55]

25.20   Section 283 explains what is meant by a special resolution:[56]

(1) A special resolution of the members (or of a class of members) of a company means a resolution passed by a majority of not less than 75%.

(2) A written resolution is passed by a majority of not less than 75% if it is passed by members representing not less than 75% of the total voting rights of eligible members (see Chapter 2).

(3) Where a resolution of a private company is passed as a written resolution—

   (a) the resolution is not a special resolution unless it stated that it was proposed as a special resolution, and

   (b) if the resolution so stated, it may only be passed as a special resolution.

(4) A resolution passed at a meeting on a show of hands is passed by a majority of not less than 75% if it is passed by not less than 75% of the votes cast by those entitled to vote.

(5) A resolution passed on a poll taken at a meeting is passed by a majority of not less than 75% if it is passed by members representing not less than 75% of the total voting rights of the members who (being entitled to do so) vote in person, by proxy or in advance (see section 332A) on the resolution.

(6) Where a resolution is passed at a meeting—

   (a) the resolution is not a special resolution unless the notice of the meeting included the text of the resolution and specified the intention to propose the resolution as a special resolution, and

---

[47] 2006 Act, s 21.

[48] 2006 Act, ss 77 and 78.

[49] 2006 Act, ss 90(1), 97(1), 105. These sections concern change of status by which a private company becomes public, a public company becomes private, and an unlimited private company becomes limited.

[50] (i) Disapplication of pre-emption rights (2006 Act, ss 569–73); (ii) reduction of capital in connection with redenomination (2006 Act, s 626); (iii) variation of class rights (2006 Act, s 630); (iv) reduction of capital (2006 Act, s 641); (v) authority for off-market purchase of a company's own shares (2006 Act, ss 694–7, 700); (vi) payment out of capital by a private company for the redemption or purchase of its own shares (2006 Act, ss 713, 716–19).

[51] 2006 Act, s 88.

[52] 2006 Act, ss 966, 967, 970–2.

[53] Insolvency Act, ss 84(1)(b) and 110.

[54] Insolvency Act, s 122(1)(a).

[55] Table A, reg 70, Model Article (pcls) 4, and Model Article (plc) 4. An ordinary resolution is sufficient if the members wish to authorize or ratify a transaction or conduct of the directors: *Bamford v Bamford* [1970] Ch 212, CA, but not if the members are adverse to the directors: *Automatic Self-Cleansing Filter Syndicate Co Ltd v Cunninghame* [1906] 2 Ch 34, CA; *Gramophone and Typewriter Co Ltd v Stanley* [1908] 2 KB 89, CA; *Salmon v Quin & Axtens Ltd* [1909] 1 Ch 311; *John Shaw & Sons (Salford) Ltd v Shaw* [1935] 2 KB 113, CA.

[56] Amended by the Companies (Shareholders' Rights) Regulations 2009 (SI 2009/1632), regs 2(2) and 5(2). 'Eligible members' are those entitled to vote on the resolution: s 289.

(b) if the notice of the meeting so specified, the resolution may only be passed as a special resolution.

Since a private company may pass a special resolution by the written resolution procedure **25.21** and the period of notice for both ordinary and special resolutions is 14 days, the differences between the two types of resolution are that (i) a special resolution requires a majority of 75 per cent rather than a simple majority, and (ii) the formalities for obtaining a special resolution are stricter than for an ordinary resolution. Where the written resolution procedure is adopted, the resolution must state that it is proposed as a special resolution.[57] Where the resolution is passed at a meeting the notice of the meeting must have included the text of the resolution and specified the intention to propose the resolution as a special resolution.[58] Once the resolution has been specified as a special resolution, it can only be passed as a special resolution.

In *Re Moorgate Mercantile Holdings Ltd*[59] Slade J held that a resolution is not validly passed **25.22** as a special resolution if there has been any departure between the text as proposed and the text of the resolution as purportedly passed, unless (i) the departure is not one of substance, such as correcting grammatical or clerical errors or making the language more formal, or (ii) all the members of the company, or relevant class of members, agree to waive compliance with the statutory requirements for a special resolution now contained in s 283. A company's articles may deal with errors in the proposal of a special resolution by providing that a special resolution proposed at a meeting may be amended by ordinary resolution if the chairman proposes the amendment at the meeting at which the resolution is proposed and the amendment does not go beyond what is necessary to correct an obvious error in the resolution.[60] A company cannot by ordinary resolution ratify and make good an invalid special resolution.[61]

(4) Informal unanimous consent

Section 281(4), quoted in paragraph 25.14 above, preserves the rule of law that the informal **25.23** unanimous consent of all the members of the company who have a right to attend and vote at a general meeting of the company can override formal, including statutory, requirements and is as effective to bind the company as a duly passed resolution.[62] The rule is founded on the dictum of Lord Davey in *Salomon v Salomon* that 'the company is bound in a matter intra vires by the unanimous agreement of its members'.[63] The rule has come to be known as the *Duomatic* principle, in reference to the case decided by Buckley J who stated the principle:

> I proceed upon the basis that where it can be shown that all shareholders who have a right to attend and vote at a general meeting of the company assent to some matter which a general

---

[57] 2006 Act, s 283(3).
[58] 2006 Act, s 283(6); *McConnell v E Prill & Co Ltd* [1916] 2 Ch 57.
[59] [1980] 1 WLR 227.
[60] Model Article (pcls) 47(2) and Model Article (plc) 40(2).
[61] *Baillie v Oriental Telephone Co* [1915] 1 Ch 503, CA.
[62] This rule of law is also recognized in 2006 Act, ss 29(1), 239(6), 257(1)(b). The government decided against codifying this rule, considering that the benefits of codification (clarity and certainty) were outweighed by the disadvantages that would result from loss of flexibility; White Paper: *Modernising Company Law* at paras 2.31–2.35; White Paper: *Company Law Reform* at para 4.2. For discussion and recommendations of the CLR, see CLR: *Developing the Framework* at paras 4.21–4.23; CLR: *Final Report* at para 2.14.
[63] [1897] 1 AC 22, 59, HL.

meeting of the company could carry into effect, that assent is as binding as a resolution in general meeting would be.[64]

The principle is most likely to be relevant to private companies where there is an identity or close connection between the directors and shareholders, but in theory it applies equally to public companies; provided in all cases that all members with a right to vote agree.[65] It has also been held to be applicable to matters affecting the class rights of particular shareholders and to shareholders' agreements.[66]

25.24 More recently Neuberger J described the *Duomatic* principle in rather wider terms:

> The essence of the *Duomatic* principle, as I see it, is that, where the articles of a company require a course to be approved by a group of shareholders at a general meeting, that requirement can be avoided if all members of the group, being aware of the relevant facts, either give their approval to that course, or so conduct themselves as to make it inequitable for them to deny that they have given their approval. Whether the approval is given in advance or after the event, whether it is characterised as agreement, ratification, waiver, estoppel, and whether members of the group give their consent in different ways at different times does not matter.[67]

25.25 The *Duomatic* principle is not a general panacea. If the shareholders are not competent to effect the act formally, the *Duomatic* principle does not enable them to do it informally without a meeting.[68] A distinction may be drawn between (i) statutory or other controls which exist for the protection of shareholders, or the relevant class, and which may be waived by the informal unanimous consent of all the shareholders or members of the relevant class and, (ii) statutory or other controls which exist to protect the interests of other persons, such as creditors, which may not be waived.[69] In each case it is necessary to consider the purpose and underlying rationale of the particular formality, statutory or otherwise, that has been overlooked.[70] The *Duomatic* principle has been invoked to validate the payment of remuneration

---

[64] See *Re Duomatic Ltd* [1969] 2 Ch 365, 373 (where the shareholders with a right to vote signed the accounts). See also *Parker Cooper Ltd v Reading* [1926] 1 Ch 975; *Re Express Engineering Works* [1920] 1 Ch 466; *Re Oxted Motor Co* [1921] 3 KB 32; *Re Bailey, Hay & Co Ltd* [1971] 1 WLR 1357 (where the assent was acquiescence); *Re Gee & Co Ltd* [1975] Ch 52; *Cane v Jones* [1980] 1 WLR 1451; *Multinational Gas and Petrochemical Co v Multinational Gas and Petrochemical Services Ltd* [1983] Ch 258, CA; *Wright v Atlas Wright (Europe) Ltd* [1999] 2 BCLC 301, CA; *Re Tulsesense Ltd* [2010] 2 BCLC 525; *Schofield v Schofield* [2011] 2 BCLC 319, CA; *Hussain and Sattar v Wycombe Islamic Mission & Mosque Trust Ltd* [2011] EWHC 971 (Ch); *Goldtrail Travel Ltd v Aydin* [2015] 1 BCLC 89: *Re Finch (UK) Plc* [2016] 1 BCLC 394.

[65] *Demite Ltd v Protec Health Ltd* [1998] BCC 638; *Knopp v Thane Investments Ltd* [2003] 1 BCLC 380; *Extrasure Travel Insurances Ltd v Scattergood* [2003] 1 BCLC 634 at para 153.

[66] *Re Torvale Group Ltd* [1999] 2 BCLC 605 (class meeting); *Euro Brokers Holdings Ltd v Monecor (London) Ltd* [2003] 1 BCLC 506, CA (shareholders' agreement, where the assent was through a corporate representative).

[67] *EIC Services Ltd v Phipps* [2004] 2 BCLC 589 at para 122. In the same report the Court of Appeal reversed the judgment of Neuberger J on different grounds.

[68] *Re New Cedos Engineering Co Ltd* (1975) [1994] 1 BCLC 797, 814, per Oliver J; approved by the Court of Appeal in *Wright v Atlas Wright (Europe) Ltd* [1999] 2 BCLC 301, 314, 315. See also *Re Tulsesense Ltd* [2010] 2 BCLC 525; *Schofield v Schofield* [2011] 2 BCLC 319.

[69] *Precision Dippings Ltd v Precision Dippings Marketing Ltd* [1986] Ch 447, CA; *BDG Roof Bond Ltd v Douglas* [2000] 1 BCLC 401; *Bairstow v Queens Moat Houses plc* [2001] 2 BCLC 531 at para 36, CA; *Kinlan v Crimmin* [2007] 2 BCLC 67. The reasoning in *Re Peak (RW) (Kings Lynn) Ltd* [1998] 1 BCLC 193 is influenced by the failure to comply with the provisions of 1985 Act, s 381A which are no longer in force. The *Peak* case was distinguished in *Dashfield v Davidson* [2008] BCC 222. See also: Jason Ellis, 'Unanimous Consent of Shareholders: A Principle Without Form?' Company Lawyer 2011, 32(9), 260–6.

[70] *Wright v Atlas Wright (Europe) Ltd* [1999] 2 BCLC 301 at 315, per Potter LJ.

to a director or of pension contribution for his benefit.[71] The court has also accepted that the members may informally but unanimously alter the articles of the company,[72] approve the reduction of the company's share capital,[73] sanction a transaction with a director,[74] or disapply pre-emption rights.[75]

In contrast, the informal unanimous assent of shareholders does not enable the company to **25.26** avoid compliance with a provision for the protection of creditors[76] or to validate an unlawful distribution.[77] Another important limitation on the ability of members to authorize or ratify transactions or conduct of the directors is where the company is insolvent or of doubtful solvency and the transaction is or may be harmful to the interests of creditors.[78] This is discussed in more detail in Chapter 20, Section D.

For the *Duomatic* principle to apply the court must be satisfied that all the shareholders **25.27** whose consent is required have in fact assented.[79] The court would not accept that assent has been given where the shareholder was unaware that his assent was necessary or being sought,[80] or where inadequate disclosure is given.[81] Since the written resolution procedure makes it simple for private companies to obtain a recorded decision of its members and companies are obliged to keep records of written resolutions and minutes of general meetings, the courts may become more sceptical about attempts to set up informal unanimous agreements that are not properly recorded, particularly when the alleged agreement is claimed to have the same effect as a special resolution.[82]

---

[71] *Re Duomatic Ltd* [1969] 2 Ch 365; *Re Horsley & Weight Ltd* [1982] Ch 442, CA.

[72] *Cane v Jones* [1980] 1 WLR 1451.

[73] *Re Barry Artist plc* [1985] BCLC 283, where Nourse J reluctantly sanctioned a reduction of capital for which a special resolution was required (now 2006 Act, s 641).

[74] Under what is now 2006 Act, Part 9, Chapter 4 (transactions with directors): *Wright v Atlas Wright (Europe) Ltd* [1999] 2 BCLC 301, CA; *NBH Ltd v Hoare* [2006] 2 BCLC 649 at para 43. Also see *Demite Ltd v Protec* [1998] BCC 638, where the alleged informal resolution did not constitute approval of the arrangement as required by the 1985 Act, s 320(1) (now 2006 Act, s 190(1)).

[75] *Pena v Dale* [2004] 2 BCLC 509.

[76] *Precision Drippings Ltd v Precision Drippings Marketing Ltd* [1986] Ch 447, CA. In *Kinlan v Crimmin* [2007] 2 BCLC 67 the informal unanimous consent of the shareholders was effective to dispense with compliance with one statutory provision for the protection of shareholders, but not another provision which had a wider purpose, including the protection of creditors.

[77] *Aveling Barford Ltd v Perion Ltd* [1989] BCLC 626; *Secretary of State for BIS v Doffman* [2011] 2 BCLC 541 at para 41.

[78] *Kinsela v Russell Kinsela Pty Ltd* [1986] 4 NSWLR 722, 732, per Street CJ; *West Mercia Safetywear Ltd v Dodd* [1988] BCLC 250, CA; *Bowthorpe Holdings Ltd v Hills* [2003] 1 BCLC 226 at paras 51–5; *Colin Gwyer & Associates Ltd v London Wharf (Limehouse) Ltd* [2003] 2 BCLC 153 at para 74; *Re MDA Management Ltd* [2004] 1 BCLC 217 at para 70; *Secretary of State for BIS v Doffman* [2011] 2 BCLC 541 at paras 44 and 45.

[79] *Re D'Jan of London Ltd* [1994] 1 BCLC 561, 564. Other cases where the court was not satisfied that assent was given are *Re Tulsesense Ltd* [2010] 2 BCLC 525; *Secretary of State for BIS v Doffman* [2011] 2 BCLC 541 at para 40; *Barnett v Rose* 21 September 2011, [2011] All ER (D) 108 (Sep), at paras 112–17; *Tayplan Ltd v Smith* [2012] BCC 523, CSIH, at paras 27, 28.

[80] *EIC Services Ltd v Phipps* [2004] 2 BCLC 589 at paras 138 and 146.

[81] *Clark v Cutland* [2004] 1 WLR 783 at para 21, CA.

[82] Section 355(1)(a) requires a company to keep records of all resolutions of members passed otherwise than at general meetings. Section 356(2) provides that the record of a resolution passed otherwise than at a general meeting, if purporting to be signed by director of the company or by the company secretary, is evidence of the passing of the resolution. 2006 Act, ss 29 and 30 requires any resolution or agreement agreed to by all the members of a company that, if not so agreed to, would not have been effective for its purpose unless passed as a special resolution (or which varies class rights) to be forwarded to the Registrar within 15 days after it is passed or made.

25.28   There is some uncertainty whether the assent must be that of the registered shareholder or whether the assent of the beneficial owner is sufficient. The orthodox position is that the consent of the registered shareholder is required.[83] However, in *Deakin v Faulding* Hart J held that the *Duomatic* principle could apply where the beneficial owner, not the registered shareholder, assented, and the beneficial owner was also regarded as acting as agent for his nominee.[84] In *Sharar v Tsitsekkos* Mann J held, for the purposes of a summary judgment application, that the proposition that the *Duomatic* principle could never apply to the consent of a beneficial, but not registered owner, was not clearly right.[85]

C. Written Resolutions

(1) General provisions about written resolutions

25.29   A written resolution is a resolution of a private company proposed and passed in accordance with Part 13, Chapter 2. A public company cannot pass a written resolution, although it could under the 1985 Act. The new written resolution provisions set out in Chapter 2 of the Act are intended to simplify procedures for private companies and should be the normal means by which members of such companies make decisions, whether by ordinary or special resolution.[86] Private companies may use the written resolution procedure to ratify acts of directors under s 239, but not to pass a written resolution to remove a director or auditor before the expiration of his term of office.[87] A written resolution may be proposed by the directors of a private company in accordance with s 291 or by the members of a private company in accordance with ss 292–5. A written resolution has effect as if passed by the company in general meeting or, as the case may be, by a meeting of a class of members of the company.[88]

25.30   A resolution proposed as a written resolution of a private company is to be circulated among the eligible members, who are the members who would have been entitled to vote on the resolution on the circulation date.[89] The circulation date of a written resolution is the date on which copies of it are sent or submitted to members (or if copies are sent or submitted to members on different days, the first of those days).[90] There is no express provision for sending or submitting the proposed written resolution to the company's auditor, but s 502 provides that the company's auditor is entitled to receive all such communications relating to the written resolution proposed to be agreed to by a private company as are required to be supplied to a member of the company.[91]

---

[83] *Domoney v Godinho* [2004] 2 BCLC 15; *Re Tulsesense Ltd* [2010] 2 BCLC 525 at paras 42 and 43.

[84] [2001] 35 LS Gaz R 32. As to exercise of rights by beneficial owners, see *Re DNick Holding plc* [2014] Ch 196.

[85] [2004] EWHC 2659 (Ch) at paras 62–7; *Re Tulsesense Ltd* [2010] 2 BCLC 525 at paras 42 and 43.

[86] 2006 Act, ss 281(1), 292(2), 283(2)–(3), 284, 288–300.

[87] 2006 Act, s 288(2).

[88] 2006 Act, s 288(5).

[89] 2006 Act, s 289(1). If the persons entitled to vote on a written resolution change during the course of the day that is the circulation date of the resolution, the eligible members are the persons entitled to vote on the resolution at the time that the first copy of the resolution is sent or submitted to a member for his agreement (s 289(2)).

[90] 2006 Act, s 290.

[91] The 2008 BERR guidance indicated that the proposed written resolution need not be sent to the auditor.

Section 300 has the effect that a private company cannot in its articles provide for an alterna-   **25.31**
tive written resolution procedure or prevent the company from using the written resolution
procedure in Chapter 2 by insisting on meetings. It states:

> A provision of the articles of a private company is void in so far as it would have the effect that a
> resolution that is required by or otherwise provided for in an enactment could not be proposed
> and passed as a written resolution.[92]

Table A, reg 53 is inconsistent with s 281(1) for private companies and s 281(2) for public companies and ceased to have effect for companies incorporated on or after 1 October
2007.[93] The Model Articles do not contain any provisions for written resolutions, since
Chapter 2 is a self-contained code. Since s 281(4) preserves the *Duomatic* principle it is possible for all the members of a private company to dispense with compliance with Chapter 2
and instead make an informal unanimous agreement in relation to the matter that might
have been proposed as a written resolution (and such a course is also available to a public
company).

(2) Circulation of written resolutions

Where the directors propose a resolution as a written resolution the company must send or   **25.32**
submit a copy of the resolution to every eligible member either (a) by sending copies at the
same time (so far as reasonably practicable) to all eligible members in hard-copy form, in
electronic form, or by means of a website, or (b) if it is possible to do so without undue delay,
by submitting the same copy to each eligible member in turn (or different copies to each of
a number of eligible members in turn), or (c) by sending copies to some members in accordance with (a) and submitting a copy or copies to other members in accordance with (b).[94]
The copy of the resolution must be accompanied by a statement informing the member how
to signify agreement to the resolution, as provided in s 296, and as to the date by which the
resolution must be passed if it is not to lapse in accordance with s 297.[95]

The members of a private company may require the company to circulate a resolution that   **25.33**
may properly be moved and is proposed to be moved as a written resolution and, if they
do, they may also require the company to circulate with the resolution a statement of not

---

[92] Attempts were made to amend s 300 prior to enactment, so as to allow private and public companies to
make alternative provisions in their articles. The government rejected these attempts on the basis that: (i) the
statute provides detailed procedures which are not onerous and therefore should be followed; (ii) for public
companies certain decisions need to be taken in a meeting rather than by written resolution, pursuant to the
Second Company Law Directive; (iii) there is nothing in the Act which stops non-statutory resolutions from
being passed in whatever way the articles envisage. If the articles require members' agreement, there is no need
to comply with the statutory procedures: see Hansard, HC Debate Day 2, col 978 (18 October 2006).

[93] Table A, reg 53 states: 'A resolution in writing executed by or on behalf of each member who would have
been entitled to vote upon it if it had been proposed at a general meeting at which he was present shall be as
effectual as if it had been passed at a general meeting duly convened and held and may consist of several instruments in the like form each executed by or on behalf of one or more members.'

[94] 2006 Act, s 291(1)–(3). Options (b) and (c) allow the company to pass round a document or email
instead of sending out several copies. Section 299 provides that where a company sends a written resolution or
a statement relating to a written resolution to a person by means of a website, the resolution or statement is not
validly sent for the purposes of Chapter 2 unless the resolution is available on the website throughout the period
beginning with the circulation date and ending on the date on which the resolution lapses under s 297. Also see
2006 Act, s 1144(2) and Sch 5, Part 3 for communications in electronic form and para 4 for communications
by means of a website.

[95] 2006 Act, s 291(4).

more than 1,000 words on the subject matter of the resolution.[96] The rights of the members to require the company to circulate the resolution and statement are subject to three restrictions.

25.34 First, the resolution and accompanying statement must command the requisite support from members. This is the threshold requirement and the company is not required to circulate the resolution and accompanying statement until it receives requests that it do so from members representing not less than the requisite percentage of the total voting rights of all members entitled to vote on the resolution.[97] The requisite percentage is 5 per cent or such lower percentage as is specified for this purpose in the company's articles.[98]

25.35 Secondly, members must not abuse their power to require the company to circulate the written resolution and accompanying statement. The resolution is not capable of being properly moved as a written resolution if (a) it would, if passed, be ineffective (whether by reason of inconsistency with any enactment or the company's constitution or otherwise), (b) it is defamatory of any person, or (c) it is frivolous and vexatious.[99] The company is not required to circulate the accompanying statement if it or any other person who claims to be aggrieved applies to the court under s 295 and the court is satisfied that the rights conferred by ss 292 and 293 are being abused.[100]

25.36 Thirdly, the members who request the company to circulate the resolution and statement under s 293 must pay the company's expenses, unless the company has resolved otherwise, and must deposit with, or tender to, the company a sum sufficient to meet the company's expenses.[101]

25.37 Not more than 21 days after it becomes subject to the requirement under s 292 to circulate the resolution, the company must send or submit to every eligible member a copy of the

---

[96] 2006 Act, s 292(1) and (3). These provisions are intended to enhance shareholder engagement: Hansard, H Comm D, col 980 (18 October 2006).

[97] 2006 Act, s 292(4). By s 292(6) the request (a) may be in hard copy form or electronic form, (b) must identify the resolution and accompanying statement, and (c) must be authenticated by the person or persons making it. As to hard copy form and electronic form, see s 1144 and Sch 4. As to authentication, see s 1146.

[98] 2006 Act, s 292(5).

[99] 2006 Act, s 292(2). If the directors take the view that the proposed resolution is ineffective, defamatory, or frivolous or vexatious and the resolution is accompanied by a statement, the issue of abuse will be determined on an application under s 295. Where there is no accompanying statement, the directors could apply to the court for a declaration that they are not liable to circulate it under s 293, or they could inform the members of their decision and leave it to the members to apply to court for an order that they do so, or require a meeting under ss 303–5, or conceivably apply to the court under s 306. Since s 292(1) requires the members to identify the resolution, rather than merely the general nature of the business to be considered (as under s 303(4)), it may be easier for directors to conclude that the proposed resolution would, if passed, be ineffective; *Isle of White Railway Co v Tahourdin* (1883) 25 Ch D 320, 329, 330, per Cotton LJ; 334, per Lindley LJ; *Rose v McGivern* [1998] 2 BCLC 593, 605–12.

[100] 2006 Act, ss 293(1) and 295(1). Section 295(1) is in similar terms to s 317(1) and may be compared with s 520(4). If the court considered that the company's application under s 295 was tactical, it might order the company to pay the members' costs on the indemnity basis; *Jarvis plc v PricewaterhouseCoopers* [2000] 2 BCLC 368, a case on 1985 Act, s 394, the predecessor of s 520 (concerning circulation of auditor's statement on ceasing to hold office). On the other hand, s 295(2) provides that the court may order members who requested the circulation of the statement to pay the whole or part of the company's costs of the application, even if they are not parties to the application. Members who support the circulation of a resolution and statement should therefore satisfy themselves that the statement is not abusive.

[101] 2006 Act, ss 293(1) and 294. A demand for an unreasonable deposit would not be regarded as compliance with s 293 (HC Comm D, col 316). Sections 316 and 340 are the equivalent provisions for general meetings and AGMs.

resolution and a copy of any accompanying statement in the same manner and with the same guidance as applies to the circulation of written resolutions proposed by the directors.[102] The duties imposed on the company (and the directors) by s 293 in respect of the circulation of the resolution proposed by members largely mirror the requirements set out in s 291 for the circulation of written resolutions proposed by directors. An additional requirement under s 293 is that the resolution must be circulated within 21 days of the request being made by the member to the company pursuant to s 292.[103]

Where the company's articles include a provision enabling a member to nominate another **25.38** person or persons as entitled to enjoy or exercise all or any specified rights of the member in relation to the company, any nominated person has the right to be sent the proposed written resolution under ss 291 and 293 and to require circulation of a written resolution under s 292.[104] If the company is a traded company, in that its shares are admitted to trading on a regulated market, a member of the company who holds shares on behalf of another person may nominate that person to enjoy information rights, which include the right to receive communications that the company sends to its members concerning written resolutions.[105]

The validity of the resolution, if passed, is not affected by a failure to comply with ss 291 or **25.39** 293.[106] If the vote is carried, it will be valid even if a member who would have been in the minority was not circulated with the proposed resolution. Such a member may have a remedy by unfair prejudice petition under the 2006 Act, Part 30. Instead, to secure compliance with ss 291 and 293, in the event of default in complying with them, an offence is committed by every officer of the company in default who is liable to a fine on conviction.[107]

(3) Agreeing to written resolutions

A member signifies his agreement to a proposed written resolution when the company **25.40** receives from him, or someone acting on his behalf, an authenticated document, which may be in hard-copy form or in electronic form, identifying the resolution to which it relates and indicating his agreement to the resolution.[108] Once agreement to the resolution has been signified to the company it cannot be withdrawn.[109]

---

[102] 2006 Act, s 293(1)–(4). The company's obligations under s 293(1) are subject to ss 294(2) (deposit or tender of sum in respect of circulation) and 295 (application not to circulate members' statement).

[103] 2006 Act, s 293(3).

[104] 2006 Act, Part 9, s 145.

[105] 2006 Act, Part 9, ss 146–8. Section 147 prescribes the form in which copies are to be provided to the nominated person.

[106] 2006 Act, ss 291(7) and 293(7). The reason for s 291(7) is that a company must have certainty to be able to pursue its business effectively and efficiently irrespective of whether or not errors are made: see Hansard, HC Standing Committee Day 5, col 306 (30 June 2006). For the same reason, the validity of a written resolution is not affected by an accidental failure to send a memorandum required under Part 10, Chapter 4 (transactions with directors requiring approval of members): s 224.

[107] 2006 Act, ss 291(5)–(6) and 293(5)–(6). For officer in default, see s 1121.

[108] 2006 Act, s 296(1) and (2). For the authentication of the document signifying consent, see s 1146. A signature is not required. For communication of the consent in hard-copy form or electronic form, see s 298, which provides that where the company has given an electronic address the document signifying agreement may be sent electronically to that address, and ss 1143, 1144(1), 1168, and Sch 4. Subject to voting agreements, a member may vote as he pleases (para 25.95 below), but on a resolution to ratify the acts of a director under s 239 the director (if a member) and members connected with him are not eligible to vote: ss 239(3) and (5) and 252.

[109] 2006 Act, s 296(3).

25.41 A written resolution is passed when the required majority of eligible members have signified agreement to it.[110] A simple majority is required for an ordinary resolution and a majority of not less than 75 per cent is required for a special resolution.[111] On a vote on a written resolution and subject to any provision of the company's articles (a) in the case of a company having a share capital, every member has one vote in respect of each share or £10 of stock held by him, and (b) in any other case every member has one vote.[112] Subject to any provision of the company's articles, where there are joint holders of shares, only the vote of the senior holder who votes may be counted.[113]

25.42 A proposed written resolution lapses if it is not passed before the end of the period specified for this purpose in the company's articles, or, if none is specified, the period of 28 days beginning with the circulation date. The agreement of a member to a written resolution is ineffective if signified after the expiry of that period.[114] This means that there is a definite date after which the company can say that a resolution with insufficient support has not been passed.

25.43 If the written resolution is passed the company must keep a record of it and if the resolution is a special resolution a copy of it must be forwarded to the Registrar within 15 days after it is passed.[115] A copy of the written resolution signed by a director of the company or by the company secretary is evidence of the passing of the resolution.[116] Where there is a record of a written resolution of a private company, the requirements of the Companies Act with respect to the passing of the resolution are deemed to be complied with unless the contrary is proved.[117]

D. Resolutions at Meetings

25.44 The default provisions for obtaining the authorization of the company at a meeting are set out in the Companies Act, Chapter 3, ss 301–5.[118] These provisions apply equally to private and public companies. Additional provisions, concerning AGMs and polls, which apply only to public companies, quoted companies, and traded companies are then set out in Chapters 4 and 5 of the Act (which are discussed in Sections E and F below).

---

[110] 2006 Act, s 296(4). Eligible members are those members who are entitled to vote on the resolution: s 289.

[111] 2006 Act, ss 282(1)–(2) and 283(1)–(2).

[112] 2006 Act, s 284(1) and (4). Account must be taken of any weighted voting rights, as in *Bushell v Faith* [1970] AC 1099. Section 287 provides that nothing in Chapter 2 affects (a) any provision of a company's articles requiring an objection to a person's entitlement to vote on a resolution to be made in accordance with the articles, and for the determination of any such objection to be final and conclusive, or (b) the grounds on which such a determination may be questioned in legal proceedings. Table A, reg 58 is a provision for deter-mining the admissibility of votes for the purposes of a meeting. Model Article (pcls) 43 and Model Article (plc) 35 provide for the determination of errors and disputes in relation to votes at meetings.

[113] 2006 Act, s 286, which is derived from Table A, reg 55. The senior holder of a share is determined by the order in which the names appear in the register of members.

[114] 2006 Act, s 297. The circulation date is identified in accordance with s 290 and is included in the 28-day period; see *Zoan v Rouamba* [2000] 1 WLR 1509, CA at para 24.

[115] 2006 Act, s 355(1)(a) and 2006 Act, ss 29 and 30. The provisions of ss 355(1)(a) and 356(2)–(3) also apply to class meetings: s 359.

[116] 2006 Act, s 356(2).

[117] 2006 Act, s 356(3).

[118] These sections derive in part from Table A, regs 37–9, 47, 48, 63. The new provisions on resolutions in general meeting reflect the fact that private companies will no longer be required to hold AGMs. 1985 Act, s 367, which gave the Secretary of State a power to call a meeting where there had been no AGM, has been repealed.

A resolution of the members of a company is validly passed at a general meeting if notice of **25.45** the meeting and of the resolution is given and the meeting is held and conducted in accordance with the provisions of Chapter 3 of the Act (and where relevant, Chapter 4) and the company's articles.[119]

(1) Calling meetings

Meetings called by the directors

The directors of a company may call a general meeting of the company or a meeting of a **25.46** class of members.[120] The directors may informally and unanimously agree to call a meeting, but if they are not unanimous they should make a majority decision in accordance with the company's articles.[121]

The directors will use the power to call a general meeting where they wish to obtain the **25.47** assent, authorization, or ratification of the members to a particular transaction or conduct and the written resolution procedure is not available and they cannot obtain the informal unanimous consent of all the members. The directors' power to call a general meeting is a fiduciary power to be exercised for the purpose for which it is conferred.[122] Pursuant to their duties to the company the directors will invariably prepare a circular explaining their opinion that the resolutions proposed by them should be supported by the members.

Meetings requisitioned by members

The members of a company may require the directors to call a general meeting of the com- **25.48** pany, but not a meeting of a class of members.[123] The company's articles may give members additional powers to call meetings.[124] Under s 303 the directors are required to call a general meeting once the company has received requests[125] to do so from members which satisfy two conditions.

First, the resolution must command the requisite support from members. The members **25.49** making the request must represent at least 5 per cent of such of the paid-up capital of the company as carries the right of voting at general meetings of the company (excluding any

---

[119] 2006 Act, s 301.

[120] 2006 Act, ss 302, 334, 335 and also Table A, reg 37. Section 335, dealing with class meetings of companies without a share capital, is a new section. Table A, reg 37 also provides that if there are not within the UK sufficient directors to call a general meeting, any director may call a meeting. The secretary of a company has no power to call a general meeting under the Companies Act or under the general law: *In re State of Wyoming Syndicate* [1901] 2 Ch 431.

[121] Table A, regs 88–98, Model Articles (pcls) 7–14 and Model Articles (plc) 7–16; *Harben v Phillips* (1883) 23 Ch D 14, *Re Haycraft Gold Reduction Co* [1900] 2 Ch 230; *Bolton Engineering Ltd v TJ Graham & Sons Ltd* [1957] 1 QB 159, CA. Irregularities in convening a general meeting may be cured by ratification by the board or provisions in the company's articles: *Hooper v Kerr Stuart & Co* (1900) 83 LT 729; *Transport v Schomberg* (1905) 21 TLR 305; *Boschoek Proprietary Co v Fuke* [1906] 1 Ch 148.

[122] 2006 Act, s 171; *Pergamon Press Ltd v Maxwell* [1970] 1 WLR 1167. The power would be abused if the directors called a meeting for a time and place when they knew that a member or members could not attend.

[123] 2006 Act, ss 303, 334(2)(a), 335(2)(a).

[124] Table A, reg 37 provides that if there are not within the UK sufficient directors to call a meeting, any member of the company may call a meeting. Model Article (plc) 28 provides that if a company has fewer than two directors, and the director (if any) is unable or unwilling to call a meeting to appoint further directors, then two or more members may call a general meeting (or instruct the company secretary to do so).

[125] A request may be in hard-copy form or in electronic form and must be authenticated by the person or persons making it (2006 Act, s 303(6)).

paid-up capital held as treasury shares).[126] If the company does not have a share capital, the requests must have been received from members who represent at least 5 per cent of the total voting rights of all members having a right to vote at general meetings.[127] Where the company's articles include a provision enabling a member to nominate another person or persons as entitled to enjoy or exercise all or any specified rights of the member in relation to the company, any nominated person has the right to require directors to call a general meeting under s 303.[128]

25.50 Secondly, the request must identify the general nature of the business to be dealt with at the meeting, and may include the text of the resolution that may properly be moved and is intended to be moved at the meeting.[129] A resolution may not be properly moved if (a) it would, if passed, be ineffective, (b) it is defamatory of any person, or (c) it is frivolous or vexatious.[130]

25.51 Directors required under s 303 to call a general meeting of the company must call a meeting within 21 days from the date on which they become subject to the requirement, and the meeting must be held on a date not more than 28 days after the notice convening the meeting.[131] Section 304(2)–(4) contains further provisions designed to ensure that the members' requests are properly considered at the meeting: (a) the notice of the meeting must include notice of any resolution identified in the request, (b) the business that may be dealt with at the meeting includes a resolution of which notice is given under s 304, and (c) if the resolution proposed is a special resolution, the directors are treated as not having duly called the meeting if they do not give the required notice of the resolution in accordance with s 283.

25.52 If the directors are required under s 303 to call a meeting, and do not do so in accordance with s 304, the members who requested the meeting, or any of them representing more than one half of the total voting rights of all of them, may themselves call a general meeting which must be called for a date not more than three months after the date on which the directors become subject to the requirement to call a meeting.[132] The meeting must be called in the same manner, as nearly as possible, as that in which meetings are required to be called by directors of the company and the notice of the meeting must include notice of any resolution included in the members' requests.[133] The business that may be dealt with at the meeting includes a resolution of which notice is given in accordance with s 305,[134] but the

---

[126] 2006 Act, s 303(2)(a) as amended by the Companies (Shareholders' Rights) Regulations 2009 (SI 2009/1632), reg 4(1) and (2), which by reg 4(1) and (3) also repealed s 303(3).

[127] 2006 Act, s 303(2)(b).

[128] 2006 Act, Part 9, s 145.

[129] 2006 Act, s 303(4). The phrase 'general nature of the business' is broader than the phrase 'objects of the meeting' in 1985 Act, s 368(3), but that flexibility is balanced by the option to include the text of the proposed resolution, which is new. If the requests merely state the general nature of the business, rather than the text of the proposed resolution, it may be more difficult for the directors to conclude that any resolution, if passed, would be ineffective; para 25.35 and n 100 above.

[130] 2006 Act, s 303(5), which is in the same terms as s 292(2) concerning written resolutions (para 25.35 above). If the resolution may not properly be moved, the directors will not act on the request, leaving it to the members to call, or purport to call the meeting under s 305 or apply to court under s 306.

[131] 2006 Act, s 304(1).

[132] 2006 Act, s 305(1) and (3).

[133] 2006 Act, s 305(2) and (4).

[134] 2006 Act, s 305(5).

members are not entitled to raise other business at the meeting that was not identified in the requests.[135]

The sanction on the directors for failing to comply with the members' requests is that the **25.53** company is obliged to reimburse the reasonable expenses incurred by the members requesting the meeting by reason of the directors' failure duly to call a meeting and any sum so reimbursed must be retained by the company out of any sums due or to become due from the company by way of fees or other remuneration in respect of the services of such of the directors as were in default.[136]

The directors should not be passive in relation to the meeting requisitioned by the members. **25.54** If the directors consider that the resolution is contrary to the best interests of the company, their fiduciary duties require them to take proper steps to oppose it, by circulating a statement of their views and soliciting votes and proxies, for which purposes they may use the company's funds.[137]

Meetings ordered by the court

Section 306 gives the court power to order a meeting of the company to be called, held, and **25.55** conducted in any manner the court thinks fit whenever it is impracticable to call or conduct a meeting, but not a meeting of holders of a class of share.[138] It provides:

(1) This section applies if for any reason it is impracticable—
   (a) to call a meeting of a company in any manner in which meetings of that company may be called, or
   (b) to conduct the meeting in the manner prescribed by the company's articles or this Act.
(2) The court may, either of its own motion or on the application—
   (a) of a director of the company, or
   (b) of a member of the company who would be entitled to vote at the meeting,
   order a meeting to be called, held and conducted in any manner the court thinks fit.
(3) Where such an order is made, the court may give such ancillary or consequential directions as it thinks expedient.
(4) Such directions may include a direction that one member of the company present at the meeting be deemed to constitute a quorum.
(5) A meeting called, held and conducted in accordance with an order under this section is deemed for all purposes to be a meeting of the company duly called, held and conducted.

The court may order a meeting to be held of its own motion, or on the application of a direc- **25.56** tor or a member who would be entitled to vote at a meeting. The jurisdiction to make an order is founded on it being for any reason impracticable to call or conduct a meeting. The circumstances in which the calling or conducting of a meeting are impracticable are unlimited and may arise from an absence of directors or members or where there are practical difficulties in giving notice to members overseas.[139] It is not, however, impracticable to conduct

---

[135] *Ball v Metal Industries* [1957] SC 315.

[136] 2006 Act, s 305(6) and (7).

[137] *Peel v London and North-Western Railway* [1907] 1 Ch 5, CA; *Wilson v London Midland and Scottish Railway Co* [1940] Ch 393, CA.

[138] 2006 Act, ss 306, 334(2)(b), 335(2)(b). The leading authority on the predecessor to s 306 is *Union Music Ltd v Watson* [2003] 1 BCLC 453, CA.

[139] *Re Consolidated Nickel Mines Ltd* [1914] 1 Ch 883; *Re Noel Tedman Holdings Pty Ltd* [1967] Qd R 561; *Harman v BML Group Ltd* [1994] 1 WLR 893, 896, CA, per Dillon LJ. In *Re British Union for the Abolition of*

a meeting simply because the chairman is a director and shareholder, giving rise to a conflict between his duty to the company and his interests as a shareholder.[140]

25.57 There have been several cases where the impracticability has resulted from a director and minority shareholder abusing the quorum provisions by absenting himself and preventing an effective meeting from taking place in which he would be removed from office or another director would be appointed. In those circumstances the court has directed that a meeting be called, if necessary with a direction that one member present shall constitute a quorum.[141] Those cases are to be distinguished from ones where the court has declined to exercise its powers under s 306, because to do so would override an entrenched or class right or affect substantive voting rights by breaking the deadlock between two equal shareholders.[142]

25.58 The following propositions may be derived from the judgment of Peter Gibson LJ in the leading authority, *Union Music Ltd v Watson*.[143]

(1) Section 306 is a procedural section intended to enable company business which needs to be conducted at a general meeting of the company to be so conducted. The management of its affairs should not be frustrated by the impracticability of calling or conducting a general meeting in the manner prescribed by the articles and the Companies Act.

(2) The section confers on the court a discretion, which must be exercised properly having regard to the relevant circumstances.[144]

(3) The fact that there are quorum provisions in the company's articles requiring two members' attendance will not in itself be sufficient to prevent the court making an order under s 306, where the applicant is seeking a proper order such as the appointment of a director, something which a majority shareholder would have the right to procure in ordinary circumstances. The order would not affect the substantive voting rights of the minority shareholder who may choose whether or not to attend the meeting.

(4) The machinery of s 306 is not to be used to override entrenched or class rights, or rights in the nature of class rights, by imposing a new shareholder agreement on the parties.[145] A quorum provision is not a class right.

Vivisection [1995] 2 BCLC 1 the court gave directions for votes to be cast by post, because there was apprehension that the meeting would be disrupted by violence.

[140] *Might SA v Redbus Interhouse plc* [2004] 2 BCLC 449. In *Monnington v Easier plc* [2006] 2 BCLC 283 the court refused an order, because it was not impracticable to call or conduct a meeting, even though the board might frustrate its intended purpose by appointing new directors, and the applicant could not use the statutory power to achieve an alteration of the company's articles.

[141] *Re El Sombrero Ltd* [1958] Ch 900; *Re HR Paul & Sons Ltd* (1974) 118 Sol Jo 166; *Re Opera Photographic Ltd* [1989] 1 WLR 634; *Re Woven Rugs Ltd* [2002] 1 WLR 324; *Union Music Ltd v Watson* [2003] 1 BCLC 453, CA; *Vectone Entertainment Holding Ltd v South Entertainment Ltd* [2004] 2 BCLC 224; *Wheeler v Ross* [2011] EWHC 2527 (Ch); *Smith v Butler* [2012] BCC 64, CA at paras 49–54.

[142] *Harman v BML Group Ltd* [1994] 1 WLR 893, CA; *Ross v Telford* [1998] 1 BCLC 82, CA. The dividing line between these cases and those in the preceding footnote is a narrow one. In *Alvona Developments Ltd v Manhattan Loft Corporation (AC) Ltd* [2006] BCC 119, on a summary judgment application, the judge held that an alleged right of a minority shareholder to be a director was a class right, which if established would prevent an order from being made. That decision is difficult to reconcile with s 168 and its predecessor, 1985 Act, s 303.

[143] [2003] 1 BCLC 453 at paras 32–43. Buxton LJ and Morland J agreed with the judgment of Peter Gibson LJ. Applied in *Vectone Entertainment Holding Ltd v South Entertainment Ltd* [2004] 2 BCLC 224; *Smith v Butler* [2012] BCC 64, CA at paras 49–54.

[144] An applicant for an order is not entitled to an order as of right, nor is the respondent entitled to resist the order as of right: *Re El Sombrero Ltd* [1958] Ch 900.

[145] Explaining *Harman v BML Group Ltd* [1994] 1 WLR 893, CA.

(5) Section 306 is a procedural section not designed to affect substantive voting rights or to shift the balance of power between shareholders where they have agreed that power should be shared equally and where potential deadlock must be taken to have been agreed for the protection of each shareholder.[146]

The existence of an unfair prejudice petition under Part 30 or the likelihood of litigation if an order is made are not factors that will prevent the court from making an order under s 306 if other circumstances justify it, but the court may impose conditions.[147]   **25.59**

(2) Notice of meetings
Length of notice

A general meeting of a private company (other than an adjourned meeting) must be called by notice of at least 14 days (excluding the day of the meeting and the day on which notice is given), but the company's articles may require a longer period.[148] A majority of the members may, however, agree to shorter notice if they are a majority in number of the members having a right to attend and vote at the meeting, being a majority who together hold not less than 90 per cent (or such higher percentage not exceeding 95 per cent as may be specified in the company's articles) in nominal value of the shares giving a right to attend and vote at the meeting (excluding any shares of the company held as treasury shares).[149]   **25.60**

A general meeting of a public company must also be called by notice of at least 14 days (excluding the day of the meeting and the day on which notice is given), but the company's articles may require a longer period.[150] A majority of the members may also agree to shorter notice if they are a majority in number of the members having a right to attend and vote at the meeting, being a majority who together hold not less than 95 per cent in nominal value of the shares giving a right to attend and vote at the meeting (excluding any shares of the company held as treasury shares).[151]   **25.61**

The AGM of a public company must be called by notice of at least 21 days (excluding the day of the meeting and the day on which notice is given), but the company's articles may require a longer period of notice.[152] The members of a public company may unanimously agree to   **25.62**

---

[146]   Referring to *Ross v Telford* [1998] 1 BCLC 82, CA.

[147]   *Re Sticky Fingers Restaurant Ltd* [1992] BCLC 84; *Re Whitchurch Insurance Consultants Ltd* [1993] BCLC 1359; *Harman v BML Group Ltd* [1994] 1 WLR 349, CA; *Re Woven Rugs Ltd* [2002] 1 BCLC 324; *Vectone Entertainment Holding Ltd v South Entertainment Ltd* [2004] 2 BCLC 224; *Wheeler v Ross* [2011] EWHC 2527 (Ch); *Smith v Butler* [2012] BCC 64, CA.

[148]   2006 Act, s 307(1) and (3), and s 360. Section 360 is a new provision, which enacts the former common law rule in *Re Hector Whaling Ltd* [1936] Ch 208, and was introduced by amendment after the Second Reading of the bill in the House of Commons: Hansard, HC Standing Committee Day 5, cols 322–3 (30 June 2006). Table A, reg 115 provides: 'A notice shall be deemed to be given at the expiration of 48 hours after the envelope containing it was posted or, in the case of electronic communication, at the expiration of 48 hours after the time it was sent.'

[149]   2006 Act, s 307(4)–(6). The reduction in the requisite percentage to 90 per cent, subject to the company's articles, is a change from the 1985 Act. See Table A, reg 38. In the case of a company not having a share capital the majority must represent not less than the requisite percentage of the total voting rights at that meeting of all the members: s 307(5)(b).

[150]   2006 Act, ss 307(2)(b), (3), and 360.

[151]   2006 Act, s 307(4)–(6). Section 307(5)(b) applies to a company not having a share capital.

[152]   2006 Act, ss 307(2)(a), (3), and 360.

shorter notice of an AGM, unless the company is a traded company, in which case they have no power to reduce the 21-day period.[153]

25.63 There are special rules about notice required of general meetings of traded companies.[154] If the traded company is an opted-in company[155] and the meeting is held to decide whether to take action that might result in the frustration of a takeover bid for the company or the meeting is held by virtue of the 2006 Act, s 969,[156] the rules about the general meetings of a public company described in paragraph 25.53 apply.[157]

25.64 For general meetings of a traded company (other than the meetings described in the preceding paragraph regarding the takeover of an opted-in company), the following rules apply:

(1) In a case where the following three conditions are met a general meeting of a trading company must be called by notice of at least 14 days, unless the company's articles require a longer period of notice.[158] The three conditions are that: (i) the general meeting is not an AGM;[159] (ii) the company offers the facility for members to vote by electronic means accessible to all members who hold shares that carry rights to vote at general meetings;[160] and (iii) a special resolution reducing the period of notice to not less than 14 days has been passed at the immediately preceding AGM, or at a general meeting held since that AGM.[161]

(2) In any other case, a general meeting of a traded company must be called by notice of at least 21 days, unless the company's articles require a longer period of notice.[162]

(3) Where a general meeting is adjourned, the adjourned meeting may be called by shorter notice than that specified in subparagraphs (1) and (2) above. Where the meeting is adjourned for lack of a quorum, this power to hold the adjourned meeting on a shorter period of notice only applies if (i) no business is to be dealt with at the adjourned meeting the general nature of which was not stated in the notice of the original meeting, and (ii) the adjourned meeting is to be held at least ten days after the original meeting.[163]

---

[153] 2006 Act, ss 307(4), (7), and 337(2), as amended by the Companies (Shareholders' Rights) Regulations 2009 (SI 2009/1632), reg 16(1)–(5).

[154] 2006 Act, ss 307(A1), (A2) and 307A, inserted by the the Companies (Shareholders' Rights) Regulations 2009 (SI 2009/1632), reg 9(1) and (2).

[155] As defined by 2006 Act, s 971(1).

[156] 2006 Act, s 969 gives the offerer the power to require a general meeting to be held, if he holds shares amounting to not less than 75 per cent in value of all the voting shares of the company.

[157] 2006 Act, s 307(A1)(b).

[158] 2006 Act, s 307A(1)(a) and (6).

[159] 2006 Act, s 307A(2).

[160] 2006 Act, s 307A(3), which also provides that this condition is met if there is a facility, offered by the company and accessible to all the members mentioned in the subsection, to appoint a proxy by means of a website. By s 360A(2), in the case of a traded company the only permitted requirements and restrictions for participation in a general meeting by electronic means are those that are necessary to ensure identification of those taking part and the security of the electronic communication and are proportionate to the achievement of those objectives.

[161] 2006 Act, s 307A(4). If the company has not yet held an AGM this condition is met if the special resolution has been passed at a general meeting (s 307A(5)).

[162] 2006 Act, s 307A(1)(b) and (6).

[163] 2006 Act, s 307A(7).

Form and content of the notice

Section 308 provides that notice of a general meeting of a company must be given in hard-copy form, in electronic form, or by means of a website in accordance with s 309.[164] Section 309 states the requirements for valid notification to a member of the presence of the notice of the meeting on the website: (i) the notification must state that it concerns a notice of a company meeting, specify the place, date, and time of the meeting, and, in the case of a public company, state whether the meeting will be an AGM; and (ii) the notice must be available on the website throughout the period beginning with the date of notification and ending with the conclusion of the meeting. The mandatory terms of s 308 would seem to preclude provision in the company's articles for giving notice of a general meeting by advertisement in an appropriate newspaper (a form of communication mentioned in s 312(3)(a) for the giving of special notice of certain resolutions). In the unlikely event that it is impracticable to give notice to all members by at least one of the three methods specified in s 308, it will be necessary to apply to the court under s 306 for directions as to the manner in which the meeting should be called. **25.65**

The notice must state the place, date, and time of the meeting and the general nature of the business to be dealt with at the meeting.[165] The notice must contain a 'fair, candid, and reasonable explanation' of the business to be dealt with at the meeting.[166] If it does not and, for example benefits to directors are concealed, any resolution purportedly passed will be invalid and the company will be restrained from acting on it.[167] **25.66**

The Notice of a general meeting of a traded company must also include:[168] **25.67**

(1) a statement giving the address of the website on which there is published (a) the matters set out in the notice of the meeting, (b) the total number of shares in the company and shares of each class in respect of which members are entitled to exercise voting rights at the meeting, (c) the totals of the voting rights that members are entitled to exercise at the meeting in respect of the shares of each class, and (d) members' statements, members' resolutions and members' matters of business received by the company after the first date on which notice of the meeting is given;[169]
(2) a statement that the right to vote at the meeting is determined by reference to the register of members or, if an election under 2006 Act, s 128B is in force in respect of the

---

[164] 2006 Act, ss 308 and 309. See also s 1144(2) and Sch 5 for communications by a company in hard-copy form, electronic form, and by means of a website.

[165] 2006 Act, s 311(1) and (2), which states provisions in 1985 Act, Table A, reg 38. Section 311(2) has effect subject to any provision of the company's articles.

[166] *Kaye v Croydon Tramways Co* [1898] 1 Ch 358, CA.

[167] *Re Hampshire Land Co* [1896] 2 Ch 743; *Kaye v Croydon Tramways Co* [1898] 1 Ch 358, CA; *Normandy v Ind Coope & Co* [1908] 1 Ch 84; *Pacific Coast Coal Mines v Arbuthnot* [1917] AC 607, PC; *Stainer v Lee* [2011] 1 BCLC 535 at para 46.

[168] 2006 Act, s 311(3) inserted by the Companies (Shareholders' Rights) Regulations 2009 (SI 2009/1632), reg 10(1)(3).

[169] 2006 Act, ss 311(3)(a) and 311A(1). Section 311A(2)–(6) specifies the requirements as to the availability and accessibility of the information on the website. Failure to comply with those requirements does not affect the validity of the meeting or of anything done at the meeting (s 311A(7)), but non-compliance is an offence committed by every officer in default punishable by a fine (s 311A(8) and (9)).

company, by reference to the register kept by the registrar under s 1080, and the time when that right will be determined;[170]

(3) a statement of the procedures with which members must comply in order to be able to attend and vote at the meeting, (including the date by which they must comply);[171]

(4) a statement giving details of any forms to be used for the appointment of a proxy;[172]

(5) where the company offers the facility for members to vote in advance or by electronic means, a statement of the procedure for doing so (including the date by which it must be done, and details of any forms to be used); and[173]

(6) a statement of the right of members to ask questions.[174]

25.68 In every notice calling a meeting of a company there must appear, with reasonable prominence, a statement informing the member of his right under s 324 to appoint a proxy and any more extensive rights conferred by the company's articles to appoint more than one proxy.[175] To achieve certainty in the outcome of the meeting, failure to comply with s 325 does not affect the validity of the meeting or of anything done at the meeting.[176] The sanction for non-compliance is that every officer of the company who is in default commits an offence and if convicted is liable to a fine.[177]

25.69 Where a traded company sends a copy of a notice of a meeting to a person nominated under s 146 the copy of the notice must be accompanied by a statement that he may have a right under an agreement between him and the member by whom he was nominated to be appointed, or to have someone else appointed, as a proxy for the meeting, and, if he has no such right or does not wish to exercise it, he may have a right under such agreement to give instructions to the member as to the exercise of voting rights. Section 325 does not apply to the copy of the notice sent to the nominated person, and the company must either omit the notice required by s 325, or include it but state that it does not apply to the nominated person.[178]

To whom notice must be sent

25.70 Notice of a general meeting must be sent to every member of the company, every director, and also to any person who is entitled to a share as a consequence of the death or bankruptcy of a member, subject to any enactment and any provision of the company's articles.[179]

---

[170] 2006 Act, ss 311(3)(b) and 360B(2) (qualified by s 360B(5)) if an election has been made under s 128, when those provisions come into effect), which provides that the time to be determined by the company must be not more than 48 hours before the time for the holding of the meeting.

[171] 2006 Act, s 311(3)(c).

[172] 2006 Act, s 311(3)(d).

[173] 2006 Act, s 311(3)(e). Section 322A deals with votes cast in advance and s 360A deals with voting by electronic means.

[174] 2006 Act, s 311(3)(f). Section 319A deals with questions at general meetings of traded companies.

[175] 2006 Act, s 325(1). Table A, reg 59 allows a member to appoint more than one proxy and regs 61 and 62 provide for the form of proxy. Model Articles (pcls) 45 and 46 and Model Articles (plc) 38 and 39 deal with the content and delivery of proxy notices.

[176] 2006 Act, s 325(2).

[177] 2006 Act, s 325(3) and (4).

[178] 2006 Act, Part 9, s 149.

[179] 2006 Act, s 310. See also Table A, reg 38, the relevant part of which provides: 'Subject to the provisions of the articles and to any restrictions imposed on any shares, the notice shall be given to all members, to all persons entitled to a share in consequence of the death or bankruptcy of a member and to the directors and auditors.' Table A, reg 112, deals with service of notices on members and provides that a member whose registered address is not within the UK is not entitled to receive any notice of the company if he does not give the company an address within the UK at which notices may be given to him, or an address to which notices may be sent using

A company's auditor is also entitled to receive all notices and communications of general meetings.[180] Notice is given to a personal representative and trustee in bankruptcy for information since the company's articles may exclude them from the meeting and they will not be counted in any vote.[181]

Where the company's articles include a provision enabling a member to nominate another person or persons as entitled to enjoy or exercise all or any specified rights of the member in relation to the company, any nominated person has the right to be sent the notice of the general meeting under s 310.[182] If the company is a traded company, a member of the company who holds shares on behalf of another person may nominate that person to enjoy information rights, which include the right to receive communications that the company sends to its members concerning notice of meetings.[183]   **25.71**

Resolutions requiring special notice

An ordinary resolution for the removal of a director or auditor or, in certain circumstances, to appoint a person as auditor in place of a person whose term of office has ended requires special notice to be given to the company.[184] By s 312(1) such a resolution is not effective unless notice of the intention to move it has been given to the company at least 28 days before the meeting at which it is moved.[185] The company must give its members notice of the resolution in the same manner and at the same time as it gives notice of the meeting, but if that is not practicable, the company must give its members notice at least 14 days before the meeting by advertisement in a newspaper having an appropriate circulation, or in any other manner allowed by the company's articles.[186] If after the notice of the intention to move the resolution has been given to the company, a meeting is called for a date 28 days or less after notice has been given, the notice is deemed to have been properly given, though not given within the time required.[187]   **25.72**

Accidental failure to give notice of resolution or meeting

Section 313(1) states the general rule that where a company gives notice of a general meeting or a resolution intended to be moved at a general meeting any accidental failure to give notice to one or more persons shall be disregarded for the purpose of determining whether notice of   **25.73**

---

electronic communications. Section 310 and the part of Table A, reg 38 quoted above, reverse the position at common law under which the personal representatives of a deceased shareholder were not entitled to receive notice: *Allen v Gold Reefs of West Africa Ltd* [1900] 1 Ch 656, CA. Table A, reg 116 deals with service of notices on personal representatives and trustees in bankruptcy. See also *Speechley v Allott* [2014] EWCA Civ 230 where there was a failure to give proper notice in respect of an unincorporated association.

[180] 2006 Act, ss 498–502 state the duties and rights of auditors.

[181] 1985 Act, Table A, reg 31 and 2006 Act, ss 282 and 283.

[182] 2006 Act, Part 9, s 145.

[183] 2006 Act, Part 9, ss 146–8. Section 147 prescribes the form in which copies are to be provided to the nominated person.

[184] 2006 Act, ss 168(2) and 511.

[185] 2006 Act, s 312.

[186] 2006 Act, s 312(2) and (3). These subsections are machinery designed to ensure that members, as well as the director or auditor concerned, have notice of the proposed resolution, but nothing in s 312 gives an individual member the right to compel inclusion in the agenda of a company meeting of a resolution of the type that requires special notice: *Pedley v Inland Waterways Association Ltd* [1977] 1 All ER 209. If the company is a traded company, a member of the company who holds shares on behalf of another person may nominate that person to enjoy information rights, which include the right to receive communications that the company sends to its members concerning notice of meetings, such as notice of a resolution requiring special notice (s 146).

[187] 2006 Act, s 312(4).

the meeting or resolution is duly given.[188] The general rule is subject to any provision in the company's articles, except that, to ensure certainty, it cannot be modified in respect of s 304 (notice of meetings required by members), s 305 (notice of meetings called by members), or s 339 (notice of resolutions at AGMs proposed by members).[189] Where information rights have been conferred on a nominated person in respect of a traded company, a failure to give effect to the rights conferred by the nomination does not affect the validity of anything done by or on behalf of the company.[190]

25.74 A person who claims that the meeting is valid has the burden of proving that the failure to give notice was accidental.[191] An accidental omission requires a genuine, but failed, attempt to serve shareholders in accordance with their rights; but a deliberate decision not to serve in accordance with the articles will not suffice.[192] So, the court has been satisfied that the failure to give notice to certain members was accidental when inadvertently records of their addresses had become separated from the rest, but a deliberate decision not to give notice to a member, based on a mistaken belief that the member is not entitled to notice is not an accidental failure.[193]

25.75 Independently of s 313, a failure to give notice to a member for any reason can be cured by the assent of all the members of the company entitled to vote[194] or by the presence at the meeting of the member who had not been given notice and his acquiescence in the business conducted at it.[195] The agreement of a member to treat the meeting as valid and effective notwithstanding lack of notice may be express or by implication, verbal or by conduct, given at the time or later, but nothing short of unqualified agreement, objectively established, will be sufficient.[196]

(3) Members' statements

25.76 The members of a company may require the company to circulate, to members of the company entitled to receive notice of a general meeting, a statement of not more than 1,000 words with respect to a matter referred to in a proposed resolution to be dealt with at that meeting, or other business to be dealt with at that meeting.[197] The rights of the members to require the company to circulate the resolution and statement are subject to three restrictions.

25.77 First, the statement must command the requisite support from members. This is the threshold requirement and the company is not required to circulate the statement until it receives

---

[188] 2006 Act, s 313(1). See Table A, reg 39, which is in these terms: 'The accidental omission to give notice of a meeting to, or non-receipt of notice of a meeting by, any person entitled to receive notice shall not invalidate the proceedings at that meeting.'

[189] 2006 Act, s 313(2).

[190] 2006 Act, s 150(6).

[191] *POW Services Ltd v Clare* [1995] 2 BCLC 435, 450.

[192] *The Peninsular & Orient Steam Navigation Co v Eller & Co* [2006] EWCA Civ 432 at paras 44–56, per Lloyd LJ; *Re Halcrow Holdings Ltd* [2011] EWHC 3662 (Ch) at para 40.

[193] *Re West Canadian Collieries Ltd* [1962] Ch 370; *Royal Mutual Benefit Society v Sharman* [1963] 1 WLR 581; *Musselwhite v CH Musselwhite & Son Ltd* [1962] Ch 964. See also *Speechley v Allott* [2014] EWCA Civ 230.

[194] This is an application of the *Duomatic* principle (paras 25.16–25.20 above): *Re Express Engineering Works Ltd* [1920] 1 Ch 466; *Re Oxted Motor Co* [1921] 3 KB 32; *Parker and Cooper v Reading* [1926] Ch 975.

[195] *Re Bailey, Hay & Co Ltd* [1971] 1 WLR 1357.

[196] *Re Tulsesense Ltd* [2010] 2 BCLC 525 at para 41; *Schofield v Schofield* [2011] 2 BCLC 319, CA at para 32, per Etherton LJ.

[197] 2006 Act, s 314(1). Members have a similar right in respect of written resolutions proposed by them: s 292(2) and para 25.33 above.

requests[198] that it do so from (a) members representing at least 5 per cent of the total voting rights of all the members who have a relevant right to vote (excluding any voting rights attached to any shares in the company held as treasury shares), or (b) at least 100 members who have a relevant right to vote and hold shares in the company on which there has been paid up an average sum, per member, of at least £100.[199] Where the company's articles enable a member to nominate another person or persons as entitled to enjoy or exercise all or any specified rights of the member in relation to the company, a nominated person may request the company to circulate the statement.[200] If the company is a traded company, a member may nominate another person to enjoy information rights, in which case the nominated person may be included among the 100 members for the purpose of requesting the company to circulate the statement if the conditions in s 153(2) are satisfied with respect to the nominated person.[201]

Secondly, members must not abuse their power to require the company to circulate a statement. The company is not required to circulate the statement if, on an application by the company or another person who claims to be aggrieved, the court is satisfied that the rights conferred by ss 292 and 293 are being abused.[202] **25.78**

Thirdly, unless the meeting to which the requests to circulate the statement relate is an AGM of a public company and requests sufficient to require the company to circulate the statement are received before the end of the financial year preceding the meeting, the members who request the company to circulate the statement must pay the companies' expenses of complying with s 315, unless the company has resolved otherwise, and must deposit with, or tender to, the company a sum sufficient to meet the company's expenses in doing so.[203] **25.79**

A company that is required under s 314 to circulate a statement must send a copy of it to each member of the company entitled to receive notice of the meeting in the same manner as the notice of the meeting, and at the same time as, or as soon as reasonably practicable after, it gives notice of the meeting.[204] There is no reason to think that failure duly to circulate the **25.80**

---

[198] By 2006 Act, s 314(4) each request (a) may be in hard-copy form or in electronic form, (b) must identify the statement to be circulated, (c) must be authenticated by the person or persons making it, and (d) must be received by the company at least one week before the meeting to which it relates. For hard-copy form and electronic form, see ss 333 and 1144(1) and Sch 4. For authentication, see s 1146.

[199] 2006 Act, s 314(2). By s 314(3) a 'relevant right to vote' means '(a) in relation to a statement with respect to a matter referred to in a proposed resolution, a right to vote on that resolution at the meeting to which the requests relate, and (b) in relation to any other statement, a right to vote at the meeting to which the requests relate'.

[200] 2006 Act, s 145.

[201] 2006 Act, ss 146 and 153, as amended by the Companies (Shareholders' Rights) Regulations 2009 (SI 2009/1632), reg 17(3).

[202] 2006 Act, ss 315(2) and 317. Section 317(2) provides that the court may order members who requested the circulation of the statement to pay the whole or part of the company's costs of the application, even if they are not parties to the application. Members who support the circulation of a members' statement should therefore satisfy themselves that the statement is not abusive. Section 295 is the equivalent provision for written resolutions, discussed in para 25.35 above.

[203] 2006 Act, ss 315(2) and s 316, which may be compared with s 294 in relation to written resolutions and statements, discussed in para 25.36 above, and s 340 in relation to public company AGMs.

[204] 2006 Act, s 315(1). The company's obligations under s 315(1) are subject to s 315(2) (deposit or tender of sum in respect of circulation) and s 317 (application not to circulate members' statement). If the company is a traded company, a member of the company who holds shares on behalf of another person may nominate that person to enjoy information rights, which include the right to receive communications that the company sends to its members concerning notice of meetings: ss 146–8.

members' statement of itself affects the validity of any resolution passed at the meeting.[205] Instead, in the event of default in complying with s 315, an offence is committed by every officer of the company in default who is liable to a fine on conviction.[206]

(4) Procedure at meetings

Attendance and business at the meeting

25.81 A company's articles invariably provide that the directors are entitled to attend and speak at general meetings even if they are not shareholders.[207] The business at the meeting will, however, be decided on by three classes of person: (i) the individual members, who are entitled to vote, (ii) representatives of companies appointed in accordance with the 2006 Act, s 323, and (iii) proxies appointed in accordance with ss 324–31.[208] A company may require reasonable evidence of the entitlement of any person who is not a member to participate in the meeting.[209]

25.82 The meeting is held at the place identified in the notice, but all the members of a company may informally agree to change the location of the meeting. With modern technology it is possible for persons located elsewhere to be connected by audio-visual links to the place of the meeting, so that they are regarded as being present.[210] Thus the 2006 Act, s 360A recognizes that a meeting may be held and conducted in such a way that persons who are not present together at the same place may by electronic means attend and speak and vote at it[211] and Model Article (pcls) 37(3) and Model Article (plc) 29(3) enable the directors to make whatever arrangements they consider appropriate to enable those attending a general meeting to exercise their rights to speak or vote at it.[212]

25.83 For a traded company there are special rules about participation at a general meeting.

(1) Such a company can only make requirements and restrictions about participation by electronic means if they are necessary to ensure the identification of those taking part and the security of the electronic communication and if they are proportionate to the achievement of those objectives.[213]

(2) Any provisions in a traded company's articles is void in so far as it would have the effect of imposing a restriction on a right of a member (i) to participate in and vote at a general

---

[205] There is no equivalent to 2006 Act, s 293(7).

[206] 2006 Act, ss 291(5)–(6) and 293(5)–(6). For officer in default, see s 1121.

[207] Table A, reg 44; Model Article (pcls) 40 and Model Article (plc) 32.

[208] Table A, regs 59–63, Model Articles (pcls) 45 and 46, and Model Articles (plc) 38 and 39 deal with proxies or proxy notices and votes by proxies. In the case of traded companies, regard should be had to the interests in the appointment of proxies of nominated persons with information rights under Part 9: ss 146 and 149. Note the obligation of a traded company to provide an electronic address for receipt of proxies and any document or information relating to proxies: s 333A, inserted by the Companies (Shareholders' Rights) Regulations 2009 (SI 2009/1632), reg 13(4).

[209] 2006 Act, s 360A(3), inserted by the Companies (Shareholders' Rights) Regulations 2009 (SI 2009/1632), reg 8.

[210] *Byng v London Life Association Ltd* [1990] Ch 170, 183, 192, CA.

[211] 2006 Act, s 360A(1), inserted by the Companies (Shareholders' Rights) Regulations 2009 (SI 2009/1632), reg 8.

[212] This issue was addressed in the CLR: *Company General Meetings and Shareholder Communication* s at paras 29–30 and the CLR: *Developing the Framework* at paras 4.30–4.35, and the White Paper: *Company Law Reform* at para 4.2.

[213] 2006 Act, s 360A(2), inserted by the Companies (Shareholders' Rights) Regulations 2009 (SI 2009/1632), reg 8. This does not affect s 360A(3).

meeting unless the member's shares have (after having been acquired by the member and before the meeting) been deposited with, or transferred to, or registered in the name of another person, or (ii) to transfer shares during the period of 48 hours before the time for the holding of the general meeting if that right would not otherwise be subject to restriction.[214]

(3) A traded company must determine the right to vote at a general meeting by reference to the register of members at a time (determined by the company) that is not more than 48 hours before the time of the holding of the meeting.[215]

All the members of a company may decide what business to conduct at a general meeting, but in the absence of unanimity, the business will be limited to the resolutions proposed, or business of the general nature described, in the notice of the meeting.[216] **25.84**

Quorum

For the purposes of the quorum provisions in s 318 a qualifying person is (i) an individual who is a member of the company, (ii) a person who is authorized to represent a corporation which is a member of the company, who has been appointed under s 323, or (iii) a person appointed as proxy for a member in relation to the meeting.[217] The quorum provisions in s 318 do not apply to a variation of class rights meeting.[218] **25.85**

In the case of a company limited by shares or guarantee which has only one member, one qualifying person present at the meeting is a quorum.[219] If the sole member does not take a decision by way of written resolution, s 357 provides that he must provide the company with details of any decision made by him that may be taken by the company in general meeting or which has effect as if agreed by the company in general meeting, so that the company has a written record of the decision.[220] Section 231 provides for a written record to be made of any contract between the company and a sole member who is also sole director which is not entered into in the ordinary course of business. There are criminal sanctions for failure to comply with ss 231 and 357, although non-compliance does not affect the validity of the transaction or decision.[221] **25.86**

---

[214] 2006 Act, s 360B(1), inserted by the Companies (Shareholders' Rights) Regulations 2009 (SI 2009/1632), reg 20. Section 360B(2) is qualified by s 360B(5) if an election has been made under s 128, when those provisions come into effect. For the purpose of calculating the period of 48 hours, no account is taken of any part of a day that is not a working day (s 360B(3)). This restriction on a traded company's articles does not affect the operation of (i) the 2006 Act, Part 22 (information about interests in a company's shares), (ii) 1985 Act, Part 15 (orders imposing restrictions on shares), or (iii) any provisions in a company's articles relating to the application of any provision of either of those Parts; nor does it affect the validity of the model articles prescribed under the 2006 Act, s 19 or articles to the same effect (s 360B(4)).

[215] 2006 Act, s 360B(2), inserted by the Companies (Shareholders' Rights) Regulations 2009 (SI 2009/1632), reg 20 (see n 214 above). For the purpose of calculating the period of 48 hours, no account is taken of any part of a day that is not a working day (s 360B(3)).

[216] 2006 Act, ss 304 and 311 and Table A, reg 38.

[217] 2006 Act, s 318(3).

[218] 2006 Act, ss 334(3)(a) and 335(3)(a); instead for a class meeting the quorum is as stated in ss 334(4) or 335(4), as the case may be.

[219] 2006 Act, s 318(1).

[220] 2006 Act, s 357 and 2006 Act, s 355(1)(c).

[221] 2006 Act, ss 231(3), (4), and (6) and 357(3)–(5). These provisions go a long way to avoiding the unsatisfactory position of a sole director and member 'purporting to continue the business and effectively bind everyone else who is interested in it by anything to which, in his private thoughts, he cares to assent', which Oliver J rejected and, with a homage to Wordsworth, described as 'the self-sufficing power of solitude'; *Re New Cedos Engineering Co Ltd* (1976) [1994] 1 BCLC 797, 813.

25.87 If a company limited by shares or guarantee has more than one member, or in any other case, subject to the provisions of the company's articles, two qualifying persons present at the meeting are a quorum. But a quorum cannot be achieved by a member appointing two or more corporate representatives or proxies.[222] A single person present in two capacities (as an individual member and as a corporate representative) counts as two persons.[223] Unlike the 1985 Act, ss 370(4) and 318(1) and (2) do not include the phrase 'personally present', which suggests that it is not necessary for the two qualifying persons to be physically present in the same meeting room.[224] The quorum provision in Table A is slightly different to s 318(1) and (2): 'Save in the case of a company with a single member two persons entitled to vote upon the business to be transacted, each being a member or a proxy for a member or a duly authorised representative of a corporation, shall be a quorum.'

25.88 No business other than the appointment of the chairman of the meeting can be transacted at a general meeting if the persons attending do not constitute a quorum and, in such a case, the meeting has to be adjourned.[225] Subject to the company's articles, the quorum has to be present for the duration of the meeting.[226] A resolution purportedly passed at an inquorate meeting will be invalid.[227] Abuse of the quorum provisions can be overcome by applying to the court under s 306 to order a meeting at which a quorum may be one person present (paragraphs 25.55–25.59 above).

Chairman

25.89 Section 319 provides a default rule for the appointment of the chairman of a general meeting, by which, subject to any provision in the company's articles, a member may be elected to be chairman by ordinary resolution of the company passed at the meeting. In fact the company's articles invariably make provision for the chairman of the board to be chairman of the meeting, or for a director to be chairman, or, in default of a director being appointed chairman, for the members to choose one of their number to be chairman.[228]

25.90 The chairman's responsibilities are to supervise the conduct of the meeting, to determine whether the meeting should be adjourned, and to take any votes that are required. It is the chairman's responsibility to secure the proper, fair, and orderly conduct of the meeting so that the meeting can make its decision on any matter before it.[229] The chairman will

---

[222] 2006 Act, s 318(2).

[223] *Neil McLeod & Sons Ltd, Petitioners* [1967] SC 16.

[224] This accords with modern commercial practice (para 25.82 above) and is reflected in Model Article (pcls) 37(4) and Model Article (plc) 29(4), which both provide: 'In determining attendance at a general meeting, it is immaterial whether any two or more shareholders attending it are in the same place as each other.'

[225] Table A, regs 40–2; Model Articles (pcls) 39(2) and 41(1) and Model Articles (plc) 31(2) and 33(1).

[226] *Sharp v Dawes* (1876) 2 QBD 26 (CA); *Re Sanitary Carbon Co* [1877] WN 223; *Re London Flats Ltd* [1969] 1 WLR 711. Table A, reg 41 provides that the meeting has to be adjourned if the meeting ceases to be quorate. Under the 1948 Table A, reg 53, if a quorum was present at the commencement of the meeting, the departure of members reducing the numbers present to below the quorum figure did not invalidate resolutions passed at the meeting: *Re Hartley Baird Ltd* [1955] Ch 143.

[227] *Re Cambrian Peat, Fuel and Charcoal Ltd* (1875) 31 LT 773.

[228] Table A, regs 42 and 43; Model Article (pcls) 39 and Model Article (plc) 31. On the power under the general law of the members present to appoint a chairman, when the chairman does not attend: *Re Salcombe Hotel Development Co Ltd* [1991] BCLC 44. A proxy may be elected chairman: s 328. In *Re Bradford Investments Ltd* [1991] BCLC 224 it was held that the members could choose a solicitor who held a proxy but was not a member to act as temporary chairman to supervise the election of a proper chairman.

[229] *National Dwellings Society v Sykes* [1894] 2 Ch 159; *Carruth v Imperial Chemical Industries* [1937] Ch 707, 761, 767, PC.

introduce any directors' report or members' statement that is to be put before the meeting. The chairman will direct the order of speeches by directors and members, corporate representatives, and proxies.[230] He may also have a discretion to allow non-members to attend and speak at the meeting.[231] Once a resolution has been properly debated, the chairman may end the debate and take the vote or close the meeting.[232]

For a general meeting of a traded company the 2006 Act, s 319A requires that the company **25.91** must cause to be answered any question relating to the business being dealt with at the meeting which is put by a member attending the meeting, unless (a) to do so would interfere unduly with the preparation for the meeting or involve disclosure of confidential information, (b) the question has already been answered on a website, or (c) it is undesirable in the interests of the company or the good order of the meeting to answer it.[233]

The company's articles usually provide that the chairman must adjourn the meeting if a quo- **25.92** rum is not present within half an hour from the time appointed for the meeting,[234] but that, where a quorum is present, the chairman may with the consent of the meeting adjourn it to a later date.[235] The chairman also has a residual power to adjourn the meeting where the circumstances are such that the consent of the meeting cannot be ascertained, but his decision to do so may be challenged on the same grounds as apply to judicial review cases.[236] If the articles provide for the chairman to have power to adjourn with the consent of the meeting, the members cannot compel an adjournment against the wishes of the chairman.[237] The new Model Articles, however, give the members an independent right to direct the chairman to adjourn the meeting.[238] If the chairman purports to adjourn the meeting without the consent of the members and leaves the meeting, declaring it closed, the members may appoint another chairman and continue the meeting.[239]

When adjourning a general meeting of a traded company note should be taken of the special **25.93** rules about notice of the adjourned meeting, as described in paragraph 25.64 above.

An adjourned meeting is a continuation of the original meeting and it will conduct the **25.94** same business as could have been conducted at the original meeting. The articles invariably

---

[230] The articles usually provide for directors to be entitled to speak, whether or not they are members: Table A, reg 44; Model Article (pcls) 40(1) and Model Article (plc) 32(1). A member has a prima facie right to speak (*Const v Harris* (1824) Turn & R 496, 525) and this right to speak is reflected in Model Article (pcls) 37(2), (3), and (5) and Model Article (plc) 29(2), (3) and (5). A corporate representative and a proxy have rights to speak on behalf of the member: ss 323 and 324.

[231] Model Article (pcls) 41(2) and Model Article (plc) 32(2).

[232] *Wall v London and Northern Assets Corp* [1898] 2 Ch 649, CA; *Carruth v Imperial Chemical Industries* [1937] AC 707, 767, PC.

[233] Inserted 2009 by the Companies (Shareholders' Rights) Regulations 2009 (SI 2009/1632), reg 12(1).

[234] Table A, reg 41 provides that the meeting shall 'stand adjourned to the same day in the next week at the same time and place or to such time and place as the directors may determine'. Model Article (pcls) 42 and Model Article (plc) 33 both provide for the meeting to be adjourned in such circumstances (subpara (1)), but the adjournment date is to be fixed in accordance with subpara (3) in the same way as for any other adjournment.

[235] Table A, reg 45; Model Article (pcls) 42(2)(a) and Model Article (plc) 33(2)(a). In *Re Abbey National plc* [2005] 2 BCLC 15 the articles required a poll on a resolution to adjourn.

[236] *Byng v London Life Association Ltd* [1990] Ch 170, CA; Model Article (pcls) 42(2)(b) and Model Article (plc) 33(2)(b).

[237] *Salisbury Gold Mining Co v Hathorn* [1897] AC 268, PC.

[238] Model Article (pcls) 42(3) and Model Article (plc) 33(3).

[239] *National Dwellings Society v Sykes* [1894] 3 Ch 159; *John v Rees* [1970] Ch 345.

provide that if the adjournment is for more than 14 days, notice should be given, but subject to that,[240] and unless the articles otherwise provide, no further notice is necessary, the quorum is the same, and the proxies for the original meeting can be used.[241] Where a resolution is passed at an adjourned meeting of a company, the resolution is for all purposes to be treated as having been passed on the date on which it was in fact passed, and is not to be deemed passed on any earlier date.[242]

Votes

25.95 The chairman is responsible for taking the vote on resolutions at the meeting. The articles usually provide that, unless a poll is duly demanded, votes shall be decided on a show of hands.[243] When the vote is on a show of hands, every member present in person has one vote, and every proxy present who has been duly appointed by one or more members entitled to vote on the resolution has one vote.[244] Where the resolution is to ratify acts of a director, the votes of the director (if a member) and persons connected with him are disregarded.[245] Articles invariably provide that in the event of equality of votes, the chairman has a casting vote, but such a provision is considered to be inconsistent with ss 281 and 282.[246] On a vote on a resolution at a meeting on a show of hands (unless a poll is demanded and the demand is not subsequently withdrawn), a declaration by the chairman that the resolution has or has not been passed, or passed with a particular majority, is conclusive evidence of that fact without proof of the number or proportion of the votes recorded in favour of or against the resolution.[247] The articles usually provide that the chairman's decision on entitlement to

---

[240] And to the special rules for traded companies mentioned in the preceding para.

[241] *Wills v Murray* (1850) 4 Ex 843; *Scadding v Lorant* (1851) 3 HLC 418; *McLaren v Thomson* [1917] 2 Ch 261. Table A, reg 45; Model Article (pcls) 42(5) and (6) and Model Article (plc) 33(5) and (6).

[242] 2006 Act, s 332.

[243] Table A, reg 46; Model Article (pcls) 42 and Model Article (plc) 34.

[244] 2006 Act, ss 284(2), as substituted by the Companies (Shareholders' Rights) Regulations 2009 (SI 2009/1632), reg 2(3), and s 285(1). The articles may provide that a share may not be voted if there are monies owed in respect of it: Table A, reg 57 and Model Article (plc) 41. There are possible difficulties of interpretation of s 284 when a corporate member appoints several representatives. Where there are joint holders of shares, only the vote of the senior holder who votes, in person or by proxy, is to be counted and seniority is determined by the order of names in the register of members: s 286, which restates Table A, reg 55. Provisions about proxies are to be found in ss 324–31; Table A, regs 59–63; Model Articles (pcls) 45, 46 and Model Article (plc) 38, 39. The right to appoint a proxy to act at a meeting is one of the rights that a nominated person may enjoy where s 145 applies. In the case of a traded company a nominated person may also be entitled to appoint a proxy, depending on his agreement with the nominee member: ss 146 and 149.

[245] 2006 Act, ss 239(4)–(5) and 252. Subject to s 239, as far as the company is concerned, if a member is entitled to vote on a resolution, he may vote as he pleases even if he is interested in the transaction being voted on: *North-West Transportation Co v Beatty* (1887) 12 AC 589, PC; *Burland v Earle* [1902] AC 83, PC; *Northern Counties Securities Ltd v Jackson & Steeple Ltd* [1974] 1 WLR 1133. A member may, however, enter into a valid agreement as to the exercise of voting rights, which may be enforced by injunction: *Russell v Northern Bank Development Corporation Ltd* [1992] 1 WLR 588, HL. (For limitations on the effectiveness of a vote, see Ch 20, Section D above.)

[246] The Tables A to F Amendment Regulations 2007 therefore delete Table A, reg 50 for companies incorporated on or after 1 October 2007. But 2006 Act Commencement Order No 5, Sch 5, para 2(b) amends 2006 Act Commencement Order No 3, Sch 3, by inserting a new para 23A, which provides that where immediately before 1 October 2007 a company's articles provided for a chairman's casting vote, unless it had subsequently been removed, such provision continued to have effect notwithstanding 2006 Act, ss 281(3) and 282.

[247] 2006 Act, s 320(1) and (3), which re-enacts 1985 Act, 378(4) and restates Table A, regs 47 and 48 with changes. Evidence tendered to the effect that the chairman's declaration was wrong is inadmissible, but the chairman's declaration can be challenged if (a) there is a manifest error on the face of the declaration (if it identifies insufficient votes for the resolution to be passed), (b) there was an error in the procedure (if a member was wrongly excluded from voting), or (c) fraud is shown: *Re Hadleigh Castle Gold Mines* [1900] 2 Ch 419; *Arnot v*

vote is final and conclusive.[248] Further, an entry in respect of the chairman's declaration in minutes of the meeting recorded in accordance with s 355 is also conclusive evidence of that fact without proof.[249]

Where the outcome or likely outcome of a vote is contentious, a poll may be demanded. **25.96** Section 321 makes void any provision in a company's articles in so far as it would have the effect of:

(1) excluding the right to demand a poll at a general meeting on any question other than the election of the chairman of the meeting or the adjournment of the meeting; and
(2) making ineffective a demand for a poll on any such question which is made—
   (a) by not less than 5 members having the right to vote on the resolution; or
   (b) by a member or members representing not less than 10% of the total voting rights of all the members having the right to vote on the resolution (excluding any voting rights attached to any shares in the company held as treasury shares); or
   (c) by a member or members holding shares in the company conferring a right to vote on the resolution, being shares on which an aggregate sum has been paid up equal to not less than 10% of the total sum paid up on all the shares conferring that right (excluding shares in the company conferring a right to vote on the resolution which are held as treasury shares).[250]

A demand by a proxy is taken into account for the purpose of determining the qualification to demand a poll under paragraphs (a)–(c) above.[251] The articles usually give the chairman and members (if certain conditions are met, which conditions cannot be less extensive than required by s 321) the right to demand a poll.[252] If the chairman has the right to demand a poll, he should exercise that right when he is unable to determine the outcome of a vote on a show of hands.[253] The demand for a poll may be withdrawn with the chairman's consent before it is taken.[254]

Subject to the provisions of the company's articles, the chairman will determine when **25.97** and how to take the poll. He may wish to have the assistance of scrutineers. The articles usually provide for the poll to be taken immediately or, if it does not concern the election of the chairman of the meeting or adjournment, at a future date within 30 days of the meeting of which at least 7 days' notice is given, and that the result of the poll shall be the decision of the meeting in respect of the resolution on which the poll was demanded.[255]

United African Lands [1901] 1 Ch 518, CA; *Re Caratal (New) Mines Ltd* [1902] 2 Ch 498; *Clark & Co* [1911] SC 243.

[248] Table A, reg 58; Model Article (pcls) 43(2) and Model Article (plc) 35(2). These provisions are effective: s 287.

[249] 2006 Act, s 320(2), which restates Table A, reg 47.

[250] 2006 Act, s 321 does not apply to variation of class rights meetings: ss 334(3)(b) and 335(3)(b).

[251] 2006 Act, s 329.

[252] Table A, reg 46; Model Article (pcls) 44(1) and (2) and Model Article (plc) 36(1) and (2). The Model Articles provide that a poll may be demanded (a) before the meeting, (b) before the show of hands, or (c) immediately after the result of the show of hands is declared. They also give a director the right to demand a poll (which may be significant on a vote for his removal).

[253] *Second Consolidated Trust v Ceylon Amalgamated Tea & Rubber Estates Ltd* [1943] 2 All ER 567.

[254] Table A, reg 48; Model Article (pcls) 44(3) and Model Article (plc) 36(3).

[255] Table A, regs 51 and 52; Model Article (plc) 37. Model Article (pcls) 44(4) provides that for private companies polls must be taken immediately and in such manner as the chairman of the meeting directs. Subject to the articles, a chairman has an inherent power to adjourn for a poll; *Jackson v Hamlyn* [1953] Ch 577.

25.98 On a vote on a resolution on a poll taken at a meeting, subject to any provisions of the company's articles, in the case of a company having a share capital, every member has one vote in respect of each share or £10 of stock held by him, and in any other case, every member has one vote.[256] When a poll is taken it is the votes conferred by each share that are counted, so that it is irrelevant whether the member is voting in person or by proxy.[257] A member who is entitled to more than one vote on a poll need not, if he votes, use all his votes or cast all the votes he uses in the same way.[258] For special provisions about polls of quoted companies, see Section F below.

25.99 A company's articles may contain a provision to the effect that on a vote on a resolution on a poll taken at a meeting, the votes may include votes cast in advance.[259] The 2006 Act regulates the power to include such a provision in two ways:

(1) In the case of a traded company any such provision in relation to voting at a general meeting may be made subject only to such requirements and restrictions as are necessary to ensure identification of the person voting and are proportionate to the achievement of that objective.[260]

(2) Any such provision is void in so far as it would have the effect of requiring any document casting a vote in advance to be received by the company or another person earlier than these times: (a) in the case of a poll taken more than 48 hours after it was demanded, 24 hours before the time appointed or the taking of the poll; (b) in the case of any other poll, 48 hours before the time for holding the meeting or adjourned meeting.[261]

Minutes of general meetings

25.100 A company must keep minutes of all proceedings of general meetings[262] and if a resolution is a special resolution a copy of it must be forwarded to the Registrar within 15 days after it is passed.[263] The minutes of proceedings of a general meeting, if purporting to be signed by the chairman of that meeting or by the chairman of the next general meeting, are evidence of the proceedings of the meeting.[264] Where there is a record of proceedings of a general meeting of

---

[256] 2006 Act, s 284(3) and (4). Cf Table A, reg 54. Note also s 285(3). Companies' articles frequently provide for weighted voting rights and effect will be given to them on a poll; *Bushell v Faith* [1970] AC 1099, HL. In *Sugarman v CJS Investments LLP* [2015] 1 BCLC 1, CA, the articles of a property management company, on their true construction, ousted the default provisions in the 2006 Act, s 284(3) and gave each member one vote at a meeting and on a poll.

[257] Hansard, HC Standing Committee Day 5, col 297 (30 June 2006).

[258] 2006 Act, s 322. It allows members who hold shares on behalf of different clients to act on their clients' instructions, by voting in different ways or not voting. Section 152 is to similar effect.

[259] 2006 Act, s 322A(1), which was inserted by the Companies (Shareholders' Rights) Regulations 2009 (SI 2009/1632), reg 5(1).

[260] 2006 Act, s 322A(2), which does not affect any power of a company to require reasonable evidence of the entitlement of any person who is not a member to vote. Cf 360A(2).

[261] 2006 Act, s 322A(3). In calculating these periods, no account is taken of any part of a day that is not a working day (s 322A(4)).

[262] 2006 Act, s 355(1)(b). The minutes must be kept for at least ten years (s 355(2)). If there is non-compliance with s 355 every officer of the company in default commits an offence, punishable by a fine (s 355(3) and (4)).

[263] 2006 Act, ss 29 and 30. If there is non-compliance with s 30 the company and every officer of the company in default commits an offence, punishable by a fine (s 30(2) and (3)).

[264] 2006 Act, s 356(4). Table A, reg 100 provides that the directors shall cause minutes to be made in books kept for the purpose of all proceedings at meetings of the company and class meetings, including the names of the directors present at each such meeting.

a company, then, until the contrary is proved the meeting is deemed duly held and convened, all proceedings at the meeting are deemed to have duly taken place, and all appointments at the meeting are deemed valid.[265]

E. Public Companies and Traded Companies: AGMs

(1) The obligation to hold an AGM

A private company does not have to hold AGMs unless it is required to do so by its memorandum or articles,[266] or it is a traded company. A public company must also hold AGMs. As described below, the Companies Act provides members of a public company or traded company with rights to probe or challenge the management of the company by requiring additional resolutions to be proposed or additional business to be discussed at the AGM if certain conditions are satisfied. **25.101**

Every public company must, by s 336(1), hold an AGM in each period of six months beginning with the day following its accounting reference date (in addition to any other meetings held during that period).[267] For a private company that is a traded company s 336(1A) extends the period to nine months.[268] If the company fails to comply with these requirements as a result of giving a notice under s 392 specifying a new accounting reference date and stating that the current accounting reference period or the previous accounting reference period is to be shortened, it will be treated as if it had complied with the subsection if it holds an AGM within three months of giving that notice.[269] **25.102**

If the company fails to comply with ss 336(1) or (1A) an offence is committed by every officer of the company in default and a person guilty of an offence is liable to a fine.[270] **25.103**

(2) Public companies

A notice calling an AGM of a public company must state that the meeting is an AGM.[271] The AGM must be called by notice of at least 21 days, and that period can only be reduced if the company is not a traded company and all the members entitled to attend and vote at the meeting agree to shorter notice.[272] **25.104**

The members of a public company may require the company to give, to members of the company entitled to receive notice of the next AGM, notice of a resolution which may **25.105**

---

[265] 2006 Act, s 356(5).

[266] 2006 Act Commencement Order No 3, Sch 3, para 32. By 2006 Act, Commencement Order No 3, Sch 3, para 32, as amended by 2006 Act Commencement Order No 5, Sch 5, para 2(b) an elective resolution under 1985 Act, s 366A is not regarded as a provision requiring a private company to hold an AGM.

[267] The 2006 Act, s 336(1) reduces the period within which the AGM must be held from ten to six months. For discussion of the reforms in relation to AGMs, see CLR: *Company General Meetings and Shareholder Communication* at paras 31, 32, 41, 46; CLR: *Developing the Framework* at paras 4.25–4.28, 4.39; CLR: *Completing the Structure* at paras 4.2–4.5; CLR: *Final Report* at paras 6.39, 7.6, 7.8; White Paper: *Company Law Reform* at para 4.2.

[268] Inserted by the Companies (Shareholders' Rights) Regulations 2009 (SI 2009/1632), reg 15(1)–(4).

[269] 2006 Act, 336(2).

[270] 2006 Act, s 336(3) and (4).

[271] 2006 Act, s 337(1).

[272] 2006 Act, ss 307(2)(a) and 337(2), as amended by the Companies (Shareholders' Rights) Regulations 2009 (SI 2009/1632), reg 16(1)–(5).

properly be moved and is intended to be moved at the meeting.[273] The proposed resolution may be supported by a members' statement under ss 314–17, subject to the restrictions there mentioned (paragraphs 25.76–25.80 above). The members' right to require circulation of a resolution for an AGM is subject to three restrictions.

25.106 First, members must not abuse their power to require the company to circulate the resolution. The resolution is not capable of being properly moved at an AGM if: (a) it would, if passed, be ineffective (whether by reason of inconsistency with any enactment or the company's constitution or otherwise); (b) it is defamatory of any person; or (c) it is frivolous and vexatious.[274]

25.107 Secondly, the resolution must command the requisite support from members. This is the threshold requirement and the company is not required to circulate the resolution until it receives requests, identifying the resolution of which notice is to be given,[275] that it do so from (a) members representing at least 5 per cent of the total voting rights of all the members who have a relevant right to vote on the resolution at the AGM to which the requests relate (excluding any voting rights attached to any shares in the company held as treasury shares), or (b) at least 100 members who have a right to vote on the resolution at the AGM to which the request relates and hold shares in the company on which there has been paid up an average sum, per member, of at least £100.[276] The level of support required for the resolution is the same as the level of support required for the circulation of a members' statement for a general meeting and nominated persons have the same rights to be included in the support for the resolution as are described in paragraph 25.77 above.[277]

25.108 Thirdly, to be effective to require the company to circulate the proposed resolution, the members' requests must be received by the company at least six weeks before the AGM to which the requests relate, or, if later, the time at which notice is given of that meeting.[278]

25.109 A company that is required under s 338 to give notice of a resolution must send a copy of it to each member of the company entitled to receive notice of the AGM in the same manner as notice of the meeting, and at the same time as, or as soon as reasonably practicable after, it gives notice of the meeting.[279] The business which may be dealt with at an AGM includes a resolution of which notice is given in accordance with s 339.[280] To secure compliance with s 339, in the event of default in complying with it, an offence is committed by every officer of the company in default who is liable to a fine on conviction.[281]

---

[273] 2006 Act, s 338(1).

[274] 2006 Act, s 338(2). This is the same restriction as applies to members' requests for circulation of a written resolution under s 292(2); see para 25.35 above.

[275] By s 338(4)(a)–(c). Each request may be in hard-copy form or in electronic form and must be authenticated by the person or persons making it. Section 338(4) may be compared with ss 292(6), 303(6), 314(4), 338A(4)–(5). For hard-copy form and electronic form, see ss 333 and 1144(1) and Sch 4. For authentication, see s 1146.

[276] 2006 Act, s 338(3).

[277] 2006 Act, ss 146 and 153. Section 153(2) states the conditions for the exercise of this right.

[278] 2006 Act, s 338(4)(d).

[279] 2006 Act, s 339(1). The company's obligations under s 339(1) are subject to s 340(2) (deposit or tender of sum in respect of expenses of circulation).

[280] 2006 Act, s 339(3).

[281] 2006 Act, s 339(4) and (5). The liability of an officer 'in default' is dealt with in s 1121.

Members who requested the circulation of the resolution do not have pay the company's **25.110** expenses of complying with s 339 if requests sufficient to require the company to circulate it are received before the end of the financial year preceding the meeting.[282] If sufficient requests are not received within that time, the members who requested the company to circulate the resolution must pay the company's expenses of complying with s 339, unless the company resolves otherwise.[283] Also, unless the company has previously so resolved, the company is not bound to comply with that section unless there is deposited with, or tendered to, the company, not later than six weeks before the AGM to which the request relates, or, if later, the time at which notice is given of that meeting, a sum sufficient to meet the company's expenses in complying with s 339.[284]

(3) Traded companies

The members of a traded company may request the company to include in the business **25.111** to be dealt with at an AGM any matter (other than a proposed resolution) which may be properly be included in the business.[285] The request must identify the matter to be included in the business and must be accompanied by a statement setting out the grounds for the request.[286]

This right to include additional business is subject to the same three restrictions as to content, **25.112** support, and level of support as apply to the right of members of a public company to require the company to circulate a resolution to be moved at the AGM, as discussed in paragraphs 25.105–25.108 above.[287]

A company that is required under s 338A to include any matter in the business to be dealt **25.113** with at the AGM must (i) give notice of it to each member of the company entitled to receive notice of the AGM in the same manner as notice of the meeting, and at the same time as, or as soon as reasonably practicable after, it gives notice of the meeting, and (ii) publish it on the same website as that on which the company published the information required by s 311A (publication of information in advance of a general meeting).[288] To secure compliance with s 340A, in the event of default in complying with it, an offence is committed by every officer of the company in default who is liable to a fine on conviction.[289]

The provisions of s 340B about the expenses of circulating members' matters to be dealt with **25.114** at an AGM are substantially the same as the provisions in relation to members' resolutions, as described in paragraph 25.110 above.

---

[282] 2006 Act, s 340(1).

[283] 2006 Act, s 340(2)(a).

[284] 2006 Act, s 340((2)(b). Section 340 may be compared with ss 294 and 316 in relation to written resolutions and statements. See paras 25.36 and 25.79 above.

[285] 2006 Act, s 338A(1). Section 338A was inserted by the Companies (Shareholders' Rights) Regulations 2009 (SI 2009/1632), reg 17(1).

[286] 2006 Act, s 338A(4)(b) and (c). A request may be in hard-copy form or electronic form and must be authenticated by the person or persons making it (s 338A(4)(a) and (d)).

[287] 2006 Act, s 338A(2), (3), and (5).

[288] 2006 Act, s 340A(1). The company's obligations under s 339(1) are subject to s 340B(2) (deposit or tender of sum in respect of expenses of circulation). Sections 340A and 340 B were inserted by the Companies (Shareholders' Rights) Regulations 2009 (SI 2009/1632), reg 18(1). For s 311A, see para 25.67 above.

[289] 2006 Act, s 340A(3) and (4). The liability of an officer 'in default' is dealt with in s 1121.

F. Quoted Companies and Traded Companies: Polls

25.115 For quoted companies and traded companies there are special rules for publication of poll results and members of a quoted company may require an independent report on a poll to ensure the validity of the decision.[290]

(1) Publication of poll results

25.116 Section 341 provides for the results of a poll taken at a meeting or class meeting of a quoted company or traded company to be made available on a website in accordance with the requirements of s 353.[291]

25.117 In relation to a quoted company that is not a traded company, the information about the results of the poll required to be made available on a website are (a) the date of the meeting, (b) the text of the resolution or description of the subject matter of the poll, (c) the number of votes cast in favour, and (d) the number of votes cast against.[292]

25.118 A traded company must ensure that, in addition to the information required in respect of a public company, the information made available on a website includes: (a) the number of votes validly cast, (b) the proportion of the company's issued share capital represented by those votes, and (c) the number of abstentions, if counted.[293] A traded company must do this by the end of 16 days beginning with the day of the meeting or, if later, the end of the first working week after the day on which the result of the poll is declared.[294]

25.119 In the event of default in complying with ss 341 and 353 an offence is committed by every officer of the company in default and a person guilty of an offence is liable to a fine.[295] Failure to comply with ss 341 and 353 does not affect the validity of the poll or the resolution or other business (if passed or agreed) to which the poll relates.[296]

(2) Independent report on poll

25.120 The members of a quoted company may require the directors to obtain an independent report on any poll taken, or to be taken, at a general meeting or class meeting of the company.[297]

---

[290] The provisions in Chapter 5 of the Act, ss 341–54 were recommended by the CLR: *Final Report* at para 6.39. By s 354 the Secretary of State may limit or extend the types of company to which the provisions of Chapter 5 apply; eg to extend it to other companies with a large shareholder base, which are not private companies, or to narrow the application of the Chapter if the definition of quoted company were to be extended; Hansard, HL, col 185 (11 January 2006).

[291] Section 352 applies s 341 to the results of a poll in respect of a class meeting. The requirements of s 353 are that (i) the website is maintained by or on behalf of the company, and identifies the company, (ii) there is no charge for access to the website or obtaining hard copies of information on it, and (iii) the information is made available as soon as reasonably practicable and remains on the website for two years.

[292] 2006 Act, s 341(1).

[293] 2006 Act, s 341(1A), which was inserted by the Companies (Shareholders' Rights) Regulations 2009 (SI 2009/1632), reg 19(1), (3). The proportion is to be determined at the time at which the right to vote is determined under s 360B(2) (qualified by s 360B(5) if an election has been made under s 128, when those provisions come into effect).

[294] 2006 Act, s 341(1B).

[295] 2006 Act, s 341(3) and (4). The liability of an officer 'in default' is dealt with in s 1121.

[296] 2006 Act, s 341(5).

[297] 2006 Act, ss 342 and 352(1A), which was inserted by the Companies (Shareholders' Rights) Regulations 2009 (SI 2009/1632), reg 19(4). Sections 342–53 were introduced to address what was said to be a lack of confidence in the integrity and effectiveness of counting proxies; CLR: *Final Report* at para 6.39(iv); White

The provisions regarding independent reports on polls are detailed. The following paragraphs focus on those provisions that directly concern directors.

The directors are only required to obtain an independent report if, in respect of each poll, **25.121** they receive requests that they do so from (a) members representing at least 5 per cent of the total voting rights of all the members who have a right to vote on the matter to which the poll (excluding any voting rights attached to any shares in the company held as treasury shares), or (b) at least 100 members who have a right to vote on the matter to which the poll relates and hold shares in the company on which there has been paid up an average sum, per member, of at least £100.[298] The level of support required to obtain the report is the same as the level of support required for the circulation of a members' statement for a general meeting and a members' resolution at an AGM[299] and nominated persons have the same rights to be included in the support for the request for a report.[300]

Unless no poll on which a report is required is in fact taken, the directors who are required **25.122** by s 342 to obtain an independent report on a poll or polls, must appoint an independent assessor to prepare a report for the company on it or them within one week after the company being required to obtain the report.[301] The directors must not appoint as the independent assessor a person who does not meet the independence requirements in s 344, or who has another role in relation to any poll on which he is to report (including, in particular, a role in connection with collecting or counting votes or with the appointment of proxies).[302] In the event of default in complying with s 343 an offence is committed by every officer of the company in default and a person guilty of an offence is liable to a fine.[303]

The independent assessor's report must state the independent assessor's name and his opin- **25.123** ion whether (a) the procedures adopted in connection with the poll or polls were adequate; (b) the votes cast (including proxy votes) were fairly and accurately recorded and counted; (c) the validity of members' appointments of proxies was fairly assessed; (d) the notice of the meeting complied with s 325 (notice of meeting to contain statement of rights to appoint proxies); and (e) s 326 was complied with in relation to the meeting (company-sponsored invitations to appoint proxies).[304] The report must give the independent assessor's reasons for the opinions stated, or record that he is unable to form an opinion on any of those matters and state his reasons for that.

Paper: *Modernising Company Law* at para 2.19; White Paper: *Company Law Reform* at para 3.1; Paul Myner's *Review of impediments to voting United Kingdom shares*; and the debate at Hansard, HL GC Day 6, vol 679, col 134 (2006); HL Report, vol 682, col 731 (2006); HC Comm D, col 336 (2006).

[298] 2006 Act, s 342(2). By s 342(4), each request (a) may be in hard-copy form or in electronic form, (b) must identify the statement to be circulated, (c) must be authenticated by the person or persons making it, and (d) must be received by the company at least one week before the meeting to which it relates. For hard-copy form and electronic form, see ss 333 and 1144(1) and Sch 4. For authentication, see s 1146.

[299] 2006 Act, s 342(1)(a) and (b). See paras 25.77 and 25.107 above.

[300] 2006 Act, ss 146 and 153. Section 153(2) states the conditions for the exercise of the right.

[301] 2006 Act, s 343.

[302] 2006 Act, s 344 identifies persons who may not be appointed as an independent assessor, having regard to specified connections of themselves or their associates (as explained by s 345) with the company. An auditor of the company is not excluded from being an independent assessor. Section 346 deals with the appointment of a partnership as an independent assessor.

[303] 2006 Act, s 341(3) and (4). The liability of an officer 'in default' is dealt with in s 1121.

[304] 2006 Act, s 347.

25.124 For the purpose of preparing his report, the independent assessor is entitled to attend the meeting at which the poll is to be taken and any subsequent proceedings in connection with the poll and to be provided with a copy of the notice of the meeting and other communications provided by the company in connection with it.[305] For the same purpose, the independent assessor (a) is entitled to access to the company's records relating to any poll on which he is to report and the meeting at which the poll or polls may be, or were, taken;[306] and (b) may require anyone who at any material time was, among others, a director or secretary of the company, to provide him with information or explanations.[307] There are two protections for persons required to give information and explanations. First, a statement made by a person in response to a requirement under s 349 may not be used in evidence against him in criminal proceedings except proceedings under s 350.[308] Secondly, the person is not required to disclose information in respect of which a claim to legal professional privilege could be maintained in legal proceedings.[309]

25.125 The independent assessor may enforce his rights under ss 348 and 349 by applying for an injunction.[310] Section 350 enforces compliance with s 349 by imposing criminal sanctions:

(1) A person who fails to comply with a requirement under s 349 without delay commits an offence, unless it was not reasonably practicable for him to provide the required information or explanation, and if convicted is liable to a fine.[311]

(2) A person commits an offence if he knowingly or recklessly makes to an independent assessor a statement, oral or written, that conveys or purports to convey any information or explanations which the independent assessor requires, or is entitled to require under s 349, and is misleading, false, or deceptive in a material particular. On conviction a person is liable to a fine or imprisonment.[312]

25.126 Section 351 provides for information about the appointment of an independent assessor to be made available on a website in accordance with the requirements of s 353 (paragraph 25.116 above). The information about the independent assessor required to be made available on the website is (a) the fact of his appointment, (b) his identity, (c) the text of the resolution or, as the case may be, a description of the subject matter of the poll to which his appointment relates, and (d) a copy of a report by him which complies with s 347. In the event of default in complying with ss 351 and 353 an offence is committed by every officer of the company in default and a person guilty of an offence is liable to a fine.[313] Failure to comply with ss 351 and 353 does not affect the validity of the poll or the resolution or other business (if passed or agreed) to which the poll relates.[314]

25.127 Sections 342–53 do not identify the civil consequences of a report by an independent assessor of inadequacies, unfairness, or procedural defects in the meeting or the taking of the poll.

---

[305] 2006 Act, s 348.

[306] 2006 Act, s 349(1).

[307] 2006 Act, s 349 (2) and (3). The other persons who may be required to provide information are: an employee of the company, a person holding or accountable for any of the company's records, a member of the company, and an agent of the company including the company's bankers, solicitors, and auditor.

[308] 2006 Act, s 349(4).

[309] 2006 Act, s 349(5).

[310] This is acknowledged by s 350(5).

[311] 2006 Act, s 350(3).

[312] 2006 Act, s 350(4).

[313] 2006 Act, s 351(3) and (4). The liability of an officer 'in default' is dealt with in s 1121.

[314] 2006 Act, s 351(5).

In a clear case, a member may be able to obtain a declaration that a resolution was not passed or other business not agreed. The admissibility of the report as evidence in civil proceedings is uncertain.[315] Civil proceedings following a critical report may not be needed, however, because an adverse report may have consequences for the company's listing unless changes are made to the governance of the company.

G. Records of Resolutions and Meetings

By s 355, every company must keep records comprising (a) copies of all resolutions of members passed otherwise than at general meetings (written resolutions and resolutions passed by informal unanimous consent), (b) minutes of all proceedings of general meetings, and (c) details provided to the company in accordance with s 357 of decisions of a sole member (paragraph 25.86 above); and these records must be kept for at least ten years from the date of the resolution, meeting, or decision.[316] Records of the resolutions, minutes, and details required to be kept under s 355 may be kept in hard-copy or electronic form, and may be arranged in such manner as the directors of the company think fit, provided that (a) the information in question is adequately recorded for future reference, and (b) records kept in electronic form are capable of being reproduced in hard-copy form.[317] Where those records are kept otherwise than in bound books, adequate precautions must be taken to guard against falsification, and to facilitate the discovery of falsification. Compliance with these provisions is enforced by criminal sanction. If the company fails to comply with them, an offence is committed by every officer of the company in default and a person guilty of an offence is liable to a fine.[318]

25.128

A company's articles will usually provide that a member has no right of inspection of company records except as conferred by statute or authorized by the directors or by ordinary resolution of the company.[319] But s 358 provides for the records of resolutions and meetings referred to in s 355 to be open to inspection. Those records relating to the previous ten years must be kept available for inspection at the company's registered office, or at an alternative inspection location.[320] By s 358(2) the company must give notice to the Registrar of the place at which the records are kept available for inspection, and of any change in that place, unless they have at all times been kept at the company's registered office. By s 358(3) the records must be open to the inspection of any member of the company without charge, and by s 358(4) any member may require a copy of any records on payment of such fee as may

25.129

---

[315] Cf 1985 Act, s 441(1), in relation to an inspector's report.

[316] 2006 Act, s 355(1) and (2). The main changes made by the 2006 Act in relation to records of resolutions and meetings are that s 355(2) requires records to be kept for at least ten years and that s 359 also applies Chapter 6 of the Act to meetings of a class of members. Table A, reg 100 requires the directors to cause minutes to be made in books kept for the purpose of, among other things, all proceedings at meetings of the company and of the holders of any class of shares in the company, including the names of the directors present at each such meeting.

[317] 2006 Act, s 1135(1) and (2).

[318] 2006 Act, ss 355(3)–(4) and 1135(3)–(4). The liability of an officer 'in default' is dealt with in s 1121.

[319] Table A, reg 109; Model Article (pcls) 50 and Model Article (plc) 83.

[320] Under the 2006 Act, s 1136, the Companies (Company Records) Regulations 2008 (SI 2008/3006), reg 3 provides that a company can specify a place situate in the part of the UK in which the company is registered, which is the same place for all the relevant provisions and which has been notified to the Registrar as an alternative inspection location.

be prescribed.[321] If default is made for 14 days in complying with s 358(2) or an inspection under s 358(3) is refused, or a copy requested under s 358(4) is not sent, an offence is committed by every officer of the company in default and a person guilty of an offence is liable to a fine.[322]

25.130 Where a special resolution is passed or any resolution or agreement is agreed to by all the members of a company that, if not agreed to, would not have been effective for its purpose unless passed as a special resolution, a copy of the resolution or agreement, or (in the case of a resolution or agreement that is not in writing) a written memorandum setting out its terms, must be forwarded to the Registrar within 15 days after it is passed or made.[323] If the company fails to comply with these requirements an offence is committed by the company and every officer of the company in default and a person guilty of an offence is liable to a fine.[324]

---

[321] A member may be accompanied by an adviser: *McCusker v McRrae* [1966] SC 253. The prescribed charge is 10p per 500 words or part thereof copied and the reasonable costs incurred by the company in delivering the copy; the Companies (Fees for Inspection and Copying of Company Records) Regulations 2007 (SI 2007/2612), reg 4.

[322] 2006 Act, ss 355(3)–(4), 1135(3)–(4), 1138(2)–(3). The liability of an officer 'in default' is dealt with in s 1121.

[323] 2006 Act, ss 29 and 30(1).

[324] 2006 Act, s 30(2) and (3). The liability of an officer 'in default' is dealt with in s 1121.

26

ACCOUNTING RECORDS
AND DISCLOSURE REQUIREMENTS

Stephen Robins

A. Introduction

(1) Scope of the chapter

The primary purpose of this chapter is to describe the functions, responsibilities, and liabi- **26.01**
lities of company directors in relation to accounting records, the requirements for disclosure
of annual accounts and reports, and audit (the 2006 Act, Parts 15 and 16).[1] This broad subject area breaks down into several parts.

---

[1] These provisions came into force on 6 April 2008 (2006 Act Commencement Order No 5, Art 3(1)(d)
and (e)), except for s 463 (liability for false and misleading statements in directors' report, etc), which came into
force on 20 January 2007 (2006 Act Commencement Order No 1, Art 3(1)(c)) and ss 417 (contents of directors' report) and 485–8 (appointment of auditors of private company), which came into force on 1 October
2007 (2006 Act Commencement Order No 3, Art 2(1)(g) and (h)).

(1) Section B of this chapter considers the functions, responsibilities, and liabilities of directors in connection with the 'raw materials'—ie the accounting records themselves—which must be kept by the company in accordance with the statutory provisions.

(2) Section C goes on to consider the functions, responsibilities, and liabilities of directors in connection with the forming of those raw materials into a finished product—ie the preparation of accounts and reports.

(3) Section D describes the additional transparency and disclosure obligations under FSMA, Part 6 and the Transparency and Disclosure Rules that apply to listed companies and those that issue securities which are transferable on a regulated market in the UK.[2]

(4) Section E returns to the annual accounts and considers the functions, responsibilities, and liabilities of directors in connection with the checking of the finished product, ie the audit. This is the work of auditors, who must be supplied with information by the company's directors.

(5) Finally, Section F considers the functions, responsibilities, and liabilities of directors in connection with the annual confirmation of the accuracy of information on the register kept by the registrar, which must be filed in accordance with the provisions of the 2006 Act, Part 24.[3] The annual conformation makes public information contained in the company's registers of members, directors, and secretaries, which the directors are responsible for maintaining and which have been discussed in Chapter 4, Section B(3) above.

26.02 This chapter highlights the criminal and civil liabilities of directors where there is a contravention of the provisions in Parts 15, 16, and 24. It should also be noted that one of the matters to which the court and the Secretary of State must have regard when determining whether a person's conduct as a director of one or more companies or overseas companies makes him unfit to be concerned in the management of a company, whether to make a disqualification order (and if so the period of disqualification), or to accept a disqualification undertaking is the extent of the director's responsibility for any material contravention or breach of any applicable legislative requirement,[4] which includes failure to keep proper accounting records in the place and for the duration required by the 2006 Act and failure to prepare, approve, or sign annual accounts. In practice, non-compliance with these requirements is a very common basis for a finding of unfitness warranting disqualification.[5]

(2) Key concepts

26.03 The provisions in the 2006 Act concerning accounts and reports make use of a number of concepts which are defined in that Act. The main distinctions for the purpose are: (1) the distinction between companies subject to the 'small companies regime' and those which are not subject to that regime; and (2) the distinction between 'quoted companies' and companies that are not quoted.

---

[2] Made under FSMA, ss 73A(3), 89A–G, 96A, 96B in order to give effect to the Transparency Directive (Directive 2004/109/EC).

[3] As substituted by SBEE Act 2015, s 92 with effect from 30 June 2016 and which replaced provisions about the annual return.

[4] CDDA, s 12C and Sch 1, paras 1, 6 as restated by SBEE Act 2015, s 106 with effect from 1 October 2015.

[5] See eg *Re New Generation Engineers Ltd* [1993] BCLC 435; *Secretary of State for Trade & Industry v Ettinger, Re Swift 736 Ltd* [1993] BCLC 896; *Re Firedart Ltd, Official Receiver v Fairall* [1994] 2 BCLC 340; *Secretary of State for Trade & Industry v Arif* [1997] 1 BCLC 34; *Re Galeforce Pleating Co Ltd* [1999] BCLC 704; *Re Artistic Investment Advisers Ltd* [2015] 1 BCLC 619. See further Ch 31 at paras 31.79, 116–20 below.

The small companies regime

The small companies regime applies to a company for a financial year in relation to which **26.04**
the company: (1) qualifies as small; and (2) is not excluded from the regime. Qualification
as 'small' is dealt with by the 2006 Act, s 382.[6] In summary, the company must satisfy[7] two
or more of the following requirements: (1) turnover of not more than £10.2 million, (2)
balance sheet total[8] of not more than £5.1 million, and (3) not more than 50[9] employees.[10]

A parent company will not qualify as a small company unless the group which it heads quali- **26.05**
fies as a small group.[11] A 'small group' is a group which meets two or more of the following
requirements: (1) aggregate[12] turnover of not more than £10.2 million net[13] (or £12.2 million gross);[14] (2) aggregate balance sheet total of not more than £5.1 million net (or £6.1
million gross); and (3) aggregate number of employees of not more than 50.[15]

A public company is not capable of qualifying as a small company.[16] The term 'public company' is **26.06**
defined in the 2006 Act, s 4(2). Furthermore, a company will be excluded[17] from the small companies regime if it is an authorized insurance company,[18] a banking company,[19] an e-money issuer,[20]

---

[6] As amended by the Companies Act 2006 (Amendment) (Accounts and Reports) Regulations 2008 (SI
2008/393), reg 3(1). There is also a concept of 'micro-entities' in the 2006 Act, s 384A. These are entities which
satisfy two or more of the following criteria: (a) turnover of not more than £632,000; (b) balance sheet total
of not more than £316,000; and (c) not more than ten employees. This concept, which was introduced by the
Small Companies (Micro-Entities' Accounts) Regulations 2013/3008, is not considered in detail in this work.
[7] If the company satisfies two or more of these requirements in its first financial year, it will qualify as
'small': see 2006 Act, s 382(1). A company qualifies as small in relation to a subsequent financial year if the
qualifying conditions are met in that year: see 2006 Act, s 382(1A). In relation to a subsequent financial year,
where on its balance sheet date a company meets or ceases to meet the qualifying conditions, that affects its
qualification as a small company only if it occurs in two consecutive financial years: see 2006 Act, s 382(2).
[8] The 'balance sheet total' is the aggregate of the amounts shown as assets in the company's balance sheet: see
2006 Act, s 382(5).
[9] The employee number must be the average number of persons employed by the company in the year,
determined in accordance with 2006 Act, s 382(6).
[10] Again the turnover and balance sheet total figures were updated by the Companies, Partnerships and
Groups (Accounts and Reports) Regulations 2015/980 with effect from 1 January 2016 at the latest (or 1
January 2015 if the directors so choose).
[11] 2006 Act, s 383, as amended by the Companies Act 2006 (Amendment) (Accounts and Reports)
Regulations 2008 (SI 2008/393), reg 3(2). A group qualifies as small in relation to the parent company's first
financial year if the qualifying conditions are met in that year: see 2006 Act, s 383(2). A group qualifies as small
in relation to a subsequent financial year of the parent company if the qualifying conditions are met in that
year: see 2006 Act, s 383(2A). However, in relation to a subsequent financial year of the parent company, where
on the parent company's balance sheet date the group meets or ceases to meet the qualifying conditions, that
affects the group's qualification as a small group only if it occurs in two consecutive financial years: see 2006
Act, s 383(3).
[12] Aggregate figures must be ascertained by aggregating the relevant figures determined in accordance with
2006 Act, s 382 for each member of the group.
[13] The term 'net' means after any set-offs and other adjustments made to eliminate group transactions.
[14] The term 'gross' means without the set-offs and adjustments mentioned in the preceding footnote.
[15] The turnover and balance sheet total figures were updated by the Companies, Partnerships and Groups
(Accounts and Reports) Regulations 2015/980 with effect from 1 January 2016 at the latest (or 1 January 2015
if the directors so choose).
[16] 2006 Act, s 384(1)(a).
[17] 2006 Act, s 384(1)(b).
[18] See 2006 Act, s 1165(2) for a definition of the term 'authorised insurance company'.
[19] The term 'banking company' is defined in 2006 Act, s 1164.
[20] 2006 Act, ss 474(1) and 539, which provides that an e-money issuer is (a) an electronic money institution, within the meaning of the Electronic Money Regulations 2011 (SI 2011/99), or (b) a person who has

a MiFID investment firm,[21] a UCITS management company,[22] or a company that carries on insurance market activity.[23]

26.07   The most significant exclusion from the small companies regime relates to members of ineligible groups. In short, the small companies regime will not apply to any company which is a member of an ineligible group.[24] A group will be ineligible for these purposes if any of its members is (inter alia)[25] a traded company.[26] This means that any company, however small, which forms part of a group headed by a public company, will be ineligible for the small companies regime.

Quoted companies

26.08   A quoted company is a company whose equity share capital:[27] (1) has been included in the official list[28] in accordance with the provisions of FSMA, Part 6; (2) is officially listed in an EEA state; or (3) is admitted to dealing on either the New York Stock Exchange or Nasdaq. Companies quoted on the AIM fall outside this definition. Perhaps unsurprisingly, an 'unquoted company' is 'a company that is not a quoted company'.[29]

Medium-sized companies

26.09   A company is 'medium sized' if two or more of the qualifying conditions are met; and it is not excluded from so qualifying. The qualifying conditions are: (1) turnover of not more than £36 million, (2) balance sheet total of not more than £18 million, and (3) not more than 250 employees.[30] A parent company will qualify as a medium-sized company only if the group which it heads is a 'medium-sized group'.[31] A group qualifies as 'medium sized' if two or more of the following conditions are met: (1) aggregate turnover of not more than £36 million net (or £43.2 million gross), (2) aggregate balance sheet total of not more than £18 million net (or £21.6 million gross), and (3) aggregate number of employees of not more than 250.[32]

---

permission under Part 4A of the Financial Services and Markets Act 2000 (c. 8) to carry on the activity of issuing electronic money within the meaning of article 9B of the Financial Services and Markets Act 2000 (Regulated Activities) Order 2001 (SI 2001/544).

[21]   2006 Act, ss 474(1) and 539, which explains the meaning of a MiFID investment firm.

[22]   2006 Act, ss 474(1) and 539, which provides that a UCITS management company is defined in the Glossary of the FCA Handbook.

[23]   2006 Act, s 1165(7) provides that insurance market activity has the meaning given in FSMA, s 316(3).

[24]   2006 Act, s 384(1)(c).

[25]   A group will also be ineligible if any of its members is a body corporate (other than a company) whose shares are admitted to trading on a regulated market in an EEA state, a person (other than a small company) who has permission under FSMA, Part 4A to carry on a regulated activity, a small company that is an authorized insurance company, a banking company, an e-money issuer, a MiFID investment firm or a UCITS management company, or a person who carried on insurance market activity; see 2006 Act, s 384(2)(b), (c), (d), (e).

[26]   2006 Act, s 384(2)(a), as amended by the Companies, Partnerships and Groups (Accounts and Reports) Regulations 2015/980, reg 4(5)(b).

[27]   2006 Act, s 385(1) and (2). The term 'equity share capital' is defined by 2006 Act, s 548 to mean a company's entire issued share capital excluding any part which has limits on the right to participate in a distribution by way of dividend or capital.

[28]   The term 'official list' has the meaning given by FSMA, s 103(1).

[29]   2006 Act, s 385(3).

[30]   2006 Act, s 465 (as amended by the Companies, Partnerships and Groups (Accounts and Reports) Regulations 2015/980). The 'balance sheet total' is the aggregate of the amounts shown as assets in the company's balance sheet; see 2006 Act, s 465(5).

[31]   2006 Act, s 466(1).

[32]   2006 Act, s 466(4) (as amended by the Companies, Partnerships and Groups (Accounts and Reports) Regulations 2015/980). By s 466(5) the aggregate figures are to be ascertained by aggregating the relevant

Public companies are expressly precluded from being medium-sized companies.[33] Further 26.10
exclusions relate to companies which have permission under FSMA, Part 4A to carry on a
regulated activity or which carry on insurance market activity.[34]

Equally significant is the fact that a company cannot be a medium-sized company if it is a 26.11
member of an ineligible group.[35] A group will be ineligible if any of its members is (inter
alia) a traded company.[36] As with the small companies regime, this means that any company
which is a member of a group headed by a public company may not take the benefit of any
provision relating to medium-sized companies.

Officer in default

The provisions of the 2006 Act, concerning accounting records, transparency, and disclo- 26.12
sure are enforced through contravention being made a criminal offence. In many cases the
offence may be committed by an 'officer in default'. The 2006 Act, s 1121 provides that
an officer includes any director, manager, or secretary and that an officer is in default if 'he
authorizes or permits or participates in, or fails to take all reasonable steps to prevent, the
contravention'. Where a company is an officer of another company, it does not commit an
offence as an officer in default unless one of its officers is in default; in which case its own
officer personally commits an offence.[37] For further discussion about a director's criminal
liability, reference should be made to Chapter 35, Section I.

B. Accounting Records

(1) Introduction

It is essential for the officers of a company to ensure that the company maintains proper 26.13
accounting records so that business decisions are made on the basis of reliable information and so that, if the business fails, the liquidator's administration of the winding up is
facilitated.[38] Provisions designed to ensure that proper records are kept may now be found
in the 2006 Act, Part 15, Chapter 2. The importance of these provisions was emphasized by
Chadwick J in *Secretary of State for Trade and Industry v Arif*:[39]

> [This legislation] has, at the least, two purposes. First, to ensure that those who are concerned
> in the direction and management of companies which trade with the privilege of limited
> liability do maintain sufficient accounting records to enable them to know what the position

---

figures for each member of the group. By s 466(6) the term 'net' means after any set-offs and other adjustments
made to eliminate group transactions and the term 'gross' means without such set-offs or adjustments.

[33] 2006 Act, s 467(1)(a).

[34] 2006 Act, ss 467(1)(b) and 1165(7) (see para 26.06 above).

[35] 2006 Act, s 467(1)(c).

[36] 2006 Act, s 467(1)(a). A group will also be ineligible if any of its members is a body corporate (other than
a company) whose shares are admitted to trading on a regulated market in an EEA state, a person (other than a
small company) who has permission under FSMA, Part 4A to carry on a regulated activity, an e-money issuer,
a small company that is an authorized insurance company, a banking company, a MiFID investment firm or a
UCITS management company, or a person who carries on insurance market activity: see 2006 Act, s 467(2)(b),
(c), (ca), (d), (e) and para 26.06 above.

[37] 2006 Act, s 1122.

[38] *Secretary of State for Trade and Industry v Arif* [1997] 1 BCLC 34; see also *Re Firedart Ltd, Official Receiver
v Fairall* [1994] 2 BCLC 340.

[39] [1997] 1 BCLC 34.

of the company is from time to time. Without that information, they cannot act responsibly in making decisions whether to continue trading. But equally important is a second purpose. If the company fails, a licensed insolvency practitioner will become office holder; as liquidator or as administrator or as administrative receiver. The office holder requires information as to the company's trading and transactions which is sufficient to enable him to identify and recover or exploit the company's assets. His task is made extremely difficult, if not impossible, if the company has failed to comply with its obligations under [the legislation].

26.14 The importance of the requirement to keep proper accounting records is emphasized by the criminal penalties imposed for non-compliance with these provisions, and also by the 2006 Act, s 498(1), which requires a company's auditors to form an opinion as to whether adequate accounting records have been kept by the company.[40] If the auditor is of the opinion that adequate accounting records have not been kept, he is required to state that fact in his report.[41]

(2) Duty to keep accounting records

26.15 Every company is required to keep adequate accounting records.[42] The accounting records must be sufficient to show and explain the company's transactions;[43] to disclose with reasonable accuracy, at any time, the financial position of the company at that time;[44] and to enable the company's directors to ensure that any accounts required to be prepared comply with the requirements of the 2006 Act.[45] The term 'accounting records' is broadly expressed and will encompass, for example, purchase invoices, sales invoices, paying-in books, and bank statements; and documents do not cease to be accounting records simply because their contents have been summarized or included in another document such as the final accounts.[46] The obligation is to ensure that the accounting records disclose the financial position at any time; in other words, they must be up to date to the current time.

26.16 It is also necessary for tax purposes, under the Finance Act 2009, for every qualifying company to appoint a 'senior accounting officer' (defined in Sch 46, para 16 as 'the director or officer who, in the company's reasonable opinion, has overall responsibility for the company's financial accounting arrangements'). The senior accounting officer of a qualifying company must take reasonable steps to ensure that the company establishes and maintains appropriate tax accounting arrangements. The senior accounting officer of a qualifying company must, in particular, take reasonable steps: (1) to monitor the accounting arrangements of the company, and (2) to identify any respects in which those arrangements are not appropriate tax accounting arrangements.

Contents of accounting records

26.17 A company's accounting records must, in particular, contain: (1) entries from day to day of all sums of money received and expended by the company and the matters in respect of

---

[40] 2006 Act, s 498(1)(a).

[41] 2006 Act, s 498(2).

[42] 2006 Act, s 386(1).

[43] 2006 Act, s 386(2)(a). See also *R v BAE Systems plc* [2010] EW Misc 16 (CC).

[44] 2006 Act, s 386(2)(b).

[45] 2006 Act, s 386(2)(c). In the case of 'publicly traded' companies, the accounting records must also be sufficient to ensure that consolidated accounts are prepared in accordance with Art 4 of the IAS Regulation: see Regulation (EC) No 1606/2002 of the European Parliament and of the Council of 19 July 2002 on the application of international accounting standards.

[46] *DTC (CNC) Ltd v Gary Sargeant & Co* [1996] 1 BCLC 529.

which the receipt and expenditure takes place; and (2) a record of the assets and liabilities of the company.[47] If the company's business involves dealing in goods, the accounting records must also contain: (1) statements of stock held by the company at the end of each financial year, (2) all statements of stocktaking from which any statement of stock has been or is to be prepared, and (3) except in the case of goods sold by way of ordinary retail trade, statements of all goods sold and purchased, showing the goods and the buyers and sellers in sufficient detail to enable them to be identified.[48]

Where and for how long records must be kept

A company's accounting records must be kept at its registered office or such other place as the directors think fit and must at all times be open to inspection by the company's officers.[49] If a company's accounting records are kept outside the UK, it will be necessary for all accounts and returns to be sent to, and kept at, a place in the UK, and the accounts and returns must at all times be open to inspection by the company's officers.[50] The accounts and returns sent to the UK must be such as to: (1) disclose with reasonable accuracy the financial position of the business at intervals of not more than six months and (2) enable the directors to ensure that the accounts required to be prepared comply with the requirements of the 2006 Act and, where applicable, Article 4 of the IAS Regulation.[51]   **26.18**

In the case of a private company, accounting records must be kept for three years from the date on which they are made.[52] In the case of a public company, accounting records must be kept for six years from the date on which they are made.[53]   **26.19**

Computerized records

The 2006 Act, s 1135(1) provides that a company's accounting records may be kept in hard-copy or electronic form, provided the information in question is adequately recorded for future reference. However, where accounting records are kept in electronic form, they must be capable of being reproduced in hard-copy form.[54]   **26.20**

Delivery of records to liquidator or administrator

It should be noted that additional requirements are imposed in the event of the company going into administration, administrative receivership, liquidation or, provisional liquidation.[55] In such circumstances, any officer or former officer of the company who has in his possession or control any books, papers, or records to which the company appears to be   **26.21**

---

[47] 2006 Act, s 386(3).
[48] 2006 Act, s 386(4).
[49] 2006 Act, s 388(1). A director has a common law right to apply to the court for an order requiring the company to make its accounting records available to him: *McCusker v Rae* (1966) SC 253; *Conway v Petronius Clothing Co Ltd* [1978] 1 WLR 72; *Berlei Hestia (NZ) Ltd v Fernyhough* [1980] 2 NZLR 150; *Wuu Khek Chiang George v ECRC Land Pte Ltd* [1999] 3 SLR 65; *Oxford Legal Group Ltd v Sibbasbridge Services plc* [2008] 2 BCLC 381, CA. However, neither the director's right under 2006 Act, s 388 to inspect the company's accounting records nor his common law right to obtain access to records oblige the company to 'answer what are in effect interrogatories arising out of the documents they have produced. The obligation is to permit inspection of documents, not to provide a narrative account of the events which the documents record': *Kang v Kang* [2013] EWHC 2828 (Ch) at para 16, per Norris J.
[50] 2006 Act, s 388(2).
[51] 2006 Act, s 388(3).
[52] 2006 Act, s 388(4)(a).
[53] 2006 Act, s 388(4)(b).
[54] 2006 Act, s 1135(2).
[55] Insolvency Act, s 234(1). See Ch 33, Section G(3) below.

entitled, or which relate to the promotion, formation, business, dealings, affairs, or property of the company, may be ordered by the court to deliver the relevant books, papers, or records to the administrator, administrative receiver, liquidator, or provisional liquidator (as the case may be).[56]

(3) Liabilities of directors in relation to accounting records

Criminal sanctions

26.22   If a company fails to keep accounting records in the form and place required by the 2006 Act, an offence is committed by every officer of the company who is in default.[57] It is a defence for a person charged with such an offence to show that he acted honestly and that in the circumstances in which the company's business was carried on such default was excusable.[58] If a company fails to keep accounting records for the duration required by the 2006 Act, an officer of the company commits an offence if he fails to take all reasonable steps for ensuring compliance with the statutory requirements.[59] The penalty for any of these offences is, on conviction on indictment, imprisonment for a term not exceeding two years or a fine or both, and, on summary conviction, imprisonment for a term not exceeding 12 months or a fine not exceeding the statutory maximum.[60]

26.23   In addition, where a company keeps accounting records in electronic form which are not capable of being reproduced in hard-copy form, an offence is committed by every officer in default.[61] The offence is triable summarily and the penalty is a fine not exceeding level 3 on the standard scale and, for continued contravention, a daily default fine not exceeding one-tenth of level 3 on the standard scale.

26.24   There are additional criminal sanctions in the event that the company is wound up. An offence is deemed to have been committed by any past or present officer who, within the period of 12 months prior to, or after, its commencement (i) conceals, destroys, mutilates or falsifies any book or paper affecting or relating to the company's property or affairs, (ii) makes any false entry in any book or paper affecting or relating to the company's property or affairs, or (iii) fraudulently parts with, alters, or makes any omission in any document affecting or relating to the company's property or affairs, or who is privy to the doing by others of any of those things.[62]

Civil liability for wrongful trading

26.25   If a company fails to keep adequate accounting records, the directors of that company may have no reliable means of assessing the company's financial position and may continue trading when in fact there is no reasonable prospect of the company avoiding insolvent liquidation. In those circumstances, in the event of the company being wound up, the directors will face the prospect of civil liability to contribute to the company's assets under the Insolvency Act, s 214.'

---

[56] Insolvency Act, ss 234(2) and 235(2)–(3).
[57] 2006 Act, ss 387(1) and 389(1). For 'officer in default', see para 26.12 above.
[58] 2006 Act, ss 387(2) and 389(2).
[59] 2006 Act, s 389(3).
[60] 2006 Act, ss 387(3) and 389(4).
[61] 2006 Act, s 1135(2), (3). For 'officer in default', see para 26.12 above.
[62] Insolvency Act, s 206. 'Book or paper' includes electronic records: *R v Taylor* [2011] 1 WLR 1809, CA. See further Ch 35, Section J(3) below, where this and other offences under the Insolvency Act are discussed.

The knowledge to be imputed in testing whether or not directors knew or ought to have **26.26** concluded that there was no reasonable prospect of the company avoiding insolvent liquidation is not limited to the documentary material actually available at the given time, but will include any information which, given reasonable diligence and an appropriate level of general knowledge, skill, and experience, would have been ascertainable by the company's directors.[63]

C. Annual Accounts and Reports

(1) Introduction

This section deals with the functions, responsibilities, and liabilities of company directors in **26.27** relation to annual accounts and reports, including: (1) the preparation of annual accounts; (2) the directors' report; (3) in the case of quoted companies, the directors' remuneration report; (4) the duty to publish accounts and reports; (5) in the case of public companies, the laying of accounts before general meeting; (6) in the case of quoted companies, approval of the directors' remuneration report; (7) the filing of accounts and reports; and (8) the revision of defective accounts and reports.

(2) Preparation of annual accounts

The 2006 Act, ss 390–414 require companies to prepare individual accounts and, in the case **26.28** of parent companies which are not subject to the small companies regime or able to take the benefit of any exemption, group accounts. These sections establish three core principles with regard to a company's or group's financial statements. First, they must comply with specific statutory requirements as to disclosure, format, and accounting principles. Secondly, the balance sheets and profit and loss accounts must give a 'true and fair view' of the company's or group's financial position and its profit or loss for a given period. Thirdly, within a group of companies, accounting standards should prima facie be consistently applied.

Duty to prepare individual accounts

The directors of every company must prepare accounts for the company for each of its **26.29** financial years[64] unless the company is exempt as a dormant subsidiary.[65] The accounts may either be prepared in accordance with the 2006 Act or IAS.[66] The former are referred to as 'Companies Act individual accounts' and the latter as 'IAS individual accounts'. Once a company has switched to IAS, all subsequent accounts must be prepared in accordance with IAS unless there is a 'relevant change of circumstance'.[67] There are also rules on consistency within groups. A company's financial year must be determined in accordance with the 2006

---

[63] *Re Produce Marketing Consortium Ltd (No 2)* [1989] BCLC 520. See further Ch 34, Section C(3) below.

[64] 2006 Act, s 394.

[65] 2006 Act, s 394A contains a conditional exemption for certain dormant subsidiaries. For a list of companies which are automatically excluded from the dormant subsidiaries exemption, see 2006 Act, s 394B.

[66] 2006 Act, s 474(1) refers to the definition in the IAS Regulation (EC) 1606/2002. This includes International Accounting Standards, International Financial Reporting Standards, and related interpretations (SICs or IFRICs) issued or adopted by the International Accounting Standards Board and adopted by the European Commission in accordance with the IAS Regulation.

[67] 2006 Act, s 395(4) provides that there is a 'relevant change of circumstance' if, broadly, the company becomes the subsidiary of another undertaking that does not prepare IAS consolidated accounts or the company (or its parent undertaking) ceases to have securities admitted to trading on a regulated market in the EEA.

Act, s 390. In summary, it will be the same as the company's accounting period,[68] subject to the directors' discretion to alter the last day of the period by plus or minus seven days. The duty to prepare accounts is an obligation of the directors and the duty is owed to the company and not to individual shareholders.[69]

Requirement for individual accounts to show a true and fair view

26.30 The directors of a company must not approve a company's individual accounts (whether Companies Act or IAS individual accounts) unless they are satisfied that they give a true and fair view of the company's assets, liabilities, financial position, and profit or loss.[70] Ultimately this will be a matter of judgment; there may be more than one method of presenting the financial position of a company in a way which is true and fair.[71] It is for the courts to decide in any given case whether the accounts do give a true and fair view. However, in deciding this question the courts look for guidance to the ordinary practices of accountants and in particular to the standards published by the relevant professional body. These published standards not only guide accountants in the preparation of accounts but also mould the expectations of those who read or use the accounts. Therefore compliance with professional standards is prima facie evidence that the accounts present a true and fair view of the assets and liabilities of the company or the group. Deviation from accepted accounting principles is prima facie evidence that the accounts do not present a true and fair view of the assets and liabilities of the company or the group.[72] For this reason, the obligation to give a true and fair view means that a company should follow any applicable accounting standard, unless there is a good reason not to do so.[73]

Contents of individual accounts

26.31 A company's individual accounts must contain a balance sheet as at the last day of the financial year and a profit and loss account.[74] In relation to Companies Act individual accounts, the balance sheet must give a true and fair view of the state of affairs of the company as at the end of the financial year and the profit and loss account must give a true and fair view of the profit or loss of the company for the financial year.[75] IAS individual accounts must achieve a fair presentation. If in any financial year a company is or has been party to arrangements that

---

[68] 2006 Act, s 391.

[69] *Devlin v Slough Estates Ltd* [1983] BCLC 497.

[70] 2006 Act, s 393(1). This provision helps to reinforce the true and fair concept for companies who prepare their accounts using IAS. IAS 1.13 requires accounts to achieve a fair presentation but does not use the 'true and fair' formulation. Particular rules apply in the case of micro-entities: see 2006 Act, s 393(1A). See *BTI 2014 LLC v Sequana SA* [2016] EWHC 1686 (Ch) at paras 370–81, 432–5 for discussion about true and fair view of contingent liabilities and relevance of professional advice.

[71] *Devlin v Slough Estates Ltd* [1983] BCLC 497 at 503. See also Financial Reporting Council, *True and Fair* (FRC, July 2011) and *DE&ES Bauunternehmung v Finanzamt Bergheim* (Case C-275/97) [2000] BCC 757.

[72] *Macquarie Internationale Investments Ltd v Glencore UK Ltd (No 2)* [2011] 1 BCLC 561, CA at paras 50–6.

[73] *Lloyd Cheyham & Co Ltd v Littlejohn & Co* [1987] BCLC 303. See also *Odeon Associated Theatres v Jones (Inspector of Taxes)* [1971] 1 WLR 442; *Gallagher v Jones (Inspector of Taxes)* [1994] Ch 107; *Revenue and Customs Commissioners v William Grant & Sons Distillers Ltd* [2007] 1 WLR 1448, HL; and *Macquarie Internationale Investments Ltd v Glencore UK Ltd (No 2)* [2011] 1 BCLC 561, CA at paras 50–6.

[74] 2006 Act, s 396(1).

[75] 2006 Act, s 396(2). See The Small Companies and Groups (Accounts and Directors' Reports) Regulations (SI 2008/409) and The Large and Medium-Sized Companies and Groups (Accounts and Reports) Regulations (SI 2008/410), both made under s 396(3) and other sections. In the case of the individual accounts of a company which qualifies as a micro-entity in relation to the financial year (see 2006 Act, ss 384A and 384B), the micro-entity minimum accounting items included in the company's accounts for the year are presumed to give the true and fair view required by subsection (2): 2006 Act, s 396(2A).

are not reflected in its balance sheet and at the balance sheet date the risks or benefits arising from those arrangements are material, information in respect of the nature and business purpose of the arrangements (and, in the case of any company which is not subject to the small companies regime, the financial impact of the arrangements on the company) must be given in notes to the company's annual accounts.[76]

The notes to a company's annual accounts must disclose the average number of persons **26.32** employed by the company in the financial year; and, in the case of a company not subject to the small companies regime, the notes to the company's accounts must also disclose the average number of persons within each category of persons so employed.[77] Except in the case of a company subject to the small companies regime, the notes to the company's annual accounts or the profit and loss account must disclose, with reference to all persons employed by the company during the financial year, the total staff costs of the company relating to the financial year broken down between (a) wages and salaries paid or payable in respect of that year to those persons, (b) social security costs incurred by the company on their behalf, and (c) other pension costs so incurred.[78]

The notes to a company's annual accounts must give information about directors' remunera- **26.33** tion and other benefits including (i) gains from the exercise of share options, (ii) benefits received or receivable under long-term incentive schemes, (iii) payments for loss of office as defined by the 2006 Act, s 215, (iv) benefits receivable, and contributions for the purpose of providing benefits, in respect of past services of a person as a director or in any other capacity while director, and (v) consideration paid to or receivable by third parties for making available the services of a person as director or in any other capacity while director.[79] A director and any person who was a director within the preceding five years has a duty to give notice to the company of such matters relating to himself as may be necessary for the notes to the company's accounts to give the required information.[80] Failure to comply with this obligation is an offence.[81]

In the case of a company which does not prepare group accounts, details of advances and **26.34** credits granted by the company to its directors, and guarantees of any kind entered into by the company on behalf of its directors, must be shown in the notes to the individual accounts.[82]

---

[76] 2006 Act, s 410A.

[77] 2006 Act, s 411(1), (1A).

[78] 2006 Act, s 411(5).

[79] 2006 Act, s 412(1), (2). For small companies the detailed information is set out in the Small Companies and Groups (Accounts and Directors' Reports) Regulations (SI 2008/409), reg 5 and Sch 3, which contains provisions about total amount of directors' remuneration, compensation for loss of office and sums paid to third parties in respect of directors' services. For large and medium-sized companies the detailed information is set out in the Large and Medium-Sized Companies and Groups (Accounts and Reports) Regulations (SI 2008/410), reg 8 and Sch 5, which contains (i) provisions about the total amount of directors' remuneration which apply to both quoted and unquoted companies, and (ii) provisions about information about highest paid director's emoluments, excess retirement benefits, compensation for loss of office and sums paid to third parties in respect of directors' services, which apply only to unquoted companies. If the requirements of these regulations are not complied with in the annual accounts, the auditor must include in his report, so far as he is reasonably able to do so, a statement giving the required particulars: 2006 Act, s 498(4).

[80] 2006 Act, s 412(5).

[81] 2006 Act, s 412(6).

[82] 2006 Act, s 413(1). See *Disclosure of Loans to Directors in Company Accounts* (DBIS, 2009).

Preparation of group accounts

26.35 If a parent company is subject to the small companies regime, the preparation of group accounts is optional.[83] Where the parent company is neither subject to the small companies regime nor otherwise exempt, the preparation of group accounts is mandatory, and, in addition to the preparation of the parent company's individual accounts, the directors are expressly required to prepare group accounts at the end of every financial year, unless the company is exempt.[84] A company is exempt from the requirement to prepare group accounts if (a) it would be subject to the small companies regime but for being a public company, and (b) it is not a traded company.[85] Further exemptions are located in s 400 (company included in the EEA accounts of larger group), s 401 (company included in non-EEA accounts of larger group), and s 402 (company none of whose subsidiary undertakings need be included in consolidation). Group accounts of UK publicly traded companies[86] are required by Article 4 of the IAS Regulation to be prepared in accordance with IAS (IAS group accounts). The group accounts of other companies may be prepared in accordance with the 2006 Act (Companies Act group accounts) or IAS.[87] Once a parent company has switched to IAS in its group accounts, all subsequent accounts must be prepared in accordance with IAS unless there is a 'relevant change of circumstance'.[88] There are also rules on consistency within groups.

Subsidiary undertakings to be included in group accounts

26.36 Where a parent company prepares group accounts, all the subsidiary undertakings of the company must be included in the consolidation,[89] unless: (1) the inclusion of the subsidiary undertaking is not material for the purposes of giving a true and fair view;[90] or (2) severe long-term restrictions substantially hinder the exercise of the rights of the parent company over the assets or management of that undertaking;[91] or (3) extremely rare circumstances mean that the information necessary for the preparation of group accounts cannot be obtained without disproportionate expense or undue delay;[92] or (4) the interest of the parent company is held exclusively with a view to subsequent resale.[93]

---

[83] 2006 Act, s 398.

[84] 2006 Act, s 399(1), (2).

[85] 2006 Act, s 399(2A).

[86] UK-incorporated companies whose securities are admitted to trading on an EU-regulated market such as the FSA's Official List.

[87] The AIM Rules require parent companies incorporated in the UK to prepare their consolidated accounts in accordance with IAS for financial years commencing on or after 1 January 2007.

[88] 2006 Act, s 403(5). There is a relevant change of circumstance if, broadly, the company becomes a subsidiary undertaking of another undertaking that does not prepare IAS group accounts, or if the company (or its parent undertaking) ceases to be an undertaking with securities admitted to trading on a regulated market in the EEA. After a financial year in which the directors of a parent company prepare IAS group accounts for the company, the directors may change to preparing Companies Act group accounts for a reason other than a relevant change of circumstance provided they have not changed to Companies Act group accounts in the period of five years preceding the first day of that financial year: 2006 Act, s 403(5A). In calculating the five-year period for the purpose of subsection (5A), no account should be taken of a change due to a relevant change of circumstance: 2006 Act, s 403(5B).

[89] 2006 Act, s 405(1).

[90] 2006 Act, s 405(2). Note that two or more undertakings may be excluded only if they are not material taken together.

[91] 2006 Act, s 405(3)(a).

[92] 2006 Act, s 405(3)(b).

[93] 2006 Act, s 405(3)(c).

Requirement for group accounts to show a true and fair view

The directors must not approve group accounts unless they are satisfied that they give a true **26.37** and fair view (as discussed in paragraph 26.30 above) of the assets, liabilities, financial position, and profit or loss of the undertakings included in the consolidation as a whole, so far as concerns members of the company.[94]

Contents of group accounts

Companies Act group accounts must comprise a consolidated balance sheet dealing with **26.38** the state of affairs of the parent company and its subsidiary undertakings and a consolidated profit and loss account dealing with the profit or loss of the parent company and its subsidiary undertakings.[95] The accounts must give a true and fair view of the state of affairs as at the end of the financial year, and the profit or loss for the financial year, of the undertakings included in the consolidation as a whole, so far as concerns members of the company.[96] IAS accounts must achieve a fair presentation.

The notes to group accounts must give the information about directors' remuneration and **26.39** other benefits described in paragraph 26.33 above.[97]

In the case of a parent company that prepares group accounts, details of any advances and **26.40** credits granted to the directors of the parent company by that company or by any of its subsidiary undertakings and any guarantees of any kind entered into on behalf of the directors of the parent company by that company or by any of its subsidiary undertakings must be shown in the notes to the group accounts.[98]

Consistency of financial reporting within group

The directors of a parent company must secure that the individual accounts of the parent **26.41** company and each of its subsidiary undertakings are all prepared using the same financial reporting framework, ie UK GAAP, or IAS, except to the extent that in the opinion of the directors there are good reasons for not doing so.[99] However, a parent company that prepares both individual and group accounts using IAS is not required to ensure that all its subsidiary undertakings use IAS, provided that they all use the same framework.[100]

Approval and signing of accounts

A company's annual accounts must be approved by the board of directors and signed on **26.42** behalf of the board by a director of the company.[101] The signature must appear on the company's balance sheet.[102] If the accounts are prepared in accordance with the provisions applicable to companies subject to the small companies regime or the micro-entity provisions,

[94] 2006 Act, s 393(1)(b); where group accounts are prepared in accordance with IAS, this is helpful to reinforce the true and fair standard.

[95] 2006 Act, s 404(1).

[96] 2006 Act, s 404(2).

[97] 2006 Act, s 412(1), (2). For small companies' group accounts the detailed information is set out in the Small Companies and Groups (Accounts and Directors' Reports) Regulations (SI 2008/409), reg 9 and Sch 3. For large and medium-sized companies' group accounts the detailed information is set out in the Large and Medium-Sized Companies and Groups (Accounts and Reports) Regulations (SI 2008/410), reg 8 and Sch 5.

[98] 2006 Act, s 413(2).

[99] 2006 Act, s 407.

[100] 2006 Act, s 407(5).

[101] 2006 Act, s 414(1).

[102] 2006 Act, s 414(2).

the balance sheet must contain a statement to that effect in a prominent position above the signature.[103]

Criminal liability of directors

26.43   If annual accounts are approved that do not comply with the requirements of the 2006 Act (and, where applicable, the requirements of the IAS Regulation), every director of the company who knew that they did not comply, or was reckless as to whether they complied, and failed to take reasonable steps to secure compliance with those requirements or, as the case may be, to prevent the accounts from being approved, commits an offence.[104] A person guilty of any such offence is liable on conviction on indictment, to a fine, or, on summary conviction, to a fine not exceeding the statutory maximum.[105]

(3) The strategic report

26.44   The directors of a company must prepare a strategic report for each financial year of the company.[106] For a financial year in which (a) the company is a parent company, and (b) the directors of the company prepare group accounts, the strategic report must be a consolidated report (a 'group strategic report') relating to the undertakings included in the consolidation.[107]

26.45   The purpose of the strategic report is to inform members of the company and help them assess how the directors have performed their duty under s 172 (duty to promote the success of the company).[108]

26.46   Accordingly the strategic report must contain (a) a fair review of the company's business, and (b) a description of the principal risks and uncertainties facing the company.[109] The review required is a balanced and comprehensive analysis of (a) the development and performance of the company's business during the financial year, and (b) the position of the company's business at the end of that year, consistent with the size and complexity of the business.[110] The review must, to the extent necessary for an understanding of the development, performance, or position of the company's business, include (a) analysis using financial key performance indicators, and (b) where appropriate, analysis using other key performance indicators, including information relating to environmental matters and employee matters.[111] The report must, where appropriate, include references to, and additional explanations of, amounts included in the company's annual accounts.[112]

---

[103]   2006 Act, s 414(3).

[104]   2006 Act, s 414(4).

[105]   2006 Act, s 414(5).

[106]   2006 Act, s 414A(1). This requirement does not apply if the company is entitled to the small companies exemption.

[107]   2006 Act, s 414A(3). A group strategic report may, where appropriate, give greater emphasis to the matters that are significant to the undertakings included in the consolidation, taken as a whole.

[108]   2006 Act, s 414C(1).

[109]   2006 Act, s 414C(2).

[110]   2006 Act, s 414C(3).

[111]   2006 Act, s 414C(4). In this context, 'key performance indicators' means factors by reference to which the development, performance, or position of the company's business can be measured effectively. It should be noted that, where a company qualifies as medium-sized in relation to a financial year (see the 2006 Act, ss 465–7), the review for the year need not comply with the requirements of s 414C(4) so far as they relate to non-financial information.

[112]   2006 Act, s 414C(12).

In the case of a quoted company the strategic report must, to the extent necessary for an **26.47** understanding of the development, performance, or position of the company's business, include (a) the main trends and factors likely to affect the future development, performance, and position of the company's business, and (b) information about (i) environmental matters (including the impact of the company's business on the environment), (ii) the company's employees, and (iii) social, community, and human rights issues, including information about any policies of the company in relation to those matters and the effectiveness of those policies.[113] In the case of a quoted company the strategic report must also include (a) a description of the company's strategy, (b) a description of the company's business model, (c) a breakdown showing at the end of the financial year (i) the number of persons of each sex who were directors of the company; (ii) the number of persons of each sex who were senior managers of the company (other than persons falling within sub-paragraph (i)); and (iii) the number of persons of each sex who were employees of the company.[114]

In the case of failure to comply with the requirement to prepare a strategic report, an **26.48** offence is committed by every person who (a) was a director of the company immediately before the end of the period for filing accounts and reports for the financial year in question, and (b) failed to take all reasonable steps for securing compliance with that requirement.[115]

(4) The directors' report

The directors of a company are required to prepare a directors' report for each financial **26.49** year of the company,[116] unless it is exempt as a small company[117] or a micro-entity.[118] Where a parent company prepares group accounts, the directors' report must be a consolidated report (a 'group directors' report') relating to the undertakings included in the consolidation.[119] A group directors' report may, where appropriate, give greater emphasis to the matters that are significant to the undertakings included in the consolidation, taken as a whole.[120]

Contents of directors' report

The directors' report must state the names of the persons who, at any time during the financial **26.50** year, were directors of the company.[121] Except in the case of companies entitled to the small companies exemption, the directors' report must also state the amount (if any) which is recommended by the directors to be paid by way of dividend.[122]

---

[113] 2006 Act, s 414C(7).
[114] 2006 Act, s 414C(8).
[115] 2006 Act, s 414A(5).
[116] 2006 Act, s 415(1). A person guilty of such an offence under this section is liable (a) on conviction on indictment, to a fine; (b) on summary conviction, to a fine not exceeding the statutory maximum.
[117] 2006 Act, s 415A.
[118] 2006 Act, s 415(1A).
[119] 2006 Act, s 415(2).
[120] 2006 Act, s 415(3).
[121] 2006 Act, s 416(1)(a). See the Small Companies and Groups (Accounts and Directors' Reports) Regulations (SI 2008/409) and the Large and Medium-Sized Companies and Groups (Accounts and Reports) Regulations (SI 2008/410), both made under s 416(4) and other sections.
[122] 2006 Act, s 416(3).

26.51   The directors' report of a small company must also disclose information about (i) political donations and expenditure, (ii) charitable donations, (iii) employment of disabled persons, and (iv) acquisition by the company of its own shares.[123]

26.52   The directors' report of a large or medium-sized company must disclose the information mentioned in the preceding paragraph and also information about (i) asset values, (ii) financial instruments, (iii) miscellaneous matters (important events affecting the company, future developments, an indication of research and development activities and foreign branches), (iv) employee involvement, and (v) the policy and practice on payment of creditors.[124]

26.53   The directors' report of a quoted company whose equity securities are admitted to trading on a regulated market must disclose, in addition to the matters in the preceding paragraph, further detailed information about or affecting its capital and securities, including the following matters about directors: (i) any rules that the company has about appointment and replacement of directors, (ii) the powers of the company's directors, including in particular any powers in relation to the issuing or buying back by the company of its shares, and (iii) any agreements between the company and its directors or employees providing for compensation for loss of office or employment that occurs because of a takeover bid.[125]

26.54   Unless a company is exempt from audit and the directors have taken advantage of that exemption, the directors' report must also contain a statement to the effect that, in the case of each of the persons who are directors at the time the report is approved, (1) so far as each director is aware, there is no information required by the auditor in connection with preparing his report of which the company's auditor is unaware, and (2) each director has taken all the steps that he ought to have taken as a director in order to make himself aware of any such information and to establish that the company's auditor is aware of that information.[126]

Approval and signing of directors' report

26.55   The directors' report must be approved by the board of directors and it must be signed on behalf of the board by a director or, alternatively, by the company secretary.[127] If the report is prepared in accordance with the small companies regime, it must contain a statement to that effect in a prominent position above the signature.[128] If there is a separate corporate governance statement (ie one which is not included in the directors' report), it must be approved by the board of directors and signed on behalf of the board by a director or the secretary of the company.[129]

Criminal liability of directors

26.56   In the case of failure to comply with the requirement to prepare a directors' report, an offence is committed by every person who was a director of the company immediately before the end

---

[123] 2006 Act, s 416(4); the Small Companies and Groups (Accounts and Directors' Report) Regulations 2008 (SI 2008/409), reg 7 and Sch 5.

[124] 2006 Act, s 416(4); the Large and Medium-Sized Companies and Groups (Accounts and Reports) Regulations (SI 2008/410), reg 10 and Sch 7, Parts 1–5.

[125] 2006 Act, s 416(4); the Large and Medium-Sized Companies and Groups (Accounts and Reports) Regulations (SI 2008/410), reg 10 and Sch 7, Part 6.

[126] 2006 Act, s 418(1), (2).

[127] 2006 Act, s 419(1).

[128] 2006 Act, s 419(2).

[129] 2006 Act, s 419A. A 'corporate governance statement' is a statement required by rules 7.2.1 to 7.2.11 in the Disclosure Rules and Transparency Rules sourcebook issued by the FCA: 2006 Act, s 472A(1).

of the period for filing accounts and reports for the financial year in question and who failed to take all reasonable steps for securing compliance with that requirement.[130] The penalty for such an offence is a fine on conviction on indictment or a fine not exceeding the statutory maximum on summary conviction.[131]

Where a directors' report contains a statement that the auditor is aware of all relevant audit **26.57** information and that the director has taken all the steps that he ought to have taken as a director in order to make himself aware of all relevant audit information and to establish that the company's auditor is aware of it, but the statement is false, every director of the company who knew that the statement was false (or was reckless as to whether it was false) and failed to take reasonable steps to prevent the report from being approved, commits an offence[132] punishable on conviction on indictment to imprisonment for a term not exceeding two years or a fine or both or on summary conviction to imprisonment for a term not exceeding 12 months or to a fine not exceeding the statutory maximum or both.[133]

If a directors' report is approved which does not comply with the statutory requirements **26.58** imposed by the 2006 Act, ss 415–19, every director of the company who knew that it did not comply (or was reckless as to whether it complied) and failed to take reasonable steps to ensure compliance with those requirements or, as the case may be, to prevent the report from being approved, commits an offence[134] punishable on conviction on indictment by a fine or on summary conviction by a fine not exceeding the statutory maximum.[135]

Civil liability of directors

Pursuant to the 2006 Act, s 463, if a company suffers loss as a result of an untrue or mis- **26.59** leading statement in a directors' report (or in a strategic report or a directors' remuneration report), or by reason of the omission from the report of anything which ought properly to have been included, any director who knew the statement to be untrue or misleading (or was reckless as to whether the statement was untrue or misleading), or knew the omission to be dishonest concealment of a material fact, will be liable to compensate the company.[136] However, no person shall be subject to any liability to any person other than the company as a result of reliance by any person on the untrue or misleading or omitted information.[137]

(5) Quoted companies: directors' remuneration report

Duty to prepare directors' remuneration report

The directors of a quoted company must produce a remuneration report for each financial **26.60** year of the company, which contains information about their remuneration and matters relevant to it, some of which must be audited.[138]

---

[130] 2006 Act, s 415(4).
[131] 2006 Act, s 415(5).
[132] 2006 Act, s 418(5).
[133] 2006 Act, s 418(6).
[134] 2006 Act, s 419(3).
[135] 2006 Act, s 419(4).
[136] 2006 Act, s 463(1), (2), (3).
[137] 2006 Act, s 463(4).
[138] 2006 Act, ss 420 and 421; the Large and Medium-Sized Companies and Groups (Accounts and Reports) Regulations (SI 2008/410), reg 11 and Sch 8. Provisions of this type were first introduced by the Directors' Remuneration Report Regulations 2002 (SI 2002/1986). Under the Financial Services Act 2010, ss 4, 5 regulations may make additional requirements for executive remuneration reports for financial services companies.

Contents of directors' remuneration report

26.61 The information contained in the directors' remuneration report which is not subject to audit is (i) the names of the directors who considered directors' remuneration and of the persons who advised or provided services to them, (ii) a statement of the company's policy on remuneration,[139] (iii) a statement of how pay and employment conditions of employees of the company and other undertakings within the same group as the company were taken into account when determining directors' remuneration for the relevant financial year, (iv) a performance graph illustrating shareholder returns compared with market performance, and (v) information about directors' service contracts.[140]

26.62 The matters in the directors remuneration report that must be audited by the auditors under the 2006 Act, ss 497 and 498(4) are (i) the amount of each director's emoluments and compensation in the relevant financial year, and (ii) information about share options, long-term incentive schemes, pensions, excess retirement benefits of directors and past directors, compensation of past directors, and sums paid to third parties in respect of directors' services.[141]

26.63 Every director of the company, and every person who was a director in the preceding five years, is under a specific statutory duty to give notice to the company of such matters relating to himself as may be necessary for the preparation of the directors' remuneration report.[142]

Approval and signing of directors' remuneration report

26.64 The directors' remuneration report must be approved by the board of directors and signed on behalf of the board, either by a director or by the company secretary.[143]

Criminal liability of directors

26.65 If a company's directors fail to comply with the requirement to prepare a directors' remuneration report, every person who was a director of the company immediately before the end of the period for filing accounts and reports for the financial year in question and who failed to take all reasonable steps for securing compliance with that requirement commits an offence punishable on conviction on indictment by a fine and on summary conviction by a fine not exceeding the statutory maximum.[144]

26.66 Additionally, any director or any person who has in the preceding five years been a director of the company will commit an offence (punishable by fine) if he fails to provide the company with such matters relating to himself as ought to appear in the directors' remuneration report.[145]

---

[139] The policy may be revised: see 2006 Act, s 422A.

[140] The Large and Medium-Sized Companies and Groups (Accounts and Reports) Regulations (SI 2008/410), reg 10 and Sch 8, Part 2. Also, if the company is a listed company and it releases an executive director to serve as a non-executive director of another company, the remuneration report should include a statement as to whether or not the director will retain his earnings from the external appointment and, if so, what the remuneration is: UK Corporate Governance Code (April 2016), D.1.2.

[141] The Large and Medium-Sized Companies and Groups (Accounts and Reports) Regulations (SI 2008/410), reg 10 and Sch 7, Part 3.

[142] 2006 Act, s 421(3).

[143] 2006 Act, s 422(1).

[144] 2006 Act, s 420(2), (3).

[145] 2006 Act, s 421(4).

If a directors' remuneration report is approved which does not comply with the requirements **26.67** of the 2006 Act, ss 420 to 422, every director of the company who knew that it did not comply (or was reckless as to whether it complied) and who failed to take reasonable steps to secure compliance or, as the case may be, to prevent the report from being approved, commits an offence punishable on conviction on indictment to a fine or on summary conviction to a fine not exceeding the statutory maximum.[146]

Civil liability of directors

If a directors' remuneration report is untrue or misleading or contains any material omis- **26.68** sion which results in the company suffering a loss, any director who knew of the untrue or misleading nature of the information (or was reckless as to whether it was untrue or misleading) or who knew the omission to be a dishonest concealment of a material fact is liable to compensate the company.[147]

(6) Duty to publish accounts and reports

The 2006 Act, Part 15, Chapter 7, ss 423–36 contain provisions for the publication of **26.69** accounts and reports. Every company[148] is required by statute to send a copy of its financial accounts and reports for each financial year to every member of the company, every debenture holder, and every person who is entitled to receive notice of general meetings.[149] The accounts and reports sent out in compliance with this requirement must identify the signatory by name on the balance sheet, directors' report, and, in the case of a quoted company, directors' remuneration report.[150] Statutory accounts must be accompanied by the auditor's report on those accounts (unless the company is exempt from audit and the directors have taken advantage of that exemption).[151] If group accounts are prepared, a company must not publish individual accounts unless they are accompanied by the group accounts.[152]

If a company publishes any financial information (non-statutory accounts) in addition to **26.70** the statutory accounts required to be filed with the Registrar of Companies, it must take care to ensure that readers of the non-statutory accounts do not confuse them with the statutory accounts. To this end, the company must state clearly that the non-statutory accounts are not the statutory accounts[153] and must ensure that the auditor's report on the statutory accounts is not published alongside the non-statutory material.[154]

---

[146] 2006 Act, s 422(2), (3).

[147] 2006 Act, s 463(1), (2), (3). Although this provision is capable of rendering a director liable in damages for untrue or misleading information or material omissions in a directors' remuneration report, it is suggested that it will be rare for a company to suffer a loss by reason of such untrue or misleading information or material omission.

[148] In *Re Allen Craig & Co (London) Ltd* [1934] Ch 483, Bennett J confirmed that the obligation is that of the company and not that of the auditors.

[149] 2006 Act, s 423, which is subject to s 426, which gives certain companies the option to provide a strategic report with supplementary material (s 423(6)). Copies need not be sent to a person for whom the company does not have a 'current address': s 423(2). The term 'current address' is defined in 2006 Act, s 423(3). Where the company's articles so provide, a member may nominate another person (typically a beneficial owner of the shares) as a person with a right to be sent a copy of the annual accounts and reports: s 145(1), (2), (3)(h).

[150] 2006 Act, s 433(1), (2), (3).

[151] 2006 Act, s 434(1).

[152] 2006 Act, s 434(2).

[153] 2006 Act, s 435(1)(a).

[154] 2006 Act, s 435(2).

26.71 In the case of a private company, the requirement to send out copies of accounts and reports must be complied with by the end of the period for filing accounts and reports (nine months after the end of the relevant accounting reference period) or, if earlier, the date on which the company actually delivers its accounts and reports to the Registrar.[155] A public company must circulate accounts and reports at least 21 days before the date of the relevant accounts meeting.[156] If a public company's accounts and reports are dispatched less than 21 days before the accounts meeting, the members may agree to waive the default at the accounts meeting, and upon such agreement the accounts and reports will be deemed to have been duly sent.[157] However, it is not possible for the members to agree prospectively to waive late service of accounts and reports which have not yet been sent out.

Option to provide strategic report with supplementary material

26.72 By the 2006 Act, s 426 a company may provide a copy of the strategic report together with the prescribed supplementary material, instead of the accounts and reports which otherwise would be required to be sent out, provided that it complies with the conditions for doing so.[158]

26.73 The supplementary material is prescribed by the 2006 Act, s 426A, which provides the supplementary material must (a) contain a statement that the strategic report is only part of the company's annual accounts and reports; (b) state how a person entitled to them can obtain a full copy of the company's annual accounts and reports; (c) state whether the auditor's report on the annual accounts was unqualified or qualified and, if it was qualified, set out the report in full together with any further material needed to understand the qualification; (d) state whether, in that report, the auditor's statement under s 496 (as to whether strategic report and directors' report consistent with the accounts) was unqualified or qualified and, if it was qualified, set out the qualified statement in full together with any further material needed to understand the qualification; (e) in the case of a quoted company, contain a copy of that part of the directors' remuneration report which sets out the single total figure table in respect of the company's directors' remuneration in accordance with the requirements of Schedule 8 to the Large and Medium-sized Companies (Accounts and Reports) Regulations 2008 (SI 2008/410).

26.74 Where a strategic report is provided with supplementary material, members and debenture holders will continue to have a statutory right to demand a copy of the full accounts and reports,[159] and accounts and reports must be sent out to any member or debenture holder or person who is entitled to receive notice of general meetings who requests them.[160]

---

[155] 2006 Act, s 424(2). See s 442 for the time for filing accounts.

[156] 2006 Act, s 424(3). In the 2006 Act, the term 'accounts meeting' means, in relation to a public company, a general meeting of the company at which the company's annual accounts and reports are to be laid in accordance with s 437: see, specifically, s 437(3). At least 21 clear days means 21 clear days' notice, excluding the day of service and the day on which the meeting is to be held: *Re Railway Sleepers Supply Co* (1885) 29 Ch D 204.

[157] 2006 Act, s 424(4).

[158] The Companies (Summary Financial Statements) Regulations (SI 2008/374), regs 4–8 state the conditions for sending out a summary financial statement.

[159] 2006 Act, ss 431 and 432.

[160] 2006 Act, s 426(2).

Quoted companies: website publication

The 2006 Act, s 430, contains a requirement for quoted companies (as defined in s 385) to **26.75** put the full accounts and reports on a website. This requirement is in addition to sending out the full accounts and reports to members under s 423. The annual accounts must be made available as soon as reasonably practicable on a website that is maintained by or on behalf of the company and that identifies the company in question. Access to the website must be available to all members of the public and not just to members, and there must be continuous access to the website without charge. The annual accounts and reports for a financial year must remain available until the accounts and reports for the next financial year are published on the website.

Rights of members and debenture holder to demand copies

In addition to their rights to receive copies of accounts and reports under the 2006 Act, **26.76** s 423 (or to a strategic report and supplementary material under s 426), a member or debenture holder is entitled to demand a copy of the company's last annual accounts, the strategic report, the last directors' report, and the auditor's report on those accounts and, in the case of a quoted company, the last directors' remuneration report and directors' report on it.[161]

Criminal liability of directors

If a company fails to circulate its accounts and reports to members, debenture holders, and **26.77** such others as may be entitled to receive notice of general meetings by the statutory deadline, an offence (punishable by way of fine) is committed by every officer in default.[162] It should be noted that in the case of a public company, which sends out its accounts and reports less than 21 days before the accounts meeting, the officers in default will be guilty of an offence unless the members agree at the accounts meeting to waive the default, in which case the accounts and reports will be deemed to have been duly sent, and the offence will no longer exist.[163]

Offences may also be committed in connection with a failure of a quoted company to make **26.78** its accounts and reports available on a website in accordance with the statutory requirements;[164] a failure by any company to identify the signatory by name on the balance sheet, directors' report, and, in the case of a quoted company, the directors' remuneration report;[165] a failure to enclose the auditor's report or, where group accounts are prepared, copies of the group accounts;[166] or a failure to comply with the statutory requirements aimed at preventing confusion between statutory and non-statutory accounts.[167] These offences are triable summarily and punishable by fine.[168]

It is a summary offence punishable by a fine not exceeding level 3 on the standard scale, com- **26.79** mitted by every officer in default, for a company to fail to comply within seven days with a demand by a member or debenture holder for a copy of accounts and reports.[169]

---

[161] 2006 Act, ss 431(1)–(2) and 432(1)–(2). Where a person holds shares, which are admitted to trading on a regulated market, on behalf of another person, he may nominate that person to enjoy the right to require copies of the accounts and reports: s 146(1), (2), (3)(i).

[162] 2006 Act, s 425(1), (2). For 'officer in default', see para 26.12 above.

[163] 2006 Act, s 424(4).

[164] 2006 Act, s 430(5), (6).

[165] 2006 Act, s 433(4).

[166] 2006 Act, s 434(4).

[167] 2006 Act, s 435(5).

[168] 2006 Act, ss 430(7), 430(5), 434(5), 435(6).

[169] 2006 Act, ss 431(3)–(4) and 432(3)–(4).

(7) Public companies: laying accounts before general meeting

26.80 The directors of a public company must lay before the company in general meeting copies of its annual accounts and reports.[170] This requirement must be complied with not later than the end of the period for filing the accounts and reports in question.[171] If this requirement is not complied with by the deadline, every person who immediately before the end of that period was a director of the company commits a summary offence.[172] However, it is a defence for a person charged with such offence to prove that he took all reasonable steps for securing that those requirements would be complied with before the end of the applicable period.[173] It is not a defence to prove that the documents in question were not in fact prepared.[174]

(8) Quoted companies: approval of directors' remuneration report

26.81 In the case of a quoted company, the directors' remuneration report for the financial year must be approved at the company's accounts meeting[175] in respect of that financial year. To that end, s 439(1) provides that a quoted company must, prior to the accounts meeting, give to the members of the company entitled to be sent notice of the meeting notice of the intention to move at the meeting, as an ordinary resolution, a resolution approving the directors' remuneration report for the financial year (other than the part containing the directors' remuneration policy[176]). The business of that meeting must then include the resolution;[177] this is the case even where the company has defaulted in sending out the resolution as required by s 439(1). Pursuant to s 439(4), the directors of a quoted company are expressly required to ensure that the resolution is put to the vote at the meeting.

26.82 If the statutory requirements are not complied with, an offence is committed by every officer in default.[178] If the resolution is not put to the vote at the meeting to which it relates, an offence is committed by every director of the company,[179] save that it is a defence for a person charged with such an offence to prove that he took all reasonable steps for securing that the resolution was put to the vote at the meeting.[180] These offences are both summary and punishable by fine.[181]

(9) Filing of accounts and reports

26.83 The directors of a company must deliver to the Registrar, for each financial year, the accounts and reports required by the 2006 Act, ss 444–7,[182] but an unlimited company is exempt from these filing obligations[183] and there are also exemptions for certain dormant subsidiaries.[184] The precise content of the filing obligation will depend on whether the company in question

---

170 2006 Act, s 437(1).
171 2006 Act, s 437(2).
172 2006 Act, s 438(1), (4).
173 2006 Act, s 438(2).
174 2006 Act, s 438(3); cf *Stockdale v Coulson* [1974] 1 WLR 1192.
175 The term 'accounts meeting' is defined in s 437(3).
176 As to which see 2006 Act, s 439A.
177 2006 Act, s 439(3).
178 2006 Act, s 440(1). For 'officer in default', see para 26.12 above.
179 2006 Act, s 440(2).
180 2006 Act, s 440(3).
181 2006 Act, s 440(4).
182 2006 Act, s 441(1).
183 2006 Act, ss 441(2) and 448.
184 2006 Act, s 448A; see also 2006 Act, s 448B–448C.

is unquoted, and if so whether it is small,[185] or medium-sized,[186] or whether it is quoted;[187] different requirements are in place for different types of company. In summary:

(1) The directors of a small company must deliver a copy of the balance sheet and the auditor's report (unless exempt from audit), but it is not mandatory to deliver a copy of the profit and loss account or the directors' report (and the balance sheet and profit and loss account may be in abbreviated form).[188]

(2) The directors of a company, which is not a small company but is entitled to the small companies exemption in relation to the directors' report, must deliver a copy of the company's annual accounts and the auditor's report (unless exempt from audit), but it is not mandatory to deliver a copy of the directors' report.[189]

(3) The directors of a medium-sized company must deliver a copy of the annual accounts, the strategic report, the directors' report, and the auditors' report (unless exempt from audit).[190]

(4) The directors any other unquoted company must deliver a copy of the annual accounts, the strategic report, the directors' report, any separate corporate governance statement, and the auditors' report.[191]

(5) The directors of a quoted company must deliver a copy of the annual accounts, the strategic report, the directors' remuneration report, the directors' report, any separate corporate governance statement, and the auditors' report.[192]

26.84 The copies of any accounts or reports of the company delivered under those provisions must state the name of the person who signed them on behalf of the board.[193] The copies of any auditor's report delivered under those provisions must state the name of the auditor or the person signing as senior statutory auditor, unless their names may be omitted in accordance with the 2006 Act, s 506.[194]

26.85 The accounts and reports required to be filed must be delivered by the directors to the Registrar by the applicable deadline.[195] For private companies, this will be nine months after the end of the relevant accounting reference period.[196] For public companies, it will be six months after the end of that period.[197] However, if the relevant accounting reference period is the company's first and is a period of more than 12 months, the deadline for the filing of accounts will be nine months (in the case of a private company) or six months (in the case of a public company) from the first anniversary of incorporation, or three months after the end of the accounting reference period, whichever is the later.[198]

---

[185] 2006 Act, s 382.

[186] 2006 Act, s 465.

[187] 2006 Act, s 385.

[188] 2006 Act, s 444(1)–(5). See also 2006 Act, s 444(5A), (5B) and (5C). 'For small companies exemption from audit, see 2006 Act, ss 476–9.

[189] 2006 Act, s 444A(1), (2), and (5).

[190] 2006 Act, s 445(1)–(2), and (7).

[191] 2006 Act, s 446(1), (2), and (5).

[192] 2006 Act, s 447(1), (2).

[193] 2006 Act, ss 444(6), 444A(3), 445(5), 446(3), 447(3).

[194] 2006 Act, ss 444(7), 444A(4), 445(6), 446(4), 447(4).

[195] 2006 Act, s 442(1). Months are to be reckoned in accordance with s 443 which reverses the 'corresponding date rule' laid down by the House of Lords in *Dodds v Walker* [1981] 1 WLR 1027.

[196] 2006 Act, s 442(2)(a).

[197] 2006 Act, s 442(2)(b).

[198] 2006 Act, s 442(3).

Criminal liabilities of directors

26.86 If the directors' duty to file accounts and reports is not complied with by the applicable dead-line, an offence is committed by every director of the company,[199] save that it is a defence for any person charged with such an offence to show that he took all reasonable steps for secur-ing that the duty would be complied with before the end of the relevant period.[200] However, it is not a defence to show that the relevant documents were not actually prepared.[201]

Civil liabilities of directors

26.87 If the directors fail to comply with the duty to file accounts and reports by the deadline, the Registrar may serve a notice requiring those duties to be complied with within 14 days.[202] If after 14 days the duty has still not been complied with, the Registrar (or any member or creditor of the company) may apply to the court for an order directing the directors, or any of them, to make good the default within such time as may be specified by the court.[203] Any director who fails to comply with such an order will be liable to be committed to prison for contempt of court. In addition, a director may be ordered to pay the costs of the proceedings.[204]

26.88 In addition, where the directors of a company fail or neglect to comply with the duty to file accounts and reports by the applicable deadline, the company is liable to pay a civil penalty which may be recovered by the Registrar, who must pay it into the Consolidated Fund.[205] The company's liability is strict and the Registrar's role is confined to recovery of the pen-alty.[206] It is no defence for the company to show that the documents in question were never prepared.[207] The quantum of the penalty is fixed by regulations and depends on the length of the default and whether the company is a private or public company.[208] The company may obtain indemnification for the penalty from its directors on the ground of negligence or breach of fiduciary duty.

(10) Revision of defective accounts and reports

26.89 Where the annual accounts, directors' remuneration report, directors' report, or strategic report of the company do not comply with the requirements of the 2006 Act (or, where applicable, with the requirements of the IAS Regulation),[209] the directors may prepare

---

[199] 2006 Act, s 451(1).

[200] 2006 Act, s 451(2).

[201] 2006 Act, s 451(3); cf *Stockdale v Coulson* [1974] 1 WLR 1192.

[202] 2006 Act, s 452(1)(b).

[203] 2006 Act, s 452(1).

[204] 2006 Act, s 452(2).

[205] 2006 Act, s 453(1), (3).

[206] In *R (on the application of POW Trust) v Chief Executive and Registrar of Companies* [2003] 2 BCLC 295, a company sought judicial review of the Registrar's decision to recover the penalty. The company contended that the liability arose by reason of the Registrar's decision, which was susceptible to judicial review. Lightman J said: 'The liability is strict: there is no defence to a claim to payment if there has been noncompliance with the filing obligation. The role of the Registrar is confined to recovery of the penalty: he has no role in respect of the liability to pay or the quantum of the penalty. I accordingly hold that the statutory penalty is immediately payable without more on non-compliance.' See also *Registrar of Companies v Radio-Tech Engineering Ltd* [2004] BCC 277.

[207] 2006 Act, s 453(4).

[208] 2006 Act, s 453(2); the Companies (Late Filing Penalties) and Limited Liability Partnerships (Filing Periods and Late Filing Penalties) Regulations (SI 2008/497).

[209] Regulation (EC) No 1606/2002 of the European Parliament and of the Council of 19 July 2002 on the application of international accounting standards.

revised versions.[210] If the accounts and reports in question have been circulated to members or filed with the Registrar, the revisions must be confined to the correction of the respects in which the previous documents failed to comply with the applicable requirements, and any necessary consequential alterations.[211]

Where the directors of a company should, but do not, take the initiative to revise defective **26.90** accounts and reports, they may find that they become subject to the unwelcome attention of the Secretary of State or the Conduct Committee of the FRC.

Involvement of Secretary of State

The 2006 Act, s 455, provides that the Secretary of State may serve a notice on the directors **26.91** of a company requiring them (1) to provide an explanation, within a period of one month, of the aspects of the accounts or reports which the Secretary of State considers to be non-compliant, or alternatively (2) to prepare revised accounts or a revised report.[212]

If the directors fail to comply with such a notice, the Secretary of State has the ability to **26.92** apply to court under s 456 for a declaration that the accounts or reports in question are defective in the manner alleged and for an order requiring the directors to prepare compliant accounts and reports.[213] On the hearing of such an application, the court may give directions as to (1) the auditing of the accounts and/or reports, (2) the revision of the accounts and/or reports, (3) the taking of steps by the directors to bring the making of the order to the notice of anyone who might rely on the defective accounts and/or reports, and (4) such other matters as the court thinks fit.[214] The court may also order the directors who were party to the approval of the defective accounts or report to pay the costs of the proceedings.[215]

The Conduct Committee

The 2006 Act, s 457, enables the Secretary of State to delegate his powers to 'a fit and proper **26.93** person'. For this purpose the Conduct Committee of the FRC is appointed to exercise the powers.[216]

The Conduct Committee has extensive powers to obtain documents,[217] information, and **26.94** explanations from the officers of the company.[218] The 2006 Act, s 459 provides that the Conduct Committee, as an 'authorized person', may require any officer, employee, or auditor of the company to produce any document, or to provide him with any information or explanations that he may reasonably require for the purpose of discovering whether there are grounds for an application to the court under s 456 or deciding whether or not to make

---

[210] 2006 Act, s 454(1). Also see the Companies (Revision of Defective Accounts and Reports) Regulations (SI 2008/373) (as amended). The ability to prepare revised accounts is limited to cases of non-compliance with mandatory requirements; accounts may not be revised on other grounds (eg inadvertent disclosure of legally privileged information): *Re a Company (No 1389920)* [2004] 2 BCLC 434.

[211] 2006 Act, s 454(2).

[212] 2006 Act, s 455(1), (2), (3).

[213] 2006 Act, ss 455(4) and 456(1).

[214] 2006 Act, s 456(3), (4).

[215] 2006 Act, s 456(5).

[216] See the Supervision of Accounts and Reports (Prescribed Body) and Companies (Defective Accounts and Directors' Reports) (Authorised Person) Order 2012/1439.

[217] For these purposes, 'document' includes information recorded in any form: s 459(8).

[218] These powers were originally introduced by the C(AICE) Act 2004 further to a recommendation of the Coordinating Group on Audit and Accounting Issues, which was established by the government following the collapse of Enron.

such an application.[219] If a person fails to comply with a request by the authorized person for documents, information, or explanations, the authorized person may apply to the court for an order requiring that the request be complied with.[220] Failure to comply with such an order will amount to contempt of court rendering the contemnor liable to be committed to prison.

D. Quoted Companies; Transferable Securities: Additional Transparency and Disclosure Requiremets

26.95 The Transparency Directive,[221] implemented in the UK through the Disclosure and Transparency Rules made by the FCA, imposes additional periodic reporting obligations on quoted companies.[222]

26.96 Such companies must produce: (1) an annual financial report consisting of consolidated audited accounts, a management report, and responsibility statement; (2) a half-yearly report consisting of condensed financial statements, an interim management report, and a responsibility statement; and (3) approximately midway through each half-year period an interim management statement. Many of the requirements overlap with existing statutory disclosure requirements.

26.97 Chapter 27, at paragraphs 27.71–27.78, discusses the Disclosure and Transparency Rules, made under FSMA, Part 6 and the powers of the FCA under those provisions. A director is exposed to penalty or censure at the instance of the FCA if, as a person discharging managerial responsibilities within an issuer, he contravenes any provision of the Disclosure Rules or if he was knowingly concerned in the contravention by the issuer or other specified person of the Disclosure or Transparency Rules.[223]

E. Audit

(1) Introduction

26.98 This section deals with the functions, responsibilities, and liabilities of company directors in relation to audit under the 2006 Act, Part 16. Specifically, it deals with: (1) the requirement for audited accounts; (2) directors' functions in relation to appointment of auditors; (3) directors' functions in relation to auditors' remuneration; (4) directors' functions and responsibilities in relation to the functions of the auditors; (5) directors' functions and responsibilities in relation to the removal or resignation of auditors; (6) in respect of quoted companies, the directors' functions in relation to the right of members to raise concerns at

---

[219] 2006 Act, s 459(1), (2), (3). 2006 Act, s 460 restricts the disclosure of information obtained under compulsory powers, but the restrictions are subject to the exceptions in s 461, by which disclosure to the Secretary of State, the Treasury, the Bank of England, the FCA, the PRA, and Commissioners for HMRC is permitted.

[220] 2006 Act, s 459(4), (5).

[221] Directive 2004/109/EC of the European Parliament and of the Council of 15 December 2004.

[222] The Disclosure and Transparency Rules in the FCA Handbook (see Ch 27 Section B(6) below) apply to issuers with securities admitted to trading on a regulated market in the UK (or outside the UK where the UK is the home state for the purposes of the Transparency Directive). This will include issuers with securities admitted to the FCA's Official List, whether incorporated in the UK or elsewhere, but not AIM issuers.

[223] See in particular FSMA, s 90A and Sch 10A.

the accounts meeting; and, finally, (7) directors' functions and responsibilities in relation to provisions protecting auditors from liability.

(2) Requirement for audited accounts

A company's annual accounts for a financial year must be audited, unless the company is **26.99** exempt from audit.[224] The statutory purpose of this provision is to secure for shareholders independent and reliable information on the true financial position of the company at the time of the audit.[225] The importance of audited accounts is now reinforced by the Fourth Company Law Directive,[226] which states that companies must have their annual accounts audited by one or more persons authorized by national law to audit accounts.[227]

The exemptions relate to small companies,[228] subsidiary companies,[229] dormant compa- **26.100** nies,[230] and non-profit-making companies subject to public-sector audits.[231] The provisions relating to qualification for exemption are considered below.

However, in the case of small companies, exempt subsidiaries, and dormant companies **26.101** which are entitled to claim exemption from audit, the members of the company representing not less in total than 10 per cent in nominal value of the company's issued share capital (or any class of it) are entitled by the 2006 Act, s 476, to serve a notice requiring that the company's accounts be audited. The notice may not be given before the financial year to which it relates and must not be given later than one month before the end of that year.[232] If such a notice is served, the directors must not claim exemption from audit, but must ensure instead that the company's accounts are audited in accordance with the requirements of the 2006 Act, Part 16.

In the case of a small or dormant company, or an exempt subsidiary where no such notice is **26.102** given by members requiring audit, and in the case of non-profit-making companies subject to public-sector audits, the right to claim exemption from audit must be exercised by election; in other words, it is an 'opt in' system, rather than an 'opt out' system. To elect to take advantage of the exemption, the directors of the company must ensure that the company's balance sheet contains a statement (which must appear above the signature)[233] that the company is exempt from audit; failure to include such a statement on the balance sheet will cause the company to lose its right to claim exemption, and the company will be liable to audit.[234] In addition, in the case of a small or dormant company, the balance sheet must record (again by way of statement appearing above the signature) that the company's members have not required the company to obtain an audit, and that the directors acknowledge their responsibilities for complying with the requirements of the Companies Act with respect to accounting records and the preparation of accounts; failure to ensure that the balance sheet

---

[224] 2006 Act, s 475(1).
[225] *Re London & General Bank (No 2)* [1895] 2 Ch 673, 682, per Lindley LJ.
[226] 78/660/EEC.
[227] Art 51(1)(a).
[228] 2006 Act, s 477.
[229] 2006 Act, s 479A.
[230] 2006 Act, s 480.
[231] 2006 Act, s 482.
[232] 2006 Act, s 476(3).
[233] 2006 Act, s 475(4).
[234] 2006 Act, s 475(2).

contains this statement will result in the company losing its exemption, and an audit will be required.[235]

Exemption from audit: small and dormant companies and subsidiaries

26.103   A company that qualifies as a small company in relation to a financial year is exempt from the requirements relating to the audit of accounts for that year.[236] A company is also exempt from the requirements of the 2006 Act relating to the audit of individual accounts for a financial year if (a) it is itself a subsidiary undertaking, and (b) its parent undertaking is established under the law of an EEA state.[237] However, this exemption for subsidiaries is conditional upon compliance with all of the specified conditions.[238]

26.104   To be exempt from audit as a dormant company, the company must have been either (1) dormant since its formation, or (2) dormant since the end of the previous financial year, provided (a) it is entitled to prepare individual accounts in accordance with the small companies regime (or would be so entitled but for having been a public company or a member of an ineligible group) and (b) it is not required to prepare group accounts for that year.[239]

26.105   A company that would otherwise qualify is excluded from the small or dormant companies exemptions if, within the financial year in question, it was (among other things) a traded company, an authorized insurance company, a banking company, an e-money issuer, a MiFID investment firm, or a UCITS management company.[240]

Exemption from audit: companies subject to public-sector audit

26.106   A non-profit-making company is not subject to the audit requirements imposed by Part 16 of the Companies Act if (but only if) its accounts are subject to public-sector audit by the Controller and Auditor General (or, in Wales, by the Auditor General).[241]

(3) Appointment of auditors

26.107   The 2006 Act, Part 16, Chapter 2, relates to the appointment of auditors. The requirement to appoint an auditor applies to both private and public companies, unless exempt from audit. In either case, failure to appoint an auditor is not an offence, but an offence is committed by any officer in default if the company fails to notify the Secretary of State that no auditor has been appointed. A person may be appointed to carry out a particular audit exercise without being appointed to the office of auditor.[242]

---

[235] 2006 Act, s 475(3).

[236] 2006 Act, s 477(1). Whether a company qualifies as a small company is to be determined in accordance with the 2006 Act, s 382(1).

[237] 2006 Act, s 479A(1).

[238] 2006 Act, s 479A(2) specifies the conditions: (a) all members of the company must agree to the exemption in respect of the financial year in question, (b) the parent undertaking must give a guarantee under s 479C in respect of that year, (c) the company must be included in the consolidated accounts drawn up for that year or to an earlier date in that year by the parent undertaking in accordance with (i) the provisions of Directive 2013/34/EU of the European Parliament and of the Council on the annual financial statements, consolidated statements, and related reports of certain types of undertakings, or (ii) international accounting standards, (d) the parent undertaking must disclose in the notes to the consolidated accounts that the company is exempt from the requirements of this Act relating to the audit of individual accounts by virtue of this section, and (e) the directors of the company must deliver the prescribed documents to the registrar.

[239] 2006 Act, s 480(1), (2).

[240] 2006 Act, ss 478, 479B, and 481. For the meaning of these terms, see para 26.06 above.

[241] 2006 Act, s 482.

[242] *Mutual Reinsurance Co Ltd v Peat Marwick Mitchell & Co* [1997] 1 BCLC 1.

Private companies

In the case of a private company, an auditor (or auditors) must be appointed for each finan- **26.108** cial year of the company, unless the directors reasonably resolve otherwise on the ground that audited accounts are unlikely to be required (ie because the company is entitled to an exemption).[243] The appointment must be made before the end of the period of 28 days beginning with the end of the time allowed for sending out copies of the company's annual accounts and reports for the previous financial year, or, if earlier, the day on which copies of the company's annual accounts and reports for the previous financial year are circulated to members (the 'period for appointing auditors').[244]

At any time before the company's first period for appointing auditors, or following a period **26.109** in which (by reason of being exempt from audit) the company did not have any auditor, or to fill a casual vacancy, the company's directors may appoint an auditor.[245] Otherwise, the audi- tor must be appointed by the members by ordinary resolution.[246] However, if auditors are not appointed by the directors or the members, the Secretary of State has power to appoint an auditor.[247] In order to ensure that the Secretary of State is aware that the power to appoint an auditor has arisen, the company is required by statute to give notice to the Secretary of State that no auditor has been appointed and that the Secretary of State's power to appoint has accordingly become exercisable.[248] Such a notice must be given within one week of the end of the period for appointing auditors.

An auditor of a private company will not take office until any previous auditor ceases to **26.110** hold office, and will cease to hold office at the end of the next period for appointing audi- tors, unless reappointed.[249] However, where no successor has been appointed, the auditor in office will be deemed to be reappointed, unless (1) he was appointed by the directors, (2) the company's articles require actual reappointment, (3) the deemed reappointment is prevented by the members (ie under s 488, which enables members representing 5 per cent of the total voting rights of all members to give notice that the auditor should not be auto- matically reappointed), (4) the members have resolved that he should not be reappointed, or (5) the directors have resolved that no auditor should be appointed for the financial year in question.[250]

Public companies

In the case of a public company, auditors must be appointed for each financial year of the com- **26.111** pany, unless the directors reasonably resolve otherwise on the ground that audited accounts are unlikely to be required.[251] The auditors must generally be appointed by the members at a meeting at which accounts are to be laid. There is no provision for deemed reappointment. The auditors of a public company will not take office until any previous auditor ceases to hold office, and will cease to hold office at the end of the accounts meeting next following

---

[243] 2006 Act, s 485(1).
[244] 2006 Act, s 485(2).
[245] 2006 Act, s 485(3).
[246] 2006 Act, s 485(4).
[247] 2006 Act, s 486(1).
[248] 2006 Act, s 486(2).
[249] 2006 Act, s 487(1).
[250] 2006 Act, s 487(2).
[251] 2006 Act, s 489(1).

their appointment, unless reappointed.[252] The requirement to notify the Secretary of State if no auditor is appointed and the power of the Secretary of State to appoint the auditor is the same for public companies as for private companies except the Secretary of State must be notified within a week of the accounts meeting.[253]

Criminal liability of directors

26.112 Failure, in respect of both private and public companies, to give the notice to the Secretary of State when required that auditors have not been appointed and that his default powers are exercisable is an offence committed by the company and every officer of the company who is in default.[254] The offence is summary and punishable by fine.[255]

(4) Auditors' terms of engagement

26.113 The terms on which the auditor is engaged are for negotiation and determination by the directors, exercising their general duties, but provisions about remuneration and liability protection are subject to particular statutory controls.

Remuneration

26.114 If the auditor is appointed by the members, the auditor's remuneration must be fixed by the members or in such manner as they may determine (which could be by the directors).[256] However, if the auditor is appointed by the directors, the directors have a specific statutory duty to fix the auditor's remuneration.[257] For these purposes, 'remuneration' includes sums paid in respect of expenses.[258]

26.115 In determining the level of remuneration payable to an auditor or negotiating the amount to be fixed by the members, the directors should take reasonable steps to ensure that the company's auditors are not remunerated in excess of the going rate.

26.116 The amount of the auditor's remuneration must be disclosed in a note to the company's annual accounts.[259]

Liability protection

26.117 The general rule is that any provision exempting an auditor from liability in connection with any negligence, default, breach of duty, or breach of trust in relation to the company occurring in the course of the audit or under which the company directly or indirectly provides the auditor with an indemnity in respect of those liabilities is void. But this is subject to two exceptions.[260]

26.118 The first exception is that the company is not prevented from indemnifying an auditor against any liability incurred by him in defending civil or criminal proceedings in which

---

[252] 2006 Act, s 491(1).

[253] 2006 Act, s 490.

[254] 2006 Act, ss 486(3) and 490(3). For 'officer in default', see para 26.12 above.

[255] 2006 Act, ss 486(4) and 490(4).

[256] 2006 Act, s 492(1).

[257] 2006 Act, s 492(3).

[258] 2006 Act, s 492(4).

[259] 2006 Act, s 494 and the Companies (Disclosure of Auditor Remuneration and Liability Limitation Agreements) Regulations 2008 (SI 2008/489), regs 4–6.

[260] 2006 Act, s 532. Cf s 232 for the comparable provision in respect of directors' liability protection, discussed in Ch 20 above.

he is successful or in connection with a successful application for relief under the 2006 Act, s 1157.[261] Even though the company may be entitled to indemnify the auditor against costs, it will be for the directors, acting in accordance with their general duties, to decide whether it is in the interests of the company that it should do so.

The second exception is where, in accordance with the 2006 Act, ss 534–6, the company and the auditor agree to a liability limitation agreement. Such an agreement is subject to a number of restrictions and controls:[262]   **26.119**

(1) It is only effective in relation to acts or omissions occurring in the course of the audit for one financial year and it must specify the year to which it relates.[263]
(2) It must be authorized by members of the company (though a private company can waive the need for approval).[264]
(3) The limitation cannot reduce the auditors' liability to less than such an amount as is fair and reasonable in all circumstances, having regard to the auditors' responsibilities, their contractual obligations to the company, and the professional standards expected of them.[265]

Again, it will be for the directors, acting in accordance with their general duties, to decide, in the case of a private company, where the members have waived the need for approval, whether the company should enter into such an agreement and, if so, what the limitation should be and, in any other case, what terms should be put to the members for approval.   **26.120**

A company which has made a liability limitation agreement must disclose in a note to its annual accounts the principal terms and the date of the resolution approving it (or in the case of a private company the date of the waiver resolution).[266]   **26.121**

(5) Auditors' functions

The auditor's report

A company's auditor must make a report to the company's members on all annual accounts of the company which are, in the case of a private company, sent out to members, or, in the case of a public company, laid before the company in general meeting.[267]   **26.122**

In order to prepare the report, the auditor must carry out such investigations as will enable him to form an opinion as to (1) whether adequate accounting records have been kept by the company and returns adequate for the audit have been received from branches not visited by him, (2) whether the company's individual accounts are in agreement with the accounting   **26.123**

---

[261] 2006 Act, s 533. Cf s 234 for qualifying third party indemnity protection for directors, discussed in Ch 20 above. For discussion of s 1157 in relation to directors, see Ch 19, Section D above.

[262] The Secretary of State may make further regulations as to the provisions of a liability limitation agreement under s 535(2) and (3).

[263] 2006 Act, s 535(1).

[264] 2006 Act, s 536. In the case of a private company the approval may be given by written resolution or by resolution passed at a meeting (ss 536(2) and 281), but approval in relation to a public company must be given by resolution passed at a meeting (s 536(3)). Note also the limited right to withdraw approval under s 535(5).

[265] 2006 Act, s 537.

[266] 2006 Act, s 538; Disclosure of Auditor Remuneration and Liability Limitation Agreements Regulations 2008 (SI 2008/489), para 8.

[267] 2006 Act, s 495(1). Particular provision is made for the case of micro-entities by 2006 Act, s 495(3A).

records and returns, and (3) in the case of a quoted company, whether the directors' remuneration report is consistent with the accounting records and returns.[268]

26.124   The report must include an introduction, which must identify the annual accounts which are the subject of the audit and the financial reporting framework which has been applied in their preparation, and a description of the scope of the audit, which must identify the auditing standards in accordance with which the audit was conducted.[269] The body of the report must state clearly whether, in the auditor's opinion, the annual accounts (1) give a true and fair view,[270] (2) have been properly prepared in accordance with the relevant financial reporting framework, and (3) have been prepared in accordance with the requirements of the Companies Act (and, where applicable, the requirements of the IAS Regulation).[271] The auditor's report must be either 'qualified' or 'unqualified' and must include a reference to any matters to which the auditor wishes to draw attention by way of emphasis without qualifying the report.[272]

26.125   In his report on the company's annual accounts, the auditor must also (a) state whether, in his opinion, based on the work undertaken in the course of the audit (i) the information given in the strategic report (if any) and the directors' report for the financial year for which the accounts are prepared is consistent with those accounts, and (ii) any such strategic report and the directors' report have been prepared in accordance with applicable legal requirements, (b) state whether, in the light of the knowledge and understanding of the company and its environment obtained in the course of the audit, he has identified material misstatements in the strategic report (if any) and the directors' report, and (c) if applicable, give an indication of the nature of each of the misstatements referred to in paragraph (b).[273] In the case of a quoted company, the auditor must also report to the members in respect of the auditable part of the directors' remuneration report; specifically, he must state whether the directors' remuneration report has been properly prepared in accordance with the requirements of the Companies Act.[274]

26.126   Where the company prepares a separate corporate governance statement in respect of a financial year, the auditor must in his report on the company's annual accounts for that year:

(a) state whether, in his opinion, based on the work undertaken in the course of the audit, the information given in the statement in compliance with rules 7.2.5 and 7.2.6 in the Disclosure Rules and Transparency Rules sourcebook made by the Financial Conduct Authority (information about internal control and risk management systems in relation to financial reporting processes and about share capital structures)—(i) is consistent with those accounts, and (ii) has been prepared in accordance with applicable legal requirements,

(b) state whether, in the light of the knowledge and understanding of the company and its environment obtained in the course of the audit, he has identified material misstatements in the information in the statement referred to in paragraph (a),

---

[268]   2006 Act, s 498(1).
[269]   2006 Act, s 495(2).
[270]   See para 26.30 above.
[271]   2006 Act, s 495(3).
[272]   2006 Act, s 495(4).
[273]   2006 Act, s 496.
[274]   2006 Act, s 497.

(c) if applicable, give an indication of the nature of each of the misstatements referred to in paragraph (b), and

(d) state whether, in his opinion, based on the work undertaken in the course of the audit, rules 7.2.2, 7.2.3, and 7.2.7 in the Disclosure Rules and Transparency Rules sourcebook made by the Financial Conduct Authority (information about the company's corporate governance code and practices and about its administrative, management, and supervisory bodies and their committees) have been complied with, if applicable.[275]

If the accounting records and returns have not been kept adequately, or if adequate returns have not been received from unvisited branches, or if the individual accounts are not consistent with the accounting records and returns, or if the auditable part of the directors' remuneration report is not consistent with the accounting records and returns, the auditor must state that fact in his report.[276] Furthermore, if the auditor fails to obtain all the information and explanations which, to the best of his knowledge and belief, are necessary for the purposes of his audit, he must state this fact in his report.[277] **26.127**

Where the company is required to prepare a corporate governance statement in respect of a financial year and no such statement is included in the directors' report, the company's auditor, in preparing his report on the company's annual accounts for that year, must ascertain whether a corporate governance statement has been prepared, and if it appears to the auditor that no such statement has been prepared, he must state that fact in his report.[278] **26.128**

Specific duties of directors in respect of the auditor's report

A company's directors are likely to be one of the auditor's main sources of information. Accordingly the directors' duties in relation to the preparation and contents of the auditors' report relate chiefly to the provision of information to the auditor. To that end, an auditor is expressly entitled to require any officer of the company to provide such information or explanations as he thinks necessary for the performance of his duties as auditor.[279] He may also ask any officer of a subsidiary undertaking to provide him with books, accounts, or vouchers relating to the subsidiary undertaking.[280] He may also require the company to obtain information from any overseas subsidiary undertaking.[281] If necessary, the auditor may apply to the court for an injunction to enforce these rights to information.[282] **26.129**

The auditor is also entitled to all communications relating to written resolutions and general meetings, to attend any general meeting and to be heard at the meeting on any part of the business which concerns him as auditor.[283] **26.130**

---

[275] 2006 Act, s 497A, as substituted by the Companies, Partnerships and Groups (Accounts and Reports) Regs 2015, SI 2015/980 as from 6 April 2015 for financial years beginning on or after 1 January 2016 and between 1 January 2015 and 1 January 2016 if the directors so decide. For the Disclosure and Transparency Rules, see the FCA Handbook.

[276] 2006 Act, s 498(2).

[277] 2006 Act, s 498(3).

[278] 2006 Act, s 498A.

[279] 2006 Act, s 499(1), (2). As to the auditor's ability to obtain audit information regarding pending legal matters, see *The Ascertainment and Confirmation of Contingent Liabilities Arising from Pending Legal Matters* (ICAEW, 1995).

[280] 2006 Act, s 499(2)(d).

[281] 2006 Act, s 500.

[282] 2006 Act, s 501(6).

[283] 2006 Act, s 502.

26.131 The obligations in the Companies Act to provide auditors with information are supported by the statement that must be included in the directors' report that, so far as each director is aware, there is no relevant audit information of which the company's auditor is unaware and that each director has taken all steps to make himself aware of any relevant audit information and to establish that the auditor is aware of such information.[284]

Criminal liability of directors

26.132 An offence is committed by any officer (or, for that matter, any other person) who knowingly or recklessly makes any statement to an auditor, whether oral or written, which conveys or purports to convey any information required by the auditor, but which is misleading, false, or deceptive in a material particular.[285] Such an offence is triable on indictment and punishable by imprisonment for up to two years or a fine or both, or summarily and punishable by imprisonment for up to 12 months or a fine not exceeding the statutory maximum or both.[286]

26.133 In addition, a summary offence punishable by fine is committed by any person who fails without delay to comply with an auditor's requirement for information, unless it was not reasonably practicable for him to provide the required information.[287]

26.134 Furthermore, where a parent company fails to comply with an auditor's request for information, a summary offence punishable by fine is committed by every officer of the company who is in default.[288]

(6) Removal or resignation of auditors

Removal of auditor from office

26.135 Under the 2006 Act, s 510, the members of a company may remove an auditor from office by ordinary resolution at a meeting, provided that the special notice required by s 511 has been (1) given to the company and (2) forwarded by the company to the auditor proposed to be removed. Where the members resolve to remove an auditor in accordance with these provisions, the company is required to give notice of that fact to the Registrar within 14 days.[289]

Resignation of auditor

26.136 A company's auditor has an express statutory right to resign at any time. The auditor must send a notice of resignation to the company.[290]

26.137 Where the company is a public interest company, the notice must also be accompanied by a statement setting out the reasons for the resignation.[291] Also, where the company is a non-public interest company, a statement of reasons must be provided in certain circumstances.[292]

---

[284] 2006 Act, s 418.
[285] 2006 Act, s 501(1).
[286] 2006 Act, s 501(2).
[287] 2006 Act, s 501(3), (5).
[288] 2006 Act, s 501(4). For 'officer in default', see para 26.12 above.
[289] 2006 Act, s 512(1).
[290] 2006 Act, s 516, as amended by Deregulation Act 2015, s 18 with effect from 1 October 2015 (as were 2006 Act, ss 518–25).
[291] 2006 Act, s 519(1).
[292] 2006 Act, s 519(2).

For these purposes, 'public interest company' means a company (a) any of whose transfer- **26.138**
able securities are included in the official list (within the meaning of FSMA, Part 6), or (b)
any of whose equity share capital is officially listed in an EEA state; and 'non-public interest
company' means a company that is not a public interest company.[293]

An auditor of a public interest company (or a non-public interest company where the audi- **26.139**
tor considers that the reasons for his resignation should be drawn to the attention of the
members) who resigns and makes a statement under s 519 may also requisition a general
meeting of the company for the purpose of receiving and considering his explanation of the
reasons for his resignation and he may request the company to circulate his statement to the
members with the notice convening the meeting.[294]

The directors, within 21 days from the date of the deposit of the requisition, must proceed **26.140**
duly to convene a meeting for a day not more than 28 days after the date on which the notice
convening the meeting is given.[295]

If the auditor's statement is not produced in time to be circulated with the notice of the **26.141**
meeting, the auditor may require his statement to be read out at the meeting and he may also
exercise his right to be heard orally.[296]

The company and other aggrieved parties can apply for a court order to prevent the audi- **26.142**
tor from abusing these provisions to secure needless publicity to defamatory material in his
statement, provided they do so within 14 days of the deposit of the statement.[297] Such an
application involves making an allegation of bad faith against the auditor.[298]

Subject to an application being made to court, in the case of a public interest company (or **26.143**
a non-public interest company where the auditor omits to state that none of the reasons for
his resignation should be drawn to the attention of the members) the company must, within
14 days of receipt of the auditor's statement, send a copy to every member of the company,
every holder of the company's debentures, and every person who is entitled to receive notice
of general meetings,[299] and the auditor must send a copy of the statement to the Registrar.[300]

If the auditor ceases to hold office (a) in the case of a private company, at any time other **26.144**
than at the end of a period for appointing auditors or (b) in the case of a public company, at
any time other than at the end of an accounts meeting, within 14 days of the sending of the
auditor's statement, the company must give notice to the audit authority[301] that the auditor has ceased to hold office and must accompany the notice with a copy of the statement
(even though there has been an application to court).[302] (However, this does not apply if the

---

[293] 2006 Act, s 519A.
[294] 2006 Act, s 518(1)–(3).
[295] 2006 Act, s 518(5).
[296] 2006 Act, s 518(8).
[297] 2006 Act, s 518(9), 520(2)–(5). The time limit is strict and cannot be extended: *P&P Design plc v PricewaterhouseCoopers* [2002] 2 BCLC 648.
[298] *Jarvis plc v PricewaterhouseCoopers* [2000] 2 BCLC 368 at para 16(2). Also see *Easier v Deloitte & Touche LLP* [2004] EWHC 3263 (Ch).
[299] 2006 Act, s 520(2) (and s 423).
[300] 2006 Act, s 521.
[301] This term is defined by 2006 Act, s 525.
[302] 2006 Act, ss 523 and 525; Statutory Auditors (Delegation of Functions etc) Order 2008 (SI 2008/496) para 5. The auditor has independent obligations to notify the Professional Oversight Board: s 522.

company reasonably believes that the only reasons for the auditor's ceasing to hold office are exempt reasons.[303])

Criminal liability of directors in relation to the auditor's statement and requisition

26.145 If the directors fail to comply with the requirement to convene a meeting pursuant to the auditor's requisition in accordance with the 2006 Act, s 518(5), an offence is committed by 'every director who fails to take all reasonable steps to ensure that a meeting was convened'.[304] The offence is indictable or triable summarily and punishable by way of fine.[305]

26.146 If the company defaults in complying with its obligation to send copies of the auditor's statement to every member, debenture holder and other person entitled to receive notice of general meetings in accordance with s 520, an offence (punishable by fine) is committed by every officer of the company who is in default.[306]

26.147 Similarly an offence (punishable by a fine) is committed by every officer of the company who is in default, if the company fails to comply with its obligation to notify the audit authority of the auditor ceasing to hold office before the end of his terms in accordance with s 523.[307] However, in each case it is a defence for a person charged with such an offence to show that he took all reasonable steps and exercised all due diligence to avoid the commission of the offence.[308]

(7) Quoted companies: right of members to raise concerns at accounts meeting

Duties in relation to website publication

26.148 Pursuant to the 2006 Act, s 527 the members of a quoted company[309] representing at least 5 per cent of the total voting rights of all members[310] (or, alternatively, at least 100 members who hold shares on which there has been paid up an average sum, per member, of £100)[311] may require[312] the company to publish on a website[313] a statement setting out any matter relating to the audit of the company's accounts or the ceasing of the auditor to hold office that the members propose to raise at the next accounts meeting of the company.[314]

26.149 The statement must be made available on the website within three working days of the company being required to publish it on a website[315] and must be kept available until after the meeting to which it relates,[316] although a failure to make information available on a

---

[303] As to which see 2006 Act, s 519A(3).
[304] 2006 Act, s 518(6).
[305] 2006 Act, s 518(7).
[306] 2006 Act, s 520(6), (8). For 'officer in default', see para 26.12 above.
[307] 2006 Act, s 523(4), (6). For 'officer in default', see para 26.12 above.
[308] 2006 Act, ss 520(7) and 523(5).
[309] For the purposes of the 2006 Act, Chapter 5, ss 527–30 a company is a quoted company if it is a quoted company in accordance with s 385 in relation to the financial year to which the accounts to be laid at the next accounts meeting relate.
[310] 2006 Act, s 527(2)(a). Beneficial owners of shares held by nominees can join in the exercise of rights under s 527 if they do so in accordance with s 153.
[311] 2006 Act, s 527(2)(b).
[312] The request may be sent to the company in hard-copy or electronic form and must be received by the company at least one week before the meeting to which it relates: s 527(4)(a), (d).
[313] The technical requirements as regards the website are contained in s 528. In short, the website must (a) be maintained on behalf of the company, (b) identify the company in question, and (c) be accessible free of charge.
[314] 2006 Act, s 527(1).
[315] 2006 Act, s 528(4)(a).
[316] 2006 Act, s 528(4)(b).

website throughout the relevant period will be disregarded if (1) the information was made available on the website for part of the period and (2) the failure is wholly attributable to circumstances that it would not be reasonable to have expected the company to prevent or avoid.[317]

It should be noted that a quoted company is not required to place on a website a statement **26.150** under this section if, on an application by the company or another person who claims to be aggrieved, the court is satisfied that the rights conferred by this section are being abused.[318]

Criminal liability of directors in respect of website publication

Where a company fails to comply with s 528 or s 529, an offence (punishable by fine) is com- **26.151** mitted by every officer in default.[319]

F. Provision of Information to the Registrar

The 2006 Act, Part 24, ss 853A–853L were introduced by the Small Business, Enterprise and **26.152** Employment Act 2015 to replace the previous provisions in Part 24, ss 854–8 in respect of a company's annual return.[320] The new Part 24 imposes a series of duties to provide relevant information to the registrar. In addition, there is a duty to confirm that the other duties have been complied with. These are explained in the following paragraphs.

(1) Delivery and notification duties

Confirmation statements

Every company must, before the end of the period of 14 days after the end of each review **26.153** period, deliver to the registrar (a) such information as is necessary to ensure that the company is able to make the statement referred to in paragraph (b), and (b) a statement (a 'confirmation statement') confirming that all information required to be delivered by the company to the registrar in relation to the confirmation period concerned under any relevant duty (i) has been delivered, or (ii) is being delivered at the same time as the confirmation statement.[321] For these purposes the relevant duties are the duties set out below.[322]

The 'confirmation statement' is (a) in relation to a company's first confirmation statement, **26.154** the period beginning with the day of the company's incorporation and ending with the date specified in the statement ('the confirmation date'); and (b) in relation to any other confirmation statement of a company, the period beginning with the day after the confirmation date of the last such statement and ending with the confirmation date of the confirmation statement concerned.[323]

The confirmation date of a confirmation statement must be no later than the last day of **26.155** the review period concerned.[324] Each of the following is a review period (a) the period of

---

[317] 2006 Act, s 528(5).
[318] 2006 Act, s 528(5).
[319] 2006 Act, s 530.
[320] SBEE Act, s 92 which fully came into effect on 30 June 2016.
[321] 2006 Act, s 853A(1).
[322] 2006 Act, s 853A(2).
[323] 2006 Act, s 853A(3).
[324] 2006 Act, s 853A(4).

12 months beginning with the day of the company's incorporation; (b) each period of 12 months beginning with the day after the end of the previous review period.[325]

26.156 Where a company delivers a confirmation statement with a confirmation date which is earlier than the last day of the review period concerned, the next review period is the period of 12 months beginning with the day after the confirmation date.[326]

26.157 For the purpose of making a confirmation statement, a company is entitled to assume that any information has been properly delivered to the registrar if it has been delivered within the period of five days ending with the date on which the statement is delivered.[327] However, this does not apply in a case where the company has received notice from the registrar that such information has not been properly delivered.[328]

Relevant events

26.158 The 2006 Act, s.853B introduces the concept of a duty to notify the registrar of the occurrence of a 'relevant event'. These duties are:

(1) to give notice of a change in the address of the company's registered office;[329]

(2) in the case of a company in respect of which an election is in force to keep membership information on the central register,[330] to deliver anything as mentioned in 2006 Act, s 128E;[331]

(3) to give notice of a change in directors or in particulars required to be included in register of directors or register of directors' residential addresses;[332]

(4) in the case of a company in respect of which an election is in force to keep information in register of directors or register of directors' residential addresses on the central register,[333] to deliver anything as mentioned in 2006 Act, s 167D;[334]

(5) in the case of a private company with a secretary or a public company, to give notice of a change in secretary or joint secretaries or in particulars required to be included in register of secretaries;[335]

(6) in the case of a private company with a secretary in respect of which an election is in force to keep information in register of secretaries on central register,[336] to deliver anything as mentioned in 2006 Act, s 279D;[337]

(7) in the case of a company in respect of which an election is in force to keep information in the PSC register (register of people with significant control) on the central register,[338] to deliver anything as mentioned in 2006 Act, s 790ZA;[339] and

---

[325] 2006 Act, s 853A(5).

[326] 2006 Act, s 853A(6).

[327] 2006 Act, s 853A(7).

[328] 2006 Act, s 853A(8).

[329] See 2006 Act, s 87.

[330] See 2006 Act, s 128B.

[331] By 2006 Act, s 128E(2): information that the company would have been obliged under the 2006 Act to enter in its register of members, had the election not been in force, except the dates mentioned in s 128E(3).

[332] See 2006 Act, s 167.

[333] See 2006 Act, s 167A.

[334] By 2006 Act, s 167D(2): changes of which the company would have been obliged to give notice under s 167, had the election not been in force, and any statement that would have had to accompany the notice.

[335] See 2006 Act, s 276.

[336] See 2006 Act, s 279A.

[337] By 2006 Act, s 279D(2): changes of which the company would have been obliged to give notice under s 276, had the election not been in force, and any statement that would have had to accompany the notice.

[338] See 2006 Act, s 790X.

[339] By 2006 Act, s 790ZA(2); information that the company would have been obliged under ss 790M–790V to enter in its PSC register, had the election not been in force.

(8) in the case of a company which keeps any company records at a place other than its registered office,[340] to give notice of a change in the address of that place.[341]

Change in company's principal business activities

26.159 Where (a) a company makes a confirmation statement, and (b) there has been a change in the company's principal business activities during the confirmation period concerned, the company must give notice to the registrar of the change at the same time as it delivers the confirmation statement.[342] In this regard it should be noted that the information as to the company's new principal business activities may be given by reference to one or more categories of any prescribed system of classifying business activities.

Statement of capital

26.160 Where a company having a share capital makes a confirmation statement, the company must deliver a statement of capital to the registrar at the same time as it delivers the confirmation statement.[343]

26.161 However, this requirement does not apply if there has been no change in any of the matters required to be dealt with by the statement of capital since the last such statement was delivered to the registrar.[344]

26.162 The statement of capital must state with respect to the company's share capital at the confirmation date (a) the total number of shares of the company, (b) the aggregate nominal value of those shares, (c) the aggregate amount (if any) unpaid on those shares (whether on account of their nominal value or by way of premium), and (d) for each class of shares (i) prescribed particulars of the rights attached to the shares, (ii) the total number of shares of that class, and (iii) the aggregate nominal value of shares of that class.[345]

Trading status of shares

26.163 Where a company having a share capital makes a confirmation statement, the company must deliver to the registrar a statement dealing with the matters mentioned set out below at the same time as it delivers the confirmation statement.[346] But this does not apply if and to the extent that the last statement delivered to the registrar applies equally to the confirmation period concerned.[347]

26.164 The relevant matters are (a) whether any of the company's shares were, at any time during the confirmation period concerned, shares admitted to trading on a relevant market or on any other market which is outside the United Kingdom, and (b) if so, whether both of the conditions mentioned below were satisfied throughout the confirmation period concerned.[348]

---

[340] In accordance with Companies (Company Records) Regulations 2008 (SI 2008/3006), made under 2006 Act, s 1136.
[341] Companies (Company Records) Regulations 2008 (SI 2008/3006), reg 3.
[342] 2006 Act, s 853C.
[343] 2006 Act, s 853D(1), (2).
[344] 2006 Act, s 853D(3).
[345] 2006 Act, s 853D(4).
[346] 2006 Act, s 853E(1), (2).
[347] 2006 Act, s 853E(3).
[348] 2006 Act, s 853E(4).

26.165 The conditions are that (a) there were shares of the company which were shares admitted to trading on a relevant market; (b) the company was a DTR5 issuer.[349]

Shareholder information: non-traded companies

26.166 Where (a) a non-traded company[350] makes a confirmation statement, and (b) there is no election in force under the 2006 Act, s 128B in respect of the company, the company must deliver the information set out below to the registrar at the same time as it delivers the confirmation statement.[351] However, this does not apply if and to the extent that the information most recently delivered to the registrar in this regard applies equally to the confirmation period concerned.[352]

26.167 The information is (a) the name (as it appears in the company's register of members) of every person who was at any time during the confirmation period a member of the company, (b) the number of shares of each class held at the end of the confirmation date concerned by each person who was a member of the company at that time, (c) the number of shares of each class transferred during the confirmation period concerned by or to each person who was a member of the company at any time during that period, and (d) the dates of registration of those transfers.[353]

Shareholder information: certain traded companies

26.168 Where a traded company[354] makes a confirmation statement, the company must deliver the following information to the registrar at the same time as it delivers the confirmation statement.[355] However, this does not apply if and to the extent the information most recently delivered to the registrar applies equally to the confirmation period concerned.[356]

26.169 The information is (a) the name and address (as they appear in the company's register of members) of each person who, at the end of the confirmation date concerned, held at least 5 per cent of the issued shares of any class of the company, and (b) the number of shares of each class held by each such person at that time.[357]

---

[349] 2006 Act, s 853E(5). For these purposes, 'DTR5 issuer' means an issuer to which Chapter 5 of the Disclosure Rules and Transparency Rules sourcebook made by the FCA (as amended or replaced from time to time) applies; and 'relevant market' means any of the markets mentioned in the Financial Services and Markets Act 2000 (Prescribed Markets and Qualifying Investments) Order 2001, article 4(1).

[350] A 'non-traded company' is a company none of whose shares were, at any time during the confirmation period concerned, shares admitted to trading on a relevant market or on any other market which is outside the UK: see 2006 Act, s 853F(2).

[351] 2006 Act, s 853F(1), (3).

[352] 2006 Act, s 853F(4).

[353] 2006 Act, s 853F(5).

[354] A 'traded company' is a company any of whose shares were, at any time during the confirmation period concerned, shares admitted to trading on a relevant market or on any other market which is outside the UK: 2006 Act, s 853G(2). However, this is subject to the proviso that a company is not a traded company if throughout the confirmation period concerned (a) there were shares of the company which were shares admitted to trading on a relevant market, and (b) the company was a DTR5 issuer.

[355] 2006 Act, s 853G(1), (4).

[356] 2006 Act, s 853G(5).

[357] 2006 Act, s 853G(6).

Exemption from Part 21A

Also, where a company (a) which is not a DTR5 issuer, and (b) to which Part 21A does not **26.170**
apply (information about people with significant control[358]), makes a confirmation statement, the company must deliver to the registrar a statement of the fact that it is a company to
which Part 21A does not apply at the same time as it delivers the confirmation statement.[359]
However, again, this does not apply if the last statement delivered to the registrar applies
equally to the confirmation period concerned.

People with significant control

Finally, where (a) a company to which Part 21A (information about people with sig- **26.171**
nificant control) applies makes a confirmation statement, and (b) there is no election in
force under the 2006 Act, s 790X in respect of the company, the company must deliver
the information stated in its PSC register[360] to the registrar at the same time as it delivers the
confirmation statement.[361] Again, however, this does not apply if and to the extent that
the information most recently delivered to the registrar applies equally to the confirmation
period concerned.

(2) Failure to deliver confirmation statement

If a company fails to deliver a confirmation statement before the end of the period of 14 **26.172**
days after the end of a review period an offence is committed by (a) the company, (b) every
director of the company, (c) in the case of a private company with a secretary or a public
company, every secretary of the company, and (d) every other officer of the company who
is in default.[362] For this purpose a shadow director is treated as a director.

A person guilty of such an offence is liable on summary conviction to a fine, and, for contin- **26.173**
ued contravention, a daily default fine not exceeding the greater of £500 and one-tenth of
level 4 on the standard scale.[363]

The contravention continues until such time as a confirmation statement specifying a con- **26.174**
firmation date no later than the last day of the review period concerned is delivered by the
company to the registrar.[364]

It is a defence for a director or secretary charged with this offence to prove that the **26.175**
person took all reasonable steps to avoid the commission or continuation of the
offence.[365]

In the case of continued contravention, an offence is also committed by every officer who is **26.176**
in default in relation to the continued contravention,[366] punishable by a fine not exceeding
the greater of £500 and one-tenth of level 4 on the standard scale for each day on which the
contravention continues and the person is in default.[367]

---

[358] 2006 Act, s 790B.
[359] 2006 Act, s 853H(1).
[360] 'PSC register' has the same meaning as in Part 21A (see 2006 Act, s 790C).
[361] 2006 Act, s 853I.
[362] 2006 Act, s 853L(1).
[363] 2006 Act, s 853L(2).
[364] 2006 Act, s 853L(3).
[365] 2006 Act, s 853L(4).
[366] 2006 Act, s 853L(5).
[367] 2006 Act, s 853L(6).

27

CAPITAL AND DISTRIBUTIONS

Stephen Robins

A. Introduction

This chapter is primarily concerned with the functions, responsibilities, and liabilities of directors in respect of shares. Sections B to F cover the statutory provisions contained in the 2006 Act, Parts 17, 18, and 20 to 23.[1]   **27.01**

Section B(6), dealing with particular rules about the issue of shares by quoted companies, discusses the provisions in FSMA of particular concern to directors.   **27.02**

---

[1] Parts 17 and 18 came into force on 1 October 2009, except for (a) s 544 (transferability of shares) which came into force on 6 April 2008, and (b) ss 641(1)(a), (2), (6), 642, 644, 652(1) and (3), 654 (enabling a private company to reduce its capital without having to obtain a court order) which came into force on 1 October 2008. Also on 1 October 2008 the restrictions in the 1985 Act, ss 151, 153, 155–8 on the giving by a private company of financial assistance for the acquisition of its own shares, including the 'whitewash' procedure, were repealed. Parts 20–3 came into force on 6 April 2008, except for ss 791–810, 811(1)–(3), 813, 815–28 (information about interests in shares) which came into force on 20 January 2007. Part 21A came into force on 30 June 2016, having been inserted by the SBEE Act 2015, s 81 and Sch 3.

B. Allotment and Issue of Shares

(1) The nature of a share

27.03   A share is personal property (not real estate)[2] in the nature of a chose in action[3] comprising 'the interest of a shareholder in the company measured by a sum of money, for the purpose of liability in the first place, and of interest in the second, but also consisting of a series of mutual covenants entered into by all the shareholders inter se'.[4] In the 2006 Act, the term 'share' in relation to a company means share in the company's share capital.[5] A certificate under the common seal of a company specifying any shares held by a member is prima facie evidence of his title to those shares.[6]

27.04   Shares in a limited company having a share capital must each have a fixed nominal value.[7] An allotment of a share that does not have a fixed nominal value is void.[8] Further, such an allotment is an offence (punishable by fine) committed by every officer in default.[9] Shares in a limited company having a share capital may be denominated in any currency, and different classes of shares may be denominated in different currencies.[10]

27.05   Each share must be designated with a specific number, unless all the issued shares in the company or in any particular class are fully paid up and rank *pari passu* for all purposes, in which case numbering is not required.[11] In order to improve transparency of ownership of companies, a company may no longer issue share warrants to bearer.[12]

27.06   For the purposes of the 2006 Act, shares in a company are taken to be allotted when a person acquires the unconditional right to be included in the company's register of members in respect of the shares or, if the company has elected to keep information on the central register, to have his name and other particulars delivered to the registrar in respect of the shares.[13] A share is not issued until the processes of application, allotment, and registration have been completed.[14]

---

[2] 2006 Act, s 541.

[3] *R v Williams* [1942] AC 541, 549; *Colonial Bank v Whinney* (1886) 11 App Cas 426.

[4] *Borland's Trustee v Steel Bros & Co Ltd* [1901] 1 Ch 279, 288, per Farwell J.

[5] 2006 Act, s 540(1). Section 540(2) provides that a company's shares may no longer be converted into stock, but this is subject to transitional provisions for conversions pursuant to company resolution made before 1 October 2009 (2006 Commencement Order No 8, Sch 2, para 41).

[6] 2006 Act, s 768(1). For articles concerning share certificates, see Table A, regs 6 and 7; Model Articles (pcls) 24 and 25; Model Articles (plc) 46 and 47. Model Article (plc) 50 contemplates that a public company may wish to issue uncertificated shares (2006 Act, ss 783–90).

[7] 2006 Act, s 542(1).

[8] 2006 Act, s 542(2).

[9] 2006 Act, s 542(4) and (5).

[10] 2006 Act, s 542(3), codifying existing practice: *Re Scandinavian Bank Group plc* [1988] Ch 87. But see s 765 (initial authorized minimum share capital requirement for public company to be met by reference to share capital denominated in sterling or euros). A company's articles usually give it power to issue shares with such rights or restrictions as the company may by ordinary resolution determine: Table A, reg 2; Model Article (pcls) 22; Model Article (plc) 43.

[11] 2006 Act, s 543.

[12] 2006 Act, s 779(4) and SBEE Act 2015, s 84 and Sch 4, which contains detailed provisions in respect of the surrender of existing warrants, with offences committed by officers in default in the event of non-compliance with those provisions. These provisions came into force on 26 May 2015; SBEE Act 2015, s 164(3)(g).

[13] 2006 Act, s 558, as amended by SBEE Act 2015, s 94, Sch 5, Part 2, paras 11, 20 with effect from 30 June 2016. For the option to keep information on the central register, see 2006 Act, ss 128A–128K.

[14] *National Westminster Bank plc v Inland Revenue Commissioners* [1995] 1 AC 119, HL.

(2) General rules

Authorization of allotment

Where a private company has a single class of shares, no specific authorization to allot shares is necessary, and the directors may exercise any power of the company to allot shares or grant rights to subscribe for or to convert any security into such shares, except to the extent that they are prohibited from doing so by the company's articles.[15]

27.07

In the case of a private company with more than one class of shares, and in the case of a public company, the position is different, and specific authorization to allot shares, or to grant subscription/conversion rights, is required, either by way of authorization in the articles, or by way of authorization by resolution.[16] Such authorization may be specific or general and conditional or unconditional.[17] The authorization must: (i) state the maximum number of shares to which it relates; and (ii) specify a date within the next five years on which the authority is to expire.[18] The shares must be allotted, or the subscription/conversion rights granted, within the period of the authorization's validity, although there is nothing to prevent the allotment of shares after the expiration of the authorization pursuant to an agreement entered into prior to that time, if the authorization itself expressly permits this.[19] In the case of subscription/conversion rights, no authority is required for the allotment of shares pursuant to exercise of the rights.[20]

27.08

In either case, the power to allot shares must be exercised bona fide in the best interests of the company as a whole and not for a collateral purpose[21] and fairly as between different shareholders.[22]

27.09

If the statutory rules relating to authorization of allotment are not observed, any director of the company who knowingly contravened the statutory requirements or permitted or authorized the contravention is guilty of an offence punishable by fine.[23] In addition, attempts by directors to use the power of allotment to increase or consolidate their own control of a company, or to prevent a rival from gaining control of a company, are likely to be held to be invalid.[24]

27.10

---

[15] 2006 Act, s 550. This is a new provision recommended by the CLR: *Final Report* at para 4.5, which only applies to existing or transitional companies if the members have resolved that the directors should be given the powers in s 550 (2006 Act Commencement Order No 8, Sch 2, paras 43 and 44). The term 'subscribe for' is considered to possess its ordinary meaning of taking shares for cash: *Government Stocks & Other Securities Investment Co Ltd v Christopher* [1956] 1 WLR 237. Table A and the Model Articles do not restrict the power of the directors to allot shares, but members of private companies may require articles containing such restrictions in order to preserve their proportionate interests in the company.

[16] s 551(1).

[17] s 551(2).

[18] 2006 Act, s 551(3). It should be noted that an authority which is about to expire may be extended for a further five years: s 551(4). A resolution renewing such authority must comply with the same requirements, ie it must state the maximum number of shares to which it relates and specify an expiry date which must be a date within the next five years: s 551(5).

[19] 2006 Act, s 550(7).

[20] 2006 Act, s 549(3).

[21] *Howard Smith Ltd v Ampol Petroleum Ltd* [1974] AC 821, PC. See also *Eclairs Group Ltd v JKX Oil & Gas Plc* [2015] Bus LR 1395, SC.

[22] *Mutual Life Insurance Co of New York v Rank Organisation Ltd* [1985] BCLC 11.

[23] 2006 Act, s 549(4) and (5).

[24] *Fraser v Whalley* (1864) 2 Hem & M 10; *Punt v Symons & Co Ltd* [1903] 2 Ch 506; *Piercy v S Mills & Co Ltd* [1920] 1 Ch 77; *Hogg v Cramphorn Ltd* [1967] Ch 254; *Bamford v Bamford* [1970] Ch 212, CA; *Howard*

Commissions etc

27.11   The general rule[25] is that a company must not apply any of its shares or capital money,[26] either directly or indirectly, in payment of any commission, discount, or allowance to any person in consideration of his agreeing to subscribe for shares in the company or procuring or agreeing to procure subscriptions.[27] To 'subscribe for' shares generally means to take up shares for cash and does not include a purchase of issued shares.[28] In deciding whether the general rule has been contravened, the court will look at the substance of the transaction, not the form.[29] Where shares are issued partly in consideration of subscribing or procuring subscriptions and partly for other consideration, the whole issue falls within the prohibition.[30]

27.12   The exception to this rule is that commissions may be paid if, but only if, the payment of commission is authorized by the company's articles and the commission does not exceed 10 per cent of the price at which the shares are issued or the amount or rate authorized by the articles, whichever is the less.[31]

27.13   It has been held that commission paid in contravention of the statutory provisions is not recoverable unless the recipient had notice of the illegality.[32] In such circumstances, it may be the case that the directors are liable in damages to compensate the company for its loss, depending on the facts.

Registration of allotment

27.14   An allotment of shares must be registered as soon as practicable and in any event within two months after the date of the allotment.[33] If the company has elected to keep information on the central register, that obligation is replaced by an obligation to deliver particulars of the allotment of shares to the Registrar in accordance with the 2006 Act, Part 8, Chapter 2A.[34] Further, the company[35] must, within one month of making the allotment, deliver a return to the Registrar[36] and the return must contain the prescribed information and must be accompanied by a statement of capital.[37]

Smith Ltd v Ampol Petroleum Ltd [1974] AC 821, PC; *Eclairs Group Ltd v JKX Oil & Gas Plc* [2015] Bus LR 1395, SC. See also 2006 Act, s 171.

[25]   Which was a rule at common law prior to its statutory formulation: see *Ooregum Gold Mining Co of India v Roper* [1892] AC 125, in which the House of Lords held that the payment of such commissions was ultra vires. See also *Australian Investment Trust Ltd v Strand & Pitt Street Properties Ltd* [1932] AC 735.

[26]   The phrase 'shares or capital money' means unissued shares or money derived from the issue of shares: *Hilder v Dexter* [1902] AC 474. Premium paid over par value falls within the scope of the term 'capital money': *Shorto v Colwill* [1909] WN 218.

[27]   2006 Act, s 552(1).

[28]   *Government Stock & Other Securities Investment Co v Christopher* [1956] 1 WLR 237.

[29]   *Booth v New Afrikaner Gold Mining Co Ltd* [1903] 1 Ch 295; *Keatings v Paringa Consolidated Mines Ltd* [1902] WN 15.

[30]   *Banking Service Corporation Ltd v Toronto Finance Corpn Ltd* [1928] AC 333.

[31]   2006 Act, s 553(2). The exception was first introduced by the Companies Act 1900. Authorization in the memorandum is not sufficient: *Re Republic of Bolivia Exploration Syndicate* [1914] 1 Ch 139. Table A, reg 4 and Model Article (plc) 44 provide for a company to which those articles apply to pay commission on subscription for its shares.

[32]   *Andreae v Zinc Mines of Great Britain Ltd* [1918] 2 KB 454.

[33]   2006 Act, s 554(1).

[34]   2006 Act, s 554(2A).

[35]   Similar provisions apply as regards unlimited companies: 2006 Act, s 556.

[36]   2006 Act, s 555(2).

[37]   2006 Act, s 555(3), which, with s 555(4), was recommended by the CLR: *Final Report* at para 7.30. It implements the requirement in the Second Company Law Directive (77/91/EEC) that 'the statutes or

If the company fails to register an allotment in accordance with s 554, an offence (punishable **27.15** by fine) is committed by every officer in default.[38] If the company fails to deliver a return of allotment containing the appropriate particulars and the statement of capital to the Registrar within one month, an offence (punishable by fine, with a daily default fine for continued contravention) is committed by every officer in default[39] although there is special provision enabling such person to apply to the court for relief on the grounds that the omission to deliver the document was accidental or due to inadvertence.[40] The court may grant such relief as it considers to be just and equitable; such relief will ordinarily take the form of an extension of time in which to deliver the document.[41] Relief may be granted on the basis of ignorance or misunderstanding of the statutory provisions.[42]

Payment for shares

The general rule is that shares must not be allotted gratuitously[43] or at a discount[44] (ie for less **27.16** than the nominal value of the shares in question). The allottee must pay at least the nominal value of the shares: 'the liability of a member continues so long as anything remains unpaid upon his shares. Nothing but payment, and payment in full, can put an end to the liability.'[45]

Any shares allotted in contravention of the Act give rise to a liability[46] on the part of the allot- **27.17** tee to pay the company an amount equal to the discount,[47] with interest.[48] Any subsequent holder of the shares will be similarly liable, save for a bona fide purchaser for value without notice of the contravention.[49] An allotment of shares at par subsequent to allotment at a premium does not constitute an allotment at a discount.[50]

A company may, if so authorized by its articles, make arrangements on the issue of shares for **27.18** a difference between the allottee shareholders in the amounts and time of payment of calls

---

instruments of incorporation of the company shall always give at least the following information ... (c) when the company has no authorised capital, the amount of the subscribed capital'. The prescribed information is specified in the Companies (Shares and Share Capital) Order 2009 (SI 2009/388), reg 3. The statement of capital must contain the usual particulars, as specified in s 555(4) (ie total number of shares, aggregate nominal value, rights attached, total number in each class, aggregate nominal value of each class, and amounts paid up). The Companies (Shares and Share Capital) Order 2009 (SI 2009/388), reg 2 states the prescribed particulars for the purposes of s 555(4)(c)(i).

[38] 2006 Act, s 554(3) and (4).

[39] 2006 Act, s 557(1) and (2).

[40] 2006 Act, s 557(3). Accordingly the legislation envisages that a person may be 'in default' within s 1121(3) by accidentally or inadvertently authorizing, permitting, participating in, or failing to take all reasonable steps to prevent the contravention.

[41] 2006 Act, s 557(3).

[42] See *Re Jackson & Co Ltd* [1899] 1 Ch 348; *Re Tom Tit Cycle Co Ltd* (1899) 43 Sol Jo 334; *Re Whitefriars Financial Co Ltd* [1899] 1 Ch 184.

[43] *Re Wragg Ltd* [1897] 1 Ch 796; *Ooregum Gold Mining Co of India Ltd v Roper* [1892] AC 125; *Re Eddystone Marine Insurance Co* [1893] Ch 9. Note that Model Article (pcls) 21 contemplates that shares in a private company will be issued fully paid up, whereas Model Articles (plc) 52–62 contemplate that a public company may issue partly paid shares (as may a company to which Table A applies (regs 8–22)).

[44] 2006 Act, s 580(1).

[45] *Ooregum Gold Mining Co of India v Roper* [1892] AC 125, 145 (Lord Macnaghten). See also *Re Eddystone Marine Insurance Co* [1893] 3 Ch 9 and *Welton v Saffery* [1897] AC 299.

[46] *Re Bradford Investments plc* [1991] BCLC 224.

[47] 2006 Act, s 580(2).

[48] 2006 Act, s 609(1). The rate of interest is 5 per cent per annum or such other rate as may be specified by order made by the Secretary of State.

[49] 2006 Act, s 588(1), (2).

[50] *Hilder v Dexter* [1902] AC 474.

on their shares and may accept payment of the amount remaining at any time.[51] Further, the company may, if so authorized by its articles, pay a dividend in proportion to the amount paid up on each share where a larger amount is paid up on some shares than on others.[52]

27.19 The general rule as to payment (subject to special rules for public companies) is that shares allotted by a company and any premium on them may be paid up in money or money's worth (including goodwill and know-how).[53] A debt due from the company and payable so that the demands could be set off will suffice,[54] as will property handed over pursuant to a binding contract.[55]

27.20 However, as Lord Watson said in *Ooregum Gold Mining Co of India v Roper*:[56]

> The court 'would doubtless refuse effect to a colourable transaction, entered into for the purpose or with the obvious result of enabling the company to issue its shares at a discount; but it has been ruled that, so long as the company honestly regards the consideration given as fairly representing the nominal value of the shares in cash, its estimate ought not to be critically examined'.

It is only where the consideration is 'colourable' or illusory or where it is manifest on the face of the instrument that the shares are issued at a discount that the court will be prepared to consider the adequacy of the consideration.[57] Whether the consideration is colourable is a question of fact in each case.[58]

27.21 Directors who allot shares at a discount are guilty of a breach of duty to the company and are liable to pay the amount of the discount and interest to the company if that amount cannot be recovered from the allottee or holder of the shares, as where the shares have passed into the hands of a bona fide purchase for value from the original allottee.[59]

Share premiums

27.22 If a company issues shares at a premium, whether for cash or otherwise, a sum equal to the aggregate amount or value of the premium on those shares must be transferred to an account called the 'share premium account'.[60] Sums transferred to the share premium account may be used to write off the expenses of issuing those shares and any commission lawfully paid on the issue of those shares.[61] The company may also use the share premium account to pay up new shares to be allotted to members as fully paid bonus shares.[62] Otherwise, and subject to specific provisions applicable in respect of group reconstruction relief[63] and merger relief,[64]

---

[51] 2006 Act, s 581.

[52] 2006 Act, s 581.

[53] 2006 Act, s 582(1). See *Drummond's Case* (1869) 4 Ch App 772; *Pell's Case* (1869) 5 Ch App 11; *Re Baglan Hall Colliery Co* (1870) 5 Ch App 346; *Schroder's Case* (1870) LR 11 Eq 131; *Jones' Case* (1870) 6 Ch App 48, *Key's Case* (1868) 16 WR 1103; *Re Wragg Ltd* [1897] 1 Ch 796.

[54] *Forbes and Judd's Case* (1870) 5 Ch App 270.

[55] *Re Baglan Hall Colliery Co* (1870) 5 Ch App 346; see also *Dent's Case* (1873) LR 15 Eq 407; *Fothergill's Case* (1873) 8 Ch App 270.

[56] [1892] AC 125, 137.

[57] *Re White Star Line Ltd* [1938] Ch 458; *Mosely v Koffyfontein Mines Ltd* [1904] 2 Ch 108; *Re Wragg Ltd* [1897] 1 Ch 769.

[58] *Re Innes & Co Ltd* [1903] 2 Ch 254.

[59] *Hirsche v Sims* [1894] AC 654.

[60] 2006 Act, s 610(1).

[61] 2006 Act, s 610(2).

[62] 2006 Act, s 610(3).

[63] 2006 Act, s 611.

[64] 2006 Act, s 612.

the balance standing to the credit of the share premium account is subject to the ordinary rules relating to reduction of capital, and the share premium account is treated for these purposes as though it were merely part of the company's paid-up share capital.[65] It follows that directors may incur civil or criminal liability in respect of the share premium account in precisely the same circumstances as may result in liability upon any unlawful reduction of the company's capital generally.

(3) Pre-emption rights

Pre-emption rights in respect of newly issued shares may exist in the company's articles or under statute. Alternatively, pre-emption rights may be excluded by the company's articles, or excluded from operating in certain circumstances, or disapplied for various reasons. These various possibilities will be considered before considering the procedure to be followed where such rights exist and apply and the liability of directors for contravention of pre-emption rights. The relevant statutory provisions, which provide the overarching code for pre-emption rights, including such rights in the articles, apply to 'equity securities' (defined to mean ordinary shares or rights to subscribe for or convert securities into ordinary shares; 'ordinary shares' being defined in turn to mean shares which are uncapped as to dividend and capital). These provisions have no application to the taking of shares by subscribers to the memorandum on the formation of the company.[66]

Pre-emption rights in the articles

In many cases, a company's articles will contain a pre-emption provision, prohibiting the company from allotting ordinary shares of a particular class unless it has offered those shares to existing shareholders.[67]

Pre-emption rights under statute

The 2006 Act, s 561(1),[68] states the general rule, giving existing shareholders a right of pre-emption in respect of equity securities:[69]

27.23

27.24

27.25

> A company must not allot equity securities to a person on any terms unless—
> (a) it has made an offer[70] to each person who holds ordinary shares in the company to allot to him on the same or more favourable terms a proportion of those securities that is as nearly as practicable equal to the proportion in nominal value held by him of the ordinary share capital of the company, and

---

[65] 2006 Act, s 610(4).

[66] 2006 Act, s 577.

[67] Such provisions fall within 2006 Act, s 568. 1985 Act Table A and the draft Model Articles do not include pre-emption provisions, leaving that matter to statutory control and to any additional provisions desired by the parties. Table A to earlier Companies Acts did include pre-emption provisions: see, eg the 1862 Table A, reg 27; the 1908 Table A, reg 42; the 1929 Table A, reg 35.

[68] 2006 Act, s 561(1). See *Re Sunrise Radio Ltd; Kohli v Lit* [2010] 1 BCLC 367 at paras 104–20, 132–5, 281–3 (issue of shares at par when a higher price was obtainable was unfairly prejudicial conduct; this holding not affected by judgment on appeal: [2014] 1 BCLC 427, CA). Note that shareholders' rights of pre-emption existing at 1 October 2009 are subject to transitional provisions (2006 Act Commencement Order No 8, Sch 2, paras 49–55).

[69] For the provisions in the 2006 Act 2006 about pre-emption rights (ss 560–77), s 560(1) provides that 'equity securities' are ordinary shares in the company and rights to subscribe for or convert securities into ordinary shares and that shares are not ordinary shares if, as respects dividends and capital, they carry a right to participate only up to a specified amount in a distribution. Section 560(2) and (3) explains the meaning of allotment of equity securities in ss 560–77.

[70] The offer may be in hard-copy or electronic form: s 562(2).

(b) the period during which any such offer may be accepted has expired or the company has received notice of the acceptance or refusal of every offer so made.

Treasury shares are disregarded for these purposes, so that the company is not treated as a person who holds ordinary shares, and any treasury shares are not treated as forming part of the ordinary share capital of the company.[71] The offer period must be at least 14 days and must not be withdrawn prior to its expiry.[72]

27.26 The pre-emption rights contained in the 2006 Act, s 561 are subject to:[73]

(1) exceptions to pre-emption rights in relation to the allotment of bonus shares, the allotment of equity securities for non-cash consideration (in whole or in part), or in the case of employees' share schemes;[74]

(2) exclusion of pre-emption rights for private companies;

(3) the disapplication of pre-emption rights in the circumstances described in paragraph 27.28; and

(4) savings in relation to pre-emption requirements under the 1985 Act.[75]

27.27 The statutory pre-emption rights are excluded in two cases:

(1) A private company's articles may exclude the provisions contained in the 2006 Act, ss 561 by provisions[76] either (a) generally in relation to the allotment by the company of equity securities, or (b) in relation to allotments of a particular description.[77] Furthermore, any requirement or authorization contained in the articles of a private company that is inconsistent with the statutory provisions is treated as excluding them.[78]

(2) Also, the pre-emption rights in s 561 do not apply where the company's articles contain a corresponding right in accordance with which the company makes an offer to allot to the holder of ordinary shares of the particular class and the holder or anyone in whose favour he has renounced his right accepts the offer.[79]

27.28 The directors of a private company that has only one class of shares may be given power by the articles, or by special resolution of the company, to allot shares/equity securities of that class as if the statutory right or pre-emption did not apply, or applied subject to modification.[80] Similarly, where the directors of a public or private company (with one or more classes of shares) are generally authorized to allot shares, they may be given power by the articles, or by a special resolution to allot equity securities pursuant to the authorization in a manner which would otherwise contravene the statutory pre-emption provisions.[81] Alternatively, where the directors of a public or private company are authorized (whether generally or specifically) to allot shares, the company may by special resolution disapply the statutory pre-emption rights, or apply them subject to modification, in respect of a 'specified allotment'

---

[71] 2006 Act, s 561(4).
[72] 2006 Act, s 562(4) and (5).
[73] 2006 Act, s 561(5).
[74] 2006 Act, ss 564–6.
[75] 2006 Act, s 576.
[76] 2006 Act, s 567(1).
[77] 2006 Act, s 567(2).
[78] 2006 Act, s 567(3).
[79] 2006 Act, s 568.
[80] 2006 Act, s 569.
[81] 2006 Act, s 570.

of equity securities.[82] A special resolution in respect of a specific allotment must not be proposed unless it is recommended by the directors[83] and before it is proposed the directors must make a written statement setting out their reasons for making the recommendation, the amount to be paid to the company in respect of the equity securities to be allotted, and the directors' justification of that amount.[84] It is an offence for a person knowingly or recklessly to authorize or permit the inclusion of any matter that is misleading, false, or deceptive in a material particular in such a statement.[85]

Where pre-emption rights apply, whether pursuant to statute or by reason of a pre-emption   **27.29**
provision in the company's articles, the statutory requirements as to communication of the pre-emption offer must be observed,[86] save to the extent that the company's articles provide otherwise.[87] Accordingly, the offer may be made in hard-copy or electronic form (or, where the holder's address is not known, by way of advertisement in the Gazette[88]) and must be open for acceptance for at least 14 days (and may not be withdrawn prior to its expiry date).[89]

Where applicable pre-emption requirements are contravened, the company and every officer   **27.30**
who knowingly authorized or permitted the contravention are jointly and severally liable to compensate any person to whom an offer should have been made in accordance with those provisions for any loss, damage, costs, or expense which the person has sustained or incurred by reason of the contravention.[90] Proceedings against the company and/or the directors must be commenced within two years.[91] In addition, there is authority to support the proposition that a failure to comply with pre-emption provisions may provide grounds for an unfair prejudice petition.[92]

(4) Private companies: prohibition of public offers

A private company limited by shares or limited by guarantee and having a share capital must   **27.31**
not offer to the public[93] any securities[94] of the company or allot or agree to allot any securities of the company with a view to their being offered to the public.[95] An offer is not regarded as an offer to the public if it can properly be regarded, in all the circumstances, as not being

---

[82] 2006 Act, s 571.
[83] 2006 Act, s 571(5).
[84] 2006 Act, s 571(6). The statement must be sent with the resolution if it is a written resolution or circulated with the notice calling the meeting: s 571(7).
[85] 2006 Act, s 572(2).
[86] 2006 Act, s 562.
[87] 2006 Act, s 567.
[88] 2006 Act, s 562(3).
[89] 2006 Act, s 562(4) and (5). The period in s 562(5) was reduced from 21 days to 14 days with effect from 1 October 2009 by the Companies (Share Capital and Acquisition by Company of its own Shares) Regulations 2009 (SI 2009/2022), reg 2, made in accordance with s 562(6) and (7).
[90] 2006 Act ss 563(2) and 568(4).
[91] 2006 Act, ss 563(3) and 568(5).
[92] *Re a Company (No 005134 of 1986) ex p Harris* [1989] BCLC 383.
[93] Or any section of the public: 2006 Act, s 756(2). See, generally, *Sherwell v Combined Incandescent Mantels Syndicate Ltd* [1907] WN 110 and *Re South of England Natural Gas & Petroleum Co* [1911] Ch 573.
[94] The word 'securities' means shares or debentures: 2006 Act, s 755(5), which came into effect on 6 April 2008.
[95] 2006 Act, s 755(1). There is a rebuttable statutory presumption that an allotment or agreement to allot securities was made with a view to their being offered to the public if an offer of the securities (or any of them) to the public is made within six months after the allotment or agreement to allot or before the receipt by the company of the whole of the consideration to be received in respect of the securities: 2006 Act, s 755(2).

calculated to result, directly or indirectly, in securities of the company becoming available to persons other than those receiving the offer or otherwise being a private concern[96] of the person receiving it and the person making it.[97] A private company will not breach the prohibition if it makes an offer to the public in good faith in pursuance of arrangements under which it is to re-register as a public company before the shares are allotted, or if it undertakes to, and does, re-register as a public company within six months of the offer being made.[98]

27.32 If it appears to the court that a private company is proposing to make an offer to the public in contravention of the prohibition, the court may restrain the company from so doing.[99] Where the contravention has already occurred, the court may make an order requiring the company to re-register as a public company[100] or make a winding-up order in respect of the company[101] or make a 'remedial order'. A 'remedial order' is an order for the purpose of putting a person affected by a contravention of the prohibition in the position he would have been in if the contravention had not occurred and may require any person knowingly concerned in the contravention to offer to purchase any of the securities at such price and on such other terms as the court thinks fit.[102] Officers of the company are obvious targets for remedial orders, but the court's powers are wide, and a remedial order may be made against any person knowingly involved in the contravention, whether or not an officer of the company.[103] Where a remedial order is made against the company itself, the court may provide for the reduction of the company's capital accordingly.[104]

(5) Public companies: particular rules

Minimum capital requirements

27.33 A public company must not do business or exercise any borrowing powers unless the Registrar has issued it with a trading certificate which will be issued on an application by the company if the Registrar is satisfied that the nominal value of the company's allotted share capital is not less than the authorized minimum.[105] The 'authorized minimum' is currently £50,000 or the prescribed euro equivalent.[106]

27.34 An application for a certificate must (1) state that the nominal value of the company's allotted share capital is not less than the authorized minimum, (2) specify the amount, or estimated amount, of the company's preliminary expenses, (3) specify any amount or benefit

---

[96] The term 'private concern' is rebuttably presumed where an offer is made to a person already connected with the company (eg an existing member or employee or family member or widow of such a person or existing debenture holder of the company: s 756(5)) or where the offer is made in the context of an employees' share scheme: s 756(4).

[97] 2006 Act, s 756(4).

[98] 2006 Act, s 755(3).

[99] 2006 Act, s 757(2). 2006 Act, ss 757–9 are new provisions, to which the Companies (Authorised Minimum) Regulations 2008 (SI 2008/729), reg 6, and the Companies (Authorised Minimum) Regulations 2009 (SI 2009/2425), reg 6, both concerning determination of exchange rates, apply.

[100] 2006 Act, s 758(2).

[101] 2006 Act, s 758(3).

[102] 2006 Act, s 759(3).

[103] 2006 Act, s 759(4).

[104] 2006 Act, s 759(5).

[105] 2006 Act, s 761(1) and (2).

[106] 2006 Act, s 763(1), (2). The Companies (Authorised Minimum) Regulations 2009 (SI 2009/2425), reg 2 prescribes €57,100 as the equivalent amount.

paid or given, or intended to be paid or given, to any promoter[107] of the company, and the consideration for the payment or benefit, (4) be accompanied by a statement of compliance, and (5) be accompanied by a statement of the aggregate amount paid up on the shares of the company on account of their nominal value.[108] It should be noted that a false representation as to the capital position for the purpose of securing a certificate is grounds for disqualification of directors under the CDDA.[109]

Once obtained, a trading certificate is conclusive evidence that the company is entitled to **27.35** do business and exercise any borrowing powers.[110] However, if a company does business or exercises any borrowing powers without a trading certificate, an offence (punishable by fine) is committed by every officer in default as well as by the company itself.[111] Furthermore, in addition to this criminal liability, the directors may incur civil liability for trading or borrowing without a trading certificate: the 2006 Act, s 767(3) provides that the directors of a public company will be jointly and severally liable to provide indemnification to any person who suffers loss by reason of the fact that the company has traded with or borrowed from such person without a trading certificate and then failed to perform the contractual obligations owed to such person and arising from such trade or borrowing within 21 days of being called on to do so.[112] The directors liable in this manner will be those who were directors at the time the company entered into the transaction in question.[113]

Liability to return allotment money when issue not fully subscribed

Where shares in a public company are offered[114] for subscription, no allotment may be made **27.36** unless the issue is subscribed in full or the offer is made on terms that the shares subscribed for may be allotted in any event or upon satisfaction of specified conditions which are in fact satisfied.[115]

If money has been received from applications for shares which are not allotted by reason of **27.37** this prohibition, that money must be repaid to the applicants forthwith (without interest).[116] If any money is not repaid within 48 days after the first making of the offer, the directors and

---

[107] The term 'promoter' is a 'short and convenient way of designating those who set in motion the machinery by which the [Companies] Act enables them to create an incorporated company': *Erlanger v New Sombrero Phosphate Co* (1878) 3 App Cas 1218, 1268, per Lord Blackburn. It is someone who 'undertakes to form a company with reference to a given project and to set it going, and who takes the necessary steps to accomplish that purpose': *Twycross v Grant* (1877) 2 CPD 469, 541, per Cockburn CJ.

[108] 2006 Act, s 762. The fifth requirement was inserted by SBEE Act 2015, s 98(1) and (3) with effect from 30 June 2016.

[109] *Re Kaytech International plc* [1999] 2 BCLC 351.

[110] 2006 Act, s 761(4).

[111] 2006 Act, s 767(1) and (2).

[112] 2006 Act, s 767(3).

[113] 2006 Act, s 767(4).

[114] Whether for cash or non-cash consideration: see 2006 Act, s 578(4). Where the shares have been offered for non-cash consideration, the provisions of s 578(5) modify the statutory language so as to make it applicable to non-cash assets. If it is not reasonably practicable to return the non-cash consideration, the company must return its value in money at the time it was received.

[115] 2006 Act, s 578(1). 2006 Act, ss 578 and 579 are subject to transitional provisions where the prospectus was issued before 1 October 2009: 2006 Act Commencement Order No 8, Sch 2, para 56.

[116] 2006 Act, s 578(2). In fact, where the money was paid into a separate account pursuant to an express term to that effect in the offer, the money may already be impressed with a trust for the applicants and should be returned to them as beneficiaries in any event, irrespective of the statutory provision to that effect: *Re Nanwa Gold Mines Ltd* [1955] 1 WLR 1080; *Moseley v Cressey's Co* (1865) LR 1 Eq 405; see also *Quistclose Investment Ltd v Rolls Razor Ltd* [1970] AC 567.

the company are jointly and severally liable to repay it together with interest at the judgment rate.[117] However, liability will not attach to any director who proves that the default in repayment was not due to any misconduct or negligence on his part.[118]

27.38 If the shares are wrongly allotted in contravention of this prohibition, the allotment is voidable (by notice[119]) at the instance of the application within one month of the date of the allotment, and not later.[120] A director of a public company who knowingly contravenes or permits or authorizes the contravention of the prohibition regarding allotment is liable to compensate the company and the allottee respectively for any loss, damages, costs, or expenses that the company or allottee may have sustained or incurred by the contravention.[121] The term 'knowingly' means with knowledge of the facts on which the contravention depends, but it does not extend to knowledge of the legal effect of the facts.[122] Proceedings to recover such loss, damages, costs, or expenses must be brought within two years or not at all.[123]

Payment for shares in cash

27.39 Additional rules apply in the case of shares in a public company. First, shares taken by a subscriber to the memorandum of a public company and any premium on the shares must be paid up in cash.[124] For the purpose of the Act, a 'cash consideration' includes a cheque received by the company in good faith that the directors have no reason for suspecting will not be paid and an undertaking to pay cash at a future date.[125] The cash need not be pounds sterling but may be in a foreign currency.[126]

27.40 Furthermore, a public company must not accept at any time, in payment up of its shares or any premium thereon, an undertaking given by any person that he or another should do work or perform services for the company or any other person.[127] If any such undertaking is accepted, s 585(2) imposes a liability[128] on the holder of the shares to pay the nominal value, any premium and interest (subject to any relief from liability which may be granted by the court; s 589). However, s 591 provides that such an undertaking will remain enforceable by the company notwithstanding the fact that it ought properly not to have been accepted by the company.[129]

---

[117] 2006 Act, s 578(3); Judgments Act 1838, s 17.

[118] 2006 Act, s 578(5).

[119] *Re National Motor Mail Coach Co Ltd* [1908] 2 Ch 228. The allotment may be avoided even where the company is in winding up.

[120] 2006 Act, s 579(1).

[121] 2006 Act, s 579(3). Where the allotment has occurred, the matter is governed by s 579, and s 578 is no longer applicable: *Burton v Bevan* [1908] 2 Ch 240.

[122] *Burton v Bevan* [1908] 2 Ch 240; see also *Twycross v Grant* (1877) 2 CPD 469; *Shepherd v Broome* [1904] C 342; *MacLeay v Tait* [1906] AC 24.

[123] 2006 Act, s 579(4).

[124] 2006 Act, s 584.

[125] 2006 Act, s 583(3). Section 583(3)(e) (payment by any other means giving rise to a present or future entitlement to a payment or a credit equivalent to payment, in cash) and s 607 (penalty for contravention) only apply in relation to consideration received pursuant to an obligation entered into on or after 1 October 2009; 2006 Act Commencement Order No 8, Sch 2, para 57. An 'undertaking to pay cash ... at a future date' does not include the assignment of an earlier debt: *System Control plc v Munro Corporate plc* [1990] BCLC 659.

[126] 2006 Act, s 583(6).

[127] 2006 Act, s 585(1).

[128] The effect is to create an immediate liability as if the allottee had agreed to take up the shares for cash: *Re Bradford Investments plc* [1991] BCC 224.

[129] 2006 Act, s 591(1).

Additionally, a public company must not allot a share except as paid up at least to one-quarter of its nominal value and the whole of any premium on it.[130] If a company allots shares in contravention of this provision, the share is to be treated as if one-quarter of its nominal value, together with the whole of any premium on it, had been received, and the allottee is liable to pay such an amount as would be required to render the shares one-quarter paid up[131] with interest.[132] Relief under s 589 is not available in such a case. **27.41**

Finally, a public company must not allot shares as fully paid up (as to their nominal value or any premium on them) otherwise than in cash if the consideration for the allotment is or includes an undertaking which is to be or may be performed more than five years after the date of the allotment.[133] If shares are allotted in contravention of this rule, the allottee is liable to pay the company an amount equal to the aggregate of their nominal value and the whole of any premium (or, if the case so requires, so much of that aggregate as is treated as paid up by the undertaking) with interest[134] (subject to any relief from liability which may be granted by the court: s 589). **27.42**

If the statutory rules relating to payment for shares and additional requirements in the case of public companies are contravened, an offence (punishable by fine) is committed by every officer in default.[135] **27.43**

Independent valuation of non-cash consideration

A public company must not allot shares as fully or partly paid up (as to their nominal value or any premium on them) otherwise than in cash unless (1) the consideration for the allotment has been independently valued in accordance with the Act,[136] (2) the valuer's report has been made to the company during the six months immediately preceding the allotment of the shares, and (3) a copy of the report has been sent to the proposed allottee.[137] **27.44**

If the allottee has not received the valuer's report required or there is some other contravention of the statutory requirements, and the allottee knew or ought to have known of the contravention,[138] then the allottee is liable to pay the company an amount equal to the aggregate of the nominal value of the shares and the whole of any premium with interest.[139] The court has power to grant relief subject to quite stringent conditions.[140] **27.45**

---

[130] 2006 Act, s 586(1). This provision does not apply to shares allotted in pursuance of an employees' share scheme: s 586(2). Model Articles (plc) 52–62 contemplate that a public company may issue partly paid shares (as does Table A, regs 8–22).

[131] 2006 Act, s 586(3).

[132] 2006 Act, s 609(1).

[133] 2006 Act, s 587(1).

[134] 2006 Act, s 587(2); for interest see s 609(1).

[135] 2006 Act, s 590(1) and (2).

[136] The valuer's report must comply with the requirements of s 596(3).

[137] 2006 Act, s 593(1). There are exceptions for takeovers, schemes of arrangement, and mergers or divisions: ss 594 and 595. Note amendments made to ss 593 and 595 by the Companies (Reporting Requirements in Mergers and Divisions) Regulations 2011 (SI 2011/1606), reg 2 as from 1 August 2011.

[138] Liability is imposed if the allottee knew or ought to have known of the facts which constitute the contravention: *Systems Control plc v Munro Corporate plc* [1990] BCLC 659. It is not a requirement that the allottee knew the requirements of the law as to valuation.

[139] 2006 Act, s 593(3).

[140] 2006 Act, s 606. See also *Systems Control plc v Munro Corporate plc* [1990] BCLC 659.

27.46 A copy of the valuer's report must be delivered to the Registrar.[141] This must occur at the same time as the filing of the return of the allotment.[142] The company's directors must ensure that this occurs. If these requirements are not satisfied, an offence (punishable by fine) is committed by every officer in default.[143] Where a director fails to file the report, it is possible to apply to the court for relief.[144] If the court is satisfied that the omission to deliver the documents was accidental or due to inadvertence,[145] or that it is just and equitable to grant relief,[146] it may make an order extending the time for delivery of the document for such period as the court thinks proper.[147]

27.47 It is important for directors of public companies to ensure that the statutory requirements as to non-cash consideration are complied with, since contravention of the statutory requirements amounts to an offence committed by every officer in default and such offence is punishable by fine.[148]

Transfer of non-cash asset in initial period

27.48 A public company formed as such must not enter into an agreement with a person who is a subscriber to the company's memorandum for the transfer by him to the company, or another, before the end of the company's initial period of one or more non-cash assets and under which the consideration for the transfer to be given by the company is at the time of the agreement equal in value to one-tenth or more of the company's issued share capital, unless (1) the requirements as to independent valuation are complied with, and (2) the requirements of member approval are complied with.[149]

27.49 The requirements for independent valuation are laid down by the 2006 Act, ss 599–600. In short, the consideration must have been independently valued, and the valuer's report must have been made to the company during the six months preceding the date of the agreement, and a copy of the report must have been sent to the proposed transferor. The specific requirements as to the contents of the valuer's report are contained in s 600.

27.50 The requirements for member approval are laid down by the 2006 Act, s 601. In summary (1) the terms of the agreement must have been approved by an ordinary resolution of the company, (2) the valuer's report must have been circulated to members, and (3) a copy of the proposed resolution must have been sent to the proposed transferor.

27.51 If the transferor does not receive the valuer's report, or if there has been some other contravention of the statutory requirements and the transferor knew or ought to have known that there was a contravention, the company is entitled to recover any consideration given by it for the transfer, and the agreement is void.[150]

---

[141] 2006 Act, s 597(1).
[142] 2006 Act, s 597(2).
[143] 2006 Act, s 597(3) and (4).
[144] 2006 Act, s 597(5).
[145] *Re Jackson & Co Ltd* [1899] 1 Ch 348.
[146] *Re Tom-Tit Cycle Co Ltd* (1899) 43 *Sol Jo* 334; *Re Whitefriar's Financial Co Ltd* [1899] 1 Ch 184.
[147] 2006 Act, s 597(6).
[148] 2006 Act, s 607(2) and (3).
[149] 2006 Act, s 598(1).
[150] 2006 Act, s 604(2).

A company that has passed a resolution under s 601 with respect to the transfer of an asset **27.52** must, within 15 days of doing so, deliver to the Registrar a copy of the resolution together with the valuer's report.[151] If the company fails to comply with this requirement, an offence (punishable by fine) is committed by every officer in default.[152] Further, any contravention of the statutory requirements amounts to an offence committed by every officer in default and such offence is punishable by fine.[153]

(6) Quoted companies and transferable securities: particular rules

Introduction

For the purposes of the 2006 Act, Part 15, concerning accounts and reports, a quoted com- **27.53** pany is a company whose equity share capital has been included in the official list in accordance with FSMA, Part 6, or is officially listed in an EEA state or is admitted to dealing on either the New York Stock Exchange or Nasdaq.[154] Other public companies, while remaining unquoted, may offer to the public securities, such as shares, which are transferable on eg AIM, PSM, or PLUS Quoted Market. FSMA, Part 6, ss 72 to 103, is headed 'Official Listing' and includes (a) listing,[155] (b) transferable securities, public offers and admission to trading,[156] (c) transparency and disclosure obligations,[157] and (d) provisions about compensation and penalties.[158]

The FCA, as the competent authority for the purposes of FSMA, Part 6, has made Part 6 **27.54** rules: listing rules, disclosure rules, prospectus rules, and also corporate governance rules.[159] These rules are to be found in the FCA handbook under the heading 'Listing, Prospectus and Disclosure':

(1) The Listing Rules apply to listing particulars in relation to the admission to the official list of securities issued by the company.[160]
(2) The Prospectus Rules apply to an offer to the public of transferable securities.[161]
(3) The Disclosure Rules and the Transparency Rules apply to traded securities.[162]

Detailed consideration of Part 6 and those rules is beyond the scope of this work, but direc- **27.55** tors need to be aware of their responsibilities and potential for liability under these provisions. Similarly directors should be aware of their potential civil liability by reason of the powers of the FCA:

---

[151] 2006 Act, s 602(1).
[152] 2006 Act, s 602(2) and (3).
[153] 2006 Act, s 607(2) and (3).
[154] 2006 Act, s 385(2).
[155] FSMA, ss 75–82.
[156] FSMA, ss 84–9.
[157] FSMA, ss 89A–89N, the Transparency Obligations Directive (Directive 2004/109/EC; see FSMA s 103(1)) and disclosure at ss 96A and 96B.
[158] FSMA, ss 90–4.
[159] FSMA, s 72A.
[160] FSMA, ss 72–82, 96; the Financial Services and Markets Act 2006 (Official Listing of Securities) Regulations 2001 (SI 2001/2956), as amended.
[161] FSMA, ss 84–9 and the Prospectus Rules made under FSMA, s 73A.
[162] FSMA, ss 89A–89G, 96A, 96B. The Disclosure Rules implement Art 6 of the Market Abuse Directive (2003/6/EC), Arts 2 and 3 of Commission Directive 2003/124/EC and Arts 5 and 6 of Commission Directive 2004/72/EC.

(1) to impose penalties on insiders and others guilty of market abuse in relation to shares and other qualifying investments admitted to trading on a prescribed market or for which a request for admission has been made[163] and

(2) to obtain from the court (a) an injunction restraining contravention of a requirement imposed by or under FSMA, (b) a restitution order against a person who has contravened a requirement by or under FSMA or who has been knowingly concerned in the contravention, or (c) a restitution order in a case of market abuse.[164]

For civil liability of directors under these provisions, reference should be made to Chapters 24, Section F(2) above and 32 below.

27.56   Finally, FSMA, Part 27 creates a number of offences in relation to misleading statements and practices, including where a person, in purported compliance with any requirement imposed by or under FSMA, knowingly or recklessly gives the FCA, PRA, or CMA information which is false or misleading in a material particular.[165] For detailed discussion of these offences and insider trading, reference should be made to Chapter 35, Section G below.

Listing

27.57   A company may apply to the FCA for securities issued by it to be included in the official list maintained by it as competent authority under FSMA, Part 6 and the Listing Rules.[166] Securities, other than those for which an approved prospectus is required by FSMA, s 85, may not be admitted to the official list unless (a) listing particulars have been submitted to, and approved by, the FCA and published, or (b) the Listing Rules provide for publication of a specified document, other than listing particulars or a prospectus.[167]

27.58   Where the issuer is a body corporate the persons responsible for the content of the listing particulars include:

(1) each person who is a director of that body at the time when the particulars are submitted to the FCA, unless the particulars are published without his knowledge or consent and on becoming aware of their publication he forthwith gives reasonable public notice that they were published without his knowledge or consent; and

(2) each person who authorized himself to be named, and is named, in the particulars as a director or as having agreed to become a director of that body either immediately or at a future time.[168]

27.59   As persons responsible for the listing particulars, directors must take steps to ensure that the company complies with the general duty of disclosure in the listing particulars. FSMA, s 80, provides that listing particulars:

---

[163] FSMA, ss 118–31A. For prescribed markets and qualifying investments s 130A(1) and the Financial Services and Markets Act 2000 (Prescribed Markets and Qualifying Investments) Order 2001 (SI 2001/996).

[164] FSMA, Part XXV, ss 380–6.

[165] FSMA, ss 398–403 and Financial Services Act 2012, ss 89–95.

[166] FSMA, ss 72–5.

[167] FSMA, s 79; Listing Rules 3 and 4.

[168] FSMA, s 79(3); Financial Services and Markets Act 2000 (Official Listing of Securities) Regulations 2001 (SI 2001/2956), reg 6.

must contain all such information as investors and their professional advisers would reasonably require, and reasonably expect to find there, for the purpose of making an informed assessment of—

(a) the assets and liabilities, financial position, profits and losses, and prospects of the issuer of the securities; and

(b) the rights attaching to the securities.[169]

In determining what information should be included in listing particulars, regard must be **27.60** had (in particular) to (a) the nature of the securities and their issuer, (b) the nature of the persons likely to consider acquiring them, (c) the fact that certain matters may reasonably be expected to be within the knowledge of professional advisers of a kind which persons likely to acquire the securities may reasonably be expected to consult, and (d) any information available to investors or their professional advisers as a result of requirements imposed on the issuer of the securities by a recognized investment exchange, by listing rules, or by or under any other enactment.[170] If the company's directors are not aware of the relevant information, they must make reasonable enquiries.[171] Supplementary listing particulars must be prepared if there is a significant change in circumstances prior to listing.[172]

A director responsible for listing particulars or supplementary listing particulars is exposed **27.61** to two forms of civil liability or penalty:

(1) First, he will be liable to pay compensation to a person who has (a) acquired securities to which the listing particulars or supplementary listing particulars apply, and (b) suffered loss in respect of them as a result of any untrue or misleading statement in the particulars supplementary particulars or the omission from the particulars supplementary particulars of any matter required to be included therein by ss 80 or 81, subject to the exemptions in s 82 and Schedule 10.[173]

(2) If the FCA considers that he was knowingly concerned in the contravention of any provision of the Listing Rules or the Disclosure Rules, it may (a) impose on him a penalty of such amount as it considers appropriate, or (b) issue a public statement censuring the person who would otherwise be liable to a financial penalty; but the FCA may not take action against a person after the end of the period of two years beginning with the first day on which it knew of the contravention unless proceedings against that person, in respect of the contravention, were begun before the end of that period.[174]

---

[169] Disclosure may be exempted under FSMA, s 82, if disclosure would be contrary to the public interest or seriously detrimental to the issuer or, in the case of securities of a kind specified in the Listing Rules, if disclosure would be unnecessary for persons of the kind who may be expected normally to buy or deal in securities of that kind. However, no exemption may be granted in respect of 'essential information'—ie information which a person considering acquiring securities of the kind in question would be likely to need in order not to be misled about any facts which it is essential for him to know in order to make an informed assessment.

[170] FSMA, s 80(4).

[171] FSMA, s 80(3).

[172] FSMA, s 81.

[173] FSMA, s 90(1)–(10).

[174] FSMA, s 91(1), (1ZA), (2)–(7). A person discharging managerial responsibilities within an issuer who has requested or approved the admission of a financial instrument to trading on a regulated market is also liable under these provisions for any contravention of the Disclosure Rules (s 91(1ZA)(b)). FSMA, s 92 provides for the FCA to give a warning notice to the person against whom it proposes to take action under s 91.

27.62 In relation to the listing particulars, a director may be guilty of an offence if he knowingly or recklessly:

(1) makes a false or misleading statement dishonestly conceals material facts or engages in conduct which creates a false or misleading impression as to the market in or the price or value of any relevant investments;[175] or

(2) gives the FCA information which is false or misleading in a material particular.[176]

Prospectus

27.63 A request for admission to trading on a regulated market (such as the London Stock Exchange's Main Markets for official listed securities) and/or an offer of securities to the public will, unless exempt, require a prospectus, which must be approved by the FCA. Detailed requirements in respect of the form and contents of a company's prospectus are contained in the Prospectus Rules. Further, if before the closure of the offer or the commencement of trading there arises or is noted a significant new factor, material mistake, or inaccuracy relating to the information included in a prospectus approved by the FCA, the person on whose application the prospectus was approved must, in accordance with Prospectus Rules, submit a supplementary prospectus containing details of the new factor, mistake, or inaccuracy to the FCA for its approval.[177]

27.64 The procedure for approval is laid down by FSMA.[178] A prospectus will not be approved unless: (a) the UK is the home state in relation to the issuer of the transferable securities to which it relates; (b) the prospectus contains the information necessary to enable investors to make an informed assessment of the assets and liabilities, financial position, profits and losses, and prospects of the issuer of the transferable securities and of any guarantor and the rights attaching to the transferable securities;[179] and (c) there has been compliance with all other applicable requirements. A prospectus must include a summary (unless the transferable securities in question are ones in relation to which the Prospectus Rules provide that a summary is not required). The summary must, briefly and in non-technical language, convey the essential characteristics of, and risks associated with, the issuer, any guarantor, and the transferable securities to which the prospectus relates.[180]

27.65 As a condition of approving a prospectus, the FCA may by notice in writing (a) require the inclusion in the prospectus of such supplementary information necessary for investor protection as the FCA may specify, (b) require a person controlling, or controlled by, the applicant to provide specified information or documents, (c) require an auditor or manager of the applicant to provide specified information or documents, and (d) require a financial intermediary commissioned to assist either in carrying out the offer to the public of the

---

[175] Financial Services Act 2012, ss 89–94.
[176] FSMA, s 398.
[177] FSMA, s 87G.
[178] See in particular ss 87C and 87D.
[179] FSMA, s 87A(1)–(4). Disclosure of information may be exempted if the inclusion of the information would be contrary to the public interest or seriously detrimental to the issuer, provided that the omission would be unlikely to mislead the public with regard to any facts or circumstances which are essential for an informed assessment, or if the information is only of minor importance for a specific offer to the public or admission to trading on a regulated market and unlikely to influence an informed assessment: see FSMA, s 87B.
[180] FSMA, s 87A(5), (6).

transferable securities to which the prospectus relates or in requesting their admission to trading on a regulated market, to provide specified information or documents.[181]

It is unlawful (a) for transferable securities to be offered to the public in the UK unless an **27.66** approved prospectus has been made available to the public before the offer is made,[182] and (b) to request the admission of transferable securities to trading on a regulated market situated or operating in the UK unless an approved prospectus has been made available to the public before the request is made.[183] There are two consequences of contravention:

(1) A person who contravenes either of these provisions is guilty of an offence.[184] A director may also be guilty of an offence if he consented to or connived in the contravention or if it was attributable to any neglect on his part.[185]

(2) Further, a contravention of these provisions is actionable, at the suit of a person who suffers loss as a result of the contravention, subject to the defences and other incidents applying to actions for breach of statutory duty.[186]

If there is an infringement of a provision in FSMA, Part 6, the Prospectus Rules or any other **27.67** provision made in accordance with the prospectus directive,[187] the FCA has power to (a) suspend or prohibit the public offering,[188] (b) suspend or prohibit admission to trading on a regulated market,[189] and (c) censure the issuer.[190]

In terms of responsibility for the prospectus or supplementary prospectus, the Prospectus **27.68** Rules draw a distinction between a prospectus relating to equity shares and a prospectus relating to other forms of transferable securities:[191]

(1) For equity shares, the persons responsible include (a) each person who is a director of the body corporate when the prospectus is published unless it is published without his knowledge or consent and on becoming aware of its publication he forthwith gives reasonable public notice that it was published without his knowledge or consent,[192] and (b) each person who authorized himself to be named, and is named, in the prospectus as a director or as having agreed to become a director of that body either immediately or at a future time.[193]

---

[181] FSMA, s 87J.

[182] FSMA, s 85(1), subject to the exemptions in ss 85(5) and 86, by which a person does not contravene s 85(1) if: (a) the offer is made to or directed at qualified investors only (as defined by s 86(7)); (b) the offer is made to or directed at fewer than 150 persons, other than qualified investors, per EEA state (subject to s 86(3) which provides that a trust, partnership or joint holders count as a single person); (c) the minimum consideration which may be paid by any person for transferable securities acquired by him pursuant to the offer is at least €50,000 (or an equivalent amount); (d) the transferable securities being offered are denominated in amounts of at least €50,000 (or equivalent amounts); or (e) the total consideration for the transferable securities being offered cannot exceed €100,000 (or an equivalent amount).

[183] FSMA, s 85(2), subject to the exemptions in s 85(6).

[184] FSMA, s 85(3). The punishments are: on summary conviction, imprisonment for a term not exceeding three months or a fine not exceeding the statutory maximum or both, or, on conviction on indictment, imprisonment for a term not exceeding two years or a fine or both.

[185] FSMA, s 400.

[186] FSMA, s 85(4).

[187] Directive 2003/71/EC, OJ 2003 L 345/63, which is implemented by Regulation (EC) 809/2004.

[188] FSMA, ss 87K and 87O.

[189] FSMA, ss 87L and 87O.

[190] FSMA, ss 87M and 87N.

[191] FSMA, s 84(1)(d) and Prospectus Rule 5.5.

[192] Prospectus Rules 5.5.3(2)(b)(i) and 5.5.6.

[193] Prospectus Rule 5.5.3(2)(b)(ii).

(2) For other forms of transferable securities, a director will only be responsible if he is stated in the prospectus as accepting responsibility for it or if he authorizes the contents of it or a specified part of it.[194]

27.69 As with listing, a director responsible for the prospectus is exposed to two forms of civil liability or penalty:

(1) He will be liable to pay compensation to a person who has (a) acquired securities to which the prospectus or supplementary prospectus apply, and (b) suffered loss in respect of them as a result of any untrue or misleading statement in the particulars or supplementary particulars or the omission from the particulars or supplementary particulars of any matter required to be included therein by ss 87A and 87G, subject to the exemptions in s 87B and Schedule 10.[195]

(2) If the FCA considers that he was knowingly concerned in the contravention of FSMA, Part 6 relating to transferable securities, the Prospectus Rules, or a provision made in accordance with the Prospectus Directive or a requirement imposed under such a provision, it may (a) impose on him a penalty of such amount as it considers appropriate, or (b) issue a public statement censuring the person who would otherwise be liable to a financial penalty; but the FCA may not take action against a person after the end of the period of two years beginning with the first day on which it knew of the contravention unless proceedings against that person, in respect of the contravention, were begun before the end of that period.[196]

27.70 In relation to statements in, or omissions from, the prospectus, a director may also commit a criminal offence as described in paragraph 27.62 above.

Transparency and disclosure

27.71 The Transparency Rules[197] apply to traded securities (although each rule should be consulted for its application) and lay down a detailed code for the provision of (for example): (a) 'voteholder information' (ie information relating to the proportion of voting rights held by a person in respect of the shares); (b) information relating to the rights attached to transferable securities, including information about the terms and conditions of those securities which could indirectly affect those rights; (c) information about new loan issues and about any guarantee or security in connection with any such issue; (d) notification of voting rights held by the issuer; and (e) notification of proposed amendments of the issuer's constitution.[198]

27.72 FSMA, s 89H–89J, enables the FCA to call for information. These provisions apply to directors and similar officers; they also apply to auditors and voteholders.[199] The FCA may by

---

[194] Prospectus Rules 5.5.4. and 5.5.8.

[195] FSMA, s 90(11). By s 90(12) a person is not to be subject to civil liability solely on the basis of a summary (or a translation of it) in a prospectus unless the summary is misleading, inaccurate, or inconsistent when read with the rest of the prospectus.

[196] FSMA, s 91(1ZA) (1A), (2)–(7). A person discharging managerial responsibilities within an issuer who has requested or approved the admission of a financial instrument to trading on a regulated market is also liable under these provisions for a contravention of the Disclosure Rules (s 91(1ZA) (b)). FSMA, s 92 provides for the FCA to give a warning notice to the person against whom it proposes to take action under s 91.

[197] FMSA, s 89A, implementing the Transparency Obligations Directive.

[198] FSMA, ss 89B–89E.

[199] The term 'voteholder' means a person who holds voting rights in respect of any voting shares or is treated as holding such rights.

notice in writing given to a person to whom the section applies require him (a) to provide specified information or information of a specified description, or (b) to produce specified documents or documents of a specified description. The FCA may also require: (a) such information to be provided in such form as it may reasonably require; (b) any information provided, whether in a document or otherwise, to be verified in such manner as it may reasonably require; and (c) any document produced to be authenticated in such manner as it may reasonably require. The FCA may also require an issuer to make public any information provided under these provisions or may itself make that information public, if the issuer fails to do so.

In case of infringement of transparency obligations the FCA has power to censure the issuer **27.73** and to suspend or prohibit trading in securities.[200]

The Disclosure Rules apply to: **27.74**

(1) issuers who have requested or approved admission of their financial instruments, including shares, to trading on a regulated market in the UK (not AIM, PSM, or PLUS Quoted Market);
(2) persons acting on behalf of or for the account of such an issuer;
(3) persons discharging managerial responsibilities within an issuer who is (a) registered in the UK and who has requested or approved admission of its shares to trading on a regulated market, or (b) not registered in the UK or in any other EEA state but who has requested or approved admission of its shares to trading on a regulated market and who is required to file annual information in relation to the shares in the UK in accordance with the Article 10 of the Prospectus Directive; and
(4) persons connected to such persons discharging managerial responsibilities.[201]

For the purposes of the Disclosure Rules a 'person discharging managerial responsibilities **27.75** within an issuer' means (a) a director, or (b) a senior executive who has regular access to inside information relating, directly or indirectly, to the issuer, and has power to make managerial decisions affecting the future development and business prospects of the issuer.[202] Schedule 11 identifies the persons connected with such a person.[203]

Persons discharging managerial responsibilities and persons connected to them must notify **27.76** the issuer in writing of the occurrence of all transactions conducted on their own account in the shares of the issuer, or derivatives or any other financial instruments relating to those shares within four business days of the day on which the transaction occurred.[204] The issuer must notify a RIS of the event by no later than the end of the business day following receipt by it of the information.[205]

The issuer of securities may be liable to pay compensation to persons who have suffered loss **27.77** as a result of a misleading statement or dishonest statement information published pursuant to the Transparency Rules (eg annual, half-yearly, or interim reports or preliminary

---

[200] FSMA, ss 89K–89N.
[201] FSMA, s 96A(1).
[202] FSMA, s 96B(1).
[203] FSMA, s 96B(2).
[204] Rules 3.1.2, 3.1.3. For persons discharging managerial responsibilities within an issuer, see FSMA, s 96B(1) and for connected persons, see s 96B(2) and Sch 11B.
[205] Rules 3.1.4–3.1.8.

statements) relating to the securities or a dishonest delay in publishing such information.[206] The issuer is so liable only if a person discharging managerial responsibilities within the issuer in relation to the publication (a) knew the statement to be untrue or misleading or was reckless as to whether it was untrue or misleading, or (b) knew the omission to be a dishonest concealment of a material fact.[207] A loss is not regarded as suffered as a result of the statement or omission in the publication unless the person suffering it acquired the relevant securities (a) in reliance on the information in the publication and (b) at a time when, and in circumstances in which, it was reasonable for him to rely on that information.[208] In this connection, if the relevant untrue or misleading statement or dishonest omission concerned the directors' report, the directors' remuneration report or a summary financial statement derived from them, the company may be able to obtain compensation from the knowing or reckless director.[209]

27.78 If the FCA considers that a director, as a person discharging managerial responsibilities within an issuer, has contravened any provision of the Disclosure Rules or was knowingly concerned in the contravention of the Disclosure Rules, it may (a) impose on him a penalty of such amount as it considers appropriate, or (b) issue a public statement censuring the person who would otherwise be liable to a financial penalty; but the FCA may not take action against a person after the end of the period of two years beginning with the first day on which it knew of the contravention unless proceedings against that person, in respect of the contravention, were begun before the end of that period.[210]

C. Alteration of Share Capital

27.79 A limited company with share capital may not alter its share capital[211] except by: (1) increase of share capital by way of allotment;[212] (2) reduction of capital;[213] (3) subdivision or

---

206 FSMA, s 90A and Sch 10A.
207 FSMA, Sch 10A, para 3(2) and (3).
208 FSMA, Sch 10A, para 3(4).
209 2006 Act, s 463.
210 FSMA, s 91(1ZA), (1A), (2)–(7). A person discharging managerial responsibilities within an issuer who has requested or approved the admission of a financial instrument to trading on a regulated market is also liable under these provisions for any contravention of the Disclosure Rules (s 91(1ZA) (b)). FSMA, s 92 provides for the FCA to give a warning notice to the person against whom it proposes to take action under s 91.
211 2006 Act, s 617(1). However, nothing in s 617 affects: (a) the power of a company to purchase its own shares, or to redeem shares, in accordance with Part 18; (b) the power of a company to purchase its own shares in pursuance of an order of the court under (i) s 98 (application to court to cancel resolution for reregistration as a private company), (ii) s 721(6) (powers of court on objection to redemption or purchase of shares out of capital), (iii) s 759 (remedial order in case of breach of prohibition of public offers by private company), or (iv) Part 30 (protection of members against unfair prejudice); (c) the forfeiture of shares, or the acceptance of shares surrendered in lieu, in pursuance of the company's articles, for failure to pay any sum payable in respect of the shares; (d) the cancellation of shares under s 662 (duty to cancel shares held by or for a public company); (e) the power of a company (i) to enter into a compromise or arrangement in accordance with Part 26 (arrangements and reconstructions), or (ii) to do anything required to comply with an order of the court on an application under that Part; (f) the cancellation of a share warrant issued by the company and of the shares specified in it by a cancellation order or suspended cancellation order made under SBEE Act 2015, Sch 4, para 6 (cancellation where share warrants not surrendered in accordance with that Schedule); (g) the cancellation of a share warrant issued by the company and of the shares specified in it pursuant to ss 1028A(2) or 1032A(2) (cancellation of share warrants on restoration of a company).
212 2006 Act, s 617(2)(a).
213 2006 Act, s 617(2)(b).

reconsolidation of shares;[214] (4) reconversion of stock into shares;[215] and (5) redenomination of shares.[216] Authorization in the company's articles is not a prerequisite.[217] A resolution of this nature may be contingent upon the happening of a future event, such as confirmation of a reduction of capital by the court.[218] As with all corporate powers, these powers must be exercised bona fide for the benefit of the company as a whole.[219]

In each case, the directors must ensure that notice is provided to the Registrar in accordance **27.80** with the statutory rules, together with a statement of capital. Notice of subdivision or consolidation or reconversion of stock must be sent to the Registrar within one month[220] and must be accompanied by a statement of capital.[221] Notice of redenomination or notice of reduction of capital in connection with redenomination must be sent to the Registrar within one month and must state the date on which the resolution was passed and be accompanied by a statement of capital.[222] Default in complying with these requirements is an offence (punishable by fine)[223] committed by every officer in default.[224]

(1) Class rights

Shares are of one class if the rights[225] attached to them are in all respects uniform.[226] However, **27.81** for this purpose the rights attached to shares are not regarded as different from those attached to other shares by reason only that they do not carry the same rights to dividends in the 12 months immediately following their allotment.[227] Any amendment of a provision contained in a company's articles for the variation of the rights attached to a class of shares (or the insertion of any such provision into the articles) is itself to be treated as a variation of those rights.[228] Variation includes abrogation.[229]

---

[214] 2006 Act, s 617(3)(a); see also s 618.

[215] 2006 Act, s 617(3)(b); see also s 620. See generally *Morrice v Aylmer* (1874) 10 Ch App 148 and *Re Home & Foreign Investment & Agency Co* [1912] 1 Ch 72.

[216] 2006 Act, s 617(4); see also ss 622 and 626.

[217] *Re Bank of Hindustan* (1873) 9 Ch App 1; *Taylor v Pilsen* (1884) 27 Ch D 268. A company's undertaking in a shareholders' agreement not to exercise these powers will be unenforceable, but the shareholders' agreement will be enforceable by the shareholders inter se: *Russell v Northern Bank Development Corp Ltd* [1992] 1 WLR 588.

[218] *Re Salinas of Mexico* [1919] WN 311; *Re Welsbach Incandescent Gas Light Co* [1904] 1 Ch 87; *Re Australian Estates & Mortgage Co Ltd* [1910] 1 Ch 414.

[219] *Allen v Gold Reefs of West Africa* [1900] 1 Ch 656, CA.

[220] 2006 Act, ss 618(1) and 621(1).

[221] 2006 Act, ss 618(2)–(3) and 621(2)–(3). The Companies (Shares and Share Capital) Order 2009 (SI 2009/388), reg 2 states the prescribed particulars for the purposes of s 621(3)(c)(i).

[222] 2006 Act, ss 625(1)–(3) and 626(1)–(3). The Companies (Shares and Share Capital) Order 2009 (SI 2009/388), reg 2 states the prescribed particulars for the purposes of s 625(3)(c)(i). A reduction is not effective until the documents are registered: s 627(5). The company must also deliver to the Registrar a statement confirming that the reduction of capital did not exceed 10 per cent of the nominal value of allotted shares immediately after reduction: s 627(6).

[223] 2006 Act, ss 619(5), 621(5), 625(5), 627(8).

[224] 2006 Act, ss 619(4), 621(4), 625(4), 627(7).

[225] See eg *Eley v Positive Government Security Life Assurance Co* (1875) 1 Ex D 20; *Rayfield v Hands* [1960] Ch 1; *Bushell v Faith* [1970] AC 1099; *Re Blue Arrow plc* [1987] BCLC 585.

[226] 2006 Act, s 629(1). See also *Cumbrian Newspaper Group Ltd v Cumberland & Westmorland Herald & Printing Co Ltd* [1987] Ch 1, 22 (Scott J). A Company's articles usually give it power to issue different classes of share: Table A, reg 2; Model Article (pcls) 22; Model Article (plc) 43.

[227] 2006 Act, s 629(2).

[228] 2006 Act, s 630(5).

[229] 2006 Act, s 630(6). See also *White v Bristol Aeroplane Co Ltd* [1935] Ch 65; *Re John Smith's Tadcaster Brewery Co Ltd* [1953] Ch 308; *Greenhalgh v Arderne Cinemas Ltd* [1946] 1 All ER 512, CA.

27.82 Rights attached to a class of shares in a company having share capital may only be varied: (1) in accordance with provision in the company's articles for variation, or (2) where the company's articles contain no such provision, if the holders of shares of that class consent to the variation in accordance with the 2006 Act, s 630.[230] That section provides that the consent must be in writing from the holders of at least three-quarters in nominal value of the issued shares of that class (excluding any shares held as treasury shares) or by way of a special resolution passed at a separate general meeting of the holders of that class sanctioning the variation.[231]

27.83 The holders of not less in the aggregate than 15 per cent of the issued shares of the class in question (being persons who did not consent to or vote in favour of the resolution for the variation) may apply to the court, within 21 days of the consent being given or the resolution passed, to have the variation cancelled.[232] If such an application is made, the variation has no effect unless and until it is confirmed by the court.[233] The court may, if satisfied having regard to all the circumstances of the case that the variation would unfairly prejudice[234] the shareholders of the class represented by the applicant, disallow the variation, and shall if not so satisfied confirm it.[235]

Functions and liabilities of directors

27.84 Where the court makes such an order, the company must within 15 days forward a copy of the order to the Registrar of Companies.[236] If this is not done, an offence (punishable by fine and daily default fine for continued contravention) is committed by every officer in default.[237]

27.85 A company must give a notice with particulars to the Registrar of Companies within one month: (1) if it assigns a name or other description (or new name or new description) to any class or description of shares;[238] (2) if the rights attached to any shares are varied;[239] (3) if, being a company not having a share capital, it creates a new class of members,[240] assigns a name or other designation (or new name or new designation) to any class of members,[241] or varies the rights of any class of members.[242] Default in complying with any

---

[230] 2006 Act, s 630(2).

[231] 2006 Act, s 630(4).

[232] 2006 Act, s 633(2). The applicants must either hold 15 per cent of the shares of the class affected or have been appointed in writing by the holders of 15 per cent at the date of the presentation of the petition and not merely when it comes on for a hearing: *Re Sound City (Films) Ltd* [1947] Ch 169; *Re Suburban & Provincial Stores Ltd* [1943] Ch 156. For this purpose any of the company's share capital held as treasury shares is disregarded.

[233] 2006 Act, s 633(3). The application must be made within 21 days after the date on which the consent was given or the resolution was passed and may be made on behalf of the shareholders entitled to make the application by such one or more of their number as they may appoint in writing for the purpose: s 633(4). See *Re Suburban & Provincial Stores Ltd* [1943] Ch 156 and *Re Sound City (Films) Ltd* [1947] Ch 169.

[234] See *British America Nickel Corp v O'Brien* [1927] AC 369.

[235] 2006 Act, s 634(5). The decision of the court on any such application is final, ie not subject to appeal, unless the reason for dismissing the application is procedural only, in which case an appeal will lie: *Re Suburban & Provincial Stores Ltd* [1943] Ch 156.

[236] 2006 Act, s 635(1).

[237] 2006 Act, s 635(2) and (3).

[238] 2006 Act, s 636(1).

[239] 2006 Act, s 637(1).

[240] 2006 Act, s 638(1).

[241] 2006 Act, s 639(1).

[242] 2006 Act, s 640(1).

of these requirements is an offence (punishable by fine)[243] committed by every officer in default.[244]

(2) Reduction of share capital

In certain circumstances, the directors of a company may legitimately form the view that the **27.86** company's capital exceeds its reasonable requirements and that it is desirable to repay a portion of the capital to the company's shareholders.[245] In other cases, the directors may take the view that there has been a loss of capital, eg through unprofitable trading, and that it is necessary to reduce the company's capital in order to restore reality to the company's accounts.[246]

A company may reduce its share capital in any way.[247] In particular it may: (1) extinguish or **27.87** reduce the liability on any of its shares in respect of share capital not paid up,[248] or (2) either with or without extinguishing or reducing liability on any of its shares, cancel any paid-up share capital that is lost or unrepresented by its available assets[249] or repay any paid-up share capital in excess of the company's wants.[250]

Private companies: reduction of capital supported by solvency statement

The 1985 Act provided that a reduction of capital could not be achieved without confirma- **27.88** tion by the court.[251] However, this procedure proved to be unduly cumbersome in cases of routine reductions by private companies, and the CLR recommended that private companies should be able to reduce share capital using a solvency statement procedure for capital reductions.[252] This recommendation was adopted by the legislature, and the solvency statement procedure for private companies, which permits a reduction of capital without court involvement, appears in ss 641 to 644 of the 2006 Act.

The solvency statement procedure involves three steps over a period of no more than **27.89** 30 days: (1) the making of a solvency statement by all the company's directors; (2) within 15 days, the passing of a special resolution;[253] and (3) within a further 15 days, the

---

[243] 2006 Act, ss 636(3), 637(3), 638(3), 639(3), 640(3).

[244] 2006 Act, ss 636(2), 637(2), 638(2), 639(2), 640(2).

[245] *British and American Trustee and Finance Corporation v Couper* [1894] AC 399, 413; *Ex p Westburn Sugar Refineries Ltd* [1951] AC 625.

[246] *Re Hoare & Co Ltd* [1904] 2 Ch 208; *Re Jupiter House Investments (Cambridge) Ltd* [1985] BCLC 222; *Re Grosvenor Press plc* [1985] BCLC 286; *Re Barrow Haematite Steel Co* [1900] 2 Ch 846.

[247] The words 'in any way' first appeared in the Companies Act 1908 to confirm that there were no limits on a company's ability to reduce capital by cancelling paid-up capital not lost or unrepresented by available assets; cf *Re Anglo-French Exploration Co* [1902] 2 Ch 845, 854; and see *Re Jupiter House Investments (Cambridge) Ltd* [1985] 1 WLR 975.

[248] 2006 Act, s 641(4)(a).

[249] 2006 Act, s 641(4)(b)(i); see also *Re Abstainers' and General Insurance Co* [1891] 2 Ch 124; *Re Barrow Haematite Steel Co* [1900] 2 Ch 846; *Re Hoare & Co Ltd* [1904] 2 Ch 208; *Re Jupiter House Investments (Cambridge) Ltd* [1985] 1 WLR 975.

[250] 2006 Act, s 641(4)(b)(ii); see also *Wilsons & Clyde Coal Co Ltd* [1949] AC 462; *Prudential Assurance Co Ltd v Chatterley Whitfield Collieries Co Ltd* [1949] AC 512; *Ex p Westburn Sugar Refineries Ltd* [1951] AC 625.

[251] 1985 Act, s 135(1). In addition, the 1985 Act provided that a reduction of capital could be achieved only if expressly permitted by the company's articles. The CLR recommended that the need for prior authorization in the articles be removed: CLR: *Completing the Structure*, para 2.15. In line with this recommendation, the need for prior authorization in the articles has not been retained, although a company may expressly prohibit or restrict a reduction of capital by making provision to this effect in its articles: see 2006 Act, s 641(6).

[252] CLR: *Final Report*, para 10.6.

[253] Companies Act 2006, s 641(1)(a).

registration of the reduction with the Registrar. The reduction takes effect when the third step is completed.[254]

27.90　The lack of judicial scrutiny of the process means that the directors' solvency statement possesses great significance. It is the means by which the process is commenced, and the primary material on which the shareholders of the company will form a view as to whether or not the reduction is viable. For this reason, the 2006 Act creates various offences in connection with the solvency statement.

27.91　A company may not reduce its share capital under the solvency statement procedure if as a result of the reduction there would no longer be any member of the company holding shares other than redeemable shares.[255]

27.92　Further, a company may not reduce its share capital (whether pursuant to the solvency statement procedure or by way of a special resolution confirmed by the court) as part of a scheme of arrangement under Part 26 by virtue of which a person, or a person together with its associates,[256] is to acquire all the shares in the company or (where there is more than one class of shares in a company) all the shares of one or more classes, in each case other than shares that are already held by that person or its associates.[257] However, this latter restriction does not apply to a scheme under which (a) the company is to have a new parent undertaking, (b) all or substantially all of the members of the company become members of the parent undertaking, and (c) the members of the company are to hold proportions of the equity share capital of the parent undertaking in the same or substantially the same proportions as they hold the equity share capital of the company.[258]

27.93　Furthermore, a special resolution for the reduction of a company's capital may not provide for a reduction to take effect later than the date on which the resolution has effect.[259] This restriction, which would operate to prevent a company passing a resolution on, say, 1 January stating that the reduction is to take effect on 1 October, is necessary to ensure that a reduction authorized at a time of solvency is not effected subsequently when the company's financial position has deteriorated. The 2006 Act, s 644(3) prescribes when the resolution takes effect—that is, when a copy of the resolution, supported by the solvency statement and a statement of capital, has been filed with and registered by the Registrar of Companies.

27.94　The 2006 Act, s 643, provides that a 'solvency statement' for these purposes is a statement that each of the directors:

(1)　has formed the opinion, as regards the company's situation at the date of the statement, that there is no ground on which the company could then be found to be unable to pay (or otherwise discharge) its debts;[260] and

---

[254] 2006 Act, s 644(4). Accordingly, under the solvency statement procedure, it is not possible to resolve that a reduction will take effect in 16 or more days' time.

[255] 2006 Act, s 641(2).

[256] The term 'associate' has the meaning given by s 988 (meaning of 'associate'), reading references in that section to an offeror as references to the person acquiring the shares in the company; 2006 Act, s 641(2C).

[257] 2006 Act, s 641(2A), inserted by Companies Act 2006 (Amendment of Part 17) Regs 2015 (SI 2015/472, reg 3(1), (2) with effect from 3 March 2015.

[258] 2006 Act, s 641(2B), inserted as for s 641(2A).

[259] 2006 Act, s 641(5).

[260] 2006 Act, s 643(1)(a).

(2) has also formed the opinion (i) if it is intended to commence the winding up of the company within 12 months of that date, that the company will be able to pay (or otherwise discharge) its debts in full within 12 months of the commencement of the winding up or (ii) in any other case, that the company will be able to pay (or otherwise discharge) its debts as they fall due during the year immediately following that date.[261]

In forming the necessary opinions, the directors must take into account all of the company's liabilities, including any contingent or prospective liabilities.[262]

27.95 The solvency statement must (a) be in writing, (b) indicate that it is a solvency statement for the purposes of s 642, (c) be signed by each of the directors, (d) state the date on which it is made, and (e) state the name of each director of the company (but there is no requirement that the directors must all be in the same location when they make this statement).[263]

27.96 If one or more of the directors is unable or unwilling to make this statement, the company will not be able to use the solvency statement procedure to effect a reduction of capital unless the dissenting director or directors resign (in which case the solvency statement must be made by all of the remaining directors).

27.97 If the directors make a solvency statement without having reasonable grounds for the opinions expressed in it, and the statement is delivered to the Registrar, an offence is committed by every officer in default.[264] The penalty on conviction on indictment is imprisonment for a term not exceeding two years or a fine or both;[265] summary conviction may also result in imprisonment, but for a maximum of 12 months, or a fine not exceeding the statutory maximum, or both.[266]

27.98 The reduction must be authorized by special resolution which must be passed not more than 15 days after the date of the making of the solvency statement.[267] Where the resolution is proposed as a written resolution, the company's directors should ensure that copies of the solvency statement are sent or submitted to every eligible member at or before the time at which the resolution is sent or submitted to him.[268] Where the resolution is proposed at a general meeting, the directors should ensure that a copy of the solvency statement is available for inspection by members at the meeting.[269]

27.99 A failure to observe these procedural requirements will not affect the validity of a resolution to reduce capital.[270] However, it is an offence committed by every officer in default for a solvency statement which was not provided to the company's members in accordance with these requirements to be filed with the Registrar.[271] Since a reduction of capital by the solvency statement procedure will not become effective unless and until the resolution and the

---

[261] 2006 Act, s 643(1)(b).
[262] 2006 Act, s 643(2).
[263] 2006 Act, s 643(3); Companies (Reduction of Share Capital) Order 2008 (SI 2008/1915), para 2.
[264] 2006 Act, s 643(4). See *BTI 2014 LLC v Sequana SA* [2016] EWHC 1686 (Ch) at paras 317–40 and in particular 327.
[265] 2006 Act, s 643(4).
[266] 2006 Act, s 644(5).
[267] 2006 Act, s 642(1)(a).
[268] 2006 Act, s 642(2).
[269] 2006 Act, s 642(3).
[270] 2006 Act, s 642(4).
[271] 2006 Act, s 644(7).

solvency statement are filed with the Registrar,[272] it is important to ensure that the solvency statement is sent to shareholders or made available at the meeting, because failure to comply with these requirements will mean that the reduction is not lawfully capable of taking effect.

27.100 Within 15 days after the date on which the resolution for reducing share capital is passed, the company must deliver to the Registrar a copy of the solvency statement and a statement of capital.[273] The statement of capital must state (with respect to the company's share capital as reduced by the resolution): (a) the total number of shares of the company; (b) the aggregate nominal value of those shares; (c) the aggregate amount (if any) unpaid on those shares (whether on account of their nominal value or by way of premium); and (d) for each class of share, particulars of the rights attached to the shares, the total number of shares of that class, and the aggregate nominal value of the shares of that class.[274] The Registrar must register these documents on receipt.[275] The reduction will take effect upon such registration.[276]

27.101 In addition, the company must deliver to the Registrar, within 15 days after the resolution is passed, a statement by the directors confirming that the solvency statement was (a) made not more than 15 days before the date on which the resolution was passed, and (b) provided to the company's members in accordance with the statutory requirements.[277]

27.102 Although the late delivery of the solvency statement and statement of capital, or the nondelivery of the statement confirming the solvency statement's compliance with the statutory requirements will not affect the validity of the resolution,[278] these defaults will give rise to an offence committed by every officer in default (and by the company itself) punishable by fine.[279] It is therefore important to ensure that the statutory requirements are strictly observed. Furthermore, an offence is committed by every officer in default if the company delivers to the Registrar a solvency statement that was not provided to members in accordance with these requirements.[280]

Reduction of capital by order of the court: private and public companies

27.103 For public companies, reduction of capital by way of a special resolution confirmed by order of the court remains the only means of lawfully achieving a reduction.[281] This route is also open to private companies, although the solvency statement procedure is used by private companies in the majority of cases.

27.104 Section 646 provides scope in certain cases for creditors to object to a reduction of capital. This section is applicable automatically where the proposed reduction of capital involves either diminution of liability in respect of unpaid share capital or the payment to a shareholder of any paid-up share capital, but the court has a power to disapply it.[282] In all other

---

[272] 2006 Act, s 644(1), (4).
[273] 2006 Act, s 644(1).
[274] 2006 Act, s 644(2), as amended by SBEE Act 2015, s 97, Sch 6, paras 1, 10 with effect from 30 June 2016. The Companies (Shares and Share Capital) Order 2009 (SI 2009/388), reg 2 specifies the prescribed particulars for the purposes of s 644(2)(c)(i).
[275] 2006 Act, s 644(3).
[276] 2006 Act, s 644(4).
[277] 2006 Act, s 644(5).
[278] 2006 Act, s 644(6).
[279] 2006 Act, s 644(9).
[280] 2006 Act, s 644(7).
[281] 2006 Act, s 641(1)(b).
[282] 2006 Act, s 645(2). The disapplication of s 646 is not an 'all or nothing' matter, since the court may, if having regard to any special circumstances of the case it thinks proper to do so, direct that s 646 is not to apply

cases, s 646 is prima facie inapplicable, although the court has power in any case to direct that it is to apply.[283]

Where the section applies automatically (and is not disapplied) or is applied by the court, **27.105** every creditor of the company who would be entitled to prove in the company's winding up[284] and who can show that there is a real likelihood that the reduction would result in the company being unable to discharge his debt or claim when it fell due is entitled to object to the reduction of capital.[285] It has been said that this is 'a high test which a creditor is likely to find difficult to overcome'.[286] Where the section calls upon a creditor to show 'a real likelihood' that the reduction 'would' result in an inability to discharge the debt when it becomes due, it is calling upon the creditor to demonstrate a particular present assessment about a future state of affairs.[287] The following points should be noted:

(1) The assessment about a future state of affairs has to be well grounded in the facts as they are now known and must avoid the purely speculative.[288]

(2) The duration of the appropriate future period will be affected by the nature and duration of the liability in question, but in general the more remote in time the contemplated event that will make payment fall due the more difficult it must be to establish the reality of the likelihood that the return of capital will itself result in inability to discharge the debt.[289]

(3) The section does not require a creditor to prove that a future event will happen: it is concerned to evaluate the chance of the event (the company's inability to discharge the debt because it has returned capital). It describes the chance as 'real likelihood'—ie beyond the merely possible, but short of the probable.[290]

(4) It is the causative link between the reduction of capital and the company's perceived future inability to discharge the debt which is crucial. An objecting creditor, ie a creditor who seeks to show that he is entitled to object, must establish a 'real likelihood' (a) that the company will be unable to pay his claim when it falls due for payment at some time in the future and (b) that that inability to pay his claim at that time in the future will result from the reduction of capital now. The test of entitlement to object is that it is the reduction of capital, as opposed to some other future event, which may result in the company's inability to discharge the debt.[291]

Where the section applies (and is not disapplied) or is applied, the court is required to settle **27.106** a list of creditors,[292] and for this purpose the court is required to ascertain the names of the creditors and the nature and amount of their debts or claims.[293] The court may also publish

---

as regards any class or classes of creditors: 2006 Act, s 645(3). See *Royal Scottish Assurance plc* [2011] CSOH 2 for guidance regarding the court's power to disapply the requirement.

[283] 2006 Act, s 645(4).

[284] ie including prospective and contingent creditors. See *Re Liberty International plc* [2010] 2 BCLC 665 at para 15, per Norris J.

[285] 2006 Act, s 646(1).

[286] *Royal Scottish Assurance plc* [2011] CSOH 2 at para 7, per Lord Glennie.

[287] See *Re Liberty International plc* [2010] 2 BCLC 665 at para 17, per Norris J.

[288] See *Re Liberty International plc* [2010] 2 BCLC 665 at para 18, per Norris J.

[289] See *Re Liberty International plc* [2010] 2 BCLC 665 at para 19, per Norris J.

[290] See *Re Liberty International plc* [2010] 2 BCLC 665 at para 20, per Norris J.

[291] *Royal Scottish Assurance plc* [2011] CSOH 2 at para 13, per Lord Glennie.

[292] 2006 Act, s 646(2).

[293] 2006 Act, s 646(3)(a).

notices fixing a day or days within which creditors must apply to be included on the list or (if they fail to apply) be excluded from the right to object to the reduction of capital.[294] If a creditor on the list does not consent to the reduction, the court may dispense with the consent of that creditor, provided that the company secures payment of his debt or claim.[295] The debt or claim must be secured by appropriating either the full amount of the debt or claim or (if the company does not admit the liability) such amount as may be fixed by the court after an enquiry.[296]

27.107   As explained above, the requirements regarding the settling of a list of creditors apply automatically in certain cases, unless disapplied by the court. In practice, the requirements are always disapplied on the following basis:

> In practice … upon it being demonstrated to the satisfaction of the court that there are no creditors whose protection requires a list of creditors to be settled, the court dispenses with the requirement to settle a list. This has become the norm … [and] no list of creditors has been settled under this section or its predecessors either in Scotland or in England since 1949. The requirement for a list of creditors has always been disapplied. What happens in practice is that the court makes an assessment of the nature and amount of debts and claims outstanding at the date of the application for confirmation of the reduction; and forms a view as to the risk, if any, that the reduction in capital might result in prejudice to some or all of those creditors. In general terms, it has become the practice of the Court of Session in Scotland and … the Companies Court in London, to dispense with settlement of a list of creditors if the court can be satisfied that there is no realistic possibility of any creditor being put at risk by the reduction … or if one or more of certain accepted methods of creditor protection are adopted. The principal methods are: (a) obtaining the consent of creditors and, where only some of the creditors consent, subordinating the claims of consenting creditors to those of non-consenting creditors; (b) setting aside cash in a blocked account in an amount sufficient to discharge the claims of non-consenting creditors; (c) the provision by a bank or other third party with a sound credit covenant of a guarantee in an amount sufficient to cover the claims of non-consenting creditors; and (d) the giving of an appropriately worded undertaking, the effect of which is to ensure that any distribution consequent upon the reduction being confirmed by the court does not reduce the net assets of the company below a figure sufficient to ensure that the claims of non-consenting creditors will be paid as they fall due.[297]

27.108   The court has no jurisdiction to confirm a reduction of capital unless it is satisfied that every creditor entitled to object has either consented to the reduction or had his debt paid or secured.[298] Where these requirements are satisfied, the court may make an order[299] confirming the reduction on such terms and condition as it thinks fit.[300] Where the court confirms the reduction, it may order the company to publish (a) the reasons for the reduction or such other information in regard to it as the court thinks expedient with a view to giving proper information to the public[301] and (b) the causes that led to the reduction.[302]

---

[294]   2006 Act, s 646(3)(b).
[295]   2006 Act, s 646(4).
[296]   2006 Act, s 646(5).
[297]   *Royal Scottish Assurance plc* [2011] CSOH 2 at para 8, per Lord Glennie.
[298]   2006 Act, s 648(2).
[299]   As to the scope of the court's jurisdiction, see *British and American Corporation v Couper* [1894] AC 399; *Poole v National Bank of China* [1907] AC 229; and *Re Grosvenor Press Ltd* [1985] 1 WLR 980.
[300]   2006 Act, s 648(1). The court may eg impose a condition that the articles shall be so altered that the shares reduced in amount shall also be reduced in voting power: *Re Pinkey & Sons SS Co* [1892] 3 Ch 125; *Re Continental Union Gas Co* (1891) 7 TLR 47.
[301]   See eg *Re Truman, Hanbury & Co* [1910] 2 Ch 498.
[302]   2006 Act, s 648(3).

The court must also approve a statement of capital[303] which must state (with respect to the **27.109** company's capital as altered by the order):

(1) the total number of shares of the company;
(2) the aggregate nominal value of those shares;
(3) the aggregate amount (if any) unpaid on those shares (whether on account of their nominal value or by way of premium); and
(4) for each class of shares, (i) prescribed particulars of the rights attached to the shares, (ii) the total number of shares of that class, and (iii) the aggregate nominal value of shares of that class.[304]

The court's order and the statement of capital must be registered[305] (subject to special provi- **27.110** sions applying where a public company's capital is reduced below the authorized minimum; see below). The reduction of capital takes effect on the registration of the order and statement of capital,[306] unless it is part of a compromise or arrangement sanctioned by the court under Part 26, in which case it takes effect on delivery to the Registrar (rather than actual registration) unless the court orders otherwise.[307]

The Registrar must certify the registration of the order and statement of capital[308] and the **27.111** certificate must be signed by the Registrar and authenticated by the Registrar's official seal.[309] Such a certificate will be conclusive evidence that the statutory requirements relating to a reduction of capital were satisfied and that the company's share capital is as stated in the statement of capital.[310]

Where by order of the court the nominal value of a public company's allotted capital is **27.112** reduced below the authorized minimum, the Registrar must not register the order unless (a) the court so directs,[311] or (b) the company is first re-registered as a private company.[312] Section 651 provides an expedited procedure for re-registration in these circumstances.

Although s 646(2) charges the court with the task of settling a list of creditors, and s 646(3) **27.113** mandates the court to find out about the company's creditors, the practical reality is that the court will be heavily dependent on information provided by the company itself. For this reason, the court will expect to be provided with full and accurate information by the company's directors.

To fortify the directors' obligation to provide the court with information, s 647 provides **27.114** that it is an offence for any officer of the company intentionally or recklessly to conceal the name of a creditor entitled to object to a reduction of capital or misrepresent the nature and

---

[303] 2006 Act, s 649(1).
[304] 2006 Act, s 649(2), as amended by SBEE Act 2015, s 97, Sch 6, paras 1, 11 with effect from 30 June 2016. The Companies (Shares and Share Capital) Order 2009 (SI 2009/388), reg 3 states the prescribed particulars for the purposes of s 649(2)(c)(i).
[305] 2006 Act, s 649(1).
[306] 2006 Act, s 649(3)(b).
[307] 2006 Act, s 649(3)(a).
[308] 2006 Act, s 649(5).
[309] 2006 Act, s 649(6)(a).
[310] 2006 Act, s 649(6)(b).
[311] See eg *Re Minster Assets plc* [1985] BCLC 2000.
[312] 2006 Act, s 650(1), (2). See also the Companies (Authorised Minimum) Regulations 2009 (SI 2009/2425), regs 3 and 5.

amount of the debt or claim of a creditor.[313] It is also an offence for any officer of the company to be knowingly concerned in any such concealment or misrepresentations.[314] These offences are punishable on conviction on indictment to a fine or on summary conviction to a fine not exceeding the statutory maximum.[315]

(3) Public companies: serious loss of capital

27.115 Where the net assets of a public company are half or less of its called-up share capital, the directors are under a statutory obligation to call a general meeting of the company to consider whether any, and if so what, steps should be taken to deal with the situation.[316] The meeting must be called (ie notice given) not later than 28 days from the earliest day on which one or more directors of the company becomes aware of the fact that the net assets are half or less of the called-up share capital[317] and must be convened for a date not later than 56 days from that date.[318] In other words, the section begins to operate from the moment a single director becomes aware of the fact. However, it will be difficult in practice to know whether or not the section applies, because difficult questions are likely to arise when making the necessary calculations, particularly having regard to the different methods of valuing assets.

27.116 If there is a failure to convene a meeting in accordance with the statutory requirements, an offence (punishable by fine[319]) is committed by each of the directors of the company who knowingly authorizes or permits the failure or (after the period during which the meeting should have been convened) knowingly authorizes or permits the failure to continue.

(4) Acquisition by limited company of its own shares

27.117 In *Trevor v Whitworth*,[320] the House of Lords held that a company could not be a member of itself, and that a purchase by a company of its own shares, although expressly authorized by its articles, was ultra vires and an unauthorized reduction of capital contrary to the interests of the creditors. A transaction which upon closer examination can be seen to involve an unlawful return of capital to a member, whether directly or indirectly, is void.[321]

27.118 The common law position has for many years been replaced by a similar statutory prohibition. The general rule is now contained in s 658 of the 2006 Act, which provides that a limited company must not acquire its own shares, whether by purchase, subscription, or otherwise, except in accordance with the provisions of Part 18 of the Act.[322]

27.119 If a company purports to acquire its own shares in contravention of this general rule, the purported acquisition is void,[323] and an offence is committed by the company and every

---

[313] 2006 Act, s 647(1)(a).

[314] 2006 Act, s 647(1)(b).

[315] 2006 Act, s 647(2).

[316] 2006 Act, s 656(1).

[317] 2006 Act, s 656(2).

[318] 2006 Act, s 656(3). The usual requirements as to notice etc must be complied with in the ordinary way.

[319] 2006 Act, s 656(5).

[320] (1887) 12 App Cas 409.

[321] *Barclays Bank plc v British & Commonwealth Holdings plc* [1996] 1 BCLC 1; *Aveling Barford Ltd v Perion* [1989] BCLC 626 (discussed and approved by Lord Walker in *Progress Property Co Ltd v Moorgarth Group Ltd* [2011] 1 WLR 1, SC at paras 20–2, 30). It should be noted that this rule has never applied to unlimited companies: see *Re Borough Commercial and Building Society* [1893] 2 Ch 242.

[322] 2006 Act, s 658(1).

[323] 2006 Act, s 658(2)(b). See eg *Vision Express (UK) Ltd v Wilson* [1995] 2 BCLC 419 and *Re R W Peak (King's Lynn) Ltd* [1998] 1 BCLC 193.

officer in default.[324] A person guilty of this offence is liable on conviction on indictment to imprisonment for a term not exceeding two years or a fine or both or on summary conviction to imprisonment for a term not exceeding 12 months or a fine not exceeding the statutory maximum.[325]

The general rule is subject to a number of important exceptions. First, s 658 of the Act does **27.120** not prohibit a limited company from acquiring any of its own fully paid shares otherwise than for valuation consideration, eg by way of legacy or gift,[326] because such an acquisition does not have the effect of depleting the company's assets. However, since the company cannot be a member of itself, the general rule is that shares must be vested in a nominee to be held on the company's behalf and may be voted as the company directs.[327] Now a company may hold treasury shares (paragraphs 27.189–27.193 below).

Secondly, the 2006 Act, s 658 does not prohibit: **27.121**

(1) the acquisition of shares in a reduction of capital duly made;[328]
(2) the purchase of shares in pursuance of an order of the court[329] under s 98 (application to court to cancel resolution for re-registration as a private company), s 721(6) (powers of court on objection to redemption or purchase of shares out of capital), s 759 (remedial order in case of breach of prohibition of public offers by private company), or Part 30 (protection of members against unfair prejudice);[330] or
(3) the forfeiture of shares, or the acceptance of shares surrendered in lieu, in pursuance of the company's articles, for failure to pay any sum payable in respect of the shares.

In each case, however, failure to comply with the correct procedure will mean that the general rule applies and the purported acquisition will be void.[331]

Additionally, a company is not precluded by s 658 from acquiring the shares of another **27.122** company in circumstances in which the sole asset of the acquired company is shares in the acquiring company.[332] However, in view of the potential for abuse and adverse consequences for shareholders and creditors, the court will look carefully at such transactions to see that the directors of the acquiring company have acted with an eye solely to the interests of the acquiring company (and not eg to the interests of the directors) and have fulfilled their fiduciary duties to safeguard the interests of shareholders and creditors alike.

Finally, and most importantly, a company will be able to acquire its own shares in accordance **27.123** with Chapter 4 of Part 18 of the 2006 Act. The provisions of Chapter 4 of Part 18, which constitute a major exception to the general principle, are considered in detail below.

---

[324] 2006 Act, s 658(2)(a).
[325] 2006 Act, s 658(3).
[326] 2006 Act, s 659(1); see also *Kirby v Wilkins* [1929] 2 Ch 444 and *Re Castiglione's Will Trusts* [1958] Ch 549.
[327] *Re Castiglione's Will Trusts* [1958] Ch 549; see also *Kirby v Wilkins* [1929] 2 Ch 444.
[328] 2006 Act, s 659(2)(a).
[329] In all of these cases, the court's power to order a company to acquire its own shares is preserved as a means of remedying some other default.
[330] 2006 Act, s 659(2)(b).
[331] *Re R W Peak (King's Lynn) Ltd* [1998] 1 BCLC 193.
[332] *Acatos & Hutcheson plc v Watson* [1995] 1 BCLC 218.

27.124   If shares are taken by a subscriber to the memorandum as nominee of the company or are issued to a nominee of the company or are acquired by a nominee of the company, partly paid up, from a third person, then the nominee is treated as holding the shares on his own account, so that the company has no beneficial interest in them.[333]

27.125   In addition, if the nominee, having been called on to pay any amount for the purpose of paying up or paying any premium on the shares, fails to pay that amount within 21 days from being called on to do so, then, in the case of shares that he agreed to take as subscriber to the memorandum, the other subscribers are jointly and severally liable with him to pay that amount, and, in any other case, the directors of the company when the shares were issued to or acquired by him are jointly and severally liable with him to pay that amount.[334]

27.126   However, if the subscriber or director acted honestly and reasonably and having regard to all the circumstances ought fairly to be relieved from liability, the court may relieve him, either wholly or in part, from his liability on such terms as the court thinks fit.[335] Similarly, any subscriber or director who has reason to apprehend that a claim will or might be made for the recovery of any such amount may apply to the court to be relieved from liability.[336]

Public companies: cancellation, re-registration

27.127   Where a public company[337] acquires a beneficial interest in its own shares in the special circumstances described in s 622(1), the company must cancel the shares and diminish the amount of its share capital by the nominal value of the shares cancelled.[338] Where the effect of such cancellation is that the nominal value of the company's allotted share capital is brought below the authorized minimum, the company must apply for re-registration[339] as a private company, stating the effect of the cancellation.[340] Cancellation must occur within a prescribed period from the date of forfeiture or surrender or acquisition (as the case may be).[341] Before such cancellation, neither the company nor its nominee may exercise any voting rights in respect of the shares[342] and any purported exercise of those rights is void.[343]

27.128   Where a company cancels shares in order to comply with this requirement, it must notify the Registrar of the cancellation within a month of the date of cancellation.[344] The notice must be accompanied by a statement of capital[345] which must state, with respect to the company's share capital immediately following cancellation:

---

[333] 2006 Act, s 660(1), (2). This section is not intended to apply to employee share schemes: see 2006 Act, s 660(3).

[334] 2006 Act, s 661(1), (2).

[335] 2006 Act, s 661(3).

[336] 2006 Act, s 661(4).

[337] Or a private company which subsequently re-registers as a public company: see 2006 Act, s 668. However, the 2006 Act, ss 622–70, do not apply to an old public company: Companies Act 2006 (Consequential Amendments, Transitional Provisions and Savings) Order 2009 (SI 2009/1941).

[338] 2006 Act, s 662(1), (2)(a).

[339] Consequential provisions relating to re-registration may be found in ss 664–5.

[340] 2006 Act, s 662(2)(b).

[341] 2006 Act, s 662(3).

[342] 2006 Act, s 662(5).

[343] 2006 Act, s 662(6).

[344] 2006 Act, s 663(1).

[345] 2006 Act, s 663(2).

(1) the total number of shares of the company;

(2) the aggregate nominal value of those shares; and

(3) for each class of shares, (a) prescribed particulars of the rights attached to the shares, (b) the total number of shares of that class, and (c) the aggregate nominal value of the shares of that class, and (d) the amount paid up and the amount (if any) unpaid on each share (whether on account of the nominal value of the share or by way of premium).[346]

Cancellation, re-registration: criminal liabilities of directors

If a public company required to cancel shares under s 662 fails to do so within the three-year time period, a summary offence punishable by fine[347] is committed by every officer in default.[348] If the company cancels the shares but fails to notify the Registrar within one month of cancellation or fails to provide a statement of capital to the Registrar together with the notice, an offence (punishable on summary conviction by way of fine[349]) is committed by every officer of the company in default.[350] Finally, if a public company cancels shares but fails within the appropriate period to re-register as a private company (in circumstances where its share capital has fallen below the 'authorized minimum' required by s 763), a summary offence punishable by fine[351] is committed by every officer in default.[352]   **27.129**

(5) Financial assistance for purchase of own shares

The giving of financial assistance by a company for the purpose of the purchase of its own shares was first prohibited by the 1929 Act, s 45, following recommendations of the Greene Committee in 1926.[353] Arden LJ summarized the legislative history in *Chaston v SWP Group plc*:[354]   **27.130**

> Section 45 of the Companies Act 1929 ... was enacted as a result of the previously common practice of purchasing the shares of a company having a substantial cash balance or readily available assets and so arranging matters that the purchase money was lent by the company to the purchaser ... The general mischief ... [is] that the resources of the target company and its subsidiaries should not be used directly or indirectly to assist the purchaser financially to make the acquisition. This may prejudice the interests of the creditors of the target or its group, and the interests of any shareholders who do not accept the offer to acquire their shares or to whom the offer is not made.

No prohibition for assistance by private company

Since 1929, the prohibition on such financial assistance has extended to public and private companies. In 2005, however, the CLR concluded that specific statutory prohibitions were   **27.131**

---

[346] 2006 Act, s 663(3). The Companies (Shares and Share Capital) Order 2009 (SI 2009/388), reg 2 states the prescribed particulars.

[347] 2006 Act, s 667(3).

[348] 2006 Act, s 667(1)(a), (2).

[349] 2006 Act, s 663(5).

[350] 2006 Act, s 663(4).

[351] 2006 Act, s 667(3).

[352] 2006 Act, s 667(1)(b), (2).

[353] See Ch 1 above at para 1.61 for the history and *Re VGM Holdings Ltd* [1942] Ch 235, 239. For more recent examples of the abuse against which the provision was directed, see *Selangor United Rubber Estates Ltd v Cradock (No 3)* [1968] 1 WLR 1555; *Wallersteiner v Moir* [1974] 1 WLR 991.

[354] [2003] 1 BCLC 675, 686, CA.

unnecessary in the case of private companies as the mischief in question could be controlled by other means:

> The provisions on financial assistance are designed to protect creditors and shareholders against the misuse and depletion of a company's assets. The CLR concluded that it was inappropriate for private companies to continue to carry the cost of complying with the rules on financial assistance as abusive transactions could be controlled in other ways, eg through the provisions on directors duties … or through the wrongful trading and market abuse provisions … Private companies will therefore no longer be prevented from providing financial assistance for the purchase of their own shares.[355]

27.132 In order to give effect to the reform recommended by the CLR the restrictions in the 1985 Act, ss 151–3 and 155–8 on the giving by a private company of financial assistance for the acquisition of its own shares, including the 'whitewash' procedure have been repealed as from 1 October 2008.[356] The relevant provisions of the 2006 Act only prohibit the giving of financial assistance in relation to acquisition of shares in public companies.[357] However, private companies will still come within the scope of the legislation where they are subsidiaries of a public company and are providing financial assistance for the purpose of an acquisition of shares in a public company, unless one of the exceptions set out in s 682 is available.[358]

Meaning of 'financial assistance'

27.133 The term 'financial assistance' is explained by s 677(1):

> (1) In this Chapter 'financial assistance' means—
>   (a) financial assistance given by way of gift,
>   (b) financial assistance given—
>   (i) by way of guarantee, security or indemnity (other than an indemnity in respect of the indemnifier's own neglect or default), or
>   (ii) by way of release or waiver,
>   (c) financial assistance given—
>   (i) by way of a loan or any other agreement under which any of the obligations of the person giving the assistance are to be fulfilled at a time when in accordance with the agreement any obligation of another party to the agreement remains unfulfilled, or
>   (ii) by way of the novation of, or the assignment (in Scotland, assignation) of rights arising under, a loan or such other agreement, or
>   (d) any other financial assistance given by a company where—
>   (i) the net assets of which are reduced to a material extent by the giving of the assistance, or
>   (ii) the company has no net assets.

---

[355] White Paper: Company Law Reform, p 41. For the history of this reform, see CLR: *Proposals for Reform of Sections 151–158 of the Companies Act 1985* (October 1993) and CLR: *Financial Assistance by a Company for the Acquisition of its Own Shares* (November 1996 and April 1997). See also CLR: *The Strategic Framework* at paras 5.4.20–5.4.25; CLR: *Company Formation and Capital Maintenance* (October 1999); CLR: *Completing the Structure* at paras 7.12–7.15; CLR: *Final Report* at para 2.30.

[356] 2006 Act Commencement Order No 5, Arts 5(2) and 8(b) and Sch 3.

[357] Attempts to reform the law relating to financial assistance by public companies are hampered by the requirements of the Second Directive on Company Law (EEC 77/91) which provides that a public company may not advance funds, nor make loans, nor provide security, with a view to the acquisition of its shares by a third party: see, specifically, Art 23.

[358] See, specifically, s 682(1)(a), (2).

Each limb of this definition reuses the term 'financial assistance' without ever defining it.[359] **27.134** This omission is particularly important in light of the broad words of paragraph (d), as Ward LJ observed in *Chaston v SWP Group plc*:[360]

> I can understand [a] to [c] and they seem all to be related to direct or indirect assistance given for the actual acquisition of the shares, that is to say help in meeting the consideration for the transaction. But [d] tells one nothing about what comprises financial assistance. The words are as wide as they can be—'any other financial assistance'. Rather it tells you when financial assistance is not financial assistance, namely when it is de minimis.

In the absence of a statutory definition, the task of explaining the meaning of the term has **27.135** been performed by the courts. Perhaps the most commonly cited explanation is that of Hoffmann J in *Charterhouse Investment Trust Ltd v Tempest Diesels Ltd*:[361]

> There is no definition of giving financial assistance in the section, although some examples are given. The words have no technical meaning and their frame of reference is in my judgment the language of ordinary commerce. One must examine the commercial realities of the transaction and decide whether it can properly be described as the giving of financial assistance by the company, bearing in mind that the section is a penal one and should not be strained to cover transactions which are not fairly within it.[362]

The meaning of the term 'financial assistance' was also considered in *MT Realisations Ltd* **27.136** *v Digital Equipment Co Ltd*,[363] in which Mummery LJ referred to the words of the Federal Court of Australia in *Sterileair Pty Ltd v Papallo*:[364] 'Assistance involves something in the nature of aid or help. It cannot exist in a vacuum; it must be given to someone.' However, it is not enough merely for there to be assistance; the section will not apply unless the assistance is financial.[365]

In most cases, the financial assistance takes the form of direct contributions towards the con- **27.137** sideration payable for the shares. Indeed, in *Brady v Brady*,[366] Lord Oliver said that the use of the target company's assets to fund the purchase price is the 'obvious mischief' at which the section is aimed.

However, as the decision of the Court of Appeal in *Chaston v SWP Group plc*[367] makes clear, **27.138** this is not the only prohibited form of financial assistance. In that case, a purchaser (SWP) wished to acquire shares in a company (DCR). SWP wished to carry out a 'due diligence' exercise. DCR paid for a firm of accountants (D&T) to carry out some of the work necessary for the 'due diligence' exercise. As a result, SWP avoided the cost of instructing its own accountants (C&L) to carry out this work. As Buxton LJ held:[368]

---

[359] *Charterhouse Investment Trust Ltd v Tempest Diesels Ltd* [1986] BCLC 1, 10; *Chaston v SWP Group plc* [2003] 1 BCLC 675, 687, CA. See also *AMG Global Nominees (Private) Ltd v Africa Resources Ltd* [2009] 1 BCLC 281.

[360] [2003] 1 BCLC 675, 694, CA.

[361] [1986] BCLC 1, 10.

[362] This passage was cited with approval by Aldous LJ in *Barclays Bank plc v British & Commonwealth Holdings plc* [1996] 1 WLR 1, 15, CA; by Arden LJ *in Chaston v SWP Group plc* [2003] 1 BCLC 675, 687, CA; and by Toulson LJ in *Anglo Petroleum Ltd v TFB (Mortgages) Ltd* [2008] 1 BCLC 185 at paras 26 and 27, CA.

[363] [2003] 2 BCLC 117, 124, CA.

[364] (1998) 29 ACSR 461.

[365] *Barclays Bank plc v British & Commonwealth Holdings plc* [1996] 1 WLR 1, 15, CA per Aldous LJ.

[366] [1989] AC 755, 780, HL.

[367] [2003] 1 BCLC 675, CA.

[368] [2003] 1 BCLC 675, 693, CA.

The first obvious conclusion was that if D&T did not do the spadework for the due diligence exercise, then SWP's accountants, C&L, would have had to dig for the information clearly thought to be material to the exercise and C&L would then have charged SWP for doing that work. DCR's incurring those liabilities and discharging part of those debts was, therefore, of financial assistance to SWP. [Therefore] SWP was helped by not having to put its hand in its pocket for part of the fees that would otherwise be incurred in the due diligence exercise.

The payment of D&T's fees by DCR was financial assistance because, as Arden LJ observed, 'both the purchaser and the vendors were relieved of any obligation to pay for this service themselves'.[369]

27.139 The Court of Appeal's conclusion in the *Chaston* case demonstrates that financial assistance is not limited to situations in which the target company actually provides the consideration payable by the purchaser in respect of the shares. It is important to emphasize, however, that each case turns on its own facts. As Arden LJ observed in *Chaston v SWP Group plc*:[370] 'Accordingly, the question whether financial assistance exists in any given case may be fact-sensitive and not one which can be answered simply by applying a legal definition.'

27.140 Financial assistance will exist where the purchaser obtains a loan to finance the acquisition which is then guaranteed by the target company.[371] Similarly, financial assistance will exist where the target company buys an asset from a potential purchaser at an overvalue in order to provide the potential purchaser with funds with which to finance the acquisition of shares in the target company.[372]

Prohibitions of financial assistance

27.141 There are four separate prohibitions. First, s 678(1) provides that where a person is proposing[373] to acquire shares in a public company, it is not lawful for that company, or a company that is a subsidiary[374] of that company, to give financial assistance directly or indirectly for the purpose of the acquisition before or at the same time as the acquisition takes place. However, s 678(1) does not prohibit a company from giving financial assistance for the acquisition of shares in it or its holding company if: (1) the company's principal purpose in giving the assistance is not to give it for the purpose of any such acquisition; or (2) the giving of the assistance for that purpose is only an incidental part of some larger purpose of the company, provided that, in either case, the assistance is given in good faith in the interests of the company.[375]

---

[369] [2003] 1 BCLC 675, 698, CA. See, by way of contrast, *Corporate Development Partners LLC v E-Relationship Marketing Ltd* [2009] BCC 295, in which a fee for identifying targets for acquisition was not 'financial assistance' because on the facts the commitment to pay the fee was not intended to and did not assist or advance the acquisition at all, and did not smooth the path towards any ultimate acquisition.

[370] [2003] 1 BCLC 675, 689, CA.

[371] *Arab Bank plc v Mercantile Holdings Ltd* [1994] Ch 71; *Coulthard v Neville Russell* [1998] 1 BCLC 143; *Re Continental Assurance Co of London plc* [1997] 1 BCLC 48; *Re Hill & Tyler Ltd* [2005] 1 BCLC 41.

[372] *Belmont Finance Corp v Williams Furniture (No 2)* [1980] 1 All ER 393.

[373] See *Estafnous v London & Leeds Business Centres Ltd* [2009] EWHC 1308 (Ch) at paras 76–77 for a discussion of the concept of 'proposing' (appeal dismissed without reference to this point: [2011] EWCA Civ 1157).

[374] In *Arab Bank plc v Mercantile Holdings Ltd* [1994] Ch 71 the question arose whether it is sufficient if the company providing the assistance is a foreign subsidiary. Millett J held that the phrase 'any of its subsidiaries' had to be construed as being limited to subsidiaries which are companies incorporated under English law, and that a foreign subsidiary was therefore not prohibited from giving financial assistance for the purpose of the acquisition of shares in its English parent company.

[375] 2006 Act, s 678(2).

Secondly, s 678(3) provides that where a person has acquired shares in a company and a liability has been incurred (by that or another person) for the purpose of the acquisition, it is not lawful for that company, or a company that is a subsidiary of that company, to give financial assistance directly or indirectly for the purpose of reducing or discharging the liability if, at the time the assistance is given, the company in which the shares were acquired is a public company. However, section 678(3) does not prohibit a company from giving financial assistance if (a) the company's principal purpose in giving the assistance is not to reduce or discharge any liability incurred by a person for the purpose of the acquisition of shares in the company or its holding company, or (b) the reduction or discharge of any such liability is only an incidental part of some larger purpose of the company, provided that, in either case, the assistance is given in good faith in the interests of the company.[376]   **27.142**

Thirdly, s 679(1) provides that where a person is acquiring or proposing to acquire shares in a private company, it is not lawful for a public company that is a subsidiary of that company to give financial assistance directly or indirectly for the purpose of the acquisition before or at the same time as the acquisition takes place. However, s 679(1) does not prohibit a company from giving financial assistance for the acquisition of shares in its holding company if (a) the company's principal purpose in giving the assistance is not to give it for the purpose of any such acquisition, or (b) the giving of the assistance for that purpose is only an incidental part of some larger purpose of the company, provided that, in either case, the assistance is given in good faith in the interests of the company.[377]   **27.143**

Fourthly, s 679(3) provides that where a person has acquired shares in a private company and a liability has been incurred by that or another person for the purpose of the acquisition, it is not lawful for a public company that is a subsidiary of that company to give financial assistance directly or indirectly for the purpose of reducing or discharging the liability. However, s 679(3) does not prohibit a company from giving financial assistance if (a) the company's principal purpose in giving the assistance is not to reduce or discharge any liability incurred by a person for the purpose of the acquisition of its shares in its holding company, or (b) the reduction or discharge of any such liability is only an incidental part of some larger purpose of the company, and, in either case, the assistance is given in good faith in the interests of the company.[378]   **27.144**

The meaning of 'purpose'

In each of the four cases identified above, the statutory prohibition will apply if the assistance was given either (a) 'for the purpose' of the acquisition,[379] or (b) for 'for the purpose' of discharging a liability incurred 'for the purpose' of the acquisition.[380] But none of the statutory prohibitions will apply if (i) the company's 'principal purpose' is not to give assistance 'for the purpose' of the acquisition or to reduce or discharge any liability incurred 'for the purpose' of the acquisition,[381] or (ii) the giving of the assistance for the prohibited purpose 'is only   **27.145**

---

[376] 2006 Act, s 678(4).
[377] 2006 Act, s 679(2).
[378] 2006 Act, s 679(4).
[379] 2006 Act, ss 678(1) and 679(1).
[380] 2006 Act, ss 678(3) and 679(3).
[381] 2006 Act, ss 678(2)(a), (4)(a) and 679(2)(a), (4)(a).

an incidental part of some larger purpose' of the company.[382] In *Anglo Petroleum Ltd v TFB (Mortgages) Ltd* Toulson LJ said:[383]

> A purpose requires a mind. The relevant purpose is that of the company or subsidiary, through its relevant officer or officers, in giving the alleged assistance … Whether the consequence [of an act] was the actor's purpose is a matter for inference from all the circumstances. There may be many situations in life in which a person does a particular act knowing that it will have a particular consequence, but without that consequence being the purpose for which he does the act.

27.146 The meaning of the word 'purpose' was considered in detail by the House of Lords in *Brady v Brady*.[384] The key passage appears in the speech of Lord Oliver:

> My Lords, 'purpose' is, in some contexts, a word of wide content but in construing it in the context of the fasciculus of sections regulating the provision of finance by a company in connection with the purchase of its own shares there has always to be borne in mind the mischief against which [the statutory prohibition] is aimed. In particular, if the section is not, effectively, to be deprived of any useful application, it is important to distinguish between a purpose and the reason why a purpose is formed. The ultimate reason for forming the purpose of financing an acquisition may, and in most cases probably will, be more important to those making the decision than the immediate transaction itself. But 'larger' is not the same thing as 'more important' nor is 'reason' the same as 'purpose'. If one postulates the case of a bidder for control of a public company financing his bid from the company's own funds—the obvious mischief at which the section is aimed—the immediate purpose which it is sought to achieve is that of completing the purchase and vesting control of the company in the bidder. The reasons why that course is considered desirable may be many and varied. The company may have fallen on hard times so that a change of management is considered necessary to avert disaster. It may merely be thought, and no doubt would be thought by the purchaser and the directors whom he nominates once he has control, that the business of the company will be more profitable under his management than it was heretofore. These may be excellent reasons but they cannot, in my judgment, constitute a 'larger purpose' of which the provision of assistance is merely an incident. The purpose and the only purpose of the financial assistance is and remains that of enabling the shares to be acquired and the financial or commercial advantages flowing from the acquisition, whilst they may form the reason for forming the purpose of providing assistance, are a by-product of it rather than an independent purpose of which the assistance can properly be considered to be an incident.[385]

27.147 In other words, the 'purpose' is the outcome sought to be facilitated or enabled by the giving of financial assistance, and the 'reason' is the statement made to explain why that outcome is being pursued. In order to apply Lord Oliver's analysis of the statutory provisions, it is necessary to ask what a company is trying to achieve by giving the financial assistance. If the company is giving the financial assistance in order to promote or enable the acquisition of shares or satisfy a liability incurred as a result of the acquisition of shares, then the financial assistance will prima facie fall within the statutory prohibition. If the company anticipates that the acquisition of shares will produce various benefits, then the company's desire to obtain these benefits is simply the company's reason or motive for seeking to promote the acquisition of shares, and the company's reason or motive is not a 'purpose' in this context.

---

[382] 2006 Act, ss 678(2)(b), (4)(b) and 679(2)(b), (4)(b).
[383] [2008] 1 BCLC 185, CA at para 35.
[384] [1989] AC 755, HL.
[385] [1989] AC 755, 779–80.

Put another way, a 'purpose' must be some additional objective which the company seeks to achieve and which exists alongside the acquisition of shares rather than simply flowing from the acquisition of shares.

In *Plaut v Steiner*,[386] on the basis of Lord Oliver's decision in *Brady*, Morritt J dismissed the **27.148** contention that the principal or larger purpose of the company was to effect the commercial division of the company. The division of the company, he pointed out, could have been effected without the financial assistance, but would never have been proposed without the contemporaneous exchange of shares. Each purpose, he held, was equally large, and neither was incidental to the other, as neither would have existed without the other.

Unconditional exceptions

The following transactions are permissible as a matter of general company law and are **27.149** expressly excluded by s 681(1) from the prohibitions in ss 678 and 679:

(1) distribution of a company's assets by way of dividend lawfully made or a distribution made in the course of the company's winding up;
(2) the allotment of bonus shares;
(3) reduction of capital under Chapter 10 of Part 17;
(4) a redemption or purchase of shares under Chapter 3 of Part 18 or a purchase of shares under Chapter 4 of Part 18;
(5) anything done in pursuance of an order of the court under Part 26 (order sanctioning compromise or arrangement with members or creditors);[387]
(6) anything done under an arrangement made in pursuance of the Insolvency Act, s 110 (acceptance of shares by liquidator in winding up as consideration for sale of property); and
(7) anything done under an arrangement made between a company and its creditors which is binding on the creditors by virtue of Part 1 of the Insolvency Act.

Conditional exceptions

The 2006 Act, s 682(2) provides for a number of limited exceptions in cases involving **27.150** (a) money-lending companies, (b) employees' share schemes, (c) acquisition of shares by employees and the relatives of employees, and (d) the making of loans to employees for the purpose of share acquisitions.

Criminal liability of directors

If a company contravenes any of the prohibitions on financial assistance, an offence is com- **27.151** mitted by the company and every officer of the company in default.[388] A person guilty of this offence is liable on conviction on indictment to imprisonment for a term not exceeding two years or a fine or both or on summary conviction to imprisonment for a term not exceeding 12 months or a fine not exceeding the statutory maximum or both.[389]

---

[386] (1989) 5 BCC 353.
[387] See *Re Uniq plc* [2012] 1 BCLC 783, in which David Richards J sanctioned a scheme which involved the giving of financial assistance, stating that 'the power of the court … to sanction financial assistance as part of a scheme is not qualified by reference to particular criteria'.
[388] 2006 Act, s 680(1).
[389] 2006 Act, s 680(2).

Civil liability of directors

27.152   A director who authorizes the giving of financial assistance in breach of the statutory provisions will be in breach of his duties to the company and liable to make good any loss suffered by the company resulting from the breach.[390]

Disqualification

27.153   Participation by directors in a scheme which contravenes the statutory provisions may be relied on by the Secretary of State in disqualification proceedings as evidence of unfitness.[391]

(6) Redemption or purchase of own shares

27.154   One of the statutory exceptions to the rule in *Trevor v Whitworth*[392] involves the redemption or purchase by a company of its own shares out of distributable profits or the proceeds of a fresh issue. In the case of redemption, there is in fact no acquisition, because the shares are merely cancelled in accordance with their terms. In either case, however, there is no reduction of capital, because the capital paid out on redemption or by way of consideration for the acquisition is either replaced by the proceeds of the newly issued shares or accounted for by a *pro tanto* reduction in the profits available for dividend. The ability of a company to issue redeemable shares was first introduced by the 1929 Act in respect of 'redeemable preference shares' (although the term 'preference' was not defined) and extended by the Act 1981 Act to enable companies to issue redeemable shares of any class. The related power given to companies to purchase their own shares was first introduced in 1981.

27.155   The detailed procedural requirements relating to redemption and purchase are set out below. Non-compliance with the central substantive requirements will not be treated as a mere irregularity capable of being waived or dispensed with or validated by unanimous agreement of all members entitled to vote at the meeting because the members are not the sole group for whose benefit the requirements have been imposed.[393] However, informal unanimous consent may be sufficient to cure 'minor' contraventions[394] (such as, perhaps,

---

[390]   *Selangor United Rubber Estates Ltd v Cradock (No 3)* [1968] 2 All ER 1073; *Steen v Law* [1964] AC 287; *Curtis's Furnishing Store Ltd v Freedman* [1966] 1 WLR 1219; *Karak Rubber v Burden (No 2)* [1972] WLR 602; *Wallersteiner v Moir* [1974] 3 All ER 217; *Belmont Finance Corp Ltd v Williams Furniture Ltd* [1980] 1 All ER 393.

[391]   *Re Dawes & Henderson (Agencies) Ltd (No 2)* [1999] 2 BCLC 317; *Re Continental Assurance Co of London plc* [1997] 1 BCLC 48.

[392]   (1887) 12 App Cas 409.

[393]   *Precision Dippings Ltd v Precision Dippings Marketing Ltd* [1986] 1 Ch 447, CA; *Re R W Peak (King's Lynn) Ltd* [1998] 1 BCLC 193; *Wright v Atlas Wright (Europe) Ltd* [1999] 2 BCLC 301, CA; *Re Torvale Group Ltd* [1999] 2 BCLC 605; *BDG Roof-Bond Ltd v Douglas* [2000] 1 BCLC 401. A statutory requirement may only be waived by the person or persons for whose benefit or protection it was introduced. This rule is commonly expressed in the Latin maxim *quilibet potest renunciare juri pro se introducto* ('Anyone may renounce the benefit of a stipulation or other right introduced entirely in his own favour'). Authoritative statements of the principle include: *Halesowen Presswork & Assembles Ltd v National Westminster Bank* [1972] AC 785, HL at pp 808–9, per Lord Simon; *Johnson v Moreton* [1980] AC 37, HL at 58–61, per Lord Hailsham; at 67–8, per Lord Simon. Rights or protections introduced for the benefit of a limited group of persons may be waived by those persons; rights or protections introduced for the benefit of a wider group of persons or for the public good generally may not be waived by a limited group of persons.

[394]   See, on this issue, *BDG Roof-Bond Ltd v Douglas* [2000] 1 BCLC 401, 417. See also *Kinlan v Crimmin* [2007] 2 BCLC 67, in which the Deputy Judge (Philip Sales QC) held at para 40 that '[t]he provision in section 164(6)(a) is ... clearly one for the protection of the members of the company rather than third parties, and hence is capable of being waived by the relevant members entitled to vote if they are unanimously in agreement that adherence to its terms is not required'. See also *Dashfield v Davidson* [2008] BCC 222.

the accidental omission of one shareholder's name from the memorandum appended to the contract under s 696(4) of the Act), because insignificant errors which prejudice no one ought not to be allowed to invalidate the whole scheme.[395] However, directors should be astute to ensure that the statutory requirements are followed, as numerous offences may be committed in relation to redemption and purchase of a company's own shares by officers in default.

Redeemable shares

The 2006 Act, s 684(1) expressly provides that a limited company having a share capital may issue shares that are to be redeemed or are liable to be redeemed at the option of the company or the shareholder. A private company's ability to issue redeemable shares does not depend on prior authorization in the company's articles. However, the articles of a private limited company may exclude or restrict the issue of redeemable shares.[396] In the case of a public company, by contrast, prior authorization in the articles is essential, and redeemable shares may not be issued unless so authorized.[397] In the case of any company, no redeemable shares may be issued at a time when there are no issued shares of the company that are not redeemable.[398] The aim of this requirement is to ensure that the company does not find itself entirely without shares, which could occur if the only shares were all redeemable. **27.156**

Terms and manner of redemption

The directors of a private or public company have the ability[399] to decide on the terms, conditions, and manner of redemption of shares, provided that the company has authorized them to do so, either in its articles or by way of a resolution.[400] Where the directors are authorized to determine the terms, conditions, and manner of redemption, they must do so before the shares are allotted.[401] It should also be noted that any obligation of the company to state in a statement of capital the rights attached to the shares extends to the terms, conditions, and manner of redemption.[402] **27.157**

Payment and financing of redemption

Redeemable shares may not be redeemed unless they are fully paid.[403] Under the 1985 Act, it was necessary for payment of the redemption monies to be contemporaneous with redemption. However, s 686 of the 2006 Act provides that the terms of redemption may provide for the amount payable[404] on redemption to be paid on a date later than the redemption date, provided that the holder of the shares is agreeable to this.[405] Where the holder of the shares **27.158**

---

[395] See *Re Willaire Systems plc* [1987] BCC 67.

[396] 2006 Act, s 684(2).

[397] 2006 Act, s 684(3).

[398] 2006 Act, s 684(4).

[399] As recommended by the CLR: *Final Report*, para 4.5.

[400] 2006 Act, s 685(1). A resolution authorizing the directors in this manner may be an ordinary resolution even though it amends the company's articles: 2006 Act, s 685(2). Where the directors are not authorized in the articles or by way of resolution to determine these matters in respect of redeemable shares, the terms, conditions, and manner of redemption must be stated in the company's articles: 2006 Act, s 685(4).

[401] 2006 Act, s 685(3)(a).

[402] 2006 Act, s 685(3)(b).

[403] 2006 Act, s 685(1).

[404] As to the meaning of payment and the possibility of non-cash consideration, see *BDG Roof-Bond Ltd v Douglas* [2000] 1 BCLC 401.

[405] 2006 Act, s 686(2).

is not agreeable to deferred payment, then the amount payable on redemption must be paid on redemption.[406]

27.159 Redeemable shares may be redeemed out of capital, provided that the statutory requirements are observed. Redemption out of capital is considered below. Otherwise, redeemable shares may only be redeemed out of distributable profits of the company or the proceeds of a fresh issue of shares made for the purpose of the redemption.[407] Use of such funds ensures that there is no erosion of the capital maintenance doctrine.[408] Further, any premium payable on redemption must be paid out of distributable profits,[409] unless the shares were issued at a premium, in which case the premium payable on redemption may be paid out of the proceeds of a fresh issue of shares made for the purposes of the redemption, up to an amount equal to the lesser of the aggregate of the premiums received by the company on the issue of the shares redeemed or the current amount of the company's share premium account (including any sum transferred to that account in respect of premiums on the new shares).[410] The amount of the company's share premium account should then be reduced accordingly.[411]

Notification of redemption: criminal liability of directors

27.160 Where shares in a limited company are redeemed, the shares are treated as cancelled, and the amount of the company's issued share capital is diminished accordingly by the nominal value of the shares redeemed.[412]

27.161 Within one month of redemption, the company must notify the Registrar of the redemption, specifying the shares redeemed.[413] The notice must be accompanied by a statement of capital[414] which must state with respect to the company's share capital immediately following the redemption:

(1) the total number of shares of the company;

(2) the aggregate nominal value of those shares;

(3) the aggregate amount (if any) unpaid on those shares (whether on account of their nominal value or by way of premium); and

(4) for each class of shares, (a) prescribed particulars of the rights attached to the shares, (b) the total number of shares of that class, and (c) the aggregate nominal value of shares of that class.[415]

27.162 If the redemption is not notified to the Registrar as required, an offence is committed by the company and every officer in default.[416] This offence is triable summarily only and

---

[406] 2006 Act, s 686(3).

[407] 2006 Act, s 687(2).

[408] See *Quayle Munro Ltd, Petitioners* [1994] 1 BCLC 410.

[409] 2006 Act, s 689(3).

[410] 2006 Act, s 688(4).

[411] 2006 Act, s 688(5).

[412] 2006 Act, s 688(6).

[413] 2006 Act, s 689(1).

[414] 2006 Act, s 689(2).

[415] 2006 Act, s 689(3), as amended by SBEE Act 2015, s 97, Sch 6, paras 1, 13 with effect from 30 June 2016. The Companies (Shares and Share Capital Order) Order 2009 (SI 2009/388), reg 2 states the prescribed particulars for the purposes of s 689(3)(c)(i).

[416] 2006 Act, s 689(4).

punishable by way of a fine not exceeding level 3 on the standard scale and, for continued contravention, a daily default fine not exceeding one-tenth of level 3 on the standard scale.[417]

Purchase of own shares: generally

Under the provisions of the 2006 Act, a limited company is able to purchase its own shares, subject to the provisions of the 2006 Act, without requiring prior authorization in its articles.[418] However, its ability to do so may be fettered by an express restriction or prohibition in the articles.[419] Further, a limited company may not purchase its own shares if as a result of the purchase there would no longer be any issued shares of the company other than redeemable shares or shares held as treasury shares.[420] **27.163**

It should also be noted that listed companies must also comply with the requirements of the Listing Rules on purchase of own shares (eg in respect of additional disclosure and notification requirements and a prohibition on redemption or purchase of a company's own shares during a 'prohibited period' as defined in the Model Code for dealings by directors set out in the Appendix to Chapter 9 of the Listing Rules). Further, it may be necessary for directors to consult the Takeover Code, which contains additional provisions governing, inter alia, the circumstances where redemption or purchase may result in an obligation to make a mandatory offer, and preventing an offeree company during the course of an offer (or at a time when the board has reason to believe that a bona fide offer might be imminent) from redeeming or purchasing any of its own shares (except in performance of an existing contract) without the approval of shareholders in general meeting. **27.164**

Payment and financing of purchase

A limited company may not purchase its shares unless they are fully paid.[421] Furthermore, where a limited company purchases its own shares, the shares must be paid for on purchase.[422] In other words, deferred consideration is not permitted, and the terms of the contract must oblige the purchaser to hand over the consideration simultaneously with the transfer of the shares.[423] The scope and rationale of the prohibition of deferred consideration was explained in the Department of Trade's consultative document *The Purchase by a Company of its Own Shares*:[424] **27.165**

> If companies were permitted to buy their own shares it would follow, in the absence of express prohibition, that they could enter into executory contracts, or obtain options, to do so. There seems to be no grounds for prohibition; indeed ... executory contracts appear to be vital if the aim is to be achieved. Performance of such contracts would necessarily be conditional on

---

[417] 2006 Act, s 689(5).

[418] Prior authorization in the articles, which was a necessity under the 1985 Act, has been removed in accordance with the recommendations of the CLR: *Completing the Structure*, para 2.15.

[419] 2006 Act, s 690(1).

[420] 2006 Act, s 690(2).

[421] 2006 Act, s 691(1).

[422] 2006 Act, s 691(2). It has been held that 'payment' in this context is not limited to payment in cash and may include a purchase of shares in return for assets: *BDG Roof-Bond Ltd v Douglas* [2000] 1 BCLC 401. Note that the requirement for the shares to be paid for on purchase does not apply in a case where a private limited company is purchasing shares for the purposes of or pursuant to an employees' share scheme: 2006 Act, s 691(3), inserted by Companies Act (Amendment of Part 18) Regs 2013 (SI 2013/999), reg 3, with effect from 30 April 2013.

[423] See *Pena v Dale* [2004] 2 BCLC 508; *BDG Roof-Bond Ltd v Douglas* [2000] 1 BCLC 401; *Kinlan v Crimmin* [2007] 2 BCLC 67.

[424] Cmnd 7944 at para 38.

its being lawful for the company to pay for the shares at the time when the contract is completed, ie on the assumption that payment could lawfully be made out of profits only, on the company's having profits available at the time or times of performance. What should happen, however, if the contract had been partly performed? Suppose, for example, that the company has 900 issued shares owned equally by three shareholders. One dies and the company agrees to buy his 300 shares for £30,000 payable by equal instalments out of the profits for the next three years. The first year's payment is made but in the second year insufficient profits are available. If this eventuality has been foreseen and dealt with in the contract all may be well. But what if it has not? It is tempting to say that the purchase of the first 100 shares for £10,000 should be completed but that would be to make a different contract for the parties and, probably, one that would not be satisfactory to either. The estate wants to get out of the company and not to be left with 200 (probably unsaleable) shares. The company has agreed the price on the basis that it is buying a holding which, through the power to block a special resolution, conferred a measure of negative control. An alternative solution (though clearly not one wholly satisfactory to the estate) would be to say that in the absence of agreement to the contrary the whole transaction should be cancelled. This might occasionally present difficulties if the personal representative had distributed the £10,000 or if the 100 shares had already been transferred to the company and cancelled. Neither solution is ideal. But all that seems to be necessary is to provide some rule which, in the absence of express agreement, would provide a workable solution if not a perfect one.

27.166 There are three means by which a private company may purchase its own shares. The first possibility is a payment out of capital in accordance with Chapter 5 of Part 18 of the 2006 Act.[425] This possibility is considered below. The second option, which exists only for private limited companies authorized by their articles to take this step, is a purchase of own shares out of capital otherwise than in accordance with Chapter 5, up to an aggregate purchase price in a financial year of the lower of—(a) £15,000, or (b) the nominal value of 5 per cent of its fully paid share capital as at the beginning of the financial year.[426] The third option is a payment out of distributable profits or the proceeds of a fresh issue of shares made for the purpose of financing the transaction.[427] Any premium payable on the purchase must be paid out of distributable profits,[428] unless the shares were issued at a premium, in which case any premium payable on their purchase may be paid out of the proceeds of a fresh issue of shares up to an amount equal to the lesser of the aggregate of the premiums received by the company on issue or the current amount of the company's share premium account (including any sums transferred to that account in respect of premiums on the new shares).[429] Whichever method is adopted, the amount of the company's share premium account should then be reduced accordingly.[430]

27.167 In addition, it should be noted that any payment apart from the purchase price (eg the price for acquiring an option to buy shares) must be made out of the company's distributable profits.[431] If this requirement is not met, then the relevant contractual right acquired by the company (eg the option) may not be exercised or relied on by the company.[432]

---

[425] 2006 Act, s 692(1).
[426] 2006 Act, s 692(1ZA); inserted by Companies Act (Amendment of Part 18) Regs 2013 (SI 2013/999, reg 4 with effect from 30 April 2013.
[427] 2006 Act, s 692(2)(a).
[428] 2006 Act, s 692(2)(b).
[429] 2006 Act, s 693(3).
[430] 2006 Act, s 693(4).
[431] 2006 Act, s 705(1).
[432] 2006 Act, s 705(2).

Authority for purchase of own shares

The procedure to be applied for the purchase by a company of its own shares will depend on **27.168** whether the purchase is a 'market purchase' or an 'off-market purchase'. In short, a purchase is a 'market purchase' if it is made on a recognized investment exchange and is subject to a marketing arrangement on the exchange.[433] The term 'recognized investment exchange' is defined in Part 18 of FSMA, but excludes an overseas exchange. A company's shares are subject to a 'marketing arrangement' on a recognized exchange if they are listed under Part 6 of FSMA or the company has been afforded facilities for dealing in the shares to take place on the exchange without prior permission for individual transactions from the authority governing the exchange and without limit as to the time during which those facilities are to be available.[434] A purchase is 'off-market' if the shares are purchased privately, ie otherwise than on a recognized investment exchange (or on a recognized investment exchange but not subject to a marketing arrangement on the exchange).[435] In other words, any private company purchasing its own shares will always make an off-market purchase.

A market purchase must be authorized in accordance with the 2006 Act, s 701.[436] This **27.169** requires the purchase to be authorized in advance by a resolution.[437] The authorization must specify the maximum number of shares authorized to be acquired and determine both the maximum and minimum prices[438] that may be paid for the shares.[439] The authorization must also specify a date on which it is to expire, which must not be later than five years after the date on which the resolution is passed.[440] The purchase must occur during this 'window of opportunity' (although it is possible for the authorization to permit the company to enter into an executory contract during the 'window of opportunity' which falls to be performed after the expiry of the period).[441]

An off-market purchase must be carried out in accordance with the 2006 Act, s 693A or **27.170** s 694.[442] Under the former, a company may make an off-market purchase of its own shares for the purposes of or pursuant to an employees' share scheme if the purchase has first been authorized by a resolution of the company under that section. Under the latter, either the terms of the contract must be authorized by special resolution prior to execution of the contract, or the contract must contain a condition precedent requiring approval by way of special resolution prior to performance.[443] In the case of a public company, the resolution must specify the date on which the authorization is to expire, which must not be later than

---

[433] 2006 Act, s 693(2), (3), (4).

[434] 2006 Act, s 693(3).

[435] 2006 Act, s 693(2).

[436] 2006 Act, s 693(1)(b).

[437] 2006 Act, s 701(1). The authority may be general or limited and may be conditional or unconditional: 2006 Act, s 701(2). It may be varied, revoked, or renewed by way of further resolution: 2006 Act, s 701(4).

[438] The authority may specify a particular sum or alternatively provide a basis or formula for calculating the amount of the price, provided that the calculation does not depend on any person's discretion or opinion: 2006 Act, s 701(7).

[439] 2006 Act, s 701(3).

[440] 2006 Act, s 701(5).

[441] 2006 Act, s 701(6).

[442] 2006 Act, s 693(1)(a); s 694(1). Section 693A was inserted by Companies Act (Amendment of Part 18) Regs 2013 (SI 2013/999), reg 7 with effect from 30 April 2013.

[443] 2006 Act, s 694(2). The ability to enter into a contract conditional on approval by shareholders is intended to save time by enabling directors to negotiate and agree a contract ahead of shareholder approval.

five years after the date on which the resolution was passed.[444] Special provisions apply in respect of voting for such a resolution. In short, any member who holds shares to which the resolution relates is unable effectively to vote for the resolution.[445]

27.171   Where a company seeks a resolution to authorize an off-market purchase, a copy of the contract[446] (or a memorandum setting out its terms,[447] if the contract is not a written contract) must be made available to the members,[448] and the resolution is not validly passed if these requirements are not satisfied.[449] Similar provisions exist in respect of the variation and release of an authorization to make an off-market purchase.[450]

27.172   The rights of a company under a contract for the off-market or market purchase of its own shares, authorized under ss 693A, 694, or 701 is not capable of being assigned.[451]

Inspection of contract: criminal liability of directors

27.173   Where a company has entered into a contract for a market purchase or an off-market purchase, it is necessary for the company to keep available for inspection at its registered office[452] a copy of the contract (or, if the contract is not in writing, a copy of the memorandum of its terms)[453] for a period of ten years commencing with the completion of purchase.[454] Every member of the company (and, in the case of a public company, every member of the public) is entitled to inspect the contract without charge.[455]

27.174   If the contract (or memorandum of its terms) is not kept available for inspection in accordance with these statutory requirements, or if an inspection requested by a person entitled to do so is refused, an offence (triable summarily and punishable by a level 3 fine with a daily fine for continued contravention)[456] is committed by every officer in default.[457] In addition, in the case of a refusal to permit inspection, the court may make an order compelling immediate inspection.[458]

Notification to register: criminal liability of directors

27.175   Where the company keeps a copy of the contract or memorandum available for inspection at a place which is not the company's registered office, it must notify the Registrar of the address

---

[444] 2006 Act, s 694(5).

[445] 2006 Act, s 695(2), (3).

[446] If the contract does not contain the names of the members holding shares to which the contract relates, it must be accompanied by a memorandum containing this information: 2006 Act, s 696(3).

[447] Such a memorandum must include the names of the members holding shares to which the contract relates: 2006 Act, s 696(3).

[448] 2006 Act, s 696(2). If the resolution is to be a written resolution, the contract or memorandum must be sent or submitted to every eligible member at or before the time at which the proposed resolution is sent or submitted to him. If the resolution is to be passed at a meeting, the contract or memorandum must be made available for inspection by members of the company both at the company's registered office for not less than 15 days ending with the date of the meeting and at the meeting itself.

[449] 2006 Act, s 696(5).

[450] See 2006 Act, ss 697, 698, 699, 700, 701.

[451] 2006 Act, s 704.

[452] 2006 Act, s 702(4).

[453] 2006 Act, s 702(2).

[454] 2006 Act, s 702(3).

[455] 2006 Act, s 702(6).

[456] 2006 Act, s 702(2).

[457] 2006 Act, s 703(1).

[458] 2006 Act, s 703(3).

of the place.[459] If the company fails to give notice to the Registrar within 15 days, an offence (punishable by fine and daily default fine for continued contravention[460]) is committed by every officer in default.[461]

Return to Registrar: criminal liability of directors

Where a company has purchased its own shares in accordance with the statutory provisions, it **27.176** must deliver a return to the Registrar within 28 days of the date on which the shares are delivered to it.[462] The return must (inter alia) state, with respect to each class of share purchased, the number and nominal value of the shares and the date on which they were delivered to the company.[463] Additional requirements apply in the case of a public company, which must state in the return the aggregate amount paid for the shares and the maximum and minimum prices paid in respect of shares of each class purchased.[464] If the return is not sent to the Registrar in accordance with these requirements, an offence (punishable by fine[465]) is committed by every officer in default.[466]

Notice of cancellation: criminal liability of directors

When a company purchases its own shares, they will be treated as cancelled, unless they are **27.177** held as treasury shares, in which case special provisions apply. Where the shares are treated as cancelled, the company must give notice of cancellation to the Registrar within a period of 28 days commencing with the date of delivery of shares, specifying the shares cancelled.[467] The notice must be accompanied by a statement of capital (except where the statement of capital would be the same as a statement of capital that is required to be delivered to the registrar under s 720B(1)),[468] which must state with respect to the company's share capital immediately following cancellation:

(1) the total number of shares of the company;
(2) the aggregate nominal value of those shares;
(3) the aggregate amount (if any) unpaid on those shares (whether on account of their nominal value or by way of premium), and
(4) for each class of share, (a) prescribed particulars of the rights attached to the shares, (b) the total number of shares of that class, and (c) the aggregate nominal value of shares of that class.[469]

If the requirements for notification accompanied by a statement of capital are not observed, an offence (triable summarily and punishable by fine[470]) is committed by every officer in default.[471]

---

[459] 2006 Act, s 702(5).
[460] 2006 Act, s 703(2).
[461] 2006 Act, s 703(1).
[462] 2006 Act, s 707(1).
[463] 2006 Act, s 707(3); see also 2006 Act, s 707(2). Particulars of shares delivered to the company on different dates and under different contracts may be included in a single return: 2006 Act, s 707(5).
[464] 2006 Act, s 707(4).
[465] 2006 Act, s 707(7).
[466] 2006 Act, s 707(6).
[467] 2006 Act, s 708(1).
[468] 2006 Act, s 708(2).
[469] 2006 Act, s 708(3), as amended by SBEE Act 2015, s 97, Sch 6, paras 1, 14 with effect from 30 June 2016. The Companies (Shares and Share Capital) Order 2009 (SI 2009/388), reg 2 states the prescribed particulars for the purposes of s 708(3)(c)(i).
[470] 2006 Act, s 708(5).
[471] 2006 Act, s 708(4).

Redemption or purchase by private company out of capital

27.178   A private company may redeem redeemable shares, or purchase its own shares, out of capital in accordance with the 2006 Act, ss 709–23. In either case, the profits available for distribution[472] and/or the proceeds of any fresh issue of shares made for the purpose of the redemption or purchase must be applied towards the payment and exhausted before capital may be utilized in this manner.[473] The 'permissible capital payment' (defined by s 710) is essentially such amount of capital as is required to make up the balance of the redemption or purchase payment once these other sources of funds have been exhausted.

27.179   In order to make a lawful redemption or purchase of own shares out of capital, four key requirements must be satisfied.[474] First, there must be a directors' statement accompanied by an auditors' report. Secondly, there must be a special resolution approving the payment out of capital. Thirdly, there must be a public notice. Fourthly, the directors' statement and the auditors' report must be available for inspection.

Directors' statement and auditors' report

27.180   The directors' statement[475] must be made by all the directors (including any de facto directors)[476] and must specify the amount of the permissible capital payment[477] for the shares in question.[478] It must also state that, having made full inquiry into the affairs and prospects of the company, the directors have formed the opinion:

(1)   as regards its initial situation immediately following the date on which the payment out of capital is proposed to be made, that there will be no grounds on which the company could then be found unable to pay its debts;[479] and

(2)   as regards its prospects for the year immediately following that date, that (having regard to (a) their intentions with respect to the management of the company's business during that year and (b) the amount and character of the financial resources that will in their view be available to the company during that year) the company will be able to continue to carry on business as a going concern (and will accordingly be able to pay its debts as they fall due) throughout that year.[480]

A declaration made without any or sufficient inquiry into the financial affairs of the company is not properly made.[481]

---

[472]   Defined by s 711 and calculated in accordance with 2006 Act, s 712.

[473]   2006 Act, s 710(1), s 711, s 712.

[474]   2006 Act, s 713(1). By s 713(2) this is subject to s 720A and to any order of the court under s 721 (power of court to extend period for compliance on application by persons objecting to payment). Section 720A sets out reduced requirements for payment out of capital for purchase of own shares for the purposes of or pursuant to an employees' share scheme out and s 720B sets out the requirements for registration of the resolution and supporting documents for such a purchase. Sections 720A and 720B were inserted by Companies Act 2006 (Amendment of Part 18) Regs 2013 (SI 2013/999), reg 12 with effect from 30 April 2013.

[475]   It is intended that the Secretary of State will make regulations regarding the precise form and content of the statement in addition to the statutory requirements: see 2006 Act, s 714(5).

[476]   *Re In A Flap Envelope Co Ltd* [2004] 1 BCLC 64.

[477]   The term 'permissible capital payment' is defined by 2006 Act, s 710.

[478]   2006 Act, s 714(2).

[479]   In forming their opinion, the directors must take into account all of the company's liabilities including any contingent or prospective liabilities: see 2006 Act, s 714(4).

[480]   2006 Act, s 714(3).

[481]   *Re In A Flap Envelope Co Ltd* [2004] 1 BCLC 64.

The statement must be accompanied by a report addressed to the directors from the company's auditor stating that (a) he has inquired into the company's state of affairs, (b) the amount specified in the statement as the permissible capital payment for the shares in question has in his view been properly calculated, and (c) he is not aware of anything to indicate that the opinion expressed by the directors in their statement is unreasonable.[482]   **27.181**

Special resolution

The payment out of capital must be authorized by a special resolution of the company[483] **27.182** which must be passed on, or within the week immediately following, the date on which the directors' statement is made.[484] It should be noted that any member who holds shares to which the resolution relates is unable to vote thereon, in the case of a written resolution, and if he votes at a meeting, the resolution (if passed) is not effective if it would not have been passed without his votes.[485] A copy of the directors' statement and auditors' report must be made available to members (either by being sent or submitted with the written resolution or by being made available at the meeting for inspection)[486] and the resolution is ineffective if this requirement is not complied with.[487]

Public notice

Within the week immediately following the date of the resolution, the company must cause **27.183** to be published in the Gazette a notice containing the following particulars: (a) a statement that the company has approved a payment out of capital for the purpose of acquiring its own shares by redemption or purchase or both (as the case may be), (b) particulars of the amount of the permissible capital payment for the shares in question and the date of the resolution, (c) the location of the place where the directors' statement and auditors' report may be inspected, and (d) a statement to the effect that any creditor may within five weeks of the date of the resolution apply to the court for an order preventing the payment.[488] The notice must also be published in a national newspaper.[489] But before any such notice is published in the Gazette or a newspaper, the company must provide the Registrar with a copy of the directors' statement and auditors' report.[490]

Inspection of statement and report

The directors' statement and auditors' report must be kept available for inspection by mem- **27.184** bers and creditors without charge[491] at the company's registered office (or such other place as may have been specified pursuant to regulations made under s 1136) until a period of five weeks has elapsed since the date of the resolution.[492] If the documents are available somewhere other than the registered office, the location of this place must be notified to the Registrar.[493]

---

[482] 2006 Act, s 714(6).
[483] 2006 Act, s 716(1).
[484] 2006 Act, s 716(1), (2).
[485] 2006 Act, s 717(1), (2), (3), (4).
[486] 2006 Act, s 718(2).
[487] 2006 Act, s 718(3).
[488] 2006 Act, s 719(1).
[489] 2006 Act, s 719(2), (3).
[490] 2006 Act, s 719(4).
[491] 2006 Act, s 720(4).
[492] 2006 Act, s 720(1).
[493] 2006 Act, s 720(3).

Right of creditors and members to object

27.185   Any creditor of the company (and any member who did not consent to, or vote in favour of, the resolution) may apply to the court within five weeks of the date of the resolution[494] for the cancellation of the resolution.[495] On being served with the application, the company must immediately notify the Registrar.[496] Similarly, within 15 days of an order by the court in respect of such an application, the company must deliver a copy of the order to the Registrar.[497]

Payment out of capital

27.186   If there is no application by any creditor or member within the five-week vulnerability period, the company may make the payment out of capital, but it must do so before the expiry of a period of seven weeks commencing with the date of the resolution.[498] In other words, if no creditor objects, the company will have a two-week window in which to make the payment. The tight timetable is designed to ensure that the payment is made before the company's circumstances change in an unexpected adverse manner such as to render the payment imprudent. However, if the company's circumstances do change for the worse in a way which was not foreseen, and the directors consider that it is necessary to renege on the payment, s 735(2) provides that the company will not be liable in damages in respect of its failure to redeem or purchase the shares, and s 735(3) prohibits the court from making an order for specific performance.

Criminal liabilities of directors

27.187   There are three relevant offences. First, if the directors' statement is made without reasonable grounds for the opinions expressed in it, an offence[499] is committed by every director who is in default.[500] Secondly, if the directors' statement and auditors' report are kept somewhere other than the registered office without notifying the Registrar within 14 days, or if a request for inspection by any member or creditor is refused, an offence[501] is committed by every officer in default.[502] Thirdly, if the company fails to notify the Registrar of an application objecting to the resolution or an order of the court in respect of such an application, an offence[503] is committed by every officer in default.[504]

Civil liabilities of directors

27.188   A director may find himself under a civil liability pursuant to the Insolvency Act, s 76, which applies where a company is being wound up and has made a payment out of capital in respect of the purchase or redemption of its own shares and the aggregate of its assets

---

[494]   2006 Act, s 721(2).

[495]   2006 Act, s 721(1).

[496]   2006 Act, s 722(2).

[497]   2006 Act, s 722(3).

[498]   2006 Act, s 723(1). By s 723(1A) the same time periods apply to a purchase for the purposes of or pursuant to an employees' share scheme under s 720A.

[499]   Punishable on conviction on indictment to imprisonment for a term not exceeding two years or a fine or both and on summary conviction to imprisonment for a term not exceeding 12 months or a fine not exceeding the statutory maximum or both: 2006 Act, s 715(2).

[500]   2006 Act, s 715(1).

[501]   Triable summarily and punishable by fine: 2006 Act, s 720(6).

[502]   2006 Act, s 720(5).

[503]   2006 Act, s 722(5).

[504]   2006 Act, s 722(4).

and the amounts paid by way of contribution is not sufficient for the payment of its debts and liabilities and the expenses of the winding up. In those circumstances, if the winding up commenced[505] within one year of the date on which the relevant payment out of capital was made, then the person whose shares were redeemed or purchased and the directors who signed the statutory declaration are, so as to enable the insufficiency to be met, liable to contribute to the company's assets.[506] Directors who can discharge the burden of proving that they had reasonable grounds for forming the opinion set out in the declaration are not liable.[507] If the person whose shares were purchased or redeemed complies with his statutory obligation to contribute to the company's assets,[508] he may apply to the court for an order requiring any director who is liable to pay him such amount as the court thinks is just and equitable.[509] Similarly, if a director who is liable and who contributes to the company's assets in accordance with such liability, he may apply to the court for an order that the former shareholder reimburse him to such an extent as the court thinks just and equitable.[510]

Treasury shares: generally

The Second Directive on Company Law required Member States to pass laws permitting listed companies to acquire and hold (without cancellation) a limited proportion of shares in themselves.[511] The relevant legislation was introduced in 2003.[512] In the 2006 Act, ss 724–32 provide for the holding of shares purchased by the company as treasury shares, rather than being cancelled.[513] Where a limited company purchases its own shares out of distributable profits, the company may hold the shares[514] or (to the extent permitted by the Act) deal with them.[515] Where the shares are held by the company, the company must be entered in its register of members (or, where the company has elected to keep information on the central register, its name must be delivered to the Registrar) as the member holding the shares.[516] (Private companies and public companies whose shares are not listed or admitted to trading on the identified markets are only able to purchase their own shares for cancellation.) **27.189**

There are a number of significant restrictions which apply to treasury shares. First, a company which holds treasury shares in itself may not exercise any right in respect of the treasury shares, and any purported exercise of such right is void.[517] Therefore, for example, the company is not permitted to vote on the shares. Secondly, a company which holds treasury shares in itself cannot pay or make any dividend or distribution on those **27.190**

---

[505] For the concept of 'commencement' of winding up, see 2006 Act, s 86 and Insolvency Act, s 129.
[506] Insolvency Act, s 76(2).
[507] Insolvency Act, s 76(2)(b).
[508] Insolvency Act, s 76(2)(a), s 76(3).
[509] Insolvency Act, s 76(4).
[510] Insolvency Act, s 76(4).
[511] 77/91/EEC, Art 19.
[512] See, for historical interest only, the Companies (Acquisition of Own Shares) (Treasury Shares) Regulations 2003 (SI 2003/1116) and the DTI's consultation paper, *Treasury Shares: A Consultative Document* (September 2001).
[513] Note that the limit on the maximum amount of treasury shares in the 2006 Act, s 725 was repealed as from 1 October 2009 by the Companies (Share Capital and Acquisition by Company of its own Shares) Regulations 2009 (SI 2009/20220), reg 5(1).
[514] However, the statutory provisions do not override anything in the company's articles to the contrary, such as a requirement to cancel shares immediately upon acquisition.
[515] 2006 Act, s 724(3).
[516] 2006 Act, s 724(4). For election to keep information on the central register, see 2006 Act, ss 128A–128K.
[517] 2006 Act, s 726(2).

shares, including a distribution of assets to members on winding up.[518] Thirdly, there are restrictions on disposal of treasury shares. Either they must be sold for a cash consideration[519] or they must be transferred for the purposes of an employee share scheme[520] and, whenever a disposal occurs, whether for a cash consideration or for the purposes of an employee share scheme, the disposal must be notified to the Registrar.[521] In addition, the Listing Rules prohibit the sale of treasury shares during a prohibited period,[522] and the Takeover Code treats any sale or transfer of treasury shares as equivalent to a new issue and imposes limits on such sales or transfers during the course of an offer or where the company has reason to believe that a bona fide offer might be imminent without the approval of the shareholders in general meeting. Fourthly, the proceeds of sale must be dealt with in accordance with the 2006 Act, s 731 which provides that such part of the proceeds as amount to a recovery of the amount paid by the company on acquisition must be treated as realized profit of the company, whilst any excess above and beyond mere recoupment of outlay must be transferred to the company's share premium account.

Treasury shares: criminal liability of directors

27.191 Where treasury shares are sold, or transferred for the purposes of an employees' share scheme, and the obligation to notify the Registrar of disposal arises, the company must deliver a return to the Registrar within 28 days of the date of disposal.[523] The return must state with respect to shares of each class disposed of (1) the number and nominal value of the shares and (2) the date of disposal.[524] Failure to comply with these requirements gives rise to an offence (punishable by fine and daily default fine for continued contravention)[525] committed by every officer in default.[526]

27.192 Treasury shares may be cancelled at any time.[527] Where treasury shares are cancelled, the company must notify the Registrar within 28 days of cancellation[528] and the return must state the number and nominal value of the shares and the date on which they were cancelled.[529] The notice must be accompanied by a statement of capital[530] which must include the particulars specified in the Act.[531] If the company fails to notify the Registrar by way of return accompanied by an appropriate statement of capital, then an offence (punishable by

---

[518] 2006 Act, s 726(3).

[519] Which includes a cheque received by the company in good faith which the directors have no reason for suspecting will not be honoured: 2006 Act, s 727(2)(b).

[520] 2006 Act, s 727(1), (2).

[521] 2006 Act, s 727(1).

[522] The Listing Rules also impose additional requirements (eg in respect of notification) designed to maintain investor protection and reduce any perceived scope for market manipulation.

[523] 2006 Act, s 728(1).

[524] 2006 Act, s 728(2). Particulars of shares disposed of on different dates may be included in a single return: 2006 Act, s 728(3).

[525] 2006 Act, s 729(5).

[526] 2006 Act, s 728(4).

[527] 2006 Act, s 729(1).

[528] 2006 Act, s 730(1).

[529] 2006 Act, s 730(2). Again, particulars of shares cancelled on different dates may be included in a single return: 2006 Act, s 730(3).

[530] 2006 Act, s 730(4).

[531] 2006 Act, s 730(5). The Companies (Shares and Share Capital Order) Order 2009 (SI 2009/388), reg 2 states the prescribed particulars for the purposes of s 730(5)(c)(i).

fine and daily default fine for continued contravention)[532] is committed by every officer in default.[533]

In addition to these two specific instances of criminal liability on the part of officers in **27.193** default, the 2006 Act, s 732 contains a 'sweep up' provision in respect of treasury shares by stating that any contravention of the statutory provisions relating to treasury shares is an offence committed by the company and any officer in default punishable by way of fine (either on conviction on indictment or on summary conviction).[534] Possible contraventions would include the sale of treasury shares for non-cash consideration and the failure to cancel treasury shares upon loss of qualifying status.

D. Transfer of Shares

(1) Directors' functions and responsibilities on allotment

Where shares are allotted by a company, the company must, within two months after the **27.194** allotment, complete (and be ready to deliver) certificates of the shares.[535] The same rule applies to debentures and debenture stock.[536] Default in complying with this requirement, as regards shares, debentures, or debenture stock, is an offence (punishable by fine)[537] committed by every officer in default.[538] Further, a shareholder may serve a notice on the company requiring the company to make good its default; failure by the company to comply within ten days of the service of the notice will enable the shareholder to apply to court to have the certificates delivered to him, and the court may make an order directing the company and any officer to make good the default.[539] Such an application may result in a costs order against the company and/or its officers.[540]

(2) Directors' functions and responsibilities on transfer

A company may not register a transfer of shares or debentures unless (a) a proper instru- **27.195** ment[541] of transfer has been delivered to it, or (b) the transfer is either exempt under the Stock Transfer Act 1982[542] or made in accordance with such regulations as may be made by

---

[532] 2006 Act, s 730(7).

[533] 2006 Act, s 730(6).

[534] 2006 Act, s 732(1), (2).

[535] 2006 Act, s 769(1). For articles concerning share certificates, see Table A, regs 6 and 7; Model Articles (pcls) 24 and 25; Model Articles (plc) 46 and 47. Model Article (plc) 50 contemplates that a public company may wish to issue uncertificated shares (2006, Act, ss 783–90).

[536] 2006 Act, s 769(1).

[537] 2006 Act, s 769(4).

[538] 2006 Act, s 769(3).

[539] 2006 Act, s 782(1), (2).

[540] 2006 Act, s 782(3).

[541] This provision was first introduced in 1929 to put an end to the practice of avoiding the payment of stamp duty by means of oral transfers. A 'proper instrument' is an instrument which is appropriate or suitable for stamping for stamp duty purposes, and a document may be a 'proper instrument' even if it omits the consideration, since that may be ascertained subsequently for the purpose of stamping: *Nisbet v Shepherd* [1994] 1 BCLC 300. See also *Re Paradise Motor Co Ltd* [1968] 1 WLR 1125 and *Dempsey v Celtic Football & Athletic Co Ltd* [1993] BCC 514. It is not possible to contract out of this requirement. If a company's articles of association purport to dispense with the need for an instrument of transfer, they will be invalid: *Re Greene* [1949] Ch 333; *Barnett v Rose* [2011] EWHC 2906 (Ch).

[542] The Stock Transfer Act 1982 provides that transfers of certain gilt-edged securities are effective without the need for an instrument in writing.

the Treasury and/or the Secretary of State under Chapter 2 of Part 21 of the Act.[543] Needless to say, this prohibition does not apply to transfers by operation of law,[544] eg to a trustee in bankruptcy pursuant to the Insolvency Act, s 306.

27.196 The shares or other interest of any member in a company are transferable in accordance with the company's articles.[545] If there are no restrictions on transfer in a company's articles or elsewhere, the company's shareholders may transfer their shares without constraint or limitation, and the directors will have no discretionary power to refuse to register a transfer made in good faith.[546] However, a company may by its articles restrict its members' right to transfer their shares and may enforce restrictions against its members.[547] Since shares are prima facie transferable, a restriction on the right of transfer must be sufficiently clear and the courts have said that a restriction may not be achieved through uncertain language of doubtful meaning.[548] The directors of a company have no power to authorize registration in circumstances where there has been a breach of the articles.[549]

27.197 Where a company's articles authorize the directors to reject transfers to transferees of whom they disapprove, the directors must, before making any decision, consider the question fairly at a board meeting.[550] Further, their decision must be embodied in a substantive resolution.[551] A power of this kind is a fiduciary power to be exercised bona fide in the best interests of the company.[552]

27.198 When a transfer of shares or debentures has been lodged with a company, the company must (as soon as practicable and in any event within two months) either (a) register the transfer, or (b) give the transferee notice of refusal to register the transfer, together with reasons for the refusal.[553] A company which refuses to register a transfer must give the transferee such further information about the reasons for the refusal as the transferee may reasonably request.[554] If the company fails to comply with these requirements, an offence (punishable by fine)[555] is committed by the company and every officer in default.[556] Again, this provision does not

---

[543] 2006 Act, s 770(1). If the company has elected to keep information on the central register, references in s 770 to registering a transfer (or a person) are to be read as references to delivering particulars of the transfer (or person) to the Registrar: s 770(3), inserted by SBEE Act 2015, s 94, Sch 5, Pt 2, paras 11 and 26 with effect from 30 June 2016.

[544] 2006 Act, s 770(2).

[545] 2006 Act, s 544(1).

[546] *Re Smith, Knight & Co, Weston's Case* (1868) 4 Ch App 20; *Re National Provincial Marine Insurance, Gilbert's Case* (1870) 5 Ch App 559, 565; *Re Cawley & Co* (1889) 42 Ch D 209; *Re Copal Varnish Co Ltd* [1917] 2 Ch 349; *Re Bede Steam Shipping Co Ltd* [1917] 1 Ch 123.

[547] *Borland's Trustee v Steel Bros & Co Ltd* [1901] 1 Ch 279; *Lyle & Scott Ltd v Scott's Trustees* [1959] AC 763.

[548] *Greenhalgh v Mallard* [1943] 2 All ER 234, 237 (Lord Greene).

[549] *Hurst v Crampton Bros (Coopers) Ltd* [2003] 1 BCLC 304; *Tett v Phoenix Property & Investments Co Ltd* [1986] BCLC 149.

[550] *Re Gresham Life Assurance Society, ex p Penney* (1872) 8 Ch App 446.

[551] *Re Hackney Pavilion Ltd* [1924] 1 Ch 276.

[552] 2006 Act, s 172; *Re Smith & Fawcett Ltd* [1942] Ch 304; *Re Coalport China Co* [1895] 2 Ch 404; *Mactra Properties Ltd v Morshead Mansions Ltd* [2009] 1 BCLC 179. Nor may it be exercised for an improper purpose: 2006 Act, s 171.

[553] 2006 Act, s 771(1). If the company has elected to keep information on the central register, references in s 771 to registering a transfer (or a person) are to be read as references to delivering particulars of the transfer (or person) to the Registrar: s 771(2A), inserted by SBEE Act 2015, s 94, Sch 5, Pt 2, paras 11 and 27 with effect from 30 June 2016.

[554] 2006 Act, s 771(2).

[555] 2006 Act, s 771(4).

[556] 2006 Act, s 771(3).

apply to transfers by operation of law;[557] nor does it apply to transfers if the company has issued a share warrant in respect of the shares.[558]

Also, subject to four statutory exceptions, the company must complete (and be ready to **27.199** deliver) within two months of the date of receipt of the transfer the appropriate certificates in respect of the shares, debentures, or debenture stock in question.[559] The statutory exceptions, where this rule does not apply, are:

(1) transfers which the company lawfully refuses to register;[560]
(2) where the conditions of the issue of the shares, debentures, or debenture stock provide otherwise;[561]
(3) transfers to financial institutions; and[562]
(4) where, following the transfer, the company has issued a share warrant in respect of the shares.[563]

In a case not falling within one of the statutory exceptions, failure to comply with its requirements is an offence (punishable by fine)[564] committed by every officer in default.[565] Further, the shareholder may serve a notice on the company requiring the default to be remedied; failure to comply with the notice will entitle the shareholder to bring the matter before the court, and the court may make an order requiring compliance and may also make a costs order against the company and/or its officers.[566]

(3) Provisions in the articles

Table A and the Model Articles contain regulations dealing with the transfer of shares and in **27.200** particular the power of the directors to refuse to register a transfer:

(1) The instrument of transfer should be in any usual form or in any other form approved by the directors and should be executed by the transferor and, if any shares are partly paid, by the transferee (Table A, reg 23, Model Article (pcls) 26(1) and Model Article (plc) 63(1)).
(2) No fee is to be charged for registering the transfer and the company may retain any instrument of transfer which is registered (Table A, regs 27 and 28, Model Article (pcls) 26(2) and (3) and Model Article (plc) 63(2) and (3)).
(3) The various standard form articles give the directors power to refuse to register the transfer, but they do so in different ways. Table A, reg 24 gives the directors a discretionary power to refuse to register the transfer (a) of a share which is not fully paid to a person

---

[557] 2006 Act, s 771(5)(a).
[558] 2006 Act, s 771(5)(b); see also s 779.
[559] 2006 Act, s 776(1).
[560] 2006 Act, s 776(2).
[561] 2006 Act, s 776(3)(a).
[562] 2006 Act, s 776(3)(b). For these purposes, 'financial institutions' are recognized clearing houses acting in relation to recognized investment exchanges, nominees of recognized clearing houses acting in relation to recognized investment exchanges designated for these purposes by the rules of the recognized investment exchange in question, and nominees of recognized investment exchanges designated for these purposes by the rules of the recognized investment exchange in question: see s 778(2); see also Part 18 of FSMA, which defines the component parts of this definition, eg 'recognized clearing house'.
[563] 2006 Act, s 776(4)(c); see also s 779.
[564] 2006 Act, s 776(6).
[565] 2006 Act, s 776(5).
[566] 2006 Act, s 782.

of whom they do not approve, (b) of a share over which the company has a lien, or (c) which fails to satisfy certain formal requirements (lodged at the correct office, of only one class of share and in favour of not more than four transferees). For public companies Model Article (plc) 63(3) is similar except that (a) there is no need for the directors not to approve of the transferee of a partly paid share (presumably because this was considered unnecessary) and (b) transfer could be refused if the transfer is not accompanied by the share certificates or other evidence of title reasonably required by the directors. For private companies Model Article 26(5) simply gives the directors a discretion to refuse to register the transfer.

(4) If the directors refuse to register they must give notice of the refusal to the transferee and return the instrument of transfer (Table A, regs 25 and 28, Model Article (pcls) 26(5) and Model Article (plc) 63(6)). The Model Articles entitle the company to retain the instrument where the directors suspect that the proposed transfer may be fraudulent.

(5) Finally Table A, reg 26 gives the directors power to suspend the register of transfers of any class of shares for up to 30 days in any year. This power is not included in the Model Articles.

E. Information about People with Significant Control

(1) The PSC register

27.201 In order to promote transparency of ownership of interests in companies and to try to prevent companies from being used for money laundering, the financing of terrorism, and other illegal activities the SBEE Act 2015 has inserted Part 21A, ss 790A–790ZG, into the 2006 Act.[567] These provisions provide for the gathering of information about persons with significant control over companies other than those to which Part 21A does not apply and for the information to be maintained in a register of people with significant control (a 'PSC register'). Alternatively a private company may elect to keep the information on the central register kept by the Registrar.[568]

27.202 These requirements apply to all companies other than DTR5 issuers and companies which have voting shares traded on a regulated market in an EEA state or on certain other markets,[569] since such companies already have to make information about their major shareholders publicly available.

27.203 The provisions for identifying the persons whose particulars should be entered on the PSC register are inevitably broad and complex, since they are designed to defeat attempts to conceal control.[570] Since the company is made responsible for identifying persons with

---

[567] SBEE Act 2015, s 81 and Sch 3, which came fully into effect on 30 June 2016. Part 21A is supported by The Register of People with Significant Control Regulations 2016 (SI 2016/339) ('Register of PSC Regulations') which also came into force on 30 June 2016.

[568] As to the alternative method of record-keeping, see ss 790W–790ZE.

[569] 2006 Act, s 790B and Register of PSC Regulations, reg 3 and Sch 1. By s 790B(3) a 'DTR5 issuer' is an issuer to which Chapter 5 of the Disclosure Rules and Transparency Rules sourcebook made by the FCA (as amended or replaced from time to time) applies.

[570] The provisions derive from the Money Laundering Regulations 2007 (SI 2007/2157) and the EC's proposal for a Fourth Money Laundering Directive.

significant control and recording their particulars on the PSC register, it is important for directors to appreciate the scope of these provisions.

(2) Persons with significant control

The persons with significant control over a company may be either individuals[571] or legal **27.204** entities.[572] Such persons may be either 'registerable', in which case their particulars must be entered on the PSC register, or they are 'non-registerable'.

Individuals

References to a person with (or having) 'significant control' over a company are to an indi- **27.205** vidual ('X') who meets one or more of the specified conditions in relation to the company.[573] The 'specified conditions' are that (i) X holds, directly or indirectly, more than 25 per cent of the shares in the company, (ii) X holds, directly or indirectly, more than 25 per cent of the voting rights in the company, (iii) X holds the right, directly or indirectly, to appoint or remove a majority of the board of directors of the company, (iv) X has the right to exercise, or actually exercises significant influence or control over the company, or (v) the trustees of a trust or the members of a firm that, under the laws by which it is governed, is not a legal person meet any of conditions (i)–(iv), in their capacity as such, or would do so if they were individuals and X has the right to exercise, or actually exercises, significant influence or control over the activities of that trust or firm.

An individual with significant control over a company is a registrable person unless he is **27.206** non-registerable, in that he does not hold any interest in the company except through one or more other legal entities over each of which he has significant control and each of which is a 'relevant legal entity' in relation to the company.[574]

The particulars of an individual who is a registrable person which must be entered on the **27.207** PSC register are (a) name, (b) a service address, (c) the country or state (or part of the UK) in which the individual usually resides, (d) nationality, (e) date of birth, (f) usual residential address, (g) the date on which the individual became a registrable person in relation to the company, (h) the nature of his or her control over that company, and (i) if, in relation to the company, restrictions on using or disclosing any of the individual's PSC particulars are in force, disclosure of that fact.[575]

---

[571] For the purposes of Part 21A the following are treated as individuals even if they are legal persons under the laws by which they are governed: (a) a corporation sole, (b) a government or government department of a country or territory or a part of a country or territory, (c) an international organization whose members include two or more countries or territories (or their governments), and (d) a local authority or local government body in the UK or elsewhere: 2006 Act, s 790C(12).

[572] A legal entity is a body corporate or a firm that is a legal person under the law by which it is governed: 2006 Act, s 790C(5).

[573] 2006 Act, s 790C(2) and (3) and Sch 1A, paras 1–6, as explained by paras 10–25.

[574] 2006 Act, s 790C(4). See Sch 1A, Pt 2, which explains when someone holds an interest in a company or holds that interest through another legal entity.

[575] 2006 Act, ss 790K(1), 790M. By s 790K(4), s 163(2) (particulars of directors to be registered: individuals) applies for the purposes of s 790K(4). If a body is treated as an individual under s 790C(12) the required particulars are: (a) name, (b) principal office, (c) the legal form of the person and the law by which it is governed, (d) the date on which it became a registrable person in relation to the company, and (e) the nature of its control over the company. For further provisions about nature of control and foreign limited partners, see Register of PSC Regulations, regs 7 and 8. For provisions about protection from disclosure of usual residential address and protection from use or disclosure of secured information, see ss 790ZF, 790ZG, Sch 1A and Register of PSC Regulations, Pts 6 and 7, regs 22–45.

Legal entities

27.208 In relation to a company, a legal entity is a 'relevant legal entity' if (a) it has significant control over the company, in that it would have come within the definition in paragraph 27.205 above if it been an individual, and (b) it is subject to its own disclosure requirements, in that Part 21A applies to it, it is a DTR5 issuer, or its voting shares are traded on a regulated market in an EEA state or on certain other markets.[576] A relevant legal entity is registrable unless it is non-registrable, in that it does not hold any interest in the company except through one or more other legal entities over each of which he has significant control and each of which is a 'relevant legal entity' in relation to the company.[577]

27.209 The particulars of a registrable relevant legal entity which must be entered on the PSC register are: (a) corporate or firm name, (b) registered or principal office, (c) the legal form of the entity and the law by which it is governed, (d) if applicable, the register of companies in which it is entered (including details of the state) and the registration number in that register, (e) the date on which it became a registrable relevant legal entity in relation to the company, and (f) the nature of its control over the company.[578]

(3) Information-gathering

27.210 A company to which these requirements applies must take reasonable steps (a) to find out if there is anyone who is a registrable person or a registrable relevant legal entity in relation to the company, and (b) if so, to identify them.[579] Without limiting the steps the company is obliged to take, it must give notice to anyone whom it knows or has reasonable cause to believe to be a registrable person or registrable relevant legal entity in relation to it, requiring the addressee, within one month, to state whether he or she is a registrable person or a registrable relevant legal entity and, in either case, to confirm or correct any particulars included in the notice and supply any that are missing.[580] The company is not obliged to take steps or give notice where it already has the relevant information.[581]

27.211 The company also has a discretion to give notice to a person if it knows or has reasonable cause to believe that the person knows (a) the identity of someone who is a registrable person or relevant legal entity in relation to the company or any entity which would have been a relevant legal entity in relation to the company, but for the fact that it is not subject to its own disclosure requirements, or (b) the identity of someone likely to have that knowledge.[582] The notice may require the addressee, within one month, to state whether or not the addressee knows of any person within (a) above or any person likely to have that knowledge.[583] The addressee is not obliged to disclose any information in respect of which a claim to legal professional privilege could be maintained in legal proceedings.[584]

---

[576] 2006 Act, s 790C(6), (7); Register of PSC Regulations, regs 3, 4 and Sch 1.

[577] 2006 Act, s 790C(8). See Sch 1A, Pt 2, which explains when someone holds an interest in a company or holds that interest through another legal entity.

[578] 2006 Act, s 790K(3). For further provisions about nature of control and foreign limited partners, see Register of PSC Regulations, regs 7 and 8.

[579] 2006 Act, s 790D(1).

[580] 2006 Act, s 790D(2)–(4), (8). For knowledge and particulars, see s 790D(13).

[581] 2006 Act, s 790D(11).

[582] 2006 Act, s 790D(5), (6).

[583] 2006 Act, s 790D(7), (8).

[584] 2006 Act, s 790D(12).

The company must also seek to keep the relevant information up to date by giving notice **27.212** to the registrable person or registrable relevant legal entity stated on the PSC register if the company knows or has reason to believe that the person or entity has ceased to be registrable in relation to the company or that the particulars have become incorrect or incomplete.[585] The notice must require the addressee to confirm whether or not there has been a change and, if so, to state the date of the change and to confirm or correct the particulars included in the notice and supply any that are missing from the notice.[586]

In addition, certain persons are obliged to supply the company with information about reg- **27.213** istrable persons and relevant legal entities and to update that information.[587]

The primary sanction for failure to comply with a notice or to supply information, is that the **27.214** company may issue a restriction notice which has the effect that with respect to the relevant interest (a) any transfer of the interest is void, (b) no rights are exercisable in respect of the interest, (c) no shares may be issued in right of the interest or in pursuance of an offer made to the interest-holder, and (d) except in a liquidation, no payment may be made of sums due from the company in respect of the interest, whether in respect of capital or otherwise.[588]

(4) Criminal liability

If a company fails to comply with these information-gathering requirements, an offence is **27.215** committed by the company and every officer in default (punishable by imprisonment, or a fine, or both).[589]

The company must maintain the PSC register[590] and make it available for inspection.[591] **27.216** Offences are committed by the company and every officer in default in the event of non-compliance with these requirements.[592]

Where a private company gives the Registrar notice of election to keep the information **27.217** about persons with significant control over it at the companies registry, the notice must be accompanied by a statement containing all the information required to be contained in the company's PSC register.[593] If the company fails to comply with these requirements, an offence is committed by the company and every officer in default, including any shadow director (punishable by imprisonment or a fine or both).[594] Offences are also committed by the company and every officer in default, including any shadow director, where there is a failure to notify the Registrar of any changes.[595] If the company fails to respond to a request for confirmation that all the information required to be delivered to the Registrar has been delivered, an offence is committed by the company and every officer in default.[596]

---

[585] 2006 Act, s 790E(1)–(5), (7). A notice is not required if the company already has the information: s 790E(8).

[586] 2006 Act, s 790E(6)

[587] 2006 Act, ss 790G, 790H.

[588] 2006 Act, s 790I, Sch B1.

[589] 2006 Act, s 790F. For 'officer in default', see para 26.12 above.

[590] 2006 Act, s 790M(1)–(11), (14).

[591] 2006 Act, s 790N(1)–(3).

[592] 2006 Act, ss 790M(12), (13), 790(N)(4), (5), 790Q, 790S. For 'officer in default', see para 26.12 above.

[593] 2006 Act, s 790X(6)–(8).

[594] 2006 Act, s 790X(9), (10). For 'officer in default', see para 26.12 above.

[595] 2006 Act, s 790ZA.

[596] 2006 Act, s 790ZB. For 'officer in default', see para 26.12 above.

F. Public Companies: Obtaining Information about Interests in Shares

27.218 A public company may give notice to any person whom the company knows or has reasonable cause to believe to be interested in the company's shares or to have been so interested at any point in the preceding three years.[597] The notice may require the recipient to confirm that fact or (as the case may be) to state (a) whether or not it is the case, and (b) if he holds, or has during the preceding three years held, any such interest, to give such further information as may be required in accordance with the Act.[598]

27.219 Where the recipient fails to comply with the notice, the company may apply to the court for an order directing that the shares in question be subject to restrictions.[599] The effect of such an order is to ensure that: (i) any transfer of the shares will be void; (ii) no voting rights may be exercised in respect of the shares; (iii) no further shares may be issued in right of the shares or in pursuance of an offer made to their holder; and (iv) except in a liquidation, no payment may be made of sums due from the company on the shares, whether in respect of capital or otherwise.[600] Due to the costs and uncertainties related to the court process, most listed companies take similar powers in their articles, which can be invoked without application to the court, subject to limitations imposed by the FCA's Listing Rules.[601]

27.220 The members of a company holding at least 10 per cent of such of the paid-up capital of the company as carries a right to vote at general meetings of the company (excluding any voting rights attached to any shares in the company held as treasury shares) may require it to issue a notice under s 793 requiring information about interests in shares.[602] If the company fails to comply with such a request, an offence (punishable by fine[603]) is committed by every officer in default.[604]

27.221 Where the company does comply with the request, ie by issuing a notice under s 793, the company must, on the conclusion of its investigation, cause a report to be prepared. The report must be made available for inspection within a reasonable period (not more than 15 days) after the conclusion of the investigation.[605] If the investigations take longer than three months, the company must prepare interim reports every three months, until the investigations are completed.[606] Failure to prepare the necessary reports is an offence punishable by fine committed by every officer in default.[607]

---

[597] 2006 Act, s 793(1).

[598] 2006 Act, s 793(2). Specifically, the notice may require the recipient to give particulars of his own present or past interest in the company's shares: 2006 Act, s 793(3). See also 2006 Act, s 793(4). See also *Eclairs Group Ltd v JKX Oil & Gas Plc* [2015] Bus LR 1395, SC.

[599] 2006 Act, s 794(1).

[600] 2006 Act, s 797(1).

[601] Listing Rule 9.3.9R. See *Eclairs Group* (n 598 above) where a case where the power in the articles was used for an improper purpose.

[602] 2006 Act, s 803(1), (2).

[603] 2006 Act, s 804(3).

[604] 2006 Act, s 804(2). For 'officer in default', see para 26.12 above.

[605] 2006 Act, s 805(1).

[606] 2006 Act, s 805(2).

[607] 2006 Act, s 806(3), (4). For 'officer in default', see para 26.12 above.

Any such reports must be retained for six years and must be kept available for inspection at **27.222** the company's registered office or such other place as may be specified in regulations under s 1136. If not kept at the registered officer, the company must notify the Registrar of the place where the reports are kept available for inspection and any change in such place.[608] If default is made for 14 days in complying with this requirement, an offence (punishable by fine) is committed by the company and every officer in default.[609]

Reports must be open to inspection by any person without charge and any person is entitled, **27.223** on request and on payment of the applicable fee, to be provided with a copy of the report or any part of it within ten days of making a request for the same.[610] Default in complying with these requirements is an offence punishable by fine committed by the company and every officer in default.[611]

In addition, the company must keep a register of information received by it in pursuance **27.224** of a requirement imposed under s 793. A company which receives any such information must, within three days of receipt, enter in the register (a) the fact that the requirement was imposed and the date on which it was imposed, and (b) the information received in pursuance of the requirement.[612] Failure to comply with this requirement is an offence punishable by fine committed by the company and every officer in default.[613]

The register must be kept available for inspection at the company's registered office or at **27.225** such other place as may be specified in regulations under s 1136. If not kept at the registered office, the company must give notice to the Registrar of the place where the register is kept available for inspection and any change in that place; however, no such notice is required if the register has at all times been kept available at the company's registered office. If default is made in complying with these requirements, an offence (punishable by fine) is committed by the company and every officer in default.[614]

Unless the register is kept in such a form as itself to constitute an index, the company must **27.226** keep an index of the names entered in it. If an alteration is made to the register, a corresponding alteration must be made to the index within ten days. The index must contain, in respect of each name, a sufficient indication to enable the information entered against it to be readily found. The index must be kept available for inspection at the same place as the register. Default in complying with these requirements is an offence punishable by fine committed by the company and every officer in default.[615]

The register and index must be open to inspection by any person without charge. Any per- **27.227** son is entitled, on request and on payment of the relevant fee, to be provided with a copy of any entry in the register. A person seeking to inspect the register or to obtain a copy of an entry must provide a request containing the particulars stipulated by s 811(4) (eg name, address). Where a company receives a request under s 811, it must comply with the request

---

[608] 2006 Act, s 805.

[609] 2006 Act, s 806(1), (2).

[610] 2006 Act, s 807(1), (2).

[611] 2006 Act, s 807(3), (4). For 'officer in default', see para 26.12 above.

[612] 2006 Act, s 808(2). See also 2006 Act, s 808(3), (4).

[613] 2006 Act, s 808(5), (6). For 'officer in default', see para 26.12 above.

[614] 2006 Act, s 809(4), (5). For 'officer in default', see para 26.12 above.

[615] 2006 Act, s 810(5), (6). For 'officer in default', see para 26.12 above.

if it is satisfied that it is made for a proper purpose or refuse to comply with the request if it is not so satisfied. A person whose request is refused may apply to the court. If the court is not satisfied that the request was made for a proper purpose, it may dismiss the application. If a request is provided under s 811 which the company considers is made for a proper purpose, but the company wrongly refuses to comply with the request, an offence punishable by fine is committed by the company and every officer in default.[616]

G. Distributions

27.228 A distribution of a company's assets to a shareholder, except in accordance with specific statutory procedures, is a return of capital which is unlawful and ultra vires the company.[617] The rule is essentially a judge-made rule, almost as old as company law itself, derived from the fundamental principles embodied in the statutes by which Parliament has permitted companies to be incorporated with limited liability.[618] The relevant provisions by which capital may lawfully be distributed to shareholders are set out below. If the company does not comply with the statutory requirements, the distribution will be unlawful.[619] It cannot therefore be made lawful by ratification. Directors may incur civil liability by reason of an unlawful distribution, and shareholders are also likely to be required to repay.

(1) Meaning of 'distribution'

27.229 The word 'distribution' is defined by the Act, s 829 to mean every description of distribution of a company's assets to its members, whether in cash or otherwise.[620] Accordingly, a distribution may include, for example, the gratuitous element in a sale at an undervalue to a member[621] or 'equity payments' to shareholders pursuant to the terms of a company voluntary arrangement.[622] Benefits in kind to members in their capacity as such may also constitute distributions.[623] The label is not determinative: for example, 'director's remuneration' paid to a director who is also a shareholder may on a closer analysis appear to be a distribution to the director qua shareholder.[624] Whether a transaction amounts to a distribution is a matter of substance, not form.[625] A mere arithmetical difference between the consideration given for the asset or assets and the figure or figures at which it or they are in subsequent proceedings valued retrospectively will not of itself mean that there has been a distribution.[626] The court's task is to inquire into the true purpose and substance of the impugned transaction—a task which calls for an investigation of all the relevant facts, which will sometimes include the state of mind of the human beings who are orchestrating the corporate activity.[627] A distribution

---

[616] 2006 Act, s 813(1), (2). For 'officer in default', see para 26.12 above.

[617] *Progress Property Co Ltd v Moorgarth* [2010] 1 BCLC 1 (CA), [2011] 1 WLR 1, SC.

[618] *Progress Property Co Ltd v Moorgarth* [2011] 1 WLR 1, SC at para 15, per Lord Walker.

[619] See eg *Precision Dippings Ltd v Precision Dippings Marketing Ltd* [1986] Ch 447; *Bairstow v Queen's Moat Houses plc* [2001] 2 BCLC 531, CA. If the distribution is in part covered by distributable profits, it may be treated as lawful to that extent: *Re Marini Ltd* [2004] BCC 172.

[620] 2006 Act, s 829(1).

[621] *Aveling Barford Ltd v Perion Ltd* [1989] BCLC 626.

[622] *Re TXU Europe Group plc* [2012] BCC 363.

[623] *Jenkins v Harbour View Courts Ltd* [1966] NZLR 1.

[624] *Re Halt Garage (1964) Ltd* [1982] 3 All ER 1016. See also *Ridge Securities Ltd v IRC* [1964] 1 WLR 479, in which excessive interest payments were held to amount to an unlawful distribution.

[625] *Progress Property Co Ltd v Moorgarth* [2011] 1 WLR 1, SC at para 16, per Lord Walker.

[626] *Clydebank Football Club Ltd v Steedman* 2002 SLT 109.

[627] *Progress Property Co Ltd v Moorgarth* [2011] 1 WLR 1, SC, at para 27, per Lord Walker.

disguised as an arm's length transaction is the paradigm example of the type of case in which such an approach is required:

> If a company sells to a shareholder at a low value assets which are difficult to value precisely, but which are potentially very valuable, the transaction may call for close scrutiny, and the company's financial position, and the actual motives and intentions of the directors, will be highly relevant. There may be questions to be asked as to whether the company was under financial pressure compelling it to sell at an inopportune time, as to what advice was taken, how the market was tested, and how the terms of the deal were negotiated. If the conclusion is that it was a genuine arm's length transaction then it will stand, even if it may, with hindsight, appear to have been a bad bargain. If it was an improper attempt to extract value by the pretence of an arm's length sale, it will be held unlawful. But either conclusion will depend on a realistic assessment of all the relevant facts, not simply a retrospective valuation exercise in isolation from all other inquiries.[628]

However, the following are expressly not distributions: an issue of shares as fully or partly paid **27.230**
bonus shares; a lawful reduction of capital in accordance with the Act; the lawful redemption or purchase of the company's own shares out of capital or unrealized profits in accordance with the Act; or a distribution of assets to members in a solvent winding up.[629]

(2) General rules

The basic rule is that a company may only make a distribution out of profits available for **27.231**
the purpose.[630] A company's profits available for distribution are its accumulated, realized profits, so far as not previously written off in a reduction or reorganization of capital duly made,[631] less its accumulated realized losses, so far as not previously written off in a reduction or reorganization of capital. The existence of a profit or loss is determined principally, but not exclusively, by reference to generally accepted accounting principles.[632] Whether a distribution may be made by a company must be determined by reference to the profits, losses, assets, liabilities, provisions, capital, and reserves as stated in the 'relevant accounts'.[633] The 'relevant accounts' may be the last annual accounts, the interim accounts, or the initial accounts.[634] Different requirements must be satisfied in each case.

If the last annual accounts are to be used, s 837 must be consulted. In short, the 'last annual **27.232**
accounts' are the individual accounts last circulated to members under s 423. The accounts must have been properly prepared in accordance with the Act or must at the very least be such that any deficiencies are immaterial.[635] In addition, the auditor must have made his report on the accounts and, if the accounts were qualified, the materiality of the matters resulting in the qualification must be addressed in the context of distributions.[636] The requirement for the auditors to state whether any qualification in their report is a material one is a mandatory

---

[628] *Progress Property Co Ltd v Moorgarth* [2011] 1 WLR 1, SC, at para 29, per Lord Walker.
[629] 2006 Act, s 829(2).
[630] 2006 Act, s 830(1).
[631] 2006 Act, s 830(2).
[632] *Gallagher v Jones* [1994] Ch 107.
[633] 2006 Act, s 836(1).
[634] 2006 Act, s 836(2).
[635] 2006 Act, s 837(2). The consequence of the accounts not being properly prepared or not giving a true and fair view is that any distribution in reliance on the accounts will be a breach of the statutory provisions and hence unlawful: see *Bairstow v Queens Moat Houses plc* [2001] 2 BCLC 531; *Allied Carpets Group plc v Nethercott* [2001] BCC 81.
[636] 2006 Act, s 837(4).

requirement for the protection of creditors, and so if it is not given before the distribution is made, then whatever the circumstances the distribution will be unlawful.[637]

27.233　Initial accounts may be used, subject to s 839 of the Act, where the company has only recently commenced trading and the distribution is proposed to be declared during the company's first accounting reference period, or before any accounts have been circulated in respect of that period. Initial accounts must enable a reasonable judgment to be made as to the amounts of the profits, losses, assets, liabilities, provisions, capital, and reserves.[638] Initial accounts will be insufficient if they fail to make provision for a tax liability which is likely to be incurred.[639] Where initial accounts are to be utilized by a public company as the basis for a distribution, additional requirements will apply.[640]

27.234　If a company has previously drawn up and circulated annual accounts, but the distribution cannot be justified by those accounts, interim accounts must be used and s 838 must be followed. In short, 'interim accounts' must be accounts which enable a reasonable judgment to be made as to the amounts of the profits, losses, assets, liabilities, provisions, capital, and reserves.[641] Where a public company intends to use interim accounts, additional requirements will apply.[642]

27.235　Specific rules apply as to successive distributions by reference to the same accounts,[643] realized losses and profits and revaluation of fixed assets,[644] realized profits and losses of long-term insurance business,[645] and the treatment of development costs.[646] Such accountancy matters fall outside the scope of this work.

27.236　The articles usually provide for the company by ordinary resolution to declare dividends in accordance with members' rights, but that no dividend should exceed the amount recommended by the directors.[647] The directors have power to decide to pay interim dividends unless preferential dividends are in arrears. Provided they act in good faith, directors do not incur liability to preference shareholders for any loss suffered by the lawful payment of an interim dividend.[648] The directors also have power to pay dividends at a fixed rate if it appears to them that the profits available for distribution justify it.[649]

---

[637] *Precision Dippings Ltd v Precision Dippings Marketing Ltd* [1986] Ch 447.
[638] 2006 Act, s 839(1).
[639] *Re Loquitur Ltd* [2003] 2 BCLC 442.
[640] 2006 Act, s 839(2)–(7). As with 'interim accounts': the 'initial accounts' must have been 'properly prepared' and must have been subject to an auditor's report (with additional requirements if that report was qualified) and must have been delivered to the Registrar.
[641] 2006 Act, s 838(1).
[642] 2006 Act, s 838(2). In short, the accounts must have been 'properly prepared' (that is to say, prepared in accordance with 2006 Act, ss 395–7, applying those requirements with such modifications as are necessary because the accounts are prepared otherwise than in respect of an accounting reference period). In addition, the balance sheet must have been signed, and a copy of the accounts must have been delivered to the Registrar.
[643] 2006 Act, s 840.
[644] 2006 Act, s 841.
[645] 2006 Act, s 843.
[646] 2006 Act, s 844.
[647] Table A, regs 102 and 104; Model Article (pcls) 30(1)–(4); Model Article (plc) 70(1)–(3). Note that there are also powers for non-cash distributions and capitalization of profits: Table A, regs 105 and 110; Model Articles (pcls) 34, 36; Model Articles (plc) 76, 78.
[648] Table A, reg 103; Model Article (pcls) 30(1), (5), and (7).
[649] Table A, reg 103; Model Article (pcls) 30(6); Model Article (plc) 70(6).

(3) Additional provisions for public companies

Additional restrictions apply in respect of public companies. A public company may only make **27.237** a distribution: (i) if the amount of its net assets is not less than the aggregate of its called-up share capital and undistributable reserves, and (ii) if, and to the extent that, the distribution does not reduce the amount of those assets to less than that aggregate.[650] For this purpose:

(1) A company's 'net assets' means the aggregate of the company's assets less the aggregate of its liabilities.[651]

(2) The term 'liabilities' here includes (a) where the relevant accounts are Companies Act accounts, provisions of a kind specified for the purposes of this subsection by regulations under s 396, and (b) where the relevant accounts are IAS accounts, provisions of any kind.[652]

(3) A company's undistributable reserves are (a) its share premium account, (b) its capital redemption reserve, (c) the amount by which its accumulated, unrealized profits (so far as not previously utilized by capitalization) exceed its accumulated, unrealized losses (so far as not previously written off in a reduction or reorganization of capital duly made), and (d) any other reserve that the company is prohibited from distributing (i) by any enactment or (ii) by its articles. The reference in this context to capitalization does not include a transfer of profits of the company to its capital redemption reserve.[653]

A public company must not include any uncalled share capital as an asset in any accounts relevant for purposes of this section.[654] Additional requirements apply in the case of investment companies.[655]

(4) Liability for unlawful dividends

Civil liability of directors at common law

A director who caused or permitted the payment of an unlawful dividend was potentially **27.238** liable to the company at common law for breach of trust or negligence.[656] Now the liability would be described as arising from a breach of one or more of the fiduciary duties stated in 2006 Act, ss 171–3 or breach of the duty to exercise reasonable care, skill, and diligence stated in s 174.[657]

---

[650] 2006 Act, s 831(1).
[651] 2006 Act, s 831(2).
[652] 2006 Act, s 831(3).
[653] 2006 Act, s 831(4).
[654] 2006 Act, s 831(5).
[655] 2006 Act, ss 832 and 833. With effect from 6 April 2012 the Companies Act 2006 (Amendment of Part 23) (Investment Companies) Regulations 2012 (2012/952) made amendments to ss 832(5) and (6) and 833(1)(b) and (2) and omitted ss 833(3), 834, and 835.
[656] This proposition was established at a very early stage in the development of company law by a long line of cases including *Evans v Coventry* (1856) 25 LJ Ch 489, 501 (Kindersley V-C) and (1857) 8 De GM & G 835, 616 (Court of Appeal); *In re Mercantile Trading Co, Stringer's Case* (1869) LR 4 Ch App 475, 487 (Selwyn LJ); *In re County Marine Insurance Co, Rance's Case* (1870) LR 6 Ch App 104, 119–20 (James LJ) and 122–4 (Mellish LJ); *Salisbury v Metropolitan Railway Co* (1870) 22 LT 839, 841 (Malins V-C); *In re National Funds Assurance Co* (1878) 10 Ch D 118, 125–9 (Jessel MR); *In re Exchange Banking Company, Flitcroft's Case* (1882) 21 Ch D 519, 525 (Bacon V-C); *In re Oxford Benefit Building and Investment Society* (1886) 35 Ch D 502, 509 (Kay J); *Precision Dippings Ltd v Precision Dippings Marketing Ltd* [1986] Ch 447, CA; *Bairstow v Queens Moat Houses plc* [2001] 2 BCLC 531, CA at paras 37–48; *Re Paycheck Services 3 Ltd* [2010] 1 WLR 2793, SC.
[657] *BAT Industries plc v Windward Prospects Ltd* [2013] EWHC 3612 (Comm) at paras 28–36 contain an outline of how an unlawful dividend claim may be made.

27.239   An early statement of principle may be found in *Evans v Coventry* per Kindersley V-C:[658]

> It does appear to me that the directors had a duty, not only to the persons who were shareholders, but a duty to the persons who effected insurances in this society—a duty which imposed on them the necessity of not misapplying the funds of this society—that is, applying them in any way not justified by the terms of the deed; still more did it impose upon them the duty of not applying those funds in any way, or from any motive which was in itself unjustifiable; and I cannot but hold that all those who were directors are liable not only to refund those dividends which they themselves received in respect of their shares, but that they are liable to refund all the dividends, as far as any of them personally were parties to the declaring of dividends or concurred in it. I must hold that they are liable to make good to the funds of the society the dividends which have thus been declared and paid.

27.240   The early cases conceptualized the director's liability purely in terms of breach of trust.[659] It was not until 1894 that Lindley and Kay LJJ explained that the trust analysis was not entirely apt, since directors were not actually trustees of the company's assets, but that, if they misapply it or deal with it in a manner which is beyond their powers, they are treated as having committed a breach of trust, just as if they had been trustees and are liable to make good the company's moneys.[660] This conclusion has been followed repeatedly.[661]

27.241   Accordingly it is arguable that the position at common law remains the same today in relation to breach of fiduciary duty claims as it was in the late nineteenth century when the position was summarized in the following terms by Kay J in *Re Oxford Benefit Building and Investment Society*:[662]

> It is settled by authorities which I cannot dispute: (1) That directors are quasi-trustees of the capital of the company. (2) Directors who improperly pay dividends out of capital are liable to repay such dividends personally upon the company being wound up. (3) This liability may be enforced by a creditor or by the liquidator ... or by the incorporated company before a winding-up. (4) The acquiescence of the shareholders does not affect the creditors in such a case. (5) Such an act is a breach of trust, and the remedy is not barred by the Statute of Limitations.[663]

Equally, however, it is arguable that a director's liability for unlawful dividends is a strict liability, which will exist in every case involving an unlawful dividend, whether or not the directors can be said to have been at fault in any way. See, for example, the decision of the Supreme Court in *Revenue and Customs Commissioners v Holland, In Re Paycheck Services 3 Ltd*,[664] in which Lord Hope identified two conflicting lines of authority as to whether the liability was strict or fault-based. Lord Hope expressed an obiter preference for the view that a director who causes an unlawful dividend to be paid is under a

---

[658]   (1856) 25 LJ Ch 489, 501, per Kindersley V-C.

[659]   See eg in *Salisbury v Metropolitan Railway Co* (1870) 22 LT 839, 841 (Malins V-C); *Wye Valley Railway Co v Hawes* (1880) 16 Ch D 489, 494 (Jessel MR); *Re Exchange Banking Company, Flitcroft's Case* (1882) 21 Ch D 519 (Bacon V-C); and *Leeds Estate Building and Investment Company v Shepherd* (1887) 36 Ch D 787, 797–8 (Stirling J).

[660]   In *Re Lands Allotment Company* [1894] 1 Ch 616, 631, per Lindley LJ; 638 per Kay LJ.

[661]   See eg *Belmont Finance Corporation Ltd v Williams Furniture Ltd (No 2)* [1980] 1 All ER 393, 405.

[662]   (1886) 35 Ch D 502, 509.

[663]   And see, more recently, *Progress Property Co Ltd v Moorgarth* [2011] 1 WLR 1, SC at para 32 per Lord Walker, approving *Clydebank Football Club Ltd v Steedman* 2002 SLT 109 at para 79 per Lord Hamilton, to the effect that '[w]hether or not they [the directors] were ... in breach [of their fiduciary duties] will involve consideration not only of whether or not the directors knew at the time that what they were doing was unlawful but also their state of knowledge at the time of the material facts'.

[664]   [2010] 1 WLR 2793, at paras 45–47 (Lord Hope), 124 (Lord Walker), and 146 (Lord Clarke).

strict liability to make good such misapplication of the company's property, subject only to relief from sanction if he establishes that he acted honestly and reasonably. In the Court of Appeal, Rimer LJ had said that he found the arguments in support of that view compelling. Lord Clarke also agreed with Rimer LJ's views at paragraph 146. At paragraph 124 Lord Walker expressed agreement with Rimer LJ on '*the other issues*' (which would apparently include this one). Accordingly there is an unresolved issue of law as to whether the liability is fault-based or strict, with high authority in support of both propositions.

At common law a director may also be held liable to pay damages to the company in tort for **27.242** negligence. Now he would liable for breach of the duty to exercise reasonable care, skill, and diligence, as stated in the 2006 Act, s 174. This analysis was considered by Stirling J in *Leeds Estate Building and Investment Company v Shepherd*:[665]

> Directors who are proved to have, in fact, paid a dividend out of capital fail to excuse themselves if they have not taken reasonable care to secure the preparation of estimates and statements of account, such as it was their duty to prepare and submit to the shareholders, and have declared the dividends complained of without having exercised thereon their judgment as mercantile men on the estimates and statements submitted to them.[666]

In *Re D'Jan of London Ltd*[667] Hoffmann LJ held that the duty of care owed by a director to a **27.243** company at common law is accurately stated in the Insolvency Act, s 214.[668] This standard is now part of the statutory code of directors' duties under the 2006 Act, s 174.

No repayment of an improperly paid dividend will, however, be ordered where the payment **27.244** was made without fault on the part of the directors.[669] This is the case whether the claim is formulated as breach of fiduciary duty or breach of the directors' contractual duty. The nature and extent of fault which has to be found against a director before he is liable to make repayment of the dividends was considered by Nelson J in *Bairstow v Queens Moat Houses plc*:[670]

> Whilst there are passages in the nineteenth century cases which suggest that the test for judging a director's conduct was at least in part objective, there is no doubt that the standard of care set was undemanding. A 'mere error of judgment' would not permit recovery and 'gross or wilful negligence' had to be established … The law has however kept pace with the changing role of directors. An executive director under a contract of service and paid substantial remuneration must be expected to bring to his work a level of competence commensurate with his responsibilities and his remuneration. As I have found earlier in this judgment in relation to the duty of skill and care generally, an executive director is to be judged at common law by the same test as set under s 214 of the Insolvency Act 1986. Thus he has to have the general knowledge, skill and experience that may reasonably be expected of a person carrying out the same

---

[665] (1887) 36 Ch D 787, 801.

[666] Lord Davey cited this statement with approval in *Dovey v Cory* [1901] AC 477 at 490, adding: 'It is by this standard that the conduct of the respondent must be judged in this case.'

[667] [1994] 1 BCLC 561.

[668] See also *Bairstow v Queens Moat Houses plc* [2000] 1 BCLC 549, 559D–E (Nelson J). For an example of a case in which the directors were held liable to pay damages to the company for negligently causing the payment of an unlawful dividend, see *Leeds Estate Building and Investment Company v Shepherd* (1887) 36 Ch D 787, 805 (Stirling J): 'Upon the whole, although the directors were, I believe, ignorant of the true state of the company's affairs, and although I find no trace of their having acted with the view of obtaining any improper benefit for themselves, I feel compelled to hold that they have fallen short of that standard of care which … they ought to have applied to the affairs of the company.'

[669] *Bairstow v Queens Moat Houses plc* [2000] 1 BCLC 549, 577 (Nelson J). His judgment on the directors' liability for paying unlawful dividends was upheld by the Court of Appeal: [2001] 2 BCLC 531.

[670] [2000] 1 BCLC 549, 559B–G.

functions as are carried out by that director in relation to the company as well as the general knowledge, skill and experience that that director has ... This modern objective test requires that a director is judged not merely by that which he knows, but also that which he ought to know as a reasonably diligent person having the knowledge, skill and experience expected of a person carrying out his task. I am satisfied that this is so whether his acts or omissions are being considered in the context of the general duty of skill and care, or his specific duties in relation to the payment of dividends. The test of culpable negligence or carelessness or gross neglect set out in the nineteenth century cases must therefore be considered in the light of the developments in the law relating to the duties of directors, and in so far as they remain extant as tests, must be assessed in relation to the modern role and function of a paid executive director.

27.245   Nelson J summarized his conclusions:[671]

[A] director who authorises the payment of an unlawful dividend in breach of his duty as a quasi-trustee will be liable to repay such dividends:
(1) if he knows that the dividends were unlawful, whether or not that actual knowledge amounts to fraud; or
(2) if he knows the facts that established the impropriety of the payments, even though he was unaware that such impropriety rendered the payment unlawful (*Re Kingston Cotton Mill Co (No 2)* [1896] 1 Ch 331 at 347 and *Precision Dippings Ltd v Precision Dippings Marketing Ltd* [1986] Ch 447 at 457);
(3) if he must be taken in all the circumstances to know all the facts which render the payments unlawful (*Precision Dippings Ltd v Precision Dippings Marketing Ltd* [1986] Ch 447 at 457);
(4) if he ought to have known, as a reasonably competent and diligent director, that the payments were unlawful (*Norman v Theodore Goddard* [1991] BCLC 1028, *Re D'Jan of London Ltd* [1994] 1 BCLC 561 and s.214 of the Insolvency Act 1986).

27.246   A director found liable in respect of unlawful dividends is obliged to account to the company for the full amount of those dividends and restore them.[672]

27.247   In a claim against directors for breach of fiduciary duty or negligence, the proper claimant before the making of a winding-up order is the company itself. A claim by the company is also possible after the making of a winding-up order. In the alternative the liquidator may bring a claim against a director under the Insolvency Act, s 212 (see Chapter 34, Section C(1) below).[673]

27.248   A director or former director who faces a claim by the company or the liquidator may be able to rely on the 2006 Act, s 1157[674] in defence to such a claim. It is not necessary for a party

---

[671] [2000] 1 BCLC 549, 559H–560B.

[672] *Revenue and Customs Commissioners v Holland, Re Paycheck Services 3 Ltd* [2010] 1 WLR 2793, SC, at para 49, per Lord Hope, following *Bairstow v Queens Moat Houses plc* [2001] 2 BCLC 531 at para 54, per Robert Walker LJ.

[673] It is well established that this section deals only with procedure and does not create any new rights. It provides a summary mode of enforcing existing rights: *City Equitable Fire Insurance Co* [1925] 1 Ch 407, 507 (Pollock MR). In *Revenue and Customs Commissioners v Holland, Re Paycheck Services 3 Ltd* there was disagreement in the Court of Appeal and the Supreme Court as to the discretion under the Insolvency Act, s 212, to reduce Mr Holland's liability if he had been liable under that section, which both Courts held he was not. In favour of the narrow view of the discretion under s 212 were Rimer LJ at [2009] 2 BCLC 309 at paras 99–102 and Lords Walker and Clarke at [2010] 1 WLR 2793 at paras 124 and 146. In favour of the broader discretion were Elias and Ward LJJ at [2009] 2 BCLC 309 at paras 129–35, 141; and Lord Hope at [2010] 1 WLR 2793 at para 49. Lords Collins and Saville did not address this issue.

[674] In *Bairstow v Queens Moat Houses plc* [2001] 2 BCLC 531 the Court of Appeal refused relief where the directors had been guilty of dishonesty in preparing the relevant accounts. See also *Re Loquitur Ltd* [2003] 2 BCLC 442; *Re Paycheck Services 3 Ltd* [2008] 2 BCLC 613; [2009] 2 BCLC 309, CA at paras 81–9, 123, 142;

to plead specially s 1157 and the section may be raised if the parties so wish for the first time at trial.[675]

Civil liability of members at common law

In many cases, directors are also members. In such cases, the directors may be liable at com- **27.249**
mon law, as members, in addition to their liabilities as directors. The common law position as regards members who receive an unlawful dividend is: (1) they may be liable to repay money had and received by reason of a mistake of fact (ie on a restitutionary claim by the company, subject to the defence of change of position); or (2) they may be held liable as constructive trustees on the grounds of knowing receipt of trust property.

The second potential ground of liability was explained in *Belmont Finance Corporation Ltd v* **27.250**
Williams Furniture Ltd (No 2):[676]

> If the directors of a company in breach of their fiduciary duties misapply the funds of their company so that they come into the hands of some stranger to the trust who receives them with knowledge (actual or constructive) of the breach, he cannot conscientiously retain those funds against the company unless he has some better equity. He becomes a constructive trustee for the company of the misapplied funds. This is stated very clearly by Jessel MR in *Russell v Wakefield Waterworks Co* (1875) LR 20 Eq 474, 479, where he said: 'In this court the money of the company is a trust fund, because it is applicable only to the special purposes of the company in the hands of the agents of the company, and it is in that sense a trust fund applicable by them to those special purposes; and a person taking it from them with notice that it is being applied to other purposes cannot in this court say that he is not a constructive trustee.'[677]

As a statement of law, this passage remains broadly accurate. However, it is submitted that **27.251**
Buckley LJ was wrong if he meant to say that *constructive* knowledge of a breach of trust would be sufficient. In fact, according to subsequent Court of Appeal authority, it appears that the true position is that a shareholder will not be held liable as a constructive trustee unless his state of knowledge at the time of the receipt of the unlawful dividend was such as to make it *unconscionable* for him to retain the benefit of the dividend.[678] A shareholder's liability as a constructive trustee was considered by Colman J in *Allied Carpets Group plc v Nethercott*:[679]

> The constructive trust is imposed on the recipient of the company's property not because he has agreed to hold it as trustee under a bare trust for some special commercial purpose but because the property has been transferred to him and to his knowledge ultra vires the powers of the company. The conjunction of want of power of disposal and knowledge of that deficiency produces the position where no beneficial interest has passed from the company to the transferee. When the company claims repayment of the unlawfully distributed dividends it is simply reclaiming its property from a transferee who, because he acquired it with knowledge that the company has been wrongfully divested of it, is under a duty to restore it.[680]

[2010] 1 WLR 2793, SC at paras 50, 124, 146 (where the claim to relief under what is now 2006 Act, s 1157 would have failed except for the few days grace the director was allowed to respond to legal advice).

[675] *Re Kirbys Coaches Ltd* [1991] BCLC 414 (Hoffmann J).
[676] [1980] 1 All ER 393, 405, CA per Buckley LJ.
[677] See also *Rolled Steel Products (Holdings) Ltd v British Steel Corporation* [1986] 1 Ch 246, 298 (Slade LJ) and 303–7 (Browne-Wilkinson LJ).
[678] *Bank of Credit and Commerce International (Overseas) Ltd v Akindele* [2001] Ch 437, CA.
[679] [2001] BCC 81.
[680] See also *Moxham v Grant* [1900] 1 QB 88, 92 (AL Smith LJ) and 94 (Collins LJ), and *Re Cleveland Trust plc* [1991] BCLC 424 (Scott J).

27.252 It is arguable that a shareholder who is also a director may be entitled to be relieved from liability under the 2006 Act, s 1157 although the position is not entirely free from doubt.[681]

Civil liability of members under statute

27.253 Further, the 2006 Act, s 847 gives companies a statutory means of recouping unlawful dividends from shareholders.[682] It provides:

(1) This section applies where a distribution, or part of one, made by a company to one of its members is made in contravention of this Part.

(2) If at the time of the distribution the member knows or has reasonable grounds for believing that it is so made, he is liable—

(a) to repay it (or that part of it, as the case may be) to the company, or

(b) in the case of a distribution made otherwise than in cash, to pay the company a sum equal to the value of the distribution (or part) at that time.

(3) This is without prejudice to any obligation imposed apart from this section on a member of a company to repay a distribution unlawfully made to him.

(4) This section does not apply in relation to—

(a) financial assistance given by a company in contravention of section 678 or 679, or

(b) any payment made by a company in respect of the redemption of purchase by the company of shares in itself.

27.254 The leading case on this provision is *It's A Wrap (UK) Ltd v Gula*,[683] in which the Court of Appeal held that for a member to have the knowledge or reasonable grounds for belief required by this provision, he need not know or have reasonable grounds to believe that the distribution will contravene the provisions of the Act, and it will be sufficient if he knows or has reason to believe the relevant facts constituting the contravention.

---

[681] In *Inn Spirit Ltd v Burns* [2003] BPIR 413 the directors of a company had taken large sums of money from the company by way of unlawful dividend. Rimer J dismissed the company's application for summary judgment, holding that the directors had a real prospect of successfully defending the claim under the 1985 Act, s 727.

[682] This section replicates (with immaterial differences) the 1985 Act, s 277, which in turn replicated the 1980 Act, s 44. The 1980 Act, s 44, which was enacted to comply with the UK's obligations under Art 16 of the Second Directive on Company Law (79/91/EEC). Prior to the 1980 Act, s 44 coming into force on 18 December 1980, a company seeking to recover unlawful dividends had to rely on its common law remedies, which have been expressly preserved by statute (1980 Act, s 44(2), 1985 Act, s 277(2), and 2006 Act, s 847(3)).

[683] [2006] 2 BCLC 634, CA.

28

REORGANIZATIONS AND TAKEOVERS

Tom Smith QC

A. Introduction

The Companies Act, Parts 26, 27, and 28, ss 895–992, contain provisions about arrange- **28.01**
ments and reconstructions, mergers and divisions of public companies, and takeovers.
Chapters 1 and 2 of Part 28, ss 942–73, concerning the Takeover Panel and impediments
to takeovers, were new provisions introduced by the 2006 Act, while the remaining sections
in these Parts restate with minor amendments provisions contained in the 1985 Act.[1] The
purpose of this chapter is to discuss the role of directors in relation to these procedures and to
identify their duties and liabilities. For this purpose each part of this chapter begins with an
introductory description of the provisions and procedures, which is followed by a discussion
of the relevant functions and duties of directors.

B. Arrangements and Reconstructions

(1) The scope of the provisions

The Companies Act, Part 26, ss 895–901, contain the established procedure whereby a **28.02**
company can propose a compromise or arrangement between itself and its creditors (or any
class of them) or its members (or any class of them).[2] If a majority in number representing

---

[1] The 2006 Act, ss 895–941 came into force on 6 April 2008: 2006 Commencement Order No 5, Art 3(1)(l)
and (mm). Sections 942–92 came into force on 6 April 2007: 2006 Commencement Order No 2, Art 2(1)(b).
[2] These provisions can be traced back to the 1870 Act, when their application was limited to companies
being wound up. The 1908 Act brought into force provisions of the 1907 Act, which extended their application
to all companies.

75 per cent in value of the creditors (or class of creditors) or members (or class of members) as the case may be, vote in favour of a compromise or arrangement then the court may sanction the compromise or arrangement. The compromise or arrangement will then have binding effect on the company and on the creditors (or class of creditors) or members (or class of members).

28.03 Directors will be concerned with proposals for schemes to effect compromises or arrangements between a company and its members, where it is desired to reorganize the capital of the company or in the context of a takeover or amalgamation.[3] They would only be concerned with schemes to effect compromises or arrangements with creditors if the company is not in administration or liquidation. If the company is or is likely to be unable to pay its debts, a company voluntary arrangement under the Insolvency Act, Part 1 may be a more advantageous procedure and the directors may well be advised to place the company in administration in order to protect its property and enable it to carry on business while the scheme is being promoted.[4] In spite of those considerations, in recent years directors have been increasingly involved in promoting schemes of arrangement outside of formal insolvency proceedings between companies and creditors in cases where the financial structure or indebtedness of the company is being reorganized[5] or where a solvent insurance company wishes to compromise policyholders' claims.[6]

---

[3] *Re Peninsular & Oriental Steam Navigation Company* [2006] EWHC 389 (Ch). In recent times, schemes of arrangement have proved to be increasingly popular as a means of effecting takeovers. The perceived advantages of schemes as a means of effecting takeovers are speed (obtaining 100 per cent control of a company will usually be quicker under a scheme than under a takeover offer) and certainty (since a scheme, if sanctioned, will deliver 100 per cent ownership of the offeree) which may, in particular, give assurance to lenders financing the deal. In addition, a scheme will normally avoid stamp duty (0.5 per cent) on the value of the offeree company's shares acquired by the offeror, as these are typically cancelled and reissued to the offeror, and no stamp duty is levied on such transaction. A scheme may also prove attractive where the offeree company has a significant number of US shareholders as a court-approved scheme is exempt from the US tender offer requirements under the US Securities Exchange Act 1934. The principal drawback with schemes is that they always require 75 per cent approval by offeree company shareholders present and voting at the relevant shareholders' meetings and are, therefore, to this extent inflexible. They are also more vulnerable to a blocking strategy as a shareholder (for example a competing offeror) with a 25.1 per cent shareholding (or, in practice, significantly lower) can prevent the necessary 75 per cent being achieved. Such a holding would not be sufficient to prevent an offeror achieving 50.1 per cent acceptance under a normal takeover offer (see para 28.86 below).

[4] However, once the promotion of the scheme for creditors is underway the court should stay executions against the company's property: *Hudson's Concrete Products Ltd v DB Evans (Bilston) Ltd* (1961) 105 SJ 281, CA; *D Wilson (Birmingham) Ltd v Metropolitan Property Developments Ltd* [1975] 2 All ER 814, CA; *Rainbow v Moorgate Properties Ltd* [1975] 1 WLR 788, CA; *Roberts Petroleum Ltd v Kenny Ltd* [1983] 2 AC 192, 207–13, HL; *BlueCrest Mercantile BV v Vietnam Shipbuilding Industry Group* [2013] EWHC 1146 (Comm).

[5] There are a large number of recent examples where the financing arrangements of English and foreign companies have been restructured using a scheme of arrangement outside of insolvency proceedings from Marconi (see *Re Marconi plc, Re Marconi Corp plc* [2003] EWHC 1083 (Ch)), Drax (see *Re Drax Holdings Ltd* [2004] 1 WLR 1049), and MyTravel (see *Re MyTravel Group plc* [2005] 2 BCLC 123) to Crest Nicholson, McCarthy & Stone, Countrywide (see *Re Castle Holdco 4 Ltd* [2009] EWHC 1347 (Ch)), and IMO Car Wash (see *Re Bluebrook Ltd* [2010] 1 BCLC 338) to more recent examples often involving foreign companies eg La Seda de Barcelona (see *Re La Seda de Barcelona SA* [2011] 1 BCLC 555), Rodenstock (see *Re Rodenstock GmbH* [2011] Bus LR 1245), Primacom (see *Re Primacom Holding GmbH* [2013] BCC 201), Vietnam Shipbuilding (see *Re Vietnam Shipbuilding Industry Group* [2014] 1 BCLC 400), Apcoa (see *Re Apcoa Parking (UK) Ltd* [2014] 4 All ER 150 and *Re Apcoa Parking Holdings GmbH* [2015] 2 BCLC 659), and Global Garden Products (*Re Global Garden Products Italy SpA* [2016] EWHC 1884 (Ch)).

[6] eg *Re Hawk Insurance Co Ltd* [2001] 2 BCLC 480, CA; *Re Pan Atlantic Insurance Co Ltd* [2003] 2 BCLC 678; and *Re Osiris Insurance Ltd* [1999] 1 BCLC 182.

Meaning of 'compromise' and 'arrangement'

A compromise is an agreement in settlement of a claim which is in doubt, dispute, or dif- **28.04** ficulty of enforcement.[7] On the other hand, an 'arrangement' has a very wide meaning.[8] The only requirement established by the case law is that an arrangement must involve an element of 'give and take';[9] beyond that, the courts have declined to attempt to define an arrangement. A moratorium on claims may constitute an arrangement.[10] Further, by s 895(2), an 'arrangement' is also specifically defined to include a reorganization of the company's share capital by the consolidation of shares of different classes or by the division of shares into shares of different classes, or by both of these methods.

Persons with whom they can be made: creditors and members

Although 'creditor' is not defined in the Companies Act, it has been held that for these **28.05** purposes (a) a creditor is any person who has a pecuniary claim against the company including those whose claims are future or contingent,[11] and (b) a creditor is not limited to those persons who would have a provable claim in the winding up of the company (though it does include all such persons).[12] A person who is the beneficiary of property held by the company on trust for his benefit is not a creditor for these purposes.[13] However, a person who has security for a debt or liability owed to him by the company remains a creditor for the purposes of the jurisdiction under Part 26.[14] Where bonds are held in an immobilized form in the clearing systems, then prima facie the depositary as the holder of the bonds will be the creditor of the company; however, the underlying bondholder may also be a creditor on the basis that it has a contingent claim against the company where it has the right to call for a definitive bond to be issued.[15]

A compromise or arrangement may properly be promoted between a company and only **28.06** some of its creditors. A class of creditors formulated for the purposes of approving a scheme of arrangement does not have to contain all the persons with similar rights who might objectively be said to fall within the class provided that the class is formulated in a commercially rational way or for good commercial reasons.[16] A company is free to select the creditors with whom it wishes to enter into a scheme of arrangement and it is not necessary for the company to include or consult any class of creditors or contributories who are not affected

---

[7] *Mercantile Investment & General Trust Co v International Co of Mexico* [1893] 1 Ch 484n, 491n, CA.

[8] *Re National Bank Ltd* [1966] 1 WLR 819, 829; *Re Calgary and Edmonton Land Co* [1975] 1 WLR 355, 363; *Re Savoy Hotel Ltd* [1981] 1 Ch 351, 359.

[9] *Re NFU Development Trust Ltd* [1972] 1 WLR 1548.

[10] *Inland Revenue Commissioners v Adam & Partners Ltd* [2001] 1 BCLC 222, CA. It is not a necessary element of an arrangement that it should alter the rights existing between the company and the creditors or members with whom it is made; provided that the context and content of the scheme are such as properly to constitute an arrangement between the company and the members or creditors concerned, it will fall within the section: *Re T&N Ltd (No 3)* [2007] 1 BCLC 563.

[11] *Re Midland Coal, Coke and Iron Co* [1895] 1 Ch 267; *Re Cancol Ltd* [1996] 1 All ER 37.

[12] *Re T&N Ltd* [2006] 1 WLR 1728 at para 40.

[13] *Re Lehman Brothers International (Europe)* [2009] EWCA Civ 1161, [2010] 1 BCLC 496.

[14] *Re Lehman Brothers International (Europe)* (n 13 above), and see *Re Alabama, New Orleans, Texas and Pacific Junction Railway Co* [1891] 1 Ch 213.

[15] *Re Dunderland Ltd* [1909] 1 Ch 446; *Re Castle Holdco 4 Ltd* [2009] EWHC 1347 (Ch). See Maunder, Bondholder Schemes of Arrangement: Playing the Numbers Game [2003] *Insolvency Intelligence* 73, and Sterling and Taylor, Issues Arising in Cross-Border Schemes of Arrangements [1994] *International Insolvency Review* 122.

[16] *Sea Assets Ltd v PT Garuda Indonesia* [2001] EWCA Civ 1696, CA; *Re Telewest Communications plc (No 1)* [2005] 1 BCLC 752 at para 57.

by the scheme, either because their rights are not altered or because they have no economic interest in the company.[17]

28.07 The meaning of 'member' does not present any difficulties. The members of a company are the subscribers of the company's memorandum of association once registered and every other person who agrees to become a member of the company and whose name is entered in the register of members.[18]

Company

28.08 A company for the purposes of the Companies Act, Part 26, means any company liable to be wound up under the provisions of the Insolvency Act or the Insolvency (Northern Ireland) Order 1989.[19] Under the provisions of the Insolvency Act both companies incorporated in England and Wales and foreign companies may be wound up.[20] A large number of schemes of arrangement have been sanctioned in respect of foreign companies, increasingly so in recent times.

28.09 The Court of Appeal has held that there are three conditions which must be satisfied for the making of a winding-up order in respect of a foreign company: (1) there must be a sufficient connection with England (which may, but does not necessarily have to, consist of assets within the jurisdiction); (2) there must be a reasonable possibility, if a winding-up order is made, of benefit to those applying for the winding-up order; and (3) one or more persons interested in the distribution of assets of the company must be persons over whom the court can exercise jurisdiction.[21] In *Re Drax Holdings plc*[22] the court held that the second and third requirements do not need to be satisfied for the court to have jurisdiction to sanction a scheme in respect of a foreign company; it is enough that a sufficient connection with England is shown. The fact that the relevant liabilities are governed by English law will give rise to a sufficient connection for these purposes.[23] Where the relevant liabilities are not governed by English law, it would be necessary to rely on other links with the jurisdiction to demonstrate a sufficient connection eg that the company's centre of main interests (COMI) is in England and Wales.[24]

28.10 In addition to the common law requirements for winding up a foreign company, the Insolvency Regulation now restricts the jurisdiction of the English court, in relation to companies with their COMI within the EU, to winding up only such companies as have their COMI or an establishment in England and Wales. However, these rules as to intra-European jurisdiction do not affect the question of whether the company is liable to be wound up for purposes of the court's jurisdiction to sanction a compromise or arrangement. In *Re Rodenstock GmbH*[25] the court held that neither the Insolvency Regulation nor the Judgments Regulation appeared on their face to be directed at restricting the English court's

---

[17] *Re Bluebrook Ltd* [2010] 1 BCLC 338; *Re Tea Corp Ltd* [1904] 1 Ch 12.
[18] 2006 Act, s 112.
[19] 2006 Act, s 895(2)(b).
[20] Foreign companies may be wound up as unregistered companies under the Insolvency Act, s 221.
[21] *Stocznia Gdanska SA v Latreefers Inc (No 2)* [2001] 2 BCLC 116, CA.
[22] [2004] 1 WLR 1049.
[23] *Re Rodenstock GmbH* [2011] EWHC 1104 (Ch), [2011] Bus LR 1245; *Re Vietnam Shipbuilding Industry Group* [2014] 1 BCLC 400.
[24] See *Re Magyar Telecom BV* [2015] 1 BCLC 418.
[25] [2012] BCC 459. Followed in *Re Primacom Holding GmbH* [2013] BCC 201 and in subsequent cases.

international jurisdiction in relation to solvent schemes and, given that all company law consolidation since either of the regulations had been implemented had re-enacted the 'liable
to be wound up' test in an unaltered form, it was improbable on a purposive interpretation
of those regulations that any such narrowing of the English court's jurisdiction had been
intended.

28.11 A further issue concerns the court's jurisdiction over some or all of the scheme creditors in
accordance with the provisions of the recast Judgments Regulation.[26] Article 4 of the recast
Judgments Regulation provides that, subject to the other provisions of the Regulation, persons domiciled in a Member State must be sued in the courts of that Member State. It has
not yet been determined in the cases whether this applies to a scheme, although it is suggested that, even allowing for the autonomous meaning of the concept of 'sued' as used in the
Judgments Regulation, it is not apt to apply to a scheme of arrangement between a company
and its creditors which does not involve the company 'suing' its creditors in any ordinary
sense. In any event, in a sequence of cases, the courts have held that, even if the Judgments
Regulation does apply, the English court will have jurisdiction pursuant to Article 25 of the
Judgments Regulation over the scheme creditors where the relevant agreements which are
the subject of the scheme contain a provision conferring jurisdiction on the English court.[27]
In *Re Vietnam Shipbuilding Industry Group*,[28] it was held this applies to both exclusive and
non-exclusive jurisdiction clauses in favour of the English courts. Similarly, the English
court will have jurisdiction, pursuant to Article 8 of the Judgments Regulation, where any of
the scheme creditors are domiciled in England.[29] In many cases, therefore, the English court
will have jurisdiction irrespective of whether the Judgments Regulation applies.

(2) Summary of the procedure

Court order for holding of meeting

28.12 The procedure for the sanction of a compromise or arrangement is begun by an application
being made to the court for an order under s 896 summoning a meeting or meetings of
creditors (or class of creditors) or members (or class of members) as the case may be. Under
s 896(2) the application may be made by (a) the company; (b) any creditor or member of
the company; (c) if the company is being wound up, the liquidator; or (d) if the company is
in administration, the administrator. The application is made by a Part 8 Claim Form and
should be supported by evidence in the form of a witness statement which describes the
company and the proposed scheme, exhibits a copy of the draft scheme and explanatory
statement, and exhibits copies of the forms of the notices of meetings and proxy and voting
forms which it is intended to send to the creditors and/or members.[30]

---

[26] See *Re Rodenstock* [2011] Bus LR 1245 at paras 57–63, *Re Primacom Holding GmbH* [2013] BCC 201 at
paras 8–17 of the second judgment, *Re NEF Telecom BV* [2012] EWHC 2944 (Ch) at paras 29–45, *Re Vietnam
Shipbuilding Industry Group* [2014] 1 BCLC 400 at paras 10–16, *Re Magyar Telecom BV* [2014] BCC 488 at
para 31; *Re Apcoa Parking Holdings GmbH* [2015] BCC 142, *Re Van Gansewinkel Groep NV* [2015] Bus LR
1046, and *Re Stemcor Trade Finance Limited* [2015] EWHC 2662 (Ch).

[27] *Re Primacom Holding GmbH* [2013] BCC 201 at paras 13–14 of the second judgment, *Re NEF Telecom
BV* [2012] EWHC 2944 (Ch) at para 41, *Re Vietnam Shipbuilding Industry Group* [2014] 1 BCLC 400 at paras
14–16, *Re Hibu Finance (UK) Ltd* [2014] EWHC 370 (Ch), and *Re Apcoa Parking Holdings GmbH* [2014]
BCC 538.

[28] [2014] 1 BCLC 400.

[29] *Re Magyar Telecom BV* [2013] EWHC 3800 (Ch) at para 31.

[30] See Practice Direction to CPR Part 49: Applications under the Companies Acts and Related Legislation.

28.13   In the case of a compromise or arrangement between a company and its creditors or members, it is the responsibility of the applicant at this stage to determine whether more than one meeting of creditors or members is required to consider the scheme and, if so, to ensure that those meetings are properly constituted by a class of creditors or members.[31] The test to be applied is that each meeting should be constituted by creditors or members whose rights against the company are not so dissimilar as to make it impossible for them to consult together with a view to their common interest.[32] The test is to be applied by analysing the rights of creditors or members which are to be released or varied under the scheme and the new rights (if any) which the scheme gives to those whose rights are released or varied.[33] Further, the fact that individuals may hold divergent views based on their private interests not derived from their legal rights against the company is not a ground for calling separate meetings.[34] Individual creditors or shareholders may exclude themselves from a meeting of creditors or shareholders (as the case may be) by voluntarily agreeing to be bound by the proposed scheme of arrangement.[35]

28.14   At the stage of applying for an order convening a meeting of creditors, it is the responsibility of the applicant by evidence in support of the application or otherwise to draw to the attention of the court as soon as possible any issues which may arise as to the constitution of meetings or creditors or which otherwise affect the conduct of those meetings (referred to as 'creditor issues').[36] For this purpose, unless there are good reasons not to do so, the applicant is required to take all steps reasonably open to it to notify any person affected by the proposed scheme of the purpose which the scheme is designed to achieve, the meetings of creditors which the applicant considers are required, and their composition.[37] Usually, this is done by writing to the affected creditors in advance of the hearing of the application for an order summoning the meeting or meetings of creditors. The purpose of this approach is to enable creditor issues going to the constitution of meetings to be identified and resolved at an early stage in the process. The extent of the notice required to be given to creditors in advance of the convening hearing will depend on the circumstances including the complexity of the scheme and the degree of urgency.[38] Where the scheme is complex and notice to creditors is being sent through the clearing systems, more than 14 days' notice may well be required.

---

[31]   Practice Statement (Companies: Schemes of Arrangement) [2002] 1 WLR 1345 at para 2.

[32]   *Re Hawk Insurance Co Ltd* [2001] 2 BCLC 480, CA at para 30, where Chadwick LJ approved the test stated by Bowen LJ in *Sovereign Assurance Co Ltd v Dodd* [1892] 2 QB 573, CA for identifying a class as being whether the rights of the creditors within the class are not so dissimilar as to make it impossible for them to consult together with a view to their common interest. See also Practice Statement (Companies: Schemes of Arrangement) [2002] 1 WLR 1345 at para 2.

[33]   In considering the rights of creditors which are to be affected by the scheme, it is necessary to use the correct comparator. In the case of an insolvent company, where the scheme is proposed as an alternative to an insolvent liquidation, it is their rights as creditors in an insolvent liquidation of the company: *Re Hawk Insurance Co Ltd* (n 27 above). However, where a company is solvent and will continue in business, it is the creditors' rights against the company as a continuing entity which are the appropriate comparator: *Re British Aviation Insurance Co Ltd* [2006] 1 BCLC 665.

[34]   *Re UDL Argos Engineering & Heavy Industries Co Ltd* [2002] 1 HKC 172, HK CFA at para 27(3), per Lord Millett. Where a member of a class of creditors has further rights against the company which some or all of other members of the class do not have (for example, where a lender has holdings in more than one class of debt) then it is suggested that this is a matter which will not normally give rise to a need for separate meetings but rather will go to the question of whether the votes of the meeting of creditors properly reflect the interests of the class.

[35]   *Re SABMiller plc* [2016] EWHC 2153 (Ch).

[36]   Practice Statement (Companies: Schemes of Arrangement) [2002] 1 WLR 1345 at para 4.

[37]   Practice Statement (Companies: Schemes of Arrangement) [2002] 1 WLR 1345 at para 4.

[38]   *Re Indah Kiat International Finance Company BV* [2016] BCC 418 at para 29.

In addition, the modern approach is to consider issues going to jurisdiction at the convening **28.15** hearing (both as to the court's jurisdiction in relation to the company and over the scheme creditors). Accordingly, issues going to jurisdiction should also be drawn to creditors' attention in the letter sent to them prior to the convening hearing.[39]

In making an order for the summoning of a meeting or meetings to consider a compro- **28.16** mise or arrangement, the court will invariably give directions as to the means by which the relevant creditors or members (as the case may be) are to be notified of the meeting or meetings and the manner in which the meeting or meetings are to be conducted. In relation to the former, the court will usually give directions for notifying the creditors or members by post or through the relevant clearing system (in the case of securities held in immobilized or dematerialized form) and at the same time for the relevant voting and proxy forms to be sent to them. In addition, it is sometimes the case (eg where the company may not have complete records of all the relevant creditors or reliable means of contacting them) for the meeting or meetings to be directed to be advertised by means of advertisements inserted in relevant publications which are likely to come to the attention of the relevant creditors or members. In relation to the meetings themselves, the court will usually direct a nominated person to act as chairman of the meetings and to report on the results to the court.

Where a majority in number representing 75 per cent in value of the creditors (or class of **28.17** creditors) or members (or class of members) as the case may be, present and voting (either in person or by proxy) at the meeting or meetings summoned by the court, agree the compromise or arrangement, then the court may, on an application, sanction the compromise or arrangement. It should be noted that the court's jurisdiction to sanction a compromise or arrangement only arises where the compromise or arrangement has been approved by a double majority at each meeting: (1) a simple majority in number of those voting and (2) a 75 per cent majority by value of those voting.

As under s 896(2) for an order convening a meeting or meetings of creditors or members, **28.18** under s 899(2) an application for sanction of a compromise or arrangement may be made by (a) the company; (b) any creditor or member of the company; (c) if the company is being wound up, by the liquidator; or (d) if the company is in administration, by the administrator. Accordingly, a compromise or arrangement can be proposed by a creditor or member as well as by the company itself. However, in *Re Savoy Hotel Ltd*[40] the court held that the approval of the company to a compromise or arrangement was essential and, therefore, the court had no jurisdiction to sanction a proposed scheme absent such approval.

The application for sanction is made by way of a Part 8 Claim Form.[41] It should be sup- **28.19** ported by evidence consisting of (a) a witness statement (which will usually be made by a director) verifying the Claim Form, briefly explaining the reasons why it is submitted that the court should sanction the scheme, and drawing any other relevant matters to the court's attention; (b) a witness statement verifying compliance with the court's directions as to the service of the scheme documents and advertisement of the meetings; and (c) a report from the chairman on the meeting or meetings of creditors and/or members verified by a witness

---

[39] *Re Van Gansewinkel Group BV* [2015] Bus LR 1046.
[40] [1981] Ch 351.
[41] See Practice Direction to CPR Part 49: Applications under the Companies Acts and Related Legislation.

statement. The report should have attached to it the printed scheme of arrangement signed by the chairman at the meeting.

28.20   The application for sanction of the scheme will then be heard by the court. On an application to sanction a scheme, the court must be satisfied that the requirements of the statute (such as the requirement that the scheme has been approved by the requisite majorities) have been satisfied so that it has jurisdiction to sanction the scheme.

28.21   In relation to the exercise of its discretion to sanction a scheme, the court must be satisfied that the arrangement is such as an intelligent, honest man acting in respect of his interest might reasonably approve.[42] But, equally, the court will recognize that creditors (and members) are invariably the best judges of what is in their commercial interest:

> If the creditors are acting on sufficient information and with time to consider what they are about, and are acting honestly, they are, I apprehend, much better judges of what is to their commercial advantage than the Court can be.[43]

Aside from reasonableness, the court may refuse to sanction a scheme where the votes cast at the meeting or meetings do not fairly represent the relevant creditors (for example, because the turnout of those entitled to vote is so low) or because it considers the scheme to be inherently unfair. Other reasons why the court may refuse to sanction a scheme, related to the question of whether the meetings fairly represented the relevant creditors, are if there was some misconduct in the holding of the meetings or defect in the provision of information to the creditors (such as that contained in the explanatory statement).

28.22   There is also a general principle that where a power is exercisable by a majority of a class then that power must be exercised by the majority in accordance with what is in the interests of the class as a whole.[44] Accordingly, the court may decline to sanction a scheme if the relevant majority creditors voted in favour of the scheme in furtherance of their own individual interests rather than the interests of the class as a whole. However, it is important to note that the requirements of this principle will be satisfied provided that the majority honestly believes that the decision it is taking is in the best interests of the class as a whole. It is therefore in general terms a subjective rather than objective test which is applied, though the lack of reasonable grounds for making a decision may indicate a lack of good faith.[45] It follows that provided that any decision by the majority is taken in good faith as being in the best interests of the class as a whole and there are reasonable grounds to support that view, then the requirements of the principle should be satisfied.

The order and its effect

28.23   A compromise or arrangement sanctioned by the court is binding on all persons subject to the proposed compromise or arrangement, namely all creditors or the relevant class of creditors or all members or the relevant class of members as the case may be.[46] The

---

[42] *Re National Bank Ltd* [1966] 1 WLR 819 approving a passage from *Buckley on the Companies Acts*.

[43] *Re English, Scottish and Australian Chartered Bank* [1893] 3 Ch 385, 409, CA, per Lindley J.

[44] *British America Nickel Corp Ltd v M J O'Brien Ltd* [1927] AC 369, 371, HL; *Redwood Master Fund Ltd v TD Bank Europe Ltd* [2006] 1 BCLC 149; *Assenagon Asset Management SA v Irish Bank Resolution Corp Ltd* [2013] 1 All ER 495; *Azevedo v Imcopa Importacao Exportacao e Industria de Oleos Ltda* [2015] 1 QB 1, CA.

[45] See *Shuttleworth v Cox Bros & Co (Maidenhead) Ltd* [1927] 2 KB 9, CA; *Citco Banking Corp NV v Pusser's Ltd* [2007] Bus LR 960, PC.

[46] 2006 Act, s 899(3).

court's order takes effect once a copy has been delivered to the Registrar of Companies.[47] Accordingly, it is the Act which gives binding force to a scheme once it has been proposed, approved by the requisite majority of creditors or members, and sanctioned by the court.[48]

Under s 900, the court has certain powers to facilitate a reconstruction of a company or **28.24** amalgamation pursuant to a compromise or arrangement which has been sanctioned. For these purposes, the essence of a 'reconstruction' of a company is that the shareholders in the new company should be the same or substantially the same as those in the old company.[49] In other words, under a 'reconstruction' substantially the same shareholders will continue to carry on the business.[50] An 'amalgamation' is an amalgamation of two or more companies. The powers under s 900 arise where it is shown that the compromise or arrangement is proposed for the purposes of, or in connection with, a reconstruction or amalgamation and under the scheme the whole or part of the undertaking or the property of any company concerned in the scheme (the transferor company) is to be transferred to another company (the transferee company).[51]

Under s 900(6), every company in relation to which an order is made under s 900 must cause **28.25** a copy of the order to be delivered to the Registrar of Companies within seven days after its making. In the event of default of compliance with this requirement, the company and every officer of the company who is in default will commit an offence.[52]

Section 901 provides that if an order under either s 899 sanctioning a scheme or under s **28.26** 900 facilitating a reconstruction or amalgamation is made which amends the company's articles of association or any resolution or agreement affecting a company's constitution, then a copy of the order must also be delivered to the Registrar of Companies, accompanied by a copy of the articles of association or the relevant resolution or agreement as amended. Further, every copy of the company's articles of association issued after the order has been made must be accompanied by a copy of the order, unless the effect of the order has been incorporated into the articles by amendment. Again, a failure to comply with these requirements will result in the company, and every officer of the company who is in default, committing an offence.

---

[47] 2006 Act, s 899(4).

[48] *Kempe v Ambassador Insurance Co* [1998] 1 WLR 271, PC.

[49] *Re MyTravel Group plc* [2005] 2 BCLC 123.

[50] *Re South African Supply and Cold Storage Co* [1904] 2 Ch 268; *Brooklands Selangor Holdings Ltd v Inland Revenue Commissioners* [1970] 1 WLR 429; *Fallon v Fellows* [2001] STC 1409.

[51] To this end, the court has power to make provision for any or all of the following matters: (a) the transfer to the transferee company of the whole or any part of the undertaking and of the property or liabilities of any transferor company; (b) the allotting or appropriation by the transferee company of any shares, debentures, policies, or other like interests in that company which under the compromise or arrangement are to be allotted or appropriated by that company to or for any person; (c) the continuation by or against the transferee company of any legal proceedings pending by or against any transferor company; (d) the dissolution, without winding up, of any transferor company; (e) the provision to be made for any persons who, within such time and in such manner as the court directs, dissent from the compromise or arrangement; (f) such incidental, consequential, and supplemental matters as are necessary to secure that the reconstruction or amalgamation is fully and effectively carried out. In s 900 'property' includes property, rights, and powers of any description, but will only include property which the company has the right to deal with without obtaining the consent of a third party (*Nokes v Doncaster Amalgamated Collieries Ltd* [1940] AC 1014 (HL)) and 'liabilities' include duties (s 900(5)).

[52] 2006 Act, s 900(7).

Recognition abroad

28.27   One issue which arises following the successful sanction of a scheme concerns its recognition and enforceability in other countries. Where a scheme is sanctioned in the context of insolvency proceedings falling within the scope of the Insolvency Regulation, and such a scheme amounts to a composition between the company and its creditors, then it should automatically be recognized and enforceable in other EU Member States pursuant to Article 25 of the Insolvency Regulation which specifically provides for the recognition of 'compositions approved by the court'.

28.28   Where the company is not in insolvency proceedings, and where the scheme is in respect of liabilities which are governed by English law, it may be possible for the effect of the scheme to be recognized abroad simply by virtue of the general principle which forms part of many legal systems that the discharge or variation of a debt or other contractual obligation in accordance with its governing law will be recognized.[53]

28.29   The more difficult question is whether a scheme qualifies as a judgment for the purposes of recognition under the provisions of the recast Judgments Regulation.[54] There is some debate as to (a) whether the Judgments Regulation applies at all to schemes and (b) whether an order of the court sanctioning a scheme constitutes a 'judgment' for these purposes. As to (a), Article 1(2)(b) excludes from the Judgments Regulation altogether 'bankruptcy, proceedings relating to the winding-up of insolvent companies or other legal persons, judicial arrangements, compositions and analogous proceedings'. However, it seems unlikely that this was intended to exclude compositions outside insolvency proceedings, not least because the Jenard Report and the case law of the European Court of Justice suggest that the exception is limited to insolvency proceedings.[55] As to (b), 'judgment' is itself widely defined in the Judgments Regulation to mean 'any judgment given by a court or tribunal of a Member State, whatever the judgment may be called, including a decree, order, decision or writ of execution'.[56] This appears to be conceptually capable of encompassing an order of the court sanctioning a scheme.[57] Further, in the context of recognition of judgments under general principles of private international law, there is some support for the proposition that an order sanctioning a solvent scheme is a judgment for these purposes.[58] It is submitted that the correct analysis is that, whilst a scheme does not fall within the jurisdictional rules of Chapter II of the Judgments Regulation, as it does not involve any defendants being 'sued',

---

[53]   See *Re Vietnam Shipbuilding Industry Group Ltd* [2014] 1 BCLC 400 at para 8, and *Re Rodenstock GmbH* [2011] Bus LR 1245 paras 76–7.

[54]   As a regulation, the Judgments Regulation has direct effect in all Member States and, unlike a directive, is not required to be implemented by domestic national legislation. Chapter III of the Judgments Regulation deals with the recognition and enforcement of judgments.

[55]   See *Gourdain v Nadler* [1979] ECR 733, and see *Re Rodenstock GmbH* [2011] Bus LR 1245.

[56]   Article 2(a).

[57]   See also Art 25 of the Insolvency Regulation pursuant to which 'compositions approved by [the] court' in the context of insolvency proceedings are to be recognized in other Member States. Pursuant to Art 25.1 of the Insolvency Regulation, the mechanism for the enforcement of such compositions is that contained in the relevant provisions of the Judgments Regulation (as the successor to the Brussels Convention). It appears to follow from this that, at least conceptually, a sanctioned scheme of arrangement is capable of being recognized and enforced under the Judgments Regulation machinery.

[58]   *Re Cavell Insurance Company Ltd*, 23 May 2006, Court of Appeal for Ontario on appeal from the Ontario Superior Court of Justice (Farwell J) upholding the decision of the lower court recognizing an order of the English court convening a meeting of creditors for the purposes of considering a scheme proposed pursuant to 1985 Act, s 425.

it nevertheless falls within the rules governing recognition and enforcement of judgments in Chapter III.

In the United States, recognition of both solvent and insolvent schemes has historically been **28.30** possible under s 304 of the United States Bankruptcy Code. Following such recognition, the United States courts may then grant relief in order to give effect to the scheme in the United States.[59] In October 2005, s 304 was replaced by a new Chapter 15 in the Bankruptcy Code, which implements the UNCITRAL Model Law on Cross-Border Insolvency. Under Chapter 15 the United States courts have continued to recognize both solvent and insolvent schemes of arrangement as 'foreign proceedings' and to grant relief in support of them.[60]

(3) Directors' particular responsibilities

In view of the complexity, directors should rely on advice from lawyers in relation to the **28.31** preparation of a scheme of arrangement and it is to be expected that such lawyers will drive the process. Directors' particular functions arise in relation to the recommendation of the scheme, the preparation of the explanatory statement, the preparation of the evidence in support of the applications for an order convening meetings and for sanction, the chairing and conduct of the meeting or meetings, and certain specific statutory duties.

Recommendation of scheme

The duties of a director include promoting the success of the company and exercising inde- **28.32** pendent judgment.[61] Accordingly, a director faced with a proposed scheme of arrangement must be satisfied, in exercise of his independent judgment, that the result to be achieved by the scheme is in the company's best interests and will promote its success. This may be because the scheme reduces the company's indebtedness and puts in place a more efficient capital structure or because the scheme facilitates a takeover which the directors consider to be in shareholders' best interests.

Aside from being satisfied as to the desirability of the general result to be achieved by a pro- **28.33** posed scheme, a director should also be satisfied that the scheme is a proper one to put to the company's creditors or members (as the case may be) and to seek orders from the court for the convening of a meeting or meetings of creditors or members and, ultimately, in respect of which to seek the sanction of the court. This involves being satisfied that the scheme itself is not inherently unfair to any parties and is such that an intelligent, honest man acting in respect of his interest might reasonably approve it.

Classes

A director of a company proposing a scheme should also be satisfied, having taken appro- **28.34** priate advice, that the classes of creditors or members in respect of which the company is proposing to convene meetings to consider the proposed scheme are properly formulated. As noted in paragraph 28.13 above, it is the responsibility of the applicant company to determine whether more than one meeting of creditors or members is required to consider

---

[59] For the old position under s 304, see *Re Board of Directors of Hopewell International Insurance Ltd* 275 BR 699 (SDNY 2002), where the US District Court affirmed the decision of Tina L Brozman, Chief Judge in the Bankruptcy Court at 238 BR 25 (Bkrtcy SDNY 1999); *Re Kingscroft Insurance Co* 138 BR 121 (Bankr SD Fla 1992).

[60] See eg *Re Magyar Telecom BV* [2015] 1 BCLC 418.

[61] 2006 Act, ss 172 and 173.

the scheme. The test to be applied is whether the rights of the creditors or members are not so dissimilar as to make it impossible for them to consult together with a view to their common interest. Inevitably, directors will need to take appropriate legal advice on this issue.

28.35 A failure to ensure that the correct number of meetings is held may result in the court refusing to sanction the scheme even if approved by the requisite majority of creditors or members. This may result in prejudice to the company in the form of wasted costs and time as well as prejudice in the fact that the scheme will not take effect. However, it does not follow that directors should always err on the side of caution and opt for more rather than fewer meetings of creditors (or members). Convening too many meetings of creditors may lead to as much prejudice as convening too few meetings because, since a scheme has to be approved by the requisite majority in each meeting, it gives a group of creditors a power to veto the scheme which they would not otherwise have. It is therefore important that the test for deciding how many meetings to convene is always applied in a neutral and balanced way.

Explanatory statement

28.36 Under s 897, where a meeting has been summoned by the court, every notice summoning the meeting that is sent to a creditor or member must be accompanied by a statement explaining the effect of the compromise or arrangement. Likewise, any notice summoning a meeting which is given by advertisement must either include such a statement or (as is more likely to be the case in practice) state where and how the creditors or members entitled to attend the meeting can obtain copies of the statement.[62]

28.37 In addition to explaining the effect of the compromise or arrangement, the statement must explain any material interests of the directors of the company (whether as directors, members, creditors, or otherwise) and the effect on those interests of the compromise or arrangement in so far as it is different from the effect on the like interests of other persons.[63] It should be noted that where there is a change of the material interests of a director as set out in the explanatory statement which is not disclosed, the court may not sanction the scheme unless satisfied that no reasonable shareholder would alter his decision as to how to act on the scheme if the changes had been disclosed.[64] In relation to the rights of the debenture holders of the company, where the compromise or arrangement affects such rights the explanatory statement must explain the effect on the interests of the trustees of any deed for securing the issue of the debentures of the compromise or arrangement in so far as it is different from the effect on the like interests of other persons.[65] If a company makes a default in complying with these requirements in relation to explanatory statements, then an offence is committed both by the company and by an officer of the company who is in default.[66] However, a person will not be guilty of an offence if he can show that the default was due to the refusal of a director or trustee for debenture holders to supply the necessary particulars of his interests.[67]

---

[62] Where a notice given by advertisement states that copies of an explanatory statement can be obtained, then any creditor or member entitled to attend the meeting is entitled to obtain a copy from the company free of charge by making application in the manner indicated by the notice (s 897(4)).

[63] 2006 Act, s 897(2). See *Coltness Iron Co Ltd, Petitioners* [1951] SC 476; *City Property Investment Trust Corp Ltd, Petitioners* [1951] SC 570; *Second Scottish Investment Trust Co Ltd* [1962] SLT 392; *Re MB Group plc* [1989] BCLC 672; *Re Heron International NV* [1994] 1 BCLC 667.

[64] *Re Minster Assets plc* [1985] BCLC 200.

[65] 2006 Act, s 897(3).

[66] An officer of the company for these purposes includes a liquidator or administrator and a trustee of a deed for securing the issue of debentures of the company (s 897(6)).

[67] 2006 Act, s 897(7).

Under s 898, it is the duty of any director of the company to give notice to the company **28.38** of such matters relating to himself as may be necessary for the purposes of the explanatory statement required by s 897. A director who makes default in complying with this section commits an offence and is liable on summary conviction to a fine not exceeding level 3 on the standard scale.[68]

As a basic rule the explanatory statement must contain sufficient information to enable the **28.39** recipient properly to make a reasonable judgment as to whether the proposed scheme is in his commercial interest or not.[69] One test of the adequacy of the information in the explanatory statement is whether any missing information would cause a creditor to change his view as to whether to consent to the scheme. In this context, it has been said that an explanation of the effects of the scheme requires an explanation of how the scheme will affect a bondholder or creditor commercially and that he needs to be given such up-to-date information as can reasonably be provided on what he can expect if the group were to go into liquidation and as to what he can expect under the scheme.[70] In this respect, where a scheme is put forward as an alternative to formal insolvency proceedings, both the explanatory statement and the evidence subsequently placed before the court should provide details as to the different predicted outcomes and as to the basis for those predictions.[71] Further, the lack of such information in the explanatory statement may be a ground for the court refusing to sanction the scheme.[72] The explanatory statement will usually conclude with a recommendation by the directors that the creditors or members, or a class of them, with whom the compromise or arrangement is proposed to be made agree to it by voting in favour of the scheme at the meeting(s) convened for the purpose.[73]

One issue in respect of which directors need to exercise particular care relates to side agree- **28.40** ments entered into between the company, or a third party acting on the company's behalf, and one or more of its creditors. Any secret deal made in connection with a compromise or arrangement pursuant to which a creditor is to receive more than the other creditors in return for supporting (or not opposing) the compromise or arrangement is illegal and void and the existence of such a deal will render the compromise or arrangement voidable at the instance of an aggrieved creditor.[74] The principles underlying this rule are that creditors of a company must be treated equally[75] and that there should be complete good faith between the debtor and his creditors in connection with a proposed compromise or arrangement.[76] It follows that directors should be careful to ensure that a company, or someone acting for the company, does not enter into such undisclosed agreements which may have the effect of voiding the proposed compromise or arrangement. However, there is nothing inherently

---

[68] 2006 Act, s 898(2), (3).

[69] *Re Indah Kiat International Finance Company BV* [2016] BCC 418 at para 41.

[70] *Re Heron International NV* [1994] 1 BCLC 667.

[71] *Re Van Gansewinkel Groep BV* [2015] Bus LR 1046 at para 24; *Re Indah Kiat International Finance Company BV* [2016] BCC 418 at para 71.

[72] *Re Heron International NV* (n 70 above).

[73] This is not a requirement under the Act and the failure to include a recommendation may not lead to the court refusing to sanction the scheme: see *Re TDG plc* [2009] 1 BCLC 445. However, it is a requirement under the Listing Rules in the case of listed companies.

[74] *Cadbury Schweppes plc v Somji* [2001] 1 BCLC 498, CA; *National Westminster Bank plc v Kapoor* [2012] 1 All ER 1201, CA.

[75] *McKewan v Sanderson* (1875) LR 20 Eq 65.

[76] *Dauglish v Tennent* (1866) LR 2 QB 49.

objectionable about a company promoting a scheme from reaching agreement with some of its creditors under which they undertake to vote in favour of the scheme.[77]

Chairing the meeting

28.41 Typically, the person nominated by the court to act as the chairman of the convened meetings of creditors or members will be a director of the company. The duties of the chairman are to hold the meeting or meetings in accordance with the directions given by the court. The chairman must ensure that the meeting is held at the correct time and place and that the votes (whether in person or by proxy) are properly admitted and counted. The latter is particularly important since the requirement that a scheme be approved by the relevant majorities goes directly to the court's jurisdiction to sanction the scheme[78] and it is therefore necessary for the court to be satisfied that the majorities have been properly constituted.[79]

28.42 The chairman should address the meeting and deal with any questions raised by the members or creditors present. The chairman should then put a resolution for approval of the proposed scheme of arrangement to the meeting. Voting at the meeting on the resolution should take place by way of poll and not by way of show of hands since the value of the claims voted is relevant to the calculation of the majorities. The chairman should ensure that all proxies received are in order.[80] If the resolution for approval of the scheme is passed, the chairman should sign a copy of the printed scheme of arrangement which was approved and adopted by the meeting.

Evidence

28.43 Finally, as set out above, the directors of a company may have an important role to play in assisting with the preparation of the applications which have to be made to the court in connection with a scheme. Typically, it will be necessary for a director to provide evidence in the form of a witness statement explaining the relevant background, the proposed scheme, and why the directors consider the scheme to be in the company's best interests. Such evidence must comply with the provisions of the CPR (ie identify the source of any knowledge and belief) and should not come from a recent appointee with no personal knowledge.[81] Where a director acts as chairman of the meetings, it will also be necessary for him to prepare a report on the meetings to the court. In practice, such evidence will be prepared in the first instance by the company's lawyers. However, it goes without saying that the relevant director must ensure that all such evidence is completely truthful and gives a full and frank account of the matters which are relevant to the court's consideration of the scheme.

---

[77] *Re British Aviation Insurance Co Ltd* [2006] 1 BCLC 665 at para 103.

[78] *Re Dorman Long & Co Ltd* [1934] Ch 635; *Re Savoy Hotel Ltd* [1981] Ch 351.

[79] In many cases the establishment of creditors' claims, which often arise in connection with financing provided to the relevant company, is straightforward. In other cases, the matter can be more complicated and many insurance schemes, in particular, contain provisions providing for the adjudication and determination of creditors' claims at the voting stage, since these claims will often be future or contingent. The provisions in the schemes sanctioned in *Hawk Insurance Co* and in *Re Pan Atlantic Insurance Co Ltd* [2003] 2 BCLC 678 are both examples of this. In the latter case, the court held that such adjudication mechanisms are not inconsistent with the basic right to a court hearing.

[80] It should be noted that directors who receive proxies for and against the proposed scheme have no option whether or not they will use them but are bound to use them to vote: *Re Dorman Long & Co Ltd* [1934] Ch 635.

[81] *Re Indah Kiat International Finance Company BV* [2016] BCC 418 at para 26.

C. Mergers and Divisions of Public Companies

(1) Scope of the provisions

Where the scheme of arrangement under s 899 concerns a private company which proposes **28.44** to effect a merger or division (within the meaning of Chapter 2 of Part 27), it can use the court's powers under s 900 to transfer to the transferee company the undertaking, property, and liabilities of the transferor company without the need for further formality. However, where the scheme involves a merger or division and is in relation to a public company the requirements of the Companies Act, Part 27 will need to be met.

Part 27 derives from the Third and Sixth EC Company Law Directives and imposes certain **28.45** specific requirements in the case of mergers and divisions of public companies in addition to those applicable to schemes generally. The aim of these directives was to harmonize national law in relation to mergers and divisions and, in relation to the former, to introduce the concept in those national law systems which did not already recognize it. Although the directives were implemented by the previous Companies Act, the provisions contained in Part 27 substantially expand on those contained in the old Act.[82]

By s 902(1) Part 27 applies where a compromise or arrangement is proposed between a **28.46** public company and its creditors (or any class of them) or its members (or any class of them) for the purposes of, or in connection with, a scheme for the reconstruction of any company or companies or the amalgamation of any two or more companies, the scheme involves a merger or division, and the consideration for the transfer (or each of the transfers) envisaged is to be shares in the transferee company (or one or more of the transferee companies) receivable by members of the transferor company (or transferor companies), without any cash payment to members.

In relation to mergers, the provisions apply to two types of merger: **28.47**

(1) *merger by absorption*: where the undertaking, property, and liabilities of the relevant public company are to be transferred to another existing public company; and
(2) *merger by formation of a new company*: where the undertaking, property, and liabilities of two or more public companies, including the relevant company, are to be transferred to a new company, whether or not a public company.[83]

A division takes place where the undertaking, property, and liabilities of the relevant public **28.48** company are to be divided among and transferred to two or more companies each of which is either an existing public company or a new company, whether or not a public company.[84] In other words, it covers the splitting up of a company and the transfer of its assets to one or more acquiring companies, whether previously existing or newly formed.

The general scheme of the rules relating to mergers and divisions of public companies con- **28.49** tained in Part 27 is that there must be compliance with both the relevant requirements of

---

[82] These provisions were inserted in the 1985 Act as s 427A and Sch 15A by the Companies (Mergers and Divisions) Regulations 1987 (SI 1987/1991) to give effect to the Third EC Directive on Mergers (Dir 78/855/EEC of 25 July 1978) and the Sixth EC Directive on Divisions (Dir 82/891/EEC of 17 December 1982).
[83] 2006 Act, s 904(1).
[84] 2006 Act, s 919(1).

Part 26, containing the rules relating to arrangements and reconstructions generally, and with the specific rules relating to mergers and divisions (as the case may be) contained in Part 27. However, certain of the rules contained in both Part 26 and in Part 27 in relation to mergers and divisions are modified or excluded in certain circumstances.

(2) Summary of the procedure for mergers

28.50 By s 907(1) the central requirement of the procedure for mergers is that, except in certain limited cases relating to mergers by absorption,[85] the scheme by which the merger is to be effected must be approved by a majority in number representing 75 per cent in value of each class of members of each of the merging companies, present and voting either in person or by proxy at a meeting. To this end, s 911(1) and (3) requires that various documents are produced and made available for inspection by the members of each of the merging companies: (a) a draft of the proposed terms for the merger; (b) an explanatory report produced by the directors; (c) an expert's report drawn up on behalf of each of the merging companies;[86] (d) the company's annual accounts and reports for the last three financial years ending on or before the first meeting of the members, or any class of members, summoned for the purposes of approving the scheme; and (e) any supplementary accounting statement required by s 910.

28.51 The expert's report which is required is a written report on the draft terms addressed to the members of the relevant company, though the court may on the application of all of the relevant merging companies approve the appointment of a joint expert to produce a single report on behalf of all of the companies.[87] The expert must be a person who is eligible for appointment as a statutory auditor[88] and must meet the independence criterion.[89] Under the requirements of the Act, his report must: (a) indicate the method or methods used to arrive at the share exchange ratio; (b) give an opinion as to whether the method or methods used are reasonable in all the circumstances of the case, indicate the values arrived at using each such method, and (if there is more than one method) give an opinion on the relative importance attributed to such methods in arriving at the value decided on; (c) describe any special valuation difficulties that have arisen; (d) state whether in the expert's opinion the share exchange ratio is reasonable; and (e) in the case of a valuation made by a person other than himself, state that it appeared to him reasonable to arrange for it to be so made or to accept a valuation so made.[90]

28.52 In addition to the expert's report, in certain cases a supplementary accounting statement may be required. The requirement to provide such a statement arises where the last annual accounts of any of the merging companies relate to a financial year ending more than seven months before the first meeting of the company summoned for the purposes of approving

---

[85] See para 28.53 below.

[86] Directive 2007/63/EC amended the Third and Sixth Directives to dispense with this requirement if all shareholders so agree. This directive was implemented by the Companies (Mergers and Divisions of Public Companies) (Amendment) Regulations 2008 (SI 2008/690) which inserted s 918A into the 2006 Act. Under s 918A if all members holding shares in, and all persons holding other securities of, the companies involved in the merger (being shares or securities that carry a right to vote in general meetings of the company in question) so agree, the requirement of s 909 (expert's report) does not apply.

[87] 2006 Act, s 909(2), (3).

[88] 2006 Act, s 1212.

[89] 2006 Act, s 909(4). In relation to the independence criterion, see ss 936 and 937.

[90] 2006 Act, s 909(5). The obligations of the expert in this regard are further set out in s 935.

the scheme.[91] The statement must include, amongst other things, a balance sheet for the company as at a date not more than three months before the draft terms for the merger were adopted.[92]

The expert's report, and the directors' explanatory report, are not required in the case of a **28.53** merger by absorption where all of the relevant securities[93] of the transferor company (or, if there is more than one transferor company, of each of them) are held by or on behalf of the transferor company.[94] In addition, in this case, the explanatory statement normally required by s 897 of the Act is not necessary.[95]

The cases where it is not necessary for the scheme to be approved by the requisite majorities of **28.54** members are set out in ss 916–18. Section 916 applies in the case of a merger by absorption where 90 per cent or more of the relevant securities of the transferor company or companies are held by or on behalf of the transferee company. In these circumstances, it is not necessary for the scheme to be approved by a meeting of members of the transferee company provided that the court is satisfied that: (a) publication of notice of receipt of the draft terms by the Registrar took place in respect of the transferee company at least one month before the date of the first meeting of members, or any class of members, of the transferor company summoned for the purpose of agreeing to the scheme; (b) the members of the transferee company were able during the period beginning one month before, and ending on, that date to inspect at the registered office of the transferee company copies of the draft terms, the requisite annual accounts and reports, and any supplementary accounting statement required by s 910 and to obtain copies of those documents or any part of them on request free of charge; and (c) one or more members of the transferee company, who together held not less than 5 per cent of the paid-up capital of the company which carried the right to vote at general meetings of the company (excluding any shares in the company held as treasury shares) would have been able, during that period, to require a meeting of each class of members to be called for the purpose of deciding whether or not to agree to the scheme, and no such requirement was made.

Section 916 does not apply where all of the relevant securities of the transferor company or **28.55** companies are held by the transferee, namely where the transferor is a wholly-owned subsidiary of the transferee. In this case, s 917 applies and provides that there is no need for the scheme to be approved by either the members of the transferor company or companies or the members of the transferee company providing that the court is satisfied as to the requirements set out in the preceding paragraph.

Finally, s 918 applies in relation to any merger by absorption, including cases where the trans- **28.56** feree company does not hold any shares in the transferor company or companies. Again, in such a case it is not necessary for the scheme to be approved by the members of the transferee company provided that the court is satisfied that the requirements set out in paragraph 28.52 above have been complied with.

---

[91] 2006 Act, s 910(1).
[92] 2006 Act, s 910(2)(a).
[93] ie shares or other securities carrying the right to vote at general meetings of the company (2006 Act, s 915(6)).
[94] 2006 Act, ss 908(3), 909(7), 915(4).
[95] 2006 Act, s 915(3).

28.57 On the sanction of a scheme involving a merger or division, the court must fix a date on which the transfer or transfers to the transferee company or companies of the undertaking, property, and liabilities of the transferor company is or are to take effect.[96] This may be done either in the order sanctioning the scheme itself or in any order made under s 900 in exercise of the court's powers to facilitate a reconstruction or amalgamation.

(3) Directors' particular functions and duties in relation to mergers

28.58 The first functions and duties of the directors of a company which is proposed to be the subject of a merger are to ensure that a draft of the proposed terms of the scheme is first drawn up and is then adopted by the directors.[97] The Act specifies the matters which must be included in the draft terms, namely: (a) the name and address of registered office of the transferor and transferee companies, and whether they are companies limited by shares or companies limited by guarantee and having a share capital; (b) the number of shares in the transferee company to be allotted to members of a transferor company for a given number of their shares (the 'share exchange ratio') and the amount of any cash payment; (c) the terms relating to the allotment of shares in the transferee company; (d) the date from which the holding of shares in the transferee company will entitle the holders to participate in profits, and any special conditions affecting that entitlement; (e) the date from which the transactions of a transferor company are to be treated for accounting purposes as being those of the transferee company; (f) any rights or restrictions attaching to shares or other securities in the transferee company to be allotted under the scheme to the holders of shares or other securities in a transferor company to which any special rights or restrictions attach, or the measures proposed concerning them; and (g) any amount of benefit paid or given or intended to be paid or given to any of the experts referred to in s 909 or to any director of a merging company and the consideration for the payment of benefit. The matters set out in points (b), (c), and (d) are not required to be stated in the case of a merger by absorption where all of the relevant securities of the transferor company (or, if there is more than one transferor company, of each of them) are held by or on behalf of the transferor company.[98]

28.59 By s 906(1) the directors are under a duty to ensure a copy of the draft of the proposed terms is delivered to the Registrar of Companies.[99]

28.60 In addition to ensuring that the draft terms are prepared and adopted, the directors of a merging company must draw up and adopt an explanatory report.[100] The report must contain the explanatory statement which is required under Part 26 in relation to an arrangement or reconstruction generally and should set out the legal and economic grounds for the draft terms and, in particular, for the share exchange ratio and specify any special valuation difficulties. However, again, this requirement does not apply in the case of a merger by absorption where all of the relevant securities of the transferor company or companies are held by or on behalf of the transferor company. In addition to the production of the explanatory report, as noted above, the directors may also be required to prepare a supplementary accounting statement to bring the last set of accounts up to date.

---

[96] 2006 Act, s 939(1).
[97] 2006 Act, s 905(1).
[98] 2006 Act, ss 905(3) and 915(1)–(2).
[99] 2006 Act, s 906(1).
[100] 2006 Act, s 908(1).

(4) Summary of the procedure for divisions

The procedure for divisions essentially follows that for mergers, although the Act does impose **28.61** some further disclosure obligations in the case of divisions in order to provide further protection for shareholders and creditors.

As with mergers, the essential feature of the procedure for divisions is that, except in certain **28.62** limited cases, the scheme by which the division is to be effected must be approved by a majority in number representing 75 per cent in value of each class of members of each of the merging companies, present and voting either in person or by proxy at a meeting.[101] Again, this central requirement is given effect to by obligations to produce and make available for inspection by the relevant members relevant documents in order that the members may evaluate the division. These documents are the draft terms (which must also be delivered to the Registrar of Companies), the directors' explanatory report, an expert's report, the company's annual accounts and reports for the last three financial years, and any supplementary accounting statement required.[102]

The members of the relevant companies may, however, agree that the explanatory report, the **28.63** expert's report, and the supplementary statement need not be produced.[103] In addition, the court has a power to disapply the requirements to deliver the draft terms to the Registrar of Companies under s 921 and to permit inspection of documents in accordance with s 926.[104] In order to exercise this power, the court must be satisfied that three conditions are fulfilled: (a) the members of the company must have received, or been able to obtain free of charge, copies of the documents listed in s 926 in time to examine them prior to the relevant meeting of members;[105] (b) the creditors of that company must have received or been able to obtain free of charge copies of the draft terms in time to examine them before the relevant meeting; and (c) no prejudice would be caused to the members or creditors of the transferor company or any transferee company by making the order in question.

The requirements of the report to be provided by the expert on behalf of each of the relevant **28.64** companies, or by a joint expert on behalf of all of the companies, are the same as those which apply in the case of a merger.[106] The report must also cover the same matters as are required in the case of a merger.[107]

In certain cases, the requirement for meetings of members may be dispensed with. Pursuant **28.65** to s 931, where all the shares of the transferor company carrying the right to vote at general meetings are held by or on behalf of one or more existing transferee companies, then it is not necessary for the scheme to be approved by the members of the transferor company if the court is satisfied that the following requirements have been satisfied: (a) publication of

---

[101] 2006 Act, s 922(1).

[102] 2006 Act, s 926(1), (3). As with mergers, the requirement to provide a supplementary statement arises where the last annual accounts of any of the companies involved in the division relate to a financial year ending more than seven months before the first meeting of the company summoned for the purposes of approving the scheme (s 925(1)). The statement has to include, amongst other things, a balance sheet for the company as at a date not more than three months before the draft terms for the merger were adopted (s 925(2)(a)).

[103] 2006 Act, s 933.

[104] 2006 Act, s 934(1).

[105] Or, in the case of an existing transferee company where no meeting is held pursuant to 2006 Act, s 932, in time to require a meeting to be held.

[106] 2006 Act, s 924(1)–(4).

[107] 2006 Act, s 924(5).

notice of receipt of the draft terms by the Registrar took place in respect of all the companies involved in the division at least one month before the date of the court's order; (b) the members of every company involved in the division were able during the period beginning one month before, and ending on, that date to inspect at the registered office of their company copies of the draft terms, the directors' explanatory report, the expert's report, the requisite annual accounts and reports, and any supplementary accounting statement and to obtain copies of those documents or any part of them on request free of charge; and (c) one or more members of the transferor company, who together held not less than 5 per cent of the paid-up capital of the company which carried the right to vote at general meetings of the company (excluding any shares in the company held as treasury shares), would have been able, during that period, to require a meeting of each class of members to be called for the purpose of deciding whether or not to agree to the scheme, and no such requirement was made.

28.66   Pursuant to s 932, it is not necessary for a scheme to be approved by members of a transferee company if the court is satisfied that the same conditions as set out in the preceding paragraph are satisfied in relation to that company. In addition, the court has the power to disapply the first and second conditions in the circumstances set out in paragraph 28.65 above.[108]

(5) Directors' particular functions and duties in relation to divisions

28.67   As with mergers, the directors of a company which is proposed to be the subject of a division are required to adopt a draft of the proposed terms of the scheme.[109] The draft must contain the same matters as are required in the case of a merger (see paragraph 28.58 above) but must also: (a) provide particulars of the property and liabilities to be transferred (to the extent that these are known to the transferor company) and their allocation among the transferee companies; (b) make provision for the allocation among and transfer to the transferee companies of any other property and liabilities that the transferor company has acquired or may subsequently acquire; and (c) specify the allocation to members of the transferor company of shares in the transferee companies and the criteria upon which that allocation is based.

28.68   By s 921(1) the directors are further under a duty to ensure a copy of the draft of the proposed terms is delivered to the Registrar of Companies. This obligation may, however, be disapplied by order of the court under s 934.

28.69   The directors of a company subject to a division must draw up and adopt an explanatory report.[110] The report must contain the explanatory statement which is required under Part 26 in relation to an arrangement or reconstruction generally and should set out the legal and economic grounds for the draft terms and, in particular, for the share exchange ratio and for the criteria on which the allocation to the members of the transferor company or shares in the transferee companies was based and specify any special valuation difficulties. It must also state whether a report has been made to any transferee company under s 593 of the Act and, if so, whether that report has been delivered to the Registrar of Companies.[111] This

---

[108] 2006 Act, s 932(5).
[109] 2006 Act, s 920(1).
[110] 2006 Act, s 923(1).
[111] 2006 Act, s 923(3).

requirement to produce an explanatory report does not, however, apply where all members holding shares (or other securities giving a right to vote in the companies involved in the division) so agree.[112]

In addition to the production of the explanatory report, as noted above, the directors may **28.70** also be required to prepare a supplementary accounting statement to bring the last set of accounts up to date. In the case of a division, the directors of the transferor company must also report to every meeting of the members (or class of members) of the transferor company summoned for the purpose of agreeing to the scheme as well as to the directors of each transferee company on any material changes in the property and liabilities of the transferor following the adoption of the draft terms.[113] The directors of the transferee companies must in turn report on these matters to their own members.[114] Again, both the supplementary accounting statement and the report on material changes can be dispensed with where the relevant members so agree.

D. Takeovers

(1) Scope of the provisions

The provisions of the Companies Act relating to takeovers are contained in Part 28, ss 942– **28.71** 91.[115] Amongst other things, these provisions implement the EC Directive on Takeovers (the Takeovers Directive).[116] The Takeovers Directive lays down minimum requirements concerning the regulation of takeovers of companies whose shares are traded on a regulated market.

The Act also places the existing Panel on Takeovers and Mergers (the Panel) on a statutory foot- **28.72** ing and confers on it various functions set out in Part 28. The Panel was established in 1968 and its main functions are to issue and administer the City Code on Takeovers and Mergers (the Takeover Code or the Code[117]) and to supervise and regulate takeovers and other matters to which the Takeover Code applies. The Code, however, had no statutory force prior to the Act coming into force[118] and one of the main functions of the provisions of the Act dealing with takeovers is now to place the Panel and the Code within a statutory framework. The intention, however, has been to preserve the existing independence and authority of the Panel.[119]

The Panel's existing function is to ensure that shareholders are treated fairly and are not denied an **28.73** opportunity to decide on the merits of a takeover and that shareholders of the same class are afforded

---

[112] 2006 Act, s 933(1).

[113] 2006 Act, s 927(1).

[114] 2006 Act, s 927(2).

[115] Chapters 1 and 2 implement provisions in the Takeovers Directive (Directive 2004/25/EC). Chapter 3 restates with minor amendments provisions contained in 1985 Act, ss 428–30F. Section 988 includes provisions restating provisions in 1985 Act, s 204.

[116] Directive 2004/25/EC. The directive was initially implemented by regulations in May 2006 and at that time only applied to companies whose shares were admitted to trading on a regulated market. In effect, therefore, the 2006 Act extends the scope of UK legislation implementing the directive to cover certain companies to which the Takeover Code applies.

[117] 10th edn, 19 September 2011.

[118] See Sir John Donaldson MR in *R v Panel on Takeovers and Mergers, ex p Datafin Ltd* [1987] QB 815: the Panel performs its functions 'without visible means of legal support'. See also *Re Expro International Group plc* [2010] 2 BCLC 514, para 11.

[119] White Paper, 3.6.

equivalent treatment by an offeror. Likewise, under the Act the central function of the Panel is to regulate takeover bids and merger transactions and other transactions that have or may have an effect on the ownership or control of companies. To this end, the Panel has been given the statutory power to make rules to assist it in the discharge of its functions, including to cover the matters dealt with by the existing Takeover Code, which rules the court is able to enforce on the application of the Panel.[120] The Panel is empowered to give rulings on the interpretation, application, or effect of the rules made by it.[121] The rules which have been made by the Panel are set out in the latest version of the Takeover Code.[122] The Panel is also given other specific statutory powers including the power to require the provision of documents and information.[123]

28.74 The power to require the provision of documents and information extends to any documents and information reasonably required in the exercise by the Panel of its functions.[124] The Panel is entitled to serve a notice on a person setting out the documents or information which it requires and such person is then obliged to comply with the notice at the place specified and within the period of time specified in the notice, provided that this is a reasonable period. Where information is provided to the Panel which relates to the private affairs of an individual or to any particular business, then the general rule is that such information cannot be disclosed without the consent of the individual or the person carrying on the business.[125] However, this rule is subject to a large number of exceptions set out in Schedule 2 to the Act and does not apply to any disclosure that is made for the purpose of facilitating the carrying out by the Panel of any of its functions.[126]

28.75 Under the provisions of s 951(1)–(3) the rules made by the Panel must make provision for the decisions of the Panel to be subject to review by a committee of the Panel (the Hearings Committee) and for there to be a right of appeal against a decision of the Hearings Committee to an independent tribunal called the Takeover Appeal Board. It seems likely that this will preserve the current position where the courts have held that the Panel is subject to judicial review but have declined to interfere with decisions made by the Panel during the course of takeovers.[127]

28.76 The Panel is able to be a party to legal proceedings in its own name[128] and is exempted from liability in damages for anything done or omitted to be done in or in connection with the discharge or purported discharge of its functions, except where such act or omission was in bad faith or where damages would be due under the Human Rights Act 1998, s 6(1).[129]

28.77 In addition to requiring bodies (such as the Panel) which regulate takeovers to be placed on a statutory footing, the Takeovers Directive contains substantive provisions which seek to remove impediments to takeovers, in other words, steps that may be taken by companies both prior to and during a takeover bid which have the aim of frustrating a bid. These types

---

[120] 2006 Act, s 955.

[121] 2006 Act, s 945.

[122] Together with the rules of procedure of the Hearings Committee.

[123] In relation to administrative matters, the Panel is given the power to collect fees and charges for the purpose of meeting its expenses (s 957(1)) and the Secretary of State is empowered to make regulations allowing for a levy to be payable to the Panel (s 958).

[124] 2006 Act, s 947(3).

[125] 2006 Act, s 948(2).

[126] 2006 Act, s 948(3).

[127] *R v Panel on Takeovers and Mergers, ex p Datafin Ltd* [1987] QB 815.

[128] 2006 Act, s 960.

[129] 2006 Act, s 961. As to the exemption from liability for acts done in bad faith, see *Three Rivers District Council v The Governor and Company of the Bank of England* [2003] 2 AC 1, HL.

of defences broadly consist of 'pre-bid defences' and 'post-bid defences'. Pre-bid defences include differential share structures under which minority shareholders exercise disproportionate voting rights; limitations on share ownership and restrictions on transfer of shares set out in the company's articles or in contractual agreements. Post-bid defences include matters such as seeking to sell key assets of the company without shareholder approval. In relation to the former, Part 28, Chapter 2 of the Act sets out rules restricting the use of pre-bid defences. However, these rules are not compulsory but only apply where a company, which has voting shares admitted to trading on a regulated market, has opted in by way of special resolution.[130]

Finally, Part 28, Chapter 3, ss 974–91 contains provisions dealing with the problems of, and for, **28.78** residual minority shareholders following a successful takeover bid by providing for 'squeeze-out' and 'sell-out' rights. Squeeze-out rights enable a successful bidder to purchase compulsorily the shares of remaining minority shareholders who have not accepted the bid. Sell-out rights enable minority shareholders to require the majority shareholder to purchase their shares.

(2) Directors' particular functions and duties

The principal responsibility of directors in relation to a takeover bid is to ensure that a **28.79** company which is either making a takeover bid or is the subject of a bid complies with the provisions of the Act and with the rules made by the Panel which will encompass the existing Takeover Code.[131] Under the Act and the Code, the Panel may give a direction restraining someone from acting in breach of the Code[132] or may order the payment of compensation for a breach of certain provisions of the Code.[133] The Panel may also apply to the court for an order enforcing compliance with a requirement under the Code.[134]

The Takeover Code applies to any directors through which a company to which the Code **28.80** applies acts.[135] All companies to which the Code applies are expected to ensure that their directors and employees receive appropriate and timely guidance in respect of the Code and a company will he held responsible for any of its directors' or employees' acts or omissions.

The Takeover Code sets out General Principles which are applicable to all takeovers.[136] **28.81** Directors of a company that is either the maker or the subject of a takeover bid are obliged to ensure that they and the company act in accordance with these principles. The General Principles are expressed in broad terms and companies are required to comply with the spirit of the principles rather than simply their literal terms. The General Principles[137] are:

(1) All holders of the securities of an offeree company of the same class must be afforded equivalent treatment; moreover, if a person acquires control[138] of a company, the other holders of securities must be protected.

---

[130] 2006 Act, s 966.

[131] 2006 Act, s 943(3). The following paragraphs refer to the 11th edition of the Takeover Code as at 20 May 2013.

[132] 2006 Act, s 946.

[133] 2006 Act, s 952(1)(a). This applies in relation to a breach of the requirements of rules 6, 9, 11, 14, 15, 16.1, or 35.3: see the Takeover Code, A19.

[134] 2006 Act, s 955.

[135] Code, A7. For the purposes of the Code, directors include persons in accordance with whose instructions the directors or a director are accustomed to act (Code, C8).

[136] Code, B1.

[137] The General Principles reflect the Takeovers Directive, Art 3.

[138] 'Control' is a key concept in the Takeover Code and is defined as meaning an interest, or interests, in shares carrying in aggregate 30 per cent or more of the voting rights of a company, irrespective of whether such interest or interests give de facto control.

(2) The holders of the securities of an offeree company must have sufficient time and information to enable them to reach a properly informed decision on the bid; where it advises the holders of securities, the board of the offeree company must give its views on the effects of implementation of the bid on employment, conditions of employment, and the locations of the company's places of business.

(3) The board of an offeree company must act in the interests of the company as a whole and must not deny the holders of securities the opportunity to decide on the merits of the bid.

(4) False markets must not be created in the securities of the offeree company, of the offeror company, or of any other company concerned by the bid in such a way that the rise or fall of the prices of the securities becomes artificial and the normal functioning of the markets is distorted.

(5) An offeror must announce a bid only after ensuring that he/she can fulfil in full any cash consideration, if such is offered, and after taking all reasonable measures to secure the implementation of any other type of consideration.

(6) An offeree company must not be hindered in the conduct of its affairs for longer than is reasonable by a bid for its securities.

The approach, announcements, and independent advice

28.82   The general rule is that any takeover offer must be made in the first instance to the board of directors of the offeree company or the company's advisers.[139] The identity of the offeror must be disclosed at the outset. Further, the board of the offeree company which is the subject of the approach is entitled to be satisfied that the offeror is, or will be, in a position to implement the offer in full. It follows that the board of a company which is the subject of an approach should request that the offeror provides this information.

28.83   A key issue prior to and following any approach to the offeree company regarding the making of an offer concerns the need for an announcement. Generally, announcements in relation to a potential takeover are required to be made at an early stage. The circumstances in which an announcement is required are set out in the Takeover Code and include when a firm intention to make an offer which is not subject to any precondition has been notified to the offeree company and when, following an approach to the offeree company, it is the subject of rumour or speculation or there is an untoward movement in its share price. Before the board of the offeree company has been approached, the responsibility for making an announcement will rest with the offeror but, following an approach having been made, primary responsibility for making an announcement will rest with the board of the offeree company.[140] Prior to an announcement being made, all price-sensitive information about a contemplated offer must be kept absolutely secret.[141]

28.84   The directors of an offeror company are plainly under an important obligation to consider carefully whether or not to make a takeover offer. Such a decision clearly falls to be taken consistently with the directors' duty to promote the success of the company. In addition,

---

[139] Takeover Code, rule 1.
[140] Takeover Code, rule 2.3.
[141] Takeover Code, rule 2.1.

the Takeover Code specifically provides that an announcement of a firm intention to make an offer should only be made when the offeror has every reason to believe that it can and will continue to be able to implement the offer.[142] Once a firm announcement has been made, an offeror must normally proceed with the offer unless the offeror is entitled to invoke a precondition or condition under rule 13 of the Takeover Code.[143] Rule 13.5 provides that an offeror should not invoke a condition or precondition so as to cause the offer not to proceed, to lapse, or to be withdrawn, unless the circumstances which give rise to the right to invoke the condition or precondition are of 'material significance' to the offeror in the context of the offer.[144] Where a person makes a statement of an intention not to make an offer then it will not be able to make an offer within six months of the date of the statement.[145]

Having received a takeover offer, the board of the offeree company is obliged to obtain **28.85** competent independent advice as to whether the financial terms of the offer are fair and reasonable.[146] The substance of the advice must be made available to shareholders. As the Code notes, the requirement for independent advice is of particular importance where the offeror is a management buy-out vehicle or where existing management or controllers are interested in the offeror. The Code advises that the board of an offeree company should appoint an independent adviser as soon as possible after it becomes aware of the possibility that an offer may be made.

Restrictions on dealings

During the period between the time when there is reason to suppose an approach or an offer **28.86** is contemplated and the announcement of the approach or offer or of the termination of the discussions, no dealings of any kind can take place in the securities of the offeree company by a person, not being the offeror, who is privy to price-sensitive information.[147] Likewise, during an offer period, the offeror (and any persons acting in concert with it) must not, except with the consent of the Panel, sell any securities in the offeree company.[148]

Mandatory offers

In certain circumstances, an obligation under the Takeover Code to make a mandatory offer **28.87** may be triggered. The purpose of the requirement to make a mandatory offer is to protect the interests of the general body of shareholders when control of a company is acquired. Under rule 9.1, the obligation to make a mandatory offer arises where:

(1) any person acquires, whether by a series of transactions over a period of time or not, an interest in shares which (taken together with shares in which persons acting in concert with him are interested) carry 30 per cent or more of the voting rights of a company; or

---

[142] Takeover Code, rule 2.7(a).
[143] Takeover Code, rule 2.7(b).
[144] By way of example, it was held by the Panel that WPP was not entitled to invoke a condition in its takeover offer for Tempus on the basis that there had been a 'material adverse change' in the prospects for Tempus following the events of 11 September 2001.
[145] Takeover Code, rule 2.8.
[146] Takeover Code, rule 3.1. Such advice will normally be obtained from an investment bank.
[147] Takeover Code, rule 4.1.
[148] Takeover Code, rule 4.2.

(2) any person (together with persons acting in concert with him) is interested in shares which in aggregate carry not less than 30 per cent of the voting rights but does not hold shares carrying more than 50 per cent of such voting rights and such person (or any persons acting in concert with him) acquires an interest in any other shares which increases the percentage of shares carrying voting rights in which he is interested.

Persons 'acting in concert' comprise persons who, pursuant to an agreement or understanding (whether formal or informal), cooperate to obtain or consolidate control of a company or to frustrate the successful outcome of an offer for a company. Amongst others, a company is presumed to act in concert with its directors (and with any close relatives or related trusts of its directors).

28.88   A mandatory offer must be made to the holders of all classes of equity share capital (whether voting or non-voting) and to the holders of any other class of transferable securities carrying voting rights to acquire their securities. The consideration offered must be in cash (or be accompanied by a cash alternative) at not less than the highest price paid by the offeror (or any person acting in concert with it) for any interest in shares of that class during the 12 months prior to the announcement of that offer.[149] For directors, it should also be noted that when directors (or their close relatives or related trusts) sell shares to a person as a result of which that person is required to make an offer under rule 9, then the directors must ensure as a condition of the sale that the person undertakes to fulfil his obligations under rule 9.[150]

Voluntary offers

28.89   In relation to voluntary offers, the terms of the offer are generally a matter for the offeror company to put forward. However, it is required to be a condition of any offer for voting equity share capital (or for any other transferable securities which carry voting rights) which, if it is accepted, would result in the offeror holding shares carrying over 50 per cent of the voting rights of the offeree company, that the offer will not become or be declared unconditional as to acceptances unless the offeror has acquired or agreed to acquire shares carrying over 50 per cent of the voting rights.[151] The purpose of this provision is to ensure that if the offeror does acquire any shares under the offer, it acquires sufficient to give it control of the offeree company.

28.90   It is also a requirement under the Code that any offer should not normally be subject to conditions or preconditions which depend solely on subjective judgements by the directors of the offeror or offeree company or the fulfilment of which is in their hands.[152] Further, where the offeree company has more than one class of equity share capital a comparable offer must be made for each class of share irrespective of whether they carry voting rights or not.[153]

---

[149] Takeover Code, rule 9.5(a).

[150] Takeover Code, rule 9.6. In addition, except with the consent of the Panel, such directors should not resign from the board until the first closing date of the offer or the date when the offer becomes or is declared wholly unconditional, whichever is later.

[151] Takeover Code, rule 10.

[152] Takeover Code, rule 13.1.

[153] Takeover Code, rule 14. A comparable offer need not necessarily be an identical offer.

Provision of information to shareholders

A key aspect of directors' duties in relation to takeovers is to keep their shareholders informed **28.91** since it is the shareholders who will ultimately decide on an offer. The general rule is that shareholders must be given sufficient information and advice to enable them to reach a properly informed decision as to the merits or demerits of an offer.[154] The Code expressly provides that no relevant information should be withheld from shareholders.[155] The information must be made available so that shareholders can make a decision in good time.

Information about companies involved in an offer must be made equally available to all **28.92** offeree company shareholders, so far as possible, at the same time and in the same manner.[156] In addition, each document or advertisement issued, or statement made, during the course of an offer must be prepared with the highest standards of care and accuracy and the information given must be fairly and adequately presented.[157] A profit forecast in particular may clearly be highly material to a takeover offer. The Code emphasizes that profit forecasts must be compiled with due care and consideration and in a manner consistent with the company's accounting policies.[158]

Board's opinion on the offer

The board of the offeree company must circulate to the company's shareholders its opinion **28.93** on the offer and must, at the same time, make known to the shareholders the substance of the advice given to the board under rule 3.1.[159] The opinion must include the views of the board on the effect of implementation of the offer on all the offeree company's interests, including specifically employment, and the offeror's strategic plans for the offeree company and their likely repercussions on employment and the locations of the offeree company's places of business. The opinion must also state the board's reasons for forming its opinion.

The requirement for the board to state its opinion on an offer is one of the central obligations **28.94** upon directors in connection with a takeover.[160] The board's opinion will be based on both the independent advice received and on the board's own commercial judgments and views, in particular, gained from their stewardship of the business. However, it is unlikely that it will be appropriate for a board to recommend an offer unless the advice received is that it is a fair one. If a board is split in its views on an offer, then the minority on the board should also publish their views.

In forming their opinion on an offer, the directors must act in accordance with their statu- **28.95** tory duties to exercise independent judgment[161] and to promote the success of the company

---

[154] Takeover Code, rule 23.

[155] It also states that the obligation of the offeror in these respects towards the shareholders of the offeree company is no less than the offeror's obligation towards its own shareholders.

[156] Takeover Code, rule 20.1.

[157] Takeover Code, rule 19.1. This applies whether it is issued by the company direct or by an adviser on its behalf.

[158] Takeover Code, rule 28.1.

[159] Takeover Code, rules 25.1, 25.2.

[160] Where a director has a conflict of interest, he should not normally join with the remainder of the board in expressing its views on the offer. A director will normally be regarded as having a conflict of interest where it is intended that he should have any continuing role (whether executive or non-executive) in either the offeror or the offeree company in the event of the offer being successful (see the Code, note 4 on rule 25.2).

[161] 2006 Act, s 173.

for the benefit of its members as a whole.[162] However, this does not mean that the directors should be solely influenced by what is in the financial best interests of the present members of the company since under the 2006 Act, s 172 they are also required to have regard to, amongst other things, the likely consequences in the long term; the interests of employees; relationships with suppliers, customers, and others; and environmental issues. These factors should all be reflected in the decision-making process by which the directors form their opinion on a takeover offer.

Restrictions on frustrating action

28.96 Although the board is required to provide its opinion on an offer, the provisions of the Takeover Code reflect the fact that it is ultimately for the shareholders to decide. The Code therefore prohibits action from being taken, once a takeover bid is imminent, in relation to an offeree company which might frustrate that decision. Accordingly, during the course of an offer (or before the date of the offer if the board of the offeree company has reason to believe that a bona fide offer might be imminent) the board must not, without approval of the shareholders in general meeting, take any action which might result in any offer or bona fide possible offer being frustrated or in shareholders being denied the opportunity to decide on its merits.[163] This would, for example, cover the situation where the offeree company proposes to sell a valuable asset. This is so even if the directors' actions would not amount to a breach of their general duties under the Companies Act. Likewise, the redemption or purchase by the offeree company of its own shares is restricted without approval of the shareholders in general meeting.[164]

28.97 It is important to note, however, that there is nothing to prevent directors of an offeree company who have received a takeover bid from searching for a competing bidder. Such steps do not frustrate the takeover offer, even though they may make it less likely that the first offer will succeed. Indeed, a competition between bidders may best serve the interests of the shareholders of the offeree company by driving up the final price. In relation to their own shareholdings, directors do not appear to be under a positive duty to accept the highest offer in respect of their own shares, but their recommendation to shareholders given in their capacity as directors should not reflect their own personal interests.[165]

28.98 Finally, under the provisions of Part 22 of the Companies Act a public company has various powers to obtain information about interests in its shares (see Chapter 27, Section E above). These powers may be of use in the context of a takeover offer or rumoured takeover proposal.

Provision of information and documentation to the Panel

28.99 In relation to the provision of information and documentation, a director may be required to comply with a notice served on him by the Panel under s 947. The Code itself requires any person dealing with the Panel to do so in 'an open and co-operative way' and that the Panel expects prompt cooperation and assistance from persons dealing with it.[166] A person who deals with the Panel is obliged to disclose to the Panel any information known to them and

---

[162] 2006 Act, s 172.
[163] Takeover Code, rule 21.1.
[164] Takeover Code, rule 37.3.
[165] *Re a Company* [1986] BCLC 382.
[166] Code, A17.

relevant to the matter being considered by the Panel (and to correct or update that information if it changes) and to take all reasonable care not to provide incorrect, incomplete, or misleading information to the Panel.[167] A failure to do so may lead to a director being the subject of a direction from the Panel requiring compliance,[168] a sanction being imposed on a director by the Panel,[169] or enforcement by the court.[170]

Squeeze-out and sell-out rights

Directors also have particular obligations under the Act in relation to the exercise of **28.100** squeeze-out or sell-out rights under Chapter 3 of Part 28 of the Act. Where an offeror serves a notice under s 979 in relation to the exercise of squeeze-out rights, it must also send a copy of the notice to the company accompanied by a statutory declaration in the prescribed form stating that the conditions for the giving of the notice are satisfied.[171] A failure to do so will be a criminal offence,[172] unless the person can prove that he took reasonable steps for complying with the section.[173] It is also an offence for a person to make the declaration knowing it to be false or without having reasonable grounds for believing it to be true. It should be noted that where the offeror is a company the declaration must be made by a director of the company.[174]

Under s 984, a shareholder can exercise sell-out rights which arise under s 983(2), (3), or **28.101** (4) by a written communication addressed to the offeror. Further, within one month of the times specified in s 983(2), (3), or (4) (as the case may be) the offeror must give any shareholder who has not accepted the offer notice in the prescribed manner of the rights that are exercisable by that shareholder under s 983(2), (3), or (4) and the period within which the rights are exercisable.[175] An offeror who fails to comply with this requirement commits a criminal offence.[176]

Implementation—schemes of arrangement

As noted above, in recent times, schemes of arrangement have proved to be increasingly **28.102** popular as a means of effecting takeovers. In addition to the provisions of the Takeover Code, there is a considerable body of law applicable to the promotion of schemes of arrangement and their consideration by the court. However, in considering the approach to adopt to any scheme of arrangement which implements a takeover, the court will be heavily influenced by the provisions of the Takeover Code. In *Re Expro International Group plc*[177] the court

---

[167] Code, A17. In addition, where a matter is determined by the Panel and the person subsequently becomes aware that information they supplied to the Panel was incorrect, incomplete, or misleading then that person must promptly contact the Panel to correct the position (Code, A18). Where a determination of the Panel has continuing effect, the party or parties to that determination must promptly notify the Panel of any new information unless they reasonably consider that it would not be likely to have been relevant to the determination.

[168] 2006 Act, s 946.

[169] 2006 Act, s 952(1)(b).

[170] 2006 Act, s 955(1)(b).

[171] 2006 Act, s 980(4).

[172] 2006 Act, s 980(6).

[173] 2006 Act, s 980(7).

[174] 2006 Act, s 980(5).

[175] 2006 Act, s 984(3). This does not apply if the offeror has given the shareholder a notice in respect of the shares in question under s 979 (s 984(4)).

[176] 2006 Act, s 984(5).

[177] [2010] 2 BCLC 514.

considered an application by certain shareholders for the adjournment of the sanctioning of a scheme of arrangement which was to implement a takeover. The purpose of the adjournment would have been to allow the possibility of an improved offer being made. The court refused the adjournment, on the basis that the shareholders had already approved the scheme with knowledge of the possibility of a further bid being made. It was stated that this result was achieved by application of the established principles applicable to the consideration of schemes of arrangement. However, the court also expressed the view that there should be a common approach to the conduct of bids, whether they are structured as an offer or as a scheme, so that the court procedure inherent in a scheme should not introduce a level of uncertainty which has otherwise been eliminated by the Takeover Code.

29

PENSION SCHEMES

Henry Legge QC

A. Overview of Pensions Law

(1) Surplus to deficit

29.01 The first decade of the new millennium saw a huge increase in the cost to companies of providing pensions for their current and former employees. Schemes which had previously been assessed as well funded and in surplus became underfunded and in deficit. The costs of funding this deficit and the accruing liabilities of the scheme can often be a very significant drain on a company's cash flow and resources. How did this happen?

29.02 Three principal factors led to this turnaround:

(1) The assumptions used to calculate mortality rates in actuarial valuation of schemes began to assume that the members of the scheme would live longer (and also often in addition that members' life expectancy would continue to increase further in the future). This meant that members' pensions were more expensive to fund, because the pensions were assumed to be in payment for a longer time.

(2) As yields on gilts and other fixed income instruments fall, the amount which actuaries assume to be required to meet future liabilities is greater than the amount which they had previously assumed to be required when yields were higher.

(3) Many of the surpluses which schemes enjoyed during the 1990s derived from gains made on equities. Similar gains (and commensurate losses) arose for investors during the first years of the new millennium. However, many schemes were unable to take advantage of these gains (but also gained protection from the worst of the losses) because a large proportion of the assets of the scheme were allocated to fixed income instruments rather than equities.

29.03 This story illustrates the nature of the liability of employers under a defined benefit contribution scheme. The liability is volatile and dependent on macroeconomic and sociological factors outside the employer's control. The value of the scheme fund is only one of the matters affecting whether or not a scheme is in surplus or in deficit. Now that the regime established by the Pensions Act 2004 has been fully implemented, there is much less scope for variance in methods of valuation than existed before the act and in practice greater oversight of trustee investment policy. However, this has not affected the essential nature of the liability of the sponsoring employer of a defined benefit scheme: the employer's obligation will normally be a current and continuing liability to meet a future and variable obligation to pay benefits to the members of the scheme, whose quantum is to a significant extent outside the employers' control.

(2) Security of members' benefits and the Pensions Act 2004

29.04 A deficit in a scheme is not just a problem for the employer. If the employer is unable to meet its liabilities to the scheme, the deficit could mean that the members of the scheme might not receive the benefits to which they are entitled under the scheme.

29.05 The regime imposed by the Pensions Act 2004 attempted to improve security of members' benefits in the following ways:

(1) By establishing a statutory fund, the Pensions Protection Fund, which (broadly) meets the liabilities for the benefits of members of schemes (but subject to a cap) where (broadly) the sponsoring employer of the scheme is insolvent. The fund is funded from two sources: first, by a statutory levy on schemes which would be eligible for the protection of the fund if their employer were to become insolvent and, secondly, by the assets of the schemes whose members' benefits are met by the fund.

(2) By increasing the costs for employers of withdrawing from a scheme. The liability incurred by an employer on withdrawal from a scheme is now valued on a basis which reflects the cost of purchasing annuities and deferred annuities to meet the pension obligations arising under the scheme. This basis is likely to be significantly more expensive for the employer than the cost of meeting the liabilities of the scheme on an ongoing basis.

(3) By imposing a more demanding statutory regime for the funding of schemes by employers on an ongoing basis, coupled with oversight by the Pensions Regulator. Trustees are therefore better equipped to demand enhanced funding from employers. The involvement of the Regulator in overseeing the funding of schemes has also incentivized trustees to adopt a more cautious approach to funding and to the investment allocation of assets within the scheme than might otherwise have been the case.

29.06 The duties and obligations of directors of trustee companies and employers to their own companies accord with their general obligations described in more detail in the rest of this book. However, in addition, the pensions legislation confers on the Pensions Regulator power to impose on directors of trustee companies and employers personal liability for civil penalties in certain circumstances where the relevant company is in breach of the provisions of the relevant Act. The Act also confers on the Regulator the 'moral hazard' powers under ss 38 and 47, which are considered in more detail below.

29.07 The regime has been broadly effective to enhance the security of the benefits accrued by existing members. However, there is good reason to think that the regime has also taken effect to accelerate the rate at which employers have closed schemes to new members and (notwithstanding the increase in the cost of withdrawal) have barred future accrual. In any event, pensions are likely to continue to cause difficulties for employers and their directors for some time to come.

(3) The types of pension promise

Companies can make pension provision for their employees in a number of different ways. **29.08**

Funded/unfunded

It is not necessary for an employer company to set aside a fund separate from the assets of **29.09** the company for the provision of pension benefits. Historically, the principal advantages of setting aside funds in that way have been twofold: first, the assets will be protected from creditors in the event of the company's insolvency and, secondly, the assets set aside receive a more favourable tax treatment in the hands of the scheme trustees than they would receive if they were part of the assets of the company (as to which, see below). However, sometimes one or both of these considerations are not of great importance. In that type of situation, pension benefits may be paid directly by an employer and the rights of the pensioner comprise merely a promise by the employer to pay. This type of arrangement is especially prevalent in the public sector and has sometimes been used in the private sector to provide 'top-up' benefits for highly paid employees.

Registered/unregistered

Prior to 6 April 2006, pensions were subject to eight different tax regimes.[1] From 6 April **29.10** 2006, the Finance Act 2004, Part 4 imposed a new regime with the intention of simplifying the taxation of pensions. Broadly, all schemes which were eligible for favourable tax treatment under the old regime as exempt approved schemes became eligible for similar treatment under the new regime as registered schemes.

The change in the tax treatment of unapproved schemes effected by the Finance Act 2004 is **29.11** likely to make it unattractive in most cases to set up new unregistered schemes, particularly funded unregistered schemes. However, unapproved schemes which have already been set up are unlikely to wind up as a result of the changes, so the distinction between registered and unregistered schemes is likely still to remain of some importance. The provisions of the Pensions Act 1995, s 75, which impose a debt on the employer, do not apply to unregistered schemes.[2]

Defined benefit/defined contribution

Under a defined benefit scheme, the benefits to be provided by members are set (as the name **29.12** suggests) with reference to the benefits to be provided to them. So, for example, the scheme might provide that a pension is to be paid to members on their normal retirement date, set at one-eightieth of their final salary for each year of pensionable service undertaken by them.

The cost of this promise can be unpredictable: the member may live long beyond normal **29.13** retirement date; the member's salary may increase; the yield on the amount put aside to meet the liability may not meet expectations. In a funded defined benefit scheme, this obligation

---

[1] Principally: exempt approved, funded unapproved, unfunded unapproved, personal pension, small self-administered scheme.

[2] Occupational Pension Schemes (Employer Debt) Regulations 2005 (SI 2005/678), reg 4(1).

is met from the trust fund and the balance of the cost above any contributions from the employees is funded by a contribution covenant from the employer. The employer therefore takes the burden (and in some cases reaps the benefit) of any fluctuations in the cost of providing the benefits promised to the member.

29.14 By contrast, in a defined contribution scheme the employer agrees with the trustees or the employee to pay an amount into the scheme, often expressed as a percentage of the employee's salary. This amount would be set aside each year as a notional or (in some cases) actual fund for the employee.

29.15 When the employee becomes entitled to the benefits (say on retirement), this fund is applied to provide whatever benefits can be purchased for the member. There is no additional obligation on the employer. The risk of adverse experience is therefore borne by the member.

29.16 Some schemes are hybrid defined contribution and defined benefit schemes. So, a scheme may be a defined benefit scheme with a defined contribution section. Equally, the terms of some schemes are written in such a way that issues arise as to whether the scheme is properly analysed as a defined benefit or defined contribution scheme. In *Aon Trust Corporation Ltd v KPMG*,[3] the Court of Appeal analysed as defined benefit a scheme with many of the characteristics of a money purchase, or defined contribution, scheme. The effect was that the employer debt provisions of the Pensions Act 1995, s 75 obliged KPMG, the employer, to underwrite any shortfall in the scheme, notwithstanding that the scheme did not include a contribution covenant and had been established long before the enactment of any statutory funding requirements.[4]

29.17 Unless the text indicates otherwise, the comments and explanations in this chapter are intended to refer to a funded registered defined benefit scheme, which is the type of scheme most frequently encountered by pensions lawyers in practice.

(4) The classic defined benefit scheme

The source of the law

29.18 The core obligation owed to the trustees of a scheme by the employer or employers sponsoring the scheme is the employer's contractual obligation to fund the scheme. Equally, the core obligation owed by the trustees of the scheme to the members and the other beneficiaries of the scheme is a fiduciary obligation deriving from the trustees' status as trustees.

29.19 However, onto these obligations (which arise as a matter of the general law) has been superimposed a detailed and complex statutory edifice. The two main pillars of that edifice are the Pensions Acts 1995 and 2004. The approach adopted under these Acts is, broadly, to provide an outline scheme of regulation, the details of which are then clarified and particularized in a series of lengthy and (as it has turned out) frequently amended statutory instruments. Not even the most enthusiastic supporter of the current state of the law would argue that the scheme of pensions legislation has progressed in such a way as to make the divination of the law easily approachable by the layman or non-specialist lawyer.

---

[3] [2006] 1 WLR 97, CA.
[4] See also *Houldsworth v Bridge Trustees Ltd* [2011] 1 WLR 1912, SC.

The cost to the employer

The classic defined benefit scheme is contributory, which means that members of the scheme **29.20** are obliged to make regular contributions to the scheme as a precondition to the provision of benefits for them. The balance of the cost of providing benefits for the members is met by the employer. However, the fact that the scheme is a funded scheme and that the vast majority of the benefits are to be paid in the future means that the assessment of the relevant cost will inevitably amount principally to an assessment of how much is presently required to meet the cost of providing those benefits in the future. This raises the question of how that cost is to be assessed.

This cost is (and has been) assessed on a number of different bases, the three most important **29.21** of which are described here. Each basis arises and is relevant in a different context

The first basis is the 'Statutory Funding Objective' (SFO), introduced by the Pensions Act **29.22** 2004, ss 221–3. This applies while the scheme is ongoing. Under the legislation the trustees and the employer, with the advice of the scheme actuary, should jointly agree on a statement of funding principles, taking into account factors relevant to the scheme itself. This will reflect, for example, the trustees' investment policy (ie the greater the proportion of growth assets, the higher the projected yield on the portfolio and the higher the discount rate) and the likely salary growth of the members of the scheme. This leads to a basis for valuing the scheme (the technical provisions) at the next valuation. This will in turn lead to the preparation of a schedule of the contributions to be paid over the next three years until the next valuation and for the period thereafter.

The second basis is the 'buy-out basis' which applies when there is a trigger event under **29.23** the Pensions Act 1995, s 75: (broadly) when a scheme comes to an end or an employer withdraws from the scheme.[5] On this basis, liabilities are calculated as if accrual had ceased on the relevant date and the liability of the employer is the amount required to buy annuities to meet those liabilities minus the value of the assets on that date.[6] The discount rate applied to the liabilities in order to produce a capital sum will therefore be the commercial rate used by insurance companies (ie one based on gilt yields) rather than the SFO rate which had been used for calculation of liabilities while the scheme was ongoing. Unless the scheme is very mature (ie with a very high proportion of members whose pensions are in payment), the liabilities of the scheme calculated on the buy-out basis are likely to be much greater than the liabilities calculated on the ongoing basis. One of the idiosyncrasies of the statutory regime is that the discount rate applied to calculate the value of the relevant annuities is not the commercial rate at the date when the annuities are to be purchased, but is rather the rate on the date when s 75 first applies (for example, the date when the employer withdraws from the scheme or becomes insolvent).[7] This date may often be many months, if not years, before annuities are in fact purchased (assuming annuities were purchased at all), so that the statutory regime builds in a variance between the amount which the scheme would need if it bought annuities and the amount it will in fact receive. This variance could run both ways: if gilt yields increased after the relevant date, the scheme could have more than it needed.

---

[5] As to which, see below.
[6] See Pensions Act 1995, s 75(4A).
[7] See *Bestrustees plc v Kaupthing Singer & Friedlander Ltd* [2012] Pens LR 187.

29.24   The third basis is the Pensions Act 2004, s 179 basis. This is a variant of the buy-out basis and (broadly) calculates the amount required to buy annuities to secure the benefits which would be payable by the Pensions Protection Fund ('the PPF') if the liabilities and the assets of the scheme were to be taken over by the PPF. This will not be the same as the buy-out figure because there is a cap on the quantum of benefits which can be paid to individual members under the PPF.

Liabilities before withdrawal

29.25   While the scheme is ongoing, the SFO and the related funding regime applies (as described above). Schemes must be valued every three years. Preparation of the triennial valuation of the scheme on the basis of the statement of funding principles leads to the calculation of a deficit or surplus. This in turn should lead to the agreement of a schedule of contributions. Where (as is currently likely) the scheme is in deficit, the trustees and the employer must agree a recovery plan. This will set a date by which the deficit is to be paid off and will set out the contributions which need to be made in the intervening period (called the 'recovery period') by the employer if that objective is to be achieved. A critical factor in assessing the appropriate length of the recovery period is the financial strength of the employer and its commitment to the scheme (often together described as the strength of the employer's covenant). The stronger the employers' covenant, the longer the recovery period and the smaller the size of the annual contributions. This therefore provides an incentive for employers to increase the likelihood that the trustees will recover the amounts due to them, thereby strengthening their covenants. Employers will accordingly often provide parent company guarantees and/or charges over company assets securing the employer's liabilities to the scheme as part of the process of agreeing the schedule of contributions. This process of agreement is overseen by the Regulator: where the Regulator intervenes in the process of valuing the scheme, the Regulator will scrutinise the technical provisions and the recovery plan and if necessary impose a schedule of contributions on the parties. Where the trustees and the employer are unable to agree, the trustees must report the matter to the Regulator.

29.26   In any event, the ultimate product of the triennial valuation of the scheme and the ensuing negotiations, with or without the intervention of the Regulator, is a schedule of contributions to be paid by the employer to the trustees. The schedule of contributions creates an enforceable obligation which can be enforced by the trustee against the employer.

29.27   In addition to the contributions to be paid direct to the scheme, the employer will be liable to pay a levy to the Pension Protection Fund. The place of the levy within the scheme of the Pensions Act 2004 is to provide funding to the PPF against the possibility of the scheme's liabilities exceeding its assets on the withdrawal of an employer. Consistently with this approach, the levy is calculated (broadly) as a function of the size of the scheme adjusted by (broadly) its chance of failure. This has meant that, again, it is often in the interests of an employer to provide or procure security for its obligations under the scheme (for example, by procuring a parent company guarantee) so as to reduce the size of the levy payable by the employer. This, of course, increases the chances that the employer's liabilities will be met on an insolvency.[8]

---

[8] This policy was for a time undermined by the basis of the assessment of the security provided by the employer, since the value of the security provided was for some time to be assessed without taking into account the failure of the employer's business.

Liabilities on withdrawal

29.28 Where a liability is triggered under the Pensions Act 1995, s 75, the employer will prima facie be liable for the full amount of the buy-out debt.[9] Critically, liability under the section is not limited to the cost of providing benefits for members who are or have been employed by the employer, but can relate also to 'orphan' members, ie members who have no employer at the time when the liability is triggered. Complex additional provisions deal with 'multi-employer' schemes, where more than one employer acts as the sponsoring employer (see below).

29.29 The code by which a liability arises under s 75 is complex. However, in outline, a liability arises in the following circumstances:

(1) where an 'insolvency event' (in practice administration or winding up) occurs in relation to one or more of the sponsoring employers;

(2) where the trustees or administrators of the scheme notify the Pensions Protection Fund under the Pensions Act 2004, s 129 that the employer is unlikely to continue as a going concern; and

(3) when, in the case of a multi-employer scheme, a sponsoring employer ceases to employ active members of the scheme.[10] For cessations of employment before April 2008, it is now clear that the applicable regulation (regulation 6(4) of the Employer Debt Regulations) in certain circumstances allowed cessation without a s 75 debt.[11] For cessation after that date an amended provision applies.

29.30 The liability under s 75 can be disapplied where a withdrawal arrangement is agreed with the Regulator.[12] This provision can be of great practical importance where the employer is sold or is restructured, since the payment of a s 75 debt on a buy-out basis would often be an obstacle to the successful completion of the deal.

29.31 Where a scheme has more than one sponsoring employer, similar considerations apply: withdrawal by each employer will trigger liability for each employer on a buy-out basis. However, in some cases there was formerly considerable scope for flexibility in the apportionment of liability between withdrawing employers.

29.32 Before 5 April 2008, when the Occupational Pension Schemes (Employer Debt and Miscellaneous Amendments) Regulations 2008[13] came into force, the withdrawing employer would in the normal case be liable to pay the proportion of the liability which 'in the opinion of the actuary after consultation with the trustees or managers, the amount of the scheme's liabilities attributable to employment with that employer (*ie the withdrawing employer*) bears to the total amount of the scheme's liabilities attributable to employment with the employers (*ie the current sponsoring employers*)'.[14] It is important to note that (as

---

[9] Occupational Pension Schemes (Employer Debt) Regulations (SI 2005/678), reg 3B, as amended by the Occupational Pension Schemes (Employer Debt etc) (Amendment) Regulations (SI 2005/2224).

[10] Occupational Pension Schemes (Employer Debt) Regulations 2005, reg 2(1) amended by the Occupational Pension Schemes (Employer Debt and Miscellaneous Amendments) Regulations 2008 (SI 2008/731).

[11] See *PNPF Trust Company v Taylor* [2010] PLR 261 and *Cemex UK Marine v MNOPF Trustees* [2009] EWHC 3258.

[12] As described in the Occupational Pension Schemes (Employer Debt) Regulations, Sch 1A.

[13] SI 2008/731.

[14] Occupational Pension Schemes (Employer Debt) Regulations 2005, reg 6(2)(a).

in the case of the single withdrawing employer) the liability of the employer was not limited to the buy-out cost of the employer's own employees, but also encompassed a proportionate part of the cost of providing benefits for 'orphan' members.

29.33   However, where the scheme conferred power to apportion contractual liability between different employers, the s 75 debt assessable on the withdrawing employer could be allocated in the same way.[15] Where such a power was available to the trustees, the trustees could therefore prima facie use this power to apportion the s 75 liability between withdrawing employers in such a way as to maximize recovery for the scheme. A notable example of this practice was the case of *Re Phoenix Ventures Holdings Ltd*,[16] relating to the restructuring of the Rover Group, in which the trustees sought to allocate (in that case unsuccessfully) as much as possible of the s 75 liability to the group holding company, which had plenty of assets but had been the employer of only very few members, rather than to the trading companies, which had employed numerous members but had few assets.

29.34   After 5 April 2008, the effect of the new regulation 6(4) of the Occupational Pension Schemes (Employer Debt) Regulations 2005 (as amended) is that scheme rules allowing trustees to apportion liability between employers in multi-employer schemes are not effective to apportion liability under s 75 if the power to apportion is exercised after that date. Instead, employers are only liable for the costs of members' accrual referable to the member's period of employment with that employer, subject to complex provisions in relation to 'orphan' members.

B. The Position of the Trustee

(1) Identity and capability of the directors

29.35   The trustee of the classic scheme will often be a company established for that purpose. Under the Pensions Act 2004, s 242 at least one-third of the directors of the company must be member-nominated directors, appointed in accordance with the requirements at s 242(5). There are detailed exceptions to this rule set out in the Occupational Pension Schemes (Member Nominated Trustees and Directors) Regulations 2006,[17] most notably in cases where the scheme is unapproved or the sole trustee is an 'independent trustee' within the Pensions Act 1995, s 23(3).[18] Failure to comply with this requirement will lead to a liability for the trust company to pay civil penalties.[19]

29.36   The Pensions Act 2004, ss 247–9 imposes an obligation on directors and other officers and employees of corporate trustees to be conversant with the following matters:

(1) the trust deed and rules of the scheme;
(2) any statement of investment principles for the time being maintained under the Pensions Act 1995, s 35;
(3) the most recent statement of funding principles;

---

[15] Occupational Pension Schemes (Employer Debt) Regulations 2005, reg 6(2)(b).
[16] [2005] 38 PBLR, [2005] EWHC 1379 (Ch).
[17] SI 2006/714.
[18] By virtue of the Pensions Act 2004, s 242(10); Member Nominated Trustee Regulations (SI 2006/714), reg 2(k); Pensions Act 1995, s 23(3).
[19] Pensions Act 2004, s 242(11).

(4) any other trustee policy document relating to the administration of the scheme;

(5) the law relating to pensions and trusts; and

(6) the principles relating to (a) the funding of occupational pension schemes, (b) the investment of the assets of such schemes, and (c) such other matters as may be prescribed.

Happily for newly appointed trustees or directors of the trustee company, they have six **29.37** months in which to familiarize themselves with these matters.[20] The scope of the understanding required of trustees by the Regulator is set out in a code prepared by the Regulator and related guidance. It is clear from these materials that a relatively high degree of competence and professionalism is expected of trustees. These requirements clearly enhance the standard of care to be expected of a trustee under the Trustee Act 2000, s 1 (ie the standard of care required of a trustee for the purposes of a claim in breach of trust).

(2) Duties of the trustee

As a matter of general trust law, the trustee owes the members of the scheme the fiduciary **29.38** obligations owed by a trustee to its beneficiaries. This obligation is glossed and amended by the imposition of specific statutory duties.

The trustee must administer the trust assets properly and consistently with the standard of **29.39** care imposed on the trustee by the Trustee Act 2000, s 1 and/or under the general law. The most important practical implications of this obligation for a pension fund trustee are set out below.

Proper investment

The wide power of investment in the Pensions Act 1995, s 34(1) confers on the trustees **29.40** power to invest in any asset, subject to the specific terms of the scheme. However, although a particular investment may well be within the trustees' powers (in the sense that the investment will not be ultra vires), the investment decision may well be a breach of trust or in breach of duty as an inappropriate or foolhardy exercise of that power.

By the Occupational Schemes (Investment) Regulations 2005,[21] reg 4 ('the Investment **29.41** Regulations'), trustees must invest the assets of the fund in the following way:

(1) in the best interests of members and beneficiaries;

(2) in the case of a potential conflict of interest, in the sole interest of members and beneficiaries;

(3) in a manner calculated to ensure the security, quality, liquidity, and profitability of the portfolio as a whole;

(4) in a manner appropriate to the nature and duration of the expected future retirement benefits payable under the scheme (in other words in such a way as to match the projected liabilities of the scheme);

(5) predominantly in investments admitted to trading on regulated markets,[22] so that any investment in assets not traded on regulated markets must be kept to a prudent level (ie

---

[20] Occupational Pension Scheme (Trustees' Knowledge and Understanding) Regulations (SI 2006/686), reg 3.

[21] SI 2005/3378.

[22] As to the definition of 'regulated market'; see Investment Regulations, reg 4(11). This definition includes collective investment schemes holding investments traded on regulated markets and certain types of insurance policy (see Investment Regulations, reg 4(9)).

in practice the trustees must be cautious about investing in untraded assets or in funds which hold untraded assets (eg some private equity funds));

(6) the assets of the scheme must be properly diversified; and

(7) investment in derivative instruments may be made only in so far as they contribute to a reduction of risks or facilitate efficient portfolio management (including the reduction of cost or the generation of additional capital or income with an acceptable level of risk) and must be made and managed so as to avoid excessive risk exposure to a single counterparty and to other derivative operations.

29.42 In addition, by the Investment Regulations, reg 12 and the Pensions Act 1995, s 40 most large schemes are unable to invest more than 5 per cent of the fund in 'employer-related investments'.[23] These provisions were introduced in order to avoid the employer using the capital of the scheme for the business, often to the serious disadvantage of the members of the scheme (eg in the Maxwell debacle).

29.43 By the Pensions Act 1995, s 47(2) trustees are obliged to appoint a fund manager. The Act makes detailed provision as to the investment management agreement by which the fund manager is to be appointed. In addition, pursuant to the Pensions Act 1995, s 36, the trustees are under an obligation to take 'proper advice' (in practice advice given by a person authorized under the FSMA) in relation to the suitability of the investments of the scheme in the light of the investment criteria set out above.

29.44 Further, by the Pensions Act 1995, s 35 and the Investment Regulations, reg 2 the trustees are obliged to prepare and consult with the employer in relation to the preparation of a statement of investment principles. The trustee must do more by way of consultation than merely giving notice to the employer of its intentions.[24]

29.45 The Pensions Act 1995, s 34 confers on the trustees wide power to delegate their investment powers (which the terms of s 47, requiring appointment of a fund manager, clearly make desirable). However, the section also provides for a limitation of the liability of the trustee in relation to investment decisions once a manager has been appointed. The trustees are not responsible for the act or default of any fund manager in the exercise of any discretion delegated to him if they have taken all such steps as are reasonable to satisfy themselves that (a) the fund manager has the appropriate knowledge and experience for managing the investments of the scheme, and (b) he is carrying out his work competently and complying with the requirements of s 36 (ie in practice complying with the investment criteria set out above).

29.46 This is just as well, because the Pensions Act 1995, s 33 curtails the application of trustee exoneration clauses in the exercise of investment powers. Trustees cannot be excused for negligence in 'the performance of their investment functions'. In the circumstances, the most likely areas in which the investment activities of trustees are likely to attract the risk of liability are where:

---

[23] Defined by Pensions Act 1995, s 40(2) and Investment Regulations, reg 11.

[24] *Pitmans Trustees v the Telecommunications Group plc* [2004] PBLR 32, [2004] EWHC 181 (Ch). See *IBM United Kingdom Holdings Ltd v Dalgliesh* [2014] Pens LR 335 at para 1543ff on what must be disclosed by a consulting party in the context of a consultation.

(1) the trustees' power of investment is limited (in such cases it is critical that the scope of the trustees' power is highlighted to the investment manager and the investment manager acts accordingly);

(2) there is a significant mismatch between the liability profile of the scheme and the assets held as investments;[25]

(3) the fund is insufficiently diversified or is held in risky investments;

(4) insufficient steps are taken by trustees to oversee the investment managers and to review their performance; and

(5) the investment management agreement with the fund manager includes provisions which are unusually onerous for the trustee or unusually lenient for the fund manager.

Collection

Another critical obligation of the trustee is to recover adequate contributions from the **29.47** employer. The statutory mechanism for the recovery of contributions is set out in outline above. Although the trustee is clearly under a duty to recover what is properly due from the employer, it is questionable whether trustees are under a duty to use every power at their disposal to maximize the amount which is due. An example of a device which the trustee might use or threaten to use is an amendment of the scheme's investment strategy so as to alter the basis of valuation of the scheme's liabilities (as in the *Pitmans* case).[26]

Payment of benefits

The trustee owes a duty to pay the correct benefits to members and dependants at the right **29.48** time. A beneficiary is entitled to information from the trustees promptly in relation to the benefits properly payable to him (or her).

If the beneficiary has been underpaid, he has a claim against the trustees for his entitlement **29.49** and against the trustees in breach of trust. If the beneficiary has been overpaid, the trustees may theoretically be able to recover the sums from the beneficiary as money paid under a mistake. However, the beneficiary may have defences based on change of position or estoppel if he has spent the money[27] and it will often be impracticable for trustees to attempt to pursue numerous beneficiaries for small sums. However, the trustees will often be entitled as a matter of law to recoup themselves from the sums payable in the future to the beneficiary. This course in turn may not be free of danger for the trustees, since it may trigger a complaint of maladministration by the beneficiary.

Making decisions

The obligation of the trustee when exercising a discretionary power is now well settled: the **29.50** trustee must 'exercise the power for the purpose for which it is given, giving proper

---

[25] In most cases a 'mismatched' investment policy of this type would be at the prompting of the employer: the greater the proportion of equities in which the fund is invested, the higher in principle the discount rate applicable on a valuation of the liabilities, so therefore the lower the value of the liabilities. However, even if an employer were able to persuade the trustees to run a significantly mismatched investment policy and the scheme actuary were willing to value the scheme using the discount rate basis implied by the scheme's asset allocation, it would still be necessary to persuade the Regulator that the technical provisions adopted by the scheme actuary were appropriate.

[26] *Pitmans Trustees v the Telecommunications Group* [2004] EWHC 181.

[27] eg *National Westminster Bank v Somer International* [2002] QB 1286, CA.

consideration to the matters which are relevant and excluding from consideration matters which are irrelevant'.[28] There is no separate overarching duty for the trustee to act fairly.

29.51 Where the trustee of the scheme is a corporate trustee, it may be difficult to piece together the reasoning to be imputed to the company for the purposes of assessing whether or not the trustee has given proper consideration to the matters which are relevant or irrelevant to the decision. Conversely, the fact that the minutes of the board are likely to have been kept and (perhaps) the board's discussion recorded may be helpful.

29.52 In many cases, the directors of the trustee company will be directly interested in the way in which a trustee exercises a discretionary power. If normal principles of fiduciary obligation were to be applied, this interest could vitiate any decision which had the effect of benefiting the director himself.[29] These principles are disapplied by the Pensions Act 1995, s 39 so that a trustee (and by extension the director of a trustee company) is not precluded from exercising trust powers in such a way as to benefit himself.

29.53 However, s 39 does not bar a challenge to a decision made by a trustee under which he in fact benefits himself. The trustee is not entitled to give undue weight to his own personal interests in reaching a decision as to the exercise of trustee powers. The trustee must still exercise the power for its proper purpose, taking into account relevant matters and not taking into account irrelevant matters in reaching his decision, within the formulation in *Edge v Pensions Ombudsman*.[30]

29.54 Further, in making decisions the trustee is not obliged to take into account only the interests of the members and the beneficiaries. The trustee can take into account the interests of the employer as well in the right type of case.[31] Examples might include decisions about the distribution of surplus, amendment, or augmentation of benefits and other matters which might take effect to increase the employer's level of contribution.

Whistle-blowing

29.55 The pensions legislation imposes on trustees an obligation to make disclosure in certain prescribed circumstances. The principal obligations are as follows:

(1) The duty to make a report to the Pensions Protection Fund where the trustees become aware that the sponsoring employer is 'unlikely to continue as a going concern'.[32]

(2) The duty under reg 2(1) of the Notifiable Events Regulations 2005[33] to report to the Regulator the occurrence of any of the prescribed Notifiable Events. These are principally aimed at events which are likely to have a dramatic effect on the funding of the scheme: for example, a decision not to enforce a debt, a substantial transfer of members

---

[28] *Edge v Pensions Ombudsman* [2000] Ch 602, 623, CA, per Chadwick LJ and see also *Pitt v Holt* [2013] 2 AC 108 at paras 41 and 73.

[29] As in *Re Drexel Burnham Lambert Pension Plan* [1995] 1 WLR 32 and the two cases of Vinelott J on the point: *Re Makin (William) & Sons Ltd* [1993] OPLR 171 and *British Coal Corporation v British Staff Superannuation Scheme Trustees Ltd* [1993] PLR 303.

[30] [2000] Ch 602.

[31] Cf *Thrells v Lomas* [1993] 1 WLR 456 and *Edge v Pensions Ombudsman* [2000] Ch 602 at 626. Difficult questions might arise as to the extent to which the trustees can properly take the employer's interests into account where the employer's actions might themselves be questionable, especially in the light of the continuing expansion of the employer's obligation of good faith (as to which, see below).

[32] Under Pensions Act 2004, s 129.

[33] SI (2005/900).

in or out of the scheme, granting benefit augmentations without the availability of adequate funding, or granting very large benefit augmentations to individual members.

(3) The duty under the Pensions Act 2004, 228(2) to report to the Regulator and the members a failure by the employer to make contributions which is likely to be material to the exercise of the Regulator's functions.

(4) The duty under the Pensions Act 2004, s 70 to inform the Regulator where the trustees have reasonable grounds to believe that there has been a material breach of the provisions of the scheme or the provisions of the legislation applicable to the scheme.

(5) There is a further scheme of notifiable events which arises after a withdrawal arrangement has been approved by the Regulator,[34] but this is outside the scope of this work.

(3) Liability of directors of trustee company

29.56 The nature of the role undertaken by a corporate trustee makes it difficult to think of circumstances in which it will ever be possible for a beneficiary to pierce the trustee company's corporate veil (so as to ascribe the actions of the company to the directors). The directors of the trustee company owe no direct fiduciary duty to the beneficiaries of the scheme.[35]

29.57 In practice, this leaves only two avenues available to a beneficiary who wishes to make a director personally liable for the actions of a corporate trustee. The first is where the circumstances justify a claim against the director as constructive trustee, most likely for dishonest assistance. In *Barlow Clowes International Ltd v Eurotrust International Ltd*[36] the Privy Council clarified the test for dishonesty in cases of dishonest assistance:

> In summary, [the judge] said that liability for dishonest assistance requires a dishonest state of mind on the part of the person who assists in a breach of trust. Such a state of mind may consist in knowledge that the transaction is one in which he cannot honestly participate (for example, a misappropriation of other people's money), or it may consist in suspicion combined with a conscious decision not to make inquiries which might result in knowledge: see *Manifest Shipping Co Ltd v Uni-Polaris Insurance Co Ltd* [2003] 1 AC 469. Although a dishonest state of mind is a subjective mental state, the standard by which the law determines whether it is dishonest is objective. If by ordinary standards a defendant's mental state would be characterised as dishonest, it is irrelevant the defendant judges by different standards. The Court of Appeal held this to be a correct statement of the law and their Lordships agree.

29.58 If a director of the trustee company has acted dishonestly in this way, then the scheme exoneration clause will not apply to relieve the trustee from liability for the actions of the dishonest director (assuming the trustee to be vicariously liable for the actions of the dishonest director). Many corporate trustees of pension schemes will now have the benefit of insurance policies against breach of trust claims, so that a claim against the trustee would have some value. The benefit of the claim against the director is therefore likely to be principally tactical (and even then it may be important to check that the necessary allegation of dishonesty does not vitiate the trustee company's insurance policy).

---

[34] Under Occupational Pension Schemes (Employer Debt) Regulations, 2005/678, regs 6C, 7.

[35] *HR v JAPT* [1997] PLR 97 and *Gregson v HAE Trustees Ltd* [2008] 2 BCLC 542.

[36] [2006] 1 WLR 1476, PC at para 10, per Lord Hoffmann. At paras 14–17 Lord Hoffmann clarified an element of ambiguity in the speech of Lord Hutton in *Twinsectra Ltd v Yardley* [2002] 2 AC 164, HL at paras 35 and 36.

29.59 However, if the trustee company is not insured in this way, a claim against the company may be valueless, either because the trustee company has no assets or because the principal employer of the scheme is also the scheme trustee (as was often the case before Pensions Act 1995) and the principal employer is insolvent (as may well be the case where the beneficiaries are looking to bring a claim against the trustee). In those circumstances, a claim against the directors of the trustee company personally may be the only way of making recovery.

29.60 The second way in which a claim might be brought against the directors of the trustee company (at least as a matter of theory) is by a 'dog leg' claim. The reasoning underlying this type of claim is as follows:

(1) The actions of the director would justify a claim against him by the trustee company in breach of fiduciary duty based on standard principles of director's liability.

(2) The benefit of the trustee company's cause of action is held by the trustee company as an asset of the scheme.

(3) Since the cause of action is a trust asset, a beneficiary is entitled to bring a claim against the trustee company for administration of the cause of action under the principle in *Hayim v Citibank*[37] on the basis that the trustee company is conflicted from bringing the claim.

29.61 The claim is brought by the beneficiary joining both the trustee company and the director. In *HR v JAPT*,[38] the court refused to strike out a 'dog leg' claim. However, despite this initial (comparative) success, it appears that no claims of this type have been brought successfully. In *Gregson v HAE Trustees Ltd*,[39] Robert Miles QC, sitting as a deputy judge of the Chancery Division, struck out a 'dog leg' claim in circumstances where the trustee company was the trustee of a number of trusts (unlike in *HR v JAPT*). The judgment of the court includes a detailed analysis of the shortcomings of the principle and includes criticism of the decision in *HR v JAPT*. Although the facts of *Gregson* are distinguishable from *HR v JAPT*, it is difficult to avoid the conclusion that *HR v JAPT* would have been decided differently had the ratio of *Gregson* been applied in that case.[40]

29.62 The Pensions Acts allow the Regulator to impose civil penalties on trustees for breaches of some of the obligations imposed by the act. The specific statutory obligations in relation to which civil penalties may be imposed are too numerous to itemize here. However, they include the following liabilities under the Pensions Acts 1995 and 2004:

(1) failure to prepare and review a statement of funding principles (the 2004 Act, s 223);

(2) failure to obtain, receive, and make available to the employer an actuarial valuation of the scheme (the 2004 Act, s 224);

(3) failure to report to the Regulator an employer's failure to pay contributions where there are reasonable grounds to believe that matter may be of material significance to the Regulator (the 2004 Act, s 228); and

(4) failure to inform the Regulator and members of the Scheme that the employer has not met contributions (the 1995 Act, s 88).

---

[37] [1987] AC 370.

[38] [1997] PLR 99.

[39] [2008] 2 BCLC 542.

[40] See also, in Jersey, *Alhamrani v Alhamrani* [2007] JLR 44.

Pensions Act 1995, s 10 and Pensions Act 2004, s 314 both provide that these civil penalties **29.63** may be imposed on a director of the trustee company personally where the act or omission on which the civil penalty is based 'was done with the consent or connivance of, or is attributable to any neglect on the part of' the relevant director. Unsurprisingly, penalties cannot be met from scheme funds (Pensions Act 2004, s 256).

C. Obligations of the Employer

(1) Duty of good faith

The general law imposes on sponsoring employers a duty to its employees 'that the employ- **29.64** ers will not, without reasonable and proper cause, conduct themselves in a manner calculated or likely to destroy or seriously damage the relationship of confidence and trust between employer and employee'.[41] The obligation applies also in relation to the exercise by the employer of its powers under the scheme, whether or not it holds those powers in a fiduciary capacity. The obligation prima facie applies also in relation to past employees like pensioners and deferred pensioners and is wide enough to allow a claim for compensation by, for example, trustees against a sponsoring employer.[42]

In *Re Prudential Staff Pension Scheme*[43] Newey J clarified the scope of this duty in the context **29.65** of pension schemes. Although he accepted the submission that the duty of good faith in the context of pensions was not restricted to the state of the employment law authorities at the time of the *Imperial Group Pension Trust* case,[44] so that subsequent authority could be taken into account, he did not go so far as to impose an overall requirement of 'fairness' on the employer in exercising its powers under the trust deed. This had been the thrust of many of the leading employment law authorities decided after the *Imperial Group Pension Trust* case.[45] Rather, in the context of the facts of the *Prudential* case, which concerned a challenge to Prudential's change of policy in augmenting members' benefits, the obligation was limited to a requirement on the part of the employer not to act irrationally or perversely.[46] The employer was entitled to take into account its own interests. Further, the fact that the members had reasonable expectations that their benefits would be increased in accordance with the previous practice did not mean that Prudential was acting in breach of the duty of good faith in bringing that practice to an end.

In *IBM United Kingdom Holdings Ltd v Dalgleish*,[47] the members were successful in arguing **29.66** that the employer had breached its obligation of good faith by resiling from statements as to its commitment to the scheme which, although they were not legally binding and were specifically stated by the employer as not to be binding, were intended to be acted upon. The case is enormously complex and as at the time of writing is subject to an appeal. Detailed

---

[41] *Imperial Group Pension Trust v Imperial Tobacco* [1991] 1 WLR 589, deriving from *Woods v WM Car Services (Peterborough) Ltd* [1981] IRLR 347, approved by the Court of Appeal in *Lewis v Motorworld Garages Ltd* [1985] IRLR 465.

[42] See eg *IBM United Kingdom Holdings Ltd v Dalgleish* [2015] Pens LR 99 at para 139.

[43] [2011] Pens LR 239.

[44] [1991] 1 WLR 589 (para 29.64 above).

[45] eg *Johnson v Unisys Ltd* [2003] 1 AC 518 and *Eastwood v Magnox Electric plc* [2005] 1 AC 503.

[46] However, see now *Braganza v BP Shipping Ltd* [2015] 1 WLR 1661, SC.

[47] [2014] Pens LR 335.

discussion of the scope of the duty is therefore best considered in the light of the judgments of the appeal court (or appeal courts) in a future edition. Readers should assume that the scope of the duty of good faith imposed on an employer in a pension context will be uncertain until the case is finally determined.

(2) Duty of disclosure

29.67 Statute imposes on employers a number of specific duties of disclosure. The principal obligations are as follows:

(1) A duty to disclose to the actuaries and auditors of the scheme on request any information which is reasonably required for the performance of the duties of the trustees and of the actuaries and auditors. This obligation applies also to the auditor of the employer.[48]

(2) In addition, the employer is obliged to disclose to the trustees without request any event whose occurrence might reasonably be believed to have an impact on the performance of the trustees' duties.[49]

(3) The disclosure obligations arising under the Notifiable Events Regulations, reg 2(2)[50] to disclose to the Regulator a number of events related to the employer which (in practice) would have a material effect on the future of the scheme. Examples are: a decision by the employer to take action which will result in a debt potentially or actually owed to the scheme not being paid in full; ceasing to carry on business in the UK; the employer being advised that it is trading wrongfully for the purposes of the Insolvency Act 1986, s 214; breach of a banking covenant; a parent company relinquishing control of the employer and conviction of a director of the employer for an offence involving dishonesty.

(4) The obligation under the Pensions Act 2004, s 70 to make a written report to the Regulator when the employer has reason to believe that the scheme is not being administered in accordance with the law in a way which would be material to the exercise by the Regulator of its duties

29.68 In situations where a company is heading towards financial difficulties, this legislative code has the potential to cause serious difficulties. The employer may be under an obligation to inform the trustees of possible future underperformance by the company under the Occupational Pension Schemes (Scheme Administration) Regulations 1996, reg 6. Once informed, the trustees may be under an obligation to inform the Pensions Protection Fund that the company is 'unlikely to continue as a going concern'.[51] In the worst-case scenario, this might in turn trigger a liability under the Pensions Act 1995, s 75, which in many cases would seal the company's fate.

29.69 A critical consideration in this type of situation is likely to be the relative size of the pensions liability. In many cases, the trustees of a company's pensions fund will be by far the company's biggest creditors. However, in that type of case the company and the trustees are necessary, if sometimes uneasy, bedfellows.

---

[48] Occupational Pension Schemes (Scheme Administration) Regulations 1996, reg 6(1)(a) and Pensions Act 1995, s 47.

[49] Occupational Pension Schemes (Scheme Administration) Regulations 1996, reg 6(1)(b).

[50] The Pensions Regulator (Notifiable Events) Regulations 2005 (SI 2005/900).

[51] Under Pensions Act, s 129.

There is little reason for the trustees to try to wind up the company when the bulk of the **29.70** scheme's liabilities may well be guaranteed by the PPF. The trustees are entitled to take into account the existence of the PPF when making decisions.[52] However, in *Independent Trustee Services Ltd v Hope*,[53] Henderson J held that a proposed exercise of the power in the scheme to secure pensions by buying annuities to apply the fund to buy annuities for some of the members in the knowledge that the benefits of the other members would be largely met by the PPF was improper as a fraud on the power and a circumvention of the scheme of the Pensions Act 2004. The same result is likely to apply in most circumstances where trustees put into effect a course of action which would be questionable in the absence of the security provided by the PPF and which resulted in increased liabilities for the PPF. The long-term interests of the members will normally lie with the trustees continuing to collect contributions from the employer and continuing to allow members to accrue service. Nevertheless, the size of the company's liability may often mean that the trustees will feel that this process is precarious.

Conversely, if the company wishes to reduce its exposure to pensions liabilities over time, **29.71** its interests are likely to lie in limiting future accrual under the scheme (for example by closing the scheme to new members) while meeting its liabilities as they arise. Immediate withdrawal may well currently be unattractively expensive, but there may come a time when financial conditions conspire to make withdrawal affordable. However, until that time, the trustees will continue to insist on (and the company will be obliged to pay) contributions on the basis that the company must over time discharge any deficit in the scheme.[54] As the scheme becomes more mature, the basis of valuation of the scheme will tend towards the gilt-based 'buy-out' basis.

(3) Powers of the Regulator: civil penalties and moral hazard

The Regulator has power to impose on employers civil penalties for breach of some of the **29.72** statutory obligations of employers under the pensions legislation. The specific statutory obligations in relation to which civil penalties may be imposed are too numerous to itemize here. However, they include failure of the employer without reasonable excuse to pay contributions under a schedule of contributions (under Pensions Act 2004, s 228(4)(b)).

The Pensions Act 1995, s 10 and Pensions Act 2004, s 314 both provide that these civil **29.73** penalties may be imposed on a director of the trustee company where the act or omission on which the civil penalty is based 'was done with the consent or connivance of, or is attributable to any neglect on the part of' the relevant director.[55]

This raises the prospect of personal liability under the section for a director of a company **29.74** which fails to meet its liabilities under a schedule of contributions. The extent to which the Regulator will use the power to impose civil penalties in this way remains to be seen.

However, powers which the Regulator certainly has exercised are the 'moral hazard' powers **29.75** set out in the code at Pensions Act 2004, ss 38–51. This code provides the Regulator with two powers to require payments to be paid to the scheme which stand outside the scope of the

---

[52] eg *L v M* [2007] PLR 11.
[53] [2009] EWHC 2810 (Ch), [2010] ICR 553.
[54] As a 'recovery plan' under Pensions Act 2004, Part 3.
[55] By virtue of Pensions Act 1995 s 10(5)(b) and (6)(a).

obligations of the employer to pay contributions under the statutory schedule of contributions. The ultimate sanction in each case is service of a contribution notice on the target, the amount specified in which is recoverable from the target as a debt in court proceedings. The power arises in the following situations:

(1) The s 38 contribution notice procedure. This applies where the target is either the employer or a person 'connected with or an associate of' the employer[56] and was 'party'[57] to an act or a deliberate failure to act whose main purpose in the Regulator's opinion was to prevent the recovery of a debt under s 75 or 'otherwise than in good faith' to prevent a debt becoming due, settle it or reduce it. Where these conditions are fulfilled, the Regulator has power to impose a contribution notice on one or more of the qualifying targets. Although the quantum of the notice is the amount which the Regulator considers to be reasonable, it is now settled that the section requires there to be a causative link between the act which the Regulator relies on and the amount of the contribution notice.[58] In practice, this regime imports a species of fault-based liability in relation to transactions which attempt to procure that an employer does not have to meet a s 75 liability owed to the scheme, whether or not that liability has in fact arisen.

(2) The s 47 contribution notice procedure. This applies where an employer is under-resourced, either because it is a service company (ie a company whose turnover derives from charges made to other members of the company's group for the services of the employer's employees[59]) or is 'insufficiently resourced'.[60] Again, the amount which can be recovered from the target is the amount which in the opinion of the Regulator is reasonable[61]. However, by contrast to the s 38 procedure, the s 47 procedure imports no requirement of fault and in principle is not limited by a requirement that the amount to be recovered by the target should have in some way have been caused by that fault. The test for the identity of targets for the procedure is similar to the test which applies in respect of the s 38 procedure but has a narrower ambit.

29.76 Both of these powers potentially have a wide application and the s 47 power imports a substantial element of discretion. It is therefore often of critical importance to know who is within the scope of the potential targets for notices.

29.77 Under the s 38 regime, only the employer in relation to the scheme or a person connected with or an associate of the employer who was party to the impugned act or failure to act can be the subject of a contribution notice.[62] The tests for 'connection' and for being an 'associate' are the wide insolvency tests in the Insolvency Act 1986, 249 and 435.[63] This means that a director or shadow director of the employer can be a target (under s 249) as can any employee of the employer,[64] or an individual who controls the employer.[65] In practice, the Regulator

---

[56] See Pensions Act 2004, s 38(3)(a).
[57] Defined at s 38(6)(a) as including those persons who knowingly assist in the act or deliberate failure to act.
[58] *Michel van de Wiele NV v Pensions Regulator* [2011] Pens LR 109.
[59] Section 44(2).
[60] Defined (broadly) as a company whose value is less than 50 per cent of the s 75 debt. The provisions were considered in detail in the Canadian case of *Nortel.*
[61] See ss 47(3) and 43(5).
[62] Section 38(3)(b).
[63] Pensions Act 2004, s 51(3).
[64] By s 435(4).
[65] By s 435(7).

has often targeted individuals in s 38 cases.[66] This clearly constitutes a significant statutory extension to the potential liability of directors in relation to the activities of companies where (as will often be the case) a pension obligation is in issue.

Equally, companies in the same group as the employer (companies under the same control **29.78** as the employer[67]) and holding companies (companies which control the employer[68]) are also potentially within the scope of the charge. However, in each case it is the relationship with the employer which is critical, so that third party purchasers who are not connected or associated with the employer are outside the scope of the charge even if the third party was in some way involved in the impugned act of failure to act.

Under the s 47 regime, the scope for the Regulator to bring claims against individuals is **29.79** much more limited, no doubt as a matter of policy, since the s 47 regime does not require proof of fault. So, the s 47 notice for support can be served on the employer, an associate of the employer or someone connected with the employer, as under the s 38 regime.[69] However, it is only if the employer is an individual that an individual can fall within the net of the section as an 'associate' or person 'connected with' the employer. Under the s 47 regime, the full breadth of the insolvency test only applies to persons who are not individuals.[70] In practice, therefore, the scope for an individual to become liable under the s 47 regime is much more limited than under the fault-based s 38 regime.

---

[66] See *Michel van de Wiele NV v Pensions Regulator* [2011] Pens LR 109, which concerned a sale of a company under a 'pre-pack', *Desmond v Pensions Regulator* [2011] WL 6943288 and the decision of the Determination Panel of the Regulator in the *Carrington Wire* case (24 April 2015), where the target was alleged to have acted in such a way as to negative the effect of a guarantee.

[67] By s 435(6).

[68] By s 435(7).

[69] Under s 43.

[70] By s 43(6).

Part VI

PUBLIC INTEREST
AND INSOLVENCY PROCEEDINGS

30

INVESTIGATIONS AND PUBLIC INTEREST WINDING-UP PETITIONS

Glen Davis QC

A. Introduction

Serious misconduct, or breaches of duty by a company or its directors affecting the company's relationships with members of the public, may trigger an investigation by the Secretary of State into the manner in which the company's business has been conducted, or even the appointment of inspectors and publication of a formal report. In an appropriate case, the Secretary of State or a regulatory authority may petition the court to wind the company up on the basis that it is 'just and equitable' to do so in the public interest. Such a liquidation need not be predicated on insolvency. A winding-up order terminates the directors' powers of management and is the logical response to misconduct or mismanagement by directors which is revealed by an inspector's report. **30.01**

Following an investigation, or where a company has become insolvent, the Secretary of State may apply for an order disqualifying the subject from acting as a director of a company or otherwise being concerned in a company's affairs. A court before whom a person is being tried for a relevant offence may also have jurisdiction to make such an order. **30.02**

The relevant statutory provisions are not among those consolidated in the 2006 Act, although they have been amended in some respects by that Act. Investigations are conducted under the 1985 Act, Part 14, which continues in force. Public interest winding-up petitions are presented, and the subsequent liquidations are carried out, under the Insolvency Act, with jurisdiction extended by relevant legislation where the company in question or the business it carries out is of a particular type (paragraph 30.55 below). **30.03**

B. Investigations

(1) Initiating an investigation

30.04   The vast majority of investigations will take the form of confidential enquiries utilizing the compulsory powers of the Secretary of State under the 1985 Act, s 447, which provides[1] as follows:

(1)   The Secretary of State[2] may act under subsections (2) and (3) in relation to a company.[3]

(2)   The Secretary of State may give directions to the company requiring it—

(a)   to produce such documents (or documents of such description) as may be specified in the directions;

(b)   to provide such information (or information of such description) as may be so specified.

(3)   The Secretary of State may authorise a person (an investigator) to require the company or any other person—

(a)   to produce such documents[4] (or documents of such description) as the investigator may specify;

(b)   to provide such information (or information of such description) as the investigator may specify.

30.05   The Court of Appeal considered the legislative history and intent of s 447 (as then enacted) in *Attorney-General's Reference (No.2 of 1998)*,[5] noting that the power to obtain documents and information from directors and officers had been introduced (originally in Companies Act 1967) following a recommendation by the Jenkins Committee in 1962,[6] and saying:

We believe the legislative history is significant in this case, for it gives insight into the legislative intention and the balance Parliament sought to achieve between important public and individual interests. It is of great public importance that the Secretary of State should be able to make inquiries into the affairs of the company before he embarks upon the appointment

---

[1]   The present form of 1985 Act, s 447 was substituted by the C(AICE) Act, s 21 as from 6 April 2005, subject to the transitional provisions in Arts 6–13 of the Companies (Audit, Investigations and Community Enterprise) Act 2004 (Commencement) and Companies Act 1989 (Commencement No 18) Order 2004 (SI 2004/3322). These broadly provide for authorizations and requirements made under the preceding provisions to continue to have effect.

[2]   The legislation refers only to 'the Secretary of State'. From 1983 to 2007, the relevant powers were exercised by the Secretary of State for Trade and Industry. From 28 June 2007 until 5 June 2009, they were exercised by the Secretary of State for Business, Enterprise and Regulatory Reform (his department being colloquially known as 'BERR'). From 5 June 2009 until 14 July 2016, they were exercised by the Secretary of State for Business, Innovation and Skills (his department being colloquially known as 'DBIS'). Since 14 July 2016, they have been exercised by the Secretary of State for Business, Energy and Industrial Strategy (his department being colloquially known as 'DBEIS').

[3]   Under the 2006 Act, the definition of a 'company' for the purposes of the Companies Acts (a term which, by 2006 Act, s 2(1)(c), includes those provisions of the 1985 Act that remain in force, ie including s 447), is a company formed and registered under the 2006 Act or an existing company (formed under the 1985 Act or earlier legislation). This definition came into force on 1 October 2009, when the definition of 'company' in the 1985 Act, s 735(1) was repealed. 1985 Act, s 453 extends these provisions so that there is power to investigate overseas companies: bodies corporate incorporated outside the UK which are or have at any time carried on business there. The powers under 1985 Act, s 431 to investigate on the application of a company or its members, and under ss 442–5 of that Act to investigate the ownership of a company, do not apply to an overseas company.

[4]   The term 'document' is given a wide definition in s 447(8) for the purposes of these provisions: it 'includes information recorded in any form'.

[5]   [2000] QB 412.

[6]   Report of the Company Law Committee (1962)(Cmnd 1749) at paras 214–5.

of inspectors which could be damaging to the interests of the company, its shareholders and others; and on the other hand there is a need to ensure that those who are asked for an explanation of documents are not subject to questioning which could expose them to penalties in circumstances in which they may not appreciate the nature and extent of the answers they are required to give.[7]

The Court of Appeal rejected an argument that s 447 as it was then drafted should be given a restricted meaning; the present provisions are anyway wider.

An investigation will usually commence as a result of a complaint from a member of the pub- **30.06**
lic or information provided by another regulator or an insolvency practitioner. The government does not randomly select companies to investigate.[8] In practice, the complaint will be investigated by the Companies Investigation Branch (CIB).[9] Published guidance indicates that CIB will investigate a limited company where there is sufficient 'good reason' and it is the public interest to do so; they may investigate if information received suggests 'corporate abuse', which 'may include serious misconduct, fraud, scams or sharp practice in the way the company operates'[10], Previous statements by CIB have indicated that there must be reasonable grounds to suspect fraud, serious misconduct, material wrongdoing or significant irregularity in a company's affairs for an investigation to take place, that they investigate 'aspects of corporate behaviour which might harm both the business community and the public generally', and that they give higher priority to 'those cases with a higher level of risk to the public'.[11] The most recent published guidance indicates that CIB will investigate where information they receive suggests corporate abuse, which 'may include serious misconduct, fraud, scams or sharp practice in the way the company operates'. The Insolvency Service aims to complete consideration of 90 per cent of complaints within two months and 90 per cent of investigations within six months.[12] The results of an investigation are not necessarily

---

[7] Per Beldam LJ at 424.

[8] There was a clear statement of this policy by the DTI, the predecessor of BERR, DBIS, and DBEIS, in the Guidance Document published in January 2005 when the C(AICE) Act 2004 came into force. This publication indicated that only some 5 per cent of complaints and referrals result in an investigation.

The Insolvency Service Annual Report for 2014–15 (published in September 2015) recorded that in the relevant year the Service had carried out 150 investigations, wound up 102 companies, disqualified 1,209 directors and obtained 578 restriction orders against insolvent individuals. The Report particularly highlighted interventions by the Insolvency Service's Public Interest Unit where the public had lost money through pressure selling of worthless carbon credit certificates and wine investment scams. One egregious example was the case of Bordeaux Fine Wines Ltd, wound up in the public interest on 26 February 2014, in which the company had sold wine worth at least £19 million to investors but failed to supply at least £9 million worth of cases.

The Annual Report for 2015–16 (published in July 2016) recorded that in that year the Service had carried out 153 investigations, wound up 131 companies, disqualified 1,208 directors and obtained 434 restriction orders against insolvent individuals, as well as making 483 criminal referrals to prosecuting authorities and 25 further disclosures to other regulators. It highlighted 'scams' such as pressure selling of coloured diamonds at inflated prices and inappropriate sales of health supplements.

[9] CIB forms part of the regulatory arm of DBEIS and is nowadays located within the Insolvency Service, an Executive Agency sponsored by DBEIS, although its remit runs wider than insolvencies. For a general account of how CIB formerly operated and the exercise of powers then contained in the Companies Act 1967, see *In re Golden Chemical Products Ltd* [1976] Ch 300.

[10] *Company Investigations—What We Do*, as updated in July 2016 and available on the Government website at <https://www.gov.uk/government/publications/the-insolvency-service-company-investigations-what-we-do>.

[11] These quotations were taken from *When Can the Service Investigate* on the Insolvency Service website as it appeared in April 2012. Earlier statements of policy in similar terms appeared on the Insolvency Service website in February 2008 under the heading *About the Companies Investigation Branch*. The documents are now preserved online in the National Archives <http://webarchive.nationalarchives.gov.uk/*/http://www.bis.gov.uk/insolvency>.

[12] *Company Investigations—What We Do*, as published in July 2016.

made public, and CIB has indicated that they will not tell the complainant whether or not they have decided to investigate or what they have found if they do investigate, but that they will normally pass on the information if they think the complainant's concerns are more appropriate for another public body, and that they issue a press release when they complete any follow-up action.[13]

30.07 There is a measure of protection under the statutory regime for 'whistle-blowers' who make a 'relevant disclosure' to the Secretary of State. Such a disclosure cannot, of and by itself, leave the discloser open to a claim for breach of an obligation of confidence.[14] This would extend to, for example, a director or other insider who wishes to alert CIB to issues of concern. To qualify, the disclosure must be 'of a kind that the person making the disclosure could be required to make' under Part 14 of the 1985 Act.[15] (The conditions which must be satisfied also include that the disclosure is made to the Secretary of State otherwise than in compliance with a requirement under Part 14, but this does not suggest that, where the disclosure is made in compliance with such a requirement, a claim for breach of confidence would arise.) The disclosure must be made in good faith and in the reasonable belief that the disclosure is capable of assisting the Secretary of State for the purpose of exercise of his functions under Part 14,[16] and it must not be more than is reasonably necessary for the purpose of assisting the Secretary of State to exercise those functions.[17] However, there will be no protection if the disclosure is prohibited by an 'enactment' (whenever passed or made),[18] or if the discloser owes an obligation of confidence in respect of the information in the capacity of banker or lawyer.[19]

30.08 The relevant statutory provisions refer to things being done and decisions being made by 'the Secretary of State', but in practice the decisions in question are made by a senior official. It is well established as a matter of public law that this is permissible and appropriate.[20]

30.09 The decision to initiate an investigation or appoint inspectors is merely an administrative decision. There is no requirement for directors and others who may be involved to be given a chance to make representations or offer explanations before such a decision is taken. This does not breach any rules of natural justice, because they should be given an opportunity

---

[13] *Company Investigations—What We Do*, as updated in July 2016 and available on the Government website at <https://www.gov.uk/government/publications/the-insolvency-service-company-investigations-what-we-do>.

[14] s 448A(1).

[15] s 448A(2)(b).

[16] s 448A(2)(c).

[17] s 448A (2)(d).

[18] s 448A(2)(e) and (3); s 448A(5), as amended by Sch 1 para 57 of The Companies Act 2006 (Consequential Amendments, Transitional Provisions and Savings) Order 2009 (SI 2009/1941) provides that 'enactment' in this section has the meaning given by s 1293 of the 2006 Act. Unless the context otherwise requires, this includes subordinate legislation, an Act of the Scottish Parliament and an instrument made under Northern Ireland legislation:

[19] s 448A(2)(e) and (4).

[20] *Carltona Ltd v Commissioners of Works* [1943] 2 All ER 560, 563, CA, per Lord Greene MR; followed by the Court of Appeal in *Lewisham BC v Roberts* [1949] 2 KB 608 and *R v Skinner* [1968] 2 QB 700. In the latter case, Widgery LJ said (at 707): 'if a decision is made on his behalf by one of his officials, then that constitutionally is the Minister's decision. It is not strictly a matter of delegation; it is that the official acts as the Minister himself and the official's decision is the Minister's decision.' This *Carltona* principle was specifically considered and endorsed in the context of CIB investigations by Brightman J in *In re Golden Chemical Products Ltd* [1976] Ch 300, but as Kennedy LJ observed in *R v Secretary of State for Social Services, ex p Sherwin* (1996) 32 BMLR 1, his decision on this point 'really adds nothing to those earlier decisions'.

to do so in the course of the inquiry. However, there must exist at least some reasonable grounds for the decision to investigate, and the decision must be made in good faith.[21] As Lord Denning MR has explained: 'the officers of the Department of Trade are appointed to examine the books, there is no need for the rules of natural justice to be applied. If the company was forewarned and told that the officers were coming, what is to happen to the books? In a wicked world, it is not unknown for books and papers to be destroyed or lost.'[22] The person taking the decision must not exceed or abuse the statutory discretion which they are given, and they must not use it for some ulterior purpose.[23]

A flawed decision to initiate an investigation would in principle be open to challenge by **30.10** judicial review, but in this context the prospects of a successful challenge are unlikely to be high.[24] In *R v Secretary of State for Trade, ex p Perestrello*[25] Woolf J, dismissing an application for judicial review in the context of exercise of powers of inspection of a company's affairs under the 1967 Act, s 109, said that talk of rules of natural justice in this context 'is not really helpful'. Before the Board of Trade exercise their powers, 'they must think there is good reason to do so', so that it is almost inevitable that, before the powers are exercised:

> the officers concerned, and through his officers, the Secretary of State, must regard the situation as one where there are matters to be investigated. They are acting in a policing role. Their function is to see whether their suspicions are justified by what they find, and that being so, it is wholly inappropriate for the case to be approached in the same way as one would approach a person performing a normal judicial role or quasi-judicial role; a situation where the person is making a determination. What is done ... is to ascertain whether there is evidence to support a prima facie view of a possible undesirable situation in relation to a company, and that being so, the role of the Department is very much the role of the potential prosecutor.

Apart from the company itself, a present or former director or other officer is within the **30.11** class of those who may be required to produce documents or provide information to an investigator. A person upon whom a requirement is imposed under s 447(3) may require the investigator to produce evidence of his authority.[26] A requirement under s 447(2) or (3) must be complied with 'at such time and place as may be specified in the directions or by the investigator (as the case may be)'.[27] This would not give an investigator carte blanche to impose an entirely unreasonable time and place for cooperation, but in a case of urgency, a person could be required to cooperate outside normal office hours.

---

[21] *Norwest Holst Ltd v Secretary of State for Trade* [1978] Ch 201, CA.
[22] *Norwest Holst Ltd* (n 21 above), 224.
[23] *R v Secretary of State for Trade, ex p Perestrello* [1981] QB 19, 35, per Woolf J.
[24] In *R v Commission for Racial Equality, ex p Hillingdon London Borough Council* [1982] QB 276, 300, CA, Griffiths LJ considered the *Norwest Holst* decision and said:

> The primary question with which the court was concerned was whether there was an obligation on the Board of Trade to give a hearing to the company before exercising their power to appoint inspectors. The court held there was no such requirement. As to the wide question whether in an appropriate case the court would have power to review the minister's decision if it could be demonstrated that there were no circumstances suggesting misconduct by the company, it is clear from the judgments of Lord Denning M.R. and Geoffrey Lane LJ, 225, 230 respectively, that they considered that the court had such a power, although there were no grounds for exercising it as the affidavit sworn on behalf of the minister in fact revealed circumstances suggesting misconduct. Again I find nothing in this authority to suggest that an administrative power can only be quashed on grounds of bad faith.

[25] [1981] QB 19, 34.
[26] s 447(4).
[27] s 447(5).

30.12   Documents which are sought in the course of an investigation may be in the hands of a third party such as a lawyer or accountant. Such a professional adviser may have a possessory lien over the documents until their bill is paid. At common law, a possessory lien is lost if the party loses possession of the item over which the lien is claimed.[28] To overcome objection on this score, s 447(6) provides that the production of a document in pursuance of s 447 does not affect any lien which a person has on the document.

30.13   Failure to comply with a requirement under s 447 is not of itself an offence, but the 1985 Act, s 453C[29] provides that the inspector, Secretary of State, or investigator may certify the fact of non-compliance to the court. If, after hearing any witnesses and any statement in defence, the court is satisfied that the offender has failed to comply with the requirement without reasonable excuse, it is punished as if the defaulter was guilty of a contempt of court.[30] It is also one of the factors which the court may take into consideration in deciding whether to make a winding-up order[31] or a disqualification order.

30.14   A person who, in purported compliance with a requirement to provide information under s 447, provides information which he knows to be false in a material particular, or who recklessly provides information which is false in a material particular, commits a criminal offence.[32] The penalty is a prison term of up to two years or a fine or both.[33]

30.15   It is also an offence for an officer[34] of a company to destroy, mutilate, or falsify a document affecting or relating to the company's property or affairs, to make a false entry in such a document, or to be privy to such a thing being done by another person. If the facts are proved, the officer is guilty 'unless he proves that he had no intention to conceal the state of affairs of the company or to defeat the law'.[35] An officer who fraudulently parts with, alters, or makes an omission in any such document,[36] or is privy to someone else doing so, also commits an offence.[37] The penalty for these offences is a prison term of up to seven years or a fine or both.[38]

30.16   Where there are reasonable grounds for believing that documents[39] exist which have not been produced in compliance with a requirement under Part 14 of the 1985 Act, and that

---

[28] Cf *Larner v Fawcett* [1950] 2 All ER 727.

[29] Inserted by the C(AICE) Act 2004, as from 6 April 2005.

[30] s 453C.

[31] Cf *Re Atlantic Property Ltd* [2006] EWHC 610 (Ch), per Lawrence Collins J at [10]–[11].

[32] s 451(1).

[33] s 447(2) as substituted by 2006 Act, s 1124 and Sch 3, para 5(1) with effect from 1 October 2007.

[34] By 2006 Act, s 1173(1) 'officer' in relation to a body corporate 'includes a director, manager or secretary'. This section replaced the definition to similar effect in the 1985 Act, s 744 with effect from 1 October 2009.

[35] s 450(1). The offences under this section are not limited to those which occur or come to light in connection with an investigation. In *R v Chauhan* [2000] 2 CR App R (S) 230, the defendants were accused of a course of conduct which created a false or misleading impression as to the market in or price of investments. The indictment included a charge under 1985 Act, s 450(1) to which the defendant pleaded guilty. He was sentenced to 18 months' imprisonment on each count, to be served concurrently, and was disqualified from acting as a director for ten years. The sentence was upheld on appeal. The Court of Appeal considered that it gave a very heavy discount for the assistance which this defendant had given to the prosecuting authorities, and in the circumstances it was 'a very lenient sentence indeed'.

[36] This reflects the wording of the Insolvency Act, s 206(10)(e) where the conduct has occurred within the 12 months immediately preceding the commencement of the winding up of a company.

[37] s 450(2).

[38] s 450(3) as substituted by 2006 Act, s 1124 and Sch 3, para 4(1) with effect from 1 October 2007.

[39] By s 448(10) 'document' is again given a wide definition for the purposes of s 448 so that it includes 'information recorded in any form'.

they are thought to be at particular premises, an application may be made to a justice of the peace under the 1985 Act, s 448 for a warrant to enter and search the premises. The information in support of the application must be verified on oath by or on behalf of the Secretary of State or by a person appointed or authorized to exercise powers under Part 14.[40] The application is self-evidently not one which would be made on notice to the company or its directors, because that would defeat its purpose.

A warrant may also be issued if, on information similarly verified on oath, a justice of the **30.17** peace is satisfied that there are reasonable grounds for believing that an offence has been committed for which the penalty on conviction on indictment is imprisonment for a term of not less than two years, that documents relating to whether the offence has been committed exist on any premises, that the Secretary of State, or the person appointed or authorized (ie inspector or investigator) has power to require production, and that there are reasonable grounds for believing that the documents would not be produced if production was required, but instead the documents would be removed from the premises, hidden, tampered with, or destroyed.[41] The warrant can also cover other documents at the premises if the justice of the peace is satisfied on the information on oath that there are reasonable grounds for believing that such other documents are also on the premises.[42]

The warrant will be valid for one month beginning with the day of issue.[43] It must name at **30.18** least one constable, and may name other persons (who would in most cases be the investigator or inspector or members of their staff). Those named in the warrant, and any other constables, are authorized under the warrant to enter the premises specified in the information using such force as is reasonably necessary for the purpose,[44] search them and either take possession of the documents or take any other steps which may appear to be necessary for preserving them or preventing interference with them.[45] They may also take copies of such documents,[46] and under s 448(3)(d) they may require any person named in the warrant to provide an explanation of the documents or to state where they may be found. It is a criminal offence[47] intentionally to obstruct the exercise of any rights conferred by the warrant, or to fail without reasonable excuse to comply with a requirement under s 448(3)(d).

Documents seized under s 448 may be retained for three months,[48] unless criminal proceed- **30.19** ings to which the documents are relevant are commenced within that period, in which case they may be retained until the conclusion of those proceedings.[49]

(2) Appointment of inspectors

Appointment by the Secretary of State

In the most serious cases, the Secretary of State will appoint inspectors under the 1985 **30.20** Act, ss 431 or 432 to investigate the affairs of a company and to report the result of their

---

[40] s 448(1).
[41] s 448(2).
[42] s 448(4).
[43] s 448(5).
[44] s 448(3)(a).
[45] s 448(3)(b).
[46] s 448(3)(c).
[47] s 448(7) and (7A). The offence is punishable by a fine.
[48] s 448(6)(a).
[49] s 448(6)(b).

investigations to him.[50] The Secretary of State is at liberty to appoint anyone he considers suitably qualified, but the usual practice has been to appoint a team comprising a senior accountant and a senior lawyer. CIB has in the past indicated that inspections are normally carried out 'where the company involved is a major plc and the matters subject to enquiry are of significant public interest'.[51] Appointments of inspectors are now rare.[52]

Appointment following application to the Secretary of State

30.21 An appointment under the 1985 Act, s 431 is made following an application to the Secretary of State by the company itself,[53] or by a specified proportion of its members. Where the company has share capital, the application must be made by not less than 200 members or members holding not less than one-tenth of the issued shares (not counting treasury shares).[54] In the case of a company not having share capital (such as a company limited by guarantee), the application must be made by not less than one-fifth of the registered members.[55]

30.22 An application must be supported by cogent evidence to show that there is 'good reason' for requiring the investigation. There is no statutory definition of what will constitute a 'good reason' for these purposes, but to justify an investigation there would need to be prima facie evidence of sufficient weight that at least some serious misconduct involving the public interest may have taken place. The applicants may also be required to give security[56] for the costs of the investigation.

Appointment of inspectors following court order

30.23 The Secretary of State is required to appoint inspectors if the court declares that the company's affairs ought to be investigated.[57] There is no limit on the court's jurisdiction in this respect, so it would appear that this is in principle something which the court could order of its own motion in any case in which it came to the conclusion that such an order is justified on the evidence in proceedings before it.

30.24 Where an application has been made to the Secretary of State who has declined to appoint inspectors or simply failed to do so, or where it is not possible for the prospective applicant to comply with the requisite conditions described above, a formal application may be made to court for a declaration that the affairs of the company ought to be investigated.[58] As the

---

[50] Powers to appoint an inspector to examine into the affairs of a company were formerly exercised by the Board of Trade, and can be traced back through the 1948 Act, s 165 and the 1929 Act, s 135 to the 1862 Act, s 56. In an early discussion of the scope of the inspector's function, Lord Esher MR said in *Re Grosvenor and West-End Railway Terminus Hotel Co Ltd* (1897) 76 LT 337, CA: 'The object of the inquiry which the Board of Trade has authority to order under s 56 is to examine into and ascertain facts to enable the inspector to make a report of his opinion to the Board of Trade. That is all.'

[51] A statement to this effect previously appeared on the Insolvency Service website.

[52] Since 2000 there have been only two appointments: Transtec plc (Hugh Aldous FCA and Roger Kaye QC appointed January 2000, report published October 2003) and Phoenix Venture Holdings Ltd and MG Rover Group Ltd (Gervase MacGregor FCA and Guy Newey QC appointed May 2005, report published September 2009). This contrasts with increasing use by the FSA (now FCA) of its powers to require a report under FSMA, s 166 on the activities of a company which is regulated under that Act.

[53] s 431(2)(c): it appears that the directors can resolve to cause the company to apply, without requiring to seek the approval of the shareholders by resolution in general meeting.

[54] s 431(2)(a).

[55] s 431(2)(b).

[56] The present limit is £5,000, but a higher amount may be specified by order: s 431(4).

[57] s 432(1).

[58] Such applications are now governed by PD49A, supplementing Part 49 CPR, entitled '*Applications under the Companies Acts and Related Legislation*' (2016 White Book at Vol 2 2G–7). Although para 5 of PD49A

procedure requires that notice is given to the Secretary of State (by service on his departmental solicitors), the Secretary of State will have an opportunity to consider making an appointment without being directed to do so by the court. Contested applications to court for appointments are understandably rare.

Discretionary appointment of inspectors by the Secretary of State

The Secretary of State also has a discretionary power to appoint inspectors if it appears to him that there are circumstances suggesting the existence of one or more of the conditions set out in the 1985 Act, subs 432(2). These are: **30.25**

(a) that the company's affairs are being or have been conducted with intent to defraud the creditors or the creditors of any other person, or otherwise for a fraudulent or unlawful purpose, or in a manner which is unfairly prejudicial to some part of its members;[59]
(b) that any actual or proposed act or omission of the company (including an act or omission on its behalf) is or would be so prejudicial, or that the company was formed for any fraudulent or unlawful purpose;
(c) that persons concerned with the company's formation or the management of its affairs have in connection therewith been guilty of fraud, misfeasance, or other misconduct towards it or towards its members; and
(d) that the company's members have not been given all the information with respect to its affairs which they might reasonably expect.

An application which is supported by an insufficient number of members to qualify under the 1985 Act, s 431 may therefore nonetheless be sufficient to trigger an appointment under s 432. **30.26**

(3) Investigation by the inspectors and report

Scope of appointment

An appointment under either s 431 or 432 is an appointment to investigate 'the affairs of the company'. The term is wide on its face, and there is no statutory definition. The natural meaning connotes the company's 'business affairs', and the expression has been held to include the company's 'goodwill, its profits or losses, its contracts and assets including its shareholding in and ability to control the affairs of a subsidiary' and extended to the activities of a receiver and manager appointed by a debenture holder who had constituted himself a director of a subsidiary and sold the shareholding in a sub-subsidiary at an undervalue.[60] **30.27**

---

suggests that this practice direction applies unless another practice direction provides otherwise, it appears that previous practice directions in this area are superseded, including the old practice direction reported at [1954] 1 WLR 563 (see notes to PD49A in the 2016 White Book at 2G–38). An application should now be commenced by Part 8 Claim Form. Although there is no specific provision in the present practice direction, the application should be supported by full evidence of all facts and matters relied on, and it should be served on the solicitor for DBIS. Evidence of such service should be filed with the court.

[59] s 432(4) provides that the reference to members in s 432(2)(a) includes a person who is not a member but to whom shares in the company have been transferred or transmitted by operation of law (as does the 2006 Act, s 994(2)).

[60] *R v Board of Trade, ex p St Martin Preserving Co Ltd* [1965] 1 QB 603, 613. For discussion of the scope of the affairs of the company in the context of an unfair prejudice petition under the 2006 Act, Part 30, see Ch 23 at paras 23.18–23.22 above.

30.28 Once inspectors have been appointed, they can extend their investigation to a subsidiary or holding company of the company under investigation, or to another member of the same group ('a subsidiary of its holding company or a holding company of its subsidiary') if they think it necessary to do so for the purposes of their investigation. They are required to report also on the affairs of the other body corporate 'so far as they think that the results of their investigation of its affairs are relevant to the investigation of the original subject company'.[61]

30.29 Changes introduced under the 2006 Act[62] have made clear that the Secretary of State has power to give the inspectors directions, and the 1985 Act, s 446A(1) provides that an inspector must comply with them. An inspector may also seek directions.[63] The general powers to give directions include:

(1) as to the subject matter of the investigation, by reference to a specified area of the company's operation, a specified transaction, a period of time 'or otherwise'; and[64]

(2) as to a particular step in the investigation which the inspector is required to take or not to take.[65]

30.30 The Secretary of State also now has power to direct that an inspector is to take no further steps in his investigation.[66] If the inspector was appointed under the 1985 Act, s 432(1) following a declaration by the court that the affairs of the company ought to be investigated,[67] the Secretary of State may only give a direction bringing an investigation to a premature end on grounds that matters suggesting that a criminal offence has been committed have come to light and been referred to the appropriate prosecuting authority.[68] In such circumstances, any requirement for the inspector to produce an interim report will lapse,[69] and the inspector will only be required to make a final report to the Secretary of State if matters suggesting criminal offences have been committed have been referred to the prosecuting authorities and the Secretary of State requires a report,[70] or the appointment followed an order of the court.[71]

Duties towards inspectors

30.31 Under the 1985 Act, s 434(1) it is the duty of all officers and agents of the company or of any other body corporate to which the investigation is extended by inspectors under the 1985 Act, s 433:

(a) to produce to the inspectors all documents of or relating to the company or, as the case may be, the other body corporate which are in their custody or power,

(b) to attend before the inspectors when required to do so, and

(c) otherwise to give the inspectors all assistance in connection with the investigation which they are reasonably able to give.

---

[61] 1985 Act, s 433.

[62] ss 446A and 446B, introduced under 2006 Act, s 1035(1) with effect from 1 October 2007 where an inspector is appointed on or after that date.

[63] s 446A(4)(c).

[64] s 446A(2)(a).

[65] s 446A(2)(b).

[66] s 446B(1).

[67] Or under s 442(3) where inspectors have been appointed to report on the ownership of a company following an application by members.

[68] s 446B(2).

[69] s 446B(3).

[70] s 446B(4)(a).

[71] s 446B(4)(b).

Under the 1985 Act, s 434(2) it is also the duty of an officer or agent of the company or body **30.32** corporate, or any other person whom the inspectors consider is or may be in possession of information relating to a matter which they believe to be relevant to their investigation to comply with a requirement by them:

(a) to produce to [the inspectors] any documents in his custody or power relating to that matter,

(b) to attend before [the inspectors], and

(c) otherwise to give [the inspectors] all assistance in connection with the investigation which he is reasonably able to give.

Amendments to the 1985 Act, s 434 made by the 2006 Act have made clear that a 'docu- **30.33** ment' for these purposes includes 'information recorded in any form'.[72] The power to require production of a document includes the power, where the document is not in hard-copy form, to require production in hard-copy form or from which a hard copy can readily be obtained.[73] The inspectors have power to take copies or extracts from a document produced pursuant to s 434.[74]

Obstruction of inspectors appointed under ss 431 or 432 is treated as a contempt of court **30.34** and punishable in the same manner.[75] This extends to:

(1) failure to comply with the duties under s 434(1)(a) and (c) to produce documents, and otherwise give all the assistance the person is reasonably able to give;[76]

(2) refusal to comply with the duty under s 434(1)(b) to attend the inspectors when required to do so or to comply with a requirement of the inspectors under s 434(2); and[77]

(3) refusal to answer any question put to the person by the inspectors for the purposes of the investigation.[78]

These provisions were considered in *Re an Inquiry into Mirror Group Newspapers plc*[79] when **30.35** inspectors referred to the court the refusal of an ex-director to answer their questions and his refusal to enter into a confidentiality undertaking not to disclose information which, in the course of their questioning, they put to him. The ex-director's excuse and explanation for his refusal to answer the questions was that the particular circumstances of the case had rendered the questioning of him by the inspectors unfair and oppressive, and he said that the inspectors had no right to require him to give a confidentiality undertaking. Sir Richard Scott V-C said:

> the assistance that those on whom the statutory obligation is placed must give is not unlim-
> ited. They must give the assistance that they are 'reasonably able to give'. The word 'rea-
> sonably' limits the extent of their obligation. To put the point another way, the inspectors
> cannot place demands on them that are unreasonable, whether as to the time they must
> expend or the expense they must incur in preparation for the questions or in any other
> respect. Inspectors must bear in mind that those summoned before them are not being

---

[72] s 434(6), amended from 1 October 2007 by 2006 Act, s 1038(1).
[73] s 434(7), added as above.
[74] s 434(8), added as above.
[75] s 436.
[76] s 436(1)(a).
[77] s 436(1)(b).
[78] s 436(1)(c).
[79] [2000] 1 Ch 194.

remunerated for their assistance and will often, perhaps usually, have to take time off their normal business of earning a living in order to provide the requisite assistance. In some cases inspectors will have reason to believe that those they summon to appear before them have committed misfeasances of one sort or another towards the company whose affairs are being investigated.

That circumstance does not, in my judgment, justify any more onerous demands than would be reasonable to make of a person under no similar cloud. The reasonableness and proportionality of inspectors' demands may depend upon the purpose of the inquiry and the nature of the office in the company held by the particular witness. Inspectors appointed, for example, to inquire into what has become of company assets that have gone missing can reasonably, in my view, place a heavy burden of assistance on directors of the company whose duty it was to manage and preserve those assets. All the circumstances must, in my judgment, be taken into account in deciding whether or not assistance which a person is, in an absolute sense, able to give is also assistance which he is *reasonably* able to give. But, if, in all the circumstances, the demands made on the person go beyond what he is *reasonably* able to give, his failure to comply with the demands will not be a breach of his statutory duty and should not be treated as a contempt of court.

Procedural fairness and the conduct of investigations by inspectors

30.36 Inspectors who are appointed under the 1985 Act or the FSMA are under a duty to act fairly towards those whose conduct they may criticize in their report.[80] One aspect of this is for such individuals to have the chance to know in advance the criticisms which may be made, and to make representations about them. As Lord Denning MR famously put it:

> The inspectors can obtain information in any way they think best, but before they condemn or criticise a man, they must give him a fair opportunity for correcting or contradicting what is said against him.[81]

30.37 The practice is for inspectors to communicate their provisional views once their report is nearing completion, so that they can take account of any responses. It is not necessarily unfair for inspectors to provide a summary of their criticisms, as long as it is sufficient for the subject to understand what they are. It is also not necessarily unfair for the inspectors to proceed to complete their report if the subject of criticisms does not respond.[82]

30.38 Where procedural unfairness has denied a party the opportunity to put before the inspectors material which might have made a real difference to their conclusions,[83] it would in principle be possible for the court to grant a declaration to the effect that the inspectors have acted unfairly. However, the courts are reluctant to grant such a declaration which could undermine a report as a whole, and are astute not to allow themselves to be cast in the role of a

---

[80] *Re Pergamon Press Ltd* [1971] Ch 388, 399, 402, 403, 407, CA.

[81] *Re Pergamon Press Ltd* [1971] Ch 388, 400A, CA; cited by Chadwick LJ in *R (Clegg) v Secretary of State for Trade* [2003] BCC 128, CA at para 2.

[82] That was the position in *Clegg* [2003] BCC 128, CA. The inspectors were appointed to investigate alleged insider dealing in the shares of Parkway Group Limited which had been the subject of an agreed takeover by Wace Group plc. Mr Clegg had been managing director of Wace Group. The inspectors' report was published on 31 August 2000. The inspectors completed their report some five years after provisional criticisms had been put to Mr Clegg. He suggested that he had been led to believe that no report would be completed without a response being received from him. The judge at first instance gave permission to proceed with judicial review, but dismissed the substantive application, and he was upheld by the Court of Appeal.

[83] It is not necessary to show that the outcome would have been different, but it is necessary to show that it might have been different, in other words that he had 'a case of substance to make': per Lord Wilberforce in *Malloch v Aberdeen Corporation* [1971] 1 WLR 1578, 1595; *Clegg* [2003] BCC 128 at para 30.

court of appeal against the findings of inspectors, particularly as Parliament itself has granted no right of appeal against such findings. A declaration would only be granted in exceptional circumstances.[84]

Confidential nature of an investigation

The investigation by the inspectors is not a judicial proceeding[85] and ought to be held in **30.39** private.[86] This is in part because it is likely to involve the consideration by the inspectors of information and evidence which is of its nature confidential and in part because the initial report of the inspector to the Secretary of State or prosecuting authorities is a confidential report and there is a risk that it may damage the company or the reputations of individuals if 'unfavourable opinions as to the financial position of the society or company ... prematurely and wrongly formed in the minds of the public or the policy-holders'.[87] In short, 'irreparable harm might unjustly be done to the reputation of a company ... by giving publicity to such preliminary investigations'.[88]

In a particular case, the inspectors may need to show a witness confidential information or **30.40** documents. If they do so, the witness is entitled to use the information to take advice or to prepare for the inspectors' questions, by consulting others who had been involved, in order to check his recollection or remedy his lack of recollection. Using the documents in this way would not be a breach of any duty to those from whom they were obtained or to the inspectors. Disclosure for some other purpose might be a breach of duty to those from whom the documents had been obtained.[89]

An inspector is entitled to the assistance of a person whose assistance is considered to be **30.41** reasonably necessary, which would include a shorthand writer to take a note of proceedings which will assist the inspector when he comes to prepare his report. An officer of the company who is required to answer questions cannot object to doing so because of the presence of such a person.[90] Similarly, parties may attend with counsel to represent them.[91]

Use of evidence in other proceedings

Under the 1985 Act, s 434(3) an inspector may examine a person on oath for the purposes **30.42** of the investigation, and it is well established that the subject cannot resist answering on the

---

[84] See comments of Stanley Burnton J quoted with approval by Chadwick LJ in *Clegg* [2003] BCC 128, CA at para 37.

[85] *In re Grosvenor and West-End Railway Terminus Hotel Co* (1897) 76 LT 337, CA, a case under the 1862 Act. In *Re Pergamon Press Ltd* [1971] Ch 388, Lord Denning MR said at 399 that the 'proceedings are not judicial proceedings ... They are not even quasi-judicial, for they decide nothing; they determine nothing. They only investigate and report. They sit in private and are not entitled to admit the public to their meetings ...'. The European Court of Human Rights has also held that the functions performed by inspectors are investigative rather than adjudicative, so that Art 6 ECHR does not apply: Case No 28/1993/423/502, *Fayed v UK* (1994) 18 EHRR 393.

[86] *Hearts of Oak Assurance Co v AG* [1932] AC 392, a case concerning examination under the Friendly Societies Act 1896, and the Industrial Assurance Act 1923, but in which the House of Lords considered the closest analogy was the appointment of inspectors under the 1929 Act, s 129; see also *Pergamon* [1971] Ch 388 and *Re an Inquiry into Mirror Group Newspapers plc* [2000] Ch 194, 211, 212, per Sir Richard Scott V-C.

[87] *Hearts of Oak Assurance Co v AG* [1932] AC 392, 397, per Lord Thankerton.

[88] *Hearts of Oak Assurance Co v AG* [1932] AC 392, 403 per Lord Macmillan.

[89] *Re an Inquiry into Mirror Group Newspapers plc* [2000] 1 Ch 194.

[90] *Re Gaumont-British Picture Corporation* [1940] Ch 506, applying *Hearts of Oak Assurance Co v AG* [1932] AC 392.

[91] *McLelland, Pope and Langley Ltd v Howard* [1968] 1 All ER 569, HL (Note).

grounds of the usual privilege against self-incrimination.[92] This does not mean that inspectors have unlimited power to pursue investigations, and there may come a point, particularly after a person has been charged with a criminal offence, where further questioning by inspectors on matters relevant to that offence would be regarded as oppressive and unfair.[93]

30.43 An answer given by a person to a question put to him in the course of an investigation by inspectors may be used in evidence against him in subsequent proceedings.[94] This formerly included in criminal proceedings,[95] but in 1996 the European Court of Human Rights found that the use of documents obtained by inspectors under compulsion had violated the defendant's right to a fair hearing under Art 6 EHRC in *Saunders v UK*.[96] The position is now governed by s 434(5A) and (5B)[97] which provides that in criminal proceedings in which the person is charged with an offence other than an offence under the Perjury Act 1911, s 2 or 5[98] (a) no evidence relating to the answer may be adduced, and (b) no question relating to it may be asked by or on behalf of the prosecution, unless evidence relating to it is adduced, or a question relating to it is asked, in the proceedings by or on behalf of that person. It should be noted that this only affords limited protection, because there is no restriction on the evidence being adduced or a question being asked by a co-defendant (for example, in the course of a 'cut-throat' defence). However, a defendant in a criminal trial cannot compel inspectors to produce witness statements made to the inspector in the course of investigation.[99]

30.44 An inspectors' report, certified by the Secretary of State to be a true copy, is admissible in any legal proceedings as evidence of the opinions of the inspectors in relation to any matter contained in the report.[100] It is also evidence of any fact stated therein for the purposes of an application by the Secretary of State for a disqualification order under the CDDA, s 8.[101] A report may also be used to support a winding-up petition by the Secretary of State, or by a contributory if the Secretary of State does not present such a petition.[102] Where the evidence is not challenged, the court may act on the basis of the report supported only by an affidavit of an official,[103] but where it is challenged more direct evidence will be required.[104]

---

[92] *R v Seelig* [1992] 1 WLR 149, CA; *Re London United Investments plc* [1992] Ch 578, CA; *R v Saunders (No 2)* [1996] 1 Cr App R 463.

[93] See comments of Dillon LJ in *Re London United Investments plc* [1992] Ch 578, 600.

[94] s 434(5).

[95] *R v Harris* [1970] 1 WLR 1252.

[96] Case 43/1994/490/572, [1998] BCLC 362. It should, however, be noted that the European Court of Human Rights did not regard the privilege against self-incrimination as absolute, saying that 'it does not extend to the use in criminal proceedings of material which may be obtained from the accused through the use of compulsory powers but which has an existence independent of the will of the suspect such as, inter alia, documents acquired pursuant to a warrant, breath, blood and urine samples and bodily tissue for the purpose of DNA testing'. The question of whether there had been an infringement of the right had to be examined in the light of all the circumstances of the particular case.

[97] Inserted by the Youth Justice and Criminal Evidence Act 1999 with effect from 14 April 2000.

[98] Or the Scottish equivalent.

[99] *R v Cheltenham JJ, ex p Secretary of State for Trade* [1977] 1 WLR 95.

[100] s 441.

[101] s 441.

[102] *Re St Piran* [1981] 1 WLR 1300.

[103] *Re Travel & Holiday Club* [1967] 1 WLR 711; *Re Allied Produce Co* [1967] 1 WLR 1469.

[104] *Re ABC Coupler Engineering Co* [1962] 1 WLR 1236.

Publication of a report

The statutory wording previously provided that the inspectors were to report on the affairs **30.45** of the subject company in such manner as the Secretary of State directs, but a change under the 2006 Act has clarified that the inspectors are to report the result of their investigations to him.[105] This has clarified that, in the first instance, the inspectors are to make an internal report to the Secretary of State. It is then for the Secretary of State (or in practice officials within his department) to decide whether or not to publish a report.[106]

The Secretary of State's powers to give a direction to the appointed inspectors[107] extends to **30.46** power to direct that a report by the inspector should include or exclude the inspector's views on a specified matter,[108] and also that the report is to be made in a specified form or manner,[109] or by a specified date.[110]

Where inspectors have been appointed pursuant to an order of the court, the Secretary of **30.47** State is obliged to furnish a copy of any report by them to the court.[111]

If he thinks fit, the Secretary of State may forward a copy of any report of the inspectors to **30.48** the company's registered office.[112] He may also, if he thinks fit, furnish a copy on request and payment of the prescribed fee to (a) any member of the company or other body corporate which is the subject of the report, (b) the person whose conduct is referred to in the report, (c) the auditors of that company or body corporate, (d) the applicants for the investigation, and (e) any other person whose financial interests appear to the Secretary of State to be affected by the matters dealt with in the report, whether as a creditor of the company or body corporate or otherwise.[113] The Secretary of State may also cause a report to be printed and published,[114] and this is the usual practice.

Expenses of an investigation

In the first instance, the expenses of an investigation under Part XIV of the 1985 Act are **30.49** defrayed by the Secretary of State[115] and met from money provided by Parliament.[116] These expenses will include such reasonable sums as the Secretary of State may determine in respect of general staff costs and overheads.

However, if a person is convicted in proceedings instituted as a result of the investigation, **30.50** they can be ordered in the criminal proceedings to pay the expenses of the investigation to the extent specified in the order.[117] A change under the 2006 Act means that this no longer only applies where the defendant has been ordered to pay the costs in the criminal proceedings.

---

[105] 1985 Act, ss 431(1) and 432(1), amended by 2006 Act, s 1035(2) and (3) respectively, with effect from 1 October 2007 and applying where an inspector is appointed on or after that date.
[106] 1985 Act, ss 473(3)(c) and 443(1); *R (Clegg) v Secretary of State for Trade and Industry* [2003] BCC 128, CA at para 5.
[107] See para 30.29 above.
[108] s 446A(3)(a) and (b).
[109] s 446A(3)(c).
[110] s 446A(3)(d).
[111] s 437(2).
[112] s 437(3)(a).
[113] s 437(3)(b).
[114] s 437(3)(c).
[115] s 439(1).
[116] s 439(10).
[117] s 439(2).

30.51   If the appointment of inspectors was ordered by the court, the company dealt with by the report is liable for the costs unless it was the applicant, and except to the extent that the Secretary of State directs to the contrary.[118]

30.52   The applicants for an investigation under ss 431 or 442(3) are liable to such extent if any as the Secretary of State may direct.[119] Where the Secretary of State has been persuaded to act of his own motion under s 432(2), there is no power to recoup the expenses of the investigation. Where the inspectors were not appointed of the Secretary of State's own motion, they may if they think fit, and must if the Secretary of State so directs them, include in their report recommendations as to how they consider the expenses of the investigation should be directed to be borne.[120]

C.   Public Interest Winding-up Petitions

(1)   Companies that may be wound up in the public interest

30.53   Where it appears to the Secretary of State that it is 'expedient in the public interest that a company[121] should be wound up', from any of the following reports or information the Secretary of State has power[122] to present a winding-up petition under the Insolvency Act, s 124A. The reports and information specified in s 124A(1) are:

(1)   any report made or information obtained as a result of investigations under Part XIV (except under s 448A) of the 1985 Act;

(2)   any report by inspectors under FSMA, ss 167, 168, 169, or 284, or, in the case of an open-ended investment company, under regulations made as a result of s 262(2)(k) of that Act;

(3)   any information or documents obtained by the FCA or PRA under FSMA, ss 165, 171–3, and 175, dealing with investigations by either regulator;[123]

(4)   any information obtained under Criminal Justice Act 1987, s 2 or the Criminal Justice (Scotland) Act 1987, s 52, dealing with investigations of fraud; and

(5)   any information obtained under the 1989 Act, s 83, dealing with powers exercisable for the purpose of assisting overseas regulatory authorities.

30.54   By the Insolvency Act, s 124B, the Secretary of State also has power to petition for the winding up of a Societas Europaea (SE) set up under Article 1 of the EC Statute for a European Company[124] which does not comply with the requirement under Article 7 of that statute

---

[118] s 439(4).
[119] s 439(5).
[120] s 439(6).
[121] Including a foreign company: *Re Delfin International (SA) Ltd* [2000] 1 BCLC 71. A public interest petition may be presented against a foreign corporation which has been dissolved in its state of incorporation: *Secretary of State for BIS v New Horizon Energy Ltd* [2015] EWHC 2961 (Ch), in which one of the respondents had been dissolved in Illinois for failure to file accounts.
[122] Under the Insolvency Act, s 124(4)(b). The Secretary of State may also present a petition under s 124(4)(a) if the ground of the petition is that in s 122(1)(b) (a public company which was registered as such on its original incorporation, the company not having been issued with a trading certificate under the 2006 Act, s 76, and more than a year has passed since it was so registered) or that in s 122(1)(c) (an 'old public company', within the meaning of Sch 3 of the Companies Act 2006 (Consequential Amendments, Transitional Provisions and Savings) Order 2009.
[123] As amended by the Financial Services Act 2012 with effect from 1 April 2013.
[124] Council Regulation 2157/2001 of 8 October 2001.

for an SE's registered office to be located in the same Member State as its head office, and it appears to the Secretary of State that it should be wound up.

The FCA and PRA have analogous powers to present a petition in respect of a company **30.55** which is authorized under FSMA, s 367,[125] and the FCA may also petition for breach of certain obligations by a European Cooperative Society.[126]

In the case of a 'community interest company' established and regulated under Part 2 of **30.56** the C(AICE) Act 2004, the Regulator of Community Interest Companies may present a winding-up petition.[127]

Such petitions are commonly referred to as 'public interest' petitions. Only the Secretary of **30.57** State (or by analogy the specified regulator) is entitled to rely solely on the public interest when seeking a winding up on 'just and equitable' grounds.[128] It is open to the Secretary of State also to rely on the insolvency of the company, but it is not necessary for him to do so. Conversely, it has been said that insolvency as such is not sufficient in itself to justify a winding up in the public interest,[129] but the reasons for and circumstances of the insolvency may be highly material.[130]

A public interest petition may be presented in respect of a foreign company.[131] However, **30.58** the court will only make a winding-up order if it is satisfied that there is sufficient connection with this jurisdiction and/or of prejudice to local public interest.[132] Because it is not necessary for a public interest petition to be founded on insolvency, such proceedings (notwithstanding that the petition and, if an order is made, the liquidation, are conducted under the Insolvency Act) do not constitute *insolvency proceedings* for the purposes of the EC Regulation on Insolvency Proceedings.[133] This means that the court is not concerned to establish that it has sufficient jurisdiction to hear a public interest petition because the *centre of main interest* of the company lies within the UK and not some other EC Member State, but it also implies that there is no automatic recognition of a public interest liquidation in other Member States.

(2) The Secretary of State's decision

The threshold requirement is that the Secretary of State has formed the opinion that it is **30.59** 'expedient in the public interest' for the company to be wound up. Forming and holding the relevant opinion give the Secretary of State standing to present his petition.[134] Although the

---

[125] Examples are: *Re Inertia Partnership LLP* [2007] 1 BCLC 739; *Re Digital Satellite Warranty Cover Ltd* [2011] Bus LR 981 (Warren J), upheld in the Court of Appeal ([2012] 2 All ER (Comm) 38), and in the Supreme Court (*Digital Satellite Warranty Cover Ltd v FSA* [2013] 1 WLR 605).

[126] Insolvency Act, ss 124(4)(AA) and 124C(1)–(2).

[127] Insolvency Act, s 124(4A) and C(AICE) Act, s 50. Note the former states that the petition may be presented in a case falling within the latter, but the latter merely states that the Regulator may present a petition for a community interest company to be wound up if the court is of the opinion that it is just and equitable that the company should be wound up, not applying if the company is already being wound up by the court.

[128] *Re Millennium Advanced Technology Ltd* [2004] 1 WLR 2177.

[129] *Re Senator Hanseatische Verwaltungsgesellschaft mbH* [1997] 1 WLR 515, CA; *Re Marann Brooks CSV Ltd* [2003] BCC 239.

[130] *Re UK-Europe Group plc* [2007] 1 BCLC 812.

[131] *Re Delfin International (SA) Ltd* [2000] 1 BCLC 71.

[132] In *Re a Company (No 007816 of 1994)* [1997] 2 BCLC 685, CA and in *Re Titan International Inc* [1998] 1 BCLC 102, CA public interest petitions failed on these grounds.

[133] *Re Marann Brooks CSV Ltd* [2003] BCC 239.

[134] *Re Walter L Jacob & Co Ltd* [1989] BCLC 345, CA.

section refers to the decision being made by the Secretary of State, there is no requirement for the decision to be made by the minister personally, and so it may properly be made by the Secretary of State acting through one of his officers.[135]

30.60 The decision must be a proper one, as a matter of public law, in that proper grounds for it must exist and be relied upon, irrelevant matters must not be taken into account, and the opinion must be one that a reasonable Secretary of State could reach. In theory, formation of that opinion is subject to judicial review. In *Re Walter L Jacob & Co Ltd*,[136] the Court of Appeal said that any challenge to the decision must be brought in judicial review proceedings, if at all, and is not a matter for the court hearing the petition. However, as Nicholls LJ pointed out, such a challenge would normally be pointless in practice, because, if no reasonable Secretary of State could have formed the requisite opinion, the petition will presumably fail on its merits in any event, so that judicial review proceedings would be idle.

30.61 The phrase 'expedient in the public interest' is a wide one. As Millett LJ made clear in *Re Senator Hanseatische Verwaltungsgesellschaft mbH*,[137] it is not confined to cases of illegality:

> The expression 'expedient in the public interest', is of the widest import; it means what it says. The Secretary of State has a right, and some would say a duty, to apply to the court to protect members of the public who deal with the company from suffering inevitable loss, whether this derives from illegal activity or not. A common case in which he intervenes is where an insolvent company continues to trade by paying its debts as they fall due out of money obtained from new creditors. The insolvency is the cause of the eventual loss, but it is the need to protect the public, not the insolvency, which grounds the Secretary of State's application for a winding up order in such cases.

(3) The court's discretion

Where the company is not already in liquidation

30.62 The court has jurisdiction to wind up the company on public interest grounds if it thinks it just and equitable to do so. The leading discussion of the principles on which the court exercises its discretion in this regard is to be found in the judgment of Nicholls LJ in the Court of Appeal in *Re Walter L Jacob & Co Ltd*.[138] In *Re UK-Euro Group plc*,[139] Edward Bartley Jones QC conveniently extrapolated from Nicholls LJ's judgment the following summary of the basic principles:

> 1 The burden of proof is on the Secretary of State. That burden of proof, on areas of disputed fact, is the normal burden in civil proceedings, namely proof on the balance of probabilities. However, to wind up an active company compulsorily is a serious step, and the Secretary of State who asserts that it is just and equitable for the court to take that step must

---

[135] *Re Golden Chemical Products Ltd* [1976] Ch 300, applying *Carltona Ltd v Commissioners of Works* [1943] 2 All ER 560, *Lewisham BC v Roberts* [1949] 2 KB 608, and *R v Skinner* [1968] 2 QB 700.

[136] [1989] BCLC 345, CA.

[137] [1997] 1 WLR 515, 526, CA.

[138] [1989] BCLC 345. For further discussion of the applicable principles in particular contexts see, among others: *Re Secure and Provide plc* [1992] BCC 405; *Re Market Wizard Systems (UK) Ltd* [1998] 2 BCLC 282; *Re a Company (No 5669 of 1998)* [2000] 1 BCLC 427; *Re Alpha Club (UK) Ltd* [2002] 2 BCLC 612; *Re a Company (No 6494 of 2003)* [2004] EWHC 126 (Ch); *Re Supporting Link Alliance Ltd* [2004] 1 WLR 1549; *Re Portfolios of Distinction Ltd* [2006] 2 BCLC 261.

[139] [2007] 1 BCLC 812 at para 16.

put forward and establish reasons which have a weight justifying the court taking that step ([1989] BCLC 345).

2 In considering whether or not to make a winding-up order, the court has to have regard to all the circumstances of the case as established by the material before the court at the hearing. In essence, this is a balancing exercise—taking into account the totality of the material before the court and carefully considering those matters which constitute reasons why the company should be wound up compulsorily, and those which constitute reasons why it should not. But it must be firmly borne in mind that, on a Secretary of State's 'public interest' petition, the reasons being put forward for a compulsory winding up are rooted in considerations of the public interest. The court, if it is to discharge its obligations to carry out the appropriate balancing exercise, must itself evaluate those 'public interest' reasons to the extent necessary for the court to form a view as to whether they do, indeed, afford sufficient reason for the making of a winding-up order (see at [1989] BCLC 351–352, 352–353).

3 Whilst the court will note that the source for the submissions that the company should be wound up is a government department charged by Parliament with wide-ranging responsibilities in relation to the affairs of companies, indeed a department which has considerable expertise in these matters and which can be expected to act with a proper sense of responsibility when seeking a winding-up order, nevertheless the cogency of the submissions made on behalf of the Secretary of State will fall to be considered and tested in the same way as any other submissions. The Secretary of State's submissions are not, ipso facto, endowed with such weight that those resisting a winding-up petition presented by him will find the scales loaded against them (see at [1989] BCLC 353).

4 At the end of the day, the court must be able, itself, to identify the aspect or aspects of the public interest which, in the view of the court, would be promoted by making a winding-up order in the particular case (see at [1989] BCLC 353); put another way, the court must be satisfied that a winding-up order is in the public interest and must identify why that is the case (see at [1989] BCLC 354).

5 For many years Parliament has recognised the need for the general public to be protected against the activities of unscrupulous persons who deal in securities. Whilst the comments of Nicholls LJ (at [1989] BCLC 359) were directed to the activities of the subject company in dealing in third party securities, I see no reason whatsoever why this proposition should not apply, in the present case, to the dealings by the company in its own securities. As I shall indicate, below, the company has been in major breach of various regulatory provisions designed to protect the public against the company's dealings in its own securities (ie its own shares).

6 The public interest requires that individuals and companies dealing in securities with the public should maintain at least the generally accepted minimum standards of commercial behaviour and that those who, for whatever reason, fall below those standards should have their activities stopped (see at [1989] BCLC 359).

7 The more unusual and speculative the investment, the heavier is the burden resting on a vendor of shares to ensure that the contents and get-up of his sales literature are not misleading (see at [1989] BCLC 359).

8 The fact that the subject company may have ceased its offending activities prior to presentation of the Secretary of State's petition is a factor, and an important factor, to be taken into account (if, indeed, the public is no longer at a risk from the offending activity) but it is by no means a crucial or determinative factor. Balanced against it must be the fact that it would offend ordinary notions of what is just and equitable that, by ceasing its offending activities on becoming aware that the net is closing around it, a company which has misconducted itself can, thereby, enable itself to remain in being despite its previous history. By winding up such a company, the court will be expressing, in a meaningful way, its disapproval of such misconduct. Further, in addition to this being a fitting outcome for the company itself, such a course has the further benefit of spelling out to others that the

court will not hesitate to wind up companies whose standards of dealing with the investing public are unacceptable (see at [1989] BCLC 360).

30.63 Each case will turn on its own particular facts. In *Re Walter L Jacob & Co Ltd*, Nicholls LJ considered that it would not be acceptable on the facts before him to leave in being a company which had raised substantial sums of money on misleading documentation, and then ceased trading, with the consequence that hundreds of investors had been left with shares of questionable value. It would be in the public interest that such a company should be wound up.

30.64 One type of business which is considered to put the public particularly at risk is the pyramid-selling scheme (which may also be impeached as unlawful gambling[140] or as an unlawful trading scheme[141]). In *Re Senator*, Millett LJ used the phrase 'inherently objectionable' to characterize a 'snowball scheme' called The Titan Business Club under which, upon payment of a fee of £2,500, an individual obtained the right to introduce others to the scheme.[142] If he recruited another member then he earned commission of £450 (thereby recouping part of his outlay). The commission rate rose the more members he introduced: and if the people whom he recruited themselves in turn recruited others, then the commission rate rose again. In his membership application each member explicitly acknowledged that 'my success depends on introducing new members'. Millett LJ described the scheme in these terms:

> The scheme is merely a device for enabling the organisers and a relatively small number of early recruits to make potentially very large profits at the expense of the much larger number of those who are recruited later. Every new participant is in truth gambling on the scheme continuing long enough for him to recover his money and, he hopes, make a profit. But the scheme is not, of course, held out to him on this basis. Schemes of this kind are inherently objectionable and the court has consistently held that it is just and equitable to wind up the companies which operate them. They tend to be sold on a false and deceptive basis, sometimes explicit but usually implicit, that they are a certain source of profit for those who join and are capable of lasting indefinitely. A particular vice of such schemes is that they encourage similar dishonesty on the part of their members, who can recover their money only at the expense of new members whom they induce to enter the scheme ...

30.65 In *Secretary of State for BERR v Amway (UK) Ltd*[143] Norris J set out some particular characteristics of businesses which had been found to be objectionable in previous decisions:

(1) operating a business that mathematically or self-evidently is bound to fail causing loss for the latest participants;[144]

(2) operating a business which consists of nothing beyond the sale of participations in the business itself with the consequence that a relatively small number of early recruits make potentially very large profits at the expense of a much larger number recruited later;[145]

(3) misrepresenting the nature of the business of the company in a serious way;[146]

---

[140] Contrary to the Gambling Act 2005 (formerly unlawful lottery contrary to Lottery and Amusements Act 1976, s 1).

[141] Contrary to the Fair Trading Act 1973, s 120.

[142] [1997] 1 WLR 515, 524, 525.

[143] [2011] 2 BCC 716 at para 14.

[144] *Re Senator* [1997] 1 WLR 515, CA; *Re Vanilla* (unrep, 1998); *Re Alpha Club* [2002] 2 BCLC 612.

[145] *Re Senator, Re Vanilla, Re Alpha Club* (n 144); *Re Delfin* [2000] 1 BCLC 71.

[146] *Re Walter Jacob* (an apparent adviser in fact operating as a share vendor); *Re Supporting Link Ltd* [2004] 1 WLR 1549 (commercial company holding itself out as a charity fundraiser); *Re UK-Euro Group* [2007] 1 BCLC 812 (principal activity of the company the raising of money not the development and sale of a product).

(4) seriously misrepresenting the product being marketed by the company;[147]

(5) promoting a business on the basis that its participants will earn a reward greater than is commensurate with the effort; and[148]

(6) by the nature of the business facilitating wrongdoing by others.[149]

Other factors which may lead to a public interest winding-up order being made include **30.66** persistent misconduct and mismanagement, inadequate record-keeping, and regular breaches of companies legislation.[150] The Court considers the evidence as a whole, and examples of the sort of misconduct which merits a winding-up order can be seen from some recent cases.

In *Re Corvin Construction Ltd*,[151] six linked construction companies were ordered to be **30.67** wound up where there was cogent evidence demonstrating that they lacked commercial probity, had failed to file full and true accounts, had allowed an undischarged bankrupt to operate as a de facto director, and had failed to cooperate with an Insolvency Service investigation. The detailed allegations included misleading statements on the companies' websites and the filing of 'dormant company' accounts by companies which were active. The deputy judge, Alison Foster QC, referred to 'a litany of complaints concerning invoicing for monies not due, persistent sub-standard workmanship, disregard of health and safety requirements, evasiveness with customers and general irresponsible behaviour'. She found that there had been 'a general picture of pervasive abrogation of responsibility and absence of transparency and probity'.

In *Secretary of State for BIS v World Future Ltd*,[152] the companies, which had been involved in **30.68** a scheme to market carbon credits, were wound up following an investigation by Company Investigations. Investors had received unsolicited phone calls and were falsely told that they could expect returns of at least 25 per cent, and in some cases as much as 50 per cent, within a year.

In *Re PAG Management Services Ltd*,[153] Norris J accepted that it was expedient in the public **30.69** interest to wind up a company operating a 'business rate minimisation scheme' which, while not unlawful, subverted the true and proper purpose of insolvency law. The scheme involved the incorporation of special purpose vehicles (SPVs) to which PAG's client companies would grant leases at a nominal rent which the landlord would waive. Contemporaneously with the grant of a lease, the SPV would be placed in a members' voluntary liquidation. As a result, the property would not be subject to national non-domestic rate ('NNDR') under the Local Government Finance Act 1988, s 45 and PAG would receive as a fee a percentage (varying between 15 per cent and 40 per cent) of the NNDR saved. Norris J accepted that, where

---

[147] *Re Walter Jacob* (unmarketable shares); *Re Vanilla* (painting 'far too rosy a picture'); *Re Supporting Link* ('local' guide produced nationally and randomly distributed); *Re Equity & Provident* [2002] 2 BCLC 78 (sale of an apparent mechanical warranty in reality no such thing).

[148] *Re Senator* [1997] 1 WLR 515, CA.

[149] *Re Senator* where Millett LJ said at [1997] 1 WLR 515, 525: 'a particular vice of such schemes is that they encourage similar dishonesty on the part of their members'.

[150] *Australian Securities Commission v AS Nominees Ltd* (1995) 1 ALR 1; for an example, see *Secretary of State for BIS v PGMRS Ltd* [2011] 1 BCLC 443.

[151] [2013] All ER (D) 07 (Jan), [2012] Lexis Citation 110.

[152] [2013] EWHC 723 (Ch).

[153] [2015] EWHC 2404 (Ch), [2015] BCC 720.

the business of the company does not involve the commission of illegal acts or breaches of regulatory requirement, the company may nonetheless be would up if its business is 'inherently objectionable' because it activities are 'contrary to a clearly identified public interest'.[154] The Judge said it could not be held that avoidance/mitigation schemes are contrary to the public interest and he was not persuaded that companies and partnerships which offer tax mitigation schemes are in general carrying on a business which is inherently objectionable even if the products are highly artificial. However, the Secretary of State succeeded because PAG's activities were 'contrary to a clearly defined public interest'; the judge said it was 'the use of the company in liquidation as an asset shelter and the inherent bias towards prolongation of the liquidation that is subversive of the true purpose and proper functioning of insolvency law'.

30.70 Failure to comply with a Companies Act inquiry is a serious matter which will be weighed against the company on a public interest petition,[155] but a minor partial failure to cooperate with an investigation would generally be regarded as insufficient to found a petition or to tip the scale if the other allegations do not justify an order.[156]

30.71 *Secretary of State v Amway* (referred to at paragraph 30.65 above) is a (comparatively rare) example of a case where a public interest petition did not succeed. At first instance, Norris J considered that the Secretary of State had failed on the balance of probabilities to prove that the company had been carrying on an unlawful lottery or conducting an unlawful trading scheme. He considered it unhelpful to substitute some concept such as 'inherent objectionability' for the 'fundamental question' of whether it was just and equitable to wind up the company.[157] He found that, in the light of a revised business model which the company had put into effect, it was not. The Secretary of State's appeal was dismissed by the Court of Appeal,[158] which reviewed the authorities on s 124A and emphasized that matters have to be looked at as at the time of the hearing of the petition and as a whole, so that a company may be able to avoid being wound up by adopting a business model that corrects past deficiencies or misconduct.[159]

30.72 Another example of a case where a public interest petition failed is *Re Portfolios of Distinction Ltd*[160] where the deputy judge, Mr John Jarvis QC, appears to have been satisfied that the company had sufficiently reformed its procedures to render a winding-up order inappropriate.

---

[154] Cf *Abacrombie & Co Ltd* [2008] EWHC 2520 (Ch), in which David Richards J held that the company's debtor advisory services, which involved selling the debtor's equity in property to the client's spouse or partner at a low price in anticipation of the debtor's bankruptcy and using the proceeds to fund excessive charges by the company, gave rise to arrangements which 'subverted the proper functioning of the law and procedures of bankruptcy'.

[155] *Secretary of State for BERR v Art It plc* [2009] 1 BCLC 262 at para 21.

[156] *Secretary of State v PGMRS Ltd* [2011] 1 BCLC 443 at para 79 (where a winding-up order was made for other reasons).

[157] [2011] 2 BCLC 716 at paras 13 and 61.

[158] [2011] 2 BCLC 716, CA.

[159] [2011] 2 BCLC 716, CA at paras 63 and 65 in the judgment of Rix LJ. In *Secretary of State for BERR v Charter Financial Solutions Ltd* [2009] EWHC 1118 (Ch), Sir Edward Evans-Lombe (sitting as a judge of the High Court) observed: 'It will be a rare case where the court declines to make a winding up order where the Secretary of State has rejected the undertakings and pressed for a winding up order. Nonetheless it is open to the court in such a rare case to do so where the facts, in the court's judgment, require it.'

[160] [2006] 2 BCLC 261.

Where the company is already in liquidation

A public interest petition may not be pursued if the company in question is already being **30.73** wound up by the court.[161] However, voluntary liquidation is no bar to a compulsory winding-up order.[162] It is open to the Secretary of State to pursue a petition, and to the court to make an order, but the fact of voluntary liquidation is one of the circumstances to be taken into account. In *Re Lubin, Rosen and Associates Ltd*,[163] Megarry J said:

> Where the results of that investigation lead the Secretary of State to the conclusion that it is expedient in the public interest that the company should be wound up, and he accordingly presents a petition for a compulsory order, I do not think that the passing of a resolution for a voluntary winding up shortly before the Secretary of State presents his petition, and the subsequent confirmation of that resolution, ought to be allowed to put the voluntary winding up into an entrenched position, as it were, which can be demolished only if the Secretary of State can demonstrate that the process of voluntary winding up will be markedly inferior to a compulsory winding up. The Secretary of State may, of course, reach the conclusion that a voluntary winding up will suffice, and so not proceed with his petition; but if he does proceed, then in my judgment the question is essentially whether, in all the circumstances of the case (including, of course, the existence of a voluntary winding up and the views of the creditors), it is just and equitable for the company to be wound up compulsorily. In addition to the suspicion of offences, the presence of foreign complications such as exist in this case, and the difference between the interests of the disappointed purchasers and those of any other creditors, seem to me to make it both just and equitable that this winding up should be conducted with the full authority and resources of the court.

One particular factor which carried weight with Megarry J in that case was that, although there was provision under the 1948 Act for a voluntary liquidator to report apparent offences, in a compulsory liquidation the official receiver came under a specific duty to submit a report to the court, setting out the state of the company and whether further inquiry was desirable. Megarry J went on to conclude that, where there were circumstances of suspicion, as there were in that case, it was highly desirable that the winding up should be by the court, with all the safeguards that this provided, including the investigation of any suspected offences. The desirability of a full and vigorous independent investigation of the company's affairs in a compulsory liquidation was also emphasized by Lightman J in *Re Pinstripe Farming Co Ltd*.[164]

A voluntary liquidator who is in office can properly appear by counsel on the hearing of the **30.74** petition, and it may be desirable and appropriate for such an office-holder to assist the court with evidence of what he has found and what the present position is, but he should not press a view one way or another.[165] There seems to be no reason in principle why the voluntary liquidator should not in an appropriate case go on to be appointed as liquidator in the compulsory liquidation; in most cases, however, the voluntary liquidator will appear to lack the necessary independence.[166]

---

[161] Insolvency Act, s 124A(2).

[162] *Re Lubin, Rosen and Associates Ltd* [1975] 1 WLR 122; *Securities and Investments Board v Lancashire and Yorkshire Portfolio Management Ltd* [1992] BCLC 281; *Re Alpha Club (UK) Ltd* [2002] 2 BCLC 612 (resolution for voluntary liquidation had been passed less than a fortnight before the hearing of the petition).

[163] A case under the 1967 Act, s 224, the predecessor of Insolvency Act, s 124A.

[164] [1996] 2 BCLC 295; cf *Re Future Trading Corp* (unrep Robert Walker J, 16 August 1996).

[165] Cf *Re Medisco Equipment Ltd* [1983] BCLC 305.

[166] *Re Pinstripe Farming Co Ltd* [1996] 2 BCLC 295; cf *Re Lowerstoft Traffic Services Ltd* [1986] BCLC 81.

(4) Provisional liquidator and procedural matters

Provisional liquidator

30.75 Pending the hearing of a public interest petition, as in the case of any other winding-up petition, in an appropriate case the court will appoint a provisional liquidator.[167] Such an appointment may be justified not only when the company is obviously insolvent or the assets are in jeopardy, but also when 'a good prima facie case'[168] for the company to be wound up on public interest grounds has been made out, even if it appears to be solvent. As Megarry J said in *Re Highfield Commodities*:[169]

> The exercise of that power [to appoint a provisional liquidator] may have serious consequences for the company, and so a need for the exercise of the power must overtop those consequences. In particular, where the winding up petition is presented because the Secretary of State considers that it is expedient in the public interest that the company should be wound up, the public interest must be given full weight, though it is not to be regarded as being conclusive.
>
> The matter may be tested by considering a well-run and prosperous company thriving on the frauds which it practices on the public. If the Secretary of State presents a winding up petition under section 35 of the Act of 1967, I cannot conceive that it would be right to say that as the company is solvent and no assets are in jeopardy, no provisional liquidator should be appointed unless the evidence of fraud is so strong at that stage that it is clear that the company is bound to be wound up. In such a case it might well be highly desirable to put a provisional liquidator in control so that no more money will be taken from the public.

30.76 The jurisdiction to appoint provisional liquidators can be exercised if the court is satisfied that a winding-up petition has been presented and is likely to be successful. 'Likelihood' in this context means demonstrating: that the petitioner is entitled to present a petition; that a material part of it is not capable of dispute; and that the petitioner has given full and frank disclosure.[170] In the context of a public interest petition following an investigation, the court is entitled to take into account that, if the company had information which met the concerns implicit in the investigation, it would have advanced that explanation to the investigators and not have concealed it.[171]

30.77 The petitioner should consider whether a remedy other than appointment of a provisional liquidator (for example, injunctive relief) would provide an adequate answer to the concerns which are raised.[172]

30.78 Notwithstanding the possibility that the company may be damaged by the appointment of a provisional liquidator, there is no requirement for a cross-undertaking in damages on an application without notice for the appointment, because the Secretary of State seeks the appointment for the purpose of enforcing the law or in the performance of a public duty: the

---

[167] *Re Highfield Commodities Ltd* [1985] 1 WLR 149.

[168] *Re Union Accident Insurance Co Ltd* [1972] 1 All ER 1105, per Plowman J; cited by Megarry J in *Highfield Commodities Ltd* [1985] 1 WLR 149, 158, 159.

[169] [1985] 1 WLR 149, 159.

[170] *Revenue and Customs Commissioners v Rochdale Drinks Distributors Ltd* [2012] 1 BCLC 748, CA; *Revenue and Customs Commissioners v Winnington Networks Ltd* [2014] BCC 675; *Secretary of State for BIS v New Horizon Energy Ltd* [2015] EWHC 2961 (Ch).

[171] Per Norris J in *Secretary of State for BIS v New Horizon Energy Ltd* [2015] EWHC 2961 (Ch), at para 27.

[172] *Re City Vintners Ltd* (Etherton J, unreported, 10 December 2001), discussed in *Mishcon de Reya v Barrett* [2007] 1 BCLC 153 at [76]–[80]; *Secretary of State for BIS v Hawkhurst Capital PLC* [2013] EWHC 4219 (Ch).

Secretary of State ought not to be dissuaded from exercising his statutory powers in this behalf by being required to give any undertaking in damages.[173] It is proper to draw the fact that no undertaking is being offered to the attention of the court, particularly when the application is made on short notice or without notice.[174]

In *Re Senator Hanseatische Verwaltungsgesellschaft mbH*, Sir Richard Scott V-C granted **30.79** injunctions to preserve the position pending the hearing of the winding-up petition. In the Court of Appeal, Millett LJ said of the injunctions and the application for the appointment of provisional liquidators:[175]

> Neither is likely to be completely effective to prevent the organisers [of the scheme] from setting up a similar scheme in the name of another entity and making use of the membership of the existing scheme to continue their activities. In the absence of suitable undertakings from the individuals behind the scheme to refrain from doing this, I would for my part have thought it much the better course to appoint a provisional liquidator. This would have a number of advantages. It would put in place an independent officer of the court to take charge of the company's activities pending the hearing of the petition and to be a focal point for the present members to turn to for advice as to their position. He would also be entitled to obtain possession of the current membership lists and ensure they could not be used, without the approval of the court, to operate similar schemes pending the hearing of the petition.

The offer of undertakings

A company which is the subject of investigation or a public interest petition sometimes seeks **30.80** to protect its position by offering undertakings, to the Secretary of State or to the court, to desist from certain practices or to change its business model. In *Re Supporting Link Ltd* Sir Andrew Morritt V-C referred to the recent cases in which undertakings had been accepted or refused,[176] and accepted that the court had power to accept undertakings and to dismiss the petition on that basis.[177] Sir Andrew Morritt V-C went on to conclude:[178]

> In my view unless the Secretary of State is content that the petition is disposed of on undertakings the court should be very slow indeed to accept them in preference to making a winding-up order. All the reasons given by Brightman J in *Re Bamford Publishers* remain as valid now as they were then. If the court is satisfied that the offending business has ceased and it is prepared to trust the existing management then it may be appropriate to dismiss the petition altogether. But if it is not so satisfied or does not trust the existing management then I find it hard to envisage a case in which it would be appropriate to dismiss the petition on undertakings as to the future conduct of the company's business.

---

[173] *Re Highfield Commodities* [1985] 1 WLR 149, 156. For the same reason, the FCA is not required to give a cross-undertaking in damages when it seeks an injunction as part of its law enforcement function: *Financial Services Authority v Sinaloa Gold plc* [2013] 2 AC 28, SC.

[174] *Secretary of State for BIS v Hawkhurst Capital PLC* [2013] EWHC 4219 (Ch).

[175] [1997] 1 WLR 515, 526, 527.

[176] [2004] 1 WLR 1549. Undertakings satisfactory to the Secretary of State were accepted in *Re Vehicle Options Ltd* [2002] EWHC 3235 (Ch); *Re Easy-Dial Ltd* [2003] EWHC 3508 (Ch); and *Secretary of State for Trade and Industry v KTA Ltd* [2003] EWHC 3512 (Ch). In *Re Equity and Provident Ltd* [2002] 2 BCLC 78 undertakings were refused by Patten J and a winding-up order was made. *Re Derek Colins Associates Ltd* [2002] EWHC 1893 (Ch) is a rare case where the judge accepted undertakings and refused to make a winding-up order where that course has been opposed by the Secretary of State.

[177] At para 55.

[178] At para 58. In so doing he relied on the decision of Brightman J in *Re Bamford Publishers Ltd*, The Times, 4 June 1977, and observations of the Court of Appeal in *Re Blackspur Group plc* [1998] 1 WLR 422, 433.

30.81 In *Secretary of State for Trade and Industry v Bell Davies Trading Ltd*,[179] the Court of Appeal endorsed the Vice-Chancellor's approach in *Re Supporting Link Ltd* and gave the following guidance:

> The judge has a discretion whether or not to make a winding-up order. As for undertakings, the court has a discretion whether or not to accept them if they are proffered and whether or not to make the giving of them a condition of dismissing the petition. In considering the exercise of his discretion the willingness or otherwise of the Secretary of State to accept undertakings, which have to be policed by the Department of Trade and Industry, is an important factor.

> Thus, in the exercise of the discretion, the judge is entitled (a) to dismiss the petition on undertakings if, for example, he is satisfied that the offending business has ceased or if the undertakings are acceptable to the Secretary of State; or (b) to dismiss the petition on undertakings, even if that course is opposed by the Secretary of State, although that will be unusual; or (c) to refuse to accept undertakings and to wind the company up, if, for example, he is not satisfied that those giving the undertakings can be trusted.

30.82 Following those decisions, in the *Amway* case, Norris J said[180] that the Secretary of State is not a licensor of approved business models or a business design consultant and is under no obligation to approve or to police a scheme of undertakings relating to the conduct of an individual company's business. To be acceptable the revised business model must be 'fully formulated, comprehensive, open and transparent, and capable of effective and ongoing implementation without the supervision of either the Secretary of State or the court'. In the Court of Appeal, after reviewing the previous authorities and stressing that the case was unusual and differed in many respects from the 'typical example of a newly incorporated business whose raison d'etre is to defraud the public and the dishonesty of whose controlling and often sole director is carried forward into the investigation and trial', Rix LJ said:

> I do not intend in any way at all to detract from the observations of previous judges about the dangers of imposing the policing of undertakings given by delinquent companies on a Secretary of State who has no obligation to compromise his petition on terms which do not seem acceptable to him. Nevertheless, where exceptionally a judge considers that undertakings can perform a useful role, it seems to me that there is nothing in past jurisprudence to prevent a judge from accepting them, even if the Secretary of State does not consent, or, as in *Addcom* and again in *Bell Davies*, would not have consented but for the court's own intervention.[181]

Procedure

30.83 In general, the procedure for a public interest petition is the same as for any other winding-up petition. The petition is verified by witness statement and filed in court under rule 4.7(1)

---

179 [2005] 1 All ER 324, CA (Note) at paras 110 and 111. In *Secretary of State for BERR v Amway (UK) Ltd* [2011] 2 BCLC 716, CA Rix LJ said at para 13 that the *Bell Davies* case is a good illustration of the balancing exercise which the court has to perform in exercising its discretion under s 124A. In *Secretary of State for BIS v KJK Investments Ltd* [2015] EWHC 1589 (Ch), concerning two companies involved in a private pension fund investment scheme, Birss J indicated that the court might very well be wary of making a winding up order if the result would be to create severe losses for the investors whereas, if there was a realistic prospect of the companies trading profitably in future, the investors might recover realistic returns on their investments despite there being a serious question over the probity of the arrangements. In this case, there was no realistic prospect of investors recovering returns on their investments and so it was in the public interest to wind up the companies.

180 [2011] 2 BCLC 716 at paras 10 and 11.

181 [2011] 2 BCLC 716, CA at para 80.

of the Insolvency Rules (and IR 2016, r 7.7 after 6 April 2017). The court fixes the venue for the hearing and the petition is then served on the company.

The petition is required to be advertised, unless the court directs otherwise under rule 4.11 **30.84** (and IR 2016, r 7.10 after 6 April 2017).[182] The onus is on the company to show sufficient cause why the petition should not be advertised. For this purpose the court would have to be satisfied that creditors are not at risk and that advertisement would cause serious damage to the reputation and financial stability of the company.[183]

Different considerations arise where a provisional liquidator is appointed urgently at the **30.85** same time as the petition is presented. These will be cases in which the court has accepted that it is necessary to intervene and take immediate control of the company's assets and business; it may be necessary to announce the appointment to protect the public or enable them to protect themselves, but it is likely that the announcement will have a severe effect on the company's ability to carry on trading. Indeed the likely consequence of the appointment is to bring the company's business to an immediate halt. In *Secretary of State for Trade and Industry v North West Holdings plc*[184] the Court of Appeal reviewed and endorsed the Secretary of State's normal practice at the time of issuing a press release announcing the provisional liquidator's appointment as soon as he agrees, but observed that in cases of difficulty the directions of the court could be obtained.

The position of contributories

A contributory has a prima facie right to appear and file evidence in opposition to a public **30.86** interest winding-up petition, even where the company itself is not opposing the petition, but only where the contributory can show that the company is solvent and that the contributory therefore has a genuine interest in the outcome.[185]

Costs

Although directors are not usually ordered to pay the costs of a company's defence against a **30.87** winding-up petition, the court has jurisdiction to order them to do so which has on occasions

---

[182] Rule 4.11 is concerned only with the advertisement required to appear in the London Gazette, and not with press releases which may be the subject of objection on other grounds: *Secretary of State for Trade and Industry v North West Holdings plc* [1998] BCC 997.

[183] *Re a Company (No 007923 of 1994)* [1995] 1 WLR 953, CA. In that case the Court of Appeal was satisfied that advertisement would do lasting damage, and granted the company's appeal against the judge's refusal to direct that the petitions should not be advertised. In the event the petition was dismissed. Although the companies had technically been guilty of aiding and abetting the carrying on of unauthorized insurance business by foreign companies in the UK, the directors had believed themselves to be acting lawfully and under the circumstances the conduct of the companies had not been intrinsically against the public interest: *Re a Company (No 007293 of 1994) (No 2)* [1995] BCC 641. An application to restrain advertisement was refused in *Secretary of State for BIS v Broomfield Developments Ltd* [2014] EWHC 3925 (Ch), where the petition alleged objectionable trading practices and provision of credit to customers without a consumer credit licence in connection with a land bank scheme. Applying the balancing exercise identified in *Re a Company (No 007923 of 1994)* the deputy judge found that the interests of the purchasers of plots of land in knowing about the petitions outweighed the alleged harm to the company, which could be mitigated by a validation order under s 127 of the Insolvency Act.

[184] [1999] 1 BCLC 425, 430, 431. Publicity protects persons dealing with the company and the provisional liquidator. Chadwick LJ said that it was desirable that the public should be made aware that the Secretary of State has concluded that the company should be wound up in the public interest and the court has been satisfied that a provisional liquidator should be appointed.

[185] *Allso v Secretary of State for Trade and Industry* [2004] 1 WLR 1566; *Secretary of State for BIS v World Future Ltd* [2013] EWHC 723 (Ch).

been exercised in the context of a public interest petition, particularly where the court considered that the directors had no bona fide belief in the defence advanced.[186]

30.88 There is Court of Appeal authority that the Secretary of State, although acting in the public interest, has no specially favourable costs regime to rely on.[187] On the other hand, there is a conflicting line of authority suggesting that, in the absence of dishonesty or lack of good faith, a costs order should not be made against a regulator unless there is some good reason to do so.[188] This point was expressly left open by the Court of Appeal in *Secretary of State for BERR v Amway (UK) Ltd*, where the argument on costs proceeded on the basis of a concession.[189]

30.89 In an appropriate case, such as where there has been a relevant change in the company's position or significant evidence filed at a late stage, it is open to the court to make a split order on costs.[190] It is sometimes suggested that, as a matter of policy, the costs of defending a petition are also to be paid as an expense of the ensuing liquidation if an order is made. However, it is open to the court to provide in the order that costs of the defendant company are not to be paid until any unsecured creditors have been paid in full.[191]

---

[186] eg *Re Aurum Marketing Ltd* [2000] 2 BCLC 645; *Re North West Holdings plc* [2001] 1 BCLC 468, CA; *Secretary of State for Trade and Industry v Liquid Acquisitions Ltd* [2003] 1 BCLC 375.

[187] *Re Southbourne Sheet Metal Co Ltd* [1993] 1 WLR 244, CA.

[188] *Gorlow v Institute of Chartered Accountants* [2001] EWHC 220 (Admin); *Bradford MDC v Booth* (2001) 3 LGLR 8; *Baxendale-Walker v The Law Society* [2007] EWCA Civ 223, [2008] 1 WLR 426.

[189] [2011] BCLC 716 at paras 91 and 92 in the judgment of Toulson LJ.

[190] *Re Xyllyx plc (No 2)* [1992] BCLC 378; *Secretary of State for BERR v Amway (UK) Ltd* [2009] BCC 781; [2011] 2 BCLC 716 aff'g; [2008] BCC 713.

[191] Cf *Re Bathampton Properties Ltd* [1976] 1 WLR 168; such an order was made by Warren J in *Re Digital Satellite Warranty Cover Limited* [2011] EWHC 124 (Ch), [2011] Bus LR 981 (appeals from the winding-up orders dismissed by the Court of Appeal ([2012] 2 All ER (Comm) 38 and by the Supreme Court ([2013] 1 WLR 605)).

31

DISQUALIFICATION PROCEEDINGS

Robert Amey

A. Introduction

Disqualification from being a director or in any way concerned in the management of a **31.01** company without the leave of the court was brought into effect by the 1929 Act following the recommendations of the Greene Committee.[1] An undischarged bankrupt was disqualified by virtue of his status[2] and the court was given power to disqualify for up to five years promoters, directors, and officers of a company ordered to be wound up who had committed

---

[1] Report of the Greene Committee at paras 56–7, 61–2. Lord Millett gives a history of directors' disqualification in *In Re Pantmaenog Timber Co Ltd* [2004] 1 AC 158, HL at paras 32–8.

[2] Until 1976 bankruptcy was of unlimited duration unless the bankrupt applied for and obtained an order for his discharge.

fraud and persons responsible for fraudulent trading.[3] The 1948 Act extended the power to disqualify to officers of the company who had been guilty of any breach of duty.[4]

31.02 Following recommendations of the Jenkins Committee[5] the court's power to make disqualification orders was extended to (i) directors of more than one company that had gone into insolvent liquidation and whose conduct made them unfit to be concerned in the management of a company;[6] (ii) persons who has been persistently in default in relation to delivery of documents to the registrar;[7] (iii) persons convicted of an indictable offence (whether on indictment or summarily) in connection with the promotion, formation, management, or liquidation of a company or with the receivership or management of a company; and (iv) persons summarily convicted for persistent default in relation to delivery of documents to the registrar.[8] Disqualification was limited to 5 years, but that limit was increased to 15 years for persons convicted on indictment, found guilty of fraudulent trading, or found guilty of any fraud in relation to the company or breach of duty.

31.03 The Cork Committee found widespread dissatisfaction with the effectiveness of the law of disqualification; it was too restricted and was not used enough.[9] The Cork Committee made a number of recommendations, including mandatory disqualification for at least two years for unfit conduct, many of which were adopted in the Company Directors Disqualification Act 1986 (CDDA).[10]

31.04 The provisions of the CDDA are discussed in the following paragraphs of this chapter. In outline, disqualification is mandatory in the cases of unfit directors of insolvent companies and companies in breach of competition law, but is otherwise a matter for the discretion of the court. Undischarged bankrupts remain disqualified from taking part in or directly or indirectly being concerned in the promotion, formation, or management of a company, as are persons subject to (i) a bankruptcy restrictions order or undertaking, (ii) a debt relief restrictions order or undertaking or to whom a moratorium period under a debt relief order applies,[11] or (iii) an order under the Insolvency Act, s 429(2) revoking a county court administration order.[12] Disqualified persons may apply to the court for permission to take part in the affairs of a company.[13]

---

[3] 1929 Act, ss 142, 217, 275.

[4] 1948 Act, s 188, following recommendations in the report of the Cohen Committee at paras 150–3.

[5] Report of the Jenkins Committee at paras 80–5.

[6] Insolvency Act 1976, s 9; later amended by the Companies Act 1981, s 94.

[7] Companies Act 1976, s 28.

[8] Companies Act 1981, s 93 which inserted a new s 188 in the 1948 Act.

[9] Cork Report at paras 1807–37.

[10] The CDDA applies to England, Wales, and Scotland, but not to Northern Ireland: s 24.

[11] CDDA, s 11, as amended by SBEE Act 2015, s 113(1), (2) with effect from 1 October 2015. The Enterprise Act 2002 reduced the normal duration of a bankruptcy from three years to one year. To deal with bankrupts whose conduct before or after the making of the bankruptcy makes it appropriate that they should be subject to the restrictions of a bankrupt for more than one year, the Enterprise Act 2002 gave the court power to make a bankruptcy restriction order for between two and 15 years: Insolvency Act s 281A. For debt relief restrictions orders and undertakings and the moratorium period under a debt relief order, see Insolvency Act, ss 251H and 251V.

[12] CDDA, s 12. By the Insolvency Act, s 429 the order revoking the county court administration order may direct that s 12 shall apply to the person for a period of up to one year.

[13] This is inherent in the terms of the disqualification order and the bankruptcy restriction in CDDA, s 11. CDDA, s 17 deals with the application for leave.

Since 1986 disqualification orders have been a regularly used tool to prevent or deter the **31.05** abuse of limited liability, whether through dishonesty, lack of probity, incompetence, or disregard of responsibilities. Between 2010 and 2015, about 1,100–1,400 disqualification orders or undertakings were made each year, of which about 80 per cent were in the form of undertakings, and the average length of disqualification was about six years.[14]

The CDDA has undergone three significant reforms since its enactment in 1986. First, to **31.06** save the costs of court proceedings, the Insolvency Act 2000 gave the Secretary of State power to accept a disqualification undertaking, which could be varied by the court.[15] Secondly, the Enterprise Act 2002 introduced competition disqualification orders and undertakings.[16] Thirdly, the Small Business, Enterprise and Employment Act 2015 (SBEE Act 2015) introduced disqualification for conviction abroad of offences connected to companies and for instructing unfit directors of insolvent companies, reformed the provisions about matters to be taken into account for determining unfitness, and introduced new provisions for compensation orders and undertakings.[17]

B. Disqualification Orders

(1) The disqualification order

CDDA, s 1(1) provides that: **31.07**

In the circumstances specified below in this Act a court may, and under sections 6 and 9A shall, make against a person a disqualification order, that is to say an order that for a period specified in the order—
(a) he shall not be a director of a company, act as receiver of a company's property or in any way, whether directly or indirectly, be concerned or take part in the promotion, formation or management of a company unless (in each case) he has the leave of the court, and
(b) he shall not act as an insolvency practitioner.

In respect of ss 2–5, 5A, 8ZA, 8ZD, and 10, any person may be subject to a disqualification order if the conditions of those sections are satisfied and the court sees fit to so order. Under ss 6 and 9A, disqualification is mandatory upon satisfaction of the relevant conditions, but it flows from those conditions that only a director may be disqualified under those sections. For the purpose of ss 6 and 9A, 'director' includes a de facto or shadow director.[18]

In the CDDA 'company' means a company registered under the 2006 Act in Great Britain **31.08** or a company that may be wound up under the Insolvency Act, Part 5, as an unregistered

---

[14] The Insolvency Service Annual Report and Accounts 2010–15. The majority of disqualification cases concern allegations of (i) non-payment of Crown debts, (ii) accounting matters, (iii) transactions to the detriment of creditors, and (iv) criminal matters.

[15] CDDA, ss 1A, 7(2A), 8A, inserted by the Insolvency Act 2000, s 6(1), (2), (3), (5) as from 2 April 2001.

[16] CDDA ss 9A–9E, inserted by the Enterprise Act 2002, ss 204(1)(2) as from 20 June 2003.

[17] CDDA ss 5A, 6(1A), (2A), 8(2A), (2B), 8ZA–8ZE, 10(3), 12C, 15A–15C inserted by SBEE Act 2015, ss 104, 105, 106, 110 as from 1 October 2015. These provisions were brought into force by The Small Business, Enterprise and Employment Act 2015 (Commencement No 2 and Transitional Provisions) Regs 2015, SI 2015/1689, para 2. For the law as it stood prior to 1 October 2015, see the second edition of this book.

[18] CDDA, ss 6(3C), 9E(5). Section 22(4) defines a director in the same terms as the 2006 Act, s 250. Section 22(5) defines a shadow director in the same terms as the 2006 Act (both as amended by SBEE Act 2015 with effect from 26 May 2015).

company.[19] A disqualification order is not limited in effect to the kind of company in connection with which it was made and the court has no power to make a disqualification order in relation to one class of company only.[20]

31.09 In the CDDA 'director' includes any person occupying the position of director, by whatever name called.[21] Section 1(1) goes wider than mere directorship and extends to being concerned or taking part in the promotion, formation, or management of a company. It does not, however, preclude all activities in connection with a company or its business. The prohibition in the order is necessarily limited and, in the context of s 2(1), the courts have recognized a distinction between 'managing certain specific aspects of the company's activities, such as production, sales, trading and the like, and the central management of the affairs of the company, that is to say the matters normally undertaken by the directors or officers of the company'.[22] This would seem to apply equally to s 1(1), although the line between prohibited and permitted activities is not precisely clear and can be difficult to draw. In circumstances in which it is unclear whether or not an activity falls within the scope of the order, a well-advised former director, or other person, should apply for leave under s 17 to carry on a particular activity, which may readily be obtained in an appropriate case. In *Re TLL Realisations Ltd*, Park J explained that:

> Section 1 of the Act does not impose an absolute prohibition on a disqualified person being concerned in or taking part in the management of a company … Indeed applications for leave are common, and an application for leave to undertake a specific job (usually, though not in this case, a directorship of an identified company) is frequently made at the same hearing as that at which the court imposes the general disqualification.[23]

The procedure and requirements for obtaining leave under s 17 are set out in Section H(1) below.

31.10 The period of disqualification will be specified in the order itself, and the order is discharged upon the lapse of that period. In connection with this, s 1(3) provides:

> Where a disqualification order is made against a person who is already subject to such an order, or to a disqualification undertaking, the periods specified in those orders or, as the case may be, in the order and the undertaking shall run concurrently.

This saving against the accumulation of periods of disqualification is, in practice, not absolute. A breach of a disqualification order, or undertaking, is treated as an aggravating factor in calculating the appropriate period of disqualification on some other ground.[24]

31.11 The Secretary of State, by the Registrar of Companies, is required to maintain a register of disqualification orders and undertakings from prescribed particulars supplied to him by

---

[19] CDDA, s 22(2). The CDDA applies to bank insolvency and bank administration (CDDA, ss 21A and 21B; Banking Act 2009, ss 121 and 155) and to building society insolvency and special administration (CDDA, s 21C and Building Societies Act 1986, s 90E). In its current form the CDDA also applies to building societies, incorporated friendly societies, NHS foundation trusts, open-ended investment companies, registered societies as defined in the Co-operative and Community Benefit Societies Act 2014, and charitable incorporated organizations (CDDA, ss 22A–22F, with the modifications there stated).

[20] *R v Goodman* [1993] 2 All ER 789, 793, CA.

[21] CDDA, s 22(4), which is in the same terms as the 2006 Act, s 250 and includes a de facto director.

[22] *R v Campbell* [1984] BCLC 83, 85, CA.

[23] [2000] BCC 998, 1003; affd [2000] 2 BCLC 223, CA.

[24] *Re Sevenoaks Stationers (Retail) Ltd* [1991] Ch 164, 174, CA.

court clerks and managers.[25] The prescribed particulars include all disqualification orders made and undertakings given and any action in consequence of which such an order, or any undertaking, is varied or ceases to be in force. The register is a public register and may currently be accessed in its electronic form without charge.

(2) Disqualification undertakings

It has been possible since 2 April 2001 for a person to offer and the Secretary of State to accept a disqualification undertaking, as an alternative to an order being made under s 6 or 8 (unfitness).[26] A disqualification undertaking is also available as an alternative to disqualification orders under ss 5A (disqualification for convictions abroad), 8ZA (person instructing unfit director of insolvent company), and 8ZD (person instructing unfit director: other cases).[27] In each case, the Secretary of State may accept the undertaking if it appears to him that it is expedient in the public interest to accept the undertaking instead of applying or proceeding with the application for a disqualification order. **31.12**

The emphasis in the section is on a subjective appraisal by the Secretary of State of what is in the public interest, and the Secretary of State is not obliged to accept an undertaking where it is considered that a trial would be preferable.[28] **31.13**

A disqualification undertaking is defined in CDDA, s 1A(1) as: **31.14**

> an undertaking by any person that, for the period specified in the undertaking, the person—
> (a) will not be a director of a company, act as receiver of a company's property, or in any way, whether directly or indirectly, be concerned or take part in the promotion, formation or management of a company unless (in each case) he has leave of a court; and
> (b) will not act as an insolvency practitioner.

The maximum period which may be specified in an undertaking is 15 years, as for an order, and the minimum period which may be specified in an undertaking under CDDA, s 7 or 8ZC, is two years.[29]

The usual practice is to provide that a relevant period of disqualification will begin 21 days after acceptance by the Secretary of State.[30] This is in part to facilitate any application for leave to act which may be contemplated. Undertakings are registered at Companies House. **31.15**

The court[31] has power to vary an undertaking to reduce the period or provide for it to cease to be in force, on application by the person who is subject to it.[32] On such an application, the Secretary of State is to appear and call the attention of the court to any matters which seem to him to be relevant.[33] On an application for an undertaking to cease to have effect, the applicant cannot resile from any previously agreed statement of fact which, but for certain **31.16**

---

[25] CDDA, s 18; Companies (Disqualification Orders) Regulations 2009 (SI 2009/2471). In *Cathie v Secretary of State for BIS* [2011] BCC 685 it was held that a disqualification order that had been stayed pending appeal did not have to be registered so long as it was stayed.

[26] CDDA, ss 7(2A) and 8(2A), inserted by the Insolvency Act 2000.

[27] As inserted by SBEE Act 2015, s 105 with effect from 1 October 2015.

[28] *Re Blackspur Group plc (No 3), Secretary of State v Davies (No 2)* [2002] 2 BCLC 363, CA.

[29] CDDA, s 1A(2).

[30] By analogy with CDDA, s 1(2); see below.

[31] The relevant court depends on the type of undertaking, and is specified in CDDA, s 8A(3).

[32] CDDA, s 8A.

[33] CDDA, s 8A(2).

theoretical differences, is treated as a binding agreement capable of rescission only on ground which would support rescission or variation of a private law contract or on some public interest ground.[34] The discretion to direct that an undertaking cease to have effect is exceptional but unfettered.[35]

(3) Periods of disqualification

31.17 The period of disqualification, or tariff, is sensitive to the facts of each case and is subject to prescribed minimum and maximum periods which vary according to the grounds upon which disqualification is ordered. In all cases, the period of disqualification begins 21 days from the date of the order.[36]

31.18 The prescribed maximum periods are:

(1) 5 years for (i) conviction by a court of summary jurisdiction for an indictable offence,[37] (ii) persistent breaches of companies legislation,[38] (iii) on summary conviction for failing to file returns, etc;[39] and

(2) 15 years for (i) conviction for an indictable offence other than by a court of summary jurisdiction,[40] (ii) fraud, etc in winding up,[41] (iii) certain convictions abroad,[42] (iv) unfit conduct,[43] (v) instructing unfit director,[44] (vi) unfit conduct in connection with a company in breach of competition law,[45] and (vii) wrongful trading.[46]

The only prescribed minimum period is two years under ss 6 (unfit directors of insolvent companies) and 8ZA (person instructing unfit director of insolvent company).[47] Where the Secretary of State accepts a disqualification undertaking, the maximum and, as the case may be, minimum period that can be specified in the undertaking is the same as that prescribed for the corresponding disqualification order.[48]

31.19 Within these confines the courts have set out guidelines as to how the appropriate tariff is to be calculated. The leading case is *Re Sevenoaks Stationers (Retail) Ltd*, in which Dillon LJ approved the then practice of the Chancery Division in relation to applications under s 6:

> I would for my part endorse the division of the potential 15-year disqualification period into three brackets … viz.:
>
> (i) the top bracket of disqualification for periods over 10 years should be reserved for particularly serious cases. These may include cases where a director who has already had one period of disqualification imposed on him falls to be disqualified yet again.

---

[34] *Re INS Realisations Ltd* [2006] 1 WLR 3433 at paras 30–1, per Hart J.
[35] *Re INS Realisations Ltd* (n 34 above) at para 43.
[36] CDDA, s 1(2).
[37] CDDA, s 2(3).
[38] CDDA, s 3(5).
[39] CDDA, s 5(5).
[40] CDDA, s 2(3).
[41] CDDA, s 4(3).
[42] CDDA, s 5A(6).
[43] CDDA, ss 6(4), 8(4).
[44] CDDA, ss 8ZA(4), 8ZD(5).
[45] CDDA, s 9A(9).
[46] CDDA, s 10(2).
[47] CDDA, ss 6(4) and 8ZA(4).
[48] CDDA, ss 1(A)(2) and 9B(5).

(ii) The minimum bracket of two to five years' disqualification should be applied where, though disqualification is mandatory, the case is, relatively, not very serious.

(iii) The middle bracket of disqualification for from six to 10 years should apply for serious cases which do not merit the top bracket.[49]

In *Re Westmid Packing Services Ltd*[50] Lord Woolf MR further refined the guidelines when he stated that: **31.20**

(1) The power to grant leave under s 17 is irrelevant to determining the proper period of disqualification.

(2) The period of disqualification must reflect the gravity of the offence and, as such, credit cannot be given for the period of effective disqualification commencing upon the bringing of proceedings and ending with the making of the order.[51]

(3) There is no room for 'plea-bargaining', but there can be negotiation as to the basis upon which an admission might be made, provided the facts are disputed and the starting point correctly reflects the gravity of the conduct.

(4) When it comes to mitigation, the court is not restricted to the facts supporting the application for disqualification in question: a wide variety of matters—including the former director's age and state of health, the length of time he has been in jeopardy, whether he has admitted the offence, his general conduct before and after the offence, and the periods of disqualification of his co-directors that may have been ordered by other courts—may be relevant and admissible in determining the appropriate period of disqualification.[52]

These include, additionally, the defendant's reliance on professional advice and proper or positive conduct such as cooperation with any office-holder or any attempt to remedy his misconduct or otherwise improve the position of creditors, for example.

The court is also entitled to consider aggravating factors such as the breach of an existing disqualification order or undertaking by the defendant,[53] or, at least in connection with disqualification proceedings under s 6, the defendant's conduct in the proceedings, including his conduct as a witness.[54] **31.21**

The appropriate tariff is a matter for the trial judge applying these guidelines. The citation of cases as to the period of disqualification is unhelpful,[55] and an appellate court may only review his decision and substitute a different period when the judge has erred in principle.[56] The following provides an indication as to how the guidelines might be applied: **31.22**

(1) The use of a company as a means of perpetrating a fraud, or a fraud in connection with the management of a company, is likely to warrant a tariff in the top bracket. In *Re*

---

[49] [1991] Ch 164, 174e–g, CA. In *Re Cargo Agency Ltd* [1992] BCLC 686, 689 Harman J observed that Chancery judges were already familiar with this division into three bands.

[50] [1998] 2 All ER 124, 131, 132, CA.

[51] Also *Secretary of State for Trade and Industry v Arif* [1997] 1 BCLC 34, 44–5.

[52] [1998] 2 All ER 124, 134, CA.

[53] *Re Sevenoaks Stationers (Retail) Ltd* [1991] Ch 164, 174f, CA.

[54] *Secretary of State v Reynard* [2002] 2 BCLC 625, 629–31, CA; *Re Godwin Warren Control Systems plc* [1993] BCLC 80, 92; *Re Moorgate Metals Ltd* [1995] 1 BCLC 503, 516–17; *Re Living Images Ltd* [1996] 1 BCLC 349, 377.

[55] *Re Westmid Packing Services Ltd* [1998] 2 All ER 124, 134, CA; *Re Civica Investments Ltd* [1983] BCLC 456, 457–8.

[56] eg *Re Swift 736 Ltd* [1993] BCLC 896, CA.

Vintage Hallmark plc, the directors were disqualified for 15 years, having fraudulently induced a subscription for shares and the purchase of the company's goods for their own benefit.[57] In *Official Receiver v Doshi*, a director was disqualified for 12 years for carrying out a fraud on the company's debt factor and having 'been shown to be capable of a level of mendacity which is breathtaking in its audacity and remarkable for its fluency'.[58] In *Secretary of State for BIS v Warry*[59] guidance was given as to periods of disqualification in a missing trader fraud. In any case where the director has been knowingly involved, and has played a significant role, in MTIC fraud, then a period of disqualification in the top bracket (of over 10 years) should be imposed. This is also likely to be appropriate in cases where the director has wilfully closed his eyes to MTIC fraud. The minimum period of disqualification will usually be 11 years where a defendant does not contest the application, and 12 years where the defendant unsuccessfully defends the application. In any case where it is proved that the respondent director did not actually know but (without wilfully closing his eyes to the obvious) ought to have known of the MTIC fraud, the period of disqualification should be within the middle bracket (of more than 5 and up to 10 years). Absent extenuating circumstances, in such a case the disqualification period is likely to fall in the top half of that bracket, and thus between seven-and-a-half and 10 years.

(2) The continued trading of a company whilst insolvent coupled with a persistent failure to keep proper accounts and file statutory accounts and returns is more likely to warrant a tariff within the middle bracket, especially where there is some aggravating impropriety, for example, a preferential payment, unfair discrimination against a particular creditor or class of creditor, or the abuse of successive phoenix companies.[60]

(3) The continued trading of a company whilst insolvent or the failure to keep proper accounts and file statutory accounts and returns is, without more, likely to warrant a tariff within the minimum bracket.[61]

31.23 These guidelines appear to apply to *all* disqualification proceedings. Indeed, it would be odd were a different approach adopted, given the overlap between the grounds for disqualification under s 6 and ss 2–5, and 10 and the overlapping jurisdiction of the civil and criminal courts. In *Re Land Travel Ltd*, Jacob J considered it 'self-evident' that civil and criminal courts should apply the same standards.[62] In the earlier criminal case of *R v Young*[63] Brooke J had adopted a different approach when he said that the sentencing power under s 2 was 'a completely general and unfettered power given by Parliament to courts on the occasion when a person is convicted of an indictable offence of that type' to which the 'jurisdiction exercised in particular by the judges of the Chancery Division' was irrelevant. A different approach

---

[57] [2007] 1 BCLC 788.

[58] [2001] 2 BCLC 235 at paras 19 and 118. Tariffs of 12 and 11 years were also imposed in *Re City Truck Group Ltd* [2007] 2 BCLC 649 and *Secretary of State for Trade and Industry v Kappler* [2008] 1 BCLC 120.

[59] [2014] EWHC 1381 (Ch).

[60] *Re Sevenoaks Stationers (Retail) Ltd* [1991] Ch 164, CA; *Re Travel Mondial Ltd* [1991] BCLC 120; *Re Tansoft Ltd* [1991] BCLC 339; *Re City Investment Centres Ltd* [1992] BCLC 956; *Re Godwin Warren Control Systems plc* [1993] BCC 80; *Re Firedart Ltd* [1994] 2 BCLC 340; *Re Britannia Homes Centres Ltd* [2001] 2 BCLC 63; *Re Bunting Electric Manufacturing Co Ltd* [2006] 1 BCLC 550.

[61] *Re New Generation Engineers Ltd* [1993] BCLC 435; *Re Linval Ltd* [1993] BCLC 654; *Re Swift 736 Ltd* [1993] BCLC 896, CA; *Re Continental Assurance Co of London plc* [1997] 1 BCLC 48; *Re Verby Print for Advertising Ltd* [1998] 2 BCLC 23; *Re Amaron Ltd* [2001] 1 BCLC 562.

[62] [1998] BCC 282, 284.

[63] [1990] BCC 549, 552–3, CA.

has, however, been taken in other more recent criminal cases[64] and so it would seem that the guidance in *Sevenoaks* is of general application.

C. Disqualification for Misconduct in Connection with Companies

Mandatory disqualification for unfitness under s 6(1) is by far the most frequently applied **31.24** ground for disqualification, but the statutory grounds considered in this Section C, which give the court a discretion to make a disqualification order, fulfil the same important policy function of protecting the public from persons whose past conduct means that they should not be allowed to be a director or concerned in the management of a company. These grounds are set out in CDDA, ss 2–5A and 10.

CDDA, s 12C(1)(b)[65] provides that where a court must determine whether to exercise any **31.25** discretion it has to make a disqualification order under CDDA, ss 2–4, 5A, or 10, as discussed below, it must:

(a) in every case have regard in particular to the matters set out in paragraphs 1 to 4 of Schedule 1 to the CDDA and which are considered in paragraphs 31.79 to 31.90 below; and

(b) in a case where the person concerned is or has been a director, or shadow director,[66] of a company or overseas company, also have regard in particular to the matters set out in paragraphs 5 to 7 of that Schedule, which are considered in paragraphs 31.91 to 31.131 below.

This requirement does not apply where the court is the one before which the person is convicted of the relevant indictable offence or, in the case of a summary conviction, any other magistrates court.[67]

(1) Conviction of indictable offence

CDDA, s 2(1) provides that: **31.26**

The court[68] may make a disqualification order against a person where he is convicted of an indictable offence (whether on indictment or summarily) in connection with the promotion, formation, management, liquidation or striking off of a company, with the receivership of a company's property or with his being an administrative receiver of a company.[69]

An 'indictable offence' means an offence which, if committed by an adult, is triable on indictment, whether it is exclusively so triable or triable either way.[70] The maximum period

---

[64] *R v Edwards* (1998) 2 Cr App R (S) 213; and *R v Millard* (1994) 15 Cr App R (S) 445.
[65] Inserted by SBEEA 2015, s 106 (1), (5), which came into force on 1 October 2015.
[66] CDDA, s 12C(5).
[67] CDDA, s 12C(2).
[68] For the purposes of s 2(1) the court means (a) any court having jurisdiction to wind up the company in relation to which the offence was committed, (a)(a) in relation to an overseas company not falling within para (a), the High Court, (b) the court by or before which the person is convicted of an offence, or (c) in the case of a summary conviction in England and Wales, any other magistrates' court acting in the same local justice area: CDDA, s 2(2). Where the application is made to the court with winding-up jurisdiction, the application may be made by the Secretary of State, the official receiver, or by the liquidator or any past or present member or creditor of any relevant company: CDDA, s 16(2). For comment on disqualification under this section in the criminal courts see Ch 35, Section K below.
[69] In CDDA, s 2(1) 'company' includes an overseas company as defined in s 22(2A): CDDA s 2(1A).
[70] CDDA, s 2(2); Interpretation Act, s 2(2) and Sch 1.

of disqualification under s 2 is 15 years unless the order is made by a court of summary juris-diction, in which case the maximum period is 5 years.[71] Where a criminal court has already declined to make a disqualification order following conviction, it is an abuse of process for the Secretary of State to rely on identical grounds in an application to the High Court for a disqualification order under s 2. Instead he could apply under s 6 (and stay the proceedings pending criminal trial) or proceed under s 4 on a sufficiently different basis from the facts of the conviction.[72]

31.27 The jurisdiction to make a disqualification order turns on whether the defendant is convicted of an indictable offence 'in connection with' one or more of the activities specified in s 2(1). It is necessary to identify the conduct which it is said makes the defendant unfit as a director. In *R v Chandler*,[73] a director had been found guilty of various strict liability regulatory offences after the Crown had abandoned the more serious allegations of fraud. A disqualification order imposed by the sentencing judge was quashed because judge had failed to identify misconduct which made the director unfit. In *R v Goodman*,[74] the relevant misconduct was found in the defendant's conviction for insider dealing contrary to the Company Securities (Insider Dealing) Act 1985. Staughton LJ explained that 'some relevant factual connection with the management of the company' was required:

> There are three possible ways of looking at the test to be applied. The first might be to say that the indictable offence referred to in the 1986 Act must be an offence of breaking some rule of law as to what must be done in the management of a company or must not be done. Examples might be keeping accounts or filing returns and such matters ... Another view might be that the indictable offence must be committed in the course of managing the company. That would cover cases such as *Georgiou, Corbin,* and *Austen*. What the defendants in all those cases were doing was managing the company so that it carried out unlawful transactions.

> The third view would be that the indictable offence must have some relevant factual connec-tion with the management of the company. That, in our judgment, is the correct answer. It is perhaps wider than the test applied in the three cases we have mentioned, because in those cases there was no need for the court to go wider than in fact it did. But we can see no ground for supposing that Parliament wished to apply any stricter test. Accordingly, we consider that the conduct of Mr Goodman in this case did amount to an indictable offence in connection with the management of the company. Even on a stricter view that might well be the case, because as chairman it was unquestionably his duty not to use confidential information for his own private benefit. It was arguably conduct in the management of the company when he did that.[75]

This test is necessarily imprecise, but it was applied in *R v Creddy* to uphold the disqualifi-cation of a solicitor who made available his client account 'as a private banking facility' for assets which were, and which he suspected were, the proceeds of crime.[76] This decision is undoubtedly correct, but, in less clear cases, it may be useful, as indicated by Staughton LJ, to apply the narrower tests first developed by the Court of Appeal as a cross-check to the broader test in *R v Goodman*.[77]

---

[71] CDDA, s 2(3).
[72] *Secretary of State for BIS v Weston* [2014] BCC 581.
[73] [2015] EWCA Crim 1825.
[74] [1993] 2 All ER 789, CA.
[75] [1993] 2 All ER 789, 792 CA.
[76] [2008] 1 BCLC 625, CA, para 14.
[77] *R v Georgiou* [1988] BCC 322, CA; *R v Austen* (1985) 7 Cr App R (S) 214; *R v Corbin* (1984) 6 Cr App R(S) 17.

(2) Persistent breaches of companies legislation

CDDA, s 3(1) provides that: **31.28**

> The court[78] may make a disqualification order against a person where it appears to it that he has been persistently in default in relation to provisions of the companies legislation requiring any return, account or other document to be filed with, delivered or sent, or notice of any matter to be given, to the registrar of companies.

The maximum period of disqualification under s 3 is five years.[79]

The focus of any complaint is likely to be a failure to file accounts and to provide information   **31.29**
to the Registrar,[80] but the scope of s 3(1) may properly include *any* return, account, or other
document to be filed with the Registrar of Companies under the 2006 Act as well as any such
provisions under the Insolvency Act, Parts 1–7 concerning company insolvency and winding
up, since the definition of 'companies legislation' for the purpose of s 3 extends to that Act also.[81]

The 'default' is that of the defendant and not the company. The companies legislation may   **31.30**
impose an obligation on the company to file a prescribed return or account, for example, but the
focus of s 3(1) is the default of the defendant under the companies legislation. The defendant's
default need not be culpable for the defendant to be liable for disqualification under s 3(1), but
his culpability is likely to be relevant to the exercise of the court's discretion.[82]

The expression 'persistently in default' is not defined, but, in *Re Artic Engineering Ltd*,   **31.31**
Hoffmann J considered that it connotes 'some degree of continuance or repetition' and an
analogy with s 3(2) provided some indication of 'the kind of conduct which the legislature
had in mind'.[83] This issue will, however, only arise where s 3(2) is not satisfied. Section 3(2)
provides that persistent default is conclusively proved upon showing that in the five years
ending with the date of the application the defendant has been 'adjudged guilty' of three or
more defaults, whether or not on the same occasion. To be treated under s 3(2) as adjudged
guilty of a default in relation to any provision of the companies legislation, the defendant
must have been:

(1) convicted of an offence consisting in a contravention of, or failure to comply with, a
    provision of the companies legislation, whether on his own part or on the part of any
    company;[84]

(2) made subject to a default order requiring delivery of company accounts, requir-
    ing the preparation of revised accounts, or enforcing the company's filing
    obligations;[85] or

---

[78] The court means (a) any court having jurisdiction to wind up any of the companies in relation to which the offence or other default has been or is alleged to have been committed, and (b) in relation to an overseas company not falling within (a), the High Court: CDDA, s 3(4). The application may be made by the Secretary of State, the official receiver or by the liquidator or any past or present member or creditor of any relevant company: CDDA, s 16(2).

[79] CDDA, s 3(5).

[80] 2006 Act, ss 441–5 (accounts) and 2006 Act, Part 24 as amended by SBEE Act 2015 with effect from 30 June 2016 (provision of information to the Registrar, formerly the annual return).

[81] CDDA, ss 3(4A) and 22(7).

[82] *Re Artic Engineering Ltd* [1986] 1 WLR 686, 691, 692.

[83] [1986] 1 WLR 686, 692.

[84] CDDA, s 3(3)(a). In CDDA, s 3 'company' includes an overseas company as defined in s 22(2A): CDDA s 3(A).

[85] CDDA, 3(3)(b)(i), (ia), and (ii), referring to 2006 Act, ss 452, 456, 1113.

(3) made subject to an order under the Insolvency Act enforcing the duty of a receiver, manager, or liquidator to make returns.[86]

(3) Fraud etc in winding up

31.32 So far as concerns directors, CDDA, s 4(1) provides that the court[87] may make a disqualification order against a person if, in the course of the winding up of a company, it appears that he:

(a) has been guilty of an offence for which he is liable (whether he has been convicted or not)[88] under section 993 of the Companies Act 2006 (fraudulent trading), or

(b) has otherwise been guilty, while an officer ... of the company ... of any fraud in relation to the company or of any breach of his duty as such officer.

The maximum period of disqualification under s 4 is 15 years.

31.33 The power to disqualify under s 4 only arises if the company is being wound up. The winding up may be compulsory or voluntary, solvent or insolvent. The section overlaps with s 10, concerning wrongful trading (paragraph 31.40 below). The conduct that may attract disqualification under s 4 is necessarily serious: fraudulent trading or fraud. The section also applies to 'any breach of duty', although the breach must be of sufficient gravity to warrant the court exercising its discretion to disqualify.[89]

(4) Summary conviction

31.34 CDDA, s 5(2) and (3) entitles a court convicting a defendant of a summary offence to make a disqualification order if during the five years ending with the date of the conviction the defendant has had made against him, or has been convicted of, in total not less than three default orders[90] and offences. The offences include the offence of which he is convicted by that court and any other offence of which he is convicted on the same occasion.

31.35 For the purposes of s 5 an 'offence' is one of which the defendant is convicted (either on indictment or summarily) in consequence of a contravention of, or failure to comply with, any provision of the companies legislation requiring a return, account, or other document to be filed with, delivered, or sent, or notice of any matter to be given, to the Registrar of Companies.[91]

---

[86] CDDA, s 3(3)(b)(iii) and (iv), referring to Insolvency Act, ss 41 and 170.

[87] Any court having jurisdiction to wind up any of the companies in relation to which the offence or other default has been or is alleged to have been committed: CDDA, s 4(2). The application may be made by the Secretary of State, the official receiver or by the liquidator or any past or present member or creditor of any relevant company: CDDA, s 16(2).

[88] Despite the reference to a director being 'guilty of an offence', the court will apply the civil standard of proof. Nonetheless, allegations of fraud require cogent evidence: *Secretary of State for BIS v Doffman (No 2)* [2011] 2 BCLC 541 at paras 29–31, per Newey J.

[89] Cf CDDA, s 6 case *Re Polly Peck International plc (No 2)* [1994] 1 BCLC 574, 580.

[90] By s 5(4) the definition of 'summary offence' in the Interpretation Act, Sch 1 applies and 'default order' has the same meaning as in CDDA, s 3(3)(b).

[91] CDDA, s 5(1). 'Companies legislation' has the same meaning as in s 3, namely the Companies Acts and the Insolvency Act, Parts 1–7: ss 5(4A) and 22(7). In s 5 'company' includes an overseas company as defined in s 22(2A): CDDA s 5(4B).

The basis for making a disqualification order under s 5 therefore overlaps substantially with that under s 3, but only the criminal courts have power to disqualify under this section; see further Chapter 35 at paragraph 34.260.

31.36

(5) Conviction abroad for offences in connection with companies

The SBEE Act 2015 inserted s 5A into the CDDA, providing for disqualification for certain convictions abroad. The Secretary of State may apply to the court for a disqualification order if he considers it expedient in the public interest.[92] The court then has a discretion whether to make an order against the person if he has been convicted of a relevant foreign offence.[93] The maximum period of disqualification under this section is 15 years.[94]

31.37

A relevant foreign offence is one which:

31.38

(a) is committed outside Great Britain,
(b) in connection with the promotion, formation, management, liquidation or striking off of a company[95] (or any similar procedure), with the receivership of a company's property (or any similar procedure) or with his being an administrative receiver of a company (or holding a similar position), and
(c) which corresponds to an indictable offence under the law of England and Wales or Scotland.[96]

Where a person convicted of a relevant foreign offence offers a disqualification undertaking, the Secretary of State may accept that undertaking if he considers it expedient in the public interest to do so.[97]

31.39

(6) Participation in wrongful trading

CDDA, s 10(1) provides that:

31.40

Where the court makes a declaration under section 213 or 214 of the Insolvency Act that a person is liable to make a contribution to a company's assets, then, whether or not an application for such an order is made by any person, the court may, if it thinks fit, also make a disqualification order against the person to whom the declaration relates.

The maximum period of disqualification under s 10 is 15 years.[98] The power to make a declaration under the Insolvency Act, s 213 or 214 is considered in Chapter 34, Sections C(2) and (3) below.

The jurisdiction to make a disqualification order under s 10 overlaps substantially with the jurisdiction under s 6 and, given the more extensive matters which may be taken into account in assessing unfitness under that section, the majority of applications for disqualification touching on fraudulent or wrongful trading will be brought under s 6. The power to disqualify under s 10 may be used where the liquidator has applied for a contribution

31.41

---

[92] CDDA, s 5A(1).
[93] CDDA, s 5A(2).
[94] CDDA, s 5A(6).
[95] 'Company' includes an overseas company: CDDA s 5A(5).
[96] CDDA, s 5A(3).
[97] CDDA, s 5A(4).
[98] CDDA, s 10(2). In s 10, 'company' includes an overseas company as defined in s 22(2A): CDDA s 10(3).

order under the Insolvency Act, s 213 or 214, but no application has been made under CDDA, s 6.[99]

D. Disqualification for Unfitness

(1) Mandatory disqualification for unfitness

31.42 CDDA, s 6(1) provides that:

> The court[100] shall make a disqualification order against a person in any case where, on an application under this section, it is satisfied—
> (a) that he is or has been a director of a company which has at any time become insolvent (whether while he was a director or subsequently), and
> (b) that his conduct as a director of that company (either taken alone or taken together with his conduct as a director of one or more companies or overseas companies)[101] makes him unfit to be concerned in the management of a company.

The applicant is the Secretary of State unless the company is or has been wound up by the court, in which case the Secretary of State may direct the official receiver to apply.[102] The minimum period of disqualification is two years and the maximum period is 15 years.[103] The court accordingly has a *duty* to disqualify for at least two years anyone whose conduct as a director of a company which has become insolvent makes him unfit to be concerned in the management of a company.

31.43 Section 6 specifically applies to directors, including shadow directors[104] and de facto directors.[105] Both types of director are discussed in Chapter 3 Section C(2) and (3) above.[106]

---

[99] In the early case of *Re Bath Glass Ltd* (1988) 4 BCC 130, 133 it was suggested that disqualification under s 10 is most likely to be ordered in a case where a claim for contribution is successfully made for a short period of wrongful trading and, as such, it is felt that a mandatory two-year disqualification is not justified. It is hard to envisage circumstances in which a court would be justified in adopting such a view, given the seriousness with which the courts view a director's failure to have regard to the interests of creditors when the company is in serious financial difficulties (paras 31.100–31.111 below) and a director's responsibility for the company becoming insolvent and failing to provide goods or services (paras 31.80–31.82 below).

[100] If the company is being or has been wound up by the court, the court is that court; in cases of voluntary winding up, administration, or administrative receivership, the court is any court with jurisdiction to wind it up: CDDA, s 6(3).

[101] The reference to overseas companies was inserted into s 6 (and other sections of the CDDA) by SBEE Act 2015 with effect from 1 October 2015. The amendment makes clear that conduct in relation to companies registered outside of the United Kingdom can form the grounds for disqualification, although in fact this was the case previously, since the definition of 'company' in s 22(2) CDDA has always included both UK-registered companies and unregistered companies which might be wound up under the Insolvency Act, Part 5.

[102] CDDA, s 7(1).

[103] CDDA, s 6(4).

[104] CDDA, s 6(3C).

[105] *Re UKLI Ltd* [2015] BCC 755.

[106] In the context of disqualification: *Re Lo-line Electric Motors Ltd* [1988] Ch 477; *Re Moorgate Metals Ltd, Official Receiver v Huhtala* [1995] 1 BCLC 503; *Re Richborough Furniture Ltd* [1996] 1 BCLC 507; *Re Sykes (Butchers) Ltd* [1998] 1 BCLC 110; *Secretary of State for Trade and Industry v Tjolle* [1998] 1 BCLC 333; *Re Kaytech International plc* [1999] 2 BCLC 351, CA; *Re UKLI Ltd* [2015] BCC 755. The leading authority on de facto directors is now *Revenue and Customs Commissioners v Holland, Re Paycheck Services 3 Ltd* [2010] 1 WLR 2793, SC, which at para 41 disapproved the reasoning of Evans Lombe J in *Secretary of State for Trade and Industry v Hall* [2009] BCC 190 at paras 13, 29–30.

The first of these conditions, s 6(1)(a), is defined by s 6(2), which emphasizes the entry of the   **31.44**
company into formal insolvency proceedings:

> For the purposes of this section, a company becomes insolvent if—
> (a) the company goes into liquidation at a time when its assets are insufficient for the pay-
> ment of its debts and other liabilities and the expenses of the winding up,
> (b) the company enters administration, or
> (c) an administrative receiver of the company is appointed.

The inability of the company to pay its debts is only relevant in the case of liquidation, which
must be an insolvent liquidation. The relevant test is balance-sheet—rather than cash-flow, or
commercial—insolvency, as indicated by 'its assets are insufficient for the payment of its debts
and other liabilities and the expenses of the winding up'.[107] The validity of the insolvency proceedings is not open to challenge in the disqualification proceedings.[108] The insolvency of a
company is merely the gateway to the bringing of disqualification proceedings, and once that
gateway has been passed, the fact that the creditors of the company have been, or might be,
paid in full should not ordinarily amount to a defence, although in making its overall assessment about whether unfitness was established the court might take that fact into account.[109]

The second condition, s 6(1)(b), is defined by s 6(1A),[110] which states that: **31.45**

> references to a person's conduct as a director of any company or overseas company include,
> where that company or overseas company has become insolvent, references to that person's
> conduct in relation to any matter connected with or arising out of the insolvency.

For the purposes of s 6 an overseas company becomes insolvent if the company enters
into insolvency proceedings of any description (including interim proceedings) in any
jurisdiction.[111]

The expression 'makes him unfit to be concerned in the management of a company' does not   **31.46**
entitle the court to find a person is not unfit because, at the time of the hearing (a) he has demonstrated in some other way that he is not unfit, or (b) the evidence in that case only proves that
his conduct was unfit in connection with the company in issue and not in relation to companies
generally. In *Re Grayan Building Services Ltd*,[112] Arden J had held that proceedings under the
Insolvency Act, s 239 had brought home to the company's former directors the consequences
of granting a preference and that, despite serious shortcomings in their conduct, they were not
unfit to be concerned in the management of a company. The Court of Appeal expressly rejected
the construction of s 6(1) said to support this conclusion. Hoffmann LJ explained that:

> It is true that the subsection uses the present tense 'makes,' but ... this means only that the
> court has to make the decision on the evidence put forward at the hearing ... The court is

---

[107] For the difference between balance sheet and cash-flow insolvency, see *BNY Corporate Trustee Services Ltd v Eurosail-UK 2007-3BL Plc* [2013] 1 WLR 1408, SC.
[108] *Secretary of State for Trade and Industry v Jabble* [1998] 1 BCLC 598, CA.
[109] *Re Normanton Wells Properties Ltd* [2011] 1 BCLC 191 at paras 21–2.
[110] Inserted by SBEE Act 2015, s 106(1), (2)(b) as from 1 October 2015. CDDA s 6(1A) replaces language that has been deleted from s 6(2), but in different terms. For authority on the former language, see *Secretary of State for Trade and Industry v Ivens* [1997] 2 BCLC 334, CA (discussing conduct in relation to the lead and collateral companies).
[111] CDDA s 6(2A) inserted by SBEE Act 2015, s 106(2)(d) as from 1 October 2015.
[112] [1995] Ch 241, CA.

concerned solely with the conduct specified by the Secretary of State or official receiver under rule 3(3) of the Insolvent Companies (Disqualification of Unfit Directors) Proceedings Rules 1987. It must decide whether that conduct, viewed cumulatively and taking into account any extenuating circumstances, has fallen below the standards of probity and competence appropriate for persons fit to be directors of companies.

… If the court always had to be satisfied at the hearing that the protection of the public required a period of disqualification, there would be no need to make disqualification mandatory … The purpose of making disqualification mandatory was to ensure that everyone whose conduct had fallen below the appropriate standard was disqualified for at least two years, whether in the individual case the court thought that this was necessary in the public interest or not. Parliament has decided that it is occasionally necessary to disqualify a company director to encourage the others.[113]

31.47   A further attempt to construe s 6(1) as conferring some residual discretion was rejected in *Re Barings plc (No 5)*.[114] Jonathan Parker J held that the court is concerned only with the conduct of which complaint is made and not with whether the person is unfit to be concerned in the management of *any* company:

In the context of an issue as to unfitness it is neither here nor there whether a respondent could have performed some other management role competently. That is not the test of 'unfitness' for the purposes of s 6 … Under s 6 the court is concerned only with the conduct in respect of which complaint is made, set in the context of the respondent's actual management role in the company. If in his conduct in that role the respondent was guilty of incompetence to the requisite degree, then a finding of unfitness will be made and (under s 6) a disqualification order must follow.[115]

31.48   The court accordingly only has 'discretion' under s 6(1) in deciding whether or not it is 'satisfied' that the defendant's conduct makes him unfit to be concerned in the management of a company. In this respect, a clear thread in the authorities is that 'whatever else is required of a respondent's misconduct if he is to be disqualified, it must at least be "serious"'.[116] If it were otherwise, the trigger for mandatory disqualification might be satisfied by a mere breach of duty. *In Re Structural Concrete Ltd*[117] Blackburne J set out a 3-stage process: '(1) do the matters relied upon amount to misconduct; (2) if they do, do they justify a finding of unfitness; and (3) if they do, what period of disqualification, being not less than two years, should result?'

31.49   The fact that a criminal court has not made a disqualification order when invited to do so at the sentencing stage is not itself a bar to a subsequent civil application by the Secretary of State.[118] Equally disqualification proceedings may be commenced when criminal proceedings may ensue or the civil proceedings may be stayed pending the criminal proceedings and then resurrected when the criminal proceedings have concluded and

---

113 [1995] Ch 241, 253.
114 [1999] 1 BCLC 433.
115 [1999] 1 BCLC 433, 485.
116 *Re Polly Peck International plc (No 2)* [1994] 1 BCLC 574, 580.
117 [2001] BCC 578, 586; followed in *Re Artistic Investment Advisers Ltd* [2015] 1 BCLC 619.
118 *Re Denis Hilton Ltd* [2002] 1 BCLC 302; *Secretary of State for BIS v Weston* [2014] BCC 581.

factors may be raised in the civil proceedings which may justify a longer period of disqualification.[119]

(2) Office-holder's report on conduct

CDDA, 7A[120] requires the office-holder[121] in respect of an insolvent company to prepare a conduct report about the conduct of each person who was a director of the company on the insolvency date or at any time in the preceding three years.[122] For the purposes of s 7A a company is insolvent if (a) it is in liquidation and at the time it went into liquidation its assets were insufficient for the payment of its debts and other liabilities and the expenses of the winding up, (b) the company has entered administration, or (c) an administrative receiver of the company has been appointed.[123] The conduct report must, in relation to each person, describe any conduct of the person which may assist the Secretary of State in deciding whether to apply for a disqualification order or accept a disqualification undertaking.[124] The report must be sent to the Secretary of State within three months of the insolvency date, or such longer period as he may allow,[125] and there is a continuing obligation to report any new information which subsequently comes to the office-holder's attention as soon as reasonably practicable.

31.50

The office-holder may disclose to the Secretary of State material, including interviews, obtained under the Insolvency Act, s 235, since the provision of such material is for the purposes of the administration.[126] The report will not be privileged and the respondent to the disqualification application will be entitled to have it disclosed.[127]

31.51

(3) Determination by the Secretary of State

In a s 6 case, forming and holding the relevant opinion that it is 'expedient in the public interest'[128] for a disqualification order to be made gives the Secretary of State standing to make the application. Although the section refers to the decision being made by the Secretary of State, there is no requirement for the decision to be made by the minister personally, and so it may properly be made by the Secretary of State acting through one of his officers.[129]

31.52

The formation of the requisite opinion and the decision to make an application for a disqualification order must be proper decisions, as a matter of public law, in that proper grounds for them must exist and be relied upon, irrelevant matters must not be taken into account, and

31.53

---

[119] CDDA, s 1(4); *Re Cedarwood Productions Ltd* [2004] BCC 65, CA.

[120] In force 6 April 2016 (replacing s 7(3), which was repealed: SBEE Act 2015, s 107). Section 7A is supported by the Insolvent Companies (Reports on Conduct of Directors) (England and Wales) Rules 2016 (SI 2016/180) which also came into force on 6 April 2016 when, subject to transitions and savings, the Insolvent Companies (Reports on Conduct of Directors) Rules 1996 were revoked.

[121] As defined in s 7A(9). See also ss 7A(7), where there is more than one office-holder.

[122] CDDA, s 7A(1). Section 7A(10) explains the meaning of 'insolvency date', read with s 7A(8).

[123] CDDA, s 7A(2), to which s 6(1A) applies. See paras 31.44 and 31.45 above.

[124] CDDA, s 7A(3).

[125] CDDA, s 7A(4).

[126] *Re Polly Peck International plc* [1994] BCC 15 (where the administrators had given assurances that the material would only be used for the purposes of the administration).

[127] *Secretary of State for Trade and Industry v Baker* [1998] Ch 356.

[128] CDDA, s 7(1).

[129] Cf *Re Golden Chemical Products Ltd* [1976] Ch 300, applying *Carltona Ltd v Comrs of Works* [1943] 2 All ER 560, *Lewisham Borough Council v Roberts* [1949] 2 KB 608, and *R v Skinner* [1968] 2 QB 700.

the opinion or decision must be one that a reasonable Secretary of State or regulator could reach. In theory, the decision is subject to judicial review. In practice, it has been difficult for prospective defendants to obtain the necessary permission to proceed with an application for judicial review.[130]

31.54 For applications under s 7 seeking disqualification under s 6, s 7(2) provides:[131]

> Except with the leave of the court, an application for the making under section 6 of a disqualification order against any person shall not be made after the end of the period of three years beginning with the day on which the company of which that person is or has been a director became insolvent.[132]

For applications for leave under this section, see Section H(1) below.

31.55 Where a person in respect of whom the conditions in section 6(1) are satisfied offers a disqualification undertaking, the Secretary of State may accept that undertaking if he considers it expedient in the public interest to do so.

31.56 Section 7(4)[133] entitles the Secretary of State or the official receiver to require any person to furnish him with information and to produce and permit inspection of books, papers, and other records as are considered by him to be relevant to that person's or another person's conduct as a director of a company which has at any time become insolvent.

(4) Expedient in the public interest

31.57 CDDA, s 8 provides that:[134]

(1) If it appears to the Secretary of State that it is expedient in the public interest that a disqualification order should be made against a person who is, or has been, a director or shadow director of a company, he may apply to the court for such an order.

(2) The court[135] may make a disqualification order against a person where, on an application under this section, it is satisfied that his conduct in relation to the company (either taken alone or taken together with his conduct as a director or shadow director of one or more other companies or overseas companies) makes him unfit to be concerned in the management of a company.

---

[130] In *R v Secretary of State for Trade and Industry, ex p McCormick* [1998] BCC 379 the Court of Appeal refused permission for judicial review of a decision to rely on transcripts of compulsory interviews by inspectors; *R v Secretary of State for Trade and Industry, ex p Eastway* [2000] 1 WLR 2222. Similarly, in *R v Secretary of State for Trade and Industry, ex p Lonrho plc* [1992] BCC 325 the applicant company failed in an attempt to challenge by judicial review the Secretary of State's decision *not* to pursue disqualification proceedings.

[131] As amended by SBEEA 2015, s 108(1) as from 1 October 2015. The previous two-year time limit applies to an application relating to a company which has become insolvent before that date; see s 108(2) and (3). There is no time limit for applications under s 8 after an investigation of the company or under s 9A for a competition disqualification order.

[132] The words 'an application for the making of an order' have the same meaning as 'the bringing of proceedings' for the purpose of the Limitation Act 1980: *Secretary of State for Trade and Industry v Vohora* [2009] BCC 369 at paras 10 and 27, per Evans Lombe J.

[133] As amended by Deregulation Act 2015, ss 19 Sch 6, Pt 4 para 11 as from 1 October 2015. Previously, the Act merely referred to the relevant insolvency office-holder rather than 'any person'. The amendment came into force on 1 October 2015 as regards companies that became insolvent on or after that date; see SI 2015/1732.

[134] As amended by SBEE Act 2015, ss 106 and 109, which came into force on 1 October 2015. The effect of the amendments is to remove the restrictions on applications for a disqualification order following an investigation, and to include reference to overseas companies. CDDA, s 6(1A) applies for the purposes of s 8: s 8(2B).

[135] The High Court: CDDA, s 8(3).

The maximum period of disqualification is fifteen years, but unlike disqualification for unfitness under s 6 there is no minimum period.[136] As with s 6, the Secretary of State has power to accept a disqualification undertaking.[137]

This confers a power to disqualify a director who is unfit but, unlike s 6, imposes no statutory **31.58** duty to do so. The power is, however, fettered to the extent that the court 'would not, having formed the view that disqualification was necessary in the public interest, be acting judicially if it did not make a disqualification order'.[138] As such, it has been *assumed* that the test of unfitness under s 8(2) is the same as that under s 6(1), although the point remains undecided. In *Secretary of State for Trade and Industry v Hollier*, Etherton J invited counsel to address him on the issue but to his 'surprise' both counsel were agreed that 'the same approach and principles should apply as in cases under s 6 in respect of the determination of unfitness and fixing the period of disqualification'.[139]

The approach taken by the court in *Hollier* is adopted here, and cases under s 8 are dis- **31.59** cussed below with the case law under s 6(1), although specifically referenced as such.[140] A ground sufficient to warrant mandatory disqualification for at least two years should at least be capable of justifying disqualification under s 8(2) and, given the approach currently adopted in practice, there appears to be no discernible difference in the way the courts have approached the issue of unfitness under either section, notwithstanding that the language of s 8(2) focuses more broadly on the defendant's 'conduct in relation to the company' and not merely his 'conduct as a director', which forms part of the test under s 6(1).

Since disqualification proceedings are civil, not criminal, the use of evidence obtained under **31.60** compulsion does not infringe the right against self-incrimination which is protected by Article 6(1) of the ECHR.[141]

(5) Persons instructing unfit directors

One of the difficulties with the law as it stood prior to 1 October 2015 was that a wrongdoer **31.61** who was not himself a director but who exercised influence over a director was not liable to disqualification unless he could be described as a shadow director. However, as Harman J held in *Re Unisoft Group Ltd (No. 3)*,[142] 'with a multi-member board, unless the whole of the board, or at the very least a governing majority of it … are accustomed to act on the directions of an outsider, such an outsider cannot be a shadow director'. Accordingly, a wrongdoer who persuaded only a minority of the directors to act unlawfully could not be a shadow director, and would therefore escape disqualification. CDDA, ss 8ZA–8ZE[143] fill

---

[136] CDDA, s 8(4).

[137] CDDA, s 8(2A).

[138] Cf *Re Grayan Building Services Ltd* [1995] Ch 241, 253g.

[139] [2007] BCC 11, paras 45–51, 59. In *Secretary of State for Trade and Industry v Ashman*, Lloyd J, 15 June 1998, (unreported), pp 13–18 of the transcript, Lloyd J recorded that there was 'no great dispute as to the relevant law' and set out the law applicable as it had then developed under s 6.

[140] *Re Samuel Sherman plc* [1991] 1 WLR 1070; *Re Looe Fish Ltd* [1993] BCLC 1160; *Re Aldermanbury Trust plc* [1993] BCC 598; *Secretary of State for Trade and Industry v Ashman*, Lloyd J, 15 June 1998 (unreported); *Re JA Chapman & Co Ltd* [2003] 2 BCLC 206; *Secretary of State for Trade and Industry v Hollier* [2007] BCC 11; *Secretary of State for BERR v Sullman* [2009] 1 BCLC 666.

[141] *R v Secretary of State for Trade and Industry, ex p McCormick* [1998] BCC 379, CA.

[142] [1994] 1 BCLC 609, 620.

[143] Sections 8ZA–8ZE were inserted into the CDDA by SBEE Act 2015, s 105, which came into force on 1 October 2015.

this lacuna, applying to a wrongdoer who exercises influence over a single director, even if the rest of the directors are uninfluenced.

31.62   CDDA, s 8ZA provides that the court may make a disqualification order against a person (P) who instructs an unfit director. The court must be satisfied:

(1)   that a disqualification order under s 6 or a disqualification undertaking under s 7(2A) has been made against a person who is or has been a director (but not a shadow director) of a company (the main transgressor); and

(2)   that P exercised the requisite amount of influence over the main transgressor.

P is deemed to have exercised the requisite amount of influence over the main transgressor if any of the conduct which resulted in the disqualification order or undertaking was the result of the main transgressor acting in accordance with P's directions or instructions.[144] The section makes clear that P will not be liable purely by reason of having given advice in a professional capacity.[145] The minimum period of disqualification under s 8ZA is two years and the maximum period is 15 years.[146]

31.63   If it appears to the Secretary of State that it is expedient in the public interest that a disqualification order should be made under s 8ZA, he may make an application to the court for such an order, or where the application for an order under s 6 against the main transgressor has been made by the official receiver, direct the official receiver to make such an application.[147] Such an application may not be made more than three years after the company in question became insolvent.[148] The power of the Secretary of State or the official receiver to require any person to furnish such information or documents as he requires under s 7(4) (discussed at paragraph 31.56 above) applies equally in this context.[149] Section 8ZC provides for the Secretary of State to accept a disqualification undertaking instead of making an application under s 8ZB.

31.64   Sections 8ZD–8ZE are almost a mirror image of ss 8ZA–8ZC, except that where ss 8ZA–8ZC provide for disqualification of a person instructing an unfit director of an insolvent company, ss 8ZD–8ZE provide for disqualification of a person instructing an unfit director in cases of disqualification where it is expedient in the public interest under s 8. Accordingly, there is no minimum period of disqualification, although the maximum period of disqualification is still 15 years.[150]

(6)   Matters for determining unfitness: the general approach

31.65   The courts have not set out precise matters for determining unfitness, but the more recent cases indicate a concern to define more precisely the standard of probity and competence to which directors must adhere. The case law prior to the introduction of mandatory disqualification under s 6(1) tended to emphasize some breach of the standards of 'commercial

---

[144]   CDDA, s 8ZA(2).
[145]   CDDA, s 8ZA(3). This reflects the position for shadow directors under CA, s 251(2) and CDDA, s 22(5).
[146]   CDDA, s 8ZA(4).
[147]   CDDA, s 8ZB(1).
[148]   CDDA, s 8ZB(2).
[149]   CDDA, s 8ZB(3).
[150]   CDDA, s 8ZD(5).

morality' or serious incompetence as the badge of unfit conduct. In *Re Dawson Print Group Ltd*, in an application under the 1985 Act, s 300, Hoffmann J stated that:[151]

> There must, I think, be something about the case, some conduct which if not dishonest is at any rate in breach of standards of commercial morality, or some really gross incompetence which persuades the court that it would be a danger to the public if he were to be allowed to continue to be involved in the management of companies, before a disqualification order is made.

In *Re Lo-Line Electric Motors*, also an application under the 1985 Act, s 300, Browne-Wilkinson J similarly considered that:

> The primary purpose of the section is not to punish the individual but to protect the public against the future conduct of companies by persons whose past records as directors of insolvent companies have shown them to be a danger to creditors and others. Therefore, the power is not fundamentally penal. But if the power to disqualify is exercised, disqualification does involve a substantial interference with the freedom of the individual. It follows that the rights of the individual must be fully protected. Ordinary commercial misjudgment is in itself not sufficient to justify disqualification. In the normal case, the conduct complained of must display a lack of commercial probity, although I have no doubt that in an extreme case of gross negligence or total incompetence disqualification could be appropriate.

Following the enactment of s 6(1), the Court of Appeal, in *Re Sevenoaks Stationers (Retail)* **31.66** *Ltd*,[152] however, objected to a gloss being placed upon the actual words of s 6(1). Dillon LJ considered that:

> [T]here seems to have been a tendency, which I deplore, on the part of the Bar, and possibly also on the part of the official receiver's department, to treat the statements as judicial paraphrases of the words of the statute, which fall to be construed as a matter of law in lieu of the words of the statute. The result is to obscure that the true question to be tried is a question of fact—what used to be pejoratively described in the Chancery Division as 'a jury question'.[153]

Descriptions of conduct as being in breach of 'commercial morality', or lacking in 'commercial probity', are accordingly 'helpful in identifying particular circumstances in which a person would clearly be unfit',[154] but are not a substitute for the statutory language, including Schedule 1.

The decisions following *Sevenoaks* have not treated the question of unfitness as simply one of **31.67** fact, but have instead concentrated on the standards of probity and competence appropriate for persons fit to be directors of companies. As Norris J said in *Secretary of State for BERR v Sullman*, 'The question for decision may be "a jury question", but the tribunal making the decision is not a jury.'[155]

In *Re Polly Peck International plc (No 2)*, Lindsay J rejected a submission to the effect that **31.68** conduct was only relevant to s 6(1) if it breached some privilege of trading through a limited

---

[151] [1987] BCLC 601, 604.
[152] [1991] Ch 164, CA.
[153] [1991] Ch 164, 176.
[154] [1991] Ch 164, 176.
[155] [2009] 1 BCLC 397 at para 3.

liability company, notwithstanding the previous (and continued) explanation of the purpose of s 6(1) in those terms:

> The Act itself suggests no such qualification and, by making consideration of breach of any duty by a director a matter to which regard is in particular to be paid by the courts (see s 9(1) of and Sch 1, Pt 1, para 1 to the 1986 Act), would seem to exclude it. There are duties, for example to apply the money of the undertaking only for the purposes of the undertaking, which would seem to me to be as applicable to, say, a partnership as to a limited company and in any event the definition of 'company' in the 1986 Act can include bodies not having limited liability: see s 22(3). I can think of few tasks less profitable in disqualification cases than an examination of whether a given shortcoming of a director could properly be said to be a consequence of or attendant upon the privilege of trading with limited liability.[156]

Similarly in *Re Grayan Building Services Ltd*, Hoffmann LJ considered that:

> The purpose of making disqualification mandatory was to ensure that everyone whose conduct had fallen below the appropriate standard was disqualified for at least two years, whether in the individual case the court thought that this was necessary in the public interest or not.[157]

31.69 In *Secretary of State for Trade and Industry v Goldberg*, Lewison J moreover suggested a principled explanation for this approach:

> [T]he identification of the standard of conduct laid down by the law is important for two reasons. First, because the question of unfitness to do something can, as it seems to me, only be judged against an expectation of what is required of a person doing, or attempting to do, that thing. Secondly, because fairness to a director, or prospective director, requires that he should know what the law expects of him both before accepting his appointment and while carrying out his duties. I am uncomfortable with the notion that an honest director may be held to be unfit on account of conduct that, many years later, a judge may consider was a breach of some indefinable standard of commercial morality.[158]

On this basis, he accepted the submission of counsel that 'commercial morality' was not the relevant test to the extent that:

> [T]he court must be very careful before holding that a director is unfit because of conduct that does not amount to a breach of any duty (contractual, tortious, statutory or equitable) to anyone, and is not dishonest.[159]

The phrase 'to anyone' is important, because the conduct alleged to be unfit may be harmful to, or directed against, third parties, such as customers or investors, as well as the company. It is not necessary to show that the company is the 'victim' of the relevant conduct.[160] The question of unfitness cannot therefore be reduced to whether or not the conduct amounts to one or more breaches of duty as a company director.

31.70 Prior to the amendments made by the SBEE Act 2015, CDDA, s 9 required the court to have regard in particular to the matters mentioned in Schedule 1 of the Act when

---

[156] [1994] BCLC 574, 579.
[157] [1995] Ch 241, 253.
[158] [2004] 1 BCLC 597, para 42.
[159] [2004] 1 BCLC 597, para 43.
[160] *Secretary of State for BERR v Sullman* [2009] 1 BCLC 397 at para 28, per Norris J. In *Cathie v SS for BIS (No 2)* [2011] BCC 685, [2012] BCC 813 (CA) the directors discriminated against the Revenue and Customs Commissioners by not paying PAYE during a period when the company was still paying other creditors and by misleading the Revenue about the company's financial situation.

determining whether a person's conduct makes him unfit to be concerned in the management of a company. The Secretary of State was also required to have regard to those matters when determining whether to accept a disqualification undertaking. The SBEE Act 2015, s 106 has repealed CDDA, s 9 and inserted a new CDDA, s 12C, with a Schedule 1 which describes matters to which regard should be had in broader terms than its predecessor.[161]

The new s 12C[162] is also broader in scope than s 9 in that it applies to: **31.71**

(1) the determination by the court (a) whether a person's conduct as a director of one or more companies or overseas companies makes the person unfit to be concerned in the management of a company, (b) whether to exercise any discretion it has to make a disqualification order under any of ss 2–4, 5A, 8 or 10, and (c) as to the period of disqualification;[163] and
(2) the determination by the Secretary of State (a) whether a person's conduct as a director of one or more companies or overseas companies makes the person unfit to be concerned in the management of a company, and (b) whether to exercise any discretion he has to accept a disqualification undertaking under ss 5A, 7 or 8.

Since the court is required to have regard to, but is not limited by, the matters in the Schedule, **31.72** the following judicial pronouncements on the old Schedule 1 will still be relevant. Indeed, in *Re Amaron Ltd*, Neuberger J said that:

[I]n setting out specific grounds in Sch I to the 1986 Act the legislature did not intend other grounds capable, on appropriate facts, of being inherently more culpable than, on other facts, some of the grounds set out in the schedule, to be of less importance. It seems to me that one takes each allegation of unfitness on its merits and considers it, irrespective of whether it falls within Sch I or not.[164]

In *Secretary of State for BERR v Sullman*, a case under s 8 which involved misleading state- **31.73** ments to investors and customers, Norris J stated that:

I do not regard a breach of an identifiable and independent duty to be a prerequisite for a finding of culpable conduct under the CDDA 1986. The Act uses the broad term 'conduct' (not 'any breach of duty'): and I consider that the authorities establish that unfitness may be demonstrated by conduct which does not involve a breach of any statutory or common-law duty, but which, for example, constitutes a failure to achieve an acceptable standard of commercial probity.[165]

Although the conduct in that case is capable of rationalization as a breach of duty by the company's directors, it being contrary to the commercial interests of the company to mislead investors and customers, such a focus would miss the basis underlying the complaint, namely an abuse of limited liability by misleading investors and customers for profit.

Finally, in reviewing this area, it should be kept in mind that the courts have been careful **31.74** not to adopt too strict an approach to the question of unfitness because of hindsight. In *Re*

---

[161] With effect from 1 October 2015. Schedule 1 may be modified by statutory instrument: s 12C(7), (8).
[162] To which s 6(1A) applies: s 12C(6).
[163] CDDA, s 12C(1); but not where the court is one mentioned in s 2(2)(b) or (c): s 12C(2).
[164] [2001] 1 BCLC 562, 568; and *Re Migration Services International Ltd* [2000] 1 BCLC 666, 677–8, in which Neuberger J accepted that Sch 1 may have been intended to draw to the attention of directors their positive duties.
[165] [2009] 1 BCLC 397 at paras 29–30. See also *Re Bradcrown Ltd, Official Receiver v Ireland* [2001] 1 BCLC 547 at para 12, per Lawrence Collins J.

Living Images Ltd, Laddie J explained that, with the benefit of knowing that the company became insolvent:

> It is very easy therefore to look at the signals available to the directors at the time and to assume that they, or any other competent director, would have realised that the end was coming. The court must be careful not to fall into the trap of being too wise after the event.[166]

This does not mean that latitude is accorded to directors but merely that the court is likely to approach each charge with caution, especially in cases which involve assessment of the quality of judgments made in the course of business.

(7) Matters for determining unfitness, etc in all cases

31.75   As explained at paragraph 31.70 above, the SBEE Act 2015 introduced significant amendments to this part of the CDDA. Previously, Schedule 1 distinguished between (a) matters applicable to all cases, and (b) matters applicable where the company had become insolvent. The new Schedule 1 distinguishes between (a) matters to be taken into account in all cases, and (b) matters to be taken into account where the person is or has been a director. This change results from the fact that, whereas the old Schedule 1 applied only to ss 6 and 9A, the new Schedule 1 applies much more widely. Being a director is not a precondition for disqualification under ss 2–5A, 8ZA, 8ZD, or 10.

31.76   The second main difference is that the new schedule uses broader categories. For example, the old paragraphs 1–5, which listed various types of unlawful conduct, are replaced with a new paragraph 1, which simply requires the court to take into account 'any material contravention by a company or overseas company of any applicable legislative or other requirement'. The one matter in the old schedule which is not found in the new schedule concerns paragraph 8 of the old Schedule 1, which required the court to take into account any transaction within ss 127, 238, or 240 IA 1986 for which the director was responsible. The old paragraph 8 has been repealed, and so such conduct will only be relevant if it involves a breach of duty, which is not always the case.

31.77   Paragraphs 1–4 of Schedule 1 concern matters to be taken into account in all cases:

(1)   The extent to which the person was responsible for the causes of any material contravention by a company or overseas company of any applicable legislative or other requirement.

(2)   Where applicable, the extent to which the person was responsible for the causes of a company or overseas company becoming insolvent.

(3)   The frequency of conduct of the person which falls within paragraph 1 or 2.

(4)   The nature and extent of any loss or harm caused, or any potential loss or harm which could have been caused, by the person's conduct in relation to a company or overseas company.

31.78   Paragraphs 5–7 concern additional matters to be taken into account where the person is or has been a director:

(5)   Any misfeasance or breach of any fiduciary duty by the director in relation to a company or overseas company.

---

[166] [1996] 1 BCLC 348, 356c.

(6) Any material breach of any legislative or other obligation of the director which applies as a result of being a director of a company or overseas company.

(7) The frequency of conduct of the director which falls within paragraph 5 or 6.

(i) Responsibility for company's contravention of legislative requirements, etc

Although SBEE Act 2015 has introduced significant amendments into Schedule 1, it is likely **31.79** that a court, when determining whether to make a disqualification order and if so for how long, will be guided by the authorities on the Act as it was prior to 2015. Schedule 1, Part I, paragraph 4[167] formerly required the court to have regard to the extent of the director's responsibility for any failure by the company to comply with provisions of the 2006 Act concerning registers of members, directors, and secretaries,[168] accounting records,[169] annual returns, (now to provide information to the Registrar)[170] and the register of charges.[171] Although '[d]efaults of this kind are not to be brushed off as trivial',[172] it has been said that '[o]n their own, although misconduct, they would not warrant a finding of unfitness. They add some weight to the other findings of misconduct when overall consideration is given to the issues of fitness and the appropriate period of disqualification.'[173]

(ii) Responsibility for company becoming insolvent

Schedule 1 paragraph 2[174] requires the court to have regard to the extent of the director's respon- **31.80** sibility for 'the causes of a company or overseas company becoming insolvent'. A company may fail for one or many reasons and this paragraph focuses on the responsibility of the director for the circumstances that brought about the particular insolvency. Although the paragraph is expressed in broad general terms and may overlap with other paragraphs, a director would not be disqualified unless his contribution to a cause of the company becoming insolvent was in some way culpable. Correspondingly, any such or other grounds for disqualification would not be absolved upon the emergence of a surplus as against unsecured creditors in the liquidation.

The courts appear to have accepted this construction. In *Re Barings plc (No 5)*, Jonathan **31.81** Parker J explained that:

> [T]he relevant inquiry is not whether the respondent has caused (in any strict legal sense) the insolvency. It raises a different and much broader question, namely: To what extent were the respondent's failings responsible for the causes of the insolvency? In my judgment in address-ing that question the court is required to adopt a correspondingly broader approach, eschew-ing nice legal concepts of causation.[175]

On this basis, he held that one of the directors in that case bore 'a heavy responsibility for the causes of the companies ... becoming insolvent' because 'had he performed his management

---

[167] In the form substituted by the Companies Act 2006 (Consequential Amendments, Transitional Provisions and Savings) Order 2009 (SI 2009/941) with effect from 1 October 2009.

[168] 2006 Act, ss 113, 114, 162, 165, 167, 275, 276.

[169] 2006 Act, ss 386 and 388.

[170] 2006 Act, Part 24 (as amended by SBEE Act 2015 with effect from 30 June 2016). See *Re Churchill Hotel (Plymouth) Ltd* [1988] BCLC 341; *Secretary of State for Trade and Industry v Goldberg* [2004] 1 BCLC 597.

[171] 2006 Act, ss 860 and 878.

[172] *Reynard v Secretary of State for Trade and Industry* (unreported, 22 June 2001, Blackburne J).

[173] *Reynard v Secretary of State for Trade and Industry* (n 172 above).

[174] As amended by SBEE Act 2015.

[175] [1999] 1 BCLC 433, 483; and *Re Skyward Builders plc*, High Court, London, 20 December 2002.

duties properly Leeson's unauthorised activities would almost certainly have come to light and the collapse of the Barings Group might have been avoided'.[176]

31.82 The cases within this category include failure to supervise a reckless trader,[177] the misselling of complex financial products with the consequence that claims against the company precipitated its insolvency,[178] and making false representations to obtain financial assistance in the acquisition of a target company which, ultimately, caused the insolvency of both companies.[179]

(iii) *Frequency of conduct*

31.83 Schedule 1 paragraph 3 requires the court to take into account the frequency of conduct of the person which falls within paragraph 1 or 2. This reflects the position in authorities decided under previous versions of Schedule 1.

(iv) *Loss and harm*

31.84 Schedule 1 paragraph 4 refers to the 'nature and extent of any loss or harm caused, or any potential loss or harm which could have been caused, by the person's conduct in relation to a company or overseas company'. There have been many disqualification cases arising out of the use of a company as a vehicle for fraud, or the commission of a fraud in the course of its business.[180] In such a case, the company is itself likely to be liable to the creditors or other persons who have been defrauded, and the directors responsible will have breached their fiduciary duties to the company. But any such breach of fiduciary duty will not be the underlying reason for disqualification: it is the commission of that fraud or falling below acceptable standards of commercial probity which renders that person unfit to be a director.[181]

31.85 The sort of commercially unacceptable conduct that merits a finding of unfitness and disqualification may be illustrated by *Secretary of State for BERR v Sullman*,[182] a s 8 disqualification case, which arose out of the collapse of the Claims Direct business, which carried on business promoting a contingency scheme to fund litigation and an 'after-the-event' insurance policy in order to take advantage of the changes to litigation funding allowed by the Access to Justice Act 1999. Norris J found that Mr Sullman was unfit in respect of the following charges:[183]

---

[176] [1999] 1 BCLC 433, 575.
[177] *Re Barings plc (No 5)* [1999] 1 BCLC 433.
[178] *Secretary of State for BIS v Aaron* [2009] EWHC 3263 (Ch).
[179] *Re Bunting Electric Manufacturing Co Ltd* [2006] 1 BCLC 550.
[180] *Secretary of State for Trade and Industry v Kappler* [2008] 1 BCLC 120; *Re City Truck Group Ltd* [2007] 2 BCLC 649; *Re Vintage Hallmark plc* [2007] 1 BCLC 788; *Re Bunting Electric Manufacturing Co Ltd* [2005] EWHC 3345 (Ch); and *Official Receiver v Doshi* [2001] 2 BCLC 235. In *Secretary of State for BIS v Corry*, 9 January 2012 at para 7 HHJ Pelling QC said that, in a missing trader inter-community fraud case, it had to be shown that (i) the company was knowingly involved in the MTIC fraud, as explained in *Kittel v Belgium* [2008] STC 1537, ECJ; and (ii) the knowledge attributed to the company was in fact knowledge of the director.
[181] *Secretary of State for BERR v Sullman* [2009] 1 BCLC 397 at paras 3, 28–30.
[182] [2009] 1 BCLC 397. Other examples of commercially unacceptable conduct include *Official Receiver v Wild* [2012] EWHC 4279 (Ch) (aggressive sales techniques, avoidance of consumer protection regimes and failure to deliver to customers); *Re UKLI Ltd* [2015] BCC 755 (unlawful collective investment scheme and improper loans and advances); *Secretary of State for BIS v Doherty* [2014] EWHC 2816 (Ch) (director fell short of the appropriate standard of probity and competence through reckless attitude towards asset funding agreements); *Re RD Industries Ltd* [2014] EWHC 2844 (Ch) (directors causing company to breach terms of invoice discounting agreement); and *Re FG Hawkes (Western) Ltd* [2015] EWHC 1585 (Ch) (misleading accounting records, which included false debts, and false VAT returns led to customers and Revenue and Customs Commissioners being harmed).
[183] [2009] 1 BCLC 397, summarized at para 117.

(1) He was very seriously at fault in seeking to establish the Claims Direct business by widespread misrepresentation of the nature of the risk which customers ran in purchasing the company's product before implementation of the 1999 Act when there was real uncertainty that the Lord Chancellor's Department would give retrospective sanction for the company's policies and then making misleading statements in an attempt to justify the company's conduct.[184]

(2) He misrepresented to the public and to underwriters and customers the failure rate of claims handled by Claims Direct; he said the failure rate was 4 per cent, when internal figures were in the range 17–37 per cent.[185]

(3) He caused Claims Direct to pay panel solicitors an unlawful referral fee and the creation of false paperwork in an endeavour to avoid acknowledged difficulties under the Solicitors' Code to mislead others in relation to costs assessment.[186]

(4) He failed in Claims Direct's prospectus to disclose to prospective investors the personal benefits that he and his fellow director would obtain from the offer.[187]

(5) He knowingly misled investors after the flotation of Claims Direct as to insurance arrangements.[188]

(6) He misconducted himself in purchasing a business from a co-director at a price that could not be justified.[189]

Without putting a judicial gloss on the words 'unfit to be concerned in the management of a company', Norris J went on to explain why that conduct demonstrated a falling below acceptable standards of commercial probity. A limited liability company should not acquire its business or capital or confer benefits on its directors through inviting sections of the public to deal with it on a false or misleading basis.[190] *Secretary of State for BIS v Aaron*[191] is a similar case, where the directors were found to be unfit because they missold complex financial products and exposed the company to financial claims that brought about its insolvency. In *Secretary of State for BIS v Doffman (No 2)*[192] the directors were unfit because they and associated companies had benefited from directors' breaches of duty and disregard of the companies' separate corporate personalities. **31.86**

Prior to 2015, Schedule 1, Part II, paragraph 7 required the court to have regard to the extent of the director's responsibility for any failure by the company to supply any goods or services which have been paid for (in whole or in part). This matter is now subsumed within the new wording of paragraph 4, although it is likely that authorities decided under the old Schedule 1 will be instructive. In *Re City Pram and Toy Company Ltd*, Judge Levy QC allowed the appeal of the Secretary of State against the refusal of Mr Registrar Rawson **31.87**

---

[184] [2009] 1 BCLC 397 at paras 12 and 27.
[185] [2009] 1 BCLC 397 at paras 41 and 43.
[186] [2009] 1 BCLC 397 at paras 51 and 55.
[187] [2009] 1 BCLC 397 at paras 59, 100–6.
[188] [2009] 1 BCLC 397 at paras 107, 110, 111.
[189] [2009] 1 BCLC 397 at paras 112–16.
[190] [2009] 1 BCLC 397 at para 118.
[191] [2009] EWHC 3263.
[192] [2011] 2 BCLC 541.

to disqualify the directors in that case. Having regard to paragraph 7 and the £31,000 shortfall to unsecured creditors in that case, he explained that:

> I am satisfied, as I have already said, that ground 1 has been made out. In these circumstances, in my judgment, it was wrong for the twins to cause or allow the company to trade. A fortiori it was wrong for the company to accept deposits from customers when they knew or ought to have known that, due to the company's financial situation, there was no reasonable prospect of the company being able to pay the goods for which the deposits were paid. The Secretary of State therefore succeeds on this count.[193]

As noted above, such conduct is likely to be construed as taking an unwarranted risk with creditors' money.

31.88   In order to avoid exposing creditors to unwarranted risks, when there is real concern about the company's solvency, deposits for orders for goods and services should be paid into a trust account.[194]

(8) Additional matters where a person is or has been a director

(v) Misfeasance or breach of fiduciary duty

Misfeasance

31.89   Misfeasance probably has the same meaning as it has in the Insolvency Act, s 212. It covers breach of trust,[195] but also extends to other acts or omissions which contravene substantive rules of company law or insolvency law. Examples of contraventions of company law that might involve misfeasance on the part of the directors responsible are (a) failure to declare an interest in an existing transaction or arrangement as required by the 2006 Act, s 182, (b) failure to obtain approval of members to transactions with directors as required by the 2006 Act, and (c) making distributions out of capital in contravention of the 2006 Act, Part 23.[196] Making a preference within the Insolvency Act, s 239 is a misfeasance on the part of the director responsible.[197] In every case, it is for the Secretary of State to prove misfeasance on the balance of probabilities but, in applying that standard, the more serious the allegation the more cogent the evidence required to prove it having regard to the inherent improbability of fraudulent conduct and serious impropriety.[198]

Misapplication of company property

31.90   Prior to 2015, Schedule 1, Part I, paragraph 2 required the court to have regard to any misapplication or retention by the director of, or any conduct by the director giving rise to an obligation to account for, any money or other property of the company.

31.91   There was an obvious overlap between this matter and misfeasance discussed in paragraph 31.89 above, and the draftsman appears to have recognized this, subsuming misapplication of company property under that broader category. Nonetheless, the many cases decided

---

[193] [1998] BCC 537, 548.

[194] *Re Kayford Ltd* [1975] 1 WLR 279; *Re Lewis's of Leicester Ltd* [1995] 1 BCLC 428.

[195] *Coventry and Dixon's Case* (1880) 14 Ch D 660, 670, CA.

[196] *Re National Funds Assurance Co* (1878) 10 Ch D 118, CA; *Re Exchange Banking Co* (1882) 32 Ch D 149, CA; *Re National Bank of Wales* [1899] 2 Ch 629, CA; *Re AG (Manchester) Ltd* [2008] BCC 497.

[197] *Re Washington Diamond Mining Co* [1893] 3 Ch 95, CA; *Re West Mercia Safetywear Ltd* [1988] BCLC 250, CA.

[198] *Secretary of State for BIS v Doffman (No 2)* [2011] 2 BCLC 541 at paras 29–31, per Newey J.

under the old schedule will continue to be relevant.[199] In *Secretary of State for Trade and Industry v Blunt*, the judge explained that:

> Misappropriation by a director is always serious. Creditors would legitimately feel aggrieved at others, particularly those responsible for the management of the company, benefiting at their expense. A deliberate and conscious decision to benefit oneself unlawfully from assets that a person knows do not belong to him is entirely unacceptable. It is a very serious allegation in respect of which disqualification is entirely justified.[200]

Misapplication of company money would also seem to properly include a payment of excessive remuneration because, although no theft is involved, the payment of excessive remuneration is a 'misapplication' of company money or property and, as such, gives rise to an obligation to account.[201] In *Re Melcast (Wolverhampton) Ltd*, Harman J described the requisite misconduct in the following terms: **31.92**

> [T]he remuneration ... cannot be said ... to amount to conduct which, to put it vulgarly, is often called living 'high on the hog' at the expense of creditors. There is no suggestion ... that the directors feathered their own nests, ran large and expensive cars, had a great deal of expensive entertaining, or pocketed large salaries on the back of the company. They do not appear to have done any of those things and this is not that sort of case at all. It is a case of gross mismanagement, of complete ignoring of the proper responsibilities of directors, and of shutting their eyes to the proper liabilities attached to the company rather than anything of a dishonest character in the sense of conduct for their own personal financial benefit.[202]

In this way, the test applied by the courts in the disqualification cases is in line with the guidance given as to the appropriate level of remuneration that might be authorized in good faith in the absence of divisible profits.[203]

Breach of fiduciary duty

Prior to 2015, Schedule 1, Part I, paragraph 1 required the court to have regard to:[204]   **31.93**

> Any misfeasance or breach of any fiduciary or other duty by the director in relation to the company, including in particular any breach by the director of a duty under Chapter 2 of Part 10 of the Companies Act 2006 (general duties of directors) owed to the company.

In accordance with the 2006 Act, the general fiduciary duties are those stated in ss 171–3 and 175–7. These duties are discussed in detail in Chapters 10–13 and 15–17 above. Misfeasance may encompass wider defaults in relation to the company. The following paragraphs consider the disqualification cases on breach of duty under the headings of the codified general duties.   **31.94**

---

[199] See eg *Secretary of State for Trade and Industry v Blunt* [2005] 2 BCLC 463; *Official Receiver v Stern (No 2)* [2002] 1 BCLC 119, CA; *Re Park House Properties Ltd* [1998] BCC 847; *Re Living Images Ltd* [1996] BCC 112; *Re Continental Assurance Co of London plc* [1997] 1 BCLC 48; *Re Tansoft Ltd* [1991] BCLC 339.

[200] [2005] 2 BCLC 463 at para 23.

[201] *Re A & C Group Services Ltd* [1993] BCLC 1297; *Re Synthetic Technology Ltd* [1993] BCC 549; *Re Cargo Agency Ltd* [1992] BCC 686; *Re Melcast (Wolverhampton) Ltd* [1991] BCLC 288; *Re McNulty's Interchange Ltd* [1989] BCLC 709; *Re Ipcon Fashions Ltd* [1989] BCC 773.

[202] [1991] BCLC 288, 291.

[203] *Re Halt Garage (1964) Ltd* [1982] 3 All ER 1016, 1038j–1039h.

[204] The words beginning at 'including' were added by the Companies Act (Consequential Amendments, Transitional Provisions and Savings) Order 2009 (SI 2009/1941) as from 1 October 2009.

Breach of fiduciary duties to act in accordance with the company's constitution or to exercise powers for proper purposes

31.95   A director may breach his fiduciary duty under the 2006 Act, s 171(a) if he fails to act in accordance with the company's constitution. It will be rare for a director to be responsible for the company acting beyond its corporate powers, since almost all companies have unrestricted objects.[205] *Re Samuel Sherman plc*[206] may be regarded as a rare example of a case in which a finding of unfitness under s 8 was justified on the basis of an act falling outside the proper scope of the company's objects. In that case, the director of a ladies' garments company had invested the proceeds of the sale of its stock and premises in a speculative oil and gas venture. The conduct was ultra vires, but the true complaint appears to have been the unsuitability of the investment in the circumstances, specifically that it was not readily realizable should its value fall, it carried a liability to put up further funds, and it was effected without recourse to shareholders. A serious disregard of the procedures laid down in the company's constitution particularly where it involves failing to consult members, could be a breach of fiduciary duty, meriting disqualification.

31.96 A director may breach his fiduciary duty under the 2006 Act, s 171(b) if he fails to exercise powers for the purposes for which they are conferred. Such a breach could be a sufficient basis for disqualification if the director's conduct can be characterized as abusive. The sale of an asset at undervalue to the director or a connected party may be analysed as a breach of several fiduciary duties, including the duty under s 171(b), but it is the prejudice caused by the transaction and any benefit derived by the director which drives the case for disqualification. In *Re Looe Fish Ltd*,[207] a case under s 8, the director abused the power to allot shares, so as to defeat attempts by a rival faction among the members to gain control of the board, and caused the company to breach the prohibition on a company acquiring its own shares under the 1985 Act, s 143. Jonathan Parker J did not regard the contravention of s 143 as sufficiently serious to warrant disqualification on the ground of unfitness, but he did consider the abuse of the power to allot shares sufficient to show unfitness meriting disqualification:

> As to unfitness, I find that in using the power to allot shares in the way he did, Mr Soady displayed a clear lack of commercial probity. He allowed his concern to keep the Cairns group from obtaining control of the company to lead him to abuse his power as a director to allot shares in the company. It is not enough for him to say that he did what he did in the best interests of LFL as he saw them. A director who chooses deliberately to play fast and loose with his powers, as Mr Soady has done in this case, in order to remain in control of the company's affairs, is in my judgment unfit to be concerned in the management of a company, and it is expedient in the public interest that a disqualification order be made against him.[208]

This was so even though there was 'no question of insolvency' and the director 'did not act out of motives of personal gain, nor did he receive any improper benefit'.[209] The reason for disqualification in *Re Looe Fish Ltd* was accordingly the abuse of a corporate power to subvert

---

[205] 2006 Act, s 31(1) (and also s 39). Under the former 1985 Act, s 3A (which came into effect on 4 February 1991) a company whose objects are stated to be those of a general trading company has power to carry on any trade or business whatsoever.
[206] [1991] 1 WLR 1070.
[207] [1993] BCLC 1160.
[208] [1993] BCLC 1160, 1172.
[209] [1993] BCLC 1160, 1172f.

the ordinary balance of power within the company. As Lord Wilberforce recognized, '[s]elf-interest is only one, though no doubt the commonest, instance of improper motive'.[210]

Similarly, participation by directors in a scheme which contravenes the statutory provisions **31.97** against a public company giving financial assistance in the purchase of its own shares (2006 Act, ss 677–83) may be relied on by the Secretary of State in disqualification proceedings as evidence of unfitness.[211] Now that the prohibition is restricted to public companies, it is less likely to feature in disqualification applications.

Breach of fiduciary duty to promote the success of the company

A director may breach his fiduciary duty under the 2006 Act, s 172 if he fails to act in the **31.98** way he considers, in good faith, would be most likely to promote the success of the company for the benefit of its members as a whole. This is a subjective good faith duty, but s 172(1) requires a director to have regard to a number of specific matters.[212] Two cases may be seen as illustrating breaches of s 172 of sufficient gravity to warrant disqualification. The first is *Re Austinsuite Furniture Ltd*,[213] where Vinelott J disqualified a director for seven years for, amongst other things, procuring the lead company to enter into a transaction with a company whose debt burden it was servicing, which had no commercial purpose and was intended solely to create a misleading impression as to the true financial position of those companies. The director in that case had insisted it was the responsibility of the lead company's auditors to object to a valuation used in the transaction if they considered it improper, but the judge held that even if true 'it does not absolve him from the charge that his conduct in relation to this transaction was so irresponsible as to evidence a failure to appreciate his duties as a director'.[214] In that case, it was estimated that the lead company would have been compelled to cease trading a year earlier had true accounts been filed.

The other case is *Re JA Chapman & Co Ltd*,[215] where the director of an insurance brokerage **31.99** company had caused it to 'gross up' premiums notified to assureds, thereby enabling it to benefit from the difference between the premium received and the true premium paid to the underwriter. This decision resulted in an immediate benefit to the company because it received income in addition to its commission, but, being contrary to accepted market practice, it ultimately resulted in expulsion from Lloyds and insolvency. It was a decision no rational company director could have made in good faith and warranted disqualification under s 8 on the ground of unfitness.

The duty to consider or act in the interests of creditors

Section 172(3) states that the duty imposed by that section has effect subject to any enact- **31.100** ment (ie wrongful trading under the Insolvency Act, s 214) or rule of law requiring directors in certain circumstances to consider or act in the interests of creditors of the company. As set

---

[210] *Howard Smith Ltd v Ampol Petroleum Ltd* [1974] AC 821, 834h (also 837e–838b), HL.

[211] *Re Dawes & Henderson (Agencies) Ltd* (No 2) [1999] 2 BCLC 317; *Re Continental Assurance Co of London plc* [1997] 1 BCLC 48. See further Ch 27, Section C(5) above.

[212] The set of specific duties flowing from the general duty under s 172 is not closed: *Item Software (UK) Ltd v Fasshi* [2005] 2 BCLC 91, 103–4, CA.

[213] [1992] BCLC 1047.

[214] [1992] BCLC 1047, 1059.

[215] [2003] 2 BCLC 206. Similarly, in *Secretary of State for BIS v Pawson* [2015] EWHC 2626 (Ch) the director was disqualified for eight years for raising investment funds for unsustainable objects, which enabled the companies to make payments for his financial benefit.

out in Chapter 12, Section E above, directors owe a duty, where the company is insolvent or of doubtful solvency (a) to take into account the interests of creditors, and (b) to direct the company in a way compatible with the requirements of the Insolvency Act, ss 214, 238, 239, and 423. A failure to comply with these general duties may result in mandatory disqualification under s 6(1) and, in this respect, cases in which disqualification has been justified on the ground of trading while insolvent to the detriment of creditors may be regarded as particular examples of the standard of conduct by which company directors must abide where the company is insolvent or where its solvency is doubtful. The detail of the disqualification case is, however, important because, in the context of disqualification, the courts have identified certain features which aggravate a breach of those general duties and which may constitute grounds for disqualification beyond those general duties.

31.101 The following three propositions, in particular, emerge from cases in which disqualification has been sought on the basis that the company traded while insolvent to the detriment of creditors:

(1) A director will not normally be at risk of a finding of unfitness, such as to lead automatically to disqualification, merely because he knowingly allows the company to trade while insolvent,[216] but there would be a finding of unfitness, leading to disqualification, if the director, while allowing the company to trade while insolvent, diverted profits to other associated companies.[217]

(2) A director will normally only be at risk of a finding of unfitness sufficient to warrant automatic disqualification where, at the time credit is taken by the company, he knows or should know that there is no reasonable prospect of the company avoiding insolvency (ie the director is guilty of wrongful trading).[218]

(3) A director will exceptionally be at risk of a finding of unfitness sufficient to warrant automatic disqualification where, notwithstanding that he reasonably believed that the company could avoid insolvency, he is responsible for some other misconduct which, in the circumstances, renders him unfit.[219] That misconduct would ordinarily involve dishonesty, want of commercial probity, or a display of incompetence to a marked degree.[220]

The 'other misconduct' referred to in proposition (3) is typically some form of 'unfair discrimination' against a particular creditor or, more usually, against a particular class of creditors such as the Crown or customers who have made prepayments or deposits for goods or services. In such cases, the company continues to pay its other creditors at the expense of the Crown, or some of its suppliers at the expense of other of its creditors for its own benefit.[221]

---

[216] *Re Uno plc* [2006] BCC 725 at para 144; *Secretary of State for Trade and Industry v Creegan* [2002] 1 BCLC 99, 101, CA; *Secretary of State for Trade and Industry v Gash* [1997] 1 BCLC 341.

[217] *Re Mea Corporation Ltd* [2007] 1 BCLC 618 at paras 109–11, per Lewison J.

[218] *Re Uno plc* [2006] BCC 725 at para 144; *Secretary of State for Trade and Industry v Creegan* [2002] 1 BCLC 99, 101, CA; *Re Sevenoaks (Stationers) Ltd* [1991] Ch 164; and *Re Bath Glass Ltd* [1988] 4 BCC 130, 133–4.

[219] *Re Uno plc* [2006] BCC 725 at paras 145–9; *Re Structural Concrete Ltd* [2001] BCC 578; *Secretary of State for Trade and Industry v McTighe* [1997] BCC 224; *Re Sevenoaks (Stationers) Ltd* [1991] Ch 164; and *Re Bath Glass Ltd* [1988] 4 BCC 130, 133–4.

[220] *Re Uno plc* [2006] BCC 725 at para 153, where Blackburne J applied *Re Grayan Building Services Ltd* [1995] Ch 241, 253, CA.

[221] *Official Receiver v Key* [2009] 1 BCLC 22 at paras 63–4 at which HHJ Mithani said that the conduct had to be sufficient to show a policy of discrimination. Such an approach was endorsed by the Court of Appeal in *Cathie v Secretary of State for BIS* [2012] BCC 813, CA, at para 39. See also *Secretary of State for Trade and Industry v Thornberry* [2008] BCC 768, where the director was unfit because he failed to make inquiries

The above propositions flow from the decision of Blackburne J in *Re Uno plc*,[222] in which the judge considered a charge of unfitness where the directors caused or allowed the companies to continue trading at the risk of customers, who paid deposits against orders for goods, at a time when the companies were insolvent but had a reasonable prospect of avoiding insolvency proceedings. **31.102**

Prior to the decision in *Re Uno plc*, the courts appeared to apply two alternative tests to determine unfitness in cases where a company had traded to the detriment of its creditors. The first test is closely analogous to the test for civil liability for wrongful trading under the Insolvency Act, s 214 in which the court focused on whether (a) the director knew or ought to have concluded that there was no reasonable prospect that the company would avoid becoming insolvent, and (b) he had taken every step with a view to minimizing the potential loss to creditors he ought to have taken.[223] Under the second test the court asked, more broadly, whether the company had taken an unwarranted risk with creditors' money by continuing to trade.[224] The second test is difficult to apply because it leaves at large the question of what makes a risk 'unwarranted'; the answer to which, by definition, has to pick out conduct that cannot be characterized as a failure to take every step a director ought to have taken in circumstances in which he knew or ought to have concluded there was no reasonable prospect that the company could avoid becoming insolvent. **31.103**

The value of the decision in *Re Uno plc* is that it focuses on specific features of insolvent trading which put a director at risk of disqualification for unfitness notwithstanding a reasonable belief that the company will not become insolvent. In his review of this issue at paragraphs 144–9 of his judgment, Blackburne J stated that: **31.104**

> [144] [A] director will not be at risk of a finding of unfitness, such as to lead automatically to disqualification, merely because he knowingly allows the company to trade while insolvent, ie he allows the company to incur credit (including, I would add, accepting a payment from a customer in advance of the supply of the relevant goods or service) even though, at the time and as he knows, the company is insolvent and later goes into liquidation. It does not add anything to the proposition to say that, in causing the company to incur credit (or accept payment in advance of the supply of the goods or service), the director was 'taking advantage' of the third party in question. In a sense, every company which incurs credit when, as its director knows or ought to know, it is insolvent, is 'taking advantage' of the third party supplier of credit. *If the director is to be found unfit there must ordinarily be an additional ingredient. Normally that ingredient is that, at the time that the credit is taken (or the advance payment received, which is in essence the same), the director knows or should know that there is no reasonable prospect of his company avoiding insolvency* ...

> [145] But ... as the court in *Creegan* recognised, it is not the case that, merely because at the time in question the directors reasonably believed that the company could avoid insolvency,

---

about the company's affairs which would have been likely to have prevented tacit discrimination against paying Crown debts over a substantial period.

[222] [2006] BCC 725 at para 140.

[223] *Secretary of State for Trade and Industry v Creegan* [2002] 1 BCLC 99, 101, CA; *Re Cubelock Ltd* [2001] BCC 523; and *Secretary of State for Trade and Industry v Gash* [1997] 1 BCLC 341, 348–9.

[224] *Re Verby Print for Advertising Ltd* [1998] 2 BCLC 23, 27–8; *Re City Pram and Toy Co Ltd* [1998] BCC 537, 539; *Re Moonlight Foods (UK) Ltd* [1996] BCC 678, 692; *Re Richborough Furniture Ltd* [1996] 1 BCLC 507, 517; *Re Living Images Ltd* [1996] 1 BCLC 348, 359; and *Re Synthetic Technology Ltd* [1993] BCC 549, 562.

they can escape a finding of unfitness in consequence of having allowed the company to trade while insolvent ...

[147] The vice of their conduct was in deliberately allowing the company's liability to the Revenue to mount while using the monies thereby saved (ie the tax deducted from its self-employed operatives) to pay its other creditors ... without taking any steps to secure the Revenue's agreement to the delayed payment of its mounting debt. They did so in circumstances where, if at any time and as eventually happened, demand was made for payment of the debt, the company had no means of payment, and an insolvent liquidation was bound to ensue. (Emphasis added.)

31.105   It is possible to identify further aggravating features in cases where an insolvent company trades to the detriment of its creditors, namely:[225]

(1)   unfair treatment of particular creditors;
(2)   the abuse of successive 'phoenix' companies, whether or not that abuse also amounts to a breach by the director of the prohibition under the Insolvency Act, s 216;[226] and
(3)   the incorporation of an under-capitalized company in circumstances in which insolvent failure is both foreseeable and likely.

The above features might also properly include the accepting of deposits or prepayments at a time when the company was without a reasonable prospect of avoiding insolvency, or the grant of a preferential payment, or the execution of a transaction at undervalue. These matters are discussed at paragraphs 31.87 and 31.88 above.

31.106   *Re Synthetic Technology Ltd*,[227] which was the originator of the test of 'the taking of unwarranted risks with creditors' money by continuing to trade', is an example of a case where unfair treatment of creditors by an insolvent company with a reasonable prospect of avoiding insolvency proceedings meant that the director responsible was unfit. In that case, the judge could not have held that the company had traded wrongfully in a way analogous to the Insolvency Act, s 214 because the company's business had been purchased from a company in administration whose administrators had produced a favourable report as to 'the rosy prospects' of the business's future success.[228] The deputy judge nevertheless found the director unfit, because he had not merely permitted the company to continue to trade whilst it was insolvent, but had done so unfairly at the expense of the Crown:

[T]he company under the management of Mr Joiner exploited the Crown together with the company's other creditors by deliberately pursuing a policy of only paying at the last minute

---

[225]   *Official Receiver v Stern (No 2)* [2002] 1 BCLC 119; *Re Windows West Ltd* [2002] BCC 760; *Secretary of State for Trade and Industry v Ivens* [1997] 2 BCLC 334, CA; *Re Swift 736 Ltd* [1993] BCLC 896; *Re Linval Ltd* [1993] BCLC 654; *Re Travel Mondial Ltd* [1991] BCC 224; *Re Ipcon Fashions Ltd* [1989] BCC 773.

[226]   A breach of the Insolvency Act, s 216 restricting the use of former company names is a discrete but related ground for disqualification: *Re Skyward Builders plc* [2002] 2 BCLC 750; *Re Migration Services International Ltd* [2000] 1 BCLC 666.

[227]   [1993] BCC 549, 562d–e.

[228]   [1993] BCC 549, 563a–c. The judge indicated his 'surprise' at the administrators' report, surmising that they had been 'over-influenced' by the director's prediction that the company would be able to obtain a share of an anticipated increase in the worldwide market for the company's product.

those creditors which were pressing, which the Crown together with the bulk of the company's other creditors were not at the material time doing or not with sufficient persistence.[229]

The abuse of successive 'phoenix' companies emerges as a distinct reason for disqualification **31.107** and not merely as a feature of certain wrongful trading cases. In *Re Windows West Ltd*, Gabriel Moss QC, sitting as a deputy judge of the High Court, explained the problem of phoenix companies in these terms:

> Although 'phoenix' companies are often a menace to the public, I would introduce one note of caution. There are also honest phoenix companies where a failure has occurred through no fault of the management and the business has been rescued into a successor company in the interests of creditors and the public. The 'bad' phoenix company is by contrast characterised by the selfish and dishonest behaviour of the management in looking after their own interests and ignoring those of the creditors and/or the public.[230]

The focus of the court's inquiry is accordingly the abuse by a director of limited liability trading, notwithstanding that the incorporation of a 'phoenix' company is not unlawful.

The incorporation of an under-capitalized company is similarly not necessarily wrongful as **31.108** there is no general capital adequacy requirement in English law,[231] but it may be improper where failure is likely and any trading can only be at the expense of creditors. In *Re Rolus Properties Ltd*, Harman J considered 'the mere fact that the company had been formed and had embarked with small capital upon a speculative venture would not by itself warrant criticism',[232] but, in the subsequent case of *Re Chartmore Ltd*, he regarded it as significant that the company's 'substantial capital liability was not met with any proper capital provision'.[233] In that case, the company had purchased the assets of the director's father's insolvent company and, in so doing, incurred a liability which could *only* be met by the funds of the company's general creditors because no other capital had been introduced.

Prior to 2015, Schedule 1, Part I, paragraph 3 required the court to have regard to the extent **31.109** of the director's responsibility for the company entering into any transaction liable to be set aside under the Insolvency Act, s 423, which is concerned with transactions defrauding creditors. What makes a transaction contrary to s 423 is considered at Chapter 34, Section E(4) below.

In *Re Diamond Computer Systems Ltd*, Jules Sher QC, sitting as a deputy judge of the **31.110** High Court, indicated that a transaction contrary to s 423 would be sufficient to warrant disqualification:

> The official receiver's complaint is that all these transactions took place at a time when Mr Brown and Mr Ballan knew that Diamond was insolvent and that the freehold properties were transferred for the purpose of putting them beyond the reach of Diamond's creditors other

---

[229] [1993] BCC 549, 562g–h. The deputy judge followed Dillon LJ in *Re Sevenoaks (Stationers) Ltd* [1991] Ch 164, 183e.

[230] [2002] BCC 760 at para 13.

[231] A minimum capital requirement exists in relation to a public company, and a failure to comply with this is likely to be regarded as serious: see *Secretary of State for Trade and Industry v Hollier* [2007] BCC 11, a case under s 8 in which the defendant had traded wrongfully and in breach of the minimum capital requirement; *Re Kaytech International plc* [1999] 2 BCLC 351, CA, in which the defendant had falsely stated the paid-up capital of the company.

[232] [1988] 4 BCC 446, 447.

[233] [1990] BCLC 673, 675.

than Direction. If these complaints are made out at trial, Mr Brown will be shown to be guilty of misconduct as a director of Diamond.[234]

The extent to which the director was responsible for the company entering into a transaction defrauding creditors now falls to be considered under the category of breach of the duty to consider or act in the interests of creditors.

31.111   Similarly, prior to 2015, Schedule 1, Part II, paragraph 8 required the court to have regard to the extent of the director's responsibility for the company entering into any transaction or giving any preference, being a transaction or preference liable to be set aside under the Insolvency Act, ss 127 and 238–40.[235] Again, this is now only relevant insofar as it involves a breach of fiduciary duty, but where a breach of duty is involved, the grant of a preference contrary to s 239,[236] or a transaction at undervalue contrary to s 238[237] is likely to be considered as a serious failure and may alone warrant mandatory disqualification.

Breach of fiduciary duty to exercise independent judgment

31.112   A director may breach his fiduciary duty under the 2006 Act, s 173 if he fails to exercise independent judgment. A failure to exercise independent judgment may warrant mandatory justification under s 6(1), but it is necessary to examine carefully the circumstances of the failure, in particular, the responsibilities with which the director was tasked in conjunction with the responsibilities of other directors, individual and collective.[238] The particular problems encountered in the cases are the dominance of the board of directors by an individual director, the minimum participation required of a company director, and the failure of a director to take proper responsibility for a duty delegated to another. The extent of this duty is considered in Chapter 13 above.

Breach of fiduciary duty in relation to conflict of interest

31.113   The 2006 Act, ss 175–7 deal with conflicts of interest in three distinct ways, as discussed in Chapters 15–17 above. First, a director will breach his fiduciary duty if, without effective authorization from the company, he fails to avoid a situation in which he has, or could have, a direct or indirect interest that conflicts, or may possibly conflict with the interests of the company—such conflict not arising in relation to a transaction or arrangement with the company.[239] The typical example of such a conflict is taking advantage of a corporate opportunity without the effective consent of the company. In *Re Park House Properties Ltd*, Neuberger J explained that 'even on its own' the conflict of interest and duty in that case warranted mandatory disqualification.[240]

---

[234] [1997] 1 BCLC 174, 178.

[235] Or in Scotland under the Insolvency Act, s 242, or s 243, or under any rule of law in Scotland.

[236] *Official Receiver v Stern (No 2)* [2002] 1 BCLC 119, CA; *Re Funtime Ltd* [1999] 1 BCLC 247; *Re Verby Print for Advertising Ltd* [1998] 2 BCLC 23; *Re Sykes (Butchers) Ltd* [1998] 1 BCLC 110; *Re Grayan Building Services Ltd* [1995] Ch 241; *Re T&D Services Ltd* [1990] BCC 592.

[237] *Re Genosyis Technology Management Ltd* [2007] 1 BCLC 208; *Re Bradcrown Ltd* [2001] 1 BCLC 547; *Secretary of State for Trade and Industry v Tillman* [2000] 1 BCLC 36; *Secretary of State for Trade and Industry v Lubrani* [1997] 2 BCLC 115; *Re Keypak Homecase Ltd (No 2)* [1990] BCLC 440.

[238] *Re AG Manchester Ltd* [2008] BCC 497, in which the judge highlighted the particular responsibilities of a finance director at para 183 of his judgment; *Re Landhurst Leasing plc* [1999] 1 BCLC 286; *Re Barings plc (No 5)* [1999] 1 BCLC 433; affd [2000] 1 BCLC 523, CA; *Re Westmid Packing Services Ltd* [1998] 2 All ER 124, CA; *Re Polly Peck International plc (No 2)* [1994] 1 BCLC 574.

[239] 2006 Act, s 175.

[240] [1997] 2 BCLC 530, 551.

Secondly, a director will also breach his fiduciary duty if he accepts a benefit from a third **31.114** party, conferred by reason of his being a director or doing, or not doing, anything as director.[241] The typical example of this is taking a bribe, which is inexcusable and almost by definition unfit conduct.

Finally, a director, who is directly or indirectly interested in a proposed transaction with the **31.115** company, will breach his fiduciary duty if he fails to declare the nature and extent of his interest to the other directors.[242] The failure to declare the director's interest involves misleading fellow directors and may well warrant mandatory disqualification under s 6(1).[243]

(vi) Material breach of legislative or other obligations

Material breach of legislative obligations

Prior to 2015, Schedule 1 Part I, paragraph 5[244] required the court to have regard to **31.116** the extent of the director's responsibility for any failure by the directors of the company to comply with provisions of the 2006 Act for (a) the preparation of annual accounts,[245] (b) the approval and signature of abbreviated accounts,[246] and (c) the name of the signatory to be stated in the published copy of the accounts.[247] Now, the new paragraph 6 requires the court to take into account any 'material breach of any legislative or other obligation of the director which applies as a result of being a director of a company or overseas company'.

The failure to maintain accounting records in accordance with the statutory rules is a matter **31.117** of complaint present in a large number of disqualification cases.[248] It is treated as a serious failure and not a mere 'venial sin'.[249] In *Re Firedart Ltd*, Arden J explained that:

> When directors do not maintain accounting records in accordance with the very specific requirements of s 221 of the Companies Act 1985, they cannot know their company's financial position with accuracy. There is therefore a risk that the situation is much worse than they know and that creditors will suffer in consequence. Directors who permit this situation to arise must expect the conclusion to be drawn in an appropriate case that they are in consequence not fit to be concerned in the management of a company.[250]

Arden J also made clear that a director cannot necessarily avoid responsibility for failure to maintain accounting records on the basis that their preparation and filing was delegated to a professional accountant with whom the director must cooperate.[251]

---

[241] 2006 Act, s 176.

[242] 2006 Act, s 177. Note that 2006 Act, s 182 deals with disclosure of a director's interest in an existing transaction or arrangement.

[243] *Re Dominion International Group plc (No 2)* [1996] 1 BCLC 572; *Re Godwin Warren Control Systems plc* [1993] BCLC 80; and *Re Tansoft Ltd* [1991] BCLC 339.

[244] Substituted by SI 2008/948 as from 6 April 2008.

[245] 2006 Act, ss 394 and 399.

[246] 2006 Act, ss 414 and 450.

[247] 2006 Act, s 433.

[248] *Official Receiver v Stern (No 2)* [2002] 1 BCLC 119, CA; *Re Park House Properties Ltd* [1997] 2 BCLC 530; *Re Firedart Ltd* [1994] 2 BCLC 340; *Re Swift 736 Ltd* [1993] BCLC 896, CA; *Re Linval Ltd* [1993] BCLC 654; *Re New Generation Engineers Ltd* [1993] BCLC 435; *Re Travel Mondial Ltd* [1991] BCC 224; *Re Tansoft Ltd* [1991] BCLC 339; *Re Sevenoaks Stationers (Retail) Ltd* [1991] Ch 164; *Re Chartmore Ltd* [1990] BCLC 673; *Re T&D Services Ltd* [1990] BCC 592; *Re Lo-Line Electric Motors Ltd* [1988] Ch 477; *Re Western Welsh International System Buildings Ltd* [1988] BCC 449; *Re Artistic Investment Advisers Ltd* [2015] 1 BCLC 619.

[249] *Re Swift 736 Ltd* [1993] BCLC 896, 900, CA.

[250] [1994] 2 BCLC 340, 352.

[251] [1994] 2 BCLC 340, 347.

31.118 In the case of a small company, the responsibility of a director for a failure to maintain accounting records may be reduced to the extent a professional company secretary is engaged. In *Re Rolus Properties Ltd*, Harman J considered that:

> [A]nyone who obtains a chartered secretary to assist in the administration of the affairs of a company, large or small, would, in my view, have reasonable grounds for saying that he had taken proper steps to provide the company with an officer who would, by definition above all others, be competent to and should be able to prepare all necessary paperwork.[252]

He accordingly reduced to two years what would otherwise have been a tariff of between four and six years.

31.119 A director is, of course, not liable to be disqualified for a professional error by the company's auditor, but a failure to maintain accounting records will be aggravated where those records were deliberately misstated, or otherwise not true and fair.[253] In *Re Austinsuite Furniture Ltd*, discussed in paragraph 31.98 above, the company entered into an uncommercial transaction in order to falsify its financial position.[254] It was estimated that the lead company would have been compelled to cease trading a year earlier had true accounts been filed.

31.120 On the other hand there may be rare cases where a failure to maintain proper accounts is inconsequential. In *Re Cargo Agency Ltd*,[255] the company failed to keep and file accounts but had it kept and filed proper accounts only three months' activity would have been recorded and the accounts would have only been available to the public for a very short time before the company in fact went into voluntary liquidation. Harman J accordingly considered that 'there was an undoubted accounting default but one which ... had almost no practical effect on the particular facts of this case and can therefore be ignored'[256] for the purpose of assessing the appropriate tariff.

31.121 A failure to cooperate with an office-holder is a particularly serious matter which is regarded as sufficient to justify disqualification on its own and, in cases of deliberate concealment, is likely to warrant a high tariff. In *Secretary of State for Trade and Industry v Blunt*, the judge explained that:

> The allegation of concealment is no less serious [than the allegation of misappropriation]. In my view, that allegation would justify disqualification on its own. The failure by a director or any other person involved in the affairs of a company to make a full and frank disclosure to an office-holder about the manner in which such affairs have been conducted may create serious difficulties for the office-holder. He will often have little information about the affairs of the company. He may therefore need to rely entirely upon the information he receives from such persons to re-constitute the affairs of the company. It is not surprising, in the circumstances, that the Insolvency Act 1986 contains numerous provisions specifically requiring directors and others involved in the affairs of a company to co-operate fully with the office-holder and to be truthful about their conduct and involvement in such affairs. Any failure by them to co-operate or to be truthful might not only be enforced by court action against them (see for

---

[252] [1988] 4 BCC 446, 448.

[253] *Secretary of State for Trade and Industry v Ashman*, High Court, London, 15 June 1998, a case under s 8 in which the accounts of a public company were grossly misstated. This case arose from the administrative receivership of Blackspur Group plc. For related disqualification proceedings see: [1998] 1 BCLC 676, CA; [2001] 1 BCLC 653; [2002] 2 BCLC 263, CA; [2006] 2 BCLC 489.

[254] [1992] BCLC 1047.

[255] [1992] BCLC 686.

[256] [1992] BCLC 686, 690–1.

example ss 234 to 236 of the Insolvency Act 1986), but could also result in their incurring criminal liability for their actions (see for example ss 206 to 211 of the Insolvency Act 1986).[257]

This approach is likely to be followed and to apply irrespective of the form of insolvency proceeding in issue. In such cases, it is no defence to assert that the false statements were made on the advice of professional advisers. It is the duty of the director to tell the truth.[258]

Material breach of other obligations

Schedule 1 paragraph 6 requires the court to take into account any 'material breach of any **31.122** legislative or other obligation of the director which applies as a result of being a director of a company or overseas company'. The one general obligation of all company directors which is not classified as a fiduciary duty is the duty to exercise reasonable care, skill, and diligence, as stated in the 2006 Act, s 174. This duty is considered in Chapter 14 above. Since the schedule refers to a 'material' breach, minor incompetence as a director is unlikely to suffice, but a serious failure by a director to exercise reasonable care, skill, and diligence, involving gross negligence or incompetence may warrant disqualification under s 6(1).

The courts have held that unfitness by reason of incompetence may be established even **31.123** without proof of a breach of duty, but such a finding is unlikely where the application is not supported by some other matter, such as unfair discrimination against a creditor or class of creditor. In *Secretary of State for Trade and Industry v Goldberg*, Lewison J accepted that the general duty as now stated in s 174 represented '[t]he general standard of competence that the law requires of a director'[259] and that '[i]ncompetence in "a marked degree" is enough to render a person unfit'[260] but he considered himself bound by the decisions in *Re Bath Glass Ltd* and *Re Barings (No 5)* to the extent 'that unfitness by reason of incompetence may be established even without proof of a breach of duty'.[261] Lewison J nonetheless considered that:

> [T]he question of unfitness to do something can … only be judged against an expectation of what is required of a person doing, or attempting to do, that thing … [T]he court must be very careful before holding that a director is unfit because of conduct that does not amount to a breach of any duty (contractual, tortious, statutory or equitable) to anyone, and is not dishonest.[262]

In this light, disqualification on the basis of incompetence is to be approached by asking **31.124** (a) whether the director breached his duty of care, skill, and diligence, or, exceptionally, whether some other misconduct is present which justifies a finding of incompetence, and (b) whether, in all the circumstances, that breach of duty or other misconduct is sufficiently serious to warrant a finding of unfitness. The second condition is particularly important because the overriding question is whether incompetence is such that the director should not be concerned in the management of a company.

---

[257] [2005] 2 BCLC 463, para 24.

[258] *Secretary of State for Trade and Industry v Blunt* [2005] 2 BCLC 463 at para 25; *Re Living Images Ltd* [1996] 1 BCLC 348, 376.

[259] [2004] 1 BCLC 597 at para 19. Lewison J in fact approved the law then stated in *Re D'Jan of London Ltd* [1994] 1 BCLC 561, 563 which phrased the standard of competence in terms equivalent to the Insolvency Act, s 214 and which has since been endorsed by the legislature under 2006 Act, s 174.

[260] [2004] 1 BCLC 597 at para 21; and *Re Sevenoaks Stationers (Retail) Ltd* [1991] Ch 164, 184.

[261] *Secretary of State for Trade and Industry v Goldberg* [2004] 1 BCLC 597 at para 28; *Re Barings plc (No 5)* [1999] 1 BCLC 433, 486; affd [2000] 1 BCLC 523, CA; and *Re Bath Glass Ltd* [1988] 4 BCC 130, 133–4.

[262] *Secretary of State for Trade and Industry v Goldberg* [2004] 1 BCLC 597 at para 43.

31.125 The cases in which a director has been disqualified for incompetence are accordingly varied and tend to overlap substantially with other, more specific grounds, such as the failure to maintain and file proper accounts and returns, because allegations of failure are often accumulated to support a finding of sufficiently serious incompetence. The more discrete complaints have included complete inactivity amounting to a total abrogation of responsibility,[263] a failure to ensure that the company received a debt due to it from the sale of its assets,[264] a failure to adequately value and capitalize the business of a target company,[265] seriously flawed judgments and valuations in relation to commercial transactions,[266] the advance of a loan to a related company which had no prospect of repayment,[267] the sale of the company's business on deferred terms without security,[268] a failure to introduce and operate appropriate financial and other controls in the management of the company's business,[269] a failure to properly monitor the carrying on of delegated activities which caused the insolvency of the company,[270] acquiescing in the payment of unlawful dividends,[271] and failing to take any steps to examine the company's affairs and so failing to prevent the tacit discrimination against payment of Crown debts over an extended period.[272]

31.126 In assessing the competence of a director, in line with the approach taken to assessing a breach of the general duty of care, higher standards of conduct are expected from more experienced directors and those having or professing competence in a particular area, for example a finance director.[273]

(vii) Frequency of conduct

31.127 Like paragraph 3, paragraph 7 obliges the court to take into account the frequency of conduct of the director which falls within paragraph 5 or 6.

E. Mandatory Competition Disqualification Orders

31.128 CDDA, s 9A provides that:[274]

(1) The court[275] must make a disqualification order against a person if the following two conditions are satisfied in relation to him.
(2) The first condition is that an undertaking which is a company of which he is a director commits a breach of competition law.

---

[263] *Re Kaytech International plc* [1999] 2 BCLC 351, CA; *Re Westmid Packing Services Ltd* [1998] 2 All ER 124, CA.

[264] *Re Tansoft Ltd* [1991] BCLC 339.

[265] *Re City Investment Centres Ltd* [1992] BCLC 956; *Re Austinsuite Furniture Ltd* [1992] BCLC 1047.

[266] *Re Aldermanbury Trust plc* [1993] BCC 598.

[267] *Re Continental Assurance Co of London plc* [1997] 1 BCLC 48.

[268] *Secretary of State v McTighe* [1996] 2 BCLC 477.

[269] *Re Landhurst Leasing plc* [1999] 1 BCLC 286.

[270] *Re Barings plc (No 5)* [1999] 1 BCLC 433; affd [2000] 1 BCLC 523, CA.

[271] *Re AG (Manchester) Ltd* [2008] BCC 497.

[272] *Secretary of State for Trade and Industry v Thornberry* [2008] BCC 768.

[273] *Re Barings plc (No 5)* [1999] 1 BCLC 433, 483–4; affd [2000] 1 BCLC 523, CA; *Re Continental Assurance of London plc* [1997] 1 BCLC 48; but cf *Secretary of State for Trade and Industry v Thornbury* [2008] 1 BCLC 139 at para 36 which regarded *Continental Assurance* as merely supporting the more general proposition that a '[l]ack of financial awareness or of a basic obligation to familiarise oneself with the company's financial position is no defence' to a charge of unfitness.

[274] Inserted by the Enterprise Act 2002, s 204 with effect from 20 June 2003.

[275] The High Court: CDDA, s 9E(4).

(3) The second condition is that the court considers that his conduct as a director makes him unfit to be concerned in the management of a company.

Conduct includes omissions.[276] Director includes a de facto director and a shadow director.[277] The application may be made by the Competition and Markets Authority (CMA) or by a specified regulator.[278] The maximum period of disqualification is fifteen years, but there is no minimum period.[279]

By s 9A(4) an undertaking commits a breach of competition law if it engages in conduct **31.129** which infringes prohibitions on agreements etc (preventing, restricting, or distorting competition),[280] or on abuse of a dominant position.[281]

For the purpose of deciding whether a person is unfit to be concerned in the management **31.130** of a company within the meaning of s 9A(3), the court must have regard to whether s 9A(6) applies to him, may have regard to his conduct as a director of a company in connection with any other breach of competition law, but must not have regard to the matters mentioned in Schedule 1.[282] Subsection 9A(6) applies to the person if, as a director of the company (a) his conduct contributed to the breach of competition law (whether or not he knew that the conduct of the undertaking constituted the breach),[283] (b) his conduct did not contribute to that breach, but he had reasonable grounds to suspect that the conduct of the undertaking constituted the breach and he took no steps to prevent it, or (c) he did not know but ought to have known that the conduct of the undertaking constituted the breach.

If the CMA or specified regulator has reasonable grounds for suspecting that a breach of **31.131** competition law has occurred it or he may carry out an investigation for the purpose of deciding whether to make an application under s 9A for a disqualification order.[284] If, as a result of the investigation, the CMA or specified regulator proposes to apply under s 9A, it must first give notice to the person likely to be affected by the application and give him an opportunity to make representations.[285]

---

[276] CDDA, s 9E(4).

[277] CDDA, ss 9E(5) and 22(4)–(5).

[278] CDDA, ss 9A(10) and 9E(2), which provides that, for the purpose of a breach of competition law in relation to a matter in respect of which he or it has a function, a specified regulator is (a) the Office of Communications, (b) the Gas and Electricity Markets Authority, (c) the Water Services Regulation Authority, (d) the Office of Rail Regulation, (e) the Civil Aviation Authority, (f) the Monitor (under the Health and Social Care Act 2012), (g) the Payment Systems Regulator established under the Financial Services (Banking Reform) Act 2013, or (h) the FCA. Section 9D gives the Secretary of State power to make regulations to co-ordinate the performance of functions under ss 9A–9C, but so far no regulations have been made.

[279] CDDA, s 9A(9).

[280] Competition Act 1998, Ch 1 and Treaty on the Functioning of the European Union, Art 101. For this purpose references to the conduct of an undertaking are references to its conduct taken with the conduct of one or more other undertakings: CDDA, s 9A(8).

[281] Competition Act 1998, Ch 2 and Treaty on the Functioning of the European Union, Art 102.

[282] CDDA, s 9A(5).

[283] CDDA, s 9A(7).

[284] CDDA, s 9C(1). For the purposes of such investigation the Competition Act, ss 26–30 apply to the CMA and the specified regulators as they apply to the CMA for the purposes of an investigation under s 25 of that Act.

[285] CDDA, s 9C(3) and (4).

31.132 The CMA or a specified regulator has power to accept an undertaking as an alternative to a competition disqualification order.[286] This is similar to the power under ss 7(2A) and 8(2A) (paragraphs 31.12–31.16 above), but the wording specified in CDDA, s 9B(3) is slightly different albeit to the same effect: that the person will not act as a director of a company or receiver of a company's property, or be concerned or take part in the promotion, formation, or management of a company. There is no automatic provision that the person may act with the leave of the court, but s 9B(4) provides that the undertaking may make such provision. The court[287] has power to vary a competition disqualification undertaking. On the application the CMA or specified regulator is to appear and call the attention of the court to any matters which appear to it or him to be relevant and may give evidence or call witnesses.[288]

F. Procedure for Obtaining Disqualification Orders

(1) Notice of intention to apply

31.133 Once the decision to proceed has been taken, CDDA, s 16(1) provides:[289]

> A person intending to apply for the making of a disqualification order shall give not less than 10 days' notice of his intention to the person against whom the order is sought …

This requirement is directory rather than mandatory,[290] so failure to give proper notice is merely a procedural irregularity which does not invalidate the proceedings. The notice does not need to set out in full the grounds on which the application is to be made.[291] However, ten clear days' notice is required.[292]

(2) Time limits

31.134 There is a three-year limitation period for applications for disqualification under ss 6[293] (unfit directors of insolvent companies) and 8ZA[294] (person instructing unfit director of insolvent company), unless the court gives leave for proceedings to be commenced out of time. The CDDA does not prescribe the factors which are to be taken into account on an application for permission to issue proceedings or to add a defendant to existing proceedings out of time.[295] Similar issues will arise when, although the proceedings were commenced within the time limit, the evidence was not ready at that time and permission is sought for an extension of time (until after the two-year period has expired) in which to serve it.[296] In *Re Probe Data*

---

[286] CDDA, s 9B.

[287] The High Court: CDDA, s 8A(3)(a).

[288] CDDA, s 8A(2A).

[289] As amended by SBEE Act 2015, s 111, Sch 7, Pt 1, para 1 as from 1 October 2015.

[290] *Secretary of State for Trade and Industry v Langridge, Re Cedac Ltd* [1991] Ch 402, CA; *Re Finelist Ltd, Secretary of State for Trade and Industry v Swan* [2004] BCC 877; *Secretary of State for BERR v Smith* [2009] BCC 497.

[291] *Re Cedac* [1991] Ch 402.

[292] *Re Jaymar Management Ltd* [1990] BCLC 617.

[293] CDDA, s 7(2), as amended by SBEE Act 2015, s 108(1) with effect from 1 October 2015. Prior to that date the limitation period was two years.

[294] CDDA, s 8ZB(2).

[295] See eg *Re Westmid Packaging Services Ltd* [1995] BCC 203.

[296] The position in *Re Blackspur Group plc, Secretary of State for Trade and Industry v Davies* [1996] 4 All ER 289, CA.

Systems Ltd (No 3),[297] Scott LJ said that the court should take into account: (a) the length of delay, (b) the reasons for the delay, (c) the strength of the case against the director, and (d) the degree of prejudice caused to the director by the delay. In *Re Blackspur Group plc*,[298] Millett LJ said that this was not exhaustive, and the court should take all relevant circumstances into account.

If an application for permission is required, the Secretary of State is expected to make it **31.135** without delay. Applications were refused in *Re Crestjoy Products Ltd*[299] where the ten-day letters had been sent shortly before the end of the two-year period but the application was not made until some ten weeks after the end of two years, there was further delay because of a fault in the form of the application, and Harman J was not satisfied that a good reason for extension of time had been shown. Similarly, in *Re Cedar Developments Ltd*,[300] permission was refused where the proceedings had not been commenced in time through an administrative oversight, although the application for permission was made less than a week after the two-year period had expired. Delay attributable to the defendant will weigh in favour of the Secretary of State.[301]

Once disqualification proceedings have been commenced, they must be progressed with **31.136** reasonable expedition. The courts will apply (with some adjustment to take account of the particular nature of the proceedings)[302] the usual principles applicable in civil litigation to cases where there is unjustifiable and excessive delay. In an extreme case the courts have the power under the CPR[303] to strike out the proceedings for want of prosecution.[304] In *Re Blackspur Group (No 4)*,[305] Arden LJ said:

> Proceedings which, as in this case, are brought at the end of the two-year period are liable to be struck out, if there is inordinate or inexcusable delay: see *Re Manlon Trading Ltd*.[306] Proceedings will be struck out if there is a substantial risk of an unfair trial but they will not be struck out simply because there has been a delay in the course of the preparations for trial or even in the trial itself: see, for example, *Re Manlon Trading Ltd* and *Re Rocksteady Services Ltd, Secretary of State for Trade and Industry v Staton*.[307]

Significant delay may also affect the right of the defendant under Article 6 of the ECHR **31.137** to have civil rights determined within a reasonable time. In *EDC v United Kingdom*,[308] the European Court of Human Rights (ECtHR) held that there had been a breach of such

---

[297] [1992] BCLC 405, CA; cf *C M Van Stillevoldt v El Carriers Inc* [1993] 1 WLR 207.

[298] [1996] 4 All ER 289, CA; followed in *Re Instant Access Properties Ltd* [2011] EWHC 3022 (Ch).

[299] [1990] BCLC 677.

[300] [1994] 2 BCLC 714.

[301] *Re Copecrest Ltd, Secretary of State for Trade and Industry v Tighe* [1993] BCLC 1118; on appeal [1994] 2 BCLC 284, CA.

[302] In *Re Manlon Trading Ltd, Official Receiver v Aziz* [1996] Ch 136, CA, Beldam LJ said that, because disqualification proceedings were brought in the public interest, not to enforce private rights, they should not be struck out lightly: the public interest nature of the proceedings was to be balanced against any prejudice suffered by the defendant.

[303] CPR, rule 3.4(2)(b) and (c).

[304] See eg *Re Noble Trees Ltd* [1993] BCLC 1185; *Official Receiver v B Ltd* [1994] 2 BCLC 1; *Re Manlon Trading Ltd, Official Receiver v Aziz* [1996] Ch 136, CA; *Secretary of State for Trade and Industry v Martin* [1998] BCC 184.

[305] [2008] 1 BCLC 153 at para 13.

[306] [1996] Ch 136, CA.

[307] [2001] 1 BCLC 84; affd [2001] BCC 467, CA.

[308] [1998] BCC 370.

rights where disqualification proceedings had not been brought to trial for some four and a half years pending determination of criminal proceedings. In *Eastaway v UK (App no 1496/01)*,[309] the ECtHR held that disqualification proceedings arising from the collapse of the Blackspur Group which had been commenced in 1992 and culminated in an undertaking by Mr Eastway in May 2001 had taken too long and so violated Mr Eastway's Article 6 rights. However, in *Re Blackspur Group (No 4)*,[310] the Court of Appeal declined to set aside the undertaking the director had given, pointing out that the fact that there has been a violation of Article 6 does not necessarily mean that there cannot be a fair trial or that the proceedings are necessarily to be struck out.[311] While the decision of the ECtHR was binding, it had made no finding that there could not be a fair trial because of the delay, and such a finding was not implicit in its judgment.

(3) Courts and applicants

31.138 The court with the power to make a disqualification order under CDDA, ss 2–4 and 6, is the court with jurisdiction to wind up the company.[312] The application for an order under ss 2–4 may be made by the Secretary of State, the official receiver, the liquidator, or any past or present member or creditor of any company in relation to which that person has committed or is alleged to have committed an offence or other default.[313]

31.139 An application for an order under s 6 is made by the Secretary of State, but, in the case of a person who is or has been a director of a company which is being or has been wound up by the court in England and Wales, the Secretary of State may direct the official receiver to apply.[314] Proceedings are not invalidated by being commenced in the wrong court, and proceedings for or in connection with a disqualification order under s 6 or in connection with a disqualification undertaking accepted under s 7 may be retained in the court in which the proceedings were commenced, although it may not have been the court in which they ought to have been commenced.[315]

31.140 The High Court has power to make a disqualification order under CDDA, s 8 on the application of the Secretary of State.[316] The High Court has jurisdiction to make a competition disqualification order under s 9A on the application of the Competition and Markets Authority or specified regulator.[317]

31.141 Where the application under the CDDA is made by the Secretary of State, the official receiver, the Competition and Markets Authority, the liquidator, or a specified regulator, the applicant is to appear and call the attention of the court to any matters which seem to him

---

[309] [2006] 2 BCLC 361.

[310] [2008] 1 BCLC 153, CA.

[311] *AG's reference (No 2 of 2001)* [2004] 2 AC 72, HL.

[312] CDDA, s 2(2) (where the Crown Court and magistrates' court also have jurisdiction), and ss 3(4), 4(2), 6(3). If an application is made under s 6 in respect of a company which is being wound up by the court, the application must be made to that court. For applications under s 6, s 6(3A) provides that the Insolvency Act, ss 117 and 120 apply with the modifications there stated. It does not matter that the company has been dissolved prior to the making of the application: *Secretary of State for Trade and Industry v Arnold* [2008] 1 BCLC 581 at paras 8, 11, 12.

[313] CDDA, s 16(2).

[314] CDDA, s 7(1).

[315] CDDA, s 6(3B).

[316] CDDA, s 8(1) and (3).

[317] CDDA, ss 9A(10) and 9E(3).

to be relevant and may himself give evidence or call witnesses, as may the respondent to the application.[318]

Disqualification orders may be made by the Crown Court or magistrates' court under ss 2 **31.142** and 5 or by the court hearing a wrongful trading application under s 11, so that the jurisdiction to make a disqualification order is an adjunct to the court's normal criminal or civil jurisdiction.

(4) General procedure

The Insolvent Companies (Disqualification of Unfit Directors) Proceedings Rules 1987 (the **31.143** 'Disqualification Rules') apply to an application under the CDDA:

(a) for leave to commence proceedings for a disqualification order after the end of the period mentioned in s 7(2);
(b) to enforce any duty arising under s 7(4) (provision of information, etc);
(c) for a disqualification order where made (i) by the Secretary of State or the official receiver under s 7(1) (disqualification of unfit directors of insolvent companies), (ii) by the Secretary of State under s 5A (disqualification for certain convictions abroad), s 8 (disqualification of director on finding of unfitness), s 8ZB (application for an order under s 8ZA), or 8ZD (order disqualifying person instructing unfit director: other cases) or (iii) by the Competition and Markets Authority or a specified regulator under s 9A (competition disqualification order);
(d) under s 8A (variation etc of disqualification undertaking); and
(e) for leave under (i) s 1A(1) or s 9B(4) (and s 17 as it applies for the purposes of either of those sections), or (ii) ss 1 and 17 as they apply for the purposes of ss 5A, 6, 7(1), 8, 8ZA, 8ZC, 8ZD, 8ZE, 9A, or 10.

The CPR and the Practice Direction: Directors Disqualification Proceedings (the **31.144** 'Disqualification PD') apply in respect of applications to which the Disqualification Rules apply, except where the Disqualification Rules make provision to inconsistent effect.[319] The Disqualification Rules do make special provision inconsistent with the CPR in the following respects:

(1) An application is to be made under the CPR Part 8 procedure or by application notice, except that the Insolvency Rules apply to an application against a liquidator, administrator, or administrative receiver to enforce a duty under CDDA, s 7(4).[320]
(2) The Insolvency Rules, rules 7.47 and 7.49 apply to appeals and applications to review orders.[321]
(3) Rules 3 to 8, discussed below, apply to applications for disqualification orders of the types described in paragraph 31.143(c) above.[322]

The Disqualification PD describes the procedure to be adopted where Disqualification **31.145** Rules, rules 3–8, apply and where they do not. It states that the proceedings are allocated to

---

[318] CDDA, s 16(1) and (3).
[319] Disqualification Rules, rule 2(1). The Disqualification PD [2015] BCC 224 is printed in Civil Procedure at 3J-1 to 3J-64.
[320] Disqualification Rules, rule 2(2), (3), and (5).
[321] Disqualification Rules, rule 2(4).
[322] Disqualification Rules, rule 2A.

the multi-track.[323] The following paragraphs outline the procedure for an application for a disqualification order in accordance with Disqualification Rules, rules 3–8.

31.146 Proceedings are commenced by Part 8 Claim Form, including endorsements informing the defendant of the maximum period of disqualification that may be imposed, that the application may be determined summarily (with a maximum period of disqualification of five years) or adjourned for substantive hearing, and notifying the defendant of the applicable time limits for evidence.[324]

31.147 The applicant is required to file evidence in court at the time the application is issued, including a statement of the matters by reference to which the defendant is alleged to be unfit to be concerned in the management of a company.[325] Evidence is to be in the form of affidavits, except that the official receiver may provide a report which is treated as if verified by affidavit.[326] A certified copy of a report by inspectors appointed under Part XIV of the 1985 Act will be admissible in evidence.[327] Three points may be made about the evidence in support of the application:

(1) There should be a clear statement of the grounds for the application and of the essential facts relied on in support.[328]

(2) In the interests of fairness, the applicant should disclose relevant materials in his possession, but not all documents that he could obtain; there was no requirement for the applicant to obtain evidence or conduct investigations.[329]

(3) There is an implied exception to the strict rules of evidence on hearsay evidence, opinion evidence, and the rule in *Hollington v Hewthorn*,[330] so that the Secretary of State could rely on a report produced by the FCA and materials obtained in its investigation as prima facie evidence, it being for the director to adduce evidence rebutting it.[331]

31.148 The applicant is responsible for serving the claim form with acknowledgement of service on the defendant.[332] Where a defendant is outside the jurisdiction, an application must be made for an order for service outside the jurisdiction in such manner as the court thinks fit.[333] The court will not permit service out of the jurisdiction where it is not satisfied that there is a good arguable case that the requisite conditions for a disqualification order to be made have been satisfied.[334]

---

[323] Disqualification PD, para 2.

[324] Disqualification Rules, rule 4; Disqualification PD, para 4.

[325] Disqualification Rules, rule 3; Disqualification PD, para 8.2.

[326] Disqualification Rules, rule 3(2); Disqualification PD, para 8.1.

[327] 1985 Act, s 441 and Disqualification PD, para 8.1.

[328] *Re Rex Williams Leisure Ltd* [1994] Ch 1, 87, 88; *Re Sutton Glassworks Ltd* [1996] BCC 174; *Re Finelist Ltd* [2004] BCC 877 at paras 17 and 21; *Secretary of State for BIS v Chohan* [2011] EWHC 1350 (Ch).

[329] *Secretary of State for BIS v Doffman* [2011] 1 BCLC 596 at para 13.

[330] [1943] KB 587, CA. The rule is to the effect that a judgment, verdict, or award of another tribunal is not admissible evidence to prove a fact in issue or a fact relevant to the issue in other proceedings between different parties. Subject to the implied exception mentioned in this paragraph, the rule applies to disqualification proceedings; *Secretary of State for Trade and Industry v Bairstow* [2004] Ch 1, CA at para 27.

[331] *Secretary of State for BERR v Aaron* [2009] 1 BCLC 55, CA.

[332] Disqualification Rules, rules 5(1) and (3); Disqualification PD, paras 6.1 and 6.2.

[333] Disqualification Rules, rule 5(2); Disqualification PD, 6.4.

[334] *Re Seagull Manufacturing Co Ltd (No 2)* [1994] Ch 91.

The defendant has 28 days after service to file any evidence on which he wishes to rely in **31.149** opposition to the application.[335] Evidence in reply is to be served within 14 days of receipt of the defendant's evidence[336] although these time periods may be extended prior to the first hearing by written agreement between the parties.[337] The Disqualification PD provides that so far as possible all evidence should be filed before the first hearing of the disqualification application.[338]

Statements made in pursuance of a requirement under specified provisions of the CDDA[339] **31.150** or under rules made for the purposes of the CDDA are generally admissible in evidence against the maker or a person who concurred in the making of the statement.[340] However, CDDA, s 20(2) provides that in criminal proceedings:[341]

(a) no evidence relating to the statement may be adduced, and
(b) no question relating to it may be asked,by or on behalf of the prosecution, unless evidence relating to it is adduced, or a question relating to it is asked, in the proceedings by or on behalf of that person.

In *Secretary of State of Trade and Industry v Crane*,[342] Ferris J discussed CDDA, s 20, which he regarded as offering an additional and substantial layer of protection in almost all cases in which there are parallel criminal and disqualification proceedings. This reasoning has been criticized,[343] on the basis that evidence a defendant may wish to rely on in disqualification proceedings is not in fact compelled, and it has also been pointed out that the bar in s 20(2) does not prevent a co-defendant in criminal proceedings from raising material in those proceedings.[344]

---

[335] Disqualification Rules, rule 6(1); Disqualification PD, para 8.4. In *Secretary of State for BIS v Potiwal* [2012] EWHC 3723 (Ch) Briggs J struck out as an abuse of process the director's evidence that he lacked knowledge of the company's VAT evasion, when the VAT tribunal had found that he did know. In so doing, Briggs J applied the principle stated in *Hunter v Chief Constable of the West Midland Police* [1982] AC 52, 536, HL that the court has an inherent power to prevent misuse of its procedure which would be manifestly unfair to a party before it or would otherwise bring the administration of justice into disrepute. In *Secretary of State for Trade and Industry v Bairstow* [2004] Ch 1 at paras 39–42, the Court of Appeal held that the Secretary of State could not rely on a judgment of a civil court to which he was not a party to prove unfitness and that it was not manifestly unfair within the *Hunter* principle for him to be required to prove his case.

[336] Disqualification Rules, rule 6(2); Disqualification PD, para 8.6.

[337] Disqualification PD, para 8.7.

[338] Disqualification PD, para 8.8.

[339] CDDA, ss 5A, 6–10, 12C, 15–15C, or 19(c), or Sch 1 (as amended by SBEE Act 2015, s 111, Sch 7, Pt 1, paras 1, 15 as from 1 October 2015.

[340] CDDA, s 20(1).

[341] Other than the limited classes of exceptions listed in CDDA, s 20(3).

[342] [2001] 2 BCLC 222.

[343] See Walters and Davis-White QC, *Directors Disqualification and Bankruptcy Restrictions*, 3rd edn (Sweet and Maxwell, 2009) at paras 7–91 and 7–92.

[344] The mere fact that a defendant might give an indication of his likely defence in prospective criminal proceedings did not debar the claimant from nonetheless pursuing civil proceedings: *Jefferson Ltd v Bhetcha* [1979] 1 WLR 898, CA. In *Re TransTec plc, Secretary of State for Trade and Industry v Carr* [2007] 1 BCLC 93, David Richards J declined to order a stay of disqualification proceedings because of pending criminal proceedings, considering that the defendants' position could be suitably protected by directions that the respondents were to serve their evidence on the Secretary of State before the start of the criminal trial but not to serve it on each other or file it and that the Secretary of State was to refrain from showing the evidence to any witness or potential witness in the criminal trial. It has been said that the Secretary of State has a public duty to apply for the disqualification of unfit directors. He cannot be held up indefinitely by other proceedings over which he has no control (see *Re Rex Williams Leisure plc* [1994] Ch 350, 368F, CA, per Hoffmann LJ).

31.151 The first hearing takes place before the Registrar,[345] not less than eight weeks after the claim form was issued.[346] At that hearing, the Registrar will either determine the application summarily or adjourn it giving such further directions as may be required so that the application may be heard at the earliest possible date.[347]

31.152 Most disqualification cases are heard by the Registrar rather than a judge. Where the application is contested, the court may order the makers of affidavits and reports to attend for cross-examination, but the court may control the scope of cross-examination.[348] Many applications are dealt with on an uncontested basis.[349] The court may make a disqualification order whether or not the defendant appears,[350] but a disqualification order made in the absence of the defendant may be set aside or varied by the court on such terms as it thinks just.[351]

(5) Appeals

31.153 It is only in exceptional cases that a disqualification order is stayed pending appeal.[352] If, however, the order is stayed, it will not be registered under CDDA, s 18.[353]

31.154 On appeal, the appeal court will normally defer to the decision of the trial judge as regards the findings of primary fact, but as regards the inferences to be drawn from the primary facts or the evaluation of such facts, for example in determining whether a reasonable director should have concluded that the company should not have traded beyond a particular point, the appellate court is in as good a position as the trial judge to draw any such inferences or to make any such evaluation: *Re Hitco 2000 Ltd.*[354]

G. Consequences of Disqualification

(1) Criminal consequences

Bankruptcy

31.155 By CDDA, s 11(1) and (2),[355] it is an offence for a person to act as director of a company,[356] or directly or indirectly to take part in or be concerned in the promotion, formation, or

---

[345] Disqualification Rules, rule 7(2); Disqualification PD, para 9.1.

[346] Disqualification Rules, rule 7(1); Disqualification PD, para 4.3.

[347] Disqualification Rules, rule 7(3); Disqualification PD, paras 9.1, 9.2.

[348] CPR 32.1(2); *Secretary of State for Trade and Industry v Gill* [2005] BCC 24. Disqualification PD, para 10 deals with preparation of documentary material for trial.

[349] See Disqualification PD, para 11. Disqualification PD, para 12 deals with *Carecraft* procedure, which is largely defunct now that disqualification undertakings can be accepted.

[350] Disqualification Rules, rule 8.1; Disqualification PD, para 8.1.

[351] Disqualification Rules, rule 8.2; Disqualification PD, para 8.2.

[352] *Secretary of State for Trade and Industry v Bannister* [1996] 1 WLR 118; *Secretary of State for BERR v Sainsbury* [2009] EWHC 3496.

[353] *Cathie v Secretary of State for BIS* [2011] BCC 685, [2012] BCC 813 (CA).

[354] [1995] 2 BCLC 63 (approved by the Court of Appeal in *Re Grayan Ltd* [1995] Ch 241, 255). In *Re Grayan Ltd*, Hoffmann LJ referred to *Benmax* v. *Austin Motor Co. Ltd.* [1955] AC 370, in which Viscount Simonds said that where an appeal concerned the proper inference to be drawn from primary facts, 'an appellate court should form an independent opinion, though it will naturally attach importance to the judgment of the trial judge'.

[355] As substituted by SBEE Act 2015, s 113(1), (2) with effect from 1 October 2015.

[356] Company includes a company incorporated outside Great Britain that has an established place of business in Great Britain: CDDA, s 11(4); inserted by the Companies Act 2006 (Consequential Amendments,

management of a company, without the leave of the court,[357] at a time when (a) he is an undischarged bankrupt,[358] (b) a bankruptcy restrictions order or undertaking is in force in respect of him,[359] (c) a debt relief restrictions order or undertaking is in force in respect of him,[360] or (d) a moratorium period under a debt relief order applies in relation to him.[361]

The object of the original prohibition in s 11 affecting undischarged bankrupts, as indicated **31.156** by the report of the Greene Committee, was to prevent a person obtaining credit and the protection of limited liability for so long as he remained an undischarged bankrupt.[362] The prohibition in s 11(1) is, for this reason, automatic and a breach an 'offence'. It has been held that even where a bankruptcy is annulled following payment in full of the relevant debts, the former bankrupt still commits an offence if he acts as a director prior to the annulment.[363] For further discussion of the criminal consequences, see Chapter 35, Section K below.

Section 11(1) and (2) reflects the current bankruptcy regime,[364] in which a person is entitled **31.157** to automatic discharge from bankruptcy within one year, unless an application is made for an order that the discharge period shall cease to run, but may be subject to specific bankruptcy restrictions upon application of the Secretary of State.[365] The minimum period of a bankruptcy restrictions order is two years and the maximum period is 15 years.[366] The court is obliged to make a bankruptcy restrictions order if it thinks it appropriate having regard to the conduct of the bankrupt, taking into account specified types of behaviour on the part of the bankrupt.[367] The Secretary of State has power to accept a bankruptcy restrictions undertaking, which has the same effect as a bankruptcy restrictions order.[368]

Failure to pay under county court administration order

Where a person fails to make any payment which he is directed to make by virtue of an admin- **31.158** istration order under Part VI of the County Courts Act 1984, the court that is administering that person's estate under the order may, if it thinks fit, revoke the administration order and make an order directing that certain credit restrictions and CDDA, s 12 shall apply to the person for a period not exceeding one year.[369] By CDDA, s 12(2) a person subject to such an order shall not, except with the leave of the court which made the order, act as director, liquidator, or directly or indirectly take part or be concerned in the promotion, formation, or management of a company. A breach of s 12(2) is an offence (see further Chapter 35, Section K below).[370]

Transitional Provisions and savings) Order 2009 (SI 2009/1941), para 85(1), (7) with effect from 1 October 2009.

[357] As defined in s 11(2A).

[358] In England and Wales, Scotland, or Northern Ireland.

[359] Under the Bankruptcy (Scotland) Act 1985, the Insolvency Act or the Insolvency (Northern Ireland) Order 1989.

[360] Under the Insolvency Act or the Insolvency (Northern Ireland) Order 1989.

[361] Under the Insolvency Act or the Insolvency (Northern Ireland) Order 1989.

[362] Paras 56 and 57.

[363] *IRC v McEntaggart* [2006] 1 BCLC 476.

[364] Introduced by the Enterprise Act 2002, s 257(2) and Sch 21, para 5, which came into effect on 1 April 2004.

[365] Insolvency Act, ss 279(1), 279(3), 281A, and Sch 4A.

[366] Insolvency Act, Sch 4A, para 4.

[367] Insolvency Act, Sch 4A, para 2.

[368] Insolvency Act, Sch 4A, paras 7–9.

[369] Insolvency Act, s 429. Note that amendments have been made to s 12 by the Tribunals, Courts and Enforcement Act 2007, ss 106, 146, and Sch 16 but they have not yet been brought into effect.

[370] CDDA, s 13.

Contravention of disqualification order

31.159 A person who acts in contravention of a disqualification order or undertaking commits an offence (see further Chapter 35, Section K).[371]

31.160 Where a body corporate is guilty of an offence of acting in contravention of a disqualification order or undertaking, any director, manager, secretary, or other similar office of the body corporate is also guilty of an offence if he consented or connived in commission of offence by the body corporate or the that offence was attributable to any neglect on his part.[372]

(2) Personal liability for company's debts

31.161 The civil consequences of acting in contravention of a disqualification order or undertaking[373] attach both to the person so acting and to anyone else involved in the management of the company[374] who acts or 'is willing to act' on instructions given without the permission of the court by a person whom he knows at the time to be the subject of a disqualification order or undertaking under the CDDA[375] or an undischarged bankrupt. Either is made personally responsible by CDDA, s 15(1) for all the relevant debts of the company. Liability is joint and several with the company and any other person who is liable under CDDA, s 15.[376]

31.162 The person who acts in contravention is liable for 'such debts and other liabilities as are incurred at a time when that person is involved in the management of the company'.[377]

31.163 The person who becomes liable by acting or being willing to act on instructions given without the permission of the court by a person whom he knows at the time to be the subject of a disqualification order or undertaking or an undischarged bankrupt is liable for such debts and other liabilities as are incurred at a time when that person was acting or willing to act.[378] There is a statutory presumption that a person involved in the management of a company who has at any time acted on the instructions given without the leave of the court by a person whom he knew at that time to be subject to a disqualification order or undertaking or to be an undischarged bankrupt was willing to act at any time thereafter on the instructions of that person.[379] The onus will therefore be on the defendant to rebut the presumption.

31.164 It appears that each relevant creditor can sue a person who is liable for a company's debts under CDDA, s 15 just as they would be able to pursue a director who is jointly and severally liable under the Insolvency Act, s 217 for the debts of a company which has been operating under a name which is prohibited in relation to them.[380]

---

[371] CDDA, s 13.

[372] CDDA, s 14(1). That sub-s applies to members who manage the body corporate's affairs as if they were directors: s 14(2).

[373] Or in contravention of CDDA, ss 11, 12A, or 12B (but not s 12(2)).

[374] CDDA, s 15(4) provides that a person is 'involved in the management of a company' if he is a director of the company or if he is concerned whether directly or indirectly or takes part in the management of the company.

[375] Or under the Company Directors Disqualification (Northern Ireland) Order 2002.

[376] CDDA, s 15(2).

[377] CDDA, s 15(3)(a).

[378] CDDA, s 15(3)(b).

[379] CDDA, s 15(5), as substituted by the Companies Act 2006 (Consequential Amendments, Transitional Provisions and Savings) Order 2009 (SI 2009/1941), Art 2(1), Sch 1, para 85(1), (9)(b) with effect from 1 October 2009.

[380] See Ch 34 at Section D(4) below; cf *Thorne v Silverleaf* [1994] 2 BCLC 637, CA.

This remedy will be of particular importance when the company debtor is insolvent and the **31.165** person liable under s 15 has assets against which a judgment can be enforced. In *Re Prestige Grindings Ltd*,[381] Judge Norris QC held that a creditor who has a relevant debt has an 'immediate and unconditional' claim against a person liable under s 15, which he can pursue for his own benefit, while the company only has a restitutionary right of contribution against that person, arising from the 'joint and several' nature of the liability but only if and when it has paid more than its share. As he put it:

> In my judgment s 15 creates two separate sets of rights. To put the matter shortly and simply, it first makes the disqualified director personally responsible for all the relevant debts; and it secondly provides that the disqualified director is jointly and severally liable with the company for those debts. The first confers on the creditor a separate statutory cause of action against the disqualified director to supplement his contractual right against the company; the second gives the company a right of contribution from someone who by statute has become its co-debtor. The section does not confer on the company (co-debtor A) the right to sue the disqualified director (co-debtor B) for the amount of the debt that is owed to C. That is what para (2) of the originating application seeks when it asks the court to make an order that Mr Yardley pay to the company the value of the relevant debts. But such a right is unknown to the general law and I hold that it cannot be spelled out of the words of the section. The personal responsibility created by the section is to the creditor and with the company. The section does confer on the company (co-debtor A) the right to recover from the disqualified director (co-debtor B) a contribution in circumstances where the general law so allows.

He therefore held that it was inappropriate for the liquidator to put himself forward as a representative of all the creditors, or for one creditor to be appointed as representative of the creditors as a whole. He could seek a declaration of prospective liability from a co-debtor[382] but the judge considered this premature (apparently because the liquidator had not yet admitted any debts to proof). HM Revenue and Customs were parties to the proceedings and could seek an immediate order to be paid by the defendants the sums due from the company. If other creditors such as the company's landlord wished to pursue claims, they would need to do so separately. In each case it would be necessary to establish: (a) that the conditions in CDDA, s 15(1) are satisfied;[383] (b) that the company owes a debt or has a liability to the relevant creditor; and (c) that the debt or liability was incurred at the relevant time.

(3) Compensation orders and undertakings

One of the major changes made by the SBEE Act 2015 was the introduction of compensa- **31.166** tion orders and undertakings. The court may make a compensation order against a person on the application of the Secretary of State if satisfied that the person is subject to a disqualification order or undertaking under the CDDA, and that the conduct for which the person is subject to the disqualification order or undertaking has caused loss to a creditor of an insolvent company of which the person has been a director.[384] It is also possible for a compensation order to be made against a person subject to a disqualification order under

---

[381] [2006] 1 BCLC 440.

[382] By analogy with the sort of declaration which might be granted to a co-surety: cf *Wolmerhausen v Gullick* [1893] 2 Ch 514.

[383] The judge seems to have contemplated that this might need to be established separately in each set of proceedings, but that if it was put in issue the claimant might seek permission to rely on a declaration under s 15 made in previous proceedings.

[384] CDDA, s 15A(3).

s 8ZA or 8ZD or a disqualification undertaking under s 8ZC or 8ZE.[385] The Secretary of State may also accept an undertaking instead of applying for an order.[386]

31.167 The Secretary of State may apply for a compensation order at any time within two years of the relevant disqualification order or undertaking.[387] Where a disqualification order has been made, the application for a compensation order must be made to the same court. In any other case, the application must be made to the High Court.[388]

31.168 A compensation order is defined in s 15B as an order to pay an amount specified in the order either to the Secretary of State (for the benefit of a creditor or creditors or a class or classes of creditor specified in the order) or as a contribution to the assets of a company specified in the order. A compensation undertaking is similarly defined. In determining the amount payable, the court (in the case of an order) or the Secretary of State (in the case of an undertaking) must have regard in particular to the amount of the loss caused, the nature of the conduct which caused the loss, and whether the person has made any other financial contribution in recompense for the conduct. Section 15C provides for the variation of a compensation undertaking on the application of the person subject to it.

31.169 The objective of compensation orders was described by the Insolvency Service in its impact assessment as being to 'effect a change of behaviour in directors by increasing the likelihood of culpable directors being called to account for their actions, whilst providing better recourse to creditors who have suffered'.[389] Whether this objective is achieved depends on how frequently these new provisions are used by the Secretary of State and how the courts respond to applications for compensation.

H. Applications for Leave

(1) Disqualification orders and undertakings

31.170 As set out above, a disqualification order is an order that the person will not act in the prohibited ways unless he has the leave of the court,[390] and there will be similar provision in an undertaking in the context of proceedings under CDDA, ss 5A, 7, 8, 8ZC, and 8ZE.[391]

31.171 Certain procedural aspects for applications for leave are to be found in CDDA, s 17 and further procedural provision is made by the Disqualification PD. It will often be convenient to make an application for leave at the time the original order is made, an approach which was endorsed by the Court of Appeal in *Re Dicetrade*[392] and *Re TLL Realisations Limited, Secretary of State for Trade and Industry v Collins*.[393] It will usually be in the director's interests because it avoids delay, and it will enable the judge who is familiar with the case to deal with the application. However, the

---

[385] CDDA, s 15A(6).
[386] CDDA, s 15A(2).
[387] CDDA, s 15A(5).
[388] CDDA, s 15A(7).
[389] Giving the court and Secretary of State a power to make a compensatory award against a director, Final Impact Assessment, 5 June 2014.
[390] CDDA, s 1(1)(a).
[391] CDDA, s 1A(1)(a), as amended by SBEE Act 2015, s 111, Sch 7, Pt 1, paras 1, 3(1), (2) as from 1 October 2015.
[392] [1994] 2 BCLC 113, CA, per Dillon LJ.
[393] [2000] 2 BCLC 223, CA, per Peter Gibson LJ.

fact that the court knows or expects that an application for leave will be made is not a reason for only imposing the minimum period of disqualification: the court starts with what it considers the appropriate period for the gravity of the allegations, and then proceeds to consider whether permission should be granted against that background.[394]

Where the disqualification order was made by a court with jurisdiction to wind up companies, **31.172** the application for permission is to be made to that court.[395] Where the order was made by a court without such jurisdiction (ie under CDDA, ss 2, 5), the application for permission is to be made to the court which would have had jurisdiction to wind up the company (or one of the companies) to which the offence related.[396]

Where an undertaking has been accepted by the Secretary of State (ie under CDDA, ss 5A, **31.173** 7, or 8), application for permission is to be made to a court to which the Secretary of State could have applied for a disqualification order.[397]

The Secretary of State is required to appear and call the attention of the court to any matters **31.174** which seem to him to be relevant,[398] except where the application was for a competition disqualification order under CDDA, s 9A.[399]

Where the undertaking was accepted by the Competition and Markets Authority or a speci- **31.175** fied regulator (ie under CDDA, s 9B), the application must be made to the High Court[400] and it is the duty of the regulator who originally applied for the order or accepted the under- taking to appear and call the attention of the court to any matters which appear to the regula- tor to be relevant.[401]

Applications for leave are governed by Part Four of the Disqualification PD. They are made **31.176** by a Part 8 Claim Form or by an application notice in existing proceedings, supported by affidavit evidence.[402] In the case of a competition disqualification order or undertaking, they are to be served on the relevant regulator; in other cases, they are to be served on the Secretary of State.[403]

Although the Secretary of State (or relevant regulator) is required to attend and draw the **31.177** court's attention to matters considered relevant, the court is not limited to considering those matters.[404] If the Secretary of State does not oppose the application, it will usually be suf- ficient for a letter to that effect to be provided to the court.[405]

In *Re Westmid Packing Services Ltd*,[406] the Court of Appeal offered guidance on the sort **31.178** of evidence which would be appropriate on an application for leave, saying that relevant

---

[394] *Re Westmid Packing Services Ltd* [1998] 2 All ER 124, CA.
[395] CDDA, s 17(1).
[396] CDDA, s 17(2).
[397] CDDA, s 17(3). For the court to which application should be made where an undertaking has been given under s 8ZC or 8ZE, see s 17(3ZA) or (3ZB).
[398] CDDA, s 17(5).
[399] CDDA, s 17(6).
[400] CDDA, s 17(3A).
[401] CDDA, s 17(7).
[402] Disqualification PD, paras 17.2 and 19.1.
[403] Disqualification PD, paras 20.1 and 20.2.
[404] *Secretary of State for Trade and Industry v Renwick* (unreported) July 1997.
[405] *Re Dicetrade Ltd* [1994] 2 BCLC 113, CA.
[406] [1998] 2 All ER 124, CA.

matters might include the director's general reputation and conduct in discharge of the office of director, his age and state of health, the length of time he had been in jeopardy, whether he had admitted the offence, his general conduct before and after the offence, and periods of disqualification of any co-directors that might have been ordered by other courts. But the court should adopt a broad-brush approach, so that detailed or repetitive evidence should not be allowed, and the citation of cases would in the great majority of cases be unnecessary and inappropriate. In *Secretary of State for Trade and Industry v Collins*,[407] Peter Gibson LJ said that the application for leave should be supported by clear evidence as to the precise role which the applicant would play in the company or companies in question and up-to-date and adequate information about that company or those companies.

31.179   The court will look closely at the conduct which led to disqualification[408] and the applicant will usually need to satisfy the court that the company in respect of which leave to act is sought is solvent and paying its debts as they fall due, and that its trading performance makes it unlikely that there will be any repetition of the misconduct which led to disqualification.[409] The applicant will also usually need to demonstrate that the company is up to date with its accounts and reporting requirements.

31.180   While each case will turn on its own particular facts, the importance of protecting the public from the consequences of possible future defaults will be a significant factor. It will be more likely that leave will be granted where the misconduct resulting in disqualification has been regarded as at the less serious end of the spectrum, particularly those cases where the disqualification period was five years or less. Guidance was given by Arden J in *Re Tech Textiles Ltd*:[410]

(1) The court must have regard to the purpose for which disqualification is imposed.[411] The purpose of s 6 is protective rather than penal, although the section also has a deterrent function.

(2) The court will have regard to two factors in particular: the protection of the public; and the need for the applicant to be a director.

(3) The 'public' for this purpose includes all relevant interest groups, such as shareholders, employees, lenders, customers and other creditors. The court must look at the grounds on which unfitness was found, and the view that the court took as to the character of the applicant, in particular his honesty, reliability and willingness to accept advice. The previous career of the applicant may also be relevant, for example, whether the applicant had had a previous disqualification order made against him.

---

[407] [2000] 2 BCLC 223, CA.

[408] See eg *Re Barings plc (No 5), Secretary of State for Trade and Industry v Baker* [2000] 1 WLR 634; *Re Morija* [2008] 2 BCLC 313, in which the judge set out a short summary of the established principles at paras 32–5 of his judgment.

[409] See eg *Secretary of State for Trade and Industry v Palfreman* [1995] BCC 193. Cf *Re Lombard Shipping & Forwarding Ltd* (unreported) Ch D 22 March 1993, in which an application for leave failed in part because one of the companies was having difficulties paying its rates bill.

[410] [1998] 1 BCLC 260, 267–9.

[411] This echoes what Sir Richard Scott V-C said in *Re Dawes & Henderson (Agencies) Ltd* [1999] 2 BCLC 317: 'In the present case, as in all cases, the reasons for the making of the disqualification order are of the greatest importance. The main reason why orders are made is for the protection of the public. An application under s 17 for leave always raises the question whether the grant of leave would be consistent with the need to protect the public.'

(4) 'Need' for this purpose, means practical need, for example where the involvement of the applicant in the capacity sought is vital to customer or investor confidence, or for some other sufficient reason.[412]

(5) As regards the company of which the applicant is to become a director, the court must consider the nature of the company's business, the size of the company, its financial position, the number of directors, the number of its employees and creditors, and the risks involved in the company's particular business. It must also look to see whether there is a potential for the matters which were held to constitute unfitness to recur.

(6) In many cases the applicant proposes that measures be put in place to protect the public and avoid recurrence, including the appointment of solicitors or accountants as directors, and the institution of a system for producing regular financial information.

(7) The court should also take into account all other relevant factors, such as the director's conduct since the matters which gave rise to the established grounds occurred, in particular since the proceedings for disqualification were begun. Thus if he has acted as a director while the proceedings were pending it will be relevant to see whether the companies have carried on business satisfactorily, for instance whether they are trading profitably, have complied with their obligations under relevant legislation and have paid liabilities as they fall due.

An order under s 17 gives leave only in respect of one or more specified companies, and may be subject to quite stringent conditions,[413] tailored to the circumstances of the particular case. Examples have included: a requirement that a named person remained a director with voting control,[414] a requirement that a chartered accountant act as co-director,[415] a ban (among other conditions) on signing cheques without a counter-signature,[416] a ban on loans to an associated company,[417] a requirement for prompt settlement of the company's debts and for regular management accounts to be prepared,[418] and restriction to performance in a subordinate capacity.[419] The court may grant leave for a time in order for specific acts to be carried out.[420] Where there is an issue as to the interpretation of an order giving leave, the normal principles of interpretation apply.[421] **31.181**

It appears that the court will not grant permission retrospectively where the applicant is subject to a disqualification order, because to do so might decriminalize past acts which would have been in breach of the restrictions.[422] **31.182**

---

[412] In *Re Streamhaven Ltd* [1998] 2 BCLC 64 Rattee J said that 'where the applicant concerned has been disqualified because of dishonesty, it is unlikely that his own needs will weigh very heavily, if at all, and it is unlikely that adequate protection to the public can be provided without the full and absolute operation of a disqualification order'. See however, R*e Liberty Holdings Unlimited and Copperidge Developments Ltd* (Chief Registrar Baister, 16 September 2015, unreported) where leave was granted to a director who had been disqualified under s 2 following his conviction and imprisonment for various dishonesty offences.

[413] *Re Westmid Packing Services Ltd* [1998] 2 All ER 124, CA; *Re Clenaware Systems Ltd* [2014] 1 BCLC 447.

[414] *Re Lo-Line Electric Motors Ltd* [1988] Ch 477.

[415] *Re Majestic Recording Studios Ltd* [1989] BCLC 1.

[416] *Re Gibson Davies Chemists Ltd* [1995] BCC 11.

[417] *Secretary of State for Trade and Industry v Arif* [1997] 1 BCLC 34.

[418] *Secretary of State for Trade and Industry v Rosenfield* [1999] BCC 413.

[419] *Re TLL Realisations Ltd* [2000] 2 BCLC 223, CA.

[420] *Secretary of State for BERR v Meade* [2011] All ER (D) 35 (Aug); *Re Portland Place (Historic House) Ltd* [2012] EWHC 4199 (Ch) (disqualified director given permission to instruct company to defend mortgage possession proceedings, where the company held the property on trust for the former director).

[421] *Feld v Secretary of State for BIS* [2014] 1 WLR 3396.

[422] *Re Brian Sheridan Cars Ltd* [1996] 1 BCLC 327.

(2) Bankruptcy

31.183   Equally, CDDA, s 11, which makes it an offence for a bankrupt (or a person subject to a bankruptcy restrictions order or undertaking, a debt relief restrictions order or undertaking, or to whom a moratorium period under a debt relief order applies) to act as a director, contemplates that the bankrupt may obtain the leave of the court to do so.[423] Where the person is an undischarged bankrupt, the application must be made to the court by which the person was adjudged bankrupt. Where the person is subject to a bankruptcy restrictions order or undertaking or a debt relief restrictions order or undertaking, the application must be made to the court which made the order or which has jurisdiction to annul the undertaking. Where there is a moratorium period, the application must be made to the court to which an application would be made under the Insolvency Act, s 251M(1).

31.184   In the case of an application for leave to act by an undischarged bankrupt, the court has no power to give leave unless notice of the application has been given to the official receiver, and if the official receiver is of the opinion that it is contrary to public interest for the application to be granted, it is his statutory duty to attend the hearing and oppose the application.[424] The applicable procedure is found in IR 6.202A–6.205.

31.185   Apart from the Australian case of *Re Altim Pty Ltd,* there is a dearth of authority on the approach of the court when considering an application under s 11. It is conceived that the court will adopt the same approach as in an application under s 17.

---

[423] CDDA, s 11(1); cf *Re McQuillan* (1989) 5 BCC 137 and the Australian case *Re Altim Pty Ltd* [1968] 2 NSWR 762.

[424] CDDA, s 11(3).

32

CIVIL PENALTIES FOR MARKET ABUSE

Glen Davis QC and Robert Amey

A. Introduction

(1) History of market abuse legislation

The English law of market abuse has a long history.[1] As early as 1285, brokers required a **32.01** license to practise in the City of London.[2] By the late seventeenth century, London was home to well-developed spot and futures markets, and the mis-selling of securities to unsophisticated investors was rife.[3] The preamble to a statute of 1697 complained that certain traders had 'unlawfully combined and confederated themselves together to raise or fall from time to time the Value of ... Stock and Bank Bills'.[4] This was injurious not only to the individuals

---

[1] For a more complete account, see Rider et al, *Guide to Financial Services Regulation* (3rd edn, 1997, CCH) Ch 1.

[2] Stat. Civitatis London: 13 Edw I stat 5: 'Ne nul abrocour ne seit denz la citee forceaus qe soent receuz e jures devant le gardeyn ou Meyre e Aldermans.'

[3] See the House of Commons Journal for 25 November 1696, which contains reports of the 'pernicious Art of Stock-jobbing', whereby shares were sold 'for much more than they are really worth' to 'ignorant Men, drawn in by the Reputation, falsly raised, and artfully spread, concerning the thriving State of their Stock'.

[4] Stat 8 & 9 Will III c 32, also known as An Act to restrain the number and ill practice of Brokers and Stock-jobbers.

deceived, but to market confidence generally. As the preamble noted, the unlawful manipulation of stock prices:

> ... is a very greate abuse ... and is extreamly prejudicial to the publick Creditt of this Kingdome and to the Trade and Comerce thereof and if not timely prevented may ruine the Creditt of the Nation and endanger the Government it selfe.[5]

The Act forbade brokers from acting as principals, required them to provide a £500 bond which would be forfeit in the event of misconduct, and to swear on oath that they would 'performe the Office and Employment of a Broker ... without Fraud or Collusion'.

32.02   The twentieth century saw a flurry of legislative activity. In the 1930s, committees chaired by Sir Archibald Bodkin and Sir Alan Anderson provided recommendations to Parliament[6] which ultimately led to the Prevention of Fraud (Investments) Act 1939. The 1939 Act was re-enacted with minor amendments under the same title in 1958. Secondary legislation passed pursuant to the 1958 Act introduced the concepts of the Chinese Wall, 'know your client' procedures and the obligation to follow 'good market practice'.[7]

32.03   In the 1980s, the UK securities markets underwent considerable modernization as Parliament intervened in what had previously been a largely self-governing industry. Concerns about restrictive practices led to the process known as 'Big Bang' in 1986. At the same time, a number of highly publicized mis-selling scandals led to Professor Gower's review of financial regulation, which ultimately led to the Financial Services Act 1986. The 1986 Act created the Securities and Investments Board, which in 1997 was re-named to become the Financial Services Authority.

32.04   On 1 December 2001, the 1986 Act was replaced by the Financial Services and Markets Act 2000. Significant amendments were later made to the FSMA regime in order to implement the Market Abuse Directive (2003/6/EC) ('MAD') on 1 July 2005.

(2) The pre-2016 FSMA regime

32.05   Since the current regime is the evolutionary successor to that introduced by MAD, it is worth examining briefly how the old regime operated. Market abuse was defined in FSMA, s 118 which described six[8] types of behaviour which would amount to market abuse, provided they occurred in relation to qualifying investments admitted to trading on a prescribed market, qualifying investments in respect of which a request for admission to trading on such a market had been made, or in certain cases, investments in relation to such qualifying investments. The six types of behaviour were:

(1) where an insider dealt, or attempted to deal, in a qualifying investment or related investment on the basis of inside information relating to the investment in question;

(2) where an insider disclosed inside information to another person otherwise than in the proper course of the exercise of his employment, profession, or duties;

---

[5] The Financial Services and Markets Tribunal gave a remarkably similar justification in its judgment in the *Philippe Jabre* case (10 July 2006): '*the reason why [insider dealing] is prohibited, is that it reduces confidence in the integrity and transparency of the market*'.

[6] Cmnd 5259 and Cmnd 5539.

[7] Licensed Dealers (Conduct of Business) Rules 1983 (SI 1983/585).

[8] Prior to 2014 there was an additional type of behaviour in s 118(4), which essentially amounted to acting upon inside information.

(3) where the behaviour consisted of effecting transactions or orders to trade (otherwise than for legitimate reasons and in conformity with accepted market practices on the relevant market) which gave, or were likely to give, a false or misleading impression as to the supply of, or demand for, or as to the price of, one or more qualifying investments, or secure the price of one or more such investments at an abnormal or artificial level;

(4) where the behaviour consisted of effecting transactions or orders to trade which employed fictitious devices or any other form of deception or contrivance;

(5) where the behaviour consisted of the dissemination of information by any means which gave, or was likely to give, a false or misleading impression as to a qualifying investment by a person who knew or could reasonably be expected to have known that the information was false or misleading; and

(6) where the behaviour was likely to give a regular user of the market a false or misleading impression as to the supply of, demand for, or price or value of, qualifying investments, or would be, or would be likely to be, regarded by a regular user of the market as behaviour that would distort, or would be likely to distort, the market in such an investment, and the behaviour was likely to be regarded by a regular user of the market as a failure on the part of the person concerned to observe the standard of behaviour reasonably expected of a person in his position in relation to the market.

Section 118A then contained supplementary provision about certain behaviour, s 118B **32.06** defined an 'insider', and s 118C defined 'inside information'. These three sections were inserted into FSMA as a direct consequence of MAD.

Section 119 obliged the FCA to issue a code containing such provisions as the FCA considered **32.07** would give appropriate guidance when determining whether or not behaviour amounted to market abuse, while sections 120–122 concerned the contents, procedure for issuing, and effect of that code. In early 2016, that code (the Code of Market Conduct) was contained in the FCA Handbook in the first chapter of the Market Conduct Sourcebook.[9] Sections 123–127 provided for FCA enforcement action against persons engaged in market abuse.

(3) 2016 reforms

On 3 July 2016, the Market Abuse Regulation ('MAR')[10] came into force[11] in the United **32.08** Kingdom. The relevant changes to domestic legislation were implemented by the Financial Services and Markets Act 2000 (Market Abuse) Regulations 2016, SI 2016/680 (the 'FSMA Regulations'), Regulation 3 of which designates the FCA as the UK's competent authority under MAR.

Since MAR is directly effective in the United Kingdom, ss 118–122 of FSMA are now **32.09** redundant, and have been repealed in their entirety.[12] The Code of Market Conduct has been replaced by a (significantly amended) chapter in the FCA Handbook simply entitled 'Market Abuse', reflecting the fact that the new chapter is simply non-binding guidance on the interpretation of MAR. In addition, the FSMA Regulations provide for further extensive

---

[9] The FCA website <https://www.handbook.fca.org.uk> contains a useful facility for viewing historic versions of the FCA Handbook and its predecessors as at any date from 1 June 2001 onwards.

[10] Regulation 596/2014, not to be confused with the FCA's Market Conduct Sourcebook, Chapter 1 of which contains guidance on the interpretation of the Regulation, and which is confusingly also known as MAR.

[11] Certain provisions relating to SMEs and OTFs came into force on 3 January 2017: Article 39(4).

[12] FSMA Regulations Reg 9(3).

amendments to FSMA and other primary and secondary legislation in order to comply with MAR.

32.10 The replacement of national primary and secondary legislation with a single Europe-wide legislative instrument was deliberate. MAR aims to create 'uniform rules and clarity of key concepts and a single rule book'[13] in order to 'avoid potential regulatory arbitrage'.[14]

32.11 MAR aims to establish a common regulatory framework on insider dealing, the unlawful disclosure of inside information and market manipulation (market abuse) as well as measures to prevent market abuse to ensure the integrity of financial markets in the Union and to enhance investor protection and confidence in those markets.[15]

32.12 The principal provisions of MAR which concern company directors are Articles 14–15. Article 14 provides that a person shall not:

    (a) engage or attempt to engage in insider dealing;
    (b) recommend that another person engage in insider dealing or induce another person to engage in insider dealing; or
    (c) unlawfully disclose inside information.

Article 15 provides that a person shall not engage in or attempt to engage in market manipulation.

(4) Scope of this chapter

32.13 MAR was enacted on the same day as the Directive on Criminal Sanctions for Market Abuse[16] ('CSMAD'). The new regime created by MAR and CSMAD is sometimes known as 'MAD II'. The United Kingdom has opted out of CSMAD and retains its own system of criminal sanctions for market abuse. For the criminal liability of directors engaged in market abuse, see Chapter 35, Section G below.

32.14 This chapter deals with the duties imposed on natural persons (who may or may not be company directors) by MAR, primarily the duties relevant to the directors of ordinary trading companies. Directors of companies whose business involves trading in financial instruments will be subject to considerable additional regulation. It goes without saying that in addition to the parts of MAR dealt with in this chapter, there is an enormous body of European and domestic law dealing with financial regulation which is outside the scope of this chapter.[17]

32.15 Similarly, conduct by a director which infringes MAR will very often also infringe some other legal rules which are outside the scope of this chapter. For example, a director who misuses inside information concerning the company of which he is a director in order to make a profit for himself not only breaches MAR, but may also be liable under the following heads:

    (1) breach of confidence;

---

[13] MAR recital 1.
[14] MAR recital 2.
[15] MAR article 1.
[16] 2014/57/EU.
[17] See Niamh Moloney, *EU Securities and Financial Markets Regulation* (3rd edn, OUP, 2014), and Barry Rider et al, *Market Abuse and Insider Dealing* (3rd edn, Tottel, 2016), both of which predate the coming into force of MAR but which nonetheless contain a valuable account of their respective areas.

(2) breach of contract to the extent that the misuse of inside information is prohibited by the contract;

(3) causing loss by unlawful means (or any of the other so-called 'economic torts'); and

(4) breach of the duties in ss 171–7 CA 2006.[18]

B. Market Abuse Regulation

MAR is substantially based on MAD and carries over a number of key concepts. However, **32.16** MAR also updates the EU market abuse framework by extending its scope to financial instruments traded on platforms other than regulated markets and over the counter and adapting rules to new technology and behaviour. It clarifies that market abuse occurring across spot commodity and related derivative markets is prohibited and tailors the rules for SME issuers.

MAR defines market abuse as 'a concept that encompasses unlawful behaviour in the finan- **32.17** cial markets' which consists of 'insider dealing, unlawful disclosure of inside information and market manipulation'.[19]

The essential characteristic of insider dealing, according to MAR, consists in an unfair **32.18** advantage being obtained from inside information to the detriment of third parties who are unaware of such information and, consequently, the undermining of the integrity of financial markets and investor confidence.[20]

MAR applies to financial instruments[21] whether: **32.19**

(1) admitted to trading on a regulated market[22] or for which a request for admission to trading on a regulated market has been made;

(2) traded on an MTF,[23] admitted to trading on an MTF or for which a request for admission to trading on an MTF has been made;

(3) traded on an OTF[24]; or

---

[18] See Part III, Chapters 10–18 above.

[19] MAR recital 7.

[20] MAR recital 23.

[21] MAR also applies to behaviour or transactions relating to the market of emission allowances or other auctioned products based thereon. The specific provisions of MAR dealing with abuse of the markets for emission allowances and related products are unlikely to be relevant to most company directors and are therefore not dealt with in detail in this chapter. As a general rule, that conduct which would amount to abuse of the market for financial instruments is also likely to be abusive if carried out in relation to the market for emission allowances.

[22] MAR Art 3(1) point (6), which refers to Article 4(1) point (21) of Directive 2014/65/EU (also known as MiFID II). A regulated market is a multilateral system operated and/or managed by a market operator, which brings together or facilitates the bringing together of multiple third-party buying and selling interests in financial instruments—in the system and in accordance with its non-discretionary rules—in a way that results in a contract, in respect of the financial instruments admitted to trading under its rules and/or systems, and which is authorized and functions regularly and in accordance with Title III of MiFID II.

[23] Multilateral trading facility, see MAR Art 3(1) point (7), which refers to Article 4(1) point (22) of Directive 2014/65/EU (also known as MiFID II). An MTF is a multilateral system, operated by an investment firm or a market operator, which brings together multiple third-party buying and selling interests in financial instruments—in the system and in accordance with non-discretionary rules—in a way that results in a contract in accordance with Title II of MiFID II.

[24] Organized trading facility, see MAR Art 3(1) point (8), which refers to Article 4(1) point (23) of Directive 2014/65/EU (also known as MiFID II). An OTF is a multilateral system which is not a regulated market or an MTF and in which multiple third-party buying and selling interests in bonds, structured finance products,

(4) not covered by point (a), (b) or (c), the price or value of which depends on or has an effect on the price or value of a financial instrument referred to in those points, including, but not limited to, credit default swaps and contracts for difference.

32.20 Financial instruments are defined as the following:[25]

(1) Transferable securities;

(2) Money-market instruments;

(3) Units in collective investment undertakings;

(4) Options, futures, swaps, forward rate agreements, and any other derivative contracts relating to securities, currencies, interest rates or yields, emission allowances or other derivatives instruments, financial indices or financial measures which may be settled physically or in cash;

(5) Options, futures, swaps, forwards, and any other derivative contracts relating to commodities that must be settled in cash or may be settled in cash at the option of one of the parties other than by reason of default or other termination event;

(6) Options, futures, swaps, and any other derivative contract relating to commodities that can be physically settled provided that they are traded on a regulated market, a MTF, or an OTF, except for wholesale energy products traded on an OTF that must be physically settled;

(7) Options, futures, swaps, forwards, and any other derivative contracts relating to commodities, that can be physically settled not otherwise mentioned in point 6 of this Section and not being for commercial purposes, which have the characteristics of other derivative financial instruments;

(8) Derivative instruments for the transfer of credit risk;

(9) Financial contracts for differences;

(10) Options, futures, swaps, forward rate agreements, and any other derivative contracts relating to climatic variables, freight rates, or inflation rates, or other official economic statistics that must be settled in cash or may be settled in cash at the option of one of the parties other than by reason of default or other termination event, as well as any other derivative contracts relating to assets, rights, obligations, indices, and measures not otherwise mentioned in this Section, which have the characteristics of other derivative financial instruments, having regard to whether, inter alia, they are traded on a regulated market, OTF, or an MTF;

(11) Emission allowances consisting of any units recognized for compliance with the requirements of Directive 2003/87/EC (Emissions Trading Scheme).

C. Unlawful Disclosure of Inside Information

(1) The general prohibition

32.21 Unlawful disclosure of inside information is prohibited by Article 14 subparagraph (c).

---

emission allowances or derivatives are able to interact in the system in a way that results in a contract in accordance with Title II of MiFID II.

[25] MAR Art 3(1) point (1), which refers to Article 4(1) of Directive 2014/65/EU (also known as MiFID II).

(2) What is inside information?

The definition of inside information under MAR is broadly the same as it was under MAD **32.22** (and so authorities decided under the old regime will continue to be of assistance) but has been widened to capture inside information for spot commodity contracts. In general, precise information which is not public but which if public would be likely to have a significant effect on the price of a financial instrument will be inside information.

The FCA Handbook, MAR1.2.12 lists a number of factors to be taken into account in deter- **32.23** mining whether or not information has been made public, such as whether the information has been disclosed to a prescribed market through a regulatory information service, whether the information is contained in records which are open to inspection by the public and whether the information can be obtained by lawful observation by the public.

MAR Article 7 identifies four types of information. **32.24**

(i) Information relating to financial instruments

This is information of a precise nature,[26] which has not been made public, relating, directly **32.25** or indirectly, to one or more issuers or to one or more financial instruments,[27] and which, if it were made public, would be likely to have a significant effect on the prices of those financial instruments or on the price of related derivative financial instruments.[28]

Information is of a precise nature if it indicates a set of circumstances which exists or which **32.26** may reasonably be expected to come into existence, or an event which has occurred or which may reasonably be expected to occur, where it is specific enough to enable a conclusion to be drawn as to the possible effect of that set of circumstances or event on the prices of the financial instruments, related derivative financial instrument, or related spot commodity contracts. In this respect, in the case of a protracted process that is intended to bring about, or that results in, particular circumstances or a particular event, those future circumstances or that future event, and also the intermediate steps of that process which are connected with bringing about or resulting in those future circumstances or that future event, may be deemed to be precise information.

In a case under the old regime, it was held that information can be of a precise nature even **32.27** though it is inaccurate.[29] It has also been held that information will be 'specific' unless it is so vague or general that it is impossible to draw a conclusion as regards its possible effect on the price; it is not even necessary for the information to indicate that the price will move in a particular direction.[30] There is no reason to suppose that the position will be any different under MAR.

As for the definition of information 'which, if it were made public, would be likely to have a **32.28** significant effect on the prices of those financial instruments or on the price of related derivative financial instruments', this is information that a reasonable investor would be likely to use as part of the basis of his investment decisions.[31] The assessment is to be made on the

---

[26] As to which, see paras 32.26–32.27.
[27] As to which, see para 32.20.
[28] As to which, see para 32.28.
[29] *Hannam v FCA* [2014] UKUT 233 (TCC); [2014] Lloyd's Rep FC 704 at para 71.
[30] C-628/13 *Lafonta v Autorité des marchés financiers* [2015] Bus LR 483.
[31] MAR Article 7(4). This mirrors the interpretation placed on the corresponding provision of MAD in *Hannam v FCA* at para 100. In the same case at para 121, it was held that 'likely' is to be read as meaning that

basis of the ex ante available information, taking into consideration the anticipated impact of the information in light of the totality of the related issuer's activity, the reliability of the source of information and any other market variables likely to affect the financial instruments or the related spot commodity contracts.[32] Ex post information can be used to check the presumption that the ex ante information was price sensitive, but should not be used to take action against persons who drew reasonable conclusions from ex ante information available to them.[33]

(ii) Information relating to commodity derivatives

32.29 This is information of a precise nature,[34] which has not been made public, relating, directly or indirectly to one or more commodity derivatives or relating directly to the related spot commodity contract, and which, if it were made public, would be likely to have a significant effect on the prices of such derivatives or related spot commodity contracts,[35] and where this is information which is reasonably expected to be disclosed or is required to be disclosed in accordance with legal or regulatory provisions at the Union or national level, market rules, contract, practice, or custom, on the relevant commodity derivatives markets or spot markets.

32.30 A commodity derivative is an instrument giving the right to acquire or sell any commodity or giving rise to a cash settlement determined by reference to commodities or other indices or measures.[36]

(iii) Information relating to emission allowances

32.31 This is information of a precise nature[37] in relation to emission allowances or auctioned products based thereon, which has not been made public, relating, directly or indirectly, to one or more such instruments, and which, if it were made public, would be likely to have a significant effect on the prices of such instruments or on the prices of related derivative financial instruments.[38] Emission allowances are any units recognized for compliance with the requirements of Directive 2003/87/EC (Emissions Trading Scheme).[39]

(iv) Information provided by a client to a broker

32.32 This is information conveyed, to a person charged with the execution of orders concerning financial instruments, by a client and relating to the client's pending orders in financial instruments, which is of a precise nature,[40] relating, directly or indirectly, to one or more issuers or

---

there is a 'real prospect' the information having a significant effect on price (which in turn means having a more than de minimis effect).

[32] MAR recital 14.
[33] MAR recital 15.
[34] As to which, see paras 32.26–32.27.
[35] As to which, see para 32.28.
[36] MAR Article 3(1) point (24), which refers to point (30) of Article 2(1) of Regulation (EU) No 600/2014 (MiFIR II), which refers to point (44)(c) of Article 4(1) and Section C of Annex I of Directive 2014/65/EU (MiFID II).
[37] As to which, see paras 32.26–32.27.
[38] As to which, see para 32.28.
[39] MAR Article 3(1) point (19), which refers to point (11) of Section C of Annex I to Directive 2014/65/EU (MiFID II).
[40] As to which, see paras 32.26–32.27.

to one or more financial instruments,[41] and which, if it were made public, would be likely to have a significant effect on the prices of those financial instruments, the price of related spot commodity contracts, or on the price of related derivative financial instruments.[42]

(3) When is disclosure unlawful?

Disclosure will be unlawful where a person possesses inside information and discloses that **32.33** information to any other person, except where the disclosure is made in the normal exercise of an employment, a profession, or duties.[43] It is also unlawful to pass on a recommendation or an inducement to trade where the recommendation or inducement is based on inside information, and the person passing on the recommendation or inducement knows the same.[44]

So if a director of a listed company became aware of a takeover offer received by the company **32.34** which is likely to cause the share price to increase when the offer is announced, he would obviously be guilty of unlawful disclosure of inside information if he shared this informa-tion with a friend, even if he did not expect the friend to deal based on the information.[45] If he told his friend instead that the friend should purchase some shares in the company, but offered no explanation at all for his recommendation, this would not itself be a disclosure of inside information, but it would be an inducement to engage in insider dealing.[46] If, how-ever, the friend, knowing that the recommendation was based on inside information, passed the recommendation to her husband so that he could trade, she would be guilty of unlawful disclosure of inside information.

If, however, a passenger on a train passing a burning factory calls his broker and tells him **32.35** to sell shares in the factory's owner, the passenger will not be using inside information. This information has been obtained by legitimate means through observation of a public event.[47]

(4) Market soundings

There was some concern at the drafting stage that market soundings could be inadvert- **32.36** ently caught within the definition of unlawful disclosure. Market soundings are defined in MAR as interactions between a seller of financial instruments and one or more potential investors, prior to the announcement of a transaction, in order to gauge the interest of potential investors in a possible transaction and its pricing, size, and structuring. They can

---

[41] As to which, see para 32.20.

[42] As to which, see para 32.28.

[43] Disclosure to a government department, the Bank of England, the Competition Commission, or any other regulatory body or authority in connection with the performance of the functions of that body or author-ity is deemed to be in the normal exercise of a person's duties: FCA Handbook MAR1.4.3. For an example of unlawful disclosure under the old regime, see *Hannam v FCA* [2014] UKUT 233 (TCC); [2014] Lloyd's Rep FC 704, where the Chairman of Capital Markets at J P Morgan, and Global Co-Head of UK Capital Markets at J P Morgan Cazenove was fined £450,000 after sending an email to a business contact. In that case, it was held at para 122 that the FCA had the burden of proving that the disclosure was outside the course of Mr Hannam's employment, profession, or duties.

[44] MAR Article 10.

[45] See FCA Handbook MAR1.4.2.

[46] See para 32.45.

[47] This example is taken from the FCA Handbook, MAR1.2.14.

involve an initial or secondary offer of relevant securities, and are distinct from ordinary trading.[48]

32.37 According to MAR, market soundings are a highly valuable tool to gauge the opinion of potential investors, enhance shareholder dialogue, ensure that deals run smoothly, and that the views of issuers, existing shareholders and potential new investors are aligned. They may be particularly beneficial when markets lack confidence or a relevant benchmark, or are volatile, and the ability to conduct market soundings is important for the proper functioning of financial markets.[49]

32.38 However, market soundings can involve the disclosure of inside information. Accordingly, MAR provides that the disclosure of inside information in the context of a market sounding shall not be unlawful provided the requirements of the Regulation are followed.

32.39 In order that the disclosure of inside information made in the course of a market sounding be deemed to be made in the normal exercise of a person's employment, profession or duties, the disclosing market participant must comply with the following requirements.

32.40 That person must, prior to conducting a market sounding, specifically consider whether the market sounding will involve the disclosure of inside information, and make a written record of its conclusion and the reasons therefor, providing such written records to the FCA upon request. This obligation shall apply to each disclosure of information throughout the course of the market sounding, and the written records must be updated accordingly. The person must also:

(1) obtain the consent of the person receiving the market sounding to receive inside information;[50]

(2) inform the person receiving the market sounding that he is prohibited from using that information, or attempting to use that information, by acquiring or disposing of, for his own account or for the account of a third party, directly or indirectly, financial instruments relating to that information;

(3) inform the person receiving the market sounding that he is prohibited from using that information, or attempting to use that information, by cancelling or amending an order which has already been placed concerning a financial instrument to which the information relates; and

(4) inform the person receiving the market sounding that by agreeing to receive the information he is obliged to keep the information confidential.

The disclosing market participant must make and maintain a record of all information given to the person receiving the market sounding, and the identity of the potential investors to whom the information has been disclosed, including but not limited to the legal and natural persons acting on behalf of the potential investor, and the date and time of each disclosure. He must provide that record to the FCA upon request.

---

[48] MAR recital 32.

[49] MAR recital 33.

[50] For a case where a person receiving inside information had specifically asked not to be 'wall-crossed' and refused to sign a non-disclosure agreement, but was nonetheless fined (along with his fund) a total of £7.2 million after he was provided with inside information against his will and traded as a result of that information, see *FSA v Einhorn* (FSA Final Notice, 15 February 2012).

D. Insider Dealing

(1) The general prohibition

Insider dealing and attempted insider dealing are prohibited by Article 14 subparagraph (a). **32.41**
Recommending that another person engage in insider dealing or inducing another person to
engage in insider dealing are prohibited by Article 14 subparagraph (b).

(2) What is insider dealing?

The definition of insider dealing under MAR is broadly the same as it was under MAD, **32.42**
except that it is clarified that use of inside information to amend or cancel an order shall be
considered to be insider dealing.

Insider dealing occurs where a person possesses inside information[51] and uses that **32.43**
information by acquiring or disposing of, for its own account or for the account of a
third party, directly or indirectly, financial instruments[52] to which that information
relates. The use of inside information by cancelling or amending an order concerning
a financial instrument to which the information relates where the order was placed
before the person concerned possessed the inside information, is also considered to be
insider dealing.

Where a person in possession of inside information deals in a related financial instrument, **32.44**
there is a rebuttable presumption that the inside information was used for the purpose of
dealing.[53] This reflects the position under MAD.[54] The presumption can be rebutted if the
dealer proves that he was engaged in 'legitimate behaviour'.[55]

A person recommends that another person engage in insider dealing where, being in posses- **32.45**
sion of inside information, he recommends, on the basis of that information, that another
person acquire or dispose of financial instruments or cancel or amend an order concerning a
financial instrument, to which that information relates. A person induces another person to
engage in insider dealing where, being in possession of inside information, he induces that
other person, on the basis of that information, to acquire or dispose of financial instruments
or to cancel or amend an order concerning a financial instrument, to which that information
relates.[56]

It is easy to see how a director might commit the latter type of conduct. Suppose a director **32.46**
of a listed company is aware of a takeover offer received by the company which is likely to
cause the share price to increase when the offer is announced. He would probably know that
he should not deal in the company's shares himself on the basis of this information. He may
also know that he must not share his knowledge of the takeover bid with his friends. But he

---

[51] See paras 32.25–32.28.
[52] As to which, see para 32.20.
[53] Recital 24.
[54] *C-45/08: Spector Photo Group and Van Raemdonck* [2011] BCC 827.
[55] See para 32.47 *et seq*.
[56] For a case under the old regime where a broker in possession of inside information advised his client to
place a trade, see *FSA v Shah* (FSA Decision Notice, 8 February 2013). In that case, the client did not know that
Mr Shah had inside information, but Mr Shah was fined £125,000 nonetheless because his recommendation
was based on inside information.

would also be liable under MAR if he simply advised his friends to purchase shares in the company, even if he did not explain why.

(3) Legitimate behaviour

32.47 Article 9 describes a number of situations in which a person who deals while in possession of inside information can rebut the presumption that he used the inside information. There are, for example, exceptions for non-natural persons who have implemented proper internal procedures to prevent market abuse,[57] and for market makers and execution-only brokers carrying out their activities in the normal course of their business.[58]

32.48 The most relevant examples for directors are as follows.

32.49 A person may well come into possession of inside information after he has entered into a contractual or other obligation to execute a trade, but before he has executed the trade. Clearly, if he then executes the trade, it should not be presumed that he is engaged in insider dealing. Accordingly, a person who trades while in possession of inside information because he came under an obligation to trade before he possessed inside information shall not be deemed to be engaged in insider dealing.[59]

32.50 In the context of a merger or acquisition, the directors of the acquirer will come into possession of information concerning the target company in the course of conducting due diligence which is not in the public domain. Insider dealing restrictions were never meant to catch such situations. Accordingly, where a person obtains inside information in the conduct of a public takeover or merger with a company and uses that inside information solely for the purpose of proceeding with that merger or public takeover, he shall not be deemed to be engaged in insider dealing, provided that at the point of approval of the merger or acceptance of the offer by the shareholders of that company, any inside information has been made public or has otherwise ceased to constitute inside information.[60] This exemption does not apply to stake-building.[61]

32.51 A person who has decided to dispose of or acquire financial instruments in large volume possesses inside information that is likely to affect the price of that instrument: he knows that his own transaction is about to take place. It would be absurd if he was prohibited from using this information when deciding how to place the relevant trades. Accordingly, a person in such a position does not commit insider dealing where he uses his own knowledge in placing the trade.[62]

32.52 All of these exceptions are subject to another exception: insider dealing may still be deemed to have occurred if the FCA establishes that there was an illegitimate reason for the orders to trade, transactions, or behaviours concerned.[63] FCA Handbook MAR1.3.15 contains a list of factors which may be taken into account in determining whether a person's behaviour is

---

[57] Article 9(1).
[58] Article 9(2).
[59] Article 9(3).
[60] Article 9(4).
[61] Defined as 'an acquisition of securities in a company which does not trigger a legal or regulatory obligation to make an announcement of a takeover bid in relation to that company': Article 3(1) point (31).
[62] Article 9(5).
[63] Article 9(6).

carried out legitimately in the normal course of that person's duties, including whether the person has complied with other regulatory duties and whether his behaviour was reasonable by the proper standards of conduct of the market concerned.

(4) Safe harbours

The prohibition of insider dealing does not apply to trading in own shares in buy-back pro- **32.53** grammes or trading in securities or associated instruments for the stabilization of securities when the conditions in MAR are met.[64]

For a buy-back programme, those conditions are satisfied where: **32.54**
(1) the full details of the programme are disclosed prior to the start of trading;
(2) trades are reported as being part of the buy-back programme to the FCA in accordance with Articles 25–26 of MiFIR and subsequently disclosed to the public;
(3) adequate limits with regard to price and volume are complied with; and
(4) it is carried out in accordance with the regulatory technical standards specified by ESMA and with the sole purpose of:
   (a) reducing the capital of an issuer;
   (b) meeting obligations arising from debt financial instruments that are exchangeable into equity instruments; or
   (c) meeting obligations arising from share option programmes, or other allocations of shares, to employees or to members of the administrative, management, or supervisory bodies of the issuer or of an associate company.

For a stabilization programme, those conditions are satisfied where: **32.55**

(1) stabilization is carried out for a limited period;
(2) relevant information about the stabilization is disclosed and notified to the FCA no later than the end of the seventh daily market session following the date of execution;
(3) adequate limits with regard to price are complied with; and
(4) such trading complies with the conditions for stabilization laid down in the regulatory technical standards specified by ESMA.

E. Market Manipulation

(1) The general prohibition

Market manipulation is prohibited by Article 15. The Regulation expressly provides that **32.56** where a non-natural person carries out market manipulation, the natural persons who participate in the decision to carry out activities for the account of the non-natural person shall also be liable.[65]

(2) What is market manipulation?

Under MAR, market manipulation comprises the following activities:[66] **32.57**

---

[64] Article 5.
[65] Article 12(4).
[66] Article 12(1).

(1) entering into a transaction, placing an order to trade or any other behaviour which:

    (a) gives, or is likely to give, false or misleading signals as to the supply of, demand for, or price of, a financial instrument or a related spot commodity contract; or

    (b) secures, or is likely to secure, the price of one or several financial instruments or a related spot commodity contract at an abnormal or artificial level;

    unless the person entering into a transaction, placing an order to trade, or engaging in any other behaviour establishes that such transaction, order, or behaviour have been carried out for legitimate reasons, and conform with an accepted market practice as established in accordance with Article 13;

(2) entering into a transaction, placing an order to trade, or any other activity or behaviour which affects or is likely to affect the price of one or several financial instruments or a related spot commodity contract, which employs a fictitious device or any other form of deception or contrivance;

(3) disseminating information through the media, including the internet, or by any other means, which gives, or is likely to give, false or misleading signals as to the supply of, demand for, or price of, a financial instrument or a related spot commodity contract, or is likely to secure, the price of one or several financial instruments or a related spot commodity contract at an abnormal or artificial level, including the dissemination of rumours, where the person who made the dissemination knew, or ought to have known, that the information was false or misleading; or

(4) transmitting false or misleading information or providing false or misleading inputs in relation to a benchmark where the person who made the transmission or provided the input knew or ought to have known that it was false or misleading, or any other behaviour which manipulates the calculation of a benchmark.

32.58 Suppose that a director of a listed company wished to inflate the value of the company's shares for his own reasons, and so he spreads false rumours that the company will soon announce a takeover bid which will result in the share price increasing. This would be an obvious example of market manipulation.

(3) Indicia of market manipulation

32.59 The Regulation gives a non-exhaustive list of indicia of market manipulation.

32.60 The following behaviour is market manipulation where it has, or is likely to have, the effect of fixing, directly or indirectly, purchase or sale prices or creates, or is likely to create, other unfair trading conditions, or has or is likely to have the effect of misleading investors acting on the basis of the prices displayed, including the opening or closing prices:

(1) the conduct by a person, or persons acting in collaboration, to secure a dominant position over the supply of, or demand for, a financial instrument or related spot commodity contracts;

(2) the buying or selling of financial instruments, at the opening or closing of the market, which has or is likely to have the effect of misleading investors acting on the basis of the prices displayed, including the opening or closing prices;[67]

---

[67] For an example of this conduct under the old regime, see the case of *Rameshkumar Goenka* (Final Notice, 17 October 2011), who was fined nearly $10 million for placing very large trades a few seconds before the close

(3) the placing of orders to a trading venue, including any cancellation or modification thereof, by any available means of trading, including by electronic means, such as algorithmic and high-frequency trading strategies, by:

    (a) disrupting or delaying the functioning of the trading system of the trading venue or being likely to do so;

    (b) making it more difficult for other persons to identify genuine orders on the trading system of the trading venue or being likely to do so, including by entering orders which result in the overloading or destabilization of the order book; or

    (c) creating or being likely to create a false or misleading signal about the supply of, or demand for, or price of, a financial instrument, in particular by entering orders to initiate or exacerbate a trend.[68]

Other behaviour which will amount to market abuse includes the taking advantage of occasional or regular access to the traditional or electronic media by voicing an opinion about a financial instrument or related spot commodity contract (or indirectly about its issuer) while having previously taken positions on that financial instrument or related spot commodity contract and profiting subsequently from the impact of the opinions voiced on the price of that instrument or spot commodity contract, without having simultaneously disclosed that conflict of interest to the public in a proper and effective way. **32.61**

MAR Annex I sets out further factors which, while not on their own constituting market manipulation, are to be taken into account when considering whether transactions or orders to trade constitute market manipulation. These factors relate to false or misleading signals, price securing, and employment of fictitious devices or other forms of deception or contrivance. They are most likely to be of interest to persons who trade professionally in financial instruments and are unlikely to be relevant to the directors of most companies. **32.62**

(4) Accepted market practices

The FCA is empowered by Article 13 to adopt established market practices. If behaviour described in paragraph 32.57 above, which would otherwise be considered market manipulation, conforms with such an established market practice and has been carried out for legitimate reasons, it will not constitute market manipulation. **32.63**

F. Managers' Transactions

(1) The obligation to disclose

As the preamble to MAR states, requiring persons discharging managerial responsibilities ('PDMRs') to disclose trades made on their own account, or by a person closely associated **32.64**

---

of the market, not for legitimate reasons, but in order to increase the closing price of the relevant instrument above a certain level so as to receive a payment under the terms of a structured product.

[68] For an example under the old regime involving so-called 'layering' or 'spoofing', see *7722656 Canada Inc (formerly Swift Trade Inc) v FSA* [2013] EWCA Civ 1662; [2014] Lloyd's Rep FC 207 where the FSA imposed a fine of £8 million, and the case of *Michael Coscia* (FCA Final Notice, 3 July 2013), a high-frequency trader who was fined over US$900 million. This case gives a definition of 'layering' and 'spoofing' at para 6, from which, in *FCA v Da Vinci Invest Ltd* [2016] Bus LR 274 Snowden J at para 22 said that 'the term "layering" refers to the placing of multiple orders that are designed not to trade on one side of the order book, and the term "spoofing" refers to the fact that the placing of such orders creates a false impression as to the person's true trading intentions.'

with them, is not only valuable information for market participants, but also constitutes an additional means for competent authorities to supervise markets.[69] Accordingly, PDMRs must notify the issuer and the FCA of every transaction conducted on their own account relating to the shares or debt instruments of that issuer or to derivatives or other financial instruments linked thereto within three business days.[70]

(2) What types of transaction should be disclosed?

32.65   Included in the definition of notifiable transactions are:

(1) pledging or lending of financial instruments by or on behalf of a PDMR or a person closely associated with a PDMR;

(2) transactions undertaken on behalf of a PDMR or closely associated person by another person, including where that other person has a discretion; and

(3) transactions made under a life insurance policy where the policyholder is a PDMR or closely associated person who bears the investment risk and who has the power or discretion to make investment decisions or to execute transactions regarding specific instruments in that life insurance policy.

32.66   There are two important qualifications to the obligation to disclose which mean that, in practice, the vast majority of transactions by company directors will not have to be disclosed.

(1) The disclosure obligation only applies in respect of issuers who have requested or approved admission of their financial instruments to trading on a regulated market; or in the case of an instrument only traded on an MTF[71] or an OTF,[72] have approved trading of their financial instruments on an MTF or an OTF or have requested admission to trading of their financial instruments on an MTF.

(2) There is a de minimis threshold of €5,000 per calendar year, which is calculated by adding without netting all notifiable transactions.[73] Accordingly, a director who buys €2,500 of shares in the company of which he is a director and then sells those shares in the same calendar year must make a notification, but if he held the shares until the next calendar year before disposing of them, he would not need to make a notification.

(3) Managers' transactions during the closed period

32.67   The 30 calendar days preceding the announcement of an interim financial report or a year-end report which the issuer is obliged to make public according to stock market rules or national law is a particularly sensitive time. Interim financial reports and year-end reports often have a significant effect on the securities issued by the company making the report, and immediately before the report is made, the company's directors are likely to be in possession of particularly sensitive inside information.

32.68   Accordingly, that period is known as the 'closed period' during which a PDMR shall not conduct any transactions on his own account or for the account of a third party, directly or

---

[69] Recital 59.

[70] Article 19(1).

[71] See fn 23.

[72] See fn 24.

[73] Article 19(8). Member states have the option of increasing the threshold to €20,000, although the FCA has indicated an intention not to do this: CP15/35.

indirectly, relating to the shares or debt instruments of the issuer or to derivatives or other financial instruments linked to them.[74]

However, the strictness of that rule is tempered by an exception allowing the issuer to permit a PDMR to trade during a closed period either: **32.69**

(1) on a case-by-case basis due to the existence of exceptional circumstances, such as severe financial difficulty, which require the immediate sale of shares; or
(2) due to the characteristics of the trading involved for transactions made under, or related to, an employee share or saving scheme, qualification or entitlement of shares, or transactions where the beneficial interest in the relevant security does not change.

G. Sanctions

(1) Relevant provisions of MAR

The question of precisely what sanction results from market abuse is left by MAR to Member States. In the UK, the sanctions most likely to be applied for market abuse are as set out in FSMA ss 56, 66, 123–123C, 129, and 380–82 (discussed at paragraph 32.75 *et seq* below). However, since domestic law will inevitably fall to be construed consistently with EU law, it is helpful to give a brief overview of the relevant provisions of MAR. **32.70**

MAR obliges Member States to make available the following sanctions for market abuse:[75] **32.71**

(1) an order requiring the person responsible for the infringement to cease the conduct and to desist from a repetition of that conduct;
(2) the disgorgement of the profits gained or losses avoided due to the infringement insofar as they can be determined;
(3) a public warning which indicates the person responsible for the infringement and the nature of the infringement;
(4) withdrawal or suspension of the authorization of an investment firm;
(5) a temporary ban of a person discharging managerial responsibilities within an investment firm or any other natural person, who is held responsible for the infringement, from exercising management functions in investment firms;
(6) in the event of repeated infringements of Article 14 or 15, a permanent ban of any person discharging managerial responsibilities within an investment firm or any other natural person who is held responsible for the infringement, from exercising management functions in investment firms;
(7) a temporary ban of a person discharging managerial responsibilities within an investment firm or another natural person who is held responsible for the infringement, from dealing on own account;
(8) maximum administrative pecuniary sanctions of at least three times the amount of the profits gained or losses avoided because of the infringement, where those can be determined;
(9) in respect of a natural person, maximum administrative pecuniary sanctions of at least:

---

[74] Article 11.
[75] Article 30.

(a) for infringements of Articles 14 and 15, €5 million or in the Member States whose currency is not the euro, the corresponding value in the national currency on 2 July 2014;

(b) for infringements of Articles 16 and 17, €1 million or in the Member States whose currency is not the euro, the corresponding value in the national currency on 2 July 2014; and

(c) for infringements of Articles 18, 19, and 20, €500,000 or in the Member States whose currency is not the euro, the corresponding value in the national currency on 2 July 2014; and

(10) in respect of legal persons, maximum administrative pecuniary sanctions of at least:

(a) for infringements of Articles 14 and 15, €15 million or 15 per cent of the total annual turnover of the legal person according to the last available accounts approved by the management body, or in the Member States whose currency is not the euro, the corresponding value in the national currency on 2 July 2014;

(b) for infringements of Articles 16 and 17, €2.5 million or 2 per cent of its total annual turnover according to the last available accounts approved by the management body, or in the Member States whose currency is not the euro, the corresponding value in the national currency on 2 July 2014; and

(c) for infringements of Articles 18, 19, and 20, €1million or in the Member States whose currency is not the euro, the corresponding value in the national currency on 2 July 2014.

32.72 When determining what sanction to impose, the FCA must take into account all relevant circumstances, including, where appropriate:[76]

(1) the gravity and duration of the infringement;

(2) the degree of responsibility of the person responsible for the infringement;

(3) the financial strength of the person responsible for the infringement, as indicated, for example, by the total turnover of a legal person or the annual income of a natural person;

(4) the importance of the profits gained or losses avoided by the person responsible for the infringement, insofar as they can be determined;

(5) the level of cooperation of the person responsible for the infringement with the competent authority, without prejudice to the need to ensure disgorgement of profits gained or losses avoided by that person;

(6) previous infringements by the person responsible for the infringement; and

(7) measures taken by the person responsible for the infringement to prevent its repetition.

32.73 The FCA is obliged to advertise the imposition of a sanction on its website for a minimum period of five years.[77] The publication of such information often causes considerable embarrassment to the individuals concerned, it may be possible to obtain an interim

---

[76] Article 31.
[77] Article 34.

injunction restraining publication until after any reference to the Upper Tribunal has been determined.[78]

In a case under the old regime, it was held that the burden of proof is on the FCA, and the **32.74** standard of proof is the ordinary civil standard (the balance of probabilities) rather than the criminal standard (beyond reasonable doubt).[79] There is no reason to believe that the position will be any different under MAR.

(2) Administrative sanctions under FSMA

Administrative sanctions for market abuse are as set out in FSMA ss 123–123C. **32.75**

Where the FCA is satisfied that a person has: **32.76**

(1) contravened Article 14 (insider dealing[80] and unlawful disclosure of inside information[81]) or Article 15 (market manipulation[82]) of MAR,
(2) contravened, or been knowingly concerned in the contravention of some other provision of MAR or a supplementary EU regulation, or
(3) not being an authorised person,[83] has contravened certain provisions of FSMA,[84]

the FCA may either impose a penalty 'of such amount as it considers appropriate', or publish a statement censuring the person.[85]

Where the FCA is satisfied that an individual has **32.77**

(1) contravened Article 14 (insider dealing[86] and unlawful disclosure of inside information[87]) or Article 15 (market manipulation[88]) of MAR,
(2) contravened, or been knowingly concerned in the contravention of some other provision of MAR or a supplementary EU regulation, or
(3) has contravened certain provisions of FSMA,[89]

the FCA may impose a temporary prohibition on the individual holding an office or position involving responsibility for taking decisions about the management of an investment firm, and/or a temporary prohibition on the individual acquiring or disposing of financial instruments, whether on his or her own account or the account of a third party and whether directly or indirectly. If the FCA is satisfied that an individual has contravened Article 14 or 15 of MAR, it may impose a permanent prohibition on the individual holding an office or

---

[78] *R (on the application of S) v X* [2011] EWHC 1645 (Admin).
[79] *Hannam v FCA* [2014] UKUT 233 (TCC); [2014] Lloyd's Rep FC 704 at paras 14 and 147–92.
[80] See para 32.41 *et seq.*
[81] See para 32.21 *et seq.*
[82] See para 32.56 *et seq.*
[83] Defined in FSMA s 31.
[84] Sections 122A, 122B, 122C, 122G, 122H, or 122I (which concern the FCA's powers to require information); 123A or 123B (which are discussed at paras 32.77–32.78) or Part 11 (Information Gathering and Investigations) insofar as any obligation imposed relates to MAR any supplementary EU regulation.
[85] FSMA s.123.
[86] See para 32.41 *et seq.*
[87] See para 32.21 *et seq.*
[88] See para 32.56 *et seq.*
[89] Sections 122A, 122B, 122C, 122G, 122H, or 122I (which concern the FCA's powers to require information); or 123B (which is discussed at para 32.79).

position involving responsibility for taking decisions about the management of an investment firm.[90]

32.78 Where the FCA is satisfied that an authorized person[91] has

(1) contravened Article 14 (insider dealing[92] and unlawful disclosure of inside information[93]) or Article 15 (market manipulation[94]) of MAR,

(2) contravened, or been knowingly concerned in the contravention of some other provision of MAR or a supplementary EU regulation, or

(3) has contravened certain provisions of FSMA,[95]

the FCA may suspend, for such period as it considers appropriate, any permission which the person has to carry on a regulated activity, and/or impose, for such period as it considers appropriate, such limitations or other restrictions in relation to the carrying on of a regulated activity by the person as it considers appropriate. The period of suspension cannot, however, last longer than 12 months.[96]

32.79 Any one or more of the powers under ss 123, 123A, and 123B may be exercised in relation to the same contravention.[97] If the FCA proposes to exercise its powers under ss 123, 123A, and 123B, it must first give the person a warning notice, stating where relevant the amount of any proposed penalty, the terms of any proposed statement, the terms of any proposed prohibition and the period for which any proposed suspension or restriction is to have effect.[98] If the FCA then decides to exercise its powers under ss 123, 123A, and 123B, it must give the person a decision notice, similarly containing the amount of any penalty, the terms of any statement, the terms of any prohibition and the period for which any suspension or restriction is to have effect.[99]

32.80 The FCA Handbook sets out the FCA's approach to the imposition of penalties in Chapter 6 of the Decision Procedure and Penalties Manual (DEPP 6).[100] DEPP 6.5.2 provides that the FCA's penalty-setting regime is based on the following principles:

(1) Disgorgement—a firm or individual should not benefit from any breach;

(2) Discipline—a firm or individual should be penalized for wrongdoing; and

(3) Deterrence—any penalty imposed should deter the firm or individual who committed the breach, and others, from committing further or similar breaches.

32.81 When calculating the total amount payable,[101] DEPP 6.5.3 provides that the total amount payable may be made up of two elements: (i) disgorgement of the benefit received as a result

---

[90] FSMA s 123A.
[91] Defined in FSMA s 31.
[92] See para 32.41 *et seq.*
[93] See para 32.21 *et seq.*
[94] See para 32.56 *et seq.*
[95] Sections 122A, 122B, 122C, 122G, 122H, or 122I (which concern the FCA's powers to require information); or 123A (which is discussed at para 32.77).
[96] FSMA s 123B.
[97] FSMA s 123C.
[98] FSMA s 126.
[99] FSMA s 127.
[100] For a discussion of DEPP 6, see *FCA v Da Vinci Invest Ltd* [2016] Bus LR 274 at para 202 *et seq.*
[101] For some examples of Upper Tribunal's approach to determining penalties, see *Massey v FSA* [2011] UKUT 49 (TCC); [2011] Lloyd's Rep FC 459; *Betton v FSA* FS/2008/0011, 19 November 2010 and *Visser and Fagbulu v FSA* [2011] Lloyd's Rep FC 551 at paras 110–26 in particular.

of the breach; and (ii) a financial penalty reflecting the seriousness of the breach. These elements are incorporated in a five-step framework, which can be summarized as follows:

(a) Step 1: the removal of any financial benefit derived directly from the breach;
(b) Step 2: the determination of a figure which reflects the seriousness of the breach;
(c) Step 3: an adjustment made to the Step 2 figure to take account of any aggravating and mitigating circumstances;
(d) Step 4: an upwards adjustment made to the amount arrived at after Steps 2 and 3, where appropriate, to ensure that the penalty has an appropriate deterrent effect; and
(e) Step 5: if applicable, a settlement discount will be applied. This discount does not apply to disgorgement of any financial benefit derived directly from the breach.

32.82 Also worth noting (although it is not a provision specific to market abuse, and applies only to authorized persons,[102] exempt persons[103] and persons to whom the general prohibition does not apply as a result of FSMA Part 20[104]) is FSMA s 56, which empowers the FCA to make a prohibition order if it appears to it that an individual is not a fit and proper person[105] to perform functions in relation to a regulated activity. The prohibition order can prohibit the individual from performing a specified function, any function falling within a specified description or any function. Once again, before it can make a prohibition order, the regulator must first give the individual concerned a warning notice setting out the terms of the proposed prohibition, and then a decision notice, naming the individual to whom the prohibition applies and setting out the terms of the order.[106]

32.83 Another provision specific to approved persons[107] or employees of relevant authorized persons[108] is s 66, which entitles a regulator to take action against a person if it appears that the person is guilty of misconduct and the regulator is satisfied that it is appropriate in all the circumstances to take action against him. The action taken by the regulator can include the imposition of a penalty, the suspension of any approval or imposition of conditions or time limit on any approval, and the publishing of a statement of the misconduct.

32.84 The exercise by the FCA of its power to issue a decision notice can, of course, be challenged in the Upper Tribunal (Tax and Chancery Chamber).[109] Such challenges are not properly described as 'appeals', since the Upper Tribunal carries out a *de novo* review of the entire case and considers the matter completely afresh,[110] conducting a complete re-hearing of the matter and considering fresh evidence if presented to it.[111] Accordingly, an FCA decision notice is not treated as a judicial decision, with the consequence that the doctrine of *res judicata* will not apply to it (although the public law duty to act rationally precludes the

---

[102] Defined in FSMA s 31.
[103] Defined in FSMA s 417.
[104] Provision of Financial Services by Members of the Professions.
[105] Defined in the FCA Handbook in the part entitled: *FIT The Fit and Proper Test for Approved Persons*.
[106] FSMA s 57. For examples of prohibition orders under s 56, and a discussion of the appropriateness of such a sanction, see *Betton v FSA* FS/2008/0011, 19 November 2010 at paras 73–9; *Massey v FSA* [2011] UKUT 49 (TCC); [2011] Lloyd's Rep FC 459 at paras 56–8 and *Visser and Fagbulu v FSA* [2011] Lloyd's Rep FC 551 at paras 108–9.
[107] Defined in FSMA s 64(13).
[108] Defined in FSMA s 66(7).
[109] FSMA ss 57(5) and 127(4). The Upper Tribunal is designated as the appropriate tribunal by FSMA s 417.
[110] *Hannam v FCA* [2014] UKUT 233 (TCC); [2014] Lloyd's Rep FC 704 at para 6.
[111] *R (Davies) v FSA* [2004] 1 WLR 185, CA at para 8 per Mummery LJ.

FCA from advancing, at the tribunal stage, a case inconsistent its own findings when issuing a notice).[112] In very limited circumstances, it is possible to challenge a decision notice in the Administrative Court by way of judicial review,[113] although a treatment of such proceedings is beyond the scope of this chapter.

(3) Injunctions under FSMA

32.85 If, on the application of the appropriate regulator[114] or the Secretary of State, the court is satisfied that there is a reasonable likelihood[115] that any person will contravene a relevant requirement,[116] or that any person has contravened a relevant requirement and that there is a reasonable likelihood that the contravention will continue or be repeated, the court may make an injunction.[117] Three types of order are available: an order restraining the contravention, an order directing remedial action to be taken when there has been such a contravention and an order freezing the assets of someone who has contravened certain requirements or been knowingly involved in a contravention. A freezing order under FSMA s 380(3) is similar to a freezing order under the court's inherent jurisdiction (formerly known as a *Mareva* injunction), apart from its timing: a *Mareva* injunction may only be applied for where court proceedings have been commenced or are imminent whereas this section gives the appropriate regulator or Secretary of State an independent power to apply to the court for a freezing order on the grounds that they believe a breach may have occurred. The power does not prevent separate applications for *Mareva* injunctions. Where an injunction is sought on an interim basis, there is no general rule that the FCA should be required to give a cross-undertaking in damages.[118]

32.86 Infringements or threatened infringements of Article 14 (insider dealing[119] and unlawful disclosure of inside information[120]) or Article 15 (market manipulation[121]) of MAR are dealt with expressly in FSMA, s 381. If, on the application of the FCA, the court is satisfied that there is a reasonable likelihood[122] that any person will contravene Article 14 or 15, or that any person has contravened Article 14 or 15 and that there is a reasonable likelihood that the contravention will continue or be repeated, the court may make an injunction restraining the contravention.[123]

32.87 On an application under ss 380–383 which relates to a market abuse requirement, the FCA may request the court to consider whether it is appropriate to impose a penalty, a temporary or permanent prohibition (if the person is an individual) and/or a suspension or restriction.[124] The court may impose any of those sanctions, but will only impose a permanent

---

[112] *Carrimjee v FCA* [2015] UKUT 79 (TCC); [2015] Lloyd's Rep FC 256.
[113] See *R (Willford) v FSA* [2013] EWCA Civ 677 for the applicable principles.
[114] Depending on the context, either the FCA or the PRA, see FSMA s 380(8)–(12).
[115] See para 32.89 for the meaning of 'reasonable likelihood'.
[116] Defined in FSMA s 380(6).
[117] FSMA s 380.
[118] *FSA v Sinaloa Gold plc* [2013] 2 AC 28, SC.
[119] See para 32.41 *et seq*.
[120] See para 32.21 *et seq*.
[121] See para 32.56 *et seq*.
[122] See para 32.89 for the meaning of 'reasonable likelihood'.
[123] FSMA s 381. For an example of a prohibitory injunction under the old regime, see *FCA v Da Vinci Invest Ltd* [2015] EWHC 2401 (Ch); [2015] Lloyd's Rep FC 540.
[124] FSMA s 129.

prohibition where it is satisfied the person concerned has contravened Article 14 (insider dealing[125] and unlawful disclosure of inside information[126]) or Article 15 (market manipulation[127]) of MAR.

The interplay between FSMA ss 129 and 381 was considered in *FCA v Da Vinci Invest Ltd.*[128] **32.88** In that case, the FCA had alleged that the defendants had engaged in market abuse, and brought a claim for a final injunction and a financial penalty against the defendants pursuant to FSMA ss 381 and 129. The court held that the power to impose a penalty under FSMA s 129 is exercisable in the same proceedings in which an injunction is sought irrespective of whether an injunction is actually granted in those proceedings.[129] Moreover, although the court is not bound by the FCA's own detailed penalty framework,[130] the framework should provide a starting point when determining a penalty under s 129.[131]

Furthermore, the court expressly rejected the submission that for there to be a 'reasonable **32.89** likelihood' of future market abuse, there must be a more than 50 per cent probability that it will occur in future.[132] The degree of potential harm caused by market abuse is sufficiently high that, when determining whether there is a reasonable likelihood that the market abuse will be repeated and whether in all the circumstances it is appropriate to grant an injunction under s 381, the test to be applied is whether the risk of repetition of market abuse is a real possibility that cannot sensibly be ignored.[133]

(4) Restitution under FSMA

If, on the application of the appropriate regulator[134] or the Secretary of State, the court is sat- **32.90** isfied that a person has contravened a relevant requirement,[135] and that profits have accrued to him or that one or more persons have suffered loss or been otherwise adversely affected as a result of the contravention, the court may order the person concerned to pay restitution to the regulator.[136]

Restitution for infringements of Article 14 (insider dealing[137] and unlawful disclosure **32.91** of inside information[138]) or Article 15 (market manipulation[139]) of MAR are dealt with expressly in FSMA, s 383. If, on the application of the FCA, the court is satisfied that a person has contravened Article 14 (insider dealing[140] and unlawful disclosure of inside information[141]) or Article 15 (market manipulation[142]) of MAR, and that profits have accrued to

---

[125] See para 32.41 *et seq.*
[126] See para 32.21 *et seq.*
[127] See para 32.56 *et seq.*
[128] [2016] Bus LR 274.
[129] [2016] Bus LR 274 at para 99.
[130] As to which, see para 32.80.
[131] [2016] Bus LR 274 at para 201.
[132] [2016] Bus LR 274 at para 256.
[133] [2016] Bus LR 274 at para 262.
[134] Depending on the context, either the FCA or the PRA, see FSMA s 382(11)–(15).
[135] Defined in FSMA s 382(9).
[136] FSMA s 382.
[137] See para 32.41 *et seq.*
[138] See para 32.21 *et seq.*
[139] See para 32.56 *et seq.*
[140] See para 32.41 *et seq.*
[141] See para 32.21 *et seq.*
[142] See para 32.56 *et seq.*

him or that one or more persons have suffered loss or been otherwise adversely affected as a result of the contravention, the court may order the person concerned to pay restitution to the regulator.

32.92 Where an authorized person[143] has contravened a relevant requirement,[144] or been knowingly concerned in the contravention of such a requirement, or where any person has contravened Article 14 (insider dealing[145] and unlawful disclosure of inside information[146]) or Article 15 (market manipulation[147]) of MAR, then the appropriate regulator[148] can require restitution to be paid directly to the victim without applying to court.[149] The regulator must first issue a warning notice specifying the amount proposed as restitution,[150] followed by a decision notice stating the amount to be paid, to whom it is to be paid and the arrangements in accordance with which the payment or distribution is to be made.[151]

32.93 In all three cases in paragraphs 32.90–32.92 above, the amount to be paid is such sum as appears to the court (or the regulator) to be just (or appropriate), having regard to the profits accrued or the loss suffered.[152] Any restitution received from the wrongdoer is ultimately paid to the victims of the contravention, ie those directly affected by the contravention, or to whom the profits may be attributed, for example because it was their funds that were used to make a particular investment which gave rise to the profits.[153] The power to grant an injunction and the power to order restitution are not mutually exclusive, and can be exercised alongside each other in appropriate cases.[154]

---

[143] Defined in FSMA s 31.

[144] Defined in FSMA s 384(7).

[145] See para 32.41 *et seq*.

[146] See para 32.21 *et seq*.

[147] See para 32.56 *et seq*.

[148] Depending on the context, either the FCA or the PRA, see FSMA s 384(9)–(13).

[149] FSMA s 384.

[150] FSMA s 385.

[151] FSMA s 386. For the right to challenge a decision notice, see para 32.81.

[152] FSMA s 382(2); ss 383(4); 384(5). See *FSA v Anderson* [2010] EWHC 1547 (Ch) for an example of the court applying these provisions in practice.

[153] FSMA ss 382(3), 383(5), 384(5).

[154] *FSA v Martin* [2006] 2 BCLC 193 (CA).

33

DIRECTORS' FUNCTIONS AND DUTIES IN INSOLVENCY PROCEEDINGS

Charlotte Cooke

A. Introduction

Since the 1844 Winding Up Act, winding-up proceedings have been a means of requiring **33.01** directors to account for their management of the business of the company, investigating the causes of failure and enabling prosecutions to be brought, and claims made, against delinquent directors.[1] These purposes underline the winding-up provisions that have been

---

[1] The 1844 Winding Up Act (7&8 Vic, Cap 111), enacted immediately after the Joint Stock Companies Act 1844 (7&8 Vic, Cap 110), was 'An Act for facilitating the winding up the Affairs of Joint Stock Companies unable to meet their pecuniary Engagements'. Directors of companies adjudged bankrupt were required to prepare and file at court a balance sheet and specified accounts (ss 12 and 13). As precursors of the provisions in the Insolvency Act, ss 235–7, the court could order the examination of persons, including directors, capable of giving information about the affairs of the company and summary delivery up of company property (ss 15, 16, 18, 19). There were penalties for concealment of company property and falsification of books (ss 17 and

incorporated into the successive Companies Acts 1862–1985.[2] The 1862 Act introduced a summary procedure, known as a misfeasance summons, for assessing damages against delinquent directors.[3] Following the report of the Greene Committee, the 1929 Act, s 275 made persons, including directors, responsible for fraudulent trading personally liable without limit for the debts of the company and also liable to criminal prosecution.

33.02   The Cork Committee recommended wide-ranging reforms to corporate and individual insolvency law, including harmonizing the two laws so far as possible. As a result, provisions about corporate insolvency were removed from the 1985 Act and are now to be found in the Insolvency Act, which adopts many of the Cork Report's recommendations.[4] The reforms made by the Insolvency Act, which are of particular concern to directors and which are discussed in this chapter are: (a) a new CVA procedure, (b) administration, (c) administrative receivership, (d) the power for directors to present a winding-up petition, and (e) improved procedures for investigating the company's affairs and getting in its property. Chapter 34 discusses the reforms relating to (a) personal liability of directors guilty of wrongful trading, (b) personal liability of persons involved in the management of a company that contravenes restrictions on reuse of a company name (the phoenix company syndrome), and (c) improved procedures for adjusting prior transactions.

33.03   The Insolvency Act 2000, ss 1–4, reformed the CVA procedure and enabled smaller companies to use a new moratorium provision instead of administration.[5] The Enterprise Act 2002, Part 10, ss 248–55, made major reforms to administration procedure and prevented holders of floating charges from appointing administrative receivers, except in prescribed circumstances.[6] Further reforms, affecting companies with cross-border affairs, have been made by the EC Regulation (Council Regulation 1346/2000/EC on insolvency proceedings) and the Cross-Border Insolvency Regulation 2006, which brought into force the UNCITRAL Model Law on Cross-Border Insolvency.[7] Finally, the Deregulation Act 2015 and the Small Business Enterprise and Employment Act 2015 have made changes to the Insolvency Act to streamline procedure and reduce cost.

33.04   The purpose of this chapter is to summarize the provisions of the Insolvency Act as amended and associated case law, which particularly affect the functions and duties of directors. Directors of a company that is, or is likely to become, unable to pay its debts, face serious consequences if they do not respond positively to the company's situation. In such a situation the directors owe a general duty to the company to have regard to the interests of its creditors (Chapter 12, Section E above), which is reinforced by the risks of being made subject to disqualification proceedings (Chapter 31 above) and of potential personal liability for fraudulent or wrongful trading (Chapter 34, Section C below), as well as criminal prosecution (Chapter 35, Section J below). The directors will need to obtain advice from lawyers

---

30). A report on the failure was to be produced to the Attorney General to enable criminal prosecutions to be brought (s 27).

   [2] The report of the Cork Committee, paras 74–99, contains a useful summary of the history.
   [3] s 165, which is the origin of the provision now in the Insolvency Act, s 212.
   [4] The Insolvency Act came into force on 29 December 1986.
   [5] These provisions came into force on 1 January 2003. Further amendments to the CVA provisions are made by SBEE Act 2015, s 126 and Sch 9, Pt 1 with effect from 26 May 2016 and by the Deregulation Act 2015, s 19 and Sch 6 with effect from 1 October 2015.
   [6] These provisions came into force on 15 September 2003.
   [7] The EC Regulation came into force on 31 May 2002 and the Cross-Border Regulations (SI 2006/1030) came into force on 4 April 2006.

and an insolvency practitioner. If the directors wish to try to secure the company's survival as a going concern, they may wish to use the CVA procedure in the Insolvency Act, Part I, to deal with the company's debts. Unless they are able to reach a standstill arrangement with the company's major creditors, the directors will need to obtain a moratorium on the payment and enforcement of debts. If the company is eligible, they can do this under the procedure in the Insolvency Act, Schedule A1. If the company is not eligible or Schedule A1 is not considered appropriate, then the company will have to go into administration or liquidation (or administrative receivership if that is an option) and management of the company's affairs will pass from the directors to a qualified insolvency practitioner.

The focus of this chapter is on the inception of insolvency proceedings, the effect of those **33.05** proceedings on directors' powers and directors' duties to provide information about the company's affairs and to assist in investigation procedures under the Insolvency Act. Chapter 34 deals with liabilities of directors arising from insolvency proceedings.

B. Company Voluntary Arrangement

(1) Proposal by directors

A voluntary arrangement under Part I made between a company and its creditors is 'a com- **33.06** position in satisfaction of its debts or a scheme of arrangement of its affairs'.[8] A composition is an agreement to pay a sum in lieu of a larger debt or other obligation, whereas a scheme of arrangement is different from a composition and may involve something less than the release or discharge of creditors' debts, such as a moratorium.[9]

A proposal for a voluntary arrangement may be made by the directors of a company (other **33.07** than one which is in administration or being wound up).[10] The proposal provides for a nominee, who must be a qualified insolvency practitioner, to act in relation to the voluntary arrangement either as trustee or otherwise for the purpose of supervising its implementation.[11]

The CVA procedure is designed to be simpler, quicker, and cheaper than the long-established **33.08** power of a company to propose a compromise or arrangement with its creditors if duly approved by the requisite majority of its creditors and sanctioned by the court under what is now the 2006 Act, Part 26 (Chapter 28, Section B above), since under the CVA procedure there is no need to consider classes of creditors and there is no court participation (beyond receiving the nominee's report) unless there is a dispute.[12]

The first formal step in the CVA procedure is the preparation of the proposal for the intended **33.09** nominee to make his report to the court, if he agrees to act.[13] In practice, the directors will

---

[8] Insolvency Act, s 1(1).

[9] *Commissioners of Inland Revenue v Adam & Partners Ltd* [2001] 1 BCLC 222, CA at paras 39 and 40, per Mummery LJ. In *Re NFU Development Trust Ltd* [1972] 1 WLR 1548, 1555C–D, Brightman J said that an 'arrangement' in what is now 2006 Act, s 895 involved 'some element of give and take' and if rights are expropriated, there must be some 'compensating advantage'.

[10] Insolvency Act, s 1(1) and (3).

[11] Insolvency Act, s 1(2).

[12] The CVA procedure is contained in the Insolvency Act, Part I, ss 1–7B and the Insolvency Rules, rules 1.1–1.54. These Rules are replaced by rules in Part 2 of the Insolvency (England and Wales) Rules 2016 (SI 2016/1024) (the IR 2016) with effect from 6 April 2017: The SBE Act 2015 (Commencement No 6 and Transition and Savings) Regulation 2016.

[13] Insolvency Act, s 2(1)–(3) and Insolvency Rules, rule 1.4 (and IR 2016 r 2.4 after 6 April 2017).

have taken advice already from an insolvency practitioner willing to act as nominee and he will assist in the preparation of the proposal. There are several matters that the directors will discuss with the proposed nominee: (a) the terms of the voluntary arrangement, (b) how to persuade creditors to accept it, (c) compliance with disclosure requirements,[14] and (d) how the company will function until the arrangement is approved and becomes binding (ie standstill arrangement or moratorium (paragraphs 33.21–33.26 below) or whether administration is necessary (Section C below)).

33.10   The terms of the proposed arrangement must be effective to enable the company to survive. There should be a realistic prospect of the company being able to meet any payment obligations, because default will lead to liquidation. Care must be taken to ensure that contingent and disputed creditors are bound into the CVA, because otherwise such creditors, once their debts are established, will be able to insist on payment in full and, if not paid, will petition for winding up.[15] The terms of the proposal should not affect the rights of secured creditors or the priority of preferential creditors unless the consents of the affected secured or preferential creditors can be obtained.[16] Also, the court may revoke the approval on a challenge under the Insolvency Act, s 6 if the terms of the voluntary arrangement are unfairly prejudicial to the interests of any creditor, member, or contributor.[17]

33.11   The directors' proposal must provide a short explanation why, in their opinion, a CVA is desirable, and give reasons why the company's creditors may be expected to concur with such an arrangement.[18]

33.12   The Insolvency Rules require the proposal to state or otherwise deal with a large number of matters which are listed in rule 1.3(2) and include details of the company's assets and liabilities and prior transactions capable of adjustment under the Insolvency Act, ss 238, 239, 244, and 245. With the agreement in writing of the nominee, the directors' proposal may be amended at any time up to delivery of the nominee's report to the court.[19] The details required by rule 1.3(2) need not include any information the disclosure of which could seriously prejudice the commercial interests of the company.[20]

---

[14] Insolvency Act, s 2(3); Insolvency Rules, rules 1.3, 1.5, and 1.6 (and IR 2016 rr 2.3, 2.6 and 2.8 after 6 April 2017).

[15] For issues concerning the inclusion of contingent claims, see the schemes of arrangement cases *Re T&N Ltd* [2006] 1 WLR 1728; *Re T&N Ltd (No 3)* [2007] 1 BCLC 563 and on contingent claims, see *Re Nortel Companies* [2014] AC 209, SC. For issues concerning the inclusion of disputed claims, see *Alman v Approach Housing Ltd* [2001] 1 BCLC 530; *Oakley Smith v Greenberg* [2005] 2 BCLC 74, CA; *El Ajou v Stern* [2007] BPIR 693. As to whether business rates are capable of being encompassed within a CVA, see *Kaye v South Oxfordshire District Council* [2014] 2 BCLC 383.

[16] Insolvency Act, s 4(3) and (4); *IRC v Wimbledon Football Club Ltd* [2005] 1 BCLC 66, CA.

[17] *SISU Capital Fund Ltd v Tucker* [2006] BCC 463 at paras 68–78, per Warren J and *Prudential Assurance Co Ltd v PRG Powerhouse Ltd* [2008] 1 BCLC 289 at paras 71–96 where Etherton J revoked approval of a CVA on the ground that a provision for release of guarantees was unfairly prejudicial to the creditors entitled to them. In *Mourant & Co Trustees Ltd v Sixty UK Ltd* [2011] 1 BCLC 383 a landlord successfully challenged a CVA which deprived him of guarantees and other rights he would enjoy in a liquidation and which treated him less favourably than associated companies. In *Re Portsmouth City Football Club Ltd* [2011] BCC 149 the Revenue's challenge to a CVA was rejected; the different treatment of creditors was not unfair because it did not arise under the CVA, which merely reflected existing football creditor rules, which applied to the company. Also see *Revenue & Customs Commissioners v Football League Ltd* [2013] 1 BCLC 285 where another challenge to the 'football creditor rule' failed.

[18] Insolvency Rules, rule 1.3(1) (and IR 2016 r 2.3 after 6 April 2017).

[19] Insolvency Rules, rule 1.3(3) (and IR 2016 r 2.3 after 6 April 2017).

[20] Insolvency Rules, rule 1.3(4) (and IR 2016 r 2.3 after 6 April 2017).

The Insolvency Rules, rule 1.5 also requires the directors to deliver to the nominee at the **33.13** same time the proposal is delivered a statement of the company's affairs, comprising the particulars specified in rule 1.5(2) and supplementing or amplifying, so far as is necessary for clarifying the state of the company's affairs, those already given in the directors' proposal. The statement of affairs shall be made up to a date not earlier than two weeks before the date of the notice to the nominee. However, the nominee may allow an extension of that period to the nearest practicable date (not earlier than two months before the date of the notice); and if he does so, he shall give his reasons in his report to the court on the directors' proposal. The statement must be verified by a statement of truth made by at least one director.[21]

If it appears to the nominee that he cannot properly prepare his report on the basis of infor- **33.14** mation in the directors' proposal and statement of affairs, he may call on the directors to provide him with (a) further and better particulars as to the circumstances in which, and the reasons why, the company is insolvent or (as the case may be) threatened with insolvency, (b) particulars of any previous proposals for a voluntary arrangement which have been made in respect of the company, and (c) any further information with respect to the company's affairs which the nominee thinks necessary for the purposes of his report. The nominee may call on the directors to inform him, with respect to any person who is, or at any time in the two years preceding the notice has been, a director or officer of the company, whether and in what circumstances (in those two years or previously) that person has been concerned in the affairs of any other company which has become insolvent, or has himself been adjudged bankrupt or entered into an arrangement with his creditors. For the purpose of enabling the nominee to consider their proposal and prepare his report on it, the directors must give him access to the company's accounts and records.[22]

Where the directors do not propose to take steps to obtain a moratorium for the company **33.15** (under the Insolvency Act, s 1A and Schedule A1) the nominee shall, within 28 days after he is given notice of the proposal for a voluntary arrangement, submit a report to the court stating (a) whether, in his opinion, the proposed voluntary arrangement has a reasonable prospect of being approved and implemented; (b) whether, in his opinion, the proposal should be considered by a meeting of the company and by the company's creditors; and (c) if in his opinion it should, the date on which, and time and place at which, he proposes a meeting of the company should be held.[23] With his report the nominee should deliver to the court a copy of the proposal (with any authorized amendments) and a copy or summary of the statement of affairs.[24]

(2) Consideration and implementation of the proposal

Where the nominee has reported to the court that the proposal should be considered by a **33.16** meeting of the company and by the company's creditors he proceeds to summon a meeting of the company and to seek a decision from the company's creditors as to whether they

---

[21] Insolvency Rules, rule 1.5(4) (and IR 2016 r 2.6 after 6 April 2017).
[22] Insolvency Rules, rule 1.6 (and IR 2016 r 2.8 after 6 April 2017).
[23] Insolvency Act, s 2, as amended by SBEE Act 2014, s 126 and Sch 9, Pt 1, paras 1, 2 from a day to be appointed. Until the amendments take effect, the creditors' decision is made at a meeting. Note that there are provisions for the replacement of the nominee: Insolvency Act, s 2(4); Insolvency Rules, rule 1.8 (and IR 2016 r 2.10 after 6 April 2017). The nominee is expected to satisfy himself that the proposal is serious and viable: *Re a Debtor (No 140 IO of 1995)* [1996] 2 BCLC 429.
[24] Insolvency Rules, rule 1.7 (and IR 2016 r 2.9 after 6 April 2017).

approve the proposal.[25] The decision of the company's creditors as to whether they approve the proposal is made by a qualifying decision procedure.[26] Notice of this procedure must be given to every creditor of the company of whose claim and address the person seeking the decision is aware.[27] The notices summoning the meetings should include (a) a copy of the proposal, (b) a copy of the statement of affairs or a summary of it, and (c) the nominee's comments on the proposal.[28]

33.17 At least 14 days' notice to attend the meetings should also be given to all directors of the company, and, if the nominee thinks that their presence is required, other officers of the company, or persons who were directors or officers of it at any time in the two years immediately preceding the date of the notice. The nominee, as chairman, may if he thinks fit exclude any of those persons from attendance at a meeting, either completely or for any part of it.[29]

33.18 The company and its creditors may approve the proposed voluntary arrangement with or without modifications.[30] The decision to approve the proposed voluntary arrangement has effect if it is taken by the meeting of the company summoned under s 3 and by the company's creditors pursuant to that section, or, subject to application to the court, by only the creditors' decision.[31] The outcome is reported to the court.[32]

33.19 Where a decision to approve the voluntary arrangement has effect, the voluntary arrangement takes effect as if made by the company at the time the creditors decided to approve voluntary arrangement and binds every person who, in accordance with the Insolvency Rules, was entitled to vote in the qualifying decision procedure by which the creditors' decision to approve the voluntary arrangement was made, or would have been entitled if he had had notice of it, as if he were a party to the voluntary arrangement.[33] The decision is, however, subject to challenge on the grounds of unfair prejudice or material irregularity.[34]

---

[25] Insolvency Act, s 3(1) and (2), as amended by SBEE Act 2015, s 126, Sch 9, Pt 1, paras 1, 3(1)(2) with effect from 6 April 2017; Insolvency Rules, rules 1.9(1) and 1.13 (and IR 2016 r 2.25 after 6 April 2017).

[26] Insolvency Act, s 3(3), as amended by SBEE Act 2015, s 126, Sch 9, Pt 1, paras 1, 3(1)(4) with effect from 6 April 2017. The qualifying decision procedure is specified pursuant to Insolvency Act, s 246ZE and Sch 8, para 8A with effect from 6 April 2017. Until that date, the creditors' decision is made at a meeting.

[27] Insolvency Act, s 3(4), as amended by SBEE Act 2015, s 126, Sch 9, Pt 1, paras 1, 3(1)(4) with effect from 6 April 2017; Insolvency Rules, rule 1.9(2) (and IR 2016 r 2.25 after that date).

[28] Insolvency Rules, rule 1.9(3) (and IR 2016 r 2.25 after that date).

[29] Insolvency Rules, rule 1.16 (and IR 2016 r 2.30 after that date).

[30] Insolvency Act, s 4(1)–(4), as amended by SBEE Act 2015, s 126, Sch 9, Pt 1, paras 1, 4(1)(8) with effect from 6 April 2017. Subs (4) restricts modifications prejudicing secured and preferential creditors without their concurrence.

[31] Insolvency Act, s 4A, as amended by SBEE Act 2015, s 126, Sch 9, Pt 1, paras 1, 5 with effect from 6 April 2017. The circumstances in which a member could successfully challenge a decision by the creditors must be rare. At a company meeting any resolution is to be regarded as passed if voted for by more than one-half in value of the members present in person or by proxy and voting on the resolution. Until the amendments to s 4A take effect, the creditors' decision is taken at a meeting at which any resolution to pass approving any proposal or modification there must be a majority in excess of three-quarters in value of the creditors present in person or by proxy and voting on the resolution: Insolvency Rules, rules 1.19(1), 1.20(1). This is subject to the detailed rules relating to voting rights and majorities set out in Insolvency Rules, rules 1.17–1.21 (and IR 2016 rr 2.25, 2.29, 2.35, 2.36).

[32] Insolvency Act, s 4(6), (6A), as amended by SBEE Act 2015, s 126, Sch 9, Pt 1, paras 1, 4(1)(6)(7) from a day to be appointed.

[33] Insolvency Act, s 5(1) and (2), as amended by the SBEE Act 2015, s 126, Sch 9, Pt 1, paras 1, 6(1)(2) from a day to be appointed. Until the amendments take effect, the voluntary arrangement takes effect as if made at the creditors meeting. As to the legal effect of approval, see *Johnson v Davies* [1999] Ch 117, 138c, CA, per Chadwick LJ; *Raja v Rubin* [2000] Ch 274, 287, per Peter Gibson LJ.

[34] Insolvency Act, s 6. On unfair prejudice, see cases in n 17 above. On material irregularity, see *Re Cranley Mansions Ltd* [1994] 1 WLR 1610; *Re Sweatfield Ltd* [1997] BCC 744; *SISU Capital Fund Ltd v Tucker* [2006]

The truth and accuracy of the representations made by the directors in the proposal, the **33.20** statement of affairs, and further information given to the nominee and at the meetings are of critical importance. This is reinforced by the Insolvency Act, s 6A(1) which provides:

If, for the purpose of obtaining the approval of the members or creditors of a company to a proposal for a voluntary arrangement, a person who is an officer of the company—
(a) makes any false representation, or
(b) fraudulently does, or omits to do, anything, he commits an offence. A person guilty of an offence under s 6A is liable to imprisonment or a fine.

(3) Moratorium

Where the directors of an eligible company intend to make a proposal for a CVA, they may **33.21** take steps to obtain a moratorium in accordance with the Insolvency Act, Schedule A1.[35] Eligible companies are small companies other than companies such as insurance companies and banks[36] which fulfil two of the following three conditions: (a) turnover less than £6.5 million, (b) balance sheet total less than £3.26 million, and (c) having fewer than 50 employees.[37] A company is also ineligible if it is in administration, liquidation, administrative receivership, provisional liquidation, subject to a voluntary arrangement, or has had the benefit of a moratorium within the previous 12 months.[38] A company is also excluded from being eligible for a moratorium if it is party to an agreement which is or forms part of certain capital market arrangements, it is a project company of a public–private partnership project which includes step-in rights, or has incurred a liability under an agreement of £10 million or more.[39]

A moratorium, which prohibits most forms of legal process against the company,[40] is only **33.22** available if (a) the nominee is satisfied that the company is likely to have funds available to it during the proposed moratorium to enable it to carry on business,[41] and (b) the directors are content to carry on managing the business of the company during the moratorium period subject to specified restrictions, enforced by criminal sanction,[42] and monitoring by the nominee.[43] It seems that few, if any, companies are able or willing to meet these requirements, since the provisions of Schedule A1 are rarely used. The out-of-court administration model is generally preferred.

BCC 463 at paras 79–81; *Re Newlands (Seaford) Educational Trust* [2006] BCC 195; *Re Gatnom Capital & Finance Ltd* [2010] EWHC 3353 (Ch); *Goldstein v Bishop* [2016] EWHC 2187 (Ch) (and for later proceedings see [2016] EWHC 2804 (Ch)).

[35] Insolvency Act, s 1A, which, with Sch A1, was introduced by the Insolvency Act 2000.

[36] Companies are ineligible if they fall within Insolvency Act, Sch A1, paras 2(1)(a) or (b), 4A (the company is party to a capital market arrangement), 4B (the company is a project company or a project which is a public–private partnership project and includes step-in rights), or 4C (the company has incurred a liability under an agreement of £10 million or more). Paras 4D–4K explain paras 4A–4C. By para 5 the Secretary of State may modify the conditions of eligibility.

[37] Insolvency Act, Sch A1, paras 2 and 3; for the requirements for being a small company, see 2006 Act, s 382 as amended by the Companies Act 2006 (Amendment)(Accounts and Reports) Regulations 2008 (SI 2008/393).

[38] Insolvency Act, Sch A1, para 4(1).

[39] Insolvency Act, Sch A1, paras 4A–4K.

[40] Insolvency Act, Sch A1, paras 12–14.

[41] Insolvency Act, Sch A1, paras 6(2)(a) and 7(1)(e)(ii).

[42] Insolvency Act, Sch A1, paras 15–23. The restrictions concern publicity of the moratorium, obtaining credit, disposing of company property, paying debts, disposing of charged property, and market contracts.

[43] Insolvency Act, Sch A1, paras 24–8.

33.23 If the directors do wish to obtain a moratorium they file at court:

    (a) a document setting out the terms of the proposed voluntary arrangement;

    (b) a statement of the company's affairs;

    (c) a statement that the company is eligible for a moratorium;

    (d) a statement from the nominee that he has given his consent to act; and

    (e) a statement from the nominee that, in his opinion (i) the proposed voluntary arrangement has a reasonable prospect of being approved and implemented, (ii) the company is likely to have sufficient funds available to it during the proposed moratorium to enable it to carry on its business, and (iii) meetings of the company and its creditors should be summoned to consider the proposed voluntary arrangement.[44]

33.24 The moratorium comes into force when these documents are filed with the court and, in broad terms, lasts until the later of the day on which the company meeting is first held and the day on which the creditors decide whether to approve the proposed voluntary arrangement, which should be within 28 days of the moratorium coming into force, unless the moratorium is extended.[45]

33.25 The procedure for the consideration and implementation of the voluntary arrangement follows the scheme applicable to CVAs under Part 1, as described above, except that there is provision for extending the moratorium and appointing a moratorium committee.[46] There is also provision for a creditor or member to apply to the court to challenge the acts or omissions of the directors during the moratorium period on the ground of unfair prejudice.[47]

33.26 Schedule A1, paragraph 41 applies where a moratorium has been obtained for a company and provides for various offences of fraud in anticipation of the moratorium, in terms similar to the Insolvency Act, s 206 in the case of winding up (Chapter 35, Section J below).

C. Administration

(1) The new administration regime

33.27 A new administration regime, contained in the Insolvency Act, Schedule B1 came into effect on 15 September 2003.[48] The original regime, contained in the Insolvency Act, ss 8–27, continues to apply with modifications to certain companies of national significance.[49] There are also a bank administration procedure,[50] an investment bank special administration

---

[44] Insolvency Act, Sch A1, paras 6 and 7.

[45] Insolvency Act, Sch A1, para 8, as amended by SBEE Act 2015, 126, Sch 9, Pt 1, paras 1, 9(1)(4) as from a day to be appointed. Until the amendments take effect, the creditors' decision is made at a meeting.

[46] Insolvency Act, Sch A1, paras 29–39.

[47] Insolvency Act, Sch A1, para 40.

[48] It was introduced by the Enterprise Act 2002, s 248. For insurers it is modified by Financial Services and Markets Act 2000 (Administration Orders Relating to Insurers) Order 2010 (SI 2010/3023), which came into force on 1 February 2011.

[49] Enterprise Act 2002, s 249. Such companies are: building societies (Building Societies Act 1986, s 90A and Sch 15A; Building Society Special Administration (England and Wales) Rules 2010 (SI 2010/2580)); water and sewage undertakers (Water Industry Act 1991, ss 23–6 and Sch 3; Water Industry (Special Administration) Rules 2009 (SI 2009/2477)); protected railway companies (Railways Act 1993, ss 59–65 and Sch 6); companies party to a public–private partnership agreement (Greater London Authority Act 1999, ss 220–4 and Schs 14 and 15); air traffic services companies (Transport Act 2000, ss 26–32 and Sch 2).

[50] Banking Act 2009, Part 3, ss 136–45 under which the court may make a bank administration order on the application of the Bank of England and the Banking Act 2009 (Parts 2 and 3 Consequential Amendments) Order 2009 (SI 2009/317), which came into force on 21 February 2009, and the Bank Administration (England

procedure.[51] There are also special administration regimes for postal service companies, energy supply companies, health care companies, and financial services infrastructure companies.[52] The following paragraphs deal only with the position of directors in relation to the administrations under Schedule B1, under which a company,[53] which is not already in administration or liquidation, may enter administration by the appointment of an administrator[54] (a) when the court makes an administration order,[55] or (b) when the appointment is made out of court by the holder of a floating charge[56] or by the company or directors.[57] The out-of-court procedure is used in the majority of cases because of the saving in time and expense, but there are occasions when an application for an administration order is necessary or desirable.

Whichever procedure is adopted by the directors or the company, there are two conditions **33.28** for the appointment of an administrator. The first is that 'the company is or is likely to become unable to pay its debts' within the meaning of the Insolvency Act, s 123.[58] The second is that the purpose of administration is reasonably likely to be achieved.[59] In an ordinary

and Wales) Rules 2009 (SI 2009/357), which came into force on 25 February 2009. These provisions also apply to building societies pursuant to Building Societies Act 1986, s 90C; as to which see Building Societies (Insolvency and Special Administration) Order 2009 (SI 2009/805), which came into force on 29 March 2009; Building Society Special Administration (England and Wales) Rules 2010 (SI 2010/2580 and Building Society Insolvency (England and Wales) Rules 2010 (SI 2010/2581), which came into force on 15 November 2010.

[51] Investment Bank Special Administration Regulations 2011 (SI 2011/245), which came into force on 8 February 2011 and the Investment Bank Special Administration (England and Wales) Rules 2011 (SI 2011/1301), which came into force on 30 June 2011.

[52] Postal Services Act 2011, Energy Act 2011, Health and Social Care Act 2012, and Financial Services (Banking Reform) Act 2013.

[53] By Sch B1, para 111(1A) 'Company' means (a) a company registered under the 2006 Act (as to which, see 2006 Act, s 1), (b) a company incorporated in an EEA state other than the UK, or (c) a company not incorporated in an EEA state but having its COMI in a Member State other than Denmark. As to companies within (c), para 111(1B) provides that in relation to a company, COMI has the same meaning as in the EC Regulation and, in the absence of proof to the contrary, is presumed to be the place of its registered office and see *Re BRAC Rent-A-Car International Inc* [2003] 1 WLR 1421; *Re Sendo Ltd* [2006] 1 BCLC 395; *Re Stanford International Bank Ltd* [2011] Ch 33, CA.

[54] Insolvency Act, Sch B1, paras 6–8 contain general restrictions on the appointment of an administrator.

[55] Insolvency Act, Sch B1, paras 11–13, 35–39 and Insolvency Rules, rules 2.2–2.14, with effect from 6 April 2017.

[56] Insolvency Act, Sch B1, paras 14–21 and Insolvency Rules, rules 2.15–2.19, with effect from 6 April 2017. *Lovett v Carson Country Homes Ltd* [2009] 2 BCLC 196, where administrators were validly appointed by the holder of a floating charge even though a director's signature on the charge had been forged. In *Re Armstrong Brands Ltd* [2015] EWHC 3303 (Ch) a floating charge signed by a director and the company secretary, but not dated until three months later, at which time the director had ceased to be a director, complied with the execution requirements of the 2006 Act, s 44 and therefore the charge was valid as a qualifying floating charge and the charge holder was entitled to appoint administrators.

[57] Insolvency Act, Sch B1, paras 22–34 and Insolvency Rules, rules 2.20–2.27.

[58] Insolvency Act, Sch B1, para 111(1). As to the definition of inability to pay debts in s 123, see *Byblos Bank SAL v Al Khudhairy* [1987] BCLC 232, CA (a pre-Insolvency Act case); *Re Imperial Motors Ltd* [1990] BCLC 29; *Re Dianoor Jewels Ltd* [2001] 1 BCLC 450; *Re Cheyne Finance Ltd (No 2)* 1 BCLC 741 [2008]; *BNY Corporate Trustee Services Ltd v Eurosail-UK 2007-3BL plc* [2013] 1 WLR 1408, SC; *Re Casa Estates (UK) Ltd* [2014] 2 BCLC 49, CA. Where application is made to the court for an administration order, the court must be satisfied that this is the case on the balance of probabilities: Insolvency Act, Sch B1, para 11(a): *Re COLT Telecom Group plc* [2003] BPIR 324; *Hammonds v Pro-Fit USA Ltd* [2008] 2 BCLC 159 (both creditors' applications). Where the appointment is made by the company or directors, there must be a statutory declaration made by or on behalf of the person who proposes to make the application to this effect: Insolvency Act, Sch B1, paras 27(2)(a), 29(2), 30(a). Where the appointment is made by the holder of a qualifying floating charge, this condition does not have to be satisfied; instead the charge must be enforceable on the date of the appointment: Insolvency Act, Sch B1, paras 16 and 18(2).

[59] Where application is made to the court for an administration order the court must be satisfied that the administration order is reasonably likely to achieve the purpose of the administration: Insolvency Act, Sch B1,

case, if these conditions are met, and an administration application made to court, the court will likely make an administration order.[60]

33.29 The redefined purpose of administration, as stated in Schedule B1, para 3, is fundamentally different from the original purposes stated in s 8(3), in that (a) the three objectives are stated in order of priority, designed to encourage rescue, and (b) the objectives contemplate distributions in the administration to secured, preferential, and unsecured creditors, rather than outside the administration, whether on survival of the company, or under a CVA or scheme of arrangement under the 2006 Act, Part 26 or in a winding up.[61] Schedule B1, para 3 provides:

(1) The administrator must perform his functions with the objective of—
   (a) rescuing the company as a going concern, or
   (b) achieving a better result for the company's creditors as a whole than would be likely if the company were wound up (without first being in administration), or
   (c) realising property in order to make a distribution to one or more secured or preferential creditors.

(2) Subject to sub-paragraph (4), the administrator of a company must perform his functions in the interests of the company's creditors as a whole.

(3) The administrator must perform his functions with the objective specified in sub-paragraph (1)(a) unless he thinks either—
   (a) that it is not reasonably practicable to achieve that objective, or
   (b) that the objective specified in sub-paragraph (1)(b) would achieve a better result for the company's creditors as a whole.

(4) The administrator may perform his functions with the objective specified in sub-paragraph (1)(c) only if—
   (a) he thinks it is not reasonably practicable to achieve either of the objectives specified in sub-paragraphs (1)(a) and (b), and
   (b) he does not unnecessarily harm the interests of the company's creditors as a whole.

(2) Appointment of administrator by directors

33.30 Where the directors consider that an administrator should be appointed out of court, they may invite the members to make the appointment if that is practicable, but they also have

---

para 11(b); Insolvency Rules, rule 2.3(5)(c) and Form 2.2B; *Re Harris Simons Construction Ltd* [1989] 1 WLR 368; *Re Lomax Leisure Ltd* [2000] Ch 502; *Re AA Mutual International Insurance Co Ltd* [2005] 2 BCLC 8; *Re Redman Construction Ltd* [2005] EWHC 1850 (Ch); *Hammonds v Pro-Fit USA Ltd* [2008] 2 BCLC 159; *Auto Management Services Ltd v Oracle Fleet UK Ltd* [2008] BCC 761; *Re Integral Ltd* [2013] EWHC 164 (Ch). Where the appointment is made by the company or directors (or by the holder of a qualifying floating charge), there must be a statement by the administrator that in his opinion the purpose of administration is reasonably likely to be achieved: Insolvency Act, Sch B1, paras 18(3)(b) and 29(3)(b); Insolvency Rules, rules 2.16(2)(a), 2.23(2)(a), and Form 2.2B. In considering whether the statutory purpose of administration can be achieved, the potential administrators do not have to consider the directors' motives in appointing them: *Re BW Estates Ltd* [2016] 1 BCLC 708.

[60] In some cases, however, even if the conditions are met, the court may not consider it appropriate to make an administration order: *Re Brown Bear Foods Ltd* [2014] EWHC 1132 (Ch).

[61] The potential for distributions to unsecured creditors is implicit in the phrase 'better result' and express provision for distributions is made by Sch B1, para 65, with the permission of the court. The objective of making distributions to secured and preferential creditors follows from administration replacing administrative receivership, which was abolished by the Insolvency Act, s 72A (added by the Enterprise Act 2002, s 250). The new administration regime is to be contrasted with the description of the former regime given by Lord Hoffmann in *Centre Reinsurance International Co v Freakley* [2006] 1 WLR 2863, HL at paras 6 and 7.

power to make the appointment themselves, acting unanimously or by resolution of the board.[62]

The power of the directors or the company to appoint an administrator out of court is restricted **33.31** in that such an appointment may not be made if:

(1) less than 12 months have elapsed since the date on which (a) the company ceased to be in administration, if an administrator had been appointed by the company or its directors or on an administration application made by the company or its directors; (b) a moratorium ended without a CVA being in force; or (c) a CVA ended if it was made during a moratorium or ended prematurely;[63]

(2) a petition for the winding up of the company has been presented and is not yet disposed of, unless the petition for the winding up of the company was presented after the person proposing to make the appointment filed the notice of intention to appoint with the court under Sch B1, paragraph 27;

(3) an administration application has been made and is not yet disposed of; and

(4) an administrative receiver of the company is in office.[64]

If a notice of intention to appoint an administrator by the company or directors has been given under paragraph 26, and accordingly an interim moratorium is in place pursuant to para 46, the appointment of an administrator may proceed, notwithstanding that a petition for winding up has been presented (in ignorance of the moratorium).[65]

If these restrictions apply the company or its directors may apply to the court for an admin- **33.32** istration order.[66] However, where there is an administrative receiver in office, the court will dismiss the administration application unless the person by or on behalf of whom the receiver was appointed consents to the making of the administration order or the court thinks that, if an administration order were made, the security by virtue of which the receiver was appointed would be liable to be released or discharged under the Insolvency Act, ss 238–40 (transactions at undervalue and preference) or avoided under s 245 (avoidance of floating charge).[67]

Where the restrictions on appointment do not apply, the company or the directors **33.33** may appoint an administrator by giving any required notices of intention to make the appointment[68] and filing the required documents at court.[69] Where there is no need to

---

[62] Insolvency Act, Sch B1, paras 22 and 105; *Re Equiticorp International plc* [1989] 1 WLR 1010; *Minmar (929) Ltd v Khalatschi* [2011] BCC 485 at paras 49–52. In *Re Melodious Corp* [2015] 1 BCLC 518 there had been no valid appointment of administrators because the meeting of the board of directors purporting to make the appointment was inquorate.

[63] Insolvency Act, Sch B1, paras 23 and 24.

[64] Insolvency Act, Sch B1, paras 25 and 25A (inserted by the Deregulation Act 2015, Sch 6, para 5 with effect from 26 May 2015). The proviso inserted by para 25A(1) does not apply if the petition was presented under a provision mentioned in Sch B1, para 42(4): Sch B1, para 25A(2).

[65] *Re Ramora UK Ltd* [2012] BCC 672; cf *Re Business Dream Ltd* [2013] 1 BCLC 456, where the directors had given notice of their intention to appoint administrators but then changed their minds and resolved instead to put the company into creditors' voluntary liquidation, and it was held that the resolution to put the company into liquidation was invalid because it was passed during the moratorium.

[66] See eg *Re Bowen Travel Ltd* [2013] BCC 182.

[67] Insolvency Act, Sch B1, para 39. *Chesterton International Group Plc v Deka Immobilien Inv GmbH* [2005] BPIR 1103.

[68] Insolvency Act, Sch B1, paras 26–8 and Insolvency Rules 2.20–2.22.

[69] Insolvency Act, Sch B1, paras 29 and 30 and Insolvency Rules 2.23–2.26.

serve anyone with notice of intention to appoint, an immediate appointment can be made.[70]

33.34 Where there is a person with a qualifying floating charge, whether or not it is enforceable, the directors must give the holder at least five business days' written notice before they can appoint an administrator.[71] The purpose of this is to give the holder an opportunity to (a) appoint an administrative receiver, if he is entitled to, (b) appoint an administrator of his choice, (c) negotiate the identity of the administrator appointed by the directors, or (d) make an administration application. In fact it is pointless for the company or the directors to propose an administrator who is not acceptable to the holder of any qualifying floating charge. The directors can proceed to appoint an administrator within the five-day period if the holders of qualifying floating charges consent.[72]

33.35 In addition the directors must also give notice of intention to appoint an administrator to: (a) any enforcement officer, to the knowledge of the person giving the notice, charged with execution or other legal process against the company; (b) any person who, to the knowledge of the person giving the notice, has distrained against the company or its property; (c) any supervisor of a voluntary arrangement; and (d) the company, if the company is not intending to make the appointment,[73] save that there is no requirement to give notice to the prescribed persons (including the company itself) where there is no qualifying floating charge holder entitled to notice.[74] There is no minimum notice period, so that once notice has been given to these persons (if there are any), an administrator can be appointed.[75] The appointment of administrators more than ten business days after filing a notice of intention to appoint (contrary to the Insolvency Act, Sch B1, para 28(2)) does not automatically invalidate the appointment, but should be treated as a curable irregularity under Insolvency Rules, rule 7.55.[76] There are conflicting decisions of the High Court as to whether failure to give notice to any of these persons invalidates the purported appointment of an administrator,[77] but the prudent course is for directors to ensure that they strictly comply with these notice requirements. Specifically, where the appointment

---

[70] Insolvency Act, Sch B1, para 30.

[71] Insolvency Act, Sch B1, paras 14, 26(1) and (3), 28(1). The notice of intention to appoint is a statutory declaration in Form 2.8B, which must be made not more than 5 days before the notice is filed with the court and should be accompanied by a copy of the resolution of the company or decision of the directors: Insolvency Rules, rules 2.20–2.22.

[72] Insolvency Act, Sch B1, para 28(1)(b).

[73] Insolvency Act, Sch B1, para 26(2) and (3); Insolvency Rules, rule 2.20–2.22; Form 2.8B. As to the persons in (a) and (b), cf rule 2.9 in relation to an administration application.

[74] Insolvency Act, Sch B1, para 26(2), as amended by Deregulation Act 2015, s 19 and Sch 6, paras 4 and 6, with effect from 1 October 2015.

[75] Insolvency Act, Sch B1, para 28(1).

[76] *Re Euromaster Ltd* [2013] Bus LR 466.

[77] In *Hill v Stokes* [2011] BCC 473, HHJ McCahill QC held that it did not, but in *Minmar (929) Ltd v Khalatschi* [2011] BCC 485, Sir Andrew Morritt C held that there must be strict compliance with Sch B1, paras 26–8 if the out-of-court appointment is to be valid. On 21 December 2011 Warren J gave judgment in *National Westminster Bank plc v Msaada Group* [2012] BCC 226, preferring *Minmar* to *Hill v Stokes*. On the same day, Norris J gave judgment in *Re Virtualpurple Professional Services Ltd* [2012] BCC 254, reaching the opposite conclusion. Subsequent cases on failure to give the required notice are: *RE MF Global Overseas Ltd* [2012] BCC 490; *Re Assured Logistics Solutions Ltd* [2012] BCC 541; *Re Ceart Risk Services Ltd* [2012] BCC 592; *Re BXL Services Ltd* [2012] EWHC 1877 (Ch); *Re Eiffel Steel Works Ltd* [2015] 2 BCLC 57 (following *Re Ceart Risk Services Ltd*).

is made by the directors, notice should be given to the company by delivering it to its registered office.[78]

Where it is necessary to give notice of intention to appoint, a copy of the notice, accompanied by specified documents, must be filed at court.[79] The company or the directors then have ten days from the date of filing of that notice within which to appoint an administrator.[80] **33.36**

The appointment of an administrator by the directors or the company takes effect when they file with the court[81] (a) a notice of appointment, which includes a statutory declaration as to prescribed matters and identifies the administrator;[82](b) a statement by the administrator that he consents to the appointment, and that in his opinion the purpose of the administration is reasonably likely to be achieved;[83] and (c) other prescribed documents.[84] The person making the appointment must notify the administrator as soon as is reasonably practicable after these requirements are satisfied.[85] The appointment does not, however, take effect if, before these requirements are satisfied, the holder of a qualifying floating charge has appointed an administrator or an administration order has been made.[86] A company's directors have the power to cause the company to challenge the appointment of administrators by a qualifying floating charge holder.[87] **33.37**

When the appointment takes effect and the company is in administration, no resolution may be passed, or order made, for the winding up of the company and the moratorium on other legal process applies.[88] **33.38**

---

[78] In *Re Bezier Acquisitions Ltd* [2012] BCC 219 Norris J accepted that service on the company's solicitors was effective service of notice on the company of the directors' intention to appoint administrators.

[79] Insolvency Act, Sch B1, para 27. The specified documents are the copy resolution of the company or decision of the directors that accompanied the notice and a statutory declaration (a) that the company is or is likely to become unable to pay its debts, (b) that the company is not in liquidation, and (c) that, so far as they are able to ascertain, the appointment is not prevented by the restrictions in para 33.31 above.

[80] Insolvency Act, Sch B1, para 28(2). Appointment after the expiry of the 10 day period is a curable irregularity: *Re Euromaster Ltd* [2013] Bus LR 466.

[81] Insolvency Act, Sch B1, paras 29 and 31; Insolvency Rules, rules 2.23–2.26; Forms 2.9B, 2.10B.

[82] The prescribed matters to be included in the statutory declaration are (a) that the person is entitled to make the appointment under para 22; (b) that the appointment is in accordance with Sch B1; and either (c) where notice of intention to appoint has been given, that, so far as the person making the statement is able to ascertain, the statements made and information given in the statutory declaration filed with the notice of intention to appoint remain accurate; or (d) where no one is entitled to notice of intention to appoint, as to the matters specified in n 82 above: Insolvency Act, Sch B1, paras 29(2) and 30.

[83] The administrator's statement is in Form 2.2B; Insolvency Rules, rule 2.23. He may rely on information supplied by the directors of the company, unless he has reason to doubt its accuracy: Insolvency Act, Sch B1, para 29(4).

[84] The other prescribed documents are: (a) the written consent of all those persons to whom notice was given in accordance with para 26(1) unless the five-day notice period has expired: Insolvency Rules, rule 2.23(2)(b); (b) where more than one administrator is appointed a statement as to which functions are to be exercised jointly and which by any or all of the administrators: Insolvency Rules, rule 2.23(2)(c) and Sch B1, para 100(2); and (c) where notice of intention to appoint an administrator has not been given, either a copy of the resolution of the company, or a record of the decision of the directors, to appoint an administrator: Insolvency Rules, rules 2.22 and 2.25.

[85] Insolvency Act, Sch B1, para 32; Insolvency Rules, rule 2.26. For notice of appointment, see rule 2.27 and Forms 2.11B and 2.12B.

[86] Insolvency Act, Sch B1, para 33.

[87] *Closegate Hotel Development (Durham) Ltd v McLean* [2014] Bus LR 405.

[88] Insolvency Act, Sch B1, paras 42 and 43. Also the administrator may require a receiver of part of the company's property to vacate office: para 41(2).

(3) Directors' application for an administration order

33.39   An administration order is an order appointing a person as an administrator of a company.[89] The court may make an administration order in relation to a company only if satisfied (a) that the company is or is likely to become unable to pay its debts, within the meaning of the Insolvency Act, s 123; and (b) that the administration order is reasonably likely to achieve the purpose of administration (paragraph 33.29 above).

33.40   An application to the court for an administration order in respect of a company, known as an 'administration application', may be made only by (a) the company, (b) the directors of the company, (c) one or more creditors of the company, (d) a magistrates' court officer in respect of fines, or (e) a combination of such persons.[90] Where the directors apply, they may act by a majority and the application is treated for all purposes as the application of the company.[91]

33.41   The directors will need to make an administration application where they are unable to make an appointment out of court, because of the restrictions mentioned in paragraph 33.31 above. Even where there are no such restrictions it may be desirable to apply for an administration order, for example where an appointment out of court might be challenged by creditors or shareholders, or where court involvement is likely to be required because of a foreign element or the need to obtain directions.

33.42   The administration application made by the company or the directors must contain a statement of the applicant's belief that the company is, or is likely to become, unable to pay its debts.[92] The application must be supported by a witness statement complying with rule 2.4 made by one of the directors, or by the secretary, stating himself to make it on behalf of the company, as to the company's financial position and whether the EC Regulation applies.[93] There must be attached to the application a written statement by each of the persons proposed to be administrator, stating (a) that he consents to accept appointment, (b) details of any prior professional relationship(s) that he has had with the company to which he is to be appointed as administrator, and (c) his opinion that it is reasonably likely that the purpose of

---

[89]   Insolvency Act, Sch B1, para 10.

[90]   Insolvency Act, Sch B1, para 12(1)(b). A 'creditor' includes a contingent and a prospective creditor; para 12(4). An administration application may also be made by: (a) the liquidator of the company (Sch B1, para 38); (b) the supervisor of a CVA, which is treated as an application by the company (s 7(4)(b) and Sch B1, para 12(5); Insolvency Rules, rule 2.2(4)); and (c) the FCA (FSMA, s 359).

[91]   Insolvency Act, Sch B1, para 105; Insolvency Rules, rule 2.3(2).

[92]   Insolvency Rules, rule 2.2(1), by which the administration application must be in Form 2.1B, and rule 2.4(1). By rule 2.3(1), the application must state the name of the company and its address for service, which (in the absence of special reasons to the contrary) is that of the company's registered office. If the application is made by the directors, rule 2.3(2) requires that it is so made under Sch B1, para 12(1)(b).

[93]   Insolvency Rules, rules 2.2(1) and (2). Rule 2.4(2) requires the witness statement in support to contain (a) a statement of the company's financial position, specifying (to the best of the applicant's knowledge and belief) the company's assets and liabilities, including contingent and prospective liabilities; (b) details of any security known or believed to be held by creditors of the company, and whether in any case the security is such as to confer power on the holder to appoint an administrative receiver or to appoint an administrator under para 14; (c) details of any insolvency proceedings in relation to the company including any petition that has been presented for the winding up of the company so far as within the immediate knowledge of the applicant; (d) where it is intended to appoint a number of persons as administrators, details of the matters set out in para 100(2) regarding the exercise of the function of the administrators; and (e) any other matters which, in the opinion of those intending to make the application, will assist the court in deciding whether to make such an order, so far as lying within the knowledge or belief of the applicant. By rule 2.4(4) the affidavit shall also state whether, in the opinion of the person making the application, the EC Regulation will apply and, if so, whether the proceedings will be main proceedings or territorial proceedings.

the administration will be achieved.[94] Evidence in support of an administration application must provide a clear account of all potentially relevant facts and circumstances and where judgments, estimates, or opinions are stated, they should be supported by the underlying material.[95] Applicants for an administration order owe a duty of candour to the court, which should look critically at the material placed before it.[96]

The application and all supporting documents are filed with the court, which fixes a venue **33.43** for the hearing.[97] Where there is no need to serve any of the persons mentioned in the next paragraph or where any such persons consent, the court may hear the application immediately. In other cases the hearing date will be fixed to allow sufficient time for service. The filing of the application brings into force an interim moratorium on insolvency proceedings and other legal process.[98] Once the application has been made it cannot be withdrawn without the permission of the court.[99]

The following must be given not less than five days' notice of the hearing of the application: **33.44** (a) any administrative receiver of the company; (b) the holder of a qualifying floating charge who may be entitled to appoint an administrative receiver or administrator; (c) the petitioner in respect of any pending winding-up petition (and any provisional liquidator); (d) any Member State liquidator appointed in main proceedings in relation to the company; (e) the person proposed as administrator; (f) the company, if the application is made by anyone other than the company; and (g) the supervisor of a CVA.[100]

In addition notice must be given to any enforcement or other officer who, to the knowledge **33.45** of the applicant, is charged with an execution or other legal process against the company or its property and any person who, to the applicant's knowledge, has distrained against the company or its property.[101]

The directors and the company may appear or be represented at the hearing of their applica- **33.46** tion, as may the persons served under paragraph 33.44 above.[102] At the hearing the court has wide powers and may: (a) make the administration order; (b) dismiss the application; (c) adjourn the hearing conditionally or unconditionally; (d) make an interim order, including one which restricts the exercise of a power of the directors of the company or makes the management of the company subject to the control of the court or an insolvency practitioner; or (e) treat the application as a winding-up petition and make a winding-up order

---

[94] Insolvency Rules, rule 2.3(5). The statement shall be in Form 2.2B.

[95] *Re Bowen Travel Ltd* [2013] BCC 182.

[96] *Cornhill Insurance plc v Cornhill Financial Services Ltd* [1993] BCLC 914, 956, 957, CA, per Dillon LJ.

[97] Insolvency Rules, rule 2.5(1)–(3). By rule 2.5(4), after the application is filed, it is the duty of the applicant to notify the court in writing of the existence of any insolvency proceedings, and any insolvency proceedings under the EC Regulation, in relation to the company, as soon as he becomes aware of them.

[98] Insolvency Act, Sch B1, paras 42–4.

[99] Insolvency Act, Sch B1, para 12(3).

[100] Insolvency Act, Sch B1, para 12(2); Insolvency Rules, rule 2.6(3). As to service, manner of service, and proof of service, see rules 2.6–2.9 and Form 2.3B.

[101] Insolvency Rules, rule 2.7.

[102] Insolvency Rules, rule 2.12. With the permission of the court any other person who appears to have an interest justifying his appearance may also appear or be represented: rule 2.12(1)(k). As to appearance by shareholders, see *Re Chelmsford City Football Club (1980) Ltd* [1991] BCC 133; *Re Farnborough-Aircraft.com Ltd* [2002] 2 BCLC 641.

under the Insolvency Act, s 125.[103] If the court makes an administration order, it takes effect at the time appointed in the order, or if no time is appointed, when the order is made and brings into effect the moratorium on insolvency proceedings and other legal process.[104]

33.47 Three particular matters affect the decision of the court on the administration application: the appointment of an administrative receiver, the rights of the holder of a qualifying floating charge, and opposition from creditors.

33.48 The issue of an administration application does not prevent the holder of a qualifying floating charge appointing an administrative receiver or such receiver carrying out his functions.[105] Where an administrative receiver is in office, whether appointed before or after the making of the administration application, the court must dismiss the application unless the person by or on behalf of whom the receiver was appointed consents to the making of the administration order or the court thinks that the security by virtue of which the receiver was appointed would be liable to be released or discharged under the Insolvency Act, ss 238–40 (transaction at undervalue or preference) or avoided under s 245 (avoidance of floating charge) if an administration order were made.[106] If the holder of the qualifying floating charge does consent to the making of an administration order, the administrative receiver vacates office, so that there is only an administrator in office.[107]

33.49 The issue of an administration application does not prevent the holder of a qualifying floating charge from appointing an administrator under paragraph 14.[108] The effect of such an appointment is that the court cannot make an administration order on the application of the company or the directors, which must therefore be dismissed.[109] Instead of appointing its own administrator out of court, the holder of a qualifying floating charge may intervene in the administration application and apply to the court to appoint a specified person as administrator instead of the person nominated by the applicant. The court must grant that application unless, because of the particular circumstances of the case, the court thinks it right to refuse it.[110]

33.50 The administration application made by the company or the directors may be opposed by creditors, who may have presented a winding-up petition. Provided that it is satisfied that there is a real prospect that the purpose of administration may be achieved, the court will be

---

[103] Insolvency Act, Sch B1, para 13, which is subject to para 39; see para 33.48 below. For an interim order, see *Re Galidoro Trawlers Ltd* [1991] BCLC 411. In *Re Ci4net.com Inc* [2005] BCC 277 a winding-up order was made on an administration application made by a creditor.

[104] Insolvency Act, Sch B1, paras 13(2), 42, 43. The administration order is in Form 2.4B. See Insolvency Rules, rules 2.12 and 2.14 for notice of the order, and rule 2.27 for notice of appointment of administrator and Forms 2.11B and 2.12B.

[105] Insolvency Act, Sch B1, para 44(7)(c) and (d).

[106] Insolvency Act, Sch B1, para 39; *Chesterton International Group plc v Deka Immobilien Inv GmbH* [2005] BPIR 1103.

[107] Insolvency Act, Sch B1, para 41(1) and (3).

[108] Insolvency Act, Sch B1, para 44(7)(b).

[109] Insolvency Act, Sch B1, para 7, which is subject to paras 90–7 and 100–3 about replacement and additional administrators. In *Re Bickland Ltd* [2012] EWHC 706 (Ch) the directors were entitled to the costs of their administration application as if they were costs of the administration where just before the hearing the holder of a qualifying floating charge appointed an administrator. Also see *Re Sykes & Son Ltd* [2012] EWHC 1005 (Ch).

[110] Insolvency Act, Sch B1, para 36; Insolvency Rules, rule 2.10. The directors have standing to cause the company to challenge the appointment of an administrator by the holder of a qualifying floating charge: *Re Stephen Petitioner* [2012] BCC 537.

disposed to make an administration order and dismiss any winding-up petition.[111] Where there is a dispute as to the identity of the administrator, the relevant factors are usually independence and cost saving.[112] Even if the directors' or company's administration application is unsuccessful, the directors will not be ordered to pay costs if they have acted in good faith in performance of their duties to the company.[113]

The appointment of an administrator takes place at the time appointed by the order, or, where no time is appointed, when the order is made.[114] This power to make a retrospective administration order (going back up to 364 days) has been used to overcome difficulties where an out-of-court appointment has been found to have been invalid.[115] In *Re Care Matters Partnership Limited* Norris J rejected the argument that the court, faced with an application for a retrospective administration order, should only consider whether the conditions for making the administration order were satisfied at the date (in the past) when the order was sought to take effect. He held that there were two relevant questions: (i) whether an administration order ought to be made at all and (ii) when it ought to take effect. Thus in order to make a retrospective administration order, the court needed to be satisfied that the conditions for making an administration order were met at the time the application is made and that they would have been met on the date the order is deemed to have taken effect.[116] In *Mond v Synergi Partners Ltd*[117] the court considered that it was appropriate to make a winding-up order, rather than a retrospective administration order. **33.51**

(4) Pre-packs

A 'pre-packaged' administration (or 'pre-pack') involves 'a sale of all or part of the business and assets of a company ... negotiated "in principle" while it is not subject to any insolvency procedure, but on the footing that the sale will be concluded immediately after the company has entered into such a procedure, and on the authority of the insolvency practitioner appointed'.[118] The pre-pack process has advantages in that it may enable the administrator to realize more for the assets, because business continuity and goodwill are preserved, whereas **33.52**

---

[111] On the making of an administration order, a petition for the winding up of the company shall be dismissed: Insolvency Act, Sch B1, para 40(1)(a), unless the petition is under s 124A (public interest), s 124B (SEs), or by the FCA under FSMA, s 367. For cases, under the original administration regime of petitions opposed by creditors, see *Re Consumer and Industrial Press Ltd* [1988] BCLC 177; *Re Land and Property Trust Co plc (No 2)* [1991] BCLC 849; *Re Arrows Ltd (No 3)* [1992] BCLC 555; *Re Structures & Computers Ltd* [1998] 1 BCLC 292; *Re Stallton Distribution Ltd* [2002] BCC 486. For such a case under the new regime, see *El Ajou v Dollar Land (Manhattan) Ltd* [2007] BCC 953.

[112] *Re Maxwell Communication Corp Plc* [1992] BCLC 465; *Re World Class Homes Ltd* [2005] 2 BCLC 1.

[113] *Re Land and Property Trust Co plc (No 4)* [1994] 1 BCLC 232, CA; *Re Tajik Air Ltd* [1996] 1 BCLC 317. In *Re Professional Computer Group Ltd* [2009] BCC 323 the company's costs of a successful application were to be paid as an expense of the administration, whereas the costs of the creditors were not to be paid as an expense, since their challenge was unsuccessful.

[114] Insolvency Act, Sch B1, para 13(2).

[115] *G-Tech Construction Ltd* [2007] BPIR 1275; *Re Derfshaw Limited* [2011] BCC 631; *Re Frontsouth (Witham) Limited* [2011] BCC 635; *Re Care Matters Partnership Limited* [2011] BCC 957; *Re Law for All* [2011] BCC 963.

[116] [2011] BCC 957 at paras 11 and 18.

[117] [2015] 2 BCLC 229.

[118] *Re Kayley Vending Ltd* [2009] BCC 578 at para 2. Cases where administration orders have been made with a view to a pre-pack include *Re Hellas Telecommunications (Luxembourg) II SCA* [2010] BCC 295; *Re Halliwells LLP* [2011] 1 BCLC 345; *Re European Directories (DH6) BV* [2012] BCC 46. In *Re Christophorus 3 Ltd* [2014] EWHC 1162 (Ch) an urgent ruling on the interpretation of security documents was given in order to facilitate a pre-pack sale.

the going-concern value of the business invariably diminishes during an administration. Also, the employees are usually transferred to the new company, so preserving jobs and avoiding wrongful dismissal and redundancy claims against the company. Pre-packs have, however, attracted criticism because of concern, particularly where directors or shareholders are interested in the purchaser, that assets may have been sold for too little, without adequately testing the market and without proper concern for the interests of creditors.

33.53 Where a pre-pack is in contemplation, particularly where they are interested in the purchaser, directors should be particularly attentive to their duties under the 2006 Act, s 172 to promote the success of the company, having regard to the interests of creditors. They should take legal advice and the advice of an insolvency practitioner, but they must satisfy themselves that the steps that they take are in the interests of creditors. They should make sure also that what is proposed is compliant with best practice.

33.54 In this regard, in response to the concerns mentioned above, the Statement of Insolvency Practice 16 (SIP 16) was introduced in January 2009 to make the process more transparent for creditors and to ensure that fair value was obtained for the assets. The most recent (third) version of SIP 16 came into force in relation to administration appointments starting on or after 1 November 2015. In particular, SIP 16:

(1) emphasizes that administrators should be mindful of the interests of unsecured creditors and clear about the nature and extent of their relationship with directors in the pre-appointment period;

(2) emphasizes that, when considering the manner of disposal of the business or assets, administrators should bear in mind the requirements of paras 3(2) and 3(4) of Schedule B1 which provide that the administrator must perform his functions in the interests of the company's creditors as a whole and, where the purpose of administration is to make a distribution to one or more secured or preferential creditors, the administrator is under a duty to avoid unnecessarily harming the interests of creditors as a whole;

(3) highlights the importance of giving unsecured creditors a detailed explanation and justification of why a pre-packaged sale was undertaken, so that they can be satisfied that the administrator has acted with due regard for their interests; and

(4) provides a detailed list of information which should be disclosed to creditors in all cases where there is a pre-packaged sale. If there are exceptional circumstances that justify not providing such information, the administrator should provide the reasons why it has not been provided.

33.55 Following the introduction of SIP 16, in *Re Kayley Vending Ltd*[119] Judge Cooke summarized the concerns about pre-packs as being that they may too easily lead the directors and the insolvency practitioner to arrive at a solution which is convenient for both of them and their interests (perhaps also satisfying a secured creditor who might be in a position to appoint his own receiver or administrator) but which harms the interests of the general creditors. He also expressed the view that in exercising its discretion in pre-pack cases, the court must be alert to see, so far as it can, that the procedure is at least not being obviously abused to the disadvantage of creditors and that for that purpose the court was likely to be assisted by the provision of (at least) the information required by SIP 16.

---

[119] [2009] BCC 578.

(5) Effect of appointment of administrator on directors' powers

An administrator is a person appointed under the Insolvency Act, Schedule B1 to man- **33.56**
age the company's affairs, business, and property.[120] He is an officer of the court, even if
appointed out of court, and must perform his functions as quickly and efficiently as reasonably practicable.[121] The administrator is empowered to do anything necessary or expedient
for the management of the affairs, business, and property of the company;[122] and he is given
a number of specific powers.[123] The administrator on his appointment takes custody or control of all the property to which he thinks the company is entitled.[124]

The administrator's powers include the power to remove or appoint a director (whether **33.57**
or not to fill a vacancy).[125] It follows that the appointment of an administrator does not,
without more, terminate the office of a director. However, a director may not exercise a
management power—which means a power which could be exercised so as to interfere with
the exercise of the administrator's powers—without the consent of the administrator.[126] It
follows that the administrator is at liberty to give a director an active role in the management
of the company.

The board of directors retains its role as an organ of the company notwithstanding the **33.58**
appointment of an administrator, and the directors continue to be subject to statutory and
common law duties. But the directors may not interfere with the management by the administrator of the company's affairs, business, and property. If they do they risk being in contempt of court, since an administrator is an officer of the court.[127]

D. Administrative Receivership

An administrative receiver can only be appointed pursuant to a qualifying floating charge **33.59**
which was created before 15 September 2003, unless one of the exceptions applies.[128] In
practice banks and other holders of qualifying floating charges created before 15 September
2003 are usually content to appoint an administrator or to concur in such an appointment
by the company or the directors. Accordingly, appointments of administrative receivers are
becoming increasingly rare.

---

[120] Insolvency Act, Sch B1, para 1(1).
[121] Insolvency Act, Sch B1, paras 4 and 5.
[122] Insolvency Act, Sch B1, para 59(1).
[123] Insolvency Act, Sch B1, para 60 as amended by SBEE Act 2015, s 129 with effect from 26 May 2015.
[124] Insolvency Act, Sch B1, para 67.
[125] Insolvency Act, Sch B1, para 61. Even though it is in administration a company must have the minimum
number of directors required by the 2006 Act, s 154.
[126] Insolvency Act, Sch B1, para 64.
[127] Insolvency Act, Sch B1, para 5.
[128] Insolvency Act, s 72A; Insolvency Act 1986, Section 72A (Appointed Day) Order 2003 (SI 2003/2095).
The exceptions, provided for by ss 72B–72H are (i) capital market arrangements; (ii) public-private partnerships with step-in rights; (iii) utility and urban regeneration projects with step-in rights; (iv) project finance
with step-in rights (*Feetum v Levy* [2006] Ch 585, CA); (v) financial market charge under the 1989 Act, s 173, a
system-charge within the meaning of the Financial Markets and Insolvency Regulations 1996 (SI 1996/1469),
or a collateral security charge within the meaning of the Financial Markets and Insolvency (Settlement Finality)
Regulations 1999 (SI 1999/2979); and (vi) a company holding an appointment under the Water Industry Act
1991, Part II, Ch 1, a protected railway company within the meaning of the Railways Act 1993, s 59 (including
that section as it has effect by virtue of the Channel Tunnel Rail Link Act, 1996, s 19), and a licence company
within the meaning of the Transport Act 2000, s 26.

33.60   An administrative receiver is the receiver and manager of the whole or substantially the whole of the company's property, which property is charged in law or equity to the holders of charges, which include a floating charge.[129] The administrative receiver's function is to get in the company's property in order to discharge, so far as possible, the secured debts. For this purpose the administrative receiver has all the powers in the debenture by which he is appointed as well as the powers contained in the Insolvency Act, Schedule 1.[130] The administrative receiver is, or is deemed to be, the company's agent unless and until the company goes into liquidation, but liquidation does not prevent the administrative receiver from exercising his powers to manage and get in the company's property in the name of the company.[131]

33.61   The appointment of an administrative receiver has no effect on the office of the directors, but the receiver replaces the board as the person having authority to exercise the company's powers, so that the board's powers are suspended and it can no longer dispose of the company's property without the consent of the debenture holder or receiver.[132]

33.62   The position is different where the receiver has no interest in taking into his possession or control a particular asset, such as a claim against the debenture holder. This was the position in *Newhart Developments Ltd v Co-operative Commercial Bank Ltd* where the Court of Appeal held that the power to bring proceedings in the name of the company conferred on receivers (in that case, by the terms of the debenture) was an enabling power; and the provision conferring that power did not 'divest the directors of their power, as the governing body of the company, of instituting proceedings in a situation where so doing did not in any way impinge prejudicially upon the position of the debenture holders by threatening or imperilling the assets subject to the charge'.[133] In *Newhart* the Court of Appeal held that the directors, who provided the company with a full indemnity for costs, were entitled to cause the company to bring proceedings against the debenture holder without having to obtain the receiver's consent. In *Tudor Grange Holdings v Citibank* Sir Nicholas Browne-Wilkinson V-C distinguished the *Newhart* case on the ground that the proceedings against the debenture holder could impinge on the property subject to the receivers' powers, since there was no indemnity against adverse costs in place, and also expressed reservations as to whether *Newhart* was correctly decided.[134]

33.63   The board may also be able demonstrate a need for information from the receivers, beyond what is contained in the receiver's statutory accounts, in order to comply with its statutory obligation to render accounts or to exercise the company's right to redeem. But even then the board's interest in obtaining the information is subordinated to the receiver's primary duty not to do anything which may prejudice the interests of the debenture holder.[135]

---

[129] Insolvency Act, s 29(2).

[130] Insolvency Act, s 42. The powers in Sch 1 apply to both administrators and administrative receivers.

[131] Insolvency Act, s 44; *Re Henry Pound Son v Hutchins* (1889) 42 Ch D 402, CA; *Gosling v Gaskell* [1897] AC 595, HL; *Goughs Garages Ltd v Pugsley* [1930] 1 KB 615, CA; *Sowman v David Samuel Trust Ltd* [1978] 1 WLR 22; *Re Beck Foods Ltd* [2002] 1 WLR 1304, CA.

[132] *Moss Steamship Co Ltd v Whinney* [1912] AC 254, 263, HL, per Lord Atkinson; *Newhart Developments Ltd v Co-operative Commercial Bank Ltd* [1978] QB 814, 819, 821, CA, per Shaw LJ; *Re Emmadart Ltd* [1979] Ch 540, 547, per Brightman J; *Gomba Holdings UK Ltd v Homan* [1986] 1 WLR 1301, 1306, per Hoffmann J; *Village Cay Marina Ltd v Acland* [1998] 2 BCLC 327, 333, PC, per Lord Hoffmann.

[133] [1978] QB 814, 819, 821, per Shaw LJ; followed in *Watts v Midland Bank plc* [1986] BCLC 15; *Sutton v GE Capital Commercial Finance Ltd* [2004] 2 BCLC 662, CA at para 45. Note the explanation of *Newhart* given by Hoffmann J in *Gomba Holdings UK Ltd v Homan* [1986] 1 WLR 1301, 1307.

[134] [1992] Ch 53, 63.

[135] *Gomba Holdings UK Ltd v Homan* [1986] 1 WLR 1301, 1307, 1308.

E. Voluntary Winding Up

(1) Voluntary winding up: general

Where the directors of a company that is, or is about to become, unable to pay its debts find that **33.64** a CVA, administration, or administrative receivership are not available options, they will have to consider liquidation. A company which is registered under the 2006 Act may be wound up voluntarily as an alternative to being wound up by the court,[136] but unregistered companies cannot be wound up voluntarily except in accordance with the EC Regulation.[137] The overwhelming majority of windings up are voluntary and the directors would only resort to winding up by the court in rare cases where the necessary resolution of the members could not be obtained or where it is desirable to obtain the immediate appointment of a provisional liquidator.

A voluntary winding up is a process initiated by a resolution of shareholders (for the pro- **33.65** cedures, see Chapter 25 above). A company may be wound up voluntarily in two circumstances: (a) when the period (if any) fixed for the duration of the company by the articles expires, or the event (if any) occurs, on the occurrence of which the articles provide that the company is to be dissolved, and the company in general meeting has passed an ordinary resolution requiring it to be wound up voluntarily; or (b) if the company resolves by special resolution that it be wound up voluntarily.[138] Where there is a holder of a qualifying floating charge, the holder must be given five days' written notice of the resolution before it is passed, unless the holder gives his written consent.[139] This is to give the holder an opportunity to appoint an administrator. After the company has entered administration or an administration application has been made, no resolution may be passed for the winding up of the company.[140]

Companies frequently go into voluntary liquidation after a winding-up petition has been **33.66** presented or threatened, usually for the legitimate reasons of expedition and saving costs, but occasionally because the directors hope that the liquidator appointed in the voluntary winding up will be more favourably disposed towards them. Voluntary winding up does not bar the right of a creditor (or contributory) to have the company wound up by the court and creditors who have concerns about the voluntary winding up may press for a winding-up order.[141] In exercising its discretion in such a case, the court takes account of the views of the majority of independent creditors, but it will also consider the reasons for creditors' views.[142]

---

[136] Insolvency Act, s 73. 2006 Act, s 1(1) identifies companies that are registered under the 2006 Act.

[137] Insolvency Act, s 221(4). In *TXU Europe German Finance BV* [2005] BCC 90 Mr Registrar Baister made an order under Insolvency Rules, rule 7.62 confirming the creditors' voluntary windings up under English law of a Dutch company and an Irish company with COMIs in England, having regard to the EC Regulation, Art 3.

[138] Insolvency Act, s 84(1). Section 84(1)(c), providing for voluntary winding up pursuant to an extraordinary resolution, was repealed with effect from 1 October 2007; 2006 Act Commencement Order No 3, Sch 4, para 39 and Sch 5.

[139] Insolvency Act, s 84(2A), (2B).

[140] Insolvency Act, Sch B1, paras 42 and 44.

[141] Insolvency Act, s 116 (and also s 124(5)).

[142] Insolvency Act, s 195; *Re JD Swain Ltd* [1965] 1 WLR 909, CA; *Re Southard & Co Ltd* [1979] 1 WLR 1198, CA; *Re Lowestoft Traffic Services Ltd* [1986] BCLC 81; *Re Palmer Marine Surveys Ltd* [1986] 1 WLR 573; *Re Falcon RJ Developments Ltd* [1987] BCLC 437; *Re MCH Services Ltd* [1987] BCLC 535; *Re Gordon & Breach Science Publishers Ltd* [1995] 2 BCLC 189; *Re Inside Sport Ltd* [2000] 1 BCLC 302; *Re Zirceram Ltd* [2000] 1 BCLC 751. The case for a compulsory order is stronger where the petition is presented in the public interest: *Re Lubin, Rosen Ltd* [1975] 1 WLR 122.

33.67 When a company has passed a resolution for voluntary winding up, the directors must ensure that (a) within 15 days after the passing of the resolution a copy of it is forwarded to the Registrar, and (b) within 14 days after the passing of the resolution notice of the resolution is advertised in the Gazette. If default is made in complying with these obligations, the company and every officer of it who is in default is liable to a fine and, for continued contravention, to a daily default fine.[143]

33.68 A voluntary winding up is deemed to commence at the time of the passing of the resolution for voluntary winding up.[144] From the commencement of the winding up the company shall cease to carry on its business, except so far as may be required for its beneficial winding up, but the company's corporate state and powers continue until it is dissolved.[145] Also, after the commencement of the winding up any transfer of shares, not being to or with the sanction of the liquidator, or alteration in the status of members is void.[146] The resolution for voluntary winding up brings into effect the statutory scheme for distributing the company's property in satisfaction of its liabilities and, subject to that and the payment of the expenses of the voluntary winding up, among the members according to their rights and interests.[147] The court is not involved in the process of the winding up unless a question is referred to it.[148]

33.69 Before the resolution for voluntary winding up is passed the directors should consider whether they are able to make a statutory declaration as regards the company's solvency. If they do make such a declaration, the winding up will be a 'members' voluntary winding up' under the control of members, who appoint the liquidator; if they do not, the winding up will be a 'creditors' voluntary winding up' under the control of creditors whose nomination of liquidator prevails over the members' choice.[149] If a members' voluntary winding up becomes insolvent it converts into a creditors' voluntary winding up.[150]

(2) Members' voluntary winding up

33.70 The statutory declaration of solvency may be made by the directors (or, in the case of a company having more than two directors, the majority of them) at a directors' meeting to the effect that they have made a full inquiry into the company's affairs and that, having done so, they have formed the opinion that the company will be able to pay its debts in full, together with interest at the official rate (as defined in s 251), within such period, not exceeding 12 months from the commencement of the winding up, as may be specified in the declaration. Such a declaration by the directors has no effect unless (a) it is made within the five weeks immediately preceding the date of the passing of the resolution for winding

---

[143] Insolvency Act, ss 84(3) and 85; 2006 Act, ss 29 and 30.

[144] Insolvency Act, s 86. In *Secretary of State for Trade and Industry v Slater* [2008] BCC 70 the court rejected an argument that for the purpose of the TUPE Regulations 2006 a creditors' voluntary liquidation had commenced at a date earlier than the meetings of the company and creditors.

[145] Insolvency Act, s 87.

[146] Insolvency Act, s 88.

[147] Insolvency Act, ss 107 and 115; Insolvency Rules, rule 4.218. As an alternative an arrangement under s 110 could be sanctioned or distributions could be made under a CVA or scheme under 2006 Act, Part 26.

[148] Insolvency Act, s 112 gives the court power to determine any question arising in the voluntary winding up or to exercise all or any of the powers which it might exercise if the company were being wound up by the court. The court may refuse to exercise its powers under the section if the procedures are inappropriate: *Re Stetzel Thomson & Co Ltd* (1988) 4 BCC 74.

[149] Insolvency Act, ss 90, 91, 100.

[150] Insolvency Act, ss 95 and 96.

up, or on that date but before the passing of the resolution; and (b) it embodies a statement of the company's assets and liabilities as at the latest practicable date before the making of the declaration. The declaration shall be delivered to the Registrar of Companies before the expiration of 15 days immediately following the date on which the resolution for winding up is passed.[151]

A declaration of solvency is not invalidated because of minor inaccuracies in the statement of assets and liabilities, provided there is something which can reasonably and fairly be described as 'a statement of the company's assets and liabilities'.[152] **33.71**

The penalties imposed on directors who fail to comply with these obligations are stringent. A director making a declaration without having reasonable grounds for the opinion that the company will be able to pay its debts in full, together with interest at the official rate, within the period specified is liable to up to two years' imprisonment or an unlimited fine, or both. If the company is wound up in pursuance of a resolution passed within five weeks after the making of the declaration, and its debts (together with interest at the official rate) are not paid or provided for in full within the period specified, it is to be presumed (unless the contrary is shown) that the director did not have reasonable grounds for his opinion. If a declaration required to be delivered to the Registrar is not so delivered within the time prescribed, the company and every officer in default is liable to a fine and, for continued contravention, to a daily default fine.[153] **33.72**

(3) Creditors' voluntary winding up

Where there is no declaration of solvency the Insolvency Act, s 98(1A) provides for the company to convene a meeting of its creditors,[154] but this section is repealed by the SBEE Act 2015 from a date to be appointed.[155] The following paragraphs describe the simplified procedure introduced by the SBEE Act 2015, which will be supplemented by new Insolvency Rules. **33.73**

By the Insolvency Act, s 99(1) the directors are under obligations, within 7 days of the date of the resolution for voluntary winding up, to: **33.74**

    (a) make out a statement in the prescribed form as to the affairs of the company, and

    (b) send the statement to the company's creditors.[156]

The statement of affairs, which must be verified by a statement of truth made by some or all of the directors, must show:

    (a) particulars of the company's assets, debts and liabilities;

---

[151] Insolvency Act, s 89(1)–(3). By s 251 the official rate of interest is the rate payable under s 189(4).

[152] *De Courcy v Clements* [1971] Ch 693; *Re New Millennium Experience Co Ltd* [2004] 1 All ER 687 at paras 107–15.

[153] Insolvency Act, s 89(4)–(6), s 430, Sch 10.

[154] Inserted by the Legislative Reform (Insolvency) (Advertising Requirements) Order 2009 (SI 2009/864), Arts 2, 3(2)(b), and 4, except where the resolution was passed before 6 April 2009. The words 'by post' were deleted from s 98(1A)(b) by the Legislative Reform (Insolvency) (Miscellaneous Provisions) Order 2010 (SI 2010/18), Arts 2 and 7, except where the resolution was passed before 6 April 2010.

[155] SBEE Act 2015, Sch 9, para 22.

[156] As amended by SBEE Act 2014, Sch 9, para 22 from a day to be appointed. While s 98 is in force Insolvency Rules, rule 4.53B provides that if the statement of affairs does not state the company's position at the date of the meeting, the directors must give a written or oral report on any material transactions between the date of the statement and the date of the meeting.

    (b) the names and addresses of the company's creditors;

    (c) the securities held by them respectively;

    (d) the dates when the securities were respectively given; and

    (e) such further or other information as may be prescribed.[157]

The reasonable and necessary expenses of preparing the statement of affairs are an expense of the liquidation.[158] If the directors without reasonable excuse fail to comply with s 99(1), (2), and (2A), they are guilty of an offence and liable to a fine.[159]

33.75   The company may nominate a person to be liquidator at the company meeting at which the resolution for voluntary winding up is passed.[160] The creditors may also nominate a person to be liquidator and the directors must seek such a nomination from the company's creditors.[161] The creditors' nomination of liquidator prevails over any appointment by the members,[162] but any director, member, or creditor of the company may apply to court to decide who should be liquidator.[163]

33.76   If a liquidator appointed by the members has been in office before the company's creditors have nominated a person to be liquidator (or the procedure by which the company's creditors were to have made such a nomination concludes without a nomination having been made), during that period he may not exercise his powers under the Insolvency Act, s 165, except for the purpose of taking the company's property into his custody or under his control, disposing of perishable goods and goods the value of which is likely to diminish if not immediately disposed of, and taking other steps to protect the company's assets.[164] Such a liquidator must apply to the court for directions if the company or the directors fail to comply with their obligations under ss 99(1), (2) or (2A), or 100(1B).[165] If the liquidator fails to comply with these obligations he is liable to a fine.[166]

33.77   If there is a liquidation committee, the liquidator must give it notice of the disposal by him of any company property to a director or other person connected with the company.[167]

(4) Effect of voluntary winding up on directors' powers

33.78   A voluntary winding up does not bring a director's office to an end; although it may well be that his employment is terminated.[168] In the rare case where no liquidator has been appointed

---

[157] Insolvency Act, s 99(2) and (2A).

[158] Insolvency Rules, rule 4.38(1).

[159] Insolvency Act, s 99(3), as amended by SBEE Act 2014, s 126, Sch 9, Pt 1, paras 1, 23(1), (3) from a day to be appointed.

[160] Insolvency Act, s 100(1), as amended by SBEE Act 2014, s 126, Sch 9, Pt 1, paras 1, 24 from a day to be appointed.

[161] Insolvency Act, s 100(1A), (1B), as amended by SBEE Act 2014, s 126, Sch 9, Pt 1, paras 1, 24 from a day to be appointed. These provisions will be supplemented by new Insolvency Rules. In their original form, they were introduced to control the abuse associated with the procedure adopted in *Re Centrebind Ltd* [1967] 1 WLR 377.

[162] Insolvency Act, s 100(2).

[163] Insolvency Act, s 100(3), (4).

[164] Insolvency Act, s 166(1)–(3), as amended by SBEE Act 2014, s 126, Sch 9, Pt 1, paras 1, 40(1), (2) from a day to be appointed.

[165] Insolvency Act, s 166(5), as amended by SBEE Act 2014, s 126, Sch 9, Pt 1, paras 1, 39 from a day to be appointed.

[166] Insolvency Act, s 166(7).

[167] Insolvency Act, s 165(6). Section 249 gives the meaning of 'connected' with the company.

[168] For effect on office, see Insolvency Act, s 114; *Midland Counties District Bank Ltd v Attwood* [1905] 1 Ch 357. For effect on employment, see *Fowler v Commercial Timber Co Ltd* [1930] 2 KB 1, 6, CA.

or nominated by the company, the powers of the directors are severely limited. Those powers may not be exercised, except with the sanction of the court or (in the case of a creditors' voluntary winding up) so far as may be necessary to ensure compliance with s 99 (statement of affairs) and s 100(1B) (nomination of liquidator by creditors).[169] This is subject to an exception allowing the directors to dispose of goods the value of which is likely to diminish if they are not immediately disposed of, and to do other things necessary for the protection of the company's assets.[170] It is an offence for a director to fail to comply with these obligations without reasonable excuse.[171]

On the appointment of a liquidator in a members' voluntary winding up, all the powers of the **33.79** directors cease, except so far as the company in general meeting or the liquidator sanctions their continuance.[172] Upon the appointment of a creditors' voluntary liquidator, all the powers of the directors cease, except so far as the liquidation committee (or, if there is no such committee, the creditors) sanction their continuance.[173] Acts of directors without the applicable sanction are not binding on the company,[174] although, where the resolution for voluntary winding up had not been registered or advertised, the company may be bound by a transaction made with a person dealing with the company in good faith and without notice of the limitation of the directors' powers.[175]

F. Winding Up by the Court

(1) Power of directors to present petition

A petition to wind up a company may be presented by the company or its directors.[176] It **33.80** is highly unusual for a company to petition, since the members may resolve to wind up voluntarily, but, as mentioned in paragraph 33.64 above, there may be rare cases where the directors, in discharge of their duties, need to petition. If so, they must either act unanimously or by a duly passed resolution at a board meeting.[177] It is, of course, more common for winding-up petitions to be presented by creditors, contributories, or the Secretary of State in the public interest. It is beyond the scope of this work to deal with the extensive law relating to winding-up petitions.[178] Instead the following paragraphs consider the effect of

---

[169] Insolvency Act, s 114(2), as amended by SBEE Act 2014, s 126, Sch 9, Pt 1, paras 1, 30 from a day to be appointed.

[170] Insolvency Act, s 114(3).

[171] Insolvency Act, s 114(4).

[172] Insolvency Act, s 91(2).

[173] Insolvency Act, s 103.

[174] *Re London and Mediterranean Bank* (1870) 5 Ch App 567 (a bill accepted by directors without sanction was not a disposition of property capable of being sanctioned under what is now Insolvency Act, s 127).

[175] *Re a Company (No 006341 of 1992)* [1994] 1 BCLC 225.

[176] Insolvency Act, s 124. The power for directors to petition was introduced by the Insolvency Act to reverse *Re Emmadart Ltd* [1979] Ch 540. For a case where the petition was adjourned where the directors were in dispute see *Re Minrealm Ltd* [2008] 2 BCLC 141. Insolvency Act, s 73 provides that a company registered under the 2006 Act may be wound up by the court. 2006 Act, s 1(1) identifies companies that are registered under the 2006 Act.

[177] *Re Instrumentation Electrical Services Ltd* [1988] BCLC 550; *Re Equiticorp International plc* [1989] 1 WLR 1010.

[178] Insolvency Act, ss 117–30; Insolvency Rules, rules 4.4–4.31. If the company is a bank, the Bank of England or the FCA may apply for a bank insolvency order: Banking Act 2009, Part 2, ss 90–129, which came into force on 21 February 2009, with the Banking Act 2009 (Parts 2 and 3 Consequential Amendments) Order 2009 (SI 2009/317); Bank Insolvency (England and Wales) Rules 2009 (SI 2009/356), which came into

the presentation of a winding-up petition on the directors' powers of management, and the effect on the directors of the appointment of a provisional liquidator or a winding-up order.

(2) Effect of petition on directors' powers of management

33.81 The Insolvency Act, s 127 provides:

> In a winding up by the court, any disposition of the company's property, and any transfer of shares, or alteration in the status of the company's members, made after the commencement of the winding up is, unless the court otherwise orders, void.

The winding up of a company is deemed to commence at the time of the presentation of the petition for winding up, unless before the presentation of a winding-up petition, a resolution has been passed by the company for voluntary winding up, in which case the winding up is deemed to have commenced at the time of the passing of the resolution.[179]

33.82 The purposes of s 127 are to prevent the directors from disposing of company property to the prejudice of creditors, and to secure the rateable distribution of the company's property, as it existed at the commencement of the winding up, among its creditors.[180] Although property is given a wide meaning by the Insolvency Act, s 436, in relation to winding up it does not include property which the company has charged or real property that the company had agreed to sell.[181]

33.83 It follows that any disposition of the company's property, whether in the course of carrying on business or otherwise, is void if a winding-up order is made on the petition unless the court orders otherwise. Payments and transfers to the company are not affected and are a good discharge of obligations owed to the company.[182] A payment out of the company's bank account, whether in credit or overdrawn, is a disposition in favour of the payee, but is not a disposition to the bank rendering the bank liable in restitution.[183] Payments into an overdrawn bank account are dispositions in favour of the bank.[184]

33.84 The court may make a validation order either in advance or after the winding-up order.[185] There are two reasons why the directors should apply for a validation in advance. The first is self-protection. If a winding-up order is made and a disposition effected by them is not

---

force on 25 February 2009. Similar provisions apply to building societies: Building Societies Act 1986, s 90C; Building Societies (Insolvency and Special Administration) Order 2009 (SI 2009/805), which came into force on 29 March 2009; Building Society Insolvency (England and Wales) Rules 2010 (SI 2010/2581), which came into force on 15 November 2010.

[179] Insolvency Act, s 129.

[180] *Re Wiltshire Iron Co* (1868) 3 Ch App 443, 447; *Re Liverpool Civil Service Association Ltd* (1874) 9 Ch App 511; *Re Civil Service and General Store Ltd* (1887) 57 LJ Ch 119; *Re Leslie Enginers Co Ltd* [1976] 1 WLR 292, 304; *Re Gray's Inn Construction Ltd* [1980] 1 WLR 711, 717, CA, per Buckley LJ; *Denney v John Hudson & Co Ltd* [1992] BCLC 901, 904, CA, per Fox LJ; *Hollicourt (Contracts) Ltd v Bank of Ireland* [2001] Ch 555, CA at paras 20–3, per Mummery LJ; *Express Electrical Distributors Ltd v Beavis* [2016] 1 WLR 4783, CA.

[181] *Sowman v David Samuel Trust Ltd* [1978] 1 WLR 22, 30; *Re Margart Pty Ltd* [1985] BCLC 314, NSW SC; *Re French's Wine Bar Ltd* [1987] BCLC 499; *Re Branston & Gothard Ltd* [1999] BPIR 466.

[182] *Re Barned's Banking Co* (1867) 3 Ch App 105; *Mersey Steel and Iron Co v Naylor, Benzon & Co* (1884) 9 App Cas 434, 440, HL.

[183] *Hollicourt (Contracts) Ltd v Bank of Ireland* [2001] Ch 555, CA at paras 31 and 32.

[184] *Rose v AIB Group (UK) plc* [2003] 1 WLR 2791 at para 11.

[185] *Re AI Levy (Holdings) Ltd* [1964] Ch 19; *Re Sugar Properties (Derisley Wood) Ltd* [1988] BCLC 146; *Practice Direction (Companies Court: Contributory's Petition)* [1990] 1 WLR 490; *Express Electrical Distributors Ltd v Beavis* [2016] EWCA Civ 765 at para 24.

validated and the property recovered, the directors may be personally liable for breach of their duties to compensate the company for loss to its estate.[186] The second reason is that, once the company's bank is on notice of the presentation of the petition, it will close the company's account unless a validation order is obtained.[187]

Where the directors consider it to be in the interests of the company and its creditors that it **33.85** should carry on business pending the hearing of the petition, they may apply for a validating order. In *Express Electrical Distributors Ltd v Beavis* [2016] EWCA Civ 765[188] Sales LJ said, in relation to a company not shown to be solvent, that

> save in exceptional circumstances, a validation order should not be made in relation to dispositions occurring after presentation of a winding up petition if there is some special circumstance which shows that the disposition in question will be (in a prospective application case) or has been (in a retrospective application case) for the benefit of the general body of unsecured creditors, such that it is appropriate to disapply the usual pari passu principle.

Earlier in *Denney v John Hudson & Co Ltd*, a case of post-winding-up order validation, Fox LJ summarized the relevant principles:[189]

(1) The discretion vested in the court by [s 127] is entirely at large, subject to the general principles which apply to any kind of discretion, and subject also to limitation that the discretion must be exercised in the context of the liquidation provisions of the statute.

(2) The basic principle of law governing the liquidation of insolvent estates, whether in bankruptcy or under the companies legislation, is that the assets of the insolvent at the time of the commencement of the liquidation will be distributed pari passu among the insolvent's unsecured creditors as at the date of the bankruptcy. In a company's compulsory liquidation this is now achieved by ... s 127 of the Insolvency Act ...

(3) There are occasions, however, when it may be beneficial not only for the company but also for the unsecured creditors, that the company should be able to dispose of some of its property during the period after the petition has been presented, but before the winding-up order has been made. Thus, it may sometimes be beneficial to the company and its creditors that the company should be able to continue the business in its ordinary course.

(4) In considering whether to make a validating order, the court must always do its best to ensure that the interests of the unsecured creditors will not be prejudiced.

(5) The desirability of the company being enabled to carry on business was often speculative. In each case the court must carry out a balancing exercise.

(6) The court should not validate any transaction or series of transactions which might result in one or more pre-liquidation creditors being paid in full at the expense of other

---

[186] *Re Neath Harbour Smelting and Rolling Works* [1887] WN 87, 121; *Re Civil Service and General Stores* (1887) 57 LJ Ch 119. Section 127 does not provide the liquidator with any cause of action against a director for any loss which the company may have sustained, but he may bring a misfeasance application under s 212 if he can show that the disposition of property involved a breach of duty by the director; *Re Oxford Pharmaceuticals Ltd* [2009] 2 BCLC 485; *Phillips v McGregor-Paterson* [2010] 1 BCLC 77.

[187] *Re Gray's Inn Construction Co Ltd* [1980] 1 WLR 711, 720, CA, per Buckley LJ; *Hollicourt (Contracts) Ltd v Bank of Ireland* [2001] Ch 555, CA at para 7, per Mummery LJ.

[188] [2016] EWCA Civ 765 at para 56.

[189] [1992] BCLC 901, 904, 905, CA. Russell and Staughton LJJ agreed with the judgment of Fox LJ. The principles were derived from the judgment of Buckley LJ in *Re Gray's Inn Construction Co Ltd* [1980] 1 WLR 711, 717–19, CA and were applied in *Rose v AIB Group (UK) plc* [2003] 1 WLR 2791 at paras 13–16. In *Express Electrical Distributors Ltd v Beavis* [2016] EWCA Civ 765 at para 55 Sales LJ described Fox LJ's proposition (7) as misleading. An order will be refused if the company is trading at a loss: *Re a Company (No 007523 of 1986)* [1987] BCLC 200. Examples of orders being refused under the 4th and 6th paras of Fox LJ's principles are: *Re Webb Electrical Ltd* [1988] BCLC 382; *Re Fairway Graphics Ltd* [1991] BCLC 468; *Re Rafidain Bank Ltd* [1992] BCLC 301.

creditors, who will only receive a dividend, in the absence of special circumstances making such a course desirable in the interests of creditors generally. If, for example, it were in the interests of the creditors generally that the company's business should be carried on, and this could only be achieved by paying for goods already supplied to the company when the petition is presented (but not yet paid for) the court might exercise its discretion to validate payment for those goods.

(7) A disposition carried out in good faith in the ordinary course of business at a time when the parties were unaware that a petition had been presented would usually be validated by the court unless there is ground for thinking that the transaction may involve an attempt to prefer the disponee—in which case the transaction would not be validated.

33.86 If the directors apply for an order validating a proposed sale of company property, the court will grant the order if satisfied that the sale is at a proper market price and is advantageous to the company and its creditors. In such a case the price replaces the property sold and there is no infringement of the *pari passu* principle.[190] The court may also make a validating order in respect of the costs of defending the petition[191] or in respect of an arrangement for funding to support litigation being pursued by the company.[192]

33.87 Where the company is solvent, the court will validate dispositions made under transactions which the directors consider necessary or expedient in the company's interest, provided that the reasons given by the directors for their opinion are ones that an intelligent and honest man could reasonably hold. In such a case, it is for those opposing ratification to satisfy the court that the proposed transactions are harmful to the company.[193]

(3) Effect of appointment of provisional liquidator and winding-up order on directors' powers

33.88 The court may at any time after the presentation of a winding-up petition appoint a provisional liquidator, who carries out such functions as the court confers on him.[194] It is common practice for a provisional liquidator to be appointed in respect of an insurance company to promote a scheme of arrangement under the 2006 Act, Part 30.[195] The provisional liquidator is usually appointed to investigate, get in, and safeguard the company's assets pending the hearing of the petition, but he would not take any major step without obtaining directions from the court and he is not responsible for making distributions.[196] An undertaking in

---

[190] *Denney v John Hudson & Co Ltd* [1992] BCLC 901, 905, CA. Examples of the court making orders validating sales are: *Re AI Levy (Holdings) Ltd* [1964] Ch 19; *Re French's Wine Bar Ltd* [1987] BCLC 499; *Re Tramway Building & Construction Co Ltd* [1988] Ch 293; *Re Sugar Properties (Derisley Wood) Ltd* [1988] BCLC 146; *Re Rescupine Ltd* [2003] 1 BCLC 661.

[191] *Re Crossmore Electrical and Civil Engineering Ltd* [1989] BCLC 137.

[192] *Richbell Information Services Inc v Atlantic General Investments Trust Ltd* [1999] BCC 871.

[193] *Re Burton & Deakin Ltd* [1977] 1 WLR 390. But an order may be refused in the case of an allegedly solvent company where the petition is presented by the Secretary of State in the public interest: *Re a Company (No 007130 of 1998)* [2000] 1 BCLC 582.

[194] Insolvency Act, s 135; *Revenue and Customs Commissioners v Rochdale Drinks Distributors Ltd* [2012] 1 BCLC 748, CA; *Revenue and Customs Commissioners v Winnington Networks Ltd* [2014] BCC 675.

[195] *New Cap Reinsurance Corp Ltd v HIH Casualty & General Insurance Ltd* [2002] 2 BCLC 228, CA at para 11, per Jonathan Parker LJ.

[196] In *Re Parkwell Investments Ltd* [2014] 1 BCLC 721 HMRC had petitioned for the winding up of a company on the basis of unpaid VAT assessments and a provisional liquidator was appointed in circumstances where there were real questions as to the integrity of the company's management, as well as evidence that the company had been used as a vehicle for VAT fraud.

damages by the applicant will usually be required.[197] Notwithstanding the appointment, the directors remain in office and may instruct solicitors on behalf of the company to oppose the petition or the appointment of the provisional liquidator.[198] The appointment, so long as it subsists, determines the power of the directors to manage the company or deal with its property.[199] In *Pacific and General Insurance Co Ltd v Hazell* Moore-Bick J held that the appointment of a provisional liquidator automatically revokes the authority of agents appointed to act on behalf of the company by or under the authority of the directors.[200]

A compulsory winding-up order has the effect of terminating the powers of the directors, so that in the words of Lord Esher MR the position of the directors is that 'they have ceased to exist'.[201] In *Measures Brothers Ltd v Measures* the Court of Appeal held that the winding-up order terminated the director's appointment and discharged him from further performance of his obligations to the company.[202]   **33.89**

G. Directors' Duties in Relation to Investigation Procedures

The following paragraphs consider directors' obligations to provide information to administrators, administrative receivers, liquidators, and provisional liquidators (office-holders). The information is required not merely for the purpose of enabling the office-holder to fulfil his function of getting in and realizing assets in the estate and identifying liabilities. Investigations by office-holders and the official receiver are also concerned with accounting for the reasons for any failure of the company and reporting on the conduct of the directors and others involved in the management. Those reports and evidence obtained may be passed on to the Secretary of State or prosecuting authorities with a view to disqualification or criminal proceedings being taken.   **33.90**

(1) Directors' duty to provide statement of affairs and accounts

Where the company proposes a CVA or goes into a voluntary liquidation the provision by the directors of a statement of affairs is an integral part of the process. When an administrator, administrative receiver, or provisional liquidator is appointed or when a winding-up order is made certain specified persons, including the directors, are under a duty on notice to provide a statement of affairs.[203] Those specified persons are (a) officers or former officers of   **33.91**

---

[197] *Abbey Forwarding Ltd v Hone (No.3)* [2015] Ch 309, CA (assessment of compensation in respect of the undertaking of damages).

[198] *Re Union Accident Insurance Co Ltd* [1972] 1 All ER 1105, 1113.

[199] *Re Oriental Bank Corporation* (1884) 28 Ch D 634, 640; *Re Mawcon Ltd* [1969] 1 WLR 78, 82; *Re Union Accident Insurance Co Ltd* [1972] 1 All ER 1105, 1113. In *Revenue & Customs Commissioners v Munir* [2015] BCC 425 the fact that directors, who had procured the company to make payments in breach of an order appointing a provisional liquidator, had not done so for their own benefit, was a factor in civil contempt proceedings which reduced the two year starting point for sentencing to six months.

[200] [1997] BCC 400, 408.

[201] *Re Ebsworth & Tidy's Contract* (1889) 42 Ch D 23, 43, CA; also *Re Oriental Inland Steam Co* (1874) 9 Ch App 557, 560; *Fowler v Broad's Patent Night Light Co* [1893] 1 Ch 724; *Re Farrow's Bank* [1921] 2 Ch 164, 173, CA.

[202] [1910] 2 Ch 248, 254, 256, 259, CA. In contrast in the early case of *Madrid Bank Ltd v Bayley* (1866) LR 2 QB 37, Blackburn J held that directors remained officers of a company after it had been ordered to be wound up for the purposes of answering interrogatories.

[203] For administration the notice is to be sent as soon as reasonably practicable: Insolvency Act, Sch B1, para 47(1); Insolvency Rules, rule 2.28 and Form 2.13B. For administrative receivership the notice must be sent forthwith: Insolvency Act, s 47(1); Insolvency Rules, rule 3.3 and Form 3.1B. For winding up by the court or on

the company, (b) certain promoters or employees of the company, and (c) certain officers or employees of a company which is an officer of the company.[204]

33.92   In each case the statement of affairs, which is to be in a prescribed form, verified, and filed, must include (a) particulars of the company's assets, debts, and liabilities; (b) the names and addresses of the company's creditors; (c) the securities held by each creditor; and (d) the dates when the securities were given.[205] The statement of affairs must be provided within 11 days in the case of administration and 21 days in the other cases, but the relevant office-holder or the court may revoke the requirement or extend the time for providing it.[206] The expenses of preparing the statement of affairs may be paid as an expense of the administration, administrative receivership, or liquidation.[207]

33.93   There are civil and criminal consequences of default. The court may make such orders as it thinks necessary to enforce the obligations to provide the statement of affairs.[208] A person commits an offence if he fails without reasonable excuse to comply with a requirement to provide a statement of affairs.[209]

33.94   The directors and other persons identified in paragraph 33.91 above may come under a duty, at the request of the official receiver in a winding up by the court and by the liquidator in a voluntary winding up, to furnish accounts of the company of such nature, as at such date, and for such period as may be specified.[210] The specified period may begin from a date up to three years preceding the date of presentation of the winding-up petition or resolution for winding up (as the case may be), or from such earlier date to which audited accounts of the company were last prepared, but in a compulsory winding up, the court may, on the official receiver's application, require accounts for any earlier period.[211] The expenses of preparing these accounts may be paid as an expense of the liquidation.[212] The official receiver

---

appointment of provisional liquidator the official receiver may give notice: Insolvency Act, s 131(1); Insolvency Rules, rule 4.32 and Form 4.16.

[204]   For administration: Insolvency Act, Sch B1, para 47(3). For administrative receivership: Insolvency Act, s 47(3). For provisional liquidation and winding up by the court: Insolvency Act, s 131(3). By the Insolvency Act, s 235 broadly the same persons are under a duty to cooperate with the office-holder.

[205]   For administration the statement of affairs is to be verified by a statement of truth in accordance with the CPR and the administrator may apply to the court for a limited disclosure order in relation to delivery to the Registrar and filing at court: Insolvency Act, Sch B1, para 47(2); Insolvency Rules, rules 2.29, 2.30 and Forms 2.14B–2.16B. For administrative receivership the statement of affairs is to be verified by a statement of truth and the administrative receiver may apply to the court for a limited disclosure order in relation to inspection of the statement: Insolvency Act, s 47(2); Insolvency Rules, rules 3.4, 3.5, and Form 3.2. For winding up by the court or on appointment of provisional liquidator the statement of affairs is to be verified by a statement of truth and the official receiver may apply for a limited disclosure order in relation to inspection of the statement: Insolvency Act, s 131(2A); Insolvency Rules, rules 4.33, 4.35, and Form 4.17.

[206]   For administration: Insolvency Act, Sch B1, para 48(1)–(3); Insolvency Rules, rule 2.31. For administrative receivership: Insolvency Act, s 47(4) and (5); Insolvency Rules, rule 3.6. For winding up by the court or on appointment of provisional liquidator: Insolvency Act, s 131(4) and (5); Insolvency Rules, rule 4.36.

[207]   For administration: Insolvency Rules, rule 2.32. For administrative receivership: Insolvency Rules, rule 3.7. For winding up by the court or on appointment of provisional liquidator: Insolvency Rules, rule 4.37.

[208]   Insolvency Rules, rule 7.20(1)(a).

[209]   For administration: Insolvency Act, Sch B1, para 48(4). For administrative receivership: Insolvency Act, s 47(6). For winding up by the court or on appointment of provisional liquidator: Insolvency Act, s 131(7).

[210]   Insolvency Rules, rules 4.39(1) and 4.40(1).

[211]   Insolvency Rules, rules 4.39(2) and (3) and 4.40(2). Note that small companies and dormant companies are exempt from audit (2006 Act, ss 477–81) and that accounts and reports of private and public companies must be filed within nine and six months of the end of the relevant accounting reference period (2006 Act, ss 441 and 442).

[212]   Insolvency Rules, rules 4.37, 4.39(4), and 4.41.

or voluntary liquidator may require the accounts to be verified and they must be delivered within 21 days of the request, unless a longer period is allowed.[213]

In a winding up by the court, the official receiver may also require the deponents of the statement of affairs or accounts, or any one or more of them, to submit (in writing) further information amplifying, modifying, or explaining any matter contained in the statement of affairs or in accounts. Again the official receiver may require the further information to be verified and they must be delivered within 21 days of the request, unless a longer period is allowed.[214] **33.95**

(2) Directors' duties in investigation procedures in winding up by the court: public examination

Under the Insolvency Act, s 132(1) the official receiver has a duty to investigate, if the company has failed, the causes of the company's failure, and generally its promotion, formation, business, dealings, and affairs and to make such report, if any, to the court as he thinks fit. The report is prima facie evidence of the facts stated in it.[215] The statement of affairs made and submitted by directors or others, with any accounts, should be a significant contribution to the investigation. The official receiver also has power under s 235 to require those persons, among others, to give such information concerning the company and its promotion, formation, dealings, affairs, and property as he may reasonably require (paragraphs 33.106–33.109 below). **33.96**

The public examination of the company's officers under the Insolvency Act, s 133 is a valuable weapon to compel the officers of the company to comply with their duties in relation to the statement of affairs and the official receiver's investigation. It applies in all cases and not merely cases where there is a report alleging fraud.[216] A public examination may form the basis of the official receiver's report concerning the affairs of the company. It is also a means of obtaining material information for the administration of the estate which cannot as well be obtained privately and giving publicity, for the information of creditors and the community at large, to the salient facts and unusual features connected with the company's failure.[217] Thus the purpose of a public examination is not merely to obtain a full and complete disclosure of the company's assets and the affairs relating to its insolvency, but to protect the public by (a) exposing serious misconduct, (b) promoting higher standards of commercial and business morality, and (c) serving as a sanction against former officers who have not adequately assisted the official receiver or liquidator in their investigations.[218] **33.97**

---

[213] Insolvency Rules, rules 4.39(5) and 4.40(3).

[214] Insolvency Rules, rule 4.42.

[215] Insolvency Act, s 132(2). As to provision of the report to creditors and contributories, see Insolvency Rules, rules 4.43–4.48.

[216] This is one of the significant changes between the terms of the Insolvency Act, s 133 and its predecessors, 1948 Act, s 270(1) and 1985 Act, s 563: *Re Casterbridge Properties Ltd* [2004] 1 BCLC 96, CA at para 49, per Chadwick LJ.

[217] Report of the Cork Committee at para 655; *Re Seagull Engineering Ltd* [1993] Ch 345, 355, CA; *Re Richbell Strategic Holdings Ltd (No 2)* [2000] 2 BCLC 794, 800; *Re Casterbridge Properties Ltd* [2004] 1 BCLC 96, CA at para 48. See the discussion of *Re Seagull Engineering Ltd* in *Masri v Consolidated Contractors International (UK) Ltd* [2010] 1 AC 90, HL, in the speech of Lord Mance at paras 20–6.

[218] *Re Pantmaenog Timber Co Ltd* [2004] 1 AC 158, HL at paras 47 and 48, per Lord Millett; at paras 77–87, per Lord Walker.

33.98 The official receiver may at any time before the dissolution of the company apply to the court for the public examination of, among others, any person who is or has been an officer of the company; and he must make such an application, unless the court otherwise orders, if requested to do so by one half in value of the company's creditors or three-quarters in value of the company's contributories.[219] An application for a public examination may also be made where the company is in voluntary liquidation pursuant to the Insolvency Act, s 112.[220]

33.99 On such an application, the court will direct that a public examination of the officer shall be held on a day appointed by the court; and the officer must attend on that day and be publicly examined as to the promotion, formation, or management of the company or as to the conduct of its business and affairs, or his conduct or dealings in relation to the company.[221] The court is thus directed to make an order for public examination, although it would not do so in the rare case where no question could properly be put to the witness.[222] These provisions for public examination are intended to ensure that those responsible for the formation and running of an English company are liable to examination in public whether or not they are within the jurisdiction of the English courts. They therefore apply to directors residing abroad.[223]

33.100 At the public examination the official receiver, liquidator, special manager, any creditor who has tendered a proof, and any contributory may take part and question the examinee.[224] The conduct of the examination is under the control of the court and the examinee must answer all such questions as the court may put, or allow to be put, to him.[225] The examinee is to give the best answers that he can and it is no objection to questions that they extend to other members of the company's group.[226] (For self-incriminatory answers, see paragraph 33.121 below.)

33.101 If a person without reasonable excuse fails to attend his public examination, he is guilty of a contempt of court and liable to be punished accordingly.[227]

(3) Directors' liability to deliver up the company's property, books, papers, and records

33.102 When the company enters administration, an administrative receiver is appointed, the company goes into liquidation, or a provisional liquidator is appointed, the relevant office-holder is entitled and bound to take the company's property into his possession or control and the directors' functions with respect to it are displaced.[228] The directors are therefore not entitled to retain any of the company's property or its books, papers, and records.

---

[219] Insolvency Act, s 133(1), (2).

[220] *Re Pantmaenog Timber Co Ltd* [2004] 1 AC 158, HL at para 56, per Lord Millett.

[221] Insolvency Act, s 133(3). For procedure in relation to the public examination, see Insolvency Rules, rules 4.211–4.217.

[222] *Re Casterbridge Properties Ltd* [2004] 1 BCLC 96, CA at paras 44, 49, 52, per Chadwick LJ. The change from 'may' in 1948 Act, s 270(1) and 1985 Act, s 563 to 'shall' in s 133(3) represents another significant change in the law.

[223] *Re Seagull Manufacturing Co Ltd* [1993] Ch 345, CA; discussed in *Masri v Consolidated Contractors International (UK) Ltd* [2010] 1 AC 90, HL, in the speech of Lord Mance at paras 20–6.

[224] Insolvency Act, s 133(4).

[225] Insolvency Rules, rule 4.215(1).

[226] *Re Richbell Strategic Holdings Ltd (No 2)* [2000] 2 BCLC 794.

[227] Insolvency Act, s 134(1).

[228] For administration: Insolvency Act, Sch B1, paras 1(2), 59, 60–9, 111(1) and Sch 1 and paras 32.56–32.58 above. For administrative receivership: Insolvency Act, s 42 and Sch 1 and paras 32.59–32.63 above.

If the directors, or anyone else, wrongly retain company property or records, the Insolvency **33.103**
Act, s 234(2) provides the office-holder with a summary remedy. It provides:

> Where any person has in his possession or control any property, books, papers or records to
> which the company appears to be entitled, the court may require that person forthwith (or
> within such period as the court may direct) to pay, deliver, convey, surrender or transfer the
> property, books, papers or records to the office-holder.

The section should only be used for the legitimate purposes of the relevant insolvency proceeding, which may include getting in and realizing the company's property for the benefit
of its creditors, achieving the purpose of administration or, in the case of books, papers
and records, furthering the public interest in investigating and reporting on the company's
affairs, with a view to disqualification proceedings or prosecution.[229]

The application should be made in the name of the relevant office-holder.[230] It should be **33.104**
made on notice to the respondent, unless giving notice would cause injustice because of
delay or risk of dissipation or destruction of the relevant property or records.[231] The section
can be used to determine disputes as to ownership or possession of property.[232] But the section does not apply where the company's right of possession depends on establishing its title
in foreign proceedings.[233] Where appropriate a costs order may be made in favour of the
office-holder.[234]

It should be noted that s 234(3) and (4) provides a measure of protection for the office-holder **33.105**
when he seizes or disposes of property which he wrongly believes belongs to the company:

> (3) Where the office-holder—
>   (a) seizes or disposes of any property which is not property of the company, and
>   (b) at the time of seizure or disposal believes, and has reasonable grounds for believing,
>   that he is entitled (whether in pursuance of an order of the court or otherwise) to seize
>   or dispose of that property, the next subsection has effect.
> (4) In that case the office-holder—

For liquidation and provisional liquidation: Insolvency Act, ss 143(1), 144(1), 247(2), and paras 32.79, 32.80,
32.89, 32.90 above; *Caldero Trading Ltd v Beppler & Jacobson Ltd* [2012] EWHC 4031 (Comm) (under the
terms of a consent order, the company's provisional liquidators were no longer entitled to all of the company's
books and records as the order had restricted their entitlement to those documents reasonably necessary for
protecting and preserving the company's assets); *Re Corporate Jet Realisations Ltd* [2015] 2 BCLC 95.

[229] *Re Pantmaenog Timber Co Ltd* [2004] 1 AC 158, HL at paras 5 and 6, per Lord Hope; at paras 51–8, per
Lord Millett; at paras 79–87, per Lord Walker; *Sutton v GE Capital Commercial Finance Ltd* [2004] 2 BCLC
662, CA at paras 33–42. In *Walker Morris v Khalastchi* [2001] 1 BCLC 1 the company's former solicitors
resisted the liquidator's request to hand over documents relating to the company except on condition that he
should not disclose the documents to the Commissioners of Inland Revenue without a court order. It was held
that the documents were the property of the company and that it was for the liquidator to decide whether to
disclose them.

[230] *Smith v Bridgend BC* [2002] 1 AC 336, HL at para 32, per Lord Hoffmann. The application would be
made under the following provisions of the Insolvency Act: Sch B1, para 63 (administration), s 35 (receivership), s 112 (voluntary winding up), s 168(3) (winding up by the court).

[231] *Re First Express Ltd* [1992] BCLC 824.

[232] *Euro Commercial Leasing Ltd v Cartwright & Lewis* [1995] 2 BCLC 618; *Re Cosslett (Contractors) Ltd*
[1998] Ch 495, CA.

[233] *Re Leyland Daf Ltd* [1994] 2 BCLC 106, CA.

[234] In *Re Land Fleet (Leicester) Ltd* [2014] EWHC 4876 (Ch) a costs order was made in favour of an administrator who made a without-notice application for an order requiring the delivery up of computers which
belonged to the company in circumstances where there had been an unreasonable refusal to return the computers and an indication that information might be deleted.

(a) is not liable to any person in respect of any loss or damage resulting from the seizure or disposal except in so far as that loss or damage is caused by the office-holder's own negligence, and

(b) has a lien on the property, or the proceeds of its sale, for such expenses as were incurred in connection with the seizure or disposal.

Although 'property' is given an extremely wide meaning by the Insolvency Act, s 436, the protection given to office-holders by this provision applies to tangible property and not to choses in action.[235]

(4) Directors' duty to cooperate with office-holder

33.106 Section 235, which applies in the same circumstances as s 234, provides that certain specified persons, including the directors, are under a duty to cooperate with the relevant office-holder. Where a winding-up order has been made in respect of the company, the official receiver is an office-holder for the purpose of the section, whether or not he is the liquidator. Those specified persons are (a) officers or former officers of the company, (b) certain promoters or employees of the company, and (c) certain officers or employees of a company which is an officer of the company.[236] Section 235(2) provides that each of those persons shall:

(a) give to the office-holder such information concerning the company and its promotion, formation, business, dealings, affairs or property as the office-holder may at any time after the effective date reasonably require, and

(b) attend on the office-holder at such times as the latter may reasonably require.[237]

33.107 In practice enforcement of the duty to provide information under s 235 is the way in which office-holders obtain information about the company from the directors and others. In *Re Arrows Ltd (No 4)* Lord Browne-Wilkinson recorded that leading insolvency practitioners attach much greater importance to the confidentiality of information obtained under s 235 than they do to information obtained under formal examination under s 236, because s 235 is the means for obtaining speedy and reliable information from those concerned with the company, whether or not they are involved in any wrongdoing.[238] In complex cases a director may be required to submit to questioning over many days.[239] The privilege against

---

[235] *Welsh Development Agency v Export Finance Co Ltd* [1992] BCLC 148, 170, 171, 179, 190, 191, CA. There are no such protective provisions except in relation to chattels because it would never have occurred to Parliament that strict liability for conversion could exist for anything other than chattels: *OBG Ltd v Allan* [2008] AC 1, HL at para 97 per Lord Hoffmann (but note Lord Nicholl's dissent at para 236).

[236] Insolvency Act, s 235(1) and (3).

[237] By s 235(4):

the 'effective date' is whichever is applicable of the following dates—
(a) the date on which the company entered administration,
(b) the date on which the administrative receiver was appointed or, if he was appointed in succession to another administrative receiver, the date on which the first of his predecessors was appointed,
(c) the date on which the provisional liquidator was appointed, and
(d) the date on which the company went into liquidation.

[238] [1995] 2 AC 75, 101, HL.

[239] In *Re an inquiry into Mirror Group Newspapers plc* [1999] 2 All ER 641, 645, Sir Richard Scott V-C recorded that office-holders had interrogated Kevin Maxwell over 28 days in relation to the insolvencies of the Maxwell Group companies. In *Re Bernard Madoff Securities LLC* [2009] 2 BCLC 78 at para 15 Lewison J noted that an office-holder may invite whoever he pleases to attend the interview, including the trustee in bankruptcy of a foreign connected company, but that questioning should be limited to the affairs of the company subject to the English insolvency proceedings; s 235 was not to be used as a short-cut to an application under the

self-incrimination is not a reasonable excuse for refusing to answer a question.[240] Nor may a director required to provide information under s 235 insist on the office-holder keeping it confidential or only using it for the purposes of the insolvency proceedings, because the duty of confidence cannot operate so as to prevent the office-holder from disclosing it to persons to whom he is required or authorized by statute to make disclosure.[241]

Section 235 should be read with s 236, but whereas s 235 contains a mandatory obligation on the director or other officer to give information reasonably required, under s 236 the court has a discretion whether to order a private examination.   **33.108**

There are civil and criminal consequences for default in complying with obligations under s 235. The office-holder may apply for an order enforcing those obligations[242] or he may apply for an order for a private examination under s 236. By s 235(5), if a person without reasonable excuse fails to comply with any obligation imposed by the section, he is liable to a fine and, for continued contravention, to a daily default fine.   **33.109**

(5) Private examination

Section 236, which applies in the same circumstances as s 234, gives the court power to compel directors, among others, to appear before it for private examination and to produce documents.[243] Where a winding-up order has been made in respect of the company, the official receiver is included as an office-holder.[244] The court's powers under s 236 are: **33.110**

(2) The court may, on the application of the office-holder, summon to appear before it—
    (a) any officer of the company,
    (b) any person known or suspected to have in his possession any property of the company or supposed to be indebted to the company, or
    (c) any person whom the court thinks capable of giving information concerning the promotion, formation, business, dealings, affairs or property of the company.
(3) The court may require any such person as is mentioned in subsection (2)(a) to (c) to submit to the court an account of his dealings with the company or to produce any books, papers or other records in his possession or under his control relating to the company or the matters mentioned in paragraph (c) of the subsection.[245]

The procedure for an examination under s 236 is set out in the Insolvency Rules, Part 9.

Cross-Border Insolvency Regulations, Art 21. For a subsequent application under Art 21, see *Picard v FIM Advisers LLP* [2011] 1 BCLC 129.

[240] *Bishopsgate Investments Ltd* [1993] Ch 1, CA.

[241] *Re Arrows Ltd (No 4)* [1995] 2 AC 75, 102, HL, per Lord Browne-Wilkinson, commenting that the dicta of Millett J, to a contrary effect, in *Re Barlow Clowes Gilt Managers Ltd* [1992] Ch 208, 217, were too wide. This includes disclosure to the prosecuting authorities, since the purpose of the statutory investigatory powers, including s 235, includes the identification of potential criminal or other misconduct and the taking of appropriate steps in relation to it by criminal prosecution and/or disqualification: *R v Brady* [2004] 1 WLR 3240, CA at paras 26 and 27.

[242] Insolvency Rules, rule 7.20(1)(c).

[243] The court's jurisdiction to order the production of documents extends only to books, papers, or other records, but, if the applicant does not know the identity of a particular document, it will suffice for the purposes of Insolvency Rules, rule 9.2(3)(d) that they are adequately described by reference to their subject matter: *Harvest Finance Ltd* [2015] 2 BCLC 240.

[244] Insolvency Act, s 236(1).

[245] By the Insolvency Act, s 236(3A)(a) the account submitted under subs (3) must be contained in a witness statement verified by a statement of truth.

Application for order

33.111 The application under s 236 may be made without notice and is supported by a confidential statement of the grounds for the application.[246] An application without notice
should be justified on the ground of urgency or because notice could frustrate the
examination by leading to the disappearance of the witness or the destruction of documents.[247] The application is supported by a confidential statement, which the examinee
cannot inspect unless on a disputed application the court is of the opinion that it will
or may be unable fairly and properly to dispose of the application, but even then the
office-holder may satisfy the court that confidentiality in whole or in part is nevertheless
appropriate.[248]

33.112 The examination may be used for the purpose of getting 'sufficient information to reconstitute
the state of knowledge that the company should possess', so as to enable the office-holder to
identify, get in, and realize its assets and identify its liabilities.[249] But this is not the limit of the
examination. It may be used to enable claims to be investigated or to enable the official receiver
to report on conduct with a view to disqualification proceedings or criminal prosecution.[250]

33.113 In *Re British & Commonwealth plc (Nos 1 and 2)* Lord Slynn said that the court's discretion
under s 236:

> must be exercised after a balancing of the factors involved—on the one hand the reasonable
> requirements of the [office-holder] to carry out his task, on the other the need to avoid making
> an order which is wholly unreasonable, unnecessary, or 'oppressive' to the person concerned ...
> The protection for the person called upon to produce documents lies, thus, not in a limitation
> by category of documents ('reconstituting the company's state of knowledge') but in the fact that
> the applicant must satisfy the court that, after balancing all relevant factors, there is a proper case
> for such an order to be made. The proper case is one where the [office-holder] reasonably requires
> to see documents to carry out his functions and the production does not impose an unnecessary
> and unreasonable burden on the person required to produce them in the light of the [office-
> holder's] requirements. An application is not necessarily unreasonable because it is inconvenient
> for the addressee of the application or causes him a lot of work or may make him vulnerable to
> future claims, or is addressed to a person who is not an officer or employee of or contractor with
> the company ... but all these will be relevant factors, together no doubt with many others.[251]

33.114 In *Re Trading Partners Ltd*[252] Patten J said that the proper approach was:

> to give s 236 the wide meaning justified by its language and to deal with each application on a
> case by case basis determining as a matter of discretion whether the order sought is one which it is

---

[246] Insolvency Rules, rule 9.2.

[247] *Re PFTZM Ltd* [1995] 2 BCLC 354; *Re Murjani* [1996] 1 WLR 1498, 1509, 1510, a case on s 366
(the bankruptcy equivalent), where Lightman J disagreed with the judgment of Vinelott J in *Re Maxwell
Communications Corporation plc (No 3)* [1995] 1 BCLC 521, 528.

[248] Insolvency Rules, rule 9.5; *Re British & Commonwealth Holdings plc (Nos 1 and 2)* [1992] Ch 342, 355,
CA, per Nourse LJ.

[249] *Cloverbay Ltd v Bank of Credit and Commerce SA* [1991] Ch 90, 102, CA, per Sir Nicholas
Browne-Wilkinson V-C.

[250] *Re British & Commonwealth Holdings plc* [1993] AC 426, 439, HL, per Lord Slynn; *Re Pantmaenog
Timber Co Ltd* [2004] 1 AC 158, HL at para 67, per Lord Millett; *R v Brady* [2004] 1 WLR 3240.

[251] *Re British & Commonwealth Holdings plc (Nos 1 and 2)* [1993] AC 426, 439, 440, HL, per Lord Slynn.
In the quotation 'office-holder' has been substituted for 'administrator'.

[252] [2002] 1 BCLC 655 at para 13; see also *Re Delberry Ltd* [2008] BCC 653. In *Re ABC Ltd* [2010] BPIR
1297 the court gave directions restricting the use to be made by liquidators of information disclosed by HMRC
under s 236, which HMRC had obtained from the Dutch prosecution authorities.

proper for the court to make or is, to use the language of Lord Slynn, unjustified as being unreasonable, unnecessary or oppressive to the respondent.

Where the examinee is a director or former director, the case for making an order under s 236 **33.115** will be stronger than it would be against a third party, since a director owes fiduciary duties and his knowledge ought to made available to the company, but even in the case of a director the balancing exercise should be undertaken.[253] The court will usually give great weight to views of the office-holder, given his knowledge of the problems that exist in relation to the company's affairs and the information required.[254] The court may regard an order for oral examination as more oppressive than an order for production of documents.[255] Issues of privilege and confidentiality may also need to be considered by the court.[256]

Orders are frequently made to enable the office-holder to investigate possible claims against a **33.116** director or others.[257] Although an examination is not to be used to obtain an unfair advantage in litigation, an examination may be ordered while proceedings are on foot against the examinee to enable the office-holders to carry out their functions. The existence of the proceedings, even if containing serious allegations, will not bar an order for examination, provided that the examination is not conducted in a way designed to give the office-holders an advantage in litigation against the examinee.[258] The court will always be alive to the dangers of the examination providing an unfair advantage in litigation.[259]

The question of whether an order for a private examination under s 236 may be served out- **33.117** side the jurisdiction in accordance with Insolvency Rule 12A.20, applying CPR Part 6, was addressed in two recent cases. Although the Court of Appeal had held that an order for a public examination may be served outside the jurisdiction,[260] there had until recently been no decision on s 236 determining the issue.[261] In *Re MF Global UK Ltd*[262] it was held that

---

[253] *Cloverbay Ltd v Bank of Credit and Commerce SA* [1991] Ch 90, 102, CA, per Sir Nicholas Browne-Wilkinson V-C; *Re British and Commonwealth Holdings plc (Nos 1 and 2)* [1992] Ch 342, 372, CA, per Ralph Gibson LJ; *Bishopsgate Investment Management Ltd v Maxwell* [1992] BCLC 470 (not appealed on this point); *Shierson v Rastoggi* [2003] 1 WLR 586, CA at paras 28–39, per Peter Gibson LJ; at paras 53–63, per Mance LJ.

[254] *Re British and Commonwealth Holdings plc (Nos 1 and 2)* [1992] Ch 342, 371, 372 CA, per Ralph Gibson LJ.

[255] *Re British and Commonwealth Holdings plc (Nos 1 and 2)* [1992] Ch 342, 371, 372 CA, per Ralph Gibson LJ. In an appropriate case an order may be made for disclosure of redacted documents: *Re Galileo Group Ltd* [1999] Ch 100.

[256] *Re Corporate Jet Realisations Ltd* [2015] 2 BCLC 95.

[257] In *Jackson v Cannons Law Practice LLP* [2013] BPIR 1020 the court ordered the disclosure of privileged documents held by a firm of solicitors where they might be of assistance in the context of an investigation into an alleged fraud.

[258] *Shierson v Rastoggi* [2003] 1 WLR 586, CA; *Daltel Europe Ltd v Makki* [2005] 1 BCLC 594; but see *Re Atlantic Computers plc* [1998] BCC 200.

[259] *Re John T Rhodes Ltd* [1987] BCLC 77; *Re Bank of Credit and Commerce International SA* [1997] 1 BCLC 526; *Re Atlantic Computers plc* [1998] BCC 200, 208–9; *Sasea Finance Ltd v KPMG* [1998] BCC 216; *Re Sasea Finance Ltd* [1998] 1 BCLC 559.

[260] *Re Seagull Manufacturing Co Ltd* [1992] Ch 128, CA; discussed in *Masri v Consolidated Contractors International (UK) Ltd* [2010] 1 AC 90, HL, in the speech of Lord Mance at paras 20–6. In connection with CPR Part 6 (which Insolvency Rule 12A.20 makes applicable), note the endorsement by Lord Mance, at para 36, of the review of the scope of what is now CPR 6.38(1) by of Tomlinson J in *Vitol SA v Capri Marine Ltd* [2009] Bus LR 271.

[261] In *Re Casterbridge Properties Ltd* [2002] BCC 453 at paras 37–45, 48, Burton J summarized the issue and the authorities, but did not have to decide the point. The issue was not raised before the Court of Appeal: [2004] 1 BCLC 96.

[262] [2016] Ch 325.

s 236 does not have extraterritorial effect and, as such, that the court did not have jurisdiction to made an order under s 236 against a French company. In *Re Omni Trustees Ltd*,[263] on the other hand, it was held that s 236(3) does have extraterritorial effect, it being said that the decision in *MF Global* failed to appreciate that the context of the Insolvency Act, s 236 was structurally different from the former s 25 of the 1914 Act with which *Re Tucker*[264] was concerned. The power in the s 25 of the 1914 Act to order the production of documents was interpreted in *Re Omni Trustees* as having been merely ancillary to, and dependent upon, the principal power to summon a respondent to attend for examination before the court, whereas s 236(3) was considered to confer a freestanding power, independent of the power to summon a person to appear before the court, to require a person to submit to the court an account of dealings and to produce books, papers, and records.. The effect of these two decisions appears to be the court does not have jurisdiction under s 236(2) to summon a person out of the jurisdiction to appear before it to be examined, but it does have jurisdiction to compel such a person to make a witness statement giving an account of his dealings with the company or to produce books, papers, and records.[265]

33.118   In any event, uncertainty as to the reach of s 236 does not seem to cause practical problems. One reason is that the court can restrain the examinee from leaving the jurisdiction until after the examination.[266] Another reason is that the court may be able to rely on assistance from foreign courts. Section 237(4) gives the court power to order an examination of a person who is not in England and Wales outside the jurisdiction, either elsewhere in the UK or in a place outside the UK. An order made under this provision would be given effect to elsewhere in the UK.[267] If the court made an order for examination at a place outside the jurisdiction, it would rely on the assistance and cooperation of the foreign court to give effect to the order.[268]

33.119   If an order is made for a person to attend for examination, he should be tendered a reasonable sum in respect of travelling expenses incurred in connection with his attendance.[269]

The examination

33.120   As to the examination itself, s 237(4) provides that any person who appears or is brought before the court may be examined on oath, either orally or by interrogatories. Insolvency Rules, rule 9.3 provides for the order to require the submission of affidavits

---

[263]   [2015] BCC 906.
[264]   [1990] Ch 148, CA.
[265]   In *Official Receiver v Sahaviraya Steel Industries plc* [2016] 1 BCLC 758 the Deputy Judge noted the two conflicting decisions and gave the liquidator permission to serve an application under s 236 out of the jurisdiction on the company's parent company in Thailand.
[266]   *Re Oriental Credit Ltd* [1988] Ch 204.
[267]   Insolvency Act, s 426.
[268]   This could be under a provision equivalent to the Insolvency Act, s 426 applicable in the foreign court, under Art 21 of UNCITRAL, or by recognition under the European Insolvency Regulation. In *Re Anglo-American Insurance Co Ltd* [2002] BCC 715 provisional liquidators applied under the inherent jurisdiction for the English court to issue letters of request to the New York and Bermuda courts for the examination of individuals in their jurisdictions. In *Re Impex Services Worldwide Ltd* [2004] BPIR 564 the Isle of Man court as a matter of comity exercised its common law jurisdiction to order an examination as if under s 236 in response to a request from the English court.
[269]   Insolvency Rules, rule 9.6(4).

and the production of books, papers, and records. In *Shierson v Rastoggi* Peter Gibson LJ said:[270]

> The court in ordering an examination does not give carte blanche to the questions which may be asked of the witness at the examination, and if a particular line of inquiry is oppressive or if there are good reasons why particular questions should not be answered it is the right and duty of the court to limit the enquiry. The procedure is governed by the Insolvency Rules 1986. By rule 9.4(1) the liquidator may put such questions to the examinee as the court may allow and by r 9.4(5) the examinee may be represented by a legal representative who may put to him such questions as the court may allow for the purpose of enabling him to explain or qualify any answers given by him and may make representations on his behalf. The court therefore has control and if it thought that a line of questioning was unfair, for example if there had been no prior notice of it and the court thought such notice appropriate, it could stop such questions until the examinee was in a proper position to answer them.

The director may not refuse to answer questions on the ground that he may incriminate him- **33.121** self.[271] In any case, evidence obtained on the examination cannot be used against a director in criminal proceedings unless he relies on it.[272] The director cannot refuse to answer questions or withhold documents on the ground of legal professional privilege, where the privilege is the right of the company, but the personal privilege of the director or a third party will be protected.[273] The director should bear in mind that the office-holder may be able to obtain evidence against him from other sources, such as regulatory or prosecuting bodies, inspectors, or other office-holders.[274]

The written record of the examination, which should be signed by the witness, may, in any **33.122** proceedings, whether under the Insolvency Act or otherwise, be used as evidence against the witness of any statement made by him in the course of his examination.[275]

Section 237(1) and (2) gives the court power, on the application of the office-holder and on **33.123** consideration of the evidence, to make orders for delivery up of property and payment of debts, but these provisions would only be used in clear cases or where admissions are made.[276]

If the examination is made necessary because the director has unreasonably failed to coop- **33.124** erate with the office-holder, the director may be ordered to pay the costs of the examination.[277] Subject to that, unless the court otherwise orders, the applicant's costs are paid out of the insolvent estate.[278] Where the applicant is the official receiver acting otherwise than as

---

[270] [2003] 1 WLR 586, CA at para 43.

[271] *Bishopsgate Investment Management Ltd v Maxwell* [1993] Ch 1, CA.

[272] Insolvency Act, s 433(2). See further, para 33.126 below.

[273] *Re Brook Martin & Co (Nominees) Ltd* [1993] BCLC 328; *Re Murjani* [1996] 1 WLR 1498, 1505, 1506; *Re Ouvaroff* [1997] BPIR 712. The director may not be able to rely on his own legal advice or litigation privilege if a prima facie case of fraud is shown: *Barclays Bank plc v Eustice* [1995] 1 WLR 1238, CA; *Kuwait Airways Corp v Iraqi Airways Co* [2005] 1 WLR 2734, CA.

[274] *Morris v Director of the SFO* [1993] Ch 373; *Soden v Burns* [1996] 1 WLR 1513; *Secretary of State for Trade and Industry v Baker* [1998] Ch 356; *Re Trading Partners Ltd* [2002] 1 BCLC 655.

[275] Insolvency Rules, rule 9.4(6) and (7).

[276] If the court makes an order under s 237(1) and (2), it may also order the person against whom the order is made to pay the costs of the application for the order: Insolvency Rules, rule 9.6(2).

[277] Insolvency Rules, rule 9.6(1); *Miller v Bain* [2002] BCC 899. In *Hunt v Renzland* [2008] BPIR 1380 the court ordered an uncooperative director to pay the liquidator's costs of obtaining the examination under s 236 and of the examination itself. In *Re Arrowfield Services Ltd* [2015] EWHC 3046 (Ch) the decision to make a costs order against a director who had failed to cooperate with the liquidator was upheld, though the costs were reduced by a third, to take account of the liquidator's conduct in relation to the venue for interviews.

[278] Insolvency Rules, rule 9.6(3).

liquidator and therefore solely in the public interest, no order for costs may be made against him.[279]

33.125 Where (a) a person without reasonable excuse fails to appear before the court when he is summoned to do so under s 236, or (b) there are reasonable grounds for believing that a person has absconded, or is about to abscond, with a view to avoiding his appearance before the court under s 236 the court may, for the purpose of bringing that person and anything in his possession before the court, cause a warrant to be issued for the arrest of that person, and for the seizure of any books, papers, records, money, or goods in that person's possession.[280]

(6) Use of evidence obtained from directors

33.126 The evidence obtained under the above provisions may be used to support a claim by the company or the office-holder. The record of an examination conducted under s 236 for the purpose of determining whether to institute proceedings is protected by legal professional privilege.[281] The office-holder may disclose documents to creditors to obtain their approval of proceedings.[282] But it is not a legitimate use of the office-holder's information-gathering powers to pass the company's confidential documents to the debenture holder or another creditor for the purpose of their proceedings in which the company is not interested.[283] By s 433(1) in any proceedings any statement of affairs or other statement made pursuant to a requirement under ss 235 and 236 is admissible as evidence against any person who made or concurred in making the statement (but see paragraph 33.128 below for criminal proceedings).[284]

33.127 The office-holder may disclose to the Secretary of State for the purpose of director dis-qualification proceedings the transcripts of interviews conducted and documents provided pursuant to the powers in s 236, because such disclosure would be for the purpose of the administration.[285] By the CDDA, s 7(4) such disclosure may be required in addition to the report made to the Secretary of State under s 7(3).[286] The transcripts of evidence obtained from a director under ss 235 or 236 may be used against him in disqualification proceed-ings.[287] The admission in evidence at the hearing of disqualification proceedings of state-ments obtained under s 235 does not necessarily involve a breach of the right to a fair trial under Article 6(1) of the Human Rights Convention since the issue of fair trial is one which must be considered in the round having regard to all the relevant factors. These factors include the fact that disqualification proceedings are not criminal proceedings and are pri-marily for the protection of the public and that there are degrees of coercion involved in dif-ferent investigative procedures available in corporate insolvency and these differences might

---

[279] Insolvency Rules, rule 9.6(5).

[280] Insolvency Act, s 236(4)–(5). In *Re Hartmayes Ltd* [2013] EWHC 4624 a director was found guilty of contempt for having failed to comply with an order requiring him to provide information in relation to the proceeds of sale of a property.

[281] *Dubai Bank Ltd v Galadari* [1990] BCLC 90.

[282] *Re ACLI Metals (London) Ltd* [1989] BCLC 749. See also *Walker Morris v Khalastchi* [2001] 1 BCLC 1; *Re Sandford Farm Properties Ltd* [2015] EWHC 2999 (Ch) (disclosure to the assignee of claims vesting in the company).

[283] *Sutton v GE Capital Commercial Finance Ltd* [2004] 2 BCLC 662.

[284] *R v Kansal* [1993] QB 244; *Re Arrows Ltd (No 4)* [1995] 2 AC 75; *R v Sawtell* [2001] BPIR 381.

[285] *Re Polly Peck International plc* [1994] BCC 15.

[286] CDDA, s 7(3) and (4) and Insolvent Companies (Reports on Conduct of Directors) Rules 1996.

[287] Insolvency Act, s 433(1).

be reflected in different degrees of prejudice involved in the admission, in disqualification proceedings, of statements obtained by such procedures. Issues of fairness should therefore generally be decided by the trial judge.[288]

Where the official receiver is satisfied that material obtained pursuant to s 235 (or s 236) is **33.128** required by another prosecuting authority for the purpose of investigating crime, he is free to disclose that material to that prosecuting authority without an order of the court or notice to the person who had provided it. The purpose of the powers under ss 235 and 236 includes the identification of potential criminal or other misconduct and the taking of appropriate steps in relation to it.[289] However, by the Insolvency Act, s 433(2), in criminal proceedings in which any person who made or concurred in the making of a statement of affairs or other statement pursuant to a requirement imposed under ss 235 and 236 is charged with an offence (other than specified offences), no evidence relating to the statement may be adduced, and no question relating to it may be asked, by or on behalf of the prosecution, unless evidence relating to it is adduced, or a question relating to it is asked, by or on behalf of that person.[290]

---

[288] *Re Westminster Property Management Ltd, Official Receiver v Stern* [2000] 1 WLR 2230, CA.

[289] *R v Brady* [2004] 1 WLR 3240, CA at paras 26 and 27. In *Re France* [2014] BPIR 1448 the court gave permission for information obtained by trustees in bankruptcy under a search order to be disclosed to the prosecuting authority in circumstances where the trustees had given an undertaking not to use the information for proceedings outside the bankruptcy without the court's permission.

[290] Insolvency Act, s 433(2)–(4) was inserted by the Youth Justice and Criminal Evidence Act 1999, ss 59, 68(3), and Sch 3, para 7(2) and (3) with effect from 14 April 2000. These subsections were inserted to meet the difficulties exposed by *Saunders v UK* (1997) 23 EHRR 313. By s 433(3) the offences to which s 433(2) does not apply include various offences under the Insolvency Act and under the Perjury Act 1911, ss 1, 2, 5.

34

DIRECTORS' LIABILITIES IN INSOLVENCY PROCEEDINGS

Charlotte Cooke

A. Introduction

This chapter discusses the liabilities of directors in consequence of a company entering insol- **34.01** vency proceedings. Sections B and C(1) concern claims which were available to the company when it entered insolvency proceedings and can be brought in its own name or by a liquidator using the summary procedure in the Insolvency Act, s 212. Sections C(2) and (3) and D consider a director's personal liability under the Insolvency Act for wrongful trading, fraudulent trading, or contravention of the restriction on reuse of a company name, which may result from the company entering insolvency proceedings. Section E discusses the impact on directors of the provisions in the Insolvency Act for adjusting prior transactions.

B. Claims against Directors Brought in the Name of the Company

(1) Power of office-holder to bring proceedings in the name of the company

Administrators, administrative receivers, and liquidators all have power to bring claims in **34.02** the name of the company against directors to obtain relief for breach of fiduciary and other duties, to recover company property in their possession or control, or to recover debts owed to the company. The proceedings are brought in the name of the company because the cause of action is vested in it and the office-holders are merely agents.[1] A provisional liquidator may be given the same litigation powers as a liquidator by the terms of the order appointing him. Whether the supervisor of a CVA has these powers depends on the terms of the CVA.[2]

34.03 Among the powers of an administrator or administrative receiver are powers (a) to take such proceedings as may seem to him expedient in order to take possession of, collect, and get in the property of the company; (b) to appoint a solicitor to assist him in the performance of his functions; (c) to bring or defend any action or other legal proceedings in the name and on behalf of the company; and (d) to refer to arbitration any question affecting the company.[3]

34.04 Liquidators have power to bring or defend any action or legal proceeding in the name and on behalf of the company.[4] In *Re Longmeade Ltd* Snowden J summarized the relevant principles:[5]

  (i) a decision by liquidators appointed by the court as to whether to commence proceedings in the name of the company is essentially a commercial decision which the liquidators are entrusted to take without obtaining sanction from the court or the liquidation committee;

  (ii) in taking that decision, the liquidators should act in what they believe to be the best interests of the insolvent company and all those who have an interest in the estate;

  (iii) the liquidators may, but are not obliged to, consult the creditors (or contributories) who have an interest in the estate;

  (iv) the liquidators should normally give weight to the reasoned views of the majority of such creditors (or contributories), provided that they are uninfluenced by extraneous considerations;

  (v) if all those who are interested in the insolvent estate are fully informed and are of the same view, the liquidators should ordinarily give effect to their wishes;

  (vi) the court should not generally become involved in giving directions to liquidators as to how to make commercial or administrative decisions; and

  (vii) the court should not generally interfere with a commercial or administrative decision of liquidators after the event, unless it is a decision that was taken in bad faith or was a decision that no reasonable liquidator could have taken.

34.05 The Insolvency Act, s 234 gives an office-holder the option of applying in his own name for an order for delivery up of property and this section can be invoked even in cases of dispute.[6] Also a liquidator has the option of applying for a summary order under s 212 (paragraphs 34.19–34.29 below). If the case is fit for summary determination there is little to choose

---

[1] Insolvency Act, Sch B1, para 69 (administrator); Insolvency Act, s 44(1) (administrative receiver). The terms of the debenture may extend or restrict the receiver's powers. After the company has gone into liquidation an administrative receiver ceases to be agent, but may continue to use the company's name, including in litigation: *Goughs Garages v Pugsley* [1930] 1 KB 615, CA. A liquidator is agent of the company and so is not personally liable for engagements made on its behalf: *Re Anglo-Moravian Railway Co* (1875) 1 Ch D 130; *Knowles v Scott* [1891] 1 Ch 717; *Stead Hazel & Co v Cooper* [1933] 1 KB 840, 843; *Butler v Broadhead* [1975] Ch 97, 108. By the Insolvency Act, s 145 the claim could be vested in the liquidator, but this section is rarely used.

[2] The CVA may appoint the supervisor trustee or give him other powers for the purpose of implementing the CVA: Insolvency Act, s 1(2).

[3] Insolvency Act, s 42, Sch B1, para 60 and Sch 1, paras 1, 4–6.

[4] Insolvency Act, s 165(2) and Sch 4, para 4 for voluntary winding up, and s 167(1) and Sch 4, para 4 for winding up by the court; as amended by the SBEE Act 2015, s 120 with effect from 26 May 2015. Previously (under s 167(1)) the liquidator in a winding up by the court had required the sanction of the court or the liquidation committee.

[5] [2016] Bus LR 506 at para 66.

[6] *Re London Iron & Steel Co Ltd* [1990] BCLC 372.

between the alternative procedures.[7] If the claim is likely to be contested on substantial grounds, the treatment of costs may be an important consideration in choosing the mode of proceeding. If the proceedings are brought in the name of the company, the defendant may apply for security for costs under CPR Part 25, rules 25.12–25.14 on the ground that there is reason to believe that the company will be unable to pay the defendant's costs if ordered to do so and the court has a discretion to make an order for security for costs.[8] But, if there are funds in the estate, such an application is usually answered by satisfying the defendant or the court that any costs that the company is ordered to pay can be paid as a priority expense.[9] Where the defendant is not satisfied in this way, he should apply for security, because if the defendant succeeds and the company is unable to pay his costs, it is most unlikely the court would think it appropriate to make an order for costs against the office-holder.[10] If the proceedings are brought in name of the office-holder he will be personally liable for costs if he loses and an order for costs is made in favour of the successful party, but the office-holder will be indemnified out of the company's assets.[11]

(2) Defence of set-off

Where the director has made loans to the company or has a claim against it for unpaid **34.06** expenses or for wrongful or unfair dismissal, the possible availability of a defence of set-off needs to be considered. It will be advantageous to the estate if the company can recover its claims against the director clear of set-off, so that the director is limited to a right of proof in the administration or liquidation. If the director is limited to a right of proof, he will not be entitled to receive a dividend until he has paid his debt to the company.[12] In consequence the liquidator may recover the debt from the director by deducting it from any dividend otherwise payable to the director.[13]

Administrative receivership

Before turning to administration, it is convenient to consider set-off where an administrative **34.07** receiver is appointed. Under the floating charge contained in the debenture, the debenture holder takes the benefit of debts owed to the company and the company's claims subject to equities affecting the debts and claims at the date of the appointment of the administrative receiver. The only rights of set-off that may be relied on as a defence to a claim by a company in administrative receivership are in respect of (a) debts that accrued due before the

---

[7] In proceedings outside the Insolvency Act, the court has ample powers to summarily determine the claim under CPR Parts 8 and 24. Note that a claim may be brought in the name of the company against a shadow director for breach of duty (see Ch 10, Section C above), but a shadow director is not within the scope of the Insolvency Act, s 212; see para 34.20 below.

[8] CPR 25.13(2)(c). The 1985 Act, s 726, which was repealed with effect from 1 October 2009, was to the same effect.

[9] For liquidations, see Insolvency Rules, rule 4.220(2); *Norglen Ltd v Reeds Rains Prudential Ltd* [1999] 2 AC 1, 20, HL, per Lord Hoffmann; *Smith v UIC Insurance Co Ltd* [2001] BCC 11.

[10] *Dolphin Quays Development Ltd v Mills* [2008] 1 WLR 1829, CA.

[11] Insolvency Rules, rule 2.67(1)(a) for administration (and IR 2016, r 3.50 after 6 April 2017). Insolvency Rules, rule 4.218(3)(a)(i) and (ii) for liquidation (and IR 2016, rr 6.42, 7.108 after 6 April 2017), which effectively reverse *Re MC Bacon Ltd (No 2)* [1991] Ch 127 and *Lewis v IRC* [2001] 3 All ER 499, CA. See also *Re Wilson Lovatt & Sons Ltd* [1977] 1 All ER 274; *Re MT Realisations Ltd* [2004] 1 WLR 1678.

[12] This follows from the rule in *Cherry v Boultbee* (1839) 4 My & Cr 442, which applies to company liquidations; *Re SSSL Realisations (2002) Ltd* [2006] Ch 610, CA; *Re Kaupthing Singer & Friedlander Ltd (No 2)* [2012] 1 AC 804, SC at paras 18–20, 53 in the judgment of Lord Walker.

[13] *Re Davies Chemists Ltd* [1993] BCLC 544. Hoffmann LJ achieved the same result in *Re D'Jan of London Ltd* [1994] 1 BCLC 561, 564.

appointment, whether or not they were payable before that date, and (b) debts which arise out of the same contract as that which gave rise to the assigned debt or are closely connected with that contract.[14]

34.08 In effect the receivership authorities recognized defences of (a) legal set-off, where the claim and the cross-claim are for debts which are liquidated or capable of ascertainment without valuation or estimation;[15] and (b) equitable set-off, where the cross-claim 'is so closely connected with [the claim] that it would be manifestly unjust to allow [the claimant] to enforce payment without taking into account the cross-claim'.[16]

Administration

34.09 In principle the defence of set-off to a claim brought in the name of the company by the administrator is restricted to cross-claims that come within the boundaries of legal and equitable set-off, as described in the preceding paragraph. But the position is complicated by the application or possible application of broader insolvency set-off, which may be brought into effect in one of three circumstances: (a) where the administrator is authorized by the court to make a distribution and has given notice that he intends to make it, the administration set-off rule contained in Insolvency Rules, rule 2.85 (and IR 2016, r 14.24 after 6 April 2017) applies as at the date of the notice;[17] (b) where the company later goes into liquidation and insolvency set-off under Insolvency Rules, rule 4.90 (and IR 2016, r 14.25 after 6 April 2017) applies; or (c) where the company makes a CVA or scheme under the 2006 Act, Part 26 replicating the rights that creditors would have in a winding-up. If the company in administration starts proceedings before those circumstances occur, a defendant with a cross-claim who cannot rely on legal or equitable set-off may argue that the proceedings should be stayed to give him the benefit of insolvency set-off, which operates at the applicable date as a discharge of the mutual debts to the extent of the set-off.[18] A director sued for breach of duty is in an especially weak position to make such an argument, because he is unlikely to be able to rely on insolvency set-off as a defence (paragraphs 34.15, 34.16, and 34.26 below).

34.10 There is one reported case under the original administration regime where insolvency set-off was unsuccessfully relied on as a ground for a staying execution of a judgment awarded to a company in administration: *Isovel Contracts Ltd v ABB Building Technologies Ltd.*[19] The case arose out of a building subcontract under which the contractor tendered a cheque to the subcontractor to make an interim payment. The subcontractor left the works, the contractor countermanded the cheque, and an administration order was made in respect of the subcontractor. The court gave the subcontractor judgment on the dishonoured cheque and refused the contractor's application for a stay of execution on the ground that it had a Part 20

---

[14] *Business Computers Ltd v Anglo-African Leasing Ltd* [1977] 1 WLR 578, which contains a review by Templeman J of the earlier authorities; *Marathon Electrical Manufacturing Corp v Mashreqbank PSC* [1997] 2 BCLC 460.

[15] *Axel Johnson Petroleum AB v MG Mineral Group AG* [1992] 1 WLR 270, CA; *Stein v Blake* [1996] AC 243, 251, HL; *Fearns v Anglo-Dutch Paint & Chemical Co Ltd* [2011] 1 WLR 366 at para 16.

[16] *Federal Commerce & Navigation co Ltd v Molena Alpha Inc* [1978] QB 927, 975, CA, per Lord Denning MR; *Geldof's Metaalconstructie NV v Simon Carves Ltd* [2010] 4 All ER 847, CA at para 43(vi); *Fearns v Anglo-Dutch Paint & Chemical Co Ltd* [2011] 1 WLR 366 at para 20.

[17] Insolvency Act, Sch B1, para 65; Insolvency Rules, rules 2.85 (substituted with effect from 1 April 2005) and 2.95 (and IR 2016, rr 14.24 and 14.29 after 6 April 2017).

[18] *Stein v Blake* [1996] AC 243, 252–5.

[19] [2002] 1 BCLC 390.

counterclaim for damages for breach of contract exceeding the amount of the cheque, which it wished to pursue with leave under the Insolvency Act, s 11. This was because (a) the contractor should not be in a better position than it would have been if it had paid the cheque before the administration, (b) a stay would not further the purpose of administration (more advantageous realization of assets), and (c) set-off under Insolvency Rules, rule 4.90 should not be extended to administration. It is respectfully suggested that the dishonoured cheque was the critical factor in the case. But for that feature, the contractor would have had a defence of equitable set-off.

The position should be the same under the new administration regime. In *Re Kaupthing Singer & Friedlander Ltd (No 2)*[20] Etherton LJ explained: **34.11**

> It is not a policy objective of the procedures for administration or the liquidation of an insolvent company to remove or diminish the indebtedness of those liable to the company. On the contrary, one of the principle objectives is to preserve, and where possible maximize, the value of the company and its assets. The provisions for insolvency set-off are intended to promote speedy and efficient administration of the assets so as to enable a distribution to be made to creditors as soon as possible and in a manner which achieves substantial justice between the parties to the set-off and, so far as practicable, equality in the treatment of creditors. The purpose of insolvency set-off has nothing to do with the release of liabilities owed to the company save to the extent necessary to achieve those objectives.

Unless the administrator has given notice to make a distribution he will continue to collect debts due to the company, subject to any defences of legal or equitable set-off that may be available to the defendant. This promotes the purpose of administration (Chapter 33, paragraph 33.29 above). The court is unlikely to respond favourably to an application by the defendant for a stay so that in the future he can benefit from the discharge of all or part of the debt claimed as a result of insolvency set-off.

The position regarding set-off changes if the administrator is authorized to make distributions in the administration and gives notice under the Insolvency Rules, rule 2.95 (and IR 2016, r 14.29 after 6 April 2017). That brings Insolvency Rules, rule 2.85 (and IR 2016, r 14.24 after 6 April 2017) into effect. It provides for set-off of all mutual credits, mutual debts or other mutual dealings as at the date of the notice in much the same way as rule 4.90 (and IR 2016, r 14.25 after 6 April 2017) does in liquidation. Thus rule 2.85 (and IR 2016, r 14.24 after 6 April 2017) contains provisions excluding from set-off debts arising out of obligations incurred, or acquired by assignment or otherwise, after the company had entered administration or liquidation or certain steps had been taken to those ends. **34.12**

Winding up

Insolvency Rules, rule 4.90 (and IR 2016, r 14.25 after 6 April 2017)[21] provides for mutual credits and set-off, subject to the exclusion of debts arising out of obligations incurred, or acquired by assignment or otherwise, after the company had entered administration or liquidation or certain steps had been taken to those ends.[22] The substantive provisions of rule 4.90 are: **34.13**

> 4.90(1) This Rule applies where, before the company goes into liquidation there have been mutual credits, mutual debts or other mutual dealings between the company and any creditor of the company proving or claiming to prove for a debt in the liquidation.

---

[20] [2011] 1 BCLC 12, CA at para 32.
[21] In the form that has been in effect since 1 April 2005: Insolvency (Amendment) Rules (SI 2005/527).
[22] Insolvency Rules, rule 4.90(2) (and IR 2016, r 14.25 after 6 April 2017).

4.90(3) An account shall be taken of what is due from each party to the other in respect of the mutual dealings, and the sums due from one party shall be set off against the sums due from the other.

4.90(8) Only the balance (if any) of the account owed to the creditor is provable in the liquidation. Alternatively the balance (if any) owed to the company shall be paid to the liquidator as part of the assets except where all or part of the balance results from a contingent or prospective debt owed by the creditor and in such a case the balance (or part of it which results from the contingent or prospective debt) shall be paid if and when that debt becomes due and payable.

Those provisions are supplemented by rule 4.90(4)–(7) and (9), which makes it clear that the set-off rule applies to future and contingent liabilities owed by or to the company, whether the liabilities are contractual, statutory, or tortious.[23]

34.14 Set-off under rule 4.90 (and IR 2016, r 14.25 after 6 April 2017) is mandatory and cannot be contracted out of.[24] It is automatic and self-executing on the company going into liquidation, so as to discharge the mutual credits and debts to the extent of the set-off, and it applies both to proof in the liquidation and to claims brought by the liquidator.[25]

34.15 There is no reason to doubt that set-off applies as between ordinary debts owed between a director and the company.[26] Authorities on misfeasance applications under the Insolvency Act, s 212 and its predecessors show that set-off is denied where the company's claim is in respect of a breach of duty (paragraph 34.26 below, and Chapter 19, Section E(2) above).

34.16 There are a number of clear cases where the director cannot assert a set-off: (a) where the company's claim against him is to recover money taken without authority (ie conversion and a void payment);[27] (b) where the company makes a proprietary claim to recover its own money or property; (c) where the director has agreed to subordinate his loan to the company until after all other debts have been paid, so that he cannot prove in respect of it; and (d) where the director has guaranteed, but not discharged, a debt of the company (eg to its bank) and the rule against double proof prevents him from claiming set-off in respect of his guarantee liability.[28]

(3) Other defences

34.17 Where the office-holder brings proceedings in the name of the company, the director may rely on the same defences as would have been available to him if the company had brought the proceedings while the directors were managing its affairs. The defences of relief from liability under the 2006 Act, s 1157 and limitation are discussed in Chapter 19, Sections D and E(1) above.

---

[23] These provisions confirm *Secretary of State for Trade and Industry v Frid* [2004] 2 AC 506, HL.

[24] *National Westminster Bank Ltd v Halesowen Presswork and Assemblies Ltd* [1972] AC 785, HL.

[25] *Stein v Blake* [1996] AC 243, 252–5, HL, per Lord Hoffmann (a case on the Insolvency Act, s 323, the bankruptcy equivalent of rule 4.90); *Re Bank of Credit and Commerce International SA (No 10)* [1997] Ch 213, 248, per Sir Richard Scott V-C; *Secretary of State for Trade and Industry v Frid* [2004] 2 AC 506, HL at para 6, per Lord Hoffmann.

[26] *Re Etic Ltd* [1928] Ch 861.

[27] *Smith v Bridgend CBC* [2002] 1 AC 336, HL at para 35 where Lord Hoffmann approved the judgment of Millett LJ in *Manson v Smith* [1997] 2 BCLC 161, 164. *Re Reliance Wholesale (Toys, Fancy Goods and Sports) Ltd* (1979) 76 LS Gaz 731, CA, is an example of set-off being denied as a defence to a claim to recover an unauthorized payment.

[28] *Secretary of State for Trade and Industry v Frid* [2004] 2 AC 506, HL at para 13, per Lord Hoffmann.

The director may defend the proceedings on the ground that the conduct complained of was **34.18** authorized or ratified by the members, either acting unanimously and informally or by duly passed resolution, so that neither the company nor the liquidator has a claim against him. The means of passing resolutions are discussed in Chapter 25, Section B(1) above. Section B(4) of that chapter deals with informal unanimous consent. Chapter 20, Section D(4) above discusses the limits on the power to ratify.

C. Claims against Directors Brought in the Liquidation or Administration

(1) Summary remedy against delinquent directors

The Insolvency Act, s 212 provides a summary remedy against delinquent directors and others **34.19** where a company has gone into liquidation and without the need for an action in the name of the company.[29] In origin this provision can be traced back to the 1862 Act, s 165. So far as relevant to directors, s 212 provides:

> (1) This section applies if in the course of the winding up of a company it appears that a person who—
>   (a) is or has been an officer of the company,
>   ...
>   (c) not being a person falling within paragraph (a) ..., is or has been concerned, or has taken part, in the promotion, formation or management of the company,
>   has misapplied or retained, or become accountable for, any money or other property of the company, or been guilty of any misfeasance or breach of any fiduciary or other duty in relation to the company.
>   ...
> (3) The court may, on the application of the official receiver or the liquidator, or of any creditor or contributory, examine into the conduct of the person falling within subsection (1) and compel him—
>   (a) to repay, restore or account for the money or property or any part of it, with interest at such rate as the court thinks just, or
>   (b) to contribute such sum to the company's assets by way of compensation in respect of the misfeasance or breach of fiduciary or other duty as the court thinks just.
>   ...
> (5) The power of a contributory to make an application under subsection (3) is not exercisable except with the leave of the court, but is exercisable notwithstanding that he will not benefit from any order the court may make on the application.

The section is a procedural section which provides a summary means of enforcing, by appli- **34.20** cation in the liquidation, rights and obligations that could have been enforced by the company itself by ordinary action against officers or former officers.[30] Officers include de facto

---

[29] It applies to a foreign company being wound up in England, although the content of the director's duties will be determined by the law of the place of incorporation: *Base Metal Trading Ltd v Shamurin* [2005] 1 WLR 1157, CA at para 67, per Arden LJ.

[30] *Coventry and Dixon's Case* (1880) 14 Ch D 660, 670, CA, per James LJ; *Cavendish Bentinck v Fenn* (1887) 12 AC 652, 669, HL, per Lord Macnaghton; *Re City Equitable Fire Insurance Co* [1925] Ch 407, 507, 527, CA, per Pollock MR and Sargant LJ; *Re Windsor Steam Coal Company (1901) Ltd* [1929] 1 Ch 151, 160, CA; *Cohen v Selby* [2001] 1 BCLC 176, CA at para 20, per Chadwick LJ; *Re MDA Investment Management Ltd* [2004] 1 BCLC 217 at paras 70–1; *Re Kudos Business Solutions Ltd* [2012] 2 BCLC 65 at para 43.

directors, but (unlike s 214) the section does not extend to shadow directors.[31] It may also be used to enforce new rights acquired in the winding up.[32] Thus the liquidator may use the section to recover compensation from a director in respect of a preference within the Insolvency Act, s 239, which the payee was unable to repay.[33] The reach of s 212(1) has been extended so that it applies to the duty to exercise reasonable skill, care, and diligence under the 2006 Act, s 174.[34] The section therefore extends to all the general duties of a director stated in the 2006 Act, Part 10, Chapter 2, ss 170–9, as well as specific duties under that Act.[35] It does not, however, cover a simple claim to recover a debt owed by a director, which involved no breach of duty.[36] The court has dismissed applications under s 212 where the directors caused the company to enter into what appeared to be a fair transaction with a director but were 'caught out by a very technical provision of the 1985 Act' concerning the redemption of shares,[37] or where a director had acted in accordance with legal advice in relation to the sale of a property, the proceeds of sale of which were misappropriated by a de facto director.[38]

34.21 Although the section is described as providing a summary remedy its use is not confined to uncomplicated cases or ones where there is no defence.[39] The section may be invoked whenever there has been misconduct within s 212(1). The remedies in s 212(3) appear to be complementary. Thus, where a director has misapplied or retained or become accountable for any money or other property of the company, the court may order him to repay, restore, or account for the money or other property, with interest. Where the director has been guilty of any misfeasance or any breach of his duties owed to the company the court may order him to contribute to the company's assets by paying compensation.[40]

34.22 The section may be invoked by the official receiver, the liquidator, or any creditor or contributory.[41] By s 212(5) a contributory can only apply with the permission of the court, but he does not have to establish a tangible interest in the outcome, namely that if the claim

---

[31] Insolvency Act, s 251 provides that ' "officer" in relation to a body corporate, includes a director manager or secretary'. The section applies to de facto directors: *Holland v HM Revenue and Customs, Re Paycheck Services 3 Ltd* [2010] 1 WLR 2793, SC (which explores the meaning of de facto directorship and is discussed in Ch 3 above). In *Gemma Ltd v Davies* [2008] 2 BCLC 281 the liquidator failed to establish that Mrs Davies was a de facto director in a case where her husband held her out as a director on company notepaper and she performed only clerical services for the company.
[32] *Re National Funds Assurance Co* (1878) 10 Ch D 118, 125; *Flitcroft's Case* (1882) 21 Ch D 519, 530, CA.
[33] *West Mercia Safetywear Ltd v Dodd* [1988] BCLC 250, CA; *Re Oxford Pharmaceuticals Ltd* [2009] 2 BCLC 485 (where the misfeasance claim failed, although the preference claim had succeeded).
[34] *Re D'Jan of London Ltd* [1994] 1 BCLC 561. The liquidator must prove that the negligence complained of caused the alleged loss: *Cohen v Selby* [2001] 1 BCLC 176, CA at para 20. The 1986 Act adds the words 'or other duty in relation to the company', without which it had been held that the predecessor provision did not apply to negligence claims: *Re B Johnson & Co Builders Ltd* [1955] Ch 634, CA.
[35] *Re Westlowe Storage and Distribution Ltd* [2000] 2 BCLC 590, 611 (s 212 covers the whole spectrum of directors' duties); *Re HLC Environmental Projects Ltd* [2014] BCC 337 (breach of 2006 Act, ss 171(b) and 172).
[36] *Re Etic Ltd* [1928] Ch 861; *Ciro Citterio Menswear plc v Thakrar* [2002] 1 WLR 2217 at para 32.
[37] *Kinlan v Crimmin* [2007] 2 BCLC 67.
[38] *Green v Walkling* [2008] 2 BCLC 332. Similarly in *Re Pro4Sport Ltd* [2016] 1 BCLC 257 the fact the director was relying on advice was an important factor in determining that he was not in breach of his duty to exercise reasonable care.
[39] *Stringer's Case* (1869) 4 Ch App 475, 493; *Rance's Case* (1870) 6 Ch App 104; *Re Kingston Cotton Mill Co (No 2)* [1896] 2 Ch 283, 288, CA.
[40] 'Misfeasance' means 'misfeasance in the nature of a breach of trust': *Coventry and Dixon's Case* (1880) 14 Ch D 660, 670, CA, per James LJ. Once the liquidator has proved that a payment or transaction occurred, the burden is on the director to explain it: *Re Idessa (UK) Ltd* [2012] 1 BCLC 80 at para 28.
[41] An assignee of a creditor has standing: *Mullarkey v Board* [2008] 1 BCLC 638.

succeeded he would receive a distribution.[42] Any recoveries are for the benefit of the liquidation, not the individual creditor or contributory that pursued the claim.[43] Recoveries in respect of a claim that the company had when it went into liquidation may be caught by charges contained in a debenture. Rather than pursuing the claim himself, the liquidator may exercise his power to sell the claim to anyone who is willing to pursue it.[44]

For discussion about directors' duties, the breach of which give rise to a misfeasance application, reference should be made to Chapters 10–17 above. The duty to the company to have regard to the interests of creditors is of particular relevance to misfeasance applications and this is discussed in Chapter 12, Section E above. Chapter 19 above discusses remedies for breach of duty and also the defences of relief from liability under the 2006 Act, s 1157, limitation, set-off, contributory negligence, and *ex turpi causa*.[45] Paragraph 34.18 above refers to the defence of authorization or ratification and identifies the other paragraphs in this work where those matters are addressed.[46] The following paragraphs draw attention to particular issues that have arisen in the context of misfeasance applications in relation to (a) relief from liability under the 2006 Act, s 1157, (b) limitation, (c) set-off, and (d) the problem that arises where the director is concurrently liable to compensate the company for misfeasance and also for wrongful or fraudulent trading.   **34.23**

The director may ask for relief from liability under the 2006 Act, s 1157 on the ground that he acted honestly and reasonably and that, having regard to all the circumstances, he ought fairly to be excused.[47] This provision may overlap with the court's discretion under s 212 itself, by which the court may limit the amount of compensation to the amount required to pay creditors in full, or otherwise as may seem just.[48] In *Re Paycheck Services 3 Ltd*[49] the application under s 212 was dismissed because the respondent was not a de facto director. Had he been a de facto director, he would have been liable to restore to the company the full amount of the unlawfully paid dividends. But Lord Hope (in the majority) agreed with Elias and Ward LJJ that under s 212(3) the court had a discretion—even where relief under the   **34.24**

---

[42] This change in the law, which reverses *Cavendish Bentinck v Fenn* (1887) 12 App Cas 652, recognizes that a contributory, even if he will not benefit personally, may be the only person able and willing to pursue a proper claim that the company may have against a director.

[43] *Oldham v Kyrris* [2004] 1 BCLC 305, CA, where a claim by an unsecured creditor, alleging breach of duty owed to him by an administrator, was struck out.

[44] *Re Oasis Merchandising Services Ltd* [1998] Ch 170, 181, CA, per Peter Gibson LJ. Insofar as the contrast drawn by Peter Gibson LJ between the power to assign a claim under s 212 and the position in relation to claims under ss 213 and 214 is concerned, Insolvency Act 1986, s 246ZD (inserted by SBEE Act 2015, s 118 with effect from 1 October 2015) gives office-holders the power to assign claims under ss 213 and 214.

[45] In *Top Brands Ltd v Sharma* [2016] BCC 1, CA a former liquidator was unable to set up this defence, because the company's illegal trading activity was background and creditors did not have to rely on it in their claim under s 212 to recover losses caused by the former liquidator's breach of duty.

[46] In *Re Finch (UK) plc* [2016] 1 BCLC 394 the directors could rely on a defence of informal authorization or assent by all the members (*Re Duomatic Ltd* [1969] 2 Ch 365) to a claim under s 212 in respect of technical breaches of the Companies Act 1985, but not to claims for making preferential payments and redeeming shares otherwise than out of available profits.

[47] In *Re Pro4Sport Ltd* [2016] 1 BCLC 257 relief would have been granted under the 2006 Act, s 1157, if the director had been found guilty of breach of duty, since, in respect of the transaction complained of, he had acted honestly, in accordance with legal advice and with the knowledge of the prospective liquidator. .

[48] *Re Home and Colonial Insurance Co Ltd* [1930] 1 Ch 102; *Re VGM Holdings Ltd* [1942] Ch 235. In exercising his discretion under 1985 Act, s 727 in *Re D'Jan of London Ltd* [1994] 1 BCLC 561 Hoffmann LJ took into account the position of the director and his wife as creditors. Also see *Re Loquitur Ltd* [2003] 2 BCLC 442 at paras 138–41, 247: *Green v Walkling* [2008] 2 BCLC 332 at paras 42–7.

[49] [2010] 1 WLR 2793, SC, by a majority affirming the decision of the Court of Appeal [2010] Bus LR 259.

2006 Act, s 1157 is refused—to limit the order to the amount of the deficiency to HMRC as the only creditor, but the discretion did not extend to refusing to make an order at all.[50] On the other hand Lord Walker (in the minority) agreed with Rimer LJ that the discretion under s 213(3) is not a wide one, that it does not replicate the power to grant relief under s 1157 and that the order should not be restricted to the deficiency.[51]

34.25 The director may raise a limitation defence. The same limitation rules apply to an application under s 212 as they would to proceedings by the company.[52] In most cases the limitation period is six years from the date when the cause of action for breach of duty accrued, but the Limitation Act, s 21 will apply if the claim is an action in respect of trust property and time may be extended by acknowledgement or part payment or for fraud, mistake, or concealment under the Limitation Act, ss 29–32.

34.26 Paragraphs 34.06–34.16 above discuss set-off after the company has entered administration, administrative receivership, or liquidation. The question arises whether there is a special rule that prevents a director from relying on set-off as a defence to a claim under s 212 (eg for repayment of a loan or damages for wrongful dismissal). Old authority indicates that set-off is not available as a defence to a claim under s 212.[53] In *Re Etic Ltd* Maugham J said that this was settled law.[54] Millett LJ endorsed this view when refusing leave to appeal in *Manson v Smith*.[55] In *Smith v Bridgend BC* Lord Hoffmann approved Millett LJ's conclusion that a director could not raise a defence of set-off against a claim that he had taken company money without authority (ie the transfer of property was void), but did not express a view on the other justifications for the rule relied on by Millett LJ.[56] In *Goldtrail Ltd v Aydin*,[57] Rose J applied Millett LJ's conclusion to prevent defendants who had received company money as a result of the director's misfeasance, in which they had dishonestly assisted, from setting-off losses they claimed to have suffered. Further, the payments made to the defendants were not 'dealings' for the purposes of rule 4.90.

34.27 Where a director is found liable for misfeasance, he may also find himself liable to pay sums to the company for wrongful or fraudulent trading (Insolvency Act, ss 213, 214). The issue then arises whether such liability is concurrent. If the misfeasance occurred after the start of the director's duty under s 214 to take steps to minimize loss, it will usually constitute a breach of that duty, so that the claims will be duplicated and any recovery under s 212 will reduce the director's liability under s 214. Thus in *Re DKG Contractors Ltd* it was ordered that liability should not be cumulative, but that payments under ss 212 and 239 were to be taken as satisfying an order made under s 214.[58] If the misfeasance occurred before the start of the

---

[50] [2010] 1 WLR 2793, paras 49–51. Lords Collins and Saville, in the majority with Lord Hope, did not address this issue.

[51] [2010] 1 WLR 2793, paras 124 and 125. Lord Clarke agreed, para 146.

[52] *Re Eurocruit Europe Ltd* [2007] 2 BCLC 598.

[53] *Pelly's Case* (1882) 21 Ch D 492, 498, 503, 507, 508, CA; *Flitcroft's Case* (1882) 21 Ch D 519, CA; *Re Carriage Co-operative Supply Association* (1884) 27 Ch D 322.

[54] [1928] Ch 861, 870, 873. In this case the secretary wished to set off a claim for salary in lieu of notice against a claim by the liquidator for sums overdrawn against future remuneration. Maugham J took into account the exclusion of set-off as a reason for limiting the scope of the misfeasance section to cases of breach of trust and true cases of misapplication or retention of company money or property (p 875).

[55] [1997] 2 BCLC 161.

[56] [2002] 1 AC 336, HL at para 35.

[57] [2015] 1 BCLC 89 at paras 162–7. But note Vos LJ's criticism of Rose J's reasoning in para 167: *Re Goldtrail Ltd* [2016] 1 BCLC 635, CA, at paras 62–6.

[58] [1990] BCC 903.

director's duty under s 214, no duplication will be involved if there is full recovery under both sections. In *Re Purpoint Ltd*, an order was made for separate payments under ss 212 and 214, subject to the proviso that the director was not required under s 212 to recoup more than was needed to meet the company's liabilities at the date on which it should have been plain to him that the company could not avoid going into insolvent liquidation.[59]

The court may order a respondent to an application under s 212 to indemnify another respond- **34.28** ent,[60] but it is considered that a respondent cannot make a CPR Part 20 claim against someone who is not a respondent.[61]

Where proceedings under s 212 are discontinued, unless the court orders otherwise, the appli- **34.29** cant is liable for the defendant's costs incurred on or before the date on which notice of discon- tinuance was served on the defendant.[62] The court may order otherwise where there has been a material change of circumstance.[63]

(2) Fraudulent trading

Since 1929 the Companies Acts have contained provisions dealing with 'fraudulent trading', **34.30** making this a criminal offence and a ground for imposing personal liability.[64] The civil sanction for fraudulent trading may only be invoked in a winding up or if the company is in administra- tion,[65] whereas the criminal sanction (now provided for in the 2006 Act, s 993) applies whether or not the company has been or is being wound up or in administration.[66] The criminal aspects of fraudulent trading are discussed in Chapter 35, Section I(4) below.

Following recommendations of the Cork Committee, as discussed in paragraph 34.49 **34.31** below, a new liability for wrongful trading was introduced by the Insolvency Act, s 214. Whilst the pre-existing civil liability for fraudulent trading has been retained with minor amendment in s 213, recourse to this provision is now relatively rare, since all cases of fraudulent trading by a director which fall within s 213 are likely to fall within the wrongful trading provisions of s 214, and the burden of establishing the claim is less onerous in relation to wrongful trading. For the same reasons, fraudu- lent trading claims brought in administration will be rare.[67] Fraudulent trading

---

[59] [1991] BCLC 491. See also *Re Idessa (UK) Ltd* [2012] 1 BCLC 80 at paras 121–35 for the working out of director's liability for misfeasance and wrongful trading.

[60] *Re Morecombe Bowling Ltd* [1969] 1 WLR 133.

[61] *Re A Singer & Co (Hat Manufacturers) Ltd* [1943] Ch 121, CA; *Re B Johnson & Co (Builders) Ltd* [1955] Ch 634, 647, CA; *Re Shilena Hosiery Ltd* [1980] Ch 219, 227. In *Re International Championship Management Ltd* [2007] BCC 95 a respondent to a s 212 application was allowed to bring a Part 20 claim for a contribution against the firm of one of the liquidators, but none of the earlier authorities appear to have been cited.

[62] CPR rule 38.6.

[63] *Teasdale v HSBC Bank plc* [2012] 3 Costs L.O. 285. In *Re Get Me Tickets Ltd* [2012] BPIR 1005 the court ordered otherwise where a liquidator discontinued proceedings against a former director following her late disclosure of a trust deed relating to a property which she had previously said she owned.

[64] 1929 Act, s 275.

[65] The SBEE Act 2015, s 117(2) inserts Insolvency Act s 246ZA with effect from 1 October 2015. Also with effect from 1 October 2015, SBEE Act 2015, s 119 inserts Insolvency Act, s 176ZB preventing the proceeds of claims under s 213 or 246ZA from going to floating charge holders.

[66] This was first provided by the 1981 Act, s 96, which reversed the decision of the House of Lords in *Director of Public Prosecutions v Schildkamp* [1971] AC 1.

[67] The SBEE Act 2015, s 117 inserts Insolvency Act s 246ZB, applying wrongful trading provisions to com- panies in administration with effect from 1 October 2015.

does, however, retain its utility, because its scope also extends to conduct by third parties.[68]

34.32 Sections 213, 214, 246ZA, and 246ZB have effect notwithstanding that the person concerned may be criminally liable in respect of matters on the grounds of which the declaration is to be made.[69] Section 213 has extraterritorial effect and a fraudulent trading claim may be brought in respect of activities that took place outside the jurisdiction.[70] There is no reason to think that section 246ZA is any different in this regard.

34.33 Section 213 provides:

(1) If in the course of the winding up of a company it appears that any business of the company has been carried out with intent to defraud creditors of the company or creditors of any other person, or for any fraudulent purpose the following has effect.
(2) The court, on the application of the liquidator, may declare than any persons who were knowingly parties to the carrying on of the business in the manner above-mentioned are to be liable to make such contributions (if any) to the company's assets as the court thinks proper.

Section 246ZA is in the same terms save that it refers to the company being in administration rather than liquidation and to the administrator rather than the liquidator. There is no reason to think that s 246ZA will be interpreted any differently to s 213 and, as such, what is said below in respect of s 213 should be equally applicable in the context of s 246ZA (with references to liquidation to be read as references to administration).

The Applicant

34.34 By s 213(2) the application for relief for fraudulent trading can only be made by the liquidator. It used to be the case that a right of action for fraudulent trading could not be assigned, but now s 246ZD(2)(a) provides that the office-holder may assign it or the proceeds of the action.[71]

Carrying on business

34.35 A company is to be considered to be carrying on business for the purposes of s 213 even though its only activity is the collection of assets and payment of debts.[72]

34.36 The carrying on of business is to be distinguished from the carrying out of business, so that it is not sufficient, for the purposes of s 213, to show that while the company was carrying on business it entered into fraudulent transactions. For example, the director of a company

---

[68] The liquidators of BCCI companies brought several fraudulent trading claims against other banks and outsiders: *Re BCCI (No 9)* [1994] 2 BCLC 636, CA; *Re BCCI (No 13), Banque Arabe International d'Investissement SA v Morris* [2001] 1 BCLC 263; *Morris v Bank of America National Trust* [2001] BCLC 771, CA; *Re BCCI (No 14), Morris v State Bank of India* [2004] 2 BCLC 236; *Re BCCI (No 15), Morris v Bank of India* [2004] 2 BCLC 279, [2005] 2 BCLC 328, CA.

[69] Insolvency Act, ss 215(5) and 246ZC (inserted by the SBEE Act 2015, s 117 with effect from 1 October 2015).

[70] *Bilta (UK) Ltd v Nazir (No 2)* [2016] AC 1 at paras 6, 10, 53, 107–110, 210–18.

[71] With effect from 1 October 2015. As to the old law, see *Re Oasis Merchandising Services Ltd* [1998] Ch 170, CA.

[72] *Morphitis v Bernasconi* [2003] Ch 552 CA at para 41, per Chadwick LJ. In *Carman v The Cronos Group SA* [2006] BCC 451 at para 37 it was held that a company cannot be regarded as carrying on business for the purposes of s 213 after a winding-up petition has been presented and its dispositions are void under the Insolvency Act, s 127.

dealing in second-hand cars who knowingly misrepresents the age and capabilities of a vehicle is not carrying on the company's business for a fraudulent purpose, although he carries out a particular business transaction in a fraudulent manner. He does not intend to defraud a creditor for the purposes of the section, because he does nothing to make it impossible for the customer, once he becomes a creditor, to recover the sum due to him as a creditor.[73]

It is, however, possible to carry on business with intent to defraud creditors where only one creditor is defrauded and by a single transaction.[74]   **34.37**

Intent to defraud

The phrases 'with intent to defraud creditors' and 'for any fraudulent purpose' require a finding of actual dishonesty, which Maugham J characterized as 'involving, according to current notions of fair trading among commercial men, real moral blame'.[75]   **34.38**

In the first case on 'fraudulent trading', *Re William C Leitch Bros Ltd*, Maugham J directed himself that 'if a company continues to carry on business and to incur debts at a time when there is to the knowledge of the directors no reasonable prospect of the creditors ever receiving payment of those debts, it is, in general, a proper inference that the company is carrying on business with intent to defraud'.[76] In *R v Grantham* the Court of Appeal did not dissent from that statement, but held that a company also carried on business with intent to defraud creditors if it incurs credit when there is no good reason for thinking that funds will become available to pay the debts when they become due or shortly thereafter.[77] To act in this way was to expose the creditors to the risk of loss which the company had no right to take. It is not necessary to prove that the director or other person alleged to have been responsible for fraudulent trading knew at the time the debts were incurred that there was no reasonable prospect of the creditors *ever* receiving payment of their debts. Further, it is not sufficient for the directors to assert that they believed that the company would be able to pay its debts; there must be a good reason for their belief.[78] Applying this approach, it has been held that deliberately setting out to cheat Her Majesty's Commissioners of Excise of large sums of VAT and failing to make any provision for PAYE on wages falls within s 213.[79]   **34.39**

The required intent to defraud is subjective rather than objective and it is necessary to show either deliberate intention or a reckless indifference whether creditors are defrauded.[80] It is not enough to show that the company is currently insolvent, because continuing to incur credit may be justifiable in reliance on a comfort letter of the parent company which is ultimately not honoured.[81] Nor is it enough to show that an insolvent company preferred to pay some creditors over others.[82]   **34.40**

---

[73] *Re Gerald Cooper Chemicals Ltd* [1978] Ch 262.

[74] *Morphitis v Bernasconi* [2003] Ch 552, CA at paras 43–6, where Chadwick LJ discusses and explains *Re Gerald Cooper Chemicals Ltd* [1978] Ch 262, 267, 268.

[75] *Re Patrick and Lyon Ltd* [1933] Ch 786, 790.

[76] [1932] 2 Ch 71, 77.

[77] [1984] QB 675, 681–4.

[78] The Court of Appeal disapproved the statement by Buckley J to a contrary effect in *Re White and Osmond (Parkstone) Ltd* (30 June 1960, unreported), which became known as the 'sunshine test' and is quoted at [1984] QB 675, 682.

[79] *Re L Todd (Swanscombe) Ltd* [1990] BCLC 454. In *Bilta (UK) Ltd v Nazir (No 2)* [2016] AC 1 a fraudulent trading claim was brought against the persons responsible for a 'missing trader' VAT fraud.

[80] *Bernasconi v Nicholas Bennett & Co* [2000] BCC 921.

[81] *Re Augustus Barnett & Sons Ltd* [1986] BCLC 170.

[82] *Re Sarflax Ltd* [1979] Ch 529.

34.41 The words 'or for any fraudulent purpose' could not be wider, and include frauds against potential creditors.[83]

Attribution of knowledge to outsider companies

34.42 Where it is alleged that an outside company was 'knowingly party' to fraudulent trading by the company, the question arises as to through whom the requisite knowledge may be attributed to the outside company. The Court of Appeal addressed this issue in *Re Bank of Credit and Commerce SA (No 15), Morris v Bank of India*.[84] The liquidators brought a claim under s 213 against the defendant bank. The relevant knowledge was 'blind-eye' knowledge, which required a suspicion that the relevant facts existed and a deliberate decision to avoid confirming that they existed.[85] The bank contended that knowledge could only be attributed to it through its directors and that no such knowledge was established against them. The Court of Appeal rejected this argument and upheld the liquidators' claim. It reasoned as follows:[86]

(1) The policy of imposing civil liability for fraudulent trading should be considered separately from the policy of imposing criminal liability. Section 213 was not a penal provision.

(2) The proper approach to the question of attribution for the purposes of s 213 turns on the construction and purpose of that section, which was to enable the liquidator to recover compensation for the benefit of those who had suffered as a result of the fraud from those who had knowingly assisted the fraudulent conduct of the business of the company in liquidation.

(3) It would be inappropriate to limit attribution for the purposes of s 213 to the board or those specifically authorized by a resolution of the board. It would ignore the reality that the relevant transactions often take place below board level and risk emasculating the policy behind s 213 if an outsider company could shelter behind an argument that the only relevant knowledge was that of its board and that it could escape liability if the board delegated decisions to senior managers and accepted their recommendations.

(4) Accordingly there was to be attributed to the outsider company the knowledge of a person within its organization who was authorized by it to deal with the company in liquidation in respect of the relevant transactions. That person was to be regarded as 'the directing mind and will' of the outsider company.

(5) But such an attribution was not to be made irrespective of the facts of the case, because otherwise an outsider company could be made liable even though it had acted in good faith and with scrupulous care. The more senior and important within the hierarchy the agent is and the greater his freedom to act, the more readily the attribution will be made. Also attribution will be made if communications from the agent put the board on inquiry.

---

[83] *R v Kemp* [1988] QB 645, CA.

[84] [2005] 2 BCLC 328, CA.

[85] The test for 'blind eye' knowledge is set out at [2005] 2 BCLC 328 at para 14. See *Alpha Sim Communications Ltd v Caz Distribution Services Ltd* [2014] EWHC 207 (Ch) at paras 62–4.

[86] [2005] 2 BCLC 328 at paras 99, 107, 108, 111, 112, 116, 118, 120, 129, 130. For the rules of attribution of knowledge to a company, see *Meridian Global Funds Management Asia Ltd v Securities Commission* [1995] 2 AC 500, 507, PC, per Lord Hoffmann and Ch 4, Section E above. Note that it may be possible to allege that a company is vicariously liable to contribute under s 213 where its employee is knowingly party to fraudulent trading: para 113.

(6) For the purpose of s 213 there was a special rule of attribution under which the knowledge of an employee or officer of an outsider company was to be attributed to it, even though that employee or officer acted dishonestly and in breach of his duties to the outsider company and in circumstances in which he would not have passed on his knowledge to the outsider company.

Limitation

A fraudulent trading application must be commenced within six years from the time when **34.43** the company goes into insolvent liquidation, namely on the day the winding-up order is made.[87]

Remedies

There has to be some nexus between the loss which has been caused to the company's credi- **34.44** tors generally by the carrying on of the business in the manner falling within s 213 and the contribution which those knowingly party to the carrying on of the business in that manner should be ordered to make to the assets. There is no power to include a punitive element in the amount of any contribution which a person should be declared liable to make to the assets of the company. The principle on which the power should be exercised is that the contribution to the assets in which the company's creditors share in the liquidation should reflect and compensate for the loss caused to those creditors by carrying on the business in the manner which gives rise to the exercise of the power.[88]

The declaration of liability ought to state the amount for which the director is liable.[89] The **34.45** order may declare that a director is liable for such amount as will suffice to repay all creditors whose debts arose during the period of trading while insolvent and direct an inquiry as to what debts did so arise.[90] The court may declare the respondents jointly and severally liable for the full loss caused to creditors or it may limit the contributions of a less culpable director.[91]

The court is empowered to order that the liability of the person declared liable for fraudulent **34.46** trading should be charged on any debt or security due to him or that the whole or part of a debt owed by the company to the director should be subordinated to the other debts owed by the company and interest on those debts.[92]

The proceeds of the fraudulent trading claim or of any assignment of the right of action **34.47** under s 246ZD are not treated as part of the company's net property which is available for satisfaction of claims by the holders of any floating charges.[93]

A person guilty of fraudulent trading may be made the subject of a disqualification order.[94] **34.48**

---

[87] *Re Overnight Ltd* [2010] BCC 787.
[88] *Morphitis v Bernasconi* [2003] Ch 552, CA at paras 53 and 55, per Chadwick LJ.
[89] *Re William C Leitch Bros Ltd* [1932] 2 Ch 71.
[90] *Re L Todd (Swanscombe) Ltd* [1990] BCLC 454.
[91] *Re Overnight Ltd (No 2)* [2010] 2 BCLC 186, [2010] BCC 796 where one director was declared to be liable for 50 per cent of the losses to HMRC from a carousel fraud while the other director was liable for 100 per cent of the losses.
[92] Insolvency Act, s 215(2) and (4). The reason for the statutory power to impose a charge on security is explained in the report of the Cork Committee at para 92.
[93] Insolvency Act, s 176ZB, inserted by SBEE Act 2015, s 119 with effect from 1 October 2015.
[94] CDDA, ss 4 and 10.

(3) Wrongful trading

34.49 The report of the Cork Committee considered that the fraudulent trading provision, then found in the 1948 Act, s 332, was inadequate to deal with irresponsible trading for which directors and others should be held personally accountable, mainly because of the strict standards of pleading and proof required in fraud cases. The Committee recommended that civil liability to pay compensation could arise where loss was suffered as a result of 'unreasonable' conduct, which they proposed should be called 'wrongful trading', and that this should include the provision for civil liability for wrongful trading.[95] The government accepted the broad thrust of the Cork Committee's recommendation when enacting the wrongful trading provisions contained in the Insolvency Act, s 214, which complement, but do not replace, s 213.[96]

34.50 Section 214 provides:[97]

(1) Subject to subsection (3) below, if in the course of the winding up of a company it appears that subsection (2) of this section applies in relation to a person who is or has been a director of the company, the court, on the application of the liquidator, may declare that that person is liable to make such contribution (if any) to the company's assets as the court thinks proper.

(2) This subsection applies in relation to a person if—

    (a) the company has gone into insolvent liquidation,

    (b) at some time before the commencement of the winding up of the company, that person knew or ought to have concluded that there was no reasonable prospect that the company would avoid going into insolvent liquidation or entering insolvent administration,[98] and

    (c) that person was a director of the company at that time; …

(3) The court shall not make a declaration under this section with respect to any person if it is satisfied that after the condition specified in subsection (2)(b) was first satisfied in relation to him that person took every step with a view to minimising the potential loss to the company's creditors as (assuming him to have known that there was no reasonable prospect that the company would avoid going into insolvent liquidation) he ought to have taken.

(4) For the purposes of subsections (2) and (3), the facts which a director of a company ought to know or ascertain, the conclusions which he ought to reach and the steps which he ought to take are those which would be known or ascertained, or reached or taken, by a reasonably diligent person having both—

---

[95] The report of the Cork Committee at Ch 44, paras 1775–806. It should be noted that the Cork Committee reported in 1982, before the decision in *R v Grantham* [1984] QB 675, and at a time when it appeared to be necessary to show that it was 'clear that the company will *never* be able to satisfy its creditors' and that directors would have a good defence if they 'genuinely believe that the clouds will roll away and the sunshine of prosperity will shine upon them again and disperse the fog of their depression'. This was 'the sunshine test' as formulated by Buckley J in the well-known but unreported case of *Re White and Osmond (Parkstone) Ltd*, 30 June 1960, which made fraudulent trading claims particularly difficult to sustain.

[96] Insolvency Act, s 214(8).

[97] The section does not apply in respect of certain specified persons while Northern Rock, Bradford & Bingley, Deposits Management (Heritable) and Dunfermline BS are owned by the Treasury: Northern Rock plc Transfer Order 2008, SI 2008/432; Bradford & Bingley plc Transfer of Securities and Property etc Order 2008, SI 2008/2546; Heritable Bank plc Transfer of Certain Rights and Liabilities Order 2008, SI 2008/2644; Amendments to Law (Resolution of Dunfermline Building Society) Order 2009, SI 2009/814.

[98] SBEE Act, s 117(3) inserts in subs (2)(b) after 'liquidation' the phrase 'or entering insolvent administration' with effect from 1 October 2015.

    (a) the general knowledge, skill and experience that may reasonably be expected of a person carrying out the same functions as are carried out by that director in relation to the company, and

    (b) the general knowledge, skill and experience that that director has.

(5) The reference in subsection (4) to the functions carried out in relation to a company by a director of the company includes any functions which he does not carry out but which have been entrusted to him.

(6) For the purposes of this section, a company goes into insolvent liquidation if it goes into liquidation at a time when its assets are insufficient for the payment of its debts and other liabilities and the expenses of the winding up.

(6A) For the purposes of this section a company enters insolvent administration if it enters administration at a time when its assets are insufficient for the payment of its debts and other liabilities and the expenses of the administration.[99]

(7) In this section 'director' includes a shadow director.

(8) This section is without prejudice to section 213.

Section 246ZB is in the same terms save that it refers to the company being in administration rather than liquidation and to the administrator rather than the liquidator. There is no reason to think that s 246ZB will be interpreted any differently to s 214 and, as such, what is said below in respect of s 214 should be equally applicable in the context of s 246ZB (with references to liquidation to be read as references to administration).

Although the marginal note indicates that s 214 is concerned with 'wrongful trading', the **34.51** expression does not appear in the section, and it may be objected that the section is vague as to what conduct falls within its scope. Instead, the court is given power to order a person to make a contribution to the company's assets if (a) the company has gone into insolvent liquidation,[100] (b) at some time the person knew or ought to have known that insolvent liquidation or insolvent administration could not reasonably be avoided, (c) at that time the person was a director of the company, and (d) the court is not satisfied that after that time the person took every step with a view to minimizing the potential loss to the company's creditors as he ought to have taken. Although it should be easier for a liquidator to establish those matters than dishonesty or reckless disregard under s 213, there appear to have been relatively few wrongful trading cases since the Insolvency Act came into force.

The applicant

By s 214(1) the application for relief for wrongful trading can only be made by the liquida- **34.52** tor. It used to be the case that a right of action for wrongful trading could not be assigned, but now s 246ZD(2)(b) provides that the office-holder may assign it or the proceeds of the action.[101]

Insolvent liquidation

Sub-sections 214(6) and (6A) provide that a company is in insolvent liquidation or enters **34.53** insolvent administration if its assets are insufficient to pay its debts and liabilities, taking into account the expenses of the liquidation or administration, as the case may be.[102] The contribution that the court may order may make good that deficiency.

---

[99] Sub-s (6A) inserted by SBEE Act 2015, s 117(3) with effect from 1 October 2015.

[100] Section 247(2) identifies when a company goes into liquidation.

[101] With effect from 1 October 2015. As to the old law, see *Re Oasis Merchandising Services Ltd* [1998] Ch 170, CA.

[102] Similar definitions appear in Insolvency Act, s 216(7) and CDDA, s 6(2)(a).

Appreciation of unavoidable insolvent liquidation or insolvent administration

34.54 There are three critical elements of a wrongful trading claim for the court to determine: (a) the time from which the company has been wrongfully trading, (b) what the director knew or ought to have been known of the company's financial circumstances at that time, and (c) whether at that time the director knew or ought to have concluded that there was no reasonable prospect that the company would avoid going into insolvent liquidation.

34.55 The liquidator must allege a particular time from which wrongful trading occurred and prove his case by reference to that time.[103] The court will not permit the liquidator to amend his case at a late stage or at trial to allege that wrongful trading occurred from some later date where that would be unjust to the respondents.[104] Although the liquidator's case will often be based on hindsight, the court has warned that 'there is always the danger of hindsight, the danger of assuming that what has in fact happened was always bound to happen and was apparent'.[105]

34.56 The fact that the director was aware that the company is insolvent on a balance sheet or cash-flow basis does not mean that he should have concluded that insolvent liquidation was unavoidable. He may properly take the view that the company will trade out of its present difficulties and in this respect he may take a realistic account of future trading prospects.[106]

34.57 In assessing the knowledge that the directors had or ought to have had and the conclusions reached or which ought to have been reached, the court is directed to apply the standards of knowledge, skill, and experience set out in s 214(4). These standards reflect the common law duty of care, now set out in the 2006 Act, s 174 (see Chapter 14 above).[107] The standard set by s 214(4)(a) is an objective minimum, and the general knowledge, skill, and experience postulated will be much less extensive in a small company in a modest way of business, with simple accounting procedures and equipment, than it will be in a large company with sophisticated procedures.[108] Likewise, the standard may be raised by s 214(4)(b) on account of the particular attributes of the director in question.[109]

34.58 A director cannot be a 'sleeping' director; so a wife whose function in the company's affairs was limited, but who was nonetheless a director and received benefits as a director, is subject to the test under s 214(4) of a reasonably diligent person who has taken on the office of director. The Insolvency Act, s 214(4)(a) indicates that where a director performs a special function, such as finance or marketing director, then the special skills expected of such a person in that capacity are to be expected of him. Section 214(4)(a) cannot be used to reduce the

---

[103] For straightforward cases, see: *Re Bangla Television Ltd* [2010] BCC 143; *Re Idessa (UK) Ltd* [2012] 1 BCLC 80; *Re Kudos Business Solutions Ltd* [2012] 2 BCLC 65.

[104] *Re Sherborne Associates Ltd* [1995] BCC 40, 42; *Re Continental Insurance Co of London plc (No 4)* [2007] 2 BCLC 287 at para 99.

[105] *Re Sherborne Associates Ltd* [1995] BCC 40, 54.

[106] *Re Ralls Builders Ltd* [2016] Bus LR 555 at paras 168–233, where Snowden J gives a helpful review of the authorities on this question: *Re CS Holidays Ltd* [1997] 1 WLR 407, 414; *Re Continental Assurance Co of London plc (No 4)* [2007] 2 BCLC 287 at para 106; *Re Hawkes Hill Publishing Ltd* [2007] BCC 937 at paras 28, 41, 45, 47; *Roberts v Frohlich* [2011] 2 BCLC 625 at paras 111–12; *Re Kudos Business Solutions Ltd* [2012] 2 BCLC 65 at paras 35, 61.

[107] *Norman v Theodore Goddard* [1991] BCLC 1028, 1030, 1031; *Re D'Jan of London Ltd* [1994] 1 BCLC 561, 563.

[108] *Re Produce Marketing Consortium Ltd (No 2)* [1989] BCLC 520, 550.

[109] In *Re Robin Hood Centre plc, Brooks v Armstrong* [2015] BCC 661, it was held that the experience of a director in a different retail field did not raise the standards expected of him.

basic standard required on the grounds that the director in question exercised no particular functions in the company's management.[110]

Section 214(5) provides that 'the reference in subsection (4) to the functions carried out in relation to a company by a director of a company includes any functions which he does not carry out but which have been entrusted to him'. The effect of this subsection is that omissions by a director are treated in the same way as commissions.

34.59

In relation to the knowledge that the directors had or ought to have had as to the company's financial position at the relevant time, the cases in which directors have been held liable are typically cases in which the directors closed their eyes to the reality of the company's position, or failed to ensure that accounting records compliant with what is now the 2006 Act, Part 15, Chapters 2–4 were kept.[111] This was the case in *Re Produce Marketing Consortium Ltd (No 2)*, where the company had kept inadequate accounting records and the court proceeded on the basis that it should assume, for the purposes of applying the test in s 214(2), that the financial results for the year in question were known at least to the extent of the size of the deficiency of the assets over liabilities.[112]

34.60

In *Re DKG Contractors Ltd* a declaration was made against the directors under s 214 because they had failed to meet the standard required by s 214(4)(a). The court said that 'Patently, [the directors'] own knowledge, skill and experience were hopelessly inadequate for the task they undertook. That is not sufficient to protect them.'[113] Nor can directors rely on the inherently risky nature of the film industry to attempt to justify committing the company to pay substantial sums under a production services agreement when funding was not in place and the lead actor was not committed to the film.[114]

34.61

On the other hand, in *Re Continental Assurance Co of London plc* an application under s 214 was dismissed.[115] The judge held that the directors took a responsible and conscientious attitude at all times from the first board meeting when major and unexpected losses were reported to them. A director expressly raised the question of whether the company could properly continue to trade; the directors considered the question directly, closely, and frequently. At every board meeting, and at times in between board meetings, they sought assurance from the finance director and others that the company was still solvent. As the financial position looked bleaker, they reduced the scale of trading to minimal and cautious levels. When it was reported to the directors that the company had become insolvent they gave instructions that it should not do any more business, and took advice from insolvency practitioners. The commencement of a formal liquidation did not happen for some time, but that was in order to keep open as long as possible the chance of selling the company. The insolvency practitioners were aware of that at the time and raised no objections.

34.62

Turning to the prospects of avoiding insolvent liquidation, the cases where wrongful trading has been established are those where the company carried on trading long after it should

34.63

---

[110] *Re Brian D Pierson (Contractors) Ltd* [2001] 1 BCLC 275, 310.
[111] *Re Continental Insurance Co of London plc (No 4)* [2007] 2 BCLC 287 at para 106; *Re The Rod Gunner Organisation Ltd* [2004] 2 BCLC 110.
[112] [1989] BCLC 520, 550, 551.
[113] [1990] BCC 903, 912.
[114] *Singla v Hedman* [2010] 2 BCLC 61.
[115] [2007] 2 BCLC 287 at paras 106, 109, 281, 378.

have been obvious to the directors that the company was insolvent and that there was no way out for it. In those cases, the directors had been irresponsible and had not made any genuine attempt to grapple with the company's real position.[116] In *Roberts v Frohlich*[117] directors of a property development company were guilty of wrongful trading from the moment that a simple comparison between the company's accounts and the professional valuation of the property would have revealed to the directors that the company could never pay it debts, even though some two months earlier the directors could make a business judgment that the company should continue with the development. On the other hand, in *Re Sherborne Associates Ltd* the court found that the directors were aware of the company's financial difficulties and responded positively and responsibly to it. The court was not prepared to find that their belief that the company could trade out of its difficulties was unreasonable or fanciful.[118]

A director at the time

34.64   Section 214(7) explicitly applies the wrongful trading provisions to shadow directors as well as appointed directors. In *Re a Company (No 005009 of 1987)*[119] the court refused to strike out a claim that the bank was liable for wrongful trading, made on the basis that the directors were accustomed to act in accordance with the bank's directions and instructions. Section 214 also applies to de facto directors, but the liquidator must plead and prove his case that the director was either an appointed director, or a shadow or de facto director.[120]

34.65   An application may be made against the foreign directors of a foreign company which is being wound up in this jurisdiction as an unregistered company.[121] The court also has jurisdiction to make an order under the Insolvency Act, s 426 in response to a request by a foreign court for assistance in enforcing a corresponding insolvency jurisdiction.[122]

34.66   The fact that a director has died before the application is heard does not deprive the liquidator of the right to seek relief against him.[123]

Limit on declaration

34.67   Once it is established that a director knew or ought to have concluded that there was no reasonable prospect that the company would avoid going into insolvent liquidation, the onus is on the director to establish that he took every step to minimize the potential loss in order to make good a defence under s 214(3).[124] In *Re Ralls Builders Ltd*[125] Snowden J said that this is a high hurdle for a director to overcome and went on to explain that for a director to make

---

    [116]   *Re Continental Insurance Co of London plc (No 4)* [2007] 2 BCLC 287 at para 106.

    [117]   [2011] 2 BCLC 625 at paras 110–13. Similarly in *Re Ralls Builders Ltd* [2016] Bus LR 555, the directors should not have concluded that insolvent liquidation was inevitable at the end of one month, but they should have reached that conclusion at the end of the next month.

    [118]   [1995] BCC 40, 54, 55.

    [119]   [1989] BCLC 13.

    [120]   *Re Hydrodam (Corby) Ltd* [1994] 2 BCLC 180. As to de facto directors and shadow directors: *Revenue and Customs Commissioners v Holland, Re Paycheck 3 Ltd* [2010] 1 WLR 2793, SC, and Ch 3, Section C above.

    [121]   *Re Howard Holdings Ltd* [1998] BCC 549. Also see *Bilta (UK) Ltd v Nazir (No 2)* [2016] AC 1, a fraudulent trading case.

    [122]   *Re Bank of Credit and Commerce International SA (No 9); Re Bank of Credit and Commerce International (Overseas) Ltd* [1994] 3 All ER 764, Rattee J and CA.

    [123]   *Re Sherborne Associates Ltd* [1995] BCC 40.

    [124]   *Re Indessa (UK) Ltd* [2012] 1 BCLC 80 at paras 113, 120; *Re Robin Hood Centres plc, Brooks v Armstrong* [2015] BCC 661 at paras 6–10 (for further proceedings, see [2016] EWHC 2893 (Ch)).

    [125]   [2016] Bus LR 555 at para 245.

good the defence, he must demonstrate 'not only that continued trading was intended to reduce the net deficiency of the company, but also that it was designed appropriately so as to minimize the risk of loss to individual creditors'.

The standards in s 214(4) apply to the defence under s 214(3). Where the directors appreci- **34.68** ate the grave financial position of the company, they invariably consult an insolvency practitioner and either put the company into an insolvency proceeding or manage the company in accordance with his advice. In those circumstances no question of wrongful trading should arise. Where the directors do not appreciate the gravity of the company's situation and carry on trading in disregard of creditors' interests, they cannot expect to bring themselves within s 214(3). Thus it has been said that the defence is intended to apply to cases where a director takes specific steps with a view to preserving or realizing assets or claims for the benefit of creditors, even if he fails to achieve that result, and does not cover the very act of wrongful trading itself, even if it was done with the intention of trying to make a profit.[126]

No defence of acting honestly and reasonably

The Companies Act, s 1157 does not apply to claims made under s 214.[127] Parliament did **34.69** not intend the essentially subjective test under s 1157 to be operated at the same time as the objective tests within s 214. In any case the court has a discretion under s 214(1) whether to order payment of a contribution and if so as to the amount.

Limitation

A wrongful trading application must be commenced within six years from the time when the **34.70** company goes into insolvent liquidation.[128]

Remedies

Where the court's discretion to make a declaration arises, the amount of the contribution **34.71** is also in the court's discretion: the amount is described in s 214(1) as 'such contribution (if any) to the company's assets as the court thinks proper'. In the first reported case, *Re Produce Marketing Consortium Ltd (No 2)*[129] Knox J recorded the argument of counsel for the liquidator, Mary Arden QC, that the extent of liability is analogous to the assessment of damages in tort, being a matter of causation not culpability, and that the discretion is intended to enable allowance to be made for questions of causation and to avoid unjust results and held that:

(1) the jurisdiction was primarily compensatory rather than penal;

(2) prima facie the appropriate amount that a director is declared to be liable to contribute is the amount by which the company's assets can be discerned to have been depleted by the director's conduct which caused the discretion under s 214(1) to arise;

(3) without limiting the factors to be taken into account for reducing the prima facie amount, it may be appropriate to consider whether the director was guilty of deliberate wrongdoing or a failure to appreciate the situation; and

(4) the jurisdiction was to be exercised in a way that will benefit unsecured creditors.

In *Re Purpoint Ltd* Vinelott J followed Knox J's approach to the prima facie amount and **34.72** observed that the purpose of s 214 is to recoup loss to creditors as a whole, so that creditors

---

[126] *Re Brian D Pierson (Contractors) Ltd* [2001] 1 BCLC 275, 309.
[127] *Re Produce Marketing Consortium Ltd* [1989] 1 WLR 745.
[128] *Re Farmizer (Products) Ltd* [1997] 1 BCLC 589, CA.
[129] [1989] BCLC 520, 553, 554.

whose debts were incurred after the company stopped trading did not have a stronger claim than creditors with existing debts. But where, because of the director's failure to ensure that proper records were kept, it was impossible to ascertain the precise extent to which the company's net liabilities were increased by the continuance of the company's trading, the loss was to be quantified as the aggregate of the debts incurred after the date when it should have been plain to the director that the company could not avoid going into insolvent liquidation.[130]

34.73　The conclusion that the jurisdiction is compensatory not penal and that there should be some connection between the loss caused by the wrongful trading and the amount of the contribution ordered to be made is supported by subsequent decisions of the Court of Appeal.[131] In *Re Continental Assurance Co of London plc* Park J expressed the view that there must be some connection between the director's wrongful conduct and the losses that the liquidator wishes to recover from him. This connection would be satisfied in the case of normal trading losses, but not for losses caused by unforeseen events not attributable to the impugned conduct, such as unexpected weather conditions or costly litigation conducted by the liquidator.[132]

34.74　Similarly in *Re Ralls Builders Ltd*[133] Snowden J concluded that the correct approach was to ascertain whether the company suffered any loss which was caused by continuing to trade after insolvent liquidation was inevitable; that the starting point was to ask 'whether there was an increase or reduction in the net deficiency of the Company as regards unsecured creditors' after that date; and that losses that would have been incurred in any event by the company going into liquidation or administration should not be laid at the door of the directors. The reference to the net deficiency against unsecured creditors is significant, because it addresses the vice that led to the introduction of the fraudulent trading provision; namely an insolvent company continuing to trade to the advantage of holders of floating charges at the expense of unsecured creditors.[134]

34.75　Where the wrongful trading claim is coupled with a misfeasance claim against a director, the court takes into account sums ordered to be repaid on account of misfeasance during the period of wrongful trading when assessing the amount of the compensation for wrongful trading.[135]

34.76　The court has the same ancillary powers to impose charges and direct subordination as it has on a fraudulent trading claim (paragraph 34.46 above).

34.77　Where wrongful trading is alleged against a number of directors, the starting point is that liability will not be joint and several, because there is no single claim against the board collectively, but rather as many claims as there are respondent directors.[136] The court has a

---

[130]　*Re Purpoint Ltd* [1991] BCLC 491, 498, 499. In *Re DKG Contractors Ltd* [1990] BCC 903, 912 the judge ordered the directors to contribute an amount equal the debts incurred after trading should have ceased.

[131]　*Cohen v Selby* [2001] 1 BCLC 176 at para 21; *Morphitis v Bernasconi* [2003] Ch 552 at para 53 (a fraudulent trading case).

[132]　[2007] 2 BCLC 287 at paras 376–81. His judgment, delivered in 2000, was adopted in *Re Marini Ltd* [2004] BCC 172 at para 68. For reducing the prima facie amount on account of unexpected events, see *Re Brian D Pierson (Contractors) Ltd* [2001] 1 BCLC 275, 311.

[133]　[2016] Bus LR 555 at paras 241, 242. See also *Re Robin Hood Centres plc* [2016] EWHC 2893 (Ch).

[134]　See Chapter 1, para 1.67 above.

[135]　*Re DKG Contractors Ltd* [1990] BCC 903, 912; *Re Continental Assurance Co of London plc* [2007] 2 BCLC 287 at para 297; *Re Idessa (UK) Ltd* [2012] 1 BCLC 80 at paras 121–35.

[136]　*Re Continental Insurance Company of London plc* [2007] 2 BCLC 287 at paras 383–7.

discretion to order two or more directors to be jointly and severally liable, but this will only arise where the court positively exercises its discretion to impose it.

The proceeds of the wrongful trading claim or of any assignment of the right of action under s 246ZD are not treated as part of the company's net property which is available for satisfaction of claims by the holders of any floating charges.[137]   **34.78**

A person guilty of wrongful trading may be made the subject of a disqualification order.[138] An application for a declaration under s 214 may be consolidated with disqualification proceedings.[139] In *Brian D Pierson (Contractors) Ltd* the court found the directors liable for wrongful trading and drew attention to its powers under CDDA, s 10. Following post-judgment discussion between the judge, counsel for the liquidator, and counsel for the directors, and in light of written comments from the Secretary of State for Trade and Industry, the judge made an order disqualifying the directors under CDDA, s 10.[140]   **34.79**

D. Liability on Contravention of Restriction on Reuse of Company Name

(1) The restriction

In the report of the Cork Committee attention was drawn to the widespread dissatisfaction at the ease with which a person trading through the medium of one or more companies with limited liability can allow such a company to become insolvent, form a new company, and then carry on trading much as before, leaving behind him a trail of unpaid creditors. It was pointed out that the dissatisfaction was greatest where the director of an insolvent company has set up business again using a similar name for the new company, and trades with assets purchased at a discount from the liquidator of the old company.[141] It appears that the Insolvency Act, ss 216 and 217 are provisions which are designed to eradicate this 'phoenix syndrome'.   **34.80**

However, these provisions as enacted apply to a wider set of circumstances than the case of a person attempting to exploit the goodwill of a previous insolvent company. In the absence of an application under s 216(3) for leave, the court is left with no discretion on the application of the sections, and a creditor of a company is entitled to take advantage of the statutory provisions, if they can be shown to be applicable.[142]   **34.81**

The provisions are an example of a limited, though significant, departure from the general principle of corporate law that a company is a legal entity separate from its directors and members, so that only the company is liable for its debts and the creditors of the company do not have a right of recourse to the assets of the directors and members for payment of the company's debts.   **34.82**

---

[137] Insolvency Act, s 176ZB, inserted by SBEE Act 2015, s 119 with effect from 1 October 2015.
[138] CDDA, s 10.
[139] *Official Receiver v Doshi* [2001] 2 BCLC 235.
[140] [2001] 1 BCLC 275.
[141] Paras 1813, 1826–37.
[142] *Thorne v Silverleaf* [1994] 1 BCLC 637, 642, 643, CA, per Peter Gibson LJ.

34.83   It appeared to Parliament that the mischief at which the Insolvency Act s 216 is directed was of such gravity that a person acting in contravention of that section should not only be subjected to criminal sanctions by s 216(3), of which the severity would depend upon the discretion of the court, but that such person should also thereby be made personally responsible by s 217(1)(a) for all debts of the company incurred at a time when that person was involved in the management of the company. It must have been supposed that such a person would, in the ordinary course of things, learn of this provision of the law or that directors of companies which go into insolvent liquidation should be left to inform themselves of the consequences in law of acting in contravention of s 216. That burden of responsibility for the debts was also imposed upon a further category of persons by s 217(1)(b), namely any person who is involved in the management of the company and who acts or is willing to act on instructions given (without the leave of the court) by a person whom he knows to be in contravention in relation to the company of s 216; but such a person is not by the words of s 216 himself caused to be in contravention of s 216 and therefore guilty of the offence created by s 216(3).[143]

34.84   By s 216(1), s 216 applies 'to a person where a company ("the liquidating company") has gone into insolvent liquidation on or after the appointed day and he was a director or shadow director of the company at any time in the period of 12 months ending with the day before it went into liquidation'.[144] For the purposes of s 216 a company goes into insolvent liquidation if it goes into liquidation at a time when its assets are insufficient for the payment of its debts and other liabilities and the expenses of the winding up.[145]

34.85   Section 216(2) explains what is meant by a prohibited name. It provides:

> (2) For the purposes of this section, a name is a prohibited name in relation to such a person if—
>
> (a) it is a name by which the liquidating company was known at any time in that period of 12 months, or
>
> (b) it is a name which is so similar to a name falling within paragraph (a) as to suggest an association with that company.

34.86   In deciding whether a company name is so similar to another as to suggest an association with it, it is necessary to make a comparison of the names in the context of all the circumstances in which they are actually used or likely to be used: the types of product dealt in, the locations of the business, the types of customers dealing with the companies and those involved in the operation of the two companies.[146] Having regard to the civil and criminal consequences of breaching the restriction on reuse of a prohibited name, the similarity between the two names must be such as to give rise to a probability that members of the public, comparing the names in the relevant context, will associate the two names with each other, whether as successor companies or as part of the same group.[147] On this basis, the court held that the

---

[143] *Thorne v Silverleaf* [1994] 1 BCLC 637, 646, CA, per Ralph Gibson LJ.

[144] The appointed day is 29 December 1986: Insolvency Act, ss 436 and 443. In s 216, 'company' includes a company which may be wound up under Part V of the Insolvency Act: s 216(8).

[145] Insolvency Act, s 216(7). This is the same test as in Insolvency Act, s 214(6) and CDDA, s 6(2)(a).

[146] *Ad Valorem Factors Ltd v Ricketts* [2004] 1 All ER 894, CA at para 22, per Mummery LJ (applied in *Revenue and Customs Commissioners v Benton-Diggins* [2006] 2 BCLC 255).

[147] *Ad Valorem Factors Ltd v Ricketts* [2004] 1 All ER 894, CA at para 30, per Simon Brown LJ. Applied in *Revenue and Customs Commissioners v Walsh* [2005] 2 BCLC 455.

name 'Air Equipment Co Ltd' was a name so similar to 'The Air Component Co Ltd' as to suggest an association with that company.[148]

Section 216(3) states the restriction which renders a person who contravenes it liable to criminal punishment under s 216(4) and civil liability under s 217. It provides: **34.87**

> Except with leave of the court[149] or in such circumstances as may be prescribed, a person to whom this section applies shall not at any time in the period of 5 years beginning with the day on which the liquidating company went into liquidation—
> (a) be a director of any other company that is known by a prohibited name, or
> (b) in any way, whether directly or indirectly, be concerned or take part in the promotion, formation or management of any such company, or
> (c) in any way, whether directly or indirectly, be concerned or take part in the carrying on of a business carried on (otherwise than by a company) under a prohibited name.

It is not therefore necessary that the person concerned should hold the position of director in the second company, only that he should be a director or shadow director of the liquidating company.[150]

References, in relation to any time, to a name by which a company is known are to the name **34.88** of the company at that time or to any name under which the company carries on business at any time.[151] A company carries on business under a prohibited name when it carries on some, but not necessarily all of its business under that name.[152]

A director is able to protect himself from the risk of committing criminal offences and from **34.89** the burden of personal liability for the debts of the successor company in two ways: he can resign his directorship and take no further part in the management of the successor company; or he can make an immediate application to the court for leave under s 216 to act in relation to a company with a prohibited name.[153]

(2) Application for leave

When considering an application for leave under s 216, the court may call on the liquida- **34.90** tor, or any former liquidator, of the liquidating company for a report of the circumstances in which that company became insolvent, and the extent (if any) of the applicant's apparent responsibility for its doing so.[154]

In *Penrose v Secretary of State for Trade and Industry* Chadwick J stated the following princi- **34.91** ples in relation to an application for leave:[155]

---

[148] *Ad Valorem Factors Ltd v Ricketts* [2004] 1 All ER 894, CA. Differences in the way the names are presented on the company's documents are irrelevant: *Archer Structures Ltd v Griffiths* [2004] 1 BCLC 201 at para 19. Also see *R (Griffin) v Richmond Magistrates' Court* [2008] 1 WLR 1525 at para 9; *First Independent Factors Ltd v Mountford* [2008] 2 BCLC 297 at paras 18–20.

[149] 'Court' means any court having jurisdiction to wind up companies; and on any application for leave under s 216(3), the Secretary of State or the official receiver may appear and call the attention of the court to any matters which seem to him to be relevant: s 216(5).

[150] *R v Doring* [2002] BCC 838, CA.

[151] Insolvency Act, s 216(6).

[152] *ESS Production Ltd v Sully* [2005] 2 BCLC 547, CA at paras 72, 95; *Glasgow City Council v Craig* [2009] 1 BCLC 742, CSOH at para 11.

[153] *Ad Valorem Factors Ltd v Ricketts* [2004] 1 All ER 894, CA at para 19, per Mummery LJ.

[154] Insolvency Rules, rule 4.227.

[155] [1996] 1 WLR 482, 489.

(1) It is wrong to treat an applicant who seeks leave under s 216 as if he were a person who had been disqualified for any of the reasons under the CDDA unless there is evidence which shows that he ought to be disqualified for one or more of those reasons.

(2) In particular, it is wrong to treat him, without evidence of misconduct, as if he were unfit to be a company director. The fact that the applicant intends to continue to trade through a company with a prohibited name does not entitle the court, without more, to impose restrictions upon him as if he were a person who had been disqualified for some form of misconduct.

(3) Unless the court is satisfied that the applicant is a person whose conduct in relation to the liquidating company makes him unfit to be concerned in the management of a company, it should exercise its discretion under s 216(3) with regard only to the purposes for which s 216 was enacted and not on the more general basis that the public requires some protection from the applicant's activities as a company director.

34.92 So, as a matter of principle, where an application is made for leave, the court should exercise its discretion to allow the director to act in relation to a company using a prohibited name, if it is satisfied that there is no risk to the creditors of the old company and no risk to the creditors of the new company beyond that which was permitted under the law relating to the incorporation of limited liability companies—that is to say, no risk beyond that which the legislature, in permitting those who are inexperienced to trade through companies which are undercapitalized, must be taken to have regarded as acceptable.[156]

34.93 In the earlier case *Re Bonus Breaks Ltd* leave was given where the director gave an undertaking that the company would not redeem any redeemable shares nor purchase its own shares out of distributable profits for a period of two years unless that was approved by an unconnected director.[157] However, the judge did not have to decide in that case whether leave would be given if the undertakings were not given. Following *Penrose*, the practice is not to require such undertakings.

(3) Excepted cases

34.94 As contemplated by s 216(3), circumstances have been prescribed which constitute exceptions to the prohibition. These exceptions are contained in the Insolvency Rules, rules 4.228–4.230 (and IR 2016, rr 22.1–22.7 after 6 April 2017). There are three excepted cases.

First excepted case

34.95 The first excepted case, rule 4.228(1) (and IR 2016, r 22.4 after 6 April 2017), applies where the insolvency practitioner sells the business of the insolvent company to the successor company and notice is given to the creditors of the liquidating company. This fulfils two purposes: preventing the assets of the liquidating company from being acquired at an undervalue or otherwise expropriated and preventing creditors of the liquidating company from being misled as to the identity of the new company.[158]

---

[156] *Penrose v Secretary of State for Trade and Industry* [1996] 1 WLR 482, 490. This was followed in *Re Lightning Electrical Contractors Ltd* [1996] 2 BCLC 302, where leave was granted in respect of certain named but then dormant companies.

[157] [1991] BCC 546.

[158] *Penrose v Secretary of State for Trade and Industry* [1996] 1 WLR 482, 489.

In its original form it was held in *First Independent Factors and Finance Ltd v Churchill* that **34.96** the first excepted case is unavailable if the director is already working with the management of the successor company.[159] The decision gave rise to a number of difficulties. For example, it made the rule inapplicable in management buy-outs. A new rule 4.228 has therefore been substituted in place of the former one.[160]

As before, the new rule makes provision for a director of a company which goes into insol- **34.97** vent liquidation to act as a director of a company with a prohibited name where that company acquires the whole or substantially the whole of the business of the insolvent company, provided certain notice requirements are complied with. Unlike the previous rule, it also provides for such a person to carry on business under a prohibited name other than by way of a company, subject to the same requirements. In the new rule the notice requirements have also been expanded. Notice must be published in the Gazette and given to all creditors whose name and address is known to the director or could be ascertained by him on making reasonable enquiries. The prescribed notice may be given before the company enters into insolvent liquidation, for example where it is in administration or administrative receivership and may go into liquidation later. In cases where the company is not in insolvent liquidation, notice can be given where the director of the insolvent company is already a director of the acquiring company. However, notice must always be given before a director acts in a way that would be prohibited by s 216.

The notice to creditors must be in Form 4.73 (for the notice after 6 April 2017, see IR 2016, **34.98** r 22.5). In all cases the notice must state the name and registered number of the insolvent company; the name of the director or shadow director; that it is his intention to act (or, where the company has not entered liquidation, to act or continue to act) in any or all of the ways specified in s 216(3) in connection with the carrying on of the business of the insolvent company; and the prohibited name, or where the company has not entered liquidation, the name under which the business is being or will be carried on which would be prohibited in the event that the company goes into liquidation.

In *Re Bonus Breaks Ltd* the applicant referred to a widely held understanding that 'the busi- **34.99** ness of the company' for the purpose of rule 4.228 must be the business comprising both assets and liabilities.[161] Morritt J, without hearing full argument, said that it seemed to him at least arguable that the purchase of a business or part of a business from an insolvency practitioner acting as liquidator of the company did not have to include the purchase of all or any of the liabilities of the company.

Second excepted case

The second excepted case is provided for by rule 4.229 (and IR 2016, r 22.6 after 6 April **34.100** 2017).[162] This provides that where a person to whom s 216 applies as having been a director or shadow director of the liquidating company applies for leave of the court under that section not later than seven days from the date on which the company went into liquidation,

---

[159] [2007] 1 BCLC 293, CA.

[160] The new rule only applies where arrangements for the acquisition of the business from the insolvent company are entered into on or after 6 August 2007: Insolvency (Amendment) Rules 2007 (SI 2007/1974), rule 3(1) and (2), as amended by Insolvency (Amendment) Rules 2010 (SI 2010/686), rule 2, Sch 1, para 258.

[161] [1991] BCC 546.

[162] As amended by Insolvency (Amendment) Rules 2010 (SI 2010/686), rule 2, Sch 1, paras 1 and 259.

he may, during the period specified in rule 4.229(2), act in any of the ways mentioned in s 216(3), notwithstanding that he has not obtained the leave of the court under that section. The period specified in rule 4.229(2) begins with the day on which the company goes into liquidation and ends either on the day falling six weeks after that date or on the day on which the court disposes of the application for leave under s 216, whichever of those days occurs first.

34.101 This second excepted case therefore enables a person seeking leave to act as a director, or in the other ways mentioned in s 216(3), pending the hearing of the application and so avoid disruption to the management of the business of the new company.

Third excepted case

34.102 The third excepted case, set out in rule 4.230 (and IR 2016, r 22.7 after 6 April 2017),[163] indicates that the mischief addressed by s 216 is not thought to exist where a company having the prohibited name has been established and has traded for not less than 12 months before the liquidating company went into liquidation.[164] Rule 4.230 provides:

> The court's leave under section 216(3) is not required where the company referred to, though known by a prohibited name within the meaning of the section—
> (a) has been known by that name for the whole of the period of 12 months ending with the day before the liquidating company went into liquidation, and
> (b) has not at any time in those 12 months been dormant within the meaning of section 1169(1), (2), and (3)(a) of the Companies Act.

34.103 The expression 'known by' in rule 4.230 has the same meaning as in s 216(6). So rule 4.230 is capable of application where a name change has taken place in the relevant period.[165]

34.104 The object of rule 4.230 is to take outside ss 216 and 217 companies which were not phoenix companies, and since companies within the same group (formal or informal) often share a common word or acronym in their names, it may be inferred that the third excepted case should cover group companies, whether the group is formal or informal.[166] The third excepted case is aimed at relieving personal liability where there was a previously established and active business trading with limited liability and it does not apply where a previously established non-corporate business is transferred to a company with limited liability.[167]

(4) Personal liability and penalty

34.105 If a person acts in contravention of s 216, he is liable to imprisonment or a fine, or both.[168] The offence is one of strict liability and *mens rea* is not necessary for reasons of social policy and prudence;[169] it is irrelevant that there has been no express misrepresentation or that no one has actually been deceived or confused into thinking that there was an association.

34.106 Notwithstanding that the legislative purpose of ss 216 and 217 is to curb the 'phoenix syndrome', if a name is a prohibited name within the natural and ordinary meaning of the

---

[163] As amended by Insolvency (Amendment) Rules 2010 (SI 2010/686), rule 2, Sch 1, para 1.
[164] *Penrose v Secretary of State for Trade and Industry* [1996] 1 WLR 482, 490.
[165] *ESS Production Ltd v Sully* [2005] 2 BCLC 547, CA at paras 62 and 81, per Arden LJ; at paras 92 and 95, per Chadwick LJ.
[166] *ESS Production Ltd v Sully* [2005] 2 BCLC 547, CA at paras 8 and 60.
[167] *First Independent Factors and Finance Ltd v Mountford* [2008] 2 BCLC 297 at paras 27–8.
[168] Insolvency Act, s 216(4).
[169] *R v Doring* [2002] BCC 838, CA.

language of s 216(2), the case is caught by the restrictions, even if it is not a 'phoenix syndrome' case.[170]

Section 217 provides for civil liability:

34.107

(1) A person is personally responsible for all the relevant debts of a company if at any time—
  (a) in contravention of section 216, he is involved in the management of the company, or
  (b) as a person who is involved in the management of the company, he acts or is willing to act on instructions given (without the leave of the court) by a person whom he knows at that time to be in contravention in relation to the company of section 216.
(2) Where a person is personally responsible under this section for the relevant debts of a company, he is jointly and severally liable in respect of those debts with the company and any other person who, whether under s 217 or otherwise, is so liable.
(3) For the purposes of this section the relevant debts of a company are—
  (a) in relation to a person who is personally responsible under paragraph (a) of subsection (1), such debts and other liabilities of the company as are incurred at a time when that person was involved in the management of the company, and
  (b) in relation to a person who is personally responsible under paragraph (b) of that subsection, such debts and other liabilities of the company as are incurred at a time when that person was acting or was willing to act on instructions given as mentioned therein.
(4) For the purposes of this section, a person is involved in the management of a company if he is a director of the company or if he is concerned, whether directly or indirectly, or takes part, in the management of the company.
(5) For the purposes of this section a person who, as a person involved in the management of a company, has at any time acted on instructions given (without the leave of the court) by a person whom he knew at that time to be in contravention in relation to the company of section 216 is presumed, unless the contrary is shown, to have been willing at any time thereafter to act on any instructions given by that person.
(6) in this section 'company' includes a company which may be wound up under Part V.[171]

There has been a steady flow of cases in which persons have been held to be personally liable for the debts of the successor company where there has been a contravention of s 216.[172] In Scotland it has been held that where the successor company carries on distinct businesses, only one of which is conducted under the prohibited name, the director is only personally liable for the debts of the part conducted under the prohibited name.[173] A person liable for a company's debts under s 217 has no right of indemnity against the company, nor can he claim contribution from other persons liable under s 217 either by reason of s 217 itself or the Civil Liability (Contribution) Act 1978.[174] It has also been held that a person's liability to a creditor of the successor company under s 217 is not reduced on account of a set-off under Insolvency Rules, rule 4.90 of a debt owed by the creditor to the successor company.[175]

34.108

---

[170] *Ad Valorem Factors Ltd v Ricketts* [2004] 1 All ER 894, CA; *First Independent Factors Ltd v Mountford* [2008] 2 BCLC 297.

[171] It includes unregistered companies.

[172] *Thorne v Silverleaf* [1994] 1 BCLC 637, CA; *Inland Revenue Commissioners v Nash* [2004] BCC 150; *Archer Structures Ltd v Griffiths* [2004] 1 BCLC 201; *Revenue and Customs Commissioners v Walsh* [2005] 2 BCLC 455; *Revenue and Customs Commissioners v Benton-Diggins* [2006] 2 BCLC 255; *First Independent Factors and Finance Ltd v Churchill* [2007] 1 BCLC 293, CA. *First Independent Factors Ltd v Mountford* [2008] 2 BCLC 297; *Glasgow CC v Craig* [2009] 1 BCLC 742; *Advocate General for Scotland v Reilly* [2011] CSOH 141.

[173] *Glasgow City Council v Craig* [2009] 1 BCLC 742, CSOH.

[174] *HM Revenue and Customs v Yousef* [2008] BCC 805.

[175] *Archer Structures Ltd v Griffiths* [2004] 1 BCLC 201. If this decision is correct, it would seem that a person may face a larger liability under s 217 than he would have done as a guarantor.

E. Liabilities of Directors in Relation to the Adjustment of Prior Transactions

34.109 The final section of this chapter deals with the provisions in the Insolvency Act for adjusting prior transactions (a) under ss 238–41 where the company enters administration or goes into liquidation and the transaction is at an undervalue or a preference, (b) under s 245 where the company enters administration or goes into liquidation and the company has created a floating charge on its undertaking or property, and (c) under s 423 where the transaction is a fraud on creditors. Remedies for transactions within ss 238–41 and 245 are directed towards achieving a *pari passu* distribution of the insolvent company's estate or furthering the purpose of administration.[176] None of the provisions in terms provides remedies for misconduct or breach of duties by directors, but they are relevant to the duties and liabilities of directors in four respects. First, the directors, or some of them, will have caused the company to enter into the impugned transaction and their conduct in doing so may expose them to personal liability to compensate the company for any loss which is not restored by an order made under these provisions of the Insolvency Act. Secondly, if the transaction is within these provisions, the director may not be protected from liability by having obtained the consent, approval, authorization, or ratification of the members. Thirdly, under ss 238–41 and 245 there are different rules for directors and other connected persons, which make transactions with them particularly vulnerable. Fourthly, transactions at undervalue and preferences within ss 238–40 are matters to which regard may be had for the purposes of disqualification for unfitness under the CDDA.[177]

(1) Transactions at undervalue

34.110 Section 238 of the Insolvency Act applies in the case of a company only where the company enters administration or goes into liquidation.[178] The administrator or liquidator may apply to the court for an order under s 238 'where the company has at a relevant time (defined in section 240) entered into a transaction with any person at an undervalue'.[179]

34.111 The SBEE Act 2015 has made three reforms in relation to s 238. First, the liquidator does not need to obtain sanction before commencing a claim under s 238.[180] Secondly, the office-holder now has power to assign a right of action, including the proceeds of an action, arising under s 238.[181] Third, it is now made clear that the proceeds of claims under s 238, or the assignment of such claims, are not part of the company's property which is available for

---

[176] Report of the Cork Committee at para 1209, discussing the earlier law.

[177] Under CDDA, s 9, Sch 1, Part II, para 8, there was explicit reference to transactions within these sections. That is not the case under the new s 12C, Sch 1, which came into effect on 1 October 2015 and which describes the conduct to which regard should be had more broadly: responsibility for causes of company becoming insolvent (para 2) and misfeasance and breach of fiduciary duty (para 5).

[178] Insolvency Act, s 238(1). Section 339 is the equivalent provision for personal bankruptcy.

[179] Insolvency Act, s 238(2).

[180] Insolvency Act, s 165(2), 167(1), as inserted by SBEE Act, s 120 with effect from 26 May 2015. The costs are recoverable as an expense under Insolvency Rules, rule 4.218(2)(a)(i) (and IR 2016, rr 6.42, 7.108 after 6 April 2017), but where the liquidator may resort to floating charge assets, he should obtain authorization or approval under IR 4.218A–218E (and IR 2016, r 7.111–7.116 after 6 April 2017).

[181] Insolvency Act, s 246ZD, inserted by SBEE Act 2015, 118 with effect from 1 October 2015. This removes the distinction between claims in respect of company property, which could be assigned, and claims available to an office-holder under the Insolvency Act, which could not: *Re Oasis Merchandising Ltd* [1998] Ch 170, CA.

satisfaction of claims of floating charge holders.[182] These new provisions reflect a public policy of facilitating the pursuit of claims for the benefit of unsecured creditors.

Section 238(3) provides that, subject to the further provisions of s 238, 'the court shall, on such an application, make such order as it thinks fit for restoring the position to what it would have been if the company had not entered into that transaction'. There are therefore four matters to be considered: (a) whether the transaction took place at a relevant time; (b) whether the transaction was at an undervalue; (c) whether the court is prevented from making an order, because the transaction was entered into in good faith and for the purpose of carrying on the company's business and there were reasonable grounds for believing that the transaction would benefit the company; and (d) the relief, if any, to be granted. **34.112**

Relevant time

Whether or not a transaction takes place at a 'relevant time' depends on two matters. The first is purely chronological. Section 240(1) provides that, subject to s 240(2), the time at which a company enters into a transaction at an undervalue is a relevant time if the transaction is entered into at a time (a) in the period of two years ending with the onset of insolvency, (b) between the making of an administration application in respect of the company and the making of an administration order on that application, or (c) between the filing with the court of a copy of notice of intention to appoint an administrator under paragraph 14 or 22 of Schedule B1 and the making of an appointment under that paragraph. **34.113**

Section 240(3) provides a definition of 'the onset of insolvency', for the purposes of calculating the two-year period in s 240(1) and also the periods for preference claims under s 239. The onset of insolvency is: **34.114**

(a) in a case where section 238 or 239 applies by reason of an administrator of a company being appointed by administration order, the date on which the administration application is made;

(b) in a case where section 238 or 239 applies by reason of an administrator of a company being appointed under paragraph 14 or 22 of Schedule B1 following filing with the court of a copy of a notice of intention to appoint under that paragraph, the date on which the copy of the notice is filed;

(c) in a case where section 238 or 239 applies by reason of an administrator being appointed otherwise than as mentioned in paragraph (a) or (b), the date on which the appointment takes effect;

(d) in a case where section 238 or 239 applies by reason of a company going into liquidation either following conversion of administration into winding up by virtue of Article 37 of the EC Regulation or at the time when the appointment of an administrator ceases to have effect, the date on which the company entered administration (or, if relevant, the date on which the application for the administration order was made or a copy of the notice of intention to appoint was filed); and

(e) in a case where section 238 or 239 applies by reason of a company going into liquidation at any other time, the date of the commencement of the winding up.

---

[182] Insolvency Act, s 176ZB, inserted by SBEE Act 2015, s 119 with effect from 1 October 2015. As regards transaction at undervalue and preference claims, this probably clarifies the law: *Re Yagerphone Ltd* [1935] Ch 392.

A voluntary winding up is deemed to commence at the time of the passing of the resolution for voluntary winding up and that remains the time of commencement even if the voluntary winding up is superseded by a winding up by the court.[183] If the winding-up order is made under Schedule B1, paragraph 13(1)(e), the winding up commences on the making of the order and in any other case, it commences at the time of the presentation of the winding-up petition.[184]

34.115 The second matter which determines whether or not a transaction takes place at a 'relevant time' relates to the company's financial position. Section 240(2) provides that where a company enters into a transaction at an undervalue in the period of two years ending with the onset of insolvency, that time is not a relevant time for the purposes of s 238 unless the company:

(a) is at that time unable to pay its debts within the meaning of section 123 in Chapter VI of Part IV, or

(b) becomes unable to pay its debts within the meaning of that section in consequence of the transaction ...;

but the requirements of this subsection are presumed to be satisfied, unless the contrary is shown, in relation to any transaction at an undervalue which is entered into by a company with a person who is connected with the company.

Section 123 includes both the cash-flow and balance sheet tests of insolvency. But the tests stand side by side and both may be applied to determine whether or not a company is unable to pay its debts at a particular time.[185] The cash-flow test looks to the reasonably near future as well as the present and involves looking at the company's business to see if the company has the resources to pay its debts as they fall due.[186] The balance sheet test looks beyond the reasonably near future; it is not an exact test, but the company will be deemed to be insolvent if '*looking at the company's assets and making proper allowance for its prospective and contingent liabilities, it cannot reasonably be expected to meet those liabilities*'.[187] It is not correct to take into account any hope or expectation that the company will obtain assets in the future where there was no right to these assets.[188] When assessing inability to pay debts for the purposes of a transaction at undervalue or preference claim, the court has the benefit of knowing what in fact happened. But Australian authority has held that ability to pay debts 'must be determined in the circumstances as they were known or ought to have been known at the relevant time, without the intrusion of hindsight ... Unexpected later discovery of a liability, or later quantification of a liability at a particular level, may be excluded from consideration if the liability was properly unknown or seen in lesser amount at the relevant time.'[189]

---

[183] Insolvency Act, ss 86 and 129(1).

[184] Insolvency Act, s 129(2) and (3).

[185] *BNY Corporate Trustee Services Ltd v Eurosail-UK-2007-3BL plc* [2013] 1 WLR 1408, SC at para 35, per Lord Walker; *Re Casa Estates (UK) Ltd* [2014] 1 BCLC 49, CA, at paras 27, 29 per Lewison LJ.

[186] *Re Cheyne Finance plc (No 2)* [2008] 1 BCLC 741, at para 51; *BNY Corporate Trustee Services Ltd v Eurosail-UK-2007-3BL plc* [2013] 1 WLR 1408, SC at paras 25, 34, and 37, per Lord Walker; *Re Casa Estates (UK) Ltd* [2014] 2 BCLC 49, CA, at paras 27 and 28.

[187] *Re Casa Estates (UK) Ltd* [2014] 2 BCLC 49, CA, at paras 27; *BNY Corporate Trustee Services Ltd v Eurosail-UK-2007-3BL plc* [2013] 1 WLR 1408, SC at paras 37, 38, and 42.

[188] *Byblos Bank SAL v Al-Khudhairy* [1987] BCLC 232, 247, CA (a pre-Insolvency Act case).

[189] *Lewis v Doran* [2005] NSWCA 243 at para 103, per Giles JA. In *The Bell Group Ltd V Westpac Banking Corp* [2008] WASC 239 at para 1119 White J adopted a similar approach, holding that account could be taken of events occurring after the relevant date 'that a reasonable observer at the relevant date, looking at all of the circumstances in which the company found itself, would have considered likely to occur'. Insolvency at a relevant date was not in issue in the appeal in the *Bell Group* case: [2012] WASCA 257.

A finding that the company was unable to pay its debts at some earlier time than its entry **34.116** into administration or liquidation has at least two additional consequences for directors, which may affect their personal liability for breach of duty in relation to the impugned transaction. The first is that from that time, if not earlier, their duty under the 2006 Act, s 172 to promote the success of the company requires them to take account of the interests of creditors (Chapter 12, Section E above). The second consequence is that they may not have the effective protection of a resolution of the members authorizing, approving, or ratifying their conduct (Chapter 12, Section E and Chapter 20, Section D above).

A person is connected with a company if he is a director or shadow director of the company **34.117** or an associate of such a director or shadow director, or an associate of the company.[190] Whether or not a person is an associate of the company is determined in accordance with the provisions of the Insolvency Act, s 435. It follows that, where a company enters into a transaction at an undervalue with a director, the burden of proving the company's inability to pay its debts shifts from the office-holder to the director. This is logical, because a director should at all times be aware of the company's financial position and therefore able to determine whether it can enter into the transaction without prejudicing the interests of creditors.[191]

Transaction at undervalue

Section 238(4) provides for the interpretation of 'transaction at undervalue': **34.118**

> For the purposes of this section and section 241, a company enters into a transaction with a person at an undervalue if—
> (a) the company makes a gift to that person or otherwise enters into a transaction with that person on terms that provide for the company to receive no consideration, or
> (b) the company enters into a transaction with that person for a consideration the value of which, in money or money's worth, is significantly less than the value, in money or money's worth, of the consideration provided by the company.

Substantially the same language is used in s 423, concerning transactions defrauding creditors (paragraph 34.158 below).

There are therefore three elements, the first of which is that there must be a transaction **34.119** entered into by the company. In all cases the first question is to identify the transaction which is under attack.[192] The word 'transaction' includes a gift, agreement, or arrangement, and references to entering into a transaction are to be construed accordingly.[193] Apart from a gift, s 238 envisages that a transaction is something which involves some element of dealing between the parties. This is implicit in the word 'transaction', and is reinforced by the references in s 238 to the 'entry into' the transaction, 'with a person', and 'on terms that provide'.[194] An arrangement is, on its natural meaning and in the context of the Insolvency Act, apt to include an agreement or understanding between parties, whether formal or

---

[190] Insolvency Act, s 249.

[191] *Re Ciro Citterio Menswear plc* [2002] 1 WLR 2217 at paras 42–7 is an example of a case where a person connected with the company discharged the burden of proving solvency.

[192] *National Bank of Kuwait v Menzies* [1994] 2 BCLC 306, 313, CA (a s 423 case); *National Westminster Bank plc v Jones* [2002] 1 BCLC 55, CA at para 26.

[193] Insolvency Act, s 436.

[194] *Re Taylor Sinclair (Capital) Ltd* [2001] 2 BCLC 176 at paras 20 and 21; *Clements v Henry Hadaway Organisation Ltd* [2008] 1 BCLC 223 at para 31; *Ailyan and Fry v Smith* [2010] BPIR 289 (a personal insolvency case).

informal, oral, or in writing.[195] Further, it must be the company itself that enters into the transaction.[196] The requirements of the section are not satisfied if the mortgagee of company property enters into the transaction.[197] But the transaction for the purposes of the section may be a wider arrangement of which a sale of property by a mortgagee forms a vital part.[198]

34.120 The second element is that the transaction must be with a person, but that person need not be the provider of all or any consideration to the company, since s 238(4) does not stipulate by what person or persons the consideration is to be provided.[199] However, the language of s 238(4) does require some engagement, or at least communication, between the parties; the mere transmission of money, without any dealing between the parties, could not constitute the entering into of a transaction.[200]

34.121 The third element is undervalue. Section 238 is concerned with the depletion of a company's assets by transactions at an undervalue. If it is a transaction at an undervalue, it may well have caused loss to the company, so exposing the directors to a breach-of-duty claim. The purpose of the section is to restore to a company for the benefit of its creditors money or other assets which ought not to have left the company. Gifts and transactions for no consideration within s 238(4)(a) do not call for further comment.[201] For the purposes of the comparison under s 238(4)(b), it is necessary to compare the value obtained by the company for the transaction and the value of consideration provided by the company. Both values must be measurable in money or money's worth and both must be considered from the company's point of view.[202]

34.122 In *Phillips v Brewin Dolphin Bell Lawrie Ltd* Lord Scott said of s 238(4):

> It simply directs attention to the consideration for which the company has entered into the transaction. The identification of this 'consideration' is in my opinion, a question of fact. It may also involve an issue of law, for example, as to the construction of some document. But if a company agrees to sell an asset to A on terms that B agrees to enter into some collateral agreement with the company, the consideration for the asset will, in my opinion, be the combination of the consideration, if any, expressed in the agreement with A and the value of the agreement with B. In short, the issue in the present case is not, in my opinion, to identify the section 238(4) 'transaction'; the issue is to identify the section 238(4) 'consideration'.[203]

34.123 In *Re M C Bacon Ltd* Millett J held that the granting of a debenture was not a transaction at an undervalue; the mere creation of a security over a company's assets did not deplete them and did not come within s 238. By charging its assets the company appropriates them to

---

[195] *Feakins v Department for Environment Food and Rural Affairs* [2007] BCC 54, CA at para 76, per Jonathan Parker LJ (a s 423 case). At para 78 Jonathan Parker LJ said: 'In some cases it may be appropriate … to treat a single step in a series of linked dealings as the relevant transaction; in others it may not.'

[196] *Re Ovenden Colbert Printers Ltd* [2014] 1 BCLC 291, CA, at paras 32–7 (unilateral misappropriation of company assets by a director is not a dealing between him and the company). In *BTI 2014 LLC v Sequana SA* [2016] EWHC 1686 (Ch) at paras 497–502 it was held that a dividend may be a transaction at undervalue.

[197] *Re Brabon* [2001] 1 BCLC 11, 43 (a personal insolvency and s 423 case).

[198] *Feakins v Department for Environment Food and Rural Affairs* [2007] BCC 54, CA at para 77.

[199] *Phillips v Brewin Dolphin Bell Lawrie Ltd* [2001] 1 WLR 143, HL at para 20, per Lord Scott.

[200] *Re Hampton Capital* [2016] 1 BCLC 374. In *BTI 2014 LLC v Sequana SA* [2016] EWHC 1686 (Ch) at paras 497–502 it was held that a dividend may be a transaction at undervalue.

[201] In *Re Barton Manufacturing Co Ltd* [1999] 1 BCLC 740 a company transferred money to a director's wife, with no intention that she should repay it. She lent the money so received to the company's parent to reduce the companies' overdraft. It was held that the transactions between the company and the wife were gifts within s 238(4)(a).

[202] *Re MC Bacon Ltd* [1990] BCLC 324, 340.

[203] [2001] 1 WLR 143, HL at para 20.

meet the liabilities due to the secured creditor and adversely affects the rights of other creditors in the event of insolvency, but it does not deplete its assets or diminish their value. It retains the right to redeem and the right to sell or remortgage the charged assets. All it loses is the ability to apply the proceeds otherwise than in satisfaction of the secured debt. That is not something capable of valuation in monetary terms and it is not customarily disposed of for value.[204] Similarly a company does not enter into a transaction at an undervalue when it establishes a trust account to pay creditors.[205]

When the court is considering the value of the consideration passing between the company **34.124** and the other party, the following principles may be derived from the speech of Lord Scott in *Phillips v Brewin Dolphin Bell Lawrie Ltd*[206] and subsequent cases:

(1) The value of the consideration in money or money's worth is to be assessed at the date of the transaction. The general rule (subject to the following paragraphs) is that where an asset is to be valued at a fixed date, no account can be taken of subsequent events.[207] Evidence of the price obtained on a subsequent sale may enable an inference to be drawn as to the market value of the asset on the valuation date, if there has been no material change in market conditions between the valuation date and the sale.[208]

(2) If at that date value is dependent on the occurrence or non-occurrence of some event and that event occurs before the assessment of value has been completed then the valuer may have regard to it. Lord Scott said that it was unsatisfactory and unnecessary for the court to pretend that it did not know what had happened.

(3) The valuer is entitled, indeed bound, to take account of all other matters relevant to the determination of value as at the date of the transaction.

(4) Where the value of the consideration provided to the company is speculative at the time of the transaction, it is for the party who relies on the consideration to establish its value.[209] So, if part of the consideration is the taking of a sublease under which no payments are in fact made to the company, its value as consideration to the company is nil.

(5) The value of an asset that is being offered for sale is, prima facie, not less than the amount that a reasonably well-informed purchaser is prepared, in arm's length negotiations, to pay for it.[210]

Whilst it is preferable for a court to arrive at a precise figure for the incoming and outgoing **34.125** values where it is possible to do so, the court is not required to ascribe a precise figure; all that is required is that the court has to be satisfied that, whatever the precise values, the incoming value is significantly less than the outgoing value. If the court considers it appropriate to do so, it may address the issue of undervalue by taking from a range of possible values those which are most favourable to the party seeking to uphold the transaction.[211]

---

[204] *Re MC Bacon Ltd* [1990] BCLC 324, 340. In *Hill v Spread Trustee Co Ltd* [2007] 1 WLR 2404, CA at [93] the Court of Appeal cautioned that Millett J did not say that the grant of security could never amount to a transaction at undervalue, but did not comment on the difficulty of valuing the consideration passing between the parties. *Re MC Bacon Ltd* was followed in *Re Mistral Finance Ltd* [2001] BCC 27.

[205] *Re Lewis's of Leicester Ltd* [1995] 1 BCLC 428, 438, 439.

[206] *Phillips v Brewin Dolphin Bell Lawrie Ltd* [2001] 1 WLR 143, HL at paras 26, 27, 30; *Re Thoars* [2003] 1 BCLC 499 at [17], per Sir Andrew Morritt V-C.

[207] *Joiner v George* [2003] BCC 298, CA at paras 68, 70, 71.

[208] *Stanley v TMK Finance Ltd* [2011] BPIR 876 at paras 15–18.

[209] *Stanley v TMK Finance Ltd* [2011] BPIR 876 (Ch) at para 7.

[210] *Re Brabon* [2001] 1 BCLC 11, 38, a case on the Insolvency Act, s 339; *Stanley v TMK Finance Ltd* [2011] BPIR 876 (Ch) at para 7.

[211] *Re Thoars, Reid v Ramlort (No 2)* [2005] 1 BCLC 331, CA at paras 102–5, per Jonathan Parker LJ (a personal insolvency case), who referred to *National Westminster Bank plc v Jones* [2002] 1 BCLC 55, CA at paras 28 and 29, per Mummery LJ (a s 423 case).

34.126   In all cases the court is concerned with the commercial reality of the consideration given and received; with the real economic benefits of the transaction and with real value, not book value or mere 'hope' value.[212] The courts have found there to have been a transaction at an undervalue:[213]

(1)   where a finance leasing company transferred its lease agreements, with the benefit of the income stream, in return for quarterly-in-arrears payments;[214]

(2)   where property subject to mortgage, but with a substantial equity of redemption, was transferred in consideration of the transferee merely undertaking to discharge the mortgage repayments;[215]

(3)   where a mortgagor of agricultural property granted a tenancy at a proper market rent, because the tenant thereby acquired additional benefits of value (surrender value, which could be claimed as a ransom from the mortgagee) which corresponded to the diminution in the value of the mortgagor's property;[216]

(4)   where the company agreed to pay interest retrospectively;[217]

(5)   where a Cuban company sold its shares in an English company at par in sterling, but to be paid in Cuban pesos, the exchange calculated at the artificial official rate, when the commercial rate was much lower;[218] and

(6)   where the company received £1 million for a going concern business that was worth £2.41 million, even though the company could not afford to carry on trading and the transferee was the only potential purchaser.[219]

Restriction on remedies

34.127   By s 238(5) the court may not make an order under s 238 if it is satisfied:

(a)   that the company which entered into the transaction did so in good faith and for the purpose of carrying on its business, and

(b)   that at the time it did so there were reasonable grounds for believing that the transaction would benefit the company.

34.128   The first of those requirements involves both subjective and objective elements. The second is entirely objective.[220] It follows that the directors may cause a company to enter into a transaction at an undervalue provided that to do so is consistent with both their fiduciary duties and their duty of care, skill, and diligence, except that any authorization or ratification by shareholders would be irrelevant to the issue under s 238(5).[221] Thus, the subsection may

---

[212] *Agricultural Mortgage Corporation v Woodward* [1995] 1 BCLC 1, 10–12, CA, per Slade LJ; *Pinewood Joinery v Starelm Properties Ltd* [1994] 2 BCLC 412, 417 (a s 423 case); *Pena v Coyne (No 1)* [2004] 2 BCLC 703 at para 114.

[213] In appropriate cases the court will grant summary judgment: *Power v Hodges* [2016] BPIR 162.

[214] *Arbuthnot Leasing International Ltd v Havelet Leasing Ltd (No 2)* [1990] BCC 636, 644 (a s 423 case).

[215] *Re Kumar* [1993] 1 WLR 224 (a personal insolvency case). *Chohan v Saggar* [1992] BCC 306, 321 is a similar case.

[216] *Agricultural Mortgage Corporation v Woodward* [1995] 1 BCLC 1, 10, 11, CA (followed in *Barclays Bank plc v Eustice* [1995] 1 WLR 1238, 1244–6, CA.) This was a case under the Insolvency Act, s 423, but the issue considered by the Court of Appeal was whether the transaction was at an undervalue.

[217] *Re Shapland* [2000] BCC 106.

[218] *Banco Nacional de Cuba v Cosmos Trading Corp* [2001] 1 BCLC 813, 815, 819, CA.

[219] *Re MDA Investment Ltd* [2004] 1 BCLC 217 at paras 73, 114–23.

[220] *Lord v Sinai Securities Ltd* [2005] 1 BCLC 295 at para 21.

[221] 2006 Act, ss 170–81.

protect a sale of an asset by a company in financial difficulties for a price which the directors consider to be an undervalue in order to raise cash to enable the company to carry on trading.

Limitation

Applications to set aside transactions under the Insolvency Act, s 238 are generally actions **34.129** on a specialty within the meaning of the Limitation Act 1980, s 8(1) and subject to a 12-year limitation period accordingly. However, where the substance of the claim is not to set aside a transaction but 'to recover a sum recoverable by virtue of' s 238, such applications will be governed by the Limitation Act 1980, s 9(1) and are subject to a six-year limitation period accordingly.[222]

Remedies

Section 238(3) provides that the court 'shall, on such an application [under s 238], make **34.130** such order as it thinks fit for restoring the position to what it would have been if the company had not entered into' the transaction.

Despite the use of the verb 'shall', the phrase 'such order as it thinks fit' confers on the court **34.131** a broad discretion as to whether it makes an order and its terms.[223] Section 241 provides a list of possible types of orders which indicate that the applicant is not entitled to any particular form of order as of right. The burden of showing that the court should not make an order under s 238 in respect of a transaction at an undervalue is on the respondent, not the office-holder.[224]

The order may be made against persons who were not party to the transaction with the **34.132** company, but s 241 contains provisions protecting persons who acquired an interest in the relevant property in good faith and for value. Directors and other persons connected with the company are presumed, unless the contrary is shown, to have received the property otherwise than in good faith.[225] An order may be made in relation to a transaction into which the company had no power to enter.[226] A person against whom a claim is brought under s 238 is not under a common liability with someone against whom a claim had not been made for the purposes of the Civil Liability (Contribution) Act 1978.[227]

The court does not start, so far as remedy is concerned, with a presumption in favour of **34.133** monetary compensation as opposed to setting aside the transaction; the court starts from no a priori position but fashions the most appropriate remedy with a view to restoring so far as practicable and just to do so the position the parties would have been in if the company had

---

[222] *Re Priory Garage (Walthamstow) Ltd* [2001] BPIR 144. See para 34.163 below for the limitation rule in relation to s 423 claims.

[223] *Re Paramount Airways Ltd (No 2)* [1993] Ch 223, 239, CA; *Phillips v Brewin Dolphin Bell Lawrie Ltd* [2001] 1 WLR 143, HL at para 34. In *Re MDA Investment Management Ltd* [2004] 1 BCLC 217 at paras 122–4, the court refused to make an order restoring the position, because if the transaction had not occurred the company would have been in a worse position. In the bankruptcy case *Singla v Brown* [2008] Ch 357 the court exercised its discretion to make no order.

[224] *Re Barton Manufacturing Ltd* [1999] 1 BCLC 740. In *Re Shapland Inc* [2000] BCC 106 (where *Re Oasis Merchandising Services Ltd* [1998] Ch 170, CA, was not cited) it was held that the fact that a secured creditor may benefit from the order is not a reason for not making it, but now Insolvency Act, s 176ZB makes it clear that the proceeds of a successful claim do not go to floating charge holders. See *BTI 2014 LLC v Sequana SA* [2016] EWHC 1686 (Ch) at para 520, which considers the possibility of a change of position defence.

[225] Insolvency Act, ss 241(2) and (2A), and 249.

[226] Insolvency Act, s 241(4).

[227] *Re International Championship Management Ltd* [2007] 2 BCLC 274.

not entered into the transaction. In deciding how to exercise its discretion in respect of the most appropriate remedy, the court must have regard to subsequent events.[228] The court's primary, and possibly only, concern under s 238(3) is the restoration of the company's position. The position of a counter-party is a matter to be considered by the court as a general matter of discretion but the court is not obliged to ensure that such a person is restored in every particular to the status quo before the transaction, since there are many cases where that will be impossible.[229]

34.134　The scope of application of s 238 is not limited territorially. If a foreign element is involved, the court has to be satisfied that, in respect of the relief sought against the defendant, the defendant is sufficiently connected with England for it to be just and proper to make the order.[230]

Summary in relation to directors

34.135　Where a company enters into a transaction with a director or person connected with him in the two-year period, the question whether the transaction was at an undervalue will be assessed on an objective basis, without regard to any weakness in the company's bargaining position. The burden is on the director or connected party to prove solvency and justify the transaction as being in the interests of the company within s 238(5). If a director uses an intermediary to acquire the property his title will be vulnerable, because it is assumed the director acted in bad faith.

(2) Preferences

34.136　Section 239 of the Insolvency Act applies in the case of a company only where the company enters administration or goes into liquidation.[231] The administrator or liquidator may apply to the court for an order under s 239 'where the company has at the relevant time (defined in [section 240]) given a preference to any person'.[232] The office-holder has power to assign a right of action, including the proceeds of an action, arising under s 240 and the proceeds of a claim do not go to floating charge holders (see paragraph 34.111 above).[233]

34.137　Section 239(3) provides that subject to the further provisions of s 239 'the court shall, on such an application, make such order as it thinks fit for restoring the position to what it would have been if the company had not given the preference'. There are therefore four matters to be considered: (a) whether the preference was given at a relevant time, (b) whether a preference was given to a person, (c) whether the company which gave the preference was influenced in deciding to give it by a desire to prefer, and (d) the relief, if any, to be granted.

---

[228] *Re Thoars, Reid v Ramlort Ltd (No 2)* [2005] 1 BCLC 331, CA (a personal insolvency case). In *Re Husky Group Ltd* [2015] BPIR 184 compensation in respect of trademarks transferred at an undervalue was assessed on the basis of their value to the transferee, rather than their value to the company which could not exploit them.

[229] *Lord v Sinai Securities Ltd* [2005] 1 BCLC 295.

[230] *Re Paramount Airways Ltd (No 2)* [1993] Ch 223, CA. By Insolvency Rules, rules 12A.16 and 20, CPR Part 6 applies to service of applications, documents relating to applications and court orders outside the jurisdiction with such modifications as the court may direct. The claim is made under an enactment within PD6B, para 3.1(2): *Erste Group Bank AG v JSC 'VMZ RE October'* [2014] BPIR 81 at para 150, [2015] EWCA Civ 379 at para 113 (a case under Insolvency Act, s 423).

[231] Insolvency Act, s 239(1). Section 340 is the comparable provision for personal bankruptcy.

[232] Insolvency Act, s 239(2). A liquidator does not need to obtain sanction to bring the claim: Insolvency Act, ss 165(2) and 167(1), inserted by SBEE Act 2015, s 120 with effect from 26 May 2015.

[233] Insolvency Act, ss 176ZB and 246ZD, which came into force on 1 October 2015.

Relevant time

Relevant time is defined in substantially the same way for a preference within s 239 as it is **34.138**
for a transaction within s 238 (paragraphs 34.113–34.117 above). There are, however, the
following differences:

(1) The two-year period in s 240(1)(a) only applies where the preference is given to a director, shadow director, or other person who is connected with the company.[234]
(2) In any other case of preference the period is six months ending with the onset of
insolvency.
(3) There is no presumption of inability to pay debts in the case of a preference of someone
connected with the company, as there is with a transaction at undervalue.[235]

Identifying the time at which a preference may be said to have been given can be difficult. **34.139**
Where the preference is the grant of security, the relevant date is when the decision to grant
it was made, not the time when the debenture was created.[236] On the other hand, where the
preference is repayment of a loan, the relevant date for the purposes of considering the debtor
company's mental state is when the decision to effect repayment was made, not some earlier
date, when the creditor had agreed with the company to defer calling in the loan for a fixed
period.[237]

Preference

Section 239(4) provides for the interpretation of 'gives a preference': **34.140**

> For the purposes of this section and section 241, a company gives a preference to a person if—
> (a) that person is one of the company's creditors or a surety or guarantor for any of the com-
> pany's debts or other liabilities, and
> (b) the company does anything or suffers anything to be done which (in either case) has the
> effect of putting that person into a position which, in the event of the company going into
> insolvent liquidation, will be better than the position he would have been in if that thing
> had not been done.

The first element of the definition is the identification of persons who may be preferred: a **34.141**
creditor, surety, or guarantor of any of the company's debts or liabilities.[238] The second element is that the company does something or suffers something to be done which produces
the effect of a preference. A company does not suffer anything to be done when a debt
owed by it is assigned by a creditor.[239] The fact that something has been done in pursuance
of the order of a court does not, without more, prevent the doing or suffering of that thing
from constituting the giving of a preference.[240] The third element is the preference effect,
which is improving the person's position in the event of the company going into insolvent

---

234 Insolvency Act, s 249 identifies other persons connected with a company.
235 Insolvency Act, s 240(2); see *Re Reynolds DIY Stores Ltd* [2014] BCC 601 (where a preference claim
against a director failed because the liquidators adduced no evidence of inability to pay debts).
236 *Re MC Bacon Ltd* [1990] BCLC 324, 336.
237 *Wills v Corfe Joinery* [1998] 2 BCLC 75, 77, 78; *Re Stealth Construction Ltd* [2012] 1 BCLC 297 at para
61. These cases follow the reasoning of *Re MC Bacon Ltd* [1990] BCLC 324, 336 and *Re Fairway Magazines
Ltd* [1993] BCLC 643, 649.
238 In *Re Thirty-Eight Building Ltd* [1999] 1 BCLC 416, it was held that the reference is to creditor in the
legal sense.
239 *Re Parkside International Ltd* [2010] BCC 309 at paras 52–63.
240 Insolvency Act, s 239(7).

liquidation. The question is whether the person's position will be better in the assumed liquidation, not that it may be better.[241]

Desire to prefer

34.142 Issues invariably arise in respect of the restriction on the court's power to make an order under s 239, which is contained in s 239(5):

> The court shall not make an order under this section in respect of a preference given to any person unless the company which gave the preference was influenced in deciding to give it by a desire to produce in relation to that person the effect mentioned in subsection (4)(b).

34.143 In *Re MC Bacon Ltd* Millett J provided an authoritative explanation of the new provision, summarized in the following subparagraphs, which has been followed in subsequent cases:[242]

(1) As to the contrast between 'desire' under sub-s 239(5) and 'intention' which had been a feature of the previous preference provisions: Intention is objective, desire is subjective. A man can choose the lesser of two evils without desiring either of them. It is not however sufficient to establish a desire to make the payment or grant the security which it is sought to avoid. There must have been a desire to produce the effect mentioned in the subsection, that is to say, to improve the creditor's position in the event of an insolvent liquidation. A man is not to be taken as *desiring* all the necessary consequences of his actions.

(2) As to commercial transactions with a company in financial difficulties: It will still be possible to provide assistance to a company in financial difficulties provided that the company is actuated only by proper commercial considerations. Under the new regime a transaction will not be set aside as a voidable preference unless the company positively wished to improve the creditor's position in the event of its own insolvency.

(3) As to proving the presence of the desire: There is of course, no need for there to be direct evidence of the requisite desire. Its existence may be inferred from the circumstances of the case just as the dominant intention could be inferred under the old law.[243]

(4) As to the influence of the desire on the transaction: subs 239(5) requires only that the desire should have influenced the decision. That requirement is satisfied if it was one of the factors which operated on the minds of those who made the decision. It need not have been the only factor or even the decisive one. In my judgment, it is not necessary to prove that, if the requisite desire had not been present, the company would not have entered into the transaction. That would be too high a test.

34.144 It is not necessary to establish that the directors knew or believed that the company was insolvent at the relevant time.[244] A finding that a company desired to put a particular creditor in a position of advantage in the event of that company's liquidation is not a finding of moral turpitude on the part of the directors of either that company or the creditor company.[245]

---

[241] *Re Ledingham-Smith* [1993] BCLC 635, 641 (a bankruptcy case). In *Re Hawkes Hill Publishing Co Ltd* [2007] BCC 937 there was no preference in fact.

[242] [1990] BCLC 324, 335, 336; *Re Oxford Pharmaceuticals Ltd* [2009] 2 BCLC 485.

[243] In *Re Transworld Trading Ltd* [1999] BPIR 628, 634 it was said that events subsequent to the grant of a preference will sometimes throw light upon what was the desire of the company when it granted the preference, and upon whether that desire influenced the company in making the grant, but it is ordinarily the evidence of events leading up to the grant which is the most relevant.

[244] *Katz v McNally* [1999] BCC 291, 296, CA.

[245] *Re Transworld Trading Ltd* [1999] BPIR 628, 635.

There is a distinction between cases where the person preferred is a director, shadow director, **34.145** or other person connected with the company and cases where the person preferred is not so connected.[246] In the former cases, s 239(6) has the effect of reversing the burden of proving the influence of the requisite desire:

> A company which has given a preference to a person connected with the company (otherwise than by reason only of being its employee) at the time the preference was given is presumed, unless the contrary is shown, to have been influenced in deciding to give it by such a desire as is mentioned in subsection (5).

Where the preferred person is connected with the company it is in practice difficult for that **34.146** person to show that the decision to repay or secure a debt owed to him was actuated only by commercial considerations and entirely uninfluenced by the requisite desire.[247] The court has found that the burden of proof was discharged where the company made an early rental payment to the landlord in respect of premises occupied by the company and let to its directors;[248] where the company created a floating charge to secure fresh advances from a director;[249] and where the director received a redundancy payment in common with other employees.[250] But the fact that at the time of the giving of the alleged preference the directors were optimistic about the prospects for rescuing the company will not be sufficient to rebut the presumption of a preference.[251]

In contrast it is less common for an office-holder to bring a preference claim against a credi- **34.147** tor who is not connected with the company or whose debt is not guaranteed by a connected person. In *Re MC Bacon Ltd* the liquidator's claim to set aside as a preference a debenture given to the bank failed.[252] The company had no choice but to grant the security insisted on by the bank as a condition of the bank continuing to provide banking facilities so that the company could continue to trade. There was no desire to prefer and, in acceding to the bank's terms, the company was actuated only by commercial considerations.

Remedies

Section 239(3) provides that the court 'shall, on such an application [under s 239], make **34.148** such order as it thinks fit for restoring the position to what it would have been if the company

---

[246] Insolvency Act, s 249, read with s 435, explains who are connected with a company. A repayment of a loan made by a directors' pension scheme was not a payment to a person connected with the company, because of the provisions of the exclusion of pension scheme trustees from being associates for the purposes of the Insolvency Act, ss 249 and 435, which is made by s 435(5): *Re Thirty-Eight Building Ltd* [1999] 1 BCLC 416; *Re Thirty-Eight Building Ltd (No 2)* [2000] 1 BCLC 201.

[247] The office-holder succeeded in recovering payments to directors or persons connected with the company as preferences in the following cases: *Re DKG Contractors Ltd* [1990] BCC 903; *Re Exchange Travel (Holdings) Ltd (No 3)* [1996] 2 BCLC 524; [1997] 2 BCLC 579, CA (payments to directors had been made by the finance director, who had no desire to prefer, but on the instructions of directors who did not discharge the burden of proving that they were not influenced by a desire to prefer); *Wills v Corfe Joinery Ltd* [1998] 2 BCLC 75; *Re Brian D Pierson Ltd* [2001] 1 BCLC 275 (but not in respect of redundancy payments); *Re MDA Investment Management Ltd* [2004] 1 BCLC 217 at paras 136–61; *Re Cityspan Ltd* [2007] 2 BCLC 522; *Re Sonatacus Ltd* [2007] 2 BCLC 627, CA; *Re Oxford Pharmaceuticals Ltd* [2009] 2 BCLC 485. In *Weisgard v Pilkington* [1995] BCC 108 leases granted to directors were set aside as a preference since the rent was applied in reduction of debts owed to the directors. In *Re Shapland Inc* [2000] BCC 106 a charge granted to a director was set aside as a preference. In *Re Conegrade Ltd* [2003] BPIR 358 a transfer of property to a director was set aside as a preference since the sale price had been applied in reduction of the debt owed to the director.

[248] *Re Beacon Leisure Ltd* [1992] BCLC 565. In *Phillips v McGregor-Paterson* [2010] 1 BCLC 72 the issue could not be determined against the director on a summary basis.

[249] *Re Fairway Magazines Ltd* [1993] BCLC 643.

[250] *Re Brian D Pierson Ltd* [2001] 1 BCLC 275, 298.

[251] *Re Conegrade Ltd* [2003] BPIR 358, 372–4.

[252] [1990] BCLC 324.

had not given the preference'. This provision corresponds to s 238(3) in the case of transactions at an undervalue, and the principles explained in paragraphs 34.130–34.134 above apply to preference claims.

Summary in relation to directors

34.149 A director or shadow director is particularly exposed to a claim under s 239 in that claims can be made in respect of preferences given within two years of the onset of insolvency (not six months) and the burden is on him to prove that (a) the company was solvent for the purposes of s 240 at the time the preference was given, and (b) the preference was not at all influenced by a desire to prefer.

34.150 If the court cannot make an effective order against someone other than the director restoring the position to what it would have been had the preference not occurred, the director may be liable to make good the loss on the ground that he was in breach of his general duties in causing or procuring the preference to be given.[253] In *Re Brian D Pierson Ltd* Hazel Williamson QC held that misfeasance or breach of duty must be positively proved and could not be established from the mere fact a preference claim had succeeded by virtue of the statutory presumption under s 239(6).[254] In *Re Oxford Pharmaceuticals Ltd* preference claims against a connected company succeeded by virtue of the presumption in s 239(6), but the claims against the directors for breach of fiduciary duty for making the preferential payments failed where the directors reasonably believed that the company would overcome its difficulties and that the payments were in the best interests of the company, since they would stabilize the group and secure the support of the bank.[255]

(3) Avoidance of certain floating charges

34.151 Even though a floating charge created by a company in favour of a director, shadow director, or other person connected with the company within two years of the onset of insolvency may not be set aside as a preference under s 239, it may be invalid under the Insolvency Act, s 245, which avoids certain floating charges created by a company that enters administration or goes into liquidation.[256]

34.152 The condition for invalidity under s 245 is simply that the floating charge was created at a relevant time. In the case of a floating charge created in favour of a director, shadow director, or other person connected with the company, the time is a relevant time if the charge is created within two years of the onset of insolvency, whether or not the company was unable to pay its debts at the time the charge was created.[257] In the case of a floating charge created in favour of any other person, the time is reduced to 12 months before the onset of insolvency, but the time is only a relevant time if the company is then unable to pay its debts within the meaning of the Insolvency Act, s 123 or becomes unable to pay

---

[253] *Re Washington Diamond Mining Co* [1893] 3 Ch 95, 115, CA; *West Mercia Safetywear Ltd v Dodd* [1988] BCLC 250, 252, CA; *Re Cosy Seal Insulation Ltd* [2016] EWHC 1255 (Ch).

[254] [2001] 1 BCLC 275, 299. In *GHLM Trading Ltd v Maroo* [2012] 2 BCLC 369 at para 168, Newey J agreed, pointing out that there may be a breach of duty where the conditions for a preference under s 239 are not all made out. In *Re Finch (UK) plc* [2016] 1 BCLC 394, there was both a preference and a breach of duty.

[255] *Re Oxford Pharmaceuticals Ltd* [2009] 2 BCLC 485 at paras 91–5.

[256] 'Floating charge' is defined by the Insolvency Act, s 251. For 'connected with the company', see s 249, read with s 435; *Re Kilnoore Ltd* [2006] Ch 489.

[257] Insolvency Act, s 245(3)(a).

its debts within that meaning in consequence of the transaction under which the charge is created.[258]

By s 245(2) a floating charge created at a relevant time is invalid except to the extent of: **34.153**

(a) the value of so much of the consideration for the creation of the charge as consists of money paid, or goods or services supplied, to the company at the same time as, or after, the creation of the charge,

(b) the value of so much of that consideration as consists of the discharge or reduction, at the same time as, or after, the creation of the charge, of any debt of the company, and

(c) the amount of such interest (if any) as is payable on the amount falling within paragraph (a) or (b) in pursuance of any agreement under which the money was so paid, the goods or services were so supplied or the debt was so discharged or reduced.

The paragraphs of s 245(2) have been drafted to ensure that a floating charge within the reach of the section is only valid to the extent of new consideration which is of real value to the company. To the extent that such a charge merely secures existing liabilities, it will be invalid.[259]

(4) Transactions defrauding creditors

The Insolvency Act, s 423 replaced the Law of Property Act 1925, s 172 (which in turn **34.154** replaced the Fraudulent Conveyances Act 1571), which avoided conveyances of property made with intent to defeat and delay creditors. Unlike the provisions of the Insolvency Act, ss 238–41, whose purpose is to assist the *pari passu* distribution of the company's property, the purpose of s 423, like its predecessors, is to protect creditors from fraud.[260] In fact, there is little evidence of the Law of Property Act, s 172 or its predecessors being used in the company context.[261] The new s 423 seems to have attracted rather more use in that context, although most of the reported cases concern individual debtors.

The court is given power to make an order under s 423 in relation to a company, if (a) the **34.155** application is made by a person qualified to make it under s 424, (b) the company has entered into a transaction at undervalue within s 423(1), and (c) the conditions for making an order under s 423(3) are satisfied.[262]

The applicant

Section 424(1) prevents an application for an order under s 423 from being made unless **34.156** the applicant is qualified to make it. If the company is being wound up or is in administration, the application may be made by the liquidator or administrator or, with the leave of the court, by a victim of the transaction.[263] In a case where a victim is bound by a CVA the

---

[258] Insolvency Act, s 245(3)(b) and (4). Whether the person is connected or unconnected, the time is also relevant if it is in the periods specified in s 245(3)(c) and (d), which are in the same terms as s 240(1)(c) and (d) (para 34.113 above). 'Onset of insolvency' is defined by s 245(5) in substantially the same terms as s 240(3) (para 34.114 above). For inability to pay debts, see para 34.115 above.

[259] *Re Fairway Magazines Ltd* [1993] BCLC 643; *Re Shoe Lace Ltd, Power v Sharp Investments Ltd* [1994] 1 BCLC 111, CA.

[260] Report of the Cork Committee at para 1209.

[261] The only reported cases appear to be *Re Lloyd's Furniture Palace Ltd* [1925] Ch 853 and *Re Shilena Hosiery Ltd* [1980] Ch 219.

[262] In the case of a company, the court is the High Court or any other court having jurisdiction to wind it up: Insolvency Act, s 423(4).

[263] *Re Ayala Holdings Ltd* [1993] BCLC 256 (leave given to victim to apply where there was an arguable case and no application by liquidator) and on appeal as *National Bank of Kuwait v Menzies* [1994] 2 BCLC 306, CA.

application may be made by the supervisor of the CVA or by any person who (whether or not so bound) is a victim of the transaction. In any other case concerning a company the application may be made by a victim of the transaction.

34.157 For the purposes of ss 423–5, s 423(5) provides that a victim of a transaction is a person who is, or is capable of being, prejudiced by it. The definition is not restricted to creditors with present or actual debts. The definition of 'victim' is employed in relation to the criteria for relief in s 423(2), but it is not used in s 423(3), which defines the necessary purpose. The person or persons who fulfil the conditions in s 423(3) may thus be a narrower class of persons than those who at the date of the transaction are victims for the purpose of s 423(5). For a person to be a 'victim' there is no need to show that the person who effected the transaction intended to put assets beyond his reach or prejudice his interests. Put another way, a person may be a victim, and thus a person whose interests the court thinks fit to protect by making an order under s 423, but he may not have been the person within the purpose of the person entering into the transaction. Prejudice or potential prejudice is a condition for obtaining relief, but that prejudice does not have to be achieved by the purpose with which the transaction was entered into, nor does the purpose have to be one which by itself is capable of achieving prejudice.[264]

Transaction at undervalue

34.158 In relation to a company s 423(1) gives substantially the same meaning of 'transaction at undervalue' as is given by s 238(4), which is discussed at paragraphs 34.118–34.126 above, to which further reference should be made.[265] It provides, so far as relevant to a company:

> This section relates to transactions entered into at an undervalue; and a person enters into such a transaction with another person if—
> (a) he makes a gift to the other person or he otherwise enters into a transaction with the other on terms that provide for him to receive no consideration; … or
> (c) he enters into a transaction with the other for a consideration the value of which, in money or money's worth, is significantly less than the value, in money or money's worth, of the consideration provided by himself.

Condition for making an order under s 423

34.159 Whereas under s 238 the power of the court to make an order in respect of a transaction at undervalue is limited by the restriction that it must have been entered into at a relevant time, under s 423 there is no restriction in terms of time. Instead the restriction is that the court may only make an order if satisfied that the purpose for entering into the transaction is within s 423(3), which provides:

As to whether leave may be granted retrospectively, see the discussion in *Dora v Simper* [2000] 2 BCLC 561, 572; *Godfey v Torpey (No 2)* [2007] BPIR 1538 at paras 38–45. These decisions may need to be reconsidered in light of *Seal v Chief Constable of South Wales* [2007] 1 WLR 1910, HL.

[264] *Hill v Spread Trustee Co Ltd* [2007] 1 WLR 2404, CA at para 101, per Arden LJ; *Giles v Rhind (No 2)* [2009] Ch 191, CA at para 13; *Curtis v Pulbrook* [2011] 1 BCLC 638 at para 51. In *Clydesdale v Smailes* [2011] 2 BCLC 405 at para 73 David Richards J said that the concept of victim is a wider category than simply creditors. See also: *4Eng Ltd v Harper* [2010] 1 BCLC 176 at para 22; *Fortress Value Recovery Fund v Blue Skye Special Opportunities Fund* [2013] 2 BCLC 351 at paras 108–12; *NGM Sustainable Development Ltd v Wallis* [2014] EWHC 2375 (Ch) at para 27; *Westbrook Dolphin Square Ltd v Friends Life Ltd* [2015] 1 WLR 1713 at paras 394–421; *Ali v Bashir* [2015] BPIR 211 at para 42.

[265] See also: *Delaney v Chen* [2011] BPIR 39; *Re Simon Carves Ltd* [2013] 2 BCLC 100; *Concept Oil Services Ltd v En-Gin Ltd* [2013] EWHC 1897 (Comm).

In the case of a person entering into such a transaction, an order shall only be made if the court is satisfied that it was entered into by him for the purpose—

(a) of putting assets beyond the reach of a person who is making, or may at some time make, a claim against him, or

(b) of otherwise prejudicing the interests of such a person in relation to the claim which he is making or may make.

After some uncertainty, the question whether the purpose specified by s 423(3) must be the dominant purpose or whether it is sufficient for it to be a substantial purpose has now been resolved by the Court of Appeal in *Inland Revenue Commissioners v Hashmi*.[266] It is now clear that putting assets beyond the reach of a potential claimant does not have to be the dominant purpose of a transaction. It is sufficient if the purpose specified in s 423(3) is a real substantial purpose and not merely a consequence or by-product of the transaction under consideration. This may be done by showing that the company or other debtor was substantially motivated by one or other of the aims in s 423(3).[267] There is, however, a distinction to be drawn between settled aims, which are required for the purposes of s 423(3) and mere hopes.[268] **34.160**

It follows that the purpose of the company or other debtor in effecting the transaction does not have to be dishonest. Nor is the presence of a purpose within s 423(3) displaced by the fact that lawyers had advised that the transaction is proper and can be carried into effect.[269] Nevertheless, in most cases a transaction within s 423 will be dishonest, because if a man 'disposes of an asset which would be available to his creditors with the intention of prejudicing them by putting it, or its worth, beyond their reach, he is in the ordinary case acting in a fashion not honest in the context of the relationship of debtor and creditor'.[270] If the circumstances in relation to setting up the transaction are shown to be sufficiently iniquitous the court may order that communications between the debtor and his legal advisers relating to the setting up of the transaction are not privileged and should be disclosed.[271] **34.161**

The entry into the transaction must have the necessary purpose,[272] but not necessarily the transaction itself. The reference in s 423(3)(b) to 'interests' shows that the statutory purpose **34.162**

---

[266] [2002] 2 BCLC 489; *Hill v Spread Trustee Co Ltd* [2007] 1 WLR 2404, CA at para 131; applied in *Papanicola v Fagan* [2009] BPIR 320; *4Eng Ltd v Harper* [2010] 1 BCLC 176; *Curtis v Pulbrook* [2011] 1 BCLC 638 at para 50. See *BTI 2014 LLC v Sequana SA* [2016] EWHC 1686 (Ch) at paras 496, 503–513 for a discussion about predominant purpose. The earlier cases are *Chohan v Saggar* [1992] BCC 306, 323; *Pinewood Joinery v Starelm Properties Ltd* [1994] 2 BCLC 412, 418; *Royscot Spa Leasing Ltd v Lovett* [1995] BCC 502, 507, CA; *Jyske Bank (Gibraltar) Ltd v Spjeldnaes* [1999] 2 BCLC 101, 120; *Law Society v Southall* [2001] BPIR 301; *Re Brabon* [2001] 1 BCLC 11, 44.

[267] *Inland Revenue Commissioners v Hashmi* [2002] 2 BCLC 489, CA at paras 21–5, per Arden LJ; at paras 32 and 33, per Laws LJ; at para 39, per Simon Brown LJ. This case was followed in *Kubiangha v Ekpenyong* [2002] 2 BCLC 597 at para 12; *Beckenham MC Ltd v Centralex Ltd* [2004] 2 BCLC 764 at para 32; *Gil v Baygreen Properties Ltd* [2005] BPIR 95 at para 24; *Hill v Spread Trustee Ltd* [2007] 1 WLR 2404, CA at paras 131–3.

[268] *Hill v Spread Trustee Ltd* [2007] 1 WLR 2404, CA at para 132.

[269] *Arbuthnot Leasing International Ltd v Havelet Leasing Ltd (No 2)* [1990] BCC 636, 644.

[270] *Lloyds Bank Ltd v Marcan* [1973] 1 WLR 1387, 1390, CA, per Russell LJ (a case on the Law of Property Act 1925, s 172). In *Barons Bridging Finance 1 Ltd v Barons Finance Ltd* [2016] EWCA Civ 550 the Court of Appeal held that, where the judge had denied a director the opportunity to put in a witness statement, adverse inferences of intent to defraud should not be drawn.

[271] *Barclays Bank plc v Eustice* [1995] 1 WLR 1238, CA. In *Royscot Spa Leasing Ltd v Lovett* [1995] BCC 502, CA, a prima facie case of substantial purpose within s 423(3) was not shown and the court refused an order for disclosure of privileged documents.

[272] In *Re Husky Group Ltd* [2015] BPIR 184 the company had the substantial purpose of putting trademarks beyond the reach of its creditors when it transferred them to its parent in the context of a restructuring. On the other hand, the substantial purpose may not be established when property is transferred in order to perform an

is concerned with the wider interests of the claimant or prospective claimant, not merely with his rights.[273] If the company or other debtor has the statutory purpose, the recipient's belief that he is receiving benefits of value is irrelevant.[274]

Limitation

34.163 Unlike the Insolvency Act s 238, ss 423–5 do not limit the time for applying for relief by identifying a relevant time when the impugned transaction must have been entered into. In *Hill v Spread Trustee Co Ltd* the Court of Appeal held that (a) a claim under s 423 was subject to a limitation period under the Limitation Act 1980; (b) if the claim is to set aside a transfer of property, it is a claim on a specialty within s 8(1) of the Limitation Act 1980 to which a 12-year limitation period applies; (c) if the claim is to recover a sum the limitation period is six years under s 9(1); and (d) time starts to run against a trustee in bankruptcy from the date of the bankruptcy order.[275] It follows that time will start to run against a liquidator from the date when the company goes into liquidation and against an administrator from the date when the company enters administration. Time starts to run against a victim from the time when he qualifies as a person capable of being prejudiced by the transaction.[276] The running of time for bringing a claim under s 423 may be postponed on the ground of concealment under the Limitation Act 1980, s 32.[277]

Remedies

34.164 Section 423(2) corresponds with ss 238(3) and 239(3), but any order made must also protect victims. It provides:

> Where a person has entered into such a transaction, the court may, if satisfied under [subsection (5)], make such order as it thinks fit for—
> (a) restoring the position to what it would have been if the transaction had not been entered into, and
> (b) protecting the interests of persons who are victims of the transaction.

34.165 Although the power to grant relief is discretionary 'the courts must set their faces against transactions which are designed to prevent plaintiffs in proceedings, creditors with unimpeachable debts, from obtaining the remedies by way of execution that the law would normally allow them'.[278] Accordingly in a s 423 case it is much less likely that a court would exercise its discretion to make no order than might be the case with an application under s 238 or 239:

> The object of ss 423 and 425 being to remedy the avoidance of debts, the 'and' between paras (a) and (b) of s 423(2) must be read conjunctively and not disjunctively. Any order made under that subsection must seek, so far as practicable, both to restore the position to what it would have been if the transaction had not been entered into and to protect the interests of the

---

existing agreement (*Williams v Taylor* [2013] BPIR 133, CA) or to discharge an existing obligation (*Withers LLP v Harrison-Welch* [2013] BPIR 145).

[273] *Hill v Spread Trustee Co Ltd* [2007] 1 WLR 2404, CA at paras 101 and 102, per Arden LJ.

[274] *Moon v Franklin* [1996] BPIR 196.

[275] [2007] 1 WLR 2404 at paras 106–18, per Arden LJ; at paras 140–51, per Sir Martin Nourse; at para 152, per Waller LJ. A claim remains a claim on a specialty even though the property whose transfer is challenged has been sold and the claim is converted into a money claim: *Giles v Rhind (No 3)* [2007] 2 BCLC 531 at para 33, affd [2009] Ch 191, CA.

[276] *Giles v Rhind (No 3)* [2007] 2 BCLC 531 at paras 27–31, affd [2009] Ch 191, CA.

[277] *Giles v Rhind (No 3)* (n 276 above) at para 41, affd [2009] Ch 191.

[278] *Arbuthnot Leasing International Ltd v Havelet Leasing Ltd (No 2)* [1990] BCC 636, 645.

victims of it. It is not a power to restore the position generally, but in such a way as to protect the victims' interests; in other words, by restoring assets to the debtor to make them available for execution by victims.[279]

The reference to execution in that passage may be extended to collective execution in a wind- **34.166**
ing up and to alternative modes of distribution to creditors through a CVA or 2006 Act, Part 26 scheme.[280]

Without prejudice to the generality of this provision, s 425(1) provides examples of the sorts **34.167**
of orders which made by made. These are in substantially the same terms as s 241 (paragraphs 34.130–34.134 above), but taking into account the fact that s 423 may be applied outside insolvency proceedings and at a time when the claimant's debt is not established.[281]

An order may affect the property of, or impose any obligation on, any person whether or **34.168**
not he is the person with whom the debtor entered into the transaction; but such an order (a) shall not prejudice any interest in property which was acquired from a person other than the debtor and was acquired in good faith, for value, and without notice of the relevant circumstances, or prejudice any interest deriving from such an interest; and (b) shall not require a person who received a benefit from the transaction in good faith, for value, and without notice of the relevant circumstances to pay any sum unless he was a party to the transaction. For these purposes the relevant circumstances in relation to a transaction are the circumstances by virtue of which an order under s 423 may be made in respect of the transaction.[282]

Summary in relation to directors

If a director causes the company to dispose of property in circumstances to which s 423 **34.169**
applies, it is almost certainly the case that he will have breached his duties to the company and be liable to compensate the company for any loss, including the amount of any undervalue, should the property not be restored to the company.

---

[279] *Chohan v Saggar* [1994] 1 BCLC 706, 714, CA, per Nourse LJ. See *BTI 2014 LLC v Sequana SA* [2016] EWHC 1686 (Ch) at para 520 for discussion of the possibility of a change of position defence.

[280] For winding up as a mode of collective execution: *Wight v Eckhardt Marine GmbH* [2004] 1 AC 147, PC at para 26, per Lord Hoffmann; *Buchler v Talbot* [2004] 2 AC 298, HL at para 28, per Lord Hoffmann.

[281] In *Moon v Franklin* [1996] BPIR 196 a declaration was made under s 423 and a freezing order was made to preserve the property pending litigation on the claimant's claim. For service of a s 423 claim outside the jurisdiction, see *Revenue and Customs Commissioners v Begum* [2011] BPIR 59; *Re Baillies Ltd* [2012] BCC 554; *Revenue and Customs Commissioners v Ben Nevis (Holdings) Ltd* [2012] EWHC 1807 (Ch) at paras 49–55; *Erste Group Bank AG v JSC "VMZ RE October"* [2014] BPIR 81 at para 150, [2015] EWCA Civ 379 at para 20. Note that *Re Phoenix Kapitaldienst GmbH* [2013] Ch 61 (where the court authorized a foreign office-holder to proceed under s 423) was held to have been wrongly decided: *Singularis Holdings Ltd v PricewaterhouseCoopers* [2015] AC 1675 at paras 95–8.

[282] Insolvency Act, s 425(2)–(3). In *Arbuthnot Leasing International Ltd v Havelet Leasing Ltd (No 2)* [1990] BCC 636, 645 the court ordered that the transferee hold the relevant leasing contracts on trust for the transferor, without prejudice to the claims of the transferee's creditors who had become creditors since the date of the transfer. In *Chohan v Saggar* [1994] 1 BCLC 706, CA, the position of a secured creditor restricted the orders that might be made.

35

CRIMINAL LIABILITY OF DIRECTORS

Clare Sibson QC

A. Introduction

(1) Scope of the chapter

Shortly put, the criminal liability of company directors is as wide as the criminal law. **35.01**
Company directors appear before the criminal courts in connection with the conduct of
their working lives on charges as varied as false accounting, harassment, corruption, and
assault.

Rather than attempt an overview of the entire body of the criminal law, this chapter will **35.02**
focus on those offences for which directors are especially vulnerable to attract liability when
carrying out their ordinary financial and fiduciary obligations.

35.03 It should be noted that cartel offences under the Enterprise Act 2002 and money laundering are specifically excluded from this chapter. In addition, this chapter will not consider the power of the courts to confiscate a convicted defendant's assets representing the value of his benefit from criminal conduct under the Proceeds of Crime Act 2002. As for the Corporate Manslaughter and Corporate Homicide Act 2007, other than a brief discussion of the new form of corporate liability contained in s 1 of that Act (as to which see paragraph 35.21 below), these new provisions will not be considered: in its final form, the Act did not create any new forms of criminal liability against individual company directors, either as primary or secondary parties.

(2) Basic principles of criminal liability

35.04 Establishing whether an individual is exposed to the risk of criminal charge and conviction is not as simple as identifying the physical and mental elements of the offence in question and determining whether these elements may be proved against the individual concerned. Outside the terms of individual statutory offences, and beyond the definition of offences proscribed by the common law, there exists a collection of principles which enlarge the ambit of liability for all crime. Before an individual may be reassured that his proposed course of conduct does not disclose a crime or that, in respect of historical behaviour, he is not at risk of criminal conviction, the effect of these principles upon the reach of the relevant offence must be considered with care. A brief statement of these principles is set out below.

Principals, secondary parties, and 'joint enterprise'

35.05 An individual becomes liable to criminal conviction if he acts as the principal party to an offence, a secondary party to an offence, or if he participates in what was until recently commonly referred to as a criminal 'joint enterprise'. A principal party is liable to conviction because he himself has carried out the act or acts constituting the physical elements of the offence with the relevant guilty state of mind. In other words, a principal is a party liable to conviction because each element of the offence can be proved against him personally.

35.06 A secondary party is a person who does not carry out the offence himself but is nevertheless liable to conviction on the basis that he 'aids, abets, counsels or procures'[1] or—broadly speaking—wilfully assists or encourages a principal party to commit a crime. The assistance or encouragement may be given during the commission of the offence or prior to it, for example where equipment or information is made available to another to enable him to commit a crime at a later date.[2] Unlike liability for an inchoate offence (as to which, see below) secondary liability of this sort depends upon proof that the principal offender in fact went on to carry out the physical elements of the offence charged.[3]

35.07 Another term, which has often been used in criminal cases in discussion of secondary liability, is the concept of 'joint enterprise', in which a group of persons acting together commits an offence. It not a legal term of art, and its application (at least in some situations, in

---

[1] Accessories and Abettors Act 1861, s 8.
[2] *Blakely v DPP* [1991] RTR 405, DC.
[3] Note, however, that since the coming into force of Part 2 of the Serious Crime Act 2007 (1 October 2008), new statutory offences have blurred the boundary between secondary and inchoate criminal liability. These provisions created new offences of 'encouraging or assisting crime' which, in terms of the conduct they embrace, resemble old fashioned (and still extant) 'aiding and abetting' (a form of secondary liability) but are in truth inchoate because they do not depend upon proof that the primary offence in fact took place (see s 49(1)).

which it has historically be used to extend secondary liability to persons who lack the *mens rea* which must be proved against the principal offender) has recently been disapproved by the Supreme Court.[4] The substance of the concept, however, at least as it is applied in the majority of cases, remains good law: if, when viewed as individuals, no one participant has committed all of the physical acts necessary to constitute the offence (and some participants have committed none), each is nevertheless liable for the acts done in pursuance of their common intention. Therefore, once the crime has been committed, each participant is liable for the full offence.

Whether responsibility for a crime is established as a straightforward principal, as a second- **35.08** ary party, or even where it is unclear which of those two roles an individual has played, the individual concerned is liable to be prosecuted and convicted for the full offence in the ordinary way. The maximum sentence available on conviction of any secondary party is exactly the same as is available in respect of a principal offender.

Secondary party liability substantially increases the vulnerability of an individual to charge **35.09** for criminal offences, particularly offences which are tightly drawn and difficult to prove.

For example, an individual purchases a large number of shares in a company shortly before **35.10** the board makes a positive announcement about recently secured, lucrative contracts. Insider dealing is suspected. In order to establish that the individual who purchased the shares was a principal offender, the prosecution would have to prove (among other things) that he possessed specific and precise inside information at the time he dealt.[5] This may be impossible to prove. However, if the prosecution can assert on the basis of circumstantial evidence that the dealer was acting in concert with a director of the company, knowing that he was in possession of price-sensitive inside information, both the dealer and the director may be liable to conviction on the basis of their common design: the director despite the fact he has not dealt in shares,[6] the dealer despite the fact he was not put in possession of the inside information itself. The prosecutor would be likely to assert that, because of their common intention, the director and the share dealer were liable for each other's conduct in relation to the offence.

Directors' liability beyond secondary participation

In relation to certain statutory offences, individual directors may be criminally liable for the **35.11** acts or omissions of other directors or officers outside the context of secondary liability. For example, the Insolvency Act, s 432 provides:

(1) This section applies to offences under this Act other than those excepted by subsection (4).
(2) Where a body corporate is guilty of an offence to which this section applies and the offence is proved to have been committed with the consent or connivance of, or to be attributable to any neglect on the part of, any director, manager, secretary or other similar officer[7] of the body corporate, or a person who was purporting to act in any such capacity, he, as well as the body corporate, is guilty of the offence and liable to be proceeded against and punished accordingly.

---

[4] *R v Jogee* [2016] 2 WLR 681, overturning the description of the common law derived from *Chan Wing-Siu v The Queen* [1985] AC 168 and followed in cases such as *R v Powell, R v English* [1999] AC 1, HL.

[5] Criminal Justice Act 1993, ss 52, 57, 56(1).

[6] This would be the case, via the doctrine of secondary liability, even if it were not for the operation of the Criminal Justice Act 1993, s 55(1)(b).

[7] See *R v Boal* [1992] QB 591, CA as to the necessary position which an officer of the corporation must have before fulfilling this description.

35.12 A director who consents to or connives in the commission of an offence would be likely to be implicated as a secondary party in the commission of the offence in any event. But the words 'attributable to any neglect' in this section, and in others like it, expand the liability of an individual director beyond the scope of the doctrine of secondary liability very considerably.

35.13 This does not represent a general principle of the criminal law and applies only where statute specifically provides it. Other examples of similar statutory provisions include the Companies Act 2006, ss 1121 and 1255; the Theft Act 1968, s 18; and the Fraud Act 2006, s 12 (although note in respect of the latter two that the words 'attributable to any neglect' do not appear). Note, in contrast, that the Corporate Manslaughter and Homicide Act 2007, s 18 specifically excludes the possibility of individual directors' liability as secondary parties to the new offence of statutory corporate manslaughter, which may only be committed by a company.

Substantive and inchoate offences

35.14 The doctrine of secondary liability applies to substantive criminal offences only: it is necessary for the prosecution first to prove that the physical elements of the offence in question were carried through to completion before establishing guilt against a secondary party. Liability for a separate group of offences exists in certain circumstances where an intention to bring about an offence is formed, but the physical elements of the offence are never carried out. Offences of the latter sort are inchoate.

35.15 An inchoate offence is committed where a person attempts to commit a crime,[8] conspires with at least one other person to commit a crime,[9] or 'does an act capable of encouraging or assisting another to commit a crime'.[10]

35.16 So far as the liability of directors is concerned, the most significant of the inchoate offences is conspiracy and in particular conspiracy to commit an offence contrary to the Fraud Act 2006 and the residual, common law offence of conspiracy to defraud. For reasons discussed in Section C of this chapter, any agreement between two directors to carry out conduct which might be said to prejudice or risk prejudice to the interests of the company, which is formed in circumstances of secrecy and therefore could be described as dishonest, might expose those directors to criminal liability for conspiracy to defraud. As with all criminal conspiracies, liability for conspiracy to defraud arises immediately upon entering into the agreement: it does not depend upon any subsequent act done in furtherance of the conspirators' plans.

Corporate criminal liability for the acts of directors: the doctrine of identification

35.17 Although vicarious liability may exist in relation to some summary offences of a regulatory or quasi-regulatory nature, there is no general doctrine of vicarious liability in the criminal law.[11] However, the acts or omissions of a director may expose the company which he represents to criminal liability by reason of the doctrine of identification.

35.18 The doctrine of identification operates to recognize the embodiment of the company in particular individuals whose acts and intentions may be attributed to it. Whether a particular individual will be identified as the company in any given situation will be a matter of fact

---

[8] Criminal Attempts Act 1981, s 1.
[9] Criminal Law Act 1977, s 1 and preservation of certain common law conspiracies in s 5.
[10] Serious Crime Act 2007, ss 44, 45.
[11] See eg *Tesco Supermarkets Ltd v Natrass* [1972] AC 153, 179F, HL, per Lord Reid.

and degree, depending on the nature of the offence charged (and, in relation to statutory offences, the intention of Parliament with regard to the way in which the provision should be applied to companies[12]), the area of the company's business in which the offence took place, and the manner in which that particular area is managed and controlled by the company, the relative seniority and ambit of responsibility of the officer or employee concerned, and all the other circumstances of the case.[13] (An example of a circumstance which might be argued to be relevant to the issue of identification is the state of mind of the individual concerned vis-à-vis the company itself: was the individual acting in the interests of the company; was he acting honestly towards the company?) Normally—although not always—the directing will and mind of a company will be identified as the board of directors, the managing director, and perhaps other superior officers of a company who carry out the function of management.[14]

In practical terms, the doctrine of identification differs from the vicarious liability of the civil law by requiring guilty participation in the criminal activity by a much more senior officer or employee within the defendant company. **35.19**

Generally speaking, the doctrine of identification operates to create corporate criminal liability only when at least one individual representing the directing will and mind of the company is demonstrably guilty of the offence himself. Individual directors of the company may of course be guilty when their conduct is viewed together, applying the principles of secondary liability; in these circumstances, the company itself is at risk of conviction. That aside, under the common law there is no generally applicable[15] means of aggregating the acts or omissions of different individuals, none of whom are individually guilty of an offence, in order to produce corporate liability for an offence.[16] **35.20**

There is now, however, an important statutory exception to the common law position of 'no aggregation' of the faults of individual directors when determining corporate criminal liability. It is provided by the Corporate Manslaughter and Corporate Homicide Act 2007. Section 1 of the Act[17] created a new offence in circumstances where the way in which the company's activities are 'managed or organised by its senior management' forms a 'substantial element' in a 'gross breach of a relevant duty of care' which is itself a cause of a person's death. This statutory means of fixing the company with criminal responsibility for death produces a much broader form of liability than the common law process of proving that any **35.21**

---

[12] See *Global Funds Management Asia Ltd v Securities Commission* [1995] 2 AC 500. Note that before asking how Parliament intended a particular provision to apply to companies, it is first necessary to ask the logically prior question, *whether* Parliament intended the provision to apply to the company at all. See *R v Olympus Corporation and Gyrus Group Ltd* CA (Crim), 16 December 2014 for demonstration that the doctrine of identification may not be used to attribute to a company a director's liability for a statutory offence if the clear will of Parliament was that the relevant provision should not apply to the company in question.

[13] *R v ICR Haulage Co Ltd* [1944] KB 551, 559, per Stable J.

[14] *Tesco Supermarkets Ltd v Natrass* [1972] AC 153, 171, HL, per Lord Reid.

[15] In relation to certain offences, it is sometimes possible to combine the *actus reus* carried out by an ordinary employee with the *mens rea* of recklessness on the part of the directing will and mind of the company in order to produce corporate liability for an offence: *Information Commissioner v Islington LBC* [2003] LGR 38, DC.

[16] The Corporate Manslaughter and Corporate Homicide Act 2007 alters this position in respect of homicide offences only.

[17] Which came into force 6 April 2008 (except in relation to anything done or omitted before that date): see s 27(3) and SI 2008/401, Art 2(1).

one individual director is guilty of manslaughter, and then attributing this guilt to the body corporate via the doctrine of identification.

B. Production of Information for Criminal Investigations

35.22 There are two principal methods via which a criminal investigator may compel the production of information from a company.

(1) PACE search warrants

35.23 The first is where police execute a warrant to enter premises in order to search for and seize material. The powers are governed primarily—although not exclusively—by the Police and Criminal Evidence Act ['PACE'], s 8. Under this section, a justice of the peace is empowered to issue a search warrant to a police constable where there are reasonable grounds to suspect (inter alia) that: (i) an indictable offence has been committed,[18] and (ii) there is material on the specified premises which is likely to constitute relevant evidence of substantial value to the investigation of the offence.[19]

35.24 Section 8 warrants are issued and executed without notice. Therefore, in order to obtain such a warrant, the police must demonstrate that it would either be impractical or pointless to gain entry to the premises with the cooperation of the occupiers of the premises.[20] This will occur, for example, where the person or persons suspected of involvement in the offence have access to the premises and might interfere with or destroy evidence if granted notice of the police's intention to conduct a search.

35.25 Once issued, a s 8 PACE warrant empowers the police to force entry to the premises in question, to search for and to seize material of the type described in the warrant. Material subject to legal professional privilege, 'excluded material',[21] and 'special procedure material'[22] is always outside the remit of a s 8 warrant.[23]

(2) Compelled information

35.26 The second method is where a criminal investigator is empowered to compel an individual either to attend for interview at a specified time and place in order to answer questions, or to produce certain documentation.

---

[18] s 8(1)(a). The grounds for retrospective challenge of a s 8 warrant are beyond the scope of this work. However, for a recent example of the importance of an investigator's accurately and openly informing a warrant issuing court of the basis for his suspicions, and any circumstances which might mitigate against those suspicions, see *R (Tchenguiz) v Director of Serious Fraud Office* [2013] 1 WLR 1634.

[19] s 8(1)(b) and (c).

[20] s 8(1)(e) and (3).

[21] Excluded material is confidential medical or quasi-medical documents, human tissue taken for diagnosis or treatment purposes, and journalistic material. See further PACE, s 11.

[22] Special procedure material is defined by PACE, s 14 as material (other than legally privileged or excluded material) which is in the possession of a person who acquired or created the material in the course of his/her occupation and who holds the material subject either to an express or implied undertaking to hold it in confidence, or to an obligation of secrecy/restriction on disclosure imposed by any enactment. This material enjoys an enhanced degree of protection under PACE. In particular, no search warrant may be granted in relation to it. Instead, a constable must make an on-notice application for a production order. If the order is made, the subject of the order will be given at least seven days in which to comply with it.

[23] s 8(1)(d).

Many investigative agencies,[24] as well as some individuals (including an office-holder **35.27** in corporate insolvency,[25] a trustee in bankruptcy,[26] or an investigator appointed by the Secretary of State under the Companies Act 1985, s 447)[27] possess compulsory powers of this kind.[28] However, in the context of criminal investigations and for the purposes of illustration it is sufficient to consider: (i) the CJA 1987, s 2, under which the Director of the SFO may require attendance at a compulsory interview or compel the production of documents, and (ii) the FSMA, Part XI, under which an investigator appointed by the Financial Conduct Authority ('FCA') or Prudential Regulation Authority ('PRA')—together, 'the Regulators'—may likewise compel attendance at an interview or the production of information including documents.

The compulsory powers of both the SFO and the Regulators may be exercised against the **35.28** person under investigation (the suspect) and/or against any other person for the purpose of the investigation (ie potential witnesses).

An important difference between these compulsory powers and PACE powers of search **35.29** and seizure is that, prima facie, both the CJA 1987, s 2 powers and FSMA, Part XI powers are exercised on notice in writing. There is no element of surprise to their execution. However, in a situation where it would be either impractical to serve notice in writing, or where it would frustrate the purpose of the investigation to give notice of a production requirement (or where a production requirement has already been issued but has not been complied with), both the SFO[29] and the Regulators[30] are entitled to seek a search warrant from a justice of the peace. Such a warrant must be executed by a police constable.

Legal professional privilege

In relation to the production of documents, as with the execution of s 8 PACE warrants, **35.30** neither the SFO nor the Regulators may require the production of material which is subject to legal professional privilege.[31] Where the privilege is that of the company, an individual director will not be able to resist production if the organ of the company (for example a new board or a liquidator) does not resist. A director will, however, be protected in respect of legal advice given to him.[32]

---

[24] Other examples include financial investigators under the Proceeds of Crime Act 2002, the Serious and Organised Crime Agency, and certain environmental agencies.

[25] Insolvency Act, s 235.

[26] Insolvency Act, s 333.

[27] Note the width of this power: *AG's Reference (No 2 of 1998)* [2000] QB 412, CA.

[28] See also Fraud Act 2006, s 13(1) which removes the privilege against self-incrimination in all civil proceedings relating to property. This has the effect of extending the entirely compulsory nature of, for example, search orders in civil proceedings from limited types of actions—such as intellectual property cases—to all actions concerning property of any kind. It will therefore no longer be possible for litigants in civil fraud cases to avoid answering questions or complying with court orders on the basis of self-incrimination.

[29] CJA 1987, s 2(4).

[30] FSMA, s 176.

[31] CJA 1987, s 2(9); FSMA, s 413.

[32] *Re Ouveroff* [1997] BPIR 712; *R (Morgan Grenfell) v Special Commissioners* [2003] 1 AC 563, HL.

Failure to comply

35.31   Failure to comply with the SFO's or the Regulators' exercise of compulsory powers without reasonable excuse is punishable by imprisonment.[33] In respect of the Regulators' powers, a company director may be punished for the non-compliance of the company.[34]

35.32   In addition, there are specific offences of intentionally or recklessly providing false or misleading information in response to a compulsory information requirement, the maximum penalty for which (on conviction on indictment) is two years.[35]

35.33   Further, any person who knows or suspects that an investigation is being conducted or is likely to be conducted by the SFO (or by the either Regulator under FSMA, Part XI) and who falsifies, conceals, or destroys a document which he knows or suspects to be relevant to the investigation (or who causes or permits another to do the same) is guilty of an offence unless he proves (on a balance of probabilities) that he had no intention of concealing the facts disclosed by the documents from persons carrying out such an investigation.[36] In respect of an investigation under FSMA, such an offence (on conviction on indictment), carries a maximum of two years' imprisonment.[37] In respect of an SFO investigation, the offence carries a maximum of a massive seven years.[38]

35.34   Finally, any act intended to destroy or alter evidence of a crime is likely to give rise to liability for a charge of perverting the course of justice, an offence against the common law for which there is no maximum penalty.[39]

Privilege against self-incrimination

35.35   It is the essence of the compulsory powers granted to investigators such as the SFO and the FCA that a person subject to their exercise must produce the information or document required, or must answer questions put to him in interview, even if in so doing he will or may incriminate himself. Without more, a desire not to incriminate oneself does not amount to a reasonable excuse for failing to produce information or to answer a question.[40]

35.36   In respect of evidential, pre-existing documents produced in response to an information or production requirement (such as company accounting documents or email correspondence) there is no restriction on the use to which that evidence may be put: it may subsequently be used against the producer in criminal proceedings. However, a restriction on evidential use is imposed upon statements actually made by a person while under compulsion. (This applies to statements made—orally or via a prepared written statement—in interview under compulsion with investigators.) This protection is provided by the common law and article 6 of the ECHR,[41] and frequently by specific statutory provisions too.

---

[33] In relation to the SFO, a specific, summary only offence is created by CJA 1987, s 2(13) the maximum penalty for which is a level 5 fine or six months' imprisonment. In relation to the FSA, failure to comply may be treated as a contempt of court, punishable by way of fine or imprisonment of up to two years. (See further FSMA, s 177.)

[34] FSMA, s 177(2).

[35] CJA 1987, s 2(14); FSMA, s 177(4) and (5).

[36] CJA 1987, s 2(16); FSMA, s 177(3).

[37] FSMA, s 177(5).

[38] CJA 1987, s 2(17).

[39] *R v Vreones* [1891] 1 QB 360; *R v Andrews* [1973] QB 422.

[40] *R v Hertfordshire County Council, ex p Green Environment Industries Ltd* [2000] 2 AC 412, HL; *Saunders v UK* (1997) 23 EHRR 313; *IJL and others v UK* (2000) 33 EHRR 11.

[41] See *R v K* [2010] QB 343.

A person who is subject to compulsory interview by the SFO or FCA, for example, enjoys **35.37** statutory protection from the prospect of his answers being used against him by the prosecution in a criminal trial for any offence other than an offence directly connected with the making of the statement itself (such as making a misleading statement under compulsion, contrary to the CJA 1987, s 2(14)).

For example, under the CJA 1987, s 2:[42]   **35.38**

> (8) A statement by a person in response to a requirement imposed by virtue of this section may only be used in evidence against him—
> > (a) on a prosecution for an offence under subsection (14)[43] below; or
> > (b) on a prosecution for some other offence where in giving evidence he makes a statement inconsistent with it.
> (8AA) However, the statement may not be used against that person by virtue of paragraph
> > (b) of subsection (8) unless evidence relating to it is adduced, or a question relating to it is asked, by or on behalf of that person in the proceedings arising out of the prosecution.

Similar provisions restrict the use in evidence of compulsory statements made under the **35.39** Insolvency Act, s 433 and the 2006 Act, s 459(6).[44] Even where no such protection exists in statutory form, it is almost inevitable that the prosecution will be prevented from using a statement made under compulsion in evidence against the maker of the statement (otherwise than on a charge under the CJA 1987, s 2(14) or equivalent) by an exercise of the judicial power to exclude evidence under PACE, s 78.[45]

European Court of Human Rights

Domestic jurisprudence in respect of compulsory powers to require answers in interview has **35.40** always been that no violation of a suspect's fundamental rights could occur unless and until any statement made by him under compulsion is used against him in criminal proceedings.[46] According to this reasoning, a defendant's privilege against self-incrimination is adequately protected by statutory (or even judicial[47]) restriction on the subsequent use of statements made under compulsion.

Authority from the European Court of Human Rights casts doubt upon this position. In **35.41** *Shannon v UK*,[48] the Court held that a suspect's Article 6 rights (specifically, his right not to incriminate himself) may be violated by a compulsory requirement that he answer questions itself, regardless of whether his answers are subsequently used against him or not. *Shannon* concerned a piece of legislation in which the protection against subsequent use by the prosecution was not as comprehensive as is the case under both the CJA 1987, s 2 and FSMA, Part XI. (The relevant piece of legislation allowed the prosecution to use the statement made under compulsion as evidence of a previous inconsistent statement in a subsequent trial.) In addition, in *Shannon* the suspect had already been charged with a criminal offence when the exercise of compulsory powers occurred. However, the decision of the court was not necessarily dependent on either of these facts. In particular, the court stressed that information

---

[42] In respect of an FCA investigation, see FSMA, s 174(2).
[43] ie making a false or misleading statement in purported compliance with a requirement under the section.
[44] See also Fraud Act 2006, s 13(2). For the effect of s 13(1), see n 28 above.
[45] *R v K* (n 41).
[46] *Ex p Green Environment Industries Ltd* (n 40 above).
[47] *Ex p Green Environment Industries Ltd* (n 40 above); also, *IJL and others v UK* (2000) 33 EHRR 11.
[48] (6563/03) (2006) 42 EHRR 265.

provided by a suspect may assist investigators even if it is not admitted into evidence against him.[49] If this is right (and it is submitted that it is right), then it may well be a basis for alleging a violation of Article 6 even where compulsory powers are exercised before charge and even where the prohibition on subsequent use in proceedings is absolute.[50]

35.42   Frequently, compulsory powers of interview are exercised against individuals whom the investigator currently views as a potential witness. In such a situation, *Shannon* will not provide a basis to argue that the privilege against self-incrimination is or should be a reasonable excuse for failure to comply. Likewise, where an investigator genuinely has an open mind—is the individual a suspect or a witness?—it might be difficult to object to the use of compulsion. However, the FCA in particular reserves the right to exercise compulsory powers against people who are definitely under investigation as suspects for criminal offences.[51] In practice, there is precedent (occurring prior to the establishment of the FCA, when its forerunner, the FSA, was responsible for supervising financial markets) for the Regulator exercising this power in circumstances where the suspect had previously undergone a PACE interview and had exercised his right to silence.[52] To date, the lawfulness of this approach has not been litigated. However, if the policy is maintained, it is possible that at some point, in light of *Shannon*, it will be subject to challenge by way of judicial review.

C. Fraud

(1) Introduction

Width and evolution of criminal fraud law

35.43   The long-standing common law offence of conspiracy to defraud criminalizes the act of agreeing to carry out conduct which would not in itself, if pursued by an individual protagonist, amount to a criminal offence (at least, not if committed prior to the coming into force of the Fraud Act 2006 on 15 January 2007). Successive reports of the Law Commission have criticized the offence as too wide;[53] successive governments have remained committed to the preservation of the offence.[54]

35.44   The offence of conspiracy to defraud is dependent, inter alia, upon proof of prejudice to the rights of another and dishonesty. Over the centuries, the standards of honesty in business have changed, as has the scope of recognized rights which may be affected by fraud. As these standards evolve, so too does the common law offence.

---

[49]   It is not difficult to imagine how: the statement may lead to other lines of fruitful enquiry, disclose the suspect's case at an early stage, or reveal that he has no answer to the potential charge, thereby encouraging the investigators to proceed against him.

[50]   The prohibition is never absolute. For example, nothing in FSMA prevents the use of statements made under compulsion against the maker of the statement at the behest of a co-defendant. It is far from fanciful to imagine a situation in which an investigator, in possession of a significant confession obtained under compulsion, would have a real forensic advantage in contemplating the use of that confession against the maker at the behest of a co-defendant in a cut-throat situation.

[51]   See the FCA's *Enforcement Guide*, para 4.23.

[52]   In almost all circumstances, the impression created is that the investigator is motivated by a specific intention to circumvent a suspect's PACE and Art 6 ECHR rights.

[53]   Law Com 276, July 2002.

[54]   Fraud Act 2006, which—contrary to the recommendation of the Law Commission—does not repeal the common law offence of conspiracy to defraud.

New substantive offences

Criminal fraud law is additionally subject to evolution thanks to the relatively recent crea- **35.45**
tion of new substantive offences of fraud.

The Fraud Act 2006 for the first time created substantive offences of fraud which are not **35.46**
dependent on proof of an agreement by two or more people to carry out the conduct concerned. This enlarged the reach of the criminal liability in respect of fraud by criminalizing
dishonest conduct pursued by one person acting alone, which previously was only subject
to criminal sanction when pursed by more than one person, following the formation of a
conspiracy.

However, the Fraud Act did not abolish the common law offence of conspiracy to defraud. **35.47**
Therefore, there will be a residual area of conduct which falls outside the statutory definition
of substantive fraud, but which will nevertheless be criminal if it is pursued by more than
one person acting in agreement. In short, the Fraud Act expands the reach of the substantive criminal law and the liability of individuals acting alone, but it does not restrict the
scope of the corresponding inchoate offence of conspiracy or the liability of groups acting
in concert.[55]

Much of the case law on criminal fraud derives from the period prior to the enactment of the **35.48**
Fraud Act and the creation of substantive criminal offences of fraud. It is therefore convenient to discuss common law fraud first, despite the fact that it is a relatively rare charge in the
criminal courts today. The Fraud Act will be considered in detail under Section C(3) of this
part of this chapter.

(2) Common law conspiracy to defraud

It is no easy thing to give a definition of the common law offence of conspiracy to **35.49**
defraud. Historically, different formulations have been used in different authorities[56]
and there has been a tendency among practitioners to blend different aspects of the various definitions, without sufficient reference to the facts underlying the decided cases.
However, it is submitted that 'to defraud' is best defined as dishonestly to prejudice
or take the risk of prejudicing another's rights or interests, having no right to do so.[57]
Conspiracy to defraud is agreeing with another or others to act in a way which may be
described in these terms.

The elements of the common law offence of conspiracy to defraud may therefore be **35.50**
isolated as: the act of entering an agreement; the terms of the agreement involving the

---

[55] This observation is subject to one caveat. Now that the Fraud Act is in force, two or more people conspire
to commit a statutory offence of fraud, then prosecutors might be called upon to justify a charge of common
law fraud rather than the alternative statutory conspiracy or a substantive statutory offence as provided by
Parliament. (See *R v Rimmington* [2006] 1 AC 459, HL; and *Deutsche Morgan Grenfell Group plc v IRC* [2007]
1 AC 558, HL.) See further the Attorney General's *Guidance on the Use of the Common Law Offence of Conspiracy
to Defraud*.
[56] *Welham v DPP* [1961] AC 103, HL; *Scott v Metropolitan Police Commissioner* [1975] AC 819, HL; *Wai
Yu Tsang v R* [1992] 1 AC 269, PC.
[57] Note that the offence is sometimes defined more widely, in particular by omitting the 'having no right
to do so' element. It is submitted that such omission is unjustified and would, if it truly represented the law,
produce absurd results, criminalizing many instances of conduct which are plainly not unlawful. Further, it
is submitted that there is no decided case in which criminal liability for fraud has been found in a situation in
which the defendant had a right to act as he did.

prejudice or risk of prejudice to another's rights/interests; circumstances in which the parties to the agreement have no right to cause such prejudice/take such risk; the state of mind of dishonesty.

The agreement

35.51 The essence of any criminal conspiracy is the act of agreement itself. The offence is complete once the agreement is formed: even if no act is done in pursuance of it; even if one or all of the parties to the agreement experience a change of heart and communicate their withdrawal from the scheme. The principle was made plain by Brett JA in *R v Aspinall*:[58]

> Now, first, the crime of conspiracy is completely committed, if it is committed at all, the moment two or more have agreed that they will do, at once or at some future time, certain things. It is not necessary in order to complete the offence that any one thing should be done beyond the agreement. The conspirators may repent and stop, or may have no opportunity, or may be prevented, or may fail. Nevertheless the crime is complete; it was completed when they agreed.

35.52 Beyond this, the term 'agreement' itself should be given its ordinary and natural meaning. Proof of an agreement does not depend upon establishing elements of offer and acceptance, consideration, or any other feature of contractual liability as recognized by the civil law.[59]

35.53 The existence of the conspiracy will continue for as long as it remains unfulfilled, and there are at least two people party to it. Therefore, a person may join the conspiracy, and become criminally liable for it, at a time after the conspiracy was formed by others.

35.54 It is relatively rare for a prosecutor to have access to direct evidence of the formation of the criminal agreement.[60] More usually, the prosecution must invite the tribunal of fact to infer the existence of the agreement from evidence of the subsequent conduct of the participants, apparently working pursuant to a common design. Therefore, although in law a criminal conspiracy to defraud is complete once the agreement is entered into, in practice, a successful prosecution for the offence will often depend upon evidence of the fulfilment, or the partial or attempted fulfilment, of the agreement in question.

Risk of prejudice to another's rights or interests

35.55 In order to amount to the common law offence of conspiracy to defraud, the agreement in question—if it were to be fulfilled—must involve the prejudice, or risk of prejudice, to the rights or interests of another person or body.

35.56 Although there is some controversy on this point within the decided cases, it is generally considered that the range of rights and interests protected by the law against conspiracies to defraud are not limited to economic rights or interests; proof of conspiracy to defraud is not dependent on proof of actual or threatened economic loss.[61]

---

[58] (1876) 2 QBD 48, 58, CA.

[59] *R v Anderson* [1986] AC 27, HL.

[60] Such evidence does sometimes exist, for example where one conspirator gives evidence for the prosecution against his co-conspirators, where the conversations and/or correspondence in which the agreement was formed have been intercepted by the authorities, or where the terms of the agreement have been reduced into writing by the participants. The latter scenario is extremely rare but not unprecedented.

[61] *Welham v DPP* [1961] AC 103, HL; *Wai Yu Tsang v R* [1992] 1 AC 269, PC. Cf the opinion of Lord Diplock in *Scott v Metropolitan Police Commissioner* [1975] AC 819, 840, 841, HL.

The best means of illustrating the breadth of the range of rights and interests recognized by the criminal law for these purposes is by way of example. Conspiracy to defraud may be alleged in law in circumstances where the terms of an agreement involve injury, or the risk of injury, to: **35.57**

(1) the right of the state, or the person or body performing a duty on behalf of the state, to have public duties properly fulfilled. (To induce dishonestly any such person or body to act in a way which would be contrary to his/its duty were he/it in possession of the true facts is to act fraudulently.[62] In practice, therefore, any dishonest agreement to conceal certain behaviour from the public authority charged with the duty of supervising such conduct, in order to prevent the authority from fulfilling its public duty to investigate or scrutinize the conduct, will amount to a fraud on that authority. For example, an agreement to conceal dishonestly the identity of a director trading in company shares in order to prevent the FCA from investigating the possibility of insider dealing or market abuse, may amount to a conspiracy to defraud the Authority, quite apart from any proof that insider dealing has in fact occurred.)

(2) the right of a principal to disclosure of the profits obtained by an agent in connection with the performance of his fiduciary duty.[63]

(3) any right or interest vested in a principal which is capable of being protected by an action for breach of trust if compromised by one fiduciary acting alone. (Such an interest will inevitably enjoy the protection of the criminal law in circumstances where the fiduciary agrees with another person dishonestly to carry out the breach of trust concerned, even if no economic loss is involved. For example, a principal's right to disclosure of a conflict of interests is a right prejudice to which may found an allegation of conspiracy to defraud.)[64]

These examples have obvious implications for the criminal liability of company directors. **35.58** Whenever a director agrees with another to take any action which will injure or risk injury to the interests of the company, in circumstances which might be described as dishonest, the director is at risk of attracting criminal liability. In addition, whenever a director agrees with another dishonestly to conceal a significant situation or fact from a body such as Companies House, Her Majesty's Customs and Excise, the FCA, the Health and Safety Executive, or an officer appointed by the court in connection with the company's affairs, it is highly likely that the director will be at risk of criminal charge.

Dishonesty

Dishonesty is an essential element of the offence of conspiracy to defraud. There is leading **35.59** authority on the offence of conspiracy to defraud which fails to mention the issue of dishonesty.[65] However, it is beyond argument that dishonesty must be proved to the satisfaction of the jury in order to support a conviction[66] and all criminal trials proceed on this basis.

---

[62] *Welham v DPP* [1961] AC 103, HL.

[63] *Adams v R* [1995] 1 WLR 63, PC.

[64] In January 2005, at Southampton Crown Court, the trial of *R v Stovold* was heard. The case concerned the role of the directors of a brokerage company within the local authority operational lease market. The SFO had indicted the defendant with conspiracy to defraud on the basis of an alleged agreement dishonestly to conceal the existence of a conflict of interests and secret profits from his principals. The trial concluded at the close of the Crown's case with the acquittal of the defendant on the direction of the judge because, taking the Crown's case at its highest, the facts of the allegation had not been made out. However, the defence conceded that the allegation, if proved, would be capable of amounting to a criminal conspiracy.

[65] *Welham v DPP* [1961] AC 103, HL.

[66] *Landy and Kaye* [1981] 1 WLR 355, CA; *Wai Yu Tsang v R* [1992] 1 AC 269, PC.

35.60   For the purposes of the criminal law, the test of dishonesty was described by Lord Lane CJ in *R v Ghosh*[67] in this way:

> In determining whether the prosecution has proved that the defendant was acting dishonestly, a jury must first of all decide whether according to the ordinary standards of reasonable and honest people what was done was dishonest. If it was not dishonest by those standards, that is the end of the matter and the prosecution fails. If it was dishonest by those standards, the jury must consider whether the defendant himself must have realised that what he was doing was by those standards dishonest.

35.61   The test of criminal dishonesty is therefore twofold, containing an objective and a subjective element. The conduct must be dishonest by ordinary, objective standards. Subjectively, the defendant must have realized that the conduct was (by those objective standards) dishonest. Therefore a defendant who personally (perhaps for peculiar ideological reasons) believes his conduct to be morally justified and honest nevertheless has a dishonest state of mind according to the criminal law if he realizes that his conduct would be judged to be dishonest by the objective standards of the reasonable man. The question of dishonesty is quintessentially a matter for the determination of a jury. Generally speaking, in a criminal trial the judge will not specifically direct a jury on the meaning of dishonesty unless there is a real issue as to the second limb of the *Ghosh* test, namely the defendant has raised the possibility that he did not know that the conduct in question was dishonest by ordinary standards.[68]

35.62   In order to make out the element of dishonesty, it is unnecessary for the prosecution to establish that any lie was told, misrepresentation was made, or act of deceit took place.[69] The content of the agreement itself may be described as dishonest, even if the suspects did not intend to deceive their victim by telling lies or actively concealing their conduct.

35.63   On the other hand, the presence or absence of attendant circumstances of lies, misrepresentation, concealment, and secrecy, may amount to powerful evidence in support of an allegation of dishonesty. As a matter of common sense, a jury will be invited to consider that such attendant lies or secrecy prove that the defendant must have known that his primary conduct was dishonest: otherwise, why would he have hidden it?

Defences

35.64   On a charge of common law conspiracy to defraud, assuming that the elements of the offence are made out, there are three principal defences which may be raised: (i) no conspiracy between spouses or civil partners, (ii) no intention to fulfil plan, and (iii) impossibility.

35.65   First, a charge of conspiracy is not made out when the agreement alleged was formed between spouses or civil partners and involved no other person.[70] This may be of relevance to family-run companies. However, if a third party joins the agreement, then a conspiracy exists and all parties to it, including the married couple, are criminally liable.

35.66   As to the second defence, under the common law, there is a defence to a charge of conspiracy in circumstances where, although the defendant expressed his agreement to the criminal

---

[67]   [1982] QB 1053, 1064, CA.

[68]   *R v Roberts (W)* (1987) 84 Cr App R 117, CA.

[69]   *Scott v Metropolitan Police Commissioner* [1975] AC 819, HL.

[70]   *Mawji v R* [1957] AC 126, PC. The effect of the law of statutory conspiracy is the same: Criminal Law Act 1977, s 2(2).

plan, his mind did not go with his expression and he had no intention that the plan be carried out.[71] This may be described as the 'fingers crossed behind the back' defence. Once it is raised, the prosecution must disprove it to the criminal standard. This the prosecution might readily accomplish by adducing evidence that the defendant did some act in furtherance of the conspiracy.

Thirdly, there is a defence to a charge of common law conspiracy[72] in circumstances where the agreement in question was incapable of fulfilment. Again, once the defence of impossibility is raised, it is for the prosecution to disprove it to the criminal standard. The leading authority on impossibility is *DPP v Nock*.[73] The case concerned an agreement to carry out a specific chemical procedure with the intention of producing cocaine. In fact, the procedure was incapable of producing the chemical: the Privy Council held that no criminal conspiracy was disclosed on the facts. **35.67**

The principle of impossibility obviously has a very limited application where the agreement in question is not an agreement to achieve a highly specific goal, such as the production of cocaine, but an agreement which has the more nebulous effect of risking injury to another's rights. It is difficult to think of many situations in which an agreement to defraud might be saved from criminal liability by reason of the impossibility of fulfilment. However, the defence will apply, for example, where the agreement is to defraud a company which (unbeknownst to would-be conspirators) no longer exists, or a person who has already died at the time the agreement is formed. **35.68**

Penalty

Conspiracy to defraud (which is an offence which may only be tried on indictment) carries an unlimited fine, or a maximum of ten years' imprisonment, or both.[74] **35.69**

(3) Fraud Act substantive fraud

Three substantive acts of fraud

The Fraud Act,[75] s 1 changed the landscape of criminal fraud by creating three substantive offences of fraud. Subsections (1) and (2) provide: **35.70**

(1) A person is guilty of fraud if he is in breach of any of the sections listed in subsection (2) (which provide for different ways of committing the offence).
(2) The sections are—
  (a) section 2 (fraud by false representation),
  (b) section 3 (fraud by failing to disclose information), and
  (c) section 4 (fraud by abuse of position).

Each substantive offence set out in ss 2, 3, and 4 proscribes a different physical act: false representation, failing to disclose information which one has a legal duty to disclose, and **35.71**

---

[71] *R v Thomas* (1965) 50 Cr App R 1. Under a charge of statutory conspiracy (ie a charge of conspiring to commit a statutory offence, contrary to the Criminal Law Act 1977, s 1(1)) the law is slightly different: *R v Anderson* [1986] AC 27, HL.
[72] But not to statutory conspiracy: Criminal Law Act 1977, s 1(2).
[73] [1978] AC 979, PC.
[74] CJA, 12(3).
[75] It came into force on 15 January 2007; Fraud Act 2006 (Commencement) Order (SO 2006/3200).

abusing one's position as a fiduciary.[76] In addition, each offence shares the requirement of proving:

(1) dishonesty[77]; and
(2) an intent to (a) make gain for oneself or another, or (b) cause loss to another or to expose another to the risk of loss.

35.72 The relevant sections read:

2 Fraud by false representation

(1) A person is in breach of this section if he—
    (a) dishonestly makes a false representation, and
    (b) intends, by making the representation—
        (i) to make a gain for himself or another, or
        (ii) to cause loss to another or to expose another to a risk of loss.
(2) A representation is false if—
    (a) it is untrue or misleading, and
    (b) the person making it knows that it is, or might be, untrue or misleading.
(3) 'Representation' means any representation as to fact or law, including a representation as to the state of mind of—
    (a) the person making the representation, or
    (b) any other person.
(4) A representation may be express or implied.
(5) For the purposes of this section a representation may be regarded as made if it (or anything implying it) is submitted in any form to any system or device designed to receive, convey or respond to communications (with or without human intervention).

3 Fraud by failing to disclose information

A person is in breach of this section if he—
    (a) dishonestly fails to disclose to another person information which he is under a legal duty to disclose, and
    (b) intends, by failing to disclose the information—
        (i) to make a gain for himself or another, or
        (ii) to cause loss to another or to expose another to a risk of loss.

4 Fraud by abuse of position

(1) A person is in breach of this section if he—
    (a) occupies a position in which he is expected to safeguard, or not to act against, the financial interests of another person,
    (b) dishonestly abuses that position, and
    (c) intends, by means of the abuse of that position—
        (i) to make a gain for himself or another, or
        (ii) to cause loss to another or to expose another to a risk of loss.
(2) A person may be regarded as having abused his position even though his conduct consisted of an omission rather than an act.

---

[76] In order to commit this type of fraud, the defendant must 'occupy a position in which he is expected to safeguard, or not to act against, the financial interests of another person': s 4(1)(a).

[77] Dishonesty for these purposes will be *Ghosh* dishonesty, as to which see paras 35.59–35.63 above.

Fraud by Misrepresentation

A representation under s 2 above must be capable of being expressed as a statement about the   **35.73**
past or present. A simple undertaking as to future action might amount to a contractual promise,
but it does not amount to a representation.[78] The provision of an undated cheque to a bank,
as security for the full value of an outstanding loan, has been held not to amount to a 'representation' (within the terms of s 2) that the cheque would be met in the event of default on the
loan.[79] This contrasts with the position where the provision of dated cheque is taken impliedly
to represent that the cheque will be 'honoured in the ordinary course'.[80] As this distinction demonstrates, the line between a 'representation' of past or present facts and a 'promise' as to future
action is blurred by recognition (both at common law, and by the terms of s 2(3) of the Fraud
Act), that a statement of present intention (as to the future) may amount to a representation.[81]

Fraud by Failing to Disclose

The most significant limitation to the ambit of this offence is the necessity for the prosecu-   **35.74**
tion to prove that the defendant was under a legal duty to disclose the particular information
which was withheld. For example, as a matter of law, an applicant for a loan or mortgage
from a bank is under no obligation to disclose that he is unemployed, and thus his failure
to mention this fact does not amount to an offence under s 3.[82] (A false representation that
he was employed would expose him to risk of prosecution under s 2, but a statement to the
effect would not be implied merely by the fact of his application. He does not, by applying
for the loan, represent that he is entitled to it.[83])

Company directors are subject to many legal duties to disclose information about the com-   **35.75**
pany, or to the company, at particular times. For example, a director may be legally compelled
to provide information to an auditor under s 499(1) of the Companies Act 2006. Failure to
meet this obligation exposes the director to potential criminal liability under s 501(3) of the
same Act. However, if the other elements of s 3 of the Fraud Act were also made out, his failure would also put him in jeopardy under that provision (for which the maximum penalty
is ten years, rather than the two year maximum attached to s 501(3) of the Companies Act).

Fraud by Abuse of Trust

In *R v Choi*[84] the Court of Appeal endorsed a first-instance decision that a defendant may   **35.76**
be guilty of abusing a position of trust within the meaning of s 4 of the Fraud Act, even if he
had left that position by the time the fraudulent act took place. A former finance officer who,
seven months after he left that post, noticed that he still had access to his former employer's
bank accounts and used that access to transfer £40,000 to his own account, committed an
offence under s 4. Not only was the offence made out, the fact that he had left the position in
which the trust had been extended to him was 'irrelevant' when it came to sentence.[85]

---

[78] *UAE v Allen* [2012] 1 WLR 3419.
[79] *UAE v Allen* (n 78 above).
[80] *R v Gilmartin* [1983] QB 953. See also *UAE v Amir* [2012] EWHC 1711.
[81] See also *UAE v Amir* (n 80 above).
[82] *R v White* [2014] 2 Cr App R 14.
[83] *R v White* (n 82 above).
[84] [2015] 2 Cr App R (S) 55.
[85] The transferred amount was repaid in full shortly after police became involved. There was significant personal mitigation. His sentence of two years' imprisonment was reduced to 18 months by the Court of Appeal.

35.77 Note that s 4 may also be used to charge a company director in circumstances where he has taken a bribe.[86]

Gain and Loss

35.78 There is one element common to all of the substantive offences contained in the Fraud Act, ss 1–4 which marks a major difference between those offences and the type of fraud which may be the subject of a common law conspiracy to defraud. As was discussed above, the common law is not restricted to prejudice to proprietary rights or economic interests; the Fraud Act is.

35.79 Under the Fraud Act, s 5(2) the terms 'gain' and 'loss' used in the definition of the offences extend only to gains or losses of money or other property (which includes things in action and other intangibles). The Fraud Act, s 5 reads:

> **5 'Gain' and 'loss'**
> (1) The references to gain and loss in sections 2 to 4 are to be read in accordance with this section.
> (2) 'Gain' and 'loss'—
>   (a) extend only to gain or loss in money or other property;
>   (b) include any such gain or loss whether temporary or permanent; and 'property' means any property whether real or personal (including things in action and other intangible property).
> (3) 'Gain' includes a gain by keeping what one has, as well as a gain by getting what one does not have.
> (4) 'Loss' includes a loss by not getting what one might get, as well as a loss by parting with what one has.

35.80 This definition is identical in its effect as the definition of 'gain' and 'loss' for the purposes of the Theft Act 1968. Therefore, case law upon gain and loss for the purpose of false accounting under that statute (as to which see Section E below) provides a useful aid to interpreting this provision of the new Fraud Act.[87]

Two types of conspiracy to defraud

35.81 Since the enactment of the Fraud Act 2006, there are two different types of conspiracy to defraud: conspiracy to commit one of the statutory forms of fraud proscribed by the Act, which would necessarily be charged under the Criminal Law Act 1977, s 1(1); and conspiracy to defraud charged under the common law. As discussed immediately above, the most significant difference between the two is that common law conspiracy to defraud is not restricted to the prejudice of economic rights.

Penalties

35.82 By the Fraud Act 2006, s 1(3) a person who is guilty of fraud is liable: on summary conviction, to imprisonment for a term not exceeding 12 months or to a fine not exceeding the

---

[86] *R v Gayle* [2008] EWCA Crim 1344.
[87] For an intriguing instance in which the effect of s 5 may have been overlooked by both parties and the courts in a criminal case, see *Idrees v DPP* [2011] EWHC 624. A defendant was convicted of fraud by misrepresentation, contrary to the Fraud Act, ss 1 and 2, on the basis that he arranged for another person to impersonate him for the purpose of sitting the written part of the driving test (which he had previously failed 15 times). The case went before the Divisional Court by way of case stated, on the grounds that there had been insufficient evidence to link the defendant to the impersonation. The Divisional Court held that this contention was unarguable. The Fraud Act, s 5 was not raised or considered and it is therefore unclear on what basis it was thought to be fulfilled. It is submitted that a charge of common law conspiracy to defraud may have been more appropriate.

statutory maximum (or to both); on conviction on indictment, to imprisonment for a term not exceeding ten years or to a fine (or to both).

D. Theft and Deception

As stated in the introduction to this chapter, an overview of the entire criminal law is beyond **35.83** the scope of this work and this comment may be repeated with specific application to the law of theft and deception. There are many specific offences under the Theft Acts, only the principal of which will be discussed here. Particular emphasis will be placed on the way in which the law has developed in relation to the liabilities of company directors.

(1) Theft

Theft is defined by the Theft Act 1968, s 1(1): **35.84**

> A person is guilty of theft if he dishonestly appropriates property belonging to another with the intention of permanently depriving the other of it; and 'thief' and 'steal' shall be construed accordingly.

Later sections of the Act elaborate on the definition of each of the constituent elements of the offence.

Appropriation

Under the 1968 Act, s 3: **35.85**

(1) Any assumption by a person of the rights of an owner amounts to an appropriation, and this includes, where he has come by the property (innocently or not) without stealing it, any later assumption of a right to it by keeping or dealing with it as owner.

(2) Where property or a right or interest in property is or purports to be transferred for value to a person acting in good faith, no later assumption by him of rights which he believed himself to be acquiring shall, by reason of any defect in the transferor's title, amount to theft of the property.

Thus the concept of appropriation is wide. Crudely speaking, theft is not limited to the act **35.86** of picking something up and walking off with it, but extends to a much wider range of conduct in which the thief acts as if the property in question was his own. 'Any assumption ... of the rights of an owner' has effectively been interpreted by the criminal courts to mean 'the assumption of *any* of the rights of an owner'. For example, the act of showing a prospective purchaser of furniture around someone else's unoccupied house for the purpose of allowing the purchaser to select items to buy will amount to an appropriation of the furniture for the purposes of theft.[88] In practice, the act of appropriation is so wide that it is rarely necessary for a prosecutor to charge an offence of attempted theft. It also ensures that there is a very considerable overlap between the offence of theft and the offence of handling stolen goods (which will not specifically be addressed in this work).

Further, an act of appropriation may be made out even where the owner of the property **35.87** in question consents to the act. The words 'without the consent of the owner' are not to be read into the statutory definition of the theft.[89] Therefore, a taxi driver who takes bank notes

---

[88] *R v Pitham and Hehl* (1976) 65 Cr App R 45, CA.
[89] *Lawrence v Metropolitan Police Commissioner* [1972] AC 626, HL; *R v Gomez* [1993] AC 320, HL.

many times in excess of the value of his rightful fare from an open wallet offered to him by a tourist who speaks no English appropriates the money, despite the fact that (on one view)[90] he takes the money with the consent of the owner. Likewise, the acceptance of a gift will amount to an act of appropriation and may found an allegation of theft if it is dishonest and accompanied by the requisite intention permanently to deprive.[91] This feature of the law of theft is responsible for a large degree of overlap between offences of theft and offences of obtaining property or services by deception.

35.88   The width of the definition of appropriation, together with the absence of a requirement to prove a lack of consent, has particular ramifications for the liability of company directors for acts of theft.

35.89   Where a company is wholly owned by its two directors, the fact that each consents to the other's act of pocketing company funds will not prevent either director from being guilty of theft. It is possible to construct an argument that this should not be so: the company directors, according to the doctrine of identification, *are* the company for the purpose of the criminal law; they consent to the act, the company consents to the act; how can they be said to have dishonestly appropriated the company's money? In *AG's Reference (No 2 of 1982)*,[92] the Court of Appeal dealt with the effect of the doctrine of identification in this way:

> The speeches in the House of Lords in *Tesco Supermarkets Ltd. v. Nattrass*,[93] merely illustrate that in situations like the present the defendants 'are' the company in the sense that any offences committed by them in relation to the affairs of the company would be capable of being treated as offences committed by the company itself. The decision has no bearing on offences committed against the company.[94]

35.90   Therefore, where shareholders or directors act illegally or dishonestly against the company itself, knowledge of that dishonesty was not to be imputed to the company. So in this case, the company could not be said to have consented or to have been party to the acts of appropriation by the directors. On this basis, the victimization of the company by the directors appeared to be what was critical in order to establish that an appropriation or—at least—that a dishonest appropriation had occurred.

35.91   However, an alternative basis on which to rationalize the court's decision that the directors' conduct was capable of amounting to theft is to return to the more basic proposition that lack of consent on the part of the company and/or its directors and officers is not a requirement of the offence of theft. The practical distinction between the two rationales is illustrated on the following theoretical facts.[95]

---

[90] A dissenting view would be that lack of consent is an essential part of dishonesty, and that the material point on these facts is that no *true* consent is present.

[91] *R v Hinks* [2001] 2 AC 241, HL.

[92] [1984] QB 624, 640 per Kerr LJ, CA.

[93] [1972] AC 153, HL.

[94] *AG's Reference (No 2 of 1982)* has recently been the subject of approving comment by the Supreme Court in *Bilta (UK) Ltd v Nazir (No 2)* [2016] AC 1 at paras 75, 90, 155, and 194 and in *Prest v Petrodel Resources Ltd* [2013] 2 AC 415, 491 at para 41.

[95] In the SFO prosecution from which this example is drawn, the facts were hotly contested, and the scenario as posited here, although considered by the trial judge and the Administrative Court for the purpose of identifying the correct terms in which to the direct the jury, did not reflect the case for the prosecution, or for the defence. The defendant director asserted that he was not party to corruption. The prosecution maintained that he was, but that he did not inform or obtain the consent of any other director. The company director was ultimately acquitted.

A company has two directors, one of whom is approached by an important customer who **35.92** makes plain that the company will only win the renewal of a supply contract—critical to the company's profitability and survival—if a large bribe is paid; the director consults with his co-director, who consents to the course of using company monies to pay the bribe. Thereafter the first director approves the transfer of the monies in order to pay the bribe. Has he appropriated the company funds? Putting aside any liability for an act of corruption, is he guilty of theft? It is difficult to see how the directors' conduct can form an act against the company so as to prevent knowledge and/or consent to the act to be imputed to the company in accordance with the rationale of *AG's Reference (No 2 of 1982)*.[96]

The question has been tested in the Administrative Court, which upheld the first-instance **35.93** decision that such facts would disclose an act of appropriation, it being a question for a jury whether the appropriation was dishonest.[97] The defence argued the contrary position, attempting to distinguish the case from classic instances of directors' theft on the basis that there was no victimization of the company here: the director acted for the company's benefit; there was therefore no basis on which to depart from the normal effect of the doctrine of identification; the director's act was the act of the company itself; the director could not be said to have appropriated the company's funds. These arguments were roundly rejected. The court was loyal to the classic position in which 'appropriation' is a neutral term, involving no trace of the concept of 'misappropriation' and entirely silent as the honesty of the perpetrator or the 'victimization' of the owner of the property.[98]

Is it then the case that every time a director uses company property for a corrupt or dishon- **35.94** est purpose, the director is guilty of stealing the property from the company? The answer is no. In the case discussed immediately above, although the Administrative Court kept the definition of 'appropriation' wide, it reintroduced the concept of 'victimization' by stressing that the prosecution was obliged to prove that the defendant was dishonest *towards* the victim of the theft, namely that the director was dishonest *towards* the company. However, the court declined to stipulate that the jury should be directed that such dishonesty could not be made out where the director has obtained the consent of his only co-director. Dishonesty was a question for the jury, and in addition to the question whether the other director had consented, the following factors might influence their deliberations: whether the company's parent company was fully informed of events; whether it could be said that the director acted in the interests of the company; and whether the long-term interests of the company were jeopardized by potential civil and criminal liabilities arising from the director's alleged corruption.

Dishonesty

In order to make out an offence of theft, the prosecution must not only prove an appropria- **35.95** tion, but also that the appropriation was a dishonest one. As discussed above, a charge of theft requires dishonesty to be directed towards the victim of the theft. Further than that, the definition of dishonesty for these purposes is as set out in the case of *Ghosh*.[99]

---

[96] [1984] QB 624, CA.
[97] *AFP Regan*, CO/1019/2001, 17/5/2001, QBD, *coram* Lord Woolf CJ and Bell J.
[98] See further *R v Gomez* [1993] AC 320, HL.
[99] [1982] QB 1053, CA. See paras 35.59–35.63 above.

35.96 Finally, the 1968 Act, s 2 sets out three specific instances of states of mind which do not amount to dishonesty for the purposes of theft, and one instance of a circumstance which will not necessarily prevent a finding of dishonesty. It provides:

(1) A person's appropriation of property belonging to another is not to be regarded as dishonest—

    (a) if he appropriates the property in the belief that he has in law the right to deprive the other of it, on behalf of himself or of a third person;

    (b) if he appropriates the property in the belief that he would have the other's consent if the other knew of the appropriation and the circumstances of it; or

    (c) (except where the property came to him as trustee or personal representative) if he appropriates the property in the belief that the person to whom the property belongs cannot be discovered by taking reasonable steps.

(2) A person's appropriation of property belonging to another may be dishonest notwithstanding that he is willing to pay for the property.

Property

35.97 By the Theft Act 1968, s 4, property includes money, things in action (including debts), and other intangible property (such as export quotas)[100] but excludes land.

35.98 Importantly, property does not include information. Confidential information cannot be the object of theft.[101]

Belonging to another

35.99 'Another' for the purposes of the Theft Act includes a company, a company being a legal person for the purpose of the criminal law.[102] The concept of 'belonging to another' is widened by the Theft Act 1986, s 5(1) to include any person having possession or control of the property, or having any proprietary right or interest in it.

35.100 Where property is subject to trust, the person to whom it belongs is regarded as the person who has the right to enforce the trust.[103] Note, however, that secret profits obtained by a trustee will be regarded as his own property and not property belonging to the beneficiary of the trust for the purposes of the law of theft.[104] The trustee will have a civil obligation to disgorge himself of the secret profits (and in some circumstances he will be guilty of an offence of fraud and perhaps false accounting)[105] but he will not be guilty of stealing from the trust or his principal.

35.101 In addition, where a person receives property from or on account of and is under an obligation to another to retain and deal with that property or its proceeds in a particular way, the property or proceeds shall be regarded (as against him) as belonging to the other.[106] Note, however, that the obligation must be a legal one, rather than a purely social or moral one.[107]

---

[100] *AG of Hong Kong v Nai-Keung* [1987] 1 WLR 1339, PC.

[101] *Oxford v Moss* (1978) 68 Cr App R 183, DC.

[102] *AG's Reference (No 2 of 1982)* [1984] 1 QB 624, CA.

[103] Theft Act 1968, s 5(2).

[104] *AG's Reference (No 1 of 1985)* [1986] QB 491, CA.

[105] In particular note how the concept of 'gain' and 'loss' for the purposes of false accounting and—it must be assumed—the new Fraud Act offences includes avoiding an obligation to account to one's principal in respect of a secret profit: *Lee Cheung Wing v R* (1991) 94 Cr App R 355, CA. See further under Section C above.

[106] Theft Act 1968, s 5(3).

[107] *R v Hall* [1973] QB 126.

The effect of this provision is to enable a suspect to be charged with theft for the act of mixing with his own money (or the money of his own business) the money received by him from his client or principal which ought to have been kept in a separate account.

Likewise, where a person receives property by another's mistake, and is under an obligation **35.102** to make complete or partial restoration of the property or its proceeds, then the property or its proceeds are to be regarded (as against him) as belonging to the other to the extent of that obligation.[108] Again, the obligation must be a legal, rather than a moral or social obligation.[109] This provision is apt to cover situations in which a director receives an overpayment from his company by way of remuneration.

Intention permanently to deprive

It has been said that there is no offence of 'dishonest borrowing' in English law. Strictly **35.103** speaking this is true. However, on a charge of theft, it is in some circumstances possible to secure a conviction despite the fact that the defendant meant ultimately to restore the property to its rightful owner.

The Theft Act 1968, s 6 reads: **35.104**

  (1) A person appropriating property belonging to another without meaning the other permanently to lose the thing itself is nevertheless to be regarded as having the intention of permanently depriving the other of it if his intention is to treat the thing as his own to dispose of regardless of the other's rights; and a borrowing or lending of it may amount to so treating it if, but only if, the borrowing or lending is for a period and in circumstances making is equivalent to an outright taking or disposal.
  (2) Without prejudice to the generality of subsection (1) above, where a person, having possession or control (lawfully or not) of property belonging to another, parts with the property under a condition as to its return which he may not be able to perform, this (if done for the purposes of his own and without the other's authority) amounts to treating the property as his own to dispose of regardless of the other's rights.

This provision will apply, and should be left to the consideration of the jury, in circumstances **35.105** where a director 'borrows' money from a company meaning one day to repay it, but intending to deal with it in the meantime in such a manner that he knows he is risking its loss. The 'critical notion' in this provision is whether the defendant intended to treat the property as his own to dispose of, regardless of the other's rights.[110]

Penalty

The maximum sentence for theft on conviction on indictment is seven years' imprisonment.[111] **35.106**

(2) Offences of deception

Pre-Fraud Act 2006

Prior to the coming into force of the Fraud Act 2006 on 15 January 2007, there were five principal **35.107** cipal deception offences under the Theft Acts of 1968 and 1978: (i) obtaining property,[112]

---

  [108] Theft Act 1986, s 5(4).
  [109] *R v Hall* [1973] QB 126.
  [110] *R v Fernandez* [1996] 1 Cr App R 175, 188, CA, per Auld LJ.
  [111] Theft Act 1986, s 7.
  [112] Theft Act 1968, s 15.

(ii) obtaining a money transfer,[113] (iii) obtaining a pecuniary advantage,[114] (iv) obtaining services,[115] and (v) evading a liability[116] by deception. Each of these offences was repealed by the 2006 Act.[117] Case law relating to these old offences, particularly in relation to the meaning of deception, remains important in respect of some other extant criminal provisions (such as directors' false accounting contrary to s 19(1) of the Theft Act 1968).

35.108 The leading authority on the meaning of deception is *DPP v Ray*.[118] Note that deception is not restricted to deliberate deception, but includes reckless deception—that is, deception caused with indifference or disregard as to whether the statement is true or false.[119] In order to make out any offence of obtaining by deception, the deception in question must be effective, namely it must operate on the mind of the person deceived so as to constitute the effective cause by which the property is obtained.[120] It follows that the deception must precede the obtaining of the property in order to make out the offence.

Post-Fraud Act 2006

35.109 In respect of conduct which takes place wholly after the coming into force of the relevant section of the Fraud Act 2006,[121] the old offences of obtaining by deception are replaced by the three new substantive fraud offences (as to which see above) and one offence of obtaining services *dishonestly*.

35.110 By the Fraud Act 2006, s 11:

(1) A person is guilty of an offence under this section if he obtains services for himself or another—
   (a) by a dishonest act, and
   (b) in breach of subsection (2).
(2) A person obtains services in breach of this subsection if—
   (a) they are made available on the basis that payment has been, is being or will be made for or in respect of them,
   (b) he obtains them without any payment having been made for or in respect of them or without payment having been made in full, and
   (c) when he obtains them, he knows—
      (i) that they are being made available on the basis described in paragraph (a), or
      (ii) that they might be, but intends that payment will not be made, or will not be made in full.

---

[113] Theft Act 1968, s 15A. The need to enact this separate offence was highlighted by the decision of the House of Lords in *R v Preddy* [1996] AC 815, HL in which it was decided that inducing a financial institution to advance mortgage monies did not involve obtaining 'property belonging to another' within the meaning of the Theft Act 1968. Rather than obtain a chose in action which belonged to someone else, the defendant had induced the bank to create a new thing in action in the form of the enlarged credit balance in his own account. Absent s 15A, the same problem would exist in relation to cheques: *R v Clark* [2001] Crim LR 572, CA.

[114] Theft Act 1968, s 16.

[115] Theft Act 1978, s 1.

[116] Theft Act 1978, s 2.

[117] Fraud Act 2006, s 14(3) and Sch 1, para 1. Each offence may still be charged, however, in relation to conduct committed or commenced prior to 15 January 2007 (Sch 2, para 3(1)). Given the length of some fraud investigations, there is still some prospect of these old provisions being used.

[118] [1974] AC 370, HL.

[119] *R v Staines* (1970) 60 Cr App R 160, CA.

[120] *R v Clucas* [1949] 2 KB 226; *R v King and Stockwell* [1987] QB 547.

[121] ie 15 January 2007.

It is probable that many instances of deceit which previously would have been charged as **35.111**
obtaining property by deception will in future be charged under the Fraud Act 2006, s 2 as
fraud by false representation.

An important contrast between the old offences of deception and the new substantive **35.112**
fraud offences is that the latter do not depend upon proof that any property was in fact
obtained as a result of the deceit. Thus the new fraud offences set out in the 2006 Act,
ss 2–4 overlap significantly with the inchoate versions of the old deception offences
(such as attempts to obtain property by deception) as well as the old deception offences
themselves.

As with other fraud offences under the new Act, an offence contrary to s 11 carries a maxi- **35.113**
mum of 12 months' imprisonment (and/or a fine) on summary conviction and ten years'
imprisonment (and/or a fine) on conviction on indictment.

E. False Accounting and Forgery

(1) Introduction

Directors' liabilities for accounting and forgery offences arise by reason of the general offence **35.114**
of false accounting, proscribed by the Theft Act 1968, the general forgery offences of the
Forgery and Counterfeiting Act 1981, and also by reason of specific liabilities imposed upon
directors under both the Theft Act 1968 and under Companies Act legislation.

(2) False accounting under the Theft Act 1968

The Theft 1968, s 17(1) provides: **35.115**

> (1) Where a person dishonestly, with a view to gain for himself or another or with intent to
>   cause loss to another—
>   (a) destroys, defaces, conceals or falsifies any account or any record or document made
>   or required for any accounting purpose; or
>   (b) in furnishing information for any purpose, produces or makes use of any account,
>   or any such record or document as aforesaid, which to his knowledge is or may be
>   misleading, false or deceptive in a material particular;
>   he shall, on conviction on indictment, be liable to imprisonment for a term not exceeding
>   seven years.

This offence is of obvious application to any act committed by a director in relation to his **35.116**
own company's accounts. However, the offence of false accounting is wider than may appear
at first glance.

Made or required for an accounting purpose

The words 'made or required' together cover any document or record which is meant for, or **35.117**
subsequently used for, an accounting purpose. A document specifically made for an accounting purpose is obviously covered, and will remain covered even if the document is never in
fact used.[122] The offence also applies to documents made for an entirely different purpose
(for example, an application form for a loan from a bank) which is subsequently used for an

---

[122] *R v Sharma* [1990] 1 WLR 661.

accounting purpose by another person (eg when the bank uses the form to input data into its own account of the transaction).[123]

35.118   In addition, it should be noted that the requirement 'for an accounting purpose' is a requirement which attaches to the nature of the document itself. Where the prosecution rely upon a false statement contained in the document, it is not necessary for the prosecution to prove that false statement in question was material to the accounting purpose.[124]

35.119   Therefore, if a company director were to insert a false particular about the company upon an application form seeking a corporate loan from a bank, so long as he had the requisite state of mind,[125] he is liable for an offence of false accounting if that application form is subsequently used by the bank to enter the details of the loan into its own internal accounts, even though the falsehood in question has no effect on the accuracy of the bank's ledger.

Gain and loss

35.120   Gain and loss are defined by the Theft Act 1968, s 34(2) in these terms:

> For the purposes of this Act—
> (a) 'gain' and 'loss' are to be construed as extending only to gain and loss in money or other property, but as extending to any such gain or loss whether temporary or permanent; and—
>   (i) 'gain' includes a gain by keeping what one has, as well as a gain by getting what one does not; and
>   (ii) 'loss' includes a loss by not getting what one might get, as well as a loss by parting with what one has …

35.121   In order to establish that the defendant acted with a view to gain for himself or another, it is not necessary for the prosecution to exclude the possibility that the defendant was lawfully entitled to the property he sought to acquire. A person who furnishes false information in order to obtain money acts with a view to gain for himself, even if the money is undoubtedly owing to him, since by his actions he converts a mere right of action in respect of the debt into obtained cash, and thereby gains more than he already had; *AG's Reference (No 1 of 2001)*.[126] This case confirmed pre-existing first-instance authority to the effect that the term 'gain' is not restricted to the idea of making a profit.[127]

35.122   Whether inducing a creditor to forbear suing on a debt may amount to a 'gain' on the part of the debtor is less clear. In *R v Goleccha*[128] the court held that a debtor acting with such a purpose did not act with a view to gain for himself. This authority was not specifically considered by the Court of Appeal in *AG's Reference (No 1 of 2001)* (above), but it must be doubted whether the earlier decision survives the later. If inducing the payment of a lawful debt may amount to a 'gain' of the subsequent cash payment, it must follow that inducing a creditor not to sue on a debt amounts to a 'loss' of cash on his part, albeit potentially only temporary loss. *Goleccha* was a curious case because the prosecution put its allegation on the somewhat

---

[123]   *AG's Reference (No 1 of 1980)* [1981] 1 WLR 84, CA.
[124]   *R v Mallet* [1978] 1 WLR 820, CA.
[125]   ie dishonesty and a view to cause gain for himself or another (including the company) or with intent to cause loss to another (including the company).
[126]   *AG's Reference (No 1 of 2001)* [2003] 1 WLR 395.
[127]   *R v Parkes* [1973] Crim LR 358, Crown Court.
[128]   [1989] 1 WLR 1050, CA.

artificial basis that the defendant, by inducing the forbearance of his creditor, 'gained' the continued existence of the provision of the credit facility. The Court of Appeal rejected that as a proper basis for a conviction, but neither the prosecution nor the court appear to have considered that, regardless of what the defendant could be said to have 'gained'[129] from deceitfully inducing forbearance of his default, he undoubtedly caused a loss to the bank. Argument before the court does not appear to have focused on those parts of s 34(2) which provide that loss need not be permanent and that loss can include not getting what one might get (such as money in repayment of a debt), as well as parting with what one already has. In a subsequent, unreported decision of the Court of Appeal,[130] *Goleccha* was described as a decision 'turning very much on its own facts'. It is submitted that *Goleccha* should not be treated as good law.

A company director who falsifies a document with a view to avoiding an obligation to account to his principal company in respect of personal profits obtained by him in the course of his activities on behalf of the company acts with a view to gain for himself, even if he has caused no loss to his principal by his activities.[131] 'Gain' of course, is defined by s 34(2) to include keeping what one has, as well as gaining what one has not.   **35.123**

A company director who creates false invoices purportedly issued by recently acquired companies with a view to mollifying his co-directors as to the wisdom of those acquisitions does not act with a view to gain for himself. It is artificial for the Crown to seek to demonstrate the contrary by speculating that the director, if his attempts at mollification failed, might have had to placate his co-directors using his own financial resources, in circumstances where he was under no legal obligation so to do.[132]   **35.124**

Falsifying

The term 'falsifies' is not defined by the 1968 Act, but s 17 does contain a deeming provision which applies to accounts and documents (but not to other, mechanical forms of record). Section 17(2) provides: **35.125**

> For the purposes of this section a person who makes or concurs in the making in an account or other document an entry which is or may be misleading, false or deceptive in a material particular, or who omits or concurs in omitting a material particular from an account or other document, is to be treated as falsifying the account or document.

Dishonesty

See generally paragraphs 35.59–35.63 above.   **35.126**

Penalty

The maximum penalty for an offence contrary to s 17 is a term of imprisonment of seven years.   **35.127**

(3) Forgery

The principal forgery offence—the offence of making a false instrument—is set out in the Forgery and Counterfeiting Act 1981 (the 1981 Act), s 1. Other offences under the same Act   **35.128**

---

[129] See further *R v Eden* (1971) 55 Cr App R 193, CA in which a defendant who was proved to have acted to 'put off the evil day of having to sort out the muddle and pay up' was held by the Court of Appeal to have acted with a view to temporary gain.

[130] *R v Masterson*, unreported, 30 April 1996, CA (94/02221/X5).

[131] *Lee Cheung Wing v R* (1992) 94 Cr App R 355, PC.

[132] *R v Masterson*, unreported, 30 April 1996, CA (94/02221/X5).

include copying,[133] using,[134] and possessing[135] a false instrument. Only the principal forgery offence will be discussed in this work.

35.129 The 1981 Act, s 1 provides:

> A person is guilty of forgery if he makes a false instrument with the intention that he or another shall use it to induce somebody to accept it as genuine, and by reason of so accepting it, to do or not to do some act to his own or any other person's prejudice.

Instrument

35.130 The offence of making a false instrument applies to a wider range of documents than the offence of false accounting (which is restricted to documents and records made or required for an accounting purpose). The anti-forgery legislation applies to all documents, be they formal or informal, and to all disks, tapes, soundtracks, and other devices used to store information.[136]

False

35.131 However, the offence of forgery is in other ways narrower than the offence of false accounting. In essence, the terms of the 1981 Act require the document in question to bear false information *about itself* (for example, that it was made by a person who did not in fact make it, or that it was made on a date on which it was not in fact made), as opposed to merely bearing false information about the person who made it (for example, that person's—or his company's—assets, liabilities, credit status, or history).[137]

35.132 Under the 1981 Act, a person is to be deemed to have 'made' a false instrument if he alters a document so as to make it tell a lie about itself in any way which would qualify to trigger the offence under the Act.[138]

Prejudice

35.133 The term 'prejudice' is given special definition under the 1981 Act. Under s 10(1), an act or omission intended to be induced is to a person's prejudice only if it is one which, if it occurs, will result in his loss of property or of opportunity to gain a financial advantage, or in his becoming liable to someone else gaining a financial advantage from him; or if it is the result of a person having accepted the false instrument as genuine in connection with his performance of a duty.

35.134 As in relation to the offence of false accounting, loss in this context embraces (under the terms of s 10) permanent and temporary loss, and includes loss by not getting what one might have gained, as well as parting with what one already has.

Penalty

35.135 A person convicted of forgery is liable summarily to 12 months' imprisonment or a fine (or both) and on indictment to ten years' imprisonment.[139]

---

133 1981 Act, s 2.
134 1981 Act, s 3.
135 1981 Act, s 5.
136 1981 Act, s 8(1).
137 1981 Act, s 9(1) and *R v More* [1987] 1 WLR 1578, HL.
138 1981 Act, s 9(2).
139 1981 Act, s 6.

(4) Directors' accounting liabilities

The Theft Act 1968, s 19(1) provides: **35.136**

Where an officer of a body corporate or unincorporated association (or a person purporting to act as such), with intent to deceive members or creditors of the body corporate or association about its affairs, publishes or concurs in publishing a written statement which to his knowledge is or may be misleading, false or deceptive in a material particular, he shall on conviction on indictment be liable to a term of imprisonment not exceeding seven years.

This liability is in addition to specific liabilities contained in the Companies Act 2006 (as   **35.137** to which see Section I below). For discussion of the concept of knowledge, see paragraph 35.197 below. Note that the words 'is or may be' in s 19 mean that the offence can be committed with a reckless state of mind in respect of the accuracy of the written statement.

In relation to deceit and deception, see paragraph 35.108 above. Note, however, that in con- **35.138** trast to some other statutory offences of deception, an offence under s 19 requires a specific intention to deceive.

F. Bribery and Corruption

(1) Introduction

The Bribery Act 2010 came into force 1 July 2011. It: **35.139**

(1) repealed the Public Bodies Corrupt Practices Act 1889, the Prevention of Corruption Act 1906, and the Prevention of Corruption Act 1916;
(2) introduced three groups of substantive offences;
(3) widened the territorial application of UK anti-corruption law; and
(4) created a new corporate offence of failure to prevent bribery.

(2) Substantive offences

The three new sets of offences created about the Bribery Act are: offences of bribery contrary   **35.140** to s 1, offences of being bribed contrary to s 2, and the offence of bribing a foreign public official, contrary to s 6.

Extraterritorial effect

The territorial application of each of the three forms of substantive offence under the 2010   **35.141** Act is governed by s 12. The application is wide. Indeed, the territorial extent of these offences is so unusual that it is worth addressing this first, before examining the elements of the substantive offences themselves.

There are two ways in which jurisdiction for these offences is triggered. The first is conven- **35.142** tional: an offence is committed in the UK if any act or omission which forms part of the offence takes place here. But alternatively, any act or omission which would form part of the offence if committed inside the UK will trigger jurisdiction if committed outside the jurisdiction by a person who has a 'close connection'[140] with the UK. Note that once UK

---

[140] '*Close connection*' is defined by s 12(4). Persons with close connections to the UK include British citizens, UK residents, and bodies incorporated in the UK.

jurisdiction is established, proceedings may be brought in the UK for the entire offence and against each of its participants, not just against the person whose act or omission triggered jurisdiction. On the face of it, if a UK resident director of a Cayman Islands company commits an act of bribery in India jointly with three other persons (none of whom is connected to the UK), the UK courts will have jurisdiction to try all four participants for that offence.

Bribing another

35.143 Under s 1, a person is guilty of bribing another if he (directly or through a third party)[141] offers, promises, or gives a financial or other advantage to another person, and either:

(1) (under sub-s 2) intends the advantage (i) to induce a person[142] to perform improperly a relevant function or activity, or (ii) to reward a person for the improper performance of such a function or activity; or

(2) (under sub-s 3) knows or believes that the acceptance of the advantage would itself constitute the improper performance of a relevant function or activity.

Being bribed

35.144 Offences of being bribed are largely the reverse image of the offences created by s 1. Under s 2, a person is guilty of being bribed if he requests, agrees to receive, or accepts a financial or other advantage and:

(1) (under sub-s 2) intends that, in consequence, a relevant function or activity should be performed improperly (by himself of another person);

(2) (under sub-s 3) the request agreement or acceptance itself constitutes the improper performance by him of a relevant function or activity; or

(3) (under sub-s 4) the advantage is as a reward for the improper performance of a relevant function or activity.

35.145 In addition, s 1(5) creates an offence where, in anticipation of or in consequence of a person's requesting, agreeing to receive, or accepting a financial or other advantage, a relevant function or activity is performed improperly either by the requestor himself, or by someone else at his request or with his assent of acquiescence. This form of the offence will bite, for example, where a gift is accepted innocently at first, but later has the effect of corrupting the performance of the relevant function.

Improper performance of a relevant function

35.146 A common feature of the each form of the first two types of offence is the concept of 'improper performance of a relevant function'.

35.147 Under s 3 of the Act, a 'relevant function or activity' is any function of a public nature, any activity connected with a business[143] or performed in the course of a person's employment, and any activity performed by or on behalf of a body of persons (whether corporate of unincorporated) which the person is expected to perform in good faith or impartially, or which otherwise puts the person performing it in a position of trust. It is obvious that all duties of a company director will fall within this definition.

---

[141] See s 1(5).

[142] In the form of the offence created by sub-s (2), it does not matter whether the person to whom the advantage is offered etc is the same person who is to perform (or has performed) the relevant function. See s 1(4).

[143] Business includes a trade or profession: s 3(7).

Under s 4, a relevant function or activity is performed improperly if it is performed in breach **35.148**
of a 'relevant expectation'. Where the person performing the activity is expected to perform
it in good faith or impartially, then that is the relevant expectation. Where the person performs the function in a position of trust, a breach of that trust is a breach of the relevant
expectation.

By s 5, the standard of expectation is: 'what a reasonable person in the United Kingdom **35.149**
would expect in relation to the performance of the type of function or activity concerned'.
Where the performance is not subject to the law of any part of the UK (for example, because
it occurs wholly outside the jurisdiction), the test remains that of the reasonable person in
the UK. Further, in such a case, s 5(2) requires the tribunal of fact to disregard any foreign
custom or practice when deciding if the UK standards of expectation have been breached,
unless that custom or practice is permitted or required by the written law[144] applicable in the
territory concerned.

Although most commentary on the 2010 Act has focused on the ways in which it has **35.150**
extended liability for corruption in the UK (both by enlarging its territorial application and
by creating the brand new corporate offence of failing to prevent corruption) the concept
of '*improper performance*' represents a narrowing of the former, early twentieth-century versions of offences of corruption. As was discussed in the previous edition of this work, there
was formerly an irrebuttable presumption that the giving of any gift or reward to an agent in
order to induce him to do or not to do anything in connection with his principal's affairs was
corrupt. This presumption has now gone. Of course, in many cases, improper performance
will readily be inferred from the size of the advantage and the circumstances in which it was
offered or given. But there are situations in which this change in the law will make a critical
difference to liability.[145] The new law also enables a much more common-sense approach to
be taken to the issue of corporate hospitality.[146] Note, however, that it remains unnecessary
for the prosecution to prove dishonesty.[147]

Bribing a foreign public official

The third type of substantive offences under the 2010 Act resembles previous English law of **35.151**
corruption more closely in that there is no requirement to prove improper performance of a
relevant function. As was generally the case under the old law, liability is established by the

---

[144] Written law includes case law published in written sources: s 5(3)(b).

[145] eg at the time of writing there is a degree of controversy in the legal profession as to the propriety of paying referral fees for work passed from insurance companies to solicitors firms, or from solicitors to counsel. In
July 2011 the Chairman of the Bar Council, Peter Lodder QC, wrote an open letter to its members stating that
'*referral fees are bribes*'. It is submitted that this view (which is a minority one) would be more easily justified
by reference to the old as opposed to the new law of corruption in the UK. Unless the professional receiving
the referral fee is specifically prevented from so doing by his regulator (such that receipt of the advantage was
itself improper), or the referral fee is paid to induce or in return for the referral of work to a professional whom
it is not in the client's interests to instruct, it is difficult to see how the 'improper performance' element of the
offence might be fulfilled. This new element of bribery offences is likely to provide many future defendants with
arguable defences, where before there was none.

[146] A common-sense approach is well supported by the Secretary of State's Guidance published under s 9
of the 2010 Act.

[147] Thus, on the specific facts of *R v Smith* [1960] 2 QB 423 (where a bribe was paid in order to expose a
public official as corrupt) it is likely that, even under the modern law, the defendant would not be entitled to
acquittal. This would be the case unless the defendant could bring himself within the very narrow defences
provided by s 13 of the Act (eg because the bribery was committed in the proper exercise of any function of the
intelligence services or armed forces when engaged on active service).

fact of the offer, promise, on gift and an intention to influence the official concerned (even if the intention is merely to induce him to do what he would in any event be duty bound to do). More specifically (and unlike the old law), the intention must also be to obtain or retain business or an advantage in the conduct of business.[148] It is incumbent on the prosecution to prove, in addition, that the official was neither permitted nor required by the written law applicable to him to be influenced by the relevant offer, promise, or gift.

(3) Failure to prevent bribery

35.152 The Bribery Act 2010 creates a new form of secondary liability for offences of bribery. Unlike substantive offences under the Act, which can be committed by individuals or by corporate bodies, this offence can only be committed by a 'relevant commercial organization'. Individual directors or officers of a company do not carry liability for this offence. It is included, however, because responsibility for ensuring that a company does not become liable under this new provision will fall upon its directors.

35.153 Section 7 of the Act provides:

> (1) a relevant commercial organisation ('C') is guilty of an offence under this section if a person ('A') associated with C bribes another person intending—
>   (a) to obtain or retain business for C, or
>   (b) to obtain or retain an advantage in the conduct of business for C.
> (2) but it is a defence for C to prove that C had in place adequate procedures designed to prevent persons associated with C from undertaking such conduct.

35.154 Under sub-s (3), bribery means an offence of bribery under ss 1 or 6 of the Act. Note that the bribery must be committed for the benefit or intended benefit of the relevant commercial organization itself. Therefore a company is not liable under this section simply because one of its directors commits an act of bribery in his private life.

Relevant commercial organization

35.155 The definition of 'relevant commercial organisation' is particularly important because the term also provides the territorial application of the failure to prevent offence. Under s 7(5), 'relevant commercial organisation' means:

> (a) a body which is incorporated under the law of any part of the United Kingdom and which carries on a business (whether there or elsewhere),
> (b) any other body corporate (wherever incorporated) which carries on a business, or part of a business, in any part of the United Kingdom,
> (c) any partnership which is formed under the law of any part of the United Kingdom and which carries on a business (whether there or elsewhere), or
> (d) any other partnership (wherever formed) which carries on a business, or part of a business, in any part of the United Kingdom.

35.156 The concept of an organization carrying on a business or part of a business within the UK is potentially very wide. It could, for example, extend jurisdictional application to companies which are incorporated and based overseas, but which market their products or services to consumers in the UK. The Serious Fraud Office has certainly indicated that it takes a 'wide view' of this term.[149]

---

[148] See s 12(2).
[149] See eg speech of Richard Alderman, Director of the SFO, Joint RBCC/Chadbourne & Park LLP Seminar, St Petersburg, 17 March 2011, available at the SFO's website. The Secretary of State has also expressed

Associated persons

The liability of a company to prevent bribery is limited to persons associated with it. **35.157**
Under s 8, a person is associated with a company (or other relevant commercial organization) if—disregarding any bribe under consideration—the person performs services
for or on behalf of the organization. The section cites, by way of example, subsidiaries,
agents, and employees as potential service providers, but this list is not exhaustive.[150]
Neither is it determinative; it would be perfectly possible for a relevant commercial
organization's subsidiary, for example, to fail the service provider test. Whether or not
the person performs services for the organization is to be determined by reference to all
the relevant circumstances and not merely by reference to the nature of the relationship
between the person and the organization.[151] Only in the case of an employee is there
a presumption that he performs services for the organization, and even then, the presumption may be rebutted.[152]

Defence of adequate procedures

Given the potential width of the failure to prevent the offence, the s 7(2) defence of adequate **35.158**
procedures is obviously of critical importance to all UK companies and overseas organizations with a significant business presence within the UK.

The Secretary of State has published guidance under s 9 of the Act about the procedures **35.159**
which organizations may put in place to prevent corruption by associated persons. All
UK companies need to pay attention to this guidance, not only as a matter of good practice, but also to protect themselves from secondary liability in the unfortunate event that
any of their associates commit bribery offences for their benefit. The guidance is available at <www. justice.gov.uk>. In short, the approach of the guidance is to advocate the
implementation of measures proportionate to the risks posed by the type and location
of business conducted by or on behalf of the organization, which risks must regularly
be assessed.

(4) Penalties

Under s 11 of the Bribery Act, an individual found guilty of an offence under ss 1, 2, or **35.160**
6 is liable on conviction on indictment to ten years' imprisonment, or unlimited fine, or
both. (Under the former, 1906 Act, the maximum penalty was one of seven years' imprisonment.) Corporate defendants found guilty of an offence under ss 1, 2, and 6 are liable
to an unlimited fine (or, in the magistrates' court, a fine up to the statutory maximum of
£5,000). The s 7 offence of failing to prevent bribery, which is only capable of commission
by organizations, may only be tried on indictment and carries the maximum penalty of
an unlimited fine.

---

an opinion. In guidance to commercial organizations published under s 9(1) of the Act (available at the
Ministry of Justice's website), he has stated that a common-sense application of the test will require proof of a
'demonstrable business presence' in the UK. It is submitted that this formulation does no more than restate the
question. In any event, the status of this guidance as an aid to statutory interpretation other than of the term
'adequate procedures' (which is the only purpose for which the guidance is mandated by ss 7(4) and 9(1) of the
Act) is questionable.

[150] See s 8(3).
[151] Sub-s (4).
[152] Sub-s (5).

G. Insider Dealing and Market Rigging

35.161 This chapter will not be concerned with the civil or regulatory liabilities which may arise under FSMA.[153] The FCA's powers to levy financial penalties against regulated and non-regulated persons for conduct amounting to market abuse is considered in Chapter 32 and will not be considered here. However, the regulatory offence of market abuse has equivalent offences under the criminal law. Regulatory market abuse translates into the criminal offences of insider dealing and market rigging, which are discussed below.

(1) Insider dealing

Introduction

35.162 Insider dealing is currently proscribed as an offence by the Criminal Justice Act 1993 (the 1993 Act), Part V. The statutory provisions are, like their predecessors,[154] technical and complicated. Until relatively recently, prosecutions for the offence were rare. For this reason there is no extensive body of case law upon the subject. However, what case law there is makes plain that the legislation should not be further complicated by an unduly technical or elaborate interpretation of its terms.[155] Instead, a purposive approach should be adopted, bearing in mind the mischief at which the legislation is aimed.[156]

35.163 The mischief at which the legislation is aimed may at least be simply stated. A 1977 White Paper, *The Conduct of Company Directors*,[157] commented that there was a need for laws which would prevent situations in which a person bought and sold securities when he, but not the other party to the transaction, was in possession of confidential information which affected the value of to be placed upon them. Lord Lowry, in *AG's Reference (No 1 of 1988)*,[158] put the matter even more succinctly: 'The mischief [at which the legislation is aimed] consists of dealing in securities while in possession of the confidential information.'[159] This purpose must be borne in mind when reading the provisions of the current statute.[160]

Offence-creating provision

35.164 The main offence-creating provision of Part V of the 1993 Act is s 52. It proscribes three forms of insider dealing: (i) where a person who has information as an insider himself deals in securities, (ii) where he encourages another to deal, and (iii) where he discloses inside information to another (other than in the proper course of his employment).

35.165 Under the Criminal Justice Act 1993, Part V, s 52:

---

[153] Financial Services and Markets Act 2000.

[154] ie the Company Securities (Insider Dealing) Act 1985 and the Companies Act 1980, ss 68–73. The latter was based upon the White Paper: *The Conduct of Company Directors*, Cmnd 7037 (1977).

[155] *AG's Reference (No 1 of 1988)* [1989] AC 971, HL; *R v Staines and Morrisey* [1997] 2 Cr App R 426, 438, CA. Both cases were decided in relation to the 1985 Act. It is submitted that they apply equally to the modern statute.

[156] *AG's Reference (No 1 of 1988)* [1989] AC 971, HL; *R v Staines and Morrisey* [1997] 2 Cr App R 426, CA.

[157] Cmnd 7037 (1977).

[158] [1989] AC 971, HL.

[159] At 735.

[160] For a further statement of the purpose of the legislation, see *R v Staines and Morrisey* [1997] 2 Cr App R 426, 430, CA, per Lord Bingham CJ.

(1) An individual who has information as an insider is guilty of insider dealing if, in the circumstances mentioned in subsection (3), he deals in securities that are price-affected securities in relation to the information.

(2) An individual who has information as an insider is also guilty of insider dealing if—

(a) he encourages another person to deal in securities that are (whether or not that other knows it) price-affected securities in relation to the information, knowing or having reasonable cause to believe that the dealing would take place in the circumstances mentioned in subsection (3); or

(b) he discloses the information, otherwise than in the proper performance of the functions of his employment, office or profession to another person.

(3) The circumstances referred to above are that the acquisition or disposal in question occurs on a regulated market, or that the person dealing relies on a professional intermediary or is himself acting as a professional intermediary.

(4) This section has effect subject to section 53.[161]

Whichever of the three forms is charged, it is the definition of 'a person who has information as an insider' which is the first, essential element of the offence.   **35.166**

Person who has information as an insider

The definition of 'a person who has information as an insider' is provided by the 1993 Act, s 57. Within the definition, reference is made to another term of art used within Part 5 of the Act: 'inside information'. The term is itself defined in s 56 of the Act. Putting the effect of ss 56 and 57 of the Act together, a person has information as an insider if and only if: **35.167**

(1) He possesses—and knows that he possesses—inside information, that is information which:

(a) relates[162] to particular securities or to a particular issuer or to particular issuers of securities and not to securities generally or to issuers of securities generally,

(b) is specific or precise,

(c) has not been made public,[163] and

(d) is price-sensitive, ie would be likely to have significant effect on the price of any securities if it were made public.[164]

(2) He has, and knows that he has, the inside information from an inside source, that is:

(a) he has it (i) through being a director, employee or shareholder of an issuer of securities,[165] or (ii) by virtue of his employment, office or profession,[166] or

(b) the direct or indirect source of the information is a person within (a) above.[167]

---

[161] See below. Section 53 sets out defences to the charge.

[162] Under s 60(4) of the 1993 Act, where an issuer of securities is a company, information shall be treated as 'relating' to the issuer not only where it is about the company, but also where it may affect the company's business.

[163] A non-exhaustive lists of instances in which information is to be treated as made public, and of matters which need not prevent information being treated as made public, are contained in s 58. The issue will be a question of fact for the jury. It is submitted that the thrust of s 58 is that whether information is made public is a function of the extent to which it is generally available.

[164] ss 57(1)(a) and 56(1)–(2).

[165] This reflects s 57(2)(a)(i) and covers people connected directly with the company—the people most literally 'inside' it.

[166] This reflects s 57(2)(a)(ii) and is apt to cover people employed outside the company itself but brought inside as professional advisors. A company's bankers, business consultants, public relations agents, accountants, and legal advisors will frequently move into the category of insiders.

[167] s 57(2)(b).

35.168 'A person who has information as an insider' is therefore a person who possesses what he knows to be inside information, from what he knows to be an inside source. Any person who fulfils this definition is subject to the s 52 prohibition against dealing, encouraging others to deal in the securities in question, or disclosing the inside information to any other person otherwise than in the proper performance of his functions of his employment, office, or profession. Whether each part of the definition of 'a person who has information as an insider' is fulfilled will be a matter of fact for the jury,[168] underlining again that the provisions of the Act should not be read in a technical or over-elaborate manner.

35.169 The purposive approach of the criminal courts in respect of this offence is well demonstrated by judicial interpretation of the statutory definition of 'inside information' in particular.

35.170 By the terms of s 56, inside information must relate to particular securities (or to a particular issuer or to particular issuers), must be specific or precise, must not have been made public, and must be price-sensitive. However, the Court of Appeal has specifically declined to read into the definition of inside information the additional requirement that the information disclosed from the inside source must, in and of itself, enable the person to whom it is disclosed to identify the securities to which it relates.[169] Therefore if an accountant tells a friend socially that he is working on a bid which one of his firm's clients is proposing to make for the publicly quoted capital of a target company and his friend subsequently uses the information provided and some further research in order to discover the name target, the friend has 'information as an insider'[170] and is subject to s 52. In reaching this conclusion, the court expressly noted that the effect of the appellant's dealing fell squarely within the type of mischief the Act was intended to prohibit and interpreted the provisions of the Act accordingly.[171] For further guidance on what amounts to 'inside information', see *Hannam v FCA*[172], in which the Upper Tribunal considered this question in the closely related context of FSMA, s 118C. Note in particular that a degree of inaccuracy within the information was held not to disqualify it from amounting to 'inside information' and that, although it was necessary for the information to be specific enough to indicate the direction in which the price of relevant security might move, it was not necessary for it to enable assessment of the extent of the possible movement.

35.171 At first glance, it might be asked what the requirement that the defendant had the inside information from an 'inside source' adds to the elements of the offence, other than an extra level of complexity. If the information in question fulfils all the necessary requirements to constitute 'inside information'—particularly the requirement that it not be public information—is it not inevitable that it will have emanated, directly or indirectly, from an inside source? The answer is no; the requirement that the defendant must have the inside information from an inside source serves an important purpose in distinguishing between legitimate and illegitimate instances of acting on non-public, price-sensitive information.

---

[168] *R v Staines and Morrisey* [1997] 2 Cr App R 426, 438.

[169] *R v Staines and Morrisey* (n 168 above).

[170] What was called 'unpublished price sensitive information' at the time of the decision in *Staines and Morrisey* (n 168 above).

[171] *Staines and Morrisey* (n 168 above) at 438.

[172] [2014] UKUT 233 (TCC). FSMA, s 118C was repealed on 3 July 2016 when the Market Abuse Regulation came into force in the UK; see Chapter 32 at Section A(3) above.

For example, a shareholder of a company is returning from holiday by train. He passes by **35.172**
the company's largest factory and sees that it is on fire.[173] The shareholder possesses inside
information within the meaning of s 56. However, he does not possess the inside information from an inside source within the meaning of s 57: he does not have it by reason of
his status as a shareholder, but by reason of his observation from the train. He is therefore
not a 'person who has information as an insider' for the purpose of s 52 of the Act and he
is perfectly entitled to call his broker and instruct him to sell his stock. This position can
be contrasted with the position of the chief executive of the company, who is informed
of the fire by an employee. The chief executive has the inside information by virtue of his
directorship, and therefore from an inside source: he is subject to the prohibition of s 52
until the information is made public. The same must be said for the shareholder's broker.
If the shareholder informs the broker why he wishes to sell his shares, the broker comes by
the inside information by virtue of his employment, and therefore from an inside source
by reason of s 57(2)(a)(ii). He is therefore a person who has information as an insider and
he too is subject to s 52.

Dealing

By s 55(1) of the 1993 Act, a person deals in securities within the terms of s 52 of the Act if **35.173**
he himself acquires[174] or disposes[175] of them (whether on his own behalf or as the agent of
another) or if he directly or indirectly procures an acquisition or disposal of the securities by
any other person.[176]

So far as the first two forms of the offence created by s 52 are concerned (dealing and encour- **35.174**
aging another to deal), the dealing in question must take place on a regulated market, relying on a professional intermediary, or where the offender is himself acting as a professional
intermediary.[177] Private, off-market transactions fall outside the scope of the Act and may
not form an allegation of insider dealing.

'Regulated market' is defined by Articles 9 and 10 of the Insider Dealing (Securities and **35.175**
Regulated Markets) Order 1994 (SI 1994/187) to be any market which is established under
the rules of an investment exchange specified in the Schedule to the Order. The list has
been expanded by subsequent amendment.[178] The list of UK markets currently covered are
OFEX and those markets established under the rules of: the London Stock Exchange; LIFFE
Administration & Management; OMLX, the London Securities and Derivatives Exchange
Limited; virt-x Exchange Limited; and CoredealMTS.

'Professional intermediary' is defined by s 59 of the Act. It is apt to cover professional share **35.176**
traders and stock brokers.

---

[173] This example is taken from the Market Conduct Manual of the FSA's Handbook (reference code MAR
1.4.8) as it was as of 1 January 2004. It does not appear in the current FCA Handbook.
[174] This includes agreeing to acquire and entering into a contract which creates the security: s 55(2).
[175] This includes agreeing to dispose and bringing an end to the contract which created the security: s 55(3).
[176] The latter alternative provides for a large margin of overlap between the first two forms of the offence of
insider dealing (dealing and encouraging another to deal) by making a person guilty of the first, perhaps as well
as the second, whenever he 'procures' another to deal in the securities.
[177] s 52(3).
[178] ie the Insider Dealing (Securities and Regulated Markets) (Amendment) Order 1996 (SI 1996/1561);
the Insider Dealing (Securities and Regulated Markets) (Amendment) Order 2000 (SI 2000/1923); the Insider
Dealing (Securities and Regulated Markets) (Amendment) Order 2002 (SI 2002/1874).

Securities to which the Act applies

35.177 The 1993 Act, Part V applies to any security which is listed within Schedule 2 and which satisfies any order made by the Treasury under s 54(1)(b). The only order currently issued is the Insider Dealing (Securities and Regulated Markets) Order 1994 (SI 1994/187) as amended. Under the terms of the Order, Part V of the Act applies only to securities which fall within Schedule 2 if they are officially listed in an EEA state or are dealt with or quoted on a regulated market.[179]

Defences

35.178 The scope of the offence is undoubtedly broad but it is narrowed in its effect by the availability of four general and several special defences.

35.179 The general defences to a charge of insider dealing are set out in s 53 of the Act. The effect of the section is as follows.

35.180 Where a person is accused of one of the first two forms of the offence (dealing or encouraging another to deal) he is not guilty if he shows that either:

(1) he did not at the time expect the dealing to result in a profit attributable to the fact that the information in question was price-sensitive information in relation to the securities;

(2) at the time he believed on reasonable grounds that the information had been disclosed widely enough to ensure that none of those taking part in the dealing would be prejudiced by not having the information; or

(3) he would have done what he did even if he did not have the information.[180]

35.181 The second of these general defences allows for a not-guilty verdict where the inside information, although not public, was nevertheless reasonably believed by the defendant to have been sufficiently widely known to prevent that particular deal being conducted on an unfair basis. The question of drawing the line between cases which fall inside and outside this defence will be an issue of fact for the jury (except, perhaps, in an extreme case, for example where, on the Crown's own evidence, the defendant trader was dealing on his own account with a professional colleague whom he reasonably believed to possess the same information as himself).

35.182 The third of the general defences represents a significant narrowing of the offence. In previous statutory incarnations of insider dealing, as now, there was also no requirement for the Crown to prove causation as part of its case, but unlike the present position, it was no defence to prove that a defendant would have done exactly as he did even had he not had the information.[181]

35.183 Where a person is accused of the third type of insider dealing (committed by disclosure of information held as an insider), he is not guilty if he shows that either:

(1) he did not at the time expect any person, because of the disclosure, to deal in securities on a regulated market or relying on or as a professional intermediary, or

---

[179] See para 35.175 above.
[180] See s 53(1) and (2).
[181] *AG's Reference (No 1 of 1988)* [1989] AC 971, HL.

(2) as per the first general defence set out in paragraph 35.180 above, although he did have such an expectation, he did not at the time expect the dealing to result in a profit attributable to the fact that the information in question was price-sensitive information in relation to the securities.

The special defences available on a charge of insider dealing are contained in Schedule 1 of **35.184** the 1993 Act and are subject to amendment by order of the Treasury.[182] At present, the special defences designated by Schedule 1 of the Act provide that an individual is not guilty of an offence of insider dealing if he shows that:

(1) he acted in good faith in the course of his business as a market maker or his employment in the business of a market maker,[183] or

(2) the information which he had was market information[184] and either:
    (a) it was reasonable for an individual in his position to have acted as he did despite having that information as an insider at the time,[185] or
    (b) that he acted in connection with and with a view to accomplishing an acquisition or disposal (or a series of such) which was under consideration or subject to negotiation, and the market information in question arose directly out of his involvement in the acquisition or disposal (or series of such),[186] or

(3) he acted in conformity with the price stabilization rules[187] or with the relevant provisions of Commission Regulation (EC) No 2273/2003.

There is no decided case upon whether the general or special defences provided by the Act are **35.185** for the defendant to prove on a balance of probabilities, or for the prosecution to disprove (if raised by the defence) to the usual criminal standard. However, similar, previous statutory provisions[188] have been held to reverse the burden, requiring the defendant to prove his defence to the civil standard.[189] This obviously provides the prosecutor with a good starting point from which to argue that, under the 1993 Act, the burden must likewise lie with the defence. However, this will not automatically follow. Previous statutory provisions were interpreted before the enactment of the Human Rights Act 1998, which requires statutes wherever possible to be interpreted compatibly with the ECHR, Article 6(2) presumption of innocence.[190] The arguments against construing a reversed burden in relation to defences

---

[182] Section 53(4) and (5). Sch 1 has to date been amended by the Financial Services and Markets Act 2000 (Consequential Amendments and Repeals) Order 2001 (SI 2001/3649), Art 341, and by the Financial Services and Markets Act 2000 (Market Abuse) Regulations 2005 (SI 2005/381), reg 3.

[183] Sch 1, Art 1. Simply put, a market maker is a person who holds himself as willing to buy and sell shares and is recognized as doing so under the rules of the market.

[184] Broadly speaking, market information is information about share trading (rather than information about the company which issued its shares or its business). Market information is defined in Sch 1, Art 4 as information consisting of one or more facts such as: particular securities have been or are to be acquired, the price (or range of prices) at which they have been or are to be acquired, and the identity of any person involved or likely to be involved in the acquisition.

[185] Sch 1, Art 2.

[186] Sch 1, Art 3.

[187] Made under FSMA, s 144(1).

[188] ie Company Securities (Insider Dealing) Act 1985, s 3(1).

[189] *R v Cross* (1990) 91 Cr App R 115, CA.

[190] For an example of a case in which, post-Human Rights Act 1998, a statutory provision has been held *not* to reverse the burden of proof (despite the use of the words, 'It is a defence for a person charged to prove that …') see *R v Carass* [2002] 1 WLR 1714, CA.

under the 1993 Act would include the fact that the defences in question are not limited to straightforward, technical questions of status, exemption, or licence, but include concepts such as good faith and reasonableness. Ordinarily, where good faith is relevant, if there is a possibility that the defendant did possess it, he ought to be entitled to be acquitted on that basis (especially where the offence is a serious one, carrying a maximum penalty of a lengthy prison sentence). Support for this argument may be derived from *R v Webster*[191] (which concerned the compatibility of a reversed burden of proof with article 6(2) of the ECHR in the context of charges of corruption).

35.186 A further limitation on the application of s 52 is provided by s 63 of the 1993 Act. Section 52 does not apply to anything done by an individual acting on behalf of a public sector body in pursuit of monetary policies or policies in respect to exchange rates or the management of public debt or foreign exchange reserves. Unlike the general and special defences mentioned above, if this issue is raised by the defence, the prosecution will bear the burden of disproving the suggestion to the criminal standard.

Jurisdiction

35.187 The territorial scope of the offence is clearly set out in s 62. Broadly, it is confined to dealing which is conducted within the UK or in relation to a market regulated in the UK, and to disclosure of information which is made or received within the UK.

Penalties

35.188 By s 61(1) the maximum penalty for insider dealing on summary conviction at the magistrates' court is a fine not exceeding the statutory maximum, or imprisonment for a term of six months, or both. On conviction on indictment before the Crown Court, a defendant is liable to an unlimited fine or imprisonment for a term not exceeding seven years, or both.

35.189 An offence of insider dealing committed by a market professional, or involving profit or loss on any sort of scale, is likely to be met by a substantial term of immediate imprisonment.[192]

(2) Market rigging

Introduction

35.190 Market rigging is currently prohibited by Part 7 of the Financial Services Act 2012 ('the FSA 2012'), which came into force on 1 April, 2013, and repealed[193] the provisions formally found in FSMA, s 397. The earliest incarnation of similar offences was contained in the Prevention of Fraud (Investments) Act 1953.

Offence-creating provision

35.191 Part 7 of the FSA 2012 creates three different offences, one of which is new. The first two offences, contained in ss 89 and 90, broadly replicate the offences which were previously contained in FSMA, s 397, but with some modification which will render the offences easier to prove; they cover misleading *statements* and dishonest concealments (s 89) and

---

[191] [2011] 1 Cr App R 16.

[192] *R v Butt* [2006] EWCA 137 (Crim); *R v Spearman*, unreported, Southwark CC, 4 June 2004. Spearman received 30 months' imprisonment for insider dealing. He and his wife had received inside information from a man who worked as a proofreader for a company which printed confidential documentation in relation to company mergers and acquisitions. He had invested over £2 million in various different stocks and had made an illicit profit in excess of £200,000.

[193] s 95.

misleading *conduct* (s 90) in relation to investments. Conduct which may be charged under s 89 includes, for example, a situation in which a director makes an unduly favourable profit forecast, realizing that this may prevent existing shareholders from disposing of their stock in the company, or where an investor lies about the cash balance of a company at a time when he is seeking to dispose of his shares. Section 90 covers misleading *practices*, such as market manipulation by the conduct of artificial trades, designed to create the impression that there is more interest in a particular stock than there truly is.

In addition to these two offences, s 91 creates a new offence of making a false or mis-   **35.192**
leading statement in relation to a relevant benchmark, which is defined[194] to include LIBOR,[195] and certain other, UK-based overnight and fixing rates. This provision was enacted as a direct response to the LIBOR fixing scandal, which broke in the summer of 2012. There was previously no specific statutory offence to cover the dishonest manipulation of such benchmark rates.[196] Since the new offence is confined to statements made 'in the course of arrangements for the setting of a relevant benchmark', it is in practice only those individuals who are closely connected with this process (for example because they are responsible for submitting a 'Panel Bank's' [197] daily rate to NYSE Euronext, for the purpose of LIBOR calculation) who are likely to be at risk of transgressing it. It is not, primarily, of concern to company directors and will not therefore be considered further as part of this work.

Misleading statements

There are three elements which the prosecution must prove to make out an offence of mak-   **35.193**
ing a misleading statement contrary to FSA 2012, s 89. The prosecution must prove that the defendant:

(1) made a misleading statement or concealed any material facts;
(2) with the requisite state of mind in relation to either the accuracy of the statement or the fact of the concealment respectively; and
(3) acted with the intention of inducing any person to act or refrain from acting in a way specified in s 89(2), or was reckless as to whether the statement/concealment would have that effect.

Where the prosecution relies on a positive, misleading 'statement', this term clearly covers all   **35.194**
formal announcements made about a company or its business by its officers. For example, public profit warnings, company reports and accounts, as well as statements made by directors in meetings with individuals or groups of investors will all fall well within the terms of the offence. However, the subsection is wide enough to embrace in addition all private remarks made about a particular investment by individual shareholders, investors, traders, or any other person.

---

[194] By s 93(4) (and by the Financial Services Act 2012 (Misleading Statements and Impressions) Order 2013/637).

[195] The London Interbank Offered Rate.

[196] Note, however, that in August 2015, Tom Hayes was convicted of eight counts of conspiracy to defraud, and was sentenced to 14 years imprisonment, for his role in orchestrating large-scale LIBOR rigging at two successive banks for which he worked in the 2000s. Other individuals are currently being prosecuted for similar alleged conduct—also under pre-existing fraud law.

[197] ie a bank which is a member of the pool of banks from whose daily submissions of offered rates LIBOR is calculated.

35.195 To make out an offence where a positive misstatement is alleged, the statement must be 'false or misleading in a material respect'. Where a series of statements are made, it would be contrary to common sense to examine each in isolation to establish whether it is misleading. It is perfectly permissible to view all of the statements together in order to determine the overall effect.[198]

35.196 The *actus reus* of s 89 is also made out where any person who conceals any material facts,[199] whether in connection with a positive statement or otherwise.[200] It is submitted that this part of the section is just as wide in its reach as the remainder of the provision; it is not restricted in its scope to directors who have positive duties in relation to the disclosure of matters concerning a company's business.

35.197 Where the prosecution relies upon a positive statement, it must prove that the defendant, at the time he made the statement, knew that it was false or misleading in a material respect, or that he was reckless to the same.[201] Knowledge means actual knowledge, as opposed to suspicion or even belief, but evidence that a person 'wilfully shut his eyes to the truth' may be treated as evidence that in fact he knew what he was attempting to ignore.[202] Recklessness in this context has been held to mean a 'rash statement ... with no real basis of fact to support it and not caring whether it was true or false': *R v Page*.[203] This case was decided in relation to the Financial Services Act 1986, and before the decision of the House of Lords in *R v G*,[204] in which various definitions of recklessness persisting in the criminal law were considered and standardized. *Page* was not considered in the opinions of their Lordships, neither was it cited in argument. An application of *R v G* to FSA, s 89 would result in the test for recklessness in this part of the section being 'that the defendant knew of the risk that the statement was misleading (false or deceptive)'. However, since this decision of the House of Lords there has been first-instance precedent of the application of *Page* to FSMA, s 397 (the legislative forerunner to the current offences).[205] It is submitted that *Page* provides a peculiarly culpable form of recklessness, and therefore a greater hurdle to the prosecution in proving the elements of its case.

35.198 Where the prosecution relies on a positive misstatement, dishonesty is not an essential element of the offence, although of course it may be present, particularly where the statement is made with knowledge as to its false nature. However, even a person who recklessly makes a false statement might in some circumstances also act dishonestly, for example if he deliberately gives the impression that he has carefully verified the accuracy of what he says.

---

[198] *Aaron's Reefs Ltd v Twiss* [1896] AC 273, HL.

[199] 'Facts' includes a person's present intention: *R v Central Criminal Court, ex p Young* [2002] 2 Cr App R 12, DC, decided in relation to the 1986 Act, s 47. Therefore a director who dishonestly conceals his own plan to take a particular position in relation to a stock falls within the terms of sub-s (1)(c), creating a significant degree of overlap between this offence and the offence under s 90, as to which see below from para 35.204 below.

[200] Sub-s (1)(c).

[201] Sub-s (1)(b).

[202] *Warner v Metropolitan Police Commissioner* [1969] 2 AC 256, 279, HL, per Lord Reid. See also re 'knowingly' (in the context of fraudulent trading) *Re Bank of Credit and Commerce International SA (No 15)* [2004] 2 BCLC 479, [2005] 2 BCLC 328, CA.

[203] [1996] Crim LR 821, CA.

[204] [2004] 1 AC 1034, HL.

[205] *R v Rigby, Bailey and anor*, Southwark Crown Court, 2005.

Where the prosecution relies on the concealment of material facts in order to prove the **35.199** charge, then it is obliged to prove that the defendant acted dishonestly.[206] Dishonesty is an issue of fact upon which no specific direction is usually given by a trial judge; where direction is required, it is the *Ghosh* test which applies.[207]

By s 89(2), a person who makes the misleading statement or dishonestly conceals the mater- **35.200** ial facts is guilty of an offence only if he acts with the intention of inducing, or is reckless as to whether he may induce, another person to either:

(1) enter into, offer to enter into, or refrain from entering or offering to enter into a relevant agreement which relates to a relevant investment;[208] or

(2) exercise, or refrain from exercising, any rights conferred by a relevant investment[209] (eg shares or stock held in the share capital of any company).[210]

The person whom it is intended to induce or who may be induced by the statement/conceal- **35.201** ment need not be the same person to whom the misleading statement was made, or from whom the material fact was concealed.[211] Further, it is not necessary for the inducement to be effective in order for the offence to be made out.

In relation to the possibility of inducement, it is submitted that the test of recklessness which **35.202** should be applied is that contained in *R v G*.[212] A person is reckless for the purpose of s 89(1) (a) and (b) if he is aware of a risk of inducement and unreasonably goes on to take that risk by making the misleading statement/concealing the material facts.

Where a person is charged with having made a statement which he knew to be false or mis- **35.203** leading in a material respect (but not where the charge is one of recklessly making a statement or dishonestly concealing material facts), sub-s (3) provides three specific defences. It is a defence for the accused to show that the defendant acted in conformity with price stabilizing rules, control of information rules, or the relevant provisions of Commission Regulation (EC) No 2273/2003. These defences are similar in their effect to one of the special defences to a charge of insider dealing provided by the Criminal Justice Act 2003, Schedule 1.[213]

Misleading practices

The second offence contained in Part 7 of the FSA 2012 applies, by s 90, to a person who **35.204** does any act, or engages in any course of conduct, which creates a false or misleading impres- sion as to the market in or the price or value of any relevant investments.[214] Conduct falling within the terms of this offence would include a major shareholder of a company who wishes

---

[206] Sub-s (1)(b).

[207] *R v Ghosh* [1982] QB 1053, CA; *R v Roberts (W)* (1985) 84 Cr App R 117, CA.

[208] s 93(3)(a) and Financial Services Act 2012 (Misleading Statements and Impressions) Order 2013/637, art. 2.

[209] s 93(3) and Financial Services Act 2012 (Misleading Statements and Impressions) Order 2013/637, art. 2.

[210] s 93(5) and Financial Services Act 2012 (Misleading Statements and Impressions) Order 2013/637, art. 4 and Financial Services and Markets Act 2000 (Financial Promotion) Order 2005/1529, Schedule 1, para 14.

[211] s 89(2).

[212] [2004] 1 AC 1034, HL.

[213] Para 35.206 below.

[214] As to the meaning of 'relevant investment', see para 35.200 above and the footnotes to that paragraph.

to sell his entire holding, but who first contrives a number of small transactions between himself and an anonymous associate, in order to give the impression that there is interest in the stock, thereby raising its value before disposing of the bulk of his shares.

35.205 In its previous incarnation (under FSMA, s 397), the offence of misleading market practices could not be committed recklessly. That position has been changed by FSA 2012, s 90 making the new version of this offence significantly wider and easier to prove. There is also, under s 90, a new form of this offence which resembles Fraud Act 2006 offences. In summary, under s 90 it is now incumbent on the prosecution to prove that the defendant:

(1) intended to create the impression and acted with the intention of inducing another person to acquire, dispose of, subscribe for, or underwrite the relevant investments, or from exercising any rights conferred by those investments, or to refrain from doing any of the above, or

(b) intended to create the impression, knowing that it was false or misleading or being reckless as to the same, and either intending or being aware that it was likely that such action would result in the making of a gain for himself or another or the causing of a loss to another.[215]

35.206 Section 90(9) creates four defences to a charge under this provision. The first provides that, where the first form of the offence described immediately above is relied on by the prosecution, it is a defence for a person to show that he reasonably believed his conduct would not create an impression that was false or misleading. Other paragraphs of sub-s (9) provide defences that are similar in terms to the defences to an offence under s 89 provided by sub-s (3):[216] they concern price stabilization, the control of information rules, and the provisions of Commission Regulation (EC) No 2273/2003.

Jurisdiction

35.207 The jurisdictional extent of offences under ss 89 and 90 is governed by ss 89(4) and 90(10). Under the former, the statement or concealment in question, or the person whom it is intended to induce or who may be induced, or the formation of the relevant agreement, must take place/be in the UK. For the false practices offence, either the defendant's conduct or the false or misleading impression created must take place in the UK.

Penalties

35.208 The maximum penalty for market rigging is, by s 92, on summary conviction in the magistrates' court a fine not exceeding the statutory maximum or imprisonment for a term not exceeding 12 months. On conviction on indictment before the Crown Court, a defendant is liable to a fine or imprisonment for a term not exceeding seven years or both. For discussion of the appropriate penalty in a case where a company director had recklessly made misleading statements see *R v Rigby and another*.[217]

---

[215] Gain and loss have the same meaning as under the Fraud Act 2006, and are limited to gain or loss of money or property of some other kind.

[216] Para 35.203 above.

[217] [2005] EWCA 3487 (Crim).

H. Causing a Financial Institution to Fail

35.209 In March 2016, an entirely new criminal offence of causing a financial institution to fail came into force, under ss 36–38 of the Financial Services (Banking Reform) Act 2013. Not all company directors will be capable of committing such an offence; it applies only to 'senior managers in relation to financial institutions'.[218] Any such manager will be liable where he takes or agrees to take a decision on behalf of the financial institution as to the way in which the business of a group institution[219] is to be carried on, or fails to take steps he could take to prevent such a decision be taken, where the implementation of the decision causes the failure of the group institution. The mental element of the offence is that the manager was (when taking the decision etc) aware of a risk that this would be the result. There is also an additional fault element: it is necessary for the prosecution to prove that the manager's conduct in relation to the decision was, in all the circumstances, far below what could reasonably be expected of a person in his position. The maximum penalty for the offence is, on summary conviction, twelve months' imprisonment and/or a fine, on indictment, seven years' imprisonment and/or a fine.

35.210 The offence carries highly specific elements, including the unusual event of the failure of a bank or other financial institution and a causation requirement. It also requires proof of a particularly egregious fault element: conduct falling 'far below' what could reasonably be expected. For all these reasons it is expected that prosecutions under this section will be few and far between.

I. Companies Act Offences

(1) Introduction

35.211 Like its predecessors, the 2006 Act contains a raft of criminal sanctions in respect of misconduct of diverse kinds and orders of seriousness. The 2006 Act contains provisions which enact (or re-enact) criminal liabilities for company directors in respect of: (i) record-keeping, (ii) accounting and auditors, (iii) disclosure of interests, (iv) wrongful disclosure of information, (v) issuing of shares, (vi) the company's acquisition of its own shares, and (vii) removal from the register.[220]

35.212 The 2006 Act also contains the principal provision in English law against fraudulent trading. This offence, which is the most serious offence under the 2006 Act, will be discussed separately below.

35.213 Many of the offences under the 2006 Act apply to both the company and 'every officer of the company who is in default'. In these sections 'officer' includes any director, manager,[221] or

---

[218] s 36(1)(a).

[219] Which could be the financial institution on whose behalf the decision is made, or any other institution within its group. See subs-s (2).

[220] Note that loans to directors and connected persons ceased to be criminal offences on 1 October 2007, when ss 330–47 of the 1985 Act were repealed by the Companies Act 2006 Commencement Order No 3, Art 8 and Sch 2.

[221] It has been held that the word 'manager' should not be too narrowly construed, that it is not to be equated with a managing or other director or general manager, and that it describes any person who in the affairs of the company exercises a supervisory control which reflects the general policy of the company for the time being or

secretary and any person who is to be treated as an officer of the company for the purposes of the provision in question and an officer is 'in default' if he authorizes or permits, participates in, or fails to take all reasonable steps to prevent, the contravention.[222] Some sections of the 2006 Act specifically provide that a shadow director is treated as an officer of the company.[223] A company may be an officer of another company. In this situation, it does not commit an offence unless one of its officers is in default and, where that is the position, both the corporate officer and its own officers are liable to be prosecuted.[224]

(2) Classification

Three classes

35.214   The wide variety of criminal provisions contained in the 2006 Act may be classified into three groups:

(1) those which create serious offences, which are triable on indictment, carrying a maximum penalty of an unlimited fine and in some cases a sentence of imprisonment, or summarily, in which case the maximum penalty is a fine not exceeding the statutory maximum (currently £5,000);[225]

(2) those which create intermediate offences, which are triable only summarily but which carry a maximum penalty of a level 5 fine;[226] and

(3) quasi-regulatory offences, which are triable only summarily and which carry a maximum penalty of a level 2 or 3 fine only.

35.215   In addition to the offences created by the Act itself, the Act contains provision for the creation of Corporate Governance Regulations by the Secretary of State.[227] These regulations may create offences, including criminal offences, but these may only be tried summarily and the maximum penalty may not exceed the statutory maximum fine.[228]

35.216   By the Criminal Justice Act 1982, s 37, the standard scale of maximum fines for summary offences is:

Level on the scale	Amount of fine
1	£200
2	£500
3	£1,000
4	£2,500
5	£5,000

35.217   Each class of offence contained within the 2006 Act is distinguished not only by the maximum sentence in terms of imprisonment or fine, but by the consequences which flow with

---

which is related to the general administration of the company: *Re a Company (No 00996 of 1979)* [1980] Ch 138, 144, CA, per Shaw LJ.

[222] 2006 Act, s 1121.
[223] eg 2006 Act, s 162(6). Shadow director is defined by 2006 Act, s 251.
[224] 2006 Act, s 1122.
[225] This is set by the Magistrates' Courts Act 1980, s 32, but a different sum may be substituted by order under s 143 of that Act.
[226] ie level 5 on the standard scale under the Criminal Justice Act 1982.
[227] s 173.
[228] s 1273(4).

regard to the Company Directors Disqualification Act 1986 (CDDA) (as to which see Section K below). Only offences in the first class of serious offences will give rise on conviction to the broad discretion to disqualify an individual from acting as a director (for up to 15 years if on indictment, five years summarily) under the CDDA, s 2. However, conviction of more than three intermediate or quasi-regulatory offences in a five-year period may also give the magistrates' court power to disqualify under the CDDA, s 5.[229]

A final distinction between the quasi-regulatory offences and the more serious offences contained in the Act is that it may be open to a prosecutor to argue that quasi-regulatory offences (punishable with a maximum of a £1,000 fine) are not criminal offences within the meaning of Article 6 of the ECHR. If such an argument were upheld in respect of any offence, the primary effect would be that statements made under compulsion (further to the exercise of a compulsory information requirement under this Act or any other statute) prima facie would be admissible in order to prove that offence against the maker of the statement.[230] **35.218**

(3) Serious offences under the Companies Act 2006

This chapter does not discuss the numerous intermediate and quasi-regulatory offences in the 2006 Act;[231] instead it concentrates on the offences contained in the 2006 Act which are classified as serious in that they may be tried on indictment. For the vast majority of these serious offences the maximum penalty is a fine, but a few carry a maximum penalty of two years' imprisonment. Some of the important features of these most serious offences are discussed in the following paragraphs. **35.219**

Accounting records

Every officer of the company in default commits an offence if the company fails to keep adequate accounting records in accordance with s 386 and fails to keep them at the registered office and available for inspection by the company's officers in accordance with s 388(1) and (3).[232] An officer charged with these offences has a defence if he acted honestly and in the circumstances in which the company's business was carried on the default was excusable.[233] An officer also commits an offence if he fails to take all reasonable steps to secure that a company's accounting records are not preserved for the applicable period (six years for a private company and 12 years for a public company) or if he intentionally causes the company to default.[234] **35.220**

Knowledge and recklessness

Several of these serious offences under the 2006 Act refer to concepts of knowledge or recklessness in relation to the provision of information or explanations to an independent person such as the independent assessor of a poll of members of a quoted company,[235] the auditors,[236] the registrar,[237] **35.221**

---

[229] Section J below.
[230] On this topic, see further paras 35.36 *et seq* above and in particular *R v K* [2010] QB 343.
[231] Many examples can be found in Ch 26 in relation to contravention of requirements about accounting records, annual accounts and reports, audit, and provision of information to the Registrar (formerly the annual return).
[232] 2006 Act, ss 387(1) and 389.
[233] 2006 Act, ss 387(2) and 389(1)
[234] 2006 Act, ss 388(4) and 389(3).
[235] 2006 Act, 350.
[236] 2006 Act, ss 418 and 501.
[237] 2006 Act, s 1112.

or an independent valuer.[238] The concepts are also used in relation to statements in the directors' report for each financial year or the directors' statement under s 571 concerning the disapplication of pre-emption rights by special resolution.[239] For a discussion of these concepts, see paragraph 35.197 above.

Misleading, false, or deceptive

35.222   The phrase 'misleading, false, or deceptive' in relation to statements or the provision of information or explanations is used frequently in the offences that carry a maximum sentence of two years' imprisonment.[240] Comment on these matters is at paragraph 35.108 above. See also paragraph 35.195 above.

Preservation of capital

35.223   The 2006 Act relaxed the procedure for private companies reducing their capital. Now they can do so without applying to court for sanction provided that the directors make a solvency statement in accordance with s 643. That section makes it an offence for a director to make a solvency statement, which is delivered to the registrar, without having reasonable grounds for the opinion expressed in it.

35.224   The company and every officer in default commits an offence if the company contravenes s 658, which prohibits a limited company from acquiring its own shares, whether by purchase, subscription, or otherwise, except in accordance with the provisions of the 2006 Act, Part 18. A private limited company may redeem or purchase its own shares out of capital, provided that, among other things, the directors make a solvency statement in accordance with s 714. The directors commit an offence if they make such a statement without having reasonable grounds for the opinion expressed in it.

Financial assistance to acquire public company's own shares

35.225   It is an offence contrary to the 2006 Act, s 680 to contravene the prohibitions contained in ss 678 and 679 against a company (or its subsidiary) giving financial assistance directly or indirectly to a person who is acquiring or proposing to acquire shares in that company, for the purpose of the acquisition before or at the same time the acquisition takes place. Unlike the equivalent, repealed offences previously contained in the 1985 Act, these provisions apply only to transactions involving a public company. They apply in two situations: (i) where the company in which shares are acquired is a public company (s 678(1) and (3)), and (ii) where the acquisition is of shares in a private company of which a public company is subsidiary. Note that the 2006 Act, s 680 (like the 1985 Act, s 151(3)) has the effect of making individual directors criminally liable for a default of these provisions, on pain of imprisonment.

35.226   The phrase 'financial assistance' does not have a technical meaning; instead the court identifies the commercial realities of the transaction, bearing in mind that the purpose of the prohibition is to prevent the resources of the target company and its subsidiaries being used directly or indirectly to assist the purchaser to make the acquisition to the possible prejudice

---

[238] 2006 Act, ss 1153, concerning independent valuations for the purposes of s 93 (re-registration as public company; recent allotment of shares for non-cash consideration), 593 (allotment of shares of public company in consideration of non-cash asset), and 599 (transfer of non-cash asset to public company).

[239] 2006 Act, ss 418 and 572.

[240] 2006 Act, ss 350, 501, 572, 747, 814, 1112.

of the creditors of the target or its group or the remaining shareholders.[241] It is not, however, necessarily detrimental to the target or its group.[242] Thus there is financial assistance where the target company pays an excessive price for an asset and the money is used to buy shares in the target;[243] where a company agrees to pay consultancy services to its shareholder directors to induce two of them to sell their shares to the third for nominal amounts;[244] or where a subsidiary pays for accountants' due diligence fees in connection with the acquisition of its parent's shares.[245] On the other hand, assistance must amount to financial help of some kind, not simply the short circuiting of process for the sake of convenience.[246] There is further discussion of these issues in Chapter 27, Section C(5) above.

Note that it is not *in itself* a defence to a charge under s 680 for a director to have acted in the best interests of the company. Motive (to benefit the company) must always be distinguished from purpose (acquisition of company shares): see *Chaston* above. However, the 2006 Act, ss 678(4) and 679(4) (like the 1985 Act, s 151) provide a defence to a charge under these provisions where the assistance is given in good faith in the interests of the company and the company's principal purpose in giving assistance was not to reduce or discharge any liability incurred by a person for the purpose of the acquisition of shares; or the reduction or discharge of any such liability was only an incidental part of some larger purpose of the company. **35.227**

Note also that the 2006 Act, ss 681 and 682 contain a number of unconditional and conditional exceptions to the prohibition on financial assistance. The unconditional exceptions include: dividends lawfully made, distribution in the course of winding up, allotment of bonus shares, a reduction of capital under Chapter 10 of Part 17, and a redemption or purchase of shares under Chapter 3 of Part 18. The conditional exceptions include transactions where: the company lends money as part of its ordinary business or the company provides financial assistance for the purposes of an employees' share scheme in good faith in the interests of the company or its holding company. **35.228**

(4) Fraudulent trading

By far the most serious offence under the 2006 Act is fraudulent trading, the maximum penalty being ten years' imprisonment. This is an increase from seven years' imprisonment, which was the maximum penalty for the equivalent offence under the 1985 Act, s 458. For the civil aspects of fraudulent trading under the Insolvency Act, s 213, see Chapter 34, Section C(2) above. **35.229**

The 2006 Act, s 993(1) and (2) provides: **35.230**

(1) If any business of a company is carried on with intent to defraud creditors of the company or creditors of any other person, or for any fraudulent purpose, every person who is knowingly a party to the carrying on of the business in that manner commits an offence.
(2) This applies whether or not the company has been, or is in the course of being, wound up.

---

[241] *Chaston v SWP Group Ltd* [2003] 1 BCLC 675, CA at paras 31 and 32, per Arden LJ; *MT Realisations Ltd v Digital Equipment Co Ltd* [2003] 2 BCLC 117, CA, at para 28.
[242] *Chaston v SWP Group Ltd* [2003] 1 BCLC 675, CA at paras 38–40, per Arden LJ; *MT Realisations Ltd v Digital Equipment Co Ltd* [2003] 2 BCLC 117, CA at para 32, per Mummery LJ.
[243] *Belmont Finance Corporation Ltd v Williams Furniture Ltd (No 2)* [1980] 1 All ER 393, CA, a case on the 1948 Act, s 54.
[244] *Macpherson v European Strategic Bureau Ltd* [2000] 2 BCLC 683, CA.
[245] *Chaston v SWP Group Ltd* [2003] 1 BCLC 675, CA.
[246] *MT Realisations Ltd v Digital Equipment Co Ltd* [2003] 2 BCLC 117, CA.

35.231 This provision is identical to the 1985 Act, s 458. Therefore, although the cases cited below pertain to the old s 458, they are equally relevant to the offence in its new statutory form. The section creates two different offences: (i) carrying on a business with intent to defraud creditors and (ii) carrying on a business for any other fraudulent purpose.[247]

Business carried on

35.232 Business may be 'carried on' even where it has ceased all trading activities, with the debt collection and the payment of creditors.[248] In addition, one large transaction may constitute the carrying on of business,[249] although the section is not aimed at individual transactions.

Knowingly party to the carrying on of the business

35.233 It was said by Lord Lane CJ in *R v Grantham*[250] that the section is intended to cover those who are 'running the business', and that 'party to the carrying on of the business' must therefore be interpreted to mean those people exercising control or management. It is submitted that the effect of this is to place a different meaning on the word 'party' in this section than is to be found elsewhere in the criminal law (where party means nothing more than an active participant, rather than someone in control).[251]

35.234 A financial adviser does not become party to the carrying on of the business by failing to advise the directors that the company is insolvent and should cease trading.[252] (It is submitted that he would be unlikely to become a party, even if the word was interpreted as it normally is in the context of the criminal law.)[253]

35.235 A problem with Lord Lane CJ's interpretation of the provision may arise when one considers the position of a person who is not responsible for or in any way involved in the management or running of the company or its business but who nevertheless knowingly participates in the fraudulent acts themselves. The view has been expressed that such a person should be, and is, covered by the terms of the section.[254]

With intent to defraud creditors

35.236 Where the prosecution relies on proving an intention to defraud creditors (as opposed to some other fraudulent purpose) it is necessary to prove intent to defraud creditors in general. Therefore evidence that, for a short period, one creditor was in fact defrauded may be insufficient to make out the offence.[255] In addition, the fraud must be aimed at actual, rather than potential creditors.[256] (In contrast, where the prosecution alleges 'any other fraudulent purpose', potential creditors may suffice.)[257] Note that, in common with common law conspiracy to defraud, but unlike modern Fraud Act offences, the required intent to 'defraud'

---

[247] *R v Inman* [1967] 1 QB 140.
[248] *Re Sarflax Ltd* [1979] Ch 140.
[249] *Re Gerald Cooper Chemicals* [1978] Ch 262.
[250] [1984] QB 675, CA. His words were later approved in *R v Miles* [1992] Crim L R 657, CA.
[251] Section A of this chapter.
[252] *Re Maidstone Building Provisions Ltd* [1971] 1 WLR 1085.
[253] Section A of this chapter.
[254] *Re Augustus Barnett & Sons Ltd* [1986] BCLC 170 per Hoffmann J.
[255] *Morphitis v Bercansoni* [2003] Ch 552.
[256] *R v Inman* [1967] 1 QB 140.
[257] *R v Kemp* [1988] 1 QB 645.

creditors is not restricted to situations in which fraud has the potential to cause a loss of (or affect) money or property.[258]

The offence requires proof of dishonesty[259] in the *Ghosh* sense.[260] Where the prosecution **35.237** alleges an intention to defraud creditors, the dishonesty must have been directed towards the creditors.[261]

In relation to 'intent to defraud' and in relation to fraudulent purpose in general, see Section **35.238** C of this chapter.

Sentencing

Doubtless because fraudulent trading always involves some form of deception of creditors, **35.239** under the 1985 Act, quite naturally many practitioners and judges took the view that *R v Clark*[262] (which sets tariff sentences for offences of theft committed in breach of trust, according to the value of the theft) was an appropriate guide to sentencing in fraudulent trading cases (substituting the value of the theft with the outstanding amount owed to creditors). However, there then came clear guidance from the Court of Appeal that this was not the correct approach: offences of fraudulent trading should be seen as less serious than offences of theft; the tariff figures contained in *Clark* should not be applied to fraudulent trading without adjustment downwards.[263] In a previous edition of this work it was submitted that this guidance will need to be reviewed in light of the increase in the maximum penalty for fraudulent trading from seven years (which was in line with the maximum penalty for theft) to one of ten years (in line with the maximum penalty for conspiracy to defraud and the new substantive fraud offences under the Fraud Act 2006). Subsequently, the Court of Appeal indicated, in *R v McCrae*[264] that it would be appropriate, in certain situations, to have regard to sentencing guidelines for confidence tricksters when sentencing for this type of offence. Since *McCrae,* the situation has changed again; in October 2014, a 'Definitive Guideline' was published by the Sentencing Council, for all offences of 'Fraud, Bribery and Money Laundering'. Although fraudulent trading is not specifically covered by the Guideline, applying the spirit of *McCrae*, it is submitted the criminal courts will have regard to it when sentencing in respect of this offence.

J. Insolvency Act Offences

(1) Introduction

There is a multiplicity of offences under the Insolvency Act 1986. This section will focus on **35.240** the principal criminal offences which may be committed by company directors specifically (as opposed to bankrupts).[265]

---

[258] See *R v Hollier* [2013] EWCA 2041, in which it was held that the fraudulent purpose, within the meaning of this offence, could take the form of disguising a particular person's ownership and control of the trading company.

[259] *R v Cox and Hodges* (1982) 75 Cr App R 291.

[260] Paras 35.59–35.63 above.

[261] *R v Smith* [1996] 2 Cr App R 1.

[262] [1998] Cr App R 137, CA.

[263] *R v Gibson* [1999] 2 Cr App R(S) 52.

[264] [2013] 1 Cr App R (S) 1.

[265] Insolvency Act, Part IX deals with offences which may be committed by bankrupts.

(2) Directors' liabilities

35.241 Under the Insolvency Act, company directors may attract criminal liability for a very wide variety of misconduct: (i) when making a statutory declaration of a company's insolvency; (ii) in relation to a company's creditors; (iii) in relation to a moratorium; (iv) in relation to winding up and liquidation; (v) in relation to the company's administrator; (vi) in relation to record-keeping.

35.242 Most of these offences may be committed by the company and by its officers. In relation to some offences, the Insolvency Act, s 432[266] makes special provision for the liability of company directors which is wider in ambit than the general doctrine of secondary liability under the criminal law.

35.243 A helpful summary of all punishable offences under the Insolvency Act 1986, together with the mode of trial and maximum penalty attaching to each offence, can be found in Schedule 10 to the Act itself. (In addition, a summary of offences under the Insolvency Rules 1986 can be found in Schedule 5 to the Rules, and from 6 April 2017 Schedule 3 of the Insolvency Rules 2016.)

(3) Principal offences under Insolvency Act, Part IV

35.244 The Insolvency Act, Part IV contains the principal offences which may be committed by company directors before and during the liquidation of the company. The offences that relate to conduct before the winding up are fraud in anticipation of winding up and transactions in fraud of creditors.[267] The offences that relate to conduct during the winding up are misconduct in course of winding up, falsification of a company's books, material omissions from a statement relating to company's affairs, and false representations to creditors.[268] Finally s 216 makes it an offence of strict liability[269] to reuse the company's name after it has gone into liquidation, except in prescribed circumstances.[270]

35.245 In relation to the offence of fraud in anticipation of winding up (s 206), note that where the prosecution rely on sub-s (1)(b) (fraudulently removing company property to the value of £500 or more), 'removing' includes diverting. Therefore, where an officer of the company transfers company money to a third party for the purpose of an honest transaction, but the transaction does not go ahead and the money is returned to the officer, the officer is liable under s 206(1)(b) if, at that point, he fraudulently fails to return the money to the company: see *R v Robinson*.[271] Note further that company property includes the fruit of company property, at least where that fruit is compiled by an officer of the company: *R v McCredie, R v French*.[272] The expression 'book or paper affecting or relating to the company's property' should be given a practical meaning, reflecting current usage, so that it includes electronic records.[273]

---

[266] Para 35.11 above.
[267] Insolvency Act, ss 206 and 207.
[268] Insolvency Act, ss 208–11.
[269] *R v Cole* [1998] 2 BCLC 234.
[270] See Ch 34, Section D above for civil implications.
[271] [1990] BCC 656.
[272] [2000] 2 BCLC 438, CA.
[273] *R v Taylor* [2011] 1 WLR 1809, CA, following *R v McCredie* [2000] 2 BCLC 438, CA, and *R (Griffin) v Richmond Magistrates' Court* [2008] 1 WLR 1525, CA.

Where misconduct in the course of winding up is charged (s 208), note that an officer of the **35.246**
company has a duty actively to disclose to the liquidator the company's property, books, and
papers, and therefore may be criminally liable for failure to meet that obligation even where
no prior request for delivery has been made: *R v McCredie, R v French*.[274]

Several of the offences contained in Part IV of the Act are subject to a provision that it is a **35.247**
defence for an accused 'to prove' that he had no intent to defraud. Note that these provisions
do not have the effect of reversing the burden of proof; the defendant is subject only to an
evidential burden to raise its lack of intent as an issue. See further: *R v Carass*.[275]

(4) Sentence

All of the offences in ss 206–11 and 216 are triable either way (that is, before the magistrates **35.248**
or before the Crown Court). With the exception of offences under ss 207 and 216 (for which
the maximum penalty on indictment is two years' imprisonment, or a fine, or both) the
maximum penalty for each offence on indictment is seven years' imprisonment, or a fine,
or both.[276]

A conviction for any offence which involves fraud by a director against the company or its **35.249**
creditors is very likely to result in the imposition of a period of immediate custody. For example, a conviction for failing to make full and true disclosure of a company's property to the
liquidator during winding up contrary to the 1986 Act, s 208(1)(a) has been held to warrant
a sentence of nine months' imprisonment (together with an order under the CDDA of two
years' disqualification).[277]

K. The Company Directors Disqualification Act 1986

(1) Introduction

The CDDA has three significant effects so far as the criminal law is concerned. First, it pro- **35.250**
vides for the penalty of disqualification to be imposed against individuals (whether they are
currently company directors or not) on conviction of criminal offences. Secondly it enacts
a further criminal offence of contravening a director's disqualification order. Thirdly, it prohibits (on pain of criminal conviction) undischarged bankrupts from acting as directors. The
civil aspects of the disqualification of directors are considered in Chapter 31.

(2) The penalty of disqualification

The CDDA, s 1(1) provides: **35.251**

> (1) In the circumstances specified below in this Act a court may, and under sections 6 and 9A
> shall, make against a person a disqualification order, that is to say an order that for a period
> specified in the order—

---

[274] [2000] 2 BCLC 438, CA. See also *R v Taylor* [2011] 1 WLR 1809, where the director was guilty of failing
to disclose vehicles which remained in the company's possession after termination of HP contracts.
[275] [2002] 1 WLR 1714, CA.
[276] See the Insolvency Act 1986, Sch 10.
[277] *R v Bevis*, The Times, 8 February 2001, CA; *R v Taylor* [2011] 1 WLR 1809 where a sentence of
16 months' imprisonment was upheld in a case where, through concealment, the director had effectively stolen
money from the company and enjoyed the use of vehicles.

> (a) he shall not be a director of a company, act as a receiver of a company's property, or in any way, whether directly or indirectly, be concerned or take part in the promotion, formation or management of a company unless (in each case) he has the leave of the court, and
>
> (b) he shall not act as an insolvency practitioner.

35.252 A disqualification order under the CDDA prohibits the subject of the order from acting as a director in fact. The effect of the order cannot be circumvented by the subject's acting unofficially or informally, or by acting as a director in fact but under a different title. This is ensured by the wide terms of s 1(1)(a) itself and by the interpretation section of the statute, which defines 'director' to include anyone who occupies the position of a director, by whatever name.[278]

Discretionary disqualification on conviction of indictable offence

35.253 The circumstances in which a court may make a disqualification order (ie an order described in the CDDA, s 1(1)) are defined by the CDDA, s 2. They exist where a person is convicted of an indictable offence (on indictment or summarily) in connection with the promotion, formation, management, liquidation, or striking off of a company; with the receivership of a company's property; or with his being an administrative receiver of a company.[279] Since 26 May 2015, the type of company to which the offence may be connected in order to trigger this power has been extended to include overseas companies.[280]

35.254 The following courts are empowered to make a discretionary disqualification order of this kind: any court having jurisdiction to wind up the company in relation to which the offence was committed; in relation to an overseas company not falling within the previous category, the High Court; the court before which the person is convicted of the offence, or (in the case of summary conviction) any other magistrates' court in the same local justice area.[281]

35.255 The maximum period of a discretionary disqualification of this kind is, before a magistrates' court, five years and in any other case, 15 years.[282]

35.256 'In connection with the promotion, formation or management' of a company has been given a wide interpretation by the courts. For example, 'management' is not limited to the internal supervision of the ordinary and legitimate affairs of a company. The correct test is whether the offence had some relevant factual connection with the company.[283] A disqualification order may therefore be made in respect of a crime committed in the course of the trading activities of a company (eg insider trading[284] or the former offence of obtaining by deception).[285]

35.257 The discretion given to the courts by the CDDA, s 2 is unlike the mandatory power exercised by judges of the Chancery Division (which requires an express finding that the person concerned is guilty of conduct which makes him unfit to be concerned in the management of a

---

[278] CDDA, s 22(4).
[279] CDDA, s 2(1).
[280] CDDA, s 2(1A).
[281] CDDA, s 2(2).
[282] CDDA, s 2(3).
[283] *R v Goodman* [1993] 2 All ER 789, CA.
[284] *R v Goodman* (n 283 above).
[285] *R v Corbin* (1984) 6 Cr App R (S) 17.

company). Section 2 gives the sentencing court a completely general discretion to impose an additional sanction in respect of criminal offences connected with the running of companies and no other condition precedent must be established in order to justify the exercise of the power.[286]

The primary purpose of a disqualification order is to protect the public and therefore a **35.258** period of disqualification may be appropriate in respect of accounting offences where there is no suggestion of dishonesty, but where there is a degree of carelessness or incompetence from which the public require protection.[287] However, disqualification also forms part of the punishment for a criminal offence and therefore its imposition and length must bear some correlation to the gravity of the offence in respect of which the defendant has been convicted. It is not appropriate, for example, to combine a disqualification order with a conditional discharge.[288] In addition, long disqualification orders (above ten years) should be reserved for particularly serious cases (including cases where the director has previously been disqualified).[289]

Note that where a criminal court does not exercise its power to order disqualification under **35.259** ss 1 and 2 of the Act (either because it not invited to do so, or declines to do so), a subsequent attempt by the Secretary of State to obtain a disqualification order via the civil courts may amount to an abuse of process.[290]

Disqualification for three default notices/failure to file returns etc

Under the CDDA, s 5, on summary conviction for an offence of contravening companies **35.260** legislation requiring a return, account, or other document to be filed with the Registrar of Companies, a person who has been convicted (on indictment or summarily) within a five-year period (ending on the date of this summary conviction but including any other qualifying offences of which he is convicted on that day) of at least three default orders and offences of the same kind may be disqualified by the magistrates' court for a period of up to five years.

(3) Undischarged bankrupts: contravention of a disqualification order

By s 11 of the CCDA 1986, it is a criminal offence for a person to act as a director of a **35.261** company[291] or indirectly or directly take part in or be concerned in the promotion, formation, or management of a company, without leave of the court, at a time when: (i) he is an undischarged bankrupt; or (ii) a bankruptcy restrictions order is in force in respect of him.

The offence is one of strict liability,[292] as Henry LJ explained in *R v Brockley*: **35.262**

> Strict liability will oblige those who have been adjudicated bankrupt to ensure that their bankruptcy has, in fact, been discharged before they engage in any of the forbidden activities in relation to a company. If mens rea were required, then a bankrupt who lay low, buried his head

---

[286] *R v Young* (1990) 12 Cr App R (S) 262.

[287] *R v Victor* [1999] 2 Cr App R (S) 102.

[288] *R v Young*, (n 286 above).

[289] *R v Millard* (1993) 15 Cr App R (S) 445. For examples of facts justifying disqualification for between eight and ten years, see *R v Devol* (1992) 14 Cr App R (S) 407; *R v Ahmed* [1997] 2 Cr App R (S) 8. For an example of facts justifying a three-year disqualification order, see *R v Thobani* [1998] 1 Cr App R 227.

[290] *Secretary of State for BIS v Weston* [2014] BCC 581.

[291] By sub-s (4), company includes an overseas company which has an established place of business within Great Britain.

[292] *R v Brockley* (1993) 99 Cr App R 385, CA; [1994] 1 BCLC 606; *R v Doring* [2003] 1 Cr App R 9, CA.

in the sand, and took part in the prohibited activities, would have a defence and an advantage not available to the responsible bankrupt who took steps to establish his position before taking part in such activities.[293]

35.263 The CDDA, s 13 provides that it is a criminal offence (inter alia) to act in contravention of a disqualification order or a disqualification undertaking.[294] The offence is punishable, on summary conviction, by imprisonment of six months, a fine up to the statutory maximum, or both. On indictment, the offence carries a maximum of two years' imprisonment, or a fine, or both.

35.264 A company is itself capable of being disqualified from acting as a director of another company. Where such an offence is committed by a company with the consent or connivance of, or was attributable to any neglect on the part of any director, manager, etc, or any person who was purporting to act in any such capacity, he as well as the company is guilty of the offence under s 13 and is liable to be punished accordingly.[295]

(4) Disqualification in respect of overseas convictions

35.265 The Small Business, Enterprise and Employment Act 2015[296] has inserted a new s 5A of the CDDA, empowering the Secretary of State to apply to the High Court for a disqualification order in respect of a person who has been convicted of a relevant foreign offence (namely, an offence which, if committed in England, would trigger a power of disqualification under s1 of the Act). Note that the Secretary of State may in some circumstances accept a disqualification order under s 1A of the Act, instead of seeking such an order from the court.

(5) Sentence

35.266 In *R v Theivendran*,[297] where the Court of Appeal reduced the sentence for eight offences of being concerned in management of a company while an undischarged bankrupt to six months, suspended. Farquharson LJ said:

> If the contravention has been flagrant, that is to say deliberate or reckless, a custodial sentence would in principle be appropriate. If, on the other hand, there are no aggravating features, such as previous offences of the same kind or personal profit gained in fraud of creditors, that may be taken into account as justifying suspension of the sentence in whole or in part.

That was a case where the defendant had pleaded guilty, there was no dishonesty, there were genuine trading activities and there was no suggestion of assets being salted away beyond the reach of creditors.

35.267 In *R v Harwood*[298] the defendant pleaded guilty to two counts of being concerned in management of a company while disqualified and one count of acting as an insolvency practitioner while unqualified. He was sentenced to a community service order and to a further period of

---

[293] [1994] 1 BCLC 606, 608, CA.
[294] As to which, see CCDA, s 1A. By s 13 a person who acts in contravention of CDDA s 12(2) (order made under the Insolvency Act, s 492(2)(b) where a person fails to pay under a county court administration order) also commits an offence.
[295] CDDA, s 14.
[296] SBEE Act 2015, s 104, which came fully into force on 1 October 2015.
[297] (1992) 13 Cr App R (S) 601.
[298] [1998] EWCA Crim 3119.

ten years' disqualification under CDDA, s 2 and appealed the latter part of the sentence. The Court of Appeal dismissed the appeal, saying:

> This court has said in particular in the guideline case of *Theivendran*[299] that a sentence of imprisonment is not wrong in principle in a case of being concerned in the management of a company when an undischarged bankrupt where no dishonesty had been established. There had been a plain flouting of the order in that case of bankruptcy.
>
> A fortiori the same applies where there is an express order for disqualification. Compliance with company directors disqualification orders is something which is very difficult to police. It should be understood that in the perhaps comparatively few cases where offenders are caught they are at risk of custodial sentences.

Other cases have confirmed that flagrant and persistent breaches of a disqualification order **35.268** or being concerned in the management of a company while an undischarged bankrupt are likely to result in a term of immediate imprisonment, but that in the absence of such aggravating features an immediate prison sentence will not be imposed:

(1) In *R v Brockley*,[300] the Court of Appeal upheld a sentence of six months' imprisonment suspended for two years for acting as a company director while an undischarged bankrupt.
(2) In *R v Ashby*,[301] the Court of Appeal upheld a sentence of four months' imprisonment for violating a disqualification order over the course of three-and-a-half years and in respect of four different companies. No fraudulent enrichment could be shown, but the defendant nevertheless demonstrated a 'serious disregard of the law'.
(3) In *R v Pidgeon*,[302] the defendant had been involved in the management of a company which designed and installed kitchens, including signing cheques, while an undischarged bankrupt. At trial he was sentenced to six months' imprisonment. The Court of Appeal considered that a custodial sentence was justified, but reduced it to two months.

For an example of a case in which an immediate sentence of imprisonment was imposed **35.269** for offences of breaching a disqualification undertaking and managing a company whilst an undischarged bankrupt, see *R v Cowley-Hurlock*.[303] A sentence of 27 months' imprisonment was reduced to 20 months on appeal.

---

[299] (1992) 13 CAR (S) 601.
[300] [1994] 1 BCLC 606.
[301] [1998] 2 Cr App R (S) 37, CA.
[302] [1999] EWCA Crim 1522.
[303] [2014] EWCA Crim 1702.

Part VII

DIRECTORS OF FOREIGN COMPANIES

36

DUTIES AND LIABILITIES OF DIRECTORS OF FOREIGN COMPANIES

Tom Smith QC

A. Introduction

One of the features of the increased globalization of the world economy is that many of **36.01** the companies which carry on business in England and Wales are companies incorporated abroad. Many of these companies may carry out a substantial part, or even all of their activities in England. The question which arises for the directors of such companies is to what extent they are subject to the provisions of the Companies Act 2006 and to the other aspects of English company law.

In general terms, the question raised by foreign companies is of identifying the system of law **36.02** which is to govern the company's affairs, including the duties and obligations of its directors. In the case of individuals, it is relatively straightforward to identify the country with which that individual is connected, for example by residence. The position in relation to companies is less straightforward since companies are of course legal rather than physical persons and thus must be linked with a particular jurisdiction by legal rather than physical concepts.[1] The treatment of companies in international law is characterized by the use of a number of different concepts to identify a company with a particular legal system. These concepts include: place of incorporation, place of registered office, seat, and centre of main interests. However, there are two main ways by which a company may be tied to a particular legal system: by its place of incorporation or by the place where its seat is located.[2]

36.03 According to the incorporation theory,[3] a foreign company created in accordance with a foreign legal system and having its statutory seat (ie registered office) in a foreign state is recognized as such by the host state in which such company operates. In other words, the company is governed by the law according to which it was duly established. The rationale for the incorporation theory is the need for certainty and maximum uniformity in the choice of law.[4]

36.04 By contrast, under the real seat (or *siège réel*) theory,[5] it is the law where the company has its 'real' seat (ie its centre of management and control) which governs the company. The advantages of the real-seat theory are said to be that it enables the authorities of the country where the company is in reality based to control the company efficiently and to safeguard the protection of the company's creditors and other interested parties. Furthermore, the theory is said to secure proper regard for the economic reality and prevent fraud on, or abuse of, the law. This is because the real-seat theory 'recognises the actual facts of the company's corporate life and therefore reduces the opportunity for the evasion of regulations under the law of the state where the corporate life of the company is actually centred and upon which state the company's activities might well have the greatest impact'.[6]

36.05 English law, however, has long preferred the certainty and uniformity offered by the use of a company's place of incorporation as the decisive factor in identifying a company with a legal system and therefore follows the incorporation theory.[7] In other words, under English choice of law rules, a company will be governed by the law of its place of incorporation. Under English law, the concepts of domicile and nationality of a company stem from the place of incorporation. Thus, a company is domiciled in England if it is incorporated in England.[8]

---

[1] For a discussion of the differing approaches to jurisdiction over companies in civil litigation, see Fawcett, 'A New Approach to Jurisdiction over Companies in Private International Law' (1988) 37 ICLQ 645.

[2] See generally Rameloo, *Corporations in Private International Law* (Oxford University Press, 2001).

[3] Countries that apply the incorporation theory include the UK, the Netherlands, Ireland, Denmark, Switzerland, the United States, and Japan.

[4] Koller, 'The English Limited Company: Ready to Invade Germany?' [2004] 11 ICCLR 334, 335.

[5] Countries that apply the real-seat theory include Austria, Belgium, France, Greece, Italy, Luxembourg, Portugal, and Spain. However, within the EU the principle of freedom of establishment has made inroads on the real-seat theory. Thus, a Member State must recognize a company formed in accordance with the law of another Member State even if it would not be recognized under its own domestic conflicts of law rules: Case C-208/00 *Überseering BV v Nordic Construction Company Baumanagement GmbH (NCC)* [2002] ECR I-9919.

[6] Clarke, 'The Conflict of Law Dimension' in *Corporate Law: The European Dimensions* (Butterworths, 1991), p 162.

[7] Cath notes that the incorporation theory is especially popular in countries with a long-standing commercial maritime tradition and where an open attitude to trade is expected to be met with reciprocity as opposed to the more mercantilist attitude adopted in other countries: Cath, 'Freedom of Establishment of Companies: A New Step Towards Completion of the Internal Market' (1986) 6 *Yearbook of European Law* 247.

[8] *Gasque v Inland Revenue Commissioners* [1940] KB 80; *The Eksbridge* [1931] P 51.

Further, neither the nationality nor the domicile of a company depends on the nationality or domicile of its members.[9]

This approach is reflected in the definition of 'company' contained in the 2006 Act, s 1.[10] **36.06** A 'company' for the purposes of the 2006 Act is defined as a company formed and registered under the Act. This includes both companies formed and registered after the commencement of Part 1 of the 2006 Act and companies that immediately before the commencement of Part 1 of the 2006 Act were formed and registered under the Companies Act 1985 or the Companies (Northern Ireland) Order 1986 or were existing companies for the purposes of the 1985 Act or the 1986 Order.

Accordingly, the general rule is that the provisions of the Companies Act 2006 apply only to **36.07** companies incorporated in the UK, including Northern Ireland.[11] Under English rules, foreign incorporation companies are regarded as being governed by the laws of their places of incorporation, irrespective of where the company's operations are in fact based. The 2006 Act, s 1(3) states that for provisions of that Act applying to companies incorporated outside the UK, reference should be made to Part 34, ss 1044–59, which is discussed in Section B below.[12]

B. Directors' Functions and Responsibilities in Relation to Registration Requirements

Part 34 of the 2006 Act applies to 'overseas companies', that is companies incorporated out- **36.08** side the UK. Under the provisions of this Part an overseas company with a branch in the UK must register with the Registrar of Companies. The provisions of Part 34 largely implement the Eleventh Company Law Directive (89/666/EEC).[13] The regulations may specify the persons responsible for complying with any specified requirements of the regulations and provide for any specified contravention to be an offence, punishable by imprisonment or a fine.[14]

Under the provisions of Part 34, the Secretary of State is given the power to make provision **36.09** by regulations requiring an overseas company to deliver to the Registrar of Companies a return in a specified form together with specified documents.[15] The regulations must require an overseas company[16] to register the particulars if the company opens a branch in the UK.[17]

---

[9] *R v Arnaud* [1946] 9 QB 806; *Jansen v Drieftein Consolidated Mines Ltd* [1902] AC 484, 497, 501, 505, HL; *Continental Tyre and Rubber Co (Great Britain) Ltd v Daimler Co Ltd* [1915] 1 KB 893, 904, CA, per Lord Reading CJ; on appeal sub nom *Daimler Co Ltd v Continental Tyre and Rubber Co (Great Britain) Ltd* [1916] 2 AC 307, 349, HL, per Lord Parmoor. Exceptionally, in times of war, an English company assumes an enemy character if it is controlled by persons resident in the enemy country or adhering to that enemy, see *Daimler Co Ltd v Continental Tyre and Rubber Co (Great Britain) Ltd* [1916] 2 AC 307, 345, HL.

[10] This came into force on 1 October 2009: 2006 Act Commencement Order No 8, art 3(a).

[11] Part 45 and s 1299. In contrast the 1985 Act, s 745(1) provided that the 1985 Act did not apply to or in relation to companies registered or incorporated in Northern Ireland or outside Great Britain, except where otherwise expressly provided.

[12] Part 34 came into force on 1 October 2009: 2006 Act Commencement No 8 Order, Art 3(q).

[13] Explanatory Notes to the Companies Act 2006, paras 1326–64.

[14] 2006 Act, s 1054.

[15] 2006 Act, s 1046(1).

[16] Except in the case of a Gibraltar company in which case the regulations may make such provision (s 1046(2)(b)).

[17] 2006 Act, s 1046(2)(a). Regulations may also require an overseas company to give notice to the Registrar if it closes its branch and ceases to have a registrable presence: s 1058.

36.10   In accordance with these powers, the Secretary of State has promulgated the Overseas Companies Regulations 2009, SI 2009/1801. Under Part 2 of the regulations, an overseas company must register prescribed particulars each time it opens an establishment in the UK.[18] The prescribed particulars include particulars of the company and particulars of the establishment.

36.11   For these purposes 'establishment' means a branch within the meaning of the Eleventh Company Law Directive (89/666/EEC) or a place of business which is not such a branch.[19] There is no definition of 'branch' in this directive but in relation to credit institutions branch has been defined as 'a place of business which forms a legally dependent part of a credit institution and which conducts directly all or some of the operations inherent in the business of credit institutions'.[20] In *Somafer v Saar-Ferngas*[21] the European Court of Justice (ECJ) ruled that:

> the concept of branch, agency or other establishment implies a place of business which has the appearance of permanency, such as the extension of a public body, has a management and is materially equipped to negotiate business with third parties so that the latter, although knowing that there will if necessary be a legal link with the parent body, the head office of which is abroad, do not have to deal directly with such parent body but may transact business at the place of business constituting the extension.[22]

36.12   The regulations require an overseas company to register its name.[23] The name may be either the company's corporate name (its name under the law of the country or territory in which it is incorporated) or an alternative name under which the overseas company proposes to carry on the business in the UK.[24] However, an EEA company (being a company governed by the law of an EEA State[25]) must always register its corporate name.[26] The registration of the name of a non-EEA company is subject to various of the restrictions which apply to the names of companies formed and registered under the Companies Acts.[27]

36.13   The other particulars of the company which are required to be registered are its legal form, the identity of any register on which the company is registered in the country of its incorporation, a list of its directors and secretary (containing specified particulars of the directors and secretary, including their names, any former names, their service address and, in the case of directors, their usual residential address, nationality, country of residence, business

---

[18] Overseas Companies Regulations 2009, reg 3.
[19] Overseas Companies Regulations 2009, reg 2.
[20] Directive 77/780/EEC, Directive 89/117/EEC.
[21] Case 33/78 [1978] ECR 2183.
[22] For a case on the meaning of 'operations of a branch, agency or other establishment', see *SAR Schotte GmbH v Parfums Rothschild SAR* [1992] BCLC 235.
[23] 2006 Act, s 1047(1); Overseas Companies Regulations 2009, reg 6(1)(a).
[24] 2006 Act, ss 1047(2) and 1048.
[25] 2006 Act, s 1170.
[26] 2006 Act, s 1047(3).
[27] 2006 Act, s 1047(4). The provisions which apply are s 53 (prohibited names), ss 54–6 (sensitive words and expressions), s 65 (inappropriate use of indications of company type or legal form), ss 66–74 (similarity to other names), s 75 (provision of misleading information), and s 76 (misleading indication of activities). The provisions of s 57 (permitted characters etc) apply in every case (s 1047(5)).

occupation, and date of birth), the extent of the powers of the directors or secretary to represent the company in dealings with third parties and in legal proceedings, and whether the company is a credit or financial institution.[28] Further particulars are also required in the case of a company in an EEA state.[29]

The particulars of an establishment which are required to be registered are the address of the **36.14** establishment, the date on which it was opened, the business carried on at it, the name of the establishment (if different from the name of the company), the name and service address of every person resident in the UK authorized to accept service on behalf of the company in respect of the establishment or a statement that there is no such person,[30] a list of every person authorized to represent the company as a permanent representative of the company in respect of the establishment, the extent of the authority of any such person including whether that person is authorized to act alone or jointly, and if the person is not authorized to act alone, the name of any person with whom they are authorized to act.[31]

An overseas company which is obliged to register particulars is also obliged to register details **36.15** of any alternations in the company's constitution or of the particulars of the company or the establishment which have been registered.[32]

In relation to the registration by an overseas company of the particulars of an individual's **36.16** usual residential address, the regulations contain provisions corresponding to the 2006 Act, Part 10, Chapter 8 concerning the circumstances in which a director's residential address is protected from disclosure (Chapter 6, Section F(3) above).[33]

The regulations also make provision for an overseas company that has an establishment in **36.17** the UK to prepare accounts and reports from the directors and auditors. If the overseas company is required by its parent law to prepare, have audited, or disclose accounts or is an EEA company and is required by its parent to prepare and disclose accounts, then the company is required to deliver to the Registrar of Companies a copy of all of the accounting documents disclosed in accordance with the parent law.[34] In the case of other overseas companies, provisions of Parts 15 (accounts and report) and 16 (audit) of the 2006 Act are applied to such companies.[35] Such companies are therefore required to prepare and deliver accounts and reports in accordance with these provisions of the Act.

The Overseas Companies (Execution of Documents and Registration of Charges) **36.18** Regulations 2009 (SI 2009/1917) further make provision for an overseas company to keep available for inspection copies of instruments creating charges and a register of charges in which the charges must be entered within 21 days of their creation.[36] The relevant charges

---

[28] Overseas Companies Regulations 2009, reg 6(1).

[29] Overseas Companies Regulations 2009, reg 5(2).

[30] 2006 Act, s 1056.

[31] Overseas Companies Regulations 2009, reg 7(1).

[32] Overseas Companies Regulations 2009, reg 13(1).

[33] Overseas Companies Regulations 2009, Part 4, regs 18–29.

[34] Overseas Companies Regulations 2009, regs 31(1) and 32(1).

[35] 2006 Act, s 1049(1), (2), (3). Overseas Companies Regulations 2009, regs 36–42. The Overseas Companies Regulations 2009, Part 6, regs 43–57, makes specific provision in the case of overseas companies which are credit or financial institutions.

[36] 2006 Act, s 1052(1); Overseas Companies (Execution of Documents and Registration of Charges) Regulations, regs 23–4, as amended by the Overseas Companies (Execution of Documents and Registration of Charges) Regulations 2011 (SI 2011/2194).

for these purposes are any charge over land situated in the UK or any interest in such land; any charge on ships, aircraft, or intellectual property registered in the UK; or any floating charge on the whole or part of the company's property or undertaking situated in the UK.[37]

36.19   In addition to the provision of particulars and the filing of accounts and reports, the Overseas Companies Regulations 2009 also require overseas companies carrying on business in the UK to provide certain information in the course of trading.[38] Specifically, an overseas company carrying on business in the UK is required to display its name and country of incorporation at every location in the UK where it carries on business and at the service address of every person authorized to accept service of documents on behalf of the company.[39] The company's name must also be stated on, inter alia, all business correspondence and websites.[40]

C. Capacity and Internal Management

36.20   The general rule of English private international law is that all matters concerning the constitution of a company are governed by the law of the place of incorporation.[41] This rule is one aspect of the general principle of English rules of conflicts of law that the law of the place of incorporation governs matters of substantive company law. This principle has been increasingly recognized and given effect to in recent authorities.[42]

(1) Capacity

36.21   The capacity of a company refers to the legal power of the company to do certain acts or exercise specific rights. For these purposes, capacity has a broad 'internationalist' meaning and includes, for example, the legal ability of a company to enter into a valid contract with a third party.[43] So far as directors are concerned, it is obviously a matter of good governance to ensure that a company acts within its capacity at all times.

36.22   As *Dicey, Morris and Collins* points out, the capacity of a company may be limited in two ways.[44] First, the company's capacity may be limited by the terms of its own constitution. For these purposes, 'constitution' is construed broadly and the source of the constitution will be the company's own constitutive documents (for example, its memorandum and articles of association) together with relevant provisions of statutory and other law of the place of incorporation which apply to the company.[45] The terms and effect of a company's constitution are governed by the law of the place of incorporation. If, under its constitution, a company

---

[37] Overseas Companies (Execution of Documents and Registration of Charges) Regulations, reg 24(1) (as amended).

[38] 2006 Act, s 1051(1); Overseas Companies Regulations 2009, part 10, regs 78–86.

[39] Overseas Companies Regulations 2009, reg 60.

[40] Overseas Companies Regulations 2009, reg 62.

[41] *Dicey, Morris, and Collins, The Conflict of Laws*, 15th edn (Sweet and Maxwell, 2012), rule 175(2).

[42] See eg *Base Metal Trading Ltd v Shamurin* [2005] 1 WLR 1157, CA; *Fiona Trust & Holding Corp v Privalov* [2010] EWHC 3199 (Comm) at para 142 *et seq*; *Haugesund Kommune v Depfa ACS Bank* [2012] QB 549 at paras 27 *et seq* and paras 155–60.

[43] *Haugesund Kommune v Depfa ACS Bank* [2012] QB 549 at para 47. See also *Standard Chartered Bank v Ceylon Petroleum Corp* [2011] EWHC 1785 (Comm) at para 391 and *Integral Petroleum SA v SCU-Finanz AG* [2014] EWHC 702 (Comm), [2015] EWCA Civ 144.

[44] *The Conflict of Laws*, 15th edn at para 30–021.

[45] *Haugesund Kommune v Depfa ACS Bank* [2012] QB 549.

lacks capacity to do a certain act then any such act which the company purports to do may be invalid and ineffective.

Secondly, the capacity of a company may be limited under the law of the country which **36.23** governs the relevant transaction. In other words, the law of the country which is applicable to the transaction under the usual principles of private international law may limit the ability of the company to enter into the transaction. Under English law, such restrictions are rare. However, this issue needs to be borne in mind where a company is entering into a transaction governed by foreign law, particularly where the transaction involves the purchase of real property abroad.

(2) Internal management

The law of the place of incorporation determines the composition and powers of the organs **36.24** of the company and the formalities and procedures laid down for them.[46] This means that the law of the place of incorporation will determine, amongst other things, whether the directors have been validly appointed and the composition of the board of directors. In *Speed Investments Ltd v Formula One Holdings Ltd*[47] the Court of Appeal accepted that this was the position.[48] This position complements the position in relation to the jurisdiction of the courts. The recast Judgments Regulation,[49] which set out the rules for the allocation of jurisdiction in proceedings against persons domiciled in the EU,[50] gives exclusive jurisdiction to the courts in which a company has its seat in relation to proceedings which have as their object the validity of decisions of a company's organs.[51]

(3) Financial assistance

The 2006 Act, Part 18, Chapter 2 contains provisions dealing with financial assistance.[52] **36.25** These provisions illustrate how the English Companies Acts do not legislate in respect of the constitutional affairs of a foreign company. The consequence is that a director of a foreign company is not obliged to secure compliance by the company with provisions of the 2006 Act concerning maintenance of a company's capital.

By its terms, the 2006 Act, s 678 applies in relation to the acquisition of shares in a public **36.26** company and the provision of assistance by that company or a subsidiary of that company for the purpose of the acquisition. 'Public company' is defined in the 2006 Act, s 4 and incorporates the definition of 'company' in s 1. Accordingly, the financial assistance provisions do not apply in relation to the acquisition of shares in a foreign public company.

In relation to the provision of assistance, it is possible that an English public company may **36.27** have a foreign subsidiary and the question is therefore whether s 678 would prohibit the giving of assistance by that company. In *Arab Bank plc v Mercantile Holdings Ltd*[53] it was

---

[46] *Grupo Torras SA v Al-Sabah* [1996] 1 Lloyd's Rep 7, 15.
[47] [2005] 1 BCLC 455.
[48] See also *Sierra Leone Telecommunications Co Ltd v Barclays Bank plc* [1998] 2 All ER 821.
[49] Council Regulation (EC) No 1215/2012 of 12 December 2012 on jurisdiction and the recognition and enforcement of judgments in civil and commercial matters.
[50] Except Denmark.
[51] Art 24(2).
[52] The provisions of the 2006 Act came into force and replaced the 1985 Act, ss 151–8 on 1 October 2009 (the 2006 Act Commencement Order No 8, Art 3(1)), but private companies became exempt from the 1985 Act provisions on 1 October 2008 (2006 Act Commencement Order No 5, Arts 5(2) and 8(b) and Sch 3).
[53] [1994] Ch 71.

held that the equivalent provision in the 1985 Act did not extend to the foreign subsidiaries of English public companies. This provision referred to the public company and 'any of its subsidiaries'. The presumption was that, in the absence of a contrary intention, the provision was not intended to have an extraterritorial effect and that the term 'any of its subsidiaries' was to be construed accordingly. The 2006 Act, s 678 now makes this clear beyond doubt by specifically referring to 'a company that is a subsidiary' thereby incorporating the definition of 'company' in s 1.

D. Execution of Documents on Behalf of a Foreign Company

36.28 The 2006 Act, s 43 provides that a company may make a contract by writing under its common seal or a contract may be made on behalf of a company by a person acting under its authority, express or implied.[54] Section 44 provides that a document is executed by a company by the affixing of its common seal or if it is signed on behalf of the company by two authorized signatories or by a director of the company in the presence of a witness who attests to the signature.[55] Sections 46 and 47 deal with the execution of deeds and other documents.

36.29 Under the 2006 Act, the Secretary of State is given power to make provision by regulations applying ss 43–52 to overseas companies subject to necessary exceptions, adaptations, or modifications.[56] Such regulations are contained in the Overseas Companies (Execution of Documents and Registration of Charges) Regulations 2009, Part 2, and apply ss 43, 44, 46, 48, and 51 of the 2006 Act to overseas companies (with relevant modifications). The effect of these regulations is that the execution of documents by and on behalf of a foreign company is governed by the law of the company's place of incorporation. A foreign company can therefore make a contract in any manner permitted by the law of the place of incorporation. The authorities suggest, however, that the Regulations are concerned only with the formalities of execution and do not affect matters such as ostensible authority.[57]

36.30 Accordingly, a contract can be executed in any manner permitted by the law of the place of incorporation and would have the same effect as a document executed by an English company.

E. Duties Owed by Directors of a Foreign Company

36.31 The duties owed by a director of a company under English law have historically arisen both at common law and in equity. A director owed a duty of care to the company at both common law and in equity.[58] In addition, a director may have owed duties under his contract of employment with the company.

---

[54] 2006 Act, ss 43, 46, 47 came into force on 1 October 2009, replacing the 1985 Act, ss 36, 36AA, 38 without changes: 2006 Act Commencement Order No 8, Art 3(d).

[55] 2006 Act, s 44 came into force on 6 April 2008: 2006 Act Commencement Order No 5, Art 3(1) and replaced 1985 Act, s 36A without change, except that sub-s (2)(b) is new.

[56] 2006 Act, s 1045.

[57] *Azov v Baltic Shipping Co* [1999] 2 Lloyd's Rep 159, 170; *Rimpacific Navigation Inc v Daehan Shipbuilding Co Ltd* [2012] 2 All ER 814 at paras 30–1; *Golden Ocean Group Ltd v Salgaocar Mining Industries PVT Ltd* [2011] 2 All ER (Comm) 95 at paras 160–1; *Habbas Sinai Ve Tibbi Gazlar Istuha Endustrisi AS v VSC Co Ltd* [2013] EWHC 4071 (Comm) at paras 122–30.

[58] *Bristol & West Building Society v Mothew* [1998] Ch 1, CA.

The duties of directors have now been codified in Part 10 of the Companies Act 2006, as dis- **36.32**
cussed in Chapters 10–17 above. These provisions apply in relation to a company as defined
in the 2006 Act, s 1, namely, a company formed or registered under the Companies Acts. The
new statutory duties therefore do not apply to directors of a foreign incorporated company.

In relation to foreign companies, as noted above, the general rule of English private inter- **36.33**
national law is that all matters concerning the constitution of a corporation are governed by
the law of the place of incorporation.[59] As a result, it has been held that the law of the place
of incorporation will govern the nature and extent of the duties owed by directors to the
corporation.[60] The position underlying this general proposition is, however, somewhat more
complex since under English rules of private international law different rules may apply
depending on whether the relevant duties of a director are said to arise at common law, in
equity, or as a matter of contract.

(1) Equitable duties

Under English law (until the 2006 Act, Part 10 came into force), a director's equitable duties **36.34**
included the equitable duty of care which he owed to exercise skill and care in relation to the
company's affairs and the fiduciary duties of fidelity and loyalty imposed on a director (now
the 2006 Act, ss 171–3 and 175–7).

The law applicable to a director's equitable duties was considered by the Court of Appeal in **36.35**
the case of *Base Metal Trading Ltd v Shamurin*.[61] The Court of Appeal held that a director's
equitable duty arises from and only from the director's relationship with the company and
that, if it does not relate to the constitution of the company, then it relates to its internal
management. Since the duty is inextricably bound up with those matters then it must be
governed by the place of the company's incorporation.[62]

This conclusion is supported by other authorities. In *Pergamon Press Ltd v Maxwell*[63] the **36.36**
court held that it was not open to the English court to control the exercise of a fiduciary
power arising in the internal management of a foreign company. In *Konamaneni v Rolls-
Royce Industrial Power (India) Ltd*[64] the court held that the extent of the duties of the director
of a foreign company was governed by the law of that country's place of incorporation and
that the point was 'unexceptional and indeed obvious'. In *Shaker v Al Bedrawi*[65] the court
proceeded on the basis that the law of Pennsylvania was the applicable law to the duties of
directors of a company incorporated there.

This conclusion also achieves the most practically desirable result. It means that it is possible **36.37**
to identify with certainty the system of law which will govern a director's equitable duties
without having to undertake a factual inquiry. As the Court of Appeal pointed out in *Base*

---

[59] *Dicey, Morris, and Collins*, rule 175(2).
[60] *Dicey, Morris, and Collins*, para 30-028; *Pergamon Press Ltd v Maxwell* [1970] 1 WLR 1167; *Konamaneni
v Rolls-Royce Industrial Power (India) Ltd* [2002] 1 WLR 1269; *Shaker v Al-Bedrawi* [2003] Ch 350, CA; *Base
Metal Trading Ltd v Shamurin* [2005] 1 WLR 1157, CA; *Debt Collect London v SK Slavia Praha-Fotbal AS*
[2010] EWHC 57 (QB); *Fiona Trust & Holding Corp v Privalov* [2010] EWHC 3199 (Comm) at para 40 *et seq.*
[61] [2005] 1 WLR 1157, CA.
[62] [2005] 1 WLR 1157, paras 56 and 69.
[63] [1970] 1 WLR 1167.
[64] [2002] 1 WLR 1269.
[65] [2003] Ch 350, CA.

Metal, any other result would have created huge uncertainty and hampered the requirement for good corporate governance and proper regulatory control.[66] In practice, however, it may be difficult for the directors of a foreign company to persuade an English court that they do not owe the company fiduciary duties under the company's law of incorporation.[67]

(2) Common law duties

36.38 In addition to equitable duties, a director owed duties at common law to the company. Under English law, such duties include the common law duty to act with reasonable care and skill in relation to the affairs of the company which is the common law counterpart of the equitable duty of care. This duty is now embodied in the duty under the 2006 Act on a director to exercise reasonable care, skill, and diligence.[68]

36.39 Under the English system, a breach of the common law duty of care is actionable by a claim in tort against the director for damages for breach of duty. The Rome II Regulation on the law applicable to non-contractual obligations does not apply to non-contractual obligations arising out of the law of companies.[69] Under English law, where the Rome II Regulation does not apply the law applicable to a claim in tort is in general determined by the provisions of the Private International Law (Miscellaneous Provisions) Act 1995.[70] The general rule is that the applicable law is the law of the country in which the events constituting the tort occur.[71] However, importantly, this general rule may be displaced if it appears that, in all the circumstances, from a comparison of (a) the significance of the factors which connect a tort with the country whose law would be applicable under the general rule and (b) the significance of any factors connecting the tort with another country, that it is substantially more appropriate for the applicable law to be the law of the other country.[72]

36.40 In the case of duties owed by directors, it may be strongly arguable that the most significant factor is the relationship between the director and the company. The essential characteristic of a claim for breach of duty is that there has been a breach by the director of the obligations which lie upon him by virtue of his office as a director. Given that the general principle of English private international law is that the law of the place of incorporation will govern matters of substantive company law, this strongly suggests that it would be substantially more appropriate for the law of the place of incorporation to apply to a tort founded on a director's breach of duty.

---

[66] [2005] 1 WLR 1157, CA, para 56.

[67] See eg Chadwick J in *Re Howard Holdings Inc* [1998] BCC 549, 555 in relation to the duties of directors where the company is insolvent: 'I find it difficult to envisage any developed system of corporate law which does not impose some obligation on those charged with responsibility of the management of a company's affairs to pay regard to the question whether or not it is, from time to time, solvent and, if insolvent, to consider what should be done about it.'

[68] Companies Act 2006, s 174(1).

[69] Regulation (EC) No 864/2007 of the European Parliament and of the Council of 11 July 2007 on the law applicable to non-contractual obligations, Article 1(2)(d).

[70] *Dicey, Morris, and Collins*, rule 256(5).

[71] Private International Law (Miscellaneous Provisions) Act 1995, s 11(1). The relevant principles governing the operation of section 11 were set out by the Court of Appeal in *VTB Capital plc v Nutritek International Corp* [2012] 2 BCLC 437 at para 148, approved on this point by the Supreme Court: [2013] 2 AC 337 at para 199.

[72] Private International Law (Miscellaneous Provisions) Act 1995, s 12(1). For discussion of choice of law in relation to tort claims and assessment of damages: *Harding v Wealands* [2007] 2 AC 1, HL; *Re T&N Ltd (No 2)* [2006] 1 WLR 1792; *Trafigura Beheer BV v Kookmin Bank Co* [2006] 2 Lloyd's Rep 455.

In *Base Metal* it was held that the tort claim for breach of duty was governed by the Russian **36.41** law, rather than by the law of the place of incorporation (Guernsey), on the basis that Russia was the place where in substance the tort had been committed since this was where, amongst other things, the directors were based. This applied the old common law test as the relevant events had occurred prior to the enactment of the 1995 Act.[73] Following the enactment of the 1995 Act, it may well be that the law of the place of incorporation will apply for the reasons discussed above.

(3) Contractual duties

A director may also owe duties to the company under a contract between himself and the **36.42** company. The rules of the Rome I Regulation[74] do not apply to determine the law applicable to such duties since this falls within the exception for company law issues contained in Article 1(2)(f) of the Rome I Regulation.[75] Accordingly, the law applicable to such duties falls to be determined in accordance with English common law rules of private international law. The general rule at common law is that the law applicable to a contract is governed by the express or inferred intention of the parties or, in the absence of such intention, by the system of law with which the contract has the closest and most real connection.[76]

It follows that duties owed by a director to the company under a contract with the company **36.43** will be governed by the law intended by the parties to govern such duties or, failing any such intention, the law with which such duties are most closely connected. Where there is an express choice of law provision in the contract this system of law is therefore likely to apply. However, in any case, it appears that these general choice of law rules are, in relation to the duties owed by a director to a company, subject to a further rule that a company and a director cannot by the terms of a contract vary the duties which the director would otherwise owe to the company under the law of the place of incorporation unless that law permits such variation.[77] Accordingly, a director can by a contract assume additional or further duties to those which he would owe under the law of the place of incorporation generally, but he cannot by a contract exclude or limit those duties.

The law applicable to the duties of a director as an *employee* of the company, as opposed to **36.44** those owed by him by virtue of his office as a director of the company, will be governed by the provisions of the Rome I Regulation. In the absence of an express choice of law provision in the contract of employment, Article 8(2) of the Rome I Regulation provides that the contract is to be governed by the law of the country in which the employee habitually carries out his work in performance of the contract.

Overall, it is possible that a director's different duties in equity, at common law, and under **36.45** contract may be governed by different systems of law. This may be regrettable but is a consequence of the recognition in English law of the possibility of concurrent causes of action in equity, tort, and contract.[78] However, in practice, it is likely that the law of the place of

---

[73] *Metall und Rohstoff v Donaldson Lufkin and Jenrette Inc* [1990] 1 QB 391, CA.
[74] Regulation (EC) No 593/2008 of the European Parliament and of the Council of 17 June 2008 on the law applicable to contractual obligations.
[75] *Base Metals Ltd v Shamurin* [2005] 1 WLR 1157, CA, para 65.
[76] *Dicey, Morris, and Collins*, para 32-005; *Bonython v Commonwealth of Australia* [1951] AC 201, PC.
[77] *Base Metals Ltd v Shamurin* [2005] 1 WLR 1157, CA, para 69.
[78] *Henderson v Merrett Syndicates Ltd* [1995] 2 AC 145, HL.

incorporation will play an increasingly important role in determining all of the duties owed by a director to a company.

(4) Effect of insolvency

36.46 Once a company is insolvent, the interests of creditors (including future creditors) displace the interests of the company itself since the creditors become prospectively entitled to displace the power of the directors and the shareholders to deal with the company's assets.[79] Accordingly, upon insolvency the directors of a company may be required to preserve the company's assets for the benefit of all creditors.[80] These issues are discussed in Chapter 12, Section E and Chapter 20, Section D above. However, the directors do not owe a legal duty to creditors, in the sense that they do to the company prior to the insolvency, which the creditors might enforce by bringing an action against the directors. Rather, the obligation on directors upon the insolvency of a company to act in the interests of creditors is enforceable by the office-holder in any subsequent insolvency using the tools available to him under the insolvency legislation or by bringing an action in the name of the company.

36.47 It follows from this that the nature and extent of the duties of directors where a company enters the zone of insolvency may in practice be influenced by the law applicable to any subsequent insolvency proceedings. Thus where insolvency proceedings are commenced in England in relation to the company, it will be English law and, in particular, the provisions of the Insolvency Act, which will determine the nature and extent of the remedies available to the insolvency office-holder, for example, in relation to setting aside transactions or for fraudulent or wrongful trading.[81] Accordingly, English law will determine the liability of a director in relation to such matters. In this way, English law will influence the duties of the directors prior to the insolvency in the sense that if a director acts in a way which triggers the remedies available to an English insolvency office-holder, he may then face liability under English law in respect of such matters.

F. Civil Litigation

36.48 One of the issues of which a director of a foreign company needs to be aware is the risk of the company being subject to civil litigation in England. If the company is unsuccessful, the director may be exposed to liability for costs, as discussed in Chapter 24, Section F above. A director of a company which unsuccessfully defends a claim may also be susceptible to the machinery which the English court makes available to a successful litigant in order to assist with the enforcement of his judgment.

36.49 The rules for jurisdiction in civil proceedings involving persons domiciled in the EU (except Denmark) are contained in the recast EC Regulation on Civil Jurisdiction and Judgments[82] (the Judgments Regulation). Under the Judgments Regulation, the general rule, subject to exceptions, is that a person domiciled in the EU may be sued in the courts of the state where

---

[79] *Kinsela v Russell Kinsela Pty Ltd (in liq)* (1986) 4 NSWLR 722, 730; *West Mercia Safetywear Ltd v Dodd* [1988] BCLC 250, CA.

[80] See 2006 Act, s 172(3).

[81] See further Section H below.

[82] Council Regulation (EC) No 1215/2012 of 12 December 2012 on jurisdiction and the recognition and enforcement of judgments in civil and commercial matters.

he is domiciled.[83] The place of incorporation is one of the tests for determining the domicile of a company (the others being place of central administration and principal place of business).[84] Accordingly, a company incorporated in a Member State may be sued in its country of incorporation under the Judgments Regulation.

The Judgments Regulation also specifically provides that proceedings which have as their **36.50** object the validity of the constitution, the nullity or the dissolution of companies or other legal persons, or the validity of the decisions of their organs are to be dealt with exclusively by the courts of the Member State in which the company or other legal person has its seat.[85] The seat for these purposes is to be determined in accordance with domestic rules of private international law. In the case of England, a company will be treated as having its seat in England if it was incorporated in England.[86]

Civil jurisdiction over companies domiciled in Denmark and in EEA states (which are, **36.51** principally, Iceland, Norway, and Switzerland) are dealt with by the Brussels and Lugano Conventions respectively.[87] Under these Conventions the seat of a company is to be treated as its domicile with the seat to be determined in accordance with domestic rules of private international law.[88] Under English rules, a company is to be treated as having its seat in the UK if it was incorporated or formed under the law of part of the UK and has its registered office or some other official address in the UK or if its central management and control is exercised in the UK.[89] The Brussels and Lugano Conventions also contained similar provisions to those contained in the Judgments Regulation reserving jurisdiction over proceedings which have as their object the validity of the constitution, the nullity or the dissolution of companies or other legal persons, or the validity of the decisions of their organs exclusively to the courts where the company has its seat.[90]

The Judgments Regulation and the Brussels and Lugano Conventions do not apply to bank- **36.52** ruptcy, proceedings relating to the winding up of insolvent companies or other legal persons, judicial arrangements, compositions, and other analogous proceedings.[91] Insolvency proceedings are subject to the EC Regulation on insolvency proceedings.[92]

In relation to companies domiciled outside the EU and EEA, the usual English rules of **36.53** jurisdiction apply. Proceedings may be served on a company in the jurisdiction by leaving them at, or sending by post to, the registered address of any person resident in the UK who is authorized to accept service of documents on the company's behalf or by sending by post to any place of business of the company in the UK.[93] In addition, the proceedings may be sent or left at any place within England and Wales where the company carries on its activities.[94] It

---

[83] Judgments Regulation, Art 4.
[84] Judgments Regulation, Art 63(1), (2).
[85] Judgments Regulation, Art 24(2).
[86] Civil Jurisdiction and Judgments Order 2001 (SI 2001/3929), Sch 1, para 10.
[87] Civil Jurisdiction and Judgments Act 1982, ss 2(1) and 3A(1); Sch 1, Sch 3C.
[88] Brussels Convention, Art 53; Lugano Convention, Art 53.
[89] Civil Jurisdiction and Judgments Act 1982, s 42(3).
[90] Brussels Convention, Art 16(2); Lugano Convention, Art 16(2); Civil Jurisdiction and Judgments Act 1982, s 43.
[91] Judgments Regulation, Art 1(2)(b); Brussels Convention, Art 1; Lugano Convention, Art 1.
[92] See para 36.73 below.
[93] 2006 Act, s 1139(2).
[94] CPR rule 6.9(2). This method of service is in addition to those specified in the Companies Act: *Sea Assets Ltd v PT Garuda Indonesia* [2000] 4 All ER 371.

also seems that proceedings may be personally served on a company by leaving the proceedings with a person holding a senior position within the company.[95]

36.54　Further, in certain circumstances, it may be possible to obtain permission from the English court to serve proceedings on a foreign company, not domiciled in the EU or EEA, outside the jurisdiction.[96]

36.55　Finally, it appears that the English court has jurisdiction to make an order under CPR Part 71 to obtain information from a judgment debtor resident outside the jurisdiction. It is clear that the court may make an order requiring a judgment debtor within the jurisdiction to answer questions about assets outside the jurisdiction.[97] There was some doubt as to whether the court also had jurisdiction to make an order against a judgment debtor or officers of a judgment debtor who are outside the jurisdiction. In the case of an individual judgment debtor an order for examination may be made under CPR rule 71.2 and served outside the jurisdiction. However, in *Masri v Consolidated Contractors*[98] the House of Lords held that in relation to a corporate judgment debtor CPR rule 71.2 did not permit an order for examination to be made against an officer of a corporate debtor who was outside the jurisdiction.

G.　Remedies of Shareholders in a Foreign Company in England

36.56　The principal right and remedy of a shareholder in a company where there has been breach of directors' duties or the company is being managed in a manner prejudicial to his interests is to exercise his rights under the constitution of the company. However, where these rights and remedies are ineffective, a shareholder may be able to commence legal proceedings. The principal forms of action available to a shareholder under English law in this regard are the commencement of derivative proceedings by the shareholder (for example, against a director of the company) or the presentation of a petition to wind up the company on just and equitable grounds, as discussed in Chapter 23, Section B above.

36.57　The further remedy which is available to a shareholder in a company formed and registered under the Companies Acts is to apply to the court for an order under Part 30 of the 2006 Act on the grounds that the company's affairs are being or have been conducted in a manner that is unfairly prejudicial to the interests of members generally or of some part of its members (discussed in Chapter 23, Section A above).[99] However, this remedy is only available to a company within the meaning of the 2006 Act, which does not include a foreign company.[100]

(1)　Derivative proceedings

36.58　The general rule is that a company is the proper claimant in an action to redress harm done to the company or to prosecute a cause of action vested in the company. However, in certain

---

[95]　CPR rule 6.5(3)(b). It is not entirely clear whether CPR rule 6.5(3)(b) was intended to apply to a foreign company. However, CPR rule 6.3(2) suggests that the term 'company' in this context can include a foreign company and in *Lakah Group v al-Jazeera Satellite Channel* [2003] EWHC 1231 it appeared to be assumed that service could be effected on a foreign company under rule 6.5(3)(b) though the point was not argued.

[96]　CPR rule 6.36.

[97]　*Interpool Ltd v Galani* [1988] QB 738.

[98]　[2010] 1 AC 90.

[99]　2006 Act, s 994(1).

[100]　2006 Act, s 994(3), s 1.

circumstances established by the case law, the courts held that a shareholder in a company could be permitted to bring proceedings by way of derivative action. The action is brought in representative form by the shareholder and the company is joined as a defendant in order for it to be bound by any judgment.

The question is whether the English court has jurisdiction to hear a derivative claim in rela- **36.59**
tion to a foreign company. In *Konamaneni v Rolls-Royce Industrial Power (India) Ltd*,[101] the claimants, minority shareholders in an Indian company, sought to bring a derivative action on its behalf against two English companies who were alleged to have paid bribes to the managing director of the Indian company. The court held that the English court had jurisdiction to hear the claim since it had jurisdiction over two of the defendants and the Indian company could be joined to the proceedings as a necessary or proper party to the proceedings.[102] However, the court also held that service of the proceedings would be set aside on the grounds that the place of incorporation of a foreign company would almost invariably be the most appropriate forum for the resolution of issues relating to the existence of the right of shareholders to sue on behalf of the company.[103]

The law and procedure in relation to derivative claims is now codified in the 2006 Act, **36.60**
Part 11, ss 260–4. However, these provisions only apply to a claim by a member of a company which, as defined in the 2006 Act, s 1, is a company formed and registered under the Companies Acts. Sections 260–4 therefore do not apply in respect of derivative claims in relation to a foreign company.

The position in relation to the jurisdiction of the English court over such claims will there- **36.61**
fore remain as the court held in *Konamaneni* at least so far as companies outside the EU are concerned. In other words, the English court will have jurisdiction over such claims provided that it has jurisdiction over one or more of the defendants in accordance with its usual rules; the foreign company may then be joined to the proceedings as a necessary or proper party.[104] The claim will thereafter be subject to the procedural filter provided for by CPR rule 19.9 (which requires the claimant to seek the permission of the court to continue the claim).

However, aside from the question of jurisdiction, where permission is sought to serve out of **36.62**
the jurisdiction on the foreign company as a necessary or proper party to the proceedings, the English court will have a discretion as to whether or not to permit such service. It will only give permission where it is satisfied that England is the proper place in which to bring

---

[101] [2002] 1 WLR 1269.

[102] CPR Part 6, Practice Direction B, para 3.1(3).

[103] The US District Court for the District of Columbia, affirmed by the US Court of Appeals for the District of Columbia Circuit, dismissed a derivative claim in respect of BAE Systems plc, an English company, on the ground that the claim was not within the exceptions to the rule in *Foss v Harbottle* without considering *forum non conveniens: City of Harper Woods Employees' Retirement System v Olver and BAE Systems plc* (2008) 577 F Supp 2d 124, affd (2009) 589 F 3d 1292. In *Tomran Inc v Passano* (2004) 159 Md App 706, 862 A 2d 453 the Court of Special Appeals of Maryland upheld the decision of the Circuit Court in Baltimore that it should not dismiss a derivative claim in respect of Allied Irish Banks, an Irish company, on the ground of *forum non conveniens*, since the conduct complained of took place in relation to a subsidiary in Maryland, but that the claim should be dismissed because (i) the plaintiff was not a shareholder, and (ii) the claim was not within the exceptions to the rule in *Foss v Harbottle*. See also the decision of the US District Court for the Southern District of New York in *Silverstein v Knief*, 11 Civ 4776.

[104] Pursuant to CPR Part 6, Practice Direction B, para 3.1(3).

the claim.[105] In this respect, it is very likely that the English court would refuse as a matter of discretion to permit service out of the jurisdiction where it was sought to bring a derivative action in relation to a foreign company. This is because the place of incorporation of the company will almost invariably be the appropriate forum for the determination of the proceedings.[106]

36.63   In particular, as the court pointed out in *Konamaneni*, the law of the place of the incorporation of a company governs the right of a shareholder to bring a derivative action in England. Although a matter of English domestic law the exceptions to the rule have been regarded as matters of procedure, their real nature is not procedural in the international context.[107] They confer a right on the shareholders to protect the value of their shares by giving them a right to sue and recover on behalf of the company. The court pointed out that it would be odd if that right could be conferred under English law on the shareholders of a company incorporated in a jurisdiction which has no such rule.

36.64   The position is more complicated where the foreign company is domiciled within the EU or EEA and one or more of the other defendants is domiciled in England. In these circumstances, the provisions of the Judgments Regulation and the Lugano Convention apply. Under the provisions of the Judgments Regulation and the Lugano Convention which permit the joinder of co-defendants to proceedings, it is arguable that the foreign company could be joined to the claim.[108]

36.65   However, it is doubtful whether this provision can be invoked to permit the English court to take jurisdiction over a derivative claim in respect of a company domiciled elsewhere in the EU or EEA. The language of the provisions, which envisage distinct claims against each of the defendants which might result in irreconcilable judgments if not heard together, is inapt to apply to a derivative claim. It must also be extremely doubtful whether it was ever the intention behind these provisions to confer jurisdiction on the courts of one Member State to hear a derivative claim in relation to a company based in another Member State. This is particularly so given that the Regulation and the Convention specifically refer matters relating to the validity of the constitution of a company to the Member State where it has its seat.[109]

36.66   Furthermore, if the provisions of the Judgments Regulation and the Lugano Convention did confer jurisdiction to determine derivative claims in relation to a company incorporated in another Member State, then it is doubtful whether the courts would have a discretion to decline to hear such proceedings. Thus the route taken in *Konamaneni* would probably not be open to the court. This, in itself, is a further indication that the provisions of the Judgments Regulation and the Lugano Convention do not confer jurisdiction to hear derivative proceedings in relation to companies in other Member States.

---

[105]   CPR rule 6.37(3).

[106]   See also *SMAY Investments Limited v Sachdev* [2003] 1 WLR 1973, para 49.

[107]   *Konamaneni v Rolls-Royce Industrial Power (India) Ltd* [2002] 1 WLR 1269, para 50; *Base Metal Trading v Shamurin* [2005] 1 WLR 1157, CA at para 68, per Arden LJ.

[108]   Art 8(1) of the Judgments Regulation (where the party is domiciled in the EU excluding Denmark) or Art 6(1) of the Lugano Convention, as enacted by the Civil Jurisdiction and Judgments Act 1982, Sch 3C (where the party is domiciled in an EEA state outside the EU).

[109]   Judgments Regulation, Art 24(2); Lugano Convention, Art 16(2).

(2) Just and equitable winding up

36.67 The further remedy potentially available to a shareholder is to present a petition for the winding up of the company on the grounds that it is just and equitable that the company should be wound up. Under the provisions of the Insolvency Act, a petition may be presented for the winding up of a foreign company on such grounds.[110]

36.68 In relation to foreign companies, it is necessary to consider the position separately in relation to companies whose seat is not in a Member State of the EU or EEA and companies whose seat is in such a country. So far as companies with their seat in the EU or EEA are concerned, as noted above, the Judgments Regulation and the Brussels and Lugano Conventions specifically confer jurisdiction over proceedings which have as their object the dissolution of a company on the state where the company has its seat.[111] It is considered that a petition for the winding up of a company on just and equitable grounds would fall within this provision.[112] Accordingly, the English court will not have a jurisdiction to wind up on just and equitable grounds a company which has its seat in another EU or EEA Member State.

36.69 In relation to foreign companies whose seats are outside the EU and EEA, there is no fetter on the English court's jurisdiction to make a winding-up order on just and equitable grounds. However, in such cases, it is likely that the court would accede to an application to stay the petition on grounds of *forum non conveniens* or would refuse to permit service of the petition out of the jurisdiction on the basis that the proper forum was the place of the company's incorporation.[113]

H. Insolvency Proceedings

36.70 A director of a foreign company may have to consider English insolvency proceedings either where the company is insolvent and requires protection from its creditors or where it is necessary to place the company into insolvency proceedings as part of a consensual restructuring. In the former context, the director may have to consider whether insolvency proceedings represent the best way of obtaining the necessary protection or, alternatively, the director may have to consider whether the company should resist an application for English insolvency proceedings brought by a creditor. In the latter context, the question may be whether English insolvency proceedings represent the most effective route of achieving the desired restructuring. In practice, the views of the company's creditors on this question will also be critical. Also a creditor may take insolvency proceedings in England against a foreign company with a view to proceedings being taken by the office-holder or the company against the director.

(1) Availability of English insolvency proceedings for foreign companies

36.71 The principal insolvency procedures available in relation to companies under the Insolvency Act, as discussed in Chapter 32 above, are: administration, creditors' voluntary liquidation,

---

[110] Insolvency Act, s 221(5)(c).

[111] Judgments Regulation, Art 24(2); Brussels Convention, Art 16(2); Lugano Convention, Art 16(2). As to the meaning of seat for these purposes, see the Civil Jurisdiction and Judgments Act 1982, s 43 and the Civil Jurisdiction and Judgments Order 2001 (SI 2001/3929), Sch 1, para 10.

[112] See *Re Senator Hanseatische Verwaltungsgeschellschaft* [1996] 2 BCLC 563.

[113] See *Re Harrods (Buenos Aires) Ltd* [1992] Ch 72, CA. Other aspects of the decision in *Re Harrods* have been overruled by the decision of the ECJ in *Owusu v Jackson* [2005] QB 801.

compulsory liquidation, and members' voluntary liquidation. The Enterprise Act 2002 reformed the administration procedure and effectively abolished administrative receivership in relation to floating charges created on or after 15 September 2003.

36.72 International insolvency proceedings are principally governed by the European Council Regulation on Insolvency Proceedings (the Insolvency Regulation) and the UNCITRAL Model Law on Cross-Border Insolvency as implemented by the Cross-Border Insolvency Regulations 2006 (the Cross-Border Regulations). In addition, the English court has the power to grant assistance in relation to insolvency matters to foreign courts in certain specified states pursuant to the Insolvency Act, s 426. The Insolvency Regulation, the Cross-Border Regulations, the Insolvency Act, s 426 together with the powers of the courts under common law,[114] essentially form a suite of measures by which the English courts can grant assistance to and cooperate with foreign insolvency proceedings.

(2) The Insolvency Regulation

36.73 The Insolvency Regulation, which came into force on 31 May 2002, is of central importance to insolvency proceedings in respect of debtors based in Europe.[115] The Insolvency Regulation governs, in relation to all Member States of the EU (except Denmark), the jurisdiction to commence insolvency proceedings and the recognition and enforcement of judgments arising from such proceedings. A recast version of Insolvency Regulation entered into force from 26 June 2015 applying to insolvency proceedings from 26 June 2017.[116]

36.74 The general scheme of the Insolvency Regulation is that the jurisdiction to open insolvency proceedings in respect of a company with its centre of main interests within the EU is conferred on the courts of the Member State where the debtor's centre of main interests is situated.[117] These proceedings are known as 'main proceedings'. In the case of companies and legal persons, it is presumed, in the absence of evidence to the contrary, that the place of the registered office is the centre of main interests.[118] Where a debtor's centre of main interests is located in a Member State, the courts of other Member States only have jurisdiction to open insolvency proceedings in relation to the debtor if he has an 'establishment' in that Member

---

[114] *Rubin v Eurofinance SA* [2013] 1 AC 236; *PricewaterhouseCoopers v Saad Investments Co Ltd* [2014] 1 WLR 4482, PC; *Singularis Holdings Ltd v PricewaterhouseCoopers* [2015] AC 1675, PC; *Stichting Shell Pensioenfonds v Krys* [2015] AC 616, PC.

[115] Council Regulation (EC) No 1346/2000 of 29 May 2000 on insolvency proceedings. See further Moss, Fletcher, and Isaacs, *The EC Regulation on Insolvency Proceedings*, 3rd edn (Oxford University Press, 2016).

[116] Council Regulation (EC) No 848/2015 of 20 May 2015 on insolvency proceedings.

[117] Art 3.1. The term 'centre of main interests' is not defined in the EC Regulation though Recital 13 suggests that it should correspond to the place where the debtor conducts the administration of his interests on a regular basis and is therefore ascertainable by third parties.

[118] Art 3.1. In *Re Eurofood IFSC Ltd* [2006] Ch 508, the ECJ held that where a debtor is a subsidiary company whose registered office and that of its parent company are situated in two different Member States, the presumption can be rebutted only if factors which are both objective and ascertainable by third parties enable it to be established that an actual situation exists which is different from that which location at that registered office is deemed to reflect. In *Interedil Srl v Fallimento Interedil Srl* [2012] BCC 851 the ECJ confirmed that where a debtor company's registered office had been transferred before a request to open insolvency proceedings was lodged, the company's centre of main interests was presumed to be the place of the new registered office. The ECJ also held that where the bodies responsible for the management and supervision of a company were in the same place as its registered office then the presumption in article 3 of the Regulation could not be rebutted. But where the debtor company's central administration was not the same as its registered office the presumption could be rebutted by factors satisfying the requirements of objectivity and ascertainability.

State;[119] the effects of such proceedings (known as 'secondary proceedings') are restricted to the assets situated in that Member State.[120]

Accordingly, for directors faced with the need to reorganize a company through insolvency **36.75** proceedings the location of the company's centre of main interests will be of critical importance. If the centre of main interests is located in another EU state, then it will not be possible to open main proceedings in England. On the other hand, if the centre of main interests is located in England it will be possible to place the company into main insolvency proceedings in England, including administration, notwithstanding that the company is incorporated elsewhere (whether in another EU state or outside the EU).[121] In appropriate circumstances, it may be possible to move a company's centre of main interests to England in order to open main insolvency proceedings in England.[122]

(3) The Cross-Border Regulations

The function of the Cross-Border Regulations differs from that of the Insolvency Regulation **36.76** in that they do not allocate jurisdiction to open insolvency proceedings but rather enable the English court to grant relief in support of foreign insolvency proceedings already taking place abroad. Where such foreign proceedings are 'main' proceedings then the effect of recognition of the foreign proceedings under the Cross-Border Regulations is to provide for an automatic stay on the commencement or continuation of actions or proceedings concerning the debtor's assets, rights, obligations, and liabilities.[123] In addition, the court may as a matter of discretion grant further forms of relief in support of the foreign insolvency.[124] Notably, this includes relief providing for the examination of witnesses; the taking of evidence; or the delivery of documents concerning the debtor's assets, affairs, obligations, or liabilities. In effect, this extends to a foreign office-holder the equivalent powers which are available to the office-holder in a domestic insolvency proceeding.[125]

(4) Section 426

Under the Insolvency Act, s 426 the English court has the obligation to grant assistance **36.77** in relation to insolvency matters to foreign courts in certain specified states (essentially Commonwealth states).[126] Section 426 provides that the English court 'shall assist' the requesting state and, in order to do so, it is given the authority to apply either English insolvency law or the corresponding insolvency law of the requesting state. The overriding consideration is to assist the foreign court unless there is a compelling reason why such assistance

---

[119] Art 3.2. An 'establishment' is defined as any place of operations where the debtor carries out a non-transitory economic activity with human means and goods: Art 2(h).

[120] Art 3.2.

[121] See *Re BRAC Rent-A-Car International Inc* [2003] 1 WLR 1421.

[122] See n 118 above.

[123] Cross-Border Regulations, Sch 1, Art 20(1).

[124] Cross-Border Regulations, Sch 1, Art 21(1).

[125] ie under the Insolvency Act 1986 s 236. See *Re Chesterfield United Inc* [2013] 2 BCLC 709.

[126] The relevant territories are the Channel Islands and the Isle of Man, Anguilla, Australia, the Bahamas, Bermuda, Botswana, Canada, Cayman Islands, Falkland Islands, Gibraltar, Hong Kong, Republic of Ireland, Montserrat, New Zealand, St Helena, Turks and Caicos Islands, Tuvalu, Virgin Islands, Malaysia, Republic of South Africa, and Brunei Darussalam: Insolvency Act, s 426(11) and Co-operation of Insolvency Courts (Designation of Relevant Countries and Territories) Order 1986 (SI 1986/2123); Co-operation of Insolvency Courts (Designation of Relevant Countries and Territories) Order 1996 (SI 1996/253); Co-operation of Insolvency Courts (Designation of Relevant Countries and Territories) Order 1998 (SI 1998/2766).

cannot be granted.[127] Section 426 is frequently invoked for the purpose of investigating or pursuing claims against directors.[128]

(5) Administration

36.78 In relation to companies with their centres of main interests outside the EU, the English court may make an administration order in respect of a company incorporated overseas pursuant to a request for assistance from a foreign court in one of the specified states pursuant to s 426.

36.79 In *Re Dallhold Estates (UK) Pty Ltd*[129] an administration order was made in England over an Australian company pursuant to a request from the Australian court made under s 426.[130] The administration order in *Dallhold Estates* was made despite the fact that in Australia there was no jurisdiction to make an equivalent order. Having identified the matters specified in the request from the Australian court, the English court identified the relevant insolvency law applicable to comparable matters falling within its jurisdiction and applied those laws to the matters falling within the request, disregarding the fact that the company which was the subject matter of the request was foreign. The court therefore treated the Australian company as if it was an English company.

36.80 However, outside s 426, the jurisdiction to place a foreign company into administration in England is circumscribed by the definition of 'company' contained in Schedule B1 to the Insolvency Act 1986.[131] Pursuant to this definition, the following types of company can be placed into administration in England: (a) a company registered under the Companies Act 2006 in England and Wales or Scotland, (b) a company incorporated in an EEA state other than the UK, and (c) a company not incorporated in an EEA state but having its centre of main interests in a Member State other than Denmark. The final category reflects the effect of the Judgments Regulation. Outside of these categories, and outside of s 426, there is no power to place a foreign company into administration in England.

(6) Winding up

36.81 Under the provisions of the Insolvency Act both companies incorporated in England and Wales and, subject to the provisions of the Insolvency Regulation, foreign companies may be wound up. In particular, foreign companies may be wound up as unregistered companies under the Insolvency Act, s 221. It follows that a foreign company with its centre of main interests outside the EU may be wound up by the English court. There are numerous cases in which the English court has in fact made a winding-up order in relation to such companies.

36.82 In *Re Latreefers Inc*[132] the Court of Appeal held that there are three conditions which must be satisfied for the making of a winding-up order in respect of a foreign company: (1) there must be a sufficient connection with England (which may, but does not necessarily have

---

[127] The principles underlying the application of s 426 are set out in the decisions of the Court of Appeal in *Hughes v Hannover Rückversicherungs-Aktiengesellschaft* [1997] 1 BCLC 497, CA; *Smith v England* [2001] Ch 419, CA; and by the House of Lords in *Re HIH Casualty and General Insurance Ltd* [2008] 1 WLR 852.

[128] *England v Smith* [2001] Ch 419, CA; *Re Trading Partners* [2002] 1 BCLC 655.

[129] [1992] BCLC 621.

[130] See also *Re Tambrook Jersey Ltd* [2014[Ch 252, CA.

[131] Insolvency Act 1986, Sch B1, para 111(1A).

[132] *Stocnzia Gdanska SA v Latreefers Inc (No 2)* [2001] 2 BCLC 116, CA.

to, consist of assets within the jurisdiction); (2) there must be a reasonable possibility, if a winding-up order is made, of benefit to those applying for the winding-up order; and (3) one or more persons interested in the distribution of assets of the company must be persons over whom the court can exercise jurisdiction.

Under the Insolvency Act, s 221, a foreign company can be wound up on grounds other **36.83** than insolvency, for example if the court is of the opinion that it is just and equitable to do so. However, in relation to European companies, Article 24(2) of the Judgments Regulation applies in relation to solvent liquidations and provides that the courts of the Member State in which the company, legal person, or association has its seat shall have exclusive jurisdiction in proceedings which have as their object the validity of the constitution, the nullity, or the dissolution of companies or other legal persons or associations of natural or legal persons, or of the validity of the decisions of their organs.[133]

(7) Company voluntary arrangements

As with the provisions relating to administration, the provisions of the Insolvency Act relat- **36.84** ing to voluntary arrangements apply to (a) a company registered under the Companies Act 2006 in England and Wales or Scotland, (b) a company incorporated in an EEA state other than the UK, and (c) a company not incorporated in an EEA state but having its centre of main interests in a Member State other than Denmark.[134] For the same reasons as discussed above in relation to administration, subject to the operation of the rules contained in the Insolvency Regulation, CVAs are therefore available in the case of companies incorporated in an EEA state and foreign companies with their centre of main interests in the UK. In addition, as with administration, the provisions relating to voluntary arrangements may be applied to other foreign companies pursuant to a request made under the Insolvency Act, s 426.[135]

(8) Schemes of arrangement

Finally, although not strictly an insolvency proceeding, schemes of arrangement under **36.85** the Companies Act 2006 Act, Part 26, ss 895–901, as discussed in Chapter 28 above, may be sanctioned in relation to a foreign company. A company for the purposes of the Companies Act, Part 26, means any company liable to be wound up under the provisions of the Insolvency Act or the Insolvency (Northern Ireland) Order 1989.[136] In *Re Drax Holdings plc*[137] the court held that the second and third requirements of the test set out in *Latreefers*[138] for winding up a foreign company do not need to be satisfied for the court to have jurisdiction to sanction a scheme in respect of a foreign company since they go to discretion rather than to jurisdiction; it is enough that a sufficient connection with England is shown.[139]

---

[133] *Re Senator Hanseatische Verwaltungsgesellschaft* [1996] 2 BCLC 563.
[134] Insolvency Act 1986, s 1(4).
[135] *Re Television Trade Rentals Ltd* [2002] BPIR 859.
[136] s 895(2)(b).
[137] [2004] 1 WLR 1049. Followed in *Re Rodenstock GmbH* [2011] Bus LR 245.
[138] Para 36.82 above.
[139] See generally *Re Rodenstock GmbH* [2011] Bus LR 245 (where the debts subject to the scheme were governed by English law), *Re Primacom Holding GmbH* [2013] BCC 201, *Re Vietnam Shipbuilding Industry Group* [2014] 1 BCLC 400, and *Re Magyar Telecom BV* [2015] 1 BCLC 418.

(9) Obligations of directors in insolvency proceedings

36.86   The provisions of the Insolvency Act which require the director of an insolvent company to cooperate with office-holders apply where a foreign company is in insolvency proceedings in England. In the case of a foreign company being wound up as an unregistered company the provisions of the Insolvency Act are specifically applied to such companies.[140] In the case of foreign companies placed into liquidation or administration in England on the grounds that their centres of main interests are here, then the relevant provisions of the Insolvency Act must be taken to apply as they would to an English company.[141] The following paragraphs deal with a director's obligations under the Insolvency Act, ss 234–6. These provisions are discussed in more detail in Chapter 33, Section G above.

36.87   Under the Insolvency Act, s 234 the office-holder is entitled to get in the company's property including its books, papers, and records and the court may order any person, including a director, to deliver such property to the office-holder. Under s 235 various persons, including officers of the company, are under a duty to cooperate with the office-holder and to give to the office-holder such information concerning the company and its promotion, formation, business, dealings, affairs, or property as the office-holder may reasonably require.

36.88   In addition to these provisions, s 236 contains important powers which enable the office-holder to seek orders from the court requiring various persons, including any officer of the company, to submit an affidavit to the court containing an account of his dealings with the company or to produce any books, papers, or other records in his possession or under his control relating to the company or the promotion, formation, business, dealings, affairs, or property of the company. Any person who is brought before the court pursuant to s 236 may also be examined orally on oath.[142] As noted above, the effect of the Cross-Border Regulations may be to make similar powers available to the office-holder in a foreign insolvency proceeding.

36.89   As well as applying where a foreign company is in insolvency proceedings in England, these provisions will apply where the relevant property or documents which the office-holders seeks to obtain are located abroad. The court has jurisdiction under s 236 to make an order requiring the production of documents located abroad where the liquidator reasonably required to see those documents in order to carry out his statutory functions and production of them does not impose an unnecessary or unreasonable burden on the person required to produce them in the light of those requirements.[143]

36.90   The more difficult question is whether an application under s 236 can be made against a person who is outside the jurisdiction. In *Re Tucker*[144] the Court of Appeal decided that the equivalent provision of the Bankruptcy Act 1914[145] in relation to personal insolvency was

---

[140]   Insolvency Act, ss 221(1) and 229(1).

[141]   Definitions for the first group of parts of the Insolvency Act relating to corporate insolvency are contained in s 251. This applies the definitions in the Companies 2006, which include the definition of 'company' in s 1, '*except in so far as the context otherwise requires*'. Where a foreign company is in liquidation or administration in England because its centre of main interests is in England then the reference to 'company' in Part VI must be read as including such a company.

[142]   s 237(4).

[143]   *Re Mid East Trading Ltd* [1998] 1 All ER 577, CA.

[144]   [1990] Ch 148, CA. See also *Re Seagull Manufacturing Co Ltd* [1992] Ch 128 dealing with the Insolvency Act 1986, s 133.

[145]   Bankruptcy Act 1914, s 25.

confined to persons in England at the relevant time who could be served with a summons of the English court in England. The language of s 236 is similar to that of the Bankruptcy Act 1914 and it might therefore be arguable that the same reasoning should apply. However, under rule 12A.20 of the Insolvency Rules 1986 the court is given power to order the service of process outside the jurisdiction and there is no suggestion that this does not include an application under s 236. Accordingly, it is suggested that an application under s 236 can be made against a person outside the jurisdiction at least insofar as it relates to the production of documents or an account of dealings with the company.[146]

36.91 The court also has jurisdiction under the Insolvency Act, s 133 to order the public examination of a director irrespective of the nationality of the director or whether he is resident or present in England.[147]

(10) Liabilities of directors arising from English insolvency proceedings

36.92 Where a foreign company is subject to insolvency proceedings in England, then it will be subject to the same provisions regarding the setting aside of antecedent transactions and the liabilities of directors as if the company was English.[148] Directors' liabilities in these respects are discussed in Chapter 33 above.

36.93 Accordingly, it has been held that the provisions of the Insolvency Act 1986 which impose liability on directors for wrongful trading may apply to the directors of a foreign company in liquidation in England.[149] This was so despite the fact that the directors were resident abroad and there was no similar liability under the law of the country in which the company was incorporated. Indeed, it is important to note that the possibility of bringing claims against the directors of a foreign company under the Insolvency Act, ss 213 and 214 (fraudulent trading and wrongful trading) may itself be a reason why it is appropriate for the English court to make a winding-up order in respect of a foreign company.[150] In addition, claims may be made against directors of a foreign company in the English court under ss 213 and 214 pursuant to s 426 where a request has been received from the courts of a relevant country or territory even though the company is not in fact in insolvency proceedings in England.[151]

36.94 The provisions relating to the setting aside of antecedent transactions on grounds that they were at an undervalue or were preferences contained in the Insolvency Act, ss 238, 239, and 423 will also apply in relation to a foreign company in insolvency proceedings in England so as to enable the court to grant relief against any person whether or not they are resident in England.[152] There is no territorial limitation on the application of these provisions. However, the relief under these provisions is discretionary and, if a foreign element is involved, the court will need to be satisfied that in respect of the relief sought against him the defendant

---

[146] This was the result in *Re Omni Trustees Ltd* [2015] BCC 906. In *Re MF Global UK Ltd* [2016] 2 WLR 588 the Court reached the contrary conclusion but, as the Court noted in *Re Omni Trustees Ltd*, the Court had not been referred to the earlier decision of the Court of Appeal in *Re Mid East Trading Ltd* [1998] 1 BCLC 240.

[147] *Re Seagull Manufacturing Co Ltd* [1992] Ch 128.

[148] See in relation to the winding up of a foreign company, Insolvency Act 1986, ss 221(1) and 229(1).

[149] *Re Howard Holdings Inc* [1998] BCC 549.

[150] *International Westminster Bank plc v Okeanos Maritime Corp* [1988] Ch 210; *Stocznia Gdanska SA v Latreefers Inc (No 2)* [2001] 2 BCLC 116, Lloyd J and CA.

[151] *Re Bank of Credit and Commerce International SA (No 9)* [1994] 2 BCLC 636.

[152] *Re Paramount Airways Ltd* [1993] Ch 223, CA. See also *Jyske Bank (Gibraltar) Ltd v Spjeldnaes* [1999] 2 BCLC 101; *Banco Nacional de Cuba v Cosmos Trading Corp* [2000] 1 BCLC 813, CA.

is sufficiently connected with England for it to be just and proper to make the order against him despite the foreign element.

36.95 The Insolvency Regulation also envisages that avoidance actions such as those available under ss 238, 239, and 423 are governed by the law of the state in which the proceedings are opened.[153] The position would be more complex where there are two sets of insolvency proceedings in different countries and the matter falls outside the scope of the Insolvency Regulation. In those circumstances, it is to be expected that the courts and the laws of the country in which the principal insolvency proceedings are based would be permitted to take the lead.[154]

36.96 In addition, where a proposed respondent to an application is located abroad it is necessary for the applicant to seek the leave of the court for service out of the jurisdiction. The Insolvency Rules 1986 make provision for service out of the jurisdiction of any proceedings arising in the course of insolvency proceedings in accordance with CPR Part 6 (rule 12A.20 and IR 2016, r 12.1 after 6 April 2017). The court will make an order under this rule where it is satisfied that there is a real issue between the claimant and the defendant which the claimant can reasonably ask the court to try.[155] Where a foreign element is involved one of the factors which the court will consider is whether the defendant has a sufficient connection with England in connection with the relief sought.[156]

36.97 In relation to the disqualification of directors under the CDDA, the provisions apply to any company wherever incorporated which could be wound up under the Insolvency Act[157] and anyone, of whatever nationality, can be disqualified for conduct rendering him unfit to be a director of a company.[158] This is irrespective of where the conduct complained of occurred. Disqualification under the CDDA is discussed in Chapter 31 above.

(11) Liabilities of directors arising from foreign insolvency proceedings

36.98 A director of a foreign company which is in insolvency proceedings abroad, and who is resident in England, may also potentially face liabilities arising out of those foreign insolvency proceedings which are recognized and given effect to in England. However, in *Rubin v Eurofinance SA*[159] the Supreme Court held that a default and summary judgment of the US Bankruptcy Court given in the context of US bankruptcy proceedings would not be recognized and enforced in England, in circumstances where the defendants had not participated in the US proceedings or submitted to the jurisdiction of the US court.

36.99 The effect of the judgment in *Rubin v Eurofinance* is that a director of a foreign company which is the subject of insolvency proceedings, and who is the subject of the claims made in those proceedings which result in a judgment being given against him, may have such

---

[153] Art 4(2)(m).

[154] *In re Maxwell Communication Corporation*, 170 BR 800 (US Bankruptcy Court for the Southern District of New York) presented an analogous problem in relation to the question of which system of law should govern the avoidability of pre-insolvency transactions, which the US bankruptcy and district courts resolved by deferring to English law and the English courts based on the finding that England was the centre of the case. This was despite the fact that US creditors would have done better if US rather than English law had been applied to the preference issue.

[155] *Re Paramount Airways Ltd* [1993] Ch 223, CA; *Re Howard Holdings Inc* [1998] BCC 549.

[156] *Re Paramount Airways Ltd* [1993] Ch 223, CA.

[157] See CDDA, ss 6(1) and 22(2).

[158] *Re Seagull Manufacturing Co Ltd (No 2)* [1994] Ch 91.

[159] [2013] 1 AC 236.

judgment enforced against him in England, only if the foreign court has personal jurisdiction over him (for example, if he had submitted to the jurisdiction of the foreign court). This is because the ordinary common law rules governing the recognition of foreign judgments applied also to judgments given in insolvency proceedings and under such rules a foreign judgment *in personam* would only be recognized if the foreign court had personal jurisdiction over the defendant in accordance with English rules of private international law. In practice, this would require the director either to have submitted to the jurisdiction of the foreign court or to have been resident in the foreign country when the proceedings commenced.

I. Foreign Disqualification

The 2006 Act, Part 40, ss 1182–91[160] contain provisions about persons subject to foreign disqualification orders, which are intended to close a gap in the previous law. Previously, a person who was disqualified from acting as a director, or subject to a similar restriction, in another country was able to act as a director of a company in the UK. Part 40 of the 2006 Act closes this gap by empowering the Secretary of State to make regulations to disqualify persons who have been disqualified in another country from acting as directors of a UK company.   **36.100**

For these purposes, a person is subject to 'foreign restrictions' if under the law of another country or territory he is, by reason of misconduct or unfitness, disqualified to any extent from acting in connection with the affairs of a company or he is, by reason of misconduct or unfitness, required to obtain permission or meet any other condition before acting in connection with the affairs of a company or he has, by reason of misconduct or unfitness, given relevant undertakings.[161] This is intended to encompass those persons who have been disqualified under, or fallen foul of, foreign laws equivalent to the Company Directors Disqualification Act 1986.[162]   **36.101**

The regulations may make any provision for any such person being disqualified from being a director of a UK company, acting as receiver of a UK company's property, or in any way, whether directly or indirectly, being concerned or taking part in the promotion, formation, or management of a UK company.[163] At the date of this edition no regulations had been made.[164]   **36.102**

---

[160] In force 1 October 2009: 2006 Act Commencement Order No 8, Art 3(w).

[161] 2006 Act, s 1182(2).

[162] Explanatory Notes to the 2006 Act at para 1508.

[163] 2006 Act, s 1184(1).

[164] But see the new CDDA, s 5A, discussed in Chapter 31, Section C(5) above, which provides for disqualification of a person who has been convicted abroad of an offence which (i) was committed outside Great Britain in connection with the promotion, formation, management, liquidation, striking off of a company (including an overseas company), the receivership of property of such a company or the administrative receivership of such a company, and (ii) corresponds with an indictable offence under the law of England and Wales.

INDEX

n = footnote.